# The Oxford Companion to Film

# THE OXFORD COMPANION TO

# FILM

## EDITED BY
## LIZ-ANNE BAWDEN

Oxford University Press · London · New York · Toronto · 1976

*Oxford University Press, Ely House, London W.1*

GLASGOW NEW YORK TORONTO MELBOURNE WELLINGTON
CAPE TOWN IBADAN NAIROBI DAR ES SALAAM LUSAKA ADDIS ABABA
DELHI BOMBAY CALCUTTA MADRAS KARACHI DACCA
KUALA LUMPUR SINGAPORE HONG KONG TOKYO

ISBN 0 19 211541 3

© Oxford University Press 1976

Filmset in Photon Times 9 pt. by
Richard Clay (The Chaucer Press), Ltd., Bungay, Suffolk
and printed in Great Britain by
Fletcher & Son Ltd., Norwich

# Contributors

MAIN CONTRIBUTORS
Liz-Anne Bawden, Elaine Burrows, Jill Dimmock, Colin Ford, Gillian Hartnoll, Sara Jolly, Karol Kulik, Sheldon Meyer, Betty Palmer, John Raisbeck, Thelma Schaverien, Kenneth Thompson, Martin Walsh, Sheila Whitaker.

SPECIAL CONTRIBUTORS
Brenda Davies (Great Britain), Thorold Dickinson, Derek Elley (Hungary), Simon Field (underground), David Fisher (technical), Anne Fleming (propaganda), Kevin Glover (documentary), Helen Harrison (newsreel), Martin Howells (copyright), David James (animation), Ruth Kreitzman (Italy), Sam Kula (USA), Ernest Lindgren (archive), Michael Moulds (Canada), Robert Morgan (technical), José Ospina (Latin America), Michelle Snapes (France), Richard Taylor (animation), Victoria Wegg-Prosser (compilation).

OTHER CONTRIBUTORS
Roy Armes, Susan Bennett, Suzanne Budgen, David Castel, Robert Culff, Claude Delmas, Elli Epp, G. M. Gidley, Kari Hanet, Jon Harris, Susan Lermon, John Pigeon, Molly Plowright, Christopher Rodrigues, Peter Sainsbury, Peter Seward, John Williams.

# Preface

The aim of the *Oxford Companion to Film* is to answer any query which may occur to the amateur of film in the course of reading or film-going, and to lead him on to topics of related interest. Cinema, being art, spectacle, mass industry, political instrument, as well as mirror of its times, casts a particularly wide net; and the scope of the book attempts to reflect this. Special attention has been given to topics on which information is not readily available elsewhere, such as propaganda, paper prints, or archives; and to individuals of whom little has been said of their particular relation to cinema, such as Scott Fitzgerald, Erik Satie, or Billy the Kid.

With such a wide field, selection is inevitable. Individual entries do not claim to be comprehensive, but rather to offer the most effective picture of the subject. No attempt has been made, for instance, to give complete lists of the films made by a particular director or played in by a particular actor. Such comprehensive lists can be found elsewhere: those selected for the *Companion* claim to be the most significant. Similarly, statistics relating to film production, audience figures, and so on, are selective rather than comprehensive.

Films are referred to by their original title wherever available, and cross-referred from their original title. Individual films have been selected for entry on grounds of their artistic, historical, or sociological interest. Film credits, again, are selective rather than complete. The date given is in each case the date of release in the country of origin: where an anomaly arises (as in the case of *Une Partie de campagne* or *Sedmikrásky*) it is explained in the text. Running times are indicated to the nearest quarter of an hour for feature films and to the nearest five minutes for short films. It was tempting to offer running times to the nearest minute, but films are so frequently shorn of footage by accident or design that such attempted accuracy would have been misplaced.

Cross-referencing in such a work is necessarily frequent. A word, name, or title printed in small capitals indicates that the subject is treated in a separate entry. The entries, as in all *Oxford Companions*, are self-indexing.

Contributors have had to combine special knowledge with a talent for succinct, expressive writing—and the second quality has been harder to find than the first. Particular emphasis has been laid on the need for accuracy; and, although no book can hope to be free from errors, inordinate pains have been taken to make the *Companion* accurate in the information it gives.

A constant problem has been keeping up to date entries which must inevitably be out of date before the book is printed. The end of 1974 was chosen as the cut-off date, and only outstanding events of 1975 can be included in this edition. (Very often, though, an entry which peters out in the fifties indicates that the subject's career did the same.) A much more serious problem in such a rapidly changing field as cinema has been whether or not to include a subject of recent development. Account has been taken of some modernist and revolutionary movements, such as the new American cinema and Latin-American revolutionary cinema. Women's cinema, on the other hand, defying as it does any but the crudest categorization, will have to wait for future editions to receive the attention it will certainly deserve.

Particular consideration has been given to the illustrations. Each illustration is a complete frame photographed from the film (rather than a publicity still taken at the time of production, which is much more usual). Each frame is reproduced in its correct aspect ratio, the shape in which it was intended to be seen on the screen; frames of the same ratio are reproduced on the same scale.

This policy has meant that each film illustrated has been lent by the distributor and photographed specially for the *Companion*. The real difficulties involved account to some extent for the comparative sparseness of the illustrations; but the notorious reluctance of some of the larger American companies to allow any reproduction at all accounts for the much more regrettable lack of balance, and American films are, as so often, sadly under-represented. We can only acknowledge all the more gratefully the generosity of those who were willing to let us illustrate their films, and hope that those who were not may perhaps allow us to remedy the present inadequacies in future editions.

Acknowledgement appropriate to all those who have helped on an undertaking of this scope is difficult to make. Outstanding among the contributors for the quality and professionalism of their work (as well as the inestimable virtue of keeping to deadlines) are Sara Jolly, Gillian Hartnoll, Jill Dimmock, Karol Kulik, Kenneth Thompson, Thelma Schaverien, and Betty Palmer. The staff of the British Film Institute, most particularly the Library and Information Department, gave help with the skill, patience, and enthusiasm for which they are deservedly well known.

I would also like to thank the Slade School, University College London, for housing the *Companion* during most of the work; and those colleagues, students, and friends who have given advice and help, particularly James Leahy, Lutz Becker, and Marian McColl. Throughout the work Frances Thorpe and her colleagues at the Slade Film History Register gave constant help and advice; so, too, in the early days, did Professor Hugh Gray of the University of California at Los Angeles.

The Oxford University Press has been a most generous and encouraging publisher, and I would like to thank those members who have contributed far more than would have been expected of them: Sheldon Meyer in particular for his warmth, support, and spirited criticism; Susan Lermon and Anne Charvet for their meticulous and constructive copy-editing; Jeffrey Sains and Susan le Roux.

No thanks can adequately acknowledge the contribution of Betty Palmer, who has from the earliest days worked with skill and devotion, ordering the mass of files, chasing and cheering contributors, editing and re-editing entries, as well as writing many. Her contribution to the *Companion* is inestimable.

So, too, is that of the consultants. The book's balance and perspective owe a great deal to the regular (and constantly constructive) criticism, the painstaking thoroughness, and the support of Brenda Davies in London, Sam Kula in Washington and Ottawa, and Sheldon Meyer in New York.

To Thorold Dickinson I owe a very special debt of gratitude. I had the pleasure and privilege of working for and with him when he was Professor of Film in the University of London and Director of Film Studies at the Slade School, and it was through his enthusiasm that the *Companion* came into being.

LIZ-ANNE BAWDEN,
The Slade School,
University College London
August 1975

British consultant

**BRENDA DAVIES**
*Head of Information and Documentation,*
*British Film Institute*

American consultant

**SAM KULA**
*Director*
*National Film Archives of Canada*
formerly
*Archivist and Assistant Director*
*The American Film Institute*

Special consultants

**THOROLD DICKINSON**    *Professor Emeritus of Film, University of London*
**SHELDON MEYER**    *Vice-President, Oxford University Press, New York*

Editorial assistant

**BETTY PALMER**

*The Oxford Companion to Film* is dedicated to
Sir William Coldstream, Slade Professor 1949–75,
who was responsible for the founding and nurturing of
film studies at University College London

ILLUSTRATIONS

Research by            Thelma Schaverien
Photographs by         Yossi Balanescu
Line drawings by       Tom Partridge

Particular thanks are due to M. François Truffaut and Films du Carrosse for the title-page illustration from *L'Enfant sauvage*; to Mr Charles Cooper of Contemporary Films Ltd for his generosity in lending us films and allowing reproduction from them and to Mrs Lottie Steinhart for her practical help; to Mr George Hoellering of Academy Cinemas Ltd; to David Francis of BBC-Television; to Mr Stanley Forman, Educational and TV Films; and to Connoisseur Films, London Films, United Artists, the Imperial War Museum, Amanda Films, Gala Film Distributors Ltd, Twentieth Century-Fox, Anthony Morris (London) Ltd.

ABBREVIATIONS

*Dir* director; *asst* assisted by; *prod* producer or production company; *scr* scriptwriter; *ph* cameraman; *mus* music; *lyr* lyrics; *chor* choreography; *des* art director; *cost* costumes; *sp eff* special effects; *ed* editor

# A

**'AA' certificate,** film category introduced by the BRITISH BOARD OF FILM CENSORS in 1970, restricting admission to persons over the age of fourteen. (See CENSORSHIP, GB.)

**ABBOTT,** BUD (1895–1974), US comic actor, came from a circus family but found his field in vaudeville. His touring double act with Lou COSTELLO met with great success, and their first film *One Night in the Tropics* appeared in 1940, to be followed by a stream of knock-about comedies sometimes amounting to four in one year. Abbott's portrayal of the thin smoothie perpetually exploiting and humiliating his fat simpleton partner was unsubtle, but they gained much popularity, taking over the audience that had enjoyed LAUREL AND HARDY. Abbott and Costello had their own names for the European market: in France they were called 'Les Deux Nigauds', in Italy 'Gianni e Pinotto'. The team split up after an unsuccessful television series in 1955, and Abbott retired the next year.

**ABC** see ASSOCIATED BRITISH CINEMAS

*A BOUT DE SOUFFLE* (*Breathless*), France, 1960. 1½hr. *Dir* Jean-Luc Godard; *prod* Georges de Beauregard; *scr* Godard, based on a story by François Truffaut; *ph* Raoul Coutard; *ed* Cécile Decugis; *mus* Martial Solal; *cast* Jean-Paul Belmondo (Michel Poiccard alias Laszlo Kovacs), Jean Seberg (Patricia Franchini), Daniel Boulanger (Police Inspector), Jean-Pierre Melville (Parvulesco).

The story (outlined by François TRUFFAUT) of a young car-thief wanted by the police for the shooting of a patrolman, and his relationship with an American student in Paris who subsequently informs on him, was GODARD's first feature film. Its stylistic devices have been so completely assimilated into the orthodoxy of commercial film-making that it is difficult to appreciate the original impact of its innovations. The film was shot entirely on location in the streets, cafés, and hotel rooms of Paris. Wherever possible, additional lighting, use of tripods, cranes, dollies, and rails was avoided: moving camera shots were hand-held and tracking was accomplished by seating the cameraman in a wheelchair. Establishing shots were eliminated in favour of jump-cutting. The dialogue was not, as is commonly believed, improvised by the actors, but written by Godard who would not, however, allow them to learn their lines but cued them during takes. The sound-track was necessarily entirely post-synchronized.

*A bout de souffle* was conceived by Godard as a break with the traditions of 'quality' film-making and a return to the directness and immediacy of the American GANGSTER movie (a title dedicates the film to MONOGRAM PICTURES).

**ABPC** see ASSOCIATED BRITISH PICTURE CORPORATION

**ABSTRACT FILM,** term used to describe a variety of experimental films of a 'non-figurative' nature. The abstract film had its origins in the AVANT-GARDE movements of the twenties; it has evolved along two main channels, between which the basic distinction is whether the foundation is photographed reality or graphic material; the latter type again divides into two main streams, one employing the standard ANIMATION technique of frame-by-frame photography, the other bypassing the camera in favour of work accomplished directly on to clear film stock.

It has been argued that films based on photographed reality are not truly abstract, but they are generally allowed into any discussion of the subject. Works in this category cover a wide range, from experiments in 'pure' cinema and 'pattern' films to the more impressionistic type of DOCUMENTARY. *Le Ballet mécanique* (Fernand LÉGER and Dudley Murphy, 1924), generally considered the first completely abstract film to be photographed as opposed to drawn, used human faces and kitchen utensils as subjects for rhythmic montage treatment. Almost contemporary with it were the 'pure cinema' experiments of Henri CHOMETTE, who photographed the shifting forms created by reflections of light in rapidly moving crystals in a film known variously as *Jeux de reflets et de la vitesse* or *Reflets de lumière et de vitesse* (1925), and the work of Man RAY, notably the surrealist ciné-poem *Emak Bakia* (1926). In 1927 Walter RUTTMANN merged abstract film and documentary in BERLIN, DIE SYMPHONIE EINER GROSSSTADT. Chomette's experiments were followed up by

MOHOLY-NAGY in Germany during the twenties with his series of *Lichtspiele* and by the Englishman Oswell Blakeston in collaboration with the Belgian Francis Brugière with *Light Rhythms* (1930); the American Douglas Crockwell experimented with shooting along the incident rays of light sources and as late as 1948 another American, James Davis, made *Light Reflections and Shadows*. Emulating Léger's use of objects, Eugene Deslaw based *La Marche des machines* (1928) on images of machinery and *La Nuit électrique* (1930) on illuminated street signs, and in America Robert FLOREY incorporated machine-age abstractions into *The Loves of Zero* (1929). Of similar but finer quality were works by the American photographer Ralph Steiner, including *$H_2O$* (1929), an abstract study of water reflections and patterns in light and shade, and *Mechanical Principles* (1930), which employed mechanical parts in motion.

Visual interpretations of music became a particular manifestation of the abstract film, both in photographic and animation form. In 1928–9 Germaine DULAC made three abstract films using photographic imagery to interpret music, *Disque 927*, *Arabesque*, *Thème et variations*, and Ruttmann used images of water for his visual counterpoint to Schumann's piano piece *In der Nacht* (1931). The possibilities of this photographic approach were limited and the genre passed out of fashion, although it was revived in America by Slavko VORKAPICH in his pictorial impressions of Wagner's *Forest Murmurs* and Mendelssohn's *Fingal's Cave*, in which striking camerawork was rhythmically and emotionally blended with the music.

The pioneers of drawn abstract film were Viking EGGELING and Hans RICHTER who in 1918 and 1920 collaborated on scroll drawings which seemed to cry out for film animation. They worked separately in film, Eggeling persisting with thousands of drawings on scrolls to make *Symphonie Diagonale* (1920–2), while Richter used animated cut-outs to make *Rhythmus 21, 23, 25* (1921–5). Richter went on to use abstract forms, symbols, and actual objects in *Filmstudie* (1926), *Inflation* (1927–8), an essay in economic inflation used as an introduction to a commercial feature film produced by UFA, and *Vormittagsspuk* (*Ghosts Before Noon* or *Ghosts Before Breakfast*, 1927–8), a grotesquely humorous study of the rebellion of everyday objects, to music by Paul Hindemith. Like Richter, Ruttmann moved from pure abstraction, in his series *Opus I, II, III, IV* (1921–4), to the abstract treatment of real objects in the 'Falkentraum' sequence in Part 1 of LANG's DIE NIBELUNGEN (1924). In 1951 Richter compiled an anthology, *Thirty Years of Experiment*, of work by Eggeling, Ruttmann, and himself.

In Germany in the early days of sound, Oskar FISCHINGER embarked on a series of what he termed 'absolute film studies' using animated abstract patterns and forms as a visual counterpart to music. His ideas were used in a diluted form in the Bach section of DISNEY'S FANTASIA (1940). The approach initiated by Fischinger was capable of more development and abstraction than photographed interpretation of music. In similar but more complex style was the work in the United States of designer Mary Ellen Bute and cameraman Ted Nemeth who in the forties made a series of films counterpointing image and music; outstanding examples are *Toccata and Fugue* (1940) and *Tarantella* (1941). Recent work in this territory has included *To Our Children's Children's Children* (1970), by John HALAS and Harold Whitaker, in which striking optical techniques create abstract shapes of pure colour with a stained-glass effect.

The painter Marcel Duchamp achieved an almost three-dimensional effect by using motorized optical devices—rotating drawings on discs of concentric or eccentric rings—in the famous anagrammatically-titled *Cinéma Anémic* (1926), made in collaboration with Man Ray and Marc ALLÉGRET. In later years Duchamp used the same kinetic methods in Richter's surrealist film *Dreams That Money Can Buy* (1944).

One of the most original pioneers of the mid-thirties was Len LYE who broke fresh ground by freeing the abstract film from photographic techniques. He made the historic *Colour Box* (1935) by working directly on film stock and developed a mathematical basis for hand-painting abstract images on film. Norman MCLAREN, working with Lye at the GPO Film Unit (see CROWN FILM UNIT), became particularly interested in synthetic sound-track. Starting with *Allegro* (1939) he followed up the experiments of Fischinger and Moholy-Nagy, physically inscribing 'noises' on the sound-track. McLaren's subsequent work for the NATIONAL FILM BOARD of Canada made his name as an animator, but has recurrently shown abstract tendencies.

The possibilities of synthetic sound were further developed in the complex post-Fischinger work of John and James WHITNEY, who have explored the use of computers, with their capacity to adopt and scan patterns of dots, to create complex abstract effects.

In the fifties Len Lye returned to the experimental field with *Colour Cry* (1952), *Rhythm* (1957), and *Free Radicals* (1958), then turned to 'tangible motion' sculptures which attempt a blend of film and kinetic art.

**ACADEMY AWARD** see OSCAR

**ACADEMY CINEMA,** London, founded in 1931 by Elsie Cohen with the object of showing interesting foreign films which were at the time almost inaccessible to the British public. The first film to be shown at the Academy was DOV-ZHENKO'S ZEMLYA (*Earth,* 1930). At first the policy was to show revivals, repeats, and major classics, but new foreign films soon made up the staple programme. The Academy was taken over by George HOELLERING in 1947. The opening of Academy Two in 1965 and Academy Three in 1967 widened the choice of programmes, and with both example and generous advice the Academy has provided a lead for ART HOUSES throughout the country.

**ACADEMY FRAME.** Frame size adopted to accommodate the sound track down one side of a 35mm print while maintaining the picture proportions of 1·33 : 1 which had become accepted before the introduction of sound (see ASPECT RATIO). The academy frame (standardized by the ACADEMY OF MOTION PICTURE ARTS AND SCIENCES) is still the standard for all films not using a WIDE SCREEN or ANAMORPHIC process.

**ACADEMY LEADER** see LEADER

**ACADEMY OF MOTION PICTURE ARTS AND SCIENCES** (AMPAS) was formed by the US film industry in 1927 with the declared aim of raising the educational, cultural, and technical standards of film-making. The original thirty-six members were drawn from the most influential production companies and also included major film personalities: the first president was Douglas FAIRBANKS. There are now members representing all branches of the industry. AMPAS owns a collection of films and an extensive library of printed matter relating to film, and is responsible for the annual presentation of OSCARS (Academy Awards) for outstanding achievement in the previous year's productions.

*ACCATONE,* Italy, 1961. 2hr. *Dir, scr* Pier Paolo Pasolini; *asst dir* Bernardo Bertolucci; *prod* Alfredo Bini; *ph* Tonino Delli Colli; *ed* Nino Baragli; *cast* Franco Citti (Accatone), Silvana Corsini (Maddalena), Franca Pasut (Stella).

PASOLINI'S first film is the story of a pimp who falls in love, and tries to earn an honest living working in a scrap-metal yard; unable to stand the job's physical hardness, Accatone turns to petty thieving; he escapes arrest but is killed in a road accident.

The film is a clear reflection both of Pasolini's novel of sub-proletarian Rome, *Ragazzi di Vita,* and his own life in Rome in the years before he began to work as a scriptwriter.

The film used no professional actors, and its antecedents in NEO-REALISM are also apparent in the depiction of Rome's vicious suburban milieu, which is ironically commented on by the J. S. Bach sound-track. But neo-realist compassion is integrated with the complex probing of the character of Accatone.

*ACCIDENT,* GB, 1967. Eastman Colour; 1¾hr. *Dir* Joseph Losey; *prod* Royal Avenue Chelsea; *scr* Harold Pinter; *ph* Gerry Fisher; *des* Carmen Dillon; *mus* John Dankworth; *cast* Dirk Bogarde (Stephen), Stanley Baker (Charley), Jacqueline Sassard (Anna), Michael York (William), Vivien Merchant (Rosalind), Delphine Seyrig (Francesca), Alexander Knox (the Provost), Ann Firbank (Laura).

The arrival of the beautiful Anna (the visitor-as-intruder is a favourite LOSEY theme) reveals the tensions lying beneath the stillness of an Oxford summer; the resulting conflicts—sexual, social, and intellectual—are subtly expressed through Harold PINTER's dialogue, which maintains a bland surface of apparent inconsequentiality. The film's dislocated time structure attests to the influence of Alain RESNAIS, fully acknowledged by Losey. Losey's visual style, often criticized as unnecessarily baroque, attained a new simplicity in Carmen Dillon's settings: the burden of expression falls on his actors, with Dirk BOGARDE and Stanley BAKER in particular giving their finest performances in any of his films.

*ACE IN THE HOLE* (or *The Big Carnival*), US, 1951. 1¾hr. *Dir, prod* Billy Wilder for Paramount; *scr* Wilder, Lesser Samuels, Walter Newman; *ph* Charles Lang Jr; *cast* Kirk Douglas (Charles Tatum), Jan Sterling (Lorraine), Bob Arthur (Herbie Cook).

The rescue of a man trapped underground is deliberately delayed by a failed news reporter (Kirk DOUGLAS) in order to heighten the story's news value. A brilliant attack on the sensation-mongering Press and the sensation-hungry public alike, the film is a reflection of WILDER's characteristically sardonic assessment of human behaviour as essentially self-serving or foolish; but this cynicism was not tempered by Wilder's customary ribald wit and flair for comic invention, and *Ace in the Hole* was a commercial disaster in spite of intensive selling by PARAMOUNT under its alternative title.

**'A' certificate,** category instituted by the BRITISH BOARD OF FILM CENSORS, soon after it was established in 1912, to designate films suitable for general public viewing. From 1921 the 'A' certificate came to describe films more suitable for adults, and children under sixteen were admitted only when accompanied by an adult. With the introduction of the 'AA' CERTIFICATE in 1970, unaccompanied children were admitted to 'A' certificate films, the category serving to indicate that some parents might consider the film not wholly suitable for children. (See CENSORSHIP, GB.)

**ACETATE** see SAFETY FILM

**ACTING.** In the earliest days of cinema it was obvious that actors should be in the main drawn from the theatre. But drawbacks quickly became apparent: particularly in the English-speaking world, films were despised by actors of any standing and they appeared on the screen only with reluctance. When they did appear, the declamatory, large-scale style of acting currently fashionable looked ridiculous when further enlarged on the cinema screen; in addition, the harsh lighting (natural or artificial) necessary with insensitive ORTHOCHROMATIC film cruelly exposed mature faces. Stage actors continued to appear in films, notably in the FILM D'ART productions in France and in the 'Famous Players in Famous Plays' series initiated by Adolph ZUKOR. These had cultural prestige, and appearances by internationally-famous stage stars (Sarah BERNHARDT, Eleonora DUSE, Beerbohm Tree) had some curiosity value. For the bulk of entertainment films, however, actors were created from raw material, chosen for youth and good looks. D. W. GRIFFITH was particularly adept at finding young girls who epitomized the innocent appeal of his heroines and at teaching them to convey feeling by facial and bodily expression: outstanding among his discoveries were Mary PICKFORD and Lillian GISH, who became the greatest actresses of the American silent cinema.

In Europe the ties between theatre and cinema were closer, although an actor would typically move from theatre to films and not vice versa. Asta NIELSEN brought screen acting to a degree of accomplishment paralleled only by Lillian Gish, and usually with much stronger material; Emil JANNINGS, although his performances now seem overstrained, acquired a large following with his energetic characterizations; and Hollywood benefited from the acquisition of a number of talented actors from Europe, including Jannings, Greta GARBO, Pola NEGRI, Charles LAUGHTON, and Lars HANSON.

Technical improvements and the development of more sophisticated audience tastes were accompanied by increasing refinement of acting style, so that by 1927 Janet GAYNOR, in F. W. MURNAU's SUNRISE, could give a performance of delicacy and conviction that remains completely acceptable to modern audiences. Garbo's silent acting had a luminous intensity that she was able to carry over into sound films, aided by a deep yet clear voice and an accent that was intriguing but comprehensible.

The introduction of sound inevitably caused some casualties among the Hollywood stars. Inadequate spoken English sent Jannings and Pola Negri back to Europe, and voices of an unattractive quality were made worse by primitive sound recording equipment: John GILBERT's career was undermined by the weakness of his voice. Not all established film actors were able to adapt from mime to spoken drama and not all stage actors could scale down their performances to the intimacy demanded by the camera. Stage actors who developed into important stars possessed a quality of personal magnetism as well as the ability to allow the camera to capture changing expressions. Bette DAVIS, Humphrey BOGART, Cary GRANT, Katharine HEPBURN, Edward G. ROBINSON, Spencer TRACY, Henry FONDA, all succeeded by this combination of distinctive personality and technical skill. TYPECASTING, however, limited the Hollywood actor's range, and valuable star properties were too often required to play variations on a successful role (see also STAR SYSTEM).

Screen comedy changed radically with the introduction of sound. The characteristic mobility and agility on which silent comedy depended could not be accommodated by the relatively static early sound camera; besides, dialogue was considered all-important in the new situation. As a result, SLAPSTICK and its derived styles of physical humour, developed by CHAPLIN, KEATON, LANGDON, LAUREL AND HARDY, was superseded by verbal, wise-cracking comedy.

Cross-fertilization between stage and screen led to the development of a subdued, naturalistic style of acting, although to later audiences the clichés and mannerisms in Hollywood films of the thirties and forties are as apparent as in earlier silent films. Male stars, in particular, cultivated a hygienic smoothness: even in scenes of physical endurance they were allowed to show only superficial signs of exertion or suffering. These conventions began to break down in the early fifties when Elia KAZAN brought a new acting style to the screen. The realistic effect of performances by Marlon BRANDO, James DEAN, and others made a tremendous impact on American film acting. Their style, derived from the teachings of STANISLAVSKY via the ACTORS' STUDIO, is as susceptible to mannerism as any other, but its introduction into Hollywood aroused a new interest in the actor's creative function.

Outside the US and Britain the boundaries between film and stage acting remained relatively undefined after the introduction of sound. Particularly in France, the actor was respected as an artist rather than a commercial commodity, and the pre-war films of Jean RENOIR gave actors a freedom in creating their roles that has rarely been equalled. The use of non-actors to play roles similar to their own in real life (which goes back to EISENSTEIN and recurred in MENSCHEN AM SONNTAG, 1929) became an important element of NEO-REALISM in post-war Italy. The idea has been taken up frequently since, especially in fiction films aiming at a documentary effect such as those of Ken LOACH. Lack of technique can make a non-professional appear more artificial than a skilled actor, but the obvious problems can be successfully overcome by an authoritative director such as Robert BRESSON.

Some of the greatest screen acting has been in films by directors who have themselves had experience as actors. Renoir and DUVIVIER in France; DE SICA and FELLINI in Italy; Carol REED in Britain; Griffith, STROHEIM, and Martin RITT in America; PUDOVKIN and Sergei BONDARCHUK in the USSR; KINUGASA and MIZOGUCHI in Japan, demonstrate that personal understanding of the actor's craft can strengthen the collaboration between director and cast. At the Moscow Film School (VGIK) students taking the directors' course are required to study acting in addition to the various technical aspects of filmmaking.

*ACTOR'S REVENGE, An,* see YUKINOJO HENGE

**ACTORS' STUDIO, The,** was founded in New York in 1947 by Elia KAZAN and Cheryl Crawford, later joined by Lee Strasberg. Strasberg, Crawford, and Harold Clurman had in the thirties created the Group Theatre, producing socially committed plays according to the precepts of STANISLAVSKY: the Actors' Studio is an extension of this. There is a limited number of full members, usually established actors, who work on their acting technique and interpretation of character, aiming at a naturalistic effect; improvisation and group discussion play an important part. The product of the approach (the 'Method' or 'Method acting' as it has come to be generally known) is shown in the screen performances of Eli WALLACH, Shelley WINTERS, Rod STEIGER, Anthony QUINN, Montgomery CLIFT, and perhaps most typically in those of Marlon BRANDO and James DEAN. In its more extreme forms it may be far removed from Stanislavsky's concept; its naturalism often descends into apparent incoherence, and the technique may become a barrier rather than an aid to convincing characterization. The Studio has a group, also limited in number, of 'observers'; among these its influence is noticeable in the work of Arthur MILLER in particular.

**ACTT** (Association of Cinematograph, Television and Allied Technicians), the British trade union representing all technical grades of film production. ACT (Association of Cine-Technicians) was formed in 1933, but the union's effectiveness dates from the appointment of George Elvin as General Secretary in 1935. Anthony ASQUITH (in 1934 the first film director to join: Thorold DICKINSON and Ivor MONTAGU were also early members) was President from 1937 until his death in 1968, when Elvin succeeded him. Renamed the Association of Cinematograph and Allied Technicians in 1947 (television was included in 1956), the union has been a political watch-dog on the film industry. ACTT is also an employment exchange, allocating technicians to jobs, but continual unemployment has made entry to the union (and thus to the industry) increasingly difficult. Its own co-operative production company produces films for the Trade Union movement and has made several features.

*ÅDALEN 31,* Sweden, 1969. Technicolor; 2hr. *Dir, scr, ed* Bo Widerberg; *prod* Svensk Filmindustri; *ph* Jörgen Persson; *cast* Peter Schildt (Kjell), Kerstin Tidelius (his mother), Roland Hedlund (Harald), Stefan Feierbach (Åke), Marie de Geer (Anna), Anita Björk (Anna's mother).

A historical episode, the suppression of a strikers' demonstration by troops in 1931, is treated from the point of view of a working-class family whose eldest son is in love with the factory owner's daughter. Returning to the social setting of KVARTERET KORPEN (1963), WIDERBERG handles this grim theme with the visual lyricism he employed in ELVIRA MADIGAN (1967).

*ADAM'S RIB,* US, 1949. 1¾hr. *Dir* George Cukor; *prod* MGM; *scr* Ruth Gordon, Garson Kanin; *ph* George J. Folsey; *des* Cedric Gibbons, William Ferrari; *mus* Miklos Rozsa; *cast* Spencer Tracy (Adam Bonner), Katharine Hepburn (Amanda Bonner), Judy Holliday (Doris Attinger), Tom Ewell (Warren Attinger), David Wayne (Kip Lurie), Jean Hagen (Beryl Caign).

TRACY and HEPBURN stylishly act out a variation on the sex-war theme: husband as prosecutor, wife as defending counsel using the courtroom as a feminist platform, carry their professional battle into their private life.

The accomplished playing and impeccable timing of the two stars is a delight; yet it is not among their most attractive comedies. CUKOR directed the film in a deliberately artificial manner, emphasizing its theatricality by the use of an immobile camera through long dialogue exchanges; and the script is only intermittently witty and inventive. The film's distinction lies in the fine acting of its stars and of some of the supporting players, notably the engaging Judy HOLLIDAY.

**ADDAMS, DAWN** (1930– ), British actress, has worked in Hollywood and England since 1950. She was chosen by CHAPLIN to star with him in *A King in New York* (1957); her other films have been less notable.

**ADDINSELL, RICHARD** (1904– ), British composer, began his career in the cinema with RKO in 1933. Returning to Britain in 1936, he wrote a number of film scores including those for *Fire Over England* (1937), *Good-bye Mr Chips* (1939), and GASLIGHT (1940); and he achieved a spectacular popular success with the 'Warsaw Concerto' in *Dangerous Moonlight* (1941), for which he received a decoration from the Polish government in exile. Other films for which he composed scores include *Blithe Spirit* (1945), *A Diary for Timothy* (Humphrey JENNINGS, 1946), *Under Capricorn* (Alfred HITCHCOCK, 1949), MACBETH (1960), *The Roman Spring of Mrs Stone* (1961).

**ADDISON, JOHN** (1920– ), British composer, a major figure in British film music since the late forties, equally adept at writing for extrovert comedies or intense dramas and thrillers. His many film scores include those for *The Guinea Pig* (1948), *Seven Days to Noon* (1950), *The Man Between* (1953), *Reach for the Sky* (1956), and *Girl with Green Eyes* (1963). He has worked frequently for Tony RICHARDSON: on *The Entertainer* (1960), A TASTE OF HONEY (1961), *The Loneliness of the Long Distance Runner* (1962), TOM JONES (1963), for which he won an OSCAR, *The Loved One* (1965), and *The Charge of the Light Brigade* (1968).

**ADDITIVE COLOUR.** When red, green, and blue lights—the additive primary colours—are projected overlapping on to a screen, they add together to produce the effect of any other colour including white, depending on their relative brightnesses. The principle is used for colour television: it was applied to motion pictures in such early processes as KINEMACOLOR (1906), CHRONOCHROME (1912), and was revived for DUFAYCOLOR (1932); but the successful use of colour in the cinema developed from the introduction of SUBTRACTIVE colour processes in 1916. (See also COLOUR.)

**ADIEU PHILIPPINE,** France, 1962. 1¾hr. *Dir* Jacques Rozier; *prod* United France, Alpha Prod, Rome–Paris Films; *scr* Michèle O'Glor, Rozier; *ph* René Mathelin; *mus* Jacques Denjean, Maxime Saury, Paul Mattei; *cast* Jean-Claude

Aimini (Michel), Yveline Cery (Liliane), Stefania Sabatini (Juliette), Vittorio Caprioli (Pachala).

A picaresque film relating the last few months of freedom of a young television technician about to be called up to serve in Algeria, and his adventures with two inseparable girls.

*Adieu Philippine* combined a fictional structure with the newly developed techniques of CINÉMA-VÉRITÉ, using concealed microphones and cameras in real locations, actors who were for the most part amateurs, and partially improvised dialogue. As in ROZIER's earlier short, *Blue Jeans* (1958), music played an important part in determining the rhythm of the editing.

With its informal spontaneity, gaiety, and cavalier attitude to the traditions of narrative cinema, the film was very much of its time, encapsulating a precise moment of contemporary French history both social and cinematic. Unfortunately, it was expensive by NOUVELLE VAGUE standards (owing mainly to the use of two cameras and chronic delays during the editing) and involved Rozier in a dispute with the original producer, Georges de Beauregard.

**ADVENTURER, The,** US, 1917. 30min. *Dir, scr* Charles Chaplin; *prod* Mutual; *ph* Rollie Totheroh, William C. Foster; *cast* Charles Chaplin (the convict), Edna Purviance (the rich girl), Eric Campbell (her suitor), Henry Bergman (her father), Frank J. Coleman (the guard), Kono (the chauffeur), Albert Austin.

The last of CHAPLIN's twelve comedies for the MUTUAL Film Corporation is unpretentious and full of good old-fashioned SLAPSTICK. That is perhaps why it is still so popular, particularly a staple favourite—like THE PAWNSHOP (1916)—at children's parties. Charlie is an escaped prisoner who, dressed in a stolen swimsuit, saves two rich women from drowning and, in their home, pretends to be as wealthy and fashionable as they. His rival—as in all the Mutual films—is burly Eric Campbell (who was killed in a car crash soon after). When he sees Charlie's picture in the newspaper, he calls the police and a typically mad, inventive chase results.

**AFFAIRE EST DANS LE SAC, L',** France, 1932. 45min. *Dir* Pierre Prévert; *prod* Pathé-Nathan; *scr* Jacques Prévert; *ph* Gibory; *mus* Maurice Jaubert; *cast* Lora Hays (Gloria), Julien Carette (Clovis), J.-P. Dreyfus (Dutilleul), Gildès (Hollister).

A satirical burlesque, in which the basic story (a bored millionaire will marry his daughter only to a man who can amuse him) erupts into all kinds of comic and surrealist incidents, including a kidnapping plot. The bold satire and irreverence for contemporary values outraged the public at the time and the film was a commercial

*L'Affaire est dans le sac* (Pierre Prévert, 1932)

failure, but in it many of the classic elements of French film comedy can be recognized.

**AFRICAN QUEEN, The,** GB, 1952. Technicolor; 1¾hr. *Dir* John Huston; *prod* Romulus–Horizon; *scr* James Agee, Huston, from the novel by C. S. Forester; *ph* Jack Cardiff; *cast* Katharine Hepburn (Rose Sayer), Humphrey Bogart (Charlie Allnutt), Robert Morley (Brother Samuel Sayer), Peter Bull (German captain), Theodore Bikel (German first officer).

Accomplished acting, skilful characterization, and fine location photography distinguish this story of a missionary's sister and the hard-bitten captain of a small trading boat involved with a German gunboat in German East Africa after the outbreak of the First World War. With his leading players, HUSTON transforms a somewhat improbable adventure-romance into a convincing story of love growing out of shared endurance, told with endearing humour.

The film is virtually a duologue between Humphrey BOGART, who, as the intrepid Charlie Allnutt, adroitly manages the change from uncouth and uncaring drifter to a man of devotion, perseverance, and courage, and Katharine HEPBURN, at her superb best as the prim spinster whose prudishness

turns into warmth and tolerance. Bogart won his only OSCAR for this performance.

**ÂGE D'OR, L',** France, 1930. 1hr. *Dir* Luis Buñuel; *prod* Vicomte de Noailles; *scr* Buñuel, Salvador Dali; *ph* Albert Dubergen; *des* Schilzneck; *mus* Wagner, Mendelssohn, Beethoven, Debussy; *cast* Gaston Modot, Lya Lys, Max Ernst, Pierre Prévert, Caridad de Laberdesque, Madame Noizet.

BUÑUEL's second film, perhaps his definitive work, in fact owes little to Salvador DALI. Two lovers (Gaston MODOT and Lya Lys) declare war on a bourgeois society intent on thwarting the fulfilment of their desire. Charged with a surrealistic glee, *L'Âge d'or* shows a blind man being beaten, a dowager being slapped, a father punishing his son for a misdemeanour by shooting him down. In the final section of the film Buñuel doffs his hat to the Marquis de Sade, whose ideas on liberty the director holds dear.

Shown at STUDIO 28, *L'Âge d'or* was officially banned after the cinema had been wrecked by a protesting mob of right-wing extremists.

**AGEE, JAMES** (1909–55), US writer. His Tennessee childhood is captured in the novel *A*

*Death in the Family* (filmed in 1963 as *All the Way Home*) and his anguished adult private life—his struggles against the pressures of money, alcohol, tobacco, and suicidal urges—is partially revealed in his *Letters to Father Flye* (published 1962). During the forties, after years of uncongenial journalistic assignments, he made his reputation as film critic for *The Nation*, at the same time working anonymously in the same capacity on *Time* (and on occasion writing contradictory reviews for the two journals). He also wrote essays on such topics as the silent screen comedians, including his hero CHAPLIN, and John HUSTON. His criticism has been admired since for its exactness of description, prose quality, eclectic sympathies, and perceptiveness. In 1941 he had collaborated with Walker Evans, the photographer, to produce a documentary book, *Let Us Now Praise Famous Men*. His first work in films was the commentary for *The Quiet One* (Sidney Meyers, 1948). He went on to write distinguished scripts, including 'The Bride Comes to Yellow Sky' (an episode of *Face to Face*, 1952), in which he played a small part, THE AFRICAN QUEEN (1952), THE NIGHT OF THE HUNTER (1955), and a major life of LINCOLN for television. Among his unproduced scripts is *Noa-Noa* (1953), which was derived from Gauguin's diaries. After his death, both criticism and scripts were collected into the two volumes of *Agee on Film*, New York, 1958; London, 1963.

**AGFACOLOR,** an early colour system developed in Germany by Agfa Filmfabrik and the ancestor of many of today's colour film stocks.

Agfacolor was first introduced as a 16mm REVERSAL film in 1936, a year later than Kodachrome. Both were multilayer films, in which three emulsions sensitive to the three primary colours were laid on a single film base. When the Second World War isolated German technology, Agfa continued to develop Agfacolor into a negative–positive process similar to EASTMAN COLOR. It was used on a number of German feature films, including Goebbels's morale-building epic *Kolberg* (1945) and the fantasy *Münchhausen* (1943). With Germany's defeat the Agfacolor patents were taken over by the Russians to form the basis of their SOVCOLOR and the East German ORWOCOLOR. In America, the Agfa subsidiary continued under US control to produce ANSCO COLOR and Anscochrome in competition with Kodak colour film stocks. In West Germany manufacture continues under the name Agfa-Gevaert.

Agfacolor and most of its derivatives are characterized by comparatively soft colours which some cinematographers consider more natural than Eastman Color.

**AGIT-PROP,** Russian term coined from *agita-tsiya-propaganda*, a means of informing and educating the masses in political principles and ideas. The cinema was used extensively for the purpose in post-revolutionary Russia, the films being known as *agitki*. NEWSREELS and DOCUMENTARIES as well as politically oriented feature films have been used to this end up to the present day.

*AGNUS DEI* see ÉGI BÁRÁNY

**AGOSTINI,** PHILIPPE (1910– ), French cameraman, chiefly notable for his work with BRESSON on *Les Anges du péche* (1943) and *Les Dames du Bois de Boulogne* (1945). The stylized imagery of these is in contrast with the sharp realism of his photography for DU RIFIFI CHEZ LES HOMMES (1955). He has also directed several films, mostly of a religious nature, such as *Le Dialogue des Carmelites* (1959).

**AHERNE,** BRIAN (1902– ), British actor, who began in the theatre and continued to act regularly on the stage until 1960. *The Squire of Long Hadley* (1925) was the first of several English films, but his Hollywood career began with *Song of Songs* (1933). He was the charming but caddish hero, a part he played very effectively in a number of films. The Emperor Maximilian in *Juarez* (1939) provided a change and an OSCAR nomination as best supporting actor. Later parts included the engaging friar/uncle in *The Swan* (1956) and an embittered King Arthur in *Lancelot and Guinevere* (1962, *Sword of Lancelot* in US).

**AIMÉE,** ANOUK (1932– ), French actress, real name Françoise Sorya. Educated in France and England, she has made films in various languages. Her first starring part was as Juliet in *Les Amants de Vérone* (PRÉVERT and CAYATTE, 1948), which was followed by a number of romantic leading roles; working with FELLINI, in LA DOLCE VITA (1960) and OTTO E MEZZO ($8\frac{1}{2}$, 1963), she emerged as an actress of real strength and sensitivity. Her work with Jacques DEMY, in LOLA (1961) and *The Model Shop* (1968), is notable, and the wide popularity of Claude LELOUCH's *Un Homme et une femme* (1966) made her an international star. She played the title role in George CUKOR's *Justine* (1969) and has also worked for DUVIVIER, DE SICA, FRANJU, and many other distinguished directors. In 1970 she married Albert FINNEY, her third husband.

*AKAHIGE* (*Red Beard*), Japan, 1965. Tohoscope; 3hr. *Dir* Akira Kurosawa; *prod* Kurosawa Films/Toho; *scr* Kurosawa, Ryuzo Kukishima, Hideo Oguni, Masato Ide, from the novel by Shugoro Yamamoto; *ph* Asaichi Nakai, Takao Saito; *cast* Toshiro Mifune (Akahige), Yuzo Kayama (Yasumoto), Kamatari Fujiwara (Rokusuke), Tsutomu Yamakazi (Sahachi), Terumi Niki (Otoyo).

Yasumoto, newly qualified as a doctor, believes he will be practising among the aristocracy but finds he is to treat poor clinic patients. Under the guidance of Akahige, the fanatical clinic head who sees the battle against disease as a fight against evil, he painfully learns to distinguish the delights of professional prestige from the rewards of healing the sick.

*Akahige* is set in the historical period of KUROSAWA's swashbuckling samurai films, but its material and treatment lie more within the style of his modern films such as IKIRU (1952) and his adaptations from Dostoevsky. The plot is long and complex, concentrating on social detail sometimes at the expense of narrative tautness. Comparisons with Western medical dramas of the Dr Kildare type are inevitable, and Kurosawa's tendency to sentimentality gives them substance; but this tendency is offset by the finely controlled visual style as well as by Toshiro MIFUNE's masterly performance as the autocratic, compassionate Akahige.

**ALAMO, The,** fort improvised from old mission buildings in San Antonio, Texas, scene in March 1836 of the desperate stand of some 180 TEXICANS and Americans (Davy CROCKETT and James Bowie among them) against General Santa Anna's Mexican army of three or four thousand men. The defenders were all killed: their action served to rally Texican forces against Santa Anna, with the cry, 'Remember the Alamo', during the remainder of Texas's struggle for independence from Mexico.

The battle has featured in many films, notably *The Last Command* (1955). John WAYNE directed a 2½-hour version of the incident, *The Alamo* (1960), in which he also played Davy Crockett. Richard WIDMARK co-starred as Jim Bowie, and Laurence HARVEY gave a chilly performance as Travis, commander of the fort. A lavish if uninspired production, the film offers in its course an adequate compound of every ingredient dear to the heart of WESTERN fans. The '1824' conspicuous on flags in the fort refers to the year in which a new, federal, constitution had been introduced in Mexico, only to be promptly abrogated by Santa Anna.

**ALAZRAKI, BENITO** (1923–  ), Mexican director and producer, first worked as producer and co-writer for Emilio FERNANDEZ's *Enamorada* (1946). He is best known for his first feature film *Raices* (*Roots*, 1955), which he also scripted in collaboration with Carlos Velo. *Raices* is composed of four short stories of Mexican Indian life, based on the writings of Francisco Gonzales. The film was internationally praised, and received a prize at CANNES in 1955, but his later films were less individual

**ALBANIA.** Film production did not begin until 1947, and Albania is the smallest film-making country in Eastern Europe. Only documentaries and newsreels were made during the first decade of production. Studios were set up in 1953, under state control, and the first Albanian feature film followed four years later. A Soviet production was actually the first feature film made in Albania, the story of a national hero, *Velikii voin Albanii Skanderbeg* (*The Great Warrior Skanderbeg*, 1954) directed by YUTKEVICH.

The production of feature films was limited to one per year until 1966, since when it has gradually increased. Although the films have tended to draw predominantly on Albanian history, contemporary themes have been dealt with, as in Dhamo's *Tana* (1958), an examination of modern rural life, and Gjika's *Horizonte të hapura* (*Broad Horizons*, 1968), which has an industrial setting.

By the mid-sixties there were seventy-six cinemas in the country, which also makes large use of a number of mobile cinemas, important in reaching remote rural areas.

Despite the small size of the industry, Albania boasts its own film archive.

**ALBATROS** see KAMENKA

**ALDO, G. R.** (1902–53), Italian cameraman, real name Aldo Graziati, went to France in 1920 intending to become an actor. He worked as a still photographer in Paris for twenty-five years before becoming a cameraman. Recognized as a master of lighting and composition, Aldo photographed among other films LA TERRA TREMA (1948), MIRACOLO A MILANO (1951), UMBERTO D (1952). He was killed in a car crash during the making of SENSO (1954).

**ALDRICH, ROBERT** (1918–  ), US director, went to Hollywood in the forties after turning his back on a successful family business. Within a comparatively short time he was working as first assistant to such distinguished directors as Jean RENOIR, Lewis MILESTONE, and William WELLMAN, but following *Abbott and Costello Meet Captain Kidd* (1952), on which he assisted Charles Lamont, he began a short career in television, which ended when METRO-GOLDWYN-MAYER asked him to direct his first feature, *The Big Leaguer*, in 1953. He became his own producer in 1955 with *Kiss Me Deadly* and *The Big Knife*. All the films over which he has had production control have been criticized for their extreme violence, in particular the bizarre *Whatever Happened to Baby Jane?* (1962) and *The Dirty Dozen* (1967), set in a military prison: both were commercially very successful.

In 1968 Aldrich opened his own independent studio. That he patently despises the Hollywood system is obvious in *The Legend of Lylah Clare* (1968) which was almost totally suppressed by the distributors, MGM. His films have also been heavily cut by the censors, particularly the explicit lesbian scenes in *The Killing of Sister George* (1968). He seems invariably to gravitate to the sensational but he has a direct and unhypocritical approach to subjects that Hollywood has traditionally handled in a genteel or blunted fashion.

**ALEA,** TOMÁS GUTIÉRREZ (1928– ), Cuban director, made amateur films while a student, including *Una Confusion cotidiana* (1948), co-directed with Nestor ALMENDROS. From 1950 he studied at the CENTRO SPERIMENTALE in Rome and on his return to Cuba co-directed with Julio Garcia Espinosa *El Mengano* (1956) about the miners of Cienaga de Zapata: the film showed considerable promise but suffered from official interference. The three-part *Historias de la Revolucion* (1961) placed him at the forefront of Cuban directors after the revolution of 1959 (see CUBA). *Las Doce Sillas* (1962), a transposition of Ilf and Petrov's novel *The Twelve Chairs* to a Cuban setting, and *Muerte de un burocrata* (1966) were vehicles for an effectively satirical attack on officialdom. World attention was caught by Alea's MEMORIAS DE SUBDESAROLLO (*Memories of Underdevelopment*, 1968) which, like the first part of *Historias de la Revolucion*, examined the role of the intellectual in the Cuban revolution. *Una Pelea Cubana contra los demonios* (*A Cuban Fight Against the Demons*, 1972) examined superstition, fear, and subjection in a seventeenth-century Cuban village.

**ALEKAN, HENRI** (1909– ), French cameraman, after working as assistant to such notable cinematographers as Georges PÉRINAL and Eugen SCHÜFFTAN, photographed several outstanding films including LA BATAILLE DU RAIL (1946) and LA BELLE ET LA BÊTE (1946). Since the early sixties he has usually worked on large-scale international productions such as *Mayerling* (1968).

***ALEXANDER NEVSKY,*** USSR, 1938. 1¾hr. *Dir, ed* S. M. Eisenstein; *prod* Mosfilm; *scr* Eisenstein, Piotr Pavlenko; *asst dir* D. I. Vasiliev;

*Alexander Nevsky* (S. M. Eisenstein, 1938)

*ph* Edvard Tissé; *des* Isaac Schpinel, Nikolai Soloviov, from sketches by Eisenstein; *mus* Sergei Prokofiev; *cast* Nikolai Cherkassov (Alexander Nevsky), Nikolai Okhlopov (Vasili Buslai), Alexander Abrikosov (Gavrilo Olexich), Dmitri Orlov (Ignat), Vasili Novikov (Pavsha).

After the series of abortive and rejected projects which had made up EISENSTEIN's working life since STAROYE I NOVOYE (*Old and New*, 1929), he was allowed to direct *Alexander Nevsky* under strict supervision from a picked team of co-workers. The result, a historical epic based on the thoroughly acceptable political theme of a people's army led by a popular hero, driving brutal Teutonic invaders from the soil of Holy Russia, was enormously popular. The film was, however, withdrawn at the time of the German-Soviet Pact in 1939 and not shown again until the German invasion of Russia.

Eisenstein's admirers abroad were disappointed by the conventional approach of *Alexander Nevsky*. But the film remains a remarkable visual experience, with tightly controlled formal composition; the battle on the ice is a *pièce de résistance*. The close collaboration of PROKOFIEV made the music an integral part of the action.

**ALEXANDROV,** GRIGORI (1903– ), Russian director, real name Mormenko, was employed at first in the theatre as an acrobat and in various back-stage capacities, including stage management at the Proletkult theatre in Moscow under Meyerhold while EISENSTEIN was director there (1920–2). He became assistant director to Eisenstein on STACHKA (*Strike*) and BRONE-NOSETS POTEMKIN (*The Battleship Potemkin*, both 1925). On OKTIABR (1928) and STAROYE I NOVOYE (*Old and New*, 1929) he co-directed and in 1929 he accompanied Eisenstein and TISSÉ to Europe and the US to study Western developments in film technique. While in France Alexandrov and Tissé collaborated on ROMANCE SEN-TIMENTALE (1930), a short non-narrative film using many of the new sound and camera techniques. On his return to the USSR Alexandrov made *Internationale* (1932), his first film as sole director.

With *Vesyolye rebyata* (*Jazz Comedy*, 1934) he introduced the big Hollywood-style musical to the USSR, using many Western techniques including filming action to a pre-recorded music track. The score was by SHOSTAKOVICH. His next films, *Tsirk* (*Circus*, 1936) and *Volga-Volga* (1938), were also musicals and starred Luba Orlova whom Alexandrov married. The films achieved enormous success throughout Eastern Europe: at one time there were 5000 copies of *Vesyolye rebyata* in circulation; the bonus from their profits made Alexandrov a rouble millionaire. He also directed documentaries at this time

and during the war years. In 1944 he succeeded Eisenstein as artistic director of Mosfilm and returned to directing fiction features with *Vesna* (*Spring*, 1947). His occasional films since have usually been of a celebratory kind, such as *Kompositor Glinka* (*Glinka, Man of Music*, 1952) and *Lenin v Polshe* (*Lenin in Poland*, 1961).

**ALEXEÏEFF,** ALEXANDRE (1901– ), French animator, was born in Russia and studied in Paris, where he became a book illustrator. After watching L'IDÉE (1934) in production in 1932 he experimented with animation techniques and invented the pin screen, a metal surface pierced by about five million tiny holes through which he pressed metal pins which, obliquely lit, created shadows with all possible gradations from black to white according to the length of pin protruding from the screen. With this method he made *Une Nuit sur le mont chauve* (1933), *Le Nez* (*The Nose*, 1963), from a story by Gogol, and the credit sequences for Orson Welles's *Le Procès* (*The Trial*, 1963); Claire Parker has been his collaborator since 1931. Alexeïeff has made many other animation films, some for advertising, and has become an authority on the theory and technique of animation. His book illustrations are often still photographs of images arranged on the pin screen; in particular, an illustrated edition of Boris Pasternak's *Doctor Zhivago*.

**ALGERIA.** A national cinema came into being almost spontaneously, in the late fifties and early sixties, during the war of liberation against the French. Its first products were anonymous or collectively made documentaries, recording and publicizing different aspects of the struggle. Films such as *Djazaïrouna* (*Our Algeria*, 1959), a compilation of newsreels by Chanderli and Hamina, and shorts such as their *Yasmina* (1961), which dealt with the sufferings of war refugees, were characteristic of the early Algerian cinema.

During the troubled years after independence in 1962 Algerian film-makers continued to devote themselves almost exclusively to the themes of war and liberation. There have been several very successful feature-length works on the subject. Among them are *Les Oliviers de la justice* (1962), directed by the American James Blue; Ahmed Rashidi's *L'Aube des damnés* (1965), a compilation work on African colonization, which contains rare archive material, held together with a fine commentary by the writer Mammeri; Jacques Charby's *Une si jeune paix* (1965), a fictional work dealing with the effect of the war on two bands of orphans; Selim Riad's *La Voie* (1968), the most violent and political of Algerian films; and Hamina's *Vent des Aurès*

(1966), generally recognized as one of the most important Algerian films to date. Two successful co-productions, Lovenzini's *Les Mains libres* (1965) and PONTECORVO'S LA BATTAGLIA DI ALGERI (1965), were made by the short-lived private company, Casbah Films.

The major weakness of the Algerian cinema has been its narrow range of themes. Only a tiny proportion of films concern themselves with modern social problems. An exception is Lallem's short film *Elles* (1968), a study of young schoolgirls and the changing position of women in Algerian society. Ghalem's *Mektoub* (1970), a critical study of the conditions of Algerian immigrant workers in France, has not been shown in Algeria.

State control of production and distribution (completed in 1969) allows the government to exercise firm left-wing censorship. A lack of technical equipment and training facilities is another factor inhibiting the growth of the Algerian cinema, considered among the most healthy and promising of the young African cinemas.

**ALICE IN WONDERLAND,** US, 1934. 1¼hr. *Dir* Norman McLeod; *prod* Paramount; *cast* Charlotte Henry (Alice), Gary Cooper (White Knight), Cary Grant (Mock Turtle), W. C. Fields (Humpty Dumpty).

The film combines episodes from both Lewis Carroll's classic books for children, *Alice's Adventures in Wonderland* (1865) and *Through the Looking-Glass* (1872). A long list of PARAMOUNT stars made unusual appearances with entertaining effect.

Other versions include a silent one-reeler by Cecil HEPWORTH (1906), Walt DISNEY's full-length cartoon (1951), and a British/French production in AGFACOLOR (1948) directed by Dallas Bower. The latter used puppets for all the characters except for Alice, who was played by Carol Marsh, and, in a prologue, Queen Victoria and Lewis Carroll played by Pamela BROWN and Stephen Murray. *Alice's Adventures in Wonderland* (1972), a British live-action version directed by William Sterling, was a faithful but unadventurous adaptation.

**ALL ABOUT EVE,** US, 1950. 2¼hr. *Dir, scr* Joseph L. Mankiewicz; *prod* Darryl F. Zanuck for Twentieth Century-Fox; *ph* Milton Krasna; *mus* Alfred Newman; *cast* Bette Davis (Margo), Anne Baxter (Eve), George Sanders (Addison de Witt), Gary Merrill (Bill Sampson), Celeste Holm (Karen), Thelma Ritter (Birdie), Marilyn Monroe (Miss Casswell).

Joseph L. MANKIEWICZ won OSCARS for both the script and the direction of this acidly accurate depiction of theatrical politics and an unscrupulous *ingénue*'s rise to stardom. In an excellent cast, Bette DAVIS gave one of her most dazzling performances.

**ALLÉGRET,** MARC (1900–73), French director. After taking a law degree he became secretary to André Gide, and his first film *Voyage au Congo* (1926) was made when he accompanied Gide on an expedition to Africa. He worked as assistant director to Robert FLOREY and August Genina, and began making his own films from 1931. Much of his work has considerable charm, notably *Fanny* (1932, see MARIUS), *L'Arlésienne* (1942), and *Le Bal du Comte d'Orgel* (1969). *Blanche Fury* (1947) and the misconceived *L'Amant de Lady Chatterley* (1955) are, less typically, sexual melodramas.

**ALLÉGRET,** YVES (1907– ), French director, first worked as assistant to various directors including RENOIR (*La Chienne*, 1931) and his brother Marc Allégret. During the thirties he was an active member of the left-wing GROUPE OCTOBRE. After making some advertising films he spent the war in Nice, directing under the name of Yves Champlain and reverting to his own name in 1943. He began to make a reputation in the late forties, particularly with *Dédée d'Anvers*, *Une si jolie petite plage* (both 1948), and *Manèges* (1949) which all starred Simone SIGNORET to whom he was for a time married. His later films show an uneasy compromise between the demands of the box-office and his own committed socialism.

**ALLEN,** FRED (1894–1956), US comic actor, worked in vaudeville, theatre, and radio before his first film appearance in *Thanks a Million* (1935). His numerous film appearances established him as an acid, tight-lipped comic in the mainstream tradition of American throwaway humour. *It's in the Bag* (1945, *The Fifth Chair* in GB) is a black comedy that successfully uses Allen's venomous asides.

**ALLIED ARTISTS** see MONOGRAM

**ALLIO,** RENÉ (1924– ), French director, worked as a painter and at the same time costume and set designer in the theatre. After 1957 he worked regularly with Roger Planchon's Théâtre de la Cité in Lyons, and became particularly associated with the design of the cultural centre there and in other places. Becoming interested in cinema, he began by animating one of his own designs and in 1963 made a short live-action film, *La Meule*. In 1965 he made his first feature film, LA VIEILLE DAME INDIGNE, a delightful account of how an old widowed lady starts behaving in a way quite unexpected by her family. Distinguished particularly by the performance of SYLVIE as the old lady, the film won several prizes, but has been little shown outside France. In 1967 Allio made *L'Une et l'autre* and in 1968 *Pierre et Paul*, both from his own scripts. Neither has been distributed outside France. *Les Camisards* (1970) was a more ambitious undertaking, a costume film involving large numbers of actors, many of them drawn from Planchon's company. Les Camisards was the name given to a group of Protestants in the Cévennes who, in the face of oppression after the revocation of the Edict of Nantes in 1685, became insurgents and for several years waged effective guerrilla warfare on the Royalist forces. Allio handled the spectacle and human drama with verve and sympathy, and the film was well received at foreign festivals; but, like his other films, it has not been widely seen. *Rude journée pour la reine* (1974) starred Simone SIGNORET as an overburdened housewife living out a dreary existence with the aid of romantic fantasies.

Allio, a self-confessed 'political' film-maker, differs from contemporaries who make political films—like GODARD, MARKER, and STRAUB—in that he seeks to subvert by diverting. His films are accessible in form, accomplished in achievement, and charming to the point of seductiveness. But in spite of his gentle approach, the theme of his work is insistent: that every social situation must be constantly questioned if human beings are to cease exploiting one another.

***ALL QUIET ON THE WESTERN FRONT,*** US, 1930. 2½hr. *Dir* Lewis Milestone; *prod* Universal; *scr* Milestone, Maxwell Anderson, Del Andrews, George Abbott, from the novel by Erich Maria Remarque; *ph* Arthur Edeson; *cast* Lew Ayres (Paul Baumer), Louis Wolheim (Katczinsky), John Wray (Himmelstoss), Raymond Griffith (Gerard Duval), George 'Slim' Summerville (Tjaden), Russell Gleason (Muller), William Blakewell (Albert), Scott Kolk (Leer).

Lewis MILESTONE's version of Remarque's novel is an anti-war declaration of power and realism which has scarcely diminished with the passage of time. It boldly depicts the German point of view in its story of seven boys taken straight from the classroom, imbued with patriotic fervour, and plunged into the horrors and miseries of trench warfare. Their experience brings disillusion, and when finally all but one of the seven have been killed, a new group of excited recruits arrives to take their place.

The film is distinguished by Milestone's grasp of the possibilities of using sound and his skilful editing of the single track which was all that was technically available to him (see SOUND). It is also remarkably effective in the staging of grimly impressive sequences of trench-warfare: this was probably the first time that the general public had been made vividly aware of the conditions under which men lived and fought in the trenches. Milestone made good use of the lavish resources he was given, including a large acreage of land and UNIVERSAL's new CRANE, to shoot battle-sequences so convincing that they have not infrequently found their way into COMPILATION films as actuality shots. In spite of the inadequate acting, the film compares well with PABST's WESTFRONT 1918, made the same year.

In Germany, the Nazis succeeded in having the film banned after staged demonstrations outside cinemas where it was showing (see PROPAGANDA).

***ALL THE KING'S MEN,*** US, 1949. 1¾hr. *Dir* Robert Rossen; *prod* Rossen for Columbia; *scr* Rossen from Robert Penn Warren's novel; *ph* Burnett Guffey; *ed* Al Clark; *mus* Louis Gruenberg; *cast* Broderick Crawford (Willie Stark), John Ireland (Jack Burden), Joanne Dru (Anne Stanton), Mercedes McCambridge (Sadie Burke), Anne Seymour (Lucy Stark).

The rise and fall of Governor Willie Stark, based on the career of Huey LONG. Robert Penn Warren's novel *All the King's Men*, with its account of political corruption, had interested ROSSEN when it was published in 1946 and awarded the Pulitzer Prize. Influenced by the Italian NEO-REALISM which had reached the US since the war, Rossen insisted on location shooting (in Stockton, California) but by no means broke away entirely from the studio. He also insisted on Broderick CRAWFORD, then comparatively unknown, for the leading role. Closely following the book, the film is hard-hitting. It was well received by public and critics, winning several awards including three OSCARS.

**ALLYSON,** JUNE (1926–  ), US actress, was taken up by METRO-GOLDWYN-MAYER, when she replaced Betty HUTTON in *Panama Hattie* on Broadway. Throughout the course of many films, at first all musicals, later in straight and dramatic roles, she established and maintained the 'girl next door' image, typified by her performance as Jo in *Little Women* (1949).

**ALMENDROS,** NESTOR (1930–  ), Spanish-born cameraman, went to Cuba in 1948. There he made amateur films with Tomás Gutiérrez ALEA and other young Cuban enthusiasts. He spent a year in Rome at the CENTRO SPERIMENTALE, then taught for a while in the US, where he became friendly with Maya DEREN, the MEKAS brothers, and other UNDERGROUND film-makers. After the revolution in 1959 he returned to Cuba and became a cameraman and director for ICAIC, but, unhappy with the organization's monolithic structure, he moved to France. He began his association with Eric ROHMER on the Rohmer and Douchet sections of *Paris vu par . . .* (1964): his first feature film and his first in 35mm was Rohmer's *La Collectionneuse* (1966). He went on to photograph the rest of Rohmer's six 'contes moraux', MA NUIT CHEZ MAUD (1968), LE GENOU DE CLAIRE (1970), and L'AMOUR, L' APRÈS-MIDI (1972). His work for Rohmer shows an intense awareness of characters within their physical environment, marked, especially in exterior scenes, by lighting of a diffused, luminous quality reminiscent of early Swedish films. He has also done distinguished work for François TRUFFAUT with a similar deceptive simplicity: the refined classicism of L'ENFANT SAUVAGE (1970), *Domicile conjugale* (*Bed and Board*, 1970), with its breathless evocation of crowded urban living, and *Les Deux Anglaises et le continent* (*Anne and Muriel*, 1971), which re-creates both the period and the visual style of paintings by Renoir and Monet.

*ALONE ON THE PACIFIC* see TAIHEYO HITOR-IBOCHI

**ALTMAN,** ROBERT (1925–    ), US director, became associated with film when he worked on industrial projects after serving in the Second World War. He trained in television, becoming director on series such as 'Combat' and 'Bus Stop', and earned a reputation for idiosyncracy and forthrightness. His uneasy relationships with producers continued in feature films, beginning with *Countdown* (1967) which was savagely cut for release in Britain—from 101 to 73 minutes. After making *That Cold Day in the Park* (1969) in Canada, he attracted critical praise and commercial success with a zany comedy M*A*S*H (1971). Altman continued to experiment with camera and sound techniques in the less successful *Brewster McCloud* (1971) and in *McCabe and Mrs Miller* (1972), an interesting reworking of classic WESTERN themes. *Images* (1972), filmed from his own script, was a remarkable exercise in psychological tension, winning for Susannah YORK the award for best actress at CANNES, and the diversity of his work was emphasized by *The Long Goodbye* (1973), an affectionate and intelligent version of Raymond CHANDLER's novel.

**ALVAREZ,** SANTIAGO, Cuban documentary director, worked for Cuban television as a music librarian. He entered film-making at the time of the revolution in 1959, taking charge of the weekly newsreel *Noticiero ICAIC* (see CUBA). Using an assemblage of live footage, stills, titles, and some animation, vigorously edited to a unified sound track including popular songs, speeches, sound effects, he has constructed some striking examples of AGIT-PROP cinema. Outstanding examples of the *Noticiero* which have been distributed abroad are *Now!* (1965), *Hanoi, martes 13* (1967), and *LBJ* (1969).

**ALWYN,** WILLIAM (1905–    ), British composer, made his first working contact with film when he appeared briefly as a flautist in a cinema orchestra at the age of fifteen. He studied at the Royal Academy of Music, where he later became Professor of Composition. Apart from his considerable output of orchestral and chamber music, Alwyn has composed many distinguished film scores, at first chiefly for documentaries such as FIRES WERE STARTED (1943) and *World of Plenty* (Paul ROTHA, 1943) and later for fiction features such as ODD MAN OUT (1947) and THE FALLEN IDOL (1948). Like other contemporary British composers he owed his introduction to film music to the Empire Marketing Board Film Unit (see CROWN FILM UNIT).

**AMANTS, Les,** France, 1958. 1½hr. *Dir* Louis Malle; *prod* Nouvelles Editions de Films; *scr* Malle, Louise de Vilmorin, from the book *Point de lendemain* by Dominique Vivant, Baron de Denon; *ph* Henri Decaë; *ed* Léonide Azar; *cast* Jeanne Moreau (Jeanne Tournier), Alain Cuny (Henri Tournier), Jean-Marc Bory (Bernard Dubois-Lambert), Judith Magre (Maggy Thièbout-Leroy), Gaston Modot (Coudray).

After the critical success of his first feature *L'ascenseur pour l'échafaud* (1957), MALLE asked Louise de Vilmorin to write with him a film from the moralistic love story *Point de lendemain*, published in 1777. With the story transposed to the modern *haute bourgeoisie*, the film is sharply satirical, not only of its milieu but also of prudish screen conventions. Jeanne MOREAU, closely associated with Malle at the time, gave a superb performance as the sensuous and wayward wife. It is hard now to believe that the film was regarded as scandalously erotic: it was, however, well received by critics (TRUFFAUT welcomed it as 'la première nuit d'amour au cinéma'), and had great commercial success, bringing international recognition to both Malle and Moreau.

**AMBLER,** ERIC (1909–    ), British writer, published the first of his spy stories in 1936. Several of these have been adapted for the screen, notably *Journey into Fear* (1942), started by Orson WELLES and completed by Norman Foster, and *The Mask of Dimitrios* (Jean NEGULESCO, 1944). Ambler himself worked as a scriptwriter on Army training films during the war. He scripted *The Way Ahead* (1944), in collaboration with Peter USTINOV; his subsequent scripts include *The Cruel Sea* (1952) and *A Night to Remember* (1957). He was the first of ten writers to work on the script of THE MUTINY ON THE BOUNTY (1962). His wife, Joan Harrison, is a film producer.

**AMBROSIO**, ARTURO (b. 1869), Italian producer, was one of the founders of the Italian film industry. He started making films in 1904, and established his own company in 1905, employing famous actors such as Eleonora DUSE, Armando Falconi, and Ermete Novelli. In 1911 Ambrosio signed a contract with Gabriele d'Annunzio for exclusive screen rights to the poet's work. Two big spectaculars, *Teodora* (1919) and *La nave* (1920), brought his active film career to a close.

**AMECHE**, DON (1910–   ), US actor, amiable and engaging in personality, handsome in a vaguely Latin style, made his screen début in 1936. His work was usually for TWENTIETH CENTURY-FOX, playing light-weight roles in musicals. When he played the inventor of the telephone in *The Story of Alexander Graham Bell* (1939), telephones became for a time popularly known in the US as 'Ameches'. He revealed himself as an unsuspectedly accomplished comedy actor in Ernst LUBITSCH's *Heaven Can Wait* (1943), but subsequently was for the most part cast in desultory roles in indifferent films. In 1951 he virtually retired from the cinema but he later made a few film appearances, looking as distinguished and elegant as ever, notably in DISNEY's *The Boatniks* (1970).

**AMERICAN FILM INSTITUTE** (AFI) was founded in June 1967 with funds from government and private sources, notably the National Foundation for the Arts, the Ford Foundation, and the MOTION PICTURE ASSOCIATION OF AMERICA (MPAA). Its headquarters are in the John F. Kennedy Center for the Performing Arts in Washington DC and it is administered by a Board of Trustees whose duties include the appointment of the Institute's director, the first being George STEVENS Jr.

AFI Archives, founded in 1968, is a member of the FÉDÉRATION INTERNATIONALE DES ARCHIVES DE FILM (FIAF), and works in collaboration with the Library of Congress where the AFI collection is held. Its major project in documentation, the AFI Catalog, is a comprehensive filmography of every film produced in the USA since 1893. AFI has operated a cinémathèque in Washington since 1969 with a cinema now located in the Kennedy Center. The Center for Advanced Film Studies in Beverley Hills, California, also established in 1969, offers

training in film-making at a professional level and conducts research which includes the compilation of an oral history of the American film based on interviews with surviving pioneers. The Center also manages an independent grant programme to assist young film-makers.

The Institute offers educational programmes and works to co-ordinate the activities of individuals and organizations in film education, training in film-making, and film preservation through seminars, conferences, and publications such as the *AFI Report*.

**AMERICAN FILM MANUFACTURING COMPANY** (American Flying A), US production company, was founded in 1910 by John R. Freuler and Samuel Hutchinson. Like most production concerns opposing the New York based MOTION PICTURE PATENTS COMPANY, American Flying A found it convenient to operate at a distance, in this case at Niles, California. Starting with Westerns shot in the open air, by 1914 the company had extended its range and acquired a studio in Chicago where a version of *The Cricket on the Hearth* was made; also dating from 1914–15 is the serial *The Diamond in the Sky*. By 1916 Flying A, releasing through MUTUAL had nine directors and nine associated companies—Clipper, Mustang, Vogue, Signal, etc—each specializing in its own type of film. With directors and stars such as Marshall NEILAN, Dean Tanner, Lottie (sister of Mary) Pickford, Irving Cummings, and Mary Mills Minter on its payroll at various times, the company remained in existence until the early twenties.

*AMERICAN IN PARIS, An,* US, 1951. Technicolor; 2hr. *Dir* Vincente Minnelli; *prod* Arthur Freed for MGM; *scr* Alan Jay Lerner; *ph* John Alton, Alfred Gilks; *des* Cedric Gibbons, Preston Ames; *sets* Edwin B. Willis, Keogh Gleason; *cost* Orry-Kelly, Irene Sharaff, Walter Plunkett; *mus* Johnny Green, Saul Chaplin; *comp* George Gershwin; *lyrics* Ira Gershwin; *chor* Gene Kelly; *cast* Gene Kelly (Jerry), Leslie Caron (Lise), Oscar Levant (Adam), Georges Guétary (Henri), Nina Foch (Milo).

Jerry, an American painter living in Paris, is loved by the wealthy Milo, but he falls in love with Lise who is engaged to Henri; eventually there is a happy ending for the painter and the French girl. The film is best known for the 17-minute ballet set to the title music, with each scene designed in the style of a particular French painter, but it also contains some of Gene KELLY's most delightful choreography in shorter numbers such as 'Love Is Here to Stay', a romantic pas-de-deux by the Seine, and the infectiously gay 'Tra-la-la-la' in which Kelly dances all over Oscar Levant's piano. The film also marked Leslie CARON's film début.

**AMERICAN STANDARDS ASSOCIATION** (ASA) is most widely known in film for its EMULSION speed rating system, which measures the relative sensitivity of film to light. The Association is also responsible for many other technical standards in use in the United States. These are normally compatible with standards established elsewhere in the world.

*AMERICAN TRAGEDY, An,* novel by Theodore Dreiser published in 1925 and based on an actual New York murder case. PARAMOUNT bought the rights and it was one of the projects offered to EISENSTEIN during his stay in Hollywood in 1930; but the studio disliked his proposed treatment. The first film version was directed by Josef von STERNBERG in 1931, under the original title and starring Phillips Holmes, Frances Dee, and Sylvia SIDNEY. A second version, A PLACE IN THE SUN (1951), was directed by George STEVENS and starred Montgomery CLIFT, Elizabeth TAYLOR, and Shelley WINTERS.

**AMFITHEATROF,** DANIELE (1901– ), Russian-born musician who studied music in Rome and became a symphony orchestra conductor before starting his association with Hollywood film music. *Lassie Come Home* (1943) was among his earlier scores, and in 1947–8 he wrote for a number of UNIVERSAL films, including LETTER FROM AN UNKNOWN WOMAN (1948) and *Another Part of the Forest* (1948). He then composed for films produced by most of the major companies, including *The Desert Fox* (1951, *Rommel, Desert Fox* in GB), *Human Desire* (1954), *Heller in Pink Tights* (1960), and *Major Dundee* (1964).

*AMICHE, Le* (The Girl Friends), Italy, 1955. 1¾ hr. *Dir* Michelangelo Antonioni; *prod* Trionfalcine; *scr* Antonioni, Suso Cecchi d'Amico, Alba De Cespedes, from a story by Cesare Pavese, 'Tra donne sole' in *La bella estate*; *ph* Gianni Di Venanzo; *des* Gianni Polidoro; *mus* Giovanni Fusco; *cast* Eleanora Rossi Draco (Clelia), Valentina Cortese (Nene), Gabriele Ferzetti (Lorenzo), Yvonne Furneaux (Momina), Franco Fabrizi (Cesare), Madeleine Fischer (Rosetta), Annamaria Pancani (Mariella).

Clelia, a poor girl who has done well in a Rome fashion house, returns to her native Turin to open a new branch. She becomes involved in the affairs of a group of women through finding one of them, Rosetta, after a suicide attempt. Different couples form and break, and finally Clelia leaves to return to Rome.

ANTONIONI adapted Pavese's story but invested it with his own distinctive view. Unlike the other women Clelia works instead of leading an idle, empty life; and she is the only one who makes any attempt to help Rosetta. The characterization is sharp and subtle: in long sequences of great complexity, camera movements and actors' movements in relation to each other and to the physical surroundings express their individuality and the shifting relationships between them. Two such sequences have become justly famous; one on a beach and one in Momina's flat. The film is unusual in giving equal emphasis to ten characters: the individual performances are excellent, with Yvonne Furneaux perhaps outstanding as the malicious Momina. Similar themes and Antonioni's masterly handling of them were to distinguish the greatest decade of his career, which opened with *Le amiche.*

**AMIDEI,** SERGIO (1904– ), Italian scriptwriter and producer, wrote his first film, *Pietro Micca,* in 1938. His talent for Italian dialect comedy was recognized some time before he found his ideal field in NEO-REALISM; working together with FELLINI on the script of ROMA, CITTÀ APERTA (1945) and PAISÀ (1947) for ROSSELLINI. Among many other films he wrote (and also produced) DOMENICA D'AGOSTO (1950) and *Parigi è sempre Parigi* (1951), both directed by Luciano EMMER.

*AMORE IN CITTÀ* (Love in the City), Italy, 1953. 1¾hr (in the version distributed abroad). *Prod* Cesare Zavattini in collaboration with Riccardo Ghione and Marco Ferreri; *scr* Aldo Buzzi, Luigi Chiarini, Luigi Malerba, Tullio Pinelli, Vittorio Vettroni; *ph* Gianni Di Venanzo; *mus* Mario Nascimbene.

ZAVATTINI, one of the major proponents of NEO-REALISM, aimed in this film to embody his definition of the main neo-realist ideas: the use of true incidents, often drawn from newspaper reports, played by amateur actors who may be the people involved in the original events, filmed in the locales where the events took place. The film consists of six episodes:

'Paradiso per tre ore' (Paradise for 3 Hours) *dir* Dino Risi; 'Tentato suicido' (Attempted Suicide) *dir* Michelangelo ANTONIONI; 'Una agenzia matrimoniale' (Marriage Bureau) *dir* Federico FELLINI; 'Storia di Caterina' (Caterina's Story) *dir* Zavattini and Francesco Maselli; 'Gli Italiani si voltano' (The Italians Turn and Stare) *dir* Alberto LATTUADA; 'L'amore que si paga' (Paid Love) *dir* Carlo LIZZANI.

Lizzani's episode was removed from the film before it was made available for showing outside Italy, as the authorities objected to its depiction of Roman prostitution.

*AMOUR, L'APRÈS-MIDI, L'* (*Love in the Afternoon*), France, 1972. Eastman Color; 1½hr. *Dir, scr* Eric Rohmer; *prod* Les Films du Losange; *ph* Nestor Almendros; *des* Nicole Rachline; *cast* Bernard Verley (Frédéric), Zouzou (Chloë), Françoise Verley (Hélène).

Happily married, Frédéric spends his lunch hours daydreaming about the women passing in the street. The equilibrium of his life is disturbed by the unexpected visit to the office of a friend's ex-mistress.

The last of ROHMER's *contes moraux* represents a development of his theme: the man is now committed to the woman he thinks he loves. *L'Amour, l'après-midi* subtly portrays Frédéric's ambivalent response to the temptation of the protean Chloë, who preys on the office-worker's weak spot, the afternoon. His role as the everyman of the *contes moraux* is charmingly shown in a fantasy sequence where the women from the earlier *contes* are drawn into his embrace as they approach him in the street. The film's apparent simplicity of intention and execution is a hallmark of the skill of Rohmer, his production team, and his actors in handling the elusive life of the mind and heart, their confusions and conflicts.

**ANAMORPHIC LENS.** The idea of an anamorphic image, with a squeezed effect achieved as in a curved mirror, was brought from China to Europe during the Renaissance, and painters made puzzle pictures by this means. The inventor of the lens was a French physicist and professor of optics at the Sorbonne, Henri Chrétien (1879–1956), who during the First World War devised this means for seeing a wide view out of the narrow aperture of the French military tank. He adapted the lens for the still camera to make aerial photography more economical. In 1927 he patented the hemispheric lens which he called Hypergonar.

In applying the principle to cinematography a curved lens is used in front of the normal lens to squeeze on to the film a distorted image twice as wide as the image received through a normal lens alone. In projection the process is reversed so that the projector throws an image on to the screen in the proportion roughly of 3 × 7 in place of the traditional 3 × 4.

An advantage of the anamorphic system is that it uses the whole area of the film frame alongside the sound track. Commercially developed as CINEMASCOPE, the anamorphic became for a time the most widely established system for films on the wide screen.

Other anamorphic processes have been developed in the USSR, in France (Dyaliscope), in Japan (Tohoscope), and elsewhere. (See also WIDE SCREEN, ASPECT RATIO.)

**ANDERSON,** GILBERT M. ('Broncho Billy'), (*c.* 1883–1971), US actor and director, real name Max Aronson. Known primarily as an actor, he also wrote and directed films. He was a travelling salesman and model before Edwin S. PORTER hired him. In Porter's THE GREAT TRAIN ROBBERY (1903), according to Anderson, he played a passenger on the train as well as the bandit who shot him. In 1907 he formed the ESSANAY Company with George K. Spoor. Tall and well-built, he adopted a distinctive costume to become the screen's first Western hero, Broncho Billy, the creation of the novelist Peter B. Kyne. *The Bandit Makes Good* (1908) was followed by some 500 one- and two-reelers during the next eight years until his retirement in 1918 in the face of competition from longer Westerns and newcomers like W. S. HART and Tom MIX. He was awarded a special OSCAR in 1957 for his 'contribution to the development of the narrative film and the emergence of the screen hero'.

**ANDERSON,** Dame JUDITH (1898–     ), Australian stage actress who has occasionally appeared in films since emigrating to the US. Her first film role was in the one-reel *Madame of the Jury* (1930); her first feature film was *Blood Money* (1933). Usually seen in small character roles, she is probably best remembered for her outstandingly evil Mrs Danvers in HITCHCOCK's REBECCA (1940) and for a similar role in Otto PREMINGER's *Laura* (1944). She played Lady Macbeth opposite Maurice Evans in MACBETH (1960); later, after a gap of five years, she returned to films as the tragic squaw Buffalo Cow Head in *A Man Called Horse* (1970), in which she coped with dialogue entirely in Sioux.

**ANDERSON,** LINDSAY (1923–     ), British director. Born in India where his father was serving in the army, Anderson received a conventional upper middle-class education at public school (Cheltenham) and Oxford. Returning to Oxford after army service in the war, he began editing and writing in SEQUENCE. He started making films in 1948 at the invitation of a Yorkshire manufacturing firm. Walter LASSALLY worked with him on one of several short films he made in the industrial north, and also on *Thursday's Children* (1953), about deaf children, which won an OSCAR in 1955 but obtained only limited release.

*O Dreamland!*, also made in 1953, an unglamorous portrayal of people in a seaside amusement park, revealed the harsh element in Anderson's perception of humanity. His best work since has been a result of the tension between this and the optimistic faith in people of *Thursday's Children* and most of his earlier films. *O Dreamland!* was shown three years later in the first FREE CINEMA programme. Throughout these years Anderson continued his hard-hitting writing about cinema (in SIGHT AND SOUND and other journals after the end of *Sequence* in 1952); he published *Making a film*, London, 1952, an account of the making of Thorold DICKINSON's *Secret People* (1952); he also made commercials and the first of five episodes of 'Robin Hood' for television.

Besides providing the main theoretical voice for Free Cinema he was active in its organization, and in 1957 made *Every Day Except Christmas*, about Covent Garden Market, at the invitation of Karel REISZ. The twenty-minute film financed by Ford's became forty minutes long, thanks to additional private backing. A projected feature for EALING STUDIOS was abandoned because Anderson refused to adapt his treatment to the studio's demands. He began directing stage plays for the Royal Court Theatre, and during the years of the British 'new wave' (see GREAT BRITAIN), his activity was confined to the theatre. Through what he has called 'the grace and insistence' of Reisz he made his first feature, THIS SPORTING LIFE, in 1963. His short film *The White Bus* (1967) was to have been part of a full-length feature planned by WOODFALL. In 1967 he was invited to direct in the theatre in Warsaw, and while he was there he made another short, *Raz Dwa Trzy* (*The Singing Lesson*).

IF . . . (1968) at last allowed Anderson the freedom he demanded, which he used to attack the educational system through which he had himself passed. He then converted the charming rebel (played by Malcolm McDowell) into the Candide-like hero of *O Lucky Man!* (1973) where his strictures are broadened to take in the whole of contemporary Western society.

Anderson's clarity and determination about his aims as critic and practising film-maker have made him more influential than any other single figure in unsettling the complacency of the British film industry. His refusal to compromise has meant that he has not made many films, but his work is consistent with the artistic principles he has never ceased to proclaim.

Anderson's articles in *Sequence* and *Sight and Sound* (particularly 'Stand Up! Stand Up!', *Sight and Sound*, Autumn 1956) are important to an understanding of his ideals and work. Elizabeth Sussex's *Lindsay Anderson*, London, 1969, is an invaluable short account of his career up to *If* . . .

**ANDERSSON,** BIBI (1935– ), Swedish actress, made her first screen appearance in Poppe's *Dumbom* (1953). She is best known for her performances in films directed by Ingmar BERGMAN, including SOMMARNATTENS LEENDE (*Smiles of a Summer Night*, 1955), DET SJUNDE INSEGLET (*The Seventh Seal*, 1957), and SMUL-TRONSTÄLLET (*Wild Strawberries*, 1957). Her conventionally cool Swedish beauty conceals reserves of passion revealed particularly in her complex role as the white-starched nurse in PERSONA (1966). She has also worked under the direction of SJÖMAN, ZETTERLING, and others as well as in the Swedish theatre since 1956. Her début outside Sweden was in *Duel at Diabolo* (Ralph Nelson, 1965).

**ANDERSSON,** HARRIET (1932– ), Swedish actress, acted first in the theatre and made her first film, *Medan staden sover* (*While the City Sleeps*), in 1950. She became internationally known with her leading role in *Sommaren med Monika* (*Summer with Monika*, Ingmar BERGMAN, 1953), which displayed to the full her unaffected sensuality. She was notable in GYCKLARNAS AFTON (*Sawdust and Tinsel*, 1953), SOMMARNATTENS LEENDE (*Smiles of a Summer Night*, 1955), *Sàsom i en spegel* (*Through a Glass Darkly*, 1961), and in other Bergman films. She has worked also for other directors such as Mai ZETTERLING, in *Älskande par* (*Loving Couples*, 1964) and Jörn DONNER, to whom she is married.

***AND GOD CREATED WOMAN*** see ET DIEU CRÉA LA FEMME

**ANDRESS,** URSULA (1936– ), Swiss actress, maintains the tradition of the 'vamp' or 'sex symbol' in the style of the sixties. Her typically nubile roles include those in *Dr No* (1962) and *She* (1965).

**ANDREWS,** DANA (1909– ), US actor, made his début in *The Westerner* (1940). He gave an impressive performance as the innocent lynch victim in THE OX-BOW INCIDENT (1943) and was particularly effective as tough but troubled heroes, like the detective in *Laura* (1944) who finds himself falling in love with a supposedly dead woman, or a returning war veteran in THE BEST YEARS OF OUR LIVES (1946). After *Boomerang* (KAZAN, 1947) his career began to decline until he was playing either leading parts in small-budget films like *Crack in the World* (1965), or supporting roles in major productions such as *In Harm's Way* (1965), in which he showed that he was still a good actor, given the opportunity.

**ANDREWS,** JULIE (1935– ), British actress and singer, made frequent radio and variety appearances as a child. She starred in the Broadway production of *The Boy Friend* in 1954, and created the role of Eliza Doolittle in MY FAIR LADY, also on Broadway, in 1956. Her films *Mary Poppins* (1964) and THE SOUND OF MUSIC

(1965) were well suited to her wholesome appeal and displayed her talents as a singer. She showed a flair for light comedy in *The Americanization of Emily* (1964) and *Thoroughly Modern Millie* (1967), but the role of Gertrude LAWRENCE in *Star!* (1968) and other mainly dramatic roles have tended to reveal her limitations as a straight actress.

*ANGEL EXTERMINADOR, El* (*The Exterminating Angel*), Mexico, 1962. 1½hr. *Dir, scr* Luis Buñuel; *prod* Gustavo Alatriste; *ph* Gabriel Figueroa; *mus* Paradisi, Scarlatti, Gregorian chants; *cast* Silvia Pinal (Laetitia), Enrique Rambal (Nobile), Jacqueline Andere (Alicia Roc), José Bavicra (Leandro), Claudio Brook (Julio), Rosa Elena Durgel (Silvia).

A group of rich supper guests find themselves mysteriously trapped, unable to leave their host's drawing-room, and over weeks gradually decline into barbarism and near-cannibalism. In some ways BUÑUEL's most baffling film, it can be read as a social allegory or as a complex exercise in the irrational, notably in the arbitrary introduction of a bear and a flock of sheep into the palatial mansion. His typical black humour is to the fore, heightened by the plain, objective visual style.

*ANGELS WITH DIRTY FACES*, US, 1938. 1½ hr. *Dir* Michael Curtiz; *prod* Warner Bros; *scr* John Wexley, Warren Duff; *ph* Sol Polito; *cast* James Cagney (Rocky Sullivan), Pat O'Brien (Jerry Connolly), Humphrey Bogart (James Frazier), Ann Sheridan (Laury Ferguson), George Bancroft (Mac Keefer).

James CAGNEY in one of his most famous gangster roles was ably seconded by Pat O'BRIEN who, a product of the same slums, has become a priest. The ending has become something of a classic sequence: Cagney is dragged screaming and struggling to the electric chair, in himself as brazen and defiant as ever but agreeing, in response to his priest-friend's plea, to a display of pretended cowardice to disillusion the slum boys who idolize him.

The film was a follow-up to DEAD END (1937) and again featured Humphrey BOGART as a racketeer and the Dead End Kids as the teenage gang. It was in turn followed by *Angels Wash Their Faces* (1939).

*ANGER*, KENNETH (1930?–    ), US director, had an early and formative introduction to the cinema when he played the little Indian boy in MAX REINHARDT'S A MIDSUMMER NIGHT'S DREAM (1935); he began making films as a child. *Fireworks* (1947) describes a dream in which the dreamer goes through a series of strange and violent rituals by which he achieves self-initiation, and marks a continuing preoccupation with ritual and ritual objects. The film was championed by Jean COCTEAU and it was partly through him that Anger worked in France for several years, finally completing *Eaux d'Artifice* (1953) after several abortive projects. He has continued to move between Europe and the US. His later films reflect an increasing involvement with the occult in the form of Aleistair Crowley's Magick: *Invocation of my Demon Brother* (1969) is entirely devoted to the ritual of raising the devil, but even the earlier films—*Inauguration of the Pleasure Dome* (1954, with a multi-screen version in 1958), SCORPIO RISING (1964), and *Kustom Kar Kommandos* (1965)—are full of Magick symbolism and ritual, as well as Anger's typical scenes of startlingly explicit sexual imagery usually associated with violent homosexual relationships. Despite the consequent obscurity, they still have a powerful effect on the uninitiated through their visual beauty, complex and violent imagery, and brilliant editing (EISENSTEIN is an acknowledged master) and are the work of an imaginative and original film-maker. He has also written a book—*Hollywood babylone* (Paris, 1959), which purports to be an exposé of the private lives of prominent Hollywood personalities.

**ANIMATION.** Cartoon films are those created by filming drawings in sequence to create the illusion of a moving picture. Animation is the technique of preparing the drawings to give this illusion of life and movement. The term is also applied to the movement of puppets or abstract three-dimensional objects in the making of PUPPET FILMS. The common factor is that each movement is photographed in separate steps— one or two frames for each fraction of movement—with the camera stopped between each drawing or each adjustment of the puppet, as opposed to conventional cinematography where the camera runs at a constant number of frames per second, recording the movements as they take place.

**Technical.** The only actual movement in animated film is the change from frame to frame specified by the animator. This requirement governs all the equipment used in the process. The film must pass through the gate evenly from frame to frame and perfect registration must be maintained between successive drawings and between each drawing and frame of film at every stage of the production process. Any transverse or panning movement of the drawing or raising and lowering of the camera is precisely controlled by machinery capable of movements calibrated in thousandths of an inch.

In the diagram, the camera (a) is shown mounted on the rostrum (US term 'animation stand'). The motor (b) which drives the camera one frame at a time is mounted alongside. The camera photographs the field (c) on the table (d). The field commanded is made smaller or larger by bringing the camera down or taking it up: this movement is produced by turning the vertical worm (e) and controlled by the guide column (f). Horizontal movement of the drawing (sideways/ and back and forth) is created by moving the sliding bars (gg) in the table by means of a horizontal worm. The drawings are fixed to the table or to the bars by 'registration pegs' (h) which are common to both the camera equipment and the artists' desks (j). The paper, card, and transparent plastic used in the process are all punched on a registration punch with holes which fit these pegs precisely.

**Stages of Production.** The film-maker sets down his idea in the form of a strip cartoon, the 'storyboard'. This details the complete action, includes the dialogue, and indicates where music and sound effects are required. The sound track (music, voices, and effects) is usually recorded first and the animation fitted to it.

The key animator plans the movements, noting on a numbered sheet—the 'dope sheet', which matches the numbered frames of the sound track—the frame on which the key positions occur, thus outlining the entire sequence of the action. The action of the figures is broken down into separate levels of drawing, each level on a separate sheet so that the body may be on one, the head on another, the arms on a third, the eyes and mouth on a fourth. It is uncommon to go beyond five levels. All the levels together make up the complete figure, and when traced on the transparent CEL do not betray the composite make-up.

Once the key animator has planned the sequence of action and drawn the principal positions, an assistant makes the intermediate drawings—'in betweens'—and the complete set is traced and coloured on the cel. The cels, the backgrounds, and the dope sheet are passed to the cameraman who reads from the dope sheet which cel is required for each frame and what camera movements, if any, are required.

This typical manufacturing process is often varied in individual cases. In particular, a filmmaker working alone or with one or two assistants may create the storyboard, make the sound track, and execute all the animation drawings directly on cel, e.g. DUNNING, HUBLEY, etc. The aim is usually to avoid the coarsening of sensitively styled drawings by less skilled assistants and tracers. It is usually practicable only on

1. Handles for controlling horizontal worms.

2. Shadow board to reduce reflection.

3. Two point lighting.

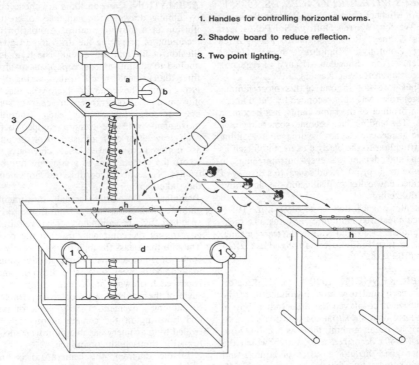

Animation table

short lengths and where the film-maker is not pressed for time. In general, a properly designed character can be handled by the varying skills of key animator, assistant, and tracer without loss of quality.

Other animation techniques include:

**Direct Drawing on Film.** Conventional animation techniques can be by-passed by drawing directly on to positive or negative film stock or on to the clear celluloid itself. Pioneers in this field were Oskar FISCHINGER and Len LYE. The effect is necessarily rather broad and crude but can be extremely lively. 'Drawn' sound tracks can be created by this means, a technique explored particularly by Norman MCLAREN.

**Cut-out Animation.** Lotte REINIGER, the pioneer of cut-out animation, used silhouettes which were as refined in action (and therefore as laborious) as cel animation. Other film-makers have used flat paper puppets with components in stock sizes and positions which can be assembled to produce all the required attitudes. These are arranged on the camera table, by-passing the use of drawings. Subtlety of movement suffers, but the method is quicker than cel animation and is useful where vigour is more desirable than polish.

**Model Animation.** Frame-by-frame animation of models is often used in live-action films where an effect would be too difficult or expensive to create full-size. In 2001—A SPACE ODYSSEY (1968) there were model animation shots, shots combining models with live-shot material, and even shots combining models, live action, and drawn animation.

**Pin Screen.** ALEXEÏEFF reproduced the effect of a screen-printed photograph by arranging millions of pins projecting through a perforated screen. By progressively altering the level of areas of pins, lit from the side to create shadows, the gradual movement of animation was achieved.

**Computers.** The radiant dots of a computer's display screen may be organized into pictures in a similar manner to Alexeïeff's pins. The frame-by-frame progression is rapid, but the style of drawing is confined to mathematical variations of a given figure and does not allow for much grace of form. The labour required to programme a computer to produce the subtleties of line and colour of which hand-drawn animation is capable makes it unlikely to rival the human animator, although the WHITNEYS have achieved rich abstract effects. It is valuable as a tool, taking the effort out of some aspects of the animation process, particularly where alterations in the size and aspect of simple three-dimensional forms is concerned: this facility is widely used in instructional films. Computers are also widely used in the mass production of conventionally animated television series, where numbered series of movement drawings are used in permutations to give stock movements of stock characters.

**Pixillation.** The use of a stop frame camera to speed up and fragment the movement of actors, creating roughly the effect of cartoon timing with living people. One of the best-known examples is McLaren's *Neighbours* (1952).

**Animated Stills.** A degree of life can be given to still photographs by photographing each one for a varying number of frames, and consequently varying fractions of a second. The technique was well used by Chris MARKER in LA JETÉE (1964).

**Graphics Films.** Pleasing results can be achieved by photographing on a rostrum camera drawings or paintings without any ingredient of movement within or between them but often using camera movement over them. This technique is the basis of those art films which deal in detail with the work of famous painters. It is also used to film old prints or photographs for inclusion in COMPILATION films on historical subjects.

By far the largest proportion of animation films produced throughout the world is devoted to advertising, propaganda, or didactic purposes. Information, whether true or false, can be conveyed with much greater speed and clarity than in a live-action film and the animated drawing can demonstrate the behaviour of objects that the camera cannot record or present an analysis of movement or change that is too fast or too slow for other forms of reproduction. This area of production gives financial support to many artists working in animation, who find in its formal qualities a means of individual expression for abstract or symbolic ideas, as well as purely aesthetic concepts, not readily available in any other medium.

## History

Devices to give drawings the illusion of movement were in use in the middle of the nineteenth century, long before the invention of cinematography. By 1882 Emile REYNAUD had combined the principle of his Praxinoscope with a projector, and in 1892 he opened the Théâtre Optique at the Musée Grévin in Paris. His device was capable of showing 'films' lasting up to fifteen minutes, and although his work was superseded by the motion photography of the LUMIÈRE brothers, EDISON, and MÉLIÈS, he had established animation as a form which predates live-action cinema in every respect.

The advent of the photographic cinema initially overshadowed the appeal of moving drawings, and animation was virtually reinvented in about 1908 through the work of J. Stuart BLACKTON in the US and Emile COHL in France. From this time the animated image was realized through photographic means, with the exception of direct work on to film stock.

**USA.** Closely following Blackton's work in the US was that of Winsor McCay, a cartoonist from the *New York Herald*. Using simple line drawings, he produced his first film, GERTIE THE DINOSAUR, in 1909 and in 1918 made the first animated feature, *The Sinking of the Lusitania*. The years 1919–20 saw the establishment of the first American cartoon production units: the result was a standardization not only of form, to a supporting component in cinema programmes, but also of manufacturing methods. The breaking down of work into stages occurred at this time, and has changed very little since. These studios produced one-reel films, about ten minutes long, each telling an adventure of some recurring character, human or animal. Max FLEISCHER'S BETTY BOOP, Koko the Clown, and, later, POPEYE, Pat Sullivan's FELIX THE CAT, and Herriman's Krazy Kat were popular examples. Towards the end of the twenties MICKEY MOUSE arrived, and the DISNEY studio began to dominate the American animation scene.

Disney's position as the colossus of the cartoon film is attributable to two qualities, his organizing ability and his feeling for a story. With Ub IWERKS, he pioneered the precise integration of the animated image with sound—particularly music—in the SILLY SYMPHONY series which began in 1928. Although newspaper cartoon characters, as well as characters from animated films, had frequently featured as stuffed toys or decorative motifs, it was the Disney studio that really developed the selling of designs to outside manufacturers to become a major source of income. The high cost and slow returns of cartoon film production make some form of interim revenue desirable: this problem became acute when the Disney studio cut back on its production of shorts to undertake the enormous task of SNOW WHITE AND THE SEVEN DWARFS (1937). The greatest effort was made at this time to sell licences for the use of Mickey Mouse and the rest—as well as the Snow White characters—as toys, children's games, puzzles, decorative transfers, and so on. This arm of the business was over the years remarkably successful, and since then no cartoon company of any size has neglected to support its income in this way.

During the thirties Disney had virtually no competition, although there were other studios at work. Max Fleischer continued to produce Popeye shorts and in 1939 followed Disney into feature production with *Hoppity Goes to Town*, notable for its direct social comment. In the forties, METRO-GOLDWYN-MAYER and WARNER BROS began to make headway against the Disney shorts with HANNA AND BARBERA'S TOM AND JERRY and Chuck Jones and Ted Avery's Bugs Bunny. These films were not unlike Disney's in style and technique, but they introduced a more anarchic approach and greater freedom in the use of ludicrous violence. The other major force at this time was UNITED PRODUCTIONS OF AMERICA (UPA), set up in 1948 by a breakaway group of Disney animators led by Stephen Bosustow. The UPA style was more gentle, more witty, and in a sense more literary than its contemporaries': its influence was felt throughout Europe as well as America, reaching its peak in the mid-fifties. At this point, the growth of television and its effect on cinema audiences reduced the market that had sustained short cartoon productions. Commercial animation studios now devote their output almost entirely to low-budget, mass-produced cartoons for television and advertising.

In contrast to this industrialized area of cartoon production, small independent groups have sprung up under animators like John HUBLEY, Ernest Pintoff, Fred Wolff and Teru Murakami, and Robert Crumb. Although their work is often termed 'experimental', they bring professionalism and artistic assurance to their individual graphic styles, and have extended the use of cartoon films as comments on the world and human behaviour. Ralph Bakshi has made animated feature films in the style of the underground press, including FRITZ THE CAT (1971) and *Heavy Traffic* (1973).

**Canada.** From its foundation in 1941, the NATIONAL FILM BOARD attracted talented filmmakers who, free from commercial restrictions, produced a number of short films of notably high standard. The animation unit was formed by Norman MCLAREN, who made the first of his remarkable series of explorations of animation technique, *Dollar Dance*, in 1943. McLaren's resistance to the concept of the animated film as a narrative vehicle has helped to encourage experiment among his colleagues at the NFB: Grant Munro has used unusual materials to good effect in several films, and Wolf Koenig advanced the technique of filming still photographs in such films as *City of Gold* (1957). The unit is similar in democratic structure to UPA, and its member animators, including Colin Low, Ryan Larkin, René Jodoin, Jim McCay, and Gerald Potterton, have collaborated on joint projects in addition to producing distinctly individual work. The few animators in Canada outside the NFB, including Cioni Carpi, the English mathematician Trevor Fletcher, Bernard Longpré, and Al Sens, have since the sixties produced work comparable in originality to that of their contemporaries at the Board.

**Great Britain.** Up to the forties, commercial animation in Britain was, as in the rest of Europe, dominated by American imports and influence. Paul Terry was at the Bray Studios from 1916, but left for the US where he became one of the creators of Krazy Kat. Anson Dyer, director of a burlesque version of *The Merchant of Venice* (1919), introduced US animation studio methods in the early thirties. At this time independent work began to appear: Georg Pal, a puppet-animator, made several competent advertising films, a form that was to become a British forte; Len LYE, at the GPO Film Unit (see CROWN FILM UNIT), pioneered new animation techniques; and in 1940 G. E. Studdy emulated the US style of presentation with Bonzo the Dog. HALAS AND BATCHELOR established what was to become by the fifties the largest animation studio in Western Europe, producing didactic, propaganda, and, by 1950, cinema shorts; at the end of the war, with the Larkins studios, they found an outlet through the Ministry of Information and industrial advertising. Apart from a short-lived attempt by the RANK ORGANISATION to set up a large Disney-like studio in the late forties, British animation has remained largely dependent on such channels, and is noted for its subtle blend of entertaining wit and clarity of message. The revenue from advertising enabled several studios to produce cartoons for the cinema, including Halas and Batchelor's *Animal Farm* (1954), the first British animated feature. Through similar means Richard WILLIAMS (*The Little Island*, 1958), George DUNNING (YELLOW SUBMARINE, 1968), Bob Godfrey, and the Biographic studios have been able to undertake interesting independent work. Britain, like other countries, has also seen exploitation of the home animation industry by US producers, who can bring a pre-designed film or series to the country and employ local facilities more cheaply than in the United States.

**France.** Cohl's pioneering work was not followed up, and French animation started to gain impetus only in the mid-thirties. The Pole Ladislas STAREVITCH made several puppet films from 1921; other individual works included BARTOSCH's L'IDÉE (*The Idea*, 1934), in woodcut style and with music by HONEGGER, and *Barbe-bleue* (1938), with animated Plasticine figures, by Jean PAINLEVÉ and René Bertrand. ALEXEÏEFF, too, made a puppet film, *La Belle dormante* (1935), with music by Poulenc, apart from the films using his painstaking pin screen technique; twenty years later he was still exploring experimental techniques like the pendulum-trace photography of *Sève de la terre* (1955).

French animation often displays a characteristic lyricism: the first film in this vein was *Joie de vivre* (1934) by the English illustrator Anthony Gross and the American Hector Hoppin. Stylistically similar was Paul GRIMAULT's *Le Petit Soldat* (1947), part of a series which culminated

in his Disney-like though sensitively controlled *La Bergère et le Ramoneur* (1953). Since the fifties there has been an increase in both individualistic work, such as that of the Hungarian Peter Foldes, who has also worked in Britain, and productions from commercial studios such as that of Jean Image and the unit at Cinéastes set up by Jim Phabian from MGM in 1955. The many animators currently working in France are encouraged by lively theoretical discussion and the practical support of festivals such as Anneçy and CANNES.

**Germany.** The first German animated film, by Julius Pinschewer, appeared around 1912. The rise of Dada and other avant-garde groups promoted several serious experiments in animated film, notably by the loosely knit group which included Viking EGGELING, Hans RICHTER, Walter RUTTMANN, and Oskar FISCHINGER (see ABSTRACT FILM). The work of Lotte REINIGER became popular in the thirties; but she, like many of her contemporaries, left Germany to escape the Nazi régime. Animated film in Germany did not gain momentum until the mid-fifties, through the work of the DEFA studios in East Germany and that of Urchs, Herbst, Euscher, and Hunger in West Germany.

**Italy.** Italian animation probably began with PASTRONE and de CHOMÓN's *La guerra e il sogno di Momi* (*The War and Momi's Dream*) in 1916, but there was little incentive to establish domestic competition with American dominance. The situation was broken by the Second World War, and the successful completion of Gino Parenti's *Brave Anselmo* in 1940 encouraged the founding of several animation studios, one of which (CAIF) produced a feature-length version of *Pinocchio* in the same year. American influence was gradually shed during the following decade. The Gaviolis' *The Magic Pot* (1956) indicates the developing self-confidence of Italian animation: their incisive and sharply designed *La lunga calza verde* (*The Long Green Stocking*, 1962) depicts the unification of Italy. The sixties saw the complete emergence of the Italian sense of elegant design, blended with the effervescent satire of Bozzetto's *West and Soda* (1965) and *Vip, mio fratello superuomo* (*Vip, My Superman Brother*, 1969), the stark comment of Manfredi's *Il muro* (*The Wall*, 1971), or the visual wit of Cavandoli's *La linea* series.

**Eastern Europe.** Here animation is generally characterized by rapid development from the early fifties, with Poland, Czechoslovakia, and Yugoslavia producing a body of work outstanding for its seriousness of content, social satire, and technical originality.

*Poland.* Several individuals emerged from the late fifties: the two who have received most critical acclaim for the originality of their ideas are Jan LENICA and Walerian BOROWCZYK, one of the few animators to move on to directing live-action films. Witold Giersz, after experimenting with broadly painted surfaces blended with superimposed animated figures in *Maly western* (*The Little Western*, 1960), has investigated the formal considerations of combining pictorial design and choreography: *Kon* (*Horse*, 1967) is one of a series of intriguing applications of animation to oil paint. Other important Polish animators working in the sixties included Szczechura, Zitman, Kotowski, Nehrebecki, and Janik.

*Czechoslovakia.* As elsewhere in Eastern Europe, little animation was produced until after the Second World War. Jíři TRNKA's *Pérak a SS* (*The Devil on Springs*, 1946) proved popular for its bitter anti-Nazi comment. Trnka became a national figure in the sixties, through his versatility in painting, design, illustration, cartoon films, and above all puppet films. His work with puppets encouraged contemporary film-makers, making it a forte of Czechoslovakian animation. The vivacious formal combinations of drawn and puppet animation in Karel ZEMAN's films, notably BLÁZNOVA KRONIKA (*The Jester's Tale*, 1964) have been occasionally echoed in the work of other animators. Brdecka, Miler, and Hofman are graphic animators whose work began in the late forties and who have kept pace with the technical resourcefulness and original wit of their contemporaries in puppet films.

*Yugoslavia.* Yugoslav animators have largely functioned as a group, often producing their most original work within a collaborative framework. In Zagreb several animated advertising and didactic films were produced by the Pole Sergei Tagatz in the twenties and a prolific number of similar films by the Maar Studios until 1936. The Zagreb animation studio was formed in 1950, and the increasing availability of UPA films at first provided a stylistic direction. The result was a series of animated advertising films produced by Kostelac, directed by Vukotić, designed by Marks, Bourek, and Kolar, and animated by Jutrisa and Kostanjsek. Zagreb Film provided funds and distribution. Extensive experiment followed, which resulted in their first narrative cartoon film *The Playful Robot* (1956), which, although less successful than the advertising films, was a useful indication of the group's potential. Vukotić and MIMICA's *Cowboy Jimmie* (1957), a satire on the Western, was the group's first real success and marked the emergence of the Zagreb characteristics: wit, pointed satire, graphic resourcefulness, and inventive animation. Films displaying these elements include Vukotić's *Surogat* (*Substitute*, 1961), Kristl's *Don Quixote* (1961), Mimica and Marks's *Muha* (*The Fly*, 1966), and Dragic's *Idu Dani* (*Passing Days*, 1969).

In the rest of Eastern Europe, the pattern of accelerated development from the fifties is similar. Bulgaria's Todor Dinov made his first film *Iunak Marco* (*Marco the Hero*) in 1955 and quickly rose to a position of international repute. Hungary's leading animator Gyula Macskassy began in 1952 with *Races in the Forest*. In Romania, POPESCU-GOPO made children's films from 1951; the general interest in animation in Romania led to the inauguration of the Mamaia animated film festival in 1966.

*USSR.* Animated films have been produced in the Soviet Union since the early twenties. Many were vehicles for propaganda like *China in Flames*, made in 1925. In the same year an animation studio was set up in Moscow, and four years later sound cartoon films such as Tsekhanovsky's *The Postman* were appearing. Pushtko's *Novyi Gulliver* (*The New Gulliver*, 1935) combined animated puppets with a live actor. In 1936 the Soviet Multfilm Studio was established and within two years had increased its output to twenty-four films a year. Most Russian animated films were in colour by this time; their style demonstrates the pervasive influence of Hollywood and particularly of Disney. Production was reduced by the war and in the fifties inspiration flagged, although Ivanov-Vano and a few other animators won international awards. Ivanov-Vano's *Leycha* (*The Mechanical Flea*, 1964) and *Secha pri Kerzhentse* (*The Battle near Kerzhentes*, 1971) are evidence of more awareness in contemporary Russian animation. A healthy decentralization process has taken place with the establishment of animation studios at Kiev in the Ukraine, Tbilisi in Georgia, Tallin in Estonia, and Tashkent in Soviet Asia.

Alongside the technical and formal progress in the sixties and early seventies in countries possessing an established tradition in animation, there is a new development of the medium in countries which, for various economic or cultural reasons, were unable to support it previously. Japan, apart from the outstanding work of Yoji Kuri, has produced little of note, having adopted a commercial Hollywood style of production and presentation; Spanish animation has been submerged in television advertising, but recent films from J. A. Sistiaga and the Moro and Marcian studios indicate new stylistic advances; some South American countries have recently formed animation units, as have New Zealand, China, Egypt, Turkey, Nigeria, Korea, and most other countries with an expanding economy and channels through which animated films can be distributed.

***ANNA KARENINA.*** Starting with a Russian production dating from 1910, fifteen screen versions of Tolstoy's novel (1878) are known to have been made. The story of the beautiful Russian noblewoman who sacrifices her child and reputation for an unworthy lover has an obvious appeal for film-makers and film audiences: GARBO appeared twice as Anna, in a silent version entitled *Love* (1928, *Anna Karenina* in GB), with John GILBERT as Vronsky, and in a widely acclaimed performance in *Anna Karenina* (1935), directed by Clarence BROWN, with Fredric MARCH as Vronsky and Basil RATHBONE as Karenin.

The only other English-language version, *Anna Karenina* (produced by Alexander KORDA, 1948), attempted to translate to the screen the author's densely populated canvas of Russian high society, aided by lavish designs by Cecil BEATON; but Julien DUVIVIER's direction failed to draw from Vivien LEIGH the doomed passion required in the title role. Kieron Moore was generally considered unequal to the portrayal of Vronsky, although Ralph RICHARDSON's Karenin was widely admired.

*Anna Karenina*, USSR, 1967, in SOVCOLOR and 70mm, was directed by Alexander Zarkhi and starred Tatiana SAMOILOVA as Anna, Vassily Lanovoi as Vronsky, and Nikolai Gritzenko as Karenin. It avoided the other film versions' restriction of the plot to Anna's love story, taking in the dense network of relationships created by Tolstoy, and especially the love affair and marriage of Levin (played by Boris Goldaiev) and Kitty (Anastasia Vertinskaya).

**ANNAKIN,** KEN (1914– ), British director, worked as a journalist, actor, and theatre director before entering films. At first his work was limited to lightweight comedies aimed at the home market, such as *Here Come the Huggetts* (1948), but in 1960 he directed his first large-scale production: *The Swiss Family Robinson.* He continued in the same style with *Those Magnificent Men in Their Flying Machines* (1965) and other big-budget co-productions.

*ANNÉE DERNIÈRE A MARIENBAD, L',* France, 1961. Dyaliscope; 1½hr. *Dir* Alain Resnais; *prod* Pierre Courau (Precitel), Raymond Froment (Terrafilm); *scr* Alain Robbe-Grillet; *ph* Sacha Vierny; *des* Jacques Saulnier; *mus* Francis Seyrig; *cast* Delphine Seyrig, Giorgio Albertazzi, Sacha Pitoëff.

Among an assembly of guests in a vast baroque mansion, the narrator/hero tries to persuade a woman that they have met before, and that she has agreed to go away with him, leaving the man (her husband perhaps), who has accompanied her to this mansion.

RESNAIS is concerned not with the objective reality of this situation, but with the expression of the subjective reality of the central characters. In *Marienbad* the convolutions of this purely mental inner reality are offered as an open-ended poetic experience; the logic and chronology of the exterior world are denied; events are mirrored, multiplied, and distorted by memory and imagination. The décor of the film (the glittering blacks and whites, the geometrical gardens, the shadowy profusion of baroque decoration, and the endless corridors) recalls the style of early German EXPRESSIONISM, and indeed seems to reflect outwardly the doubts and obsessions of the main characters.

With its haunting, dream-like rhythm and its icy formal beauty, its intricate and insoluble ambiguities, *Marienbad* continues to excite great critical debate, and has attracted numerous explanations and definitions.

**ANN-MARGRET** (1941– ), Swedish-born US actress, real name Ann-Margaret Olsson, was noticed singing with a group in Las Vegas. Her first film was *Pocketful of Miracles* (Frank CAPRA, 1961). At first limited to dumb blonde roles, she sidled and occasionally sang her way through a number of films of the sixties including *Bye Bye Birdie* (George Sidney, 1963) and *The Cincinnati Kid* (Norman JEWISON, 1965). Her performance as a blowsy sex kitten in *Carnal Knowledge* (Mike NICHOLS, 1971) revealed her as a promising actress, but *The Train Robbers* (Burt Kennedy, 1972) gave her less scope.

**ANOUILH,** JEAN (1910– ), French playwright, adapted and directed the film versions of his own plays *Le Voyageur sans bagages* (1943) and *Deux sous de violettes* (1951). He has written dialogue for several films, notably MONSIEUR VINCENT (1948) and adapted ANNA KARENINA for the version directed by Julien DUVIVIER in 1948. Film adaptations in English from his plays include *The Waltz of the Toreadors* (1962) and *Becket* (1964).

*A NOUS LA LIBERTÉ,* France, 1931. 1½hr. *Dir, scr* René Clair; *prod* Tobis; *ph* Georges Périnal; *des* Lazare Meerson; *mus* Georges Auric; *cast* Raymond Cordy (Louis), Henri Marchand (Émile), Rolla France (Jeanne).

In his first departure from the sparkling *divertissements* of his early career CLAIR comments ironically on modern industrial society. Two ex-gaolbirds, one working on the production line of the other's profitable gramophone factory, finally abandon their soulless existence to live as joyous vagabonds. Clair's resourceful use of sound parallels life in confinement and in 'free' society: the clamour of the city and factory is deliberately similar to the metallic background noises of prison. The film was considered subversive in Hungary and Portugal where it was banned

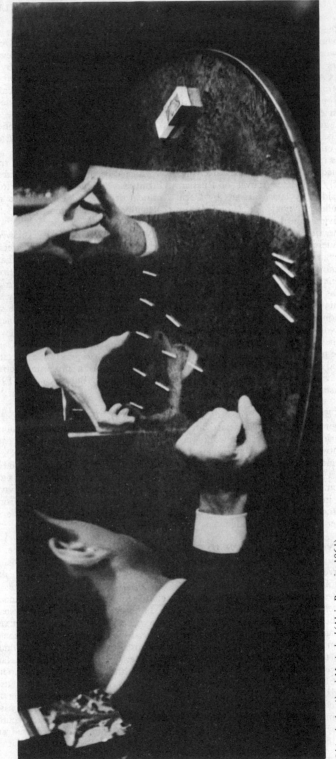

*L'Année dernière à Marienbad* (Alain Resnais, 1961)

outright, and its liberal ideas started Clair's breach with TOBIS.

CHAPLIN'S MODERN TIMES (1936) used virtually the same theme; Tobis wanted to sue but Clair gracefully chose to regard this as a tribute rather than a plagiarism.

**ANSCO COLOR,** a colour REVERSAL film used in the US in the forties and fifties, and one of the many stocks derived from the German AGFACOLOR. In 16mm it was a competitor of Kodachrome; in 35mm it was occasionally used for feature film production. (See COLOUR.)

**ANSTEY,** EDGAR (1907–   ), British documentary director and producer, joined the Empire Marketing Board in 1931 (see CROWN FILM UNIT) and edited FLAHERTY'S INDUSTRIAL BRITAIN (1933) under GRIERSON's supervision. His films as director at this time included *Granton Trawler* (with Grierson, 1934) for the EMB, and *Six-Thirty Collection* (1934) for the GPO. He organized the SHELL FILM UNIT in 1934. With Arthur ELTON, Anstey produced for the gas industry a series of films with a direct approach to social problems (see DOCUMENTARY), notably *Housing Problems* (1935) and his own *Enough to Eat* (also entitled *Nutrition*, 1936) with commentary by Julian HUXLEY. Anstey was THE MARCH OF TIME's London Director of Productions (1936–8), and for a period its Foreign Editor in New York. During the war, he produced documentaries for the Ministry of Information through Film Centre, a consultative agency, and was the *Spectator*'s film critic (1941–6). He remained with Film Centre until becoming head of British Transport Films in 1949, where his productions include John SCHLESINGER's *Terminus* (1961). Anstey in recent years has particularly encouraged scientific film work.

**ANSWER PRINT,** the first complete, corrected print with sound-track made by a LABORATORY from the negative of a completed film. The producer's sometimes unspoken doubts about the final appearance of the film are in effect answered, although it may have to be remade several times before he accepts the answer. (In Britain it is sometimes called the first show print and in the US first trial print.) The answer print marks the end of production: prints made prior to it have been silent RUSHES worked on by the editor; prints made after it will be RELEASE PRINTS, produced in bulk for distribution. (See also GRADING.) A DUPE negative is usually accompanied by an answer print, to provide means of checking the quality of the negative.

**ANTOINE,** ANDRÉ (1858–1943), French director and writer. After a distinguished career in the theatre (he was twice director of the Théâtre de l'Odéon), Antoine worked in Paris from 1915 to 1922, directing screen versions, often scripted by himself, of books by French authors, Hugo, Dumas, Zola, etc. He spent his last twenty years as a critic, writer, and respected authority on film and theatre.

**ANTOINE DOINEL,** character created by François TRUFFAUT and observed in a series of films. Having chosen Jean-Pierre LÉAUD for the part in his first feature film, LES QUATRE CENTS COUPS (1959), Truffaut developed, during the shooting and after, a relationship with the boy which reflected and extended his own with André BAZIN (to whose memory *Les 400 coups* is dedicated). The story of the growing boy was taken up again in 1962 in *L'Amour à vingt ans*, an EPISODE film with other contributions from Renzo Rossellini, Marcel OPHULS, Andrzej WAJDA, and Shintaro Isahara. In Truffaut's episode, Antoine/Léaud is seventeen: he is in a job and falls in love for the first time, but makes more headway with the parents of his girl-friend than with her. He reappears in *Baisers volés* (*Stolen Kisses*, 1968), having just completed his military service and ready to sample what he can of life. He falls in love with Christine Darbon (played by Claude Jade), tries a variety of jobs, is hired by a detective agency, gets off with the woman he is meant to watch (superbly played by Delphine SEYRIG), is fired by the agency, and ends up with Christine again. In *Domicile conjugal* (*Bed and Board*, 1970), Antoine and Christine are married and he is trying to settle himself into a lucrative job. Christine is expecting a baby, and Antoine, with his characteristic blend of diffidence and solemnity, has an affair with a Japanese girl. He cannot keep away from his newly made home, however, and rejoins Christine and his baby son, Alphonse.

The films have been—since *Les 400 coups*—very light-hearted and even slight in incident, but in them Truffaut has captured the unease and euphoria, the irresponsibility and the seriousness of adolescence and youth. Léaud, playing the role of each age as he reached it, developed Antoine as an engaging, spontaneous, wistful young man doing his best not to be cramped by the society he finds himself in. The series is unique as a biography of a screen character, and was brought to an end by Truffaut at the point where Antoine's questing for his personality had to come to an end.

Truffaut, ed, *Les aventures d'Antoine Doinel*, Paris, 1970.

**ANTONIONI,** MICHELANGELO (1912–   ), Italian director, developed his interest in theatre and cinema while a student at Bologna University and began writing for a newspaper published in his native Ferrara. He continued to do so until the late thirties, severely criticizing the Italian films of the WHITE TELEPHONE era. His first essay in cinema was a documentary in a mental hospital, never completed. In 1939 he moved to Rome to work on the universal exhibition planned to take place in 1943, and began contributing articles to CINEMA. The following year he enrolled as a student of directing at the CENTRO SPERIMENTALE. His career proper began in 1942, with his collaboration on the script of ROSSELLINI's *Un pilota ritorna*: in the same year he worked on the script of Enrico Fulchignoni's *I due foscari* (on which he was also assistant director) and spent some time working with CARNÉ on LES VISITEURS DU SOIR. His own first film, *Gente del Po*, a documentary about life in the Po valley, was begun in 1943. It was partly lost in processing and storage, and the final version in 1947 was edited from barely half the original footage. In 1947 he worked on the script of DE SANTIS's CACCIA TRAGICA, and in 1948 he made two short films, one about city cleaners and one about rural superstitions. On these two films he began the collaboration with the musician, Giovanni FUSCO, whose work was to make a considerable contribution to his later career.

His next short film, *L'amorosa menzogna* (1949), attacking the false glamour of the *fumetti*, magazine photo-strips, foreshadowed his participation as co-scriptwriter in 1952 for LO SCEICCO BIANCO, FELLINI's attack (though a more light-hearted one) on the same subject, and underlined his detestation of vulgarized art. Antonioni made three more short films before getting the opportunity to direct his first feature, *Cronaca di un amore* (1950), starring Lucia Bosè, which marked a departure from the tenets of NEO-REALISM within which he had worked as a documentarist. The story of a rich married woman, her poor lover, and the death of her husband in a car crash, it drew directly on the American thriller conventions which had inspired OSSESSIONE (1942). Many qualities were already apparent which were to distinguish Antonioni's later work: the haunting imagery of city streets, some sequences of remarkably complex camera movements, the element of unsolved mystery, and above all the confrontation of a beautiful, erotic woman with an impoverished lover. Several critics, especially in France, noticed the film with enthusiastic approval. His next film, *I vinti* (1952), returned nearer the documentary spirit in treating the activities of young delinquents in episodes set in Italy, France, and England. The film had difficulties with censorship in Italy, where Antonioni's proposed depiction of neo-Fascist activity had to be watered down, and in France, where the film was banned.

In 1953 he contributed 'Tentato suicido' to the EPISODE film AMORE IN CITTÀ. Suicide was to be another theme recurring in his work, and at this time Antonioni denied the assertion made by some critics that this was connected with the writer Pavese's preoccupation with suicide. During the same year he directed *La signora senza camelie*, with Lucia Bosè as a shop-girl who is transported to stardom on the screen then reduced, after an ambitious failure, to playing pulp roles. The workings of the film industry are viewed with an acrid eye reminiscent of Antonioni's distaste for the *fumetti*, and the treatment of failed glamour recalls Scott FITZGERALD, whose work Antonioni admires. Above all, the imagery of the film, with the characters viewed in relation to the physical surroundings of the studio and the streets of Milan, showed Antonioni's developing assurance.

His next film, LE AMICHE (1955), the only one of his films adapted directly from a literary work, the story 'Tra donne sole' by the misogynist Pavese, is a beautifully controlled study of the relationships between a group of women and their men-friends. Although no moral pronouncement is explicit, and the film is informed by a taste for women characteristic of Antonioni and quite foreign to Pavese, the characters' manoeuvres and the film's culmination in a suicide clearly express a condemnation of society's prescriptions for human relationships. Antonioni's scathing view of male inadequacy in particular was the dramatic focus for IL GRIDO (1957). Less at ease in the worker's milieu and hampered perhaps by the international cast imposed on him, Antonioni achieved a film of much less complexity and effectiveness: but the full power of his experience was realized in L'AVVENTURA (1960). The film is irradiated by the performance Antonioni drew from Monica VITTI, one of great vitality and eroticism; and he became an international success overnight, helped by the outcry with which the audience at CANNES greeted the film's elusive mixture of mystery, eroticism, and implicit social comment.

For his next two films, which pursued the themes of *L'avventura* so that the three are often spoken of as a trilogy, he was able to command the cream of international stars. In LA NOTTE (1961), Jeanne MOREAU and Marcello MASTROIANNI played a couple confronting the stresses arising in their marriage and finding nothing more than a tenuous solution. In L'ECLISSE (1962) Monica Vitti once again assumed a central role, enacting with Alain DELON the final drifting into nothingness of a relationship. The films of this remarkable series are all characterized by two particular stylistic hall-marks of Antonioni: formal visual beauty, and an increasingly assured use of pacing and

*La notte* (Michelangelo Antonioni, 1961)

rhythm in which, instead of the manipulation of time according to cinematic conventions comfortable for the spectator, dramatic ellipsis alternates with sequences where natural time is inexorably observed.

IL DESERTO ROSSO (*The Red Desert*, 1964) gave Antonioni his first opportunity to relate his characters to their environment through the use of colour. Typically, he imposed his own vision on landscapes and interiors, so that the settings reject naturalism to become a visual metaphor for despair. The film's lack of conviction stems as much perhaps from the failure of Monica Vitti to sustain the demanding central neurotic role as from the aridity of the generalizations about man's alienation in industrial society.

Antonioni's move to production abroad coincided with a point in his career at which he had exhaustively pursued the theme preoccupying him since his first feature, the inadequacy of human roles and attitudes. It was also the point at which his artistic relationship with Vitti, so fruitful during his later Italian films, had broken down, and at which the use of colour dictated radical stylistic departures for him. He directed an episode, 'Prefazione', in Dino DE LAURENTIIS's *I tre volti* (1965), and in the same year he made, under contract to METRO-GOLDWYN-MAYER, BLOW-UP (released 1967). Although there is a sense of strain about the excesses of swinging London and unease in the performances of his stars, the film makes accomplished use of pop art modes and carries sharp observations about the reality of an artist's relation to society.

Antonioni's next assignment took him to California, where he spent two years preparing and shooting ZABRISKIE POINT (1970). Critics who had, not without justification, pointed to self-indulgent mannerisms in *Blow-up* were even more hostile in their reception of *Zabriskie Point*, which contains nevertheless sequences of great beauty and is a resounding condemnation of materialistic values. In 1973, after a visit to China, Antonioni returned to London to make *The Passenger* (1975).

Antonioni's greatest achievement was in those films of the decade between '*Le amiche* and *Il deserto rosso* in which his lucid pessimism found assured dramatic and visual expression. In a body of work almost devoid of light-heartedness and humour, he has shown himself to be a sensitive and profound moralist.

The most consistently perceptive among Antonioni's critics have been Paul-Louis Thirard (*M. A. Antonioni*, Premier Plan No 15, Paris, 1960) and Ian Cameron, whose *Antonioni*, written with Robin Wood, London, 1968 and 1971, and New York, 1969, is an excellent account, with full bibliography which includes the published scripts.

*APA* (*Father*), Hungary, 1967. 1½hr. *Dir, scr* István Szabó; *prod* Mafilm Studio 3; *ph* Sándor Sára; *mus* János Gonda, Mahler's First Symphony; *cast* Miklós Gábor (father), Klári Tolnay (mother), András Bálint (Takó, the son), Dani Erdélyi (young son), Kati Sólyom (Anni).

In spite of the success of his first feature,

*Álmodozások kora* (*The Age of Daydreaming*, 1964), it was with *Apa*, the following work, that SZABÓ attracted world attention. It perfectly synthesizes two facets of Hungarian cinema—concern for the younger generation and memories of the past—into a work which both dazzles the senses by its technical mastery and is genuinely moving. Szabó follows, in fragmentary style, the growth of a boy to early adulthood, portraying Takó's dreams as he attempts to expunge the legend of his dead father. By stressing both the boy's need to prove himself and his perverse reliance on his father's memory, Szabó crystallized, with humour and feeling, many of his generation's neuroses.

**APARTMENT, The,** US, 1960. Panavision; 2hr. *Dir* Billy Wilder; *prod* Mirisch; *scr* Wilder, I. A. L. Diamond; *ph* Joseph LaShelle; *des* Alexander Trauner; *cast* Jack Lemmon (C. C. Baxter), Shirley MacLaine (Fran Kubelik), Fred MacMurray (J. D. Sheldrake).

C. C. Baxter's attempts to advance his career by lending his appartment to executives for their sexual intrigues forms the basis of this typical WILDER film. The New York office milieu is evoked with mordant detail, and the switch from harsh comedy to near-tragedy is judged with the assuredness that is a hall-mark of his best work.

Wilder and DIAMOND's script is full of characteristically satirical thrusts at corporate ethics and personal morality. Shirley MACLAINE and Jack LEMMON are perfectly matched in conveying the fine balance between black humour and despair.

**A PROPOS DE NICE,** France, 1930. 45min. *Dir, ed* Jean Vigo; *ph* Boris Kaufman.

VIGO's first film is built up from shots of Nice in the 'candid camera' manner of Dziga VERTOV, contrasted with shots which add pungent comment. (KAUFMAN is Vertov's youngest brother, and Vigo had known and admired Vertov's work for some years.) In incorporating material he had filmed previously at the Paris zoo, Vigo was emulating the practice as well as the principle of the Russian MONTAGE he admired so much. The film tends to be overrated today from an excess of piety. It has considerable originality, but is most interesting as an indication of Vigo's developing power and the sources of his cinematic inspiration (RICHTER and RUTTMANN as well as Vertov, and René CLAIR).

Some shots (e.g. the nude at the café table), though included in the 16mm print, are missing from the 35mm print current in Great Britain. This is because 16mm film is not subject to censorship (see CENSORSHIP, GB).

*A propos de Nice* (Jean Vigo, 1930)

**ARBUCKLE,** ROSCOE ('Fatty') (1881–1932), US comic actor, worked in vaudeville, then joined Mack SENNETT, appearing with the KEYSTONE Kops and CHAPLIN, and moving with Sennett to Jesse L. LASKY's Artcraft in 1917. He exploited the typical humour of the greedy fat man, developing the spontaneity, improvisation, and timing that characterized the best performers of Sennett's team. His talent was able to sustain feature-length films, notably three directed in 1921 by James CRUZE: *Crazy to Marry*, *Gasoline Gus*, and *The Dollar-a-Year Man*.

Scandals in his private life abruptly killed Arbuckle's popularity in 1921, and had some bearing on the formation of the MPPDA the following year (see MOTION PICTURE PRODUCERS ASSOCIATION). Under the pseudonym of William Goodrich he directed *The Red Mill* (1927), starring Marion DAVIES, and worked occasionally with Buster KEATON. In his last years he also used the sadly joking credit Will B. Good.

**ARCHIVE.** The term 'film archive', in the strict sense, means a collection of films of all categories preserved as documents for purposes of academic and historical research, and for public education. In this sense it is synonymous with 'film museum' and with the various forms of 'cinémathèque' ('cineteca', 'filmoteca', 'kinoteka', etc). The film archive may be more justly likened to a museum than a library and, like a museum, it is perpetually harassed by the conflicting interests of the protection of its collection and the public's requirements of access. The high cost of acquiring and preserving film is a considerable factor in the difficulty of reconciling these interests. The financial and technical resources needed to acquire, store, preserve, and catalogue film collections, and to make them publicly available, can usually be provided only by government subsidy; the major film archives are therefore usually national collections. In many countries steps are being taken to add the preservation of television material to the archive's responsibilities.

The work of a film archive consists of:
**Selection.** As, for considerations of space and cost, not every film can be permanently stored, it is the archivist's task to decide whether a given film is a justified choice for his collection. Fiction and actuality films may present conflicting claims for preservation.
**Acquisition.** Statutory deposit is required in those countries having a nationalized film industry and in a few others (e.g. Denmark, Italy). Elsewhere, archives must depend on voluntary donation of copies, so that even such films as are selected for a collection may not in

fact be made available; also, the quality of donated prints may be poor.
**Preservation.** Master copies are stored and should be used only for striking DUPE negatives: ideally they should never be projected. Storage of film is an expensive and specialized process: to delay deterioration, colour stock is usually stored at a temperature of −4°C and a relative humidity of 15%: modern colour processes use fugitive dyes and the long-term effectiveness of cold storage is not yet ascertainable; the dyes used in three-strip TECHNICOLOR positive prints are relatively stable, but the unequal shrinkage rates of PANCHROMATIC and ORTHOCHROMATIC stock presents special preservation problems for the original negatives. Black-and-white acetate stock is stored at 13°C, relative humidity 55%. NITRATE stock storage requirements are similar to those of acetate, but its combustible nature makes special fire precautions essential. Frequent checking of nitrate stock for signs of decay is also necessary, and the eventual transfer of nitrate prints on to acetate (safety) film.
**Cataloguing.** An exhaustive catalogue is an obvious necessity.
**Access.** All archives should have means of making their collections available to interested persons, and should preferably have their own viewing rooms. In addition, most archives are linked to a full-time cinema whose programmes regularly include duplicate copies of films from the archive.
**Documentation.** A supporting collection of documentary information (which may include scripts, stills, scores, publicity material) is an essential part of a film archive.

The capacity of film to record and preserve contemporary life and events was recognized very early in the history of cinematography. Shortly after Gladstone's funeral in 1898, a writer in the British periodical *Truth* pleaded for 'a kind of national gallery . . . for the collection of films of all public events', and in 1906 *The Optical Lantern and Cinematograph Journal* contained a proposal for the deposit of films in the British Museum and other statutory deposit libraries. In 1918 the Imperial War Museum was founded in London, with a section devoted to films and still photographs from the First World War. It was not until the early thirties, however, that the first practical steps were taken towards establishing film archives. As a result of recommendations made in 1932 by the British Commission on Cultural and Educational Films in its report *The Film in National Life*, the NATIONAL FILM ARCHIVE was started in 1935 within the BRITISH FILM INSTITUTE. Elsewhere, the stimulus came not from historians but from film enthusiasts, who were possibly influenced by the threatened disappearance of silent film masterpieces. In 1933 Einar Lauritzen in Stockholm created Filmhistoriska Samlingarna (later absorbed into SVENSKA FILMINSTITUTET); in 1935 Iris BARRY and John Abbott set up the Museum of Modern Art Film Library (now Department) in New York; and in Paris in 1936 Henri LANGLOIS developed the CINÉMATHÈQUE FRANÇAISE from his own private collection. In Berlin the Reichsfilmarchiv came into existence in 1935, but did not survive the Second World War. Since the end of the war similar film archives have been established in many parts of the world, particularly in Eastern Europe where state control of film production and distribution was introduced. In the Soviet Union, where nationalization had been in force since 1920, the official archive, Gosfilmofond, was not founded until 1948; but, initially drawing on a rich store of material from the Russian studios and distribution agencies, it has become one of the most important film archives in the world, covering 150 acres at Bielye Stolbi near Moscow and employing a staff of 600.

The work of film archives is co-ordinated internationally by the FÉDÉRATION INTERNATIONALE DES ARCHIVES DE FILM (FIAF).

**ARGENTINA.** Film-making began in Argentina in the 1890s, but during the silent era the national product was eclipsed by the success of more sophisticated foreign films, particularly those from the US. The coming of sound, however, allowed an indigenous, Spanish-language cinema to grow and flourish during the thirties; during this decade the Argentinian film began to have great commercial success, rivalling MEXICO in the Latin-American market, and drawing its strength from the exploitation of folk themes and national qualities. Typical of this era were the many films on the theme of the tango. Among the best of the popular film-makers was José A. Ferreya, who made several films with the famous tango singer Libertad Lamarque; the most successful of these was *Ayudame a vivir* (1935). His contemporary, Leopoldo Torres Rios, was another prominent figure among the veterans of the Argentine cinema, although his prolific output was of uneven quality. During the thirties two of the most important production companies were established, Argentine Sono Films and the now defunct Lumiton.

An intellectual cinema with a literary emphasis was developing alongside the more popular films. There were several important literary adaptations, including Mario Soffici's *Prisioneros de la Tierra* (1939) and Lucas Demare's *La Guerra gaucha* (1942), the first production of Artistas Argentinas Asociados, a quality production company formed by a nucleus of directors, actors, and writers. Leopoldo TORRE NILSSON, the son of Torres Rios, dominated Argentinian cinema in the forties and fifties with a succession of orthodox but powerful social dramas. His talented contemporary Fernando Ayala also reflected the literary tradition in such films as *El Jefe* (1953).

Despite these occasional successes, cinema languished during the Peronist era (1946–55), menaced by economic crises and government interference. In 1957, new legislation on film set up the Instituto Nacional de la Cinematografia to supervise all matters pertaining to the cinema, including financing, and revised the QUOTA regulations. Annual film festivals were instituted in 1959, and there were signs of an upsurge of talent. The poets Manuel Antin, Fernando Birri, and David José Kohon began making films. Other young directors began making films more socially oriented than those of their predecessors. Simon Feldman (*El Negocion*, 1959), Lautaro Murua (*Shunko*, 1960), and Rodolfo Kuhn (*Los Jovenes Viejos*, 1961) all showed promise. Birri, influenced by NEO-REALISM, made *Los Inundados* (1962), dealing with the lumpen minorities of the country, which was banned.

Meanwhile a group of political film-makers set up an independent co-operative Cine Liberacion, working closely with the Confederacion General de Trabajodores and linked to the Peronist party. The group includes Humberto Rios (*El Grito de este Pueblo*, 1972), Gerardo Vallejo (*Camino hacio la muerte del viejo Reales*, 1971), Raul de la Torre, Alberto Fisherman, and Juan José Stagnaro. The leading figure is Fernando Solanas, whose *La Hora de los Hornos* (*The Hour of the Furnaces*, 1969), a three-part film essay on the anti-colonialist struggle of Argentinian workers, comes close to realizing the 'aesthetic of violence' called for by Glauber ROCHA. The film was probably the main stimulus for the passing of a new and rigorous censorship law which effectively prevented public exhibition of political films; Cine Liberacion severed its connection with commercial outlets but managed to maintain a well-organized network of unofficial distribution.

**ARLEN,** HAROLD (1905–   ), US songwriter, real name Hyman Arluck, wrote many of his best songs for Hollywood films. His music, heavily jazz-accented, contained melodies of unusual structure and length. Among his best known songs are 'Over the Rainbow' (THE WIZARD OF OZ, 1939), 'Blues in the Night' (*Blues in the Night*, 1941), 'That Old Black Magic' (*Star Spangled Rhythm*, 1942), 'One for My Baby' (*The Sky's the Limit*, 1943), and 'The Man That Got Away' (A STAR IS BORN, 1954).

Arletty in *Les Enfants du Paradis* (Marcel Carné, 1945)

**ARLETTY** (1898–    ), French actress, real
name Arlette-Léonie Bathiat, was a comedy
actress on the stage for ten years before starring
in her first film, *Un Chien qui rapporte* (Jean
Choux, 1930). Dissatisfied with her performance
in this, she accepted only minor roles for some
time in order to learn the craft of film acting. She
found her perfect medium in the succession of
PRÉVERT-CARNÉ films which made her internationally famous, especially LE JOUR SE LÈVE
(1939), LES VISITEURS DU SOIR (1942), and LES
ENFANTS DU PARADIS (1945).

Arletty has rarely made films outside France:
an exception is *The Longest Day* (Ken ANNAKIN,
1962).

**ARLISS,** GEORGE (1868–1946), British actor
who made his stage début in 1886 and from
1901 spent most of his career in America. His
screen début was in 1921 in *The Devil* followed
by the title part in *Disraeli*, a role he repeated in
the sound version (1929) which won him an
OSCAR. His sardonic Rajah of Rukh in *The
Green Goddess* (1923) was also recreated in a
sound remake (1930). Arliss remained essentially a stage actor and his performances in films,
although held in immense popular respect, now
appear flamboyantly theatrical in style, especially

his frequent affectation of a monocle. Most of his
films were historical romances, *Alexander
Hamilton* (1931), *Voltaire* (1933), *Cardinal
Richelieu* (1935), and *The Iron Duke* (1935), in
which he played Wellington. His last screen appearance was the title role in *Dr Syn* (1937). He
wrote two autobiographical books: *Up the years
from Bloomsbury* (1927) and *George Arliss by
himself* (1940).

**ARNHEIM,** RUDOLF, German-born psy-
chologist and aesthetician, Professor of Psychology of Art at Harvard University. His interest in the cinema and his influence in the realm of
film aesthetics dates from the era of silent films.
Besides numerous articles in journals such as
FILM CULTURE and SIGHT AND SOUND, his major
publications have been *Film als kunst* (Berlin,
1932), *Film* (London, 1933), *Radio* (London,
1936), *Art and visual perception* (London,
1956), and *Film as art* (London, 1958), a translation of *Film als kunst* with selections from
*Film*. Arnheim's central thesis with regard to
cinema is that a clear differentiation exists between the world of the senses, and the world that
we perceive on the two-dimensional surface of
the cinema screen: *Film as art* analyses the
disparity between real and artistic experience,

and proves that the creative film-maker is concerned not with placid registration of events before the camera but with the creative interpretation of these events, a process which demands both conceptual intelligence and technical mastery of the medium. In all this theorizing, Arnheim's contemporaneity has been tempered by a concern for the fundamentals of the medium; his essays on sound and on colour for instance, evince a mature grasp of the potential of each, even at the moment of their adoption by the industry. Arnheim has written extensively on the psychology of art, and its relation to the *gestalt* theory of expression. (See also CRITICISM.)

**ARNOLD,** EDWARD (1890–1957), US actor, real name Gunther Schneider, who began his film career in the early thirties. He appeared with Mae WEST in *I'm No Angel* (1933), and soon in leading roles: as the detective in James WHALE's *Remember Last Night?* (1935), in the title part of *Diamond Jim* (1935), as Inspector Porfiry in CRIME AND PUNISHMENT (Josef von STERNBERG, 1935), and as John Sutter in *Sutter's Gold* (1936). He was also in several Frank CAPRA films (*You Can't Take It With You*, 1938; MR SMITH GOES TO WASHINGTON, 1939; *Meet John Doe*, 1941). He renewed his interpretation of Diamond Jim Brady in *Lillian Russell* (1940) and played the Devil in *All that Money Can Buy* (William DIETERLE, 1941). With his solid build and unmistakable features, he was often cast as a plutocrat, but he was a versatile actor, adept both in comedy and in heavier character roles. He remained a familiar figure on the screen until 1956.

**ARNOLD,** MALCOLM (1921–  ), British composer, has had a prolific output of concert music including seven symphonies and eight concertos and has written frequently for films, winning an OSCAR for his score for THE BRIDGE ON THE RIVER KWAI (1957).

**AROMARAMA,** invented by Charles Weiss, was first used to accompany a travelogue, *The Great Wall of China* (1959). Mike TODD backed a system called Glorious Smell-O-Vision with a thriller, *The Scent of Mystery* (1960). But the first use of scent with films was at the climax of *The Broadway Melody* (1929) at its presentation on Broadway, when synthetic orange-blossom perfume belched out of the auditorium's ceiling. Attempts to intensify the effect of films by accompanying sequences with appropriate scents wafted through the cinema's air-conditioning system have been unsuccessful, not least among the problems involved being the difficulty of eliminating each scent before the introduction of the next.

*AROUND THE WORLD IN EIGHTY DAYS*, US, 1956. Todd-AO; 3hr; Eastman Color. *Dir* Michael Anderson; *prod* Michael Todd; *scr* S. J. Perelman, James Poe, John Farrow, from the novel by Jules Verne; *des* James Sullivan, Ken Adams; *mus* Victor Young; *cast* David Niven (Phileas Fogg), Cantinflas (Passepartout), Robert Newton (Inspector Fix), Shirley MacLaine (Princess Aouda).

Mike TODD brought a characteristic flamboyance to his exuberant screen version of Jules Verne's accelerated travelogue. The film's main appeal to audiences lay in the sight of a remarkable number of famous names—including Noël COWARD, Marlene DIETRICH, FERNANDEL, John GIELGUD, Buster KEATON, George RAFT, Frank SINATRA, and Ava GARDNER—in cameo roles; the extravagant production values and tongue-in-cheek treatment of fantasy did not entirely compensate for the over-inflation of the subject. Among generally stylish performances, the much-heralded CANTINFLAS failed to live up to his reputation.

**ARRIFLEX,** the world's first practical mirror reflex camera produced by the Munich-based company, Arnold & Richter. The 35mm model, the Arriflex 35, was first shown at the Leipzig Trade Fair in 1937 and was quickly and widely adopted because of its compactness and lightness, which made it suitable for hand-holding. Being powered by its own battery, the Arriflex was much used as a wartime newsreel camera and has since, in both 35mm and 16mm versions, become one of the most widely used cameras in the world. A development from the basic design is the Arriflex 16BL (later also produced in 35mm) which, being sound insulated or 'blimped', is suitable for synchronous sound shooting. The worldwide acceptance and success of the range of cameras was marked by the presentation of a special OSCAR to Arnold & Richter in 1966 for the design and development of the Arriflex 35. One of the first American films to be shot almost entirely with an Arriflex was Robert FLAHERTY's LOUISIANA STORY (1948). (See CAMERA.)

**ARTAUD,** ANTONIN (1896–1948), French actor and writer, appeared in two films directed by Abel GANCE, *Mater Dolorosa* (1917) and *Napoléon* (1927). His best-known performance is the compassionate Massieu in DREYER's LA PASSION DE JEANNE D'ARC (1928). During the twenties Artaud developed into a melancholic poet, closely associated with contemporary avant-garde movements, particularly with SURREALISM and the 'Theatre of Cruelty'. He wrote the scenario for LA COQUILLE ET LE CLERGYMAN (1928), but although the film was presented by

Germaine DULAC as 'un rêve d'Antonin Artaud' he repudiated her treatment of his ideas.

**ARTCRAFT** see FAMOUS PLAYERS

**ART DIRECTION,** term applied only in cinema to the design of settings, costumes, and accessories. The *art director*, sometimes credited as the *production designer* (see below), fills the same basic role as the designer in the theatre, although, as the resources of photography, lighting, and special effects have developed, the demands on him have become infinitely more complex and varied.

The earliest film-makers paid little special attention to settings. EDISON and LUMIÈRE were concerned only with reproducing reality. MÉLIÈS showed a precocious awareness of the potential of cinema to create magical effects, but his spectacles and fantasies used the backdrops and props customary in variety theatres: the designs have both humour and a primitive charm but no special adaptation to the needs of the camera. When narrative films became the general order, theatrical design conventions were long-lasting. ZECCA's 'filmes réalistes' were played out before painted canvas flats, as were the interiors of POR-TER's THE GREAT TRAIN ROBBERY (1903). The FILM D'ART, such as *L'Assassinat du Duc de Guise* (1908) had magnificent designs by Emile Bertin, but still within the established theatrical manner. FEUILLADE was one of the first directors to break away from conventional set design: FANTÔMAS (1913–14), LES VAMPIRES (1915–16), and JUDEX (1916) had shadowy rococo interiors designed by Robert Jules Garnier, GAUMONT's head of design, combined with exteriors which, shot in the streets of Paris, achieved a feeling for the strange beauty discernible in everyday surroundings.

A virtually immobile camera made three-dimensional detail unnecessary: painters skilled in *trompe l'oeil* techniques could produce a wholly convincing effect from a static middle-distance view. The monumental conception of PASTRONE's CABIRIA (1914) demanded a new approach to film design. Solid sets of unprecedented size were built and the exploratory eye of the moving camera was thereby encouraged to display the settings to greater advantage; once CAMERA MOVEMENTS became an accepted element of film style the function of the designer was definitively severed from that of his counterpart in the theatre. INTOLERANCE (1916) brought together the styles of film design then current. 'The Fall of Babylon', taking account of the recently aroused interest in archaeological discovery, outdid *Cabiria* in historical splendour; 'The Massacre of St Bartholomew' now appears like the last flowering of the *film d'art*; 'The

Mother and the Law' adopted the everyday realism, or 'verismo' which was the main trend in Italy in opposition to historical spectacle (see ITALY).

During the years immediately after the First World War the main advances in film design took place in Germany, partly under the influence of EXPRESSIONISM (which had been at its strongest there), partly through actors, directors and designers who had worked in the theatre with REINHARDT and carried his ideas into films. LUBITSCH's early work was striking for its design quality: *Madame Dubarry* (1919, *Passion* in US), designed by Karl Machus, achieved a combination of opulence and intimacy; in *Das Weib des Faraon* (1921) Ernst Stern produced a more consciously aesthetic effect, placing richly decorated costumes in stark, massive sets. These trends were paralleled in Hollywood, where STROHEIM's silent films echoed and exaggerated the former style while DEMILLE created a fantasy world of glamour and wealth.

Expressionism, although a brief movement in its fully developed form, had a long-term effect on film design and, especially, lighting. In DAS CABINETT DES DR CALIGARI (1919) Hermann WARM, Walter RÖHRIG, and Walter Reimann (all originally painters) abandoned realism and attempted to convey a tortured vision through painted canvas sets and stylized costumes and make-up. This extreme approach was short-lived; but the characteristic diagonal lines and hallucinatory perspectives were carried on through DER GOLEM (1920, designer Hans Poelzig), LANG's *Der müde Tod* (1921, designed by Röhrig and Robert Herlth), NOSFERATU (1922), filmed entirely out of doors but in locations carefully chosen by the designer Albin Grau, and WIENE's *Raskolnikoff* (1923, designer André Andreiev). Lang's training as a painter and architect is evident in all his German films, especially DIE NIBELUNGEN (1924), which realized paintings by Böcklin, and METROPOLIS (1926), with its geometric, futuristic forms. Both films were designed by Otto Hunte, Erich Kettelhut, and Karl Vollbrecht, and they demonstrate the virtuosity of German studio craftsmanship at its peak. The main concurrent style, the KAMMER-SPIELFILM, demanded greater naturalism, a restrained stylization of familiar surroundings, and conformability of scale with the human figure. The fluid, subjective camera movements best exemplified by DER LETZTE MANN (1924, designed by Herlth and Röhrig) necessitated solid, three-dimensional constructions and correct perspectives. The twenties saw the acknowledged pre-eminence of German designers and craftsmen and the most routine productions were endowed with remarkably accomplished settings. The German studios were especially adept at creating perspective in shallow sets with painted back-drops and at reducing three-dimensional models: they reputedly peopled the 'distances' of such sets with children and even dwarfs, dressed as adult extras, to maintain correct scale.

The silent period in French commercial cinema was marked only by the adventurousness of Abel GANCE. In general stock scenery was used, although some of the Impressionism in vogue with the AVANT-GARDE filtered into the studio. The flood of Russian *emigrés* who worked on films produced by Alexandre KAMENKA for Albatros brought an exotic flavour, heavily influenced by the orientalism of Diaghilev's Ballets russes. Marcel L'HERBIER was one of the first French directors to appreciate fully the importance of design: *L'Inhumaine* (1924, designer Robert Mallet-Stevens) had sets of startling modernist simplicity and in *Feu Mathias Pascal* (1925) CAVALCANTI, assisted by Lazare MEERSON, took up and refined Expressionist techniques to convey the dislocated world of Pirandello.

In the Soviet Union didactic aims and restricted means imposed a documentary style on silent films, except in the early experiments of both PROTAZANOV and the FEKS group which were influenced by FUTURISM and the circus. PUDOVKIN and, later, DOVZHENKO made lyrical use of outdoor locations; EISENSTEIN's settings extended sober actuality into the realms of symbolism.

Hollywood art direction was in the main notable for technical expertise. Teams of plasterers, carpenters, painters, upholsterers, and decorators carried out the designers' instructions with speed and a high degree of craftsmanship; but there was in general little concern with matching design to a particular film, and the designer's name carried little weight. There were however exceptional art directors who helped to gain recognition for their craft. Richard Day gained his early experience with Stroheim, concocting settings of elaborate decadence, worked in a quasi-documentary manner on GANGSTER FILMS for WARNER BROS in the thirties, and carried on into stark realism for films by KAZAN including A STREETCAR NAMED DESIRE (1951) and ON THE WATERFRONT (1954). Hans Dreier brought from Germany an extraordinary combination of the baroque and the expressionistic: his best work is seen in the over-heated romances of STERNBERG

*Das Cabinett des Dr Caligari* (Robert Wiene, 1919)

and, in contrast, the mannered wittiness of films by Lubitsch, especially TROUBLE IN PARADISE (1932); he was later responsible for the gloomy settings of SUNSET BOULEVARD (1950). Cedric GIBBONS was the doyen of Hollywood art directors, placing an entirely characteristic gloss on films made by METRO-GOLDWYN-MAYER during his long career there. Van Nest Polglase, who devised the misty, minimal settings of THE INFORMER (1935), collaborated closely with Gregg TOLAND to supply the detail demanded by the camera's intense probing in CITIZEN KANE (1941). Most respected of all was probably William Cameron MENZIES who was credited on GONE WITH THE WIND (1939) as production designer; the term was an innovation, indicating that sets, costumes, and all aspects of design and decoration were parts of an over-all design plan for which he carried the ultimate responsibility: until this time, in the big studios, the separate design skills had operated with a greater or lesser degree of fragmentation. The production designer in his palmy days had a certain inhibiting effect on the film-making process. In *Gone with the Wind* the design element was paramount so that camera angles, the positioning of actors, and inevitably even the editing were deployed to suit the designer's aims.

Political pressures in Germany, Italy, and the Soviet Union in the thirties affected the visual style of films as much as their subjects. Meanwhile in France, great strides were made, especially in suiting the style of design to the subject and mood of a given film. Lazare Meerson working with CLAIR and FEYDER refused to take refuge in empty spectacle or generalization: in UN CHAPEAU DE PAILLE D'ITALIE (1927) the interiors wittily parody the décors of PATHÉ films of the turn of the century; SOUS LES TOITS DE PARIS (1930) applied a kind of fairy-tale formality to authentic reproductions of street scenes; and LA KERMESSE HEROÏQUE (1935) brought Flemish domestic painting to life. The last two also demonstrate Meerson's skill with the use of miniatures to create extended perspective. CARNÉ, with his designer Alexandre TRAUNER, aimed at an effect labelled 'poetic realism' which has endured less successfully than other work of the period: QUAI DES BRUMES and *Hotel du Nord* (both 1938) look uncomfortably artificial today. RENOIR, whose greatest films were designed by Eugène Lourié, leaned more towards realism than poetry, placing his characters in environments that were solidly convincing without obtruding the designer's ideas.

Britain, like America, benefited during the thirties and forties from the arrival of *emigré* film artists from Europe. Vincent KORDA, who had started his film career in France with MARIUS (1931), specialized in the domestic side of historical spectacle—THE PRIVATE LIFE OF HENRY VIII (1933), REMBRANDT (1936)—creating rich effects with comparatively limited means. Alfred JUNGE (who had also worked on *Marius*) was based in Britain from 1932. His fertile imagination created detailed settings ranging from period drama in *The Iron Duke* (1935) to the elaborate fantasy of *A Matter of Life and Death* (1946, *Stairway to Heaven* in US), and the lush Himalayan scenery of *Black Narcissus* (1947). Hein HECKROTH, Junge's costume designer on the latter two, was, like many European designers, a disciple of Gordon CRAIG. His designs for THE RED SHOES (1948) and *The Tales of Hoffmann* (1951) effectively used colour to indicate subjective states.

Other British art directors who made an impression during the forties included Paul Sheriff, best known for his lively, artificial designs for HENRY V (1944), and his assistant on that film, Carmen Dillon, who realized the misty-edged, brutal masses of Elsinore in OLIVIER'S HAMLET (1948). During the course of a distinguished career she was also responsible for the elegantly Edwardian decorative style of ASQUITH'S *The Importance of Being Earnest* (1952).

Up to this time studio shooting was the rule in all film-making countries, except for sequences in Westerns and other action films. Unwieldy equipment and the difficulty of sound recording away from the sound stage or the studio 'lot' made location work an unrewarding exercise, and the great accomplishment of designers and craftsmen must also have inhibited any impulse to use natural surroundings. This skill, both technical and aesthetic, was part of a continual process of improvement on established methods: there were no real innovations until a new direction was given by Italian film-makers during and immediately after the Second World War, where the financial and political exigencies that gave rise to NEO-REALISM compelled them to use real locations out-of-doors and in actual houses, churches, and farms. This gave substance to the raw realism of their themes and the freshness of their work sent film-makers all over the world out into the open in the hope of escaping the artificiality of studio-made settings.

The hope was not always realized. The art director, still needed to transform reality into acceptable realism, often expended considerable efforts to bring real locations up to the standards of studio settings. Young European film-makers, led by the French NOUVELLE VAGUE and not trained in studio methods, made exciting use of real settings for their early films but quickly realized that reality could be adapted to carry a subjective dimension: GODARD in PIERROT-LE-FOU (1965) and DEMY in *Les Demoiselles de Rochefort* (1966), like ANTONIONI in IL DESERTO

ROSSO (*The Red Desert*, 1964), demanded that buildings, objects, even trees should be painted in colours that emphasized their emotional significance.

The availability of studio facilities has meanwhile diminished radically and films that could well have been completely studio-made twenty years ago are now made on location as a matter of course—but the art director's function is still vital. Comparison of two films by Joseph LOSEY, THE SERVANT (1963) designed by Richard Macdonald and ACCIDENT (1967) designed by Carmen Dillon, show how a director's style can be modified by his collaborators. Close collaboration between director and designer (as with other members of the team—cameraman, editor, scriptwriter) can help greatly in giving coherence to the finished work: regular partnerships between director and designer, in addition to those already mentioned include FELLINI and Piero Gherardi, COCTEAU and Christian BÉRARD, MALLE and Bernard Evein. A consistent visual style has run through the JAMES BOND films thanks to the extravagantly fantastic designs of Ken Adam. (See also EFFECTS.)

**ART HOUSE,** term of US origin (equivalent to the French 'cinéma d'art et d'essai') to describe cinemas showing classic films and new films of limited commercial appeal. The art house movement began in France when Jean TEDESCO turned the avant-garde Théâtre du VIEUX COLOMBIER into the Cinéma d'Avant Garde in 1924. Several art houses flourished in Paris in the twenties, notably STUDIO DES URSULINES and STUDIO 28. They formed, together with the ciné-clubs, an outlet for the work of avant-garde film-makers as well as neglected films of pioneers. Art houses continue to flourish in France, encouraged by the cultural climate sympathetic to film and, since 1958, by government subsidy of the exhibition of 'quality' films. In Britain, the FILM SOCIETY in the twenties played the role of the French art houses, showing films from Germany and the USSR which had no commercial outlet. The oldest British art house is the ACADEMY, closely followed by the EVERYMAN.

In the US the art house, or 'little cinema', movement is considered to have originated with Michael Mindlin (president of the 5th Avenue Playhouse Group) who had presented the first American commercial showing of a foreign 'art movie'—DAS CABINETT DES DR CALIGARI (1919) —in 1920. With Symon Gould (founder in 1925 of the International Film Arts Cinema Guild and owner of the Cameo Theater and Film Guild Cinema) Mindlin introduced repertory exhibition, revivals of Hollywood classics, and premières of foreign films, sometimes the only showing they received in the US. The early American art houses were chiefly associated with the mature silent cinema and few survived the coming of sound. The movement was revived in the early fifties by Amos Vogel, founder of Cinema 16, with the aim of showing significant foreign films and avant-garde work of American or foreign origin, all unlikely to obtain commercial distribution in the US. In California, Pauline KAEL ran the Berkeley Cinema Guild for fifteen years, providing a model for American art houses with repertory presentations of classics, retrospectives, and the avant-garde for a minority audience.

The Confédération Internationale des Cinémas d'Art et d'Essai (CICAE) exists to facilitate and co-ordinate the work of art houses. Of recent years this work has been expanded and to some extent taken over by the cinemas of the various national film institutes.

**ARTHUR,** JEAN (1905–   ), US actress, real name Gladys Georgianna Greene, played her first film role in John FORD's *Cameo Kirby* (1923). Her husky voice came to be an important part of her attractively distinctive personality, but ironically it was just this which at first prevented her finding good roles in the early days of sound. Not until Ford's *The Whole Town's Talking* (1935) was she given an appropriate part as the timid hero's down-to-earth but good-natured colleague, and she became skilled in playing the tough, soft-hearted working girls who received much screen attention in Hollywood films of the thirties. MR DEEDS GOES TO TOWN (1936) was the first of three CAPRA films which gave her similar parts, and she was the classic HAWKS woman in *Only Angels Have Wings* (1939). Despite considerable success, she was painfully shy and virtually retired on the expiry of her COLUMBIA contract in 1944. Since then she has appeared only in *A Foreign Affair* (1948) and SHANE (1953), although she has made infrequent theatre and television appearances including a comedy series, 'The Jean Arthur Show'.

**ARTS COUNCIL OF GREAT BRITAIN, The,** established in 1945, developed from the wartime Committee for the Encouragement of Music and the Arts (CEMA). Its purpose is 'developing and inspiring a greater knowledge, understanding, and practice of the arts' and in furtherance of this aim it has sponsored films on art and artists for several years. Notable among these are *Turner* (1966) and *The Pre-Raphaelite Revolt* (1967), both directed by David Thompson, and *The Secret World of Odilon Redon* (Stephen Cross, 1973). An Art Film Committee was formed in 1968 and since then a number of short films on individual painters and sculptors has been financed by the Council. The films are most frequently used by educational establishments, but are also occasionally shown in supporting programmes in ART HOUSES and some have been seen on television abroad.

**ARZNER, DOROTHY** (1900–   ), America's most successful woman director, started in films by typing scripts, but soon progressed to editing. She edited *Blood and Sand* (1922) and created the bull-fighting sequences out of STOCK footage and some matching shots of VALENTINO, but is best known for her work on THE COVERED WAGON (1923). *Fashions for Women* (1927) was her first film as a director, and later films included *Wild Party* (1929), a rather innocent romance, despite its title, which co-starred Fredric MARCH and Clara BOW. Many of her films were romantic dramas like *Christopher Strong* (1933) in which Katharine HEPBURN suffered through an unhappy love affair with a married man. After directing *First Comes Courage* (1943) she went to work in the American Department of Education, later becoming a lecturer in the film department at the University of Southern California.

**ASC** (American Society of Cinematographers) may be seen on credit titles after the name of the cameraman or director of photography. Membership of the society is by invitation only and is confined to craftsmen working in Hollywood; it was founded in 1918, its aim being 'to advance the art and science of cinematography'.

**ASHES AND DIAMONDS** see POPIÓL I DIAMENT

**ASPECT RATIO,** the physical proportions of the image projected on to the cinema screen. In the early years of cinema the desirable proportion was generally accepted as 1·33:1, derived from the picture shape adopted by EDISON for his KINETOGRAPH. Various attempts to expand the image, either by all-round enlargement or by altering the width/height ratio met with little success, mainly because of the technical problems involved (see WIDE SCREEN).

The first important (although short-lasting) change in aspect ratio came with the introduction of sound. The area of film available for the image was narrowed to allow for the printing of a single optical sound track along one side, creating a picture with the proportions 1·2:1. This was so nearly square as to be unpleasing aesthetically and from 1932 the practice of masking the camera aperture, so as to reduce the height of the image and maintain the accepted ratio (the 'academy frame'), was adopted internationally.

With the introduction of CINEMASCOPE in 1953, and successive versions of ANAMORPHIC

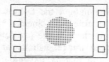

35mm. full screen aperture (silent): aspect ratio 1·33:1 approx.

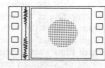

35mm.original sound aperture:aspect ratio approx.1·2:1,centre line of picture shifted to right.

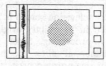

35mm. academy aperture:aspect ratio 1·33:1

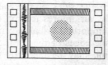

35mm. masked for widescreen:aspect ratio 1·85:1. Sometimes shot as academy aperture and masked to 1·85:1 in projection.

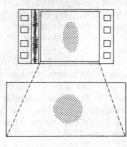

35mm. anamorphic (CinemaScope, Panavision) squeezed image, squeezed 2:1(width of objects is half normal width). Projected appearance of 35mm. anamorphic image unsqueezed 2:1: aspect ratio 2·35:1

70mm. non-anamorphic with stereophonic magnetic tracks (left, right, centre, control or back-of-cinema): aspect ratio 2·2:1; five perforations high. No squeeze.

and wide screen processes, a multiplicity of aspect ratios came into common use, from the traditional 1·33:1 to the 2·7:1 of Ultra-Panavision and others. Well-equipped cinemas are provided with electrically controlled black masking which adjusts the screen to the exact ratio of any film. Unfortunately, the failure to make such equipment available in all cinemas has led to a serious abuse: a mask in the projector arbitrarily sets the screen image, usually at a ratio of 1·85:1. This practice is particularly objectionable when a film with the academy aspect ratio is shown; the cropping of the upper and lower edges of the frame makes the film as seen a travesty of the original. 'Flat' (i.e. non-anamorphic) 16mm prints of films shot in scope processes also distort the original image by cropping the sides of the frame.

The aspect ratio of the television screen is 5:4 and no film can be seen in its exactly original form without costly re-processing. Since the preponderance of commercial films are now made in wide screen or anamorphic processes, television showing with the sides of the frame omitted can give only an impression of the original's effect. When important visual information is placed at the side edges of the composition, some compensation may be made by the use of devices incorporated in the TELECINE machine which selectively PAN across the frame; but in practice this amounts to a virtual re-editing of the film and must be considered undesirable.

Spectators puzzled by differences and discrepancies on the screen can learn more from *Behind the screen* by Kenneth MacGowan, New York, 1967, *The Focal encyclopedia of film and television techniques*, London, New York, 1969, and *A Discovery of cinema* by Thorold Dickinson, London, New York, 1971.

Commoner anamorphic and wide screen processes with their aspect ratios:

*anamorphic:*

| | |
|---|---|
| CinemaScope | 2·55:1 with stereo sound |
| | 2·35:1 with single track sound |
| SuperScope | 2:1 and 2·35:1 |
| Technirama | 2:1 |
| Techniscope | 2·35:1 |
| Ultra-Panavision | 2·7:1 |

*wide screen:*

| | |
|---|---|
| Todd-AO | 2·2:1 |
| VistaVision | 1·85:1 |

Non-anamorphic 35mm prints for general distribution usually have an aspect ratio of 1·85:1. (See also DYNAMIC FRAME, PROJECTORS.)

*ASPHALT JUNGLE, The*, US, 1950. 1¾hr. *Dir* John Huston; *prod* MGM; *scr* Huston, Ben Maddows, from the novel by W. R. Burnett; *ph* Harold Rosson; *mus* Miklos Rozsa; *cast* Sterling Hayden (Dix Handley), Louis Calhern (Alonzo D. Emmerich), Jean Hagen (Doll Conovan), James Whitmore (Gus Minissi), Sam Jaffe (Reimenschneider).

HUSTON brought an authentic style to this vivid account of a minutely planned jewel robbery and its sour aftermath of double-cross. The treatment incorporated a convincing account of police activity but largely avoided the then fashionable semi-documentary approach to concentrate on the criminal mind and the characters of the criminals. This new approach was much admired and had considerable influence on subsequent crime films, many of which borrowed unashamedly from it.

Sterling HAYDEN had the star role as a killer who loves horses and dreams of his childhood home, but the players who commanded most attention were Louis CALHERN as a crooked lawyer and Sam Jaffe as the criminal mastermind. Marilyn MONROE made one of her earlier appearances in the supporting cast.

**ASQUITH,** the Hon. ANTHONY (1902–68), British director, was a son of Herbert Asquith, British Prime Minister 1908–15 and later created Earl of Oxford and Asquith. He learned about film-making on a visit to Hollywood, and on his return to England made three distinguished silent films, all thrillers with strong atmospheric effects: *Shooting Stars* (1927), *Underground* (1928), and *A Cottage on Dartmoor* (1930). *Tell England* (1931, *Battle of Gallipoli* in US) was his first sound film (although *A Cottage on Dartmoor* had some sound sequences added before release), and it added lustre to his reputation with its authenticity and technical command. Asquith's next major success was his brilliant adaptation of Shaw's PYGMALION (1938) which was followed the next year by *French Without Tears*, the first of his successful collaborations with Terence RATTIGAN. During the war he divided his activities between polished entertainment films (*Quiet Wedding*, 1940; *Fanny by Gaslight*, 1944, *Man of Evil* in US) and semi-documentary war dramas (*We Dive at Dawn*, 1943; *The Way to the Stars*, 1945). In later years he specialized almost entirely in adaptations from stage plays: Rattigan's *The Winslow Boy* (1948) and *The Browning Version* (1951), an elegant and sparkling version of WILDE's *The Importance of Being Earnest* (1952), Shaw's *The Doctor's Dilemma* (1958) and *The Millionairess* (1960) were all excellent transcriptions of theatrical material in cinematic terms. His last two films, *The VIPs* (1963) and *The Yellow Rolls Royce* (1964), both from scripts by Rattigan, had a faded elegance which recalled the appeal of his best films but which was out of key with audiences of the sixties.

Asquith gave much of his time to trade union and social and political activities on behalf of his fellow technicians and was the first president of the ACTT. Commemorating his interest in film music the SOCIETY OF FILM AND TELEVISION ARTS has established an annual Anthony Asquith Memorial Award for the year's best film score.

**ASSEMBLY,** the first stage in cutting film. All shots are joined together in script order. The SLATE and camera flashes are removed but no attempt has yet been made to make accurate cuts.

**ASSOCIATED BRITISH CINEMAS** (ABC), British cinema circuit, the exhibition arm of Associated British Picture Corporation. Founded in 1928, the company took over the thriving Union Cinemas Ltd in 1937, resulting in a total of 431 cinemas under its control. Now a part of Electrical and Musical Industries (EMI), the circuit is still a powerful group and the only serious rival to the RANK chain.

**ASSOCIATED BRITISH PICTURE CORPORATION** (ABPC), the production division of the Associated British organization was incorporated in 1926 but did not become active until 1932. It then replaced British International Pictures (BIP), which had produced all the more notable British films since 1927 at its studios in Elstree. At the same time PATHÉ replaced Wardour Films which over the preceding few years had become a major British distribution force. ABPC as producers, Pathé as distributors, and ABC (Associated British Cinemas) as exhibitors became sister companies. (Associated British Film Distributors, formed in 1932, was not linked to the consortium, but to Associated Talking Pictures which later became EALING STUDIOS.)

During the thirties and forties ABPC produced chiefly lightweight comedies and thrillers at its Elstree and Welwyn studios. Few remarkable films emerged, some exceptions being *Jamaica Inn* (Alfred HITCHCOCK, 1939); *Piccadilly Incident* (Herbert WILCOX, 1946), which made Michael WILDING a star; Thorold DICKINSON's THE QUEEN OF SPADES (1948); Alberto CAVALCANTI's *For Them That Trespass* (1949); *Stage Fright* (Hitchcock, 1950); and *The Dam Busters* (Michael Anderson, 1955), an outstandingly successful war film. Feature film production was gradually abandoned in the late fifties and the distribution arm became Warner-Pathé in 1960. In 1969 the consortium was taken over by Electrical and Musical Industries (EMI) who resumed production at Elstree; several striking successes included *The Railway Children* (1970) and THE GO-BETWEEN (1971) as well as a number of films based on popular television series. The distribution company handled METRO-GOLDWYN-MAYER releases in 1970–4 as MGM-EMI, then became Anglo-EMI when MGM withdrew from the film business.

**ASTAIRE,** FRED (1899–    ), US dancer, singer, and actor, real name Fred Austerlitz, who had a long and successful stage career with his sister Adele, beginning when they were small children. When Adele, on marrying, retired, he accepted an offer from RKO, his film début being a guest appearance in *Dancing Lady* (1933). He was featured with Ginger ROGERS in *Flying Down to Rio* (1933), and the show-stopping success of their number 'The Carioca' led to the delightful series which set a standard for screen musicals of the thirties (see MUSICALS). All their films had the same basic plot, a light-hearted romance acted by what became a recognizable stock company; their enduring appeal is in the Astaire–Rogers partnership and particularly in the range and invention of the choreography for which (although he did not take screen credit) Astaire was largely responsible, helped usually by Hermes Pan. The elegance and precision of his solo number 'Top Hat, White Tie and Tails' in TOP HAT (1935), the virtuosity of 'Bojangles of Harlem' and the sheer exuberance of 'Pick Yourself Up', both from SWING TIME (1936), and the romantic sweep of the ballroom dancing numbers in all these early films demonstrate aspects of his dancing versatility. Although his voice, a light, reedy tenor, was apparently unpromising, he was almost equally successful as a singer because of his skill at pointing and phrasing a lyric. Some of the best song-writers of the thirties wrote especially for him: the quintessential Cole PORTER–Fred Astaire number 'Night and Day' was written for the Broadway show which was filmed as *The Gay Divorcee* (1934); *Roberta* (1935) included 'I Won't Dance' by Jerome KERN; *Follow the Fleet* (1936) had several memorable numbers by Irving BERLIN; George GERSHWIN's 'A Foggy Day' originated in *Damsel in Distress* (1937); *Shall We Dance?* (1937) featured the nostalgic 'They Can't Take That Away from Me', one of Gershwin's (and Astaire's) best songs.

After *The Story of Vernon and Irene Castle* (1939) the Astaire–Rogers partnership ended, to be revived once more in *The Barkleys of Broadway* (1949). Astaire's success in musicals continued with other partners, notably Judy GARLAND in EASTER PARADE (1948) and Cyd CHARISSE in THE BAND WAGON (1953) and *Silk Stockings* (1957) which added modern ballet to his accomplishments.

By now in his late fifties (although this was not apparent from his dancing) Astaire turned to straight dramatic parts with *On the Beach* (1959). He continued to dance in a number of successful musical television spectaculars and sang and danced a little in COPPOLA's excellent *Finian's Rainbow* (1968). He published a modest and likeable autobiography called *Steps in time* in 1959.

**ASTOR,** MARY (1906–  ), US actress, real name Lucile Langhanke, whose long, full career included type-casting as the beautiful defence-less heroine, as in *Don Juan* (1926) with John BARRYMORE, and as the sympathetic mother, notably in MEET ME IN ST LOUIS (1944). Her range was far wider, however, and her most famous role is probably the beautiful, lying vil-lainess in THE MALTESE FALCON (1941), although her only OSCAR (1941, for Best Supporting Actress) was for her performance in an eternal triangle story, *The Great Lie* (1941).

**ASTRUC,** ALEXANDRE (1923–  ), French critic and director, studied law and literature, then worked as a journalist and as assistant to Marcel Achard, Marc ALLÉGRET, and Marcel PAGLIERO. His début as a serious film director was a short film, *Le Rideau cramoisi* (1952), a stylized adaptation from the first 'Diabolique' of Barbey d'Aurevilly which, although it won critical recognition, was not successful commer-cially. His later work has been similarly received, and there have been long intervals in which he has not worked on films.

His first full-length feature, *Les Mauvaises Rencontres* (1955), was followed by *Une Vie* (1958), from a short story by Maupassant; *La Proie pour l'ombre* (1960), notable for the per-formance of Annie GIRARDOT, was Astruc's first film from an original script. After *L'Education sentimentale* (1962), adapted from Flaubert's novel, he made two war films: *La Longue Marche* (1966) and *Flammes sur l'Adriatique* (1968).

He is best known as a critic, especially for his theory of the 'caméra-stylo', a film language that would be the equal of literature in suggestiveness and subtlety. His own films, however, tend to wordiness and reliance on surface imagery.

*ATALANTE, L'* (*Le Chaland qui passe*), France, 1934. 1½hr. *Dir* Jean Vigo; *prod* J. L. Nounez for Gaumont; *scr* Vigo, Albert Riera; *ph* Boris Kaufman, Louis Berger; *des* Francis Jourdain; *ed* Louis Chavance; *mus* Maurice Jaubert; *cast* Jean Dasté (Jean), Dita Parlo (Juliette), Michel Simon (le Père Jules), Gilles Margaritis (ped-lar), Louis Lefevre (boy).

A banal story about a young barge-master and his bride, chosen by his producer after the trouble caused by ZÉRO DE CONDUITE (1933), was very freely treated by VIGO. The character of le Père Jules in particular, as seen by Vigo and brought to life by Michel SIMON, gave scope for surrealist fantasy as well as humour and warmth.

The exteriors were shot in the winter of 1933–4 around the canals north-east of Paris. The exceptionally severe weather caused not only the final breakdown of Vigo's health but also great difficulties in shooting; but the result is often a lyricism and beauty rarely surpassed. Details of life on the barge are simple and realis-tic; back in the studio, Vigo insisted on shooting within the cramped confines of an exact replica of the barge's interior, refusing the usual facilities of studio construction. He collapsed before the final aerial shots were completed, but was able to discuss their editing.

The film was very coldly received on its first presentation. Before GAUMONT would undertake distribution they insisted on crucial cuts. They foisted on the film in place of JAUBERT's delicate music the popular song 'Le Chaland qui passe', and issued the mutilated film under that title, but even this version had no success.

In 1940 the stoppage of American imports into France aided efforts to secure the film's re-release. A reconstituted version, restoring some cut sequences, Jaubert's music, and the original title, enjoyed a moderate success. Devoted efforts have been made since the war to restore *L'Atalante* to the form Vigo intended. Not all the defects in structure and continuity are attribut-able to mutilation: some were problems which Vigo himself failed to solve. Nevertheless, *L'Atalante* can now be seen as the work of one of the most original artists in cinema.

*ATLANTIDE, L',* France, 1921. 3½hr. *Dir* Jacques Feyder; *prod* Thaelmann; *scr* Feyder, from the novel by Pierre Benoît; *ph* Georges Specht; *des* Manuel Orazi; *cast* Stacia Napier-kowska (Antinea), Jean Angelo (Captain Mor-hange), Georges Melchior (Lt de St Avit), Marie-Louise Iribe (Tanit Zerga), Mohammed Ben Nuri (Bon Djema).

Two soldiers serving in Africa rediscover the lost city of Atlantis. The queen of the city, Antinea, has the power to make all men fall in love with her, but Morhange resists her charms with disastrous consequences.

FEYDER shot most of the film on location in the desert near Algiers, deriving spectacular effects from the vast plains of shimmering sand. A slight story was amply compensated for the public by the romantic exoticism of the atmo-sphere and the extravagance of the production; *L'Atlantide* was extremely successful, continuing to attract an audience even after a sound version had been made by PABST in 1932.

***ATONEMENT OF GOSTA BERLING, The,*** see GÖSTA BERLINGS SAGA

**ATTENBOROUGH,** RICHARD (1923– ), British actor, producer, and director. His first film, IN WHICH WE SERVE (1942), established him as a player of youthful, often weak, characters, a type which tended to dominate his career for almost twenty years. One notable exception was his performance as Pinkie, the vicious young thug in *Brighton Rock* (1947). Since founding his own production companies, Beaver Films (with Bryan FORBES) and Allied Film Makers (with Forbes, Basil DEARDEN, and others), he has shown unusual willingness as a producer to tackle bleak topics in films such as *The Angry Silence* (1960), *Séance on a Wet Afternoon* (1964), and *10 Rillington Place* (1970), all of which have extended his acting range into character roles. His first film as director was OH! WHAT A LOVELY WAR (1969).

**AUDRAN,** STÉPHANE, French actress, has usually appeared under the direction of Claude CHABROL whom she married in 1964. Her assurance and subtle expressiveness have illuminated very varied kinds of female psychology, and their partnership has resulted in some films of outstanding quality, notably *Les Biches* (1968), *La Femme infidèle* (1968), LE BOUCHER (1969), and JUSTE AVANT LA NUIT (1971). She also brought a vitally cryptic quality to BUÑUEL'S LE CHARME DISCRET DE LA BOURGEOISIE (1972).

**AUDRY,** JACQUELINE (1908– ), French director who worked as a continuity girl before directing her first film—a short called *Les Chevaux du Vercors* (1943). She made her name with GIGI (1949) the first of a trilogy based on stories by COLETTE, all starring Danièle DELORME. Her later films include *Huis Clos* (1954), from Sartre's play, and *Les Petits Matins* (1961).

**AURIC,** GEORGES (1899– ), French composer, a member of the group known as 'Les Six', has written the scores for many films. He has done distinguished work in France (A NOUS LA LIBERTÉ, 1931), Britain (DEAD OF NIGHT, CAESAR AND CLEOPATRA, both 1945, THE QUEEN OF SPADES, 1948), and the US (ROMAN HOLIDAY, 1953). His waltz theme from MOULIN ROUGE (1952) became very popular in its own right.

**AURIOL,** JEAN-GEORGE (1907–50), French critic and essayist who in 1927 founded the magazine *Du Cinéma*, which became *La Revue du Cinéma* (1929–31). He participated in founding the avant-garde Paris cinema STUDIO 28. From 1933 to 1944 he was a critic and scriptwriter of such films as L'HERBIER's *L'Honorable Catherine* (1942). In 1946–9 he resumed publication of *La Revue du Cinéma*, which was devoted to critical research into the history of the cinema. After his death in a car crash his work was continued by André BAZIN and DONIOL-VALCROZE in CAHIERS DU CINÉMA.

**AUSTRALIA.** The strong Australian tradition of reporting, documentary, and ethnographic film began as early as 1896 when a LUMIÈRE representative filmed the Melbourne Cup yacht race. The following year a newsreel on aboriginals was made and in 1901 Sir William Baldwin Spencer began to film aboriginals in Central Australia. *The Story of the Kelly Gang*, a sixty-six-minute fiction film which was premièred at the Melbourne Town Hall on Boxing Day 1906, is believed to be the world's first feature film: many other films about the Australian folk-hero have been made.

Cut off from the European product by the First World War, Australia found her own industry burgeoning. Raymond Longford, the most distinguished director of these days, had made nineteen features by 1920 when he directed *The Sentimental Bloke* which had international distribution, becoming a notable financial and artistic success in Britain. Charles CHAUVEL began his thirty years as a director with *Moth of Mombi* (1926). However, like other countries, Australia became a ready market for Hollywood in the mid-twenties and the domestic industry declined: the occasional features produced included *Out of the Shadows* (1930), Australia's first sound film. The death-blow to virtually all home production came in the late forties, when one of the two exhibition circuits was taken over by the American Hoyt's and the other by RANK's Greater Union. The programmes they showed were almost entirely American or British: Chauvel had some success with *The Rats of Tobruk* (1948), about the Australians besieged in that town in 1942, but *Jedda* (1953), which tackled the aborigine problem, found no favour with Australian audiences. There was a temporary vogue for filming British and American productions in Australia, the best of which were THE OVERLANDERS (1946) and *Eureka Stockade* (1948), both directed by Harry WATT for EALING STUDIOS, *Bush Christmas* (1947), directed by Ralph Smart for Rank, and *The Shiralee* (1957), directed by Leslie Norman for Ealing. Another version of *Ned Kelly* (1970) was made in Australia, directed by Tony RICHARDSON with Mick Jagger of the Rolling Stones in the title role.

The National Film Board was set up in 1945, charged with producing documentaries about Australia and importing educational films for Australian distribution. The Board governs the Commonwealth Film Unit which makes the films and is financed solely by the government through the News and Information Bureau. The opportunities for creative film-making have proved limited, and sometimes only three or four non-educational films a year have been possible. Recently, however, new ideas have started to flow and Ian DUNLOP, the distinguished ethnographer, has been joined at the Unit by other adventurous film-makers such as Stefan Sargent and Rhonda Small. Travelling scholarships have enabled film-makers to make contact with their counterparts in other countries.

From the late sixties feature production began to show signs of a revival, but few Australian films have been seen abroad. An exception is *The Adventures of Barry McKenzie* (Bruce Beresford, 1972), based on a comic strip in the satirical magazine *Private Eye*, which, after tremendous success with Australian audiences, was given some international distribution.

**AUSTRIA.** The first Austrian film, *Von Stufe zu Stufe*, was directed in 1908 by Anton Kolm. In 1910–11 Alexander Count Kolowrat founded the production company Sascha and the Film-Count studios at Sievering where Austria's first feature film, *Der Millionenonkel* (1913), was made. Until his death in 1927 Kolowrat proved the most dynamic figure in the Austrian film industry; in 1918 he amalgamated most of the other existing companies and started the first Austrian newsfilm company, Sascha Woche.

Austrian film was able to draw on the rich theatrical tradition of the Austro-Hungarian Empire. Adaptations of operas and operettas were frequently made as silent films with accompanying music played by a live orchestra: Richard Strauss's *Der Rosenkavalier* was produced in this way in 1926, directed by Robert WIENE (see OPERA FILMS). But the impoverishment of Austria after the division of the Empire combined with the increasing power of the German industry to prevent the growth of a distinctive Austrian cinema. Austrian film-makers who were attracted to work in Germany included Fritz LANG, G. W. PABST, Karl GRÜNE, and Willi FORST, and from the late twenties Austrian studios were used mainly to make German-backed films including Max OPHULS' LIEBELEI (1932) and Forst's *Maskerade* (1934). During the Second World War the Austrian companies were taken over by the Germans and produced light entertainment films in the Viennese tradition. After 1945, with the exception of Pabst (*Der Prozess*, 1948) and Walter Kolm (*Eroica*, 1949), Austrian film-makers maintained the formula of musicals and popular entertainment films until the mid-fifties. Subsequently Austrian cinema rapidly stagnated and the studios are mostly rented by German television companies. Die Entwicklung, the Austrian underground, is however emerging as an alternative to commercial cinema.

There are two archives, the official Österreichisches Filmarchiv at Laxenburg and the State-aided but independent Österreichisches Filmmuseum which holds screenings at the Albertina Gallery in Vienna. Austria holds a leading position in the field of film education. As early as 1907, Dr Arche, with the firm Lechner, received official encouragement to organize classroom films. Today there are more than a hundred educational film libraries. Since 1956 the association Aktion der gute Film has actively promoted the exchange and discussion of cultural films, including the distribution of foreign films.

**AUTANT-LARA,** CLAUDE (1903– ), French director, worked as a set designer during the twenties and directed an experimental short *Fait divers* (1923). He also experimented with the ANAMORPHIC lens in *Construire un feu* (1927) (see also WIDE SCREEN).

With the coming of sound he spent two years in Hollywood directing French versions of American films. He returned to France to make the film operetta *Ciboulette* (1933). He became really established during the war with several elegant films starring Odette Joyeux, all as light and insubstantial as their titles suggest: *Le Mariage de Chifon* (1942), *Lettres d'amour* (1942), *Douce* (1943), on which he established the script-writing team Aurenche and Bost, who collaborated on almost all his subsequent films, and *Sylvie et le fantôme* (1945).

LE DIABLE AU CORPS (1947), a more serious work, was one of his most successful films. Its exploration of love in opposition to social conventions introduced a theme often repeated in later works, and one which brought him frequently into conflict with conservative opinion. He followed this with two farces, the light but very effective *Occupe-toi d'Amélie* (1949), adapted from Feydeau, and *L'Auberge rouge* (1951), starring FERNANDEL as a distinctly unholy monk. After directing the 'Orgueil' ('Pride') episode in *Les Sept Péchés capitaux* (1951) and *Le Bon Dieu sans confession* (1953), he adapted COLETTE's novel for *Le Blé en herbe* (1954), which deals with the triangular relationship between a pair of teenage lovers and an older woman. Adaptations from the classics— Stendhal's *Le Rouge et le noir* (1954) and Dostoevsky's *Le Joueur* (1958)—were less successful and most of his later films were made specifically for the commercial market, but in the anti-military *Non uccidere* (*Thou Shalt Not Kill*, 1961) and *Journal d'une femme en blanc* (1965), which dealt with abortion, he reverted to his favourite radical preoccupations.

During his long and uneven career Autant-Lara has been attacked on the one hand for his courageous treatment of anti-establishment themes and on the other for his completely traditional approach to film-making. His handling of actors, however, particularly in romantic situations, has produced some work of enduring quality.

**AUTEUR THEORY,** method of criticism derived from and extending BAZIN's view of realism, introduced by the writers in CAHIERS DU CINÉMA during the fifties. Its basis was the claim that a film-maker should be considered in the light of thematic consistency and development throughout his work; and its great virtue was that it allowed serious consideration to be given to many Hollywood directors previously outside the pale of the 'cinema as art' school of criticism. The *auteur* critics, TRUFFAUT, GODARD, ROHMER, CHABROL outstanding among them, developed the theory to embrace the Hollywood directors they particularly enjoyed and whose work was to influence their own films: HITCHCOCK was the brightest star in their galaxy and closely clustered round him were MINNELLI, PREMINGER, HAWKS, and Nicholas RAY. Other Hollywood directors, particularly those of 'B'-PICTURES, became susceptible of serious treatment. Some European directors were admitted, for different reasons: RENOIR, ROSSELLINI, and BRESSON were outstanding among these, the first finding a place mainly because earlier critics had failed to accommodate him in their theory.

As the *Cahiers* critics abandoned writing for film-making the *auteur* theory was taken up in England by the young contributors to *Movie* in the early sixties and it was launched in the US with a flourish by Andrew SARRIS. The pantheon was at first consolidated rather than expanded, but the *auteur* theory, aided by some extraneous refinements, lurched sideways in the late sixties to include such directors as Budd BOETTICHER, Douglas SIRK, and Samuel FULLER.

Essentially idealist and humanist, the theory served its purpose in generating new insights, but is in the process of being overtaken by more rigorous and analytical critical approaches.

**AUTRY,** GENE (1907– ), singing cowboy, was a railway telegrapher when Will ROGERS, who liked his singing, suggested he become a professional entertainer. From 1928 he sang on radio and soon began to make records. In 1934 he had two small singing parts in Westerns and he became a popular success with *Tumblin' Tumbleweeds* (1935), in which he starred with his horse Champion and Smiley Burnette. They made a long series of musical Westerns for REPUBLIC, notably *Carolina Moon* (1940) and *Back in the Saddle* (1941), before Autry joined the US Air Corps in 1942, when his place was filled by Roy ROGERS. He enjoyed continuing success in Hollywood after the war and branched out into television in 1950 to make 'The Gene Autry Show' and to produce several other successful series.

**AUTUMN AFTERNOON, An,** see SAMMA NO AJI

**AVANT-GARDE,** term used loosely to describe any experimental movement in the arts, working outside or in opposition to accepted forms, dealing with subjects which may be considered unsuitable or offensive by contemporary standards, and essentially hostile to commercial considerations. In cinema, the term is often applied specifically to the various radical experimentalists active in France and Germany in the period 1918–30 as well as later modernist movements.

In France several experimental schools emerged. The first of these owed much to Impressionism: soft focus, superimposition, and striking camera angles were its main features. Abel GANCE, Germaine DULAC, Louis DELLUC, Jean EPSTEIN, Marcel L'HERBIER, Jean RENOIR, Alberto CAVALCANTI, and Jean GRÉMILLON were the principal representatives of this school. From 1925 to 1930 *cinéma-pur*, an essentially nonnarrative form deriving from the work in Germany of Viking EGGELING and Walter RUTTMANN, drew several French film-makers into the field of ABSTRACT FILM: they included Henri CHOMETTE, Grémillon, Marcel Duchamp, Dulac, Fernand LÉGER, and Eugene Deslaw. During this time the Surrealists seized on film as the perfect medium (see SURREALISM): Man RAY, René CLAIR, Dulac, Jacques PRÉVERT, Jean COCTEAU, Salvador DALI, Luis BUÑUEL, and Jean VIGO all contributed to the expression of Surrealist ideas through film. In Germany Oskar FISCHINGER maintained the development of abstract film into the early thirties, while Ruttmann, who had moved into the field of semi-documentary, applied the aesthetics of abstraction to social milieu. During the period of artistic ferment that followed the Revolution, the Russian avant-garde expressed itself in films chiefly through experimental MONTAGE and dramatic caricature in the work of KOZINTSEV and TRAUBERG, KULESHOV, VERTOV, EISENSTEIN, and PROTAZANOV. In Great Britain, Len LYE was almost alone in working experimentally in film, using techniques of drawing directly on to film stock, but some of the visual effects achieved by other members of the GPO Film Unit (see CROWN FILM UNIT) were influenced by the European avant-garde.

The rapid dwindling of experimental cinema in

Europe during the early thirties was caused, apart from the effects of political ideology in Germany and the USSR, by the increased complexity of working with sound. The avant-garde in the US was, like commercial cinema, immeasurably enriched by many artists exiled from Europe. EXPRESSIONISM (although it had been commercially accepted in Germany and was therefore not part of the true avant-garde) formed one branch of the experimental stream in America: representative films were *The Last Moment* (Paul FÉJOS, 1927) and *The Life and Death of 9413, A Hollywood Extra* (Robert FLOREY, 1928). The Russian experiments in montage were emulated in a number of 'cine poems' including *Footnotes to Fact* (Lewis JACOBS, 1932). In contrast, the abstract movement had its followers including Ralph Steiner ($H_2O$, 1929) and survived into the sound era with many attempts to synthesize visual and musical rhythms. Fischinger, now working in the US, also continued to work on abstract films and was influential in the attempt to make abstraction commercially viable in FANTASIA (1940). Surrealism, which was to some extent rapidly absorbed into commercial cinema, was slower to emerge in the American avant-garde: it is best represented in the post-war work of Maya DEREN and Kenneth ANGER and continues to be an important element in American UNDERGROUND cinema. Unlike avant-garde movements in other countries, the American experimental cinema has maintained a lively and continuing development, partly attributable to improvements in cheap, simple equipment (see 8MM, 16MM). Elsewhere, the avant-garde spirit is now most active in the use of film as a political tool by GODARD, STRAUB, MARKER, and other committed film-makers.

Many new fields first explored by avant-garde film-makers have widened the horizons of commercial cinema, for in film, as in all the other arts, the existence of a vigorous experimental element is essential to the acceptance of new thematic and stylistic ideas in the body of generally accepted work.

*AVEU, L'* (*The Confession*), France/Italy, 1970. Eastman Color; $2\frac{3}{4}$hr. *Dir* Costa-Gavras; *prod* Films Corona/Films Pomereu (Paris)/Fono Roma/Selena Cinematografica (Rome); *scr* Jorge Semprun, based on the book by Lise and Artur London; *ph* Raoul Coutard; *cast* Yves Montand (Artur London), Simone Signoret (Lise), Gabriele Ferzetti (Kouhoutek), Michel Vitold (Smola).

The false confession of treason forced from the Czech Cabinet Minister Artur London for the purposes of staging a show trial in 1951 forms the basis of the book, which the film follows closely. Unlike z (1968), *L'Aveu* makes no pretence at being fiction and COSTA-GAVRAS's attack on the abuses of Communist government is as unsparing as his account of political murder under right-wing totalitarianism.

*AVVENTURA, L'*, Italy/France, 1960. $2\frac{1}{4}$hr. *Dir* Michelangelo Antonioni; *prod* Produzioni Cinematografiche Europee (Rome), Société Cinématographique Lyre (Paris); *scr* Antonioni, Elio Bartolini, Tonino Guerra; *ph* Aldo Scavarda; *des* Piero Poletto; *ed* Eraldo Da Roma; *mus* Giovanni Fusco; *cast* Monica Vitti (Claudia), Lea Massari (Anna), Gabriele Ferzetti (Sandro), Dominique Blanchar (Giulia), James Addams (Corrado), Esmeralda Ruspoli (Patrizia), Renzo Ricci (Anna's father), Dorothy De Poliolo (Gloria Perkins), Lelio Luttazzi (Raimundo).

Anna and Sandro go for a trip among the islands off Sicily with a group of friends. After an argument with Sandro, Anna disappears. Claudia joins Sandro in his search for her on the mainland and they become lovers. This daring use of a minimal plot, and ANTONIONI's refusal to explain Anna's disappearance, outraged audiences at CANNES. Some critics castigated the film as monotonous and boring, but it survived initial incomprehension to become an international success.

*L'avventura* took up and developed themes and techniques already apparent in Antonioni's work. The inadequacy of moral codes to support human relationships, and the failure of the artist who compromises with materialistic values had been cogently expressed in LE AMICHE (1955). Antonioni's style of expressing character through visual means—by camera and group movements—was also already well developed, as well as the rhythm of his cutting and certain dramatic devices like leaving a mystery unsolved. In spite of great difficulties in production, causing real hardship among the cast and crew, the film brilliantly assembles all Antonioni's best elements; and he used to the full the advantage of his first wide screen. The acting is excellent: Gabriele FERZETTI repeats and develops his role from *Le amiche* of the inadequate male/artist, the amateur James Addams (father of Dawn ADDAMS) gives a crisply cut performance as Corrado, and Lea Massari is beautifully convincing as the unpredictable Anna. The touchstone of the film, however, is Monica VITTI's performance, which is not so much an achievement of acting as one of those occasions comparatively rare in film history when an actor's response to a director's needs illuminates a whole film.

*AWFUL TRUTH, The*, US, 1937. $1\frac{1}{2}$hr. *Dir* Leo McCarey; *prod* Columbia; *scr* Vina Delmar, from a play by Arthur Richman; *ph* Joseph

Walker; *cast* Irene Dunne (Lucy Warriner), Cary Grant (Jerry Warriner), Ralph Bellamy (Daniel Leeson).

An elemental battle of the sexes is fought between the estranged Warriners, each flaunting suitors in the other's face, but ultimately they are reconciled. Irene DUNNE and Cary GRANT keep their sang-froid in spite of the unflagging pace and the constant physical action. Ralph Bellamy's stuffy, callow 'other man' is a perfect foil.

A remake, *Let's Do It Again* (1953), starred Ray MILLAND, Jane Wyman, and Aldo Ray.

**AXELROD,** GEORGE (1922– ), US writer and director, became an overnight success in 1952 with his stage play *The Seven Year Itch*. His first film script was *Phfft* (1954). The following year he adapted THE SEVEN YEAR ITCH for the cinema. He wrote the screen versions of BUS STOP (1956) and his own stage play *Will Success Spoil Rock Hunter?* (1957), also *Breakfast at Tiffany's* (1961) from the story by Truman CAPOTE, and THE MANCHURIAN CANDIDATE (1962). He was responsible for the script of *How to Murder Your Wife* (1964), a frenetic black comedy starring Jack LEMMON. Axelrod became director/producer/writer with *Lord Love A Duck* (1965) and in 1968 made *The Secret Life of an American Wife* with the same independence.

Axelrod's original work creates its effect by brash, irreverent treatment of such nervous subjects as sex, domesticity, and material success. As a director he tends to be heavy-handed: his scripts work best in the hands of an experienced and authoritative director. His adaptations show considerable resourcefulness: in particular, John FRANKENHEIMER has acknowledged Axelrod's contribution to *The Manchurian Candidate*, on which they worked in close collaboration.

**AYRES,** LEW (1908– ), US actor, real name Lewis Ayer, originally a musician and band leader, made his film début opposite Greta GARBO in *The Kiss* (Jacques FEYDER, 1929) and especially won acclaim at the time for his performance in ALL QUIET ON THE WESTERN FRONT (Lewis MILESTONE, 1930). He had periods of relegation to 'B' pictures, but became widely popular as the title character in the 'Dr Kildare' series (1938–41). His pacifist stand during the Second World War lost him much popularity, but he scored a minor success (again as a doctor) in *Johnny Belinda* (1948). By the mid-fifties he had virtually retired from the screen, but reappeared in *Advise and Consent* (1961) and *The Carpetbaggers* (1963).

**AZNAVOUR,** CHARLES (1924– ), French actor and singer, real name Aznavurjan. During the forties, he wrote songs for Edith Piaf and Maurice CHEVALIER, before his own establishment as France's most popular male vocalist with his appealing ugliness and winsome charm. In films, he has worked for a number of notable directors, including Georges FRANJU, in LA TÊTE CONTRE LES MURS (1958), Jean-Pierre MOCKY, in *Les Dragueurs* (*The Young Have no Morals*, 1959), and Jean COCTEAU, in LE TESTAMENT D'ORPHÉE (1960); but his best characterization undoubtedly remains the complex, sensitive Charlie Kohler in TRUFFAUT's TIREZ SUR LE PIANISTE (1960). His recent international films include *The Adventurers* (1970) and *The Games* (1969).

# B

**BABY DOLL,** US, 1956. 1¾hr. *Dir, prod* Elia Kazan; *scr* Tennessee Williams, from his plays *The Long Story Cut Short* and *27 Wagons Full of Cotton*; *ph* Boris Kaufman; *mus* Kenyon Hopkins; *cast* Karl Malden (Archie), Carroll Baker (Baby Doll), Eli Wallach (Silva Vacarro), Mildred Dunnock (Aunt Rose Comfort), Lonny Chapman (Rock).

Tennessee WILLIAMS constructed from two of his stage plays a story of sexual tensions which lead to destruction and havoc; KAZAN transmuted this into an astutely observed, funny, and sensual film. The atmosphere of a Southern US community, with its inherent oppressiveness and stress, was remarkably well conveyed, supported by fine acting particularly by Carroll BAKER and Eli WALLACH, both in their first important film roles.

**BACALL,** LAUREN (1924– ), US actress, real name Betty Joan Perske, was working as a model when she was noticed by Howard HAWKS and offered a film contract. Her first screen part, when she was brilliantly cast opposite Humphrey BOGART in TO HAVE AND HAVE NOT (1944), allowed her immediately to establish a strikingly smouldering and intelligent personality. She married Bogart; although their screen partnership was a delicious blend of edgy wise-cracking and romantic intensity, the other films in which she appeared with him, THE BIG SLEEP (1946) and *Key Largo* (1948), gave her little opportunity to develop her acting range. *How To Marry A Millionaire* (1953) and *Designing Woman* (1957) among others have shown her to be a very polished *comédienne* with a talent for acid wit. She appears regularly on television and in the theatre and was particularly successful in the 1970 Broadway musical *Applause!* which was based on ALL ABOUT EVE (1950).

**BACK PROJECTION** or rear projection, a method of showing a film with the projector on the opposite side of a translucent screen from the audience. Used in a cinema, back projection provides a bright image without completely darkening the house and was used for a time in several small US 'newsreel theaters'. Used in film production, it is the oldest and simplest method of filming actors against a moving background photographed elsewhere.

Until recently the latter application was denoted by the screen credit 'process photography'. A typical example is the interior of a moving car in which the actors converse while the street can be seen receding through the rear window. A special cutaway car is placed in front of the camera, with the translucent screen behind it and the projector behind that in line with the camera lens. The film of the street background, shot earlier from the back of a camera car, is projected on the screen; the image, seen through the window, is photographed simultaneously with the car and actors. Thus dialogue can be recorded in studio silence (and the engine sound added later); lighting can be studio-perfect

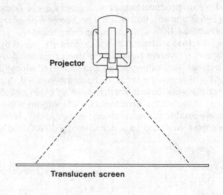

Projector

Translucent screen

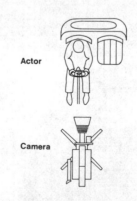

Actor

Camera

Back projection

(although it must not spill on to the screen surface); and the projected background will remain the same from rehearsal to final take. The illusion is completed by rocking the dummy car and moving tree branches past the studio lights.

Once the early problems of even screen illumination and synchronization of camera and projector shutters had been solved, back projection became the standard method of filming actors against distant locations, hazardous action, or even studio sets—when retakes were needed after the set was knocked down. Back projection is now being supplanted by FRONT PROJECTION, which provides greater flexibility in a smaller studio area. Other methods of achieving similar effects are the DUNNING PROCESS and the travelling MATTE. (See EFFECTS.)

**BACON, LLOYD** (1890–1955), US director who started as an actor, appearing in many CHAPLIN films of both the ESSANAY and MUTUAL periods. He later worked for Mack SENNETT, and directed Lloyd Hamilton comedies. His career as a feature film director spanned thirty years, and included *The Singing Fool* (1928), 42ND STREET (1933), GOLDDIGGERS OF 1937 (1936), *A Slight Case of Murder* (1938), *The Oklahoma Kid* (1939), *Action in the North Atlantic* (1943), *The Sullivans* (1944). His later work included Lucille BALL comedies—*Miss Grant Takes Richmond* (1949, *Innocence is Bliss* in GB), *The Fuller Brush Girl* (1950, *The Affairs of Sally* in GB), and *The French Line* (1954).

**BAD AND THE BEAUTIFUL, The,** US, 1952. 2hr. *Dir* Vincente Minnelli; *prod* John Houseman for MGM; *scr* Charles Schnee, from a story by George Bradshaw; *ph* Robert Surtees; *des* Cedric Gibbons, Edward Carfagno, Edwin B. Willis, Keough Gleason; *mus* David Raksin; *cast* Kirk Douglas (Jonathan Shields), Lana Turner (Georgia Lorrison), Walter Pidgeon (Harry Pebbel), Dick Powell (James Lee Bartlow), Barry Sullivan (Fred Amiel), Gloria Grahame (Rosemary Bartlow), Gilbert Roland (Gaucho Ribera).

One of a number of films of the period which purported to reveal the reality of Hollywood, *The Bad and the Beautiful* is the story of Jonathan Shields, formerly a successful film producer, who tries to make a come-back through an actress, a writer, and a director whose careers he has made at the expense of their friendship. A series of flashbacks in which these three celebrities describe Shields's career reveal Hollywood as a microcosm where ruthlessness is a necessity for success, where the bad is an inevitable corollary to the beautiful.

The film itself has an elegant glitter which preserves and glorifies the Hollywood myth rather than undermining it.

**BAKER, CARROLL** (1932?– ), US actress who gave an impressive performance as the child wife in BABY DOLL (1956). With a few exceptions, including *The Big Country* (1958), she has been limited since then to playing various oversexed ladies in films like *The Carpetbaggers* (1963) and *Il dolce corpo di Deborah* (*The Sweet Body of Deborah*, 1967).

**BAKER, JOSEPHINE** (1906–75), US revue artist, who appeared all over the world, but was most closely associated with the Folies Bergère. She was one of the earliest black entertainers to attain international stardom. She made several French musical films in the twenties and thirties beginning with *La Revue des Revues* (1927). For many years she devoted herself to a large family of orphans of various races.

**BAKER, STANLEY** (1927– ), Welsh actor. His first important role as the bullying Lieutenant Bennett in *The Cruel Sea* (Charles FREND, 1952) convinced him that the best parts always go to the villain. He has been a tough and intelligent HEAVY in numerous thrillers. *Blind Date* (1959) began his association with Joseph LOSEY, which continued in THE CRIMINAL (1960), *Eva* (1962), and ACCIDENT (1967). He has formed his own film and television production company and was co-producer of *Zulu* (1963) and *Robbery* (1967).

**BÁLAZS, BÉLA** (1884–1949), Hungarian writer and film theorist, published novels, plays, and poems before and during the First World War, and also wrote libretti and ballet subjects for musicians, Béla Bartók among them. Closely associated with the Commune, Bálazs had to leave the country when it was overthrown by Horthy in 1919. Living in Austria and then Germany, he developed his critical theories about cinema, publishing *Der sichtbare Mensch* in Vienna in 1924 and *Der Geist des Films* in Berlin in 1930. The importance of his writings lay mainly in his insistence that it was necessary to elaborate a new aesthetic for the new art, and in his proposal that cinema, particularly in its use of close-up and MONTAGE, made the world newly visible. He was one of the founders of the left-wing co-operative Volksverbund für Filmkunst, with PABST, Piscator, and others. He also worked with BRECHT on the script of DIE DREIGRO-SCHENOPER (1931—neither was credited), and on the script of Leni RIEFENSTAHL's *Das blaue Licht* (1932). The rise of Nazism forced him to leave Germany: until 1945 he lived in the Soviet Union, working mainly as a teacher of film theory. He returned to Hungary in 1945 and took part in the restoration of the shattered film industry, working on the script of VALAHOL

EURÓPÁBAN (*Somewhere in Europe*, 1947), the first post-war Hungarian film to catch international attention. He became once again an influential theorist and teacher, working not only in Budapest but also in Prague. His *Film—Werden und Wesen einer neue Kunst* (1948), an attempt to synthesize his life-long aesthetic views, was published in English as *Theory of the film: character and growth of a new art*, trans. Edith Bone, London, 1952, New York, 1972.

**BÁLAZS BÉLA STUDIO,** an organization within the Hungarian film industry designed to help young film-makers. Originally set up in 1958, it made an unpromising start because of lack of agreement on policy, and the few short films produced lacked enterprise. A new start was made in 1961 when the emergence of 'new waves' in other countries provided stimulus for change in Hungary and an enterprising generation graduated from the Film Academy. Judit ELEK, Pál GÁBOR, and István SZABÓ were among those who joined the Studio and helped bring about a change in its constitution: the true existence of the Studio is reckoned from that year. An agreed sum is allocated annually by the industry for the production of short films by the Studio, and production policy is decided by an elected leadership in consultation with all members. A critical difference in procedure from that of the production groups in the main industry is that projects are agreed at the planning stage rather than on the basis of a prepared script, so that the film-maker has more freedom in the execution of his project.

The first great success was Szabó's *Te* (*You*, 1963), probably Hungary's most-awarded short film. A steady production of successful short films included Sándor SÁRA's *Ciganyok* (*Gypsies*, 1962) and Ferenc Kardos's *Miénk a világ* (*On Top of the World*, 1963). In 1963–5 the Studio's policy came under strain as the film-makers sought opportunities for feature-length production, but the policy of shorts has prevailed, and later productions include Judit Elek's *Meddig él az ember?* (*How Long Does a Man Matter?*, 1967) and Ferenc KÓSA's *Öngyilkosság* (*Suicide*, 1967).

The idea behind the setting up of the Studio has been triumphantly vindicated by its results. Young film-makers not yet able to command feature-length resources are able to start directing, and in conditions of freedom which encourage enterprise. By showing up the stagnation in the rest of the industry and by earning Hungarian films a good reputation abroad, the Studio materially contributed to the upsurge of Hungarian films during the sixties.

**BALCON,** MICHAEL (1896–    ), British producer, after working as a film salesman, started making short advertising films in partnership with Victor SAVILLE. They went into feature production with *Woman to Woman* (1923), directed by Graham Cutts assisted by Alfred HITCHCOCK. The film was a great success and, undeterred by the comparative failure of their second venture *The White Shadow* (1924), Balcon formed his own production company, GAINSBOROUGH PICTURES, in 1924. In 1932 he was invited to take over the rebuilt GAUMONT BRITISH studios at Shepherd's Bush and was director of production both there and at Gainsborough for some years. Under him both companies flourished with a number of popular successes; he also took the gamble of backing FLAHERTY'S MAN OF ARAN (1934).

At the end of 1936 Balcon left Gainsborough and Gaumont British and was for a time a producer for METRO-GOLDWYN-MAYER at the new studios at Denham. In 1938 he joined the board of EALING STUDIOS and personally supervised the production of the many successful films made by that company during the forties and early fifties. He arranged the removal of Ealing's production to the RANK ORGANISATION studios at Pinewood and after Ealing ceased operation in 1955 he continued to produce for Rank; but the lack of independence he inevitably suffered there led to his leaving in 1959 to become chairman of Bryanston Films, a consortium of small independent film-making companies (one of which was his own company Michael Balcon Productions) whose films were to be released through BRITISH LION. In 1964 he became chairman of the board of directors of British Lion, but resigned in 1968 because he considered the company's production policy unenterprising. He was also head of Anglo Enterprise Film Productions until 1967, on the board of a commercial television company, and a governor of the BRITISH FILM INSTITUTE, as well as chairman of the BFI production board.

Balcon's life-long enthusiasm for the cinema and his conviction of the value of film as a medium of high-quality popular entertainment have made him a moving force in British cinema for fifty years. He was knighted in 1948 in recognition of his influence. He has written a lively autobiography, *Michael Balcon presents a lifetime of films*, London, 1969.

**BALL,** LUCILLE (1910–    ), US actress whose work as a model led to a bit part in *Roman Scandals* (1933). Early films like *Follow the Fleet* (1936) showed a *comédienne* of wit and presence, and leading parts followed in films such as *Dubarry Was a Lady* (1943) and *Sorrowful Jones* (1949). In 1951 she began the 'I Love Lucy' series and her comic timing, penetrating voice, and apparently boundless energy made her

*Ballada o soldate* (Grigori Chukrai, 1959)

one of television's most successful stars. For several years, after her marriage to Desi Arnaz ended in 1962, she was in sole control of Desilu Productions and its studio, one of the largest television production companies in Hollywood.

***BALLADA O SOLDATE*** (*Ballad of a Soldier*), USSR, 1959. 1½hr. *Dir* Grigori Chukrai; *prod* Mosfilm; *scr* Chukrai, Valentin Yoshov; *ph* Vladimir Nikolayev, Era Saveleya; *ed* M. Timofeieva; *mus* Mikhail Ziv; *cast* Vladimir Ivashev (Alyosha), Antonina Maximova (Alyosha's mother), Sharma Prokhorenko (Shura), Nikolai Kruchkov (General), Yevgeni Urbanski (invalid soldier).

A young soldier, Alyosha, refuses a medal and instead takes leave from the front to visit his mother. During his travels by train, truck, and on foot, he meets many people, all affected by the war; a crippled veteran, a comic sentry, faithful and faithless wives, and of course a girl, Shura, with whom he falls in love.

CHUKRAI directs simply and at times naïvely, but there is no denying the technical polish of the film. This was the first film that the Soviet Union entered in any American film festival (San Francisco, 1960) and it won first prize. It also took a prize at CANNES in the same year.

**BALLARD,** LUCIEN (1908–   ), US cameraman, started as a member of a camera crew at PARAMOUNT, then as assistant to Lee GARMES on MOROCCO (1930). He became a protégé of STERNBERG and acquired much of his skill in such films as *The Devil is a Woman* (1935) and CRIME AND PUNISHMENT (1935). Some of Ballard's most creative later work has been in Westerns, particularly working with BOETTICHER and PECKINPAH, where his sensitive use of colour is evident. Notable is Ballard's 'period' lighting for RIDE THE HIGH COUNTRY (1962, *Guns in the Afternoon* in GB), and his creation of atmosphere and use of the TELEPHOTO lens in THE WILD BUNCH (1969). As in all his work, Ballard's skill brings significant qualities to the films. His other work includes *Buchanan Rides Alone* (1958), *The Rise and Fall of Legs Diamond* (1959), *Will Penny* (1967), and *True Grit* (1969).

**BALLET FILMS** as such are largely a post-war phenomenon, but the association of the two arts goes back much further to include some sketchy film of Pavlova dancing in Mary PICKFORD's private studio, which was included in a rather poor documentary about her entitled *The Immortal Swan* (1936). This record of her dancing was generally held to diminish her reputation and for many years other ballet dancers, notably Margot Fonteyn, were discouraged from allowing themselves to be filmed. Despite this, there is an obvious advantage to the ballet profession in having film records of dancers and ballets, and the New York Public Library Dance Collection includes over one million feet of film of this nature. Pavlova also appeared in a non-dancing role in *The Dumb Girl of Portici* (1916) and a number of other ballet dancers have worked as film actors, most notably Leslie CARON. Hollywood musicals began to incorporate ballet sequences recruiting ballet dancers such as Zorina and Cyd CHARISSE and leading American choreographers such as Balanchine (ballets in *Goldwyn Follies*, 1938, and *On Your Toes*, 1939) and Agnes DeMille (*Oklahoma!*, 1955). There were also films with a ballet setting like *La Mort du cygne* (1937), remade as *The Unfinished Dance* (1947); ballet in the cinema was really established by the commercial success of one of these, THE RED SHOES (1948), which starred Moira Shearer, a leading ballerina with the Sadlers Wells Ballet, and which featured a twenty-minute ballet especially choreographed by Robert Helpmann with the intention of making full use of the potential of the film medium.

The first films devoted to ballet performances specially staged for the camera appear to be *Le Lac des cygnes* and *Graduation Ball* directed by Boris Zatouroff in France in 1939, closely followed by Léonide Massine's adaptation of his ballets *Gaîeté Parisienne* and *Capriccioso Espagnol*, directed by Jean NEGULESCO in Hollywood in 1941. In the fifties the Russians began their successful and continuing series of filmed ballets, usually studio restagings of Bolshoi and Kirov Ballet productions, and of these the early *Romeo and Juliet* (1954) with Ulanova is still probably the outstanding example. The Russians were emulated in Britain by Paul CZINNER who appropriately began with *The Bolshoi Ballet* (1957) which was shot as a theatre performance using multiple cameras. Later films with the Royal Ballet and starring Margot Fonteyn were shot in a studio. In 1958, Margaret Dale began directing BBC television performances by British ballet companies and many of these were also distributed as films. The growing popularity of ballet in Germany led to a number of German television ballet films, which were also given cinema exhibition, but were unfortunately often printed on a wide screen ratio, with a resulting, and sometimes disastrous, 'topping and tailing' of the dancers. The popularity and development of American ballet is also reflected in films like that of the New York City Ballet dancing Balanchine's A MIDSUMMER NIGHT'S DREAM (1966). In France a feature-length film was made of four

Roland Petit ballets entitled *Un, Deux, Trois, Quatre!* (*Black Tights*, 1960).

The balance between respect for the original stage production and producing something which works as cinema is not easily achieved. Perhaps the most successful attempt is the German film of Nureyev's production of *Schwanensee* (*Swan Lake*, 1966), which is also one of the few films to succeed in conveying something of the excitement which ballet can arouse in the theatre. José Limon's *The Moor's Pavane* (1950), photographed by Walter Strate, is also said to succeed in this by photographing the dancers against an unlit background. Too often, though, insensitive editing and framing destroy the rhythm of the dancing and mask movement which should be seen.

While it is enormously valuable to have films of major theatre ballets, both as a record and as a means of making them available to a wider audience, the real development must lie in original film ballets. So far, this has mainly taken the form of ballets within feature films such as AN AMERICAN IN PARIS (1951) and *The Red Shoes* although some experimental short films have been made, notably Maya DEREN's *The Very Eye of Night* (1959). Gene KELLY's *Invitation to the Dance* (1956) was a full-length, although three-part, dance film, but it was not accounted a success; Sir Frederick Ashton's *The Tales of Beatrix Potter* (1971, *Peter Rabbit and Tales of Beatrix Potter* in US) fared better, as did *Don Quixote* (1973) co-directed in Australia by Robert Helpmann and Rudolf Nureyev. There have been some very interesting original television ballets, John Cranko's *Eugene Onegin* (1966) being an excellent example.

**BANCROFT,** ANNE (1931–    ), US actress, real name Italiano, was brought to Hollywood after making a reputation in television. She appeared in some undistinguished films during the fifties, then for a time worked only in the theatre where she quickly established herself as an actress of considerable power. She returned to films to repeat her stage success in *The Miracle Worker* (Arthur PENN, 1962); her subsequent appearances on the screen have been infrequent but prestigious, notably as the distraught, absent-minded housewife in *The Pumpkin Eater* (Jack CLAYTON, 1964) and as the sardonic older woman in THE GRADUATE (Mike NICHOLS, 1967).

*BANDIT, The,* see CANGACEIRO, O'

*BANDITI A ORGOSOLO* (*The Bandits of Orgosolo*), Italy, 1961. 1¾hr. *Dir* Vittorio De Seta; *prod* Titanus; *scr* De Seta, Vera Gherarducci; *mus* Valentino Bucchi; *cast* Michele

Cossu (shepherd), Peppeddu Cuccu (his brother), Vittorina Pisano (the girl), and other Sardinian shepherds.

A young shepherd gets involved with the police; accompanied by his twelve-year-old brother, he tries to take his flock to freedom. The sheep die, and he becomes a bandit. DE SETA's first feature film is remarkable for its documentary quality and fine photography.

**BAND WAGON, The,** US, 1953. Technicolor; 1¾hr. *Dir* Vincente Minnelli; *prod* Arthur Freed for MGM; *scr* Betty Comden, Adolph Green; *ph* Harry Jackson; *ed* Albert Akst; *des* Cedric Gibbons, Preston Ames; *cast* Fred Astaire (Tony Hunter), Cyd Charisse (Gaby), Jack Buchanan (Jeffrey Cordova), Oscar Levant (Lester Marton), Nanette Fabray (Lily Marton).

A happy film from the great period of METRO-GOLDWYN-MAYER MUSICALS. Its slick action and quick-fire dialogue were supplemented by effective dance numbers (with inventive choreography by Michael Kidd) and, among its set-pieces, a transformation-scene fiasco and a travesty of detective drama à la Mickey Spillane. The film was based on the successful Broadway show of the thirties with much of the original Schwartz–Dietz score retained. Of the songs the biggest hits were 'Dancing in the Dark' and the comedy number 'Triplets'. The film was equally happy in its casting, with a zestful quintet of principals.

**BANK DICK, The,** US, 1940. 1¼hr. *Dir* Edward Cline; *prod* Universal; *scr* Mahatma Kane Jeeves; *ph* Milton Krasner; *cast* W. C. Fields (Egbert Sousé), Cora Witherspoon (Agatha Sousé), Una Merkel (Myrtle Sousé), Evelyn Del Rio (Elsie Mae Adele Brunch Sousé), Jessie Ralph (Mrs Hermisillo Brunch), Franklin Pangborn (J. Pinkerton Snoopington).

W. C. FIELDS had virtually complete freedom in making *The Bank Dick*—he wrote the script under one of his various pseudonyms—and the film demonstrates his screen character in its most fully developed form. The hen-pecked husband in an atrocious American family, he gains a fortune as a screenwriter by exploiting his natural idleness, bibulousness, cowardice, gullibility, and cunning. There is also an evocation of the classic silent film chase directed by Edward Cline, a graduate of the Mack SENNETT school.

**BANKHEAD,** TALLULAH (1902–65), US actress of considerable talent and beauty (she was not unlike GARBO in profile), who had an attractive husky drawl which was much imitated. Her best work was done in the British and American theatre, notably in *The Little Foxes* and *The Skin of Our Teeth*, but she had an intermittent film career notably in *Tarnished Lady* (1931),

HITCHCOCK's *Lifeboat* (1944), in which she gave her best film performance as the wise-cracking reporter, and LUBITSCH's *A Royal Scandal* (1945, *Czarina* in GB), in which she succeeded in turning Catherine the Great into a variation of the traditional Bankhead role. Latterly her career suffered from the effects of a hectic private life, recounted with some frankness in her autobiography *Tallulah* (London, 1952).

**BARA,** THEDA (1890–1955), US actress, real name Theodosia Goodman, a tailor's daughter from Cincinnati, began her stage career with small parts under the name of Thedosia De Coppett. She was discovered for the part of the 'vampire' for '*A Fool There Was*' (1915), and put under contract by William FOX. Fox organized for her the first full-scale publicity campaign to create a star image. Every detail of her background (daughter of a sheikh and a princess, or alternatively a French artist and a mysterious Arab; born in the shadow of the Pyramids; hobbies, distilling perfumes and astrology, and so on) and of her appearance was tailored to fit the role of a sex siren. The fact that her new name is an anagram of 'death arab' was probably noticed only after its adoption, but was fully exploited. She was only the first of many stars to find that grooming for a particular role cruelly absorbed much of her private life and personality. (See STAR SYSTEM.) During her five years with Fox she made some forty films; all were variations on the role of the fatal woman whose sexual magnetism leads to the destruction of the men entrapped by her, and gave currency to the term 'vamp'. She applied this stereotype to many of the famous women of history and literature, including CARMEN (1915), Lady Isobel in *East Lynne* and Juliet in ROMEO AND JULIET in 1916, CAMILLE and *Cleopatra* in 1917, *Madame Dubarry* and *Salome* in 1918. Her screen career ended as abruptly as it began, when her contract with Fox expired; she returned to the stage but was unable to break out from the restrictions imposed upon her by her image.

**BARBARO,** UMBERTO (1902–59), Italian critic and director, made *I cantieri dell' Adriatico*, a documentary, in 1933, and his only feature film, *L'ultima nemica*, in 1937. After teaching at the CENTRO SPERIMENTALE and translating PUDOVKIN's books, he scripted DE SANTIS's CACCIA TRAGICA (1947). He edited BIANCO E NERO in 1945–8 and wrote several novels.

**BARBERA,** JOSEPH, see HANNA AND BARBERA

**BARDEM,** JUAN ANTONIO (1922– ), Spanish director, studied at the Madrid film school (IIEC) while qualifying as an agricultural

engineer. At the film school he met Luis BER-
LANGA and, with a group of friends, they completed their first joint project *Esa pareja felix*
(*That Happy Couple*) in 1951. Bardem was not
awarded the film school's diploma, possibly
because his political views were already clear,
and for a time had to work as an engineer, but
after selling one of the several scripts they had
written while at IIEC, Berlanga was able to film
BIENVENIDA MR MARSHALL (*Welcome Mr Marshall*). This was well received at CANNES in 1953
and Bardem's MUERTE DI UN CICLISTA (*Death of
a Cyclist*) had equal success two years later. The
emergence of committed, realistic films from
Franco's Spain aroused wide interest in Bardem's work. When in 1956 he was arrested during the filming of *Calle Mayor* and imprisoned
on political grounds, there was an international
outcry and he was released after a fortnight. His
next film was heavily censored and converted
from a critical study of peasant life, to be called
*Los Segadores* (*The Reapers*), into a conventional melodrama. Under the title *La Venganza*
(*Vengeance*), foisted on it by the authorities, it
was coolly received at Cannes in 1958. In that
year Bardem helped to found a production company, UNINCI, of which he became president.
As well as directing for them he became a
producer, notably of VIRIDIANA (1961), becoming involved in the political and religious uproar
that BUÑUEL's film aroused and which forced the
company to close down. After directing a film in
Argentina, Bardem returned to Spain, continuing
his courageous attempts at a realistic and critical
examination through film of contemporary Spanish life.

**BARDOT,** BRIGITTE (1934–   ), French
actress from a well-to-do family, studied dancing
and posed as a photographic model before trying
to get parts in film. An early introduction to
Marc ALLÉGRET led not to parts but to an
acquaintance with Roger VADIM, who saw Bardot's star potential and eventually married her.
She got parts at first in lightweight films (including one in GB, *Doctor at Sea*, 1955), and
gradually evolved her image. Cool, sexy
insolence was the keynote, conveyed by the careful insouciance of her appearance—fringe and
pony-tail, very often jeans and bare feet—and
her complete lack of conventionality or prudery.
Allégret had some hand in the evolution of the
Bardot image, giving her a part in *Futures
vedettes* (1954), and René CLAIR noticed her
beauty, giving her a small part in the polished
*Les Grandes Manoeuvres* (*Summer Manoeuvres*,
1955), in which she remained firmly buttoned up
to the neck. The sexy image was virtually complete in *La Lumière d'en face* (*Light across the
Street*, Georges Lacombe, 1955), but the full

impact burst on enthusiastic audiences in
Vadim's ET DIEU CRÉA LA FEMME (*And God
Created Woman*, 1956). Bardot became the great
sex symbol of the next decade, one of the very
few to be created and exploited as such outside
Hollywood, and significant because of the new
type of femininity to which she gave currency:
amoral and anti-conformist, jaunty and indifferent, but still, with her *gamine* appeal, capable of
being forgiven as a childish innocent. In a series
of films, mostly sexy comedies, she exploited and
expanded her myth, which fed at the same time
on the well-publicized tempestuousness of her
private life. Several directors tried to use her in
more mature dramatic roles: CLOUZOT in *La
Vérité* (1960), Vadim in *Le Repos du guerrier*
(1962), MALLE in *Vie privée* (1962), and GODARD
in LE MÉPRIS (1963). But her talent was not for
drama: it was for the exposition of her particular
brand of sex-appeal and for the horse-play
comedies which she graced with gusto and style.
Malle gave her her best role in VIVA MARIA!
(1965), where the mixture of fun, adventure, and
sexiness suited her talents and she found an
admirable foil in Jeanne MOREAU.

Bardot the phenomenon attracted a good deal
of attention from sociologists and psychologists,
and in *Brigitte Bardot and the Lolita syndrome*
(1959) Simone de Beauvoir published a rather
solemn but acute analysis of her enormous
success. Jacques ROZIER made a pleasing short
film about her, *I paparazzi* (1963), and she appeared as herself in *Dear Brigitte*, made in the
US in 1965.

**BARKER,** WILL G. (1867–1951), British
producer, was one of the most successful and
colourful figures of the early years of British
cinema. Starting as a travelling salesman, he
became in 1906 managing director of the Warwick Trading Co, where his enthusiasm for news
and actuality films created large profits. In 1908
he set up his own company, Barker Motion
Photography, and the following year built a
studio in the London suburb of Ealing. As late as
1914 he was still claiming that actuality was the
only valid use of film, but he had also a distinct
flair for spectacle as well as a shrewd business
sense. His version of Sir Herbert Beerbohm
Tree's stage production of Shakespeare's *Henry
VIII* in 1911 was probably the first British film
to be rented to exhibitors instead of sold
outright: only six weeks after its first release
Barker publicly burned the twenty distribution
copies as a protest against the practice of
repeatedly showing films in a disgracefully worn
state.

While maintaining his chief output of films of
actual events and 'interest' subjects—*Who's
Who In Doggieland* (1912) was a popular guide

to various breeds—Barker also made occasional lavish historical dramas. *Sixty Years a Queen* (1913) was a haphazard summary of Victoria's reign, enjoyably lumping together grand state occasions and sentimental domestic scenes. *East Lynne* (1913), lasting nearly two hours, was the most elaborate of many versions of the well-loved pathetic novel. The acting is stilted but the film shows considerable polish for its time in the establishing of visual continuity and emotional rhythm. From 1913 Barker concentrated on a very successful series of 'London Melodramas'—thrillers which used his favourite London backgrounds and actuality street scenes to give verisimilitude to their complicated action.

Barker retired from films in 1918, while still very successful, aware that audience tastes were changing and that the British industry was fast failing to meet the increased competition from America.

**BARNET,** BORIS (1902–65), Russian director and actor, trained in Lev KULESHOV's workshop and appeared in films made under Kuleshov. His strength as a director of satirical comedies emerged in his first film *Devushka s korobkoi* (*The Girl with the Hat Box*, 1927), starring Anna STEN. *Moskva v oktiabre* (*Moscow in October*, 1927), one of the films commissioned to celebrate the tenth anniversary of the Revolution, is less characteristic, but *Dom na Trubnoi* (*The House on Trubnaya Square*, 1928) reverted to the sharp observation of comically entangled relationships. He appeared in PUDOVKIN's POTOMOK CHINGHIS-KHANA (*The Heir to Genghis Khan*, 1928) and continued to direct comedies, notably *Okraina* (*Patriots*, 1933) which, with its delicate balance of humour and pathos in a provincial setting, has overtones of Chekhov. Barnet made short films for the Fighting Film Albums during the Second World War and directed a few feature films in the post-war years.

**BARONCELLI,** JACQUES DE (1881–1951), French director, had a prolific career, making over sixty films between 1915 and 1947, with subjects ranging from melodrama and romance —*Ramuntcho* (1919), *La Femme et le Pantin* (1929)—to adaptations of literary classics—*Le Père Goriot* (1923)—and action dramas— *L'Homme du Niger* (1939). His films, although designed as straightforward entertainment, were nevertheless elegant and well-made.

**BARRANDOV,** main production studios of Czechoslovakia, originally designed by Max Urban, architect and film pioneer, and built in 1932–3. The studios stand on a small plateau on the west side of Prague, named after Joachim

Barrande (1799–1883), the French geologist who classified the Silurian fauna, especially trilobites, of the magnificent limestone cliffs exposed by a sweep of the Vltava. (The annual award made by the studio is the Golden Trilobite, *Zlaté Trilobit*.) During the thirties, Barrandov was the best-equipped studio complex in central Europe, and attracted a good deal of foreign production: UFA, METRO-GOLDWYN-MAYER, and PARAMOUNT all developed their own distribution systems in Czechoslovakia. The Germans took over the studios in 1940, and towards the end of the war their production was of necessity based almost entirely on Barrandov, which was enlarged and improved for the purpose. Although rivalled now by the studios built by other nationalized industries in Eastern Europe since the war, Barrandov remains the most sophisticated.

**BARRAULT,** JEAN-LOUIS (1910– ), French actor and stage producer, began his career at the Atelier Theatre in 1930; he joined the Comédie Française in 1940, leaving six years later to form his own company (Barrault-Renaud) with his wife. The best-known contemporary actor/producer in France, he was director of the Théâtre de France until 1968, when he was dismissed after the political upheavals.

Although cinema has always taken second place, he has played some memorable film roles. His early film appearances include parts in CARNÉ's *Jenny*, *Mademoiselle Docteur* (both 1936), and *Drôle de drame* (1937). During the forties he played a series of heroic leads: Napoleon in *Le Destin fabuleux de Desirée Clary* (1942), Berlioz in *Symphonie Fantastique* (1941), the blind sculptor in *L'Ange de la nuit* (1944). Most outstanding however was his performance as the mime Debureau in LES ENFANTS DU PARADIS (1945). His other films include LA RONDE (1950) and RENOIR's *Le Testament du Docteur Cordelier* (1959).

**BARRETO,** LIMA (1905– ), Brazilian director. His early films include two documentaries, *Painel* (1951), which dealt with the fresco of Portinari, and *Santuario* (1951), on the baroque sculptures of Aleijadinho. His first feature film, O' CANGACEIRO (1953), told the story of a group of north Brazilian bandits, and was highly successful internationally. The following year he made *São Paulo en festa*, and in 1961 directed *A Primera missa*, on the religious vocation of a young boy, which did not meet with the success of his previous films.

**BARRY,** IRIS (1896–1969), British-born film historian and writer who worked mainly in the US. She was a founder member of the London

FILM SOCIETY in 1925, and is best known for her work as a director of the Museum of Modern Art Film Library in New York (from 1935) where she initiated and directed the first successful effort to preserve American films and was instrumental in saving examples of world cinema. She was author of a number of books on film, including *D. W. Griffith: American film master*, New York, 1965.

**BARRY, JOHN** (1933– ), British musician and composer who began writing for films with *Beat Girl* (1959), though his reputation more especially dates from 1962 when he wrote and directed the score for *The Amorous Prawn*, composed the jazz music for *The L-Shaped Room*, and wrote the distinctive music for *Dr No*; he was retained on the team for the late JAMES BOND films. His other scores include *Zulu* (1963), *Séance on a Wet Afternoon* (1964), *The Ipcress File* (1965), THE KNACK (1965), *King Rat* (1965), *Born Free* (1965), THE CHASE (1966), *The Whisperers* (1966), *Dutchman* (1966), *The Lion in Winter* (1968), and *Monte Walsh*, *Walkabout*, MIDNIGHT COWBOY (all three 1970).

**BARRYMORE, ETHEL** (1879–1959), US actress, real name Blythe, sister of John and Lionel Barrymore, had a long and distinguished career in the theatre. She appeared on the screen as early as 1909, in *The Divorcee*, and her occasional films included *Life's Whirlpool* (1917), written and directed by Lionel. The eminent trio appeared together in only one film, *Rasputin and the Empress* (1932, *Rasputin* in GB), after which Ethel acted only on the stage until *None but the Lonely Heart* (1944), for which she won an OSCAR. Her innate dignity, personal integrity, and masterful delivery of often banal dialogue added lustre to a score of films in the forties and fifties, notably *The Farmer's Daughter* (1947), *Portrait of Jennie* (1948), *Pinky* (1949), *Kind Lady* (1951), and *Young at Heart* (1954)

**BARRYMORE, JOHN** (1882–1942), US actor, real name Blythe, brother of Ethel and Lionel Barrymore. His early films were farces, but DR JEKYLL AND MR HYDE (1920) established him in the cinema as *Hamlet* established him on the stage two years later. His swashbuckling performances in films such as *Don Juan* (1926) and *The Beloved Rogue* (1927) for WARNER BROS made him a romantic idol. He made several films with his brother, including GRAND HOTEL (1932) which co-starred him with Greta GARBO. His best roles were in films like *A Bill of Divorcement* (1932), TWENTIETH CENTURY (1934), and *Midnight* (1939) in which he could display his sardonic wit and good comic timing. He was a splendid Mercutio in ROMEO AND JULIET (1936).

His last film, *Playmates* (1942), was one of several in which he parodied his own tragedy by playing a drunken actor. He wrote an autobiography, *Confessions of an actor* (London, 1926); a biography, *Good night sweet prince* by Gene Fowler, was published, London, 1944. His daughter Diana's autobiography, *Too much too soon* (London, 1957), was filmed in 1958 with Errol FLYNN as Barrymore.

His son, John Drew Barrymore (1932– ), has starred in several films, notably LOSEY's *The Big Night* (1951).

**BARRYMORE, LIONEL** (1878–1954), US actor, real name Blythe, brother of Ethel and John Barrymore, started his long and successful film career with D. W. GRIFFITH in 1911. At first he combined stage and screen acting, but from 1926 he concentrated on films; he also directed occasionally, notably *Madame X* (1929). A character actor who was also a star, he gave many outstanding performances, particularly in *Sadie Thompson* (1928), *A Free Soul* (1931), *Rasputin and the Empress* (1932, *Rasputin* in GB), the only film in which Ethel, John, and Lionel Barrymore appeared together, DINNER AT EIGHT (1933), *A Family Affair* (1937), the first of the HARDY FAMILY series in which he created the role of Judge Hardy, and *You Can't Take It With You* (1938). From 1938 he was confined to a wheelchair, but his career continued undiminished. He was in fourteen of the popular 'Dr Kildare' series, *It's a Wonderful Life* (1946), DUEL IN THE SUN (1946), and *Key Largo* (1948), among many others.

**BARTHELMESS, RICHARD** (1895–1963), US actor, gave two outstanding performances for D. W. GRIFFITH: as the Chinaman in BROKEN BLOSSOMS (1919) and in the quite different character of an unsophisticated American boy in WAY DOWN EAST (1920). The latter image was the one with which he became widely popular in the earlier part of his career, notably in TOL'ABLE DAVID (1921). With changing tastes he moved on to tougher, more complex roles such as those he played in *The Dawn Patrol* (1930) and *Only Angels Have Wings* (1939).

**BARTHOLOMEW, FREDDIE** (1924– ), British child actor, chiefly in Hollywood, became world-famous for his first starring part, the title role in DAVID COPPERFIELD (1934). The remarkable quality of this and later performances, notably in ANNA KARENINA (1935), *Captains Courageous* (1937), and *Little Lord Fauntleroy* (1937), is indicative of real talent; but his few appearances in adult roles were disappointing and he retired from acting in 1950. (See also CHILD STARS.)

**BARTOSCH,** BERTHOLD (1893–1968), animator of Czech origin, worked during the twenties in Berlin as assistant and later collaborator to Lotte REINIGER, providing the background to some of her later films, particularly *Die Abenteuer des Prinzen Achmed* (*The Adventures of Prince Achmed*, 1926). Around 1930 Bartosch moved to Paris and worked on publicity films and especially on L'IDÉE (1934).

**BARZMAN,** BEN (1912– ), Canadian scriptwriter whose work in Hollywood included the script for Joseph LOSEY's first feature *The Boy with Green Hair* (1948). He left America at the time of the Hollywood investigations of the UNAMERICAN ACTIVITIES COMMITTEE. Films he wrote in Europe included *Celui qui doit mourir* (*He Who Must Die*, 1956), *Time without Pity* (1957), *Blind Date* (1959), and *The Heroes of Telemark* (1965); he co-scripted *The Fall of the Roman Empire* (1964) and *The Blue Max* (1966).

**BASEHART,** RICHARD (1919– ), US stage actor who made his film début with WARNER BROS in *Cry Wolf* (1947) and quickly achieved stardom in a succession of TWENTIETH CENTURY-FOX films; among his best performances at this time was the would-be suicide in *Fourteen Hours* (Henry HATHAWAY, 1951). He appeared in films by a variety of leading Hollywood directors, including Robert WISE, Samuel FULLER, John HUSTON, Richard BROOKS, and Martin RITT. He has worked in Europe, notably in two FELLINI films, LA STRADA (1954) and IL BIDONE (1955).

**BASS,** SAUL (1920– ), US graphics designer who began a very successful and influential career in film CREDITS when Otto PREMINGER commissioned him to design the titles for *Carmen Jones* (1954). He worked on Preminger's next eight films, among them THE MAN WITH THE GOLDEN ARM (1955) with its distinctive angular designs, but he is probably best known for the black alley cat credit sequence in *Walk on the Wild Side* (1962) which, like all his best work, brilliantly and economically establishes the predominant theme of the film. He has also designed specific sequences in several films, notably the shower murder in PSYCHO (1960), and directed his own films including *Why Man Creates* (1968), which won an OSCAR for the best documentary short.

**BATAILLE,** SYLVIE (1912– ), French actress, studied with Charles Dullin, and acted with the Compagnie des Quinze. She started her cinema career with small parts in silent films, but it was not until the introduction of sound that she began to be really successful. In 1934 she played in *La Voix sans visage* and *Adémai aviateur*, and was noticed by RENOIR; she played Edith in LE CRIME DE MONSIEUR LANGE (1936). Her most successful role was that of Henriette in his UNE PARTIE DE CAMPAGNE (1936), where her fresh-faced beauty perfectly suited the part. She also played the lead in CARNÉ's *Jenny* (1936), and took a small part in his *Les Portes de la nuit* (1946). She retired from acting shortly after the war, having appeared in only twenty-four films throughout her career.

**BATAILLE DU RAIL, La,** France, 1946. 1½hr. *Dir, scr* René Clément; *prod* Co-operative Générale du Cinéma Français, for the Railway Resistance Movement and Ciné Union; *ph* Henri Alekan; *cast* Salina (Athos), Daurand (Camargue), Lozach (Louis), French railwaymen.

CLÉMENT's tribute to the wartime resistance operated by French railway workers continues to bear comparison with the best films of its kind, such as ESPOIR (1939) and ROMA, CITTÀ APERTA (1945). Avoiding false drama and telling his story with admirable directness, he was particularly successful in his handling of the many non-professional actors who re-enacted their real exploits for the film. *La Bataille du rail* won the Grand Prix at CANNES, 1946.

**BATCHELOR,** JOY, see HALAS AND BATCHELOR

**BATES,** ALAN (1930– ), British actor who was first widely noticed as the working-class hero of *A Kind of Loving* (SCHLESINGER, 1962). He played the tramp in *Whistle Down the Wind* (1962) and the sardonic host to the tramp in Clive DONNER's film of PINTER's *The Caretaker* (1963). He was a blithely satirical go-getter in the same director's *Nothing But the Best* (1964). Some of his most effective performances have been achieved in unsatisfactory films: *Zorba the Greek* (1965), as the anxious Englishman whose passions are released by his encounter with primitive simplicity, *Georgy Girl* (1966), DE BROCA's *Le Roi de Coeur* (*King of Hearts*, 1966), and Schlesinger's *Far from the Madding Crowd* (1967). *The Fixer* (1968) gave him a powerful role as the suffering victim of prejudice. The brooding sensuality of Birkin in *Women in Love* (1969) was a simplified version of Lawrence's complex original and THE GO-BETWEEN (1971) gave him little opportunity to develop a rounded characterization. A serious and versatile actor, he has perhaps yet to find a director who can fully realize his power on the screen.

**BATHING BEAUTIES, Mack Sennett's,** see KEYSTONE

*BATTAGLIA DI ALGERI, La* (*The Battle of Algiers*), Algeria/Italy, 1965. 2hr. *Dir* Gillo Pontecorvo; *prod* Casbah Films (Algiers)/Igor Films (Rome); *scr* Franco Solinas; *ph* Marcello Gatti; *des* Sergio Canevari; *mus* Ennio Morricone, Pontecorvo; *cast* Jean Martin (Colonel Mathieu), Yacef Saadi (Saari Kader), Brahim Haggiag (Ali la Pointe), Tommaso Neri (Captain Dubois), Fawzia El Kader (Halima), Michèle Kerbash (Fathia), Mohamed Ben Kassen (Little Omar).

To portray a major event in the conflict between the Algerians and the French, which culminated in Algeria's independence in 1962, PONTECORVO exploited the expressive possibilities of the Casbah's dingy backstreets (contrasted with the Haussmann-like avenues of the French quarters), as well as the audience's familiarity with newsfilm, its black and white grainy texture, depth of field, dramatic close-ups, and detached reporting of events.

At the same time, by emphasizing the complexity of the situation traced through the careers of leading individuals and amplified by the haunting score, the film disallows snap judgements and makes the justification of torture by the French disarmingly persuasive, if not ultimately excusable.

*BATTLESHIP POTEMKIN, The,* see BRONENOSETS POTEMKIN

**BAXTER,** WARNER (1893–1952), US actor, made his film début in 1918, and after 1921 appeared in many silent successes including Maurice TOURNEUR's *Aloma of the South Seas* (1926). In Raoul WALSH's *In Old Arizona* (1929) he played the Cisco Kid, a character he repeated in sequels (*The Arizona Kid*, 1930; *The Cisco Kid*, 1931; *Return of the Cisco Kid*, 1939). He reached the height of his career in the thirties; prominent among his films were *The Squaw Man* (Cecil B. DEMILLE, 1931), 42ND STREET (1933), *Broadway Bill* (Frank CAPRA, 1935), and *The Prisoner of Shark Island* (John FORD, 1936). Most of his films until 1939 had been for TWENTIETH CENTURY-FOX; but his career waned, and with COLUMBIA in the forties he was relegated to 'B' pictures, notably the Crime Doctor series.

**BAZIN,** ANDRÉ (1919–58), French critic and theorist. A speech handicap prevented his entry into the teaching profession, but he taught film appreciation and ran a film society at the Maison des Lettres which provided informal educational facilities for young people in Paris during the German occupation. After the war he worked at the INSTITUT DES HAUTES ÉTUDES CINÉMATO-GRAPHIQUES (IDHEC) and took an active interest in film societies and youth clubs. He wrote for newspapers and periodicals of very varied political and Catholic opinions, including *La Revue du cinéma*. In 1951, with Lo Duca and DONIOL-VALCROZE, Bazin started CAHIERS DU CINÉMA to replace *La Revue*, which had collapsed in 1949. He was co-editor of *Cahiers* until his death, and his involvement with the formulation of a systematic theory of cinema with which to counter EISENSTEIN's theory of MONTAGE greatly influenced a whole generation of film criticism in France.

Although his writing lacks rigour and is often imbued with a pseudo-mystical vocabulary borrowed from the Catholic philosopher Emmanuel Mounier, Bazin was conscious of most of the current issues concerning film theory. Like his predecessor and mentor Roger LEENHARDT, he based his criticism on the films actually made rather than on any preconceived aesthetic or sociological principles. He particularly admired STROHEIM and DREYER, and praised RENOIR as a link between these silent masters and the more direct and conscious representation of reality which he perceived in the work of WELLES, VISCONTI, and ROSSELLINI. He considered that the realistic nature of the film image was best evolved through '*plans-séquences*', extended shots edited in the camera rather than in the cutting-room. His interest in the naturalistic cinema led him to focus attention on Hollywood films, greatly influencing the NOUVELLE VAGUE film-makers.

Bazin's monumental critical work *Qu'est ce le cinéma?* was planned in four volumes: I *Ontologie et langage*, dedicated to Leenhardt and to Bazin's protégé François TRUFFAUT, and II *Le Cinéma et les autres arts* were published in Paris, 1958, 1959; III *Cinéma et sociologie* in 1961 and IV *Une Ésthetique de la réalité: le néo-réalisme* in 1962. At the time of his death he was working on a film script, *Les Églises romanes de Saintonge*, and a book, *Renoir*, which was published in Paris, 1972, edited by Truffaut (English translation, London, 1974).

*What is cinema?*, Berkeley, Cambridge, 1968, 1971, contains a selection of Bazin's criticism in English translation.

**BEATLES, The,** British pop music group consisting of George Harrison (1943–   ), John Lennon (1940–   ), Paul McCartney (1942–   ), and Ringo Starr (1940–   ), real name Richard Starkey, which during the sixties enjoyed phenomenal popularity. They appeared as themselves in A HARD DAY'S NIGHT (1965), *Help!* (1965), both directed by Richard LESTER, *Magical Mystery Tour*, made for television, and *Let It Be* (1970). All these used a slender plot as a vehicle for cheeky humour, fantasy, and songs, and the Beatles happily transferred to the screen their energy and insouciance. Their numbers formed the basis for the animated film YELLOW SUBMARINE (1968). John Lennon also appeared in Lester's *How I Won the War* (1967) and Ringo Starr in *Candy* (1968) and *That'll Be the Day* (1973).

**BEATON,** CECIL (1904– ), British stage designer and still photographer whose film work began as costume designer for *Dangerous Moonlight* (1941). He designed costumes for major productions by the RANK ORGANISATION (*Beware of Pity,* 1946) and by KORDA'S LONDON FILMS (*An Ideal Husband,* 1947, ANNA KARENINA, 1948). In later years he extended his film activity to overall production design, notably in Hollywood with GIGI (1958) and the sumptuous MY FAIR LADY (1964).

**BEAT THE DEVIL,** GB, 1953. 1½hr. (82 min in US). *Dir* John Huston; *prod* Romulus-Santana; *assoc prod* Jack Clayton; *scr* Truman Capote, Huston, from the novel by James Helvick; *ph* Oswald Morris; *mus* Franco Mannino; *cast* Humphrey Bogart (Billy Dannreuther), Jennifer Jones (Gwendolen Chelm), Gina Lollobrigida (Marian Dannreuther), Robert Morley (Petersen), Peter Lorre (O'Hara).

Inconsequential humour characterized HUSTON's ironic burlesque of crime-and-adventure melodrama. The plot incorporated a welter of deliberate misunderstandings and complications, turning into something of a tortuous maze.

The film met with no more than a lukewarm critical reception when it first appeared, but its stock has risen. It is now viewed as Huston's send-up of the thriller, aided by a splendid cast: BOGART in one of his best parts, Jennifer JONES in an unaccustomed comedy role, Robert MORLEY as the leader of a group of crooks.

**BEATTY,** WARREN (1937– ), US actor, real name Beaty, brother of Shirley MACLAINE. His first film was *Splendour in the Grass* (Elia KAZAN, 1961), and Kazan had an immediate influence on his intense approach to acting. His stature grew through performances in *Lilith* (Robert ROSSEN, 1964) and *Mickey One* (Arthur PENN, 1965), and stardom came with Penn's BONNIE AND CLYDE (1967), which Beatty also produced. His recent films have included *McCabe and Mrs Miller* (Robert ALTMAN, 1972) and *Dollars* (1972, *The Heist* in GB), in which he exhibited a capable maturity as the smooth, unruffled bank-robber who cases a job from the inside.

**BEAU SERGE,** Le, France, 1959. 1½hr. *Dir, scr* Claude Chabrol; *prod* AJYM/CGCF; *ph* Henri Decaë; *cast* Gérard Blain (Serge), Jean-Claude Brialy (François), Bernadette Lafont (Marie), Michèle Meritz (Yvonne), Claude Cerval (the priest).

François, returning to his native village, finds his talented childhood friend Serge has become a hopeless drunk. His well-meant attempts to help do more harm than good: finally he risks his life to reconcile Serge with his estranged wife.

*Le Beau Serge* was made on location in CHABROL's own village, using unknown actors and local people in the supporting roles. Not strictly autobiographical, it is nevertheless a very personal film. It was financed by Chabrol's first wife and he thus had complete independence. Its success gave him similar independence in making LES COUSINS (1959) and also in supporting the work of other young French directors. It is uneven in quality, very much a young man's film; its main importance lies in being the first feature film of the NOUVELLE VAGUE.

**BECH,** LILI (1885–1939), Danish-born actress chiefly in Sweden, enjoyed much popularity in the early years of Swedish cinema. She is now mainly remembered in Mauritz STILLER's *Vampyren* (*Vampires,* 1913) and as the second wife of Victor SJÖSTRÖM.

**BECKER,** JACQUES (1906–60), French director, worked from 1932 as an assistant to Jean REŇOIR, whose benevolent influence may be traced throughout his films. Work on his first film as director, *L'Or du Cristobal,* was interrupted by the outbreak of war: his first completed film was a thriller, *Dernier Atout* (1942). His second, GOUPI-MAINS-ROUGES (1943), had tremendous success in occupied France, with its realistic portrayal of rural life, reminiscent of PAGNOL, and the close, sympathetic observation of people and their relationships which was to become Becker's hall-mark. *Falbalas* (also shot during the Occupation in 1944, but first shown in 1945) is the beginning of Becker's exploration of the Paris milieu that was to be developed further in his next three films, *Antoine et Antoinette* (1947), *Rendez-vous de juillet* (1949), and EDOUARD ET CAROLINE (1951). Each of these three films studies in intimate detail a group of people, exploring with gently humorous penetration their conventions of behaviour and the shifts of their relationships. The plot in each case is slender in the extreme, for Becker's concern is with character rather than with reaction to events imposed by a script. The conviction of the performances reflects his own interest in acting as a craft and the close relationship he was able to establish with his actors.

CASQUE D'OR (1952) is also set in Paris but at the turn of the century, and Becker evoked with meticulous detail the surroundings and manners of the period as successfully as he had done in his modern Paris settings. The script was largely written by Becker himself, using contemporary law reports, and *Casque d'or* is perhaps for this reason his most enduring film.

*Touchez pas au grisbi* (1954) is a return to modern life, a gangster story from a *serie noire* novel by Albert Simonin, who also wrote DU RIFIFI CHEZ LES HOMMES (1955). These two films both had an influence on the vogue for the FILM NOIR, but Becker's account of robbery and gang warfare is more concerned with the complexities of character than with the efficient exercise of violence. The thoughtful rhythm of the film gave the actors (outstandingly Jean GABIN in one of his most mature characterizations) the opportunity to portray their roles in depth.

*Ali Baba et les quarante voleurs* (1954), a vehicle for FERNANDEL, *Les Aventures d'Arsène Lupin* (1956), a light period comedy about a gentleman thief, and *Montparnasse 19* (1957), a biography of the painter Modigliani, gave Becker little opportunity to explore further his particular interests. However, LE TROU (1960), his last film, has not only the strengths of his earlier work but is an indication of new directions. The subject, a prison escape, the use of non-professional actors, the concentrated austerity of the camera style, and the marvellous creation of atmosphere make *Le Trou* an interesting comparison with BRESSON's UN CONDAMNÉ A MORT S'EST ÉCHAPPÉ (1956), although Becker's film is humanist rather than spiritual in tone.

Becker's films, and particularly *Goupi-mains-rouges*, have been undeservedly neglected. His best films (*Goupi-mains-rouges*, *Edouard et Caroline*, *Casque d'or*, *Le Trou*) show him to have been a master in the use of film to convey aspects of human character and behaviour with unsentimental warmth and concern. His control of each film's individual rhythm was outstanding: much of his ability to reproduce detailed social milieux is in the cutting and juxtaposition of shots. This technical accomplishment was, however, never allowed to take the place of intelligent observation of men and women in relation to each other and their surroundings.

**BEERY, NOAH** (1884–1946), US actor, brother of Wallace Beery, went into films in 1910 after several years' stage experience. He became one of the silent screen's best-loved villains in such films as TOL'ABLE DAVID (1921), *The Spoilers* (1922), and *Beau Geste* (1926). His career was overshadowed by that of his brother, but Noah continued to work regularly until his death. His many other films include *The Mormon Maid* (1918), *The Mark of Zorro* (1920), *The Four Feathers* (1929), *She Done Him Wrong* (1933), *The Girl of the Golden West* (1938), *This Man's Navy* (1945).

**BEERY, WALLACE** (1886 or 1889–1949), US actor, progressed from railway worker to training circus elephants before becoming a stage actor. In 1914 he was hired by ESSANAY to act and direct: while with them he made his popular *Swedie* series, short SLAPSTICK comedies in which he played a Swedish housemaid. In 1916 he moved to Hollywood, where he worked for UNIVERSAL and KEYSTONE: his elopement with Gloria SWANSON in 1917 caused a breach with the latter company.

He played the villain in a number of popular films, including Maurice TOURNEUR's *The Last of the Mohicans* (1921), breaking out of type when Douglas FAIRBANKS gave him the part of Richard the Lionheart in ROBIN HOOD (1922), and starring with VALENTINO in THE FOUR HORSEMEN OF THE APOCALYPSE (1922). With Raymond Hatton, another popular HEAVY, he made a series of comedies, notably *We're in the Navy Now* (1928). He gave a powerful performance as a ferocious thug in *The Big House* (1930), a prison drama. This success gave him a long-term contract with METRO-GOLDWYN-MAYER and he became one of the company's most important stars, remaining with them until his death. Among his notable films were King VIDOR's *The Champ* (1931), two earthy comedies with Marie DRESSLER, *Min and Bill* (1931) and *Tugboat Annie* (1933), GRAND HOTEL (1932), DINNER AT EIGHT (1933), and *Port of the Seven Seas* (1938), a remake of MARIUS (1931) in which he played the role created by RAIMU. In all he appeared in over 200 films, in parts designed to suit his great height and weight but of considerable variety, and holding his own alongside some of Hollywood's outstanding stars. He appeared occasionally with his brother Noah.

**BEGGAR'S OPERA, The,** GB, 1953. Technicolor; 1¼hr. *Dir* Peter Brook; *prod* Laurence Olivier, Herbert Wilcox; *scr* Dennis Cannan, from the ballad opera by John Gay; *additional dialogue and lyrics* Christopher Fry; *ph* Guy Green; *des* W. C. Andrews; *mus* (arrangements) Sir Arthur Bliss; *cast* Laurence Olivier (Macheath), Dorothy Tutin (Polly), George Devine (Peachum), Stanley Holloway (Lockit), Daphne Anderson (Lucy Lockit). All the cast except Laurence Olivier and Stanley Holloway have their voices dubbed for the songs.

Peter BROOK made an impressive début as a feature film director with a lavish adaptation of Gay's ballad opera. For all its failure to solve the main problem of the musical, the transition from speech to song, the film has an exciting sense of drama and movement. Among the prestigious cast there were some excellent acting performances, notably Laurence OLIVIER's swashbuckling Macheath and Dorothy TUTIN's sweetly sentimental Polly Peachum. (See also DIE DREIGROSCHENOPER.)

**BELAFONTE,** HARRY (1927– ), West Indian actor and singer whose first film appearance was a supporting part in *Bright Road* (1953), in which Dorothy Dandridge played the female lead. He co-starred with her in his next film, the all-Black *Carmen Jones* (1954), and scored an even greater popular success with both his performance and his singing of the title song in *Island in the Sun* (1957). After *Odds Against Tomorrow* (1959), he disappeared from the screen for a decade, resuming his film career in *The Angel Levine* (1970). His career, like Sidney POITIER's, has reflected Hollywood's attempts to propitiate the Civil Rights movement by giving starring roles to acceptably handsome black actors.

**BELGIUM.** The principle of PERSISTENCE OF VISION (one of the bases of cinematography) was first formulated by a Belgian, A. F. PLATEAU, who put the principle into practice in his Phantascope (1832). The first film to be shot in Belgium was also of an innovatory nature: the balloon descent to the Grande Place in Brussels used by GRIMOIN-SANSON in his CINÉORAMA (1900). A studio was built on the outskirts of Brussels in 1908 and native production companies began to emerge after the First World War, but Belgium, with its small population and cultural and linguistic divisions, has been unable to sustain a large film industry. French-speaking film workers such as Jacques FEYDER and Charles SPAAK have tended to transfer their talents to the richer film world of France. Belgium's strength has lain chiefly in short films and documentary, with Henri STORCK achieving international status as a documentary director. Art films have continued and illuminated the Belgian tradition in the graphic arts: André Cauvin, Paul Haesaerts, and François Weyergans have made important contributions in this area. In 1953–62 only forty-eight full-length features were produced (400–600 films are imported each year) but co-productions have in recent years helped to give opportunities to Belgian film-makers. One newcomer to have made an impact in this way is Harry Kümel, whose baroque fantasies, notably *Monsieur Hawarden* (1968), have earned international praise. Belgium has become a centre for experimental film since the first festival held at Knokke-le-Zoute in 1949, sponsored by the Belgian Cinémathèque. There is a national film school, the Institut Supérieur des Arts du Spectacle et Techniques de Diffusion, and a flourishing system of ciné-clubs.

**BELL,** MARIE (1900– ), French actress who began her career in the early twenties, notably in silent films by Henry-Roussell and Gaston Ravel, including the latter's version of *Madame Récamier* (1928). She reached the height of her fame in the thirties. Among films that attained international reputation were *Le Grand Jeu* (Jacques FEYDER, 1934), *Légions d'honneur* (Maurice Gleize, 1938), *La Charrette fantôme* (Julien DUVIVIER, 1938), and *Le Colonel Chabert* (René Le Hénaff, 1943). The film with which she is above all associated is Duvivier's *Un Carnet de bal* (1937). She also gave a powerful performance in VISCONTI's VAGHE STELLE D'ORSA (1965).

***BELLE ET LA BÊTE, La,*** France, 1946. 1¾hr. *Dir, scr* Jean Cocteau, from the fairy-tale by Mme Leprince de Beaumont; *prod* André Paulvé; *ph* Henri Alékan, supervised by René Clément; *des* Christian Bérard; *mus* Georges Auric; *cast* Jean Marais (The Beast/Avenant), Josette Day (Belle), Mila Parély, Nane Germon (her sisters), Marcel André (her father).

In his first film after LE SANG D'UN POÈTE (1930), COCTEAU adapted the old legend to his personal mythology, in particular creating ambiguity through Jean MARAIS's playing both the Beast and Avenant. The film is stylistically varied, moving from comic farce in the scenes with the Belle's sisters to dream-like slow-motion photography in the Beast's castle. Here, as in ORPHÉE (1950), Cocteau came near to realizing his aim of creating a visual equivalent of poetic experience.

***BELLES DE NUIT, Les,*** France/Italy, 1952. 1½hr. *Dir* René Clair; *prod* Franco London Film-Rizzoli; *scr* Clair, J.-P. Grédy, P. Barillet; *ph* Armand Thirard, Robert Juilliard, Louis Née; *des* Léon Barsacq; *mus* Georges Van Parys; *cast* Gérard Philipe (Claude), Martine Carol (Edmée), Gina Lollobrigida (Leila), Magali Verdeuil (Suzanne).

Claude, a gauche young music teacher, finds in dreams that draw him back through history, the romantic adventures that his everyday life lacks. As his real life improves the compensatory dreams turn to nightmares, culminating in a slapstick chase from the Stone Age back to the present. CLAIR establishes an internal logic in the film, avoiding the dangers of indulgence in pure fantasy: each dream event is stimulated by an image or reference in Claude's waking hours and real acquaintances figure as characters in his dreams. Not just a witty extravaganza, the film carries an ironic comment on the myth of the good old days.

***BELLISSIMÀ,*** Italy, 1951. 2hr. *Dir* Luchino Visconti; *prod* Bellissimà Films; *scr* Suso Cecchi d'Amico, Francesco Rosi, Visconti, from a story by Zavattini; *ph* Piero Portalupi, Paul Ronald; *ed* Mario Serandrei; *cast* Anna Magnani (Maddalena), Walter Chiari (Alberto), Tina Apicella (Maria), Gastone Renzelli (Spartaco), Alessandro Blasetti (himself).

Maddalena is ready to stop at nothing to make a film star of her daughter, Maria, but, becoming disillusioned with the world of CINECITTÀ, finally refuses the screen test offered to the child. VISCONTI's use of an untypically spare and realistic visual style is offset somewhat by the rambling denouement and by Anna MAGNANI's bravura performance.

**BELLOCCHIO,** MARCO (1939– ), Italian director, interrupted his philosophical studies to follow courses in acting and directing at the CENTRO SPERIMENTALE. He made three short films and spent the year 1964–5 studying under Thorold DICKINSON at University College, London. While living in London, he completed the script for I PUGNI IN TASCA (*Fists in the Pocket*, 1966). He returned to Italy to raise the money to make the film—it cost only £28,000, much of it lent by his family—which was a great critical success and won several prizes. *La Cina è vicina* (*China is Near*, 1968) was less successful. Bellocchio's political views made him unpopular with potential backers and his next feature film, *In nome del padre*, did not appear until 1971.

**BELMONDO,** JEAN-PAUL (1933– ), French actor, trained for the classical theatre and after several small stage parts played his first film role for CARNÉ in *Les Tricheurs* (*The Cheaters*, 1958). The film which brought him international notice was A BOUT DE SOUFFLE (1960). It led, with his other appearances for GODARD in *Une femme est une femme* (1961) and PIERROT-LE-FOU (1965), to the danger of his being typed as an appealing outlaw, the latter-day equivalent of BOGART and GABIN, both of whom he greatly admires. *Borsalino* (1970), which he co-produced with his co-star Alain DELON, embodies many of the myths which have accrued to him and his delight in the Hollywood legends of the thirties.

Belmondo's acting parallels the stylistic techniques of the NOUVELLE VAGUE: he makes use of the audience's knowledge of his own character, often giving an impression of improvisation, and makes frequent references to his screen idols. But that he is capable of a wider range of interpretation than is popularly attributed to him is evinced by his portrayal of a petty criminal in MALLE's *Le Voleur* (1967), a thoughtful and original interpretation, and in the title role of LÉON MORIN, PRÊTRE (1961) where he gave a fine,

deeply-felt performance. His ability as an actor has won him a reputation that will endure as well as the star popularity that his distinctive personal magnetism has won on the international circuit. He has written an autobiography, *Trente ans et vint-cinq films* (Paris, 1963).

**BENCHLEY,** ROBERT (1889–1945), US humorist whose most celebrated film work was in a sporadic but long-lived series of comedy sketches in the form of 'scientific' lectures, graced by such titles as *The Sex Life of the Polyp*. One of these, *How to Sleep* (1935), won an OSCAR. He also appeared in comedy character parts in a number of feature films, including *The Major and the Minor* (1942), *I Married a Witch* (1942), and *It's in the Bag* (1945, *The Fifth Chair* in GB).

**BENDIX,** WILLIAM (1906–64), US actor whose distinctive rasping voice with its thick Brooklyn accent, sturdy build, and craggy features made him a specialist in tough-guy roles after he attracted attention in a supporting part in *The Glass Key* (1942). He was comparatively versatile, however, equally at home in comedy as genial or dim-witted characters. Only occasionally was he cast in leading roles: *Brooklyn Orchid* (1942) was an indifferent film, but his performance as the stoker in the film version of Eugene O'Neill's *The Hairy Ape* (1944) was memorable and possibly his finest achievement on the screen. Among other good parts at this period were those in *Lifeboat* (1944), *The Blue Dahlia* (1946), and *The Web* (1947). In 1951, he made a characteristic contribution to the excellent *Detective Story* and redeemed *Macao* (STERNBERG, 1952), which had the formidable co-starring team of Robert MITCHUM and Jane RUSSELL, from disaster. He visited Britain to appear in *The Rough and the Smooth* (1953) and in addition to film work starred in a successful television series, 'The Life of Riley'.

**BENEDEK,** LASZLO (1907– ), Hungarian director in the US, Germany, and Britain. The two films which made his name, *Death of a Salesman* (1952) and *The Wild One* (1953), were distinguished chiefly by the performances of Fredric MARCH and Marlon BRANDO respectively.

**BEN-HUR,** US, 1925. 2¼hr. *Dir* Fred Niblo; *prod* MGM; *ph* Percy Hilburn, Rene Guissart, Charles Struss, Clyde de Vinna; *cast* Ramon Novarro (Ben-Hur), Francis X. Bushman (Messala), Frank Currier (Quintus Arrius), May McAvoy (Esther), Carmel Myers (Iras).

*Ben-Hur* (published 1880), the best-selling novel by General Lew Wallace (1827–1905), having become a tremendous success in a stage adaptation in which W. S. HART appeared as Messala, was in demand for film adaptation as early as 1907, when the makers of a two-reel version were sued in the first COPYRIGHT case arising out of a film. The company, KALEM, lost at a cost variously reported between $25,000 and $50,000, the case having taken four years to conclude.

In 1921 Abraham Erlanger, the impresario who already owned the stage rights of *Ben-Hur*, set up the Classical Cinematograph Corporation for the sole purpose of securing the film rights. Having achieved this at a cost of $600,000, he then coolly offered them for sale at $1 million, an unprecedented sum that was not forthcoming, but in 1922 the Goldwyn company (see METRO-GOLDWYN-MAYER) came to an arrangement with Erlanger to produce the film and divide the profits on an equal basis. Shooting started in Italy, where political unrest and unsatisfactory workmanship caused mounting costs. The director, Rex INGRAM, was replaced, first by Charles Brabin, then by Fred NIBLO; George Walsh, originally cast as Ben-Hur was, after much wasted time, dismissed in favour of Ramon NOVARRO. Shooting of the sea battle sequences at Livorno was accompanied by highly coloured reports of accidents and loss of lives which, even if exaggerated, helped to increase the unit's difficulties and heightened the atmosphere of scandal that created a legend around *Ben-Hur* before it ever appeared on the screen. Finally the team returned to Hollywood to complete the film. It was greeted with acclaim, particularly for Francis X. BUSHMAN's performance as Messala and for the brilliantly filmed chariot race. B. Reeves EASON, the SECOND UNIT director, was mainly responsible for this and his considerable experience in Westerns came into full play in creating a remarkable cinematic *tour de force*. At a considerable expenditure of film, horses, time, and money he created a totally new film experience, and *Ben-Hur* has a place in cinema history by virtue of this sequence alone. Costing $4 million and taking three years to make, dogged with mishaps from the start, it may be said to have set the pattern for future mammoth productions.

*Ben-Hur*, US, 1959. Todd-AO Panavision; 3½hr; Technicolor. *Dir* William Wyler; *prod* Sam Zimbalist for MGM; *scr* Karl Tunberg; *ph* Robert L. Surtees; *cast* Charlton Heston (Ben-Hur), Stephen Boyd (Messala), Jack Hawkins (Quintus Arrius), Haya Harareet (Esther).

The sophisticated modern techniques, including STEREOPHONIC sound, available for the remake of *Ben-Hur* failed to lift it out of the class of routine epic productions of the fifties. The film was, however, redeemed by the literate additional dialogue by, among others, the English playwright Christopher Fry. Charlton HESTON gave a performance of much dignity and restraint.

**BENNETT,** CONSTANCE (1905–65), US actress, sister of Joan Bennett and daughter of Richard Bennett. Her first major film role was in *Cytherea* (1924); during the silent period she played mainly melodramatic or flapper parts; but by the early thirties she had become a popular star, specializing in playing sophisticated ladies of doubtful morals, notably in *The Affairs of Cellini* (Gregory LA CAVA, 1934). Later she was able to exploit her talent for comedy, and is above all remembered as the attractive heroine of the amusing *Topper* (1937) and *Topper Takes a Trip* (1939). After a lengthy absence from the screen, she made a reappearance shortly before her death in the 1965 remake of *Madame X*.

**BENNETT,** JOAN (1910–    ), US actress, sister of Constance Bennett, had her first film role in *Bulldog Drummond* (1929). She appeared in a variety of films, many of indifferent quality even after her performance as Amy in *Little Women* (George CUKOR, 1933). Hitherto as delightfully blonde as her sister, she became and remained black-haired. She played Dumas heroines in *The Man in the Iron Mask* (1939) and *Son of Monte Cristo* (1940), both opposite Louis Hayward, and appeared in two Fritz LANG films, *The House Across the Bay* (1940) and *Manhunt* (1941). Again under Lang's direction, she gave two of her best performances as corrupt temptresses in *The Woman in the Window* (1944) and *Scarlet Street* (1945), and she worked for Jean RENOIR in *The Woman on the Beach* (1947). In contrast with these 'vamp' parts were her performances in light comedy: she made the most elegant of mothers as she shared family trouble with Spencer TRACY and Elizabeth TAYLOR in *Father of the Bride* (1950) and *Father's Little Dividend* (1951). None of her subsequent films did her justice.

**BENNY,** JACK (1894–1974), US comedian specializing in the 'slow burn'—a brand of humour depending on skilled timing. Most of his jokes are constructed around his self-allegedly mean, cowardly, incompetent personality. His films, mostly musicals, did little more than exploit his popular vaudeville and radio act, but *To Be or Not To Be* (LUBITSCH, 1942), which co-starred Carole LOMBARD, showed his capabilities as a stylish comic actor. From the mid-fifties, apart from a few guest appearances in films, he worked in television.

**BENOIT-LÉVY,** JEAN (1888–1959), French director of more than three hundred educational or documentary films, began his career in the early twenties. In 1922 he made *Pasteur* with Jean EPSTEIN, and later worked closely with the latter's sister, Marie Epstein, who wrote most of his scripts. Their best-known film was *La Maternelle (The Nursery School*, 1933). After spending the war years in America he directed the film services of the United Nations, 1946–9. A proponent of educational cinema, he wrote many books on the subject, including *Les Grandes Missions du cinéma* (Montreal, 1945).

**BÉRARD,** CHRISTIAN (1902–49), French designer, who worked for many years in the theatre with Louis JOUVET and others, creating both period and realistic settings with the utmost flair. Although he worked briefly with both KORDA and CARNÉ in the forties, his only film work that reached fruition was with Jean COCTEAU, with whom he first worked in 1930, on the stage production of *La Voix humaine*. His three films for Cocteau, LA BELLE ET LA BÊTE (1946), *L'Aigle à deux têtes* (1947), and LES PARENTS TERRIBLES (1948), are indicative of his great range of ability; indeed, the first and last may be considered in some respects almost as much the achievement of Bérard as of Cocteau.

**BERGGREN,** THOMMY (1937–   ), Swedish actor, apart from a leading role in Jörn DONNER'S *En sondag i september (A Sunday in September*, 1963), has made his most notable appearances in films directed by Bo WIDERBERG. His intelligent simplicity and direct emotional appeal allied with considerable personal charm added much to the effectiveness of KVARTERET KORPEN (*Raven's End*, 1963), ELVIRA MADIGAN (1967), and *Joe Hill (The Ballad of Joe Jill*, 1971).

**BERGMAN,** INGMAR (1918–   ), Swedish director, born in Uppsala of an austerely strict evangelical family; his father was a Lutheran pastor. While at university he directed student theatre productions, then worked in amateur experimental theatre. He began work as a theatre director in 1944 at the City Theatre, Hälsingborg, and when he moved to the Göteborg City Theatre in 1946 his reputation was firmly established. During this period he edited scripts for SVENSK FILMINDUSTRI which was making efforts to encourage new talent in the Swedish cinema (see SWEDEN). Bergman's first screen credits were as scriptwriter and assistant director on Alf SJÖBERG'S HETS (*Frenzy*, 1944). The following year he directed his first film *Kris (Crisis)*, for which he also wrote the script, followed by *Det Regnar på vår kärlek (It Rains on Our Love*, 1946). He also scripted *Kvinna utan ansikte (Woman Without a Face*, 1947), directed by Gustaf MOLANDER.

Bergman then directed *Skepp till Indialand (A Ship to India*, 1947), which continued his common theme of this period—the young desperately battling with a cruel, often hopeless, adult society. Bergman here used his characteristic device of separate narratives which cross and interact. In *Hamnstad (Port of Call*, 1948) Bergman acknowledged the influence of Italian NEO-REALISM and struck an almost documentary note seldom noticeable in his other work. The culmination of these obsessive adolescent themes came with *Fängelse (Prison* or *The Devil's Wanton*, 1949), a despairing story of a young prostitute and the circumstances leading to her suicide.

With *Törst (Thirst* or *Three Strange Loves*, 1949) Bergman introduced a theme which he has developed in depth—the inward experiences of women and their essential loneliness. His films exploring this subject include *Sommarlek (Summer Interlude* or *Illicit Interlude*, 1950), KVINNORS VÄNTAN (*Waiting Women* or *Secrets of Women*, 1952), *Sommaren med Monika (Summer with Monika* or *Monika*, 1953), *Kvinnodröm (Journey into Autumn* or *Dreams*, 1954), *Nära livet (So Close to Life* or *Brink of Life*, 1957); SOMMARNATTENS LEENDE (*Smiles of a Summer Night*, 1955) touches on the same theme in a comedy vein. Here the actress in the Bergman film becomes of great importance; in fact the stages of his development can to a degree be charted through his association with various actresses—Mai-Brit Nilsson, Harriet ANDERSSON, Eva DAHLBECK, Bibi ANDERSSON, Ingrid THULIN, Liv ULLMANN, Mai ZETTERLING. The continuing importance of women in Bergman's films is, however, balanced by the valuable contribution of actors, notably Max VON SYDOW and Gunnar BJÖRNSTRAND.

One of Bergman's most intriguing works, GYCKLARNAS AFTON (*Sawdust and Tinsel* or *The Naked Night*, 1953) introduced circus performers as a metaphor for the artist in society; its other major theme—sexual humiliation—was to become increasingly important in Bergman's introspective vision. *En lektion i kärlek (A Lesson in Love*, 1956), although a light-hearted comedy, was not free of his despairing view of sexual relations.

Bergman achieved world-wide critical success with DET SJUNDE INSEGLET (*The Seventh Seal*, 1957), which conveys a modern philosophy of despair through its powerful evocation of the horrors of medieval life. SMULTRONSTÄLLET (*Wild Strawberries*, 1957), set in modern times, is a profound study of man's isolation. It further enhanced Bergman's reputation. In *Jungfrukällen (The Virgin Spring*, 1960) he returned to a medieval setting, using images of limpid beauty or dark menace to create a tale of brutal crime and sadistic retribution. Bergman's conception of God as an implacable silence is vital to all three films, notwithstanding the relative calm at the close of both *Smultronstället* and *Jungfrukällen*. The visual element of Bergman's work has become increasingly powerful. He has built on the Swedish tradition of superb camerawork, adding to the skill of his most frequent cameramen, Gunnar FISCHER and Sven NYKVIST, a penetrating imagery where the underlying significance of objects, the hostility of natural surroundings, or the painful fragility of human flesh tellingly supplement his narrative. His symbolism is frequently derived from Jungian dream analysis, nowhere more clearly than in his trilogy of the early sixties. The three films use separate subjects to illustrate the loneliness and vulnerability of modern man, starved of faith and love: *Såsom i en spegel* (*Through a Glass Darkly*, 1961) is a drama of close family relationships, Strindbergian in its analysis of mutual destruction; *Nattvardgästerna* (*Winter Light* or *The Communicants*, 1963) presents the hopeless search for divine love that turns men away from human contact; *Tystnaden* (*The Silence*, 1963) carries isolation to its ultimate point, placing a dying woman and her sister, tortured by frustrated desires, in a foreign country with no means of communication.

Bergman's obsession with the psycho-sexuality of women began, in *Tystnaden*, to turn away from consideration of women in relation to men to women closeted with other women (though this was discernible as early as *Kvinnors väntan* and *Nära livet*). PERSONA (1966), perhaps the most engrossing of his later films, places two women in neurotic intimacy, dissecting their mutual responses with cruel objectivity. The performances of Liv Ullmann and Bibi Andersson argue rare devotion to their director and identification with his aims.

Although an intensely personal film-maker whose themes and expressive ideas have remained remarkably consistent, Bergman has shown a concern to identify himself with the avant-garde. *Persona* has a prologue which emphasizes the physical properties of the medium (he specified that stills from the film must be reproduced with the sprocket holes to underline the same idea); and a television sequence of the Vietnam war sits uneasily in his private world. *Vargtimmen* (*Hour of the Wolf*, 1968), his most explicit study of the artist at odds with society, uses a fragmented narrative style. *Skammen* (*Shame*, 1968), shot in the grainy style associated with newsreel, attempts a political statement about individual responsibility in a totalitarian state, but is most notable for revealing a further development in Bergman's pessimism about human relationships. *En Passion*

(*A Passion* or *Passion of Anna*, 1969), beautifully filmed in desaturated colour, re-examines the themes of the artist's function and of the impossibility of human trust; sequences where the actors abandon their roles to address the camera directly tend to weaken the film: a masterly story-teller, Bergman betrays his talent in attempting to exploit techniques of alienation. *Viskingar och Rop* (*Cries and Whispers*, 1972) again places a group of women in a confined situation, exploring their emotional interaction with appalling intensity. The increasingly permissive climate allowed the sado-erotic element often hinted at earlier to emerge fully: rich colour links the visual content to the narrative with Bergman's characteristic skill.

*Scener ur ett aektenskap* (*Scenes from a Marriage*, 1974), derived from a six-part series made for Swedish television, returned to the examination of relationships between men and women, in particular the enclosed world of middle-class married life. It was notable for its spare, almost documentary visual style and for a performance of great sensibility from Liv Ullman.

Bergman's dominance in Swedish cinema was unchallenged until the early sixties when young critics led by Bo WIDERBERG attacked his preoccupation with private, inner turmoil. However justified such strictures may be, his consistently striking work over thirty years has made him a giant of the cinema. The coherence of his works extends to the theatre which he has never abandoned, taking his company to Stockholm every winter to mount productions of Strindberg, Ibsen, and other classics, and to the Swedish islands and countryside in the summer for filming. His extraordinarily close relationship with his actors has inspired selfless and sometimes great performances, without which his vision might have lost its intensity.

Robin Wood, *Ingmar Bergman*, New York, 1970, Birgitta Steene, *Ingmar Bergman*, New York, 1968.

**BERGMAN,** INGRID (1915– ), Swedish actress, trained at the Royal Dramatic Theatre School in Stockholm. Early in her career she played small parts in films for SVENSK FILM-INDUSTRI and also for UFA in Berlin. Her first starring role was in INTERMEZZO (1936), which was seen by a representative of David O. SELZNICK; as a result she was invited to Hollywood to make an English-language version of the same subject co-starring Leslie HOWARD: *Intermezzo* (1939, *Escape to Happiness* in GB). It is generally supposed that Selznick was hoping to launch a second GARBO: for some years she was hired out to other companies while he searched for appropriate subjects for her. During this period she starred in *Adam Had Four Sons* (1940) for COLUMBIA, DR JEKYLL AND MR HYDE (1941) for METRO-GOLDWYN-MAYER, CASA-BLANCA (1943) for WARNER BROS, and *For Whom the Bell Tolls* (1943) for PARAMOUNT. For MGM she then appeared in the remake of GASLIGHT (1944) and for Selznick in two films directed by HITCHCOCK, *Spellbound* (1945) and NOTORIOUS (1946).

The image built up during this time of a radiant natural beauty with total personal integrity was reinforced by her appearance as an up-to-date nun in *The Bells of St Mary's* (1945), but it was her triumphant success in the title role of Maxwell Anderson's *Joan of Lorraine* on Broadway that established her exalted image with the American public. Her own production JOAN OF ARC (1948) was, however, artistically and commercially a failure.

Bergman left Hollywood for England to make her third film with Hitchcock, *Under Capricorn* (1949); shortly after its completion the publicity surrounding her relationship with Roberto ROS-SELLINI created an uproar in Europe and even more in the US. Their first child was born while she was still married to her first husband, and this dealt a lasting blow to her popularity. Unfortunately, the films she made under Rossellini's direction were far from successful. For some years after their marriage ended she worked in Europe, returning to Hollywood only to receive an OSCAR for her performance in *Anastasia* (1956). Subsequent films made in Europe, including *Indiscreet* (1958), a sophisticated comedy co-starring Cary GRANT, and *The Inn of the Sixth Happiness* (1958), in which she played an English missionary in China, went a long way towards re-establishing her popularity. *Cactus Flower* (1969) gave her the role of a plain woman emerging into beauty and amorous success, and she handled its combination of comedy and charm with endearing conviction.

**BERGNER,** ELISABETH (1900–    ), Austrian actress, had already earned a considerable reputation in the theatre especially in the plays of Shaw before gaining great popularity in Germany with such films as *Der Geiger von Florenz* (1926), *Ariane* (1931), and *Der träumende Munde* (1932). With her husband and director Paul CZINNER she left Germany for England in the early thirties and under his direction made *Catherine the Great* (1934), with Douglas FAIRBANKS, the very successful *Escape Me Never* (1936), *As You Like It* (1936), with Laurence OLIVIER, and an English version of *Ariane: Stolen Life* (1939). Her fragile beauty and sensitive acting won her a large following.

**BERKELEY,** BUSBY (1895–    ), US dance director, real name William Berkeley Enos. A celebrated Broadway stage director, he was brought to Hollywood by Florenz Ziegfeld and Samuel GOLDWYN to stage the production numbers for the Eddie CANTOR musicals including *Whoopee* (1930) and *Roman Scandals* (1933). Much of his best work is in the WARNER BROS musicals, including 42ND STREET (1933) and the GOLDDIGGERS series (1933–7).

In his musical numbers Berkeley made many innovations in production technique, pre-planning every action from the camera's viewpoint so tightly that the editor needed only to connect each piece of film with the next, and using only one very mobile camera instead of four or five stationary cameras as had been the usual practice. His camera was always on the move—panning, changing angles, shooting from above—and the screen was filled with hundreds of leggy, scantily dressed girls on revolving floors or futuristic platforms. The famous Berkeley kaleidoscope effect, where the dancers performed in concentric circles to a camera perched directly above them, graced almost all his films of the thirties. He treated people strictly as components in mobile patterns comparable at times with those created by Leni RIEFEN-STAHL. His style may well be criticized as vulgar and ornate, but the inventiveness of his camera work broke new ground in the MUSICAL and influenced his successors (DONEN, MINNELLI, Gene KELLY) in their further developments of the genre.

He made some uncharacteristic excursions into dramatic subjects, notably *They Made Me a Criminal* (1939) starring John GARFIELD; then with the changing style of screen musicals in the forties, Berkeley turned to directing the cheerfully routine Judy GARLAND–Mickey ROONEY musicals and others including *For Me and My Gal* (1942). These demonstrate his limitations in treating people as characters. The musical numbers, although often successful, increasingly show a flagging of invention occasionally almost amounting to unintentional self-parody. He later directed production numbers in occasional films including *Rose Marie* (1954) and *Billy Rose's Jumbo* (1962). In the late sixties a widespread vogue for thirties kitsch helped popularize his work with a new generation of film-goers. At seventy-five he staged a Broadway revival of *No, No, Nanette* starring Ruby KEELER, who had made her name in his early film musicals.

**BERLANGA,** LUIS GARCIA (1921–    ), Spanish director, studied at the Madrid film school (IIEC) where he met Juan Antonio BAR-DEM. They collaborated on several scripts, then co-wrote and co-directed *Esa pareja felix* (*That Happy Couple*, 1951). Berlanga's first important film was BIENVENIDA MR MARSHALL (*Welcome Mr Marshall*, 1953), a sharply satirical look at the effect of the announcement of American aid on a backward Spanish town. Apart from a period when, under the influence of ZAVATTINI, he tried to force the themes and techniques of NEO-REALISM into Spanish film-making, he has specialized in picaresque satires on modern Spanish life. *Placido* (1962) shows all his preoccupations, and in EL VERDUGO (*The Executioner*, 1964) they are to be found in the macabre instruction of a reluctant apprentice hangman. As with other adventurous Spanish film-makers, Berlanga's work has suffered considerably from political and religious censorship.

**BERLIN, IRVING** (1888–    ), Russian-born US song-writer, real name Israel Baline. A very prolific and versatile composer, he provided the songs for many screen musicals. Outstanding among them are three that teamed Fred ASTAIRE and Ginger ROGERS: TOP HAT (1935), featuring the songs 'Cheek to Cheek', 'Isn't it a Lovely Day', and 'Top Hat, White Tie and Tails'; *Follow the Fleet* (1936), with 'Let's Face the Music and Dance'; and *Carefree* (1938), which included 'Change Partners'. *On the Avenue* (1937) had 'I've Got My Love to Keep Me Warm'; *Alexander's Ragtime Band* (1938) was built around the number with which Berlin had revolutionized popular song-writing in 1911; and in *Holiday Inn* (1942), Bing CROSBY sang the indestructible 'White Christmas' for the first time. Berlin made a guest appearance in *This is the Army* (1943), singing 'Oh How I Hate to Get Up in the Morning'. *Blue Skies* (1946) and EASTER PARADE (1948) are among his other enduring scores. He also wrote many stage musicals, a number of which became successful films, among them *Annie Get Your Gun* (1950) and *Call Me Madam* (1953).

**BERLIN—DIE SYMPHONIE EINER GROSSSTADT**, Germany, 1927. 1¼hr. *Dir* Walter Ruttmann; *scr* Ruttmann, Karl Freund, from an idea by Carl Mayer; *ph* Freund, Reimar Kuntze, Robert Baberske, Laszlo Schäffer.

Carl MAYER, in his desire to get away from the studio-bound atmosphere of contemporary German cinema, conceived this film as a documentary about a day in the life of the city, which would reflect the city's beauty, but also raise issues of social importance. Karl FREUND obtained some very sensitive stock which enabled him to shoot without artificial light. Shooting began in 1926, and Freund and the other cameramen began their filming enthusiastically, often concealing the camera in suitcases and the like so as to photograph people unawares. But as soon as the editing began the difference between Mayer's approach and RUTTMANN's became apparent. Ruttmann was interested in formal rather than sociological aspects. Mayer objected to this attitude towards a reality that cried out for criticism and interpretation, and asked to be dissociated from the whole project. Edmund Meisel composed music for the film and Ruttmann worked with him during the editing.

Influenced by, and developing, the ideas of MONTAGE of EISENSTEIN and VERTOV, Ruttmann constructed the film through the careful editing of patterns of movement, the symphonic form, with its rhythmic and structural demands, taking precedence over content so that the film does not reproduce the city's own rhythm, but imposes a rhythm upon it. Social contrasts are featured, but they are a formal expedient rather than a protest. The film is less a documentary than a development of the absolute or ABSTRACT film, using people and objects as well as patterns and shapes. As such it is successful. It led to a number of similar films and influenced many of the social films of the period.

CAVALCANTI's *Rien que les heures*, a film in a similar style about Paris, was made at the same time.

**BERLIN FILM FESTIVAL.** Partly to reassure the West Berliners that they were still a part of the international scene in spite of their geographical isolation, the festival was established in 1951 under the directorship of Dr Alfred Bauer. The west supported it largely out of political sympathy; the socialist countries of Eastern Europe would not participate, although they sent observers until the building of the Berlin wall in 1961. Prizes were awarded both by public ballot and by an international jury until 1957 when public participation was discontinued.

The festival quickly became an international showcase and by 1956 was acknowledged by world producers as comparable with CANNES and VENICE. The tendency was, however, more towards the independent or non-commercial film: documentary had always held an important place and a youth section was instituted in 1961. In the mid-sixties the festival acquired some notoriety for the sensationalism and political extremism of some of the entries and in 1970 political activists succeeded in stopping proceedings. Berlin has, however, prospered, with participating nations increasing yearly. The countries of Eastern Europe now send entries and the festival is noted for showing films from the emergent nations.

The Berlin festival is held in midsummer. Awards for the best feature, documentary, and short films are the Goldener Bär (Golden Bear) and Silberner Bär (Silver Bear). Gold and Silver

Bears may also be awarded for direction and acting.

**BERNHARDT,** SARAH (1844–1923), real name Sarah Henriette Rosine Bernard, famous French stage actress who made a number of early silent films. These include *Hamlet–duel scene* (1900, see HAMLET), *La Dame aux camélias* (1912), and LA REINE ELISABETH (1912), the latter being one of several films directed by Louis MERCANTON. Her performances look extremely overemphatic on film and can only poorly represent her prowess as an actress.

**BERNSTEIN,** ELMER (1922– ), US composer-conductor who began writing film scores in the early fifties and who, particularly after THE MAN WITH THE GOLDEN ARM (1955), emerged as one of the leading American film composers. Film music was becoming widely diffused by the issue of sound-tracks on long-playing records, and Elmer Bernstein's score for *The Ten Commandments* (1956) was—exceptionally for its time—issued at length on two discs. Among numerous notable scores were those for *Desire under the Elms* (1958); THE MAGNIFICENT SEVEN (1960) and both its sequels; and *To Kill a Mockingbird* (1962). *Thoroughly Modern Millie* (1967) earned him an OSCAR.

**BERNSTEIN,** LEONARD (1918– ), US musician, for many years conductor of the New York Philharmonic and composer of opera and major symphonic works besides two eminently successful Broadway musicals: the joyously exuberant ON THE TOWN (filmed 1949) and WEST SIDE STORY (filmed 1961). He also wrote the score for ON THE WATERFRONT (1954).

**BERNSTEIN,** SIDNEY LEWIS (Baron Bernstein of Leigh) (1899– ), head of the Granada cinema circuit and Granada Television, who was one of the founders of the original FILM SOCIETY in 1925. During the Second World War he was a Films Adviser to the Ministry of Information and in later years produced three films, including HITCHCOCK's *Rope* (1948). He was created a life peer in 1969.

**BERRY,** JULES (1883–1951), French actor, real name Jules Paufichet, who first appeared in *L'Argent* (Marcel L'HERBIER, 1928). He became especially famous as the smooth, wide-mouthed villain of many French films of the thirties and forties. Those of international reputation include LE CRIME DE MONSIEUR LANGE (Jean RENOIR, 1936), *Le Voleur des femmes* (Abel GANCE, 1937), and *Carrefour* (Kurt Bernhardt, 1938); but perhaps his most famous roles were in two films by Marcel CARNÉ, as the malevolent dog-trainer in LE JOUR SE LÈVE (1939) and as the devil in LES VISITEURS DU SOIR (1942).

**BERTINI,** FRANCESCA (1888– ), Italian actress who became Italy's first film star with *Assunta spina* (1915). In 1918 a company, Bertini Film, was formed to produce films exploiting her tragic beauty. She enjoyed enormous popularity until her semi-retirement in 1921 on her marriage to a Swiss nobleman. She continued to appear occasionally in films up to 1975.

**BERTOLUCCI,** BERNARDO (1940– ), Italian director, son of the poet Attilio Bertolucci, was interested in film-making from his teens. His first job in films was assistant to PASOLINI on ACCATONE (1961). The first film he made himself was *La commare secca* (1962), a Pasolini subject, but treated very differently from its author's intentions. *Prima della rivoluzione* (*Before the Revolution*, 1964), an explosive mixture of radical politics and raw emotion, aroused much controversy. During the next two years Bertolucci worked on a three-part television documentary on petrol, *La via del petrolio*. In 1967 he made a film about the Living Theatre, in collaboration with its director Julian Beck, which formed a part of an EPISODE film *Vangelo 70* produced by Carlo LIZZANI. *Partner* (1968), loosely based on the Dostoevsky story 'The Double', showed how heavily Bertolucci had come under GODARD's influence during their close friendship, which ended in political differences; but *La strategia del ragno* (*The Spider's Strategy*, 1970) and IL CONFORMISTA (*The Conformist*, 1970) have a striking confidence and maturity. The element of autobiography in *Prima della rivoluzione* is still apparent, particularly in the treatment of the father/son relationship, but Bertolucci's handling of the complex and emotional topic of Fascism in pre-war Italy is impressive. LAST TANGO IN PARIS (1972) took up a new theme, the cruelty generated by suffering, expressed with the authority now expected from him.

**BEST YEARS OF OUR LIVES, The,** US, 1946. 3hr. *Dir* William Wyler; *prod* Samuel Goldwyn; *scr* Robert E. Sherwood, from *Glory For Me* by McKinlay Kantor; *ph* Gregg Toland; *mus* Hugo Friedhofer; *cast* Myrna Loy (Milly Stephenson), Fredric March (Al Stephenson), Dana Andrews (Derry), Teresa Wright (Peggy Stephenson), Virginia Mayo (Marie Derry), Hoagy Carmichael (Butch Engle), Harold Russell (Homer Parrish).

After reading a feature on demobilization in *Time Magazine*, Samuel GOLDWYN commissioned McKinlay Kantor to base a film story on the idea. The result was *Glory For Me*, a 434-

page essay in blank verse which was adapted for the screen by Robert E. Sherwood. The plot is deliberately schematic: the three returning veterans represent the three armed services and three social classes, with a neat inversion in Derry's descent from officer to near-destitute unemployment.

Goldwyn's customary polish was here applied to a sombre subject and a realistic depiction of small-town America. His remarkable cast included Harold Russell, a veteran who had lost both hands and whose skill with the prosthetic hooks had led to an appearance in the War Department's *The Diary of a Sergeant* (1945). There were doubts as to whether the film could appeal to a war-weary public, but William WYLER's accomplished direction skirted sentimentality to create a resounding success. The film won seven OSCARS.

***BÊTE HUMAINE, La,*** France, 1938. 1¾hr. *Dir* Jean Renoir; *prod* Paris Film Production; *scr* Renoir, from the novel (1890) by Emile Zola; *ph* Curt Courant; *des* Eugène Lourié; *ed* Marguerite Renoir, Suzanne de Troyes; *mus* Joseph Kosma; *cast* Jean Gabin (Lantier), Simone Simon (Séverine), Fernand Ledoux (Roubard), Julien Carette (Pecqueux), Jenny Halia (Pecqueux's friend), Colette Régis (Pecqueux's wife), Blanchette Brunoy (Flore), Jacques Berlioz (Grandmorin).

RENOIR's second adaptation of Zola—he filmed *Nana* in 1926—is a modernization made with an evident sense of fidelity to the author: the credits conclude with a quote from the novel, Zola's signature, and his portrait. The weight of a lengthy novel can be sensed behind the film's succession of murders and attempted killings, despite the skill with which the incidents are fitted together. Lantier (Jean GABIN), a train driver struggling to control his homicidal urges, falls in love with Séverine (Simone SIMON). Her attempts to persuade him to dispose of her husband and his increasing obsession with the murder in which she had been an unwilling accomplice culminate on the evening of the railwaymen's ball. While the sound of a popular song lingers in the air, Lantier kills Séverine; and next morning he plunges to his own death from a speeding locomotive.

*La Bête humaine* is a classic example of literary adaptation. Renoir shaped his material so as to produce a quartet of excellent acting roles—for Fernand LEDOUX as Séverine's husband and Julien CARETTE as Lantier's fireman as well as for the two principals. Many of the individual sequences are among the most powerful that Renoir created—the opening scene shot on the footplate of Lantier's engine, the love scene in the rain and the attempted murder of the husband, the ball and the killing of Séverine. Renoir is here

closest to the black world of Marcel CARNÉ and Julien DUVIVIER, where an obscure fate drives a potentially good man to murder and self-destruction.

**BETTY BOOP,** created in 1915, the flapper heroine of numerous Max FLEISCHER cartoons, satirized by turns the various sex symbols of the thirties. This gold-digging good-time girl was finally killed off by the Hays Office (see CENSORSHIP, US) but was later resurrected on television. (See ANIMATION.)

**BEVAN,** BILLY (1887–1957), Australian-born actor, real name William B. Harris, who pursued his career in Hollywood. He established his reputation as a comedian with Mack SENNETT in the golden age of SLAPSTICK, becoming a leading comic in the Sennett films of the PARAMOUNT period, including *Lizzies of the Field* (1924) and *The Golf Nut* (1927). He later became a character actor, appearing in *Riley the Cop* (John FORD, 1928) and various films of the thirties, including Ford's THE LOST PATROL (1934), and was frequently seen in small parts in the forties.

***BEZHIN LUG*** (*Bezhin Meadow*) see EISENSTEIN

***BIANCO E NERO,*** Italian monthly film journal, first published January 1937, by the CENTRO SPERIMENTALE DI CINEMATOGRAFIA, edited until 1951 by Luigi CHIARINI.

One of the first Italian publications to promote the study of film aesthetics and serious criticism, the range of *Bianco e nero* has always been wide and international. In addition to authoritative signed articles on all aspects of the cinema, film reviews, and festival reports, complete screenplays are often published.

In 1964 an *Antologia di Bianco e nero 1937–1943* was published in four volumes, an anthology of the most important earlier articles, criticisms, theories, and screenplays.

**BIBERMAN,** HERBERT J. (1900–71), US scriptwriter, producer, and director, worked first in the theatre as actor and stage manager. In 1935 he went to Hollywood under contract to COLUMBIA. He was founder of the Hollywood Anti-Nazi League and wrote and directed *Master Race* (1942), a protest against Fascism. He also produced films for UNITED ARTISTS. One of the Hollywood Ten (see UNAMERICAN ACTIVITIES), he was convicted of contempt of Congress in 1950 and served a six-month prison sentence. He was among the group of left-wing film-makers who collaborated on SALT OF THE EARTH (1953) and he wrote and directed *Slaves* (1969) which draws parallels between the condition of slaves in the Kentucky of the 1850s and the modern Black Power movement.

**BICKFORD,** CHARLES (1889–1967), US actor. After appearing in *Dynamite* (1929) he had a large number of supporting and, later, character actor roles. His rugged features and air of dependability made him ideal for portraying sturdy, reliable, outdoor, or rough types. One of his rare leading roles was opposite Greta GARBO in *Anna Christie* (1930). He appeared in almost every kind of film; among many notable performances were those in *Mutiny in the Big House* (1939), *The Song of Bernadette* (1943), DUEL IN THE SUN (1946), *Johnny Belinda* (1948), and *The Big Country* (1958). He also worked in television in 'The Virginian' series.

*BICYCLE THIEVES* see LADRI DI BICICLETTE

**BICYCLING,** a dubious procedure employed during the silent and early sound film period, when prints were often in short supply, to permit showing the same print in two or even three cinemas the same evening. When the first reel of a film had ended, it was hastily rewound and handed to a messenger who rushed it on his bicycle to another cinema (where the programme had been advertised as beginning later). The messenger bicycled back to the first cinema in time to be handed reel two. If the film's distributor happened to be unaware of the practice, he would receive only one rental fee for more than one showing. The plot of Renato CASTELLANI's *Sotto il sole di Roma* (1948) touches on such shady proceedings.

The term 'bicycle print' is sometimes still used for any spare print.

*BIDONE, Il,* Italy/France, 1955. 1¾hr. *Dir* Federico Fellini; *prod* Titanus; *scr* Fellini, Ennio Flaiano, Tullio Pinelli; *ph* Otello Martelli; *des* Dario Cecchi; *mus* Nino Rota; *cast* Broderick Crawford (Augusto), Richard Basehart (Picasso), Franco Fabrizi (Roberto), Giulietta Masina (Iris).

Augusto, middle-aged and going to seed, works with a group of small-time crooks who use a variety of confidence tricks to extort money from poor people. The film begins and ends with an elaborate trick, but the sense of fun pervading the earlier adventures has been dissipated by the end; Augusto's moral collapse is completed, and he dies alone on a stony hillside.

ZAVATTINI had criticized FELLINI for what he considered a betrayal of NEO-REALISM: in *Il bidone* Fellini replied by casting the film visually in the neo-realist mould but exposing the sentimentality of the neo-realist films which stopped short of showing the degrading effects of poverty. Like LA DOLCE VITA (1960), *Il bidone* may be considered a possible sequel to I VITEL-

LONI (1953): these crooks are what the Vitelloni might have grown into.

*BIENVENIDO MR MARSHALL,* Spain, 1953. 1¼hr. *Dir* Luis Berlanga; *prod* UNINCI; *scr* Berlanga, Juan Antonio Bardem; *ph* Manuel Berenguer; *cast* Lolita Sevilla (Carmen Vargas), Manolo Moran (Manolo), José Isbert (Don Pablo), Alberto Romea (Don Luis), Elvira Quintilla (Señorita Eloisa).

The news that a Marshall Plan commission is to visit their village galvanizes its inhabitants to present their surroundings so as to gain maximum aid. Their dreams of what the expected dollars will buy are shattered when the official convoy sweeps through without stopping. The slight plot is given substance by the film's pointed observation; the sharply written script of BERLANGA and BARDEM, influenced by NEO-REALISM and with flashes of malicious humour, held out hopes that these adventurous young film-makers would be able to break through the restrictions that had long inhibited Spanish cinema.

*BIG BROADCASTS,* four lavish film revues produced by PARAMOUNT in the thirties, featuring radio personalities and recording stars of the time, a popular format already used in *Paramount on Parade* (1930), and which borrowed from the style set by METRO-GOLDWYN-MAYER's BROADWAY MELODY (1929). *The Big Broadcast* (1932) was directed by Frank Tuttle, with a story revolving round a bankrupt radio station saved by an amateur who organizes the 'Big Broadcast': among those featured were Bing CROSBY crooning 'Where the Blue of the Night Meets the Gold of the Day' and Cab Calloway and his orchestra inimitably rendering 'Minnie the Moocher'. *The Big Broadcast of 1936* was directed by Norman Taurog, with a plot involving George Burns and Gracie Allen and a television-like invention called the 'Radio Eye', which could conjure up talent from across the globe. The cast again included Bing Crosby, plus the Vienna Boys Choir, Lyda Roberti, and Ethel Merman doing a number with a troupe of trained elephants. Song-writers included Ralph Rainger and Dorothy Parker.

*The Big Broadcast of 1937* was directed by Mitchell Leisen. As usual the plot concerned a radio station, and the talent aired included Benny Goodman and Jack BENNY; other attractions were the début of Bob 'Bazooka' Burns and an injection of the classics with Leopold Stokowski conducting Bach's Fugue in G Minor. Leisen also directed the last of the series, *The Big Broadcast of 1938*, which marked W. C. FIELDS's return to the screen after illness. The story this time involved a race between ocean liners, and found room for Martha Raye, and Dorothy LAMOUR. It also included the only film appearance of Kirsten Flagstad, rendering Brünhilde's battle cry from Wagner's *Die Walküre*, and the first screen appearance of Bob HOPE singing 'Thanks for the Memory' with Shirley Ross.

**BIG HEAT, The**, US, 1953. 1½hr. *Dir* Fritz Lang; *prod* Columbia; *scr* Sidney Boehm, from the novel by William P. McGivern; *ph* Charles Lang; *cast* Glenn Ford (Dave Bannion), Gloria Grahame (Debby Marsh), Jocelyn Brando (Kate Bannion), Alexander Scourby (Mike Lagana), Lee Marvin (Vince Stone).

A young police officer conducts a personal crusade against the corruption prevalent in the town, with added single-mindedness after the death of his wife (Marlon BRANDO's sister Jocelyn in one of her rare film appearances) in a booby-trap designed for him.

The characterization is conventional, apart from the gangster's moll, impressively played by Gloria Grahame. Lee MARVIN is notably repellent as a political strong-arm man. LANG's frequent themes of violence and revenge are treated with a cold, savage skill. There is no indulgence in the violence; only in the idealized portrayal of the policeman's happy family life.

**BIG PARADE, The**, US, 1925. 2¼hr. *Dir* King Vidor; *prod* MGM; *scr* Laurence Stallings; *cast* John Gilbert, Renée Adorée, Tom O'Brien, Karl Dane.

Presaging the attitudes of ALL QUIET ON THE WESTERN FRONT (1930), VIDOR's film gave a realistic account of an American private soldier's experience of the Great War and its immediate aftermath. It came at the beginning of a swing against the romantic view of war: public opinion was ready to see it depicted with truth and intelligence, and *The Big Parade* added visual beauty to these qualities, while the cutting of the battle scenes is still an example of editing at its most skilled. It was an enormous popular success in the US (although not in the UK, where critics sneered at the implication that the Americans had won the war).

**BIG SLEEP, The**, US, 1946. 2hr. *Dir, prod* Howard Hawks for Warner Bros; *scr* William Faulkner, Leigh Brackett, Jules Furthman, from the novel by Raymond Chandler; *ph* Sid Hickox; *cast* Humphrey Bogart (Philip Marlowe), Lauren Bacall (Vivian), John Ridgeley (Eric Mars), Martha Vickers (Carmen), Charles Waldren (General Sternwood).

An almost unfathomable plot begins with the engagement of Philip Marlowe by the wealthy, moribund General Sternwood to find a potential blackmailer who turns out to have been mur-

dered. The greatest strength of HAWKS's objective version of the first-person narrative was the incisive dialogue—as much William FAULKNER's as CHANDLER's. Humphrey BOGART, playing opposite Lauren BACALL, was a satisfying embodiment of Chandler's cynical hero.

**BILLANCOURT,** French production studios beside the Seine, in the suburbs of Paris, built in 1920 by Henri Diamant-Berger for *Vingt ans après*. During the twenties it was known as the Abel Gance Studios and was almost wholly staffed by White Russian émigrés, for whose benefit a large icon was installed. The cost of sound film equipment ruined the managing company, Braunberger-Richebé, in 1933. The Société Lauer took over, but BRAUNBERGER remained manager of the production company, Société Anonyme Paris-Studio-Cinéma. During the Second World War, the German-owned company CONTINENTALE was based there. On average twenty films a year are shot in these well equipped studios which are partly occupied by ORTF. Films made at Billancourt include GANCE's NAPOLÉON (1927), RENOIR's LA GRANDE IL-LUSION (1937), CARNÉ's LE JOUR SE LÈVE (1939), as well as Eddie CONSTANTINE's films.

**BILLY THE KID** (1859–81) was born Henry McCarty in New York City, but went most of his life under the name of William H. Bonney. The murders which made him a legend took place during a cattle vendetta. He was killed unheroically by Sheriff Pat Garrett as he entered a darkened room in Fort Sumner, New Mexico. He has been played on the screen by Johnny Mack Brown in *Billy the Kid* (1930), Roy ROGERS in *Billy the Kid Returns* (1939), Robert TAYLOR in a big-budget *Billy the Kid* (1941), and Audie Murphy in *The Kid from Texas* (1949), all of which show little concern for historical reality. Paul NEWMAN, in THE LEFT-HANDED GUN (1958), gave a more searching portrayal. PECK-INPAH's *Pat Garrett and Billy the Kid* (1973) went a little way towards demythologizing the legend, particularly in the accurate portrayal of his death.

**BIOGRAPH,** properly the American Mutoscope and Biograph Company, founded in 1896 by W. K. L. DICKSON, H. N. Marvin, and H. Casler to market the MUTOSCOPE (a peep-show device for penny arcades similar to EDISON's Kinetoscope) and the Biograph (a camera and projector in one). The company soon began to make films to meet the growing demand, and in 1897 constructed a small studio on the roof of an office block in Manhattan. The famous studio at 11 Fourteenth Street was opened in 1906, and in 1910 the company followed the general move of film production companies to California, dividing its activities thereafter between New York and Los Angeles. In 1908–13 D. W. GRIFFITH made about 400 short films for Biograph, developing his craft and building up a stock company of actors which included Mary PICKFORD, Lillian and Dorothy GISH, Mack SENNETT, Mae MARSH, Robert Harron, and Florence LAWRENCE. To keep costs down, Biograph refused to give these players name billing or to back Griffith's projects for longer and more expensive films. After Griffith left to join MUTUAL in 1913, taking his cameraman Billy BITZER and many of his players, Biograph never recovered and two years later went into liquidation.

The Biograph Company was one of the nine members of the MOTION PICTURE PATENTS COMPANY, set up in 1908 to corner the rights to existing patents.

**BIOSCOPE, The,** independent weekly trade journal published in London 1908–32. In earlier years there was much emphasis on new technical developments and advice to readers on such matters as opening new cinemas, also occasional features on the purposes and achievements of the cinema from the sociological viewpoint.

Current releases and films in production were listed in each issue for the information of cinema managers, and full synopses of releases were given. Provincial coverage was exhaustive. The *Bioscope* was the first trade journal to review films; it also carried influential discussion of current and proposed legislation relating to the film industry. The educational and scientific use of film was featured from an early stage.

The name and goodwill were bought by Odham's Press after the *Bioscope* went into voluntary liquidation in 1932, but no further issues appeared.

**BIRTH OF A NATION, The,** US, 1915. 2¼hr. *Dir* D. W. Griffith; *prod* Epoch (Griffith, Harry E. Aitken); *scr* Griffith, Frank E. Woods, Thomas Dixon Jr, based on Dixon's *The Clansman* and *The Leopard's Spots*; *ph* G. W. Bitzer; *cast* Henry B. Walthall (Ben Cameron), Mae Marsh (Margaret Cameron), Ralph Lewis (Phil Stoneman), Lillian Gish (Elsie Stoneman), George Siegman (Silas Lynch), Walter Long (negro soldier), Josephine Crowell (Mrs Cameron), Miriam Cooper, Spottiswoode Aitken, Elmer Clifton, Robert Harron, Wallace Reid, Joseph Henaberry, Donald Crisp, Elmo Lincoln, Raoul Walsh, Eugene Pallette, Sam de Grasse.

GRIFFITH's epic account of the American Civil War uses the interwoven story of two families, the Southern Camerons, and the Northern Stone-

mans. After the victory of the North, Phil and Elsie's father, a congressman, inaugurates an equality programme in the South, with the aid of his half-caste henchman, Silas Lynch. During the anarchic period of the reconstruction, Ben Cameron's younger sister dies after a negro soldier attempts to rape her. In order to avenge her death, Ben becomes a leader of the Ku Klux Klan. The Cameron family are besieged by a negro army, there is a last-minute rescue by Ben and the Klan, finally North and South are reunited.

The making of *The Birth of a Nation* was a magnificent effort of sustained creativity. Nothing on such a scale had been attempted in the cinema before, and every aspect of the production, from the raising of finance to the organization of huge crowds of extras, depended on Griffith's personal efforts and supervision. No actual script was used during shooting, Griffith carrying a vast general plan in his head and working mainly through controlled improvisation.

Originally entitled *The Clansman*, the film followed its source novel in its bias towards the White Southern viewpoint (Griffith's father had been a veteran of the Confederate army). It was acclaimed for its outstanding merits—richly organized structure, dynamic editing, and dramatic use of screen space—but there was an outcry against its offensive portrayal of the negro, especially in the film's later scenes. The National Association for the Advancement of Coloured People (NAACP) launched an effective boycott and continued to picket cinemas where it was being shown until the Second World War. Hurt and surprised, Griffith wrote a defensive pamphlet, *The Rise and Fall of Free Speech in America*; his next film, INTOLERANCE (1916), was in part inspired by the more violent expressions of opinion and attempts to ban *The Birth of a Nation*.

A special issue of FILM CULTURE (1965, no 36) by Seymour Stern describes in detail the making and reception of the film.

**BIRUMA NO TATEGOTO** (*The Burmese Harp*), Japan, 1956. 2hr. *Dir* Kon Ichikawa; *prod* Nikkatsu; *scr* Natto Wada; *ph* Minoru Yokoyama; *des* Takashi Matsuyama; *ed* Masonori Truju; *mus* Akira Ifukube; *cast* Rentaro Mikuni (Captain Inouye), Shoji Yasui (Private Mizushima), Tatsuya Mihashi (Defence Commander), Taniye Kita Bayashi (old woman), Yunosuke Ito (village head).

Mizushima is a musician member of the defeated Japanese army in Burma. On the Japanese capitulation, he volunteers to persuade a remaining outpost to surrender. They refuse and are shelled; encountering their bodies and those of other Japanese forces, Mizushima decides to remain in Burma as a mendicant priest to bury as many of the bodies as he can, while his unit returns to Japan.

ICHIKAWA's moving treatment of the story is not naturalistic; for him, the idea of the unbreakable continuity of the past, the present, and the future is more important than the realistic rendering of day-to-day wartime.

**BISON,** trade-mark of WESTERNS produced by Kessel and Baumann's New York Motion Picture Company. Bison films were issued by Carl LAEMMLE's IMP, later UNIVERSAL, 1909–12, by MUTUAL 1912–15, and thereafter by TRIANGLE. Their extreme popularity dated from 1911 when Thomas INCE became supervising director and reached its peak in 1914–15 when the Bison marked films starring (and in effect directed by) W. S. HART. The mark became defunct with the collapse of Triangle.

**BITTER RICE** see RISO AMARO

**BITZER,** BILLY (1874–1944), US cameraman, real forenames Gottlieb Wilhelm, worked with W. K. L. DICKSON on the development of the MUTOSCOPE and continued with the Mutoscope and BIOGRAPH company as a cameraman. He filmed the McKinley Presidential nomination in 1896 and the Jeffries–Sharkey championship fight in 1899, probably the first successful filming by artificial light. After D. W. GRIFFITH joined Biograph in 1908, Bitzer photographed nearly all his films until 1924. Their collaboration produced many new and improved techniques of artificial lighting, camera movement, and masking; the variety of vignette effects produced by Bitzer's use of the IRIS was particularly characteristic. All these techniques reached their peak in THE BIRTH OF A NATION (1915), especially the fast extended tracking shots in the battle scenes. INTOLERANCE (1916) was shot entirely by natural light, but displays extraordinary camera virtuosity, including the use of a DOLLY 140 feet high and even balloon shots. Bitzer accompanied Griffith to Europe to film sequences for HEARTS OF THE WORLD (1918) which, with BROKEN BLOSSOMS (1919), shows Bitzer's romantic use of lighting, particularly the ethereal effects achieved for Lillian GISH by back-lighting and over-exposure. WAY DOWN EAST (1920) was largely shot on location in conditions of extreme cold: he made use of a carbide bicycle lamp attached to the camera to counteract the static electricity caused by the cold, dry atmosphere. Bitzer's last film with Griffith was *America* (1924); his subsequent work cannot be compared with his earlier films and he died in obscurity. His importance as a

pioneer was later recognized, and the Hollywood cameramen's union have instituted a Billy Bitzer Award in recognition of distinguished work in the field.

His reminiscences were published as *Billy Bitzer: his story*, New York, 1973.

**BJÖRK,** ANITA (1923–  ), Swedish actress, trained at the Royal Dramatic Theatre School, Stockholm. Her elegant and passionate film performances are best exemplified by *Himlaspelet* (*The Road to Heaven*, Alf SJÖBERG, 1942), FRÖKEN JULIE (1951), KVINNORS VÄNTAN (*Waiting Women*, 1952), and ÅDALEN 31 (1969). She has worked occasionally outside Sweden.

**BJÖRNSTRAND,**  GUNNAR  (1909–  ), Swedish actor, made his film début in *Falske millionären* (Paul Merzbach, 1931). A polished and versatile actor, Björnstrand has had a varied and distinguished career in films and theatre, but his wide fame rests chiefly on the films in which he has worked under the direction of Ingmar BERGMAN, the first of which was *Det regnar på vår kärlek* (*It Rains on Our Love*, 1946). Other outstanding  performances  under  Bergman include those in GYCKLARNAS AFTON (*Sawdust and Tinsel*, 1953), SOMMARNATTENS LEENDE (*Smiles of a Summer Night*, 1955), DET SJUNDE INSEGLET (*The Seventh Seal*, 1957), SMULTRONSTÄLLET (*Wild Strawberries*, 1957), and *Nattvardgästerna* (*Winter Light*, 1963). Björnstrand has also worked under the direction of MATTSSON, SJÖBERG, and others.

**BKSTS** see BRITISH KINEMATOGRAPH SOUND AND TELEVISION SOCIETY

**BLACKBOARD JUNGLE, The,** US, 1955. 1¾hr. *Dir, scr* Richard Brooks from the novel by Evan Hunter; *prod* Pandro Berman for MGM; *ph* Russell Harlan; *mus* Bill Haley and the Comets; *cast* Glenn Ford (Richard Dadier), Anne Francis (Anne Dadier), Sidney Poitier (Gregory Miller), Vic Morrow (Artie West).

BROOKS's melodrama of a harassed New York teacher's fight for survival and communication with his pupils shocked contemporary audiences by its exposure of urban teenage violence, sexuality, and racialism. Haley's 'Rock Around the Clock' virtually introduced rock 'n' roll to the screen.

**BLACKMAIL,** GB, 1929. 1½hr. *Dir* Alfred Hitchcock; *prod* British International Pictures; *scr* Hitchcock, Benn W. Levy, Charles Bennett, from a play by Bennett; *ph* Jack Cox; *des* Wilfred C. Arnold; *mus* Campbell and Connelly; *cast* Anny Ondra (Alice White), Sara Allgood (Mrs White), Charles Paton (Mr White), John

Longden (Frank, the detective), Donald Calthrop (Tracy), Cyril Ritchard (the artist).

A girl stabs an artist who has tried to rape her and her police detective boy-friend conceals his knowledge of her guilt. Victimized by a blackmailer, they call his bluff, and after a chase through the British Museum he falls to his death from a roof.

*Blackmail* was the first British sound film: HITCHCOCK has variously described it as being shot silent then mostly remade with sound and as having been made as a sound film from the outset, but without the producers' knowledge. In addition to the technical problems of the new medium, Anny ONDRA spoke English badly and her lines were read off-camera by Joan Barry.

In spite of the difficulties Hitchcock succeeded in making imaginative use of the new dimension, at one point creating a kind of sound montage in which the word 'knife', heard in a breakfast-time conversation the morning after the murder, echoes and re-echoes in the guilty girl's mind. The film contained a number of trick shots, notably in the British Museum sequence where the SCHÜFFTAN PROCESS was used but (again ac-

cording to Hitchcock) kept a secret from the producers.

A success with both critics and public, *Blackmail* did much for the prestige of British films and confirmed Hitchcock's talent after the promise of his earlier films.

**BLACK ORPHEUS** see ORFEU NEGRO

**BLACKTON,** JAMES STUART (1868 or 1875–1941), British-born US pioneer producer and director, worked as a journalist and cartoonist in New York. Thomas EDISON filmed him at work in *Blackton the Evening World Cartoonist* (1896). Blackton acquired a KINETOGRAPH and with Albert E. Smith launched the VITAGRAPH company, a leading independent challenge to Edison's monopoly. Their first productions, the usual brief dramas and actuality scenes, caught the public taste and Blackton's shrewd awareness of the right moment to expand into more ambitious projects invariably paid dividends: two of their major early successes were *Raffles* (1905), which Blackton probably directed, and *The Life of Moses* (1910). With their comparatively light-

*Blackmail* (Alfred Hitchcock, 1929)

weight Vitagraph camera, Blackton and Smith became pioneer NEWSREEL cameramen. Although many of the events they presented were faked, as was customary, they travelled as far as Cuba for actuality footage. Blackton also developed ANIMATION techniques through stop-motion photography, and his early cartoons had a seminal influence on Emile COHL and other European animators. During the First World War Blackton had particular success with jingoistic dramas such as *The Battle Cry of Peace* (1915) starring Norma TALMADGE. From 1917, a year after Vitagraph bought out LUBIN, SELIG, and ESSANAY and became VLSE, Blackton made films as an independent, while retaining an interest in the new company. In the early twenties he worked in Britain, where his most notable film was in PRIZMACOLOUR, *The Glorious Adventure* (1921), starring Victor MCLAGLEN and Lady Diana Manners. In 1926, three years after his return to the US, VLSE was taken over by WARNER BROS and Blackton retired as a millionaire, but he was ruined in the Wall Street crash of 1929.

**BLAIR,** BETSY (1923–    ), US actress who has been particularly successful in portraying women whose lives are drab and unhappy, notably in *Another Part of the Forest* (1948) and MARTY (1955) for which she won several awards. She was also in *The Snake Pit* (1948), a horrific drama set in a mental hospital, and ANTONIONI's IL GRIDO (1957), but has seldom appeared since her marriage to Karel REISZ in 1963.

**BLANCHAR,** PIERRE (1892–1963), distinguished French stage actor, who became one of the leading French stars of the thirties with his performances in *Les Croix des bois* (1932), *Crime et châtiment* (1935), in which he played Raskolnikov, *Un Carnet de bal* (1937), and many others. He successfully exploited a breathless manner of speaking and intense gaze which were in fact a result of his having been gassed in the First World War. He directed two films, *Secrets* (1942) and *Un seul amour* (1943), in both of which he also appeared. He was a member of the Resistance group responsible for the film *La Libération de Paris* (1944), for which he spoke the commentary in exemplary fashion.

**BLASETTI,** ALESSANDRO (1900–    ), Italian director. A film critic during the thirties, he founded a cinema co-operative 'Augustus' in 1928 and made his first film *Sole* (*Sun*) in 1929. A story of the reclamation of the Pontine marshes, it showed strong visual influences from the silent Soviet cinema and had considerable influence on young Italian film-makers. In 1932 he founded, as part of the Rome music academy,

the predecessor of the CENTRO SPERIMENTALE DI CINEMATOGRAFIA. During the thirties he had a lively output, alternating costume dramas such as the very successful *1860* (1933) with light comedies, but he also occasionally returned to realistic subjects such as *Vecchia guardia* (1935). *La corona di ferro* (1941), a grandiose allegory, was sharply attacked by the critics: this led him back to realism with *Quattro passi fra le nuvole* (*Four Steps in the Clouds*, 1942), a light comedy co-scripted by ZAVATTINI which in many ways anticipated aspects of NEO-REALISM. Although *Un giorno nella vita* (*A Day of Life*, 1946) told of a German massacre of a convent of enclosed nuns, Blasetti's post-war work has been mainly in the extravagant historical style or in the vein of light comedy. It was this aspect of his career that was portrayed when he played himself in VISCONTI's BELLISSIMÀ (1951).

***BLAUE ENGEL, Der*** (*The Blue Angel*), Germany, 1930. 1¼hr. *Dir* Josef von Sternberg; *prod* Erich Pommer, for UFA; *scr* Carl Zuckmayer, Karl Vollmüller, Robert Liebmann, from the novel *Professor Unrath* by Heinrich Mann; *ph* Gunther Rittau, Hans Schneeberger; *des* Otto Hunte; *mus* Friedrich Hollander; *lyrics* Robert Liebmann; *cast* Emil Jannings (Professor Immanuel Rath), Marlene Dietrich (Lola-Lola Frölich), Kurt Gerron (Kiepert, a magician), Rosa Valetti (Guste, his wife), Hans Albers (Mazeppa).

Professor Rath, a middle-aged schoolmaster, becomes infatuated with and later marries Lola-Lola, a singer in a sleazy café, and is increasingly degraded by her until he is completely humiliated as an abused stage clown. When Lola finally leaves him for another man, he returns a broken old man to his school, and dies at his desk.

For years the decadence and sadism of *Der blaue Engel* established it in the popular mind as a 'daring' example of sex on the screen: even today the prevailing image is that of the silk hat, black stockings, suspenders, and bare thighs of Marlene DIETRICH; and the song known in its English version as 'Falling in Love Again' is the one primarily associated with the star's huskily distinctive singing voice. Dietrich became a star overnight in the role of Lola; JANNINGS's performance was in a characteristically heavy, expressionistic style which even by 1930 seemed outmoded. STERNBERG's direction was almost as heavy as Jannings's performance, but the film remains notable for its pictorial composition, elaborate settings, and profusion of detail. It was made in two versions, German and English.

***BLÁZNOVA KRONIKA*** (*The Jester's Tale*), Czechoslovakia, 1964. 1½hr. *Dir* Karel Zeman; *prod* Gottwaldov Film Studios; *scr* Pavel Juráček, Zeman; *ph* Václav Hunka; *des* Zdeněk

Rozkopal; *mus* Jan Novák; *cast* Petr Kostka (Petr), Miroslav Holub (Matěj), Emilie Vašáryová (Lenka), Valentina Thielová (Veronika).

A young farmer, forcibly conscripted during the Thirty Years War, accompanies a girl disguised as a jester on a search for a country without war. ZEMAN mounted his tale, a combination of romantic fantasy and pacifist comment, in a typically witty, decorative style. The film is a culmination of his experiments with mixed techniques—live action, ANIMATION, PIXILLATION, painted scenery, real locations; it is most successful where artifice is openly acknowledged and extended to create magical and beautiful effects.

**BLIMP,** a sound-proof enclosure for the motion picture camera which prevents its noise from being picked up by the microphone when synchronized sound is being recorded. In the early days of sound film the camera and its operator were shut up together in an immobile, sound-proof booth to ensure silence; the development of the blimp freed the operator from this claustrophobic situation and allowed the camera to move again. The bulk and weight of a blimped camera, however, preclude its use for hand-held shots: a sturdy DOLLY or CRANE is required to move camera and operators about. The blimp is slowly being superseded by 'self-blimped' cameras which are lighter and noiseless in operation, like the ARRIFLEX BL. The term 'blimp' was used by obvious analogy with the unwieldy non-rigid airship to which it was originally applied.

**BLOCK BOOKING,** system of supporting the distribution of films with poor commercial prospects by grouping them with others of assured drawing power. Exhibitors wishing to rent box-office successes (particularly those with popular stars) would be forced by each production company to take features less likely to be profitable as part of a package deal, thus greatly inflating the value to the studio of an important property (star or film). The practice was initiated by PARAMOUNT in 1915–16 and was made illegal in the US in 1948 as part of the separation of production and exhibition interests.

**BLOCKBUSTER,** a term which came into increasing use in the sixties, denoting a major film, invariably very long and in spectacular or ornate style, handsomely mounted, and with glossy production values, usually with a star-studded cast and representing a huge financial investment on the part of its producers. Blockbusters are almost always subjected to initial ROAD-SHOW presentation as HARD TICKET attractions. They were temporarily an effective answer to the problem of recapturing some of the cinema's lost audience.

**BLONDELL,** JOAN (1909–  ), US actress, began her stage career as a child. Her first film was *Sinner's Holiday* (1931) with JAMES CAGNEY, both in roles they had played on the stage. With considerable comic flair, she played the dizzy blonde, especially in musicals such as *Footlight Parade* (1933) and GOLDDIGGERS OF 1933 (1933). As well as working for television, she has remained active in films in character roles. Not all have done her justice, but she made memorable appearances in the TRACY–HEPBURN comedy *The Desk Set* (1957, *His Other Woman* in GB), *Angel Baby* (1961), and *The Cincinnati Kid* (1965).

**BLOOM,** CLAIRE (1928–  ), British actress, made her theatre début in 1947; later, her casting by CHAPLIN in LIMELIGHT (1952) gave her an international reputation. Her stage career continued, mostly in classical roles, while her range of screen parts expanded, revealing an exceptional sensual quality beneath her cool beauty. Her films include *Richard III* (1955), *The Brothers Karamazov* (1957), LOOK BACK IN ANGER (1959), *The Chapman Report* (1961), *The Spy Who Came in from the Cold* (1965), *Three into Two Won't Go* (1969), and *A Doll's House* (Patrick Garland, 1973).

***BLOW-UP,*** GB, 1967. Eastman Color; 1¾hr. *Dir* Michelangelo Antonioni; *prod* Bridge Films (Carlo Ponti) for MGM; *scr* Antonioni, Tonino Guerra, inspired by a short story by Julio Cortazar; *ph* Carlo Di Palma; *des* Assheton Gorton; *mus* Herbert Hancock; *cast* Vanessa Redgrave (Jane), David Hemmings (Thomas), Sarah Miles (Patricia), Peter Bowles (Ron).

In his first film made abroad since the non-Italian episodes of *I vinti* (1952) and his tenth feature, ANTONIONI confirmed the stylistic departures marked by his last Italian film, IL DESERTO ROSSO (1964). He reintroduced a vestigial plot line in the story of the apparent crime photographed by Thomas, a successful fashion photographer, and his attempts to establish through enlargements whether or not a crime had been committed. Along this slender thread are slung the incidents and associations by which Antonioni observes the artist's and the individual's role in society. The central character is, for the first time since IL GRIDO (1957), a man, and one who is pursuing his career with gusto and success. The episodes are lively, the editing brisk, and in spite of an air of gratuitous trendiness not eased by an embarrassing performance from Vanessa REDGRAVE as the girl who offers her all to get the photographs back, the film has a sense of vigour uncommon in Antonioni's work. It was his first international success in commercial cinemas.

*BLUEBEARD'S EIGHTH WIFE*, US, 1938. 1½hr. *Dir, prod* Ernst Lubitsch for Paramount; *scr* Charles Brackett, Billy Wilder, from the play by Alfred Savoir; *ph* Leo Tover; *cast* Claudette Colbert (Nicole de Loiselle), Gary Cooper (Michael Brandon), Edward Everett Horton (Marquis de Loiselle), David Niven (Albert de Regnier).

The Bluebeard of the title, played by Gary COOPER, is a much-married American millionaire who finally succumbs to the daughter of an impoverished French marquis. An elegant trifle, typical of LUBITSCH's polished frivolity, the film was enormously popular. Its sophistication is less shocking now, but the witty dialogue is still effective.

An earlier version was directed by Sam WOOD in 1923.

**BLUE SCREEN PROCESS** is used to combine foreground action with background material shot elsewhere. It is the most common form of travelling MATTE and is achieved by photographing the foreground action against a uniformly blue background, with colour negative in the camera. By the use of colour filters in later printing, MATTES can be made from the foreground which are used in combining the two images on one DUPE negative.

Blue screen is now being challenged by FRONT PROJECTION. A similar process to the travelling matte, known as chroma-key, is much used in television and works on the blue screen principle although the effect is achieved electronically and colours other than blue can be used.

**BOETTICHER,** BUDD (1916– ), US director, progressed from assistant director to director in 1944. His first real success was his eleventh film, *The Bullfighter and the Lady* (1951). His early interest in bull fighting and a period as a professional matador helped him to transcend the 'B' feature material he was usually given and led to a position as technical adviser on the remake of *Blood and Sand* (1955). Also in 1955 he directed another bull-fighting film, *The Magnificent Matador* starring Anthony QUINN, and a thriller, *The Killer Is Loose*. He then made the series of seven WESTERNS known as the Ranown cycle, which revitalized the career of Randolph SCOTT, who played the central figure as well as co-producing with Harry Joe Brown. 'B' Westerns in scale, each made in twelve to eighteen days, they followed a classic formula; but Boetticher (and Burt Kennedy, the main scriptwriter) elaborated on the formula to produce some perfect examples of the genre: *Seven Men From Now* (1956), *The Tall T* (1957), *Ride Lonesome* (1959), *Comanche Station* (1959). This cycle was to provide the model

for PECKINPAH's RIDE THE HIGH COUNTRY (1962, *Guns in the Afternoon* in GB) which also starred Randolph Scott. Boetticher's recurrent examination of an isolated, self-reliant individual was extended again in *The Rise and Fall of Legs Diamond* (1959); aided by the photography of his frequent collaborator Lucien BALLARD, this successfully re-created the visual style of GANGSTER FILMS of the thirties.

In 1963–8 Boetticher worked independently and under great hardship on a dramatized documentary *Arruza* (1968), about the Mexican bull-fighter Carlos Arruza. After his own script for *Two Mules for Sister Sara* (1969) had been, against his wishes, assigned to Don SIEGEL, he returned to Hollywood and the Western with *A Time for Dying* (1969).

**BOGARDE,** DIRK (1921– ), British actor, made his film début in *Esther Waters* (1947). For some years he was popular as a romantic lead in films of little substance, but he also played more interesting and varied roles, including young delinquents in *The Blue Lamp* (1949) and *Hunted* (1952), and a suspected homosexual in *Victim* (1961). *Darling* (John SCHLESINGER, 1965) gave him a strong and sympathetic role, but his increasing versatility and skill became particularly evident in films directed by Joseph LOSEY: THE SERVANT (1963), *King and Country* (1964), *Modesty Blaise* (1966), and ACCIDENT (1967). His close association with VISCONTI, in *La caduta degli Dei* (*The Damned*, 1970) and MORTE A VENEZIA (*Death in Venice*, 1971), has perhaps been less happy, leading to a degree of self-indulgence.

**BOGART,** HUMPHREY (1899–1957), US actor, appeared in films from 1930. His first real impact was made in *The Petrified Forest* (1936), repeating his stage success as Duke Mantee, and for the next five years he was identified with the coldly ruthless gangster, a figure made more menacing by the peculiarity of a slight lisp. Among his memorable roles at this time are those in *Kid Galahad* (1937), DEAD END (1937), and THE ROARING TWENTIES (1939). In *They Drive by Night* (1940) he played the first of the more sympathetic criminals that made a transition from outright villains to heroes. The best of these attractive gangsters (based on DILLINGER, whom Bogart somewhat resembled) was in *High Sierra* (1941).

Sam Spade, the private detective in THE MALTESE FALCON (1941) marked a real advance for Bogart and for detective films. It was the first of the classic Bogart roles: the man just outside conventional society, reckless, amoral by accepted standards, yet with a personal code of honour and strong sentiments. His evolution to

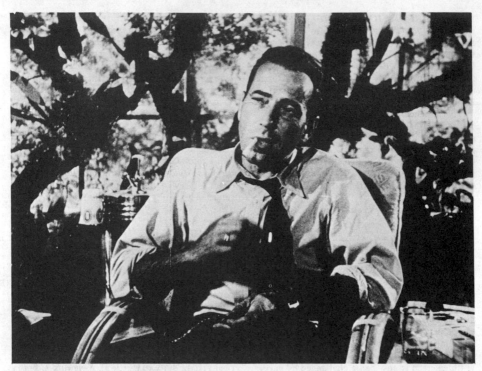

*Humphrey Bogart in The Big Sleep* (Howard Hawks, 1946)

romantic hero was completed in CASA-BLANCA (1943) in which Bogart's distinctive, enduring combination of toughness and vulnerability is definitively deployed. In TO HAVE AND HAVE NOT (1945) and THE BIG SLEEP (1946) he further developed the kind of character later labelled the anti-hero or outsider—although the Bogart formula was endowed with a romantic appeal lacking in later versions. Both films co-starred Lauren BACALL, his wife, and their partnership brought to a high level the effectiveness of crackling sexual attraction behind a façade of wisecracks and edged banter.

Bogart's career continued with undiminished success until his death. Outstanding among his later roles were the seedy alcoholic trader in THE AFRICAN QUEEN (1951), for which he won his only OSCAR, the psychotic Captain Queeg in *The Caine Mutiny* (1954), and a reversion to the professional criminal in *The Desperate Hours* (1955). But it is for his films of the forties that he is chiefly remembered and admired. The best of them re-appear with consistent success, both theatrically and on television, and the Bogart *persona* that they created has become a part of cinema mythology. Their conventions and imagery recur repeatedly, notably in the work of

MELVILLE and other exponents of the FILM NOIR, more recently in the British *Gumshoe* (1972), a film constructed around the hero's passion for old Bogart movies.

**BOGDANOVICH,** PETER (1940–   ), US director and critic, while still in his early twenties wrote monographs to accompany Museum of Modern Art seasons of films by WELLES (1961), HAWKS (1962), and HITCHCOCK (1963). His books *Allan Dwan: the last pioneer* (London, 1971), *John Ford* (London, Berkeley, 1967), and *Fritz Lang in America* (London, 1968; New York, 1969) reveal an eye for visual style and enthusiasm for the great days of Hollywood.

He worked with Roger CORMAN, notably on *Wild Angels* (1967) and Corman backed his first film as director, *Targets* (1967). This was a low-budget feature with Boris KARLOFF in his last role playing an ageing horror star who is eventually shot down by a pathological killer. *The Last Picture Show* (1971), about a declining Texas town in the mid-fifties, has fewer explicit allusions to Hollywood, but carefully and affectionately renders the details and atmosphere of the period in grainy black and white. *What's Up,*

*Doc?* (1972), freely based on BRINGING UP BABY (1938), is the essential SCREWBALL comedy of the thirties seen from a seventies standpoint, and *Paper Moon* (1973) returned to the thirties, whimsically presenting the adventures of an attractive con-man and a precocious orphan girl.

Bogdanovich has also directed a feature-length study of John FORD, *Directed by John Ford* (1971), narrated by Orson Welles and financed by the AMERICAN FILM INSTITUTE.

**BOHDIEWICZ,** ANTONI (1906–70), Polish director and teacher, studied and worked in Paris during the thirties. When he returned to Poland in 1936 he was closely associated with the START group and produced some short films. After the liberation he organized a Young Directors Workshop in Kraków, and from 1949 directed feature films. His influence on the younger generation of Polish film-makers has, however, been less through his films than by his teaching at the film school at LÓDŹ.

**BOLIVIA.** One of the least developed countries in Latin America, Bolivia had little indigenous film production until 1960. Some documentaries and newsreels were made by the Bolivian Cinematographic Institute, founded in 1943, but all features were imported, the majority from the US.

In 1952 the nationalist government of Paz Estenssoro came to power. With government backing, Jorge SANJINES, Oscar Soria, and Ricardo Rada made *Revolucion* (1963), a documentary on the social changes that were taking place. The following year Estenssoro was overthrown by General Barrientos, but Sanjines retained government approval and in 1965 was appointed head of the Film Institute. He and his collaborators continued to make films, incurring official disapproval with *Ukamau* (1966). The Institute was disbanded and the group set up Ukamau Films, for which Sanjines directed his best-known film *Yawar Malku* (*Blood of the Condor*, 1969). With financial backing from Italian television and helped by the relaxation of censorship after the rise to power of General Torres, he made his first colour feature *La Noche de San Juan* (1971) at Ukamau's independent production centre at La Paz; but with the overthrow of Torres by Colonel Hugo Banzer soon after, Bolivian film production again came to a halt.

**BOMBSHELL** (*The Blonde Bombshell* in GB), US, 1933. 1¼hr. *Dir* Victor Fleming; *prod* MGM; *scr* Jules Furthman, John Leo Machin, from a play by Caroline Francke and Mack Crane; *ph* Chester Lyons; *cast* Jean Harlow (Lola Burns), Lee Tracy (Space), Frank Morgan (Pops), Franchot Tone (Gifford Middleton), Pat O'Brien (Brogan), Una Merkel (Mac).

This early SCREWBALL comedy devastatingly exposes the goldfish world of the Hollywood star. Jean HARLOW's bewildered, endearing star combines forthright sex appeal with an honest individuality and touching vulnerability. Her shameless, fast-talking press agent is vividly portrayed by Lee Tracy.

**BOND, The,** US, 1918. 10min. *Dir, scr* Charles Chaplin; *ph* Rollie Totheroh; *cast* Charlie Chaplin, Edna Purviance, Sydney Chaplin, Albert Austin.

Though CHAPLIN was widely criticized for not joining the armed forces during the First World War, he did make a propaganda short for the British war effort (with Harry Lauder) and he toured the US for two months in 1918 (with Mary PICKFORD and Douglas FAIRBANKS) selling Liberty Bonds. He then made for the Liberty Loan Committee this semi-serious half-reel, now one of the rarest Chaplins, for free distribution. It exhorted its audiences: 'There are different kinds of Bonds: the Bond of Friendship; the Bond of Love; the Marriage Bond; and most important of all—the Liberty Bond.'

**BOND,** WARD (1903–60), US character actor, a veteran of over 200 feature films. During the thirties he frequently played small parts for John FORD, but remained in relative obscurity until 1957, when he starred in the popular television series 'Wagon Train', which was developed from one of Ford's best post-war films WAGONMASTER (1950). His sudden transformation from anonymity to household fame was cut short by his death from a heart attack. Bond was as devoted to American patriotism as he was to acting, and often sponsored anti-communist activities.

**BONDARCHUK,** SERGEI (1920–   ), Russian actor and director of Ukrainian birth, trained as a stage actor and served in the Theatre of the Soviet Army during the war. His interest in cinema was aroused on a visit to GERASIMOV's acting class at VGIK: he enrolled there and his fine diploma performance as a young resistance fighter in Gerasimov's *Molodaya gvardiya* (*The Young Guard*, 1948) showed promise of his future stature. During the last years of Stalinism rewarding parts were rare, but Bondarchuk steadily gained prestige as an actor of both power and sensitivity. He played the lead in two patriotic biographies of national figures: *Michurin* (1948), DOVZHENKO's first colour film, and *Taras Shevchenko* (1951), directed by Igor Savchenko. In the latter, an impressive study in ageing, he played the revered poet, philosopher, and soldier who was oppressed under the Tsarist régime and exiled to Siberia in the 1840s. In contrast, *Poprigunia* (*The Grasshopper*, 1953) gave him the role of the shy, sensitive Dimov and showed his awareness of the nuances of Chekhov's characterizations. He made his first impact on western audiences in OTHELLO (1955), with a performance that combined animal strength, intellectual power, and emotional delicacy; but it was spoiled in English-speaking countries by inept DUBBING.

After several less distinguished films Bondarchuk appeared in a short film *Stranitsi rasskaza* (*Pages from a Book*, 1957). This was an account of how Mikhail Sholokhov's much-loved novel *Sudba cheloveka* (*Destiny of a Man*) came to be written and was a COMPILATION of wartime newsreel material with acted sequences from the story, in which Bondarchuk played the hero, Solokov. *Stranitsi rasskaza* was not in itself important, but it impelled Bondarchuk, against considerable official resistance, to make his own film version of SUDBA CHELOVEKA (1959). This first enterprise as director (he also again played Solokov) demonstrated his peculiar combination of strength and sensitivity, particularly in his controlled use of a potentially explosive visual style. His debt to his fellow-Ukrainian Dovzhenko is also in evidence, in his integration of characters with their surroundings and the constant awareness of the proximity of life and death.

This striking proof of his capacities led to his being given the direction of the four-part VOINA I MIR (*War and Peace*, 1966–7). What could have been a mere demonstration of enormous resources became, under Bondarchuk's control, a fine transcription in cinematic terms of Tolstoy's conception, balancing the grandeur and tragedy of the cosmic view with intimate observation of individual characters. As well as directing he played the part of Pierre with insight and authority.

*Waterloo* (1970), a Mosfilm/DE LAURENTIIS co-production, gave him a further opportunity to work on a large scale, but it was lacking in interest on the intimate level and the inevitable difficulties of collaborating with an international team made the film a far less substantial achievement than *Voina i mir*. His performance in *Dyadya Vanya* (*Uncle Vanya*, 1971) shows again his subtle control as an actor. With all his virtuosity in the use of visual techniques, Bondarchuk is essentially an actor's director, working in the STANISLAVSKY tradition of character revelation through a complete knowledge of the actor's craft.

**BONHEUR, Le**, France, 1964. Eastman Color; 1½hr. *Dir, scr* Agnès Varda; *prod* Parc Film; *ph* Jean Rabier, Claude Beausoleil; *des* Hubert

Montloup; *mus* Mozart; *cast* Jean-Claude Drouot (François), Claire Drouot (Thérèse), Sandrine Drouot (Gisou), Olivier Drouot (Pierrot), Marie-France Boyer (Emilie).

François, a carpenter, lives contentedly with his wife and young children. When he falls in love with a post office clerk, Emilie, this does not conflict with his married happiness, merely complements it. He explains this to his wife who is found drowned shortly afterwards. After a time he marries Emilie and the happy family life continues as before.

Despite the lyricism of the film, demonstrated by self-conscious colours and the music of Mozart, the theme of happiness is treated with an almost cruel detachment. The schematic structure of the story and deliberate lack of realism give it the disturbingly abstract quality which runs through VARDA's work.

**BONNEY, WILLIAM H.**, see BILLY THE KID

**BONNIE AND CLYDE**, US, 1967. Technicolor; 1¾hr. *Dir* Arthur Penn; *prod* Warren Beatty; *scr* David Newman, Robert Benton; *ph* Burnett Guffey; *mus* Charles Strouse; *cast* Warren Beatty (Clyde Barrow), Faye Dunaway (Bonnie Parker), Michael J. Pollard (C. W. Moss), Gene Hackman (Buck Barrow), Estelle Parsons (Blanche).

The exploits of a pair of small-time criminals of the Depression era, many of the events drawn from fact (the posed snapshots, Bonnie's poem sent to the newspapers). Both the story and the milieu, re-created through costumes, music, and the ever-present consciousness of social injustice, are viewed through a contemporary fusion of nostalgia and psychological interpretation.

*Bonnie and Clyde* had been offered first to GODARD then to TRUFFAUT by its producer and star Warren BEATTY. It was Arthur PENN's first completely successful film, displaying all the imaginative flair of *Mickey One* (1965) and THE CHASE (1966) with more control than either. The wayward young couple and their inefficient collaborators are depicted with comical affection coloured as the film progresses by the increasing threat of bloody retribution: the moments of realistic violence are tellingly modulated within the overall sense of childish fantasy.

Other films based on the Bonnie and Clyde case include *You Only Live Once* (Fritz LANG, 1937), with Henry FONDA and Sylvia SIDNEY; *Gun Crazy* (Joseph H. Lewis, 1949), with John Dall and Peggy Cummins; and *The Bonnie Parker Story* (William Witney, 1958), with Dorothy Provine.

**BOORMAN, JOHN** (1933–    ), British director, worked from 1962 for BBC television, gaining critical attention with his series of documentaries 'Citizen '63'. His awareness of the disparity between what people say and what they do gave the series considerable power; the same consciousness informs his feature films. 'Citizen '63' was followed in 1964 by 'The Newcomers', a six-part study of a couple in Bristol.

The following year Boorman made his first feature film *Catch Us If You Can*, a vehicle for the pop group The Dave Clark Five. The film was shot in Bristol and, like his next film *Point Blank* (1967), made in Los Angeles, was notable for its resourceful use of urban locations. *Point Blank* is a violent parable in which Lee MARVIN plays a gangster whose attempts to subvert organized society, represented by the hierarchy of the criminal underworld, meet only with frustration. *Hell in the Pacific* (1968), starring Toshiro MIFUNE and Marvin as a Japanese and an American soldier marooned on a Pacific island, explored the ways in which conditioned social responses pervert instinctive feelings. *Leo the Last* (1969) starred Marcello MASTROIANNI as a minor European prince living in a back street of London's multi-racial Notting Hill Gate. Technical brilliance and a fertile imagination could not entirely reconcile the elements of allegory, social commentary, and psychological drama.

*Deliverance* (1972) was more successful on all levels. Four city men go for a weekend's canoeing down a wild Appalachian river which is due to be destroyed in the construction of a reservoir. Their trip becomes a test of endurance, operating at once as allegory and adventure story. The more grandiose *Zardoz* (1974), however, set in a totalitarian future where ageing has been brought under control, carried Boorman's ideas on society and the individual uneasily into the realm of science fiction.

**BORGNINE**, ERNEST (1917– ), US actor of Italian extraction, was for much of his early career type-cast in tough, unsympathetic roles, notably in FROM HERE TO ETERNITY (1953). In MARTY (1955) he played the gentle, ordinary leading man in an unglamorized love story in which his sensitive acting won wide acclaim. He has since established himself as a steady, dependable actor, appearing in a wide variety of films, notably *The Best Things in Life are Free* (1956), the Biblical spectacular *Barabbas* (1961), *Ice Station Zebra* (1968), and THE WILD BUNCH (1969). In Robert ALDRICH's *The Legend of Lylah Clare* (1968) he gave a striking performance as a wicked Hollywood tycoon. He has also had a successful television career.

**BORINAGE** see MISÈRE AU BORINAGE

**BORN YESTERDAY**, US, 1951. 1¾hr. *Dir* George Cukor; *prod* Columbia; *scr* Albert Mannheimer, from the play by Garson Kanin; *ph* Joseph Walker; *mus* Frederick Hollander; *cast* Judy Holliday (Billie Dawn), William Holden (Paul Verral), Broderick Crawford (Harry Brock).

George CUKOR effectively translated Garson KANIN's popular stage play to the screen with Judy HOLLIDAY re-creating her Broadway role of the dumb blonde who, with the help of a newspaperman, becomes too educated for her *nouveau riche* boy-friend. Excellent dialogue and Judy Holliday's particular talent make it a sharp and highly entertaining film.

**BOROWCZYK**, WALERIAN (1923– ), Polish animator and director, worked as a lithographic designer and experimented with painting directly on to film. During a visit to Paris in 1952 he made two shorts, *Photographies vivantes* and *L'Atelier de Fernand Léger*. He collaborated with Jan LENICA on *Byl sobie raz* (*Once Upon a Time*, 1957) and *Dom* (*House*, 1958) and was animation consultant on Stanislaw Jedryka's *Stadion* (1958). The following year he returned to Paris where he made *Terra Incognita*, using the pin screen technique developed by ALEXEÏEFF.

He continued to work in France, making *L'École* (1958), *L'Encyclopédie de grandmaman* (1963), *Renaissance* (1963), the destruction of strange objects filmed in reverse motion, and his most intense film *Les Jeux des anges* (1964). His emerging style showed bitter humour, ironic surrealism, and a sense of cruelty and fear conveyed through fine line drawing. More recently he has directed live-action feature films in France: *Goto, l'île d'amour* (1968), is a surreal allegory set in a fictional totalitarian state, and *Blanche* (1971), is a medieval tale of sexual passion. *Contes immoraux* (*Immoral Tales*, 1973) consists of four separate studies of erotic perversion depicted with Borowczyk's characteristic visual richness.

**BORZAGE**, FRANK (1893–1961), US director who made his début in 1920 following eight years as an actor. His earlier silent films were made for PARAMOUNT; then he made a number for FIRST NATIONAL including pictures starring Norma TALMADGE (*Secrets*, 1924; *Lady*, 1925). But better known is his work for FOX, notably the succession of romances featuring the popular co-starring team of Janet GAYNOR and Charles Farrell ('America's Favourite Lovebirds'), including *Seventh Heaven* (1927), which won the first OSCAR for a film, and *Street Angel* (1928).

Prominent among his sound films were *A Farewell to Arms* (1933), based on Ernest

HEMINGWAY's novel and starring Gary COOPER and Helen HAYES; *Man's Castle* (1933), a bold romantic drama of love and unemployment during the Depression, with Spencer TRACY and Loretta YOUNG; *Desire* (1936), co-directed with Ernst LUBITSCH; *The Big City* (1937), co-starring Spencer Tracy and Luise RAINER, plus Jack Dempsey heading a group of champion boxers who come to the aid of the hero in a dockside climax which was a glorious mixture of pugilism and slapstick comedy; some Joan CRAWFORD vehicles, including *Mannequin* (1938) and *Strange Cargo* (1940); and one of the Deanna DURBIN films, *His Butler's Sister* (1944).

Most of his later work, which ranged from a swashbuckler, *The Spanish Main* (1945), to a religious spectacle, *The Big Fisherman* (1959), is of marginal interest, but during his best years Borzage was undoubtedly one of Hollywood's great romanticists. He dealt by preference with the triumph of love over adversity and drew from actors of widely varying talent performances of attractive warmth.

**BOSSAK,** JERZY (1910–   ), Polish documentary director, was one of the founders of START and, with Aleksander FORD, organized the film unit of the Polish Army in the USSR during the war. In 1948 he became controller of the documentary film studio in Warsaw, shortly afterwards resigning to concentrate on film production. His work has had much influence on the style of Polish documentary films. Among his outstanding work, *Powodz* (*The Flood*, 1947) won a prize at CANNES and the feature-length *Pokoj zwyeciezy swiata* (*Peace Conquers the World*, 1951) was co-directed by Joris IVENS. He has also been a professor at LÓDŻ and artistic director of the Warsaw documentary studio.

**BOSUSTOW,** STEPHEN, see UNITED PRODUCTIONS OF AMERICA (UPA)

**BOUCHER,** *Le* (*The Butcher*), France/Italy, 1969. Eastman Color; 1½hr. *Dir, scr* Claude Chabrol; *prod* Films la Boétie (Paris)/Euro-International (Rome); *ph* Jean Rabier; *cast* Stéphane Audran (Hélène), Jean Yanne (Popaul), Antonio Passalia (Angelo), Mario Beccaria (Léon Hamel).

After Hélène, the beautiful but frigid schoolmistress, has gently rejected the advances of Popaul, the local butcher, the town is shocked by a succession of brutal sex murders. CHABROL handles the thriller elements of his tale with characteristic skill, particularly the discovery of a mutilated body by a school party and the gradual revelation to Hélène of Popaul's guilt. Moreover he invests the narrative with compassionate perceptiveness, so that the teacher's withdrawal and the butcher's savagery are alike seen as expressions of erotic frustration; Stéphane AUDRAN and Jean Yanne convey complex emotions with unusual subtlety. The drama is solidly rooted in the society of a small Périgord town with local people playing their real-life roles, and Jean RABIER's sunny photography heightens the grim theme.

**BOUDU SAUVÉ DES EAUX** (*Boudu Saved From Drowning*), France, 1932. 1½hr. *Dir, scr* Jean Renoir; *prod* Michel Simon, Jean Gehret; *ph* Marcel Lucien; *des* Hughes Laurent, Jean Castanier; *ed* Marguerite Renoir, Suzanne de Troyes; *mus* Raphael, Johann Strauss; *cast* Michel Simon (Boudu), Charles Granval (Lestingois), Marcelle Haina (Mme Lestingois), Séverine Lerczinska (Anne-Marie).

*Boudu sauvé des eaux* demonstrates RENOIR's ability to depict the ambiguities of personal relationships within a theatrically formalized social scheme, a world divided between master and servants. It delineates a marriage through the responses of women capable of reacting to the appeal of two entirely contrasting men, the bourgeois bookseller Lestingois and the tramp Boudu. In Renoir's view the relationship between these two, born when Lestingois plunges into the Seine to save Boudu from drowning, is supreme, surviving even Boudu's anti-social behaviour and his seduction of his benefactor's wife and mistress.

Made a year after *La Chienne*, this splendidly amoral tale is a high point of Renoir's collaboration with the actor Michel SIMON and a good example of his experiments with DEEP FOCUS. Its combination of farce and seriousness and its conscious flouting of the canons of good taste make it characteristic of French cinema of the early thirties: the figure of the tramp and the irresponsible evasion at the end recall René CLAIR's A NOUS LA LIBERTÉ, made the previous year, while Simon's performance anticipates the role he played for Jean VIGO in L'ATALANTE (1934). Renoir's film shares with these a vein of anarchic poetry and glorification of the individual struggle against social pressures.

**BOULTING BROTHERS.** Twin brothers JOHN and ROY (1913–   ) who have worked together since the late thirties, interchanging the responsibilities of producer and director, but with Roy the more active as director. Their early work included *Trunk Crime* (1939), a strange psychological thriller; *Inquest* (1940), a murder drama commenting on coroners' courts; *Pastor Hall* (1940), from Ernst Toller's play based on the experiences of the Nazi-defying pastor Niemöller; and *Thunder Rock* (1942), a moral fantasy set in a lonely lighthouse. During the

*Boudu sauvé des eaux* (Jean Renoir, 1932)

war, John served with the RAF and directed *Journey Together* (1945), while Roy was in the army working on *Desert Victory* (1943) and similar documentary features of wartime campaigns.

Returning to civilian life, the brothers resumed collaboration in a number of notable films including *Brighton Rock* (John, 1947), *Fame is the Spur* (Roy, 1947), *The Guinea Pig* (Roy, 1948), and *Seven Days to Noon* (John, 1950). In the fifties they abandoned the seriousness of purpose that had always characterized their work, and *Seagulls over Sorrento* (Roy, 1954), the inordinately popular *Private's Progress* (John, 1956), *Lucky Jim* (1957), and *I'm All Right Jack* (1959) are notable among the comedies and farces which have constituted their main output since. In 1955 both brothers were appointed to the board of BRITISH LION and John became managing director in 1969. They resigned in 1973 and returned to independent production and direction.

John Boulting is married to Hayley MILLS.

**BOUQUET,** MICHEL, French actor whose stage career has been particularly associated with

plays by Anouilh, Osborne, and Pinter. He played small parts in films for some years, including CLOUZOT's *Manon* (1948) and GRÉMILLON's *Pattes blanches* (1949) and spoke the commentary for RESNAIS's NUIT ET BROUILLARD (1955). CHABROL gave him his first leading role in *La Femme infidèle* (1968), and Bouquet emerged as an actor of unusual subtlety, conveying complex emotions with apparently total passivity. As another justified murderer, tortured by guilt, in Chabrol's companion-piece JUSTE AVANT LA NUIT (1971) he again partnered Stéphane AUDRAN to striking effect. Meanwhile his reputation was established with a number of other films, including TRUFFAUT's *La Mariée était en noir* (*The Bride Wore Black*, 1967) and *La Sirène du Mississippi* (*Mississippi Mermaid*, 1969). In 1972 he had important roles in six films including *L'Attentat* (*Plot*) based on the Ben Barka affair.

**BOURVIL** (1917–70), French actor, real name André Raimbourg, who took his professional name from Bourville in Normandy where he was brought up. He became immensely popular with

French radio audiences in the late forties singing his own pithy songs. His film appearances usually failed to exploit his particular talents, but he gave good comic performances for CLOUZOT in *Miquette et sa mère* (1950), Sacha GUITRY in *Si Versailles m'était conté* (1954) and *Si Paris nous était conté* (1955), and Renė CLAIR in *Tout l'or du monde* (1961). His best-known film abroad was probably AUTANT-LARA's *La Traversée de Paris* (1956), in which Bourvil played a conscientious little black marketeer, skilfully combining straight-faced farce, black comedy, and outright tragedy.

**BOW,** CLARA (1905–65), US actress whose sex appeal (she was Elinor GLYN's IT GIRL) and gay, at times almost frenetic, manner made her one of the most popular stars of the twenties. Films like *Mantrap* (1926) show her ability to give performances of considerable depth and feeling, but she is best remembered as the expressive-eyed, cupid-bow-mouthed flapper of films like *It* (1927) and *The Wild Party* (1929). A series of scandals in 1930 and 1931 destroyed her career, although she continued to work in films for a time afterwards.

**BOYD,** WILLIAM (1898–1972), US actor, first appeared as Clarence E. Mulford's Western hero, Hopalong Cassidy, in 1935. He had previously enjoyed a minor screen reputation, appearing frequently in Cecil B. DEMILLE's films during the twenties. Between 1935 and 1940 Boyd made twenty-six Hopalong Cassidy WESTERNS, in which his distinctive appearance—white hair, black hat and costume, white horse—and sincere smile as he battled against the forces of evil, made him an international celebrity. Boyd's continued success was assured when he began a television series in the late forties, followed by massive sales of cowboy-suits and toy revolvers marketed by his own Hopalong Cassidy Enterprises. In 1953 he worked again for DeMille, making a guest appearance in *The Greatest Show on Earth*.

**BOYER,** CHARLES (1897–　), French actor, first appeared on the screen in the twenties, in such films as *L'Homme du large* (Marcel L'HERBIER, 1920) and *Le Capitaine Fracasse* (Alberto CAVALCANTI, 1927). He went to Hollywood in the early sound era and thereafter divided his career between America and France. Notable among his continental films were *L'Epervier* (L'Herbier, 1933), *Le Bonheur* (L'Herbier, 1934), *La Bataille* (Nicolas Farkas, 1934), *Mayerling* (Anatole LITVAK, 1936), *Orage* (Marc ALLÉGRET, 1938), *Madame de ...* (Max OPHULS, 1953), and *LOLA MONTÈS* (Ophuls, 1955).

Supporting roles in *The Trial of Mary Dugan* (1929) and *The Big House* (1930) were among his earlier American appearances, and within a few years he was a top Hollywood star whose suave charm, delightfully accented voice, and considerable versatility won him tremendous popularity. Particular successes at this period were in *The Garden of Allah* (1936), and opposite GARBO in *Tovarich* (1937) and *Conquest* (1937, *Marie Walewska* in GB) in which he was a convincing Napoleon. He took the role of PÉPÉ-LE-MOKO in the American remake *Algiers* (1938), and his many other Hollywood films included *History Is Made at Night* (1937), *Love Affair* (1939), GASLIGHT (1944, *The Murder in Thornton Square* in GB), *Cluny Brown* (1946), *Arch of Triumph* (1948), and *The Cobweb* (1955).

He became increasingly distinguished and poised with maturity, and his fame scarcely abated in the sixties (*Paris brûle-t-il?*, 1965; *How to Steal a Million*, 1966; *Barefoot in the Park*, 1967; *The Madwoman of Chaillot*, 1969). He also appeared in the prestigious cast of the musical remake of *Lost Horizon* (1972) and gave an admired performance in RESNAIS's *Stavisky* (1974).

**'B' PICTURE,** term coined in the US to denote a feature film made at low cost and of modest length (55 to 75 minutes), usually with a minor star or perhaps a couple of fading ones. Designed to fill in the second half of the programme, hence also known as a 'second' or 'supporting' feature, they were usually booked for a fixed fee rather than a percentage of the gross receipts. They were a staple product, providing full employment in an industry otherwise subject to wide fluctuations: certain Hollywood companies, in particular MONOGRAM PICTURES, specialized in producing 'B' pictures and were respected for their skill in creating this utility form of entertainment. Jean-Luc GODARD dedicated his first full-length film A BOUT DE SOUFFLE (1960) to Monogram Pictures. The role of 'B' pictures in the entertainment industry has been taken over by the low-budget television series. (See DOUBLE FEATURE.)

**BRADLEY,** DAVID (*c.* 1920–　), US director whose reputation rests on his work as an amateur. He made his first film while still at school (the same school attended by Orson WELLES).

During war service he worked on the films of the Nuremberg trials. As a student at Northwestern University, Illinois, he directed several feature-length films in 16mm including JULIUS CAESAR (1949), which starred Charlton HESTON, then a fellow-student. *Julius Caesar* was widely noticed and prompted Dore SCHARY to invite Bradley to Hollywood. He directed *Talk About a Stranger* (1951) for METRO-GOLDWYN-MAYER, but has since only sporadically made feature films.

**BRAKHAGE,** STAN (1933–  ), US avant-garde film-maker, in work completed since the mid-fifties has made interesting and seminal contributions to the development of non-narrative film. Although not publicly shown, films such as *Flesh of Morning* (1956–7), *Anticipation of the Night* (1958), and *Dog Star Man* (1959–64), with their fragmentary editing, multiple superimpositions, and variably exposed sequences, as well as in their rejection of conventional attitudes, have had considerable influence on the American UNDERGROUND. Brakhage's statement of aesthetics, *Metaphors on vision*, was published by FILM CULTURE in 1963.

**BRANDO,** MARLON (1924–  ), US actor, trained at the ACTORS' STUDIO, whose 'method' his acting style was to epitomize in the public mind. His first major success was in 1947 as Stanley Kowalski in the stage production of Tennessee WILLIAMS's *A Streetcar Named Desire*, after which he was brought to Hollywood by Stanley KRAMER to star in *The Men* (Fred ZINNEMANN, 1950). Brando was well suited to the role of a paraplegic soldier whose physical frustrations echo his cultural limitations. The impression of suppressed power, conveyed by hesitant speech with explosions of painful violence became his forte, particularly under the direction of Elia KAZAN in the film version of A STREETCAR NAMED DESIRE (1951) and in ON THE WATERFRONT (1954). Brando's style provided an easy target for traditionalists but the intelligence underlying his apparent incoherence was evident in VIVA ZAPATA! (1952), in which his portrayal of the revolutionary leader was subdued and well modulated, and in JULIUS CAESAR (1953), in which he was powerfully moving as Mark Antony. In strong contrast to these, *The Wild One* (1953) showed him as the leader of a gang of leather-jacketed young thugs. The film's violence was deplored at the time (in Britain it was banned for several years) but it set a fashion for many others with the same theme and treatment. His influence on acting styles, not only in Hollywood but in Britain and Europe, was largely based on these early films in which conventional attractiveness is set aside in favour of brutal conviction. This contrast with the polished artificiality fashionable in films up to the time is heightened by scenes of physical suffering which his performances almost invariably include.

With all his advantages as an actor, his career has been punctuated with mediocre performances. His excursions into costume drama (*Desirée*, 1954, in which he played Napoleon) and musical (GUYS AND DOLLS, 1955) were misjudged; his only Western, ONE-EYED JACKS (1960) which he also directed, was commercially a failure although admired by connoisseurs of the genre. It betrayed an element of artistic self-indulgence that also led to the difficulties he created during the shooting of THE MUTINY ON THE BOUNTY (1962), which were not justified by his own performance. He made a return to earlier form in THE CHASE (1966), but CHAPLIN's *A Countess from Hong Kong* (1966) and *Candy* (1968) were mistaken attempts at light comedy.

Brando's political involvement and his identification with the cause of racial minorities has perhaps contributed to the uncertainties of direction in his career. This concern undoubtedly led him to accept the leading role in Gillo PONTECORVO's *¡Queimada!* (1968), which deals with negro revolution in the Caribbean. In THE GODFATHER (1971) he played the head of a Mafia-like 'family' with an authority that dispelled doubts as to the development of his unusual talent; and in LAST TANGO IN PARIS (1972) he powerfully succeeded in conveying within the character of a middle-aged widower the painful alienation of his earlier roles.

Brando's sister Jocelyn (b. 1920) has also pursued an acting career. Her occasional film appearances include THE BIG HEAT (1953) and THE CHASE (1966).

**BRASSEUR,** PIERRE (1905–  ), French actor of considerable if occasionally undisciplined talent, made intermittent film appearances from 1925. His first memorable role was as the snivelling crook in QUAI DES BRUMES (1938); this was in striking contrast to the part which earned him lasting fame, the swaggering actor Fernand Lemaître in LES ENFANTS DU PARADIS (1945). His bravura characterizations include leading roles in *Les Fortes de la nuit* (1946), PORTE DES LILAS (1957), LES YEUX SANS VISAGE (1959), and *Il bell' Antonio* (1960).

**BRAULT,** MICHEL (1928–  ), Quebec director and cameraman, one of the pioneers of the Candid-Eye movement at the NATIONAL FILM BOARD of Canada, particularly with *Les Raquetteurs* (1958, with Gilles Groulx and *La Lutte* (1960, with Claude JUTRA). He worked as a cameraman with Jean ROUCH in Africa and with Mario Ruspoli. He collaborated with Pierre PERRAULT to make *Pour la suite du monde* (1963). Many of the best recent Quebec films have been distinguished by his photography.

**BRAUNBERGER,** PIERRE (1905–  ), French producer, distributor, exhibitor, and pioneer of the ART HOUSE movement, launched his first production, RENOIR'S *La Fille de l'eau*, in 1924 and went on to produce most of Renoir's early films, including *Tir au flanc* (1928), *La Chienne* (1931), and UNE PARTIE DE CAMPAGNE (1936). Many of the shorts with which the NOUVELLE VAGUE directors, including GODARD, RESNAIS, and TRUFFAUT, began their careers were produced by his Films de la Pléiade as well as many outstanding feature films such as TIREZ SUR LE PIANISTE (*Shoot the Pianist*, 1960) and VIVRE SA VIE (1962). He has also backed documentaries with a social orientation (MOI UN NOIR, 1958; CUBA SI!, 1961) and documentaries about the other arts (GUERNICA, 1950).

Braunberger's eclecticism, his ability to pick out the most promising young talents of the time, and his willingness to give young directors complete freedom, have made him an important figure in French cinema. He is the only producer to have been awarded the Louis DELLUC prize three times.

**BRAZIL.** Antonio Leal, a Portuguese, filmed in Rio de Janeiro in 1908 and an Italian, Paolo Benedetti, made films from 1910, first in Barbacena then in Rio. Vittorio Capellaro, an Italian actor working in Sâo Paulo, had some success with literary adaptations in the manner of the FILM D'ART—*Inocência* (1915), *O Mulato* (1916), *Iracema* (1918)—but Brazilian cinemas were flooded with French and Italian films, later superseded by films from Hollywood.

Such local production as managed to persist was fragmented between three localities, Catagueses, Recife, and Campinas, each with its characteristic style. Catagueses proved the most fertile ground, from which emerged Brazil's most influential director, Humberto Mauro whose career lasted from 1925 to the mid-fifties. The important films of his early career include *Na Primavera da Vida* (1925) and *Ganga Bruta* (1933), which combined clear observation of Brazil's social conflicts with subjective symbolism and forceful narrative. International attention was briefly drawn to Brazilian cinema by *Limite* (1929), the only film made by Mario Peixoto, composed of the mental images of three people adrift at sea.

The introduction of sound caused a near-collapse in the industry; *Alô, alô, Brasil?* (1934), a musical, launched Carmen MIRANDA'S career, but cinemas were in the main given over to American imports until, towards the end of the thirties, French films began to gain popularity. Mauro, who in 1936 became head of the Instituto Nacional de Cinema Educativo, continued to direct films including *Descubrimento do Brasil* (1937), with music by Villa-Lobos.

The late forties saw attempts to stimulate a national film industry with QUOTA legislation and the reconstitution in 1949 of the Vera Cruz production company, originally dating from 1925. Alberto CAVALCANTI was invited to take charge of splendid new studios at Sâo Bernardo da Campo, but the company's reliance on foreign directors and techniques restricted opportunities for Brazilian film-makers. Cavalcanti himself directed a few films for Vera Cruz, but the company's policy was nervously divided between encouraging an indigenous film style and capturing mass audiences, and it failed in both. Lima BARRETO'S O' CANGACEIRO (*The Bandit*, 1953) created an international stir: it combined a genuine feeling for national cultural and social identity with a vigorous romanticism that gained a fervent following. A large proportion of the film's profits, however, went to the distributors, COLUMBIA.

Independent film-makers began to make their mark in the fifties, especially Nelson Pereira dos Santos with *Rio, Quaranta Graus* (1953) which compassionately traced the course of a love-affair in a poor area of Rio. Santos, his brother Robert Santos, Ruy Guerra, and Glauber ROCHA came together in the CINEMA NOVO co-operative which initiated exciting developments in Brazilian cinema and inspired political film-makers all over Latin America. Brazil's urban problems reached the commercial screen only with ORFEU NEGRO (*Black Orpheus*, 1958), a French/Italian co-production filmed in Rio at carnival time. The effects of the military coup in 1964 gradually stifled the political voice of Cinema Novo and since Rocha's departure from Brazil in 1969, independent cinema there has lost much of its impetus.

**BRECHT,** BERTOLT (1898–1956), German playwright and poet who in his plays during the twenties developed his influential theory of 'alienation' by which the creation of illusion is deliberately avoided, so that the audience shall not be manipulated emotionally but remain capable of intelligent appraisal. After settling in Berlin in 1924, Brecht worked for a time as assistant to Max REINHARDT. His first real success was DIE DREIGROSCHENOPER in 1928, which PABST filmed in 1931. Brecht subsequently repudiated Pabst's film, initiating a long and costly law suit on the grounds that the film subverted his original design. His own involvement with film was more overtly political: he worked with Slatan DUDOW on the latter's short film *Seifenblasen* (1929) and with Ernst Ottwald wrote the script for Dudow's KÜHLE WAMPE (1932).

His left-wing and pacifist views forced him to flee from Germany in 1933. He lived in Switzerland, Denmark, and Finland, and finally went to California in 1941, where he settled uneasily in

Hollywood. He wrote a script for LANG, *Hangmen also Die* (1943), which led to a repetition of his law suit with Pabst. He felt that his·intentions had not been respected in the finished film and he won a decision in court allowing him a credit distinguishing his script from the shooting script. There was an abortive project for a film about JOAN OF ARC with Leon Feuchtwanger, who had staged Brecht's first play in Munich in 1922, and he was employed as a writer by various studios for the sake of his famous name; but none of his scripts reached the screen unmodified. In 1947 Joseph LOSEY directed a stage production of Brecht's *Galileo Galilei*, with Charles LAUGHTON in the lead. It was not a great success.

Brecht became involved in the hearings of the UNAMERICAN ACTIVITIES Committee in 1947 and although no charge was brought against him he left the US for Switzerland. During these years of exile he had written what are generally considered his most important plays, *Mother Courage*, *Galileo*, *The Good Woman of Setzuan*, and *The Caucasian Chalk Circle*. He was invited to East Germany to set up a theatre company, the Berliner Ensemble. The last films he worked on as a writer were Joris IVENS's *Lied der Ströme* (1953) and *Herr Puntila und sein Knecht Matti* (1955), directed by CAVALCANTI.

**BRENNAN**, WALTER (1894–1974), US actor who entered films in 1923 and became a leading and unusually versatile character actor able to play roles from outright comedy parts to villainous heavies, but best remembered as the hero's crony in many Westerns. He won three OSCARS for supporting roles (*Come and Get It*, 1936; *Kentucky*, 1938; *The Westerner*, 1940), and was even more memorable in MY DARLING CLEMENTINE (John FORD, 1946). He was prominent throughout the fifties (including *Bad Day at Black Rock*, 1954; RIO BRAVO, 1959); in the sixties he divided his time between films and television.

**BRESSON**, ROBERT (1907–    ), French director. After a childhood spent alternating between his native Auvergne and Paris, he took a degree in literature and philosophy. He worked as a painter for a while and made his first film in 1934, *Les Affaires publiques*. No copies of the film are known to exist, but according to the main protagonist, Gilles Margaritis, it was a short satirical comedy, whose cerebral humour had affinities with that of René CLAIR. Bresson worked on the scripts of *Les Jumeaux de Brighton* (Claude Heymann, 1936, with RAIMU and Michel SIMON) and of *Courrier Sud* (1937), and was working as Clair's assistant on the preparation of *Air pur* when the outbreak of war stopped its production.

Bresson spent eighteen months as a prisoner of war, returning home in 1941. In 1943 he made his first feature-length film, *Les Anges du péché*, a spiritual drama centred on a convent. In spite of its moral seriousness, the film had some popular success, and Bresson was able to make *Les Dames du Bois de Boulogne* (1945). He adapted the story from Diderot's *Jacques le Fataliste*: COCTEAU wrote the dialogue and Maria CASARÈS gave a fine performance in the central role. The film was well received by the critics but not by the public, and Bresson was unable to find backing for another film until he was given the opportunity of making JOURNAL D'UN CURÉ DE CAMPAGNE (1951), from the novel by Bernanos. Bresson's renunciation of the use of professional actors dates from this film, which also marked a heightening of austerity in his methods. Once again he had to face a gap of five years before he could make another film: he actually started *La Princesse de Clèves* in colour, and worked on an adaptation of Lancelot of the Lake, but neither project was completed at the time.

UN CONDAMNÉ A MORT S'EST ÉCHAPPÉ (1956) was a full and masterly achievement of the difficult aim Bresson has always pursued in his films, that of expressing a state of mind in visual terms. It had a modest commercial success, and since then Bresson has contrived to work more regularly. *Pickpocket* (1959), written by Bresson on a theme which is close to that of *Crime and Punishment*, was not well received. Bresson's spareness fails to carry conviction here and degenerates into over-solemnity. The singleness of his vision was once again triumphantly vindicated, however, in LE PROCÈS DE JEANNE D'ARC (1962), a subject which naturally attracted Bresson but constituted a particular challenge in view of the great number of film versions already made.

*Au hazard, Balthazar* (1966) was one of the Franco-Swedish co-productions undertaken on the initiative of SVENSKA FILMINSTITUTET (the Swedish Film Institute). The donkey, Balthazar, is subjected to the brutal treatment that man tends to deal out to his fellow-man. The influence, perhaps, of the Alpine locations in which the film was mainly shot introduced a lyricism new for Bresson; never gratuitous, but serving to underline the harshness of the film's burden in a way which is repeated in MOUCHETTE (1966). For the subject of *Mouchette* Bresson returned to the work of Bernanos. He showed a rare touch of mellowness in transposing the location from the north to Provence for the sake of the good weather for filming, but there is little mildness in the film itself, a beautifully controlled, inexorable account of suffering which ends, as most of his subjects do, with the arbitrary closure of death.

In his next film, *Une Femme douce* (*A Gentle Creature*, 1969), he used colour for the first time. This film and his *Quatre Nuits d'un rêveur* (*Four Nights of a Dreamer*, 1971) are based on stories by Dostoevsky (*Quatre Nuits* being the latest of four screen versions of 'White Nights'): both films are transferred to a modern Parisian setting and are treated with less asceticism than his earlier films. *Une Femme douce* in particular suffers from the transposition of time and place: in a modern situation the story loses its motivation. He finally realized a long-cherished project with *Lancelot du lac* (1974) which richly re-created the Arthurian legend at a point where the Grail quest is abandoned as vain.

Bresson's Catholic beliefs are vital to the thematic coherence of his work: a state of grace or holiness is achieved through sin and suffering. His people are defined existentially through their actions (depicted with fastidious respect for detail: the minutiae of escape preparations, methods of pickpocketing, etc), using the minimum of verbal exposition and avoiding psychological explanations. His narrative is pared down to focus on the implicit moral. His subjects, treated with a sensitive economy scarcely paralleled in cinema, are often placed within spatio-temporal structures of classical severity (prisons, prescribed lengths of time), and emphasis is always by elimination rather than accumulation. To intensify the clarity of his statements, he has increasingly refused to allow his actors to make a creative contribution; they must execute his instructions with the utmost fidelity. An artist of refined vision, he has won a hard core of devotees who unhesitatingly claim him among the masters of cinema.

Bresson's work has been the subject of a large body of good criticism. The most perceptive single work is perhaps Michel Estève's *Robert Bresson*, Cinéma d'Aujourd'hui, no. 8, Séghers, Paris, 1962. A useful work in English is *The Films of Robert Bresson* by Amédée Ayfre and others, London, 1969, New York, 1970, which has an excellent bibliography.

**BRICE,** FANNY (1891–1951), US stage entertainer, real name Fanny Borach, who became one of Florenz Ziegfeld's biggest Broadway stars in the twenties, capitalizing on her plain looks and dry, Jewish humour. During the thirties she was immensely popular on radio. She made film appearances in *My Man* (1929), named after her famous torch song, *The Great Ziegfeld* (1936), and *Ziegfeld Follies* (Vincente MINNELLI, 1946), the latter giving rise to her memorable description of Esther WILLIAMS: 'Wet she is a star, dry she ain't'. Films based on her life include *Rose of Washington Square* (1939), with Alice FAYE, and *Funny Girl* (William WYLER, 1968), for which Barbra STREISAND won an OSCAR.

**BRIDGE ON THE RIVER KWAI, The,** GB, 1957. CinemaScope; 2¾hr; Technicolor. *Dir* David Lean; *prod* Sam Spiegel; *scr* Pierre Boulle, from his own novel; *mus* Malcolm Arnold; *cast* William Holden (Shears), Alec Guinness (Colonel Nicholson), Jack Hawkins (Major Warden), Sessue Hayakawa (Colonel Saito), James Donald (Major Clipton).

The first of David LEAN's epic films was adapted from an anti-war novel by Pierre Boulle. (Boulle himself is credited with the screenplay, though there is some controversy about who was really responsible for it; Carl FOREMAN among others certainly being involved.) Though it loses some of the irony of the original, and has a somewhat confused ending, it is a visually beautiful and stirring film for which Lean won his first OSCAR. The best parts of the film study two fanatics: the Japanese prison commander who must have a railway bridge built by his prisoners in the Siamese jungle and the stiff-necked and stubborn British colonel who gets his men to do it in an incredible three months, only for it to be blown up by commandos. The fine performances of Alec GUINNESS and Sessue HAYAKAWA under Lean's skilled direction carry the main weight of the film.

**BRIEF ENCOUNTER,** Britain, 1945. 1¾hr. *Dir* David Lean; *prod* Noël Coward, Anthony Havelock-Allen, Ronald Neame; *scr* Coward, from his one-act play *Still Life*; *ph* Robert Krasker; *mus* Rachmaninov's Second Piano Concerto; *cast* Celia Johnson (Laura Jesson), Trevor Howard (Alec Harvey), Stanley Holloway (Albert Godby), Cyril Raymond (Fred Jesson), Joyce Carey (Myrtle Bagot).

This account of a passionate yet unconsummated relationship between a married woman and a married man created a great impression both in Britain and abroad: it won the Grand Prix de la Critique at the first CANNES Festival. Script, direction, and acting all combined to depict deep emotional involvement against a realistic English suburban background; the film may be seen as the apotheosis in British films of the idea that non-heroic events in everyday settings can supply excellent cinematic material. Rachmaninov's music was skilfully used to heighten the romantic effect.

**BRIGHTON SCHOOL,** an informal group of pioneer British film-makers working on the south coast around 1900 led by G. A. SMITH and James WILLIAMSON. The term was not assumed by the group itself, but was used for convenience and given currency by the historian Georges

SADOUL. His *British creators of film technique*, London, 1948, deals specifically with the group.

**BRINGING UP BABY,** US, 1938. 1¾hr. *Dir, prod* Howard Hawks for RKO; *scr* Dudley Nichols, Hager Wilde, from a story by Wilde; *ph* Russell Metty; *cast* Cary Grant (David Huxley), Katharine Hepburn (Susan), Charles Ruggles (Major Horace Applegate), May Robson (Aunt Elizabeth).

The 'Baby' of the title, an untrained leopard which is substituted for the pet belonging to Susan (Katharine HEPBURN), is the focus of strife between her and the anthropologist played by Cary GRANT.

This joyful paean to eccentricity tilts at a society that discourages individuality. Despite her unladylike behaviour, which at times is plainly anti-social, the irresponsible upper-class heroine is applauded as a point of sanity in an insane world.

Peter BOGDANOVICH drew freely on *Bringing Up Baby* in *What's Up, Doc?* (1972).

**BRITISH BOARD OF FILM CENSORS** was set up in 1912 to approve films for public viewing. The operation of the Cinematograph Act of 1909 had established the right of local authorities to ban films on grounds of impropriety; the variety of decisions taken across the country led to a chaotic situation, and the film trade itself, led by the Cinematograph Exhibitors Association and the main producing companies, took steps to set up a central censoring body whose decisions should be valid throughout Britain. ('Topicals'— i.e. NEWSREELS—were excluded from the Board's jurisdiction and have remained so except when the country was at war.) Local councils were slow to surrender their authority, but in 1921 the London County Council (now the Greater London Council) enacted by-laws which specified that only films passed by the Board might be shown in cinemas licensed by them. Other authorities gradually followed this lead, but they still retain the right to ban a film which has been passed by the Board or to permit the showing of a film which has been refused a certificate.

The Board consists of a President and Secretary appointed by the film industry, examiners, readers (of scripts submitted in advance of production), and clerical staff. The Presidents, who have usually been unconnected with the cinema, are chosen for their high public reputation; the appointment is approved by the Home Secretary. Although the President's signature appears on the Board's certificates, actual decisions regarding the award or refusal of a certificate rests with the Secretary, who also discusses with producers the cutting of objection-

able sequences and speaks for the Board in any public discussion of contentious matters. The Board's work is financed by viewing fees based on running time.

The Board works independently of the industry and of government, but it is essential for it to maintain good relations with both, as well as the goodwill of local authorities. General reluctance to strengthen arguments for state censorship in Britain has encouraged close co-operation between the Board and the government. At the instigation of the Foreign Office, *Dawn* (Herbert WILCOX, 1928), a film about Edith Cavell, was refused a certificate for fear of offending Germany; in the twenties the Board respected the government's desire to prohibit the public showing of the new 'revolutionary' films from Soviet Russia; and during the Second World War security censorship was undertaken by the Board on behalf of the government.

Until the sixties the Board's decisions tended to lag behind public opinion and its image of old-fashioned paternalism gave rise to many colourful but apocryphal tales of the censor's ineptitude; but John Trevelyan, Secretary from 1958 to 1971, changed its style. Trevelyan encouraged and participated in open debate on the Board's decisions and encouraged film-makers to work closely with the Board during production so as to avoid the necessity of cuts after a film's completion. Concern with violence and, more recently, drug abuse, as much as with sexual matters, was emphasized; and the changing social climate was more readily acknowledged. The censors' decisions inevitably came under attack from either side, being too liberal for many and still too restrictive for others; and a certain reaction towards caution took place after Trevelyan's retirement. But the general trend would appear to be a progression towards a relaxation of censorship of films intended for adult audiences while maintaining a protective policy towards children.

*What the censor saw* by John Trevelyan, London, 1973, is a personal and entertaining account of the workings of the British Board of Film Censors.

(See CENSORSHIP, GB; 'AA' CERTIFICATE, 'A' CERTIFICATE, 'H' CERTIFICATE, 'U' CERTIFICATE, 'X' CERTIFICATE.)

**BRITISH FILM ACADEMY** see SOCIETY OF FILM AND TELEVISION ARTS

**BRITISH FILM INSTITUTE, The,** was founded in 1933, drawing its funds from government sources and members' subscriptions: it is now financed mainly by the government through the Department of Education and Science. For the first part of its existence, the organization had a strong bias towards educational films which was reflected in its magazines SIGHT AND SOUND (taken over from the British Institute of Adult Education) and the *Monthly Film Bulletin* (founded in 1934 and now largely devoted to reviews, plot synopses, and full credits of all feature films trade-shown in Britain). For a time local branches were in operation throughout Britain, some of which joined to form the basis of the Scottish Film Council. The National Film Library, later re-named the NATIONAL FILM ARCHIVE, was established in 1935 with a responsibility for maintaining a national repository of films of permanent historical, social, or artistic value. The Lending Section of the National Film Library was started in 1938, but gradually grew to include films from other sources and eventually became a separate department as the BFI Film Distribution Library.

Screenings of films selected from the Archive had begun in 1936. The need for an Institute-owned cinema was met when the Telekinema (built for the Festival of Britain in 1951) was passed to the BFI to become the first NATIONAL FILM THEATRE. The Information Department and Book Library house one of the world's largest collections of printed material on films and work in co-operation with a considerable Stills Collection.

The BFI Production Fund helps to finance films by new directors and has of late contributed to some distinguished work including Bill Douglas's *My Childhood* (1972) and *My Ain Folk* (1973) and Peter K. Smith's *A Private Enterprise* (1974).

The Institute has been the subject of controversy for much of its career, attacks published in 1936 reading remarkably like those of recent years. Controversy arises from the nature of the Institute, uncomfortably combining the roles of a public body and a private members' club, as much as from questions of policy.

Ivan Butler, *To encourage the art of the film*, London, 1971, gives an account of the BFI's history.

**BRITISH FILM PRODUCTION FUND,** an arrangement devised by a Treasury official Sir Wilfred Eady in 1950, and known colloquially as the Eady Plan, to provide a levy on cinema admissions in Britain for the benefit of British film production. Originally a voluntary scheme, it became statutory under the Cinematograph Films Act 1957. The levy is collected from cinemas by HM Customs & Excise and the proceeds handed over to the British Film Fund Agency. The Fund is distributed to British film-makers in proportion to their films' earnings in Britain. The present rate of levy is one-ninth of the excess over 7½p charged for cinema admission.

**BRITISH KINEMATOGRAPH, SOUND AND TELEVISION SOCIETY,** a professional society founded in 1931, devoted to technical and scientific progress in the film and television industries. The Society arranges lectures and exhibitions, promulgates technical standards, and publishes a monthly journal on current technical developments. Membership, principally in the UK, is by election from those working in cinematography, sound recording, or television. Members who have attained positions of responsibility in one of these industries are entitled to the letters MBKS after their names.

**BRITISH LION,** originally a production company which functioned briefly from about 1919. The famous production–distribution company was founded by Sam W. Smith in November 1927; incorporated as British Lion Film Corporation, it flourished from the mid-thirties as the British distributors of REPUBLIC PICTURES. With Shepperton as its main studios, it was active in British production. Early in 1946, control of British Lion was acquired by LONDON FILMS, with Alexander KORDA himself as production adviser and chairman of the company which ran the Shepperton studios. In the following years high production losses were incurred, and the position was worsened late in 1950 when Republic brought to an end its relationship with British Lion and set up its own distribution concern in Britain. The government had lent British Lion £3 million through the NATIONAL FILM FINANCE CORPORATION, and the company's financial crisis reached a peak in the spring of 1954 when the NFFC called in the loan and appointed a receiver and manager: it was then disclosed that all British Lion's share capital of £1,205,000 had been lost. With the old company wound up, British Lion Films Ltd was formed in January 1955 to take over the assets of its insolvent predecessor; its main function was not film production but the provision of distribution and financial guarantees for independent producers. Among those appointed to a reorganized board of directors were practical film-makers—the BOULTING Brothers, Frank LAUNDER and Sidney GILLIAT. The company's financial standing then seemed to improve steadily, and early in 1961 there was a new departure in the joint formation by British Lion and COLUMBIA of BLC Films, to be responsible for marketing the films of both constituents in the UK, an arrangement which lasted until 1967. In 1963 the company reported its fourth profitable year in succession and the fact that £600,000 of the government loan had been paid off. Early in 1964, however, the government sold the company back to private enterprise, to a group headed by Michael BALCON, in spite of considerable opposition within the film industry. There was a drop in profits of £86,000 in the first year under private enterprise. In September 1965, Balcon was succeeded as chairman by Lord Goodman. An increase in the company's profits was announced in 1967; in the following year the BBC bought British Lion's library of feature films; and by 1969, with John Boulting as managing director, it appeared that the company was in a healthy financial condition, though the number of new films distributed was becoming fewer, and by 1971 there was scarcely more than a trickle. A new and as yet uncertain chapter in the organization's history was opened in April 1972 when Barclay Securities, headed by the financier John Bentley, took over British Lion.

**BRITTEN,** BENJAMIN (1913– ), British composer, studied first under Frank Bridge and later at the Royal College of Music under John Ireland. He composed the music for several documentary films, notably *Coal Face* and NIGHT MAIL (both 1936), and *The Tocher* (1938), which was produced by Lotte REINIGER for the GPO Film Unit (see CROWN FILM UNIT). Britten's Variations and Fugue on a Theme by Purcell was written for a Crown Film Unit production *Instruments of the Orchestra* (1946): the commentary written for the film is often used in concert and recorded performances of the work under the title *The Young Person's Guide to the Orchestra.*

**BROADWAY MELODY,** a cycle of 'backstage' musicals produced by METRO-GOLDWYN-MAYER. They created a style for the film musical which dominated the thirties, becoming a formula: a plot concerning the trials and tribulations involved in putting on a Broadway show, leading up to the grand finale of opening night. They began with *The Broadway Melody* (1929), made in 1928 when sound was revolutionizing the industry. Irving THALBERG hired two young song-writers, Arthur FREED and Herb Nacio Brown, to write original numbers for this, MGM's first film musical. Heralded as '100% All Talking, 100% All Singing . . .', it was a tremendous success, won the OSCAR for best film of the year, and was acclaimed for its use of sound. Directed by Harry Beaumont, it starred Bessie LOVE, Anita Page, and Charles King, and told the story of two sisters from vaudeville who make it to Broadway, romance, and success. Executed on a sumptuous scale, its original numbers

included 'The Wedding of the Painted Doll', a ballet sequence in TECHNICOLOR, 'Broadway Melody', and 'You Were Meant for Me'. MGM immediately followed it with *Hollywood Revue of 1929*, released the same year, which introduced 'Singin' in the Rain'.

The second of the series was *Broadway Melody of 1936* (1935), directed by Roy del Ruth, also with original songs by Freed and Brown, including 'You Are My Lucky Star', and 'Broadway Rhythm', which introduced Eleanor POWELL's tap-dancing. The plot revolved round a young producer set to make a hit with his first Broadway musical, and featured Jack BENNY, Robert TAYLOR, and Vilma and Buddy Ebsen, with a script by Moss Hart. *Broadway Melody of 1938* (1937), was again directed by Roy del Ruth, with Eleanor Powell, Robert Taylor, Sophie Tucker, and a fourteen-year-old Judy GARLAND in her first feature film, singing 'You Made Me Love You' to a photograph of Clark GABLE. The plot concerned a Broadway production, and the cast also included Robert BENCH-LEY, with much of the score again by Freed and Brown. *Broadway Melody of 1940* (1939), directed by Norman Taurog, starred Fred ASTAIRE, Eleanor Powell, and George Murphy; the music and lyrics by Cole PORTER included his haunting 'I Concentrate on You'. This told the story of a pair of male vaudeville dancers, and how one found fame on Broadway. Astaire and Powell danced 'Begin the Beguine', and the reputedly biggest set ever made was built entirely of mirrors for the lavish production. It was re-issued in 1948, entitled simply *Broadway Melody*. The original *Broadway Melody* (1929), was also used as a basis for *Two Girls on Broadway* (*Choose Your Partners* in GB) in 1940, with Joan BLONDELL, Lana TURNER, and George Murphy.

**BROKEN ARROW,** US, 1950. Technicolor; 1½hr. *Dir* Delmer Daves; *prod* Twentieth Century-Fox; *scr* Michael Blankfort, from the novel *Blood Brother* by Elliott Arnold; *ph* Ernest Palmer; *cast* James Stewart (Tom Jeffords), Debra Paget (Conseeahray), Jeff Chandler (Cochise).

The first Western for twenty years to depict the Red Indian in a sympathetic light and to portray love between the races, *Broken Arrow* derives its standpoint from DAVES's early encounter with Navaho and Hopi Indians. Its success prompted a succession of pro-Indian films, exploiting the commercial rewards of social comment.

**BROKEN BLOSSOMS,** US, 1919. 1¾hr. *Dir, prod* D. W. Griffith for United Artists; *scr* Griffith, based on 'The Chink and the Child'

*Broken Blossoms* (D. W. Griffith, 1919)

from Thomas Burke's *Limehouse Nights*; *ph* G. W. Bitzer; *sp eff* Hendrick Sartov; *musical accompaniment* Louis F. Gottschalk; *cast* Lillian Gish (the girl), Richard Barthelmess (the Chinese), Donald Crisp (the girl's father).

In the Limehouse district of London, a Chinese boy falls in love with a young girl who lives in terror of her father, a boxer. After losing a match, the father returns home, and beats his daughter to death. Discovering this, the Chinese boy kills the father, and then himself.

GRIFFITH made of this raw melodrama a violent and yet tender tragedy, meticulously controlled. Griffith's Limehouse is a gloomy, fog-bound quarter, which permeates the whole story with its melancholy atmosphere. Lillian GISH gave one of her most affecting performances, ably partnered by Richard BARTHELMESS, whose reputation is chiefly based on *Broken Blossoms* and TOL'ABLE DAVID (1921).

*Broken Blossoms*, GB, 1936. 1½hr. *Dir* John (Hans) Brahm; *scr* Emlyn Williams, from the story by Thomas Burke; *cast* Emlyn Williams (the Chinese), Dolly Haas (the girl), Arthur Margetson (the father).

When the British sound version was planned, Griffith was invited to supervise the production, but resigned after a short time. The later version had little commercial success.

**BRONCHO BILLY** see ANDERSON, G. M.

*BRONCO BULLFROG*, GB, 1970. 1½hr. *Dir*, *scr* Barney Platts-Mills; *prod* Andrew St John for Maya Films; *ph* Adam Barker-Mill; *mus* Howard Werth, Tony Connor, Keith Gemmell, Trevor Williams; *cast* Del Walker (Del), Anne Gooding (Irene), Sam Shepherd (Bronco Bullfrog), Freda Shepherd (Irene's mother), Dick Philpott (Del's father).

Two East End teenagers fall in love and run away from home and parental disapproval. They hide out with Bronco Bullfrog, a local hero who has just escaped from Borstal. A police sergeant is knocked out when he comes to take Irene home; the film ends here, leaving its young characters apparently trapped in a dead-end of delinquency.

The film was largely improvised, played by local people PLATTS-MILLS had met while working with Joan LITTLEWOOD, and used authentic locations.

Despite considerable critical interest the film did not gain general release outside London.

*BRONENOSETS POTEMKIN* (*The Battleship Potemkin*), USSR, 1925. 1¼hr. *Dir, scr, ed* S. M. Eisenstein; *prod* Goskino; *ph* Edvard Tissé; *asst dir* Grigori Alexandrov; *cast* A. Antonov (Vakukinchuk), Vladimir Barski (Golikov), Grigori Alexandrov (Gilyarovski), M. Gomorov (Matyushenko), sailors of the Red Navy, citizens of Odessa, members of the Proletkult Theatre.

Instructed to make a film commemorating the 1905 revolution, EISENSTEIN chose to base his script on the mutiny on board the battleship *Potemkin* of the Black Sea Fleet, somewhat adapting the historical facts to create an inspired combination of propaganda and art.

The clarity and effectiveness of *Potemkin* derives from the simple, forceful narrative which justifies Eisenstein's use of 'types' rather than fully rounded characters whose complexity might obscure the film's message. TISSÉ, as well as capturing the stylized visual element of Eisenstein's conception, developed new techniques to film the inexperienced players and, especially, the

brilliant sequence of the massacre on the Odessa steps; he is also credited with inventing the brief, effective series of shots showing stone lions apparently rising in support of the people. The film's enduring power lies in Eisenstein's command of rhythmic editing which binds all the elements into a controlled scheme (fully discussed in his essay on *Potemkin*, published in *Notes of a film director,* translated by X. Danko, London, 1959, New York, 1970).

*Potemkin* was an immediate and enduring international success. In Germany it was presented with an accompanying musical score composed by Edmund Meisel and approved by Eisenstein. Modern prints incorporate this score as a sound-track.

**BROOK,** PETER (1925–  ), British director, has worked in the theatre with great distinction since the age of twenty, directing a wide range of plays and operas in London, Paris, and New York. His first film was *A Sentimental Journey* (1943), adapted from Laurence Sterne's novel (1768): he then directed short films for Gaumont British Instructional. His other films show a predilection for literary sources, notably THE BEGGAR'S OPERA (1953), MODERATO CANTABILE (1960), and LORD OF THE FLIES (1963).

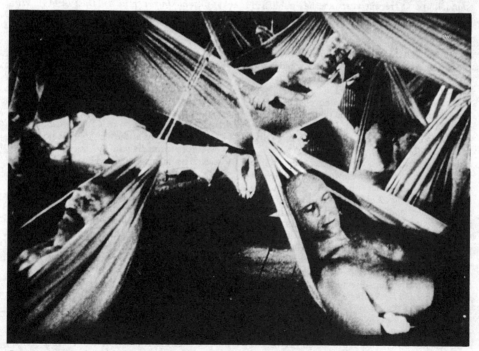

*Bronenosets Potemkin* (S. M. Eisenstein, 1925)

*Marat/Sade* (1966), from the play by Peter WEISS, and *Tell Me Lies*, a protest against the war in Vietnam (1967), were film adaptations of his own stage productions. His *King Lear* (1970), starring Paul SCOFIELD, was the first sound film version of one of SHAKESPEARE's most difficult plays. As a film-maker, Brook has not been unambitious in his choice of subjects, but he is essentially a theatre director.

**BROOKS,** LOUISE (1906–   ), US actress, was a moderately successful star during the twenties. She quarrelled with her studio, PARAMOUNT, and accepted an offer from G. W. PABST who had noticed her in Howard HAWKS's *A Girl in Every Port* (1928). Her performance as the destructively beautiful Lulu in DIE BÜCHSE DER PANDORA (*Pandora's Box*, 1928) was almost universally disliked at the time of the film's first release: few critics appreciated the strong sense of evil and corruption that her passivity conveyed. But on the strength of this one performance she has become a legend and her calm, pale face framed by smooth, bobbed hair has become part of the iconography of cinema. GODARD echoed it in Anna KARINA's make-up and hair-style in part of VIVRE SA VIE (1962). After another silent film for Pabst, *Tagebuch einer Verlorenen* (*Diary of a Lost Girl*, 1929), Louise Brooks returned to Hollywood but failed to establish herself in sound films. Of recent years she has published articles which show her to be a shrewd observer of Hollywood.

**BROOKS,** RICHARD (1912–   ), US director and writer, began by writing scripts for radio and worked briefly in the theatre before transferring to the cinema. His film scripts include John HUSTON's *Key Largo* (1948). As a novelist he is best known for *The Brick Foxhole* (filmed to his own script as *Crossfire* in 1947), *Boiling Point*, and a Hollywood novel, *The Producer* (New York, 1951, London, 1969).

Brooks's work as a director has been prolific and efficient. *Crisis* (1950), with Cary GRANT in a serious part, and the authentically gory buffalo slaughter of *The Last Hunt* (1956) attracted some notice, and the popular success of THE BLACKBOARD JUNGLE (1955), the story of a teacher in a New York slum school, gave him greater freedom in his work. Since 1962 he has been his own producer and his continuing interest in literary subjects is shown in the number of films which as writer–director he has taken from such sources: *The Brothers Karamazov* (1957), *Cat on a Hot Tin Roof* (1958), *Elmer Gantry* (1960), *Sweet Bird of Youth* (1961), *Lord Jim* (1964), and IN COLD BLOOD (1967). He married Jean SIMMONS in 1960 and directed her in *The Happy Ending* (1969).

**BROWN,** CLARENCE (1890–   ), US director who began his Hollywood career in 1915 as assistant to Maurice TOURNEUR. His earlier films include *Smouldering Fires* (1924), starring Pauline FREDERICK, *The Goose Woman* (1925), and *The Eagle* (1926) with Rudolph VALENTINO. In a long career with METRO-GOLDWYN-MAYER he became noted for the visual elegance of his style as Greta GARBO's favourite director, launching her Hollywood career with *Flesh and the Devil* (1927), followed by *Woman of Affairs* (1928), *Romance* (1930), *Anna Christie* (1930), *Inspiration* (1931), ANNA KARENINA (1935), and *Conquest* (1937, *Marie Walewska* in GB). Garbo's co-star in *Romance* was Clark GABLE, and Clarence Brown frequently directed Gable later, including *Possessed* (1931), *Night Flight* (1933), *Wife vs. Secretary* (1936), *Of Human Hearts* (1938), *Idiot's Delight* (1939), *They Met in Bombay* (1941), and *To Please a Lady* (1950). He directed most of MGM's other top stars, notably Joan CRAWFORD (*Chained*, 1934; *The Gorgeous Hussy*, 1936); Spencer TRACY (*Edison the Man*, 1940; *Plymouth Adventure*, 1952); James STEWART and Hedy LAMARR (*Come Live with Me*, 1941); Elizabeth TAYLOR (*National Velvet*, 1944); and Katharine HEPBURN (*Song of Love*, 1947). Notable among his numerous other films were *Ah! Wilderness* (1935), *The Rains Came* (1939), *The Yearling* (1946), and *Intruder in the Dust* (1949). With their soft-focus pictorial quality, Brown's films often verge on the sentimental, but they have a good sense of personal relationships and even his glossy, large-budget productions retain a human dimension.

**BROWN,** JOE E. (1892–1973), US comedian, joined a circus at the age of nine, later becoming a professional baseball player and a vaudeville artist. His first film was *Crooks Can't Wait* (1928), and he was at the height of his popularity as a screen comedian in the thirties and early forties. His talents extended to acrobatics and novelty dancing, but he was particularly famous for his clown-like features, above all his extraordinarily wide mouth to which reference was sometimes made in the titles of his films (*Funnyface*, 1935; *Wide Open Faces*, 1937; *Shut My Big Mouth*, 1941). In later years he appeared in supporting parts, including roles in SOME LIKE IT HOT (1959) and *Comedy of Terrors* (1963).

**BROWN,** PAMELA (1917–75), British actress, whose main reputation was made on the London stage, but whose infrequent screen appearances were invariably striking. She was an overpowering presence in *I Know Where I'm Going* (1945), and her unusual looks, acting talent, and personal magnetism gave weight to minor roles, particularly in *The Tales of Hoffmann* (POWELL, 1951), *Richard III* (OLIVIER, 1955), *Becket* (1964), and *Secret Ceremony* (LOSEY, 1968).

**BROWNING,** TOD (1882–1962), US director, went to Hollywood in 1914 and worked for a time for D. W. GRIFFITH. In 1917 he directed his first film, *Jim Bludso.* His unique combination of eerie mysticism and macabre humour began to make itself felt in *The Unholy Three* (1925). This concerned a ventriloquist, a dwarf, and a giant, and starred Lon CHANEY who was in several successful Browning films. An armless knife-thrower was the villain of *The Unknown* (1927). *London after Midnight* (1927), a story of murder and hypnosis, again starred Lon Chaney. In 1931 Browning directed the definitive version of DRACULA, with Bela LUGOSI, and the following year FREAKS, in which all but two of the actors are physically deformed. He re-worked the Dracula theme in *The Mark of the Vampire* (1935). *Devil Doll* (1936), a tale of telepathy and devious revenge, was co-scripted by Erich von STROHEIM. *Miracles for Sale* (1939), set in the world of conjuring and illusionism, was Browning's last film: he sank into obscurity and his death was erroneously announced in 1944.

**BROWNLOW,** KEVIN (1938– ), British producer–director. An ardent film collector and amateur film-maker, he entered the industry as an assistant editor in 1955. He edited documentaries, including Lindsay ANDERSON's *The White Bus* (1967), and Tony RICHARDSON's feature *The Charge of the Light Brigade* (1968). Besides his first feature film IT HAPPENED HERE (1966), Brownlow has made several documentaries. *Abel Gance, the Charm of Dynamite* (1968), which contains extracts from J'ACCUSE (1919), LA ROUE (1922), and NAPOLÉON (1927), is a tribute to GANCE, to whom Brownlow also dedicated his book *The parade's gone by*, London, 1969, a re-appraisal of the silent era in the American cinema.

**BRUNIUS,** JACQUES (1906–67), French director whose other activities included those of writer, broadcaster, actor, and critic. After studying aeronautics, Brunius entered the cinema in the late twenties as an assistant to René CLAIR, Luis BUÑUEL, and Jean RENOIR, appearing in a leading role in the latter's UNE PARTIE DE CAMPAGNE (1936). In the thirties Brunius was a member of the Surrealist group (see SURREALISM) and was, with the PRÉVERT brothers, a moving spirit of the left-wing GROUPE OCTOBRE.

Jacques Brunius in *Une Partie de campagne* (Jean Renoir, 1936)

He escaped to Britain in 1940 and worked with the Free French on radio programmes laced with cryptic information for the French Resistance. He settled in Britain and later appeared in several British films, notably *The Wooden Horse* (1950).

His first film as director was *Autour d'une évasion* (1933), and he also made a number of short films, notably *Violons d'Ingres* (1937), *Somewhere to Live* (1952), and *The Blakes Slept Here* (1954). He contributed an important chapter on the silent avant-garde French film to Roger MANVELL's *Experiment in the film* (1949), wrote for SIGHT AND SOUND, and made many intellectually stimulating contributions to radio programmes on the arts.

**BRYNNER,** YUL (1916– ), US actor of Russian origin, made his film début in *Port of New York* (1944) then disappeared from the screen until he repeated his stage success in the RODGERS and HAMMERSTEIN musical *The King and I* (1956). Depending more upon chilly mannerisms and on the fascinatingly perverse trademark of a totally bald head than on his acting resources, his field has been limited; but he was notable as the leader of a band of Western samurai in THE MAGNIFICENT SEVEN (1960).

**BUCHANAN,** JACK (1891–1957), British musical comedy actor who, during the twenties and thirties, was immensely popular as a debonair leading man of stage musicals and revues. He made films in both Britain and Hollywood but his particular charm transferred uneasily to the screen. By co-starring him with Fred ASTAIRE in THE BAND WAGON (1953), Vincente MINNELLI brought Buchanan back to public notice and his career revived in the last years of his life.

***BÜCHSE DER PANDORA, Die*** (*Pandora's Box*), Germany, 1928. 1½hr. *Dir* G. W. Pabst; *prod* Nero-Film; *scr* Laszlo Wajda, from *Die Büchse der Pandora* and *Erdgeist* by Franz Wedekind; *ph* Günther Krampf; *cast* Louise Brooks (Lulu), Fritz Kortner (Dr Schön), Franz Lederer (Alva Schön), Carl Goetz (Schilgoch), Alice Roberts (Anna), Gustav Diessi (Jack the Ripper).

Lulu, the sensual yet untouchable woman whose type appeared frequently in Wedekind's plays, spreads emotional and physical destruction before meeting her own fate at the hands of Jack the Ripper. PABST used the story to develop two of his favourite themes: the social breakdown of the post-war years and the exploration of various aspects of female eroticism. *Die Büchse der Pandora* was far from successful, with the critics who felt that a silent film could not possibly be made from such a literary source

as Wedekind's work, and with the German public who deeply resented the temerity of an American actress in playing 'our Lulu': they dismissed Louise BROOKS's haunting subtlety as simply bad acting. Like most of Pabst's films it was heavily censored in many countries: in France, among other changes, the ending omitted Jack the Ripper and showed Lulu being converted by the Salvation Army.

**BUCZKOWSKI,** LEONARD (1900–66), Polish director, whose career from 1923 until his death spanned not only the transition from silent to sound films but also the difficult years of political upheaval in Poland. He directed *Zakazane piosenki* (*Forbidden Songs*, 1947), the first feature film of the newly nationalized film industry, *Skarb* (*The Treasure*, 1949), a delightful comedy, and many other popular fiction films as well as shorts and documentaries.

**BUFFALO BILL,** stage name of William Frederick Cody (1846–1917), an Indian scout who became a hero of dime-novels and then many Westerns, among them *The Plainsman* (1937) and *Pony Express* (1953): his broad-brimmed hat was the prototype of the Stetson. His Wild West Show toured Europe as well as the United States (a command performance was given at Windsor Castle at Queen Victoria's Golden Jubilee Celebrations) and helped to establish the myth adopted by the American cinema from its earliest days. He founded the town of Cody, Wyoming, a few miles east of the Yellowstone Park, which he helped to popularize.

**BUGS BUNNY,** created in 1936, was a wisecracking Brooklyn rabbit, the indomitable hero of many WARNER BROS cartoons. He was created by a team of three: Chuck Jones, Tex Avery, and Fritz Freleng; his voice was that of Mel Blanc, like all the other Warner cartoon characters. (See ANIMATION.)

**BULGARIA.** Because of economic backwardness and political vicissitudes, film production began late and remained small and uneven until nationalization after the Second World War. Foreign films were projected in some of the cities from 1897, but the first Bulgarian film was not made until 1910: *Bulgaran e galant*, a Max LINDER-inspired comedy by Vasil Gendov, then aged nineteen. Gendov, working with much enthusiasm but small means, battled for thirty years to create a national industry, and was recognized as an honoured artist when the state finally took over production. Nationalistic themes, particularly anti-Turkish, dominated such production as there was between the wars, with Gendov remaining the moving spirit and making films of all kinds, from comedy to social and political observation. His *Diavolat v Sofia* (*The Devil in Sofia*, 1922) was a satire, and *Bunt rabov* (*The Revolt of the Slaves*, 1934), one of the first two Bulgarian sound films, was an account of the life of the revolutionary Vasil Levski which was banned and released only after severe cutting. During the thirties the emerging movement among intellectuals and artists against Fascism struggled to find expression, and in 1931 Boris Greshov made *Beskrastni grobovi* (*Tombs without Crosses*); but although the movement intensified after the stirring speech by Gheorghi Dimitrov (later President of the Socialist state) at the Comintern of 1935, cinema offered little outlet, and Greshov's remained the only overtly anti-Fascist film.

In 1939 Bulgarsko Dĕlo was formed for the production of weekly newsreels of the same name, and it became the organization within which resistance was secretly fostered. Production during the war became more consistent, with a certain amount of anti-government propaganda slipping into the routine historical and folk-lore themes which were predominant. The radical reorganization in 1948, with the establishment of the Socialist state and nationalization of the film industry, gave Bulgaria the opportunity of building an industry virtually from scratch. Unlike the other Eastern European countries, Bulgaria did not set up a film school, preferring to rely on those in other countries, particularly Russia. Soviet production naturally provided the pattern for the new industry, which gradually increased annual feature production to ten by 1960. Anti-Nazi and socialist-realist themes dominated until, towards the end of the fifties, a new generation of film-makers tried to evolve a more complex approach.

*Zvezdi* (*Stars*, 1959, a co-production with East Germany directed by Konrad Wolf) gave impetus to the movement in its attempt to personalize its evaluation of Nazism, and at about the same time the films of Ranghel Vulchanov dealt with more personal themes. His *Slantzeto i siankata* (*Sun and Shadow*, 1962) was, with *Zvezdi*, one of the first films to be fairly widely seen outside Bulgaria. Foreign attention and the emergence of 'new waves' in other countries had their effect, and the opening of the studio complex at Bojana near Sofia in 1963 gave impetus to further production, which rose to twenty-five in 1970. Vulo Radov developed a poetic and humanistic style with several films during the sixties, including *Kradetzat na praskovi* (*The Peach Thief*, 1964) and *Nai dalgata noset* (*The Longest Night*, 1967). His *Cernite angheli* (*Black Angels*, 1970), however, in romanticizing the murder of Fascists by a cheerful young Resistance group during the war, falls into a very

innocuous pattern to which the only objection might be that, like BONNIE AND CLYDE (1967), it glamorizes violence.

Other outstanding directors of the sixties are Grisha Ostrovski and Todor Stoyanov who with the writer and poet Blaga Dimitrova made *Otklonenie* (*Side-tracked*, 1967), remarkable for its sophisticated structure with flashbacks. Binka Zheliazkova also dealt with contemporary themes in *Prizurvaniat balon* (1967), which was quickly withdrawn after its first release and held up for several years. In 1969 two other films questioned oppression, one a first feature by Gheorghi Stoyanov, a mixture of fantasy and black comedy about brutal treatment of revolutionaries, *Ptitzi i hrutki* (*Birds and Greyhounds*), and the other *Bialata staia* (*The White Room*) by Metodi Andonov. Even older directors like Borislav Shariliev turned, in the late sixties, to personal subjects, as in his *Sbogom Prijateli!* (*Goodbye, chums*, 1969), examining personal relationships between teachers and pupils. Among the general run of thrillers, comedies, and historical dramas, the theme of resisting oppression recurs in the work of some directors: Milen Nikolov's *Gola savest* (*Naked Conscience*, 1971), although set before the war and safely within the anti-Fascist pattern, is concerned with oppression in a wider context. Khristo Khristov's *Posledno lyato* (*The Last Summer*, 1973) examines individual resistance from another standpoint.

The production of documentary and popular science films has been fostered by the nationalized industry, and in the past twenty years a lively animation studio has developed, largely in the wake of the great success in 1955 of *Iunak Marco* (*Marco the Hero*) by Todor Dinov, who has remained outstanding in the animation field, and has also in *Ikonostasat* (*Ikonostasis*, 1969, with Khristo Khristov) started working in features. Endowed with fine actors who alternate between stage and screen, and building on its experience since 1948, the Bulgarian industry has established itself as a thriving and lively national enterprise.

**BUÑUEL, LUIS** (1900– ), Spanish director of cultured bourgeois family, was educated first at a Jesuit school where the totally repressive system of instruction made a lasting impression on him. Although ostensibly a well-behaved pupil he has acknowledged various bizarre and blasphemous activities outside school hours. At the University of Madrid, where he studied in 1920–3, he met Salvador DALI and the poet García Lorca. In 1925 he went to Paris. Fritz LANG's *Der müde Tod* (1921) turned his interest to film-making: he became a pupil at the Académie du Cinéma and worked for Jean EPSTEIN on

*Mauprat* (1926) and *La Chute de la maison Usher* (1928). He was also an assistant on Etievant and Malpas's *La Sirène des tropiques* (1928). Buñuel soon fell out with Epstein and, using money sent by his mother, he made his first film, UN CHIEN ANDALOU (1928), in collaboration with Dali. The film is a demonstration of automatism— the release of irrational, inconsequential associations—much in vogue among the Surrealists at the time. The influence on Buñuel of SURREALISM was fundamental and lasting, although Epstein warned him against having anything to do with it. In October 1930 L'ÂGE D'OR opened at STUDIO 28. It caused a scandal and was quickly withdrawn. In the film desire and love (*l'amour fou* of the Surrealists) bring about the downfall of the order of the day. There are important references to the Marquis de Sade, whose revolutionary ideas about the fulfilment of desire have meant much to Buñuel. Buñuel claims that his ideas have not changed since *L'Âge d'or* was made.

At the time of the *L'Âge d'or* scandal Buñuel was in Hollywood. Back in Spain, financed by winnings from a lottery, he made LAS HURDES (*Land Without Bread*, 1932) a documentary about the sufferings in Las Hurdes, an impoverished region of Spain. The images in the film are terrifying: the chronically sick, the poor and the deranged, the dead and decaying in their hovels are contrasted with the rich trappings of the Church. A fierce exposure of extreme inhumanity and injustice, the film has had very limited circulation.

After *Las Hurdes* Buñuel worked at dubbing for PARAMOUNT in Paris and for WARNER BROS in Spain. He had a hand in the COMPILATION *Madrid '36* (1937) about the Spanish Civil War. He was invited to New York to make anti-Nazi films and later documentaries for the American army, but, after being accused by his old friend Dali of being an atheist he was dropped from the project. In 1945 he was working as a producer for Warner Bros. With the money he earned he left for Mexico, where he directed a musical, *Gran Casino* (1947), which was a box-office failure. His next film, a comedy called *El gran calavera* (*The Great Madcap*, 1949), was very successful and this allowed Buñuel to make one of his greatest films, LOS OLVIDADOS (*The Young and the Damned*, 1950). He became regarded in Mexico as a competent director, equally at home with the fierce social criticism of *Los Olvidados* or silly melodramas like *Susana* (1951).

From this time his increasing independence allowed him to place his personal stamp on his

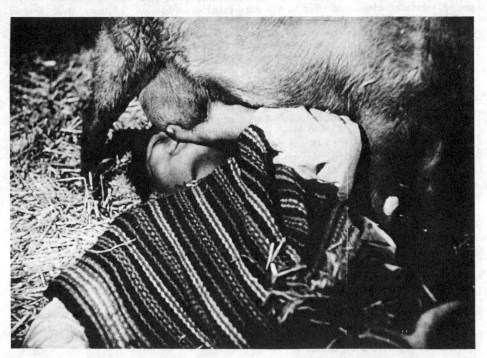

*Los Olvidados* (Luis Buñuel, 1950)

films. In *Subido al cielo*, his fourth film of 1951, he imbued a picaresque melodrama with the sort of black humour that the Surrealists prescribed as an antidote to bourgeois seriousness and sentimentality. *El Bruto* (1952), like *L'Âge d'or*, emphasizes the liberating force of sexual passion. ROBINSON CRUSOE (1952) incorporates much of his characteristic imagery, especially dreams and insects. In *El* (1952) Buñuel recapitulates his ideas of the subversive powers of love, and *l'amour fou* is also the subject of *Abismos de pasión* (1953), an adaptation of WUTHERING HEIGHTS. The last film of Buñuel's prolific and propitious period in Mexico was ENSAYO DE UN CRIMEN (*The Criminal Life of Archibaldo de la Cruz*, 1955), a film of delirious eroticism, full of the blackest humour.

In 1955 he returned to France, where he was swamped with offers from producers. He chose to make *Cela s'appelle l'aurore*, about revolutionary loyalty and social struggle. In his next film, *La Mort en ce jardin* (1956), Buñuel introduced the figure of the priest who, although likeable, is ineffective and is ultimately forced to admit that it is impossible to live a pure Christian life. Buñuel was to develop this idea in later films, including NAZARÍN (1958) in which the priest of the title comes to the conclusion that to practise religion adds to, not diminishes, suffering. After two lesser works, *La Fièvre monte à El Pao* (1959) and *La Joven* (*The Young One*, 1960), Buñuel directed one of his most important films, VIRIDIANA (1961), where his iconoclastic humour reaches its height in the tramps' 'Last Supper'. *Viridiana* was Buñuel's first opportunity to work independently in Spain since the horrific exposures of *Las Hurdes*; it was immediately banned there.

He returned to Mexico to make EL ANGEL EXTERMINADOR (*The Exterminating Angel*, 1962), in which a group of socialites, mysteriously trapped in a single room for several days, are gradually stripped of the protective veneer of civilized life. Buñuel's treatment of LE JOURNAL D'UNE FEMME DE CHAMBRE (*Diary of a Chambermaid*, 1964) conveys provincial sexual repression through a humorous approach to the characters' foibles and habits which serves to make the film's climactic cruelty all the more shocking. *Simon del desierto* (*Simon of the Desert*, 1965) has again the theme of the ultimate failure of absolute piety. His most recent films, *Belle de jour* (1966), LA VOIE LACTÉE (*The Milky Way*, 1969), *Tristaña* (1970), LE CHARME DISCRET DE LA BOURGEOISIE (1972), and *Le Fantôme de la liberté* (1974), have increasingly reverted to the anecdotal structure of his earliest work in order to comment ironically on man's bizarre attempts to civilize the irrational.

Because he abhors any institution or dogma that in effect destroys human freedom—he fell foul of the Catholic Church at an early age—Buñuel is much concerned with the problems posed by Christian faith. The weapons with which he attempts to destroy moral and physical constraint include blasphemy, eroticism, the fulfilment of desire, anti-clericalism, black humour, and the resources of the unconscious mind. To him, also, middle-class morality is immoral because it is founded on social injustice: the only road a man can travel is the road of rebellion.

Although he has usually had to work within a limited budget, the unpretentious visual style of his films is deliberate and is an important element in his greatness: he avoids any display of bravura technique.

His high status among discriminating audiences is in part an acknowledgement not only of the personal integrity which has carried him through the years of commercial restraints with his aims and beliefs intact but also of the high level of achievement of many of his films. Ironically, the arch-enemy of any kind of established society has become an admired and respected figure in the development of cinema.

**BURKE,** BILLIE (1884–1970), US actress, made her first big success in London in 1903. There followed a series of Broadway appearances and she married Florenz Ziegfeld in 1914. A lovely redhead, she was lured into films as early as 1916, but her parts were so poor that she returned to the stage where her success in *The Vinegar Tree* led to the type-casting from which she never really escaped. So good were her portrayals of fluffy, pretty, bird-brained ladies that she repeated them in dozens of films, including DINNER AT EIGHT (1933), *Topper* (1937), THE WIZARD OF OZ (1939), THE MAN WHO CAME TO DINNER (1942), *Father of the Bride* (1950). She published an autobiography, *With a feather on my nose*, London, 1950.

**BURMESE HARP, The,** see BIRUMA NO TATEGOTO

**BURTON,** RICHARD (1925– ), Welsh actor, real name Richard Jenkins, was one of thirteen children of a South Wales coal-miner. After service with the RAF he became involved with undergraduate theatricals while a student at Oxford. He earned a considerable reputation in the London theatre, particularly in the Shakespearian roles he played at the Old Vic. Although his first film appearance was in *The Last Days of Dolwyn* (1948) it was several years—interspersed with several miscast roles in Hollywood films and two marriages, particularly his well-publicized marriage to Elizabeth TAYLOR—

before his good looks and vigorous acting ability became well-known to cinema audiences.

His films include THE ROBE (1953), LOOK BACK IN ANGER (1959), *Becket* (1964), Martin RITT's *The Spy Who Came in from the Cold* (1965), and *Anne of the Thousand Days* (1969). Latterly he has often co-starred with Elizabeth Taylor, most notably in CLEOPATRA (1962), *Who's Afraid of Virginia Woolf?* (1966), THE TAMING OF THE SHREW (1967), and *The Comedians* (1967). He co-directed *Dr Faustus* (1967), a film record of his Oxford stage production, and John GIELGUD's Broadway production of 1964 in which Burton played HAMLET was also filmed.

**BUSHMAN,** FRANCIS X. (Xavier) (1883–1966), US actor famous during the silent era. Handsome and muscular, he began his career with the ESSANAY Company in 1911. Metro's ROMEO AND JULIET (1916) was one of several films in which he appeared with Beverly Bayne as an early 'love team'. Bushman blamed the disclosure that they were married for the subsequent blight on his career. He made a comeback in 1925, however, in BEN-HUR as the villainous Messala. After another period of film inactivity he played in supporting roles in a number of mainly undistinguished sound films until the year of his death.

*BUS STOP,* US, 1956. CinemaScope; 1½hr; Eastman Color. *Dir* Joshua Logan; *prod* Twentieth Century-Fox; *scr* George Axelrod, based on the play by William Inge; *ph* Milton Krasner; *cast* Marilyn Monroe (Cherie), Don Murray (Bo), Arthur O'Connell (Virgil), Betty Field (Grace), Hope Lange (Elma).

The handsome, randy virgin Bo, on a visit to Phoenix to ride in a rodeo and provide himself with a woman, abducts a torch-singer, although with honourable intentions. Because of the coarseness of its handling of sexual drives, *Bus Stop* fails in its apparent aim of being a joyously bawdy romp, but Marilyn MONROE's wistful, untalented Cherie was one of her most substantial performances.

*BUTCH CASSIDY AND THE SUNDANCE KID,* US, 1969. Panavision; 2hr; De Luxe Color. *Dir* George Roy Hill; *prod* Twentieth Century-Fox/Campanile Productions; *scr* William Goldman; *ph* Conrad Hall; *mus* Burt Bacharach; *cast* Paul Newman (Butch Cassidy), Robert Redford (the Sundance Kid), Katherine Ross (Etta Place), Strother Martin (Percy Garris), Jeff Corey (Sheriff Bledsoe), George Furth (Woodcock).

A high-spirited story of two bank robbers and their audacious methods of robbing the Union Pacific Railroad—twice. At the second attempt their plans misfire and they flee to Bolivia, where they continue their activities until killed in a gun battle with the Bolivian Army.

The film gives a highly romanticized version of the exploits of two real outlaws: the chase which comprises most of the second part of the film being completely fabricated. NEWMAN and REDFORD are likeable rogues, and the film is visually striking, making interesting use of montage effects. Cheerfully eclectic in style, and reminiscent of a range of films which includes JULES ET JIM (1961) and BONNIE AND CLYDE (1967), it achieves its own distinctive charm and poignancy, with added appeal from its musical score and theme song, 'Raindrops'.

The making of the film is interestingly documented in *The Making of 'Butch Cassidy and the Sundance Kid'* (1972) a forty-minute film made by Robert Crawford.

*BUTCHER, The,* see BOUCHER, LE

# C

**CABARET,** US, 1972. Technicolor; 2hr. *Dir, choreo* Bob Fosse; *scr* Jay Presson Allen, from the musical play by Joe Masteroff, John Kandor, Fred Ebb; *ph* Geoffrey Unsworth; *mus* Kandor; *lyr* Ebb; *cast* Liza Minnelli (Sally Bowles), Michael York (Brian Roberts), Helmut Griem (Maximilian von Heune), Joel Grey (Master of Ceremonies).

Based directly on Christopher Isherwood's *Goodbye to Berlin* (1939) and less on John Van Druten's adaptation of that book for the stage, *I Am a Camera* (filmed in Britain in 1955), *Cabaret* is shaped round a young Englishman's summer in Berlin in the thirties, his meeting with an American cabaret singer, Sally Bowles, and their relationship with a rich German baron.

The cabaret itself is the film's centrepiece, reflecting the frenetic and ugly nature of German society at that time more emphatically than the interpolated Nazi incidents. The songs, impressively staged and filmed, provide pungent comment on the situation. Structure, camerawork, and editing are incisive. The performances are outstanding: Joel Grey as the insidious, repellent Master of Ceremonies, Michael YORK as Brian, and Liza MINNELLI, who won an OSCAR, capturing the recklessness and fragility of Sally Bowles.

**CABINETT DES DR CALIGARI, Das** (*The Cabinet of Dr Caligari*), Germany, 1919. 1¼hr. *Dir* Robert Wiene; *prod* Erich Pommer for

*Das Cabinett des Dr Caligari* (Robert Wiene, 1919)

Decla; *scr* Carl Mayer, Hans Janowitz; *des* Walter Röhrig, Walter Reimann, Hermann Warm; *ph* Willy Hameister; *cast* Werner Krauss (Caligari), Conrad Veidt (Cesare), Lil Dagover (Jane), Friedrich Feher (Francis).

Caligari is a hypnotist whose somnambulist, Cesare, kills the hero's friend and carries off his girl. Having exposed Caligari, the hero is himself revealed as an inmate of a lunatic asylum where Caligari is director.

*Caligari*'s reputation is based on its position in the development of EXPRESSIONISM in the German cinema. The style of design in particular, sets painted mainly flat with distortions of perspective emphasized by grotesquely angled lighting, became known as 'Caligarism' and had a great influence on German films of the next decade, although its long-term effect has tended to be overrated.

The original outline by MAYER and JANOWITZ represented Caligari unequivocally as the insane villain: the framework, which by representing the hero as mad reverses the authors' intentions, was added by POMMER. Fritz LANG, who was originally to have directed, and WIENE both accepted Pommer's version against the bitter protests of the authors.

After the National Socialist Government implemented a policy of Germanizing words derived from French, the film became generally known as *Das Kabinett des Dr Caligari*.

A parody, *Das Kabinett des Dr Larifari* (1930), was directed in Germany by Robert Wolmuth; an American remake, *The Cabinet of Dr Caligari* (1962), was a poor pseudopsychological melodrama.

**CABIN IN THE SKY**, US, 1943. 1½hr. *Dir* Vincente Minnelli; *prod* Arthur Freed for MGM; *scr* Joseph Schrank, based on the musical play by Lynn Root; *ph* Sydney Wagner; *lyr* John Latouche; *mus* Vernon Duke; *additional mus and lyr* E. T. Harburg, Harold Arlen, Duke Ellington; *cast* Ethel Waters (Petunia), Eddie 'Rochester' Anderson (Little Joe), Lena Horne (Georgia Brown), Louis Armstrong (Trumpeter), Rex Ingram (Lucifer Jr), Duke Ellington and his orchestra, the Hall Johnson Choir.

While unconscious after a brawl, Little Joe dreams of the struggle for his soul between his wife, Petunia, and Lucifer Jr. Petunia's prayers triumph, and Joe gets another chance.

Despite its exploitation of negro stereotypes, MINNELLI's musical fantasy succeeded, aided by the highly stylized production and the fine music and playing by the all-Black cast. Ethel Waters re-created her stage role, and notable numbers included her 'Happiness Is Just a Thing Called Joe' and Lena Horne and Eddie Anderson in the duet 'Life's Full of Consequences'.

**CABIRIA**, Italy, 1914. 2¼hr. *Dir, scr* Piero Fosco (Giovanni Pastrone); *prod* Itala Film; *ph* Segundo de Chomón, Giovanni Tomatis, Augusto Batagliotti, Natale Chiusano; *literary adviser* Gabriele d'Annunzio; *cast* Italia Almirante Mazzini (Sophonisba), Lidia Quaranta (Cabiria), Umberto Mozzato (Fulvio Axilla), Bartolomeo Pagano (Maciste), Vitale De Stefano (Massinissa).

The film, following the adventures of the slave girl Cabiria during the Second Punic War, was inspired by the novel *Carthage in Flames* by Emilio Salgari. Its original running time was more than four hours.

PASTRONE was to an astonishing extent the sole author of this massive film. His name remained unknown at first (not until the sound re-issue of 1931 was his pseudonym attached to the film); this was because d'Annunzio's name had been bought for prestige reasons. In fact d'Annunzio's handsomely paid contribution was limited to the wording of the titles and the choice of some of the characters' names. The scale on which the production was financed was unprecedented, surpassing even that of QUO VADIS (1913). Shooting took six months, in the studios and in locations carefully picked in Sicily, the Alps, and Tunisia. Pastrone and his chief cameraman Segundo de CHOMÓN made some revolutionary technical innovations. The camera was moved on a DOLLY and on a primitive CRANE. There were innovations in lighting, notably lighting from below. The original film was tinted, and Pastrone commissioned a 'Sinfonia del fuoco' (Symphony of Fire), to be performed during projection by an orchestra of eighty and a choir of seventy.

*Cabiria* had a tremendous reception from the public and critics alike, and was the occasion for the first complete film review in the Italian press—three-quarters of a column in the *Corriere della sera*. It was the first film to be shown in a fashionable New York theatre, the Astor, and the film world was startled by its success with sophisticated audiences. It confirmed and enlarged the impression made by its precursors, *Quo Vadis*, Capellani's LES MISÉRABLES (1912), and CASERINI's *Gli ultimi giorni di Pompeii* (*The Last Days of Pompeii*, 1913). Its success enabled GRIFFITH to gain support for his large-scale projects: he is said to have acquired a print for himself and studied it. It also created the character of MACISTE, who has remained a favourite subject of popular Italian films.

**CABIRIA** (Fellini) see NOTTI DI CABIRIA

**CACCIA TRAGICA** (*Pursuit*), Italy, 1947. 1½hr. *Dir* Giuseppe De Santis; *prod* G. Giorgio

Agliani; *scr* Carlo Lizzani, De Santis, Cesare Zavattini, Michelangelo Antonioni, Umberto Barbaro; *ph* Otello Martelli; *ed* Mario Serandrei; *mus* Giuseppe Rosati; *cast* Vivi Gioi (Daniela), Andrea Checchi (Alberto), Carla Del Paggio (Giovanna), Vittorio Duse (Giuseppe), Massimo Girotti (Michele), Checcho Rissone (Mimi), Guido Dalla Valle (the German).

The action is set in the Romagna district shortly after the Liberation. A lorry is ambushed, a bride kidnapped, and money that will buy tools for a collective farm is stolen: the peasants unite to hunt down the bandits. DE SANTIS' fluid camera movement (with frequent crane shots, a rarity in post-war Italy) and attractive groupings within the frame add a slightly melodramatic vitality to his serious treatment of Italy's post-war ills.

**CACOYANNIS,** MICHAEL (1922–   ), Greek Cypriot director, studied law in London and spent the war years with the BBC Greek Service. After the war he worked as an actor on the London stage and developed an interest in directing. In 1953 he went to Athens to direct his first film, *Kyriakatiko xypanima* (*Windfall in Athens*). *Stella* (1955) starred Melina MERCOURI as a Carmen-like figure in a contemporary Athenian setting. In his next two films, TO KORITSI ME TA MAVRA (*The Girl in Black*, 1955) and TO TELEFTEO PSEMMA (*A Matter of Dignity*, 1957), as in his first, his perceptive direction was greatly aided by the striking performance of Ellie LAMBETTI; the addition of Walter LASSALLY as cameraman to his team gave the films a distinctive visual stamp.

Cacoyannis's last few years in Britain had coincided with the questioning and ferment which resulted in the FREE CINEMA movement: his talent found its best expression in pithy and affectionate observation of everyday Greek life. The hard facts of international distribution perhaps conspired with later political developments to prevent the full development of the cinematic flair which had already, with *To telefteo psemma*, acquired bite and maturity. In 1960 he made one more modern film in Greece, *Eroica* (*Our Last Spring*), with an international cast and English dialogue, then went to Italy to make *Il relitto* (*The Wastrel*).

*Elektra* (1961), starring Irene PAPAS, photographed by Lassally, and with music by Mikis THEODORAKIS, was the first of a trilogy from Euripides. Then, after the considerable international success of *Zorba the Greek* (1965), an action extravaganza starring Anthony QUINN, Cacoyannis made *The Day the Fish Came Out* (1967), a strangely heavy-handed allegory. The second part of the Euripides trilogy followed, *The Trojan Women* (1971), an international co-production starring Katharine HEPBURN, Vanessa REDGRAVE, and Irene PAPAS.

**CAESAR AND CLEOPATRA,** GB, 1945. Technicolor; $2\frac{1}{4}$hr. *Dir, prod, scr* Gabriel Pascal, from the play by George Bernard Shaw; *ph* F. A. Young, Robert Krasker, Jack Hildyard, Jack Cardiff; *des* Oliver Messel; *mus* Georges Auric; *cast* Vivien Leigh (Cleopatra), Claude Rains (Caesar), Flora Robson (Ftatateeta), Stewart Granger (Apollodorus), Basil Sydney (Rufio), Cecil Parker (Britannus).

It was claimed that $£1\frac{1}{4}$ million was spent on Gabriel PASCAL's lavish production (including, reputedly, a portable Sphinx introduced to the Egyptian location) which was in part intended to demonstrate the potential of the British film industry early in its post-war resurgence. However, in spite of the film's elaborate settings and distinguished acting performances, Shaw's mannered dialogue was uneasily grafted on to a conventional film treatment.

**CAGNEY,** JAMES (1904–   ), US actor, made his film début in *Sinner's Holiday* (1931) after some years in vaudeville as a singer and soft-shoe dancer, and achieved instant notoriety when he ground half a grapefruit into Mae Clarke's face in PUBLIC ENEMY (1931). He became identified with the small-time crook, aggressive as a fighting cock and as amoral, in films like *G-Men* (1935), ANGELS WITH DIRTY FACES (1938), THE ROARING TWENTIES (1939), and *Each Dawn I Die* (1939). One aspect of the quintessential Irish-American, pugnacious and cock-sure, was embodied in these typical characterizations; it contrasted with the kind of decent, warm-hearted Irishness conveyed by Pat O'BRIEN who often played the cop, warder, or priest to Cagney's criminal.

As the style of GANGSTER FILMS changed Cagney's standard roles became more vicious and psychotic, for example in *White Heat* (1949), *Kiss Tomorrow Goodbye* (1950), and *Love Me or Leave Me* (1955).

All Cagney's performances depended on a range of mannerisms—staccato delivery, curling lip, edgy, explosive movements—which added up to a kind of violent sex-appeal that greatly helped his popularity. They were carried wholesale into more sympathetic roles such as Bottom in A MIDSUMMER NIGHT'S DREAM (1935) and George M. Cohan in *Yankee Doodle Dandy* (1942)—another legendary Irish-American, and a reversion to his earlier song-and-dance roles for which he won his only OSCAR. In *One, Two, Three* (1961), Billy WILDER allowed the Cagney characteristics to dominate the film, a frenetic and violent farce.

Cagney has directed one film, *Short Cut to Hell* (1957), a remake of *This Gun for Hire* (1942).

**CAHIERS DU CINÉMA**, French film review born out of *La Revue du cinéma*, first published in 1951 under the editorship of André BAZIN, Lo Duca, and Jacques DONIOL-VALCROZE.

Bazin gave *Cahiers* his own aesthetic, the idea of a popular cinema that countered the element of pretentiousness then current in film criticism. His recognition of the merits of Hollywood films, in particular, led to a revaluation of the contribution made by the commercial industry to film art.

In 1955 there began to emerge a new generation of cinema-conscious writers, some of whom were to become film-makers of the NOUVELLE VAGUE, among them Domarchi, GODARD, RIVETTE, Scherer, CHABROL, and in particular TRUFFAUT. The group developed the '*politique des auteurs*' (see CRITICISM, AUTEUR THEORY), a polemical stance which involved the formation of a pantheon of hitherto neglected directors, mainly American, with HITCHCOCK at their head, and the developing of a critical vocabulary including such terms as *auteur* and *mise-en-scène*. Over-enthusiastic application of the method led to some exaggerated conclusions, but *Cahiers*' influence on both film-makers and the young cinema audience was considerable. FILM CULTURE in the US and *Movie* in Britain took up and developed the 'auteur' method; it was challenged by *Positif*, which stood for social commitment in cinema.

In the sixties, after Bazin's death and under the influence of structuralism, *Cahiers* narrowed its approach to film criticism. In answer to *Cinéthique*'s polemical criticism, *Cahiers* clearly defined its policy as Marxist, political, and 'scientific' in an elaborate editorial, 'Cinéma/Idéologie/Critique', in October 1969.

*Cahiers*' contribution to film theory has continued to increase, mainly through the writings of J. L. Comolli, J. Narboni, J. P. Oudart, P. Bonitzer, and others.

There was a short-lived attempt to produce a translated version: *Cahiers du Cinéma in English*, ed. Andrew Sarris, 1965–7.

**CAINE, MICHAEL** (1933–  ), British actor, real name Maurice Micklewhite, appeared unbilled in his first film, *A Hill in Korea*, in 1956. His first big role, the laconic hero in *The Ipcress File* (Sidney J. FURIE, 1965), with its two successors *Funeral in Berlin* (Guy Hamilton, 1966) and *Billion Dollar Brain* (Ken RUSSELL, 1967), made him popular, but with his performance as a working-class Casanova in *Alfie* (1966), he became a considerable star with his own farouche style. His recent work has included *Too Late the Hero* (Robert ALDRICH, 1969), *Zee & Co* (1972), *Pulp* (1972), as a bemused pulp fiction writer involved with Maltese mafiosi, and a virtuoso performance opposite Laurence OLIVIER in *Sleuth* (1973).

**CALAMAI, CLARA** (1915–  ), Italian stage actress who enjoyed great popularity in Italy during the war years. Her most famous film role was that of the adulterous wife in OSSESSIONE (1942), a part originally intended for Anna MAGNANI. She appeared again for Visconti in LE NOTTI BIANCHI (*White Nights*, 1957). Her other films were unremarked abroad.

**CALAMITY JANE** (*c.* 1852–1903), probable real name Martha Jane Canarry, who during her lifetime was depicted in newspapers and dime novels as an embodiment of frontier womanhood, fearless, aggressive, and hard-drinking. She grew up in mining camps in Montana, Wyoming, and Utah. A skilled horsewoman and expert with a gun, she is believed to have been at one time a scout for General CUSTER. In 1875 she moved to Deadwood City, Dakota, where she lived during the Gold Rush, and became a notorious local character. She later married and went to Texas, but in 1903 returned with her daughter to Deadwood, where she died. She is buried near the grave of Wild Bill HICKOCK.

She has been portrayed in several films including: *The Plainsman* (1937), by Jean ARTHUR, *The Badlands of Dakota* (1941), by Frances Farmer, *The Paleface* (1948), by Jane RUSSELL, *Calamity Jane and Samm Bass* (1950), by Yvonne De Carlo, the musical *Calamity Jane* (1953), by Doris DAY, and the remake of *The Plainsman* (1966), with Abby Dalton and Evelyn Ankers.

**CALHERN, LOUIS** (1895–1956), US actor, after working in the theatre in the early part of his career, soon established himself in films as a player of stately character parts. This dignified image could be ridiculed to advantage, as in DUCK SOUP (1933), or given the overtones of evil, as in THE ASPHALT JUNGLE (1950). He was appropriately and successfully cast in the title role of JULIUS CAESAR (1953).

**CALVERT, PHYLLIS** (1915–  ), British actress, real name Phyllis Bickle, made her mark as the innocent heroine of GAINSBOROUGH costume melodramas such as *The Man in Grey* (1943) and *Fanny by Gaslight* (1944) both with James MASON. After a short period in Hollywood in the late forties she returned to England and continues to appear in films, theatre, and television.

**CAMBRIDGE, GODFREY** (1929–  ), US comedian, a cynical and satirical observer of American racial problems from the Black viewpoint. His films include *The Biggest Bundle of Them All* (1967), *The President's Analyst* (Theodore J. FLICKER, 1967), to which he contributed a masterful performance as a US government agent, and *Watermelon Man* (1970), a satire about what happens to a white bigot when his skin turns black overnight.

**CAMERA.** The motion picture camera differs from the still camera in only one important respect: the film is mechanically carried through the apparatus, halting 24 times a second (in sound filming), moving on while the shutter is closed. The earliest equipment (EDISON's KINETO-GRAPH, LUMIÈRE's Cinématographe) combined camera and projector in one piece of apparatus. Since the separation of the two functions the camera has remained unaltered in basic principles: development has been almost entirely towards smaller size, greater convenience, and compatibility with sound equipment.

The introduction of SOUND forced the first major changes in camera design. The unwieldy BLIMP was used to silence the camera's mechanical noise while retaining freedom of movement, and motors finally ousted hand cranking to ensure the constant running speeds necessary for sound recording. In recent years various electronic refinements have simplified the shooting of picture and sound in SYNCHRONIZATION, but the camera continues to be a recorder of pictures only—although in such fields as newsfilm the sound recorder may be incorporated in the camera itself.

Half the bulk of the motion picture camera is still taken up by the MAGAZINE or film chamber which, in professional 35mm cameras, contains sufficient film for up to eleven minutes' shooting (see REEL). The viewfinder is nowadays commonly a reflex finder which allows the operator to follow the framing and focus as seen by the lens. Improvements in optical technology have been relevant to both still and cine cameras. WIDE ANGLE, TELEPHOTO, and especially ZOOM lenses are now common in cinematography, and oddities such as the fish-eye lens may be employed for special purposes. The full range of FILTERS used by still photographers is available to motion picture cameramen. The cine camera's main limitation in comparison with the still camera is the absolute limit set to EXPOSURE by the fixed shutter speed; this may be to some extent overcome by the use of variously sensitive film stocks.

The motion picture camera is thus a relatively simple mechanical device, incapable of playing tricks, conveying a message, or expressing emotion. Its power derives from the manner in which it is operated or moved (see CAMERA MOVEMENTS, CRANE, DOLLY, ZOOM), from the

images which are presented to it (see ACTING, ART DIRECTION), from the skill of the CAMERA-MAN or DIRECTOR employing it, and from the techniques which accompany or transform the simple images it records (see EDITING, EFFECTS, MATTE, SOUND).

**CAMERAMAN.** There is rarely one single person concerned with the camera, except on the smallest of productions. The camera department as a whole is responsible not only for the operation of the camera itself, but for all aspects of photography, including the lighting. This can involve a sizeable crew on a feature film. In overall charge is the lighting cameraman or cinematographer, in the US often called the Director of Photography. His responsibility is to achieve the photographic images and effects desired by the DIRECTOR and he thus usually concentrates mainly on the lighting. The camera is in the control of the camera operator, who looks through the viewfinder during a TAKE, checking the framing and focus and moving the camera as desired. The operator's assistant is the focus-puller, whose main function is to adjust the focusing when the camera, or the subject in the frame, moves. A second assistant, the clapper-loader or CLAPPER-BOY, holds up the SLATE at the start of the shot, loads film into the MAGAZINES, keeps a record of the footage shot and other technical details, and generally assists on more menial tasks.

On smaller productions these functions may be amalgamated and a camera crew of one, two, or at most three is common for documentary and television film shooting. The same crew may also fulfil certain other functions, which in features would be carried out by specialist teams. Equipment is carried around by the GRIPS, who also lay tracks for the DOLLY which they then push. In American usage the head of this team is called the key grip. Lighting is set according to the lighting cameraman's instructions by electricians or 'sparks' whose foreman is called the 'gaffer'.

On large, multi-million-dollar productions, the camera department and electricians may account for at least fifteen crew members. In addition, there may be special EFFECTS and rostrum cameramen, usually based in a studio, and sometimes a whole SECOND UNIT.

The distinction between the roles of members of the camera department grew up as productions became more complex and expensive and as trade unions were formed to protect film technicians. Pioneer cameramen were usually the engineers who made the cameras or showmen for whom the camera also served as a projector. All over the world, major developments in both aesthetics and techniques have been made by cameramen: Segundo de CHOMÓN and Rudolf MATÉ in

Europe made major advances, but only the work of certain Hollywood cameramen is well recorded. Billy BITZER, for example, began his career in the movies as an engineer and electrician with BIOGRAPH. The GRIFFITH/Bitzer partnership made use of each new technique, inventing or adapting many of their own. Credit is difficult to apportion, but it was on their jointly made films that close-ups, lighting effects, and MATTES were successfully used, as were back-lighting, the IRIS, the camera matte box, and shooting from moving vehicles, all of which helped to separate the cinema from theatrical tradition. Given that a whole new world was opening up before him, Bitzer probably added more effects to the cameraman's repertoire than anyone else.

Great photographic achievements were often the product of collaboration between a brilliant director and an inventive cameraman. The challenge of the director's vision seems to have pushed the cameraman to his finest efforts. Many examples could be quoted, from the camera CRANE, developed at UNIVERSAL by Hal Mohr with director Paul Fejos and used in *Broadway* (1929), to Geoffrey Unsworth's work on KUBRICK'S 2001: A SPACE ODYSSEY (1968). Most notable between these two is probably Gregg TOLAND, whose films include THE GRAPES OF WRATH (1940), WUTHERING HEIGHTS (1939) for which he won an OSCAR, and CITIZEN KANE (1941). His main contribution was the extended depth of field achieved by using wider angle LENSES than were normal, which is one of the many impressive features of *Citizen Kane*.

A less well-known contemporary of Toland, Don Norwood, also made an important contribution by devising the photosphere, an attachment enabling more rapid assessment of the overall lighting of a scene. This invention is typical of the work of the great pioneering cameramen whose efforts do not always show directly on the screen. It is technical advances which underlie stylistic innovations like hand-held techniques, depth of field photography, zooming, craning, and shooting by available light at night.

Like most other people behind the camera, the cameraman rarely achieves much public recognition. Perhaps it is the very unobtrusiveness of their efforts which brings this situation about; the greatest cameramen are often the ones who blend most easily into the team.

**CAMERA MOVEMENTS.** The camera can be rotated in a horizontal plane (PAN right or left) or a vertical plane (tilt up or down); it can move along its direction of view (DOLLY in or out) or at right angles to it (crab right or left); and it can rise or fall from its normal height (CRANE up or down). When mounted on a large studio crane it can perform all these movements, simultaneously if necessary. It is not normally considered a camera movement when both camera and principal subject ride on the same moving vehicle.

All these movements can be used for the obvious purpose of shifting the view from one part of the scene to another, or to follow action which would otherwise move out of FRAME. Less obvious is the way a director can subtly focus attention by excluding detail or including it just in time to catch the viewer's eye. Carried further, movements can add life to an otherwise static scene or explore an environment as the viewer would if present. Movements in which the camera changes its position in space (dollying, crabbing, and craning) even have the technical function of increasing the viewer's perception of depth and dimension, since parallax causes near objects to move past more rapidly than distant ones. (Conversely, camera movements are usually impossible when special EFFECTS are being used to simulate depth, since the trick would be exposed.)

The ability of the motion picture camera to change its direction of view and its point of view during a shot is the only basic attribute that sets it apart from the still-picture camera, other than the obvious fact that it can record the movements of its subject. Yet camera movements were the last of the fundamental cinematic principles to come into general use, and the relatively static camera remained standard practice until well into the twenties. The use of the mobile camera to intensify the spectator's experience, as opposed to enlarging his physical view, was also slow in developing. Giovanni PASTRONE, in CABIRIA (1914), consciously used camera movements to heighten the three-dimensional effect of his elaborate sets, but even such pioneers in the use of camera mobility as D. W. GRIFFITH and Erich von STROHEIM were primarily concerned with following the action and giving the audience a privileged view rather than involving it subjectively. Probably the first film to investigate such possibilities was MURNAU'S DER LETZTE MANN (*The Last Laugh*, 1924). Carl MAYER'S script specified the camera's involvement in the action: sometimes it even assumes the protagonist's viewpoint (the 'subjective camera'), as in the famous drunk scene.

From the twenties, apart from the brief period when the exigencies of early sound processes virtually immobilized the camera (see SOUND), the use of camera movements for both observation and dramatic effect increased. The technique found its most flamboyant exponent in Orson WELLES, who shot entire sequences with the actors composing and recomposing themselves within a fluidly moving frame. In less skilled hands the mobile camera, used continually without dramatic justification or sufficient technical accomplishment, can be both irritating and distracting. The difficulty of rehearsing and shooting moving-camera shots, especially with the increase in LOCATION work, has made them less fashionable today, although the ZOOM lens and the hand-held camera have become simpler substitutes.

**CAMÉRA-STYLO** see ASTRUC, CRITICISM

**CAMERINI, MARIO** (1895–      ), Italian director, started work in film in the early twenties, directing his first film, *Jolly, clown da circo* in 1923, and has directed over forty features, mainly comedies. In DE SICA, Camerini found the actor he needed for a series of comedies in the thirties, that included *Gli uomini che mascalzone* (1932) and *Daro un milione* (1935). His best-known films of recent years include *Molti sogni per le strade* (1948), and *Il brigante Musolino* (1951), but he is important chiefly for giving opportunities to newcomers such as ZAVATTINI and CASTELLANI.

**CAMILLE**, US, 1936. 1¾hr. *Dir* George Cukor; *prod* MGM; *scr* Joe Akins, Frances Marion, James Hilton, from the novel and play by Alexandre Dumas *fils*; *ph* William Daniels; *ed* Margaret Booth; *cast* Greta Garbo (Marguerite Gautier), Robert Taylor (Armand Duval), Lionel Barrymore (Duval *père*).

Dumas's romantic tragedy of the self-sacrificing demi-mondaine provided a fitting vehicle for GARBO's art. Her luminous beauty and extraordinary sensuality override the banal material and frequent revivals of the film have proved consistently popular with her many admirers.

Other American film versions of *Camille* include one by FOX in 1917 starring Theda BARA, NAZIMOVA's own production of 1921 in which she starred with VALENTINO, and Fred NIBLO's version in 1927, with Norma TALMADGE.

**CAMMINO DEGLI EROI, Il** (*The Path of the Heroes*), Italy, 1937. 1¼hr. *Prod* Instituto Nazionale Luce (East African Cinematograph Section).

A documentary sponsored by the Fascist government, recording the Italian invasion of Abyssinia in 1935, and a precursor of the German combat films of the Second World War.

For a showing by the FILM SOCIETY in London in 1937, reels of *Il cammino degli eroi* were alternated with reels of the Russian *Abyssinia* (1936) filmed during the same events, under the title *A Record of War*. This juxtaposition of two viewpoints provides a classic illustration of the use of film in PROPAGANDA.

**CAMMINO DELLA SPERANZA, Il** (*The Road to Hope*), Italy, 1950. 1¾hr. *Dir* Pietro Germi; *prod* Lux Films; *scr* Federico Fellini, Tullio Pinelli, Germi; *ph* Leonido Barboni; *mus* Carlo Rustichelli; *ed* Rolando Beneditti; *cast* Raf Vallone (Saro), Elena Varzi (Barbara), Saro Urzi (Ciccio), Franco Navarra (Vanni), Liliana Lattanzi (Rosa), Mirella Giotti (Lorenza).

The film tells of the desperate journey made by a group of Sicilians in search of work; they struggle to the northern borders of Italy, and then illegally into France, despite being tricked, beaten, and robbed en route. The film is neo-realist in style and subject, with characteristic hints of melodrama.

**CAMPANADAS A MEDIANOCHE** (*Chimes at Midnight* in GB; *Falstaff* in US), Spain/Switzerland, 1966. 2hr. *Dir, scr* Orson Welles, adapted from *Richard II*, *Henry IV Parts I and II*, *Henry V*, *The Merry Wives of Windsor* by William Shakespeare; *prod* Internacional Films Española (Madrid)/Alpine (Basle); *ph* Edmond Richard; *narr* from Holinshed's *Chronicles*, spoken by Ralph Richardson; *cast* Orson Welles (Falstaff), Keith Baxter (Prince Hal), John Gielgud (Henry IV), Margaret Rutherford (Mistress Quickly), Jeanne Moreau (Doll Tearsheet), Norman Rodway (Henry Percy), Marina Vlady (Kate Percy), Alan Webb (Justice Shallow).

In the most successful of his SHAKESPEARE films, Orson WELLES took the bold course of extracting material from five plays to construct an examination of the character of Falstaff and his relationship with Prince Hal. Any notion of the original plots and their structure is necessarily lost: instead the film gives a new and valid view. According to Welles's interpretation Falstaff's buffoonery is a shield against a changing world (mirrored in the changes in his friendship with the young prince) where chivalry is giving way to the chilly manoeuvres of power politics. Financial stringency hampered the production, and technical imperfections are particularly marked in the sound-track. However, in many sequences Welles made a virtue of necessity, succeeding through imagination and his thorough command of the medium in achieving effects usually lacking in more ambitious film adaptations from Shakespeare. Welles's own performance is one of his finest, and Margaret RUTHERFORD is outstanding in one of her rare serious roles.

**CAMPBELL**, Mrs PATRICK (1865–1940), British actress, *née* Beatrice Stella Tanner, whose first stage appearance was in 1888. Prominent among the roles she played in a long and brilliant theatre career were Lady Macbeth, Mélisande, Paula Tanqueray, and Electra, and in 1914 she was the original Eliza Doolittle in Shaw's *Pygmalion*. In her last years she went to Hollywood and appeared in a few films including *Riptide* (1934), *One More River* (1934, *Over the River* in GB), *Outcast Lady* (1934), and *Crime and Punishment* (Josef von STERNBERG, 1935). Unfortunately her film appearances give little idea of the extraordinary personality and caustic wit that made her famous.

**CAMUS,** MARCEL (1912– ), French director. A painter and sculptor, he began in films as assistant to FEYDER, ASTRUC, and BUÑUEL and made his first short film, *Renaissance du Havre*, in 1950. In 1956 he made *Mort en fraude*, a protest against the war in Indo-China. ORFEU NEGRO (*Black Orpheus*, 1958) is a modern version of the Orpheus myth filmed in Rio de Janeiro during the carnival, and exemplifies Camus's talent for capturing the spectacular and exotic. Awarded first prize at CANNES in 1959, it enjoyed considerable international success. *Os Bandeirantes* (*The Pioneers*, 1960) was also set in Brazil, and *L'Oiseau de paradis* (1962) dealt with Cambodia. *Le Chant du monde* (1965), an adaptation of a story by Jean GIONO, was followed by *L'Homme de New York* (1967) and *Vivre la nuit* (1968).

**CANADA.** The close proximity of the US, a relatively small and scattered population, and the cultural gulf between French- and English-speaking groups have combined to inhibit the development of a Canadian film industry. Foreign-owned distributors had no incentive to offer outlets for locally made films, and many talented directors and actors left to make their mark outside Canada. However, one constant and positive element of Canadian cinema has always been the documentary. One of the first examples of the use of film was by the Canadian Pacific Railway Co who set up the Bioscope Company in 1900 with the purpose of making films to encourage immigration. The same motive in 1903 prompted the start of the *Living Canada* series, directed by Guy Bradford. The first known feature film was *Evangeline* (1914). Both documentary and feature made much of the picturesque harshness of Canadian geography, lumbering, wolves, the cold and the snow.

Ernest Shipman was one of the more successful early producers with films such as *Cameron of the Royal Mounted* (1921) and *The Man from Glengarry* (1922). Something might have been built on these modest beginnings had it not been for the failure of *Carry on Sargeant!* (Bruce Bairnsfather, 1928), an expensive ($500,000)

silent comedy which could not compete with the newly arrived sound film. Perhaps the only early Canadian feature to achieve classic status is *The Viking* (Varick Frissell and George Melford, 1931). Filmed on location in Newfoundland, the authentic drama of seal fishing more than compensates for the contrived romantic interest. The same year Gordon Sparling joined the Canadian branch of Associated Screen News and started to direct a succession of good quality shorts in the *Canadian Cameo* series (1931–54), such as *Grey Owl's Little Brother* and *Acadian Spring Song*. Government sponsorship was mainly in the hands of the Motion Picture Bureau but production was also carried out by other departments. In 1939, to counteract the prevailing dominance of Hollywood and to co-ordinate all government film activity, the NATIONAL FILM BOARD was set up under John GRIERSON. This move not only made possible Canada's leading role as a source of war propaganda, but also had a profound effect in the long term on the Canadian cinema. Through its distribution system people in even the most remote areas have come to accept film as a normal means of communication. Its most important influence however has been on the Canadian film-makers, few of whom have not worked at some time or another for the Board.

After the war francophone Canadians began making feature films, notably *Tit-Coq* (Gratien Gélinas and René Delacroix, 1953), but the most important films of the post-war period were still shorts. *The Loon's Necklace* (1948) was an immensely popular sponsored short film based on an Indian legend. Norman MCLAREN had built up a strong animation department at the NFB and was creating a series of minor masterpieces using techniques of drawing directly on film. The mainstream of the NFB, influenced by the demands and techniques of television, turned to the production of films with more popular appeal using as their material the life around them. *Paul Tomkowicz* (Roman Kroiter, 1953) and *Corral* (Colin Low, 1954) were the signposts which led, via the *Candid Eye* series, to the development of the *cinéma-direct* movement by the French Canadian film-makers at the NFB. This movement, influenced by Jean ROUCH, found its first expression in *Les Raquetteurs* (1958) and was a vital force for many years. In different ways, but still unmistakably, it was evident in two key films which appeared in 1963. *Pour la suite du monde* (Pierre PERRAULT and Michel BRAULT), showing the lives of fishermen in a remote community, is a fine example of poetic documentary. On the other hand, *A tout prendre* (Claude JUTRA) although semi-autobiographical, belongs to a region where fact and fiction overlap.

The NFB's first feature film was made in

1962. *Drylanders* (Don Haldane) was a semi-documentary story of a farming family in Canada between the early 1900s and 1930. By 1964 the Board was firmly involved in the production of feature films, both in English and in French: *Le Chat dans le sac* (Gilles Groulx) and *Nobody Waved Good-bye* (Don Owen). Both these films are concerned with the problems of youth but they reflect the profound differences between the Quebec and English traditions, differences which have become more noticeable as Canadian film-makers have found the confidence and the language to express themselves. A satirical view of Canadian life was ironically expressed by Gilles Carle in *La Vie heureuse de Léopold Z* (1965).

In 1967 the Canadian Film Development Corporation was set up with a fund of $10 million to promote the feature film industry. In the area of film production it has had a significant influence and has helped to finance some good films which would otherwise not have been made. It has not made a comparable effort in the field of distribution which remains firmly in the hands of foreign interests. As a result the audiences for the rich variety of films made in recent years have been smaller than the films deserved, but Canadian films are gradually gaining a foothold in the big towns. Financial support from the state has been accompanied by an encouraging increase in popular knowledge and appreciation. Jutra's *Mon oncle Antoine* (1971), a beautifully acted study of adolescence in rural Quebec, enjoyed long runs in Montreal and, more surprisingly, Toronto. Other outstanding recent Quebec films include Gilles Carle's *La Vraie Nature de Bernadette* (1972) and Denys Arcand's *Réjeanne Padovani* (1973).

English Canadian directors have yet to show the assurance and artistic maturity of the best Quebec films. Interesting work, however, has been produced by Allan King (*A Married Couple*, 1969), Don Shebib (*Goin' Down the Road*, 1970), William Fruet (*Wedding in White*, 1972), and Eric Till (*A Fan's Notes*, 1972). *The Apprenticeship of Duddy Kravitz* (Ted Kotcheff, 1974) was widely seen and earned an international success unprecedented in Canadian cinema.

*CANGACEIRO O'* (*The Bandit*), Brazil, 1953. 1½hr. *Dir* Lima Barreto; *prod* Vera Cruz; *scr* Rachel De Queiroz, Barreto; *ph* Chick Fowle; *des* Pierrino Massenzi; *mus* Gabriel Migliori; *cast* Alberto Ruschel (Theodoro), Marisa Prado (Olivia), Milton Ribeiro (Galdino), Vanja Orico (Maria-Clodia).

Produced by the studio set up by CAVALCANTI in 1951, the film deals with a group of Cangaceiros, north Brazilian bandits of the Robin Hood type; one of the bandits falls in love with a schoolmistress captured by his group, and meets his death as a result. Drawing on a background of national legend, the film had an important role in the development of Brazilian cinema, and was a prizewinner at CANNES in 1953, receiving special mention for its music, based on folk themes. The film was re-issued as *The Bandit* in a dubbed English version in 1962.

**CANNES FILM FESTIVAL.** Originally planned for the autumn of 1939, the first film festival at Cannes took place in 1946 leading the rapid post-war development of film festivals all over the world. Until 1950 the Cannes festival was held in the early autumn; from 1951 it took place in spring to avoid clashing with its chief rival VENICE. Since 1946 two years were missed (1948 and 1950) owing to a combination of shortage of funds and political conflicts within the French film industry. The festival of 1968 was abandoned mid-way following demonstrations (supported by film-makers of the calibre of GODARD and TRUFFAUT) against the display of brash commercialism at a time of serious political upheavals.

Cannes has maintained its place among the leading festivals of the world (Venice, BERLIN, and MOSCOW are its closest rivals). It is essentially a market-place, providing publicity and sales opportunities for films and talent alike. Each country selects its own entries, both feature-length and short films. The main award, for the best film, is the Palme d'or (Golden Palm): other awards are made for best direction, best actor, and best actress. At the discretion of the judges awards are on occasion made for best script, décor, poetic humour, human document, etc, and a Special Jury Prize is sometimes brought in for films which deserve acknowledgement.

**CANTINFLAS** (1911– ), Mexican comic actor, forename Mario-Moreno, of enormous popularity in his native country. His many films made there are unknown abroad, but he was seen more widely in leading roles in Mike TODD's AROUND THE WORLD IN EIGHTY DAYS (1956) and in *Pépé* (1960).

**CANTOR,** EDDIE (1893–1964), US comedian nicknamed 'Banjo-eyes', because they always appeared to be popping out of his head. Success in a number of Ziegfeld shows and enormous popularity on radio led to his first film, *Kid Boots* (1923), and his screen career flourished in the thirties with films like *The Kid from Spain* (1932) and *Roman Scandals* (1933). He was portrayed by Keefe Braselle in *The Eddie Cantor Story* (1953).

**CANUTT,** YAKIMA (1895– ), US stuntman, actor, and director, real name Enos Edward

Canutt, was born in Washington of German/ Scots parentage, and is not half-Indian as widely believed. He began his career as a rodeo cowboy, and was World Champion 1917–23. He acquired the nickname 'Yakima' in 1914, when, after he took a dramatic fall from a bronco, a newspaper wrongly headlined 'Cowboy from Yakima takes flight'. In 1924 he entered films, first as an actor, then as stuntman, appearing in scores of silent Westerns. He organized stunt teams for mass action scenes, and by the thirties was an acknowledged expert in the field. During this period he also worked on a series of Westerns for MONOGRAM with John WAYNE, often as double and villain simultaneously. In Ford's STAGECOACH (1939), among other stunts, Canutt was the man who fell under a wagon's wheels and galloping horses' hooves; he can just be seen getting to his feet at the end of the shot. He remained an active stuntman to the remarkable age of fifty.

In 1944 he became a SECOND UNIT director, organizing stunts and mass action scenes, also directing some films, including *Oklahoma Badlands* (1948). His sons Tap and Joe are both professional stuntmen, often in scenes directed by their father, as in *Fall of the Roman Empire* (1964), *Where Eagles Dare* (1968). Canutt's considerable work as second unit director of stunts and action scenes includes: *Ivanhoe* (1953), BEN-HUR (1959), SPARTACUS (1960), EL CID (1961), *Rio Lobo* (1970). In 1967 Canutt was awarded an honorary OSCAR. He invented many stunt devices, including wagons rigged to disintegrate on cue and a dubious device of trip wires to make horses fall in shot, and he perfected the technique of film fist fights.

**CAPONE,** AL (1899–1947), Italian-born US gang leader who virtually controlled Chicago's underworld in the late twenties, known as 'Scarface Al' from injuries acquired in a bar fight. He deposed Johnny Torrio, head of Chicago's largest gang, and in 1927–30 ran most of the illegal operations in the city. Gang rivalry was strong, and Capone was no doubt involved in the renowned St Valentine's Day massacre of 1929. In 1931 he was gaoled for eleven years on Federal tax evasion charges. He served eight years, but was released in 1939, mentally and physically ill, and retired to Miami, Florida. His screen portrayals include LITTLE CAESAR (1930) by Edward G. ROBINSON, SCARFACE (1932) by Paul MUNI, *Al Capone* (1959) by Rod STEIGER, and *The St Valentine's Day Massacre* (1967) by Jason ROBARDS Jr. (See also GANGSTER FILM.)

**CAPOTE,** TRUMAN (1925– ), US author born in New Orleans whose writing embraces novels, stories, a musical called *House of Flowers*, and journalism on varied topics. He has a sharp sense of the topical and has been criticized for his clinical detachment.

Films made from his works include *Breakfast at Tiffany's* (1961) with Audrey HEPBURN as the wayward Holly Golightly and IN COLD BLOOD (1967). He has also written television plays and the scripts for BEAT THE DEVIL (1953) and *The Innocents* (Jack CLAYTON, 1961).

**CAPRA,** FRANK (1897– ), US director of Italian origin, bluffed his way into directing one-reel versions of famous poems. After completing the first of these in 1923 he went to work with Harry LANGDON and had considerable part in establishing the character of the simpleton triumphant with which Langdon had much success.

In 1928 Capra started his long association with COLUMBIA, directing cheap 'quickies'. When the company started to gamble on larger projects, he was ready for the challenge and quickly established Columbia as a major force with a series of popular successes including *Rain or Shine* (1930), his only musical, and *Platinum Blonde* (1931), starring Jean HARLOW. His conscious involvement with social themes as the basis for undeniably sentimental dramas began with *American Madness* (1932), about the runs on banks initiated by rumour and panic withdrawals. His lovable characters placed in situations based on topical realities and provided with contrived optimistic resolutions of their problems achieved tremendous popularity with audiences escaping from the hardships of the Depression. IT HAPPENED ONE NIGHT (1934), the quintessential SCREWBALL comedy, was an enormous success. MR DEEDS GOES TO TOWN (1936) and MR SMITH GOES TO WASHINGTON (1939), beneath their overt attack on corruption, carry a comforting belief in the power of simple honesty and individualism. *Lost Horizon* (1937), a truly escapist romance, and the OSCAR-winning *You Can't Take It With You* (1938), were unqualified hits. Capra's films of the thirties were strengthened by a sharp sense of characterization and skilled control of comic pace, well served by the scripts written by his frequent collaborator, Robert RISKIN.

Capra left Columbia at the expiry of his contract in 1939 and formed his own company, which produced two films before America's entry into the war. *Meet John Doe* (1941) has the typical Capra hero, personified like Mr Deeds by Gary COOPER, fighting the threat of Fascism. *Arsenic and Old Lace*, made in 1941 but not released until 1944, was a fairly direct, and very funny, adaptation of the stage success. In 1941 Capra, with the rank of Major, was made head of the US War Department's film-making. He supervised, and in part personally directed, the WHY WE FIGHT series (1942–5), which is still highly regarded for its effective use of film technique for persuasive purposes.

Returning to independent production in 1945, Capra formed Liberty Films in partnership with William WYLER, George STEVENS, and Samuel Briskin. *It's a Wonderful Life* (1946), *State of the Nation* (1948), *A Hole in the Head* (1959), and *A Pocketful of Miracles* (1961), a remake of his earlier success *Lady for a Day* (1933), all show his gift for sharp delineation of character, but their sentimentality found less favour with a changing audience.

Always a thorough craftsman, Capra campaigned for some years for the recognition of directors' rights over the finished form of their films. He was instrumental in setting up the Directors' Guild and became its first President. *The name above the title* (New York, 1971) is an energetic if erratic autobiography.

**CARABINIERS, Les** (*The Soldiers* in GB, *The Riflemen* in US), France/Italy, 1963. 1¼hr. *Dir* Jean-Luc Godard; *prod* Georges de Beauregard, Carlo Ponti; *scr* Godard, Jean Gruault, Roberto Rossellini, based on the play *I carabinieri* by Benjamin Joppolo; *ph* Raoul Coutard; *ed* Agnès Guillemot; *mus* Philippe Arthuys; *cast* Marino Masè (Ulysse), Albert Juross (Michel-Ange), Geneviève Galéa (Vénus), Catherine Ribero (Cléopâtre).

Lured by promises of booty, Ulysse and Michel-Ange leave their mother and sister and go off to fight for king and country. But the king signs a peace treaty with the enemy and the two peasants receive their reward for faithful service at the hands of a firing squad.

The critical reaction against *Les Carabiniers* was so violent that the film was withdrawn almost immediately after its release. Some interpreted GODARD's Brechtian detachment as callous indifference to his subject, others accused him of technical incompetence: the film was said to be poorly written, photographed, and edited. In fact Godard had taken more care over the preparation of his script than ever before, and the primitive visual quality of the film was the result of much experiment with unorthodox processing techniques to reproduce the strongly contrasted, grainy image associated with old newsreel footage. This hostile rejection of his film provoked Godard to reply to his critics in an article (*Cahiers du Cinéma* 146) in which he concluded that the misunderstanding had arisen over his objective treatment of a subject usually treated subjectively. Nevertheless in his next film, LE MÉPRIS (1963), he returned to a form that was, at least superficially, more conventional.

**CARDIFF,** JACK (1914–  ), British cameraman who earned a high reputation by his virtuoso use of colour in a number of British films by POWELL and PRESSBURGER including *A Matter of Life and Death* (1946, *Stairway to Heaven* in US), *Black Narcissus* (1947), for which he won an OSCAR, and THE RED SHOES (1948). Since 1958 he has directed, mainly action stories and thrillers, but also *Sons and Lovers* (1960), a distinguished adaptation of D. H. Lawrence's novel; *Young Cassidy* (1964), a good evocation of Dublin at the turn of the century; and *Girl on a Motorcycle* (1968), which he also produced and co-scripted.

**CARDINALE,** CLAUDIA (1939–  ), Italian–French actress, was born in Tunisia of Italian parents. In 1957 she won a competition to discover 'the most beautiful Italian girl in Tunisia'; the prize was a visit to the VENICE Film Festival, during which she attracted much attention. She was taken up by the Italian producer Franco Cristaldi (whom she later married), whose declared aim was to make her an Italian Brigitte BARDOT. While she has not achieved Bardot's international success, Cardinale has progressed steadily from her first film, *Goha le Simple* (1957), through appearances in films by directors who include VISCONTI (ROCCO E I SUOI FRATELLI, 1960 and IL GATTOPARDO, 1963) and FELLINI (OTTO E MEZZO, 1963) to some stature in both the comic and dramatic fields.

**CARETTE,** JULIEN (1897–1966), French character actor, a clown of the first quality who has contributed memorable supporting roles to notable French films. He appeared in 115 films in 1932–64, the first being L'AFFAIRE EST DANS LE SAC (Jacques PRÉVERT, 1932). He became one of Jean RENOIR's regular team, in LA GRANDE ILLUSION (1937), *La Marseillaise* (1938), LA BÊTE HUMAINE (1938), and as the poacher in LA RÈGLE DU JEU (1939). Some of his last work was for Claude AUTANT-LARA—in *La Jument verte* (1959) and *Vive Henri IV, vive l'amour* (1961). He died from burns received in an accident caused by a cigarette.

**CAREY,** JOYCE (1898–  ), British actress, real name Joyce Lawrence, daughter of Lilian Braithwaite. She was essentially a stage actress until the forties when she played character roles in IN WHICH WE SERVE (1942) and *Blithe Spirit* (1945). She is particularly remembered as the railway-station refreshment-room dragon in BRIEF ENCOUNTER (1945). She has continued to appear frequently in minor roles in British films.

**CAREY,** PATRICK (1916–  ), Irish director and cameraman born in London, whose interest in cinema took him back to Britain, as there was virtually no film-making in Eire; he made his first documentary for the RAF. He worked in India, Persia, and Indonesia, and was with the unit that filmed the ascent of Mount Everest in 1953. After another three years in Britain he joined the NATIONAL FILM BOARD of Canada; for the Board he photographed the dreamily beautiful *Sky* (1962).

Carey's study of Celtic myth and legend and his affinity with primitive natural forces resulted in four fine short films: *Yeats Country* (1965), *Mists of Time* (1968), *Errigal* (1968), and *Oisin* (1970), Eire's contribution to European Conservation Year. *Oisin* is the most moving of Carey's films and, like *Yeats Country*, won several awards. Carey photographed the British documentary *Wild Wings* (1967) and also works as a cameraman and SECOND UNIT director on features, notably Fred ZINNEMANN's *A Man for All Seasons* (1966).

**CARLSEN,** HENNING (1927–   ), Danish director, from 1947 made numerous shorts and documentaries. His first feature, the anti-apartheid *Dilemma* (*A World of Strangers*, 1962), was shot clandestinely in South Africa. He is best known in Britain for *Sult* (*Hunger*, 1966), a portrait of a writer literally driven mad by starvation, drawn from a novel by Knut Hamsun first published in 1890. After *Mennesker modes og sod musik opstaar i hjertet* (*People Meet*, 1967), an unsuccessful excursion into light comedy, Carlsen returned to documentary with *Er i bange?* (1971), about a Maoist commune in Copenhagen, before making another feature, *Man sku' vaere noget ved musikken* (1972) which is reminiscent of the work of Miloš FORMAN in its observation of social behaviour.

**CARMEN.** Prosper Mérimée's story of the turbulent loves of the gypsy tigress was popular with film-makers long before the introduction of sound made a screen version of Georges Bizet's opera possible. France produced silent versions in 1909 and 1926, the latter shot in Spain and co-directed by Jacques FEYDER and Françoise ROSAY; the story was also filmed in Spain in 1910 and 1914. Hollywood's first Carmen was Marguerite Snow (1913), after which Mérimée's tale frequently appeared in the American silent cinema. Cecil B. DEMILLE imported the operatic star Geraldine Farrar in 1915 and in the same year Theda BARA played the role under the direction of Raoul WALSH. In CARMEN (*Charlie Chaplin's Burlesque on Carmen*, 1916), Edna PURVIANCE's attempt at a serious performance is interrupted by CHAPLIN. Walsh returned to the subject with *The Loves of Carmen* (1927), starring Dolores DEL RIO. In Germany Pola NEGRI

played the title role under the direction of Ernst LUBITSCH (1918, released in the US in 1921 as *Gypsy Love*). A ten-minute silhouette film (1933) by Lotte REINIGER used Bizet's music as accompaniment.

Viviane Romance and Jean MARAIS enacted the fatal love story in a French version (1942) which combined Mérimée and Bizet in equal parts, but the music was not predominant in *The Loves of Carmen* (1948) in which a sultry Rita HAYWORTH taunted Glenn FORD. Otto PREMINGER restored the music with his all-Black, updated *Carmen Jones* (1954), in which Dorothy Dandridge mimed to the singing of Marilyn Horne. An Italian updating, *Carmen di Trastevere* (1962), with Giovanna Ralli, was far less successful. The Carmen story was the basis for one of Radley Metzger's erotic films, *Carmen, Baby* (1967) and the same year a film was made of Herbert von Karajan conducting a Salzburg Festival production of Bizet's opera with Grace Bumbry singing Carmen. The popularity of the opera has made it a great favourite for films with a back-stage or musical setting, and the punning possibilities of the title have not been ignored by the makers of short cartoons—*Carmen Get It* (1963) and *Carmen's Veranda* (1964) being among the less painful.

**CARMEN** (*Charlie Chaplin's Burlesque on Carmen*), US, 1916. 1hr. *Dir, scr* Charles Chaplin; *prod* Essanay; *ph* Rollie Totheroh; *cast* Charlie Chaplin (Darn Hosiery), Edna Purviance (Carmen), Ben Turpin (Renendados), Jack Henderson, Leo White, John Rand, May White, Bud Jamison, Wesley Ruggles.

CHAPLIN rarely made parodies, the favourite standbys of most other silent comedians. This burlesque of DEMILLE's film (1915) (see CARMEN) was shot just before Chaplin left ESSANAY, and the company tried to make the most of its investment by adding a new sub-plot with Ben Turpin and including much footage that Chaplin would undoubtedly have rejected. What finally appeared was twice as long—and presumably half as funny—as Chaplin's intended two-reeler.

**CARMICHAEL,** HOAGY (1899–   ), US composer, pianist, singer, and actor. In 1928 he wrote 'Stardust', dedicated to his friend the jazz musician Bix Beiderbecke. Carmichael's hit songs by now included 'Two Sleepy People', 'Georgia On My Mind', and 'Old Rocking Chair'. He entered films with a bit part in *Topper* (1937) and then returned to composing and arranging until he was featured in HAWKS's TO HAVE AND HAVE NOT (1944), singing his 'Hong Kong Blues'. In 1951 he won an OSCAR for his song 'In the Cool, Cool, Cool of the Evening' written for *Here Comes the Groom* (1951). He appeared in THE BEST YEARS OF OUR LIVES (1946), and the films for which he has written songs include GENTLEMEN PREFER BLONDES (1953).

**CARNÉ, MARCEL** (1909–    ), French director, was born and brought up in Montmartre, and it was intended that he should follow his father's trade as a cabinet-maker: instead, he trained as a cameraman in his spare time. Between 1928 and 1936 he worked as assistant to René CLAIR on SOUS LES TOITS DE PARIS (1930), and to FEYDER on *Les Nouveaux Messieurs* (1929), *Le Grand Jeu* (1934), and LA KERMESSE HÉROIQUE (1935). During this period he also worked as a film journalist and made a short documentary, *Nogent, Eldorado du dimanche* (1929).

In 1936 he had his first chance to direct a full-length film when Feyder went to England, leaving the making of *Jenny* in Carné's sole charge. Carné, who had admired Jacques PRÉVERT's work on the script of LE CRIME DE MONSIEUR LANGE (1936), brought him in to work on *Jenny*. Although the film had only a mediocre success, it marked the beginning of a highly productive partnership between Prévert and Carné which was to last over ten years. In 1937 they made the farcical *Drôle de drame*. The designer TRAUNER, whose sets were to be one of the distinctive features of Carné's films, first worked with him on this occasion.

In QUAI DES BRUMES (1938) Carné began to show the perfection of his craftsmanship, particularly in his masterly evocation of the gloomy, mist-shrouded atmosphere of the story. The fatalistic encounter of lovers doomed to only a brief moment of happiness, a theme which they first explored in this film, was to form one of the central preoccupations of the Carné–Prévert films. Jean GABIN and Michèle MORGAN first appeared together in *Quai des brumes*, giving memorable performances under Carné's meticulous direction.

After the unexceptional *Hôtel du Nord* (1938) on which Prévert did not collaborate, they worked together on LE JOUR SE LÈVE (1939). In many ways the most accomplished of Carné's films, it is a tightly constructed and minutely controlled work. In it, as in *Quai des brumes*, the social realism of the subject-matter is invested with a poetic quality, mainly through the conscious artifice of the sets and dialogue, and the music of Maurice JAUBERT. His next two films were made during the Occupation, when it was no longer possible to deal effectively with contemporary social subjects, and LES VISITEURS DU SOIR (1942) and LES ENFANTS DU PARADIS (1945) are both set in the past. The latter, with its powerful evocation of theatrical society in nine-teenth-century Paris, has proved to be the most enduring of Carné's films. Although made under great difficulties, its combination of spectacle and romantic passion has continued to fascinate audiences.

After *Les Portes de la nuit* (1946) the partnership with Prévert broke up, and Carné's subsequent work has rarely approached the quality of his earlier films. His post-war films include: *La Marie du port* (1950), *Juliette ou la clef des songes* (1951), THÉRÈSE RAQUIN (1953), *Les Tricheurs* (1958), and *Trois chambres à Manhattan* (1965).

Even the best of Carné's work, that of the 1936–46 period, has undergone considerable revaluation during recent years. The studio-bound artistry, the rehearsed perfection of his films, and the fatalistic outlook which they present, make them seem cold and outmoded in the context of the flexibility and freedom of modern cinema; but he was one of the finest craftsmen of the French cinema, holding a dominant position among film-makers of the thirties and forties.

**CAROL, MARTINE** (1922–67), French actress, real name Marie-Louise-Jeanne Mourer, made her reputation mainly in films directed by her husband, CHRISTIAN-JAQUE, and later had parts in films of more standing, including LES BELLES DE NUIT (1952) and LOLA MONTÈS (1955).

**CARON, LESLIE** (1931–    ), French dancer and actress, danced leading roles with the Ballet des Champs Elysées in Paris before joining METRO-GOLDWYN-MAYER for AN AMERICAN IN PARIS (1951). She has starred in musicals including GIGI (1958) and has made a transition to straight acting with, among others, FANNY (1960) and *The L-Shaped Room* (1962).

**CARRADINE, JOHN** (1906–    ), US actor, who made his name on the stage as a Shakespearian actor. He entered films in 1935, and his gaunt face led him to be cast in many horror films, including several made by UNIVERSAL: *Bride of Frankenstein* (1935) was one of his earliest films, and numerous others included *House of Frankenstein* (1945) in which he played DRACULA. His commanding presence made him ideal for villainous but gentlemanly character parts. In the course of an active screen career he appeared in films by a variety of leading directors, from Cecil B. DEMILLE to Jean RENOIR and Fritz LANG, but he was in particular a familiar figure in many of John FORD's films. These included *The Prisoner of Shark Island* (1936), *The Hurricane* (1938), STAGECOACH (1939), THE GRAPES OF WRATH (1940), and more recently THE MAN WHO SHOT LIBERTY VALANCE (1962) and *Cheyenne Autumn* (1964).

**CARRIÈRE, JEAN-CLAUDE** (1931– ), French scriptwriter, humorist, novelist, and playwright, became connected with the cinema when Jacques TATI commissioned him to write book versions of LES VACANCES DE MONSIEUR HULOT (1951) and MON ONCLE (1958). He went on to co-script and co-direct *Rupture* (1961) and *Heureux Anniversaire* (1961) with Pierre ÉTAIX, and later co-scripted several of Étaix's feature films. Carrière has worked as scriptwriter for Louis MALLE (VIVA MARIA!, 1965; *Le Voleur*, 1967), Jacques Deray (*Borsalino*, 1970), and Miloš FORMAN (*Taking Off*, 1971) among others. His work with BUÑUEL has been particularly striking: LE JOURNAL D'UNE FEMME DE CHAMBRE (1964), *Belle de jour* (1966), LA VOIE LACTÉE (1969), and LE CHARME DISCRET DE LA BOURGEOISIE (1972) display acute wit and an essentially surrealist vision. For *La Voie lactée* Carrière conducted an impressive amount of research into the dogmas and heresies of the Catholic Church; he also played the role of Priscillian. He played a leading role opposite Anna KARINA in *L'Alliance* (Christian de Chalonges, 1971), based on his own novel, and has directed a short film, *La Pince à l'ongles* (*The Nail Clippers*, 1968), which is a succinct, elegant, and very funny surrealist joke.

**CARROLL, MADELEINE** (1906– ), gracious British-born stage and screen actress whose first film was *The Guns of Loos* (1928). She was in two HITCHCOCK thrillers, THE THIRTY-NINE STEPS (1935) and *Secret Agent* (1936), and her success as the prototype of Hitchcock's cool blonde heroines led to stardom in Hollywood during the early forties.

**CARRY ON**, British-made series of formula comedy films that started in 1958 with *Carry On, Sergeant*. By the end of 1974, twenty-six had been completed, all produced by Peter Rogers and directed by Gerald Thomas; during this time only two scriptwriters have been used, Norman Hudis, on the first five, and Talbot Rothwell since. Kenneth Williams, Charles Hawtrey, Sid James, Hattie Jacques have acted in most of the films, consistently playing predictable roles. This quality has contributed to *Carry On*'s continued success at the box-office, as the audience knows what to expect—a prerequisite for a formula comedy series that relies on burlesque, double-entendre, and parody of cinema clichés.

**CARSON, JACK** (1910–63), Canadian-born actor who began his Hollywood career in *Stage Door* (1937). Burly and ebullient, he specialized in comedy roles of a voluble kind. He was prominent in WARNER BROS films of the forties, including *Mildred Pierce* (1945) and several others directed by Michael CURTIZ, sometimes in leading parts in films such as *April Showers* (1948), opposite Ann SOTHERN, and *The Groom Wore Spurs* (1951), opposite Ginger ROGERS. His later films included A STAR IS BORN (1954), *Cat on a Hot Tin Roof* (1958), and *The Bramble Bush* (1959).

**CARSON, KIT** (1809–68), US frontiersman famed as a trapper, hunter, guide, and soldier. After working as a teamster and cook on a wagon train, he became a beaver trapper in the Rockies, moving from California to Wyoming, Idaho, and Colorado. In 1842 in Missouri he met John Charles Frémont, the military explorer, and became his guide on an expedition to California, then in 1843 to Oregon to chart the mouth of the Columbia River, and again in 1845 to California. Carson also carried Frémont's dispatches to Washington, and through these reports became nationally famous. He fought in the Mexican War, and in 1853–60 was Indian Agent for the Utes and Apaches around New Mexico. During the Civil War he served with the Union, and rose to the rank of brigadier-general. In 1867 he resigned from the army and wrote *Kit Carson's own story*. Carson City, Nevada, is named after him. Film versions of his adventures include *Kit Carson* (1928), with Fred Thomson; *The Painted Stallion* (1938), a serial, with Sammy McKim; *Kit Carson* (1940), with Jon Hall; and a fifties televison series with Bill Williams.

**CARSTAIRS, JOHN PADDY** (1910–70), British director, son of the entertainer Nelson 'Bunch' Keys, began his career as a camera assistant in 1927. He directed his first film, *Holiday's End*, in 1937 and quickly established himself as a versatile film-maker, particularly skilled in comedy. His best-known films are *Spare a Copper* (1940), *The Chiltern Hundreds* (1949), and the series which established the comedian Norman Wisdom, beginning with *Trouble in Store* (1953). In all, Carstairs directed forty-five feature films, worked for television, and also wrote over thirty books. He painted, and had an exhibition at the Royal Academy.

**CARTIER-BRESSON, HENRI** (1908– ), French still photographer, studied painting before travelling in 1930 to the Ivory Coast where he took his first photographs. He travelled all over the world, rapidly building up a reputation as a humane and perceptive observer. During the Spanish Civil War he did some filming in Republican hospitals. He worked as an assistant to RENOIR on *La Vie est à nous* (1936), UNE PARTIE DE CAMPAGNE (1936), and LA RÈGLE DU JEU (1939), in which he also appeared. During the war he was taken prisoner, but escaped to become an active member of the Resistance, setting up a film unit for them. After the Liberation he worked on two documentaries for the wartime US Office of War Information (*Les Services Americaines d'Information*), one of which was the masterly LE RETOUR (1947). In 1970 he directed, for American television, a film 'essay' called *California Impressions*, without sound and with colour only in tints. Economy and humanism are the marks of Cartier-Bresson's work, in both still photography and film.

**CARTON**, PAULINE (1888–1974), Swiss-born actress with a long career in French films since the silent days, including a part in *Feu Mathias Pascal* (Marcel L'HERBIER, 1925). She is reputed to have appeared in over a hundred films since the advent of sound; certainly she was a familiar figure as a character actress on the French screen, particularly in films written and directed by Sacha GUITRY, including the popular *Le Roman d'un tricheur* (*The Cheat*, 1936).

**CARTOON** see ANIMATION

*CASABLANCA*, US, 1943. 1¾hr. *Dir* Michael Curtiz; *prod* Warner Bros; *scr* Julius J. Epstein, Philip G. Epstein, Howard Koch, from the play by Murray Burnett and Jean Alison; *ph* Arthur Edeson; *cast* Humphrey Bogart (Rick), Ingrid Bergman (Ilsa Lund), Paul Henreid (Victor Laszlo), Claude Rains (Capt Renault), Conrad Veidt (Major Strasser), Sydney Greenstreet (Señor Ferrari), Peter Lorre (Ugarte), Dooley Wilson (Sam).

Humphrey BOGART, as the cynical yet vulnerable owner of Rick's Bar in wartime Casablanca, discovers that a Resistance worker whose escape to the US he is aiding is the husband of his lost love. *Casablanca* has all the qualities of romantic Hollywood films at their best: a tightly worked out plot, crisp dialogue, satisfyingly predictable characterizations, and the polish of a well-knit studio team working together. Bogart's tough-guy qualities were admirably teamed with Ingrid BERGMAN's luminous beauty, and Claude RAINS gave an excellent performance as the devious French police captain.

Bogart's much quoted 'Play it again, Sam' is incorrect; he in fact says 'Play it, Sam', the song being 'As Time Goes By' by M. K. Jerome and Jack Scholl.

**CASARÈS**, MARIA (1922– ), Spanish actress, went to France as a refugee in 1936, and has enjoyed a distinguished career there in both theatre and films. Her magnificently expressive features and dark beauty have lent themselves particularly to tragic parts, including that of the abandoned wife in LES ENFANTS DU PARADIS (1945), the vengeful Hélène in *Les Dames du Bois de Boulogne* (1945), and Death in ORPHÉE (1950) and LE TESTAMENT D'ORPHÉE (1960).

**CASERINI**, MARIO (1874–1920), Italian director, originally a painter, one of the pioneers of Italian cinema and among its most important directors during the years before the First World War. He made more than seventy films in his fifteen-year career including an early *Viaggio al centro della luna* (1905). He was a leading director of the immensely popular costume spectacles of the time, his contributions to the genre including *Giovanna D'Arco* (1908), *Beatrice Cenci* (1909), *Catalina, Lucrezia Borgia* (both 1910), *Gli ultimi giorni di Pompeii* (*The Last Days of Pompeii*, 1913). He then moved on to emotional dramas built around the cult of 'divismo' (see ITALY), such as *Il treno degli spettri* (1912) and *Ma l'amore mio non muore* (1913) starring Lyda Borelli.

*CASQUE D'OR* (*Golden Marie*), Francè, 1952. 1½hr. *Dir* Jacques Becker; *prod* Speva Films/Paris Films; *scr* Becker, Jacques Companeez; *ph* Robert LeFèbre; *mus* Georges Van Parys; *cast* Simone Signoret (Marie), Serge Reggiani (Manda), Claude Dauphin (Leca).

Manda, an honest workman, is drawn by his passion for Marie into the world of petty criminals, pimps, and prostitutes. He is driven twice to murder and dies on the guillotine.

BECKER's evocation of turn-of-the-century Paris is masterly, in the detailed settings and the behaviour of his characters. In spite of the sordid events of the plot, which are nowhere glossed over, the film has a quality of affirmation, particularly in the open-air scenes, which owes much to the glowing sensuality of Simone SIGNORET's performance in the title role.

**CASSAVETES**, JOHN (1929– ), US actor and director of great sensitivity and intelligence, first attracted wide attention in *Edge of the City* (Martin RITT, 1956, *A Man is Ten Feet Tall* in GB). His independent production SHADOWS (1960) enjoyed qualified commercial success, but had considerable influence on independent low-budget film-making. Work as a director within the studio system, on *Too Late Blues* (1961) and *A Child is Waiting* (1962), clashed with his individual temperament; the latter film was completed by Stanley KRAMER. Performances in *The Dirty Dozen* (Robert ALDRICH, 1967), ROSEMARY'S BABY (1968), and the long-running television series *Johnny Staccato* have helped to finance his own directing projects. FACES (1968), *Husbands* (1970), and *Minnie and Moskowitz* (1971) betray the over-indulgence of a director/actor too attached to his material, but they contain strong performances and uncompromising examination of personal relationships.

**CASSEL,** JEAN-PIERRE (1932–   ), French actor discovered by Gene KELLY for *The Happy Road* (1956). He was the engaging, inept hero of Philippe DE BROCA's *Les Jeux de l'amour* (1960) and *L'Amant de cinq jours* (1961); these, with Jean RENOIR's *Le Caporal epinglé* (*The Vanishing Corporal*, 1962), established him as a screen actor and he was soon representing France in international productions like *Those Magnificent Men in Their Flying Machines* (Ken ANNAKIN, 1965) and OH! WHAT A LOVELY WAR (Richard ATTENBOROUGH, 1969). He is perhaps best known for his appearance in René CLAIR's *Les Fêtes galantes* (1965) and in France he has a strong reputation as a night-club entertainer. His Gallic charm is strengthened by intelligent playing of difficult roles as in *Baxter!* (Lionel Jeffries, 1972) and BUÑUEL's LE CHARME DISCRET DE LA BOURGEOISIE (1972).

**CASTELLANI,** RENATO (1913–   ), Italian director, started work in the thirties as a scriptwriter, working with SOLDATI, BLASETTI, and CAMERINI. *Un colpo di pistola* (1941) was his first film; it gained immediate critical recognition which was strengthened by his neo-realist trilogy *Sotto il sole di Roma* (1948), *E primavera* (1949), and *Due soldi di speranza* (1952). (See NEO-REALISM.) In 1954 he made his first colour film, *Giulietta e Romeo*, in which Shakespeare's lovers were played by the appropriately young Laurence HARVEY and Susan Shentall. His recent films lack the warmth and lightness of touch which earlier gave him an international reputation. In 1971 he wrote and directed a series on Leonardo Da Vinci for Italian television.

**CASTLE,** IRENE and VERNON, US dancing team, American Irene Foote (1893–1968) and British Vernon Blythe (1885–1918). They made only one feature film as a team—*The Whirl of Life* (1915); but Irene made several films, mostly after Vernon's death in a training plane crash. Fred ASTAIRE and Ginger ROGERS portrayed them in their last RKO musical, *The Story of Vernon and Irene Castle* (1939).

*CAT PEOPLE,* US, 1942. 1¼hr. *Dir* Jacques Tourneur; *prod* Val Lewton for RKO Radio; *scr* DeWitt Bodeen; *ph* Nicolas Musuraca; *des* Albert S. D'Agostino, Walter B. Keller; *ed* Mark Robson; *mus* Roy Webb; *cast* Simone Simon (Irena Dubrovna), Kent Smith (Oliver Reed),

Tom Conway (psychiatrist), Jane Randolph (Alice Moore), Jack Holt (Commodore).

A neat variation on the lycanthropy theme, with Simone SIMON as a convincingly feline heroine, *Cat People* is possibly the best of the LEWTON–TOURNEUR horror films of the early forties. The plot is of little consequence; but the treatment, relying on suggestion to the extent of never showing the 'monster', was both original and effectively macabre. The film's success led to a sequel, *The Curse of the Cat People* (1944), also produced by Lewton but directed by Robert WISE.

**CAVALCANTI,** ALBERTO DE ALMEIDA (1897–   ), Brazilian producer and director, in 1922 entered the commercial film industry in Paris as a set designer, after studying architecture in Geneva. In Paris he worked with, among others, Marcel L'HERBIER, Louis DELLUC, Jean RENOIR, and George PEARSON, and eventually became a director and producer himself. Cavalcanti had maintained an active interest in the Parisian AVANT-GARDE, and his first notable film was a highly original study of Paris and its inhabitants, *Rien que les heures* (1926). He worked on many films in France, including foreign-language versions of American films for PARAMOUNT, but most significantly *En Rade*, which he directed in 1928.

In 1933, Cavalcanti moved to England and was employed by John GRIERSON in the GPO Film Unit (see CROWN FILM UNIT). He directed *Pett and Pott* (1934) and he was able to apply his theories of commentative sound with particular success in such films as *Coal Face* (1936), which he also directed, and NIGHT MAIL (1936). Cavalcanti gradually assumed Grierson's role as producer-in-chief for the Unit. As producer he was responsible for many of the important British DOCUMENTARY films of the thirties and forties, such as *BBC: The Voice of Britain* (Stuart LEGG, co-producer Grierson, 1935), *North Sea* (Harry WATT, 1938), and *Spare Time* (Humphrey JENNINGS, 1939).

He joined Michael BALCON at EALING STUDIOS in 1940 as an associate producer. He produced several documentaries for Ealing, including a COMPILATION lampooning Mussolini, *Yellow Caesar* (1941). He influenced the introduction of a documentary realism into British feature films, such as *The Foreman Went to France* (Charles FREND, 1942), of which Cavalcanti was the associate producer. The first completely fictional film to be directed by Cavalcanti in Britain was *Went the Day Well?* (1942). This was the first of several distinguished films, made during and immediately after the war, which in effect mark the peak of Cavalcanti's career as a director, and include two episodes in DEAD OF NIGHT (1945),

Nicholas Nickleby (1947), and They Made me a Fugitive (1947). During the war Cavalcanti also compiled Film and Reality (1942), possibly the first film anthology, for the BRITISH FILM INSTITUTE.

Cavalcanti returned to Brazil in 1950 and became head of the Vera Cruz production company. He produced or directed several features and documentaries, including Painel (1951), an award-winning documentary directed by Lima BARRETO, and directed three films; but the company never became commercially viable, and in 1955 he went to East Germany to collaborate with Bertolt BRECHT on Herr Puntila und sein Knecht Matti. Cavalcanti has since worked in Spain, Israel, and Italy. He has produced plays, directed The Monster of Highgate Ponds (1960) for the CHILDREN'S FILM FOUNDATION in Britain, and lectured on film art at UCLA.

**CAYATTE,** ANDRÉ (1909– ), French director, trained as a lawyer and journalist. He began directing during the forties and made his reputation with Les Amants de Vérone (1948), which was written by Jacques PRÉVERT. Thereafter he made a series of films dealing with social and legal problems, all written by Charles SPAAK and including Justice est faite (1950), Nous sommes tous des assassins (1952), Avant le déluge (1953), and Le Dossier noir (1955). Le Passage du Rhin (1960) is a compelling story of French prisoners of war escaping from Germany. He shook off the sombre influence of the war years with La Vie conjugale (1963). This consisted of two 95-minute films, shown separately, recounting a marriage breakdown, one from the point of view of the husband the other from that of the wife. Cayatte's didactic tendencies lead to a sober realistic style with little cinematic excitement, but his best work has a muscular intelligence.

**CAYROL,** JEAN (1911– ), French novelist, scriptwriter, and director. Originally a poet, and writer of the 'nouveau roman' school, Cayrol is one of an increasing number of French writers who have turned to the cinema. For Cayrol, writing and making films are two aspects of the same search, and the themes of memory and adjustment to the past are central to his work in both fields. He first worked in the cinema as a scriptwriter, collaborating with RESNAIS on NUIT ET BROUILLARD (1955), a documentary on concentration camps. (Cayrol had himself been a prisoner in one for three years.) He then directed several short films himself, collaborating with Claude Durand. These include On vous parle (1959), La Frontière (1960), made secretly in Spain, Madame se meurt (1961), and De tout pour faire un monde (1963). With Durand he also wrote a book on the cinema, Le Droit du

regard (Paris, 1963). In the same year Cayrol wrote the script for Resnais's MURIEL. He directed his own full-length feature Le Coup de grâce in 1965. This deals with the return of a man to Bordeaux twenty years after he has betrayed Resistance workers there. As in Muriel, the interest centres on a group of people haunted by memories, and the return of a central character after a long absence. The film met with a very mixed reception from the critics, and caused offence in Bordeaux. In 1966 Cayrol wrote the script for Orgen Roos's Sincerely Yours, and also directed a short feature of his own, La Déesse, in which a boy deserts from the army and steals a car in order to rejoin the girl he loves.

**CECCHI D'AMICO,** SUSO (1914– ), Italian scriptwriter, real forename Giovanna, worked during the war on several theatrical productions with her father Emilio Cecchi, who had also worked in cinema as writer and producer. In 1945 she was offered her first script; this was soon followed by VIVERE IN PACE (1946), which won a prize for its script. She became acknowledged as one of the leading scriptwriters for the neo-realist directors, working almost always in collaboration with a team in the approved neo-realist way (see NEO-REALISM). She has worked with Italy's most important directors, including VISCONTI, DE SICA, and ANTONIONI. Among her best-known films are LADRI DI BICICLETTE (1948), MIRACOLO A MILANO (1951), BELLISSIMÀ (1951), LE AMICHE (1955), and ROCCO E I SUOI FRATELLI (1960).

**CEL** or cell, the name given in ANIMATION to the acetate sheet (originally celluloid) on which each drawing of an animated image is made. Five seconds of continuous action requires up to sixty different drawings, which would be impracticable if the artist had to re-draw the entire picture each time. Cel animation allows him to draw stationary elements only once for each scene; only moving images are drawn sixty times on sixty cels. Not only the characters moving in the foreground, but the room furniture and décor shifting in the middle ground can be on cels, sometimes eight or more thick, with different parts of the scene showing through wherever the cel has been left unpainted. The cel is not only an important labour-saving device; it made possible 'full animation' with realistic use of perspective and complex action of the kind brought to a high level in DISNEY feature-length cartoons.

**CENDRARS,** BLAISE (1887–1961), French writer, real name Frédéric Sauserhall, was a poet and journalist. His work in the cinema was exclusively in collaboration with Abel GANCE; he wrote J'ACCUSE (1919), was Gance's assistant on LA ROUE (1922), and wrote *La Fin du monde* (1931), which he adapted from his own novel. He also published *ABC du cinéma* (1926) and *Hollywood la Mecque du cinéma* (1936). His novel *L'Or, la merveilleuse histoire du Général Johann August Suter* (1925) was one of the abortive projects undertaken by EISENSTEIN in Hollywood. The film version, *Sutter's Gold*, was finally directed by James CRUZE in 1936.

**CENSORSHIP** of films has been an almost universally accepted necessity from the earliest days of cinema. The vividness of the medium and, even more, the accessibility of the cinema to a much wider audience than had ever been exposed to the theatre, literature, or even the music-hall, alerted the authorities to the risks of dangerous influences. The kind of danger feared most has varied; thus, in different countries, the censor's activity may be directed at sex, violent crime, politics, or even stylistic expression. It has been unusual for all these elements to be equally sensitive, an exception being the Soviet Union during the thirties and forties. Only Belgium has never instituted pre-censorship of films for adults; Denmark and Uruguay abandoned it in recent years. The film censor is an agent of the government in all countries except Britain, the US, Germany, and Japan, where a recognized system of pre-censorship is operated by the film industry itself.

The most effective form of censorship is what may be called 'auto-censorship', representing built-in reaction and sensibility to prevailing opinion and feelings. Times of crisis, of which war is the most obviously recognizable, produce reactions in public opinion which are reflected in all media of expression. The costliness of films has made them unusually vulnerable in the matter of auto-censorship and this, combined with their unique power of mass persuasion, has made them peculiarly sensitive indicators of prevailing opinion. Striking examples include the abrupt swing from isolationism to belligerence in American films immediately before the nation's engagement in the First World War; the rallying of the British film industry during the Second World War; and the unity of tone in films from socialist countries, largely attributable to a sense of being embattled societies which has been with them throughout their existence (see also PROPAGANDA).

**Great Britain** has no film censorship established by statute. The Cinematograph Act 1909, the legal starting-point for the existing system, was framed to protect audiences against material risk, most particularly—following disasters in Paris and elsewhere—against fire. Local authorities were charged with licensing buildings where inflammable film was projected for public entertainment and with enforcement of stringent safety regulations. Although there had been murmurings against the sensationalism of some films, notably *The Life of Charles Peace* (1905), no provision was made in the Act for control of the content of films; but immediately the new law came into force local councils began to bring, and win, cases against licensees on the grounds of impropriety in films being shown. The diversity of objections raised in various areas led to agitation from the industry itself for some centralized system of censorship. In 1912, chiefly at the instigation of the Cinematograph Exhibitors' Association and major producers, the BRITISH BOARD OF FILM CENSORS was set up. Local councils were at first reluctant to surrender their authority over films shown in their areas, but gradually accepted the principle that a film passed by the Board could be shown without fear of prosecution under the 1909 Act. They retain, however, the right to pass for local showing a film that has been refused a certificate by the Board or to ban a film that has been passed by the Board.

Except during the two world wars, NEWSREELS have always been exempt from examination by the BBFC, to avoid delay in bringing them to the screen and to maintain the freedom traditionally accorded to journalism. Attempts to impose censorship on newsreels, especially during the thirties, may have contributed to the bland, non-controversial tone of British newsreels in general.

The rise of the film-society movement in the mid-twenties, led by the FILM SOCIETY in London, presented new problems. Their object was to bring non-commercial films before audiences interested in cinema as an art. In fact, many films brought into Britain in this way were refused certificates when they were later submitted to the Board: they include EISENSTEIN'S STACHKA (*Strike*) and BRONENOSETS POTEMKIN (both 1925), PUDOVKIN'S MAT (*Mother*, 1926), and DULAC'S LA COQUILLE ET LE CLERGYMAN (*The Seashell and the Clergyman*, 1928). Recognizing the seriousness of intent of the film societies, most local authorities instituted special conditions under which films could be shown to members and guests.

Since powers of censorship had developed from legislation intended to deal with fire risks from inflammable film (see NITRATE), they could not be applied to 16mm safety film (introduced in 1923). Interesting anomalies have resulted: 16mm prints of VIGO'S A PROPOS DE NICE (1930), for example, include a shot of a nude woman which has been excised from 35mm copies. The inadvertent protection of 16mm film from censorship was, however, of little concern to film societies owing to the limited supply of narrow-gauge prints. The greatly increased use of 16mm film during the war years was one of the main stimuli to new legislation; another was the change to acetate (safety) film for all commercial 35mm prints, completed in the early fifties. To meet the new situation, the Cinematograph Act 1952 brought all commercial film showings within the local authorities' licensing powers without reference to the inflammability of film. The Act confirmed the status of film societies and commercial film clubs and their exemption from censorship, subject to specified conditions of membership; and for the first time Scotland was brought into line with England and Wales.

BBFC certificate classifications had for some time proved inadequate in the face of changing film styles. The 'H' certificate, introduced in 1930 to prohibit children from seeing horror films, was suspended in 1942 when the Board decided to ban all such films: this left only two certificate categories, 'U' (universal, i.e. unrestricted admission) and 'A' (adult) to which children in adult company could be admitted. Two films which strengthened dissatisfaction with this situation were *Forever Amber* (1947), a lusty Restoration romance, and *No Orchids for Miss Blandish* (1948), a violent crime thriller. After a period of experiment, the 'X' certificate was introduced in 1951 for films suitable only for adult audiences. In 1970 the 'AA' certificate introduced a lower age limit of fourteen and the 'A' became unrestricted but warned parents of possible grounds for objection.

If the need for film censorship is admitted, the British model has much to recommend it. Films are submitted voluntarily to the BBFC, and the absence of a formal code has allowed the Board to act pragmatically in response to changes in public taste and opinion. Certainly the Board is vulnerable to pressure from both official and unofficial sources. It appears likely that the government was directly concerned in the banning of certain films, including the great revolutionary statements of Eisenstein and Pudovkin and, during the period of appeasement, films with an anti-German bias such as PROFESSOR MAMLOCK (1938). After the comparative freedom of the sixties, when hitherto unacceptable topics were dealt with in all media with increased frankness, a strong reaction took place, led by a group calling itself the Festival of Light. Films like KUBRICK'S A CLOCKWORK ORANGE (1971) and BERTOLUCCI'S LAST TANGO IN PARIS (1972) were classed with the proliferating backstreet sex films in an attempt to force a resumption of the more restrictive attitudes of earlier years. A response to this feeling was indicated by recurrent attempts to introduce legislation making both film societies and commercial film clubs

subject to the current obscenity laws as well as prohibiting the advertising of films not carrying a BBFC certificate.

**United States of America.** No Federal legislation has been enacted on the question of film censorship, although a variety of local laws have existed at both State and municipal level. In the years immediately after the First World War, Hollywood became a byword for licentious conduct. Growing public disapproval of well-publicized scandals and the variety of local judgements on the acceptability of particular films induced producers to create in 1922 a self-regulating body, the Motion Picture Producers and Distributors of America (MPPDA, later the MOTION PICTURE PRODUCERS OF AMERICA—MPPA), with Will H. HAYS as its first head. This action at first placated the critics of Hollywood's dubious morals; and in fact no film censorship laws were passed by individual States after the formation of the MPPDA. But members of the association did not willingly co-operate with the recommendations of the Studio Relations Committee (the 'Hays Office'), set up in 1926 to guard against indecency in films. Public criticism again increased, culminating, in 1934, in the formation of the Legion of Decency, inspired by American Roman Catholic bishops but supported by other religious denominations. The Legion's importance was confirmed by a Papal Encyclical of 1936. Its power to influence cinema takings by boycotting objectionable films swiftly brought the producers into line with the Production Code (the 'Hays Code') which had been drawn up in 1930 by Martin Quigley, a Roman Catholic publisher, and Daniel Lord, SJ.

The Code set out in considerable detail the limits to be observed in depicting sexual, social, and criminal behaviour. It was enforced by the Production Code Administration, whose most influential officer, Joseph I. Breen, implemented the Code in 1933–54 with complete faith in its sufficiency. Only in 1956, when Breen had retired, was the Code revised to accommodate changed social and economic conditions.

The Hays Code, regarded from the more sophisticated stand-point of the sixties and later, has been derided for the simplicity of its standards. Criminals, adulterers, and other wrongdoers could not be seen to benefit from their misdeeds, family life was an obvious force for good, religious and ethnic minority groups must not be offended. But the economic structure of the American film industry in the thirties and forties was based on the loyalty of a mass audience, cutting across age and social and cultural groups. Although the Code probably did less to raise or uphold the nation's moral tone than its creators had hoped and although it unquestionably inhibited the realistic treatment of serious topics, it helped to ensure a regular family audience which could depend on a steady flow of high-quality, inoffensive entertainment.

The Production Code Administration worked with producers at all stages, from the selection of a basic story, through scrutiny of the shooting script, to approval of the completed film. From 1934 a seal of approval was given to films passed by the PCA and no member of the MPPDA might release a film without the seal. The following year PCA procedures were offered to non-member producers.

As in Britain, the prevailing obscenity laws were deemed sufficient to deal with the import of, and inter-state commerce in, offensive films: EX-TASE (1933), from Czechoslovakia, was banned in this manner in 1935. Prosecutions were also brought under local censorship or obscenity laws and were usually successful. Pleas of free expression based on the First and Fourteenth Amendments of the Constitution were rejected until 1952, when Roberto ROSSELLINI's L'amore (1948) was banned by the New York City licensing authorities on the grounds of blasphemy. The New York Court of Appeal reversed this verdict and expressly brought films (hitherto classed with items of commerce) within the constitutional freedoms allowed to the arts in general; this judgement was confirmed by a number of cases concerning, for example, Pinky (Elia KAZAN, 1949), LA RONDE (1950), M (Joseph LOSEY, 1951), The Moon Is Blue (Otto PREMIN-GER, 1953), Le Blé en herbe (AUTANT-LARA, 1954).

Preminger was at this time deliberately defying the Production Code: The Moon Is Blue, a comedy about virginity, was distributed without a seal of approval and proved that the seal was not essential to either commercial success or security from censorship; and THE MAN WITH THE GOLDEN ARM (1955) was awarded a seal although it contained explicit depictions of drug addiction. The Code's ban on nudity was undermined by The Pawnbroker (Sidney LUMET, 1964), which was passed by the PCA uncut in consideration of the dramatic justification for a scene in which a woman stripped to the waist.

The Legion of Decency, renamed the National Catholic Office for Motion Pictures in 1965, continued to review films, classifying their recommendations under six headings; but the Church's influence was weak. The PCA, too, began to classify films bearing its seal. After some experiment the rating became in 1972: 'G' (general) all ages admitted; 'PG' parental guidance suggested; 'R' (restricted) parent or adult guardian must accompany persons under seventeen; 'X' persons under seventeen not admitted. Operation of the ratings is voluntary on the part of the exhibitor and no machinery exists to enforce them.

The market for pornography of a more or less extreme character expanded rapidly from the late sixties. Films which had found an audience only in back-street areas began to be shown more widely. Action taken under the obscenity laws varied according to locality, with Boston the most active in attempting to suppress objectionable matter. A Congressional Committee was appointed in 1968 to examine the legal, social, and psychological effects of pornography. Its majority conclusion, that no strengthening of legal controls was either desirable or necessary, was rejected by President Johnson and by his successor President Nixon: public disquiet on the subject became vocal and by the early seventies there was again agitation for Federal legislation on censorship.

**Soviet Union and other socialist countries.** Countries with a nationalized film industry operate their own system of censorship. A film's general topic and treatment will be scrutinized before a start can be made and supervision is carried on throughout production, fluctuating in severity according to the prevailing political climate.

The Russian film industry was nationalized in 1919 and, by a statute of 1922, censorship powers were placed with the Commissariats of Education of the various republics. Undesirable elements were described in general terms, with an emphasis on ideological purity and a total ban on 'pornography'. The scope of the censor's duties was thus open to wide interpretation. For a few years after the Revolution a remarkable degree of freedom was accorded to all artists. Auto-censorship was at full strength, with revolutionary themes taking up almost the entire output of films, but little restraint appears to have been placed on artistic modes of expression until the end of the New Economic Policy in 1928.

The first Five Year Plan brought a tightening of controls, both financial and ideological, and the film industry was re-structured under the management of Soyuzkino, which took the final decision about the acceptability of any part of a film. Each studio was given an artistic political council, with members appointed by Soyuzkino, to supervise sensitive matters during the course of production. SOCIALIST REALISM became the only acceptable narrative mode and Eisenstein in particular was repeatedly censured for his experimental 'formalism'. Moral standards were rigidly enforced. Two sequences of DOVZHENKO's beautiful and politically irreproachable ZEMLYA (Earth, 1930) were cut: a naked woman's hysterical mourning and a group of workers happily urinating into a tractor's radiator.

From the mid-thirties until the death of Stalin

in 1953 restrictions on subjects, personnel, treatment, and every other element in each film increased, resulting in a state of near-stagnation in Russian film production. In 1950 only six feature films survived this multiple censorship process. After 1954 the situation eased and directors like KALATOZOV and HEIFITS were able to deal with human relationships outside the context of the workers' struggle or national glorification. Although extremes of personal expression have continued to be discouraged this relaxation has persisted. At all times, certain films have been passed for export but not for home exhibition: a recent example is TARKOVSKY's *Andrei Rublev*, made in 1966, shown at foreign festivals from 1969, but not released in the Soviet Union until 1971.

In other Socialist countries, where the film industry is modelled on that of the Soviet Union, censorship is implemented in a similar manner. Reflection of current political tendencies is very apparent, particularly in the emergence of a 'new wave' in CZECHOSLOVAKIA during the sixties. The later films of Dusan MAKAVAJEV, totally banned in Yugoslavia, have perhaps misled foreign audiences as to the degree of frankness in sexual and political comment permitted there.

*Film censors and the law* by Neville March Hunnings, London, 1967, is an authoritative account of censorship legislation in several countries.

**CENTRE NATIONAL** du Cinéma Français, organization set up in Paris in 1947 as a watchdog over the fortunes of the French cinema industry. The Centre's control of the financing of authorized films and the receipts of all films shown in France, gives it disciplinary powers useful in its attempts at co-ordinating various branches of the industry. The CINÉMATHÈQUE FRANÇAISE and the INSTITUT DES HAUTES ÉTUDES CINÉMATOGRAPHIQUES (IDHEC) are also under its wing. It publishes *Bulletin d'Information*, a statistical survey of French and European cinema. (See FRANCE.)

**CENTRO SPERIMENTALE DI CINEMATOGRAFIA,** founded in 1932 by Alessandro BLASETTI as a department of the Rome Academy of Music, emerged as an independent establishment under its present name in 1935. From 1937 the Centro published the influential journal BIANCO E NERO and in 1940 the school moved to premises close to CINECITTÀ. Although founded by the Fascist Government, the Centro managed during the war years to create an independent, experimental spirit that greatly enriched the quality of Italian post-war films and contributed directly to the rise of NEO-REALISM.

A two-year course offers training in directing, production, camerawork, sound, acting, set design, and costume design. Classes on the history of cinema, theatre, and music are also held. Candidates for directing and production must have a university degree; for other courses, university entrance qualifications are required. Foreign students are admitted in limited numbers. The work is divided equally between theory and practice, second-year students participating in film-making. The notably well-equipped studio with two stages is used by the students and is also rented to commercial producers; students work as apprentices on professional productions, and a number of major films have been made in this way.

Many distinguished Italian film-makers have been associated with the Centro and visiting lecturers from abroad have included Charles CHAPLIN, René CLAIR, Jean RENOIR, and Robert BRESSON. The Centro's many distinguished graduates include Michelangelo ANTONIONI, Pietro GERMI, Giuseppe DE SANTIS, and Giorgio ZAMPA. (See FILM SCHOOLS.)

*CERTO GIORNO, Un* (*One Fine Day*), Italy, 1968. Eastman Color; $1\frac{3}{4}$hr. *Dir, scr* Ermanno Olmi; *prod* Cinema-Italnoleggio/Cinematografico-Instituto Luce; *ph* Lamberto Caimi; *mus* Gino Peguri; *cast* Brunetto Del Vita (Bruno), Lidia Fuortes (girl interviewer), Vitaliano Damioli (Davoli), Giovanna Ceresa (account executive), Raffael Modugno (artist), Maria Crosignani (Elena).

The first of OLMI's films to deal with the company executive as opposed to the 'insignificant' employee. It examines, not without irony (the product being promoted is 'Job Dinner'), the disorienting and dehumanizing effects of business pressures on the character of an advertising man, showing the dishonesty of his personal relationships as a reflection of the claustrophobia and tensions of his office life. Only a car crash brings him to a pessimistic awareness of his situation.

Olmi's command of his material is as discreet as ever, but the relationship between the individual condition and that of society is more overt than in his earlier films. The final shot, an explosion in a landscape watched on television by the executive, draws a clear parallel between his spiritual state and the devastation of the land.

**CERVI,** GINO (1901–74), Italian actor, was already well known in Italy when post-war screenings of BLASETTI's *Quattro passi fra le nuvole* (*Four Steps in the Clouds*, 1942) brought him international critical attention. He achieved world renown in the French/Italian co-production *Le Petit Monde de Don Camillo* (*The Little World of Don Camillo*, 1951), in which

FERNANDEL was the redoubtable Catholic priest and Cervi his obstinate Communist opponent, Peppone. The success of their teaming led to five further 'Don Camillo' films between 1953 and 1970.

**CÉSAR** see MARIUS

**CHABROL, CLAUDE** (1930– ), French director, worked as a publicity officer for TWENTIETH CENTURY-FOX in Paris and made his name as a member of the group of young critics who revitalized CAHIERS DU CINÉMA in the fifties. With Eric ROHMER he published *Hitchcock* (Paris, 1957), an intense study of the director's work from a moral, indeed Catholic, standpoint; the subject-matter of Chabrol's films repeatedly shows his admiration of HITCHCOCK.

LE BEAU SERGE (1959), generally acknowledged as the first feature film of the NOUVELLE VAGUE, indicates Chabrol's major interest: the detailed social milieu which gives solidity to a melodramatic plot usually involving or culminating in murder. His second film, LES COUSINS (1959), applied this approach to student life in Paris; it was critically acclaimed and very successful commercially.

For the next ten years his output was prolific but uneven, following the currently fashionable FILM NOIR in various directions: straight thrillers, studies of the falsity of bourgeois relationships, unpretentious spy spoofs. He also contributed a sketch, 'La Muette', to *Paris vu par . . .* (1964), in which his main preoccupations are encapsulated; Chabrol himself played opposite his wife, Stéphane AUDRAN, in a savagely ironical look at middle-class marriage.

The increasing prominence of Stéphane Audran in Chabrol's films has accompanied their increasing intellectual strength. In *Les Biches*, *La Femme infidèle* (both 1968), *Que le bête meure (Killer!)*, LE BOUCHER (both 1969), *La Rupture* (1970), JUSTE AVANT LA NUIT *(Just Before Nightfall*, 1971), and *La Décade prodigieuse (Ten Day's Wonder*, 1971), he studies, often with great intensity, personal relationships within the enclosed settings of family, village, or house party, using violent death as the central point or resolution of his tale. Thematic consistency, reiterated motifs such as the family meal or celebration, and the permutation of certain names among his leading characters (Charles, Paul, Hélène) have stimulated weighty critical analysis, which he perhaps mischievously encourages. His best films lend themselves to various levels of appreciation. They have a narrative tension which makes them engrossing entertainment. The obviously inspiring working relationship with Audran has produced studies of feminine psychology remarkable for their subtle complexity, but his selection and direction of other actors has been equally successful, resulting in perceptive and detailed characterizations. With his cameraman Jean RABIER he has developed a sophisticated visual style that emphasizes or contrasts ironically with his themes: bright, springlike simplicity for *La Femme infidèle*, pastoral sunshine for the horrors of *Le Boucher*, tight geometrical compositions for *Juste avant la nuit*. In 1974 he expressly abandoned the bourgeois milieu to depict a group of revolutionary guerrillas; *Nada* tilts at both established and alternative society, coldly demonstrating the suspect motivation and bungling methods of both.

**CHAGRIN ET LA PITIÉ, Le** (*The Sorrow and the Pity*), Switzerland, 1969. 4½hr. *Dir* Marcel Ophuls; *prod* TéléVision Rencontre (Norddeutscher Rundfunk/Société Suisse de Radiodiffusion); *scr, interviews* Ophuls, André Harris; *ph* André Gazut, Jürgen Thieme.

Using extended interviews and newsreel footage to illuminate its emotional topic, *Le Chagrin et la Pitié* is a thoughtful and authoritative documentary study in depth of the German occupation of Clermont-Ferrand, showing with clarity and objectivity not only that not all Frenchmen resisted the enemy, but that many were active collaborators.

The film was originally planned by French television (ORTF), but on leaving France to work in Germany Marcel OPHULS took the project to Norddeutscher Rundfunk and the film was eventually made as a German/Swiss coproduction. It was refused by ORTF who were inevitably accused of wishing to maintain the myth of universal French resistance to the German forces. It became a *succès de scandale* in Paris, where it ran for months to packed audiences in two cinemas, and it was shown on television in most European countries.

**CHAIR, The,** US, 1963. 1¼hr. *Dir, ph, ed* Robert Drew, Richard Leacock, Donn Alan Pennebaker, Greg Shuker, Jim Lipscombe, Hope Ryden; *prod* Drew for Drew Associates.

Shot in 16mm with the light, mobile, synchronized equipment developed for DREW ASSOCIATES, *The Chair* was released in syndication as part of the CBS-TV 'Living Camera' series. Its success, and its reputation as one of the best examples of DIRECT CINEMA, are based on its intelligent and immediate reporting of a life-and-death crisis: the hearing at which a young defence lawyer attempts to save his black client, Paul Crump, from the electric chair.

**CHALAND QUI PASSE, Le,** popular song and the title under which L'ATALANTE was first released in 1934. The song (English version, 'Love's last word is spoken, chéri') was originally Italian, and popularized in *Gli uomini che mascalzoni* (Mario CAMERINI, 1932), in which Vittorio DE SICA played the romantic lead.

**CHALIAPIN,** FEODOR (1873–1938), Russian bass, then at the height of his fame, appeared in a disastrous silent film version of Rimsky-Korsakov's opera *Pskovityanka*, made in 1915. He then avoided films until almost the end of his career, when he played the leading role in *Don Quichotte* (1934), directed by PABST, with music by Jacques IBERT. It was made in two versions, French and English. Normally in such a film the singer mimes the action to a pre-recorded music track: Chaliapin refused to accept this method, and insisted on genuinely singing throughout the many takes. This placed an undue strain on the ageing singer's voice, with the result that he was unable to sing again in public.

**CHALLENGE FOR CHANGE,** project initiated in 1967 by the NATIONAL FILM BOARD of Canada in co-operation with Federal government departments, which pioneered the principle of citizen participation in community television (a phenomenon made possible by the development of cable television in North America), since emulated by programmes such as *Catch 44* in Boston, USA. The project's founder John Kemeny, and a team which included Colin Low and later George STONEY, began by making influential films about problems of poverty, unemployment, housing, racial discrimination, but gradually withdrew into an advisory capacity as their former subjects assumed full editorial control and eventually technical responsibility, using film, half-inch videotape (cheap and simple to operate), and 'live' transmission with audience participation possible by telephone. *Challenge for Change* and its francophone equivalent *Société Nouvelle* demonstrate a democratic alternative to the present oligarchy of huge networks.

**CHAMBARA** films. Japanese period films about samurai, in which swordfights play an important part.

**CHANDLER,** JEFF (1918–61), US actor, real name Ira Grossell, whose first film was *Johnny O'Clock* (1947); his performance as Cochise in BROKEN ARROW (1950) made him a popular star, and he retained a considerable following until his final appearances in *Return to Peyton Place* (1961) and *Merrill's Marauders* (1962).

**CHANDLER,** RAYMOND (1888–1959), US author, born in Chicago of an American Quaker father and an Irish Quaker mother, went to an English public school and finished his education in Germany and France. After a varied career, including working as a journalist in England, he settled in Southern California. Apart from his film scripts he wrote several books, creating something of a revolution in his own genre, the thriller. His cynical 'private eye', Philip Marlowe, became a prototype which dominated thriller-writing for fifteen years. The role was played on the screen by, successively, George MONTGOMERY, Dick Powell, Robert MONTGOMERY, Humphrey BOGART, James GARNER, and Elliott Gould.

Several of Chandler's novels were made into films: *The High Window* (Robert Stevenson, 1943), remade in 1947 as *The Brasher Doubloon* (*The High Window* in GB), THE BIG SLEEP (1946), *Farewell My Lovely* as *Murder My Sweet* (Edward DMYTRYK, 1945, *Farewell My Lovely* in GB), the most Chandleresque of all the Marlowe films, and *The Little Sister* as *Marlowe* (1969). *Farewell My Lovely* was used as the basis of *The Falcon Takes Over* (1942) without the character of Marlowe. A seventies treatment of the material was introduced by Robert ALTMAN in *The Long Goodbye* (1973), restoring to Marlowe some of the less 'heroic' traits of the original character that were lost in earlier transitions to film where he was shaped to the current cinematic conventions.

Chandler's story *Lady in the Lake* was the subject of the first film (1946) to be made entirely in the first person with the camera representing the eye of the detective. The director was Robert MONTGOMERY, who appeared as the detective only in shots looking into a mirror.

His original film scripts include DOUBLE INDEMNITY (1943), *The Blue Dahlia* (George MARSHALL, 1946), and STRANGERS ON A TRAIN (1951).

Chandler's books were ideal material for screen adaptation, with their detailed observation, fast dialogue, and coolly detached attitude to violent crime, but their transference to the screen was marred, except in *Murder My Sweet*, *The Big Sleep*, and *The Long Goodbye*, by inept casting and a failure to convey the Chandler milieu or his command of narrative pace.

**CHANEY,** LON (1886–1930), US actor, was born of deaf and dumb parents. From an early age he was therefore used to expressing himself in mime, an asset which he developed to a high degree after embarking on a film career in 1913. He was also highly skilled in make-up, justly earning the title of 'The Man with a Thousand Faces', but his successes in the portrayal of grotesques were based not only on external distortion: his sensitive acting brought a quality of humanity to the most warped and terrifying creatures. Particularly famous among his silent roles were Quasimodo in *The Hunchback of Notre Dame* (1923) and the mysterious presence with the face of a living skull in *The Phantom of the Opera* (1925), culminating in the hideous vampire of *London after Midnight* (1927).

Chaney was at first reluctant to appear in talking pictures, but the 1930 remake of his successful *The Unholy Three* (1925) showed that his vocal talents well matched his physical versatility. He was about to embark on the title role of UNIVERSAL'S DRACULA (1931) at the time of his early death from throat cancer.

**CHANEY,** LON, Jr (1915–73), US actor, real name Creighton Chaney, assumed his father's famous name in 1937, although he had been playing small film roles since 1932. Apart from his well-received performance as Lennie in *Of Mice and Men* (1939) he was limited to 'monster' roles, mostly those made famous by Boris KARLOFF and Bela LUGOSI in the thirties.

*CHANG,* US, 1927. 1½hr. *Dir, ph* Ernest B. Schoedsack, Merian C. Cooper; *prod* Paramount; *titles* Achmed Abdullah.

Having achieved recognition with *Grass* (1925), the directors went into the jungles of northern Siam and, after some two years' work, brought back enough footage to make another documentary feature, *Chang*. The material was capably edited into a coherent narrative, telling how Kru, a Lao tribesman, and his family leave their village, make a clearing in the jungle, struggle against both vegetation and wild animals, and domesticate an elephant. The film was both an artistic and financial success.

A climax in the form of an elephant stampede was made more impressive by the use of Magnascope, an early large-screen process by which the image was magnified four times by a supplementary lens on the projector. Several other films were shown in this enlarged form at first-run cinemas, but the size of the screen entailed loss of a satisfactory view from rear seats under balconies and the consequent reduction in revenue killed the system.

**CHANGING BAG,** a light-proof cloth bag for removing exposed film from the camera MAGAZINE and loading fresh stock. Professional film stock is not supplied on daylight-loading spools and would be ruined by light if some sort of portable darkroom were not available. The clapper-loader inserts his arms into elastic 'sleeves' and manipulates the film and magazine inside the bag by touch alone.

*CHAPAYEV,* USSR, 1935. 1½hr. *Dir, scr* Sergei and Georgy Vasiliev, based on writings by D. A.

Furmanov and A. N. Furmanova; *prod* Lenfilm; *ph* Alexander Sigayev, A. Xenofontov; *cast* Boris Babochkin (Chapayev), B. Blinov (Furmanov), Vavara Myasnikova (Anna), Leonid Kmit (Petka), Illarion Pevstov (Col Borozdin).

Chapayev was a Red Army commander who fought against Czech and Kolchak forces in the Civil War. He was killed in action, and became a folk-hero when a book about him was published in the early twenties by his political commissar, D. A. Furmanov. Furmanov also submitted a film treatment to the Leningrad studio in 1924, but this was put aside and forgotten. In 1932 Furmanov's widow submitted her own treatment, and the recent changes brought about by the introduction of the first Five Year Plan (see SOVIET UNION) made the subject more acceptable.

The VASILIEVS' film, made with a single soundtrack, deals with the hero's exploits in an uncomplicated way. The symbolic burden of the film is the Communist Party's role in the Civil War, and in the constant friction between the hero and his commissar it is the former who is shown to be human and fallible. His role as leader is also underlined, foreshadowing Stalin's personality cult, although less baldly than in SHCHORS (1939).

*Chapayev* was screened as the highlight of the celebrations to mark the fifteenth anniversary of Soviet cinema held in January 1935, and of the International Film Festival in Moscow the following month. It was received in the USSR with enormous enthusiasm. The ideological demands of the State were met, and the public welcomed with relief a film so much less demanding than those they were offered by EISENSTEIN and DOVZHENKO. Audiences abroad, however, who had learnt to look for explosive ideas in Soviet silent cinema, were disappointed; and *Chapayev* remains of interest in the context of SOCIALIST REALISM rather than for intrinsic merit.

*CHAPEAU DE PAILLE D'ITALIE, Un* (*An Italian Straw Hat*), France, 1927. 1½hr. *Dir, scr* René Clair, from the play by Labiche and Michel; *prod* Albatros; *ph* Maurice Desfassiaux, Nicolas Roudakoff; *des* Lazare Meerson; *cast* Albert Préjean (Fadinard), Olga Chekova (Anaïs de Beauperthuis), Marise Maia (the bride), Yvonneck (Norancourt).

The popular stage farce deals with the disastrous results to Fadinard when his horse chances to eat the straw hat of an errant wife who happens to be at the time in a mildly compromising situation with a cavalry officer. The hilarious events of the search for an identical replacement before Fadinard can get to his wedding form the body of the plot. CLAIR choreographed this piece of charming nonsense into a comedy of classical elegance, swiftly-paced and maintaining the element of comic suspense throughout. The wittily accurate nineties costumes and settings heighten the film's humour. IBERT's incidental music to the play was sometimes used to accompany the film.

**CHAPLIN,** CHARLES (1889–    ), British actor and director whose parents were music-hall performers. Born in the slums of Lambeth, London, he was five when he first appeared on the stage with his father, an alcoholic who died soon after. Charlie was sent to a home with his elder half-brother Sydney (son of a different father) but returned to the stage when he was seven. Ten years later he followed Sydney into the famous Fred KARNO company; he stayed with the company for seven years, touring England, Europe, and the US where, in 1913, Mack SENNETT recruited him for his successful KEYSTONE Studio by offering him $150 a week.

He made thirty-five SLAPSTICK comedies at Keystone starting with *Making a Living* (1914), where he appears as an impoverished English dandy, one of his favourite stage personae. All but one (TILLIE'S PUNCTURED ROMANCE, 1914) ran for two REELS or less. Most of them featured the Tramp, who was first seen in KID AUTO RACES AT VENICE (1914) and remained his usual characterization for more than thirty years. Chaplin's style was less knockabout than Sennett's and he ran into difficulties with Mabel NORMAND who directed some of his films. As he began to settle down, the Tramp's individual character emerged: the waddling walk, the dandy air sustained in spite of his unkempt clothes, the combination of gallantry and rakishness in his attitude to women, his fierce independence and endless resourcefulness. He became so successful that other companies outbid Sennett for his services. In January 1915 he went to ESSANAY for $1250 a week making in a year fourteen films, still slapstick but gradually becoming less frenzied. In February 1916 he joined MUTUAL at a salary guaranteeing him $670,000 annually; he had multiplied his earnings by ten each year since arriving in Hollywood.

Chaplin lavished time and care on the Mutual films, and the qualities that had begun to emerge at Essanay—pathos, irony, satire—featured even more as the Tramp became less unscrupulous, less ready to kick children or cheat colleagues. Intellectuals began to analyse films like EASY STREET and THE IMMIGRANT (both 1917) seriously—perhaps too seriously, for it would appear that Chaplin found more and more truth in their discovery of significance in his work. Realizing that his audience was changing, and maturing both as an individual and an artist, he began to stray from his popular roots—Max

LINDER as well as the music hall—and his genius for mimed comedy.

There were now so many Chaplin imitators that when he joined FIRST NATIONAL in 1918, with a contract to make eight films for $1,000,000, he prefaced each with the title 'None genuine without his signature'. The signature symbolized that, as producer, director, scriptwriter, star, he had a freedom rarely granted by Hollywood, earned by an international popular success which has rarely been equalled. Songs were sung about him, children's games alluded to him, statuettes of him sold at $1 each. On a visit to Europe in 1921, 'Charlot' was hysterically fêted by public and notables alike. His enormous popularity sprang from the universality of his appeal. Class barriers were transcended by his appearance, which could be seen as reduced gentility or ambitious poverty; cultural differences by the classic simplicity of his plots; and the normal bias in favour of the underdog was satisfied, in his earlier work, by his invariable triumph over bullying, rich, or glamorous adversaries while never changing his seedy appearance. The grace and timing of his mime were equally effective as pathos took an increasingly important part in his work, reaching a peak in THE KID (1920).

In 1919 Chaplin had joined D. W. GRIFFITH, Mary PICKFORD, and Douglas FAIRBANKS to form UNITED ARTISTS. He wrote and directed A WOMAN OF PARIS (1923), showing remarkable subtlety and skill in handling visual narrative and accomplished control of his actors. Then, while scandal raged on the subject of his first divorce, he made the three films that mark the peak of his career: THE GOLD RUSH (1925), THE CIRCUS (1928), and CITY LIGHTS (1931). Although the last appeared after the introduction of sound, Chaplin used it only for music and effects. Words finally came from his mouth in MODERN TIMES (1936), but only in a gibberish song, and he did not speak until THE GREAT DICTATOR (1940). Significantly, these two films marked the end of the Tramp ('the little fellow' as Chaplin called him). His creator was right to distrust the use of words in his characterization, but there was no other persona he could assume that would capture the sympathy the Tramp had earned; Chaplin's achievement and success, based on one character and on his genius for mime, began to decline.

Meanwhile Chaplin's off-screen activities slowly eroded his popularity. His life was punctuated by four marriages (to Mildred Davis, Lita Grey, Paulette GODDARD, and Oona O'Neill, all teenagers except Goddard), three divorces, and countless scandals. He was charged with evading income tax and plagiarizing the plot of *The Great Dictator*. In 1942 he urged American friendship with Russia—advice later used to brand him a Communist. Most damning of all, he never took American citizenship and, after MONSIEUR VERDOUX (1947) which the popular press found disgusting and intolerable, he was threatened with having to appear before the UNAMERICAN ACTIVITIES Committee. When he visited Europe in 1952 to publicize LIMELIGHT, he was warned that if he returned he would be charged with 'moral turpitude and Communist sympathies'. He settled in Switzerland with his fourth wife. After twenty years and two comparatively unsuccessful European films (*A King in New York*, 1957; *A Countess from Hong Kong*, 1966) Hollywood proffered an olive branch and he was given a tumultuous reception at the 1972 OSCAR ceremony. He retired a wealthy man, having shrewdly maintained absolute rights over most of his films which he maintained until 1972, when they were sold to Black Ink Films, a company set up for the purpose. His son by Lita Grey, Sydney Jr (b. 1926), and one of his daughters by Oona O'Neill, Geraldine (b. 1944), are film actors.

It is unlikely that Chaplin was ever a Communist. His childhood made him sympathetic to the poor and down-trodden, of whom he had a rather Dickensian view, and he naturally assimilated some of the radical ideas of the writers and artists who discovered intellectual content in his films. But what he valued most was the freedom of the individual—a theme central to *Shoulder Arms*, *Modern Times*, and *The Great Dictator*, for instance; his life, his beliefs, and his films all illustrate the battle of the little man against the impersonal 'them'. If, towards the end of his long career, adulation and artistic freedom led him too far away from the instinctive, simple, and graceful comedy with which he began, his legacy nevertheless includes some of the greatest screen comedies ever made.

He has published three autobiographical volumes: *Charlie Chaplin's own story*, Indianapolis, 1916; *My trip abroad*, New York, 1930; *My autobiography*, London, 1964; New York, 1966. He was knighted in 1975.

**CHAPLIN,** SAUL (1912– ), US songwriter, wrote lyrics for Sammy Fain's songs in films of the early forties, but is best known as musical arranger on films such as *Cover Girl* (1944), *The Jolson Story* (1946), *Summer Stock* (1950, *If You Feel Like Singing* in GB), AN AMERICAN IN PARIS (1951), SEVEN BRIDES FOR SEVEN BROTHERS (1954), and WEST SIDE STORY (1961). He was also co-producer of *Les Girls* (1957), *West Side Story*, and THE SOUND OF MUSIC (1965).

**CHARISSE,** CYD (1924– ), US dancer and actress, real name Tula Ellice Finklea, trained as a dancer, and toured Europe with the de Basil Ballets Russes. She joined METRO-GOLDWYN-MAYER in 1945, appearing in several musicals, notably SINGIN' IN THE RAIN (1952), *It's Always Fair Weather* (1955), and *Silk Stockings* (1957), Rouben MAMOULIAN's remake of NINOTCHKA (1939), in which she played the role created by GARBO. Her career has progressed to straight acting in films such as TWO WEEKS IN ANOTHER TOWN (1962).

**CHARLIE CHAN,** character drawn from a series of books by Earl Derr Biggers about an inscrutable Chinese detective, who was the subject of just under fifty films. The adaptations were launched with a serial in 1926 and the series proper began when Warner Oland played the part in *Charlie Chan Carries On* (1931) and continued to play it for a further sixteen films. After his death in 1938, he was succeeded by Sidney Toler who made twenty-two Chan films before his death in 1947, when the role was taken over by Roland Winter, whose last Chan film was *Sky Dragon* (1949). J. Carroll Naish continued the tradition in thirty-nine television films (1957–8).

**CHARLOT,** name given by French distributors to the personality incarnated in his early films by Charlie CHAPLIN. Thus, for example, SHOULDER ARMS (1918) became in France *Charlot, soldat*. Chaplin himself coined the verb *charlotter* to describe the enthusiastic reception accorded him on personal appearances in France.

**CHARME DISCRET DE LA BOURGEOISIE,** *Le* (*The Discreet Charm of the Bourgeoisie*), France/Spain/Italy, 1972. Panavision; 1¾hr; Eastman Color. *Dir* Luis Buñuel; *prod* Greenwich Film (Paris)/Jet Film (Barcelona)/Dean Film (Rome); *scr* Buñuel, Jean-Claude Carrière; *ph* Edmond Richard; *cast* Fernando Rey (Ambassador), Delphine Seyrig (Mme Thévenot), Paul Frankier (M Thévenot), Stéphane Audran (Mme Sénéchal), Jean-Pierre Cassel (M Sénéchal), Bulle Ogier (Florence), Julien Bertheau (Bishop), Michel Piccoli (Home Secretary).

Six representatives of the *haute bourgeoisie* make repeated attempts to take a meal together: on each occasion their plans are disrupted by events that range from the terrifying to the ludicrous.

This basic framework inverts the situation of EL ANGEL EXTERMINADOR (1962), where a number of wealthy dinner guests are prevented from concluding their social engagement and which also contains a swingeing attack on bourgeois values. But there is an even closer relationship with LA VOIE LACTÉE (1969), which dissects

BUÑUEL's other lifelong bugbear, religion and the Church, with the same gleeful precision that he here applies to powerful, polite society. A similar fragmentary structure is used in the two films, with 'reality' interrupted by fantasy sequences (flashbacks in *La Voie lactée*, dreams in *Le Charme discret de la bourgeoisie*), all presented with a surreal intensity characteristic of Buñuel's mordant humour; and both are notable, compared with his Mexican films, for the polished quality of his spare technique and the accomplished acting of his players.

**CHARPIN,** FERNAND (1887–1944), French actor, born in Marseilles, specialized in roles requiring a meridional accent. While playing the lead in Roger Ferdinand's play *Chotard et Cie* at the Odéon he was seen by RAIMU who asked him to play Panisse in Marcel PAGNOL's *Marius*. Charpin, whose career had been modest until this time, never forgot that it was Raimu who gave him his great chance and the two remained close friends until Charpin's death. His success in the film of MARIUS (1931) was the first of thirty character roles in some of the best French films of the thirties, including Marc ALLÉGRET's *Fanny* (1932), DUVIVIER's *La Belle Equipe* (1935) and PÉPÉ-LE-MOKO (1936), and Pagnol's *César* (1936) and LA FEMME DU BOULANGER (1938).

**CHARULATA,** India, 1964. 2hr. *Dir, scr, mus* Satyajit Ray, based on the novel by Rabindranath Tagore; *prod* R. D. Bansal; *ph* Subrata Mitra; *des* Bansi Chandragupta; *ed* Dulal Dutta; *cast* Madhabi Mukherjee (Charulata), Sailen Mukherjee (Bhupati), Soumitra Chatterjee (Amal).

RAY's unerring social observation combines here with his warm interest in human relationships to create a rounded picture of a marriage nearing breakdown. The husband, Bhupati, involved with his political journal, has neglected Charulata; from loneliness and boredom, she almost persuades herself into an affair with his younger brother, and Bhupati for the first time becomes aware of the possibility of betrayal. The couple's final attempt at reconstructing their relationship is summed up in the final frozen shot of their hands not quite meeting—a grave comment on the falsity of easy happy endings. Soumitra Chatterjee gives probably his best performance for Ray as the light-hearted young poet who is caught up in emotions too powerful for him.

**CHASE, The,** US, 1966. Panavision; 2¼hr (2hr in GB); Technicolor. *Dir* Arthur Penn; *prod* Sam Spiegel for Columbia; *scr* Lillian Hellman, from the novel and play by Horton Foote; *ph* Joseph LaShelle, Robert Surtees; *cast* Marlon Brando (Sheriff Calder), Jane Fonda (Anna Reeves), Robert Redford (Bubber Reeves), E. G. Marshall (Val Rogers), Angie Dickinson (Ruby Calder).

The escape of Bubber Reeves from a State prison has dramatic and violent consequences. In his Texan home town, vested interests and prejudice are easily activated on a drunken Saturday night against the handful of people, including the sheriff, who would give Bubber a fair hearing.

Despite an over-insistence on the town's total corruptness, *The Chase* is a powerful film; its explicit violence and explosive and cynical climax do not seem gratuitous. The end, however, reminiscent of Lee Harvey Oswald's assassination, aroused criticism at the time. In comparison with PENN's next film, BONNIE AND CLYDE (1967), *The Chase* has perhaps been unjustly neglected.

**CHASE,** CHARLEY (1893–1940), US comedian and director, real name Charles Parrott, who appeared in over 200 short films and directed about 100. He began in vaudeville, but by 1914 he was at the Mack SENNETT Studios first as an actor working with CHAPLIN and ARBUCKLE, then from 1915, as a director using his real name. He started working for Hal ROACH in 1921, and was joined later by his brother James who worked principally as a director but also did some acting under the name of Paul Parrott and is often confused with his brother. In 1923 Charley began a successful and long running series in which he played a dapper innocent constantly getting into trouble. Some of the best films were directed by Leo MCCAREY: later Charley and his brother took over the direction. When Roach stopped making short films in 1936, Charley moved to COLUMBIA where he continued making comedy shorts until his death.

**CHAUVEL,** CHARLES (1897–1959), Australian director whose activity as a film-maker (producer and writer as well as director) dates back to the twenties: his best known silent film is *Moth of Mombi* (1926). He became known outside Australia with *Forty Thousand Horsemen* (1942) and *Rats of Tobruk* (1948). Other well-known examples of his work are *The Rugged O'Riordans* (1948) and *Jedda* (1953).

**CHAYEFSKY,** PADDY (1923–    ), US playwright and scriptwriter, real forename Sidney. He made his reputation with plays for television, moving into films in the fifties when straight drama began to disappear from the American television screen. MARTY (1955), *The Bachelor Party* (1957), and *Middle of the Night* (1959) were all adapted from his television work: they demonstrate his ability to portray ordinary, inarticulate people and a preference for limited physical surroundings. His later screenplays written directly for films deal with larger subjects; they include *The Goddess* (1958), *The Americanization of Emily* (1964), *Ice Station Zebra* (1968), and *Paint Your Wagon* (1969).

***CHELOVEK S KINOAPPARATOM*** (*Man with a Movie Camera*), USSR, 1929, 1½hr. *Dir* Dziga Vertov; *asst* Elizaveta Svilova; *ph* Mikhail Kaufman.

VERTOV's last silent feature film presents a montage of city life, but his aim is less to document Moscow than to reveal all the technical possibilities of the camera, which becomes the hero of the film. The film goes beyond KINO-GLAZ in its attempt to give its audience the role of director: film footage here becomes, as Vertov hoped, as rapid as the thoughts of its audience.

The film was criticized, notably by EISEN-STEIN, for the formal virtuosity of its technique, but it was a revelation of the tenuous relation between reality, perceived reality, and filmed reality: moreover, Vertov maintains from the opening shot a disarming mood of infectious gaiety.

**CHERKASOV,** NIKOLAI (1903–66), Russian actor of broad range and great intellectual power, began his career in music-hall as a comic actor. He was brought to fame by his role as the 75-year-old Professor Polezhayev in HEIFITS's *Deputat Baltiki* (*Baltic Deputy*, 1937), and he went on to play the leading roles in EISENSTEIN's ALEXANDER NEVSKY (1938) and the two-part IVAN GROZNYI (*Ivan the Terrible*, 1944–58), where his exceptional height and deep voice were of great advantage. He did not, however, always see eye to eye with Eisenstein, whom he criticized for being more interested in visual effects than in allowing his actors to give good performances. He also played the part of Gorky in ROMM's *Lenin v 1918 godu* (1939).

His later films include *Stalingradskaya bitva* (*Battle of Stalingrad*, 1950), *Rimsky-Korsakov* (1952), *Don Quixote* (1956), and *Vsyo ostayotsia lyudyam* (*Legacy*, 1963). He also worked in the theatre and wrote several articles and books, including *Notes of a Soviet actor*. He was a prominent public figure and served as a deputy in the Supreme Soviet.

**CHEVALIER,** MAURICE (1888–1972), French entertainer, gained an international reputation in the Paris music halls of the twenties. With Jeanette MACDONALD as his leading lady, he lent charm and distinction to early Hollywood musicals, especially LUBITSCH's THE LOVE PARADE (1930) and *One Hour With You* (1932) and MAMOULIAN'S LOVE ME TONIGHT (1932), in

which he sang the song always identified with him, 'Mimi'. He made a film come-back in WILDER's *Love in the Afternoon* (1957) and was particularly successful as the ageing roué in GIGI (1958), where his insouciant manner was revealed at its best in the songs 'I Remember It Well' and 'Thank Heaven for Little Girls'.

**CHIARINI,** LUIGI (1900–   ), Italian critic and film theorist, began in journalism and worked on the Fascist literary magazine *Quadrovia*. In 1935 he founded the CENTRO SPERIMENTALE DI CINEMATOGRAFIA and started the journal BIANCO E NERO which he edited until 1951. He published *Cinque capitoli sul film* in 1941 and, in 1949, *Film nei problemi dell'arte*, perhaps his most influential work, in which he expounded his theory of the cinema as an art of collaboration and defined the role of the director as the unifying force among the mass of disparate contributors. In 1952 he founded *Rivista del cinema italiano*; during these years he also wrote critical articles for CINEMA, *Cinema nuovo*, and *Il contemporaneo*. In 1959 he was appointed Professor of Film at the University of Pisa and he was director of the VENICE Film Festival, 1963–9.

Chiarini has also been practically involved in film-making, as scriptwriter with DE SICA on *Stazione termine* (1953), with BLASETTI on *La fiammata* (1953) and *Tempi nostri* (1954), and on AMORE IN CITTÀ (1963). His films as director, including *Via delle cinque lune* (1942), *La Bella addormentata* (1942), and *Patto col diavolo* (1950), are all adaptations from literary sources: they reveal a cold, formal style that is not engaging.

***CHIEN ANDALOU, Un,*** France, 1928. 25min. *Dir* Luis Buñuel; *prod, scr* Buñuel, Salvador Dali; *ph* Albert Dubergen; *des* Schilzneck; *mus* Beethoven, Wagner, a tango; *cast* Simone Mareuil, Pierre Batcheff, Jaime Miravilles, Salvador Dali, Luis Buñuel.

Salvador DALI and Luis BUÑUEL conceived their first collaboration as a series of jokes. Their intention was that nothing in the film should be capable of rational explanation but should have the logic of a dream. *Un Chien andalou* is an exposition of automatism, a technique suggested by André Breton, SURREALISM's spokesman, as a means of tapping a rich supply of images from the unconscious mind. Some of the film's images recur with remarkable consistency through Buñuel's mature work.

The music chosen to accompany the silent film was added as a sound-track in 1960.

**CHILDREN'S FILM FOUNDATION.** The long-standing popularity in Britain of children's matinées held, usually on Saturday mornings, in

*Un Chien andalou* (Luis Buñuel, 1928)

local cinemas, prompted J. Arthur RANK to set up in 1944 a Children's Entertainment Films Division of the RANK ORGANISATION. Mary Field was appointed director and in 1951 was awarded the OBE in recognition of her work. In that year the British film industry took over the project under its present name, with Rank as chairman, succeeded by John Davis in 1960, and with Mary Field as Executive Officer. The Cinematograph Films Act, 1957, guaranteed the CFF an annual grant (amount unspecified) from the BRITISH FILM PRODUCTION FUND: this, together with reduced fees to actors and directors, agreed in co-operation with the unions, subsidizes the production of low-budget features (usually about an hour long), shorts, and serials aimed at the 7–13 age group. This system of production of children's films is unique to Britain. From the earliest days under the Rank Organisation, the production committees have aimed at films with a healthy moral (but not moralizing) content. As the films are shown only at children's matinées and for servicemen's families in forces' camps, never at ordinary public shows or on television, it is difficult to assess how they would compare with films made for a competitive commercial market.

**CHILD STARS.** Hollywood producers in the twenties quickly discovered that films featuring small, winsome children had an almost unlimited appeal for the public; for two decades child performers were a valuable property in the film world. They became an important element in the STAR SYSTEM, with the benefits and tribulations that accrued to adult stars; but the greater vulnerability of children sometimes led to even more serious exploitation. Within a few years a child actor could acquire a huge fortune and as quickly lose it again to greedy relatives. Their success was often attributable to the kind of driving ambition ironically portrayed in VISCONTI'S BELLISSIMÀ (1951). Exploitation was rife on the emotional as well as the financial level.

Mary PICKFORD was one of the earliest child stars, featured in fifteen of GRIFFITH's shorts in 1909. She enjoyed a long career, playing the role of a ringleted innocent well into adulthood in spite of her attempts to be accepted in mature roles. Jackie COOGAN rapidly became famous for his performance as the appealing urchin in CHAPLIN'S THE KID (1920). He was immediately signed up by FIRST NATIONAL and featured in a series of films, usually as a pathetic waif. For a short time Coogan became an international idol, with events such as his first short haircut becoming headline news. By the time he was thirteen, however, his stardom was over and he was later obliged to sue his mother and stepfather to recover the remains of his fortune.

Freddie BARTHOLOMEW specialized in demure roles such as DAVID COPPERFIELD (1934) and *Little Lord Fauntleroy* (1937). His earnings amounted to a million dollars, but lengthy legal wrangles between his aunt (who had managed his career and who wished to adopt him) and his parents dissipated most of his fortune. Mickey ROONEY became famous as the young ANDY HARDY. His undoubted talent was never fully developed, but there is lasting quality in the films he made co-starring Judy GARLAND. The latter was one of the child stars to suffer most bitterly from the pressures of exploitation: her whole life, while she was under contract to METRO-GOLDWYN-MAYER, was unscrupulously manipulated, and her adult career was marred by several severe breakdowns. Deanna DURBIN became a star at fourteen years old in *Three Smart Girls* (1936), a film which saved UNIVERSAL from bankruptcy. Jackie Cooper made his name in *Skippy* (1930) and counted among his other successes *The Champ* (1931) and *Treasure Island* (1935). He was particularly notable for his ability to cry convincingly and his films usually featured scenes of copious weeping.

Shirley TEMPLE, most famous of all child stars, was for a decade TWENTIETH CENTURY-FOX's biggest earner, being number one box-office attraction in America 1936-8 leading from Clark GABLE, Mae WEST, Joan CRAWFORD, and Bing CROSBY. During the dreary years of the economic slump she became the idol of America, and was even thanked by President Roosevelt for 'bringing America through the Depression with a smile'. She was also awarded a special OSCAR in 1934 'in grateful recognition of her outstanding contribution to screen entertainment'.

Bobby Breen, Bonita Granville, Baby Leroy (Winnebrenner), Jane Withers, and the various children who starred in Hal ROACH's *Our Gang* films from 1922 onwards were other well-known stars of the time. The child star, whose own name was a box-office draw, was a strictly American phenomenon, although at least one attempt was made in Britain to compete with Hollywood's profitable properties with Binkie Stewart. Their popularity was limited to the twenties and thirties, a time of economic depression when the need for escapist entertainment responded to the fairy-tale quality of their films.

The glib professionalism of the Hollywood child stars contrasts with the outstandingly authentic performances which some European directors have drawn from child actors, although in both traditions of film-making the child has most frequently been portrayed as the victim of oppression. Directors such as DE SICA, in SCIUSCIÀ (1946) and LADRI DI BICICLETTE (1948), and

TRUFFAUT, in LES QUATRE CENTS COUPS (1959) and L'ENFANT SAUVAGE (1970), have directed children with extraordinary success. Other films with excellent child performances include LES JEUX INTERDITS (1952) and KES (1970).

**CHILE.** A short documentary made in 1916 was the start of Chilean cinema, but the industry remained undeveloped through lack of technique, shortage of funds, and American competition: in 1917–29 only 78 films were made. Jorge Délano was a pioneer, first improvising a studio in his own home and then establishing one at Santa Elena. His *Juráme no volver a amar* launched Guillermo Janquez, an actor who became exceedingly popular, and *La Calle del ensueño* (1929) was so successful it was shown at Seville where it won a prize.

Film-making continued sporadically after sound was introduced in 1934. *Hollywood es asi* (1944) was a notable success. Chile Films, financed by the Radio Corporation of Chile, government funds, and public subscription, came into being in 1944 and founded a studio outside Santiago. After producing only nine films they went bankrupt in 1947. There were a few co-productions with Mexico, Argentina, and Brazil.

An actively political group of film-makers emerged under the banner of Salvador Allende's Frente Revolucionario de Alianza Popular. Strongly influenced by recent developments in Latin American cinema, especially in BRAZIL and CUBA, they made short films supporting Allende's candidacy for the 1964 presidential election, later forming themselves into an independent co-operative, Cinematografia Tercer Mundo. Their two most remarkable films, both made in 1969, were Aldo Francia's *Valparaiso mi amor*, attacking discrimination against the lower classes in the legal system, and Miguel Littin's *El Chacal de Nahueltero (The Jackal of Nahueltero)*, a semi-documentary reconstruction of the case of a peasant, brutalized by the aimless poverty of his class, who committed a futile mass murder.

Chilean cinema was nationalized soon afterwards, when Allende became president. The new Chile Films produced documentaries and newsreels, renting its studio and technical facilities for independent feature production. The documentaries made by Littin have a relaxed, accessible style, avoiding the pamphleteering of many political film-makers. No steps were taken to restrict the import of foreign films, and the young Chilean industry seemed to promise an unusual balance of politics and entertainment. The military coup of 1973, however, resulted in an extreme right-wing government, and at present the future of the cinema in Chile is far from promising.

CHIMES AT MIDNIGHT see CAMPANADAS A
MEDIANOCHE

CHINA. The first films seen in China were of
French and American origin, both shown in
Shanghai, in 1896 and 1897 respectively. The
first film-makers were foreigners, shooting scenes
of everyday life and of the Russo-Japanese War
for exhibition in Europe and America. Some
small companies were formed (mostly with foreign capital) in the early years, filming scenes
from Peking operas, one of which formed the
basis of the first Chinese fiction film, Ting-chun
Shan (Tingchun Mountain, 1908), or making
slapstick comedies in imitation of those being
imported. It was not until an American, Benjamin Polaski, set up the Asia Motion Picture
Company in co-operation with two Chinese in
1908 that original films, such as Pu Hsi Erh (The
Unfilial Son), and Hsi T'ai Hou (The Widowed
Empress), both made in 1909, were regularly
produced for home distribution. In 1917, the
Commercial Press, a Shanghai publishing company, set up a film department which, besides
making entertainment films, began to produce
newsreels and documentaries, some of which
were distributed as part of a mass education and
literacy programme conducted by Sun Yat-sen's
revolutionary forces.

The first all-Chinese film company was Ming
Hsing (Star), established at Shanghai in 1922.
This company made some of the best films of the
silent period, including Ku Erh Chiu Tsu Chi
(Orphan Rescues Grandfather, 1923), directed
by Cheng Chen-chin.

Inflation caused a crisis in the industry in
1925 and conditions were still unstable when
sound films were first introduced into the
country. Few companies were financially able to
change to the new medium, but in 1931 Ming
Hsing released the first Chinese sound film, Sing-
song Girl Red Peony. In Shanghai talking pictures were in Mandarin (or Peking) Chinese,
not in the local dialect, which meant that few of
the audience could understand them. Small
companies started up in Hong Kong and Canton
making films in Cantonese. These were
distributed in China, and also in large numbers
to Chinese communities abroad.

The political upheavals of the late twenties and
early thirties—the beginning of the Civil War,
Chiang Kai-shek's coup d'état in 1927, and the
Japanese attacks on Shanghai, Manchuria, and
Central China—did much to encourage a growing social realism in Chinese films. The first
important film from this movement was Wild
Torrent (1933), directed by Cheng Bu-kao, about
the oppression of the peasants by landlords and
authorities after the flooding of the Yangtse river.
One of the most noted directors of the period was

Tsai Chu-sheng, who made The Song of the
Fishermen (1934), showing the hardships of the
Yangtse fishermen. A great success in China, this
was the first film to gain acclaim abroad, being
awarded a prize at the Moscow Festival of 1935.
Other films which broke away from the theatre-
based romantic costume dramas and violent
sword-play adventures include Shen Hsi-ling's
Crossroads (1937), about unemployed ex-
students.

When the Japanese invaded Shanghai in 1937,
many film-makers left for Hong Kong or Taiwan,
but others followed the government, first to
Hankow and then to Chungking. The Japanese
took over, or built, studios as they advanced and
used Chinese actors and technicians who had
stayed in Shanghai to make propaganda co-
productions such as Song of the White Orchid
(1939, directed by Kunio Watanabe) about a
Manchurian girl and a Japanese immigrant, and
Sorrows Left at Spring River (1944, directed by
Hiroshi Inagaki and Yueh Feng) about the Tai-
ping rebellion. Several patriotic films, such as Sai
Shan Feng Yün (Storm on the Border, 1940),
directed by Ying Yun-wei, were made in
Chungking. But perhaps more important was a
small group of film-makers who followed the
Communist forces to Yenan. The first film made
there, Yenan Yü Pa Lu Chün (Yenan and the
Eighth Route Army, 1939), was followed by
several documentaries recording the activities of
the Communists at this time.

After the war, the left-wing groups produced
the best films of the pre-Republic period I Kian
Ch'un Shui Hsiang Tung Liu (Spring River
Flows East/Tears of the Yangtse, 1947), directed
by Tsai Chu-sheng, Ch'iao (The Bridge, 1949),
directed by Wang Pin, and Cheng Chun-li's
Crows and Sparrows (1949).

After the establishment of the Republic in
October 1949 the film industry was nationalized.
A Film Bureau was set up under the Ministry of
Culture, and was made responsible for the six or
seven major studios and those that made news-
reels, documentaries, and educational and other
shorts. The first film from the People's Republic
of China was Chung Kuo Jen Min Ti Shen Li
(Victory of the Chinese People, 1950), made with
technical and financial assistance from the Soviet
Union and directed by Leonid Varlamov and
Liu Pai-yu. Some of the studios were closed
during the Cultural Revolution of 1966 and film
production continued at a much reduced rate.
Other government organizations include the
Film Archive of China, founded in 1957, and the
Chinese Film Workers' Association which pub-
lishes several magazines on film theory.

The feature films of New China are frequently
propagandist, many based on the theme of the
armed struggle of the peasants under the leader-

ship of the Communist Party, showing how any obstacle can be overcome by following the teachings of Chairman Mao Tse-tung. Others portray events from Chinese history: peasant workers oppressed by cruel landlords and overseers or exploited by Western capitalists. Many of these films are adapted from new or 'revised' Peking operas, a form still very popular with audiences, or from literary works. Some of the more important films made before the Cultural Revolution include *Hsin Erh Yü Yin Hsiung Chu'an* (*New Heroes and Heroines*, 1950), directed by Shih Tung-shan; *Liang Shan-po and Chu Ying-tsi* (1953), by Sang Hu and Huang Sha; *Li Shuangshuang* (*The Peasant Hsiang Lin's Wife*, 1962) by Lu Jen; *Serfs* (1964), by Li Chung, about the conditions of the Tibetan peasants; and *The East is Red* (1965), the film of a four-hour pageant held in 1964 to mark the fifteenth anniversary of the Republic. After the Cultural Revolution, 'revised' versions were made of some popular films, for example, *Chih Ch'ü Hua Shan* (*Taking Tiger Mountain by Strategy/The Capture by Stratagem of Mount Hua*, 1970), originally filmed in 1953. *Pai Mao Nü* (*The White-Haired Girl*), first produced as an opera in 1949 and based on an actual event, was filmed in 1950. The opera was rewritten after the Cultural Revolution and a film of this version was released in 1972.

China has long realized the value of the cinema as a medium for propaganda and instruction. Many documentary and educational shorts are made each year; while some are straightforward exhortations to follow the Party line, others may induce pride in China's cultural heritage or give instruction, particularly in agricultural subjects. The films are shown in cinemas, clubrooms, factories, at fixed points in rural areas, and from about 8000 mobile units in the less accessible country districts. The development of a new 8·75mm gauge has meant that these mobiles can use cheaper and lighter equipment than was previously possible.

Chinese film-makers have been active in the Third World countries of Asia, Africa, and Latin America, helping with the production of films locally, showing Chinese films, and making films about the developing nations for home distribution. Films from Taiwan, much aided by American finance, have mostly tried to copy the commercial style of HONG KONG, but have had little success abroad.

*Dianying: electric shadows* by Jay Leyda (Boston, 1972) is the first comprehensive history in English of the Chinese cinema.

**CHOMETTE,** HENRI (1891–1941), French director, brother of René CLAIR, worked during the twenties as assistant to Jacques de BARON-CELLI and Jacques FEYDER, but was at that time more interested in his own theories of 'pure cinema'. Three short films, *Jeux de reflets et de vitesse* (1925), *Cinq minutes de cinéma pur* (1925), and *A quoi rêvent les jeunes filles* (1927), put into practice his ideal of editing isolated images into an abstract, rather than a narrative, sequence. He never associated himself with any AVANT-GARDE group and his experiments met with little success. During the thirties he directed a few light comedies, but they lacked the grace and originality of his brother's films.

**CHOMÓN,** SEGUNDO DE (1871–1929), Spanish cameraman, director, and technical innovator, trained as an engineer and was interested in cinema from its earliest days. He set up his own company in Barcelona in 1902, at first for manufacture and processing, later expanding into documentary production. PATHÉ became interested in his TINTING process and commissioned him to colour prints of their films for Spanish distribution. In 1906 he joined Pathé in Paris. While working there he investigated various devices including the process later to become Pathécolor, animation techniques, a form of superimposition, a camera DOLLY, and various kinds of masking. His enterprise and ingenuity were remarkable, but his talents as a director were limited. In 1910, again in Barcelona, he set up another independent company whose output was prolific but mediocre. The offer of a generous contract by ITALA FILM took him in 1912 to Italy where for several years he collaborated with Giovanni PASTRONE, notably on CABIRIA (1914). From 1919 he was in demand as chief cameraman and special effects consultant in Italy and in France, where he worked on NAPOLÉON (1927) for Abel GANCE.

**CHRÉTIEN,** HENRI see ANAMORPHIC LENS

**CHRISTENSEN,** BENJAMIN (1879–1959), Danish director known as Christianson in Germany and the US, trained as a singer and turned to acting when his voice failed. He first worked in cinema as a writer, in 1912, and as an actor from 1913. In 1915 he wrote, directed, and acted in *Haevnens nat* (*Night of Vengeance*) in Denmark, later moving to Sweden where, between 1918 and 1921, he made his most famous film HÄXAN (*Witchcraft through the Ages*, 1922). He went to Germany in 1924 and worked for UFA, acting and directing; in 1926 he was invited to work in Hollywood. The mystery comedies he directed there, including *The Haunted House* (1928) and *The House of Horror* (1929), both with Chester CONKLIN, were craftsmanlike representatives of the genre. Shortly before the outbreak of war he returned to Denmark. He directed three films on social problems and a thriller in the early forties and spent the last seventeen years of his life as manager of a Copenhagen cinema, benefiting from the municipality's enlightened policy towards distinguished former film workers (see DENMARK).

**CHRISTIAN-JAQUE** (1904– ), prolific French director, real name Christian Maudet, has been directing since 1932. He first attracted serious attention with *Les Disparus de Saint-Agil* (1938), a blend of mystery and satirical comedy starring Erich von STROHEIM and Michel SIMON and set in a boys' boarding school. His wartime work included the extraordinary *L'Assassinat du Père Noël* (1941), *La Symphonie fantastique* (1941), a biography of Berlioz, and a CARMEN (1942) with the smouldering Viviane Romance in the title role. *Boule de Suif* (1945) and *Un Revenant* (1946), with its superb performance by Louis JOUVET, gained him critical esteem, and he hit a successful streak in the early fifties with *Fanfan la Tulipe* (1951), the star-studded *Souvenirs perdus* (1951), and *Adorables créatures* (1953). His wife Martine CAROL frequently starred in his films.

**CHRISTIE,** JULIE (1940– ), British actress, was first widely noticed as the hero's unattainable ideal girl in *Billy Liar* (John SCHLESINGER, 1963). Schlesinger's *Darling* (1965), in which she played a fashion model unscrupulously making use of her charms, made her an international success. Her acting style is poised and modern; she was somewhat out of key both in the future of TRUFFAUT's *Fahrenheit 451* (1966) and in the period settings of DOCTOR ZHIVAGO (1966) and *Far From the Madding Crowd* (Schlesinger, 1967). She gave a fine performance, however, in THE GO-BETWEEN (1971) as a complacent Edwardian beauty, calmly exploiting other people for her own pleasure; and in *Don't Look Now* (Nicholas ROEG, 1973) she was convincing as a sensual, impulsive woman caught up in mysterious events.

*CHRONIQUE D'UN ÉTÉ,* France, 1961. 1½hr. *Dir* Jean Rouch, Edgar Morin; *prod* Argos Films; *ph* Roger Morillers, Raoul Coutard, J-J. Tarbes, Michel Brault; *ed* Jean Ravel.
Jean ROUCH had studied and recorded on film the effects of European culture on African societies; Edgar MORIN had been stimulated by ROGOSIN's ON THE BOWERY (1957) and REISZ's *We Are the Lambeth Boys* (1959) to apply an ethnographic approach to the lives of groups of Parisians; recent improvements in 16MM synchronous units allowed informal, flexible filming. About twenty-five hours of interviews with factory workers, students, and artists were filmed,

but disagreement arose over the editing. The producers demanded a smooth, conventional flow of sequences, Rouch preferred an objective, biographical approach, and Morin's aim was a philosophical dialectic based on the question 'Are you happy?' The finished film betrays these conflicting approaches; and although Rouch and Morin themselves appear frequently in the interviews, the tone is one of detachment from the people who are its subjects.
The term CINÉMA-VÉRITÉ was coined by the producers to publicize the film and later extended to describe a new philosophy of documentary film-making. (See also DIRECT CINEMA, DOCUMENTARY.)

**CHRONOCHROME,** an early three-colour ADDITIVE process for producing colour motion pictures, dating from 1912. (See COLOUR.)

**CHUKRAI,** GRIGORI (1921– ), Russian director born in the Ukraine, started in films as a pupil of Mikhail ROMM. His first full-length film *Nazar Srodolia* (1954) was adapted from the play of the same name by Taras Shevchenko. He attracted a great deal of attention with his second film SOROK PERVYI (*The Forty-First*, 1956), an adaptation of one of Lavrenev's stories, which had already been filmed once, silent, by PROTAZANOV in 1928. This was a barely concealed attack on the already dying cult of the hero, which had been promulgated and encouraged by Stalin. His next film BALLADA O SOLDATE (1959) drew on his own experiences of the misery and waste of war and the confusion of the aftermath. Official repudiation of Stalinism enabled Chukrai to make a direct attack upon it in his next film *Chistoye nebo* (*Clear Skies*, 1961). This is a much more politically opportunist film and lacks the warmth and lyricism of his earlier work. His latest film to reach the West is *Zhili-bili starik so starukhoi* (*There was an old man and an old woman*, 1965).

**CHURCHILL,** WINSTON SPENCER (1874–1965), an avid film fan and noted dilettante, signed a contract with Alexander KORDA's LONDON FILMS in 1934 and worked as a writer and adviser on films like *The 25-Year Reign of George V* (uncompleted) and *Conquest of the Air* (1938). He was largely responsible for the script of *Lady Hamilton* (1941) which Korda took with him to Hollywood. A feature documentary, *The Finest Hours* (1964), and an American television series, *The Valiant Years* (1960), were centred on him, and he was, of course, portrayed often in films dealing with wartime Britain. Richard ATTENBOROUGH's *Young Winston* (1972) was an account of his early life.

**CHYTILOVÁ, VĚRA** (1929–    ), Czech director, studied philosophy and architecture and worked as technical draughtsman and fashion model before getting a job at BARRANDOV as continuity girl. She rose fast to assistant director (on *Ztracenci*, *Three Men Missing*, Makovec, 1957), and in the same year enrolled at FAMU, the Prague film school. Her time there coincided with that of SCHORM, NĚMEC, and of other future directors of Czechoslovakia's new wave. Her graduation film, *Strop* (*Ceiling*, 1962), was a medium-length which marked her immediately as one of the first formalists of the new wave, although the story remained in line with acceptable socialist-realist tenets: a pretty medical student drops into the world of fashion shows and finally realizes the vacuity of her existence when she boards a train and meets simple, hard-working country people. The fashion-show sequences, in particular, show the influence that CINÉMA-VÉRITÉ had on Chytilová and her contemporaries, and official misgivings on the score of the film's formalism were overborne by approval for its content. Her next film, also 1962, *Pytel blech* (*A Bag of Fleas*), about textile workers, was more ostensibly in the *cinéma-vérité* style. The story of a sixteen-year-old girl who puts her boy-friend before her work was filmed in a direct manner, and, although the action was in fact entirely staged, non-actors were used throughout and a certain amount of the dialogue improvised. The portrait of factory officials (played by themselves) aroused opposition which delayed the film's release for a year.

Traits already evident in Chytilová's work became prominent in her next film, her first feature-length film from her own story and script, *O něčem jiném* (*Another Way of Life* or *About Something Else*, 1963). *Cinéma-vérité* technique and preoccupation with formal articulation of philosophical statement, besides an emerging feminism, were apparent in the juxtaposed stories of two very different women's lives (one of them Eva Bosáková, world record-holder in gymnastics, the other a dissatisfied housewife). Chytilová's interest in pop music had already been hinted at in *Pytel blech*, in the controversial passages about the young workers' liking for 'eccentric western dances', and her next project was a reaction to the official war on popular jazz and pop singers. She wrote a film which was to feature one of two women singers who had been prosecuted and banned from singing: not surprisingly, the script was turned down out of hand.

The importance of the pop music world for Czechoslovak film-makers was, however, one of the strands woven into her next individual project, SEDMIKRÁSKY (*Daisies*, 1966). (She was one of the directors contributing to the PONTI-sponsored *Perličky na dně*, *Pearls of the Deep*, 1965, having characteristically chosen a weird story about a bride.) Except for one or two sequences and the retention of non-actors, the *cinéma-vérité* technique was abandoned in *Sedmikrásky*, which was instead conceived in a dazzlingly sophisticated formal structure. Ester KRUMBACHOVÁ's designs and the photography of Jaroslav KUČERA (whom Chytilová had recently married) brilliantly support her organization of her own preoccupations into a film which is one of the most extreme statements to come from a socialist country and which is masterly by any standards. The not-very-convincing framework of nuclear destruction did not save the film from inevitable official condemnation. Political tension over the growing freedom of expression among artists remained high: *Sedmikrásky* shared the fate of Němec's O SLAVNOSTI A HOSTECH (*The Party and the Guests*) and Schorm's *Návrat ztraceného syna* (*The Return of the Prodigal Son*, both the same year) in being refused release. The ban on *Sedmikrásky* was lifted in 1967, but the embargo on funds for Chytilová remained, and her next film was financed by the Belgian company Elisabeth Films. *Ovoce stromu rajskych jime* (*The Fruit of the Trees of Paradise*, 1970), with Krumbachová once again collaborating on the design and script and Kučera on the photography, was shown at the 1970 CANNES Festival. Colour, music, and visual metaphors are again brilliantly woven in a complex symbolic structure, now very far removed from Chytilová's documentary beginnings. She has stayed in Czechoslovakia, but has been unable to make a film since.

**CINECITTÀ** film studios were built on the outskirts of Rome to replace the CINES studio destroyed by fire in 1935. The project was backed by an industrialist, Carlo Roncoroni, who died shortly after the building was completed; the government took over the studios and ran them directly. During the war Cinecittà was bombed and then used as a transit camp, but by 1950 the damage had been repaired and the studios were running at full efficiency. Claimed to be the biggest studio in Europe, Cinecittà offers a vast industrial complex with fourteen stages of various dimensions and three pools, the largest of which measures $62 \times 165$ metres. Cinecittà was the setting for parts of VISCONTI's BELLISSIMÀ (1951) and ANTONIONI's *La signora senza camelie* (1952). It has frequently been used for international productions, especially for large-scale projects such as BEN-HUR (1959), CLEOPATRA (1962), and FELLINI's *Roma* (1972).

**CINECOLOR,** a two-colour film process used considerably in the late thirties as a cheaper substitute for TECHNICOLOR. It had an emulsion on both sides of the film, toned orange and blue-green; these characteristic colours became widely associated with 'B' pictures and Westerns. (See COLOUR.)

**CINEMA.** Buildings designed exclusively for the showing of films did not appear until well after the turn of the century. The earliest films, regarded as a passing novelty, were shown in gaudily decorated fairground booths, or projected in theatres and music halls between the acts of the main entertainment. There were also mobile projection booths which projected their films on to outdoor screens in public squares.

Films found their first permanent home in crudely converted shops, the nickelodeons of the US, the 'penny gaffs' of England. As the popularity of films grew, larger buildings, old factories, skating rinks, or theatres, were converted for use as cinemas, also popularly known as bioscopes or electric theatres.

It is thought that Central Hall, Colne, in Lancashire, built for the showman Joshua Duckworth in 1907, was the first building in Britain specifically designed and constructed for the showing of films. Cinemas proliferated throughout the provinces, as well as London, where Leicester Square had early established itself as a centre of film entertainment with shows at two variety theatres, the Empire Music Hall, and the Alhambra. The West End Cinema (c. 1912), later the Rialto, was probably the first auditorium to be designed as a cinema in London.

The hybrid origins of the cinema as a building are reflected in the heterogeneous style characteristic of early picture-house design. If the gaudy and elaborately decorated façade bore witness to a fairground origin, the neo-classical décor, the red plush and the crystal chandeliers (all borrowed from the variety theatre), strove to conceal the cinema's vagabond beginnings. Indeed, interiors at first closely resembled those of conventional theatres, even down to the provision of an orchestra pit, a stage, and dressing rooms for the live performers who preceded the film show.

The British Cinematograph Act of 1909 laid down certain regulations which helped shape the design of cinemas. These required the provision of a separate fireproof projection box, freedom of access, adequate exits, and the provision of fire appliances. Similar laws were passed in the United States at the same time.

Cinema design in the US developed rapidly after 1912, the picture houses became increasingly elaborate and luxurious, evolving into the fantastic 'movie palaces' of the twenties. Thomas Lamb was the first major architect to distinguish himself in cinema design. His early buildings included the Regent (1913), the Strand Theater (1914), the Rialto (1916), and the Rivoli (1917), all in New York and under the flamboyant management of S. L. Rothafel (Roxy). Resolutely neo-classical exteriors were matched by luxurious interiors, perhaps in Adam or Empire style, designed with elaborate attention to detail and effect. By 1921, Lamb had designed over 300 picture palaces, which introduced a new scale of opulence to the cinema.

In 1914–20, war-imposed building restrictions prevented the development of British cinema architecture. When expansion recommenced, the American influence, and particularly that of Lamb, was dominant, although the British approach tended to be haphazard, even unprofessional, at least until the thirties. There were exceptions, as in the work of Robert Atkinson, who was closely acquainted with American cinema design, and who introduced a new standard of functional efficiency into British cinema building with his Brighton Regent (1921). Frank T. Verity's Shepherd's Bush Pavilion, opened in 1923, distinguished itself by winning the RIBA's annual London Street Architecture award.

American picture-palace architecture reached unparalleled extravagance during the twenties. John Eberson specialized in 'atmospheric' design in which the auditorium seemed to be set out of doors in some exotic locality: the Majestic, Houston (1923), the Bronx Paradise (1925), and the Chicago Paradise (1928) were various expressions of Italianate rococo built for Loew's Inc. Meyer and Holler designed the two most famous Hollywood cinemas: Grauman's Egyptian (1922) reflected the current rage for the relics of Ancient Egypt and Grauman's Chinese (1927) exploited the possibilities of chinoiserie. It is best known now for the cement impressions of the hands and feet of film stars, instituted at the cinema's opening by Norma TALMADGE. C. W. and George L. Rapp, too, specialized in cinema architecture, including the Chicago Oriental (1925) for Balaban and Katz and the Brooklyn Paramount (1928) with its Florentine flavour; they also designed the Balaban family mausoleum in Chicago.

Rothafel's New York Roxy (1927), the 'cathedral of motion pictures' designed by Walter Ahlschlager and decorated by Harold Rambusch, enshrined the glittering excesses of the American picture palaces of the twenties. 'Roxy' was also entrusted with the creation of Radio City Music Hall (1932), a prime example of art deco. Apart from their decorative attractions, all these major cinemas were provided with elaborate electrical and mechanical equipment to mount the stage shows that were a part of the programme, as well as the essential cinema organ—the 'Mighty Wurlitzer', rising up from the orchestra pit bathed in multi-coloured changing lights. (Even when the introduction of sound made musical accompaniment unnecessary, the organ interlude remained a major attraction.) The largest picture palaces retained in addition a resident orchestra, choir, and *corps de ballet*.

The great decade of American cinema design was the twenties, that of Britain the thirties. The introduction of sound necessitated more care about the design of the auditorium, and many of the basic technical aspects of design became standardized at this period. Three types of auditorium predominated: the single-floored, flat, or slightly raked type for the small cinema; the stadium type with raised rear tier; and the 'super' cinema, with single balcony, which was the principal development in the thirties. The super cinema was generally designed to seat between 1500 and 2000 to provide for heavy demand at weekends: full houses from Friday to Sunday covered running costs for the whole week. Lighting became more sophisticated, and played an important part in interior design. Other important design factors were the lay-out of increasingly complex projection rooms, heating and ventilation systems, and the placing of the giant electric organs.

Structured steel was preferred to reinforced concrete in the building of cinemas, as it is more economical. Brick, at first a favourite facing, was later superseded by more varied materials, including faience tiling, terracotta, and white precast concrete slabs.

In London, prominent cinema architects of the thirties included Edward A. Stone (the Astorias at Brixton, Finsbury Park, Streatham, and the Old Kent Road); George Cole (the Trocadero at Elephant and Castle and the remarkable Gaumont State, Kilburn, 1937); and Robert Cromie (Gaumont Palace—now Odeon—Hammersmith, 1932). Drury and Gomersall of Manchester were responsible for a number of important provincial cinemas, including the Regent, Fallowfield, 1929, and the Regal, Altrincham, 1931. Komisarjevsky, a former theatrical set-designer, created fanciful, impressionistic interiors, as in the Moorish-style décor of the Dover Granada (1930) and the Gothic Granada, Tooting.

The ODEON organization, headed by Oscar Deutsch, was foremost in establishing a coherent approach to cinema design in the thirties. The firm's principal architect was Harry W. Weedon, who designed the first Odeon at Perry Barr, Birmingham, in 1930. The Odeons were characterized by their single tower design, cream faience tiling, and characteristic plain lettering on an illuminated background. Weedon's famous black granite Odeon, built on the site of the old Alhambra, Leicester Square, was opened in 1937.

Cinemas in Europe had, from the outset, a quality and sophistication rarely found in the baroque palaces and pavilions of England and the United States. Architects of the Modern Movement, in search of a style of architecture which would express the technological age, designed cinemas where elegant simplicity derived from essential functionalism. The best of these buildings made a genuine contribution to modern architecture. They include Asplund's Stockholm Skandia (1922), and Erich Mendelsohn's Universum (Luxor Palast) in Berlin, completed in 1929. Its outstanding feature was the horseshoe-shaped auditorium, subsequently adopted by UFA in many of their cinemas. Another prominent UFA architect was Fritz Wilms. In France, Belloc's cubistic reconstruction of the Gaumont Palace in Paris was particularly impressive.

During the thirties the influence of European Functionalism began to make itself felt in British cinema design, as in the austerely beautiful CURZON, Mayfair (1934), designed by Sir John Burnet, Tait and Lawn, which was replaced in 1966.

The spread of television after the Second World War resulted in a decline in cinema building. Many existing cinemas were converted to other uses such as bingo clubs or bowling alleys. In the decade 1955–65 the number of cinemas in Britain was reduced by more than half. Most new post-war cinemas have been sponsored by the RANK ORGANISATION, including the Odeon, Elephant and Castle, designed by Erno Goldfinger. The introduction of CINEMASCOPE did not result in any radical changes in cinema design, but CINERAMA, needing a vast curved screen, and a projection booth large enough to house three linked projectors, entailed considerable design alteration.

While the post-war era has seen the decline of the mass-cinema, the specialized cinema, whether the European ART HOUSE, or the American DRIVE-IN, has continued to expand and flourish. Even the small news theatres, put out of business by television, have often survived as centres for pornographic films. An important trend in both Britain and the US has been the conversion of large cinemas into three or four small auditoria each showing a different programme, often equipped with automatic 16mm projection.

Don Sharp: *The picture palace and other buildings for the movies*, London, 1969; Ben M. Hall: *The best remaining seats*, New York, 1961.

**CINEMA,** Italian monthly film journal, first published July 1936, ceased publication 1956, edited from the beginning by Luciano de Feo. With the rise of Fascism, and the creation of the CENTRO SPERIMENTALE DI CINEMATOGRAFIA in

1937, Mussolini appointed his son Vittorio as a co-editor.

Nevertheless *Cinema* had already gathered a group of leftist-minded young critics to its columns, including VISCONTI, ANTONIONI, and DE SANTIS; and its young editorial staff managed to make it a vehicle for new ideas, at the same time subtly anti-Fascist.

Many new theories were discussed in its columns, and much of its interest now lies in the fact that the majority of the writers and directors who later created the Italian school of NEO-REALISM at one time wrote for *Cinema*.

**CINEMA NOVO,** Brazilian film co-operative, emerged from the upsurge of Brazilian nationalism in the late fifties. The group, led by Glauber ROCHA, aimed at an economically viable indigenous film culture, freed from the foreign and especially the North American influence that had hitherto dominated the scene. To this end, a co-operative agency, Difilms, was also set up to handle distribution through both commercial cinemas and the film society and trade union network. Apart from Glauber Rocha, the group's main directors included Nelson Pereira dos Santos (*Vidas secas*, 1962) and Ruy Guerra (*Os Fuzis*, 1963). Cinema Novo has always been criticized by the activist left wing for its concern with aesthetics as much as revolutionary effect and for its readiness to work within the structure of the established film industry. Since the military coup of 1964, independent film production in Brazil has been fraught with an increasing number of problems and since 1969 Glauber Rocha himself has worked abroad, but the best work of Cinema Novo has had a profound influence on film-makers in other Latin American countries. (See BRAZIL.)

**CINEMASCOPE,** the name given to the anamorphic process developed by Henri Chrétien when TWENTIETH CENTURY-FOX bought the patent rights in 1952 and developed the process commercially. (See ANAMORPHIC LENS, WIDE SCREEN.)

**CINÉMATHÈQUE FRANÇAISE,** under its director Henri LANGLOIS, has been an important factor in the creation of France's exceptionally lively cinema culture. It was founded with private funds in 1936 by Langlois in association with Georges FRANJU and Jean MITRY. The original purpose was to save silent classics threatened by the coming of sound; since then it has acquired a large collection of films and two cinemas which between them show six different films a day. During the war Langlois, his assistants Lotte EISNER and Mary Meerson, and the Cinémathèque staff hid hundreds of films from the occupy-

ing forces. Langlois was later decorated for his part in the rescue operations and the Cinémathèque began receiving a grant from the government. Retrospective seasons of Hollywood films were to have a strong influence on the NOUVELLE VAGUE directors, first in their writing in CAHIERS DU CINÉMA and later in their films. Seasons showing the entire works of particular directors drew critical and public attention to the role of the director in the creation of a film while at the same time introducing the public to new styles of film-making. In this Langlois's eclectic taste and faith in his intuitions about unknowns was of leading importance. Ingmar BERGMAN, Norman MCLAREN, DE SICA, KUROSAWA, and MIZOGUCHI were among the directors who became well known in France through seasons of their work at the Cinémathèque. Langlois's unorthodox administrative methods, however, made him unpopular in official quarters. In 1960 he broke with the FÉDÉRATION INTERNATIONALE DES ARCHIVES DE FILM (FIAF), and later fell out with the French government itself. In February 1968 he and his staff were dismissed. French and foreign film-makers immediately announced that they would not permit the new administration to screen their films and the demonstrations outside the Cinémathèque were one of the first reflections of the state of ferment in Paris in 1968. By April the scandal was such that the authorities decided to reinstate Langlois and his staff but to withdraw their subsidy. A new government archive was established in 1969 at Bois d'Arcy outside Paris.

The reputation of the Cinémathèque remains undimmed, however, and its cinemas continue to run with as much panache as ever.

The Cinémathèque's Musée du Cinéma was opened at the Palais de Chaillot in Paris in 1972. The creation of Langlois who has been gathering material since before the Second World War, it houses only a tenth of the collection held by the Cinémathèque, though this is neither evident nor significant as the museum is not attempting to impose on film history an analysis or interpretation, but to convey a living impression of cinema since its inception. (The theft of a camera and a Theda BARA dress shortly after it opened is regarded as a tribute to its achievement.) The chronological organization starts from the beginning of photography (with an original REYNAUD print, and Daguerrotypes) including the earliest moving pictures. EDISON's first motion picture machine is there. LUMIÈRE's *L'Arrivée d'un train en Gare de la Ciotat* runs continuously. A Meccano-like half-size skeleton of MÉLIÈS' studio has been built. Hermann WARM has reconstructed the set for DAS CABINETT DES DR CALIGARI (1919). Models—the robot from METROPOLIS (1927), the houses from SOUS LES TOITS DE PARIS (1930), spacecraft from 2001: A SPACE ODYSSEY

(1968)—scripts, sketches, posters, costumes—
Ivan the Terrible's finery, Buster KEATON's hat,
Moira Shearer's red shoes, dresses worn by Marlene DIETRICH, Marilyn MONROE, Bette DAVIS,
STROHEIM's helmet and greatcoat—make up the
majority of the exhibits. But the museum's
success lies less in a catalogue of outstanding
items than in its re-creation of the dream world
of cinema.

**CINEMATOGRAPHY**, the technical process of
photography applied to moving images; the term
derives from the machine (the Cinématographe)
patented by the LUMIÈRE brothers in February
1895. The process is concerned with three basic
elements: the synthesis of movement; photography; and projection.

Projection was the first element for which a
practical solution was found. Forms of magic
lantern were known in ancient Egypt and Rome,
and reappeared in post-Renaissance Europe. The
magic lantern proper was perfected in France
and Italy in the seventeenth century and by
the eighteenth century magic lantern shows
were a modestly popular spectacle. The Belgian
physicist Robert (known as Robertson, 1763–
1837) developed a sophisticated version of the
magic lantern which he called the 'Phantascope'
or 'Fantascope' (presented to the public in
1798).

Chinese shadow shows also grew rapidly in
popularity after their introduction in Germany
in the eighteenth century. From the court at
Versailles, Séraphin's famous Chinese shadow
theatre went to the Palais-Royal in 1784 and
took hold in Paris as a public attraction.

Photography was developed between 1816
and 1839 by Niepce and Daguerre in France,
Fox-Talbot in Britain, and others working
independently and concurrently. By the 1850s
photographs were being used for magic lantern
slides, and the introduction of electricity allowed
for stronger and more constant light for the
projection apparatus.

The question of the persistence of an image on
the retina had been considered by scientists from
Newton on. Roget and Faraday both furthered
research in England during the early nineteenth
century and the Belgian PLATEAU enunciated a
definitive theory of the PERSISTENCE OF VISION.
In 1825 an optical toy, the 'Thaumatrope', had
been launched commercially by J. A. Paris,
based on a process developed by the astronomer
Herschel and William Fitton, with cardboard
discs revolved by pulled strings. In 1829 Plateau
developed his 'Phénakistiscope', which he perfected and renamed 'Phantascope' in 1832. A
disc with eight vertical apertures revolved in
front of another disc bearing representations of
eight consecutive stages of a movement. At about

the same time, a German 'Stroboscope' was marketed, and the 'Zoetrope' (or 'Daedalum' or
'Wheel of Life') was developed on the same principle by William Horner; and over the next
decades a variety of 'Kinetescopes', 'Bioscopes',
'Stereophantascopes', and so on added refinements to the basic principle.

The problem of the analysis of movement was
pursued by many scientists from the time that
photography was invented. An outstanding contribution came from Thomas Du Mont, who
patented in London in 1859 a 'camera zoo-
tropica', capable of reproducing the phases of
a movement in twelve successive images. The
astronomer Pierre Jules-César Janssen developed
the method to track the course of the planet
Venus; and his technical innovations were further refined by the physiologist Etienne-Jules
MAREY, who in 1882 built his 'photographic
gun'. Improvements on the original 'gun' led
Marey to develop a fixed 'Chronophotographe',
and in collaboration with Georges DEMENY he
continued during the eighties and nineties to perfect techniques for both the analysis and synthesis of movement.

Analytical studies were also being pursued
in the US, notably by Eadweard MUYBRIDGE,
although on different principles. Muybridge also
solved the problem of re-synthesizing (by
projecting) his successive images, at first with
his 'Zoogyroscope' but finally with the
'Zoopraxograph', based on the 'Praxinoscope'
projector developed by Emile REYNAUD during
the eighties. The registration and reproduction of
movement were further perfected by Thomas
Alva EDISON working with W. K. L. DICKSON,
with their 'KINETOGRAPH', to which George
EASTMAN adapted the flexible roll film which he
had introduced for use in the still camera: the
Kinetograph, integrated with the 'Kinetoscope'
viewing apparatus, was launched commercially
at the Chicago Exhibition of 1894.

Other pioneers who independently paralleled
some of the apparatus developed in France and
the US include the Czech inventor Purkyně;
the Russians Lyubimov and Timchenko, who in
1893 built a more advanced version of the Kinetoscope than Edison's; and the German brothers
Skladanowsky who in 1895 patented a 'Bioskop'
for projecting moving images, similar to Reynaud's device. Some 125 machines of greater or
lesser sophistication were constructed at about
the same time in Europe and the US, all by now
combining the recording, reproduction, and
projection of images: but the Lumières' Cinématographe, more compact and efficient than
its competitors, rapidly conquered world markets.

A detailed account of these early years is
given in Jacques Deslandes, *Histoire comparée*

*du cinéma*, vol. I 1826–96, vol. II 1896–1906 (Tournai, 1966, 1968).

In modern parlance the term *cinematography* has come to mean all the work, creative and technical, performed by the CAMERAMAN during production of a film.

In photography a complete work may be as little as a single photograph; in cinematography a complete work is the film as a whole, and the shot is only an element in it. Thus cinematography deals with relationships between shots and between groups of shots (scenes or sequences). A scene may be lighted so that the faces of some characters are in total blackness (the 'love nest' confrontation in TOLAND'S CITIZEN KANE, 1941, for example), and the result on its own violates a principle of good photography; but in the context of the whole film we have already seen the faces many times, and the lighting provides a contrast and makes the point that the people are now behaving as mindless stereotypes. Good cinematography avoids the outstanding individual shot and achieves an overall integration of mood and unity of style.

Cinematography also differs from photography in that it demands a higher degree of collaboration. The cinematographer's artistic and technical authority is subordinate to the producer's and director's (and sometimes to the star's). Further, his work must take into account the other functions involved: his lighting must avoid casting shadows from the microphone, his camera can move only as the set allows, his exposure must suit the laboratory's processing baths. A good cinematographer plans his work with the director and designer, collaborates with the sound mixer and the editor, and understands the needs of the actor and the stills photographer. If he tries to achieve good results without creative consultation, other aspects of the film suffer and his own work is diminished by association.

By contrast, the technical details of cinematography have much in common with still photography. Lighting is controlled to illuminate detail and separate planes, to suggest locale and time of day, and to sketch a mood or atmosphere. Composition within the FRAME directs attention to particular persons or objects, always with the qualification that the size and proportion of the motion picture frame do not change during the course of the film. Colour is used and controlled to create emotional connotations and for simple identification, but always in collaboration with the art director. EXPOSURE, for the cinematographer, is not a creative choice but a mechanical requirement for continuity of brightness between shots in the same sequence. This, and the fixed shutter speed, make focus a considerable prob-lem in cinematography, and considerable ingenuity is needed to keep the centre of interest always sharp (see DEEP FOCUS). Like the still photographer, the cinematographer has at his disposal a range of lenses and he will use his expertise to select the most appropriate to achieve his aims (see CAMERA, ZOOM).

*CINÉMA-VÉRITÉ*, 'film truth' or KINO-PRAVDA, the concept originally evolved in theory and practice by Dziga VERTOV, was adopted to describe Jean ROUCH and Edgar MORIN's CHRONIQUE D'UN ÉTÉ (1961); the term has come to describe a stylistic school of film-making mainly concerned with DOCUMENTARY.

The style developed in the late fifties and early sixties concurrently with DIRECT CINEMA in America. The two movements sprang from the same roots, and although declaring two distinct philosophies the resulting films have many similarities. Rejecting both the idealism of FLAHERTY and the didacticism of IVENS, LOR-ENTZ, and GRIERSON, the new documentarists threw themselves into social issues, aiming at the immediacy of television while attacking its superficiality. On both sides of the Atlantic, the recent improvements in portable cine and sound equipment (see 16MM) gave impetus to mobile, flexible filming: the new lightweight equipment made it possible to reduce the film crew to cameraman and sound man, one of whom would characteristically be the director, although playing a completely different role from that of the director of the conventional, scripted documentary. The principal difference in approach between direct cinema and *cinéma-vérité* was in the function of the film-maker himself: while the 'direct' film-maker claimed to take an objective stance, merely standing by in the hope that a situation already tense would resolve itself in a dynamic, enlightening crisis, the practitioner of *cinéma-vérité* deliberately intervened, hoping that greater spontaneity and truth would be stimulated by the participation of the film-maker in the event filmed.

Apart from Rouch, major figures in *cinéma-vérité* have been François REICHENBACH (*Un Coeur gros comme ça*, 1961), Mario RUSPOLI (*Regards sur la folie*, 1961), and Jean Herman (*Les Chemins de la mauvaise route*). The style spread widely during the sixties: young Canadian film-makers who had worked in France carried it back to Canada, resulting in depictions of Québecois life by Michel BRAULT and Pierre PERRAULT and stimulating the CHALLENGE FOR CHANGE programme; Grigori CHUKRAI applied the principles in *Pamyat* (*Memory*, 1969).

*Cinéma-vérité* was not so much a self-contained movement with a coherent and sustained philosophy as a manifestation of current questioning of conventional patterns of audience participation and the social and political uses of film. The wedding of sociology to a radical film aesthetic, although not altogether successful in the quality of individual works produced, was a significant step towards widening the horizons of cinema. Its influence was profound. Chris MARKER, although rejected by the theorists of *cinéma-vérité* for his personal and poetic application of their methods, has produced a fine body of political films. In fiction films, Jacques ROZIER's ADIEU PHILIPPINE (1962), with its use of improvised dialogue, lightweight cameras, and hidden microphones, clearly bears the impress of *cinéma-vérité*; TRUFFAUT'S LES QUATRE CENTS COUPS (1959) has similar characteristics and a spontaneity that owes much to the general artistic and social climate from which *cinéma-vérité* drew its inspiration; and GODARD has perhaps done most to explore in fiction films the use of the camera as participant rather than observer.

**CINEMIRACLE** see CINERAMA

**CINÉORAMA,** a process patented in 1897 by Raoul GRIMOIN-SANSON, was presented at the Paris Exhibition of 1900. The audience entered a circular building which contained a cylindrical screen 330 feet in circumference. Ten synchronized projectors in a circular booth projected a continuous moving image on to the screen. The audience climbed on to a platform on the roof of the booth, arranged to resemble the basket of a huge balloon, with the ceiling of the building shaped like the balloon's underbelly. The films, hand-coloured, depicted balloon journeys from Paris to Brussels and elsewhere. The effect of the performance in the darkened hall was physically sensational, but the heat generated by the projectors under the audience constituted a fire risk and led to the closing of the building after only three performances.

**CINERAMA.** Fred Waller, director of special effects at PARAMOUNT, was convinced that much effectiveness of projected film was lost because the old 3 × 4 screen (see ASPECT RATIO) occupied only a small part of the 130°–160° which is the angle of vision of an average spectator. Called in by the oil industry to deal with an awkward space in the New York World Fair of 1939, Waller devised a system which he called Vitarama, with eleven 16mm projectors throwing images on to a half-dome. The system was developed during the war as the Flexible Gunnery Trainer, with five 35mm projectors. After the war the system was further refined to three projectors and three screens curved to cover 140°, together with stereophonic sound;

and *This is Cinerama* was launched by the Cinerama Corporation on Broadway in September 1952. The film made an impact in its own right and successfully attracted attention to the new process.

From the beginning Cinerama projection suffered from the serious drawback of the images' joining unevenly on the screen. To overcome this, the device of the jiggolo, or gigolo, was developed. This was a pair of saw-toothed masks vibrating between each pair of images to blur the images and conceal any uneven junction.

For a short time Cinemiracle (announced in 1955 by the National Theaters Corporation) tried to better the Cinerama system by using one projector (instead of Cinerama's three) with mirrors throwing the right- and left-hand images horizontally on to the screen. The technical difficulties, including making allowance in printing for loss of light caused to the side-images by the mirrors, proved too formidable, and after one film, *Windjammer* (1958), the company abandoned the process.

Apart from problems of film printing and projection, Cinerama relied too much on factual presentation of a visually sensational nature (such as roller-coasting, etc) whose novelty soon began to wear off. By the time that the Cinerama Corporation had turned to fiction in filming HOW THE WEST WAS WON (1962), the 70MM systems, starting with TODD-AO, were challenging Cinerama's superiority in giving the illusion of peripheral vision on a single image and a single screen, and the process was discarded in favour of the more manageable systems, notably PANAVISION. 2001: A SPACE ODYSSEY (1968), for instance, was shot and projected on 70mm Panavision, with the 35mm prints reduced for ANAMORPHIC projection. Naturally, the Corporation continues to use the term Cinerama as its trade-mark for its presentations on 70mm.

**CINÉ-ROMAN,** French term coined around 1904 to characterize novelettish films including SERIALS. It was synonymous with FEUILLETON-CINÉMA, magazines which published the episodes of a serial in comic strip form in parallel with cinema showings. PATHÉ produced a series of romantic films which they called *ciné-romans*, starting with *Roman d'amour* (1905) directed by Lorant Heilbronn. *Ciné-roman* was later sometimes applied to stories written with a view to screen adaptation, and published scripts of films illustrated with stills may also be so described.

**CINES,** Italian company founded in 1906 to produce films and manufacture equipment, made a number of successful costume dramas in its early years, often under the direction of Mario

CASERINI. The company was important enough to be represented at the CONGRÈS DES DUPES in 1909. In 1911, following the severe recession in the European film industry, Cines became the newly-financed Società Italiana Cines Anonima Roma, which had diverse interests in the development and marketing of cinematographic equipment as well as in film production. QUO VADIS (1913), in length, costliness, and spectacle, initiated a worldwide revolution in feature film production and with LES MISÉRABLES (1912) led the recovery of the European industry. Cines attempted to recover from the losses incurred during the First World War by entering the Unione Cinematica Italiana, but in 1921 ceased operation.

The name Cines was resurrected in 1929 and again in 1949. The company now bearing the name is in part state-owned.

**CIRCARAMA.** A means of projecting a 360° image, devised for Walt DISNEY's Disneyland amusement park. The screen, 8 feet high × 130 feet in circumference, receives images projected simultaneously by eleven 16mm projectors. Problems of matching the joining edges of the images are avoided by dividing the screen into eleven panels by dark vertical strips.

**CIRCUS, The,** US, 1928. 1¾hr. *Dir, prod, scr* Charles Chaplin, assisted by Harry Crocker; *ph* Rollie Totheroh, Jack Wilson, Mark Marklatt; *cast* Charlie Chaplin (the Tramp), Allan Garcia (the circus owner), Merna Kennedy (his daughter), Henry Crockford (tightrope walker), Henry Bergman (old clown), Doc Stone (prize-fighter).

The last of CHAPLIN's silent films has Charlie as a circus hand who becomes a clown by accident. Though there are some tragic elements, he here returned from the drama of A WOMAN OF PARIS (1923) and the comparative seriousness of THE GOLD RUSH (1925) to the much simpler comedy of the earlier years: memorable comic sequences include his first attempt at performing on a trapeze and his reaction to being trapped in a lion cage—with the lion. In the first year in which the American ACADEMY OF MOTION PICTURE ARTS AND SCIENCES made its awards, Chaplin won an OSCAR 'for versatility and genius in writing, acting, directing, and producing *The Circus*'. Chaplin re-issued the film in 1970, with a sound track produced, as usual, by himself.

**CITIZEN KANE,** US, 1941. 2hr. *Dir* Orson Welles; *prod* RKO; *scr* Herman J. Mankiewicz, Welles; *ph* Gregg Toland; *mus* Bernard Herrmann; *ed* Robert Wise (and Mark Robson, uncredited); *cast* Orson Welles (Kane), Agnes Moorehead (his mother), Dorothy Comingore (Susan Alexander), Joseph Cotten (Jedediah Leland), Everett Sloane (Bernstein).

Press magnate Kane dies in his west-coast palace of Xanadu, murmuring the word 'Rosebud'. A reporter of a news magazine like THE MARCH OF TIME is charged with discovering the significance of the word; and, in interviewing several people closely connected with Kane, discovers that the magnate's public-spirited image by no means corresponds with the private view that these different people have of him.

The similarity between Kane and the newspaper publisher William Randolph HEARST caused a considerable scandal and led to a delay in the film's release. The Hearst papers launched a crusade against the film which ranged from demands that it be banned to an absolute refusal to mention or advertise it. It was finally press-shown only after RKO had been threatened by WELLES with a law-suit. The Hearst papers ignored it but the rest of the press was enthusiastic if puzzled. In New York (where it won the Film Critics' Award) and the larger towns the film did fair business: in the smaller towns it flopped. Some exhibitors, indeed, paid for the film in a block of RKO bookings (see BLOCK BOOKING) and preferred not to screen it. At the end of the year it won two critical awards and an OSCAR for the best original screenplay of 1941. Welles's difficulties with RKO had begun while the film was in the making, and its comparative commercial failure spelt the end of his artistic freedom in Hollywood.

The film's influence on Hollywood was nevertheless profound. The most obvious and immediate was in the construction of the script. The earlier precedent for a series of recollections out of chronological order, in William K. HOWARD's THE POWER AND THE GLORY (1933), had passed largely unnoticed; but MANKIEWICZ and Welles effectively released scriptwriters thenceforth from the convention of strict chronology. Welles's use of wide-angle and deep-focus LENSES, made possible through the work of his cameraman Gregg TOLAND, pointed the way to the development of action within a single frame. This same effect had been achieved by RENOIR in his films throughout the thirties; but Welles's handling of movement and composition within the frame was essentially formal. The formal element was seized on and hardened in Hollywood into increasing rigidity, which was broken only by the impact of Italian post-war NEO-REALISM. *Citizen Kane* also made innovations in the use of sound which Welles sought to carry further in his later films.

Apart from its resounding influence, the film claims an enduring place in world cinema by its sheer exuberance, and in particular that of

Welles's own performance. It repeatedly appears highly placed in polls of the best films ever made.

**CITY LIGHTS**, US, 1931. 1½hr. *Dir, prod, scr* Charles Chaplin, assisted by Harry Crocker, Henry Bergman, Albert Austin for United Artists; *ph* Rollie Totheroh, Gordon Pollock, Mark Marklatt; *des* Charles D. Hall; *mus* Charles Chaplin; *cast* Charlie Chaplin (the Tramp), Virginia Cherrill (the blind girl), Harry Myers (the millionaire), Henry Bergman, Albert Austin, Robert Parrish, Jean Harlow.

CHAPLIN started work on this story of the Depression almost as soon as THE CIRCUS (1928) was finished, but the introduction of sound made him stop production. He sensed, rightly, that words would weaken the effectiveness of much of his comedy, and would certainly lessen his international appeal. When he resumed filming, he had decided to use no dialogue, but to incorporate music and realistic sound effects. The anachronistic mixture worked surprisingly well; this story of a tramp who, by a series of lucky accidents, is able to restore the sight of a blind flowergirl, competes with THE GOLD RUSH (1925) as the most consistently successful and popular of his films (on its first release, it made a profit of over $5 million). There are classic comic sequences—the near-balletic boxing match, the drunken spaghetti-confetti-eating scene, the catastrophic effects when Charlie swallows a whistle at a musical soirée—but the genuine pathos of the story (for which Virginia Cherrill as the blind girl must take a share of the credit) is most remembered.

**CITY STREETS**, US, 1931. 1½hr. *Dir, prod* Rouben Mamoulian for Paramount; *scr* Max Marcin, Oliver H. P. Garrett, based on a story by Dashiell Hammett; *ph* Lee Garmes; *cast* Gary Cooper (the Kid), Sylvia Sidney (Nan), Paul Lukas (Big Fella Maskal), Guy Kibbee (Pop Cooley), William Boyd (McCoy).

Nan's father persuades her to take the blame for a murder which he has committed, assuring her that the gang will not let her go to prison. The scene where the Kid visits Nan in prison and they try to embrace through the wire mesh is justly famous and much imitated; the sequence in which Pop's murder is carried out is a masterpiece of delicate understatement and control. *City Streets* is often described as one of the first GANGSTER FILMS, but it is more concerned with the effect of the gang on the two young people than with the gang itself.

**CIVILIZATION, or HE WHO RETURNED**, US, 1916. 2¼hr. *Dir, prod* Thomas H. Ince for Triangle; *scr* C. Gardner Sullivan; *ph* Irvin Willat; *cast* J. Barney Sherry, Enid Markey, Howard Hickman, Lola May.

America's transition from pacifism to militarism between 1914 and 1917 is nowhere more clearly reflected than in the films of those years. Indeed, Hollywood was ahead of government and public thinking and helped stimulate pro-war opinion. *Civilization*, in which Christ returns as a submarine engineer to preach peace, was the last and most commercially successful of the pacifist films; anti-German sentiment was however conspicuous enough in it for Sweden to ban the film. An epilogue showing President Wilson giving INCE his blessing was claimed by the Democrats to have contributed to his re-election in 1916. Despite proficient use of GRIFFITH's techniques, Ince's film lacks enduring human quality, and its interest today lies mainly in its historical importance.

**CLAIR**, RENÉ (1898– ), French director, real name Chomette, was born in Paris. Rather than follow the family business, he became a journalist and in 1920 was persuaded, reluctantly, to take part in a film. Like GRIFFITH, he took a pseudonym because the cinema seemed no more than a temporary expedient for him. He acted in several films as a *jeune premier*—including some directed by FEUILLADE, whom he greatly admired—and began to take a serious interest in cinema, especially CHAPLIN. Not content with his (rather mediocre) acting, he got his first chance of direction with ENTR'ACTE (1924), which was followed by *Paris qui dort* (1924). He continued meanwhile as a journalist, writing film criticism and keeping in touch with much of the literary and artistic activity of Paris at the time. His later full-length silent films, *Le Fantôme du Moulin Rouge* (1924), *Le Voyage imaginaire* (1925), *La Proie du vent* (1926), UN CHAPEAU DE PAILLE D'ITALIE (1927), and *Les Deux Timides* (1928), were all produced by KAMENKA's Albatros Films: it is ironical that Clair, generally thought of as essentially French in style, was backed by foreign companies (Albatros in the twenties and the German TOBIS for his sound films). The fantastic nature of his films contains some elements of SURREALISM, but humour and burlesque is always at their core. He developed the instinct for dance movement—expressed early in *Entr'acte*—which runs right through his films. Décor and music contribute to the choreography which is his hall-mark.

He was dismayed by the coming of sound, but commented: 'It is not impossible that a real art of talking films (*un art propre au film parlant*) should emerge.' He himself went on, with SOUS LES TOITS DE PARIS (1930) and LE MILLION (1932) in particular, to create 'un art propre au film parlant'. In 1931 he made a satire on modern industrial life in A NOUS LA LIBERTÉ. Chaplin's MODERN TIMES (1936) followed the theme and even some of the ideas so closely that Clair's production company, Tobis, wanted to take legal action. Clair protested, saying: 'The whole of the cinema has learned lessons from Chaplin. . . . If he was inspired by my film, that's an honour for me.'

His liberal ideas estranged his German backers, and the French Fascists created a scandal around LE DERNIER MILLIARDAIRE (1934), which was produced with French backing, forcing him to seek backing abroad. In 1935 he had a success with *The Ghost Goes West*, made for Alexander KORDA in London. After breaking his contract with Korda and forming a company briefly with Jack BUCHANAN, he returned to France and was working on a short film *Air pur*, when war began. He accepted an invitation to go to Hollywood; but like Jean RENOIR he was unable happily to transplant his talent to the soil of Hollywood. He made several undistinguished films, and found his old touch again only when he returned to France to make *Le Silence est d'or* (1947). In 1950 he made *La Beauté du diable* in Italy, and returned to his particular brand of fantasy in LES BELLES DE NUIT (1952). Since then he has made several elegant films, including *Les Grandes Manoeuvres* (1955) and *Porte des Lilas* (1957).

Clair will undoubtedly endure as one of the outstanding figures of cinema. He is unusual among directors for having written penetratingly about cinema, and more importantly for having achieved in his best films the creation of an original world. His achievement in cinema was uniquely recognized by the Académie française in 1960, and he remains the only member of that august body to have been elected on his film record alone.

Clair's many published works include *Réflexion faite*, Paris, 1951, translated by Vera Traill as *Reflections on the cinema*, London, 1953, and *Cinéma d'hier, cinéma d'aujourd'hui*, Paris, 1970.

***CLAIRE'S KNEE*** see GENOU DE CLAIRE, LE

**CLAPPER-BOARD**, a small board on which are chalked the name of the film, the name or number of the scene, the number of the take, and the names of director, cameraman, and production company. An arm, painted with diagonal black-and-white stripes, is hinged on top of the board. The arm may be closed on to the board with a sharp noise—hence the name. The board is held in front of the camera at the beginning and end of each take; the information written on it serves to identify the piece of film at the editing stage, and the sharp noise serves as a precise point for the synchronization of sound.

The clapper-boy, who wields the board, is a lowly figure in the production hierarchy: his position is often spoken of, literally and figuratively, as the starting-point in a film-making career.

**CLARKE,** SHIRLEY (1925–   ), US director whose training in modern dance gave rise to her early short films *Dance in the Sun* (1953), *Bullfight* (1955), *Moment in Love* (1959), and *Bridges-Go-Round* (1958), a lyrical, 'dancing' film in the tradition of the 'city symphony'. Her first feature *The Connection* (1961) was a film of the Living Theatre's production of Jack Gilbert's play about drug addiction. *The Cool World* (1963) also dealt with the harsh realities of city life. Its subject—the frustrated ghetto life of the young black—was approached from a very different direction in *Portrait of Jason* (1967) in which an extrovert black homosexual delivers an extended monologue to an immobile camera; the film's purely functional style and use of 'real' time comment on and extend the notion of CINÉMA-VÉRITÉ. Clarke now works largely with video. She appeared as herself in *Lions Love* (Agnès VARDA, 1969).

**CLARKE,** T. E. B. (1907–   ), British scriptwriter, entered films after working in journalism. His scripts for EALING STUDIOS helped form the company's style: witty accounts of bizarre events taking place among ordinary people against well-observed naturalistic backgrounds. His best films include *Hue and Cry* (1947), PASSPORT TO PIMLICO (1949), and THE LAVENDER HILL MOB (1951). He is rare among British scriptwriters in having made his name with original screenplays, but after a five-year absence he returned to films scripting *A Tale of Two Cities* and *Gideon's Day* (both 1958) and co-scripting *Sons and Lovers* (1960), all literary adaptations.

**CLAYTON,** JACK (1921–   ), British director and producer, whose first short film, *The Bespoke Overcoat* (1955), was widely admired and won a prize at VENICE. His first feature as director was ROOM AT THE TOP (1958) which, with its uncompromising handling of topics hitherto avoided in British cinema, caused something of a sensation. His films since, although uneven in quality, are polished and intelligent. *The Innocents* (1961) validly used modern insights into psychology to give substance to Henry James's 'The Turn of the Screw' (described by its author as simply an *amusette*) while losing none of the original's eerie atmosphere. In *The Pumpkin Eater* (1964), scripted by Harold PINTER from Penelope Mortimer's novel, Clayton's liking for fast, fragmentary cutting effectively conveys the subjective view of the heroine, magnificently played by Anne BAN-

CROFT. *Our Mother's House* (1967) is less assured than Clayton's earlier films although it has considerable originality, particularly in the attempt to show how, in crisis conditions, children may assume the responsibility of adults while adults behave like children. Clayton's film version of *The Great Gatsby* (1974) was generally disappointing, yielding too much of the original's sensitivity to glossy production values.

**CLÉMENT**, RENÉ (1913–  ), French director, studied architecture, but transferred his interest to the cinema around 1934, working as a cameraman and assistant director. During the thirties he made a number of short documentary films, developing a spare and realistic directing style which served him well in his best feature films, LA BATAILLE DU RAIL (1946) and LES JEUX INTERDITS (1952). These two war stories are treated with a compassionate intimacy which makes them memorable, and Clément's handling of mostly non-professional actors is masterly. *Gervaise* (1956), an adaptation of Zola's *L'Assommoir*, is a harsh, convincing reproduction of a period and a situation, greatly aided by Maria Schell's acting in the title role. His later work on big international co-productions has been less effective: such films as *Barrage contre le Pacifique* (1958) and *Paris, brûle-t-il?* (1965), with all-star casts, are successful only as well-made commercial entertainments.

**CLÉO DE CINQ A SEPT**, France/Italy, 1962. 1½hr. *Dir, scr* Agnès Varda; *prod* Bruno Drigo, Rome-Paris Films; *ph* Jean Rabier; *des* Bernard Evein; *mus* Michel Legrand; *cast* Corinne Marchand (Cléo), Antoine Bourseiller (Antoine), Dorothée Blank (Dorothée), Dominique Davray (Angèle), Michel Legrand (Bob), José-Luis De Villalonga (Cléo's lover).

The film records ninety minutes (screen time equalling real time), in the life of a night-club singer, as she awaits a diagnosis which may tell her she has cancer. The camera observes Cléo's feelings and reactions as she wanders through Paris encountering friends and strangers, her whole attitude coloured by the threat of death and solitude. The carefully observed real time contrasts with Cléo's experience of it, trivial events taking on a grotesque importance. The film has great visual elegance, and Paris itself, beautifully photographed, perhaps rivals Cléo as the centre of interest.

**CLEOPATRA**, US, 1962. Todd-AO; 2¾hr; De Luxe Color. *Dir* Joseph L. Mankiewicz; *prod* Walter Wanger for Twentieth Century-Fox; *scr* Mankiewicz, Ranald McDougall, Sidney Buchman, from Plutarch, Suetonius, Appian, and C. M. Franzero's *The Life and Times of Cleopatra; ph* Leon Shamroy; *cast* Elizabeth Taylor (Cleopatra), Richard Burton (Mark Antony), Rex Harrison (Julius Caesar), Roddy McDowell (Octavian).

An opulent and spectacular account of most of the traditionally accepted ideas about the life of Cleopatra, notable for the many vicissitudes of the production. It took over four years to shoot at a cost of approximately 40 million dollars. At first it was to be made on a 3-million dollar budget in England, but after six months' work, with Peter FINCH as Caesar, various setbacks including Elizabeth TAYLOR's critical illness caused the project to be temporarily abandoned. Rouben MAMOULIAN, who had directed up to this point, resigned and his place was taken by Joseph L. MANKIEWICZ who re-wrote the script, continuing to do so almost from day to day after shooting recommenced in Rome. Much adverse publicity surrounded the project when the romantic relationship between Elizabeth Taylor and Richard BURTON became public knowledge, and spiralling costs made *Cleopatra* the most expensive film production to date. Although by the end of 1968 the film had earned 26 million dollars, placing it tenth in the list of highest-earning films, it failed to make a profit. The drain on TWENTIETH CENTURY-FOX's finances at a critical time was nearly disastrous and finally unseated Spyros SKOURAS from control of the company.

**CLIFFHANGER,** the device that creates suspense between episodes in a SERIAL. At the end of every episode the hero or heroine is placed in an impossibly dangerous situation the happy outcome of which is divulged at the beginning of the next episode, when the audience's memory is also refreshed by a recapitulation of the major incidents that led up to the problematic situation. To make the action run on smoothly, the cliffhanger is shot twice, once for the end of the episode, and again for the beginning of the next.

**CLIFT,** MONTGOMERY (1920–66), US actor on the professional stage from the age of thirteen. He was a brooding, introspective actor, often at odds with himself and his craft. Encouraged by Elia KAZAN, he used the ACTORS' STUDIO 'method' to explore the characters he portrayed; all his film performances were distinguished by an intelligent command of his role. Among his many fine performances those in RED RIVER (1948), *The Heiress* (William WYLER, 1949), A PLACE IN THE SUN (1951), *I Confess* (Alfred HITCHCOCK, 1953), FROM HERE TO ETERNITY (1953), and *Freud* (John HUSTON, 1962) are outstanding, but perhaps his most persuasive and engaging role was Perce Howland, the hapless cowboy drifter in THE MISFITS (1961).

**CLOCKWORK ORANGE, A,** GB, 1971. (Colour process not credited); 2¼hr. *Dir, prod* Stanley Kubrick for Warner Bros/Polaris; *scr* Kubrick from the novel by Anthony Burgess; *ph* John Alcott; *mus* Rossini, Purcell, Elgar, Rimsky-Korsakov, Beethoven, Walter Carlos, etc; *cast* Malcolm McDowell (Alex DeLarge), Patrick Magee (Mr Alexander), Adrienne Corri (Mrs Alexander), Carl Duering (Dr Brodsky), Miriam Karlin (Cat Lady).

In an unnamed city of the future, Alex leads a teenage quartet indulging in rape, robbery, destruction, and gang warfare. A course of aversion therapy is imposed upon him by the authorities but, deprived of his capacity for violence, he cannot survive in a society based on violence. Driven to near-suicide by one of his previous victims, he recovers his previous personality, together with the ability to manipulate the social system.

KUBRICK transposed Anthony Burgess's novel to the screen with little alteration of the plot, and vividly depicted the setting, a materialistic urban environment where the only colour and vitality is provided by groups of young thugs dressed in perversely-styled uniforms. The film's message— that free will and individuality must be preserved at all costs—is unexceptionable; the argument is perhaps weakened by its presentation. Characterization is sacrificed to the demands of a thesis. The delinquent Alex has a perverse attractiveness and his violent acts, although explicitly shown, are given a stylized unreality; Alex the victim of society becomes appealingly vulnerable, so that real conflict is evaded. Kubrick's habitual pessimism here takes on a cynical tone.

However, with his usual technical accomplishment, Kubrick makes stunning use of colour— harsh and glossy for the first part of the film, muted and naturalistic when Alex has been subjugated. The use of music is characteristically inventive and iconoclastic, particularly the choral movement of Beethoven's Ninth Symphony which becomes Alex's stimulation to sadistic pleasures.

*A Clockwork Orange* was released in Britain at a time when energetic reaction against the relaxation of film CENSORSHIP was taking place. It acquired a notoriety which polarized audiences, undoubtedly contributing to its enormous commercial success but to a degree inhibiting serious examination of the director's intentions and methods.

**CLOSE-UP,** a shot taken close to a face or object which is therefore seen greatly magnified on the screen. In sensitive hands the close-up of an expression or object significant for development of the plot can have great dramatic impact.

**CLOSE-UP,** journal published monthly in London from July 1927 to December 1933. The proprietor Bryher (a novelist whose real name is Winifred Ellerman, daughter of the multi-millionaire shipowner, Sir John Ellerman) was at first assistant editor to her husband Kenneth MacPherson. Later Oswald Blackeston joined them, also as assistant editor. *Close-Up* was the first journal in English to take film seriously as an art. Its scope was international, including for example detailed studies of the cinema in Germany, Japan, and the Soviet Union. Its aim, to explore every possible aspect of the cinema from a wide cultural point of view, was ambitious and successful. Typical titles of articles, often written by distinguished people such as EISENSTEIN, Robert Herring, Dorothy Richardson, and Upton SINCLAIR were 'The Cinema and the Classics', 'Nature and Human Fate', 'What the Critics don't know', and 'The Negro Actor and the American Movies'. The journal also gave up-to-date information on current film production, the opening of new cinemas, etc. Poetry and creative writing, for example by Gertrude Stein, were also included.

Reprint published Geneva, London, 1969.

**CLOUZOT,** HENRI-GEORGES (1907– ), French director, worked in the thirties as assistant director and scriptwriter and spent a short time in Berlin directing French versions of German productions. His first feature, *L'Assassin habite au 21* (1942) was a polished thriller. It was followed by *Le Corbeau* (1943) around which a scandal developed: it was produced by the German-owned CONTINENTALE FILMS, and it was alleged that the depressing view of French provincial life depicted in it was used as German propaganda. As a result Clouzot did not direct until 1947 when he won first prize at VENICE with QUAI DES ORFÈVRES, an underworld drama with a realistic Paris setting, very reminiscent of the pre-war work of CARNÉ and DUVIVIER. The pessimism allied with technical expertise which runs through all of Clouzot's work, including *Manon* (1948), a modernized version of the eighteenth-century classic *Manon Lescaut*, culminated in LE SALAIRE DE LA PEUR (*The Wages of Fear,* 1953). After an effective excursion into the horror thriller, with the technically brilliant *Les Diaboliques* (1955), he directed *Le Mystère Picasso* (1956), an impressive study of the artist at work which owes as much to Claude RENOIR's beautiful photography as to the direction.

Largely because of his ill health Clouzot's work has been irregular and uneven in quality. Since *Le Salaire de la peur* his only important film has been *La Vérité* (1960) which deals, like *Manon*, with amoral urban youth and sets his lonely and misunderstood heroine (excellently played by Brigitte BARDOT) in a social context of violence and hopelessness. An heir to the pre-war tradition of French cinema, rather than part of its post-war renaissance, Clouzot's best work is memorable for its concern with the outsider struggling to survive in a hostile world.

**COBB,** LEE J. (1911–   ), US actor, worked with Group Theatre during the thirties and made his film début in *North of the Rio Grande* (1937). He has portrayed on the screen a series of powerful, usually villainous, characters, including virtuoso performances in *Johnny O'Clock* (Robert ROSSEN, 1947), ON THE WATERFRONT (1954), TWELVE ANGRY MEN (1957), and *Party Girl* (Nicholas RAY, 1958). Of late he has played more patriarchal roles in EXODUS (1960), HOW THE WEST WAS WON (1962), and others.

**COBURN,** CHARLES (1877–1961), US actor, originally a Shakespeare specialist, who first appeared on screen in 1938 and became famous in the forties and fifties as a rotund character player. Although effective as crusty or irate types, he is most associated with benevolent comedy characters, epitomized by his OSCAR-winning performance opposite Jean ARTHUR and Joel MCCREA in *The More the Merrier* (George STEVENS, 1943). In his later years he made one or two films in Britain and often appeared on television.

**COBURN,** JAMES (1928–   ), US actor, made his film début in *Ride Lonesome* (BOETTICHER, 1959), and was for some time typed in Westerns including THE MAGNIFICENT SEVEN (1960). His flair for comedy in adventure tales was attractively deployed in *The Great Escape* (1962), *Charade* (1963), *The Americanization of Emily* (1964), and *A High Wind in Jamaica* (1965) and he began to be widely noticed with his creation of a super-spy in two outrageous parodies, *Our Man Flint* (Daniel MANN, 1966) and *In Like Flint* (Gordon Douglas, 1967). He played a role with more bite in Theodor FLICKER's *The President's Analyst* (1967).

**COCTEAU,** JEAN (1889–1963), French director and scriptwriter, was involved with the artistic avant-garde from an early age. After seeing action in the First World War he served in a private ambulance corps and in 1915 met Erik SATIE. They collaborated on a ballet for Diaghilev, *Parade*, with sets by Picasso. This atmosphere of creative ferment encouraged Cocteau's wide artistic range, and over the next forty-five years he wrote novels, poems, and plays, produced ballets, and even painted a little.

He himself commented, 'for me the cinematograph is only one medium of expression among others'.

His films reflect his variety of abilities. Some, such as *L'Aigle à deux têtes* (1947) and LES PARENTS TERRIBLES (1948), are straight transpositions of his plays, adapted for the screen and directed by himself. LES ENFANTS TERRIBLES (1950), although adapted by Cocteau, was directed by Jean-Pierre MELVILLE. He did not wish to build a reputation as a commercial director and was always content to work as a scenarist: during the Occupation he was involved as a scriptwriter on a number of films including Jean Delannoy's *L'Eternel Retour* (1943) and Robert BRESSON's *Les Dames du Bois de Boulogne* (1945); later he wrote the script of Georges FRANJU's THOMAS L'IMPOSTEUR (1965).

In 1946 Cocteau directed his own film adaptation of Madame Leprince de Beaumont's LA BELLE ET LA BÊTE, which showed lucidly how poetry derives from the ordinary and everyday rather than from the obscure. This principle is central to the three films on which Cocteau's reputation as a film-maker mainly rests: LE SANG D'UN POÈTE (1930), ORPHÉE (1950), and LE TESTAMENT D'ORPHÉE (1960). These intensely personal and original films deal with the role of the artist and the nature of his inspiration, Cocteau's recurrent preoccupation. They mingle myth and reality, often by the use of trick photography.

Always a provocative and stimulating artist, Cocteau finally won the official recognition of election to the Académie française in 1955. His contribution to cinema, although not great in quantity, was characteristically original.

**CODY,** WILLIAM, see BUFFALO BILL

**COHL,** ÉMILE (1857–1938), French animator, was a pupil of André Gill, the celebrated cartoonist. By 1885 he had become a fashionable photographer as well as a leading cartoonist. His first animated film, *Fantasmagorie*, was completed in 1908. Over the next ten years he made more than a hundred cartoon films, using technical innovations that greatly extended the resources of ANIMATION: frame-by-frame animation of line drawing, combinations of animation and live action, stop-frame animation, etc. In *Le Cauchemar du Fantoche* (1908), Cohl created a character (Fantoche) who became a prototype for all the later 'little men' of the cartoon world. He worked in the US from 1913 to 1915 on the *Snookums* series, but his interests in France were ruined by the war: he died in extreme poverty. His metamorphic and marvellous world is as fresh today as it was then.

**COHN,** HARRY (1891–1958), US producer of German/Polish origin, after working as a song-plugger entered films in 1918 as secretary to Carl LAEMMLE. With his brother Jack (1889–1956) and Joe Brandt he founded CBC Sales Corporation in 1920 which expanded into COLUMBIA PICTURES in 1924. Unusually, Harry Cohn was president as well as head of production of Columbia, whose modest studios he ruled as absolute dictator until his death. His overbearing attitude towards his employees made him unpopular, but he made Columbia a major force in Hollywood during the thirties and forties. He shrewdly followed up the box-office success of Frank CAPRA's early films by giving Capra unusual freedom, and the director's career was at its height during this period. Other outstanding films made under Cohn's control include ALL THE KING'S MEN (1949), BORN YESTERDAY (1951), and FROM HERE TO ETERNITY (1953). He had a flair for turning attractive starlets into box-office stars; Robert ALDRICH's *The Legend of Lylah Clare* (1968) is assumed to be based on his grooming of Kim NOVAK, and he was also personally responsible for the popular success of Rita HAYWORTH.

*King Cohn* by Bob Thomas, New York, 1967, gives a lively picture of this important and unpleasant autocrat.

**COLBERT,** CLAUDETTE (1905–    ), French-born US actress, real name Lily Chauchoin, whose round cheeks, large expressive eyes, and lively manner suited the comedy parts in which she excelled. She was at the height of her career in the thirties and early forties with comedies like the charming *Three-Cornered Moon* (1933), IT HAPPENED ONE NIGHT (1934), for which she won an OSCAR, and Mitchell Leisen's *Midnight* (1939) in which she more than held her own in a talented cast including John BARRYMORE at the top of his form. She made over sixty films and these also included *The Sign of the Cross* (DEMILLE, 1932) with her famous asses' milk bath and John FORD's beautiful DRUMS ALONG THE MOHAWK (1939) in which she played a young bride plunged into the dangers of eighteenth-century frontier life. Her career began to decline at the end of the war with a number of routine thrillers and comedies, among them *Sleep My Love* (1948) and *The Egg and I* (1947), one of seven films with Fred MACMUR-RAY. Her last film was *Parrish* (1961) but she has continued to work in the theatre.

*COLD DAYS* see HIDEG NAPOK

**COLETTE** (Gabrielle-Sidonie Colette, 1873–1954), French writer, took an active interest in film throughout her working life. She was film critic for the Paris journal *Film* 1916–18, and adapted and scripted many of her own books for the screen, starting with *La Vagabonde* (Italy, 1918). She wrote the French dialogue for MÄDCHEN IN UNIFORM (1931) and collaborated with OPHULS on the adaptation of *La Divine* (1935). Among the screen adaptations of her books are 'La Chatte' an episode in *Les Sept Péchés capitaux* (1951), and two versions of GIGI (1949 and 1958).

**COLLINGE,** PATRICIA (1894–1974), Dublin-born actress whose long stage career began in London in 1904 but was mostly spent in the US. Her most memorable film role was also her first, Birdie Hubbard in THE LITTLE FOXES (William WYLER, 1941), which she had already played on the New York stage. Her next film was *Shadow of a Doubt* (Alfred HITCHCOCK, 1943); others included *Tender Comrade* (1943), *Casanova Brown* (1944), *Teresa* (1951), *Washington Story* (1952), and *The Nun's Story* (1958). Her film appearances were in character parts, often of an eccentric nature.

**COLMAN,** RONALD (1891–1958), US actor, was born in Britain and served with the British Army in the First World War. He went to the US in 1920 and was noticed by Lillian GISH when he played a supporting role in *La Tendresse* on Broadway. He played opposite her in *The White Sister* (1924), but it was with *Arrowsmith* (1931), co-starring Helen HAYES and directed by John FORD, that Colman gained wide popularity, establishing a reputation as a sophisticated romantic lead, his distinctive voice becoming a hall-mark of the type. He is chiefly remembered for his appearances in *A Tale of Two Cities* (1935), *Lost Horizon, The Prisoner of Zenda* (both 1937), and *Random Harvest* (1942), and for the unusually dramatic performance which won him his only OSCAR in *A Double Life* (1948) (see OTHELLO).

**COLOMBIA** has had a well-documented history of film production since 1914, but foreign influences have always predominated. The small domestic output continues to be swamped by imported features, mostly from the US. In 1942 a law for the protection of the national cinema offered some advantages to producers, but lack of technical facilities presented problems that have still not been overcome.

The first films to express a national viewpoint were *Raíces de piedra* (1962) by the Spanish-born José Maria Arzuaga, *Tres cuentos colombianos* (1963) by Julio Luzardo and Alberto Meija, and Julio Brach's *Cada voz lleva su angustia* (1965). Political cinema began in 1968 with Arzuaga's *Pasado el meridiano*, which was censored. Other short political films, usually shot silent on 16mm, include Gabriela Samper's *El hombre de sal* (1968) and Meija's *¿Bolivar, donde estas que no te veo?*, and *29 de febrero* (1970). The leader of this 'third cinema' group is Carlos Alvarez, whose *Asalto* (1967), *Colombia '70* (1969), and *¿Que es la democracia?* (1971) were judged by the government to be 'insulting to the politicians in power'. His wife, Julia de Alvarez, has made *Un dia yo pregunte* (1970).

A new Cinema Act was passed in 1971, lowering the import duty on basic materials and instituting a 10 per cent QUOTA. Lack of quota enforcement powers, paucity of processing facilities, and stringent censorship have, however, combined to hold back film production. In 1972 the three main figures of progressive Colombian cinema, Julia de Alvarez, Carlos Alvarez, and Gabriela Samper, were arrested for alleged complicity with the guerrilla group ELN.

**COLONIAL FILM UNIT,** was founded by William Sellers in 1939, as part of Britain's wartime information services. Throughout the thirties, as Propaganda Officer to the Medical Health Service in Nigeria, he had experimented with educational films, principally on health and hygiene. Financed by the Colonial Development Fund, the Colonial Film Unit produced and distributed information and propaganda films for the British Colonial Territories. George PEARSON contributed his extensive professional experience, and training courses encouraged local film-making. Mobile cinema vans catered for average audiences of 2,000 (the record was 15,000), with spontaneous commentary in local dialects. A quarterly publication, *Colonial Cinema*, was produced from 1942 until shortly before the Unit's closure in 1955. (See also CROWN FILM UNIT.)

**COLOUR** in motion pictures, as in all photography, is practicable only because the human eye and brain are capable of perceiving the same colour in different ways. Light is a form of radiant energy which travels in waves of varying lengths, and the eye is sensitive to a small spectrum of wavelengths ranging from red (long wavelengths) through yellow, green, and blue to violet (short wavelengths). If, for example, a sodium-vapour streetlamp emits light of wavelengths near the middle of the spectrum, the eye sees it as yellow. And if red and green lights are projected together on a screen they combine additively and the eye again perceives yellow. If white light, which contains all the colours of the spectrum, falls on a wall painted yellow, the paint absorbs all other colours and reflects only yellow back to the eye. Fortunately, all these ways of perceiving yellow, and many more, can be accurately counterfeited on film in a single way: a coloured dye in the film subtracts all colours except yellow from the white light of the projector, so that screen images of the streetlamp, overlapping spotlights, and painted wall each appear yellow. All modern colour films work in this way.

Historically, colour appeared in photography even before motion pictures, but the various methods in use were ill-adapted to the requirements of the cinema, to which colour was first introduced in an artificial form. Most feature films during the silent period were tinted to produce an overall colour thought to be symbolic of the action: blue for a night scene, red for a holocaust, straw for a sunny day. Many important films had one or two reels tinted in several simultaneous colours by stencils, painstakingly cut by hand and run past dye rollers in contact with the print. In the final reel of *Gli ultimi giorni di Pompeii* (*The Last Days of Pompeii*, 1913) the eruption of Vesuvius in red and orange flame against a dark blue sky can still dazzle a modern audience.

Natural colour photography came to the screen by way of a series of primitive processes which appeared and disappeared in nervous succession. First came the ADDITIVE colour processes such as KINEMACOLOR (1906), CHRONOCHROME (1912), and PRIZMACOLOR (1918); all were generally limited to short one-reel subjects. A much later additive process was DUFAYCOLOR, which achieved some popularity in the late thirties. None of the additive colour systems was successful, chiefly because their use demanded modifications to the cinema projector.

It was SUBTRACTIVE colour which offered the possibility of lifelike effects from ordinary projectors. However all the early subtractive processes were two-colour systems which omitted one of the three primary colours needed for accurate reproduction. The first of these was an improved Prizmacolor. Another was an early and clumsy version of TECHNICOLOR, in which two coloured prints were cemented back-to-back and run through the projector together; it was used for the colour sequences in BEN-HUR (1925) and for the Douglas FAIRBANKS film *The Black Pirate* (1926). The most popular of all was CINECOLOR, which had a blue-green emulsion on one side of the film and an orange one on the other. From about 1935 it was widely used as a cheap colour process for 'B' pictures and Westerns, possibly because it photographed skies and tanned faces well, if little else.

Natural colour cinematography came of age in 1935 with MAMOULIAN's *Becky Sharp*, the first live-action feature made entirely in three-strip Technicolor. (Walt DISNEY had used the process for animation in *Flowers and Trees* two years earlier, and there had been sequences in *The House of Rothschild* and *Kid Millions*, 1934.) From its early two strip versions, Technicolor had evolved into a mature three-strip process. Three films ran through the huge camera, each recording one of the primary colours; these were converted into dye images which were printed on to a single film for projection. The system, while complex and expensive, was capable of considerable subtlety in colour reproduction. For nearly twenty years it was refined and improved until the very name Technicolor, often coupled with the adjective 'glorious', became virtually a synonym for any colour motion picture.

Meanwhile the Eastman Kodak Company had introduced Kodachrome to the amateur market. Unlike Technicolor it was a multilayer film, in which the three colour-sensitive emulsions were all placed on a single film base which could be used in an ordinary 16mm camera. Then in 1952 the multilayer principle was applied to professional films and EASTMAN COLOR appeared. It immediately superseded both the Technicolor three-strip process and the improved Technicolor 'monopack' and became the standard colour film for professional use. The simplicity and speed of Eastman Color made possible the WIDE SCREEN and ANAMORPHIC films in colour which appeared shortly afterwards.

In the years preceding the Second World War a similar film, AGFACOLOR, was developed in Germany. All the colour film stocks in use today are lineal descendants of either Agfacolor or Eastman Color. ANSCO COLOR, Gevacolor, Ferraniacolor, and SOVCOLOR are all essentially regional variants of the subtractive negative-positive colour process in which most modern films are photographed.

The use of colour as a stylistic element of motion pictures has been characterized by a succession of stubborn dogmas. At first, largely for technical reasons, colour was limited to short items of scenic interest, with the outstanding exception of Kinemacolor's coverage of the *Delhi Durbar* (1911). In the first years of sound, colour sequences were interpolated into many musical films. As techniques improved and colour spread to feature films, it was reserved almost exclusively for musicals and costume epics in which brilliant hues and startling contrasts were used to make the most of the medium. Colour was sometimes used only in parts of a film to contrast the mundane and the extraordinary, as in THE WIZARD OF OZ (1939). This cliché was brilliantly inverted in *A Matter of Life and Death* (1946, *Stairway to Heaven* in US), where wartime England was shot in Technicolor and the glories of Heaven in black-and-white to underline the hero's reluctance to depart this life. The often-criticized brashness of colour in

films was not attributable to technical limitations but rather to its application by designers (following the demands of producers) to brilliant artificial scenery and costumes. This limited policy made creative cameramen, such as James Wong HOWE and Lucien BALLARD, reluctant to work in colour: thus, although considerations of cost limited its use, it also came to be regarded as inappropriate to serious or realistic subjects. This attitude was so strong that even TWENTIETH CENTURY-FOX was forced to rescind its original decree that all CINEMASCOPE films must be made in colour. Not until the sixties, when colour became ubiquitous in television, magazines, and amateur photography, did it become acceptable on the screen as naturalism. Designers and cameramen then turned the earlier philosophy on its head and evolved an equally unreal style of neutral greys and muted tints to keep colour from distracting attention.

There have been comparatively few creative landmarks in the history of colour films; most colour experiments were artistic failures and were not repeated. In 1954 William Clothier photographed *Track of the Cat* in what amounted to monochromatic colour: only Robert MITCHUM's red hunting jacket stood out against a world of white snow, black firs, and grey skies. John HUSTON experimented imaginatively with colour in MOULIN ROUGE (1952) and commissioned a special Technicolor process for *Moby Dick* (1956) to suggest old whaling prints. And in IL DESERTO ROSSO (1964), ANTONIONI painted natural objects in unnatural colours to alter their emotional connotations. VISCONTI has, with various cameramen, attained remarkable control of rich colour compositions, outstandingly in IL GATTOPARDO (*The Leopard*, 1963) and MORTE A VENEZIA (*Death in Venice*, 1971). Such special cases aside, colour motion pictures have in general remained artistically inferior to the best contemporary still photography.

Considerable problems are presented by processing. Strict technical control and supervision are required to ensure prints of good quality. Unfortunately, only a few prints of any film are made to a high standard, for show in first-run cinemas: the bulk of release prints are mass-produced and consequently tend to vary in quality. Colour prints also deteriorate far more quickly than black-and-white, the magenta tones increasing while the others fade. In theory this loss can be retarded by refrigerated storage, but this is normally only provided by established film ARCHIVES.

*The international encyclopedia of film*, ed. Roger Manvell, London, 1972, contains a useful illustrated history of colour processes.

**COLPI**, HENRI (1921– ), French editor and director, after studying at the INSTITUT

DES HAUTES ÉTUDES CINÉMATOGRAPHIQUES (IDHEC) worked as a journalist on the *Ciné-Digest*, publishing a book, *Le cinéma et ses hommes* in 1947. He then began working in films as an editor, and rapidly established himself as one of the finest in France. During the fifties he worked with several distinguished directors, including RESNAIS, VARDA, CHAPLIN, and CLOUZOT, and directed several short films. In 1961 he directed his first feature, *Une Aussi Longue Absence*, written by Marguerite DURAS, which won the DELLUC prize and the Grand Prix at CANNES for that year. The following year he made *Codine*, a beautifully-realized adaptation of a novel by the Romanian Panaït Istrati, and the first Franco-Romanian co-production. Two further features followed, *Pour une étoile sans nom* (1966), and *Heureux qui comme Ulysse* (1969). Colpi has also written an important book on the function of music in the cinema, *Défense et illustration de la musique dans le film* (Lyons, 1963).

**COLUMBIA PICTURES,** US production company. In 1920 Harry COHN, his brother Jack Cohn, and Joseph Brandt—who had worked previously at UNIVERSAL—founded their own film-making company which they called CBC Sales Corporation. At its 'Poverty Row' studio in Hollywood, CBC began producing shorts and two-reel comedies, earning the company its industry nickname, the 'Cornbeef and Cabbage Company'. In an attempt to upgrade the studio's reputation, the three executives changed the company's name to Columbia Pictures in 1924 and began a policy drive towards better feature and co-feature films. Although Brandt was company president 1924–32, the real force behind Columbia's gradual rise to a position alongside the major Hollywood studios was the tough and vulgar Harry Cohn, president from 1932 until his death in 1958.

Columbia's first break-through occurred in the late twenties when Cohn hired Frank CAPRA as a director of studio comedies. Capra made a succession of films which earned critical acclaim: their financial success secured Capra a degree of independence not usually allowed under Cohn's domineering rule. These films included IT HAPPENED ONE NIGHT (1934), MR DEEDS GOES TO TOWN (1936), *Lost Horizon* (1937), *You Can't Take It With You* (1938), and MR SMITH GOES TO WASHINGTON (1939). At the same time other directors like Howard HAWKS and stars like Cary GRANT provided Columbia with equally successful light comedies such as THE AWFUL TRUTH (1937), HOLIDAY (1938), and HIS GIRL FRIDAY (1940).

After Capra's departure in 1939 the studio fell into a slump, turning out undistinguished films by contract directors; top film-makers were reluctant to work for the notorious Cohn. During the forties Columbia's only notable features included *A Song to Remember* (1944), *The Jolson Story* (1946), and the films of Columbia superstar Rita HAYWORTH. The studio's recovery in the early fifties came mainly through backing independent producers and directors like Sam SPIEGEL, David LEAN, Otto PREMINGER, Robert ROSSEN, Elia KAZAN, and Fred ZINNEMANN who made a number of impressive films for Columbia distribution: ALL THE KING'S MEN (1949), BORN YESTERDAY (1951), FROM HERE TO ETERNITY (1953), ON THE WATERFRONT (1954), *The Caine Mutiny* (1954), *Picnic* (1956), THE BRIDGE ON THE RIVER KWAI (1957), and LAWRENCE OF ARABIA (1962).

Under Cohn's successors, Abe Schneider and Leo Jaffe, the studio embarked on even more adventurous plans, particularly with respect to overseas productions. British films like *The Pumpkin Eater* (1964), *Georgy Girl* (1966), *Oliver!* (1968), and THE GO-BETWEEN (1971) were all Columbia-financed, as were several unconventional American films such as EASY RIDER (1969). Columbia's trade-mark, based on the Statue of Liberty and unmistakably conveying a reference to 'Hail Columbia', has been the target for clever spoofing as in such Columbia releases as *The Mouse That Roared* (1959), *Strait-jacket* (1963), and *Cat Ballou* (1965).

One of the few studios known solely for its film-making rather than for its theatre properties or conglomerate takeovers, Columbia has also fully exploited the area of television, making series and movies for television through its subsidiary Screen Gems. Columbia's inability to keep its large studio space occupied in the late sixties has resulted in the closure of the Columbia lot and the move in April 1972 of both Columbia and Screen Gems to the WARNER BROS studio. The two companies are now amalgamated as Columbia-Warner.

**COMBINED PRINT** see MARRIED PRINT

**COMDEN,** BETTY (1916– ), real name Elizabeth Cohen, and **GREEN,** ADOLPH (1915– ), US scriptwriters and lyricists whose first major success was the Broadway musical *On the Town* (1945), in which they also appeared. This success brought them to Hollywood and METRO-GOLDWYN-MAYER where their first film-writing assignment was *Good News* (1947). Their lyrics for *Take Me Out to the Ball Game* (1949, *Everybody's Cheering* in GB) marked the beginning of their professional association with Gene KELLY and Stanley DONEN, with whom Comden and Green worked on the brilliant trio of film musicals ON THE TOWN (1949), SINGIN' IN THE RAIN (1952), and *It's Always Fair Weather*

(1955). Their other film work includes scripting *The Barkleys of Broadway* (1949) and *Auntie Mame* (1958) and writing script and lyrics for *Bells Are Ringing* (1960) and *What a Way To Go* (1963). Comden and Green's witty, pungent scripts and lyrics have contributed much to the work of MINNELLI, Kelly, and Donen. In THE BAND WAGON (1953) they wrote themselves into the script as the Oscar Levant/Nanette Fabray characters, the difference being that Comden and Green are not married to each other.

**COME BACK AFRICA**, US, 1959. 1½hr. *Dir, prod* Lionel Rogosin; *scr* Rogosin, Lewis N'kosi, Bloke Modisane; *ph* Ernest Artaria, Emil Knebel.

The title, a translation of an African National Congress slogan, sets the tone for a vivid denunciation of apartheid by observation of the practical and moral effects of the system on Black South Africans. The film tells the story of a poverty-stricken farmer, Mgabi, who leaves his village and tries to find work. He is sacked from a variety of jobs before reaching Sophiatown, a slum suburb of Johannesburg. The ending reinforces the pervasive pessimism of the film: he returns from a prison sentence to find his wife strangled. In his agony and rage he demolishes the shanty.

The film was shot in secret and with limited means, disguised for the benefit of the authorities as a musical. Although it is technically crude and its amateur acting frequently stilted, it provides useful documentary background to the plight of Black South Africans. The staged incidents are the least successful. Among noteworthy scenes that are improvised is one showing a group of black intellectuals drinking together illegally in a shebeen.

**COMMAG PRINT,** a print with picture and magnetic sound combined on the same piece of film. The term is BBC coinage, a contraction of 'combined magnetic'; elsewhere it is called a STRIPED print. Related terms of similar origin are COMOPT, SEPMAG, and SEPOPT; see also MARRIED PRINT.

**COMMANDON,** JEAN (b. 1877), French doctor of medicine and pioneer in scientific film. In 1908, backed by Charles PATHÉ, he constructed equipment for filming microscopic life and in 1912 made the first films of X-rays. He also made over a hundred short films on zoological, botanical, medical, and surgical subjects.

**COMOPT PRINT,** a print with picture and optical sound combined on the same piece of film, otherwise known as a MARRIED PRINT. See COMMAG, SEPMAG, SEPOPT.

**COMPILATION,** film assembled from footage made for another purpose and which has usually been released as part of an earlier film. The limits of content for compilation are endless, but compilation films are almost always non-fiction. Their purpose may be to educate, inform, influence, and/or entertain their audience.

Neither the English term nor the French (*film de montage*) is entirely satisfactory since both are frequently applied to non-fiction films or television programmes which use predominantly unissued footage, which may or may not have been specifically shot for the production. Compilation often makes up a sequence in a documentary film, but that does not permit the term to be applied to the entire film. The term is also misapplied to feature-length assemblages of short fiction stories, properly called EPISODE films.

The technical aspects of compilation can be daunting. Silent film must be stretched so that it may be projected at sound speed with film shot at sound speed (see STRETCHING). DUPE negatives or FINE GRAINS must be taken so that the original material can survive intact for future use, and it was not until 1926 that Agfa and Eastman discovered satisfactory commercial methods of making dupe negatives. Colour film and black-and-white and colour videotape cause further printing complications, and the editing of one with the other can present aesthetic problems. Another such problem is presented by the brevity (as little as four seconds) of newsreel shots and the difficulty of cutting them acceptably into longer shots.

Finding, documenting, and authenticating the original material has always been the most time-consuming task for the compilation film maker. ARCHIVES and news film libraries have now lessened this burden to a certain degree, with the result that research today has become a much more meticulous and scrupulous affair than it used to be.

COPYRIGHT clearance should be obtained, although in the past it has often been ignored. Royalty, access, and search fees may add to the high cost of printing a substantial proportion of film over and above the expected length of the finished production. Nevertheless, compilation films are on average cheaper than new productions and, as such, they have always had a commercial appeal to the producer which has been rewarded by enthusiasm from the general public.

As soon as a satisfactory film cement had been developed, producers experimented with the compilation film as a substitute for news footage they could not photograph. In 1898 Francis Doublier released a news story purporting to show scenes of the arrest and imprisonment of DREYFUS in 1894, made up of shots from

Doublier's library. Other producers followed his example and used footage from productions to make new films, such as *The Life of an American Fireman* (1903) by Edwin S. PORTER and *Reptiles and their Greedy Ways* (1908) by Charles URBAN. The early newsreels used considerable amounts of previously issued footage and its authenticity was not questioned for some time (see NEWSREEL).

During the First World War, the potential of the compilation film as a means of interpreting historical events was fully realized (see PROPAGANDA). Typical examples, released in 1917, were *America's Answer to the Hun, Under Four Flags*, and *The Military Power of France*, and in 1919 British Famous Films released the British compilation *The World's Greatest Story*.

The editing techniques of such films were straightforward and unsophisticated. In post-revolutionary Russia, however, shortage of raw stock made editors work with used footage and the compilation film was admirably suited to current experiments in MONTAGE, aspiring to become an art form in its own right. In 1921 Dziga VERTOV compiled a thirteen-reel *Istoriya grazhdanskoi voini* (*History of the Civil War*) and used issued footage in many of his *Kino* magazines. Sovkino Studios commissioned their editor Esther SHUB to undertake a massive project, finding and viewing thousands of feet of film on Russian history from 1896, and compiling three statements in the cause of the Revolution, *Padeniye dinasti Romanovikh* (*Fall of the Romanov Dynasty*, 1927), *Velikii put* (*The Great Road*, 1927), and *Rossiya Nikolaya II i Lev Tolstoy* (*The Russia of Nicholas II and Leo Tolstoy*, 1928). Inspired by the power of actuality on the screen, she felt that in comparison with historical reconstruction it had a conviction that could neither pale nor age. This is the continuing attraction of compilation to a film-maker.

In Western Europe and the US, the trend in the twenties was towards biographical and historical compilations of a less didactic nature, such as Cecil M. HEPWORTH's *Through Three Reigns* (1922); *The March of the Movies* (1927) by Otto Nelson and Terry Ramsaye; *Charles A. Lindbergh's Triumph of the Air* (1928) by A. E. Hancock; *Conquest* (1929) by Basil WRIGHT; and numerous newsreel tributes to the year, the decade, public figures, such as *Earl Haig, The Soldier and the Man*.

As the euphoria of peace waned, several film-makers began to analyse the effects of the First World War and compilation was naturally the technique which most of them employed. The eloquence and commitment of Shub's compilations were rivalled by Henri STORCK's influential *Histoire du soldat inconnu* (1932), Louis DE ROCHEMONT's *The Cry of the World* (1932), Norman Lee's *Forgotten Men* (1934), and other works of lesser stature concentrating on the anti-war theme. In Germany Walter RUTTMANN and Hans RICHTER experimented with the compilation as an analytic form, while *Der Weltkrieg* (*Behind the German Lines*, 1927), *Blutendes Deutschland* (1933), and *Bilddokumente* (1935) reinforced the contention that the Allies had planned the destruction of Germany throughout the First World War and the Weimar Republic.

The coming of sound prompted Hollywood to plunder the archives for jokey compilations on the silent era. However, the immediacy of world crises allowed the compilation film to concentrate, as in the past, on interpreting current events. The major studios used footage from their newsreels to produce biographies on the leading politicians of the day: and THE MARCH OF TIME (1931–51) relied on issued shots for much of its material. Commentary dominated the visual images, and it was only in the hands of accomplished film-makers that sound and picture were juxtaposed creatively. In 1937 Luis BUÑUEL helped compile *Madrid '36* from official Republican footage of the outbreak of the Spanish Civil War which makes emotive use of Beethoven's symphonies on the sound track. Esther Shub's classic compilation *Ispaniya* (*Spain*, 1939) combined a wealth of newsreel material shot by Roman KARMEN and Boris Makaseyev during the war, a subtle use of music, composed by Gavril Popov, and a powerful commentary written and spoken by the playwright Vishnevsky.

The best compilation films to date have dealt with clear-cut ideological conflicts, and the Second World War provided a huge impetus to the development of the form. Film libraries increased dramatically in size, and government finance was forthcoming for classic propaganda compilations such as *Sieg im Westen* (Germany, 1940), *Yellow Caesar* (GB, 1941), *The Ramparts We Watch* (*The March of Time*, US, 1940), *The World at War* (US, 1943), and *Bitva za nashu Sovietskuyu Ukrainu* (*The Fight for Our Soviet Ukraine*, USSR, 1943).

Each country exploited news footage of their allies or opponents and it was easy to expose the enemy to ridicule, as Charles Ridley, an editor at British Movietone News did in *Germany Calling: the Lambeth Walk* (1940). Frank CAPRA's WHY WE FIGHT series (1942–5) achieved a new peak for the compilation film, revealing an enlightened and instructive use of source materials. WORLD IN ACTION (1942–5) began in 1941 as a local Canadian series *Canada Carries On*, written and supervised by Stuart LEGG although John GRIERSON was responsible for the general guide-lines. It was remarkable for its assumption that its audience would welcome, as they did, its intelligent, even intellectual, approach. The theatres of war were fully explained, and from 1943 several editions were devoted to predicting the effects of peace.

One outstanding series of compilation films which inherited techniques from the British documentary movement of the thirties, and became a model of its kind for future compilations, particularly on television, was Paul ROTHA's government-sponsored trilogy on the post-war problems of food and famine, *World of Plenty* (1943), *Land of Promise* (1945), and *The World is Rich* (1947), which illustrated the comments of experts with relevant archive footage, and managed to convey abstract concepts with specific visual sequences.

In the immediate post-war period recrimination, reconstruction, and nostalgia were the dominant themes of the compilation film. *The True Glory* (1945) by Carol REED and Garson KANIN, was the most popular compilation on the war, earning critical acclaim for its humanity and honesty. Few compilations before or since have concentrated so successfully on the personal angle of the ordinary soldier's experiences in wartime.

In 1947 Henri CARTIER-BRESSON and Richard Banks compiled issued and newly shot footage for LE RETOUR, about the liberation of French prisoners from concentration camps and their return to France. Its understated emotion and eloquence contrasts with the other, longer compilations on the theme of Nazi crimes, such as WARNER BROS' *Hitler Lives* (1945), Karmen and Elizaveta Svilova's *Sud narodov* (*Trial by the Peoples*, 1947), the THORNDIKES' *Archiv sagen aus* (*The Archives Testify* series, late fifties), *Svĕdectvi* (*Evidence/The Czechoslovak Story*, 1961), and *Der Nürnberger Prozess* (*Nazi Crimes and Punishment*, 1958). Only Alain RESNAIS's essay on Auschwitz, NUIT ET BROUILLARD (1955), surpasses *Le Retour* in its sense of tragedy unmarred by sensationalism or distortion.

Understandably, nostalgia was not limited to the war period. Pathé's *Scrapbook for 1922* (1947) and *The Peaceful Years* (1948) in Britain, *Cavalcata di mezzo secolo* (*Cavalcade of Half a Century*, 1951) in Italy, and *Fifty Years Before Your Eyes* (1950) in the US were a few of the more memorable compilations on the past which were released at this time. Nicole VEDRÈS in PARIS 1900 (1948) proved that audiences could be enchanted by early film of such personalities as Monet, Renoir, Bernhardt, Carpentier, Melba, without resorting to an explanatory or superior commentary. A musical score by Guy Bernhardt played an important role in this expert compilation film, as did Malcolm ARNOLD's score for

*Powered Flight* (1953). This is a scholarly but exciting history of aviation by Stuart LEGG for the SHELL FILM UNIT, made with the co-operation of the Royal Aeronautical Society, one of the first of many academic bodies to become interested in the potential of archive film, and to lend their support to its responsible exploitation.

The East German film studios, DEFA, were particularly adept in using the compilation form to present a doctrinaire view of recent history. Two of their editors, Andrew and Annelie Thorndike, became the best exponents of the feature-length, investigative, and accusatory compilation film, based on exhaustive film research. *Wilhelm Pieck: das Leben unseres Präsidenten* (1951) was followed by *Du und mancher Kamerad* (*The German Story*, 1956), two episodes of the *Archiv sagen aus* series, and *Das russische Wunder* (*The Russian Miracle*, 1963) each of which, if biased in content, is nevertheless a masterly summary of a viewpoint utilizing archive footage.

The phenomenon of Nazi Germany and its vast wealth of historical film has been a constant attraction to the compilation film-maker, which shows no signs of abatement today. Erwin Leiser, a German working in Sweden, has concentrated on making films about this one topic, producing in 1960 *Den blödiga Tiden* (also known as *Mein Kampf*), in 1961 *Eichmann und das dritte Reich*, *Waehle das Leben* (referring also to the atom bomb), and in 1962 *Deutschland erwache*, a rare example of an attempt to examine a régime through its feature film content.

Paul Rotha in 1961 might have been thought to have made the definitive compilation on Hitler, *Das Leben von Adolf Hitler*, for which he viewed 2,500,000 feet of archive film; but as history is constantly being re-interpreted, it too has come in for criticism and, in some areas, ridicule. The dependence of the compilation film-maker on copyright clearance is well illustrated by this film—Rotha was allowed access to official Bonn government film on condition he did not mention the Krupp family—and by *All'armi, siamo fascisti* (1962) an Italian production on the rise of Fascism which was refused the use of any of the footage preserved at the Instituto Luce (see ITALY).

The discovery of untapped film sources, the expiration of film rights, and the re-assessment of history will always guarantee work for compilation film makers. In 1965 Mikhail ROMM, who had worked on compilations in the Soviet Union since 1948, found a market for an attack on Nazi Germany concentrating on familiar atrocity footage entitled *Obyknovenyi fashizm* (*Ordinary Fascism*, shown commercially as *Echo of the*

*Jackboot*). In recent years, the emphasis has for-tunately moved away from political exposé to-wards the human angle. Two British productions in 1973, Lutz Becker's *The Double Headed Eagle* and Philippe Mora's *Swastika* both em-ploy forgotten film, such as Eva Braun's home movies and local Party documentaries, to present the authentic, unofficial face of Nazism. A similar technique is used in the French production *Le Bonheur dans vingt ans* (*Happiness in Twenty Years*, 1971) by Albert Knobler, which relates events in Czechoslovakia in 1948–68 as they affected ordinary people.

Compilations for the commercial cinema in the post-war period were not limited to nostalgia or retrospectives on the causes and progress of the Second World War. In 1953, Joris IVENS and Vladimir Pozner produced for DEFA a memor-able documentary which relied almost entirely on archive footage, *Lied der Ströme* (*Song of the Rivers*). The project arose out of the World Congress of Trade Unions held in Vienna in 1953 and attempted, largely successfully, to por-tray the workers of the world and their progress towards self-sufficiency within the context of the trade union movement. The polemical content is, as might be expected, high, but the level of pictorial journalism is outstanding. Ideological commitment was also the main motivation for George Morrison's *Mise Eire* (*I am Ireland*, 1959) and *Saoirise?* (*Freedom*, 1961), two parts of a planned trilogy on twentieth-century Ireland. The result is a moving history as well as a political statement about the nature of the Irish problem. Similar efforts to persuade by implica-tion, rather than by direct statement, were made by Frédéric ROSSIF in MOURIR A MADRID (*To Die in Madrid*, 1962), the first feature-length non-fiction film on the Spanish Civil War since Shub's *Ispaniya*, which rivals the passion and beauty of its predecessor.

The post-war conflicts in the THIRD WORLD are also being recorded in compilation film. Few examples from China have been seen in the West, apart from *Storm in Asia* (1960) which includes footage from FRONTIER FILMS' *China Strikes Back* (1938). Here, as with many Soviet Union compilations, it is more interesting to note which films have been excluded, rather than included, as the history books are re-written.

The existence of a Latin American political cinema owes much to the revolution in Cuba and to the influential achievements of the Instituto Cubano del Arte y Industria Cinematografica (ICAIC). The impressive work of Santiago ALVAREZ includes many films which use compila-tion sequences to put their message in historical perspective. *Now* (1965) and *LBJ* (1969) use montage of stills (in itself a type of compilation) to attack the American political system, while

other eloquent films deal with Vietnam (*Hanoi, martes 13*, 1967; *79 Primeveras*, 1969) and Bolivia (*Hasta la Victoria Siempre*, 1967).

The effect of television on the development of compilation as a cinematic form has been slight, but in terms of output and commercial viability its impact has been enormous. Many of the tech-nical flaws in archive film, and the awkward switching, in one compilation programme, be-tween different film and video gauges and be-tween various colour and sound processes, are less apparent on the small screen.

Predictably, the two world wars have been the most popular topic for television compilations in Europe and the US. By the early fifties *The March of Time: Crusade in the Pacific* had introduced the long compilation series to American television viewers, quickly followed by NBC's *Victory at Sea* (1952/3) and Second World War sea battles. CBS's *The Twentieth Century* (1957/61) devoted a disproportionate number of its 104 episodes to the two wars, reflecting public interest in the subject as well as the wealth of relevant archive footage. ABC's *The Valiant Years* (1960), an ambitious visualization of Winston Churchill's memoirs, began the trend towards an academic rather than nostalgic approach to the treatment of history on television, although the American productions are in general more biased than their British equivalents. The editing and film research in CBS's *World War I* (1964), for example, are impeccable, but the script is verbose and histrionic.

In Britain the BBC and major ITV companies have vied with each other for high audience rat-ings and academic prestige in their presentation of compilation series. Out of numerous produc-tions, the most memorable are BBC's *The Great War* (1964) and *The Lost Peace* (1966), super-vised by Tony Essex; Granada's *Cities At War* (1968); and Thames's *The Day Before Yesterday* (1970) and *The World at War* (1973/4), produced by Jeremy Isaacs.

The debate surrounding the ethics of film research and distortion has become more and more complicated, indicating historians', academics', and film aesthetes' growing interest in these television series. In 1964 Tony Essex felt entirely justified in reversing shots where neces-sary so that the Germans would always be seen moving from right to left and the Allies from left to right. By 1973 such techniques in the cause of continuity were frowned upon and much of the praise for *The World at War* series is based upon the producers' scrupulous regard for accuracy in their use of film as evidence.

The tendency to use the reminiscences of eyewitnesses in television compilations is increasing. The important film LE CHAGRIN ET

LA PITIÉ (1969), by Marcel OPHULS, cannot be termed a compilation film, when a major proportion of its running time is devoted to the reminiscences of those who experienced Vichy France and its liberation. More use of issued footage is made in his *A Sense of Loss* (1973), about the conflicts in Northern Ireland (which has still to be shown in Britain).

No director in Britain has built his reputation on the compilation form, perhaps because the financiers of such films are mainly television companies whose structure demands a team effort. In the US, however, where there is more scope for the independent producer to make films and then sell them to a television station, two names have dominated the form—David Wolper and Emile de Antonio. Wolper is the more commercial and less committed of the two, and his output is more prolific. His tastes are catholic and his compilations range from nostalgic tributes to Hollywood and Marilyn MONROE, to journalistic studies on American current affairs, such as *The Race for Space* (1958) and *The Making of the President* (1960 and 1964) which won prestigious American cinema and television awards. De Antonio has used the form to make immediate political comments on recent events in American history, such as *Point of Order* (1963), which unravels the intricacies of the Army McCarthy hearings, *In the Year of the Pig* (1968), surveying the history of Vietnam over the last forty years, and *Millhouse, A White Comedy* (1971), one of the best satirical attacks on a political leader.

After seventy-five years of cinema, the compilation form has proved to be an enduring one, feeding on extant film sources and the public's nostalgia and curiosity about the past. Historians have ceased to deride archive film as a source material, and in Europe and the US groups of academics are forming production companies to compile films as well as books about the past. These productions are not as biased as those produced for ideological purposes by the Third World or East European countries, and they are relieved of the commercial pressures which can force Western film or television producers to compromise. Nevertheless, and indeed as a result of their impartiality, they rarely aspire to the levels of passionate commitment or lyrical beauty achieved by the key compilations in the past.

Jay Leyda, *Films beget films*, London, 1964; Arthur Elton, *Film as source material for history*, London, 1955.

**COMPOSITE PRINT,** the US term for a print with picture and sound combined on the same piece of film. In the UK it is called a MARRIED PRINT.

*CONDAMNÉ A MORT S'EST ECHAPPÉ, Un* (*A Man Escaped*: Bresson's alternative title *Le Vent souffle où il veut*), France, 1956. 1¼hr. *Dir* Robert Bresson; *prod* Société Nouvelle des Etablissements Gaumont/Nouvelles Editions de Film; *scr* Bresson, from the account by André Devigny; *ph* Léonce-Henry Burel; *des* Pierre Charbonnier; *ed* Raymond Lamy; *mus* Mozart, Mass in C minor; *cast* François Leterrier (Fontaine), Charles LeClainche (Jost), Roland Monod (priest), Jacques Ertaud (Orsini), Maurice Beerblock (Blanchet).

BRESSON read in the *Figaro littéraire*, November 1954, an account by André Devigny, who had been condemned to death by the Gestapo in 1943 and imprisoned in the Fort de Montluc in Lyons, from which no prisoner had ever escaped. He escaped only a few hours before his execution was due. Bresson set his face against any kind of sensationalism. The title denies the possibility of suspense in its conventional usage: the film is full of suspense, but it arises from the tension of Fontaine's moral and physical effort. Bresson paid meticulous attention to realistic details. He wanted to make the film in the actual prison cell, and being denied permission had it reconstructed in the studio. Not only were the measurements precise, but real materials were used rather than the usual studio imitation. Devigny was engaged to supervise the exactness of every detail in the film.

In making the film, Bresson refined the methods he had used 'in JOURNAL D'UN CURÉ DE CAMPAGNE (1951). All the actors were non-professional and the demanding central role of Fontaine was played by a twenty-seven-year-old philosophy student. The film concentrates on Fontaine, and is confined to the barest essentials: momentous action such as the attempted escape at the beginning and the killing of the sentry is suggested rather than shown. A strong sense of isolation from the outside world, and of oppression and death within the prison, is built up by visual hints supported by a skilful sound-track. As in all the best of Bresson's work, the effect is achieved by elimination of the unnecessary: the economy with which he makes implications allows him to concentrate on the moral force of Fontaine's determination to escape.

*CONFORMISTA, Il* (*The Conformist*), Italy/France/West Germany, 1970. Technicolor; 1¾hr. *Dir, scr* Bernardo Bertolucci, from the novel by Alberto Moravia; *prod* Mars Film (Rome)/Marianne (Paris)/ Maran (Munich); *ph* Vittorio Storaro; *mus* Georges Delerue; *cast* Jean-Louis Trintignant (Marcello), Stefania Sandrelli (Giulia), Enzo Taroscio (Quadri), Pierre Clémenti (Lino), Dominique Sanda (Anna Quadri).

In an attempt to repress the memory of childhood traumas, Marcello offers his services to the Fascists and is deputed to assassinate his former professor. He realizes that conformism, the surrender of personal responsibility, cannot compensate for emotional insecurity: the end of the film shows him attempting to come to terms with his latent homosexuality.

The Freudian preoccupations that run through BERTOLUCCI's work are here assimilated into an ironic study of pre-war European society, a society evoked by the oppressive use of dark and light. Marcello travels in closed vehicles and inhabits a world of heavily furnished apartments, artificially lit or sunlit only through slatted shutters. He is the outsider amongst occupants involved in baffling, disturbing pursuits. Aided by Jean-Louis TRINTIGNANT's tense conviction in the title role, the evocation of a system based on the willing co-operation of the weak with a brutal régime is remarkably complete.

**CONGRÈS DES DUPES,** name given at the time in *Ciné-Journal* to the Premier Congrès International des Fabricants de Film which met in Paris in February 1909 under the presidency of Georges MÉLIÈS. The principal manufacturers and producers of France, England, Germany, Italy, Denmark, and Russia, suffering from the short-lived but severe crisis from 1907, had been further alarmed by the manoeuvrings in the US which led to the setting-up of the MOTION PICTURE PATENTS COMPANY and its attempt to monopolize the US market. They were joined at the conference in Paris by George EASTMAN, who hoped to be able to repeat in Europe the deal by which he had become exclusive supplier of film stock to the MPPC in the US. In Paris, however, he found a formidable competitor in Charles PATHÉ. The struggle between Eastman and Pathé for control over supply of stock, and the substitution of film hire for the sale of prints which was the main preoccupation of the conference (see DISTRIBUTION), led to the erection of a structure in the European industry which has endured until recent years without radical change. An immediate effect was the squeezing out of small companies, that of Méliès sadly and ironically among them. Other less dramatic but far-reaching decisions of the conference affected standardization of film stock.

*CONGRESS DANCES* see KONGRESS TANZT, DER

**CONKLIN,** CHESTER (1886–    ), US actor, a key performer in Mack SENNETT's KEYSTONE comedies. A former circus clown, he used a cross-eyed stare and an air of monumental ineptitude as his principal comic devices. He later appeared in GREED (1923), MODERN TIMES (1936), and THE GREAT DICTATOR (1940).

**CONNERY,** SEAN (1930–    ), Scottish actor usually identified with JAMES BOND in the films of Ian Fleming's spy thrillers. His sang-froid and debonair charm ideally fitted Bond's character in *Dr No* (1962), *From Russia With Love* (1963), *Goldfinger* (1964), *Thunderball* (1965), and *You Only Live Twice* (1967). He refused the next Bond film (*On Her Majesty's Secret Service*, 1969) but returned in *Diamonds Are Forever* (1971). Connery has tried to escape this typecasting and succeeded best in *The Hill* (LUMET, 1965), as the labour agitator in *The Molly Maguires* (RITT, 1969), and in the tough thriller *The Anderson Tapes* (Lumet, 1971). He was less at ease than usual in John BOORMAN's excursion into science fiction, *Zardoz* (1974).

**CONNOLLY,** WALTER (1887–1940), US actor, of stage background, who went to Hollywood in 1932 and became familiar in character roles, especially in irate or apoplectic parts. He was Claudette COLBERT's father in IT HAPPENED ONE NIGHT (1934) and his best remembered screen appearance was in another characteristic role—as the editor in NOTHING SACRED (1937).

**CONSTANTINE,** EDDIE (1917–    ), US actor who has achieved considerable fame working in French films where he was much in demand, particularly during the fifties, for tough-guy roles in crime melodramas such as *Du Rififi chez les femmes* (1959). He became associated particularly with Peter Cheyney's character Lemmy Caution, a role he played, in an appreciably different context, in Jean-Luc GODARD's *Alphaville* (1965). He has occasionally made films in Britain, including *SOS Pacific* (1959).

**CONTINENTALE FILMS.** Nazi-controlled production company, set up in Paris in 1941 under the direction of Graven (Paris representative of Goebbels's Propaganda Ministry), to produce French films of a diverting nature. Continentale Films produced thirty of the 220 films made in France during the Occupation, and the firm had its own circuit (cinemas confiscated from Jewish owners such as Siritsky and Jacques Haik). Directors who worked for the company include Henri Decoin—*Premier rendezvous* (1941) and *Les Inconnus dans la maison* (1942) —CHRISTIAN-JACQUE, André CAYATTE, and H.-G. CLOUZOT—*Le Corbeau* (1943). Those who worked with the German company became extremely unpopular with their compatriots, and Clouzot in particular was virtually blacklisted for a time.

**CONTINUITY GIRL,** the member of a film production team who keeps a written record of all details of the action in each shot so that they can be precisely matched in later shots of the same action. In Hollywood and France she is called the script girl. She is in effect the editor's secretary: she notes the position of an ashtray, the length of the cigarette in it, and with which hand the actor picks it up, so that continuity is maintained when the editor cuts between two shots of the action. (See MATCHING.) The job is basic to the fragmented nature of film production and has no exact parallel in the other performing media.

**COOGAN,** JACKIE (1914–    ), US actor, who became a CHILD STAR in CHAPLIN'S THE KID (1920), after which his little tramp role was exploited in many films: *Peck's Bad Boy* (1921), OLIVER TWIST (1922), *Little Robinson Crusoe* (1924), *Old Clothes* (1925), *Tom Sawyer* (1930), *Huckleberry Finn* (1931), among them. In 1937 he was involved in a famous court case against his mother and stepfather, to gain possession of some of his childhood earnings. This led to agitation for legislation to protect the earnings of child actors. He enjoyed something of a hit in the ghoulish television serial *The Addams Family* (1964–5). He continues to play small parts in films and television.

**COOK Jr,** ELISHA (1907–    ), US actor, began his career on the stage at the age of fourteen. He signed a contract with PARAMOUNT in 1936 and appeared in a number of little-remembered films: he achieved his major break-through for WARNER BROS as Wilmer, the Fat Man's white-faced, gun-happy but not always effective thug in John HUSTON'S THE MALTESE FALCON (1941). He successfully exploited his physical limitations (smallness, croakily whining voice, and pinched features); gangsters and gunmen became his speciality, but he avoided type-casting except in being largely restricted to unpleasant characters. As well as thrillers like *Dillinger* (1945) and THE BIG SLEEP (1946), he found a place in Danny KAYE comedy (*Up in Arms*, 1944), Boris KARLOFF horror (*Voodoo Island*, 1957), and in many Westerns including SHANE (1953).

**COOPER,** GARY (1901–61), US actor, started in films as an extra, usually in WESTERNS. A supporting role in *The Winning of Barbara Worth* (1926) led to leading parts; his first all-talkie *The Virginian* (1929) made him a star and established the kind of character for which he is chiefly remembered—tough, reticent, brave, and laconic. Although he is mainly associated with Westerns, many of his best films were action dramas or comedy-romances. He starred opposite Marlene DIETRICH in Josef von STERNBERG's MOROCCO (1930), and in MAMOULIAN's CITY STREETS (1931) he played the inexperienced pawn of city racketeers. Ernest HEMINGWAY considered him the ideal actor for the hero in *A Farewell to Arms* (1933), but he also made an agreeable White Knight in the 1934 version of ALICE IN WONDERLAND. LIVES OF A BENGAL LANCER (1935), an enormous popular success, was in vigorous contrast to his stylish comedy performances in Frank BORZAGE's *Desire* (1936), again opposite Dietrich, and in MR DEEDS GOES TO TOWN (1936) as the honest, unaffected Longfellow Deeds. *The General Died at Dawn* (1936) gave him a crusading role as an American adventurer toppling a Chinese war-lord; the same year he returned to the Western as Wild Bill HICKOCK in the Cecil B. DEMILLE epic *The Plainsman* (1937). He was the much-married millionaire in BLUEBEARD's EIGHTH WIFE (1938) and a gallant English aristocrat in *Beau Geste* (1939), and typically sensitive and courageous in William WYLER's intelligent *The Westerner* (1940).

Cooper's popular success was confirmed by his first OSCAR, for the title role in Howard HAWKS's *Sergeant York* (1941). He was another Hemingway hero in *For Whom the Bell Tolls* (1943). Apart from another romantic role in *Saratoga Trunk* (1944), the next ten years failed to provide him with parts of significant quality, but his second Oscar justly rewarded one of his best characterizations: Will Kane, the ageing Marshall who stands alone against a vicious gang in HIGH NOON (1952). His last films gave him two quietly appealing roles, a Quaker in Wyler's *Friendly Persuasion* (1956) and Audrey HEPBURN's middle-aged lover in Billy WILDER's bitter-sweet *Love in the Afternoon* (1957), and two more notable Westerns, *Man of the West* (1958) and *The Hanging Tree* (1959).

Cooper's acting ability was limited—he could never have played an outright villain—but he brought to each role a studied sincerity that quickly established and sustained the characterization. His popularity and standing as a great Hollywood star endured until his death.

**COOPER,** MERIAN C. (1894–    ), US director and producer who, after flying service in the First World War, became a journalist and then an explorer. The latter interest led to the production of his first film *Grass* (1925), with Ernest B. SCHOEDSACK as his cameraman. It was one of the few documentary films to have real commercial success, and Cooper and Schoedsack followed it with CHANG (1927), one of the first features shot on PANCHROMATIC stock and again very profitable. The partnership succeeded again with the first film adaptation of A. E. W. Mason's novel

*The Four Feathers* (1929), and Cooper's enjoyment in filming the animal sequences led him to make KING KONG (1933), in spite of initial disapproval from David O. SELZNICK, at the time a producer at RKO. Cooper and Schoedsack collaborated equally in the direction of *King Kong*, their last joint venture, and this culmination of their partnership was another box-office hit and proved lastingly influential in the fantasy field. After *King Kong* Cooper became a producer.

The rest of his career was spent mostly in collaboration with John FORD, who became his partner in Argosy Pictures. Their first productions were STAGECOACH (1939) and *The Long Voyage Home* (1940). Cooper served in the USAAF throughout the Second World War, resuming his association with Ford after the war to make *The Fugitive* (1947), *Fort Apache* (1948), SHE WORE A YELLOW RIBBON (1949), *Rio Grande*, and WAGONMASTER (both 1950). Argosy dissolved very successfully in 1956 and Cooper became director of production for CINERAMA.

**COPLAND,** AARON (1900–   ), US composer whose film scores, few in number but high in quality, date mainly from the forties. They include music for *Of Mice and Men* (1939), *North Star* (1943), *The Heiress* (1949), for which he won an OSCAR, and documentaries including Willard VAN DYKE's *The City* (1939). Especially well known is his reticent but effective music for *Our Town* (Sam WOOD, 1940), which has been issued as a gramophone recording; and also his score for *The Red Pony* (1949), from which a children's suite was adapted for concert performance.

**COPPOLA,** FRANCIS FORD (1933–   ), US director, trained in film at the University of California at Los Angeles. After writing a prizewinning script he entered the industry, like others of his generation, through work with Roger CORMAN. He was an assistant director and writer before directing his first feature, *Dementia 13* (1963, *The Haunted and the Hunted* in GB), then returned to writing for a period. In 1966 he was allowed to direct his own project *You're a Big Boy Now*, one of the earliest and more interesting of Hollywood's examinations of the young generation. Although it was overshadowed by THE GRADUATE (1967) it proved Coppola's ability to work within a low budget and encouraged WARNER BROS to trust him with *Finian's Rainbow* (1968). With the help of Fred ASTAIRE, Coppola made this one of the few recent examples of the Hollywood MUSICAL to show real vitality. Success within the commercial system allowed him to experiment with his own subjects: *The Rain People* (1969), concerning a young married woman trying to escape from emotional responsibility, was shot entirely on location between New York and Los Angeles, using a small crew. For this and other independent productions Coppola formed American Zoetrope, his own production unit with complete film-making facilities. He also continued to write screenplays: *Patton: Lust for Glory* (Franklin SCHAFFNER, 1969), which he co-wrote, won an OSCAR for its screenplay. THE GODFATHER (1971) broke box-office records and also proved Coppola's ability to handle a large-budget production while endowing the story of syndicated crime with a feeling for character and family relationships. *The Conversation* (1974), a smaller-scale film, thoughtful and innovatory, was followed by another box-office triumph, *The Godfather, Part II* (1975).

Coppola has applied his considerable profits to promoting film distribution and exhibition and to backing projects by promising newcomers.

**COPYRIGHT** is a protection legislated by governments primarily for the benefit of their own nationals in their own countries, to enable them to have the exclusive right to use, to lease, and to receive payment for the use of, any original ideas which they have created and expressed in an identifiable form, and to enable them to take legal action for the recovery of damages against anyone infringing this right. The term copyright (or author's rights) covers both copying and performing rights.

There are basically two laws governing film copyright in Great Britain, the Copyright Act of 1911 which is applied to films made before 1957 and the Copyright Act of 1956 covering those made from 1957 onwards. Neither Act, however, was framed to deal specifically with films, and their application to this field has led to many anomalies. A Parliamentary Committee (the Whitford Committee) has recently been charged with investigating the copyright law including its functioning with regard to films, television, and video.

The 1911 Act did not grant copyright to film *per se* but as a dramatic work. This means, in practice, that the term of copyright is the usual one of 50 years from the death of the author— the author being the person who plans the work and employs others to compose the different parts—normally the producer but not the production company, since only a natural person can be a dramatic author. If the author contracted the rights to another person, this could only be for a period not exceeding 25 years after the death of the author—the Act stipulated that in such circumstances the rights must revert to the heirs of the author for the remainder of the copyright period (i.e. the remaining 25 years).

In addition to the author, there may be other owners of copyright in parts of the film-script, photographs, music, etc, but in all probability these rights will have been assigned to the film company. Very few of the production companies of the thirties or earlier still exist, and even those that do have not kept adequate records; this combined with the disposal of assets of liquidated companies leads to a potentially chaotic situation.

The 1911 Act quite clearly applied to fiction films; documentaries and newsreels might arguably be termed 'non-dramatic' works and legal opinion seems quite firmly to agree that newsreel, to the extent to which it is unedited sequences of photographs, is covered by the same law as news photographs—its copyright life is 50 years from the date of the events depicted. However, this opinion seems never to have been tested in a court of law.

The 1956 Copyright Act created for the first time in British law a specific film-copyright, which applies to films made from 1957 onwards (British films made after 31 May 1957 and foreign films made after 26 September 1957). The new term of copyright became 50 years from publication—the date of publication is taken to be that on which the film was registered under the Quota Acts, or, if the film is not so registrable, the date on which the film was first published. It is in this very important area of publication that film differs from every other kind of copyright work. Publication of a film is not the same as exhibition, except when the trade showing of a film is taken to mean that the film is being offered for hire or, exceptionally, for sale. In fact, films are sold (in the sense of being offered for sale on the open market as with, for example, 8mm films) so rarely that the whole concept of the copyright period may be meaningless if, at the end of it, the public have no access to copies of the film. There is nothing in British copyright law that places the onus on copyright holders to release copies of films once they have come into the public domain.

Since the 1911 Act copyright period of the life of the author plus 50 years was replaced in the 1956 Act by just 50 years, the definition of author has now to be extended to include not only individuals but companies as 'makers' of a film. The 1956 Act also provides that on expiry of the copyright period of a film, the film may be exhibited in public without infringing any of the other copyrights residual in the film (e.g. musical, literary). On the other hand, certain anomalies may arise if the screen rights in a literary work have been assigned for a period shorter than the copyright life of the film. In these circumstances the film must be withdrawn from commercial distribution unless the owner of the rights in the original literary work gives permission for further commercial exploitation. The 1956 Act does however distinguish between the public and other (domestic and private and educational) exhibition of film. It is only the public exhibition of film which is an infringement of copyright: the screening of a film to a domestic and private or school audience is not an infringement. This very important aspect of the 1956 Act has so far been totally ignored by the film industry.

The copyright situation in the US is both more formal and simpler than in Britain. Films enjoy copyright only if they are registered with the Copyright Office of the Library of Congress *before* publication. Early practice followed the law applying to still photographs, and the deposition of films printed in the form of positive strips has fortuitously resulted in the unique collection of very early films at the Library of Congress (see PAPER PRINTS). To discourage pirating, producers of this period often incorporated their trade mark in the set decorations of the films—the MÉLIÈS star was one notable example. Since the US Copyright Law of 1912 recognized films in their own right, two copies of the best edition of the film registered (e.g. 35mm rather than 16mm) must be deposited with the Copyright Office; but in practice lack of storage and preservation facilities led to the acceptance of willingness to deposit as sufficient. The films enjoy a copyright period of 28 years, with an optional further 28 years which may be taken up only by the copyright holder. Additionally, every copy of a film registered in copyright must bear notice of copyright, e.g. © John Doe 1969. The use of this particular form of notice may result in securing copyright in countries outside the United States under the provisions of the Universal Copyright Convention.

Historically, there have been two international copyright systems operating since the end of the last century: the Berne Convention (or Union) dating from 1886 and amended every twenty years and the Pan American Union. The majority of European countries including Britain, France, Germany (but not the Soviet Union) belong to the Berne Convention and the United States (but not Canada) to the Pan American Union. In 1952 the Universal Copyright Convention was drawn up by UNESCO and since the US joined this convention, the former subterfuge of 'simultaneous' publication in the US and Canada (a Berne Convention member) is no longer necessary for a film to enjoy copyright in both the US and Berne Convention countries. In fact the minimum requirement for a film to be in copyright under the terms of the Universal Copyright convention is that it should carry a copyright notice as described above.

In countries which maintain a nationalized film industry, copyright is vested in the state. The Soviet Union is now a signatory of the 1952 Convention, but the position of other Socialist countries in relation to international copyright is undefined and it is not yet clear whether the rights in their films are subject to the normal time limits or whether they are held in perpetuity by the producing country.

The use of copyright material as the basis for a film is subject to the normal laws. Two early cases defined this principle in the US and in Europe: KALEM, as the makers of the first film version of BEN-HUR (1907), were successfully sued by the heirs of the author, General Lew Wallace; and the widow of Bram Stoker won an action to have all the official copies of MURNAU's NOSFERATU (1922) destroyed for infringement of the copyright on DRACULA.

Distribution rights are vested in the purchaser of those rights, which apply to a specified geographical area and period. At the expiry of such a contract the distributor is required to surrender or destroy all prints in his possession. During his ownership of rights he may deny exhibition of a film; and this has led to serious abuse when distribution rights are taken up by a production company in order to suppress competition with its own remake. Numerous examples of this practice include the withdrawal of PAGNOL's MARIUS trilogy (1931–6) by WARNER BROS to benefit Joshua LOGAN's FANNY (1960), of Thorold DICKINSON's GASLIGHT (1940) by METRO-GOLDWYN-MAYER in favour of George CUKOR's *Gaslight* (1944, *The Murder in Thornton Square* in GB), and of Marcel CARNÉ's LE JOUR SE LÈVE (1939) by RKO, who remade it as *The Long Night* (Anatole LITVAK, 1947).

**COQUILLE ET LE CLERGYMAN, La** (*The Seashell and the Clergyman*), France, 1928. 45min. *Dir* Germaine Dulac; *scr* Antonin Artaud; *ph* Paul Parguel; *cast* Alex Allin, Gerica Athanasiou, Bataille.

Antonin ARTAUD had intended to direct and play the lead in this typically surrealist revelation of subconscious urges through automatic associations in the mind of a frustrated priest. The film developed as a collaboration between Artaud and Germaine DULAC, but Artaud withdrew and repudiated it. When Dulac presented the film as 'un rêve d'Antonin Artaud' at the STUDIO DES URSULINES, the affronted Surrealists stormed out of the cinema, leaving the lay audience, who were totally baffled by the film, in a state of uproar. In Britain, it was refused a certificate by the censors on the grounds that 'This film is so cryptic as to be almost meaningless. If there is a meaning, it is doubtless objectionable.' (See CENSORSHIP, GB.)

*La Coquille et le Clergyman* is now recognized as an enduring example of AVANT-GARDE film: in addition to its imaginative qualities it has a technical ease attributable to Dulac's experience in commercial cinema. (See also SURREALISM.)

**CORMAN,** ROGER (1926–    ), US director and producer. After starting as a messenger boy for TWENTIETH CENTURY-FOX in 1948, he set up Roger Corman Productions in 1953. In the next five years he produced and directed a number of second features made cheaply on location or using rented studio space. Feature productions of the sixties included a series of adaptations from stories by Edgar Allan Poe, in which Corman showed a distinctive talent for the elegantly macabre: *The Masque of the Red Death* (1964) is an outstanding representative of the genre. It is notable that he still worked within schedule and with remarkable economy: *The Terror* (1963) was written and filmed in three days left over from the shooting schedule of *The Raven* (1963), using the same sets and costumes.

After the Poe cycle Corman devised and directed *The Wild Angels* (1966), an examination of youthful violence which was extreme enough to be banned in the UK, *The Trip* (1967), concerned with the use of the hallucinogenic drug LSD, and his first big-budget studio production *The St Valentine's Day Massacre* (1967). *Bloody Mama* (1969), starring Shelley WINTERS as the matriarch of a gang of violent criminals, capitalized on the success of BONNIE AND CLYDE (1967), but won critical acclaim. In Britain it was quite severely cut by the censors before release.

Throughout his career as producer and director Corman has been particularly generous in giving opportunities to newcomers such as Peter BOGDANOVICH and Francis Ford COPPOLA.

**CORNELIUS,** HENRY (1913–58), South African-born director who studied under Max REINHARDT and worked in Germany and France before moving to Britain in the mid-thirties. He entered films in the editing department of KORDA's LONDON FILMS and later joined EALING STUDIOS. His reputation as a director rests on half a dozen films, in particular two comedy successes, PASSPORT TO PIMLICO (1949) and *Genevieve* (1953). His later films showed little of the *élan* of his earlier work. His last film, *Law and Disorder* (1958), was completed by Charles CRICHTON.

**CORTEZ,** STANLEY (1908–    ), US cameraman, real name Stanley Krantz, worked with several portrait photographers in New York, then moved to Hollywood where he became an assistant cameraman for Cecil B. DEMILLE. He is one of Hollywood's most respected and professional cameramen: among his outstanding films are THE MAGNIFICENT AMBERSONS (1942) and THE NIGHT OF THE HUNTER (1955). He also worked with Samuel FULLER on *Shock Corridor* (1963) and *The Naked Kiss* (1964).

**COSTA-GAVRAS,** COSTI (1933– ), director of Russo-Greek parentage, resident in France since childhood. He first worked as an assistant to René CLÉMENT on *Le Jour et l'heure* (1963) and his own work shows its debt to Clément's predilection for films which are spectacular and yet socially aware. With Yves MONTAND, Simone SIGNORET, and the writer Jorge Semprun as co-producers, Costa-Gavras directed his first film *Compartiments tueurs* (*The Sleeping Car Murders*, 1965), a stylish thriller owing much to the American 'B' feature.

z (1968), a crime story with a polital background based on the assassination of the Greek liberal Lambrakis, showed similar efficiency and polish in its treatment. It became an international success, combining as it does entertainment with an irreproachable message. A similarly uncomplicated view was turned in L'AVEU (*The Confession*, 1970) on left-wing totalitarianism. *État de siège* (*State of Siege*, 1973) observed the tactics of South American urban guerrillas. The casting of Montand (the socialist hero-victim of both *Z* and *L'Aveu*) as a kidnapped CIA agent gave the film a political ambivalence not apparent in Costa-Gavras's previous work.

**COSTELLO,** LOU (1906–59), US comic actor, real name Louis Francis Cristillo, trained as a boxer, then worked as a newsboy and bar-tender before forming a comedy double act with Bud ABBOTT. The act had considerable success touring the US, and was transferred virtually unchanged to the screen. Costello's portrayal of a fat, sensitive simpleton perpetually tormented and exploited by his smooth, overbearing partner was skilfully worked out. Many of their films were SLAPSTICK parodies of perennially popular subjects such as TARZAN, WESTERNS, science fiction. After the team split up in 1955, Costello continued as a solo act, making one feature film, *The Thirty-Foot Bride of Candy Rock* (1959).

**COTTAFAVI,** VITTORIO (1914– ), Italian director, was assistant director to Vittorio DE SICA and Augusto Genina, and directed his first feature *I nostri sogni* in 1943. Apart from working extensively for television, he is best known for his contributions to the Italian hokum films of the early sixties, including *La vendetta di Ercole* (*Goliath and the Dragon*, 1960) and *Ercole alla conquista di Atlantide* (*Hercules Conquers Atlantis*, 1961), to which he brought a distinctively personal style with visual flair, flamboyant cutting, and notably ebullient handling of trivial material.

**COTTEN,** JOSEPH (1905– ), US actor worked in the theatre, including Orson WELLES's Federal Theaters productions and Mercury Theater of the Air, before beginning his screen career to remarkable effect in Welles's first two films, CITIZEN KANE (1941) and THE MAGNIFICENT AMBERSONS (1942). He scripted and played in *Journey into Fear* (1942), begun by Welles but finished by Norman Foster. A reliable if not a particularly versatile actor, Cotten went on to make numerous films. Among his notable parts were those in *Shadow of a Doubt* (Alfred HITCHCOCK, 1943), DUEL IN THE SUN (1946), THE THIRD MAN (1949), and *Under Capricorn* (Hitchcock, 1949). His more recent films have included *Hush ... Hush Sweet Charlotte* (1964) and *The Oscar* (1965).

***COUNTERPLAN*** see VSTRECHNYI

**COURANT,** CURT (or Kurt, Curtis) (*c.* 1895– ), German-born cameraman. His early work included LANG's *Hilde Warren und der Tod* (1917), which he co-photographed, HAMLET (1920), and QUO VADIS? (1925). In 1933, under the threat of Nazi interference, he left Germany to work in France and England. He was one of the finest cameramen of the thirties, this period of his work including *Perfect Understanding* (1933), THE MAN WHO KNEW TOO MUCH (HITCHCOCK, 1934), LA BÊTE HUMAINE (Jean RENOIR, 1938), LA FEMME DU BOULANGER (PAGNOL, 1938) and LE JOUR SE LÈVE (CARNÉ, 1939). In 1947 he collaborated on MONSIEUR VERDOUX with CHAPLIN. Semi-retirement was interrupted by *It Happened in Athens* (Andrew Marton, 1961).

**COURTENAY,** TOM (1937– ), British actor, began his acting career in the theatre in 1959. His first screen performance in *The Loneliness of the Long Distance Runner* (1962) established him as a serious actor, skilled at portraying dogged suffering. *Billy Liar* (John SCHLESINGER, 1963) was an excursion into comic fantasy: in *King and Country* (Joseph LOSEY, 1964) he played a frightened soldier summarily court-martialled and executed. He was the haggard revolutionary Pasha in DOCTOR ZHIVAGO (1966) and the prisoner-victim of the Soviet authorities in *One Day in the Life of Ivan Denisovich* (1971). His stage career has continued with roles ranging from Shakespeare via Ibsen and Chekhov to *Charley's Aunt*.

**COUSINS, Les,** France, 1959. 1¾hr. *Dir, prod, scr* Claude Chabrol; *ph* Henri Decaë; *cast* Gérard Blain (Charles), Jean-Claude Brialy (Paul), Juliette Mayniel (Florence), Claude Cerval (Clovis), Guy Decomble (bookseller).

CHABROL's second film explored the relationships of LE BEAU SERGE (1959) by inverting them. Here it is the country boy, Charles, who is innocent and idealistic, encountering his hedonistic, amoral city cousin; the variation on a basic theme is further emphasized by the reversal of the casting—Brialy becoming the corrupt, Blain the simple, character. Chabrol's picture of student life in Paris is well sustained, with much keenly-observed detail. *Les Cousins* was awarded first prize at the BERLIN Film Festival, 1959.

**COUSTEAU,** JACQUES-YVES (1910– ), French director. A naval officer keenly interested in underwater exploration, Cousteau began using a camera under water in 1939 as an aid to his research, modifying the equipment himself as necessary. His first short film *Par dix-huit mètres de fond* was released in 1943, and aroused a great deal of interest. Other shorts recording underwater expeditions followed, including *Epaves* (1945), *Au large des côtes tunisiennes* (1949), *Les Phoques du Rio de Oro* (1949), *Carnets de plongée* (1950), and *Un Musée sous la mer* (1953). In 1956 he made a full-length documentary in colour, *Le Monde du silence* (*The World of Silence*) with Louis MALLE as assistant director. The film, which won a Golden Palm at CANNES, went far beyond the bounds of a scientific documentary, capturing the fantastic poetry of the underwater world. Following the great success of this film, Cousteau made *Le Monde sans soleil* in 1964, and has since made several series for television.

**COUTARD,** RAOUL (1924– ), French cameraman, was a photographer with the army, then became a photo-reporter for several magazines including *Paris-Match* and *Life*. He started working in cinema in 1957 and quickly became one of the favourite cameramen of the directors of the NOUVELLE VAGUE. His most remarkable characteristics have been resourcefulness and adaptability, from joining lengths of fast still film stock not then available as cine film for A BOUT DE SOUFFLE (1960), his first feature film, to the use of improvised vehicles for hand-held tracking shots—notably the bath-chair at Orly airport in *Une Femme mariée* (1964). Coutard's style is often loosely described as that he most often used for GODARD, with very flat lighting: in fact his style varies considerably according to the needs of different directors. Besides photographing most of Godard's films, he has worked with TRUFFAUT on TIREZ SUR LE

PIANISTE (1960), JULES ET JIM (1961), and *La Peau douce* (1963), with Jacques DEMY on LOLA (1961), with Jean ROUCH on CHRONIQUE D'UN ÉTÉ (1961), and with COSTA-GAVRAS on Z (1968) and L'AVEU (1970). He has directed several short films and a feature-length documentary on Vietnam, *Hoa Binh* (1970).

**COVERED WAGON, The,** US, 1923. 2¼hr. *Dir, prod* James Cruze for Paramount; *scr* Jack Cunningham, from the novel by Emerson Hough; *ph* Karl Brown; *cast* J. Warren Kerrigan, Lois Wilson, Alan Hale, Ernest Torrence, Tully Marshall.

The very size of the undertaking is perhaps the main contribution to the genre of this epic reconstruction, shot largely on location, of one of the great nineteenth-century treks across the American continent. The enormous critical and commercial success brought a doubling of WESTERN production the following year (the year of John FORD's artistically superior THE IRON HORSE), and the ideas and techniques introduced have been used in hundreds of subsequent films; indeed, CRUZE may be seen as the founder of an 'odyssey' tradition in the American Western.

**COWARD,** NOËL (1899–1973), British writer, actor, composer, and director, who began as a child actor in the theatre, making his first film appearance in a brief scene in HEARTS OF THE WORLD (1918). Most of his work has been in the theatre and several of his plays have been adapted for the screen. These include *Private Lives* (1931), with Norma SHEARER and Robert MONTGOMERY, Ernst LUBITSCH's slickly sophisticated version of *Design for Living* (1933), and the patriotic epic *Cavalcade* (1933), directed with éclat by Frank LLOYD. His musical play *Bitter Sweet* was filmed by Herbert WILCOX in 1933 and by W. S. VAN DYKE in 1940.

Coward's stylish, irreverent wit is typified by his part in the HECHT–MACARTHUR film THE SCOUNDREL (1935), but the serious side of his character was revealed by IN WHICH WE SERVE (1942), a patriotic tribute to the Royal Navy which he produced and co-directed with David LEAN, for which he wrote the script and music, and in which he starred. It was followed by three further films as producer and scriptwriter, with David Lean as sole director. *This Happy Breed* (1944) and BRIEF ENCOUNTER (1945) reflected the more serious aspect of his work; *Blithe Spirit* (1945) was a delightful comedy which launched Margaret RUTHERFORD on a successful film career. After the war his work in the cinema was principally as an actor playing sophisticates and eccentrics in films like *Our Man in Havana* (1959), *Bunny Lake Is Missing* (1965), and *Boom* (1968).

**CRAB DOLLY** see DOLLY

**CRAIG,** EDWARD GORDON (1872–1966), British stage designer, real name Henry Edward Gordon Godwin Wardell, was the son of Ellen Terry and the architect Edward Godwin. His work in stage direction and design was and remains influential in all fields of drama and has had particular influence on art direction in the cinema. The set designs in Douglas FAIRBANKS's ROBIN HOOD (1922) were directly derived from Craig's ideas. These were expressed in several books, notably *Towards a new theatre* (1912) and *Design in the theatre* (1927), and in his quarterly review *The Mask* (1908–31).

His son Edward Carrick (b. 1905) has had a long and honourable career as an art director in British studios.

**CRANE,** a wheeled camera platform with a boom arm, used for moving-camera shots vertically as well as horizontally. The camera and its operators ride on a platform at the end of the counterweighted boom; during the shot they can rise to heights of 20 feet or more, descend to floor level, or perform the usual movements of a DOLLY while cantilevered just over the heads of actors. The crane may be driven manually, hydraulically, or electrically, depending on the crane and the requirements of the shot.

Traditionally crane shots have been most effectively used in large-scale studio spectacles such as musicals, where often the camera moved gracefully through eight or ten precise positions in space during a single long take. Lately the availability of the ZOOM lens has both added to the versatility of the crane and reduced the frequency of its use. (See CAMERA MOVEMENTS, GRIP.)

**CRANES ARE FLYING, The**, see LETYAT ZHUR-AVLI

**CRAWFORD,** BRODERICK (1910– ), US actor, son of vaudeville and stage stars Helen Broderick and Lester Crawford. Discovered by Samuel GOLDWYN, he made his screen début in *Woman Chases Man* (1937) and followed this with numerous tough roles, mainly in crime films and Westerns. More outstanding were his comic performance in BORN YESTERDAY (1951) and his thoughtful portrayal of Willie Stark in ALL THE KING'S MEN (1949), for which he won an OSCAR. He played a leading role in IL BIDONE (1955) and starred in the successful television series 'Highway Patrol' (1955–9).

**CRAWFORD,** JOAN (1908– ), US actress, real name Lucille Le Sueur, was a chorus girl on Broadway before gaining a contract with METRO-GOLDWYN-MAYER, at first appearing chiefly in musicals under her real name. Determined attention to her career soon made her one of that studio's outstanding team of stars during the thirties, usually playing career women who surrender emotional fulfilment for material gain. The first of her successful films in this vein was *Paid* (1930), which was followed by many others, gaining her a large public following. She was outstanding, in spite of formidable competition, in the star-studded GRAND HOTEL (1932). Her insistence on playing the prostitute Sadie Thompson in *Rain* (Lewis MILESTONE, 1933) temporarily alienated many fans; her performance can now be seen as a remarkably mature piece of acting, but it was necessary for her to retreat into more sympathetic roles for a time and most of her films of this period are routine. After seventeen years with MGM she went to WARNER BROS where she made a startling comeback in *Mildred Pierce* (Michael CURTIZ, 1945), for which she won her only OSCAR. Her energetic performance as a totally ruthless woman set the style for many subsequent roles.

Joan Crawford's skill in using her advancing years to advantage has been seen in *The Damned Don't Cry* (1947), *The Story of Esther Costello* (1956), and many other starring parts; latterly her scriptwriters have often used the device of madness to add strength to her characterizations. One of Hollywood's most enduring box-office stars, she has often been compared with Bette DAVIS, particularly for her skill in transforming basically novelettish material into performances of considerable power. The two appeared together to considerable effect in the ghoulish *Whatever Happened to Baby Jane?* (Robert ALDRICH, 1962).

**CREDITS,** properly *credit titles*, the titles at the beginning or end of a film listing the actors and technicians who have worked on it, often fulfilling by their design, layout, and backgrounds the subsidiary function of establishing style or atmosphere. Credits, to the people whose names appear in them, are as vital as money; they are the visible proof of work performed and can ensure continuity of employment. Artists consider them so essential that their contracts specify the form, size, duration, and priority of their names on the screen.

Early films contained no credits at all, but the popularity of certain actors led producers to draw attention to their presence. Credits other than artists' were for many years limited to director and producer, until the growing power of trade unions forced other technical functions on to the screen. Hollywood films in particular can be dated within a few years by the precise form and placing of their credits. They should not however be regarded as wholly factual: many a credit conceals an unrecorded injustice such as a department head fronting for talented underlings or a writer fired and stripped of credit after a disagreement. Conversely an innocuous technical credit such as 'second-unit direction by Andrew Marton' can conceal, from the layman, a distinguished and major contribution to the film.

The 'pre-credit sequence' became fashionable from the early fifties, the film opening without warning on a section of narrative or a generalized sequence indicating the film's setting or subject. The credits, inserted at the end of this sequence, may mark a point of suspense. The convention can be effective in capturing the audience's attention, but can equally be merely irritating when used in an arbitrary or inept manner.

The design of credits has sometimes been brought to a high degree of accomplishment by specialists who are themselves usually uncredited, one outstanding exception being Saul BASS.

**CRETINETTI** see DEED, André

**CRICHTON, CHARLES** (1910– ), British director, started with film editing before directing a short film *Young Veterans* (1941); his first feature was *For Those in Peril* (1944). He became one of the EALING STUDIOS team with *Hue and Cry* (1947): this, with other films that he directed, notably THE LAVENDER HILL MOB (1951), was typical of the Ealing comedies which won wide praise. His later films include *The Battle of the Sexes* (1959) and *He Who Rides a Tiger* (1965).

**CRIME AND PUNISHMENT**, the novel by Dostoevsky, was published in 1865. This massive psychological study of a poor student, Raskolnikov, who murders and robs an old moneylender and her sister, has been filmed a number of times. The density of Dostoevsky's exposition is probably impossible to parallel in film terms: screen adaptations have generally dealt with the earlier, more eventful, sections of the story and avoided both the Nietzschean theorizing with which the murderer attempts to justify his act and his purifying experience of imprisonment in Siberia.

Apart from Alexander Drankov's Russian film of c.1906, the only notable silent version is Robert WIENE's *Raskolnikoff* (1923), which used exiled actors of the Moscow Art Theatre. The hero's emotional disturbance was conveyed by ruthless editing and Andrei Andreiev's sets made a significant contribution to Wiene's Expressionist conception. This remains one of the most successful attempts.

The first American version, Josef von STERN-BERG's *Crime and Punishment* (1935), illustrates the immense difficulties of condensing the original in spite of moving performances by Edward ARNOLD and Peter LORRE. In the same year, in France, Pierre Chenal directed *Crime et châtiment*, concentrating on the battle of nerves between Raskolnikov and the examining magistrate and drawing magnificent performances from Pierre BLANCHAR as the hero and Harry Baur as the magistrate. The music for this version was by Arthur HONEGGER.

A Swedish version, *Brott och Straff* (1945), was directed by Hampe Faustman and a Mexican one, *Crimen y Castigo* (1951), by Fernando de Fuentes. *Crime et châtiment* (1956), directed by Georges Lampin, transposed the story to contemporary France: it is remarkable only for Claude RENOIR's camerawork. A contemporary American transposition, *Crime and Punishment USA* (1958), was an underrated experiment made on a low budget.

The Soviet Union did not attempt the subject until 1969. *Prestuplenye i nakazanye* had an appropriate length of 200 minutes, and it was typical of many Russian literary adaptations in being academically loyal to the text. Among the cast, Innokenti Smoktunovsky stood out as society's spokesman, relentlessly hunting down the outsider.

**CRIME DE MONSIEUR LANGE, Le** (*The Crime of Monsieur Lange*), France, 1936. 1½hr. *Dir* Jean Renoir; *prod* Obéron; *scr* Renoir, Jacques Prévert, Jean Castanier; *ph* Jean Bachelet; *des* Castanier, Robert Gys; *ed* Marguerite Renoir; *mus* Jean Wiener, Joseph Kosma; *cast* Jules Berry (Batala), René Lefèvre (Lange), Florelle (Valentine), Nadia Sibirskaïa (Estelle), Sylvie Bataille (Edith), Henry Guisol (young Meurnier), Marcel Levesque (concierge), Odette Talazac (his wife).

A group of workers take over a publishing house when its crooked owner, Batala, absconds. After they have made a success of the enterprise he returns to re-assume control and one of the workers, Lange, kills him to save the collective. The story is told in flash back as Lange and his girl friend Valentine put their case to a group of workers who have recognized them as they try to escape across the frontier.

The tone is markedly different from that of TONI, made a year earlier. In *Le Crime de Monsieur Lange*, RENOIR, working with members of the left-wing GROUPE OCTOBRE, found himself politically committed almost without any conscious decision on his part. In this sense the film looks forward to *La Vie est à nous* which Renoir, although not a Party member, made for the Communist Party in 1936. His involvement with the Popular Front also brought about the collaboration with Jacques PRÉVERT which gives *Le Crime de Monsieur Lange* a foretaste of Prévert's later work with Marcel CARNÉ, notably in the figures of the sardonic Batala and Lange, the good man driven to murder. But the mood is one of optimism and there is hope at the end that working-class solidarity will prevail and the lovers will escape to freedom.

**CRIME WITHOUT PASSION,** US, 1934. 1¼hr. *Dir, scr* Ben Hecht, Charles MacArthur; *prod* Hecht, MacArthur for Paramount; *ph* Lee Garmes; *spec eff* Slavko Vorkapich; *des* Albert R. Johnson; *cast* Claude Rains (Lee Gentry), Margo (Carmen Brown), Whitney Bourne (Katy Costello), Stanley Ridges (Eddie White), Paula Trueman (Buster Malloy), Leslie Adams (O'Brien).

When Ben HECHT and Charles MACARTHUR left Hollywood to set up their own company in New York, *Crime Without Passion* gave them an excellent start with its story of a cunning lawyer who uses his professional skills to build up a false alibi when he accidentally shoots his mistress, but ends up trapping himself in an even worse situation. Claude RAINS was outstanding as the lawyer whose personality splits as his legal brain counsels him in the crises, and Margo was acclaimed as an important discovery in her first screen part as the lawyer's ex-mistress.

**CRIMINAL, The** (*The Concrete Jungle* in US), GB, 1960. 1½hr. *Dir* Joseph Losey; *prod* Merton Park Studios; *scr* Alun Owen; *ph* Robert Krasker; *des* Richard MacDonald; *mus* Johnny Dankworth; *cast* Stanley Baker (Johnny Bannion), Sam Wanamaker (Mike Carter), Margit Saad (Suzanne), Patrick Magee (Chief Warder Barrows), Gregoire Aslan (Frank Saffron), Jill Bennett (Maggie).

LOSEY's first major critical success after leaving America was derived from a banal and melodramatic story of prison life and the London underworld. After extensive rewriting by the playwright Alun Owen, the script gained in realism and idiomatic authenticity; Losey added his own view of power structures, represented by the prison environment, and of the isolation of the individual in a society of interlocking monopolies, in this case the world of organized crime. Losey's acknowledged debt to Stanley KUBRICK is evident in this film with its echoes of *The Killing* (1956).

**CRIMINAL LIFE OF ARCHIBALDO DE LA CRUZ, The**, see ENSAYO DE UN CRIMEN

*Le Crime de Monsieur Lange* (Jean Renoir, 1936)

**CRIN BLANC, CHEVAL SAUVAGE** (*The Wild Stallion*), France, 1953. 40min. *Dir, prod, scr* Albert Lamorisse for Films Montsouris; *ph* Edmond Sechan; *mus* Maurice Le Roux; *cast* Alain Emery (the boy), Pascal Lamorisse (his little brother), *gardiens* of the Camargue.

The story of a boy's efforts to gain the affection and preserve the liberty of a wild white stallion, told with the combination of poetic fantasy and documentary realism that became LAMORISSE's hall-mark, attracted much attention. *Crin blanc* was awarded the Jean VIGO prize for 1953, and has remained deservedly popular.

**CRISP,** DONALD (1880–1974), British-born actor and director, went to the US in 1906 and pursued most of his career in Hollywood, first in opera, then as a stage director, before becoming a staff player with BIOGRAPH. He was one of D. W. GRIFFITH's assistants, notably on THE BIRTH OF A NATION (1915) in which he also played the role of General Grant and he was a memorable villain in BROKEN BLOSSOMS (1919). During the twenties, he was a director, his best-remembered film being the Douglas FAIRBANKS swashbuckler *Don Q, Son of Zorro* (1925) in which he also took an acting role. Later he devoted himself to acting, and for over three decades was a familiar screen figure in featured and character roles, playing gentlemen of either benign or stern temperament. He was the patriarch in *How Green Was My Valley* (1941) and he was in several of Elizabeth TAYLOR's early films: *Lassie Come Home* (1943), *National Velvet* (1944), and *Courage of Lassie* (1946).

**CRITICISM.** Discussion of films was slow to gain respectability in mass circulation periodicals, and trade papers generally carried only the descriptions of films provided by the producers or distributors: THE BIOSCOPE was exceptional in offering its readers objective reviews of new films. Not until the twenties did serious newspapers in Britain and the US recognize the necessity of publishing regular film reviews: James AGEE in the US, Graham GREENE, E. Arnot ROBERTSON, and C. A. LEJEUNE in Britain, were in the forefront of journalists who gave films the consideration accorded to books, music, and the theatre. Good film reviewers—their number of recent years including Pauline KAEL, Dilys POWELL, Parker TYLER—have done much to educate and inform the film-going public; they can also wield considerable power: the praise or condemnation of a journalist like Bosley Crowther of the *New York Times* can materially affect a film's success.

The main impetus towards serious criticism (as opposed to useful but ephemeral reviewing or reporting) came in the early decades of the century, from artists who recognized in the new medium potentially new forms of expression. In Italy, Marinetti in a manifesto of 1916 hailed cinema as an ideal vehicle for the mechanistic doctrines of FUTURISM. In Germany the Expressionist painters recognized film's potential for their own very different aims. In France, where Louis DELLUC led the debate in his journal *Cinéa*, the AVANT-GARDE argued out the theories they were putting into practice on film. During the twenties the Hungarian Béla BÁLAZS straddled France and Germany and was the leading voice of the European clamour for film to be recognized as an art form.

The most radical consideration of film theory, however, took place in Russia in the years following the Revolution. There the conventions of the nineteenth-century novel and theatre which cinema had rapidly absorbed and adapted were challenged by the new generation of film-makers, KULESHOV, PUDOVKIN, EISENSTEIN, and VERTOV pre-eminent among them. MAYAKOVSKY and the critic Viktor Shklovsky were leading figures in the debate which raged around the doctrines of the Futurists and Formalists, and Eisenstein and Vertov both formed part of the Left Front in Art group which published those doctrines in the journals *Lef* and *Novyi Lef*. In essence, they asserted that the old forms of narrative were obsolete and proposed that cinema should serve revolutionary ends by exploiting time and space in new ways: for Eisenstein it was to be the potential shock of MONTAGE ('Kino-fist'); for Pudovkin the building of new concepts using sequences as 'bricks'; for Vertov a new view of the world and society through the infinitely perfectible vision of the 'Kino-eye' (see KINO-GLAZ).

The artistic debate was leading to irreconcilable positions by the end of the twenties, before it was definitively brought to a close by the official adoption of SOCIALIST REALISM as the yardstick for cultural correctness. Formalism was condemned and only after Stalin's death in 1953 and the Twentieth Party Congress in 1956, when Khrushchev first publicly denounced Stalinist oppression, was there any opportunity for artists of Socialist Eastern Europe to escape from the prescribed forms of socialist realism.

In Western Europe, in the meantime, the writings of Bertolt BRECHT took up and developed some of the arguments raised by the Russians a decade before. The coming of sound at the end of the twenties caused a flurry of comment—mostly protest—from film-makers in east and west alike (CLAIR and PAGNOL in France, the Eisenstein–Pudovkin–Alexandrov manifesto of 1929 in Russia). During the thirties, alongside the practice of restoring fluidity of movement (particularly developed in the work of RENOIR—see PLAN-SÉQUENCE), an emerging philosophy of cinema as primarily the recorder of physical reality was voiced by Rudolph ARNHEIM. The stylistic innovations of Orson WELLES in the early forties and the upsurge of NEO-REALISM in Italy inspired a new era of critical philosophy of which André BAZIN was the arch-priest.

The touchstone of Bazin's belief was film's power to reveal situations and relationships by reproducing them within a representation of 'real' space. Siegfried KRACAUER attempted an aesthetic justification of these notions in his *Theory of film*. Bazin's emphasis was primarily sociological and metaphysical, and his laurels were denied to any film which did not conform to his prescribed canons. At the same time his work, in its rejection of the 'film as art' approach, had the great merit of offering a method of seriously considering Hollywood films which had hitherto been outside the critical pale. This virtue was welcomed by his followers, particularly the critics writing in CAHIERS DU CINÉMA, who developed the AUTEUR THEORY further to expand and formalize the criticism of popular films. During the fifties and early sixties the *auteur* theory embraced an ever-wider range of directors who were admitted to the pantheon.

The arguments of the Russians during the twenties, pushed aside (in spite of Brecht) by the main streams of realist criticism in both east and west, were revived during the late sixties and swept back into favour in the wake of the 'nouvelle critique' and of the Marxist revival, debated particularly by the 'Tel Quel' group in France and taken up decisively by *Cinéthique* and *Cahiers du cinéma* after 1968. Those questions raised by the Russian Formalists are being pursued by means of enquiry into the fundamental elements of film form: Noel Burch has offered the most succinct account of the approach in *Theory of film practice* (London, 1972). A new basis was concurrently given to the discussion by the emergence of semiology or semiotics—the attempt to apply to cinema objective methods within the science of signs postulated in the early twenties by Saussure and elaborated in the fifties and sixties by Roland Barthes. The most important protagonist of this line has been Christian Metz, who has sought to adapt and extrapolate from the linguistic models to specifically cinematic phenomena. Peter Wollen was instrumental in bringing the semiotic method before the English-speaking public in his book *Signs and meanings in cinema* (3rd rev. ed. London, 1972).

Semiotics offers a search for scientifically discernible codes of cinema and their interactions: it has been extended into a Marxist reinterpretation of Freudian psychoanalysis in the wake of work by Jacques Lacan and Julia Kristéva. The notion of realism, kept under question by Brecht, is under searching enquiry. Other models and methods are being impressed from the Marxist sociology of Lukács and the work of Lucien Goldmann. Thus critical enquiry in the seventies is taking shape in several specialized modes, the major ones placing strong emphasis on formalist doctrine: *Screen*, a journal published by the Society for Education in Film and Television under the auspices of the BRITISH FILM INSTITUTE, has given extensive coverage of the dominant lines of current debate.

**CROCKETT, DAVY** (1786–1836), US Congressman 1827–31 and 1833–5 and hero of folk-legend created for political purposes and probably with the help of Crockett himself. He left his native Tennessee in pique at not being re-elected in 1836, and died in the defence of the ALAMO. In his role of bear-hunter and glamorous frontiersman he has been portrayed in several WESTERNS, notably DISNEY's *Davy Crockett, King of the Wild Frontier* (1955) and John WAYNE's *The Alamo* (1960), in which Wayne played Crockett.

**CROMWELL, JOHN** (1888–    ), US director who began as an actor and producer in the theatre and whose film career dates from the early days of sound. His sympathy and tact with actors drew many outstanding performances from his players including those of Bette DAVIS in *Of Human Bondage* (1934), Ronald COLMAN and Douglas FAIRBANKS Jr in *The Prisoner of Zenda* (1937), Raymond Massey in *Abe Lincoln in Illinois* (1939, *Spirit of the People* in GB) and Kim Stanley in *The Goddess* (1958). He was still acting on the American stage into his eighties.

**CROSBY, BING** (1901–   ), US singer and actor, real name Henry Lillis Crosby, acquired his professional name at school from his avid reading of a comic strip, 'The Bingville Bugle'. He worked with jazz bands during the thirties, developing the style which in his first radio series in 1931 brought him nation-wide success. PARAMOUNT signed him on, and he became a box-office draw with a wide popular audience.

Crosby's mild humour and sentimentality appealed to public taste at a time when films were essentially family entertainment: *Going My Way* (1944), in which he played a singing priest, was typical. The series of *Road* films (1940–51) gained astringency from the presence of Bob HOPE without damaging the Crosby style. In all he has appeared in sixty-eight feature films and about twenty shorts; his later career includes non-singing parts, such as his starring roles in *The Country Girl* (1954) and the remake of STAGECOACH (1966).

**CROSBY, FLOYD** (*c.*1900–    ), US cinematographer who won an OSCAR for his photography

*Csillagosok, katonák* (Miklós Jancsó, 1967)

of F. W. MURNAU's TABU (1931). He differs markedly from other top Hollywood cameramen in his evident preference for working on a large number of low-budget or unpretentious films rather than fewer but large-scale or ambitious productions. A particularly fine exponent of black-and-white photography, he turned to colour later than most cameramen, but his colour work has been equally remarkable.

**CROWN FILM UNIT.** In existence under this name from 1940 to 1951, the unit was the successor to the Empire Marketing Board and GPO Film Units. Work by all three units is often referred to as being by the Crown Film Unit.

The EMB was set up in 1928 to give attention to food supplies within the British Empire. The Film Unit was fostered from the first, thanks largely to the foresight of Sir Stephen Tallents. John GRIERSON was, with Walter Creighton, one of the original joint officers of the Unit, and Grierson's personality contributed vitally to the Unit's policy and progress. In 1933 the EMB was abolished as a whole, but happily the GPO took over the Unit and its by now considerable library. The GPO Film Unit was taken over by the Ministry of Information in September 1939, and was re-named the Crown Film Unit in April 1940. In April 1946 the Ministry of Information became the Central Office of Information with the CFU continuing as production unit for its Films Division. When the Conservative Government returned to power in 1951, the Unit was disbanded. Since then there has been no government film unit, and the gap in production left by the CFU's disappearance has only to a limited extent been filled by productions sponsored by the COI and those of the film units of nationalized industries and large private companies.

Grierson directed one film, *Drifters*, in 1929, then became producer of the Unit until he resigned in 1937. Early recruits included Arthur ELTON, Basil WRIGHT, and Stuart LEGG. The 'Grierson school' found their main sources of influence in the unlikely combination of EISENSTEIN and FLAHERTY (the latter made one film, INDUSTRIAL BRITAIN, for the Unit in 1931, released 1933): they also looked to such continental influences as Walter RUTTMANN and Joris IVENS. They welcomed the early Soviet socialist realist films like VSTRECHNYI (1932) and CHAPAYEV (1934), and provided an outlet in the UK for the political idealism which was the British version of SOCIALIST REALISM.

At a time when economic depression made the life of an artist peculiarly difficult, many artists were glad to work for the Unit. This, together with the Unit's enlightened policy of seeking fresh talents in all fields, brought into its service a considerable number of young artists. Alberto

CAVALCANTI joined the Unit in 1934, and initiated experiments in sound which were the most exhilarating in Britain in the thirties. John Taylor, Paul ROTHA, and Edgar ANSTEY were among the Unit's directors; Benjamin BRITTEN, William ALWYN, W. H. Auden, and William Coldstream were among artists in other media who worked for the Unit. Among the films produced during the Unit's hey-day of the thirties were SONG OF CEYLON (1934), NIGHT MAIL (1936), and *Coal Face* (Cavalcanti, 1936).

Grierson's resignation in 1937 modified the idealistic policies of the Unit, and the outbreak of war brought information films into a new prominence in Britain as in all belligerent countries. Harry WATT, Jack Lee, Jack Holmes, and Pat Jackson were among the Unit's directors during and after the war. It was also at this time that the brightest talent of British documentary film-making emerged: that of Humphrey JENNINGS, who directed for the Unit one of Britain's most distinguished wartime documentaries FIRES WERE STARTED (1943).

Grierson's early policy of encouraging talent left its mark until the Unit's demise: after the war, for instance, Ken Cameron developed advanced sound equipment and its use at the Unit's Beaconsfield studio. Britten's *Young Person's Guide to the Orchestra* was originally written for *Instruments of the Orchestra* (1946). (See also DOCUMENTARY.)

**CRUZE,** JAMES (1884–1942), US director born in Utah of Danish parents, worked as a film actor from 1908. From 1918 he directed more than a hundred films, of which the most notable is THE COVERED WAGON (1923). *Sutter's Gold*, which was one of EISENSTEIN's projects rejected by PARAMOUNT, was directed by Cruze in 1936.

*CSILLAGOSOK, KATONÁK (The Red and the White)*, Hungary/USSR, 1967. Agascope; 1¼hr. *Dir* Miklós Jancsó; *prod* Mafilm Studio 4/ Mosfilm; *scr* Georgi Mdivani, Gyula Hernádi, Jancsó; *ph* Tamás Somló; *ed* Zoltán Farkas; *cast* Tatyana Konyukova (Yelizaveta), Krystyna Mikolajewska (Olga), Mikhail Kasakov (Nestor), Viktor Ardyushko (Ivan), Bolot Beyshenaliyev (Chingiz), József Madaras (Commander), Tibor Molnár (András), András Kozák (László), Jácint Juhász (István).

The first Russian-Hungarian co-production, arranged for the fiftieth anniversary of the Russian Revolution, the film is set in Central Russia during 1918 when Hungarians were fighting in the International Brigade of the Red Army. *Csillagosok, katonák* (which literally translates as *Stars, Soldiers*) showed JANCSÓ broadening his examination of human tenacity into large-scale set-pieces which made full use of the horizontal aspect of the scope screen and the possibilities of human groupings in open spaces. A less claustrophobic work than his preceding SZEGÉNY-LEGÉNYEK (*The Round-Up*, 1965), its wartime setting allowed Jancsó's interest in contrasts full rein: the mounted rider against the infantryman; domination and submission; man as a unit or pack-member; the plain and the town. With the minimum of dialogue he welded these elements into a filmic hymn of celebration, his laterally-tracking camera providing the ground rhythm.

**CUBA.** In 1897 a five-hour film show was put on by a Frenchman, Gabriel Vayre, who also made the first film there, *Documental sobre extinctión de incendios* (1897, 1 minute). By 1899, José Catassus, a Mexican, was carrying a portable camera round the country. Cinema quickly became a favourite diversion, which it has remained. In 1906 Enrique Díaz Quesada made *Parque de Palatino*. Until 1920 he was almost Cuba's only film director, usually concentrating on social or revolutionary themes, but Juan Angelo directed the best known Cuban film of this period about the national hero *Marcel García* (1913), which displayed his belief in the political function of film. In the twenties the only director of any note was Ramón Péon, whose successful *Realidad* (1920) enabled him to build Golden Sun Pictures studios. *La Virgen de la caridad* (1929) was probably his most visually imaginative work.

Although a few short sound films were made in the early thirties, Cuba's first sound feature was not produced until 1937: *La Serpiente roja* directed by Ernesto Caparros. Its success stimulated the founding of Película Cubano, which brought back Péon after several years working in Hollywood and Mexico. His *El Romance de palmar* (1938) remains one of the best films made in Cuba. Increasing domination by Mexico and later the US depressed production; such Cuban films as were made consisted mainly of trivial comedies and musicals, and the war brought production almost to a standstill.

After 1945 the industry revived, but it still, as in the gangster film *Siete muertes a plazo fijo* (1948), imitated American models. In 1954 there was an attempt to portray a Cuban subject in *La Rosa blanca*, made for Jose Marti's centenary, but, directed by and starring Mexicans, financed by an obligatory levy organized by Batista, and suffering from official interference, it is hardly distinguishable from its forebears.

However, encouraged by the Club Foto de Cuba, formed in 1943, and the Sociedad Cultural Nuestro Tiempo, amateur film-making flourished. In that year Placido Gonzales Gomez made a colour film, *Un dia cazando palomas*.

Tomás Gutiérrez ALEA made two shorts (*La Caperucita roja* and *Un Fakir*, 1946), then joined with Nestor ALMENDROS to make *Una Confusion cotidiana* (1948) from a Kafka story. *El Mengano* (1956), a documentary by Alea with the Nuestro Tiempo group on the coalminers and peasants of the Cienaga de Zapata, was confiscated by the Batista government.

The revolution of 1959 was followed by immediate and sweeping reforms in the film industry. ICAIC (Instituto Cubano del Arte y Industria Cinematografica) was set up and took over all foreign production and distribution agencies, confiscating equipment and prints. A new, well-equipped studio was built and production teams were trained with the aid of crash courses by Czechoslovak personnel. By 1969 ICAIC had produced 45 features, 85 documentaries, 49 cartoons, and 450 newsreels. The distribution arm, Departamento de Divulgacion Cinematografica, controls numerous outlets— 100 cinemas in Havana, including a 1500-seat archive cinema, 100 cinemas elsewhere, and 100 *ciné-moviles*. As well as domestic and imported entertainment features, programmes normally include political documentaries and a newsreel.

Newsreel production has flourished in Cuba since the early days of sound, and it became an important agitational tool of the revolutionary government. Santiago ALVAREZ directed the weekly *Noticiero ICAIC*, issues of which have been distributed internationally, including *Hanoi, martes 13* (1967), *Now!* (1965), and *LBJ* (1969).

Several film-makers, finding the monolithic structure of ICAIC frustrating, have left Cuba: they include Eduardo Manet (*El Negro*, 1960), Fausto Canal (*Hemingway*, 1962), and Almendros, who has achieved notable success as a cameraman in France. Alea has become Cuba's leading feature director: his *Muerte de un Burocrata* (*Death of a Bureaucrat*, 1966) and MEMORIAS DEL SUBDESAROLLO (*Memories of Underdevelopment*, 1968) suggest that Castro's government is not attempting to stifle lively and critical film-making. *Lucia* (Humberto Solas, 1969), an ambitious film on the position of women in Cuba past and present, shows perception, humour, and freedom of expression, and Pastor Vega's *De la Guerra Americana* (1970) drew international attention.

Foreign film-makers who have worked in Cuba since 1959 include Cesare ZAVATTINI (script for Espinosa's *Un Joven rebelde*, 1961), Chris MARKER (CUBA, SI!, 1961), Mikhail KALATOZOV (*Soy Cuba*, 1966), Felix Greene (*Cuba Va!*, 1971), Joris IVENS, Agnès VARDA.

***CUBA SI!***, France, 1961. 1hr. *Dir, scr, ph* Chris Marker; *prod* Films de la Pléïade; *Cuban collab-*

orators Saul Yelin, Eduardo G. Manet, Selma Diaz.

Shot in Cuba in January 1961 during the second anniversary of the Revolution, *Cuba si!* is a homage to the new Cuban nation and reflects the faith and hopes which Castro raised among the French Left at that time. It contains two very direct interviews with Fidel Castro and an account of the early days of the Revolution in the Sierra Maestra. True to MARKER's film style, *Cuba si!* combines earnestness and honesty with poetry and irony. During the cutting, the US landing at the Bay of Pigs (17 April) took place. With the help of newsreel shots and documents sent from Cuba, Marker ended his film with the failure of this aggression, leaving no doubt where his sympathies lay; the film was banned in France until 1963.

**CUKOR**, GEORGE (1899– ), US director, came to Hollywood from Broadway, where he had worked as a stage manager and director. He started as a dialogue director on several films, including ALL QUIET ON THE WESTERN FRONT (1930), before directing his first film, *Tarnished Lady* (1931), with Tallulah BANKHEAD, which showed great distinction; but his first big chance came when LUBITSCH, obliged to re-cut *Broken Lullaby* (1932, *The Man I Killed* in GB), handed over to him the direction of *One Hour With You* (1932), which starred Jeanette MAC-DONALD and Charles BOYER. This auspicious start established Cukor from the outset as one of Hollywood's most proficient film-makers. His adaptations for the screen of material from other sources, for example DINNER AT EIGHT (1933), DAVID COPPERFIELD (1934), and ROMEO AND JULIET (1936), are remarkably faithful to the originals while exploiting their cinematic possibilities, and he has drawn excellent performances from actors of the first rank including GARBO, in CAMILLE (1936), Katharine HEPBURN, in several films including THE PHILADELPHIA STORY (1940), Spencer TRACY, and Ronald COLMAN.

Cukor was originally chosen to direct GONE WITH THE WIND (1939) but was replaced by Victor FLEMING, and his first opportunity to handle a very large-scale production came much later with A STAR IS BORN (1954); his resounding success with this lavish but intelligent musical was consolidated by *Les Girls* (1957), starring Gene KELLY, and MY FAIR LADY (1964). His many other films include the remake of GASLIGHT (1944, *The Murder in Thornton Square* in GB), BORN YESTERDAY (1951), *Bhowani Junction* (1956), with Ava GARDNER in one of her best roles as an Anglo-Indian girl, and *Justine* (1969).

**CUL-DE-SAC**, GB, 1966. 1¾hr. *Dir* Roman Polański; *prod* Gene Gutowski for Compton; *scr*

Polański, Gerard Brach; *ph* Gilbert Taylor; *mus* Krzysztof Komeda; *cast* Donald Pleasence (George), Françoise Dorléac (Teresa), Lionel Stander (Richard), Jack MacGowran (Albert).

As in NÓŻ W WODZIE (*Knife in the Water*, 1962), the action centres on a married couple and an intruder who are removed from the social ties of the world (the film's location was Holy Island, Northumberland). Tension is built up through shifts of dominance between the three; unlike the earlier film the relationships are finally resolved in violence.

Although it was written before REPULSION (1965) it was the success of the latter that enabled POLAŃSKI to raise backing for *Cul-de-Sac*. It was awarded the Golden Bear at the BERLIN Festival, 1966.

**CUNY**, ALAIN (1908– ), French actor, whose first contact with cinema was as a costume designer for directors such as CAVALCANTI, FEYDER, and RENOIR. He became a stage actor and played small roles in films: his first major film role was in LES VISITEURS DU SOIR (1942). Since appearing in Malaparte's *Il cristo proibito* (1950), Cuny has had a successful career in both French and Italian films: they include ANTONIONI's *La signora senza camelie* (1952), MALLE'S LES AMANTS (1958), and FELLINI'S LA DOLCE VITA (1960), in which he played the suicidal friend of the central character. BUÑUEL cast Cuny with particular effectiveness as the mysterious, incantatory Man in the Cape in LA VOIE LACTÉE (1969).

**CURE, The**, US, 1917. 30min. *Dir, scr* Charles Chaplin; *prod* Mutual; *ph* Rollie Totheroh, William C. Foster; *cast* Charlie Chaplin (the patient), Edna Purviance (the girl), Eric Campbell (the man with gout), Henry Bergman (the masseur).

Perhaps the best of CHAPLIN's films made under his contract with MUTUAL, particularly memorable for his involvement with a revolving door. 'The cure' (drinking water) is intended to get rid of the hero's alcoholic habits, but he only succeeds in getting most of the nursing home's other patients, and some of the staff, drunk. For once, Charlie wears a light-coloured suit and straw boater instead of tail coat and bowler hat.

**CURTIS**, TONY (1925– ), US actor, real name Bernard Schwarz, gained his early acting experience in amateur productions during his service with the US Navy. He played small supporting roles in *Gilda* (1946) and *Criss Cross* (1948), and his looks, athleticism, and good-humoured personality soon won him wide popularity. He has appeared in widely differing films with equal success, notably *The Vikings*

(1957), THE DEFIANT ONES (1958), SOME LIKE IT HOT (1959), and *The Boston Strangler* (1969).

**CURTIZ,** MICHAEL (1888–1962), US director, real name Kertész, began his film career in his native Hungary and also worked for UFA in Berlin and in Britain. He was imported to Hollywood by WARNER BROS to direct *Noah's Ark* (1928).

Curtiz exemplified the craftsmanlike studio director who brought technical proficiency and polish to the varied material he was given. His contribution to Warner's GANGSTER cycle included *20,000 Years in Sing-Sing* (1933) and ANGELS WITH DIRTY FACES (1938). He showed his ability to pace action swiftly in Errol FLYNN's best films, *Captain Blood* (1935), *The Charge of the Light Brigade* (1936), *The Adventures of Robin Hood* (1938, co-directed), and *The Sea Hawk* (1940), and he tackled more serious themes with sincerity and feeling, as in *Cabin in the Cotton* (1932) and *Mission to Moscow* (1942). He could extract good performances from actors, and he directed two of Warner's contract players to their only OSCARS: James CAGNEY in *Yankee Doodle Dandy* (1942) and Joan CRAWFORD in *Mildred Pierce* (1945). Perhaps his most memorable single film is CASABLANCA (1943), a wartime romance representative of Hollywood at its best.

**CURZON,** London art house opened in 1934. Its programmes were chosen by its joint owner, the Marquis de Case Maury, whose showmanship was outstanding: in 1936, for example, he bought the English rights of Sacha GUITRY's *Bonne Chance* (1935) for £500 and took £13,000 during its run at the Curzon alone. In 1951 LA RONDE (1950) opened and ran for 76 weeks—a notable record. During the war years the Curzon was requisitioned by the War Office, opening daily from 8 a.m. to 1 a.m., the longest hours of performance known for a London cinema. The original cinema, an outstanding example of thirties architecture, was demolished in 1966 and rebuilt in an office block.

**CUSTARD PIE** throwing as a comic gag was allegedly invented by the KEYSTONE company. SENNETT's own version in his autobiography, that Mabel NORMAND one day in 1913 spontaneously threw a custard pie which happened to be handy at Ben TURPIN as he was working out a comic routine, cannot be absolutely accurate, as Turpin did not join Keystone until 1917. Other accounts vary as to who threw the first pie at whom. Undoubtedly, though, the gag arose spontaneously, and the first Keystone pie on film record was thrown by Mabel Normand at Fatty ARBUCKLE in *A Noise from the Deep* (July 1913).

The gag became a favourite with Keystone, who bought their pies from a store on the corner. Although later pies were specially made for the purpose, Keystone pies were often the real thing, with blackberries and whipped cream particularly favoured by Keystone's acknowledged champion, Del Lord. Keystone discovered that for comic effect surprise was essential, and developed a wide range of variations on the basic gag.

The possibilities of pie throwing appealed to and were exploited by most comedians of the silent screen. One of the best-remembered setpieces in pie throwing is the last third of LAUREL AND HARDY's *The Battle of the Century* (1927, two reels), in which a couple of dozen people and some 3,000 pies were involved. (The sequence is often referred to as a complete film, having been extracted for inclusion in the COMPILATION, *The Golden Age of Comedy*, 1958.)

The term custard-pie has gained currency in ordinary speech to denote the kind of simple, purely physical, humour involved.

**CUSTER,** General GEORGE ARMSTRONG (1839–76), achieved notoriety, and provided subject-matter for several WESTERNS, through his monumental blunder at the Battle of the Little Bighorn, where he and 224 others were slaughtered by Indians. D. W. GRIFFITH's *The Massacre* (1913) depicted the incident. In films, Custer has generally been sympathetically portrayed, by Ronald REAGAN (*Santa Fe Trail*, 1940), Erroll FLYNN (*They Died With Their Boots On*, 1942), and others. Henry FONDA's characterization in John FORD's *Fort Apache* (1948) was less reverent, and as played by Richard Mulligan in Arthur PENN's *Little Big Man* (1971) Custer emerged as a ludicrously vain blunderer.

**CUTTING COPY,** called a 'work print' in the US, the print of a film used during production by the editor to make all cuts, and as a guide in preparing optical EFFECTS, DUBBING, and MIXING sound. The negative (or reversal original) is not projected or cut by the editor; any damage is thus confined to the cutting copy. There is no sound on the cutting copy; it is on a separate magnetic film, cut parallel with the picture. After the cutting copy and track have been screened on a DOUBLE HEAD projector and the work approved, the negative is cut (not edited) to match the cutting copy exactly. Prints subsequently made from the cut negative are MARRIED sound prints and are of much better quality than the worked-over cutting copy, which has no further use. (See EDITING.)

**CYBULSKI,** ZBIGNIEW (1927–67), Polish actor, played a creative role in both theatre and cinema. With fellow-actor Bogumil Kobiela he founded two experimental theatrical groups. He shared an auspicious feature film début with Roman POLAŃSKI in WAJDA'S POKOLENIE (*A Generation*, 1954). Cybulski frequently denied comparisons with James DEAN, but not only his status as a cult-figure justified these. His characterization of Maciek in Wajda's POPIÓL I DIAMENT (*Ashes and Diamonds*, 1958), the rebel doubting the continuing validity of his cause, brought international renown. Maciek's mode of dress and tinted glasses were eagerly emulated.

In the course of almost forty films, Cybulski worked with Aleksander FORD in *Osmy dzien tygodnia* (*The Eighth Day of the Week*, 1957); with Wajda again in *Niewinni czarodzieje* (*Innocent Sorcerers*, 1959); and with Wojciech HAS in *Rekopis znaleziony w Saragossie* (*The Saragossa Manuscript*, 1964). Again with Kobiela, he co-scripted Morgenstern's *Do widzenia do jutra* (*See You Tomorrow*, 1960), in which both appeared. Outside Poland, his work included *Att älska* (*To Love*, Jörn DONNER, Sweden, 1964) and the Wajda episode in *L'Amour à vingt ans* (France, 1962).

Cybulski's death in a train accident inspired Wajda's film-within-a-film, *Wszystko na sprzedaz* (*Everything for Sale*, 1968), in which the dead actor's spiritual heir is played by Daniel Olbrychski (b. 1945), who has largely assumed Cybulski's role in Polish theatre and cinema.

**CZECHOSLOVAKIA** can claim one of the pioneers in the technical development of cinema in the physiologist Purkynĕ, who during the 1840s and 1850s perfected various forms of moving-image machines for his scientific work and even looked forward to their being put to artistic uses. The first Czech films were made and projected in 1898 by Jan Křiženecký, with LUMIÈRE equipment which he had bought in Paris. During the next few years films were shot and projected fairly widely, at first in Czech territory and later in Slovakia. The first permanent film theatre was opened in Prague in 1907 by the conjuror Ponrepo. Regular production began in 1910 with the founding of Kinofa, a company devoted primarily to actuality and scientific film. One of the most effective pioneers was the architect Max Urban, who started making films in 1910, and in 1911 married the well-known actress Anna Sedláčková who played in most of his films. His Fotokinema company (1911) became in 1912 ASUM-Film, from the combination of their initials. Based at BARRANDOV on the outskirts of Prague, the company maintained a brisk output for a few years and was finally wound up in 1917. In 1913 Alois Jalovec founded Illusionfilm, which specialized in producing dramatic films with popular actors.

Native production did not flourish in the face of competition from imported films, but film-going took a firm hold on the public: in 1913, more than one-third of the 700 cinemas of the Austro-Hungarian Empire were on Czech territory.

Such production as there was languished during the First World War, but at the same time there was a growing interest in film among intellectuals and actors. The formation of the independent Czechoslovak republic in 1918 brought new stimulus to production and furthered attempts to develop cinema as part of national culture. In 1923 the Film Museum (Čescoslovenskyé filmové museum) was founded by Jindřich Brichta for the encouragement of interest in cinema, one of the first such institutions in the world. Competition from foreign films, especially German and American, was severe, and by 1923 the newly-revived industry had been brought to a state of crisis. Only eight Czech films were produced in 1924. A revival towards the end of the twenties (35 films in 1929) was brought to a halt by the American slump just as sound was coming in (eight films in 1930).

Production during the twenties was dominated by themes of nationalist interest, particularly historical reconstructions. Comedies, characteristically, flourished, particularly those with the actor Vlasta Burian. The success of German and American films led also to imitation by Czechoslovak film-makers. Two notable achievements towards the end of the decade were Gustav MACHATÝ's *Erotikon* (1929) and Curt Junghans's TAKOVÝ JE ŽIVOT (*Such is Life*, 1930). The former marked the beginning of international appreciation of Machatý, the latter did not receive the attention it deserved because it was shot silent at a time when sound had already arrived in the US and Western Europe.

The introduction of sound brought to Czechoslovakia as to other small film-producing nations the problem of language restriction. The country reacted vigorously, in two distinct ways. On the one hand, the industry aimed for the international market with a diet of operettas and light comedies: on the other, a more serious stimulus was received from the activities of a lively avant-garde movement in the arts. The critic Karel Teige in particular was influential in fostering the strain of social awareness already emerging in the twenties, and a more light-hearted dose of social and political satire was injected into cinema from the Liberated Theatre (Osvobozené Divadlo) in the films of Voskoveč and Werich. Strong popular support for the film industry helped to induce the government in the early days of sound to introduce a subsidy for films of a certain quality; this, again, was probably the first of its kind in the world. The fund from which subsidies were to be made was supported in part by a tax levied on the import of foreign films. This served, too, to appease popular resentment against foreign and especially German films. At the same time as the introduction of the subsidy, a QUOTA restriction was imposed by which at least eight films of home production had to be screened by each cinema during a year.

The studios at Barrandov, built 1932–3, were the most advanced in central Europe, and attracted many foreign productions and co-productions. Together with these, increasing home production (from 8 films in 1930 to 54 in 1937) made Czechoslovakia the liveliest centre of film-making in central and eastern Europe during the thirties.

Machatý's international reputation received a further boost with EXTASE, shown at Venice in 1933. Machatý had also made an important early contribution in sound to the developing stream of social comment with Ze Soboty na Neděli (From Saturday to Sunday, 1931). Martin FRIČ, whose silent Varhanik u Sv Víta (The Organist of St Vitus's Cathedral, 1929) had inaugurated the stream, continued to contribute to it, but received much wider recognition for his films on historical and nationalist themes. His Jánošik (1935), about a Slovak hero of the Robin Hood type, was one of the most popular films of the decade, at home and abroad. He also filmed Voskoveč and Werich, and had started the decade with a sound version of Dobrý Voják Švejk (The Good Soldier Schweik, 1931) from Jaroslav Hašek's greatly-loved book (published 1924), which had already been filmed in serial form in silent days by Machatý and Karel Lamač, with Anny ONDRA in her first screen part. Lamač specialized in light comedies, many of them starring Anny Ondra, and worked in Berlin, Paris, and Vienna as well as in Prague. Karel Anton was another prolific director, whose most important film, Tonka Šibenice (Tonischka, 1929–30), had been made silent and had sound added. Other outstanding directors of the thirties were Vladislav Vančura, Jindřich Honzl, and Otakar VÁVRA, the latter specializing in adaptations from literary and historical classics which showed a high degree of craftsmanship. Josef Rovenský, though less prolific in output, made an important contribution, particularly with his Řeka (The River, 1933), to what became recognized as the 'Czech style' of lyricism and beautiful photography, with which the names of the cameramen Jan STALLICH and Otto HELLER are deservedly associated. Towards the end of the decade a considerable amount of documentary film was also emerging, in which Karel Plicka and Alexander Hackenschmied (later Hammid) were outstanding. Two young directors who made a beginning in this school were Jiří Weiss, who worked on documentaries in Prague for two years before leaving for England in 1938, and Elmar KLOS.

The Nazi occupation of Czech territory and the setting up of the puppet Slovak state in 1939 following the Munich Agreement brought to an abrupt end the thriving activity of the Czech film industry. Czechoslovak production slumped from 40 films in 1940 to 9 in 1944. The Germans used for themselves the well-developed production facilities, and towards the end of the war added greatly to the capacity of Barrandov, where they could make films, as the Czechs express it, amid far less noise than at home in Germany.

During this war, however, as during the first, serious consideration was being given to the future of Czechoslovak film. The national film archive was founded in 1943, and, even more important, plans were being prepared by a group led by Vávra and Klos for the nationalization of the film industry as soon as the Nazis should withdraw. When the social democratic republic was re-established in 1945, the first decree for nationalization (in August) dealt with the film industry. Three important features of the new system were the establishment of new studios for puppet and animation films, the introduction of group production for feature films, and the establishment of the Film School, FAMU, in Prague. Slovak cinema, with its own feature and documentary studios, was given separate recognition in 1947. Decrees confirming the organization of the film industry were among the earliest issued when the Communist Party took over government in February 1948: the Czechs are justifiably proud that the advantages of the socialist system of production were developed in their country first in eastern Europe.

Early evidence was given of the benefits of nationalization. Production had fallen to three films in 1945, but in 1947 Karel Steklý's Sirena (The Strike) won the Golden Lion at VENICE, and the same year saw the production of Jiří TRNKA's Spalíček (The Czech Year), as well as the first Slovak film. Vávra, Weiss, and Klos (teamed after 1952 with Ján KADÁR), with Frič and the two newcomers Trnka and Karel ZEMAN, continued as the most productive directors during the difficult post-war years when Stalinism and the demands of the newly-socialist state restricted the scope of Czech cinema. Trnka in particular was able to achieve in his puppet films a breadth of subtle vindication of human values, and it is no accident that his most creative period was precisely the time, in the early fifties, when the scope for feature films was most circumscribed.

Production fluctuated at the beginning of the fifties, but by the end had begun to rise steadily (27 Czech films and 4 Slovak in 1960; 32 and 7 in 1965; 33 and 7 in 1967) to stabilize around the 40 mark; documentary and animation output also rose steadily. More striking even than the rise in production was the emergence of a new generation of film-makers who were able in the relaxed atmosphere of the late fifties and sixties to produce a 'new wave' of lively, imaginative films with contemporary themes. The period of political relaxation inaugurated by the Twentieth Congress in Moscow in 1956 coincided with the new generation emerging from FAMU: they found an excellently organized industry awaiting them, giving rise to one of the most stimulating periods of activity in European cinema.

Vojtěch Jasný's *Zářijové noci* (*September Nights*, 1957) gave a glimpse of what was to come, criticizing personality cult in the army; the same year saw Weiss's *Vlčí jáma* (*Wolf Trap*). Jasný followed with *Touha* (*Desire*, 1958), the first film overtly expressing anxiety about contemporary life. The early experiments of Věra CHYTILOVÁ in Prague and Stefan Uher in Bratislava did not at first meet with official approval, but these two were soon joined by other young film-makers no longer content to accept official stereotypes. As in the thirties, the avant-garde of film-makers pursued their ideas in close association with the other arts, and in particular worked with and drew inspiration from the 'little theatre' groups such as Semafor.

Miloš FORMAN (*Černý Petr*, *Peter and Pavla*, 1963; *Lásky jedné plávovlasky*, *A Blonde in Love*, 1965; HOŘI, MÁ PANENKO, *The Firemen's Ball*, 1967), Ivan PASSER (INTIMNÍ OSVĚTLENÍ, *Intimate Lighting*, 1966), and Jiří MENZEL (OSTŘE SLEDOVANÉ VLAKY, *Closely Observed Trains*, 1966) excelled in social observation, sometimes satirical, sometimes gentle, always sharp. Another group experimented with film form to express abstract ideas: Evald SCHORM (*Každý den odvahu*, *Everyday Courage*, 1964), Jan NĚMEC (*Démanty noci*, *Diamonds of the Night*, 1964; O SLAVNOSTI A HOSTECH, *The Party and the Guests*, 1966), Pavel Juráček (co-dir *Josef Kilian*, 1963), with Chytilová herself directing perhaps the boldest experiments. In Slovakia, Solan and Barabáš were among the young directors who joined Uher in the upsurge of the early sixties. Between 1962 and 1968, some sixty new directors got their chance to make films, in an atmosphere characterized by a strong sense of mutual encouragement and enthusiasm: these years were marked, too, by many international prizes for Czech films. Vávra, Klos, and Kadár among the older directors remained closely associated with the new wave,

and the contribution of Alfred RADOK should be acknowledged: primarily a theatrical experimenter, he became interested in film in 1947, and has helped and encouraged many of the newcomers to cinema. His *Dědeček automobil* (*Old Man Motor-Car*, 1956), in breaking with accepted form, seemed to them to point to new possibilities. He was also the main developer of the charming LATERNA MAGICA (Magic Lantern).

The existence of a fine cadre of actors, trained in the Prague Academy and practised in a lively experimental theatre was an important contributing factor to the success of the decade, as was the cross-fertilization between cinema and television, where exciting film work was being done especially in the field of popular music. The strong tradition of pre-war Czech cinema and the cultural importance which the Czechoslovak public has always accorded cinema also helped all these new factors to coincide and thrive in producing films of vitality and enduring quality.

The invasion of August 1968 interrupted one of the happiest periods of film production that the world has yet seen. Since the return of rigid censorship there has been a dearth of available subject matter and few directors are able to express themselves fully within the available bounds. A few interesting films from Czechoslovakia have been seen in the West since 1968: they include *Valerie a týden divu* (*Valerie and her Week of Wonders*, 1970), *Apozdravuju vlastovky* (*And My Love to the Swallows*, 1972), and *Lidé z metra* (*People of the Metro*, 1974) by Jaromil Jures, charming fantasies marked by precise surrealist imagery, and Juraj Herz's *Petrolejové lampy* (*Oil Lamps*, 1971), a period romance of great visual richness. Karel Kachyna directed *Uz zaze skacu kaluze* (*I'm Jumping Over Puddles Again*, 1970), a children's film of unashamed sentimentality but considerable technical accomplishment that won admiration abroad, as did *Dny zrady* (*Days of Betrayal*, 1973), Vávra's grey reconstruction of the Munich crisis. Frantisek Vlačil has directed historical epics at once grandiose and thoughtful, and Jaroslav Papoušek, a former collaborator of Forman, is popular for his sharp black comedies about a middle-aged family man called Homolka.

Josef Skvorecky, *All the bright young men and women*, Toronto, 1971; Langdon Dewey, *Outline of Czechoslovakian cinema*, London, 1971; Antonín J. Liehm, *Closely watched films*, New York, 1974.

**CZINNER, PAUL** (1890–1972), Hungarian-born British director, made several films starring his wife, Elisabeth BERGNER, in pre-war Germany. In 1930 they took refuge in Britain, where he directed her in *Catherine the Great* (1934), *Escape Me Never* (1936), and *As You Like It* (1936) co-starring Laurence OLIVIER. He latterly concentrated on filming OPERA and BALLET productions, rather as a valuable record of great contemporary performances than as films in their own right: these include *The Bolshoi Ballet* (1957), *The Royal Ballet* (1959), *Der Rosenkavalier* (1961), and *Romeo and Juliet* (1966).

# D

**DAGOVER,** LIL (1897– ), German actress, real name Martha Maria Liletts, became involved in the theatre after her marriage in 1917 to the German actor Fritz Daghofer (1872– 1936). The marriage lasted only two years, but she had been noticed by the director Robert WIENE, who recommended her to LANG for the leading role in *Kara Kiri* (*Madam Butterfly*, 1919). Her most famous film was Wiene's DAS CABINETT DES DR CALIGARI (1919), but during the height of her career she also appeared with distinction in films directed by MURNAU and MOLANDER, and made one film in Hollywood: *The Woman from Monte Carlo* (1931).

**DAHLBECK,** EVA (1920– ), Swedish actress, trained at the Royal Dramatic Theatre School in Stockholm and continued as one of the Royal Theatre's leading actresses, particularly in plays by Ibsen and Strindberg. Her first film was *Rid i natt* (*Ride Tonight*, 1942), directed by Gustaf MOLANDER and she has also worked in Sweden for such directors as SJÖBERG and Mai ZETTERLING and in France for Agnès VARDA in *Les Créatures* (1965). Her first film for Ingmar BERGMAN was KVINNORS VÄNTAN (*Waiting Women*, 1952) and her warmth and maturity has been shown to advantage in other films directed by him, notably SOMMARNATTENS LEENDE (*Smiles of a Summer Night*, 1955), and *Nära livet* (*Brink of Life*, 1957).

**DAIEISCOPE,** WIDE SCREEN process adopted by the Daiei Company as the Japanese licensees of PARAMOUNT'S VISTAVISION process. It is identical with VistaVision.

*DAISIES* see SEDMIKRÁSKY

**DALI,** SALVADOR (1904– ), Spanish painter noted in cinema chiefly for his collaboration with Luis BUÑUEL on two films: UN CHIEN ANDALOU (1928) and L'ÂGE D'OR (1930). Dali collaborated on the scenario of *Un Chien andalou*, and his involvement with *L'Âge d'or* was even slighter. He was, moreover, 'frightfully disappointed' by the work. In 1944 Dali, by then a fashionable figure among Hollywood society (he had left France in 1939), contributed a dream sequence to HITCHCOCK's *Spellbound* (1945).

**DALIO,** MARCEL (1900– ), French actor of Romanian origin, went to the Paris Conservatoire in 1916, but was called up for military service soon afterwards. After the war he appeared in cabaret and revue, and also in serious plays. His first film part was in *Mon Chapeau* (1933), and he worked in both theatre and cinema throughout the thirties. His short and swarthy physique would have limited a less skilled actor, but his subtlety of characterization and an air of delicacy and reserve produced some memorable performances. His films in this period include PÉPÉ-LE-MOKO and LA GRANDE ILLUSION (both 1937), *Les Pirates du rail* (1938), and LA RÈGLE DU JEU (1939). After working in the theatre in Canada, he went to Hollywood, where he appeared in such films as *The Shanghai Gesture* (1941), CASABLANCA (1943), *The Song of Bernadette* (1943), and TO HAVE AND HAVE NOT (1944). He returned to France in 1946, and has since worked mostly there and in the US. His most recent roles have been in *Catch-22*, *The Great White Hope* (both 1970), and *Aussi loin que l'amour* (1971).

*DAMA S SOBACHKOI* (*The Lady with the Little Dog*), USSR, 1959. 1½hr. *Dir, scr* Josif Heifits, from the story by Chekhov; *prod* Lenfilm; *ph* Andrei Moskvin, D. Meschiev; *cast* Ya Savvina (Anna Sergeievna), Alexei Batalov (Dmitri Gourov), Ala Chostakova (Mme Gourova).

Anna and Dmitri, no longer young and each trapped in a meaningless marriage, meet on holiday in Yalta and fall in love. Their attempts to overcome their increasing passion fail, and after returning home they continue their affair, meeting in a drab hotel room in Moscow; the end of the film promises no resolution of their problem. The leading players perfectly portray characters locked in an inertia induced by rigid convention. HEIFITS's sensitive direction is a superb visualization of the muted tone of Chekhov's prose, conveying with extreme subtlety the surroundings and social ambience of Yalta in summer and Moscow in winter.

**DANIELS,** BEBE (1901–71), American actress who began acting as a child, making her first film, *The Common Enemy*, in 1908. Dark and

*Dama s sobachkoi* (Josif Heifits, 1959)

lively, she became one of the most popular *comédiennes* of the silent era, but had her greatest successes in musicals, including *Rio Rita* (1929) and 42ND STREET (1933). At the beginning of the war she and her husband Ben LYON moved to England where she wrote and appeared with him in several successful radio comedy series including 'Hi Gang' and 'Life with the Lyons', before succumbing to the long period of ill-health which preceded her death.

**DANIELS, WILLIAM** (1895–1970), US cameraman whose work on two STROHEIM films, FOOLISH WIVES (1921) and GREED (1923), brought him to the forefront of his profession. He was head cameraman for METRO-GOLDWYN-MAYER, 1924–46, and is probably best remembered for the characteristic sheen, suggestive of mystery and luxury, which he brought to most of Greta GARBO's Hollywood films, outstandingly *Flesh and the Devil* (1927), QUEEN CHRISTINA (1934), and CAMILLE (1936). Other examples of his professional versatility are DINNER AT EIGHT (1933), *Winchester 73* (1950), *The Glenn Miller Story* (1953), and *Cat on a Hot Tin Roof* (1958).

**DANKWORTH, JOHN** (Johnny) (1927– ), British jazz musician who in the late fifties turned to composing film scores, quickly becoming one

of the foremost British composers in this field. His scores include SATURDAY NIGHT AND SUNDAY MORNING (1960), THE CRIMINAL (1960), THE SERVANT (1963), *Darling* (1965), MORGAN ... A SUITABLE CASE FOR TREATMENT (1966), *Modesty Blaise* (1966), ACCIDENT (1967), *The Magus* (1968), *The Engagement* (1970), *Perfect Friday* (1970). He is married to the jazz singer Cleo Laine.

**DAQUIN, LOUIS** (1908– ), French director whose reputation outside his native country rests almost entirely on the first film he directed, *Nous les gosses* (*Us Kids*, 1941), which reached English-speaking countries soon after the war. Daquin handled his predominantly juvenile cast beautifully in this engaging story of the inventive stratagems adopted by a group of schoolchildren to raise money to pay for a broken window. Only a few of Daquin's subsequent films (including a version of Maupassant's *Bel-Ami*, 1955) have been widely seen and none attracted comparable attention. He was for some years head of the French film workers' trade union and has written a book, *Le Cinéma, notre métier* (Paris, 1960).

**DARRIEUX, DANIELLE** (1917– ), French actress, made her first film, *Le Bal* (1931), at the age of fourteen. She was soon established as an *ingénue* lead and starred in many romantic vehicles and sophisticated comedies in the thirties and forties. Her special blend of wit, beauty, and aristocratic romanticism found its best medium in such films as *Occupe-toi d'Amélie* (AUTANT-LARA, 1949) and LA RONDE (1950), with a late and nostalgic flowering in Jacques DEMY's *Les Demoiselles de Rochefort* (1966).

**DARWELL,** JANE (1880–1967), US character actress, real name Patti Woodward, made her first film appearance in the silent days, when her films included *Master Mind* (1920) and the 1921 version of *Brewster's Millions*. She appeared in matronly roles in many films of the thirties and forties, becoming particularly associated with films by John FORD and winning an OSCAR for her performance as Ma Joad in THE GRAPES OF WRATH (1940). Her other films with Ford included *Three Godfathers* (1948), WAGON-MASTER (1950), *The Sun Shines Bright* (1952), and, in a small part which gave her little to do, MY DARLING CLEMENTINE (1946). She remained active in the sixties, her later films including *Mary Poppins* (1964).

**DASSIN,** JULES (1911– ), US director who has occasionally scripted and acted in his own films. His earlier work includes *Nazi Agent* (1942), *Brute Force* (1947), with Burt LANCASTER, *Naked City* (1948), a realistic police thriller which inspired an imitative television series, and *Thieves' Highway* (1949). In 1950 Dassin was forced out of Hollywood by the blacklisting that followed the investigations of the UNAMERICAN ACTIVITIES Committee and went to France. His first film after several years' inactivity was DU RIFIFI CHEZ LES HOMMES (*Rififi*, 1955) which immediately re-established his international reputation. It was followed by the equally successful *Celui qui doit mourir* (*He Who Must Die*, 1956). POTE TIN KYRIAKI (*Never on Sunday*, 1959) and *Phaedra* (1961) were devoted to his wife, Melina MERCOURI; Dassin resumed his speciality, the crime thriller, with *Topkapi* (1964). He returned to the US to make *Uptight* (1968), a new version of THE INFORMER (1935), set in the context of Black revolutionary activity.

**DASTÉ,** JEAN (1904– ), French actor, was already established in the theatre when he made his screen début in Jean RENOIR's BOUDU SAUVÉ DES EAUX (1932). An actor of gentle subtlety, often with a diffident air, he appeared intermittently in films until 1944, his most fruitful work being for Jean VIGO, in ZÉRO DE CONDUITE (1933) and L'ATALANTE (1934), and for Renoir, in LE CRIME DE MONSIEUR LANGE (1936) and LA GRANDE ILLUSION (1937). Dasté maintained his allegiance to the theatre, managing his

own stage company in the late forties and early fifties. He has occasionally appeared on the screen in recent years, notably in MURIEL (1963), Z (1968), and L'ENFANT SAUVAGE (1970).

**DAVES,** DELMER (1904– ), US director, as a young man lived among the Navaho and Hopi Indians for a time. He began his career in films as a property boy on THE COVERED WAGON (1923), then worked as a scriptwriter until his début as director with *Destination Tokyo* (1943). In 1950 he made his first Western, BROKEN ARROW, one of the first films to take a pro-Indian standpoint. All his Westerns, including *The Last Wagon* (1956), which he also wrote, 3.10 TO YUMA (1957), and *The Hanging Tree* (1959), have social realism allied to a quality of allegory, an approach which, from the early fifties, was an essential part of the development of the genre. Daves's other films, covering a wide range of subject matter, are weak in comparison with his Westerns.

***DAVID AND LISA,*** US, 1962. 1½hr. *Dir* Frank Perry; *prod* Paul M. Heller; *scr* Eleanor Perry; *cast* Keir Dullea (David), Janet Margolin (Lisa), Howard da Silva (Alan).

An actual case history of two emotionally disturbed adolescents who find their way to stability through mutual love and trust was closely adapted for the screen.

An example of American independent cinema made on a small budget by a team for the main part new to commercial film-making, the film caused something of a stir and won a prize at VENICE.

***DAVID COPPERFIELD.*** Screen adaptations of Charles DICKENS's semi-autobiographical novel published in 1849–50 include: a US version made in 1911; an early British six-reeler directed by Cecil HEPWORTH in 1913, with Eric Desmond, Kenneth Wall, Alma Taylor, and Tom Butt; a Danish adaptation directed by A. W. Sandberg (1922); and the most successful to date, the 1934 METRO-GOLDWYN-MAYER classic directed by George CUKOR from a sensitive and literate script by Hugh Walpole. This captured excellently the flavour of the novel, with a strong sense of social milieu, sharp contrasts of mood and character, and sentimentality ultimately held in check. Cukor's strength as a director of actors was particularly evident in the performances of Freddie BARTHOLOMEW as the young David and W. C. FIELDS as Mr Micawber; the excellent cast also included Basil RATHBONE (Murdstone), Edna May OLIVER (Betsy Trotwood), Lionel BARRYMORE, Lewis Stone, Roland YOUNG, and Maureen O'SULLIVAN. Dickens's original title was used: *The Personal History, Adventures,*

*Experience and Observations of David Copperfield, the Younger.*

Delbert MANN directed the 1970 British version which was intended primarily for American television. The prestigious cast included Michael REDGRAVE, Ralph RICHARDSON, Laurence OLIVIER, Edith EVANS, and Richard ATTENBOROUGH. This adaptation leaned heavily on flashbacks to accommodate the long, complicated plot, and emphasized Dickens's sentimentality at some cost to his astringent observation.

**DAVIES, MARION** (1898–1961), US actress, real name Marion Douras, started her stage career as a chorus girl. She was taken up by William Randolph HEARST, who became determined to make her a romantic film star, however great the cost; this relationship was developed in CITIZEN KANE (1941). WELLES's untalented and disenchanted Susan Alexander is, however, no close transcript of her original. After several films financed by Hearst, the only successful one of which was *When Knighthood was in Flower* (1922), Marion Davies found her real medium in comedy, exploiting her delicate prettiness in hilariously inappropriate slapstick and parody, and reaching her peak in two films directed by King VIDOR, *The Patsy* (1927) and *Show People* (1928). Her career continued successfully into the sound era and she retired in 1937 to live with Hearst, until his death in 1951, at his mansion San Simeon, in an atmosphere far removed from the gloom of Kane's Xanadu.

**DAVIS, BETTE** (1908– ), US actress, began her career successfully in the theatre, but made an inauspicious film début in *The Bad Sister* (1931) and had no opportunity to show her ability until her seventh film *The Man Who Played God* (1932). She signed a long-term contract with WARNER BROS, but the relationship was a stormy one, erupting into a court case in 1936. Even after her triumph as the cockney prostitute in *Of Human Bondage* (1934), the studio continued to cast her in second-rate parts. Only after her brilliant performance in *Jezebel* (1938), as a headstrong Southern belle who drives away the man she loves and then repents too late, was she able to control her career, to excellent effect. Her parts included a wealthy socialite who learns to face a fatal illness with courage, in *Dark Victory* (1939), and an unmarried mother forced to watch a rival win her unacknowledged daughter's love while she becomes the child's spinster aunt, in *The Old Maid* (1939). In both films, Edmund GOULDING's skill as a director and the detail and conviction of Bette Davis's acting combine to transform apparently novelettish plots into credible and moving

stories. She gave equally successful performances in THE LITTLE FOXES (1941) and *Now Voyager* (1942) among many other films, but since her success as the fading star in ALL ABOUT EVE (1950), her career has been uneven and her appearances less frequent. Her appearance as the insane, ageing child star in *Whatever Happened to Baby Jane?* (1962) brought her back into the limelight and is typical of the larger-than-life characters and performances in which she has more recently specialized.

**DAVIS, SAMMY, Jr** (1925– ), American entertainer, singer, and actor, of enormous vitality, formerly married to the Swedish actress Mai Britt. Born in Harlem, of show-business parents, Davis joined their double act at the age of four. From 1947 to 1954 he successfully toured the night-club circuit, becoming a friend of Frank SINATRA, and a member of the famous 'Clan'.

Despite losing an eye in a car crash in 1954, Davis made his Broadway début in the musical *Mr Wonderful* (1956). During this time he became a convert to Judaism, and has since used the ebullient self-description of 'a one-eyed Negro Jew'.

With Sinatra and Dean MARTIN he appeared in what have become known as the 'Clan' films, *Ocean's Eleven* (1960), *Sergeants Three* (1961), *Robin and the Seven Hoods* (1964). Other film appearances include *Anna Lucasta* (1959), *Die Dreigroschenoper* (1962) directed in West Germany by Wolfgang STAUDTE, *Sweet Charity* (1968). *Yes I Can* (New York, London, 1965), written with Jane and Burt Boyar, is a racy, entertaining autobiography.

**DAY, DORIS** (1924– ), US singer and actress, real name Doris Kappelhoff, worked as a vocalist with various dance bands including Les Brown's before making her first film *Romance on the High Seas* (1949, *It's Magic* in GB). Her fresh and unaffected personality gained immediate popularity with mass audiences, and this was maintained by musicals such as *Calamity Jane* (1953) and Stanley DONEN's *Pajama Game* (1957), and straight thrillers such as THE MAN WHO KNEW TOO MUCH (1956). Her appearances in such potentially suggestive 'sex war' comedies as *Pillow Talk* (1959), *Lover Come Back* (1961), and *That Touch of Mink* (1962) added the element of hygienic innocence necessary to make them acceptable to a wide US public. She has a thoroughly professional approach, both as singer and actress, and is an accomplished *comédienne*. Her films under Norman JEWISON's direction, *The Thrill of it All* (1963) and *Send Me No Flowers* (1964), bear comparison with the best comedies of the thirties.

**DAY AT THE RACES, A,** US, 1937. 1½hr. *Dir* Sam Wood; *prod* MGM; *scr* Robert Pirosh, George Seaton, George Oppenheimer; *ph* Joseph Ruttenberg; *cast* Groucho Marx (Dr Hugo Z. Hackenbush), Chico (Tony), Harpo (Stuffy), Allan Jones (Gil), Maureen O'Sullivan (Judy), Margaret Dumont (Mrs Upjohn).

*A Day at the Races* displays the MARX BROTHERS' frenetic humour in classic style, notably in a water ballet, a voodoo episode, and a dentistry sequence. Chico and Harpo demonstrate seven ways to sabotage a horse-race with devastating lunacy, and as wall-paper hangers frustrate Groucho's attempted seduction of a luscious blonde. Groucho, as a horse doctor in charge of a nursing home, woos the only rich patient (Margaret DUMONT) with typically mordant wisecracks. These moments stand out against a sentimental sub-plot of the kind that marred most of their later films.

**DAY FOR NIGHT** see NUIT AMÉRICAINE, LA

**DAY OF WRATH** see VREDENS DAG

**DEAD END,** US, 1937. 1½hr. *Dir* William Wyler; *prod* Samuel Goldwyn; *scr* Lillian Hellman, Sidney Kingsley, from their stage play; *ph* Gregg Toland; *des* Richard Day; *cast* Sylvia Sidney (Drina), Joel McCrea (Dave), Humphrey Bogart (Baby Face Martin), Claire Trevor (Francey), Allen Jenkins (Hunk), Billy Halop (Tommy), Hunz Hall (Dippy), Bobby Jordan (Angel), Leo Gorcey (Spit).

*Dead End* was intended as a stringent examination of urban slums as breeding places for crime, but the incipient delinquents became colourful, engaging characters cutely working their way through a gangster melodrama. The film succeeded by the strength of its performances and William WYLER's skilled direction. The juveniles scored such a success that they appeared together as the Dead End Kids in such films as ANGELS WITH DIRTY FACES (1938) and, with changes in personnel and an increasing accent on comedy, survived for well over a decade, first as the East Side Kids, then as the Bowery Boys.

**DEAD OF NIGHT,** GB, 1945. 1¾hr. *Prod* Michael Balcon; *scr* John V. Baines, Angus McPhail; *ph* Douglas Slocombe; *mus* Georges Auric.

The five episodes in this highly effective exercise in the supernatural are: 'The Hearse Driver' (Basil DEARDEN), 'The Christmas Party' (CAVALCANTI), 'The Haunted Mirror' (Robert HAMER), 'The Ventriloquist's Dummy' (Cavalcanti), and 'Golfing Story' (Charles CRICHTON). Excellent teamwork avoided the fragmentary effect of many EPISODE films; the cast was of a uniformly high standard, with memorable performances from Googie WITHERS in the third sequence and Michael REDGRAVE in the fourth, which is generally considered the most successfully gripping.

**DEAN,** JAMES (1931–55), US actor, attended drama classes at UCLA before moving to New York. He appeared on television and in off-Broadway plays and attended the ACTORS' STUDIO for a short time. In 1953 he attracted considerable notice as the Arab boy in a dramatized version of Gide's *The Immoralist* and won several awards. As a result he was brought to Hollywood by Elia KAZAN under a seven-year contract with WARNER BROS.

Kazan's skill at discovering actors of a new and unusual stamp was already well known. Dean followed Marlon BRANDO and Montgomery CLIFT in the succession of farouche males who set up a new romantic ideal for a public used to the polished leading men of the thirties and forties. Dean's particular appeal was youth: in his three films EAST OF EDEN (1955), REBEL WITHOUT A CAUSE (1955), and *Giant* (1956), he embodied vulnerable adolescent uncertainty and social destructiveness, creating a figure with which a restless younger generation could identify. His popularity was immediate and overwhelming; his clothes and mannerisms set a fashion that outlasted his life. His obsession with speed was part of the image, and his death when his sports car crashed while travelling at 115mph was, while hysterically mourned, regarded as in a sense fitting.

The few examples of his work can give only a limited idea of Dean's potential as an actor, but his stature as a generation's idol grew for some years after his death. Most of the available unused film of him was included in a documentary, *The James Dean Story* (1957).

**DEARDEN,** BASIL (1911–71), British director, gained his early film experience as assistant director on Will HAY and George FORMBY comedies. His own features have, however, shown a more serious approach, often with a semi-documentary treatment of topical social problems. Among these are *The Bells Go Down* (1943), *The Captive Heart* (1946), *Frieda* (1947), and *The Square Ring* (1949); later examples include *Sapphire* (1959), about black immigrants in Britain, and *Victim* (1961), dealing with the blackmailing of homosexuals. A lighter element was introduced with *The Smallest Show On Earth* (1957), which was followed by, among many others, the fashionable comedy-thrillers *The League of Gentlemen* (1960) and *Only When I Larf* (1968).

*DEAREST LOVE* see SOUFFLE AU COEUR, LE

*DEATH IN VENICE* see MORTE A VENEZIA

*DEATH OF A CYCLIST* see MUERTE DE UN CICLISTA

**DEBRIE,** ANDRÉ (1880–1967), French inventor and engineer who, following in his father's footsteps, constructed the Parvo camera (1908), one of the world's standard 35mm cameras until the advent of modern reflex cameras. (See CAMERA.) At twenty-eight the director of a large company, Debrie continued to invent and perfect many pieces of filming equipment: high-speed cameras, a universal tripod, sound projectors, microfilm cameras, etc. He worked with Abel GANCE on the development of the triptych sequences in NAPOLÉON (1927).

**DE BROCA,** PHILIPPE (1920– ), French director, was an assistant on CHABROL's first three films and made his début as director under the auspices of Chabrol's own company. *Les Jeux de l'amour* (1960) marked de Broca's particular talent for sparkling comedy with an almost balletic formality and perfectly exploited the volatile personality of his leading actor, Jean-Pierre CASSEL. His second film, *Le Farceur* (1960), again featuring Cassel, further developed this individual, sparkling style, and *L'Homme de Rio* (1964) was a frenetic spoof of the current spy/chase genre. *Le Roi de Coeur* (*King of Hearts*, 1966), a wild farce set in the First World War, is perhaps less successful than de Broca's earlier films in combining hilarious comedy with an underlying seriousness of intent.

**DECAË,** HENRI (1915– ), French cameraman whose experimental styles anticipated the requirements of the NOUVELLE VAGUE directors. He has directed a number of short films in France and collaborated with Jean-Pierre MELVILLE, using a hand-held camera technique for *Le Silence de la mer* (1948). The critics-turned-directors lent heavily on the established professionals for technical advice and Decaë's work on *L'Ascenseur pour l'échafaud* (Louis MALLE, 1957) placed him in great demand, for black-and-white photography—notably LES QUATRE CENTS COUPS (François TRUFFAUT, 1959)—and for colour—*Plein soleil* (René CLÉMENT, 1959). He has continued to work frequently for Malle (VIVA MARIA!, 1965) and Melville (*Le Samourai*, 1967 and *Le Cercle rouge*, 1970).

**DECLA BIOSCOP,** German production company. Decla, sister company to the French Eclair, was founded in 1916 by Erich POMMER; it merged with Bioscop in 1919. Before it was absorbed into UFA in 1923, the company was responsible for several major films including WIENE's DAS CABINETT DES DR CALIGARI (1919), MURNAU's *Schloss Vogeloed* (1921), and LANG's DR MABUSE DER SPIELER (1922).

**DEED,** ANDRÉ (b. 1884), French actor, real name Chapuis, who, after appearing as a singer and acrobat at the Folies-Bergère and Chatelet music halls, ventured into films in 1905, when he became a member of a troupe that worked for the PATHÉ studio. He worked briefly for Georges MÉLIÈS. Then, in 1906, he was offered the lead in a number of spectacular, acrobatic comedies that were to gain rapid and great popularity, particularly *Boireau démenagé* and *Les Apprentissages de Boireau* (1907). By the end of 1908 he had changed names again to become 'Cretinetti', this time working for the Italian company, ITALA. He was to remain so called (in Britain 'Cretinetti' was known as 'Foolshead'; in France as 'Gribouille') until the end of a very successful international career in 1915, the year that Charlie CHAPLIN and Mack SENNETT burst upon the European scene. He died some time after 1930, a poor and forgotten man.

**DEEP FOCUS,** popular term describing photography which displays great DEPTH OF FIELD, with close and distant objects all equally sharp. The term came into general use to characterize Gregg TOLAND's photography of CITIZEN KANE (1941), which revived deep focus in feature films after a long absence. (See ORTHOCHROMATIC FILM, PANCHROMATIC FILM.)

**DEFA** (Deutsche Film Aktien Gesellschaft), East German state-owned production company. In August 1945 film-makers returning to Soviet-occupied Germany set up, under the auspices of the Soviet Military Administration, the Filmaktiv, an association to re-establish the German film industry. The improvised first production, the first German-made newsreel after the war, was set up in the Althoff Studios in Berlin. This was followed by documentaries and in 1946 by the first post-war German feature film, DIE MÖRDER SIND UNTER UNS (*The Murderers Are Among Us*). In May of that year the Filmaktiv became DEFA; which was and remains the only film company in East Germany. In spite of the lack of studio facilities and shortages of electricity and film stock, DEFA's output during its first two years was promising, but the gradual hardening of political censorship led to an inevitable falling-off. By the end of the forties 80% of DEFA's shares were held by the Ministry of Film Production of the USSR and the company was managed by Stalinist hard-liners. The number of entertainment films was reduced and the political message enforced. The more creative artists left to work in the West and the promising developments of the immediate post-war years were not maintained.

**DEFIANT ONES, The,** US, 1958. Wide screen; 1½hr. *Dir, prod* Stanley Kramer; *scr* Nathan E. Douglas, Harold Jacob Smith; *ph* Sam Leavitt; *cast* Tony Curtis (Jackson), Sidney Poitier (Cullen), Theodore Bikel (Sheriff), Lon Chaney Jr (Big Sam).

The escape of two prisoners from a chain gang provides a framework for an examination of racial prejudice: the four-foot chain which links the two men unwillingly together and symbolizes the inescapable inter-dependence of human beings is replaced by voluntary co-operation at the end of the film. This dramatic argument for tolerance and humanity, like so much of KRAMER's work, succeeded in combining liberal idealism with popular appeal: it was awarded two OSCARS, for photography and script, and Sidney POITIER was voted the best actor at the BERLIN Film Festival in 1958.

**DE HAVILLAND, OLIVIA** (1916– ), US actress, was noticed by a REINHARDT talent scout and appeared in Reinhardt's Hollywood Bowl production of A MIDSUMMER NIGHT'S DREAM. She was offered a role in the WARNER BROS film of 1935, together with a seven-year contract. Throughout her time with Warners she was unhappy with the parts she was given, mostly in light historical romances opposite Errol FLYNN, except when she was loaned to SELZNICK to play Melanie in GONE WITH THE WIND (1939). She had many disagreements with the studio and was suspended for a total of six months: when her contract expired she successfully fought a legal battle against the studio's attempt to add the suspension period to the initial seven-year agreement.

Working as a free-lance she played more serious dramatic parts such as those in *To Each His Own* (1946) and *The Heiress* (1949), for each of which she won an OSCAR, and in the terrifying *Snake Pit* (1948), set in a mental hospital. Her performance in *Lady in a Cage* (1964) was greatly admired, although the film's extreme violence was at the time generally disliked.

**DEHN, PAUL** (1912– ), British writer, worked as a film critic for the *News Chronicle* and *Daily Herald*. He and James Bernard won the Best Original Story OSCAR for *Seven Days to Noon* (Roy and John BOULTING, 1950), and Dehn wrote another good thriller, *Orders to Kill* (1958), for Anthony ASQUITH; but it was not until 1964 that Dehn gave up criticism to con-

centrate on screenplays. He quickly made his name as an inspired spy-story writer, co-writing *Goldfinger* (Guy Hamilton, 1964), and scripting *The Spy Who Came in from the Cold* (Martin RITT, 1965) and the underrated *The Deadly Affair* (Sidney LUMET, 1966). He also wrote the three sequels to the highly successful PLANET OF THE APES (1968). Dehn was associate producer on *Fragment of Fear* (1970), and also wrote the screenplay with its bemusing open-ended climax.

**DE LAURENTIIS, DINO** (1919– ), Italian producer, after acting in a few films turned to production in 1940. He married Silvana MANGANO in 1949 and collaborated with Carlo PONTI, 1950–4. During the early part of his career he backed a few films of great artistic merit, notably RISO AMARO (*Bitter Rice*, 1949), EUROPA '51 (1952), LA STRADA (1954), and LE NOTTI DI CABIRIA (1957). He has also been associated with large-budget co-productions including *War and Peace* (King VIDOR, 1956), *La Bibbia* (*The Bible*, John HUSTON, 1966), and *Waterloo* (Sergei BONDARCHUK, 1970). Dinocittà, the studios near Rome which he owned until 1971, rank second to CINECITTÀ in their facilities.

**DELERUE, GEORGES** (1924– ), French composer, prominent in film music since the mid-fifties. He composed the waltz for HIROSHIMA MON AMOUR (1959) and attracted wide attention with his bitter-sweet music for JULES ET JIM (1961). He worked with TRUFFAUT again on *La Peau douce* (1963), *Les Deux Anglaises et le continent* (*Anne and Muriel*, 1971), and LA NUIT AMÉRICAINE (*Day for Night*, 1973). He has composed the music for films by GODARD (LE MÉPRIS, 1963), Louis MALLE (VIVA MARIA!, 1965), and BERTOLUCCI (IL CONFORMISTA, 1970). In England he worked with Ken RUSSELL on *French Dressing* (1963) and *Women in Love* (1969) and composed music in a sixteenth-century idiom for *A Man for All Seasons* (1966) and *Anne of the Thousand Days* (1969).

**DEL GIUDICE, FILIPPO** (1892–1961), Italian-born British producer, a former lawyer. A refugee from Fascist Italy, Del Giudice settled in England in 1934 and in three years had established a production company, TWO CITIES FILMS (i.e. Rome and London), which was later financed and in 1943 absorbed by the RANK ORGANISATION. He was responsible for backing many of Britain's finest films of the forties, among them Noël COWARD's IN WHICH WE SERVE (1942) and *Blithe Spirit* (1945), HENRY V (1944), *The Way Ahead* (1944), and ODD MAN OUT (1947), giving film-makers the opportunity to work untroubled by financial considerations. In 1947 he broke away from Rank, forming a new company, Pilgrim Pictures. After *The Guinea Pig* (1948), however, ill-health ended his career.

**DELLUC,** LOUIS (1890–1924), French critic, director, and pioneer of the ciné-club movement. He edited the magazine *Le Film*, 1917–19; was film critic of the daily *Paris-Midi*, 1919–23; he edited *Le Journal du Ciné-Club*, 1920–1; in 1921 he founded the weekly *Cinéa* and edited it for two years. With Léon MOUSSINAC he instituted a school of independent film criticism, as against the publicity criticism then current. He was one of the first critics to work out a coherent theory of film; in his books *Cinéma et cie* (Paris, 1919) and *Photogénie* (Paris, 1920) and in his articles he fought for the recognition of film as an art form, attacked the theatrical approach to film, and emphasized its rhythmical and lyrical elements. These principles were consciously pursued in his own films.

Delluc's first work in the cinema was as script-writer for Germaine DULAC's *La Fête espagnole* (1919): it featured Delluc's future wife Eve Francis who was to appear in practically all his films. His films, including *Fumée noire* and *Le Silence* (both 1920), *Fièvre* and *Le Chemin d'Ernoa* or *L'Americain* (both 1921), and the elegiac *La Femme de nulle part* (1922), intermingle past and present with an increasingly refined use of flashbacks and explore the relationship of man and his environment. His last film, *L'Inondation* (1924), was partly influenced by SJÖSTRÖM and STILLER. He wrote all his films: four of his scripts, *La Fête espagnole*, *Le Silence*, *Fièvre*, and *La Femme de nulle part*, were published as *Drames de cinéma* (Paris, 1923).

The Prix Louis Delluc, honouring his memory, has been awarded annually since 1937 (except during the war years) to an outstanding French film of the current year. The first to receive the prize was *Les Bas-fonds* (1936); other winners have been ESPOIR (1945) and *L'Ascenseur pour l'échafaud* (Louis MALLE, 1957).

**DELON,** ALAIN (1935– ), French actor, discovered at the 1957 CANNES Festival and offered a Hollywood contract, decided instead to accept apprentice roles with European directors. In 1960 he played Rocco in ROCCO E I SUOI FRATELLI for VISCONTI and a year later appeared in L'ECLISSE for ANTONIONI. He has since starred in several international co-productions and become, with Jean-Paul BELMONDO, the foremost *jeune premier* in French cinema. In roles such as Jeff Costello in Jean-Pierre MELVILLE's *Le Samourai* (1967) he personifies the ritual mythology of the FILM NOIR. *Borsalino* (1970), produced by his own company, is a more light-hearted gesture to the French delight in gangsters and Marseilles.

**DELORME,** DANIÈLE (1926– ), French actress, real name Girard, began her career on the stage at the age of sixteen and made her film début in 1942 with a small part in Marc ALLÉGRET's *Félice Nanteuil*. She is particularly associated with films by Jacqueline AUDRY in which she personified some of COLETTE's celebrated characters (GIGI, 1949; *Minne, l'ingénue libertine*, 1950; *Mitsou*, 1956).

**DELPHIN** (1882–1938), French actor, real name Jules Sirveaux, was a dwarf as a result of an accidental fall in childhood. He became a successful stage actor specializing in juvenile roles but appeared in only two films, as the headmaster in VIGO's ZÉRO DE CONDUITE (1933) and as the Fool in FEYDER's LA KERMESSE HÉROÏQUE (1935). His temperamental behaviour under Vigo's direction led to several crises and more than once Henri STORCK had to conduct peace negotiations.

Delphin gassed himself in the apartment he had furnished to his own scale, leaving as a suicide note one of Pascal's *Pensées*: '*Tout le malheur des hommes vient de ne pas savoir se tenir au repos dans leur chambre.*'

**DEL RIO,** DOLORES (1905– ), Mexican actress, real name Dolores Asúnsolo Martinez, was discovered by the American director Edwin Carewe, in whose *Joanna* (1925) she made her début. A classically beautiful, if limited, actress, she achieved fame in Raoul WALSH's *What Price Glory?* (1926). Her other Hollywood films include *The Loves of Carmen* (1927), *Resurrection* (1928), *Flying Down to Rio* (1933). Working for the Mexican director Emilio FERNÁNDEZ, she revealed a profounder style in several films, including *María Candelaria* (1943).

**DE LUXE COLOR.** The screen credit 'Color by De Luxe' identifies a film photographed in EASTMAN COLOR and processed by De Luxe Laboratories of New York, a subsidiary of TWENTIETH CENTURY-FOX. The stock is identical with Eastman Color.

**DEMENY,** GEORGES (1850–1917), French inventor who in 1892, following up the laboratory experiments of E. J. MAREY, introduced the Phonoscope. This projected animated drawings, including brief close-ups of faces articulating words which could be lip-read. In 1895 Demeny developed an improved version of Marey's Chronophotograph which virtually duplicated LUMIÈRE's Cinématographe.

**DEMILLE,** CECIL B. (1881–1959), US producer-director whose parents were professional actors. He wrote plays, sometimes in collaboration with his brother William, acted, and

Delphin in *La Kermesse héroïque* (Jacques Feyder, 1935)

worked in opera, before forming the Jesse Lasky Feature Play Company jointly with Jesse LASKY, Samuel Goldfish (later GOLDWYN), and Arthur FREED. His first film as director was the very successful *The Squaw Man* (1913); he soon broke away to become an independent producer and director, usually releasing through PARAMOUNT. In 1915 he created in CARMEN the first of the lavish spectacles that were to become synonymous with his name. The DeMille formula was completed when the first of many bathtub scenes was plumbed into *Old Wives for New* (1923) 'to help tell the story'. The prize-winning entry in a newspaper's film idea competition became *The Ten Commandments* (1923), his best-known film which he remade more than thirty years later.

From 1932 DeMille worked under contract to Paramount. *The Plainsman* (1937) and *Union Pacific* (1939) demonstrated that he saw the Western as a variation of his historical spectacles. The Bible was his favourite source material. *Samson and Delilah* (1949) starred Victor MATURE ('the essence of maleness') and Hedy LAMARR; and DeMille stated modestly of the climactic destruction of the temple: 'Credit is due

to the Book of Judges, not to me.' *The Greatest Show on Earth* (1952) was the only contemporary subject in the last twenty years of his career.

During the thirties and forties DeMille's rightwing political views brought him into frequent conflict with trade unions to which he was totally opposed. His anti-union activities effectively debarred him from radio and television work, but he continued to be a major figure in Hollywood and often played cameo roles in Paramount films. His most interesting appearance was probably in SUNSET BOULEVARD (1950) in which he played the veteran director visited by Gloria SWANSON, whose real career had in fact been established by working with DeMille in 1919–21.

Although DeMille's films may be dismissed for naïvety of characterization and plot, they contain scenes of truly epic quality such as the building of the pyramids in *The Ten Commandments* (1956). The quintessential Hollywood showman, he displayed a skill in creating spectacular effects and in handling crowds that has not been matched.

**DEMY,** JACQUES (1931–   ), French director, married to Agnès VARDA. After directing three short films in the fifties, he made a considerable impression with his first feature, LOLA (1961). This had been planned as a musical, but backing for the more expensive project was not available until, after the success of *La Baie des Anges* (1963), a light-hearted romance starring Jeanne MOREAU, he made LES PARAPLUIES DE CHERBOURG (1964) which, using a plot reminiscent of PAGNOL's MARIUS trilogy (1931–6), created a fairy-tale romance where even the most prosaic exchanges were sung to LEGRAND's music. It was very successful, but Demy's attempt to confirm his standing as a director of musicals with *Les Demoiselles de Rochefort* (1966) was disappointing in spite of a strong cast which included Catherine DENEUVE, Françoise DORLÉAC, and Gene KELLY. A continuation of the story of *Lola*, *Model Shop* (1968), made in the US and with Anouk AIMÉE in the lead was, however, much admired. Two outright fairy-tales, *Peau d'âne* (*The Magic Donkey*, 1970) and *The Pied Piper* (1971), were an uneasy blend of sophistication and whimsy. Demy's unashamed preference for light-hearted nostalgia is in contrast to the preoccupations of his contemporaries. His work is totally apolitical, but he shares with them a love and knowledge of cinema which shows in his work, in references or tributes to earlier films (*Lola* is dedicated to Max OPHULS), and his grasp of the techniques of film-making is entirely authoritative.

**DENEUVE, CATHERINE** (1943–   ), French actress, real name Dorléac, sister of Françoise DORLÉAC. Her somewhat conventional beauty has not been allowed to overshadow her considerable and versatile acting powers, which have been admired by such important directors as POLAŃSKI (REPULSION, 1965), BUÑUEL (*Belle de Jour*, 1966; *Tristaña*, 1970), and TRUFFAUT (*La Sirène du Mississippi*, 1969).

**DENHAM,** British film studios, opened in 1936, when KORDA made THINGS TO COME, and closed in 1953 after DISNEY had completed ROBIN HOOD. In the intervening years over 150 films were produced, among them DICKINSON's GASLIGHT (1940), *The Life and Death of Colonel Blimp* (Michael POWELL, 1943), OLIVIER's HENRY V (1944) and HAMLET (1948), and REED's ODD MAN OUT (1947). The RANK ORGANISATION sold the 160-acre studio, which had been the focus of British film aspirations (and had seen the production of Britain's first TECHNICOLOR film), in order to consolidate its production activities at PINEWOOD.

**DENMARK.** In 1903 Peter Elfet, court photographer, made Denmark's first film, *Henrettelsen* (*The Execution*); the following year the first permanent cinema, Kosmorama, was opened. In 1906 Ole Olesen formed Nordisk Film (now the world's oldest production company) and his films, directed by Viggo Larsen, competed in world markets. Olesen set up several branches abroad, including Berlin, London, and the US, where his Great Northern Film Company joined the resistance to the MOTION PICTURE PATENTS COMPANY. *Løvejagten* (*Lion Hunt*, 1907) was an early hit. In 1909 Nordisk's first studio was built and the same year Biorama and Fotorama were established, the latter producing *Heksen og Cyklisten* (*The Witch and the Cyclist*), a beautifully constructed film using trick photography. Fotorama also produced *Den hvide Slavehandel* (*The White Slave Trade*, 1910) which was such a success that Nordisk released an identical film four months later, and which led to an international vogue for films on similar subjects. Like *Afgrunden* (*The Abyss*, 1910), starring Asta NIELSEN and directed by Urban Gad, it exceeded the currently usual length of 200 metres. So did Nordisk's *Atlantis* (August Blom, 1913) and a half-length version was insisted on for US distribution. It was an extraordinarily advanced film about a sinking liner starring Olaf Fønss who was to play the title role in the German HOMUNCULUS (1916).

Nordisk remained the most prolific Danish company throughout the war, its position partly maintained by its strong distribution system. It failed, however, to adapt to the new wartime audience, and in 1916 Carl DREYER was engaged to advise on policy. He suggested films from literary sources and A. W. Sandberg, noted for his popular success *Klovnen* (*The Clown*, 1917) starring Valdemar Psilander, filmed several DICKENS novels. One exceptional Nordisk film was August Blom's *Verldens Undergang* (*The End of the World*, 1916). Nordisk failed to exploit the talent of Benjamin CHRISTENSEN, whose *Det hemmelighedsfulde X* (*The Mysterious X*, 1913) and *Haevnens nat* (*The Night of Vengeance*, 1915) displayed new camera angles and editing techniques; Christensen did most of his important work abroad.

Danish films of the twenties were generally unimaginative. Lau Lauritzen's Long and Short films (Fyrtanet og Bivognen) anticipating LAUREL AND HARDY, Storm Petersen's animation films, and the work of Dreyer were of higher quality, although Dreyer, like Christensen, was already doing his most important work abroad.

Denmark's first full-length sound film was George Schneevoigt's *Eskimo* (1930). Schneevoigt followed this with literary films such as *Hotel Paradis* (1931) then turned to light comedy. Poul Henningsen's critical film about contemporary Denmark, *Danmarksfilm* (1935), was a forerunner of the documentaries of the forties and was cited by Theodore Christensen and Karl Roos in their book *Film* (1936) as the kind of film, technically and thematically, Danish film-makers should be making. Benjamin Christensen returned and made *Skilsmissens Børn* (*Children of Divorce*, 1939).

The hard reality of occupation produced a flourishing documentary movement. Ministeriernes Filmudvalg (The Film Committee of the Departments of State) was set up in 1941 as a production unit headed by Mogens Skot-Hansen. Documentaries were made by Karl Roos, his brother Jorgen Roos, Theodore Christensen, Astrid and Bjarne Henning-Jensen, Ole Palsbo, Dreyer, and others. Feature films made during the war include Dreyer's VREDENS DAG (*Day of Wrath*, 1943), Johan Jacobsen's *Otte Akkorder* (*Eight Chords*, 1944), and French-inspired gangster films started by *Afsporet* (*Derailed*, 1942), co-directed by Lau Lauritzen Jr and Bodil Ipsen; Lauritzen and Alice O'Frederick's *Affaeren Birthe* (*The Affair of Birth*, 1945) showed an actual child-birth. Also in 1945 came several resistance films such as J. Jacobsen's *Den Usynlige Haer* (*The Invisible Army*), Lauritzen and Mrs Ipsen's *De røde Enge* (*The Red Meadows*), and T. Christensen and K. Roos's *Detgaelder din Frihed* (*Your Freedom is at Stake*), a COMPILATION of film shot by Resistance workers. The bitterest post-war film was Palsbo's *Ta'hvad du vilha* (*Take What You Want*, 1947).

Since then Danish cinema has tended to retreat from serious contemporary issues into mediocre comedy, heavy moralizing, or glamorous escapism. More outstanding films include Henning-Jensen's *Hvor Bjergenesejler* (*Where Mountains Float*) which won the documentary prize at Venice in 1955, the year Dreyer was awarded the Golden Bear at BERLIN for ORDET (*The Word*); Eric Balling's *Kispus* (*Tricks*, 1956) was recognized at Berlin for its inventive use of colour. Henning CARLSEN's *Sult* (*Hunger*, 1966) starred Per Oscarsson and, like his *Klabauten mander* (*We Are All Demons*, 1969) was a Scandinavian co-production. Peter BROOK's *King Lear* (1970), was a British/Danish co-production with a Danish state subsidy.

Denmark's film organization is notable. Since 1922 a licence has been required to open a cinema. The licensee, who may be an individual, an organization, a municipal authority, or a production company, may not hold more than one cinema. He is appointed by the Secretary of Justice on the recommendation of the Film Council, whose members include two representatives of cinema licensees and five members elected by cultural organizations. It has become customary to appoint as managers to municipal cinemas distinguished former film workers such as Asta Nielsen and Carl Dreyer. The Film Council also manages Statens Filmfond (the Film Fund) and Statens Filmcentral. The former's revenue derives from a tax on cinema licences and takings emulating that instituted in Sweden in 1963 (see SVENSKA FILMINSTITUTET). It subsidizes Dansk Kulturfilm, a production company formed in 1932 to make educational films, feature films with an educative slant, and feature films for children. It is run by an assembly of representatives of state educational administration and educational and cultural organizations. The Fund also finances Ministeriernes Filmudvalg, the Statens Filmcentral (in part state subsidized) established in 1938 to handle distribution for Dansk Kulturfilm and Ministeriernes Filmudvalg, and the national ARCHIVE, Dansk Filmmuseum, founded in 1941. A national film school (Danske Filmskole) was established in 1966.

Despite such well-planned organization, Danish cinema has not maintained an output significantly superior in quality to that in countries where low artistic standards have been attributed to commercial domination. It has, however, because of moderate production costs and large home audiences, been able to support a constantly active industry. Film CENSORSHIP was abolished in 1969, and with the relaxation of censorship regulations in many other European countries Denmark has maintained a profitable output of sex films for domestic and overseas distribution.

**DEPTH OF FIELD,** the range of distances from the camera lens within which a subject remains in acceptably sharp focus. Depth of field is increased by moving the subject further from the lens or by using a wider-angle lens (either of which makes the subject appear smaller), or by using a smaller lens aperture (which requires more light or a more sensitive film stock). For 35mm filming, depth of field is limited and the big screen demands critical sharpness; these factors force the camera and actors to move within precise marks on the studio floor, and make the focus-puller an indispensable member of the camera crew. For small-format films shown on small screens, depth of field is much greater; 8mm photographers can usually ignore it. (See CAMERA.)

**DEPTH OF FOCUS,** the range of distances behind the camera lens within which the image of a given subject remains in acceptably sharp focus. The extent of this range is determined by the type of lens in use. It should not be confused with DEPTH OF FIELD. (See CAMERA.)

**DEREN,** MAYA (1908–61), US director, dancer, and author who emigrated from Russia in

1927 and became a seminal figure in the early American UNDERGROUND film. *Meshes of the Afternoon* (1943), made in collaboration with her husband Alexander Hammid, and *At Land* (1944), in both of which she also acted, are romantic and surrealist fantasies of the subjective imagination. In her later films, beginning with *A Study in Choreography for the Camera* (1945), while retaining a romantic emphasis, Deren experimented with the formal properties of the medium and its capacity to manipulate space and time. *Meditation on Violence* (1948) transforms the movements of a boxer into a dance.

Her last completed film *The Very Eye of Night* (1959) takes choreographed dance as its point of departure and endows it with supernatural qualities of lightness and grace. In personally arranging the distribution and exhibition of her films she advanced the commercial independence that now underpins the underground film movement, and through her Creative Film Foundation she provided early financial support for some of its most important members.

**DERNIER MILLIARDAIRE, Le,** France, 1934. 1½hr. *Dir, scr* René Clair; *prod* Pathé Natan; *ph* Rudolph Maté; *des* Lucien Aguettand; *mus* Maurice Jaubert; *cast* Max Dearly (Banco), Renée Saint-Cyr (Princess Isabelle), Marthe Mellot (the Queen).

The liberal sentiments of A NOUS LA LIBERTÉ (1931) had injured CLAIR's standing with TOBIS, his German producers, and the openly anti-Fascist satire of *Le Dernier Milliardaire* led to their refusal of the project. Clair found French backing, but the film although often very funny lacks the grace and rhythmic assurance of his earlier comedies. It was howled down by right-wing demonstrators at the first showing and the hostility it brought him caused Clair's first departure to work outside France.

**DE ROBERTIS,** FRANCESCO (1902–59), Italian director who, after a naval career, began directing government-sponsored films in 1940. *Mine in vista* (1940) and *Uomini sul fondo* (1941) were both naval stories, the second shot entirely on board a submarine. In his use of non-actors and documentary techniques he crucially influenced ROSSELLINI (who worked as an assistant on *Uomini sul fondo*) and other adherents of NEO-REALISM. Rossellini's *La nave bianca* (1941), about a hospital ship, was commissioned, co-scripted, and supervised by De Robertis. After the war he wrote and directed occasional fiction features including *Gli amanti di Ravello* (1950).

**DE ROCHEMONT,** LOUIS (1899–    ), US producer who in 1917–23 was in the US Navy as a communications expert and made a series of recruiting films. In 1923 he became an associate editor on W. Randolph HEARST's International Newsreel, then in 1927 became European editor for Pathé Newsreel. In 1928–34 he was short-subject editor for Fox's Movietone News, and in 1934 made two series of shorts, *The Adventures of a Newsreel Cameraman*, and *The Magic Carpets of Movietone*. In 1934, with Roy Larsen of Time Inc, De Rochemont conceived a new kind of monthly news magazine, THE MARCH OF TIME. The series ran until 1951, with De Rochemont producing the regular issues until 1943, as well as many noted war-time documentaries. In 1944 he became a producer at TWENTIETH CENTURY-FOX, and brought his semi-documentary style to such features as *The House on 92nd Street* (1945), based on a story of FBI infiltration of a US-based Nazi organization, and *Boomerang* (KAZAN, 1947), based on a real murder case.

In 1947, he formed an independent production and distribution company, Louis De Rochemont Associates, and in 1948–52 produced the documentary series *The Earth and Its Peoples*. Their first feature film was *Lost Boundaries* (1949), about a negro doctor who passed for white in a small New England town, and was discovered after twenty years' service to the community, again based on fact. In 1955 De Rochemont produced *Cinerama Holiday*, the second CINERAMA film and in 1958 *Windjammer*, the only film made in the Cinemiracle process. His other productions include *The Fighting Lady* (1944), *13 Rue Madeleine* (1947), *The Whistle at Eaton Falls* (1951), *Martin Luther* (1953), *The Roman Spring of Mrs Stone* (1961).

**DE SANTIS,** GIUSEPPE (1917–    ), Italian director, studied for some time at the CENTRO SPERIMENTALE before writing film criticism for the Italian review CINEMA, which was influential in the articulation of the notion of NEO-REALISM. In 1942 De Santis collaborated on the script of VISCONTI's OSSESSIONE, and then on ROSSELLINI's *Desiderio* (1946, completed by PAGLIERO), by which time the neo-realist movement was firmly established. In the following year De Santis directed his own first film, CACCIA TRAGICA, whose tendencies towards sentimentality were reinforced by RISO AMARO (*Bitter Rice*, 1949), which was chiefly notable for the presence of Silvano MANGANO and the impact it made abroad. In 1950 he directed *Non c'è pace tra gli ulivi*, which was followed by *Roma, ore 11* (1952) and *Una strada lunga un anno* (1958); only *Roma, ore 11* shows any distinction, in so far as its dramatic flair is free from political didacticism.

**DESERTO ROSSO, Il** (*The Red Desert*), France/Italy, 1964. Technicolor/Eastman Color;

2hr. *Dir* Michelangelo Antonioni; *prod* Films Duemila (Rome)/Francoriz (Paris); *scr* Antonioni, Tonino Guerra; *ph* Carlo Di Palma; *des* Piero Poletto; *mus* Giovanni Fusco; *cast* Monica Vitti (Giuliana), Richard Harris (Corrado), Carlo Chionetti (Ugo), Xenia Valderi (Linda), Rita Renoir (Emilia), Aldo Grotti (Max).

Giuliana, married to an engineer, Ugo, and living in a world of industrial landscapes and dominant machinery, is in a state of neurotic crisis. ANTONIONI appears to suggest that she is in fact the only character struggling for warm human individuality in face of the remorseless uniformity of the machine age. The role demanded from Monica VITTI a degree of professional technique she could not command, and Richard HARRIS was unable to give adequate support. This was Antonioni's first colour film, and he assumed at once a total control: beautiful subdued reds and greens dominate the shots of the all-important landscape, and bright colours are reserved for the moments of fantasy and hope for Giuliana. Colour is the dominant element of the film, and it exists almost as a beautiful visual abstraction.

**DE SETA,** VITTORIO (1923–    ), Italian director, studied architecture at Rome University, and started making documentary films after working as scriptwriter and assistant director for LE CHANOIS in *Village magique* (1954). His colour documentaries, shot chiefly in Sicily and Sardinia, gained him critical recognition and international awards; of particular merit were *Lu tempu di li piscispata* (1954), *Isole di fuoco* (1955), and *Pescherecci* (1959). The coherence and integrity of these films was largely facilitated by De Seta's complete control over them, producing, directing, writing, photographing, and editing all the material. De Seta's first feature, BANDITI A ORGOSOLO (1961), co-scripted with his wife Vera Gherarducci, bears the same stamp of intellectual honesty and technical proficiency. The film won prizes both in Italy and abroad, but the critics had to wait five years for his next film, *Un uomo a meta* (1966) which marks a new direction in De Seta's career: instead of the analysis of social character that was at the heart of the documentaries and *Banditi a Orgosolo*, there is a concern for the past and the mistakes of the past, which lead to the anguish of modern living.

**DE SICA,** VITTORIO (1901–74), Italian director and actor, trained as an accountant and made several appearances in amateur dramatics, including performances for his regimental dramatic company during his military service. In 1922 he began work as a stage-hand, and from 1923 he acted with several professional companies; in 1925 he joined that of Luigi Almirante, with whom he had his first great success two years later, in the Za-Bum revues.

Although De Sica's first film part had been in *L'affare Clémenceau* (1922), it was another ten years before he established himself as a film actor, in CAMERINI's *Gli uomini che mascalzoni* (1932) which popularized the song 'Le Chaland qui passe' (see also L'ATALANTE). For the next ten years De Sica was extremely successful as an actor, appearing in almost forty films, and leading his own theatre company from 1935.

Dissatisfaction with Carmine Gallone's direction of him in *Manon Lescaut* (1939) led De Sica to film direction, and in 1940 he co-directed and acted in a screen version of an earlier stage success, *Rose Scarlette*. The success of this sentimental drama enabled De Sica to direct three more films in the next eighteen months, including *Teresa Venerdi* (1941), with Anna MAGNANI. But it was not until *I bambini ci guardano* (*The Children Are Watching Us*, 1942) that De Sica gave proof of his dramatic (as opposed to comic) power; it was also his first important collaboration with the scriptwriter Cesare ZAVATTINI (who had written Camerini's *Daro un milione*, 1935, in which De Sica acted). Zavattini had worked uncredited on the script of *Teresa Venerdi*; but in De Sica's subsequent films, Zavattini's contribution was virtually as important as that of De Sica himself. Zavattini's political awareness crystallized De Sica's humane psychological understanding into a specific social context, that of occupied and post-war Italy.

*I bambini ci guardano*, showing the break-down of a middle-class marriage through a child's eyes, did not bring financial success, but De Sica and Zavattini were able to work on a project for the Centro Catolico Cinematografico, *La porta del cielo*. Courageously shot in 1944, during the German occupation, and evincing De Sica's maturing eye for authentic observation and detail, the film met with the Vatican's disapproval, and it was not shown until 1948, in Paris. By this time, De Sica had established an international reputation, as SCIUSCIÀ (*Shoeshine*, 1946) had, along with ROSSELLINI's ROMA, CITTÀ APERTA (1945), been hailed as the beginning of a new cinematic style, NEO-REALISM. It was also the first film of De Sica's cinematic maturity, and like neo-realism itself, was prompted by the social realities of post-war Italy, whose material poverty intruded upon the process of film-making, involuntarily adding to the films' neo-realist character.

De Sica's next film, LADRI DI BICICLETTE (*Bicycle Thieves*, 1948), is his best known work. No Italian producer would finance it, and David O. SELZNICK's offer to back it bore one condition that De Sica refused: a star actor such as Cary

GRANT. De Sica eventually raised the money himself, as he has often done since, earning sufficient money from his acting performances to continue directing films; in the years 1950–60, he acted in more than fifty films, from comedies to Rossellini's *Il generale della rovere* (1959). *Ladri di biciclette*, despite its critical recognition, brought political pressure upon De Sica and Zavattini, because its denunciation of social conditions was thought to be against the interests of the Italian nation; the Italian Home Office had already refused to send *Sciuscià* to the CANNES Festival in 1946, on grounds of the film's 'immorality'. The political pressures naturally discouraged producers from financing neo-realist films, and De Sica's next two productions, MIRACOLO A MILANO (1951) and UMBERTO D (1952) were financed largely by De Sica himself, and also marked the end of his most creative directing. Both films continue De Sica's examination of the problematic relationship between the individual and his social environment; in later years such frankness was impossible, both because of political conditions, and because Hollywood's capitalization upon the Italian film industry sapped even De Sica's strength of purpose. He continued to work with Zavattini, and his composer, Alessandro Cicognini, but their films evince an increasing elegant glossiness and a growth in the sentimentality which slightly mars even his best work. *Stazione termini* (1953) was partly financed by Selznick, and starred Jennifer JONES and Montgomery CLIFT; but the American version was heavily cut, re-edited (without De Sica's permission), and released, as *Indiscretion of an American Wife*. *Il Tetto* (1956), drawn from the problems of housing shortage, describes how a group of friends build a bungalow for a young couple, taking advantage of the regulation that a new house could not be officially torn down if the roof was complete at dawn. A slight but charming piece, it was De Sica's last film in the neo-realist manner. In 1960 he won an OSCAR for *La Ciociara* (*Two Women*), starring Sophia LOREN.

In 1959 De Sica acted in a British television production, *The Four Just Men*, with Jack HAWKINS, partly, he said, to get away from the comedy roles he always played in Italian productions. He has since acted in several English-language films, including ASQUITH's *The Millionairess* (1960). Since he abandoned the controversial social issues of his neo-realist work, De Sica has had less difficulty in finding producers for his films. These include a film adaptation of a play by Sartre, *I sequestrati di Altona* (*The Condemned of Altona*, 1962), and the amusing episodes in *Ieri, oggi, domani* (*Yesterday, Today, To-morrow*) also in 1963, which won another Oscar. In 1964 he filmed an effective adaptation

of Eduardo di Filippo's *Filumena Marturano*, starring Sophia Loren and Marcello MASTROIANNI, under the title *Matrimonio all' Italiana* (*Marriage, Italian Style*). This was followed by *Un mondo nuovo* (*A New World*) and *Caccia alla volpe* (*After the Fox*) in 1966, and similar romantic pieces in recent years.

*Il giardino dei Finzi-contini* (1970) represented a return to social and political themes, the Nazi treatment of Italian Jews. Visual and aural glossiness and a less than perceptive depiction of the pre-war world mar the film's conviction. De Sica will be remembered for those films in which he and Zavattini fused social, psychological, and political insights in their period of artistic creativity.

**DESIGN** see ART DIRECTION

**DESTINY OF A MAN** see SUDBA CHELOVEKA

**DESTRY RIDES AGAIN,** US, 1939. 1½ hr. *Dir* George Marshall; *prod* Joe Pasternak for Universal; *scr* Felix Jackson, Henry Mayers, Gertrude Purcell, from the novel by Max Brand; *ph* Hal Mohr; *ed* Milton Carruth; *des* Jack Otterson; *mus* Frank Skinner; *cast* James Stewart (Tom Destry), Marlene Dietrich (Frenchy), Charles Winniger (Wash Dimsdale), Brian Donlevy (Kent), Una Merkel (Lilybelle Callahan), Mischa Auer (Boris Callahan).

While sacrificing nothing of the drama and action traditional in the Western, *Destry Rides Again* introduced a new style with its debunking of the genre and its snappy dialogue. James STEWART's engaging performance wittily parodied the typical Western hero, and Marlene DIETRICH's singing (including the famous 'The Boys in the Back Room'), and even more her fighting, created something of a sensation.

UNIVERSAL made two other films from Max Brand's book. The first, directed by Ben Stoloff in 1932, marked a come-back by Tom MIX. ZaSu PITTS and Andy DEVINE had the main character roles. *Destry* (1954) was designed as a vehicle for Audie Murphy; George MARSHALL again directed, but unsurprisingly failed to re-create the impact of his own classic. Nevertheless, it was among the best of the many Westerns Audie Murphy made for Universal.

**DEUXIÈME SOUFFLE, Le** (*Second Breath*), France, 1966. 2½ hr. *Dir* Jean-Pierre Melville; *prod* Les Productions Montaigne; *scr* Melville, from the novel by José Giovanni; *ph* Marcel Combes; *cast* Lino Ventura (Gu Minda), Paul Meurisse (Inspector Blot), Raymond Pellegrin (Paul Ricci), Christine Fabrega (Manouche).

Gu, a gangster of declining skill and reputation, breaks jail, joins a gang who carry out a robbery, and is trapped by the police into betraying his friends and his honour. Beneath its surface realism, particularly in the planning and execution of the robbery, the film examines comradeship and betrayal with MELVILLE's typical black wit and prodigality of visual invention.

*DEUX OU TROIS CHOSES QUE JE SAIS D'ELLE* (*Two or Three Things I Know About Her*), France, 1966. Techniscope; 1½hr; Eastman Color. *Dir, scr* Jean-Luc Godard; *prod* Anouchka Films/Argos-Films/Les Films du Carrosse/Parc Film; *ph* Raoul Coutard; *ed* Françoise Collin; *mus* Beethoven; *cast* Marina Vlady (Juliette Janson), Anny Duperey (Marianne), Roger Montsoret (Robert Janson), Jean Narboni (Roger), Raoul Lévy (John Bogus).

Juliette Janson, who with her husband and young child has been rehoused in one of the high-rise 'grands ensembles' recently built in the suburbs of Paris, spends one day each week in the city centre where she prostitutes herself to improve her family's standard of living. But the 'elle' of the title refers not to Juliette but to Paris. The film was inspired by an inquiry in *Le Nouvel Observateur* into casual prostitution in the new suburban housing complexes. This linked up with one of GODARD's pet theories, that in order to live in modern society one is forced to prostitute oneself in some way, as for example doing an unsatisfying job simply for the money. The story of the film is subordinate to the sociological analysis, but at the same time the very process of film-making is questioned, with Godard's voice on the soundtrack asking why he has chosen these particular images and debating various alternatives.

**DEVINE**, ANDY (1905– ), US character actor of rotund build and croakily high-pitched voice. He began his film career in 1926 as an extra and became one of the most familiar of featured players, appearing in countless films and working for practically every major Hollywood studio, sometimes in major productions like John FORD's STAGECOACH (1939) or John HUSTON's THE RED BADGE OF COURAGE (1951), but mostly in 'B' pictures as the hero's comic sidekick. Westerns were his particular speciality, but especially in his forties heyday with UNIVERSAL (often partnering Richard Arlen) he was equally to be found in boxing, mining, oilfield, and lumberjack dramas.

**DE WILDE**, BRANDON (1942–72), US actor who deservedly made a great impact on the public with his restrained performance as the bespectacled John Henry in THE MEMBER OF THE WEDDING (1953), a role which he had also played on the stage. He was again impressive as the devotion-filled boy in SHANE (1953). Star billing quickly followed, but apart from HUD (1963) his later performances failed to sustain the éclat of his initial appearances.

*DIABLE AU CORPS, Le,* France, 1947. 1¾hr. *Dir* Claude Autant-Lara; *prod* Transcontinental Films; *scr* Jean Aurenche, Pierre Bost, from the novel by Raymond Radiguet; *ph* Michel Kelber; *des* Max Douy; *mus* René Cloërec; *cast* Micheline Presle (Marthe Grangier), Gérard Philipe (François Jaubert), Jean Debucourt (Jaubert), Denise Grey (Mme Grangier), Jean Varas (Jacques).

The film's subject, an adulterous affair between a seventeen-year-old student and an older woman whose husband is serving at the Front, was less startling to contemporary audiences than AUTANT-LARA's treatment which, following Radiguet's own attitude in the original novel, was tender, humorous, and totally without condemnation. The love scenes, explicit for the time, are still striking for their truthful depiction of physical passion. The film's strength owes much to the First World War setting and the sense it conveys of life continuing in spite of distant carnage. The acting, too, is impressive, in particular Gérard PHILIPE's performance as the capricious boy bewildered by his own emotions.

**DIAMOND**, I. A. L. (1920– ), US scriptwriter whose family emigrated to America from Romania in 1929. His first name was then Itek, which was reportedly changed to Isadore during schooldays; he added the initials A.L. when he began writing at COLUMBIA. Diamond worked as a contract writer for various studios, including METRO-GOLDWYN-MAYER and PARAMOUNT; his earlier films include *Murder in the Blue Room* (1944), *Never Say Goodbye* (1946), *Let's Make it Legal* (1951). In 1954 he wrote some satirical sketches for a Hollywood writers' dinner, which was attended by Billy WILDER, and this led to their successful collaboration on films displaying a notably sharp and irreverent wit. Together they wrote *Love in the Afternoon* (1957), SOME LIKE IT HOT (1959), and *Avanti!* (1972). On some of their later films, including THE APARTMENT (1960), *One, Two, Three* (1961), *Irma La Douce* (1963), *The Private Life of Sherlock Holmes* (1970), Diamond was also co-producer.

*DIARY OF A CHAMBERMAID* (Buñuel) see JOURNAL D'UNE FEMME DE CHAMBRE, LE

*DIARY OF A COUNTRY PRIEST* see JOURNAL D'UN CURÉ DE CAMPAGNE

**DICKENS**, CHARLES (1812–70), English novelist. His novels have been a popular source of film plots from the early days of the cinema. The first seems to have been *Nicholas Nickleby* (1903), made in America and consisting of a single scene set in Dotheboys Hall. About 1915 the Danish director A. W. Sandberg became something of a specialist in filming Dickens. There have been over seventy films, based on some seventeen different novels, including *Barnaby Rudge* (1915) starring Chrissie White and *Great Expectations* (1917) starring Jack Pickford. A 1922 version of *Oliver Twist* starred Jackie COOGAN as Oliver and Lon CHANEY as Fagin, and there have been ten films of *A Christmas Carol*, including a musical version, *Scrooge* (1970) with Albert FINNEY in the title role. *The Only Way* (1925) was the first version of the stage play of *A Tale of Two Cities* and starred Sir John Martin Harvey as Sydney Carton, a part which was subsequently played by Ronald COLMAN in 1935 and Dirk BOGARDE in 1958. DAVID COPPERFIELD (1934) directed by George CUKOR, and David LEAN's GREAT EXPECTATIONS (1946) and *Oliver Twist* (1948) are the Dickens films most generally admired for fidelity to their originals (Lean called Dickens 'the perfect screenwriter'); but the most successful adaptations have probably been the various BBC television serials, which are in a form well suited to novels originally published in parts, and at a length which permits time to do justice to Dickens's rich and varied characterizations. Lionel Bart's stage musical *Oliver!* was filmed by Carol REED in 1968 with great popular success.

**DICKINSON, THOROLD** (1903–    ), British director, went to Paris in 1925 to work as interpreter on George PEARSON's *Mr Preedy and the Countess*. He soon became a competent picture- and sound editor. He directed his first film, *The High Command*, in 1936, then went to Spain and with Sidney Cole made *Spanish ABC* (1938) about the Civil War.

*The Arsenal Stadium Mystery* (1939) was followed by GASLIGHT (1940). *The Next of Kin* (1941), an anti-'careless talk' military training film for the War Office, was considered so useful that it was put on general release by the Ministry of Information. In 1942 he organized the new Army Kinematograph Service's production programme and supervised the making of seventeen training films. *Men of Two Worlds* (1946) was a semi-documentary collaboration on an African subject between the Ministry of Information and the Colonial Office. In 1948 he made THE QUEEN OF SPADES, a highly atmospheric adaptation of Pushkin's story. *Secret People* (1951) presaged

*The Queen of Spades* (Thorold Dickinson, 1948)

the urban violence which was to become routine among revolutionary activists; its filming was documented by Lindsay ANDERSON in his book *Making a film: the story of 'Secret People'* (London, 1952). *Hill 24 Doesn't Answer* (1955), made in Israel, was a passionate account of an incident in the Arab-Israeli war of 1948.

In 1956–60 Dickinson headed the Film Section of the United Nations Office of Public Information, which under his aegis produced such films as *Out* (1956), the controversial *Blue Vanguard* (1957) about the UN action in the Gaza Strip after the Anglo-French landings at Suez in 1956, and *Power Among Men* (1958). In 1960 he returned to England to take up a newly-created university post in film studies and in 1967 became Britain's first Professor of Film, retiring in 1971.

**DICKSON,** W. K. L. (1860–1935), British inventor who emigrated to the US and in 1882 sought employment with EDISON who engaged him for electrical research and experiment in his laboratory. Within five years Dickson had become Edison's laboratory chief, less concerned with electricity than with photography, notably working on the development of the KINETO-GRAPH and Kinetoscope (1888–92). As a result of this work, he became the author of the first textbook on cinematography, *History of the kinetograph, kinetoscope and kinetophonograph,* which he wrote with his sister Antonia in 1895. *The Edison motion picture myth* by Gordon Hendricks (Berkeley, 1961) explains the important contribution made by Dickson to the innovations usually attributed solely to Edison.

**DIETERLE, WILLIAM,** originally Wilhelm (1893–1972), German director and actor, acted with REINHARDT. He directed and starred in *Die Menschen am Wege* (*Man by the Roadside,* 1923), from a Tolstoy story, with Marlene DIE-TRICH, and acted in DAS WACHSFIGURENCABIN-ETT (*Waxworks,* 1924). He went to Hollywood in 1929 to direct German-language versions of American films, later graduating to English ones. He collaborated with Reinhardt on A MIDSUM-MER NIGHT'S DREAM (1935). His *Satan Met a Lady* (1936) was a lame version of Dashiell HAMMETT'S THE MALTESE FALCON. The biographical films he directed for WARNER BROS during the late thirties, including *The Story of Louis Pasteur* (1936) and *The Life of Emile Zola* (1937), were the best of his prolific Hollywood career: *Magic Fire* (1955), based on Wagner's life, carried less conviction. In 1958 he returned to Europe, working in the theatre as well as occasionally directing films.

**DIETRICH, MARLENE** (1902–  ), German-born actress, real name Marie Magdelene von Losch, whose long career in films began obscurely in about 1922. Although she has herself expressed doubt as to whether she appeared in some films attributed to her—PABST'S DIE FREUDLOSE GASSE (*Joyless Street,* 1925), for instance—she was well enough known by 1928 to be considered for the lead in that director's DIE BÜCHSE DER PANDORA (*Pandora's Box*). In 1930 Josef von STERNBERG cast her as the fatal Lola-Lola in DER BLAUE ENGEL (*The Blue Angel*); Emil JANNINGS was the nominal star, but she was so successful that the film continues to be identified with her. At once signed on by PARAMOUNT, and drastically remodelled and refined, she embarked on a series of films in which Sternberg transformed her into an aloof, talking mask, beautiful and perverse, and suggestive of all manner of erotic sophistications. MOROCCO (1930), DISHONORED (1931), SHANGHAI EXPRESS, *Blonde Venus* (both 1932), THE SCARLET EMPRESS (1934), and *The Devil is a Woman* (1935) were all in their time attacked by the critics, but have gradually gained esteem. The ending of their partnership saw a decline in Sternberg's career, but Dietrich remained a popular star. Most of her films attempted to build on the strong element of sexuality and fatal love that had characterized her roles for Sternberg, but *Angel* (Ernst LUBITSCH, 1937) and DESTRY RIDES AGAIN (George MARSHALL, 1939) gave her the opportunity to display both sophisticated wit and her notably beautiful legs. During the war she concentrated on fund-raising appearances and entertaining servicemen and her film appearances since then have been intermittent. They include leading roles in *Martin Roumagnac* (1946), made in France, in which she appeared opposite Jean GABIN, Billy WILDER'S *A Foreign Affair* (1948), and Fritz LANG'S *Rancho Notorious* (1952), as well as a number of cameo roles. Since the early fifties she has enjoyed an outstanding success in international cabaret to which she brings a characteristic aura of ageless glamour, sleek sophistication, and worldly charm.

**DIFFUSER,** a sheet of cotton or gauze placed over a light source to soften or diffuse the light falling on the scene to be photographed. Early silent film studios, built with glass roofs to admit daylight, had huge diffusers which could be pulled across the glass on rope rigging to control bright sunlight. Modern diffusers, placed over individual lights to control intensity and remove hard shadows, are called wires, gauzes, etc, depending on the material used.

**DIFFUSION,** a photographic method of softening detail and creating radiant highlights, once used extensively for romantic CLOSE-UPS. The effect is created by placing a diffusion filter over the camera lens. Diffusion is subtly different from soft focus, with which it is often confused.

**DILLINGER, JOHN** (1903–34), US criminal who, in a period of only fourteen months, accomplished a series of daring bank raids and prison escapes in the mid-West which displayed imagination, skill, and a legendary stylishness. Dillinger (pronounced with a hard 'g') did not indulge in the indiscriminate slaughter common among gangsters of the time, but several brutal shootings were attributed to him by the authorities who were unnerved by his near-heroic status with the American public. The FBI mounted the biggest manhunt in its history and, after being betrayed by a brothel-keeper, he was shot down outside a Chicago cinema.

Direct portrayal of Dillinger on the screen was prohibited by the Production Code (see CENSORSHIP, US) for more than ten years, but veiled references to his exploits appear in several GANGSTER FILMS of the thirties. *High Sierra* (1941) is based on his career and starred Humphrey BOGART (who resembled Dillinger) in one of his most memorable roles. Later overt film accounts include *Dillinger* (1945), *I Died a Thousand Times* (1955), a remake of *High Sierra*, *Guns Don't Argue* (1955), *The FBI Story* (1959), *Young Dillinger* (1964), and *Dillinger* (1973).

**DINNER AT EIGHT,** US, 1933. 1¾hr. *Dir* George Cukor; *prod* MGM; *scr* Frances Marion, Herman J. Mankiewicz, from the play by George S. Kaufman and Edna Ferber; *ph* William Daniels; *ed* Ben Lewis; *cast* Marie Dressler (Carlotta Vance), John Barrymore (Larry Renault), Wallace Beery (Dan Packard), Jean Harlow (Kitty Packard), Lionel Barrymore (Oliver Jordan), Billie Burke (Millicent Jordan).

Largely unappreciated at the time of its initial appearance as an uncinematic adaptation of a sophisticated stage play, the film later acquired an almost legendary reputation as one of the best Hollywood films of the early thirties, notable for the ingenious construction and deft exposition of its multi-stranded story, the brilliance of its dialogue and characterization, with virtuoso performances by some of METRO-GOLDWYN-MAYER's top stars, and the skill of CUKOR's direction.

**DIRECT CINEMA** like its European cousin CINÉMA-VÉRITÉ is both a distinct historical movement and a diffuse style of documentary film-making. The name was given by Albert MAYSLES to the approach developed in America during the early sixties by the group of film-makers—notably Drew, LEACOCK, PENNEBAKER, and the Maysles brothers—who had worked together as DREW ASSOCIATES. Influenced more directly by the concerns of photo-journalism than by those of the conventional documentary, their interest in mobility, invisibility, and immediacy led them to develop new equipment and new methods of teamwork, innovations that linked them to those other documentary movements—NATIONAL FILM BOARD work in Canada, FREE CINEMA in Britain, *cinéma-vérité* in France—most sensitive to the new era of television.

Direct cinema is direct in the sense that technical professionalism is secondary to the effort to record the feel of an event or situation; hence the erratic lighting and camerawork, the avoidance of narration and interpretive editing, and the preponderance of long takes that characterize it as a style. The film-maker tries to work without preconceived ideas and to find what is inherently dramatic in the situation filmed rather than imposing a structure on it. This particular ideal, part of the American documentary tradition that began with FLAHERTY and runs through STONEY and the FRONTIER FILMS group, leads film-makers to work without a shooting script, like news reporters, trusting themselves to catch the unconsidered gestures and words through which people betray themselves. In order not to direct events and so falsify their position as quasi-researchers, some of the Drew group refuse even to use interviews.

Films like THE CHAIR (1963), *Crisis: Behind a Presidential Commitment* (1963), and Arthur and Evelyn Farron's *Birth and Death* (1969) lend themselves effectively to this approach, because they deal with high-tension situations. So do character studies like Pennebaker's *Don't Look Back* (1967) and the Maysles brothers' *Salesman* (1969) whose success depends on the sensitivity and initiative of individual cameramen and sound recordists.

Critics of the Direct Cinema approach point out that it claims an objectivity which is impossible because the film-makers' presence in the situation filmed must inevitably influence their material. But in fact the method has worked out valuable techniques for working with near-invisibility, and its efforts to develop a non-narrative form have contributed a genuinely useful style of film-making.

**DIRECTOR,** the principal creative artist involved in the making of any film; the artistic supervisor of the work performed by the other artists and technicians, and of the form and content of the film itself.

This definition of the director's function has only comparatively recently been accepted. In the commercial industry the director was for many years an employed member of a team; his judgement was rated no higher than that of other members and was in general subordinate to that of the PRODUCER. There were exceptions from the very beginning. The names of GRIFFITH, SENNETT, and INCE would sell a film to the audience (and, of course, CHAPLIN, but as an actor not as a director). Producers engaged directors like MURNAU, LUBITSCH, or CAPRA on the basis of their previous successes but the public, apart from an informed minority, chose its films by the star or the subject. Not until the inescapable stamp of HITCHCOCK became widely recognized did the general public go to see a particular director's films and John FORD was probably the next director to make films that sold by virtue of his own name.

Perhaps a surprising number of directors succeeded in giving an individual creative flavour to their work. Recognition of their achievement is in the main a post-1950 phenomenon, following in the wake of reassessment of earlier films by French critics (see AUTEUR THEORY). General acceptance of this change of values is indicated by advertising: often the names of FELLINI, LOSEY, RUSSELL, and other important contemporary directors are given more space in posters than that of the star.

The word director has almost as many meanings as there are film directors. The director of a COMPILATION film may simply select existing STOCK shots and write an accompanying commentary, while the director of a mammoth musical may be an organizer, writer, *metteur-en-scène*, musician, choreographer, editor, and publicist. Only on the smallest and least complex of films is it possible to consider the director the 'maker' of the film; almost always he is the leader of a team of artists and technicians whose work he shapes and controls in accordance with his vision of the finished film, and in all matters entailing the spending of money he is normally subordinate to the producer.

Ideally the director becomes involved at the earliest stage of making a film—called 'pre-production'—as part of a vital trio: producer, director, writer. Any one of these may have conceived the idea and set the production wheels in motion. The director may be the writer or producer of a given film or he may combine all three roles; he may also be credited as co-writer or co-producer or both. However organized, the decisions made during this stage, incorporated in the script and production plan, largely determine the character of the eventual film and are surprisingly difficult to alter later on.

During production the director comes into his own. He may or may not have been allowed a voice in casting, choosing locations, and hiring the crew; but once filming begins he is responsible for the best creative use of his cast, crew, and facilities. (The producer should intervene only where money is concerned: David O. SELZNICK was a notorious exception to this rule.) However expert the director and however careful the planning, there is always an element of improvisation during filming, and it is here that a director can keep the film consistent with his original concept or introduce a personal style to a script he did not conceive or write.

After shooting, in the 'post-production' stage, the director may well have no further control over the film; this was common in the heyday of the Hollywood studio system but is less so today. If the director does participate in the editing, it is again as a supervisor who outlines his intentions to the editor but leaves their execution to him. The editor's skill and experience are as necessary to the director as those of the cameraman, art director, and all the other members of the film-making team. Sometimes the director is contractually guaranteed 'first cut', after which the film may be re-cut to the producer's or distributor's preference.

***DISHONORED***, US, 1931. 1½hr. *Dir* Josef von Sternberg; *prod* Paramount; *scr* Daniel N. Robin, from an original story by Sternberg; *ph* Lee Garmes; *des* Hans Dreier; *cast* Marlene Dietrich (X 27), Victor McLaglen (Lt Kranau), Lew Cody (Col Kovrin), Gustav von Seyffertitz (Secret Service Head), Warner Oland (General von Hindau).

The plot, with Marlene DIETRICH as a prostitute in the Austrian Secret Service unmasking a Russian spy and pursuing him in a variety of disguises, finally being court-martialled herself, and making a grand exit to face the firing-squad, is unlikely if not absurd, and the film's atmosphere is seldom convincing geographically. But its stature in the STERNBERG canon has tended to increase in recent years, perhaps partly because it displays both the director's obsession with decorative effect and his wry humour, but particularly on account of a resplendent performance by Dietrich.

**DISNEY, WALT** (1901–66), US animator and producer, worked initially in a commercial art studio in Kansas City where he met Ub IWERKS, whose superior drawing and technical skill were to make his first successes possible. By 1923 Disney, his brother Roy (who became financial overseer), and Iwerks were in Hollywood: their first series, *Alice in Cartoonland* (1924–5), which combined a live actress with animated cartoon animals, was in all respects unsuccessful, but *Oswald the Lucky Rabbit* (1928) was an improvement, owing largely to Disney's constant, and costly, efforts to perfect his methods. MICKEY MOUSE was designed in the same year, when Disney was also involved in a copyright dispute with his distributor, the Winkler Organization. Animated by Iwerks, Mickey starred in *Plane Crazy*, *Gallopin' Gaucho*, and STEAMBOAT WILLIE _(all 1928) which, through Disney's optimistic foresight and the technical enterprise of Iwerks and Wilfred Jackson, was the first cartoon with sound. Its immediate success prompted the SILLY SYMPHONY series (1929), involving the Three Little Pigs who rivalled Mickey in popularity.

Disney's immediate application of other new techniques, such as the first use of three-strip TECHNICOLOR in *Flowers and Trees* (1933), his flair for story-telling, and untiring organizing ability all helped to establish a virtual monopoly for the Disney animation studios in the thirties. He was the perfectionist overseer of a studio which worked to an industrialized production-line system: by 1934 he had a production staff of 700 and had opened distribution offices in London and Paris. A large-scale merchandizing programme augmented direct profits from the films. Disney characters promoted the sales of toys, watches, T-shirts, and many other products. In the Christmas season of 1933, for instance, 250,000 Mickey Mouse railway engines were sold. The scheme not only earned a large revenue, but also maintained the continuing popularity of the Disney creations.

In 1934 Disney threw all his resources into the production of the first feature-length cartoon with sound and colour, and SNOW WHITE AND THE SEVEN DWARFS was released in 1937, to great success. During its production Iwerks developed the MULTIPLANE camera, for which the Disney studios won a special OSCAR. Apart from the quasi-STEREOPHONIC sound of FANTASIA (1940), this was Disney's last major technical breakthrough. After the release of *Pinocchio* and *Fantasia* in 1940, *Dumbo* (1941) looked back to the broad humour and caricature of his earlier work. The war interrupted work on *Bambi* (1943), but new outlets were found in the production of training films such as *Victory through Air Power* (1943). The building of the Burbank studio checked profits, and a studio strike in 1941, occasioned by Disney's implacable authoritarianism, led to the establishment of a group of animators in stylistic opposition, UNITED PRODUCTIONS OF AMERICA (UPA). After the war, the naturalistic precision heralded by *Bambi* increased: *The Three Caballeros* (1944) combined animation with live-action and in 1950 Disney produced his first live-action feature, *Treasure Island*. A number of such films were made, including *20,000 Leagues under the Sea* (1954), *Westward Ho the Wagons* (1956), and *Old Yeller* (1957), as well as a series of nature documentaries, beginning with *Seal Island*

(1949) and including *The Living Desert* (1953) and *The African Lion* (1955). All Disney films, cartoons, live-action, and documentaries, combined technical polish with wholesome, energetic narrative, a form aimed specifically at the family audience which, from the fifties, received decreasing attention from other Hollywood producers.

Disneyland, in California, was opened in 1955. An amusement park incorporating all the elements of Disney fantasy, it was to become one of the biggest tourist attractions in the world, although Disney himself visualized it as a prototype for urban community planning. From 1959 work progressed on a second Disneyland in Florida, opened in 1971.

Meanwhile the studio was still producing feature cartoons like *Cinderella* (1950), ALICE IN WONDERLAND (1951), *Peter Pan* (1953), and *Lady and the Tramp* (1955). *The Sleeping Beauty* (1958) was unsuccessful, but family audiences continued to be served with a series of cheerful comedies starring Fred MACMURRAY, the best of which was *The Absent Minded Professor* (1960). In terms of box-office success, Disney made a triumphant come-back with *Mary Poppins* (1964), starring Julie ANDREWS, but only *Jungle Book* (1967), released after Disney's death, recalls the inventive unpretentiousness of the pre-war era and points again to the fact that his creative strength lay in his flair for story-telling, which, in later years, was swallowed up in the management of a multi-million-dollar entertainment enterprise.

By his will, the California Institute of the Arts received $4 million to endow the Disney Foundation. (See also ANIMATION, especially US.)

**DISSOLVE,** a photographic effect in which one shot appears to dissolve slowly into the next. In the UK the term 'mix' is often used for the same effect. Conventionally the dissolve is employed as a transition between scenes to suggest a lapse of time or a change of place; it is considered to be more emphatic than a cut and less than a FADE. The dissolve is also the basis for trick shots in which a person or object slowly disappears: it is done by dissolving from the shot including the person to an identical shot without him. Professional dissolves are now made by OPTICAL PRINTING after filming is complete, not in the camera as with amateur films. (See EFFECTS.)

**DISTRIBUTION,** the stage in the economy of cinema between production and EXHIBITION. Film is now subject to COPYRIGHT: distributors buy from the producers the right to distribute a film in an agreed territory for a defined period (usually five or seven years). The distributor supplies the film to the EXHIBITOR and licenses him to show it, and the payment by the exhibitor to the distributor is commonly known as film hire or film rental. The term renter is frequently used for a distributor. As well as negotiating bookings with exhibitors, the distributor is responsible for the supply of prints and for publicity material. Distributors have to varying extents engaged in the functions of exhibition and especially production, and have become the dominant element in countries where the film industry is not nationally owned or oriented. The influence of the distributors has been largely conservative, yielding to change only when one of their number has decided to support an innovation or a novelty to entice back a dwindling audience.

In the early days of cinema the middle stage of distribution did not exist. There was a factory where the films were made and a shop where copies were sold, usually priced per foot, irrespective of subject unless the matter and manner were unusually ambitious. Travelling showmen bought enough single copies of different films to provide five or six different programmes and showed them round the countryside until they wore out. Even in towns fixed cinemas were so rare that they could maintain the same group of programmes for months on end.

As the number of fixed cinemas proliferated, there arose an increasing need for more changes of programme to encourage the habit of regular visits to the same local cinema, and for exclusivity of product to ensure that competing cinemas did not show the same programme. Middlemen, calling themselves renters or distributors, began buying many copies of films and hiring them to exhibitors, who could rely on them for frequent changes of programme. But producers found that some distributors would buy one copy of a film and make copies from a negative struck off the original print. Moreover, instead of making a fixed hire charge, they began to demand a percentage of the takings at the box-office on the grounds that in doing so they were sharing the risks with their clients and thus justifying a share of the gains.

To counteract these trends, many of the larger producers became their own distributors and in the US banded themselves into a trust—the MOTION PICTURE PATENTS COMPANY (1909). European producers attempted to form a similar association at a conference known as the CONGRÈS DES DUPES; it broke up without achieving a European trust, but nevertheless it put paid to the efforts of the smaller producers (including MÉLIÈS, ironically chairman of the conference) to maintain a system of outright sales, and it encouraged distribution by or through a few major producers. Although the effect of the new arrangements drove out the small artist-businessman like Méliès and obliterated the itinerant showman, the stability they brought established financial confidence in the industry. The resultant expansion in production resolved the problems which had bedevilled the years since 1907, and was in part responsible for the increase in length and quality of films.

The main US distributors based on New York developed into a series of vertically integrated trusts, owning studios, production companies, and circuits of cinemas throughout the country, with further circuits bound by preferential contracts. Their power was weakened after the Second World War by the exercise of the Sherman Anti-Trust Act (1890) under which, by the PARAMOUNT consent decree (1949), exhibition in the US was divorced from production and distribution. BLOCK BOOKING of films had already been forbidden by law, and individual films were now able to be rented on their own merit. In Britain vertical integration persists, with domination of the trade and industry by a duopoly consisting of the RANK ORGANISATION and Anglo-EMI (see ASSOCIATED BRITISH). Even where there is no vertical integration, the importance of a guarantee of distribution for raising money ensures that distributors still have a considerable influence on production.

The major American distributors built up organizations throughout the world, functioning in each territory (i.e. country or group of smaller countries) according to the conditions of company law in each situation. But even in countries like Britain where the company has to be registered as being under British control, all major decisions are dictated by New York or Hollywood.

Alongside commercial or 'theatrical' distribution to audiences who pay to see a programme, usually in an established cinema or theatre, non-theatrical distribution to all other (usually non-paying) audiences such as film societies, schools and universities, and industrial audiences now accounts for a very high proportion of production in all the advanced countries, usually on 16MM or smaller gauges. The earlier system of a fixed rental fee still operates in non-theatrical distribution in Great Britain.

**DI VENANZO,** GIANNI (1920–66), Italian cameraman, began work as an assistant cameraman on CASTELLANI's *Un colpo di pistola* (1941). Over the next ten years he worked on a number of distinguished films with the directors VISCONTI, ROSSELLINI, and DE SANTIS, and the cameramen Aldo TONTI, Otello MARTELLI, and G. R. ALDO. In 1952 he became a lighting cameraman, and quickly evolved the style that lends his work distinction: cool, precise, with a fine sense for white light: sun-filled courtyards with hard-lined shadows. The other part of his greatness lay in his ability to subsume his style into the textures demanded by the director. Few artists could work with such distinction for directors as diverse as ANTONIONI, ROSI, LOSEY, and FELLINI. Among his finest films are LE AMICHE (1955), LA NOTTE (1961), SALVATORE GIULIANO (1962), L'ECLISSE (1962), LE MANI SULLA CITTÀ (1963), OTTO E MEZZO (1963), and GIULIETTA DEGLI SPIRITI (1965).

**DJIM CHUANTE** (*Sol Svanetii, Salt for Svanetia*), USSR, 1930. 50min. *Dir, scr* Mikhail Kalatozov from an idea by Sergei Tretyakov; *prod* Goskinprom, Georgia; *ph* Kalatozov, M. Gegelashvili.

Although its political message is, like that of TURKSIB (1929), the economic necessity of opening up a geographically isolated area (in the Caucasus), this film is more often compared with BUÑUEL'S LAS HURDES (1932). KALATOZOV's documentary depicts with almost surreal intensity the cultural conflict between pagan and Christian, and the social conflict between primitive and modern.

**DMYTRYK,** EDWARD (1908–   ), Canadian-born director who began his Hollywood career with PARAMOUNT in 1923 and was a film editor throughout the thirties. His work as director began in earnest in 1940, and in four years he made sixteen films, including contributions to the popular 'Boston Blackie' and 'FALCON' series. *Hitler's Children* (1943) is his most admired film of this period, but he attracted even greater attention with *Murder My Sweet* (1945, *Farewell My Lovely* in GB), his adaptation of Raymond CHANDLER's novel in which Dick POWELL surprised everybody with his performance as the tough private eye, Philip Marlowe. At his peak in the forties, Dmytryk continued to win critical acclaim, notably with *Crossfire* (1947) and *Give Us This Day* (1949), the latter one of several films he made in Britain as a temporary casualty of the American witch-hunting period (see UNAMERICAN ACTIVITIES). After *The Sniper* (1952), he seemed to lose much of his individuality; his later work, from *The Young Lions* (1958), through *The Carpetbaggers* (1963) to *Shalako* (1968), has not added appreciably to his reputation.

**DOCKS OF NEW YORK, The,** US, 1928. 2hr. *Dir* Josef von Sternberg; *prod* Paramount; *scr* Jules Furthman; *ph* Harold Rosson; *des* Hans Dreier; *cast* George Bancroft (Bill Roberts), Betty Compson (Sadie), Olga Baclanova (Lou), Clyde Cook ('Sugar' Steve).

A ship's stoker rescues a girl from suicide, marries her on impulse and promptly deserts her; but he jumps ship to return to her, confesses to a crime for which she has been arrested and serves a prison sentence, the girl promising to wait for him. The film, received as a realistic drama of life in the raw, was strengthened by convincing acting. It is often regarded as a silent precursor of the thirties cycle of GANGSTER FILMS, but STERNBERG treated the settings of docks and low life with soft lighting and formal pictorial effect.

**DR JEKYLL AND MR HYDE,** by R. L. Stevenson (1850–94), published in 1886 as *The Strange Case of Dr Jekyll and Mr Hyde,* has provided the basis for a number of screen adaptations.

*Der Januskopf* (1920) was freely adapted from Stevenson's book by Hans JANOWITZ. The dual leading role was played by Conrad VEIDT and the director was F. W. MURNAU.

In the same year in the US, two versions appeared starring Sheldon Lewis and John BARRYMORE respectively. Barrymore's performance was a *tour de force* of acting, the transformations from the good to the evil personification of the character being effected by facial distortion without the aid of trick photography. The treatment of the story has echoes of *The Picture of Dorian Gray,* even to the extent of borrowing some of Oscar WILDE's epigrams for the subtitles. This version was directed by John Stuart Robertson.

In PARAMOUNT's version of 1932 Rouben MAMOULIAN maintained his reputation as an experimenter with some startlingly effective innovations. At the opening of the film the camera took the place of the leading character, driving up to the club in a carriage, from which it descended and entered the building, then swinging to look at itself in a mirror, at which point Fredric MARCH, as Dr Jekyll is first seen. (This device was repeated in Jerry LEWIS's *The Nutty Professor,* 1963, French title *Docteur Jerry et Mister Love,* a successful lampoon, often as funny as many horror films succeed in being unintentionally.) In the transformation scenes the camera for the first time revolved 360° on its axis to give an effect of vertigo, recorded heartbeats (Mamoulian's own) were synchronized with gong-strokes to build up tension, and successive layers of specially coloured make-up were revealed by the use of colour filters to avoid the necessity for cuts and optical dissolves. Fredric March, so far best known in comedy roles, gained an OSCAR for his portrayal of the extremes in the leading part.

Mamoulian's version proved difficult to surpass. METRO-GOLDWYN-MAYER's 1941 production, directed by Victor FLEMING, relied on Spencer TRACY's not entirely adequate command of facial expression, rather than on make-up and camera tricks, to effect the transformations. Ingrid BERGMAN scored a personal triumph as Ivy, Hyde's pathetic victim.

RENOIR's *Le Testament du Dr Cordelier* (1959, *Experiment in Evil* in the US) brought the theme into the contemporary idiom with its translation of the bestial Hyde into the anarchic killer/clown memorably played by Jean-Louis BARRAULT. In this film Renoir experimented with multi-camera photography.

*The Two Faces of Dr Jekyll* (1960, *House of Fright* in the US), a routine HAMMER FILMS production, added little to previous developments of the theme, which has been burlesqued in an inevitable *Abbott and Costello meet Dr Jekyll and Mr Hyde* (1956), with Boris KARLOFF, a dismal parody.

**DR MABUSE DER SPIELER**, Germany, 1922. Part I: DER GROSSE SPIELER—*Ein Bild der Zeit* (*The Great Gambler—Image of a Generation*). 1½hr. Part II: INFERNO—*Menschen der Zeit* (*Inferno—People of a Generation*). 1¾hr. *Dir* Fritz Lang; *prod* Erich Pommer for UFA; *scr* Lang, Thea von Harbou, based on the novel by Norbert Jacques; *ph* Carl Hoffmann; *des* Otto Hunte, Stahl-Urach; *cast* Rudolph Klein-Rogge (Dr Mabuse), Alfred Abel (Count Told), Aud Egede Nissen (Cara Carozza), Gertrude Welcker (Countess Lucy Told), Paul Richter (Edgar Hull), Bernhard Goetzke (Von Wenck).

*Dr Mabuse* was made at a time of political unrest and rapid economic inflation in Germany. While the main theme is the battle of wits between Mabuse the master-criminal and Von Wenck, LANG was obviously concerned with portraying the decadence of the contemporary social atmosphere. The two feature-length parts are complementary and were intended for showing on consecutive evenings. However, after initial showings in Europe, slightly cut, when the film reached the US in 1927 it had been heavily edited into one feature—later released as *The Fatal Passions*—and has only comparatively recently been seen again in the original version.

Lang revived Mabuse in his last pre-war German film DAS TESTAMENT DES DR MABUSE (1932) and again in *Die tausend Augen des Dr Mabuse* (1960).

**DR STRANGELOVE: OR HOW I LEARNED TO STOP WORRYING AND LOVE THE BOMB**, GB, 1963. *Dir*, *prod* Stanley Kubrick; *scr* Kubrick, Terry Southern, Peter George, from the novel *Red Alert* by Peter George; *des* Ken Adam; *cast* Peter Sellers (Mandrake, President Muffley, Dr Strangelove), George C. Scott (General Turgidson), Sterling Hayden (General Ripper), Keenan Wynn (Colonel Guano).

KUBRICK's version of the events leading to the final nuclear holocaust is recounted with biting satire, using a spare visual style reminiscent of newsreel photography. An unusual unity of approach among the cast (with perhaps the exception of Peter SELLERS) helped to consolidate this wry exposition of the probable fate of humanity in the age of technology.

**DOCTOR ZHIVAGO**, US, 1966. Panavision 70; 3¼hr; Metrocolor. *Dir* David Lean; *prod* Carlo Ponti; *scr* Robert Bolt; *ph* F. A. Young; *mus* Maurice Jarre; *cast* Omar Sharif (Zhivago), Julie Christie (Lara), Geraldine Chaplin (Tonya), Tom Courtenay (Pasha/Strelnikov), Ralph Richardson (Alexander), Siobhan McKenna (Anna), Rita Tushingham (the girl), Rod Steiger (Komarovsky), Alec Guinness (Yevgraf).

Until this glamorized version of the novel which won Boris Pasternak a Nobel Prize, David LEAN still seemed the British cinema's best director and Robert Bolt, who had rescued the script of LAWRENCE OF ARABIA (1962) for him, its most promising writer. Shot mainly on location in Spain, amid acres of simulated snow, the lavish production has all Lean's customary polish. But all the great events of the novel go for nothing in a welter of episodes, as do its dominant themes of destiny and the overriding importance of the individual in relation to the society in which he lives. Only F. A. YOUNG's distinguished photography and the acting of some of the cast lift the mammoth enterprise out of the slush of Maurice JARRE's score. The popularity of his 'Lara' theme, however, combined with the star cast and visual appeal, made the film an enormous commercial success.

**DOCUMENTARY.** The early curiosity value of cinema—moving pictures of real-life scenes—was rapidly superseded by the dramatized narrative. Actuality film (known variously as *actualités*, *documentaires*, topicals, travel films), after dominating the cinema for its first few years, became a subsidiary part of programmes after 1908, in the form of NEWSREELS. The few exceptions included Herbert Ponting's records of SCOTT's EXPEDITION to the South Pole and Charles URBAN's KINEMACOLOR presentation of the *Delhi Durbar* (1911), which lasted 2½ hours and was a considerable commercial success. These, however, were plainly presented, with minimal structuring of the material. Even during the First World War, when the cinema began to play an important role in PROPAGANDA campaigning, the treatment of actuality film was primitive in comparison with the techniques used in fiction films.

The first advance in the structuring of

actuality film was made in the SOVIET UNION. A critical shortage of film stock after the Revolution forced editors to use even the shortest lengths, and startling new possibilities were revealed by cutting together brief sequences. Dziga VERTOV made important experiments with these new techniques in his KINO-PRAVDA newsreels and constant cross-fertilization took place with fiction films, becoming particularly evident in the work of EISENSTEIN. The great Russian silent films were to have unparalleled influence on documentary film-makers in other countries.

Meanwhile a different approach to the presentation of actuality film was revealed by Robert FLAHERTY in NANOOK OF THE NORTH (1922). The reflective, lyrical tone of *Nanook* founded a style complementary to the energetic didacticism of films following the Russian model: the two streams have continued to the present day. The unexpected box-office success of *Nanook* encouraged commercial producers to back a number of films about primitive peoples during the twenties; among the most memorable are COOPER and SCHOEDSACK's *Grass* (1925) and CHANG (1927) and Flaherty's MOANA (1926). Short programme-fillers also began to gain currency, but these were generally of a more pedestrian quality.

The Russian example was seized upon by AVANT-GARDE film-makers in Germany and France. CAVALCANTI's *Rien que les heures* (1926), a portrait of Paris, Walter RUTTMANN's BERLIN, DIE SYMPHONIE EINER GROSSSTADT (1927), and Jean VIGO's A PROPOS DE NICE (1930), made in collaboration with Vertov's brother Boris KAUFMAN, all display the formal inspiration of contemporary Russian directors. In the Soviet Union itself, Vertov's theories culminated in CHELOVEK S KINOAPPARATOM (*Man with a Movie Camera*, 1929). Common characteristics began to emerge: a general rejection of the artistic and political values of the commercial cinema as represented by Hollywood; an absolute belief in film as an art form (film societies were formed to bring the work of film artists before a serious audience and were themselves modest but adventurous sponsors of new films); a political bias for the most part towards the left. Stylistically their work was characterized by a new freedom for the camera—the ever-inquiring, all-seeing camera-eye, rejoicing in its own versatility. They aspired to the condition of music, creating rhythm and counterpoint by conscious application and development of the principles of MONTAGE and the dynamics of the framed image. There was a new energy in formal composition, seeking the abstract in the actual, creating totally subjective film records.

In Britain John GRIERSON as Films Officer of the Empire Marketing Board (see CROWN FILM UNIT) sought to convince politicians and civil servants of the cinema's massive potential for public education and persuasion. His group, which included Basil WRIGHT, Paul ROTHA, Arthur ELTON, Stuart LEGG, Edgar ANSTEY, had little or no prior experience of film-making. They shared a leftist ideology, but this was expressed with moderation in their work: government-backed films could not make an outright attack on the existing order. Although the contribution of the avant-garde was acknowledged, overt aestheticism was discouraged; films like SONG OF CEYLON (1934) and NIGHT MAIL (1936) owe more to Flaherty, the Russians, and some Hollywood directors—John FORD and James CRUZE, for example. Grierson intended the films to play an educational rather than a theatrical role, and the use of cheap, non-inflammable 16MM film stock gave them currency in schools, clubs, and film societies. A notable series of films depicting social problems was produced for the Gas Industry: *Housing Problems* (Anstey and Elton, 1935), *Enough to Eat* (Anstey, 1936), *Children at School* (Wright, 1937), *The Smoke Menace* (John Taylor, 1937). These found ready audiences not only in trade union halls and Left Book Club study groups, but in all manner of political, cultural, and charitable organizations. From the mid-thirties they were strongly influenced stylistically by THE MARCH OF TIME.

American documentary films of the thirties were, as far as the general public was concerned, chiefly travelogues and ten-minute 'interest' films like PETE SMITH SPECIALTIES. The travelogues became rigidly repetitive in form, taking a cursory tourist's-eye-view of romantic places with commentaries whose clichés, especially the valedictory '. . . and so as the sun sinks slowly in the west . . .', became common currency. The resistance of commercial interests to government-sponsored film-making delayed until the mid-thirties the setting up of official units to make films about the Depression and the New Deal. Hollywood profitably channelled its social comment and reformist energy into the melodramatic 'realism' of the GANGSTER movies and Darryl ZANUCK's series of social-conscience productions, notably *I Am a Fugitive from a Chain Gang* (Mervyn LEROY, 1932). A more characteristic reaction was Busby BERKELEY's 'Forgotten Man' routine for LeRoy's GOLD-DIGGERS OF 1933—a peculiar form of knowing escapism. The only activist films came from the left-wing Film and Photo League. Like their British counterparts who formed a Film and Photo League affiliated to the Left Book Club discussion groups, they lacked finance, expertise, and effective distribution, but from this background came Seymour Stern and Leo HURWITZ. Ralph STEINER, Willard VAN DYKE, and Paul

STRAND were established still photographers who moved into the documentary cinema, strongly influenced by the Russians. In fact, the most influential 'documentary' movement in the US was that of the still photographers, organized under Roy E. Stryker of the Rural Resettlement Administration (just as actors and directors were mobilized by President Roosevelt in Federal Theater projects). Their efforts were supported by a lively tradition of photo-journalism, substantiated by the appearance of *Life* in 1936 (in Britain the equivalent, *Picture Post*, was not published until 1938).

The first US government film project, also for the Resettlement Administration, was assigned to a devoutly New Deal Democrat, Pare LORENTZ, whose first film was THE PLOW THAT BROKE THE PLAINS (1936). Lorentz had to contend first with the political dissension of his collaborators and then with the opposition of Hollywood, which was against the New Deal in general and government film-making in particular. However, THE RIVER (1937) obtained wide theatrical release and its international success led directly to the establishment of the US Film Service in 1938. Lorentz's lyrical approach suited his ecological subjects but fitted no leftist's idea of social criticism, a role filled for the radical by FRONTIER FILMS and for the liberal moderate by *The March of Time*.

In the Soviet Union during the thirties, documentary film languished, as did the feature film, under the restrictions of SOCIALIST REALISM. Vertov's 'formalism' was totally discredited: his last film to meet with official approval was the moving TRI PESNI O LENINYE (*Three Songs of Lenin*, 1934). Socialist ideas were disseminated through the cinema by a small and scattered avante-garde in Britain (Ivor MONTAGU and others); in the US (Frontier Films); Spain (BUÑUEL'S LAS HURDES, 1932, and the pro-Republican films of the Civil War); Poland (the START group); and France (RENOIR's work for the Front Populaire). But the representative political film-maker of the thirties and beyond is Joris IVENS; his films are like a historical map of socialist causes: *Pesn o geroyakh* (*Song of Heroes*, USSR, 1932), MISÈRE AU BORINAGE (Belgium, 1933), THE SPANISH EARTH (1937), and *The 400 Million* (1938), about the Japanese invasion of China.

Documentary film in the non-commercial sense has in the main been characterized by a left-wing political allegiance. The principal exception occurred in Nazi Germany, where documentaries were an important part of the highly-organized propaganda machine. Leni RIEFENSTAHL emerged as a documentary film-maker with an absolute mastery of spectacle: in TRIUMPH DES WILLENS (*Triumph of the Will*,

1934) she did with Nazi uniforms what Busby Berkeley did with chorus-girls, she provided an escape from political and economic insecurity in the dream-geometry of perfect order. OLYMPIA (1938) is still among the best of many Olympics documentaries. The brilliant editing and the total mastery of rhythm and movement poeticized both the human form and the political machine. The campaign films made by the German Propaganda Ministry after the outbreak of war, notably *Feuertaufe* (*Baptism of Fire*, 1941), depicted the early victories of the German forces with terrifying effect, chiefly attributable to the virtuosity of German editors.

The war effort in the Allied countries took film-makers of both documentary and feature films into the propaganda field. Enduring documentaries made during the war include Harry WATT's *Target for Tonight* (1940) and Humphrey JENNINGS's moving, unsentimental observations of ordinary people under war conditions. America's most striking contribution to the war documentary was the WHY WE FIGHT series (1942–5), supervised by Frank CAPRA; directors of note such as John FORD, John HUSTON, and William WYLER also made campaign films for public release. The experienced documentarists, such as Lorentz, were used in the field of public and military education and 'orientation'. Paul Strand's NATIVE LAND (1942) was a reminder to the war generation that democratic slogans had flesh and blood correlatives in human rights, but the film received only limited distribution. Important Soviet directors such as DOVZHENKO, PUDOVKIN, and Roman KARMEN worked on footage from the front line, assembling it into campaign films.

In the post-war years commercial sponsorship increased and creative talents had to comply with the specific demands of backers. Among the notable successes was Flaherty's beautiful swansong LOUISIANA STORY (1948), financed by the Standard Oil Company of New Jersey. RANK's *This Modern Age* (1946–50), fifteen-minute films on serious topics written by leading journalists and filmed by first-rate documentary craftsmen, emulated *The March of Time*. Routine travelogues continued to appear, usually sponsored by national tourist boards. Some striking documentaries were produced by the United Nations, including *Power Among Men* (1958). DISNEY's feature-length nature documentaries gained a following among family audiences, and MONDO CANE (1961), with its emulators, exploited the sensationalism that could be injected into the travelogue formula. Rank's *Look at Life* (1959–69), a weekly series of ten-minute films usually on trivial topics, went into competition with the long-established *Pathé Pictorial* (1918–69). But in Britain and the US the inroads of television on cinema audiences was reducing the outlets for documentary films even below pre-war levels.

Elsewhere, however, the whole concept of documentary (Grierson's 'creative interpretation of reality') was undergoing change. In Italy the humanist aesthetic of documentary evolved into NEO-REALISM, neither fiction nor fact. The dramatic impact of ROSSELLINI's films, in particular, was reflected in a move to social realism in Hollywood, notably in *The House on 92nd Street* (Henry HATHAWAY, 1945) and *Boomerang* (Elia KAZAN, 1947). This trend was short-lived; independent films like Hurwitz's *Strange Victory* (1949) and BIBERMAN's SALT OF THE EARTH (1953) showed that the forebodings of *Native Land* were becoming reality.

French documentarists, even PAINLEVÉ and GRÉMILLON, worked on the obligatory official war retrospectives, and René CLÉMENT made effective use of the technique of factual reconstruction in his tribute to the Resistance movement, LA BATAILLE DU RAIL (1946). Fitting successors to the films of Flaherty were Georges ROUQUIER's FARREBIQUE (1946), Arne SUCKS-DORFF's *Det stora aventyret* (*The Great Adventure*, 1953), and Bert HAANSTRA's *Alleman* (*The Human Dutch*, 1963). Short factual films became a training-ground for directors later to achieve distinction. Films about artists and their works proliferated and still constitute a thriving cottage industry for artists, poets, and musicians, occupying film-makers of the calibre of Henri STORCK, Grémillon, Wright, and Don LEVY. Alain RESNAIS began his documentary career with a series of art films, dramatically re-creating the spatial dynamics of the original works within the different dimensions of his own framed images. GUERNICA (1950) extended the interpretation of a work of art into a personal political statement, and in NUIT ET BROUILLARD (1955), like Georges FRANJU in LE SANG DES BÊTES (1949) and HÔTEL DES INVALIDES (1951), Resnais presented a raw vision of inhumanity inconceivable in the cinema of Grierson, Jennings, Flaherty, or Lorentz.

The increasingly imprecise and devalued application of the term 'documentary' led to its rejection by recent movements: FREE CINEMA in Britain, DIRECT CINEMA in the US, CINÉMA-VÉRITÉ in France. All these movements were aided by the rapid improvement during and after the war of light-weight 16mm equipment which offered cheapness and flexibility to the independent film-maker working for the most part on location. Perhaps the most important contribution of *cinéma-vérité* was the interview film, most successful in ROUCH's CHRONIQUE D'UN ÉTÉ (1961) and MARKER's LE JOLI MAI (1963). Both the methods and philosophy of *cinéma-vérité* have influenced the directors of the NOUVELLE VAGUE, GODARD in particular; and Marcel OPHULS further extended the form in LE CHAGRIN ET LA PITIÉ (*The Sorrow and the Pity*, 1969).

Direct cinema sprang from the work of radical film-makers like Lionel ROGOSIN, but DREW ASSOCIATES reached a wider audience through television with a remarkable series of films by Richard LEACOCK, Donn PENNEBAKER, Albert MAYSLES, and others. *Woodstock* (Mike Wadleigh, 1970), possibly the most profitable documentary of all time, combined *vérité* photography with a brilliantly fluent editing technique, and began a vogue for films recording pop music festivals and concerts.

The NATIONAL FILM BOARD of Canada, with important projects such as CHALLENGE FOR CHANGE, continues to be the most progressive and influential production agency of any capitalist government, and Canada has produced three accomplished practitioners of *cinéma-vérité*—Allan King, best known for *Warrendale* (1967), and the French-Canadians Michel BRAULT and Pierre PERRAULT.

In Britain as in the US, television solved the problem of the sponsorship and distribution of documentaries. From the established tradition of British documentary, only Rotha and Grierson worked extensively in television, and their roles were tributes to the past: television documentary owes more to radio and to journalism than to Grierson's movement. Outside the important but ephemeral journalistic field, British television has produced a new generation of film-makers including John SCHLESINGER, Ken RUSSELL, Clive DONNER, and John BOORMAN. Peter WATKINS has successfully applied the techniques of television reportage to the historical past (*Culloden*, 1964) and to the hypothetical future (*The War Game*, 1965). Kenneth LOACH has based a very promising film career on his television compounds of drama and documentary such as *Cathy Come Home* (1966).

As the focal point of the liberal conscience in the sixties, Vietnam attracted the attention of many film-makers. *Loin du Viet-nam* (*Far from Vietnam*, 1967) impressively combined the talents of Marker, Resnais, Claude LELOUCH, Agnès VARDA, Godard, and Ivens, while Pierre SCHOENDORFFER's *The Anderson Platoon* (1967) won a richly-deserved OSCAR. Ivens, Marker, and Varda have also worked in CUBA, where the revolutionary government has used educational and propagandist film in an original and purposeful way, and which has in Santiago ALVAREZ an artist in the vital tradition of Vertov. (See also NEWSREEL, PROPAGANDA, COMPILATION.)

Erik Barnouw, *Documentary: a history of the non-fiction film*, New York, London, 1975.

**DOLBY SYSTEM,** a proprietary noise reduction system, first developed for tape and cassette recording and now applied to 35mm film OPTICAL SOUND tracks. The electronic circuit not only reduces unwanted noise and hiss, but makes possible the first important improvement in professional sound standards since the early thirties. 'Dolbyized' tracks sound 'cleaner' and clearer than ordinary tracks. A later addition to the system introduced stereophonic sound on optical tracks, previously available only in cinemas with 70MM projection and magnetic sound reproducers.

**DOLCE VITA, La,** Italy/France, 1960. Total-scope; 3hr. *Dir* Federico Fellini; *prod* Riama (Italy)/Pathé Consortium Cinema (France); *scr* Fellini, Ennio Flaiano, Tullio Pinelli, Brunello Rondi; *ph* Otello Martelli; *des* Piero Gherardi; *mus* Nino Rota; *cast* Marcello Mastroianni (Marcello), Anouk Aimée (Maddalena), Yvonne Furneaux (Emma), Anita Ekberg (Sylvia), Alain Cuny (Steiner), Annibale Ninchi (Marcello's father), Valeria Ciangottini (Paola).

Marcello is a gossip journalist with aspirations to being a serious writer. Through a series of events—his wife's attempted suicide, his meeting with an American film star, a patently bogus miracle, a visit from his father, elaborate parties—Marcello's life is shown to be rich in incident but poor in true relationships and personal satisfactions.

The film may be considered a possible sequel to I VITELLONI (1953); Marcello is what Moraldo might have become.

*La dolce vita* caused a considerable sensation. It was shot in an atmosphere of scandal and its revelations about Roman society, many members of which appeared in the film, were eagerly seized on by the world press. The open hostility of the Vatican further enhanced the notoriety through which the phrase 'la dolce vita' passed into other languages besides Italian. The film was immensely successful in the US and a dubbed version went on general release in Britain.

**DOLLY,** properly speaking a wheeled camera platform used for moving-camera shots such as the dolly shot or tracking shot. The camera, operator, and focus-puller ride together on the dolly, propelled usually by muscle power rather than a motor for the sake of silence and accuracy. So smooth must the movement be that special rails or tracks are laid for the dolly to follow when filming outdoors or on rough floors. On these occasions the camera is angled upwards or to one side to avoid photographing the tracks.

The standard studio dolly is a bulky affair and difficult to move freely in a confined space. To accommodate it, sets are sometimes constructed with wild walls that can be swung away to let the dolly pass. The introduction of the crab dolly, narrower and with all four wheels steerable, made such gymnastics unnecessary. It allowed the camera to glide through doorways and circumnavigate tables—and to move crabwise, thus coining a new cinema term, the crab shot. (See CAMERA MOVEMENTS, CRANE, GRIP.)

**DOMENICA D'AGOSTO** (*Sunday in August*), Italy, 1950. 1½hr. *Dir* Luciano Emmer; *prod* Sergio Amidei for Colonna Films; *scr* Franco Brusati, Luciano Emmer, Giulio Macchi, Cesare Zavattini, from a story by Sergio Amidei; *ph* Domenico Scala, Leonida Barboni, Ubaldo Marelli; *ed* Jolanda Benvenuti; *mus* Roman Vlad; *cast* Anna Baldini (Marcella), Franco Interlenghi (Enrico), Elvy Lissia (Luciano), Massimo Serato (Roberto), Correda Verga (Baron), Marcello Mastroianni (Ercole), Ave Ninchi (Fernanda Meloni).

Made on location with a partly amateur cast, the film traces the ordinary lives of five groups of people on one Sunday, when they leave Rome for the beach resort of Ostia. The diffuseness of the plot is problematic (there is little connection between the five groups), but EMMER's eye for character delineation, skilful editing, and the acting of Anna Baldini give this gentle realist film considerable charm and merit.

**DONALD DUCK,** famous DISNEY cartoon character, who first appeared in 1934 in *The Wise Little Hen*, in which he had only one line ('Who—me? Oh no! I got a bellyache!'). His lines were quacked by Clarence Nash. His body was remarkable for its plasticity—a rubbery rear and twistable neck, topped by a big mouth. (See also ANIMATION.)

**DONAT, ROBERT** (1905–58), British actor, earned the respect and affection of a wide public in many fine stage and screen performances in spite of the handicap of chronic asthma. He gained wide attention, especially in the US, in THE PRIVATE LIFE OF HENRY VIII (1933). In such films as THE THIRTY-NINE STEPS (1935), *Knight Without Armour* (1937), *Goodbye Mr Chips* (1939), for which he won an OSCAR, *The Winslow Boy* (1948), and *Lease of Life* (1954) he established his reputation for great delicacy and restraint. In *The Inn of the Sixth Happiness* (1958) his ill health was severe enough to be apparent to audiences, adding poignancy to his last appearance on the screen.

**DONEN, STANLEY** (1924– ), US director, began his career as a dancer and choreographer. After working with Gene KELLY on the choreography of *Cover Girl* (1944) and *Anchors*

*Aweigh* (1945) he went on to co-direct and choreograph ON THE TOWN (1949) with Kelly. His first solo as director was *Royal Wedding* (1951, *Wedding Bells* in GB), a pleasant Fred ASTAIRE–Jane Powell vehicle which drew its inspiration in part from Astaire's early career and gave Sarah Churchill her only musical role. SINGIN' IN THE RAIN (1952) and *It's Always Fair Weather* (1955) reunited Donen with Kelly: their collaborations revolutionized the Hollywood musical, integrating music and dance with the customary vestigial plot so that the songs and dances were the story (see MUSICALS).

Donen's later musicals, for which others received the choreography credits, include the energetic SEVEN BRIDES FOR SEVEN BROTHERS (1954), FUNNY FACE (1957), *Pajama Game* (1957), and *Damn Yankees* (1958, *What Lola Wants* in GB). Since 1958 he has worked in Britain making films for his own companies. *Indiscreet* (1958) and *Charade* (1963), sophisticated comedies starring Cary GRANT, *Two for the Road* (1966), an intricately constructed social comedy starring Albert FINNEY and Audrey HEPBURN, and *Bedazzled* (1967), a surrealistic modern morality play, show Donen working towards a comedy format that allows him to make serious social comment.

**DONIOL-VALCROZE,** JACQUES (1920– ), French director, critic, and actor. After editing J.-G. AURIOL's *La Revue du cinéma* (1947–9), he founded CAHIERS DU CINÉMA with André BAZIN, becoming editor-in-chief. In his critical writing he contributed enthusiastically to the birth of the NOUVELLE VAGUE. He appeared as an actor in Jean COCTEAU's ORPHÉE (1950), Pierre KAST's *Le Bel Âge* (1959) and *Vacances Portugaises* (1963), and ROBBE-GRILLET's *L'Immortelle* (1963). His first film as director, *L'Eau à la bouche* (1959), showed a polish that has continued through his subsequent work. *Le Viol* (1967), in particular, is a strikingly elegant film which, like *L'Immortelle*, coolly questions the nature of reality.

**DONLEVY,** BRIAN (1899–1972), Irish-born actor, made his film début in 1929 and became well-known for his distinctive voice and fast, terse mode of dialogue delivery. He tended to be type-cast as fast-talking politician, tough, crook, or racketeer: he scored particular successes as a politician in Preston STURGES's THE GREAT MCGINTY (1940) and as a Czech Resistance worker in Fritz LANG's *Hangmen Also Die* (1943). One of the best of his crisp performances was again as a politician in *The Glass Key* (1942); but he firmly grasped a rare opportunity to escape from such parts as a poor immigrant who rises to success and wealth in King VIDOR's *An American Romance* (1944). He later played roles in Britain, including the title role in the first two Quatermass films.

**DONNER,** CLIVE (1926– ), British director, began as an assistant editor in 1942, working under David LEAN and Carol REED. As an editor from 1951, he worked particularly with Henry CORNELIUS and Ronald Neame. From 1956, Donner made second features, then documentary and television films. He returned to feature films with *Some People* (1962), and a low-budget version of Harold PINTER's *The Caretaker* (1963). His reputation was established internationally with two comedies, *What's New Pussycat?* (1965) and *Here We Go Round the Mulberry Bush* (1967), but an epic *Alfred the Great* (1969) was not so successful. Donner also teaches filmmaking and directs for the theatre.

**DONNER,** JÖRN (1933– ), Finnish director, was a writer and film critic in his native country before moving to Sweden in the early sixties. There he became film critic for the Stockholm *Dagen Nyheter*: his unsparing criticism of Ingmar BERGMAN for the latter's refusal to relate his dramatic problems to the contemporary situation made him well known. His first four features as director, made in Sweden, all star his wife Harriet ANDERSSON, whose qualities as an actress strongly appeal to Donner. He shows great strength in his handling of actors: Thommy BERGGREN and Zbigniew CYBULSKI have also worked with him to great effect, in *En sondag i september* (*A Sunday in September*, 1963) and *Att älska* (*To Love*, 1964) respectively. The emotional conflicts of Donner's characters—he writes all the scripts of his films—are firmly placed within contemporary social dilemmas: *Här börjar äventyret* (*Adventure Starts Here*, 1965), in particular conveys personal disorientation with the aid of dialogue in four languages. After the comparative failure of *Tvarbälk* (*Rooftree*, 1967), Donner returned to Finland. His films made there show a more strongly personal flavour, and in *Mustaa Valkoisella* (*Black on White*, 1967) and *69* (1969) he plays the leading role himself.

**DONSKOI,** MARK (1901– ), Russian director of Ukrainian birth, came from a revolutionary family and was imprisoned for a time during the Civil War. He entered the Moscow Film School (VGIK) in 1926 and began work as a director the following year. His first film to attract wide attention was *Pesnya o schastye* (*Song of Happiness*, 1935), dealing with the life of the Mari people on the Volga. In 1938 he began work on an adaptation of Maxim GORKY's memoirs, which became the trilogy *Detstvo Gor-*

*kovo* (*The Childhood of Gorky*, 1938), *V lyud-yakh* (*My Apprenticeship*, 1939), and *Moi universiteti* (*My Universities*, 1940). The trilogy was one of the outstanding works of the thirties and is probably Donskoi's finest achievement. Much of its success springs from the immense sympathy felt by Donskoi for Gorky's philosophy; he considered himself a spiritual disciple of the writer, sharing his fervent humanism and love of his native country. He obtained excellent performances from his cast and particularly the children in the first and second parts. The Volga landscape of Gorky's youth, which Donskoi had already used to great effect in *Pesnya o schastye*, invested the films with a distinctive beauty; the relation of characters to landscape and an eloquent use of cinematic space were characteristic of Donskoi's directing.

He went on to direct some of the best of the Soviet films made during the Second World War, notably *Kak zakalyalas stal* (*How the Steel was Tempered*, 1942). He returned to Gorky with MAT (*Mother*, 1956), keeping much closer to the original than had PUDOVKIN. His later films have included a further Gorky adaptation, *Foma Gordeiev* (1960), the story of a young bourgeois in revolt against his wealthy background. His *Chaliapin* (1969) was a life of the famous singer.

**DORLÉAC,** FRANÇOISE (1941–67), French actress, sister of Catherine DENEUVE. Her fragile sensuality, compassionately observed by TRUFFAUT in *La Peau douce* (1963), emerged as mere prettiness in *Les Demoiselles de Rochefort* (DEMY, 1966). She was killed in a car crash.

**DOUBLE-8,** an alternative term for 8 MM film, referring to the double row of 8mm pictures photographed on 16 MM film and slit in half after processing.

**DOUBLE FEATURE** or double bill. Term describing a cinema programme consisting of two full-length feature films which came to replace the programmes presenting films with a stage show. A few palatial cinemas prided themselves on booking the two most important films in current release, but the vast majority were less ambitious and booked one big (or 'A') picture or first feature, against a percentage of the gross receipts, and one 'B' PICTURE or second feature for a fixed fee, often for convenience booking both from the same distributor. The conventional length of programme being three hours, exhibitors encouraged 'A' pictures running about 90 minutes and 'B' pictures running about 75 minutes, to allow time for newsreels, trailers, and possibly an animated cartoon. The double feature habit discourages the booking of short films unless the main feature is of great length, allow-

ing only for a 'full supporting programme'. (See also EXHIBITION.)

**DOUBLE HEAD,** a method of screening a film during production. The picture and sound are originated separately, one on film and the other on magnetic tape which is re-recorded on magnetic film; this separation is maintained throughout production to allow them to be edited and manipulated independently. When during this time it is necessary to screen the film, it is shown on a double head projector which runs the picture and sound on separate reels locked in synchronization. Only when the film is completed are the picture and sound brought together on one piece of film—a MARRIED PRINT in UK terminology.

Double head projection is a widespread practice in television, especially for news and documentary, where a married print may not be necessary or possible in the time available.

**DOUBLE INDEMNITY,** US, 1943. 1¾hr. *Dir* Billy Wilder; *prod* Paramount; *scr* Wilder, Raymond Chandler, based on the story by James M. Cain; *ph* John F. Seitz; *mus* Miklos Rozsa, with César Franck's Symphony in D minor; *cast* Fred MacMurray (Walter Neff), Barbara Stanwyck (Phyllis Dietrichson), Edward G. Robinson (Burton Keyes).

The title refers to the double insurance benefit paid out for accidental death: the victim's wife and her lover plan to pass off the murder of her husband as an accidental fall from a train, but the crime is solved by an insurance claims investigator (Edward G. ROBINSON). The entire film is narrated as a flashback, a fact that is recurrently lost sight of until the final climax, but a sharply witty script, tremendous suspense, and unsparing realism, and the superb performances of Robinson and Fred MACMURRAY, combined to give WILDER his first big box-office success.

**DOUGLAS,** KIRK (1916– ), US actor and producer, real name Yssur Danilovitch Demsky, returning after war service to a promising stage career, was noticed by Hal WALLIS and offered a part in *The Strange Love of Martha Ivers* (Lewis MILESTONE, 1946). His first leading part was in *Champion* (Mark ROBSON, 1949), and he soon became an established star, combining toughness with much intelligence in his choice and interpretation of parts. Throughout the fifties he made numerous appearances, working with such respected directors as William WYLER (*Detective Story*, 1951), Billy WILDER (ACE IN THE HOLE, 1951), Vincente MINNELLI (THE BAD AND THE BEAUTIFUL, 1952; *Lust for Life*, 1956), and John STURGES (GUNFIGHT AT THE OK CORRAL, 1956), and was widely admired in PATHS OF GLORY

(1957), which was produced by Douglas's own company, Bryna. Such films as SPARTACUS (1960), TWO WEEKS IN ANOTHER TOWN (1962), and SEVEN DAYS IN MAY (1964), have continued to show him as an actor of considerable intelligence, although his ability does not always prove adequate to the parts he chooses.

**DOUGLAS,** MELVYN (1901– ), US actor, real name Melvyn Hesselberg, whose first film was *Tonight or Never* (1931). In his second film, *As You Desire Me* (1932), he co-starred with GARBO, but otherwise his first few years on the screen were marked by unrewarding parts. *She Married Her Boss* (1935) and, particularly, *Theodora Goes Wild* (1936), revealed a talent for sophisticated comedy which he brought to a high degree of polish in many films, of which NINOTCHKA (1939), *Third Finger, Left Hand* (1940), and *That Uncertain Feeling* (LUBITSCH, 1941) were excellent examples. Besides Garbo, with whom he co-starred in *Two-Faced Woman* (1941) as well as *Ninotchka*, his leading ladies included Myrna LOY, Rosalind RUSSELL, Jean ARTHUR, Loretta YOUNG, Joan BLONDELL, Norma SHEARER, and Joan CRAWFORD. By 1942, he had made about fifty films, but after demobilization in 1946, he appeared in only a few more before abandoning Hollywood for stage and television. When he returned to the screen in 1962 (initially in *Billy Budd*) he emerged as an outstanding character actor. He won an OSCAR for his supporting performance as the father in HUD (1963), brought distinction to the role of the hotelier in *Hotel* (1967), and triumphed as the self-centred old man in *I Never Sang for My Father* (1969).

**DOUGLAS,** PAUL (1899–1959), US actor who came into prominence from the later forties in numerous TWENTIETH CENTURY-FOX films. Solidly built (he had been a professional footballer as well as a broadcaster) and with a countenance that could positively beam, he was equally at home in comedy or dramatic roles. Prominent among his films were *A Letter to Three Wives* (Joseph L. MANKIEWICZ, 1949), *Panic in the Streets* (Elia KAZAN, 1950), *Fourteen Hours* (Henry HATHAWAY, 1951), and *Joe Macbeth* (Ken Hughes, 1955).

**DOVZHENKO,** ALEXANDER (1894–1956), Russian director, worked in Soviet embassies in Warsaw and Berlin, studied painting, and on his

*Zemlya* (Alexander Dovzhenko, 1930)

return to his native Ukraine became a newspaper cartoonist. A committed Communist, he rejected painting as a revolutionary medium and joined VUFKU (All-Ukrainian Photo-Cinema Administration) as a scriptwriter in 1925. His first script, which he later repudiated, was for *Vasya—reformator* (*Vasya the Reformer*, 1926); he wrote and directed a comedy, *Yagodki lyubvi* (*Love's Berries*), in the same year; in 1927 he directed and acted in a political thriller, *Sumka dipkur'era* (*The Diplomatic Pouch*).

He first began to realize his capacity in ZVEN-IGORA (1927), a complex experimental work made towards the close of the period of artistic freedom that ended with the rigorous censorship enforced during the first Five Year Plan (see SOVIET UNION). *Arsenal* (1929) treated more directly a theme of great political immediacy, the Ukrainian class struggle during the Civil War. The subject of collectivization brought together Dovzhenko's two main passions, reverential love for his homeland and the formation of a Socialist society. ZEMLYA (*Earth*, 1930) endowed the conflict between peasants and kulaks with a lyrical sensuality that shocked the Russian authorities; it nevertheless established Dovzhenko as the representative artist of the Ukraine and electrified minority audiences abroad after it was shown at VENICE in 1932.

Dovzhenko's first sound film, *Ivan* (1932), was another political poem, about the hydro-electric project on the Dnieper river. He extended the deliberation of his visual imagery to the use of dialogue, and the spareness of style maintains the intensity of *Zemlya*. In 1935 he went to Siberia to direct *Aerograd* for the Mosfilm studios, returning to the Ukraine to make SHCHORS (1939) in the new studio built for him by the Ukrainian government.

Like other major Russian directors, Dovzhenko spent the war years directing or supervising documentaries, notably *Osvobozhdenie* (*Liberation*, 1940), *Bitva za nashu Sovietskuyu Ukrainu* (*The Fight for our Soviet Ukraine*, 1943), and *Pobeda na pravoberezhnoi Ukraine* (*Ukraine in Flames*, 1945); he also worked as a front line war correspondent. His later projects were subjected to the rigid censorship imposed during the last years of Stalin's rule: his colour film *Michurin* (*Life in Blossom*), about the famous horticulturalist, was made in 1946 but not released until 1948. A planned trilogy about the development of a Ukrainian village from 1930 was completed after his death by his widow, Yulia Solntseva: *Poema o more* (*Poem of the Sea*, 1958), *Povest plammennykh let* (*The Flaming Years*, 1960), and *Zacharovannaya Desna* (*The Enchanted Desna*, 1965).

A selection of Dovzhenko's writings on cinema, translated and edited by Marco Carynnyk, were published as *Alexander Dovzhenko: poet and film-maker* (Cambridge, Mass, and London, 1974).

***DRACULA***, by Bram Stoker (1847–1912), published in 1897, first appeared on the screen as NOSFERATU (1922), directed by F. W. MURNAU. Stoker's widow brought a successful action for breach of COPYRIGHT and official prints of the film were destroyed.

*Dracula* (Tod BROWNING, 1931), with FRANK-ENSTEIN (1931), established UNIVERSAL as the leading producers of horror films and was commercially very successful, both on its first release and when it was re-issued in a double bill with *Frankenstein* in 1938. The title role had been played in the 1927 stage version by Bela LUGOSI, and on the death of Lon CHANEY, who had originally been intended for the lead, Lugosi was cast for the film. Its success was due mainly to his performance and the impression of total evil it conveyed, apparently much to the public's taste, for at the height of his popularity Lugosi had a following as great as that of any romantic screen idol. *Dracula's Daughter* (1936) was an honourable sequel, though much less successful at the box-office than its forerunner.

Routine HAMMER FILMS remakes of the subject appeared: *Dracula* (1958, *Horror of Dracula* in US) and *Dracula, Prince of Darkness* (1965). The character has appeared in many other horror films such as *House of Dracula* (1945). A British *Dracula* (1973), directed by Dan Curtis, was made for American television and starred Jack PALANCE in the title role.

***DREIGROSCHENOPER, Die,*** Germany, 1931. 1¾hr. *Dir* G. W. Pabst; *prod* Warner Bros/Tobis/Nero; *scr* Leo Lania, Béla Bálazs, Ladislaus Vayda, from the stage play by Bertolt Brecht and Kurt Weill; *ph* Fritz Arno Wagner; *des* A. Andreiev; *cast* Rudolf Forster (Mackie Messer), Caroline Neher (Polly), Lotte Lenya (Jenny), Waleska Gert (Mrs Peachum).

The film version of BRECHT and WEILL's very successful adaptation (1928) of *The Beggar's Opera* disregards the episodic structure and shock tactics of the original and thereby sacrifices to a large extent Brecht's theory of alienation. Weill's songs, which were pivots of the stage play, are less vital to the film and some are omitted. PABST's realistic treatment was ideally suited to the beggars' demonstration, but jarred with the stylized sets and lighting of the rest of the film. Brecht's withdrawal from the project before completion of the script may have contributed to this strange confusion of styles, which muffled the film's social impact. The political satire is, however, still sharp (the film was banned in Britain after one showing by the

FILM SOCIETY), and the mobility of WAGNER's camera gives the film pace and attack.

The film was made simultaneously in French and German. *Die Dreigroschenoper* was filmed again as a West German/French remake in 1962, directed by Wolfgang STAUDT, with Curd JURGENS as Mackie Messer and Hildegarde KNEF as Jenny. Striking use was made of colour, harking back to the Expressionist paintings of the twenties. (See also THE BEGGAR'S OPERA.)

**DRESSLER, MARIE** (1869–1934), US actress, made her name in musical comedy and her first film, TILLIE'S PUNCTURED ROMANCE (1914), co-starring CHAPLIN and Mabel NORMAND, was based on one of her stage successes. It was enormously popular, but her other silent films were less so and her stage career also declined, partly because of her whole-hearted involvement with trade-unionism in the theatre. With the coming of sound her popularity revived and she became a star character actress, specializing in tough, elderly pessimists of wide girth and broad humour. By 1933 she was named as the year's top box-office draw in both the *Motion Picture Herald* and the *Hollywood Reporter*. Among her most successful films were *Anna Christie* (1930), with Greta GARBO, *Tugboat Annie* (1933) with Wallace BEERY, a perfect foil, and the all-star production DINNER AT EIGHT (1933).

**DREW ASSOCIATES,** US production–distribution company started in 1959 by Robert Drew who acts as executive producer to a group of film-makers whose work was the foundation of the movement which became known as DIRECT CINEMA.

While still working as a photo-journalist on *Life*, Drew was examining the problems of making a film in the on-the-spot manner of *Life* reporting. Impressed by Richard LEACOCK's television film *Toby* (1954), he joined forces with Leacock to form an association that would work towards the creation of a new kind of television journalism. They were joined by others, mostly ex-journalists: Donn Alan PENNEBAKER, James Lipscombe, Gregory Shuker, Hope Ryden, Al MAYSLES. Time-Life supplied the funds they needed to develop lighter, more mobile, less conspicuous equipment. By the time they shot *Primary* (1960), they had perfected a silent hand-held 16MM camera and a light self-powered tape-recorder, the two linked by an accurate cable-less system of synchronization invented by Leacock. They had also perfected a method: two-person units consisting of a sound man and a camera-man were sent out to shoot the footage; then everyone collaborated to edit it. *On the Pole* (*Eddie Sachs*) (1961) and *Football* (1962) are among their early films made in this way and

screened as part of the CBS-TV 'Living Camera' series whose most influential single film was THE CHAIR (1963).

*The Children Were Watching* (1960)—a study of de-segregation battles in New Orleans shot by Leacock as one of four *Close-Up!* documentaries made in co-production with John Secondari of ABC-TV—and *Crisis: Behind a Presidential Commitment* (1963)—the last film made by Drew Associates before Leacock and Pennebaker left—were extremely inflammatory examples of direct cinema journalism. Contrary to television's conventionally impartial approach to controversy, Drew Associates used the same approach to news reports as they did to their character studies: they were interested, not in a general dispassionate truth, but in the specific emotional truth of a given person in a given situation.

At its best the Drew Associates' effort to remain open to their subject-matter has resulted in really original perceptions and a genuinely useful style of film-making.

**DREYER, CARL THEODOR** (1889–1968), Danish director whose distinguished contribution to the art of film spans over fifty years. Born of a Swedish mother, he was orphaned as a baby and adopted by Danish parents. After writing theatre criticism in Copenhagen, he came to the cinema in 1912 as a scriptwriter; up to 1918 he wrote over twenty films, including adaptations from Zola and Balzac. (The films he later directed all had literary sources.) He worked for Nordisk from 1916: they financed his first film *Praesidenten* (*The President*, 1920), after he had proved himself as both scriptwriter and editor. A rather contrived thriller, the film demonstrates Dreyer's early infatuation with D. W. GRIFFITH, whose INTOLERANCE (1916) he had just seen. The plot is built up in flashbacks, a technique he borrowed from Griffith, but it does prefigure characteristics of Dreyer's maturity in a pre-occupation with matters of conscience and a meticulous attention to authenticity in the décor. His second film, *Blade af Satans Bog* (*Leaves from Satan's Book*, 1921) was a yet more slavish imitation of Griffith. Modelled on *Intolerance*, it has four episodes concerned with the recurrent prevalence of evil, although the four stories are not interwoven as in the Griffith film. Again, great trouble was taken over the sets, and the rhythmic sense that Dreyer developed in the editing helped to redeem the film. It was photographed by George Schneevoigt, who worked again with Dreyer on *Prästänkan* (*The Parson's Widow*, 1920) and *Der var engang* (*Once Upon a Time*, 1922). *Prästänkan* was shot on location in Norway for the Swedish company SVENSK FILMINDUSTRI, and marks the appearance of

Dreyer's characteristic concern with real people, rather than the melodramatic caricatures of his first two films: the acting is strikingly naturalistic for its time. The film's humour and lyricism demonstrate the influence of SJÖSTRÖM and STILLER and contradict accusations that Dreyer lacked a sense of humour.

In 1921 he went to Berlin to make *Die Gezeichneten* (*Love One Another*, 1922), a denunciation of anti-Semitism made with a cosmopolitan cast. Despite the melodramatic characterization, Dreyer's handling of the complex plot is firm. This period of apprenticeship closed with the elegant but thin *Der var engang*, for which Dreyer returned to Denmark.

Dreyer's first work of real accomplishment came in 1924 with *Mikaël*, an UFA production co-written by Thea von HARBOU. The interiors were photographed by Karl FREUND and it was produced by Erich POMMER: not surprisingly, contemporary German critics classed it with the KAMMERSPIELFILM. But this story of an artist's unfulfilled love for his adopted son is told with such an eye for detail and observation of people that the film's Expressionist qualities constitute its surface rather than its substance. Dreyer returned to Denmark to make *Du Skal aere din hustru* (*Master of the House*, 1925), for which he had a composite four-roomed apartment built in the studio; this concentration of the drama within cramped physical surroundings recurs constantly and gives Dreyer's work much of its emotional intensity. The story of the taming of a tyrannical husband by his family is distinguished also by its naturalistic detail, and in its emphasis on the narrative power of faces and gestures it prefigures LA PASSION DE JEANNE D'ARC, made two years later. On the strength of the success of *Du Skal aere din hustru* he re-visited Norway to make the humorous folk-tale *Glomdalsbruden* (*The Bride of Glomdal*, 1926), a deceptively relaxed pause before the intensity of *La Passion de Jeanne d'Arc* (1928), the first film of Dreyer's full maturity.

He had suggested three historical heroines: Catherine de Medici, Marie-Antoinette, and Joan of Arc. The last-named was approved, and Dreyer based his script, for the only time in his career, not on a fictional source but on actual transcripts of the trial, concentrating the suffering and humiliation of Joan's twenty-nine examinations into one day. The anguish of FALCONETTI's only film appearance has become one of cinema's most enduring achievements. The film was a critical success but a financial disaster and Dreyer sued the production company for breach of contract. It was not until 1931 that he managed to finance his next film, VAMPYR (1932), his first sound film. This was a critical as well as a financial failure and for the next eleven years

Dreyer was forced to return to journalism in Denmark. VREDENS DAG (*Day of Wrath*, 1943) became his first popular success because analogies were drawn between his account of seventeenth-century witch hunting and the sufferings of occupied Denmark: although Dreyer disclaimed any allegorical plan, he was forced to take refuge in Sweden until the end of the war. *Vredens dag* looks back to *La Passion de Jeanne d'Arc* in its unsparing depiction of cruelty and humiliation.

While in Stockholm he directed *Två människor* (*Two People*, 1945) which he refused to have shown publicly during his lifetime. ORDET (*The Word*, 1955), however, is in the mainstream of his work, in its confined atmosphere, its measured pace, and its intense examination of emotion; but here the emotions are less restricted to the area of suffering than in some of his earlier work, and the film has a rare quality of spiritual optimism. *Ordet* won the Golden Lion at VENICE, two years after Dreyer had been honoured by the award of the lease of one of Copenhagen's largest cinemas, according to the municipality's policy towards distinguished Danish film workers (see DENMARK).

Although the supernatural has no place in Dreyer's last film GERTRUD (1964), it continues the stylistic and thematic lines of *Ordet* in its visual stillness and its examination of the nature of love. Largely disliked on its first appearance, *Gertrud* has gradually acquired great esteem.

Dreyer's work lies outside the direct line of the development of film: for one who was above all a man of cinema, his rejection of the usual preoccupation with visual mobility is remarkable. His refusal to compromise his artistic integrity meant that in forty-five years he directed only fourteen feature films; but his best work has a timelessness that is a result of his superb visualization of emotions and ideas.

**DREYFUS, ALFRED** (1859–1935), French officer of Jewish descent unjustly sentenced to Devil's Island for treachery but reprieved after lengthy legal proceedings (1894–1906). He gained the support of Emile Zola who wrote *J'accuse*, a pamphlet exposing the anti-Semitic army conspiracy behind the Dreyfus case, for which he himself was tried. *Dreyfus* (1898) purported to show scenes of Dreyfus's arrest and imprisonment, and Georges MÉLIÈS, an ardent Dreyfusard, made *L'Affaire Dreyfus* in eleven scenes in 1899. The British *Dreyfus* of 1931 directed by F. W. Kraemer, with Cedric HARDWICKE as Dreyfus, gives a straightforward account taken from the play *The Dreyfus Case* by Herzog and Rehfisch. William DIETERLE's *The Life of Emile Zola* (US, 1937) is a tribute to Zola's endeavour to bring about justice. Paul MUNI plays Zola and

Joseph Schildkraut Dreyfus. *I Accuse* (1958), directed by José FERRER who also played Dreyfus, focuses on the man, a dull and dedicated patriot as mirrored in Nicholas Halasz's book *Captain Dreyfus, a study in mass hysteria*.

Abel GANCE made two anti-war films (1919 and 1938) which bear the same title as Zola's exposure.

**DRIVE-IN,** a form of outdoor cinema in which patrons watch the film from their own cars, parked in semicircular bays before an oversized screen. Sound is provided by captive loudspeakers placed inside each car so that windows may be closed. Factors such as weather, screen illumination, and time of sunset make drive-in presentation generally inferior to that of conventional cinemas, but these problems are balanced by the privacy and social intimacy they afford. Drive-ins originated in the US and have only spread to areas where climate and automobile density are favourable.

*DRUMS ALONG THE MOHAWK,* US, 1939. Technicolor; 1¾hr. *Dir* John Ford; *prod* Darryl F. Zanuck for Twentieth Century-Fox; *scr* Lamar Trotti, Sonya Levien, from the novel by Walter D. Edmunds; *ph* Bert Glennon, Ray Rennahan; *mus* Alfred Newman; *cast* Claudette Colbert (Lana Best Martin), Henry Fonda (Gilbert Martin), Edna May Oliver (Mrs McKlennan), Eddie Collins (Christian Reall), John Carradine (Caldwell).

During the American War of Independence a group of secessionist farmers courageously withstands the repeated attacks of Indians who are in the pay of the British government.

John FORD's first colour film embodies his recurrent elemental themes: birth, death, and the pioneer's deep devotion to his land. He made dramatic use of the somewhat crude TECHNICOLOR available, especially in the beautifully paced sequence where Henry FONDA, as the dogged, sensitive settler, is hunted through the dawn by three Indian braves. Claudette COLBERT gave a spirited performance as the hero's gently-bred wife at the stockades.

**DUBBING,** the process of adding dialogue or other sounds to the sound-track of a film after the picture itself has been shot. Normally in West European and US production, the actors' voices are recorded simultaneously with the photography, and this 'sync' sound is heard on the final track. (See SYNCHRONIZATION.) But if for various reasons the dialogue must later be altered, the picture is not re-shot; new dialogue is dubbed. The film is broken into short scenes of less than a minute, running continuously in endless loops.

The actors watch each loop projected in a dubbing theatre and after many repetitions they record the words as their lips move on the screen. The procedure bears little resemblance to acting and many actors never master it.

Dubbing is most familiar to the filmgoer as a means of translating foreign films into his own language. This is usually done after the film is completed, outside the country of origin, and without the supervision of the original director. The translator concerns himself primarily with writing lines which can be spoken in the same length of time as the original lines and with roughly similar lip movements; sometimes he must sacrifice the literal meaning for an approximation. The actors who dub the voices are not highly-paid stars and do not receive screen credit; lacking such motivations, they rarely equal the original performances. (Occasionally, in a film with a multilingual cast, each star dubs his own voice for the version shown in his home country.) When the voices have been recorded, the dubbing mixer combines them with a music-and-effects track supplied by the original producer. Only the sounds from this 'M&E' track remain from the original film; any footsteps or 'atmosphere' that were recorded along with the original dialogue are lost in the dubbed version (unless painstakingly re-created and dubbed in again). The sound-track that eventually results from all this is often a pale shadow of the original, and sophisticated audiences have come to prefer SUBTITLES to dubbing. But when dubbing is carried out by artists as dedicated as those who made the film, as in the case of the English dubbed version of HIROSHIMA MON AMOUR (1959), the effect may be superior to subtitling.

Dubbing is frequently employed in the original language version of a film for technical reasons. Sound tracks of scenes shot on location can be marred by the sound of aircraft or traffic out of camera range. Wide shots uncluttered by furniture may afford no place to conceal a microphone close enough to pick up voices intelligibly. In such cases a guide track is recorded which audiences will never hear; the original actors dub their own voices, speaking the same words and listening to the guide track through earphones. Sometimes minor script changes are necessary to avoid referring to action which has ended on the cutting-room floor. New words will then be dubbed against the old lip movements, usually undetected.

In some European countries dubbing is a habit rather than a resort. All Italian feature films are dubbed, usually by a totally different cast. Some directors justify this by pointing to the technical and artistic freedom it allows them, but the practice owes more to conditions during and after the

Second War when studios and equipment were in short supply. Lack of the expensive equipment which makes flexible synchronous shooting possible may also be a reason for dubbing, especially in those countries where production is still predominantly studio-based, as it is, for instance, in Eastern Europe.

In the UK the term 'dubbing' is commonly applied to the process of MIXING or re-recording the various voice, effects, and music tracks into a single master track, which occurs in all films.

***DUCK SOUP***, US, 1933. 1¼hr. *Dir* Leo McCarey; *prod* Paramount; *scr*, *mus*, *lyrics* Bert Kalmar, Harry Ruby; *ph* Henry Sharp; *cast* Groucho Marx (Rufus T. Firefly), Harpo (Pinkie), Chico (Chicolini), Zeppo (Bob Rolland), Margaret Dumont (Mrs Teasdale), Louis Calhern (Ambassador Trentino).

*Duck Soup* is a short tightly-made comedy of the MARX BROTHERS' vintage period which lampoons the war films and Ruritanian romances of the early sound era. Groucho, as the indigent president of Freedonia, wins the rich Mrs Teasdale (Margaret DUMONT at her most statuesque) with a repertoire of bland insults and outwits the inefficient scheming of Harpo and Chico, agents of a neighbouring state. Mock heroics abound: Harpo's ride of Paul Revere ends abruptly at the sight of a blonde in a négligé. The culminating battle sequences, in particular, are a fine example of inspired satirical lunacy.

**DUDOW**, SLATAN (1903–63), German director born in Bulgaria, studied architecture in Berlin and became director of a workers' theatre group. He visited the USSR in 1929 and in the same year collaborated with Bertolt BRECHT on the script of an experimental short film *Seifenblasen* (*Soap Bubbles*, often known by its French title *Bulles de savon*). He also worked with Brecht on the script of DIE DREIGROSCHENOPER (1931), and Brecht co-scripted Dudow's first and best-known feature film, KÜHLE WAMPE (1932). Dudow's Communist sympathies exiled him from Germany from 1935 to 1945: he made no more films until he settled in East Germany as one of DEFA's most esteemed directors. The films of this last stage of his career include *Unser täglich Brot* (*Our Daily Bread*, 1949), about post-war reconstruction in East Berlin; *Frauenschicksale* (*A Woman's Destiny*, 1952), a Cold War drama containing some uncharacteristically Expressionist effects; *Stärker als die Nacht* (*Stronger than Night*, 1954), a bitter denunciation of Nazism; and *Der Hauptmann von Köln* (*The Captain of Cologne*, 1956).

***DUEL IN THE SUN***, US, 1946. Technicolor; 2¼hr. *Dir* King Vidor; *prod* Selznick International; *scr* David O. Selznick, Oliver H. P. Garrett; *ph* Lee Garmes, Hal Rosson, Ray Rennahan; *des* J. McMillan Johnson; *ed* Hal C. Kern; *mus* Dmitri Tiomkin; *cast* Jennifer Jones (Pearl Chavez), Joseph Cotten (Jesse McCanles), Gregory Peck (Lewt McCanles), Lionel Barrymore (Senator McCanles), Herbert Marshall (Scott Chavez), Lillian Gish (Mrs McCanles), Walter Huston (The Sinkiller), Charles Bickford (Sam Pierce).

The plot embraces most of the ingredients of melodrama, including adultery, miscegenation, execution, seduction, treachery, and murder; it also allows splendid visual set-pieces, notably the wrecking of a train carrying explosives and expansive vistas of herds of cattle and hordes of horsemen. SELZNICK's grand conception was admirably executed by King VIDOR and a distinguished cast; but the film's pretensions to daring realism appeared somewhat naïve even in its own time. The protracted, quasi-erotic finale, in which the two wounded lovers crawl interminably closer to die in each other's arms, became celebrated and earned the film the sobriquet 'Lust in the Dust'.

**DUFAYCOLOR**, colour film process of the thirties notable chiefly for its use in Humphrey JENNINGS's *Design for Spring* (1938). Dufaycolor was an ADDITIVE process incorporating in the stock a finely-ruled screen of red, green, and blue lines. (See COLOUR.)

**DULAC**, GERMAINE (1882–1942), French director, worked as a journalist on the feminist newspaper *La Française* from 1909. From 1915 to 1920 she directed films for her own company, Delia Film, financed by her husband Albert Dulac, an agricultural engineer. Her first film was *Les Sœurs ennemis* (1916); the best-remembered from this commercial period is *La Fête espagnole* (1919), from a scenario by Louis DELLUC and starring Delluc's wife Eve Francis. After her marriage ended in 1920 Dulac continued to direct at least one film a year until 1929, becoming increasingly involved with current AVANT-GARDE movements—SURREALISM, ABSTRACT FILM, pure cinema. *La Souriante Madame Beudet* (1923) is a subjective, impressionistic study of the bored wife of a provincial merchant; LA COQUILLE ET LE CLERGYMAN (1928) is generally accepted as the first Surrealist film, although it was dismissed by the Surrealist group at the time. In 1928–9 she made three abstract films, but ill health and her apprehensions regarding the expense and inhibiting effect of working with sound, halted her career as a director, although she continued to work on newsreels in an advisory capacity.

Dulac became founder and president of the

Fédération française des ciné-clubs in 1925 and also made many contributions to the lively debates on film aesthetics during the thirties and forties: as a theorist she has been ranked with the important critics of her day.

**DUMONT**, MARGARET (1889 or 1890–1965), began as a singer, first joining the MARX BROTHERS in their stage show *Cocoanuts* (1928). She appeared in seven of the Marx Brothers' thirteen films, a pillar of rectitude, responding with sympathetic fortitude to Groucho's mixture of insults and amorous advances. Her success as the perfect comic foil led to numerous other films with such comedians as W. C. FIELDS, LAUREL AND HARDY, Danny KAYE.

**DUNAWAY**, FAYE (1941– ), US actress who came to Hollywood via the theatre. The success of BONNIE AND CLYDE (1967) and her performance as Bonnie established her as a star, and her assured, mocking beauty appeared to advantage in *The Arrangement* (KAZAN, 1969) and *The Thomas Crown Affair* (JEWISON, 1968). In *Little Big Man* (1970) she displayed a flair for the comic irony demanded by PENN's conception.

**DUNLOP**, IAN (1927– ), Australian documentary director, was born in London of a Scottish father and an Australian mother. In 1948 he went to Australia and studied anthropology at the University of Sydney, where he was also active in the University Film Group.

Though primarily an anthropologist, at twenty-five he decided to become a film-maker. After three years with the Australian Broadcasting Commission he joined the Commonwealth Film Unit as a production assistant and a year later, in 1957, went into the Western Desert to direct his first film, about a weather station. The profound effect of the locale and nomadic aborigines led him to embark on his major work: an expedition in 1965 into the Western Desert which resulted in a series of films under the general title *People of the Australian Western Desert* (1966–70). This was not only an extraordinary piece of observation but a moving study of the instincts and emotions that hold all men together despite cultural differences. Its quality was recognized by several awards.

Dunlop is now a recognized authority on ethnographic film; since 1969 he has extended his field to include the people of Papua, New Guinea.

**DUNNE**, IRENE (*c.* 1904– ), US actress and singer, originally trained for grand opera, then began her career in musicals. Her success in the stage production of *Show Boat* in 1929 led to a contract with RKO, where she made her film début in *Leathernecking* (1930) and her first big

success in *Cimarron* (1931). She appeared in many sentimental and romantic comedies, usually typed in genteel lady-like roles, and became closely associated with the music of Jerome KERN in such musicals as *Roberta* (1935) and *Show Boat* (1936). Apart from some witty romantic comedies such as *Theodora Goes Wild* (1936) and THE AWFUL TRUTH (1937) she is perhaps best remembered for her more mature performances in *Anna and the King of Siam* (1946), *Life with Father* (1947), and as Queen Victoria in *The Mudlark* (1950). She retired from films after appearing in *The Grass is Greener* (1952).

**DUNNING**, GEORGE (1920– ), Canadian animator. After his early work from 1942, largely with the NATIONAL FILM BOARD of Canada, he joined UNITED PRODUCTIONS OF AMERICA (UPA) and in 1957 formed his own production company TV Cartoons (now TVC) in London with former UPA staff. His animated films since then have been divided between commercial work and experimental shorts, the latter characterized by his free use of techniques normally foreign to ANIMATION, such as glass painting (*The Flying Man*, 1962) and pencil on paper (*Damon the Mower*, 1971). These experiments were reflected in his imaginative reinterpretation of the Lennon–McCartney lyrics in the popular and commercial YELLOW SUBMARINE (1968).

**DUNNING PROCESS,** an early method of filming actors in the studio against a moving background photographed elsewhere. The actors and foreground objects were illuminated with yellow light and stood before a blank screen illuminated with blue light. In the camera, the unexposed film was placed in contact with a print of the moving background toned yellow-and-white rather than black-and-white. Wherever blue light from the screen passed through the print it was filtered by the yellow-toned areas, producing an image of the print. Wherever yellow light from the actors passed through the print it passed unhindered, producing an image of the actors only. The use of colour to separate foreground from background made the Dunning process unsuitable for colour filming, and it was superseded by BACK PROJECTION and the travelling MATTE. (See EFFECTS.)

**DUPE NEGATIVE,** a copy or duplicate of the original negative, normally made via a FINE-GRAIN print or a colour interpositive. A dupe negative may be made of an entire film as protection against damage to the original or to allow simultaneous printing on more than one machine. Dupe negatives of individual shots may be required to correct errors, to superimpose titles,

*Le Voyage dans la lune* (Georges Méliès, 1902)

*Yukinojo henge* (Kon Ichikawa, 1963)

or to introduce optical EFFECTS. During the thirties when, particularly in the US, large numbers of prints were needed for distribution, the original negative was used only to process show prints for large cities and a fine-grain print for each distribution area. From the latter, dupe negatives were struck to supply general release prints; to see a good original print, it was necessary to pay for a seat at a 'first run' cinema.

A dupe negative is invariably inferior in photographic quality to the original: there may be losses of sharpness and steadiness coupled with increases in contrast and grain. Keeping these to a minimum is not difficult in black-and-white, but colour dupe negatives appear noticeably coarser than originals and often have distorted hues. Since optical effects are made on dupe negatives, they are unhappily obvious in colour films and have gone out of fashion in recent years. Since about 1970 a new development, colour reversal intermediate film, has allowed colour dupe negatives to be made directly (not via an interpositive) from the original negative with negligible colour losses, but it has only limited application to optical effects. (See OPTICAL PRINTING.)

**DUPONT,** EWALD ANDRÉ (1891–1956), German director, started in films as a scriptwriter. His first important film was *Das alte Gesetz* (*The Ancient Law*, 1923, also known as *Baruch*). The sensational success of VARIÉTÉ (1925) brought him a contract with UNIVERSAL, but Dupont directed only one film in Hollywood, *Love Me and the World is Mine* (1927), then returned to Europe. He worked in both Germany and England and directed Europe's first all-talkie, *Atlantic* (1929), in German and English. He worked again in Hollywood as a director, 1933–9, left the film industry for the next ten years, then from 1951 directed a few more low-budget features.

**DURAS,** MARGUERITE (1914–   ), French novelist, scriptwriter, and director, published her first novel *Les Impudents* in 1943; she has since produced over a dozen other works including plays, novels, television dramas, and film scenarios. She has frequently used one idea in various forms, as in *La Musica*, which she wrote originally as a television drama, then as a theatre piece, a novel, and finally as a film script. One of the central themes of her work is concerned with the crisis point in a relationship, with the account of a vital meeting or parting between two individuals. Dialogue is the central mode of narration in her novels, and several have been made into films: *Barrage contre le Pacifique* (1958) by René CLÉMENT, *10.30 pm Summer* (1966) by Jules DASSIN and *The Sailor from Gibraltar*

(1966) by Tony RICHARDSON. These were all made without the direct collaboration of Duras.

Duras first became directly involved in cinema when she wrote the original script for HIROSHIMA MON AMOUR (1959). Her nuanced and subtly expressive dialogue, delicately counterpointing RESNAIS's images, finally established her already growing reputation as a writer; some critics, however, find that her work balances on the edge of thinness and banality.

In 1960, with Gérard Jarlot, she adapted her novel MODERATO CANTABILE for a film by Peter BROOK, and the following year collaborated again with Jarlot on the script for COLPI's *Une Aussi Longue Absence*. In 1966 she wrote the scenario for Jean Chapot's *La Voleuse* and also collaborated with Paul Seban on the film of *La Musica*.

She directed her first film in 1969, an adaptation of her novel written in the same year, *Détruire dit-elle*. A study of the interflow of identity between a group of characters, the film makes oblique reference to the political upheavals in Paris during May 1968 and is, according to Duras, a deeply political film. She had similar aims in *Jaune le soleil* (1971) which suffered, however, from the co-operative manner in which it was made. *Natalie Granger* (1972) is more justly representative of Duras' talent.

**DURBIN,** DEANNA (1922–   ), US singer and actress born in Canada, made her feature-film début in *Three Smart Girls* (Henry Koster, 1936). Her second film, *One Hundred Men and a Girl* (1937) also directed by Koster, created a minor musical sensation in featuring as her co-star the conductor Leopold Stokowski, then at the height of his fame. Her singing voice and open-hearted charm made her a popular favourite for several years: her films of this period include *Mad About Music* (1938), *Three Smart Girls Grow Up* (1939), *Spring Parade* (1940), and *It Started with Eve* (1941). After Joe Pasternak, her producer at UNIVERSAL, moved to METRO-GOLDWYN-MAYER, the quality of her films gradually declined and she retired in 1949.

***DU RIFIFI CHEZ LES HOMMES*** (*Rififi*), France, 1955. 2hr. *Dir* Jules Dassin; *prod* Indus Films/SN Pathé Cinéma/Prima Film; *scr* René Wheeler, Dassin, Auguste le Breton, from the novel by le Breton; *ph* Philippe Agostini; *mus* Georges Auric; *cast* Jean Servais (Tony), Carl Mohner (Jo), Robert Manuel (Mario), Perlo Vita (César).

A closely-knit group of likeable criminals plan and execute a jewel robbery. The Paris underworld is shown in impeccable detail, and the film's high spot is the half-hour sequence which shows (without dialogue) the efficient carrying out of the crime which is said to have inspired several real robberies. DASSIN himself played the part of César under the pseudonym Perlo Vita.

**DURYEA, DAN** (1907–68), US actor, a specialist in dark scowl and evil grin which, coupled with his rasp-like delivery, led him to become one of the screen's top villains. He had small parts in William WYLER'S THE LITTLE FOXES (1941), in which he had also played on the New York stage, and in Howard HAWKS's *Ball of Fire* (1941); but he more markedly attracted attention in two of Fritz LANG's best films of the period, *The Woman in the Window* (1944) and *Scarlet Street* (1945). His speciality tended to be blackmailers or other brutal, sadistic villains; after *Winchester '73* (1950) he frequently played in Westerns.

**DUSE, ELEONORA** (1858–1924), Italian actress, after achieving international success in both classical and modern roles, retired from the stage in 1911. She was persuaded by Arturo AMBROSIO and Febro Mari to appear in one film, *Cenere* (1916), on which she collaborated on both script and direction. Duse was dissatisfied with the result and managed to have the film withdrawn; fortunately, copies still exist in film archives and provide a unique impression of the depth and restraint of her art. She returned to the stage in 1921, but no other film record of her acting was made.

**DUVIVIER, JULIEN** (1896–1967), French director, after a short career as a stage actor, directed his first film *Haceldama ou le prix du sang* in 1919. His active career, which ended with *Diaboliquement votre* (1967), thus spanned nearly fifty years. He is generally considered to have reached his peak of achievement with PÉPÉ-LE-MOKO and *Un Carnet de bal* (both 1937). He directed *Lydia* (1941), starring Merle OBERON, in Britain, then worked in Hollywood. At the end of the war he returned to France; thereafter his only English-language film was ANNA KARENINA (1948). With *Sous le ciel de Paris* (1951) he once more approached the style of poetic realism which he had achieved in the late thirties; of his other late films *Le Petit Monde de Don Camillo* (1951) and *Le Retour de Don Camillo* (1953) were the only ones to achieve wide success, chiefly for FERNANDEL's superb interpretation of the belligerent priest.

**DWAN, ALLAN** (1885–    ), Canadian-born director with a prolific career in Hollywood from 1909. He began as a writer for ESSANAY and became a director of one-reelers for the AMERICAN FILM COMPANY in 1911, subsequently moving to UNIVERSAL where he directed many short films including *Richelieu* (1914). Following periods with FAMOUS PLAYERS, TRIANGLE, and Artcraft, he directed Douglas FAIRBANKS in ROBIN HOOD (1922). In 1923–6 he was with Famous-Players-Lasky (see FAMOUS PLAYERS) where he made eight films with Gloria SWANSON, including *Zaza* (1923) and *Manhandled* (1924). During the early sound period he worked mainly for FOX and FIRST NATIONAL, but he also directed another Fairbanks film, *The Iron Mask* (1929). In the early thirties he made three films in Britain, and on returning to Hollywood worked principally at TWENTIETH CENTURY-FOX until 1941, notably on a succession of films starring Claire TREVOR, several Shirley TEMPLE vehicles, and one of the studio's major productions, *Suez* (1938).

After some comedies produced by Edward Small for UNITED ARTISTS release, he joined REPUBLIC in 1945 and remained until 1954, making films which included *Sands of Iwo Jima* (1949). His later work included several films for RKO and television productions.

*Allan Dwan—the last pioneer*, by Peter Bogdanovich, London, 1971 is a valuable study.

**DYNAMIC FRAME.** Early motion picture systems had differing shapes and sizes of FRAME and it was largely because of the commercial ascendency of systems such as EDISON'S KINETOGRAPH that the shape was fixed in the horizontal four-by-three ratio derived from classical proportions dating back to the ancient Greeks. (See ASPECT RATIO.)

In his essay 'The Dynamic Square' (published in CLOSE-UP, March–June, 1931), EISENSTEIN bemoaned this dominant aspect ratio and did not regard experiments with WIDE SCREEN formats to be an improvement. He wanted a format in which the shape and size of the projected image could be matched to the requirements of the subject. Film-makers who have occasionally attempted to break from convention have, for technical reasons, always done so by masking off part of the normal frame or by using more than one projector.

Perhaps the most far-reaching but least-used technique involves a constantly changeable shape and size of image. The technique, called the Dynamic Frame in the only example of its kind, *The Door in the Wall*, directed by Glen Alvey Jr, can be used to isolate parts of a larger frame in a manner similar to the IRIS, or to create different shapes according to composition possibilities or the director's aesthetic whim. *The Door in the Wall*, produced under the auspices of the BRITISH FILM INSTITUTE's Experimental Film Fund in 1955, achieved its effect by preparing a separate masking film which, when printed over the edited original, left visible only those parts of the frame which were required. It would also be possible to use a system of hard masks in front of the camera lens, which could be manipulated during shooting to the shapes required. The inflexibility and technical difficulties of this latter method make it generally undesirable.

The subsequent disregard of the dynamic frame may be attributed to two factors: the development of multiple image techniques used in films such as *The Boston Strangler* (Richard FLEISCHER, 1969) and the widespread belief that a good director can achieve everything he wishes within the bounds of the ACADEMY or scope frame.

# E

**EADY PLAN/MONEY** see BRITISH FILM PRODUCTION FUND

**EALING STUDIOS,** British production company in operation 1931–55. The studios were built in the western suburbs of London by Associated Talking Pictures, a company formed by Reginald Baker, Samuel Courtauld of the famous textile family, and Basil Dean, a successful theatre impresario; Baker alone remained on the board of Ealing Studios throughout its life as a company.

During the thirties the company was modestly successful with films aimed at the home market, particularly those built around popular stars of the music hall such as Gracie FIELDS and George FORMBY. Michael BALCON joined the company as a board member and head of production in 1938, and the outbreak of war brought a change of emphasis in the company's productions. Thorold DICKINSON's *The Next of Kin* (1941) was made as a military training film for the War Office: it was later shown publicly under the auspices of the Ministry of Information; the very successful *The Foreman went to France* (1942) was directed by Charles FREND, one of the many young directors who gained their early experience at Ealing, and produced by Alberto CAVALCANTI.

The company's consistent policy was to maintain a regular production team and to recruit new talent from among its ranks. Other directors who started in this way include Charles CRICHTON, Robert HAMER, and Alexander MACKENDRICK. The team also included a group of very talented scriptwriters, T. E. B. CLARKE, John Dighton, Robert Hamer, and William Rose among them; without doubt this use of a homogeneous team contributed largely to the distinctive quality of Ealing films during the forties and fifties. A memorable product of this teamwork is DEAD OF NIGHT (1945).

The 'Ealing comedies' of the post-war years earned wide and well-deserved popularity. With the exception of WHISKY GALORE (1949, *Tight Little Island* in the US) which was adapted from a novel by Compton Mackenzie, they used original scripts from the company's own writers, often drawn from real-life incidents. Their distinctive flavour was created by the development of bizarre events in ordinary, closely-observed surroundings—the realist approach developed during the war is noticeable. *Hue and Cry* (Crichton, 1947), PASSPORT TO PIMLICO (1949), THE LAVENDER HILL MOB (1951), THE MAN IN THE WHITE SUIT (1951), and *The Ladykillers* (Mackendrick, 1955), all represent this short and distinguished period in British film-making. An exception to the usual approach is KIND HEARTS AND CORONETS (1949), probably the first British black comedy.

The general impression of the Ealing style its heyday was one of English domesticity, an impression reinforced by the suburban studio itself—an unpretentious set of buildings with pleasant gardens and even beehives—and the friendly informality that prevailed among the studio personnel. This image was not affected by the excellent action films produced during and after the war, including *San Demetrio, London* (1943), *Scott of the Antarctic* (1948), and *The Cruel Sea* (1952), all directed by Charles Frend. During the post-war years an attempt was made to extend Ealing's activities abroad. THE OVERLANDERS (1946) and *Eureka Stockade* (1948) both made in Australia and directed by Harry WATT, had some commercial success, but plans to operate a subsidiary production company with studios in Australia failed to materialize.

During the forties and fifties the increasing domination of British film production and distribution by the RANK ORGANISATION presented distribution difficulties to independent companies; an agreement drawn up in 1944 between Ealing and Rank, by which Ealing gained advantageous distribution terms while retaining total production autonomy, covered the company's most fertile period, artistically and commercially, and protected it from the problems of a small company in a situation of near-monopoly.

However, in 1952, financial problems led to the selling of the studios to the BBC and the concentration of Ealing production at Rank's Pinewood Studios. The loss of independence which this move entailed was probably inevitable; and the company was wound up in 1955.

*EARLY SPRING* see SOSHUN

**EARP,** WYATT (1848–1929), served as a law officer in Wichita and Dodge City before moving with his brothers Virgil and Morgan to Tombstone, Arizona, where Virgil was made Marshall and where the famous gun battle with the Clantons took place in 1881. The best-known portrayals of his exploits are by Henry FONDA in MY DARLING CLEMENTINE (1946), Burt LANCASTER in GUNFIGHT AT THE OK CORRAL (1956), and James STEWART in John FORD's *Cheyenne Autumn* (1964). In his later years Earp acted as technical adviser to W. S. HART. His friendship with 'Doc' HOLLIDAY has been elaborated upon in films and television series including 'Gunsmoke', one of the longest-running series on US television.

*Wyatt Earp: Frontier Marshall* by Stuart N. Lake (Boston, New York, 1931) gives an account of Earp's exploits that is sometimes in conflict with contemporary accounts. *Tombstone* by O. B. Faulk (London, New York, 1973) is a valuable history of the place and the myths attached to it.

*EARTH* see ZEMLYA

**EASON,** B. REEVES (1886–1956), US director of many low-budget features and serials. He is best remembered as SECOND UNIT director for spectaculars which include the celebrated chariot race in Fred NIBLO's BEN-HUR (1925), the land rush sequences in Wesley RUGGLES's *Cimarron* (1931), and the tournaments and duels in Keighley and CURTIZ's *The Adventures of Robin Hood* (1938). Eason was an expert horseman, but ruthless in achieving the effects he wanted. The carnage associated with his sequences in Curtiz's *The Charge of the Light Brigade* (1936) contributed to the passage of legislation to protect animals used in films. His last film was *Rimfire* (1949). His son, B. Reeves Eason Jr, appeared in Westerns as an actor.

*EASTER PARADE*, US, 1948. Technicolor; 1¾hr. *Dir* Charles Walters; *prod* Arthur Freed for MGM; *scr* Sidney Sheldon, Frances Goodrich, Albert Hackett; *ph* Harry Stradling; *mus, lyr* Irving Berlin; *cast* Fred Astaire (Dan Hughes), Judy Garland (Hannah Brown), Peter Lawford (Jonathan Harrow), Ann Miller (Nadine Hale).

Fred ASTAIRE was in semi-retirement when Gene KELLY, originally cast for the leading role, was injured during rehearsals. Astaire was persuaded to return to the screen, and danced with his usual precision and grace. With Judy GARLAND giving a witty performance as the raw chorus girl who blossoms into a star, the result was a skilful musical with some outstanding numbers, including the famous 'We're a Couple of Swells' and Astaire's hectic 'Drum Crazy' solo.

**EASTMAN,** GEORGE (1854–1932), US industrialist who in 1879 developed an improved photographic plate. Realizing that photography could be made available to a much wider public, he worked towards the introduction of a flexible roll film on paper (1884), a simple box camera, the Kodak (1889), and a transparent celluloid roll film (1889). He probably patented his celluloid film with still photography in mind, and its application to the motion picture camera was developed by W. K. L. DICKSON working with EDISON. Eastman gave away millions of dollars, especially to the arts and to dentistry. His home, Eastman House, Rochester, New York, became a film museum and archive.

The Eastman Kodak Company continued to be a major force internationally in the development and manufacture of photographic equipment. Its first real impact on motion pictures was with the introduction of 16mm Kodachrome in 1935. From 1943 35mm Kodachrome was used in the TECHNICOLOR monopack system, but this became obsolescent with the development of EASTMAN COLOR negative film.

**EASTMAN COLOR,** colour negative film from which positive prints can be made, a close relative of the Kodacolor film used for snapshots. Introduced by the Eastman Kodak Company in 1952, it rapidly superseded TECHNICOLOR, until then the only entirely successful colour process applied to motion pictures. Used in an unmodified camera and capable of being processed in an ordinary laboratory, Eastman Color proved cheaper and infinitely more flexible than either Technicolor's three-strip process with its specially-built camera or Technicolor monopack, processed as three colour separation negatives. Successive improvements in speed and grain have offered cameramen increasing freedom in the creative use of colour.

Today almost every colour feature film produced in the US and Western Europe is photographed on Eastman Color negative and printed on Eastman Color print film; it may appear on credits as METROCOLOR, WARNERCOLOR, or Color by DE LUXE. Even films bearing the credit 'Color by Technicolor' will usually have been photographed on Eastman Color negative but printed by the Technicolor laboratories. (See COLOUR.)

*EAST OF EDEN*, US, 1955. CinemaScope; 2hr; Warnercolor. *Dir, prod* Elia Kazan for Warner Bros; *scr* Paul Osborn, from the novel by John Steinbeck; *ph* Ted McCord; *ed* Owen Marks; *cast* James Dean (Caleb Trask), Julie Harris (Abra), Raymond Massey (Adam Trask), Jo Van Fleet (Kate Trask), Richard Davalos (Aron Trask), Burl Ives (sheriff).

*East of Eden* was KAZAN's first film using CINEMASCOPE and colour, and for all its grandeur it was a more controlled work than ON THE WATERFRONT (1954). It was also the first of his explorations of adolescence and of father–son relationships. Kazan himself worked on the script which, following Steinbeck's novel, is derived from the story of Cain and Abel. James DEAN was impressive in his first starring role as the complex, anguished younger son, and his scenes with Julie HARRIS as his brother's sweetheart have great poignancy.

**EASTWOOD,** CLINT (1930–  ), US actor, was signed by UNIVERSAL in 1954; a bit part in *Francis in the Navy* (1955), in the series starring Donald O'CONNOR and Francis the Talking Mule, was followed by *The First Travelling Saleslady* (1955). In 1959 Eastwood went to CBS-TV for the Western series 'Rawhide' which ran for seven years. He gained international recognition in Sergio LEONE's trio of Italian-made Westerns beginning with *Per un pugno di dollari* (*For a Fistful of Dollars*, 1964), and his abilities were further extended in films directed by Don SIEGEL including *Coogan's Bluff* (1968), *Two Mules for Sister Sara* (1969), and *Dirty Harry* (1971). Also in 1971 Eastwood made his first film as director, *Play Misty for Me*.

**EASY LIVING,** US, 1937. 1½hr. *Dir* Mitchell Leisen; *prod* Arthur Hornblow Jr for Paramount; *scr* Preston Sturges from a story by Vera Casparay; *ph* Ted Tetzlaff; *cast* Jean Arthur (Mary Smith), Edward Arnold (J. B. Ball), Ray Milland (John Ball Jr), Luis Albernini (Mr Louis Louis).

This SCREWBALL comedy makes the most of an absurd basic device: Edward ARNOLD petulantly flings his wife's new sable coat out of his New York penthouse window; it lands on Jean ARTHUR riding to work on the top of a Fifth Avenue bus; compromised, she is forced to pose as his mistress. The film effectively juxtaposes extreme opulence with the poverty of Depression America, especially in the contrast between Arnold as the blustering banker and Jean Arthur's bewildered heroine.

**EASY RIDER,** US, 1969. Technicolor; 1½hr. *Dir* Dennis Hopper; *prod* Peter Fonda; *scr* Fonda, Hopper, Terry Southern; *ph* Laszlo Kovacs; *cast* Peter Fonda (Wyatt), Dennis Hopper (Billy), Antonio Mendoza (Jesus), Phil Spector (Connection), Robert Walker (Jack), Jack Nicholson (Hanson).

An examination of contemporary America in the framework of a motor-bike Odyssey ends with the shooting down of the two voyagers, Billy and Wyatt, by a truck driver who dislikes their life-style. The beauty and potential richness of the country is repeatedly set against the stupidity, corruption, and violence of its people. Made independently, inexpensively, and informally, in a style deriving from DIRECT CINEMA, the film was an outstanding box-office success. It led to a temporary vogue for low-budget films, made by newcomers but commercially backed. The folk-rock sound-track featuring many currently popular performers also became a model to be imitated for a time.

**EASY STREET,** US, 1917. 25min. *Dir, scr* Charles Chaplin; *prod* Mutual; *ph* Rollie Totheroh, William C. Foster; *cast* Charlie Chaplin, Edna Purviance, Albert Austin, Eric Campbell, James T. Kelley, Henry Bergman, John Rand, Charlotte Mineau, Frank J. Coleman.

One of the most interesting of CHAPLIN's MUTUAL films, *Easy Street* is unique in making the Tramp uphold the law instead of opposing it. Down and out at the beginning of the film, he steals the collection box from the Easy Street Mission. Reformed by the minister and his assistant (that she is the beautiful Edna PURVIANCE helps bring about the transformation), his first act is to return the collection box. Soon he is so firmly on the side of law and order that he becomes a policeman. Single-handed, he defeats the local bully (Eric Campbell, as usual in the Mutual films), cleans up Easy Street and then, with a self-satisfied smirk, walks sedately with the rest of the now highly respectable citizens of the area to attend service at the Mission.

**ECLISSE, L'** (*The Eclipse*), Italy/France, 1962. 2hr. *Dir* Michelangelo Antonioni; *prod* Robert and Raymond Hakim for Interopa Film/Cineriz (Rome)/Paris Film Production (Paris); *scr* Antonioni, Tonino Guerra, Elio Bartolini, Ottiero Ottieri; *ph* Gianni Di Venanzo; *des* Piero Poletto; *ed* Eraldo Da Roma; *mus* Giovanni Fusco; *cast* Monica Vitti (Vittoria), Alain Delon (Piero), Francisco Rabal (Riccardo), Lilla Brignone (Vittoria's mother), Louis Seignier (Ercoli).

The affair between Vittoria and Riccardo has ended and they part in the dawn. Riccardo tries to renew the relationship, but Vittoria recognizes that it is over. She meets Piero and starts an affair with him, which he wants to turn into marriage but she refuses.

*L'eclisse* is often regarded as the third of a trilogy begun with L'AVVENTURA (1960) and LA NOTTE (1961). It picks up themes and situations from them, and provides a sense of completion by Vittoria's reversal of the choices made by the protagonists of the earlier films. In particular, she seems to prefer solitude to a failing relationship, and the only moments in the film where she seems happy are when she is alone.

The streets and buildings of Rome, characteristically depicted with austere beauty, echo the alienation of ANTONIONI's people. Stylistically the film marks something of a departure for Antonioni: it is much more fragmented than his previous films, and the ending is a remarkable sequence of fifty-eight shots which encapsulates the emptiness of Vittoria and Piero's relationship—and that of all the couples before them.

**EDDY,** NELSON (1901–67), US singer who achieved great popularity on the screen in the thirties, especially in romantic musicals directed by W. S. VAN DYKE and co-starring Jeanette MACDONALD: *Naughty Marietta* (1935), *Rose Marie* (1936), and *Sweethearts* (1938), as well as *Rosalie* (1938) in which he was partnered by Eleanor POWELL. The teaming with MacDonald also flourished under other directors, in such films as *Maytime* (1937), *The Girl of the Golden West* (1938), and *New Moon* (1940), but his popularity declined after the partnership broke up in 1942.

**EDIPO RE** (*Oedipus Rex*), Italy, 1967. Technicolor; 1¾hr. *Dir, scr* Pier Paolo Pasolini; *prod* Alfredo Bini; *ph* Giuseppe Ruzzolini; *cast* Franco Citti (Oedipus), Silvana Mangano (Jocasta), Carmelo Bene (Creon), Julian Beck (Tiresias), Pier Paolo Pasolini (High Priest).

Although the text of *Edipo Re* (translated by PASOLINI himself) is faithful to Sophocles, its structure and emphases are not. The most overt change is the addition of a prologue and epilogue, set in modern times, extending the myth into the present. While pointing out that the motives of an ancient tragedy still exist today, it enables Pasolini to make explicit the autobiographical element of the film. He also plays the part of the High Priest.

Pasolini filmed in Morocco, exploiting to the full the vast, bleak stretches of desert. The use of primitive music emphasized the primeval reverberations of his subject.

**EDISON,** THOMAS ALVA (1847–1931), US inventor, began his working life as a railway worker and was later a telegraph operator. He took out his first patent in 1868, on an electric registering device known as a 'stock-ticker' which was installed at the Wall Street Stock Exchange. His subsequent inventions included a much refined telegraph (1871), the phonograph (1877), and the electric light (1879). By 1894 Edison's Western Electric Company was one of the most powerful in the US.

On 6 October 1889 motion pictures were projected in Edison's New Jersey laboratory. In 1891 Edison, with an employee W. K. L. DICKSON, perfected and patented the KINETOGRAPH.

The first pictures were of dancing girls, performing animals, and men at work. Attempts at synchronizing the kinetoscope and the phonograph were made.

Edison's interest in motion pictures was always peripheral to his other concerns, and after Dickson left him in 1897 to market his own MUTOSCOPE he made no more important advances in the field. However, the Edison patents on most motion picture camera and projection devices were the basis of the attempt by the MOTION PICTURE PATENTS COMPANY to establish a monopolistic trust.

**EDITING,** the process of assembling the individual shots and sound tracks made for a film into a coherent whole. At its narrowest, editing amounts to a mere splicing together of shots in a predetermined order; at its widest, editing embraces the whole range of post-production techniques and can create meaning out of miscellany.

The editor's technique is as much art as craft, and it is mostly uncodified. Working with one or more assistants, he receives the RUSHES from the laboratory and synchronizes the picture and sound. He then begins a series of cuts, each a step nearer the final form of the film. The first ROUGH CUT is usually no more than a routine assembly of the film's component shots and is usually made to the director's instructions. In succeeding versions material is added or removed and rhythm and timing are altered until the editor, director, and others concerned are satisfied with its shape.

Finally the editor carries out or supervises the post-production operations that turn the film from a worn and much-spliced copy into a finished print: sound effects tracks are added alongside the main dialogue or commentary track; music, having meanwhile been written and recorded, is added; and all these parallel tracks are finally mixed into a master magnetic sound track (see MIXING). Special EFFECTS shots or INSERTS may be added to the picture; titles may be cut in; opticals are placed to link scenes (see DISSOLVE, WIPE). Then the negative film is cut— so far all operations have been carried out on replaceable work prints—and the ANSWER PRINT or first graded print is made by the laboratory. Much of the final work is carried out by assistants or specialists, but the editor oversees and co-ordinates it all.

Not until the answer print is screened is the film viewable in its final form; anticipating and predicting this final form, and the effect it will have on the audience, is perhaps the editor's most valued and delicate skill.

Film-makers early grasped the new medium's narrative and dramatic potential. Effects achieved visually, ranging from all the tricks of which film is capable (superimposition, disappearance/reappearance, etc) to the effects achieved by composition, lighting, and acting, could be employed and gradually developed. But almost from the beginning the most powerful means of cinematic expression was seen to be the cutting together—or editing—of separate pieces of film.

The very earliest films were simple uncut shots strung together. Foremost among those who developed film narrative by cutting were Edwin S. PORTER (*The Life of an American Fireman* and THE GREAT TRAIN ROBBERY, both 1903) and Cecil HEPWORTH (*Rescued by Rover*, 1905). By 1910, the narrative uses of ellipsis and continuity were well established. D. W. GRIFFITH developed them further and added parallel cutting between concurrent events as well as enormously extending the range of dramatic and expressive possibilities of close-ups, lighting, acting, and so on.

Griffith's insistence on the effectiveness of shots rather than scenes was carried over into Russian cinema after 1917. The comparative newness of film made it attractive to artists fervently seeking revolutionary potential in art forms; and the film-makers of the twenties in Russia—EISENSTEIN, KULESHOV, PUDOVKIN, and VERTOV foremost among them—seized on the power of the shot in relation to other shots as the basis of their use of the medium. Eisenstein's theories of MONTAGE became widely known and influential among artists abroad. In France the AVANT-GARDE questioned established narrative forms as radically as the Russians. Elsewhere, especially in Germany and the US, dramatic effect was developed mainly through expressive sets, lighting, and acting, and by greater use of camera movement (MURNAU, LANG, PABST) and editing was generally used to strengthen these elements.

The coming of sound tended to reinforce the narrative conventions as accepted mainly in the US: visual metaphor was considered unnecessary when dialogue could explain states of mind or off-screen events. The main aim of editing was now to produce dramatic effects while maintaining at all costs smoothness of continuity. In the thirties and forties directors both in Europe and the US filmed extended action through long takes and DEEP FOCUS (sometimes described as 'editing in the camera'): pre-eminent among these were Jean RENOIR, following in the steps of STROHEIM, and Orson WELLES. The connotative use of montage was perpetuated in commercial cinema chiefly through the 'montage sequence', where rapid conventional images give an impression of contracted narrative—newspaper headlines dissolving into moving train wheels superimposed over applauding hands, for example. These sequences were the work of specialist craftsmen (the best known is Slavko VORKAPICH) and were usually outside the control of the film's director.

The anti-narrative influence of montage was carried on mainly among documentary filmmakers, notably GRIERSON's group in Britain. The special demands of documentary continue to necessitate the combination of montage and narrative continuity. Often the separate shots are visually unrelated and the editor must create or impose a meaning by the way he juxtaposes them; equally, a documentary has a narrative structure, and the editor must make it flow as smoothly and convincingly as a feature film.

In commercial cinema editing remains a narrative tool, chiefly employed to reinforce the impression of 'reality'—in whatever form it has been currently accepted. This potential was extended in the wake of RESNAIS's HIROSHIMA MON AMOUR (1959), questioning the status of reality in terms of time, memory, and fantasy: unheralded FLASHBACKS and unexpected juxtapositions of shots in such films as L'ANNÉE DERNIÈRE A MARIENBAD (1961) and OTTO E MEZZO (1963) effected a change in narrative techniques without basically altering established conventions.

Real challenge to these conventions re-emerged in the late sixties in both the US and Europe, in the American UNDERGROUND and in the films of GODARD and, later, STRAUB. Filmmakers of the current modernist movements have returned to the concerns of the post-1917 Russians in seeking fundamental reconsideration of the formal potential of film, and in the overt rejection of 'editing' in the classic or conventional sense. Mainstream cinema continues to be concerned mainly with dramatic narrative, with editing striking, as it always has, a balance between ellipsis and continuity which shifts with increasing audience sophistication and technical development.

**EDITOR,** the member of the film production team responsible for cutting or EDITING the film. Under ideal conditions his creative contribution can be as important as the director's. In conventional feature film practice the editor's work begins during shooting, when he synchronizes the RUSHES from each day's work. As shooting progresses he assembles the film into a ROUGH CUT, and after shooting is completed he polishes his work to produce the fine cut, sometimes under the director's supervision. Finally he prepares the picture for optical EFFECTS and the sound-tracks for MIXING. On an important film these duties may be divided among several assistant editors, a supervising editor, music editor, dubbing editor, etc.

***EDOUARD ET CAROLINE,*** France, 1951. 1¾hr. *Dir* Jacques Becker; *prod* UGC; *scr* Annette Wademant, Becker; *ph* Robert le Fèbre; *cast* Daniel Gélin (Edouard), Anne Vernon (Caroline), Jacques François (Alain), Jean Galland (Claude Beauchamp), Jean Toulut (Barville), Betty Stockfeld (Mme Barville).

The best of BECKER's comedies with a modern Parisian setting, *Edouard et Caroline* achieves its effect not by plot development but by humorous and perceptive examination of people in a naturalistic situation. Its sympathetic warmth, which never descends into sentimentality, makes it an elegant piece of social observation, often directly reminiscent of LA RÈGLE DU JEU (1939).

**EDWARDS,** BLAKE (1922– ), US writer, producer, and director, married to Julie ANDREWS. He worked as a radio writer, then moved to television as a writer and occasional director, creating the private eye Peter Gunn for a long-running series. In the early fifties he began a successful collaboration with Richard QUINE, for whom he wrote *My Sister Eileen* (1955). Turning to direction, he demonstrated his talent for comedy in *Breakfast at Tiffany's* (1961).

Edwards's characters usually show lightness and constraint, but he is also capable of blending compassion with drama, as in *Days of Wine and Roses* (1962), about alcoholism, and creating tension as in *Experiment in Terror* (1962, *The Grip of Fear* in GB). His later films include *The Pink Panther* (1963, which he also scripted), *The Great Race* (1965), and *Darling Lili* (1969) both of which he wrote, produced, and directed.

**EFFECTS,** a general term applied in filmmaking to the simulation of actions or appearances, as opposed to simply photographing actuality. Effects, however accurate, have by definition no place in true documentary films. In film CREDITS a distinction is made between 'special effects' which are physically created in front of the camera and 'special photographic effects' which are produced optically or photographically on the film itself.

'Special effects' appear more frequently than most cinema-goers realize. Violent and catastrophic events such as storms, fires, and explosions are almost always created by effects experts, to render them safe and repeatable. But milder and more common items are also effects: fog is chemically generated to the required degree of murkiness, durable cobwebs are spun from spray guns, fountains are made to spurt without a sound to mar the dialogue. An entire subcategory of special effects embraces the model shot, where the scaled-down miniatures must appear to live in the same world with scaled-down water, smoke, and fire.

'Special photographic effects' also occur frequently, and not only in expensive films with violent action. Studio-made features usually include sequences in which actors are artificially placed against a moving background photographed elsewhere. This can be done by BACK PROJECTION or FRONT PROJECTION: a film of the background action is projected on a screen behind the actors in the studio. A similar effect can be achieved by travelling MATTE: here the actors perform before a blank screen and the background is printed in by the laboratory. Most of the obvious trick effects are produced photographically. The appearances and disappearances of THE INVISIBLE MAN (1933) were created by travelling matte (but the objects he handled while invisible were manipulated by wires).

The dedicated student of special effects has never been presented with a better textbook than Stanley KUBRICK's 2001 : A SPACE ODYSSEY (1968). Here the effects were more than trappings required by practical and economic necessity; they formed the imaginative core of the film. The techniques employed are virtually a catalogue: back projection, front projection, models, travelling matte, multiple printing, ANIMATION, and more. Kubrick himself created and supervised the effects (with more care than directors usually devote to actors) and awarded himself a separate screen credit saying so. (See also DUNNING PROCESS, OPTICAL PRINTING.)

**EGGELING,** VIKING (1880–1925), Swedish painter who worked in Paris from 1897. He collaborated with Hans RICHTER on researches into the relationship between images and time sequences by means of abstract drawings on scrolls: both, working separately, extended their experiments into the field of film. Eggeling completed only two films, *Orchestre Horizontal-Vertical* (1919) and *Symphonie Diagonale* (1924), and his work was seen by only a limited audience; but his ideas on rhythm, movement, abstract imagery, and the relationship of all three to organized sound (musical accompaniment) influenced Richter, RUTTMANN, FISCHINGER, and other European abstract film-makers. (See also ABSTRACT FILM, AVANT-GARDE.)

*ÉGI BÁRÁNY* (*Agnus Dei*), Hungary, 1970. 1½hr; Eastman Color. *Dir* Miklós Jancsó; *prod* Mafilm Studio 1; *scr* Jancsó, Gyula Hernádi; *ph* János Kende; *ed* Zoltán Farkas; *cast* József Madaras (Father Varga), Márk Zala (Priest), Lajos Balázsovits (Canon), András Kozák (Bearded Young Man), Anna Széles (Mária), Jaroslava Schallerová (Magdalena), Daniel Olbrychski (Daniel).

Using a small, intensely religious peasant community as a microcosm, JANCSÓ abstracts the events of the period after August 1919, when the Whites under Admiral Horthy were seizing power from the Red Republic of Councils under Béla Kun. The community is invaded first by one side, then by another, until finally an inspired leader (Daniel) emerges from the Horthy ranks, kills the peasants' fanatical Father Varga, and departs triumphant.

Jancsó's second film in colour perfectly combines his perennial concern with authoritarianism with his more recent interest (since switching from monochrome) in celebration through song and dance. Most of the dialogue is in the form of direct quotation from the Bible or national songs. Whereas in *Fényes szelek* (*The Confrontation*, 1968) Jancsó was concerned with political dogma, here he shows the tyranny and hypocrisy of religious dogma, epitomized in a sequence of compressed sadism in which a young girl is stripped and made to hear a description of torture. The film's great visual beauty and symbolic use of song and ritual do not mask Jancsó's cold view of human submission and domination.

**EGYPT.** A small but regular output of feature films has been produced in Egypt since 1918. Aimed at local audiences, they have consisted chiefly of melodramas using romanticized Bedouin or Ancient Egyptian settings and, after the introduction of sound, musical romances using indigenous singing and dancing. During the Second World War a realist vein began to emerge which became stronger after the revolution of 1952. However, official censorship, which has always been strict and which may ban films on political as well as moral grounds, has largely prevented film-makers from dealing with topics of a critical nature. Government measures introduced in 1957 attempted through a system of loans to stimulate higher artistic quality in films, but also increased the censor's powers. Foreign productions were also encouraged, including *The Ten Commandments* (1956), *Khartoum* (1965), *La Bibbia* (*The Bible*, 1966), and *The Sailor from Gibraltar* (1967).

A film school was set up in Cairo in 1959, and the sixties saw a few films of real quality beginning to emerge. Hussein Kamal attracted international attention with *Al Mostaheel* (*The Impossible*, 1965) and *El Boustagi* (*The Postman*, 1967). Shadi Abselam's *El Mumia* (*The Night of Counting the Years*, 1969) was acclaimed at VENICE in 1970 for its beauty and seriousness.

With the hardening of hostilities against Israel, Egyptian censorship was extended to prohibit Jewish elements in foreign films (about three hundred are imported annually); CLEOPATRA (1962) was banned because Elizabeth TAYLOR had been converted to Judaism. The only product of the Egyptian cinema to have made any international impact is the actor Omar SHARIF.

*8½* see OTTO E MEZZO

**8MM,** the smallest standard film width, nominally eight millimetres. Introduced in 1932 as an amateur film, 8mm soon replaced 9·5MM in worldwide popularity. Because of its cheapness, and despite its poor definition, it was also used for educational films and for rented cartoons and shorts, sometimes with a MAGNETIC sound stripe. In 1965 8mm was itself replaced by SUPER-8, and is now obsolescent.

**EIRE.** Creative cinema has not taken root in the Republic, largely because the country has until recently been comparatively poor; but both the basically verbal nature of Irish culture and strict moral censorship may have inhibited the development of the medium. Newsreel material has been filmed, usually by foreign companies, from 1896; some was used in George Morrison's COMPILATIONS *Mise Eire* (*I Am Ireland*, 1959) and *Saoirse?* (*Freedom*, 1961), which impressively depict events in Irish history 1893–1918 and 1918–22. The documentary films of Patrick CAREY have also been widely seen and admired outside Ireland.

Although there has been little indigenous film-making, the growth of a film culture has been furthered by the national Film Institute (set up in 1945 by a Roman Catholic action group), and by the Cork Film Festival, established in 1956. The Ardmore studios near Dublin were opened in 1958, chiefly to offer foreign companies facilities for location shooting. (As early as 1944, the Agincourt scenes of HENRY V were shot in Ireland, because of the ready availability of horses.) British and American producers have taken advantage of the comparatively cheap labour and spectacular scenery. There has also been a small but regular output of information and short films, mostly for home distribution.

**EISENSTEIN,** SERGEI MIKHAILOVICH (1898–1948), Russian director. His mother was Russian, his father of German-Jewish stock, both from a solidly bourgeois, cultivated background. From childhood he showed a talent for drawing, especially for caricature: he entered university in Petrograd to study for his father's profession of civil engineering but soon changed over to architecture, which came closer to his artistic interests. At this time Eisenstein remained apolitical; he witnessed the risings of 1917 but did not take part. However, when civil war broke out in 1918, he joined his fellow-students in enlisting in the Red Army. He was posted to the Eastern Front, at first building defence works, then designing and making propaganda posters.

While still in the army, Eisenstein came in contact with Japanese culture. This made a deep and lasting impression on him, particularly the discovery of Japanese graphics and writing. Much of his later work, both practical and theoretical, was an attempt to understand and extend the effect of the ideogram—the written character which by combining the symbols for different concepts creates a separate, independent meaning.

Eisenstein went to Moscow after demobilization, planning to study Japanese, but he needed to find work in order to obtain a ration card. A chance meeting with the actor Maxim Straukh resulted in Eisenstein's being taken on at the Proletkult Theatre as a scene painter and designer, from which he soon progressed to direction. His work with the Proletkult, and later with Vsevolod Meyerhold's theatre, indicated the direction of his creative tendencies: an attempt to construct new forms of dramatic realism through generalization, stylization, and caricature. Like his fellow-workers in these theatres (who held an aesthetic position in extreme opposition to STANISLAVSKY's Moscow Art Theatre), Eisenstein saw the function of art within the revolution as an iconoclastic force, attacking the traditions of conventional bourgeois art; this attitude, while it inclined him to experiment freely, conflicted to some extent with his feeling for the great art of the past.

In 1924, for the Proletkult, he staged Sergei Tretyakov's play *Gas Masks* in the Moscow Gas Factory. The juxtaposition of his conception of dramatic realism (the play) with actual reality (the factory setting) convinced him that the theatre was too inflexible a medium for his work. With the Proletkult team, notably Grigori ALEXANDROV who worked with Eisenstein continually until 1932, he embarked almost immediately on his first film STACHKA (*Strike*, 1925).

Eisenstein's previous contact with cinema had consisted of the use of film sequences in theatre productions and of working with Esther SHUB on the preparation of Fritz LANG's DR MABUSE DER SPIELER (1922) for release in the Soviet Union. He was also familiar with the newsreel techniques of Dziga VERTOV. *Stachka* combines characteristics derived from Eisenstein's work in the theatre (de-personalization, caricature) with structured editing using contrasting images to create metaphor or comment which was the main experimental concern of Shub and Vertov. He was particularly fortunate in having the talented cameraman Edvard TISSÉ to help in the execution of his ideas.

*Stachka* was received in the Soviet Union with some bewilderment: abroad it had a marked success and the Russian authorities chose Eisenstein to direct a film commemorating the revolution of 1905. From the proposed eight-part scenario, simply called *1905*, Eisenstein finally chose

to concentrate on one section: the mutiny on a battleship of the Black Sea fleet which, with some alteration of historical facts, emerged as BRONENOSETS POTEMKIN (*The Battleship Potemkin*, 1925). *Potemkin* is probably the most complete expression of Eisenstein's ideas on cinema; it was certainly the most immediately successful of his films. His creative editing, his insistence on using carefully chosen 'types' rather than professional actors, and his obsession with both emotional and compositional stylization, were eminently suited to the simple, forceful narrative. The film was a considerable success when it opened at the Bolshoi Theatre in December 1925. Abroad its impact was explosive, especially in Germany, in France (where Eisenstein gained particular support from the eminent critic Léon MOUSSINAC), and in Britain (where it was presented by the FILM SOCIETY). Douglas FAIRBANKS and Mary PICKFORD saw *Potemkin* in Moscow in 1926 and, on their return to America, spread word of the extraordinary upsurge of talent currently taking place in Russian cinema.

The appearance of PUDOVKIN's MAT (*Mother*, 1926) shortly after *Potemkin* not only confirmed the remarkable quality of the new Russian films, but set off a lasting controversy about the two directors. Their opposing methods were crystallized by Eisenstein himself. It was a question of how MONTAGE should be used—his own 'collision' of images was intended to stimulate the spectator to new, startling responses, while Pudovkin's 'linkage' aimed to draw the audience along a smooth narrative line. The personal rancour of their differences may have been exaggerated, but their relationship was always cool, and the consistent success of Pudovkin's films in the Soviet Union gave the authorities a standard against which to set Eisenstein's less popular work.

Eisenstein and Pudovkin were each instructed to make a film commemorating the 1917 Revolution, to be shown in the tenth anniversary year. Eisenstein broke off a project about collectivization, *Generalnaya Linya* (*The General Line*), to work on OKTIABR (*October*), an account of the October Revolution distantly related to John Reed's book *Ten Days That Shook the World*. (The film is sometimes known by this title in the US.) Like Pudovkin, who was working at the same time on KONYETS SANKT-PETERBURGA (*The End of St Petersburg*, 1927), Eisenstein was given both freedom and all possible facilities to make *Oktiabr*, but political events worked against him and shortly before the film's completion Trotsky, whom Eisenstein had shown as a central figure of the revolution, fell into disfavour. Complete re-editing was necessary to bring the film into line and it was not ready for showing until March 1928. Meanwhile Pudovkin's film had been seen and admired: his presentation of a grand theme—the revolution —as seen through the eyes of one worker had an immediate popular appeal which Eisenstein's intellectual view of human endeavour had not. *Oktiabr* was admitted to be a striking visual experience and Eisenstein's handling of great masses of people was particularly impressive; but his advanced experiments with visual metaphor were far beyond the average Russian audience of the time and the film lacked narrative coherence, possibly as a result of the unplanned re-editing. Abroad, too, *Oktiabr* was not as well received as *Potemkin*.

Eisenstein returned to *Generalnaya Linya*, now re-titled STAROYE I NOVOYE (*Old and New*, 1929). It is in some ways his most approachable film, containing an appealing central human figure: the peasant woman who becomes committed to collective agriculture. Eisenstein chose Marfa Lapkina for the role on the basis of his theory of 'typage', but her warmth takes equal place with the film's aesthetic qualities: ironically, *Staroye i novoye* was the most fiercely attacked, on the grounds of formalism, of all Eisenstein's silent films. But before it had been publicly shown in the Soviet Union, Eisenstein, with his collaborators Alexandrov and Tissé, had left on an officially approved visit to study film technique abroad, paying their way by lecturing and filming.

Since working in the theatre, Eisenstein had been pursuing theoretical studies and publishing essays on aesthetics. One of the most important, stimulated by the introduction of sound in the US, was 'The Sound Film', published in *Zhizn Iskusstva* (Leningrad, 5 August 1928) and signed jointly by Eisenstein, Alexandrov, and Pudovkin. It condemned the early Hollywood approach, which largely depended on synchronous sound, as a kind of cinematic tautology and urged that the sound-track should be treated as an element in montage, deliberately avoiding the illustrative function so as to create 'an orchestral counterpoint of visual and aural images'. The statement became known as the 'Sound Manifesto' and translations appeared the same year in the *Vossische Zeitung* (Berlin), *New York Herald Tribune*, *New York Times*, CLOSE-UP, and, in 1930, in *Cinéa-Ciné* (Paris). It may therefore be assumed that the official purpose of the tour was to examine sound equipment. Also, Eisenstein had received an offer from Joseph SCHENCK to direct a film in Hollywood and was eager to take this up. Schenck's offer was later withdrawn, and during his travels in Europe Eisenstein conducted various negotiations to work in Hollywood.

The three Russians visited Germany, Switzerland (for the first Avant-Garde Congress at Geneva), England (where Eisenstein's lectures to the Film Society had considerable influence on British film-makers), and France (where he lectured at the Sorbonne). Everywhere they were greeted with delight by film enthusiasts and harassed by government agencies who, with the increasing political isolation of the Soviet Union, regarded the film-makers as undesirable visitors.

Finally a firm offer from PARAMOUNT came while Alexandrov and Tissé were working in Paris on ROMANCE SENTIMENTALE (1930). (Eisenstein allowed his name to be attached to this film at the producer's stipulation, but it held no interest for him and he had little or no hand in its making.) Eisenstein was greeted in the US by full-scale studio publicity treatment and, simultaneously, an anti-Communist, anti-Semitic campaign to have him deported: he attempted to ignore both and start work on a film. Two projects were turned down by Paramount: an adaptation of the novel *L'Or* by Blaise CENDRARS about the California Gold Rush, under the title *Sutter's Gold*; and Theodore Dreiser's AN AMERICAN TRAGEDY, for which Eisenstein prepared a treatment which had the novelist's full approval. The mutual inability of director and producers to recognize each other's aims, Paramount's current internal conflicts, with Jesse L. LASKY who had invited Eisenstein fighting B. P. SCHULBERG for control, and the continuing campaign of slander against Eisenstein, resulted in the cancelling of his contract.

The company made every attempt to send Eisenstein back to Russia immediately. But he cherished a long-standing ambition to make a film in Mexico and, on the advice of Charles CHAPLIN, approached the left-wing novelist Upton SINCLAIR for funds. Sinclair's wife in fact backed the project financially, appointing her brother Hunter Kimbrough as producer.

*Que Viva Mexico!* was planned as four separate but thematically related episodes with a prologue and epilogue. Material was shot for all except one episode. Eisenstein intended the film to be a celebration of the peculiar spirit of Mexico, embodying the nation's typically clashing forces: life and death, beauty and corruption, freedom and oppression, paganism and Christianity. The plan was far more grandiose than the Sinclairs had foreseen, and the project was probably doomed from the start. Conflicting accounts, with accusations and self-justifications from all parties have been fully documented in Marie Seton's biography of Eisenstein and in *The making and unmaking of Que Viva Mexico!*, ed. Harry M. Geduld and Ronal Gottesman (Bloomington, Indiana, and London, 1970). Certainly Eisenstein greatly exceeded his schedule and modest budget. All his footage was sent back to Hollywood for processing, and this unedited material appeared to Sinclair both inconsequential and dangerously ambivalent in political and

*Que viva Mexico!* (S. M. Eisenstein, 1932)

religious matters. Kimbrough, the nominal producer, knew nothing of film-making and quarrelled incessantly with Eisenstein's methods. When the Sinclairs finally withdrew their backing, Eisenstein, Alexandrov, and Tissé were hurried back to Russia via the US. Eisenstein was refused access to his Mexican footage: it was understood that it was to be sent after him for editing, but he in fact never saw any of the material, disclaiming further interest when it was cleared for despatch to him in 1939. Sinclair released one episode as *Thunder over Mexico* (1933) and scenes from the epilogue as *Death Day* (1934), both edited by Sol LESSER, in spite of impassioned protests from Eisenstein's supporters in the US and abroad, which culminated in a petition against Sinclair's nomination for the Nobel Prize for Literature. In 1939 Marie Seton and Paul Burnford used substantial amounts of the original footage for *Time in the Sun*, which they edited in accordance with Eisenstein's verbal description of his intentions. *Mexican Symphony*, a series of educational shorts put together by various hands from the material not used by Lesser, was issued in 1941–2. These assemblages reveal elements in Eisenstein's vision which had so far been only implied—an obsession with weird, savage imagery, grotesque humour, a dis-

tinctly ambiguous feeling towards religion and its trappings—and a singular strain of eroticism was introduced.

On his return to the Soviet Union in 1932, Eisenstein found himself in a difficult position. Although his international reputation could not be ignored, his involvement in the Mexican scandals, his extended absence and consequent rumours of defection, and his fracas with Sinclair, a distinguished American radical, made him politically suspect. During his absence the direction of artistic development had changed under the Stalinist régime from the postrevolutionary style of free-wheeling experiment to the sober conventions of SOCIALIST REALISM. Films were expected to be either healthy, lightweight entertainment (a field in which Alexandrov was to excel) or the heroic, realistic dramas primarily directed towards underpinning the new social order and exemplified by VSTRECHNYI (*Counterplan*, 1932). Eisenstein, the speculative, cultured experimentalist, was treated with reserve. He worked as a scenario consultant at various studios and was appointed to teach at VGIK, using his lectures to conduct further explorations of aesthetic theory, but his various suggestions for film subjects were turned down. Among these was a life of Toussaint

L'Ouverture, liberator of Haiti, with Paul ROBESON in the lead.

In January 1935, at the fifteenth anniversary celebrations of the founding of the Soviet film industry, Eisenstein was severely castigated for his unconventional attitudes and lack of creative activity. His few supporters included the veteran director Lev KULESHOV and Lebedev, head of the Institute of Scientific Cinematographic Research: Lebedev perceptively (and courageously) asserted that all Eisenstein's films could be regarded as practical experiments testing theoretical work, and that there was a place in the arts as well as in science for pure research. But generally Eisenstein was in disgrace; at the end of the celebrations he was included in the lowest order of awards, that of Honoured Art Worker.

He submitted with dignity to his critics and within weeks started work on his first sound film, *Bezhin Lug* (*Bezhin Meadow*), the story of a Young Pioneer who was killed by his own father while guarding the collective harvest from the retrogressive kulaks. Work on the film was interrupted by Eisenstein's illness, but he managed to complete the shooting in spite of growing official displeasure at his handling of the subject. In March 1937 work on the editing of *Bezhin Lug* was halted and a three-day conference of film workers was called to examine the film in the light of the criticism it had already received. As with *Staroye i novoye*, Eisenstein was accused of placing his personal preoccupations above truthful representation of the problems of collectivization; of 'formalism'—stylistic experiment at the cost of clear exposition; of transforming the theme into allegory by representing the boy as a religious martyr; and doubts were cast on his commitment to socialism. The case became a *cause célèbre* abroad, but again Eisenstein was compliant and, in a statement published that year, accepted his colleagues' accusations and repudiated *Bezhin Lug*.

As a result of his co-operative attitude Eisenstein was appointed to direct ALEXANDER NEVSKY (1938)—but under strict supervision from a picked team of co-workers. His assistant director, D. I. Vasiliev, was particularly charged with holding him to a clear narrative unobscured by stylistic experiments. Large financial and technical resources were lavished on the film, which was an immediate and resounding success. Eisenstein's admirers outside the Soviet Union were less impressed: in spite of its dramatic power, striking imagery, and imaginative use of PROKOFIEV's music, *Alexander Nevsky* could not compare with the stimulating experimentalism of his early work. Eisenstein's docility and the film's success were unfortunately off-set by external events. A patriotic spectacle depicting the defeat of Teutonic invaders, it became an embar-rassment to the signatories of the German–Soviet Pact of 1939 and was withdrawn until the USSR joined forces with the Allies.

In 1940, as a compensatory gesture, Eisenstein mounted an impressive production of Wagner's *Die Walküre* at the Bolshoi Theatre. In 1943 the 'reformed' Eisenstein, who seemed to be working more or less to order, was trusted with what was intended to be another splendid historical drama IVAN GROZNYI (*Ivan the Terrible*). The popular star Nikolai CHERKASOV was again specified for the lead, but the script and shooting were not as closely supervised as for *Alexander Nevsky*: because of wartime conditions, the film was made at the Alma-Ata Studios in Kazakhstan. Part 1 was completed within the year and shown in 1944: it met with mixed reactions, but Stalin's personal approval meant that work could continue on Part 2. The Stalin Prize, first class, was awarded to Eisenstein, Cherkasov, Tissé, Prokofiev, and other members of the production team. But as work proceeded on Part 2, doubts about Eisenstein's handling of the subject became stronger. Stalin completely reversed his opinion as the presentation of Ivan's character became more complex. Eisenstein was attacked for distorting historical facts, for re-interpreting character (and, worse, in a distinctly Freudian light), and for the disconcerting visual stylization reminiscent, in its KABUKI-like formality, of his interest in Japanese art. Part 2 was not released until 1958, five years after Stalin's death and ten years after Eisenstein's. A third part had been planned but was never begun.

Early in 1946, just after cutting Part 2 of *Ivan*, Eisenstein suffered a major heart attack from which he never completely recovered. He was able to teach a little and to work on essays on film theory, but did not achieve his aim of assembling his theoretical writings into a single, massive work on film aesthetics. Eisenstein's films should be considered in the context of his theoretical work which, although not finally formulated, raises many important questions. The montage theory is the most widely recognized of his speculations, but his wide knowledge of the arts and of religion, anthropology, and psychology, led him to investigate many areas of human perception and response. He was convinced that film offered the ultimate synthesis of all kinds of art and education, and he underlined the importance of cinema in revolutionary activity.

Essays by Eisenstein available in English: *The film sense* (New York, 1942; London, 1943); *Film form* (New York, 1949); *Film essays with a lecture* (London, 1968; New York, 1970), all translated and edited by Jay Leyda; *Notes of a film director*, translated by X. Danko (London, 1959; New York, 1970). *Kino: a history of the Russian and Soviet film* by Jay Leyda (London and New York, 1960) contains personal reminiscences of Eisenstein, as do *Sergei M. Eisenstein: a biography* by Marie Seton (London, 1952; New York, 1960) and *With Eisenstein in Hollywood* by Ivor Montagu (Berlin, 1968; New York, 1969).

**EISLER, HANNS** (1898–1962), German composer, studied under Schönberg and first made an impression with 'musical cartoons' based on current events. All his published work was destroyed when the Nazis came to power and he spent the years 1937–48 in the US, working on film and concert music; but before leaving Europe he had composed the music scores for KÜHLE WAMPE (1932) and Joris IVENS's *Pesn o geroyakh* (1932), among others, and had collaborated on songs and theatre music, with Bertolt BRECHT. His expulsion from the US followed on his protests against the denunciation of CHAPLIN by the UNAMERICAN ACTIVITIES Committee; during his final years in Europe he worked with several directors including Chaplin and RESNAIS (NUIT ET BROUILLARD, 1955). His book *Composing for the films* was published in London, 1947.

**EISNER, LOTTE,** German-born author and critic, studied history of art and archaeology before entering journalism and becoming a film and theatre critic. She left Berlin for Paris in 1933, where she worked as a correspondent for *World Film News* and other publications. In 1945 she joined the CINÉMATHÈQUE FRANÇAISE, working with Henri LANGLOIS, programming festivals, exhibitions, and lectures. Apart from articles for film magazines, she has written *L'Écran démoniaque* (1952), a study of EXPRESSIONISM in the German cinema, translated into English as *The haunted screen*, London and Berkeley, 1969, and *F. W. Murnau*, London, 1972.

**EKK, NIKOLAI** (1902– ), Russian director, worked in Meyerhold's theatre as actor and stage manager. After graduating from the State Film School (VGIK) he directed silent documentaries. His first sound film, *Putyovka v zhizn* (*Road to Life*, 1931), dealing with the gangs of vagrant youths that caused a problem in Russia after the Revolution, was a considerable achievement, technically, dramatically, and politically. *Grunya kornakova* (*The Nightingale*, 1936), the first Soviet colour film, lacked the quality of Ekk's previous work. In 1939 he made two further colour films and has since done little work in the cinema. He is also a playwright and has written some screen plays.

**EKMAN, GÖSTA** (1890–1938), Swedish actor of great distinction and popularity in the theatre

appeared also in a number of films. The best-known abroad was INTERMEZZO (1936), in which his romantic intensity contributed much to the film's success. He also worked in Germany for MURNAU in *Faust* (1926).

**EKMAN, HASSE** (1915– ), Swedish actor and director, son of Gösta EKMAN, had a prolific output during the forties, demonstrating his versatility in war stories, *Första divisionen* (*First Division*, 1941), thrillers, *Lågor i dunklet* (*Flames in the Dark*, 1942), and gentle romances, *Ombyte av tåg* (*Changing Trains*, 1943). Ekman has habitually scripted and controlled the production of his films; his strength in the direction of actors was displayed in *Flicka och hyacinter* (*Girl with Hyacinths*, 1950), a story of loneliness and suicide.

**EKTACHROME** was introduced by the Eastman Kodak company in 1958 as a low contrast colour stock and gradually replaced Kodachrome, which had been in use as an amateur 16mm stock since 1941. Two new faster (i.e. more sensitive to light) Ektachrome films were introduced in the late sixties and shorter processing time was developed. Ektachrome is now widely used for professional 16mm production, especially when only small quantities of prints are needed.

**EL CID,** US/Italy, 1961. 70mm Super-Technirama; 3hr; Technicolor. *Dir* Anthony Mann; *prod* Samuel Bronston Productions/Dear Film; *scr* Philip Yordan, Fredric M. Frank; *ph* Robert Krasker; *mus* Miklos Rozsa; *cast* Charlton Heston (Rodrigo Diaz de Bivar), Sophia Loren (Chimene), John Fraser (King Alfonso), Raf Vallone (Count Ordonez), Geneviève Page (Queen Urraca), Gary Raymond (King Sancho), Herbert Lom (Ben Yussaff).

A spectacle about the exploits of the knight Rodrigo, known as El Cid, who devoted his energies to driving the Moors from eleventh-century Spain. The film carried its marathon length better than the majority of elephantine productions which for a time seemed the answer to cinema's dwindling audiences, and gave scope to Anthony MANN's flair for filming action previously developed mainly in Westerns. Its main attraction was its pictorial magnificence and spectacular splendour, particularly in the siege of Valencia, and Charlton HESTON's outstanding performance.

**ELEK, JUDIT** (1937– ), Hungarian director, enrolled at the Academy for Film Art in 1956, where she remained until 1961. During the middle sixties she made three shorts for the BÉLA BÁLAZS STUDIO which dealt directly with the problems she was later to enlarge upon in her first feature *Sziget a szárazföldön* (*The Lady from Constantinople*, 1968)—loneliness, old age, and the difficulties of reconciling the past with the present. Her unforced visual style owes much to her documentary training, and the uncompromising approach of her first feature showed surprising maturity.

**ELEPHANT BOY**, GB, 1936. 1½hr. *Dir* Robert J. Flaherty, Zoltan Korda; *prod* Alexander Korda for London Film Productions; *asst dir* David Flaherty; *scr* John Collier, Akos Tolnay, Marcia De Silver; *ph* Osmond Borrodaile; *cast* Sabu (Toomai), Walter Hudd (Petersen), Wilfred Hyde White (Commissioner).

The only commercial fiction feature undertaken by the great documentary film-maker, *Elephant Boy* can hardly be compared with the best of FLAHERTY's work. Ostensibly adapted from Kipling's *Toomai of the Elephants*, *Elephant Boy* was a full two years in production (1935–6). The footage shot in India by Flaherty is barely visible in the final version, for Alexander KORDA insisted on extensive changes once the unit returned to England—revisions which ranged from an entirely new plot to additional elephant sequences composed mainly of gigantic rubber elephant feet. The one contribution of Flaherty's which remained in the film was his discovery and casting of SABU in the leading role.

Even though the film was mildly successful— winning, ironically enough, a best direction prize at VENICE (1937)—it is an example of the extreme difficulty in mixing documentary and commercial goals and styles within the same film. An excellent account of the filming of *Elephant Boy* (and the hazards of producing for Flaherty) can be found in Arthur Calder Marshall's biography of Flaherty, *The innocent eye*, London, 1963, New York, 1966.

**ELTON,** Sir ARTHUR (1906–73), British producer and director of documentaries, entered the film industry via the script department of GAINSBOROUGH PICTURES, and joined John GRIERSON at the Empire Marketing Board (see CROWN FILM UNIT) in 1931, there directing several documentaries, notably *Aero-Engine* (1934), a silent film. In 1935, he and Edgar ANSTEY directed *Housing Problems*. With Grierson, Elton was in 1938 a founder of Film Centre Ltd, a consultancy and co-ordinating organization, and concentrated on production. Supervisor of Films at the Ministry of Information 1941–5, he later worked as an adviser and film production consultant for numerous commercial and international organizations. He was a hereditary baronet.

**ELVEY,** MAURICE (1887–1967), British director, worked with the experimental Stage Society before entering the film industry. His prolific career, stretching over nearly fifty years, resulted in a large number of reliable, entertaining films ranging from an early version of *The Hound of the Baskervilles* (1921), through Gracie FIELDS vehicles such as *Sally in Our Alley* (1931), to farces like *Dry Rot* (1956). His best work appeared in the forties, notably *Salute John Citizen* (1942) and *The Gentle Sex* (1943), which he co-directed with Leslie HOWARD.

**ELVIRA MADIGAN**, Sweden, 1967. Eastman Color; 1½hr. *Dir, scr, ed* Bo Widerberg; *prod* Europa Film; *ph* Jorgen Persson; *mus* Mozart's Piano Concerto No. 21 in C major K467, Vivaldi Violin Concerti; *cast* Pia Degermark (Elvira), Thommy Berggren (Sixten), Lennart Malmer (Kristoffer), Cleo Jensen (Cook), Nina Widerberg (little girl).

The true story of a Swedish nobleman who eloped with a tightrope dancer to spend a romantic summer in Denmark, finally committing suicide when their money was exhausted, is treated with a tender lyricism which avoids sentimentality. The film's strength lies in its visual beauty: people and settings are handled with great sensibility and the colour is delicately controlled. The music, too, is used sparingly but to remarkable effect in heightening the poignancy of the story. This was the first of WIDERBERG's films to achieve success with an international audience.

**EMBEREK A HAVASON** (*People on the Mountain/Men in the Mountains*), Hungary, 1942. *Dir* István Szőts; *scr* József Nyirö, Szőts; *ph* Ferenc Fekete; *des* Imre Sörés; *mus* Ferenc Farkas; *cast* Alice Szellay, János Görbe, József Bihary, Lajos Gárday.

This tragic story of a poor couple in the Transylvanian mountains appeared at a time when Hungarian production, though rising in quantity to over forty features a year, was generally low in quality. The first feature of the young Szőts (whose only other work a few years later was banned), it showed an appreciation of the cinema's artistic resources and paved the way for further explorations of peasant life.

**EMMER,** LUCIANO (1918–   ), Italian director who scripts his own films. He gained an international reputation with his delightful first feature DOMENICA D'AGOSTO. A supporting role was played by the then little-known Marcello MASTROIANNI, who appeared in Emmer's next two films *Parigi è sempre Parigi* (1951) and *Le ragazze di Piazza di Spagna* (1952). These failed to maintain the humorous alternations of mood so successful in *Domenica d'agosto*. *Il* *bigamo* (1956), a strident comedy co-starring Mastroianni and Vittorio DE SICA, did little to enhance the director's reputation. As well as a number of other features, Emmer has made several distinguished art films on the work of Giotto, Bosch, Goya, and others.

## EMPIRE MARKETING BOARD FILM UNIT
see CROWN FILM UNIT

**EMSHWILLER,** ED (1925– ), US UNDER-GROUND director, worked as a science-fiction illustrator before making his first film *Dance Chromatic* (1959). This was the first of a series of films exploring his obsession with the movement of dancers. He rapidly established himself as one of the most accomplished and imaginative technicians in the underground movement, through his use of single frame time exposures and superimpositions. He directed *Thanatopsis* (1960–2) which was followed by *Totem* (1962–3), a complex interpretation of a performance by the Alwin Nicolais Dance Company and photographed HALLELUJAH THE HILLS (1963). *Relativity* (1963–6), made with the aid of a Ford Foundation grant, aims to elucidate the concept of man's place in the universe and shows a development of his earlier, entirely visual and abstract, work. *Branches* (1971) uses creative editing to restructure figurative material.

**EMULSION,** the photosensitive layer of film STOCK. By varying the ways in which it is manufactured, it is possible to change its characteristics, notably the relative sensitivity to light. These variations from one emulsion to another are measured as the film's 'speed' and given a corresponding index number on the ASA (American Standards Association) or DIN (Deutsche Industrie Normal) scale. Emulsion is made by suspending light-sensitive particles, normally of silver bromo-iodide, in gelatine. Minute quantities of dyes may be added to achieve sensitivity to particular parts of the colour spectrum—usually to make it sensitive over as wide a range as possible. In colour films, three or more layers of emulsion are used, between which are filters to control the light reaching each layer.

**END OF ST PETERSBURG, The,** see KONYETS SANKT-PETERBURGA

**ENFANT SAUVAGE, L',** France, 1970. 1½hr. *Dir* François Truffaut; *prod* Les Films du Carrosse/Les Artistes Associés; *scr* Truffaut, Jean Gruault, from *Mémoire et rapport sur Victor de l'Aveyron*, by Jean Itard; *asst dir* Suzanne Schiffman; *ph* Nestor Almendros; *ed* Agnès Guillemot, asst by Yann Dedet; *mus* Vivaldi,

under direction of Antoine Duhamel; *cast* Jean-Pierre Cargol (Victor), François Truffaut (Itard), Françoise Seigner (Madame Guerin), Jean Dasté (Pinel), Paul Villé (le vieux Rémy).

TRUFFAUT's script is faithfully based on the account published in 1806 by the young doctor Itard who in 1797 took pity on a wild boy found in the Aveyron, took him into his home, and undertook to civilize him.

The film is dedicated to Jean-Pierre LÉAUD, and most clearly reflects Truffaut's compassionate concern with children and with education. It reflects his belief that respect for individuals must be combined with faith in civilization, and that the potential loss to the boy of primitive freedom is outweighed by the precious gift of communication. The painstaking, sometimes painful, steps by which Itard tries to teach the young Victor to speak are shot with economy and restraint: the film's classic lucidity is achieved with the help of Nestor ALMENDROS' beautiful black-and-white photography and of Vivaldi's music under the direction of Antoine Duhamel. Warmth and a powerful sense of personal involvement are conveyed by Truffaut's delicate performance as Itard—his first major acting role.

**ENFANTS DU PARADIS, Les,** France, 1945. 3¼hr. *Dir* Marcel Carné; *prod* Pathé Cinéma; *scr* Jacques Prévert; *ph* Roger Hubert; *des* Alexander Trauner; *mus* Maurice Thiriet, Joseph Kosma, G. Mouque; *cast* Arletty (Garance), Jean-Louis Barrault (Debureau), Pierre Brasseur (Frédéric Lemaître), Maria Casarès (Nathalie), Marcel Herrand (Lacenaire), Louis Salon (Comte Edouard de Montray), Pierre Renoir (Jericho).

A rich and colourful evocation of theatrical society in nineteenth-century Paris, the film centres on the love between the famous mime Debureau and the beautiful Garance who is also loved by an aristocrat, a criminal, and an actor.

The film, which took three years to make under the difficult conditions of the Occupation, contains some superb set-pieces of spectacle and is a work of immense emotional power. The performances of ARLETTY, BARRAULT, and BRASSEUR in roles based on historical figures are of memorable quality, and *Les Enfants du paradis* continues to exercise a spell over audiences at frequent and popular revivals, at a time when CARNÉ's other films tend to be out of favour.

**ENFANTS TERRIBLES, Les** (*The Strange Ones*), France, 1950. 1¾hr. *Dir, prod* Jean-Pierre Melville; *scr* Jean Cocteau from his novel; *ph* Henri Decaë; *ed* Monique Bonnot; *des* Mathys; *cast* Nicole Stéphane (Elisabeth), Edouard Dermithe (Paul), Renée Cosima (Agathe), Jacques Bernard (Gérard), the voice of Jean Cocteau.

*Les Enfants du paradis* (Marcel Carné, 1945)

Paul and Elisabeth, brother and sister, create a private, enclosed world of their own in the single room which they share and which reflects the disorder of their lives and emotions. Their complex emotional and erotic manoeuvres culminate inevitably in suicide.

This claustrophobic COCTEAU fantasy, made on a very small budget, was shot mainly on the stage of the Théâtre Pigalle. It is a strange and variable work; in particular it failed to support the tragic dénouement. The film's use of baroque music, Vivaldi's Concerto in A minor for two violins and strings (from L'Estro Armonico, Op.3) as transcribed by Bach, was an original idea at the time, attracting both attention and imitation.

**ENGEL, ERICH** (1891–    ), German director, after considerable experience in the theatre, made his first film *Funf von der Jazz-band* (1932) in a light escapist vein, a style which he maintained throughout the thirties and during the war years. During the post-war period which he spent in East Germany he turned to more serious subjects, as in *Affaire Blum* (1948), but on moving to West Germany he returned to his earlier style.

**ENGEL, MORRIS** (1918–    ), US director, has been influential in the establishing of the new American approach to film production, making independent low-budget films in New York. *The Little Fugitive* (1953), a humane and authentic depiction of American family life, won much admiration, and he has successfully adapted television techniques in making *Lovers and Lollipops* (1956), entirely on location, and *Weddings and Babies* (1958).

**ENRICO, ROBERT** (1931–    ), French director, trained at the INSTITUT DES HAUTES ÉTUDES CINÉMATOGRAPHIQUES (IDHEC) and served with the French army film unit before working in television and sponsored documentaries. His *Thaumetopoea* (1960), about the menace of the Procession Moth, won many awards. A fictional short, LA RIVIÈRE DU HIBOU (*Incident at Owl Creek*, 1961), is still Enrico's best-known work. His first feature, *La Belle Vie* (1963), concerned the Algerian troubles. This and subsequent features, more obviously commercial, have failed to fulfil the shorts' early promise—even given the talents of BELMONDO (*Ho!*, 1968), BARDOT (*Boulevard du Rhum*, 1971) and Maurice RONET (*Une Peu, beaucoup, passionnément*, 1971).

***ENSAYO DE UN CRIMEN*** (*The Criminal Life of Archibaldo de la Cruz*), Mexico, 1955. 1½hr.

*Dir* Luis Buñuel; *prod* Alianza Cinematográfica; *scr* Buñuel, Eduardo Ugarte; *ph* Augustín Jiménez; *cast* Ernesto Alonso (Archibaldo), Miroslava Stern (Lavinia), Rita Macedo, Ariadna Welter, Rodolfo Landa.

Archibaldo is by intention a psychopathic woman-killer, but he is balked in every planned murder but one by the intervention of some other violent death to the intended victim. *Ensayo de un crimen* is a compendium of BUÑUEL images —including women's shoes, insects, wedding gowns—and is jokingly structured around his major preoccupations, derived from SUR-REALISM, *l'amour fou* interwoven with *l'acte gratuit*. It is Buñuel genially poking fun at himself.

**ENTR'ACTE**, France, 1924. 20min. *Dir* René Clair; *scr* Francis Picabia; *ph* Jimmy Berliet; *mus* Erik Satie; *cast* Jean Borlin, Man Ray, Marcel Duchamp, Erik Satie, Georges Charensol, Rolf de Maré.

The iconoclastic painter and poet Francis Picabia conceived *Entr'acte* to fill a fifteen-minute intermission between the two acts of the Dada ballet *Relâche*. The film, full of exuberant and absurd humour, was shot in three weeks by René CLAIR on the stage and terrace of the Théâtre des Champs-Elysées, Luna Park, and elsewhere in Paris; the cast includes many leading personalities of the Paris avant-garde. According to Clair, it was intended as an exercise in style and a homage to the pioneers of screen comedy—the LUMIÈRE Brothers of *L'Arroseur arrosé*, MÉLIÈS, and certain American comedians. Erik SATIE's inconsequential music was played in accompaniment to the silent film.

**EPISODE FILM.** A collection of short fiction films by one or more directors, usually grouped by a common theme or author to form a feature-length film. They are sometimes incorrectly termed COMPILATION films. INTOLERANCE (1916) was an early and distinguished example (although unusual in the interweaving of the episodes), but the form has not been a popular one in the United States. The isolated examples include *If I Had a Million* (1932), two Julien DUVIVIER films, *Tales of Manhattan* (1942) and *Flesh and Fantasy* (1943), and *O. Henry's Full House* (1952, *Full House* in GB). The form enjoyed a vogue in the British cinema in the late forties and early fifties, notably with three films based on short stories by Somerset Maugham: *Quartet* (1948), *Trio* (1950), and *Encore* (1951). There was also a number of films of an episodic

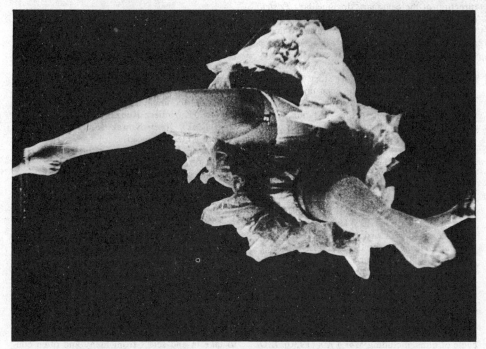

*Entr'acte* (René Clair, 1924)

nature in which several stories were pulled together by a common setting or event as in *Bond Street* (1948) and *Train of Events* (1949), in which a train crash provided the climax to three different stories. These films had been preceded by the eerie DEAD OF NIGHT (1945) and in more recent years this tradition has been continued by a series of episodic horror films including *Dr Terror's House of Horrors* (1965) and *Vault of Horror* (1973).

The form has enjoyed considerable success on the continent, although OPHULS' *Le Plaisir* (1952), based on Maupassant stories, provides the only major example of an episode film based on a single author. In the same year ANTONIONI directed his episode film *I vinti*, but more recently the films have been packages of episodes by different directors, including TRUFFAUT and WAJDA (*L'Amour à vingt ans*, *Love at Twenty*, 1962); GODARD, ROSSELLINI, PASOLINI and Gregoretti (*RoGoPaG*, 1962); VISCONTI and Bolognini (*Le streghe*, 1967); CHABROL and POLAŃSKI (*Les Plus Belles Escroqueries du monde*, 1963); and Chabrol and ROHMER (*Paris vu par...*, 1964). One of the most accomplished episode films is KOBAYASHI'S KWAIDAN (1964).

**EPSTEIN, JEAN** (1897–1953), French director and theoretician, first worked as assistant to DELLUC on *Le Tonnerre* (1921), progressing to the direction of the centenary documentary *Pasteur* (1921). On the strength of its favourable reception PATHÉ offered him a contract (terminated after four films by mutual agreement), as director.

His first film for Pathé, *L'Auberge rouge* (1923), adapted from a short story by Balzac, was a promising attempt to open up the possibilities of novel dramatic constructions and subtle rendering of atmosphere; his next film, *Coeur fidèle* (1923), established his reputation as one of the leading experimental film-makers in France.

Following the Pathé contract, he made four commercial-type films for KAMENKA'S Albatros, one of which, *Le Lion des Mogols* (1924), was adapted from a script by MOZHUKIN, who played the lead.

In *La Glace a trois faces* (1927) Epstein put into practice theories which he had been developing in a number of articles and books such as *Bonjour Cinéma* (Paris, 1921) and *Le Cinématographe vu de l'Etna* (Paris, 1926). There was a continual exchange between his theory and practice. For instance, in *La Chute de la maison Usher* (1928), on which BUÑUEL worked as an assistant, he used slow motion for a dramatic purpose, possibly for the first time.

FINIS TERRAE (1929) marks the beginning of a cycle of films, including *Mor'Vran* (1930), *L'Or des mers* (1933), and *Le Tempestaire* (1947),

centred on Brittany and notable for their sympathetic observation and attempts at integration of sound and imagery.

One of the first theoreticians of the cinema, Epstein clarified and emphasized the significance of the close-up and camera angles and, most importantly, envisaged film as capable of altering traditional modes of thinking.

**ERMLER, FRIEDRICH** (1908–67), Russian director, was interested in films from childhood. In 1924 he joined the Leningrad Film School where he countered the FEKS group's principle of revolution through form by organizing the KEM (Experimental Film Workshop), which more conventionally advocated revolution through content. Ermler's silent films, including *Oblomok Imperii* (*Fragment of an Empire*, 1929), have a directness and humanity which ensured their wide popularity. After a hiatus in his career at the coming of sound he was persuaded by YUTKEVICH to co-direct VSTRECHNYI (*Counterplan*, 1932). Ermler's political dependability (he had been a member of the Communist Party since 1919) and preference for simplicity of technique ensured official approval: at the 1935 celebrations commemorating fifteen years of Soviet cinema, when EISENSTEIN was humiliated, he received the Order of Lenin. He went on to a stable and productive career which lasted into the sixties.

*EROICA*, Poland, 1957. 1½hr. *Dir* Andrzej Munk; *prod* WFF Lódź, WFD Warsaw; *scr* Jerzy S. Stawiński, from his novels *Wegrzy* (*The Hungarians*) and *Ucieczka* (*Escape*); *ph* Jerzy Wójcik; *mus* Jan Krenz; *cast* Part 1 'Scherzo alla Polacca', Edward Dziewonski (Dzidzius), Barbara Polomska (his wife), Kazimierz Opalinski (regional commandant); Part 2 'Ostinato lugubre', Kazimierz Rudzki (Turek), Josef Kostecki (Zak), Josef Nowak (Kurzawa), Roman Klosowski (Szpakowski).

*Eroica*, subtitled *Symfonia bohaterska w dwoch czesciach* (*Heroic symphony in two movements*), has the nature of a diptych, each self-contained part illuminating the other. The irony of the title as applied to the two stories, one of comically reluctant, the other of romantically useless, heroism, has itself the ambivalence of MUNK's view. Completely without the romanticism of his contemporaries, he nevertheless observes acts of courage with admiration, whatever their motives or results. His balanced objectivity is conveyed through a fluid and complex camera style, using long sequences with constant movement in both the subject and the point of view and in the use of DEEP FOCUS and numerous long shots which compel the spectator to take in and select from many and often conflicting visual impressions.

**EROTIKON**, Sweden, 1920. 1¾hr. *Dir* Mauritz Stiller; *prod* Svensk Filmindustri; *scr* Stiller, Gustaf Molander from the play by Franz Herzeg; *ph* Henrik Jaenzon; *cast* Lars Hanson (Preben Wells), Anders de Wahl (Professor Charpentier), Tora Teje (Irene), Karin Molander (Marthe).

STILLER's best-known comedy was also his last before he went over to more sombre themes. It achieved international success: its elegant sexual manoeuvres have been compared with SOMMAR-NATTENS LEENDE (*Smiles of a Summer Night*, 1955), but its graceful wit has none of BERGMAN's acid overtones.

**ESPOIR**, France, 1945. 1½hr. *Dir, scr* André Malraux; *mus* Darius Milhaud.

*Espoir*, originally titled *Sierra de Teruel*, was begun in 1938 with the blessing of the Spanish Republican Government. It was shot from an original script not based on MALRAUX's novel *L'Espoir* (published in 1937) except for one episode, the bombing of a Nationalist airfield, and was intended as a propaganda film to win support for the Republican cause. Confusion with the novel has led to the film's being frequently referred to as *L'Espoir*. Shooting in the Madrid and Barcelona studios was only three-quarters finished in January 1939 when Franco's troops took Barcelona. Malraux completed some of the shooting and the editing in Paris, and the film was to have appeared in 1939 under its original title but was prevented by the outbreak of war. In 1945, a LAVENDER PRINT was found to have escaped the Germans' systematic destruction. The film was distributed as *Espoir* after some mutilation and the addition of a presentation by Maurice Schumann stressing the similarities between the Spanish Republican's fight and that of the French Resistance; it won the Prix Louis DELLUC, 1945. Malraux, who was still at the front, was not consulted; when in 1969 he saw the film for the first time since 1939 he did not recognize his original cutting.

The narrative technique and structure of *Espoir* are well ahead of its time; but one of the film's chief merits is perhaps that, although it was a careful, elaborate studio production with professional actors, it gives the illusion of real war caught by the eye of a concealed camera.

**ESSANAY**, US film company founded 1907 by George K. Spoor and Gilbert M. ANDERSON, the name derived from the initials of the founders. The company's emblem was a Red Indian's head. It had branch offices in London, Paris, Berlin, and Barcelona.

At first Essanay made Westerns, of which the most famous were the Broncho Billy series, directed and acted by Anderson. He made approximately one Broncho Billy film a week, the total amounting to 376. The best-known Essanay players of the period 1910–14 were J. Warren Kerrigan, Francis X. BUSHMAN, Beverley Bayne, and Wallace BEERY.

In 1914 the company signed on Charlie CHAPLIN, fresh from success with KEYSTONE, for one year. During this year, Chaplin made fifteen films, mainly two-reelers including *The Champion*, A NIGHT IN THE SHOW, and *Work*. His leading lady in those films was Edna PURVIANCE.

Early in 1915, the English branch of Essanay announced their intention of abandoning their previous 'open market' policy and of renting films to the theatres as 'exclusives' (see EXHIBITION, DISTRIBUTION). They made this move because of Chaplin's enormous popularity and the desire to keep all his Essanay productions under immediate control of the company. This meant that Chaplin's films were elevated to the rank of features, obtainable only from one distributor, at an increased fee. In the same year, 1915, Essanay was incorporated with VITAGRAPH, LUBIN, and SELIG, in a combination known as the VLSE.

In 1916 Spoor let Chaplin go at the end of his contract. He also bought out Anderson and with EDISON founded a new company known as Perfection Pictures in 1917. At this time the English branch of Essanay reorganized itself and became known as Film Booking Offices—FBO. After the departure of Chaplin and Anderson, the company lingered on, but produced no films of any distinction.

**ÉTAIX**, PIERRE (1928–   ), French director and actor, appeared in music hall and worked in films as a gag-man, notably for Jacques TATI on MON ONCLE (1958). In 1959 he played the third thief in BRESSON's *Pickpocket*. In collaboration with Jean-Claude CARRIÈRE he scripted and directed two short films, *Rupture* (1961) and *Heureux Anniversaire* (*Happy Anniversary*, 1961), and his first feature *Le Soupirant* (*The Suitor*, 1962). He has since written, directed, and appeared in *Insomnie*, *Yoyo*, and *Tant qu'on a la santé* (all 1965), *Le Grand Amour* (1969), and *Pays de Cocagne* (1970). Étaix's early ambition was to be a circus clown, and all his films are constructed around physical, virtually non-verbal humour allied with a controlled elegance reminiscent of Max LINDER and Buster KEATON; they also owe much to the style of Tati, but without attempting Tati's wry social comment. In 1967–8 Étaix worked with the clowns of the Bouglione circus and he and his wife, Annie Fratellini, appeared in FELLINI's *I clowns* (1970).

**ET DIEU CRÉA LA FEMME** (*And Woman . . . Was Created* or *And God Created Woman*),

France, 1956. CinemaScope; 1½hr; Eastman Color. *Dir* Roger Vadim; *prod* Iena Film UCIL/Cocinor (Raoul Lévy); *scr* Vadim, Raoul Lévy; *ph* Armand Thirard; *cast* Brigitte Bardot (Juliette), Curt Jurgens (Eric), Christian Marquand (Antoine), Jean-Louis Trintignant (Michel).

VADIM's first film was shot on location in St Tropez and largely improvised. It established his own reputation, as well as that of Brigitte BARDOT whose sultry eroticism as a young woman having an affair with her husband's brother was at the time sensational. The film features the glamorous surroundings and sexual daring that typify Vadim's work. Its popularity and the wide publicity it achieved helped to pave the way for the NOUVELLE VAGUE by proving to French film financiers that young directors could make commercial successes.

*ETERNAL JEW, The,* see EWIGE JUDE, DIE

**EVANS,** EDITH (1888–  ), British actress, established a brilliant reputation in the theatre early in her career. Apart from appearances in *A Welsh Singer* (1915) and *East is East* (1916), however, her first film role was in THE QUEEN OF SPADES (1948). She has followed this with a short but admirable list of character parts in films, outstandingly in *The Importance of Being Earnest* (1952) and *The Chalk Garden* (1964), both parts with which she had had enormous success on the stage. For her remarkable performance in *The Whisperers* (1966) she received the award for best actress at the BERLIN Film Festival. She was awarded the DBE in 1946.

**EVERYMAN,** Hampstead, London cinema formerly a theatre, became one of the most famous of ART HOUSES. It was founded by James Fairfax-Jones in 1933, opening on Boxing Day with LE MILLION (1932). Although primarily a repertory cinema, the Everyman has achieved some distinguished British premières including LA RÈGLE DU JEU (1939) and DONSKOI's Maxim GORKY trilogy (1938–40), and presented the first commercial screening of ZÉRO DE CONDUITE (1933). Retrospective seasons of directors' work are held, as well as explorations of areas such as Ealing Comedies or Underrated Films.

*EWIGE JUDE, Der (The Eternal Jew),* Germany, 1940. 1hr. *Dir* Fritz Hippler, from an idea by Dr E. Taubert; *prod* DFG; *ph* A. Endrejat, A. Hafner, etc; *mus* Franz R. Friedl; *ed* Hans Dieter Schiller, Albert Baumeister.

An extreme example of Nazi PROPAGANDA film, *Der ewige Jude,* purporting to be a documentary justifying the National Socialist policy towards the Jews, was issued in Germany and in some occupied European countries during the war. By a not unskilful juxtaposition of archive material, footage especially shot in the occupied Warsaw ghetto, and unacknowledged extracts from feature films, a viciously emotive argument is built up, supported by a continuous commentary largely made up of distortions and falsehoods. Much play is made of the Jewish sources of 'degenerate' modern art: the film cites and shows Max REINHARDT, Ernst LUBITSCH, Charlie CHAPLIN, and Peter LORRE, an extract from whose performance in M (1931) is shown in such a way as to identify the actor with the psychopathic character portrayed.

*EXECUTIONER, The,* see VERDUGO, EL

**EXHIBITION,** the projection of films to a paying audience. For non-commercial exhibition, to a non-paying or membership audience, see DISTRIBUTION.

The independent showman who bought and later rented films for display in fairground booths or penny arcades was rapidly superseded by the owner or manager of the small fixed cinema who rented films from exchanges, later called distribution companies. As the distributors became richer they moved into production and, controlling the marketable product, were in a position to force out the independent exhibitor. In spite of recurrent attempts to legislate against such monopolies, vertical integration persisted in the US until 1949 and still exists in Britain. The cinema manager within a large chain is not even nominally the exhibitor and is responsible only for the efficient day-to-day running of the cinema; he has no say in choice of programmes, length of run, or seat prices. His position is similar in countries with a nationalized industry where the important decisions are taken by the municipality in consultation with the central organization.

Earlier exhibition methods survived in some countries. The travelling showman became an agent of AGIT-PROP in the immediate aftermath of the Russian Revolution, when agit-trains toured remote areas with films and educational literature. The touring film show is still a commonplace in rural districts of less developed countries.

The independent cinema owner continues to prosper in countries which are not dominated by the American or Socialist models of a production/distribution/exhibition network. In France, in particular, the persistence of a thriving film culture may be in part attributable to the number of independent outlets available to film-makers. The decline of the regular mass audience in the fifties accompanied the increase of specialized cinemas and ART HOUSES whose owners are able to exercise the special skills of a cinema exhibitor, notably the choice of a particular film for a particular audience: a film's potential success can be undermined by mounting it in the wrong area or even in the wrong cinema, and only considerable expertise can judge whether to continue the run of a film which has had a slow start at the box-office. Publicity and exploitation, usually handled by the distributor, may be taken on by the art house manager, especially in the case of a revival or retrospective season. (See also CINEMA, DISTRIBUTION.)

**EXHIBITOR,** one who exhibits films to a paying audience—usually, therefore, a cinema proprietor or owner. The booking manager of a large circuit is regarded as the exhibitor for all the circuit's individual cinemas. Exhibition interests are represented by the Cinematograph Exhibitors' Association in Britain and the National Association of Theater Owners in the US.

*EXODUS*, US, 1960. Super Panavision 70; 3¼hr; Technicolor. *Dir, prod* Otto Preminger (Carlyle Alpina Productions); *scr* Dalton Trumbo, from the novel by Leon Uris; *ph* Sam Leavitt; *mus* Ernest Gold; *des* Richard Day; *cast* Paul Newman (Ari Ben Canaan), Eva Marie Saint (Kitty Fremont), Ralph Richardson (General Sutherland), Peter Lawford (Major Caldwell), Lee J. Cobb (Barak Ben Canaan), Sal Mineo (Dov Landau), John Derek (Taha), Hugh Griffith (Mandria).

An account of the escape to Palestine of a group of Jews interned by the British in Cyprus in 1947. Although focusing on a group of central characters, *Exodus* is unashamedly an epic and the real political issues of the situation are avoided. The film marks a departure from the more enclosed dramas of PREMINGER's earlier work. Dalton TRUMBO received screen credit on *Exodus* (and on SPARTACUS in the same year) after some years' blacklisting (see UNAMERICAN ACTIVITIES).

*EXPLOITS OF ELAINE, The,* US, 1914, 14 episodes. *Dir* Louis Gasnier, George B. Seitz; *prod* Pathé Company; *cast* Pearl White, Creighton Hale, Arnold Daly, Sheldon Lewis, Floyd Buckley.

*The Exploits of Elaine* followed hard on the heels of the enormously successful *The Perils of Pauline*, with Pearl WHITE once more playing the heroine, this time on the track of her father's murderer. As before, Pearl White managed to get into impossible situations, only to be saved from certain death at the last moment (see CLIFFHANGER). Indeed in one episode she was pronounced dead but was brought back to life the following week. Elaine's exploits were popular enough—the serial showed a profit of a million dollars—for the PATHÉ Company to produce *The New Exploits of Elaine* (1915) and *The Romance of Elaine* (1915). (See SERIAL.)

**EXPOSURE,** as in still photography, the degree to which the film is exposed to light. Theoretically exposure can be controlled both by the amount of light admitted through the lens (the diaphragm or *f*-stop) and by the length of time for which it falls on the film (the shutter speed). However in practice the cinematographer is severely limited in his use of these controls. His shutter speed is fixed at a maximum of about 0·02 seconds because his film must run constantly at 24 frames per second; and his diaphragm is usually set as small as possible to maintain DEPTH OF FIELD. Therefore he tends to control exposure principally by altering the amount of light actually falling on the scene. An additional consideration not common to still photography is that he must equalize exposure in successive shots to avoid sudden changes of brightness on the screen. Thus he usually strives for consistent, rather than correct, exposure, and alters the light falling on any area which as a result appears too light or too dark. Extreme exposures may, however, be used for aesthetic purposes, as in the pale, drained, flashback sequence of BERGMAN's GYCKLARNAS AFTON (*Sawdust and Tinsel/The Naked Night*, 1953).

**EXPRESSIONISM,** a movement in the graphic arts, literature, drama, and film which flourished in Germany 1903–33. Its main aim was the external representation of man's inner world, particularly the elemental emotions of fear, hatred, love, and anxiety.

In film the movement is recognized as beginning with WIENE's DAS CABINETT DES DR CALIGARI (1919), although Expressionist elements can be traced earlier, in HOMUNCULUS (1916) for example. Certain aspects, the concern with the dual nature of man, the power of fate, the fascination of monstrous or sub-human creatures, were directly derived from the pessimism and morbidity of the German Romantic tradition; more prosaically, economic stringency was instrumental in establishing a characteristic visual style. The artificiality of painted sets and the obscurity that resulted from power shortages were justified in *Caligari* and its early successors by the distortion of external objects to represent man's psychic condition; the oblique shadows that continued to be typical of the genre indicated the haunted world of the films' protagonists.

Most of the major directors of German silent cinema contributed to the Expressionist group of films. Wiene spanned the whole period with

*Caligari, Genuine* (1920), *Raskolnikoff* (1923), and ORLACS HÄNDE (1925). WEGENER'S DER GOLEM (1920), a prototype of the monster film, used chiaroscuro lighting inspired by the magical effects of REINHARDT's stage productions, to soften the harsh contrasts of typical Expressionism, and Martin's *Von morgens bis Mitternacht* (1920) was adapted from an Expressionist play. LENI's *Hintertreppe* (*Backstairs*, 1921) and DAS WACHSFIGURENCABINETT (*Waxworks*, 1924) and PICK's SCHERBEN (1921) and SYLVESTER (1923) placed the apocalyptic doctrine of Expressionism in the enclosed world of the KAMMERSPIELFILM, while Grüne's *Die Strasse* (1923) began to direct it to the comparative reality of the STREET FILMS. ROBISON's *Schatten* (*Shadows*, 1923) was entirely created from the most characteristic visual element of Expressionist cinema.

MURNAU and LANG pursued strikingly similar courses. Murnau's NOSFERATU (1922) endowed the vampire myth with menacing shadows to indicate impending doom; DER LETZTE MANN (1924) moved towards social criticism while still conveying the enigmatic pessimism of the Expressionist vision; *Faust* (1926) emphasized the duality of man and his ultimate subjection to fate. Lang skilfully manipulated the supernatural in *Der müde Tod* (1921), made economic disaster the work of a Mephistophelean madman in DR MABUSE DER SPIELER (1922), and used his characters as a mechanistic element in overpowering décors in DIE NIBELUNGEN (1924) and METROPOLIS (1927).

DUPONT's VARIÉTÉ (1925) was one of the last full manifestations of Expressionism in the cinema: it starred Emil JANNINGS who specialized in stylized representations of men crushed by fate. Carl MAYER, who as scriptwriter had been a moving force in the development of the form, had by this time become more concerned with the cinema's potential to examine social reality. Expressionism gave way to the Neue Sachlichkeit (New Objectivity) of films by PABST and others: both styles were finally suppressed by the Nazi régime in favour of heroic 'realism' and

*Nosferatu* (F. W. Murnau, 1922)

trivial entertainment. As an influence on visual style in the cinema, however, Expressionism was of continuing importance. Pabst, Lang, and STERN-BERG continued to exploit the atmospheric qualities of lighting and set design to various ends, and the migration of many German film artists to Hollywood helped to carry its conventions into American films. The GANGSTER FILMS and horror cycles of the thirties are especially marked by Expressionism, and oblique lighting, angular compositions, and menacing objects have continued to be accepted devices in conveying suspense, fear, and abnormal mental states.

Lotte Eisner, *The haunted screen*, London and Berkeley, 1969.

*EXTASE*, Czechoslovakia, 1933. 1½hr. *Dir* Gustav Machatý; *scr* Machatý, from a story by Vítěslav Nezval; *ph* Jan Stallich; *des* Bohumil Heš; *starring* Hedy Kiesler, later Lamarr.

Nezval's simple story of an adulterous triangle in a pastoral setting was shot partly on location in Slovakia, and is invested with great lyrical beauty by STALLICH's photography. MACHATÝ expressed to the full his preoccupation with eroticism, exploring the psychological representation of physical desire in symbolic and naturalistic sequences. The famous nude shots of Hedy Kiesler (soon to become Hedy LAMARR in Hollywood) seem innocuous today but caused outrage at the time, and were cut from most of the versions widely seen in Europe and the US. Despite protests from the Pope, the film had a triumphant reception at the VENICE festival in 1934. Hedy Lamarr's husband unsuccessfully tried to buy up prints of the film and the nude photographs, but in spite of his efforts and the censors', *Extase* has continued to enjoy a well-deserved reputation for stylish eroticism and lyricism. Hedy Lamarr published her account of it in *Ecstasy and Me* (1966).

(The date given for the film's production varies. It was completed in 1932 and given its first showing in Prague in January 1933.)

**EXTERIOR,** any shot or scene in a film which purports to take place out of doors, in natural illumination as opposed to artificial light. The term does not necessarily indicate that the shot will in fact be made out of doors; exteriors are frequently photographed in the studio to allow control of light, weather, and extraneous sound. (See LOCATION.)

*EXTERMINATING ANGEL, The,* see ANGEL EXTERMINADOR, EL

# F

**FÁBRI, ZOLTÁN** (1917– ), Hungarian director, studied drama and Fine Arts. After working as a comedian, stage manager, and set designer (a role he still undertakes on many of his films), he became artistic director of the Hunnia studios in 1949. A director since 1952, he first attracted attention with *Körhinta* (*Merry-Go-Round*, 1955), shown at Cannes in 1956, a work which contributed to the brief renaissance of the Hungarian cinema in the fifties and launched the career of the actress Mari Törőcsik. Successive films showed his wide-ranging interests, most especially his sensitive depiction of country life and people, and the sixties saw no diminution in his standards; with films such as *Husz óra* (*Twenty Hours*, 1964), *Utószezon* (*Late Season*, 1967), and *Plusz-minusz egy nap* (*One Day More or Less*, 1972) he has maintained his place in Hungarian cinema while adapting his individual style to the modern idiom.

**FABRIZZI,** ALDO (1905– ), Italian actor and director, left school at an early age and after a variety of jobs acted in a local dialect play and then joined a vaudeville company playing between showings at cinemas. He began his film career with *Avanti c'è posto* (1942) and has continued to appear regularly, but his international reputation rests on two roles, the priest in ROSSELLINI'S ROMA, CITTÀ APERTA (1945), for which he received second prize at CANNES, and Uncle Tigna in ZAMPA'S VIVERE IN PACE (1946). He began directing films in 1948 with *Emigrantes* and has since continued to direct occasionally in addition to acting.

**FACE IN THE CROWD, A,** US, 1957. 2hr. *Dir, prod* Elia Kazan; *scr* Budd Schulberg, from his story *Your Arkansas Traveller*; *ph* Harry Stradling, Gayne Rescher; *ed* Gene Milford; *songs* Tom Glazer, Schulberg; *cast* Andy Griffith (Lonesome Rhodes), Patricia Neal (Marcia Jeffries), Anthony Franciosa (Joey Kiely), Walter Matthau (Mel Miller), Lee Remick (Betty Lou).

With *A Face in the Crowd*, the story of a folk singer's meteoric and gratuitous rise to national television fame, his increasing megalomania, and his ultimate downfall, KAZAN showed the power of television, then still hardly realized. The inherent dangers of personality-building, and the exploitation of the gullible viewing public, were explored with humour, bitterness, and sharp observation. Andy Griffith gave a good performance in his film début as the brash Rhodes, and Patricia NEAL brought her accustomed insight and depth to the woman who finally destroys the monster she helped to create.

**FACES,** US, 1968. 2¼hr. *Dir, scr* John Cassavetes; *prod* Maurice McEndree; *ph* Al Ruban; *ed* Ruban, McEndree; *cast* John Marley (Richard Forst), Gena Rowlands (Jeannie Rapp), Lynn Carlin (Maria Forst), Fred Draper (Freddie), Seymour Cassel (Chet).

With subtle realism *Faces* covers thirty-six hours in the lives of a couple whose marriage has gone sour, using a film-within-the-film structure to strengthen the audience's identification with the characters. The candid examination of two affairs, one tender, one sordid, traces the undignified disintegration of these middle-aged products of American suburbia. The film is remarkable for the appearance of complete spontaneity in both acting and shooting, which can in fact have been achieved only through skill and control.

**FAIRBANKS,** DOUGLAS (1883–1939), US actor, real name Julius Ullman, went to Hollywood from a successful career in the theatre. Like many stage actors he affected to despise the medium, claiming to be attracted to California by the climate; nevertheless he quickly became a success in light satirical comedies mostly written by Anita LOOS. In these early films he was already displaying his acrobatic talents, but after he formed UNITED ARTISTS in 1919 with Charlie CHAPLIN, D. W. GRIFFITH, and Mary PICKFORD (whom he married in 1920) he embarked on the series of action spectaculars that made him a celebrity. Fairbanks was a real impresario, taking a hand in all the departments of film-making. He was particularly interested in set design: the lavishness of his sets, though impressive was never vulgar. *The Mark of Zorro* (1920), ROBIN HOOD (1922), THE THIEF OF BAGDAD (1924), and *The Black Pirate* (1926) were vehicles built around Fairbanks's muscular athleticism and were commercially very successful, straightforwardly appealing to a wide family audience. He carried the clean-living image depicted in these films into his private life, assuming the position of exemplar to the nation's youth. During this time he and Mary Pickford, from their famous residence 'Pickfair', virtually ruled the social life of Hollywood. THE TAMING OF THE SHREW (1929), the only film in which he starred opposite Mary Pickford, was also one of his best; in his last films he was unable to come to terms with encroaching age and he retired in 1934.

**FAIRBANKS Jr**, DOUGLAS (1908– ), US actor, son of Douglas Fairbanks by his first marriage, made his film début in 1923 in *Stephen Steps Out* and made numerous film and stage appearances in both the United States and Britain. He came to the fore in the thirties, his earlier talkies including *The Dawn Patrol* (Howard HAWKS, 1931) and THE SCARLET EMPRESS (Josef von STERNBERG, 1934). He went to Britain to co-star with Elisabeth BERGNER in Alexander KORDA's production of *Catherine the Great* (1934). Perhaps his most famous screen role was as Rupert of Hentzau in *The Prisoner of Zenda* (John CROMWELL, 1937), a memorable performance amid a cast including Ronald COLMAN, Madeleine CARROLL, Raymond MASSEY, C. Aubrey Smith, David NIVEN, and Mary ASTOR. *Gunga Din* (George STEVENS, 1939) and *Green Hell* (James WHALE, 1940) are among his other well-remembered films. In the later forties he worked with both OPHULS and LUBITSCH, with Maria Montez in the former's *The Exile* (1947) and with Betty GRABLE in the latter's *That Lady in Ermine* (1948). Among his athletic roles in the swashbuckling tradition of his father was the title part in *Sinbad the Sailor* (1947). In the early fifties he settled in Britain, and after a few appearances in British films became involved with the production of films for television, notably the series 'Douglas Fairbanks Presents'. In 1949 he was made an honorary KBE.

*FALCON, The.* A popular series of crime-and-detection films made by RKO. The Falcon, operating outside the law to right wrongs and dispense justice, was created by Michael Arlen. He was played in the first three films (*The Gay Falcon*, 1941, *The Falcon Takes Over*, and *The Falcon's Brother*, 1942) by George SANDERS. Tom Conway (Sanders's brother in real life as well as in the latter film) successfully carried the role through a number of sequels in the next few years. In the late forties, John Calvert played the lead in a new but less distinguished series whose titles (e.g. *Appointment with Murder*, 1948) strangely failed to indicate their Falcon affiliation.

**FALCONETTI**, RENÉE (1901–46), French actress, was a successful and respected stage actress before and after appearing in her only film. This was LA PASSION DE JEANNE D'ARC (1928), in which Falconetti gave a sensitive and moving performance as St Joan, valiantly submitting to the physical indignities to which DREYER found it necessary to subject her.

*FALCONS, The,* see MAGASISKOLA

*FALLEN IDOL, The,* GB, 1948. 1½hr. *Dir, prod* Carol Reed for London Films; *scr* Graham Greene, from his short story 'The Basement Room'; *ph* Georges Périnal; *mus* William Alwyn; *cast* Ralph Richardson (Baines), Michèle Morgan (Julie), Bobby Henrey (Felipe), Sonia Dresdel (Mrs Baines).

By restricting himself to a small cast and a limited locale—a near-deserted embassy—Carol REED here achieved an effect of meticulous miniaturism. He drew from his cast low-key performances of remarkable homogeneity: his skilled direction and editing of the untrained child actor Bobby Henrey as the lonely little boy and Ralph RICHARDSON's quietly strained manner, as the kindly butler who is suspected of his wife's murder because of the child's efforts to protect him, are notable.

*FALSTAFF* see CAMPANADAS A MEDIANOCHE

**FAMOUS PLAYERS,** US production company formed in 1912 by Adolph ZUKOR. Having successfully distributed in the US LA REINE ELIZABETH (*Queen Elizabeth*, 1912) starring Sarah BERNHARDT, Zukor conceived the idea of a company specializing in 'Famous Players in Famous Plays'. He soon perceived that filmed theatre would not sustain large popular audiences and shrewdly embarked on building a team of film actors to star in the dramas, romances, and comedies that were the basis of the company's success. In 1914 he drew Mary PICKFORD from BIOGRAPH with a $2,000 a week contract and name billing. Besides this important property his stars included the *ingénue* Marguerite Clark, Pauline FREDERICK for strong dramatic roles, Hazel Dawn, a tomboyish *comédienne*, and Marie Doro in adventure stories. John BARRYMORE, already established on the stage, made some of his early films for Zukor, and Tyrone Power Sr was one of the team. Edwin S. PORTER was with Famous Players from the beginning and directed some of the earliest productions, but the company's main strength continued to be its players.

In 1916 Zukor re-signed Mary Pickford to a two-year contract which guaranteed her over a million dollars as well as a bonus of up to $3,000 based on film profits. In the same year Famous Players merged with the Jesse LASKY Feature Play production company to form Famous Players–Lasky Corporation with Zukor as president, Lasky as head of production, and, briefly, Samuel Goldfish (later GOLDWYN) as studio manager. Also in 1916 Artcraft Pictures Corporation was formed, initially to distribute Mary Pickford's films. The following year the cream of the waning TRIANGLE company, including D. W. GRIFFITH, Thomas INCE, Mack SENNETT, Douglas FAIRBANKS, and Anita LOOS, was acquired by Zukor for Artcraft: by the end of 1917 Cecil B. DEMILLE, Maurice TOURNEUR, and Allan DWAN were the most important Artcraft directors, but the subsidiary company lost its separate identity in 1918.

Both Zukor and Lasky had throughout released through W. W. Hodkinson's Paramount Pictures distribution concern. In 1918, with Famous Players–Lasky in a position of increasing strength and paying attention to exhibition outlets, Paramount became part of the consortium.

By now the company's additional star players included William S. HART, Florence Vidor, Elsie Ferguson, Jack Holt, Dorothy Dalton, Gloria SWANSON, and Dorothy GISH; Ince and J. Stuart BLACKTON were among its production supervisors; directors now associated with the company included Victor Schertzinger, Fred NIBLO, James CRUZE, Sam WOOD, and Donald CRISP. By 1922 most of the original Zukor and Lasky stars had gone, but the company remained stable and prosperous. Ethel Clayton had become an important star and conspicuous names now included Richard BARTHELMESS, Agnes Ayres (notably opposite Rudolph VALENTINO in The Sheikh, 1921), Bebe DANIELS, Marion DAVIES, Thomas Meighan, Lila Lee, and Betty Compson. Important directors now with the company included Victor FLEMING and George Fitzmaurice; the latter made Three Live Ghosts (1922), with Anna Q. Nilsson, which was then considered the best production to emerge from the Famous–Lasky British studios. By 1925 Ernst LUBITSCH was directing for the company, whose new acquisitions included Pola NEGRI, Adolphe MENJOU, Ricardo Cortez, Warner BAXTER and Edward Everett HORTON.

In 1927 the company was re-established as PARAMOUNT Pictures Corporation, although Famous Players–Lasky continued in Britain, where the change of name to Paramount did not take place until 1930.

**FANCK,** ARNOLD (1889–1974), German director who, after working as a ski instructor, embarked on filming with *Wunder des Schneeschuhe* (*Marvels of Ski*, 1920). At a time when most German films were made entirely in the studio, he created the 'mountain film', training a team of technicians who were expert alpinists and skiers to capture the most grandiose aspects of nature. His foremost collaborators were Leni RIEFENSTAHL, Luis TRENKER, and Sepp Allgeier. Fanck's fiction films, including *Die weisse Hölle von Pitz Palü* (*The White Hell of Pitz Palü*, 1929), *Der weisse Rausch* (*The White Frenzy*, 1931), and *SOS Eisberg* (1933), are all remarkable for their location photography. As part of a co-production agreement between Germany and Japan he directed *Die Liebe der Mitsu, Tochter des Samurai* (*The Love of Mitsu, Daughter of the Samurai*, 1937), a vehicle for Nazi propaganda in a Japanese setting, and during the war he made some competent documentaries on German art.

**FANNY,** US, 1960. Wide screen, 2¼hr; Technicolor. *Dir, prod* Joshua Logan for Mansfield; *scr* Julius Epstein; *ph* Jack Cardiff; *mus* Harold Rome; *cast* Maurice Chevalier (Panisse), Charles Boyer (César), Leslie Caron (Fanny), Horst Buchholz (Marius).

LOGAN's *Fanny* incorporates in its 2¼ hours the story of PAGNOL's trilogy, MARIUS (1931), *Fanny* (1932), and *César* (1936). The original was closely studied for costume, mannerisms, etc. The main outline of the story of Marius and Fanny is followed, that of César transposed almost beyond recognition. Any attempt at reproducing the original in another language must have been doubtful of success: Logan's film lacks conviction even within his own terms. *Fanny* had only moderate success in the US and elsewhere.

**FANNY** (Pagnol) see MARIUS

**FANTASIA,** US, 1940. Technicolor; 2hr. *Prod* Walt Disney; *story dir* Joe Grant, Dick Huemer; *ed* Stephen Ceillag; *mus dir* Edward H. Plumb; *conductor* Leopold Stokowski, with the Philadelphia Orchestra; *narrative introductions* Deems Taylor; sequences based on: *The Nutcracker Suite* (Tchaikovsky), *Toccata and Fugue in D Minor* (J. S. Bach), *The Sorcerer's Apprentice* (Dukas), *The Rite of Spring* (Stravinsky), *Symphony No. 6 in F Major, The Pastoral* (Beethoven), *Dance of the Hours* (Ponchielli), *Night on the Bare Mountain* (Mussorgsky), 'Ave Maria' (Schubert).

The technical culmination of the SILLY SYMPHONY experiments in linking the animated image with music, *Fantasia* is a series of sequences in which musical classics are interpreted by cartoon animation. The result varies from the inventive, abstract shapes (based on the work of FISCHINGER) of the Bach Toccata and Fugue, to the embarrassingly cute centaurs of the

Beethoven *Pastoral Symphony*: apart from such subjective judgements, the film has aroused controversy as to the validity of any visual interpretation of music. Stokowski collaborated with Disney at each stage of the production and was mainly responsible for the attempt to achieve STEREOPHONIC sound.

Although a commercial failure on its release, *Fantasia* has enjoyed frequent revivals and in the early seventies was something of a cult among members of drug-orientated groups seeking psychedelic experiences.

**FANTÔMAS**, France, 1913. 1¼hr. *Dir, scr* Louis Feuillade; *prod* Gaumont; *ph* Guérin; *cast* René Navarre (Fantômas), Breon (Inspector Juve), Georges Melchior (Fandor), Renée Carl (Lady Beltham), Jane Faber (Princess Danidoff).

Based on the first of thirty-two volumes of an immensely popular series of detective novels written by Pierre Souvestre and Marcel Allain, FEUILLADE's film in three episodes, a forerunner of the SERIAL, met with similar success. Fantômas is a diabolical criminal and master of disguise, against whom the detective Juve and ace-reporter Jérôme Fandor pit their wits in vain. In 1913–14 Feuillade went on to film, with characteristic élan, four more Fantômas stories, in four or six parts each. After Feuillade's death the character was periodically revived, but none of the later films is comparable with the original.

**FARREBIQUE; ou, Les Quatres Saisons**, France, 1946. 1¼hr. *Dir* Georges Rouquier; *prod* Jacques Giraud for L'Écran Français and Films Etienne Lallier; *scr* Rouquier, from an idea by Claude Blanchard; *ph* André Dantan; *time lapse ph* Daniel Sarrade, Maurice Delille (filmed at the Jardin des Plantes, Paris); *mus* Henri Sauguet.

*Farrebique* depicts the life of a peasant family in south-western France from December 1944 to November 1945. Around this theme ROUQUIER built a loving and detailed record of life on a farm in the district where he was born, using as his actors a family well known to him.

This record of a way of life that had changed very little for more than a century is a valuable social document. DOVZHENKO's ZEMLYA (*Earth*, 1930) showed a similar community of peasant farmers, but was mostly interested in the impact of progress and political events. Rouquier, on the other hand, was more concerned to present the land and its traditions. Following two short films on country crafts, *Farrebique*, Rouquier's first full-length film was his greatest and most affectionate tribute to the strength he saw in French rural traditions.

**FARRELL**, GLENDA (1904–71), US actress, made her film début in LITTLE CAESAR (1931)

and appeared opposite Paul MUNI in *I Am a Fugitive from a Chain Gang* (1932). In *The Mystery of the Wax Museum* (1933) she played a wise-cracking girl reporter who saves Fay WRAY from a molten-wax fate at the hands of villainous Lionel Atwill. This type of part became her speciality, particularly in the title role of the 'Torchy Blane' series (begun in 1939). She never attained the status of a front-rank star but was a talented and individual player. After a brief absence from the screen, she returned in character parts, and she has also done much television work.

**FARROW**, MIA (1945– ), US actress, daughter of director John Farrow and actress Maureen O'SULLIVAN. She became well known through her appearances in the American television series 'Peyton Place' and a much-publicized romance and marriage with Frank SINATRA. Hypersensitive in appearance, she excelled as the terrified wife in ROSEMARY'S BABY (1968) and the deceptive, elusive Cenci in *Secret Ceremony* (LOSEY, 1968), but was less successful as the innocent sophisticate Daisy in *The Great Gatsby* (Jack CLAYTON, 1974). She is married to André PREVIN.

**FASSBINDER**, RAINER WERNER (1946– ), German actor and director, studied acting and in 1967 joined the Munich Action Theatre. With friends from this group he began making films in 1969. One of his first films *Katzelmacher* (1969), in which he also acted, is an attack on the inhuman treatment of foreign workers in Germany, but the film makes it clear that its lessons can be universally applied. *Warum läuft Herr R. Amok* (*Why Does Herr R. Run Amok?*, 1969), which brought Fassbinder to world attention, attacks the conformity and dullness of everyday life. *Warnung vor einer heiligen Nutte* (1971) is a statement about the impossibility of collective film-making. In *Der Händler der vier Jahreszeiten* (*Pedlar of the Four Seasons*, 1971), which has been very popular in Germany, Fassbinder charts his main character's progression from discontent to despair with great skill. Recent films to receive international acclaim are *Die bittren Tränen der Petra von Kant* (*The Bitter Tears of Petra von Kant*, 1972) and *Angst essen Seele auf* (*Fear Eats the Soul*, 1974).

Fassbinder makes four to five films a year and inevitably their quality varies. His best films are marked by compression and directness, underlined by a sparse décor. The characters are often distanced from the audience by their mask-like faces and the monotone of their dialogue, and yet in their plight they can be both moving and amusing.

**FATHER** see APA

**FAULKNER, WILLIAM** (1897–1962), US novelist and scriptwriter whose deliberately sensational novel *Sanctuary* (published 1931) first attracted the attention of Hollywood to his work. He wrote periodically for films over a period of twenty years, then turned to television writing. *Sanctuary* was filmed as *The Story of Temple Drake* (1933), but Faulkner's first assignment was the dialogue for Howard HAWKS's *Today We Live* (1933), based on his story 'Turnabout' (published 1950). He went on to script Hawks's TO HAVE AND HAVE NOT (1944), THE BIG SLEEP (1946), and *Land of the Pharaohs* (1955), all of which demonstrate the ease with which Faulkner adapted his writing to the demands of cinema. Like other Hollywood writers, he also worked on numerous scripts for which he received no screen credit and his adaptations of his own major novels were never used. He captured the seamier side of Hollywood in his story 'Golden Land'.

Several of his novels have been made into films of varying quality. They include *Intruder in the Dust* (published 1948, filmed 1949, directed by Clarence BROWN), filmed in Oxford, Mississippi, Faulkner's home town and the setting for most of his novels; THE LONG HOT SUMMER (1958), based on *The Hamlet* (published 1940), and *The Sound and the Fury* (published 1929, filmed 1959), both directed by Martin RITT; another version of *Sanctuary* (1960) by Tony RICHARDSON; and *The Reivers* (published 1962, filmed 1969, directed by Mark Rydell).

**FAURE, ÉLIE** (1873–1937), French left-wing philosopher, art historian, and writer whose writings on film, although limited, are noteworthy for the contention that cinema is a collective activity possessing an international language which will play a part in the collectivization that is bound to succeed capitalism. His book on film aesthetics was published in English as *The art of cineplastics*, Boston, 1923. Many perceptive comments on the cinema were scattered through his various writings on art and philosophy. A selection was edited by his son, Jean-Pierre Faure, and published as *Fonction du cinéma*, Paris, 1964.

**FAYE, ALICE** (1915– ), US actress, real name Alice Jeanne Leppert, blonde heroine and singing star of a number of musicals and light comedy-dramas, made her screen début in *George White's Scandals* (1934). She spent most of her career with TWENTIETH CENTURY-FOX, scoring many successes in the thirties and early forties in films with a period flavour and nostalgic appeal. In one of her most popular films, *Rose of Washington Square* (1939), she played a singer modelled on Fanny BRICE. Don AMECHE partnered her in several films, and Tyrone POWER, Carmen MIRANDA, John Payne, and Jack Oakie were featured more than once. Following the uncharacteristic *Fallen Angel* (1945) she retired on her marriage to the band-leader Phil Harris, to reappear only for a remake of STATE FAIR (1962). Her singing voice was pleasant but almost styleless and her acting ability was limited; but she had a likeable personality and a charm that endeared her to many filmgoers.

**FEATURE FILM,** a full-length entertainment film, usually fictional. (Full-length non-fiction subjects are normally described as *feature-length* documentaries.) The term derives from the selling of films on the basis of an attraction—star, subject, sensational passages—that could be 'featured' in publicity. As films of more than two reels became in themselves an attraction, 'feature film' came to be recognized as an indication of length. The first feature tops the bill in a double feature programme; it is usually longer than the 'B' FEATURE, or supporting feature; and it is rented in return for a percentage of the box-office takings, not hired for a fixed sum as is the rest of the programme.

In British law a feature film is defined by a minimum length of three reels (3000 ft) or $33\frac{1}{3}$ minutes running time (see REEL). In practice, during the heyday of double-feature programmes for mass audiences, the first feature usually lasted 90 minutes and the second feature some 70 minutes. More recently, and especially with the decline of the 'B' feature, a feature film may have a running time of anything from 100 minutes to three hours. The convention that a feature film should run for not less than 90 minutes has created problems of distribution for shorter features; often a subject may be stretched beyond its best length by the necessity of filling the accepted running time.

**FÉDÉRATION INTERNATIONALE DES ARCHIVES DE FILM** (FIAF), the international federation of film archives, was created in Paris in 1938 by the joint action of the four major film archives then existing, the CINÉMATHÈQUE FRANÇAISE, New York's Museum of Modern Art Film Department, the NATIONAL FILM ARCHIVE in London, and the Reichsfilmarchiv in Berlin. Its first Congress was held in New York in 1939. Further development was interrupted by the Second World War, as a result of which the Reichsfilmarchiv disappeared, but the three remaining founder members came together in Paris in 1946 to re-establish the federation. It immediately began to attract new members, particularly from those countries in Eastern Europe where post-war reorganization brought film production and distribution under State ownership. One of the founding members, the Cinémathèque française, resigned in 1960: apart from this the membership has steadily grown. FIAF is an independent body financed solely by annual contributions from its members and governed by officers and Executive Committee elected annually. Until 1969 the headquarters were in Paris; since then they have been in Brussels.

The purposes of FIAF are to facilitate communication and exchange between its members; to maintain a common code of conduct for all members, to ensure both the rights of individual archives and those of copyright owners of films in their collections; to promote the international standardization of such essential archival procedures as preservation and cataloguing; to study common problems of customs, insurance, copyright, statutory deposit, etc; to provide staff training by study courses and exchange of personnel; to negotiate with other interested bodies such as the International Federation of Film Societies and International Federation of Film Producers; to stimulate the formation of film archives in countries where they do not already exist; and, in general, to promote every conceivable interest of film archives at the international level.

**FEHER,** FRIEDRICH (1895–    ), German director, appeared as an actor in DAS CABINETT DES DR CALIGARI (1919); he later claimed to have had a large hand in directing it. He directed several films in Germany, including *Der Haus ohne Turen und Fenster* (1921) which shows the direct influence of EXPRESSIONISM and later worked in England and Hollywood on various films including *The Robber Symphony* (1935), which was reminiscent of PABST'S DIE DREI-GROSCHENOPER (1931).

**FEHÉR,** IMRE (1926–    ), Hungarian director, born in Romania. He joined the Budapest Academy of Film Art in 1946, and after graduating four years later worked for a time as producer, scriptwriter, and assistant director. He is best known for his first feature film *Bakaruhában* (*A Sunday Romance*, 1957), which holds a major place in the cultural thaw of the mid-fifties for its undogmatic treatment of middle-class society. He has never equalled the international success of that work despite further films during the late fifties and well into the sixties.

**FEKS** (Fabrika eksentricheskovo aktyora—Factory of the Eccentric Actor) was founded in 1921 in Leningrad by KOZINTSEV, TRAUBERG, and YUTKEVICH (Yutkevich left the group shortly after) with the aim of reforming the entire Socialist theatre along the lines of circus and vaudeville. One of their first presentations was a staging of Gogol's *Zhenit'ba* (*Marriage*), using some film sequences. In 1923 they attracted the attention of Sevzapkino with their play *Foreign Trade at the Eiffel Tower* and were invited to make a short comedy on a similar fantastic plane. *Pokhozhdeniya Oktyabrini* (*Adventures of Oktyabrina*, 1924), an eccentric fantasy, was unsuccessful, but it enabled Kozintsev and Trauberg to explore, discover, and even invent elements of cinema which were to prove fruitful in their later work. Their first film to find success with the public was *Chyortovo koleso* (*Devil's Wheel*, 1926), and in the same year they made *Shinel* (*The Cloak*).

The group, which included the actors GERASIMOV and Kouzmina and the cameraman MOSKVIN, believed in a cinematic art which was neither literary nor theatrical, and required cinema to begin afresh and to show the everyday world in a more revealing light: they often placed an object in an unusual setting to make the audience more aware of it. In some of their ideas they were influenced by the Italian futurist Marinetti. Several films were made by members of the FEKS group, although not actually produced by FEKS: of these the most notable was NOVYI VAVILON (*New Babylon*, 1929).

In time Kozintsev and Trauberg came to feel that eccentricity and aestheticism were driving them away from social reality and they felt the need to come to grips with more concrete problems: FEKS was disbanded in 1929.

**FELIX,** MARIA (c. 1916–    ), Mexican actress of striking beauty, starred in several Mexican films, the most notable being *Maria Candelaria* (1943), directed by Emilio FERNÁNDEZ, then worked in Spain, Italy, and France before playing La Belle Abbesse in RENOIR'S *French Cancan* (1955). Still in France, she appeared in *Les Héros sont fatigués* (1955) and she co-starred with Gérard PHILIPE in BUÑUEL'S *La Fièvre mont a El Pao* (1959), a Franco-Mexican co-production. She has retired to Mexico and rarely makes films.

**FELIX THE CAT,** US cartoon character created by the Australian animator Pat Sullivan (1887–1933) about 1921 and taken over on Sullivan's death by his partner Otz Messmer until 1935. Felix was one of the original cartoon animal stars, paralleling the cinema clown-heroes of the twenties. Simple outline drawing and graphic visual puns were used to depict his unperturbed saunter with his 'hands' behind his back through disastrous adventures; his signature tune 'Felix Keeps on Walking' became a popular hit.

**FELLINI,** FEDERICO (1921–    ), Italian director, worked in Rome as a journalist, caricaturist, writer of songs and sketches, and gag-man. In

*Otto e mezzo* (Federico Fellini, 1963)

1939 he began a long apprenticeship as co-writer of film scripts: the most important were ROSSELLINI'S ROMA, CITTÀ APERTA (1945) and PAISÀ (1947). He also acted, opposite Anna MAGNANI, in the section 'Il miracolo' of Rossellini's *L'amore* (1948). He was in the main stream of NEO-REALISM, collaborating on scripts for LATTUADA and GERMI as well as Rossellini, and often working as assistant director.

Fellini's first film as director was LO SCEICCO BIANCO (*The White Sheikh*, 1952), a farce drawn from his experience as a journalist. I VITELLONI (1953), set in a sea-side town like Rimini (Fellini's birthplace), is more openly autobiographical. With its social observation and affectionate humour it attracted international attention. In the same year Fellini directed 'Un'agenzia matrimoniale', an episode of AMORE IN CITTÀ.

After the success of *I vitelloni*, Fellini was given bigger resources to make LA STRADA (1954), which both confirmed his own standing and made a star of his wife, Giulietta MASINA. This intensely personal film was attacked by ZAVATTINI for betraying the principles of neo-realism: Fellini replied with IL BIDONE (1955), which by implication criticized the sentimental element in neo-realism.

LE NOTTI DI CABIRIA (1956) again centred on Giulietta Masina and Fellini then wrote a starring vehicle for her, *Fortunella* (Eduardo De Filippo, 1958). By now his considerable reputation had earned him the chance of a big-budget production and he justified it with LA DOLCE VITA (1960), an international success both critically

and commercially. OTTO E MEZZO ($8\frac{1}{2}$, 1963) marked a peak in his career and a culmination of his quasi-autobiographical films (*I vitelloni, Il bidone, La dolce vita*). Here he worked with absolute control, moving freely among the inventions of his own imagery; and he carried the new strain of fantasy into the third of his films designed for Masina, GIULIETTA DEGLI SPIRITI (*Juliet of the Spirits*, 1965).

*Fellini-Satyricon* (1969), drawn from Petronius, was markedly different from Fellini's other work in its classical setting, hysterical flamboyance, and determined sensationalism. He returned to autobiographical concerns with *I clowns* (1970), made for Italian television, which celebrates his life-long enchantment with circus people. Direct experience was the key to his next two films, *Roma* (1972), an episodic study of the great city, and *Amarcord* (*I Remember*, 1974), which returns to the Rimini of Fellini's youth.

While Fellini's films have become more personal and rich in imaginative fantasy, they have maintained throughout his career a coherent pattern of imagery and reference. His preference for working with a stable team—Tullio Pinelli and Ennio FLAIANO as writers, Gianni DI VENANZO and Giuseppe Rotunno as cameramen, Pietro Gherardi as designer, Nino ROTA as composer—has also helped to give his films consistency. His flair for the cinematic expression of personal obsessions is unparalleled: he may sometimes be accused of self-indulgence, but his gusto, humour, and perceptive delineation of character have resulted in some remarkable films whose

*Sedmikrásky* (Věra Chytilová, 1966)

*Sedmikrásky* (Věra Chytilová, 1966)

flaws contribute to, rather than undermine, their success.

*Fellini* by Suzanne Budgen (London, 1966) and *Federico Fellini* by Gilbert Salachas translated by Rosalie Siegel (New York, 1969) provide useful insights into Fellini's work up to *Giulietta degli spiriti*.

**FEMME DU BOULANGER, La,** France, 1938. 2hr. *Prod, dir, scr* Marcel Pagnol, from a story by Jean Giono; *ph* G. Benoit; *mus* Vincent Scotto; *cast* Raimu (the baker), Jeanette Leclerc (his wife), Charles Moulin (the shepherd), Robert Vattier (the priest), Robert Bassac (the schoolmaster), Charpin (the Marquis), Charles Blavette, Edouard Delmont.

The attractive young wife of a village baker runs off with a handsome shepherd. The baker is too distracted to bake bread, and the villagers help to find his wife and bring about her return. PAGNOL's company gave one of their most successful and sympathetic presentations of Provençal life and humour in this entertaining film. RAIMU's performance is perhaps the most impressive of his cinematic career.

**FERNANDEL** (1903–71), French comedian from Marseilles, real name Fernand-Joseph-Désiré Contandin, was a star for over forty years. His immense popularity, which made his name, face, and voice known abroad even to those who never saw him perform, began in 1932 with *Le Rosier de Madame Husson* as a play and a film, and survived through an unceasing spate of films, including *Un Carnet de bal* (Julien DUVIVIER, 1937). During the difficult time of the war he co-directed several films, amongst them *Simplet* (1942) and *Adrien* (1943). In the fifties his fame spread further with his portrayal of Don Camillo in a series of films. He had a long horseface which usually drooped lugubriously but was transformed by a radiant grin revealing a very large mouthful of teeth.

**FERNÁNDEZ,** EMILIO (1904–   ), Mexican director and actor. His films of the forties, among them *Maria Candelaria* (1943), *La Perla* (1946), and *Maclovia* (1948), all photographed by Gabriel FIGUEROA and starring Pedro Armendariz, helped to establish Mexico as a significant force in Spanish-speaking countries. His work displays a visual style that became characteristic of many Mexican films, with carefully composed long shots, dramatically-lit close-ups, and interiors that employ stark contrasts in light and shadow. He remade his own *Enamorada* (1946) in Hollywood as *The Torch* (1950). As an actor, one of his major roles was, in *The Gaucho* (1928), but he is best known for his appearances in American productions filmed in Mexico such

as *Return of the Seven* (1966) and THE WILD BUNCH (1969).

**FERRER,** JOSÉ (1912–   ), US actor, director, and producer, was well known as an actor and director in the theatre before embarking on a film career. He carried his serious and progressive approach over into such performances as the title role in *Cyrano de Bergerac* (1950), and Toulouse-Lautrec in John HUSTON's MOULIN ROUGE (1952). Among the films he has directed are *The Shrike* (1955), *The Great Man* (1956), and *I Accuse* (1958), a re-telling of the DREYFUS case made with great honesty and conviction. He was married to the singer and actress Rosemary Clooney.

**FERRER,** MEL (1917–   ), US actor, originally intended to be a writer, but after appearing in summer stock he worked on Broadway as a dancer and actor before moving to Hollywood. He gained much popularity in Fritz LANG's *Rancho Notorious* (1952) and his almost balletic performance in *Scaramouche* (1953) was very successful. After marrying Audrey HEPBURN he directed her in one film, *Green Mansions* (1959), then worked for a time chiefly in Europe, returning to Hollywood in 1968 after his marriage ended.

**FERZETTI,** GABRIELE (1925–   ), Italian actor, real forename Pasquale, trained at the Rome Academy of Dramatic Art. He first attracted the critics' attention in 1953 when he appeared in SOLDATI's *La provinciale* with Gina LOLLOBRIGIDA; since then he has acted in many films, including *Puccini* (1953), *Il sole negli occhi* (1953), and two by ANTONIONI, LE AMICHE (1955), and L'AVVENTURA (1960). He has appeared in both European and Hollywood films.

**FESTIVALS.** The first film festival took place in 1932 when VENICE included cinema in the Biennale of that year. After the Second World War the concept spread on an international scale with CANNES leading the way in 1946.

A film festival is a prominent cultural event, besides giving commercial advantages to the town or city involved. National tourist boards may help with finance to draw extra visitors and extend the tourist season. The number of festivals now fluctuates around 200, some taking place only once, others becoming regular events.

The major festivals—Venice, Cannes, and BERLIN in Western Europe, MOSCOW and Karlovy Vary in Eastern Europe—set the general pattern. The prime function is to provide an international showcase for national film industries. The prestige attached to prize-winners is important for the film-makers and actors

*Le Feu follet* (Louis Malle, 1963)

involved and helps to attract foreign markets. Festivals also provide an excellent opportunity for publicity. In competitive festivals films are entered by the producing country. Increasingly, 'fringe' activities have sprung up, showing films submitted by producers, directors, etc, and these may attract as much attention as the official festival programme.

The more modest festivals fall into two categories. Those on the same pattern as the five giants but avoiding the worst commercial and political excesses include Edinburgh, Cork, London, Mar del Plata, New York, Rio de Janeiro, and San Francisco. There are also specialized festivals which concentrate on a single area of film, such as science fiction (Trieste), educational films (Pisa), short films (OBERHAUSEN), the new avant-garde or UNDERGROUND (Knokke-le-Zoute), animation (Annecy). Non-competitive festivals like London do not enjoy the prestige and publicity that awards bring and cater more for local audiences than for foreign visitors.

**FEU FOLLET, Le** (*A Time to Live and a Time to Die*), France, 1963. 1¾hr. *Dir, scr* Louis Malle, from the novel by Drieu la Rochelle; *asst dir* Volker Schloendorff; *prod* Nouvelles Editions de Films; *ph* Ghislain Cloquet; *ed* Suzanne Baron; *des* Bernard Evein; *mus* Erik Satie's 'Gymnopédies' and 'Gnossiennes'; *cast* Maurice Ronet (Alain), Léna Skerla (Lydia), Bernard Noël (Dubourg), Jeanne Moreau (Jeanne), Alexandra Stewart (Solange), Henry Serre (Frédéric).

The central character of Drieu la Rochelle's novel, published in 1931, was a drug-addict, living out his last few disillusioned days before killing himself. MALLE changed him to an alcoholic and added two significant sequences (one referring to the Algerian war, the other reproducing a scene in a bar from Scott FITZGERALD's story, 'Babylon Revisited'): otherwise the film closely follows the structure of the book. The skills acquired during the making of such apparently disparate films as LES AMANTS (1958) and ZAZIE DANS LE MÉTRO (1960) are quietly evident in the remorseless view of the people and objects surrounding Alain, and particularly in the brilliant editing. Maurice RONET's fine performance is crucial to the creation of sympathy with Alain in the face of his own self-destructiveness. Erik SATIE's music beautifully underlines the haunting, tragic mood of the film. *Le Feu follet* shows a perception of pain and tragedy astonishing in a young director: it is a rare achievement, of enduring stature.

**FEUILLADE, LOUIS** (1873–1925), French director, was taken on as a scriptwriter by GAUMONT in 1905. He replaced Alice GUY-BLACHÉ as the company's artistic director and at first made chiefly farces. From this early period the lyricism of *Prométhée* (1908) is outstanding. In 1910 he instituted Le Film Ésthétique, to compete with PATHÉ'S FILM D'ART. A shrewd businessman, he produced a series of sentimental films featuring children, including *Bébé apache* (1910) and *Bout-de-Zan* (1913). *Les Vipères* (1911), another series, consisted of realistic but mediocre thrillers. In 1913 Gaumont bought the screen rights of the popular series of books featuring the diabolical criminal Fantômas. Feuillade filmed five of the series, starting with FANTÔMAS (1913). After a short period of war service, he directed several patriotic films, then, prompted by the popularity of *The Perils of Pauline* (1914), he made LES VAMPIRES (1915–16), a SERIAL in ten episodes. Its phenomenal success led to JUDEX (1916), this time in twelve episodes, followed by *La Nouvelle Mission de Judex* (1917). He concentrated on serials until the end of his career—*Tih Minh* (1918), *Barabbas* (1919), *Les Deux Gamines* (1920), *L'Orpheline* and *Parisette* (1921), and *Le Fils du flibustier* (1922).

During his fourteen years' activity Feuillade made more than 450 films, the best of them alive with inventiveness, spontaneity, and great lyrical charm. The ease with which he combined the real and the fantastic, his gay and inconsequential manipulation of the medium, give his films a sense of enjoyment of cinema which is still fresh today.

**FEUILLETON,** French term for an illustrated adventure story in serial form that evolves daily in a newspaper. In 1912 an American magazine, *The Ladies' World*, ran a feature called *What Happened to Mary*, the main incidents of which were recapitulated in a monthly series of films of the same title. This promotional device developed into the SERIAL, with newspaper instalments and film episodes appearing simultaneously (*The Adventures of Kathlyn*, 1913–14; *The Perils of Pauline*, 1914). (See also CINÉ-ROMAN.)

**FEUILLÈRE,** EDWIGE (1907– ), French actress, real name Caroline Cunati, showed early promise as an actress but her career had a slow start. She played small parts in stage farces and in lightweight film comedies during the late twenties using the sobriquet Cora Lynn: her marriage to Pierre Feuillère in 1931 provided her with the name later to become famous as that of 'la grande dame du cinéma français'. She appeared with the Comédie française, 1931–3, playing small roles in their lighter productions, but her starring part in *Stradivarius* (1935) brought her to the forefront of her profession. Her stage career took a new direction, and she appeared in such moving tragedies as *L'Aigle à deux têtes* (COCTEAU), *La Dame aux camélias* (Dumas), and *Partage de midi* (Claudel). Her films, from *La Duchesse de Langeais* (1942), show to advantage her talent for the portrayal of regally tragic women in the true romantic idiom: among the most outstanding are *L'Aigle à deux têtes* (1947), *Adorables créatures* (1952), *Le Blé en herbe* (1953), and *Olivia* (1956).

**FEYDER,** JACQUES (1887–1948), Belgian director, real name Jacques Fréderix, after starting his career as a stage actor in Paris, began playing small parts in films by FEUILLADE and MÉLIÈS. In 1915 he directed his first film, *Monsieur Pinson policier*. He developed a thorough knowledge of technique in a succession of short films before starting on a long and varied career of full-length works. Feyder always considered himself primarily as a craftsman; his work includes a wide range of styles and treatment and, while rarely brilliant, he made a solid contribution to early cinema.

His first full-length film, L'ATLANTIDE (1921) was an adaptation of a novel by Pierre Benoît. In 1923 he filmed an adaptation of Anatole France's story *Crainquebille*, and the following year *Visages d'enfants*, the only film of which he was the complete author. Shortly after this Feyder was offered the post of artistic director for the new Vita Films studios in Vienna, together with a contract to make three films. Feyder decided to make *L'Image* (1926) in colour. The film was a disastrous failure and he returned to Paris where he made *Gribiche* (1926) starring his wife Françoise ROSAY, and CARMEN (1926). In 1928 Feyder went to Berlin where he made one of his finest films, THÉRÈSE RAQUIN, from the story by Zola. The expressionist style of the film with its sinister shadow effects and claustrophobic atmosphere powerfully captures the horror of Zola's story. After *Les Nouveaux Messieurs* (1929) Feyder spent a period in Hollywood. He directed GARBO in *The Kiss* (1929) but most of his work consisted of directing foreign-language versions of American films. Disillusioned with the Hollywood system he returned to France in 1933. He then made three films with Charles SPAAK as his co-scriptwriter, *Le Grand Jeu* (1934), *Pension Mimosas* (1935) and LA KERMESSE HÉROÏQUE (1935). The last was particularly successful, but after this Feyder's career gradually declined. He made *Knight Without Armour* for Alexander KORDA in 1937, *Les Gens du voyage* (1939), *Une Femme disparaît* (1941), *La Loi du nord* (1942), *Maturareise* (1943), and *Macadam* (1946), working in Switzerland during his last years.

His marriage to Françoise Rosay was an enduring partnership of great value to both in their artistic careers. They also collaborated on a book, *Le Cinéma notre métier*, Geneva, 1944.

**FIAF** see FÉDÉRATION INTERNATIONALE DES ARCHIVES DE FILM

**FIDANZATI, I,** Italy, 1963. 1¼hr. *Dir, scr* Ermanno Olmi; *prod* Titanus Sicilia/22 Dicembre; *ph* Lamberto Caimi; *des* Ettore Lombardi; *mus* Gianni Ferrio; *cast* Carlo Cabrini (Giovanni), Anna Canzi (Liliana).

The relationship between Giovanni and Liliana, his fiancée, is revitalized through their enforced separation when Giovanni has to leave her in Milan to go and work in Sicily.

OLMI's discreet use of flashback and social comment enriches and articulates the relationship of an undistinguished but compassionately drawn couple. Close observation of the hot, hostile, newly industrialized environment in which Giovanni finds himself further defines Olmi's preoccupation with work.

The film was made, with Olmi's usual economy, in six weeks, using a crew of eight.

**FIDO,** Film Industry Defence Organisation, operated from 1959 by British RENTERS and EXHIBITORS to restrict the sale of feature films to television.

**FIELDS, GRACIE** (1898–    ), British music-hall singer, whose legendary popularity during the thirties was supported by several films which exploited her combination of sentimentality and common sense, and incidentally established the early fortunes of EALING STUDIOS. *Sing As We Go* (1934), written by the novelist J. B. Priestley, gave her an ideal role (as a Lancashire mill-girl) and a signature tune; but in spite of efforts first by METRO-GOLDWYN-MAYER, then by TWENTIETH CENTURY-FOX to widen her audience, her appeal was almost entirely ineffective outside Britain. She has been semi-retired since the early fifties.

**FIELDS, W. C.** (1879–1946), US comedian, born of an English cockney father and an American mother, real name William Claude Dukinfield, made his name as a comedy juggler and became a star of vaudeville and musical comedy. He toured Europe in 1901 and in 1915 he joined the Ziegfeld Follies and also made his first film, *Pool Sharks*. His first real success in films came in the mid-twenties with *Sally of the Sawdust*, (D. W. GRIFFITH, 1925) and *So's Your Old Man* (Gregory LA CAVA, 1926) which display the impeccable comic timing he had developed in vaudeville. The introduction of sound gave his unprepossessing and bibulous appearance the support of his deadpan, gravel voice with its perfect control of inflection and delivery. His films with Allison Skipworth, notably *Million Dollar Legs* and *If I Had a Million* (both 1932) were successes and his screen career was established by four two-reelers made by Mack SENNETT: *The Dentist* (1932), *The Fatal Glass of Beer*, *The Pharmacist*, and *The Barber Shop* (all 1933).

He was ideally cast as an overbearing Humpty Dumpty in ALICE IN WONDERLAND (1934), and DAVID COPPERFIELD (1934) gave him an opportunity for real acting: his characterization of Micawber stands out from the self-caricature he usually played. But he won the hearts of millions by his suspicious hatred of such hallowed objects as children, animals, and Christmas, and by his battling (with never-failing presence of mind and every mean trick) against natural enemies like policemen, bank managers, and golf caddies. In films like *The Old-Fashioned Way* (1934), *Poppy* (1936), from his stage success which had also been filmed in 1927, *You Can't Cheat an Honest Man* (1939), THE BANK DICK, MY LITTLE CHICKADEE (both 1940), and *Never Give a Sucker an Even Break* (1941), he did the outrageous things most people would love to do but dare not, and the audiences shared vicariously in his unvirtuous triumphs.

Fields was a great eccentric: his public and private personalities were closely linked. He claimed to have, for example, some seven hundred bank accounts, many in fictitious names, and wrote many of his scripts under such pseudonyms as Otis Criblecoblis and Mahatma Kane Jeeves. He died, with a final irony, on Christmas Day.

A biography, *W. C. Fields, his follies and fortunes* by Robert Lewis Taylor (New York, 1966), is usefully supplemented by *W. C. Fields* by J.-P. Coursodon (Paris, Anthologie du Cinéma no. 32, 1968).

**FIGUEROA, GABRIEL** (1907–    ), Mexican cameraman, studied violin and contemporary design before entering Mexican cinema in 1932. In 1935 he studied in Hollywood for four months. His first film credit was *Alla en el Rancho Grande* (1936). He collaborated with Emilio FERNÁNDEZ on many films, the first being *Flor Silvestre* (1943), and worked for John FORD, notably in *The Fugitive* (1947), and John HUSTON. He is skilled in the use of filters and in achieving nuances of light and shadow. He worked on several of BUÑUEL's Mexican films, including LOS OLVIDADOS (1950), *El* (1952), NAZARÍN (1958), and EL ANGEL EXTERMINADOR (1962), where the simplicity of his photography is in striking contrast to his academic elegance for other directors.

**FILM CULTURE,** US journal started in 1955 by Jonas MEKAS, with his brother Adolfas also a member of the editorial board. After appearing at first as a bi-monthly then for a short time as a monthly, the journal since 1958 has been issued, in Mekas's words, 'on an unperiodical basis'.

From its beginning, *Film Culture* was the only journal to take the experimental American films seriously (see UNDERGROUND), and after a few years of mainly sharp criticism deliberately became the main vehicle for the views and assessment of independent film-makers. Mekas himself, Hans RICHTER, and Stan BRAKHAGE are among the film-makers, and Parker TYLER and P. Adams Sitney among the writers, who contributed to the consistent critical evaluation of the American avant-garde.

At the same time, *Film Culture* through the writings of Andrew SARRIS was mainly responsible for introducing the AUTEUR THEORY to America. In this, as in the exchange between theory and practice, it was attempting to take on in the American context the role that CAHIERS DU CINÉMA had played in the fifties in France.

A representative selection of articles from *Film Culture* was published as *Film Culture Reader*, New York, 1970, London, 1971.

**FILM DAILY YEAR BOOK,** US trade annual originally published in 1918 as *Wid's Year Book*, named after its proprietor F. C. (Wid) Gunning who also published *Wid's Daily*, later the *Film Daily*, a trade paper. It became the *Film Daily Year Book* in 1924, under the editorship of Joseph Dannenberg. It was a comprehensive and detailed annual survey of the motion picture industry, with an editorial review of the year and articles on specific items concerning film-makers such as the Hays Code (see CENSORSHIP, US). Statistical data on production, distribution, and exhibition were included, lists of actors and their recent work, information on studios, their production, and the studio personnel. Earlier issues included lists of feature films separately indexed under star and director. It ceased publication in 1971. The first volumes—*Wid's Year Book 1918–22*—were reprinted in 1971 by the Arno Press, New York.

**FILM D'ART, Le,** French production company founded in 1908 in order to attract wealthier and more educated audiences by making films on scripts commissioned from writers of good standing such as Anatole France and Edmond Rostand. Top stage designers and composers were engaged, and some of the best actors of the day took part (Le Bargy, Mouny-Sully, Réjane), causing an early breach in the anonymity of film players. Le Film d'Art's first film, shown in December 1908, was *L'Assassinat du Duc de Guise*, a great success unmatched by their subsequent films. Charles PATHÉ was enthusiastic and bought the exclusive rights, and the company's policy was for a time emulated by many French, Italian, and Danish companies. The term 'film d'art' came to be adopted for films of some cultural pretension, using prestigious scripts and actors drawn from the theatre. MERCANTON'S LA REINE ELISABETH (1912), CAPELLANI'S LES MISÉRABLES (1912), and FEUILLADE'S 'Films Esthétiques' are leading examples. Adolph ZUKOR's 'Famous Players in Famous Plays' attempted to adapt the formula to the American market. As a company Le Film d'Art continued in existence until the introduction of sound, but, apart from some early work by Abel GANCE, its later output was undistinguished.

**FILM NOIR,** term used by French critics (notably Nino Frank) to describe a particular kind of dark, suspenseful thriller. The term gained currency in the years after the Second World War, when Hollywood thrillers such as THE MALTESE FALCON (1941) could be seen in French cinemas. It derived from the *roman noir*, the term used in the nineteenth century to describe the English romantic horror novel. German film-makers pioneered a form of horror film (such as NOSFERATU, 1922) using oblique lighting and compositional tension rather than physical action to create a nightmare world of violence (see EXPRESSIONISM), and these elements were fed into the Hollywood GANGSTER tradition by the German directors and cameramen who went to the US.

A certain blackness of physique—of dark, wet, city streets or of the play of shadows—tended to be an important element in the *film noir*, as well as the depiction of a dark world of corruption and crime. In France during the Second World War the genre provided a vehicle for films of high quality that were not objectionable to the occupying authorities. It became very popular with the French post-war generation of film-goers and was enthusiastically adopted by some film-makers, particularly MELVILLE. GODARD's ALPHAVILLE (1965) is his tribute to the *film noir*.

**FILM QUARTERLY,** US journal first published in 1945 as the *Hollywood Quarterly* under the joint sponsorship of the University of California and the Hollywood Writers Mobilization, which set out to emphasize the social function of film and radio, and in presenting a record of research and study of film to provide a basis for evaluation of economic, social, aesthetic, educational, and technical trends. Under a joint editorship headed by Samuel Farquhar, various committees dealt with all aspects of the media. Among those on the first committees were Abraham POLONSKY, Edward DMYTRYK, Farciot Edouart, and Orson WELLES. In Autumn 1951, to avoid the geographical association with Hollywood, the journal changed its name to the *Quarterly of Film, Radio and Television*, and then in 1958 became *Film Quarterly*, published by the University of California Press. From the beginning the articles have been varied, detailed, authoritative, and have helped establish a new mode of critique of the cinema in America, withstanding the changes of title and modifications of scope over the years.

**FILM SCHOOLS.** With the exception of VGIK, established in Moscow in 1919, film schools were slow to spring up. Hostility from the commercial industry was in the main responsible: academic study of film-making was dismissed in favour of *ad hoc* apprenticeship or the import of experienced directors, writers, and actors from the theatre. This lack of co-operation meant that a student would have little opportunity of practical work in a commercial studio and no guarantee of employment after graduating; and the considerable cost of founding and equipping a film school could not reasonably be contemplated under such conditions. Countries in which film was regarded as ephemeral entertainment have been particularly slow to accord the official recognition implied by the setting up of national film schools.

Countries with a state-controlled film industry or a totalitarian government led the way in formal film training. The obvious benefits to be derived from the investment were increased control over films and film workers and a degree of cultural prestige. These factors contributed to the foundation in Rome of the CENTRO SPERIMENTALE DI CINEMATOGRAFIA in 1935 and were even more important in the case of the Deutsche Film-Akademie, set up by Goebbels in 1938. But even in Germany under the Third Reich, the established industry was resistant to the idea of a film school and in 1940 control of training was handed over to UFA.

The INSTITUT DES HAUTES ÉTUDES CINÉMATOGRAPHIQUES was a going concern in Paris by 1943, but apart from France, Germany, Italy, and the USSR, acceptance of the need for national film schools has been a post-war phenomenon. In Eastern Europe, political reorganization has invariably included nationalization of film production, leading naturally to the setting up of film schools: most are modelled on VGIK and have a similar close liaison with the professional studios. Outstanding among them are the Polish film school at LÓDŹ and those of Hungary, Czechoslovakia, and Romania, which have all made vital contributions to their respective national cinemas. Bulgaria has no national film school, but sends students to VGIK and IDHEC.

Apart from the US, virtually all the main producing countries now have national film schools, financed by government funds, by grants from the film industry, or by a combination of the two. In Sweden, for example, the Filmskolan is operated under the auspices of SVENSKA FILM-INSTITUTET which is financed by a tax on cinema admissions. In Britain the doubts of commercial film-makers and the trade unions were finally overcome and government support obtained. In 1971 the National Film School was opened at Beaconsfield Studios: until that time, the only courses in film-making available in Britain were those operated by the Film and Television Department of the Royal College of Art and the independent London Film School. In America film training has for some years been available through various university departments, notably the University of Southern California, the University of California at Los Angeles (UCLA), New York University, and the College of the City of New York, but without assured co-operation from the film industry. However, in 1969, a Center for Advanced Film Studies was opened by the AMERICAN FILM INSTITUTE with the aid of a Ford Foundation grant. As the AFI has close ties with the major American production companies, the school has the necessary support of the industry.

Film school courses vary widely in length, aims, teaching methods, and technical facilities, and in their differing emphasis on technical training, aesthetic studies, encouragement of individual creative potential, and the production of employable craftsmen. The Centre International de Liaison des Écoles de Cinéma et de Télévision (CILECT) was formed in 1955 to promote film teaching, discussion of methods and technical advances, and student exchanges.

**FILM SOCIETY, The,** the first group of its kind in the world, was founded in London in 1925 to promote the intellectual respectability of the cinema by showing important and influential films denied commercial exhibition. The original council comprised Iris BARRY, Sidney Bernstein, Frank Dobson, Hugh Miller, Walter Mycroft, Adrian Brunel and, perhaps the main driving force behind the society, Ivor MONTAGU. Founding members included Maynard Keynes, H. G. Wells, and G. B. Shaw. Despite the fact that a number of film-makers such as George PEARSON, John GRIERSON, and Thorold DICKINSON became associated with the society, it was regarded with some hostility by the trade who, rightly, saw its existence as an implicit criticism of current exhibition policy. In fact, Brunel was forced by his employers, GAINSBOROUGH, to sever all official connections with the society. Although the Film Society is best known for its championing of German Expressionist and Russian films, its range was wide. Among the films shown at its Sunday performances held in the New Gallery Kinema were NOSFERATU (1922), GREED (1923), BRONENOSETS POTEMKIN (1925), LA PASSION DE JEANNE D'ARC (1928), and *Drifters* (1929). The last of the society's 108 programmes was presented on 23 April 1939.

**FILTER,** a thin sheet of coloured gelatine, sometimes cemented between glass, placed over the camera lens to alter the colour of the light reaching the film. In black-and-white cinematography filters are often used to control the rendering of coloured objects. A yellow filter, for example, darkens blue skies and accentuates clouds; a red filter lightens freckles so that they disappear against the skin tone. In colour cinematography filters are usually restricted to correcting the general colour content of the lighting to match the colour sensitivity of the film, as when a film stock balanced for studio lights is used for exterior photography in daylight. Sometimes large sheets of gelatine are placed over the light sources instead of the camera lens. Faced with the problem of shooting an interior lit both by artificial lights and by daylight coming through windows, a cameraman may elect either to bring the lights up to daylight colour with blue filters, or to bring the daylight down to the colour of the artificial lighting by taping huge sheets of reddish gelatine over the windows. Besides such routine applications, filters can be used to produce subtle or spectacular distortions of natural colours. In MOULIN ROUGE (1952) extensive use was made of filters to evoke the Paris of Toulouse-Lautrec. (See COLOUR, DIFFUSER.)

**FINCH,** PETER (1916– ), Australian actor, moved to England after appearing in the British/ Australian production *Eureka Stockade* (1948). He gained popularity in war films such as *The Wooden Horse* (1950) and *A Town like Alice* (1956, *The Rape of Malaya* in US). He has developed as an actor of intelligence and sensitivity, perhaps tending to be underrated because of his good looks. He is particularly noted for his reticent characterizations of publicly successful men whose emotional life is in some way flawed: outstanding examples are Oscar WILDE in *The Trials of Oscar Wilde* (1960), the novelist in *Girl with Green Eyes* (1963), the Jewish doctor in *Sunday, Bloody Sunday* (John SCHLESINGER, 1971), and Lord Nelson in *Bequest to the Nation* (1973). He has also worked in Hollywood and has had a distinguished stage career.

**FINE CUT,** the stage in EDITING at which the picture is completely edited to the satisfaction of both director and editor. After this, the sound editing is completed and the original master is cut in accordance with the fine cut.

**FINE-GRAIN PRINT,** also called a master positive or a LAVENDER, a positive copy of a film made from the original black-and-white negative. From the fine-grain one or more DUPE negatives can be made, either to incorporate optical EFFECTS or to safeguard the original negative. (Thus, possession of a fine-grain is archivally the next best thing to possession of the original.) A fine-grain is lower in contrast than a normal print, as well as having a finer grain structure; these characteristics compensate for inevitable losses in the duplicating process. It is also widely known as the Insurance Fine Grain and its manufacture and safe deposit are often stipulated in insurance contracts.

***FINIS TERRAE,*** France, 1929. 1hr. *Dir* Jean Epstein. Shot in the islands of Ouessant and Bannec, Brittany, with fishermen and their boats as actors.

Following EPSTEIN's experimental, avant-garde films, *Finis Terrae* belongs to his documentary period; but it nevertheless betrays his continued preoccupation with aesthetics and style, and the human element is kept at a distance. His direction of non-professional actors was particularly successful. Epstein returned to Brittany and its fishermen with *Mor'Vran* (*La Mer aux Corbeaux*, 1930).

**FINLAND.** The population of Finland is small and this, combined with the language barrier which prevented much distribution abroad, hindered the growth of the cinema in Finland, and sent many directors such as Mauritz STILLER and Jörn DONNER to work in Sweden.

Films were first shown in Finland by the LUMIÈRE brothers in 1896, but although cinemas were built from about 1901, they usually showed Swedish films. Short actualities were made sporadically from 1904, but it was not until 1906, when Karl Emil Ståhlberg set up his company Apollo Atelier, that regular production began. Ståhlberg produced the first Finnish fiction film, *Salaviinapolttajat* (*The Moonshiners*, 1907), which was directed by Teuvo Puro and Louis Sparre. Puro was one of the more prominent directors throughout the silent period, making films typical of the industry at that time: dramas of country life and adaptations from plays and novels such as *Sylvi* (*Sylvie*, 1913). In 1919, Puro founded Suomi Filmi, the first production company of any importance (and one which still exists today) in conjunction with Erkki Karu. Among other films that Karu made for Suomi Filmi were a documentary, *Finlandia* (1922) sponsored by the Ministry of Foreign Affairs, and one of the classics of Finnish silent films, *Nummisuutarit* (*The Village Shoemakers*, 1923).

In 1930, Yriö Norta made the first Finnish sound film, a short called *Sano se Suomeski* (*Say it in Finnish*), which was soon followed by others, including Karu's version of *Tukkipojan morsian* (*The Bride of the Lumberjack*, 1931), but the coming of sound increased the problems of distribution outside the country. During the thirties Finland began to make films comparable to those produced by larger industries. The most important director of the period was Nyrki Tapiovaara, whose work includes *Juha* (1935), and *Miehen Tie* (*The Way of Man*, 1940). *Miehen Tie* was photographed (and completed when Tapiovaara vanished on a wartime mission) by Erik Blomberg; Blomberg was also cameraman on Risto Orko's bootlegger thriller *VMV 6* (1935), and went on to direct popular comedies starring his wife, Mirjami Kuosmanen, as well as some notable films in the fifties, such as *Valkoinen Peura* (*The White Reindeer*, 1952).

Production fell during the Second World War from about 10 films a year to 4–5, but the industry expanded again, reaching its peak in the fifties, with about 25 films a year. This was the heyday of Finnish films, and several well-known directors came to prominence then. Besides Blomberg, there was Roland af Hällström, with such films as *Tukkijoella* (*The Log-drivers*, 1951) and *Ryysyrannen Jooseppi* (*Joseph of Ryysyranta*, 1956), and Matti Kassila with *Tyttö Kunnisillalta* (*The Girl from the Moon Bridge*, 1953). Edvin Laine is still a popular director in the traditional style: his best known films, such as *Tuntematon sotilas* (*The Unknown Soldier*, 1955), *Täällä pohjantähden alla* (*Here, Beneath the North Star*, 1968), and *Akseli ja Elina* (*Akseli and Elina*, 1970), are all adaptations from novels by Vaïno Linna.

The change in the structure of Finnish society from a rural to an urban economy, which began in the sixties, and the success of the Popular Front in 1966, have been reflected in the social and political themes now appearing in the work of many directors: Risto Jarva with *Onnenpeli* (*A Game of Chance*, 1965) and *Työmiehen päiväkirja* (*A Worker's Diary*, 1967); Mikko Niskanen with *Käpy selän alla* (*Skin to Skin/Under Your Skin*, 1966) and *Kahdeksan surmanluotia* (*Eight Deadly Shots*, 1972), which he made originally for television. Perhaps the best-known of modern directors is Jörn Donner who made such films as *Mustaa valkoisella* (*Black on White*, 1967), and *Perkele! Kuvia Suomesta* (*Fuck Off! Images from Finland*, 1971). Donner was one of a group of film enthusiasts who in 1957 founded Suomen Elokuvaarkisto, the Finnish Film Archive, which seeks to encourage film art and since 1971 has promoted Finnish films abroad. In 1969, the Ministry of Education, together with three film trade organizations, set up Suomen Elokuvasäätiö, the Finnish Film Foundation. Through this foundation (which publishes several film journals in English and other languages) state grants are now being made to film-makers.

**FINNEY, ALBERT** (1937– ), British actor, gained a considerable reputation in modern and classical stage roles before his first screen appearance in SATURDAY NIGHT AND SUNDAY MORNING (1960), for which he received both critical and popular acclaim. His brilliantly realistic portrayal of a hedonistic factory worker contrasted with the flamboyant title role of TOM JONES (1963), proving him versatile as well as talented. He co-starred with Audrey HEPBURN in Stanley DONEN's imaginative comedy-romance *Two for the Road* (1966). Finney's increasing engagement with the cinema resulted in his setting up a production company, Memorial Enterprises, which has been responsible for several unusual films. These include *Charlie Bubbles* (1967), which Finney directed as well as playing the lead, IF . . . (1968), *Loving Memory* (1970) never released commercially probably because only one hour long, and *Gumshoe* (1972). Finney has always maintained his involvement with the theatre. He is married to Anouk AIMÉE.

**FIREMAN'S BALL, The,** see HOŘÍ, MÁ PANENKO

**FIRES ON THE PLAIN** see NOBI

**FIRES WERE STARTED** (*I Was a Fireman*), GB, 1943. 1¼hr. *Dir, scr* Humphrey Jennings; *prod* Ian Dalrymple for Crown Film Unit; *ph* Cyril Pennington-Richards; *ed* Stewart McAllister; *mus* William Alwyn; *cast* members of the National Fire Service.

The film depicts twenty-four hours in the life of a sub-station of the National Fire Service during the London blitz. JENNINGS used no formal script, and although the dialogue today seems stilted an extraordinary truth is captured by the beauty of the photography and simplicity of approach.

**FIRST NATIONAL,** US company founded in 1917 by John D. Williams and Thomas L. Tally, was at first a distributive channel formed to combat the growing practice of BLOCK BOOKING instituted by PARAMOUNT. It also established studios of its own, signing on some of the best talent then available. This included D. W. GRIFFITH, Mary PICKFORD, and Charles CHAPLIN, to whom the company gave a famous contract to make eight films for $150,000 each. Two of Chaplin's most successful and enduring films were made at First National: SHOULDER ARMS (1918) and THE KID (1920). Other famous FN releases were *Daddy-Long-Legs* (1919), TOL'-ABLE DAVID (1921), *The Sea Hawk* (1924), *The*

*Dark Angel* (1925), and *Long Pants* (1927). The company merged with Associated Producers in 1921 to form Associated First National which, in 1929, was absorbed by WARNER BROS.

**FISCHER,** GUNNAR (1910–   ), Swedish cameraman, joined SVENSK FILMINDUSTRI as an assistant to Julius Jaenzon in 1935. In 1942 he became director of photography and worked on a number of films including DREYER's *Två mån-niskar* (*Two People*, 1945). In 1948 he filmed BERGMAN's *Hamnstad* (*Port of Call*) and was to remain Bergman's regular cameraman on a dozen films until he was succeeded by Sven NYK-VIST on completion of *Djävulens öga* (*The Devil's Eye*, 1960). Among the films that he has shot for Bergman are SOMMARNATTENS LEENDE (*Smiles of a Summer Night*, 1955), DET SJUNDE INSEG-LET (*The Seventh Seal*, 1957), and SMULTRON-STÄLLET (*Wild Strawberries*, 1957). Since leaving Bergman his talents for creating dramatic photographic contrasts have been under-used. He has himself directed a few shorts and is known as an illustrator of children's books.

**FISCHINGER,** OSKAR (1900–67), German-born animator. A disciple of Walter RUTTMANN and Viking EGGELING, he attempted to interpret music using in the main non-objective forms. His earliest films, made in Germany in 1925–32, were issued as a numbered series (Studies 1–12). From the same period date his special effects for several films, including those for Fritz LANG's *Die Frau im Mond* (1929). In 1933 his *Komposi-tion im Blau*, in GASPARCOLOR, won a special prize at VENICE, and he was invited to go to Hollywood. His contribution to Walt DISNEY's FANTASIA (1940) was eliminated, however, as being too abstract. Other films made in US include: *Allegretto* (1936), *An American March* (1940), and *Motion Painting No 1* (1947), which was awarded the Grand Prix at the Brussels Exhibition, 1949. (See also ABSTRACT FILM, ANIMATION, AVANT-GARDE.)

*FISTS IN THE POCKET* see PUGNI IN TASCA, I

**FITZGERALD,** BARRY (1888–1961), Irish character actor, real name William Shields, associated with the Abbey Theatre in Dublin before going to Hollywood in the mid-thirties. He there appeared in small parts in a variety of films, including BRINGING UP BABY (1938). After a short period of maritime bias (*The Long Voy-age Home*, 1940; *The Sea Wolf*, 1941), he attained real fame with his OSCAR-winning performance as the benevolent Irish priest in *Going My Way* (1944). Among the more important of his later films were *Naked City* (1948),

*Union Station* (1950), and *The Quiet Man* (1952).

**FITZGERALD,** F. SCOTT (1896–1940), US writer, saw himself and was widely accepted as spokesman for the 'Jazz Age' following the First World War. Attracted by sophisticated city life, he was determined to write his way to fame and fortune. He successfully published *This Side of Paradise* (1920) and short stories—of which three were filmed in 1920–2—and in 1922 he soared to fame with his second novel, *The Beautiful and Damned*. A film version, directed by William Seiter, was made of it in the same year. Fitzgerald's next novel, *The Great Gatsby*, was published in 1925, and was recognized by critics as a much more considerable work. It did not have great popular success, however, although Owen David's play from it, produced in New York by George CUKOR in 1926, was very successful commercially, as was the film made the same year from the play; it was directed by Herbert Brenon, with Warren Baxter as Gatsby, Lois Wilson as Daisy, and William POWELL as Wilson.

Fitzgerald and his wife, Zelda, had by this time established the pattern of frenetic living, heavy drinking, and wild extravagance that was the material of his books, and he was to spend the rest of his life struggling to maintain it. In the late twenties, they spent part of their time in Europe, both to live more cheaply and to find treatment for Zelda's mental disorders. Fitzgerald made his first visit to Hollywood in 1927: on this trip, as on his next in 1931, what he wrote was not used. In 1934 he published *Tender is the Night*, based with agonizing closeness on his and Zelda's experience. It was a failure both critically and financially. Zelda was now seriously ill and Fitzgerald drinking uncontrollably. He was still struggling to earn money by writing stories, and in 1936 wrote the series of essays, *The Crack-up*. In 1937 he returned to Hollywood, under contract to METRO-GOLDWYN-MAYER.

For a time, under the influence of Sheilah Graham, he worked conscientiously, but nothing he wrote was ever used untouched. He worked on *The Women* (1939) and GONE WITH THE WIND (1939) but the material was not used: the only film on which he received a (co-) credit was *Three Comrades* (Frank BORZAGE), 1938). The changes made to the script by the producer, Joseph L. MANKIEWICZ, upset Fitzgerald's precarious balance, and in December 1938 his contract was not renewed. His work with Budd SCHUL-BERG on *Winter Carnival* (1939) later inspired Schulberg's novel, *The Disenchanted* (1950). During the last few months of his life, Fitzgerald worked on *The Last Tycoon*, based on his experience at MGM and in particular of Irving

THALBERG. The novel was only half-finished when he died in December 1940. A less substantial but more realistic memorial to his Hollywood experience was the series of seventeen Pat Hobby stories, written in 1939 and 1940 and published in *Esquire*, five of them posthumously.

His literary reputation remained at a very low ebb throughout the forties. Film rights in the story 'Babylon Revisited' had been bought for $300 in 1940, but were not taken up by MGM until 1954, when the story was rewritten to take place in Paris after the Liberation, and became *The Last Time I saw Paris*, directed by Richard BROOKS. In 1948 David O. SELZNICK decided to make *Tender is the Night* with his wife, Jennifer JONES, as Nicole, but the project was put off, and Selznick sold the rights to Fox in 1959. By the time the film was made, in 1961, Jennifer Jones was forty-two, and Jason ROBARDS Jr, playing Dick Diver, was thirty-eight: even Henry KING's respectful direction could not save the project from inevitable disaster. A second version of *The Great Gatsby*, directed in 1949 by Elliot Nugent, was pedestrian, although Alan LADD as Gatsby gave one of his more thoughtful performances, and Betty Field was an authentic Daisy. The third version, in 1974, was directed by Jack CLAYTON, with Robert REDFORD as Gatsby and Mia FARROW as Daisy. In 1959, Fitzgerald's own life was the subject of *Beloved Infidel*, directed with delicacy by Henry King. Based on the book by Sheilah Graham and Gerold Frank about Fitzgerald's most dissipated years, and starring Gregory PECK and Deborah KERR, the film could only be a distressing reminder of the havoc of his life.

That life, and the sense Fitzgerald himself had of representing a generation, have had considerable appeal for film-makers. References to him by other film-makers have served him more truly than the films made of his work or life: nowhere perhaps more than in MALLE's LE FEU FOLLET (1963), whose allusions poignantly reflect the transient glamour and the self-destructiveness of Fitzgerald's life.

Two books among those written on Fitzgerald deal with his Hollywood career: *Crazy Sundays* by Aaron Latham, New York, 1971, and *The far side of paradise* by Arthur Mizener, London, 1951.

**FIVE BOYS FROM BARSKA STREET** see PIATKA Z ULICY BARSKIEJ

**FLAHERTY,** ROBERT J. (1884–1951), US documentary film-maker brought up and educated in Canada, in his youth explored and mined in the wilderness of Canada with his father. In 1914 he married Frances Hubbard who was to remain his constant inspiration and collaborator until his death. In 1910–16 he led four expeditions into sub-arctic Canada under the sponsorship of Sir William Mackenzie, exploring and mapping the archipelago in the Hudson Bay known as the Belcher Islands (the largest of which now bears Flaherty's name), the Baffin Land region, and the northern Ungava area.

On one of these expeditions Flaherty took with him a motion picture camera and printing equipment: his only training had been a three-week course in New York. His first subjects were the people of the North among whom he had grown up—Indians, fur traders, and, in particular, the Eskimos. Unfortunately, the film he shot during his 1913–14 and 1915–16 expeditions was destroyed when he dropped a cigarette in his editing room. After four years of searching for a backer, Flaherty persuaded Revillon Frères, the fur traders, to sponsor his next project, which was filmed in 1920–2. In NANOOK OF THE NORTH (1922) his aim was to communicate the place of primitive human life within the natural environment, a theme which was to dominate most of his films. The difficult conditions under which he worked were to be reflected in his chosen methods of film-making for the next twelve years. *Nanook* had considerable critical and commercial success, and Flaherty found himself acclaimed as a major DOCUMENTARY film-maker. In 1923, after having written a memoir *My Eskimo Friends*, he was approached by Jesse L. LASKY of PARAMOUNT to make a 'Nanook' of the South Seas and he spent the next two years in the Samoan Islands filming MOANA (1926). (See also PANCHROMATIC FILM.) Following the limited commercial success of this film—the result of inadequate publicity and exploitation—he made two short sponsored documentaries, *The Pottery Maker* and *Twenty-Four Dollar Island*, both in 1926.

He embarked on his next two main projects in partnership with other directors. For WHITE SHADOWS IN THE SOUTH SEAS (1928) METRO-GOLDWYN-MAYER engaged him to work in collaboration with W. S. VAN DYKE, but once in Tahiti for the filming Flaherty felt that he was making no contribution and left. He began work on a film for FOX about the Pueblo Indians of New Mexico; the company abandoned the project and Flaherty went into partnership with F. W. MURNAU to make TABU (1931), again in Tahiti. The two directors could not work co-operatively and Flaherty sold his share of the company to Murnau.

After unrealized projects with the USSR and in Berlin, Flaherty went to Britain in 1931 at the invitation of John GRIERSON, who felt that the 'master' could instruct his group in natural observation. The resulting film INDUSTRIAL BRITAIN (1933) was finally assembled by Grierson's team. In MAN OF ARAN (1934), financed by

GAINSBOROUGH, Flaherty returned to the themes of family, daily life, and man against nature which had proved so successful in *Nanook* and *Moana*; again he spent two years living with the Aran Islanders in order to make the film. In 1935 he went to India to shoot ELEPHANT BOY (1936) for Alexander KORDA. Although he was unhappy with the co-directors sent from London to keep him working to schedule, he remained on the film until it was complete, even through the shooting in London of re-takes and filling-in sequences (such as rubber elephant feet for the elephant dance).

After *Elephant Boy* Flaherty was once more in financial difficulties with no prospect of a producer. He wrote two rather poor adventure novels in 1938; in 1939 Pare LORENTZ, then head of the US Film Service, invited him to the US to make THE LAND (1941). For about a year Flaherty worked with Frank CAPRA at the War Department Films Division, but he was never at home with propaganda films and had neither the ability nor the desire to tell a conventional story in film. Until the end of the war he was in a state of unwilling retirement, occasionally advising on or supervising others' films. His last film was generously financed by the Standard Oil Company of New Jersey as a prestige documentary. The editing by Helen VAN DONGEN, who had worked with him on *The Land*, contributed towards making LOUISIANA STORY (1948) what some considered Flaherty's finest film.

Flaherty's film career was constantly hindered by his cheerful inability to come to terms with the inevitable commercial pressures. (He never worked twice for the same backers.) When filming one of his chosen projects he was totally immersed in the subject and was difficult to work with; but he was universally admired. He was a first-rate cameraman, who believed in trying to do everything possible within the camera itself rather than in the editing process. An uncompromising film poet, more at ease in silent than in sound films, his need to live with his subjects and to develop his story from them rather than for them goes far towards explaining the immediate, humanistic appeal of his work.

Frances Hubbard Flaherty, *The Odyssey of a film-maker: Robert Flaherty's story*, Urbane (Illinois), 1960, New York, 1972; Arthur Calder-Marshall, *The innocent eye: the life of Robert Flaherty*, London, 1963, New York, 1966; Richard Griffith, *The world of Robert Flaherty*, New York, Boston, 1953.

**FLAIANO,** ENNIO (1910– ), Italian scriptwriter, began work as an architect before becoming a journalist and essayist. His first forays into the cinema were in the forties, with PAGLIERO and LATTUADA, but in 1952 he began his long collaboration with FELLINI, on LO SCEICCO BIANCO; he worked on the scripts of all Fellini's films up to GIULIETTA DEGLI SPIRITI (1965).

**FLASHBACK,** a narrative device in which chronological continuity is broken to show earlier events. In silent cinema direct story-telling was rarely complicated by the use of flashbacks; when they occurred they were usually clearly signalled by subtitles. An exception is VARIÉTÉ (1925), in which the substance of the film is recalled by a convict at the time of his discharge from prison.

The flashback was a frequent feature of Hollywood films of the thirties: action being preferable to description, it replaced the verbal recollection of past events customary in the theatre. Certain conventions were observed: if a film contained more than one flashback, they were placed in relative chronological order within the main narrative; transitions were clearly signalled by introductory dialogue, by optical techniques such as the ripple-dissolve, by the sound-track, or by any combination of these; the information contained in the flashback was objectively true within the terms of the story. THE POWER AND THE GLORY (1933) created some interest by disregarding the first of these conventions, but Orson WELLES's free-wheeling treatment of past events in CITIZEN KANE (1941) was hailed as a revolution in narrative cinema. However, the other conventions continued to be observed: the transitions between 'then' and 'now', as well as the factual contents of the flashback, were unambiguous. Alfred HITCHCOCK, in *Stage Fright* (1950), even caused some offence with a 'lying' flashback, which confused the plot of a conventional thriller without any artistic justification. RASHOMON (1950) successfully exploited the 'lying' flashback in showing four contradictory accounts of the same event without any indication of their respective probability; but still the relative standing of 'then' and 'now' was clearly maintained.

Two adaptations from stage plays showed an innovatory trust in the cinema audience's capacity to interpret the collision of remembered events with the narrative present. Laszlo BENEDEK's *Death of a Salesman* (1952) and Alf SJÖBERG's FRÖKEN JULIE (*Miss Julie*, 1951) both allowed characters from the past to enter the same shot, and even the same frame, as the person recalling them: so that in *Fröken Julie*, for instance, the child and the adult Julie are seen together, apparently existing on the same level of reality but with no confusion as to their respective function in the narrative.

The dogma that simple, linear narrative was necessary to retain an audience's attention took considerably longer to break down in the cinema than in the other story-telling arts—literature and the theatre. Although television has helped to educate audiences in the potential of visual fluidity, Alain RESNAIS is the director mainly responsible for erasing the clear line hitherto drawn in mainstream cinema between 'now' and 'then', 'true' and 'false'. In HIROSHIMA MON AMOUR (1959) the heroine's mind moves from present to remembered experience with complete psychological conviction. Often, the temporal status of a scene is not immediately apparent, and it is the viewer's task to elucidate the trigger-mechanism that arouses each memory. In L'ANNÉE DERNIÈRE A MARIENBAD (1961) conventional narrative form is abandoned in favour of dream-like ambiguity. The flashback as a rigid convention has since become virtually obsolete, and the structural possibilities of narrative cinema immeasurably enriched.

**FLEISCHER,** DAVE (1894–    ) and MAX (1889–1972), US animators, both started as cartoonists: Max was the first to work in animation, making instructional films for the US Army from 1915. After the war the brothers joined forces, with Max as artistic and technical director and Dave as producer. They had immediate success with their first series of short cartoon films, *Out of the Inkwell* (1921), which featured Koko the Clown. They also created BETTY BOOP and POPEYE. Betty Boop's career was short, as her 'immorality' gave offence to various moral watchdogs, but Popeye, introduced in 1933, retained his popularity until 1947. At a time when Walt DISNEY, their only serious competitor, was aiming at the family audience, the Fleischers' cheerfully robust humour appealed to the adult cinema-goer, but their attempt to compete with Disney's full-length cartoon features, with *Gulliver's Travels* (1939) and *Mr Bug Goes to Town* (1941), was a commercial failure. They split up in 1942; Dave became director of the animation department at COLUMBIA and Max formed his own company to make industrial films.

**FLEISCHER,** RICHARD (1916–    ), US director, son of Max Fleischer. During the Second World War he made shorts and newsreels for RKO. *Child of Divorce* (1946) was the first of his many 'B' features for that company, though in 1948 he won an OSCAR for best documentary feature with *Design for Death* which he coproduced. Fleischer's first big film was *The Happy Time* (1952) for Stanley KRAMER, and his handling of DISNEY's epic *20,000 Leagues under the Sea* (1954) led to other commercially respectable commissions. From 1955 he worked mainly for TWENTIETH CENTURY-FOX, notably on *Compulsion* (1959) and *Crack in the Mirror*

(1960), both with Orson WELLES. A brief flirtation with Dino DE LAURENTIIS to make *Barabba* (1962) was unsuccessful and Fleischer returned to Hollywood. *Dr Dolittle* (1967), although an interesting film, was a commercial flop on a grand scale; this was probably beneficial to Fleischer, as it led him from lavish film-making to smaller-scale subjects. *The Boston Strangler* (1968), his best film, was the first of a series of tightly controlled dramas, and allowing for the interruption of *Tora! Tora! Tora!* (1970)—reputed to have cost Fox $20 million—he continued this trend with *10 Rillington Place* (1970); *The Last Run* (1971), taking over from John HUSTON; *The New Centurions* (1972, *Precinct 45: Los Angeles Police* in GB); and *Soylent Green* (1973), a harsh science-fiction story. In his best films, tightly-scripted crime dramas which examine the society that creates violence as well as the violence itself, Fleischer has proved himself an efficient director with a discerning eye for the foibles of both the hunters and the hunted.

**FLEMING,** VICTOR (1883–1949), US director, started as a cameraman with TRIANGLE, where he worked with GRIFFITH and FAIRBANKS before becoming a director in 1919. During his long and very productive career he made a number of films that will be remembered with affection, notably *The Virginian* (1929), with Gary COOPER, THE WIZARD OF OZ (1939), with Judy GARLAND, and DR JEKYLL AND MR HYDE (1941). He directed the greater part of GONE WITH THE WIND (1939), and was chosen by Ingrid BERGMAN to direct her independent production JOAN OF ARC (1948).

**FLICKER,** THEODORE J. (1930–    ), US director. Versatile all-rounder—actor, writer, satirist, night-club comedian, architect, and director of New York's Premise Theater Company—he later worked extensively as a director of television film. He wrote and directed *The Troublemaker* (1964) and *The President's Analyst* (1967), between which he worked as Alexander MACKENDRICK's assistant on *Don't Make Waves* (1967). *Up in the Cellar* (1970, *Three in the Cellar* in GB), satirizing campus revolution, gave scope to his sharp observation and wry humour.

**FLICKERS,** early slang term for motion pictures derived from the flickering effect produced by primitive projection.

Flicker is produced in the main by slow shutter speed. In early silent days the projector's shutter closed once for every FRAME, while the movement on to the next frame was taking place. The problem was improved by closing the shutter momentarily once while the film is moving on and twice while the frame is stationary in the projector: three closures for each frame at 16 frames per second. At sound projection speed (24 frames per second), two closures per frame is normally satisfactory. With the projector shutter thus closing nearly 50 times a second, flicker should be eliminated.

It can, however, still occur if the projector lamp is too strong or the print too bright. Modern projectors, which do not have mechanically-driven shutters, are capable of blacking out the screen image for fractions of a second with varying frequency according to need. (See PERSISTENCE OF VISION.)

**FLOREY, ROBERT** (1900– ), French director, after brief experience in the GAUMONT and PATHÉ studios, went to Hollywood in 1921 and spent most of his working life there. His first film *The Life and Death of 9413, a Hollywood Extra* (1928), made on a very low budget, was designed by Slavko VORKAPICH and photographed by Gregg TOLAND: it created something of a sensation, but his subsequent work, though prolific, has been unmemorable apart from *The Cocoanuts* (1929), the first MARX BROTHERS film, and *The Beast with Five Fingers* (1947), an effective exercise in the horror genre. He has made over a hundred films for television and has published an excellent book of reminiscences: *Hollywood d'hier et d'aujourd'hui* (Paris, 1948).

**FLYNN, ERROL** (1909–59), US actor, was born in Antrim, N. Ireland, not, as he preferred it to be known, in Tasmania. It was, however, in Australia that he made his first film, playing the part of Fletcher Christian in *In the Wake of the Bounty* (1934). He then moved to Hollywood and starred in *Captain Blood* (1935), which brought him worldwide popularity. It has been said that Flynn played many roles but only one part—himself; certainly his range was usually limited to the heroic leads of romantic costume dramas, but most of his films, notably *The Charge of the Light Brigade* (1936) and *The Adventures of Robin Hood* (1938) were good examples of the polished entertainment at which Hollywood excelled. Much of Flynn's popularity can be attributed to his colourful private life, which he made no attempt to keep private: his autobiography *My wicked, wicked ways* (London, 1960) probably embroiders the already eventful story. In his last film, *Too Much Too Soon* (1958), he departed from his usual swashbuckling role to portray his, in a sense, predecessor, John BARRYMORE.

**FONDA, HENRY** (1905– ), US actor, who attracted wide notice on the stage in *The Farmer Takes a Wife*; his first screen role was in 1935 in an adaptation of the play with Janet GAYNOR,

directed by Victor FLEMING. While he is by no means incapable of the lighter touch, he has become identified with the man of conscience, resisting ignorance, oppression, and prejudice, as in THE GRAPES OF WRATH (1939), TWELVE ANGRY MEN (1957), and Otto PREMINGER's *Advise and Consent* (1961), or with the clear-eyed WESTERN hero, tough but never brutal, of MY DARLING CLEMENTINE (1946) or Anthony MANN's *The Tin Star* (1956).

**FONDA, JANE** (1937– ), US actress, daughter of Henry Fonda, was a model and stage actress before becoming a screen star with polished performances in *The Chapman Report* (1961) and *Walk on the Wild Side* (1962). She appeared for Roger VADIM (whom she married in 1965) in LA RONDE (1964) and *La Curée* (1966) and scored a particular success in *Cat Ballou* (1965). In *They Shoot Horses Don't They?* (1969) and *Klute* (1971) she revealed hitherto unrecognized acting ability. She has been active in radical politics in the US and starred opposite Yves MONTAND in *Tout va bien* (1972) for GODARD, who in the same year launched an attack on her political integrity in the short film *Letter to Jane*.

**FONDA, PETER** (1939– ), US actor, son of Henry Fonda, has gained a reputation as representative of the younger generation of America with his performances in *Lilith* (Robert ROSSEN, 1964), *The Wild Angels* (Roger CORMAN, 1967), and especially in EASY RIDER (1969), which he also produced.

**FONTAINE, JOAN** (1917– ), US actress of British origin, real name Joan de Havilland, is the sister of Olivia DE HAVILLAND; both sisters received their early acting training from their mother. Reluctant to use the same name as her sister, who had made a successful start in films, Joan Fontaine appeared in various supporting stage roles as Joan St John and Joan Burfield: it was under the latter name that she appeared in her first film *No More Ladies* (George CUKOR, 1935). In 1937 she took her stepfather's surname, Fontaine, and after a successful appearance in the play *Call it a Day* was signed by RKO. Except for *Quality Street* (1937) her films for this company were unmemorable; after she left them she was chosen by SELZNICK to appear opposite Laurence OLIVIER in REBECCA (1940), and her second HITCHCOCK film SUSPICION (1941) won her an OSCAR. Olivia de Havilland was in the same year's nominations and signs of coolness between the sisters were inflated by the popular press into a 'feud' which had at least the merit of sustaining public interest in their work. Apart from the title role in *Jane Eyre* (1944) opposite Orson WELLES, her most successful appearance of later years was in OPHULS' LETTER FROM AN UNKNOWN WOMAN (1948). Illness prevented her from appearing regularly after 1958, although she played a supporting role in *Tender is the Night* (1961).

**FOOLISH WIVES**, US, 1921. 2hr (but see below). *Dir, scr* Erich von Stroheim; *prod* Universal; *ph* Ben Reynolds, William Daniels; *des* Stroheim, Richard Day; *cast* Stroheim (Karamzin), Maude George (Princess Olga), Mae Busch (Princess Vera), George Christians (Howard Hughes), Miss Dupont (his wife), Cesare Gravina (Gaston), Malvine Polo (his daughter), Dale Fuller (chambermaid).

Planned by STROHEIM as a two-part film to take the whole of the normal double feature programme, *Foolish Wives* was cut by the producers from its original five hours to less than half and then further truncated by the censor. Using a theme that he had already explored, American naïvety in a decadent European setting, Stroheim plays the cynically amoral Count who attempts to seduce the wife of the American ambassador to Monaco while carrying on a long-term affair with his own chambermaid and planning to rape the half-witted daughter of Gaston, a counterfeiter. Like most of Stroheim's heroes, the Count comes to a grisly end, stabbed by Gaston and disposed of in a sewer. The loss of large sections of sub-plot confuses the story line, but what remains is remarkable for the detailed observation of social milieu and its bitingly witty attitude to sex.

**FOOLSHEAD** see DEED, André

**FORBES**, BRYAN (1926– ), British actor, writer, director, and producer, real name John Theobald Clark. From a successful career as a supporting actor, he progressed to even greater success as a scriptwriter, notably in *The Angry Silence* (1960), a serious attempt to study aspects of British trade unionism, which he also co-produced. In his first film as director, *Whistle Down the Wind* (1961), he treated a difficult theme—a group of children mistake a criminal on the run for Jesus Christ—with some delicacy. His best films, including *The L-Shaped Room* (1962), *Séance on a Wet Afternoon* (1964), *King Rat* (1965), which was made in Hollywood, and *The Whisperers* (1966), with its impressive leading performance by Edith EVANS, use his own scripts; they demonstrate his sympathetic handling of actors as well as his preference for human dramas in drab settings.

In 1969 Forbes was appointed head of production for EMI (see ASSOCIATED BRITISH). In spite of some successes, including an excellent children's film, *The Railway Children* (Lionel Jeffries, 1970), a BALLET film, *Tales of Beatrix Potter* (Reginald Mills, 1971), and his own *The Raging Moon* (1970, *Long Ago, Tomorrow* in US), about the love affair between two paraplegics, the company's dissatisfaction with his box-office achievements led to his resignation in 1971. He has written a novel about the film industry, *The distant laughter*, London, 1972, and an autobiography, *Notes for a life*, London, 1974.

**FORD**, ALEKSANDER (1908– ), Polish director, was co-founder in 1930 of the START group. His pre-war work included two outstanding films in documentary form: *Legion Ulicy* (*Legion of the Street*, 1932), about newsboys, and *Sabra* (1933), a pro-Jewish film made in Palestine. Ford fled from the Nazis to the USSR, where he formed the Polish Army Film Unit, producing newsreels, the COMPILATION *Bitwa pod Lenino* (*Battle of Leningrad*, 1943), and *Majdanek, oboz smierci* (*Majdanek, Extermination Camp*, 1944). With the destruction of Poland's pre-war film industry, this unit provided the foundation of Film Polski. *Ulica Graniczna* (*Border Street*, 1948) was the first of three postwar features by which Ford dominated Polish cinema. *Młodość Chopina* (*Young Chopin*, 1952) and PIATKA Z ULICY BARSKIEJ (*Five Boys from Barska Street*, 1953), on which WAJDA was Ford's assistant, continued his characteristic concern for youth. Ford had encouraged the new generation of Polish directors—he was artistic supervisor on Wajda's POKOLENIE (*A Generation*, 1954)—but his own prominence declined as that of Wajda and MUNK increased. His infrequent films since the mid-fifties have included *Osmy dzien tygodnia* (*The Eighth Day of the Week*, 1957), a West German-Polish co-production featuring CYBULSKI; *Krzyzacy Granwald* (*Knights of the Teutonic Order*, 1960), a historical epic which was commercially very successful in the west; and *Pierwszy dzien wolnosci* (*First Day of Freedom*, 1965). During the political upheavals of 1968 Ford was dismissed from his position in the LÓDŹ film school; he now lives in Israel.

**FORD**, CHARLES (1908– ), French journalist and historian, began reviewing films in 1925. Since then he has become a prolific writer and broadcaster. He has written for numerous magazines and published several books, many of them (e.g. *Histoire encyclopédique du cinéma*, 5 vols, Paris, 1947–62) co-written with René Jeanne. Ford's Catholic background is most evident in his *Le cinéma au service de la foi* (Paris, 1953).

**FORD**, GLENN (1916– ), Canadian-born actor, real forename Gwyllyn, popular star of many Westerns. His first film was *Heaven with a Barbed Wire Fence* (1939), and he later worked for Charles Vidor, notably in *Gilda* (1946). During the Second World War, he served in the US marines, training French resistance fighters. During the fifties he was a resident leading man at METRO-GOLDWYN-MAYER. His extensive career has taken in over a hundred film appearances, including THE BIG HEAT (Fritz LANG, 1953), THE BLACKBOARD JUNGLE (Richard BROOKS, 1955), *Pocketful of Miracles* (Frank CAPRA, 1961), which Ford co-associate produced, and recent work for Burt Kennedy. Ford is a Commander in the US Naval Reserve, and served in Vietnam 1967–8. From 1943 to 1959 he was married to Eleanor POWELL.

**FORD**, JOHN (1895–1973), US director, born Sean Aloysius O'Feeny (originally O'Fearna), in Cape Elizabeth, Maine, thirteenth and youngest child of Irish immigrant parents. The family moved to Portland, where his father owned a saloon, from there making trips home to Galway, Ireland. After graduating from high school in 1913, Sean went to Hollywood where an older brother, Francis, having adopted the name Ford, was a contract writer/actor/director with UNIVERSAL. Sean was Anglicized to John and taking his brother's new surname, he began work as Jack Ford as prop boy, labourer, stunt man, and bit actor in his brother's films. He appeared in dozens of films, and was a Ku Klux Klansman in THE BIRTH OF A NATION (1915). By 1915 he was also working as an assistant director, making a film a week, with titles such as *The Lumber Yard Gang* (1915), *Peg o' the Ring* (1916). The pace and energy of these early days in the industry helped breed the professionalism that marked his career.

Ford's first film as director/writer was *The Tornado* (1917), a bank robbery Western, in which he also played the stunt-riding hero. With *The Soul Herder* (1917) Ford began a successful series starring Harry CAREY as Cheyenne Harry; other films in this series included *Cheyenne's Pal* (1917), *Wild Women* (1918), *Marked Men* (1919). By the time *The Outcasts of Poker Flat* appeared in 1919, Ford was receiving critical notice for his style of direction. His first non-Western subject was a New York-Irish story, *The Prince of Avenue A* (1920), starring the boxer 'Gentleman' Jim Corbett.

In *Action* (1921), Francis Ford first appeared in a film of his brother's, and that year Ford left Universal for FOX, where he worked exclusively for the next ten years. He was first credited as John Ford on *Cameo Kirby* (1923), starring John GILBERT; the next year he made THE IRON HORSE (1924). This story of the American transcontinental railroad, of pioneering enterprise and

achievement, firmly established Ford as one of the leading directors in the industry. Already he was concerned with subjects and themes that were to recur in his later more celebrated works. In *Three Bad Men* (1926), a story of the Dakota Land Rush of 1876, he evoked the spirit of the pioneers, and *Four Sons* (1928) told the story of a family uprooted by external events. *Hangman's House* (1928) saw John WAYNE in a bit part in his first Ford film. Ford's first talkie was *Napoleon's Barber* (1928).

*Men without Women* (1930) marked the beginning of Ford's collaboration with the scriptwriter Dudley NICHOLS, with whom he made some of his most admired films of the thirties. THE LOST PATROL (1934) was a particular success and its reception finally persuaded RKO to allow them to film a project for which they had long been pressing: an adaptation of Liam O'Flaherty's novel of the Irish troubles, THE INFORMER (1935). The film's critical acclaim and enthusiastic public reception, as well as the four OSCARS it was awarded, made Ford a major Hollywood figure.

Ford's other assignments of the late thirties included *Wee Willie Winkie* (1937), a vehicle for Shirley TEMPLE over which he nevertheless managed to cast his own style. Then, within a year, he made four films of outstanding creative achievement: STAGECOACH (1939), the classic Western and his first to be shot in Monument Valley, Arizona; *Young Mr Lincoln* (1939); DRUMS ALONG THE MOHAWK (1939), his first film in colour; and THE GRAPES OF WRATH (1940). These films encapsulate Ford's devotion to America, its legends, history, and customs, and his feeling for the family and the importance of the community, all conveyed with admiration, tenderness, and humour. No film-maker has caught the frontier experience as profoundly and dramatically.

During the Second World War he was with the US Navy, as Chief of the Field Photographic Branch. His work included the first US war documentary *The Battle of the Midway* (1942), filmed during the actual battle. The METRO-GOLDWYN-MAYER feature *They Were Expendable* (1945), about the US defeat in the Philippines, was conceived as propaganda but achieved enduring quality. Ford's first film after the war was MY DARLING CLEMENTINE (1946), one of his most visually poetic works. In 1946 he formed an independent production company with Merian C. COOPER, Argosy Pictures, and made a long-cherished project *The Fugitive* (1947), from Graham GREENE's novel *The Power and the Glory*. It was commercially unsuccessful, and Ford returned to the Western with *Fort Apache* (1948), *Three Godfathers* (1948), a remake of his *Marked Men* (1919), dedicated to the memory of his old friend Harry Carey, and SHE WORE A YELLOW RIBBON (1949). Following WAGONMASTER (1950), Argosy produced *Rio Grande* (1950), and *The Quiet Man* (1952), a story of an Irish-American returning to the land of his fathers, told with humour and a love of Ireland deeply rooted in Ford's own sensibilities. During the fifties Ford's values were deemed unfashionable in a wave of socially 'realistic' themes and spectacular productions. In 1955 he made his first film in CINEMASCOPE, the meandering *The Long Gray Line* about West Point. In THE SEARCHERS (1956) an embittered Civil War veteran's search for his nieces captured by Indians embodies Ford's vision of the end of the old West, and THE MAN WHO SHOT LIBERTY VALANCE (1962) again shows him regretting the passing of an old order.

Ford is often dubbed reactionary and indeed tended to use stereotypes. But his was a contradictory vision, in which the needs of progress conflict with the values and spirit of the past, and the care with which he created his characters outweighed his sometimes naïve sentiments. The people remain the essential factor in all his works: whatever the plot, the love and humour with which he presented his characters, and the dignity which he imparted to them, made Ford an acknowledged master. He made over a hundred films, including *Up the River* (1930), *Judge Priest* (1934), *The Whole Town's Talking* (1935), *The Prisoner of Shark Island* (1936), *Tobacco Road* (1941), *The Sun Shines Bright* (1952), *Mogambo* (1953), *The Last Hurrah* (1958), *Two Rode Together* (1961), *Cheyenne Autumn* (1964), *Seven Women* (1965), *Vietnam, Vietnam* (1971).

Of importance, too, is Ford's stock company of actors used repeatedly over the years, including Francis Ford, Jane DARWELL, John CARRADINE, Hoot GIBSON, Ben Johnson, Harry Carey Jr, Thomas MITCHELL, Victor MCLAGLEN, Ward BOND, J. Farrell McDonald, Jack Pennick, and particularly Henry FONDA, John Wayne, and James STEWART. Full details of Ford's films may be found in *John Ford*, by Peter Bogdanovich, London, 1967, Berkeley, 1968.

**FOREIGN VERSIONS** were a result of the film industries' attempt to enlarge the potential audience for talking pictures. Silent films were marketable internationally at minimal cost by replacing the original intertitles with translations, but the introduction of sound necessitated new techniques if the revenue from foreign distribution was to continue. America and Germany were the principal producers of foreign versions, taking advantage of the hesitation of most European producers to instal sound recording equipment. Hollywood studios imported actors,

writers, and directors from every European country, while PARAMOUNT fitted out the old PATHÉ studios at Joinville near Paris specifically for the production of foreign-language versions. On the stages of this notorious 'Babel-sur-Seine', teams of actors performed successively on the same set until as many as a dozen versions of each film were obtained. The first feature film emerged from the Paramount production line in March 1930, with the first year's target set at ninety features and fifty short supporting films. Not surprisingly, the films made under these conditions were unremarkable and within two years Paramount abandoned its attempt to dominate the European market. The economics of 'versions' were unstable: few could be guaranteed to recoup even the modest sums spent on them except those in Spanish which reached large audiences in Latin America. With the introduction of re-recording producers soon realized that DUBBING, although in some cases even less satisfactory than 'versions', was a very much more viable proposition.

**FOREMAN, CARL** (1914–    ), US scriptwriter, producer, and director, was associated for most of his Hollywood career with films produced by Stanley KRAMER, notably *Champion*, *Home of the Brave* (both 1949), and HIGH NOON (1952). He also adapted *Cyrano de Bergerac* for the screen in 1952. The committed flavour of most of his work brought him into disfavour with the UNAMERICAN ACTIVITIES Committee: he was blacklisted and moved to England. He collaborated (without credit) on the script of THE BRIDGE ON THE RIVER KWAI (1957) and was executive producer of *The Key* (Carol REED, 1957), then formed his own production company. His productions are mainly large-scale action and entertainment films, including *The Guns of Navarone* (1961), *The Victors* (1963), which he also directed, *Born Free* (1965), *Living Free* (1971), and *Young Winston* (1972). Foreman has played an active part in British cinema outside the field of commercial production: he has been a Governor of the BRITISH FILM INSTITUTE and was a member of the committee formed to set up the British National Film School in 1971.

**FORMAN, MILOŠ** (1932–    ), Czech director, orphaned at an early age, his parents having been arrested and killed by the Nazis. He was brought up by an uncle. He enrolled at FAMU (the Prague film school) as a scriptwriter, and while he was still a student there in 1955 worked on a script for Martin FRIČ. In 1956 he was assistant director to Alfred RADOK on *Dědeček automobil* (*Old Man Motor-Car*), and in 1957 scripted and assisted in the direction of Ivo Novak's *Štěnata*

(*Puppies*), a gentle, humorous film about young people which foreshadowed one of the main themes of his later work. Forman wanted to direct as well as write, but for the next few years he worked with Radok on the LATERNA MAGICA, during its most experimental period. He was active in the lively cultural life of Prague, frequenting the Semafor theatre and meetings held by Jan Werich (of the famous satirical pair of the thirties, Voskovec and Werich). At Semafor, he worked with Jiří Šlitr and Jiří Suchý, whose partnership carried on the tradition of the earlier pair.

When he returned to film work proper in 1962, Forman's first assignment was on a fairly routine anti-Fascist film, *Tam za lesem* (*Beyond the Wood*). At this time he directed his first film, *Konkurs* (*Talent Competition*, 1963), which started from the idea of a documentary about the Semafor. Sham auditions were announced for a girl singer, and Forman filmed the results on 16mm. A sympathetic representative of the studio had them printed on 35mm, and Forman edited in a fictional anecdote. He then filmed a contest of brass bands in a provincial town, again giving the documentary material fictional shape with a simple anecdote. *Konkurs* and *Kdyby ty muziky nebyly* (*If It Weren't for All Those Bands*) were put together and issued as a single

feature after the release of *Černý Petr* (*Peter and Pavla*, 1963).

*Konkurs* exemplified the main pattern of Forman's preoccupations and methods of working. The influence of CINÉMA-VÉRITÉ was evident, particularly in his use of documentary and of non-actors for the fictional framework. His firm rooting in the fine Czech traditions of black comedy and of mutual nourishment between the arts is indicated by the participation of Suchý and Šlitr, who also wrote the music for *Konkurs*. His collaborator on the subject was Ivan PASSER, with whom he was to work on his next four films, and his cameraman was Miroslav ONDŘIČEK. The fictional themes he injected were both about the conflict between the generations. Above all, his unrelenting eye for grotesquerie and posturing was revealed as his most distinctive hallmark.

These themes were elaborated in *Černý Petr*, the story of a young shop apprentice taken from a novel by the sculptor Jaroslav Papoušek, who joined Forman and Passer to write the script. The story concerns the clash of the mutually uncomprehending worlds of the young generation and the old, the latter splendidly personified by Peter's father, played by Jan Vostřcil, the conductor of one of the bands from *Konkurs*. The acrid, humorous view of the boy's distaste for his work ran counter to all socialist realist tenets,

*Lásky jedné plavovlásky* (Miloš Forman, 1965)

and the script was frowned on by the authorities, but the finished film won the Czechoslovak Film Critics' prize for 1963 and other awards abroad.

The same team of Forman, Passer, and Papoušek wrote (and Ondříček photographed) Forman's next film *Lásky jedné plavovlásky* (*A Blonde in Love*, 1965). A young girl's first love-affair was again treated with anecdotal direct-ness, sympathy for the young, and eye for the grotesque: the same official criticism and popular success greeted it, and Forman's reputation became firmly established at home and abroad. In 1966 he returned to the Semafor for a film for television based on a successful 'jazz opera' by S and S, who also starred in it. With his next feature film, HOŘI, MÁ PANENKO (*The Firemen's Ball*, 1967), Forman, working again with Passer, Papoušek, and Ondříček, made a criticism of society which was unsoftened even by the inclusion of sympathetic central protagonists. Early in 1968 Forman left for the US to make a film for PARAMOUNT, and showed in *Taking Off* (1971) that his talent for observation was by no means confined to his own society. Ondříček worked with him on the film, and, like him, Forman has not yet returned to Czechoslovakia. In 1973 he made a contribution to the film of the Munich Olympics, *Visions of Eight*.

**FORMBY**, GEORGE Jr (1904–61), British comedian, was primarily a music hall star, but a number of films were made around his formula of simple north-country humour and mildly sug-gestive songs which he accompanied on the ukelele. They were mostly broad satires on cur-rent fads—motor-cycle racing in *No Limit* (1935), the RAF in *It's in the Air* (1938), for example—and were popular enough to main-tain the fortunes of EALING STUDIOS which had earlier been established by Gracie FIELDS. His naïve appeal was less popular in the post-war years and he made no more films after 1947, but he continued to appear in music hall and in stage musicals until shortly before he died.

**FORST**, WILLI (1903– ), Austrian director and actor, real name Wilhelm Frohs, acted in the Austrian and German theatre and in films from 1922. He played chiefly in light comedy and operetta, often under the direction of E. A. DUPONT, and in 1933 became a director in his own right. He specialized in romantic escapism: his films, usually set in turn-of-the-century Vienna, have unmistakable polish and elegance. Notable among his very popular output (which continued until 1955) are *Maskerade* (1934) and *Bel Ami* (1939).

**FORTY-FIRST, The**, see SOROK PERVYI

*42ND STREET*, US, 1933. 1½hr. *Dir* Lloyd Bacon; *prod* Darryl F. Zanuck for Warner Bros; *scr* James Seymour, Rian James, from the novel by Bradford Ropes; *ph* Sol Polito; *chor* Busby Berkeley; *des* Jack Okey; *cost* Orry-Kelly; *songs* Al Dubin, Harry Warren; *cast* Warner Baxter (Julian Marsh), Bebe Daniels (Dorothy Brock), George Brent (Pat Denning), Una Merkel (Lor-raine Fleming), Ruby Keeler (Peggy Sawyer), Guy Kibbee (Abner Dillon), Dick Powell (Billy Lawler), Ginger Rogers (Ann Lowell 'Anytime Annie').

*42nd Street* inaugurated Busby BERKELEY's sensationally successful career with WARNER BROS; his staging of 'Shuffle off to Buffalo', inside a Pullman railway carriage, and '42nd Street', where the Manhattan skyline itself dances—each chorus girl bearing a section of sky-scraper—established him as a major figure in screen musicals. The songs, by Al Dubin and Harry Warren, also included 'You're Getting to Be a Habit with Me' and 'Young and Healthy'.

The film introduced Ruby KEELER to the screen in the classic role of the chorus girl who takes over the leading part at the last minute when the star falls ill, simultaneously winning success and the leading man, Dick Powell, who was to co-star with her in a series of musicals. Ginger ROGERS and Una Merkel played the wise-cracking but good-hearted chorus girls, who were to become familiar stereotypes in the flood of musicals which followed in the wake of *42nd Street*'s success.

**FOSCO**, PIERO, see PASTRONE, Giovanni

**FOSSE**, BOB (1925– ), US choreographer, actor, and director with a theatrical family back-ground, worked extensively as a dancer and choreographer on the New York stage. He danced and acted in the films *The Affair of Dobie Gillis*, *Kiss Me Kate* (both 1953), and *Give a Girl a Break* (Stanley DONEN, 1955). He then choreo-graphed films, including *My Sister Eileen* (Rich-ard QUINE, 1955), *Pajama Game* (Donen and George Abbott, 1957), and *Damn Yankees* (Donen and Abbott, 1958; *What Lola Wants* in GB). He directed his first film, *Sweet Charity*, in 1968. An adaptation of his own stage musical, it was critically acclaimed but unhappily failed at the box-office. His first big commercial success was CABARET (1972), which introduced a new style of musical drama in the cinema.

*FOUR HORSEMEN OF THE APOCALYPSE, The*, US, 1922. 2¼hr. *Dir*, *prod* Rex Ingram for Metro; *scr* June Mathis, from the novel by Vin-cente Blasco Ibañez; *ph* John Seitz; *ed* Grant Whytock; *cast* Rudolph Valentino (Julio Des-noyers), Alice Terry (Marguerite Laurier),

Pomeroy Cannon (Madariaga), Joseph Swickard (Marcelo Desnoyers), Virginia Warwick (Chichi), Wallace Beery (Colonel Von Richthofen).

Two sisters marry a Frenchman and a German and the two families find themselves on opposing sides in the First World War. Rudolph VALENTINO became a star with his performance as Julio, the son of the French family, who has a love affair with a married woman. She atones for her sin by becoming her husband's nurse when he is blinded in the war, while Julio joins the army and dies encountering his German cousin. The film contains INGRAM's talent for precise recreation of another time and place, including some brilliantly photographed and realized war sequences, which have rarely been equalled.

The remake directed by Vincente MINNELLI in 1961, starring Glenn FORD, Ingrid THULIN, Charles BOYER, and Paul HENREID, was on all counts less striking than the earlier version.

**FOX FILM CORPORATION,** US production, distribution, and exhibition company. Theatre owner William FOX established a film-making company, Box Office Attractions, in 1913. Renamed Fox Film Company in 1915 and supported by a distribution branch (Fox's Greater New York Film Rental Company), the firm set up a studio in Hollywood and became famous with 'vamp' pictures starring Theda BARA, Westerns with Tom MIX and Buck JONES, and big-budget features like THE IRON HORSE (1924), *What Price Glory?* (1926), and *In Old Arizona* (1929). Under the management of Fox and his vice-president Winfield Sheehan, Fox Films pioneered the Case-Sponable sound-on-film process in 1927 (re-christened Fox Movietone) and also bought the patent rights of the German Tri-Ergon sound process. The government forced the dismantling of Fox's trust-like empire in the late twenties, and the corporation was able to survive the 1929 crash only because of a financial agreement made by Fox with the New York financiers Harold Stuart and John Otterson. This agreement resulted in an ownership struggle which led to the notorious ousting of William Fox from his own company in 1931. In 1935 Fox Films was merged with Darryl F. ZANUCK's and Joseph SCHENCK's Twentieth Century Pictures to form TWENTIETH CENTURY-FOX Film Corporation.

**FOX, WILLIAM** (1879–1952), US producer of Hungarian origin, worked in the garment trade then, after owning a penny arcade, developed a chain of fifteen cinemas and in 1912 went into production with his own company which in 1915 became the FOX FILM CORPORATION. An independent and adventurous business man, he was, with Carl LAEMMLE, a leading contender against the MOTION PICTURE PATENTS COMPANY. He was also one of the earliest producers to experiment with sound film and wide screen. Financial interests forced him out of his own company after the Wall Street crash and he spent the last twenty years of his life in retirement. For a contemporary view, see *Upton Sinclair presents William Fox*, written and published by Upton Sinclair in 1933 (reprinted, New York, 1970).

**FRAME.** Artistically, the rectangle within which the moving picture appears, and which defines the limits of the original subject visible to the audience. Technically, the smallest temporal unit of film measurement, representing, for sound film, $\frac{1}{24}$ of a second of screen time.

The physical size of the film frame is determined by the width of the film in use and the length of the film that is advanced after each individual exposure is made. The original ratio between the frame's height and width was established at about 3:4 by EDISON's original KINETOGRAPH and remained the same for the first half century of film history. The look of the traditional motion picture, its style, and even much of its content were therefore largely determined by what could be comfortably 'framed' in a 3 × 4 rectangle.

The considerable power of the cinema to move and influence audiences depends greatly upon the way in which the frame rigidly limits what they can see. Movement is perceived in relation to the frame's edges, and can be emphasized by enlarging the movement relative to the frame or diminished by panning the frame with the movement. Outside the frame, a world exists but cannot be perceived except in sound, and movement there is assumed to continue unchanged since it was last seen until it is seen again. In skilled hands, this selectivity of the sharply-defined frame is an important factor in the cinema's power to influence audiences. (See also ASPECT RATIO, DYNAMIC FRAME.)

**FRANCE**'s achievements in the invention and the development of cinema can be traced back to the 1880s with the experiments of the physiologist Etienne MAREY, and the 1890s, with the Théâtre Optique of Emile REYNAUD. The official birth of French (and, with it, world) cinema was on 28 December 1895, when the LUMIÈRE brothers presented to the Parisian public the films they had made the year before with their newly-patented invention, the Cinématographe. Their team of cameramen travelled the world, using the camera to record what they saw, thus becoming the first newsreel cameramen. For the Lumières, the Cinématographe was merely a scientific curiosity and even when it became an obvious success in all the major cities of Europe and America they refused to exploit its commercial and artistic potential. They made documentary and newsreel films until 1900, unwilling to change their style. It was a man of the theatre, an illusionist, George MÈLIÈS, who used film creatively and gave it life.

In 1896, two enterprising men, Léon GAUMONT and Charles PATHÉ, set about popularizing film on a grand scale. By 1914 they had established large companies to produce, distribute, and exhibit films, with subsidiaries abroad. Gaumont began by producing films with the help of his secretary, Alice GUY-BLACHÉ, to whom he entrusted the production. She became the first woman director and moved on to be head of his largest studio in Paris. Two talented film-makers appeared, Ferdinand ZECCA, who worked for Pathé from 1891, and Louis FEUILLADE, who went from Pathé to Gaumont. In one of Zecca's most inventive films, *Histoire d'un crime* (1901), the technique of flashback was used to reconstruct the story of a crime, as told by the murderer to the court. Feuillade, who made some 800 films in 1905–22, is best remembered for his serials, FANTÔMAS (1913), LES VAMPIRES (1915–16), and JUDEX (1916). In 1908, the brothers Lafitte formed FILM D'ART, a company which produced stage classics on film using actors from the theatre, who brought to film acting a badly needed artistic quality. Cinema itself formed new talent such as Max LINDER, who became the best paid and most sought-after comic star of the pre-war period. He developed a comic style combining subtlety and sobriety which inspired Charles CHAPLIN.

After the First World War, the prosperity of the film industry in France was eclipsed by increased imports of American films. During the years 1916–17, cinema had become a popular and accepted form of entertainment in France. In contrast, the industry suffered from the general economic malaise of the post-war period in France. Production fell, as did the standard of film-making.

The early twenties brought about a completely new approach to film. This was due primarily to two film theoreticians, Ricciotto Canudo, who created the Club des Amis du 7e Art, and Louis DELLUC, who founded the ciné-club movement. By their writings in art and film magazines they helped publicize films as an art form among artistic and intellectual circles, attracting a new public to the cinema. Delluc with some new directors such as Marcel L'HERBIER, Jean EPSTEIN, Abel GANCE, and Germaine DULAC made films in which they explored some of the theories they had developed. Delluc's aim was the creation of a psychological atmosphere best achieved in his films *Fièvre* (1921) and *L'Inondation* (1924);

Dulac sought for 'visual music' in 'pure cinema'. She made one surrealistic film LA COQUILLE ET LE CLERGYMAN (1928) based on a script by Antonin ARTAUD.

With the development of Dada and SURREALISM in the arts the late twenties saw the affirmation of the AVANT-GARDE in French cinema. The main films were Fernand LÉGER's *Le Ballet mécanique* (1924), Man RAY's *Le Retour à la raison* (1923), René CLAIR's ENTR'ACTE (1924), Jean COCTEAU's LE SANG D'UN POÈTE (1930), and in particular Luis BUÑUEL's UN CHIEN ANDALOU (1928) and L'ÂGE D'OR (1930). Although they were non-commercial ventures, avant-garde films were widely seen in ciné-clubs. They impressed commercial producers who then backed some of these independent productions.

In France as elsewhere, the years 1927–9 marked the classic age of silent film. Many directors achieved a high degree of sophistication in film technique and handling of actors who gave magnificent performances such as Albert PRÉJEAN in Clair's UN CHAPEAU DE PAILLE D'ITALIE (*An Italian Straw Hat*, 1927), Gina Manes in Jacques FEYDER's adaptation of Emile Zola's novel THÉRÈSE RAQUIN (1928), and FALCONETTI in Carl DREYER'S LA PASSION DE JEANNE D'ARC (1928). In 1927 Abel Gance presented his masterpiece NAPOLÉON in which he anticipated CINERAMA by using a triple screen.

In the thirties, the coming of sound brought a revolution to French cinema. Some film-makers, such as Dulac and Epstein, disappeared from the public eye while others who had made silent films confirmed their talent, such as Clair, Feyder, and Jean RENOIR. Apart from Clair and DUVIVIER, 1930–4 was a bleak period in the commercial cinema. Dialogue became the most important aspect of film, and to overcome the language barrier many films were made in multi-language versions (see FOREIGN VERSIONS). For some producers, sound film was a way to make quick money by filming popular theatrical productions. Marcel PAGNOL and Sacha GUITRY adapted their works for the screen and Pagnol declared outright that the role of sound film was to publicize the theatre. Only René Clair in SOUS LES TOITS DE PARIS (1930), LE MILLION (1931), and A NOUS LA LIBERTÉ (1932), and Jean VIGO in ZÉRO DE CONDUITE (1933, banned until 1945 but shown in ciné-clubs), and L'ATALANTE (1934), managed to preserve their originality and achieved a continuity of style. In 1934, Clair left France for England, and Vigo, one of the most promising film-makers of this period, died.

In 1936, the CINÉMATHÈQUE FRANÇAISE was founded by Henri LANGLOIS, Jean MITRY, and Georges FRANJU. Its immediate task was to save from destruction old films, particularly silent ones whose future was threatened by the coming of sound. The mid-thirties initiated one of the richest periods in French cinema, which gave rise to such talents as Renoir, Marcel CARNÉ, Jean GRÉMILLON, and Duvivier. As actors learnt to work with sound film, talented scriptwriters such as Jacques PRÉVERT, Charles SPAAK, and Henri Jeanson liberated film still further from theatrical influence. Production increased rapidly reaching, in the late thirties, an average of 130 films per year.

All types of films were made, from the historical reconstruction of Feyder's LA KERMESSE HÉROÏQUE (1935) to the psychological drama of Grémillon's *Remorques* (1941). Carné and Prévert together made the fatalistic QUAI DES BRUMES (1938) and LE JOUR SE LÈVE (1939) starring Jean GABIN. Renoir reflected the political climate of contemporary France (particularly the Popular Front) in such films as LE CRIME DE MONSIEUR LANGE (1936), *La Vie est à nous* (1936), and *La Marseillaise* (1938), and made the two most important films of the thirties, LA GRANDE ILLUSION (1937) and LA RÈGLE DU JEU (1939).

The Second World War necessarily ended this period of artistic expansion. Clair and Renoir left France to take refuge in Hollywood. In 1940, the French film industry fell under German control and conditions of work altered considerably under the new censorship measures. By 1942 a new system of finance and control was set up with the Comité d'Organisation de l'Industrie Cinématographique (COIC) directly responsible to the Ministry of Information. A total of 354 feature films were produced in France in 1939–45. To avoid censorship directors chose nonpolitical subjects sometimes recalling a distant past such as in Carné's LES VISITEURS DU SOIR (1942) and LES ENFANTS DU PARADIS (1945). Jean Cocteau transposed to modern times the legend of Tristan and Isolde in a film directed by Jean Delannoy, *L'Eternel Retour* (1943). Psychological films were made by Henri-Georges CLOUZOT with *Le Corbeau* (1943), a gripping thriller which, because it was produced by the German-owned CONTINENTALE FILMS, was later banned, and by Robert BRESSON with *Les Anges du péché* (1943) and *Les Dames du Bois de Boulogne* (1945). Directors such as Claude AUTANT-LARA and Jacques BECKER also made their first feature films during the war. The French film school, INSTITUT DES HAUTES ÉTUDES CINÉMATOGRAPHIQUES, was created in 1943 by Marcel L'Herbier.

After the Liberation, the COIC was replaced by the Comité de Libération du Cinéma Français (CLCF) which purged the industry of collaborators. In 1946, the CLCF was dissolved and the CENTRE NATIONAL du Cinéma Français (CNC)

was established. It incorporated all the various professional organizations of the French industry. One of its immediate actions was to protect the industry against the influx of foreign films, particularly American, by reinforcing the QUOTA system. It also initiated co-productions, especially between France and Italy, and generally helped to finance independent productions. As a result, the French film industry was protected from company monopoly. Directors who had worked with German support during the war were given a cold reception, but after a few years most of them resumed their careers.

In 1947–57 the CNC's protective measures facilitated a return to film production in spite of a shortage of materials and the general economic crisis in the country. The French films made at this time expressed the social and political climate of the post-war years with a return to realism. The experiences of the war were recalled in Resistance films such as René CLÉMENT's LA BATAILLE DU RAIL (1946). The trend of FILM NOIR which had started during the war continued with Yves ALLÉGRET's *Dedée d'Anvers* (1948), Clouzot's *Les Diaboliques* (1955), André CAYATTE's *Nous sommes tous des assassins* (1952), and Jean-Pierre MELVILLE's *Bob le flambeur* (1955). Jacques Becker made a comedy *Antoine et Antoinette* (1947) and went on to more violent films portraying the underworld with CASQUE D'OR (1952), and *Touchez pas au grisbi* (1954).

The literary tradition was pursued by Autant-Lara in LE DIABLE AU CORPS (1947), and *Le Rouge et le noir* (1954). Bresson resumed work in 1951 with JOURNAL D'UN CURÉ DE CAMPAGNE (*Diary of a Country Priest*, 1951). The comedy genre was represented by the Prévert brothers in *Adieu Léonard* (1943) and a new film-maker Jacques TATI in JOUR DE FÊTE (1947) and LES VACANCES DE MONSIEUR HULOT (*Monsieur Hulot's Holiday*, 1951). A documentary movement flourished, headed by Georges ROUQUIER and Jean PAINLEVÉ, and influenced emerging film-makers of the fifties, particularly Georges Franju and RESNAIS.

By 1950 French cinema was firmly established commercially as directors of the forties launched themselves into big-budget films. Renoir, back in France, used colour most effectively in *French Can-can* (1955) and *Éléna et les hommes* (1956). Max OPHULS who had also returned from Hollywood gained international repute with LA RONDE (1950) and particularly LOLA MONTÈS (1955). In 1951 a group of film critics gathered around André BAZIN and called for changes, using the magazine CAHIERS DU CINÉMA as a forum for their campaign. François TRUFFAUT led the development of the AUTEUR THEORY, demanding a more personal approach to film-making. By 1955 most of these critics had put their ideas into practice by making short films, taking advantage of newly-introduced government aid and of the patronage offered by enlightened producers such as Pierre BRAUNBERGER. Claude CHABROL was the first to break into feature films with LE BEAU SERGE (1959), followed by Truffaut with LES QUATRE CENTS COUPS (1959), and Jean-Luc GODARD with A BOUT DE SOUFFLE (1960).

This generation of film-makers became known as the NOUVELLE VAGUE. The French film industry reacted favourably to this new development and backed it financially. While in 1957 there had been a decrease in film attendances, the years 1958–9 brought a renewed interest in film with the development of 'art et essai' cinemas, specialized cinemas receiving government subsidies (see ART HOUSE), and the opening of 25 new ciné-clubs. The doors were opened to many other new film-makers. By 1960 some eighteen directors had made their first feature film: apart from those already mentioned there were Alexandre ASTRUC, Jacques DEMY, Franju, Marcel Hanoun, Louis MALLE, Chris MARKER, Jean-Pierre MOCKY, Gérard Oury, Resnais, Jacques RIVETTE, Roger VADIM, and Agnès VARDA. These directors had little in common except that they turned professional at roughly the same time and were advocating new ideas. As their careers developed thoughout the sixties most of them retained their independent approach, as shown in such films as Demy's LES PARAPLUIES DE CHERBOURG (1964), Godard's PIERROT-LE-FOU (1965), Resnais's MURIEL (1963), Rivette's La Religieuse (1965), and Varda's LE BONHEUR (1964).

The CINÉMA-VÉRITÉ movement, led by Jean ROUCH put forward theories and new approaches to documentary film-making. Another distinctive development during the sixties was the rapprochement of film and literature through the films of such 'nouveaux romanciers' as Alain ROBBE-GRILLET (L'Immortelle, 1963; Trans-Europ-Express, 1966) and Marguerite DURAS (Détruire dit-elle, 1969). The CNC's scheme for helping independent production by advances against box-office receipts proved its success as many other new directors emerged throughout the sixties.

The political events of May 1968 had repercussions in the film industry. The CANNES film festival was abandoned, and in Paris film-makers of various backgrounds jointly suggested, in a document called 'les États-Généraux du Cinéma', a complete reorganization of the film industry and its nationalization. Although none of these ideas was implemented they nevertheless reflected the political consciousness of many French directors, such as René ALLIO, Marin Karmitz, Malle, Resnais, and others. As a result, some turned to making strictly political films such as Marker working in collaboration with the company SLON, and Godard with the group 'Dziga Vertov'.

Generally speaking, the early seventies showed an increased interest in comedy and satire with Truffaut's Domicile conjugal (Bed and Board, 1970), Claude Berri's Sexshop (1972), Jean Yanne's Tout le monde il est beau, tout le monde il est gentil (1972), René Gilson's L'Escadron Volapuk (1970), and Buñuel's LE CHARME DISCRET DE LA BOURGEOISIE (1972). Eric ROHMER switched to feature films in the last films of his series 'Six Contes Moraux'. The best and most popular thrillers were those of Melville, Le Cercle rouge (1970) and Un Flic (1972). Co-productions with a political message were made by COSTA-GAVRAS with his films Z (1968) and L'AVEU (1970). The industry looked very prosperous with a steady production of some 130 films a year, an increase in film attendance figures, and a new film production agreement between the CNC and the nationalized television company ORTF. Among the many new directors who made particularly striking films were Allio, Maurice Pialat, Jean-Louis Bertucelli, Walerian BOROWCZYK, Alain JESSUA, and Claude Sautet. Directors of the 'alternative cinema' whose approach to film remained non-commercial include Duras, Luc Moullet, Jean Eustache, and Philippe Garrel.

**FRANCESCO, GIULLARE DI DIO,** Italy, 1950. 1¼hr. *Dir* Roberto Rossellini; *prod* Rizzoli Amato; *scr* Rossellini, Federico Fellini, Felix Morlion, Antonio Benvenuti; *mus* Renzo Rossellini; *cast* Aldo Fabrizzi (Nicolaio), Arabella Lemaître (Chiara), Fra Nazario (Francesco).

Set in the thirteenth century, the film illustrates the life of St Francis of Assisi in a documentary style that achieves a lyrical but unsentimental evocation of the possibilities of saintliness.

**FRANCIS,** KAY (1899–1968), US actress, real name Katharine Gibbs, whose first film was *Gentlemen of the Press* (1929), followed by a supporting part in the first MARX BROTHERS film *The Cocoanuts* (1929). She became a popular star of the thirties with the reputation of being the best-dressed star in Hollywood, though her charm and immaculate grooming were not matched by her acting talent. Among her best-known films were TROUBLE IN PARADISE (1932), in which her performance was stiff despite being directed by LUBITSCH, *Cynara* (1932), *The White Angel* (1936), and *The Feminine Touch* (1941). Her last film was *Wife Wanted* (1946).

**FRANJU,** GEORGES (1912–   ), French director. In 1934, Franju met Henri LANGLOIS; in that year they made a short 16mm film, *Le Métro*, and in 1936 they founded the CINÉMATHÈQUE FRANÇAISE. In 1938 Franju became secretary of FIAF (FÉDÉRATION INTERNATIONALE DES ARCHIVES DE FILM), holding the post until 1945; he was secretary of the Institut de Cinématographie Scientifique 1945–53.

Franju's short documentaries are among his finest films: they gave him an international reputation which derived principally from his ability to infuse the documentary mode with intensely personal expression. In LE SANG DES BÊTES (1949), set in an abattoir, his juxtaposition of the macabre, the incongruous, the purely banal, gives rise to contradictory emotions. The lack of hysterical outrage is a characteristic of his work: in *En passant par la Lorraine* (1950) and HÔTEL DES INVALIDES (1951) the calm commentary belies the visual contradictions of horror and beauty. His next two films, *Le Grand Méliès* (1952) and *Monsieur et Madame Curie* (1953), are warmer in tone although the pathos of mutability lends a sadness to both these portraits of pioneers. He made eight more short films, among them *Les Poussières* (1954), *Le Théâtre National Populaire* (1956), and *Notre Dame, Cathédrale de Paris* (1957).

Franju's first feature film was LA TÊTE CONTRE LES MURS (1958). He had collaborated with Maurice JARRE in several of his documentaries and Jarre produced a fine score for this as well as for some of his best features including LES YEUX SANS VISAGE (1959). *Pleins feux sur l'assassin* (1960) is a conventional thriller, with only Jarre's music and Fradetal's photography to commend it, but THÉRÈSE DESQUEYROUX (1962) powerfully transferred François Mauriac's novel to the screen. JUDEX (1963) echoes *Le Grand Méliès* in its tribute to a previous era. (Franju had wanted to remake FEUILLADE'S FANTÔMAS, 1913, but was offered *Judex*, 1916, instead.) The film's surrealist overtones are stressed by Fradetal's recreation of the starkly contrasting blacks and whites of ORTHOCHROMATIC film stock. THOMAS L'IMPOSTEUR (1965) was adapted by Jean COCTEAU from his own novel. The project had been planned in 1952, but Franju had to wait twelve years before a producer could be found to finance it. His next major work was not until 1969 when Jacques PRÉVERT adapted Zola's novel *La Faute de l'Abbé Mouret*. *L'Homme sans visage* (*The Man without a Face*, 1974) brought Franju back to the fantasy-thriller.

Although the bulk of his work is contemporary with that of the NOUVELLE VAGUE directors, his style is closer to that of an earlier generation, that of VIGO and the surrealists.

**FRANKEL,** BENJAMIN (1906–73), distinguished British composer who has written much film music. He began composing songs for various films in 1935 and later started writing background scores. Among his many film scores were: *The Seventh Veil* (1945), *Mine Own Executioner* (1947), *London Belongs to Me* (1948), *So Long at the Fair* (1950), THE MAN IN THE WHITE SUIT (1951), *The Importance of Being Earnest* (1952), *The End of the Affair* (1954), *A Kid for Two Farthings* (1955), and *Summer of the Seventeenth Doll* (1959). In his last years he virtually retired from film work to devote himself to symphonic and other forms of composition.

**FRANKENHEIMER,** JOHN (1930– ), US director, was first an actor, then a television director notably with CBS. His first film, *The Young Stranger* (1957), was an adaptation of a television production on a theme of adolescent problems. *The Young Savages* (1961), starring Burt LANCASTER, combined backstreet juvenile delinquency with courtroom drama. In *All Fall Down* (1961) Angela LANSBURY gave one of her memorable performances as a possessive mother, a type which recurred, played by Thelma RITTER, in the factually-based *Bird Man of Alcatraz* (1962) which again starred Burt Lancaster. THE MANCHURIAN CANDIDATE (1962) confirmed Frankenheimer's promise as a director of unusual talent. SEVEN DAYS IN MAY (1964) was a political thriller, largely conceived in terms of dialogue, but splendidly cumulative in its increasing tension; *The Train* (1964), a French Resistance story, was particularly remarkable for its convincing railway atmosphere and detail: both again starred Burt Lancaster who, like Angela Lansbury, has given some outstanding performances under Frankenheimer's direction.

*Grand Prix* (1966), a mammoth glorification of the racing car, presented its big set-pieces with visual flair but in other respects was tedious. *The Extraordinary Seaman* (1967), a satirical comedy, was followed by *The Fixer* (1968), an intense but dull adaptation of Malamud's novel. The almost reticent *The Gypsy Moths* (1969) seemed something like a return to form; but since 1964 Frankenheimer's work has proved increasingly uneven in quality and neither *I Walk the Line* nor *The Horsemen* (both 1971) proved comparable with his earlier work.

**FRANKENSTEIN,** or *The Modern Prometheus* by Mary Shelley (1797–1851), published 1818, has provided the starting-point for many films in the horror tradition, although few have felt the need for close fidelity to the original.

UNIVERSAL established a reputation for horror films of quality chiefly on the basis of *Frankenstein* (James WHALE, 1931), starring Boris KARLOFF as the man-made monster (which is not as is commonly believed called Frankenstein—this is the name of the monster's creator). This version was a coldly effective exercise in terror, not indulging in obviously gruesome detail but gaining its effects with an impressive reticence. It was re-issued with DRACULA (1931) in 1938, and repeated its great commercial success. Universal continued to use the successful monster in such come-backs as *The Ghost of Frankenstein* (1942), *Frankenstein Meets the Wolf Man* (1943), and *House of Frankenstein* (1945), in which an attempt was made to increase the formula's effectiveness by bringing together characters from various horror stories in an unconscious parody of the genre.

*I Was a Teenage Frankenstein* (1957) astonishingly achieved its aim of reaching a younger age group. Its burlesque approach was very successful and it briefly established a fashion for teenage monsters.

Among several other uses of the man-made monster idea, *The Curse of Frankenstein* (1957) is memorable for establishing HAMMER FILMS as the heirs to Universal's lead in the horror field. A polished and only slightly satirical version, it earned a profit for its producers of over $1 million in the US alone, and was the first of a highly remunerative series of films which made the name of Hammer synonymous with horror.

**FREAKS**, US, 1932. 1½hr. *Dir* Tod Browning; *prod* MGM; *scr* Willis Goldbeck, Leon Gordon; *ph* Merrit B. Gerstad; *des* Cedric Gibbons; *cast* Leila Hyams (Venus), Wallace Ford (Phroso), Olga Baclanova (Cleopatra), Henry Victor (Hercules), Johnny Eck (The Half Man), Daisy and Violet Hilton (the Siamese twins), Randion (The Living Torso), Harry Earles (Hans).

*Freaks* was made in secret and was until recently seldom shown. Instead of using actors to impersonate the freaks, Tod BROWNING used all manner of deformities: cretins, Siamese twins, the limbless, dwarfs, a hermaphrodite, to achieve this superb realization of the grotesque. Within the film's context it is the freaks who possess integrity and solidarity: their community, peopled as it is by the abnormal, is an ideal one. 'Normal' humans—represented by Cleopatra, an acrobat, and Hercules, the strong man—are evil, avaricious, and cruel. In the macabre and violent climax the freaks wreak a terrible revenge on the two transgressors who have conspired in the degradation and robbery of the midget, Hans.

**FREDERICK**, PAULINE (1883–1938), US actress, made her screen début in 1915, in Edwin S. PORTER's version of Hall Caine's novel *The Eternal City*. A mature and intelligent actress, she was one of the few successes of Adolph ZUKOR's 'Famous Players in Famous Plays' policy (see FAMOUS PLAYERS). Her films include:

*Lydia Gilmore* (1915), *Resurrection* (1918), *Madame X* (1920), *Smouldering Fires* (1924), *On Trial* (1928), *This Modern Age* (1931).

**FREE CINEMA**, title adopted for a series of six programmes screened at the NATIONAL FILM THEATRE 1956–9 and for the movement in Britain to which they gave both impetus and expression. The first programme, in February 1956, consisted of: *Momma Don't Allow* (1955), co-directed by Tony RICHARDSON and Karel REISZ, about a North London jazz club; Lindsay ANDERSON's *O Dreamland* (1953), about a Margate amusement park; and *Together* (1955), by Lorenza Mazzetti with Anderson's help in editing, about two deaf-mutes played by Eduardo Paolozzi and Michael Andrews in an East End setting. Further programmes during the next three years showed comparable work from filmmakers abroad as well as in Britain: Norman MCLAREN's *Neighbours* (1952), Lionel ROGOSIN's ON THE BOWERY (1957), FRANJU's LE SANG DES BÊTES (1949), POLAŃSKI's *Dwaj ludzie z szafa* (*Two Men and a Wardrobe*, 1958), and *Nice Time* (1957), by Alain Tanner and Claude Goretta, were included in Free Cinema programmes.

In a series of statements accompanying the programmes, the makers defined their aims, which challenged orthodoxy in society as well as in cinema. They wished to re-emphasize the social responsibility of the artist, to free filmmaking from the trammels of commercial production, and above all to stimulate liveliness and personal expression in recognizing 'the significance of the everyday'.

The majority of the British films made under the banner of Free Cinema were descriptions of actual people and places: the makers acknowledged the term 'documentary' uneasily, because of its connotations of glossy distortion. Anderson's *Every Day except Christmas* (1957), about the workings of Covent Garden market, and Reisz's *We Are the Lambeth Boys* (1959), about a South London youth club, represent the spirit of the movement. The way had been prepared by the SEQUENCE group, led by Anderson. An important feature of the movement was that its films were made outside the normal framework of production, although, as the makers acknowledged, not without its help. Several of the people involved were working professionals, most notably Walter LASSALLY, who photographed *Momma Don't Allow* and *Every Day except Christmas*, and John Fletcher, who recorded the sound-tracks of several of the films. The support of the BRITISH FILM INSTITUTE's Experimental Fund was crucial to several of the films, and another hopeful feature was the money raised, without any strings attached, from the Ford

Mctor Co for *Every Day except Christmas* and *We Are the Lambeth Boys*.

The movement, closely connected with concurrent revolts against orthodoxy in the theatre and literature, represented one of the rare occasions in Britain when a group of artists identified common aims and together sought to put them into practice. It brought a refreshing new stream into British cinema, and its best work will endure among Britain's most notable short films. The movement's spirit was carried over into commercial fiction films made by several of its leading directors when the movement was declared closed by its instigators. A statement signed by Anderson, Reisz, Lassally, and Fletcher, accompanying the last programme in March 1959, aptly proclaimed 'Free Cinema is dead. Long live Free Cinema!' (See also DOCUMENTARY.)

**FREED,** ARTHUR (1894– ), US producer, real name Grossman, whose songwriting career led him to METRO-GOLDWYN-MAYER where he became the guardian angel of men like MINNELLI, KELLY, and DONEN, bringing them to the studio and giving them the opportunity to make the string of successful MUSICALS which emerged in the forties and fifties. Among them was SINGIN' IN THE RAIN (1952) which featured his own songs.

**FREND,** CHARLES (1909– ), British director, started his film career as an editor. His talents as a director of action films was demonstrated during the war years with such realistic dramas as *The Foreman went to France* (1942) and *San Demetrio, London* (1943). After the war he continued to work for EALING STUDIOS, directing, among others, a light-hearted comedy, *The Magnet* (1949); but his particular style is best displayed in accounts of human endurance like *Scott of the Antarctic* (1948), *The Cruel Sea* (1952), and *Cone of Silence* (1960).

*FRENZY* see HETS

**FRESNAY,** PIERRE (1897–1975), French actor, real name Pierre-Jules-Louis Laudenbach, made his stage début at the age of fifteen and at eighteen appeared in his first film, *France d'abord!* (1915). His stage career flourished, but he appeared only occasionally on the screen during the silent era. The title role of MARIUS (1931) and his continuation of the role in *Fanny* (1932: see MARIUS) launched him as a film actor. Although the only one of the leading players in PAGNOL's trilogy not native to the Midi, the vitality and conviction of his characterization earned him both popularity and respect. He visited England to play a leading part in THE MAN WHO KNEW TOO MUCH (1934) and returned to France to star

in, among others, *La Dame aux camélias* (1934, opposite his wife Yvonne PRINTEMPS, and *Koenigsmark* (Maurice TOURNEUR, 1935). *César* (see MARIUS) was filmed in 1936, again with Fresnay as Marius, and in the same year the peak of his film career was reached with the role of the aristocratic army officer Boïeldieu in LA GRANDE ILLUSION (1937).

His parts since have varied from an exuberant Offenbach in *Trois Valses* (1939) to a tough Parisian police inspector in CLOUZOT's *L'Assassin habite au 21* (1942) and the shell-shocked hero of ANOUILH's *Le Voyageur sans bagages* (1943). He scored an outstanding success as St Vincent de Paul in MONSIEUR VINCENT (1947). He appeared progressively less in films, but remained a popular and distinguished stage actor.

*FREUDLOSE GASSE, Die* (*Joyless Street*), Germany, 1925. 1¾hr. *Dir* G. W. Pabst; *prod* Hirschel-Sofar; *scr* Willi Haas, from the novel by Hugo Bettauer; *ph* Guido Seeber, Kurt Oertel; *des* Sohnie and Otto Erdmann; *cast* Asta Nielsen (Marie Leschner), Greta Garbo (Greta Rumfort), Valeska Gert (the Greifer), Werner Krauss (the butcher).

PABST's account of Vienna during inflation, laying emphasis on the ruin of middle-class families, has a strongly melodramatic flavour but was realistic enough to shock his contemporaries: it was banned outright in England and radically cut in Italy, France, Austria, and elsewhere. His gift for the direction of actresses is here already highly developed, contrasting the still virtually unknown Greta GARBO and Asta NIELSEN, then at the peak of her fame. He also made effective use of Valeska GERT, the popular cabaret artist, as the madam of a brothel.

**FREUND,** KARL (1890–1969), German-born cameraman, entered the film industry as a projectionist at the age of fifteen. Within two years he became a cameraman, making films in Berlin, Vienna, and Belgrade. He was responsible for the photography of all Asta NIELSEN's German films as well as WIENE's *Eva* (1917) starring Emil JANNINGS. In the post-war years he was closely associated with such pioneers of EXPRESSIONISM as MURNAU, LANG, and WEGENER; he was cameraman on DREYER's *Mikaël* (1924), on which the second unit cameraman was Rudolph MATÉ, and on DER LETZTE MANN (1924).

Freund was production head of Fox-Europa, 1926–9, then went to Hollywood and worked on a number of films for UNIVERSAL including Tod BROWNING's DRACULA (1931). Lew AYRES supported the story that Freund was responsible for the 'butterfly' sequence ending ALL QUIET ON THE WESTERN FRONT (1930). He became a director with *The Mummy* (1933), continuing to direct after moving to METRO-GOLDWYN-MAYER in 1935 and maintaining his association with the macabre with *Mad Love* (1935, a remake of ORLACS HÄNDE, 1925), on which the cameraman was Gregg TOLAND.

Freund continued with MGM as a cameraman until 1947. He was awarded an OSCAR for THE GOOD EARTH (1937), and although William DANIELS is credited with the photography of CAMILLE (1936) Freund appears to have been responsible for the greater part of it. Among a long list of films made during the thirties and forties ZINNEMANN's *The Seventh Cross* (1944) is outstanding. After three years with WARNER BROS, Freund left films in 1950 to work in television and to concentrate on his Photo Research Corporation.

**FRIČ, MARTIN** (1902–68), Czech director, started his career as a stage actor, began designing posters for film, then worked in a laboratory, and graduated to cameraman, scriptwriter, and film actor. He worked during the twenties with Karel Lamač and Josef Rovenský, and first made his name as director with *Varhaník u sv Víta* (*The Organist of St Vitus's Cathedral*, 1929), for which the poet Vítěslav Nezval wrote his first film script. After the coming of sound, Frič developed his flair for comedy, becoming particularly associated with the famous pair, Jiří Voskovec and Jan Werich, founders of Prague's political and satirical theatre. Outstanding among the films in which he directed them were *Hej rup!* (*Heave-Ho*, 1934) and the anti-Fascist satire, *Svět patří nám* (*The World Belongs to Us*, 1937). The latter drew a note of protest from the German embassy, together with Hugo Haas's film of the same year, *Bílá nemoc* (*The White Disease*), based on Čapek's play. Frič also worked with Haas during the thirties, and directed the most widely popular of Czech comedians, Vlasta Burian, notably in *Katakomby* (*Catacombs*, 1940). He also made the first—and only successful—Czech screwball comedy, *Eva tropí hlouposti* (*Eva Is Fooling*, 1939).

Comedy was in fact to dominate his prolific output of nearly a hundred films, but he also earned a special place as founder of Slovak cinema, making *Jánošik* in 1935. Much of this film about the legendary Slovak outlaw hero was shot on location in Slovakia. Its fine sense of spectacle won it an award at VENICE, and helped the international reputation of Czech film as well as giving a boost to Slovak sentiment.

During the German occupation, Frič continued to direct drawing-room and detective comedies, and after the war was, with Otakar VÁVRA, one of the main organizers of the newly nationalized film industry and its production groups. In 1947 he was entrusted with the direction of the first feature film to come from the new Slovak production unit, *Varúj* (*Warning*) about a returned American immigrant; and in 1950 he made his contribution to the era of socialist realism with *Pašt* (*The Trap*) about the Czech underground during the occupation, and *Zocelení* (*Steel Town*) about steel workers in the thirties. More characteristically, in 1951 he directed Jan Werich's first post-war return to the screen in *Cíšaŕuv pekaŕ* (*The Emperor's Baker*) and *Pekaŕuv cišaŕ* (*The Baker's Emperor*), a two-part satirical comedy based on the old Prague legend of the GOLEM, with Werich in the double role of the Emperor Rudolph and a baker's apprentice.

Frič continued to the end of his life to make comedies (*Král Králu, King of Kings*, 1963, and *Nejlepši ženská mého živote, The Best Girl of my Life*, 1967) among more serious films such as *Hvězda zvaná Pelyněk* (*A Star Named Wormwood*, 1964). He died of a heart attack on 21 August 1968, the day the first Soviet tanks moved into Prague.

**FRIESE-GREENE, WILLIAM** (1855–1921), British photographer, real name William Green, a man of considerable energy and enterprise whose flow of ideas led to his registration of seventy-nine British patents. Mcst of these grew out of his photographic business in Bath and Bristol (and, later, in Plymouth and London), but others were for such inventions as cigar lighters and inkless printing.

Some of Friese-Greene's ideas worked but he seems to have lacked the scientific knowledge and technical ability to carry most of them into practice (according to his obituary in *The British Journal of Photography*, he had 'the very slightest acquaintance with the scientific elements of chemistry and physics'). This certainly applies to the 'invention' of cinematography claimed for him as the result of his Patent No. 10131 (21 June 1889) for a moving picture camera and projector. His epitaph 'His genius bestowed upon humanity the boon of commercial cinema photography of which he was the first inventor and patentee' has become part of the mythology of cinema history, especially in Britain, firstly through a romanticized biography published in 1948 (*Friese-Greene, close-up of an inventor*, by Ray Allister) and then through the prestigious Festival of Britain film based on it, *The Magic Box* (John BOULTING, 1951). The image of Friese-Greene (Robert DONAT) demonstrating the first moving pictures to an open-mouthed Cockney policeman (Laurence OLIVIER) is attractive but there is no evidence that Friese-Greene ever succeeded in projecting his pictures. Even his motion picture camera, much more closely described in the 1889 patent than the projector, was the result of working with Mortimer Evans, one of Friese-Greene's many collaborators. Friese-Greene, imaginative as he was, is in fact a marginal figure in cinema history.

'William Friese-Greene and the origins of cinematography', by Brian Coe (*Photographic Journal*, March and April 1962) is a careful investigation into Friese-Greene's claims.

*FRITZ THE CAT*, US, 1971. De Luxe Color; 1¼hr. *Dir, scr* Ralph Bakshi, based on the comic strip by Robert Crumb; *mus dir* Ed Bogas, 'Yesterdays' by Jerome Kern sung by Billie Holiday, 'Mamblues' written and performed by the Carl Tjader Band.

*Fritz the Cat*, a stimulating departure from the cute, animal fantasy cartoon style, uses full ANIMATION that is lively and technically complex. Against finely-drawn backgrounds derived from enlarged photographs, Robert Crumb's anti-hero encounters a selection of 'underground' characters and engages in a variety of outrageously unconventional episodes. The loose narrative and rock music backing brought comparison with EASY RIDER (1969): the cartoon satire does not always avoid the naïve poignancy of the earlier film.

*Fritz the Cat* was the first animated feature to be given an 'x' CERTIFICATE in Britain, reawakening the question of CENSORSHIP in animation films.

**FROELICH, CARL** (1875–1953), German director, joined Oskar MESSTER's company as a cameraman in 1903. He directed films from about 1910, including a version of *The Brothers Karamazov, Die Brüder Karamasoff* (1920). Froelich was primarily a skilled director of actresses: in 1921 he made *Der Idiot* (THE IDIOT) starring Asta NIELSEN, and *Luise Millerin—Kabale und Liebe* with Lil DAGOVER. A succession of immensely popular romances starring Henny PORTEN established his reputation and his own company flourished as a part of UFA until 1940. *Luise Königen von Preussen* (1931), which Porten produced and starred in was notable among the grandiose historical dramas which fed the nationalistic spirit of the time in Germany. In the same year he supervised Leontine SAGAN's direction of MÄDCHEN IN UNIFORM and he presented his own view of boarding-school experiences in *Reifende Jugend* (1934), again starring his discovery Herthe Thiele. In 1939 he was made head of the REICHSFILMKAMMER and he continued to direct films until 1951.

*FRÖKEN JULIE* (*Miss Julie*), Sweden, 1951. 1¼hr. *Dir* Alf Sjöberg; *prod* Sandrews; *scr* Sjöberg, from the play by Strindberg; *ph* Göran Strindberg; *cast* Anita Björk (Miss Julie). Ulf Palme (Jean), Märta Dorff (Kristin), Anders Henrikson (the Count), Lissi Alandh (the Countess).

SJÖBERG's adaptation, while faithful to the original, transfers the action from a single claustrophobic room to various parts of the Count's mansion and estate, where tortured passions are played out in a midsummer setting, photographed with a brilliant clarity that throws the sombre narrative into high relief. Past events described in the play are depicted in flashbacks which are integrated into the main plot: sometimes characters from the past appear in the same scenes as the person remembering them, underlining Strindberg's insistence on the importance of past influences on emotional development.

*FROM HERE TO ETERNITY*, US, 1953. 2hr. *Dir* Fred Zinnemann; *prod* Columbia; *scr* Daniel Taradash, based on the novel by James Jones; *ph* Burnett Guffey; *cast* Burt Lancaster (Sgt Warden), Montgomery Clift (Prewitt), Deborah Kerr (Karen), Frank Sinatra (Private Maggio), Donna Reed (Lorene).

While many of the extremes of violence in the novel were omitted from the film, the result is a tough account of relationships in a unit of the US Army in peacetime, culminating in the Japanese attack on Pearl Harbor. Much of the film's initial impact lay in the casting of Deborah KERR in a role far removed from her usual well-bred style, and the come-back of Frank SINATRA in his first dramatic part.

The acting and direction were highly praised, and the film's popularity proved the viability of comparatively low-budget productions at a time when major companies were fighting the counter-attraction of television with large-scale spectaculars.

**FRONTIER FILMS**, US production cooperative set up in New York in 1936 by Paul STRAND, was at the heart of the politically leftist, socially committed DOCUMENTARY movement which grew up in New York in the Depression of the early thirties. Its approach was influenced by FLAHERTY and EISENSTEIN and by the contemporary developments of Roy Stryker's Rural Resettlement Administration still photography unit in the US, and GRIERSON's documentary movement in Britain.

Notable Frontier Films productions were *The Heart of Spain* (1937), *China Strikes Back* (1938), and NATIVE LAND (1942). Members of the co-operative included Leo HURWITZ, Lionel Berman, John Howard LAWSON, Robert Stebbins, David Wolf, Eugene Hill, and Irving Lerner; but Ralph Steiner, who had worked with Strand and Hurwitz on Pare LORENTZ's

THE PLOW THAT BROKE THE PLAINS (1936) and whose interests and approach resembled those of Frontier Films, refused to join because of political differences with Strand, and instead formed a group of his own which eventually produced Willard VAN DYKE's *The City* (1939).

**FRONT PAGE, The,** US, 1931. 1¾hr. *Dir* Lewis Milestone; *prod* United Artists; *scr* Bartlett Cormack, Charles Lederer, from the stage play by Ben Hecht and Charles MacArthur; *ph* Glen MacWilliams; *cast* Adolphe Menjou (Walter Burns), Pat O'Brien (Hildy Johnson), Mary Brien (Peggy), Edward Everett Horton (Bensinger), Walter Catlett (Murphy).

HECHT and MACARTHUR's story of newspaper reporters and political grafters initiated a vogue for dramas of newspaper life, although the main setting was not a newspaper office but the criminal court where reporters are gathered for the execution of a murderer. The film also introduced a style of dialogue, often broad and *risqué*, with much repartee, backchat, and wisecracking, which was to become a conspicuous feature of sophisticated Hollywood comedy and was more effectively rendered in Howard HAWKS's adaptation HIS GIRL FRIDAY (1940) with Pat O'BRIEN's role rewritten as a woman reporter.

Billy WILDER directed a second remake in 1974 under the original title, with Jack LEMMON as the ace reporter and Walter MATTHAU as his overbearing editor.

**FRONT PROJECTION,** a method of photographing actors in a studio combined with a moving background photographed elsewhere. It is now increasingly used in preference to BACK PROJECTION, the earlier and simpler method.

The camera is set up facing the actors and the screen behind them. But the background film cannot be simply projected on the screen as in a cinema: it would also be projected on to the actors, and they would cast shadows on the screen. (These problems originally led to the adoption of back projection.) Front projection avoids the shadows by placing the projector optically in the same position as the camera, via a small semi-silvered mirror; from the camera's point of view each shadow is hidden behind the actor casting it. The image projected on to the actors is 'drowned' by the normal studio lights; they would drown the image on the screen too, except that it is made of a special beaded material which, like cats' eyes, effectively magnifies the light reflected directly back towards the camera. Since camera and projector are on the same side of the screen, front projection requires less

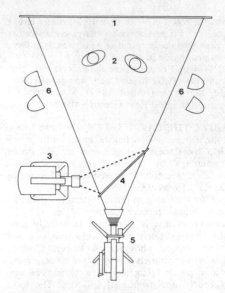

1 Screen: highly directional reflectivity
2 Actors
3 Projector
4 Semi-silvered mirror
5 Camera
6 Lighting

Front projection

studio space than back projection. Otherwise it is used in the same way as back projection, with similar or better results. (See EFFECTS.)

**FUJICOLOR,** a negative/positive and reversal colour film process introduced for professional cinematography by Fuji Photo Company in Japan in 1955.

**FULLER, SAMUEL** (1911–   ), US director, was a newspaper copy boy then crime reporter before his short stories and novels led to work as a scriptwriter in the late thirties. After the Second World War, in which he served as an infantryman in North Africa and Europe, he returned to Hollywood, where he directed his first film, a Western, *I Shot Jesse James*, in 1948. His subsequent work, much of which he wrote and produced, as well as directed, endeared him to the AUTEUR theorists of CAHIERS DU CINÉMA, and he spent some time in Paris during the sixties, appearing in Luc Moullet's *Brigitte et Brigitte* (1966) and Jean-Luc GODARD's PIERROT-LE-FOU (1966), where he pronounced his cinematic credo: 'The film is like a battle-ground: love, hate, action, violence, death . . . In one word, Emotion'. All of these are thematically at the centre of his films, whether

Westerns (*Run of the Arrow*, 1956; *Forty Guns*, 1957), war (*The Steel Helmet*, 1950; *Fixed Bayonets*, 1951; *China Gate*, 1957; *Verboten*, 1958; *Merrill's Marauders*, 1962), or crime (PICKUP ON SOUTH STREET, 1952; *House of Bamboo*, 1955; *The Crimson Kimono*, 1959; *Underworld USA*, 1960; *Shock Corridor*, 1963; *The Naked Kiss*, 1964). Beside these themes, common in the US action genres, there is a consistent preoccupation with those who stand outside society, either as members of the underworld or of another race, that is closely linked to a recurrent examination of nationality. His frequently sordid subject-matter, often drawn from his experiences as a crime reporter and a soldier, have tended to make his work rather less popular with the general public than with French intellectuals.

*FUNNY FACE*, US, 1957. VistaVision; 1¾hr; Technicolor. *Dir* Stanley Donen; *prod* Paramount; *scr* Leonard Gershe from his own story; *ph* Ralph June; *mus, lyr* George and Ira Gershwin (additional *mus* and *lyr* Edens and Gershe); *cast* Audrey Hepburn (Jo), Fred Astaire (Dick Avery), Kay Thompson (Maggie Prescott), Michel Auclair (Emile Flostre), Robert Flemyng (Paul Duval).

Based on a 1927 Broadway musical, the film retains little besides the memorable GERSHWIN score. A Cinderella tale that satirizes the world of fashion, it presents Fred ASTAIRE in a part based on the fashion photographer Richard Avedon, who as consultant was responsible for the stunning Paris settings and elegant design. Audrey HEPBURN's gamine charm contrasts brilliantly with Astaire's assured elegance, while Kay Thompson's fashion editor adds brittle humour.

**FURIE**, SIDNEY J. (1933–    ), Canadian director, studied scriptwriting and direction at the Carnegie Institute of Technology, then worked in Canadian television. His first film was the low-budget feature *Dangerous Age* (1957). In England he directed films aimed at a youthful market, including two vehicles for the pop singer Cliff Richard and *The Leather Boys* (1963) starring Rita TUSHINGHAM. *The Ipcress File* (1965), a spy thriller, was very successful and he moved to Hollywood to direct *The Appaloosa* (1966, *Southwest to Sonora* in GB). His films are noted more for the bravura of their camerawork and quickness at following current fashions than for lasting content.

**FURTHMAN**, JULES (1888–1960), US script-writer, real name Julius Grinell Furthmann, started writing scripts in 1915 under his own name. From 1918 to 1920 he wrote under the name Stephen Fox because of anti-German feel-ing. He worked for several major film companies during the twenties, writing scripts for Henry KING, John FORD, Maurice TOURNEUR, and Clarence BROWN among others, and directing one film himself: by the time of his first collaboration with Josef von STERNBERG, UNDERWORLD (1927), he was one of Hollywood's most craftsmanlike and respected scriptwriters and from 1933 was a free-lance, choosing his own subjects.

Furthman's reputation rests largely on his collaborations with Sternberg, often not fully acknowledged, and, later, Howard HAWKS. The films he scripted for Sternberg, notably *Underworld*, DOCKS OF NEW YORK (1928), MOROCCO (1930), and SHANGHAI EXPRESS (1932), have a formal narrative structure which adds discipline and strength to Sternberg's baroque tendencies.

After *Blonde Venus* (1932) Furthman worked once more for Sternberg, collaborating on the script of *The Shanghai Gesture* (1941). Meanwhile he built up with Hawks a relationship that was as successful and apparently less uneasy. Furthman was responsible, solely or in collaboration, for the scripts of some of Hawks's best film, *Come and Get It* (1936), *Only Angels Have Wings* (1939), TO HAVE AND HAVE NOT (1944), THE BIG SLEEP (1946), and RIO BRAVO (1959), his last script.

Other notable films written by Furthman include *Hotel Imperial* (Mauritz STILLER, 1927), THE MUTINY ON THE BOUNTY (1935), and *The Outlaw* (Howard HUGHES, 1946).

*FURY*, US, 1936. 1½hr. *Dir* Fritz Lang; *prod* Joseph L. Mankiewicz for MGM; *scr* Lang, Bartlett Cormack, from the story 'Mob Rule' by Norman Krasna; *ph* Joseph Ruttenberg; *cast* Spencer Tracy (Joe Wheeler), Sylvia Sidney (Katherine Grant), Walter Abel (District Attorney), Bruce Cabot (Kirby Dawson), Walter Brennan (Bugs Mayers), Frank Albertson (Charlie), George Walcott (Tom).

*Fury* was LANG's first film in America. Taking a serious contemporary social problem—lynching—it developed into a study of both unreasoning crowd psychology and the calculated pursuit of personal revenge. The film first shows enraged ordinary citizens turning into a savage mob, then examines the destructiveness of a single-minded passion for revenge in one man; the total view finally condemns both. The somewhat cosy ending was added by the studio after Lang had completed his work.

**FUSCO**, GIOVANNI (1906–    ), Italian composer who has written extensively for films. He has long been associated with Michelangelo ANTONIONI: he worked on almost all Antonioni's feature films from *Cronaca di un amore* (1950) to IL DESERTO ROSSO (1964). He has also written music for films by Alain RESNAIS: HIROSHIMA MON AMOUR (1959), in collaboration with Georges DELERUE, and LA GUERRE EST FINIE (1965).

**FUTURISM,** an artistic movement which began in Italy during the first decade of the twentieth century, led by Filippo Marinetti. It rejected traditionalism and all attempts to preserve the past, and glorified the machinery and technology of the modern world which had brought about changes in perception. The cinema was hailed as the new means of expression; the manifesto on Futurist cinema, published in 1916, rejected logic and proportion, and counselled animation of objects, emphasis on technical devices, and the fragmentation and reconstruction of the world according to whim, marking a move away from the realism of the narrative cinema. In spite of its obvious suitability as a medium for Futurist ideas, film held no real interest for Marinetti; only two films were made by Italian members of the group, Ginna's *Vita futurista* and Bragaglia's *Il perfido incanto* (*Wicked Enchantment*), both in 1906, the latter only disputedly Futurist. The movement's influence was greater in post-revolutionary Russia where the Futurists, with MAYAKOVSKY at their head, were the first to offer their services to the Revolution. VERTOV, with his emphasis on the unstaged, on man as master of the machine, and on technical devices, was partly influenced by the Futurists, as were EISENSTEIN and the FEKS group. Futurist ideas, along with those of the Formalists and Constructivists, were discussed and developed in the journals *Lef* and *Novyi Lef*, but a Futurist cinema as such never really evolved.

# G

**GAÁL, ISTVÁN** (1933– ), Hungarian director, was an electro-technician before joining the Academy for Film Art. After making his diploma film *Pályamunkások* (*Surfacemen*, 1957)—photographed by Sándor SÁRA, with whom he worked much during the sixties—he graduated in 1959 and later studied for four terms at the CENTRO SPERIMENTALE in Rome. Throughout his features he has shown a basic interest in the conflict of the individual and the community, while his style has hardened from the early beauty of *Sodrásban* (*Current*, 1964), *Zöldár* (*Green Years*, 1965), and *Keresztelö* (*Baptism*, 1967) into the more formal and menacing manner evident in MAGASISKOLA (*The Falcons*, 1970) and *Holt vidék* (*Dead Landscape*, 1971).

**GABIN, JEAN** (1904– ), French actor, real name Jean-Alexis Moncorgé, appeared in cabaret, music-hall, and at the Folies-Bergère and was for a time leading man to Mistinguett at the Moulin Rouge. He acted in films from 1930, becoming well known in films by DUVIVIER: *Marie Chapdelaine* (1934), *Golgotha* (1935), *La Bandera* and *La Belle Equipe* (both 1935). He first appeared for RENOIR in *Les Bas-fonds* (1936); and he became a star with Duvivier's PÉPÉ-LE-MOKO (1937).

Gabin's screen personality was already defined—tough and defiant but always with a hint of sensitivity: his brusqueness concealed a basic vulnerability and his offhand speech an avoidance of self-exposure. Renoir brought out his gentler side in LA GRANDE ILLUSION (1937).

Jean Gabin (right) with Pierre Fresnay in *La Grande Illusion* (Jean Renoir, 1937)

Gabin's Maréchal is a plain man, brave and loyal without posturing, susceptible to the homely warmth of the woman who aids his escape. In QUAI DES BRUMES, LA BÊTE HUMAINE (both 1938), and LE JOUR SE LÈVE (1939) he was again the social outcast, ultimately losing his fight against authority but always retaining sympathy for his predicament.

After a short and unsuccessful period in Hollywood during the early part of the war, Gabin joined the Free French Navy, winning the Médaille Militaire and the Croix de Guerre; he was later awarded the Légion d'Honneur. He returned to the cinema with *Martin Roumagnac* (1946). His acting career declined for a time, his films lacking the quality of his pre-war successes, but he recaptured his following in Jacques BECKER's excellent thriller *Touchez pas au grisbi* (1954) and contributed a genially nostalgic performance to Renoir's *French Can-can* (1955). Two films directed by Claude AUTANT-LARA, *La Traversée de Paris* (1956) and *En cas de malheur* (1958) gave scope to his characteristic style, but most of his films since have been routine—although invariably good entertainment. With FERNANDEL in 1963 he set up Gafer, a joint production company which made *L'Âge ingrat* (1964) in which they co-starred. In *L'Affaire Dominici* (1973) Gabin again created a stir: as the fierce patriarch Gaston Dominici, accused of murdering the English Drummond family, he gave a performance of uncompromising naturalism wholly in accord with the film's documentary manner.

GABLE, CLARK (1901–60), US actor, did various jobs before becoming established as an actor in the theatre. During this period he did some work as an extra and played bit parts in Hollywood, making his first screen appearance in a supporting role in STROHEIM'S THE MERRY WIDOW (1925). His first featured part was in *The Painted Desert* (1931). METRO-GOLDWYN-MAYER put him under contract and gave him a starring role in *Laughing Sinners* (1931), but his next film, *A Free Soul* (1931), in which Clarence BROWN directed him as a gangster hero who knocks his girl-friend (Norma SHEARER) about, really established him. In three years, 1931–4, he starred in over thirty films, playing opposite some of the most popular stars including Jean HARLOW and Greta GARBO: his air of tough arrogant masculinity combined with a straightforward, easygoing manner appealed to both men and women. After the success of IT HAPPENED ONE NIGHT (1934) he came top of an Ed Sullivan poll for the 'King of Hollywood' and was known as 'The King' for the rest of his life. GONE WITH THE WIND (1939) gave him his greatest role as Rhett Butler. After the death of his second wife

Carole LOMBARD in 1942 he joined the USAAF. In 1945 he returned to MGM but was dissatisfied with the parts he was given, and in 1954 became free-lance. *Mogambo* (1953), John FORD's remake of Gable's earlier success *Red Dust* (1932), broke a succession of rather undistinguished appearances. Happily his last film was also one of his best. The ill-starred THE MISFITS (1961) gave him a part, as a tough ageing cowboy, which suited him perfectly. He died shortly after the film was completed.

GÁBOR, PÁL (1932–  ), Hungarian director, after university and a spell of teaching in a provincial town, enrolled at the Academy of Film Art, graduating in 1961. Although he made three shorts during the early sixties, he spent the greater part of the decade acquiring practical experience as first assistant to such directors as Zoltán FÁBRI, Ferenc KÓSA (TÍZEZER NAP, *Ten Thousand Suns*, 1967), and Márta MÉSZÁROS (*Eltávozott nap, The Girl*, 1968). His feature début with *Tiltott terület* (*Forbidden Ground*), shown at VENICE in 1969, heralded a director with a documentary attitude towards the problems of modern society, and although in the succeeding *Horizont* (*Horizon*, 1971) and *Utazás Jakabbal* (*Journey with Jacob*, 1973) this original approach has not been maintained, his concern remains with the intimate portrayal of modern reality.

GAINSBOROUGH PICTURES, British production company formed in 1924 by Michael BALCON and initially based at Islington Studios. Its first film was *The Passionate Adventure* (1924), produced by Balcon and directed by Graham Cutts assisted by Alfred HITCHCOCK. A critical situation in the British film industry at the time led Balcon to arrange with Erich POMMER to film *The Blackguard* (1925) at the UFA studios at NEUBABELSBERG; this too was directed by Cutts with Hitchcock as assistant. Hitchcock made his début as director with a co-production made in Munich, *The Mountain Eagle* (1926, *Fear o' God* in the US). He made his first important film, *The Lodger* (1926), for Gainsborough and directed one more film, *Downhill* (1927, *When Boys Leave Home* in US), before leaving the company in 1927.

In the late twenties and early thirties the company maintained a brisk production based mainly on talent from the popular theatre, such as Ivor Novello, Yvonne Arnaud, Jack Hulbert, and Cicely Courtneidge. When GAUMONT BRITISH began production at Shepherd's Bush in 1932, Gainsborough and G-B became sister companies under Balcon as head of production. In 1937, after Balcon left, G-B collapsed as a production company but Gainsborough survived to enter its most flourishing period. Hitchcock returned to make THE LADY VANISHES (1938) before leaving for Hollywood. Marcel Varnel and Walter Forde were responsible for several broad comedies starring popular radio and music hall comedians; Anthony ASQUITH made some of the company's best serious films: *Cottage to Let* (1941), *Uncensored* (1942), and *We Dive at Dawn* (1943).

The most characteristic Gainsborough output was the series of romantic films of the mid-forties built on a group of stars known (misleadingly) as the 'Gainsborough Foursome': Margaret LOCK-WOOD, Jean Kent, Patricia Roc, Phyllis CAL-VERT, James MASON, and Stewart GRANGER. The prototype was *The Man in Grey* (Leslie Arliss, 1943); *Fanny by Gaslight* (Asquith) followed in 1944, and the very popular recipe was repeated with variations, reaching its apotheosis in *The Wicked Lady* (Arliss, 1945). With a few happy exceptions, such as *Miranda* (1948) and *The Astonished Heart* (1950), the company's later films were unremarkable and it ceased production in the early fifties.

The trademark, based on Gainsborough's portrait of Mrs Siddons, existed in three versions: a reconstruction with Glenis Lorrimer, a reproduction of the original, and Thelma Cuthbert, graciously nodding to the audience. The accompanying 'Gainsborough Minuet' was composed by Louis Levy.

**GALEEN,** HENRIK (1882–1949), Dutch-born actor, scriptwriter, and director, worked for most of his life in Germany. He entered cinema in 1910 as an actor. His first important film was DER GOLEM (1914) which he co-directed with Paul WEGENER and scripted. The following year he scripted and acted in Rye's *Peter Schlemihl* and in 1920 he wrote the script for Wegener's second film based on the Golem legend, *Der Golem; wie in der Welt kam.* MURNAU, recognizing Galeen's talent for the macabre film, approached him to write the script for NOSFERATU (1922) from Bram Stoker's novel DRACULA. The adaptation was endowed with Galeen's own ideas, in particular the demonstration of the supernatural power of love through telepathy. In 1924 he scripted LENI'S DAS WACHSFIGUREN-CABINETT. His best work was DER STUDENT VON PRAG (1926), which he directed and scripted and which combined a superb narrative structure with beautiful pictorial composition. Still keeping within the realm of fantasy Galeen directed *Alraune* (1928), the story of a woman created by artificial impregnation. In the same year Galeen made *After the Verdict* in Britain. After this his work was of little significance. In 1933 he migrated to the US.

**GANCE,** ABEL (1889– ), French director, published a volume of poems, wrote for the theatre, and played small parts before his first film appearance in Léon Perret's *Molière* (1909). He acted in a series of films with Max LINDER. In 1910 he was writing scripts for GAUMONT; by 1911 he had established his own—short-lived—company, Le Film Français, and produced *La Digue ou pour sauver la Hollande* (1911). After working in the Service Cinématographique et Photographique de l'Armée (1914–15) he joined LE FILM D'ART whose director, Louis Nalpas, allowed Gance to shoot *Un Drame au Château d'Acre* (or *Les Morts reviennent-ils?*, 1915) from his own script. Impressed, Nalpas then produced *La Folie du Docteur Tube* (1915) in which, four years before DAS CABINETT DES DR CALIGARI, Gance used the camera subjectively and experimented with distorting mirrors. Naples was alarmed by the film's innovations, and it was not released at the time. Gance pursued his innovatory techniques in *Le Droit à la vie* (1917), *Mater Dolorosa* (1917), *La Zone de la mort* (1917), and *La Dixième Symphonie* (1918).

His first successful film was J'ACCUSE (1919), a cinematically impressive pacifist statement. In LA ROUE (1922) he developed rapid cutting and quick MONTAGE techniques. He worked again with Max Linder on *Au secours* (1923), which Gance co-scripted and directed.

In 1925 he began NAPOLÉON, an ambitious conception full of vigorous innovations including triple screen (his POLYVISION), superimpositions, extensive use of the hand-held camera, and the brachyscope, a wide-angle lens he and his cameraman Kruger constructed. Financial difficulties postponed completion until 1927. It was shown at the Opéra as *Napoléon vu par Abel Gance*. The first of the five chronological episodes in the original script was published by Plon as *Napoléon vu par Abel Gance*, épopée cinématographique, and *Le Rouge et le Noir*, in the following year, published an extract from the shooting script in a special issue on the cinema. Jean Arroy, Gance's assistant, wrote *En tournant Napoléon avec Abel Gance*; he may also have made the film *En tournant Napoléon* (1925–6) which shows Gance at work. Gance played Saint-Just in *Napoléon*; in his first sound film *La Fin du monde* (1931), he took the part of Christ. *La Fin du monde* used optical effects as in *La Folie du Docteur Tube*.

About 1934 he synchronized *Napoléon* with crude stereophonic effect. From then on, except for a remake of *J'accuse* in 1938, his films were either routine or entirely experimental. With Angénieux he built the Pictographa (1938), a system which gave infinite depth of focus by the simultaneous use of different corrective lenses.

*Magirama* (1956), a collection of shorts, used WIDE SCREEN techniques.

He did manage a come-back in the sphere of period spectacle, scripting a version of Dumas's novel *La Reine Margot* (1953) and directing three features: *La Tour de Nesle* (1954, his first colour film), *Austerlitz* (1960), and *Cyrano et d'Artagnan* (1964). In 1966 he made *Marie Tudor* for television. André MALRAUX then initiated a re-edition of *Napoléon*: now entitled *Napoléon cet inconnu* (1971), it is the latest contribution to cinema from a prolific, energetic, and undisciplined film-maker who has always been his own avant-garde.

*J'accuse, d'après le film d'Abel Gance*, Paris, 1922, is a narration illustrated with stills from the film. Critical writings include: *Le Temps de l'image est venu*, Paris, 1926; *Prisme*, Paris, 1930; *Le Temps de l'image éclatée*, in *Abel Gance, hier et demain* by Sophie Darie, Paris, 1959. The last chapter of *The parade's gone by* by Kevin BROWNLOW, London, 1968, is devoted to Gance, and Brownlow's COMPILATON film *Abel Gance, The Charm of Dynamite* (1968) is another tribute to this idiosyncratic figure.

**GANGSTER FILM** as a distinct genre was a phenomenon of Hollywood during the thirties and forties, although urban crime had naturally provided material for the cinema from early days: D. W. GRIFFITH's *Musketeers of Pig Alley* (1912) showed criminal activity on an organized scale. The introduction of Prohibition in 1920 gave increased scope to gang operations and accustomed the average citizen to illegal activity in order to obtain a drink; throughout America, but especially in Chicago, bootlegging became an efficiently organized business. Criminal methods and gang warfare were given extensive newspaper publicity; this endowed gangsters with a kind of glamour, and the Depression made crime seem an almost acceptable way of defying the impersonal forces of economics.

Only a few silent films, including UNDERWORLD (Josef von STERNBERG, 1927) and *The Racket* (Lewis MILESTONE, 1928), dealt effectively with organized crime, but the introduction of sound provided the necessary dimension for the development of the gangster film, and the first one, WARNER BROS' *The Lights of New York* (Mervyn LEROY, 1928), achieved a new realism with its naturalistic settings and everyday sounds.

Although the vogue for crime plays on Broadway undoubtedly influenced the wave of gangster films that began in 1930, the genre was strikingly untheatrical. Prominent playwrights who moved to Hollywood, including Ben HECHT and Norman Krasna, concentrated as much on action and the dramatic use of sound—guns blazing, cars screeching—as on fast-paced, tough, and slangy dialogue. Gangster films had a strong sense of milieu: wet, obliquely-lit streets, dark warehouses and wharves, shadowy pool-rooms, were contrasted with glittering night-clubs and luxurious apartments. Actual events provided plot sources: audiences would have no difficulty in identifying Edward G. ROBINSON in LITTLE CAESAR (1930) as the archetypal gang leader Al CAPONE, and incidents such as the St Valentine's Day Massacre provided the climax for several dramas of gang warfare. PUBLIC ENEMY (William WELLMAN, 1931) portrayed another thinly-disguised gang leader, Hymie Weiss, and gave James CAGNEY the first of many roles as a small-time 'hood'. SCARFACE (Howard HAWKS, 1932), another version of the Capone saga with Paul MUNI in the title role, which appeared just as a public reaction against gangster films was gaining force, met with widespread disapproval.

The moralistic pressures that had established a new code for Hollywood films in 1930 (see CENSORSHIP, US) forced a change in the style of gangster films, and the social and political ideals embodied in the New Deal were reflected in their content. Implicit parallels between organized crime and big business gave way to depictions of individual outlaws based on John DILLINGER, 'Baby Face' Nelson, 'Pretty Boy' Floyd, Bonnie and Clyde, and others, and of the effects of slum environments and social injustice in forming criminals. Warner Bros again led the way with *I Am a Fugitive from a Chain Gang* (LeRoy, 1932). DEAD END (Wyler, 1937) and its successor ANGELS WITH DIRTY FACES (Michael CURTIZ, 1938) established many of the basic attributes of the type. John GARFIELD played society's victim in several films, notably *They Made Me a Criminal* (Busby BERKELEY, 1939). Prison films used the same theme, abandoning the more straightforward brutality of earlier examples like *The Big House* (George Hill, 1930) to show the 'con' as a product of society's failings.

Every major studio made gangster films during the thirties, and some lesser ones like MONOGRAM based much of their production on them. But Warner Bros retained the lead, largely because their leading players, Cagney and BOGART in particular, were readily identified with the genre. The whole cycle was summed up in THE ROARING TWENTIES (Raoul WALSH, 1939).

The Second World War eclipsed the gangster film, although Mark HELLINGER continued to produce films in the classic tradition including *High Sierra* (Walsh, 1941), THE KILLERS (Robert SIODMAK, 1946), and *Brute Force* (Jules DASSIN, 1947). Post-war crime films increasingly concentrated on explicit violence, often dealing

with psychopathic characters like Richard WID-
MARK in KISS OF DEATH (Henry HATHAWAY,
1947). Cagney's post-war gangsters followed this
trend, notably in *White Heat* (Walsh, 1949) and
*Kiss Tomorrow Goodbye* (Gordon Douglas,
1950). By the late fifties the 'Roaring Twenties'
had receded into the nostalgic past, providing the
basis for a successful television series, 'The
Untouchables', and for Billy WILDER's affectionate, hilarious parody SOME LIKE IT HOT (1959).
A cycle of gangster films followed, drawing their
inspiration from the twenties and thirties, culminating in BONNIE AND CLYDE (1967) with
its sympathetic hero-victims. THE GODFATHER
(1971) proved the continuing viability of the
subject of organized crime, treated with contemporary style and relevance.

The post-war period also produced the 'caper'
or 'heist' film, with a gang carrying out a daring,
ingenious robbery which eventually fails. THE
ASPHALT JUNGLE (1950) established the basic
elements and DU RIFIFI CHEZ LES HOMMES (1955)
started a similar trend in Europe.

France had its own tradition of crime films in
the thirties, but directors of the post-war generation (Jean-Pierre MELVILLE, François TRUFFAUT,
Jean-Luc GODARD) paid conscious homage to the
Hollywood gangster film, now labelled FILM NOIR
by critics. Indeed, Godard dedicated A BOUT
DE SOUFFLE (1960) to Monogram and Jean-Paul
BELMONDO modelled his performance in this and
other films on Bogart.

John Baxter, *The gangster film* (London,
1970), is a useful reference book.

**GARBO, GRETA** (1905– ), Swedish actress,
real name Greta Gustafsson, appeared first in
advertising films for the store in which she
worked as a sales-girl. She trained at the Royal
Dramatic Theatre School, Stockholm, where
she encountered Mauritz STILLER who was to
become the most important influence on her career. He changed her name and directed her in
her first important film GÖSTA BERLINGS SAGA
(1924). A grandiose project for a film to be made
in Turkey fell through; they broke their return
journey to Sweden in Germany, where Garbo
appeared in DIE FREUDLOSE GASSE (1925). Louis
B. MAYER, hunting for European talent had
meanwhile seen *Gösta Berlings Saga*. He was
determined to bring Stiller to Hollywood and
Stiller insisted that Garbo should accompany
him: he placed them both under contract and
transported them to the US.

Garbo was unhappy in Hollywood and when
Stiller's disputes with METRO-GOLDWYN-MAYER
took him first to PARAMOUNT and then home to
Sweden her loneliness and shyness increased.
Her reserve was built by the studio into a
mystery to which the public responded

enthusiastically and her parts were skilfully
chosen to support the new myth. In nearly all her
films she was able to present an irregular love life
as essentially tragic (*The Temptress*, 1927; *Flesh
and the Devil*, 1927; *Love*, 1928, *Anna Karenina*
in GB) thus satisfying both the Production Code
(see CENSORSHIP, US) and the audience. Her extraordinary talent was for expressing sensuality
clouded by a weary sense of inevitable disaster.

She made the transition to sound films without
difficulty. In *Anna Christie* (1930) her deep, accented voice was immediately acceptable and she
went on to even greater success with GRAND
HOTEL (1932), the only occasion on which she
spoke the often-attributed line 'I want to be
alone', and QUEEN CHRISTINA (1934), for which
she insisted on her co-star of the silent days, John
GILBERT. By now she had perfected the performance of tragic heroines (ANNA KARENINA,
1935; CAMILLE, 1936, among them).

The threat and the outbreak of war was a
major factor in the ending of Garbo's film career.
The commercial success of her films had always
leaned on the European market and the attempt
to Americanize her appeal in NINOTCHKA (1939)
and *Two Faced Woman* (1941) was a financial
failure. Shrewd investment of her earnings had
made her financially independent and she retired.

Garbo's great beauty had a special luminous
quality in close-up which made her performances
transcend the routine, even vulgar, material of
most of her films. This timeless sensuality has
increased in appeal and she has an enthusiastic
following, not least in America, where re-issues
of her films attract audiences much larger than
during her active career.

**GARDIN, VLADIMIR** (1877–1965), Russian
actor and director, acted in provincial theatres
before entering the cinema in 1913. He directed
several films, some with PROTAZANOV, including
*Peterburgskiye trushchobi* (*Petersburg Slums*,
1915) and VOINA I MIR (*War and Peace*, 1915).
In 1919 he helped found the first Soviet Film
Academy (see VGIK), which was attended
by PUDOVKIN, who assisted Gardin on *Serp i
molot* (*Hammer and Sickle*, 1921) and *Golod
—golod—golod* (*Hunger—Hunger—Hunger*,
1921). Among the films in which he acted are
VSTRECHNYI (*Counterplan*, 1932) and *Sekretnaya
missiya* (*Secret Mission*, 1950).

**GARDNER, AVA** (1922– ), beautiful American actress with a distinctive cleft chin, whose
early roles in the forties, including her first important part in THE KILLERS (1946), usually only
required her to look darkly seductive. With *The
Barefoot Contessa* (1954), *Bhowani Junction*
(1956), and SEVEN DAYS IN MAY (1964), however, she emerged as an actress of some ability.

**GARFIELD,** JOHN (1913–52), US actor, real forename Julian. After a childhood in the slums of New York, he progressed through the left-wing Group Theatre of the thirties to playing supporting roles on Broadway as Jules Garfield. He was widely noticed in Clifford ODETS's play *Golden Boy* (1937) and as a result was offered a contract by WARNER BROS. After an impressive screen début as a misunderstood young man in *Four Daughters* (1938) he was almost invariably type-cast as the sympathetic criminal pushed on to the wrong side of the law by underprivilege or bad luck. *They Made Me a Criminal* and *Dust Be My Destiny* (both 1939) made him a popular star, and were followed by many parts of the same kind. He was discontented with these restrictions, considering that Warners regarded him merely as a poor man's BOGART or CAGNEY. Twice, while on loan to METRO-GOLDWYN-MAYER for *Tortilla Flat* (1942) and THE POSTMAN ALWAYS RINGS TWICE (1946), he showed his real strength as an actor, but his studio still refused to let him vary his parts and on the expiry of his contract he left to set up his own production company. *Body and Soul* (ROSSEN, 1947) gave him one of his best roles as an inarticulate boxer. In *The Breaking Point* (1950), from HEMINGWAY's novel *To Have and Have Not*, he gave a fine performance as the lonely and disillusioned hero—the kind of part more often associated with Bogart. Ironically, the film was made by Warners.

Because of his suspected left-wing sympathies Garfield was blacklisted in Hollywood (see UNAMERICAN ACTIVITIES). He was about to play the lead in a Broadway revival of *Golden Boy* when he died of a heart attack.

**GARLAND,** JUDY (1922–69), US singer and actress, real name Frances Gumm, started as a small child in a vaudeville singing act with her sisters. At thirteen she was put under contract by METRO-GOLDWYN-MAYER who were at first slow to recognize her talent and kept her in reserve in their group of potential CHILD STARS. Her first success was a number in BROADWAY MELODY OF 1938 (1937): a version of 'You Made Me Love You' re-written as a birthday greeting for Clark GABLE.

After several featured roles she made the first of her HARDY FAMILY films opposite Mickey ROONEY in 1938. Her first memorable part was in THE WIZARD OF OZ (1939). This led to a succession of starring roles including *Babes in Arms* (1939) and *For Me and My Gal* (1942). MEET ME IN ST LOUIS (1944) and *The Pirate* (1948), both directed by Vincente MINNELLI, the second of her five husbands, and EASTER PARADE (1948), are among Hollywood's great musicals; and her particular blend of vigour and poignancy contributed much to their success. At this time

her personal problems were beginning to be widely publicized. Dominated since early adolescence by her status as a valuable studio property, she was unable to cultivate the toughness necessary to resist the exigencies of the STAR SYSTEM. In 1949 she was replaced in *The Barkleys of Broadway* by Ginger ROGERS and in *Annie Get Your Gun* (1950) by Betty HUTTON.

In the early fifties she made successful solo stage appearances in London and New York and was recalled to Hollywood for A STAR IS BORN (1954). This was an unqualified success for Garland, revealing her as an actress of maturity no loss of skill in putting over a musical number. But producers still lacked confidence in her dependability and she returned to the theatre and cabaret for the next six years. Her last three films, *Judgement at Nuremberg* (Stanley KRAMER, 1961), *A Child is Waiting* (John CASSAVETES, 1962), and *I Could Go On Singing* (Ronald Neame, 1963) gave her good parts but failed to re-establish her as a star. She died as a result of an accidental overdose of sleeping pills. Her daughter Liza MINNELLI has shown herself to have inherited many of her mother's talents, combined with a greater resilience.

**GARMES,** LEE (1898–    ), US cameraman, first worked for Thomas H. INCE as a painter and property boy. He gained his early experience as a cameraman in one- and two-reel slapstick comedies from 1916 to 1924, making his first real success with *The Grand Duchess and the Waiter* (1926), which was widely praised for its aesthetic low-key lighting plan.

His preference for 'north' light (either natural or artificial) and an economical chiaroscuro effect derives from an admiration of the paintings of Rembrandt. He used this personal style effectively in several films directed by Josef von STERNBERG, including MOROCCO (1930) and SHANGHAI EXPRESS (1932), and in the HECHT–MACARTHUR films CRIME WITHOUT PASSION (1934) and THE SCOUNDREL (1935); he was also assistant director on the latter two.

Garmes has used colour to rich effect, as in the first part of GONE WITH THE WIND (1939) and *Land of the Pharaohs* (Howard HAWKS, 1955). In *Lady in a Cage* (1964) he used a harsh documentary style well suited to the film's violent realism.

He has co-directed two feature films: *The Sky's the Limit* (1937), with Jack BUCHANAN, and *Angels over Broadway* (1940), with Ben Hecht.

**GARNETT,** TAY (1892–    ), US scriptwriter, director, and producer, who entered the film industry in 1920 as a stuntman, after being a flying instructor during the First World War. He then began writing titles for SENNETT, and by 1926 was scriptwriting. After two years as a contract writer for PATHÉ–DEMILLE, he wrote and directed *Celebrity* and *Flying Fool* (both 1929). From 1936 he began also to produce. Garnett's output has been varied and prolific, including witty comedies: *Her Man* (1930), *Joy of Living* (1938); adventures: *China Seas* (1935); unusual war stories: *Cross of Lorraine* (1943), set in German-occupied France, and *One Minute to Zero* (1952), a Korean war drama. Garnett has also done television work, including the series 'Wagon Train', 'Riverboat', 'Gunsmoke', 'Rawhide'. His many other films include: *One-Way Passage* (1932), *Slightly Honorable* (1939), which he also wrote, *Seven Sinners* (1940), *Bataan* (1943), THE POSTMAN ALWAYS RINGS TWICE (1946), *Guns of Wyoming* (1963, *Cattle King* in GB).

**GARNETT, TONY** (1936– ), British producer of television and feature films, studied psychology at university, then worked as an actor until he joined the BBC team that produced a series of contemporary dramas under the general title 'The Wednesday Play'. During 1966 and 1967 his productions, mostly directed by Ken LOACH, made a lasting impact on British television drama: they include *Cathy Come Home*, an attack on the poor provision of housing for low-income families; *Up the Junction*, a study of London working-class life; *In Two Minds*, a fictional case-history of schizophrenia supporting the theories of Laingian psychology.

After these successes, Garnett and Loach set up an independent production company, Kestrel Films. It has produced television films as well as features: *The Body* (1970), a documentary, KES (1970), and *Family Life* (1971), based on *In Two Minds*.

The feature film *Up the Junction* (1967) was, like the television play, based directly on Nell Dunn's book but was not made by Loach and Garnett.

**GARSON, GREER** (1906– ), US actress, was born in Northern Ireland and appeared on the London stage from 1932. She was noticed by Louis B. MAYER and in 1938 went to Hollywood under contract to METRO-GOLDWYN-MAYER although her first film, *Goodbye Mr Chips* (1939) with Robert DONAT, was in fact made in London: while it was being made she appeared in some of the earliest BBC television programmes. Her screen début drew immediate attention, as did her performance as Elizabeth Bennet in *Pride and Prejudice* (1940). She was soon established in the public's mind as a beautiful, intelligent woman of high principle with such films as *Mrs Miniver* (1942) and *Madame Curie* (1943); the

brief role of Calpurnia in JULIUS CAESAR (1953) accorded well with this pattern, which culminated in her portrayal of Mrs Eleanor Roosevelt in *Sunrise at Campobello* (1960).

**GASLIGHT,** GB, 1940. 1½hr. *Dir* Thorold Dickinson; *prod* British National; *scr* A. R. Rawlinson, Bridget Boland, from the play by Patrick Hamilton; *ph* Bernard Knowles; *des* Duncan Sutherland; *mus* Richard Addinsell; *cast* Anton Walbrook (Paul Mallen), Diana Wynyard (Bella Mallen), Frank Pettingell (Rough), Robert Newton (Bella's cousin).

The first film version of *Gaslight* retains the claustrophobia and suspense of the stage play, a stylish psychological thriller. The film's remarkable sense of period atmosphere is achieved largely through fluid camerawork: the opening scene, which is silent, has an intricate interplay of moving camera, moving actors, and (it almost seems) moving sets, worthy of the best French cinema of the thirties. METRO-GOLDWYN-MAYER bought the rights to remake it in 1944: the remake, known in Britain as *The Murder in Thornton Square*, was directed more lavishly and less tautly by George CUKOR, but there are effective leading performances from Ingrid BERGMAN (who won an OSCAR) and Charles BOYER. DICKINSON's version was for years a legend because the American company was supposed to have destroyed all the copies, but fortunately some prints were later found to have survived.

**GASNIER,** LOUIS (1882–1962), French director, joined PATHÉ in 1908 and directed some of the first Max LINDER films. He was sent to manage Pathé's New York office and from 1912 started to direct comedies starring Pearl WHITE and Henry B. WALTHALL; his most resounding successes were the famous SERIALS starring Pearl White, which began in 1914 with *The Perils of Pauline* and *The Clutching Hand*. Released in France under the general title *Les Mystères de New York*, Gasnier's serials became the rage: Pearl White was idolized by the young army recruits and her adventures were fanatically admired by the Dadaists and the literary avant-garde, who considered them the epic of 'l'acte gratuit' (see SURREALISM). Their popularity was immediately countered by FEUILLADE with LES VAMPIRES (1915–16).

Gasnier continued to direct serials until 1920, then made feature films in Hollywood until 1941, except for three films made in France including the first version of PAGNOL's *Topaze* (1933). He supervised a remake of *The Perils of Pauline* directed by George MARSHALL in 1947.

**GASPARCOLOR,** COLOUR print process developed in England by Bela Gaspar and introduced in 1934. It was one of the first three-colour systems and involved the bleaching out of the unwanted EMULSION layers on a single film base.

## GATE OF HELL see JIGOKUMON

*GATTOPARDO, Il* (*The Leopard*), Italy/France, 1963. Technirama; 3½hr; Eastman Color. *Dir* Luchino Visconti; *prod* Titanus/SNPC/SGC; *scr* Suso Cecchi d'Amico, Pasquale Festa Campanile, Enrico Medioli, Massimo Franciosa, Visconti, from the novel by Lampedusa; *ph* Giuseppe Rotunna; *cast* Burt Lancaster (Prince Salina, the Leopard), Alain Delon (Tancredi), Claudia Cardinale (Angelica), Serge Reggiani (Don Ciccio), Leslie French (Chevalley).

Prince Salina is an ironic spectator of his class's decline during the *risorgimento*. The final ball, lasting an hour's screen time in the uncut version, conveys in visual terms the long interior monologue in which the Prince, aware of his approaching death, watches the death of his world. VISCONTI evokes a splendid, decaying society with rich detail and shows an intriguing ambivalence towards the political issues of his subject.

Lampedusa's novel was treated with a fidelity unusual in Visconti's literary adaptations. The film, in the original version shown at CANNES, was received with enthusiasm. Trouble arose, however, over the copies distributed by TWENTIETH CENTURY-FOX in Britain and the US as part of the co-production deal. The length was cut by some forty-four minutes and the DUBBING of the non-English-speaking actors was clumsy. The prints made from a DUPE negative by the Fox subsidiary company De Luxe Laboratories were, in Visconti's view, sadly inferior to the prints processed by TECHNICOLOR in Italy. He took the greatest exception to the gross distortions of his meticulous colour compositions and, in letters to the London *Times* and *Sunday Times*, disclaimed authorship of the film as seen in Britain.

**GAUMONT,** LÉON (1863–1946), French producer, was a manufacturer of photographic equipment before entering the business of film production and exhibition in 1896. He built a small studio at Buttes Chaumont in 1898, handing over the production of fiction films to his secretary Alice GUY-BLACHÉ. The studio was rebuilt in 1905, becoming the largest film production centre in Europe. Regular NEWSREELS were instituted in 1908 when Gaumont Actualités began to appear soon after the first issues of Pathé Journal.

An inspired entrepreneur, Gaumont left the creative side of production to his directors who included, besides Guy-Blaché, Louis FEUILLADE, Victorin Jasset, and the animator Emile COHL. Production and distribution branches were set up in America, Russia, and England, and with PATHÉ FRÈRES Gaumont held undisputed primacy in the European film industry until the First World War.

After 1918 the French companies could no longer compete with American expansion. Léon Gaumont retired in the late twenties and in 1928 his company was in part absorbed by METRO-GOLDWYN-MAYER, the production arm becoming part of Gaumont-Franco Film-Aubert until that consortium went into liquidation in the early thirties. The famous name was perpetuated by Société Nouvelle des Établissements Gaumont (SNEG), still in existence, and by GAUMONT BRITISH.

**GAUMONT BRITISH.** The London branch established by Léon GAUMONT in 1898 as the Gaumont Film Company was initially a distribution company, not only for Gaumont's films but also for other major French, American, and British producers. Film production gradually increased, with films directed by Alfred Collins and Walter Haggar, and a regular NEWSREEL, Gaumont Graphic, was issued from 1910. George PEARSON started his career as a director making documentaries for the company. In 1911–12 considerable resources were invested in building a Gaumont cinema chain and studios were built at Shepherd's Bush in 1914 and at Lime Grove in 1915.

In 1927 the company severed its connection with the struggling Gaumont organization in France and was renamed Gaumont British. It was still an important distributor of British, French, and American films, but productions were sporadic until the new Shepherd's Bush studios were opened in 1932. Gaumont British then became linked with GAINSBOROUGH, with Michael BALCON as head of production for both companies. Major successes included film versions of Aldwych farces, romantic dramas, several of which starred Conrad VEIDT, and the best of Alfred HITCHCOCK's British films: THE MAN WHO KNEW TOO MUCH (1934), THE THIRTY-NINE STEPS (1935), *The Secret Agent* (1936), and SABOTAGE (1936, *A Woman Alone* in US). Other box-office draws were *Evergreen* (Victor SAVILLE, 1934) with Jessie MATTHEWS; *Bulldog Jack* (Walter Forde, 1935) with Jack and Claude Hulbert, Fay WRAY, and Ralph RICHARDSON; and *Rhodes of Africa* (Berthold Viertel, 1936) with Walter HUSTON.

After Balcon left the company in 1936, Gaumont British collapsed as a production and distribution company, but various other branches of the organization continued for some time. Gaumont British Picture Corporation maintained an important cinema chain until the early forties when it was absorbed into the RANK ORGANISATION; Gaumont British News continued to appear regularly until 1959; and smaller offshoots produced educational, scientific, and advertising shorts, under the Gaumont British name, into the fifties.

**GAYNOR, JANET** (1906–   ), US actress, who started as an extra and became one of FOX's most important stars during the late twenties and early thirties. Her special quality of innocent charm was most memorably employed by MURNAU in SUNRISE (1927); for this performance she won the first OSCAR for best actress. Successfully managing the transition to sound films she became immensely successful in winsome parts such as the orphan schoolgirl in *Daddy-Long-Legs* (1931), to which her tiny physique was suited, inheriting from Mary PICKFORD the title of 'America's Sweetheart'. She starred with Charles Farrell in a successful series of romantic films in the thirties; although she fought against TYPE-CASTING, she had little opportunity to vary her parts until she left Fox and made A STAR IS BORN (1937) for SELZNICK. This moving story of a Hollywood marriage destroyed by the changing fortunes of the partners' careers gave her her best role since *Sunrise*. After two more films she retired on her marriage to Adrian (METRO-GOLDWYN-MAYER's chief dress designer) and has made only one film appearance since, in *Bernadine* (1950), but she continues to act occasionally on television.

**GAYNOR, MITZI** (1930–   ), US actress, real name Francesca Mitzi Marlene de Charney von Gerber. Trained in opera and ballet, she displayed talent and charm in musicals like *There's No Business Like Show Business* (1954) and *Les Girls* (1957). In the somewhat leaden film version of *South Pacific* (1958) she gave a creditable performance in the role made famous by Mary MARTIN on the stage.

**GAZZARA, BEN** (1930–   ), US actor of Sicilian parentage who attracted Hollywood's attention by his performance in an ACTORS' STUDIO production of *End As a Man* and subsequently played the sadistic hero Jacko in a film version entitled *The Strange One* (1957, *End As a Man* in GB). Later films, to which he usually contributed vivid performances, include *Anatomy of a Murder* (Otto PREMINGER, 1959) as the suspected murderer, *A Rage to Live* (1965), and *Husbands* (John CASSAVETES, 1970) in which he drew on his experience of improvisation. He has worked mostly in the theatre or for television where he appeared in the series 'Run for Your Life'.

**GELATINE** see FILTER

**GÉLIN, DANIEL** (1921–   ), French actor and poet, trained in Paris under Louis JOUVET, but had a considerable struggle to establish himself in cinema. Jacques BECKER gave him the lead in *Rendez-vous de juillet* (1949) and in the charming EDOUARD ET CAROLINE (1951). These roles, together with the lead in OPHULS' LA RONDE (1950), finally established Gélin's popularity and he enjoyed several years as a romantic lead with an appealing diffidence. He has acted in some seventy films as well as on the stage, and for several distinguished directors: PABST (*La Voix du silence*, 1953), Sacha GUITRY (*Napoléon*, 1955), HITCHCOCK (THE MAN WHO KNEW TOO MUCH, 1956), COCTEAU (LE TESTAMENT D'ORPHÉE, 1960), and René CLÉMENT (*Paris brûle-t-il?*, 1965). During the sixties he appeared in Becker's television serial, 'Les Saintes chéries', and he gave a fine performance as the tetchy father in MALLE's LE SOUFFLE AU COEUR (1971).

**GEMINI SYSTEM,** a proprietary method of linking a 16mm film camera to a television camera. Both cameras see the action through the same lens, and their pictures are simultaneously recorded on film and videotape. The Gemini system was used in the late sixties primarily to make films for television. When several cameras are used (as in television practice) each film camera records a picture continuously, whether or not its corresponding television picture is being transmitted. Later these films, showing the same action from different angles, can be edited at leisure by ordinary film techniques. Improved methods of editing videotape and transferring it to film have made the Gemini system redundant since about 1970.

**GENERAL, The,** US, 1926. 1½hr. *Dir* Buster Keaton, Clyde Bruckman; *prod* Joseph P. Schenck; *scr* Al Boasberg, Charles Smith; *ph* Bert Haines, J. D. Jennings; *cast* Buster Keaton (Johnnie Gray), Marion Mack (Annabelle Lee), Glen Cavender (Capt Anderson), Jim Farley (Gen Thatcher), Frederick Vroom (Southern General).

One of the great and enduring silent comedies, *The General*, like THE NAVIGATOR (1924), takes its title from the machine around which the action evolves. A railway engine, stolen by Federal troops and rescued (with the heroine) by the Southern hero, is the focus of the action; unlike the ocean liner of the earlier film The Machine stands for no hostile environment to be subdued but for a treasured responsibility equal in Johnnie Gray's affections to the disdainful Annabelle.

Whereas   *The   Navigator*   depends   on

disproportion or on confronting the hero with improbable and unfamiliar situations, the humour of *The General* is heightened by setting events of wild comedy in a conscientiously authentic historical reconstruction. It is often of great pictorial beauty, recalling Mathew Brady's Civil War photographs.

*The great locomotive chase* by William Pittenger, an account of the incident on which the film was based, was adapted for Walt DISNEY's film of the same name (1956), far less memorable than KEATON's. The original incident took place in 1862: James J. Andrews with Union soldiers in civilian clothes stole the General, a locomotive of the Western & Atlantic railroad, which was recaptured after a chase led by Captain W. A. Fuller. Andrews and seven of his men were hanged in June 1862.

**GENERAL FILM COMPANY** see MOTION PICTURE PATENTS COMPANY

**GENERALNAYA LINYA** (*The General Line*) see STAROYE I NOVOYE

**GENERATION, A,** see POKOLENIE

**GENOU DE CLAIRE, Le** (*Claire's Knee*), France, 1970. Eastman Color; 1¾hr. *Dir, scr* Eric Rohmer; *prod* Les Films du Losange; *ph* Nestor Almendros; *cast* Jean-Claude Brialy (Jérôme), Aurora Cornu (Aurora), Béatrice Romand (Laura), Laurence de Monaghan (Claire), Michèle Montel (Mme Walter), Gérard Falconetti (Gilles).

Jérôme visits Annecy to sell his estate before his marriage. Encouraged by Aurora, a Romanian novelist and old friend whom he meets accidentally, he half-jokingly pursues each of his landlady's teenage daughters; his ultimate ambition being to caress Claire's knee.

The holiday setting of ROHMER's fifth *conte moral*, precisely captured in Nestor ALMENDROS' photography, provides both the occasion and the relaxed atmosphere for the test of Jérôme's fidelity. The ambivalence of his interest in Laura and Claire, his constant articulation of what he believes to be his attitude, the undefined nature of his relationship with Aurora, her role in manipulating his situation, give the film its tension; the enigmatic figure of Claire, the hints of action outside the frame, the undercurrent of holiday activities, add to the fascination of Rohmer's exploration of the elusive area of truth lying between words and actions.

**GENTLEMEN PREFER BLONDES,** US, 1953. Technicolor; 1½hr. *Dir* Howard Hawks; *prod* Twentieth Century-Fox; *scr* Charles Lederer, from the play by Anita Loos and Joseph Fields; *ph* Harry J. Wild; *songs* Jules Stein, Leo Robin, Hoagy Carmichael, Harold Adamson; *cast* Jane Russell (Dorothy), Marilyn Monroe (Lorelei Lee), Charles Coburn (Sir Francis Beekman), Tommy Noonan (Gus Esmond).

Anita LOOS's comic novel telling the adventures of Lorelei Lee, the archetypal wide-eyed, gold-digging blonde, was adapted by the author as a stage musical: this forms the basis of HAWKS's film version. The story leans heavily on exaggeration and caricature—particularly well exploited in the brash musical numbers. Marilyn MONROE spoke Lorelei's ungrammatical aphorisms with guileless innocence and Jane RUSSELL was her perfect foil as the wise-cracking Dorothy.

Loos herself scripted the version filmed in 1928, directly from the novel. It was directed by Malcolm St Clair and starred Ruth Taylor as Lorelei.

**GERALD McBOING-BOING** see UNITED PRODUCTIONS OF AMERICA

**GERASIMOV,** SERGEI (1906– ), Russian director, actor, and scriptwriter, studied at the Leningrad Institute of Stage Art. He began his career as an actor and was closely involved with FEKS. As a director he maintained his interest in acting, particularly in the training of young people as film actors, and is still the chief of the Joint Acting and Directing Workshop at VGIK.

In 1938, using a young cast, he made *Komsomolsk*, a socialist realist drama, which proved to be typical of many of his later films in its concern for contemporary themes and interest in the psychology of the characters. *Uchitel* (1939) drew attention to a critical situation in the Soviet educational system. In 1941 he directed part of the first Fighting Film Album and the following year co-directed with KALATOZOV *Nepobedimye* (*The Invincible*), a documentary on the siege of Leningrad. In 1944 he was made head of the documentary film studios, where he made a policy of giving assignments to directors new to this kind of work. At the Cultural and Scientific Conference for World Peace held in New York in 1949 he made a famous speech criticizing the low moral standards of American films. He made a documentary on China in 1950 and in 1958 he made *Tikhi Don* (*Quiet Flows the Don*), a film in three parts based on Sholokhov's novel. Among his later films are *Lyudi i zveri* (*Men and Beasts*, 1962) and *Zhurnalist* (*The Journalist*, 1967).

**GERMANIA, ANNO ZERO** (*Germany, Year Zero*), Italy, 1947. 1¼hr. *Dir* Roberto Rossellini; *prod* Tevere Film, Sadfilm; *scr* Rossellini, Carlo Lizzani, Max Kolpet; *ph* Robert Juillard; *ed* Eraldo Da Roma; *mus* Renzo Rossellini; *cast*

Edmund Moeschka (Edmund), Franz Kruger (his father), Barbara Hintz (Eva), Werner Pittschau (Karlheinz), Erich Guhne (the professor).

A boy in occupied Berlin, trying to feed his family from whatever resources the black market can provide, follows the advice of his former teacher (now a black marketeer) and poisons his father to lighten the family burden. Following the principles of NEO-REALISM, ROSSELLINI used only one professional actor (Franz Kruger) and shot the exteriors on location in Berlin.

**GERMANY.** The first films shown to a paying audience in Germany were presented by the Skladanowsky brothers as part of the variety bill at the Berlin Wintergarten on 1 November 1895, several weeks before the first public LUMIÈRE showing in Paris. The following year Oskar MESSTER opened the first 'movement' theatre in Germany and began to produce films: by 1897 he had 84 of his own films on the market. French, Italian, and American films soon began to pour into the country and there was a rapid growth of production companies, distributors, cinemas, and a star system, with Henny PORTEN one of the first personalities to become well known to the public.

By 1910 the two major production companies were Messter's, where Carl FROELICH was already working, and Paul Davidson's Projektion-AG Union. Davidson, wishing to film reputable stage plays, pursued reluctant stage directors and actors and formed a working relationship with REINHARDT which was to prove vital to the development of German cinema. Reinhardt himself directed some films and many of his actors began to appear on the screen. Davidson also imported the Danish actress Asta NIELSEN who in 1911 settled in Berlin with her husband, the director Urban Gad, and who made many films for Davidson's company. Meanwhile a start was made on Germany's first film studios, in Berlin.

*Der Andere* (1913) was one of the first German films to attract serious critical attention. Based on a stage play and starring a stage actor, Albert Bassermann, it was directed by Max Mack who even at this early period laid emphasis on the need for good scripts. But most films were of the kind popular in all film-producing countries—comedies, melodramas, Westerns, and detective stories, the latter often serials. The demands on home production grew enormously when imports were stopped by the outbreak of war; as well as the 2,000 cinemas flourishing in Germany there were temporary cinemas set up behind the front lines. New companies sprang up to meet this demand, their number rising from 25 in 1913 to 250 in 1919. Government finance helped to set up BUFA and DEULIG, both charged with producing films supporting the war effort.

The most enduring films of this period were tales of the supernatural such as Rye's DER STUDENT VON PRAG (1913), WEGENER and GALEEN's DER GOLEM (1914), and Rippert's HOMUNCULUS (1916). LUBITSCH, LANG, POMMER, and JANNINGS had begun to establish themselves, together with a number of artists from Austria who were to make a considerable contribution to the development of German cinema (see AUSTRIA).

UFA, later to become Germany's biggest production company, was in operation by the end of the war, delighting a weary public with costume dramas such as Lubitsch's CARMEN starring Pola NEGRI and MAY's *Veritas Vincit* (both 1918). As part of the brief post-war upsurge of liberalism, censorship was abolished in 1918: it was reintroduced two years later, but meanwhile a new type of film had emerged which was to become something of a German speciality, the quasi-educational treatise on sex as a cloak for mild pornography; Oswald's *Prostitution I & II* (1919) is an early example. Serials maintained their popularity, with Lang's *Die Spinnen* (1919–20) and May's *Herrin der Welt* (1920) among the best.

Two German films of 1919 attracted much attention abroad, Lubitsch's *Madame Dubarry* (*Passion* in the US) and WIENE's DAS CABINETT DES DR CALIGARI. *Caligari* is now seen as the first complete example of EXPRESSIONISM in the cinema, a movement consolidated by such talented directors as MURNAU, Lang, LENI, PICK, DUPONT, GRÜNE, ROBISON, and von Gerlach, and by the scriptwriter Carl MAYER. The Expressionist period culminated in DER LETZTE MANN (1924) and VARIÉTÉ (1925), but its influence on the cinema was long-lasting both in Germany and elsewhere.

Films of this quality formed only a small part of the total annual output of 200–300 features (one of the highest production figures outside Hollywood). There was a constant stream of nationalistic historical dramas, many starring Otto Gebühr who made a career of portraying Frederick the Great on the screen. There were also some delightful escapist films like Berger's *Der verlorene Schuh* (*Cinderella*, 1923) and the mountain films of Arnold FANCK. No films of this time attempted to come to terms with post-war social reality.

In 1924, after the stabilization of the mark, Hollywood companies bought up cinemas in Germany and flooded the country with American films. The government introduced a QUOTA system whereby one German film (known as Kontingentfilm) had to be made for every film imported, but as usual many films were made simply to acquire the quota certificates: some were never distributed and American companies produced films in Germany solely to fulfil the quota. UFA was in such financial straits that it was forced to negotiate large loans from PARA-MOUNT and METRO-GOLDWYN-MAYER (the Para-fumet agreement) on terms so unfavourable that by 1927 the company was again almost bankrupt.

PABST'S DIE FREUDLOSE GASSE (*Joyless Street*, 1925) initiated a period of greater awareness of social problems known as Neue Sachlichkeit (New Objectivity). Pabst, LAMPRECHT, Jutzi, and a few others depicted the age with a realism unprecedented in the German cinema. Outside the commercial cinema a strong AVANT-GARDE movement grew up. Its exponents, led by EGGEL-ING, RICHTER, FISCHINGER, and METZNER, concentrated on film form and techniques, and particularly on editing. There were also experimental documentaries including RUTTMANN'S BERLIN, DIE SYMPHONIE EINER GROSSSTADT (1927) and the co-operatively made MENSCHEN AM SONNTAG (*People on Sunday*, 1929). The animator Lotte REINIGER worked in both the commercial and avant-garde areas.

The Volksverbund für Filmkunst (Popular Association for Film Art) was formed in 1928 by Pabst, Piscator, and others to encourage artistic and progressive films and in 1929 the Deutsche Liga für unabhängigen Film (German League for Independent Film) was created to resist the glorification of war and increasing official censorship. By that year Lubitsch, Negri, Buchowetski, Dupont, Pick, Leni, Murnau, Jannings, and Pommer had left Germany. German cinema was inevitably diminished even though the move was not in all cases permanent.

Germany developed its own sound system (see TOBIS); the first German features with sound were Ich küsse Ihre Hand Madame (*I Kiss Your Hand, Madame*) and Ruttmann's MELODIE DER WELT (*World Melody*) both in 1929. With the new possibilities offered by sound, operettas became particularly popular, especially those in the Viennese tradition like DER KONGRESS TANZT (*Congress Dances*) and Zwei Herzen im Dreivier-teltakt (*Two Hearts in Waltz Time*) both in 1931. Many were made in foreign language versions, usually French or English.

Films of the early sound era which show an awareness of social and political trends include Pabst's WESTFRONT 1918 (1930), KAMERAD-SCHAFT (1931), DIE DREIGROSCHENOPER (1931), Oswald's Der Hauptmann von Köpenick (*The Captain from Köpenick*, 1931), SAGAN'S MÄD-CHEN IN UNIFORM (1931), and DUDOW'S KÜHLE WAMPE (1932). STERNBERG'S DER BLAUE ENGEL (*The Blue Angel*, 1930) and Lang's M (1931) were also important for their imaginative use of sound. These films which displayed leftist sympathies were on all counts superior to the many

nationalistic films such as Ucicky's Das Flöten-konzert von Sanssouci (1930) and York (1931) and TRENKER's Der Rebell (1932).

The Nazi Party gained a foothold in the cinema from about 1927. They made many election-eering and propaganda shorts which officially could only be shown privately, but cinema managers were bribed to include them in public programmes. The party also made use of mobile cinemas as well as organizing 'spontaneous' demonstrations against films they disliked, including ALL QUIET ON THE WESTERN FRONT (1930) and Kühle Wampe.

When the Nazis came to power in 1933 Goebbels was given the responsibility for all propaganda, and it was largely due to his efforts that film played a vital role in the Third Reich. The proportion of films devoted to overt propaganda was in fact small: the bulk of production was well-made light entertainment on trivial themes. But all films were closely supervised from script to screen and newsreels, sometimes as much as an hour long and carrying the main burden of propaganda, were a part of every cinema programme. The REICHSFILMKAM-MER, founded in 1933 as part of the Kulturkam-mer, implemented a series of controls which gradually spread through the whole industry; by the time the cinema was fully nationalized in 1942 many films made before 1933 were banned, film criticism was censored, assessment of audience reaction was carried out, and the industry had been 'purged' of Jews. Many other film workers had voluntarily left the country.

The work of Leni RIEFENSTAHL and in particular TRIUMPH DES WILLENS (*Triumph of the Will*, 1934) stands out among Nazi propaganda films. There were also youth films, SA-Mann Brand (1933), HITLERJUNGE QUEX (1933); tributes to national figures, Bismarck (1940), Der grosse König (1942); brilliant campaign films such as Feuertaufe (*Baptist of Fire*, 1911) exposures of so-called Allied atrocities like the anti-British OHM KRÜGER (1941). Most notorious of all are the anti-Semitic films JUD SÜSS (1940), Die Rothschilds (1940), and the vicious, perverse 'documentary' DER EWIGE JUDE (*The Eternal Jew*, 1940). The spectacular Münch-hausen (1943), made to celebrate UFA's twenty-fifth anniversary, was the most extravagant production of the era, using remarkable trick shots and special effects. In all, some 1,100 feature films were made under the Nazi régime.

When Germany was occupied at the end of the war a number of films and certain film-makers, including Riefenstahl and HARLAN, were blacklisted. In the few cinemas left standing the Allies, and especially the Americans, showed their own films, chosen to further their aim of de-Nazification. Almost all the production facilities, including the UFA and Tobis studios, were in the Russian zone and these were taken over in 1946 by the newly-formed State film company DEFA which had considerable backing from the Soviet Union. In the western zones licences were granted to individual film-makers and companies and Pommer was brought back to help reorganize the industry, but no financial aid was given.

The immediate post-war period was marked by films with a strong sociological content, attempts to come to terms with recent and current events. The most significant films were made by DEFA—STAUDTE'S DIE MÖRDER SIND UNTER UNS (*The Murderers Are Among Us*, 1946), ENGEL's *Affaire Blum* (1948), and Maetzig's *Ehe im Schatten* (*Marriage in the Shadow*, 1947). From the west came Brauner's *Morituri* (1947), Stemmle's *Berliner Ballade* (1948) and Pabst's *Der Prozess* (*The Trial*, 1948).

With the currency reform of 1949 and the formal separation of East and West Germany the two industries developed separately. DEFA continued to concentrate on anti-Fascist themes and films dealing with the working-class struggle such as *Das Lied der Matrosen* (*Sailors Song*, 1958) and *Stärker als die Nacht* (*Stronger than Night*, 1954), or with contemporary individual problems. Animated films, children's films, documentaries, and COMPILATIONS all constitute an important part of production, the last category best represented by the work of Andrew and Annelie THORNDIKE. An annual festival of short films and documentaries is held in Leipzig. Staudte continued to direct for DEFA until the early fifties, then settled in the West; Dudow worked in East Germany until his death. Since a political crisis in the industry in the early fifties a new generation of film-makers has emerged, but comparatively few of their films are seen outside Eastern Europe.

In West Germany, with the encouragement of the BERLIN Festival instituted in 1951, production rose rapidly: 108 feature films were made in 1954. Commercial motives were paramount; heavy sentimentality and conventional lyricism were characteristic of most films and the 'educational' sex film was revived. A thoughtful exception to the general run was Wicki's documentary-style *Die Brücke* (*The Bridge*, 1959). Lang and THIELE returned to Germany, but made no films of any merit. New stars evolved: Horst Buchholz, Curd JURGENS, Maria Schell, and Romy SCHNEIDER all gained international currency. Competition from television in the sixties led to an increase in sex and sensation, to more co-productions, but to a decrease in the number of films made. Only a quarter of the films distributed were German. Government awards were offered in an attempt to encourage creativity, but the prizes were often withheld.

In 1962 a group of young film-makers who had been working outside the commercial system stormed the OBERHAUSEN Festival with a manifesto criticizing 'Papas Kino' and promising to make good films at half the usual cost. Mainly through the efforts of Alexander KLUGE the Federal Government began to provide funds for promising young directors, a film school was established, and a number of promising new directors began to emerge. Leading figures, many of whom produce and distribute their own films, include the Schamoni brothers, Senft, SCHLÖNDORFF, Kluge, STRAUB, FASSBINDER, HERZOG, Schaaf, and Reitz. Although they are loosely referred to as a group their work bears no common stamp: Straub is probably the most original and influential, Fassbinder and Herzog the most accessible.

An avant-garde movement has separated itself from the independent main stream, with co-operative groups working in Hamburg and Cologne. A variety of experimental work is being carried out by Schroeter, von Praunheim, Nekes, Dore O., Costard, and others.

Television now lends support to the film industry by commissioning films, often of a highly experimental nature, and German critics have proved receptive to new films from both commercial and avant-garde sources.

**GERMI**, PIETRO (1914–74), Italian director, studied acting at the CENTRO SPERIMENTALE after a period at naval school. In 1946 he made *Il testimonio* (*The Witness*), and followed it with three films that firmly established him in the forefront of NEO-REALISM: *Gioventu perduta* (*Lost Youth*, 1947), *In nome della legge* (*In the Name of the Law*, 1949), and IL CAMMINO DELLA SPERANZA (*The Road to Hope*, 1950).

These early films show his preoccupation with the moral dilemmas of post-war Italy, and their lack of extraneous decoration places them clearly within the Italian post-war film tradition (although Germi disliked being called neo-realist). He continued in a similar style in *La città si defende* (1951), and *La presidentessa* (1952), before acting in his own *Il ferroviere* in 1956. The film's feeling for humanity clashed uneasily with Germi's doctrinaire inclinations, and after *L'uomo di paglia* (1958), in which he also acted, he turned his attention to satirical comedy, making the successful OSCAR-winning *Divorzio all'italiano* (*Divorce Italian Style*, 1961), with Marcello MASTROIANNI and Daniella Rocca playing the leading roles. *Sedotta e abbandonata* (*Seduced and Abandoned*, 1963) and *Signore e signori* (1966) similarly revealed his talent for humour, and the latter gained the Palme d'or at CANNES.

**GERSHWIN,** GEORGE (1898–1937), US composer, wrote many concert works combining the jazz and classical idioms, notably *Rhapsody in Blue* (1924) and *An American in Paris* (1925). He also wrote the scores of several musical films, including *King of Jazz* (1930) and LOVE ME TONIGHT (1932). AN AMERICAN IN PARIS (1951) and FUNNY FACE (1957), used music by Gershwin and his 1935 Negro folk opera *Porgy and Bess* was filmed (1959) by Otto PREMINGER.

**GERT,** VALESKA (1900– ), German dancer and singer, real name Gertrud Anderson, capitalized with style and wit on her physical ugliness and gained notoriety in Berlin cabaret in the twenties, at first for her expressionistic dancing and later for her singing. Although not a regular actress, she was well used in several German films in the twenties, starting with her performance as Puck in Neuman's parody version of *Ein Sommernachtstraum* (A MIDSUMMER NIGHT'S DREAM, 1925). She had parts in RENOIR's *Nana* (1926), GALEEN's *Alraune* (1928), and Junghans's TAKOVÝ JE ŽIVOT (*Such is Life*, 1930). Characteristically, PABST gave her the opportunity for full expression of her blend of sinister grotesquerie and verve in DIE FREUDLOSE GASSE (1925), as the madam of a brothel with GARBO as a potential recruit, and in *Tagebuch einer Verlorenen* (*Diary of a Lost Girl*, 1929), as the principal of a girls' remand home with Louise BROOKS as an inmate. Pabst also gave

her the part of Mrs Peachum in DIE DREIGROS-CHENOPER (1931), her only role in sound film (apart from her unlikely appearance in CAVAL-CANTI's *Pett and Pott*, 1934) until her singular appearance as the medium in FELLINI's GIULIETTA DEGLI SPIRITI (1965). She had to leave Germany when the Nazis came to power, went to the US, and after some years of hardship established herself in the Beggars' Bar in New York. She returned to Europe after the war, successfully running bars in various cities (one called the Witches' Kitchen among them). In her present establishment in Kampen, she is still singing her macabre songs.

She has published several books, all reminiscences of her remarkable career: *Mein Weg* (1929), *Die Bettlerbar von New York* (1950), *Ich bin eine Hexe* (1968), and *Katze von Kampen* (1973).

**GERTIE THE DINOSAUR,** US, 1909, was made independently by the famous newspaper strip cartoonist of *Little Nemo in Slumberland*, Winsor McCay, and was presented as a novel turn in vaudeville, with the artist himself supplying a commentary and sound effects. Though drawn animated films had previously been made by both James Stuart BLACKTON and Emile COHL, McCay must be considered the true father of the anthropomorphic animal cartoon.

**GERTRUD,** Denmark, 1964. 2hr. *Dir, scr* Carl Dreyer, from the play by Hjalmar Söderberg;

*Gertrud* (Carl Theodor Dreyer, 1964)

*prod* Palladium Films; *ph* Henning Bendtsen; *des* Kai Rasch; *mus* Jorgen Jersild; *cast* Nina Pens Rode (Gertrud), Bendt Rothe (Gustav Kanning), Ebbe Rode (Gabriel Lidman), Baard Owe (Erland Jansson), Axel Strøbye (Axel Nygren).

Gertrud, seeking her conception of perfect love, is seen defying convention and rejecting three men in succession. She finally accepts the fact that her ideal will never be realized; in the film's postlude she is old and alone but resignedly murmuring 'I have known Love'.

DREYER's characteristic style produces a work of stately formality which is often of great beauty. Long takes, often with a nearly immobile camera, heighten the effect of the actors' severely controlled movements and impose an introspective stillness on the duologues between Gertrud and her men which form the substance of the film. The hysterical condemnation with which a number of critics received the first showing of *Gertrud* has given way to respectful, and sometimes enthusiastic, consideration of Dreyer's last film.

**GIBBONS,** CEDRIC (1893–1956), US art director, studied art in Europe and America, then joined the Thomas A. Edison Studios as assistant art director in 1914. In 1916 he became supervising art director of Goldwyn Pictures Corporation, later METRO-GOLDWYN-MAYER, a position which he held until his death. His contract stated that Gibbons's name would appear on the CREDITS for all MGM films made in the US, even when he was not wholly or solely responsible for the designs.

Gibbons's earlier work included *The Return of Tarzan* (1920) and BEN-HUR (1925). The introduction of PANCHROMATIC film and incandescent lighting enabled him to exploit the effectiveness of large areas of plain white, notably in *The Merry Widow* (1934). In his set designs for ROMEO AND JULIET (1936) and *Marie Antoinette* (1938), both starring Norma SHEARER, he used a highly cinematic stylization rather than accurately copying the periods and locales involved.

Gibbons directed one film, *Tarzan and his Mate* (1934), which is remarkable for its aesthetic visual quality. Extracts from the crocodile sequence in this film were re-used in several later TARZAN films.

He worked on many other large-scale productions, among them THE WIZARD OF OZ (1939), *The Yearling* (1946), *Show Boat* (1951), and QUO VADIS (1951). In all his work won him 11 OSCARS.

**GIBSON,** 'HOOT' (1892–1962), US cowboy star, real forenames Edmund Richard, ran away to join a circus at the age of thirteen. He worked as a cowboy, then in a Wild West Show, before making his first film appearance in *Shotgun Jones* (1911). The 'World's Champion Cowboy' of 1912 appeared unnoticed in many one-reelers until 1916, when he starred in a series of two-reelers for UNIVERSAL. *Action* (1921) brought him fame, and was followed by a string of Western successes throughout the twenties. In 1936 he returned to the circus. He made a minor comeback in the early forties and brief reappearances in *The Marshall's Daughter* (1953) and *The Horse Soldiers* (1959).

**GIELGUD,** JOHN (1904– ), British actor, one of the most respected leaders of the British theatre, most famous for his performances in the classics. His first film was *Who is the Man?* (1924) and he played several rather undistinguished juvenile leads during the thirties, including that in HITCHCOCK's *Secret Agent* (1936). Extracts from his legendary interpretation of HAMLET are included in Humphrey JENNINGS's *A Diary for Timothy* (1945). With JULIUS CAESAR (1953), in which he gave an impressive performance as Cassius, his screen career took on new impetus and he has since made distinguished appearances in films which include *Richard III* (1955), *Becket* (1964), CAMPANADAS A MEDIANOCHE (*Chimes at Midnight*, 1966), *The Charge of the Light Brigade* (1968), and OH! WHAT A LOVELY WAR (1969). He played the title role in a new version of *Julius Caesar* (1970). In 1953 he received a knighthood.

**GIGI,** US, 1958. CinemaScope; 2hr; Metrocolor. *Dir* Vincente Minnelli; *prod* Arthur Freed for MGM; *scr* Alan Jay Lerner, from the novel by Colette; *ph* Joseph Ruttenberg; *des* Cecil Beaton, William A. Horning; *mus* Frederick Loewe; *lyr* Lerner; *mus dir* André Previn; *cast* Leslie Caron (Gigi), Maurice Chevalier (Honoré Lachaille), Louis Jourdan (Gaston Lachaille), Hermione Gingold (Madame Alvarez), Isabel Jeans (Aunt Alicia).

MINNELLI's musical version of COLETTE's story contained polished performances, in particular by Maurice CHEVALIER, Hermione Gingold, and Leslie CARON, elegant costumes and sets which were effectively displayed on the wide screen, and some memorable songs, such as 'Thank Heaven for Little Girls' and 'I Remember it Well'. However, the surface glitter failed to mask a certain soft-centredness.

A French film from the same story was directed by Jacqueline AUDRY in 1949.

**GIGOLO** see CINERAMA

**GILBERT,** JOHN (1897–1936), US actor, worked as an actor and scriptwriter for INCE, TOURNEUR, and FOX from 1915 but attracted little notice until his performance in *His Hour* (1924), for which he was coached in romantic appeal by Elinor GLYN, from whose book the film was adapted. During his time with METRO-GOLDWYN-MAYER he was built up as a successor to VALENTINO: Gilbert's success came with appearances opposite Greta GARBO in several films, including *Flesh and the Devil* (1927) and *Love* (1928), adapted from ANNA KARENINA, and with the usual rumours of a romantic relationship between the stars. However, he is chiefly remembered as one of the major casualties of the coming of SOUND: when dialogue was added to *His Glorious Night* (1929) his high-pitched voice was ridiculed by the critics, and his various attempts at a come-back failed. Garbo's insistence on his being her leading man in QUEEN CHRISTINA (1934) resulted in a subdued but competent performance indicating that, but for his early death, he might well have adjusted, with improved sound recording, to the transition from silent films.

**GILLIAT,** SIDNEY (1908– ), British director and scriptwriter, began as a writer with GAUMONT BRITISH and from *Rome Express* (1932) collaborated, often with Frank LAUNDER, in the scripts of many of the best British comedies and thrillers of the time. After co-directing *Millions Like Us* (1943) with Launder, Gilliat directed his first feature film, *Waterloo Road* (1944). For their own production company, founded in 1945, Launder and Gilliat collaborated closely on production while directing individually. Gilliat's films as director include the witty and entertaining *The Rake's Progress* (1946), *Green for Danger* (1946), *London Belongs to Me* (1948), and *State Secret* (1950). These four films compare well with others made during the British industry's most fertile period; his later work, including *The Story of Gilbert and Sullivan* (1953) and *Only Two Can Play* (1961), is less even in quality.

*GION NO SHIMAI* (*Sisters of the Gion*), Japan, 1936. 1¼hr. *Dir* Kenji Mizoguchi; *prod* Masaichi Nagata; *scr* Mizoguchi, Yoshikata Yoda; *ph* Minoru Miki; *cast* Isuzu Yamada (elder sister), Yoko Umemura (younger sister).

Made at the time of the rise of realism in Japanese films the story contrasts the respective modern and traditional attitudes of two geisha sisters to their profession.

In his somewhat schematic presentation, MIZOGUCHI remains impartial and by the end of the film when both sisters have been exploited (one injured by a jealous ex-lover, the other deserted by a lover to whom she had shown great kindness) it is ultimately the society which makes geishas necessary that is condemned.

The film successfully evokes the red light area of Kyoto; the urban setting and claustrophobic atmosphere provide an interesting contrast to Mizoguchi's period films.

**GIONO,** JEAN (1895–1971), French author of Italian parentage, made his name as the creator of philosophical rural tales, mostly set in his native Provence. In the thirties he adapted several of his stories for filming by PAGNOL, notably LA FEMME DU BOULANGER (1938). A convinced pacifist, Giono aligned himself with the Vichy Government during the war and after the Liberation suffered a degree of ostracism. During the fifties he founded his own film production company in order to control screen adaptations of his work, and directed one film himself: *Crésus* (1960), starring FERNANDEL. This and other productions of Films Jean Giono were undistinguished, with the exception of the unjustly neglected *Un Roi sans divertissement* (1964), directed by François LETERRIER.

**GIRARDOT,** ANNIE (1931– ), French actress, appeared with the Comédie Française after training at the Paris Conservatoire. She appeared in several undistinguished films from 1955, and first attracted wide notice for her performance in ROCCO E I SUOI FRATELLI (1960). She has since appeared in French and Italian films, notably *Vivre pour vivre* (Claude LELOUCH, 1968).

*GIRL IN BLACK, The,* see KORITSI ME TA MAVRA, TO

**GISH,** DOROTHY (1898–1968), US actress, appeared on the stage at the age of four as Little Willie in *East Lynn*. She made her first screen appearance in D. W. GRIFFITH's *The Unseen Enemy* (1912) and acted in a number of his films. The best known are HEARTS OF THE WORLD (1918) and *Orphans of the Storm* (1922), both with her sister Lillian, but she was more usually cast in light comedies which exploited her gay, rather mischievous personality. She visited England in 1926 to make *Nell Gwyn* and *London*, and returned to the American theatre in 1928 continuing there for most of the rest of her career. She returned to the screen as the hero's mother in *The Cardinal* (1964), which showed her acting skills were undiminished.

**GISH,** LILLIAN (1899– ), US actress, was a successful child actress before appearing in films by D. W. GRIFFITH. She became one of his chief stars with leading parts in THE BIRTH OF A NATION (1915), HEARTS OF THE WORLD (1918), *True Heart Susie* (1919), and *Orphans of the Storm* (1922). Her delicate beauty, exploited by

Lillian Gish in *Broken Blossoms* (D. W. Griffith, 1919)

Griffith in roles of injured innocence, disguised a strength and resilience that emerged in the intensity with which she played the scenes of madness in BROKEN BLOSSOMS (1919), and which carried her through the making of WAY DOWN EAST (1920), when she almost lost her life filming on a frozen river. On INTOLERANCE (1916) she was involved in the production and research, virtually acting as Griffith's assistant director, accompanying him on the set and selecting RUSHES; she also appears as the woman rocking the cradle. She continued to take part in all aspects of film-making and directed *Remodelling Her Husband* (1920), which starred her sister Dorothy. After leaving Griffith, she made for METRO-GOLDWYN-MAYER a remarkable series of films that perhaps contains her finest performances, in particular *The White Sister* (1923) directed by Henry KING, and *The Scarlet Letter* (1926) and THE WIND (1928), both directed by Victor Seastrom (SJÖSTRÖM). In more recent years she has made several notable appearances: as the mother in DUEL IN THE SUN (1946), as the indomitable Rachel in THE NIGHT OF THE HUNTER (1955), and again as the mother in *The Unforgiven* (1960). She has written an autobio-

graphy *The Movies, Mr Griffith and Me* (London, 1969) which concentrates on her career in the silent cinema.

*GIULIETTA DEGLI SPIRITI* (*Juliet of the Spirits*), Italy/France, 1965. Technicolor; 2¾hr. *Dir* Federico Fellini; *prod* Federiz (Rome)/Francoriz (Paris); *scr* Fellini, Ennio Flaiano, Tullio Pinnelli, Brunello Rondi; *ph* Gianni Di Venanzo; *des* Piero Gherardi; *mus* Nino Rota; *cast* Giulietta Masina (Giulietta), Mario Pisu (Giorgio), Sandra Milo (Suzy/Iris/Fanny), Valentina Cortese (Val), Caterina Boratto (Giulietta's mother), Valeska Gert (Bhishma).

FELLINI's third film to draw on Giulietta MASINA for inspiration has many parallels with LA DOLCE VITA (1959) and OTTO E MEZZO (8½, 1962) but uses a static pace and descriptive tone in the portrayal of Giulietta's subconscious fears and fantasies. It is Fellini's first full-length colour feature: both design and photography are memorable, although they convey the impression that the images are perhaps Fellini's rather than Giulietta's.

**GLYN,** ELINOR (1864–1943), British writer, became a celebrity on the publication in 1907 of her novel *Three Weeks*. She followed up its success with many others in the same wildly romantic vein and in 1920 was invited to work for PARAMOUNT in Hollywood. Finding that the studio was interested merely in using her name, she moved to METRO-GOLDWYN-MAYER in 1923, where she became an accepted authority on love. She also scripted the film versions of her novels *Three Weeks* (1924), *It* (1927), and *Red Hair* (1927). Clara BOW, who was taken on by Elinor Glyn as pupil and protégée, became the 'It Girl', embodying the author's theories of sexual magnetism and temporarily giving a new term to the English language. On her return to England in 1929, Elinor Glyn tried her hand at independent film production but without success.

**GO-BETWEEN, The,** GB, 1971. Technicolor; 2hr. *Dir* Joseph Losey; *prod* MGM–EMI/World Film Services; *scr* Harold Pinter, based on the novel by L. P. Hartley; *ph* Gerry Fisher; *des* Carmen Dillon; *mus* Michel Legrand; *cast* Julie Christie (Marian Maudsley), Alan Bates (Ted Burgess), Dominic Guard (Leo Colston), Margaret Leighton (Mrs Maudsley), Michael Redgrave (Leo as an old man), Michael Gough (Mr Maudsley), Edward Fox (Hugh Trimingham).

An unusually close transcription of a novel in cinematic terms, *The Go-Between* maintains the dislocated time structure of L. P. Hartley's book as well as describing the action entirely through the experiences of the narrator. LOSEY reveals his own favourite themes in the text—intrusion, initiation, class differences—and expresses them with subtlety and elegance: the nuances indicated in his Hollywood work, operating through physical gesture as much as through dialogue, here reach a remarkable degree of accomplishment. The film was awarded a richly-deserved Grand Prix at CANNES.

**GODARD,** JEAN-LUC (1930– ), French director, first became involved with cinema in 1950, acting in short films by Jacques RIVETTE and Eric ROHMER. With them he founded *La Gazette du cinéma* of which only five monthly issues were published. In 1952 Godard wrote his first articles for CAHIERS DU CINÉMA, but became a regular contributor only in 1956. During this time he made two short films, *Opération Béton* (1954) about the construction of a dam on which he was working as a labourer, and *Une Femme coquette* (1955) based on the story *Le Signe* by Guy de Maupassant. Some of the innovatory stylistic devices of his early feature films are prefigured in this short: jump-cutting, handheld camera, flash-shots, and disregard for continuity.

He made *Tous les garçons s'appellent Patrick* (1957) from a script by Rohmer, followed by *Charlotte et son Jules* (1958), in which Jean-Paul

BELMONDO worked with Godard for the first time, and *Une Histoire d'eau* (1958), an improvisation abandoned by TRUFFAUT and finished by Godard who also added a contrapuntal commentary. By 1959, the year of the emergence of the NOUVELLE VAGUE, Godard's polemical, often obscure, and frequently outrageous AUTEUR-orientated criticism was a regular feature of *Arts* as well as *Cahiers*. His first feature, A BOUT DE SOUFFLE, appeared in March 1960. LE PETIT SOLDAT (1960) was banned by the French authorities because of its treatment of the Algerian question; his next film, *Une Femme est une femme* (1961), took a more light-hearted view of life and is one of the rare examples in his work of the male–female relationship resolving itself satisfactorily.

Godard's main themes had already emerged. His protagonists are outsiders: foreigners (Jean SEBERG, Anna KARINA, Marina Vlady, Laszlo Szabo, etc), gangsters, prostitutes, political extremists, isolated from family or social ties and living as transients in hotel rooms or impersonal apartments. Prostitution in its broadest sense (surrender of integrity for material gain) became increasingly important, used literally in VIVRE SA VIE (1962), metaphorically in LES CARABINIERS and LE MÉPRIS (both 1963). *Bande à part* (1964) developed the theme of the outsider through a group of petty criminals in rebellion against the greyness of suburban life; *Une Femme mariée* (1964) depicted woman reduced to an object through the pressures of modern life, exemplified by advertising; these two views came together in PIERROT-LE-FOU (1965), with a hero who escapes from the materialistic demands of wife and job to become the essential Godard outsider. In *Alphaville* (1965), the city of the future, individuality has finally been expunged.

Godard's elliptical narrative style (one of the most influential elements of his work) was to some extent maintained in *Masculin-féminin* (1966). In *Made in USA* (1966), however, the story of a young woman's attempt to discover the identity of her lover's murderer is no more than a pretext for the exploration of the film's double theme—the Ben Barka murder and the assassination of Kennedy. Comprehension of the plot is hindered by the extreme fragmentation of the narrative, the deliberate inaudibility of parts of the sound-track, and sundry interventions like the song by the Japanese girl and Laszlo Szabo's mimicry of cartoon characters. In DEUX OU TROIS CHOSES QUE JE SAIS D'ELLE (1966) the demand for narrative is satisfied only by sequential events of a day in the life of the principal character. In contrast to *Vivre sa vie* it is unashamedly a *film à thèse* using prostitution as a symptom of the condition of modern life.

Meanwhile, Godard's political commitment

was becoming more overtly expressed in his films. In *La Chinoise* (1967) his generally sceptical tone gave way to a systematic Marxist–Leninist critique of society. WEEK-END was more conventionally constructed and presented than anything since *Masculin-féminin*, but the three films made in 1968 explicitly deny the 'bourgeois' device of narrative or plot. *Le Gai Savoir* is set in a darkened studio where Jean-Pierre LÉAUD and Juliet Berto discuss communication and try to invent a language of images and sounds. *Un Film comme les autres* would appear to have been started during or immediately after the 'events' of May 1968. Shot in 16mm, it is very much in the spirit of May, being a record of a discussion between workers from the Renault car factory and revolutionary students. Godard's own involvement in the May revolt included the production of several *ciné-tracts*, three-minute propaganda tracts on 16mm black-and-white film, consisting mainly of a montage of still photographs with graphic inter-cuts.

*One Plus One* was an unsatisfactory project from the outset. Godard had been hired to direct a film in England about abortion, but the relaxation of the abortion laws necessitated a hurried change of plan. Godard said he would still make a film in England on condition that either the BEATLES or the Rolling Stones would appear in it. Accordingly the Rolling Stones were hired and Godard came to England on 30 May, at a time when all his thoughts were on the events in Paris. Shooting dragged on into August, delayed by the arrest of Brian Jones (the Stones' bass player), a fire in the recording studio, and persistent rain. The result was Godard's most disjointed film to date: long takes of the Stones recording the song 'Sympathy for the Devil' (the film's alternative title); shots of a group of Black Power militants in a Battersea car-breaker's yard; an interview with 'Eve Democracy' (Anne Wiazemsky) about the relationship between culture and revolution; and sequences in a pornographic bookshop—each introduced by slogans spray-painted on hoardings, walls, cars, and any other convenient surfaces.

In 1969, after experimenting with television and video-recording both in Quebec and at home in Paris, Godard returned to England to film *British Sounds* for London Weekend Television. The result, filmed on the production line of a car factory and at the University of Essex, was a kind of treatise on student and worker participation which recalls *Un Film comme les autres*. As with *Le Gai Savoir*, the television company which commissioned the film refused to transmit it. In the same year *Vent d'est* continued to experiment with the fragmentation of narrative and to exploit the dialectical play of image and sound.

Godard went to Prague to make *Pravda* (1969), an hour-long examination of revisionism and the capitalist motive in the 'socialist bloc', setting a hypothetical debate between Lenin and Rosa Luxemburg against images of Czechoslovakia since the Russian invasion. Godard and Jean-Pierre Gorin (who had been his associate since 1968 in the Groupe Dziga Vertov which had produced *Un Film comme les autres*, *British Sounds*, and *Pravda*) made a film for Italian television which, predictably, was not transmitted. *Lotte in Italia* (1969) is the story of the transformation of a girl who says she is involved in the revolutionary movement and is a Marxist. The film has three parts. The first demonstrates that in various aspects of her life there is a victory of the bourgeois ideology and the second and third parts try to explain how this has happened.

Since 1969 Godard and Gorin have collaborated on numerous projects, some of them unfinished, many not distributed in France or abroad. Available information about these films is in most cases limited to their titles (*Communication, Vladimir et Rosa, 18 Brumaire, Jusqu'à la victoire*, etc).

After sustaining serious injuries in a road accident in 1971, Godard returned to directing with *Tout va bien* (1972). This was in complete contrast to his work since 1968, a full-scale feature starring Yves MONTAND and Jane FONDA as a one-time *nouvelle vague* director and an American journalist who find themselves imprisoned with a factory owner in his office during a five-day strike. Although the film's form is comparatively conventional, its content is obviously political in aim and Godard presumably chose his stars for their known left-wing political leanings: a monologue by Montand is a synthesis of elements from his own life and from that of Godard. It would appear, though, that Godard became disillusioned with his female star: *Letter to Jane* (1972) is a forty-five minute diatribe on a photograph of Jane Fonda in North Vietnam which was published in *L'Express*. The narration calls attention to her facial expression which, Godard claims, differs from that of a North Vietnamese soldier in the background because she is the product of a jaded, capitalist society.

All Godard's later films, and especially the overtly political tracts, are ephemeral, usually deliberately so. They are intended as interventions in a continuing argument—and retrospectively can themselves appear as stale as old arguments. Certainly among the most significant film-makers of his generation, he has introduced into cinema the concept of a dialectical framework, continually setting up philosophical oppositions in the context of a shapely polemic. His influence on cinema has been fundamental. Although his stylistic innovations have frequently been used in a careless, merely voguish, manner, his reconsideration of traditional cinematic aims and forms has given rise to exciting developments in the work of ALEA, BERTOLUCCI, OSHIMA, and other politically-oriented directors.

Godard has also contributed sketches to: *Les Sept Péchés capitaux* (1961), *RoGoPaG* (1962), *Les Plus Belles Escroqueries du monde* (1963), *Paris vu par . . .* (1964), *Le Plus Vieux Métier du monde, ou l'amour à travers les âges* (1967), *Vangelo '70* (1967), and *Loin du Viet-nam* (1967).

Richard Roud, *Jean-Luc Godard*, second ed, London, 1970; Philip French and others, *The films of Jean-Luc Godard*, second ed, London, 1969; Toby Mussman (ed), *Jean-Luc Godard*, New York, 1968; Jean Collet, *Jean-Luc Godard*, Éditions Seghers' Cinéma d'Aujourd'hui (in English), New York, 1970. For a severely critical view of Godard's work which underlines its tendency to appear obscure or pretentious, see 'Godard and the Godardians; a study in the New Sensibility' in John Simon, *Private screenings*, New York, 1967, pp 272–96. Godard's critical articles and interviews until August 1967 are collected and translated into English in Tom Milne (ed), *Godard on Godard*, London, 1972. A comprehensive bibliography was compiled in January 1972 by the British Film Institute.

**GODDARD,** PAULETTE (1911– ), US actress, made famous by CHAPLIN (to whom she was for a time married) with MODERN TIMES (1936) and THE GREAT DICTATOR (1939). Most of her films were made at PARAMOUNT beginning with *The Cat and the Canary* (1939) opposite Bob HOPE. A vivacious, attractive brunette, she demonstrated a flair for zany comedy in such films as *Nothing but the Truth* (1941), *So Proudly We Hail* (1943), and *My Favorite Brunette* (1947). She appeared as a blonde in the title role of her best film, RENOIR's *The Diary of a Chambermaid* (1946). She has virtually retired since her marriage in 1958 to the novelist Erich Maria Remarque.

**GODFATHER, The,** US, 1971. Technicolor; 3hr. *Dir* Francis Ford Coppola; *prod* Paramount; *scr* Mario Puzo, Coppola, from Puzo's novel; *ph* Gordon Willis; *mus* Nino Rota; *cast* Marlon Brando (Don Vito Corleone), Al Pacino (Michael), James Caan (Sonny), Richard Castellano (Clemenza), Al Martino (Johnny Fontane).

Mario Puzo's saga of an Italian-American criminal organization and its autocratic chief was a sensational success, selling 500,000 hardcover and 10 million paperback copies. PARAMOUNT's choice of Francis Ford COPPOLA to direct the film version of this valuable property, after refusals by Richard BROOKS, Peter YATES, and COSTA-GAVRAS, was surprising; his main reputation so far was as a screenwriter and his films as director had been commercially unsuccessful.

The production was beset with harassments. Before filming started the Italian-American Civil Rights League held a rally in Madison Square Garden and raised $600,000 towards attempts to stop the film which they claimed was a slur on their community. There were bomb threats and the producer's car was fired on. Coppola met the League and agreed to delete the words 'Mafia' and 'Cosa Nostra' from the script (it later appeared that 'Mafia' had never been used and 'Cosa Nostra' only once); to engage some people from the League; and to donate proceeds from the film's première to the League's hospital fund. Among other incidents, Frank SINATRA abused Puzo publicly because of the resemblance between his career and that of the character Johnny Fontane, and Vic Damone withdrew from playing Fontane in consideration of his own Italian descent.

Such episodes presumably helped the film's success, aided by an increasing public interest in the Mafia. But the initial impact was sustained by its superb professionalism: Coppola's adaptation, faithful to the book, compelled attention throughout the considerable length and was strikingly successful in conveying the hierarchical structure of tribal groupings. Marlon BRANDO's performance in the title role was justly acclaimed and his temporarily declining career took on new impetus. His performance, the direction, and the screenplay all won OSCARS, and within months *The Godfather* had broken all box-office records.

A run of Mafia films followed *The Godfather*, including *Cosa Nostra* (*The Valachi Papers*, 1972) and *Honor Thy Father* (1973), but its success was rivalled only by *The Godfather Part II* (1975), also directed by Coppola.

**GOLD,** ERNEST (1921– ), Viennese-born US composer who began a Hollywood career in the early fifties, working on a wide variety of films ranging from cartoons (*Gerald McBoing-Boing on Planet Moo*, 1955) to horror (*The Screaming Skull*, 1958), and TARZAN (*Tarzan's Fight for Life*, 1958) besides more substantial features (*Running Target*, 1956; *Too Much Too Soon*, 1957). From 1959 he worked on major productions, including Stanley KRAMER's *On the Beach* (1959), *Inherit the Wind* (1960), *Judgement at Nuremberg* (1961), *A Child Is Waiting* (1962), *It's a Mad, Mad, Mad, Mad World* (1963), and *The Secret of Santa Vittoria* (1969). His score for EXODUS (1960) won an OSCAR.

**GOLDDIGGERS.** *Golddiggers of Broadway* (1929), based on a Broadway play (first filmed in 1923) about a group of girls in search of rich husbands, was the first in a series of successful MUSICALS produced by WARNER BROS. It was directed by Roy Del Ruth with choreography by Larry Caballos and included the enormously popular song 'Tiptoe through the Tulips'. Its four successors were all choreographed by Busby BERKELEY (only the songwriter Al Dubin worked on all five), and the series contained some of Berkeley's most remarkable production numbers. *Golddiggers of 1933* (Mervyn LEROY, 1933) included 'We're in the Money', a stunning opening featuring Ginger ROGERS garbed in gold dollars; the pre-Hays Code 'Pettin' in the Park'; 'The Shadow Waltz', with sixty illuminated violins weaving a violin-shaped pattern against a darkened background; and the finale, 'Remember My Forgotten Man', an elaborately mounted number inspired by unemployment during the Depression.

*Golddiggers of 1935* (1935) was directed as well as choreographed by Berkeley and included 'The Words Are in My Heart', with fifty-six white pianos, each with its chorus girl, moving around in waltz time, and the brilliant 'Lullaby of Broadway', opening with the face of Wini Shaw, a white dot on a black screen, moving forward into close-up, and ending with the same singer falling to her death from a skyscraper. The big production number in *Golddiggers of 1937* (Lloyd BACON, 1936) was the quasi-military 'All's Fair in Love and War'. By now the formula— hard-up show-girls living in shabby rooming-houses while rehearsing a show of unbelievable extravagance—was beginning to pall. The series ended with *Golddiggers in Paris* (Roy Enright, 1938), in which Rudy Vallee replaced Dick Powell as the regular romantic lead.

**GOLD RUSH, The,** US, 1925. 2¼hr. *Dir, scr, prod* Charles Chaplin for United Artists, assisted by Chuck Riesner, Henry d'Abbado d'Arrast; *ph* Rollie Totheroh, Jack Wilson; *cast* Charlie Chaplin (the prospector), Mack Swain (Big Jim), Georgia Hale (Georgia), Bert Morissey (her friend), Henry Bergman (Hank Curtis), Malcolm Waite (Jack Cameron).

CHAPLIN's most famous film, reputed to have cost $800,000, which he himself has called 'the picture I want to be remembered by'. Charlie is a prospector in the Alaska Gold Rush of 1898 who suffers from hardship and the greed of his fellow prospectors—all, of course, bigger and stronger than he. The film is full of masterly and memorable comic sequences all set in a basically tragic situation: the log cabin dangerously balanced on a cliff edge; the shoe served as a gourmet turkey dinner, complete with bent nail

wishbone and shoelace spaghetti; a New Year's Eve dinner without any guests at which Charlie delicately evokes a saloon dance with two bread rolls stuck on the forks.

What is important about these sequences is not their originality (the teetering log cabin owes much to Harold LLOYD, whose *Safety Last*, 1923, had been a huge popular success the year before *The Gold Rush* was started, while at least one writer says that the bread roll business was invented by Fatty ARBUCKLE), but the grace and timing with which Chaplin performs them. After many setbacks, Charlie gets his girl, although some critics find this happy ending contrary to the atmosphere of the rest of the film.

Chaplin re-issued *The Gold Rush* in 1942 with a music track and commentary by himself; this was the first in a systematic release, under Chaplin's careful control, of his major silent films with sound added.

**GOLDWYN,** SAMUEL (1882–1974), US producer, real name Samuel Goldfish. With his brother-in-law Jesse LASKY, a Polish glove manufacturer, Goldfish co-founded a film production company called Lasky Feature Plays in 1910. Three years later he produced the company's first Hollywood-made feature film, *The Squaw Man* (1913), directed by the third partner Cecil B. DEMILLE. In 1916 the company merged with Adolph ZUKOR's FAMOUS PLAYERS, forming Famous Players-Lasky, and Goldfish left Lasky to form a new film-making company with the Selwyn Brothers. The new unit was called Goldwyn Pictures, from which Goldfish took his now-famous name in 1918. Goldwyn broke away from the Selwyn group in 1922, finally being bought out of the company after the merger in 1924 with the Metro and Mayer production concerns (see METRO-GOLDWYN-MAYER).

By 1925 Goldwyn had become an independent producer, owning his own studio and supporting his own stable of stars. He produced and released his films in association with larger companies like RKO and UNITED ARTISTS (in which he later became a partner and which he unsuccessfully attempted to take over in 1937). His early productions included melodramas such as *Stella Dallas* (1925), *The Dark Angel* (1935), and DEAD END (1937). Vilma Banky and Anna STEN were two of the female stars whose careers he launched. He was justly proud of his bevy of female contract players, called 'Goldwyn Girls', and showcased them in productions like *Goldwyn Follies* (1938) and the series of musicals starring Eddie CANTOR. His fracturing of English was a byword. Goldwynisms like 'Include me out' became common usage, although many phrases attributed to him were pure fabrication.

For thirty years Goldwyn maintained his position as one of Hollywood's top producers always laying equal emphasis on a high technical standard amounting to glossiness and a concern for moral tone. WUTHERING HEIGHTS (1939), *The Westerner* (1940), and THE LITTLE FOXES (1941) are among the enduring films he produced; his most celebrated effort was William WYLER's THE BEST YEARS OF OUR LIVES (1946), which swept that year's OSCAR awards and earned Goldwyn himself the Irving THALBERG Award for his exemplary work as a producer. He claimed to be concerned more with providing wholesome entertainment than with earning large profits: a characteristic expression of this concern was 'I don't care whether *The Best Years of Our Lives* makes money as long as everybody in the United States sees it.' This attitude was difficult to maintain in post-war years, and after a few more successes—THE SECRET LIFE OF WALTER MITTY (1947), *Hans Christian Andersen* (1952), GUYS AND DOLLS (1955), *Porgy and Bess* (1959)— Goldwyn retired from film-making. Nevertheless, the Samuel Goldwyn Studio is still in operation for independent production.

Goldwyn wrote a book about his early filmmaking experiences in Hollywood, *Behind the screen* (New York, 1923).

**GOLEM, Der,** Germany, 1914. ¾hr. *Dir* Paul Wegener, Henrik Galeen; *ph* Guido Seeber; *des* R. A. Dietrich, Rochus Gliese; *cast* Paul Wegener (Golem).

The first screen version of an ancient Jewish legend deals with events subsequent to those in WEGENER's 1920 film, with the Golem, resurrected after the Rabbi's death, in the hands of an antique dealer with whose daughter it falls in love. Wegener imaginatively exploits screen effects in the creation of fantasy through which psychological themes can be explored.

*Der Golem: wie in die Welt kam,* Germany, 1920. 1½hr. *Dir* Paul Wegener, Carl Boese (special effects); *prod* UFA; *scr* Wegener, Henrik Galeen; *ph* Karl Freund; *des* Hans Poelzig; *cost* Rochus Gliese; *cast* Paul Wegener (Golem), Albert Steinrück (Rabbi Loew), Lyda Salmonova (Miriam).

Wegener returns to the creation of the Golem by the ·Rabbi Loew and the victorious fight against the Emperor's expulsion of the Jews from the Prague ghetto. The Expressionist sets in Gothic baroque style—narrow streets, crazy pointed rooftops, and chiaroscuro lighting—aid the convincing portrayal of magic in medieval surroundings. Wegener's Golem served as a model for future film monsters.

Other films based on the legend include: *Golem und die Tänzerin* (1917), by Wegener and Gliese, *Golem* (1936) made in Prague by Julien DUVIVIER and starring Harry Baur, *Le Golem* (1966) made for French television by Jean Kerchbron, and a version made in Israel by Ilan Eldad.

**GONE WITH THE WIND,** US, 1939. Technicolor; 3¾hr. *Dir* Victor Fleming; *prod* David O. Selznick; *scr* Sidney Howard, from the novel by Margaret Mitchell; *ph* Ernest Haller, Ray Rennahan; *prod des* William Cameron Menzies; *mus* Max Steiner; *cast* Vivien Leigh (Scarlett O'Hara), Clark Gable (Rhett Butler), Leslie Howard (Ashley Wilkes), Olivia de Havilland (Melanie Wilkes), Thomas Mitchell (Gerald O'Hara), Hattie McDaniel (Mammy).

Margaret Mitchell (1900–49) published her best-selling novel in 1936, but the interest it had aroused even before publication inevitably led to competition for the screen rights, which were finally bought by David O. SELZNICK. Selznick intended to make the film as an independent production for release through UNITED ARTISTS; but the popular decision to cast Clark GABLE in the role of Rhett Butler necessitated an agreement with METRO-GOLDWYN-MAYER to whom Gable —a valuable property—was under contract. Production had to be postponed until Selznick's distribution contract with United Artists had expired and it was arranged that MGM should distribute the film and take an equal share of the profits. Public interest in the project was maintained by a much-publicized search for an actress to play Scarlett O'Hara: the desire for novelty was combined with the demands of economy, for the budget could not stand the cost of another major star.

The production was dogged by many of the problems associated with BLOCKBUSTERS. Costs spiralled; several writers, including Scott FITZGERALD and Ben HECHT, had a hand in reducing the long novel to a manageable screenplay; the original director, George CUKOR, was replaced by Victor FLEMING, whose ill health during shooting made it necessary to engage Sam WOOD to help complete the film. (In fact all the work was closely supervised by Selznick himself.) All the difficulties were, however, justified by the film's unprecedented commercial success. For many years it was the top grosser, only to be ousted from first place by THE SOUND OF MUSIC (1965), and there were further returns from the version reprocessed in 70MM and released in 1968.

After thirty years *Gone with the Wind* still compels admiration even while its weaknesses are acknowledged. The issues of the American Civil War are treated with naïvety and the use of TECHNICOLOR is often self-consciously aesthetic; but the prodigal use of spectacle is impressive, particularly in the famous Atlanta scenes which deserve their place in film history. It is a prime example of the 'designed' film, with every other consideration subordinated to the lavish sets and costumes. Gable, Leslie HOWARD, Thomas MITCHELL, and Hattie MCDANIEL give admirably polished versions of characterizations which they had all played many times before, but two performances are outstanding: Vivien LEIGH's, though uneven, was a remarkable achievement for a young actress comparatively new to films and Olivia DE HAVILLAND brought to a potentially colourless role a warmth and honesty which carry total conviction.

The negative of *Gone with the Wind* is stored in a golden canister. Representing as it does the culmination of the Hollywood glamour of the thirties, this extravagant gesture would seem wholly appropriate.

David O. Selznick's *Memo* (New York, 1972), gives some revealing insights into the film's production.

**GOOD EARTH, The**, US, 1937. 2½hr. *Dir* Sidney Franklin; *prod* MGM; *scr* Talbot Jennings, Tess Schlesinger, Claudine West, from the novel by Pearl S. Buck; *ph* Karl Freund; *montage* Slavko Vorkapich; *des* Cedric Gibbons; *cast* Paul Muni (Wang), Luise Rainer (O-Lan), Walter Connolly (Uncle), Tilly Losch (Lotus), Charley Grapewin (Old Father).

This adaptation of Pearl Buck's tale of a poor Chinese farmer whose rise to success and wealth is followed by disaster, was among the most famous and successful Hollywood prestige productions of the thirties; it has stood the test of time, even without the advantage of the amber-tinted prints in which it was initially released.

Paul MUNI gave a much-admired performance in the central role and Luise RAINER's sensitive and splendidly controlled playing won her an OSCAR. The convincing locust plague sequence, which was one of the most extravagant special EFFECTS set-pieces of the era, was achieved by superimposing coffee grounds floating downwards over fields of ripe wheat drenched in crude oil.

**GORDON, RUTH** (1896– ), US actress and writer, made her stage début in *Peter Pan* in 1915, since when she has been consistently involved in the theatre. She made her first major film appearance, as Mary Todd in *Abe Lincoln in Illinois* (1939, *Spirit of the People* in GB). She was also in *Dr Ehrlich's Magic Bullet* (1940) and *Two Faced Woman* (1941). She married Garson KANIN in 1942 (her second marriage). In 1944 she wrote and acted in the stage play *Over 21*. Many of the details of her acting career were included in her autobiographical play *Years Ago* (1946). She then, with her husband, wrote the screenplays for *A Double Life* (1948), ADAM'S

RIB (1949), *The Marrying Kind* (1952), *Pat and Mike* (1952), and *The Actress* (1953), an adaptation of *Years Ago*. She returned to the cinema screen after twenty-two years in *The Loved One* (1965). She has increasingly appeared in films, usually as grotesque characters, particularly since receiving an OSCAR for best supporting actress for her role in ROSEMARY'S BABY (1968).

**GORKY, MAXIM** (1868–1936), Russian novelist, real name Alexei Peshkov: the nom de plume means 'bitter'. Brought up by his grandparents in Nizhni Novgorod, Gorky had an extremely hard childhood. He became a tramp at twenty, wandering through Southern Russia, publishing stories in local newspapers. He drew heavily on his early experiences in his writing and rapidly became famous as the first truly proletarian writer, peopling his stories with strong and colourful portraits and vivid scenes of working-class life. He became a Marxist in 1899, participated actively in the October Revolution, and became the first president of the Soviet Writers Union.

He took a keen interest in film, writing two perceptive articles on the possibilities of cinema after seeing LUMIÈRE's early films. In 1919 he conceived the idea of a mammoth series of films to recount the history of human culture. This project was never realized although his idea for the film *Den novovo mira* (*A Day in a New World*) was taken up in 1940. The film, which was designed to 'tell something about modern Soviet life' was a COMPILATION of footage shot by a hundred cameramen in different parts of the USSR on the same day.

His novels provided a rich source for film adaptations; MAT (*Mother*, 1907) was adapted by both PUDOVKIN and DONSKOI. The latter also made a trilogy from Gorky's autobiography, *Detstvo Gorkovo* (*The Childhood of Gorky*, 1938), *V lyudyakh* (*My Apprenticeship*, 1939), and *Moi universiteti* (*My Universities*, 1940), and filmed from an early novel, *Foma Gordeiev* (1960).

**GOSHO, HEINOSUKE** (1902– ), Japanese director, entered the Shochiku Tokyo studio at twenty-one and worked as assistant director to Yasujiro Shimazu until 1925. Shimazu was a pioneer in selecting realistic contemporary subjects for his films and Gosho followed this example, confining himself to the *shomin-geki*, the drama of common people, and bringing to the form a quality of compassion and human warmth which has established him as one of the great Japanese directors; 'Goshoism' has become an accepted critical term indicating 'something that makes you laugh and cry at the same time'. Few of Gosho's very large output of films (he has made more than 150 features) have been seen in the West, the best known outside Japan being *Entotsu ni Mieru Basho* (*Four Chimneys* in GB; *Where Chimneys are Seen* in US, 1953) and *Osaka no Yado* (*An Inn at Osaka*, 1954).

**GOSPEL ACCORDING TO ST MATTHEW, The,** see VANGELO SECONDO MATTEO, IL

**GÖSTA BERLINGS SAGA** (*The Atonement of Gösta Berling*), Sweden, 1924. 2¾hr (but see below). *Dir* Mauritz Stiller; *prod* Svensk Film-industri; *scr* Stiller, Ragnar Hyltén-Cavallius, from the novel by Selma Lagerlöf; *ph* J. Julius Jaenzon; *cast* Lars Hanson (Gösta Berling), Gerda Lundeqvist (Margareta Samszelius), Sixten Malmerfeldt (Melchior Sinclair), Karin Swanström (Gustava), Jenny Hasselqvist (Marianne), Ellen Cederström (Märta Dohna), Mona Mårtensson (Ebba Dohna), Greta Garbo (Elisabeth).

To transfer Selma LAGERLÖF's long novel to the screen was a major undertaking: STILLER's original version lasted 3½ hours and was shown in two parts. This version, no longer in existence, was cut by Stiller for export purposes and much of the rhythm and power of the original must have been lost in the process. To the modern view *Gösta Berlings saga* lacks coherence, but there are some impressive sequences: the expulsion of the dissipated priest from his church and the burning of Ekeby Manor in particular. This was the film which introduced Greta GARBO to international audiences; her warm and sparkling performance is in contrast to her later, more famous, tragic roles.

**GOULDING,** EDMUND (1891–1959), British-born US director. After a time as scriptwriter for Henry KING, notably on TOL'ABLE DAVID (1921) and *The White Sister* (1924), and as an actor, he made his début as a director in the mid-twenties for METRO-GOLDWYN-MAYER and before long was directing GARBO in *Love* (1928), a free version of ANNA KARENINA released in Britain under that title. In the early days of sound he co-directed THE BROADWAY MELODY (1929) with Harry Beaumont before his first solo talking picture, *The Trespasser* (1929), an emotional drama starring Gloria SWANSON. *Reaching for the Moon* (1931), a musical comedy-drama with Douglas FAIRBANKS Jr and Bebe DANIELS, backed by Edward Everett HORTON in one of his valet roles, was played against settings then considered remarkably ultra-modern. A better-remembered film of similar vintage was GRAND HOTEL (1932) with its assortment of MGM's top stars.

In the mid-thirties, Goulding moved to WARNER BROS and made a speciality of directing Bette DAVIS: a remake of *The Trespasser* entitled

*That Certain Woman* (1937), *Dark Victory* (1939), *The Old Maid* (1939), and *The Great Lie* (1941). Goulding's association with romantic or emotional drama was maintained in *The Constant Nymph* and *Claudia* (both 1943), the latter following his move to TWENTIETH CENTURY-FOX where he remained until his death. He directed two of Tyrone POWER's less characteristic films, *The Razor's Edge* (1946) and *Nightmare Alley* (1948). Prominent among his later films was an episodic bumper-bundle, *We're Not Married* (1952), with an all-star cast including Ginger ROGERS, Eve Arden, Marilyn MONROE and Zsa Zsa Gabor. His last film was *Mardi Gras* (1958), an insipid musical revolving round a military cadet and a Hollywood film star.

**GOUPI-MAINS-ROUGES,** France, 1943. 1½hr. *Dir* Jacques Becker; *prod* Minerva; *scr* Pierre Véry, Becker, from the novel by Véry; *ph* Jean Bourgoin, Pierre Montazel; *cast* Fernand Ledoux (Goupi-mains-rouges), Georges Rollin (Goupi-Monsieur), Robert Le Vigan (Goupi-Tonkin), Arthur Devère (Goupi-mes-sous), Maurice Schutz (Goupi-Empéreur).

Four generations of the bickering Goupi family, who dominate their village in the manner of royalty, present a united front when one of their number is killed and another suspected of the crime. The film's realism (it was shot on location in the Charente), authentic description of rural life and manners, and warm humour recall BECKER's lasting debt to RENOIR. It was welcomed in France as a re-affirmation of national identity during the bleak time of the Occupation; its enduring quality has been undervalued abroad.

**GO WEST,** US, 1925. 1¾hr. *Dir, scr* Buster Keaton; *prod* Joseph M. Schenck; *ph* Elgin Lessley, Bert Haines; *cast* Buster Keaton (Friendless), Howard Truesdale (owner of the Diamond Bar Ranch), Kathleen Myers (his daughter), Ray Thompson (foreman), Brown Eyes (herself).

Friendless, an inept and lonely ranch-hand, finds a companion in a small brown heifer: in saving her from slaughter he saves the town from a cattle stampede. Coming between THE NAVIGATOR (1924) and THE GENERAL (1926), *Go West* is in marked contrast to those two peaks of KEATON's achievement. But although it lacks their comic invention and breathtakingly timed acrobatic jokes it has its own humorous charm.

**GO WEST,** US, 1941. 1½hr. *Dir* Edward Buzzel; *prod* MGM; *scr* Irving Brecher; *ph* Leonard Smith; *cast* Groucho Marx (S. Quentin Quale), Chico (Joe Panello), Harpo (Rusty Panello),

John Carroll (Terry Turner), Diana Lewis (Eve Wilson).

The essentially urban humour of the MARX BROTHERS transferred into a conventional Western melodrama gives rise to some memorable set pieces, notably in Groucho's impudent confidence trick, played on a queue of passengers at a railway station, in Harpo's confrontation with a desk, and in a hilarious burlesque (planned and timed with the utmost skill) of the traditional train chase.

**GPO FILM UNIT** see CROWN FILM UNIT

**GRABLE,** BETTY (1916–73), US actress, appeared on the screen from the age of thirteen in the chorus of musicals produced by FOX, METRO-GOLDWYN-MAYER, and RKO. Her career progressed slowly during the thirties, but she won great popularity during the war years, especially with the US forces, with such films as *Million Dollar Legs* (1939), *Down Argentine Way* (1940), and *Coney Island* (1943). Apart from an amusing performance in *How to Marry a Millionaire* (1953), with Marilyn MONROE, her postwar films were undistinguished and she retired from the screen in 1955, confining her appearances to cabaret and television.

**GRADING,** the process of correcting the colour and brightness of each shot when making a print of the completed picture. (It is called timing in the US.) Since each shot in a film is made separately over a period of weeks or months, exposure and colour balance may vary widely; different lenses, lighting, and film stocks also contribute to this. These differences must be eliminated by the laboratory when the first print is made. The grader (who has never seen the film before) examines the negative on a specially adapted colour television monitor and adjusts each shot until it appears correct, taking particular care to match consecutive shots of the same set or location. He enters the results of his judgement on a punched tape which automatically varies the colour and brightness of the printer light at the beginning of each shot. Less automated methods involving considerable guesswork are still used in grading black-and-white films. The first print (the ANSWER PRINT or grading print) lets the producer and director see the grader's work and add their opinions to his; several more grading prints may be produced until all are satisfied. All RELEASE PRINTS should be identical with the last grading print.

**GRADUATE, The,** US, 1967. Panavision; 1¾hr; Technicolor. *Dir* Mike Nichols; *prod* Embassy/ Lawrence Turman; *scr* Calder Willingham, Buck Henry; *ph* Robert Surtees; *ed* Sam O'Steen; *mus* Paul Simon; *cast* Anne Bancroft (Mrs Robin-son), Dustin Hoffman (Ben Braddock), Katharine Ross (Elaine Robinson), William Daniels (Mr Braddock), Murray Hamilton (Mr Robinson), Elizabeth Wilson (Mrs Braddock).

Ben Braddock, coming down from college, is the victim of his parents' affluence, an object to be paraded before their friends. He is sexually initiated by Mrs Robinson, a frustrated neighbour, and falls in love with her daughter.

*The Graduate* was an immediate success, critically and commercially. NICHOLS's racy, elliptical narrative style and use of witty, brittle dialogue won him personal recognition and an OSCAR, while his view of middle-class aspirations gained him a following among young audiences who saw the film as enunciating the generation gap. The record of Simon and Garfunkel's music became a hit, especially the 'Mrs Robinson' track. Within a year the film was fourth in the list of North American box-office successes and still held fifth place five years later.

**GRANDE ILLUSION, La,** France, 1937. 2hr. *Dir* Jean Renoir; *prod* Réalisations d'Art Cinématographique; *scr* Charles Spaak, Renoir; *ph* Christian Matras; *des* Eugène Lourié; *ed* Marguerite Renoir; *mus* Joseph Kosma; *cast* Jean Gabin (Maréchal), Pierre Fresnay (Boïeldieu), Erich von Stroheim (von Rauffenstein), Marcel Dalio (Rosenthal), Dita Parlo (Elsa), Julien Carette (the actor), Gaston Modot (the engineer), Jean Dasté (the teacher).

After celebrating the ideal of working-class solidarity in LE CRIME DE MONSIEUR LANGE and *La Vie est à nous* (both 1936), RENOIR attempted to counter currently hardening nationalism with *La Grande Illusion*, looking back to the internationalist optimism so far best represented in cinema by PABST's KAMERADSCHAFT (1931). The adept combination of French, German, and English in the dialogue heightens the comparison.

Three French prisoners of war, an aristocrat Boïeldieu, an officer of proletarian origin Maréchal, and a Jew Rosenthal, demonstrate that patriotic duty must act against deeper allegiances: Boïeldieu's true affinity is with the commandant of the prison camp, von Rauffenstein, Maréchal's with the homely German woman who aids his escape, Rosenthal (absent from the original, more schematic, script) clings to no class or national identity.

By using the romantic world of the First World War cavalry officer Renoir blurred his intended message, instead becoming engagingly caught up in the details of aristocratic refinement and their contrast with the sturdy independence of the proletariat. Even the realistic representation of prison life is diluted by fluid camerawork and the interplay created by the use of DEEP FOCUS. The film's ambiguities probably helped its wide popularity: it appealed to Mussolini and won a special prize at the VENICE Film Festival in 1939—although it was later banned by the Nazis. Its enduring appeal is attributable, not to a secure political or social message, but to its irrepressible romanticism, sustained by performances of high quality by FRESNAY, GABIN, and STROHEIM.

**GRAND HOTEL**, US, 1932. 1¾hr. *Dir* Edmund Goulding; *prod* MGM; *scr* William A. Drake, from the novel by Vicki Baum; *ph* William Daniels; *cast* Greta Garbo (Grusinskaya), John Barrymore (Baron von Gaigern), Lionel Barrymore (Kringelein), Joan Crawford (Flaemmchen), Wallace Beery (Preysing).

Vicki Baum's novel, constructed from various stories occurring among the residents of a Berlin hotel, was well suited to the display of METRO-GOLDWYN-MAYER stars which was the film's purpose. *Grand Hotel* provided typical roles for the company's major talents, and it was the prototype in films of the popular device of bringing together a disparate group whose lives intersect in a coincidental way. The sharpness of Joan CRAWFORD's performance as the poor but self-reliant stenographer is outstanding; GARBO's moments of exquisite desolation compensate for her lamentable miscasting.

A German/French remake, *Menschen im Hotel* (Gottfried Reinhardt, 1959) starred Michèle MORGAN as the ballerina.

**GRANDSCOPE**, ANAMORPHIC WIDE SCREEN process developed in Japan by the Shochiku Company. It was designed to be compatible with CINEMASCOPE and has the same ASPECT RATIO, 2·35:1.

**GRANGER**, STEWART (1913– ), British actor, real name James Stewart, whose screen career began in 1938 with *So This is London*. His roles in a succession of GAINSBOROUGH melodramas, including *The Man in Grey* (1943) and *Fanny by Gaslight* (1944), made him a popular romantic star. He married Jean SIMMONS in 1950 (divorced 1960) and they left Britain for Hollywood where he branched out as a more energetic and polished actor, particularly in cheerful swashbuckling roles such as the white hunter in *King Solomon's Mines* (1950), *Scaramouche*, and *The Prisoner of Zenda* (both 1953). After more than ten years in Hollywood he worked in Italy and Germany before returning to British films. He has also worked in television, including playing Old Shatterhand in the German-made 'Winnetou' series.

**GRANOVSKY**, ALEXANDER (1890–1937), Russian-born director who was director of the

Jewish theatre in Moscow before making some silent films in the USSR, among them *Yevreiskoye schastye* (*Jewish Luck*, 1925) from a story by Sholem Aleichem. From the late twenties he worked first in Germany, then in France. *Les Aventures du roi Pausole* (1933), after Pierre Louÿs, is probably his best-known film: it was made in two versions, French starring André Berley, and German with Emil JANNINGS. *Les Nuits muscovites* (1934) was remade in England by Anthony ASQUITH as *Moscow Nights* (1935) with the same star, Harry Baur, and Laurence OLIVIER. Baur also starred, with Danielle DARRIEUX, in Granovsky's version of *Tarass Boulba* (1935).

**GRANT**, CARY (1904– ), US actor born in England, real name Alexander Archibald Leach. After playing supporting roles in stage musical comedies, he was offered a contract by PARAMOUNT and assumed the name by which he became famous.

He appeared in seven films in 1932, his first year in Hollywood, including *Blonde Venus*, with Marlene DIETRICH; his 'amiable assurance' was remarked on by a critic after his performance in *This Is the Night* and remained a hallmark of his style. It attracted Mae WEST who chose him to set off her own colourful personality in *She Done Him Wrong* (1933). In 1937 his contract with Paramount expired and he became Hollywood's first free-lance star.

Always considered the epitome of traditional Hollywood sophistication, especially in his partnerships with Katharine HEPBURN in HOLIDAY (1938) and THE PHILADELPHIA STORY (1940), Grant has perhaps received less credit for his talent as a comedian of rigorously controlled nonchalance. It is particularly evident in his films for Howard HAWKS, BRINGING UP BABY (1938), HIS GIRL FRIDAY (1940), and *I Was a Male War Bride* (1949, *You Can't Sleep Here* in GB), where the comedy is heightened by contrast with the essentially conventional characters. He was equally successful as the charming innocent caught up in mysterious and threatening events in films directed by HITCHCOCK: SUSPICION (1941), NOTORIOUS (1946), TO CATCH A THIEF (1955), and NORTH BY NORTHWEST (1959). *None but the Lonely Heart* (Clifford ODETS, 1944) gave him one of his rare tragic roles.

Grant's skilled technique and professionalism have earned the esteem of his fellow workers. He has also earned a reputation for helping newcomers by working with untried directors such as Delmer DAVES (*Destination Tokyo*, 1943), Richard BROOKS (*Crisis*, 1950), and Blake EDWARDS (*Operation Petticoat*, 1959). In 1968 he received the Producers Guild of America's annual Milestone Award for 'historic contributions to the motion picture industry' and in 1970 a special OSCAR for his contribution to American cinema. His second marriage (1942–5) was to the millionairess Barbara Hutton, his third (1949) to the film actress Betsy Drake.

**GRAPES OF WRATH, The,** US, 1940. 2¼hr. *Dir* John Ford; *prod* Darryl F. Zanuck for Twentieth Century-Fox; *ph* Gregg Toland; *scr* Nunnally Johnson, from the novel by John Steinbeck; *mus* Alfred Newman; *cast* Henry Fonda (Tom Joad), Jane Darwell (Ma Joad), John Carradine (Casey), Charley Grapewin (Grampa Joad), Dorris Bowdon (Rosasharn), Russell Simpson (Pa Joad), O. Z. Whitehead (Al), John Qualen (Muley), Zeffie Tilbury (Grandma Joad), Frank Darien (Uncle John).

The adaptation of John STEINBECK's novel of an impoverished dustbowl family's struggle to reach the orchards of California, and of the exploitation which awaited them, provided the material for one of the earliest Hollywood films to reveal a genuine social conscience and to attempt a realistic treatment of ordinary people. FORD drew uniformly notable performances from his excellent team of actors and was able to make effective use of studio 'exteriors' thanks to the beautifully lit and composed photography of Gregg TOLAND.

**GRAY,** ALLAN (1904–   ), Polish-born British composer who began writing film music for UFA in Berlin in 1931 and moved to England in 1936. After *Emil and the Detectives* (1936), he composed for numerous other British films of the period, but became particularly prominent in the mid-forties with his association with Michael POWELL and Emeric PRESSBURGER, including *The Life and Death of Colonel Blimp* (1943), *I Know Where I'm Going* (1945), and *A Matter of Life and Death* (1946, *Stairway to Heaven* in the US). His later scores included *Mr Perrin and Mr Traill* (1948), *The Late Edwina Black* (1951), and THE AFRICAN QUEEN (1952).

**GREAT BRITAIN.** The early history of cinema in Britain is bedevilled by claims and counter-claims. The first commercial showing has, however, been clearly established. This was in February 1896 when the work of the LUMIÈRE brothers was demonstrated before a paying audience at the Regent Polytechnic, London. Two British pioneers with a claim to have preceded this by private demonstrations were Birt Acres and R. W. PAUL. Acres also made the first British newsreel (of the Derby in 1895), and gave the first Royal Command Performance, at Marlborough House, in July 1896. Paul, a scientific instrument maker, gave the first commercial showing of a British-made film at Olympia in March 1896 and also seems to have been the first to sell films and cinema apparatus.

By the turn of the century films were being made and sold all over the country, mainly actualities and comedies with an average length of fifty feet. Films were sold directly by producer to exhibitor and were shown in fairgrounds, disused shops, and music halls. When exhibitors began to accumulate stocks of old films the idea of film rental was born and the first company to exploit the market was Walker and Turner who had been touring the music halls with the EDISON kinetoscope and phonograph since 1896. The company was reorganized as Walturdaw in 1905 and was active in distribution for many years. One of the first British production companies was founded as early as 1898 by Charles URBAN, an American emigré.

Technical innovations during the early years included various systems of synchronized disc recording, hand colouring as used by Paul, and the use of tinted stock. In 1906 a colour process, KINEMACOLOR, was patented by G. A. SMITH and was launched by the Urban Trading Co in 1908. Smith shares with Paul the credit for being an early exponent of trick films.

During its second decade the British film industry could be said to have established itself: trade associations were formed, the BRITISH BOARD OF FILM CENSORS was founded (in 1912) and the first cinema legislation, the Cinematograph Act 1909 was passed. The Act was mainly concerned with cinema licensing and safety precautions which were considered to be necessary because of the inflammable nature of NITRATE film.

Films themselves were becoming longer and more elaborate. Cecil HEPWORTH, who was one of the first to realize the imaginative possibilities of the medium, had made story films such as *Rescued by Rover* as early as 1905, and was now producing more ambitious subjects like *Black Beauty* (1907) and DAVID COPPERFIELD (1913) which ran to over two hours. Well-known theatre players were appearing in films, often screen adaptations of their stage successes and Forbes Robertson appeared in a Hepworth production of HAMLET in 1913. But the importation of foreign films was already causing a depression in the industry (it was estimated that only 15% of the films released in 1910 were British made) and the tendency was worsened by the outbreak of the First World War. An Import Tax was imposed in 1915 and in 1916 an Entertainments Tax had a severe effect on cinemas in the poorer districts. The open market system had come to an end and BLOCK BOOKING and the even more deplorable 'blind booking', in which films were sometimes booked before they had even been made, were now the rule. The quality of the British product was low and by the end of the war American films had obtained a stranglehold on the market.

Nevertheless there was a brighter side. Cecil Hepworth was still active and two important names had entered the scene: Maurice ELVEY, one of the most prolific of all British directors, and George PEARSON, a former schoolmaster, who made the first of the SHERLOCK HOLMES films, *A Study in Scarlet* (1914). Newsreels and actuality were being extensively used for PROPAGANDA purposes and this demand gave a boost to the documentarists. Britain's first film knight, Sir William Jury, was honoured for his services in the topical film and D. W. GRIFFITH was brought over, with the agreement of the War Office, to make HEARTS OF THE WORLD (1918).

The immediate post-war period was a depressing one, with American dominance continuing. Even successful British films, such as Pearson's cockney 'Squibs' comedies, starring Betty Balfour, were of limited value because they could not penetrate the American market. But it was during the apparently unproductive twenties that several men came into the industry who were later to help it to achieve international acclaim. They included Michael BALCON, who had his first success with *The Rat* (1925), Alfred HITCHCOCK whose first feature, *The Pleasure Garden*, also produced by Balcon, appeared in 1925, Thorold DICKINSON who began working with Pearson, Victor SAVILLE, Herbert WILCOX, and Graham Cutts. Wilcox and Cutts had a big success with *The Wonderful Lie* (1922) and Cutts was also the director of *Woman to Woman* (1923) which actually did well in the United States. It was financed by two more important newcomers, C. M. Woolf and Oscar Deutsch. In the late twenties Anthony ASQUITH, Adrian Brunel, and Walter Forde, also a popular comedian, made their first feature films.

In an effort to counter the overwhelming dominance of America the Cinematograph Films Act 1927 introduced a British QUOTA for the first time. Exhibitors were obliged to show a 5% quota of British films in the first six months, increasing by annual stages to 20% by 1935. The Act also outlawed block and blind booking. The defensive quota produced a great increase in British production but its long-term effect was to encourage the making of cheap and inferior films simply to fill the quota—the notorious 'quota quickies' of the thirties. The Act was also responsible for the beginning of 'vertical integration' in the industry, with large companies controlling production, distribution, and exhibition. 1927 saw the floating of the huge GAUMONT BRITISH Picture Corporation as well as the formation of British International Pictures and the BRITISH LION Film Corporation. This can now be

seen as the beginning of the establishment of the powerful circuits which were eventually to dominate releases in Britain.

An interesting development in the twenties was the setting up in London in 1925 of the FILM SOCIETY by a group of intellectuals who were aware of developments in the cinema outside the English-speaking world and were anxious to see the best of European and Russian cinema. One of the Society's programmes included John GRIERSON's *Drifters* (1929), a study of North Sea fishing which was to be a seminal influence on the British documentary movement of the thirties. Similar societies were springing up in universities and in the provinces. They were the forerunners of the film society movement which, until the coming of television, provided the only means by which British filmgoers could see anything outside the normal run of commercial releases.

The coming of sound was as traumatic in Britain as everywhere else. The success of 'all-talking, all-singing' films from America resulted in a wild scramble to wire studios and cinemas for the new techniques. The first British talkie was Hitchcock's BLACKMAIL (1929) which made intelligent use of the new possibilities, but the effect of sound on most producers was to make them rely more heavily than ever on theatrical successes and on actors from the West End. An early exception was Asquith's *Tell England* (1931, *Battle of Gallipoli* in US) and it was followed by three Saville successes *Sunshine Susie* (1932), *The Good Companions* (1933), and *Evergreen* (1934) in all of which stage players were disciplined to the demands of the medium. Hitchcock too was going his triumphal way with a series of thrillers—THE MAN WHO KNEW TOO MUCH (1934), THE THIRTY-NINE STEPS (1935), and SABOTAGE (1936, *A Woman Alone* in US). Stars from the music-hall also made notable contributions to popular screen entertainment and the thirties saw successful films featuring George FORMBY, Gracie FIELDS, and Will HAY.

Meanwhile Grierson and his team at the Empire Marketing Board, and later the GPO Film Unit, were establishing the mainstream of British documentary with such films as SONG OF CEYLON (1934), *Coal Face*, and NIGHT MAIL (both 1936). Industrial sponsorship was also responsible for a number of good films of the period such as *Housing Problems* (1935), *Children at School* (1937), and *The Future is in the Air* (1937).

The outstanding figure in the entertainment film at this time was a Hungarian emigré, Alexander KORDA, who produced and directed THE PRIVATE LIFE OF HENRY VIII (1933), an exuberant romp bearing a minimal relation to history but having the gloss and panache to make it a box-office success on both sides of the Atlantic. This success enormously increased the self-confidence of British producers. Korda himself, a man of immense charm and persuasiveness, obtained a loan from the Prudential Assurance Company and set about building expensive studios at Denham. His spirit of adventure inspired others and the next few years saw the success of Saville's *The Iron Duke* (1935), Wilcox's *Sorrell and Son* (1934) and *Nell Gwyn* (1934) and, from Korda's LONDON FILMS itself *The Scarlet Pimpernel* (1934), *Sanders of the River* (1935), *The Ghost Goes West* (1935), THINGS TO COME (1936), and REMBRANDT (1936). A curious sideline of the Korda enterprise was the commissioning of Robert FLAHERTY to go to India to film, in collaboration with Zoltan KORDA, a spectacular Kipling story, ELEPHANT BOY (1936). Its leading man, a young Indian called SABU, became one of the cinema's more unlikely stars.

The boom in expensive productions was short-lived. War clouds were gathering over Europe and native production was most successful when it was most typically British, as in Saville's *South Riding* (1938), Carol REED's *Bank Holiday* (1938), and Asquith's PYGMALION (1938). There was a brief period of American activity in British studios when METRO-GOLDWYN-MAYER set up production in England and made three curious 'mid-Atlantic' films featuring American stars in British settings. They were *A Yank at Oxford* (1937), *The Citadel* (1938), and *Goodbye Mr Chips* (1939). All three were popular successes in Britain.

The outbreak of war put a stop to all such activity and more than half of the country's studio space was taken over by the government for the making of propaganda films. The GPO Film Unit was transferred to the Ministry of Information and became the CROWN FILM UNIT. The years of training in documentary began to pay dividends. Not only were straight propaganda films of real merit being produced—*London Can Take It* (1940), *Target for Tonight* (1940), *Coastal Command* (1942)—but the spirit and vitality of the documentary movement spilled over into the feature field inspiring such films as Thorold Dickinson's *The Next of Kin* (1941), Leslie HOWARD's *The First of the Few* (1942), Charles FREND's *The Foreman Went to France* (1942). The movement also produced, in Humphrey JENNINGS, a poet of the documentary whose best work, LISTEN TO BRITAIN (1942) and FIRES WERE STARTED (1943) summed up the spirit of Britain at war. The patriotic propaganda impulse which was responsible for some of the best films of the time was also essentially the force which enabled Filippo DEL GIUDICE, an Italian producer, to raise the funds to back

HENRY V (1944). Laurence OLIVIER was released from the navy to direct and star in this expensive and spectacular version of Shakespeare's play. The film was distributed by the RANK ORGANISATION, which developed into a huge vertical combine with J. Arthur RANK chairman of Gaumont-British and the ODEON group. Some other names which came into prominence during the war included David LEAN—IN WHICH WE SERVE (1942), BRIEF ENCOUNTER (1945); POWELL and PRESSBURGER—*49th Parallel* (1941), *A Matter of Life and Death* (1946); Carol Reed—*Kipps* (1941), *The Way Ahead* (1944).

At the end of the Second World War Britain could be said to have achieved a genuinely indigenous school of film-making. Attendances at the country's 4,700 cinemas had risen to 1,462 millions in 1947 and there was pressure on the government to release studio space. But although production began to climb many of the films were expensive prestige productions such as Gabriel PASCAL's CAESAR AND CLEOPATRA (1945) which did not achieve the hoped-for financial returns. Films about the war continued to be popular at British box-offices and this trend continued into the late fifties. A whole generation of actors grew up in uniform, displaying the stiff upper lip in such films as *The Captive Heart* (1945), *The Wooden Horse* (1950), *Odette* (1950), *Angels One Five* (1952), *The Colditz Story* (1955), *The Dam Busters* (1955), *Reach for the Sky* (1956), THE BRIDGE ON THE RIVER KWAI (1957).

In 1947 the government imposed a 75% tax on foreign film imports and the United States promptly placed an embargo on the export of films to Britain. The sudden shortage of American films was a challenge to British production and the new Cinematograph Films Act put the British quota up to 45%. But production costs were high and the emphasis was still on lavish, spectacular productions, with disastrous results. When an agreement was signed with the MOTION PICTURE ASSOCIATION OF AMERICA in 1948 a flood of American films suddenly hit the market and at the same time the Americans were obliged to spend 75% of their British earnings to make American films in British studios. The British industry was in its familiar state of crisis. Nevertheless the still faithful audiences were able to see such genuine British films as Reed's ODD MAN OUT (1947) and THE FALLEN IDOL (1948), Lean's GREAT EXPECTATIONS (1946) and OLIVER TWIST (1948), Olivier's HAMLET (1948), and Powell and Pressburger's THE RED SHOES (1948).

The middle forties also saw the emergence of the Ealing film. Balcon had now gathered around him at EALING STUDIOS a team of directors, writers, and technicians who believed that the way to the international market was to capture and exploit the essential national spirit, with all its oddities and humour. For ten years (1946–56) they produced a series of successes, mainly comedies, such as *Hue and Cry* (1947), KIND HEARTS AND CORONETS (1949), THE LAVENDER HILL MOB (1951), THE MAN IN THE WHITE SUIT (1951), and *The Ladykillers* (1955).

Meanwhile, in 1949, the NATIONAL FILM FINANCE CORPORATION, a government-sponsored bank to advance loans for independent production, was inaugurated and in 1950 came the BRITISH FILM PRODUCTION FUND (also known as the Eady levy) whereby a voluntary levy on box-office receipts is returned to the producer. Under the 1957 Cinematograph Films Act this levy became statutory. But none of these aid schemes altered the hard fact that in order to cover its cost a British film must succeed in foreign markets, particularly in the United States.

In addition to its other troubles the industry was now facing increasing competition from television. In 1958 an organization FIDO (Film Industry Defence Organization) was set up to buy television rights of cinema films in order to prevent their transmission on the small screen.

The depressed state of production in the fifties gave rise to efforts by young film-makers to make reputations outside the industry. This was the impulse behind the FREE CINEMA movement which used the NATIONAL FILM THEATRE to show independently made films, not only from Britain, but also from France, Poland, and America. Among the film-makers whose early films were publicized in this way were Roman POLAŃSKI, Claude CHABROL, Lindsay ANDERSON, Karel REISZ, and Tony RICHARDSON.

But the influence which really changed the face of the British film in the late fifties came not from the film-makers themselves, however talented. It came from literature and the theatre, where a new group of young writers, dubbed 'angry young men' by journalists, had successfully broken with West End tradition and were setting their novels and plays among the provincial working class. Ironically enough the first breakthrough film was made by a traditional mainstream producer-turned-director, Jack CLAYTON, and produced by John Woolf, son of pioneer C. M. Woolf. ROOM AT THE TOP (1958), adapted from John Braine's novel about a north-country careerist, was remarkable in its day for the frankness of its treatment of class, money, and sex. Its people fornicated, drank, brawled, and worked for a living. Tony Richardson's film of the seminal play of the time, OSBORNE'S LOOK BACK IN ANGER followed in the same year. After that, the floodgates were open and Britain's 'new wave' rolled on with Reisz's SATURDAY NIGHT AND SUNDAY MORNING (1960), Richardson's A

TASTE OF HONEY (1961), Lindsay Anderson's THIS SPORTING LIFE (1963), John SCHLESINGER'S *A Kind of Loving* (1962). All of these dealt with working-class life in industrial areas and all were adaptations from other mediums.

Mainstream production went on however with such respectable costume dramas as Asquith's *The Doctor's Dilemma* (1959), Ken Hughes's *The Trials of Oscar Wilde* (1960), and Jack CARDIFF's *Sons and Lovers* (1960). There was also a continuance of the steady stream of horror movies, largely produced by HAMMER FILMS. These were so expertly made (often by Terence Fisher) that they were very profitable in foreign markets and even became the subject of a minor cult in France. But the outstanding popular successes of the period were TOM JONES (1963) in which Tony Richardson and his leading actor, Albert FINNEY, suddenly deserted contemporary realism for a joyful period romp, and Terence Young's *Dr No* (1962), the first of the JAMES BOND spy thrillers which became annual money-makers for the next ten years and made an international star out of an obscure Scots actor, Sean CONNERY.

The Bond phenomenon was an early indication of the rush of American capital and influence into British cinema in the sixties. American producers were attracted to London by Eady money, by England's convenience as a European centre, by the common language and by the high standard of British actors and technicians. For a while London became the film capital of the world and in 1968 nearly 90% of the capital invested in British features was American. But the boom was short-lived; America soon had her own balance of payments problems, indigenous US production suddenly improved and the American companies began to withdraw not only their production activities but also their distribution bases. Cinema attendances continued to decline through the sixties and by 1970 the number of theatres was down to 1,529. Twinning and tripling of cinemas had by 1973 just begun to increase the number of screens available, although in smaller auditoriums, and the admissions figure for 1974 showed the first increase (from 142 to 143 millions) in over twenty years.

Inevitably, the preponderance of American and other foreign participation during the sixties and seventies has meant that very few films could be described as genuinely British. Outstanding among the expatriates working in England are Joseph LOSEY—THE SERVANT (1963), ACCIDENT (1967), THE GO-BETWEEN (1971); · Richard LESTER—A HARD DAY'S NIGHT (1965), *How I Won the War* (1967); Stanley Kubrick—2001: A SPACE ODYSSEY (1968), A CLOCKWORK ORANGE (1971); Roman Polański—CUL DE SAC

(1966), MACBETH (1971). British directors who consolidated their careers in this period include Anderson, Reisz, Schlesinger, and Bryan FORBES, who for a brief period headed production at Elstree. New reputations have been made by John BOORMAN—*Catch Us if You Can* (1965), *Zardoz* (1974); Ken RUSSELL—*Women in Love* (1969), *The Boy Friend* (1971), *Mahler* (1974); and Ken LOACH—KES (1970), *Family Life* (1971). All three obtained their early experience in television.

An oddity of the situation in the mid-seventies is that while studio space is being cut to a minimum films are being made in Britain for US television or for subscription showing in US theatres. It seems unlikely that these will ever be shown on the two main commercial circuits which still dominate the exhibition scene but they may eventually be seen on television where much of the best of world cinema is already being shown. Meanwhile the commercial producers continue to seek the safe subject, preferably with an all-star cast, which can be sold all over the world. A successful example is the thriller *Murder on the Orient Express* (1974).

It could be said that there has been very little change in the seventy-odd years of British cinema. It still depends on American markets, relies on pre-digested subjects from other arts and still tends to drive its best talents to seek better outlets across the Atlantic.

Raymond Durgnat, *A mirror for England*, London, 1970; Denis Gifford, *British film catalogue, 1895–1970*, Newton Abbot, 1973; Rachael Low, *The history of the British film*, 4 vols, London, 1948–71; Political and Economic Planning, *The British film industry*, London, 1952; Alexander Walker, *Hollywood, England*, London, 1974.

**GREAT DICTATOR, The,** US, 1940. 2hr. *Dir, prod, scr* Charles Chaplin, assisted by Dan James, Wheeler Dryden, Bob Meltzer; *ph* Rollie Totheroh, Karl Struss; *des* J. Russell Spenser; *ed* William Nico; *mus* Charles Chaplin; *cast* Charlie Chaplin (Hynkel and the barber), Paulette Goddard (Hannah), Jack Oakie (Napaloni), Reginald Gardner (Schultz), Henry Daniell (Garbitsch), Billy Gilbert (Herring).

CHAPLIN's first film to use sound fully has as its subject Hitler and Nazi Germany and is the most direct attack in any of his films. While it was being made, most Americans still thought their country would never go to war against Germany. War was declared during production but, as with SHOULDER ARMS (1918), Chaplin pressed on. Again he was right and only in Chicago was the film refused a licence (perhaps because of the large German population there).

Chaplin plays a dual role—as Hynkel, dictator of Tomania, a brilliant impersonation of Hitler, and a ghetto barber who has more than a hint of the Tramp. When the barber is mistaken for the Dictator, the persecuted Jew has the opportunity to speak to the world. His six-minute speech, the climax of the film, is a strong plea for tolerance, humanity, peace, and individual freedom.

The film's ultimate failure lies in its remoteness from the intense personal experience which informs his best films and in its confused tone, which shifts uneasily between slapstick, satire, pathos, and anger. But the sequences conceived in silent film terms, especially Hynkel's megalomaniac balloon dance with a globe, display Chaplin's early mastery of the medium, and Jack Oakie's caricature of Mussolini is memorable.

**GREAT EXPECTATIONS,** GB, 1946. 2hr. *Dir* David Lean; *prod* Lean, Ronald Neame for Cineguild; *scr* Lean, Neame, from the novel by Charles Dickens; *ph* Guy Green; *des* John Bryan; *mus* Walter Goehr; *cast* John Mills (Pip), Valerie Hobson (Estella), Finlay Currie (Magwitch), Francis L. Sullivan (Jaggers), Bernard Miles (Joe Gargery), Alec Guinness (Herbert Pocket), Martita Hunt (Miss Havisham), Anthony Wager (Pip as a boy), Jean Simmons (Estella as a girl), Freda Jackson (Mrs Gargery).

Directed by David LEAN with great intelligence and narrative skill, Charles DICKENS's over-sized characters are effectively reduced to cinema scale: the acting and dialogue (much of it taken directly from the novel) avoid the theatricality of so many British adaptations of the kind. The film's good looks were recognized in the OSCARS won by its photographer Guy Green and designer John Bryan. The scenes on the Medway saltings and in the cobweb-draped house of the eccentric Miss Havisham are especially memorable. The many excellent performances include Alec GUINNESS's first screen appearance.

Other film adaptations of *Great Expectations* include: a FAMOUS PLAYERS production of 1917, starring Jack Pickford; a Danish version of 1923; a worthy if dispirited version from UNIVERSAL in 1934; and a Swiss production directed by Leopold H. Ginner and shown at the San Remo Festival in 1971.

**GREAT McGINTY, The** (*Down Went McGinty* in GB), US, 1940. 1½hr. *Dir, scr* Preston Sturges; *prod* Paramount; *ph* William Mellor; *cast* Brian Donlevy (Dan McGinty), Muriel Angelus (Catherine), Akim Tamiroff (the boss), William Demarest (the politician), Allyn Joslyn (George).

The naïve McGinty is elected governor by

corrupt means. After an attempt to clean up the local intrigues, he is forced to abandon the political arena.

Preston STURGES's first film sets the style of his best work in the brilliance of its comic timing and the sharpness of the script (which won an OSCAR). It remains one of the best satires on American politics.

**GREAT TRAIN ROBBERY, The,** US, 1903. 10min. *Dir* Edwin S. Porter; *prod* Edison Co; *cast* George Barnes, Frank Hanaway, G. M. Anderson, Marie Murray, A. C. Abadie.

The hold-up and robbery of a train and the pursuit and defeat of the bandits is told in fourteen scenes, each continuous and unedited but skilfully balanced to provide a strong narrative flow. All the scenes are in long-shot except the last, a close-up of the gang leader firing point-blank at the audience; exhibitors were recommended to use this startling device at either the beginning or end of the film.

*The Great Train Robbery* was one of the most successful and profoundly influential of the early narrative films and PORTER's style of story-telling was widely emulated for some years. It launched Broncho Billy ANDERSON, the screen's first cowboy hero.

**GREDE,** KJELL (1936–   ), Swedish director. Originally a teacher of maladjusted children, Grede worked as an assistant to BERGMAN before directing his first feature film, a study of the friendship of two lonely children *Hugo och Josefin* (1968). The film appealed successfully to both child and adult audiences, and received critical praise for its delicate, unsentimental handling, and lyrical visual style. His second film, *Harry Munter* (1969), explores the life of an adolescent who tries to adjust to the world by helping a series of misfits he collects around him. *Klara Lust* (1972) has a similar theme, and again Grede attempted to invest the real world with a quality of child-like fantasy. Both *Harry Munter* and *Klara Lust* met with a rather uneasy critical reception, although confirming Grede as an original and thoughtful new contributor to the Swedish cinema.

**GREECE.** The first Greek film appeared in 1912, but the development of a film industry there was beset by difficulties: a small and poor country, Greece has been recurrently ravaged by war and political turmoil. In the ten years from 1922 there were fourteen changes of government: there could be little investment in the cinema in these unsettled conditions, and production during this decade averaged only two or three films a year. The introduction of sound accentuated the problem. Lacking the funds for sound equipment, Greek studios settled for a system of post-synchronization which was often carried out abroad. Production reached its lowest point during the German occupation (only one film was made between 1940 and 1942), but after the war a more hopeful epoch began. Studios were equipped efficiently for the first time and the output of films rapidly increased: 6 films were made in 1947, 28 in 1957, and by 1967 over 70 films a year were being produced. Film criticism, although it had begun in 1919, started to flourish after 1945. In 1950 the Union of Athens Film Critics was formed, together with the first Greek ciné-club, and the Greek Ciné-mathèque was founded in 1957. The first Greek film school had been formed in 1920 but had rapidly collapsed, and it was not until 1951 that an efficient film school was set up, Lycourgos Stavrakos's Film Academy. Other schools opened during the fifties, but all are severely hampered by lack of funds.

Despite the lack of government aid, the relatively long post-war period of political stability contributed to the emergence of a real Greek cinema. The influence of Italian NEO-REALISM was readily absorbed and given a strongly national flavour in the work of the so-called Athenian school; some of their best films were *Pikro psoni* (*Bitter Bread*) directed by Grigoriou in 1951, Iliadis's *Necropolitis* (*The Dead City*, 1951), the first Greek film to be presented at CANNES, Greg Tallas's *The Barefoot Battalion* (1953), Tzavellos's *Kalpike liva* (*The Counterfeit Sovereign*, 1955), CACOYANNIS's *Stella* (1955) and TO KORITSI ME TA MAVRA (*The Girl in Black*, 1955), and the films of Koundouros, such as *Magici polis* (*The Magic City*, 1954) and *To Potami* (*The River*, 1960). For the most part, Greek film-makers have been reticent in drawing on classical literature; because of the exigencies of political censorship, they have equally avoided subjects from Greece's more recent history, Kanellopoulos's *Sky* (1962) dealing with the Italian invasion and Ado KYROU's *Bloko* (1965) set during the German occupation being notable exceptions.

During the sixties the growth of commercial cinema made it increasingly difficult for serious young film-makers to find producers. The commercial mainstream is of a low standard, consisting largely of melodramas and Westerns transposed to a local setting which are vastly popular in the villages where there is still a high rate of semi-literacy. In 1960 the state began to take an interest in the industry and passed legislation to foster national production and to encourage foreign investment. The relatively cheap production costs—$100,000 to make POTE TIN KYRIAKI (*Never on Sunday*, 1959)—and ideal climatic conditions attracted a spate of co-productions including *The Guns of Navarone* (1961), *It Happened in Athens* (1961), and *Zorba the Greek* (1965). While these foreign productions have done much for the Greek tourist trade, truly Greek films have made little international impact.

**GREED**, US, 1923. 2½hr (but see below). *Dir*, *scr* Erich von Stroheim, from the novel *McTeague* by Frank Norris; *prod* MGM; *ph* Ben Reynolds, William Daniels; *des* Stroheim, Richard Day; *cast* Gibson Gowland (McTeague), ZaSu Pitts (Trina), Jean Hersholt (Marcus), Cesare Gravina (Zerkow), Dale Fuller (Maria), Chester Conklin (Popper Sieppe), Sylvia Ashton (Mommer Sieppe), Tempe Piggott (McTeague's mother).

STROHEIM filmed Norris's novel with absolute fidelity and ended up with a film ten hours long. The film's completion coincided with the merger of the Goldwyn Co that resulted in the formation of METRO-GOLDWYN-MAYER and brought Stroheim's old enemy Irving THALBERG in as head of production. He insisted that Stroheim shorten the film which, at 24 reels instead of the original 42, was then handed over to Rex INGRAM who edited it down to 18 reels (4½hr); it was then passed by the producers to an anonymous studio cutter who reduced it to its present length.

The surviving version of *Greed* can therefore give only an outline of Stroheim's conception. Both sub-plots, intended to counterpoint the main story of McTeague's marriage and gradual degradation, were excised; but the closely-knit nature of the narrative leaves confusing references to these sub-plots in the remaining parts. Cesare Gravina's role disappeared altogether although his name is retained on the credits. Even in its mutilated form *Greed* is an undeniably powerful work and Stroheim's skill is here probably at its best in depicting character against meticulously-observed settings (the film was made almost entirely in the locations described in the novel) and there are fine performances from his company of favourite actors including ZaSu PITTS in her first serious role.

*The complete Greed*, Herman G. Weinberg (New York, 1972).

**GREEN**, ADOLPH, see COMDEN AND GREEN

**GREENE**, GRAHAM (1904– ), British novelist, journalist, and playwright. His novels, with their racy plots and seedy milieux, have frequently been adapted for the screen. *This Gun For Hire* (1942), *The Ministry of Fear* (1944), *Confidential Agent* (1945), *The Fugitive* (1947) from *The Power and the Glory*, *The End of the Affair* (1954), *The Quiet American* (1958), and *Travels with My Aunt* (1972) are among the

films derived from his work; but the theme of spiritual redemption through degradation which is a vital element of his Catholic philosophy has usually been neglected by film-makers. His most successful film collaborations were with Carol REED, for whom he wrote THE FALLEN IDOL (1948) and THE THIRD MAN (1949). Among his other original screenplays are *Twenty-One Days* (1940), adapted from John Galsworthy's *The First and the Last*; *Went the Day Well?* (Alberto CAVALCANTI, 1942); and Otto PREMINGER's *Saint Joan* (1957, see JOAN OF ARC); he also scripted *Brighton Rock* (1947), *Our Man in Havana* (1959), and *The Comedians* (1967) from his own novels. He appeared, incognito, in a small role in LA NUIT AMÉRICAINE (*Day for Night*, 1973).

Greene was a perceptive film critic, notably for the *Spectator* 1935–40. He was also literary editor of the short-lived magazine *Night and Day*, which was forced to close after two costly lawsuits. In one of these, Greene's review of *Wee Willie Winkie* (1937) was sued by TWENTIETH CENTURY-FOX, acting for Shirley TEMPLE, for libel; the case, settled out of court, cost the magazine £3,500.

A selection of his film reviews has been published as *The Pleasure Dome* (London, 1972).

**GREENSTREET**, SYDNEY, later Sidney (1879–1954), British actor who worked on the American stage from 1905. He made a sensational film début as the Fat Man in John HUSTON's THE MALTESE FALCON (1941). His individual personality and forceful presence enabled him to overcome the limitations imposed by his considerable bulk, which largely confined him to variations of the Fat Man role. He was featured in a long succession of WARNER BROS films of the forties, among the best-known being *Across the Pacific* (1942), CASABLANCA (1943), *Passage to Marseilles*, and *The Mask of Dimitrios* (both 1944).

**GREENWOOD**, JOAN (1921– ), British actress, started her stage career at seventeen. Since her first screen appearance, in *John Smith Wakes Up* (1940), she has attracted a comparatively small but discriminating following with her witty, intelligent performances in such films as KIND HEARTS AND CORONETS (1949), THE MAN IN THE WHITE SUIT (1951), *The Importance of Being Earnest* (1952), and TOM JONES (1963).

**GREGOR**, NORA (d 1949), Austrian actress, played mainly on the stage in Vienna during the twenties, but also had parts in several silent films in Germany, including CZINNER's *Der Geiger von Florenz* (1926), with Conrad VEIDT and Elisabeth BERGNER. In 1924 she acted in DREYER's *Mikaël*, made in Germany, and she had parts in five German sound films, three of them German versions made in Hollywood. She also appeared in *But the Flesh is Weak* (1932). An actress without obvious glamour and of some reserve, reflecting perhaps her role in real life as Princess Stahrenberg, wife of an Austrian diplomatist, she is best known for her role as the Marquis's wife in RENOIR'S LA RÈGLE DU JEU (1939), which she invested with dignity and warm simplicity. She committed suicide in 1949.

**GRÉMILLON, JEAN** (1901–59), French director, studied music and became a violinist in the small orchestras of various Paris cinemas. He was later to write the music for many of his films. In 1923 he started, in collaboration with a friend, a series of documentaries, and made an ABSTRACT FILM *Photogénie mécanique* (1924). Throughout his career he was equally at home with documentary, *Bobs* (1928), *Haute Lisse* (1956), or melodrama, *Les Gardiens de la phare* (1928), *L'Amour d'une femme* (1953). During the war he worked in Vichy France, directing *Lumière d'été* (1942) and *Le Ciel est à vous* (1943). He was president of the CINÉMATHÈQUE FRANÇAISE 1943–8. He made a number of short films, among them *Le Six Juin à l'aube* (1945), a bitter record of the Allied landings in northern France, and *André Masson et les quatre éléments* (1959). Grémillon's gently dogged independence limited his opportunities and such films as he made are all too rarely seen. His reputation is not as high as the quality of his films deserves.

**GRIDO, Il** (*The Cry*), Italy, 1957. 1¾hr. *Dir* Michelangelo Antonioni; *prod* SPA Cinematografica; *scr* Antonioni, Ennio De Concini, Elio Bartolini; *ph* Gianni Di Venanzo; *des* Franco Fontana; *ed* Eraldo Da Roma; *mus* Giovanni Fusco; *cast* Steve Cochran (Aldo), Alida Valli (Irma), Betsy Blair (Elvira), Dorian Gray (Virginia), Gabriella Pallotta (Edera), Lynn Shaw (Andreina).

Aldo, working in a sugar refinery in the Po valley, lives with Irma, whose husband has long deserted her. Irma learns of her husband's death and tells Aldo she wants to marry another man. He beats her in front of the village and goes away with their daughter, drifting from place to place and from woman to woman: when he returns and is rejected by Irma, he falls to his death from a tower of the refinery.

*Il grido* reverses ANTONIONI's preoccupation with women and their relationships with men to focus on the man, showing him lost and ineffectual when he can no longer take the traditional role *vis-à-vis* women. DI VENANZO's photography beautifully conveys the bleakness of Aldo's physical and mental landscape; but, partly because of

inadequate acting in some important roles and partly because the preoccupations seem too rarefied for a working man's life, the film does not carry great conviction.

**GRIERSON, JOHN** (1898–1972), British documentary producer. Grierson's film career began when he went to America in 1924 to study the relationship between the mass media and public opinion, in particular Hollywood's potential for mass persuasion and education. While there he translated the subtitles of BRONENOSETS POTEMKIN (1925), met Robert FLAHERTY, and in a review of MOANA in 1926 first applied the word 'documentary' to cinema.

On returning to Britain in 1927, Grierson became Films Officer to the Empire Marketing Board, having persuaded Stephen Tallents, Secretary of the EMB, of the value of film as a tool of democracy; in an increasingly complex society film could disseminate information in a form accessible to everyone. Grierson devised a programme of appropriate films including *Potemkin* and BERLIN, DIE SYMPHONIE EINER GROSSSTADT (1927) and himself made *Drifters* (1929), a study of herring-fishers in the North Sea. Following its success he founded, with himself as producer, the EMB Film Unit (see CROWN FILM UNIT). Flaherty's INDUSTRIAL BRITAIN (1933) was made under its auspices with Grierson supervising the film's completion. The Unit was moved to the General Post Office in 1933.

Aware of the importance of publicizing their activities Grierson and his disciples gave lectures and wrote regularly for *Cinema Quarterly* (1932–5) and *World Film News* (1936–8). A report by Grierson in 1933 led to the foundation of the SHELL FILM UNIT; the creation of Film Centre, a consultative and administrative agency, by Grierson, Arthur ELTON, Stuart LEGG, and J. P. R. Golightly, furthered documentary's expansion into non-government areas. SONG OF CEYLON (1934) and NIGHT MAIL (1936), consolidated documentary's aesthetic achievement.

Grierson resigned from the GPO in 1937. Already consultant to THE MARCH OF TIME and production adviser to the Films of Scotland Committee, Grierson was invited to Canada in 1938 to assess the possibilities of government film production there; the NATIONAL FILM BOARD of Canada resulted, with Grierson as Film Commissioner. He was General Manager of the Canadian Wartime Information Board 1942–3.

Resigning in 1945, Grierson formed International Film Associates in New York with Legg and Raymond SPOTTISWOODE, to promote the internationalist concept of documentary. However, the conviction of a former NFB secretary for espionage involved Grierson in the ensuing anti-Communist scare. In 1947 he went to Paris as Director of Mass Communications and Public Information for UNESCO, but was frustrated by lack of funds. After two years as Film Controller of the British Central Office of Information, hindered by the controlling bureaucracy, Grierson became involved in 1951 in fiction film as an executive producer with GROUP THREE. From 1955 he served on the reconstituted Films of Scotland Committee, and he presented selections of excerpts from international documentary for Scottish Television in 'This Wonderful World' 1957–68.

His direct participation in film-making was always limited to ships and the sea: *Drifters*; an unfinished project, *The Port of London*; *Granton Trawler* (with Edgar ANSTEY, 1934); a small photographic contribution to Julian HUXLEY's *Private Life of the Gannets* (1934); and the treatment for *Seawards the Great Ships* (Hilary Harris), which won an OSCAR in 1961. A selection from his many theoretical, historical, and critical writings has been published in *Grierson on documentary* (London, 1946, revised ed, 1966), edited by Forsyth Hardy.

**GRIFFITH,** DAVID WARK (1875–1948), US director, one of the most significant figures in the history of film, became involved with the cinema almost unwillingly. His ambition was to be a writer, and after a somewhat impoverished childhood in Kentucky, he left home at an early age to join a travelling theatre company as an actor and would-be playwright.

His first contact with the movies was in 1907, when the financial failure of his play, *A Fool and a Girl*, forced him into the more lucrative, if disreputable, occupation of selling plots and synopses to film companies. He was soon recruited as an actor at the BIOGRAPH Company, where he had successfully sold several stories, and appeared in Edwin S. PORTER's *Rescued from an Eagle's Nest* (1907). In 1908 Biograph, which had not yet found a satisfactory director, offered Griffith the chance of making a film. He approached the task with characteristic energy, thoroughness, and ambition. He briefed himself thoroughly on the technical aspects from one of the Biograph cameramen, Billy BITZER, who was to become one of his closest collaborators, and cast the film with particular care. Although *The Adventures of Dolly* (1908) was no better than the average one-reel melodrama of the time, it convinced Biograph of Griffith's competence. He rapidly established himself as the company's chief director, and within a couple of years Biograph films were being recognized, by critics and public alike, as far superior to rival products.

Griffith's understanding of the medium was precocious; almost from the outset his films were infused with a remarkable inventive energy and creative intuition. In the hundreds of one-reelers which he turned out in the months following *The Adventures of Dolly*, he began to discover the elements and essence of cinematic expression. His early work at Biograph includes innovations such as the change of camera set-up within a scene, and the use of the full-shot (*For Love of Gold*, 1908); the expressive use of the close-up—formerly seen only as a stunt effect in THE GREAT TRAIN ROBBERY (1903)—in *After Many Years* (1908); dramatic lighting in *The Drunkard's Reformation* (1909) and *Pippa Passes* (1909). In *The Lonely Villa* (1909) and *The Lonedale Operator* (1911) he developed the technique of crosscutting, integral to the construction of his own major works and indeed to the development of the narrative film.

Ironically, it was Griffith, the man of the theatre, who did most to free the cinema of its heritage as the poor relation of the theatre. His discoveries led him further and further away from the static, theatrical style of construction and presentation characteristic of the early cinema. Griffith established the shot, rather than the scene, as the basis of cinematic construction and made editing a crucial component. He discovered that camera movement was a major means of expression, and that the cinema could rival the fluid narrative rhythm of a novel.

As he moved the camera nearer to his actors, Griffith became aware of the need for a more naturalistic style of acting. He had a gift for discovering acting talent, and built up a fine stock company. Mary PICKFORD, Blanche SWEET, Mabel NORMAND, the GISH sisters, and Mae MARSH became famous as the waif-like heroines of Griffith's films. Among leading male actors were Donald CRISP, Henry B. WALTHALL, Robert Harron, and Lionel BARRYMORE. Unlike other pioneer directors, he was meticulous in rehearsing his actors and paid good wages.

In 1910 Griffith began taking his company to winter in California where he found the rich variety of natural location stimulating. He began to discover how to create atmosphere on film. *The Thread of Destiny* (1910), probably the first film to attempt an evocation of atmosphere, built up the religious setting required by the story through an accumulation of purely descriptive shots of the location, an old Mission building.

He was ready to expand his range of expression beyond the confines of the one-reel film. Ignoring the protests of his Biograph producers, he made the first American two-reeler, *Enoch Arden*, in 1911. This was an expanded version of his earlier success, *After Many Years*.

Having established this new freedom, he embarked on an ambitious project—a film dramatization of Darwin's theory of evolution. In retrospect, the main merit of *Man's Genesis*

(1912) is that it gained a certain intellectual prestige for the movies, proving that they could aspire to deal with serious topics. Also in 1912 he made *Musketeers of Pig Alley*, set in a New York slum.

Among the numerous films he made in 1913, *The Massacre*, a historical reconstruction of Custer's last stand, and *The Mothering Heart* were particularly sophisticated in execution. These two films, the one historical epic, the other sentimental drama, are representative of the two genres which predominate in Griffith's work. In his later films individual, intimate drama is played against, or juxtaposed with, epic spectacle.

Griffith was already acknowledged as the master of American cinema, but his fame was temporarily eclipsed by the irruption of European films on to the American market. Examples of the FILM D'ART, and more particularly the Italian epic QUO VADIS (1913), were found impressively sophisticated by American audiences. Griffith in turn was stimulated to produce his most grandiose work yet. *Judith of Bethulia* (1914), an elaborate and tautly constructed version of a Biblical story, was based on a four-part structure which anticipated the formal design of INTOLERANCE (1916). The first American four-reeler, *Judith* was extremely costly and Griffith's reckless over-expenditure on the budget caused a rupture with Biograph. He left the company before the film was released, and at the end of 1913 joined the newly formed MUTUAL Film Corporation as head of production taking with him most of his actors and his cameraman, Bitzer.

After making a handful of pot-boilers in 1914—*The Battle of the Sexes*, *The Escape*, *Home Sweet Home*, and *The Avenging Conscience*—Griffith concentrated all his energies into the creation of his epic of the American Civil War, THE BIRTH OF A NATION (1915), which crystallized into a highly complex narrative form the elements of construction which Griffith had been exploring during his five years at Biograph. The film had a vast popular success, was richly praised by critics of film, but was reviled by Black and Liberal opinion for its gross prejudice against negroes. The film even caused race riots, and it was censored in some states. Griffith's response to attempts to suppress the film was to publish a pamphlet, *The Rise and Fall of Free Speech in America*. The pamphlet linked the idea of censorship with intolerance, which was to be the subject of Griffith's second great film, *Intolerance*, which incorporated four separate stories interwoven to illustrate the abstract theme of the title. Unlike his previous film, it had no success with the public, who found the four-part structure incomprehensible. An unprecedentedly grandiose project, it brought Griffith near financial ruin. He was, however, still America's most prestigious director, and as such was invited to go to Europe and make films for the war effort. HEARTS OF THE WORLD (1918) combined documentary material and studio reconstruction to give an emotional picture of a French village under German occupation. *The Great Love* (1918) was filmed in England and incorporated footage of society celebrities in a melodramatic story of a young American who enlists in the British army.

In 1915 Griffith had become a partner in the TRIANGLE Company, together with Mack SENNETT and Thomas INCE. He had supervised several productions for the company, and had written some original scenarios under the pseudonym Granville Warwick. Most of his time, however, had been devoted to the making and marketing of the separately-financed *Intolerance*. In 1917 he transferred his allegiance to Adolph ZUKOR's Artcraft company for which *The Great Love* was his first film. Griffith's films for Artcraft, including *The Greatest Thing in Life* (1918), *A Romance of Happy Valley*, *The Girl Who Stayed Home*, *True Heart Susie*, and a Western, *Scarlet Days* (all 1919), were characterized by intimate themes and a comparatively simple style. In 1919 he joined with CHAPLIN, Mary Pickford, and Douglas FAIRBANKS to form the UNITED ARTISTS CORPORATION and his first production for release by the company was BROKEN BLOSSOMS (1919), one of his finest films.

Griffith was at this time building his own studio at Mamaroneck, New York, and because of heavy financial commitments he undertook three films for the rapidly expanding FIRST NATIONAL. These were hastily made, mediocre efforts, but his reputation was vindicated by his next film for United Artists, WAY DOWN EAST (1920), a decided critical success. He continued to explore both the domestic drama—*Dream Street* (1921), *The White Rose* (1923)—and the grandiose historical epic—*Orphans of the Storm* (1922), a drama of the French Revolution with moving performances by the Gish sisters, and *America* (1924), a tableau of American Revolutionary themes. *One Exciting Night* (1922) was a complicated thriller with heavy-handed comic touches.

*Isn't Life Wonderful?* (1924) was Griffith's last film for United Artists in its original form and virtually his last fully independent production. Set in the ruins of post-war Germany, using urban locations and local people in minor roles, the film showed a new side of Griffith reaching out for stark naturalism and social concern. Financially desperate, he renewed his contract with Zukor and made three films for PARAMOUNT,

*Sally of the Sawdust* (1925), chiefly memorable for its revelation of W. C. FIELDS's comic skills, *That Royle Girl*, and *The Sorrows of Satan* (both 1926).

Although Griffith returned to United Artists in 1927, the company no longer offered him creative freedom and, as at Paramount, he was in the position of an ordinary studio director obliged to work on assignments. He was as unable to accept his changed status and strict studio control of his budgets as to adapt his preferred subjects to developing audience tastes. The last films have little to distinguish them: they include *Drums of Love* (1928), a remake of *The Battle of the Sexes* (1928), and *Lady of the Pavements* (1929).

With *Abraham Lincoln* (1930) Griffith briefly found renewed inspiration, stimulated by a subject which appealed to him and by the challenge of his first all-sound film. Although slow-moving, it was an evocative portrayal of LINCOLN's career with a fine leading performance by Walter HUSTON. Griffith's last film, *The Struggle* (1931), was financed mainly from his own resources; the melodramatic tale of a drunkard, it was a humiliating failure. He went into a long and lonely retirement and died in Hollywood virtually forgotten by the film world.

It has been a critical commonplace to view Griffith's career after the failure of *Intolerance* as an almost unremitting decline. The late sixties, however, saw a revival of interest in his later work, with some critics evaluating *True Heart Susie*, *Dream Street*, and *Orphans of the Storm* as underrated masterpieces. What is indisputable is his influence: both the Russian development of MONTAGE and the narrative traditions of America and Europe have their roots in Griffith's work which holds a key position in the history of cinema.

Iris Barry, *D. W. Griffith, American film master*, New York, 1965; Robert M. Henderson, *D. W. Griffith, his life and work*, New York, 1972.

**GRIMAULT,** PAUL (1905– ), French animator who from 1937 was influential in turning the style of French cartoon films from caricature towards poetic satire. *Le Petit Soldat* (1947) was a landmark in the history of animation in France: Grimault's images combined with a script by Jacques PRÉVERT and music by Joseph KOSMA to produce a telling protest against the subjugation of the individual. In 1947–53 Grimault worked, again with Prévert and Kosma, on *La Bergère et le ramoneur*, the first French animated feature; but the producer interfered with the finished film and Grimault and Prévert lost an action to retrieve their work, the film coming out with scenes added contrary to Grimault's intentions. Grimault returned to working on publicity cartoons.

**GRIMOIN-SANSON,** RAOUL (1860–1941), French engineer and inventor who claimed to have perfected the cinematographic projector in advance of the LUMIÈRE brothers. The incorporation of the MALTESE CROSS device by Grimoin-Sanson and his collaborator Etienne MAREY certainly improved the regulation of film passing through the projector and it remained in common use until 1963, but the refinement was devised at about the same time by other workers in the field. Grimoin-Sanson's most notorious innovation was the CINÉORAMA, the first panoramic moving picture system. (See also WIDE SCREEN.) After the failure of this enterprise he recouped his financial losses by inventions in other fields though he always maintained his interest in cinema. His memoirs, *Le Film de ma vie*, were published in Paris in 1926.

**GRIP,** a film equivalent of the stagehand, principally responsible for the execution of CAMERA MOVEMENTS other than PANS and tilts. As their title suggests, grips do the heavy work of shifting the camera and its support to new positions, and also move the DOLLY or CRANE under the control of the camera operator. (Electrically driven equipment is operated not by grips but electricians.)

**GROUPE OCTOBRE,** radical French theatre group formed in 1933. Its aim was to express the vital political issues of the time to a proletarian audience, and to break away from the traditions of the bourgeois theatre.

Many of the actors involved began as non-professionals, and its members included Guy Decombres, Raymond Bussières, Jacques BRUNIUS, Fabien Lorris, Sylvie BATAILLE, Marcel Duhamel, CARTIER-BRESSON, Sylvain Itkine, Lou Tchimoukov, and Jacques PRÉVERT. The group took their works to factories, shops, and strike meetings. It broke up in 1936, mainly for financial reasons, but it had a marked effect on French cinema of the thirties; many of the actors from the group worked in the films of RENOIR, CARNÉ, and later BECKER, and the influence of its style and ideals is particularly evident in Renoir's LE CRIME DE MONSIEUR LANGE (1936) and *La Marseillaise* (1938), the latter financed by money from the trade union movement.

**GROUP THREE** was established in 1951 by the NATIONAL FILM FINANCE CORPORATION as an outlet for young feature film-makers (mainly from documentary) and actors. John Baxter, an experienced feature director, was production controller, John GRIERSON executive producer, and Michael BALCON chairman (succeeded by David Kingsley in 1954). The products were low-budget second features, parochial melodramas and comedies, aimed squarely at a popular market. Though financially unsound owing to distribution difficulties, the project successfully introduced to the screen actors Kenneth More, Peter FINCH, Peter SELLERS, and Tony Hancock, and directors such as Lewis Gilbert and Philip Leacock, whose dramatic reconstruction of a mining disaster, *The Brave Don't Cry* (1952), was the Group's most striking film. Ironically, the documentary *Conquest of Everest* (Thomas Stobart, commentary by Louis MacNeice, 1953) was its most profitable. Group Three closed down in 1955.

**GRÜNE,** KARL (1885–1962), German director, began acting with Max REINHARDT and started film-making in 1920. His *Die Strasse* (*The Street*, 1923), from a Carl MAYER story and without titles, introduced the STREET theme into German film. In the same year he directed *Schlagende Wetter* (*Firedamp*), about a mining disaster, which may have influenced PABST'S KAMERADSCHAFT (1931). His later work in the twenties covered a wide range of subjects from Freudian psychology to social problems, including *Arabella* (1925), a melodramatic story seen through the eyes of a horse, in which Mae MARSH starred as a ballerina. He finally settled for historical drama with *Königin Luise* (*Queen Louisa*, 1928) and a curious version of *Waterloo* (1929), both acclaimed for their luxurious settings and not without psychological interest. Although he continued working into the thirties, he failed to come to terms with sound.

**GUERNICA,** France, 1950. 11min. *Dir* Alain Resnais; *prod* Les Films du Panthéon; *scr* Robert Hessens; *commentary* Paul Éluard (spoken by Maria Casarès and Jacques Pruvost); *ph* Henri Ferrand; *mus* Guy Bernard.

Picasso's *Guernica*, painted after the destruction of that town in the Spanish Civil War, forms the central theme of the film. *Guernica* does not, however, take the form of a conventional art film; details from the painting are interwoven with many other elements (photographs, newspaper headlines, other paintings and sculptures by Picasso), the whole forming a statement on the reality behind the suffering depicted in Picasso's painting. A vital unifying element in this fragmented composition is the commentary of Paul Éluard, surrealist poet, a close friend of Picasso.

One of RESNAIS's earlier films, *Guernica* already shows some of the rhythmic assurance which characterizes his major work.

**GUERRE EST FINIE, La** (*The War is Over*), France/Sweden, 1966. 2hr. *Dir* Alain Resnais; *prod* Sofracima (Paris)/Europa Film (Stockholm); *scr, narr* Jorge Semprun; *ph* Sacha Vierny; *mus* Giovanni Fusco; *cast* Yves Montand (Diego), Ingrid Thulin (Marianne), Geneviève Bujold (Nadine), Paul Crauchet (Roberto), Jean Bouise (Ramon), Jean Dasté (the Chief), Jacques Rispal (Manolo).

Diego, a Spanish exile and revolutionary, is forced to re-examine his political and emotional commitments; the film's conflict derives from the tension between Diego's experience of actual revolution in the Spanish Civil War and the theorizing of his exiled compatriots. This is the first time RESNAIS concentrated on a single individual in depth, and the first of his films to take a clear political standpoint. In its elliptical visual style, however, and the constant counterpoint between inner and objective reality, *La Guerre est finie* is closely related to his other films.

**GUINNESS,** ALEC (1914– ), British actor, joined the Old Vic in 1936, playing various roles in the classical repertoire and establishing a considerable reputation. It was not until 1946 that his gift for brilliant and detailed characterization became known to film audiences when he appeared as Herbert Pocket in GREAT EXPECTATIONS; his Fagin in OLIVER TWIST (1948) was a *tour de force*. KIND HEARTS AND CORONETS (1949) displayed his talents in the roles of eight noble English eccentrics, a feat making him internationally famous. This flavour of eccentricity is to be found in most of his best performances, as in THE MAN IN THE WHITE SUIT, THE LAVENDER HILL MOB (both 1951), and *The Ladykillers* (1955). In THE BRIDGE ON THE RIVER KWAI (1957), *The Horse's Mouth* (1958), LAWRENCE OF ARABIA (1962), and DOCTOR ZHIVAGO (1966) he played a range of parts with invariable accuracy and reserve. He made a notable excursion into farce when he repeated his stage success *Hotel Paradiso* (1966, 1971 in GB). His film career has been paralleled by a succession of distinguished stage performances. He received a knighthood in 1959.

**GUITRY,** SACHA (1885–1957), French director, actor, and playwright, a prolific and immensely successful writer of light and witty plays, in which he acted with his successive wives (he was married five times). Guitry had also a long career in cinema, although his attitude to the medium was somewhat ambivalent. He at first regarded the advent of cinema as a possible threat to the theatre. (Although he made his first film, *Ceux de chez nous*, in 1915, it was in the sphere of documentary rather than entertainment, a reportage on various Paris celebrities of the period, including Pierre Renoir, and his own father, the actor Lucien Guitry.)

Later his attitude changed, and like PAGNOL he saw in film the possibility of preserving the ephemeral theatrical performance. Many of his films are thus straight adaptations of his plays, such as *Bonne Chance* (1935), *Pasteur* (1935), *Le Nouveau Testament* (1936), *Faisons un rêve* (1936), *Les Perles de la couronne* (1937), *Le Diable boiteux* (1948), *Debureaux*, and *Tu m'as sauvé la vie* (both 1950).

Guitry shocked the theorists of 'pure cinema' by refusing to make concessions in adapting his plays to film, and his concern as a director was always primarily with the actor's performance and comfort. He used three cameras to film *Le Diable boiteux*, and in the three films he wrote for Michel SIMON, *La Poison* (1951), *La Vie d'un honnête homme* (1952), and *Les Trois font la paire* (1957), he is reputed, at Simon's request, to have allowed only one take for each scene.

He had popular success in the fifties with a series of colourful and theatrical historical films, *Si Versailles m'était conté* (1954), *Napoléon* (1955), and *Si Paris nous était conté* (1955).

Guitry's reputation was somewhat tarnished through alleged collaboration during the German Occupation, and the value of his theatrical films is a matter of critical debate; the film for which he is undoubtedly remembered, however, is his early *Le Roman d'un tricheur* (1936), in which, exceptionally, he bypassed theatre altogether, constructing a film where the narrator's commentary entirely replaced dialogue. In his original use of commentary and in his love of actors and the theatrical he was an important influence on Alain RESNAIS.

**GUNFIGHT AT THE OK CORRAL.** In 1881 at Tombstone, Arizona, as the climax of a long-standing feud, US Marshall Virgil EARP, with his brothers Morgan and Wyatt (created deputies by their brother) and 'Doc' HOLLIDAY, faced the Clanton gang, probably unarmed, behind a livery stable known as the OK Corral. The result of the confrontation was the deaths of all but one of the Clanton gang. Virgil and Morgan Earp and Holliday were injured; only Wyatt was unhurt.

The many films featuring variously roman-ticized versions of the event include: *Frontier Marshall* (Allan DWAN, 1939), MY DARLING CLEMENTINE (John FORD, 1946), *Gunfight at the OK Corral* (John STURGES, 1956); Sturges reconstructed the incident again in *Hour of the Gun* (1967).

*Wyatt Earp: Frontier Marshall* by Stuart N. Lake, Boston and New York, 1931, gives Earp's version of the incident, though documentary evidence provides conflicting reports.

O. B. Faulk, *Tombstone*, London, New York, 1972, provides a detailed account of the fight and its background.

***GUNFIGHTER, The,*** US, 1950. 1½hr. *Dir* Henry King; *prod* Twentieth Century-Fox; *scr* William Bowers, William Sellers, from a story by Bowers and André De Toth; *ph* Arthur Miller; *cast* Gregory Peck (Johnny Ringo), Karl Malden (Mac), Jean Parker (Molly), Skip Homier (Hunt Bromley).

Probably the first WESTERN to enlist the audience's sympathies in the cause of an anti-hero, a tired gunfighter unable to escape his reputation as a killer.

An intelligent script, austere photography, and Gregory PECK's excellent performance created a new realism in a genre not hitherto given to regard for facts. The atmosphere of a newly civilized frontier town is carefully evoked in dirty streets, humble buildings, shabby clothes, and unshaven faces.

***GUNS IN THE AFTERNOON*** see RIDE THE HIGH COUNTRY

**GUY-BLACHÉ,** ALICE (1873–      ), French director and producer who, as secretary to Léon GAUMONT, was put in charge of Gaumont's production of fiction films from about 1897–8. She appears to have directed all the films herself up to about 1904, notably *La Fée aux choux*, her first undertaking. During the latter part of this period she was often assisted by Ferdinand ZECCA. Following the trend towards increasingly ambitious subjects, she directed *Esmeralda* (1905), an adaptation of Victor Hugo's *Notre Dame*, running about ten minutes, and *La Vie du Christ* (1906), running about twenty-five minutes, both of which have been attributed to her assistant Victorin Jasset. At this time she was instrumental in bringing Louis FEUILLADE into the Gaumont company.

In 1907 she went with her husband Herbert Blaché to New York, where he took charge of Gaumont's distribution branch. Her independent production company Solax was set up in 1910: she herself directed its first release, *A Child's Sacrifice* (1910), and in the company's three years of existence probably directed as many as fifty of its films. She gained a following through the popular press who featured her as the world's first and only woman director: she was in addi-tion an enterprising business woman, her com-pany forming part of the organized resistance to the MOTION PICTURE PATENTS COMPANY.

Solax became Blaché Features Inc in 1913, with Herbert Blaché as president and Alice Guy-Blaché as vice-president. The new company produced only serious dramas, in contrast to the varied output of Solax; nine of its fourteen releases were directed by Alice Guy-Blaché. A year later it was replaced by the Blachés' new enterprise US Amusement Corporation which set out, like FILM D'ART and FAMOUS PLAYERS, to bring reputable literary and theatre pieces to the screen with prestigious actors. This company lasted until 1917 with Alice Guy-Blaché as vice-president and one of its team of directors. Her last films, released through PATHÉ, were *The Great Adventure* (1918), starring Bessie LOVE, and *Tarnished Reputations* (1920). She then retired from film-making; Herbert Blaché continued to direct for various producers until the introduction of sound.

**GUYS AND DOLLS**, US, 1955. CinemaScope; 2½hr; Eastman Color. *Dir, scr* Joseph L. Mankiewicz, from the stage musical by Jo Swerling and Abe Burrows; *prod* Samuel Goldwyn; *ph* Harry Stradling; *mus, lyrics* Frank Loesser; *chor* Michael Kidd; *cast* Marlon Brando (Sky Masterson), Jean Simmons (Sarah Brown), Frank Sinatra (Nathan Detroit), Vivian Blaine (Adelaide), Stubby Kaye (Nicely-Nicely Johnson).

*Guys and Dolls* opened on Broadway in 1950 and was an immediate smash hit. The film rights were bought by Samuel GOLDWYN, who also signed Vivian Blaine and Stubby Kaye from the original cast but called in established stars for the leading roles. The choice of Joseph L. MANKIEWICZ as director of a musical based on a story by Damon Runyon was surprising, and he failed to translate the original into fully cinematic terms; but Runyon's humorously mannered dialogue was maintained, contrasting piquantly with Frank Loesser's vigorous jazz-based score. Michael Kidd's athletic choreography was outstanding.

**GWENN, EDMUND** (1875–1959), gently-spoken British actor. In the twenties he was essentially a theatre actor, but during the thirties his film work increased. He was a notable Jess Oakroyd in *The Good Companions* (1933) and played George Radfern in *Laburnum Grove* both on the stage and in the film version (1934). He then went to Hollywood and appeared in *Sylvia Scarlett* (1935), *Anthony Adverse* (1936), and *Parnell* (1937), returning to Britain for a few films, including *South Riding* (1938). In 1939 he settled in the US and took part in many films, his particularly well-known roles including Mr Bennet in *Pride and Prejudice* (1940) and Santa Claus in *Miracle on 34th Street* (1947, *The Big Heart* in GB) for which he won an OSCAR. Per-

Harriet Andersson in *Gycklarnas afton* (Ingmar Bergman, 1953)

haps the most memorable of his later performances was in Alfred HITCHCOCK's THE TROUBLE WITH HARRY (1955).

**GYCKLARNAS AFTON** (*Sawdust and Tinsel* in GB; *The Naked Night* in US), Sweden, 1953. 1½hr. *Dir, scr* Ingmar Bergman; *prod* Rune Waldekranz for Sandrews; *ph* Sven Nykvist, Hilding Bladh; *ed* Carl-Olof Skeppstedt; *cast* Åke Grönberg (Albert Johansson), Harriet Andersson (Anne), Hasse Ekman (Frans), Anders Ek (Frost), Gudrun Brost (his wife), Annika Tretow (Agda Johansson), Gunnar Björnstrand (Sjuberg).

A circus troupe passing through a provincial town becomes a study in frustrated ambition and sexual humiliation. Albert, the posturing ringmaster, is rejected by his frigid wife and subjected to jealous rages by his mistress, Anne. Anne is seduced by the suave actor Frans. In a flashback, the clown Frost is shamed by his blowsy wife and his forgiveness is portrayed as a Calvary.

BERGMAN's recurrent preoccupations—the artist's isolation and the wounds inflicted by sexual congress—here burst out in complex imagery ranging from the over-exposed pallor of the silent flashback to the expressionistic, angular compositions of the theatre scenes. A complete failure on its first appearance, *Gycklarnas afton* is now seen as a milestone in his development.

# H

**HAANSTRA,** BERT (1916– ), Dutch documentary director, worked as a photographer for the Dutch Resistance during the Second World War and began making short documentaries in 1949. He has won over sixty international awards for shorts like *Spiegel van Holland* (*Mirror of Holland*, 1950), *Strijd zonder einden* (*The Rival World*, 1958), and *Glas* (*Glass*, 1959); his feature films include *Fanfare* (1958) and *Alleman* (*The Human Dutch*, 1966). He collaborated with his close friend Jacques TATI during the first eighteen months of the making of TRAFIC (1971). Haanstra's characteristic style, lyrical, witty, and observant, also manifests a deep, unsentimental affection for the natural world, given full expression in *Bij de Beesten Af* (*Ape and Super-Ape*, 1972), a study of ethological theories and man's brutality to animals. His work has had considerable influence on the flourishing school of Dutch documentary film.

**HACKMAN,** GENE (1931– ), US actor, was first widely noticed in *Lilith* (Robert ROSSEN, 1964). He gave an excellent performance as Clyde Barrow's inept brother in BONNIE AND CLYDE (1967) and built a reputation as a capable character actor in *Downhill Racer* (Michael RITCHIE), *The Gypsy Moths* (John FRANKEN-HEIMER), *Marooned*, and *I Never Sang for My Father* (all 1969). He is the antithesis of the conventional Hollywood leading man, with almost sour-faced looks, but is a determined craftsman of the highest order. With *The French Connection* (1971) he achieved star status, winning an OSCAR for his performance as the indomitable Detective Doyle chasing drug peddlars, and he scored another success as a seedy eavesdropper in COPPOLA's *The Conversation* (1974).

**HADJIDAKIS,** MANOS (1925– ), Greek composer. His best-known and most popular scores are for DASSIN's POTE TIN KYRIAKI (*Never on Sunday*, 1959), which won him an OSCAR, and *Topkapi* (1964). Others include CACOY-ANNIS's *Stella* (1955); TO TELEFTEO PSEMMA (*A Matter of Dignity*, 1957); *It Happened in Athens* (1961); KAZAN's *America, America* (1963, *The Anatolian Smile* in GB); and *Blue* (1968).

**HAIL THE CONQUERING HERO,** US, 1944. 1¾hr. *Dir, scr* Preston Sturges; *prod* Paramount; *ph* John Seitz; *cast* Eddie Bracken (Woodrow), Ella Rains (Libby), Bill Edwards (Forrest Noble), William Demarest (Sergeant), Franklin Pangborn (Chairman of the Reception Committee).

Woodrow, superbly played by Eddie Bracken, is unwillingly set up as a war hero in his home town, a situation created and maintained by a sentimental army sergeant (William Demarest). Here Preston STURGES successfully exercises his talent for fast-paced comic satire on both hysterical hero-worship and parochial politics, with the American cult of motherhood thrown in for good measure.

**HAKIM,** ROBERT (1907– ), and RAYMOND (1909– ), French producers, formed their own production company, Paris-Film-Production, in 1934. Their first big success was PÉPÉ-LE-MOKO (1937), which was followed by a series of distinguished productions, among them RENOIR's LA BÊTE HUMAINE (1938), BECKER's CASQUE D'OR (1952), CARNÉ's THÉRÈSE RAQUIN (1953), CLÉMENT's *Plein soleil* (1959), ANTONIONI's L'ECLISSE (1962), and LOSEY's *Eva* (1962).

A third brother, André (1915– ), married Darryl F. ZANUCK's daughter and became a producer for TWENTIETH CENTURY-FOX; the fourth, Raphael, is a film exporter.

**HALAS,** JOHN (1912– ) and **BATCHELOR,** JOY (1914– ), British animated film producers. Halas arrived in Britain from Hungary in 1936 and worked with Joy Batchelor as an animator and commercial artist; they set up the Halas and Batchelor animation studios in 1940, founding their reputation on wartime PROPAGANDA and information films. They married in 1941. They continued to make commissioned advertising and instructional films after the war, by this means supporting the production of independent animated films. Their first independent short film, *Magic Canvas* (1951), set abstract images to music by Matyas Seiber. *The Owl and the Pussy Cat* (1953), *The History of the Cinema* (1956), and *Automania 2000* (1963) followed the simplified graphic style of UNITED PRODUCTIONS OF AMERICA (UPA). *Animal Farm* (1954), the first British animated feature film, met with mixed critical reactions. Since the mid-fifties their work has found its main outlet in television.

**HALL,** CONRAD (1926– ), US cameraman. Failing to get into IATSE, the established Hollywood union, he formed, with four or five others, the Association of Film Craftsmen Union, which they managed to affiliate with NABET, the TV Projectionists Union, and in this way were allowed to work in the industry. He then worked on sections of DISNEY animal features, including *The Living Desert* (1953). His career as a cameraman really began when, with others, he formed Canyon Films to make *My Brother Down There* (1956) and they drew lots for the photography. In 1965 he photographed his first feature, *The Wild Seed*. He made distinguished contributions to *Morituri* (1965, *Code Name—Morituri* in GB), *The Professionals* (1966), IN COLD BLOOD (1967), and won an OSCAR for BUTCH CASSIDY AND THE SUNDANCE KID (1969). His recent work includes *Fat City* (John HUSTON, 1972) and *Catch My Soul* (1973).

**HALL,** PETER (1930– ), British director best known for his work in the theatre, especially at the Royal Shakespeare Theatre and the Royal Opera House, Covent Garden. He directed his first film, *Work is a Four Letter Word*, in 1967 and has since made occasional films, including a Royal Shakespeare Company production of A MIDSUMMER NIGHT'S DREAM (1968) and *Three into Two Won't Go* (1969). His film work took a new direction with *Akenfield* (1974), a semi-documentary reconstruction of life over three generations in his native rural Suffolk. He was married to Leslie CARON.

*HALLELUJAH*, US, 1929. 1¾hr. *Dir* King Vidor; *prod* MGM; *scr* Wanda Tuchock, Richard Schayer; *ph* Gordon Avil; *mus* Irving Berlin, with negro spirituals; *cast* Daniel L. Haynes (Seke), Nina Mae McKinney (Chuck), William Fountain (Hot Shot), Dixie Jubilee Singers.

Seke, repenting of the accidental killing of his brother in a dispute over the semi-prostitute Chuck, becomes a revivalist preacher. Under VIDOR's direction this naïve plot supported one of the first important MUSICALS and the first sound film with an all-black cast. The characters are within the Hollywood stereotype of inferior beings, but the exhilaration of the musical numbers, and the religious passages in particular, created an impression in both America and Europe.

*HALLELUJAH THE HILLS*, US, 1963. 1½hr. *Dir, scr* Adolphas Mekas; *prod* David C. Stone;

*Hallelujah the Hills* (Adolfas Mekas, 1963)

*ph* Ed Emschwiller; *ed* Jonas Mekas; *mus* Meyer Kupferman; *cast* Peter H. Beard (Jack), Martin Greenbaum (Leo), Sheila Finn (Vera—winter), Peggy Steffans (Vera—summer), Jerome Raphael (father), Blanche Dee (mother), Jerome Hill, Taylor Mead (convicts), Ed Emschwiller (Gideon).

Jack and Leo, both in love with Vera, woo her for seven years; she finally bestows herself on the bearded Gideon.

MEKAS's vivacious *jeu d'esprit*, shot on location in Vermont on a minimal budget, is an excuse for a succession of cheerful parodies on cinematic styles ranging from slapstick via Japanese samurai fights to a friendly send-up of ANTONIONI. The acting is fresh and the photography often beautiful.

**HALLER,** ERNEST (1896–1970), US cameraman, began work as an actor at BIOGRAPH. His first known work as cameraman was on *The Hazards of Helen* (1915); in 1920–64 he shot approximately 150 films. They include *Stella Dallas* (1926), *The Dawn Patrol* (1930), *The Great Garrick* (1937), *Jezebel* (1938), THE ROARING TWENTIES (1939), GONE WITH THE WIND (1939), for which he received a joint OSCAR, REBEL WITHOUT A CAUSE (1955), *Man of the West* (1958), and *Whatever Happened to Baby Jane?* (1962).

**HALLO, SISTER!** (*Walking Down Broadway*), US, 1933. 1½hr. *Dir* Erich von Stroheim (uncredited); *prod* Fox; *scr* Stroheim, from the play by Dawn Powell; *ph* James Wong Howe; *cast* James Dunn (Jimmy), Boots Mallory (Peggy), ZaSu Pitts (Millie), Terence Ray (Mac).

*Walking Down Broadway*, STROHEIM's last film as director and his only sound film, was issued in a mutilated form as *Hallo, Sister!*; it is commonly referred to by its working title. No director's credit was given: Stroheim had refused to be associated with the film as issued. The production troubles were created not, as in the case of most of his other films, by his own intransigence, but by studio conflicts unconnected with the film itself. Uncharacteristically, he seems to have worked with moderation and speed, but was dismissed before shooting was completed. It was thought that the whole film was re-shot, but a print discovered in the FOX vaults in 1969 shows that, although his planned ending was changed and the material he had completed was badly edited, the overall conception is unmistakably his.

In its contemporary American setting *Hallo, Sister!* recalls GREED (1923): its complex characterizations of two newcomers to New York, Peggy and Milly, their rivalries and jealousies, and the sexual manoeuvres reflect the preoccupations of much of Stroheim's work.

**HAMER,** ROBERT (1911–63), British director, worked as an editor for Alexander KORDA and later became a scriptwriter. His first work as director was on an episode of DEAD OF NIGHT (1945), a distinguished début. His talent for suspense, elegance, and an acid wit was displayed in KIND HEARTS AND CORONETS (1949), which he also wrote, and is also in evidence in such films as *Pink String and Sealing Wax* (1945), *Father Brown* (1954), and *The Scapegoat* (1959).

**HAMLET.** SHAKESPEARE's most famous play has appealed to film-makers since the earliest days. Numerous versions of the play, or extracts from it, exist, some of the most valuable being those which provide records of the great actors of the past. These include Sarah BERNHARDT in the duel scene, shown at the 1900 Paris Exhibition, a ninety-minute version of Sir Johnston Forbes-Robertson's farewell performance directed in 1913 by E. Hay Plumb supervised by Cecil HEPWORTH, and a screen test made in 1933 by John BARRYMORE. Extracts from John GIELGUD's stage appearance as Hamlet are included in Humphrey JENNINGS's *A Diary for Timothy* (1945).

The first British *Hamlet* was made in 1908 by W. G. BARKER with Charles Raymond in the title role. Shooting was completed in two days at a cost of £180. Also about 1908 CASERINI directed a version for CINES. For his 1910 Danish production August Blom conducted fruitless negotiations to engage Sarah Bernhardt to play Hamlet. His film was entirely shot at Kronberg Castle (Shakespeare's Elsinore); a very long and detailed version, it was cut to one reel for distribution.

In 1948 the first important sound film of *Hamlet* was produced and directed by Laurence OLIVIER who also played the lead. The cast included Basil Sydney (Claudius), Eileen Herlie (Gertrude), and Jean SIMMONS (Ophelia). The over-use of cinematic techniques (camera mobility in particular) in contrast with the theatrical style of the interior sets and costumes detracts from the effect of the text, but the film is a permanent record of a great contemporary actor.

The 1964 stage production of *Hamlet*, starring Richard BURTON and directed by John GIELGUD, was filmed by a process derived from television (Electronovision), in which a number of small electronic cameras were placed in the theatre during an actual performance. The resulting film was shown simultaneously for two days at 1,300 cinemas in the US and then withdrawn from circulation.

The Russian *Hamlet* (1964), directed by KOZINTSEV, was widely admired. With his intimate knowledge of Shakespeare's plays, the director made a personal but effective interpretation, creating awareness of the state of Denmark and its relation to the central drama. Hamlet was played by Innokenti Smoktunovsky, Claudius by Mikhail Nazvanov, Gertrude by Elsa Radzin, and Ophelia by Anastasia Vertinskaya. The music was by SHOSTAKOVICH. In contrast, Tony RICHARDSON's 1970 film of his stage production with Nicol Williamson as Hamlet and Marianne Faithfull as Ophelia concentrated on individual psychology. The visual and dramatic economy of this version made it possible to give to the text a close attention unusual in film versions of Shakespeare.

Among many 'fringe' versions based or loosely based on the play (*Hamlet Made Over*, US, 1916; *A Sage Brush Hamlet*, US, 1919; *Hamlet and Eggs*, US, 1937; *Ophelia*, France, 1961), the German production directed in 1920 by Sven Gade and starring Asta NIELSEN is notable. The screenplay was based on the *Saxo Grammaticus* (the original source of the story), *Fratricide Punished* (a German text thought to be a pirated version of Shakespeare's play), and E. P. Vining's book *The mystery of Hamlet* in which the author put up the theory that Hamlet was really a woman. There was also a Ghanaian version transposed into a tribal setting, *Hamile* (1964).

**HAMMER FILM PRODUCTIONS,** British production company founded in 1948 under the chairmanship of James Carreras and based at Bray Studios near Windsor. In its early years the company specialized in routine second-feature productions, becoming associated with the horror and science fiction genres only after the success of *The Quatermass Experiment* (1954). They then concentrated more on the remunerative horror formula, often using established figures such as FRANKENSTEIN and DRACULA, and on versions of popular classics: *The Hound of the Baskervilles* (1959), *The Two Faces of Dr Jekyll* (1960) (see DR JEKYLL AND MR HYDE), and *She* (1965). As well as these and various other thrillers, some more prestigious productions have appeared, notably Joseph LOSEY's *The Damned* (1961) and two films starring Bette DAVIS: *The Nanny* (1965) and *The Anniversary* (1967). Hammer's output has been high (119 features in twelve years) and extremely profitable. In 1968 the company was awarded the Queen's Award for Industry in recognition of its earnings in foreign currency: James Carreras was knighted for the same reason in 1969.

**HAMMETT,** DASHIELL (1894–1961), US author, mainly during the thirties, of tough, unglamorous detective novels, often featuring Sam Spade as the private eye. Notable among the numerous films of Hammett's works are W. S. VAN DYKE's THE THIN MAN (1934), with William POWELL, which inspired several series of imitations, and HUSTON's version of THE MALTESE FALCON (1941), with BOGART as Spade. Hammett's own work in Hollywood includes the script for MAMOULIAN's CITY STREETS (1931).

**HANDS OF ORLAC, The,** see ORLACS HÄNDE

**HANDS OVER THE CITY** see MANI SULLA CITTÀ, LE

**HANNA,** WILLIAM (1920– ) and **BARBERA,** JOSEPH (1911– ), US cartoon film producers. From 1932, Barbera was a writer for the van Beuren studios on the TOM AND JERRY series and from 1937 an animator at METROGOLDWYN-MAYER. Hanna joined Leon Schlesinger's company in 1938, as a writer and director of the MGM cartoons. Hanna and Barbera first collaborated in 1940, on *Gallopin' Gals*. From 1957, their output has become increasingly geared to the demands of commercial television. They use a computerized production system, the sound-track providing codes for a stock number of movements, eye-blinks, lip-movements, shock-vibration, etc. Such productions include *The Flintstones*, *Huckleberry Hound*, *Yogi Bear*, and *Quick Draw McGraw*.

**HANSON,** LARS (1886–1965), Swedish actor, particularly remembered for his leading performances for Mauritz STILLER, in EROTIKON (1920) and GÖSTA BERLINGS SAGA (1924), and for Victor SJÖSTRÖM, in *The Scarlet Letter* (1926) and THE WIND (1928).

**HARA-KIRI** see SEPPUKU

**HARBOU,** THEA VON (1888–1954), German novelist and screenwriter, was already an established author before she began her collaboration with Fritz LANG, whom she married in 1921. She adapted or wrote scripts for all Lang's films from 1920 (*Das wanderne Bild*) to 1932, including DIE NIBELUNGEN (1924), METROPOLIS (1927), *Spione* (1928), and M (1931). They were divorced in 1934, after Lang had left Germany. She directed *Elisabeth und der Narr* and *Hanneles Himmelfahrt* (both 1934), and continued her film and writing career in Germany during the war, often in collaboration with Veit HARLAN. After the war she wrote several successful novels and some film scripts.

**HARD DAY'S NIGHT, A,** GB, 1965. 1¼hr. *Dir* Richard Lester; *prod* Walter Shenson; *scr* Alun Owen; *ph* Gilbert Taylor; *mus, lyrics* John Lennon, Paul McCartney; *cast* John Lennon (John), Paul McCartney (Paul), George Harrison

(George), Ringo Starr (Ringo), Wilfrid Brambell (Grandfather), Norman Rossington (Norm), Victor Spinetti (TV director).

Released at the height of 'Beatlemania', the film effectively transformed a teenage craze into a serious adult enthusiasm. Presenting a thirty-six hour period in the group's life, it draws strongly on the appealing, spontaneous performances of the BEATLES, an offbeat, irreverent screenplay, and LESTER's freewheeling direction. The songs dominated the pop charts at the time.

**HARDING,** ANN (1902–  ), US actress, real name Dorothy Walton Gatley, made her film début in *The Trial of Mary Dugan* (1929), released a few months before *Paris Bound* (1929). Sleek and demure, and notable at the time for keeping her blonde hair long, she became a popular favourite of the thirties in such films as *The Animal Kingdom* (1932), *When Ladies Meet* (1933), and *Peter Ibbetson* (1935), but after coming to Britain to star in the suspense thriller *Love from a Stranger* (1937) she disappeared from the screen for several years. She returned in *Mission to Moscow* (1942), *North Star* (1943), *Those Endearing Young Charms* (1945), and others.

**HARD TICKET,** US trade term to describe a method of promoting major productions, usually of BLOCKBUSTER proportions, on lines of increased admission prices, bookable seats, and separate instead of continuous performances. With a few exceptions (e.g. GONE WITH THE WIND, 1939) this is a post-war development, in part aimed at recapturing dwindling audiences.

**HARDWICKE,** Sir CEDRIC (1893–1964), British character actor who, except for one or two appearances in silent films, began his screen career in DREYFUS (1931). He appeared in many of the most notable British films of the thirties, ranging from horror (*The Ghoul*, 1933), through the historical phase of WILCOX-NEAGLE pictures (*Nell Gwyn*, 1934; *Peg of Old Drury*, 1935) to *Jew Süss* (1935) and THINGS TO COME (1936). In the better and more faithful version of *King Solomon's Mines* (1937) he was a splendid Allan Quartermaine. He spent the war years in Hollywood: after his return to Britain he appeared in *Nicholas Nickleby* (1947), *The Winslow Boy* (1948), and *Richard III* (1955). His last film was *The Pumpkin Eater* (1964).

**HARDY FAMILY,** for ten years (1937–47) and fifteen films America's, and METRO-GOLDWYN-MAYER's, favourite mythical family, representing the wholesome, overly sentimental, mid-western image of family life. The principals included father Judge Hardy, Lionel BARRYMORE in the

first film then Lewis Stone, mother Fay Holden, daughter Cecilia Parker, aunt Sara Haden, and the excitable Andy Hardy played by Mickey ROONEY. Andy's heart-to-heart talks with the Judge formed a vital part of each film. The series often featured young stars like Judy GARLAND, Ann Rutherford, and Lana TURNER as Andy's girl-friends. Although modestly budgeted and rather pedestrian in their execution—serial king George Seitz directed several—the films tapped the seemingly inexhaustible vein of middle-class situation comedy-drama that was to become the mainstay of American television. They were awarded a special OSCAR in 1942 for 'furthering the American way of life', a tribute much appreciated by Louis B. MAYER who took the films much too seriously anyway.

**HARDY,** OLIVER, see LAUREL AND HARDY

**HARLAN,** VEIT (1899–1964), German actor and director, who in 1937 was given the honorary title of Professor, only two years after making his first film. His many films varied considerably in quality: one of the best was *Die Reise nach Tilsit* (*The Journey to Tilsit*, 1939) based on the same story as MURNAU's SUNRISE (1927).

His most notorious propaganda film was JUD SÜSS (1940) for which he was tried by the Allies for crimes against humanity. (He was not convicted owing to lack of evidence.) He also directed *Kolberg* (1945), a spectacular historical epic in colour, conceived and promoted by Goebbels as a morale-raising exercise.

After being blacklisted by the Allies Harlan was allowed to return to film-making in 1950 and made several more features.

**HARLINE,** LEIGH (1907–  ), US composer who began work in the early thirties as arranger and scorer for Walt DISNEY. He wrote songs for SNOW WHITE AND THE SEVEN DWARFS (1937) and won an OSCAR for 'When You Wish Upon a Star', written for *Pinocchio* (1940). He wrote music for some of the classic Hollywood comedies of the forties, including HIS GIRL FRIDAY (1940) and *The More the Merrier* (1943). He was active in films until the mid-sixties, his other scores including *The Boy with Green Hair* (1948), *Monkey Business* (1952), PICKUP ON SOUTH STREET (1952), *Broken Lance* (1954), *Good Morning, Miss Dove* (1955), *10 North Frederick* (1958), *Guns of Diablo* (1964).

**HARLOW,** JEAN (1911–37), US actress, real name Harlean Carpenter, who became one of the most popular stars of the thirties with her first starring role in *Hell's Angels* (Howard HUGHES,

1930). *Platinum Blonde* (1931) gave her a nickname, but miscast her as a spoilt society girl, though she wore her characteristically clinging clothes in it. In 1932 she went to METRO-GOLDWYN-MAYER and it was here that she was most successful, especially teamed opposite Clark GABLE, whose male arrogance matched her provocative and outspoken sex-appeal, notably in *Red Dust* (1932) in which she played the wise-cracking Vantine with the traditional heart of gold. BOMBSHELL (1933) showed her considerable abilities as a *comédienne*, and is one of the best Hollywood comedies of the early thirties. She was working on *Saratoga* (1937), her fifth film with Gable, when she died of cerebral oedema. Her reputation has suffered from highly-coloured and probably largely inaccurate accounts of her life, among them *Harlow* which was filmed in 1965 with Carroll BAKER in the title role; but it seems her friends and close colleagues have pleasanter memories of her.

**HARRIS,** JULIE (1925– ), American stage actress who made her film début when she repeated her stage performance as the twelve-year-old Frankie in THE MEMBER OF THE WEDDING (1953) and consolidated her reputation with EAST OF EDEN (1955) and as Sally Bowles in *I Am a Camera* (1955). She makes few films, tending to specialize in vulnerable eccentrics like the neurotic Alison in *Reflections in a Golden Eye* (1967).

**HARRIS,** RICHARD (1932– ), Irish actor often cast as the stormy rebel, a part he also plays in real life. His first film was *Alive and Kicking* (1958). After his strong performance in THIS SPORTING LIFE (1962), ANTONIONI chose him to play opposite Monica VITTI in IL DESERTO ROSSO (*The Red Desert*, 1964). He played King Arthur in *Camelot* (Joshua LOGAN, 1967), the strike-breaker in Martin RITT's *The Molly Maguires* (1969), and an English aristocrat initiated as an Indian brave in *A Man Called Horse* (1970). In 1969 he took over the direction of *Bloomfield* (released in GB 1972), a disappointingly self-indulgent début as director.

**HARRISON,** KATHLEEN (1898– ), British actress who made her film début in *Hobson's Choice* (1931) and later came to specialize in Cockney character parts although she is of Lancashire birth. She repeated her role in the play NIGHT MUST FALL in the film version (1937). She won great popularity, especially as Mrs Huggett in a series of family comedies which began with *Holiday Camp* (1947). She has remained active as a character actress, and has been popular on both radio and television.

**HARRISON,** REX (1908– ), British actor having already made his mark as a stage actor made his first film appearance in 1937 in Alexander KORDA's *Men are not Gods*. He early perfected his debonair, ironic style in such films as *School for Husbands* (1937), *The Citadel* (King VIDOR, 1938), and MAJOR BARBARA (Gabriel PASCAL, 1941). After wartime service in the RAF he appeared with much success in *Blithe Spirit* (David LEAN, 1945) and *The Rake's Progress* (Sidney GILLIATT, 1946), in which his first wife Lilli PALMER also appeared. He continued his stage and film career in the US, where he maintained his considerable popularity with *Anna and the King of Siam* (1946), *The Ghost and Mrs Muir* (Joseph L. MANKIEWICZ, 1947), UNFAITHFULLY YOURS (Preston STURGES, 1948), and many others. His resounding success as Professor Higgins in the stage production of MY FAIR LADY was repeated in the 1964 film version, for which he won an OSCAR; his other roles include Caesar in CLEOPATRA (1962) and the title role in *Dr Doolittle* (1967). After the death of his second wife Kay Kendall in 1959 he was married to Rachel ROBERTS.

**HART,** LORENZ (1895–1943), US lyricist, who wrote in collaboration with Richard RODGERS. Though temperamental opposites, they formed one of the most creative musical partnerships, which lasted until Hart's death. Hart's lyrics were consistently sophisticated, witty, sensitive, and literate—'I Wish I Were in Love Again', 'My Funny Valentine', 'Where or When', 'The Lady is a Tramp'—but in films they are only to be heard in the versions prepared for radio and records, many of the original stage versions being considered too *risqué* for mass audiences. Hart collaborated with Gus Kahn on *The Merry Widow* (1934): for details of his other work see Richard Rodgers. Mickey ROONEY played Hart in the 'biography' film *Words and Music* (1948).

**HART,** WILLIAM SURREY (not Shakespeare as he liked it to be known) (1870–1946), US actor and director, worked as a cowboy and spent twenty years on the New York stage, becoming a leading actor. He also worked in films, appearing in BEN-HUR (1907) and *The Squaw Man* (1913). His first starring role was in *The Bargain* (1914), which he wrote with C. Gardiner SULLIVAN, who scripted many of his later films. The character of Rio Jim, the 'good badman', created by Hart in such films as *The Disciple* (1915) and *Hell's Hinges* (1916), brought him enormous success and he became the first cowboy star. The originality of his WESTERNS lay in the characterization of the hero and the faithful reconstruction of the Old West.

In 1917 Hart moved to PARAMOUNT where he made twenty-seven more Westerns, but his popularity declined, and he left films to write books about the West. He returned to the cinema when UNITED ARTISTS offered him considerable resources for *Tumbleweeds* (1925) in an attempt to match the epic splendour (and success) of THE COVERED WAGON (1923); but the film did not meet expectations.

**HARVEY, LAURENCE** (1927–73), British actor, real name Larushka Skikne, born in Lithuania. His film career began with *House of Darkness* (1948); he first attracted wide notice as Romeo in ROMEO AND JULIET (1954). He progressed to star status in Britain and Hollywood in such films as *The Alamo* (John WAYNE, 1960), *Butterfield 8* (1961), with Elizabeth TAYLOR, THE MANCHURIAN CANDIDATE (John FRANKENHEIMER, 1962), THE OUTRAGE (Martin RITT, 1964), and *Darling* (John SCHLESINGER, 1965). He produced and directed *The Ceremony* (1963) in which he also starred. He was married to the actress Margaret Leighton.

**HARVEY, LILIAN** (1907–68), British actress, singer, and dancer, originally in ballet and revue. She pursued the greater part of her film career in Germany and she was popular as a vivacious star in the early thirties, especially teamed with Willy Fritsch in films directed by Wilhelm THIELE (*Drei von der Tankstelle*, 1930; *Liebeswalzer*, 1931). Her greatest success was in Erik Charrell's DER KONGRESS TANZT (*Congress Dances*, 1931). She then made a few films in Hollywood and Britain, and retired after *Sérénade* (1939), a French film directed by Jean Boyer.

**HAS, WOJCIECH** (1925– ), Polish director, in 1946 graduated from the Kraków Film Institute (see LÓDŹ) to a distinguished career in documentary and educational film production. His first feature, *Pętla* (*The Noose*, 1957), was immediately successful. There followed *Pożegnania* (*Farewells*, 1958) and *Rozstanie* (*Parting* or *Goodbye to the Past*, 1960); their theme, the wary assimilation of bourgeois intellectuals into post-war Polish society, was well suited to Has's rather literary style. Like KAWALEROWICZ, he has avoided his contemporaries' specific preoccupation with the war though *Jak być kochana* (*How to be Loved*, 1962) looked back to the war from a present-day viewpoint. He acted in *Zloto* (*Gold*, 1961). CYBULSKI starred in his *Szyfry* (*The Code*, 1966) and in his best-known film, *Rekopis znaleziony w Saragossie* (*The Saragossa Manuscript*, 1964), an exotic, dream-like work. *Lalka* (*The Doll*, 1968), Has's first colour film, emulated its stunning visual qualities, but represented no stylistic advance.

**HASEGAWA, KAZUO** (1908– ), Japanese actor, trained for the KABUKI theatre but entered films in 1926. He appeared in many films directed by KINUGASA (at first credited as Nagamaru or Chojiro Hayashi) and has frequently worked for MIZOGUCHI. Dozens of film roles have made him an immensely popular star in Japan, but his best-known films abroad are JIGOKUMON (*Gate of Hell*, 1953), in which he played the ruthless Moritoh, and YUKINOJO HENGE (*An Actor's Revenge*, 1963), in which he gave a dual performance of extraordinary accomplishment and power.

**HASSELQVIST, JENNY** (1894– ), Swedish actress who at first pursued a successful career in ballet. Her first screen appearance was in Mauritz STILLER's *Balettprimadonnan* (1916) and her other films include LUBITSCH's *Sumurun* (1920) and Stiller's GÖSTA BERLINGS SAGA (1924).

**HATHAWAY, HENRY** (1898– ), US director, entered films in 1908 as a child actor, later becoming a property man. In the twenties he began many years' association with PARAMOUNT by directing Westerns; LIVES OF A BENGAL LANCER (1935) and sea stories such as *Souls at Sea* (1937) and *Spawn of the North* (1938) established him as a reliable contract director with a flair for action films.

He moved from Paramount to TWENTIETH CENTURY-FOX, where he worked from 1940 to 1960. There he introduced a new kind of thriller with a journalistic approach, the 'semi-documentary' style which was a speciality of Fox in the forties. The film setting the style was Hathaway's *The House on 92nd Street* (1945), a spy story treated from the standpoint of FBI investigations with a wealth of behind-the-scenes detail which captured the public's imagination. Its success inevitably led to more films in this vein: *The Dark Corner* (1946), *13 Rue Madeleine* (1947), KISS OF DEATH (1947), in which Richard WIDMARK made a striking début as a psychopath with an evil snigger, *Call Northside 777* (1948), and *Fourteen Hours* (1951).

Hathaway directed the greater part of HOW THE WEST WAS WON (1962) and the circus epic *The Magnificent Showman* (1964), and returned to Westerns with *The Sons of Katie Elder* (1965), *Nevada Smith* (1966), and *True Grit* (1969), from which none of his old panache is missing. His work has been uneven but distinguished by a flair for milieu and characterization, backed by a professionalism developed by long experience.

**HAWKINS, JACK** (1910–73), British actor, made his screen début in *Birds of Prey* (1930) and appeared in numerous films of the thirties. Except for a part in *The Next of Kin* (Thorold DICKINSON, 1941), his career was interrupted by wartime service. He returned to the screen in 1948 in THE FALLEN IDOL, *Bonnie Prince Charlie*, and *The Small Back Room*, still in supporting or featured roles. His rise to stardom came in the fifties, throughout which he was much in demand, winning great popularity with his solid, dependable personality. The corvette commander in *The Cruel Sea* (1952) was one of his most famous roles; he played the title part in *Gideon's Day* (1958, *Gideon of Scotland Yard* in US) and the mastermind in the highly successful *The League of Gentlemen* (1960). He appeared in various large-scale productions, including THE BRIDGE ON THE RIVER KWAI (1957), LAWRENCE OF ARABIA (1962), *Zulu* (1963), and OH! WHAT A LOVELY WAR (1969). After recovering from an operation for throat cancer he continued to appear occasionally but with his lines dubbed, often by Charles Gray.

**HAWKS,** HOWARD (1896–    ), US director, began his film career in the property department of the Mary PICKFORD Company. From the cutting-room he went to scriptwriting and was in charge of PARAMOUNT's story department 1924–6. He directed his first feature, *The Road to Glory*, in 1926. He has made outstanding films in every genre to which he has turned his hand. *The Dawn Patrol* (1930), *Only Angels Have Wings* (1939), and *Air Force* (1943), drawing on his own experience as an airman in the First World War, demonstrate his ability to handle fast-moving action with economy and visual assuredness—attributes permeating all his films, even the mutilated SCARFACE (1932). THE BIG SLEEP (1946), the best film rendering of a CHANDLER novel, although baffling in the complexity of its plot, retains the punchy pace of the original.

Hawks brought a characteristic sharpness of visual and verbal humour to SCREWBALL comedy and its derivatives in TWENTIETH CENTURY (1934), BRINGING UP BABY (1938), HIS GIRL FRIDAY (1940), *I Was a Male War Bride* (1949, *You Can't Sleep Here* in GB), and GENTLEMEN PREFER BLONDES (1953). In contrast, his WESTERNS, RED RIVER (1948) and RIO BRAVO (1959) in particular, use the conventions of the genre with imagination, tautness, and visual strength. Drawing on his own experiences in the field, his films about motor-racing—*The Crowd Roars* (1932) and *Red Line 7000* (1965)—are gripping and authentic.

His long and distinguished record of films demonstrates above all his flair for narrative, with controlled pace and effective dramatic or comic development complemented by incisive dialogue (he has had a hand in writing all his films), allied to a masterly use of the means offered within the structure of a commercialized film industry. Recurrent themes are prevalent in his work, such as the continual sex-war waged in his comedies and the heroism and male camaraderie of his war films and Westerns: his films consequently lend themselves to theorizing along AUTEUR lines, perhaps at the expense of examination of Hawks's considerable cinematic achievements.

Robin Wood's *Howard Hawks*, London, Garden City (N.Y.), 1968, examines Hawks's work from the *auteur* standpoint.

*HÄXAN* (*Witchcraft through the Ages*), Sweden, 1922. *Dir* Benjamin Christensen; *prod* Svenska; *ph* Johan Ankerstjerne; *cast* Maren Pedersen, Clara Pontoppidan, Elith Pio, Oscar Stribolt, Tora Teje, Benjamin Christensen, John Andersen, Astrid Holm, Poul Reumert, Alice O'Fredericks.

Benjamin CHRISTENSEN's most famous film is a documentary-style study of the practice and punishment of medieval witchcraft, taking the form of carefully reconstructed tableaux reminiscent of Brueghel and Bosch. The witch is shown to have been nothing more than a harmless hysteric who had the misfortune to fall prey to an order—the Church—that was both superstitious and repressive.

Unfortunately, the sound copy issued by Anthony Balch in 1968 has a superfluous commentary by the writer William Burroughs and a strident jazz score.

**HAY,** WILL (1888–1949), British music-hall comedian and accomplished amateur astronomer, who began his screen career in 1933. In his best GAINSBOROUGH comedies he was splendidly partnered by Moore Marriott and Graham Moffatt (*Oh, Mr Porter!*, 1937; *Convict 99*, 1938; *Old Bones of the River*, 1938; *Ask a Policeman*, 1939; *Where's That Fire?*, 1939). His later films, from *The Ghost of St Michael's* (1940) to *My Learned Friend* (1944), were made by EALING STUDIOS, and he co-directed several of them with Basil DEARDEN.

**HAYAKAWA,** SESSUE (1889–1973), Japanese actor who had a distinguished career in US, French, and Japanese films. Thomas INCE, seeing him act in Shakespeare, brought him to the screen in *The Typhoon* (1914). He achieved international fame when Cecil B. DEMILLE cast him as the oriental lover who brands his mistress in *The Cheat* (1915). Other films include *Black Roses* (1921), *La Bataille* (1923), *The Great Prince Shan* (1924), *Three Came Home* (1950), THE BRIDGE ON THE RIVER KWAI (1957).

**HAYDEN,** STERLING (1917–   ), US actor, first attracted attention by his striking appearance and fine physique in *Bahama Passage* (1941), a romance set in the West Indies. He tended to be a limited actor, usually cast as sturdily virile or morose characters; but given a chance by a good director he could give an impressive performance, as his interpretation of the strong-arm man in John HUSTON's THE ASPHALT JUNGLE (1950) showed. Other of his notable films include *Johnny Guitar* (Nicholas RAY, 1954) and *The Killing* (Stanley KUBRICK, 1956). His best role was undoubtedly the psychotic, terrifyingly comic general in Kubrick's DR STRANGELOVE, OR HOW I LEARNED TO STOP WORRYING AND LOVE THE BOMB (1963). He wrote a striking autobiography, *Wanderer* (New York, 1963).

**HAYES,** 'GABBY' (1885–1969), US actor, forenames George Francis, spent many years in vaudeville before going to Hollywood in the late twenties. In 1933 he joined John WAYNE for a long series of 'quickie' Westerns, then partnered first William (Hopalong Cassidy) BOYD, then Roy ROGERS, earning his nickname as a voluble old-timer. He retired from films in 1956.

**HAYES,** HELEN (1900–   ), US actress whose reputation is founded on a distinguished stage career. She has always expressed dissatisfaction with her infrequent films, although she gave fine dramatic performances in *Arrowsmith* (1931) and *A Farewell to Arms* (1933) and was dignified and moving as the Grand Duchess in *Anastasia* (1956).

**HAYS OFFICE/CODE** see CENSORSHIP, US

**HAYS,** WILL H. (1879–1954), was Postmaster-General under the Republican President Warren Harding. In 1921 he was invited by the major studio heads to become first president of the Motion Picture Producers and Distributors of America Inc (later MOTION PICTURE ASSOCIATION OF AMERICA) and remained the industry's official spokesman and arbiter of taste until his retirement in 1945. His singular power led to the MPPDA's being generally known as the Hays Office, and the Production Code on matters of morality as the Hays Office Code (see CENSORSHIP, US); although the Code was not formulated by Hays himself, its provisions were accorded with his small-town Presbyterian mode of thought, and throughout his tenure of office he conscientiously attempted to mould the Hollywood product into a wholesome and totally inoffensive form of family entertainment. After his retirement from the presidency he was a special adviser to the MPAA for a five-year period during which he used his considerable influence in support of the anti-Communist scare which shook Hollywood at that time (see UNAMERICAN ACTIVITIES).

**HAYWARD,** SUSAN (1918–   ), US actress, real name Edythe Marrener, whose thick red hair, tip-tilted nose, and heavily lashed eyes helped to bring her a number of parts as spirited heroines in films like *Tulsa* (1949) and *Untamed* (1955). She also loved and lost very effectively in *My Foolish Heart* (1949). She finally won an OSCAR, after her fifth nomination, for her performance as a murderess in *I Want to Live* (1958).

**HAYWORTH,** RITA (1918–   ), US actress, real name Margarita Cansino, was her father's partner in a Spanish dancing cabaret act; later she was offered a contract with FOX. She appeared in supporting roles under her real name, but her contract was cancelled when Fox merged with Twentieth Century in 1935, and it was not until she was taken up by COLUMBIA that she acquired the name and personality that made her widely popular. *Blood and Sand* (Rouben MAMOULIAN, 1940) exploited her widely advertized 'gipsy' qualities to the full. Her turbulent private life (including a brief and highly-publicized marriage to Prince Aly Khan) and frequent disputes with Columbia kept her very much in the public eye. *Gilda* (1946) confirmed the legendary status that she briefly held as a sex goddess, but THE LADY FROM SHANGHAI (1948), directed by Orson WELLES, her second husband, was less appealing and her career declined during the fifties.

**'H' certificate,** category introduced by the BRITISH BOARD OF FILM CENSORS in 1930 to describe films dealing with the horrific or supernatural and considered unsuitable for children. From 1951 the 'H' certificate was discontinued, and films of this nature were included in the new 'X' CERTIFICATE category. (See CENSORSHIP, GB.)

**HEARST,** WILLIAM RANDOLPH (1863–1950), US newspaper tycoon, wielded much political and business influence through his ownership of numerous newspapers and magazines. Always interested in the cinema, he formed Cosmopolitan Pictures in 1919 for the purpose of making a star of Marion DAVIES. The company moved from New York to California in 1924, operating from METRO-GOLDWYN-MAYER's studios until 1934, then from WARNER BROS. His power to make or ruin films and reputations through his newspapers may have been exaggerated; nevertheless, throughout the twenties and thirties he was one of the most feared men in the industry. He was the inspiration for CITIZEN KANE (1941), which he tried unsuccessfully to have suppressed.

W. A. Swanberg, *Citizen Hearst* (New York, 1961, London, 1962).

**HEARTS OF THE WORLD**, US, 1918. 2hr. *Dir, prod* D. W. Griffith; *scr* M. Gaston de Tolignac, translated into English by Capt Victor Marier (pseudonyms of Griffith); *ph* Billy Bitzer; *technical supervisor* Erich von Stroheim; *mus accompaniment* Carli Elinor, Griffith; *cast* Adolphe Lestina (the Grandfather), Josephine Cromwell (the Mother), Lillian Gish (the Girl), Robert Harron (the Boy), Jack Cosgrave (the Father of the Boy), Kate Bruce (the Mother of the Boy), Ben Alexander (the Littlest Brother), Dorothy Gish (the Little Disturber), Erich von Stroheim and Noël Coward uncredited.

With America's entry into the war the film industry threw itself into PROPAGANDA activity, supporting the official line with entertainment films of an extreme anti-German character. As one of the American cinema's most prestigious figures, GRIFFITH was invited by the British Government to make a film partly financed by the Ministry of Information. He was joined in London in early 1917 by his cameraman Billy BITZER and by Lillian GISH and her mother, who also played a small part in the film. They paid a brief visit to the battle front in France where some material was shot, although not by Bitzer whose German name precluded his admission to the combat areas; on their return to America in October 1917, a large amount of footage of the German army on manoeuvres was privately bought. Probably two-thirds of the film was made in the usual way in the California studios.

*Hearts of the World* is set in an occupied French village: the enemy is never actually named but is clearly Germany. The story reflects the style of its time, with near-caricatures of the barbaric Hun, and inevitably culminates in Lillian Gish's narrow escape from rape by a jack-booted officer. The film is outstanding for her performance and for Griffith's use of the French and German actuality footage which added a startling dimension of reality. Its immense public success went a long way towards restoring faith in Griffith after the disastrous failure of INTOLERANCE (1916).

**HEAVY**, term applied mainly in GANGSTER and WESTERN films to the male roles incorporating either the amoral hero who shoots in the back, hits women, and betrays his best friend (typified by James CAGNEY) or the sidekick strong man to the criminal boss. These characters are often psychopaths who break out into uncontrolled violence, and are usually played by actors who can produce mean facial expressions, and have scars or squints. Many actors have built a career on such roles, for example Richard Boone, Ray Danton, Jack Elam, Richard Jaeckel, Ralph Meeker, Richard Rust, Lee VAN CLEEF, Dan DURYEA, and Jack PALANCE.

Some actors have succeeded in breaking out from 'heavy' secondary roles to stardom, including Lee MARVIN, the personification of evil in THE BIG HEAT (1953) and THE KILLERS (1964), and Richard WIDMARK who became widely known as a giggling sadist in KISS OF DEATH (1947) and *No Way Out* (1950).

Ian and Elizabeth Cameron, *The heavies*, London, 1967.

**HECHT**, BEN (1894–1964), US writer whose parents were Jewish immigrants from Russia. After working as a journalist, mainly on the Chicago *Daily News*, he made his name in 1928 with a stage play, THE FRONT PAGE, written with Charles MACARTHUR, with whom Hecht frequently collaborated thereafter. *The Front Page* became a successful film in 1931 and Hecht became a screen writer, notably with SCARFACE (1932) and TWENTIETH CENTURY (1934) for Howard HAWKS, until disenchantment with Hollywood caused him and MacArthur to embark on independent film production. Their first co-scripted, co-produced, and co-directed film, CRIME WITHOUT PASSION (1934), pleased only the critics; the second was shelved; but the third, THE SCOUNDREL (1935), with Noël COWARD in his first major film role, established their position as distant from conventional American cinema as their Long Island studio was from Hollywood. The sharp naturalism of their dialogue, spiced with acid wit, helped to introduce a new style of writing to Hollywood; their black humour startled and delighted more sophisticated audiences. *Soak the Rich* (1936) was the last of their independent ventures, but their collaboration continued. NOTHING SACRED (1937) was one of Carole LOMBARD's best comedies, and they reputedly wrote the script for WUTHERING HEIGHTS (1939) during a trans-American train journey.

In 1948, Hecht's active opposition to British policy in Palestine, including a campaign against the distribution of British films in the US, led to a temporary ban by the British Cinematograph Exhibitors Association on all films with which he was connected.

**HECKROTH**, HEIN (1897–      ), German art director who became a stage designer at the age of twenty and moved to Britain to be one of the designers for Gabriel PASCAL's CAESAR AND CLEOPATRA (1945). He was associated with the productions of Michael POWELL and Emeric PRESSBURGER, initially as costume designer for *A Matter of Life and Death* (1946, *Stairway to Heaven* in US) and *Black Narcissus* (1947), then as production designer, his work on THE RED SHOES (1948) winning him an OSCAR.

**HEFLIN**, VAN (1910–71), US actor who made his film début in *A Woman Rebels* (1936). After winning an OSCAR for the best supporting performance in *Johnny Eager* (1942), and despite wartime interruption of his career, he soon rose to stardom in a number of METRO-GOLDWYN-MAYER films, including *Presenting Lily Mars* (1942), *Green Dolphin Street* (1947), *Act of Violence* (1948), *The Three Musketeers* (1948), and *Madame Bovary* (1949). He appeared in several UNIVERSAL films, *Tap Roots* (1948), *Tomahawk* (1951), and *Weekend with Father* (1951), and also in Joseph LOSEY's *The Prowler* (1950). Probably his most impressive performance was as the rancher in SHANE (1953), a role which made full use of his rugged, earnest quality. Notable among his later films were 3.10 TO YUMA (Delmer DAVES, 1957), *They Came to Cordura* (Robert ROSSEN, 1959), *Five Branded Women* (Martin RITT, 1960), and *Airport* (George Seaton, 1969).

**HEIFITS**, JOSIF (1906– ), Russian director, joined the Lenfilm studios as an apprentice during the twenties. Most of his films until 1950 were co-directed by Alexander Zarkhi. *Deputat Baltiki* (*Baltic Deputy*, 1937) and *Chlen pravitelstva* (*Member of the Government*, 1940), both of which portrayed the involvement of an individual in the revolutionary cause, were acclaimed in the Soviet Union. His later films include *Vo imya zhini* (*In the Name of Life*, 1947), *Bolshaya semya* (*The Great Family*, 1954), *Delo Rumyantseva* (*The Roumiantsev Case*, 1955), and *Dorogoi moi chelovek* (*My Dear Man*, 1958). He has also filmed adaptations of two stories by Chekhov: DAMA S SOBACHKOI (*The Lady with the Little Dog*, 1959), from the story of the same name, and *V gorode 'S'* (*In the Town of S*, 1966), from the story 'Ionych'. Heifits's style, with its leisurely narrative pace and acute observation of detail, lends itself admirably to the form of the short story, and these adaptations show delicacy and warmth in translating to the screen the qualities of Chekhov's work. Out of the wide range of films he has made, these two are perhaps his finest achievement.

***HEIR TO JENGHIS KHAN, The,*** see POTOMOK CHINGHIS-KHANA

**HELLER**, OTTO (1896–1970), Czech cameraman who began working in the industry in 1922

(there is a story that he embarked accidentally on his career when he was a soldier in the Austrian army, and had a camera thrust into his hands at the funeral of Franz-Josef). He worked in Czechoslovakia during the twenties, making his name mainly with Karel Lamač: he became known as one of 'the big four' of Czech cinema, together with Lamač, Anny ONDRA, and scriptwriter Václav Wassermann. As sound came in, they all worked increasingly in Germany and France, but Heller made some distinguished films in Prague, including Martin FRIČ's *Hej rup!* (*Heave-Ho*, 1934). He visited London in 1936, and continued working in western Europe before the war, escaping from Paris in 1940 to join the Czech air force in Britain. After the war he settled in Britain, and was regularly engaged on films. His most distinguished work includes DICKINSON's THE QUEEN OF SPADES (1948), *The Ipcress File* (1965), and *Alfie* (1966).

**HELLINGER**, MARK (1903–47), US writer, journalist, and producer. A journalist from 1923, he based his first script *Night Court* (W. S. VAN DYKE, 1932) on his own play; further scripts included *Broadway Bill* (Frank CAPRA, 1935) and THE ROARING TWENTIES (Raoul WALSH, 1939). He left journalism to become an associate producer with Hal WALLIS at WARNER BROS, and worked on *Torrid Zone* (1940). He was production supervisor for *Brother Orchid* (Lloyd BACON, 1940) and then associate producer for four Raoul Walsh films, including *High Sierra* (1941). He began producing for TWENTIETH CENTURY-FOX in 1941 with *Rise and Shine* (Allan DWAN), then returned to Warners, was a war correspondent in the South Pacific, and finally joined UNIVERSAL in 1946. Two powerful Burt LANCASTER films resulted: THE KILLERS (Robert SIODMAK, 1946) and *Brute Force* (Jules DASSIN, 1947). Hellinger died before the release of his last production, the remarkable *Naked City* (Dassin, 1948).

**HELLMAN**, LILLIAN (1905– ), US playwright and scriptwriter whose work, usually dealing with controversial subjects, has frequently been transferred to the screen. Her own adaptation was used for *These Three* (1936), from her play *The Children's Hour*, which was filmed again in 1962 under the original title (changed to *The Loudest Whisper* in GB), directed by William WYLER. She also adapted her play THE LITTLE FOXES for Wyler in 1941. Among her other plays which have been filmed are *Watch on the Rhine* (1943), scripted by Dashiell HAMMETT, *Another Part of the Forest* (1948), and *Toys in the Attic* (1963). Her original film scripts include *Dark Angel* (1935), Wyler's DEAD END (1937), *North Star* (Lewis

MILESTONE, 1943), and THE CHASE (Arthur PENN, 1966).

**HELLZAPOPPIN'**, US, 1941. 1½hr. *Dir* H. C. Potter; *prod* Universal; *scr* Nat Perrin, Warren Wilson; *ph* Woody Bredell; *ed* Milton Carruth; *special effects* John Fulton; *cast* Ole Olsen (Ole), Chic Johnson (Chic), Martha Raye (Betty), Mischa Auer (Pepi), Jane Frazee (Kitty), Hugh Herbert (Quimby), Robert Paige (Jeff).

Olsen and Johnson's film version of their long-running Broadway success was something of a novelty: scarcely anything comparable in zany eccentricity and near-surrealist humour had been seen on the screen since the MARX BROTHERS' early films. They made resourceful use of special effects, including an out-of-rack stunt in which, with the frame divided in the middle, their legs were at the top of the picture, their faces at the bottom, whereupon they hurled abuse at the bungling projectionist.

Hugh Herbert bumbled and burbled, Mischa Auer as an exiled Russian was a delight (even his simple request for a portion of bread created difficulties), and in particular the wide-mouthed, high-decibel Martha Raye was in full flight: her energetic volatility was an enlivening asset and her 'Watch the Birdy' number was a show-stopper.

Olsen and Johnson never repeated the success of *Hellzapoppin'*; their follow-up film (*Crazy House*, 1944) was tame by comparison, and they soon faded from the scene.

**HELM**, BRIGITTA (1906– ), German actress, real name Gisele Eve Schiltenhelm, whose film career lasted only eleven years before she retired in 1936 to marry a wealthy industrialist. LANG gave her her first screen part in the dual role of the heroine and her robot double in METROPOLIS (1927). Her strikingly distinctive face with its strong profile made her particularly successful in the roles of dominating women with almost hypnotic power over men. She made several films for PABST; in *Die Liebe der Jeanne Ney* (1927) she was uncharacteristically cast as a lonely blind girl; in *Abwege* (*Crisis*, 1928) she gave a powerful performance as the embittered wife. Other films include *L'Argent* (1928), *Alraune* (1928), and *The Blue Danube* (1932), which she made in England for Herbert WILCOX.

**HEMINGWAY**, ERNEST (1898–1961), US author whose public image, arising from his exploits in war and hunting, and his friendships with well-known personalities, was closely identified with his fictional heroes. Because of their strong active plots and his spare, visually exact prose style, very many of his novels and stories have been adapted for the screen, some more

than once. Among the film versions are *A Farewell to Arms* (1933), starring Hemingway's hero, Gary COOPER, remade in 1957; TO HAVE AND HAVE NOT (HAWKS, 1944), remade as *The Breaking Point* (1950) and *The Gun Runner* (1956); THE KILLERS (1946 and 1964), in which Hemingway's original dialogue and setting were reproduced with unusual exactness; and *The Old Man and the Sea* (1958), with Spencer TRACY. From his experiences in the Spanish Civil War Hemingway wrote *For Whom the Bell Tolls* (filmed in 1943 by Sam WOOD) and the script for Joris IVENS's documentary THE SPANISH EARTH (1937). Footage from the latter is included in Fausto Canel's *Hemingway* (1962), made in Cuba where Hemingway lived for many years. His house features in ALEA'S MEMORIAS DEL SUBDESAROLLO (*Memories of Underdevelopment*, 1968).

**HENIE**, SONJA (1912–69), Norwegian ice-skating champion, broke into films with *One in a Million* (1936) and for a time her wholesome appeal and ice-skating expertise were very popular. Her acting talent was, however, limited and of her dozen or so films only *Sun Valley Serenade* (1941) is memorable, chiefly for Glenn Miller's music.

**HENREID**, PAUL (1908– ), Italian-born Austrian actor who made his stage début in Vienna. After playing in Austrian films and on the New York stage, he visited England to appear in Carol REED's *Night Train to Munich* (1940). He then went to Hollywood where he became a devastating romantic hero in a number of WARNER BROS productions, including *Now Voyager* (1942) and CASABLANCA (1943). He later assumed a more swashbuckling guise in *The Spanish Main* (1945), *Last of the Buccaneers* (1950), and *Pirates of Tripoli* (1955), and also turned to direction (*For Men Only*, 1952). In later years he was particularly concerned with directing television films.

**HENRY V**, GB, 1944. Technicolor; 2½hr. *Dir* Laurence Olivier; *prod* Two Cities; *scr* Olivier, Alan Dent from Shakespeare's play; *ph* Robert Krasker; *des* Paul Sheriff; *mus* William Walton; *cast* Laurence Olivier (Henry V), Robert Newton (Pistol), Renee Asherson (Princess Katherine), Leslie Banks (Chorus), Esmond Knight (Fluellen).

Generally acknowledged as one of the most imaginative screen adaptations of Shakespeare, *Henry V* was Laurence OLIVIER's first film as director. Stylistically it is symmetrical in structure. Opening as a performance of the play in the Globe Theatre of Shakespeare's time, the film moves out of the theatre via stylized sets, with flattened perspective and bright colours copied from medieval illuminations, to the Battle of Agincourt which was shot on location. Then stylization takes over once more and the final scene ends in the Globe.

The Battle of Agincourt, inspired jointly by Uccello's painting *The Rout of San Romano* and the battle on the ice from EISENSTEIN's ALEXANDER NEVSKY (1938), was shot in neutral Eire using 500 men borrowed from the Eirean Home Guard.

Costing nearly half a million pounds, raised by the producer Filippo DEL GIUDICE, *Henry V* was made at a time when Britain was preparing to invade German-occupied France. Both at its release and well into the austere post-war period it proved a great success with a British public no doubt eager to escape into a more flamboyant age. In a less emotional climate the flaws have become more apparent. Stylization and naturalism are uneasily mated, not only in the art direction but, more importantly, in the performances which remain solidly within the conventions of the classical theatre.

**HEPBURN,** AUDREY (1929–   ), US actress, real name Edda Hepburn van Heemstra, was born in Belgium of Irish–Dutch parentage. She trained as a dancer in London and in 1951 appeared in THE LAVENDER HILL MOB and *Secret People* (Thorold DICKINSON) before achieving wide popularity with her starring part in ROMAN HOLIDAY (William WYLER, 1953). To this slight but charming romantic comedy she brought an individual quality of freshness and innocence which was maintained and developed in *Sabrina* (Billy WILDER, 1954) against the formidable competition of such experienced players as Humphrey BOGART and William HOLDEN. In *War and Peace* (King VIDOR, 1956) she gave a creditable performance as Natasha, but Stanley DONEN's FUNNY FACE (1957) showed off her personality to the full: her tomboyish charm was combined with a grace and elegance which pointed the way in which her style would develop.

*Green Mansions* (1959), directed by Mel FERRER, then her husband, was not well received, but in Fred ZINNEMANN's *The Nun's Story* (1959) she gave a performance of great sensitivity and warmth. By now she was a recognized and very popular star and as Eliza Doolittle in MY FAIR LADY (1964) she was justly acclaimed for the style and polish of her performance. Such a success was hard to follow up and her subsequent films, such as *Two for the Road* (Donen, 1966), with Albert FINNEY, have been less popular, but the increasing maturity of her acting shows that she has successfully progressed past the limitations of the *ingénue* roles that initiated her success.

**HEPBURN,** KATHARINE (1909–   ), US actress, began her acting career on Broadway in 1929 in *Night Hostess*. She made an exciting film début in *A Bill of Divorcement* (1932), with John BARRYMORE; her next film, *Morning Glory* (1933), won her the first of eleven OSCARS and in the same year she played Jo in *Little Women*.

In her early films the astringent quality of her performances, together with her far from glamorous looks, limited her public appeal. The studio heads at one time considered her 'box office poison' and resented her determination to fight their domination of her career, but over a period of several years her versatility in comedy and drama and the vivid intelligence of her acting gradually won her a large following.

She has managed not only to maintain her stage career but also to make the difficult transition from the romantic leads of her early films to maturer characters in her more recent work. Of the romantic roles she is best remembered in BRINGING UP BABY (1938), HOLIDAY (1938), and THE PHILADELPHIA STORY (1940), in all of which she co-starred with Cary GRANT; in films such as THE AFRICAN QUEEN (1952), *Summertime* (1955, *Summer Madness* in GB), and *The Rainmaker* (1956) she played, with a combination of dry wit and touching gaucheness, variations on the stock character of an older, inexperienced woman unexpectedly meeting with romantic adventures. In the sixties she was offered a greater variety of characterization: the neurotic Mrs Venable of *Suddenly Last Summer* (1960), the morphine addict of *Long Day's Journey into Night* (1962), the middle-class 'liberal' of *Guess Who's Coming to Dinner* (1967), Eleanor of Aquitaine in *The Lion in Winter* (1968), the eccentric *Madwoman of Chaillot* (1969), and Hecuba in *The Trojan Women* (1971).

Of her screen partners none was a better match for her than Spencer TRACY, with whom she made a number of films, including WOMAN OF THE YEAR (1942), ADAM's RIB (1949), *Pat and Mike* (1952), and *Desk Set* (1957, *His Other Woman* in GB). The rapport which they achieved in these films was a reflection of their own close personal relationship. She has worked with some of the world's best-known directors, including John FORD, John HUSTON, George CUKOR, and David LEAN, as well as some of the newer directors such as Bryan FORBES, Stanley KRAMER, and Sidney LUMET.

**HEPWORTH,** CECIL (1874–1953), British producer/director. The son of a magic lantern operator, Hepworth entered the film business by designing some hand-fed arc lamps and selling them to the pioneer exhibitor R. W. PAUL, for his Theatrograph. He became a travelling showman himself and in 1897 published probably the first book devoted to the cinema, *Animated Photography, or the ABC of the Cinematograph.* In 1895 he set up his laboratory and Hepwix Studio—its size variously quoted by him as 15ft × 8ft and 10ft × 6ft—at Walton-on-Thames and by the turn of the century was making a hundred films a year there. Perhaps the most famous film attributed to Hepworth was *Rescued by Rover* (1905), a seven-minute sentimental thriller with a total budget of less than £8. It showed his already maturing narrative and editing skill (as well as, incidentally, his family's acting ability) and sold a record 395 copies.

Paul retired in 1910, but Hepworth and those he had gathered round him led a revival based on efficient publicity and the creation of a British star system with such actors as Chrissie White, Alma Taylor, and Stewart Rome. In 1923, at the height of his success, he made *Comin' Thro' the Rye,* his second version of the subject. With its then-enormous budget of £10,000, he finally over-reached himself and, within six months, was declared bankrupt. Though Hepworth continued to work in educational films and in various Commonwealth countries, he was never an important film-maker again. His many writings include an autobiography, *Came the dawn,* London, 1951.

*HERR ARNES PENGAR* (*Sir Arne's Treasure*), Sweden, 1919. 1¾hr. *Dir* Mauritz Stiller; *prod* Svenska Bio; *scr* Stiller, Gustaf Molander, from the novel by Selma Lagerlöf; *ph* J. Julius Jaenzon; *cast* Hjalmar Selander (Sir Arne), Richard Lund (Sir Archie), Mary Johnson (Elsalill).

Originally to have been directed by Victor SJÖSTRÖM, *Herr Arnes pengar* drew STILLER away from the elegant comedies in which he had so far specialized. Powerfully fatalistic, the story is played out against a snow-bound landscape: the procession of black-robed figures following the coffin of the young girl, Elsalill, across the frozen lake is particularly memorable.

**HERRMANN, BERNARD** (1911– ), US composer and conductor, worked from 1933 for CBS writing background music for radio programmes. The score of CITIZEN KANE (1941) was his distinguished début in films: since then he has become established as one of America's most professional and prolific film composers, with a craftsmanlike knack of creating music that complements a film's visual content and faithfully carries through the director's intention. The films for which he has composed include THE MAGNIFICENT AMBERSONS (1942), *Anna and the King of Siam* (1946), using authentic Siamese scales, and *The Day the Earth Stood Still* (1951), with electronically amplified instrumental sounds used in fragmentary melodic structures. He has become associated with suspense films, largely through his collaborations with HITCHCOCK which include THE MAN WHO KNEW TOO MUCH (1956), in which part of the score for the original (1934) version was retained, NORTH BY NORTHWEST (1959), and PSYCHO (1960), in which he achieved chilling effects limiting himself to a string orchestra. No music was used in *The Birds* (1963), but Herrmann collaborated on the electronically-produced effects track. He has also worked with TRUFFAUT on *Fahrenheit 451* (1966) and *La Mariée était en noir* (1967).

**HERSKÓ, JÁNOS** (1926– ), Hungarian director, who began by studying philosophy, aesthetics, and the history of art at university before enrolling at the Academy for Film Art. After graduating in 1949 and a spell of short film work, he won a scholarship in 1951 and went to study at VGIK in Moscow. On his return he made his feature début with *A város alatt* (*Under the City,* 1953). With *Párbeszéd* (*Dialogue,* 1963) his stature was revealed as one of the middle-generation directors (along with Károly MAKK, Miklós JANCSÓ, András KOVÁCS, etc) who gave Hungarian cinema of the sixties a confident new approach from which to develop its present idiom. His work behind the scenes includes positions as Professor of Film Direction and Assistant Director at the Academy, and artistic director of Mafilm Studio 3. His work as a director has necessarily been sporadic, but he returned in 1970 with a brilliantly ironic comedy *N.N. a halal angyala* (*Requiem in the Hungarian Manner*), later emigrating with his family to Sweden.

**HERZOG, WERNER** (1942– ), German director, studied literature, theatre, and history in Pittsburgh and Munich. He began his career in the cinema with short films, *Herakles* (1963, remade in 1965) and *Spiel im Sand* (1966). His first full-length feature was *Feuerzeichen* (1967), later renamed *Lebenszeichen* (*Signs of Life*), which was followed by *Auch Zwerge haben klein engefangen* (*Even Dwarfs Started Small,* 1970), set on an island where dwarfs act out an obscene parody of everyday life. *Fata Morgana* (1971), shot in the Sahara, is an abstract parable of man's life on earth; in the same year he made another allegory using deaf mutes, *Land des Schweigens und der Dunkelheit* (*The Land of Darkness and Silence*). On a much larger scale, *Aguirre, der Zorn Gottes* (*Aguirre, Wrath of God,* 1973) uses the exploits of the Spanish *conquistadores* to illustrate the depravity of imperialism.

Herzog's work shows an originality and imagination central to the recent resurgence of German cinema.

**HESSLING, CATHERINE,** French film actress, real name Andrée Heuschling. She was model for some of Auguste Renoir's last paintings and married his son Jean in 1920. It was for her that Jean RENOIR wrote and produced *Une Vie sans joie* (also known as *Catherine*) in 1924. She was the star of four of the first five films he directed—including *Nana* (1926), from Zola's novel. She also acted in several shorts made by their friend Alberto CAVALCANTI in the late twenties, but her career was virtually at an end when she separated from Renoir in 1930.

**HESTON, CHARLTON** (1924– ), US actor whose first film appearance was as Peer Gynt in an experimental production by David BRADLEY in 1941. In the late forties he established himself as a stage actor, playing both modern and Shakespearian roles. His television appearances at this time included *Jane Eyre* (1948) and *Macbeth* (1950) directed by Franklin SCHAFFNER and he played Mark Antony in David Bradley's amateur film of JULIUS CAESAR (1949). Heston's distinctive voice, deep and well modulated, was well suited to the role of Moses in Cecil B. DEMILLE's *The Ten Commandments* (1956), in which he was also heard as the voice of God. His features and physique were, early in his film career, regarded as especially suited to ranchers, planters, military men, and adventurers. He was in King VIDOR's *Ruby Gentry* (1952) and gave a performance of outstanding integrity as the incorruptible investigator Vargas in TOUCH OF EVIL (1958). For a time he became widely identified with leading roles in historical epics such as BEN-HUR (1959), for which he won an OSCAR, and EL CID (1961). In the sixties he worked fruitfully again with Schaffner in *The War Lord* (1965) and PLANET OF THE APES (1968) and the decline in popularity of epic productions gave him the opportunity to turn from heroic to more complex characters such as General Gordon in *Khartoum* (1966), Major Dundee in Sam PECKINPAH's film of the same name (1964), and the grizzled cowpuncher in *Will Penny* (1967). In 1970 he again played Mark Antony in a British film version of *Julius Caesar* directed by Stuart Burge. A well-known liberal, Heston has been active in the Civil Rights Movement and is much admired in the industry for his scrupulous professionalism. He is President of the Screen Actors Guild of Hollywood.

*HETS* (*Frenzy*), Sweden, 1944. 1¾hr. *Dir* Alf Sjöberg; *prod* Svensk Filmindustri; *scr, asst dir* Ingmar Bergman; *ph* Martin Bodin; *ed* Oscar Rosander; *cast* Stig Jarrel (Caligula), Alf Kjellin (Jan-Erik), Mai Zetterling (Bertha), Olof Winnerstrand (headmaster).

The adolescent Jan-Erik, victimized at school by the sadistic master nicknamed Caligula and misunderstood at home, turns to a young alcoholic prostitute for affection. Her terror of an unknown man ends in her death at the hands of Caligula. Jan-Erik enters adult life lonely but free.

In spite of its schematic plot and conventional characterization, the story is carried by a powerfully expressionistic visual style. Jan-Erik's isolation and humiliation are characteristic of SJÖBERG's work; they also prefigure aspects of BERGMAN's later preoccupations.

*Hets* caused some stir abroad as an indication of the resurgence of Swedish cinema. The film also helped Mai ZETTERLING on her way to becoming an international star.

**HICKOCK, JAMES BUTLER ('WILD BILL')** (1837–76), soldier, scout, Indian fighter, lawman, vagrant, and Wild West Show star, shot in the back while playing poker. In 1923 he was played by W. S. HART in *Wild Bill Hickock*, directed by Hart with Wyatt EARP as technical adviser, in 1937 by Gary COOPER in DEMILLE's *The Plainsman*, and in 1953 by Howard Keel in *Calamity Jane*.

*HIDDEN FORTRESS, The,* see KAKUSHI TORIDE NO SAN-AKUNIN

*HIDEG NAPOK* (*Cold Days*), Hungary, 1966. Agascope; 1¾hr. *Dir, scr* András Kovács; *prod* Mafilm; *ph* Ferenc Szécsenyi; *cast* Zoltán Latinovits (Büky), Iván Darvas (Tarpataki), Tibor Szilágyi (Pozdor), Margit Bara (Büky's wife), Eva Vas (Edit), Irén Psota (Betty).

In January 1942, extreme pro-German elements in the Hungarian garrison of Ujvidék (Novi Sad) in Yugoslavia undertook a purge of Serbian partisans in the town: the so-called mopping-up operation resulted in the indiscriminate slaughter of 3,309 people.

The film recapitulates the event through the memories and mutual recriminations of four men in a prison cell, awaiting sentence for implication in the atrocity. Through flashbacks, an unusually complex narrative is built up, where separate incidents are progressively expanded, unfolding the horror with unflinching gravity. KOVÁCS draws from his players performances of outstanding conviction; the film is also notable for its chilly visual beauty and for the uncompromising acknowledgement of individual responsibility for collective crimes.

*HIGH NOON*, US, 1952. 1½hr. *Dir* Fred Zinnemann; *prod* Stanley Kramer; *scr* Carl Foreman from a story 'The Tin Star' by John W. Cunningham; *ph* Floyd Crosby; *mus* Dmitri

Tiomkin; *cast* Gary Cooper (Will Kane), Grace Kelly (Amy Kane), Thomas Mitchell (Jonas Henderson), Lloyd Bridges (Hervey Pell), Katy Jurado (Helen Ramirez).

On the day of his marriage to a strict Quaker and his retirement as Marshall of a small frontier town, Will Kane is warned that a group of gunmen who have previously terrorized the community will return on the noon train. The local worthies refuse to risk standing by him against the threatened violence and he faces the danger alone. Gary COOPER, at his quiet best in the leading role, won an OSCAR as did Dmitri TIOMKIN for the pulsing theme tune which became a popular hit.

An intelligent Western, *High Noon* earned much popularity, especially in France where it was highly praised by, among others, André BAZIN. Its impact was sharpened by the comment intended by FOREMAN on the effects of McCarthyism, and it stimulated much discussion on the use of the WESTERN genre.

*HIGH SOCIETY*, US, 1956. VistaVision; 1¾hr; Technicolor. *Dir* Charles Walters; *prod* MGM; *cast* Bing Crosby (C. K. Dexter-Haven), Frank Sinatra (Mike Connor), Grace Kelly (Tracy Lord), Louis Armstrong, Celeste Holm (Liz Imbrie).

A musical remake of THE PHILADELPHIA STORY, faithful to the original plot, but setting the events at the time of the Newport Jazz Festival in order to feature the playing and singing of Louis Armstrong.

*HIGH, WIDE AND HANDSOME*, US, 1937. 1¾hr. *Dir* Rouben Mamoulian; *prod* Arthur Hornblow Jr for Paramount; *scr, lyr* Oscar Hammerstein II; *ph* Victor Milner; *mus* Jerome Kern; *cast* Irene Dunne (Sally), Randolph Scott (Peter Cortlandt), Dorothy Lamour (Molly), Charles Bickford (Red Smith), Alan Hale (Brennan), Raymond Walburn (Doc Watterson), Akim Tamiroff.

A spectacular melodrama interwoven with music and romance concerns the struggle by prospectors in the Pennsylvania oilfields in 1859 against the railroad tycoons, trying to prevent the construction of a pipe-line. MAMOULIAN handled the elaborate plot with skill (including a scene where a circus—with elephants—becomes involved in a fight), ably supported by the performances of Irene DUNNE and Randolph SCOTT. Original songs written for the film include 'Can I Forget You' and 'The Folks Who Live on the Hill'.

**HILL,** GEORGE ROY (1922– ), US director, after serving in Europe during the Second World War, remained to study in Dublin, becoming an

actor with Cyril Cusack's company at the Abbey Theatre. After returning to the US he worked for many years in the theatre and television, scoring his first Broadway success as a director with *Look Homeward Angel* in 1957.

His first feature film was *Period of Adjustment* (1962), from the play he had directed on the stage; his second film, *Toys in the Attic* (1963), was also from a stage play. He then formed an independent company, Pan Arts, with his exagent Jerry Hellman, and made *The World of Henry Orient* (1964), a story of adolescent girls in New York with a theme of fading innocence found in much of his work. *Thoroughly Modern Millie* (1967), starring Julie ANDREWS, was a moderate success; but Hill became an important box-office name with BUTCH CASSIDY AND THE SUNDANCE KID (1969), which teamed Paul NEWMAN and Robert REDFORD in a cheerfully eclectic, stylish Western. The trio repeated this success with *The Sting* (1973), in which Hill managed a convoluted tale of confidence tricksters, as well as the marvellously chiming personalities of his two stars, with remarkable skill and lightness of touch.

**HILLER,** WENDY (1912– ), British actress, started her distinguished stage career in 1922. Among her several outstanding film appearances she is remembered chiefly in two adaptations from plays by SHAW: PYGMALION (1938) and MAJOR BARBARA (1941), but she has also given memorable performances in *Separate Tables* (1958) and *Toys in the Attic* (1963).

**HIRD,** THORA (1914– ), British actress. Lancashire-born, she made her film début in a Will HAY film, *The Black Sheep of Whitehall* (1941), and became a favourite comedy-character actress. Much in demand for films, she has also pursued a successful career on both stage and television. Her daughter is the actress Janette Scott.

*HIROSHIMA MON AMOUR*, France/Japan, 1959. 1½hr. *Dir* Alain Resnais; *prod* Argos Films, Como Films, Daiei Motion Pictures, Pathé Overseas; *scr* Marguerite Duras; *ph* Sacha Vierny, Takahashi Michio; *des* Esaka, Mayo, Petri; *mus* Giovanni Fusco, Georges Delerue; *cast* Emmanuele Riva (the actress), Eiji Okada (the Japanese), Bernard Fresson (the German), Stella Dassas (the mother), Pierre Barbaud (the father).

A French actress filming in Hiroshima has a brief affair with a Japanese she meets there. Images of love and death commingle in this town haunted by its tragic past, and the affair brings back memories of a previous love to the actress: during the war, in her home town Nevers, she had been in love with a German soldier and had

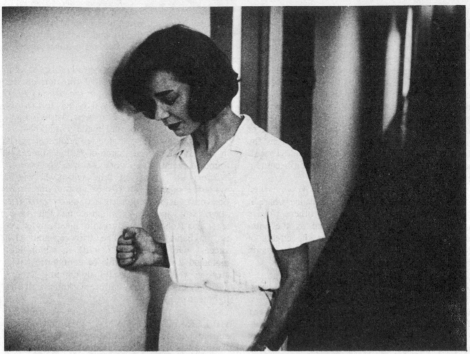

*Hiroshima mon amour* (Alain Resnais, 1959)

undergone a crisis of madness after he had been shot.

Nevers and Hiroshima, personal and universal tragedy, memory and oblivion, these themes evolve from the essentially simple love story. RESNAIS's first feature film, *Hiroshima* contains remarkable innovations, and reveals the possibilities of a new literary cinema, which could incorporate elaborate written texts and yet remain wholly cinematic. Sound, instead of merely explaining and supporting the visual story, is conceived as a vital and independent component; word, image, and music stand in a contrapuntal relationship, giving a new expressive resonance. The film, in its juxtaposition of remembered images with those of the present, in its mingling of different time sequences, reaches towards a portrayal of subjective time, a theme which Resnais developed in his later films.

**HIS GIRL FRIDAY**, US, 1940. 1½hr. *Dir, prod* Howard Hawks; *scr* Charles Lederer, from the play *The Front Page* by Ben Hecht and Charles MacArthur; *ph* Joseph Walker; *cast* Cary Grant (Walter Burns), Rosalind Russell (Hildy Johnson), Ralph Bellamy (Bruce Baldwin).

Howard HAWKS's adaptation into a SCREW-BALL comedy of THE FRONT PAGE was con-siderably more successful than Lewis MILE-STONE's (1930), despite the latter's ostensible closeness to the original. Although one of the leading male roles was rewritten for a woman (Hildebrand Johnson becoming Hildegard), the film is faithful to the fast-talking pace and tone of the play, the sex-war element serving to heighten the shrewd, ironic drama of American newspaper life. Cary GRANT's performance, as the editor, has a sharpness and strength largely responsible for the film's effectiveness.

**HIS NEW JOB**, US, 1915. 30min. *Dir, scr* Charles Chaplin; *prod* Essanay; *ph* Rollie Totheroh; *cast* Charlie Chaplin (the actor), Ben Turpin (his rival), Charlotte Mineau (the actress), Leo White (an actor), Gloria Swanson (a typist).

CHAPLIN's first film for ESSANAY was the only one he made in their Chicago studio before moving back to California where he felt more at home. In this satire on film-making (at the 'Lockstone Studios', an obvious reference to the KEY-STONE Company which he had just left), Chaplin first worked with Ben TURPIN, and first had as cameraman Rollie Totheroh, who worked on every one of his subsequent films up to and including LIMELIGHT (1952).

HITCHCOCK, ALFRED (1899– ), British director, after a Jesuit education and a short period in advertising, went to work for Famous Players-Lasky when they opened their studio at Islington, London, in 1920. His first job was lettering and designing the backgrounds for silent film titles. When Michael BALCON took over the studio in 1922, Hitchcock worked there as assistant director, art director, and scriptwriter to Graham Cutts. His early experience included work at the UFA studios in Germany (during the slump that preceded the first British QUOTA legislation) and the style of his early films reflects this contact with EXPRESSIONISM as well as a natural Anglo-American influence.

After several apprentice works of little distinction, Hitchcock directed *The Lodger* (1927), the tale of a family who suspect their lodger of being a latter-day Jack the Ripper. This is his first film to contain the basic characteristics of his developed style: the ordinary person caught up in extraordinary events; the suspense story that has provided the basis of nearly all his films; and exuberantly imaginative cinematic effects (including the famous shot through a glass floor of the lodger pacing his room above the family sitting-room, eloquently conveying the impression of sound). Because of a temporary shortage of extras, Hitchcock himself appeared in *The Lodger*; subsequently a glimpse of his rotund form became an obligatory gag, occurring in almost all his films.

BLACKMAIL (1929) was the first British feature film with synchronous sound; and already showed the characteristic interplay of sound-track and editing that distinguishes his work throughout his career. It introduced his recurrent motif of the chase, which he has developed with great expertise by the dramatic use of rapidly changing settings and a blend of realism and intense stylization that achieves the vivid impact of a nightmare. Following the success of *Blackmail*, Hitchcock directed a variety of films including some routine theatrical adaptations and even a musical, *Waltzes from Vienna* (1933). His outstanding films of the thirties were all thrillers: THE MAN WHO KNEW TOO MUCH (1934), THE THIRTY-NINE STEPS (1935), SABOTAGE (1936, *A Woman Alone* in US), and THE LADY VANISHES (1938). Apart from demonstrating his increasing skill in manipulating the conventions of suspense drama, these show him introducing humour as an off-setting device to increase tension. In *The Lady Vanishes* he also set himself the problem of limiting the action to a restricted setting, to which he was to return later.

Shortly before the outbreak of war, Hitchcock went to Hollywood under contract to David O. SELZNICK. Ironically, his first film there was a British subject, REBECCA (1940), an impeccable adaptation of Daphne du Maurier's romantic mystery story, with an all-British cast that included Joan FONTAINE and Laurence OLIVIER. It introduced a more psychological approach into Hitchcock's work; stylistically, too, it was a new departure for him, building suspense by the use of a tracking camera rather than by cutting. SUSPICION (1941) similarly used the fear-inducing properties of unspoken doubts: it was weakened by the producers' insistence on a happy ending, but marked the beginning of several successful collaborations between Hitchcock and Cary GRANT. *Shadow of a Doubt* (1943) also dealt with the growth of suspicion— in this case well-founded—and is one of the few Hitchcock films in which the central character is also the villain of the piece. Its well-rounded small-town setting is another unusual feature in his work.

In *Lifeboat* (1944) Hitchcock set himself the immensely difficult task of shooting a murder mystery within the confines of a ship's lifeboat. The action was conveyed chiefly in close-up, so that the drama became one of nine characters in conflict (Hitchcock himself making his appearance in a newspaper photograph); the film's aim of providing a parable of current international strife was not entirely realized.

*Spellbound* (1945), a murder story with a voguish flavour of psychoanalysis, used dream sequences designed by Salvador DALI and images derived from Freudian symbolism. Ingrid BERGMAN, who had notable success working for Hitchcock, starred in *Spellbound* and again in NOTORIOUS (1946). *Notorious* has a visual sophistication and clarity of construction which combine with the excellent casting to make it one of Hitchcock's most satisfying films.

In 1948, with *Rope*, Hitchcock became his own producer. Apart from its being his first colour film, the interest of *Rope* lies in its experimental shooting technique. The action, which takes place entirely in one room, was filmed in one continuous shot, interrupted only to reload the camera at ten-minute intervals; for conventional cutting Hitchcock substituted total camera mobility. The experiment was interesting if unsuccessful. Instead of heightening the intensity and unity of the drama, the technique produced a contrived and monotonous effect. He used a similar fluid camera style to a lesser extent in *Under Capricorn* (1949).

*Stage Fright* (1950), in which he deliberately confused the plot with a 'lying' FLASHBACK (conventionally considered a solecism), was one of his less popular films. His success was wholly re-established, however, by STRANGERS ON A TRAIN (1951), a classic example of the 'perfect crime' story. In *I Confess* (1953) a priest, played with sombre intensity by Montgomery CLIFT, is accused of murder and cannot reveal the real criminal without violating the secrecy of the confessional. This (with *The Wrong Man*, 1957; *Frenzy*, 1972) is the most overt expression of a theme central to many Hitchcock films, the 'exchange of guilt' whereby one man is suspected or accused of another's crime. REAR WINDOW (1954) presented another self-imposed physical problem: the viewpoint is that of a convalescent who, passing his time observing his neighbours, chances to witness a murder. It starred James STEWART, like Cary Grant remarkably effective as the puzzled hero caught up in bewildering events, a constantly recurring character in the Hitchcock canon. *To Catch a Thief* (1955), with Cary Grant as another Hitchcock hero, made exciting use of a glossy Riviera setting, particularly in the car chase sequences.

In 1956 Hitchcock remade *The Man Who Knew Too Much* in big-budget Hollywood style. It was at first received as a pale shadow of the original British version, but with revaluation of his later films its merits have gained recognition. THE TROUBLE WITH HARRY, released in the same year, was a macabre story depicted in exquisite autumnal settings and handled with a whimsical humour that was received with extremes of delight and detestation. Hitchcock ended the decade with two major films which sum up the two main trends in his work: NORTH BY NORTH-WEST (1959) capping all his previous chase films in its extravagant fantasy, which had more than a touch of self-parody, and PSYCHO (1960), a horror story with all the trappings of melodrama and one of the most successful of his psychological thrillers.

*The Birds* (1963) was an attempt to derive horror from an unexplained natural source (a vicious attack on the human race by flocks of birds) rather than a human villain; *Marnie* (1964) dealt with the psychological explanation of criminal acts by a pretty young woman; *Torn Curtain* (1966), a spy story set in East Germany, returned to the chase formula, and *Topaz* (1969) again used a spy story, but without the climactic action sequences that audiences have come to expect. In his thriller *Frenzy* (1972) Hitchcock returned to London, but the Agatha Christie-like atmosphere combines uneasily with the explicit unpleasantness of the murders committed.

He has also produced, introduced, and intermittently directed two successful television series, using them to try out new ideas and apparently deriving much enjoyment from his role as 'host'.

Hitchcock's concentration on the suspense thriller and his exploration and development of the genre is probably unique. His films are characteristically invested with his personal quality of sly humour, resourceful and imaginative use of technique, and sense of the visually dramatic. Although he has very often worked from literary sources, the original is invariably fully assimilated into his cinematic approach. His lengthy and uneven career is reflected in the variety of critical response to his films; sometimes his British films are rated highest, at others his work of the forties or his big-budget productions of later years. Many French critics, particularly those of the early period of CAHIERS DU CINÉMA, class him as a leading AUTEUR with his own distinctive film language and as such he had considerable influence on the NOUVELLE VAGUE: the films of CHABROL, in particular, contain many touches of homage to Hitchcock. His four films of the sixties, which were received with disappointment in Britain and America, were hailed in France as confirmation of the view that he continued to be in a class of his own.

Hitchcock himself, in spite of all that his admirers claim on his behalf, maintains a steady unpretentiousness, prosaically claiming a place as a skilled entertainer—which he undoubtedly and superbly is—content to work within the commercial system. Although the plots of his films frequently resolve themselves into schematic and implausible intrigues where depth of characterization is sacrificed to dramatic development, the exuberance of his technical invention and his use of montage and visual stylization to manipulate audience emotion and to create and intensify pure sensation in the spectator is unrivalled.

Claude Chabrol and Eric Rohmer, *Hitchcock*, Paris, 1957; Peter Bogdanovich, *The cinema of Alfred Hitchcock*, New York, 1962; François Truffaut, *Le Cinéma selon Hitchcock*, Paris, 1966, published in English as *Hitchcock*, New York, 1967, London, 1968; Robin Wood, *Hitchcock's films*, London, 1965, New York, 1969.

**HITLERJUNGE QUEX**, Germany, 1933. *Dir* Hans Steinhoff; *prod* Karl Ritter for UFA; *scr* K. A. Schenzinger, B. E. Lüthge; *ph* Konstantin Irmen-Tschet; *des* Benno von Arent, Arthur Gunther; *cast* a Hitler Youth (Quex), Heinrich George (his father), Bertha Drews (his mother), Claus Clausen.

Heini Völker, nicknamed Quex (mercury), the son of dedicated Communists, is converted to the cause of Nazism. While distributing election leaflets in Berlin he is stabbed by Communists and becomes a hero-martyr of the Hitler Youth.

*Hitlerjunge Quex* combined aggressive emotionalism—the youth and fragility of Quex, the poverty which has induced misguided political allegiance in his parents—with the technical accomplishment characteristic of German films of the time. It was one of the first avowedly PROPAGANDA films following Hitler's rise to power, at a time when the bulk of German film production was light, escapist fare. With OHM KRÜGER (1941) it established Hans Steinhoff as a leading director of propaganda films in the Third Reich.

**HLADNIK,** BOŠTJAN (1929– ), Yugoslav director, studied in Paris at the INSTITUT DES HAUTES ÉTUDES CINÉMATOGRAPHIQUES (IDHEC) and became assistant to CHABROL, DE BROCA, DUVIVIER, and SIODMAK. His documentary *Fantastic Ballade* (1957) had a striking experimental quality which runs through his later work which also shows a French influence. His main concern is with problems of personal alienation, particularly in his two best known films, *Ples na kiši (Dance in the Rain,* 1961), on the theme of youth, and *Peščeni grad (Sandcastle,* 1962), which looks at war through the hallucinations of a young woman.

**HOBSON,** VALERIE (1917– ), Irish-born British actress, made her film début in *Path of Glory* (1934), and went to Hollywood under contract to UNIVERSAL, appearing in quick succession in *The Mystery of Edwin Drood, The Bride of Frankenstein,* and *Werewolf of London* (all 1935). She returned to Britain in 1937 and until retiring in the mid-fifties appeared frequently in roles of an elegant, glacial nature. Her best-known films include *The Drum* (1938), *The Spy in Black* (1939), GREAT EXPECTATIONS (1946), *Blanche Fury* (1947), KIND HEARTS AND CORONETS (1949), and *The Card* (1952).

**HOELLERING,** George (1900– ), Hungarian producer, director, and editor of *Hortobagy* (1937), a Hungarian film shot on the great Hortobagy plain. He migrated to England in 1937. Since 1947 he has been in control of the ACADEMY CINEMA, one of London's first and most important ART HOUSES. He also produced and directed the film version of T. S. Eliot's *Murder in the Cathedral* (1951).

**HOFFMAN,** DUSTIN (1937– ), US actor who made a late transition from Broadway to films. His film début was in *Madigan's Millions* (1967, released 1969), but he shot to fame in THE GRADUATE (1967). With MIDNIGHT COWBOY (1970) and *Little Big Man* (1970) he established himself as a fine actor with an unusually wide range who also commands a considerable commercial pull. He gave a stalwart performance in Sam PECKINPAH's controversial *Straw Dogs* (1971), but his intense nervous qualities and puckish sense of humour particularly suited him to the part of Georgie Soloway in *Who is Harry Kellerman and Why is He Saying Those Terrible Things about Me?* (1972).

**HOLDEN,** WILLIAM (1918– ), US actor, real name William Beedle, was discovered in an amateur theatrical performance in 1938 by a PARAMOUNT talent scout. He has since worked chiefly for Paramount, although his screen début was for COLUMBIA in *Golden Boy* (1939). Holden has maintained his star status from the start, playing modern roles of a virile and romantic nature. His performances in SUNSET BOULEVARD (1950) and THE BRIDGE ON THE RIVER KWAI (1957) were outstanding: his other major films include *Our Town* (1940), BORN YESTERDAY (1951), *Stalag 17* (1953), *Executive Suite* (1954), *Sabrina* (1954), *Picnic* (1956), *The Key* (1957), and THE WILD BUNCH (1969).

*HOLIDAY,* US, 1938. 1½hr. *Dir* George Cukor; *prod* Columbia; *scr* Donald Ogden Stewart, Sidney Buchman from the play by Philip Barry; *ph* Franz Planer; *cast* Katharine Hepburn (Linda Seton), Cary Grant (Johnny Case), Doris Nolan (Julia Seton), Lew Ayres (Ned Seton), Edward Everett Horton (Nick Porter), Henry Kolker (Edward Seton).

Philip Barry's successful play about a young man who is determined to enjoy life while young rather than make money was first filmed in 1930, with Ann HARDING and Mary ASTOR as the Seton sisters, but the remake has established an enduring reputation on the basis of CUKOR's adroit direction, Katharine HEPBURN's vibrantly intense heroine, and Cary GRANT's suave, devil-may-care hero.

**HOLLAND.** Public film showings were held in Holland from 1896 and film production began in 1902. Two production companies, Albert Frères (1902) and Hollandia (1910), had modest initial success and flourished during the First World War when French and American films were unobtainable, but after the war home production foundered under American competition.

The Nederlandse Filmliga (Dutch Film League) inaugurated in 1927 achieved some success in stimulating interest in the cinema. Joris IVENS, a founder member, became one of the world's greatest documentary film-makers and had a profound influence on young directors who had drawn their first inspiration from the Filmliga. National temperament and a shortage of funds made a natural climate for documentary filming; after the ravages of the Second World War the Dutch resumed their position as respected makers of documentary and short films.

The Nederlandse Filmacademie was founded in 1958, originally to encourage the production of feature films; but although students emerged with some theoretical knowledge the country has lacked sufficient professional openings to give them practical experience. Like other small countries, Holland cannot support much domestic production and film-makers tend to go into television. The occasional features made, like Fons RADEMAKERS's *Dorp aan de riveir* (*Doctor in the Village*, 1958), maintained a background sense of documentary truth and immediacy combined with a characteristic intensity of emotion.

The French NOUVELLE VAGUE affected Dutch film-makers deeply, and many began to work in an informal manner, compensating for limited budgets with unusually creative scripts. With remarkable generosity, the Dutch government began putting up half the funds for a feature film if a backer or foreign co-producer could be found to guarantee the balance. This has helped stimulate feature production without imposing official controls on choice or treatment of subject-matter. Recent Dutch films to have received international attention include Bert HAANSTRA's *Fanfare* (1958), Nicolai van der Heyde's *Un Printemps en Holland* (1966), Adriaan van Ditvoorst's *Paranoia* (1968), and Harry Kumel's *Monsieur Hawarden* (1968), a Belgian co-production. Pim de la Parra and Wim Verstappen's Scorpio company has made the greatest impact abroad with films that include *De minder gelukkige terugkeer van Josef Katus naar het land van Rembrandt* (1966) and *Blue Movie* (1971).

**HOLLANDER,** FREDERICK (1896–    ), London-born German composer who studied music in Berlin where, after theatre work, he began his association with films. Soon after working on DER BLAUE ENGEL (*The Blue Angel*, 1930), he went to the US where his numerous scores included *Desire* (1936), *Victory* (1940), THE MAN WHO CAME TO DINNER (1942), *Walk Softly Stranger* (1950), *Androcles and the Lion* (1952), *Phffft* (1954), and *We're No Angels* (1955). In addition to his background scores, he was often active in songwriting for films, among them DESTRY RIDES AGAIN (1939) which included 'See What the Boys in the Back Room Will Have'.

**HOLLIDAY,** JOHN H. ('Doc') (1850–85), dentist and gambler, owes his fame to his friendship with Wyatt EARP, at whose side he fought at the OK Corral. His screen appearances have thus usually been alongside Earp, as in MY DARLING CLEMENTINE (1946), GUNFIGHT AT THE OK CORRAL (1956), and *Cheyenne Autumn* (1964).

**HOLLIDAY,** JUDY (1923–65), US actress, real name Judith Tuvim, started with a successful career in Broadway revues. Her first film part was in ADAM's RIB (1949). Her comic talent was fully realized as the dumb blonde in BORN YESTERDAY (1951). Other films included *The Marrying Kind* (1952), *It Should Happen to You*, *Phffft* (both 1954), *The Solid Gold Cadillac* (1956), *Full of Life* (1958), and *Bells Are Ringing* (1960).

Her peculiar brand of foolish innocence greatly endeared her to a particular audience, but she did not achieve the wide popularity that her talent deserved.

**HOLLYWOOD,** California, chiefly famous as the centre of the US motion picture industry, a district of the city of Los Angeles situated about eight miles north-west of the city centre. The first recorded building in the area was an adobe built by a Don Tomas Urquides in 1853. During the 1870s homesteaders began to settle the area, finding the climate unusually equable with breezes from the Pacific tempering the heat of the desert. Mrs Horace H. Wilcox, the wife of an early real estate developer, named the area Hollywood in the 1880s. In 1903 it was incorporated as a city but, mainly because of the problem of water supplies, the citizens voted in 1910 to become a district of Los Angeles.

Southern California appealed to film-makers from as early as 1907: they found that the area could provide almost ideal working conditions, with a maximum of sunshine for outdoor shooting, and scenery that ranged from snow-capped mountains to harsh desert. In 1908 *The Count of Monte Cristo*, begun in Chicago by SELIG, was completed in California by Francis Boggs; D. W. GRIFFITH filmed there regularly from 1910. When the MOTION PICTURE PATENTS COMPANY was set up in 1909 independent producers found it convenient to operate at a distance from New York and close to the Mexican border, and the nucleus of a film production industry began to grow up on the West Coast. The first studio in Hollywood was established in 1911 by David Horsley for the Nestor Company at the corner of Gower Street and Sunset Boulevard and by the end of the year fifteen other independent companies had studios close by. By the time the MPPC had collapsed independents had begun to dominate the industry, men like Jesse LASKY, Samuel GOLDWYN, and Cecil B. DEMILLE who jointly produced *The Squaw Man* (1913), one of America's first important films in terms of box-office success. With others such as William FOX, Carl LAEMMLE, Adolph ZUKOR, Thomas INCE, and Louis B. MAYER they developed a unique community devoted to an industry that was sustained by forceful and imaginative business acumen and by a supply of creative talent and glamour of all varieties.

America's comparative isolation during the First World War, and the international success of films by Griffith, DeMille, and others, helped Hollywood to establish a position from which it could dominate world markets. When peace came the major studios rapidly expanded, importing, chiefly from Europe, talented workers in all fields and formalizing the STAR SYSTEM on which much of the audience's loyalty depended. During this period real estate boomed, oil was discovered in the area, and people from all over the US flocked to Southern California in the hope of escaping from the hardships of the post-war and Depression years into a more glamorous world. This shifting population, the concentration of polyglot talent and temperament, and the luxurious excesses perhaps exaggerated by the press, created an impression of Hollywood as the epitome of sophistication: recurrent scandals were a source of vicarious delight to people leading duller lives all over America (and beyond) and stimulated frequent attacks on the example given to the nation which culminated in the formation of the Hays Office in 1926 and the Legion of Decency in 1934 (see CENSORSHIP, US).

The introduction of sound in 1926 and the general economic recession created a temporary crisis in Hollywood. After the unqualified success of THE JAZZ SINGER (1927) all the studios were equipped for sound and, although some old talents disappeared, there was a demand for new technicians, writers, directors, and stars. New blood was brought in from both the American and British theatre. Hollywood's image changed owing to the influence of the Hays Office and the acquisition of a family audience, but glamour was even more important to America in the Depression than during the twenties. Hollywood purveyed luxurious visions that shaped the popular imagination of the time, and an undercurrent of scandal persisted: there was an avid public for highly-coloured gossip columns devoted to Hollywood. But studio publicists played on the domestic virtues of film personalities rather than their exotic qualities, and this was the heyday of CHILD STARS.

The thirties also saw the Hollywood studio system at its peak, with each major company developing a distinctive house style. Each had its own stable of stars, a permanent team of supporting players, and complex assembly-line working methods to maintain a constant stream of main and supporting features to supply the theatre chains it controlled. The BLOCK BOOKING system, which persisted until 1948, helped sustain the power of the big producers.

During the Second World War the US was again virtually the only country to continue with full-scale production. After the war, however, a variety of forces began to alter the Hollywood of legend. The industry in Europe recovered more quickly than in the twenties and there was a new generation of directors demanding personal authority over their films. By 1950 television had become a serious competitor, despite investment in counter-attractions such as ever wider screens, STEREOSCOPIC films, STEREOPHONIC sound, and more desperate novelties such as AROMARAMA. Court decisions breaking the monopolistic control of chains of cinemas by producing companies, currency and tax restrictions including the freezing of dollar funds abroad, cheaper production costs overseas, all eroded the economic basis of Hollywood production, and there was a certain drain of talent and adverse publicity owing to the machinations of the UNAMERICAN ACTIVITIES Committee. Control of major studios began to pass from individual moguls to consortia of bankers, investment advisers, and big business interests. Studios sold their backlog of films to television, incidentally making many films available to audiences who would never otherwise have had the opportunity of seeing them. As home film production declined television increasingly absorbed writers and technicians, as well as much of the equipment and facilities of the large studios; but there was also a fertile exchange process, writers and directors trained in the intimate field of television drama moving into film-making proper.

Since the mid-fifties American financiers have, by shrewd business methods, managed to maintain a considerable degree of control in world production, investing heavily in international co-productions which employ cheap local personnel and use refined DUBBING techniques to combine the drawing power of stars of various nationalities. With the growth of television, and particularly colour television, more features are made with television showing in view: in the US the average time lapse between theatrical release and television showing is about one year as compared with three years in Britain, creating a constant demand for new features and a new industry for the companies based in Hollywood and Los Angeles.

Even now the word 'Hollywood' evokes, rather than a physical locality, a film style characterized by professionalism, dramatic realism, pace, a straightforward narrative mode, and usually a star name. In some genres, particularly the MUSICAL, the WESTERN, and sophisticated comedy, Hollywood has never been bettered. The area itself retains much of its glamour, the luxurious houses in Beverly Hills, Grauman's Chinese Theater, the stars set in the pavement of Hollywood Boulevard, even the bus tours of UNIVERSAL Studios (now entirely given over to television feature production) give a hint of the flavour of the old days. Hollywood at its height has inspired fascination, revulsion, and sometimes a combination of the two in many writers and directors.

Novels which attempt to convey its unique quality include H. L. Wilson's *Merton of the Movies* (1922), Nathanael West's *The Day of the Locust* (1939), Scott FITZGERALD's *The Last Tycoon* (1941), Budd SCHULBERG's *What Makes Sammy Run?* (1941), Norman MAILER's *The Deer Park* (1955), Gore Vidal's *Myra Breckinridge* (1968). In films Hollywood has obsessively returned to self-contemplation, with viewpoints that range from the zany HELLZAPOPPIN' (1941) to the tragic A STAR IS BORN (1937 and 1954), and all stages between—SULLIVAN'S TRAVELS (1941), SUNSET BOULEVARD (1950), *In a Lonely Place* (1950), THE BAD AND THE BEAUTIFUL (1952), SINGIN' IN THE RAIN (1952), *Inside Daisy Clover* (1966), *The Legend of Lylah Clare* (1968).

**HOLLYWOOD QUARTERLY** see FILM QUARTERLY

**HOLLYWOOD TEN** see UNAMERICAN ACTIVITIES

**HOLM,** CELESTE (1919– ), US actress in theatre and films, specializing in a sharp, fast wit and unruffled demeanour used to conceal emotion. She won an OSCAR as supporting actress in *Gentleman's Agreement* (KAZAN, 1947) and also appears to advantage as the sympathetic friend in ALL ABOUT EVE (1950) and as Frank SINATRA's side-kick in HIGH SOCIETY (1956).

**HOLT,** SETH (1923–71), British editor and director, began working for Strand films in 1942 as assistant editor. In 1944 he joined EALING STUDIOS. Films he edited include KIND HEARTS AND CORONETS (1949), THE LAVENDER HILL MOB (1951), and SATURDAY NIGHT AND SUNDAY MORNING (1960). In 1958 he directed his first and unsuccessful feature, *Nowhere to Go*. After *Taste of Fear* (1961) and *Station Six Sahara* (1962) he made his best-known film for HAMMER, *The Nanny* (1965) with Bette DAVIS, a work rich in horror and suspense. In 1967 he made *Danger Route* and was working on *Blood from the Mummy's Tomb* when he died; it was completed by Michael Carreras. Holt's films are marked by tautness of structure and psychological insight.

**HOLOGRAPHY** is an unusual form of photography in that no actual pictorial image is recorded and no lenses are used. Light is simultaneously beamed on to the subject and directly on to the photographic emulsion, producing a complex pattern of light waves. The light reflected from the subject interferes with the direct beam and creates a pattern on the emulsion. This pattern, the hologram, when viewed bears no resemblance to the original subject. The system relies on a powerful single-frequency (monochrome) light source and was impractical until the invention of the LASER in 1960.

To reconstitute the image, laser light is directed on to the processed photographic record and diffraction of the light caused by the patterns in the emulsion creates, on the same side of the hologram as the light source, an image which can be seen by the viewer. Because the image is composed of light reflected at all angles from the subject, the illusion produced is one of STEREOSCOPY. Other systems have been developed which do not require a laser in the viewing process.

In motion pictures the duration of each successive 'exposure' must be very short indeed (around one-fifth of a millionth of a second) and from an extremely powerful light source. However, the same emulsion can be used to record a number of simultaneous images. Each image can be seen by altering the angle at which light strikes the emulsion during viewing.

Limitations on the size of image which can be recorded and viewed make it likely that holography will be applied most readily to television. For cinema presentation, a form of enlarging projection would be necessary, one which is capable of magnifying in three dimensions without distortion: as yet no such system exists. A further problem is that, for optimum results, the size of the original subject and the reconstituted image should be the same, which makes cutting between long shot and close-up impossible.

**HOMBRE,** US, 1967. Panavision; 2hr; De Luxe Color. *Dir* Martin Ritt; *prod* Ritt, Irving Ravetch for Hombre Productions; *scr* Ravetch, Harriet Frank Jr, based on the novel by Elmore Leonard; *ph* James Wong Howe; *cast* Paul Newman (John Russell), Fredric March (Dr Favor), Richard Boone (Cicero Grimes), Diane Cilento (Jessie Brown), Barbara Rush (Audra Favor), Martin Balsam (Mendez).

The *hombre* of the title, a white man reared by the Apache and now living with them by choice, is thrown together with a group of travellers. Reluctantly, he shares their ordeal when they are attacked by bandits and finally sacrifices his life for members of the society by which he is rejected.

In Martin RITT's first Western he worked with the talented team of THE LONG HOT SUMMER (1958) and HUD (1963). The film is distinguished by James Wong HOWE's beautiful photography, and by the finely developed character clashes between the travelling companions.

**HOMOKY NAGY,** ISTVÁN (1914– ), Hungarian director of nature films who from the early fifties developed his own techniques for lighting and photographing animals. He made an important contribution to the emergence of the fine body of popular science films which are widely enjoyed in Hungary.

**HOMOLKA,** OSCAR (1901– ), Viennese-born actor who made his stage début in 1918 and worked on the Continent, in Britain, and in the US. His film career began about 1929 in Austrian and German films, including DREYFUS (1930) and other films directed by Richard Oswald. He visited Britain to play the title role in *Rhodes of Africa* (1936) and the saboteur in Alfred HITCHCOCK's SABOTAGE (1936, *A Woman Alone* in US). He then began his Hollywood career with *Ebb Tide* (1937). With his strong build, bushy eyebrows, wickedly twinkling eyes and gravelly voice he became an outstanding and eminently likeable character actor. Among his earlier roles, the most famous was the blustering but kindly uncle in *I Remember Mama* (George STEVENS, 1948). His films of the fifties ranged from the comedy THE SEVEN YEAR ITCH (1955) to the epic *War and Peace* (1956), in which he played General Kutuzov. In his more recent work he has been prominent in two of the Harry Palmer adventures, *Funeral in Berlin* (1966) and *Billion Dollar Brain* (1967).

**HOMUNCULUS,** Germany, 1916. 6-part serial, each part lasting 1hr approx. *Dir* Otto Rippert; *scr* Rippert, Robert Neuss; *ph* Karl Hoffmann; *cast* Olaf Fønss (Homunculus).

This successful serial follows the story of a man created in a retort by a professor and his assistant. He develops a high intellect and indomitable will but when he learns of his origin feels an outcast. Despising all mankind he becomes a dictator and precipitates a world war before being killed by a thunderbolt.

The film anticipates the German Expressionist cinema in its chiaroscuro, acting style, and organization of mass movements (see EXPRESSIONISM). It is also marked by a strong sadism and appetite for destruction.

It was condensed into three parts and revived in 1920.

**HONEGGER,** ARTHUR (1892–1955), French composer of Swiss parentage, studied in Zurich and Paris and became one of the group of French composers known as 'Les Six'. He was already associated with films during the silent era, composing scores to accompany LA ROUE (1922), NAPOLÉON (1927), and AUTANT-LARA's *Fait divers* (1923). Among his fine scores for sound films are *Les Misérables* (1934), *Mayerling* (1936), and PYGMALION (1938); his score for L'IDÉE (1934) introduced to the screen the electronic musical instrument, the Theremin. PACIFIC

231, a tone-poem composed in 1923 and based on his music for *La Roue* was used as the basis of a short film by the Russian director Tsekhanovsky in 1931 and by Jean MITRY in 1949, and his oratorio *Jeanne au bûcher* (*Joan of Arc at the Stake*), composed in 1935, was recorded on film in 1954 by Roberto ROSSELLINI with Ingrid BERGMAN in the (speaking) title role. *Arthur Honegger* (Georges ROUQUIER, 1955) is a short film about the composer's life and work.

**HONG KONG** has one of the world's most prolific film industries, rivalled only by India and catering for vast audiences in the Far East and Chinese communities all over the world. Its films are banned in China.

The biggest studios are those of Shaw Brothers and the Cathay Organization. Shaw Brothers (Run Run and Runme Shaw) control the largest and most prolific privately-owned film studio in the world. With their circuit of cinemas, extending throughout non-Communist Asia and as far as the US, they distribute their own and also foreign, notably American, films. Television has had little impact on the industry. Strict censorship and simple tastes dictate the type of product—moralistic and sentimental, made to proven plot-formulae (swordsmen-movies are particularly popular), conservative and apolitical, usually including song-and-dance interludes very much in the manner of Indian films. Production methods are by Hollywood out of General Motors: a three-shift, conveyor-belt system produces cheap films very quickly. Approximately 80 per cent of production is in Cantonese and 20 per cent in Mandarin, with some dual-language productions using different casts. In the early seventies films from Hong Kong began to find a footing in the West, particularly 'kung-fu' (martial arts) dramas. Bruce Lee, an American actor of Chinese extraction, attained a mythical status with *The Big Boss* (1971) and *Enter the Dragon* (1973) which was enhanced by his early death.

**HOPALONG CASSIDY,** cowboy character created in the books of Clarence E. Mulford, played on the screen from 1935 by William BOYD.

**HOPE,** BOB (1903– ), US comedian, real name Leslie Townes Hope, was born in Britain: his family emigrated to the US when he was four years old. He had already achieved much popularity in stage musical comedies and revues before his film début in a series of shorts made in 1934. His first starring role was in *The Big Broadcast of 1938*; the same year saw his first appearance with Bing CROSBY in a golfing short *Don't Hook Now*, in which both stars played themselves. *The Cat and the Canary* (1939) defined Hope's comic style, dry, allusive, and typically American, and gave him the character, faithfully maintained throughout his films, of a humorously cowardly incompetent, always cheerfully failing in his attempts to become a romantic hero. The very successful series of 'Road' films, in which he starred with Crosby, consolidated this character and also instituted a series of 'private' jokes between the two stars to which reference is made even in the Hope films where Crosby does not appear. *The Paleface* (1948), with Jane RUSSELL, was one of the more successful burlesques of the classic Western. Since the late fifties he has largely confined himself to television.

**HOPKINS,** MIRIAM (1902–72), US actress, real forename Ellen, whose stage career led her to Hollywood. She made her first film appearance in *Fast and Loose* (1931), closely followed by two films that properly established her—*The Smiling Lieutenant* (1931) and DR JEKYLL AND MR HYDE (1932), in which she played the unfortunate Ivy. She gave an excellent comedy performance in TROUBLE IN PARADISE (1932), and her slightly acid quality contributed to her effectiveness as *Becky Sharp* (1935) and as Bette DAVIS's cousin and rival in *The Old Maid* (1939); in both roles ostensible sweetness disguised an acquisitive and ruthless nature. She returned to the theatre in the forties, but made further films including two for William WYLER— *Carrie* (1952) and *The Children's Hour* (1962, *The Loudest Whisper* in GB); she had played a leading part in Wyler's earlier version of the latter, entitled *These Three* (1936). Her last film appearance was in THE CHASE (1966).

**HOPPER,** HEDDA (1890–1966), US actress and columnist, real name Edna Furry, who acquired a reputation for her wardrobe of astonishing hats as well as for her gossip writing. Her columns and radio broadcasts were syndicated throughout the US and, at a time when studios were jealous of the public image of their contracted stars, her threats (or promises) to expose details of their private lives gave her some personal power in Hollywood. As with her chief rival Louella PARSONS this power was probably exaggerated even at the time; and with the decline of the STAR SYSTEM gossip writing lost its appeal. As an actress she appeared in silent films and, concurrently with her writing career, in *As You Desire Me* (1932), *The Women* (1939), *Reap the Wild Wind* (1942), and played herself in SUNSET BOULEVARD (1950). She compiled some of her observations in two books, *From under my hat* (1952) and *The whole truth and nothing but* (1962), and a dual biography *Hedda and Louella*

was written by George Eells, New York, 1972. Her son William (1915–70) was a film and television actor, notably in the 'Perry Mason' television series.

*HOŘÍ, MÁ PANENKO* (*The Firemen's Ball*), Czechoslovakia, 1967. Eastman Color; 1¼hr. *Dir* Miloš Forman; *scr* Forman, Ivan Passer, Jaroslav Papoušek; *ph* Miroslav Ondříček; *des* Adolf Böhm; *ed* Miroslav Hájek; *mus* Karel Mares; *cast* Jan Vostrčil (Chairman of Ball Committee), Josef Kolb (Josef), Josef Svet (old man), Frantisek Debelka, Josef Sebánek, Karel Valnoha, Josef Rehorek (committee members), Václav Stöckel (retiring brigade commander).

After three films in which satirical observation was tempered with sympathetic humour, FORMAN and his team made a biting political satire in *Hoří, má panenko*—which means literally '(My heart's) on fire, my doll', the first line of a popular love song. The occasion of the presentation of a commemorative axe to a dying old fireman was used to reveal the hypocrisy and callousness of human and social relations; observed, characteristically, with penetrating humour, but unrelieved by the presence of sympathetic protagonists as in his earlier films. The political allusions were necessarily inconspicuous but clear enough to read: the argument over the returning of a stolen 'head-cheese' (potted meat, something between a brawn and a haggis) in particular underscoring the political arguments of the sixties about behaviour during the Stalinist fifties. President Novotný caused the film to be held up, and indignant reaction from firemen launched Forman on an explanatory tour of the country. He was criticized, as he had been before, for ridiculing 'ordinary' people and presenting them in an 'anti-humanitarian' way; criticisms at home found echoes abroad for the film's uncompromising exposure of pettiness and grotesquerie. The film remains, however, the most powerful expression of the satirical element informing the work of a most attractive director.

*HORSE FEATHERS*, US, 1932. 1¼hr. *Dir* Norman McLeod; *prod* Paramount; *scr* Bert Kalmar, Harry Ruby, S. J. Perelman; *ph* Ray June; *mus, lyrics* Bert Kalmar, Harry Ruby; *cast* Groucho Marx (Professor Wagstaff), Harpo (Harpo), Chico (Chico), Zeppo (Zeppo), Thelma Todd (Connie Bailey), David Landa (Jennings).

In *Horse Feathers* the MARX BROTHERS used all the conventions of American college life in a splendidly subversive comedy. As college president, Groucho delivers his presidential address in vaudeville style and when required to woo the rich widow Mrs Bailey, does so with rigid formality. Chico and Harpo produce a repertoire of insane devices to disrupt the institutional football game.

**HORTON,** EDWARD EVERETT (1886–1970), US supporting actor with a film career lasting from 1916 to the mid-sixties. A master of the comic 'double-take', he usually played dithering, flustered characters. He was at his best as Fred ASTAIRE's companion/adviser in *The Gay Divorce* (1934), *Shall We Dance?* (1937), and especially TOP HAT (1935).

**HOSSEIN,** ROBERT (1927– ), French actor and director. After some experience as a stage actor Hossein made his film début in DU RIFIFI CHEZ LES HOMMES (1955). He subsequently wrote, directed, and starred in several films of his own which show the influence of the FILM NOIR. Hossein has starred in many other films, playing Raskolnikov in Lampin's *Crime et châtiment* (1956), and taking a leading role in three of VADIM's films: *Sait-on jamais* (1957), *Le Repos du guerrier* (1962), and *Le Vice et la vertu* (1962). His film roles cover a catholic range, from Joffrey De Peyrac in the *Angélique* series, to the hero of DURAS' *La Musica* (1966).

*HÔTEL DES INVALIDES*, France, 1951. 20 min. *Dir, scr* Georges Franju; *prod* Forces et Voix de la France; *ph* Marcel Fradetal; *mus* Maurice Jarre; commentary spoken by Michel Simon and museum guides.

FRANJU's favourite among his short films explores military relics of the First World War, accompanying horrifying images with a typically unemotional commentary and thus making an oblique but bitter comment on the tragic waste of war.

**HOUDINI,** HARRY (1874–1926), real name Ehrich Weiss, American escapologist and debunker of spiritualism. His only appearance in films was in a serial, *The Master Mystery* (1919), which had an automaton as the villain and Houdini as the hero. He is credited with giving Buster KEATON his nickname after witnessing Keaton, as a baby, negotiating a spectacular fall. Tony CURTIS played the lead in a film biography, *Houdini* (1953).

**HOWARD,** LESLIE (1893–1943), British actor of Hungarian extraction, real name Leslie Howard Stainer, after his film début in *Outward Bound* (1930) divided his career in the pre-war years between England and the US; in both countries he soon became a popular star in the theatre and films. Outstanding among his earlier screen appearances are those in *Of Human Bondage* (1934), with Bette DAVIS, *The Petrified Forest* (1936), ROMEO AND JULIET (1936), with Norma

SHEARER, and PYGMALION (1938), which he co-directed with Anthony ASQUITH. His status as an internationally famous romantic lead was confirmed by GONE WITH THE WIND (1939). With the outbreak of war he returned to Britain where he appeared in *The First of the Few* (1942) which he also directed. While returning from a visit to Lisbon to promote his film *Pimpernel Smith* (1941), he was killed when his aircraft was destroyed by enemy action.

**HOWARD,** TREVOR (1916– ), British actor, after appearing on the stage with much success from 1933, made a distinguished screen début in *The Way Ahead* (1944) and has since concentrated on films. For some time his range was restricted to the kind of sensitive romantic role which he played with great success in BRIEF ENCOUNTER (1945) or the phlegmatic British officer, as in THE THIRD MAN (1949), but of latter years his performances have shown increasing maturity and versatility, as in *Sons and Lovers* (1960) and *The Charge of the Light Brigade* (1968).

**HOWARD,** WILLIAM K. (1899–1954), US director. In the silent era he was particularly associated with Westerns, including adaptations of Zane Grey novels for PARAMOUNT: *Border Legion* (1925) and *Thundering Herd* (1925), for example, were both noted for their exterior work and magnificent scenery; and the latter contained a spectacular buffalo stampede sequence. His early films also included *Volcano* (1926), starring Bebe DANIELS, Ricardo Cortez, and Wallace BEERY, a drama set in Martinique and containing carnival, volcano, and earthquake scenes, and a boxing drama, *Main Event* (1927).

He is particularly remembered for his films of the thirties, notably *Transatlantic* (1931), a drama set on board an ocean liner with a cosmopolitan passenger list, starring Edmund Lowe and with Myrna LOY among the featured players; SHERLOCK HOLMES (1932) with Clive Brook in the title role; and the interesting and unorthodox THE POWER AND THE GLORY (1933). *Evelyn Prentice* (1934) was a courtroom drama co-starring William POWELL and Myrna Loy. He visited England to make *Fire Over England* (1937) with its formidable cast headed by Flora ROBSON, Raymond MASSEY, James MASON, and Leslie Banks, with Laurence OLIVIER and Vivien LEIGH.

Howard was for long a half-forgotten figure among Hollywood directors; but recent revivals of some of his films and growing interest in his work are replacing past neglect.

**HOWE,** JAMES WONG (1899– ), US cameraman, real name Wong Tung Jim, was born in Canton, China, moving with his family to the US at the age of five. From 1917 he was an assistant cameraman for Cecil B. DEMILLE and in 1922 he became chief cameraman for FAMOUS PLAYERS under the name of James Howe: METRO-GOLDWYN-MAYER persuaded him to add the Chinese patronymic in 1933 for publicity purposes.

An early and productive partnership with Herbert Brenon resulted in *The Spanish Dancer* (1923), with Pola NEGRI, *The Alaskan*, *Peter Pan* (both 1924), and others. In these and in his many other silent films Howe explored to the full current developments in film stock, camera mobility, and lighting techniques. He refused to accept the restrictions on camera movements which accompanied the coming of sound. *Transatlantic* (William K. HOWARD, 1931) used for its time revolutionary techniques: WIDE-ANGLE LENSES, DEEP FOCUS, and ceilinged sets to give the claustrophobic feeling of shipboard.

Howe was one of the earliest cameramen to use a handheld camera: in *Body and Soul* (Robert ROSSEN, 1947), he shot the boxing scenes while being pushed around on roller skates. In *He Ran all the Way* (1951) he used the trick, later employed by COUTARD, of seating the cameraman in a wheelchair to give greater flexibility of movement. THE SWEET SMELL OF SUCCESS (1957) shows his work at its most sophisticated: here his photography has a hard and glossy quality which satisfyingly underlines the film's theme and background.

He has in recent years made a marked contribution to films directed by Martin RITT: the harsh visual effect of HUD (1963) is one of his most substantial achievements, and in THE OUTRAGE (1964), a remake of RASHOMON (1950), he faithfully transcribed much of KUROSAWA's original imagery, skilfully re-composed for the wide screen. Like many creative cameramen, Howe professes a strong preference for black-and-white photography. With the introduction of fast colour stock, however, he has done some impressive work in colour notably in HOMBRE (1967) and *The Molly Maguires* (1969), both again for Ritt. He has directed two feature films: *Go, Man, Go* (1954) and *The Invisible Avenger* (1957).

**HOW THE WEST WAS WON**, US, 1962. Cinerama; 2½hr; Technicolor. *Dir* Henry Hathaway, John Ford, George Marshall; *prod* MGM/Cinerama; *scr* James R. Webb; *ph* William Daniels, Milton Krasner, Charles Lang Jr, Joseph LaShelle; *ed* Harold F. Kress; *des* George W. Davis, William Ferrari, Addison Hehr; *mus* Alfred Newman; *narr* Spencer Tracy.

The first fiction film to be presented in CINERAMA, this episodic panorama of the West, spanning a period of fifty years, was not deficient in appropriately spectacular visual elements— buffalo stampede, Indians attacking a wagon train, Civil War scenes, raft caught in tremendous rapids, and plentiful eye-catching scenery.

HATHAWAY directed the entire first half and the final sequence; the Civil War episode was by John FORD; and a railway sequence (including the buffalo scene) was directed by George MARSHALL. The cast was almost entirely composed of established stars and included Agnes MOOREHEAD, Carroll BAKER, James STEWART, Gregory PECK, John WAYNE, Richard WIDMARK, Henry FONDA, Eli WALLACH, and Lee J. COBB.

In Britain, the film was generally released in a CINEMASCOPE version in 1964.

**HUBLEY, JOHN** (1914– ), US animator, worked for Disney on SNOW WHITE AND THE SEVEN DWARFS (1937), *Pinocchio* (1940), FANTASIA (1940), *Dumbo* (1941), and *Bambi* (1943). He left the Disney studios as a result of the animators' strike in 1941 and in 1945 became one of the original members of UNITED PRODUCTIONS OF AMERICA (UPA). He made some of UPA's most successful early films, including *Ragtime* (1949) and *Rooty Toot Toot* (1952). However, Hubley's graphic style with its detailed drawing and delicate colours conflicted with the characteristic UPA spareness: in 1956 he formed his own studio, Storyboard, in collaboration with his wife Faith. From his first independent films, *Adventures of an Asterisk* (1956), *Harlem Wednesday* (1958), based on the negro portraits of Gregorio Prestopino, and *Moonbird* (1960), he has developed into the descriptive 'documentary' style seen in *Of Stars and Men*, *The Hole* (both 1962), and *The Hat* (1964).

**HUD**, US, 1963. Panavision; 1¾hr. *Dir* Martin Ritt; *prod* Ritt, Irving Ravetch for Salem-Dover; *scr* Ravetch, Harriet Frank Jr, from the novel *Horseman, Pass By* by Larry McMurty; *ph* James Wong Howe; *cast* Paul Newman (Hud Bannen), Melvyn Douglas (Homer Bannen), Patricia Neal (Alma), Brandon De Wilde (Lou Bannen).

Hud Bannen, impatient for control of his grandfather Homer's cattle ranch, initiates legal proceedings against him. The herd is destroyed by foot-and-mouth disease, Homer dies heartbroken, and Hud is left alone on the desolated ranch.

RITT skilfully develops the complex conflict between Hud, the cynical realist, and Homer, the ageing idealist, in bitter opposition yet bound by deep affection. Ritt's direction and James Wong HOWE's photography of the cattle slaughter is masterly: no cattle are seen to die, but the tragedy is plain. Paul NEWMAN is a moving and convincing Hud, and Patricia NEAL, Melvyn DOUGLAS, and Brandon DE WILDE all place their intense relationships with Hud within developed characterizations.

**HUDSON,** ROCK (1925–  ), US actor, réal name Roy Fitzgerald, signed with Raoul WALSH in 1948 and made a minor appearance in *Fighter Squadron* (1948). He was sold a year later to UNIVERSAL where, working with Budd BOET-TICHER, Walsh, and Douglas SIRK, he played numerous parts with distinction, including a demanding dramatic role in *Giant* (George STEVENS, 1956). His sixth film for Sirk was the splendid Hollywood tear-jerker *Written on the Wind* (1956), and he became a big, money-spinning name in similar romances, often partnering Lana TURNER, for example *Imitation of Life* (1959). He proved an excellent light comedian opposite Doris DAY in *Pillow Talk* (1959), *Lover Come Back* (1961), and *Send Me No Flowers* (1964). In *Seconds* (John FRANKENHEIMER, 1966) he reverted to dramatic acting, but after several failures at the box-office Hudson moved into television, his work there including the series 'McMillan and Wife'.

**HUGHES,** HOWARD (1905–  ), US producer, already a millionaire by inheritance when he set up in Hollywood as an independent producer while still in his early twenties. His third film, *Hell's Angels* (1930), which he also directed, was a great success and he followed it up with others as producer, including THE FRONT PAGE (1931) and SCARFACE (1932). With *The Outlaw* (1946) he made a star of Jane RUSSELL as he had of Jean HARLOW in *Hell's Angels*. Hughes's business interests were more diverse than those of most Hollywood producers; he owned civil aviation and engineering companies and these, with his extravagant way of life, probably dissipated his interest in films. He owned RKO during one of its most unsuccessful periods (1948–57), before selling out and abandoning Hollywood to become one of the world's most sought-after recluses.

**HUNGARY.** The first films in Hungary were shown at the Velence Café in 1896. Two years later its owner formed the first Hungarian film company, Projectograph, which made films, ran a cinema, sold and rented projectors and cameras, and rented foreign films to provincial cinemas. By about 1912 there were 270 permanent cinemas in Hungary, but in the early years production hardly developed and even Projectograph became mainly a distributor. Exhibitors hired mostly French, Italian, Danish, and American films.

The first film studio, Hunnia, was completed in 1912, with Miklós Faludi, director of the Gaiety Theatre (Vigszínház) in Budapest, as director. The company was a failure, but the studio building remained. In the same year there appeared the first regular film review in a daily paper (*Világ*); its writer, Sándor (later Alexander) KORDA, also co-founded a film weekly, *Pesti Mozi*. During the next two years film companies sprang up like mushrooms, the most remarkable of which was Corvin, founded by Jenő Janovics, director of the National Theatre of Kolozsvár. By 1918 there were fifteen professional film directors in Hungary. Of these, Mihály Kertész (later Michael CURTIZ) was head of Phönix, formed from Projectograph, and Korda was head of Corvin.

At the end of 1918 Korda was given the task of reorganizing the industry, but in April 1919 the government briefly fell to the Communists and for five months Hungary had the first nationalized film industry. A great reorganization took place; a central scripting department, a register of actors, and a comprehensive programme of subjects—all based on literary classics—were among the new dispositions.

The twenties saw the virtual collapse of the industry, and in 1929 film production ceased altogether. Film theory, however, flourished. Béla BÁLAZS, living in exile, and Iván Hevesy in Budapest were both examining film as an autonomous art form (1924–5), and Lajos Kassak, the avant-garde painter and poet, in his journal *Ma*, published articles from artists and critics all over Europe. He also published, in 1924, a script by MOHOLY-NAGY dated 1921–2 and called *Dynamics of a Metropolis*, antedating both RUTT-MANN and Dziga VERTOV.

In the early thirties the state-owned Hunnia studio (managed by János Bingert) attracted foreign producers, and a number of German, Austrian, Czech, French, and American films were made there. Bingert obtained a levy on foreign films and a QUOTA system favouring home production. American pressures resulted in the quota's being abolished and the levy, paid into the Film Industry Fund, could only assist, not support, production. No producer, however, could manage without either this help or the state-owned studio, so that although the cinema was not nationalized the government controlled production.

The first two Hungarian talking films were made in 1931. *Hyppolit a lakáj* (*Hippolit the Butler*, István Székely, in Hollywood Steve Sekely) was an outstanding success, launching a style which persisted throughout the thirties. It featured recognizable people and places, talked in Budapest Hungarian, and was played with great comic verve, especially by Gyula Kabos. From 1934 to 1939 there was a boom in Hun-

*Csillagosok, katonák* (Miklós Jancsó, 1967)

garian films exported to the US, largely for the Hungarian immigrant population. New quota decrees gradually helped to strengthen production. The Second World War, by cutting down the influx of foreign films, saved the home industry, the American market being replaced by Italy and the Balkans. Production increased to some 40–50 films a year. The state now took open control: the Film Industry Fund was replaced by the National Film Committee which, while giving no subsidy, exercised rigid political control over script, cast, and technical staff. The introduction of anti-Semitic legislation greatly impoverished the industry.

EMBEREK A HAVASON (*People in the Alps*, István Szőts, 1942), struck an isolated note of protest against the lot of the poor, and with the Liberation in 1945 Hungarian cinema began a slow move forward. Béla Bálazs came back and began teaching both audience and film-makers, and recent films from abroad were publicly shown. VALAHOL EURÓPÁBAN (*Somewhere in Europe*, 1947), directed by Géza Radványi from a script by Bálazs, was a landmark. In 1947 the Communists returned to power and early the following year the cinema was again nationalized; it made a promising start with *Talpalatnyi föld* (*The Soil under your Feet*, Frigyes Bán), a story of the misery among peasants before the Liberation which reflects, with a romantic and passionate intensity, the history of Hungary itself. Hungary's first colour film, *Ludas Matyi* (*Mattie the Goose Boy*, Kálmán Nádasdy and Laszló RÁNODY, 1949), freshly explored the Hungarian countryside and village life.

In 1954 Zoltán Várkonyi's *Simon Menyhért születése* (*The Birth of Menyhert Simon*) re-examined the concerns of *Talpalatnyi föld*. *Körhinta* (*Merry-Go-Round*, 1955) confirmed Zoltán FÁBRI as a director of talent and distinction. His *Hannibál, tanár ur* (*Professor Hannibal*, 1956), set in the white terror of the twenties, led the way in the critical examination of recent events which characterizes the new Hungarian cinema. *Egy pikoló világos* (*A Glass of Beer*, Félix MÁRIÁSSY, 1955) caused a stir by presenting everyday life with a neo-realist truthfulness.

In the mid-fifties reform within the Film Academy and the founding of the BÁLAZS BÉLA STUDIO gave much-needed impetus. With *Megszállottak* (*The Fanatics*, Károly MAKK, 1961), *Oldás és kötés* (*Cantata*, Miklós JANCSÓ, 1963), and *Párbeszéd* (*Dialogue*, János HERSKÓ, 1963), film-making took on a contemporary relevance and immediacy, characterized by a preoccupation with moral survival and embodied in works of intellectual and visual intensity. The director became of paramount importance, led by Jancsó, whose SZEGÉNYLEGÉNYEK (*The Round-Up*,

1965) attracted worldwide attention, and András KOVÁCS, whose HIDEG NAPOK (*Cold Days*, 1966) splendidly exemplifies the Hungarian preoccupation with recent history. A personal and original talent is that of György Révész, who in *Egy szerelem három éjszakaja* (*Three Nights of One Love*, 1967) united apparently disparate elements into a homogeneous work. Other major directors include Ferenc KÓSA, István SZABÓ, István GAÁL, Márta MÉSZÁROS, and Sándor SÁRA.

Production, amounting to about twenty feature films a year, is organized in the group system prevailing in most of the Eastern European countries under the administration of the Board of Film. It is divided between Mafilm (feature films) and Pannonia (puppet and animation film). Hungarofilm deals with export and import of films and external distribution, Mokep with internal distribution.

**HURDES, Las** (*Land without Bread*), Spain, 1932. 30min. *Dir* Luis Buñuel; *prod* Ramón Acín; *comm* Pierre Unik; *ph* Eli Lotar; *mus* Brahms.

BUÑUEL's third film exposed with biting irony the sickness, poverty, and degradation of the Hurdanos of northern Spain. Horrifying images contrasting the riches of the Church with the sufferings of the poor are underlined by the carefully neutral commentary. The film was banned in Spain and Buñuel was unable to direct there again until he made VIRIDIANA (1961).

**HURWITZ, LEO** (1909–    ), US director, pioneered left-wing documentary in the US, beginning with *Hunger* (1932) and *Scottsboro* (1934). He worked on LORENTZ's THE PLOW THAT BROKE THE PLAINS (1936), but renounced its politics. A founder of FRONTIER FILMS, he co-directed with Paul STRAND *Heart of Spain* (1937) and NATIVE LAND (1942). Wartime informational and propaganda work for the US Army was followed by the characteristically polemical *Strange Victory* (1949), contrasting the US's professed war ideology with continuing racial persecution in American society. *Verdict for Tomorrow* (1961) studied the Eichmann trial and its implications. Hurwitz has also worked in television.

**HUSTLER, The,** US, 1961. CinemaScope; 1½hr. *Dir, prod* Robert Rossen for Twentieth Century-Fox; *scr* Rossen, Sidney Carroll, based on the novel by Walter Tevis; *ph* Gene Shufton (Eugen Schüfftan); *ed* Deedee Allan; *cast* Paul Newman (Eddie Felson), Jackie Gleason (Minnesota Fats), George C. Scott (Bert Gordon), Piper Laurie (Sarah Packard).

Eddie is a professional pool player, dedicated to beating the great Minnesota Fats. After Fats coolly defeats him in a marathon match, Eddie is manipulated into accepting a challenge from a rich playboy at straight billiards. He wins—and with renewed confidence, returns to tackle Fats again.

ROSSEN skilfully creates the harsh and grimy city world of the pool shark, and excitingly conveys the atmosphere and tension of a game played by men whose professional reputations are at stake. Paul NEWMAN's complete portrayal of Eddie—with self-assured pride in his talent and compulsion to prove himself the best—was supported by fine performances from Jackie Gleason as the acknowledged master, George C. SCOTT as the gambler who makes himself Eddie's manager, and Piper Laurie as the girl whose relationship with Eddie ends in disaster.

**HUSTON,** JOHN (1906–   ), US director, son of Walter HUSTON. His first important film work was as a writer, collaborating on the screenplays of several WARNER BROS films, including *The Amazing Dr Clitterhouse* (1938), *Juarez* (1939), *Dr Ehrlich's Magic Bullet* (1940), *High Sierra* (1941), and *Sergeant York* (1941). Few directors have made such a brilliant début as Huston with THE MALTESE FALCON (1941); after this the emotional melodramatics of *In This Our Life* (1942) seem slight despite the virtues of Bette DAVIS as the cruel but attractive younger sister and Olivia DE HAVILLAND as the kind and long-suffering elder one. *Across the Pacific* (1942) attempted, with some measure of success, to apply the 'black' thriller style of *The Maltese Falcon* (aided by the same star trio of Humphrey BOGART, Mary ASTOR, and Sydney GREENSTREET) to an espionage drama of army intelligence versus Japanese plotters.

During the war Huston wrote, directed, and photographed two outstanding documentaries for the US Army Pictorial Service. *The Battle of San Pietro* (1944) recounts an incident from the Italian campaign, showing by implication both the glory and the futility of war. *Let There Be Light* (1945) shows servicemen, emotionally damaged by their experience of combat, undergoing psychiatric treatment; the film's spareness makes it painfully effective and it was withdrawn from public circulation by the US War Department. He made a magnificent return to feature films with THE TREASURE OF THE SIERRA MADRE (1948).

After a tense version of Maxwell Anderson's *Key Largo* (1948) and *We Were Strangers* (1949), a drama of Cuban revolutionaries, came three notable films in succession: THE ASPHALT JUNGLE (1950), THE RED BADGE OF COURAGE (1951), and THE AFRICAN QUEEN (1952). In comparison, MOULIN ROUGE (1952) is uneven, and it is possible to prefer the less pretentious but hugely entertaining BEAT THE DEVIL (1953). His

noble attempt at the filmically near-impossible, *Moby Dick* (1956), was a disappointment if not a disaster. *Heaven Knows, Mr Allison* (1957) treated with humorous irony an artificial character conflict between a nun (Deborah KERR) and a marine (Robert MITCHUM). *The Barbarian and the Geisha* (1958) was beautifully photographed but generally dull; *The Roots of Heaven* (1958) was a cluttered and verbose account of Romain Gary's novel, partly scripted by the author. A large-scale Western, *The Unforgiven* (1960), with curious casting (Audrey HEPBURN, Burt LANCASTER, Audie Murphy) was dominated by the performance of Lillian GISH.

THE MISFITS (1961) was a return to form with a particular interest of its own. It was followed by a singular biographical film, *Freud* (1962), and an outlandish but enjoyable thriller, *The List of Adrian Messenger* (1963), with George C. SCOTT as Anthony Gethryn, writer Philip Macdonald's upper-crust detective. After *Night of the Iguana* (1964), a glib but amusing version of Tennessee WILLIAMS's play, Huston occupied himself with *La Bibbia (The Bible ... In the Beginning*, 1966), memorable only for Huston's own rumbustious performance as Noah. After directing part of *Casino Royale* (1967, see JAMES BOND), he made an arresting and visually remarkable though ultimately repelling version of Carson McCullers's *Reflections in a Golden Eye* (1967) followed by another complete contrast, the slender but diverting *Sinful Davey* (1968). *The Kremlin Letter* (1970) was a complex thriller, slightly too stylish. His special talent re-emerged in *Fat City* (1972), in which the apparent subject—second-rate boxers and their promoters—was the framework for a penetrating study of personal and professional failure.

Huston is a superb director of actors: outstanding examples are Humphrey Bogart and Mary Astor in *The Maltese Falcon*, Bogart and Walter Huston in *The Treasure of the Sierra Madre*, Bogart and Katharine HEPBURN in *The African Queen*, Clark GABLE and Marilyn MONROE in *The Misfits*. His best films have a strong sense of irony. He prefers to deal with men of fierce independence facing danger with courage and fatalism: romance and sentimentality take second place in his world.

**HUSTON,** WALTER (1884–1950), US actor, worked in touring companies and vaudeville, before becoming a leading actor on Broadway in the twenties. His first film was *Gentlemen of the Press* (1929), and it may be that this late arrival in Hollywood protected him from the dangers of type-casting as well as preventing him from attaining real stardom. His fine presence and the mature intelligence of his acting resulted in some fine performances, particularly in *Abraham Lin-*

coln (1930), *The Beast of the City, American Madness* (both 1932), and *Dodsworth* (1936). The latter was praised by the critics but had only modest commercial success and Huston returned to the theatre where he played Othello and in Kurt WEILL's *Knickerbocker Holiday*. It was in Weill's play that he first sang 'September Song' which had great success when he recorded it some years later. In the last ten years of his career he was particularly associated with supporting roles, finely played, in films directed by his son, John HUSTON. The most memorable of these is without doubt his powerful performance in THE TREASURE OF THE SIERRA MADRE (1948).

**HUTTON,** BETTY (1921–   ), US actress, real name Elizabeth June Thornburg, whose first screen appearance as the high-spirited, noisy, and man-mad Bessie in *The Fleet's In* (1942) was typical of the performances which earned her the title of the Blonde Bombshell. She was at her best in THE MIRACLE OF MORGAN'S CREEK (1944). Her greatest success was as the tomboy heroine of the musical *Annie Get Your Gun* (1950), but *Dream Girl* (1948) showed her in a gentler vein as the day-dreaming heroine. Her last major film was *Somebody Loves Me* (1952), after which she quarrelled with her studio and left Hollywood.

**HUXLEY,** Sir JULIAN (1887–1975), British biologist and educator, was general supervisor of biological films for Gaumont-British Instructional (1933–6) and for Zoological Film Productions (1937), overseeing a classic zoological film series for higher educational use. *The Private Life of the Gannets* (1934; OSCAR for best one-reel short subject, 1937), which Huxley directed, brought aesthetic appreciation to scientific observation. (It was produced by Alexander KORDA, who intended the title to echo his popular success THE PRIVATE LIFE OF HENRY VIII, 1933.) Huxley devised a film series on evolution, produced by Stuart LEGG, and provided the commentary for Edgar ANSTEY's *Enough to Eat* (1936). As UNESCO's first Director-General (1946–8), Huxley appointed John GRIERSON Director of Mass Communications.

**HYDE-WHITE,** WILFRID (1903–   ), British character actor who began his stage career in 1925 and made his first film appearance in REMBRANDT (1936). A virtually incessant demand developed for his portrayal of smooth, dulcet-toned, impeccable Englishmen of the traditional 'old school tie' kind, usually in light comedies but to particularly happy effect in THE THIRD MAN (1949), as the hypocritical headmaster in *The Browning Version* (1951), and as Colonel Pickering in MY FAIR LADY (1964).

# I

**IBERT,** JACQUES (1890–1962), French composer, studied at the Paris Conservatoire under Fauré. His *Divertissements*, well known as a concert work, was written for the play UN CHAPEAU DE PAILLE D'ITALIE by Labiche and has occasionally been used to accompany René CLAIR's film of 1927. His film scores include several for DUVIVIER, among them *Golgotha* (1935) and *La Charette fantôme* (1938), PABST's *Don Quichotte* (1934), and Orson WELLES's MACBETH (1948). He also wrote the music for one section of Gene KELLY's ballet film *Invitation to the Dance* (1956).

**ICHIKAWA,** KON (1915–   ), Japanese director, was first involved with cinema in 1933 as a cartoonist for the JO Studios in Kyoto. During the post-war occupation of Japan, he left animation in order to make puppet films, one of which, *Musume Dojoji (A Girl at Dojo Temple*, 1946), a puppet version of a KABUKI play, was banned by the occupying American authorities because its script had not been submitted for approval. Although soon to abandon this genre of cinema, he never lost his interest in the cinematic possibilities of the cartoon and puppet-theatre.

In 1947, Shintoho—an offshoot from the Toho studios—chose Ichikawa to direct their, and his, first feature film, *Toho senichi-ya (1,001 Nights with Toho)*. This was followed by the melodramatic *Sanhyaku-roku-yogo ya (365 Nights*, 1948) and, in 1953, by two comedies, *Ashi ni sawatta onna (The Woman Who Touched the Legs)*, a free remake of Yutaka Abe's successful silent film, and *Pu-san (Mr Pu)*, a satirical look at contemporary Japanese life based on a cartoon character. The influence of the American cinema on Ichikawa is evident in these films, for he greatly admires American comedies and was dubbed by the critics the 'Japanese Frank Capra'.

Ichikawa won the San Giorgio Prize at VENICE in 1956 with BIRUMA NO TATEGOTO *(The Burmese Harp)*. In the same year he joined Daiei and for them directed many films dealing with the humorous and the bizarre, including *Enjo (Conflagration*, 1958), about an acolyte who sets fire to the famous Kyoto Pavilion; *Kagi (Odd Obsession*, 1959), a 'savage sex comedy' which won the Venice Grand Prix; and NOBI *(Fires on the Plain*, 1959), Ichikawa's own disturbing vision of hell. On all these films and all his later works, Ichikawa collaborated with his wife, Natto Wada, one of Japan's foremost scriptwriters, as well as with Japan's greatest cameramen, such as Setsuo KOBAYASHI and Kazuo Miyagawa.

Ichikawa's increasing international success can be attributed to his three major works of the sixties: TAIHEYO HITORIBOTCHI *(Alone on the Pacific*, 1963), YUKINOJO HENGE *(An Actor's Revenge*, 1963), and especially TOKYO ORINPIKKU *(Tokyo Olympiad*, 1965). In these films Ichikawa explores his conviction that man struggles against himself more than against nature or others, in order to reach a chosen goal. He never misses an opportunity to expose the comedy, the isolation, or the irony involved in that struggle. His attitude towards Japanese life, in particular the close family ties, is more ambivalent, for in *Ototo (Younger Brother*, 1960) he approvingly shows the devotion of an elder sister to her tubercular brother, while in the same year in *Bonchi* (roughly translatable as 'eldest son') he offers a brutal picture of a matriarchal family system.

His other films include *Hakai (The Sin*, 1962), *Watashi wa nisai (Being Two Isn't Easy*, 1962), *Zeni no odori (Money Talks*, 1964), and *Matatabi (The Wanderers*, 1973).

Although a very versatile director in terms of subject-matter, Ichikawa's trademark—a sensitive cinematic eye for colour, architecture, and composition—is visible in each of his films. Less known and acclaimed than OZU or KUROSAWA, Ichikawa ranks alongside them as one of the finest Japanese directors.

***IDÉE, L'*** *(The Idea)*, France, 1934. 30min.

A film by Berthold BARTOSCH, based on a book of the same title by Frans Masereel, composed entirely of woodcuts. Bartosch worked with animated shapes moved on three layers of glass sheet, lit from underneath or from the side. The style, derived directly from Masereel but evolving during the film, is highly Expressionistic, coming some years after the direct influence of EXPRESSIONISM had passed out of German films.

The music for the film, written by Arthur HONEGGER, was played by a small orchestra (Les

Ondes Musicales) with a solo performance on the Theremin, an early electronic instrument designed by Professor Theremin, a Russian emigré working in Berlin. (See also ANIMATION.)

**IDHEC** see INSTITUT DES HAUTES ÉTUDES CINÉMATOGRAPHIQUES

*IDIOT, The.* Although many films bear this title, relatively few are adapted from Dostoevsky's novel, *The Idiot* (1868–9). Two silent versions were made: the first, a Russian film, was directed by Piotr Chardnin in 1910. The other appeared in Germany in 1921; *Der Idiot* (or *Irrende Seelen*) was produced by Russofilm, directed and scripted by Carl FROELICH with Asta NIELSEN, Alfred Abel, and Walter Janssen.

The first really successful adaptation, however, appeared in France in 1947. *L'Idiot* was directed by George Lampin with Gérard PHILIPE and Edwige FEUILLÈRE brilliantly playing the parts of Prince Mishkin and Nastasia. KUROSAWA's *Hakuchi* (1951) is a transcription in Japanese terms of Dostoevsky's novel, with Masayuki Mori (Kameda) and Toshiro MIFUNE (Akama); it was never a public success and was drastically cut even in Japan. The full version was screened in Germany in 1959 and at the New York and London festivals (1963). The Russian colour version, *Nastasia Filipovna* (1958) directed and scripted by Ivan Pyriev, with Yuri Yakovliov (Prince Mishkin) and Yulia Borisova (Nastasia) is adapted from the first part of the novel. Unlike Lampin's version it does not emphasize the pathological and abnormal side of Mishkin but stresses instead his sensitivity, honesty, and humanity.

*IF . . . ,* GB, 1968. Eastman Colour and black and white; 1¾hr. *Dir* Lindsay Anderson; *prod* Michael Medwin, Anderson for Memorial Enterprises; *scr* David Sherwin, from original script *Crusaders* by Sherwin and John Howlett; *ph* Miroslav Ondříček; *ed* David Gladwell; *mus* Marc Wilkinson plus 'Sanctus' from *Missa Luba*; *cast* Malcolm McDowell (Nick), David Wood (Johnny), Richard Warwick (Wallace), Christine Noonan (the girl), Robert Swann (Rowntree), Hugh Thomas (Denson), Peter Jeffrey (Headmaster).

Three boys turn violently against the system of their English public school. Like ZÉRO DE CONDUITE (1933), *If . . .* was intended as a metaphor for rebellion in a wider context of society; there are references to the earlier film in the somewhat unwieldy use of 'chapters' and in the closing sequence.

At the time of its appearance, *If . . .* stood out among current British films as an attempt to exploit the visual rather than the literary poten-

tial of cinema. It encountered production and distribution problems. Memorial Enterprises took the project over from Seth HOLT, but economy forced the shooting of some scenes in black and white; this created confusion in a work where the relation between fantasy and reality is not clearly conceived. The lack of stars, too, made the distributors initially wary: it was to some extent their caution which brought the film into prominence. Loud critical acclaim and a successful run at PARAMOUNT's London West End cinema eventually led to general release.

*If . . .* won first prize at CANNES in 1969 and launched Malcolm McDowell as an appealing rebel/victim: he played similar roles in KUBRICK's A CLOCKWORK ORANGE (1971) and ANDERSON's *O Lucky Man* (1973).

*IKIRU* (*Living*; initially shown in Europe as *Doomed*), Japan, 1952. 2½hr. *Dir* Akira Kurosawa; *prod* Toho; *scr* Shinobu Hashimoto, Hideo Oguni, Kurosawa; *ph* Asaishi Nakai; *cast* Takashi Shimura (Kanji Watanabe), Nabuo Kaneko (his son), Kyoko Seki (his daughter-in-law), Miki Odagiri (Toyo), Yunosuke Ito (novelist).

Discovering that he is in the terminal stages of cancer, Watanabe spends his last months in search of a meaning to life. After an uncomprehending pursuit of pleasure has failed he finds self-realization in forcing through the building of a children's playground in the slums and dies quietly.

KUROSAWA used the old man's quest to illuminate the sterility of modern city life, the erosion of family structures, and the abuses of bureaucratic government. Low-key photography and a fragmented narrative build up a mood of despair which is subtly transformed by the dogged idealism of the meek old man, played with touching simplicity by Takashi SHIMURA, one of Kurosawa's favourite actors.

*IMMIGRANT, The,* US, 1917. 30min. *Dir, scr* Charles Chaplin; *prod* Mutual; *ph* Rollie Totheroh, William C. Foster; *cast* Charlie Chaplin, Edna Purviance, Albert Austin, Henry Bergman, Eric Campbell.

The first half of *The Immigrant* is an early example of the social comment discernible in CHAPLIN's later films. The opening shots of immigrants arriving in New York on a crowded ship and being herded on to Ellis Island are full of the images found in the contemporary photographs of actual scenes by Jacob Riis and Lewis Hine. The second half takes place in a restaurant, and revolves around Charlie's problems in paying the bill.

**INCE, THOMAS HARPER** (1882–1924), US director, first worked in the theatre. After appearing in several films he was taken on as a director by Carl LAEMMLE, but he moved to Kessel and Baumann's Bison-Life Motion Pictures shortly after, where in 1911–12 he directed some one hundred films, mostly Westerns, and began supervising the work of other directors. Impressed by the success of Broncho Billy ANDERSON, Ince renewed a friendship struck up in the theatre with W. S. HART, whose potential as a Western star he shrewdly discerned. Ince supervised Hart's films, which were directed initially by Reginald Barker, and then by Hart himself. Ince's Westerns were a major factor in the success of the MUTUAL distribution company; his prestige was such that when TRIANGLE was formed in 1915, Ince, with SENNETT and GRIFFITH, was a main asset of the new company.

The supervision of films by others became Ince's most important activity, and between July 1915 and March 1918, he directed only three films; one of these, CIVILIZATION (1916), is generally considered to be his greatest achievement. His later work is undistinguished. He died in mysterious circumstances aboard the yacht of William Randolph HEARST.

*INCIDENT AT OWL CREEK* see RIVIÈRE DU HIBOU, LA

*IN COLD BLOOD*, US, 1967. 1½hr. *Dir* Richard Brooks; *prod* Brooks for Columbia; *scr* Brooks from Truman Capote's book; *ph* Conrad Hall; *des* Jack Ahern; *mus* Quincy Jones; *cast* Robert Blake (Perry Smith), Scott Wilson (Dick Hickock), John Forsythe (Alvin Dewey), Paul Stewart (reporter).

The film is faithful to Truman CAPOTE's 'non-fiction novel' about the senseless-seeming multiple murder of a Kansas farm family in 1959. By using relatively unknown principals and actual neighbours of the victims in the cast, and the authentic scene of the crime, BROOKS strained for a severely documentary effect. Like the original book, which aroused much controversy, the film's objectivity—flinching at neither the murders nor the execution of Perry and Dick— has given rise to the complaint that it is unshaped by anything more than its aesthetic structure (exemplified in the inter-cutting between the killers and their victims prior to the crime). The film's supporters, however, while agreeing that it is a presentation without meaning and an inquiry yielding no answers, have insisted that life itself is like that. The quality of Conrad HALL's photography is outstanding, revealing a very high degree of perceptiveness and skill. This adds, ironically, to the sense of strain between the documentary and dramatic effects.

**INDIA.** In a country where television is still at the experimental stage, and among a population of widespread illiteracy, film is foremost among popular entertainments, reaching even the smallest village through the travelling cinema or the 'temporary' cinema, an open structure thatched with palm found all over South India. In large urban areas there are not enough cinemas to meet demand, and the opening of a new film can cause near riots, such is the rush for admission.

Film production established itself rapidly in India, after the envoys of LUMIÈRE reached Bombay in' 1896. Most prominent among early producer/directors was Dadasaheb Phalke, a MÉLIÈS-like character who introduced the genre of mythological films, peopled by gods and goddesses of the Hindu pantheon which is still being successfully exploited today. An indefatigable experimenter, Phalke was ruined by the introduction of sound.

The arrival of sound in a country with twenty-six main linguistic areas inevitably resulted in the fragmenting of the industry and its dispersal to different language markets. Bombay, the original centre of the industry, continued to dominate, concentrating on the production of films in Hindi, the most widely spoken Indian tongue and since Independence the official language. Chief producers at Bombay include B. R. Chopra, S. Mukherjee, and Raj Kapoor. In the south, Madras developed its own massive industry with the production of films in Tamil, the chief southern language. There, production is dominated by companies such as A.V.M., Gemini, Vasu Menon, and Vijaya.

These two categories, the Hindi film in the north and the Tamil film in the south, constitute the popular mainstream of Indian cinema. Such films, the staple diet of the mass audience, are all too easily categorized. In an industry dominated by a Hollywood-type star system, a film must conform to a well-tried formula for success. It must boast a couple of well-known stars, a profusion of songs, a variety of dance numbers, and it must by Western standards be very long. Traditionally, Indian drama has always incorporated dance and music, and the origin of the popular Indian film can be linked with the now virtually extinct folk-music dramas of the nineteenth century. The commercial necessity of building a film round a collection of songs has clearly been instrumental in preventing the development of the popular cinema beyond its present frivolous state. Neither creating a coherent imaginative world of its own nor reflecting the social reality of India, the popular Indian film creates a limbo of song and dance, of sentiment and melodrama, which is comfortably flattering to the wealthy among the audience, seductively escapist for the poor. Valuable foreign currency is earned by the export of Hindi and Tamil films to South Asian emigrant communities abroad, especially in Britain and East Africa.

Since the beginnings of the Hindi cinema there has, however, been a frail but persistent tradition of socially aware films. The famous Bombay Talkies Studio, founded in 1934, produced films such as *Achhut Kanya* (*Untouchable Girl*, 1936), which dealt with the bitter issue of caste. Bimal Roy's Hindi *Do Bigha Zamin* (*Two Acres of Land*, 1953) had a neo-realist quality about it, and won the Prix International at the 1954 CANNES Festival. Another of his films, *Sujata* (1959), dealt with the caste problem in an equally realistic way. K. A. Abbas, while often working within the commercial tradition, collaborating with the star Raj Kapoor on successes such as *Awara* (*The Vagabond*, 1951) and *Shri 420* (*Mr 420*, 1955), also made more experimental films such as *Dharti ke Lal* (*Children of the Earth*, 1949), which used non-professional actors, and *Munna* (1954), the first Hindi film ever made without songs and dances. Although critically admired at home and abroad, it was not a financial success.

Under the British there was a flourishing documentary production group modelled on the CROWN FILM UNIT, but this did not survive Independence.

Among minority language cinemas, the only one of any importance to date is the Bengali cinema. Since the international success of Satyajit RAY has proved that it is possible to work outside the commercial system, the nucleus of an independent—and mainly political—cinema has developed in Calcutta, in the work of young directors such as Mrinal Sen, Ritwik Ghatak, Hrishikesh Mukherjee, and Salil Chowdhury. The American James IVORY has drawn on the contradictions of modern Indian society in films like *Shakespeare-Wallah* (1965) and *Bombay Talkie* (1970).

The fostering of film culture in India has been hindered by the severe restrictions imposed on film clubs: unlike most other countries, India does not exempt film club showings from its highly conservative censorship. Moreover, films imported for club showings are subject to the same high import duties as films commercially imported. The national film school in Poona is one of the best equipped in the world, but it makes no attempt to educate its students beyond the demands of the commercial industry.

***INDUSTRIAL BRITAIN***, GB, 1931; released 1933. 20min. *Prod* John Grierson for Empire Marketing Board Film Unit; *ph* Robert Flaherty, John Grierson, Basil Wright, Arthur Elton; *ed* Grierson, Edgar Anstey.

FLAHERTY's first film in Britain was intended by GRIERSON as a tribute to industrial craftsman-

ship. Predictably, Flaherty spent a great deal of time and money on shooting test material for the film. This test footage plus additional sequences filmed by Grierson's crew had to be combined by Grierson in the final product, which was distributed as the first in a series of six documentaries, called the 'Imperial Six'. Evidence of Flaherty's cinematic eye can be seen here and there in *Industrial Britain*, but it is basically a product of the dedicated social consciousness of Grierson and his followers.

***INFORMER, The***, US, 1935. 1½hr. *Dir, prod* John Ford for RKO; *scr* Dudley Nichols, from the novel by Liam O'Flaherty; *ph* Joseph H. August; *des* Van Nest Polglase, Marc Lee Kirk; *mus* Max Steiner; *cast* Victor McLaglen (Gypo Nolan), Heather Angel (Mary McPhillip), Una O'Connor (Mrs McPhillip), J. W. Kerrigan (Terry).

After the success of THE LOST PATROL (1934) FORD and NICHOLS were able to embark on *The Informer*, which had been a cherished project for five years. The use of minimal, impressionistic sets and misty lighting created an effective stylization of O'Flaherty's tragic story of betrayal during the Irish troubles. The film was enormously successful, both critically and commercially: OSCARS were awarded to Victor MCLAGLEN for his portrayal of the slow-brained stool pigeon, and to Ford, Nichols, and Max STEINER. This success initiated a literary vein in Ford's work, sometimes with less happy results.

This was the second film adaptation of the novel. A British silent version was directed by Arthur ROBISON in 1929.

**INGRAM, REX** (1893–1950), Irish-born US director, real name Reginald Ingram Montgomery Hitchcock, began in films in 1915 as an actor. He also worked as a designer and a scriptwriter, and directed his first film, *The Great Problem*, in 1916. The films which followed made little impact at the time, but THE FOUR HORSEMEN OF THE APOCALYPSE (1922) established him as a leading director and launched Rudolph VALENTINO as a major star. (The leading lady, Alice Terry, became Ingram's wife and was the star of many of his later films.) He made six more films in Hollywood, including a successful version of *Scaramouche* (1923), then left in search of greater independence, eventually setting up his own studio in Nice. *Mare Nostrum* (1926) was the first film made there; a spy story involving German submarines, it included a number of the exotic settings to which Ingram was attracted throughout his career, and the carefully composed and beautifully lit images which characterized his best work. Other films included *The Magician* (1926), remade as *The Garden of*

*Allah* (1927), and his only sound film, *Baroud* (1931). This was his last film and he was both the star and the director.

**INGRAM,** REX (1895–    ), US actor, a former doctor who made his film début in 1918 in TARZAN films starring Elmo Lincoln, and subsequently appeared in such silent classics as *The Ten Commandments* (1923) and THE BIG PARADE (1925). His most famous roles were De Lawd in *Green Pastures* (1936) and the giant genie in THE THIEF OF BAGHDAD (1940). Numerous other films include CABIN IN THE SKY (1943) and, in recent times, *Hurry Sundown* (1967). Ingram and Paul ROBESON were the only black actors to attain a degree of stardom in the thirties and forties and to escape, to some extent, the permissible racial stereotype.

*INNOCENCE UNPROTECTED* see NEVINOST BEZ ZAŠTITE

**INSERT,** a CLOSE-UP of some detail of the action, photographed separately and cut into the film. Typical inserts might be the fatal telegram or the scientist's view of the unexpected virus through the microscope. Such shots, which require technical expertise rather than creative inspiration, are often made in insert studios by specialists, who must take care to match the lighting with that of the rest of the sequence. The hand holding the telegram is usually not the star's hand, and the director is rarely present to supervise.

The term 'insert' is also used by Metz to describe one of his semiological units (see CRITICISM).

**INSTITUT DES HAUTES ÉTUDES CINÉ-MATOGRAPHIQUES** (IDHEC) was founded in Paris in 1943 under Marcel L'HERBIER: the director from 1951 to 1968 was Rémy Tessonneau. It was a development of the Centre Artistique et Technique des Jeunes de l'Écran (CATJE) which had flourished in Nice from 1941, training young film-makers entirely through short film.

IDHEC is subsidized by the French Government through the CENTRE NATIONAL DU CINÉMA and has the dual purpose of training filmmakers and developing film appreciation at all levels. Foreign students are accepted, entry to the two-year course being by competitive examination for both French and foreign applicants who must hold qualifications equivalent to university entrance standards. In accord with the general tendency of education in France, a high level of academic achievement is required.

There are courses for: directors, producers, cameramen, designers, sound operators, continuity girls, editors. Although there is no script-writers' course, students are encouraged to write their own scripts for their diploma films. Students of all disciplines work together, the aim being to avoid narrow specialization. Studies in film history and aesthetics are obligatory and rigorous: visiting lecturers have included Georges SADOUL and Jean MITRY.

Collective agreements exist with the trade unions to maintain professional standards. Efforts are made to balance the student intake against the state of the industry and openings for employment.

In spite of working within a tight budget, IDHEC offers not only a comprehensive range of technical facilities for its students but lectures, classes, and courses for various public groups, emphasizing its outgoing attitude to cinema education. The old IDHEC did not survive the upheavals of 1968: a reconstituted IDHEC opened in 1970 under new management. (See FILM SCHOOLS.)

**INTERLENGHI,** FRANCO (1930–   ), Italian actor, one of Rome's street urchins, who played one of the two boys in SCIUSCIÀ (1946). While most of his school companions who appeared in the film were never seen on the screen again, Interlenghi managed to establish a firm footing in the industry in subsequent years. In 1947 he played in BLASETTI's *Fabiola*, and then in Luciano EMMER's DOMENICA D'AGOSTO (1950) and *Parigi è sempre Parigi* (1951). He appeared as Moraldo in FELLINI's I VITELLONI (1953) and in the late fifties worked under Mauro Bolognini in *Giovani mariti* (1957) and *La notte brava* (1959), which he followed with a part in ROSSELLINI's *Viva l'Italia* (1960).

*INTERMEZZO,* Sweden, 1936. *Dir* Gustaf Molander; *prod* Svensk Filmindustri; *scr* Molander, Gösta Stevens; *ph* Åke Dahlquist; *cast* Gösta Ekman (Holger Brandt), Ingrid Bergman (Anita Hoffman), Inga Tidblad (Mrs Brandt), Hasse Ekman (their son).

The romantic love affair between Brandt, a renowned violinist, and his daughter's music teacher was handled by MOLANDER with sensitive directness. The film marked the first stirrings of new artistic life in the Swedish industry (see SWEDEN) and was well received abroad. Its success took Ingrid BERGMAN to Hollywood, where her first film was a remake, *Intermezzo* (1939, *Escape to Happiness* in GB), in which she repeated her original role opposite Leslie HOWARD.

**INTERNEGATIVE** see DUPE

*IN THE HEAT OF THE NIGHT,* US, 1967. De Luxe Color; 1¾hr. *Dir* Norman Jewison; *prod*

Walter Mirisch; *scr* Stirling Silliphant; *ph* Haskell Wexler; *cast* Sidney Poitier (Virgil Tibbs), Rod Steiger (Bill Gillespie), Warren Oates (Sam Wood).

A thriller set in a small Mississippi town; local police chief Bill Gillespie arrests Virgil Tibbs, a negro who happens to be passing through, on suspicion of the murder of a white man, only to find that Tibbs is a police detective.

A tense, taut film, ably controlled by JEWISON, who maintains a fine balance between the mystery and racial ingredients. WEXLER's photography captures perfectly the dry heat and dusty atmosphere of the deep south. It deservedly won three OSCARS: best film, best screenplay, best actor—Rod STEIGER, whose police chief, a basically decent though indolent man conditioned by a racialist society, is a brilliant characterization. Its undoubted distinction was overshadowed by the resounding success of BONNIE AND CLYDE, released at the same time.

Sidney POITIER repeated the role of the self-contained detective in *They Call Me MISTER Tibbs!* (1970) and *The Organization* (1971), neither of which displayed the qualities of *In the Heat of the Night*.

***INTIMATE LIGHTING*** see INTIMNÍ OSVĚTLENÍ

***INTIMNÍ OSVĚTLENI*** (*Intimate Lighting*), Czechoslovakia, 1966. 1¼hr. *Dir* Ivan Passer; *scr* Passer, Jaroslav Papoušek, Václav Sasek; *ph* Miroslav Ondříček, Jan Strecha; *ed* Jiřina Lukesová; *mus* Oldrich Korte; *cast* Věra Kresadlová (Stepa), Zdeněk Bezusek (Peter), Jan Vostřcil (grandfather), Karel Blazek (Bambas), Jaroslava Stedrá (Marus), Vlastimila Vlková (grandmother), Karel Uhlik (the chemist).

A professional cello player comes to a provincial town to visit an old friend who teaches in a local school. His fiancée comes with him, the friends get drunk together, remember old times, and play in a quartet together: the film celebrates the normal, in short, but with pith and resonance deriving from PASSER's own gentleness, acuity, and humour. The production was something of a happy accident: Passer volunteered to direct a script already accepted by one of the production groups, and worked on it with his friend and fellow-collaborator with FORMAN, Jaroslav Papoušek. The leading part of the fiancée is played by Forman's second wife, Věra Kresadlová, and Jan Vostřcil, leader of one of the brass bands from Forman's first film, also figures.

***INTOLERANCE***, US, 1916. 3¼hr. *Dir, prod, scr* D. W. Griffith for Wark Productions; *ph* G. W. Bitzer, Karl Brown; *cast* 'The Mother and the

*Intimní osvětlení* (Ivan Passer, 1966)

Law' Robert Harron (The Hero), Mae Marsh (The Dear One), Miriam Cooper (The Friendless One), Walter Long (The Musketeer of the Slums), Sam de Grasse (The Mill Owner), Ralph Lewis (Prison Governor); 'The Nazarene' Howard Gaye (Jesus), Erich von Stroheim (Pharisee), Gunther von Ritzan (Pharisee), Lillian Langdon, Olga Grey, Bessie Love; 'The Medieval Story' Margery Wilson (Brown Eyes), Spottiswoode Aitken (Her Father), Ruth Handforth (Her Mother), Eugene Pallette (Her Fiancé), Josephine Crowell (Catherine de Medici), Frank Bennett (Charles IX); 'The Fall of Babylon' Tully Marshall (The High Priest of Baal), Elmer Clifton (The Rhapsode), Alfred Paget (Prince Belshazzar), George Siegmann (Emperor Cyrus), Elmo Lincoln (Belshazzar's bodyguard), Constance Talmadge (The Mountain Girl); Lillian Gish (The Girl Who Rocks the Cradle).

Stung by the accusations of racial prejudice that had followed the release of THE BIRTH OF A NATION (1915), GRIFFITH attempted to abstract and universalize the theme of intolerance by intercutting four illustrative stories from different periods. 'The Mother and the Law', set in the present, contrasts the treatment of capitalist and worker by the law; 'The Nazarene' recounts Christ's crucifixion; 'The Medieval Story' recounts the massacre of Protestants in Paris on St Bartholomew's Day 1572; 'The Fall of Babylon' the betrayal of Prince Belshazzar to the Persians. The symbolic image of a woman rocking a cradle which punctuates the film is intended to unite the separate episodes. This complex structure disconcerted audiences of the time and the overblown grandeur of the Babylon story upset the balance of the film.

In addition its release was untimely: the pacifist tone was unwelcome when general opinion in America was in favour of entering the First World War. 'The Fall of Babylon' in particular was immensely expensive to film and later it and 'The Mother and the Law' (which had been the starting-point of the whole project) were released as individual films in an attempt to recoup some of the vast losses incurred. Producers were to be considerably more cautious in the film's wake.

Despite its lack of popular success, *Intolerance* exerted an enormous influence, especially in the Soviet Union where a copy was smuggled through the blockade by the German Socialists in 1919. With *The Birth of a Nation* it is now acknowledged as Griffith's finest work, advancing the techniques of set design, treatment of masses of extras, and camera mobility with power and originality.

A useful shot-by-shot analysis by Theodore Huff was published by the Museum of Modern Art, New York, in 1966.

**INVISIBLE MAN, The,** US, 1933. 1¼hr. *Dir* James Whale; *prod* Universal; *scr* R. C. Sherriff, based on the novel by H. G. Wells; *ph* Arthur Edeson, John Mescall; *sp eff* John P. Fulton; *mus* Charles Previn; *cast* Claude Rains (Jack Griffin, the Invisible Man), Gloria Stuart (Flora Cranley), William Harrigan (Dr Kemp), Henry Travers (Dr Cranley), Una O'Connor (Mrs Hall), Forrester Harvey (Mr Hall).

Jack Griffin (Claude RAINS) develops a drug that renders him invisible. He then succumbs to megalomania, sets out to terrorize the world into submission and is eventually destroyed himself. The magical ending has the Invisible Man's body gradually reappearing as life is leaving it. James WHALE'S film is notable for its superb trick EFFECTS and its humour bordering on slapstick.

**IN WHICH WE SERVE,** GB, 1942. 2hr. *Dir* Noël Coward, David Lean; *prod, scr, mus* Coward; *ph* Ronald Neame; *cast* Noël Coward (Captain 'D'), John Mills (Shorty Blake), Bernard Miles (Walter Hardy), Celia Johnson (Mrs Kinross), Kay Walsh (Freda Lewis), Richard Attenborough (young stoker).

Inspired by the personality of Lord Louis Mountbatten, *In Which We Serve* reconstructs in flashbacks the backgrounds of different crew members of a destroyer sunk (like Mountbatten's *Kelly*) in the Mediterranean. Fine individual performances were competently directed in the documentary manner that war brought to the British feature film, and the film deservedly enjoyed great success at the time; but its unquestioning acceptance of the existing social order is usually embarrassing to an audience not subject to the original conditions of crisis. On board HMS *Torrin* each man from the captain down knows his place; there are those who lead and those who follow, and absolute loyalty and devotion to duty are required of each. Even the unfortunate man who panics and deserts his post under fire ultimately redeems himself by dying a hero's death. The behaviour of the entire crew was presented as the ideal model for the behaviour of a society at war. In the Soviet Union the film was apparently accorded more serious consideration than any other foreign-produced feature film, and no less an authority than PUDOVKIN praised its psychological effectiveness. It is perhaps one of the best examples of how public response to certain films is governed by the prevailing emotional mood.

**IRELAND, JOHN** (1915– ), US actor who after a stage career went to Hollywood, making his début in *A Walk in the Sun* (Lewis MILESTONE, 1945). He pursued an active career in films, usually in intense or dour roles, predominantly in Westerns, including RED RIVER (1948) and GUNFIGHT AT THE OK CORRAL (1956). His most substantial part was as Willie Stark's accomplice in ALL THE KING'S MEN (1949).

**IRIS,** a transition analogous to the FADE, used in early silent films to indicate the beginning or end of a scene. For an iris-in, the image was revealed within an expanding circle, eventually filling the frame; for an iris-out the circle would contract until the screen was entirely black. As a regular convention of cinematic punctuation it was supplanted by the greater flexibility of optical effects (see OPTICAL PRINTING).

Iris shots were always produced in the camera, by mounting the iris in front of the lens and shooting through it. During its currency numerous variations—squares, star-shapes, ogives, off-centre irises—were developed. D. W. GRIFFITH led the way in using it as a story-telling device; his cameraman, Billy BITZER, is sometimes credited with inventing the apparatus. Griffith liked to use the effect as a moving frame-within-the-frame, for example beginning a scene by opening the iris half-way to reveal a single person, then widening it fully to disclose the setting. (See DYNAMIC FRAME.) Similar selective framing without cutting is now achieved by the use of the ZOOM lens.

The term 'iris' can also refer to the diaphragm *inside* the lens, which is structurally identical. In this position, however, it simply varies the overall amount of light reaching the film, without producing a circular image.

**IRON HORSE, The,** US, 1924. 2¾hr. *Dir* John Ford; *prod* Fox; *scr* Charles Kenyon, from a story by Kenyon and John Russell; *ph* George Schneiderman, Burnett Guffey; *cast* George O'Brien (Davy Brandon), Madge Bellamy (Miriam Marsh), Judge Charles Edward Bull (Abraham Lincoln), William Walling (Thomas Marsh), Fred Kohler (Deroux), Gladys Hulette (Ruby).

John FORD's first major success used a story based on the race between Union Pacific and Central Pacific to lay tracks for the first transcontinental railroad, and his handling of this epic of pioneer days brought him general acclaim. His mastery in blending human characterizations with scenic spectacle was already evident. The film was shot almost entirely on location in Nevada where, in the harshest conditions, the unit had virtually to build their own town. It considerably exceeded its budget and FOX's continued support was undoubtedly sustained by the success the previous year of PARAMOUNT's THE COVERED WAGON.

**ISRAEL.** In the years immediately after Israel's foundation in 1948, film production was confined to newsreels, information shorts, and occasional low-budget features. The first Israeli feature film to attract international attention was *Hill 24 Doesn't Answer* (1955), which Thorold DICKINSON was invited to direct. In a country with a population of under three million, films made in Hebrew were regarded as a poor risk and film-making facilities were built up with the aim of attracting foreign companies. The government offered loans and tax reliefs for both co-productions and domestic production, and also set up a centre to co-ordinate the help a foreign producer might require from the armed forces, police, municipalities, etc. There have been co-productions with French, Swedish, West German, and Belgian companies and films made in Israel include EXODUS (1960), *Cast a Giant Shadow* (1966), and *Jesus Christ Superstar* (1973).

In 1960–70 sixty features were made, increasing to twenty in 1971 alone. Audiences have increasingly welcomed films drawn from Israeli themes and Jewish folk-lore and although the introduction of television in 1968 caused some reduction in audiences, government support and a cinema-minded public promise well for a small but lively industry.

**ITALA FILM,** Italian production company founded in Turin in 1908 by Giovanni PASTRONE and a group of colleagues including three cameramen from PATHÉ. During its short life the company was dominated by the personality of Pastrone; but apart from his own films, notably CABIRIA (1914) and the early MACISTE adventures, the company had much success with short comedies, particularly those of André DEED in his 'Cretinetti' role. In 1919 Itala Film became part of the Unione Cinematografica Italiana, but Pastrone remained its artistic director until his retirement in 1923.

**ITALIAN STRAW HAT, An,** see CHAPEAU DE PAILLE D'ITALIE, UN

**ITALY.** The birth of cinematography in Italy occurred on 11 November 1895 when Filoteo Alberini patented his Kinematografo Alberini, for taking, printing, and projecting films. His device was superseded by LUMIÈRE's Cinématographe which was popularized in Rome by Leopoldo Fregoli, a music-hall impersonator who, after meeting Lumière in 1896, began to film his own music-hall turns using trick shots and even reverse motion. In 1905 the first Italian studios were founded by Alberini and his colleague Santoni. During 1904–5 the first Italian newsreels were filmed in Turin by Roberto Omegna under the auspices of Arturo AMBROSIO, while the first costume spectacular, *La presa di*

*Roma*, was made in Rome by Alberini. In 1906 Alberini and Santoni's company became CINES and Ambrosio founded his own production company in Turin; by the following year there were 500 cinemas. Also in 1907 the first Italian film publication *La Lanterna* was issued in Naples with the aim of popularizing the cinema, and another film review was started by Pietro Tonini in Milan.

Another important production company, ITALA, was founded in Turin in 1908 by Sciamengo and PASTRONE. By this time, with the expertise of foreign technicians and increased investment, the industry was blossoming. Films drew heavily on historical and literary subjects; literary classics—Shakespeare, Dante, Tasso, Manzoni, etc—were much used, and popular historical subjects included the fall of Troy, the Odyssey, the destruction of Pompeii. Comedies, dramas, and actuality films were made, but the market was dominated by the costume film, inspired by the Italian theatrical and operatic tradition.

The Italian costume film is perhaps best represented by the 1913 version of QUO VADIS directed by Guazzoni for Cines, in which massive crowds, monumental sets, and real lions all created an unprecedented wealth of spectacle. The following year saw the production of Pastrone's CABIRIA; the public success of this grandiose enterprise encouraged D. W. GRIFFITH to embark on large-scale production. The scenario of *Cabiria* is credited to d'Annunzio, but he apparently wrote only the titles. His influence lent respectability to the Italian cinema: the popular films of 'passion' sprang from d'Annunzio's affection for the 'bourgeois' drama and the exaggerated gestures with which he endowed it. CASERINI's *Ma l'amore mio non muore* (1913) was a prototype of the film of passion. This genre, which thrived alongside the costume epic, directly gave rise to the cult of 'divismo' which elevated stars like Francesca BERTINI and Lyda Borelli to the status of goddesses. Divismo had economic importance: although by 1914 Italy had captured world markets, costume films required phenomenal budgets which could be offset by the less costly melodramas; but it soon rebounded as the stars demanded increasingly large fees, and within a few years the industry was near bankruptcy.

Two other genres emerged around 1914. The 'commedia brillante' (light comedy) drew heavily on Italian operatic traditions; one of its best exponents was Lucio D'Ambra, who transposed operettas to the screen using the scores as musical accompaniment. A more significant style was the 'verismo' popularized in Italian, and notably Sicilian, literature of the nineteenth century. Verismo was adopted by films which

insisted on naturalistic settings, costumes, and plots; and it is here that the roots of NEO-REALISM are to be found, in the milieu and characters of *Sperduti nel buio* (1914), filmed in Naples by Nino Martoglio, *Assunta Spina* (1915), by Gustavo Serena, and *Cenere* (1916) by Febo Mari, filmed in Sardinia. Most of the films in this vein were adapted from existing literary texts; concurrently the Futurist group was pressing for a cinema which would realize its independent potential. Theory became practice in only one film, *Vita futurista* (1916) on which members of the group collaborated, and although Futurist ideas foreshadowed later developments elsewhere they never influenced the Italian cinema (see FUTURISM).

Film production in Italy reached a peak in 1914; the outbreak of war did not at first halt work and the golden age of Italian cinema continued, although with decreasing output and income. The economic effects of the war and increasing competition, especially from America, caused a drop in foreign sales that put an end to prosperity; in a few years production was halved and by 1921 a crisis had set in. The Unione Cinematografica Italiana, the most powerful film consortium in the world, founded in 1918, went bankrupt. By 1922 almost all the Italian film studios had closed down, and during the mid-twenties only about ten films a year were made, most with foreign collaboration.

The Instituto LUCE, which in 1925 became the state documentary and newsreel company, was used to diffuse Fascist propaganda during the thirties. The industry began to prosper again in the early years of sound, primarily because the government took charge of its finances. Production leapt from seven films in 1930 to eighty-seven in 1939, but enduring works were few and all were controlled by strict censorship. Light comedies and WHITE TELEPHONE films, superficial tales which ignored contemporary reality, were a staple product. There were many propagandistic films like *Camicia nera* (1935) by Forzano, and historically-based topics that looked back to the glory of Rome, for example *Scipione l'Africano* (1937) directed by Gallone or *Bengasi* (1942) by Augusto Genina. The few notable exceptions include the films of Alessandro BLASETTI such as *Sole* (1929) and Mario CAMERINI's *Rotaie* (1929), which dealt with current social problems. The founding of CENTRO SPERIMENTALE DI CINEMATOGRAFIA in 1935 and CINECITTÀ in 1937, both supported by Mussolini, ensured increased production. An interest in film theory was meanwhile growing, and two influential film journals, BIANCO E NERO and CINEMA, began publication in Rome. In opposition to the explicitly Fascist cinema, some directors looking for escapist subjects again turned to nineteenth-century literature, to the evocation of refined, bourgeois, provincial elegance. These directors, including Mario SOLDATI, Renato CASTELLANI, and Alberto LATTUADA, became known as the 'Calligrafisti' from their stylistic formality; they did, however, form a bridge between the early verismo and the later neo-realists, in their hints of a political, social, and cultural need to rediscover the 'true' Italy.

A turning-point for Italian cinema came in 1942 and the years following. VISCONTI'S OSSESSIONE (1942), although severely cut by the censor, was shown clandestinely in its full form and its concern with social authenticity was taken up by other film-makers. Economic stringency forced them out into the streets, sometimes using non-actors and taking for their subjects the world about them—war, Occupation, Resistance, and their aftermath—clearly shown in the films of ROSSELLINI: ROMA, CITTÀ APERTA (1945), PAISÀ (1947), GERMANIA, ANNO ZERO (1947). Soon other social topics became their concern: unemployment in DE SICA'S LADRI DI BICICLETTE (Bicycle Thieves, 1948); peasant exploitation in CACCIA TRAGICA (1947) and RISO AMARO (Bitter Rice, 1949), both directed by Giuseppe DE SANTIS; the Mafia and poverty in Sicily in In nome della legge (1949) and IL CAMMINO DELLA SPERANZA (1950), both by Pietro GERMI. Cesare ZAVATTINI, a key figure of the movement, propagated neo-realist principles through journalism and lecturing, and contributed to the scripts of some of the most important films.

Although neo-realist films drew world attention to the Italian cinema they formed only a small proportion of production. They suffered from a lack of financial and technical resources and made little appreciable profit: the Italian public in general, after years of hardship, looked for more light-hearted entertainment. By 1950 neo-realism had begun to decline and was frequently forced to make compromises; the limping industry had to surrender independence in return for government support, and the unpopularity of comment on social problems is illustrated by the official opposition to De Sica's UMBERTO D (1952). As Italy gradually recovered from the war commercial producers had turned to light comedies, melodramas, and costume films: in spite of economic instability, companies still plunged into grand historical reconstructions, continually staving off American competition, and production generally revived (ten features in 1949, twenty-five in 1953) helped by co-production agreements with other European companies. The leaders of neo-realism— Rossellini, De Sica, Visconti—were still active, FELLINI and ANTONIONI were beginning to establish reputations, and interesting films continued to come from directors like Germi, Carlo LIZ-

ZANI, Franco ROSSI, and Curzio Malaparte, whose Il Cristo proibito (1950) was a bitter treatise on the return of a prisoner-of-war. But in the forefront of production—and mostly co-production—were the hokum spectaculars, the inevitable MACISTE epics, and exotica. Italy's female stars, who usually broke into films by winning beauty contests, took a world lead in cinematic pulchritude, notable among them Silvana MANGANO, Gina LOLLOBRIGIDA, Claudia CARDINALE, and Sophia LOREN. There was a vogue for EPISODE films, with sections by famous and lesser-known directors as in AMORE IN CITTÀ (1953, Antonioni, Fellini, Lattuada, Lizzani, Maselli, Risi), Siamo donne (1953, Visconti, ZAMPA, Rossellini, Francolini), and RoGoPaG (1962, Rossellini, GODARD, PASOLINI, Gregoretti).

A resurgence began in 1960, signalled by the presentation at CANNES of L'AVVENTURA and LA DOLCE VITA: Antonioni's film was booed and Fellini was threatened with excommunication. Both films were making a conscious break with mainstream cinema in their rejection of conventional narrative, their length, and their consideration of what became a major theme of the sixties, social breakdown and alienation in a materialistic society. Both directors rapidly consolidated their achievement, and the sixties also saw the emergence of several exciting new directors with various preoccupations, from the Resistance film, revived in Nanni LOY's Quattro giornate di Napoli (1962) and Gianfranco Bosio's Il terrorista (1962), to the return of social criticism, best exemplified in the fine films of Francesco ROSI, SALVATORE GIULIANO (1962) and LE MANI SULLA CITTÀ (Hands over the City, 1963). The effects of neo-realism could still be found everywhere, especially in the marvellous, humane films of Ermanno OLMI—IL POSTO (1961), I FIDANZATI (1963)—and in the earlier work of Pasolini, such as ACCATONE (1961) and Mamma Roma (1962) about the Roman proletariat. The films of Petri, BELLOCCHIO, BERTOLUCCI, Zurlini, criticisms of bourgeois life in industrial Italy, reflect the political and social climate of the sixties and early seventies.

Economic vigour was injected into the industry by the 'spaghetti Western' whose main exponents are Sergio LEONE and Sergio Corbucci. Competing with Hollywood Westerns seemed an impossible venture, but Leone's films caught the public imagination and established the Italian Western as a witty, entertaining style. In terms of profitability it has for the moment replaced the costume epic which had re-emerged in the sixties under the label 'neo-mythologism', coined by one of the directors Vittorio COTTOFAVI.

The competition between television and cinema

has given rise to a significant compromise in Italy, important directors being financed or subsidized by the state broadcasting authority to make films for cinema and television showing. Rossellini now devotes himself to television films, while others including Bertolucci, Petri, Olmi, Risi, Liliana Cavani, Adriano Aprà, and Gianni Amico have directed some excellent films for television.

The Instituto LUCE remained the national archive until the sixties when it was replaced by the Cineteca Nazionale (founded in 1949) but it still has a unique collection of documentary and newsreel material from the inter-war years. A third major film archive, the Cineteca Italiana founded in 1938, is based in Milan.

Pierre Leprohon, *The Italian Cinema*, London, 1972.

**IT GIRL,** created by Elinor GLYN and personified by Clara BOW, was for a time during the twenties the current ideal of sex appeal.

**IT HAPPENED HERE,** GB, 1966. 1½hr. *Dir, prod, scr* Kevin Brownlow, Andrew Mollo; *des and military consultant* Mollo; *ed* Brownlow; *ph* Peter Suschitzky; *mus* Jack Beaver with excerpts from Bruckner's Ninth Symphony and the German march 'People to Arms'; *commentators* Frank Phillips, Michael Mellinger, John Snagge, Alvar Lidell; *cast* Pauline Murray, Sebastian Shaw.

A fantasy of Nazi-occupied Britain, this first film by semi-professionals took seven years to shoot (1956–63); distribution was delayed and a sequence alleged to be anti-Semitic was cut. The uncut version was shown at the festivals of Cork, Mannheim, London (1964), and CANNES (1965) where it won the Prize for Youth.

*How it happened here*, London, 1968, describes the making of the film.

**IT HAPPENED ONE NIGHT,** US, 1934. 1¾hr. *Dir* Frank Capra; *prod* Columbia; *scr* Robert Riskin, adapted from 'Night Bus' by Samuel Hopkins Adams; *ph* Joseph Walker; *cast* Clark Gable (Peter), Claudette Colbert (Ellen Andrews), Walter Connolly (Alexander Andrews), Ward Bond (bus driver).

The encounter on a bus journey of a runaway heiress and an attractive vagrant (a newspaperman in disguise) provided the plot for one of the most popular SCREWBALL comedies of the thirties; the strong sex undertone, established by Claudette COLBERT and Clark GABLE in possibly their best roles, reaches its height in the suggestive 'Walls of Jericho' sequence where, having to share a bedroom, they coyly undress using blankets as a screen. The evocation of the American countryside and CAPRA's combination of

madcap comedy and technical skill created a lasting success. The film won four OSCARS.

**IVAN GROZNYI** (*Ivan the Terrible*), USSR, Part 1 1944, Part 2 1958. 1½hr each part. *Dir, scr, ed* S. M. Eisenstein; *prod* Alma-Ata and Mosfilm Studios; *ph* Edvard Tissé (exteriors), Andrei Moskvin (interiors); *des* Y. Spinel and Leonid Naumov, from sketches by Eisenstein; *mus* Sergei Prokofiev; *cast* Nikolai Cherkasov (Ivan), Ludmilla Tselikovskaya (Anastasia Romanovna), Serafima Birman (Euphrosyne Staritsky), Pavel Kadochnikov (Vladimir Staritsky), Mikhail Nazvanov (Prince Andrei Kurbsky), Andrei Abrikosov (Boyar Fyodor Kolychev, later Philip, Metropolitan of Moscow), Alexander Mgebrov (Pimen, Archbishop of Novgorod), Vsevolod Pudovkin (Nikola).

After the resounding success of ALEXANDER NEVSKY (1938), EISENSTEIN was trusted to make another splendid historical drama from the story of the sixteenth-century Tsar Ivan IV who created a unified Russia from a fragmentary collection of feudal holdings. Part 1 deals with Ivan's struggle to establish himself as Tsar, aided by his love for the Tsaritsa Anastasia: it ends with her death by poisoning, turning Ivan's energies solely to his political aims. The ruthlessness of his measures against the boyars and his conflicts with the Church are the subject of Part 2: 'Boyarskii zagovor' (The Boyars' Plot).

Eisenstein's stylized treatment of history conflicts with his attempts to endow Ivan's character with psychological complexity. It was this increasing departure from the conventional view of the national hero (*groznyi* is more properly translated as formidable or respected) that turned Stalin against Part 2 of the film after his approval of Part 1. As a result, Part 2, although completed shortly before Eisenstein's death, was withheld until ten years later, five years after the death of Stalin.

CHERKASOV's extraordinary performance in the title role is one of the film's most memorable qualities. The strange combination of opulence and rigidity in Eisenstein's conception is disturbingly ambiguous, but results in images of bizarre beauty. A sequence in Part 2 is the only example of Eisenstein's using colour.

**IVAN THE TERRIBLE** see IVAN GROZNYI

**IVENS, JORIS** (1898–     ), Dutch documentary director, studied commerce and economics in Rotterdam; in Germany, 1923–4, he gained experience in the technical aspects of photography which was to be useful when he returned to Holland and entered his father's business, which dealt in photographic equipment.

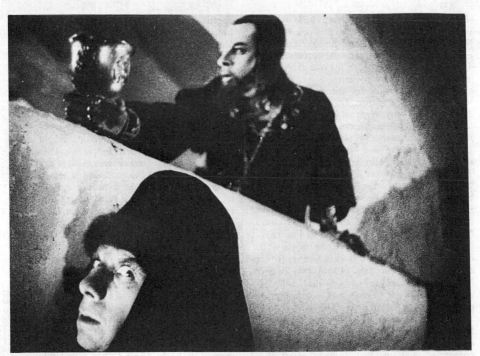

*Ivan groznyi* (S. M. Eisenstein, 1944, 1958)

He began to make films in 1928 and in the same year founded with friends the Filmliga, the first Dutch ciné-club, which was to have incalculable influence on the development of independent film-making in Holland. His first short films were exercises in patterns of movement, notably *De Brug* (*The Bridge*, 1928) and *Regen* (*Rain*, 1929) which showed the sympathetic and patient observation which was to be one of the hallmarks of his work. In 1930 he was commissioned by the Dutch Building Workers Trade Union to make an anniversary film, *Wij Bouwen* (*We Are Building*). His first sound film, commissioned by Philips Radio, *Philips-Radio* (or *Industrial Symphony*, 1931), also emphasized the visual and rhythmic qualities of his subject.

Ivens had visited the Soviet Union in 1929–30 at the invitation of PUDOVKIN who had seen *De Brug* and *Regen*. He went back in 1932 to make *Pesn o geroyakh* (*Komsomol* or *Song of Heroes*) which depicted the construction of a blast furnace. On returning to Holland he made NIEUWE GRONDEN (*New Earth*, 1934) which, starting as a celebration of the reclamation of the Zuider Zee, became a bitter denunciation of the inhumane effects of international economics. With Henri STORCK he made MISÈRE AU BORINAGE (1934), a passionate portrayal of the aftermath of a strike by Belgian miners.

Ivens's reputation had by now reached the US,

and he was invited by a group of left-wing intellectuals, Contemporary Historians, to make THE SPANISH EARTH (1937) supporting the Republican cause in the Spanish Civil War. The same group, as History Today, financed his study of contemporary China, *The Four Hundred Million* (1938), which disturbed American audiences with its reserved attitude to the merits of Chiang Kai-shek.

The success of both these films prompted the US government to offer work to Ivens, who made *Power and the Land* (1940). He stayed on in the US, making *Our Russian Front* (1941) and *Action Stations!* (1943), the latter for the NATIONAL FILM BOARD of Canada. He moved to Hollywood, working with Helen VAN DONGEN and Carl FOREMAN on *Know Your Enemy— Japan* (1944, not released) for the CAPRA unit and was writer and adviser on a feature film, *The Story of GI Joe* (William WELLMAN, 1945). In 1944 he was appointed Film Commissioner for the Netherlands East Indies; as the struggle for Indonesian independence emerged, he resigned his post and set up a unit under trade union auspices in Australia to make *Indonesia Calling* (1946), supporting the insurgents against colonialism.

From 1947 to 1955 Ivens directed or supervised a number of films for Polish and East German production companies, including *Lied der Ströme* (*Song of the Rivers*, 1953), a lyrical depiction of the international working class. With the help of CAVALCANTI he co-ordinated the episodes of the internationally-produced *Die Vind Rose* (1957), showing the role of women in various countries and societies.

After a short lyrical documentary based on an idea of Georges SADOUL, *La Seine a rencontré Paris* (1957), Ivens directed two films on China and an Italian television documentary, *L'Italia non è un paese povere* (1960). Two Cuban films, *Carnet de voyage* and *Cuba, pueblo armado* (both 1961), were followed by two films made in 1963 with the Institute of Experimental Film at the University of Chile: . . . *a Valparaiso*, with a commentary by Chris MARKER, described Valparaiso and its port and *Le Petit Chapiteau* showed the reactions of children at a circus. Since then he has made one film in France, *Le Mistral* (1965), which showed the effects of the mistral wind on people's lives, a film on Rotterdam, *Rotterdam-Europoort* (1966), two films on Vietnam, *Le Ciel, le terre* (1965) and *Dix-septième Parallèle* (1968), and contributed an episode to *Loin du Viet-nam* (1967).

Although Ivens's later films have received little distribution in western Europe, he has justly earned a name as a consistently generous, committed, and imaginative documentary film-maker. His memoirs, started in the US during the war, lost during his travels, found in 1965 in a literary agency in London, were brought up to date and published as *The camera and I*, Berlin, DDR, 1969.

**IVORY, JAMES** (1928–   ), US director whose first four feature films were made in India by the company he set up with the producer Ismail Merchant. *Gharbar* (*The Householder*, 1963), about the early problems of marriage, *Shakespeare-Wallah* (1965), telling the adventures of an English touring company in India, *The Guru* (1968), showing an encounter between Western pop culture and Eastern mysticism, and *Bombay Talkie* (1970), a satire on the Hindi film industry, were all written by Ruth Prawar Jhabvala, the British-born novelist; and they reflect the writer's as well as the director's delight in the contradictions of modern Indian life. The charm of Ivory's Indian films derives in large part from the photography of Subrata Mitra, the frequent collaborator of Satyajit RAY. Ray composed the music for *Shakespeare-Wallah*, and his influence as a film-maker is observable throughout Ivory's Indian work. Ivory returned to the US to make *Savages* (1971), an allegory of human civilization strikingly different from his earlier work.

**IWERKS, UB** (1901–71), US animator, met Walt DISNEY in 1919 and worked with him from 1923 on the *Alice in Cartoonland* and *Oswald the Rabbit* series. He animated entirely the first MICKEY MOUSE short, *Plane Crazy* (1927), and was closely involved with the SILLY SYMPHONY series (1929). In 1930, Iwerks founded his own studio to produce *Flip the Frog* and *Willie Whopper* but the two series were only mildly successful and he re-joined Disney in 1940 and formed the company's Special Process Laboratory. Iwerks contributed greatly to the technical aspects of the Disney productions, for which he won two OSCARS, in 1959 and 1965.

# J

**J'ACCUSE!,** France, 1919. 2½hr. *Dir, scr* Abel Gance, from the play *Miracle at Verdun* by Hans Chlumberg; *prod* Pathé; *asst* Blaise Cendrars; *ph* Burel, Bujart, Forster; *cast* Séverin Mars (Jean Diaz), Maryse Dauvray (Edith), Romuald Joube (her husband).

*J'accuse!* opens on a multitude of soldiers coming together to form the letters of the title; it ends with a split screen sequence contrasting a Parade of the Dead with the Victory Parade through the Arc de Triomphe. The film was actually shot during the war and released soon after it ended: no doubt because of GANCE's remarkable cinematic treatment of the inhumanity of war (the real subject beneath the melodramatic love story) it was an immediate worldwide success.

Gance directed a second, less successful, version in 1938. It was again based on Chlumberg's play, but used it to show the efforts of a veteran to avert the horrors of another war.

**JACKSON,** GLENDA (1936– ), British actress with wide experience on the stage, particularly with the Royal Shakespeare Company. She first appeared on film in Peter BROOK's record of *Marat/Sade* (1966); her performance as Gudrun Brangwen in *Women in Love* (Ken RUSSELL, 1969) brought her international recognition as well as an OSCAR for best actress. She has since had a prolific output of films and television work, her sudden rise to stardom being consolidated by her rumbustious portrayal of Elizabeth I in a BBC television series. Her professional and intelligent approach to acting has given her a formidable range, and enabled her to impart dignity even to roles where grotesquerie is required of her, as in Russell's *The Music Lovers* (1970). Her recent films have included *Sunday, Bloody Sunday* (John SCHLESINGER, 1971) and *A Touch of Class* (1972); Elizabeth I's mantle fell on her again in *Mary Queen of Scots* (1972), but *The Triple Echo* (1972) was a better display of her considerable talent.

**JACOBS,** LEWIS (1906– ), US film historian and film-maker, who trained as a painter. In 1930 he founded *Experimental Cinema*, a radical journal committed to the study and promotion of film as a progressive social force; only five issues were published, the last in 1934. He worked with Joseph Schillinger and Mary Ellen Bute on *Synchronization* (1934) and made other experimental films during the thirties. In 1939 he published the book for which he is best known, *The rise of the American film*, which still remains a standard work. He was a scriptwriter in Hollywood 1943–5, and since then has continued as director and writer of independent documentary, educational, and experimental films. He has edited numerous books, including *The emergence of film art* (1968) and *The documentary tradition* (1971). The issues of *Experimental Cinema* were republished in book form in 1969.

**JAKUBOWSKA,** WANDA (1907– ), Polish director, studied history of art at Warsaw University and began film-making in 1929. A year later she was a founder member of START, becoming production manager of its production group. The same year she collaborated on two documentary shorts, *Reportage No. 1* and *Reportage No. 2*. During the thirties she continued in documentary and in 1934 worked with Aleksander FORD on *Probuzeni (Awakening)*. In 1939, in the cadre of the Co-operative of Film Authors of which she was a co-founder, she made a full-length feature, *Nad Niemnen (On the Niemen River)*, with K. Szolowski.

During the hostilities she worked with the Resistance until she was arrested by the Germans in 1942 and deported. What she endured in Auschwitz and Ravensbrück resulted in OSTATNI ETAP (*The Last Stage*, 1948); a penetrating and tragic study of life in a concentration camp with its undercurrents of collaboration and passivity, it won international acclaim. She has continued to make features, which have included the highly praised *Zolnierz zwyciestwa (The Soldier of Victory*, 1953). Her distinguished work has strongly influenced many Polish feature films about the Second World War.

**JAMES BOND,** fictional British Secret Service agent, hero of a succession of novels by Ian Fleming (1908–64). The film adaptations, fairly loosely based on the novels but retaining the original titles, have no pretensions to anything but fast-paced, extravagant entertainment. They suited the public taste for glamorized violence in the sixties and provided the context for some exhilarating film-making. The Bond films produced by Harry Saltzman and Albert R. Broccoli are: *Dr No* (Terence YOUNG, 1962), *From Russia with Love* (Young, 1963), *Goldfinger* (Guy Hamilton, 1964), *Thunderball* (Young, 1965), *You Only Live Twice* (Lewis Gilbert, 1967), *Diamonds Are Forever* (Hamilton, 1971), all with Sean CONNERY playing Bond; *On Her Majesty's Secret Service* (Peter Hunt, 1969), with George Lazenby in the lead; *Live and Let Die* (Hamilton, 1973), starring Roger Moore. *Casino Royale* (1967), produced by Famous Artists, boasted five directors led by John HUSTON and no less than six James Bonds including Peter SELLERS. It was in fact a parody of the Bond films, a pointless exercise since these were themselves made from an ironical standpoint.

**JAMES,** JESSE (1847–82), US bank robber, rode with Quantrill's Raiders in his teens, then worked in partnership with his brother Frank (1843–1915). His career ended when he was shot in the back by his friend, Bob Ford, an incident which provided the basis for Samuel FULLER's *I Shot Jesse James* (1948). In other versions of his exploits he has been played by Tyrone POWER (*Jesse James*, 1939), Roy ROGERS (*Days of Jesse James*, 1939; *Jesse James at Bay*, 1941), and Audie Murphy (*Kansas Raiders*, 1950).

**JANCSÓ,** MIKLÓS (1921–    ), Hungarian director, successively studied law, ethnography, and history of art before enrolling at the Academy for Film Art, where he graduated in 1950. After four years of making newsreels he turned to documentaries (several concerned with art), eventually making his first feature in 1958. *A harangok Rómába mentek* (*The Bells Have Gone to Rome*) showed Jancsó's interest in war as a theatre for working out his ideas, but as yet his idiosyncratic style was barely evident. After directing the first part of *Három csillag* (*Three Stars*, 1960) and some more shorts, he made *Oldás és kötés* (*Cantata*, 1963), which indicates the future development of his visual style: the country scenes appear to prefigure his later work, although there are few hints as to the increasingly schematic style he was to form, starting with *Így jöttem* (*My Way Home*, 1964) and consolidated in SZEGÉNYLEGÉNYEK (*The Round-Up*, 1965), which caused a sensation at CANNES in 1966 and laid the foundations of his now international reputation.

Jancsó's cinema is as immediately recognizable as a composer's music—an artistic affinity he shares through his use of long compositional paragraphs, recurrent motifs, and rhythmic character movement. His use of the camera is an end in itself, tracking, encircling, and observing his players in the conscious role of a dispassionate third party. Dialogue and characterization are replaced by officialese, songs, and a view of man as a pack-member, pursued when alone, steadfast when in groups. Jancsó's view of war and man is essentially pessimistic, although his films pay abundant tribute to heroism in all its forms: with sudden death a commonplace, the harassed central characters of *Így jöttem* and *Csend és kiáltás* (*Silence and Cry*, 1968) are still propelled to continue living. Jancsó's elaborate hymns to the tenacity of the human spirit employ consistent imagery: nudity as a symbol of submission or humiliation (rarely sexual); the use of persecutor and supporter as symphonic subjects (frequently the Reds and the Whites); the bare Hungarian plains as exposed settings for the ritualistic life-and-death games; the mounted horseman as a figure of power and menace.

*Csend és kiáltás* was Jancsó's severest essay in monochrome. In *Fényes szelek* (*The Confrontation*, 1969), ÉGI BÁRÁNY (*Agnus dei*, 1970), and *Még kér a nép* (*Red Psalm*, 1971) he made use of colour and expanded the celebratory aspect of his works with frequent national songs. At the same time his schematism hardened to the extent that no definite central character emerges from the mass of players, and his camera choreography and use of long takes bordered, in the opinion of some, on sterile affectation (twenty-nine takes in *Égi bárány*; only thirteen in *Sirokko*, 1969). His use of key points in the development of Hungarian socialism as skeletal subject-matter—the fall of the Red Republic of Councils in 1919 (*Csend és kiáltás*, *Égi bárány*), Hungarians in the Internationalist Brigades during 1918 (CSILLAGOSOK, KATONÁK, *The Red and the White*, 1967), the Kossuth revolution of 1848 (*Szegénylegények*), the last days of the Second World War (*Így jöttem*)—is, however, a clear indication of his national inspiration, a view supported by two disappointing foreign excursions, *La pacifista* (1971) and *La tecnica e il rito/Il giovane Attila* (1972).

**JANNINGS,** Emil (1886–1950), German actor, born in New York, his parents taking their family back to Germany while he was a child. He played boys' parts in touring companies and became friendly with Werner KRAUSS who arranged for Jannings to study with Max REINHARDT.

Jannings was early in the influx of talent from theatre to films in Germany. He made his first films in 1914 and two years later worked for the first time for LUBITSCH in *Vendetta*. Lubitsch's *Madame Dubarry* (1919, *Passion* in the US) first

Emil Jannings in *Der letzte Mann* (F. W. Murnau, 1924)

brought Jannings (as well as Pola NEGRI) to the attention of the American public, and most of his subsequent films had considerable success in the US.

He specialized in portraying larger-than-life figures from history: Henry VIII in *Anna Boleyn*, *Danton* (both 1920), the Emperor Nero in QUO VADIS? (1925), as well as OTHELLO (1923), in which he played the suffering Moor as a massive wounded animal. He conveyed pathos through characters whose once great strength is impotent or outworn; and this enabled him to sustain the demands of the leading role in DER LETZTE MANN (*The Last Laugh*, 1924). He received further acclaim in his next four films, Paul LENI'S DAS WACHSFIGURENCABINETT (*Waxworks*, 1924); MURNAU's version of *Tartüff* (1925), in the title role; again for Murnau, in *Faust* (1926), as Mephistopheles; and in VARIÉTÉ (E. A. DUPONT, 1925). The last had immense success in the US and Jannings was invited to join PARAMOUNT at a salary reported as being $10,000 a week.

In Hollywood he played many roles based on the successful one in *Der letzte Mann*, ageing and broken men such as the film extra who has been a Russian general in *The Last Command* (STERN-

BERG, 1928). Although he was seen in only a limited range of parts, the power and pathos he readily conveyed made him a popular box-office star in the short period between his arrival in Hollywood and the introduction of sound. His poor command of English then necessitated his return to Germany, where he had one more big success in DER BLAUE ENGEL (*The Blue Angel*, 1930). He stayed in Germany for the rest of his career, but he was unable to adapt his acting style to the needs of sound films and his later work is unmemorable. In 1940 he was appointed head of UFA and in the following year appeared in the title role of OHM KRÜGER, an anti-British film set in the Boer War. Because of his co-operation with the Nazi Ministry of Propaganda he was blacklisted by the Allies, and spent his last years in retirement in Austria.

**JAPAN.** The success of the LUMIÈRE films and the EDISON Vitascope shown in Japan in 1896 and 1897, encouraged Tsunekichi Shibata, employed by a Tokyo store's photographic department, to film short actualities—Tokyo street scenes and sections from KABUKI plays—from 1898. In 1912 some of the earliest companies were formed into Nikkatsu, the first of the parent trusts, having studios in Tokyo which made *gen-dai-geki* (modern-style films), and studios in Kyoto which specialized in JIDAI-GEKI (historical films set mostly in the Togukawa era). These two types of films have always formed the basis of Japanese cinema.

Traditional theatrical influence in the cinema (from Kabuki and NOH) was slight, but the acting style of the modern *shin-geki* theatre was soon adopted by film actors. The *shin-geki* repertoire led to film adaptations from Russian and other European literatures, as, for example, Eizo Tanaka's *Ikiru Shikabane* (*The Living Corpse*, 1917) from Tolstoy, and these became as popular as the samurai and other sword-fight tales. Theatrical traditions that were carried over into the cinema were the *onnagata* (or *oyama*, female imperson-ator), and the *benshi* (speaker). As realism in films increased, it became clear that the *onnagata* was out of place. In 1921, Minoru Minata dir-ected *Rojo no Reikon* (*Souls on the Road*), the first important film to use actresses, and by the following year the popularity of female stars was so great that they took over completely from *onnagata*. The *benshi*, who narrated the stories of films while they were being shown, were far more damaging to the cinema than *onnagata* and more tenacious. Local *benshi* were very popular, and constituted a strong enough group to prevent the showing of films they did not like. Developments in cinematic narrative were clearly a threat to their existence, and for many years film-makers were afraid to try innovations. Despite the efforts of such directors as Tanaka and Kenji MIZOGUCHI to dispense with them, *benshi* remained entrenched until well into the sound period.

After the disastrous Kanto earthquake of 1923, which devastated Tokyo and with it most of Japan's film industry, large numbers of foreign films were imported until production could be re-established. The curious result of the catastrophe was that film-making took a completely new di-rection: the *shomin-geki* (films about the middle classes). Leader of this movement was Minoru Minata, with *Seisaku no Tsuma* (*Seisaku's Wife*, 1924), and he was followed by such directors as Heinosuke GOSHO, Mizoguchi, and Yasujiro OZU, who began to portray everyday life in Japan. Other film-makers were not content simply to observe, and started to criticize what they saw: capitalist and upper-middle-class cor-ruption and increasing right-wing political trends. Many of their films, like Daisuke Ito's *Gero* (*Servant*, 1927), were disguised as period drama, but audiences were quick to see compari-sons with their own society.

Sound films were not such a novelty in Japan as they had been elsewhere, because the audiences were used to hearing the *benshi* or even actors speaking the dialogue from behind the screen. Many production companies were then in financial difficulties, and exhibitors found that *benshi* were less expensive than sound equip-ment. It was not until 1931 that the first success-ful sound film, Gosho's *Madamu to Nyobu* (*The Neighbour's Wife and Mine*), was brought out, and silent films were still made on a compara-tively large scale until the mid-thirties. During the twenties and thirties foreign audiences were for the most part unaware of Japanese films. One director briefly attained international status—Teinosuke KINUGASA, with two strikingly Expressionist films: *Kurutta Ippeiji* (*A Page of Madness*, 1926) and *Jujiro* (*Crossways*, 1928). But Japanese isolationism persisted until the mid-thirties when there were some propaganda-style co-productions with Germany including *Die Liebe der Mitsu, Tochter des Samurai* (*The Love of Mitsu, Daughter of the Samurai*, 1937) direc-ted by Arnold FANCK. With the increasing militarism of Japanese society after Japan over-ran Manchuria in the first phase of the Sino-Japanese War (1931), a certain reaction had set in. There were more films critical of traditional values, such as Mizoguchi's GION NO SHIMAI (*Sisters of the Gion*, 1936); humanist ideas were even carried on into the war, by directors like Tomotaka Tasaka, with *Go-nin no Sekkohei* (*Five Scouts*, 1939), and Kimisaburo YOSH-IMURA, with *Nishizumi Senshacho-den* (*The Story of Tank Commander Nishizumi*, 1940). The authorities soon discouraged the use of per-iod films by 'committed' directors, but tried the same technique themselves with Hiroshi Inagaki's *Edo Saigo no Hi* (*The Last Days of Edo*, 1941). At the same time, they encouraged films like *Boro no Kesshitai* (*Suicide Troops of the Watchtower*, 1942), directed by Tadashi Imai, and *Nichijo no Tatakai* (*The Daily Battle*, 1944), by Yasujiro Shimazu, which showed the 'correct' attitude among troops or on the home front. Other wartime film-makers, such as Kajiro Yamamoto with *Kato Hyabusa Sentotai* (*General Kato's Falcon Fighters*, 1944), drew on documentary techniques developed in films like Tomu Uchida's *Tsuchi* (*Earth*, 1939).

Just as directors had sought refuge in the *jidai-geki* before and during the war, many were forced to do the same thing under the American Occupation. At the same time, Japan was again flooded with American films that were supposed to show the people a modern, democratic way of life. The Occupation also split up the trusts, in order to leave the small companies 'free' to do as they pleased. Many could not survive without backing from the parent organization, and closed; combined with this, vastly increased taxes and, in the case of the largest company,

Toho, industrial disputes severely curtailed production. The trusts were re-formed after Occupation officially ceased in 1952. Despite these problems, new directors, like Keisuke KIN-OSHITA and Akira KUROSAWA became established. Kinoshita began to make satires like *Karumen Kokyo no Kaeru* (*Carmen Comes Home*, 1951), the first Japanese colour film, and Kurosawa was responsible for the film that drew the attention of Western audiences to Japan, RASHOMON (1950), which won the Grand Prix at VENICE in 1951. Others, such as Kon ICHIKAWA, with BIRUMA NO TATEGOTO (*The Burmese Harp*, 1956), and NOBI (*Fires on the Plain*, 1959), and Masaki KOBAYASHI, with his trilogy *Ningen no Joken* (*The Human Condition*, 1959–61), opened up a new area of socially conscious films, many with pacifist themes, which began to explore individuality in a way never before attempted in Japan.

During the fifties, an increase in the popularity of period films, like Kinugasa's JIGOKUMON (*Gate of Hell*, 1953), and Kurosawa's KUMO-NOSU-JO (*Throne of Blood/Cobweb Castle/The Castle of the Spider's Web*, 1957), coincided with a general expansion of the industry. The complexity of Japanese society is reflected in its films: reverence for traditional values conflicts with the urge to compete with the West on advanced industrial terms, and the use of historical settings (often of the Togukawa period, *c.* 1616–1868) often parallels the questionings and upheavals of the twentieth century. As with all consumer goods, the rate of film production increased rapidly and for a time Japan overtook India as the largest film producer in the world. There were vast home audiences for quickly-made films, repetitive tales of crime and sadistic violence. Inoshiro Honda specialized in 'monster' films, starting with *Godzilla* (1954), which had a considerable following in Japan and abroad. Many of the threatening creatures in these films were radioactive mutations, indicating the pervasive effect of Hiroshima on Japanese consciousness.

This boom ceased in the early sixties, owing largely to the growth of television, and as a result the big companies' grip on production weakened. There was also a sharp increase in the crime rate. The film industry was quick to take advantage of all these things, and in the sixties many small companies were set up to compete with the large studios in making gangster films. Most were simply designed to make money but some directors used the form to carry social or political statements: among the best were Nagisa OSHIMA with *Ai to Kibo no Machi* (*A Town of Love and Hope*, 1959) and Masahiro Shinoda with *Kawaita Hana* (*Pale Flower*, 1964). As interest in gangster films waned a similar process took place with sex films. Originally aimed at the widest commercial market, 'eroductions' also became a means of political protest with such films as Kaneto SHINDO's *Kagero* (*Heat-wave Island*, 1969) and Yoshishige Yoshida's *Eros + Gyakusatsu* (*Eros + Massacre*, 1969).

Although Oshima and other contemporary directors such as Hiroshi TESHIGAHARA and Yasuzo Masumura protest strongly about their society, their work is firmly rooted in an industry that accurately reflects that society, its traditions and its present problems. The pre-eminent importance in Japan of group loyalty, which was instrumental in the growth of the industry with its structure of large parental companies and the pupil–teacher relationship between younger and older generations of film-makers, has begun to diminish. The Japanese in general have begun to value individuality, and the most recent trends indicate that Japanese films are beginning to turn away from traditional attitudes.

Joseph L. Anderson and Donald Richie, *The Japanese film: art and industry*, Rutland, Vermont, Tokyo, 1959; Donald Richie, *The Japanese movie: an illustrated history*, London, Tokyo, 1966; Arne Svensson, *Japan*, London, New York, 1971.

**JARRE,** MAURICE (1924– ), French composer, first became known as musical director of the Théâtre National Populaire, Paris, and as the author of three film scores for FRANJU: HÔTEL DES INVALIDES (1951), LA TÊTE CONTRE LES MURS (1958), and LES YEUX SANS VISAGE (1959). He composed the very effective music for MOURIR A MADRID (1962) and achieved international status with his work on large-scale productions such as LAWRENCE OF ARABIA (1962), DOCTOR ZHIVAGO (1966), and VISCONTI's *La caduta degli dei* (*The Damned*, 1970).

**JAUBERT,** MAURICE (1900–40), French composer, in his brief career wrote the music for some of the most important French films of the thirties. Outstanding among his many sensitive and intelligent scores are those for ZÉRO DE CONDUITE (1933), LE DERNIER MILLIARDAIRE (1934), L'ATALANTE (1934), and *Un Carnet de bal* (1937), the 'Valse Triste' from which made him internationally famous. He also composed remarkable scores for some of Jean PAINLEVÉ's semi-abstract scientific films. He was killed in action early in the war.

**JAZZ.** With the introduction of sound, jazz became an element in many Hollywood films. The actual presentation of jazz or jazz musicians was for some time largely confined to speciality numbers in musicals, typically in *Hollywood Hotel* (1937) with Benny Goodman's quartet and orchestra playing some of their most popular numbers. Duke Ellington's orchestra was featured in *Check and Double Check* (1930), *The Belle of the Nineties* (1934), CABIN IN THE SKY (1943), and a number of other films, Thomas 'Fats' Waller in *King of Burlesque* (1936), Jimmy Lunceford in *Blues in the Night* (1941), and Count Basie in *Top Man* (1943). Howard HAWKS remade his comedy *Ball of Fire* (1941) as *A Song is Born* (1948); Benny Goodman had an acting role as a timid professor and there were musical performances from Louis Armstrong, Lionel Hampton, Tommy Dorsey's band, and Benny Carter.

Louis Armstrong has frequently had speaking parts in films, but his talents as a singer and entertainer have been used more than his trumpet playing. After his first appearance in *Pennies from Heaven* (1936) with Bing CROSBY, he and Crosby played together in a number of films down to HIGH SOCIETY (1956). Armstrong also re-created his famous rendition of the title song for the film version of *Hello Dolly* (1969).

Acknowledgement of jazz as an art led to several films purporting to tell the story of jazz. *Syncopation* (1942) was based on the early chapters of *Jazzmen* by Fredric Ramsey Jr and Charles Edward Smith. Jackie Cooper played a character based on Leon 'Bix' Beiderbecke; Rex Stewart, a trumpeter from Duke Ellington's band had a role based on 'King' Oliver. *New Orleans* (1947) featured Armstrong, singer Billie Holiday, Woody Herman's band, and boogie-woogie pianist Meade Lux Lewis.

Virtually every major swing band appeared in speciality numbers in musicals of the late thirties and early forties. The Glenn Miller Orchestra, in particular, was prominent in films. *Sun Valley Serenade* (1941), ostensibly a Sonja HENIE vehicle, contained several numbers written for the film, some of which, such as 'Chattanooga Choo-Choo', were subsequently among the band's popular successes. *Orchestra Wives* (1942) was partly based on the band's career. James STEWART later played Miller in a sentimental but effective biography, *The Glenn Miller Story* (1953).

Many films have been based on the lives of real jazz musicians: *Young Man with a Horn* (1950) used Dorothy Barker's fictionalized biography of 'Bix' Beiderbecke and Danny KAYE played the trumpeter 'Red' Nichols in *Five Pennies* (1959). The lurid, partly distorted film life of Billie Holiday, *Lady Sings the Blues* (1972), was saved by Diana Ross's portrayal and brought an expansion of interest in the great jazz singer. Fictional stories of jazzmen have occasionally been more successful in conveying the real flavour of their world, notably *Pete Kelly's*

*Blues* (Jack WEBB, 1955) and *Paris Blues* (Martin RITT, 1961).

But the best screen representations of jazz have been in short films devoted to the musicians themselves. Dudley Murphy's *St Louis Blues* (1929) contains an overwhelming performance by Bessie Smith, the only known record of how the great blues singer actually performed. In the same year Duke Ellington's orchestra was featured in *Black and Tan Fantasy*, with numbers they played at the Cotton Club in Harlem. Ellington made a number of short films, including *Bundle of Blues* (1933), *Hot Chocolate* (1941), and *Flamingo* (1942), but his most memorable appearance was in Murphy's *Symphony in Black* (1935) in which Billie Holiday also appeared and which won a short subject OSCAR. *Smash Your Baggage* (1933) demonstrated the spectacular trumpet-playing of Roy Eldridge with Elmer Snowden's orchestra. Perhaps the best film portrait of a jazz musician—tenor saxophonist Lester Young— was in Gjon Mili's *Jammin' the Blues* (1944). *Django Reinhardt* (1958), written by Chris MARKER and directed by Paul Paviot, was a moving posthumous tribute to the great French guitarist. JAZZ ON A SUMMER'S DAY (1960) contained performances by musicians appearing at the Newport Jazz Festival.

The main effect of jazz on films was indirect, firstly through its influence on the screen MUSICAL, later through the use of jazz-derived scores for dramatic films. Ever since 42ND STREET (1933) musical films have been heavily jazz-accented; Fred ASTAIRE and other dancers of the period drew heavily on jazz sources, especially in tap-dancing numbers. Astaire paid homage to the great tap-dancer Bill 'Bojangles' Robinson with the number 'Bojangles of Harlem' in SWING TIME (1936): ironically Robinson's own film appearances were as the traditional deferential black, usually in Shirley TEMPLE vehicles. Effective scores by jazz musicians for dramatic films include: *Paris Blues* and *Anatomy of a Murder* (1959) by Ellington; SHADOWS (1960) by Charlie Mingus; *Sait-on jamais* (*No Sun in Venice*, Roger VADIM, 1957) and *Odds Against Tomorrow* (Robert WISE, 1959) by the Modern Jazz Quartet; *L'Ascenseur pour l'échafaud* (*Lift to the Scaffold*, Louis MALLE, 1957), where Miles Davis and a group of European jazz musicians created a brilliantly improvised musical background while watching a complete screening of the film; NÓŻ W WODZIE (*Knife in the Water*, 1962) by K. T. Komeda; and *Mickey One* (Arthur PENN, 1965) by Eddie Sauter with tenor saxophone solos by Stan Getz. Scores derived from jazz material have largely replaced the concert music styles of the thirties for contemporary dramatic subjects: notable examples are Alex North's score for A STREET-CAR NAMED DESIRE (1951), Elmer BERNSTEIN's for THE MAN WITH THE GOLDEN ARM (1955), Johnny Mandel's for *The Sandpiper* (1965), André PREVIN's for *Harper* (1966, *The Moving Target* in GB), and John Barry's scores for the JAMES BOND films. In Malle's LE SOUFFLE AU COEUR (*Dearest Love*, 1971), the music of Charlie Parker and Sidney Bechet is used to underline the period and content of the film.

BFI pamphlet, *Jazz in the movies* by David Meeker; Marshall and Jean Stearns: *Jazz dance: the story of American vernacular dance* (New York, 1968).

*JAZZ ON A SUMMER'S DAY*, US, 1960. De Luxe Color; $1\frac{1}{2}$hr. *Dir, prod* Bert Stern; *scr, cont* Albert D'Anniable; *ph* Stern, Courtney Hafela, Ray Phelan.

During four days of the 1958 Newport Jazz Festival, the camera moves from performers to audiences to crowds in the streets, cutting in episodes from the America's Cup yacht trials. There are notable performances from, among many others, the Jimmy Giuffre Trio, the Chico Hamilton Quintet, Anita O'Day, and a nostalgic appearance by Louis Armstrong with Jack Teagarden.

Stern, previously known as a still colour photographer, made of this film a polished and euphoric entertainment with both visual and sound elements attaining a high degree of vigour and immediacy.

*JAZZ SINGER, The*, US, 1927. $1\frac{1}{2}$hr. *Dir* Alan Crosland; *prod* Warner Bros; *scr* Al Cohn; *ph* Hal Mohr; *ed* Harold McCord; *sound* George R. Groves; *cast* Al Jolson (Jakie Rabinowitz/Jack Robin), May McAvoy (Mary Dale), Warner Oland (Cantor Rabinowitz), Eugenie Besserer (Sara Rabinowitz).

Al JOLSON played a Cantor's son in a story of pronounced Jewish sentiment and pathos involving parental disapproval and the conflict between religious tradition and the central character's career as a jazz singer. In normal circumstances the film would undoubtedly have made little impression; with Jolson singing and above all speaking two lines of dialogue, it emerged as the first part-talkie and revolutionized film history (see SOUND). It also stabilized the financially insecure WARNER BROS whose gamble on the talking picture and the VITAPHONE process paid off handsomely, placing the company among the great Hollywood production concerns.

The film was first shown at the Warner Theater in New York on 6 October 1927; although its British première did not take place until almost a year later (27 September 1928, Piccadilly Theatre), it remained the first feature film with synchronous sound to be shown publicly in Britain.

**JENNINGS,** HUMPHREY (1907–50), British documentary film-maker, studied at Cambridge where he showed great academic ability and a flair for poetry and painting. He joined the GPO Film Unit (see CROWN FILM UNIT) in 1934 as a designer and directed one film *Post Haste* (1934), possibly the first film to be composed entirely of prints and drawings. He left the Unit to make a puppet film with Len LYE and to follow up his work with Mass Observation which made close records of the day-to-day activities of ordinary people. This interest was reflected in his first film after rejoining the Unit in 1938. *Spare Time* (1939), a fifteen-minute documentary with a commentary by the poet Laurie Lee, was judged by some of Jennings's colleagues as satirical and in bad taste: in an objective study of the industrial landscape of Britain and the quality of the lives passed against it, he made no attempt to idealize the working class or to take a didactic stance.

*The First Days* (1939) and *London Can Take It* (1940), both co-directed by Harry WATT, inaugurated Jennings's most fertile period. His wartime work is at its best in these and similar observations of the Home Front, with the prosaic courage of the civilian population illustrating his deeply-held belief in the basic unity of the British spirit. After Watt moved into feature films Jennings was the leading British director of 'public information' films, many aimed specifically at American audiences: *London Can Take It* was planned around a dispatch by Quentin Reynolds, and Ed Murrow provided the commentary for *The Eighty Days* (1944) about the V2 offensive.

Jennings worked best in an allusive, non-narrative style with commentary kept to a minimum or totally eliminated. *Words for Battle* (1941) uses well-known passages of poetry and prose to enrich the imagery of wartime Britain; in LISTEN TO BRITAIN (1942) the sound-track consists of a montage of natural and created sound. His only full-length film FIRES WERE STARTED (1943) does, however, successfully employ a narrative structure. Subsequent attempts at narrative were less successful and for his last two war films Jennings returned to the associative documentary form of his earlier work. *The Eighty Days* is almost spare. In contrast, *A Diary for Timothy* (1945) uses the complex style of *Listen to Britain*, but the film's visual fluidity is uneasily matched with a somewhat over-written commentary by the novelist E. M. Forster.

The ending of the war deprived Jennings of the stimulus which had inspired his best work. Instead of celebrating and recording a national mood, in *The Cumberland Story* (1947) and *Dim Little Island* (1949) he appears to be attempting to impose unity on a society no longer interested. *Family Portrait* (1950) had a commentary by Jennings himself: it contains some fine writing but is not supported by visual material of comparable quality. Shortly before it was released, Jennings went to Greece to shoot a film for a series entitled *The Changing Face of Europe* and, while researching material, was killed by a fall from a cliff.

**JESSUA,** ALAIN (1932– ), French director, after working as assistant to OPHULS, BECKER, and CARNÉ, made a prize-winning short *Léon la lune* in 1956. In 1964 he made *La Vie à l'envers* (*Life Upside Down*), which he wrote and produced as well as directing. The story of a young man who gradually rejects the unsatisfying outer reality of his life for an inner world of fantasy, the film has a wry humour, sensitively and intelligently handling the theme of alienation.

In Jessua's second feature, *Jeu de massacre* (*Comic Strip Hero*, 1967), the juxtaposition of fantasy and reality is also the theme; a rich young man meets the creators of his favourite strip cartoon, and begins to live out the fantasies they create for him, in a film where colour and trick photography are exploited to rich effect.

**JESTER'S TALE, The,** see BLÁZNOVA KRONIKA

**JE T'AIME, JE T'AIME,** France, 1968. Eastman Color; 1½hr. *Dir* Alain Resnais; *prod* Parc Film/Fox Europa; *scr* Jacques Sternberg; *ph* Jean Boffety; *des* Jacques Dugied and Pace; *mus* Krzysztof Penderecki; *cast* Claude Rich (Claude Ridder), Olga Georges-Picot (Catrine), Anouk Ferjac (Wiana), Van Doude (Rouffers), Dominique Rozan (Haesserts, the doctor).

After a failed suicide attempt, Claude Ridder agrees to undergo an experiment, in which he will be projected back into one precise minute of his past. The time machine goes wrong, and incidents from Ridder's past surge up in disordered fragments. In particular he relives moments of a love affair with a woman called Catrine and the moment of her death. Out of the ambiguous and incomplete fragments offered, the spectator creates for himself a picture of the man's existence.

At once science-fiction and a love story, showing the influence of MARKER'S LA JETÉE (1964), *Je t'aime, je t'aime* relates to RESNAIS's earlier films in its exploration of time and the subjective consciousness; it is the first time that an element of humour figures in Resnais's work, reflecting the influence of the scriptwriter Sternberg, a humorous novelist.

**JETÉE, La,** France, 1964. 30min. *Dir, scr* Chris Marker; *prod* Argos; *ph* Jean Chiabaud; *ed* Jean Ravel; *mus* Trevor Duncan.

Made simultaneously and in contrast with MARKER's long reportage LE JOLI MAI (1963), *La Jetée* is a 'photo-roman' made up of still photographs except for one brief moving shot. It uses the technique of comic strips which Marker, like RESNAIS, holds in high regard. Spoken commentary and music link the frozen images into a kind of poem telling of man's search for an escape through time out of the ruins of a third world war. Less a science fiction story than a meditation on images and their power, on the greatness of man, and on his restrictions and his suffering, the film has great lyrical beauty and the compelling intensity of a dream.

*La Jetée* won the Prix Jean VIGO, 1963.

**JEUX INTERDITS, Les** (*The Secret Game*), France, 1952. 1½hr. *Dir* René Clément; *prod* Silver Films; *scr* Jean Aurenche, Pierre Bost, Clément, from the novel by François Boyer; *ph* Robert Juillard; *cast* Brigitte Fossey (Paulette), Georges Poujouly (Michel), Lucien Hubert (his father), Suzanne Courtal (his mother).

*Les Jeux interdits* is without doubt one of the most striking films ever made on the subject of the effects of war. Paulette's parents have been killed in an air attack on a refugee column (a sequence tellingly realistic in its photography and editing), and she is taken in by a peasant family. With their younger son she plays out gently obsessive fantasies of death and funeral rites using dead animals which he obtains for her. CLÉMENT's direction of the young children is remarkable: five-year-old Brigitte Fossey, in particular, played the part of Paulette with disturbing naturalness.

**JEWISON,** NORMAN (1926– ), Canadian-born director and producer, who has worked extensively in the US and England. After graduating from Toronto University, he went to London to write scripts and act for the BBC. He returned to Canada where he established himself as a talented television director before moving to New York to join CBS in 1958. During the next few years, he was executive producer on eight Judy GARLAND spectaculars, and directed musical programmes with Garland, Harry BELAFONTE, and Danny KAYE. His first film was *Forty Pounds of Trouble* (1963), and he then made two sparkling comedies with Doris DAY before taking over the direction of *The Cincinnati Kid* (1965) from Sam PECKINPAH. His films of the sixties often involved social or political comment, the two most successful being the outstanding *The Russians are Coming, The Russians are Coming* (1966) and IN THE HEAT

OF THE NIGHT (1967). Jewison returned to the musical background of his early television successes, to produce and direct *Fiddler on the Roof* (1971), in which an emotive and dramatic plot was successfully overlaid with musical numbers, without the latter becoming dominant, and *Jesus Christ Superstar* (1973).

**JIDAI-GEKI** (period film), probably the most popular film genre in JAPAN, usually set in the Togukawa era (*c.* 1616–1868), before the opening of Japan to Western influence. A typical example intended for local distribution consists of a traditional tale about samurai, with much realistic and bloodthirsty detail. The *jidai-geki* has also provided the basis for films of high artistic quality, notably KUROSAWA's RASHOMON (1950) and SHICHININ NO SAMURAI (*The Seven Samurai*, 1954), MIZOGUCHI's UGETSU MONOGATARI (1953), and KOBAYASHI's SEPPUKU (*Hara-Kiri*, 1962) and JOI-UCHI (*Rebellion*, 1967).

**JIGGOLO** see CINERAMA

**JIGOKUMON** (*Gate of Hell*), Japan, 1953. Eastman Color; 1½hr. *Dir* Teinosuke Kinugasa; *prod* Daiei; *scr* Kinugasa, from a novel by Kan Kikuchi; *ph* Kohei Sugiyama; *des* Kisaku Itoh; *cast* Kazuo Hasegawa (Moritoh), Machiko Kyo (Kesa), Isao Yamagata (Wataru), Yataro Kurokawa (Shigemori), Kotaro Bando (Rokuroh).

While conforming to the traditional conventions of the JIDAI-GEKI, *Jigokumon* created an impression as the first Japanese film to use a Western colour process: KINUGASA's skill in using EASTMAN COLOR to reproduce the pictorial qualities of traditional Japanese art was remarkable. Machiko KYO gave an impressive portrayal of the ideal Japanese wife, beautifully conveying the reserves of courage and passion behind the appearance of impassive submissiveness, and Kazuo HASEGAWA provided a disturbingly menacing element.

**JOAN OF ARC** is, with the exception of Christ, the religious figure most often portrayed in films. The earliest version was probably the French *Jeanne d'Arc* directed by Georges Hatot for PATHÉ in 1898. This was followed by Georges MÉLIÈS' characteristically ambitious *Jeanne d'Arc* (1900), consisting of twelve tableaux and boasting (according to the Méliès catalogue) a cast of over five hundred.

The story of St Joan was a favourite subject for the makers of the historical dramas in vogue at the beginning of the century in France and Italy. In France Albert Capellani made *Jeanne d'Arc* (1908), again for Pathé; in Italy Mario CASERINI's film for the CINES company in 1909 was followed by Nino Oxilia's *Giovanna D'Arco*

(1913) starring the celebrated diva Maria Jacobini.

In 1916 Cecil B. DEMILLE made *Joan the Woman* starring the opera singer Geraldine Farrar; the framing of the main story by episodes of contemporary trench warfare suggests that one of the film's main objectives was pro-French propaganda.

The late twenties saw two films on the subject made in France: DREYER's monumental LA PASSION DE JEANNE D'ARC (*The Passion of Joan of Arc*, 1928) and *La Merveilleuse Vie de Jeanne d'Arc* (*Saint Joan the Maid*) directed by Marco de Gastyne in 1929. Gustav Ucicky's *Das Mädchen Johanna* (*Joan of Arc*, 1935), made in Germany, shifted attention away from Joan to Charles VII, portrayed here as a cool, far-sighted politician.

Ingrid BERGMAN has twice played St Joan on the screen. In Victor FLEMING's *Joan of Arc* (1948) the warrior in Joan was emphasized at the expense of her spirituality: Bergman's boisterous tomboy contrasts strongly with her more reflective playing of the role in Roberto ROSSELLINI's *Giovanna D'Arco al rogo* (*Joan of Arc at the Stake*, 1954), a filmed record of a performance of Arthur HONEGGER's oratorio *Jeanne au bûcher*.

*Destinées* (*Love, Soldiers and Women*, France, 1954), a three-part film, included an episode *Jeanne*, directed by Jean Delannoy, with Michèle MORGAN as Joan.

Otto PREMINGER took a calculated gamble by casting a total newcomer, Jean SEBERG, as the star in his *Saint Joan* (1957); her obvious sincerity cannot be said to have outweighed her lack of acting experience. The film was far more restrained than Fleming's strident version, and had a literate screenplay by Graham GREENE based on Bernard Shaw's play.

Since Robert BRESSON's austere LE PROCÈS DE JEANNE D'ARC (*The Trial of Joan of Arc*, 1962) there has to date been a further version of the story of St Joan, freely adapted to express radical ideas about art and society: Piero Heliczer's *Joan of Arc* (US, 1967), which numbered among its cast the underground film-makers Jack SMITH and Andy WARHOL.

Some filmographies mention Bebe DANIELS as having played Joan on the screen, a misconception arising from her having attended a fancy-dress party in the guise of Joan of Arc.

A filmography, 'Jeanne d'Arc à l'écran', by V. Pinel, was published in *Études Cinématographiques*, 18–19, 1969.

**JOHNS,** GLYNIS (1923– ), daughter of Mervyn Johns, South African-born actress whose wide eyes and husky voice are engaging characteristics. She made her film début in 1936 with KORDA'S LONDON FILM PRODUCTIONS, graduated to featured roles in such films as EALING's *The Halfway House* (1945) in which she appeared alongside her father, and scored a starring success as the mermaid in the title role of *Miranda* (1948). She maintained popularity in numerous films of the fifties, notably *The Card* (1952) co-starring with Alec GUINNESS. She last appeared on the screen in *Lock Up Your Daughters* (1968), and has recently settled in the US, often appearing on television there.

**JOHNSON,** CELIA (1908–   ), British actress, started her stage career in 1928. Her comparatively infrequent film appearances have been of a distinguished order, particularly those in three films based on works by Noël COWARD: IN WHICH WE SERVE (1942), *This Happy Breed* (1944), and BRIEF ENCOUNTER (1945). More recently she gave a fine character performance as the headmistress in *The Prime of Miss Jean Brodie* (Ronald Neame, 1969).

**JOHNSON,** NUNNALLY (1897–   ), US scriptwriter, producer, and director. A prolific writer throughout his career, Johnson contributed forceful scripts for such films as FORD's THE GRAPES OF WRATH (1940) and *Tobacco Road* (1941), and worked as both writer and producer on numerous films, including Henry KING's THE GUNFIGHTER (1950). He later combined writing with directing to make many films, including *The Man in the Grey Flannel Suit* (1956), about corporation life, and *The Three Faces of Eve* (1957), with Joanne WOODWARD as a woman with a split personality.

**JOHNSON,** VAN (1916–   ), US actor, first noticed with Gene KELLY in the stage musical *Pal Joey*, for a time epitomized one variety of the Hollywood leading man—youthful, good-humoured, uncomplicated. He has made very creditable attempts at more dramatic roles, for instance in *The Caine Mutiny* (1954), *The End of the Affair* (1954), and *Action of the Tiger* (1958).

**JOINVILLE** see FOREIGN VERSIONS

*JOI-UCHI* (*Rebellion*), Japan, 1967. Tohoscope; 2hr. *Dir* Masaki Kobayashi; *prod* Mifune Productions/Toho; *scr* Shinobu Hashimoto, from a novel by Yasuhiko Takeguchi; *ph* Kazuo Yamada; *cast* Toshiro Mifune (Isaburo), Takeshi Kata (Yogoro, his son), Michiko Otsuka (his wife), Yoko Tsukasa (Ichi), Tatsuya Nakadai (Tatewaki Asano).

Yogoro, forced to marry Ichi, the overlord's mistress, is later ordered to give her back when her son becomes heir to the overlord. He refuses, supported by Isaburo, and in the ensuing conflict only the infant daughter of Yogoro and Ichi survives.

As in SEPPUKU (*Hara-Kiri*, 1962), KOBAYASHI questions traditional codes of honour and obedience when they conflict with human feelings. Characteristically, the film has great visual beauty, particularly in the composition of the shots, and a rhythmic control achieved by the alternation of stillness and explosive bursts of action.

*JOLI MAI, Le,* France, 1963. 2¼hr. *Dir* Chris Marker; *prod* Sofracima; *scr* Marker, Catherine Varlin; *ph* Pierre Lhomme; *mus* Michel Legrand; commentary spoken by Yves Montand (French version), Simone Signoret (English version).

In the spring of 1962 the director and cameraman (who are credited on the film as co-authors) shot fifty-five hours of interviews with ordinary people in the streets of Paris speaking about their lives and their feelings about living in France at that time. The interviewer, always invisible, was often MARKER himself; the use of the commentary that links the interviews is characteristic of his style, perpetually counterpointing word and image. The film is direct, yet at the same time complex and funny. It was attacked by the proponents of CINÉMA-VÉRITÉ as being neither reportage nor art: in fact, as a documented point of view in which one Frenchman holds up a mirror to other Frenchmen and sympathetically helps them to look at themselves, it stands outside the declared aims of *cinéma-vérité*.

In the English version, the song which links the film's two sections was omitted and many interviews were cut, reducing the running time by thirty minutes.

**JOLSON,** AL (1883–1950), US singer, real name in doubt: Joseph Rosenblatt or Asa Yoelson. His success as a stage entertainer was already established when he made film history by appearing in the first publicly-performed sound film, THE JAZZ SINGER (1927). He played in a few undistinguished films in the thirties, then returned to the stage, to make only one more brief appearance on the screen in *Rhapsody in Blue* (1945). Larry Parks played Jolson in two somewhat fictionalized film biographies: *The Jolson Story* (1946) and *Jolson Sings Again* (1949), with the songs dubbed by Jolson himself.

**JONES,** ALLAN (1908–   ), US singer whose voice earned him considerable popularity in the thirties, compensating for a somewhat colourless personality and limited acting ability. His three most famous films were among his earliest: A NIGHT AT THE OPERA (1935) and A DAY AT THE RACES (1937), in which he played straight man to the MARX BROTHERS, and *The Firefly* (1938), with his famous rendering of the 'Donkey Serenade'.

**JONES,** BUCK (1891–1942), US cowboy star, real name Charles Frederick Gebhart. Following his discharge from the Army, he rode in circuses, then worked as an extra at UNIVERSAL. After starring in FOX's *The Last Straw* (1919) he became a great rival to Tom MIX and eventually outshone him. By 1940 his popularity had waned, but in 1941 he began with Tim McCoy and Ray Hatton the 'Rough Riders' series, ended by his death from burns received in a nightclub fire.

**JONES,** JENNIFER (1919–  ), US actress, real name Phyllis Isley, had her first starring role in *The Song of Bernadette* (1943), in which she earned great popularity. Later appearances, under the close guidance of David O. SELZNICK, whom she subsequently married, projected a more sultry image in melodramas such as DUEL IN THE SUN (1946), *Gone to Earth* (1951), and *Ruby Gentry* (1952). Under firm direction, for example in Vincente MINNELLI's *Madame Bovary* (1952) and Henry KING's *Tender is the Night* (1961), she can put up a creditable performance.

**JOUR DE FÊTE,** France, 1947. 1¼hr. *Dir* Jacques Tati; *prod* Cady Films (Fred Orain); *scr* Tati, Henri Marquet; *ph* Jacques Mercanton; *des* René Moulaert; *mus* Jean Yatove; *cast* Jacques Tati (François), Guy Decomble (Roger), Paul Frankeur (Marcel), Santa Relli (showman), Maine Vallée (Jeanette), Roger Rafal (hairdresser), Beauvais (café owner), Delcassan (old gossip).

A travelling fair visits a small French village, and among its entertainments is a documentary film on the high-speed delivery of mail in America. The local postman, encouraged by the villagers, decides to emulate the American system. With destructive ineptitude he and his ancient bicycle become involved in some disastrous adventures as a result. The inspired insanity of TATI's first full-length film re-created the great comic style of the silent era with its emphasis on slapstick and purely visual gags. The film was shot in a new colour process which proved unsatisfactory, but a black-and-white negative had also fortunately been made.

**JOURNAL D'UN CURÉ DE CAMPAGNE** (*Diary of a Country Priest*), France, 1951. 2hr. *Dir* Robert Bresson; *prod* Union Générale Cinématographique; *scr* Bresson, from the novel by Georges Bernanos; *ph* Léonce-Henry Burel; *ed* Paulette Robert; *des* Pierre Charbonnier; *mus* Jean-Jacques Grünenwald; *cast* Claude Laydu (curé of Ambricourt), Nicole Ladmiral (Chantal), Nicole Maurey (Louise), Marie-Monique Arkell (Countess), Jean Riveyre (Count), Armand Guibert (curé of Torcy).

Bernanos' book about the work of a young, dying priest in a small village is not at first sight a likely subject for cinema, being concerned with spiritual struggle. Shortly after 1945 (the book was published in 1936), two adaptations were in fact proposed to Bernanos, who rejected them as falsifying the spirit of his work. Bernanos died in 1948, but his literary executor, after initial misgivings, was finally satisfied by the fidelity of BRESSON's film.

Although the physical setting is no more than the background to the inner drama, Bresson characteristically insisted on scrupulously reproducing the setting of the book. The abstract themes of solitude, illness, and anguish are conveyed by shots of the characters in isolation (there are very few general shots in the film), the monologue of the priest as he reads his diary, and a beautifully calculated use of sounds.

The remarkable achievement of the film is its presentation of an inner or spiritual drama by means of outward appearance and behaviour. Bresson elucidated the themes of Bernanos and developed them round the figure of the young priest. Concentration, both visual and dramatic, on the priest is intense. For his method to succeed, Bresson felt he must be in full control, and therefore chose a non-professional to interpret the demanding central role. Most of the supporting roles were also played by non-professionals (only the doctor, played by Antoine Balpêtré, was a professional actor), and their success in this film led Bresson to intensify his use of non-professionals.

**JOURNAL D'UNE FEMME DE CHAMBRE,** Le (*Diary of a Chambermaid*), France/Italy, 1964. Franscope; 1½hr. *Dir* Luis Buñuel; *prod* Speva/Filmalliance/Filmsonor/Dear; *scr* Buñuel, Jean-Claude Carrière, from the novel by Octave Mirbeau; *ph* Roger Fellous; *cast* Jeanne Moreau (Célestine), Michel Piccoli (M Monteil), Georges Géret (Joseph), Françoise Lugagne (Mme Monteil), Daniel Ivernel (Captain Mauger).

The second film version of Mirbeau's novel (the other was directed by RENOIR in 1945) converts the bourgeois circle in which Célestine becomes involved into a text-book assortment of erotic perversions. Jeanne MOREAU's cool insolence as she manipulates the weaknesses of her employers, the bailiff, and the prosperous neighbour she finally marries, perfectly embodies BUÑUEL's objective contempt for false social values. The shouts of '*vive Chiappe*' at the Fascist demonstration that ends the film immortalize the prefect of police who banned L'ÂGE D'OR in 1930.

*Jules et Jim* (François Truffaut, 1961)

*JOUR SE LÈVE, Le,* France, 1939. 1½hr. *Dir* Marcel Carné; *prod* Vog-sigma; *scr* Jacques Viot, Jacques Prévert; *ph* Curt Courant; *des* Trauner; *mus* Maurice Jaubert; *cast* Jean Gabin (François), Arletty (Clara), Jules Berry (Valentin), Jacqueline Laurent (Françoise).

François, a worker in an iron-foundry, and Valentin, a showman, are rivals in love: Françoise, the flower seller whom François loves, is fascinated by Valentin, while François becomes involved with Valentin's mistress, Clara. In a jealous confrontation between the two men François shoots Valentin. He then barricades himself into his room. During the night, as the police besiege him, François relives the memories of the events leading up to the murder. As dawn breaks and he can no longer hold out against the police he shoots himself.

The story is recounted in a series of flashbacks, dramatically juxtaposed with the central situation of François besieged in his room. It was one of the first films to make use of a consistent form of cinematic 'punctuation', indicating a change in time by the use of a slow DISSOLVE, and a change in place by the use of a WIPE.

The film epitomizes the poetic realism characteristic of the CARNÉ–PRÉVERT films, and is often considered to be their finest work. RKO bought up the rights, destroying all the prints they could obtain, and issued a remake in 1947 (*The Long Night* directed by Anatole LITVAK, with Henry FONDA and Vincent PRICE). (See COPYRIGHT.)

**JOUVET,** LOUIS (1887–1951), French actor of unusual subtlety and accomplishment. In his early career he worked as an actor and director in the theatre, including the Comédie Française, and held a professorship at the Conservatoire. He entered films in 1933 in PAGNOL's *Topaze,* followed by *Knock* (1933) which he co-directed: he also starred in a remake in 1950. With the role of the sly priest in LA KERMESSE HÉROÏQUE (1935) he began a succession of appearances which included several outstanding works of prewar French cinema. They included *Les Basfonds* (Jean RENOIR, 1936), *Un Carnet de bal* (Julien DUVIVIER, 1937), *Drôle de drame* (Marcel CARNÉ, 1937), *La Marseillaise* (Renoir, 1938), *Hôtel du Nord* (Carné, 1938), and *La Fin du jour* (Duvivier, 1938). He spent the war years in neutral countries, resuming his career with *Un Revenant* (CHRISTIAN-JAQUE, 1946); but although his performances were as stylish as ever, his films were not of the same calibre as those he made in the thirties. The best was undoubtedly QUAI DES ORFÈVRES (Henri-Georges CLOUZOT, 1947). His last appearance was in *Une Histoire d'amour* (1951).

*JOYLESS STREET* see FREUDLOSE GASSE, DIE

*JUDEX,* France, 1916. 10 episodes, total running time 4½hr. *Dir* Louis Feuillade; *prod* Gaumont; *scr* Arthur Bernède, Feuillade; *ph* Klausse, A. Glattli; *cast* René Cresté (Judex), Musidora (Diana Monti, Mlle Verdier), Bout de Zan (Réglisse), Edouard Mathé (Roger de Trémeuse), Gaston Michel (Kerjean), Yvonne Dario (Comtesse de Trémeuse).

The Minister of the Interior had complained about the criminal character of FEUILLADE's previous SERIAL, LES VAMPIRES (1915–16), and a different hero, a champion of good causes, was invented for *Judex.* The series was successful enough to prompt Feuillade to direct a sequel serial, *La Nouvelle Mission de Judex* (1917). Since Feuillade's death in 1925 two sound versions of *Judex* have appeared, both of them based on the original script: the first was directed by Maurice Champreux (Feuillade's son-in-law and cameraman) in 1933, and the second by Georges FRANJU in 1963.

*JUD SÜSS* (*Jew Süss*), Germany, 1940. 1½hr. *Dir* Veit Harlan; *ph* Bruno Mundi; *scr* Harlan, Ludwig Metzger, Eberhard Möller; *mus* Wolfgang Zeller; *cast* Werner Krauss (Loew), F. Marian (Süss).

This anti-Semitic propaganda film, which bears little resemblance to the original novel by Lion Feuchtwanger, traces the rise to power of Süss Oppenheimer, the financial adviser and collector of taxes for the Duke of Württemberg. On the death of the Duke there is a revolt against Süss who is tried and hanged. After his execution all Jews leave the country.

Although HARLAN claimed that he was forced to make the film he was tried after the war by the Allies for crimes against humanity; the charges were dropped for lack of conclusive evidence. The choice of *Jud Süss* as a test case was somewhat strange, as DER EWIGE JUDE, made in the same year, was a much more outrageous attack upon the Jews.

*Jud Süss,* which included vicious rape and torture scenes, was shown to the troops, the SS, the police, and often to the Aryan population in Eastern Europe when resettlements for the death camps were imminent.

Sir Cedric HARDWICKE starred in the British version of *Jew Süss* (1935).

*JULES ET JIM,* France, 1961. Franscope; 1¾hr. *Dir* François Truffaut; *prod* Les Films du Carrosse, SEDIF; *scr* Truffaut, Jean Gruault, from the novel by Henri-Pierre Roché; *ph* Raoul Coutard; *ed* Claudine Bouché; *mus* Georges Delerue; *cast* Jeanne Moreau (Catherine), Oskar Werner (Jules), Henri Serre (Jim), Marie Dubois (Thérèse), Vanna Urbino (Gilberte), Boris Bassiak (Albert), Sabine Haudepin (Sabine).

Jules, a German, and Jim, a Frenchman, are close friends in Paris before the First World War. They both fall in love with Catherine, and seek to share her as they share all their other experiences. Jules, however, marries her and takes her back to Germany. When the friends meet again after the war Catherine, now mother of Sabine, changes partners between them and a third man, Albert. Resolution of the shifting relationships can be achieved only through death.

TRUFFAUT reconstructed and tightened the events yet remained remarkably true to the spirit of the novel by Henri-Pierre Roché, dandy turned art-dealer, friend of Apollinaire, Duchamp, and Brancusi, whose first novel, *Jules et Jim* (published 1953) was racy and alive with the flavour of the years of his youth. He was delighted with Truffaut's handling of his work, but sadly did not live to see the film finished. Truffaut still considers *Jules et Jim* his favourite novel, and sought once again, in *Les Deux Anglaises et le continent* (1971), to pay tribute to Roché's work.

His realization of *Jules et Jim* impeccably combines the sense of period with contemporary relevance. He uses a wide range of technical devices with ease and assurance: the ANAMORPHIC lens lends grotesqueness to the actuality shots of the war in which the two friends find themselves enemies, and the camera, admirably directed by Raoul COUTARD, swoops, pans, and lingers to underline the shifting moods of the film and its characters. Conscious homage is paid to Jean RENOIR, who said 'Il y a certains plans de *Jules et Jim*, je mourais de jalousie: c'est pas lui qui aurait dû le faire, c'est moi.' The sense of exhilaration and lyricism, alternating with wistfulness and sadness, are beautifully reinforced by Georges DELERUE's music.

From the three principal actors and from the child, Truffaut drew remarkable performances. Under his sympathetic direction, indeed, Jeanne MOREAU gave one of the most attractive performances of her distinguished career. She also helped to finance the film and, together with the rest of the team of actors and technicians, contributed to the development of scenes. The sense of a happy and creative production permeates the film: the clothes were jointly designed, and, like those of BONNIE AND CLYDE (1967), caused a minor revolution in fashion. The song, 'Le Tourbillon', written for Jeanne Moreau by Boris Bassiak, became a best-seller, and Delerue's incidental music widely popular. When the film was given its première, the audience rose and applauded for a full fifteen minutes. It went on to receive prizes from festivals all over the world and an affectionate acclaim from critics and public which remains undiminished.

**JULIET OF THE SPIRITS** see GIULIETTA DEGLI SPIRITI

**JULIUS CAESAR,** with the exception of some early Italian shorts and latter-day epics such as CLEOPATRA (1962), has appeared in films chiefly through the medium of SHAKESPEARE's play.

Although records exist of ten silent film adaptations, from a version by LUBIN in 1908 to a comic one by Weston (another American production company) in 1915, it was thirty-five years before the subject was again attempted. *Julius Caesar* (US, 1949) was adapted from Shakespeare and directed by David BRADLEY, who also played Brutus, with Harold Tasker as Caesar and Charlton HESTON as Mark Antony. This was a student production, not commercially released.

The 1953 US version, adapted and directed by Joseph L. MANKIEWICZ, was unusually successful in transferring a Shakespeare play to the screen: by refusing to subordinate the text to the spectacular element, Mankiewicz was able to bring out the personal conflicts and motivations which are the core of the drama. There were some fine performances, from John GIELGUD (Cassius), James MASON (Brutus), and Edmond O'BRIEN (Casca) in particular; Marlon BRANDO's aggressive and physical interpretation of Mark Antony proved hard to accept for those with a traditional approach to Shakespeare, but for many it was a definitive performance, intelligent, and at times deeply moving.

The 1970 British *Julius Caesar*, directed by Stuart Burge, with Gielgud as Caesar, Heston again playing Antony, Jason Robards (Brutus), and Richard Johnson (Cassius), provides an interesting comparison with the 1953 version. The conventional use of TECHNICOLOR and WIDE SCREEN, though aiding the action sequences, tended to overshadow the human element.

**JUNGE,** ALFRED (1886–1964), German production designer who after a period with UFA in Germany spent most of his career in Britain, working on such films as DUPONT's *Moulin Rouge* (1928) and *Piccadilly* (1928) and on many of the most famous British pictures of the thirties. In 1942 he began an important phase of his career as production designer for Michael POWELL and Emeric PRESSBURGER, winning an OSCAR for *Black Narcissus* (1947). In 1947 he joined METRO-GOLDWYN-MAYER British Studios, remaining there throughout the fifties and designing films ranging from *Ivanhoe* (1953) to *The Barretts of Wimpole Street* (1957).

**JURADO,** KATY (1927– ), Mexican actress, real name Maria Jurado Garcia. Her Hollywood career has been largely confined to Westerns (where she has played Indian squaws as well as Mexicans), although occasional films such as the Biblical epic *Barabba* (Richard FLEISCHER, 1961) have offered a change of location and nationality. With the opportunity of something more than stereotype she has proved herself a fine actress. Her performance in ONE-EYED JACKS (1960) is outstanding.

**JURGENS,** CURD or CURT (1912– ), German actor, appeared in stage and film operettas from 1935. He spent part of the war in a concentration camp because of a derogatory remark about Goebbels. After the war he starred in many West German and Austrian films, becoming an international celebrity in 1955 on his marriage to the much-publicized Eva Bartok, his third wife, whom he later directed in *Ohne Dich wird es Nacht* (1956). His excellent performance as a Nazi in *Des Teufels General* (*The Devil's General*, 1955) also helped to gain him the role of a Teutonic HEAVY in films made in many countries, and in *The Blue Angel* (1958), the misconceived Hollywood remake of DER BLAUE ENGEL (1930), he played the part created by Emil JANNINGS.

*JUSTE AVANT LA NUIT* (*Just Before Nightfall*), France/Italy, 1971. Eastman Color; $1\frac{3}{4}$hr. *Dir* Claude Chabrol; *prod* Films la Boétie/Columbia (Paris)/Cinegai (Rome); *scr* Chabrol, from the novel *The Thin Line* by Edward Atiyeh; *ph* Jean Rabier; *cast* Stéphane Audran (Hélène), Michel Bouquet (Charles), François Périer (François), Anna Douking (Laura), Marina Ninchi (Gina).

In *La Femme infidèle* (1968), Charles Desvallées murders the lover of his wife, Hélène: in *Juste avant la nuit*, Charles Masson, married to another Hélène, kills his mistress. Other parallels abound: the murders are subordinate to their effect on conventional bourgeois marriage; both couples live at Versailles; both are affectionate but passionless, inexperienced in violent emotions; the leading roles in both films are played by Stéphane AUDRAN and Michel BOUQUET.

CHABROL's reworking of the earlier film's themes is justified by his refinement of both form and content. Uneasy moments of farce and 'quotes' from his admired HITCHCOCK are abandoned in favour of serious exploration of a relationship in crisis; and the divergent values of the Massons is more coldly credible than the strengthening of the Desvallées' attachment. Visually, too, *Juste avant la nuit* demonstrates the increasing accomplishment of both the director and his cameraman Jean RABIER, emphasizing the isolation of Charles's guilt with geometric composition, wintry lighting, and empty distances.

**JUTRA,** CLAUDE (1930– ), Quebec director, graduated in medicine but immediately turned to work in film and television. He worked in Africa, *Le Niger—jeune république* (1961) with Jean ROUCH, and in France, *Anna la bonne* (1959). He acted major roles in his first feature film *A tout prendre* (1963), an interesting experiment in autobiography, and in his best film to date *Mon Oncle Antoine* (1971). His most recent film is *Kamouraska* (1973).

# K

**KABUKI,** the most popular theatrical form in Japan, was established, according to tradition, in 1586 by a temple-dancer named O Kuni. After her death the style went through several changes until, by the middle of the seventeenth century, it achieved something like its modern form, with men playing all the parts. At this time Bunraku (puppet theatre) was at the height of its popularity, and Kabuki began to draw on Bunraku stories as well as on the older NOH theatre to extend its own repertoire.

It was natural because of classical theatrical traditions in general for women's parts in early Japanese films to be played by men—the *onnagata*, or female impersonators—but Kabuki itself has had comparatively little influence on the Japanese cinema as a whole. Its highly stylized and exaggerated acting style is much too 'big' for the close scrutiny of the camera: the kind of acting seen in many period films owes more to the natural behaviour of the samurai, and to Japanese emotionalism generally. The establishment of the modern *shin-geki* (new drama) style of theatre in the early 1900s brought new realism to Japanese acting. This realism, soon transferred to the cinema, could not co-exist with the spectacular elements of music and dance so necessary to Kabuki; one or two film directors have however drawn upon the traditions of Kabuki to outstanding effect. Whereas early Chinese filmmakers shot scenes from theatre and opera for general entertainment, early films of Kabuki—the first being scenes from *Momiji-gari* (*Maple Viewing*), and *Ni-nin Dojo* (*Two People at Dojo Temple*), filmed about 1900 by Tsunekichi Shibata—were regarded more as records of plays and actors, and were frequently used by provincial troupes to advertise their forthcoming performances.

Of the Kabuki plays that have been adapted for the screen, *Kanadehon Chushingura* (*The Syllabary of the Loyal Retainers*) first performed in the Kabuki theatre in 1748, is easily the most popular. Many versions, usually known simply as *Chushingura* (*The Loyal Forty-Seven Ronin*), have been made by such directors as KINUGASA (1932), Inagaki (1934, as *Tenpo Chushingura*, and again in 1962), and Kajiro Yamamoto (1939). MIZOGUCHI adapted another version of the play, *Genroku Chushingura*, in 1942. In

1964, Daisaku Shirakawa directed a full-length cartoon, *Wanwan Chushingura* (*Doggy March*) featuring forty-seven dogs.

KUROSAWA's *Tora no O o Fumu Otokotachi* (*The Men Who Walk on the Tiger's Tail/ Walkers on Tiger's Tail*, 1945) was based on *Kanjincho* (*The Subscription List*), first produced as a Kabuki play in 1810. *Narukami*, originally performed in 1684, was up-dated when filmed by Kimisaburo YOSHIMURA as *Bijo to Kairyu* (*The Beauty and the Dragon*, 1955); the film constantly swings between stage performance and 'reality'. Kon ICHIKAWA's first film was a puppet version of *Musume Dojo-ji* (*The Girl from Dojo Temple*, 1946), which entered the Kabuki repertoire in 1758; his YUKINOJO HENGE (*An Actor's Revenge*, 1963), makes full use of the ambiguities and paradoxes of the *onnagata* role, as well as using the outlines of the Kabuki stage to change the dimensions of the screen shape. KINOSHITA's *Narayama Bushi-ko* (*The Ballad [Song] of the Narayama*, 1958) was based on an allegorical story by Shichiro Fukagawa, and he used the theatricality (and the technical realities) of Kabuki to underline the legendary elements of the story.

In 1955, Satsuo Yamamoto made *Ukigusa Nikki* (*Duckweed Diary/Diary of Umagoro's Travelling Theatre*), in which a provincial Kabuki touring company comes into close contact with a group of striking miners. The miners give the actors a left-wing political education, and teach them a realistic *shin-geki* acting style. The whole film is propaganda for the left-wing theatre, and against the classical traditions in general. In a similar vein, Masahiro Shinoda's *Buraikun* (*The Scandalous Adventures of Buraikun/Outlaws*, 1970), while keeping closely to an original Kabuki play in both story and style, used the theme of nineteenth-century repression as an allegory for the condition of present-day Tokyo and, at the same time, parodied other period films.

EISENSTEIN's early interest in Japanese ideograms was extended by the acting style which he discovered when a Kabuki company visited Mcscow in 1928. The stylized, consecutive stages of emotion, 'cutting' from one idea to the next, helped him in formulating his ideas of MONTAGE. The formal exaggeration of character and emotion in IVAN GROZNYI (*Ivan the Terrible*, 1944, 1958) indicates direct borrowing from the Kabuki tradition.

**KADÁR, JAN** (1918–   ) and **KLOS, ELMAR** (1910–   ), Czech directors who for most of their career worked together in an unusual partnership; they shared responsibility for all facets of directing and did not divide functions. Although not experimental or challenging in their approach, they believed in what they called 'film-discussion', i.e. 'engaged' cinema, and always dealt with their subjects in a topical and thought-provoking way. This, together with their consistently excellent craftsmanship, earned them a respected place in Czech cinema.

Kadár gave up law studies in 1938 to learn film-making in Bratislava. He worked in Nazi labour camps during the war, and returned to the Short Film Studio founded in Bratislava in 1945. In the same year he made one of the first films produced there, a short about repairing the ravages of war in Slovakia. In 1947 he went to Prague, and started as scriptwriter and assistant director at BARRANDOV. In 1950 he directed *Katka* (*Katya* or *Cathy*), a Slovak comedy which for all its earnestness was frowned on by the authorities.

Klos started in cinema through helping his scriptwriter uncle on several films in the late twenties, and by acting small parts. He founded and directed the film studio run during the thirties by the Bata shoe company in Zlín (now Gottwaldov). During the war he was one of the group who secretly prepared plans for the postwar nationalization of cinema, of which he became in 1945 one of the chief administrators.

He met Kadár in 1947 on the production of a film of which Kadár was assistant director. Their first film together was a political thriller, *Únos* (*Kidnap* or *The Hijacking*, 1952), which met some official opposition. Their next film was a musical in colour, *Hudba z Marsu* (*Music from Mars*, 1954); but still the political undertones brought official criticism. *Tam na konečné* (*The House at the Terminus*, 1957), a psychological drama which included an attempted suicide, escaped criticism, but their next film, *Tři přání* (*Three Wishes/The Third Wish*, 1958) earned them a two-year suspension.

In fact they did not make another film for five years, and then in *Smrt si říká Engelchen* (*Death is called Engelchen*, 1963), made perhaps their finest film, an unsentimental, sharply-observed story about Slovak guerrillas during the war. In *Obžlovaný* (*The Accused* or *The Defendant*, 1964) they questioned the nature of responsibility in socialist society, giving conventional cinematic treatment to an unconventional plot based on a fine novel.

Their work was already gaining recognition abroad, and their next film, *Obchod na korze* (*Shop on the High Street* in GB; *Shop on Main Street* in US, 1965), was the first Czech film to win an OSCAR. Their by now considerable experience had been applied to a fine script from a good novel, with an excellent team of actors; and the result was a moving, authoritative account of the nightmare experience of living under Fascist rule in the independent Slovak state. In 1968 they started *Adrift*, a Czech/American co-production with an international cast. Shooting was interrupted by the invasion, and the film was not finished until 1969. Kadár left for the US, where he made *The Angel Levine* (1970), from a story by Bernard Malamud. Klos, for long regarded with VÁVRA as one of the grand old men of Czech cinema, stayed in Czechoslovakia.

**KAEL, PAULINE** (*c.* 1919–   ), US critic who has written regularly for a number of magazines including *Partisan Review* and the *New Yorker*. She was dismissed from the fashion magazine *McCalls* following protests from TWENTIETH CENTURY-FOX at her merciless criticism of THE SOUND OF MUSIC (1965). Noted for her biting wit, which she directs at her fellow critics as much as at the films she is discussing, she writes with great courage and perception about the films she admires. Three collections of her writings and broadcasts have been published—*I Lost It at the Movies* (1965), *Kiss Kiss Bang Bang* (1968), and *Going Steady* (1970)—and she has made some experimental films. In *The Citizen Kane Book: raising Kane* (Boston, 1971) she caused some consternation by attempting to show that MANKIEWICZ's contribution to CITIZEN KANE (1941) was at least as important as WELLES's.

**KAKUSHI TORIDE NO SAN-AKUNIN** (*The Hidden Fortress/Three Bad Men in a Hidden Fortress*), Japan, 1958. Tohoscope; 2¼hr. *Dir* Akira Kurosawa; *prod* Masumi Fujimoto, Kurosawa for Toho; *scr* Shinobu Hashimoto, Ryuzo Kikushima, Hideo Oguni, Kurosawa; *ph* Ichio Yamasaki; *cast* Toshiro Mifune (General Rokurota), Misa Uehara (Princess Yukihime), Takashi Shimura (General Nagakura), Susumu Fujita (General Tadokoro), Minoru Chiaki (Tahei), Kamatari Fujiwara (Matakishi).

One of KUROSAWA's most cheerfully energetic samurai films, involving hidden treasure, an incognito princess, and a pair of comic deserters among its many delights. Toshiro MIFUNE slaughters traitors by the dozen, while maintaining a typical air of suppressed exasperation. The film exemplifies Kurosawa's characteristically dynamic visual style, which is admirably suited to the wide screen, his insouciant attitude to the conventions of Japanese historical drama, and

*Kakushi toride no san-akunin* (Akira Kurosawa, 1958)

his acknowledged debt to Hollywood action films.

**KALATOZOV,** MIKHAIL (1903–73), Russian director, real name Kalatozishvili, learned camera and editing techniques in the Georgian film studio. His first film *Ikh tsarstvo (Their Kingdom*, 1928), a montage of documentary material, was followed by the documentary DJIM CHUANTE (*Salt for Svanetia*, 1930) and *Gvozd v sapoge (A Nail in a Boot*, 1932) which was censored by the Soviet military authorities. Nevertheless, Kalatozov was appointed administrative head of the Georgian studio where he worked with Sergei GERASIMOV on *Nepobedimye (The Unconquerable*, 1942) about Leningrad's struggle against the blockade. He was head of the chief administration of Soviet feature production 1942–6, then becoming Deputy Minister of Cinematography for four years.

He returned to direction with the anti-American *Zagovor obrechennykh (The Conspiracy of the Doomed*, 1950). In LETYAT ZHURAVLI (*The Cranes are Flying*, 1957), his best-known work, which achieved considerable fame in the west, he took advantage of the more relaxed atmosphere to produce a charming and delicate love-story in which his sensitive cameraman's eye is apparent; *Neotpravlennoye pismo (The Unsent Letter*, 1960) proved a disappointing follow-up. His last two films were made abroad, *Soy Cuba (I am Cuba*, 1966, a Cuban co-production) and *Krasnaya palatka (The Red Tent*, 1969, an Italian co-production) with Peter FINCH and Claudia CARDINALE.

**KALEM,** US production and distribution company set up in 1905 by George Kleine, Samuel Long, and Frank Marion, the name being an acronym of their initials. Kalem's most successful period dated from 1906, when Sidney OLCOTT joined the company as director. By 1909 Kalem was important enough to be one of the members of the MOTION PICTURE PATENTS COMPANY.

Olcott directed the first film version of BEN-HUR (1907), which was to establish the validity and continuity of the underlying literary COPYRIGHT in a film adaptation. As importantly, he made location shooting an accepted practice, first in Florida, then in Europe, and, for *From Manger to the Cross* (1912), in the Holy Land. This Biblical subject aroused much controversy, particularly in Britain where it reinforced demands for film censorship, the dramatic representation of Christ being still widely regarded as blasphemous. Olcott's work gave Kalem a high reputation for socially conscious stories set in authentic surroundings, but the company also produced the usual popular melodramas, serials, and series films.

Kalem did not long survive the departure of Olcott in 1913 and the increasing domination of the American film industry by larger companies and consortia: in 1916 it was taken over by VITAGRAPH.

**KAMENKA,** ALEXANDRE (1888–1970), Russian émigré producer, studied acting, directing, and theatre administration while at university in St Petersburg. In 1920, visiting Paris, he met Joseph Ermolieff and together they formed Ermolieff-Cinéma, establishing themselves in the studios at Montreuil with the help of PATHÉ. They were joined by the directors PROTAZANOV, Volkov, Nadejdine, and Tourjansky, and the stars MOZHUKIN, Lissenko, Nathalie Kovako, Nicolas Rimsky, and Nicolas Koline. In 1922 Ermolieff went to Berlin and new ventures, leaving Kamenka in control of the company which he re-named Société des Films Albatros. Although staffed almost completely by Russians, Albatros made no attempt to isolate itself from French film-makers. L'HERBIER, EPSTEIN, FEYDER, and CLAIR all worked for Kamenka with more artistic licence than they could expect to receive from his competitors, for Kamenka did not expect all his films to show a profit, and was prepared to subsidize prestige productions from the income of his commercially successful ventures. As a result of this enlightened policy a number of the best French films of the twenties and thirties bear the Albatros trade-mark, including L'Herbier's *Feu Mathias Pascal* (1925) and Clair's UN CHAPEAU DE PAILLE D'ITALIE (1927). After the Second World War Kamenka formed another company, Société des Bas-Fonds, which later became Films Alkam.

**KAMERADSCHAFT,** Germany, 1931. 1½hr. *Dir* G. W. Pabst; *prod* Nero-Film; *scr* Laszlo Wajda, Karl Otten, Peter Martin Lampel; *ph* Fritz Arno Wagner, Robert Baberske; *des* Ernö Metzner, Karl Vollbrecht; *cast* Alexander Granach (Kasper), Fritz Kampers (Wilderer), Ernst Busch (Kaplan), Elizabeth Wenst (Françoise), Gustav Puttjer (Jean), Daniel Mendaille (Emil).

Based on an actual disaster in 1906 at Courrières, on the Franco-German border, where German miners came to the rescue of their French comrades, the film brings the action up to date in order to point up the unreasonableness of political frontiers. PABST's faith in universal brotherhood and the solidarity of the workers may now seem naïve; but the film, made entirely in the studio, conveys the physical conditions of mining with the utmost realism. *Kameradschaft* is a superb example of technical means well understood and used, both in photography and in the use of sound. The use of both German and

French in the dialogue was an innovation, with great dramatic effect.

**KAMMERSPIELFILM** (chamber film). The term *Kammerspiel*, given currency by Max REIN- HARDT, was applied to a play designed for a small intimate theatre. The principles of the *Kammerspielfilm* were enunciated by the Austrian scriptwriter Carl MAYER; they resulted in a cinematic style quite different from his ex- pressionistic DAS CABINETT DES DR CALIGARI (1919).

The films of the genre are naturalistic, middle- class dramas, characterized by their unity of time, place, and action. The décor is sparse and there is a limited number of characters, who are generally nameless and referred to only by their roles. The films have a concise and intimate psy- chological content which is revealed by the camera as it lingers on actions and expressions. The surroundings are dark, bleak, and dreary and are often used to reflect the characters' sub- conscious. Significance is given to objects so that they seem to take on a life of their own. The most novel aspect of these films is their suppression of narrative titles, which gives great advantage in pace, visual fluidity, and dramatic tension. Con- versely, the main disadvantages of the absence of titles (oversimplified characterization, motiva- tion, and narrative development) are also appar- ent. The key films, all scripted by Mayer, are: *Hintertreppe* (*Backstairs*, 1921); *Scherben* (*Shattered*, 1921); SYLVESTER (1923); DER LETZTE MANN (*The Last Laugh*, 1924). *Nju* (1924) also belongs to the genre but was scripted by its director Paul CZINNER. The STREET FILMS are a development from the *Kammerspielfilm*.

**KANAL,** Poland, 1957. 1½hr. *Dir* Andrzej Wajda; *prod* Kadr Unit, Film Polski; *scr* Jerzy Stefan Stawinski, from his novel *Kloakerne*; *ph* Jerzy Lipman; *ed* Halina Nawrocka; *mus* Jan Krenz; *cast* Teresa Izewska (Daisy), Tadeusz Janczar (Korab), Wienczyslaw Glinski (Zadra), Emil Karewicz (Madry), Wladyslaw Sheybal (composer).

The second film in WAJDA's wartime Resis- tance trilogy, *Kanal* (literally translated 'sewer') is set in the Warsaw rising of 1944. A detach- ment of the nationalist Home Army is forced into the sewers, a setting used less effectively in Aleksander FORD's PIATKA Z ULICY BARSKIEJ (*Five Boys from Barska Street*, 1953). This claus- trophobic environment tightly contains the psy- chological reactions of the victims below ground to the physical pressures of their German per- secutors above. Wajda's technical assurance, demonstrated in the remarkable opening tracking shot, had obviously increased since POKOLENIE (*A Generation*, 1954) but his dramatization

seems weaker, diluted by misjudged sentimen- tality (the romance between Korab and Daisy) and unnecessary gestures towards a wider significance (in the primarily symbolic charac- ter of the composer and his references to Dante's *Inferno*). The film, however, first revealed to western audiences the new potential of Polish cinema.

**KANIN, GARSON** (1912–   ), US writer, dir- ector, and producer, joined Samuel GOLDWYN's production staff, having previously been a jazz musician and a stage actor and director. A year later he went to RKO where he directed *A Man to Remember* (1938), written by Dalton TRUMBO. War service interrupted his film career, but in 1945 he co-directed with Carol REED *The True Glory*, the OSCAR-winning official record of 'Operation Overlord' commissioned by General Eisenhower.

He returned to the stage in 1946 with his play BORN YESTERDAY (filmed in 1951 by George CUKOR and directed by Kanin himself on television in 1956) and with *Years Ago*, written by his wife Ruth GORDON. He resumed his film career writing *A Double Life* (1948) with his wife. Film scripts which typified his fast, wise- cracking style were ADAM'S RIB (1949), *The Marrying Kind* (1952), *Pat and Mike* (1952), *It Should Happen to You* (1954), all directed by Cukor, and *The Girl Can't Help It* (1957), directed by Frank TASHLIN. In 1969 he wrote and directed *Some Kind of Nut* and *Where It's At*.

His book *Tracy and Hepburn* (New York, 1970) is an intimate memoir of Spencer TRACY and Katharine HEPBURN, based on their close friendship with him and his wife.

**KARINA, ANNA** (1942–   ), Danish-born actress, made her film début in *Pingin og Skoenne* (1959), a prize-winning short directed by Ibs Smede. She was working in Paris as a model in fashion photographs when she was noticed by Jean-Luc GODARD who offered her a part in A BOUT DE SOUFFLE (1960). She refused it, but appeared in his LE PETIT SOLDAT (1960). They were married from 1961 to 1967 and she played leading roles in *Une Femme est une femme* (1961), VIVRE SA VIE (1962), *Bande à part* (1964), *Alphaville* (1965), PIERROT-LE-FOU (1965), which perhaps best reveals her consider- able talent, and *Made in USA* (1966). She has also worked with other directors, notably Agnès VARDA and Roger VADIM, and appeared in three films made in Britain: *She'll Have to Go* (1962), *Before Winter Comes* (1969), and *Laughter in the Dark* (1969). She has directed a film, *Vivre ensemble* (1973), in which she also starred.

**KARLOFF,** BORIS (1887–1969), British-born US actor, real name William Henry Pratt. Having refused to follow his English family's traditional profession, the diplomatic service, Karloff was sent to Canada where he achieved his early ambition by joining a stock company as character actor. His early years in theatre and films were precarious, but his success in a 1930 play *The Criminal Code*, for which he devised a gruesome make-up, resulted in his being cast in the film version of the play. This was followed by *Graft* (1931), in which he was noticed by James WHALE who cast him for the part of the monster in FRANKENSTEIN (1931), a part which Bela LUGOSI had refused on the grounds that the heavy make-up would render him unrecognizable. Karloff's horrifying yet sympathetic portrayal of the man-made monster placed him at once in the forefront of UNIVERSAL's team of horror players. Although his name is chiefly associated with this genre he was in fact an actor of much skill and versatility as evidenced by his performances in *Unconquered* (1947), in which he played a Red Indian chief, and *Tap Roots* (George MARSHALL, 1948). His last film appearance was in *Targets* (1967), the first feature directed by Peter BOGDANOVICH.

**KARMEN,** ROMAN (1906– ), Russian cameraman and documentary film-maker worked first as a magazine photographer. After graduating from VGIK as a cameraman he began work in the documentary film studios making newsreels. In this capacity he spent a year in Spain (1936–7) and recorded the resistance in Madrid. He was engaged in similar work in 1938 in China.

In 1939 he returned to Russia and in 1941 went to the front. He filmed the siege of Leningrad and much of this footage he used in his film *Velikaya Otechestvennaya* (*The Great Patriotic War*, 1965). He was also the chief cameraman for *Razgrom nemetskikh voisk pod Moskvoi* (*Defeat of the German Armies near Moscow*, 1942), and many other films have used his material. After the war he directed *Sud narody* (*Judgement of the People*, 1947), about the Nuremburg trials. In 1958 he made *Shiroka strana moya* (*How Broad is Our Country*), for which he developed a method similar to CINERAMA, filming with three linked cameras.

His recent films have included documentaries on India, Cuba, and Spain.

**KARNO,** FRED (1866–1941), director of an English pantomime troupe that spawned such talents as Charlie CHAPLIN and Stan LAUREL. SLAPSTICK comedy was popularized by Fred Karno before being taken up by HOLLYWOOD and Mack SENNETT. The Karno troupe made tours of the US in 1911 and 1913. On the second of these Chaplin was hired by the KEYSTONE Company to make films. Karno himself worked briefly, but unhappily, for Hal ROACH in 1930.

**KAST,** PIERRE (1920– ), French director, worked as a critic on CAHIERS DU CINÉMA for a short period and was assistant director to GRÉMILLON in 1948. They collaborated on a short film, *Les Charmes de l'éxistence* (1950), and Kast went on to make several more shorts including a study of Goya, *Les Désastres de la guerre* (1952). His first feature was *Un Amour de poche* (1957), a delicate fantasy. Most of his subsequent films, including *Le Bel Âge* (1959) and *Les Vacances portuguaises* (1963), are immensely civilized comedies of manners, but the short (26-minute) *La Brûlure de mille soleils* (1966) is a poetic science-fiction fantasy of great beauty and *Drôle de jeu* (1967) is a Resistance drama. He has also made a documentary in Brazil, *Un Drapeau blanc d'Oxala* (1969).

**KAUFMAN,** BORIS (1906– ), Polish-born cameraman. The youngest of the three Kaufman brothers returned to Poland from Russia with his parents in 1919. His brothers Denis (Dziga VERTOV) and Mikhail KAUFMAN stayed to work in the Soviet Union, corresponding with Boris on their theories of documentary cinema. He went to live in France where he met Jean VIGO who greatly admired Vertov; Boris became Vigo's cameraman on A PROPOS DE NICE (1930), ZÉRO DE CONDUITE (1933), and L'ATALANTE (1934). In 1942 he emigrated to America: his distinguished work there includes films directed by Elia KAZAN—ON THE WATERFRONT (1954), BABY DOLL (1956)—and Sidney LUMET—TWELVE ANGRY MEN (1957), *Long Day's Journey into Night* (1962), *The Pawnbroker* (1964), and *The Group* (1966).

**KAUFMAN,** MIKHAIL (1897– ), Russian cameraman, second of the three Kaufman brothers. He joined his elder brother Denis (Dziga VERTOV) as chief cameraman on the KINO-PRAVDA newsreel when he was demobilized from the Russian Army in 1922. Though he made a few documentaries himself—*Moscow* (1924), *Crèche* (1929), and, perhaps the best, *Spring* (1930)—it is as his brother's cameraman, on virtually all his films and newsreels, that he is best known. Many of the tricks and special effects on the famous CHELOVEK S KINOAPPARATOM (*The Man with a Movie Camera*, 1929) are obviously of his devising.

**KAWALEROWICZ,** JERZY (1922– ), Polish director, scriptwriter, and artistic supervisor of the Kadr Unit since 1955, studied art and then cinema, at the Kraków Film Institute (see LÓDŻ), and worked as a scriptwriter and assistant director before his first feature (from his own script), co-directed with K. Sumerski, *Gromada* (*A Rural Community*, 1952). A two-part film from a novel by Newerly set in pre-war capitalist Poland was released under the separate titles of *Celuloza* (*Cellulose* or *A Night of Remembrance*, 1954) and *Pod gwiazda frygijska* (*Under the Phrygian Star*, 1954); in spite of the prevailing ideology, traces of the liberating influence of NEO-REALISM were evident. *Cień* (*The Shadow*, 1956) and *Prawdziwy koniec wielkiej wojny* (*The Real End of the Great War*, 1957) established Kawalerowicz, with other members of his Kadr Unit (WAJDA, MUNK, KONWICKI) as a leader of the post-Gomulka Polish renaissance, although he is least typical of its national (specifically wartime) obsessions, being preoccupied rather with the uneasy balance between realism and fantasy; this psychological insight informs *Pociag* (*Baltic Express*, 1959) and his most successful work MATKA JOANNA OD ANIOŁÓW (*Mother Joan of the Angels*, 1961). This and Kawalerowicz's ornate, epic-scale *Faraon* (*Pharaoh*, 1965) were scripted by Konwicki; together they brought a rare intelligence and restraint to the historical drama. Never readily categorized, Kawalerowicz returned to a more intimate psychological study with *Gra* (*The Game*, 1968). His wife, Lucyna Winnicka, has acted in many of his films.

**KAYE,** DANNY (1913–  ), US comedian, real name David Daniel Kaminsky, enjoyed much popularity during the late forties and early fifties. His first film, *Up in Arms* (1944), established his wildly humorous style and his genius for 'scat'—brilliantly inventive word-play—but his basically gentle approach lacked variety and bite. THE SECRET LIFE OF WALTER MITTY (1947) used Kaye's talents to the full and was very successful in blending fantasy and pathos, but later films, notably *Hans Christian Andersen* (1952), descended into a sentimentality that became less acceptable at a time when public taste was tending towards more astringent forms of humour. Of late he has appeared regularly on television and has devoted much time and energy to the work of UNICEF.

**KAZAN,** ELIA (1909–  ), US stage and film director, actor, writer, and producer, was born Elia Kazanjoglou in Istanbul, Turkey. His family, of Armenian descent, emigrated to the US in 1913. In 1932 he joined Group Theater, run by Lee Strasberg, and rose from stage manager and property man to director, going on to act and direct with other radical theatre groups such as League of Workers' Theater, Theater of Action, and working with Clifford ODETS, Martin RITT, and Nicholas RAY. He was a member of the Communist Party from 1934 to 1936, and his first film, co-directed with Ralph Steiner, was a fund-raising short *Pie in the Sky* (1934), marked by high-spirited comedy and improvisation: Kazan also played a leading role. He again collaborated with Steiner on a short documentary about Tennessee miners, *People of the Cumberlands* (1937); his first film as solo director was *It's Up To You* (1941), on food rationing, made for the US Department of Agriculture. His début as a film actor was in *City for Conquest* (Anatole LITVAK, 1940) and he played another small role in Litvak's *Blues in the Night* (1941).

By the time he directed his first feature film, *A Tree Grows in Brooklyn* (1945) about growing up in a New York slum, Kazan had achieved a considerable reputation as a stage actor and director. His notable Broadway productions included Arthur MILLER's *All My Sons* and Tennessee WILLIAMS's *A Streetcar Named Desire*, both in 1947; in the same year he directed two films, *Boomerang*, dealing with obstruction of the US judicial system by party politics, and *Gentleman's Agreement*, intended as an indictment of anti-Semitism. With the proceeds from the latter Kazan set up the ACTORS' STUDIO in 1948 with Cheryl Crawford and, later, Lee Strasberg. He then took over from John FORD the direction of *Pinky* (1949), a drama about colour prejudice.

With *Panic in the Streets* (1950), an urban sociological thriller, Kazan began to display a more consciously cinematic style, as opposed to his hitherto theatrical approach. The screen version of A STREETCAR NAMED DESIRE (1951) and VIVA ZAPATA! (1952), both starring Marlon BRANDO, exemplify the oppositions in his work, the literary, even theatrical flavour especially noticeable when he worked from a Tennessee Williams source, and a more fluid, dynamic style which never entirely replaced it.

Also in 1952, at the height of the McCarthy era, Kazan testified before the UNAMERICAN ACTIVITIES Committee, naming (sometimes with their authority) his ex-Party comrades. Some critics later interpreted ON THE WATERFRONT (1954) as a defence of his testimony and beliefs.

In EAST OF EDEN (1955) he observed the conflict between an individual and his environment. With BABY DOLL (1956) he returned to a typical Tennessee Williams subject, contorted sexual relations in the Deep South; in contrast, A FACE IN THE CROWD (1957) was a brassy attack on exploitation of the mass media. In *Wild River* (1960) he examined a struggle between old individualism and New Deal social reform. *America, America* (1963, *The Anatolian Smile* in GB) was an adaptation of Kazan's semi-autobiographical novel. His virtual retirement from film-making was interrupted by *The Visitors*

(1972), shot in 16mm, which he directed from a script by his son Chris.

Kazan's films of the fifties made a considerable impact on American cinema. Working in New York, he both avoided many of the pressures of the studio system and became skilled in the use of urban locations. His attempts to present difficult social themes to a wide audience and, more especially, his handling of actors helped to establish new attitudes in Hollywood. The performances of Brando in *A Streetcar Named Desire*, Brando and Rod STEIGER in *On the Waterfront*, and James DEAN in *East of Eden* justify Kazan's readiness to allow actors to develop their roles on camera; but his methods have sometimes resulted in over-indulgence and lack of control.

Kazan's first wife, the playwright Molly Kazan, died in 1963 and he is now married to Barbara LODEN. He has published novels, including: *America, America*, New York, 1961, London, 1963; *The Arrangement*, New York, London, 1967, which he directed as a film in 1969; *The Assassins*, New York, 1972.

**KEATON,** BUSTER (1895–1966), US comic actor and director, real name Joseph Francis Keaton, the son of successful vaudeville performers. He learned the acrobatic comedian's craft from his parents and by the age of seven his skill was such that it was rumoured that he was in fact a midget. The family act broke up in 1917 as a result of Keaton senior's increasing drinking; Buster Keaton turned to films.

Keaton gained a grounding in film-making from 'Fatty' ARBUCKLE whose loyal friend he remained throughout the scandals that ended Arbuckle's career. The technical aspects of studio work immediately fascinated Keaton and he was at once able to adapt his technique to the demands of the camera. In his first film, *The Butcher Boy* (1917), the economy of his humour contrasts conspicuously with the excesses of the other performers. He continued with Arbuckle until 1920 when, with Joseph P. SCHENCK as producer, he set up his own company.

Although Keaton quickly saw there was a market for full-length comedy features, Schenck insisted that he stick to the proved two-reel formula. During the next three years he turned out a number of memorable shorts, including *The Boat* (1921), in which the usually solitary Keaton is a family man whose disastrous attempts to sail a home-made boat are gravely observed by two miniature Busters and a similarly restrained wife. In the short films he explored and evolved the main aspects of his comic appeal: an insistence on avoiding the impossible or ridiculous (any element of fantasy is invariably confined to a dream sequence) and his own emotional restraint which establishes an essential calm among the wildest events. Stoical recognition of the inevitable gives Keaton's greatest performances a melancholy flavour; only in GO WEST (1925) does he slip into pathos. 'The Great Stone Face', as he came to be known, was a misnomer: his facial expressions cover the actor's full range but are refined to minute muscular contractions which convey a powerfully comic effect by their very delicacy in response to often monumental disasters. In many of these early shorts, particularly *The Saphead* (1920), *The Boat*, and *The Electric House* (1922), he used the theme he developed fully later: the ineffective, handsome young man battling against a world of intractable mechanical matter and winning through by a combination of ingenuity, daring, and complete unawareness.

In 1923 Keaton embarked on feature productions; he never returned to shorts. *The Three Ages* (1923) pokes mild fun at GRIFFITH's INTOLERANCE (1916), with three 'romantic' stories taking place in the Stone Age, ancient Rome, and modern times; basically made up of three two-reel comedies, it is not as accomplished structurally as his later films, though full of virtuoso comic action. *Our Hospitality* (1923) marks a leap forward in assurance and polish. Keaton observed meticulous accuracy in the settings and costumes for his historically-based subject. The film, largely made on location in Oregon, is visually very beautiful; it has an intrinsic dramatic logic; and the wildly funny action is set satisfyingly in this thoroughly refined framework. Here his two major props are put to full use: the train, with its repertoire of comic/calamitous situations, and water, in a long sequence involving a river, a waterfall of apparently Niagara-like dimensions, a canoe, and a fragile heroine, who, like all his leading ladies, gallantly co-operates in the physical hazards that form the basis of Keaton's comedy.

Keaton's artistic and popular success continued to grow: SHERLOCK JUNIOR (1924), in which an extended dream sequence shows off his command of trick photography, THE NAVIGATOR (1924), and THE GENERAL (1926) are outstanding among the ten feature films he made and released between 1923 and 1928. These films raised him to the stature of a great humorist, rivalled only by CHAPLIN in his mastery of screen comedy. Keaton's style was unique: in the construction of a comic sequence, the total integrity of his performances, the subtlety and grace of his physical humour, and his almost impersonal characterization, he was inimitable.

During this period he worked with complete independence, his productions being released by METRO-GOLDWYN-MAYER under an amicable and successful agreement. When he decided to surrender his independence and transfer his productions to MGM the limitations of big studio methods crushed the spontaneity of his work: Irving THALBERG even expected him to work to an approved script. In spite of these disagreements and the increasing unhappiness of his private life the two films he made at MGM, *The Cameraman* (1928) and *Spite Marriage* (1929), are fresh and inventive. He was anxious to use sound on *Spite Marriage*, but he was not permitted to experiment with the expensive new process. His career was ultimately undermined by outright conflict with Louis B. MAYER and by his personal problems: at thirty-three he was finished as a film-maker. During the next twenty-five years he made low-budget shorts and intermittent guest appearances including brief and touching sequences in SUNSET BOULEVARD (1950) and LIMELIGHT (1952).

The undistinguished *Buster Keaton Story* (1957), which starred Donald O'CONNOR, helped to restore his finances and at the end of his life his career briefly revived with *The Railrodder* (1965) made for Canadian television, Samuel Beckett's silent *Film* (1965), and Dick LESTER's *A Funny Thing Happened on the Way to the Forum* (1966). These performances bear only the most shadowy resemblance to his great work, but the timeless quality of his silent films has made him and them consistently popular.

**KEELER,** RUBY (1910–   ), Canadian-born actress and dancer, who in a short career danced from Broadway to Hollywood stardom in the Busby BERKELEY musicals—42ND STREET (1933), her first film and the first of her successful collaborations with Dick POWELL, GOLD-DIGGERS OF 1933, *Footlight Parade* (1933), and *Dames* (1934). She was married to Al JOLSON. She retired from films in 1941, but returned to Broadway in 1970 in a revival of *No, No, Nanette* directed by Berkeley.

**KELLY,** GENE (1912–   ), US dancer, actor, and director, scored his most complete successes in three musicals directed by Vincente MINNELLI, *The Pirate* (1948), AN AMERICAN IN PARIS (1951), and *Brigadoon* (1954), and in three directed by Stanley DONEN: ON THE TOWN (1949), SINGIN' IN THE RAIN (1952), and *It's Always Fair Weather* (1955). In all these, Kelly brought a distinctive wit and intelligence to his choreography and to his own performances; but he has at times revealed a vein of pretentiousness as in the dance film which he devised and directed himself: *Invitation to the Dance* (1956). His straight acting parts, which include a leading role in *Inherit the Wind* (Stanley KRAMER, 1960), have not shown him to great advantage, and he has of late concentrated on direction with *Gigot* (1963), *Hello Dolly* (1969), and others.

**KELLY,** GRACE (1928–   ), US actress. Apart from her somewhat insipid performances in HIGH NOON (1952) and HIGH SOCIETY (1956), among others, she scored a certain success under the direction of HITCHCOCK in *Dial M for Murder*, REAR WINDOW (both 1954), and TO CATCH A THIEF (1955). *The Swan* (1956) provided perhaps her ideal role as a modern fairy-tale princess. She retired from films on her marriage to Prince Rainier III of Monaco.

**KEM** see ERMLER

**KENNEDY,** JOSEPH P. (1888–1969), US producer of Irish immigrant stock whose family has taken on an almost legendary quality through his sons John F. and Robert Kennedy, was a cinema owner and film distributor before spending some years producing second features in Hollywood. In the early twenties he managed the series of mergers that led to the formation of the vast RKO Radio Corporation. In 1928 he financed the unfinished QUEEN KELLY, produced by Gloria SWANSON and directed by STROHEIM. Later he abandoned films for a career in banking and diplomacy.

***KERMESSE HÉROÏQUE, La,*** France, 1935. 2hr. *Dir* Jacques Feyder; *prod* Films Sonores Tobis; *scr* Charles Spaak and Jacques Feyder, from a novel by Charles Spaak; *ph* Harry Stradling; *des* Lazare Meerson; *mus* Louis Beydts; *cast* Françoise Rosay (Cornelia), Jean Murat (the Duke), André Alerme (the Mayor), Micheline Cheirel (Siska), Bernard Lancret (Jean Breughel), Louis Jouvet (the chaplain), Delphin (the Fool).

A farce in mock-heroic style, the film is set in a small town in Flanders at the beginning of the seventeenth century. Spanish troops, renowned for their cruelty, are to be billeted in the town. The Mayor, terrified, decides to pretend he has just died. The townsmen follow his example, and try to hide themselves away, leaving their wives to deal with the unwelcome visitors. Naturally the plan does not turn out as expected.

The charm of this light-hearted comedy lies in its brilliant evocation of the world of the Flemish genre painters. The sets and costumes, the skilful disposition of characters, and the general gaiety and robustness of the production pay a constant homage to Brueghel and his contemporaries. The film caused violent offence in Belgium for showing the Flemish people in a less than heroic light, but it has always been very popular elsewhere. A German-language version was made simultaneously, also starring Françoise ROSAY. It was favourably looked on by the Nazi authorities, allowing as it does a sympathetic interpretation of collaboration.

*La Kermesse héroïque* (Jacques Feyder, 1935)

**KERN, JEROME** (1885–1945), US composer who by 1924 was acknowledged as the leading American composer of show music. In 1927 he wrote the score for the classic stage musical *Show Boat* which has been filmed three times— 1929, 1936, 1951. His second film was based on the stage show *Sally* (1929) and included 'Look for the Silver Lining'. *Sunny* (1930) was the first film for which he composed a new song—'I Was Alone'. Other films from his stage shows were *Music in the Air* and *Sweet Adeline* (both 1934). The words for all these were written by Oscar HAMMERSTEIN II, his most frequent lyricist. From 1935 Kern wrote almost exclusively for films: *Roberta* (1935), starring Fred ASTAIRE and Ginger ROGERS, included the songs 'Lovely to Look At', 'I Won't Dance', and 'Smoke Gets in Your Eyes'; SWING TIME (1936), which Kern wrote with Dorothy Fields, won an OSCAR for 'The Way You Look Tonight'. In 1939 Kern and Hammerstein made a brief return to Broadway with *Very Warm for May*; the film *Broadway Rhythm* (1944) was based on it, but used only 'All the Things You Are' from the original score. In 1940 they wrote the poignant song 'The Last Time I Saw Paris' which was used in *Lady Be Good* (1941). With Johnny Mercer, Kern wrote *You Were Never Lovelier* (1942), which included 'Dearly Beloved', and with Ira GERSHWIN *Cover Girl* (1944), with the lilting 'Long Ago and Far Away'. In 1945 he collaborated on his own screen biography, *'Till the Clouds Roll By*, which had the usual glamorized facts but also a wealth of Kern melodies. His last complete film score was *Centennial Summer* (1946). He died while working with Dorothy Fields on a project for *Annie Get Your Gun*, which was finally filmed in 1950.

**KERR, DEBORAH** (1921–    ), British actress, made her film début in Gabriel PASCAL'S MAJOR BARBARA (1941). After regular appearances in British films during the war her notable success in *Black Narcissus* (Michael POWELL, 1947) led to a Hollywood contract and she has since worked mainly in American films. Her lady-like presence and formality of diction constituted her particular appeal to Hollywood producers; FROM HERE TO ETERNITY (1953) was a gallant attempt at a part outside her usual range. Her scope is limited, but in roles which exploit her capacity for moral fervour and restrained passion she can be very moving: *Tea and Sympathy* (Vincente MINNELLI, 1956), *Separate Tables* (Delbert MANN, 1958), *Heaven Knows Mr Allison* (John HUSTON, 1957), and *Bonjour Tristesse* (Otto PREMINGER, 1958) were typical of her successes. In *The Innocents* (Jack CLAYTON, 1961) she was outstanding as the repressed governess battling against mysterious evil forces.

**KERSHNER,** IRVIN (1923–  ), US director, worked on documentaries for the US Information Service and was director and cameraman on the West Coast television series 'Confidential File'. His first feature film, also co-written by him, made for Roger CORMAN's production company, was *Stake-Out on Dope Street* (1958). His close friend Haskell WEXLER was cameraman on this film and their collaboration resulted in the sophisticated experimental treatment of mixed moods and tensions in *The Hoodlum Priest* (1961) and *A Face in the Rain* (1963). In Canada, Kershner directed *The Luck of Ginger Coffey* (1964). *Loving* (1970), a discordant and abrasive film, deals with his favourite topic—the born loser, here a corrupted commercial artist, trying to live in a ruthlessly impersonal world, and *Up the Sandbox* (1973) starred Barbra STREISAND in the fantasy life of a New York housewife.

**KES,** GB, 1970. Technicolor; 2hr. *Dir* Ken Loach; *prod* Tony Garnett for Kestrel Films; *scr* Loach, Garnett, Barry Hines, based on Hines's novel *A Kestrel for a Knave*; *ph* Chris Menges; *cast* David Bradley (Billy Caspar), Lynne Perrie (Mrs Caspar), Colin Welland (Mr Farthing), Freddie Fletcher (Jud).

The story of a boy who temporarily escapes the miserable limits of his home and school life by catching and training a kestrel, made entirely on location in Barnsley, Yorkshire. The only professional actor in the cast was Colin Welland; Billy's mother and brother were played by comedians from the northern club circuit and Billy by a fourteen-year-old schoolboy. To preserve the carefully-observed quality of the novel from which the film was adapted, LOACH worked closely with Barry and Richard Hines, both natives of Barnsley.

*Kes* was shown at the London Film Festival in November 1969. Some months later it was given a very limited release in the North of England and broke all box-office records. A few lines of dialogue were re-recorded and the film received a warm reception throughout the country and abroad. It was screened during the CANNES Semaine de la Critique 1970 and won first prize at Karlovy Vary in the same year.

**KEYSTONE FILM CO,** US production company. Kessel and Baumann, having withdrawn from UNIVERSAL and joined MUTUAL in 1912, wanted to complete the range of Mutual's production with a company for comedy. They agreed with Mack SENNETT, an acquaintance from their book-making days who was then directing comedies at BIOGRAPH, to set up the Keystone Film Company, announced in August 1912 as a separate company whose production would be released through Mutual. Kessel and Baumann put up the money, and Sennett, with a one-third interest, was to run the company in Los Angeles.

Sennett started production in the old BISON studio at Edendale, taking with him from Biograph Mabel NORMAND, Fred Mace, and Ford Sterling. The first Keystone production, *Cohen Collects a Debt* and *The Water Nymph* (September 1912) was an immediate success, and every week until January 1913 a new reel containing two comedies was issued to an appreciative public. Mabel Normand was in all of them; Sennett directed most and, in these early days, found time to act in some. In February 1913 a second unit was set up under Henry (Pathé) Lehrman, who joined Keystone from Biograph. Production was doubled, with one full-reeler a week as well as the split-reelers: by mid-1913 the split-reeler was virtually phased out. (See REEL.)

The essential characteristics of the Keystone style were established from the start: speed, zaniness, and irreverence. With unaccustomed modesty Sennett disclaimed the credit for originating the screen's SLAPSTICK comedy, acknowledging his own debt to French film comedies, particularly those of PATHÉ. Keystone developed slapstick, exploiting the combination of ludicrous characters, costumes, situations, and props with the possibilities offered by camera and editing tricks. Nothing and nobody was sacred: Jews and negroes were zestfully burlesqued along with parsons, widows, landlords, firemen, and, of course, cops. The famous troupe of Keystone Kops emerged gradually from December 1912 on. Sennett named seven originals, with Ford Sterling as their 'chief', but the members changed continuously, with Sennett using apprenticeship in the troupe to test his new comedians' talent. The CUSTARD PIE and the chase also became almost invariable ingredients in the Keystone recipe. Sennett's sharp and shapely editing, learnt from GRIFFITH at Biograph, restored the public's jaded interest in the chase. Pace and timing were an essential part of Keystone's success: speeded-up action as well as reverse motion and other tricks enabled Sennett to exploit to the full the death-defying thrills at crossroads and railway-crossings which were always well planned and executed with flair by the comedians who were also their own STUNT MEN.

During 1913, these staple Keystone products were augmented by a series of comic melodramas, burlesquing stage drama and rival film productions. Mabel Normand and Fatty ARBUCKLE became an immensely popular team in such films as *Mabel's Awful Mistake*: audiences gave an enthusiastic welcome alike to *A Life in the Balance* and to Griffith's *A Miser's Heart*, which it parodied. Keystone's production continued to grow in quantity as in ingenuity. By 1915 there were nine units operating. Sennett retained overall control, but had several regular directors, with Del Lord as his fastest and most trusted. By the end of 1914, too, several of his best actors were directing their own films, especially Mabel Normand, Arbuckle, Sterling, and Charlie CHAPLIN, who, after a sticky start, was rapidly becoming one of Keystone's most popular comedians. The other regulars now included Mack Swain, Hank Mann, Minta Durfee (Fatty Arbuckle's wife), Chester CONKLIN, Slim Summerville, Sid Chaplin, and Eddie Cline. Production continued to be mainly of one- and, increasingly, two-reelers, with still the occasional documentary as there had been from the start. In 1914 Sennett, knowing Griffith's *The Clansman* (later THE BIRTH OF A NATION, 1915) to be in preparation, chanced a six-reeler comedy, TILLIE'S PUNCTURED ROMANCE, with Marie DRESSLER, Chaplin, Mabel Normand, and Mack Swain, and was rewarded with great success.

In 1915 Kessel and Baumann left Mutual to form TRIANGLE with Harry Aitken, and Keystone under Sennett became part of the new company. New recruits included Buster KEATON, Ben TURPIN, Wallace BEERY, Frank CAPRA (at first as gag-man), and, briefly and unsuccessfully, Harold LLOYD. At the end of 1915 Sennett introduced the famous Bathing Beauties who in their daring costumes contributed more to popular appeal than to action. Marie Prevost was among the actresses who launched their careers through the Bathing Beauties. Gloria SWANSON was not actually a member of the troupe as is often stated: she posed for bathing-beauty publicity pictures, but was signed for leading roles and quickly achieved considerable success in them. Production costs were rising rapidly, and Keystone's product was becoming generally more polished and sophisticated, with more emphasis on carefully developed plots.

In 1917 Sennett sold his interest in the company, keeping the (now enlarged) studio but was unable to persuade Kessel and Baumann to part with the trade-mark Keystone. A large number of the contract players stayed with the company, but without Sennett's vital contribution the comedies which were produced were only mediocre, and Keystone shared Triangle's gradual collapse. Several of Keystone's brightest stars, including Keaton and Arbuckle, went with Sennett to PARAMOUNT, where he continued producing brilliantly successful comedies.

Sennett's excellent organizing ability, his inventiveness and geniality, had undoubtedly been the mainspring of Keystone's vitality and success. He contrived to create and maintain an atmosphere in which comic talent could flourish: real life at Keystone, where practical jokes on and off the lot were à regular feature, was scarcely distinguishable from Keystone films. Sennett enjoyed encouraging newcomers to enter into the frenetic atmosphere and develop their own brand of crazy humour. During the five years of Sennett's time at Keystone the company had in some five hundred films raised to its peak the particular brand of fast-moving visual humour with which its name is indissolubly associated, and had launched on their careers the most famous names of the next great decade of American silent comedy. Made at a time before the full Hollywood system had come into being, by methods which encouraged mutual fostering of inspiration among individual artists, the Keystone films represent one of cinema's original creations.

Mack Sennett's (dictated) autobiography, *King of comedy*, New York, 1954, gives a colourful account of Keystone. *Kops and custard*, by Kalton C. Lahue and Terry Brewer, Oakland, 1968, is a sympathetic but more sober account, and gives a full list of Keystone's known production.

**KHEIFITZ** see HEIFITS

**KID, The,** US, 1920. 1½hr. *Dir, scr* Charles Chaplin, assisted by Chuck Riesner; *prod* First National; *ph* Rollie Totheroh; *cast* Charlie Chaplin (the Tramp), Jackie Coogan (the Kid), Edna Purviance (his mother), Carl Miller (the man), Chuck Riesner (the bully), Tom Wilson (the policeman).

CHAPLIN took almost a year to make this rather episodic film, the first feature which he both wrote and directed. Far more serious than any of its predecessors, *The Kid* was at least partly autobiographical, showing life among the poor in the London slums through slightly rose-coloured spectacles, with the Kid as a smaller version of Charlie, the Tramp. Chaplin first saw Jackie COOGAN, aged six at the time of the film, in a variety act in Los Angeles, though he had appeared in an ESSANAY film, *Skinner's Boy*, in 1917. The extraordinary rapport established between the two gave *The Kid* its strength; the film proved the popularity of the new, sentimental Chaplin, making a profit of $1,000,000, a figure which had been passed only by THE BIRTH OF A NATION (1915). Jackie Coogan became a star overnight.

**KID AUTO RACES AT VENICE,** US, 1914. 5 min. *Dir* Henry Lehrman; *prod* Keystone; *ph* Frank D. Williams; *cast* Charlie Chaplin, the

Keystone Kids (Billy Jacobs, Thelma Salter, Gordon Griffith, Charlotte Fitzpatrick).

CHAPLIN's second film was made only a week or so after his first (MAKING A LIVING) but it marks a dramatic and decisive advance. By combining standard items from the KEYSTONE wardrobe—over-size shoes, baggy trousers, shrunken tails and bowler, a cane, and a toothbrush moustache—he found the costume and characterization of the Tramp. This little film was made on location at Venice, a seaside suburb of Los Angeles, and shows a real pedal-car race for children, with the efforts of a mock cameraman and director (played by Frank Williams and Henry Lehrman themselves) to film it being constantly frustrated by Charlie.

**KIEPURA,** JAN (1902–66), Polish-born tenor, active as a recording star in the thirties when he appeared in a number of German, Italian, and French films, making his Hollywood début in 1936 opposite operatic soprano Gladys Swarthout in *Give Us This Night*. After the war he appeared in *Addio Mimi* (1947) in Italy, *La Valse brillante* (1949) in France, and *Das Land des Lächelns* (*The Land of Smiles*, 1952) in Germany.

**KILLERS, The,** US, 1946. 1¾hr. *Dir* Robert Siodmak; *prod* Mark Hellinger for Universal-International; *scr* Anthony Veiller, from a short story by Ernest Hemingway; *cast* Burt Lancaster (Swede), Ava Gardner (Kitty), Edmond O'Brien (Reardon), Albert Dekker (Colfax), Sam Levene (Lubinsky).
The Killers, US, 1964. Pathécolor; 1½hr. *Dir* Donald Siegel; *prod* Donald Siegel for Universal-International; *scr* Gene L. Coon, from a short story by Ernest Hemingway; *cast* Lee Marvin (Charlie), Clu Gulager (Lee), John Cassavetes (Johnny North), Angie Dickinson (Sheila Farr), Ronald Reagan (Browning).

In both versions HEMINGWAY's story of a man's execution by hired killers occupies only the first reel. The rest of the film examines the motives bèhind the victim's acquiescence. Don SIEGEL had worked on the adaptation of the story for the 1946 film and his remake, although initially made for television, is considerably better than the original. His familiarity with the material is apparent in his handling of situation and character. The portrayal of the two professional killers, definitively played by Lee MARVIN and Clu Gulager, is a stylish attempt to penetrate the criminal psyche.

**KIND HEARTS AND CORONETS,** GB, 1949. 1¼hr. *Dir* Robert Hamer; *prod* Michael Balcon; *scr* Hamer, John Dighton; *ph* Douglas Slocombe; *cast* Alec Guinness (the Duke, the Banker, the Parson, the General, the Admiral, Young Ascoyne, Young Henry, Lady Agatha), Dennis Price (Louis), Valerie Hobson (Edith), Joan Greenwood (Sibella), Miles Malleson (the hangman).

Although the basic idea was drawn from a novel by Roy Horniman, the tone of the film was quite different from that of the original. Robert HAMER's very individual comedy made a wide impact at the time of its first appearance, not least because of the striking contrast it made to the already established EALING style of warm-hearted humour and naturalistic social settings. Alec GUINNESS gave a virtuoso performance of eight relations all destined to become the victims of a gentlemanly murderer, impeccably played by Dennis PRICE, but astonishing as was this *tour de force* the success of the film lies mainly in the astringency of its script and the polished direction. The pace, in particular, is impeccable, maintaining a measured development that heightens both the stylish comedy and the sense of period.

**KINEMACOLOR,** the first viable 'natural colour' process used in motion pictures, was announced by Charles URBAN and G. Albert SMITH in 1906, and by 1909 their catalogue contained dozens of short subjects. Their 2½-hour documentary on the 1911 Delhi Durbar was a brilliant success. Kinemacolor was an ADDITIVE process in which alternate frames were photographed at double speed through a rotating red-and-green filter on black-and-white stock and projected in the same way. (See COLOUR.) *The first colour motion pictures* by D. B. Thomas, a Science Museum monograph, London, 1969, gives a detailed history of the process.

**KINEMATOGRAPH RENTERS SOCIETY,** British trade organization established by major distribution companies in 1915. Its twelve articles of intent included mutual protection of trade interests, suppression of piracy or duplication of films, the adoption of legal and equitable forms of contract and other documents used in the trade, and consultation with County Councils, Local Boards, and other public bodies on matters affecting trade. It has continued on these lines, and its membership still comprises all the major distribution companies. The restrictive and protective tendencies of its practices have repeatedly brought the KRS under attack from more progressive elements in the British film industry.

**KINESCOPE,** or 'kine', a contraction of 'kinescope recording', the US term for a TELE-RECORDING. A motion picture camera photographs the television programme as it appears on the face of a television tube, thus producing a film record which can be shown on ordinary projectors. Both the camera and the tube—the kinescope tube—are specially designed to convert the 30-frame-per-second television picture into a 24-frame-per-second film recording. 16mm kinescopes made in this way were widely used in the fifties for delayed re-broadcast of programmes before videotape recording became possible.

During the same period the 'hot kine' was developed to permit closed-circuit television programmes such as boxing matches to be exhibited on cinema screens almost simultaneously. The film was fed continuously from the camera through a rapid processor and dryer and into the cinema projector. The knockout punch would appear on the screen about two minutes after it had occurred.

**KINETOGRAPH,** the first practicable motion picture camera, patented in 1891 by EDISON and his laboratory staff, notable among whom was W. K. L. DICKSON, the chief engineer largely responsible for the Kinetograph's development. The camera was the first to use EASTMAN's celluloid-base flexible film in the dimensions which are still standard: 35mm wide with four sprocket holes on either side of each frame. However, the film moved horizontally rather than vertically. The resulting images were viewed in the Kinetoscope, a peep-show device first shown publicly in 1893, in which a 50-foot loop of film gave continuous viewing. This was the first commercially successful film viewing apparatus, but Edison's insistence that it should be electrically driven made it unwieldy, and it was soon superseded by LUMIÈRE's Cinématographe.

**KINETOSCOPE** see KINETOGRAPH

*KINE WEEKLY,* British trade journal, began life in June 1889 as *The Optical Magic Lantern Journal and Photographic Enlarger.* In May 1904 it became the monthly *Optical Lantern and Kinematograph Journal* and in May 1907 launched into weekly publication as *The Kinematograph and Lantern Weekly.* The first sixteen-page issue consisted of technical articles, renters' advertisements, and news of latest productions. By 1920, under its new name of *The Kinematograph Weekly,* the journal had swollen to over a hundred pages and carried synopses and reviews of new releases for the benefit of exhibitors.

Although the *Kine* took a keen interest in current developments in cinematography, it seemed little aware of the significance of a film called THE JAZZ SINGER (1927) which in 1928 it described rather patronizingly as 'especially good for Jewish areas'. This lapse was however untypical and the *Kine* generally kept well abreast of such technical and economic questions as STEREOSCOPICS, ASPECT RATIOS, and the QUOTA

system. In 1956 it began a regular television column which at first mentioned the cinema's growing rival only in so far as it publicized films but later came to recognize it as an autonomous medium.

The *Kine* ceased publication in September 1971 and was incorporated into *Today's Cinema* (later *Cinema and TV Today*).

**KING,** HENRY (1892–    ). US director, had already spent some years in films as actor and director when he made TOL'ABLE DAVID (1921), an effectively simple drama of rural American life which was hailed by PUDOVKIN as an object lesson in film-making. He also worked in Italy, making *The White Sister* (1924) and *Romola* (1924) with Lillian GISH. A typical, reliable Hollywood craftsman with a long and honourable career, King's tastes have always been censor-proof, often sentimental (*Stella Dallas*, 1925) or moral (*The Song of Bernadette*, 1943). Two of his films that achieved real merit were *Twelve O'Clock High* (1949), an air force story, and THE GUNFIGHTER (1950). His later films included two adaptations from HEMINGWAY, *The Snows of Kilimanjaro* (1953) and *The Sun Also Rises* (1958), and *Tender is the Night* (1961), from Scott FITZGERALD.

*KING KONG,* US, 1933. 1½hr. *Dir, prod* Ernest B. Schoedsack, Merian C. Cooper; *scr* James Creelman, Ruth Rose; *ph* Edward Lindon; *sp eff* Willis O'Brien; *des* Carroll Clark, Al Herman; *mus* Max Steiner; *cast* Fay Wray (Ann Darrow), Robert Armstrong (Carl Denham), Frank Reicher (Englehorn), Bruce Cabot (Driscoll), Sam Hardy (Weston).

Behind a high wall on Skull Island lives King Kong, a gargantuan ape. His sexual instincts aroused by the arrival of Fay WRAY, the ape goes on the rampage, but is captured and taken to New York. He escapes to meet a spectacular death on top of the Empire State Building.

The trick photography, including the early use of BACK PROJECTION to reduce the human scale, is still impressive, especially sequences where Kong wrestles with an assortment of dinosaurs. With DRACULA and FRANKENSTEIN (both 1931) it is an archetypal Hollywood horror film: it has had continued success and influence.

Following in Kong's footsteps have been *Son of Kong* (1933), *Mighty Joe Young* (1949), and *Konga* (1961). Footage from *King Kong* was used in MORGAN...A SUITABLE CASE FOR TREATMENT (1966).

*KINO-GLAZ* (Film Eye). Term invented by Dziga VERTOV to describe both his ideology of film and the group of film-makers who shared it. The group is also sometimes referred to as

*Kinoki*—Film Eyes. *Kino-glaz* was also the title of one of the group's most representative films, made in 1924.

**KINO-PRAVDA** (*Film Truth*), newsreel journal of twenty-three issues directed by VERTOV from 1922 to 1925. Vertov organized units of cameramen throughout Russia to film a record of Soviet life which he edited into a unique genre of mixed DOCUMENTARY, ANIMATION, and reviews. It was popular, providing for its audience a regular chart of the Revolution's social achievements.

*Kino-Pravda*'s experimental methods of shooting and MONTAGE influenced many other documentary directors and were later used by Vertov in full-length films.

**KINOSHITA,** KEISUKE (1912– ), Japanese director, studied at a photographic school before going to work in the technical department of the film company Shochiku in 1933, where he became an assistant cameraman and then assistant director to Yasujiro Shimazu. His first film as a director was *Hana Saku Minato* (*Port of Flowers/The Blossoming Port*, 1943), a light comedy about islanders who reform two confidence men, and establish a shipping company to help the war effort. This, with KUROSAWA's first film, *Sanshiro Sugata* begun in the same year, gave new direction to the Japanese cinema which had lost impetus with the outbreak of war.

Kinoshita never confined himself to any particular kind of film. His satires include *Karumen Junjosu* (*Carmen's Pure Love*, 1944), and *Karumen Kokyo no Kaeru* (*Carmen Comes Home*, 1951), the first Japanese colour film. He has made social-realist films such as *Nippon no Higeki* (*A Japanese Tragedy*, 1953), on the breakdown of the Japanese system of family obligation, and *Nijushi no Hitomi* (*Twenty-Four Eyes*, 1954), which shows the effects of the events of the thirties and forties on the lives of a woman teacher and her pupils. In the same year, Kinoshita made a study of the emotional problems of girls in an upper-class boarding school, *Onna no Suna* (*The Eternal Generation/Garden of Women*).

Another film which shows Kinoshita's preoccupation with the image and status of women in Japanese society was *Narayama Bushi-ko* (*Ballad* [*Song*] *of the Narayama*, 1958). In this he used KABUKI settings to emphasize the legendary qualities of the story.

**KINUGASA,** TEINOSUKE (1896– ), Japanese director, having been a child actor, became a leading *oyama* (female impersonator) at the Nikkatsu studios and in 1922 led a walk-out of *oyama* in protest against the employment of actresses. His earliest films as a director were undistinguished, but in *Kurutta Ippeiji* (*A Page of Madness*, 1926) and *Jujiro* (*Crossways*, 1928) his experiments with Western techniques of fragmentary close-ups and impressionistic cutting achieved expressionistic effects that created a sensation both in Japan and Europe. After three years in Europe, during which he studied for a time with EISENSTEIN, Kinugasa returned to Japan and directed *Reimei Izen* (*Before Dawn*, 1932) which, although a period drama, was in the current Japanese fashion of social commentary, dealing in this case with prostitution.

Since the coming of sound he has confined himself to the JIDAI-GEKI. His first film of this type, *Chushingura* (*The Loyal Forty-seven Ronin*, 1932), is based on a KABUKI play filmed more than any other Japanese source; his fidelity to the traditional arts of Japan has been maintained ever since, not only in his choice of subjects but in the formal visual style of his work. JIGOKUMON (*Gate of Hell*, 1953) particularly exemplifies this approach: while its stylistic formality has its own appeal, its limitations have kept Kinugasa in the second rank when compared with such masters of the *jidai-geki* as KUROSAWA, KOBAYASHI, and MIZOGUCHI.

**KIRSANOFF,** DMITRI (1899–1957), French director of Russian origin, who worked on the fringe of the AVANT-GARDE movement in the twenties. *Ménilmontant* (1925) was one of the most striking of the experimental French films of its time, and remains his most widely-known work. His earlier *L'Ironie du destin* (1922–3) has not apparently survived. Both featured Nadia Sibirskaïa, who also appeared in most of Kirsanoff's films until the mid-thirties. The director's reputation rests essentially on *Ménilmontant* and *Brumes d'automne* (1927), ciné-poems distinguished by remarkable visual sense, beautiful photography, and the acting of Sibirskaïa. After *Rapt* (1933), Kirsanoff lost personal artistic control of his work, and his later, almost entirely commercial films are little known.

**KISS OF DEATH,** US, 1947. 1½hr. *Dir* Henry Hathaway; *prod* Twentieth Century-Fox; *scr* Ben Hecht, Charles Lederer, from a story by Eleazar Lipsky; *ph* Norbert Brodine; *cast* Victor Mature (Nick Bianco), Brian Donlevy (D'Angelo), Coleen Gray (Nettie), Richard Widmark (Tom Udo), Taylor Holmes (Earl Howser).

A convict gains his release from prison by turning state's evidence to help convict a psychopathic killer. When the killer is unexpectedly acquitted, the ex-convict lures the killer into a police trap by setting himself up as a target and so gains his freedom and permanent safety.

The film was photographed clearly and unglamorously in the kind of realistic settings that were a TWENTIETH CENTURY-FOX trade-mark in the late forties—New York's prisons, streets, tenements, and dives. In his best screen role, MATURE made a believable hero out of a stool pigeon and admirably conveyed the emotional conflicts of a hunted man. WIDMARK, in his screen début, portrayed with devastating effect a blood-thirsty, pathological killer, speaking falsetto baby talk with a nervous giggle.

**KLANGFILM,** German production company formed in 1928 by the electrical companies AEG, Siemens, and Polyphone, anxious to protect their interests at a time when they played an important role in the provision of sound equipment. The following year the company went into partnership with TOBIS.

**KLEIN,** WILLIAM (1926–   ), US director, living and working in Paris. He studied painting under Fernand LÉGER, then took up photography, publishing photographic journals of several large cities. He directed his first short film, *Broadway by Light*, in 1960, was artistic consultant on ZAZIE DANS LE MÉTRO (1960), and directed several television documentaries, including one on Cassius Clay (Muhammad Ali). He began feature film direction in 1966 with *Qui êtes-vous, Polly Magoo?* which, set in the world of fashion models, drew on his experiences as a fashion photographer for *Vogue*. He directed an episode of *Loin du Viet-nam* (1967). His *Mr Freedom* (1968) is a highly critical allegory of the international role of the US.

**KLINE,** HERBERT (1909–   ), US producer, director, and scriptwriter, in the early part of his career worked exclusively in political documentary. *Heart of Spain* (with STRAND and HURWITZ, 1937) and *Return to Life* (with CARTIER-BRESSON, 1938), both produced by FRONTIER FILMS, dealt with medical services in Spain. Kline made *Crisis* (1939) about Munich and the plight of Czechoslovakia with Alexander Hackenschmied (later Hammid) himself a Czech, and in *Lights Out in Europe* (1940), documenting the outbreak of war, and *The Forgotten Village* (with John STEINBECK, 1941), about the conflict between superstition and health education in Mexico they continued the partnership. Kline directed the first Israeli feature-length film, *My Father's House* (1947). Subsequent feature films, as director or writer, have abandoned documentary for melodrama, and include *The Kid from Cleveland* (1949), *The Fighter* (1952) and, as writer, *Prince of Pirates* (Sidney Salkow, 1953).

**KLOS,** ELMAR (1910–   ), Czech director, all of whose post-war films have been directed in collaboration with Jan KADÁR.

**KLUGE,** ALEXANDER (1932–   ), German director, practised law before entering the cinema in 1958 as an assistant to Fritz LANG. Since 1960 he has made short films, including *Brutalität in Stein* (1960), about Nazi architecture, *Lehrer (im Wandel)* (1963), and *Feuerlöscher E. A. Winterstein* (1967). In 1962 he was the leading spokesman of a group of young German film-makers who went to the OBERHAUSEN Festival to protest against the low quality of 'Papa's cinema'. His first feature was *Abschied von gestern* (*Yesterday Girl*, 1966), based on a story he wrote himself. Kluge attempts to reproduce reality by continual shifting of the plot into documentary reportage, so that authentic scenes and played scenes merge into a collage, a method which is also used in his best-known feature *Artisten in der Zirkuskuppel: ratlos* (*Artists at the Top of the Big Top—Disoriented*, 1968). His films include *Der grosse Vernau* and *Willy Tobler und der Untergang der sechsten Flotte* (both 1971), and *Gelegenheitsarbeit einer Sklavin* (*Occasional Work of a Female Slave*, 1974). Most of his films star his sister Alexandra.

**KNACK, The,** GB, 1965. 1¼hr. *Dir* Richard Lester; *prod* Woodfall; *scr* Charles Wood, based on the play by Ann Jellicoe; *ph* David Watkin; *cast* Rita Tushingham (Nancy), Ray Brooks (Tolen), Michael Crawford (Colin), Donal Donnelly (Tom).

Tolen has the knack (of successful seduction), Colin earnestly tries to acquire it, Nancy longs to be subjected to it. Richard LESTER's treatment, although lacking the serious implications of the original play, was startling for its time in the exercise of many cinematic tricks: the film's pace and enthusiasm were hailed as a novelty in British cinema.

**KNAVE OF HEARTS** or *Monsieur Ripois*, GB/France, 1954. 1¾hr. *Dir* René Clément; *prod* Paul Graetz/Transcontinental; *scr* Hugh Mills, Clément, dialogue Raymond Queneau, Mills, from *Monsieur Ripois et son Némésis* by Louis Hemon; *ph* Oswald Morris; *cast* Gérard Philipe (André Ripois), Valerie Hobson (Catherine), Joan Greenwood (Norah), Natasha Parry (Patricia).

André Ripois, an amoral Frenchman in London, adroitly woos a succession of ladies, but is rejected by the woman for whom he feels, for the first time, genuine affection. Feigning suicide in order to win her over, he falls from a balcony and breaks a leg.

At the time the film's insouciance was considered shocking: in Britain it received an 'x' CERTIFICATE. There were protests in America that the ending was insufficiently retributive and it was suggested that Ripois should break his back; the Legion of Decency insisted that, in justice, his neck too should be broken (see CENSORSHIP). The film's appeal now rests, not on its impropriety but on the stylish leading performance by Gérard PHILIPE and on CLÉMENT's witty evocation of London life, achieved by shooting on location with a concealed camera.

**KNEF, HILDEGARD** (1925– ), German actress, began her career with UFA in Berlin in 1942. In 1946 she starred in DEFA's DIE MÖRDER SIND UNTER UNS (*The Murderers Are Among Us*) and she had a scandalous success in the title role of *Die Sünderin* (*The Sinner*, 1951). Renamed Neff in the US, she was again impressive in Anatole LITVAK's *Decision Before Dawn* (1951), and in 1952 made six films including a third German version of *Alraune* (1928, 1930) with Erich von STROHEIM, *The Snows of Kilimanjaro* and *Diplomatic Courier* in Hollywood, and *La Fête à Henriette* for DUVIVIER in France. She worked in Britain in *The Man Between* (Carol REED, 1953) and *Svengali* (1954). After a Broadway success in *Silk Stockings*, a musical comedy version of NINOTCHKA (1939), she returned to Germany as the first star of the new UFA, but their first effort, *Madeleine und der Legionär* (1958) was a failure. She has since appeared in CHABROL's *Landru* (1962); as a lesbian Countess in *Lulu* (1962), a remake of DIE BÜCHSE DER PANDORA (1928); as Jenny in the 1962 remake of DIE DREIGROSCHENOPER (1931); and in *The Lost Continent* (1968). She concentrates equally on a flourishing career as writer and singer of cabaret songs and had considerable success with her memoirs, published in English as *The gift horse* (London, 1971).

***KNIFE IN THE WATER*** see NÓŻ W WODZIE

**KNIGHT, ARTHUR** (1916– ), US critic and historian, joined the staff of the Museum of Modern Art, New York in 1935 and was assistant curator of the Film Library 1939–49. During this time he became a professional writer, contributing to such magazines as *New Movies* (later *Films in Review*) and the *Saturday Review* for which he has written a regular film column for over twenty years. In recent years he has divided his time between writing and teaching. He has published numerous books; the best known, *The liveliest art* (New York, 1957), is a history of the cinema.

**KOBAYASHI, MASAKI** (1916– ), Japanese director, entered Shochiku's Ofuna Studios in 1941 but was conscripted the following year, spending some time overseas as a prisoner-of-war. He returned to Shochiku in 1943 and worked as assistant to KINOSHITA, making his first film, *Musuko no Seishun* (*His Son's Youth*) in 1952. He concerned himself from the first with social and political problems, as in *Kabe Atsuki Heya* (*Room with Thick Walls*, 1953) about war criminals. *Kuroi Kawa* (*Black River*, 1957), showing the dark side of life on a military base, made a star of Tatsuya NAKADAI and inaugurated a fruitful partnership. Kobayashi's early films showed a formal debt to Kinoshita, but his trilogy *Ningen no Joken* (*The Human Condition*, 1959–61) established his independent stature. The story of a peaceable young man of left-wing inclinations, traced through his experiences with dictatorial employers, in the army as a conscript, and as a prisoner-of-war, expresses a despairing view of modern humanity.

SEPPUKU (*Hara-Kiri*, 1962), Kobayashi's first CHAMBARA film and his first to be shown in the West, caused a sensation in Japan, where he was hailed as one of the great makers of samurai films and where the partnership of Kobayashi and Nakadai was welcomed as offering the first serious rival to the KUROSAWA–MIFUNE team. He was given what was then the biggest budget ever granted in Japan for KWAIDAN (1964), an anthology of ghost stories. JOI-UCHI (*Rebellion*, 1967) was justly praised for its thoughtful examination of traditional loyalty. Kobayashi returned to the present day with *Kaseki* (1974), tracing the European travels of a Japanese business man who is fatally ill. Kobayashi's films are very beautiful, with controlled composition and a satisfyingly expansive use of the wide screen; sound and music are used with imagination and refinement. They are imbued with a passionate concern for human dignity, especially that of the individual bound by the traditions of a formal social structure.

**KOBAYASHI, SETSUO** (1920– ), Japanese cameraman, went to work for the Nikkatsu company when he graduated in 1941. After serving in the army, 1942–9, he joined the Daiei studios in Tokyo, where his first film, *Ana* (*The Hole*, 1957), was directed by ICHIKAWA. The best of his earlier work—NOBI (*Fires on the Plain*, 1959), an episode of *Jokyo* (*The Woman's Testament*, 1959), and YUKINOJO HENGE (*An Actor's Revenge*, 1963)—was for the same director. After *Yukinojo Henge* Kobayashi did not work for Ichikawa again until 1973, when he was director of photography on *Matatabi* (*The Wanderers*). Kobayashi has worked most with Yasuzo Masumura, including *Manji* (*Passion*, 1964), *Chijin no Ai* (*An Idiot in Love*, 1967), and *Senbazuru* (*Thousand Cranes*, 1969), from the novel by Kawabata, among others.

**KOCH, CARL** (1892–1963), German director, made his first short, *Kind und Welt*, a documentary on educational methods, in 1922. Several further documentaries followed, including *Journey in Egypt* (1926), and *Nippon* (1929). Married to Lotte REINIGER, Koch was himself extremely interested in trick photography, and in 1929 made *Die Jagd nach Gluck* (*The Hunt For Happiness*), which combined silhouette animation and naturalistic photography, and featured Jean RENOIR and Catherine HESSLING as actors. Renoir was a close friend and collaborator, and Koch worked on many of his films, including *Madame Bovary* (1934), LA GRANDE ILLUSION (1937), and LA RÈGLE DU JEU (1939). When Renoir emigrated to the US in 1940, Koch completed *Tosca* (1941). During the war he emigrated to Britain, where he spent the rest of his life; he worked a great deal for television.

**KONGRESS TANZT, Der** (*Congress Dances*), Germany, 1931. 1¾hr. *Dir* Erik Charrell; *prod* Erich Pommer for UFA; *scr* Norbert Falk, Robert Liebmann; *ph* Carl Hoffmann; *des* Walter Röhrig, Robert Herlth; *mus* Werner R. Heymann; *cast* Lilian Harvey (Chrystal), Willy Fritsch (Tsar Alexander and his double), Conrad Veidt (Metternich), Lil Dagover (the Countess), Adele Sandrock (the Princess).

The setting of *Der Kongress tanzt* is the 1814 Congress of Vienna where, according to this frothy musical, the new frontiers of Europe were decided against a background of romance and (anachronistic) Viennese waltzes.

The organizing genius of Erich POMMER brought together a skilled team, notable among them Erik Charrell, a successful director of stage operettas. Charrell made the transfer to the film medium with ease, and the film's witty elegance made it an immediate success. The harmonious flow of music and images set a new and long-lasting style for screen MUSICALS.

English and French versions were shot simultaneously with the original German. The cast remained the same, except that in the exported version Henri Garat replaced Willy Fritsch.

**KONWICKI,** TADEUSZ (1926–   ), Polish scriptwriter and director, initially a film critic. He wrote *Kariéra* (*The Career*, J. Koecher, 1955) and *Zimowy zmierzch* (*Winter Dusk*, S. Lenartowicz, 1957), and was literary director of the renowned Kadr Unit. His first work as co-director with Jan Laskowski, *Ostatni dzień lata* (*The Last Day of Summer*, 1958) is still his most substantial and best-known film. With script, direction, and photography by himself and Laskowski, and a cast of two, it is a personal evocation of the aftermath of war, social insecurity, and personal loss. Its intellectual pessimism found a sympathetic audience in a period of change and uncertainty. With other works such as WAJDA's KANAL (1957), it revealed to the West the creative potential of Polish cinema. Konwicki has since scripted two films by KAWALEROWICZ, MATKA JOANNA OD ANIOŁÓW (*Mother Joan of the Angels*, 1961) and *Faraon* (*Pharaoh*, 1965), and *Jowita* (J. Morgenstern, 1967). His other films as director—*Zaduszki* (*Hallowe'en*, 1961), *Salto* (1965), an episode in the French, West German, and Polish co-production *Augenblick des Friedens* (*A Moment of Peace*, 1965), and his first film in colour *Jak daleko stad, jak blisko* (*How Far It Is and Yet How Near*, 1972)—have failed to achieve the poetic intensity of his first film. Konwicki has also established a considerable reputation as a novelist.

**KONYETS SANKT-PETERBURGA** (*The End of St Petersburg*), USSR, 1927. 2hr. *Dir* V. I. Pudovkin; *prod* Mezhrabpom-Russ; *scr* Nathan Zarkhi; *ph* Anatoli Golovnya; *des* Sergei Kozlovsky; *cast* A. P. Khristiakov (workman), Vera Baranovskaya (his wife), Ivan Chuvelov (peasant boy), V. Obolenski (Lebedev).

*Konyets Sankt-Peterburga* was commissioned, like OKTIABR (*October*, 1928), as part of the tenth anniversary celebrations of the Russian Revolution. PUDOVKIN at first intended to use a two-hundred-year history of St Petersburg as his subject, but this grandiose scheme had to be abandoned in favour of an account of the impact of the events of 1917 on an uneducated peasant boy. The film was made concurrently with *Oktiabr*, using the same sites; it was more successful than EISENSTEIN's, both with the public and officially, for its directness and emotional appeal. The two films provide an interesting comparison of their respective directors' approach.

**KORDA,** ALEXANDER (1893–1956), Hungarian-born producer and director, real name Sándor Kellner. His passion for the cinema began early, and by 1912 he was co-editor of a weekly film magazine *Pesti Mozi* (Budapest Cinema) in which he signed a comment column with the phrase 'Sursum Corda'. Two years later he directed his first film, *A becsapott úiságíró* (*The Duped Journalist*, 1914). By 1917 Korda had become Hungary's boy-genius film-maker; he had produced or directed twenty feature films and owned in partnership and ran one of Budapest's largest studios, Corvin. During the political upheavals of 1919 he left Hungary with his wife, the film star Maria Corda, and during the next ten years travelled extensively, making films in Vienna, Berlin, and Hollywood. His only memorable film of these years, *The Private Life of Helen of Troy* (1927), made in Hollywood, was a historical romance that set a pattern for many of his later films.

*Konyets Sankt-Peterburga* (V. I. Pudovkin, 1927)

After a brief stay in Paris in 1930, when he directed MARIUS (1931), Korda settled in England and formed his own production company LONDON FILM PRODUCTIONS. Seven films later he produced and directed THE PRIVATE LIFE OF HENRY VIII (1933) which put Korda and British films back into the struggle for international markets. Its success (on which he attempted to capitalize in *The Private Life of Don Juan* and *The Private Life of the Gannets*, both 1934) earned Korda a partnership in UNITED ARTISTS and secured the financial backing to assemble a stable team of talented technicians, directors, and stars to make a succession of extravagant films. The best of these include *Catherine the Great, The Scarlet Pimpernel* (both 1934), *Sanders of the River, The Ghost Goes West* (both 1935), REMBRANDT, THINGS TO COME, ELEPHANT BOY (all 1936), *Knight Without Armour* (1937), and *The Drum* (1938). Many of these were made at DENHAM STUDIOS, built by Korda, which rivalled Hollywood in grandiose facilities.

Korda's boost to British film production was spectacular, but by 1939 he had over-extended himself and his financial backers. He lost Denham Studios in that year and spent the first part of the war in Hollywood, finishing THE THIEF OF BAGHDAD (1940) and making *Lady Hamilton* (1941), *Lydia* (1941), starring his second wife Merle OBERON, and *Jungle Book* (1942). In 1942 he returned to England and received the first knighthood granted to a film-maker, as much for war services as for his contributions to the British cinema. He re-floated London Films, initially in partnership with METRO-GOLDWYN-MAYER-British (*Perfect Strangers*, 1945, was the only film completed under this organization), and then as an independent company much like his earlier London Films. He acquired Shepperton Studios, bought a controlling share in BRITISH LION, and again assembled an able team.

Although *An Ideal Husband* (1947) was the last film directed by Korda himself, he must be given credit for producing or assisting with other productions from his studio, including ANNA KARENINA, THE FALLEN IDOL (both 1948), THE THIRD MAN (1949), *The Sound Barrier* (1952), *Hobson's Choice* (1954), and *Richard III* (1955). He must also be held at least partly responsible for losing almost all the £3 million lent by the government to British Lion in 1948. In 1954 Korda once more lost control of a film empire which he had created. He has been blamed for the flamboyance of his business methods, but he was undoubtedly responsible for many of the British films that achieved international recognition in the thirties and forties.

**KORDA,** VINCENT (1897–    ), Hungarian-born art director. Youngest brother of Alexander and Zoltan Korda, Vincent left a promising career as a painter to become an art director for many of his brothers' films. His first film credit was for MARIUS (1931), but his best work can be seen in THE PRIVATE LIFE OF HENRY VIII (1933), REMBRANDT (1936), THE THIEF OF BAGHDAD (1940), and THE THIRD MAN (1949).

**KORDA,** ZOLTAN (1895–1961), Hungarian-born director. Following in his brother Alexander's footsteps, Zoltan directed films in Hungary and eventually in Britain for LONDON FILM PRODUCTIONS. He specialized in exotic adventure stories such as *Sanders of the River* (1935), ELEPHANT BOY (1936), which he co-directed, *The Drum* (1938), *The Four Feathers* (1939)—and co-directed its remake *Storm Over the Nile* (1955)—*Jungle Book* (1942), *Sahara* (1943), and *Cry the Beloved Country* (1952).

**KORITSI ME TA MAVRA, To** (*The Girl in Black*), Greece, 1955. 1½hr. *Dir, scr* Michael Cacoyannis; *prod* Ermis Films; *ph* Walter Lassally; *mus* Manos Hadjikakis; *cast* Ellie Lambetti (Marina), Dimitri Horn (Pavlo), George Foundas (Christo).

Marina is persecuted by her island neighbours for her widowed mother's indiscretions. A visiting writer tries to take her back to the mainland, but his attempt to save her is ineffective. CACOYANNIS's observation of character and relationships offsets the potentially melodramatic plot and, particularly, the violent, tragic ending. His controlled direction is notably supported by Ellie LAMBETTI's moving portrait of doomed gentility, enduring insult and oppression, and by Walter LASSALLY's spacious camerawork.

**KÖRKALEN** (*Thy Soul Shall Bear Witness*), Sweden, 1921. 1½hr. *Dir, scr* Victor Sjöström, from the novel by Selma Lagerlöf; *prod* Svenska Bio; *ph* J. Julius Jaenzon; *des* Alexander Bakó, Axel Esbensen; *cast* Victor Sjöström (David Holm), Hilda Borgström (Mrs Holm), Tore Svennberg (Georg), Astrid Holm (Sister Edith).

Oddly combining the supernatural with scrupulous attention to social detail, *Körkalen* is eerily effective within its own terms. The flexible camera movements and the sophisticated special effects demonstrate SJÖSTRÖM's directorial skill, and his performance in the leading role is impressive.

There have been two remakes, *La Charrette fantôme* (Julien DUVIVIER, 1938) and *Körkalen* (Arne MATTSSON, 1958); both are undistinguished in comparison with the original version.

**KORNGOLD,** ERICH WOLFGANG (1897–1957), Czechoslovak composer, a child prodigy who at the age of eleven had an opera staged in Vienna and, the following year, an orchestral work conducted by Nikisch in Leipzig. His later works did not sustain his early celebrity, but he made a successful career in film music after going to Hollywood with Max REINHARDT for A MIDSUMMER NIGHT'S DREAM (1935). He settled in the US, and composed music for numerous WARNER BROS productions. He won OSCARS for *Anthony Adverse* (1936) and *The Adventures of Robin Hood* (1938), and among his other film scores were those for *The Green Pastures* (1936) and *Kings Row* (1942).

**KORTY,** JOHN, US director whose early short films include animation and *The Language of Faces* (1961) a documentary against nuclear war. He both directed and photographed his first feature, *The Crazy Quilt* (1965) and two subsequent features. *Funnyman* (1967) concerns a successful cabaret performer who, dissatisfied, attempts to become a more serious artist. The more successful *Riverrun* (1968) is centred on the rivalry of a father and a lover for the affections of a pregnant girl, and *The Autobiography of Miss Jane Pitman* (1973) traces the life up to the present day of a black woman born into slavery. These loosely structured films are characterized by Korty's affection for his central characters.

**KÓSA,** FERENC (1937–    ), Hungarian director, was born in the Nyíregyháza region, of peasant stock, and after various jobs finally entered the Academy of Film Art in 1959, graduating in 1963. His three short films made there show an inquiring interest in visual effects, particularly *Fény* (*Light*, 1962) and *Jegyzetek egy tó történetéhez* (*Notes on the History of a Lake*, 1962). His talent for composition was realized in his first feature TÍZEZER NAP (*Ten Thousand Suns*, 1967), which showed the years of struggle for land and security preceding the rise of the present younger generation. He attempted to develop the themes of change and revolution in his second feature, *Ítélet* (*Judgement*, 1970), a somewhat laboured co-production with Romania and Czechoslovakia; *Nincs idő* (*Beyond Time*, 1974), set in a prison, is more justly representative of his talent.

**KOSMA,** JOSEPH (1905–    ), French composer born in Hungary, studied music at the Budapest Academy and moved to France in 1933. He began working on films in 1936 with

CARNÉ's *Jenny* and RENOIR's LE CRIME DE MON-SIEUR LANGE. He continued to work extensively with these two directors, composing the music for Renoir's UNE PARTIE DE CAMPAGNE (1936), LA GRANDE ILLUSION (1937), *La Marseillaise* (1938), LA RÈGLE DU JEU (1939), and *Le Déjeuner sur l'herbe* (1959) and for Carné's LES ENFANTS DU PARADIS (1945), *Les Portes de la nuit* (1946), and *Juliette ou la clef des songes* (1951) which was awarded the prize for best film music at CANNES.

Kosma also wrote the scores for two outstanding short films, GRIMAULT's cartoon *Le Petit Soldat* (1947) and FRANJU's LE SANG DES BÊTES (1949). He has composed for over a hundred films in all and has also written ballet and concert music and an oratorio.

**KOVÁCS, ANDRÁS** (1925– ), Hungarian director, graduated from the Budapest film school and was head of the script department of the Hunnia studios 1951–8. He was influential in the reorganization of the industry in the early fifties. He directed his first film in 1960 and, after a period of study in France, attracted great attention with *Nehéz emberek* (*Difficult People*, 1964): the title added a new phrase to current Hungarian speech. Using CINÉMA-VÉRITÉ techniques, the film examined the cases of five Hungarian inventors whose valuable work was never used at home through bureaucratic restrictiveness. This articulate and courageous film set the tone of Kovács's work. HIDEG NAPOK (*Cold Days*, 1966) attracted world attention and played a large part in establishing the reputation of the new Hungarian cinema. *Falak* (*Walls*, 1968) concentrates on a group of successful professional people and examines the dangers inherent in prosperity and security. *Staféta* (*Relay Race*, 1970) uses a group of young people to study the contradictions in contemporary Hungarian society.

**KOZINTSEV, GRIGORI** (1905–73), Russian director, studied at the Leningrad Academy of Fine Arts. In 1921, with TRAUBERG and YUT-KEVICH, he founded FEKS and began his long collaboration with the former. Their first film, produced by FEKS, *Pokhozhdeniya Oktyabrini* (*The Adventures of Oktyabrina*, 1924), was an experimental comedy about an attempted bank robbery and contained several fantastic scenes, including a crowd cycling over roof-tops. Their next film, *Chyortovo koleso* (*The Devil's Wheel*, 1926), used more realistic material but was still eccentric in treatment. *Shinel* (*The Cloak*, 1926) revealed the extent to which the two directors had been tempered by German EXPRESSIONISM: the décor created a dreamlike atmosphere; the photography turned events into demonic and grotesque happenings; and the acting was stylized and acrobatic. After *Bratishka* (1927) and *SVD* (*The Club of the Big Deed*, 1927) they made the successful NOVYI VAVILON (*New Babylon*, 1929). Their next film *Odna* (*Alone*, 1931) which was made silent and then synchronized with fragments of dialogue, had considerable psychological depth in its portrayal of a woman schoolteacher. The fanciful and eccentric elements in Kozintsev and Trauberg's earlier work were now giving way to more warmly human qualities: this development is clearly shown in the Maxim trilogy, *Yunost Maksima* (*The Youth of Maxim*, 1935), *Vozvrashcheniye Maksima* (*The Return of Maxim*, 1937), *Vyborgskaya storona* (*The Vyborg Side*, 1939), tracing the revolution through the political education of a young worker, which is distinguished for its penetrating realism and clarity of style.

During the war Kozintsev directed some shorter features about the heroic exploits of the Soviet people in wartime; after the war he worked mainly on his own. *Don Quixote* (1956) has elements of a historical romance, but nevertheless catches something of the spirit of Cervantes. Following this most of Kozintsev's time was spent preparing for his HAMLET (1964); during this period he wrote a book on Shakespeare which appeared in English as *Shakespeare: time and conscience* (London, 1967). His last film was *Korol Lir* (*King Lear*, 1972). Kozintsev has also written *The deep screen* on his experiences as a director and his views on the importance of depth in the image.

**KRACAUER, SIEGFRIED** (1889–1966), German-born writer, was cultural affairs editor of *Frankfurter Zeitung* 1920–33, then left Germany to escape the Nazis. Before he went to Paris, he had published a novel *Ginster* (1928) and some sociological work, including *Die Angestellen* (1930), a study of the German white-collar worker. While in Paris, he completed *Orpheus in Paris: Jacques Offenbach and the Paris of his time* (1937).

In 1941 he went to America where he remained for the rest of his life. He was appointed special assistant to the Curator of the Museum of Modern Art Film Library, and commissioned to analyse Nazi war film propaganda, which resulted in the publication of *Propaganda and the Nazi war film* in 1942. With the aid of a Guggenheim fellowship, he wrote *From Caligari to Hitler* (1947) which embodied the bold and unique idea of examining the development of the German national psyche through the content of German films.

Kracauer's most crucial work, *The nature of film* (1960) has its central thesis implicit in its subtitle, *The redemption of physical reality*. His conviction that the film medium's essential role is the reproduction or presentation of real events and people polarizes the oft-stated belief that theatricality and formalism have no place in the cinema, that realist cinema is the only true cinema. His arguments give rise to many profound insights, but the attempt to endow his conception of 'the properties of the medium' with absolute aesthetic value is a process which he is unable to sustain even within his own terms of reference. (See also CRITICISM.)

**KRAMER,** STANLEY (1913– ), US producer and director, joined METRO-GOLDWYN-MAYER in 1934 as an editor and later scriptwriter. During the war he directed training films for the US Army. He was an independent producer from 1948, his films including, notably, *The Men* (1950) and HIGH NOON (1952), both directed by Fred ZINNEMANN, and from 1955 he both directed and produced a number of films that exploit the inherent dramatic value of moral conflict without disturbing too many preconceptions. His treatments of racialism (THE DEFIANT ONES, 1958, and *Guess Who's Coming to Dinner*, 1967), the nuclear threat (*On the Beach*, 1959), religious prejudice (*Inherit the Wind*, 1960), and Nazism (*Judgement at Nuremberg*, 1961) were commercially very successful. His big-screen comic film *It's a Mad, Mad, Mad, Mad World* (1963) was far removed in both style and content from his other work; *The Secret of Santa Vittoria* (1969), a war story, was remarkable chiefly for a typical performance from Anna MAGNANI, but *Oklahoma Crude* (1973), with a strong cast including George C. SCOTT, Faye DUNAWAY, and Jack PALANCE, was a pithy tale of oil exploiters in the early years of the century, free from the moralizing of his earlier films.

Kramer received the Irving THALBERG Award in 1961 for consistently high quality in filmmaking.

**KRASKER,** ROBERT (1913– ), Australian-born cameraman, began assisting Georges PÉRINAL on KORDA productions including THINGS TO COME (1936). His own ability became apparent in such different films as HENRY V (1944) and BRIEF ENCOUNTER (1945) and particularly in two he photographed for Carol REED, ODD MAN OUT (1947) and THE THIRD MAN (1949), the latter winning him an OSCAR. He worked for VISCONTI on SENSO (1954) and for Anthony MANN on EL CID (1961). More recently he has worked on less memorable films, although his black-and-white photography for *Billy Budd* (1962) sensitively visualized Melville's story, and *The Collector* (William WYLER, 1965) again showed him working to advantage in colour.

**KRASNA,** NORMAN (1909– ), US producer, scriptwriter and playwright who began his career in journalism, entering films as a publicist. He wrote the original stories for two Fritz LANG films, FURY (1936) and *You and Me* (1938), and wrote or collaborated on a number of screenplays, including *Bachelor Mother* (1939), *The Flame of New Orleans* (1941), and *The Devil and Miss Jones* (1941). In 1943 he wrote and directed *Princess O'Rourke*, which won him an OSCAR.

**KRAUSS,** WERNER (1884–1959), German actor, started with Max REINHARDT. His brusque style suited the role of the insane doctor in DAS CABINETT DES DR CALIGARI (1919). He played Jack the Ripper in LENI'S DAS WACHSFIGUREN-CABINETT (*Waxworks*, 1924), the butcher, opposite GARBO, in PABST'S DIE FREUDLOSE GASSE (*Joyless Street*, 1925), Bottom, in the coarse 1925 version of *Ein Sommarnachtstraum* (A MIDSUMMER NIGHT'S DREAM) and was in REN-OIR'S *Nana* (1926). He starred in the notorious anti-Semitic JUD SÜSS (1940).

***KRIEMHILDS RACHE*** see NIBELUNGEN, DIE

**KRS** see KINEMATOGRAPH RENTERS SOCIETY

**KRUMBACHOVÁ,** ESTER (1923– ), Czech designer, scriptwriter, and director, as a young girl was a member of the anti-Nazi underground, and spent some time in a Gestapo prison. After the war she studied as a painter, and began designing costumes, at first in the theatre and then for film. Her career during the days of Stalinist repression was not smooth, because of her outspokenness, but she survived the punishments (including a spell as a bricklayer) to establish herself as a designer of distinction, working especially with Karel Kachyňa during the late fifties and early sixties. Her lively sense of colour and visual impact made her contribution noticeable in any film she worked on: extravagant hats in particular became a kind of jocular hall-mark of her work. Her originality, as well as her personal wit and beauty, established her as one of the leading group who formed the new wave of the sixties, even though she was one of the very few in that group not to have been at FAMU, the Prague film school.

She rewrote the script of Zbyněk Brynych's *. . . a pátý jezdec je strach* (*The Fifth Horseman is Fear*, 1964), and designed *Démanty noci* (*Diamonds of the Night*, 1964) for Jan NĚMEC. She made a distinctive contribution to both script and design of Věra CHYTILOVÁ'S SEDMIKRÁSKY (*Daisies*, 1966). Her collaboration with Němec was intensified when for a few years they were married: she worked with him on the script of O SLAVNOSTI A HOSTECH (*The Party and the Guests*, 1966), adding a touch of elegant venom to Němec's hatred of injustice. After their collaboration on his *Mučednici lásky* (*Martyrs of Love*, 1967), their marriage broke up, and Krumbachová's next important work was for Jaromil Jireš, co-scripting and designing his *Valerie a týden divu* (*Valerie and her Week of Wonders*, 1968), a controversial work of fantasy based on a novel by the surrealist poet Nezval. She also worked again with Chytilová on her first film since *Sedmikrásky*, *Ovoce stromu rajskych jíme* (*The Fruit of the Trees of Paradise*, 1970), and the same year directed her own first film, *Vražda Ing Ďábla* (*The Murder of Mr Engineer Devil*). The film's ridicule of traditional feminine daydreaming, sharp but not harsh, is characteristic of Krumbachová's preoccupations, and the richness of colour and design is appropriate from a director who, through her visual creativeness, has been one of the most original contributors to Czech films of the sixties.

**KUBRICK**, STANLEY (1928–   ), US director. His first two short films, *Day of the Fight* (1948) and *Fear and Desire* (1953), were made independently while he was working as a journalist on *Life*; both showed a hostile society trained against a solitary individual, prefiguring his main preoccupation. *The Killing* (1956), a thriller in form, had a similarly acerbic approach. Its crucial and popular success led to two successful collaborations with Kirk DOUGLAS. In PATHS OF GLORY (1957) a monstrously unjust court martial and execution in France during the First World War restates Kubrick's distrust of society and its treatment of the individual; SPARTACUS (1960), too, within the trappings demanded by the commission, shows the thinking man in conflict with an oppressive social environment.

After *Spartacus* Kubrick moved to Britain where he has continued to work, the change of location not apparently affecting the coherence of his development. The protagonist in LOLITA (1962), adapted from Nabokov's novel, is destroyed by his own conviction that his irresistible urges render him a social outcast. More sardonic and in sharper focus, DR STRANGELOVE, OR HOW I LEARNED TO STOP WORRYING AND LOVE THE BOMB (1963) brings Kubrick's dislike of modern society fully into the open, as well as an increasingly explicit denigration of the individual. Its satire on a world where the future lies in technological advance which will be pursued whatever the cost to humanity, was succeeded by 2001: A SPACE ODYSSEY (1968), his view of man as a puppet of technology controlled by superior powers to an unknown end. In A CLOCKWORK ORANGE (1971) the perversion of man by society is complete.

Besides its thematic unity, black humour, and striking cinematic quality, Kubrick's work is distinguished by penetrating application of music: popular songs and well-known classics are used to point up ironies and ambiguities in themselves as well as in the visual images. He has a remarkable ability to handle not only the large-scale requirements of an epic such as *Spartacus*, but also the massive technological resources demanded by *2001* and to a lesser extent by *A Clockwork Orange*. Kubrick's public popularity has grown even as his statements become more cynically pessimistic.

*KÜHLE WAMPE* (*Whither Germany?* in US), Germany, 1932. 1½hr. *Dir* Slatan Dudow; *prod* George Hoellering, Scharfenberg; *scr* Bertolt Brecht, Ernst Ottwald; *mus* Hanns Eisler; *lyrics* Helen Weigel; *cast* Hertha Thiele (Anni), Ernst Busch (Fritz), Adolf Fischer, Martin Wolter.

*Kühle Wampe* was made as a co-operative venture and precise credits cannot therefore be established. Put together under difficult conditions, with limited private and Communist Party backing and the continual threat of political interference, it used a story of individual unemployed workers to mount a fierce attack on capitalism and to create rhapsodic propaganda for a Communist revolution. Some passages testify to DUDOW's skill in the use of purely cinematic means to convey a social situation and to inspire emotional response; but the inclusion of ballads in the manner of BRECHT's theatre pieces tends to weaken the effect. The film should not, however, be judged in its known form: it was savagely cut by the German censors at the time of its original release and, as it also suffered official mutilation abroad, no complete version is known to exist.

**KULESHOV**, LEV (1899–1970), Russian director, began as a designer and made his first film *Proyekt inzhenera Praita* (*Engineer Prite's Project*) in 1918, when he also began publishing theoretical articles. After working on the agit-trains (see SOVIET UNION), he formed a film collective (including PUDOVKIN) which without film stock created stylized 'film' shows rehearsing a MONTAGE method based on American and French chase films. This was the method Kuleshov used in *Neobychainiye priklucheniya Mistera Vesta v stranye bolshevikov* (*The Extraordinary Adventures of Mr West in the Land of the Bolsheviks*, 1924) and *Luch smerti* (*The Death Ray*, 1925) original in its prediction of Fascism and its use of mobile cameras and quick cutting.

After *Po zakonu* (*By the Law*, 1926), a strong attack on capital punishment, Kuleshov met with the same production difficulties as EISENSTEIN. He was forced to work without his group until 1932 when he made *Gorizont* (*Horizon*) and *Velikii uteshitel* (*The Great Consoler*, 1933) which experiment with sound perspective. They were criticized for their intellectualism and American elements and at thirty-four Kuleshov was prevented from directing important films. As head of VGIK, from 1944, he published and taught film study programmes.

Kuleshov has been one of the most neglected among major Russian directors. His contribution to Soviet cinema was a method of montage ('creative geography') constructing spatial continuity from random film and a method of filming editorially which manipulated the actor within a perfectly rehearsed scenario. As a seminal theoretician his ideas of frame composition and cutting were used by Pudovkin and Eisenstein.

*KUMONOSU-JO* (*The Throne of Blood* in GB; *The Castle of the Spider's Web*/*Cobweb Castle* in US), Japan, 1957. 1¾hr. *Dir* Akira Kurosawa; *prod* Shujiro Motoki, Kurosawa for Toho; *scr* Shinobu Hashimoto, Ryuzo Kikushima, Hideo Oguni, Kurosawa, from Shakespeare's *Macbeth*; *ph* Asaichi Nakai; *cast* Toshiro Mifune (Taketoki Washizu), Isuzu Yamada (Asaji, his wife), Minoru Chiaki (Yoshiaki Miki, his friend), Akira

Kubo (Yoshiteru, Miki's son), Takamaru Sasaki (Kunihari Tsuzuki), Yoichi Tachikawa (Kunimaru, Kunihari's son), Takashi Shimura (Norujaru Odagura), Chieko Namira (the Witch).

In his adaptation of MACBETH Kurosawa follows the original with only minor differences, while introducing elements of the NOH theatre, most prominent in the physical appearance and movements of Isuzu Yamada in the Lady Macbeth role, and in the conception of the Witch.

The grainy contrast of white mist over black soil together with the atmospheric treatment of forest and castle create an eerie mood, while the prevalence of long shots, as well as heightening the theatrical effect, makes the final close-ups of Toshiro MIFUNE, his body bristling with arrows, all the more powerful.

**KUROSAWA, AKIRA** (1910– ), Japanese director, joined the Toho film company as an assistant director at the age of twenty-six after studying Western painting. He also worked as a scriptwriter before being allowed to direct his first film, *Sugata Sanshiro* (*Sanshiro Sugata*, 1943), from his own script: the martial, nationalistic theme was considered proper for a wartime production. The ten films he made during the next seven years established him in Japan; and RASHOMON (1950), which won the Grand

Toshiro Mifune in *Kumonosu-jo* (Akira Kurosawa, 1957)

Prix at VENICE in 1951, introduced him to the West.

His continuing popularity in the US and Europe is founded essentially on his CHAMBARA (sword-fight) films; the affinity of these lively, battle-centred, costume dramas to the WESTERN has led to several being remade in Western form: SHICHININ NO SAMURAI (*The Seven Samurai*, 1954) as THE MAGNIFICENT SEVEN (1960), *Yojimbo* (1961) as *Per un pugno di dollari* (*For a Fistful of Dollars*, Sergio LEONE, 1964), and *Rashomon*, though not a *chambara* film, as THE OUTRAGE (1964). KAKUSHI TORIDE NO SANAKUNIN (*The Hidden Fortress*, 1958) and *Tsubaki Sanjuro* (*Sanjuro*, 1962), two other outstanding examples of the genre, show Kurosawa at his story-telling best, extracting every possible advantage from the medium with visual elegance and refinement, sometimes reaching epic proportions, and with a persistent sense of mocking and affectionate humour.

A constant factor in Kurosawa's period films has been the presence of Toshiro MIFUNE in a central role; this fruitful partnership forms a link with the concurrent strand in Kurosawa's work—the treatment of modern themes, mainly of social injustice, and his literary adaptations. In the former category are IKIRU (*Living*, 1952), AKAHIGE (*Red Beard*, 1965), with Mifune, and the less satisfactory *Dodeska-den* (1970), his first colour film. For adaptation he has used sources as varied as Dostoevsky (*Hakuchi*, THE IDIOT, 1951), Gorky (*Donzoko*, THE LOWER DEPTHS, 1957), SHAKESPEARE (KUMONOSU-JO, *The Throne of Blood*, 1957, from MACBETH), all with Mifune, and Ed McBain (*Tengoku to Jigoku, High and Low*, 1963, from the novel *King's Ransom*).

Kurosawa has always emphasized the importance of the script, and most of his films have been based on his own original ideas. But not less important to his films are the camerawork and editing: the use of several cameras simultaneously to exploit every viewpoint; the drastic paring of material; the contrasting of textures; the bombardment of the spectator with a succession of flashing images alternating with the use of extended takes, are stylistic features that can be traced from his earliest work.

### KVARTERET KORPEN (*Raven's End*), Sweden, 1963. 1¾hr. *Dir, scr* Bo Widerberg; *prod* Europa Film; *ph* Jan Lindeström; *cast* Thommy Berggren (Anders), Keve Hjelm (Father), Emy Storm (Mother), Ingvar Hirdwall (Sixten), Christina Frambäck (Elsie).

WIDERBERG observes the spiritual famine of working-class conditions in the Sweden of the thirties Depression: a young would-be writer, his drunken father, and worn-out mother, in a dingy tenement, try to believe in their different ways that their conditions are alterable; the conflict of Fascism and socialism provides background comment. For Anders flight seems to be the only, and—in the film's terms—doubtful, solution.

If Widerberg does not entirely establish that the family's problems are caused by social conditions rather than by the father's alcoholism, he nevertheless creates a moving picture of the family and its environment. The film, with its social concerns, was welcomed as a departure from the preoccupations of BERGMAN which had dominated Swedish cinema for the preceding ten years.

### KVINNORS VÄNTAN (*Waiting Women* in GB; *Secrets of Women* in US), Sweden, 1952. 1¾hr. *Dir, scr* Ingmar Bergman; *prod* Svensk Filmindustri; *ph* Gunnar Fischer; *ed* Oscar Rosander; *mus* Erik Nordgren; *cast* Anita Björk (Rakel), Mai-Britt Nilsson (Marta), Eva Dahlbeck (Karin), Gerd Andersson (Maj), Aino Taube (Anita).

While a group of women wait for their husbands to join them for the summer, three of them relate decisive incidents in their married lives. The film displays BERGMAN's recurrent concern with the psychology of women, exploring the change in relationships and the compromises brought about by time and maturity, set against the ideals of a young girl and her expectations of love. In each case the emphasis is on the maternal roles into which the women have fallen, either through choice or necessity. The first of the three tales is an adaptation of Bergman's own play *Rakel och Biografvaktmästaren* (*Rachel and the Cinema Doorman*), produced in 1945 at Malmö.

### KWAIDAN, Japan, 1964. Tohoscope; 2½hr (2hr in Europe); Eastman Color. *Dir* Masaki Kobayashi; *prod* Ninjin Club/Bungei; *scr* Yoko Mizuki from stories by Lafcadio Hearn; *ph* Yoshio Miyajima; *cast* I 'Kurokami' (The Black Hair): Rentaro Mikuni (samurai), Michiyo Aratama (first wife), Misako Watanabe (second wife); II 'Yuki-onna' (The Woman of the Snow): Keiko Kishi (woman), Tatsuya Nakadai (Minkichi); III 'Minimashi Hoichi' (Hoichi the Earless): Katsuo Nakamura (Hoichi), Rentaro Mikuni (samurai), Ganjiro Nakamura (head priest), Takashi Shimura (priest), Joichi Hayashi (Yoshitsune); IV 'Chawan no naka' (In a Cup of Tea): Ganemon Nakamura (Kannai), Noborn Nakaya (Heinai). In Europe 'Yuki-onna' was released separately.

The four tales that make up *Kwaidan* (the title translates as 'ghost story'), although drawn from a Western source are entirely transmuted into traditional Japanese idiom. The heroes are samurai, Buddhist monks, or woodcutters, their supernatural encounters taking place in palaces, temples, or snowy forests. In this stylized context magic has its own incontestable logic, and the spectator is caught up in a remote world of ritual and formal beauty.

KOBAYASHI'S command of composition, colour, and sound gives substance to this world; the film contains sequences of remarkably controlled richness, often derived from classical Japanese graphic art.

*Kwaidan* took five years to prepare and one to shoot and was then the most expensive film ever made in Japan.

**KYO, MACHIKO** (1924– ), Japanese actress, after some years as a dancer, entered the Daiei studios in 1949. Her performances in RASHOMON (1950), UGETSU MONOGATARI (1953), and JIGOKUMON (*Gate of Hell*, 1953) earned her great popularity in many countries; she appeared less felicitously in Daniel MANN's *Teahouse of the August Moon* (1956), afterwards resuming her successful career in Japan.

**KYROU,** ADO(NIS) (1923– ), writer and film-maker, born in Greece where he was a member of the Resistance, moved in 1946 to Paris. An ardent Surrealist (championing, among others, the work of W. C. FIELDS and the MARX BROTHERS), he is best known for his writing, particularly *Le Surréalisme au cinéma* (1952) and *Amour-érotisme et cinéma* (1957). He has been actively involved with other Surrealists, including Luis BUÑUEL, on whose work he wrote *Luis Buñuel*, 1962. In 1951 he started, with Robert Benayoun, the magazine *L'Âge du cinéma*, which he also edited, but it foundered after only six issues. His major importance lies in his role as co-founder, in 1952, and member of the editorial board of the magazine *Positif* which fulfilled an important function in French cinema culture, opposing the critical stance of André BAZIN and CAHIERS DU CINÉMA, attacking their Catholicism and Bazin's notion of 'ontological realism' by arguing for the poetic and profoundly fantastic (i.e. sur-real) nature of the cinema. Kyrou has directed several films including *Le Moine* (1973), from the novel *The Monk* by M. G. Lewis; the film was scripted by Kyrou in collaboration with Buñuel who had intended to direct it.

# L

**LA CAVA,** GREGORY (1892–1949), US director, at first a cartoonist who worked in the silent days on animation, including *Mutt and Jeff* cartoons. He became a scriptwriter, making his début as a director with *Womanhandled* (1926). His best period came in the thirties: the political drama *Gabriel over the White House* (1933), with Walter HUSTON as the President, attracted attention; the satirical comedy *The Affairs of Cellini* (1934) had a notable cast in Fredric MARCH (as Benvenuto Cellini), Constance BENNETT, Fay WRAY, and Louis CALHERN; another fine cast was assembled for *Private Worlds* (1935), with Claudette COLBERT, Charles BOYER, Joel MCCREA, and Joan BENNETT.

La Cava's particular talent was for SCREW-BALL comedy, at its best in *She Married Her Boss* (1935), co-starring Claudette Colbert and Melvyn DOUGLAS, and MY MAN GODFREY (1936), with William POWELL and Carole LOMBARD. He also made the notable comedy-drama of theatrical life *Stage Door* (1937), with Katharine HEPBURN, Ginger ROGERS, and Adolphe MENJOU, and again directed Ginger Rogers in *Fifth Avenue Girl* (1939) and *The Primrose Path* (1940).

**LADD,** ALAN (1913–64), US actor, had a minor role in CITIZEN KANE (1941), before gaining wide popularity with his portrayal of a baby-faced murderer in *This Gun for Hire* (1942), in which he was teamed with Veronica LAKE. Their attempt to build up an acting partnership in *The Glass Key* (also 1942) was not repeated; but Ladd retained a large public following in the forties and fifties with a steady output of action films and Westerns in which he played slight variations of the tough but sensitive hero. More notably, he contributed an intelligent performance to the title role of *The Great Gatsby* (1949). The peak of his career came with SHANE (1953) in which he played the archetypal lone hero with admirable restraint. In his last film, *The Carpet-baggers* (Edward DMYTRYK, 1963), he gave a mature performance as a cowboy turned film star who becomes submerged in Hollywood intrigue.

**LADRI DI BICICLETTE** (*Bicycle Thieves*), Italy, 1948. 1½hr. *Dir, prod* Vittorio De Sica; *scr* Cesare Zavattini, Oreste Biancoli, Suso Cecchi d'Amico, Adolfo Franci, De Sica, based on a story by Luigi Martolini; *ph* Carlo Montuori; *mus* Alessandro Cicognini; *cast* Lamberto Maggiorani (the father), Lianella Carell (the wife), Gino Saltamarenda, Giulio Chiari, Vittori Antonucci.

Antonio, an unemployed labourer, is offered a job which he can accept only if he has a bicycle. He retrieves his own from the pawnbroker, but on his first day at work it is stolen. With his small son he spends his Sunday searching for it, but without success.

Shot in the poorer parts of Rome with a cast of non-actors, the film epitomizes much of NEO-REALISM, especially in the development of an impasse situation. The tight structure and the quietly effective social criticism are enriched by the gently romantic vein which enables DE SICA to avoid the stridency of SCIUSCIÀ (*Shoeshine*, 1946). Awarded many prizes including an OSCAR, *Ladri di biciclette* powerfully criticizes the forces—the Church among them—which reduce people to disillusion and despair, it remains both sharp and relevant, despite its apparently dated conventions.

**LADY EVE, The,** US, 1941. 1½hr. *Dir, scr* Preston Sturges; *prod* Paramount; *ph* Victor Milner; *cast* Barbara Stanwyck (Jean), Henry Fonda (Charles), Charles Coburn ('Colonel' Harrington), Eugene Pallette (Mr Pike), William Demarest (Muggsy).

Cardsharpers on a luxury liner fail to outwit Henry FONDA, successfully cast in an untypically glamorous role. A delightful sex comedy, *The Lady Eve* has the crisp scripting and cutting typical of Preston STURGES's best films.

**LADY FROM SHANGHAI, The,** US, 1948. 1½hr. *Dir* Orson Welles; *prod* Columbia; *scr* Welles, based on the novel *If I Die before I Wake* by Sherwood King; *ph* Charles Lawton Jr; *cast* Rita Hayworth (Elsa Bannister), Orson Welles (O'Hara), Everett Sloane (Arthur Bannister), Glenn Anderson (Grisby).

A sailor, O'Hara, becomes embroiled in the

murderous intrigues of the crippled Bannister, his beautiful wife, and his vicious partner Grisby. Plot and counter-plot result in violent death; O'Hara escapes untouched.

The narrative is so elliptical as to be confusing: this has been attributed to studio cutting, but it resembles WELLES's handling of similar material in TOUCH OF EVIL (1958). Notable for its exciting visual effects, particularly in the final fun-house sequence (which required the camera operator to slide 125 feet down a helter-skelter to achieve a stunning subjective shot) and in the culminating shoot-up in a hall of mirrors, the film displays the kind of grotesque brilliance for which Welles is justly famous.

**LADY VANISHES, The**, GB, 1938. 1½hr. *Dir* Alfred Hitchcock; *prod* Gainsborough Pictures; *scr* Sidney Gilliat, Frank Launder, from the novel by Ethel Lina White; *ph* Jack Cox; *mus* Louis Levy; *cast* Margaret Lockwood (Iris Henderson), Michael Redgrave (Gilbert), Paul Lukas (Dr Hartz), Dame May Whitty (Miss Froy), Googie Withers (Blanche), Cecil Parker (Mr Todhunter), Linden Travers (Mrs Todhunter), Basil Radford (Charters), Naunton Wayne (Caldicott).

An old lady, played with engaging dottiness by Dame May Whitty, mysteriously disappears on a trans-continental train; a girl who has been travelling with her attempts a search with the help of another passenger and they find themselves in the thick of a spy intrigue.

A slight story, combining elements of comedy, mystery, and high drama, directed with a deft elegance, the film was a skilful technical achievement; the action, which almost all takes place on the train, was photographed mainly on a ninety-foot-long set, with miniatures and transparencies ingeniously giving the impression of a real train. Using a pair of giant tumblers, HITCHCOCK gave an original touch to a drink-doping scene, by filming part of it through the glasses. Naunton WAYNE and Basil RADFORD, as a pair of archetypal Englishmen abroad, provide one of the film's lasting pleasures.

**LADY WITH A LITTLE DOG** see DAMA S SOBACHKOI

**LAEMMLE**, CARL (1867–1939), US producer of German origin, emigrated to the US in 1884 and worked his way up as a clerk and bookkeeper in various small businesses. He ventured into the NICKELODEON business in 1906, expanding into DISTRIBUTION with the Laemmle Film Service. He stood out against the monopolistic practices of the MOTION PICTURE PATENTS COMPANY, tirelessly defending the lengthy series of lawsuits they brought against him and waging an effective war of ridicule through press advertisements. In 1909, as part of the battle, he formed his own film production company, Independent Motion Picture Company (IMP) and launched the STAR SYSTEM by hiring Florence LAWRENCE, the 'BIOGRAPH Girl' and identifying her by name as the 'Imp Girl'. IMP became the nucleus of an anti-Trust consortium that was consolidated in 1912 as UNIVERSAL Pictures. Laemmle produced STROHEIM's first films, *Blind Husbands* (1918), *The Devil's Passkey* (1919), and FOOLISH WIVES (1921), but they parted company over Stroheim's extravagance on *Merry-Go-Round* (1922). Although he remained studio head until 1936, when he was forced out by the company's financial backers, Laemmle's interest in film-making diminished: production management was in the hands of his son, Carl Laemmle Jr (1908– ), during 1929–36. Universal's most important films, including ALL QUIET ON THE WESTERN FRONT (1930), were in the main Carl Jr's achievement. Laemmle's major interest at this period was philanthropic work, chiefly in Germany; this is fully recorded in his official biography *The life and adventures of Carl Laemmle* by John Drinkwater (London, 1931), which depicts him as diminutive and genial, a byword for nepotism (prompting Ogden Nash's lines 'Uncle Carl Laemmle/has a very large faemmle'), and as one of the few major Hollywood tycoons to be remembered with more affection than fear.

**LAGERLÖF**, SELMA (1858–1940), Swedish novelist who had much influence on the cinema in Sweden, particularly in its early years. Much of her somewhat earthy material was drawn from folk-tales of her native province. Outstanding films based on her books include HERR ARNES PENGAR (1919), KÖRKALEN (1921), and GÖSTA BERLINGS SAGA (1924).

**LAI**, FRANCIS (*c.* 1933– ), French composer, became famous with his individual and appealing score for Claude LELOUCH's *Un Homme et une femme* (*A Man and a Woman*, 1966), and had a similar success with his music for the same director's *Vivre pour vivre* (1968). He enjoyed further success with *Love Story* (1970). Among his other film scores are *Masculin-féminin* (GODARD, 1966), *Mayerling* (1968), *La Leçon particulière* (1968), *Three Into Two Won't Go* (1969), *La Vie, l'amour, la mort* (1968), and again for Lelouch, *Le Voyou* (*Simon the Swiss*, 1970).

**LAKE**, VERONICA (1919–73), US actress, real name Constance Ockelman, popular during the forties as one of Hollywood's quintessential vamps. Her appeal owed less to talent than to her intriguing hair-style which hid half her face: during the height of her fame there were several accidents in munitions factories to women workers trying to copy her. However, in SULLIVAN'S TRAVELS (1941) she responded to Preston STURGES's direction with an excellent performance. The peak of her brief career was in 1942 when with Alan LADD, in *This Gun for Hire* and *The Glass Key*, she formed the kind of partnership later perfected by Humphrey BOGART and Lauren BACALL, and also made her best film, *I Married a Witch*, directed by René CLAIR.

**LAMARR,** HEDY (1914– ), US actress of Austrian origin, real name Hedwige Kiesler, appeared in a number of films in Europe under the name of Hedy Kieslerová, including the sensational EXTASE (1933). From 1938 she appeared regularly under her new name in Hollywood films built around her exotically glamorous appeal. She was cast opposite Victor MATURE in DEMILLE's *Samson and Delilah* (1949).

**LAMBETTI,** ELLIE (1930– ), Greek actress, became a star of the Athens stage at the age of fifteen, earning recognition as the most talented and popular actress of her generation. Her first film appearance was in *Adouloti sclavi* (1946); she caught international attention for her starring role in *Kyriatiko xyprima* (*Windfall in Athens*, 1953), directed by Michael CACOYANNIS. This was followed by TO KORITSI ME TA MAVRA (*The Girl in Black*, 1955) and TO TELEFTEO PSEMMA (*A Matter of Dignity*, 1957), both for the same director; in the latter, particularly, she portrayed with warmth and conviction the dilemma of contemporary Greek women confronting traditional attitudes, and won worldwide acclaim for her talent and her great beauty. Critics invoked the names of GARBO and MAGNANI; but a brief bid by Hollywood to develop her potential as a star failed, mainly because of her lack of English. She has unhappily vanished from the screen, continuing to act on the stage with her own company, formed in the early fifties with Dimitri Horn (who also acted with her in the first two films).

**LAMORISSE,** ALBERT (1922–70), French director, remembered mainly for his short films CRIN-BLANC (1953) and *Le Ballon rouge* (*The Red Balloon*, 1956). His particular use of documentary techniques to create a poetic fantasy world worked less well in his full-length films *Le Voyage en ballon* (*Stowaway in the Sky*, 1960) and *Fifi-la-plume* (1965), but his integrity and independence were acknowledged. He was skilled in filming from helicopters which he used extensively in his documentaries *Versailles* (1967) and *Paris jamais vu* (1969); he was killed in a helicopter crash while filming.

**LAMOUR,** DOROTHY (1914– ), US actress, real name Dorothy Kaumeyer, became typed as Hollywood's idea of a South Seas beauty from her first film, *The Jungle Princess* (1936). She is especially remembered for the series of 'Road' films (1939–52) in which, with her spirited good humour, she was well teamed with Bing CROSBY and Bob HOPE. She retired in 1953, making occasional guest appearances since.

**LAMPRECHT,** GERHARD (1897– ), German director and film historian studied history of art before entering the cinema as a scriptwriter. His first important film was *Buddenbrooks* (1923), an adaptation of Thomas Mann's novel. In 1925 he directed *Die Verrufenen*, a social study of life in the Berlin slums which was built around observations and drawings by Heinrich Zille, followed by *Die Unehelichen* (1926), set in a similar milieu. His most famous film was *Emil und die Detektive* (1931), based on the classic children's adventure story by Erich Kästner, where Lamprecht showed a real flair for directing children. In 1937 he made *Madame Bovary* with Pola NEGRI in the title role. He directed several films during the war and immediately afterwards returned to his social preoccupations with *Irgendwo in Berlin* (1946), which deals with the problems of young people and soldiers after the defeat.

Lamprecht's cinema archive was bought by the Berlin Senate and formed the basis of the Deutsche Kinemathek founded in 1962 with Lamprecht as its first director. His own historical research, completed in 1970, has resulted in a mammoth catalogue of German silent films, *Deutsche Stummfilme 1903–1931*, published in nine volumes by the Deutsche Kinemathek, Berlin, 1967.

**LANCASTER,** BURT (1913– ), US actor, made his first film, THE KILLERS, in 1946. His roles have varied widely: those films which exploit his gritty personality include FROM HERE TO ETERNITY (1955), *The Rose Tattoo* (1955), THE SWEET SMELL OF SUCCESS (1957), *Elmer Gantry* (1960), IL GATTOPARDO (*The Leopard*, 1963). Originally a vaudeville and circus acrobat, Lancaster did most of his own stuntwork until he was over fifty, and among the films which have given scope to his athleticism and muscular physique are *The Crimson Pirate*

(SIODMAK, 1952, a remake of FAIRBANKS's *The Black Pirate*, 1926), *Trapeze* (1956), and GUNFIGHT AT THE OK CORRAL (1956). Probably his best performances have been for John FRANKENHEIMER in *Bird Man of Alcatraz* (1962), SEVEN DAYS IN MAY (1964), and *The Train* (1964). With Harold Hecht and James Hill he formed the company Hecht–Hill–Lancaster which has produced a number of his films including *Airport* (1969), an all-star BLOCKBUSTER designed mainly as a vehicle for Lancaster.

**LANCHESTER, ELSA** (1902–   ), British-born actress, real name Sullivan, who began acting after founding the Children's Theatre in 1918. She often appeared opposite her husband Charles LAUGHTON: as, for example, Anne of Cleves in THE PRIVATE LIFE OF HENRY VIII (1933). They both went to Hollywood where she played the dual role of Mary Shelley and the Bride in James WHALE's classic horror film *The Bride of Frankenstein* (1935), then returned to England for REMBRANDT (1936). Since 1940, she has spent most of her time in Hollywood, becoming an American citizen in 1950, and has specialized in playing eccentrics such as the witch, Queenie, in *Bell, Book and Candle* (1959). She wrote *Charles Laughton and I*, London, 1938.

**LAND, The**, US, 1939–41 (limited release 1942–4; withdrawn from circulation 1944). 45min. *Dir, scr, ph* Robert J. Flaherty; *prod* Douglas Baker for Agricultural Adjustment Agency (US Dept of Agriculture); *ed* Helen van Dongen; *mus* Richard Arnell.

Asked by the US government to make a film in support of New Deal agricultural policies, FLAHERTY travelled three times across the States, making a personal record of his journeys. Narrated by Flaherty himself, the film expresses his concern with a land where starvation, unemployment, and erosion occur amidst affluence and plenty. The government suppressed the film, at home because of its supposed obsolescence (the outbreak of war having reduced unemployment to a negligible amount), and abroad because of its probable harm to the war effort.

**LAND WITHOUT BREAD** see HURDES, LAS

**LANG Jr, CHARLES B.** (1902–   ), US cameraman worked for PARAMOUNT 1929–52. His first major assignment was *Tom Sawyer* (1930), and he won an OSCAR for *A Farewell to Arms* (Frank BORZAGE, 1933). He has worked particularly on Westerns and thrillers. ONE-EYED JACKS (Marlon BRANDO, 1960) contains some of his finest photography, showing the dusty hills

and the cliffs and beaches of Monterey. He has worked recently for Richard QUINE—notably on *Hotel* (1967); for Robert MULLIGAN—*Inside Daisy Clover* (1966) and the stunningly filmed *The Stalking Moon* (1968); and for Terence YOUNG on *Wait until Dark* (1967), a claustrophobic thriller.

**LANG, FRITZ** (1890–   ), Austrian-born director and writer, studied architecture and painting in Vienna and in 1910 began to travel extensively—to Russia, North Africa, China, and Japan—supporting himself by odd jobs. On the outbreak of war in 1914, he was arrested in Paris as an alien, escaped, and joined the Austrian Army. While convalescing in Vienna from wounds received in action, he met JOE MAY for whom Lang wrote his first film scripts, *Die Hochzeit im Ekzentrikklub* (*Marriage in the Club of the Eccentrics*) and *Hilde Warren und der Tod* (*Hilde Warren and Death*, both 1917). In the latter film Lang also acted at least four parts. He went to Berlin in 1918, joining the DECLA company as a story editor and reader; he also did some film cutting and was promoted to director.

Lang's first film as director/writer was *Halbblut* (*The Half-Breed*, 1919), in which a man is destroyed by his love for a woman. This was followed by *Der Herr der Liebe* (*The Master of Love*, 1919) and a two-part adventure serial *Die Spinnen* (*The Spiders*, 1919–20). The first section of *Die Spinnen* was so successful that although Lang had begun to direct DAS CABINETT DES DR CALIGARI (1919) he was replaced by Robert WIENE, so that he could quickly complete the second part. Lang co-scripted *Das wanderne Bild* (*The Wandering Image*, 1920) with Thea von HARBOU, whom he later married and who collaborated on all his films up to 1932. These early dramas already showed Lang's distinctive style and his view of the individual in relation to, and in conflict with, his environment.

Lang's first major critical success was *Der müde Tod* (1921), about a girl attempting to bargain with Death to save her lover. It was shown in Britain under the title *Destiny*; its release (as *Between Two Worlds*) was delayed in the US until 1923 because Douglas FAIRBANKS had promptly bought the rights and copied many of its special effects for his THE THIEF OF BAGDAD (1924). Lang's social and political concerns became more apparent in his first Dr Mabuse film, DR MABUSE DER SPIELER (*Dr Mabuse the Gambler*, 1922), which contained pointed allusions to the post-war social and economic conditions in Germany. In DIE NIBELUNGEN (1924) Lang and von Harbou turned to a thirteenth-century German poem and the Norse sagas. The traditional and persistent nature of the myth in Germany aided the film's success, on the strength of which UFA allowed Lang a free hand to make METROPOLIS (1927), his futuristic projection of contemporary social and political systems. UFA's most expensive film to date, its slow commercial take-off nearly bankrupted the company. Lang now formed his own company to make *Spione* (1928), concerning a crippled super-criminal masterminding an international spy network; it too had allegorical overtones.

Lang refused to add sound effects to *Die Frau im Mond* (*The Woman in the Moon*, 1929), already in production when the change-over to sound took place; but in M (1931) he made masterly use of the new medium to heighten tension and atmosphere. He followed this treatment of a psychopathic child killer with a return to Dr Mabuse, but DAS TESTAMENT DES DR MABUSE (*The Last Will of Dr Mabuse*, 1932) was not acceptable to the Nazis, who banned it in 1933. Lang fled to France, leaving his wife who was by then a Party member; she divorced him the same year.

Lang made one film in France, *Liliom* (1935), before going to Hollywood, having been signed up by David O. SELZNICK for METRO-GOLDWYN-MAYER. There was no sharp break in his work in either theme or style, although a slight loosening-up might be perceived, a greater concern with narrative detected. FURY (1936), his first completed work in the US, dealing with mob psychology and personal revenge, was an immediate commercial and critical success. *You Only Live Once* (1937), starring Henry FONDA as a petty criminal accused of a crime he did not commit, includes one of the most elegant and succinct of Hollywood bank raids—filmed from above.

He showed his versatility as a craftsman in two commercially successful Westerns, *The Return of Frank James* (1940), his first film in colour, and *Western Union* (1941). He set up an independent company to make *Hangmen Also Die* (1943), an anti-Nazi film written by himself and Bertolt BRECHT, set in Czechoslovakia just after the assassination of Heydrich. After *The Woman in the Window* (1944), he formed another short-lived company, with Walter WANGER and Dudley NICHOLS; their first film, *Scarlet Street* (1945), a remake of RENOIR's *La Chienne* (1931), concerned a middle-aged artist who, having avoided the legal penalty for murder, is reduced to degradation by guilt and grief.

*Rancho Notorious* (1952) was Lang's finest Western and THE BIG HEAT (1953), a grim thriller of revenge and corruption, his best film of the period; but he was becoming increasingly frus-

trated by the lack of personal control over his own work. After *While the City Sleeps*, a cynical story of journalistic in-fighting, and *Beyond a Reasonable Doubt* (both 1956) he returned to Germany where he made a two-part film *Der Tiger von Eschnapur* (*The Tiger of Eschnapur*) and *Das indische Grabmal* (*The Indian Tomb*, 1959), based on scripts Lang and von Harbou had written for Joe May in 1920. The two parts were intended for consecutive showings and were thus seen in Europe; in the US they were considerably mutilated and shown as one feature *Journey to the Lost City*. This version was also seen in Britain as *Tiger of Bengal*. He refused offers to remake some of his silent films, instead undertaking a last Dr Mabuse story, *Die tausend Augen des Dr Mabuse* (*The Thousand Eyes of Dr Mabuse*, 1960), showing the master criminal at work in a modern environment with technologically sophisticated weaponry to hand. Lang appeared as himself in GODARD's LE MÉPRIS (1963).

Lang's work, over fifty years and on both sides of the Atlantic, shows consistency of style and themes accompanying an extraordinary adaptability: to sound, to changed political circumstances, to a new country and language, to different genres, to commercial demands. If his later films do not reach the stature of his silent masterpieces or the classic *M*, they nevertheless indicate his unfailing cinematic sensibility, his ability to handle actors, his skill in exposition, and his architect's eye for design.

Peter Bogdanovich, *Fritz Lang in America*, London, 1968; New York 1969; Paul M. Jensen, *The cinema of Fritz Lang*, London, New York, 1969.

**LANGDON, HARRY** (1884–1944), US comedian, spent many years in vaudeville and later appeared (often anonymously) in many Mack SENNETT comedies. His special appeal lay in a combination of child-like innocence and a morose, somnambulistic manner comically at variance with everyday reality: he was a passive figure around whom chaos regularly descended, producing a slow, uncomprehending attempt to adjust to each new disaster.

Langdon's talent was a fragile commodity, and he needed a strong script and very careful direction to sustain a feature-length comedy. His last short for Sennett, *Saturday Afternoon* (1925), combined the writing and directing talents of Frank CAPRA, Arthur Ripley, and Harry Edwards who together developed his individual qualities to a high level. Four features resulted from their collaboration, *Tramp, Tramp, Tramp* (1926), *The Strong Man* (1926), *Long Pants* (1927), and *His First Flame* (1927), and placed Langdon in the first rank of silent film comedians. Capra perceptively commented: 'If there was a rule for writing Langdon material, it was this: his only ally was God. Langdon might be saved by the brick falling on the cop, but it was *verboten* that he in any way motivate the brick's fall.'

Unhappily, Langdon insisted on taking over as director. The three features he directed himself were failures, and his sound film appearances were undistinguished. In 1939 he briefly replaced Stan Laurel in the LAUREL AND HARDY comedy team, but never regained his earlier popularity.

**LANGLOIS,** HENRI (1914– ), French film collector born in Turkey. He was a passionate collector of films from his schooldays and in 1935 with Georges FRANJU he started the *Cercle du cinéma* to screen his collection of silent films. In 1936 they founded the CINÉMATHÈQUE FRANÇAISE with Langlois as director. During the war, Langlois organized secret screenings and with help from friends was able to hide and so save thousands of films from destruction. A controversial figure with a life-long devotion to cinema, Langlois is held in affection by the film-makers of the NOUVELLE VAGUE who rallied to his support during the upheavals of 1968 (see CINÉMATHÈQUE FRANÇAISE).

**LANSBURY,** ANGELA (1925– ), British-born actress who has spent most of her screen career in Hollywood. She made her film début in GASLIGHT (1944, *The Murder in Thornton Square* in GB) and had supporting or featured roles in a number of films including *National Velvet* (1944), *The Harvey Girls* (1946), and *Samson and Delilah* (1949). After playing an avaricious and dangerous woman in *Mutiny* (1952) and a sinister villainess in *Remains to be Seen* (1952), she co-starred with Randolph SCOTT in a Western, *A Lawless Street* (1955), and had leading parts in some other minor films. But in major films she tended to remain in featured roles to which she brought some dynamic performances, notably the wilful princess in *The Court Jester* (1956), the matrimony-minded mistress in THE LONG HOT SUMMER (1958), and the possessive mother in *All Fall Down* (1961). Having attracted a considerable reputation among discerning audiences, she confirmed her reputation with a brilliant characterization in THE MANCHURIAN CANDIDATE (1962). Since then she has rarely had parts of appropriate worth: *Something for Everyone* (1970, *Black Flowers for the Bride* in GB) was interesting only for her performance, and *Bedknobs and Broomsticks* (1971) was even more a waste of her talent.

**LANZA,** MARIO (1921–59), US tenor, real name Alfred Cocozza, who after *That Midnight Kiss* (1949) became one of the bright stars in the METRO-GOLDWYN-MAYER firmament, winning an enormous and adulatory following in several musicals. He is particularly remembered for the title role in *The Great Caruso* (1951).

**LARDNER** Jr, RING (1915– ), US scriptwriter, son of one of America's greatest humorists, whose first screenplay, WOMAN OF THE YEAR (1942) written in collaboration with Michael Kanin, was a notable success, though his follow-ups were disappointing. In 1950 he was imprisoned as one of the Hollywood Ten (see UNAMERICAN ACTIVITIES) and was blacklisted. He scripted one film produced in Switzerland in that year but, apart from *Virgin Island* (1959) which was credited pseudonymously, he was unable to work again in Hollywood until he wrote *The Cincinnati Kid* (Norman JEWISON, 1965). Lardner's name came back triumphantly to notice with M*A*S*H (1971): his script is remarkable for the startlingly modern and naturalistic dialogue which is as strikingly up-to-date as that of *Woman of the Year* in its own time.

**LASER** (Light Amplification by Stimulated Emission of Radiation). A high-energy light source with many applications in science. Research is in progress for using lasers for telecommunications and in HOLOGRAPHY. Lasers are also used in certain video disc players, notably the Philips VLP and MCA Discovision.

**LASKY,** JESSE (1880–1958), US executive, a former vaudeville impresario who entered the film-making business in 1913 when, with Samuel Goldfish (later GOLDWYN) and Cecil B. DEMILLE, he formed the Jesse Lasky Feature Play company. Two major successes, *The Squaw Man* (1913) and *The Virginian* (1914) both starring Dustin Farnum, gave the company a strong start. DeMille and Oscar Apfel as principal writer–directors, a fine cameraman in Alvin Wyckoff, and, in addition to Farnum, such stars as Blanche SWEET, Wallace Reid, Geraldine Farrar, and Sessue HAYAKAWA gave Lasky bargaining power when in 1916 his company merged with Adolph ZUKOR'S FAMOUS PLAYERS. Goldfish left and Lasky became head of production, a post he maintained when the company became PARAMOUNT Pictures in 1927 and until he was forced out in 1932. He later produced films for most of the major Hollywood studios and was president of the short-lived Mary PICKFORD–Jesse Lasky Corporation. His autobiography

*I blow my own horn* was published in 1957 (London).

**LASSALLY,** WALTER (1926– ), German-born British cameraman, made his name with CACOYANNIS on TO KORITSI ME TA MAVRA (*The Girl in Black*, 1955). Lassally's visual style, with sharp blacks and whites, became identified with the lyrical realism of Cacoyannis's Athenian films; but working in Britain, where he was closely associated with FREE CINEMA, he was equally successful in filming the greyly naturalistic *We Are the Lambeth Boys* (REISZ, 1959), A TASTE OF HONEY (1961), and *The Loneliness of the Long-Distance Runner* (1962), both for Tony RICHARDSON. This ability, shown by the best lighting cameramen, to adapt to the needs of varying subjects, was also evident in the visual opulence and subdued colour of TOM JONES (1963), for which he won an OSCAR, and again for Cacoyannis in the diffused black and white of *Zorba the Greek* (1965). In 1967 he photographed *Labyrinth*, an experimental MULTI-SCREEN film made by the NATIONAL FILM BOARD of Canada for Expo '67 in Montreal.

**LASSIE,** in fact a male collie dog, real name Pal, first appeared in *Lassie Come Home* (1943), co-starring Elizabeth TAYLOR. He immediately attained a popularity comparable with that of his predecessor RIN-TIN-TIN. He lived like a star in £2,000 worth of air-conditioned kennels with private grounds and staff, including a hairdresser and chiropodists. Succeeded by his son, he appeared in a string of sentimental film vehicles for his intelligence, courage, and resourcefulness; the character was used in a children's television series into the seventies and in a series of short cartoons made for television.

*LAST LAUGH, The,* see LETZTE MANN, DER

*LAST STAGE, The,* see OSTATNI ETAP

*LAST TANGO IN PARIS,* Italy/France, 1972. Technicolor; 2hr. *Dir* Bernardo Bertolucci; *prod* PEA Cinematografica (Rome)/Les Artistes Associés (Paris); *scr* Bertolucci, Franco Arcalli; *ph* Vittorio Storaro; *ed* Franco Arcalli; *mus* Gato Barbieri; *cast* Marlon Brando (Paul), Maria Schneider (Jeanne), Jean-Pierre Léaud (Tom), Darling Legitimus (concierge), Maria Michi (Rosa's mother), Veronica Lazare (Rosa).

A middle-aged expatriate American and a young Frenchwoman meet by accident in an empty flat. They embark on an affair which, at the man's insistence, is exclusively physical and impersonal: not even names are exchanged. But ultimately it is he who demands a fuller relationship.

The explicit scenes of brutal sexual intimacy with which the callousness of the affair is emphasized made *Last Tango in Paris* a subject of furious attacks at a time when film CENSORSHIP was a noisy public issue. They were claimed to exemplify the dangers of increasing outspokenness and the film was classed in some quarters with the concurrent boom in commercial erotica. In Britain an unsuccessful action under the Obscene Publications Act was brought by a private individual against the exhibitors.

The scandalized reaction undoubtedly contributed to the film's commercial success, while muffling discussion of its purpose. As a study of the pain, both inflicted and endured, inevitably associated with egotism, it goes beyond Paul's sadistic treatment of Jeanne. Paul's wife has crippled him emotionally by her cold secretiveness, finally and inexplicably committing suicide; Jeanne's fiancé Tom, an aspiring film director, treats her as the subject for an exercise in style; Jeanne kills Paul, not in self-defence but to escape his demands on her emotions; even the peripheral characters are isolated within themselves, unable to comprehend the suffering of others.

BERTOLUCCI handles his uncompromising thesis with remarkable maturity: in particular the individual talent of Marlon BRANDO is carefully deployed to heighten the film's conviction. But *Last Tango in Paris* fails to attain tragic stature, perhaps because it lacks contrast; the insistence that human relations consist only of loneliness, cruelty, and suffering makes it instead a statement of heavy pessimism.

**LATERNA MAGICA** (Magic Lantern), a combination of film and live action developed for the Czechoslovak pavilion at the Brussels Exhibition of 1958. Its principal developer was Alfred RADOK, primarily a theatre director and indefatigable experimenter. The brilliant display of visual conjuring tricks was achieved not, as was widely supposed, by elaborate electronic controls, but rather by the precision, skill, and timing of the protagonists combining their action on the stage with images from two film projectors and one slide projector (at Brussels: more were used in later performances in other cities). Many ingenious and entertaining sequences posed questions about space and illusion, with characters stepping into and out of the screen, live dancers dancing with screen partners, and sound, too, switching from actual to recorded. The early programmes were boldly experimental: Miloš FORMAN and Ivan PASSER were among the young film-makers who worked with Radok on them. The enormous popular appeal of the Laterna Magica continued unabated, but Radok left it after a film he made for a later programme was banned, and the programmes, although still entertaining, have become more banal in content.

**LATTUADA, ALBERTO** (1914– ), Italian director whose father, the composer Felice Lattuada, has scored most of his films. Alberto Lattuada directed his first film in 1942; he gained considerable attention with *Il bandito* (1946) and *Senza pietà* (1947), both in the mainstream of NEO-REALISM. In 1950 he co-directed with FELLINI *Luci del varietà*. He again attracted international notice with *La mandragola* (*The Mandrake*, 1965), from the play by Machiavelli. Lattuada founded, and is president of, the Cineteca Italiana in Milan.

**LAUGHTON, CHARLES** (1899–1962), British-born actor, made his first film appearances in 1928 in three short silent comedies starring Elsa LANCHESTER (whom he married in 1929), and directed by Ivor MONTAGU from stories by H. G. Wells: *Bluebottles*, *The Tonic*, and *Daydreams*. These led to small parts in feature films such as *Piccadilly* (1928) and *The Old Dark House* (1932), Laughton's first film in Hollywood.

Laughton was never type-cast, although all his characters have a larger-than-life feel; and all were created with overwhelming enthusiasm and attention to detail. His appearance and approach lent themselves to tyrannical roles: the king in THE PRIVATE LIFE OF HENRY VIII (1933), for which he won an OSCAR (the first for a performance in a British film); the overbearing Captain Bligh in THE MUTINY ON THE BOUNTY (1935). His greatest talent lay in portraying more complex personalities, sometimes hidden behind simple, almost child-like, façades. In *Ruggles of Red Gap* (1935), he played the unassuming English manservant who is transformed into the ideal American. Following the title role in Alexander KORDA's uncompleted *I, Claudius* (1936), he conveyed with conviction the artist's twenty-five years of physical and mental struggle in REMBRANDT (1936).

In 1938, Laughton founded Mayflower Pictures with Erich POMMER and in that year the company made its only films: *The Vessel of Wrath* (*The Beachcomber* in US), *St Martin's Lane* (*Sidewalks of London* in US), and *Jamaica Inn*. In Hollywood throughout the forties and fifties—having become an American citizen in 1940—he played many parts, most conforming to his basic idea that personal integrity must be preserved at all costs. He returned to the British

Charles Laughton in *Rembrandt* (Alexander Korda, 1936)

cinema with *Hobson's Choice* (1954) and in 1958 he created the role of Sir Wilfrid Robarts, the shrewd and cantankerous lawyer in *Witness for the Prosecution*. During this period he also co-directed some of *The Man on the Eiffel Tower* (1948) with Burgess MEREDITH; his only full-length film as sole director was THE NIGHT OF THE HUNTER (1955). His last screen appearance was a typically robust performance as Senator Sheb Cooley in *Advise and Consent* (1961).

**LAUNDER, FRANK** (1907– ), British director and scriptwriter, in the thirties wrote scripts for GAUMONT BRITISH and GAINSBOROUGH, often working with Sidney GILLIAT. Their writing partnership reached its peak with HITCHCOCK's THE LADY VANISHES (1938) and their work for TWENTIETH CENTURY-FOX, *Kipps* (1941) and *The Young Mr Pitt* (1942). They then collaborated as directors on *Millions Like Us* (1943), a story of working-class people in Britain conducting the war on the Home Front with courage and common sense. In 1945 they formed their own company, Individual Pictures (later Launder and Gilliat Productions). Although the two worked closely together, directing was on an individual basis, with Launder making *I See a Dark Stranger* (1946) and *Captain Boycott* (1947). *The Happiest Days of Your Life* (1950), an uninhibited and highly successful farce initiated a series of St Trinian's films which alternated with such films as *Geordie* (1955), *The Bridal Path* (1959), and *Joey Boy* (1965). In 1966 Launder and Gilliat reverted to co-direction for another of their popular series, *The Great St Trinian's Train Robbery*.

**LAUREL AND HARDY,** US comedians. Stan Laurel (1890–1965), real name Arthur Stanley Jefferson, was born in England and appeared with Fred KARNO's troupe. He remained in the US after a Karno tour (although he never relinquished British citizenship) and made his first film, *Nuts in May*, in 1917. In the same year he made a film with Hardy, *Lucky Dog*. Oliver Hardy (1892–1957) trained as a singer, ran a cinema, and entered films in 1913, working at first mainly with Larry SEMON, notably as the Tin Man in THE WIZARD OF OZ (1925). The two joined Hal ROACH separately in 1926 and established their partnership the following year, initiating a brilliant series of shorts with *Putting Pants on Philip* (1927).

Almost from the first they played the complementary characters Stan and Ollie. Hardy was the pompous father-figure, respectable, respectful of authority, confiding his apprehensive exasperation to the audience with his famous 'slow-burn' look at the camera; Laurel was the child, literal,

irresponsible, and destructive, unable to interpret events and tearful in a crisis. Whoever nominally directed the films, effective control lay with Laurel, who insisted on shooting in sequence and improvising freely from a vestigial script. They made the transition to sound undiminished and with their comic style virtually unchanged, making brilliant use of off-screen noises to suggest visions of unnameable disaster and using dialogue economically for plot development.

Their first feature appeared in 1931, although they continued making shorts until 1935. Notable among their feature films are the only ones to be billed as 'A Stan Laurel Production': *Our Relations* (1936) and *Way Out West* (1937), both fully integrated comedies. In 1940 they left Roach and worked for TWENTIETH CENTURY-FOX and METRO-GOLDWYN-MAYER; but the constraint of elaborate scripts and formal studio conditions is reflected in the poor quality of their later films.

*Laurel and Hardy* by Charles Barr, London, 1967; Berkeley, 1968, is both affectionate and informative.

**LAVENDER** or lavender print, colloquial term for a lavender-tinted, high-quality positive film stock from which DUPE negatives were made. It was in use from 1929 to 1940 when it was replaced by the FINE-GRAIN print still in use. Any fine-grain print may still be referred to as a 'lavender'.

**LAVENDER HILL MOB, The,** GB, 1951. 1¼hr. *Dir* Charles Crichton; *prod* Michael Balcon; *scr* T. E. B. Clarke; *ph* Douglas Slocombe; *mus* Georges Auric; *cast* Alec Guinness (Holland), Stanley Holloway (Pendlebury), Sidney James (Lackery), Alfie Bass (Shorty).

The theft of gold bullion by a meek middle-aged Bank of England messenger (a minutely-observed performance by Alec GUINNESS) and its export in the form of souvenir models of the Eiffel Tower is the framework of this typical EALING comedy. The film's unabashed insularity contributed largely to its wide success, while the sedate performances of the leading actors heightened the comedy of the fantastic plot. In the comic scenes set on the Eiffel Tower effective use was made of the travelling MATTE.

**LAWFORD,** PETER (1923– ), US actor born in Britain, appeared as a child in *Poor Old Bill* (1931) before moving to Hollywood. His career became established with *Mrs Miniver* (William WYLER, 1942) and he has since appeared regularly in more sophisticated roles, notably in *Advise and Consent* (Otto PREMINGER, 1961).

LAWRENCE, FLORENCE (1888–1938), US actress, known as the first American film star, because she was initially the only actress to be called by her own name instead of by that of the film company for which she worked. Already popular as the BIOGRAPH Girl, she was signed up in 1910 by Carl LAEMMLE who publicized her identity in the form of a false story of her death. Her films included *Lady Helen's Escapade* (1909) and *Resurrection* (1910). Paralysis caused by injuries sustained in a studio fire in 1915 stopped her career for several years, and when she returned to acting she was no longer a star. She was under contract to METRO-GOLDWYN-MAYER when she killed herself.

LAWRENCE, GERTRUDE (1898–1952), British stage actress, a stylish *comédienne* primarily associated with various Noël COWARD plays, she began appearing in films in the early days of sound, in a straightforward singing performance in a Fox-Movietone one-reeler (*I Don't Know*, 1929), and in a comedy by Coward, *Early Morning* (1929). Notable among her films were *Aren't We All?* (1932), *Lord Camber's Ladies* (1932), *Mimi* (1935), a version of *La Bohème*, REMBRANDT (1936), and *Men Are Not Gods* (1937). *Star!* (Robert WISE, 1968) was a film version of her life, in which she was impersonated by Julie ANDREWS, with little success.

*LAWRENCE OF ARABIA*, GB, 1962. Super Panavision 70; 3¾hr; Technicolor. *Dir* David Lean; *prod* Sam Spiegel for Horizon Pictures; *scr* Robert Bolt; *ph* F. A. Young; *mus* Maurice Jarre; *cast* Peter O'Toole (Lawrence), Alec Guinness (Prince Feisal), Anthony Quinn (Auda Abu Taji), Jack Hawkins (General Allenby), Omar Sharif (Sherif Ali), José Ferrer (Turkish Bey), Anthony Quayle (Colonel Brighton), Claude Rains (Mr Dryden).

Lawrence the man of action brought out the best in David LEAN; the man of mystery and psychological confusion defeated him. As with so many of Lean's works, this is scrupulously reconstructed and filmed, skilfully put together, and beautiful to look at, especially in the desert scenes. Typical of F. A. YOUNG's brilliant photography is the first sight of Sherif Ali, at first a mere dot on the screen, riding into full view out of a mirage. Peter O'TOOLE gives one of his most convincing performances, undoubtedly fortified by both his striking facial resemblance to Lawrence and Robert Bolt's intelligent script. But the film, in spite of these merits, fails to convey any insight into Lawrence's tortured character or any coherent thread to link the many episodes and sustain a length of nearly four

hours. It depends on the whole-hearted endorsement of a popular myth, and as such won enormous popular success as well as seven OSCARS.

LAWSON, JOHN HOWARD (1895–   ), US playwright and scriptwriter. His successful Broadway plays of the thirties displayed proletarian sympathies which were carried over into his film scripts. These include *Dynamite* (1930), *Heart of Spain* (Paul STRAND, 1937), *Algiers* (1938, the remake of PÉPÉ-LE-MOKO, 1937), *Blockade* (1938), about the Spanish Civil War, and *Counter-Attack* (1943), the last of three which attempted to boost the American/Soviet wartime alliance. He was a founder-member of the Screen Writers Guild, and in 1947 was called before the UNAMERICAN ACTIVITIES Committee as one of the group which became known as the Hollywood Ten. During his years on the blacklist he wrote books on films, on propaganda, and on writing for the stage and the cinema.

LEACOCK, RICHARD (1921–   ), US documentary film-maker, was brought up on his father's banana plantation where he made his first film, *Canary Island Bananas* (1935). Robert FLAHERTY was impressed by the film and later invited Leacock to work with him on LOUISIANA STORY (1948).

Leacock's first television film *Toby* (1954) led to the formation of DREW ASSOCIATES. He worked on all the important Drew documentaries, notably *Primary* (1960) and THE CHAIR (1963), up to *Crisis: Behind a Presidential Commitment* (1963). He left Drew Associates to set up a production–distribution partnership, Leacock–Pennebaker Inc, with Donn Alan PENNEBAKER. Leacock worked independently on *Happy Mother's Day* (1964, not shown in America) which revealed the commercial exploitation of the birth of quintuplets in a small-town community, and *Igor Stravinsky* (1966). He also continued to work with Pennebaker and other members of the Drew Associates team on two pop music films, *Monterey Pop* (1968) and *Sweet Toronto* (1970). In 1970, the Leacock–Pennebaker partnership broke up. He is an outstanding theorist on DIRECT CINEMA and has made important contributions to developing or adapting the light-weight equipment that is essential to this type of film-making (see 16MM).

LEADER, the length of film which precedes the actual picture on each reel to protect it from damage and to permit the film to be threaded into a projector. It also bears a printed legend identifying the film's title, version, and reel number. Following this is a sequence of numbers at

16-frame intervals which 'count down' to indicate the beginning of the actual picture and the sound. Cinema projectionists use this section—the 'academy leader', after the ACADEMY OF MOTION PICTURE ARTS AND SCIENCES which designed it—to effect a smooth change-over between reels.

In the US the word 'leader' is used for any blank film used in editing, known as 'spacing' in Britain.

**LEAN, DAVID** (1908– ), British director, entered films in 1927 as a number-board boy under Maurice ELVEY at Lime Grove Studios. Rising rapidly through the ranks as a technician, he soon made a reputation in the cutting room. He progressed to editing feature films, notably PYGMALION (1938) and MAJOR BARBARA (1941), and his work on these led Noël COWARD to invite him to co-direct IN WHICH WE SERVE (1942). He formed his own production company, Cineguild, with Coward and Ronald Neame, and directed three more Coward subjects for it, *This Happy Breed* (1944), *Blithe Spirit* (1945), and BRIEF ENCOUNTER (1945). He then turned to filming DICKENS, whom he called 'the perfect screenwriter', and made outstandingly successful versions of GREAT EXPECTATIONS (1946) and OLIVER TWIST (1948). His next three films all starred his then wife Ann TODD: *The Passionate Friends* (1949), *Madeleine* (1951), and *The Sound Barrier* (1952).

The exciting aerial sequences of *The Sound Barrier*, which Lean also produced, gave him the taste for spectacular production and big budgets which has characterized his work since. He has concentrated entirely on BLOCKBUSTERS: THE BRIDGE ON THE RIVER KWAI (1957), LAWRENCE OF ARABIA (1962), DOCTOR ZHIVAGO (1966), and *Ryan's Daughter* (1971), four films which have reputedly earned eight million dollars for Lean personally and made him, according to VARIETY, top Hollywood 'grosser' of all time.

All Lean's films are essentially straightforward narratives about simple emotions, made with an almost obsessive technical skill. His virtues and faults are perhaps summed up in *Ryan's Daughter*, the only one of the four epics which was an original screen subject. Though Lean called it 'a simple British love story', it took thirteen million dollars and three years to make; though it is shot entirely on location (mainly on the west coast of Ireland), such skill and care is lavished on the timing and composition of the exteriors that it looks almost as if it had been made on a gigantic studio set. Lean has perhaps been Britain's most solidly professional director since the Second World War, but he would seem to have little to say with the impressive tools at his command.

**LÉAUD, JEAN-PIERRE** (1944– ), French actor, was introduced to the screen and a particular kind of stardom by François TRUFFAUT in LES QUATRE CENTS COUPS (1959). His career has been shaped by the role he developed with Truffaut as ANTOINE DOINEL (after *Les Quatre cents coups* in *L'Amour à vingt ans*, 1962, *Baisers volés*, 1968, and *Domicile conjugale*, 1970), that of the engaging, bewildered innocent-at-large. With the sort of complicity characteristic of the NOUVELLE VAGUE, GODARD used him as an actor in *Masculin-Féminin* (1966), *Made in USA* (1966), *La Chinoise* (1967), WEEK-END (1967), and *Le Gai Savoir* (1968): he worked as second assistant to Godard on *Alphaville* (1965) and PIERROT-LE-FOU (1965). He also assisted Truffaut on *La Peau douce* (1963), and Jean-Louis Richard on *Mata-Hari* (1964), which Truffaut scripted. Other films in which Léaud has acted include COCTEAU's LE TESTAMENT D'ORPHÉE (1960), SKOLIMOWSKI's *Le Départ* (1966), PASOLINI's IL PORCILE (*Pigsty*, 1969), Glauber ROCHA's *Der Leone Have Sept Cabezas* (1970), and BERTOLUCCI's LAST TANGO IN PARIS (1972). His latest appearances for Truffaut have been not as Antoine Doinel but as people very like him in their scatter-brained diffidence, in *Les Deux Anglaises et le continent* (1971) and LA NUIT AMÉRICAINE (1973). Léaud disarmingly insists that he lacks the professionalism of a trained actor: his career has been of interest in its connection with Truffaut's work and its reflection of a total absorption in and devotion to cinema.

**LE CHANOIS, JEAN-PAUL** (1909– ), French director, real name Dreyfus, after working as an editor and assistant director, directed a successful comedy, *L'Irrésistible Rebelle* (1939). During the war he made a film about a group of Resistance fighters, which could not be released until 1946; *Au coeur de l'orage* was almost the only film record of the Resistance, and as such is a valuable document. Since the war Le Chanois has maintained a steady output of films, in most of which he tended to treat a specific social problem clothed in fictional form.

**LEE, CHRISTOPHER** (1922– ), British actor, descended from Italian nobility, who has specialized in fantasy and horror, most notably as the stylish Count in HAMMER's DRACULA (1958, *Horror of Dracula* in US), its many sequels, and the independent Spanish production, *Count Dracula* (1969, released 1972). Anticipating the growth of European co-production, Lee filmed extensively on the continent during the sixties, and became a leading, worldwide box-office star, appearing in well over a hundred films. He formed his own company in partnership with Anthony Nelson-Keys and they made *Nothing But the Night* (1972) as their first film.

**LEE, PEGGY** (1920–   ), US singer, actress, and lyricist, real name Norma Dolores Egstrom, made her first film appearances as vocalist with the Benny Goodman Orchestra. Her first major role was in the remake of *The Jazz Singer* (1952), for which she wrote some lyrics, followed by *Pete Kelly's Blues* (Jack WEBB, 1955). Her films as a lyricist include DISNEY's *Lady and the Tramp* (1956), in which she sang on the sound-track, and *tom thumb* (1958). With her warm, strong voice and intelligent assurance, she is an outstanding singer of jazz and standard popular music.

**LEENHARDT, ROGER** (1903–   ), French director, began his career as a journalist, and is a distinguished film critic as well as a producer and director. He began making short films in 1934 with *Le Vrai Jeu* and *L'Orient qui vient*, and although he has directed two interesting feature films, *Les Dernières Vacances* (1947) and *Le Rendezvous de minuit* (1962), he has worked almost exclusively on shorts, making nearly fifty including several biographies, *Victor Hugo* (1951), *François Mauriac* (1954), *Jean-Jacques* (1958) on J.-J. Rousseau, *Paul Valéry* (1960), *L'Homme à la pipe* (1962) on Courbet, and *Corot* (1966). His other films cover subjects ranging from the development of cinema, *La Naissance du cinéma* (1946), to new agricultural methods in Morocco, *La Fugue de Mahmoud* (1950).

**LEFÈVRE, RENÉ** (1898–       ), French actor, gained notice in the leading role in *Jean de la lune* (1931) followed by the leading role in LE MILLION (1931). After some mediocre films he played the attractive central character in LE CRIME DE MONSIEUR LANGE (1936). He has continued to play parts of solid merit and also wrote several scenarios, notably that of Marc ALLÉGRET's *Parade de sept nuits* (1941). In 1942 he wrote and directed *Opéra Musette* in which he also acted.

***LEFT-HANDED GUN, The,*** US, 1958. 1¼hr (1½hr in GB). *Dir* Arthur Penn; *prod* Warner Bros; *scr* Leslie Stevens, from the play by Gore Vidal; *ph* J. Peverell Marley; *cast* Paul Newman (William Bonney), Lita Milan (Celsa), John Dehner (Pat Garrett), Hurd Hatfield (Moultrie), James Congdon (Charlie), James Best (Tom), Colin Keith-Johnston (Tunstall), John Dierkes (McSween).

Arthur PENN's first film was an intelligent study of BILLY THE KID, placing the notorious outlaw's career in a social and psychological

framework. Paul NEWMAN's performance gave the well-told story the depth lacking in less considered versions, aided by the stark, demystifying black-and-white photography. The film indicates Penn's concern with real personages who have acquired legendary status and with the moral implications of a social order based on force.

**LÉGER, FERNAND** (1881–1955), French painter and film-maker. Léger's discovery of CHAPLIN's comedies precipitated his interest in the cinema. In collaboration with Dudley Murphy, he made *Le Ballet mécanique* (1924), an ABSTRACT film reminiscent of his Cubist painting. In 1940 he left France for America and in 1944 completed an episode in Hans RICHTER's *Dreams That Money Can Buy*. His death interrupted the making of *Le Ballet des couleurs*. His films, like his paintings, were inspired by the machinery and ephemera of modern life.

**LEGG, STUART** (1910–   ), British documentary director, producer, and author, joined British Instructional Films in 1931, and in 1932 the EMB, subsequently GPO, Film Unit (see CROWN FILM UNIT), for whom he produced a series of documentaries on communications, culminating in *BBC: The Voice of Britain* (1935). He co-authored *Money behind the screen* (1937), which drew attention to the unsound financial basis of the British film industry. As co-founder of Film Centre, a consultative agency, he functioned chiefly as a producer. In 1939 he joined GRIERSON at the NATIONAL FILM BOARD of Canada. He initiated the monthly *Canada Carries On* series and was responsible for the highly successful WORLD IN ACTION. Legg returned to Britain in 1948 as the Crown Film Unit's producer. He joined Film Centre International in 1950, becoming chairman in 1957, and his productions include his classic COMPILATION film *Powered Flight* (1953) and *Song of the Clouds* (John Armstrong, 1956), both for the SHELL FILM UNIT. Legg now devotes himself to historical authorship.

**LEGION OF DECENCY** see CENSORSHIP, US

**LEGRAND, MICHEL** (1932–   ), French composer and conductor, emerged as an individual writer of film music mainly through his scores for Jacques DEMY's LOLA (1961) and *La Baie des anges* (1963), followed by the same director's two unusual musicals LES PARAPLUIES DE CHERBOURG (1964) and *Les Demoiselles de Rochefort* (1966). Among other internationally-known films for which he wrote the music at this period were CLÉO DE 5 A 7 (VARDA, 1962), VIVRE SA VIE (GODARD, 1962), *Eva* (LOSEY, 1962), LE JOLI MAI

(MARKER, 1963), and *Bande à part* (Godard, 1964). In his music for *The Thomas Crown Affair* (1968) he scored a popular success with his song 'Windmills of the Mind', and his recent work has included *La Dame dans l'auto avec des lunettes et un fusil* (1970), *Summer of '42* (1971), and the persistent theme of THE GO-BETWEEN (1971).

**LEIGH,** JANET (1927– ), US actress, real name Jeanette Morrison, was noticed by Norma SHEARER and in 1947 signed a contract with METRO-GOLDWYN-MAYER. After making her screen début in *The Romance of Rosy Ridge* (1947), with Van JOHNSON, she appeared regularly in routine studio productions. Her films include several for some of Hollywood's best-known directors, including WELLES'S TOUCH OF EVIL (1958), HITCHCOCK'S PSYCHO (1960), and FRANKENHEIMER'S THE MANCHURIAN CANDIDATE (1962).

**LEIGH,** VIVIEN (1913–67), British actress, real name Vivien Hartley, apart from her screen successes was a popular and respected stage actress. Her early career in films reached its peak with GONE WITH THE WIND (1939), for which she received an OSCAR, CAESAR AND CLEOPATRA (1945), and ANNA KARENINA (1948); in these films the leading part ideally suited her talent for combining a fragile appearance with inner strength, even ruthlessness. Her later appearances were limited by ill health, but she adapted her natural talents to older, tragic roles: in A STREETCAR NAMED DESIRE (1951) her brilliant and moving performance won her a second Oscar. She was for twenty years married to Laurence OLIVIER.

**LEJEUNE,** Caroline (C. A.) (1897–1973), English critic, after graduating from Manchester University introduced film criticism to the pages of the *Manchester Guardian* in 1922. Six years later she joined the *Observer* where she remained film critic until 1960. Her film reviewing was always perceptive and enlivened with a trenchant, though never cruel, wit. One of her main contributions to the cinema was her championship of emerging European directors whose films she saw at the FILM SOCIETY during the twenties and thirties, though she tended to undervalue the Hollywood tradition. Her books include *Chestnuts in her lap* (1947), a collection of reviews, and *Thank you for having me* (1964), an autobiography.

**LELOUCH,** CLAUDE (1937– ), French director, probably the only contemporary commercial director to operate his own camera. He began making films at the age of nineteen with three short documentaries, *USA en vrac* and *Une Ville pas comme les autres*, both made in the US, and *Quand le rideau se lève*, made in Moscow. All three seem to have been banned, for political reasons according to Lelouch. He worked for the army film unit during his military service, then went into independent production. After making five modest features he gained international acclaim, a share of the first prize at CANNES, and two OSCARS with *Un Homme et une femme* (1966). A slender love story, with admirable performances by Anouk AIMÉE and Jean-Louis TRINTIGNANT, was embellished by the director with a glossy visual style. A certain lack of maturity was again evident in *Vivre pour vivre* (1968), which was supported mainly by the professional playing of Yves MONTAND and Annie GIRARDOT, but *Le Voyou* (1970) was an ingeniously constructed thriller made with much greater sharpness and wit and less self-indulgence. *La Bonne Année* (1974) treated a crime drama in the romantic style of his earlier successes.

**LEMMON,** JACK (1925– ), US actor and director of vaudeville and stock experience, made his first, and highly successful, appearance in *It Should Happen to You* (George CUKOR, 1954). *Phffft* (Mark ROBSON, 1954), with Judy HOLLIDAY, was less entertaining, but Lemmon won an OSCAR for his lecherous Ensign Pulver in John FORD and Mervyn LEROY's *Mister Roberts* (1955). In Billy WILDER's SOME LIKE IT HOT (1959) and THE APARTMENT (1960) his always slightly diffident underplaying was a triumph. As an alcoholic in *Days of Wine and Roses* (Blake EDWARDS, 1962) he demonstrated his ability in a serious dramatic role. He returned to farce in *How to Murder Your Wife* (Richard QUINE, 1964), produced by his own company.

Wilder's underrated *The Fortune Cookie* (1966, *Meet Whiplash Willie* in GB) inaugurated the Lemmon/Walter MATTHAU partnership. This was brilliantly exploited in *The Odd Couple* (Gene Sachs, 1967), in which their shared *ménage* becomes a satire on the marital relationship, with Lemmon as the masculine equivalent of the fussy housewife and Matthau as the complete male slob. They continued their collaboration with Lemmon as director and Matthau playing the lead in *Kotch* (1971). Lemmon appeared for Wilder again in *Avanti!* (1972) and played a harassed, confused business man in *Save the Tiger* (1973). In Wilder's remake (1974) of THE FRONT PAGE Lemmon, as the star reporter, and Matthau, as the odious newspaper editor, again made use of their special capacity for savage comic sparring.

Lemmon's comic acting is marked by an

underlying sense of pain which gives unusual tension to his performances. He employs a deceptively natural style which, with its subtlety of response and perfectly controlled timing, is the product of a high degree of professional skill.

**LENI,** PAUL (1885–1929), German director. Former poster and set designer for Max REIN-HARDT, Leni believed the film designer's role vital, demonstrating his ideas in DAS WACHS-FIGURENCABINETT (*Waxworks*, 1924). He had previously collaborated with Leopold Jessner on *Hintertreppe* (*Backstairs*, 1921), a KAMMER-SPIELFILM marred by the conflict of expressionist and realist styles, but interesting for its use of objects in a dramatic role. In Hollywood Leni's style crystallized in four thrillers—*The Cat and the Canary* (1927), remade twelve years later as a comedy with Bob HOPE, *The Man Who Laughed* (1928), *The Chinese Parrot* (1928), *The Last Warning* (1929). His shock techniques, including horror-provoking sets, were germane to HITCHCOCK's development.

**LENICA,** JAN (1928–   ), Polish animator, was a poster designer before three film collaborations with BOROWCZYK, including *Dom* (*House*, 1958), *Monsieur Tête* (France, 1959) and *Nowy Janko Muzykant* (*Janko the Musician*, 1960), established his artistic individuality. *Labirynt* (*Labyrinth*, 1962), his best-known work, brought international recognition. The Ionesco-inspired *Die Nashörner* (*Rhinoceros*, 1963) and *A* (1964) were made in West Germany. Lenica's films are short surrealist fables, strongly influenced by absurd theatre. An eclectic style utilizes cut-outs and collage; his figures range from primitives in heavy black lines to the graceful dignity of the bowler-hatted Icarus-figure in *Labirynt*. Lenica has also written and illustrated books for children.

**LENIN,** pseudonym of Vladimir Ilyich Ulyanov (1870–1924), Russian statesman. The few news-reel shots that survive of Lenin were collected by Mikhail ROMM in 1948 in the COMPILATION film *Vladimir Ilyich Lenin*. The first fiction film to include a portrayal of him was EISENSTEIN's OKTIABR (*October*, 1927), in which he made a brief, dramatic appearance. Since then many attempts have been made to portray him on the Russian screen, the most famous by the actors Boris Shchukin in Romm's LENIN V OKTIABRYE (*Lenin in October*, 1937) and *Lenin v 1918 godu* (*Lenin in 1918*, 1939) and Maxim Straukh in YUTKEVICH's *Chelovek s ruzhyom* (*Man with a Gun*, 1938), *Rasskazy o Leninye* (*Stories about Lenin*, 1958). *Lenin v Polshe* (*Lenin in Poland*, 1965), and in the third of the Maxim trilogy by

KOZINTSEV and TRAUBERG: *Vyborgskaya storona* (*The Vyborg Side*, 1939). The films of the thirties, in keeping with the ideals of SOCIALIST REALISM, depicted him in a simple, heroic light, stressing his leadership. In the cautious atmosphere of the fifties and sixties, the trend was to concentrate on his personal life. Mark DONSKOI's *Serdtse materi* (*Heart of a Mother*, 1966) and *Vernost materi* (*A Mother's Devotion*, 1967) dealt with his youth. The films of this period are romantic and humane in tone, but like those of the thirties, tend to neglect Lenin's intellectual stature, and the complexity of the political issues he faced. A hopeful exception, however, appeared in 1968: Karasik's *Shestoye iulya* (*The Sixth of July*). Based on a play by Mikhail Sha-trov which aroused considerable controversy in Russia, it shows Lenin grappling with the problems of statecraft within a complex and unusually subtle political framework.

***LENIN IN OCTOBER*** see LENIN V OKTIABRYE

***LENIN V OCTIABRYE*** (*Lenin in October*), USSR, 1937. 1½hr. *Dir* Mikhail Romm; *prod* Mosfilm; *scr* A. Kapler; *ph* B. Volchok; *des* B. Dubrovsky-Eshke; *mus* A. Alexandrov; *cast* Boris Shchukin (Lenin), I. Golshtab (Stalin).

The first sound film to portray LENIN deals with his early life. His character is recreated with great conviction, showing him as the guiding genius of the Revolution; the film moves smoothly from the intimate scenes to the large-scale epic ones where the interrelation between Lenin and the masses is well worked out.

Boris Shchukin, who had never seen Lenin, had been preparing for such a part for years by watching newsreels and studying carefully the cadences of Lenin's speech, and the film owes much to his performance.

The success of the film led to a sequel: *Lenin v 1918 godu* (1939).

**LENYA,** LOTTE (1900–   ), Austrian actress and singer, real name Karoline Blamauer, who married Kurt WEILL in 1926 and devoted most of her career to becoming a brilliant exponent of his work, mainly in the theatre. She played Jennie in the film of DIE DREIGROSCHENOPER (*The Threepenny Opera*, 1931), and returned to the cinema as the corrupt Contessa in *The Roman Spring of Mrs Stone* (1961). She played the sadistic villainess in *From Russia with Love* (1963) and the madam of a brothel in *The Appointment* (1968).

**LEONE,** SERGIO (1921–   ), Italian director and son of a pioneer film-maker, entered the film industry in 1939. He worked as first assistant, on over eighty features and short films, with many reputable Italian directors, including CAMERINI and DE SICA, in whose LADRI DI BICICLETTE (*Bicycle Thieves*, 1948) he also had a small acting part; and during the fifties with numerous American directors filming in Italy, including LEROY (QUO VADIS, 1951), WISE (*Helen of Troy*, 1955), WYLER (BEN-HUR, 1959). Leone's first film as director was *Il Colosso di Rodi* (*The Colossus of Rhodes*, 1960). Following its commercial success, Leone refused opportunities to make MACISTE epics, and became second-unit director on ALDRICH's *Sodom and Gomorrah* (1961). In the early sixties, following a widely popular German television series ('Winnetou'), Italian producers began to show an interest in Westerns. In 1964 Leone finished *Per un pugno di dollari* (*For a Fistful of Dollars*), inspired by KUROSAWA's *Yojimbo* (1961). It was shot in two languages, the cast and crew using anglicized pseudonyms—Leone was Bob Robertson. Distributors were reluctant to touch it, but on release it broke box-office records and a boom in Italian Westerns began. Leone completed a trilogy with *Per qualche dollari in più* (*For a Few Dollars More*, 1965), *Il buono, il bruto, il cattivo* (*The Good, the Bad and the Ugly*, 1966). Leone's feeling for the genre, his insistence on historical accuracy, and Clint EASTWOOD's poker-faced yet expressive 'Man With No Name' have contributed to the establishment of the spaghetti Western. Leone's other films include: *C'era una volta di West* (*Once Upon A Time in the West*, 1968), *Giu' la testa* (*Duck, you Sucker* or *A Fistful of Dynamite*, 1971).

**LÉON MORIN, PRÊTRE**, France/Italy, 1961. 2hr. *Dir* Jean-Pierre Melville; *prod* Rome–Paris Films; *scr* Melville, from the novel by Béatrix Beck; *ph* Henri Decaë; *cast* Jean-Paul Belmondo (Léon Morin), Emmanuele Riva (Barny), Irène Tunc (Christine), Marielle Gozzi (France), Patricia Gozzi (France, when older).

Barny, a young widow, Communist and anticlerical, proceeds through theological argument with a young priest to fall in love with him and unsuccessfully attempts to seduce him. By his strength of faith and warm humanity he transforms their relationship into the friendship they both need. MELVILLE's brisk but sympathetic direction of an uncharacteristic subject controls the explosive mixture of sex and religion and draws from his leading players performances of complete integrity, and Henri DECAË's low-key photography conveys well the drab atmosphere of occupied France.

**LEOPARD, The,** see GATTOPARDO, IL

**LERNER,** ALAN JAY (1918– ), US lyricist and 'book' or scriptwriter of Broadway and Hollywood musicals. Lerner wrote the screenplay for *Royal Wedding* (1951, *Wedding Bells* in GB) and the lyrics for *Belle of New York* (1952), but his best-known and most successful work has been with the composer Frederick Loewe. Of their four stage musicals—*Brigadoon* (1947, filmed 1954), *Paint Your Wagon* (1951, filmed 1969), MY FAIR LADY (1956, filmed 1964), *Camelot* (1960, filmed 1967)—*My Fair Lady* was the only success as a film, winning an OSCAR. Two other films for which Lerner wrote scripts won Oscars: AN AMERICAN IN PARIS (1951), which used George GERSHWIN's music, and GIGI (1958), another Lerner–Loewe collaboration. Lerner's stage musical *On a Clear Day You Can See Forever* (1965), with music by Burton Lane, was filmed by MINNELLI in 1970, starring Barbra STREISAND.

**LEROY,** MERVYN (1900– ), US director and producer. LeRoy's career began with the coming of sound; his first success was LITTLE CAESAR (1930), and his early reputation was sealed with *I Am a Fugitive from a Chain Gang* (1932) and GOLDDIGGERS OF 1933 (1933). Since 1927 he has made over seventy films including *They Won't Forget* (1937), WATERLOO BRIDGE (1940), *Random Harvest* (1942). His remake of QUO VADIS (1951) showed a talent for the spectacular elements of film. He has also produced films, including THE WIZARD OF OZ (1939).

**LESSER,** SOL (1890– ), US producer. The president of a corporate chain of cinemas linked to RKO, he took in hand the task of assembling EISENSTEIN's *Que Viva Mexico!*, abandoned by the director in 1932. Much against the wishes of Eisenstein's backer Upton SINCLAIR, Lesser made and released three films made up of this material, the most notable being *Thunder Over Mexico* (1933). Other Lesser productions include a series of TARZAN films (1933–53), *That Uncertain Feeling* (Ernst LUBITSCH, 1941), *Stage Door Canteen* (Frank BORZAGE, 1943) and, in more recent years, a documentary of the Kon-Tiki expedition.

**LESTER,** RICHARD (1932– ), US director working mostly in Britain, made television commercials and comedy programmes in America and Britain (where he worked on the television 'Goon Show' series), before directing an independent short comedy *The Running Jumping and Standing Still Film* (1959). This enjoyed unexpected popularity and commercial success, and Lester went on to direct comedy feature films including two starring the BEATLES, A HARD DAY'S NIGHT (1964) and *Help!* (1965), THE KNACK (1965), *How I Won the War* (1967), and *The Bed Sitting Room*

(1969). All were uneven in achievement, sometimes less than happy in their combination of fantasy and social comment; they betray Lester's dependence on cinematic tricks (slow and speeded-up motion, jump cutting, surrealist juxtapositions) rather than control at the time of shooting. *The Three Musketeers* (1974), with an all-star cast, was however an unqualified success, completely realizing Lester's aim of moulding Dumas's romance into a blend of burlesque and satire.

**LETERRIER,** FRANÇOIS (1929–  ), French actor and director, while a student was chosen by BRESSON to play the lead in UN CONDAMNÉ A MORT S'EST ÉCHAPPÉ (1956). After this first contact with cinema Leterrier gave up his studies to become a director; he began as assistant to MALLE, working on *L'Ascenseur pour l'échafaud* (1957) and LES AMANTS (1958). He also worked as assistant to Rappeneau, Etienne Périer, Roger LEENHARDT, and the ALLÉGRET brothers. His first film was an adaptation of Vailland's novel *Les Mauvais Coups* (1960). In 1964 he directed a striking adaptation of a GIONO novel, *Un Roi sans divertissement*.

**LETTER FROM AN UNKNOWN WOMAN,** US, 1948. 1½hr. *Dir* Max Ophuls; *prod* John Houseman for Universal; *scr* Howard Koch, based on the story by Stefan Zweig; *ph* Frank (Franz) Planer; *des* Alexander Golitzen; *cost* Travis Banton; *mus* Daniele Amfitheatrof; *cast* Joan Fontaine (Lisa Berndle), Louis Jourdan (Stefan Brand), Mady Christians (Frau Berndle), Marcel Journet (Johann Stauffer), Art Smith (John), Carol Yorke (Marie).

A bitter-sweet story of unrequited love with Joan FONTAINE giving a touching performance as Lisa, the young girl who hero-worships her handsome neighbour, Stefan. When they meet a few years later, she willingly succumbs to what proves to be a short-lived affair and he disappears from her life again. The film opens with Stefan reading her dying letter to him telling her story and ends with him setting out for almost certain death in a duel with her widowed husband. The ending is OPHULS': in Zweig's original, Stefan still cannot remember who she is.

One of Ophuls' most haunting films, it suggests brilliantly the romantic dream world which Lisa, blind to reality, inhabits. With its evocative re-creation of turn-of-the-century Vienna it is far closer in mood to Ophuls's European work than to the rest of his Hollywood films.

**LETYAT ZHURAVLI** (*The Cranes are Flying*), USSR, 1957. 1½hr. *Dir* Mikhail Kalatozov; *prod* Mosfilm; *scr* V. Rosov; *ph* S. Urusevsky; *cast* Tatiana Samoilova (Veronica), Alexei Batalov (Boris), A. Shvorin (Mark), Vasily Merkuryev (Fyodor Ivanovich).

The story of a love affair destroyed by war, the film won acclaim in the West, and the top prize at CANNES in 1958 as the first evidence of life stirring in Russian cinema in the short liberal respite after 1956. It has no pretentions to making profound statements, but the warm-hearted story, touching or sentimental according to taste, is executed with great exuberance. Some remarkable camera movements are exhilarating, the handling of crowd scenes is assured, the acting of a high standard, and Tatiana SAMOILOVA's performance deservedly brought her international recognition.

**LETZTE MANN, Der** (*The Last Laugh*), Germany, 1924. 1¾hr. *Dir* F. W. Murnau; *prod* Decla Film der UFA; *scr* Carl Mayer; *ph* Karl Freund; *des* Walter Röhrig; *cast* Emil Jannings (the Doorman), Maly Delschaft (his daughter), Hans Unterkirchen (Hotel Manager), Georg John (Night Watchman).

*Der letzte Mann* concerns the spiritual breakdown of an old man after his demotion from hotel porter to lavatory attendant; the loss of uniform deprives him of the focus of his self-respect. The unlikely happy ending was added at the insistence of the producer, Erich POMMER, who felt the film's unrelieved pathos to be dangerously uncommercial.

*Der letzte Mann* excited much attention, and made MURNAU's international reputation, by its technical virtuosity; it is probably the best-known silent film without titles. The use of the moving and subjective camera, hitherto virtually unexploited, are highly developed, allowing a freedom from conventional editing. The film answers to Carl MAYER's specifications for the KAMMERSPIELFILM: dealing with common people and events, observing the classical unities of time, place, and action; but it has a stylization in pictorial composition, settings, and acting harking back to EXPRESSIONISM in films.

**LEVINE,** JOSEPH E. (1905–  ), US executive. Formerly a film exhibitor and distributor, Levine developed into one of America's major foreign film importers when, during the post-war years, he recognized the potential of NEO-REALISM, and brought in numerous Italian films. In 1959 he founded Embassy Pictures Corporation and, in a notoriously extravagant

*Der letzte Mann* (F. W. Murnau, 1924)

nation-wide campaign, promoted the modest Italian spectacle *Hercules* (1959), making a fortune. Levine has since financed many overseas productions, notably OTTO E MEZZO ($8\frac{1}{2}$, 1963) and *La Ciociara* (*Two Women*, 1961), as well as personally producing several Hollywood films, such as *The Carpetbaggers* (1963). In 1968 Embassy Pictures became a subsidiary of the Avco Corporation with Levine maintaining his executive position in the company.

**LEVY,** DON (1932– ), Australian-born director, after studying at the universities of Sydney, Cambridge, and London, made TIME IS (1964), a striking half-hour exposition of the nature of time. His only feature-length film, *Herostratus* (1968), drew considerable acclaim from avant-garde film-makers and critics, even though the delay of two years spent in meticulous editing robbed the film of much of the impact of its genuine originality. His refusal to compromise with commercial standards has made it difficult for him to develop within the industry, although two short films made for Expo '67 at Montreal, *Opus* (not finished by Levy) and *Sources of Power*, a MULTI-

SCREEN production, showed that his early talent was far from exhausted.

**LEWIN,** ALBERT (1895–1968), US producer, director, and writer. During the thirties he was a production executive with METRO-GOLDWYN-MAYER, concerned with THE MUTINY ON THE BOUNTY (1935) and THE GOOD EARTH (1937) among other films. For a short time he was connected with UNITED ARTISTS; one result was *The Moon and Sixpence* (1942), which he wrote and directed. Returning to MGM, he directed *The Picture of Dorian Gray* (1944) from his own script. His later films, which he also produced, were *The Private Affairs of Bel Ami* (1947), *Pandora and the Flying Dutchman* (1951), *Saadia* (1954), and *The Living Idol* (1957); they are marked by an ornate but sometimes fascinating treatment of themes bordering the perverse.

**LEWIS,** JERRY (1926– ), US comedian, real name Joseph Levitch, began his career in cabaret in partnership with Dean MARTIN with whom he went into films in 1949. They made appearances together in *My Friend Irma* (1949), *That's My Boy* (1951), and *Artists and Models* (1955). After they separated, in 1956, Lewis appeared alone in offbeat comedies, some directed by Frank TASHLIN, others by himself. The best of these combine a slapstick skill that matches the masters of silent comedy (in *The Bellboy*, 1960, he remains inarticulate until the final seconds) with an astute social awareness, but often in his own films this is compounded with sentimentality. Films he has directed include *Ladies' Man* (1961), *The Nutty Professor* (1963, see DR JEKYLL AND MR HYDE), *The Patsy* (1965). During the sixties more extreme adherents of the AUTEUR THEORY compared Lewis's work with that of BRESSON and GODARD.

**LEWTON, VAL** (1904–51), US producer, real name Vladimir Leventon, as a child accompanied his mother to the US to join her sister, the actress Alla NAZIMOVA. Before working in the publicity department at METRO-GOLDWYN-MAYER, he was a journalist and popular novel writer. He became a story editor for David O. SELZNICK, then moved to RKO as a producer in 1942.

He was put in charge of a unit to make low-budget horror films; the demands of economy as well as his own narrative flair gave a characteristic stamp to the eleven films he produced in the next four years. They suggested rather than depicted horror, playing on the fear of the undefined instead of depending on shock effects. Jacques TOURNEUR, the director, contributed to the special style of the Lewton films in CAT PEOPLE (1942), *I Walked with a Zombie*, *The Leopard Man*, and *Seventh Victim* (all 1943). *The Curse of the Cat People* (Robert WISE, 1944) was an unusual sequel that focused on a child's imagination; *Isle of the Dead* (Mark ROBSON, 1945) captured the horror of being buried alive. The last films in the series, the costume dramas *The Body Snatchers* (Wise, 1945) and *Bedlam* (Robson, 1946), both contain excellent performances by Boris KARLOFF as well as a feeling for historical period.

Lewton moved to MGM, then to UNIVERSAL, and was briefly associated with Robson and Wise in independent production, but failed to regain the creative liberty which he had enjoyed at RKO.

Joel E. Siegel, *Val Lewton, the reality of terror*, London, 1973.

**LEYDA, JAY** (1910– ), US film historian, studied film-making in the USSR 1933–6 under EISENSTEIN and became his close friend. On his return to the US he devoted much of his time to publishing Eisenstein's theoretical writings. He worked in film archives 1957–69, including Peking and East Berlin, and has lectured in film studies. His published works include *Film form* by Eisenstein, trans and ed Leyda, 1941; *The film sense* by Eisenstein, trans and ed Leyda, 1943; *Kino: a history of the Russian and Soviet film*, 1960; *Lessons with Eisenstein*, by V. Nizhny, trans and ed Leyda and Ivor MONTAGU, 1962; *Films beget films*, an analysis of the COMPILATION film, 1964; *Film essays and a lecture by S. Eisenstein*, trans and ed Leyda, 1970; *Dian ying: electric shadows* (Cambridge, Mass; London, 1972) about Chinese film; and books on Herman Melville, Emily Dickinson and Sergei Rachmaninov.

**L'HERBIER, MARCEL** (1880– ), French director, considered the most representative of the 'Impressionist' group (see AVANT-GARDE), who helped to establish the equality of cinema with other arts. While DELLUC concentrated on the scenario, L'Herbier gave form prominence over content, searching for stylistic innovations, perfect camera angles, and plastic beauty of imagery; he was the first to make systematic use of the blurred image (*flou*). *Eldorado* (1921), about a young Swedish painter, is one of his most successful films. *L'Inhumaine* (1924) was an ambitious film which failed completely, despite the collaboration of Mallet-Stevens, CAVALCANTI, Darius MILHAUD, and Fernand LÉGER. *Feu Mathias Pascal* (1925), after a novel by Pirandello with MOZHUKIN and Michel SIMON in his first film role, was well received; it was less coldly cerebral than his other films, which inspired respect rather than pleasure. L'Herbier succeeded in imposing his own subjective view on the apparent realism of scenes shot in genuine exteriors. The influence of German EXPRESSIONISM unsettled L'Herbier, although he made many films in the thirties. He was founder in 1943 of the INSTITUT DES HAUTES ÉTUDES CINÉMATOGRAPHIQUES (IDHEC). After 1954 he worked for television.

***LIAISONS DANGEUREUSES, Les***, France, 1959. 1¾hr. *Dir* Roger Vadim; *prod* Les Films Marceau; *scr* Roger Vailland, Vadim, Claude Brulé, from the novel (1782) by Choderlos de Laclos; *ph* Marcel Crignon; *cast* Gérard Philipe (Valmont), Jeanne Moreau (Juliette), Annette Vadim (Marianne Tournel), Jeanne Valerie (Cécile Volanges), Simone Renant (Mme Volanges).

Valmont and his wife Juliette encourage each other's infidelities in order to enjoy discussing them. The lightly humorous tone is dissipated when in a series of betrayals the wife is disfigured, the husband murdered, and a virtuous young mother whom he had deserted goes mad. *Liaisons* are indeed *dangeureuses*.

As usual with VADIM, the settings are glamorous, the subject is sex, and his current wife provides anatomical interest. Like the eighteenth-century classic on which it is based, the film aspires after a moral effect but with even less conviction. It has however a visual elegance and engaging style which combine with the fine performances of Gérard PHILIPE and Jeanne MOREAU to make it one of Vadim's more interesting films.

*LIEBELEI*, Germany, 1932. 1½hr. *Dir* Max Ophuls; *prod* Elite-Tonfilm; *scr* Hans Wilhelm, Curt Alexander, from the play by Arthur Schnitzler; *ph* Franz Planer; *mus* Theo Mackeben; *cast* Wolfgang Liebeneiner (Fritz Lobheimer), Magda Schneider (Christine Weiring), Luise Ullrich (Mizi Schlager), Willy Eichberger (Theo Kaiser), Paul Hoerbiger (Hans Weiring), Gustaf Gründgens (Baron Eggerdorff), Olga Tschechowa (Baroness Eggerdorff).

A romantic story of a brief love affair between a young girl and a young officer, ending in tragedy when he is killed in a duel over a married woman. The outstanding film of OPHULS' early (German) career, its most famous sequence, encapsulating the young couple's happiness and love, is a sleigh ride through the snowy woods. Other remarkable passages capture the atmosphere of the relationship almost without dialogue, demonstrating the visual strength of Ophuls' work which, combined with sensitive use of music and sound, helped him to work successfully in a variety of countries and languages.

*LIMELIGHT*, US, 1952. 2½hr. *Dir, prod, scr* Charles Chaplin for United Artists; *asst dir* Robert Aldrich; *ph* Karl Struss, Rollie Totheroh; *des* Eugène Lourié; *ed* Joe Inge; *chor, mus* Chaplin; *cast* Charlie Chaplin (Calvero), Claire Bloom (Terry), Sydney Chaplin Jr (Neville), Nigel Bruce (impresario), Buster Keaton (Calvero's partner).

*Limelight* was CHAPLIN's last film made in the US, the last in which he was in full command of his great acting ability, and the last which merits serious consideration. It is a moving although sometimes over-emphatic portrait of Calvero, once a famous music-hall comedian. Through his friendship with a young and struggling ballet dancer, Terry, he makes a temporary come-back but this is short-lived and he dies of a heart attack in the wings of the stage where Terry is enjoying a triumph. One of the more sentimental of Chaplin's endings, it is appropriate to the backstage story of old talent being inevitably replaced by new. The film is surprisingly verbose, coming from a master of silent film techniques, but it contains the only joint appearance of Chaplin and Buster KEATON in a brief music-hall routine.

Chaplin's theme song 'Eternally' was a great hit, which helped the film's success in Europe, although it failed in the US owing to Chaplin's personal unpopularity at the time.

**LINCOLN, ABRAHAM** (1809–65), sixteenth President of the United States, was portrayed on the screen in the comparatively early years of the American silent film, including an interpretation by Joseph Henaberry incorporated in the vast canvas of GRIFFITH'S THE BIRTH OF A NATION (1915). In a full-scale biography, *Abraham Lincoln* (1924), Lincoln was played by George A. Billings: according to one account, the actor's performance was so impressive that 'he might have been born for the part'. Judge Charles Edward Bull played Lincoln in John FORD'S THE IRON HORSE in the same year. Griffith directed a biography in the early sound period (*Abraham Lincoln*, 1930); it featured a splendid performance by Walter HUSTON, much footage of Civil War action, and a reconstruction of Sheridan's ride. The late thirties saw a number of screen Lincolns, among them John CARRADINE in *Of Human Hearts* (1938), Raymond MASSEY in *Abe Lincoln in Illinois* (1939, *Spirit of the People* in GB), and Henry FONDA in *Young Mr Lincoln* (John Ford, 1939). There have been several films dealing with Lincoln's assassination, including *Suddenly* (1964).

**LINDBLOM, GUNNEL** (1931– ), Swedish actress, made her film début for Gustaf MOLANDER in *Kärlek* (*Love*, 1952). She is particularly associated with films directed by Ingmar BERGMAN, who made good use of her earthy qualities in SMULTRONSTÄLLET (*Wild Strawberries*, 1957), DET SJUNDE INSEGLET (*The Seventh Seal*, 1957), *Jungfrukällen* (*The Virgin Spring*, 1959), *Tystnaden* (*The Silence*, 1963), and *Nattvardsgästerna* (*Winter Light*, 1963). *Rapture* (1965) is her only American film to date. Since 1968 she has worked chiefly in the theatre; her occasional films including Mai ZETTERLING's *Flickorna* (*The Girls*, 1968) and Alf SJÖBERG's *Fadren* (*The Father*, 1969).

**LINDER, MAX** (1883–1925), French comic actor, real name Gabriel Leuvielle, played secondary roles in stage melodramas before joining the PATHÉ company in 1905. He made a number of short comedy films for them, the most important being *Les Débuts d'un patineur* (1908), in which the character of Max the bemused dandy first appeared. After André DEED left France to work in Italy, Linder replaced him as Pathé's chief comedy star. By 1910 he was making a film a week, all featuring Max the impeccable bachelor, living in the lap of luxury, his comic adventures usually sparked off by his pursuit of well-bred, pretty young ladies. At the end of 1910 a Max Linder cinema opened in Paris. Shortly afterwards, the first of several severe illnesses interrupted his film-making and audiences grew uneasy when the supply of fresh films (*Max cherche sa fiancée, Max se marie*) ran out. To reassure his public he appeared in a documentary explaining his absence from the screen (*Max dans sa famille*, 1911). He soon returned in triumph, supplementing his films with personal appearances in the principal cities of Europe. By 1914 he was world-famous: later he became his own producer, selling his films to Pathé by the foot.

At the outbreak of the First World War Linder became a soldier and was slightly wounded while serving at the front. The mere rumour of his death was enough to send France into mourning for a time. In 1916 he left for the US, having signed a contract to make eight films with the ESSANAY company. Only three were completed before he was obliged to return to Europe suffering from pleurisy. In Paris Linder made *Le Petit Café* (1919) before returning to Hollywood where he completed three films, one of which was *The Three Must Get Theres* (1922). In 1923 he made *Au secours!* co-scripted by Abel GANCE. His last completed film, *Le Roi du Cirque* (1924), was made in Vienna. Back in France Linder's health continued to decline and he ultimately committed suicide.

Linder's influence on the development of screen comedy has been widely acknowledged, notably by CHAPLIN. His work is known today chiefly through the COMPILATION film *En Compagnie de Max Linder* (*Laugh with Max Linder*, 1963) assembled by his daughter.

**LINDGREN, ERNEST** (1910–73), British archivist, founder and creator of the NATIONAL FILM ARCHIVE and a pioneer of the international film archive movement (see FÉDÉRATION INTERNATIONALE DES ARCHIVES DE FILM). He joined the newly-formed BRITISH FILM INSTITUTE in 1934, with special responsibility for building a National Film Library. He pioneered the principles of preservation of film material, and throughout his devoted and upright career was associated primarily with those principles, although he was keenly aware of the need for distribution as well as preservation of film. He published many articles on the practice and principle of storing film, and also published *The art of the film* (London, 1948), an introduction to film aesthetics of a scope rare at the time.

**LISTEN TO BRITAIN**, GB, 1942. 20min. *Dir, ed* Humphrey Jennings, Stewart McAllister; *prod* Crown Film Unit; *ph* H. E. Fowle; *sound* Ken Cameron.

In *Listen to Britain*, JENNINGS blended sound and image to create an emotional portrait of Britain at war. Natural sounds, popular songs, and classical music, as well as snatches of 'overheard' conversation, skilfully complement the film's visual element: there is no commentary. Only the addition of an unfortunately tedious spoken prologue mars a powerful and influential film.

**LITTLE CAESAR**, US, 1930. 1¼hr. *Dir* Mervyn LeRoy; *prod* Hal B. Wallis for Warner Bros; *scr* Francis Faragon, based on the novel by W. R. Burnett; *ph* Tony Gaudio; *cast* Edward G. Robinson (Rico Bandell 'Little Caesar'), Sidney Blackner ('Big Boss'), Glenda Farrell (Olga Strassoff), Douglas Fairbanks Jr (Joe Massara), William Collier (Tony Passa), Ralph Ince (Pete Montana).

*Little Caesar*, one of the most influential of the early Hollywood GANGSTER FILMS, shows the rise and fall of a gang boss closely modelled on Al CAPONE. Mervyn LEROY's economical direction, using a restrained, fast-paced, narrative style interspersed with flashes of violence, gives the film lasting quality. Most outstanding, however, is Edward G. ROBINSON's performance, which adds psychological complexity to Rico's vanity and ruthlessness.

**LITTLE FOXES, The**, US, 1941. 2hr. *Dir* William Wyler; *prod* Samuel Goldwyn for RKO Radio; *scr* Lillian Hellman; *ph* Gregg Toland; *des* Stephen Goosson; *cast* Bette Davis (Regina Giddens), Herbert Marshall (Horace Giddens), Teresa Wright (Alexandra Giddens), Richard Carlson (David Hewitt), Patricia Collinge (Birdie Hubbard), Dan Duryea (Leo Hubbard), Charles Dingle (Ben Hubbard).

Lillian HELLMAN herself scripted the adaptation of her stage play about the hollow triumph of a vicious and avaricious woman in a small Southern town. An example of GOLDWYN's lavish precision at its finest, *The Little Foxes* has lost nothing with the passing of time: it may be regarded as both WYLER's best film and Bette DAVIS's best performance.

In addition to Bette Davis's *tour de force*, the film was remarkable for its dramatic power, period detail, high pictorial quality (superb photography by Gregg TOLAND), and the strength of the supporting performances.

**LITTLEWOOD, JOAN** (1916– ), British theatre director chiefly known for her Theatre Workshop, a left-wing theatre group in the East End of London. She directed the film version of *Sparrows Can't Sing* (1963) and films have been made of other Theatre Workshop productions, notably OH! WHAT A LOVELY WAR (1969).

**LITVAK, ANATOLE** (1902– ), Russian-born director whose early work in Germany in the twenties featured stars such as Lilian HARVEY and Jan KIEPURA. He worked in France, notably on *L'Équipage* (1934) with Annabella and Jean-Pierre Aumont and his famous version of *Mayerling* (1936) with Danielle DARRIEUX and Charles BOYER. He then moved to Hollywood, making first *The Woman I Love* (1937, *The Woman Between* in GB), an emotional drama set in wartime France with aerial sequences as its big action set-pieces, starring Paul MUNI and Miriam HOPKINS. Between 1938 and 1941 he directed a number of films for WARNER BROS, including *Tovarich* (1937) with Claudette COLBERT and Charles Boyer; *The Amazing Dr Clitterhouse* (1938) and *Confessions of a Nazi Spy* (1939), both with Edward G. ROBINSON; and two Bette DAVIS films, *The Sisters* (1938) and *All This and Heaven Too* (1940). During the war Litvak collaborated with Frank CAPRA on the WHY WE FIGHT series. In 1947 he directed *The Long Night*, a remake of LE JOUR SE LÈVE (1939), and informed opinion vehemently attacked the vandalism that suppressed CARNÉ's film in the interests of the Hollywood version. *Sorry, Wrong Number* (1948), an overblown version of a dramatic short radio play, contrasted poorly with the tense original in spite of a good performance by Barbara STANWYCK, but Litvak caused something of a stir the same year with *The Snake Pit*, a clinical case history implicitly condemning American mental hospital treatment, with a strong performance by Olivia DE HAVILLAND.

In 1955 Litvak directed *The Deep Blue Sea* in Britain and in the sixties largely returned to filming in Europe, where his work has included *The Night of the Generals* (1966) and *La Dame dans l'auto avec des lunettes et un fusil* (1970). He has with some justice been termed an 'international' director: he is an aloof figure, independent of current fashion, whose work is generally well, if not highly, regarded.

*LIVES OF A BENGAL LANCER, The,* US, 1935. 1¾hr. *Dir* Henry Hathaway; *prod* Paramount; *scr* Waldemar Young, John L. Balderstone, Achmed Abdullah; *ph* Charles Lang; *cast* Gary Cooper (Lt McGregor), Franchot Tone (Lt Forsythe), Richard Cromwell (Lt Stone), Sir Guy Standing (Col Stone), C. Aubrey Smith (Maj Hamilton), Kathleen Burke (Tania Volkanskaya), Douglas Dumbrille (Mohammed Khan), Monte Blue (Hamzulla Khan), Colin Tapley (Lt Barrett), Akim Tamiroff (Emir), Lumsden Hare (Maj-Gen Woodley).

A full-blooded and highly popular adventure film set on the North-West Frontier, and based (remotely) on a somewhat mystical novel by Major W. Yeats-Brown. Its stiff-upper-lip story of life in the 41st Bengal Lancers, handled by the leading players with a nicely judged bantering air, included capture, imprisonment, and torture; a cavalry charge and the destruction of the enemy stronghold form the climax. The location work was reputedly by Ernest B. SCHOEDSACK who is said to have shot some 200,000 feet of film over a period of eight months spent in Peshawar, Afghanistan, and the Khyber Pass region.

*LIVING* see IKIRU

**LIZZANI, CARLO** (1917– ), Italian director, initially a journalist, began his film career as a scriptwriter, collaborating with DE SANTIS and ROSSELLINI in the late forties. His best film was his first, *Achtung banditi!* (1951) with Gina LOLLOBRIGIDA. Since then his Marxist ideology has disturbed the balance of his work.

**LLOYD, FRANK** (1889–1960), Scottish-born US director, began his career as an actor in England but worked in Hollywood from 1910. During the First World War he directed a number of Westerns starring William Farnum, or his brother Dustin, including *The Virginian* (1914), and he became associated with well-made commercial films. His work was diverse but showed an evident predilection for literary subjects (including *A Tale of Two Cities*, 1917; *Les Misérables*, 1918; *Oliver Twist*, 1922), and for costume pieces set at sea or with a firm action basis (*Eagle of the Sea*, 1926; THE MUTINY ON THE BOUNTY, 1935; *Under Two Flags*, 1936). He continued to make Westerns, notably *Wells Fargo* (1937). Other important films included his versions of Noël COWARD's *Cavalcade* (1933) and Rex Beach's gold-rush story *The Spoilers* (1942), starring Marlene DIETRICH, John WAYNE, and Randolph SCOTT.

**LLOYD, HAROLD** (1893–1971), US comedian, appeared on the stage from the age of four. In 1914, with Hal ROACH, he set up a production company (Rolin) to make short comedy films. He also appeared for a time as a member of Mack SENNETT's comedy troupe. 'Lonesome Luke', Lloyd's screen character, was at first much influenced by Charlie CHAPLIN, but by the end of 1917 he had adopted the straw hat, horn-rimmed glasses, and conventional suit that became his trade-mark. Between 1917 and early 1919 he made a hundred or so shorts and then embarked on features: among the best were *Grandma's Boy* (1922), *Safety Last* (1923), *The Freshman* (1925), *For Heaven's Sake* (1926), and *The Kid Brother* (1927). He cultivated the screen personality of the clean-cut American boy, a trifle clumsy, apparently a loser in the race for success and the hand of a fair maiden (Bebe DANIELS in earlier films, later Mildred Davis). By sheer energy, inspired invention, and dogged determination, however, he always wins through. Lloyd was an expert STUNTMAN, performing his athletic gags without a double in spite of severe injuries to one hand incurred early in his career when a property bomb exploded prematurely.

Unlike many silent screen comedians, Lloyd achieved the transition to sound, complementing his carefully developed gags with a bland, boyish voice that suited his screen personality. *Movie Crazy* (1932), in particular, bears comparison with the best of his silent work. *The Sins of Harold Diddlebock/Mad Wednesday* (1947), directed by Preston STURGES, was a screwball comedy, a departure from Lloyd's usual type of humour. The image that endures is of Lloyd hanging on with diffident aplomb to the face of a skyscraper over a giddy drop: in fact, of the three hundred films he made only five have such sequences, but their preponderance in the two compilations he made from his films, *World of Comedy* (1963) and *Funny Side of Life* (1963), has tended to exaggerate their actual frequency.

Lloyd was an efficient business man—like Chaplin he retained the rights of his films—and at the time of his death owned one of the largest estates in Hollywood. He was active in support of Republican politics in California and was president of the Shriners.

**LOACH,** KEN (1936– ), British director, worked with the BBC in the sixties, and gained experience and distinction in television drama, particularly with *Up the Junction*, *The Big Flame*, and *In Two Minds*, all produced by Tony GARNETT as part of the Wednesday Play series. Another Wednesday Play, *Cathy Come Home* (1966), a documentary-style drama about homelessness, brought him the Italia Festival Prize, an international reputation, and, eventually, backing for his first feature film *Poor Cow* (1968).

Loach left the BBC in 1968 to set up Kestrel Films, taking with him a group of people, Tony Garnett among them, who shared his democratic approach to film-making and his radical attitude to political issues such as housing, education, and workers' control. His work with Kestrel has included a number of television plays as well as the feature films KES (1970) and *Family Life* (1971); the latter uses the theories of Laingian psychiatry to indicate the possible causes of mental breakdown.

Loach's work is best characterized by his stated desire 'to clarify the lives of ordinary people'. He prefers to work on location, often using non-actors.

**LOCATION,** any place other than the studio where filming occurs. A film crew working indoors or in the open air away from the studio or its grounds (known as 'the lot') is said to be 'on location'. That a term for non-studio photography exists at all suggests the degree to which the fictional cinema has in the past avoided filming under conditions of reality.

Early film-makers, seeking sunlight to register on their insensitive negative stock, shot out of doors wherever possible. The exteriors of THE GREAT TRAIN ROBBERY (1903) were made on location near West Orange, New Jersey. Most of the classic silent comedy chases took place in the streets of Los Angeles and its suburbs among real traffic and pedestrians. But as lighting and scene design techniques improved, producers increasingly abandoned the uncertainties of location work and took refuge in the controllable conditions of the studio. The introduction of sound made location shooting, with its extraneous noise, impossible for a time except for long shots and action shots without dialogue. During the twenties, thirties, and forties directors like F. W. MURNAU and Alfred HITCHCOCK went so far as to build elaborate models rather than venture out of doors (as in SUNRISE, 1927, and most of THE LADY VANISHES, 1938). It was considered revolutionary when in 1945, under the influence of Italian NEO-REALISM, *The House on 92nd Street* included a number of shots photographed on New York's 92nd Street, although the interiors were shot in a Hollywood studio. After the Second World War a movement back to location filming began, partly in reaction to television competition, and by the sixties it was common for entire films to be made away from the studio, sometimes under unbearably difficult conditions. WIDE-ANGLE LENSES and portable lights made it possible to shoot even in cramped apartments and moving vehicles. Today most directors prefer location filming for the stimulation afforded by the presence of reality. But reality can still be avoided, even on location: for a large-budget film a street, village, or part of a city may be constructed in some scenic area and destroyed afterwards, or donated to the local authority as in David LEAN's *Ryan's Daughter* (1971).

The complexity of filming makes extended location work a difficult logistical exercise for the producer and often the physical organization is undertaken by a sub-contractor. He must provide full technical equipment, with spares in case of breakdown, and facilities for viewing the RUSHES regularly. All modern conveniences must be available for the cast and crew, temporarily deprived of their home life and unused to roughing it. Despite the difficulties, location work is often welcomed as an escape from management interference and private responsibilities. The holiday atmosphere can spiral out of control, with delightful or disastrous consequences for the film.

**LOCKWOOD,** MARGARET (1916– ), British actress of conventional brunette beauty, who enjoyed a considerable vogue as the stereotyped villainess of *The Man in Grey* (1943), *The Wicked Lady* (1945), and other GAINSBOROUGH costume melodramas. She made valiant efforts to widen her range of parts, but most of her later films were mediocre and she gave up the cinema for theatre and television. Her daughter Julia (b. 1941) is also an actress.

**LODEN,** BARBARA (1936– ), US actress and director, made her Broadway début in an *ingénue* part in *Compulsion* (1957). Her most important stage role was that of Maggie—the character based on Marilyn MONROE—in Arthur MILLER's play *After the Fall* (1964). Her first film appearance was in *Wild River* (1960), directed by Elia KAZAN, whom she later married. She also appeared in his *Splendour in the Grass* (1961). In 1970 she produced and directed her own film *Wanda*, a perceptive and moving study of an inarticulate, inept, yet undespairing woman drifting through a vapid existence.

**LÓDŹ** FILM SCHOOL (Panstwowa Wyzsza Szkola Teatraina Filmowa) was set up by the Polish government in 1947, at first in Kraków, then in Lódź; the production departments were later moved to Warsaw. Its establishment was a part of the acknowledgement of the importance of cinema in Polish political and cultural life and was a vital part of the remarkable recovery of the film industry in Poland after the Second World War.

Students, who must have a good general education, are selected by individual interview and examination to assess their potential as creative artists. Foreign students are accepted. The course lasts six years in all, the last two years being spent working under supervision in the studios of Film Polski. Teamwork is emphasized: a student, however brilliant, unable to work within a group would be unlikely to survive the first probationary year. Courses are conducted in directing, production, camerawork, acting, film theory. Students begin working in short film, some of their exercises attaining a standard high enough for commercial distribution. A diploma from Lódź is necessary for anyone wishing to enter the industry.

The teachers at Lódź are all professional filmmakers: they have included Aleksander FORD, Wanda JAKUBOWSKA, and Antoni BOHDIEWICZ. Among former students who have returned to teach are Andrzej WAJDA, Andrzej MUNK, and Roman POLAŃSKI. In its early years Lódź was shaped by its first principal Jerzy Toeplitz assisted by Jerzy BOSSAK: Toeplitz became a world authority on film education. Neither remained at Lódź after the political upheavals of 1968, when Toeplitz was succeeded by Boleslav Lewicki. (See FILM SCHOOLS.)

**LOEW,** MARCUS (1870–1927), US executive, began acquiring theatre property in 1899. In collaboration with Joseph and Nicholas SCHENCK and Adolph ZUKOR, Loew built up a vast theatre chain which in 1910 became Loew's Consolidated Enterprises (re-named Loew's Incorporated in 1919). Loew bought the Metro production company in 1920 and presided over its merger with the Goldwyn and Mayer firms. Loew's Inc became the parent company of the METRO-GOLDWYN-MAYER studio and one of America's largest theatre-owning organizations.

**LOGAN,** JOSHUA (1908– ), US director, best known for his translations of successful stage plays to the screen. *Picnic* (1955), BUS STOP (1956), and *South Pacific* (1958), all of which he had directed on Broadway, showed his skill in handling actors, but he is not always able to make his preferred theatrical material entirely viable in cinematic terms. The large-scale productions he has specialized in, including *Sayonara* (1957), FANNY (1960), and *Camelot* (1967), have tended to weightiness; *Paint Your Wagon* (1969), an extravagant musical costing over $20 million, failed to convey the vigour of the original stage play.

*LOLA,* France/Italy, 1961. Franscope; 1½hr. *Dir, scr* Jacques Demy; *prod* Rome-Paris Films/ Euro-International; *ph* Raoul Coutard; *mus* Michel Legrand, Beethoven, Bach, Mozart, Weber; *cast* Anouk Aimée (Lola), Marc Michel (Roland), Jacques Harden (Michel), Elina Labourdette (Mme Desnoyers).

A dream-like story of love lost and found, *Lola* brought international recognition to Jacques DEMY as a young director of individuality and skill. The film is dedicated to Max OPHULS, and in its structural formality is reminiscent of LA RONDE (1950); but the seriousness underlying Demy's fairy-tale is entirely his own. Anouk AIMÉE's performance is integral to the film's particular quality. She repeated the role in a continuation of the story, *The Model Shop* (1968), made in the US.

*LOLA MONTÈS,* France/West Germany, 1955. CinemaScope; 2¼hr; Eastman Color. *Dir* Max

Ophuls; *prod* Gamma Films-Florida/Oska Films; *scr* Ophuls and Annette Wademant from the story by Cecil St-Laurent; *ph* Christian Matras; *des* Jean d'Eaubonne; *cost* Marcel Escoffier, Georges Annenkov; *mus* Georges Auric; *cast* Martine Carol (Lola Montès), Peter Ustinov (Circus Master), Anton Walbrook (King Ludwig), Ivan Desny (James), Oskar Werner (the student).

The film opens with Lola Montès reduced to appearing in a circus and answering the audience's questions about her 'notorious past'. As she answers, flashbacks show her unhappy marriage and her affairs with Liszt, Ludwig of Bavaria, and a young student. At the close of the film, she is seen seated in a cage outside which a queue waits to kiss her hand for the price of a dollar.

For many years OPHULS' last film was shown only in a heavily cut ninety-minute version that dispensed with the vital flashback structure. The original dream-like conception has since been restored, but the full 140-minute version seems to be lost. With the aid of his cameraman Christian MATRAS, Ophuls made brilliant use of the new facilities of CINEMASCOPE and colour (it was his only colour film), using masking and other devices to vary the screen area. The elaborate camera movements typical of Ophuls' films include here a 360° camera revolve around Lola as she begins her first flashback reminiscence and a remarkable series of vertical crane shots as she goes to meet the man her mother intends her to marry. Although weakened by the performance of Martine CAROL and, perhaps, over-praised because of the circumstances surrounding its first appearance, it nonetheless provided a worthy end to a distinguished career.

**LOLITA**, GB, 1962. 2½hr. *Dir* Stanley Kubrick; *prod* James B. Harris; *scr* Vladimir Nabokov, from his novel; *ph* Oswald Morris; *cast* James Mason (Humbert Humbert), Shelley Winters (Mrs Haze), Peter Sellers (Quilty), Sue Lyon (Lolita).

The screen adaptation of Nabokov's study in perverse love demanded concessions to public and official sensibilities, particularly in raising the age of the 'nymphet' heroine to make her acceptable as the romantic object of a middle-aged man. This moved the emphasis of the plot from Humbert's fatal passion to his fear of disapproving society and in particular to his nightmare flight from his rival, Quilty. The journey across America, forming the central section of the film, provides the basis for KUBRICK's characteristically wry observation of the rootlessness of contemporary American society.

**LOLLOBRIGIDA**, GINA (1927–  ), Italian actress, after winning a beauty contest, was given small parts in several Italian films. Howard HUGHES invited her to Hollywood, but she refused a long-term contract, preferring to return to Italy, where she appeared in *Achtung banditi!* (Carlo LIZZANI, 1951), and, among others, *La città si difende* (Pietro GERMI, 1951). In *Fanfan la Tulipe* (CHRISTIAN-JAQUE, 1951) and René CLAIR's LES BELLES DE NUIT (1952) she was widely admired for the warmth of her acting allied to her physical attractions and she reached international star status, working in Italy, France, and the US, including an appearance for John HUSTON in BEAT THE DEVIL (1953).

**LOMBARD**, CAROLE (1908–42), US actress, real name Jane Alice Peters, who appeared as a child in Allan DWAN's *A Perfect Crime* (1921). She returned to films in 1925 and made two-reelers with Mack SENNETT in 1927–8, before moving on to some initially rather undistinguished feature films. A distinctive beauty and *comédienne*, she played a wide range of successful parts, but is best remembered for a brilliant series of SCREWBALL comedy performances. TWENTIETH CENTURY (1934), in which she played a temperamental actress, made her a star; three other films mixed comedy with varying amounts of pointed satire, about American society in MY MAN GODFREY (1936) and NOTHING SACRED (1937), and more seriously in her last film LUBITSCH's *To Be or Not To Be* (1942) about Nazi-occupied Poland. She was killed in an air crash while touring America to sell War Bonds. She was married to Clark GABLE.

**LONDON FILM PRODUCTIONS,** British production company, formed in 1932 by Alexander KORDA, the actor George Grossmith, the author Lajos Biro, and several British financiers. It infused new life into the ailing British film industry with productions such as THE PRIVATE LIFE OF HENRY VIII (1933), THINGS TO COME (1936), and REMBRANDT (1936). Briefly lodged at Korda's DENHAM STUDIOS, the company attracted able people from Britain, Hollywood, and Europe; producers included Erich POMMER and Victor SAVILLE; directors, Paul CZINNER, Jacques FEYDER, and Robert FLAHERTY; writers, Graham GREENE and H. G. Wells; and actors such as Elisabeth BERGNER, Marlene DIETRICH, Robert DONAT, Charles LAUGHTON, Vivien LEIGH, Laurence OLIVIER, and Conrad VEIDT.

Dissolved in 1939 and re-formed after the war, the second London Films provided a temporary home (Shepperton Studios) for independent film-makers: among them, Carol REED, David LEAN, Frank LAUNDER and Sidney GILLIAT, Michael POWELL and Emeric PRESS-

BURGER, and the BOULTING brothers. The most notable productions of the post-war years included ANNA KARENINA (1948), THE FALLEN IDOL (1948), THE THIRD MAN (1949), *Hobson's Choice* (1954), *Summer Madness* (1955, *Summertime* in the US), and *Richard III* (1955).

London Film Productions was strictly speaking a one-man operation, and on Korda's death in 1956 the company ceased production. The name London Films was revived in 1961 for a company distributing Korda's films.

## LONDON FILM SOCIETY see FILM SOCIETY

**LONG,** HUEY P. (1893–1935), Governor of Louisiana 1928–33, published his autobiography *Every man a king* in 1933. He served as a Senator from 1931 until his assassination in 1935: he was active in public works and was frequently criticized for corrupt practices. Several novels based on his life were published, including Robert Penn Warren's ALL THE KING'S MEN (1946), filmed under the same title by Robert ROSSEN in 1949.

***LONG HOT SUMMER, The,*** US, 1958. CinemaScope; 2hr; Eastman Color. *Dir* Martin Ritt; *prod* Twentieth Century-Fox; *scr* Irving Ravetch, Harriet Frank Jr, based on *The Hamlet* by William Faulkner; *ph* Joseph LaShelle; *cast* Paul Newman (Ben Quick), Joanne Woodward (Clara Varner), Anthony Franciosa (Jody), Orson Welles (Varner), Angela Lansbury (Minnie).

Disparate incidents from short stories by William FAULKNER are intelligently amalgamated to depict conflict within the family of Varner, town boss of a small Mississippi community. Although undeniably an actors' piece, *The Long Hot Summer* shows how perceptively Martin RITT handles intimate relationships.

***LOOK BACK IN ANGER,*** GB, 1959. 1¾hr. *Dir* Tony Richardson; *prod* Woodfall; *scr* Nigel Kneale from the play by John Osborne; *ph* Oswald Morris; *cast* Richard Burton (Jimmy Porter), Claire Bloom (Helena Charles), Mary Ure (Alison Porter), Edith Evans (Mrs Tanner), Gary Raymond (Cliff).

John OSBORNE's play brought the phrases 'angry young man' and 'anti-hero' into common usage, and the character of Jimmy Porter and the events that befall him—his rejection of his upper-class wife and the values she represents, his affair with the friend who urged the separation, the wife's miscarriage and their tentative reconciliation—were moulded into a fine screenplay by Nigel Kneale. The play had laid greater stress on the attitudes of the characters and the poses they struck, but the film was content to concentrate on the human relationships. Richard BURTON's assumption of a star role unfortunately upset the film's balance. However, the work was seen as a promising beginning for Tony RICHARDSON.

**LOOP.** In CAMERAS and PROJECTORS, the loop is the length of slack film between the upper sprocket and the gate and between the gate and the lower sprocket. This slack allows the film to change from continuous motion through the sprocket to intermittent motion at the gate and back again, without being torn.

In production, a length of film spliced head to tail in a continuous loop is often used where a shot or sequence must be repeated regularly

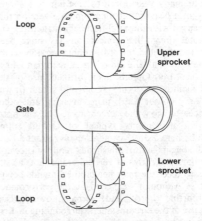

without pause for rewinding. With very short films such as television commercials, this permits sound DUBBING or MIXING, and bulk release printing, with little waste of time. Short educational films are similarly printed in bulk on loops lasting four minutes (often known as 'concept loops' because they deal with a single subject or concept). These must be shown through a special projector.

**LOOS,** ANITA (*c.*1893– ), US writer, sold her first screenplays while still in her teens. The first to be filmed was *The New York Hat* (1912), directed by D. W. GRIFFITH and starring Mary PICKFORD. Griffith engaged her as a staff writer at BIOGRAPH and she later moved with him first to MUTUAL, then to TRIANGLE, but he did not direct any more of the light satirical comedies that were her forte. Douglas FAIRBANKS was the perfect exponent of her tongue-in-cheek romances: they were directed by John Emerson whom she later married and who generally received a co-writer's credit. She also wrote narrative titles, notably for MACBETH and INTOLER-

ANCE (both 1916). In the mid-twenties Loos and Emerson left Hollywood and she wrote only sporadically for films. Her famous novel GENTLEMEN PREFER BLONDES was published in 1925; it was an immediate hit and was filmed twice, in 1928 and in 1953. Her autobiography *A girl like I* (New York, 1966) gives a racy, witty, and astute picture of the jazz age; *Kiss Hollywood goodbye* (London, 1974) entertainingly recalls her time in films.

**LORD OF THE FLIES**, GB, 1963. 1¼hr. *Dir* Peter Brook; *prod* Allen Hodgson/Two Arts; *scr* Peter Shaffer; *ph* Tom Hollyman, Gerald Feil; *cast* James Aubrey (Ralph), Tom Chapin (Jack), Hugh Edwards (Piggy).

William Golding's novel had a chequered career before falling into the hands of Peter BROOK who finally co-wrote, directed, and edited the film. EALING STUDIOS originally bought the property and re-sold it to Sam SPIEGEL for $60,000; Spiegel originally intended to produce the film himself, but ultimately relinquished his rights and allowed the young producer Lewis Allen to take over. The film was shot on a minute budget on location in Puerto Rico and neighbouring islands and edited in France. After a two-year struggle, the film opened to mixed reviews.

Golding's allegory about a group of schoolchildren who survive a plane crash and are reduced to savages in an embryo society transferred uneasily to the screen. The film had undeniable dramatic power, but it was marred by the awkwardness of an amateur cast and the feeling that it had become so much of a *cause célèbre* that Brook was no longer able to be as objective in his direction as was necessary.

**LOREN**, SOPHIA (1934– ), Italian actress, real name Sophia Scicoloni, after winning a beauty contest, appeared as an extra for some time before progressing to supporting roles. She first attracted wide notice in *La donna del fiume* (*Woman of the River*, Mario SOLDATI, 1955), and has since earned respect in both dramatic and comedy parts. Among the former *La Ciociara* (*Two Women*, Vittorio DE SICA, 1961), is outstanding, while in *The Millionairess* (Anthony ASQUITH, 1960) her performance had a rare quality of elegant slapstick. A versatile and professional actress, Loren has also worked for other notable directors including Carol REED (*The Key*, 1958), Anthony MANN (EL CID, 1961), and CHAPLIN (*A Countess from Hong Kong*, 1966), and has beome one of the major box office stars. She married Carlo PONTI in 1957.

**LORENTZ**, PARE (1905– ), US director and producer of documentaries, was originally a journalist and film critic. His first film, THE PLOW THAT BROKE THE PLAINS (1936), was made for a government department, the Resettlement Administration, concerned with the agricultural and concomitant social problems of the Dust Bowl. THE RIVER (1937) was another plea for conservation. In these films Lorentz made a distinct contribution to documentary technique by his use of rhythmic editing, meticulously matching the narration and images to Virgil THOMSON's music. In 1938, at the instigation of President Roosevelt, the United States Film Service was founded, with Lorentz as director—the first such organization in the US. Lorentz's final major film as a director was the feature-length *The Fight for Life* (1940), which dramatically depicted the work of the Chicago Maternity Centre amidst the social problems of malnutrition and slum housing.

The US Film Service produced two more films. In *Power and the Land* (1940), Joris IVENS advocated the increased electrification of agriculture. Robert FLAHERTY dealt with the problem of soil erosion and techniques of conservation in THE LAND (1941). Long resented by Hollywood and accused of New Deal propagandizing, the Film Service was closed by Congress in June 1940. During the war, Lorentz and his cameraman Floyd CROSBY produced training films for the US Air Corps. In 1946, he became Chief of Motion Pictures, Music, and Theatre in US-occupied Germany, and produced *The Nuremberg Trials*. He has since controlled a film consultancy business in New York.

**LORRE**, PETER (1904–64), Hungarian-born actor, real name Laszlo Löwenstein, ran away from home at fifteen to become an actor. After some lean early years he worked in theatres in Vienna and Zurich. His first film part was in Germany in *Frühlingserwachen* (*Spring Awakening*, 1928). Fritz LANG gave him the major role in M (1931) where his small stature and protruding eyes contributed to his sad and memorable portrait of a sexual psychopath.

He left Germany for Britain in 1933 and played the anarchist in HITCHCOCK's THE MAN WHO KNEW TOO MUCH (1934). In 1935 he went to Hollywood where he appeared in STERNBERG's CRIME AND PUNISHMENT (1935) and played John Marquand's Oriental detective in the MR MOTO film series (1937–9). John HUSTON cast him as Joel Cairo in THE MALTESE FALCON (1941); his cruel yet child-like suavity attracted attention and brought him featured roles in such films as CASABLANCA (1943), *Arsenic and Old Lace* (1944), and *Confidential Agent* (1945). Unhappy with his career, however, he went back to Europe in 1949 and in Hamburg wrote, produced, and directed *Der Verlorene* (*The Lost*

*One*, 1951) about a homicidal Nazi scientist; he returned to Hollywood in 1953. Films of the later part of his career include BEAT THE DEVIL (1953), *Silk Stockings* (1957), *A Comedy of Terrors*, and *The Raven* (both 1963).

**LOSEY**, JOSEPH (1909– ), US director, worked on a number of Federal-backed theatre projects during the thirties and supervised educational films for the Rockefeller Foundation before making a short film *Pete Roleum and his Cousins* in 1939. In 1947 he directed a stage production of BRECHT's *Galileo Galilei*, then went to Hollywood to make his first feature film *The Boy with Green Hair* (1948), an allegory about racial intolerance and the effects of war. This was followed by four thrillers with social themes: *The Lawless* (1950, *The Dividing Line* in GB), *The Prowler* (1951), M (1951), a remake of Fritz LANG's film, and *The Big Night* (1951). Losey's left-wing sympathies and his association with, among others, Brecht and Adrian Scott, one of the Hollywood Ten, led to his being blacklisted (see UNAMERICAN ACTIVITIES). He moved to Europe where, after making three films under various pseudonyms, he was able to direct *Time without Pity* (1957) in England under his own name. The melodramatic *The Gypsy and the Gentleman* (1958) and *Blind Date* (1959), a thriller, were both concerned with aspects of the British class system, a theme recurrent in his work. THE CRIMINAL (1960), a tough crime drama, was followed by *Eva* (*Eve*, 1962), which the French producers mercilessly cut and dubbed.

Losey returned to England to make THE SERVANT (1963) which established him as a director of considerable importance. The film was criticized in some quarters for its pessimism and, with some justice, for the ornate character of its visual style. *The Servant* was Losey's first film to be written by Harold PINTER; Dirk BOGARDE, who has given some of his best performances for Losey, played a leading role, and the designer was Richard MacDonald, another frequent collaborator.

*King and Country* (1964) again starred Bogarde as the defending officer in a First World War court-martial; a grim, relentless work, like *The Criminal* it demonstrates Losey's debt to Stanley KUBRICK. *Modesty Blaise* (1966), a comic-strip parody of spy thrillers, superficially uncharacteristic, can be seen as an ironic thrust at contemporary values. ACCIDENT (1967), Losey's next collaboration with Pinter, did not entirely penetrate the social milieu under scrutiny, though the camerawork was less assertive than in *The Servant*. His more flamboyant style was resumed for the baroque *Boom* and *Secret Ceremony* (both 1968), enjoyable extravaganzas dealing with domination and madness respectively and both containing opulent performances by Elizabeth TAYLOR. *Figures in a Landscape* (1970), a generally underrated film, returned to the master–slave relationship explored in *The Servant*, though placing it in a different class; it is unusual in Losey's work in being placed in exterior and characterless locations rather than the enclosed interiors he appears to prefer. THE GO-BETWEEN (1971) was Losey's first film to meet with unanimous critical praise. It marks a culmination of Losey's interest in English class structures, hitherto an important but uneasily-expressed part of his work. Since then he has directed *The Assassination of Trotsky* (1972) and an adaptation of Ibsen's *A Doll's House* (1973).

Losey has become skilled in choosing regular collaborators—Bogarde, Pinter, MacDonald, Stanley BAKER, John DANKWORTH, cameraman Gerry Fisher, playwright Alun Owen, designer Carmen Dillon, among them—who, talented in their own right, are ready to subsume their abilities into his characteristic vision. His career has shown a remarkable consistency of thematic content: domination, intrusion, corruption have recurrently been used to illustrate the social determination of moral choices. His examination of human psychology, is, however, sometimes inhibited by his essentially pessimistic philosophy and distracted by his camera's concentration on the superficial. His best achievements, with the possible exception of *The Go-Between*, have eschewed the subject of English upper-class life.

**LOST PATROL, The**, US, 1934. 1¼hr. *Dir* John Ford; *prod* Merian C. Cooper for RKO Radio; *scr* Dudley Nichols, Garrett Fort, from the story *Patrol* by Phillip MacDonald; *ph* Harold Wenstrom; *mus* Max Steiner; *cast* Victor McLaglen (Sergeant), Boris Karloff (Sanders), Wallace Ford (Morelli), Reginald Denny (George Brown), J. M. Kerrigan (Quincannon), Billy Bevan (Herbert Hale), Alan Hale (Cook), Brandon Hurst (Bell).

During the First World War, a British patrol goes astray in the Mesopotamian desert. Unseen Arab snipers pick them off, until only the Sergeant remains alive. John FORD's first collaboration with Dudley NICHOLS to receive critical notice used fine character studies to convey the men's plight. The film was shot on location in the Yuma desert in only two weeks; this economy, and that of the narrative construction, adds to the suspense a sense of grim inevitability.

**LOST WEEKEND, The**, US, 1945. 1¾hr. *Dir* Billy Wilder; *prod* Paramount; *scr* Charles Brackett, Wilder, from the novel by Charles R.

Jackson; *ph* John F. Seitz; *cast* Ray Milland (Don Birnam), Jane Wyman (Helen), Howard da Silva (Nat), Philip Terry (Wick Birnam), Doris Dowling (Gloria).

Hollywood's first film to deal seriously with alcoholism was shocking for its time and succeeded (in spite of an unconvincingly optimistic ending) by its uncompromisingly unromantic approach. WILDER's control of narrative pace, inexorably slow in contrast to the crackling speed of his comedies, and his authoritative handling of location shooting in the New York streets and a hospital for alcoholics, marked his emergence as a director of unusual skill. Ray MILLAND, usually a romantic leading man, gave his best performance as the alcoholic and was awarded one of the film's four OSCARS.

**LOTAR,** ELI (1905– ), French cameraman and director, who began his career in the cinema in 1925 as an extra before becoming the photographer of such films as CAVALCANTI's *Le Petit Chaperon rouge* (1929), Joris IVENS's *Zuiderzee* (1930), and Luis BUÑUEL's LAS HURDES (*Land Without Bread*, 1932). As director, Lotar has made many short films, often for publicity purposes, the most notable being his documentary *Aubervilliers* (1945), scripted by Jacques PRÉVERT.

**LOUISIANA STORY,** US, 1948. 1¼hr. *Dir, prod* Robert J. Flaherty for Standard Oil Company (US); *scr* Frances and Robert J. Flaherty; *ph* Richard Leacock; *ed* Helen van Dongen; *mus* Virgil Thomson; *cast* Joseph Boudreaux (boy), Lionel LeBlanc, Frank Hardy.

FLAHERTY's last film describes the coming of oil men to the swamplands of Louisiana as seen through the eyes of a young boy, Alexander Napoleon Ulysses Latour. With rhythmic, poetic images, the film sets up the mood and atmosphere of the swamps and explains the intricate technical process of oil-drilling. In translating his story to the screen, Flaherty was greatly assisted by his cameraman, Richard LEACOCK, his editor, Helen VAN DONGEN and his composer, Virgil THOMSON. It is an appropriate footnote to the film that when the young hero grew up, he became an oil driller himself.

*LOVE* see SZERELEM

**LOVE,** BESSIE (1898– ), US actress, real name Juanita Horton, who made her first film appearance in INTOLERANCE (1916). She has had a long and remarkably varied career as a star in America and as a supporting actress in England where she moved in 1935. She was often cast in childish or tomboy roles, such as the crippled orphan in *Forget Me Not* (1922); other parts

included a drug-addicted mother in *Human Wreckage* (1923) and a gangster's moll in *Those Who Dance* (1924). With the coming of talkies she had considerable success as a musical star beginning with, and especially in, THE BROADWAY MELODY (1929). In recent years her distinctive voice with its attractive gurgle has become very familiar in British theatre and television, as well as films, notably *Isadora* (Karel REISZ, 1968), in which she played Isadora's mother, and *Sunday, Bloody Sunday* (John SCHLESINGER, 1971).

**LOVE IN THE AFTERNOON** see AMOUR, L'APRÈS-MIDI, L'

*LOVE ME TONIGHT,* US, 1932. 1½hr. *Dir, prod* Rouben Mamoulian for Paramount; *scr* Samuel Hoffenstein, Waldemar Young, George Marion Jr, based on the play by Leopold Marchand and Paul Armont; *ph* Victor Milner; *mus, lyrics* Richard Rodgers, Lorenz Hart; *cast* Jeanette MacDonald (Princess Jeanette), Maurice Chevalier (Maurice Courtelin), Charles Ruggles (Vicomte Gilbert de Vareze), Charles Butterworth (Count de Savignac), Sir C. Aubrey Smith (the Duke), Myrna Loy (Valentine).

A beautiful but mysteriously ailing Ruritanian princess finds her life transformed by the arrival at her father's castle of a Parisian tailor masquerading as a nobleman.

Under MAMOULIAN's direction Maurice CHEVALIER gave a restrained performance and Jeanette MACDONALD evinced evident enjoyment in parodying her own style. The musical score, which includes one of RODGERS and HART's most famous songs 'Lover', was prerecorded, and this contributed to the flowing blend of music, dialogue, and camera movements; the sequence in which the song 'Isn't It Romantic' is carried around the city, introducing the various characters in the story, is justly famous.

*LOVE PARADE, The,* US, 1930. 2hr. *Dir* Ernst Lubitsch; *prod* Paramount; *scr* Ernest Vajda, Guy Bolton, from the play *Prince Consort* by Leon Xanrof and Jules Chancel; *ph* Victor Milner; *des* Hans Dreier; *mus* Victor Schertzinger; *lyr* Clifford Grey; *cast* Maurice Chevalier (Count Alfred), Jeanette MacDonald (Queen Louise), Lupino Lane (Jacques), Lillian Roth (Lulu), Eugene Pallette (Minister of War), Lionel Belmore (Prime Minister).

In LUBITSCH's first sound film, a musical comedy about the marital problems of the Queen of Sylvania, he made resourceful and creative use of the new medium. A great popular success, the film was a sophisticated satire, full of saucy innuendo, lavish settings, and catchy melodies, including 'Dream Lover', and the 'March of the

Grenadiers'. It was Jeanette MACDONALD's first film appearance, and she made a charming partner to Maurice CHEVALIER, who showed himself a fine comedian as the philandering Prince.

**LOWER DEPTHS, The.** There have been to date five film versions of Maxim GORKY's play. A recording was made in 1912 of a performance of the play by the Imperial Theatre of St Petersburg. Seven years later Rudolf Meinert directed a German adaptation, *Nachtasyl*. Gorky himself prepared a scenario in the early thirties, but this has remained unused and it was only with the 1952 Mosfilm recording of a production by the Moscow Art Theatre that the play was filmed again in Russia.

The two most important adaptations of *The Lower Depths* are Jean RENOIR's *Les Bas-fonds* which won the first Prix Louis DELLUC in 1936 and Akira KUROSAWA's *Donzoko* (1957). Gorky took a great interest in the script for *Les Bas-fonds* but died before the film was completed. Although Renoir was at that time sympathetic to the French Communist Party and at their earnest suggestion set the film in Russia, it related far more closely to the France of 1936 and to Renoir's previous work than to orthodox SOCIALIST REALISM. Like Renoir's previous film, LE CRIME DE MONSIEUR LANGE (1936), *Les Bas-fonds* is concerned with the relationship between a small community and the outside world (the play was opened up considerably) but whereas in the earlier film the workers are able to form a successful co-operative, the only hope in *Les Bas-fonds* lies with the hero and heroine who escape from the derelict community and take to the road.

Unlike Renoir, Kurosawa kept close to Gorky's play, maintaining the act divisions of the original and emphasizing its claustrophobia with the very first shots of high cliffs enclosing the shanty town in which the entire action is set. He drew highly theatrical performances from his actors, allowing sustained playing by his customary use of long takes shot with two or three cameras running simultaneously. Although the play is commonly regarded as sombre, Kurosawa has described it as 'very funny' and indeed *Donzoko* includes elements of broad comedy lacking in either the Mosfilm production or the Gorky scenario.

**LOY, MYRNA** (1902–   ), US actress, real name Myrna Williams, started her long and successful career with Cecil B. DEMILLE in *The Ten Commandments* (1923). During the thirties she was one of Hollywood's most popular box-office stars. She gave effective performances in many dramatic roles, but is best remembered in the THIN MAN series (1934–47) with William POWELL and in other sophisticated comedies such as *Mr Blandings Builds his Dream House* (1948), with Cary GRANT. In recent years she has devoted much time to the work of UNESCO.

**LOY, NANNI** (1925–   ), Italian director, worked as assistant to Luigi ZAMPA and made his first film, *Parola di ladro* (1957), in collaboration with Gianni Puccini. Loy is best known for *Le quattro giornate di Napoli* (1962) which, with its assertive realism, has been compared with the best work of Francesco ROSI. He has worked in television as well as directing occasional films, notably *Made in Italy* (1965), and teaches directing at the CENTRO SPERIMENTALE.

**LUBIN, SIGMUND** (c.1850–1923), US producer, began his film career in 1897, when he faked the Corbett–Fitzsimmons prize-fight in a studio and sold the film as fact. He formed the Lubin Company, which became one of the seven members of the MOTION PICTURE PATENTS COMPANY. In 1918, during the slump at the end of the war, Lubin merged with VITAGRAPH, SELIG, and ESSANAY to form VLSE.

**LUBITSCH, ERNST** (1892–1947), US director of German birth, entered the film industry in Berlin in 1909; he played small parts, then joined Max REINHARDT's stage company, returning to films as an established actor. By 1914 he was acting, writing, and directing for the newly-formed Union company, mostly comedies centred on the character (played by Lubitsch himself) of Meyer, the small Jewish business man. With the success of these sharp, controlled, comic pieces, Lubitsch was entrusted with bigger productions, grand historical romances such as *Madame Dubarry* (1919), *Sumurun* (1920), and *Das Weib des Pharaohs* (1921), in which Reinhardt's example is apparent in Lubitsch's handling of set-pieces with large crowds.

The popularity of *Madame Dubarry* in the US, where it was shown as *Passion*, brought Lubitsch (and its star, Pola NEGRI) to Hollywood. His first American film, *Rosita* (1923), was received with little enthusiasm, probably owing to the conflicts that arose between the director and his star, Mary PICKFORD, but the series of sophisticated comedies that followed made his name legendary. *The Marriage Circle*, *Forbidden Paradise* (both 1924), *Lady Windermere's Fan* (1925), are outstanding examples of his ability to convey verbal wit in silent films.

With the coming of sound, Lubitsch tackled the new medium with a musical, THE LOVE PARADE (1930). His immediate command of its possibilities and his awareness of the dramatic potential of musical numbers led to several film operettas, mostly starring Maurice CHEVALIER and Jeanette MACDONALD (not always together).

He continued to develop his own brand of ironic humour in TROUBLE IN PARADISE (1932), BLUE-BEARD'S EIGHTH WIFE (1938), and NINOTCHKA (1939). From 1936 he worked increasingly as producer as well as director. In 1937 he was awarded a special OSCAR for 'twenty-five years' contribution to the motion pictures'.

*The Shop around the Corner* (1940) showed a gentler side of Lubitsch's humour, but *To Be or Not To Be* (1942) had all his essential sharpness. The timing of his satire on Nazism was widely felt to be unfortunate, but it contains Carole LOMBARD's last film appearance (and one of her best), and an excellent performance by Jack BENNY. *Heaven Can Wait* (1943) and *Cluny Brown* (1946) had both warmth and wit, but Lubitsch's health deteriorated rapidly during the forties and his last undertaking, *That Lady in Ermine* (1948) was completed by Otto PREMIN-GER.

The 'Lubitsch touch', a particular brand of amoral wit, usually expressed with a polish and control that enables the humour to shock while rarely giving offence, was influential in American comedy, and Lubitsch's insistence on overall control of his films did much to establish in Hollywood the conception of a director's author-ity. His influence is apparent in the films of Preminger and Joseph L. MANKIEWICZ, who both worked under Lubitsch's supervision; and Billy WILDER, in his best work, shows the contempor-ary evolution of Lubitsch's good-humoured, sar-donic vision of the human condition.

**LUGOSI,** BELA (1888–1956), Hungarian-born US actor, real name Béla Lugosi Blasko, trained at the Theatre Arts Academy, Budapest. From 1915 he appeared in Hungarian films under the name Aristid Olt. He supported Béla Kun in the 1919 uprising, after which he escaped to Ger-many where he appeared in MURNAU's *Der Januskopf* (1920) (SEE DR JEKYLL AND MR HYDE). Soon afterwards he emigrated to the US and appeared on the stage and in films, including *The Last of the Mohicans* (1923); his sensational success as DRACULA in the stage adaptation gained him the lead in the 1931 film version. The role type-cast Lugosi for the rest of his career; his aristocratic appearance and mellifluous ac-cent gave an exotic flavour to his portrayals of macabre characters, and gained him a large pub-lic following. His comic performance in NIN-OTCHKA (1939) shows that he was capable of a wider variety of parts than those offered by the run of routine horror vehicles for which he is chiefly remembered.

**LUKAS,** PAUL (1895–1971), Hungarian-born actor, real name Pal Lukacs, went to the US in 1925, and appeared on the New York stage. His earlier films include CITY STREETS (1931), *Little Women* (George CUKOR, 1933), and *Dodsworth* (1936). He appeared in Alfred HITCHCOCK's last pre-war British film, THE LADY VANISHES (1938), and in Anatole LITVAK's anti-Nazi film *Con-fessions of a Nazi Spy* (1939). His suave, dominating manner lent a sinister attraction to his performances and inevitably led to his being type-cast as a variety of foreign villains. In 1943 he won an OSCAR for his performance in *Watch on the Rhine*, directed by the noted stage producer Herman Shumlin. Among later films were *Experiment Perilous* (1945) and *Berlin Express* (1948), both directed by Jacques TOUR-NEUR, *Kim* (1951), and *20,000 Leagues Under the Sea* (1954).

*LULU* see BÜCHSE DER PANDORA, DIE

**LUMET,** SIDNEY (1924–   ), US director, was a child actor in the theatre and continued to act in theatre and television before becoming a widely respected director of television plays. From his first film TWELVE ANGRY MEN (1957), which was adapted from a play he had directed for television, nearly all his subjects have been taken from established material, plays or novels. His earlier films, all in black and white and harshly naturalistic in style, deal largely with problems of human obsession and conflict (*The Fugitive Kind*, 1960; *Long Day's Journey into Night*, 1962; *Fail Safe*, 1964; *The Pawnbroker*, 1964; and others). They show a personal bias in the choice of subject, together with faithful adap-tation of the originals.

Latterly he has directed films in colour and with a more delicate and humorous approach. *The Group* (1966), from Mary McCarthy's novel, *Bye Bye Braverman* (1969), a Jewish black comedy, and *The Appointment* (1968), all explore the haunting effect of the past on the characters involved. *The Seagull* (1968), from Chekhov's play, shows Lumet making a new departure in choosing a subject from a European classic; he shows his usual respect for the original, although the film is not entirely success-ful in cinematic terms. In the seventies Lumet again changed direction, making *The Anderson Tapes* (1971), a taut thriller starring Sean CON-NERY, and *Serpico* (1974), a vigorous adaptation of a best-selling book about a New York policeman's campaign against corruption. He deftly controlled an all-star cast in *Murder on the Orient Express* (1974).

**LUMIÈRE,** AUGUSTE (1862–1954) and LOUIS (1864–1948), French inventors and pioneers of cinema. The two brothers worked in their father Antoine Lumière's photographic sup-plies factory in Lyons, where Louis made important advances in the development of dry photographic plates. By the mid-nineties Lumière products were rivalling those of George EASTMAN's Kodak company.

In 1894 EDISON's Kinetoscope (see KINETOGRAPH) was shown in Paris and Louis Lumière began work on a machine to compete with Edison's expensive device. The Cinématographe, initially camera and projector in one, was patented in the brothers' joint names on 13 February 1895; it combined the experiments and results of many earlier pioneers, the only original contribution being the system of claws which moved the film. Louis was mainly responsible for the work, starting with emulsioned paper strips which were later replaced by celluloid imported from the US. He cut and perforated the strips himself and made a dozen or so films each fifty feet long (the capacity of the spool-boxes holding the negative stock). He developed the films by hand in enamelled iron buckets and made positives using a sunlit white wall as a light source. The films were shown to various learned societies; the first demonstration was in Paris in March 1895, when *La Sortie des usines* was shown as a novelty supplementing a lecture by Louis Lumière on his primary interest, colour photography.

The first public performance of the Cinématographe took place on 28 December 1895, at the Salon Indien in the Grand Café, on the boulevard des Capucines in Paris. A number of journalists and directors of Parisian theatres (among them Georges MÉLIÈS) were present. The first day's takings amounted to 33 francs; three weeks later the daily receipt was 2,500 francs. The programme of ten films lasted twenty minutes, and there were twenty screenings a day. Although there is some confusion as to the actual films shown, the likely programme seems to have been: *La Sortie des usines*, *La Voltige*, *La Pêche aux poissons rouges*, *Arrivée des Congressistes à Neuville-sur-Saône*, *L'Arroseur arrosé*, *Les Forgerons*, *Le Repas en famille*, *Le Saut à la couverture*, *Place des Cordeliers à Lyon*, and *La Mer*. Other well-known films made by Louis Lumière between 1895 and 1897 include *Barque sortant du port*, *La Partie d'écart*, *L'Arrivée d'un train en gare*, *La Démolition d'un mur*, and *Le Repas de bébé*. All these early efforts were observations of everyday events recorded with a static camera (although with occasional panning) limited by the conventions of still photography. But *L'Arroseur arrosé*, showing a gardener receiving a jet of water in the face, is in a sense a constructed narrative, and one of the earliest film comedies.

*Barque sortant du port* (Lumière, 1896)

*La Démolition d'un mur* used reverse motion to 're-build' the wall.

Louis Lumière was sceptical of the future of motion picture photography. From 1898 he made no more films himself. However, he shrewdly refused to sell his invention and instead employed a group of cameramen (there were a hundred of them, the most famous being Mesguisch and Promio) to travel all over the world filming, processing, and projecting actuality scenes with the versatile Cinématographe.

Meanwhile the Lumières had, in 1896, opened a second cinema to show imported films which were arriving in increasing numbers. Soon the public grew tired of the limited and repetitive subjects of the early films and Louis Lumière's attempts at 'historical' subjects, including *La Vie et la Passion de Jésus-Christ* (1897) failed to preserve the Lumière monopoly from the growing competition of PATHÉ, GAUMONT, and, later, Méliès. In the hope of reviving his lead, Louis planned for the 1900 Paris Exhibition a giant screen mounted between the feet of the Eiffel Tower, on which a 70MM film could be projected. Objections by the local authorities led to a compromise whereby a screen one-third the size was mounted in the Champ de Mars. By now convinced of the ephemeral nature of his invention, he thereafter devoted himself to the improvement of raw stock and the development of colour photography and stereoscopic cinema. During the First World War he worked on ways of heating aircraft. In 1919 he was elected a member of the Académie des Sciences, and in 1920 he retired. There is now a museum and archive at the Lumière factory in Lyons, and the gates featured in *La Sortie des usines* are still in place.

**LUPINO,** IDA (1918– ), US actress born in Britain of a famous family of music-hall artists, appeared in films from the age of fifteen, first in Britain, then in Hollywood. She showed herself an actress of some strength in *High Sierra* (1941), opposite Humphrey BOGART, but, under contract to WARNER BROS, was generally treated as a second string to Bette DAVIS. Later she turned to production, *Not Wanted* (1949), and direction, *Never Fear* (1950), *Outrage* (1951),

and others. She has continued to act and direct for television and for the cinema.

**LUTYENS,** ELISABETH (1906– ), British composer whose conventional film music differs appreciably from the tough, twelve-note idiom characteristic of most of her work. She began writing for films in the mid-forties, and for many years remained associated almost entirely with documentaries; but more recently she has been in demand for fantasy and horror films, including *Dr Terror's House of Horrors*, *The Earth Dies Screaming* (both 1964), *The Skull* (1965), *Spaceflight IC-L* (1965), and *Theatre of Death* (1966).

**LYE,** LEN (1901– ), New Zealand artist, invented the technique known as 'direct film', of painting designs on to film stock without using a camera. Lye's first film *Tusalava* (1929) was sponsored by the FILM SOCIETY. The GPO (see CROWN FILM UNIT) commissioned *Colour Box* (1935), *Rainbow Dance* (1936), and *Trade Tattoo* (1937), experiments with abstract film which inspired Norman MCLAREN and others. During the war, Lye made animated and live-action films for the Ministry of Information including *When the Pie Was Opened* (1941), on making a vegetable pie, and *Kill Or Be Killed* (1943), an army training film, both live-action and both conveying a strangely surrealist atmosphere. Work for THE MARCH OF TIME led him to the US in 1944. Direct films produced there include *Rhythm* (1957) and *Free Radicals* (1958). Lye now makes Tangible Motion Sculptures in stainless steel, some of which he used in a one-minute film *Peace* (1959), made for the United Nations.

**LYON,** BEN (1901– ), US actor, was a successful leading man in Hollywood, notably in Howard HUGHES's *Hell's Angels* (1930), before moving with his wife, Bebe DANIELS, to Britain in 1939. They courageously and cheerfully identified themselves with the British in the war, becoming popular radio performers for twenty years. Two films were based on their comedy series, 'Hi Gang' (1940) and 'Life with the Lyons' (1954).

# M

**M,** Germany, 1931. 1½hr. *Dir* Fritz Lang; *prod* Nero; *scr* Lang, Thea von Harbou; *ph* Fritz Arno Wagner; *des* Karl Vollbrecht, Emil Hasler; *mus* Adolf Jansen, with 'In the Hall of the Mountain King' from Grieg's *Peer Gynt* Suite; *cast* Peter Lorre (the murderer), Ellen Widman (the mother), Inge Landgut (Elsie), Otto Wernicke (Commissar Lohmann), Gustav Gründgens (gang leader).

Based on a series of actual child-killings in Düsseldorf, *M* uses a potentially horrific theme to carry ironic social comment. Public hysteria is depicted, foreshadowing FURY (1936), and the efficient organization of the underworld in tracking down the murderer is set against the incompetence of the police force. The grim humour of this contrast is developed to the full, and *M* is often surprisingly funny.

In his first sound film LANG used the medium with great virtuosity; music and voices are employed as suggestively as images. Visually *M* has affinities with PABST'S DIE DREIGROSCHENOPER (1931), particularly in the final scenes where the tribunal of the underworld meets in an abandoned warehouse, with Hollywood GANGSTER FILMS, and in some sequences with the chiaroscuro effects of EXPRESSIONISM.

Peter LORRE's performance brought him wide acclaim and he ran the risk for a time of being typed as a psychopathic killer.

Joseph LOSEY's 1951 remake of *M* effectively transferred the action to Los Angeles and if anything emphasized compassion for the killer.

**MacARTHUR,** CHARLES (1895–1956), US playwright and scriptwriter, wrote the play THE FRONT PAGE in collaboration with Ben HECHT. Following the filming of their play by Lewis MILESTONE in 1931, MacArthur and Hecht established their own film production company which made CRIME WITHOUT PASSION (1934) and THE SCOUNDREL (1935), both full of irreverent wit and displaying a scathing view of conventional society. Other scripts written by MacArthur in association with Hecht include TWENTIETH CENTURY (1934) and WUTHERING HEIGHTS (1939), and among films he scripted individually are *Rasputin and the Empress* (1932) and *Gunga Din* (1939). He was married to Helen HAYES.

**MACBETH,** with its combination of violence and poetry, has had considerable appeal for filmmakers. In 1908 it was the first of the prestigious and successful series of SHAKESPEARE films issued by VITAGRAPH. The following year saw an elaborate Italian version directed by Mario CASERINI for CINES and in 1910 FILM D'ART issued another. The production by Sir Frank Benson's company at the Shakespeare Memorial Theatre, Stratford, was filmed in 1911, the well-known British actor Arthur Bourchier directed a version for a German company in 1913, and Sir Herbert Beerbohm Tree appeared in a TRIANGLE Fineart production in 1916. Another French version was directed in 1916 by Georgette Leblanc-Maeterlinck.

The first sound film of *Macbeth* appears to have been the amateur production directed by Thomas Blair in 1946. In 1948 Orson WELLES undertook a version for REPUBLIC, based on his Mercury Theatre production. The film was made on a low budget and, like Welles's other Shakespeare films, suffers from a poor sound-track. Welles's demonic, tormented performance in the title role accords with his interpretation of the play as a depiction of a barbaric society in decay.

In 1960, two distinguished stage actors, Judith ANDERSON and Maurice Evans, appeared in a version made for US television but also distributed theatrically. Roman POLAŃSKI's version, made in Britain (1971), is probably the most successful direct film adaptation so far. The protagonists' youth caused some surprise, but the film as a whole was both harsh and controlled; as in other Polański films, evil is powerfully present and is enigmatically attributable to either supernatural or rational causes.

The basic plot of *Macbeth* was used in KUROSAWA'S KUMONOSU-JO (*Throne of Blood*, 1957), a classically formal tragedy, using elements from the NOH drama, in which violence predominates; in *Le Rideau rouge* (1952), a modern version starring Michel SIMON and Pierre BRASSEUR; and in *Joe Macbeth* (GB, 1955), which places the action in the modern criminal underworld. *Sibirska Ledi Magbet* (*The Siberian Lady Macbeth*, 1961), directed in Yugoslavia by Andrzej WAJDA, is a powerful tragedy based on a short story by the Russian writer Leskov, not on Shakespeare's play.

**McCAMBRIDGE**, MERCEDES (1918– ), US actress, apart from a successful stage career, attracted a discriminating following with her intermittent but striking appearances in films. ALL THE KING'S MEN (1949) showed her to be a polished and intelligent actress with a talent for the wry or caustic characterizations she also projected in *Johnny Guitar* (1954) and *Angel Baby* (1960). In TOUCH OF EVIL (1958) she made an effective brief appearance.

**McCAREY**, LEO (1898–1969), US director, began his film career in 1918, making his name at Hal ROACH Studios on short comedies with Charlie CHASE and others. He was responsible for some of the best of LAUREL AND HARDY's two-reelers, including *The Battle of the Century* (1927) and *Two Tars* (1928). He established himself as a feature film director with *Roadhouse* (1928), *The Sophomore*, and *Red Hot Rhythm* (both 1929); during the thirties his comedies starred numerous top comedians, including Eddie CANTOR (*The Kid from Spain*, 1932), the MARX BROTHERS (DUCK SOUP, 1933), W. C. FIELDS (*Six of a Kind*, 1934), and Harold LLOYD (*The Milky Way*, 1936). Equally notable at this period were *Belle of the Nineties* (1934), with Mae WEST; *Ruggles of Red Gap* (1935), with Charles LAUGHTON; and THE AWFUL TRUTH (1937), with Cary GRANT and Irene DUNNE.

McCarey wrote and produced most of his films. He was particularly adept at handling actors, bringing conviction to the increasingly sentimental bias of his films, shown in *Make Way for Tomorrow* (1937), *Love Affair* (1939), starring Charles BOYER and Irene Dunne, which he remade in 1957 as *An Affair to Remember*, with Cary Grant and Deborah KERR, and in the two popular box-office successes with Bing CROSBY, *Going My Way* (1944) and *The Bells of St Mary's* (1945). He continued to specialize in comedy, including *The Cowboy and the Lady* (1938), with Gary COOPER and Merle OBERON, and *My Favorite Wife* (1940), another featuring his favoured co-starring team of Cary Grant and Irene Dunne. He directed less frequently after the mid-forties: his last films were *Rally Round the Flag Boys* (1958) and *Satan Never Sleeps* (1962).

**McCREA**, JOEL (1905– ), US actor, appeared in *Wells Fargo* (1937), followed by a starring role in Cecil B. DEMILLE's *Union Pacific* (1939). Although these successes were matched by fine performances in such different films as SULLIVAN'S TRAVELS (1941) and *Foreign Correspondent* (1940), he is best known as a star of Westerns, among them *Buffalo Bill* (1944), Raoul WALSH's underrated *Colorado Territory* (1949), *The Outriders* (1950), *Stranger on Horse-*back (1955), and, most notably, Sam PECKINPAH's RIDE THE HIGH COUNTRY (1962, *Guns in the Afternoon* in GB).

**McDANIEL**, HATTIE (1895–1952), US character actress, during the thirties and forties established a near-monopoly in genial black servant roles. For her performance in GONE WITH THE WIND (1939) she received the first OSCAR to be awarded to a black artist.

**MacDONALD**, JEANETTE (1902–65), US singer and actress, enjoyed much popularity in the many film operettas in which she starred during the thirties. Particularly successful were several appearances opposite Maurice CHEVALIER, including THE LOVE PARADE (1930), her first film, and LOVE ME TONIGHT (1932), and with Nelson EDDY in, among others, *Rose Marie* (1936) and *New Moon* (1940).

**McDOWALL**, RODDY (1928– ), British actor who having appeared in British films from 1936, became a child star in Hollywood following his evacuation to the US in 1940. Especially well-remembered appearances were in *How Green Was My Valley* (1941), *My Friend Flicka* (1943), and *Lassie Come Home* (1943). In the fifties he left films for Broadway but returned to the screen in the sixties, specializing in sullen or waspish characters, notably in *Inside Daisy Clover* (Robert MULLIGAN, 1966) and *Lord Love a Duck* (George AXELROD, 1965). He also appeared in PLANET OF THE APES (1968) and its sequels.

**MacGOWAN**, KENNETH (1888–1963), US producer, was a reviewer, publicist, and stage producer until, in 1932, he joined David O. SELZNICK at RKO, as a story editor, then associate producer. His first major film was *Topaze* with John BARRYMORE and Myrna LOY, and his first big success *Little Women* (both 1933). In 1934 he produced *La Cucaracha*, the first live-action film made in three-strip TECHNICOLOR, and *Becky Sharp*, the first three-strip Technicolor feature, as well as making his only film as director, *Anne of Green Gables*. In 1935 he joined TWENTIETH CENTURY-FOX where his productions included *This is My Affair* (1937), with Robert TAYLOR, *Four Men and a Prayer*, *In Old Chicago* (both 1938), *Young Mr Lincoln* (1939), and *Man Hunt* (1941). He then took leave of absence from Fox to work under Nelson Rockefeller producing educational and propaganda films for Latin America. He returned to Fox in 1942 and his productions included *Lifeboat* (1944) directed by HITCHCOCK. He produced one film for PARAMOUNT (*Easy Come Easy Go*, 1947), then went to the University of California at Los Angeles to found a theatre arts department. In 1945 he established the *Hollywood Quarterly* (see FILM QUARTERLY) and his book *Behind the screen: the history and techniques of the motion picture* was published posthumously in 1965.

**McGUIRE,** DOROTHY (1919–   ), US actress whose quiet, appealing charm made her a popular star of the forties and fifties. She first appeared in *Claudia* (1943), playing the title role which she had created on the stage. After *A Tree Grows in Brooklyn* (Elia KAZAN, 1945), she scored a great success in the romantic drama *The Enchanted Cottage* (1944) and in the suspense thriller *The Spiral Staircase* (1945). She was in the sequel to her first success, *Claudia and David* (1946), and several other films including *Gentleman's Agreement* (Kazan, 1947). In later years she played maternal roles; her last appearance was as the Virgin Mary in *The Greatest Story Ever Told* (1965).

**MACHATÝ,** GUSTAV (1901–63), Czechoslovak director, began his film career as an actor and quickly moved to scriptwriting and directing, working with his friend Karel Lamač and the latter's wife and collaborator, Anny ONDRA. He went to Hollywood in 1920, and is said to have been in contact with GRIFFITH and STROHEIM (although there is no evidence for the assistant directorship of FOOLISH WIVES, 1921, with which he is sometimes credited). Certainly he shared with Stroheim a taste for the erotic. After his return to Prague he raised money to make *Kreutzer Sonata* (1926), which was successful enough for him to be given in 1927 direction of the last of the series of Švejk films started by Lamač in 1925. Machatý, however, had little talent for comedy: his real flair was for stylish eroticism, which brought him great success and reputation in *Erotikon* (1929). Stylistically the film showed Russian influence in its alternation of naturalistic with symbolic sequences, and the international cast headed by the Yugoslav Ita Rina reflected Machatý's cosmopolitan tendencies. The story was written by the poet Vitěslav Nezval, and Machatý achieved much of the erotic effect by symbolic imagery: this was also the first time a nude appeared on the Czech screen. Machatý's first sound film was *Ze soboty na neděli* (*From Saturday to Sunday*, 1931), again based on a story by Nezval, an account of a young girl's attempt to find glamour in a drab world. Deriving from the stream of social consciousness which distinguished Czech cinema in the twenties, this film has not received the attention it deserves, probably because Machatý's name is more readily associated with *Erotikon* and with his next film (after another unsuccessful comedy), the notorious EXTASE (1933). Here his preoccupation with sexual tensions found full expression, and the scandals caused by the film no less than its great visual beauty made Machatý's name resound internationally.

His career had, however, reached its peak: he was unable to find backing in Czechoslovakia, and made his next two films in Italy, running into more censorship problems with the second, *Ballerina* (1936), but failing to please the audience at VENICE who expected another *Extase*. He returned to Hollywood and worked on various films, usually standing in for an indisposed director (as in THE GOOD EARTH, *Madame X* and *Born Reckless*, all 1937, and after the war for Clarence BROWN). His only full US credit was for *Jealousy* (1945), an unconvincingly naïve story about a Czech immigrant. In 1950, after his wife's suicide, he returned to Europe, writing a script for PABST, *Es geschah am 20 Juli* (*It happened on 20 July*, 1955), and making one film in Germany. Two brief visits to Prague failed to secure him any work, and he died in Munich.

**MACISTE,** a character in PASTRONE'S CABIRIA (1914), played by Bartolomeo Pagano (1878–1947), a semi-literate Genoese docker of Herculean proportions. As a result of his enormous popularity in the role he appeared in many films featuring Maciste, and the character was taken up in the silent films of other Latin countries. The tradition is comparable with that of TARZAN and similar Maciste-figures have to the present day remained consistently popular in Italian spectacular productions.

**MacKENDRICK,** ALEXANDER (1912–   ), British director, born in the US, entered films in 1937, working at PINEWOOD STUDIOS as scriptwriter and assistant director on shorts: during the war he worked on documentaries in Italy. After the war MacKendrick went to EALING STUDIOS, where he directed several films including WHISKY GALORE (1949), THE MAN IN THE WHITE SUIT (1951), for which he also collaborated on the script, and *The Ladykillers* (1955). These were all within the Ealing style of bizarre plots set against closely-observed social backgrounds. THE SWEET SMELL OF SUCCESS (1957), made in Hollywood, marked a sharpening of observation and comment. Since 1957 MacKendrick has worked in theatre and television in the US and Britain. In 1969 he was appointed first dean of the film department of the new California Institute of the Arts.

**McLAGLEN,** VICTOR (1886–1959), British-born actor, began his screen career in A. E. Coleby's *The Call of the Road* (1920) and with Lady Diana Manners in J. Stuart BLACKTON'S

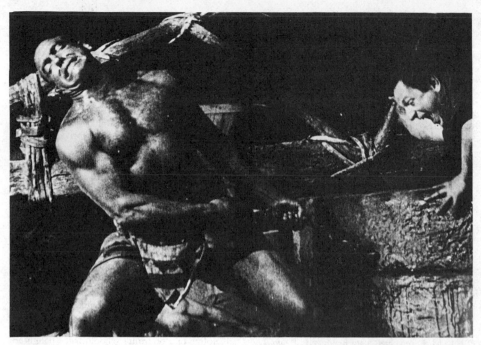

Maciste in *Cabiria* (Giovanni Pastrone, 1914)

PRIZMACOLOR film *The Glorious Adventure* (1921), before going to Hollywood. His massive build and craggy face, with a broken nose, made him ideal for burly sergeant roles or tough guys (usually warm-hearted)—parts which mainly confined him to the ranks of featured players. But on occasion he was given star roles, including the blustering sergeant in George STEVENS's *Gunga Din* (1939). He often worked with John FORD, notably as the simple-minded betrayer in THE INFORMER (1935). McLaglen did many fight scenes in the course of his career: particularly memorable was his battle with John WAYNE in another Ford film, *The Quiet Man* (1952).

**MacLAINE,** SHIRLEY (1934– ), US actress, real name Shirley Maclean Beaty (sister of Warren BEATTY), whose first film, THE TROUBLE WITH HARRY (1955) established her as an engagingly off-beat personality. *Some Came Running* (1958) gave her the opportunity to display her dramatic abilities in the first of several parts in which she has played a rather dumb floozie (*Sweet Charity*, 1968, provided a more recent variant of the role) but probably her best dramatic performance was as the tragic lesbian in *The Children's Hour* (1963, *The Loudest Whisper* in GB). Her talent as a *comédienne* is

too often betrayed by poor material, but *Ask Any Girl* (1959) and THE APARTMENT (1960) were exceptions. She published *Don't fall off the mountain* in 1971.

**McLAREN,** NORMAN (1914– ), Scottish-born animator and innovator, experimented at art school with film as an abstract medium. In 1937 he joined John GRIERSON's GPO Film Unit (see CROWN FILM UNIT), which was sponsoring Len LYE's experiments with direct film, a technique of inscribing designs directly on to clear film stock. Like Lye, McLaren was not restricted to ANIMATION: he made straightforward documentaries such as *Book Bargain* (1937) as well as animated fantasies, including *Love on the Wing* (1939). He experimented with a sonic equivalent of direct film, by working directly on to an OPTICAL track.

In 1939 McLaren went to New York, resuming his abstract experiments on colour film. In 1941, he joined Grierson at the newly-formed NATIONAL FILM BOARD of Canada, where he has remained and where he formed and trained a distinguished animation unit, though always maintaining a prolific personal output. McLaren is still perhaps best known for his many variations on direct film technique: *Dollar Dance* (1943), *Fiddle-de-Dee* (1947), *Blinkity-Blank*

(1954), *Short and Suite* (1959), *Mosaic* (1965), and many more. In *Begone Dull Care* (1949) frame divisions were ignored to achieve a new fluidity in linear composition, further developed by the experiments of *Lines Horizontal* and *Lines Vertical* (1960). These films achieve their effects at an almost subconscious level, emulating the rhythm and fluidity of music. Music itself, frequently composed by Maurice Blackburn, is important as a rhythmical basis for interpretation and response.

In *Alouette* (1944) McLaren animated cut-out shapes, a method pioneered by Emile COHL. Similar in technique were *Rhythmetic* (1956) and *Le Merle* (*The Blackbird*, 1958). *La Poulette grise* (1946) gently interpreted a French-Canadian lullaby with simple pastel drawings. *Neighbours* (1952), a relentless allegory of the futility of violence, won an OSCAR in 1953. McLaren here, and in *Two Bagatelles* (1952), used PIXILLATION, 'animating' human actors. In *Chairy Tale* (1957) and *Opening Speech* (1960) the technique is applied humorously to inanimate objects. *Canon* (1964) combines all of these techniques in a visual depiction of musical form. *Pas de Deux* (1968) used multiple-image photography of the human figure to beautiful effect. McLaren has also produced *Around is Around* (1951), a three-dimensional animated film for the Festival of Britain. He has twice worked for UNESCO, in China (1949–50) and in India (1952–3), demonstrating the mass-educational potential of his animation techniques.

McLaren followed the first great generation of experimenters—EGGELING, RICHTER, FISCHINGER, Lye—but more than any of these he has demonstrated extraordinary technical virtuosity; he has won a greater number of awards than any other film-maker.

**MacMURRAY, FRED** (1908–   ), US actor, originally a band musician and singer. His earliest films include *The Gilded Lily* (Mitchell Leisen, 1935) in company with Ray MILLAND opposite Claudette COLBERT. With a strong personality as his main asset, he was equally at home in straight dramatic roles (notably in Billy WILDER's DOUBLE INDEMNITY, 1943) and in Westerns, but he was especially adept in comedy and particularly associated with films by Leisen: *The Lady is Willing* (1942), *Take a Letter, Darling* (1942, *Green-Eyed Woman* in GB), and *No Time for Love* (1943). In the sixties he appeared in a number of films produced by Walt DISNEY; of these, *The Absent-Minded Professor* (1960) and a sequel, *Son of Flubber* (1963), were popular successes. His television series 'My Three Sons', started in 1960, ran with immense popularity for many years.

**McQUEEN, STEVE** (1930–   ), US actor, made his first film appearances in *Never Love a Stranger* (1957) and *The Blob* (1958). THE MAGNIFICENT SEVEN (1960) established his screen persona—the laconic rebel combining toughness with ingenuousness. In 1965 he formed his own production company, Solar Inc, which co-produced Robert MULLIGAN's *Baby the Rain Must Fall* (1965). When he did some of his own stunt work for *Bullitt* (1968) it added credence to the impression that McQueen's private life and liking for racing cars and motor cycles is reflected in the characters he portrays. *The Great Escape* (1962), *Junior Bonner* (1972), and *The Getaway* (1973) provide further examples of his deceptively casual acting.

**MÄDCHEN IN UNIFORM,** Germany, 1931. 1½hr. *Dir* Leontine Sagan; *prod* Deutsche Film–Gemeinschaft; *scr* Christa Winsloe, F. D. Adam, from the former's play *Gestern und Heute*; *ph* Reimar Kuntze, Franz Weihmayr; *cast* Emilia Unda (headmistress), Dorothea Wieck (Fräulein von Bernburg), Hedwig Schlichter (Fräulein von Kosten), Hertha Thiele (Manuela von Meinhardis), Ellen Schwanneke (Ilse von Westhagen).

*Mädchen in Uniform* deals with the oppressive discipline of a boarding school for the daughters of Prussian army officers and its results in the formation of a lesbian relationship between a sensitive pupil and one of the teachers. Leontine SAGAN's direct handling of highly emotional material aroused wide attention. This was the first professional German film to be collectively produced by those who worked on it; these included Carl FROELICH who supervised the direction.

There was a German remake, directed by Géza Radványi, in 1958.

**MAGASISKOLA** (*The Falcons*), Hungary, 1970. Eastman Color; 1½hr. *Dir, scr* István Gaál based on the novel by Miklós Mészöly; *prod* Mafilm Studio 4; *ph* Elemér Ragályi; *mus* András Szöllősy; *cast* Ivan Andonov (Gábor), György Bánffy (Lilik), Judit Meszléri (Teréz).

*Magasiskola* brought GAÁL international recognition, while showing a move in style away from his more lyrical and relaxed early works. Set in a falcon training camp (the title actually translates as *High School*) ruled by the iron disciplinarian Lilik, the film is a condemnation of any way of life which requires blind obedience and restraints to survive; the visiting Gábor finally flees in horror, but is pursued in the final shot by the vibrating telephone wires. Surface similarities to JANCSÓ are evident only in the film's formality and atmosphere of menace; Gaál's work is clearly distinguished by its concern for the individual.

**MAGAZINE,** the light-proof box containing film stock which is attached to the camera before filming. The magazine is the two round projections on top of the camera; unexposed stock feeds from the rear portion and exposed film is taken up in the front portion. It usually holds 1,000 feet (11 minutes) of 35mm film, which determines the maximum length of a take. (See also REEL.)

**MAGNANI,** ANNA (1909–73), Italian actress, appeared on the stage and in films from the age of eighteen. Her unusual talents first found full expression in ROSSELLINI's ROMA, CITTÀ APERTA (1945) where the essential Magnani, powerful, passionate, coarse, struck an earthy blow at the conventional film star concept. She worked again with Rossellini in *L'amore* (1948); this was a two-part film consisting of COCTEAU's 'La voce humana' (*La Voix humaine*), a solo *tour de force*, and 'Il miracolo' in which she played a simpleton who is seduced by a passing stranger (played by Federico FELLINI) in the belief that he is St John the Baptist. Her breach with Rossellini led to some lean years artistically. She gave energetic life to BELLISSIMÀ (1951), VISCONTI's sour look at commercial film-making, but her greatest role of this period was in RENOIR's delightful *Le Car-*

*rosse d'or* (1953). In almost a parody of her serious roles she is wooed by every desirable man, becoming in turn capricious, cunning, emotional, but sharper, wittier, more intelligent than any of them. Her films in Hollywood displayed her good command of English but, apart from a towering performance in *The Rose Tattoo* (Daniel MANN, 1955), failed to offer her appropriate parts. She made her mark as an actress at a mature age, conveying through her uninhibited, sometimes undisciplined, talent humour, sensuality, and inner strength. PASOLINI celebrated her unique qualities in *Mamma Roma* (1962).

**MAGNASCOPE** see CHANG

***MAGNIFICENT AMBERSONS, The,*** US, 1942. 1½hr. *Dir* Orson Welles; *prod* RKO; *scr* Welles, from the novel by Booth Tarkington; *ph* Stanley Cortez; *ed* Robert Wise, Mark Robson; *mus* Bernard Herrmann; *cast* Joseph Cotten (Eugene), Dolores Costello (Isabel), Anne Baxter (Lucy), Tim Holt (George), Agnes Moorehead (Fanny).

The portrait of an aristocratic family in decline, *The Magnificent Ambersons* convincingly re-creates the milieu of late nineteenth-

Anna Magnani in *Bellissimà* (Luchino Visconti, 1951)

century America with its social and emotional stresses.

After the scandals surrounding CITIZEN KANE (1941) and its lack of commercial success, WELLES worked under close observation and within restrictions that had not previously been applied to him. Cut from 131 to 88 minutes and with a finale made without his supervision or permission, *The Magnificent Ambersons* is a flawed but still powerful work. Although highly stylized, the film has a maturity which is in striking contrast to the almost gothic tone of *Citizen Kane*. The camera movements and sound-track in particular reflect Welles's exuberant enjoyment of filming and show that, by his second film, he had attained considerable expertise.

**MAGNIFICENT SEVEN, The,** US, 1960. Panavision; 2¼hr; De Luxe Color. *Dir, prod* John Sturges for Mirisch Alpha; *scr* William Roberts, from Kurosawa's film *Shichinin no Samurai*; *ph* Charles Lang; *mus* Elmer Bernstein; *cast* Yul Brynner (Chris), Eli Wallach (Calvera), Steve McQueen (Vin), Charles Bronson (Bernardo), Horst Buchholz (Chico), James Coburn (Britt), Brad Dexter (Harry), Robert Vaughn (Lee).

The formal and narrative similarity of KUROSAWA's samurai films to the WESTERN has made them the source of several remakes, the first such attempt being *The Magnificent Seven*, based on SHICHININ NO SAMURAI (*The Seven Samurai*, 1954). STURGES's version is probably least successful when most faithful: Kurosawa's leisurely narrative here seems slack and his delicate touches of social behaviour are clumsily transposed to a Mexican setting. The best sequence is an original addition—the Boot Hill funeral procession which opens the film and establishes character and relationships.

**MAGNUSSON,** CHARLES (1878–1948), Swedish producer, trained as a cameraman and also directed some of the early films of Svenska Bio which he joined as production manager in 1909. His skill for discovering new talent brought Victor SJÖSTRÖM and Mauritz STILLER into films and he acquired for the company the screen rights of all Selma LAGERLÖF's work—a rich source for film adaptations. He remained production head after Svenska Bio's expansion into SVENSK FILMINDUSTRI in 1919 until 1928, and was largely responsible for the high artistic quality of the company's early films.

**MAILER,** NORMAN (1923– ), US author. His first novel, a war book, *The Naked and the Dead* (1948; filmed 1958), brought him instant success. Later novels include *The Deer Park* (1955), a satire on Hollywood, and *An American Dream* (1965; filmed 1966, *See You in Hell*,

*Darling* in GB). Since the publication of *Advertisements for Myself* (1959) Mailer has increasingly seen himself as protagonist: in writing; in politics, as New York mayoral candidate; in documentaries, such as Dick Fontaine's *Will the Real Norman Mailer Please Stand UP?* (1969); as an actor in his own low-budget films, including *Beyond the Law* (1968) and, with Rip Torn, *Maidstone* (1970), which in their deliberate avoidance of sophisticated techniques and manipulation of actual events are akin to much of the American UNDERGROUND cinema. His *Marilyn: a biography of Marilyn Monroe* was published in 1973.

**MAJOR BARBARA,** GB, 1941. 2hr. *Dir, prod* Gabriel Pascal; *asst dir* Harold French, David Lean; *scr* George Bernard Shaw, from his stage play; *ph* Ronald Neame; *des* Vincent Korda, John Bryan; *cost* Cecil Beaton; *ed* Charles Frend; *mus* William Walton; *cast* Wendy Hiller (Major Barbara), Rex Harrison (Adolphus Cusins), Robert Morley (Andrew Undershaft), Robert Newton (Bill Walker), Emlyn Williams (Snobby Price), Sybil Thorndike (the General), Deborah Kerr (Jenny Hill), Marie Lohr (Lady Britomart).

Gabriel PASCAL's second film from Shaw was coolly received after the acclaim that had greeted PYGMALION (1938). Perhaps the subject, inherently less engaging, was also untimely: the moral conflict between non-violent religion and the manufacture of sophisticated armaments could not be viewed objectively by an embattled society, and Shaw's coruscating, inconclusive arguments might seem only flippant or teasing.

At a less emotional time *Major Barbara* appears the more successful of the two films, living up to a list of credits which includes many of the brightest talents of British cinema. The quirky tale was played out with gusto, especially by Rex HARRISON, ironically demure, Wendy HILLER, whose film acting had matured remarkably since *Pygmalion*, and Robert MORLEY, a delicately Mephistophelean armourer. The attempt to 'open out' the play was, however, a weakness, leading to a rushed and garbled conclusion of a witty, provoking polemic.

**MAKAVAJEV,** DUSAN (1932– ), Yugoslav director, studied philosophy and film technique at Belgrade and was a journalist and film critic. His films are among the few from Yugoslavia to have gained international distribution and recognition. *Čovjek nije tica* (*A Man is not a Bird*, 1965), concerning the dehumanizing of the workers, and *Ljubavni slučaj ili tragedija službenice PTT* (*The Switchboard Operator*, 1967), comparing humans and rats, were made in the deliberately paradoxical style of free association that has become his hallmark. NEVINOST BEZ ZAŠTITE (*Innocence Unprotected*, 1968), originally directed in 1942 by Dragolub Aleksič, was resurrected by Makavejev and re-edited with actuality footage, resulting in a funny and loving tribute to a Serbian folk hero.

Makavejev's independence, irony, and gusto are considered typically Serbian. He delights in startling juxtapositions: new and old, science and eroticism, love and crime; and he particularly enjoys satirizing the more solemn aspects of formal Communism. His films have met with popular success and some official disapproval: WR—MISTERIJE ORGANIZMA (*WR—Mysteries of the Organism*, 1971) was banned from the Pula festival of Yugoslav films.

**MAKK,** KÁROLY (1925–  ), Hungarian director, started as an assistant on the first version of the experimental *2 × 2* (1944), later working on the reshooting with Zoltán Várkonyi after the Liberation (thanks to the recommendation of László RÁNODY). Enrolling at the Academy for Film Art, he came under the guidance of Géza Radványi, for whom he worked as an assistant, along with Félix MÁRIÁSSY, on VALAHOL EURÓPÁBAN (*Somewhere in Europe/Kuksi*, 1947). After graduation in 1949 and newsreel, short film, and assistant director experience—notably with Várkonyi on *Simon Menyhért születése* (*The Birth of Menyhért Simon*, 1954)—he made his first feature *Liliomfi* in 1954, a work that contrasted strongly with the overtly propagandist cinema of the early fifties. His deft and observant handling of comedy in *Liliomfi* was sustained but not developed in *Mese a 12 találatról* (*Tale of the Twelve Points*, 1956), and in the following *Ház a sziklák alatt* (*The House under the Rocks*, 1958) his underlying interest in people trapped in hopeless situations (social or otherwise) was allowed free expression. His work during the sixties was generally undistinguished, apart from *Megszállottak* (*The Fanatics*, 1961) showing an individual at odds with bureaucracy, and was frequently attacked in the Hungarian press. His international reputation, however, was triumphantly restored with SZERELEM (*Love*, 1971), a work which demonstrated a new maturity in its detailed observation of people's private struggles.

**MALDEN,** KARL (1914–  ), US actor, real name Mladew Sekulovich. His early career as a stage actor culminated in the role of Mitch in the New York production of Tennessee WILLIAMS's *A Streetcar Named Desire* in 1947. The play was directed by Elia KAZAN, in whose film *Boomerang* (1947) Malden made his first film appearance. He won an OSCAR when he repeated his performance as Mitch in Kazan's film adaptation

of A STREETCAR NAMED DESIRE (1951). His prematurely weathered face, combined with his solid acting ability, has led to his casting in unsympathetic roles, such as two-faced Dad Longworth in ONE-EYED JACKS (1960) and Shooter, a weak double-dealer, in *The Cincinnati Kid* (1965), but a notable exception was the tough dockland priest in ON THE WATERFRONT (1954). He has directed one film, *Time Limit* (1957).

**MALLE,** LOUIS (1932–  ), French director, son of a manufacturing family which resisted his early passion for cinema, but allowed him to abandon conventional studies and enter the INSTITUT DES HAUTES ÉTUDES CINÉMATOGRAPHIQUES (IDHEC) in 1950. Two years later, COUSTEAU chose him as assistant to work on an underwater film, and insisted that Malle's contribution earned him the credit of co-director on the finished film, *Le Monde du silence* (1956).

Malle was then taken on by the producer Jean Thuillier to be assistant director to BRESSON on UN CONDAMNÉ A MORT S'EST ÉCHAPPÉ (1956). Malle found he had no inclination for the role of assistant, even to someone of Bresson's stature, and Bresson agreed with him. *Paris-Match* gave him another underwater assignment, but he damaged his ears diving and could do no more underwater photography. He tried unsuccessfully to get to Budapest during the Hungarian uprising in 1956, and when he returned to France Thuillier offered him the direction of a feature film. Together they chose the subject of *L'Ascenseur pour l'échafaud* (1957). It had considerable success, gaining Malle the unique honour of winning the Prix DELLUC with a first feature at the age of twenty-five. The film revealed not only his own talent but also that of Jeanne MOREAU and of his cameraman, Henri DECAË. A year later came LES AMANTS, which caused considerable scandal but put Malle and Moreau on the international map.

From this point he could clearly count on a commercial career, but characteristically refused to repeat the formula of success. In ZAZIE DANS LE MÉTRO (1960), he experimented more audaciously and gaily than perhaps anyone since silent days, and met with a baffled response from critics and public. *Vie privée*, which followed in 1962, was also received with disappointment: Brigitte BARDOT starred in a story about a star, and Malle did not offer the expected sensationalism. His attempt to portray Bardot as an innocent at large in stardom was not entirely successful, but the film demonstrated his increasing assurance. In 1962 he filmed the Tour de France, and in 1963 made LE FEU FOLLET; a sombre film about the last few days in the life of an alcoholic, it showed astonishing perception and authority. It was well received by critics increasingly baffled by Malle's range of subjects. In the meantime, Malle went to south-east Asia: a film on Bangkok resulted, broadcast on television in 1964. In the same year he directed a production of Strauss's *Der Rosenkavalier* at the festival of Spoleto, an experience which inspired the germ of his next film, VIVA MARIA! (1965). The lavish production on an international scale, co-starring Bardot and Moreau, caused indignation among critics hitherto merely puzzled: some, however, perceived the film's audacity and intelligence, and the public was in no doubt about enjoying the spectacle and the fun.

In 1967 Malle directed Jean-Paul BELMONDO in a spoof FILM NOIR, *Le Voleur*, and made an episode, 'William Wilson' with Alain DELON, in *Histoires extraordinaires* (*Tales of Mystery*: other episodes by VADIM and FELLINI). At the end of 1967 he left for India, and spent six months there with only one or two companions and a 16mm camera. He spent a year cutting the very considerable footage shot into one film, *Calcutta* (1969), and seven television programmes, *L'Inde fantôme*, which were greeted with admiration when they were broadcast in France, Britain, and the US. In LE SOUFFLE AU COEUR (1971), Malle returned to a subject very close to his own experience, and made a film of warmth and delicacy, once again handled with supreme assurance. It is characteristic of him that a potentially scandalous subject was treated without a hint of sensation (as in *Les Amants* and *Vie privée*). The same quality is evident in *Lacombe Lucien* (1974), about a young French labourer who gains self-esteem by becoming a collaborator. Malle has been criticized for a certain reserve or hauteur, but he has made films with a most lively sense of fun, at the same time consistently calling in question cinematic conventions. He has not been afraid, either, to deal with unpopular subjects and through seeking always to stretch his own potential from film to film has acquired an authority sometimes masked by the charm and gaiety of his films.

Remarkably little has been published on Malle. *Louis Malle*, by Henry Chapier, in the Cinéma d'Aujourd'hui series, Paris, 1964, is the only book published to date. A perceptive article was written by Pauline KAEL in the *New Yorker*, 23 October 1970.

**MALRAUX,** ANDRÉ (1901– ), French writer known for his novels and works on the history of art, as well as for his political career (he served as Minister of Cultural Affairs during the government of de Gaulle, whom he first met at the première of GANCE'S NAPOLÉON, 1927). In 1939 Malraux wrote an *Esquisse d'une psychologie du cinéma* published in 1946, and reprinted in *André Malraux* by Denis Marion (Cinéma d'Aujourd'hui series, Paris, 1970). Always anti-Fascist and politically active, he was a volunteer in the International Brigade and Commander-in-Chief of the International Airforce in the Spanish Civil War. He made his only film ESPOIR in Madrid, Barcelona, and Paris in 1938–9, but it was not released until 1945.

**MALTESE CROSS,** or Geneva movement, a mechanism employed in 35mm projectors to produce the intermittent motion of the film which is the basis of the motion picture illusion. (See PERSISTENCE OF VISION.) A wheel driven by the projector motor bears a pin, which enters one of the slots of the cross-shaped wheel (hence the name). The pin rapidly rotates the cross a quarter-turn and slides out of the slot, leaving the cross stationary until the pin completes its rotation and enters the next slot. The cross is coupled to a sprocket which pulls the film past the gate. Thus the motor's continuous rotation is changed into a stop-and-go motion. During the time the cross is stationary the shutter opens and light passes through the film to the screen. Cameras and 16mm projectors use a very different form of intermittent movement. (See PROJECTOR.)

**MALTESE FALCON, The,** US, 1941. 1¾hr. *Dir* John Huston; *prod* Warner Bros; *scr* Huston, from the novel by Dashiell Hammett; *ph* Arthur Edeson; *cast* Humphrey Bogart (Sam Spade), Mary Astor (Brigid O'Shaughnessy), Sidney Greenstreet (Kasper Gutman), Peter Lorre (Joel Cairo), Elisha Cook Jr (Wilmer).

John HUSTON's adaptation of Dashiell HAMMETT's classic of detective fiction was his first film as director. The script, notably faithful to Hammett's dialogue, the outstanding casting (particularly Humphrey BOGART as Sam Spade, a part for which the producers had originally wanted George RAFT), and Huston's sharp, decisive narrative style, combined to make an equally classic film. It inaugurated a succession of thrillers centred on the hard-boiled detective, with WARNER BROS in the vanguard.

The film gave a new direction to Bogart's career and launched Sidney GREENSTREET on a screen career of numerous repetitions of the 'Fat Man', homage to which was paid in *Gumshoe* (1972).

Huston's film largely eclipsed a version of 1931, also from Warner Bros, directed by Roy del Ruth with Ricardo Cortez as Sam Spade and Bebe DANIELS as Miss O'Shaughnessy. Another version was directed by William DIETERLE in 1936 under the title *Satan Met a Lady*, starring Bette DAVIS.

**MAMOULIAN,** ROUBEN (1898–      ), US director born in Tblisi (Tiflis), left the Soviet Union for London as a young man, shortly afterwards going on to America. He spent three years directing opera and operetta for the American Opera Company before moving to the commercial theatre in New York. His career in the theatre has been distinguished, his work including *Porgy* (1928) for the Theatre Guild, and the original productions of *Porgy and Bess* (1935), *Oklahoma* (1943), and *Carousel* (1945).

He was one of several theatre directors who were invited to Hollywood at the beginning of the sound era; he refused to be hamstrung by cumbersome sound equipment and his first film, *Applause* (1929), indicates the fluid, rhythmic style which was to become his hallmark. He is credited with being the first director to use two microphones: he continued to be a technical innovator (he directed *Becky Sharp*, 1935, the first feature film in three-strip TECHNICOLOR), his innovations always furthering his overall conception of a film.

Mamoulian was also a skilled director of actors and, more particularly, actresses. *Applause* contains a remarkable performance by the blues singer Helen Morgan as an ageing, sluttish, but warm-hearted vaudeville performer. Among those who have appeared at their best in Mamoulian's films are Sylvia SIDNEY in CITY STREETS (1931), Miriam HOPKINS in DR JEKYLL AND MR HYDE (1932) and *Becky Sharp*, Marlene DIETRICH in *Song of Songs* (1933), and Greta GARBO in QUEEN CHRISTINA (1934) which contains the most famous of all Garbo images—the final close-up as she stands at the ship's prow, her face, according to Mamoulian's instructions, a perfect blank into which the audience might read what it would.

His background in the theatre helped to make him an outstanding director of film MUSICALS. His first, LOVE ME TONIGHT, made as early as 1932, remains a model for the genre, with an excellent RODGERS and HART score perfectly interwoven into the action. This flair was also demonstrated in *The Gay Desperado* (1936) and HIGH WIDE AND HANDSOME (1937). Similar polish was displayed in two swashbucklers starring Tyrone POWER: *The Mark of Zorro* (1940) and *Blood and Sand* (1940). The ability to use musical numbers to forward characterization and plot is again in evidence in Mamoulian's last two completed films, *Summer Holiday* (1947), a musical version of Eugene O'Neill's *Ah! Wilderness*, and *Silk Stockings* (1957). Neglect of the latter results perhaps from undue reverence for NINOTCHKA (1939) on which it was based.

Tom Milne, *Rouben Mamoulian*, London, 1969; Bloomington, 1970.

**MANCHURIAN CANDIDATE, The,** US, 1962. 2hr. *Dir* John Frankenheimer; *prod* George Axelrod, Frankenheimer; *scr* Axelrod, from the novel by Richard Condon; *ph* Lionel Lindon; *cast* Frank Sinatra (Bennet Marco), Laurence Harvey (Raymond Shaw), Janet Leigh (Rosie), Angela Lansbury (Raymond's mother), Henry Silva (Chunjin), James Gregory (Senator John Iselin).

Shaw, brainwashed as a prisoner in Korea, is conditioned to carry out a series of assassinations. His fellow-veteran Marco, whose treatment has been less effective, realizes the danger, sees that Shaw's mother is manipulating events for her own purposes, and manages to avert disaster.

Working in close collaboration with George AXELROD, FRANKENHEIMER succeeded in transforming the implausible plot into a memorable thriller by the controlled *élan* of his direction. The film's explosive impact and remarkable commercial success were in part attributable to some fine performances, particularly that of Angela LANSBURY as the ruthlessly possessive mother.

**MANCINI,** HENRY (1922–     ), US conductor, composer, and song-writer who in the earlier part of his career was an arranger for Glenn Miller. He started his association with films with UNIVERSAL; his work included musical arrangements for *The Glenn Miller Story* (1953) and *The Benny Goodman Story* (1956). He then began writing background scores, among them TOUCH OF EVIL (1958), and in 1961 won an OSCAR for *Breakfast at Tiffany's* (1961) with its hit song 'Moon River'. He quickly became one of the most successful and popularly known of film composers, excelling at mellifluous writing, sweet idiom, and orchestration. Among his scores are *Charade* (1963), *The Great Race* (1965), *Arabesque* (1966), *The Molly Maguires* (1969), *I girasoli* (*Sunflower*, 1969), *Darling Lili* (1969).

**MAN ESCAPED, A,** see CONDAMNÉ A MORT S'EST ÉCHAPPÉ, UN

**MANGANO,** SILVANA (1930–   ), Italian actress, entered films after winning a beauty competition. She drew international attention in RISO AMARO (1951), where she combined the lack of inhibition popularized by Anna MAGNANI with a more conventional physical attractiveness. Later appearances in Italy and Hollywood have made her an international star. She has appeared in several PASOLINI films, including EDIPO RE (1967), and TEOREMA (1968), and in VISCONTI's MORTE A VENEZIA (*Death in Venice*, 1971). She is married to Dino DE LAURENTIIS.

**MAN IN THE WHITE SUIT, The,** GB, 1951. 1½hr. *Dir* Alexander MacKendrick; *prod*

Michael Balcon for Ealing Studios; *scr* Roger MacDougall, John Dighton, and MacKendrick; *ph* Douglas Slocombe; *mus* Benjamin Frankel; *cast* Alec Guinness (Sidney Stratton), Joan Greenwood (Daphne Birnley), Cecil Parker (Alan Birnley), Michael Gough (Michael Corland).

Untypical in having an undercurrent of serious, even satirical, social comment, *The Man in the White Suit* stands out from the cosy self-confidence of the other EALING comedies. It contains impeccable performances, notably that of Alec GUINNESS as the lonely inventor whose discovery of a dirt-repelling fabric brings upon him the wrath of both capital and labour.

*MANI SULLA CITTÀ*, Le (*Hands Over the City*), Italy, 1963. 1¾hr. *Dir* Francesco Rosi; *prod* Galatea; *scr* Rosi, Raffaele La Capria, Enso Provencale; *ph* Gianni Di Venanzo; *ed* Mario Serandrei; *mus* Piero Piccioni; *cast* Salvo Randone (Belsamo), Rod Steiger (Eduardo Nottola), Guido Alberti (Maglioni), Marcello Cannavale (De Vita).

Using mainly unknown or amateur actors, and set in Naples, the film examines the personality of Nottola (played with remarkable conviction by Rod STEIGER), a corrupt building contractor and councillor who changes his political allegiance to subvert the city's development plan for personal profit. As in SALVATORE GIULIANO (1962), ROSI's neo-realist roots are in evidence: the opening sequence of a collapsing building, in particular, strikingly repays the planning which was needed to shoot it. Throughout, Rosi's terse, economical narrative style is matched by the camerawork of DI VENANZO; the film won the Golden Lion at VENICE in 1963.

MANKIEWICZ, HERMAN (1898–1953), US writer, brother of Joseph L. Mankiewicz. After acquiring a considerable reputation as dramatic editor on the *New York Times* and the *New Yorker* he moved to Hollywood, the first of a number of Broadway writers and journalists to enter films. His first Hollywood venture was *Road to Mandalay* (1926) for Lon CHANEY, and he continued to write story construction and titles. On the advent of sound, his reputation as an accomplished writer of comedy grew with credits such as *The Royal Family of Broadway* (1930) directed by George CUKOR, *Monkey Business* (1932), and HORSE FEATHERS (1932), on both of which he was also associate producer, and DINNER AT EIGHT (1933) also directed by Cukor. With Orson WELLES he wrote CITIZEN KANE (1941) for which he received an OSCAR. A famous Hollywood wit, he continued to write for films until his death. In 1971 Pauline KAEL published *The Citizen Kane Book* which included the

shooting script and cutting continuity of the completed film, and in which she attempts to prove that Mankiewicz's contribution to the film has been severely underestimated.

MANKIEWICZ, JOSEPH L. (1909– ), US producer, director, and scriptwriter, first worked as a journalist and went to Berlin in 1920 for the *Chicago Tribune*; while there he worked for UFA translating silent film titles. On his return to America in 1929 he did similar work for PARAMOUNT, progressing to dialogue (*Fast Company*, 1929), then scriptwriting (*Skippy*, 1931). He scripted comedy (*If I Had a Million*, 1932; *Manhattan Melodrama*, 1934) and drama (FURY, 1936; *Three Comrades*, Frank BORZAGE, 1938), and produced the last two. He also adapted ALICE IN WONDERLAND for the screen (1934). Until 1942 he wrote scripts for Paramount, RKO, and METRO-GOLDWYN-MAYER and produced THE PHILADELPHIA STORY (1940) and WOMAN OF THE YEAR (1942).

Mankiewicz's first film as director was *Dragonwyck* (1945), starring Walter HUSTON and Gene TIERNEY and produced by LUBITSCH. His work during the forties and fifties, particularly *Letter to Three Wives* (1949), ALL ABOUT EVE (1950), and *Five Fingers* (1952), created an impression mostly through his accomplished direction of dialogue. *All about Eve* also evinced his delight in the New York theatrical milieu, and is memorable for Bette DAVIS's star performance. In his sober adaptation of JULIUS CAESAR (1953), he resisted the temptation to undue spectacle, and this ranks as one of the most successful film adaptations from SHAKESPEARE.

Later films include *The Barefoot Contessa* (1954), *The Quiet American* (1958), *Suddenly Last Summer* (1960), and his only musical GUYS AND DOLLS (1955). Mankiewicz took over the direction of CLEOPATRA (1962) after the retirement of Rouben MAMOULIAN from the direction. He completed the film after himself rewriting the script, almost from day to day.

Mankiewicz approaches film making as a writer of intelligence. He gains his effects through speech, and reaction to speech—an essentially theatrical approach, with less emphasis on cinematic possibilities.

MANN, ANTHONY (1906–67), US director, real name Emil Bundsmann, an actor and director on the New York stage before becoming a film casting director. He worked as Preston STURGES's assistant on SULLIVAN'S TRAVELS (1941), and directed his first feature, *Dr Broadway*, a year later. *Devil's Doorway* (1950) was his first Western, and between 1950 and 1960 out of eighteen films, eleven were in the Western genre. Five of these, *Winchester 73* (1950), *Bend of the River* (1951), *The Naked Spur* (1952), *The Far Country* (1955), and *The Man from Laramie* (1955), starred James STEWART, with whom Mann enjoyed a fruitful partnership, not only in Westerns, but in such different subjects as *The Glenn Miller Story* (1953) and *Strategic Air Command* (1955). From the Western Mann moved to the epic, successfully with EL CID (1961), less so with *The Fall of the Roman Empire* (1964). He died while shooting a fashionable spy story, *A Dandy in Aspic* (completed by Laurence HARVEY, 1968).

**MANN,** DANIEL (1912– ), US director, started as a band musician, actor, and producer of television plays. He directed *Come Back, Little Sheba* on Broadway before making a successful screen version in 1952. He made two further film adaptations of stage plays: *About Mrs Leslie* (1954) and *The Rose Tattoo* (1955); the latter, based on Tennessee WILLIAMS's play, introduced Anna MAGNANI to Hollywood. Mann showed more technical assurance as a film-maker with *Butterfield 8* (1961) and *Ada* (1961), but he remained primarily a theatrical director, as evidenced by *Willard* (1971), a disappointing science-fiction story about rats, and a Western *The Revengers* (1972).

**MANN,** DELBERT (1920– ), US film and television director. In 1949 he became an assistant director with NBC television, and within a year was promoted to full director. His major success at this time was in the 'TV Playhouse' series, 1949–55. His first film MARTY (1955), which he had also directed on television, won an OSCAR, and was produced by Harold Hecht and Burt LANCASTER, with a screenplay by Paddy CHAYEFSKY. He also worked with Chayefsky on *The Bachelor Party* (1957) and *Middle of the Night* (1959). His other films include *Separate Tables* (1958), *The Dark at the Top of the Stairs* (1960), *Lover Come Back* (1961), DAVID COPPERFIELD (1969), and *Jane Eyre* (1971). Much of Mann's film work demonstrates his taste for domestic realism.

*MAN OF ARAN*, GB, 1934. 1¼hr. *Dir, ph* Robert J. Flaherty; *prod* Michael Balcon for Gainsborough; *scr* Robert, Frances, and David Flaherty; *ed* John Goldman; *mus* John Greenwood; *cast* Colman 'Tiger' King (Man of Aran), Maggie Dirrane (wife), Michael Dillane (son).

Given a free hand by Michael BALCON to make his first sound film, FLAHERTY chose as his setting the impoverished Aran Islands off the west coast of Ireland. He chose three islanders to represent a typical family, showing in close and reverent detail their everyday struggle with their harsh environment, much as he had observed the Eskimos in NANOOK OF THE NORTH (1922). As in the earlier film, and in MOANA (1926), he resurrected an obsolete practice—here the hunting of the basking shark—into which his players threw themselves with enthusiasm. Perhaps Flaherty's greater intimacy with the Arctic and its people made *Nanook* a more personal film; *Man of Aran* concentrates more on awesome natural forces, especially the sea, than on the islanders. The music, based on Irish folk songs, is strikingly successful; the dialogue suffers from being re-recorded in a London studio. However, Flaherty produced sequences of remarkable beauty.

As usual Flaherty found it impossible to conform to a production schedule, and his extensive material was edited into its final form by John Goldman. The film was a great commercial success and won first prize at VENICE, 1934, an unusual accolade for a documentary film.

**MANSFIELD,** JAYNE (1932–67), US actress, real name Jayne Palmer, whose exaggerated physical proportions made her the butt of tasteless humour in most of her films, typically *The Girl Can't Help It* (1957) and *Will Success Spoil Rock Hunter?* (1957). Her death in a car crash was exploited with the same ruthless publicity as her life had been.

*MA NUIT CHEZ MAUD* (*My Night with Maud*), France, 1968. 2hr. *Dir, scr* Eric Rohmer; *prod* Films du Losange/Films du Carrosse/Les Films de la Pléiade and others; *ph* Nestor Almendros, Emmanuel Machuel; *cast* Jean-Louis Trintignant (Jean-Louis), Françoise Fabian (Maud), Marie-Christine Barrault (Françoise), Antoine Vitez (Vidal).

Jean-Louis, a practising Catholic with high ideals of womanhood, meets Maud, beautiful, intellectual, and free-thinking. She is willing to sleep with him, but he holds to his principles and woos Françoise whom he has noticed in church.

Maud, Jean-Louis, and their Marxist friend Vidal argue out their principles in characteristic ROHMER fashion, articulate and witty but with an underlying depth of feeling. All is not as it seems: the doctrinaire Vidal is fundamentally uncertain, the high-minded Jean-Louis behaves deviously, Françoise is not an untouched innocent, and only the promiscuous Maud speaks and behaves with total candour. The audience is drawn into their social and sexual manoeuvres, the limpid camerawork of Nestor ALMENDROS echoing Rohmer's shrewd observation and humorous analysis of character and motivation, while the players assume their complex roles with remarkable ease and integrity.

*Ma nuit chez Maud* (Eric Rohmer, 1968)

**MANVELL, ROGER** (1909–  ), British film historian and writer, has published many books on the cinema. They include *History of the British Film 1896–1906* (London and New York, 1948) with Rachael Low, *The German Cinema*, *Shakespeare and the Film* (both London and New York, 1971), and, as general editor, *The International Encyclopedia of Film* (London, 1972). He has scripted informational and animated films, the latter for HALAS AND BATCHELOR, and is editor of the journal of the SOCIETY OF FILM AND TELEVISION ARTS.

**MAN WHO CAME TO DINNER, The**, US, 1942. 2hr. *Dir* William Keighley; *prod* Warner Bros; *scr* Julius J. and Philip G. Epstein, from the stage play by George S. Kaufman and Moss Hart; *ph* Tony Gaudio; *cast* Bette Davis (Maggie Cutler), Ann Sheridan (Lorraine Sheldon), Monty Woolley (Sheridan Whiteside), Richard Travis (Bert Jefferson), Jimmy Durante (Banjo), Billie Burke (Mrs Stanley).

Sheridan Whiteside breaks his hip while on a lecture tour with his secretary, Maggie, and is obliged to stay with the Stanley family in a small American town, where his love of mischief and total dedication to self cause trouble and confusion for all around him. Monty Woolley enthusiastically recreated his stage performance and Bette DAVIS skilfully portrayed the secretary; the film bears the marks of its stage origins but William Keighley maintained an effectively frantic comic pace. The original, very successful, Broadway comedy, was supposedly based on the character of the columnist and wit, Alexander Woollcott.

**MAN WHO KNEW TOO MUCH, The**, GB, 1934. 1¼hr. *Dir* Alfred Hitchcock; *prod* Michael Balcon for Gaumont British; *scr* A. R. Rawlinson, Edwin Greenwood; *ph* Curt Courant; *des* Alfred Junge, Peter Proud; *mus* Arthur Benjamin; *cast* Leslie Banks (Bob Lawrence), Edna Best (Jill Lawrence), Peter Lorre (Abbott), Frank Vosper (Ramon Levine), Hugh Wakefield (Clive), Nova Pilbeam (Betty Lawrence), Pierre Fresnay (Louis Bernard).

A young couple on holiday in Switzerland with their small daughter, discover a plot to kill an ambassador in London. The assassins kidnap the couple's daughter to buy their silence, and they attempt to rescue their child and save the ambassador, whose shooting is planned for an Albert Hall concert, on a certain clash of the cymbals. HITCHCOCK's method of building up this climax, shot by the SCHÜFFTAN PROCESS contains the essence of his suspense technique; the film ends with the besieged assassins being smoked out of their hide-out, a sequence based on the Sidney Street siege.

The film's effectiveness derived largely from the tension between melodrama and understatement. It introduced a favourite Hitchcock device, the innocent bystander suddenly caught up in an extraordinary adventure.

The Man Who Knew Too Much, US, 1956. Technicolor; 2hr. Dir, prod Alfred Hitchcock for Paramount; scr John Michael Hayes, Angus McPhail; ph Robert Burks; des Hal Pereira, Henry Bumstead, Sam Comer, Arthur Krams; mus Bernard Herrmann; cast James Stewart (Ben McKenna), Doris Day (Jo, his wife), Daniel Gélin (Louis Bernard), Brenda de Banzie (Mrs Drayton), Ralph Truman (Inspector Buchanan), Mogens Wieth (the ambassador).

While the remake is essentially the same story, there are various differences in detail to suit the different cast and an American audience: Doris DAY's role was altered to that of a former Broadway star, and her singing plays a vital part in the rescue of her child. The original version started in Switzerland; the remake had a more exotic opening, in Morocco. The celebrated Albert Hall sequence closely resembled the original, even retaining Arthur Benjamin's original music, but is given a more humorous treatment, though losing none of its tension.

MAN WHO SHOT LIBERTY VALANCE, The, US, 1962. 2hr. Dir John Ford; prod Ford Productions/Paramount; scr Willis Goldbeck, James Warner Bellah, from a story by Dorothy M. Johnson; ph William H. Clothier; cast John Wayne (Tom Doniphon), James Stewart (Ransom Stoddard), Vera Miles (Hallie), Lee Marvin (Liberty Valance), Edmond O'Brien (Dutton Peabody), Andy Devine (Link), Woody Strode (Pompey).

Senator Stoddard returns to Shinbone for the pauper's funeral of Tom Doniphon, and relates the true story of a legendary event. The essence of the film is the inevitable replacing of the forces of order of the old West by the formalities of democracy and constitutional power, seen with affectionate regret. While the character of Ransom Stoddard carries the story line, Doniphon is the pivot; condemning himself to obscurity by anonymously destroying the vicious menace of Liberty Valance, he preserves Stoddard to build his success on a false reputation. In the words of Edmond O'BRIEN's newspaperman, '... When the legend conflicts with the facts, print the legend'. James STEWART gives a characteristically fine performance, principled, sincere, and bemused. John WAYNE confidently exploits his tough, humorous screen persona, and the film epitomizes the FORD—Wayne nostalgia for a world that never was.

MAN WITH A MOVIE CAMERA see CHELOVEK S KINOAPPARATOM

MAN WITH THE GOLDEN ARM, The, US, 1955. 2hr. Dir, prod Otto Preminger; scr Walter Newman, Lewis Meltzer, from the novel by Nelson Algren; ph Sam Leavitt; des Joe Wright, Darrell Silvera; mus Elmer Bernstein; cast Frank Sinatra (Frankie Machine), Kim Novak (Molly), Eleanor Parker (Zosch), Arnold Stang (Sparrow), Darren McGavin (Louis), Robert Strauss (Schwiefka), George Mathews (Williams).

Set in a seedy Chicago underworld of cardsharpers and drug pushers, the film shows the struggle of a professional gambler to cure his drug addiction. A grim portrayal of squalor and suffering with a performance of harrowing conviction by Frank SINATRA, it was refused a Code Seal by the MOTION PICTURE ASSOCIATION OF AMERICA, on the grounds that it dealt with a banned subject, narcotics. UNITED ARTISTS, the distributor, then resigned from the MPAA and submitted the film to local State censors, most of whom gave it a certificate (see CENSORSHIP, US). Elmer BERNSTEIN's wailing jazz score was a marked strength of the film.

MARAIS, JEAN (1913–   ), French actor, has divided his career between theatre and cinema, and owes much of his success in both fields to a crucial meeting with COCTEAU in 1937. For some years he worked almost exclusively in films written and/or directed by Cocteau, establishing himself as an archetypal romantic hero as Tristan in Delannoy's L'Éternel Retour (1943). He played a dual role in LA BELLE ET LA BÊTE (1946), and had leading parts in Ruy Blas (1947), L'Aigle à deux têtes (1947), LES PARENTS TERRIBLES (1948), ORPHÉE (1950), Éléna et les hommes (1956), Un Amour de poche (1957), LE NOTTI BIANCHI (1957), LE TESTAMENT D'ORPHÉE (1960), La Princesse de Clèves (1962), and Le Gentleman de Cocody (1965).

MARCH, FREDRIC (1897–1975), US actor, real name Frederick McIntyre Bickel. At first he was usually cast in romantic parts. His performance in DR JEKYLL AND MR HYDE (1932) showed his capacity for dramatic roles; other notable appearances include those in The Barretts of Wimpole Street (1934), as Robert Browning, and in ANNA KARENINA (1935). Later parts in a long and distinguished career were in Inherit the Wind (Stanley KRAMER, 1960), SEVEN DAYS IN MAY (John FRANKENHEIMER, 1964), and HOMBRE (Martin RITT, 1967).

MARCH OF TIME, The, a series of twenty-minute film magazines of current events issued monthly in the US 1935–51. The producer was Louis DE ROCHEMONT and technical management was first by Jack Bradford, later taken over by Lothar Wolff. Initially each issue dealt with several subjects; later the number was reduced until each concentrated on one topic only. The series had a distinct political standpoint, following the editorial policies of the influential journals *Time*, *Life*, and *Fortune*, and it has been widely criticized for the often irresponsible combination of ARCHIVE and STOCK footage, newly-shot actuality material, and staged scenes with actors. It was nevertheless a skilled, professional production, adept at blending diverse material to convey its message, and specially-shot sequences were composed and lit to feature-film standards. Issues of the thirties illuminate current American preoccupations: its comments on the state of Europe may have helped swing American opinion against isolationism, especially *Inside Nazi Germany* (1938), *The Ramparts We Watch* (1940), and *America Speaks Her Mind* (1941).

The FRONTIER FILMS series *The World Today*, in a similar format, took a more positively left-wing stance. The NATIONAL FILM BOARD of Canada's THE WORLD IN ACTION (1941–5), used similar techniques to produce a skilled and sober means of informing the public on the progress of the war as a supplement to *Canada Carries On*, which dealt with domestic topics. In Britain, RANK's THIS MODERN AGE (1946–50) attempted to emulate *The March of Time*'s success, but with a less defined editorial policy.

**MAREY**, ÉTIENNE-JULES (1830–1904), French physiologist who studied and photographed animal and human locomotion, evolving a technique of recording successive phases of motion on a single circular plate. In 1882 he developed the 'photographic gun' which took twelve photographs a second, and in 1887 his Chronophotographe, a camera capable of taking about a hundred pictures a second, which was further developed over the next decade by Georges DEMENY. A pioneer in working with rolls of paper film instead of plates, Marey experimented with celluloid stock. He was largely responsible for evolving the motion-picture camera as such, and his demonstration to the Académie des Sciences in Paris in October 1888 was the first presentation of moving pictures recorded on film.

**MÁRIÁSSY**, FELIX (1919–75), Hungarian director, studied in Italy and made his way in the film industry from 1939 as editor and assistant director, not as designer as he had originally hoped. In 1947 he worked on the production of Géza Radványi's VALAHOL EURÓPÁBAN (*Somewhere in Europe*), and in the same year became a teacher in the newly-founded film section of the Academy of Dramatic Art. Together with Zoltán FÁBRI, he became one of the most influential directors in the re-building of the post-war industry. His first film, *Szabóné* (*Anna Szabo*, 1949), was the first to deal with a contemporary problem in realistic terms: it was about the dullness of women's work in a factory, and although conforming in its principles to the rallying tone of socialist realism it treated the human dimension with warmth and was distinctive for a style strongly reminiscent of LADRI DI BICICLETTE (*Bicycle Thieves*, 1948). During the early fifties Máriássy continued to develop an individual style and to deal with contemporary subjects in a rare spirit of criticism. His particular concern with women's problems may have been inspired by his wife, who wrote many of his scripts.

The high point of his directorial career came in 1955, with two films:. one was *Budapesti tavasz* (*Budapest Spring*), made to celebrate the tenth anniversary of the siege and liberation of the city, and alleviating the potential solemnity of the subject with delicately observed human scenes. The other, *Egy pikoló világos* (*A Glass of Beer*), still informed by the spirit of NEO-REALISM, was notable for its sympathetic observation of the difficulties and temptations of a worker's family in a socialist society. It brought Máriássy wide recognition in Eastern Europe and won the Grand Prix at Karlovy Vary in 1956. Although he continued to make films, his work was overtaken in immediacy and experimentation by the younger generation whom he inspired and helped to train. His cosmopolitanism—he strikingly resembled, in both appearance and manner, DALIO as the Count in LA RÈGLE DU JEU (1939)—and commitment made him a favourite ambassador for the Hungarian cinema.

*MARIUS*, France, 1931. 2hr. *Dir* Alexander Korda; *prod* Paramount; *scr* Marcel Pagnol; *ph* Ted Pahle.
*Fanny*, France, 1932. 2hr. *Dir* Marc Allégret; *prod, scr* Marcel Pagnol; *ph* Nicolas Toporkoff. *César*, France, 1936. 2hr. *Dir, prod, scr* Pagnol; *ph* Willer.
*cast* (for the trilogy) Raimu (César), Charpin (Panisse), Orane Demazis (Fanny), Pierre Fresnay (Marius), Alida Rouffe (Honorine), Robert Vattier (M Brun).

Fanny is deserted by Marius, who is unable to resist the call of the sea. In the second film of the trilogy she marries Panisse, old friend of Marius' father César, to save her honour. In the third part Panisse dies and Fanny and Marius are re-united.

The extraordinary success of *Marius*, which had opened on the Paris stage in 1929, moved

PARAMOUNT to engage Alexander KORDA to direct the film version at their Joinville studios. PAGNOL, however, kept considerable control over his work, as he did when Marc ALLÉGRET directed *Fanny* the next year. The success of *Fanny* enabled Pagnol to build his own studios near Marseilles and *César* was filmed there with Pagnol himself directing. The text of *César*, prefaced by a statement of Pagnol's views on cinema, was published in 1937; the play was not performed on the Paris stage until 1945.

The trilogy's enduring appeal is in the humour, gusto, and sympathy with which Pagnol presents Marseilles life. *Marius*, as the least self-consciously cinematic of the three films, best embodies these qualities: nearly all the events take place in Marius' café, the centre both of the action and of comment on the action. RAIMU, particularly in this film and ably supported by CHARPIN and most of the cast, admirably exploits Pagnol's sharp dialogue which, more than the plot, sustains the interest.

The Marseillais trilogy enjoyed great popularity throughout the thirties. Several FOREIGN VERSIONS were made at the time (with Emil JANNINGS playing in the German version of *Fanny*). Joshua LOGAN bought the rights for a remake of the trilogy as FANNY (1960), preventing Pagnol's originals from being seen outside France for a term of years (see COPYRIGHT).

**MARKER, CHRIS** (1921– ), French director, real name Christian François Bouche-Villeneuve, was studying philosophy when the Second World War broke out; during the Occupation he joined the Maquis, then enlisted in the American air force as a paratrooper. After the Liberation he joined the regular staff of the neo-Catholic review *Esprit*, which leaned towards Marxism in an era of Communist witch-hunting. He wrote political commentaries, poems, articles on music, short stories, humorous and biting columns on topical events, and shared the film reviewing with André BAZIN. He was a contributor to CAHIERS DU CINÉMA from its early days. In 1950 he published *Le Coeur net*, a novel about aviation which was favourably compared with Saint-Exupéry. An inveterate traveller with a still camera, he launched a modestly priced, though lavishly illustrated, series of books collectively entitled 'Petit Planète': each volume described a foreign country, giving a subjective impression supported by facts and figures.

In the summer of 1952 Marker went to Helsinki to shoot his first film *Olympia 52*. The same year he wrote the commentary for *Les Statues meurent aussi*, made with Alain RESNAIS, which was banned for ten years as an attack on French colonialism. A number of travel films were commissioned from him by various cultural associations, including *Dimanche à Pékin* (1955) which showed the emergence of a new social order in China. In *Lettre de Sibérie* (1958) the commentary no longer coincided with the images but followed a parallel, literary and poetic, line of its own. A sequence repeated three times, each with a different commentary, and the reflection on the non-objectivity of cinema which this invited, was hailed as a stroke of genius. Marker's collaboration was sought by many film-makers and he agreed, sometimes reluctantly, to write commentaries for films not his own. At this time he began publishing books of still photographs with commentaries, which amount to film in book form: *Corréennes* (1959), *Commentaires* (1961), *Commentaires II* (1967), can all be read visually.

In 1960 Marker made *Description d'un combat* in Israel and in 1961 went to Cuba to make CUBA SI!, a celebration of Castro's revolution. Unfortunately, the Bay of Pigs landing, at the time when Marker was editing his material in Paris, moved him to add an anti-American section that was unacceptable to the French government. The film was banned and Marker published the text and stills in *Commentaires*. LE JOLI MAI (1963), generally classed as CINÉMA-VÉRITÉ, differs from the current *cinéma-vérité* film in its personal flavour and contrapuntal commentary. At the same time Marker made LA JETÉE (1963), a kind of science-fiction poem made up of still photographs.

In 1967 Marker formed a film co-operative SLON (Société pour le Lancement des Oeuvres Nouvelles) to produce a film embodying the protests of five directors—GODARD, IVENS, KLEIN, LELOUCH, and RESNAIS—against the continuation of the war in Vietnam. *Loin du Vietnam* (1967) marked an important stage in his career, not only because with his noted friendliness he managed to reconcile artistically the very different sections and their authors, but because it was his first experience of collective film-making. SLON was revived after the political upheavals of May 1968 and Marker turned from individual film-making to become the moving spirit of the co-operative.

As well as attempting to involve industrial workers by placing film-making facilities in their control, SLON issues two series of short bulletins on current events, *Nouvelle Société* and *On vous parle*. Individual films made by the group include: *La Sixième Face du Pentagone* (Marker and REICHENBACH, 1968), about the peace march on Washington; *La Bataille des dix millions* (Marker and Mayoux, 1970), about the shortfall in the Cuban sugar crop; and Marker's *Le Train en marche* (1971), which combined archive material on the Russian agit trains and an interview with the veteran Soviet director MEDVEDKIN to make a prologue to Medvedkin's rediscovered silent comedy *Schastye* (*Happiness*, 1934).

An elusive and secretive man, Marker has recently tried to merge into the SLON collectivity. But he still holds an exceptional place in French cinema (even though he has never directed a feature film), not only for the quality of his work but for the force and influence of his personality.

**MARKOPOULOS,** GREGORY J. (1928–  ), US director, a personal film-maker since his childhood, and now one of the leading figures in American UNDERGROUND films, has lived in Europe since 1967. Many of his films centre on the theme of homosexual love (male and female), particularly as developed through Greek mythology. His first serious film was a trilogy, *Du Sang de la volupté et de la mort* (1948), with the individual titles *Psyche*, *Lysis*, and *Charmides*. Using a very individual style involving clusters of single frames, superimpositions, and in-camera editing, he has elaborated a narrative style that in *Twice a Man* (1963) allowed a remarkable intermingling of memory and reality further developed in *Prometheus Bound—The Illiac Passion* (1966). His control of sound, colour, and composition continued to evolve in numerous films including the short *Ming Green* (1966), *Himself as Herself* (1966), *Gammelion* (1967), and two series of film portraits *Galaxie* (1966) and *Political Portraits* (1969).

**MARRIED PRINT,** a print with picture and sound combined on the same piece of film. During editing, picture and sound are kept separate for convenience and flexibility; once the film is completed, the MAGNETIC track is converted into an OPTICAL track and printed alongside the picture. The first such print is the ANSWER PRINT. ('Married' is British cinema terminology; 'comopt' is used in British television, 'composite' or 'combined' in the US.)

There were no married prints of the first commercial sound films; in the VITAPHONE process the sound came from a disc precariously synchronized with the picture. The limitations of this system were quickly recognized and 'sound-on-film' became standard. With sound married to picture, no amount of breakage or projectionist's error could destroy SYNCHRONIZATION. Even if a length of film is deliberately cut out of the print, an equal length of sound is cut out with it; synchronization is restored as soon as the splice has passed through both picture gate and sound head. (See COMMAG, STRIPED PRINT, DOUBLE HEAD, PROJECTOR.)

**MARSH,** MAE (1895–1968), US actress whose early career, beginning in 1912, was closely as-

sociated with D. W. GRIFFITH. She starred in his *Man's Genesis* (1912) opposite Bobby Harron, with whom she was afterwards often teamed. Her appearance as Flora Cameron in THE BIRTH OF A NATION (1915) and as 'The Little Dear One' in INTOLERANCE (1916), made her famous. Her unusually expressive face helped give her a reputation equal to that of Lillian GISH, although she was less successful in managing her career away from Griffith. In 1917 she joined Samuel GOLDWYN's new company and made *Polly of the Circus* and *The Cinderella Man* (both 1917). She made two films in England with Herbert WILCOX, before returning to Griffith for *The White Rose* (1923). From 1932 she played supporting parts in over forty films, nine of which, including her last, *Two Rode Together* (1961) in which she played a crazed Indian captive, were directed by John FORD.

**MARSHALL,** GEORGE (1891–1975), US director who worked mainly on short films from 1914 until the early thirties. His many feature films cover virtually every available subject, but he tended to specialize in comedy (with LAUREL AND HARDY and W. C. FIELDS, among others) and in Westerns: the two styles were effectively combined in his best-known film, DESTRY RIDES AGAIN (1939). Marshall also directed the remake, *Destry* (1954), and part of HOW THE WEST WAS WON (1962).

**MARSHALL,** HERBERT (1890–1966), British-born actor, became a popular success in Hollywood during the thirties and early forties in spite of losing a leg during the First World War. He had an individual, rather blasé voice and clipped delivery. Among his best-remembered films are *Blonde Venus* (Josef von STERNBERG, 1932), TROUBLE IN PARADISE (Ernst LUBITSCH, 1932), *Foreign Correspondent* (Alfred HITCHCOCK, 1940), and THE LITTLE FOXES (William WYLER, 1941). He was active in featured roles during the fifties: his later films include *The List of Adrian Messenger* (John HUSTON, 1963).

**MARTIN,** DEAN (1917–  ), US actor and singer, real name Dino Crocetti, had a varied career before teaming up with Jerry LEWIS, with whom he made a successful series of comedies. On his own he has made many popular films, which include Westerns (RIO BRAVO, 1959; *Sergeants Three*, 1961; *Four for Texas*, 1963; *The Sons of Katie Elder*, 1965, and others) and more recently spy spoofs (the Matt Helm films). Several of his film appearances have been with Frank SINATRA's clan. In Billy WILDER's *Kiss Me Stupid* (1964), Martin successfully parodied his public persona.

**MARTIN,** MARY (1913– ), US musical comedy actress who has had an extremely successful career in the theatre. She made a few film musicals, notably *The Great Victor Herbert* (1939) and *The Birth of the Blues* (1941); but in spite of her prettiness and outstanding versatility she was surprisingly neglected by Hollywood.

*MARTY,* US, 1955. 1½hr. *Dir* Delbert Mann; *prod* Harold Hecht–Burt Lancaster Production; *scr, assoc prod* Paddy Chayevsky; *ph* Joseph LaShelle; *cast* Ernest Borgnine (Marty), Betsy Blair (Clara), Esther Minciotti (Mrs Pilletti), Joe Mantell (Angie).

A subtle study of the attachment between two lonely, undistinguished people, *Marty* originated as a television play by Paddy CHAYEVSKY; both the original play and the film were directed by Delbert MANN; Esther Minciotti and Joe Mantell appeared in both versions. Ernest BORGNINE won an OSCAR for his performance as the plain, awkward hero (played on television by Rod STEIGER), and the film won the Grand Prix at the 1955 CANNES Festival. Some of the enthusiasm it aroused might be ascribed to the novelty of its theme and treatment: it maintains its reputation as an attractive and shrewdly-observed film.

As well as initiating a vogue for essentially small-scale drama, emphasizing intimate emotions and ordinary human situations, *Marty* brought a flood of new talent into the cinema. A fresh approach to film-making was initiated by a number of television-trained writers and directors, including Sam PECKINPAH, Arthur PENN, John FRANKENHEIMER, Sidney LUMET, and Franklin SCHAFFNER.

**MARVIN,** LEE (1924– ), US actor, began acting while convalescing from a wound received during the Second World War. His early film roles were of a morose or brutal nature, that in THE BIG HEAT (1953) being perhaps the most notorious. A part as a comic heavy in *The Comancheros* (Michael CURTIZ, 1961) widened his scope, but he returned to type in THE MAN WHO SHOT LIBERTY VALANCE (1962) and THE KILLERS (1964), giving extraordinarily menacing and powerful performances as professional killers. He achieved star status with *Cat Ballou* (1965), in a hilarious double role as an extravagantly evil gunman and the drink-sodden old marksman hired to deal with him.

John BOORMAN has been the director most skilled in using Marvin's special combination of savagery and bewilderment. *Point Blank* (1967) provided a tough, avenging role; *Hell in the Pacific* (1968), in which he and Toshiro MIFUNE were the only actors, depended on the intelligent portrayal of two soldiers, divided by enmity and language, marooned on a Pacific island.

Since these films, and *The Dirty Dozen* (Robert ALDRICH, 1967), Marvin has been much in demand, but the musical *Paint Your Wagon* (Joshua LOGAN, 1969) and numerous other vehicles have failed to provide the harsh, sardonic roles in which he has been most successful, and his comic talents have been largely wasted.

**MARX BROTHERS, The,** US comedy team consisting of CHICO (1891–1961), real name Leonard; HARPO (1893–1964), real name Adolph; GROUCHO (1895– ), real name Julius; and ZEPPO (1900– ), real name Herbert. Their vaudeville act, which originally included a fifth brother GUMMO (1901– ), real name Milton, was built up under the guidance of their mother, Minnie Marx, into a highly individual comedy team. Three musicals established their stage reputation: *I'll Say She Is* (1924), *The Cocoanuts* (1925), and *Animal Crackers* (1928). *The Cocoanuts* was filmed at PARAMOUNT's Long Island studios in 1929, directed by Robert FLOREY. It is a direct record of a Broadway hit of the twenties and of the last great days of vaudeville. In it the brothers helped to smooth the path of true love while deflating the dignity of an obstructive world represented by the intrepid Margaret DUMONT, an application of their particular humour that was roughly repeated in their subsequent films.

The distinctive personality that each had assumed during their vaudeville days was carried intact into their films. Groucho, with his large moustache, spectacles, long cigar, and ill-fitting suit, wore a parody of the uniform of the society which he attacked with shatteringly irreverent wisecracks delivered in a dry and objective tone. Chico's character was based on the traditional Italian street vendor: his motley assortment of clothes and inefficient scheming were combined with an exaggerated accent and a penchant for outrageous puns. Harpo (like Chico a musician of no mean talent) played the harp and never spoke, although he was not in fact dumb. In his total lack of inhibition he represented sheer zaniness. He communicated by hooting a car horn, wore a woolly wig, and cultivated the character of an eccentric and mischievous satyr. Zeppo's character was less extreme than the others; in their first five films he was an awkwardly romantic straight man, then he retired from films.

*Animal Crackers* was filmed, again in New York, in 1930, then, as a result of the recession in the theatre caused by the 1929 Wall Street crash, they moved to Hollywood. For Paramount they made *Monkey Business* (1931), HORSE FEATHERS (1932), and DUCK SOUP (1933), all embodying their typically anarchic humour.

However, these films had little success outside the big cities. After DUCK SOUP Zeppo became an agent and the three remaining Marx Brothers moved to METRO-GOLDWYN-MAYER at the invitation of Irving THALBERG. In A NIGHT AT THE OPERA (1935) and A DAY AT THE RACES (1937), which Thalberg produced, he built up the romantic story line and interpolated production numbers, successfully making them films of general family entertainment (in the best MGM tradition) but in the process diluting their sharp ghetto humour. This tendency continued in *Room Service* (1938), made for RKO, and, again for MGM, *At the Circus* (1939), GO WEST (1940), and *The Big Store* (1941), although there are occasional masterpieces of comic invention. The formula was for a time successful at the box-office, but their popularity rapidly declined: *The Big Store*, in particular, has little to commend it apart from the song 'The Tenement Symphony', which is memorable for its banality.

In 1946 they made *A Night in Casablanca* and in 1949 *Love Happy*. They then split up, making occasional separate guest appearances in films and television. In 1951 Groucho began a successful and long-running television series, nominally a quiz show but in fact a vehicle for his particular brand of wise-cracking insults. His memoirs, *Groucho and me* (London, 1959) and *Memoirs of a mangy lover* (New York, 1964), like Harpo's, *Harpo speaks!* (New York, 1961), are, although low in factual information, very entertaining. In recent years there has been a resurgence of interest in the films and in the brothers themselves. The publication of *The Groucho letters* (London and New York, 1967) and *Why a duck?* (New York, 1971, London, 1972) have both exploited and encouraged their renewed popularity.

**M\*A\*S\*H**, US, 1971. Panavision; 2hr; De Luxe Color. *Dir* Robert Altman; *prod* Ingo Preminger for Twentieth Century-Fox; *ph* Harold E. Stine; *scr* Ring Lardner Jr; *cast* Donald Sutherland (Hawkeye Pierce), Elliott Gould (Trapper John McIntyre), Tom Skerritt (Duke Forrest), Sally Kellerman (Major Hot Lips).

The initials stand for Mobile Army Surgical Hospital and LARDNER's screenplay focuses on the antics of a trio of surgeons forced to work in appalling conditions immediately behind the lines in the Korean war. The matter-of-fact approach to hospital horrors made it a landmark in iconoclastic comedy—establishment-baiting and casually salacious. The most notable feature of ALTMAN's direction was his persistent and effective use of sound overlaps, running four or five conversations simultaneously to simulate the bustle and chaos of the life, which made SUB-TITLES almost impossible. A television series

based on the same setting and characters had considerable success from 1972.

**MASINA, GIULIETTA** (1920–  ), Italian actress, played Pallina in a radio series *Cico e Pallina* written by Federico FELLINI whom she married in 1943. She entered the cinema with a fleeting appearance in ROSSELLINI's PAISÀ (1947) but her first major part was in LATTUADA's *Senza pietà* (1947) for which she was awarded the Italian Silver Ribbon for best character actress. In 1950 she again won this award in *Luci del varietà* directed by Lattuada and Fellini. She has had an active stage and screen career, but her reputation abroad rests largely on her performances in films directed by her husband: LO SCEICCO BIANCO (1952), LA STRADA (1954), IL BIDONE (1955), LE NOTTI DI CABIRIA (1957), for which she won the best actress award at CANNES, and GIULIETTA DEGLI SPIRITI (1965). *Cabiria* especially displays her shrewd, funny, and touchingly vulnerable personality: she has not unjustly been described as a female CHAPLIN. She appeared in *The Madwoman of Chaillot* (1969), her only English-speaking role.

**MASON, JAMES** (1909–  ), British actor. During the thirties he appeared in a number of QUOTA quickies. His first role to attract attention was in *I Met a Murderer* (1939). International recognition came with leading parts in romantic melodramas made by GAINSBOROUGH including *The Man in Grey* (1943), *Fanny by Gaslight* (1944), and *The Seventh Veil* (1945). He became typed as a brutal lover, but his performance as the wounded IRA man on the run in ODD MAN OUT (1947) indicated his real acting capacity. After expressing publicly his dissatisfaction with the monopolistic British film industry he went to Hollywood where he appeared for OPHULS in *The Reckless Moment*, MINNELLI in *Madame Bovary* (both 1949), and MANKIEWICZ in *Five Fingers* (1952). He twice played Rommel, in *The Desert Fox* (Henry HATHAWAY, 1951) and *Desert Rats* (Robert WISE, 1953). His outspoken criticisms of commercial film production, in Hollywood as well as Britain, may have inhibited his development into a major star; but his stature as an actor, assisted by his distinctive voice and attractiveness, has steadily increased. He has become skilled in portraying deeply flawed characters, conveying, notably in JULIUS CAESAR (1953), A STAR IS BORN (1954), and LOLITA (1962), a convincing sense of suppressed anguish.

**MASSEY, RAYMOND** (1896–  ), Canadian-born actor who began his career on the London stage in 1922 and has continued to work on the British and American stage. His aristocratic

Giulietta Masina in *La strada* (Federico Fellini, 1954)

bearing, saturnine face, and expressive voice have brought distinction to a variety of roles including SHERLOCK HOLMES in *The Speckled Band* (1931), *The Scarlet Pimpernel* (1934), the visionary scientist in THINGS TO COME (1936), a particularly devious Richelieu in *Under the Red Robe* (1937), and Abraham LINCOLN in *Abe Lincoln in Illinois* (1939, *Spirit of the People* in GB). Since taking American nationality in 1944 he has worked mostly in the US, but he played the bitterly anti-British Prosecutor in *A Matter of Life and Death* (1946, *Stairway to Heaven* in US). His other post-war films include *Mourning Becomes Electra* (1947), *Prince of Players* (1955), as Junius Brutus Booth, and *The Queen's Guards* (1960), in which his son was played by his real son Daniel Massey (b. 1933); but he is probably best known of recent years as Dr Gillespie in the television series 'Dr Kildare'. His daughter Anna Massey (b. 1937) is an actress.

**MASSINGHAM,** RICHARD (1898–1953), British actor, producer, and director, best remembered for his short wartime PROPAGANDA films. A qualified doctor, he made his first two films, *Tell Me If It Hurts* (1935) and *And So to Work* (1936), in his spare time while a senior resident at the London Fever Hospital. In 1940 he gave up medicine, and founded Public Relationship Films to make sponsored shorts, mainly for government ministries, on subjects ranging from salvage collection and preventing rumours to psychology. Typical was *The Five-Inch Bather* (1942), for the Ministry of Fuel, reminding the public of the need to save water. Massingham appeared as the bulky bather, with the regulation amount of water, soaping himself generously and cheerily rendering 'Drunken Sailor'. His other films include: *Fear and Peter Brown* (1940), *Who'll Buy a Warship* (1942), *Coughs and Sneezes* (1945), *What a Life* (1948). Massingham's films conveyed their message with great sympathy and humour, and as star of most of them he gave a gentle caricature of 'Mr Average Citizen', harassed by, yet coping with, the practicalities of wartime living.

**MASTER POSITIVE** see FINE-GRAIN PRINT

**MASTROIANNI,** MARCELLO (1924–    ), Italian actor, after appearing in *I Miserabili* (1947), a film adaptation of Victor Hugo's LES MISÉRABLES, returned to the stage, playing in a wide range of plays, from Shakespeare to Arthur Miller, before embarking on a film career which has made him an international star. His early work for Luciano EMMER—DOMENICA D'AGOSTO (1950), *Parigi è sempre Parigi* (1951),

Marcello Mastroianni with Jeanne Moreau in *La notte* (Michelangelo Antonioni, 1961)

*Le ragazze di Piazza di Spagna* (1952), *Il bigamo* (1956), Carlo LIZZANI—*Cronache di poveri amante* (1954), and Luchino VISCONTI—LE NOTTI BIANCHI (1957), established him as a sensitive actor. FELLINI's LA DOLCE VITA (1960) made him a worldwide success, but he has continued to work in Europe and chiefly in Italy, where his best films have been made. These include *Il bell'Antonio* (1960), *L'assassino*, LA NOTTE, *Divorzio all'Italiana* (all 1961), *Cronaca familiare* (1962), OTTO E MEZZO (*8½*, 1963). Outside Italy he appeared for Louis MALLE in *Vie privée* (1962) and for John BOORMAN in *Leo the Last* (1969). Mastroianni is skilled at portraying essentially modern men caught in comic, dramatic, or otherwise disorienting circumstances: his performances have a conviction and a quality of intimacy that make him one of the world's outstanding actors.

**MAT** (*Mother*), USSR, 1926. 1½hr. *Dir* V. I. Pudovkin; *prod* Mezhrabpom-Russ; *scr* Nathan Zarkhi, from the novel by Maxim Gorky; *ph* Anatoli Golovnya; *des* Sergei Kozlovsky; *cast* Vera Baranovskaya (Pelageya Vlasova, the mother), A. P. Khristiakov (Mikhail, her husband), Nikolai Batalov (Pavel, the son), Ivan Koval-Samborski (Pavel's friend), Anna Zemtsova (girl student), Pudovkin (police officer).

Zarkhi, working closely with PUDOVKIN, created from GORKY's long and loosely-structured novel a simplified, closely-knit narrative. Set at the time of the abortive 1905 revolution, *Mat* shows the mother's conversion to Communism through her experience of the suffering and injustice caused by the Tsarist régime. The theme is treated with the directness and humanism typical of Pudovkin's silent films. The film's appearance is remarkable: the composition of each individual shot, with its deep focus, impresses every step of the tragedy, giving it a classical movement; his use of water imagery helps maintain a structure that the camerawork and editing might have undermined. Pudovkin achieves, too, an extraordinary illusion of sound. *Mat* earned great and lasting popularity both in the USSR and abroad and brought Baranovskaya international recognition.

**MATCHING.** The production of film has always been a fragmented process. Shots made minutes or months apart in time, in the next studio or the next continent, may appear adjacent in the finished film. Since the juxtaposition would immediately expose any inconsistencies, filmmakers apply the technique of matching, unique to the film medium. When successful, the result is called continuity.

Details of action, costume, and setting are monitored by the CONTINUITY GIRL so that different angles of the same action will match. Scenes shot partly on LOCATION and partly in the studio are matched by making still photographs of the location to be duplicated by scenic artists. The editor matches one take to another to produce action that appears continuous across a cut. The DUBBING mixer adjusts the quality of a studio-recorded voice to match the same voice recorded elsewhere. The grader matches the colour values of successive shots photographed under different conditions. Matching is, in fact, so routine in film production that ideally the audience should never be aware of continuity lapses.

The term matching is also applied to the process of cutting the negative to conform with the cutting copy or work print prepared by the editor.

**MATÉ,** RUDOLPH (or Rudi) (1898–1964), Polish-born cameraman whose reputation is based on his earliest work, particularly DREYER'S LA PASSION DE JEANNE D'ARC (1928), with its alternation of static bleakness and giddy tracking shots, and René CLAIR'S LE DERNIER MILLIARDAIRE (1934). He went to Hollywood in 1935 and, although he collaborated with directors of the calibre of LUBITSCH and HITCHCOCK, his work there was far less distinguished. From the late forties he directed films of little importance.

***MATKA JOANNA OD ANIOŁÓW*** (*Mother Joan of the Angels*, also *The Devil and the Nun*), Poland, 1961. 2hr. *Dir* Jerzy Kawalerowicz; *prod* Kadr Unit, Film Polski; *scr* Tadeusz Konwicki and Kawalerowicz, from the novel by Jarosław Iwaszkiewicz; *ph* Jerzy Wójcik; *des* Roman Mann and Tadeusz Wybult; *cast* Lucyna Winnicka (Matka Joanna), Mieczysław Voit (Suryn), Anna Ciepielewska (Malgorzata).

For both director and Polish cinema, this film represented a decisive break from preoccupation with the war, anticipating such works as HAS's *Rekopis znaleziony w Saragossie* (*The Saragossa Manuscript*, 1964). The story of the Devils of Loudun, also the subject of Aldous Huxley's novel, John Whiting's play, Ken RUSSELL's film *The Devils* (1971), and an opera by Krzysztof Penderecki, is transposed to seventeenth-century Poland. KAWALEROWICZ's highly stylized narrative, austerely designed and composed in hard blacks and whites, inevitably aroused indignation in the Church. The American distributor added a question-mark to the English title.

**MATRAS,** CHRISTIAN (1903–   ), French cameraman who first worked as a newsreel photographer and successfully applied the technique of plain observation to feature films in the thirties. Outstanding among them are Jean EPSTEIN's *L'Or des mers* (1933) and RENOIR's LA GRANDE ILLUSION (1937). Matras has, however, shown himself able to adapt to developing techniques as well as to the demands of varied directors. He photographed Max OPHULS' last films, LA RONDE (1950), *Le Plaisir* (1952), with Philippe AGOSTINI, *Madame de . . .* (1953), and LOLA MONTÈS (1955), all notable for their complex, mobile camerawork, as well as several films for CHRISTIAN-JAQUE and, in wide screen and colour, BUÑUEL's LA VOIE LACTÉE (1969).

**MATTE,** a mask used either in original photography or in OPTICAL PRINTING to expose one area of the film and leave the rest unexposed. The matte may be a sheet of cardboard or metal with an opening cut in it: this is placed in front of the camera ( in the 'matte box') and the scene is shot through it. Such common effects as the keyhole shot or the view through binoculars are made in this way. More often, the matte is a photographic image on film, so dense that no light passes through the opaque part: this is placed in the light path of an optical printer to expose one part of the picture, then the negative of the matte

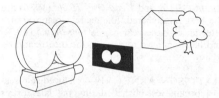

'Binocular' matte

(clear where the positive was opaque and vice versa) is similarly placed to expose the remaining part. By this method the lower half of a shot containing moving actors is combined with an upper half painted by an artist; the irregular dividing line between the two is defined by the matte. Better yet, the matte itself may move: an actor is photographed before a coloured screen and the matte is made by special printing methods so that it changes its shape as the shape of the screen seen behind the actor changes. This method, called travelling matte because the film bearing the matte image travels through the printer, is frequently used to print in a moving background behind a moving actor, when the two cannot be photographed together in the normal way. (See EFFECTS.)

***MATTER OF DIGNITY, A,*** see TELEFTEO PSEMMA, TO

**MATTHAU,** WALTER (1920–   ), US actor, former boxing instructor and basketball coach, made his first film appearance as a heavy in *The Kentuckian* (Burt LANCASTER, 1955), followed by similar roles which he was often able to enrich with a distinctive comic style. He became established as a comic actor in Billy WILDER's *The Fortune Cookie* (1966, *Meet Whiplash Willie* in GB) and with Jack LEMMON in *The Odd Couple* (1967) he particularly excelled as the slob in the partnership. His later films include *The Secret Life of an American Wife* (George AXELROD, 1968), *Cactus Flower* (1969), and the charmingly underplayed *A New Leaf* (Elaine May,

1970), in which Matthau's indolent demeanour was well suited to the part of an ageing, impecunious playboy. He played a straight role as a Los Angeles cop in *An Investigation of Murder* (1974). He directed *Gangster Story* (1961).

**MATTHEWS**, JESSIE (1907–  ), British actress, singer, and talented dancer. She was on the stage from 1917, in revues and musicals in both Britain and the US. She appeared in one or two silent films but her main screen career did not begin until 1931; she quickly rose to stardom, notably in musicals of which *The Good Companions* (1933), *Evergreen* (1934), *It's Love Again* (1936), and *Head Over Heels* (1936) are the best remembered. She made a reappearance after an eighteen-year gap in *tom thumb* (1958) and has continued to work in the theatre and on radio.

**MATTSSON**, ARNE (1919–  ), Swedish director, became established during the late forties with competent thrillers. *När kärleken kom till byn* (*When Love Came to the Village*, 1950) showed a sensitivity to Swedish rural life reminiscent of SJÖSTRÖM. *Hon dansade en sommar* (*One Summer of Happiness*, 1951) created a sensation with its frankness. In *Salka Valka* (1954), set in Iceland, personal drama is again closely related to natural forces in the true Swedish tradition; the film is striking for its visual beauty. His films since the mid-fifties have been polished thrillers or erotic dramas lacking the personal quality of his earlier work.

**MATURE**, VICTOR (1916–  ), US actor, after some stage experience, went to Hollywood in 1939. He was first widely noticed as a mute caveman in *One Million BC* (1940). His best performance was as Doc HOLLIDAY in John FORD'S MY DARLING CLEMENTINE (1946); KISS OF DEATH (Henry HATHAWAY, 1947) and *The Last Frontier* (Anthony MANN, 1956) also gave him a chance to act. But the majority of his films—*Samson and Delilah* (1949), THE ROBE (1953), *The Egyptian* (1954), for example— allowed him merely to display a fine physique and a flashily handsome face. His last two films, *Annibale* (1959) and *Caccia alla volpe* (1966), were made in Italy.

**MAY**, JOE (1880–1954), German director, real name Joseph Mandel. An early maker of melodramas and thrillers, including a series of detective films (in 1913–19), often written by Fritz LANG, about Joe Deeds, he then turned to spectaculars, directing *Veritas Vincit* (1918). His two-part *Das indische Grabmal* (1921), with a

Victor Mature (left) in *My Darling Clementine* (John Ford, 1946)

script by Lang, was notable for its high cost, partly accounted for by the hire of elephants, tigers, and rats, these last to gnaw through the hero's fetters. May's *Heimkehr* and *Asphalt* (both 1928) show the superficial influence of both EX-PRESSIONISM and the STREET FILMS. *The House of Seven Gables* (1940) and *Johnny Doesn't Live Here Any More* (1944) are among numerous films he made in Hollywood.

**MAYAKOVSKY,** VLADIMIR (1894–1930), Russian dramatist, poet, and scriptwriter. He joined the Futurists in 1911 and in 1913 wrote his first film criticism, attacking theatrical films and urging this modern art form to come out into the streets and revolutionize man's view of the world around him. His interest in film increased after the October Revolution of 1917, and in 1918 he scripted and played the leading role in three films *Nye dlya deneg rodivshisya* (*Creation Can't Be Bought*), based on Jack London's *Martin Eden*; *Barishnya i khuligan* (*The Young Lady and the Hooligan*); and *Zakovannaya filmoi* (*Shackled by Film*). Mayakovsky complained that Turkin, the director of two of the films, was unsympathetic towards his ideas and had made no attempt to transfer the Futurist experiments to the screen. Disappointed by this experience Mayakovsky withdrew from films for a time, apart from an article, written in 1922, which attacked the capitalist cinema and looked forward to a revolutionary cinema which would be non-narrative, unemotional, and realistic. He also worked for a short time with Lunacharsky on plans to reorganize the Soviet film industry.

In 1927 VUFKU, the national film company of the Ukraine, asked him to write some film scripts. He wrote nine but they were badly received and only two, both rewritten by other people, were produced. One criticism of the scripts was that they would not be understood by the masses. When other studios also turned them down, Mayakovsky ceased to play an active role in the cinema although he remained intensely interested in it, publicly expressing his criticisms. His plays *Bathhouse* and *Bedbug* were based on rejected film scripts.

**MAYER,** CARL (1894–1944), Austrian scriptwriter, worked as an actor and painter before meeting Hans Janowitz with whom he collaborated on the script for DAS CABINETT DES DR CALIGARI (1919). The subversive elements developed in Mayer's later work are already present in the original version of the script. The success of *Caligari* led to WIENE's engaging Mayer to write his next film *Genuine* (1920). After scripting MURNAU's *Schloss Vogeloed* (1921) Mayer wrote the scenario for Jessner's *Hintertreppe* (*Backstairs*, 1921), the first of his

KAMMERSPIELFILME. SCHERBEN (*Shattered*, 1921) and SYLVESTER (1923), both directed by Lupu PICK, who was in sympathy with Mayer's ideas, reveal Mayer's social awareness. In *Sylvester* he planned much of the lighting, and the use of the mobile camera can be traced to his suggestions. After *Die Strasse* (1923), Mayer wrote DER LETZTE MANN (*The Last Laugh*, 1924), his most enduring work. His detailed script specified the fluid camera movements (worked out in consultation with the cameraman, Karl FREUND) which give the film its penetrating quality, slowly and inevitably detailing the doorman's psychological collapse. Again for Murnau he then adapted *Tartüff* (1925) from Molière's play.

The showing of BRONENOSETS POTEMKIN (*The Battleship Potemkin*, 1925) in Germany inspired Mayer to move away from the studio-bound atmosphere of German film to make documentaries. His idea for a film on Berlin, however, was thwarted by RUTTMANN and he dissociated himself from BERLIN, DIE SYMPHONIE EINER GROSS-STADT (1927).

When Murnau went to Hollywood Mayer was asked to write the script for SUNRISE (1927), which he did on the condition that he could remain in Europe. He worked next with Paul CZINNER and Elisabeth BERGNER on *Ariane* (1931) and *Der träumende Mund* (*Dreaming Lips*, 1932), then moved to England where he worked with Paul ROTHA and was adviser to the TWO CITIES production company. The scripts he wrote in England were never filmed.

Mayer had an extraordinary visual imagination. He was sensitive to the broad range of camera styles and aware of the importance of the camerawork and setting as vital dramatic elements. His scripts were written in great detail with an acute sense of rhythm, describing each shot and containing meticulous directions to the director and cameraman. A script would sometimes take him a year to write and he always kept in close touch with the shooting and the editing, over which he often had the final word. He was completely devoted to the cinema and never wrote for any other medium.

**MAYER,** LOUIS B. (1885–1957), US executive, at one time a scrap dealer, began his career in films as an exhibitor and distributor, making a fortune by acquiring the New England distribution rights of THE BIRTH OF A NATION (1915). After producing several films for the Alco Company, Mayer moved to Los Angeles where he set up his own production company and where, in 1924, he and Samuel GOLDWYN initiated the merger which resulted in the formation of METRO-GOLDWYN-MAYER. For twenty-seven years head of production, Mayer was responsible for moulding the MGM 'image', often with the assistance of vice-presidents like Irving THALBERG and Dore SCHARY. A devout Republican and for years the highest paid individual in the country, Mayer ran the studio with paternalistic authority: the majority of films made accorded with his personal taste for lavish and at the same time wholesome entertainment. He built up the MGM 'stable' of players, grooming promising newcomers to succeed established stars, as well as the teams of contract technicians whose proficiency added gloss to MGM productions. By 1951, however, he was no longer in touch with changing tastes and commercial conditions; he resigned in that year and subsequently became an adviser for the CINERAMA group. A characteristic biography of Mayer is provided in Bosley Crowther's *Hollywood Rajah* (New York, 1960).

**MAYSLES,** DAVID and AL, US documentary film-making team formed in 1962 when Al left DREW ASSOCIATES. David is reporter-soundman, businessman, and (with Charlotte Swerin) editor; Al is cameraman. The first film they made as a team, *Showman* (1962), brought an invitation from GODARD to shoot a sequence in *Paris vu par ...* (1964) with Maysles's own specially-designed 16MM equipment. *Salesman* (1969) was one of the first feature-length DIRECT CINEMA studies to receive wide distribution and brought the methods introduced by Drew Associates before the general public. *Gimme Shelter* (1971) was also widely shown and, particularly for a scene in which a young man is knifed and dies before the camera during a pop concert, aroused much discussion, both within and without the film, of the film-maker's responsibility in remaining a detached observer.

**MEDVEDKIN,** ALEXANDER (1900–    ), Russian director, was a member of the Red Army cavalry during the Civil War. He directed some satirical plays during the early twenties and in 1927 left the army to become editor and assistant director to Okhlopov. During 1931 he made a remarkable series of short satirical films on social and political subjects and, as a result, was appointed to take charge of the film train organized following an order of December 1931. The three-carriage train was designed as a complete moving studio, with a crew of 32, projection and animation facilities, and fully equipped laboratories. During 1932 and 1933 the train travelled to different parts of the Soviet Union, making films on the spot, showing them to the local people and encouraging them to raise and discuss the problems they themselves found important. Medvedkin's vein of satire and enthusiasm informed the work, and such of the films as found their way into national distribution were welcomed by officialdom and public alike. Some hundreds of short films were made during the two years, of which many were thrown away as their immediate object was fulfilled.

Sound was never added to the train's facilities and Medvedkin's first feature-length film, *Styazhateli* (literally *Snatchers*, better known as *Schastye*, *Happiness*) was also silent. Made in 1934, it was released in 1935 and it dealt with the by then forbidding subject of collective farming. Using fantasy, burlesque, vaudeville, even surrealism, Medvedkin made it one of the most original films of Soviet cinema, at a time of severe orthodoxy (see SOCIALIST REALISM); audiences were delighted with its mixture of amusement and instruction. After another feature film in 1936 he returned to making documentaries and continued to do so until the early seventies.

Medvedkin remained virtually unknown outside the Soviet Union until *Styazhateli* was revived by Chris MARKER and the SLON group in 1971, on the occasion of Medvedkin's visit to Paris. Marker made a short film, *Le Train en marche* (1971), to celebrate the work of the film train and its particular brand of satirical-political comment.

**MEERSON,** LAZARE (1900–38), Russian émigré designer, left Russia at the time of the Revolution and made his way via Germany to France. He joined KAMENKA's Société des Films Albatros and worked on Marcel L'HERBIER's *Feu Mathias Pascal* (1925) as assistant to the designer Alberto CAVALCANTI. His ability was quickly recognized and, working with FEYDER and CLAIR, he proved himself the best designer working in France. He moved to TOBIS with Clair, working with him on SOUS LES TOITS DE PARIS (1930), A NOUS LA LIBERTÉ (1931), LE MILLION (1932) and *Quatorze juillet* (1933). After a further association with Feyder, *Le Grand Jeu* (1934) and *Pension Mimosas* (1935), Meerson accepted an offer from KORDA to work for LONDON FILMS but the methods of production at Denham did not appeal to him and he planned to return to France. This ambition was never realized but one of his last assignments reunited him with Clair, working in England on *Break the News* (1938). His widow, Mary, has for some years worked with Henri LANGLOIS at the CINÉMATHÈQUE FRANÇAISE.

**MEET ME IN ST LOUIS,** US, 1944. Technicolor; 2hr. *Dir* Vincente Minnelli; *prod* Arthur Freed for MGM; *scr* Irving Brecher, Fred F. Finklehoffe; *ph* George Folsey, Henri Jaffe; *des* Cedric Gibbons, Lemuel Ayers, Jack Martin Smith, Edwin B. Willis, Paul Holdchinsky; *cost* Irene Sharaff; *mus* Hugh Martin, Ralph Blane;

*chor* Charles Walthers; *cast* Judy Garland
(Esther Smith), Margaret O'Brien, Lucille
Bremer, Joan Carroll (her sisters), Mary Astor
(Mrs Smith), Leon Ames (Mr Smith), Tom
Drake (John Truett), Marjorie Main (Katie).

A classic MUSICAL, its numbers are perfectly
assimilated into a charming family story set in
St Louis, just after the turn of the century. The
film nostalgically maintains the period flavour
without lapsing into sentimentality. It also
includes one of Judy GARLAND's finest performances and her famous 'Trolley Song'. There is a
marvellously natural performance from the child
star Margaret O'Brien, notably in the Hallowe'en
sequence.

**MEKAS, ADOLFAS** (1925–  ), US critic and
director who came to New York with his brother
Jonas in 1950, and served on the editorial board
of FILM CULTURE in the mid-fifties. In 1961 he
made *Let's Cry*, which he followed in 1963 with
the surrealist comedy HALLELUJAH THE HILLS; in
1964 he edited the sound in his brother's *The
Brig*. He also appeared as an actor in Jonas's
*Guns of the Trees* (1961).

**MEKAS, JONAS** (1922–  ), US critic and director, was born in Lithuania and came to New
York in 1950, where he started his film activities,
both critical and practical. He founded FILM CUL-
TURE in 1955, and in 1960 helped to form the
New American Cinema Group. Two years later
he was the inspiration behind the establishment
of the Film-Makers' Co-operative, which soon
became the major distributing system for the
American UNDERGROUND. The majority of his
films are documentary in style and intention
(such as *Film Magazine of the Arts*, 1963, and
*The Millbrook Report*, 1966), but after writing
in support of independent features, he made the
experimental *Guns of the Trees* (1961), an
elliptical, disjointed narrative, and in 1964
*The Brig*, his best known film. *The Brig* was a
straight record of the Living Theatre's
production of Kenneth Brown's play, but the
economical CINÉMA-VÉRITÉ approach to
military brutality which Mekas employed
endowed the film with such claustrophobic
power that it won a documentary award at
VENICE in 1964. He has been a film columnist
for the *Village Voice*.

**MÉLIÈS, GEORGES** (1861–1938), French director, was the youngest son of a wealthy footwear
manufacturer, who pressed him into the family
business where he gained useful experience with
the factory's machines. He spent 1884 in London
and saw the famous conjurors Maskelyne and
Devant who inspired him to become a conjurer
himself. He also began drawing caricatures under

the anagrammatic pseudonym 'Geo Smile' for
the satirical journal *La Griffe*. In 1888 he bought
the Théâtre Robert-Houdin and until 1895 gave
all his time to running it as inventor, mechanic,
stage designer, and illusionist. A studio above the
theatre was rented to Antoine LUMIÈRE; Méliès
was present at the first public presentation of
the Cinématographe and was greatly excited by
it. The Lumières refused to sell their apparatus,
but Méliès bought a similar machine from
R. W. PAUL in London and on 4 April 1896
opened his Théâtre Robert-Houdin as a cinema.
During that year he made seventy-eight films in
the Lumière manner, as well as constructing
France's first film studio at Montreuil, near
Paris.

In 1898 the shutter of his camera jammed
while he was filming a street scene and Méliès
quickly realized the potential of trick photography to create magical effects. He developed a
repertoire of devices, including superimposition
and stop-motion: in 1898 he made *La Boîte
mystérieuse* using six trick effects. *L'Affaire
Dreyfus* (1899), a reconstruction of events from
the DREYFUS case, was followed by *Cendrillon* in
his more characteristic vein of fantasy. In 1900
he founded the first Chambre Syndicale des
Éditeurs Cinématographiques, holding the office
of president until 1912, and in 1909 he was
chairman of the CONGRÈS DES DUPES. Among
the numerous films he made during his heyday
were *Barbe-bleue* (1901), *Le Voyage dans la lune*
(1902), *Le Voyage à travers l'impossible* (1904),
*Deux Cent Milles Lieues sous les mers*, *Le Tunnel sous la Manche* (both 1907), *La Civilisation
à travers les âges*, *New York–Paris en automobile* (both 1908), all pervaded with humour
and invention.

In 1903 Méliès fought his imitators in America by opening STAR-FILM in New York, managed
by his brother Gaston, and in 1908 went over to
renting rather than selling films. From the same
year Star-Film produced Westerns and actuality
films as well as distributing Méliès' French
productions. In 1911 Méliès formed an alliance
with PATHÉ FRÈRES to distribute for Star-Film
and borrowed large sums from them to produce
his last films, including *La Conquête du Pôle*
(1912) and *Le Voyage de la famille Bourrichon*
(1913), for a rapidly developing industry engen-
dering new tastes had left him behind. His films
failed and he lost almost everything; the American company also collapsed. Méliès converted
one of his studios into the Théâtre des Variétés
Artistiques and performed there as a comedian
until 1923 when he was declared bankrupt. His
1,200 films were melted down into a substance
used in the manufacture of footwear, but at a gala
evening for Méliès held at the Salle Pleyel in
1928 a recently-discovered cache of his films

was shown. Shortly afterwards he retired to a retreat for 'cinématographistes'.

Méliès was a man of startling virtuosity and astounding energy whose influence on the fantasy film was seminal. He took the paraphernalia of the popular theatre of illusionism, spectacle, and pantomime wholesale into film, transforming it into cinematic terms through resourceful use of the camera's potential to play tricks. Some of his 'magic' effects still puzzle experts. He himself appeared in many of his films as the Devil, Mephistopheles, Faust, an alchemist, or a magician. Only about a hundred of his films have survived; there are also compilations comprising various shorter, and sections from longer, works. In 1952 Georges FRANJU, who had brought Méliès his last medicines, made *Le Grand Méliès* with Méliès' widow and his son André.

**MELODIE DER WELT** (*World Melody*), Germany, 1929. 1¾hr. *Dir, scr* Walter Ruttmann (from material made available by the Hamburg Amerika shipping line); *prod* Tobis Tonbild Syndikat; *ph* Reimar Kuntze, Wilhelm Lehne, Rudolph Rathmann, Paul Holzki; *mus* Wolfgang Zeller; *cast* J. Kowal Samborsky (the sailor), Renée Stobrawa (the woman).

Germany's first full-length sound feature, *Melodie der Welt* is an interesting piece of pioneering. The aim was to encompass the sum total of human activities and achievements by offering a cross-section of the world served by the sponsors' liners. The content of the film tends to be overwhelmed by the impressive structure. Thematically it is loosely constructed to cover topics such as religion, means of transport, sports, etc; formally it is more unified, the images deliberately colliding or linking. Its rhythmic MONTAGE is applied to both sound and image and the musical sound-track is integrated with natural sounds, such as ships' sirens, engines, and anchor chains.

**MELVILLE,** JEAN-PIERRE (1917–73), French director and producer, real name Grumbach, whose early and enduring enthusiasm for American culture moved him to change his name to that of his favourite writer, Herman Melville. In 1946 Melville started his own production company and made *Vingt-Quatre Heures de la vie d'un clown* (1946) and *Le Silence de la mer* (1948); he also directed LES ENFANTS TERRIBLES (1950) for COCTEAU.

Cocteau's influence on Melville, together with that of the American gangster novel, gave his most typical films a curiously stylized shabbiness. *Bob le flambeur* (1955), *Le Doulos* (1962), LE DEUXIÈME SOUFFLE (1966), and *Le Samourai* (1967), all gangster stories, did much to maintain the artistic respectability of the FILM

NOIR. A departure from his usual themes was LÉON MORIN, PRÊTRE (1961), a moving study of internal conflict, which gave BELMONDO one of his best roles. His *L'Armée des ombres* (1969) made memorable use of the topography of old Lyons.

Melville's aloof independence—he worked in his own studio and was uncommitted to the commercial distribution system—as well as his appreciation of American popular art, made him an idol among the young directors of the NOUVELLE VAGUE. He played a cameo role for GODARD in A BOUT DE SOUFFLE (1960) wearing the white stetson that became his trade-mark and that of his isolated heroes.

**MEMBER OF THE WEDDING, The,** US, 1953. 1½hr. *Dir* Fred Zinnemann; *prod* Stanley J. Kramer; *scr* Edna and Edward Anhalt, from the book and play by Carson McCullers; *ph* Hal Mohr; *cast* Julie Harris (Frankie), Ethel Waters (Berenice), Brandon de Wilde (John Henry).

Frankie, caught in confused adolescent emotions, waits for her adored elder brother's wedding, naïvely convinced that she will play a major role in the occasion. Carson McCullers had adapted her own book for the stage, and the film was based closely on this stage version; for the first time in Hollywood all the leading actors in the play were also in the film version. ZINNEMANN's delicate direction of moving interpretations vindicates the often-criticized 'canned theatre', successfully maintaining the enclosed atmosphere and dependence on dialogue of the play.

**MEMORIAS DEL SUBDESAROLLO** (*Memories of Underdevelopment*), Cuba, 1968. 1¾hr. *Dir, scr* Tomás Gutiérrez Alea, from the novel by Edmund Desnoes; *prod* Miguel Mendoza; *ph* Ramon Suarez; *ed* Nelson Rodriguez; *mus* Leo Bower; *cast* Sergio Corrieri (Sergio), Daisy Granados (Elena), Eslinda Nunez (Laura), Beatriz Ponchola (Noemi).

The first feature film to emerge from Castro's CUBA was warmly welcomed. Sensitively transposing Desnoes's novel to the screen, ALEA examines the dilemma of the intellectual in postrevolutionary Cuba (expressed by Desnoes himself in a scene at a writers' conference). A mature and ironical film (pointed up by a visit to Hemingway's house on the island), it conveys the atmosphere of the new Cuba shrewdly and humanely.

**MEMORIES OF UNDERDEVELOPMENT** see MEMORIAS DEL SUBDESAROLLO

**MENJOU,** ADOLPHE (1890–1963), US actor, appeared in many silent films including *The*

*Sheikh, The Three Musketeers* (both 1921), *The Marriage Circle* (1923), A WOMAN OF PARIS (1924), and *Serenade* (1927), usually playing a caddish matinée-idol type. He had a long career after the arrival of sound, progressing with ease to character parts, and playing in dramas, comedies, and musicals: his films include MOROCCO (1930), THE FRONT PAGE (1931), *A Farewell to Arms* (1933), GOLDDIGGERS OF 1935 (1935), *Stage Door*, A STAR IS BORN (both 1937), *Goldwyn Follies* (1938), *Roxie Hart* (1942), *Dancing in the Dark* (1949), PATHS OF GLORY (1957). Menjou was known as the screen's best-dressed man; he achieved another kind of publicity by co-operating with the UNAMERICAN ACTIVITIES Committee.

**MENSCHEN AM SONNTAG** (*People on Sunday*), Germany, 1929. 1hr (but see below). *Dir* Robert Siodmak, Edgar Ulmer; *scr* Billy Wilder; *ph* Eugen Schüfftan; *des* Moritz Seeler.

These are the credits given in Borde, Buache, Courtade, *Le Cinéma réaliste allemand* (Paris, 1965). Fred ZINNEMANN's name is also associated with the film, and the idea is attributed to Béla BÁLASZ. SIODMAK has said that WILDER was only peripherally involved, and in a co-operative venture of this sort the participants' roles were probably undefined.

The film details twenty-four hours in the lives of a group of working-class Berliners, observed with freshness and a dry humour. It owes much to the documentary approach of RUTTMANN; while using a structured story, the players are non-professionals re-enacting their real-life roles.

Like many silent films made after sound had been introduced, *Menschen am Sonntag* should be projected at sound, rather than silent, speed. The effect when it is projected at silent speed is ponderous and misleading.

**MENZEL, JIŘÍ** (1938–   ), Czech director, worked with CHYTILOVÁ at the Prague film school, FAMU, assisting on and acting in her graduation film. Menzel continued acting in the films of other directors (including SCHORM's *Každý den odvahu, Everyday Courage*, 1964, and *Návrat ztraceného, Return of the Prodigal Son*, 1966) as well as in his own films. His first venture in direction was a contribution to *Perličky na dně* (*Pearls of the Deep*, 1965): his episode, 'The Grand Prix', was a beautifully visualized short story by Bohumil Hrabal. Working with Josef Skvorecky, Menzel made the first —and funniest—episode of *Zločin v dívčí skole* (*Crime in the Girls' School*, 1965), starring Věra Kresadlová, FORMAN's second wife. In OSTŘE SLEDAVONÉ VLAKY (*Closely Observed Trains*, 1966), Menzel brought to a culmination the anti-heroic trend which characterized so much of the

literature and cinema of the sixties. The film's gentle black humour won it enormous popularity in Czechoslovakia, an OSCAR in the US, and condemnation in the USSR as being insulting to the anti-Nazi movement.

The same laconic humour was apparent in *Rozmarné léto* (*Capricious Summer*, 1968), based on a work by Vladislav Vančura about three ageing Lotharios idling by a swimming pool. Menzel learnt to walk the tight-rope for a part in the film: and repeated the feat in his next film, *Zločin v šantánu* (*Crime in the Night-club*, also 1968). This, too, was made with Josef Skvorecky, and was planned to be a combination of CHAPLIN, W. C. FIELDS, and Jean HARLOW. The concoction was devised for the pop singer Eva Pilarová and the satirical pair Suchý and Šlitr (with whom Menzel has regularly worked at the Semafor Theatre). The film was one of the best-attended during the months which followed the invasion of August 1968. Menzel's next film, *Skřivánci na niti* (*Skylarks on a String*), again based on Hrabal's work and again starring Věra Kresadlová, was completed in 1969 and banned in the spring of 1970: it remains unreleased.

**MENZIES, WILLIAM CAMERON** (1896–   ), US art director who defined and established the position of 'production designer', responsible for the overall appearance of a film: art direction, set design, costumes, etc. In this capacity he was responsible for the costly, yet controlled, design of GONE WITH THE WIND (1939). He worked on such films as THE THIEF OF BAGDAD (1924), Howard HAWKS's *Fig Leaves* (1926), ALICE IN WONDERLAND (1934), and Lewis MILESTONE's *Arch of Triumph* (1948), and has been particularly associated with films directed by Sam WOOD: *Our Town* (1940), *The Devil and Miss Jones* (1941), *Kings Row* (1942), and *For Whom the Bell Tolls* (1943). Intermittently he has been a director, initially with *The Spider* (1931), and in this role is best known for THINGS TO COME (1936) in which design was a paramount feature.

**MÉPRIS, Le** (*Contempt*), France/Italy, 1963. Franscope; 1¾hr; Technicolor. *Dir* Jean-Luc Godard; *prod* Georges de Beauregard, Carlo Ponti, Joseph E. Levine; *scr* Godard, based on the novel *Il disprezzo* by Alberto Moravia; *ph* Raoul Coutard; *ed* Agnès Guillemot; *mus* Georges Delerue; *cast* Michel Piccoli (Paul Javal), Brigitte Bardot (Camille Javal), Jack Palance (Jeremy Prokosch), Fritz Lang (himself), Giorgia Moll (Francesca).

The story of a wife's increasing contempt for her husband and his efforts to understand why she despises him takes place in the milieu of international film-making in Italy. *Le Mépris* is itself a truly international film, with each star speaking his native language and communicating through Giorgia Moll's quadrilingual interpretation. This, together with the star cast, the use of colour and wide screen, and the more conventional narrative structure (the screenplay adheres closely to the novel from which it is adapted), suggests that the film was intended for wider distribution than any of GODARD's preceding work. The confidence of Raoul COUTARD's photography, particularly in the climactic marital quarrel, the striking use of primary colours, and Georges DELERUE's music contribute handsomely to the film's accomplishment.

**MERCANTON,** LOUIS (d.1932), Swiss-born French director, worked in the theatre notably with Sarah BERNHARDT. He became a prolific film-maker, strongly influenced by the FILM D'ART, and he co-directed LA REINE ELISABETH (1912), starring Bernhardt. During the First World War he worked in London; he directed an important PROPAGANDA film, *Mères françaises* (1917), again starring Bernhardt. *Bouclette* and *Le Torrent* (both 1918, made with his life-long collaborator Hervil) had the young Marcel L'HERBIER as scriptwriter. *Miarka, la fille de l'ours* (1920), with Réjane, is generally considered his best film. From 1925 he worked on Anglo-French co-productions and on two-language versions of films at PARAMOUNT's Joinville studios (see FOREIGN VERSIONS) including *Le Mystère de la Villa Rose* (1930) again with Hervil. Mercanton was a theoretician of the cinema, with views close to those later taken up by the neo-realists: he persisted in working in genuine locations after most film-makers had changed over to studio filming.

**MERCHANT,** VIVIEN (1929– ), British actress, has become one of the leading interpreters, on television as well as in the theatre, of Harold PINTER's work (she married him in 1956). Her films include *The Way Ahead* (1944), *Alfie* (1966), ACCIDENT (1967), and *Alfred the Great* (1969).

**MERCOURI,** MELINA (1925– ), Greek actress and singer. Daughter of a mayor of Athens, she trained with the Greek National Theatre Company and had a successful stage career before her first film part in *Stella* (CACOYANNIS, 1955). She worked for Jules DASSIN on *Celui qui doit mourir* (1956), an association continued in the internationally successful POTE TIN KYRIAKI (*Never on Sunday*, 1960), *Phaedra* (1961), and *Topkapi* (1964). Only her screen appearances for Dassin, whom she married, showed the control and discipline necessary for so theatrical a personality. Her active campaigning

against the Greek junta resulted in the confiscation of her passport in 1967; in exile she was an even more vocal critic of the régime until her return to Greece in 1974.

**MEREDITH,** BURGESS (1909– ), US actor, accomplished and versatile, of distinctive voice, distinguished in the theatre before his first film appearance in the leading role in *Winterset* (1936), a part he had played on the Broadway stage. Particularly notable were his performances as an American war correspondent in William WELLMAN's *The ·Story of GI Joe* (1945), of which he was also co-producer, and in Lewis MILESTONE's film of John STEINBECK's *Of Mice and Men* (1939). He has been equally effective in comedy (including Garson KANIN's *Tom, Dick and Harry,* 1941; and Ernst LUBITSCH's *That Uncertain Feeling,* 1941) and even in a Fred ASTAIRE musical, *Second Chorus* (1940). Memorable among his sporadic later performances was his hostile and unbalanced witness in Otto PREMINGER's *Advise and Consent* (1961).

**MERRY WIDOW, The,** US, 1925. 2½hr. *Dir* Erich von Stroheim; *prod* MGM; *scr* Stroheim, Benjamin Glazer, from the operetta by Franz Lehár and Leo Stein; *ph* Oliver T. Marsh, Ben Reynolds, William Daniels; *des* Stroheim, Richard Day; *cast* John Gilbert (Prince Danilo), Mae Murray (Sally O'Hara), Roy D'Arcy (Prince Mirko), Tully Marshall (Baron Sadoja).

In spite of cuts demanded by the producers, *The Merry Widow* is the only major STROHEIM film to have been released in a form approximating to his intentions. His version is far from Lehár's popular operetta, the plot of which is not indicated until the last third of the film: instead he creates another version of the decadent Ruritania that is a major theme of his early work. The film constantly refers back to FOOLISH WIVES (1921) and forward to THE WEDDING MARCH (1926–8) and QUEEN KELLY (1928), particularly in its lavishness of décor and ironical observation of sexual peccadilloes.

A more direct film version of *The Merry Widow* was directed by LUBITSCH in 1934, starring Maurice CHEVALIER and Jeanette MACDONALD.

**MESSTER,** OSKAR (1866–1943), German inventor, producer, and director, set up his own film production company in 1896 using equipment he had invented himself. He experimented with speeded-up effects, close-ups, and animation, and attempted a crude form of synchronization in his filmed operettas by using records. In 1910 he founded a company for the manufacture of film equipment and in 1914 he began the first German NEWSREEL, *Messter Woche.* This was often little more than staged propaganda, with extras dressed as British. In 1917 all his companies came under the control of UFA.

**MÉSZÁROS, MARTA** (1931– ), Hungarian director, daughter of the sculptor László Mészáros, moved with her family to the Soviet Union, returning to Hungary in 1946. She studied film at VGIK in Moscow and afterwards gained experience in Budapest and Romania. In her considerable output of short films two themes dominate—art (e.g. *Festők városa—Szentendre, Szentendre—Town of Painters*, 1964) and children (e.g. *Bóbita, Blow-Ball*, 1964). Since 1968 she has directed features, showing particular interest in the metaphysical problems of young people—*Eltávozott nap* (*The Girl*, 1968), *A 'holduvar'* (*Binding Sentiments*, 1969), *Szép lányok, ne sírjatok* (*Don't Cry, Pretty Girls*, 1970), *Szabad léglegzet* (*Riddance*, 1973); her films are characterized by an unobtrusive, fluid visual style. She is married to Miklós JANCSÓ.

**METHOD** see ACTORS' STUDIO

**METROCOLOR,** a name used to identify films photographed on EASTMAN COLOR stock and processed by METRO-GOLDWYN-MAYER.

**METRO-GOLDWYN-MAYER,** US production company known as MGM, trademark a roaring lion encircled by a banner reading *ars gratia artis*. MGM was formed in 1924 with the merging of the three companies that constitute its title.

In 1916, J. Robert Rubin and Louis B. MAYER had helped found Metro Pictures Corporation as a successor to the failing Alco Company. Metro was taken over in 1920 by the exhibitors Loew's Inc. Rubin and Mayer had also established the Louis B. Mayer Pictures Corporation in 1918. This Hollywood-based company provided films for Metro and attracted Irving THALBERG from UNIVERSAL in 1923. Another producer, Samuel Goldfish, on leaving FAMOUS PLAYERS–Lasky, joined the Selwyn brothers in 1916 to set up Goldwyn Picture Corporation. The Goldwyn Studios in Culver City, once the home of TRIANGLE, eventually became the Hollywood headquarters of MGM. By the time of the merger, Samuel Goldfish was no longer active in the Goldwyn company having left to become an independent producer under his new name— Samuel GOLDWYN. Marcus LOEW, president of Loew's Inc, organized the triple merger—first, the 1924 purchase of Goldwyn Studios by Metro, then the acquisition of the Mayer group by Metro-Goldwyn in the same year.

When these transactions became final, Mayer was appointed studio head of MGM, a position which he held for the thirty years during which the company was the most important Hollywood studio. The administrative triumvirate of Mayer, Thalberg, and Harry Rapf was responsible for early successes such as *He Who Gets Slapped* (1924), THE BIG PARADE, BEN-HUR (both 1925), THE BROADWAY MELODY (1929), and GRAND HOTEL (1932). 'More stars than there are in the heavens' was MGM's catch-phrase, and numbered among the contract players were Greta GARBO, John GILBERT, Norma SHEARER, Clark GABLE, Joan CRAWFORD, the BARRYMORES, Lewis STONE, Jean HARLOW, Elizabeth TAYLOR, Judy GARLAND, Katharine HEPBURN, Spencer TRACY, and Greer GARSON. Directors and producers associated with the studio include George CUKOR, Clarence BROWN, Victor FLEMING, Mervyn LEROY, Vincente MINNELLI, Busby BERKELEY, David O. SELZNICK, and Arthur FREED.

MGM's executives made it clear that their primary concern was to attract the widest possible audience, regardless of the restrictions this policy might entail. The nonconformist talents of men like Erich von STROHEIM, Buster KEATON, Robert FLAHERTY, Rex INGRAM, and the MARX BROTHERS were not only unappreciated but often suppressed or destroyed. Indicative of all this was the standard studio policy of never allowing the lighting to be below a certain wattage so that all their films could be shown even in the poorest equipped cinemas.

Mayer and company devised the formula of providing idealistic, folksy films of Americana for home consumption and profit, and romantic screen classics for foreign distribution and prestige. Thus it was possible for the studio to be producing simultaneously the HARDY FAMILY series and the Garbo films. Shrewd, too, was Mayer's offer of MGM as home for the newspaper publisher William Randolph HEARST's Cosmopolitan Pictures Corporation and its star, Marion DAVIES, ensuring, as it did, a good press for MGM films in the Hearst papers.

MGM survived the coming of sound and an attempted takeover by William FOX early in 1929, and prospered during the Depression reaching the height of its success between 1935 and 1945, largely because of the conservative economics exercised in the New York office run by Nicholas SCHENCK. Before the war the studio produced most of its finest films—DAVID COPPERFIELD (1934), THE MUTINY ON THE BOUNTY (1935), the THIN MAN series, THE WIZARD OF OZ and GONE WITH THE WIND (both 1939). The need for escapist entertainment during the war carried MGM up to the mid-forties, a time when, deprived of its male stars, the studio exploited its CHILD STARS and actresses, in such films as *Mrs Miniver* (1942), *Lassie Come Home* (1943), and MEET ME IN ST LOUIS (1944). (MGM always catered especially for a female audience, earning it the title of the 'Woman's' studio.)

During this period MGM, having previously made its own FOREIGN VERSIONS in Hollywood, ventured into full-scale overseas production. Loew's Inc had for a long time been acquiring foreign cinema chains and film exchanges, and in 1937 MGM, worried by the Anglo-American film situation in Britain (see GREAT BRITAIN), founded MGM British Ltd, under the management of Ben Goetz at the DENHAM Studios. Some notable films were produced by MGM British, such as *Goodbye, Mr Chips* (1939); but, unfortunately, Mayer preferred to bring new English discoveries to Hollywood, rather than use them in London, and his attempts to lure British producers like BALCON and KORDA to MGM British were always short-lived.

The studio's gradual decline began after the war when Mayer was reigning alone—Thalberg had died in 1936, and no replacement for him was found until Dore SCHARY arrived at MGM in the late forties. Friction grew between Schenck, Mayer, and Schary and, in 1951, Mayer resigned. A year later, under the dictation of the Sherman Anti-Trust legislation, Loew's were forced like other companies to divorce their production and distribution interests (i.e. MGM) from their exhibition company. Schary remained head of MGM until 1956, but he and his successors lacked the kind of autocratic control necessary to make a monolithic studio function. Except for a few, often contrived, attempts at regaining prestige—the Gene KELLY musicals, the remakes of BEN-HUR (1959) and THE MUTINY ON THE BOUNTY (1962), DOCTOR ZHIVAGO (1966), 2001: A SPACE ODYSSEY (1968), and ZABRISKIE POINT (1970)—the MGM lion was no longer king of the Hollywood jungle.

Trying to offset heavy financial losses in the late sixties, MGM changed management three times in ten months and was finally bought by Kirk Kerkorian, a Las Vegas financier. The company, under the guidance of James Aubrey, an ex-president of CBS-TV, managed to make a profit by selling to an auctioneer old properties and costumes from the MGM stock, by selling off land and closing down their overseas studio at Borehamwood, England, and by cutting back production to low-budget films for non-road show or television audiences. MGM withdrew from the film business entirely in 1974.

**METROPOLIS,** Germany, 1927. 4$\frac{1}{4}$hr. *Dir* Fritz Lang; *prod* UFA; *scr* Lang, Thea von Harbou; *ph* Karl Freund, Günther Rittau; *des* Otto Hunte, Erich Kettelhut, Karl Vollbrecht; *cast* Brigitte Helm (Maria), Gustave Froehlich (Freder), Alfred Abel (his son), Rudolph Klein-Rogge (Rotwang), Heinrich George (Contrem), Fritz Rasp (Grot).

LANG was given a budget unprecedented in Germany to create a futuristic city-factory in which the working masses are slaves of the few rich masters. Like DIE NIBELUNGEN (1924), *Metropolis* represents the peak of his architectural achievement in the cinema: in settings of mammoth proportions, inspired by the skyscrapers of New York but with touches of expressionist grotesquerie, an allegory of totalitarianism takes place culminating in the revolt of the slaves, handled with a masterly sense of rhythm and control The apparent naïvety of the resolution, where love across class barriers unites the people with their rulers, may have been necessary in the political climate of the time.

*Metropolis* introduced the SCHÜFFTAN PROCESS, in an impressive sequence of flying machines moving between towering buildings.

**METZNER, ERNÖ** (1892–    ), German painter and art director, made one short experimental film, *Überfall* (*Accident*, 1929), a mystery story using Russian-style MONTAGE and distorted images. He was art director on *Die weisse Hölle von Pitz Palü* (*The White Hell of Pitz Palü*, 1929), one of Arnold FANCK's 'mountain' films, but as a designer he is best remembered for his work for PABST. Abandoning his earlier EXPRES″ SIONISM for the intensified naturalism that was the hallmark of German studio production during the late twenties and early thirties, he designed the sets for Pabst's *Das Tagebuch einer Verlorenen* (*Diary of a Lost Girl*, 1929), WESTFRONT 1918 (1930), KAMERADSCHAFT (1931), with its impressive reconstruction of a coal-mine, and *L'Atlantide* (1932). Like other Jewish artists, Metzner left Germany in 1933 and worked in France and Britain, notably on *The Robber Symphony* (Friedrich FEHER, 1935), before going to Hollywood where he spent the rest of his career as a set designer.

**MEXICO.** Feature films were made in Mexico from about 1917, mostly popular melodramas with a patriotic flavour. Development of a national film industry was handicapped by competition from American films which increased with the introduction of sound when, as in other South American countries, the cinemas were flooded with Spanish-language versions of Hollywood successes. Many of Mexico's more talented actors, including Ramón NOVARRO and Dolores DEL RIO, went to work in Hollywood. The thirties were chiefly notable for the work of foreigners: in 1931 EISENSTEIN visited Mexico to film his abortive *Que Viva Mexico!* and Fred ZINNEMANN's *Redes* (*The Wave*, 1934), with its passionate involvement with the lives of poor fishermen and the lyrical camerawork of Paul STRAND, had considerable influence on Mexican film-makers. Reaction against the domination of Hollywood was growing and resulted in a number of films using traditional or nationalistic themes. The number of Mexican-made features increased annually, aided by American investment and by government finance initiated during the presidency of General Cárdenas (1936–40).

Emilio FERNÁNDEZ, a Mexican Indian, working with the talented cameraman Gabriel FIGUEROA, directed some of the best films of the forties, including *Maria Candelaria* (1943) which passionately depicted the poverty of the peasant classes. In 1946 BUÑUEL settled in Mexico and, within the restrictions of the commercially-oriented production system, made some of his most characteristic films, including LOS OLVIDADOS (1950), ENSAYO DE UN CRIMEN (*The Criminal Life of Archibaldo de la Cruz*, 1955), NAZARÍN (1958), and EL ANGEL EXTERMINADOR (*The Exterminating Angel*, 1962).

As a whole, however, Mexican cinema has not been artistically outstanding. The formation of the Union of Mexican Film Workers (Sindicato de Trabajadores de la Producion Cinematografica Mexicana) in 1945 resulted in a virtual closed shop, and the established directors continued making traditional melodramas and homely comedies for the mass market. The fifties saw the beginnings of an independent cinema with Benito ALAZRAKI's *Raices* (*Roots*, 1955), but in 1960 the two largest exhibition circuits and the bigger studios were nationalized and this, combined with strict moral and political censorship, again threatened the growth of independent film-making. In 1964 a Film Studies Centre was set up at the University of Mexico and annual competitive film festivals began. After the violent repression of student revolts in 1968 the film festival was banned, but this did not prevent the emergence of Mexico's first political films; a collective film in two parts, *L'Agression* and *La Riposte*, was followed by another, also dealing with the revolt, *El Grito* (*The Cry*), directed by Leobardo Lopez. Both have been banned in Mexico. In 1969 a group of young film-makers, Felipe Cazals, Rafael Castanedo, Arturo Ripstein, Alexis Grivas, and Pedro Miro, formed a co-operative, Cine Independiente.

As in other politically repressed and financially backward countries, cinema in Mexico has until recently consisted largely of second-rate commercial productions, although a distinctive Spanish/Indian flavour has recurrently been discernible. The artistic achievements of the sixties have sprung from an atmosphere of political revolt, tolerated to some degree because such films buy cultural prestige internationally.

Production of films for home distribution and export to other Spanish-speaking countries has increasingly flourished, and Mexico has the most prolific Spanish-language cinema in the world.

**MICKEY MOUSE,** famous DISNEY cartoon character, who first appeared as *Mortimer Mouse* in 1927. For the next decade he remained one of the staple figures of Disney's growing reputation. Always drawn by Disney's indispensable ally, Ub IWERKS, the settings for Mickey's cocky, cruel, but bright character extended from the South Seas to the Sahara, his roles from explorer to convict, clock-cleaner, and Arab. Disney himself always spoke the sound-track for Mickey's voice. (See also ANIMATION.)

*MIDNIGHT COWBOY*, US, 1970. De Luxe Color; 2hr. *Dir* John Schlesinger; *prod* Jerome Hellman; *scr* Waldo Salt from the novel by James Herliky; *ph* Adam Holender; *ed* Hugh A. Robertson; *des* John Robert Lloyd; *mus* (supervisor) John Barry; *cast* Jon Voight (Joe Buck), Dustin Hoffman (Ratso Rizzo).

The story traces the growth of a friendship between Joe Buck, who has come to New York from Texas dressed as a cowboy to make money as a professional stud, and Ratso Rizzo, a sick con-man who dreams of going to Florida to recover his health. Business goes badly for both of them and when winter makes Ratso's condition worse, Joe steals to buy two bus tickets to Florida, but as they reach Miami Ratso dies.

The neon brashness of New York, and its complete indifference to its inhabitants, is captured, perhaps overemphatically, through a series of quick cuts, superimpositions, and other technical effects. The script although full of caustic humour, is somewhat romanticized and too neatly resolved. The pervading mood is of sadness rather than of anger or protest and the film is permeated by SCHLESINGER's sympathy for his characters in their losing battle with life. The film's commercial success is in part attributable to the sound-track, which featured a number of currently popular rock groups.

*MIDSUMMER NIGHT'S DREAM, A.* SHAKESPEARE's fairy-tale romantic comedy would seem, with its potential for fantastic treatment, ideal film material; and a number of adaptations have been filmed.

The first appears to have been in 1909, one of the numerous Shakespeare films made by VITAGRAPH around that time. It was in thirteen scenes, all except the last photographed in a real woodland setting. It was widely admired and seems to have achieved a notable degree of visual charm. About 1913 an Italian production, parts

Toshiro Mifune in *Kakushi toride no san-akunin* (Akira Kurosawa, 1958)

of which survive, showed technically advanced camerawork and sensitive use of rustic scenery. Two other known silent versions were made in Germany, and both were less than faithful to the original. Deutsche Bioscop's *Ein Sommarnachtstraum* (1913) was re-written as a modernized, grotesque tale reminiscent of E. T. A. Hoffmann; Neuman, in 1925, produced an even stranger parody starring Werner KRAUSS as Bottom and Valeska GERT as Puck. Ribaldry was a stronger element than fantasy in this version and the censors passed it for exhibition to adults only.

WARNER BROS' *A Midsummer Night's Dream* (1935) is justly the best known of all the screen versions, if only for being Max REINHARDT's only sound film. Co-directing with William DIETERLE, Reinhardt put his famous talent for spectacle to good use and created a fairy-tale romp in fantastic settings. The casting gave rise to some disapproval among conventional lovers of Shakespeare: it included Dick Powell (Lysander), Olivia DE HAVILLAND (Hermia), James CAGNEY (Bottom), Joe E. BROWN (Flute), and Mickey ROONEY, aged eleven, as Puck (and, incidentally, Kenneth ANGER in his first film appearance). But in spite of the initial shock of hearing revered lines spoken in a variety of American accents, the energetic comedy was in the main in accordance with accepted readings of the play. The only other sound film of the play to date is Peter HALL's production for the Royal Shakespeare Company, made in 1968.

Jiří TRNKA's puppet film, in CinemaScope and Eastman Color (Czechoslovakia, 1958), abandoned the text to give an enchanting dance/pantomime version of the story. Unfortunately, the prints circulated in English-speaking countries were dubbed with a narration and extracts from the play, contradicting the director's intentions. Balanchine's ballet based on the play and performed by the New York City Ballet was filmed in 1966.

**MIFUNE, TOSHIRO** (1920– ), Japanese actor, was born in Tsingtao, China. In 1945, with no previous acting experience, he entered a Toho talent contest and was given a small part in Yamamoto's *Shin Baka Jidai* (*The Foolish Times* or *The New Age of Fools*, 1946). KUROSAWA made him a star in *Yoidore Tenshi* (*Drunken Angel*, 1948) and their partnership resulted in fifteen films of striking quality; they include RASHOMON (1950), which brought both Kurosawa and Mifune to international attention, SHICHININ NO SAMURAI (*The Seven Samurai*, 1954), KUMONOSU-JO (*The Throne of Blood*, 1957), *Donzoko* (THE LOWER DEPTHS, 1957), KAKUSHI TORIDE NO SAN-AKUNIN (*The Hidden Fortress*, 1958), *Yojimbo* (1961), *Tsubaki Sanjuro* (*Sanjuro*, 1962), and AKAHIGE (*Red Beard*,

1965). Mifune's flair for comedy, ranging from the savage clowning of *Shichinin no samurai* to the stylish irony of *Tsubaki Sanjuro*, was particularly exploited by Kurosawa. MIZOGUCHI's *Saikaku Ichidai Onna* (*The Life of Oharu*, 1952) and KOBAYASHI's JOI-UCHI (*Rebellion*, 1967) gave him more serious roles, making full use of his commanding presence.

In 1963 Mifune formed a production company under his own name and the same year made his first film as director, *Goju Man-Nin no Isan* (*The Legacy of the 500,000*). Among international productions he has appeared in are *Grand Prix* (1966), John BOORMAN's *Hell in the Pacific* (1968), with Lee MARVIN, and *Soleil rouge* (*Red Sun*, 1971).

**MILESTONE, LEWIS** (1895– ), US director born in Russia, began work as a film editor. His second film as director, *Betrayal* (1929), featured Emil JANNINGS and, in a supporting role, Gary COOPER. His first sound film, *New York Nights* (1930), was followed by two major, although very different, achievements: ALL QUIET ON THE WESTERN FRONT (1930) and THE FRONT PAGE (1931). He went on to direct Joan CRAWFORD as Sadie Thompson in *Rain* (1933) and Al JOLSON in *Hallelujah, I'm a Bum* (1933, *Hallelujah, I'm a Tramp* in GB). Milestone continued to make a wide range of workmanlike films during the thirties, culminating in a convincing adaptation of John STEINBECK's *Of Mice and Men* (1939), in which Lon CHANEY Jr grasped one of his rare opportunities for a serious acting performance.

After working on the documentary *Our Russian Front* (1941) with Joris IVENS, Milestone directed grimly dramatic war films, but his sensitive and compassionate *A Walk in the Sun* (1945) compares with *All Quiet on the Western Front*. He returned to Erich Maria Remarque with an adaptation of *Arch of Triumph* (1948). His later work, including *Ocean's Eleven* (1960), a vehicle for the SINATRA clan, and the remake of THE MUTINY ON THE BOUNTY (1962), tends to lack the distinction of some of his earlier films.

**MILHAUD, DARIUS** (1892–1974), prolific and influential French composer, was a member of the group known as 'Les Six'. His concert works, ballet scores, and incidental music for the theatre often show jazz influences. He wrote occasionally for films from 1923, the most important being ESPOIR (1945).

***MILKY WAY, The,*** see VOIE LACTÉE, LA

**MILLAND, RAY** (1905– ), US actor born in Wales, has spent the greater part of his career, first in Britain and from 1931 in Hollywood, playing well-groomed leading men, often with a hint of caddishness. He proved himself a more than competent actor with THE LOST WEEKEND (1945) in which, under Billy WILDER's direction, he gave a harrowing performance as an alcoholic. His subsequent parts have been less rewarding but he has continued to make frequent polished appearances and has shown talent as a director with films including an unusual Western, *Bugles in the Afternoon* (1952).

**MILLER, ARTHUR** (1915–   ), US playwright whose tense dramas dealing with the values of modern America have been translated into notable films including *All My Sons* (1948), *Death of a Salesman* (1952), with Fredric MARCH, and *Les Sorcières de Salem* (*The Witches of Salem*, 1956), made in France starring Yves MONTAND and Simone SIGNORET, based on *The Crucible*, an allegory of the McCarthy witch-hunts. During his marriage to Marilyn MONROE (1956–61) he wrote scenes for her in *Let's Make Love* (1960) and a complete screenplay, THE MISFITS (1961). Miller's semi-autobiographical play, *After the Fall* (1964), reviews the tensions of their celebrated marriage.

**MILLER, ARTHUR C.** (1895–1970), US cameraman, began his career at the age of fourteen with Fred Balshofer in New York, afterwards joining Edwin S. PORTER. He was then a newsreel cameraman for PATHÉ, for whom he photographed *The Perils of Pauline* (1914). In 1916 he joined FAMOUS PLAYERS in Hollywood with George Fitzmaurice, and in 1918 they set up the Famous Players studios in Islington, London, where he shot *Three Live Ghosts* (1922). He photographed Fitzmaurice's *The Eternal City* (1923) on location in Rome and smuggled the negative out of Italy when Mussolini ordered them to leave the country. He worked for Cecil B. DEMILLE and William Seiter and in 1931 began a long period of work at FOX, where he shot all the Shirley TEMPLE films, and worked with John FORD (who regarded him as one of his best cameramen) on *Wee Willie Winkie* (1937), *Submarine Patrol* (1938), some of *Young Mr Lincoln* (1939) (not credited), *Tobacco Road* (1941), and *How Green Was My Valley* (1941) which brought him his first OSCAR. He received two further Academy Awards, for *The Song of Bernadette* (1943) and *Anna and the King of Siam* (1946). Other credits include THE OX-BOW INCIDENT (1943), *Letter to Three Wives* (1949), and THE GUNFIGHTER (1950). After contracting tuberculosis he retired in 1951, and held office in various professional organizations including the American Society of Cinematographers. He established a museum of early motion-picture cameras for the Society, and was its curator

until his death. In 1967 he collaborated with Fred Balshofer on *One Reel a Week*, an account of early movie-making, and just before his death he completed a 22-minute documentary *The Moving Picture Camera* to illustrate the camera's evolution.

**MILLION, Le,** France, 1932. 1½hr. *Dir, scr* René Clair; *prod* Tobis; *ph* Georges Périnal, Raulet; *des* Lazare Meerson; *mus* Armand Bernard, Philippe Parès, George Van Parys; *cast* Annabella (Béatrice), René Lefèvre (Michel), Vanda Gréville (Vanda), Louis Allibert (Prosper), Paul Olivier (Crochard), Constantin Stroesco (Sopranelli), Odette Talazac (Prima Donna).

Like UN CHAPEAU DE PAILLE D'ITALIE (1927), *Le Million* deals with the pursuit of an object—in this case a winning lottery ticket. It has the pace and comic invention of the earlier film, but CLAIR set out to bend the sound process to the medium of a true film operetta with the action integrated with, and reflected in, the music. It was influential in the development of the screen MUSICAL, and Clair's inventiveness and artistic control of the difficult single track (see SOUND) make it also an outstanding early example of good use of sound. Happily, *Le Million* was reissued in 16mm with the original ASPECT RATIO and visual quality maintained.

**MILLS, JOHN** (1908–   ), British actor, became established in the thirties in numerous films including *Goodbye Mr Chips* (1939). After army service (he was wounded in 1942) he attracted much popularity in films such as IN WHICH WE SERVE (1942), *We Dive at Dawn* (1943), and *This Happy Breed* (1944). This identification with quiet heroism has persisted: he played the title role in *Scott of the Antarctic* (1948) and has appeared in many war films including *The Colditz Story* (1955). He has contributed thoughtful performances to several literary and stage adaptations, notably GREAT EXPECTATIONS (1946), *The History of Mr Polly* (1949), *The Rocking Horse Winner* (1949), and *Hobson's Choice* (1954). His character roles in recent years range from comedy—*The Wrong Box* (1966)—to high romance—*Ryan's Daughter* (David LEAN, 1971): he won an OSCAR for his portrayal of a village idiot in the latter film.

Mills is married to the writer Mary Hayley Bell. Their two daughters are both actresses. Hayley (b. 1946) has been the more prominent in films, scoring a success as a teenage star, notably in *Tiger Bay* (1959) in which she appeared with her father, and *Whistle Down the Wind* (1961). She won a special Oscar for *Pollyanna* (1960). She married John BOULTING in

*Ivan groznyi* (S. M. Eisenstein, 1944, 1958)

*Kwaidan* (Masaki Kobayashi, 1964)

1966. Juliet (b. 1941) has also made a number of films since her first appearance in *No My Darling Daughter* (1961) and was particularly effective in Billy WILDER's *Avanti!* (1972).

**MIMICA**, VATROSLAV (1923– ), Yugoslav director, after directing three features became one of the leading figures in the Zagreb animation studio. He scripted eight cartoon films including Zagreb's first successful production *Cowboy Jimmie* (1957). With the designer Aleksandar Marks he co-directed *Samac* (*Alone*, 1958), *Perpetuum & Mobile Ltd* (1961), and *Mala kronika* (*Everyday Chronicle*, 1962), commenting on individual isolation in a technological society. Their *Tifusaria* (*Typhus*, 1963) was a tribute to the partisan war dead.

Mimica returned to live-action feature direction in 1965 with *Prometej sa otoka Viševeca* (*Prometheus from the Isle of Viševeca*) which explored the mind of a revolutionary turned bureaucrat. His probing approach has become increasingly personal in *Poneldeljak ili utorak* (*Monday or Tuesday*, 1966), examining thoughts and memories, *Kaja, ubit ću te* (*Kaya, I'll Kill You*, 1967), experimenting with the use of colour, and *Dogadaj* (*An Event*, 1969), an adaptation from Chekhov.

**MINNELLI**, VINCENTE (1913– ), US director who worked in the theatre as an art director and director of ballets and musicals before being brought to Hollywood by Arthur FREED. Five of his first six films were musicals, beginning with the all-negro fantasy CABIN IN THE SKY (1943) and including MEET ME IN ST LOUIS (1944), his first colour film, and he is usually associated with the genre, although it represents only a third of his total output. His first non-musical was the charming wartime love story *The Clock* (1944, *Under the Clock* in GB). In both these 1944 films Minnelli produced outstanding performances from Judy GARLAND to whom he was married for a time.

Minnelli's musicals are notable for the way he integrates the musical numbers into the action of the film, using them to advance characterization and plot. Examples are 'Nina' in *The Pirate* (1948), in which Gene KELLY swings his way around the town square introducing himself to all the pretty girls, the enchanting 'Love is Here to Stay' duet in AN AMERICAN IN PARIS (1951), and 'I Want To Be By Myself', danced by Fred ASTAIRE among 42nd Street's penny arcades in THE BAND WAGON (1953).

They are also characterized by their brilliant use of colour, as are all his colour films. He consistently uses a carefully limited range of colours, often using black and white or very muted tones to set off strong primaries, as in *Ziegfeld Follies* (1946), where slate blue costumes and sets are highlighted by the scarlet worn by the principals in 'Limehouse Blues', and in TWO WEEKS IN ANOTHER TOWN (1962), in which the predominant colours are muted browns, golds, and blues with a selective use of red, usually in association with the film world. This quality helped to make his film about Van Gogh, *Lust for Life* (1956), one of the few films about an artist which are worthy of their subject.

THE BAD AND THE BEAUTIFUL (1952), exaggerated and garish, was a powerful study of Hollywood. His many stylish light comedies include *Father of the Bride* (1950), *The Reluctant Debutante* (1958), and *Goodbye Charlie* (1965), in which a man is reincarnated as the delightful Debbie REYNOLDS, presenting some problems for his best friend Tony CURTIS. *On a Clear Day You Can See Forever* (1970) demonstrated, notably in the 'Come Back to Me' sequence, that he has lost none of his skill with comedy and musical numbers.

Liza Minnelli (b. 1946), the daughter of his marriage to Judy Garland, is an actress and singer of talent. She has successfully overcome the inevitable comparisons with her mother's performances and made a particular impact in CABARET (1972).

**MIRACLE OF MORGAN'S CREEK, The,** US, 1944. 1½hr. *Dir, scr* Preston Sturges; *prod* Paramount; *ph* John Seitz; *cast* Eddie Bracken (Norval Jones), Betty Hutton (Trudy Kockenlocker), Diana Lynn (Emmy Kockenlocker), William Demarest (Officer Kockenlocker), Brian Donlevy (Governor), Akim Tamiroff (the boss).

Betty HUTTON, with an ideal role as the brash, bewildered Trudy, attempts to find a substitute father for her expected baby. Eddie Bracken's aghast confrontation with the results of a multiple birth and the resulting hysterical publicity provide the climax of the plot. The film's pace and comic timing make it one of Preston STURGES's best satires on small-town America.

**MIRACOLO A MILANO** (*Miracle in Milan*), Italy, 1951. 1½hr. *Dir* Vittorio De Sica; *prod* De Sica ENIC; *scr* Cesare Zavattini, Suso Cecchi d'Amico, Mario Chiari, Aldolfo Franci, based on Zavattini's novel; *ph* G. R. Aldo; *ed* Eraldo Da Roma; *mus* Alessandro Cicognini; *cast* Francesco Golisano (Toto), Emma Gramatica, Brunella Bovo, Paolo Stoppa.

An orphan, Toto, on leaving the orphanage, goes to live in an appalling shanty-town on the outskirts of Milan where he proceeds to work miracles, in a fantasy world that is savage only towards the capitalist financiers. DE SICA considers the film largely as an experiment designed to show that NEO-REALISM could be applied even to the most fanciful subjects; underlying the child-like magic there is an attitude of bitter sophistication.

**MIRANDA,** CARMEN (1914–55), US musical actress of Portuguese origin, real name Maria de Carmo Miranda de Cunha, enjoyed much popularity during the forties in musicals exploiting the vogue for Latin-American dance music. She was known as the 'Brazilian Bombshell'; her engaging humour and towering, eccentric head-dresses ensured the success of a number of films including *Down Argentine Way* (1940) and *Copacabana* (1947).

**MIRANDA,** ISA (1909– ), Italian actress, real name Ines Isabella Sanpietro, first widely noticed in OPHULS' *La signora di tutti* (1934), became a popular dramatic star in Italy during the thirties. She subsequently became internationally known, particularly in Ophuls' LA RONDE (1950), *Summertime* (David LEAN, 1955, *Summer Madness* in GB), and *The Yellow Rolls Royce* (Anthony ASQUITH, 1964).

**MIRISCH CORPORATION,** US production company. Established in September 1957 by the three Mirisch brothers—Harold (1907–68), Marvin (1918– ), and Walter (1921– )—as an independent production company whose aim was 'to become pre-eminent as *the* quality independent film-maker', the Mirisch Corporation attracted many of Hollywood's best directors after its initial success with Billy WILDER's SOME LIKE IT HOT (1959). Having had previous experience in exhibition and production, the brothers were able to achieve their 'pre-eminent' position through careful budgeting and a simplicity of operation which allowed complete autonomy for the film-makers involved. The Mirisch film-makers included, besides Wilder, John STURGES, Robert WISE, Blake EDWARDS, John HUSTON, and Norman JEWISON. They provided the company with several outstanding productions, notably THE APARTMENT (1960), THE MAGNIFICENT SEVEN (1960), WEST SIDE STORY (1961), *The Russians Are Coming . . .* (1966), and IN THE HEAT OF THE NIGHT (1967). In 1963 ownership of the company was bought by UNITED ARTISTS, although the Mirisch brothers retained administrative control.

**MISÉRABLES,** Les, twelve-volume novel by Victor Hugo published in 1862, which combines lyricism with realistic description of the working class and attempts to scan the whole range of human existence. It has been the subject of a very great number of film adaptations. Capellani's version of 1912, produced by PATHÉ is the most

famous. Made in four episodes (distributed in the US as a single three-hour film in 1913) and inspired by the original illustrations of the novel approved by Hugo, it featured Marie Ventura and Mistinguett and proved one of the most successful of the FILMS D'ART of the period. Henri Fescourt's *Les Misérables* (France, 1925) is regarded as the best silent screen adaptation. Raymond Bernard's version appeared in 1934 in the period of unrest preceding the Popular Front, with a distinguished cast headed by Harry Baur and music by Arthur HONEGGER. It was distributed in two episodes. Of the four American adaptations, the best was that of 1935, directed by Richard Boleslawski and starring Fredric MARCH and Charles LAUGHTON. An Egyptian version, *El Boassa*, directed by Kamal Selim, appeared in 1944. The first colour production was directed in 1958 by J. P. LE CHANOIS, in two sections and starred Jean GABIN, BOURVIL, Bernard Blier, and Sylvia Montfort.

**MISÈRE AU BORINAGE,** Belgium, 1933. 35min. *Dir* Joris Ivens; *co-dir* Henri Storck. Commissioned by the Belgian Club de l'Écran.

Henri STORCK approached IVENS to help make a film showing the aftermath of the 30,000-strong strike of miners in the Borinage district, the despair and appalling conditions which prevailed during the ensuing repression: blacklisting, eviction from company houses, martial law, hunger, and constant harassing by police and *gendarmerie*. Van Gogh had once gone to the Borinage as a student evangelist to heal wounds: Storck and Ivens went to expose them, and they understood why Van Gogh had started to paint in the harsh, grimy Borinage landscape.

This was Storck's first serious subject. For Ivens, just returned from Moscow, it marked a turning-point. Ivens took responsibility for the entire production but, as a foreigner, he had to ensure that no camera was ever found with him by the police; Storck as a Belgian citizen had more freedom of movement. They carried on as if making a resistance film, always keeping a few paces ahead of the police, sending film to Brussels every day by messenger. They restricted themselves to severe and strictly orthodox camera angles: this simplicity was a deliberate stylistic revolution, not, as critics have claimed, necessitated by poor equipment. Their original aim was to present the miners' sufferings honestly and objectively, but the two film-makers, sharing the miseries and hardships of the miners, changed their aims; the film emerged as a fighting point of view rather than a factual record.

*Borinage* was never permitted regular distribution; it was banned by Dutch and Belgian censors and shown only in ciné-clubs. It was treated only as a political statement, not as a work of art, but its influence on documentary film has been acknowledged by GRIERSON and others.

**MISFITS, The,** US, 1961. 2hr. *Dir* John Huston; *prod* Seven Arts; *scr* Arthur Miller; *ph* Russell Metty; *mus* Alex North; *cast* Clark Gable (Gay Langland), Marilyn Monroe (Roslyn Taber), Montgomery Clift (Perce Howland), Eli Wallach (Guido), Thelma Ritter (Isabelle Steers).

Three failed men take up with a lonely *divorcée* hoping to gain new purpose from her spontaneity. Their callousness, at a shabby local rodeo and a round-up of horses to be slaughtered for pet food, repels her, leading to a confrontation between their spurious pretensions and her intuitive humanism.

The superbly shot sequences of rodeo riding and particularly of the pursuit and roping of wild mustangs were outstanding visual set-pieces in contrast to Arthur MILLER's copious dialogue and lachrymose philosophy.

The unhappy concomitants are well known: the film was the swan song of both Clark GABLE, who died a few weeks after shooting was completed, and Marilyn MONROE whose untimely death shortly followed. Gable's performance was among the best and certainly the most mature of his career; and Monroe, grappling with a complex part written for her by her third husband, rose to some moving moments.

**MISS JULIE** see FRÖKEN JULIE

**MR DEEDS GOES TO TOWN,** US, 1936. 2hr. *Dir*, *prod* Frank Capra for Columbia; *scr* Robert Riskin, adapted from 'Opera Hat' by Clarence Budington Kelland; *ph* Joseph Walker; *cast* Gary Cooper (Longfellow Deeds), Jean Arthur (Babe Bennett), George Bancroft (MacWade), Lionel Stander (Cornelius Cobb).

The fable of the naïve country cousin thrown into New York, and the attempts of cynical people to fleece him, carries some telling comments on cosmopolitan materialism and on the force wielded by the unintimidated individual (one of CAPRA's recurrent themes). The film's wide popularity was helped by the intriguing casting against type of Gary COOPER and Jean ARTHUR.

One of Longfellow Deeds's Vermont traits which outraged the city slickers originated the verb 'to doodle', a term that has now gained general currency.

**MR MAGOO,** created by Pete Burrows in the early fifties, appeared in numerous UNITED PRODUCTIONS OF AMERICA (UPA) cartoons and in one feature—*1001 Arabian Nights* (1961). His myopic geniality and bumbling voice (Jim Backus) were for a time very popular. (See ANIMATION.)

**MR MOTO,** the Japanese police sleuth created by the novelist John P. Marquand, was featured in a series of films made by TWENTIETH CENTURY-FOX in 1937–9. They all starred Peter LORRE and were mostly directed by Norman Foster who was also responsible for the same company's CHARLIE CHAN series. One of the best, if the wildest in story, was *Mr Moto's Last Warning* (1939), set in Port Said and about a plot to blow up the French fleet: the cast was considerable, including besides Lorre, George SANDERS, Ricardo Cortez, John CARRADINE, and Robert Coote.

**MR SMITH GOES TO WASHINGTON,** US, 1939. 2hr. *Dir*, *prod* Frank Capra for Columbia; *scr* Sidney Buchman, from a story by Lewis R. Foster; *ph* Joseph Walker; *cast* Jean Arthur (Saunders), James Stewart (Jefferson Smith), Claude Rains (Senator Joseph Price), Edward Arnold (Jim Taylor).

CAPRA's exposure of the effect of a totally honest Senator on the dealings of the US government created something of a sensation. Congress was moved to threaten retaliatory legislation, but the public was delighted with this fable of the triumph of simple goodness over corrupt power. The film has Capra's usual sharp sense of characterization and considerable authority in his control of comic pace.

**MITCHELL,** THOMAS (1892–1962), US actor who worked on Broadway as a reporter, playwright, and actor before appearing in *Craig's Wife* (1936). A versatile character actor, he took a wide variety of roles in almost sixty films. In 1939 alone he played the alcoholic doctor in STAGECOACH, for which he won an OSCAR, the hero's loyal friend, whose death scene has become something of a classic, in *Only Angels Have Wings*, and Scarlett O'Hara's weak father in GONE WITH THE WIND. His last role was as Apple Annie's supposed husband in *Pocketful of Miracles* (1961).

**MITCHELL,** YVONNE (1925– ), British actress, who began her career on the stage, making her first film appearance as the countess's companion in THE QUEEN OF SPADES (Thorold DICKINSON, 1948). An accomplished actress, her screen fortunes have fluctuated: wasted in *Turn the Key Softly* (1953), she was much admired for her performance in *Woman in a Dressing Gown* (1957). She has also had some success as a novelist.

**MITCHUM,** ROBERT (1917– ), US actor, played bit parts in HOPALONG CASSIDY films, then had a featured role in *We've Never Been Licked* (1943). His first substantial part, and an excellent performance, was in *The Story of GI Joe* (William WELLMAN, 1945), and his reputation grew with *Rachel and the Stranger* (1948) and *The Red Pony* (Lewis MILESTONE, 1949). Contrary to the predictions of the gossips, his arrest and imprisonment on a narcotics charge in 1949 did nothing to decrease his popularity; the fifties saw some of his best performances, in *The Lusty Men* (Nicholas RAY, 1952), *Track of the Cat* (Wellman, 1954), and THE NIGHT OF THE HUNTER (Charles LAUGHTON, 1955). Mitchum wrote the screenplay for *Thunder Road* (1958), which introduced his elder son Jim to the screen, and had a brief production association with Raymond Stross in 1959. More notable among his later performances were those in *Cape Fear* (1962), *Two for the Seesaw* (Robert WISE, 1963), which demonstrated his flair for wry comedy, *Secret Ceremony* (Joseph LOSEY, 1968), and *Ryan's Daughter* (David LEAN, 1971). Mitchum's proclaimed unconcern with the actor's craft, his relaxed style, and sleepy-eyed mannerisms, often cloak a thoughtful and perceptive approach to his roles.

**MITRY, JEAN** (1907–    ), French theoretician and historian, real name Jean René Pierre Goetgeluck le Rouge Rillard des Acres de Presfontaines, took a degree in philosophy and physics. He participated in the cinema in various capacities: as assistant and scriptwriter (with GANCE and L'HERBIER), actor (*La Nuit du carrefour*, Jean RENOIR, 1932), editor (*Le Rideau cramoisi*, Alexandre ASTRUC, 1952), and experimental film-maker (PACIFIC 231, 1949; *Images pour Debussy*, 1951; *Symphonie mécanique*, 1953).

From 1925 to 1932 Mitry was secretary-general of the Tribune Libre du Cinéma (one of the first ciné-clubs in France), and was one of the co-founders of the CINÉMATHÈQUE FRANÇAISE. Since 1944 he has taught at the INSTITUT DES HAUTES ÉTUDES CINÉMATOGRAPHIQUES and, in 1968, took a Chair in Film Studies in Montreal.

As a historian he has written several monographs as well as *Histoire du cinéma: art et industrie* (Paris, 1967). His most important work is probably the theoretical *Esthétique et psychologie du cinéma* (Paris, vol I, 1963, vol II, 1965). An exhaustive study, it continues, refines, and develops the work of such theoreticians as BÁLAZS, ARNHEIM, EPSTEIN, EISENSTEIN, BAZIN, Cohen-Séat, Laffay, and MORIN. Mitry always returns to his central thesis on the unique logic of film implied by the linear succession of images and insists continually on the importance of its narrative element.

**MIX,** TOM (1880–1940), US actor and director, born in Pennsylvania (not in a log-cabin north of El Paso, as he liked it to be known). After a career in the US and British armies he toured the States with a Wild West show, riding in rodeos. He had an encounter with the cinema, when SELIG made a documentary at his ranch. Shortly afterwards Mix joined Selig's staff. Between 1911 and 1917 he directed and acted in almost a hundred low-budget one- and two-reelers, but he did not achieve stardom until he moved to FOX in 1917, making more than sixty feature-length Westerns, characterized by spectacular photography and scenery, and dazzling horsemanship. Mix set a good example to youth, never smoking or drinking, or fighting without just cause. In the twenties his popularity was enormous, but with the advent of sound he left films to join a circus with his equally popular horse, Tony.

In 1932 he made a comeback with DESTRY RIDES AGAIN for UNIVERSAL. After *The Miracle Rider* (1935) he left films to form his own circus. He died in a car crash.

**MIXING,** the process of re-recording all original dialogue, music, and sound effects on to a single master sound-track. The individual components of the eventual track are as far as possible recorded separately, and in mixing their relative volume and pitch can be adjusted to produce the desired blend of sound. (In Britain mixing is often called DUBBING, a term which properly applies only to the addition of synchronized dialogue or effects after the scene has been shot.)

Mixing is actually an extension of the editing process, since the editor has prepared the various tracks and has thus predetermined the result. But the star of the occasion is the mixer (dubbing mixer in Britain), who, like the cameraman and editor, must be both technician and artist. Seated at the mixing desk in a special theatre, he watches the picture on the screen and adjusts the balance of each track relative to the whole as the master is recorded. He is guided by the editor's chart showing exactly when, and on which track, each sound begins and ends. He may also apply special processing to some sounds, such as adding echo to footsteps or filtering a voice to simulate a telephone conversation. Complex films may require many more than the usual three or four tracks to be mixed; he will then pre-mix groups of related sounds separately and finally mix the pre-mixes. Laymen are usually unaware of the mixer's contribution since his work is best when it conceals its presence. But mixers are highly regarded and chosen with great care for a production.

Mixing has been common to all sound films since the earliest abortive attempts to record all sounds on the original track, which left no latitude for changes or creative editing. The

*Moana* (Robert Flaherty, 1926)

advent of magnetic sound released mixing from the technical limitations of OPTICAL SOUND, and in the last decade ROLL-BACK MIXING has eliminated the demanding necessity of recording an entire REEL—11 minutes—in one take without errors.

The term mixing is also applied to earlier stages in sound work, when several microphones are combined in recording dialogue or music. 'Mix' is also used in the US to mean a DISSOLVE between pictures. (See SOUND.)

**MIZOGUCHI,** KENJI (1898–1956), Japanese director, came to films after working as a painter and journalist. He was an actor at the Nikkatsu studios in Tokyo in 1922 when the *oyama* (female impersonators) walked out in protest against the employment of actresses: the resulting staff shortage gave him the opportunity to direct.

His early films dealt with contemporary society, critically yet compassionately observing the suffering of women in particular, as in GION NO SHIMAI (*Sisters of the Gion,* 1936). With the increase of nationalism and the restrictions imposed on the choice of subjects, he turned like other Japanese directors to the JIDAI-GEKI (period drama) which, being politically innocuous, allowed him to work out his themes.

Of some eighty films that Mizoguchi directed, only a handful have been seen in the West, yet his work is highly regarded for its beauty and clarity. *Saikaku Ichidai Onna* (*The Life of Oharu,* 1952), UGETSU MONOGATARI (1953), SANSHO DAYU (*Sansho the Bailiff,* 1955), and *Yokihi* (*The Princess Yang Kwei Fei,* 1955) demonstrate remarkable formal and thematic consistency. All have a meditative visual style, with long takes, a relatively immobile camera, a minimum of close-ups, and frequent slow dissolves. His concern with and admiration for women is a persistent element: he often introduces the purifying or sacrificial nature of women's love. His last film, *Akasen Chitai* (*Street of Shame,* 1956), returned to prostitution in a modern setting.

**MOANA,** US, 1926. 1½hr. *Dir, scr, ph* Robert J. Flaherty, Frances H. Flaherty; *prod* Jesse Lasky for Famous Players-Lasky; *cast* Ta'avala, Fa'angase, Tu'ungaita.

*Moana* was originally planned as a South Seas successor to FLAHERTY'S NANOOK OF THE NORTH

(1922), an unexpected commercial success which temporarily gave Hollywood producers a taste for exotic documentaries. A glorification of primitive harmony with nature, the film recorded with unqualified admiration not only the intricate processes involved in the Samoan islanders' daily pursuits of cooking, cloth-making, hunting, and fishing, but also the almost defunct tattooing ceremony.

The film's special importance lies in Flaherty's successful experiment with PANCHROMATIC stock after disappointing results with the then standard ORTHOCHROMATIC film. He shot scenes only in the early morning or late afternoon to take advantage of long shadows for depth and perspective, and also used close-ups and free camera movement to explore in detail the activities observed.

On its initial release (with the sub-title *A Romance of the Golden Age*) the film was not a commercial success, but it established Flaherty's reputation. After some years PARAMOUNT destroyed the original negative of *Moana*, so that prints from a DUPE negative—with the consequent loss of brilliance—are all that can be seen today.

**MOCKRIDGE**, CYRIL (1896– ), British-born composer settled in the US and began working in films in the early days of sound. He and Alfred NEWMAN were the mainstays of TWENTIETH CENTURY-FOX's music department: Newman was usually responsible for high-powered, major productions, while Mockridge generally composed for the company's secondary films or lighter entertainment, with an emphasis on comedy. Scores include those for *The Sullivans* (1944), MY DARLING CLEMENTINE (1946), *Cheaper by the Dozen* (1950), HOW TO MARRY A MILLIONAIRE (1953), *The Solid Gold Cadillac* (1956), *Rally Round the Flag, Boys* (1958). He retired in the early sixties; THE MAN WHO SHOT LIBERTY VALANCE (1962) was among his last scores.

**MOCKY**, JEAN-PIERRE (1929– ), French actor and director. A successful film actor, who took the lead in the French episode of ANTONIONI's *I vinti* (1952), Mocky also played a leading part in FRANJU's LA TÊTE CONTRE LES MURS (1958), which he had originally intended to direct: he himself directed his first film the following year, *Les Dragueurs* (*The Young Have No Morals*). A great commercial success, it was followed by *Un Couple* (*The Love Trap*, 1960), written by Raymond QUENEAU. He has continued regularly to direct films since then, including *La Bourse et la vie* (1965), starring FERNANDEL. His work, characterized by a rather savage satirical humour, has been of uneven quality, often marred by a careless style of direction.

*MODERATO CANTABILE* (*Seven Days... Seven Nights...*), France/Italy, 1960. CinemaScope, 1½hr. *Dir* Peter Brook; *prod* Iéna, Raoul J. Lévy (Paris)/Documento Films (Rome); *scr* Marguerite Duras and Gérard Jarlot from Duras' novel; *ph* Armand Thirard; *ed* Albert Jürgenson; *des* Jean André; *mus* Diabelli; *cast* Jeanne Moreau (Anne Desbarèdes), Jean-Paul Belmondo (Chauvin), Didier Haudepin (son), Valeric Doubouzinsky (murderer), Pascale de Boysson (café proprietor), Colette Régis (Mlle Giraud).

Anne, the wife of an industrialist, has a brief affair with a worker in her husband's factory. This was Marguerite DURAS' second excursion into cinema (after HIROSHIMA MON AMOUR, 1959): the intellectual aspirations of the film together with the presence of BELMONDO and Jeanne MOREAU (who won an award for her performance at CANNES in 1961) earned it a considerable reputation. Lyrical photography and a sense of tedium established by the slow pace are effective in creating the atmosphere of a provincial French town, but BROOK's theatrical direction was not best calculated to allow for the play of ideas which was Duras' intention.

*MODERN TIMES*, US, 1936. 1½hr. *Dir, prod, scr, mus* Charles Chaplin, assisted by Carter de Haven, Henry Bergman, for United Artists; *ph* Rollie Totheroh, Ira Morgan; *des* Charles D. Hall; *cast* Charlie Chaplin (a worker), Paulette Goddard (the orphan), Henry Bergman (café owner), Chester Conklin (mechanic), Louis Natheaux (burglar), Allan Garcia (president of steel corporation).

*Modern Times* marks the end of the Tramp and the end of CHAPLIN's attempt to hold back the coming of sound. There is no synchronized dialogue; Chaplin impersonates a singing waiter, but the words are gibberish. The opening images of workmen at the factory gates intercut with shots of pigs lead one to expect a satire on the social problems of the industrial age and mass production (it was banned in Germany and Italy for Communist 'tendencies' and in the US it apparently offended industrialists); but Chaplin cannot stop being a clown for long, and the film turns out to be the familiar, and very effective, mixture of comedy and mime, fragmentary in spite of being the first of Chaplin's films with a prepared shooting script.

The film's obvious debt to René CLAIR'S A NOUS LA LIBERTÉ (1931) was regarded as plagiarism by TOBIS, who wanted to sue Chaplin; but Clair expressed himself honoured that Chaplin should be inspired by his work.

**MODOT**, GASTON (1887–1970), French actor, first appeared in the Onésime comedy series for GAUMONT in 1909. Parts in DELLUC's *Fièvre* (1921) and BUÑUEL's L'ÂGE D'OR (1930) began a long and impressive career under leading French directors, Modot becoming one of the best-known actors in the French cinema. He worked for CLAIR (SOUS LES TOITS DE PARIS, 1930), DUVIVIER (PÉPÉ-LE-MOKO, 1937), CARNÉ (LES ENFANTS DU PARADIS, 1945), BECKER (*Antoine et Antoinette*, 1947; CASQUE D'OR, 1952), and MALLE (LES AMANTS, 1958). Most frequently, and spanning the careers of both men, Modot was used by Jean RENOIR. Besides LA RÈGLE DU JEU (1939), in which he portrayed the surly, brutal Alsatian gamekeeper, he played in Renoir's *La Vie est à nous* (1936), LA GRANDE ILLUSION (1937), *La Marseillaise* (1938), *French Can-can* (1955), *Éléna et les hommes* (1956), and *Le Testament du Dr Cordelier* (1959), Modot's last film.

**MOHOLY-NAGY,** LÁSZLÓ (1895–1946), Hungarian-born painter, greatly influenced by the Constructivists, is known chiefly for his experiments with film and transparent material to explore properties of light and space. From 1923 to 1928 he taught at the Bauhaus, experimenting with 'photograms'. Early in the twenties he wrote a script, never filmed, which foreshadowed RUTTMANN's treatment of a city. He also made designs for Piscator's theatre. Among the films he made were *Lichtspiel* and *Architects' Congress*, both in the early thirties. He settled in the US in 1937, founding a school which he called the New Bauhaus in Chicago. His *Malerei, Photographie, Film* was published as a Bauhaus booklet in 1927, and revised and translated as *The new vision* (1947).

*MOI, UN NOIR,* France, 1958. Agfacolor; 1¼hr. *Dir, ph* Jean Rouch; *prod* Les Films de la Pléiade; *cast* Oumaru Ganda, Petit Toure, M. Gambi.

Disturbed by African criticism of his anthropological films, Jean ROUCH invited a group from Treichville, a suburb of Abidjan, to show him how they would like their lives recorded by the camera. He followed them not only through the everyday events of work and family but through the acting out of their fantasies, in which there are indications of the corrupting influence of Western commerce. *Moi, un noir* is an infectious, energetic film: it paved the way for less spontaneous experiments in CINÉMA-VÉRITÉ such as CHRONIQUE D'UN ÉTÉ (1961).

**MOLANDER,** GUSTAF (1888–    ), Swedish director born in Helsinki. Initially an actor and scriptwriter, he wrote SJÖSTRÖM's *Terje Vigen* (1917) and STILLER's HERR ARNES PENGAR (1919). He attracted international atten-

tion with INTERMEZZO (1936); its romanticism was given strength by Molander's sensitive direction. This conviction showed again in the historical drama of revolution *Rid i natt!* (*Ride Tonight!*, 1942). He had a prolific output during the forties and fifties, including an adaptation of ORDET (*The Word*, 1943) which provides an interesting contrast to DREYER's later version.

*MONDO CANE* (*A Dog's Life*), Italy, 1961. Technicolor; 1¾hr. *Dir, ed, comm* Gualtiero Jacopetti; *prod* Cineriz; *ph* Antonio Climati, Benito Frattari; *mus* Nino Oliviero, Riz Ortolani.

A veneer of impartiality masks a zestful collection of outré, repellent, or misguided examples of human behaviour in various parts of the world. The content includes such titbits as religious self-mutilation in Lent, goring bulls running amok, and the beheading of bulls. Jacopetti followed it up with further pseudo-documentary investigations (including *Africa addio*, 1965), and a number of imitations ensued. The original film appeared in Britain in 1963 but was not granted a certificate by the BRITISH BOARD OF FILM CENSORS.

*MONITOR,* a fortnightly BBC television programme which, running intermittently between February 1958 and July 1965, pioneered British television's presentation of the arts. Huw Wheldon's very flexible 'magazine' format contained interviews, talks, discussions, and original films, and offered a degree of creative freedom rare in professional film-making to then little-known artists like John SCHLESINGER and Ken RUSSELL.

**MONOGRAM** Picture Corporation, US production company founded in 1937. It flourished in the forties with an annual output of about thirty low-budget 'B' pictures, rarely exceeding seventy-five minutes in length. The company sometimes employed waning stars, among them Jean Parker and Kay FRANCIS, and occasionally called in personalities like Boris KARLOFF, Bela LUGOSI, Margaret DUMONT, and ZaSu PITTS, but it had its own team of frequently-used players, often employed in SERIES films.

Monogram took over the CHARLIE CHAN series from TWENTIETH CENTURY-FOX, but the films deteriorated, leaning on unsophisticated comedy rather than suspense. They also took over Leo Gorcey and Huntz Hall, with other members of the Dead End Kids whom WARNER BROS had featured in a series following their original hit in DEAD END (1937). They appeared for several years under the Monogram banner as the East Side Kids, became the Bowery Boys in *Live Wires* (1946), and continued to be popular through a long series of comedies. Western series, too, were an important part of Monogram's output. With affectionate irony, GODARD dedicated A BOUT DE SOUFFLE (1960) to Monogram Pictures.

Allied Artists Productions was created in 1946 as a subsidiary of Monogram, designed to put out prestige productions. The company gathered strength during the fifties and in 1953 Monogram was absorbed into the company, which became Allied Artists Pictures Corporation. In 1954, the company signed up three distinguished directors, John HUSTON, Billy WILDER, and William WYLER. Films such as Wilder's *Love in the Afternoon* (1957), and Wyler's *Friendly Persuasion* (1956), were among the company's most successful ventures. Recently the company has become particularly involved in television production.

***MON ONCLE***, France, 1958. Eastman Color; 2hr. *Dir* Jacques Tati; *prod* Specta Films/Gray Film/Alter Film; *scr* Tati, Jacques Lagrange; *ph* Jean Bourgoin; *des* Henri Schmitt; *mus* Franck Barcellini, Alain Romains; *cast* Jacques Tati (Monsieur Hulot), Jean-Pierre Zola (Monsieur Arpel), Adrienne Servatie (Madame Arpel), Alain Becourt (Gérard), Lucien Fregis (Monsieur Pichard), Betty Schneider (Betty), Yvonne Arnaud (Georgette).

The Arpels live a modern, gadget-ordered existence, and their small son much prefers to spend his time with his eccentric uncle, Monsieur Hulot, in an old picturesque *quartier*. When the Arpels try to find a job and a wife for Hulot, their plans naturally misfire, but by the time they gratefully dispatch Hulot abroad, they have at least established a closer relationship with their son. TATI's second film featuring Monsieur Hulot has less pure farce than LES VACANCES DE MONSIEUR HULOT (1951), and the comedy depends more on a satire evolving from the social situation than on Hulot's clowning. The difference between the soulless modern environment of the Arpels and the haphazard warmth of Hulot's surroundings is emphasized by carefully-planned contrasts in the use of colour and sound effects.

**MONROE, MARILYN** (1926–62), US actress, real name Norma Jean Baker, spent her childhood in a Los Angeles orphanage and a succession of foster-homes. Her work as a photographer's model led to a contract with TWENTIETH CENTURY-FOX. Small roles in THE ASPHALT JUNGLE and ALL ABOUT EVE (both 1950) did little more than display her physical charms, and in 1953 the studio began the systematic promotion of a new sex goddess: *Niagara*'s publicity depended on exploitation of her bodily attractions, but GENTLEMEN PREFER BLONDES, with

Howard HAWKS's direction, revealed her unique combination of vulnerability and sexuality. HOW TO MARRY A MILLIONAIRE (1953) attracted considerable attention, as did her marriage in that year to the popular baseball star Joe DiMaggio.

The stresses of the STAR SYSTEM now began to tell: an obsessive perfectionism meant that the exquisite naïvety of her performances in THE SEVEN YEAR ITCH (1955), BUS STOP (1956), and SOME LIKE IT HOT (1959) was achieved at the cost of continual friction with the studio and much personal unhappiness. Aware that her appeal could not outlast her looks she enrolled at the ACTORS' STUDIO, hoping to become accepted as a serious actress, and Arthur MILLER (her third husband) wrote one screenplay for her, THE MISFITS (1961): shortly after the film's completion they were divorced.

Her unhappy life and her death from an overdose of barbiturates were used to castigate Hollywood and its system of production. Ironically, the myths surrounding Marilyn Monroe have lived on; interest in her has increased, though she has received hardly more compassionate treatment since her death.

Norman MAILER's *Marilyn: a biography of Marilyn Monroe* was published in 1973.

***MONSIEUR RIPOIS*** see KNAVE OF HEARTS

***MONSIEUR VERDOUX***, US, 1947. 2hr. *Dir, prod, scr, mus* Charles Chaplin, assisted by Robert Florey, Wheeler Dryden, for United Artists; *ph* Rollie Totheroh, Curt Courant, Wallace Chewing; *des* John Beckman; *ed* William Nico; *cast* Charlie Chaplin (Verdoux), Martha Raye (Annabella), Isabella Elsom (Marie), Mady Corell (Mona), Allison Roddan (her son), Robert Lewis (Maurice), Audrey Betz (his wife), Helen Heigh (Yvonne), Margaret Hoffman (Lydia).

CHAPLIN's sense of humour has often been ahead of his audience's and the public of 1947 was not ready for this black comedy on a Bluebeard theme, which is said to be based on an idea by Orson WELLES, and which is open to interpretation as the ultimate extension of the Tramp's anti-social conduct. Chaplin's messages, on the other hand, are usually rather naïve for his audiences and, if the courtroom and death cell speeches which he makes in the character of the wife-killing Verdoux contain the moral of the film, it was perhaps an untimely sermon against the unscrupulous business of war. *Monsieur Verdoux* was Chaplin's first financial flop and it left his reputation at its lowest ebb. Partly to redress this, CITY LIGHTS (1931) was re-issued in 1950. It won over a new generation of film-goers to Chaplin, and *Monsieur Verdoux* was forgotten. But the subtle comic skill of Chaplin's acting makes it perhaps his best performance.

*MONSIEUR VINCENT*, France, 1947. 2hr. *Dir* Maurice Cloche; *prod* EDIC/UGC; *scr* Jean Bernard Luc, Jean Anouilh; *ph* Claude Renoir; *cast* Pierre Fresnay (Vincent de Paul), Aimé Clariond (Cardinal de Richelieu), Jean Debucourt (de Gondi), Lise Delamare (Mme de Gondi), Germaine Dermoz (Anne of Austria).

The sixteenth-century priest Vincent de Paul, a pioneer of social welfare, became one of the Church's best-loved saints. The film describes part of his life and works. It is notable for the unforced beauty of the photography and particularly for the performance of Pierre FRESNAY, portraying Vincent's dedication and humility. The film was largely backed by subscriptions from members of French Catholic cinéclubs.

**MONTAGE** has two related but distinct meanings. It is the term employed to describe sequences designed to compress background information or provide atmosphere by combining a number of images in quick succession. Much used in Hollywood features until the early sixties, though latterly mainly in gangster films, montages are characterized by newspaper headlines spiralling into view, falling calendar leaves, clock faces, train wheels, place names flashing by, and a profusion of WIPES and DISSOLVES. An archetypal montage sequence in *Babes in Arms* (1939) uses shots of different phases of a vaudeville act in circular MATTES cut out of newspapers published in different American cities. During the sequence, Mickey ROONEY ages considerably. Montage work was handed over to a special EFFECTS team and noted creative workers in this field include Slavko VORKAPICH.

Montage also describes a theory of EDITING rationalized on the basis of practical experiments, notably by EISENSTEIN, though dating back to KULESHOV's experiments with PUDOVKIN. In order to convey ideas and to emphasize intellectual rather than emotional points, the strict narrative form of film was modified to include images not necessarily related to the dramatic development. Eisenstein used the analogy of overtones in music to explain the concept and also used, as a more concrete example, the parallel with oriental calligraphy: the characters for 'dog' and 'mouth' when combined mean 'bark' rather than just 'dog's mouth'. Examples abound in Eisenstein's work, most notably in OKTIABR (*October*, 1928). Other directors have applied the theory to greater or lesser degrees: Chaplin in MODERN TIMES (1936) equates commuters with sheep and French NOUVELLE VAGUE directors used montage for comic effects as in TRUFFAUT'S TIREZ SUR LE PIANISTE (1960), in which a gangster says 'May my mother die if I am lying' and a cutaway shows an old lady falling down. Such breaks in strict chronological narrative partially paved the way for the erosion of the conventional FLASHBACK.

**MONTAGU, IVOR** (1904– ), British man of cinema, working variously as film editor, distributor, scriptwriter, director, producer, and critic. Son of a banking family elevated to the peerage, he developed at Cambridge a commitment to left-wing politics which was to be life-long. In 1925, with Sidney BERNSTEIN, he founded the FILM SOCIETY, with the main aim of exhibiting the German and Russian films which misplaced patriotism and political antipathy excluded from regular commercial distribution. He worked as a film editor, importer, and titler in partnership with Adrian Brunel and Frank Wells, son of H. G. Wells, and persuaded the latter to provide him with stories for his first three short comedies, *Bluebottles*, *Daydreams*, and *The Tonic* (all 1928). Charles LAUGHTON, Elsa LANCHESTER, and F. A. YOUNG were among the youthful team working on these films, which had, however, small success (except in Germany, where they were distributed by Carl KOCH).

Montagu's admiration for the Russians led him to translate PUDOVKIN's *Film technique* in 1929 and EISENSTEIN's lectures on *Film form* in 1935; in his own films he often emulated Eisenstein's editing techniques. When Eisenstein visited Berlin and Paris in 1929 with ALEXANDROV and TISSÉ, Montagu joined them and arranged Eisenstein's visit to London in 1930. He preceded the Russians to Hollywood and worked with them there.

After a period working with HITCHCOCK in England, Montagu went to Spain in 1938 during the Civil War to make PROPAGANDA films for the Republicans. On his return he directed *Peace and Plenty* (1939), a scathing COMPILATION comparing still photographs and film of leaders of the National Government with social conditions. During the war he worked for the Ministry of Information and afterwards joined EALING STUDIOS, where he wrote the script of *Scott of the Antarctic* (Charles FREND, 1948).

Montagu's politics were certainly part of the reason he never achieved his aim of becoming a regular director. Through his writings he has remained an active if marginal force, an impish and stimulating figure in British cinema. His publications include *Film world* (London, 1964) and *With Eisenstein in Hollywood* (Berlin DDR, 1968).

**MONTAND, YVES** (1921– ), Italian-born actor and singer, real name Ivo Livi, who has lived and worked chiefly in France. Following periods in vaudeville and, from 1943, the Paris music hall, his career was encouraged by Edith

Piaf. Their partnership culminated in the film *Étoile sans lumière* (1946), but it was Montand's second film *Les Portes de la nuit* (Marcel CARNÉ, 1946) which established him as a popular actor and singer. A taut performance in LE SALAIRE DE LA PEUR (*The Wages of Fear*, 1953) made him an international star and his success was confirmed by *Marguerite de la nuit* (Claude AUTANT-LARA, 1955) and *Les Sorcières de Salem* (*The Witches of Salem*, 1956) in which he starred opposite Simone SIGNORET whom he had married in 1951. Essentially a European actor, he was less happily placed in two Hollywood films, *Let's Make Love* (George CUKOR, 1960), in which he co-starred with Marilyn MONROE, and *Sanctuary* (Tony RICHARDSON, 1960).

Montand's fruitful collaboration with the director COSTA-GAVRAS began in 1965 with his appearance as the police inspector in *Compartiments-tueurs* (*The Sleeping Car Murders*). His performances in Costa-Gavras's three political films, Z (1968), L'AVEU (1970), and *État de siège* (*State of Siege*, 1973), gave them a solid strength and won international critical acclaim. During this period he worked with other important directors including Alain RESNAIS, John FRANKENHEIMER, Claude LELOUCH, and Jean-Pierre MELVILLE. He also returned to Hollywood to co-star with Barbra STREISAND in Vincente MINNELLI's light-hearted *On a Clear Day You Can See Forever* (1970) which, like *César et Rosalie* (1973), gave him a romantic role in contrast to his more intense characterizations of honourable, determined men under conditions of stress.

**MONTGOMERY**, ROBERT (1904– ), US actor, achieved popularity chiefly as leading man to some of METRO-GOLDWYN-MAYER's most noted women stars, including Norma SHEARER in *Their Own Desire* and *The Divorcee* (both 1930), Greta GARBO in *Inspiration* (1931), and Joan CRAWFORD in *Forsaking All Others* (1934) and *The Last of Mrs Cheyney* (1937). His enthusiastic work in establishing the Screen Actors' Guild made him unpopular with the studio and casting him in NIGHT MUST FALL (1937) was intended to alienate his public; but his convincing performance as a homicidal maniac increased his following. His problems with MGM continued. After war service he made two important films for them, John FORD's *They Were Expendable* (1945), and *The Lady in the Lake* (1946), which Montgomery directed. This adaptation of Raymond CHANDLER's novel was recounted in the first person, the camera's viewpoint being that of the detective throughout; it attracted much notice but little approval. After this he left MGM to act and direct first for UNIVERSAL and then for WARNER BROS. After directing and starring in *Your Witness* (1949) he

virtually abandoned films for television. He was the first show-business personality to be engaged to advise an American President (Eisenhower) on television appearances.

**MOORE**, GRACE (1901–47), US singer, appeared in opera and operetta before her film début in *A Lady's Morals* (1930), a fictionalized biography of Jenny Lind. This was followed by *New Moon* (1931), in which she starred with Laurence Tibbett. In *One Night Of Love* (1934), directed by Victor Schertzinger, himself a skilled musician, music from grand opera was introduced to cinema audiences with unexpected success. She retired from films in 1937, but continued to make opera and concert appearances until her death in an air crash. Kathryn Grayson starred in a film biography of Grace Moore, *So This Is Love* (1953).

**MOOREHEAD**, AGNES (1918–74), US character actress, began her career on the stage and was discovered by Orson WELLES who featured her in CITIZEN KANE (1941) and THE MAGNIFICENT AMBERSONS (1942). She appeared in a large number of films: the quality of her material was variable, though not her standard of performance; and she was particularly effective as sharp-featured, unpleasant, or neurotic characters. In recent years she was in the long-running television series 'Bewitched'.

*MÖRDER SIND UNTER UNS, Die* (*The Murderers Are Amongst Us*), Germany, 1946. 1½hr. *Dir, scr* Wolfgang Staudte; *prod* DEFA; *ph* Friedl Behn-Grund, Eugen Klagemann; *cast* Hildegard Knef (Susanna Wallner), Ernst Fischer (Dr Mertens), Arno Paulsen (Brückner), Robert Forsch (Mondschein), Albert Johann (Herr Timm).

From a group of people trying to resume their normal lives in occupied Berlin, the film highlights and concentrates on the doctor whose unwilling participation in a wartime atrocity has made him incapable of returning to his peacetime occupation.

The first feature film to be produced in postwar Germany, *Die Mörder sind unter uns* was made by DEFA under difficult conditions, both practically and politically; its technical accomplishment and thoughtfulness were a welcome surprise.

**MOREAU**, JEANNE (1928– ), French actress born in Paris of a French father and English mother, became on her twentieth birthday the youngest member of the Comédie Française. After four years she moved to the Théâtre National Populaire, with whom the following year she scored a great personal success in

L'Heure éblouissante, becoming for a time the star of the company. From the beginning of her career she took screen roles, finally catching critical and public attention in MALLE's L'Ascenseur pour l'échafaud (1957). In LES AMANTS (1958) Malle drew from her the sultry eroticism that forms a large part of her muted but undisguisable magnetism, and in VADIM's LES LIAISONS DANGEUREUSES (1959) she and Gérard PHILIPE gave a beautifully controlled portrait of wickedness. After MODERATO CANTABILE (1960) she reached the apogee of her sombre, erotic roles with ANTONIONI's LA NOTTE (1961), which also gave her some telling scenes with Monica VITTI.

Working happily on JULES ET JIM (1961) with François TRUFFAUT (for whom she had already made a brief appearance in LES QUATRE CENTS COUPS, 1959), she discovered a light-hearted vein which extended her range and resulted in one of the cinema's more memorable performances. She appeared in LOSEY's Eva (1962), DEMY's Baie des anges, Marcel OPHULS' Peau de banane, and, momentarily, for Malle again in LE FEU FOLLET (all 1963), before finding in BUÑUEL another director demanding the full range of expression at her command: her detachment, insolence, eroticism, and humour are finely combined in LE JOURNAL D'UNE FEMME DE CHAMBRE (1964).

She played the title role in the light-hearted Mata-Hari (1964) for Jean-Louis Richard (to whom she was for a time married), then starred with Brigitte BARDOT in VIVA MARIA! (1965); working once again with Malle, Moreau's polish and daring were at the core of an entertaining and accomplished success. After roles in Orson WELLES's CAMPANADAS A MEDIANOCHE (Chimes at Midnight) and Tony RICHARDSON's Mademoiselle and The Sailor from Gibraltar (all 1966), she returned to Truffaut who gave her the opportunity in La Mariée était en noir (The Bride Wore Black, 1967) to play another femme fatale, though with the delicate irony that had distinguished Mata-Hari. Her first American film was Monte Walsh (1970), co-starring Lee MARVIN. Nathalie Granger (1972) brought Moreau into contact with Marguerite DURAS, who wrote and directed this intimate, domestic piece. Moreau has pursued a successful side-career as a singer which began with a best-selling record of songs by Boris Bassiak launched in the wake of his 'Le Tourbillon', written for her in Jules et Jim.

Moreau's success is in part attributable to her mature eroticism, helped by her sultry, down-turned mouth, but her professional and versatile skill has underpinned her whole career. Working with Malle, Truffaut, and Buñuel in particular, she has proved herself an actress of delicacy and power as well as a star with an international following.

**MORGAN... A SUITABLE CASE FOR TREATMENT**, GB, 1966. 1½hr. Dir Karel Reisz; prod Leon Clore for Quintra Productions; scr David Mercer, from his own television play; ph Larry Pizer, Gerry Turpin; ed Victor Proctor; des Philip Harrison; cast David Warner (Morgan), Vanessa Redgrave (Leonie), Robert Stephens (Napier), Irene Handl (Mrs Delt).

An account of an attractive young schizophrenic in the throes of becoming unmarried from his society wife, the film is uncertain both of its theme and treatment. David Mercer's original television play was more narrowly concerned with schizophrenia: the film's extension to take in other fashionable topics makes it diffuse, but also allows for considerable fun and enjoyment. REISZ's direction is similarly uneven. Morgan is an interesting development of the 'angry young man' hero of earlier British films of this period.

**MORGAN, MICHÈLE** (1920– ), French actress, real name Simone Roussel, was launched as a star by Marc ALLÉGRET in Gribouille (1937) and, opposite Charles BOYER, in Orage (1938). Her best-remembered appearance of this period was with Jean GABIN in QUAI DES BRUMES (1938). She spent the war years in Hollywood, where her films included Higher and Higher (1943), with Frank SINATRA, and Passage to Marseille (1944), with Humphrey BOGART. In 1942 she married William Marshall (their son Mike Marshall became an actor): her husband's company produced the film version of André Gide's La Symphonie pastorale (Jean Delannoy, 1949), and she won the CANNES award for best actress for her performance as the blind girl. Her subdued emotionalism was well suited to the style of Carol REED's THE FALLEN IDOL (1948).

During the fifties Michèle Morgan was the most popular actress in France, icily beautiful in the episode 'L'Orgueil' of Les Sept Péchés capitaux (The Seven Deadly Sins, 1951) and romantically reunited with Gabin in La Minute de la vérité (The Moment of Truth, 1952); she also appeared in René CLAIR's graceful Les Grandes Manoeuvres (Summer Manoeuvres, 1955) and AUTANT-LARA's Marguerite de la nuit (1955), a version of the Faust story. She revisited Hollywood to play a French peasant woman in The Vintage (1957) and had a more than usually melodramatic role in André CAYATTE's Le Miroir à deux faces (1958). In the German remake of GRAND HOTEL (1932), Menschen im Hotel (1959), she was well chosen for the part of the ageing ballerina originally created by GARBO. Her infrequent recent appearances include an aristocratic widow in Lost Command (1966) and a melancholy eighteenth-century countess in Benjamin (1969).

**MORIN,** EDGAR (1921–   ), French film theorist. After wartime resistance work he became a sociologist, journalist, and political commentator. In 1956 he was appointed to the Centre National de Recherche Scientifique (sociology section). In the same year his 'anthropological essay', *Le Cinéma ou l'homme imaginaire*, was published. In considering film as a tool for anthropologists and in its pioneering investigation of the psychological effects of the screen image and the process of perception, it has proved a seminal work. He extended his theoretical interest in film by collaborating, in the capacity of sociologist, with Jean ROUCH on the making of CHRONIQUE D'UN ÉTÉ (1961). Although the outcome was not altogether happy it marked a significant step towards the integration of theory and practice within the CINÉMA-VÉRITÉ movement.

Morin is also the author of a study of the star system, *Les Stars* (1957).

**MORLAY,** GABY (1897–1964), French actress, real name Blanche Fumoleau, first appeared on the screen in *Le Sandale rouge* (1913), in which she had appeared on stage. Her silent films ranged widely from Max LINDER's recruiting film *Le 2 août 1914* (1915) to Jacques FEYDER's *Les Nouveaux Messieurs* (1929). She later became associated with films by Marcel L'HERBIER—*Le Scandale* (1934), *Le Bonheur* (1934), *Nuits de feu* (1938), *Entente cordiale* (1939), *La Mode rêvée* (1940)—and appeared in two of Jacqueline AUDRY's adaptations from COLETTE, GIGI (1949) and *Mitsou* (1956). She pursued a successful career in the theatre as well as making over a hundred films; her effervescent personality and unforced conviction earned her enduring popularity.

**MORLEY,** ROBERT (1908–   ), British actor. Having established a considerable reputation as a character actor in the theatre, he made his first film appearance in *Marie Antoinette* (1938). He has appeared in over forty films, notably MAJOR BARBARA (1941), in which he was a strikingly enigmatic Undershaft, *The Young Mr Pitt* (1942), *Edward My Son* (1949), THE AFRICAN QUEEN (1952), *The Outcast of the Islands* (1951), BEAT THE DEVIL (1953), *Oscar Wilde* (1960), in the title role, a part he had played on the stage in London and New York, and *The Loved One* (1965). In his recent films he has tended to be type-cast as a blustering, pompous, and eminently foolish English gentleman.

*MOROCCO,* US, 1930. 1½hr. *Dir* Josef von Sternberg; *prod* Paramount; *scr* Jules Furthman, from the play *Amy Jolly* by Benno Vigny; *ph* Lee Garmes; *des* Hans Dreier; *cast* Gary Cooper (Tom Brown), Marlene Dietrich (Amy Jolly), Adolphe Menjou (La Bassière).

*Morocco,* with a story which follows the tortuous course of the romance between a legionnaire and a cynical cabaret singer, initiated the American series of STERNBERG–DIETRICH films that followed their collaboration on DER BLAUE ENGEL (1930) in Germany. The film is notable for the introduction of Sternberg's celebrated light-and-shade effect provided by slatted shutters and doors, and for his imaginative use of natural sound in spite of the restrictions of the single track system (see SOUND).

**MORRICONE,** ENNIO (1928–   ), Italian composer, began writing film music in 1961. He became internationally known with his assertive music for spaghetti Westerns, especially Sergio LEONE's *Per un pugno di dollari* (*For a Fistful of Dollars*, 1964), *Il buono, il bruto, il cattivo* (*The Good, the Bad, and the Ugly*, 1966), and *C'era un volta di West* (*Once Upon a Time in the West*, 1968). He has also written for more serious films, including BELLOCCHIO's I PUGNI IN TASCA (1966), PONTECORVO's LA BATTAGLIA DI ALGERI (1965) and *¡Queimada!* (1968), and PASOLINI's TEOREMA (1968).

*MORTE A VENEZIA* (*Death in Venice*), Italy, 1971. Panavision; 2½hr; Technicolor. *Dir* Luchino Visconti; *prod* Alfa Cinematografico; *scr* Visconti, Nicola Bandalucco, from the novel by Thomas Mann; *ph* Pasquale De Santis; *des* Ferdinando Scarfiotti; *cost* Piero Tosi; *mus* Mahler's Third and Fifth Symphonies; *cast* Dirk Bogarde (Gustave von Aschenbach), Björn Andresen (Tadzio), Silvana Mangano (Tadzio's mother), Marisa Berenson (Frau von Aschenbach), Mark Burns (Alfried).

VISCONTI followed the events of Mann's story closely, but changed Aschenbach from a writer to a composer based on Gustav Mahler (who was the original inspiration for the character). Mahler's music is felicitously used in alternation with the multilingual hum of the luxury hotel. The evocation of *fin de siècle* Venice is one of Visconti's most successful achievements, contrasting the heavy richness of the seaside hotel, photographed in muted autumnal colours, with the decay and corruption in the city, and Dirk BOGARDE's performance as the doomed artist was widely admired. The film was awarded a Special Jury Prize at CANNES, 1971.

**MOSCOW FILM FESTIVAL.** The first international film festival in Eastern Europe was held in Moscow in February 1935. Among the foreign films to receive prizes were CLAIR's LE DERNIER MILLIARDAIRE and VIDOR's OUR DAILY BREAD (both 1934).

The festival was revived in 1957 as part of the World Festival of Youth and Sport. It is now held in the summer, alternating biennially with the film festival at Karlovy Vary (Carlsbad), Czechoslovakia, in existence since 1954. Gold medals are awarded in a wide variety of categories: feature, documentary, animation, children's film, popular science, anti-Fascist, anti-imperialist, etc; direction, acting, etc. Moscow is naturally the principal showcase for films from the Socialist countries, but it also draws a large number of African and Asian films and has always attracted support from the West.

**MOSKVIN,** ANDREI (1901–61), Russian cameraman, began his career with the FEKS group and photographed most of KOZINTSEV and TRAUBERG's films. His other work, including IVAN GROZNYI II (*Ivan the Terrible*, Part II, 1946), *Pirogov* (1947), *Don Quixote* (1956), *and* DAMA S SOBACHKOI (*Lady with a Little Dog*, 1959), demonstrates his skill at executing the needs of very different directors. He died while filming HAMLET (1964) and the camerawork was completed by his pupil Gricius.

*MOTHER* see MAT

*MOTHER JOAN OF THE ANGELS* see MATKA JOANNA OD ANIOŁÓW

**MOTION PICTURE ASSOCIATION OF AMERICA** founded in 1921 as the Motion Picture Producers and Distributors of America. Wide public antagonism aroused by the raffishness of the film industry, together with charges of the corrupting effect of films on the fast-growing audience, had led to demands for government control; to avoid this, major company heads (including William FOX, Carl LAEMMLE, Samuel GOLDWYN, Adolph ZUKOR, and Lewis J. SELZNICK) formed the MPPDA as a self-regulating body for the industry, inviting Will H. HAYS to become president. Apart from valuable contributions on the administrative level—the introduction of the Central Casting Bureau, title registration, and the Labor Committee, and the investigation of fraudulent practices among exhibitors—the Hays Office, as it came to be known, became responsible for the moral standing of the film industry in public and private. The Production Code, also referred to as the Hays Office Code, was taken from a formula drafted in 1929 by two Roman Catholics, one a priest, the other a publisher of influential film trade magazines; in 1934, because of continuing criticism from religious bodies, particularly the National Legion of Decency, it became mandatory on all members of the MPPDA (see CENSORSHIP, US). Hays's retirement from the presidency coincided with the separation of production from distribution interests and the renaming of the Association. He was succeeded in 1945 by Eric A. Johnston and in 1966 by Jack Valenti, both, like him, closely associated with the White House.

**MOTION PICTURE PATENTS COMPANY** (MPPC). A trust formed in January 1909 in an attempt to stabilize and monopolize the frenetically-developing US industry. Seven major manufacturers of equipment and films, EDISON, BIOGRAPH, VITAGRAPH, ESSANAY, SELIG, LUBIN, and KALEM, were joined by the distributor George Kleine and the French companies, PATHÉ and MÉLIÈS' STAR-FILM, who provided some seventy per cent of the US product, Pathé alone distributing twice as much footage as the combined output of the US industry.

Members of the MPPC agreed to pool their patent claims, and each received a licence to manufacture films. Edison was acknowledged as the basic owner of the patents, and was to be paid a royalty. In an attempt to create a monopoly, the nine companies agreed that no licence to manufacture should be issued except to their own members, and further contracted with the EASTMAN Kodak Company, the largest manufacturer, that film stock should be supplied only to MPPC members.

In an attempt to control EXHIBITION as well as production, the MPPC proposed a system of charges which exhibitors were to pay for the right to use projectors as well as to hire films exclusively from members of the trust. They relied on the threat of removing machinery as well as cutting off film supply for the enforcement of their system. To control DISTRIBUTION it became necessary to establish a national film exchange (the General Film Company, founded 1910) which by 1912 had swallowed up fifty-seven of the fifty-eight existing licensed exchanges.

The one distribution company which did not succumb was William FOX's Greater New York Film Rental Company. Fox's ownership of film theatres in New York and his move into production enabled him to withstand the trust, and he became effectively the leader of widespread and bitter opposition to it in the four or five years following its formation. Although over 10,000 small exhibitors were forced to sign contracts with the trust members, its impositions were fiercely resented. Bootlegging of films and equipment quickly started and flourished. Many protective associations of independent companies were formed, most important among them Carl LAEMMLE's Motion Picture Distributing and Sales Company. Competition, instead of being crushed, was in fact fostered by the trust's activities. During the years of resistance, in which lawsuits proliferated alongside acts of sabotage and open violence, the independents successfully challenged the Trust with increased production, cheaper prices, and films which were better and longer. By the time Fox brought an action in 1913 under the Sherman anti-trust law, the MPPC had already ceased to be effective. It rapidly disintegrated, although it was not formally declared illegal until 1917.

**MOUCHETTE**, France, 1966. 1½hr. *Dir* Robert Bresson; *prod* Argos Films, Parc Film; *scr* Bresson, from the novel *Nouvelle Histoire de Mouchette* by Georges Bernanos; *ph* Ghislain Cloquet; *ed* Raymond Lamy; *des* Pierre Guffroy; *mus* Monteverdi, 'Magnificat', song by Jean Wiener; *cast* Nadine Nortier (Mouchette), Jean-Claude Guilbert (Arsène), Maria Cardinal (mother), Paul Hébert (father), Jean Vimenet (Mathieu), Marine Trichet (Louisa).

Like his earlier film based on a book by Bernanos, JOURNAL D'UN CURÉ DE CAMPAGNE (1951), *Mouchette* was a commission for BRESSON, not his own choice. It had already appealed to other film-makers: GODARD almost made it the basis of his first film, and ASTRUC wanted to film it. Unlike his faithful representation of the earlier book, Bresson's film is a free adaptation of the *Nouvelle Histoire de Mouchette*. Another interesting departure from his earlier practice of reproducing as strictly as possible the authentic setting of his subject was his choice of Provence

for the location of *Mouchette*, rather than the northern village of the book. The lyricism of the images afforded by the southern countryside contrasts sharply with the harshness of the young girl's isolation and defiance, and the almost unwitting cruelty with which she is treated.

Bresson's problem was to present the story without softening it and yet without making it unbearable. He treats the incidents with more richness of detail than had been his earlier austere practice, allowing a few rare glimpses of psychological motivation. Yet it is the restraint and economy of his method, together with the sense he imparts of grace won through suffering, that saves the film from being a hopeless indictment of the human condition, and makes it a deeply moving work.

**MOULIN ROUGE**, GB, 1952. Technicolor; 2hr. *Dir* John Huston; *prod* Romulus/John Huston; *assoc prod* Jack Clayton; *scr* Anthony Veiller, Huston from the book by Pierre La Mure; *ph* Oswald Morris; *des* Paul Sheriff; *mus* Georges Auric; *cast* José Ferrer (Toulouse-Lautrec/his father), Colette Marchand (Marie), Suzanne Flon (Myriamme), Zsa Zsa Gabor (Jane Avril), Katherine Kath (La Goulue), Claude Nollier (Comtesse de Toulouse-Lautrec), Muriel Smith (Aicha).

In this film transcription of a fictionalized account of the life of Toulouse-Lautrec, HUSTON balanced the unhappy biographical content by

*Mouchette* (Robert Bresson, 1966)

creating a kaleidoscope of Paris in the gay nineties. The lengthy, flamboyant opening sequence of can-can abandon in the Moulin Rouge was a *tour de force* of imagery and cutting. The film is remarkable for the unusual use of controlled colour, with occasionally bizarre effects produced by tinting whole scenes. José FERRER gave a memorable portrayal of the deformed painter.

**MOURIR A MADRID** (*To Die in Madrid*), France, 1962. 1½hr. *Dir* Frédéric Rossif; *prod* Ancinex; *scr* Madeleine Chapsal; *ed* Suzanne Baron; *mus* Maurice Jarre.

A COMPILATION of newsreel and documentary footage of the Spanish Civil War, combined with newly-shot sequences to present an atmospheric account of the siege of Madrid. ROSSIF makes no claim to historical objectivity, and the film's emotional anti-Fascism is emphasized by music based on Spanish folk themes and by the narration (spoken in the English version by John GIELGUD and Irene Worth). Old wounds were reopened by the film; East Germany replied with *Unbändiges Spanien* (*Untameable Spain*, 1962), made up of similar material assembled to attack the Allied governments for ignoring the cause of democracy in Spain, and a Spanish compilation, *Morir en España* (1965), attempted to deny the association of Franco's régime with Fascism in Germany and Italy.

**MOUSJOUKINE** see MOZHUKIN

**MOUSSINAC**, LÉON (1890–1964), French critic and theoretician, was film critic for *Mercure de France* 1920–8, and wrote for *L'Humanité* 1921–32. In 1926 he introduced BRONENOSETS POTEMKIN (*The Battleship Potemkin*, 1925) to France and the next year founded 'Les Amis de Spartacus' for private showings of censored Soviet films. He was director of the INSTITUT DES HAUTES ÉTUDES CINÉMATOGRAPHIQUES 1946–60. He wrote several books, among the best known of which are *Naissance du cinéma* (Paris, 1925), *Le Cinéma soviétique* (Paris, 1928), and *L'Âge ingrat du cinéma* (Paris, 1946).

Concurrently with DELLUC he was one of the first to work out a coherent theory of film and was especially influential in popularizing Swedish and Russian films.

**MOVIOLA.** Outside the US all editing machines are usually called Moviolas, but the Moviola is actually an American device first made for viewing silent films and later elaborated to accommodate sound. The modern Moviola consists of side-by-side picture and sound 'heads' which may be operated separately or locked together to run synchronously. Single shots are run forward or backward through the picture head—essentially a highly simplified projector—or stopped to locate a particular frame. Magnetic soundtracks are handled similarly on the sound head. Film is not actually cut on the machine, only marked and removed for cutting later.

Although many editors refuse to work on any other machine, the Moviola's small picture and low-fidelity sound have increasingly limited its usefulness for wide screen films and stereophonic sound. In the last decade a number of second-generation editing machines have been evolved, providing high-quality picture and sound and considerable flexibility for the editor. The latest Moviola has followed this trend and no longer resembles its predecessors. (See EDITING.)

**MOZHUKIN**, IVAN (1890–1939), Russian actor, famous before the Revolution, emigrated in 1919 and became the dominant figure of a group of Russian actors, directors, and producers in Paris. Mozhukin acted in films by EPSTEIN, L'HERBIER, Tourjansky, and Volkoff (*Kean, ou désordre et génie*, 1923) and was specially acclaimed in *Le Brasier ardent* (1923) which he co-directed with Volkoff. Romanticism, violence, and refinement carried to extremes were the characteristics of his style. In 1927 he signed a contract to work in Hollywood but had little success there. Moreover, an unfortunate plastic surgery operation deprived his facial expression of some of its singularity. He returned to Paris in 1931 but the advent of sound meant that, as a Russian speaker, there was little opening for him.

**MUERTE DE UN CICLISTA** (*Death of a Cyclist*), Spain/Italy, 1955. 1¾hr. *Dir* Juan Antonio Bardem; *prod* Suevia Films/Trionfalcine; *scr* Bardem from a story by Luis de Igoa; *ph* Alfredo Fraile; *cast* Lucia Bose (Maria Jose), Alberto Closas (Juan), Carlos Casaravilla (Rafael), Otello Toso (Miguel), Bruna Corra (Matilde).

Juan, a university professor, driving with his mistress, Maria Jose, knocks down a worker on a bicycle. Fearing that their affair will be discovered, they leave the scene and later learn that the man has died. When Juan tries to convince Maria Jose that they must confess she runs him down, then is killed when she swerves to avoid another cyclist.

Censorship obliged BARDEM to punish the 'adulterous woman', which accounts for the melodramatic ending. Nevertheless, the moral, social, and political implications of the film offer a scathing comment on contemporary Spanish life.

**MULLIGAN, ROBERT** (1932– ), US director who came to the cinema from television and worked with producer Alan PAKULA. Their first production, *Fear Strikes Out* (1957), was followed by a succession of films, the best of which are *To Kill a Mockingbird* (1962), *Inside Daisy Clover* (1966), *Up the Down Staircase* (1967), and *The Stalking Moon* (1968). Mulligan's recent independent work has included *Summer of '42* (1971) and an eerie thriller in a New England setting, *The Other* (1972). His best work is characterized by sensitive observation of relationships and a quiet directorial hand.

**MULTIPLANE CAMERA,** a special animation rostrum devised by the Walt DISNEY Studios to produce realistic effects of depth and perspective for certain shots in their animated films. Because of its complexity the multiplane shot has been rarely used by other studios and is no longer seen even in current Disney cartoons.

In normal ANIMATION the CELS and backgrounds are all photographed flat, lying on the same plane. This is satisfactory as long as the camera remains stationary; but when it moves, the entire picture moves past it or towards it at the same speed, making the flatness apparent. To overcome this, Disney built the huge multiplane camera, occupying an entire room and operated by four or five skilled cameramen. The scene was painted on several sheets of glass—say, foreground trees on the nearest sheet, a woodland glade on the next sheet, distant mountains as the background. A complex rigid framework supported each glass sheet at the correct distance from the camera and allowed minutely controlled sidewise movements of the sheets. Cels bearing animated figures could be placed on any plane. Then the entire scene could be moved past the camera, each plane at a different speed, simulating the real-life effect of parallax where nearby objects pass rapidly while distant ones hardly seem to move at all.

Multiplane animation can be seen at its best in the feature films of Disney's heyday: the lyrical tracking shots through a classical landscape in the Pastoral Symphony sequence of FANTASIA (1940); the circus train in *Dumbo* (1941) puffing through hills and tunnels; and the first-day-of-school sequence in *Pinocchio* (1940), where the camera first hovers above the rooftops of the town, then descends past chimneys and gables directly into the street teeming with animated life.

**MULTI-SCREEN.** Like most 'novelty' effects, multi-screen presentation is almost as old as the cinema itself. It is unusual in having been developed and demonstrated under the auspices of various international exhibitions. The earliest was seen at the Paris Exposition Universelle of 1900, in which Raoul GRIMOIN-SANSON demonstrated CINÉORAMA, a system he had patented three years earlier.

In 1921, George W. Bingham took out patents on his Widescope. Double-width camera stock (70mm) was used for the shooting and then split during processing. The two resulting 35mm films were laced on interlocked projectors. (An almost identical system, Thrillerama, was tried out in 1956 but after a week in Houston, Texas, it was abandoned for mechanical reasons.)

The next attempt at a multi-screen system produced the most celebrated film of its kind, Abel GANCE's NAPOLÉON (1927). Under the name POLYVISION, Gance's method employed three projectors which were used sometimes discretely and sometimes to form a single wide image. For these panoramic vistas, three synchronized cameras were used during production.

Vitarama used eleven interlocked films, projected on to a curved arc with a quarter dome above it. The only known film in Vitarama was made for the Petroleum Industry exhibit at the New York World's Fair of 1939. Its inventor, Fred Waller, persevered and thirteen years later introduced a much improved version, renamed CINERAMA, using only three projectors.

The commercial breakthrough of Cinerama provided the impetus for other systems, though still used mainly for exhibition purposes. In 1959 the Ford Motor Company's Quadravision (four images projected simultaneously on to four screens) was employed in their *Design for Suburban Living* show and in the same year the US Information Service launched its Septorama (seven 35mm images shown on a geodesic dome in two rows of three and four screens). Then IBM sponsored a film by Charles and Ray Eames called *Think* for their pavilion at the New York World Fair of 1964. The seventeen different-sized screens were used for, among other purposes, the simultaneous demonstration of alternatives.

By the time of Expo '67 in Montreal, the application of multi-screen techniques had reached staggering proportions. Many exhibits included such experiments, though perhaps no others on the scale of the display of the NATIONAL FILM BOARD of Canada. Called *Labyrinth*, it comprised three chambers, in two of which film was used. In the first chamber there were two screens, one on the wall opposite the audience and one on the floor below the audience gallery. In the third chamber, five screens were arranged in cruciform, sometimes used for one large image, at other times for individual images, changing in rotational sequence.

Multi-screen techniques have been adopted latterly for tape–slide presentation, using mosaics of transparencies (sometimes more than 100 simultaneously) synchronized to a tape recording, usually in multi-track form. These are increasingly common in exhibitions for many applications. Multi-screen narrative films are comparatively dormant, except for occasional ventures by experimental film-makers. Notable among the latter is Andy WARHOL's *Chelsea Girls* (1966); other directors have tried, usually without success, to overcome the limitations of projection by printing all images on to one film. The so-called 'London version' of Kenneth ANGER's *Inauguration of the Pleasure Dome* (1958) was thus treated.

**MUNI, PAUL** (1895–1967), US actor of Austrian origin, real name Muni Weisenfreund, appeared in 1918–26 with the New York Yiddish Theatre. He had a distinguished film career during the thirties, starring in SCARFACE (1932), *I Am a Fugitive from a Chain Gang* (Mervyn LEROY, 1932), and THE GOOD EARTH (1937); he won particular acclaim for his portrayals of Pasteur in *The Story of Louis Pasteur* (1936) and Zola in *The Life of Emile Zola* (1937). His later film appearances were less frequent, although he continued to act regularly in the theatre.

**MUNK, ANDRZEJ** (1921–66), Polish director, graduated from LÓDŹ as director and cameraman in 1952. He made several distinguished documentaries which, while adhering to ideological principles (Munk was a committed Communist), brought a heightened dramatic quality to the reconstruction of real events such as railway reconstruction in *Kolejarskie slowo* (1953) and coal mining in *Gwiazdy musza plonac* (1954). His first fiction feature, *Czlowiek na torze* (*Man on the Track*, 1957), also had a railway setting: an elderly worker is killed in an accident, three sets of evidence are considered, and the question of responsibility is left open. Munk's ironical probing into wartime resistance in EROICA (1957) was ambivalent enough to disconcert audiences more used to WAJDA's passionate treatment of such topics. On a similar note, the hero of *Zezowate szczeście* (*Bad Luck*, 1960) lives through the explosive history of Poland from the thirties to the fifties, blandly embodying the national talent for survival. PASAŻERKA (*Passenger*, 1963) was interrupted by Munk's death in a car crash. In the form assembled by his friends it has greater harshness than his previous work, but its exploration of layers of truth is a direct development of his earlier ideas.

In the mainly romantic upsurge of Polish cinema in the fifties, Munk was outstanding for his irony, economy, and clarity, and his few films class him as a director of international stature.

**MURDERERS ARE AMONGST US, The,** see MÖRDER SIND UNTER UNS, DIE

**MURDER IN THORNTON SQUARE, The,** see GASLIGHT

**MURIEL, OU LE TEMPS D'UN RETOUR,** France, 1963. Eastman Color; 2hr. *Dir* Alain Resnais; *prod* Argos Films/Alpha Productions/Éclair/Les Films de la Pléiade/Dear Films (Rome); *scr* Jean Cayrol; *ph* Sacha Vierny; *des* Jacques Saulnier; *mus* Hans Werner Henze (sung by Rita Streich); *cast* Delphine Seyrig (Hélène), Jean-Pierre Kerien (Alphonse), Nita Klein (Françoise), Jean-Baptiste Thierrée (Bernard), Laurence Badie (Claudie), Martine Vatel (Marie-Do), Jean Champion (Ernest), Claude Sainval (de Smoke), Jean Dasté (l'homme à la chèvre).

Hélène invites Alphonse, her lover twenty years earlier, to stay with her in Boulogne. He arrives accompanied by Françoise, ostensibly his niece. Bernard, Hélène's stepson, is also staying with her, having recently returned from military service in Algeria. Just as Hélène and Alphonse are overshadowed by their past, so Bernard is haunted by the memory of a girl in Algeria, Muriel. The meeting provokes a kind of crisis, where each is forced to try to come to terms with his own past.

Although at first sight much more realistic than RESNAIS's previous films, *Muriel* is in fact a highly stylized work, evoking the disrupted universe of the characters through its own fragmented form, and offering the spectator mere glimpses of their existence. The restless rhythm, the operatic music, the colour, and the overlapping of dialogue from one scene to another all undermine the 'realism' of the story.

*Muriel* is a central film in Resnais's work; while it represents a further step in his experiments with narrative form, it also marks a broadening out in subject-matter. There is a development away from the intense subjectivity of HIROSHIMA MON AMOUR (1959) and L'ANNÉE DERNIÈRE A MARIENBAD (1961), and towards the overtly political preoccupations of LA GUERRE EST FINIE (1966).

**MURNAU, FRIEDRICH WILHELM** (1888–1931), German director, real name F. W. Plumpe, studied philosophy, music, and art at Heidelberg, later becoming an actor with Max REINHARDT. He came to commercial cinema after making propaganda films for the German embassy in Switzerland. His early films display the currently fashionable taste for the supernatural, and he collaborated with some of the

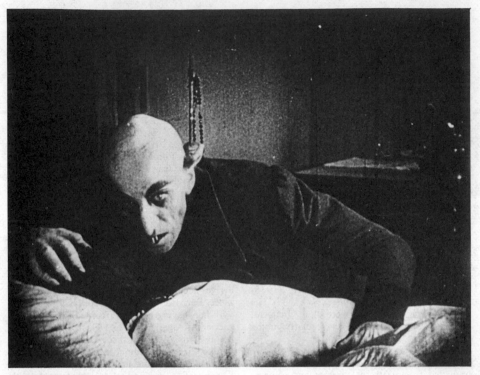

*Nosferatu* (F. W. Murnau, 1922)

major figures of the German cinema: Karl FREUND as cameraman on *Satanas* (1919), Carl MAYER as scriptwriter on *Der Bucklige und die Tänzerin* (*The Hunchback and the Dancer*, 1920), Freund on *Der Januskopf* (1920), a pirated version of DR JEKYLL AND MR HYDE, Fritz Arno WAGNER as cameraman on *Schloss Vogeloed* (*The Haunted Castle*, 1921) and NOS-FERATU, EINE SYMPHONIE DES GRAUENS (*Nosferatu, A Symphony of Terror*, 1922), which initiated a long succession of screen vampires.

The peak of Murnau's German career came with the merging of DECLA-BIOSCOP with UFA in 1923, which brought together the best film artists and technical resources of Germany. DER LETZTE MANN (*The Last Laugh*, 1924), again with Mayer and Freund and with Emil JAN-NINGS's impressive performance in the leading role, attracted wide attention. Striking cinematic devices (the mobile camera, the subjective shot, the flashing editing of the drunken dream), many of which were specified in the script, were used by Murnau with complete assurance. His last two films in Germany, *Tartüff* (1925) and *Faust* (1926), were lavish studio productions, both again starring Jannings.

Murnau left for Hollywood in 1926, and his prestige prompted William FOX to provide enormous resources for SUNRISE (1927), a strange and beautiful film, which curiously blends German and Hollywood styles and is marked by the long, fluid shots which had become his hallmark. Murnau initially found little difficulty in transferring to Hollywood and accommodating his producers' demands, but after the disappointing financial return on *Sunrise* both *Four Devils* (1928), a remake of VARIÉTÉ (1925), and *Our Daily Bread* (1929), released as *City Girl*, suffered from studio interference. The introduction of sound made both films commercially obsolete almost before they were completed; both were released with awkward sound sequences grafted on. *Our Daily Bread* shows Murnau filming on location among the Dakota farmers, competently handling the pictorial demands of a semi-documentary approach; it reflects a radical move away from literary subjects and artificial surroundings.

In spite of his ability to work with gifted collaborators, Murnau was essentially a solitary man. In 1928 he set up a production company with Robert FLAHERTY who, after MOANA (1926), wanted to make another South Seas film;

but their aims were fundamentally different and Flaherty abandoned the partnership in 1930, leaving Murnau a free hand in making TABU (1931). A silent film with a synchronized score, its haunting exoticism and visual beauty caught the public's imagination and it was his only film to achieve worldwide success. Unhappily, Murnau died in a car crash a week before the première.

Lotte Eisner, *F. W. Murnau*, London, 1972.

**MURRAY,** MAE (1889–1965), US actress, real name Marie Adrienne Koenig, whose distinctive appearance—parted lips, frizzily curled usually blonde hair, and exotic wardrobe—featured in nearly forty films between 1916 and 1931, several of them directed by her husband Robert Z. Leonard. She gave her best performance in STROHEIM's THE MERRY WIDOW (1925). Her showgirl background contributed to her dancing skills, but a growing reputation for being difficult apparently ended her career, just when the studios were embarking on musicals. Her rather sensational life is described in Jane Ardmore's biography *The self-enchanted* (New York, 1965).

**MUSIC.** A musical accompaniment was from the earliest days a part of film presentations: at the LUMIÈRES' first showing a piano was used, to counteract the noise of the projector as well as to support the sense and mood of the scenes depicted. The solo pianist in the cheap local cinema is perhaps better remembered than the small instrumental ensembles which were as customary, or the large orchestras that were taken for granted in de luxe picture houses; music for silent films in fact ranged from the pianist's improvisations through sometimes indiscriminate use of existing concert works to specially arranged scores, often with sound effects incorporated.

Among its many striking features, THE BIRTH OF A NATION (1915) marked an important step forward in the creative and precise use of film music. D. W. GRIFFITH and J. C. Breil together constructed an elaborately cued score made up of original passages and traditional American tunes. Other directors who worked closely with composers include Abel GANCE with Arthur HONEGGER on LA ROUE (1922) and NAPOLÉON (1927), Marcel L'HERBIER with Darius MILHAUD on *L'Inhumaine* (1924), and KOZINTSEV and TRAUBERG with SHOSTAKOVICH on NOVYI VAVILON (*New Babylon*, 1929). A major film composer of the twenties was Edmund Meisel, whose score for RUTTMANN's BERLIN, DIE SYMPHONIE EINER GROSSSTADT (1927) was an integral element of the film. Meisel also created powerful, large-scale scores to accompany the German release versions of EISENSTEIN's BRONENOSETS POTEMKIN (*The Battleship Potemkin*, 1925) and OKTIABR (*October*, 1928).

Recurrent attempts were made to replace cinema musicians with gramophone records, and in 1926 WARNER BROS issued *Don Juan* in their VITAPHONE sound-on-disc process, signalling the end of live film music. Some films which were shot silent but issued after sound equipment had been widely installed were given music tracks similar in style to the elaborate accompaniments that had become common: MURNAU's TABU (1931), with music by Hugo Reisenfeld, is a successful example of this compromise. Before sound MIXING became practicable (see SOUND) many narrative films dispensed with music altogether; notable exceptions were HITCHCOCK's BLACKMAIL (1929), which incorporated music sparingly but with dramatic justification, and MILESTONE's ALL QUIET ON THE WESTERN FRONT (1930). René CLAIR, in spite of his declared scepticism as to the aesthetic validity of the sound film, made delightful use of songs and background music in SOUS LES TOITS DE PARIS (1930). In STERNBERG's DER BLAUE ENGEL (*The Blue Angel*, 1930) and Pabst's KAMERADSCHAFT (1931) music was used only where it occurred realistically within the narrative. This approach has occasionally been used since, but has never superseded the use of background music for dramatic or atmospheric effect.

As Hollywood went over to sound, each major studio set up its own music department with a musical director responsible for all the company's productions. The creation of a film score, needing split-second timing of musical phrases to fit the screen image, was an entirely new branch of musical composition, but the composer's name was often omitted from credits; the only person named, as musical director or conductor, might be responsible for composition, arrangement, and scoring, or these functions might be carried out by various unnamed personnel. Film scores tended to be of routine quality, their style an extension of the 'mood' music of silent films on a more opulent scale. An influx of talented musicians, many of them refugees from Europe, helped to extend the scope of Hollywood film music, notably Max STEINER, whose scores for KING KONG (1933) and THE INFORMER (1935) show an adventurous approach to the relation of music and image. Other new arrivals who were to prove influential in the field included Dmitri TIOMKIN, Franz WAXMAN, Miklos ROZSA, Erich Wolfgang KORNGOLD, Frederick HOLLANDER, Alfred NEWMAN, and Victor YOUNG.

Away from the highly organized production system of Hollywood a number of composers were exploring the aesthetic possibilities of film music. Maurice JAUBERT provided delicate scores for classic French films such as Clair's

*Quatorze juillet* (1933), VIGO'S ZÉRO DE CON-DUITE (1933) and L'ATALANTE (1934), and CARNÉ'S LE JOUR SE LÈVE (1939). Joseph KOSMA sensitively underlined the bitter-sweet, romantic quality in many of RENOIR'S films. Documentary films attracted composers of considerable stature, including Virgil THOMSON whose best film work was with Pare LORENTZ in the thirties and, later, with FLAHERTY. In 1935 CAVALCANTI joined the GPO Film Unit (see CROWN FILM UNIT) where he encouraged the adventurous use of music: the following year Benjamin BRITTEN wrote distinguished scores for NIGHT MAIL and *Coal Face*. Also in 1935, Muir Mathieson joined KORDA'S LONDON FILMS where he had a long and influential career. A landmark of British film music was Bliss's exciting score for THINGS TO COME (1936); striking music was also composed by VAUGHAN WILLIAMS for *49th Parallel* (1941) and *Scott of the Antarctic* (1948), by William WALTON for HENRY V (1944), and by Peter Maxwell Davies for Ken RUSSELL'S *The Devils* (1971); all five scores were later reworked for concert performance.

PROKOFIEV'S collaboration with Eisenstein on ALEXANDER NEVSKY (1938) was a magnificent attempt to match visual and aural patterns, but although the music functions with complete success in the conventional manner, the formal correspondence between music and image is evident only from study of the score. Such correspondence is more easily achieved in ANIMATION, and the field has been profitably explored by many AVANT-GARDE artists including BARTOSCH, FISCHINGER, MCLAREN, LYE, ALEXEÏEFF, and the WHITNEY brothers. Walt DISNEY brought the matching of music and image to a high degree of skill, although with a naïve anthropomorphism that could be irritating: this predictable emphasis has become known as 'mickey mousing'.

By the fifties, the musician's role in Hollywood was accorded greater status and it was becoming customary to credit composition as well as musical direction. Film music began to be issued regularly on gramophone records, providing a useful supplementary income, and the provision of a theme song, even in a straight dramatic film or comedy, gradually became almost obligatory as an aid to publicity. The practice became common after the enormous popular success of the title songs from HIGH NOON (1952) and *Three Coins in the Fountain* (1954). By the end of the sixties the sale of records and performing rights of background music and theme songs was an important element in film budgeting. From the fifties, too, JAZZ played an important role in the background scores of dramatic films, especially after PREMINGER'S *Anatomy of a Murder* (1959) with music by Duke Ellington. Bill Haley provided the rock music for THE BLACKBOARD JUNGLE (1955), but otherwise rock or pop was for some time restricted to films featuring stars such as Elvis PRESLEY or the BEATLES and to documentaries on pop festivals—PENNEBAKER'S *Monterey Pop* (1968), *Woodstock* (1970), and the MAYSLES' *Gimme Shelter* (1971), all of which had enormous box-office success. From the late sixties, and especially after THE GRADUATE (1967), EASY RIDER (1969), and MIDNIGHT COWBOY (1970), pop soundtracks became customary in films with a contemporary setting.

Some directors have a highly developed consciousness of the contribution music can make to their work. Alain RESNAIS, in particular, chooses his composer early in the production and collaborates closely on relating music, dialogue, natural sound, and image. Some of the most successful film music is, however, drawn from existing works. The use of well-known classical music has to a large extent been avoided in American films except when needed in 'biographies' of composers—*The Great Waltz* (1938) about Johann Strauss, *A Song to Remember* (1944) about Chopin—but it has been used with considerable effect elsewhere. Well chosen sequences reinforce the emotional tone of the images with perhaps surprising power: passages from Saint-Saëns and Mozart in RENOIR'S LA RÈGLE DU JEU (1939), Rachmaninov in LEAN'S BRIEF ENCOUNTER (1945), Mozart in BRESSON'S UN CONDAMNÉ A MORT S'EST ECHAPPÉ (1956), Brahms in MALLE'S LES AMANTS (1958), Mozart in WIDERBERG'S ELVIRA MADIGAN (1967), Vivaldi in TRUFFAUT'S L'ENFANT SAUVAGE (1970), and Mahler in VISCONTI'S MORTE A VENEZIA (*Death in Venice*, 1971). In contrast, KUBRICK has shown a grim, satirical gift for using pre-existing popular music, setting a vacuous song like Vera Lynn's 'We'll Meet Again' against the dropping of a nuclear bomb in DR STRANGELOVE (1963) or Gene KELLY'S 'Singin' in the Rain' against rape in A CLOCKWORK ORANGE (1971).

Outside Europe and America, the potential use of indigenous music in films has often been corrupted by Western influences, most strikingly in Japan where even the delicate refinement of OZU'S films is sometimes disconcertingly accompanied by music reminiscent of routine Western romances. KOBAYASHI and, frequently, KUROSAWA have used Japanese classical music to marvellously atmospheric effect in their period films.

Music, although not indispensable, has become an accepted part of most films. In practice the music track can range from the unnoticeable through the irritatingly distracting to being, with imagery, dialogue, and sound effects, an integral part in the creation of an aesthetic whole. (See also JAZZ, MUSICALS, OPERA FILM.)

**MUSICALS.** The history of the screen musical is essentially that of the American musical: the outstanding examples of the genre have been made in Hollywood and only the American industry has consistently produced musicals throughout the sound era. Indeed, with the WESTERN, the musical could be claimed as Hollywood's outstanding contribution to the history of cinema. Not all films with songs or even production numbers may be defined as musicals. The injection of such material into a MARX BROTHERS comedy, or to heighten the sexuality of Marlene DIETRICH or the winsome appeal of Shirley TEMPLE, does not allow their films' inclusion in this category: the musical can only be defined as such if the elements of song and dance are so essential that to remove them would leave little or nothing.

Although the various sound-on-disc systems attempted during the silent era included brief musical numbers, usually featuring established stage personalities, the screen musical became possible with the introduction of sound by WARNER BROS into THE JAZZ SINGER (1927). (*The Jazz Singer* with its ten interpolated songs is not a musical in the full sense. *The Singing Fool*, 1928, again with JOLSON, put its songs into the action and, despite the hackneyed plot, achieved even greater popular success.) THE BROADWAY MELODY (1929), the first 'all-talking, all-singing, all-dancing' film, was directly derived from the backstage story as a vehicle for musical revue which was currently popular in the theatre. Its success stimulated a flood of Hollywood musicals: in the year following its release no less than seventy new musicals appeared. Broadway musical performers rushed to Hollywood, but most could not adapt to the demands of the camera and from the beginning Hollywood was forced to develop its own musical talent. Charles 'Buddy' Rogers and Nancy Carroll became the first popular musical team in films like *Illusion* (1929) and *Close Harmony* (1930). Most early musicals, however, were revues that paraded Broadway, Hollywood, radio, and vaudeville stars in lavishly-staged musical numbers interspersed with comic sketches, like *Hollywood Revue*, *The Show of Shows* (both 1929), *King of Jazz*, *Paramount on Parade*, and *Happy Days* (all 1930). The formula remained a staple of the musical, reaching its apogee with Vincente MINNELLI's *Ziegfeld Follies* (1946).

Early Hollywood musicals also reflected the popularity of stage operettas; the creative contribution of two major directors, Ernst LUBITSCH and Rouben MAMOULIAN, and the appeal of stars like Jeanette, MACDONALD, Maurice CHEVALIER, and Nelson EDDY, made the film operetta or musical comedy a viable and successful form though it hardly survived the Second World War.

Many of the early musicals were made wholly or partly in TECHNICOLOR or the rival Multicolor, but with the Depression economic stringency forced the producers to avoid technical innovations. Not until THE WIZARD OF OZ (1939) was colour used to full effect in a musical: it then became a necessary ingredient of the genre.

Song-writers were also imported from Broadway. Some, like Richard RODGERS and Cole PORTER, dabbled in film but continued to write mostly for stage shows. Irving BERLIN and Jerome KERN both devoted their attention to Hollywood for some years from 1933 creating their most memorable scores for Fred ASTAIRE and Ginger ROGERS films. George GERSHWIN wrote only four film scores, but his songs were frequently used. Two outstanding musicals made after his death, AN AMERICAN IN PARIS (1951) and FUNNY FACE (1957), had scores based entirely on his work. Hollywood also created its own song-writers, notably Jimmy Van Heusen, Harold ARLEN, and Harry WARREN. Other accomplished song-writers who worked extensively in Hollywood include High Martin, Hoagy CARMICHAEL, Walter Donaldson, Jimmy McHugh, Richard Whiting, and Frank Loesser.

The early film revues and operettas, reflecting the popular Broadway shows of the twenties, began to give way to the distinct film musical styles initiated in 1933 by 42ND STREET and *Flying Down to Rio*. *42nd Street* introduced a real jazz beat and made tap-dancing the basis for its dances. It also gave prominence to the dance director Busby BERKELEY, whose lavish, formalized production numbers became a unique feature of the big Hollywood musical. *Flying Down to Rio* was the first important film in Fred Astaire's career. Astaire's intimate elegance and Berkeley's extravagance characterized the two basic kinds of film musical that commanded enormous popularity into the forties.

Virtually every studio had its musical star during the thirties and forties. PARAMOUNT with Bing CROSBY, UNIVERSAL with Deanna DURBIN, TWENTIETH CENTURY-FOX with Alice FAYE and Betty GRABLE, although they made few enduring contributions to the genre, maintained a profitable output of musicals. METRO-GOLDWYN-MAYER's musicals had a distinctive style, based partly on the almost unlimited resources available for any individual film. Even more important was the teamwork of the talented people involved—designers, cameramen, song-writers, musical directors, and, perhaps above all, dance directors. After Busby Berkeley, MGM's most valuable musical property was Judy GARLAND who developed into an extraordinary screen personality. Her first starring role in *The Wizard of Oz* displayed the unique combination of energy and vulnerability that maintained her large following in a number of musicals during the next fifteen years.

The associate producer of *The Wizard of Oz*, Arthur FREED, was to a large extent responsible for establishing the characteristics of the best Hollywood musicals of the forties: lavish but tasteful production, effective use of colour, original screenplays with musical numbers completely integrated with the story, excellent music. He encouraged the talent of Minnelli, which resulted in such classic musicals as MEET ME IN ST LOUIS (1944), *An American in Paris*, and THE BAND WAGON (1953), and of Gene KELLY, as a dancer in *Anchors Aweigh* (1945) and *An American in Paris*, and as co-director, with Stanley DONEN, and a star of ON THE TOWN (1949), SINGIN' IN THE RAIN (1953), and *It's Always Fair Weather* (1955); and persuaded Rouben Mamoulian to direct two more fine musicals, *Summer Holiday* (1948) and *Silk Stockings* (1956). The high spots of MGM's best musicals were gathered into a COMPILATION *That's Entertainment* (1974).

By the end of the fifties increasing costs and the declining mass audience were making elaborate musicals uneconomic. Popular taste was changing: the quality of fairy-tale exuberance that distinguished musicals of the thirties and forties was being replaced in the theatre by musical plays which emphasized intimacy, sentimentality, and a kind of realism; and although Hollywood producers spent largely on the rights of successful stage shows like *Oklahoma!* (filmed 1955) and *South Pacific* (filmed 1958) it was found that they transferred uneasily, blown out of proportion on the screen. Successful film musicals became increasingly sporadic. Stanley Donen showed that stage adaptations could retain their proper dimensions with *Pajama Game* (1957) and *Damn Yankees* (1958, *What Lola Wants* in GB), but the big box-office success of WEST SIDE STORY (1961), MY FAIR LADY (1964), and THE SOUND OF MUSIC (1965) owed as much to their reputation as stage musicals as to their quality as films. DISNEY's highly successful *Mary Poppins* (1964) and the even more profitable *The Sound of Music*, both starring Julie ANDREWS, brought a wave of lavish musicals trying to duplicate their success. Such attempts were generally disastrous, with the exception of Francis Ford COPPOLA's delightful *Finian's Rainbow* (1968). *Star!* (1968), *Darling Lili* (1969), *Paint Your Wagon* (1969) lacked wit and coherence, partly because costs had rocketed so dramatically that each film needed BLOCKBUSTER selling and therefore had to carry the weight of lengthy running time and ex-travagant production values. But Robert FOSSE, once a choreographer with Donen, indicated a possible new development of the form. CABARET (1972), although not a musical in the accepted sense of the term, showed how imagination, taste, and an original conception could use elements of the genre to create a contemporary equivalent with both wit and style.

Outside America, the musical film has generally had little intrinsic importance, being derived from stage successes with some influence from Hollywood. Film operetta flourished consistently in Germany, but except for some early examples, most strikingly DER KONGRESS TANZT (*Congress Dances*, 1931), has had little circulation abroad. Only France has made notable contributions to the genre, with René CLAIR's early sound films, astonishingly fluent in their integration of music and action, and the distinctive musical fairy-tales of Jacques DEMY in the sixties. Britain has almost invariably depended on stage adaptations, commercially viable but cinematically uninspired, with Jessie MATTHEWS the most popular star in films usually directed by Victor SAVILLE, including *Evergreen* (1934). One interesting oddity emerged in 1971, when Ken RUSSELL transformed a modest stage musical *The Boy Friend* into an elaborate *hommage* to the American film musicals of the thirties.

**MUSIDORA** (1889–1957), French actress, real name Jeanne Roques, who began as a singer and dancer in the Parisian theatre. She starred in many of Louis FEUILLADE's films; her appearance in black tights and cloak in LES VAMPIRES (1915–16) electrified audiences of the time. She disappeared from the cinema in 1927, to reappear in 1951 in a documentary on the history of the film *La Magique Image*. The last years of her life were spent as a secretary at the CINÉMATHÈQUE FRANÇAISE, and in writing a number of articles on the early cinema.

**MUTINY ON THE BOUNTY, The.** Captain William Bligh in HMS *Bounty* was on a voyage in the Pacific with the purpose of transporting breadfruit plants from Tahiti to the West Indies when a mutiny broke out near the Friendly Islands on 28 April 1789. It seems likely that the mutiny was caused less by tyranny on Bligh's part than by reluctance on the part of the crew to leave the women with whom they had been comfortably established in Tahiti while the plants were loading. Twenty-five mutineers, led by the master's mate, Fletcher Christian, put Bligh and eighteen non-mutineering seamen in an open boat, and took the *Bounty* back to Tahiti. Some of them stayed there (ten of them were ultimately court-martialled in England and three executed in 1792): Christian, however, in 1790 led a group of Englishmen and Polynesian men and women who took possession of the Pitcairn Islands. There they burned the *Bounty*, and tried to found a thriving community. The experiment was not entirely successful, according to visitors' reports of debauchery and disorder. Christian, ill, lived only for some three more years, and by 1800 all the original men were dead except one Englishman who raised the young generation. Bligh and his companions, meanwhile, after a remarkable voyage in the open boat of some 4,000 miles, had made a landfall at Timor in the East Indies. Bligh returned to England in 1790, and completed a distinguished career.

Three novels by Charles Nordhoff and James Norman Hall published in the early thirties gave the impetus for the first of the two mammoth films made by METRO-GOLDWYN-MAYER. *The Mutiny on the Bounty* (1935) was based on the first of the novels. It was produced by Irving THALBERG, directed by Frank LLOYD, and starred Charles LAUGHTON as the brutish yet indomitable Bligh and Clark GABLE as Christian. Franchot TONE played a leading mutineer. The production was on a considerable scale, and the $2\frac{1}{4}$hr film was two years in the making. Although some background scenes were shot in Tahiti, the greater part is an example of Hollywood studio craftsmanship at its most accomplished. The lavish publicity material included a 'Teachers' Manual', which contrived ingeniously to gloss over the adjustments made to the story for the sake of dramatic impact.

The second version was made on an even more lavish scale, and was beset with troubles which led to comparisons with CLEOPATRA (1962). *The Mutiny on the Bounty* (1962, 3hr) starred Marlon BRANDO as Fletcher Christian and Trevor HOWARD as Bligh. The original script was written by Eric AMBLER on the basis of the same novels (this time all three), but several writers worked over it before the final screenplay credit was given to Charles Lederer. Carol REED took over early as director, but after nearly two years' location shooting in Tahiti resigned because of difficulties with Brando and was replaced by Lewis MILESTONE. Although Brando's interpretation was complex and fascinating, it distorted the conflict between Christian and Bligh and the film failed to achieve the effective balance of the earlier version. Not all the advantages of TECHNICOLOR and 70mm PANAVISION, the specially-built replica of the *Bounty*, the $27m budget, and the fine performances from Trevor Howard and a stalwart supporting cast of actors (including Hugh Griffith and Richard HARRIS) could make the troubled production the equal of its predecessor.

**MUTOSCOPE.** In 1895 W. K. L. DICKSON left EDISON, for whom he had been working, and sought commercial backing for the production of 'riffle' books of photographs, to operate within a new kind of peep-show, the Mutoscope. Avoiding Edison's patent rights, Dickson made a camera that took pictures 2in × $2\frac{3}{4}$in to print on cardboard. The device was superior to Edison's Kinetoscope (see KINETOGRAPH) in that the pictures could be viewed by natural light, instead of having to be enlarged, and illuminated by battery-powered lamps. The KMCD (Koopman, Marvin, Casler, and Dickson) Syndicate, formed to exploit Mutoscope, next produced a camera and projector, the BIOGRAPH, which was the subject of a patents case brought against them by Edison.

Joseph Jefferson appeared for Mutoscope in several brief scenes from his hit *Rip Van Winkle* (1897), becoming the first stage star to pose for motion pictures; and the Mutoscope record of the Jeffries–Sharkey fight (November 1899), filmed by Billy BITZER under artificial lights, was an important step forward in the history of the cinema. Renamed Mutoscope and Biograph, the company developed into the BIOGRAPH production company.

**MUTUAL,** US distribution company founded in 1912. Five major producers, Harry Aitken (Reliance and Majestic), John R. Freuler (AMERICAN FILM MANUFACTURING CO), Charles J. Hite (Thanhouser), Adam Kessel and Charles O. Baumann (BISON, K-B, and KEYSTONE), formed Mutual to market their products and to compete with the increasing dominance of Carl LAEMMLE. When the other executives refused to back Aitken in financing THE BIRTH OF A NATION (1915) he took the gamble alone: the film's phenomenal success moved him to leave Mutual (taking with him Kessel and Baumann) to form TRIANGLE. Mutual never recovered from the loss of its driving force and that of its major assets, GRIFFITH, INCE, and SENNETT, though it had a short association with Charlie CHAPLIN in 1916. The company finally collapsed in 1919.

**MUYBRIDGE,** EADWEARD (1830–1904), English-born photographer and investigator of animal locomotion, real name Edward James Muggeridge. Muybridge went to America as a young man and, after a commercial career, became Director of Photographic Surveys to the United States Government. While surveying the Pacific coast in 1872, he was asked by Leland Stanford, then Governor of California, to photograph a horse in motion (most versions of the story say he was asked to do this to settle a $5,000 bet, but there is no evidence for this). He made the first successful experiment at Sacramento and over the next eight years, on Stanford's stud farm and at his expense, developed a system using twenty-four cameras operated by the horse itself passing across trip threads. With exposures as short as one six-thousandth of a second, the resulting pictures were the first analysis of the way a horse moved at speed. The early pictures were published in *The Horse in Motion* (1878) and in ensuing years Muybridge published photographs of many other animals, including human beings. In 1880, he invented the Zoopraxiscope to project the pictures and recreate the movements he had photographed and this he showed to scientific bodies all over Europe and America. It was the most sophisticated projector of successive photography until the arrival of EDISON's Kinetoscope (see KINETOGRAPH) twelve years later. He continued his work at the University of Philadelphia before retiring to his birthplace, Kingston-upon-Thames.

Kevin McDonnell, *Eadweard Muybridge: the man who invented the moving picture*, London, 1972.

**MY DARLING CLEMENTINE,** US, 1946. 1¼hr. *Dir* John Ford; *prod* Twentieth Century-Fox; *scr* Samuel Engel, Winston Miller, based on the book *Wyatt Earp, Frontier Marshall* by Stuart N. Lake; *ph* Joseph P. MacDonald; *cast* Henry Fonda (Wyatt Earp), Victor Mature (Doc Holliday), Walter Brennan (Clanton), Tim Holt (Virgil Earp), Ward Bond (Morgan Earp), Cathy Downs (Clementine Carter), Linda Darnell (Chihuahua), John Ireland (Billy Clanton), Grant Withers (Ike Clanton).

In an account of Wyatt EARP's days in Tombstone, John FORD's characteristic admiration and affection is brought to bear on central events of the American frontier myth: the GUNFIGHT AT THE OK CORRAL (shown as a precise military action), the raising of Tombstone's first church, and the celebration dance, simultaneously beautiful, funny, and loving. Henry FONDA's fine performance typically conveys quiet integrity and Victor MATURE grasped a rare acting opportunity to portray the consumptive Doc HOLLIDAY.

**MY FAIR LADY,** US, 1964. Super Panavision 70; 2¾hr; Technicolor. *Dir* George Cukor; *prod* Warner Bros/First National; *scr* Alan Jay Lerner, from his musical play based on G. B. Shaw's *Pygmalion*; *ph* Harry Stradling; *mus* Frederick Loewe; *lyr* Alan Jay Lerner; *cost* Cecil Beaton; *des* Gene Allen; *mus dir* André Previn; *cast* Audrey Hepburn (Eliza; sung by Marni Nixon), Rex Harrison (Professor Higgins), Stanley Holloway (Alfred Doolittle), Wilfrid Hyde-White (Pickering), Jeremy Brett (Freddie), Gladys Cooper (Mrs Higgins).

*My Darling Clementine* (John Ford, 1946)

A successful stage show made into a lavishly expensive and stylish MUSICAL garnished with talent, *My Fair Lady* reaped the expected financial benefit and four OSCARS. Rex HARRISON won an Oscar for repeating his stage role, and held the entire production together with his idiosyncratic, domineering, yet charming Higgins, relishing each Shavian insult. Audrey HEPBURN fully justified selection for Eliza in preference to Julie ANDREWS who had taken the part on stage.

**MY LITTLE CHICKADEE**, US, 1940. 1¼hr. *Dir* Edward Cline; *prod* Universal; *scr* W. C. Fields, Mae West; *ph* Joseph Valentine; *cast* W. C. Fields (Cuthbert J. Twillie), Mae West (Flower Belle Lee), Joseph Calleia (the masked bandit).

The explosive combination of the unique personalities of W. C. FIELDS and Mae WEST in a burlesque Western of striking vulgarity emerged rather as two simultaneous solo performances than as a duet; as such, the film is a prime example of each artist's essential quality: Fields's drunken, anti-social cowardice, and Mae West's blatant sexuality. The comedy leans on the audience's familiarity with these established personalities (the predictability of each joke heightening its impact) until the pay-off, where their catch-phrases 'Come up and see me some time' and 'All right, my little chickadee' are neatly transposed.

**MY MAN GODFREY**, US, 1936. 1½hr. *Dir, prod* Gregory La Cava for Universal; *scr* Morrie Ryskind, Eric Hatch, La Cava from a story by Hatch; *ph* Ted Tetzlaff; *cast* William Powell (Godfrey Parke), Carole Lombard (Irene Bullock), Alice Brady (Angelica Bullock), Gail Patrick (Cornelia Bullock), Jean Dixon (Molly), Eugene Pallette (Alexander Bullock), Alan Mowbray (Tommy Gray).

William POWELL plays an unflappable butler in a New York mansion in a variation on *The Admirable Crichton*. Discovered living in a shanty town of unemployed men by society revellers on a scavenger hunt, he is installed as butler and promptly straightens out the lives of the entire Bullock family. The SCREWBALL comedy exposes the 'daffy' rich in merciless but affectionate fashion. Carole LOMBARD contributes the strongest comic performance as the featherbrained, appealing daughter of the household.

Henry Koster's remake in 1957 starred David NIVEN and June ALLYSON.

**MY NIGHT WITH MAUD** see MA NUIT CHEZ MAUD

# N

**NAKADAI,** TATSUYA (1930–   ), Japanese
actor, joined the Shochiku company in the early
fifties. There he began the association with
Masaki KOBAYASHI which brought him recognition as the idealist Kaji in the trilogy *Ningen no
Joken* (*The Human Condition*, 1959–61). His
other films for Kobayashi include SEPPUKU
(*Hara-Kiri*, 1962), 'Yuki-onna' (*Woman of the
Snow*), an episode of KWAIDAN (1964), JOI-UCHI
(*Rebellion*, 1967), and *Inochi Bonifuro* (*Inn of
Evil/At the Risk of My Life*, 1971). Nakadai has
been more successful than many Japanese actors
in playing in both period and modern films; but
he is best known outside Japan for his appearances in KUROSAWA's period adventure stories
*Yojimbo* (1961) and *Tsubakai Sanjuro* (*Sanjuro*,
1962) as Toshiro MIFUNE's antagonist: lean and
catlike, he counterbalances Mifune in appearance
and character. He has, however, given effective
performances in modern psychological dramas
such as ICHIKAWA's *Enjo* (*Conflagration/The
Flame of Torment*, 1958) and TESHIGAHARA's
*Tanin no Kao* (*The Face of Another*, 1966).

**NANOOK OF THE NORTH,** US, 1922. 1hr.
*Dir, scr, ph* Robert J. Flaherty; *titles* Flaherty,
Carl Stearns Clancy.

FLAHERTY spent sixteen months living with
the Eskimos in northern Canada, working in
dramatically difficult conditions, trying to capture on film a vanishing way of life. The devotion
he inspired in the Eskimos, particularly in
Nanook and his family, enabled him to record
their daily activities closely and with understanding; they were even prepared to endanger their
lives in a walrus-hunt (a pursuit already dying
out under white influence) for the sake of the
film.

Flaherty's difficulties in financing the film
before Révillon Frères, a fur company, provided
funds, were repeated when it came to distribution. PATHÉ eventually exhibited it in New York.
The critical and public response was sensational,
for here was an intimate, sensitive, and extraordinarily beautiful study of living people:
Flaherty's fluid camerawork, sharp editing, and
humane observation transformed the DOCUMEN-
TARY film. *Nanook* remains fresh and its classic
status undisputed, although audiences may now
be more wary of Flaherty's romantic outlook.

A fifty-minute sound version was issued in
1947, using narration and music by others.

**NAPOLÉON,** France, 1927. 4hr (but see below),
*Dir, scr* Abel Gance; *prod* Westi/Société géné-
rale des films; *ph* Jules Kruger; *des* Alexandre
Benois, Pierre Schildknecht; *mus* Arthur
Honegger; *cast* Albert Dieudonné (Napoléon),
Abel Gance (Saint-Just), Antonin Artaud
(Marat), Gina Manès (Joséphine).

GANCE's most ambitious and personal film
freely twisted history to present Napoleon as a
Nietzschean superman. More importantly, it displayed the director's vigorous and resourceful
use of cinematic techniques, including rapid cutting, tinting, superimposition, wide-angle lens, unrestrained use of the handheld camera, and a new
triple-screen process (see POLYVISION). After the
first presentation it was released in a truncated
version from which the triptych sequences had
been removed: Gance, disappointed by the poor
reception, destroyed much of the original footage, including some of the triptych. In 1936 he
assembled a new version with post-
synchronization and crude stereophonic effects
in which HONEGGER's original accompanying
score was replaced by music composed by Henri
Verdun.

The surviving triptych scenes were shown at
Venice in 1953 and Gance was encouraged to
edit an abbreviated version which appeared in
1955. At the instigation of André MALRAUX and
with Claude LELOUCH as producer, he prepared
another, more complete, version which appeared
in 1971. This runs to $4\frac{1}{2}$ hours and includes
sequences not seen since the first showing, sections from the 1936 version, and some new
material. Some of the post-synchronization was
retained (including ARTAUD's voice), while
Gance and Dieudonné renewed the dubbing of
their parts. There is also a prologue in colour, in
which Gance introduces the film. The original
script was published as *Napoléon vu par Abel
Gance* (Paris, 1927).

**NATIONAL FILM ARCHIVE,** London, was
established in 1935 as the National Film Library
under Ernest LINDGREN. In 1938 it was a founder member of the FÉDÉRATION INTERNATIONALE
DES ARCHIVES DE FILM (FIAF). Its collection

was originally housed in rented vaults, but the Second World War precipitated the purchase of premises at Aston Clinton, where specially-designed vaults for housing NITRATE film were built, more recently supplemented by vaults for acetate and colour films at new quarters in Berkhamsted. In 1961 the Articles of Association of the BRITISH FILM INSTITUTE (the Archive's parent body) were extended to include television, and the Archive began to select and acquire television material for preservation (see ARCHIVE).

**NATIONAL FILM BOARD** of Canada was set up in May 1939 as a result of a report by John GRIERSON (who became its first chairman) and the Canadian Government Film Commissioner. Grierson, continuing his role as the impresario of the documentary, gathered round him talent that was to make the NFB internationally known in the field of propaganda during the Second World War. He brought Stuart LEGG, Stanley Hawes, and Raymond SPOTTISWOODE from England, Joris IVENS and John Fernhout (also known as Ferno) from Holland, Irving Jacoby from New York, and Norman MCLAREN, who built up the well-known and respected animation department.

Wartime needs were served by two series: WORLD IN ACTION (1942–5) and *Canada Carries On* (from 1940) which were shown theatrically throughout Canada and in many other parts of the world. During this period young Canadians who later became the strength of the NFB's production staff learned their craft. The problem of distribution was also faced at this time, and a system of itinerant projectionists was set up to bring film to the most remote places. In later years this system was replaced by encouraging community groups to form Film Councils, using projection facilities in schools and public libraries.

After the war Grierson returned to England and the character of the NFB changed. Since most of the wartime films were no longer relevant, their place had to be filled with films to satisfy the needs of education and the community. The arrival of television in 1953 placed new demands on the NFB film libraries and influenced the introduction of a new style of filmmaking, more immediate in appeal, using techniques of CINÉMA-VÉRITÉ. A unit headed by Tom Daly as producer and including Wolf Koenig, Roman Kroiter, and Terence Macartney-Filgate, developed teamwork to a high degree and produced some short films of outstanding quality such as *The Days before Christmas* (1958), *Glenn Gould* (1959), and *Lonely Boy* (1962). Another director who came to prominence at this time was Colin Low whose work includes two of the best-known films made by the Board: *City of Gold* (1957, with Wolf

Koenig) and *Universe* (1960, with Roman Kroiter).

In 1956 the NFB moved from Ottawa to Montreal and gave increasing support to production in French. *Les Raquetteurs* (Michel BRAULT and Gilles Groulx, 1958), marked the true beginning of the NFB's French Unit and these directors, with Claude Fournier, Claude JUTRA, and Arthur Lamotte formed the nucleus of Quebec cinema.

The NFB became involved in feature-length production with *Drylanders* (Don Haldane, 1962) and *Pour la suite du monde* (Pierre PERRAULT and Brault, 1963) and the following year with *Le Chat dans le sac* (Gilles Groulx) and *Nobody Waved Goodbye* (Don Owen). A good deal of criticism attended these and other early efforts in feature film making. Such achievement as *Mon Oncle Antoine* (Jutra, 1971) and *Le Temps d'une chasse* (Francis Mankiewicz, 1972) have, however, justified the policy. The NFB has been important for the fostering of talent and craftsmanship. It should take a large measure of credit for making possible the present thriving film industry, which is now, it is hoped, being further underpinned by the CHALLENGE FOR CHANGE/Société Nouvelle programme, a huge investment in film and video-making on the community level.

**NATIONAL FILM FINANCE CORPORATION,** a statutory body under the British government's Department of Trade and Industry with a revolving loan fund available for independent British film productions. Established by the Cinematograph Films (Special Loans) Act 1949, the Corporation was originally intended to provide production finance at a time of shortage, in the hope that private capital would be encouraged to return to the industry and thus make the NFFC unnecessary. This has never been totally realized and subsequent legislation, including the Films Act 1970, continued and extended the Corporation's powers to 1980. However, in 1970 the government announced its intention to withdraw gradually from the financing of films and a handing over of the NFFC to private interests with progressively diminishing supporting loans from public funds.

**NATIONAL FILM THEATRE,** a club cinema established and run by the BRITISH FILM INSTITUTE, took over and rebuilt the Telekinema, which had been built on the south bank of the Thames for the Festival of Britain in 1951. Films of importance are shown under various headings or as part of film-makers' retrospectives; screenings now average thirty-two a week in two auditoria. The London Film Festival, inaugurated in 1957 during James Quinn's directorship, presents a selection of films from other festivals plus some additional films, and the John Player lectures, 1968–73, extended an existing tradition of visits by film personalities.

**NATIVE LAND**, US, 1942. 1½hr. *Dir, scr* Leo Hurwitz, Paul Strand; *prod* Frontier Films; *ph* Paul Strand; *comm* David Wolff, spoken by Paul Robeson; *mus* Marc Blitzstein.

The last production by FRONTIER FILMS was a savage account in semi-documentary form of anti-union oppression in America. Representative anecdotes, re-enacted by professional actors, were bound together into a documentary generalization by the commentary. The film took three years to make and was finally released at a time when the various interests were united against a common enemy; criticism of right-wing activity at home was courageous but unwelcome, and *Native Land* has received minimal distribution.

**NAVIGATOR, The**, US, 1924. 1hr. *Dir* Buster Keaton, Donald Crisp; *prod* Joseph M. Schenck; *scr* Jean C. Havez, Joseph A. Mitchell, Clyde Bruckman; *ph* Elgin Lessley, Byron Houck; *cast* Buster Keaton (the Young Millionaire), Kathryn McGuire (the Young Millionairess), Frederick Vroom (the Father), Noble Johnson (Native Chief).

As with THE GENERAL (1926), Buster KEATON's other outstanding silent film, the title refers not to the leading actor but to the machine, here an ocean liner, which provides the film's setting and *raison d'être*. The film is packed with comic invention: notably in the sequence in which the hero and heroine search for each other on the deserted ship and, later, where Keaton repairs the hull, conveying his usual nuances of expression while wearing a deep-sea diving suit. The comedy of disproportion and Keaton's passion for the Machine are epitomized when the two young people try to cook breakfast in a ship's galley designed for mass catering.

**NAZARÍN**, Mexico, 1958. 1½hr. *Dir* Luis Buñuel; *prod* Manuel Barbachano Ponce; *scr* Buñuel, Julio Alejandro; *ph* Gabriel Figueroa; *cast* Francisco Rabal (Nazarín), Marga López (Beatrice), Rita Macedo (Andara), Jesús Fernandez (Ujo, the dwarf), Noe Murayama (El Pinto).

Nazarín, the unworldly priest, attempts to live in all respects according to the precepts of Christianity. Every well-intentioned act leads to disaster, for himself and for others, but the end of the film shows him reluctantly accepting a kindness from another human being. BUÑUEL's attack on both formal and individual faith has his usual dispassionate irony, which gives *Nazarín* a certain ambiguity: the International Catholic Cinema Office awarded the film a prize. It was also awarded the Special Jury Prize at CANNES, 1959.

**NAZIMOVA,** ALLA (1879–1945), US actress born in Russia, appeared for STANISLAVSKY at the Moscow Art Theatre, becoming famous as a tragedienne, particularly in plays by Ibsen. She went to the US in 1905, after incurring the disfavour of the Tsarist Government, and rapidly achieved success with her powerfully naturalistic performances. Her first film was *War Brides* (1916), an adaptation of one of her stage successes. She made intermittent screen appearances until 1926, including CAMILLE (1921), with Rudolph VALENTINO, and *A Doll's House* (1922), from Ibsen's play. She retired from the stage in 1939, but returned to films occasionally during the early forties.

**NEAGLE,** ANNA (1904–    ), British actress, real name Marjorie Robertson, was a stage dancer and made her first film appearances in musicals. Her major roles were divided between more or less respectable historical heroines— *Nell Gwyn* (1934), Peg Woffington in *Peg of Old Drury* (1935), Queen Victoria in *Victoria the Great* (1937) and *Sixty Glorious Years* (1938), *Nurse Edith Cavell* (1939), Amy Johnson in *They Flew Alone* (1942), a French Resistance worker in *Odette* (1950), Florence Nightingale in *The Lady with a Lamp* (1951)— and romantic leads in musical comedies—*Bitter Sweet* (1933), *No, No, Nanette* (1940), *Spring in Park Lane* (1948), and its successors co-starring Michael WILDING, and *King's Rhapsody* (1956). To all these characters she brought an indomitable gentility and cheerful vitality that increased with the years. She was for a time a producer of films starring the popular singer Frankie Vaughan and appeared for five years in the stage musical *Charlie Girl*. Most of her films were produced by her husband Herbert WILCOX; she was made a DBE in 1969.

**NEAL,** PATRICIA (1926–    ), US actress, appeared on Broadway before her first film role in *John Loves Mary* (1948). Her sensitivity and increasing maturity as an actress enabled her to bring distinction to parts in films such as A FACE IN THE CROWD (1957) and *Breakfast at Tiffany's* (1961) which won her acclaim and an appreciative following, topped by an OSCAR for her portrayal of the tough, disillusioned housekeeper in HUD (1963). In 1967 she suffered a series of radical strokes, from which she made a courageous recovery. She is married to the writer Roald Dahl.

**NEBENZAL, SEYMOUR** (1898–1961), US producer, taken by his family to Berlin after the First World War, where in 1924 he founded with Richard Oswald the NERO-FILM company. Nebenzal, as the guiding light of the company, was bold and imaginative in his selection and approval of projects by directors like PABST, LANG, and CZINNER. Pabst, who worked with him at the time of the transition to sound, praised him as a collaborator who allowed complete artistic freedom. When the Nazis came to power he was forced to leave Germany for France, where he produced *Mayerling* (Anatole LITVAK, 1936) and films by Max OPHULS and Fedor Ozep. In 1938 he went to Hollywood and became an executive producer with METRO-GOLDWYN-MAYER. Among his Hollywood films are *Summer Storm* (Douglas SIRK, 1944) and *The Chase* (1946). He also produced a remake of *M* (1951), directed by LOSEY. In the US, however, he evinced none of the artistic flair he had shown in Germany. He spent his last few years in Europe.

**NEFF, HILDEGARDE**, see KNEFF

**NEGRI, POLA** (*c*.1897–       ), Polish-born actress, real name Appolonia Chalupek, worked first for Max REINHARDT's company in Berlin. After her success in LUBITSCH's *Madame Dubarry* (1919, *Passion* in the US) she went to PARAMOUNT in 1922. The first European to be given star treatment in Hollywood, she brought a flavour of unrestrained exoticism that was for a time sensationally popular. For Lubitsch, in *Forbidden Paradise* (1924), and STILLER, in *Hotel Imperial* (1927), she gave performances of wit and sophistication, but, unable to transpose her essential vampish approach to the changing styles of the late twenties, and, anticipating the inevitable problems created for foreign actresses by the introduction of sound, she returned to Europe in 1929. She made *A Woman Commands* (1932) in Hollywood, but this was unsuccessful. In 1934 she returned to Germany, where she found herself victim of a campaign to brand her as Jewish. After a direct appeal to Hitler her racial purity was established and she was restored to international fame with *Mazurka* (Willi FORST, 1935). She went on to make *Moskau-Shanghai* (1936) which was re-released in 1950 as *Der Weg nach Shanghai*. In the title role of *Madame Bovary* (LAMPRECHT, 1937) she played with a subtlety and complexity far removed from her earlier style. On the outbreak of war she returned to the US. Her most recent film was *The Moonspinners* (1964) for Walt DISNEY.

**NEGULESCO, JEAN** (1900–       ), US director born in Romania, was at first a painter and theatrical designer in Paris. He emigrated to the US in 1927 and directed his first film, *Kiss and Make Up*, in 1934. During the forties and fifties he was particularly known for his skill with romantic dramas and light comedies: notably successful films include *The Mask of Dimitrios* (1944), *Humoresque* (1947), *Johnny Belinda* (1948), *The Mudlark* (1950), *How to Marry a Millionaire* (1953), *Three Coins in the Fountain* (1954), *Daddy-Long-Legs* (1955), *Count Your Blessings*, and *The Best of Everything* (both 1959).

**NEILAN, MARSHALL A.** (1891–1958), US actor and director, became a film actor in 1911, first in juvenile roles and later as leading man. He began directing in 1914 and made a number of shorts for various companies before directing his first feature film in 1916. His best known films are those he made with Mary PICKFORD, including *Rebecca of Sunnybrook Farm* (1917) and *M'Liss* (1918), characterized by their idealized view of America's past. By the late twenties his flamboyant personality and irreverent treatment of producers had earned him a reputation for unreliability and the new demands of sound saw a further decline in his career. He directed his last film in 1937.

**NĚMEC, JAN** (1936–       ), Czech director, characteristically began his career by falling out with the authorities even while he was a student at FAMU, the Prague film school. An admirer of the work of Arnost Lustig (novelist and scriptwriter of Brynych's influential *Transport z ráje*, *Transport from Paradise*, 1963), Němec persisted in adapting a work of Lustig's—in spite of earlier denials by the school authorities—for his graduation film: *Scusto* (literally *The Morsel*; alternatively *The Loaf* or *A Bite to Eat*, 1962) was based on Lustig's story of an episode during the transportation of prisoners between concentration camps. It won a prize at a festival of student films in Amsterdam later the same year.

Němec's first feature, *Démanty noci* (*Diamonds of the Night*, 1964), was again based on a story by Lustig, about two young men trying to escape from one of the death marches for prisoners organized by the Nazis during the last days of the war. The film was, however, an attempt to capture a mental state, the result of fear and hallucination, rather than to give a naturalistic representation in socialist realist terms. The bold mixture of delusion and reality, dreams and hallucination, marked Němec as one of the foremost experimenters with form of the emerging new wave of Czech directors: and again his film earned prizes abroad and criticism at home.

In 1965 he contributed an episode to PONTI's *Perličky na dně* (*Pearls of the Deep*). His deep resentment of the evils of tyranny next combined with the sharp elegance of Ester KRUMBACHOVÁ, during their short-lived but creative association, to produce O SLAVNOSTI A HOSTECH (*The Party and the Guests*, 1966). The displeasure of the authorities which had simmered since his first two films fairly erupted: the film, together with CHYTILOVÁ's SEDMIKRÁSKY (*Daisies*, 1966), led the list of films denounced in the National Assembly in May 1967 as works which would poison the minds of the workers. While the film was held up, Němec and Krumbachová devised *Mučednici lásky* (*Martyrs of Love*, 1967), in which again Krumbachová's designs stressed the visual aspect of the three stories of shy lovers' day-dreaming. The official reception was again chilly, not on political grounds but because the film was found incomprehensible. Němec also made *Mother and Son* in Belgium in 1967 without official approval.

Meanwhile, as political events changed, *O Slavnosti a hostech* was sent to CANNES in 1968 and released in Prague: and in the spring of 1968 Němec made a series of short films for television. The star was the popular singer, Marta Kubisová, who was banned from singing after the arrival of the Russians, and whom Němec later married. During the summer of 1968 he was working happily with Josef Skvorecky on a film intended to celebrate swing music. They were also working on a documentary about Prague, which eventually turned into *Oratorio for Prague*, an account of the arrival of the Russian tanks in August which found its way to festivals in western Europe. Němec did not make any films after 1968 and in 1974 he was permitted to leave for France.

**NEO-REALISM.** The origins of neo-realism are traceable to the 'realist' or verismo style cultivated in the Italian cinema between 1913 and 1916, when films inspired by the writings of Verga and others dealt with human problems in natural settings (see ITALY). These were the themes to which the neo-realists of the forties returned, reacting against the banality that had for long been the dominant mode of Italian films and against prevailing social conditions. Neo-realism was not only a cinematic style but a whole social, moral, and political philosophy.

The term 'neo-realism' was first applied by the critic PIETRANGELI in an article · in CINEMA (1942, 146, p. 394) to VISCONTI's OSSESSIONE (1942). At the time *Ossessione* was circulated clandestinely, but its social authenticity had a profound effect on young Italian directors. DE SICA and ZAVATTINI adopted a similarly uncompromising approach to bourgeois family life in *I bambini ci guardano* (*The Children Are Watching Us*, 1942). The style came to fruition

in ROSSELLINI's three films dealing with the war, the Liberation, and post-war reconstruction: ROMA, CITTÀ APERTA (1945), PAISÀ (1947), and GERMANIA, ANNO ZERO (1947). With minimal resources, Rossellini worked in real locations using local people as well as professional actors; the films conveyed a powerful sense of the plight of ordinary individuals oppressed by political events. The roughness and immediacy of the films created a sensation abroad although they were received with indifference in Italy.

Experiences of the war and the resistance inspired the majority of early neo-realist films: outstanding representatives were *Il sole sorge ancora* (Aldo Vergano, 1946), *Il bandito* (Alberto LATTUADA, 1946), and *Senza pietà* (Lattuada, 1947). War themes gave way to social issues; De Sica attacked an uncaring society through abandoned children in SCIUSCIÀ (*Shoeshine*, 1946) and through unemployment in LADRI DI BICICLETTE (1948). A spate of films dealt with the extreme problems of Sicily, Visconti's LA TERRA TREMA (1948) and Pietro GERMI's *In nome della legge* (1949) and IL CAMMINO DELLA SPERANZA (1950) among them. Giuseppe DE SANTIS showed the exploitation of rural workers in RISO AMARO (1949) and *Non c'è pace tra gli ulivi* (*No Peace Among the Olives*, 1950).

By 1950 the impetus of neo-realism had begun to slacken. The burning causes that had stimulated the movement were to some extent alleviated or glossed over by increasing prosperity; and neo-realist films, although highly praised by foreign critics, were not a profitable undertaking: audiences were not attracted to realistic depictions of injustice played out by unglamorous, ordinary characters. De Sica's UMBERTO D (1952) was probably the last truly neo-realist film: the production was harassed by a government that had moved away from liberal post-war aims, and the finished film betrayed a sentimentality that had threatened to emerge in even its most distinguished predecessors.

Although the movement was short-lived, the effects of neo-realism were far-reaching. Its influence can be traced across the world from Hollywood, where stylistic elements in films about social and political problems echoed those of the neo-realists, to India, where Satyajit RAY adopted a typically neo-realist stance in his early films. In Italy itself neo-realist principles have been perpetuated by, among others, Ermanno OLMI, with his compassionate studies of working life, and Francesco ROSI, with his vigorous attacks on the misuse of power.

**NERO-FILM,** German production company founded in 1924 by Seymour NEBENZAL and Richard Oswald. Nebenzal eventually took over the company and produced about sixty silent films, the most outstanding being PABST'S DIE BÜCHSE DER PANDORA (1928). The company earned a high reputation for polished productions which, allied with the freedom given to creative directors, resulted in many enduring films. With the arrival of sound Nebenzal continued the association with Pabst, allowing him complete artistic freedom to make WESTFRONT 1918 (1930), DIE DREIGROSCHENOPER (1931, with WARNER BROS and TOBIS), KAMERADSCHAFT (1931), and *L'Atlantide* (1932). Nero-film also produced Paul CZINNER's *Ariane* and offered LANG the opportunity to make his first sound film M (both 1931). The company's last film was Lang's DAS TESTAMENT DES DR MABUSE (1933). Production ceased that year, when Nebenzal left Germany.

**NEUBABELSBERG,** German film studios founded in 1911, in Babelsberg on the outskirts of Berlin by the film company Deutsche Bioscop. After the merger of DECLA-BIOSCOP with UFA in 1923, the studios, often referred to as the UFA-Stadt, became the finest in Europe, with ample space and facilities for indoor and outdoor work. The amenities included rivers, lakes, a collection of railway carriages, and a zoo. In 1938 a film school was founded there which had to close down after two years. Damaged in the war, the studios were taken over in 1946 by DEFA.

*NEVER ON SUNDAY* see POTE TIN KYRIAKI

*NEVINOST BEZ ZAŠTITE* (*Innocence Unprotected*), Yugoslavia, 1968. Part Eastman Color; 1¼hr. *Dir, scr* Dusan Makavejev; *prod* Avala Film; *ph* Brank Perak, Stevan Misković; *cast* Dragolub Aleksič (himself), Ana Milosavljević (the Orphan), Vera Jovanović (the Wicked Stepmother), Bratoljub Gligorijević (the Rich and Ugly Mr Petrović).

The original *Nevinost bez zaštite* was made clandestinely in 1942 by Aleksič, a circus strong-man. Delightfully unselfconscious in story and execution, and incorporating narrative and aesthetic devices which now appear startlingly advanced for the time, it was enormously popular until confiscated by the occupying Germans. MAKAVEJEV resurrected the film and re-cut it with actuality footage, animation, and newly shot material using the original actors when possible. The film is a funny and loving homage to a Serbian folk hero; in Makavejev's conception unprotected innocence is no longer represented by the pretty orphan saved from an unpleasant suitor, but by the brave and simple Aleksič himself.

*NEW BABYLON* see NOVYI VAVILON

*NEW EARTH* see NIEUWE GRONDEN

**NEWLEY, ANTHONY** (1931– ), British actor and song-writer, appeared as a child in OLIVER TWIST (David LEAN, 1948), then progressed to second leads during the fifties and sixties. He wrote and directed *Can Hieronymus Merkin Ever Forget Mercy Humpe and Find True Happiness?* (1969), in which he also appeared.

**NEWMAN, ALFRED** (1901– ), US musical director, began composing for films in the early thirties and has written a large number of film scores, including DEAD END (1937), WUTHERING HEIGHTS (1939), THE ROBE (1953), and BUS STOP (1956). He became musical director first for UNITED ARTISTS, then for Samuel GOLDWYN, and achieved particular fame through his long association with TWENTIETH CENTURY-FOX. He won OSCARS as music director for *Alexander's Ragtime Band* (1938), *Tin Pan Alley* (1940), *With a Song in My Heart* (1952), *Call Me Madam* (1953), *Love is a Many Splendored Thing* (1955), and *The King and I* (1956). Newman's scores and arrangements have a lushly romantic quality that epitomizes Hollywood film music at its most polished.

**NEWMAN, PAUL** (1925– ), US actor, director, and producer. After appearing in repertory and on television, he enrolled at the ACTORS' STUDIO in 1952. His Broadway success in William Inge's *Picnic* in 1953 led to a contract with WARNER BROS, where his film career began inauspiciously as a Greek slave in *The Silver Chalice* (1955), but *The Rack* (1956) provided a role with more scope. With *Somebody Up There Likes Me* (1955) his star quality was recognized. His acting style and a certain facial resemblance to Marlon BRANDO (except for Newman's startlingly blue eyes) led to his being for a time promoted as Brando's successor.

In 1958 he married Joanne WOODWARD and that year they co-starred for Martin RITT in THE LONG HOT SUMMER. Newman maintained the association with Ritt in *Paris Blues* (1961), HUD (1963), THE OUTRAGE (1964), and HOMBRE (1967), Ritt helping to develop the characteristic Newman—apparently cool, with an ironic detachment masking a certain idealism. Concurrently Newman worked for various other directors, most notably in THE HUSTLER (1961), *Sweet Bird of Youth* (1961), in which he repeated his Broadway role, *Torn Curtain* (Alfred HITCHCOCK, 1966), *Cool Hand Luke* (1967), the underrated *The Secret* (or *Private*) *War of Harry Frigg* (1968), *The Life and Times of Judge Roy Bean* (1972), and *The Mackintosh Man* (1973), the last two directed by John HUSTON. In both BUTCH CASSIDY AND THE SUNDANCE KID (1969) and *The Sting* (1973), Newman co-starred with Robert REDFORD under George Roy HILL's direction and the combination of stars and unpretentious, well-made entertainment proved the cinema's continued drawing power.

RACHEL, RACHEL (1968), starring Joanne Woodward, was Newman's first film as director and *WUSA* (1970), an attack on right-wing control of the media in the US, was his first independent production. He produced, directed, and acted in *Sometimes a Great Feeling* (1971, *Never Give an Inch* in GB), and was producer/director of *The Effect of Gamma Rays on Man-in-the-Moon Marigolds* (1972), again starring Joanne Woodward, a piece of social observation marked by his characteristic sensitivity to tangled human emotions.

Newman's dazzlingly successful career is distinguished not only by good looks and professionalism, but by intelligence, discrimination, and an endearingly mischievous irreverence which pervades many of his performances; only as a director is he invariably serious.

**NEWSREEL.** The LUMIÈRE brothers, needing material to use in demonstrations of their equipment, employed a team of cameramen to film topical events and scenes of general interest. Between 1896 and 1905 their team, including Mesguisch, Promio, Florman, Doublier, and Moisson, were covering events in London, Germany, Austria, Switzerland, Ireland, Italy, New York, and the East. The profitability in cinemas of news reporting was quickly evident: R. W. PAUL filmed the Derby in 1897, events of the Boer War were recorded, as were the coronation of Tsar Nicholas II in 1896 and the funeral of Queen Victoria in 1901. In Germany, MESSTER filmed the Kaiser at Stettin in 1897 and Bismarck in retirement. In America, Thomas EDISON, J. Stuart BLACKTON, BIOGRAPH, and VITAGRAPH were all filming actual events; President McKinley's inauguration (1897) and funeral (1901) received newsreel coverage as well as the Galveston cyclone in 1900 and the San Francisco earthquake in 1906: as in any form of journalism, disasters have always been a vital constituent of newsreels. Reconstruction of topical events was common, whether declared as such or purporting to be an actual record. Georges MÉLIÈS staged a re-enactment of the coronation of Edward VII in 1902, scenes from the Boer War were performed for the cameras on Hampstead Heath, and Edward H. Amet, using model boats in his bath, made a convincing film of the destruction of the Spanish fleet in the Spanish-American War of 1898. Early faked newsfilm is usually readily identifiable as such; later, more expert, examples may generally be classed as PROPAGANDA.

The early 'topicals' were very short, often less than a minute long, each dealing with a single event. The regular issue of newsreels in the conventional sense—several short items grouped under no general heading other than topicality—was begun by PATHÉ in 1908. *Pathé Journal* was followed in the same year by *Gaumont Actualités* (see GAUMONT), by Société Éclair in 1909, and by Eclipse in 1910. Pathé pioneered British newsreels from 1909 with *Pathé Gazette*. Drankov issued newsreels in Russia from 1908 to the Revolution, *Messter Woche* prospered in Germany from 1910, and the Topical Budget film company was active in Britain from 1913, but Europe was in general dominated by the French companies with offices in London, Berlin, St Petersburg, Milan, and Barcelona. The US, too, felt the French influence, although Edison, Biograph, and Vitagraph continued to distribute newsreels.

The delay entailed by official inspection was recognized as undesirable in the case of newsreels, and CENSORSHIP was not applied to them except in countries where all news media were subject to political control and elsewhere when the nation was at war.

The outbreak of the First World War at first placed the newsfilm reporting of the Allied nations at a disadvantage. The French and British governments at first refused access to cameramen, fearing that their reports would demoralize audiences and give away strategic information. The German High Command, in contrast, gave every encouragement to the Messter cameramen from the first months of the war; when BUFA (Bild- und Filmamten) was set up in 1916 to make government-sponsored newsreels, these experienced combat cameramen provided a nucleus of its staff. German editors rapidly became skilled in using newsreel footage to carry a propaganda message, and their war reports became a powerful psychological tool at home and in neutral countries. French cameramen were allowed at the front from 1915, with military restrictions on what they were allowed to photograph. The resulting newsreel, *Annales de Guerre*, was assembled with government approval from footage shot by cameramen from the several companies who formed the Service Photographique et Cinématographique de l'Armée. In 1916 the British military authorities allowed newsreel cameramen to film war action and the War Office Cinematograph Committee superseded the Cinematograph Trade Topical Committee, a joint effort set up by several production companies in the previous year. The *Topical Budget*, issued by the War Office, became the official newsreel; in the last year of the war, the Ministry of Information rounded off news bulletins with TRAILERS—two minutes of

*Il deserto rosso* (Michelangelo Antonioni, 1964)

*Elvira Madigan* (Bo Widerberg, 1967)

live or animation film carrying a direct message.

The extraordinary impetus given to Russian cinema immediately after the Revolution (see SOVIET UNION) was especially evident in the newsreel. Edvard TISSÉ learned his craft in the field, and Dziga VERTOV became the most influential figure in actuality film in the twenties, initially through his KINO-PRAVDA newsreel series (1922–5).

Silent newsreels were issued with leading titles to explain each item. After the introduction of sound, 'headline' titles were still used, but progressively lessened in frequency and duration, allowing more picture time. The cumbersome nature of early sound equipment created problems in the recording of synchronous soundtracks, but spoken commentary added to the effectiveness of filmed reports. American companies were the first to add sound to newsreels, closely followed by the French. With the exception of British Movietone (1928), British newsreels did not adopt sound until 1931–2. In Germany the Deulig company's Wochenschau became Tonwoche in January 1932, with a sound system considered the best of its time.

During the thirties the conventional newsreel form became established, with characteristic features including frequency, length, content, and style. Newsreels appeared regularly and at relatively short intervals—once or twice a week in England and America—to maintain topicality. Issues were normally available for three-day runs, with the charges decreasing after the third day when a new issue was made available or the news had lost its immediacy. The overall length of an issue was constant at about fifteen minutes: programme planning was facilitated by a fixed timing; cutting and printing were simplified by the regular framework; and many shipping problems were eliminated by restricting newsreels to one REEL. Each issue contained several items, not necessarily related: current events, general interest reports, perhaps about different cultures or traditional ceremonies and festivals, sporting fixtures. Many such events could be programmed in advance, but the unforeseen disaster or unscheduled political drama presented problems of coverage and often provided a scoop for the luckily-placed cameraman. Usually there were about six items in an issue with a balance of the serious and the silly, longer reports and quick news flashes. Material was edited to reconstruct a sequence of events and focus the viewer's attention, but the style was on the whole noncommittal, avoiding contentious subjects, unlike news magazines and documentaries which tended to be didactic or interpretative. The news magazine, also issued at regular intervals, dealt with a single subject in each issue. THE MARCH OF TIME, introduced in 1934, was one of the most

successful; it dealt with a wide range of social and political issues, using a combination of newsreel footage, stock material, and specially-shot sequences.

Apart from the Soviet Union, where all news media were subject to political control from the time of the Revolution, the main exception to the objective style of newsreels occurred in Germany. From 1927 UFA newsreels displayed a nationalistic bias and in 1933 Goebbels took over a ready-made propaganda machine in the combination of UFA and Deulig. In 1934 the REICHSFILMKAMMER regulations specified that all cameramen operating in Germany must be members of the government film organization, in effect banning foreign newsreel crews.

The outbreak of the Second World War brought newsreels in all combatant countries under government supervision once more. As in the First World War, a propagandistic slant was widely adopted. In Britain a new rota system was adopted to save costs and conserve raw stock. A government order reduced the running time of newsreels, stock was rationed among producers, and one team was assigned to each event, the film being made available to other companies. Another type of rota system produced British News, compiled by the Central Office of Information from film shot in turn by several newsreel companies and distributed mainly in Commonwealth countries. German newsreels during the war included Tobis Wochenschau, Deulig, Die Deutsche Wochenschau, and UFA Wochenschau, all of outstanding technical quality but operating virtually wholly as propaganda. The French Service Photographique et Cinématographique de l'Armée working from the Gaumont offices managed to produce some issues of the Journal de Guerre up to the time of Dunkirk. Another newsreel, France Actualités, was given exclusive rights by the Vichy Government in 1941 and continued until 1945, when it was replaced by the resistance product France Libre Actualités. Russian cameramen were active on all fronts as well as behind the enemy lines filming partisans, and American newsreel cameramen filmed in both the European and Pacific theatres of war.

Newsreel footage amassed in all countries was used in COMPILATION form for short and feature-length films about the war. Many of the most distinguished Russian directors—including DOVZHENKO, GERASIMOV, PUDOVKIN, and YUTKEVICH—worked on such films, and the German combat films used footage shot by newsreel cameramen, sometimes with additional material. Perhaps the most outstanding use of newsreel material in this manner was the WHY WE FIGHT series (1942–5) supervised by Frank CAPRA.

The tenacity and courage of newsreel cameramen of all nationalities has only occasionally been fully acknowledged. One of the first to be killed in action was the Frenchman J. A. Dupré who fell at Verdun in 1916; his early semi-automatic camera briefly continued to record the battle after his death. An issue of *War Pictorial News* in January 1945 paid tribute to Damien Parer, an Australian who, after filming in action throughout the war, was killed in the Pacific in December 1944. The Russian film *Frontovoi Kinooperator* (*Cameraman at the Front*, 1946) was a compilation of footage secured by Vladimir Sushinsky, killed in action in Poland. As recently as 1973, television viewers saw film shot by a Swedish cameraman during an abortive military coup in Chile: the troops being filmed were seen to warn and then shoot down the cameraman himself.

The post-war growth of television rapidly eroded the viability of cinema newsreels: *British Movietone* is the only surviving cinema newsreel in Britain. Television news coverage was, like cinema newsreels, shot on 35mm film until the introduction of light-weight, high-quality 16 MM equipment in the mid-fifties. The delay entailed by processing was at first common to both media; but, with the development of an electronic system which, projecting negative film, transmits a positive image, television outstripped cinema newsreels in immediacy. For a time the use of colour gave cinemas some advantage, but it was principally used for news magazines. Newsfilm material is now increasingly supplied by a few companies comparable with the agencies that syndicate written news. At first these newsfilm agencies resisted co-operation with television companies, but an arrangement has been arrived at whereby agency material is made into news magazines for cinema release and the supply of topical news is handled jointly by the agencies and the various television networks.

Television has continued to use 16mm film for news reporting, but with improvements in light-weight equipment videotape has recently begun to replace film. Its many advantages include cheapness and versatility: it can offer live transmission, if necessary with the use of communications satellites, or storage for later broadcasting, and tapes can be wiped and re-used. The current trend indicates further developments in portable video equipment which will undoubtedly supersede the traditional camera for on-the-spot reporting.

The immediacy of television news coverage has had a profound effect on audience response to political events: the detailed coverage of the Vietnam War, for example, and especially the impact of war reports in colour, aroused public awareness to an unprecedented degree. The worldwide transmission of the assassination of John F. Kennedy and the extraordinary on-camera shooting of Lee Harvey Oswald by Jack Ruby were events that may be said to represent a change in the character and aims of newsreel reporting. (See also CENSORSHIP, COMPILATION, DOCUMENTARY, PROPAGANDA.)

**NEWTON, ROBERT** (1905–56), British actor. His film appearances were most frequent in the late thirties: in 1937 he played in seven films, among them Alexander KORDA's *Fire over England* and the abortive *I, Claudius*; the following year he acted with Charles LAUGHTON in *Vessel of Wrath* and in 1939 in *Jamaica Inn*. He had sympathetic roles in GASLIGHT (1940) and *This Happy Breed* (1944), but, with his swarthy face and menacing voice, he usually played villains as in MAJOR BARBARA (1941), as a Cockney thug, HENRY V (1944), as Pistol, ODD MAN OUT (1947), as a crazy artist, and OLIVER TWIST (1948), as Bill Sykes. He brought effective exaggeration and caricature to the role with which he was popularly most associated—Long John Silver in *Treasure Island* (1950). His last film appearance was as Inspector Fix in AROUND THE WORLD IN EIGHTY DAYS (1956).

**NEW WAVE** see NOUVELLE VAGUE

**NIBELUNGEN, Die,** Germany, 1924. Part I: *Siegfried*; Part II: *Kriemhilds Rache* (*Kriemhild's Revenge*). 3hr. *Dir* Fritz Lang; *prod* UFA; *scr* Lang, Thea von Harbou; *ph* Carl Hoffman, Günther Rittau, 'Falkentraum' sequence by Walter Ruttmann; *des* Otto Hunte, Erich Kettelhut, Karl Vollbrecht; *cast* Paul₁ Richter (Siegfried), Margaret Schön (Kriemhild), Hanna Ralph (Brunhild), Bernhard Goetzke (Volker), Theodor Loos (Gunther), Hans Adalbert von Schlettow (Hagen).

After his successes of the immediate post-war years, LANG was entrusted with a major project in a version of the ancient Nibelungen saga. *Siegfried* traces the story of the hero's journey with the captive Brunhild, her betrayal of Siegfried, and his murder by Hagen. *Kriemhilds Rache* shows how Siegfried's widow is avenged, culminating in a forty-five-minute battle with no survivors.

The characters are deliberately depersonalized: they represent heroism, vengeance, barbarism, and may not express spontaneous emotion; Lang's favourite theme of destiny rules the film. *Die Nibelungen* epitomizes his command of the architectural and spatial resources of cinema: it is a striking instance of German studio craftsmanship, particularly in the stylized settings which have a quality of legend that dwarfs the actors both literally and figuratively. Part I is the more impressive in this respect, especially the fairy-tale forest constructed in a zeppelin hangar and the splendid dragon whose fight with Siegfried is the high point of the film.

**NIBLO,** FRED (1874–1948), US director whose first films, from 1918, featured his wife, Enid Bennett. His best work was accomplished in the twenties, initially with two Douglas FAIR-BANKS adventure-spectacles, *The Mark of Zorro* (1920) and *The Three Musketeers* (1921), and the Rudolph VALENTINO success, *Blood and Sand* (1922); but he is principally remembered as the director of METRO-GOLDWYN-MAYER's spectacular BEN-HUR (1925). His work included two GARBO films, *The Temptress* (1927) which he co-directed with Mauritz STILLER and *The Mysterious Lady* (1928), and a version of CAMILLE (1927) starring Norma TALMADGE.

**NICHOLS,** DUDLEY (1895–1960), US writer, began his career as a journalist. He wrote fiction for magazines, appearing regularly in the *Saturday Evening Post* and *New York Times Magazine*, before going to Hollywood in 1929. His first film script was *Men Without Women* (1930) directed by John FORD, with whom Nichols's name is most often linked; not always to his credit as he is generally held responsible for the elements of earnestness and sentimentality that run through their work. Between them they created fourteen films, including THE LOST PATROL, *Judge Priest* (both 1934), *Steamboat Round the Bend*, THE INFORMER (both 1935), *Mary of Scotland* (1936), STAGECOACH (1939), *The Long Voyage Home* (1940), and *The Fugitive* (1947). His career has also been involved with other important directors, such as Howard HAWKS (BRINGING UP BABY, 1938; *Air Force*, 1943; *The Big Sky*, 1952), Fritz LANG (*Man Hunt*, 1941; *Scarlet Street*, 1945), and Jean RENOIR (*Swamp Water*, 1941; *This Land is Mine*, 1943). He also directed some of his own scripts, including *Mourning Becomes Electra* (1947), but with little success. He was President of the Screenwriters' Guild 1938–9.

**NICHOLS,** MIKE (1931– ), US director and actor, born in Germany, real name Michael Igor Peschkowsky. In 1954, after studying psychiatry, he formed a cabaret double act with Elaine May, using their original material; the successful partnership lasted some years. Their New York stage début in 1960 was directed by Arthur PENN. Nichols went on to direct several Broadway successes before making the film version of *Who's Afraid of Virginia Woolf?* (1966), a remarkable transposition of Albee's play. In 1967 he directed THE GRADUATE, for which he received an OSCAR for best director; its box-office success firmly established him in a film-making career. He continued his cynical commentary on contemporary life with *Catch–22* (1970), unfortunately severely cut on release, and *Carnal Knowledge* (1971).

**NICHOLSON,** JACK (1937– ), US actor, worked for Roger CORMAN and for Monte Hellmann, appearing in the latter's *The Shooting* (1966), a quiet, uncompromising Western which Nicholson also produced. He attracted attention for his performance as the alcoholic Southern lawyer in EASY RIDER (1969), and the following year he starred in Bob Rafaelson's *Five Easy Pieces*, playing opposite Karen Black whom he directed in the pleasantly rambling *Drive, He Said* (1970). Both films were notable for their astute psychological observation, restraint, and the high standard of acting. After *Carnal Knowledge* (Mike NICHOLS, 1971) Nicholson worked again for Rafaelson in *The King of Marvin Gardens* (1972). In *The Last Detail* (1973) his performance as a US naval officer, which won him the best actor award at Cannes, confirmed his versatility and perceptiveness. Nicholson's talent has gained him a wide following, in spite of his apparent preference for tackling unusual subjects with lesser-known directors.

**NICK CARTER,** the American sleuth, first appeared on the screen in two French series made in 1908 and 1909 by Victorin Jasset. An American series of thirty two-reel adventures was issued in 1921–2. The best-known Nick Carter adventures were in three films made by METRO-GOLDWYN-MAYER in 1939–40, starring Walter PIDGEON with Donald Meek as his stooge. Popular as they were, they failed to equal the success of the same studio's THIN MAN series.

**NICKELODEON,** a primitive form of cinema, immensely popular, and widespread in the United States by 1905, consisting of a long narrow room furnished with wooden bench seating, and crudely equipped for film projection. It was frequently a converted shop or store.

The term is thought to have been coined by a showman, John P. Harris, combining the Greek for theatre with the slang term for the five cents charged for entry.

The English equivalent was known as the penny gaff.

**NIELSEN,** ASTA (1883– ), Danish actress whose stage reputation was already considerable when she made her first film *Afgrunden* (*Abyss*, 1910) under the direction of Urban Gad, who became her first husband and managed her career until his death. Her success in *Afgrunden* and two other Danish films attracted attention abroad, and she was invited with Gad to Berlin in 1911. Until the late twenties she was one of the most popular film actresses in Germany, her expressive dark eyes and skill at wordlessly conveying deep feeling being ideally suited to silent films. She played the title role in HAMLET (1920), but is mostly associated with tragic heroines such as Strindberg's *Fräulein Julie* (1922), Mary Magdalen in Robert WIENE's *INRI* (1924), and Ibsen's *Hedda Gabler* (1925). In DIE FREUDLOSE GASSE (*Joyless Street*, 1925) and similarly in *Dirnentragödie* (*Tragedy of the Street*, 1927) she played a fallen woman, driven to murder by her lover's betrayal. With the introduction of sound her career suffered a check, but she made one sound film in Germany, *Unmögliche Liebe* (1932), before the rise of Nazism caused her to return to Denmark. She retired from acting in 1939 and spent some years as manager of a Copenhagen cinema under the municipality's enlightened policy towards distinguished former film workers (see DENMARK).

***NIEUWE GRONDEN*** (*New Earth*), Holland, 1934. 25min. *Dir, scr* Joris Ivens; *prod* Capi-Amsterdam; *ph* Ivens, John Fernhout, Joop Huisken, Helen van Dongen; *ed* Helen van Dongen; *mus* Hanns Eisler.

The film shows the reclamation of the Zuider Zee, culminating in a brilliantly edited sequence of the final closing of the dam against the North Sea. The exhilaration induced by the success of the project is deliberately subdued by the last part of the film which shows the economic results: thousands of men who had been employed on the project thrown out of work and the first rich harvest a glut on depressed world markets. IVENS's didactic skill with images is supported by a complex sound-track created by Helen VAN DONGEN and the excellent score by Hanns EISLER.

***NIGHT AND FOG*** see NUIT ET BROUILLARD

***NIGHT AT THE OPERA, A,*** US, 1935. 1½hr. *Dir* Sam Wood; *prod* Irving Thalberg for MGM; *scr* James Kevin McGuinness; *ph* Merritt B. Gerstad; *cast* Groucho Marx (Otis B. Driftwood), Chico (Fiorello), Harpo (Tomasso), Kitty Carlisle (Rosa), Allan Jones (Riccardo), Margaret Dumont (Mrs Claypool).

The plot, concerning Groucho's efforts to persuade the wealthy Margaret DUMONT to invest in a failing opera house and Allan JONES's leap to stardom as an operatic tenor, serves as a framework for some of the MARX BROTHERS' classic comic set pieces. Perhaps the most memorable is the sequence in which Groucho, occupying a tiny

cabin which already holds three stowaways, calls on all the various room service staff simultaneously; with hilariously surrealist logic the cabin is steadily packed with squirming humanity. In the film's climax the brothers join forces to wreck a performance of *Il trovatore*, exploiting the inherent absurdities of opera to hilarious effect.

***NIGHT IN THE SHOW, A,*** US, 1915. 30min. *Dir, scr* Charles Chaplin; *prod* Essanay; *ph* Rollie Totheroh; *cast* Charlie Chaplin, Dee Lampton, John Rand, Leo White, Edna Purviance.

Several of CHAPLIN's early films derive from Fred KARNO sketches and this is closely based on 'Mumming Birds', the most popular item in the company's US tour on which Mack SENNETT first saw Chaplin perform (in the US, it was known as 'A Night in an English Music Hall'). Chaplin plays a double role—as Mr Pest, a well-dressed but scarcely sober gentleman in the front stalls, and Mr Rowdy, an ill-kempt and no less disruptive layabout in the gallery. Between them, they manage hilariously to ruin the evening for music-hall performers and audience alike.

***NIGHT MAIL,*** GB, 1936. 25min. *Dir, scr* Basil Wright, Harry Watt; *prod* John Grierson for the GPO Film Unit; *ph* H. E. Fowle, Frank 'Jonah' Jones; *ed* R. Q. McNaughton; *sound dir* Alberto Cavalcanti; *cast* workers of the Travelling Post Office; workers of the LMS Railway.

The nightly journey of the Postal Special from London to Glasgow is lucidly depicted, the workers performing their tasks for the camera. Benjamin BRITTEN and W. H. Auden provided music and verse, a partnership which began with CAVALCANTI's *Coal Face* (1936). *Night Mail*, and particularly the section during which Auden's poem is spoken by Stuart LEGG, remains a fine example of imaginative DOCUMENTARY film-making, a worthy product of the best aspirations of GRIERSON and his colleagues at the GPO Film Unit (see CROWN FILM UNIT).

***NIGHT MUST FALL,*** US, 1937. 2hr. *Dir* Richard Thorpe; *prod* MGM; *scr* John Van Druten, from the play by Emlyn Williams; *ph* Ray June; *ed* Robert J. Kern; *cast* Robert Montgomery (Danny), Rosalind Russell (Olivia), Dame May Whitty (Mrs Bramson), Kathleen Harrison (Mrs Terence).

The screen version of Emlyn Williams's suspense melodrama equalled the play's success largely by virtue of its stylish performances. The choice of Robert MONTGOMERY to play a psychopathic killer was surprising, but it became one of his best-remembered roles. Dame May Whitty was equally memorable in the character she had created on the stage in London (1935) and New York (1936). Kathleen HARRISON appeared in the comedy role she had played in the former stage production.

A British remake directed by Karel REISZ in 1964, with Albert FINNEY as Danny, updated the original unashamed thriller into a clinical study of a psychopath, swamping the plot with significant imagery.

*NIGHT OF THE HUNTER, The,* US, 1955. 1½hr. *Dir* Charles Laughton; *prod* United Artists; *scr* James Agee, from the novel by Davis Grubb; *ph* Stanley Cortez; *des* Hilyard Brown; *mus* Walter Schumann; *cast* Robert Mitchum (Preacher Harry Powell), Shelley Winters (Willa Harper), Lillian Gish (Rachel), Billy Chapin (John), Sally Jane Bruce (Pearl), Evelyn Varden (Icey), James Gleason (Birdie).

A psychopathic 'preacher', Harry Powell, obtains money for 'the Lord's work' by marrying and murdering rich widows. The children of his last victim find refuge with Rachel, who organizes his eventual capture. Obsessive evil and sturdy goodness are represented in fine performances by Robert MITCHUM and Lillian GISH.

*The Night of the Hunter* is close in style to the German Expressionist films of the twenties. Atmospheric photography and the unusual use of music give it a timeless and dreamlike quality which emphasizes the complex allegory of good and evil; and LAUGHTON used characters and settings to explore ideas developed in his own acting roles. The film's stylization may be the reason for its failure on first release: it has since gained a considerable following.

This was the only film Laughton directed on his own and the last written by James AGEE.

**NILSSON,** TORRE, see TORRE-NILSSON

**9·5MM** film was introduced in France around 1922–3, and was one of the earliest narrow gauge films designed for use by amateurs. Like the earlier but very short-lived 11mm, it had a single perforation in the centre of the film on the line between each frame. 9·5mm remained popular in Europe for a number of years until it was superseded by the more universal 8 MM. 9·5mm has retained a few admirers and prints on 9·5mm are still available.

*NINOTCHKA,* US, 1939. 1¾hr. *Dir* Ernst Lubitsch; *prod* MGM; *scr* Charles Brackett, Billy Wilder, Walter Reisch; *ph* William Daniels; *des* Cedric Gibbons; *cast* Greta Garbo (Ninotchka), Melvyn Douglas (Leon), Ina Claire (Swana), Bela Lugosi (Razinin), Sig Rumann (Iranoff), Felix Bressart (Buljanoff), Alexander Granach (Kupalski), Gregory Gaye (Rakonin).

Ninotchka, a Soviet commissar sent to Paris to supervise three comrades seduced by the glamour of capitalist society, herself succumbs via a love affair with Leon. This was not in fact (as advertised) the first film in which GARBO laughed; it was however the first time she was used in an American comedy. The sharply-written script and LUBITSCH's typically ironical handling of potentially offensive humour carry the film on to the level of sophisticated farce.

**NITRATE FILM,** or more correctly nitrate base, was the standard film STOCK base for 35mm until 1951. Cellulose nitrate was discovered by early inventors to be a suitable medium on which to coat EMULSION and was used by George EASTMAN for his first flexible roll film in 1889. It continued in use for 60 years despite considerable fire risks resulting from the film's tendency to ignite when run at speed through projectors, cameras, or editing equipment. It has been completely replaced by less flammable materials, known generically as SAFETY FILM.

Although no longer a problem in production, nitrate film causes severe problems for film libraries and ARCHIVES. Large parts of historical collections are, of course, still on nitrate film. After a time, old stocks are liable to decompose rapidly, first becoming sticky then powdery. In this state they are even more of a fire risk, and precautions have to be taken to prevent both decomposition and danger to other films in the archive. Special isolation vaults are usually necessary and regular rewinding of the rolls of film must be carried out, both as a check and to guard against the accumulation of gases between the layers of the film. Most archives have a policy of copying nitrate film on to safety film which is much easier to store and has a longer stable life.

**NIVEN,** DAVID (1909–   ), Scottish-born actor who made his first film appearance in Hollywood in *Rose Marie* (1936). Further Hollywood films at this period include *The Charge of the Light Brigade, Dodsworth* (both 1936), *The Prisoner of Zenda* (1937), BLUEBEARD'S EIGHTH WIFE, *The Dawn Patrol* (both 1938), and WUTHERING HEIGHTS (1939). He made one film in Britain during this time (*Dinner at the Ritz,* 1937), but in 1939 he returned for army service from which he was released to appear in a few wartime films, notably *The First of the Few* (1942) and *The Way Ahead* (1944). After the war he became a familiar screen figure, not only continuing his Hollywood career but more frequently making films in England. Although effective in roles calling for a military bearing, his forte has been dashing, debonair, romantic leads; he is particularly adept in comedy, for which he invariably reveals a nice sense of timing, and was suitably imperturbable as Phileas Fogg in AROUND THE WORLD IN EIGHTY DAYS (1956) and in the title role of MY MAN GODFREY (1957). He won an OSCAR for his restrained performance in a more serious role in *Separate Tables* (1958). He has written a best-selling autobiography, *The moon's a balloon* (London, 1971).

*NOBI* (*Fires on the Plain*), Japan, 1959. Daiei-scope; 1¾hr. *Dir* Kon Ichikawa; *prod* Masaichi Nagata for Daiei; *scr* Natto Wada, from the novel by Shohei O-oka; *ph* Setsuo Kobayashi; *mus* Yasushi Akatagawa; *cast* Eiji Funakoshi (Private Tamura), Mantaro Ushio (sergeant), Yoshihiro Hamaguchi (officer), Osamu Takizawa (soldier A), Micky Curtis (soldier B), Asao Sano (soldier C), Kyu Sazanka (surgeon).

*Nobi* describes the life of the defeated Japanese troops during the last days of the Philippine campaign. Using a minimum of dialogue, ICHI-KAWA created a highly visual film which handles the repellent subjects of death and cannibalism with dignity and honesty. As in BIRUMA NO TATEGOTO (*The Burmese Harp*, 1956), he observes the experiences of ordinary people caught up in horrifying events with compassion and with contemplative wonder.

**NOH** theatre developed from songs and dances performed at fairs, originally by entertainers who came to Japan from China via Korea, and owes its present form to Zeami Motokiyo (1362–1443), a player invited to stay at the court of the Shogun. The atmosphere of the court brought great refinement to Noh, which became the preserve of aristocrats, intellectuals, and those who saw in it the essence of Japanese culture. The present-day audience is small, most Japanese preferring the extravaganza of the KABUKI.

There are about 250 plays in the modern Noh repertoire (and about the same number of comic interludes) which take their themes from myths, folk stories of gods and demons, war romances, classical Japanese and Chinese literature, and stories of women. Most of the plays relate events that have already happened, unlike Kabuki, which shows situations as they occur. The chief character is usually disguised in the first part of the play, to be revealed in the second part as perhaps a god, a demon, or the ghost of a dead hero; the actor wears masks corresponding to the two aspects of the character. Stage settings and properties are sparse, and frequently symbolic—a scarf can represent a sword, a pipe, or even running water. The actors perform in a highly stylized way, using refined, symbolic gestures—the lifting of the mask indicates a smile, the raising of the arm shows that the character is weeping, and one step may represent a journey of

many miles. The literary importance of the plays has long taken second place to the emotional atmosphere created by the actors: the language is formal and not readily understood by a modern audience, speeches are full of literary allusions and quotations, and, in addition, the stylized speech can make many words inaudible.

Noh has had little influence on the Japanese film. Adaptations from Noh plays are rare because the stories themselves are slight, and the cinema can add nothing to the stylized atmosphere, but one or two of the more popular plays, such as *Hagoromo* (*The Feathered Robe*), have been filmed simply as introductions to the art of the theatre. In 1972, Kaneto SHINDO adapted *Kanawa* (*The Iron Crown*), blending three elements—scenes from a stage performance of the play, a representation of the events described (with the text of the play as commentary), and a modern story, similar to the theme of the Noh drama, of a middle-aged woman taking revenge on her husband and his mistress. He drew a parallel between some of the magical torments used by the woman in the play and the modern woman's harassment of the couple by anonymous telephone calls, and heightened the atmosphere with the supernatural elements of the drama.

Some directors have deliberately introduced Noh elements into their films. This is most frequent when the stories have a supernatural theme, and the appearance of many ghosts is similar to those of the Noh stage. All the spectres in KOBAYASHI's KWAIDAN (1964), for example, have their counterparts in the theatre, and one of the episodes—'Minimachi Hoichi' (*Hoichi the Earless*)—has a formal structure that resembles that of a Noh play.

KUROSAWA, a great Noh enthusiast, has made by far the most use of Noh in the Japanese cinema. His *Tora no O o Fumu Otokotachi* (*The Men Who Walk on the Tiger's Tail*/*Walkers on Tiger's Tail*, 1945) is based on a Kabuki play, which, in turn, was based on the Noh drama *Ataka*. Kurosawa uses a chorus in the manner of both Noh and Kabuki, and some Noh music; Denjiro Okochi (as Benkei) speaks in the guttural bass of a Noh actor. In SHICHININ NO SAMURAI (*The Seven Samurai*, 1954), Kurosawa used more Noh music, such as the flute that accompanies the waking of the woman as the bandits' stronghold is set on fire. KAKUSHI TORIDE NO SAN-AKUNIN (*The Hidden Fortress*, 1958) is structured like a Noh play: the whole story is a fairy-tale in which, in the first part, the princess is disguised, and, in the second part, is revealed as her true self; there is continuous use of Noh music, frequently connected with the princess, and her singing of the festival song has a Noh-like intonation.

Kurosawa's greatest tribute to the Noh theatre is in his version of MACBETH: KUMONOSU-JO (*The Throne of Blood/Cobweb Castle/The Castle of the Spider's Web*, 1957). He uses a number of Noh elements, chiefly the chorus narrative, and the appearance and surroundings of both the Lady Asaji (Isuzu Yamada) and the Witch (Cheiko Naniwa), who can be compared to the two aspects of the chief Noh character. Lady Asaji's face resembles a Noh mask for a young woman, and she moves in the same controlled way as Noh actors; all her scenes with her husband, Washizu (Toshiro MIFUNE), are arranged to look like Noh stagings; the hand-washing scene is a direct reminder of the symbolic mime of the theatre. The Witch looks rather like a Noh ghost, and lives in a hut very similar to a stage property; she speaks in the flat monotone of a Noh actor, and the rustling and the clacking spinning-wheel are the sort of sounds that would be heard at a theatrical performance.

**NORMAND, MABEL** (1894/5–1930), US actress, real name Fortescue, began her film career at VITAGRAPH, then moved to BIOGRAPH where she met and worked for Mack SENNETT. A clever, pretty, and vivacious *comédienne*, she left Biograph with him in 1912 and became a popular star under his guidance, first in the Keystone Kops films (see KEYSTONE) and then as co-star (and sometimes director) of Charlie CHAPLIN, notably in the feature-length TILLIE'S PUNCTURED ROMANCE (1914). In 1916, she finally persuaded Sennett to produce another feature for her, though she went to work with GOLDWYN before the very successful *Mickey* (1918) was released. Her poor health and her connection with two major Hollywood scandals had a bad effect on her career; she returned to Sennett, but even pictures like *The Extra Girl* (1923) and a later two-reeler series for Hal ROACH were unsuccessful. She died of tuberculosis.

**NORTH BY NORTHWEST**, US, 1959. Technicolor; 2¼hr. *Dir, prod* Alfred Hitchcock for MGM; *scr* Ernest Lehman; *ph* Robert Burks; *des* Robert Boyle; *mus* Bernard Herrmann; *cast* Cary Grant (Roger Thornhill), Eva Marie Saint (Eve Kendall), James Mason (Philip Vandamm), Jessie Royce Landis (Clara Thornhill), Leo G. Carroll (the Professor), Philip Ober (Lester Townsend).

Thornhill, an advertising executive, is kidnapped by an espionage organization, who mistake him for a mythical agent, invented by the CIA to run the gang into a trap. The intrigue is thus typical of HITCHCOCK's technique of building an elaborate story round a 'non-plot', or 'Macguffin' as he calls it.

The most colourful and baroque of Hitchcock's chase films, its structure is very similar to that of his earlier THE THIRTY-NINE STEPS (1935). Thornhill, played with debonair assurance by Cary GRANT, is subjected to a hair-raising succession of adventures. He is framed for a murder in the United Nations building, pursued across an empty prairie by a crop-dusting aircraft, becomes involved with an attractive double agent, and the film culminates in a showdown with the spies among the gigantic carved-out heads of presidents on Mount Rushmore. A tongue-in-cheek extravaganza, *North by Northwest* is extremely successful within its own terms, although critics have not always recognized Hitchcock's sly humour in it.

**NORWAY.** Exhibition in Norway is largely in the hands of local authorities, who also license all cinemas. In 1917 the Communal Exhibitors Association (Komunale Kinematografers) was established, and in 1919 a communal distribution company, Kommunernes Filmcentral A/S. Half the latter's capital is owned by Oslo Commune, and the balance by other local authorities, and it handles 40 per cent of total distribution. Import of films is controlled by a committee on which all interests are represented; American companies, which distribute their own product, account for approximately half the foreign films. Despite its small population (just over 3,000,000) Norway does produce films although on a small scale; only twenty films were produced between 1907 and 1920. The Communal Exhibitors Association raised a production fund in 1920, and in 1932 founded Norsk Film A/S, which between 1920 and 1945 produced thirteen of the total sixty-nine films made. It also owns the only studio in Norway, at Jar near Oslo, and has been the only constant force in production. In recent years the government has acquired an interest in the company and also become involved in other aspects of the industry, largely through the Government Film Board (Statens Filmråd). Norwegian films are, however, still mainly of local interest and no director of international stature has emerged. The only man to maintain any consistent career was Tancred Ibsen, grandson of the dramatist, who began in the thirties, recommencing after the war.

Censorship is applied on a national basis, and no film may be shown to children under sixteen unless it has a special certificate, nor may they enter cinemas after 8 pm unless accompanied by an adult.

**NOSFERATU, EINE SYMPHONIE DES GRAUENS** (*Nosferatu, a Symphony of Terror*), Germany, 1922. 1½hr. *Dir* F. W. Murnau; *prod* Prana Film; *scr* Henrik Galeen, from Bram Stoker's *Dracula*; *ph* Fritz Arno Wagner; *cast* Max Schreck (Count Orlock, Nosferatu),

*Nosferatu* (F. W. Murnau, 1922)

Alexander Granach (Knock), Gustav von Wangenheim (Hutter), Greta Schroeder (Ellen, Hutter's wife).

Nosferatu was pirated from Bram Stoker's DRACULA, and a successful action for breach of COPYRIGHT resulted in the destruction of official prints. Its importance lies mainly in introducing the vampire to the screen and in demonstrating MURNAU's concern for visual effect and his exploration, with his cameraman Fritz Arno WAGNER, of film technique; negative film was used to suggest an eerie journey and speeded-up motion for ghostly beings. The film still retains a certain power and is a worthy representative of Murnau's developing skill.

**NOTHING SACRED,** US, 1937. Technicolor; 1¼hr. *Dir* William Wellman; *prod* David O. Selznick; *scr* Ben Hecht; *ph* W. Howard Greene; *ed* Hal Kern; *cast* Carole Lombard (Hazel Flagg), Fredric March (Wally Cook), Charles Winninger (Dr Downer), Walter Connolly (Stone), Sig Rumann (Dr Eggelhoffer).

A small-town girl, diagnosed by the alcoholic local doctor as suffering from radium poisoning, becomes the subject of a publicity stunt by a New York reporter.

*Nothing Sacred* is strikingly uncharacteristic of William WELLMAN's films. Its real strength lies in Ben HECHT's script, which turned an apparently downbeat plot into one of Hollywood's classic sophisticated comedies. His acid satire on the popular press and its gullible public was supported by witty performances from Carole LOMBARD and Fredric MARCH in the leading roles.

**NOTORIOUS,** US, 1946. 1¾hr. *Dir*, *prod* Alfred Hitchcock for RKO; *scr* Ben Hecht; *ph* Ted Tetzlaff; *cast* Ingrid Bergman (Alicia Huberman), Cary Grant (Devlin), Claude Rains (Alexander Sebastien), Louis Calhern (Paul Prescott), Leopoldine Konstantine (Mrs Sebastien).

A spy drama set in Argentina, with Claude RAINS as a Nazi agent and Cary GRANT representing the American Secret Service. HITCHCOCK treated a conventional theme with assured restraint, concentrating on the tensions between the characters: the torrid love scenes between Grant and Ingrid BERGMAN were heightened by their cool under-playing elsewhere. The film has little violence, but it culminates in a magnificent final shoot-up in a wine cellar.

***NOTTE, La,*** Italy/France, 1961. Wide screen; 2hr. *Dir* Michelangelo Antonioni; *prod* Nepi-Film, Silva-Film (Rome)/Sofitedip (Paris); *scr* Antonioni, Ennio Flaiano, Tonino Guerra; *ph* Gianni Di Venanzo; *des* Piero Zuffi; *ed* Eraldo Da Roma; *mus* Giorgio Gaslini; *cast* Jeanne Moreau (Lidia), Marcello Mastroianni (Giovanni), Monica Vitti (Valentina), Bernhard Wicki (Tommaso), Rosy Mazzacurati (Rosy), Vincenzo Corbella (Gherardini).

The film shows twenty-four hours in the life of Giovanni and Lidia Pontano, in which the incidents—a visit to a dying friend, a night out at a night-club and a party, various erotic encounters—serve to underline the growing emptiness of their marriage.

*La notte* extends and particularizes the examination of relationships which preoccupied ANTONIONI since his first feature and was given full expression in L'AVVENTURA (1960). The focus this time is on a married couple; characteristically, Antonioni uses the streets and buildings of Milan, photographed as always with cold beauty, to convey emotions and interactions. Jeanne MOREAU, under Antonioni's exacting direction, portrays with finesse Lidia's anguish in the face of the muted incomprehension of MASTROIANNI's Giovanni. An unexpectedly refreshing note is provided by Valentina, played with verve by Monica VITTI, and the sequences between the three characters are outstanding.

***NOTTI BIANCHI, Le*** (*White Nights*), France/Italy, 1957. 1¾hr. *Dir* Luchino Visconti; *prod* CIAS/Vides (Rome)/Intermondia (Paris); *scr* Suso Cecchi d'Amico, Visconti, from a short story by Dostoevsky; *ph* Giuseppe Rotunno; *des* Mario Chiari; *mus* Nino Rota; *cast* Maria Schell (Natalia), Marcello Mastroianni (Mario), Jean Marais (lodger), Clara Calamai (prostitute).

VISCONTI's version of Dostoevsky's story is dreamlike and elegiac, using deliberately artificial settings and soft, grainy photography. It was initially received with hostility and treated as a rejection of the principles of NEO-REALISM; although a minor film, it is an interestingly romantic interlude in Visconti's work.

Other film versions of the story are *Beliye nochi* (*White Nights*, USSR, 1959) directed by Ivan Pyriev and *Quatre Nuits d'un rêveur* (*Four Nights of a Dreamer*, France, 1971) directed by Robert BRESSON.

***NOTTI DI CABIRIA, Le*** (*Nights of Cabiria*), Italy/France, 1957. 2hr. *Dir* Federico Fellini; *prod* Dino De Laurentiis for Film Marceau; *scr* Fellini, Ennio Flaiano, Tullio Pinelli; additional dialogue, P. P. Pasolini; *ph* Aldo Tonti; *des* Piero Gherardi; *mus* Nino Rota; *cast* Giulietta Masina (Cabiria), François Périer (Oscar), Amadeo Nazzari (the actor), Franca Marzi (Wanda).

Cabiria, a prostitute, rescued from the water where her lover has thrown her, courageously starts afresh, but is repeatedly reminded that she is of no account in the world. She is taken advantage of by Oscar, and ends up where she started.

This is the second film in which FELLINI finds his main inspiration in Giulietta MASINA. As in

*La notte* (Michelangelo Antonioni, 1961)

the first, LA STRADA (1954), he pursues the idea of apparent contradiction: in this case that of purity as the mainspring of a disordered life.

**NOUVELLE VAGUE,** journalists' term to designate the 'new wave' of directors making their first feature films in France in the years following 1958–9. (It has since been used to describe any new movement in a national cinema, as for example in Czechoslovakia in the sixties and even, retrospectively, FREE CINEMA and after in Britain.) The main impetus for the movement in France came from the critics of CAHIERS DU CINÉMA seeking to turn director TRUFFAUT, RIVETTE, GODARD, and CHABROL foremost among them. As writers they had condemned the 'well-made' film, pleading instead for a 'personal style' in direction and extolling American cinema. HITCHCOCK was pre-eminent among the gods of the new pantheon erected by the journal's *politique des auteurs*, and his influence was to be seen in several of the *nouvelle vague* films, especially those of Chabrol. Among the few European directors conceded admiration were RENOIR, later ROSSELLINI, and BRESSON.

Two main factors made possible the transition of the *nouvelle vague* from theory to practice. One was the state of crisis in the French film industry at the time, making producers willing to back modest undertakings; and the other was the chance use of private money for a few of the first productions. The earliest film to draw attention was Chabrol's LE BEAU SERGE (1959), although it was not widely successful at first. The real breakthrough came with the success at CANNES in 1959 of Truffaut's LES QUATRE CENTS COUPS (prize for direction) and Alain RESNAIS'S HIROSHIMA MON AMOUR (International Critics' prize). This gave the necessary encouragement to producers (among whom Pierre BRAUNBERGER deserves honourable mention) to back the newcomers: in 1959 twenty-four directors made their first feature film, and in 1960 a further forty-three. Chabrol's LES COUSINS (1959) and Godard's A BOUT DE SOUFFLE (1960) were both outstanding commercial successes, but for the most part the producers' gamble failed to pay off, and within two years the financial impetus was lost.

Several of the new directors were launched on successful careers, however; and, with the notable exception of Godard, they quickly graduated to full-scale commercial budgets. The *nouvelle vague* was scarcely a coherent aesthetic movement: the films made by its directors had as common ground only the 'personal', informal approach, with a mobile, often hand-held, camera as a particular hall-mark; a preference for shooting out in the streets (and especially through the windscreens of cars) as well as in real houses;

and a not unattractive habit of referring to the work of each other and of earlier, favoured, directors. A noticeable lack of political engagement was quickly commented on by the left-wing critics: and, again, it was only Godard who gradually developed a passionate political commitment, becoming by the end of the sixties the only revolutionary (in the cinematic sense) to have emerged from the *nouvelle vague*.

**NOVAK, KIM** (1933–   ), US actress, real first name Marilyn. After winning a beauty contest she was placed under contract by Harry COHN with the intention of creating a new star to succeed Rita HAYWORTH. During her time with COLUMBIA he ruled her private life as well as personally choosing her wardrobe, make-up, and hair-style. Under direction from Richard QUINE (*Pushover*, 1954; *Bell, Book and Candle*, 1959), Otto PREMINGER (THE MAN WITH THE GOLDEN ARM, 1955), Joshua LOGAN (*Picnic*, 1956), George Sidney (*Pal Joey*, 1957), and Alfred HITCHCOCK (*Vertigo*, 1958), she gave acceptable performances, but she lacked the talent and personality to sustain star status. Most interesting was her role in *The Legend of Lylah Clare* (1968), Robert ALDRICH's violent attack on the worst excesses of the Hollywood system, in which she played out events reminiscent of her own career.

**NOVARRO, RAMON** (1899–1968), US actor, real name Ramón Samaniegos, who became a star when Rex INGRAM selected him as a possible successor to VALENTINO and cast him in *The Prisoner of Zenda* (1922). He appeared as romantic heroes in four more Ingram films before playing his most famous role in BEN-HUR (1925). During this time he was an immensely popular romantic star, with an enthusiastic fan club that outlasted his death. He was GARBO's co-star in *Mata Hari* (1942) and continued to star though less successfully until the early forties, and also did some directing. His last part was a small one in *Heller in Pink Tights* (1960). He was murdered in 1968.

**NOVYI VAVILON** (*New Babylon*), USSR, 1929. 1¾hr. *Dir, scr* Grigori Kozintsev, Leonid Trauberg; *asst dir* Sergei Gerasimov; *prod* Sovkino; *ph* Andrei Moskvin, Yevgeni Mikhailov; *des* Yevgeni Enei; *mus* (for accompaniment) Dmitri Shostakovich; *cast* Elena Kuzmina (Louise Poirier), Piotr Sobolevskii (Jean), D. Gutman (store owner), V. I. Pudovkin, S. Gerasimov.

Based on various isolated events of the Paris Commune of 1871, the film centres on the conflict between the bourgeoisie and the working class of Paris. The heroine is a salesgirl in a luxury store—the New Babylon—who forms a link between the two classes. When the Germans advance the patriotism of the poor and the cowardly behaviour of the rich are contrasted. The final scenes deal with the failure of the Commune.

Technically the film is skilfully realized and employs the advanced forms of montage which were developed by KULESHOV and PUDOVKIN. The lighting is especially skilled, and the atmosphere it conveys, particularly in the scenes dealing with the bourgeoisie, is vital to the film. In spite of the symbolic nature of the characters the performances have a remarkable warmth, in contrast to the directors' earlier work with the FEKS group.

*NÓŻ W WODZIE* (*Knife in the Water*), Poland, 1962. 1¼hr. *Dir* Roman Polański; *prod* ZRF Kamera; *scr* Polański, Jerzy Skolimowski, Jakub Goldberg; *ph* Jerzy Lipman; *mus* Krzysztof Komeda; *cast* Leon Niemczyk (Andrzej), Jolanta Umecka (Christine), Zygmunt Malanowicz (the boy).

Apparently the mere record of a sailing trip by a married couple and a boy they have picked up, *Nóż w wodzie* is an astute, spare analysis of personality conflicts.

This was POLAŃSKI's first feature film, shot with an economy and boldness which is echoed in the remarkable music. Leon Niemczyk is the only professional actor and Polański dubbed his own voice for the part of the boy. The film was awarded the Fipresci prize at the VENICE festival, 1962.

*NUIT AMÉRICAINE, La* (*Day for Night*), France/Italy, 1973. Panavision; 1¾hr; Eastman Color. *Dir* François Truffaut; *prod* Les Films du Carrosse/PECF (Paris)/PIC (Rome); *scr* Truffaut, Suzanne Schiffman, Jean-Louis Richard; *ph* Pierre-William Glenn; *ed* Yann Dedet, Martine Barraque; *des* Damien Lanfranchi; *mus* Georges Delerue; *cast* Jacqueline Bisset (Julie), Valentina Cortese (Séverine), Jean-Pierre Aumont (Alexandre), Jean-Pierre Léaud (Alphonse), François Truffaut (Ferrand), Jean Champion (Bertrand), Dani (Liliane), Alexandra Stewart (Stacey), Nathalie Baye (Joëlle, continuity girl), Bernard Menez (props man), Henry Graham, i.e. Graham Greene (insurance representative).

'La nuit américaine'/day for night, the technical term for simulating night by the use of filters in daylight, neatly reflects the film's purpose, a loving and light-hearted homage to the cinema. While *Meet Pamela* is being filmed, with Ferrand (TRUFFAUT) as director, at the Studio de la Victorine in Nice, the techniques of filmmaking are discreetly presented: how crowds are organized, how crane shots and tracking shots are set up, dialogue agreed, stars placated, props gathered, stunting carried out. In a sequence derived from his *La Peau douce* (1964), Truffaut shows the problems of introducing animals and makes dramatic use of a perverse kitten—in itself something of an achievement. He wittily exploits the relationship between the audience, the film, and the film within the film, dovetailing the practical and emotional crises into the process of shooting.

The gaiety and spontaneity of *La Nuit américaine* derive also from the relaxed performances of the 'stars' (Jean-Pierre LÉAUD, Valentina Cortese, Jean-Pierre Aumont, Jacqueline Bisset) and the production team, in particular the continuity girl, a point of stability throughout, and the endlessly inventive props man; and from DELERUE's music, which points up the action with passages of springy vitality.

The film abounds with references to films, film-makers, books. Special tribute is paid to Hollywood, overtly in the dedication to Lillian and Dorothy GISH and in the studio production of *Meet Pamela*, which mirrors Hollywood methods rather than Truffaut's own.

*NUIT ET BROUILLARD* (*Night and Fog*), France, 1955. Eastman Color and black and white; 30min. *Dir* Alain Resnais; *prod* Argos Film, Como Film; *commentary* Jean Cayrol (spoken by Michel Bouquet); *ph* Ghislain Cloquet, Sacha Vierny; *mus* Hanns Eisler.

A documentary on Nazi concentration camps, the film juxtaposes colour scenes of the present-day ruins of Auschwitz with black-and-white archive material recording the horrific reality of the former camps. The film is remarkable for its sensitive and unusual approach to the subject. Grim images of torture and death are treated with sober control, unfolding against a background of wistful music and the thoughtful commentary by Jean CAYROL, himself a victim of deportation. Instead of isolating the death camps as a single historical event, *Nuit et brouillard* seeks to be a reminder of an ever-present threat to humanity. Many of RESNAIS's stylistic and thematic preoccupations are already apparent in this film.

**NUMBER BOARD,** the generic name for the board on which the number of the shot is written during production. It is usually in the form of a board with a hinged arm, known popularly as a CLAPPERBOARD, but more commonly called the SLATE in film production circles.

**NYKVIST, SVEN** (1923– ), Swedish cameraman, after studying photography, working as an assistant cameraman, and spending a year at CINECITTÀ, joined the Swedish production company Sandrews in 1941 as a director of photography. He filmed BERGMAN's GYCKLARNAS AFTON (*Sawdust and Tinsel*), produced by Sandrews in 1953, and with *Jungfrukällen* (*The Virgin Spring*, 1960) he succeeded Gunnar FISCHER as Bergman's regular director of photography at SVENSK FILMINDUSTRI. He has worked on over a dozen films for Bergman, including *Nattvardgästerna* (*Winter Light*, 1963), *Tystnaden* (*The Silence*, 1963), PERSONA (1966), *Viskingar och rop* (*Cries and Whispers*, 1973). His films for Bergman are marked by distinctive lighting techniques (he has often experimented with coated stock) and by a controlled observation of landscape. In a Bergman film he operates the camera himself, to maintain the closest possible contact with the director's instructions.

Nykvist has recently worked on international productions, including *Erste Liebe* (*First Love*, 1970), *One Day in the Life of Ivan Denisovich* (1971), *Siddartha*, and *The Dove* (both 1974). He has directed a few films, notably *Lianbron* (*The Vine Bridge*, 1965).

# O

OBERHAUSEN Film Festival was started in 1955 by Helmar Hoffman who had determined when a prisoner-of-war in Scotland to launch a project to bring nations together in friendship. Oberhausen quickly became the most distinguished festival in Europe for short films, until then neglected by festivals. Subjects were restricted to those of political or social commitment; because of the friendship theme, little was rejected, and over-permissive films and student excesses almost wrecked the event in 1969, but the festival has since slowly re-established its position.

Oberhausen is held annually in the spring; money prizes are awarded. There is also a festival of films about sport every autumn.

OBERON, MERLE (1911– ), US actress born in Tasmania, real name Estelle Merle O'Brien Thompson. Of a curiously Oriental beauty, she was discovered working in London as a film extra and dance hostess by Alexander KORDA, to whom she was married 1939–45. He gave her the role of Anne Boleyn in THE PRIVATE LIFE OF HENRY VIII (1933), which made her a star overnight. She consolidated her success with *The Scarlet Pimpernel* (1934), before working in Hollywood for Samuel GOLDWYN in *The Dark Angel* (1935) and two films directed by William WYLER, *These Three* (1936) and WUTHERING HEIGHTS (1939). In between she played Messalina in Korda's *I, Claudius*, abandoned after she was injured in a car crash, although remnants were salvaged and shown on television as *The Epic That Never Was* (1965). She accepted small parts in the wartime morale-boosters *The Lion Has Wings* (1939), *Stage Door Canteen*, and *Forever and a Day* (both 1943), meanwhile appearing in DUVIVIER's *Lydia* (1941), as George Sand in *A Song to Remember*, and in *The Lodger* (both 1944). Notable post-war appearances include Josephine opposite Marlon BRANDO's Napoleon in *Desirée* (1954) and the Duchess in *Hotel* (1967).

O'BRIEN, EDMOND (1915– ), US actor, played bullying HEAVIES with such bravura that a switch to roles of more intentional humour was inevitable. His portrayal of a gangster, Marty 'Fats' Murdock, in *The Girl Can't Help It* (Frank TASHLIN, 1957) brilliantly parodies one of Hollywood's stock characters, as do his 'old-timers' in THE MAN WHO SHOT LIBERTY VALANCE (1962) and THE WILD BUNCH (1969). For MANKIEWICZ he gave two remarkable performances, in JULIUS CAESAR (1953) and *The Barefoot Contessa* (1954). He co-directed *Shield for Murder* (1954, with Howard W. Koch) and directed *Mantrap* (1961).

O'BRIEN, PAT (1899– ), US actor whose long and distinguished film career began with THE FRONT PAGE (1931). He became a featured player in numerous films, specializing in tough, wisecracking, characters. He was frequently teamed with James CAGNEY, playing the warm-hearted cop, priest, or prison warder to Cagney's thug, typically in ANGELS WITH DIRTY FACES (1938). His heyday was the thirties and forties, but his later appearances included roles in Joseph LOSEY's *The Boy with Green Hair* (1948), John FORD's *The Last Hurrah* (1958), and Billy WILDER's SOME LIKE IT HOT (1959).

O'CONNOR, DONALD (1925– ), US actor. A talented CHILD STAR who could sing, dance, and clown, he appeared in the RODGERS and HART musical *On Your Toes* (1939). Essentially a supporting actor, although he played the lead in *Francis* (1950) and five more films in the series, he was especially effective as Gene KELLY's sidekick in SINGIN' IN THE RAIN (1952), particularly in the comic dance routine 'Make 'em Laugh'. He played opposite Ethel Merman in *Call Me Madam* (1953) and Mitzi GAYNOR in *There's No Business Like Show Business* (1954), but was disappointing in the title role of *The Buster Keaton Story* (1957). Latterly he has concentrated on cabaret and television.

*OCTOBER* see OKTIABR

*ODD MAN OUT*, GB, 1947. 2hr. *Dir* Carol Reed; *prod* Two Cities; *scr* F. L. Green, R. C. Sherriff, from the novel by Green; *ph* Robert Krasker; *mus* William Alwyn; *cast* James Mason (Johnny), Robert Newton (Lukey), Robert Beatty (Dennis), F. J. McCormick (Shell), Fay Compton (Rosie), W. G. Fay (Father Tom).

The last hours of a wounded Irish gunman on

the run were treated by Carol REED as an odyssey with mythic and metaphysical overtones. The film, with its expressionist lighting and camera angles, was hailed as an artistic breakthrough in British cinema. It retains much power, particularly in the quality of the acting.

**ODEON CINEMAS,** the largest cinema chain in Great Britain, was started in 1933 by Oscar Deutsch, a leading film renter and exhibitor, with UNITED ARTISTS as shareholders. The name Odeon, although probably not chosen on this basis, was interpreted by an inspired publicist as an acronym: 'Oscar Deutsch Entertains Our Nation'. The cinemas themselves were innovatory in being built to a standard design, with a single rectangular tower bearing the name Odeon in squared illuminated lettering on cream faience tiling; the Odeon in Leicester Square, London, followed the same shape but was finished in black granite. Local Odeons were built and run by independent consortia under concession from Deutsch, whose organization handled the programming for the owners.

In 1939, J. Arthur RANK became a member of the board and a number of cinemas owned by PARAMOUNT were acquired. When Deutsch died in 1941, Rank became chairman and within a year or two both the Odeon and GAUMONT circuits were absorbed into the RANK ORGANISATION.

**ODETS,** CLIFFORD (1906–63), US writer. His earlier work as a playwright for New York's Group Theater, especially *Waiting for Lefty* (1935), revealed strong proletarian sympathies. *Golden Boy* (1937), about a slum boy torn between his love of music and his success as a boxer, was adapted for the screen by Odets himself in 1939. Later plays include *The Big Knife* (1948; filmed to Odets's own script by Robert ALDRICH, 1955), about an actor's corruption by financial success in Hollywood, and *The Country Girl* (1950; filmed to his own script, 1954).

Odets also wrote a number of original screenplays, including MILESTONE's *The General Died at Dawn* (1936), a fable about the fight of an idealistic American (Gary COOPER) against oppression in China; *None But the Lonely Heart* (1944), which he also directed; *Deadline at Dawn* (1946); NEGULESCO's *Humoresque* (1947); THE SWEET SMELL OF SUCCESS (1957); and *The Story on Page One* (1960), a rather flat vehicle for Rita HAYWORTH which he directed himself.

*OEDIPUS REX* see EDIPO RE

**O'HARA,** MAUREEN (1920–    ), Irish-born actress, made her first film appearance in Britain

in *Jamaica Inn* (1939). She spent most of her career in Hollywood, at first with RKO (*The Hunchback of Notre Dame*, 1939; *A Bill of Divorcement*, 1940) then with TWENTIETH CENTURY-FOX, beginning with *How Green Was My Valley* (John FORD, 1941). A fiery redhead, she made a strikingly attractive leading lady in swashbucklers and Westerns, and became particularly identified as a Ford heroine, especially in *Rio Grande* (1950) and *The Quiet Man* (1952) which allowed her to display her Irish mannerisms and flamboyant temper.

*OHM KRÜGER* (*Uncle Krüger*), Germany, 1941. 2¼hr. *Dir* Hans Steinhoff; *prod* Emil Jannings for Tobis; *scr* H. Bratt, K. Henser from the novel by A. Krieger; *ph* Fritz Arno Wagner; *mus* Theo Mackeben; *cast* Emil Jannings (Ohm Krüger), Franz Schafheitlin (Kitchener), Ferdinand Marian (Cecil Rhodes), Gustav Gründgens (Chamberlain), Hedwig Wangel (Queen Victoria).

An account of the Boer War seen through the eyes of the Boer hero and Führer figure Ohm Krüger. British missionaries are shown inciting the natives to violence; Kitchener is shown as a heartless butcher and Cecil Rhodes as a cunning schemer; Queen Victoria is shown swigging whisky; and the British are given the credit for inventing concentration camps (with a commandant resembling Winston CHURCHILL).

The film gave JANNINGS one of his most impressive roles and contains some excellent photography. Unsurprisingly, it was selected as the best foreign film at the VENICE Festival. With HITLERJUNGE QUEX (1933), *Ohm Krüger* established Hans Steinhoff as a leading director of PROPAGANDA films in the Third Reich.

*OH! WHAT A LOVELY WAR*, GB, 1969. Panavision; 2½hr; Technicolor. *Dir* Richard Attenborough; *prod* Brian Duffy, Attenborough; *ph* Gerry Turpin; *des* Don Ashton; *mus* Alfred Ralston.

Richard ATTENBOROUGH's first film as director was an adaptation of Joan LITTLEWOOD's 1963 stage musical, itself developed from a radio programme by Charles Chilton. Like the stage version, it employed a deliberately non-naturalistic style to present a panoramic history of the First World War, built around popular songs of the time. The enormous cast was largely made up of major stars whose individual contributions were small. Star-studded and lavishly produced, the film lacked the sharpness of the original with its bitter humour. It was, however, a striking commercial success.

*OKTIABR* (*October*), USSR, 1928. 2¾hr. *Dir, scr, ed* S. M. Eisenstein, from the book *Ten Days*

*Ohm Krüger* (Hans Steinhoff, 1941)

*That Shook the World* by John Reed; *asst dir* Grigori Alexandrov; *prod* Sovkino; *ph* Edvard Tissé; *cast* Nikandrov (Lenin), Vladimir Popov (Kerensky), Boris Livanov (Tereshchenko), soldiers of the Red Army, sailors of the Red Navy, citizens and workers of Leningrad.

After the resounding success of BRONENOSETS POTEMKIN (1925), EISENSTEIN was an obvious choice to direct one of the films for the tenth anniversary of the 1917 revolution. (Other filmmakers instructed to make commemorative films were PUDOVKIN, Boris BARNET, and Esther SHUB.) *Oktiabr* was completed on schedule, but the official rejection of Trotsky, who had figured largely in the film, necessitated complete re-editing and it was not ready for the celebrations in December 1927. When it was shown early the following year, it met with a puzzled and largely unfavourable response. Eisenstein had used the large resources placed at his disposal to tremendous effect in his crowd scenes, notably the storming of the Winter Palace; but his objective view and particularly his use of visual metaphor—Kerensky's peacock-walk up the palace stairs, the dismemberment and re-assembly of the Tsar's statue, the lingering examination of a variety of religious images—baffled and affronted his audience. *Oktiabr* may now be seen as a

testing-piece for various ideas that preoccupied Eisenstein throughout his work, particularly the possibility of conveying abstract concepts through the juxtaposition of contrasting images—a conviction which is central to his theory of MONTAGE.

A shortened, re-edited version of *Oktiabr* was prepared for release in the US as *Ten Days That Shook the World*, but the introduction of sound prevented its showing. Modern prints of the original film have a sound-track using music specially composed by Dmitri SHOSTAKOVICH.

**OLCOTT,** SIDNEY (1873–1949), US director of Irish-Canadian parentage, was a stage actor before joining BIOGRAPH in 1904. Two years later he went to KALEM as a director and his work was an important factor in the company's early success. He directed the first BEN-HUR (1907), which starred W. S. HART as Messala, and the following year went on location to Florida where he shot *Florida Crackers*, an indictment of social conditions there. In 1911 he took his team to Ireland and made a number of films among which *Rory O'More* and *Ireland the Oppressed*, set in the Irish rebellion of 1790, expressed his continuing interest in social topics. He spent the next two years in Europe making fiction films and travelogues for American consumption. *From Manger to the Cross* (1912), filmed in the Holy Land, led to a breach between Olcott and Kalem; it was, however, very successful commercially, probably in part because of the controversy it aroused as to the suitability of depicting Christ on the screen, however reverently.

Olcott worked on his own for a time after leaving Kalem. In 1920 he re-appeared as a distinguished director of features with *Scratch My Back*, starring Will ROGERS. During the twenties he made some notable films, including VALENTINO's *Monsieur Beaucaire* (1924). In 1927 Olcott went to Britain to become production director for the newly-formed BRITISH LION; he retired soon after the introduction of sound.

*OLD AND NEW* see STAROYE I NOVOYE

**OLIVER, EDNA MAY** (1883–1942), US actress, real surname Nutter, whose first film was *Icebound* (1924). She came to the fore as a character actress in the thirties when she appeared in numerous films, including *Cimarron* (1931), *Ladies of the Jury* (1932), *Little Women* (1933), ALICE IN WONDERLAND (1934), and *A Tale of Two Cities* (1935). She was a notable Betsy Trotwood in DAVID COPPERFIELD (1934), and her Lady Catherine in *Pride and Prejudice* (1940) was a memorable performance, although an exaggeration of Jane Austen's conception. Her last appearance was as the grandmother in Julien DUVIVIER's *Lydia* (1941). She capitalized (often gloriously) on her unprepossessing countenance, and was invariably effective as formidable, caustic old ladies.

**OLIVER TWIST**, Charles Dickens's melodramatic tale (published 1837–8) of a London waif who falls among thieves but eventually lands on his feet, has often been filmed. Principal versions include one made by VITAGRAPH in 1909, with Elita Proctor; a PATHÉ adaptation of the following year; and in 1916 another American version with Marie Doro, Tully Marshall, Raymond Hatton, Hobart Bosworth, and James Neil.

In 1922, following his success in THE KID (1920), Jackie COOGAN played the title role in a Sol LESSER–FIRST NATIONAL production. Lon CHANEY was a more than usually sinister Fagin; Frank LLOYD and Harry Weil directed.

MONOGRAM's 1933 version, with a somewhat well-fed Dickie Moore had Irving Pichel and William BOYD in the cast. Though not entirely successful, it was re-issued in 1947.

The most outstanding adaptation to date is undoubtedly David LEAN's 1948 version for Cineguild. Beautifully photographed in black and white by Guy Green, and finely designed by John Bryan to evoke the mood of the book, the cast included John Howard Davies (Oliver), Robert NEWTON (Sykes), Alec GUINNESS (Fagin), Kay Walsh, and Francis L. Sullivan.

In 1968 an OSCAR-winning version in Technicolor and Panavision 70, based on Lionel Bart's stage musical *Oliver!*, was made with Carol REED as director. The cast included Mark Lester (Oliver), Ron Moody (Fagin), Shani Wallis, Oliver REED, Harry Secombe, Peggy Mount, and Hugh Griffith.

**OLIVIER, LAURENCE** (1907–  ), British actor and director, internationally famous as a Shakespearian actor and producer of the first rank, has also had a considerable career in the cinema since 1929. He worked in Hollywood 1931–2, returning to England as Gloria SWANSON's leading man in *Perfect Understanding* (1933). During the thirties he combined an active career in the theatre with several more film roles, but it was not until his return to Hollywood in 1939 that he began to have real success in the cinema. Three major roles, in WUTHERING HEIGHTS (1939), REBECCA, and *Pride and Prejudice* (both 1940), established him. Back in England, while serving with the Fleet Air Arm he acted in two British war films, *49th Parallel* (1942) and *The Demi-Paradise* (1943). In 1944 he produced, co-directed, and starred in HENRY V, and in 1948 directed HAMLET, again playing the leading role. In 1955 he directed and starred in *Richard III*, and it is these SHAKESPEARE adaptations which form Olivier's main contribution to cinema.

Other films which demonstrate his versatile acting range are THE BEGGAR'S OPERA (1953), *The Prince and the Showgirl* (1957), which he directed, co-starring with Marilyn MONROE, SPARTACUS (1960), *The Entertainer* (1960), and *Term of Trial* (1962); he also played cameo character roles in *The Magic Box* (1951), *Bunny Lake is Missing* (1965), and OH! WHAT A LOVELY WAR (1969).

As an actor of the great tradition, with a speaking voice of notable beauty and power, he is better suited to the theatre than cinema. The film versions of *Richard III*, OTHELLO (1965), and *The Three Sisters* (1970) are valuable records of some of his impressive stage performances.

Olivier, who was director of the National Theatre 1963–73, was knighted in 1947 and created a life peer in 1971. He was for twenty years married to Vivien LEIGH: although their acting partnership on the stage was close and very popular, they made only three films together, *Fire over England* (1937), *Twenty-One Days* (1940), and *Lady Hamilton* (1941). He is now married to the stage actress Joan Plowright.

OLMI, ERMANNO (1931–   ), Italian director, worked from 1955 for the film section at Edisonvolta and in the next eight years made about forty documentaries which gave an intelligent and frank picture of the workers in a big commercial plant. In 1959 he persuaded the company to finance his first feature, *Il tempo si è termato* (*Time Stood Still*), a psychological examination of two men isolated on a mountain side in winter, guarding a dam. The older protagonist was the real guardian of the dam and the young man was a member of the Edison staff. The film won prizes at VENICE in 1959; IL POSTO (1961) established Olmi as a humane and perceptive observer of white-collar workers.

Olmi was one of a number of young writers and technicians who came together in Milan to make independent, low-budget films. He produced, wrote, directed, and on occasion photographed his own work while helping to run the group '22 Dicembre', which among other films backed De Bosio's *Il terrorista* (1962) and Olmi's I FIDANZATI (1963). He first used professional actors (Rod STEIGER and Adolpho Celi) in *E venne un uomo* (*A Man Called John*, 1965), about Pope John XXIII. More satisfactory was UN CERTO GIORNO (*One Fine Day*, 1968), his second colour feature, beautifully photographed by his frequent collaborator Lamberto Caimi.

The film again showed Olmi's preoccupation with people earning their living and the way their work affects their lives: his films are distinguished by a sense of human dignity and integrity, reminiscent of the best examples of NEO-REALISM.

Olmi has made several short films for television and his full-length television features, *I recuperanti* (*The Scavengers*, 1969), *Durante l'estate* (*During One Summer*, 1971), and *La circostanza* (*The Circumstance*, 1974), have had theatrical release.

***OLVIDADOS, Los*** (*The Young and the Damned*), Mexico, 1950. 1½hr. *Dir* Luis Buñuel; *prod* Ultramar Films; *scr* Buñuel, Luis Alcoriza; *ph* Gabriel Figueroa; *cast* Alfonso Mejía (Pedro), Roberto Cobo (Jaibo), Estela Inda (Pedro's mother), Miguel Inclán (the blind man).

Within a framework of social comment, on juvenile delinquency in city slums, BUÑUEL imbues the story of Pedro's destruction by Jaibo with his characteristic private mythology and dark humour. FIGUEROA's photography was appropriately plain and detached in its observation of Mexico City, surrealist and expressionist in the dream sequences, and though the film's objective cruelty was horrifying at the time, *Los Olvidados* brought Buñuel back to the attention

*Los Olvidados* (Luis Buñuel, 1950)

of world audiences as one of cinema's great individualists. It won the first prize for direction at CANNES, 1951.

**OLYMPIA**, Germany, 1938. 3½hr. *Dir* Leni Riefenstahl; *prod* Tobis; *ph* Hans Ertl, Walther Freutz, Guzz Lantscher, Kurt Neubert, Hans Scheib; *mus* Herbert Windt.

A record of the Olympic Games held in Berlin in 1936, made in two parts—*Fest der Völker* (Festival of the Nations) and *Fest der Schönheit* (Festival of Beauty). The first part opens in ancient Greece, glorifying both the architecture and the beauty of the human form. This is followed by the carrying of the Olympic flame to Berlin and the parade before Hitler (parts of which are cut in some prints). The rest is devoted to track and field events. The second part starts with sequences in the Olympic village, then covers the rest of the games.

English, French, and German versions were made; owing to outside interference the order of the sporting events is different in each one. On completion, after two years' editing, the film was accepted as the official film of the Olympic Committee.

RIEFENSTAHL captured both the beauty and the exhilaration of the occasion. The grace of the high divers and figures photographed against the sunlight is contrasted with quivering flags and torches which seem to be caught up in the excitement. Her close-ups of athletes' faces, which make them look like statues, and above all her sense of form and balance give the film grandeur and magnificence. The post-synchronized soundtrack also plays an important part.

Riefenstahl claims that the film is apolitical, but a strong Nazi bias is apparent in its celebration of sport as a heroic, superhuman feat and in its sections portraying Hitler and his entourage. It is nevertheless a monumental study in athletics.

**ONDRA**, ANNY (1903– ), real name Ondraková, Polish-born actress who worked mainly in Czechoslovak and German films. Trained for the theatre, she began acting in films in 1919, and became particularly associated with the actor-director Karel Lamač, whom she married. Lamač starred her in *Gilly v Praze* (1920), which began her career as one of the brightest stars of Central European cinema in the twenties, specializing in stylish comedy. She and Lamač, with the scriptwriter Václav Wassermann and cameraman Otto HELLER became known as the 'big four' of Czech silent cinema, working in Prague, Berlin, and Vienna. In some thirty silent films she also worked for other directors, including Rovensky and Kolar, and in dramatic and romantic roles, but her best work

was for Lamač. In 1929 she worked in France and Britain, starring in BLACKMAIL (1929) for HITCHCOCK. In 1930 she and Lamač founded their own company, most of their sound films being produced in Germany. Comedies and romances continued, but they specialized in operettas during the thirties. Anny Ondra stayed in Germany during the war, and acted in a few films.

**ONDŘIČEK**, MIROSLAV (1934– ), Czech cameraman, followed up his childhood enthusiasm for film by becoming a technician in a laboratory and then joining the training school at the BARRANDOV studio. In 1958 he worked as assistant cameraman on a film on which Ivan PASSER was assistant director, and through him met Miloš FORMAN, joining him on the work which led to Forman's first film *Konkurs* (1963). He became one of the favourite cameramen for the directors of the new wave, photographing *Démanty noci* (*Diamonds of the Night*, 1964) and *Mučednici lásky* (*Martyrs of Love*, 1967) for NĚMEC, and INTIMNÍ OSVĚTLENÍ (*Intimate Lighting*, 1966) for Passer. His closest association remained that with Forman, most of whose subsequent films he photographed. In 1966, although he was unable to speak English, Lindsay ANDERSON invited him to England to make *The White Bus* (1967), and the collaboration was so successful that Anderson used him for IF . . . (1968). Ondřiček left Czechoslovakia with Forman to make *Taking Off* (1971) in the US, and has since continued to work abroad.

**ONE A.M.**, US, 1916. 20 min. *Dir, scr* Charles Chaplin; *prod* Mutual; *ph* Rollie Totheroh, William C. Foster; *cast* Charlie Chaplin, Albert Austin.

CHAPLIN'S fourth film for MUTUAL is a virtuoso performance in which he is alone on the screen for almost the whole two reels. In the early hours of the morning after the night before, a drunkard, in elegant evening dress, tries to get into his friend's house without a key and to climb a double flight of stairs to bed. Chaplin's battles with inanimate objects—especially the folding wall bed (the Murphy bed) which he finally reaches—are here almost in the style of Buster KEATON.

**ONE-EYED JACKS**, US, 1960. VistaVision; 2¼hr; Technicolor. *Dir* Marlon Brando; *prod* Paramount; *scr* Guy Trosper, Calder Willingham, from the novel, *The Authentic Death of Hendry Jones*, by Charles Neider; *ph* Charles Lang Jr; *cast* Marlon Brando (Rio), Karl Malden (Dad Longworth), Pina Pellicer (Louisa), Katy Jurado (Maria), Ben Johnson (Bob Amory), Slim Pickens (Lon), Larry Duran (Modesto), Sam Gilman (Harvey).

Originally to have been made by Stanley KUBRICK, and containing a sequence allegedly directed by Sam PECKINPAH, *One-Eyed Jacks* was harshly judged by critics, perhaps taken aback by Marlon BRANDO's choosing a Western for his début as director. None the less, the classic story of revenge, the epigrammatic dialogue, the excellence of the cast, the strikingly unusual coastal landscape, superbly photographed by Charles LANG Jr, and the recurrent explosions of violence, combine to make it an unusual but excellent representative of the genre. Brando's only venture behind the camera was conducted with so large a degree of improvisation that the ending of the film was changed by popular ballot among the unit.

*ONE FINE DAY* see CERTO GIORNO, UN

*ON THE BOWERY*, US, 1957. 1hr. *Dir, prod* Lionel Rogosin, assisted by Mark Sufrin and Richard Bagley; *ph* Bagley; *ed* Carl Lerner; *mus* Charles Mill.

*On the Bowery* was, for its time, a starkly realistic portrayal of mental and physical degradation in the heart of an affluent city. ROGOSIN, using a semi-fictional story acted by real tramps and drunks and contrasted with the skyscrapers of Wall Street and Manhattan, tried to investigate the causes of social alienation. The film, shot under the difficult conditions that accompanied all location filming before the development of light-weight 16MM equipment, is awkward and somewhat naïve in comparison with the DIRECT CINEMA films it anticipated; but it stands as a courageous attempt to break through the limitations of the traditional documentary.

*ON THE TOWN*, US, 1949. Technicolor; 1¼hr. *Dir* Gene Kelly, Stanley Donen; *prod* Arthur Freed for MGM; *scr, lyr* Adolph Green, Betty Comden, from their musical play; *ph* Harold Rosson; *mus* Leonard Bernstein, Roger Edens; *cast* Gene Kelly (Gabey), Frank Sinatra (Chip), Betty Garrett (Brunhilde Esterhazy), Jules Munshin (Ozzie), Vera-Ellen (Ivy), Ann Miller (Claire).

*On the Town* was KELLY and DONEN's first film with full directing credit, and from the opening number, 'New York, New York', their inventive techniques created a funny, original, and fluently executed musical using contemporary city surroundings. All the numbers fitted well into the story of three sailors on twenty-four hours' leave in New York, and equal weight was given to all the cast, aided by COMDEN and Green's witty script. Memorable numbers included Betty Garrett's forthright 'Come Up To My Place' and the riotous 'Prehistoric Man' led

by Ann Miller, although little else of Leonard BERNSTEIN's score for the successful stage musical (in turn derived from his ballet *Fancy Free*) was retained.

*ON THE WATERFRONT*, US, 1954. 1¾hr. *Dir* Elia Kazan; *prod* Sam Spiegel; *scr* Budd Schulberg; *ph* Boris Kaufman; *ed* Arthur E. (Gene) Milford; *mus* Leonard Bernstein; *cast* Marlon Brando (Terry Malloy), Eva Marie Saint (Edie Doyle), Karl Malden (Father Barry), Lee J. Cobb (Johnny Friendly), Rod Steiger (Charley Malloy).

Shot on location in New York, from a script by Budd SCHULBERG based on a series of Pulitzer Prize-winning articles by Malcolm Johnson about the work of a Jesuit priest, Father Corridan, *On the Waterfront* shows KAZAN's technical mastery in dealing with realistic settings and individual life-styles and conflicts. The naturalistic, improvisatory style of acting which Kazan brought into the cinema from his work with the Group Theater and the ACTORS' STUDIO is here used to remarkable effect, particularly in the performances of Karl MALDEN as a forthright priest and Rod STEIGER as a corrupt labour leader; and Marlon BRANDO's inarticulate, deeply-felt characterization dominates the film. The quality of Boris KAUFMAN's photography enhances the grim mood.

An introductory title extols the virtues of American democracy, and claims that the story will show how corruption can be defeated by constitutional means: but the controlling source of corruption within the longshoremen's trade union is never exposed, and the drama in fact evolves from the individual characterizations.

Schulberg later expanded his script and published it in the form of a novel.

**OPERA FILM.** Films bearing the titles of famous operas appeared frequently on the silent screen. Many were dramatic adaptations of the original novels or plays on which operas had been based, but both cinema musicians and audiences benefited from the availability of suitable musical accompaniments in the opera score. CARMEN was the most frequently filmed opera subject, giving a start to the film career of Geraldine Farrar, the American opera star, in 1915 and providing Pola NEGRI with one of her best roles in LUBITSCH's German film of 1918 (released in the US as *Gypsy Love*). A less obvious subject was *The Dumb Girl of Portici*, the basis of Auber's opera known as *Masaniello* but more correctly called *La Muette de Portici*, filmed by UNIVERSAL in 1916 starring Anna Pavlova (see also BALLET FILM). *La Bohème* (1926), starring Lillian GISH, John GILBERT, and Renée Adorée, was based on Henri Murger's novel rather than Puccini's opera, like a German version of the same year starring Wilhelm DIETERLE.

Attempts at translating opera to silent film even included Wagner, with an American version of *The Flying Dutchman* (1923) and in one of a series of British shorts called 'Music Masters' (1925): this issue claimed to deal with Wagner's life and to include 'scenes from the operas'—in one reel. Another British series, of twelve two-reelers, appeared in 1927 under the title 'Cameo Operas'. These condensed opera stories were designed for live vocal participation: as a trade journal commented, 'Much will depend on the singers and their ability to fit in with particular scenes'.

Normally, however, opera or quasi-opera on the silent screen was voiceless, even the prestigious Austrian version of *Der Rosenkavalier* (Robert WIENE, 1926), which had the active participation of both composer, Richard Strauss, and librettist, Hugo von Hofmannsthal. The film was designed as 'a pictorial accompaniment to a special arrangement of the opera': Strauss composed a new march especially for the film and various story changes were made. In the last act, instead of the inn scene, a fête complete with dominoes, masks, and dancers, was introduced; battle scenes were dragged in, and a new ending romantically reconciled the Marschallin with her husband, home from the wars.

With the introduction of sound, famous opera singers were used in one-reelers designed to show off the new wonder. Fox-Movietone presented Bonelli and Warner-Vitaphone had both Gigli and Martinelli as well as a performance of the quartet from *Rigoletto* sung by Marion Talley, Jeanne Gordon, Gigli, and Giuseppe De Luca. An aria sung by Tito Schipa was included by RCA in a demonstration of their Photophone VARIABLE AREA recording system which challenged the prevailing VARIABLE DENSITY system.

But the advent of sound did little to stimulate the production of opera films in America. Hollywood's attitude was ambivalent: opera was not commercially viable, yet it represented prestige and cultural tone. A compromise policy was to turn distinguished singers, mainly associated with the Metropolitan Opera, into film stars. Grace MOORE was the first, making her film début in *A Lady's Morals* (1930), based on the life of Jenny Lind. She later went to France to appear opposite the tenor Georges Thill in Abel GANCE's film version of Charpentier's *Louise* (1938). Gladys Swarthout, another Metropolitan star, also appeared in a number of Hollywood films in the thirties and other established singers who followed a subsidiary Hollywood career later included Lauritz Melchior and Ezio Pinza. There was no genuinely operatic Hollywood film

until *Carmen* was revived in the all-black but musically authentic *Carmen Jones* (Otto PREMINGER, 1954).

In Britain, apart from a version of *Pagliacci* (1937), starring Richard TAUBER, there was little of note until Michael POWELL and Emeric PRESSBURGER's version of Offenbach's *The Tales of Hoffman* (1951), an ambitious failure. Pre-war Germany concentrated on operetta; an exception was Max OPHULS' *Die verkaufte Braut* (1932), from Smetana's *The Bartered Bride*.

Italy has, predictably, a strong opera film tradition. Carmine Gallone specialized in directing opera adaptations and his work in the thirties included several films with Gigli and Maria Cebotari. He also directed films starring Tito Gobbi (*Rigoletto*, 1946; *La forza del destino*, 1948) and an interesting Italian–Japanese co-production of *Madama Butterfly* (1955) photographed in Technicolor by Claude RENOIR. Equally unsurprisingly, films about Verdi have been made in Italy, including Gallone's *Giuseppe Verdi* (1938), with Gigli and Cebotari, and *Giuseppe Verdi* (Raffaello Matarazzo, 1954), with Mario Del Monaco. There was a spectacular but silly *Aïda* (1953), co-starring Sophia LOREN in black-face as Aïda and Lois Maxwell as Amneris, dubbed respectively by Renata Tebaldi and Ebe Stignani.

DUBBING the voices of distinguished singers on to roles played by actors became common in the fifties. Some unusual subjects received this treatment, including a German film of Nicolai's *Die lustige Weibe von Windsor* (*The Merry Wives of Windsor*, 1953) with the Wagnerian soprano Marthe Mödl among the dubbed singers, and from Russia Rimsky-Korsakov's *Sadko* (1952). Other Russian productions included excerpts from Glinka's *Ivan Susanin* in *Concert of Stars* (1952), *Kompozitor Glinka* (1952), a biographical film, directed by Grigori ALEXANDROV, a film about the composition and production of Mussorgsky's *Boris Godunov* (1955), and Tchaikovsky's *Eugene Onegin* (1958), beautifully photographed in delicate pastel colours. An exotic rarity was a Chinese opera film, *Shan-Po and Ying-Tai* (1953).

As well as genuine opera, older-style biographical films continued. *The Great Caruso* (1951) rocketed Mario LANZA to stardom; Kathryn Grayson played Grace Moore in *So This is Love* (1953); an Austrian film *Du bist die Welt für mich* (*The Richard Tauber Story*, 1953) starred the tenor Rudolph Schock, not yet at the height of his fame.

By the late fifties, two approaches to film opera had emerged, attempts to develop a fully cinematic treatment contrasting with direct records of stage productions. Integral performances became customary, but 'doctored' versions still appeared: in *Figaro, il barbiere di Siviglia* (1956), Rossini's score was cut and the recitatives replaced by spoken dialogue; Tito Gobbi (Figaro) and Giulio Neri (Don Basilio) both acted and sang their roles, but Irene Genna (Rosina) was dubbed by Giulietta Simionato. Transcriptions of stage productions became the speciality of Paul CZINNER, who used a multiple-camera technique to record ballet productions as well as opera (*Don Giovanni*, 1955; *Der Rosenkavalier*, 1961).

Opera film has rarely overcome two main problems. The poor quality of the sound recording, and an apparently inevitable sound-track hiss, falls far short of the standards of modern stereophonic gramophone records. The essentially stylized quality of operatic convention suffers from the lack of both 'live' presence and the distancing effect of theatre productions: frequent objections to 'close-ups of singers' tonsils' are not without justification. The Russian film of Shostakovich's *Katerina Ismailova* (1966) tackled these problems with considerable success; but was understandably less popular than yet another *Carmen* (1967) conducted by Herbert von Karajan. In spite of the difficulties of the form there appears to be a growing audience for filmed opera; possibly future developments will lie with works such as Britten's *Owen Wingrave* (1970), conceived specifically for television but using cinematic techniques.

**OPHULS,** MARCEL (1927–  ), French director, real name Oppenheimer, born in Germany, left for France with his parents in 1933 then lived in the US 1941–9, returning to France in 1950. After working as an assistant to John HUSTON, Anatole LITVAK, Julien DUVIVIER, and his father Max OPHULS (on LOLA MONTÈS, 1955), he became a television director in Germany, France, and Switzerland. During this time he also made two features for the cinema, *Peau de banane* (1963) and *Feu à volonté* (1964). His television documentary LE CHAGRIN ET LA PITIÉ (1969) created a considerable stir, both in France and abroad, by its frank yet humane handling of the tender subject of French reaction to the German occupation. His documentary on the troubles in Ulster, *A Sense of Loss* (1973), has received only limited exhibition.

**OPHULS,** MAX (1902–57), German-born director, real name Oppenheimer, began his career in the German theatre, first as an actor and then as a successful director. He left Germany in the early thirties, having already directed five films including *Die verkaufte Braut* (1932), a delightful version of Smetana's *The Bartered Bride*, and LIEBELEI (1932), adapted from Schnitzler's play; Ophuls' softening of this ironic love story

typified his approach throughout his career. He spent eight years in France, going to Italy to direct *La signora di tutti* (1934), a film which bore the hallmarks of his style—extensive use of music, long, elaborate takes with flowing camera movements, extended flashbacks. In 1941 he went to America, where he later made some of his best films, in particular LETTER FROM AN UNKNOWN WOMAN (1948), *Caught* (1949), which was more American in flavour, and *The Reckless Moment* (1949), a masterly story of blackmail with Joan BENNETT and James MASON.

Returning to Paris in 1949 for an abortive project with Mason and GARBO, Ophuls instead made LA RONDE (1950), an evocative, effective film which was also a commercial success. *Le Plaisir* (1952) was based on three stories by Maupassant. *Madame de . . .* (1953) marked a return to high romance and contained a fine performance by Danielle DARRIEUX in the title role. His last film, LOLA MONTÈS (1955), was probably his finest, but suffered for many years from being shown in a heavily cut version.

Ophuls' autobiography *Spiel im Dasein: eine Rückblende* (Stuttgart) was published two years after his death.

**OPTICAL PRINTING,** a method of printing used to introduce EFFECTS into a film, or to enlarge or reduce from one gauge to another (see REDUCTION PRINT). Ordinary prints for showing in cinemas are made by moving the negative continuously past a light aperture in contact with the raw stock; but optical printing is performed intermittently, one frame at a time, with the picture actually projected through an optical system and photographed by a camera. This procedure, sometimes called 'step printing', permits each frame to be individually controlled and allows more than one exposure on each frame of raw stock. A shot can be faded out by progressively reducing the printing light; distorted by introducing irregular glasses into the optical path; or selectively printed by blocking out portions of the frame with a travelling MATTE. Such optical printing usually produces not a print but a DUPE NEGATIVE, incorporating the effects, which can be intercut with the negatives of ordinary shots in the film.

Optical printing is currently in the process of being supplanted for many purposes by electronic video processing. Complex effects are produced on videotape by television methods and transferred to film by advanced techniques of telerecording. (See FINE-GRAIN PRINT, STRETCHING.)

**OPTICAL SOUND,** the type of sound-track most commonly used for prints carrying both picture and sound on the same film. The optical track is recorded along the edge of the film by making the sound signal vary the width of an illuminated slit as the film passes it (see SOUND CAMERA). The light exposes the negative film in the pattern of a jagged stripe which can be printed to a positive. When the print is run past another illuminated slit in a projector, the track varies the amount of light passing through the film; this is picked up by a photocell, reproducing the original sound signal. Such tracks are called VARIABLE AREA tracks; another type, the VARIABLE DENSITY track, is now rarely used. 'Phonofilms', invented by Lee DeForest in 1922, were basically the system adopted by the industry.

Optical sound recording first made possible the MARRIED PRINT, where synchronization with the picture could not be lost, and the earlier system of reproduction from a separate disc was abandoned. Independent EDITING and MIXING of sound during production also became practical. Because the optical track can be printed photographically, in the same way and at the same time as the picture, it is economical and is still in worldwide use in the 35mm and 16mm gauges. However magnetic sound is now used for original recordings, during production, on 8mm films, and even on larger gauges when better quality is required (see STRIPED PRINT). Optical sound prints cannot equal the high fidelity of modern disc recordings, but they are usually considered satisfactory in a medium dominated by the picture.

**ORDET** (*The Word*), Denmark, 1955. 2hr. *Dir*, *scr* Carl Dreyer, from the play by Kaj Munk; *prod* Palladium Film; *ph* Henning Bendtsen; *des* Erik Aaes; *mus* Poul Schierbeck; *cast* Henrik Malberg (Morten Borgen), Emil Hass Christensen (Mikkel), Preben Lerdorff Rye (Johannes), Cay Kristiansen (Anders), Birgitte Federspiel (Inger), Ejner Federspiel (Peter Skraedder).

In the second film version of Munk's play (the first was by Gustaf MOLANDER in 1943), DREYER reshaped the narrative considerably, removing Johannes as the central focus, and concentrating instead on the figure of Inger. A study of spiritual faith and love, it tells of the death of Inger in childbirth and her resurrection, a miracle that is seen as the result of human love. The measured pace of the film and Dreyer's rejection of conventional mobility in camera handling and editing have led to accusations of theatricality; but his concentrated examination of human emotion is deeply moving. Munk's widow helped plan the location shooting in his home village.

**ORFEU NEGRO**, France/Italy, 1958. Eastman Color; 1¾hr. *Dir* Marcel Camus; *prod* Dispatfilm Paris/Gemma Cinematografica; *scr*

Jacques Viot; *ph* Jean Bourgoin; *mus* Antonio Carlos Jobim, Luis Bonfa; *cast* Brenno Melio (Orpheus), Marpessa Dawn (Eurydice), Ademar Da Sylva (Death), Lourdes De Oliveira (Mira), Lea Garcia (Serafina).

A modern version of the story of Orpheus and Eurydice, set in Rio de Janeiro at Carnival time, with the hero a black tram driver. The tragic myth is movingly re-enacted in the colourful and exciting atmosphere of the festival, and much of the film's success was due to the vivid scenes of spectacle captured by CAMUS.

**ORLACS HÄNDE** (*Hands of Orlac*), Austria, 1925. 1½hr. *Dir* Robert Wiene; *prod* Pan Film; *scr* Ludwig Nerz, from the novel by Maurice Renard; *ph* Günther Krampf, Hans Andreschin; *des* Stefan Wessely; *cast* Conrad Veidt (Orlac), Alexandra Sorina (his wife).

A pianist loses his hands in a railway accident. New hands are successfully grafted but he becomes obsessed by the idea that they belonged to a murderer. This delusion changes his character and he becomes afraid of succumbing to their evil influence. He finally discovers that they were the hands of an innocent person.

Shadowy streets, dimly-lit inns, strange characters, and other Expressionist elements pervade the film but it never rises above the level of melodrama. There is nevertheless some cleverly contrasted lighting and VEIDT's powerful performance provides moments of great intensity.

The remake, *Mad Love* (1935, *Hands of Orlac* in GB) introduced Peter LORRE to Hollywood as a psychopathic doctor who performs the grafting: here the hands are indeed those of a murderer. This was one of Karl FREUND's occasional films as director and it maintains the Expressionist style of the earlier version. Other versions are *Hands of a Stranger* (US, 1960), directed by Newton Abbot, and *Les Mains d'Orlac* (France/ GB, 1960), directed by Edmond Gréville and starring Mel FERRER.

**ORPHÉE**, France, 1950. 2hr. *Dir*, *scr* Jean Cocteau; *prod* André Paulvé-Films du Palais Royal; *ph* Nicolas Hayer; *des* D'Eaubonne; *mus* Georges Auric; *cast* Jean Marais (Orphée), François Périer (Heurtebise), Maria Casarès (the Princess), Edouard Dermithe (Cégeste), Marie Déa (Eurydice).

*Orphée*, a reworking of COCTEAU's one-act play written in 1925, forms the central pillar of the director's Orphic trilogy completed by LE SANG D'UN POÈTE (1930) and LE TESTAMENT D'ORPHÉE (1960). In this modern account of the Orpheus myth Orphée is a celebrated poet, his 'death' is represented by a mysterious Princess who commands as her lethal agents two black-clad motor cyclists, while the Bacchantes have been transformed into a group of militant feminists.

The film deals with several of the themes recurrent throughout Cocteau's work; narcissism, a Romantic obsession with death, and, in particular, the portrayal of the poet as one who is torn between the 'real' world and that of the spirit and imagination. Thus when Orphée enters the Zone (the Underworld) it is as much in pursuit of the Princess as to reclaim Eurydice.

Cocteau went to considerable trouble to achieve the trick effects he required, using negative images and reversed slow motion and even filling a tank with mercury in order to film Orphée's hand passing into a mirror. A strikingly beautiful film, *Orphée* was immediately acclaimed as a masterpiece, winning the International Grand Prix at the VENICE Festival.

**ORTHOCHROMATIC FILM,** black-and-white film STOCK which is sensitive only to blue and green light, and records no red at all. For this reason its tonal rendering of coloured objects appears incorrect to the eye, and it has long been superseded by the modern PANCHROMATIC negative film.

The name orthochromatic (from Greek, meaning 'correct colour') suggests that it was an improvement over the stocks sensitive only to blue that had been used in the earliest films. Red still photographed as black, but faces, which suffered most, could be made up to look normal. Nevertheless the use of ortho film stock accounts for much of the 'soot and whitewash' appearance of silent films up to about 1926. It also accounts for the overall sharpness of the pictures: ortho was relatively 'fast' (sensitive to light) and cameramen could use small lens apertures which kept both close and distant objects in focus (see DEPTH OF FIELD, DEEP FOCUS). This advantage was lost when the subtler, but slower, panchromatic stocks were introduced.

**ORWOCOLOR,** East German colour REVERSAL film evolved from AGFACOLOR and manufactured at the Wolfen factory taken over from Agfa at the end of the Second World War. The name is derived from Original Wolfen. (See COLOUR.)

**OSBORNE, JOHN** (1929–   ), British playwright whose first successful stage play, *Look Back in Anger* (1956), made a very considerable impact on the English theatre. Osborne's play provided a focus for the emerging voice of protest, that of the 'Angry Young Men' who in the late fifties injected into British theatre, literature, and eventually cinema a vigorous new note of social realism (see GREAT BRITAIN). Tony RICHARDSON, associated with Osborne at the Royal Court Theatre, made LOOK BACK IN ANGER (1959) as his first feature film, and WOODFALL FILMS, founded by Richardson and Osborne in 1958, was influential in the development of the new school in British cinema. Osborne's *The Entertainer* (1957) was filmed by Richardson in 1960 and his *Inadmissible Evidence* (1964) was filmed in 1968 by Anthony Page who had directed the original stage production. Osborne wrote the scripts for the filmed versions of his plays and for TOM JONES (1963).

**OSCAR** (Academy Award). Prize in the form of a gold statuette, awarded annually by the American ACADEMY OF MOTION PICTURE ARTS AND SCIENCES. The statuette was executed by George Stanley from rough sketches made by Cedric GIBBONS: there are varied and conflicting accounts of how its popular name gained currency, of which the best-known is that the statuette reminded Margaret Herrick, then librarian at AMPAS and later its Executive Director, of her uncle Oscar.

Eleven awards for different categories were made in the first year (1929) for achievement in 1927–8. The categories vary from year to year, and may include direction, acting, story and screenplay, art direction, music, and various technical aspects of film-making. Nominations are made by members of AMPAS, all of whom may vote on the final list, and to be nominated for an Oscar is second only in prestige to actually receiving an award. The award is restricted to American films, but there is an annual award for the best foreign film.

BEN-HUR (1959), with eleven awards, holds the record number of Oscars so far presented to one film.

**OSHIMA, NAGISA** (1932–   ), Japanese director, graduated in law from Kyoto University where he specialized in political history, particularly the history of the Russian Revolution. In 1955 he joined Shochiku as an assistant director; he also wrote scripts and edited a critical review. His first film as director was *Ai to Kibo no Machi* (*A Town of Love and Hope*, 1959). *Nihon no Yoru to Kiri* (*Night and Fog in Japan*, 1960) was withdrawn by the producers after a few showings, ostensibly because it was uncommercial, more probably because its handling of Japanese student unrest at the time of the security treaty between Japan and the US was considered politically extreme. Oshima left Shochiku and became an independent director with *Amakusa Shiro Tokisada* (*The Rebel*, 1962). He formed his own production company, Sozosha, and made *Etsuraku* (*The Pleasures of the Flesh*, 1965). Since then he has regularly made two or three films a year: among the few to reach the West are *Koshikei* (*Death by Hanging*, 1968),

*O slavnosti a hostech* (Jan Němec, 1966)

*Shinjuku Dorobo Nikki* (*Diary of a Shinjuku Thief*, 1968), *Shonen* (*Boy*, 1969), and *Gishiki* (*The Ceremony*, 1971). Like GODARD, Oshima rejects conventional forms of film narrative, using the medium to present his own political analysis of established Japanese values.

**O SLAVNOSTI A HOSTECH** (*The Party and the Guests*), Czechoslovakia, 1966. 1¼hr. *Dir* Jan Němec; *scr* Němec, Ester Krumbachová; *ph* Jaromír Sofr; *ed* Miroslav Hájek; *mus* Karel Mares; *cast* Ivan Vyskocil (the Host), Jan Klusák (Rudolf, the Host's Adoptive Son), Jiří Němec (Josef, the Yesman), Zdenka Skvorecká (Eva, the Coquette), Helena Pejsková (Marta, the Sexy Girl), Karel Mares (the Protesting Guest), Jana Pracharová (the Hare-brained Woman), Evald Schorm (the Guest who Refused to be Happy).

The party of the title takes place in a beautiful forest glade, with the Host constantly reassuring the guests that his only wish is that they should be happy. One by one, as the feast proceeds, they assure him that they are indeed so. Only one man refuses to be happy, and when he silently leaves he is pursued by the Host's Adoptive Son and all the other guests with tracker dogs.

Made during NĚMEC's brief association with Ester KRUMBACHOVÁ, the film is a biting political allegory that merges Němec's strong hatred of oppression with Krumbachová's elegant venomousness. Most of the characters are played by their friends, so that the film to an extent represents a communal endeavour by Prague's artists and intellectuals. Krumbachová's influence is particularly felt in the strongly pictorial conception, with many scenes designed from well-known paintings and press photographs. Such references, together with the allegorical nature of the film, make it difficult even for Czech audiences. The authorities, however, had no difficulty in recognizing the implicit criticism: for two years the film remained unreleased and the target for bitter attacks, ostensibly on grounds of being incomprehensible. Němec fought to have it submitted for VENICE in the autumn of 1967, but without success. Finally, it was sent to CANNES in 1968, but was unhappily a victim of the 'events' of that year's festival.

**OSSESSIONE**, Italy, 1942. 2½hr. *Dir* Luchino Visconti; *prod* ICI Rome; *scr* A. Pietrangeli, G. Puccini, G. De Santis, Visconti, from the novel *The Postman Always Rings Twice* by James M. Cain; *ph* Aldo Tonti, Domenico Scala; *des* Gino

Franzi; *mus* Giuseppe Rosati; *cast* Massimo Girotti (Gino), Clara Calamai (Giovanna), Juan De Landa (her husband), Elio Marcuzzo (Lo Spagnolo).

*Ossessione* retains only the outline of the original novel: in particular, the dramatic balance is altered by the introduction of a new character, Lo Spagnolo, whose presence after the two lovers have murdered the woman's husband further disrupts their already guilt-ridden relationship.

The subject was suggested to VISCONTI by RENOIR, and Visconti's sympathy for American realistic literature and for Renoir's methods of working with which he had been involved, led him to use actual settings and to develop characters at a level of society outside the romantic conventions of the current WHITE TELEPHONE films. PIETRANGELI coined the term NEO-REALISM to describe the film, although the working out of a well-defined plot, the use of professional actors, and Visconti's visual formality make it less strictly neo-realist than its successors.

The finished film was unacceptable to the censors, and it was reduced to under half its length before limited release in Italy; but private screenings of the complete film stimulated young Italian film-makers, frustrated by the restrictions of Fascist censorship, to work along similar lines. As it was wartime, Visconti was unable to buy the rights from America where the novel was filmed as THE POSTMAN ALWAYS RINGS TWICE (1946), and *Ossessione* has thus remained in limited circulation.

*OSTATNI ETAP* (*The Last Stage*), Poland, 1948. 2hr. *Dir* Wanda Jakubowska; *prod* Film Polski; *scr* Jakubowska, Gerda Schneider; *ph* Borys Monastyrski; *ed* R. Pstrokońska; *cast* Wanda Bartówna (Helena), Huguette Faget (Michèle), Barbara Drapińska (Marta).

An account of Oswiecim (Auschwitz) concentration camp, filmed in the women's section of the actual camp, in which both JAKUBOWSKA and Schneider had been prisoners, made under the auspices of the United Nations Organization with an international cast. The 'last stage' is the final journey—to gas chambers and crematoria.

The needs of plot and 'human interest' remove this film from the stark immediacy of the original newsreels (or RESNAIS's NUIT ET BROUILLARD, 1955), but physical closeness in time, place, and personal experience guarantees a degree of realism and feeling inevitably lost to later directors who have portrayed concentration camps, such as MUNK and WAJDA. The film won the Golden Lion at the 1948 VENICE Festival; this and its subsequent international success drew attention to the renascent Polish film industry.

*OSTŘE SLEDOVANÉ VLAKY* (*Closely Observed Trains*), Czechoslovakia, 1966. 1½hr. *Dir* Jiří Menzel; *scr* Menzel, Bohumil Hrabal, from the novel by Hrabal; *ph* Jaromír Sofr; *ed* Jirina Lukesová; *cast* Václav Neckár (Miloš), Jitka Bendová (Máša), Vladimír Valenta (Stationmaster), Josef Somr (Hubicka), Vlastimil Brodský (Zednićek), Jiří Menzel (Dr Brabec).

The adolescent Miloš becomes a trainee at a country railway station. His diffident yet desperate attempts to lose his virginity are chronicled against a background of Czechoslovakia under German occupation, described with ironic humour.

MENZEL's first feature attains a sure balance between comedy and sadness: he had wanted to use a comic happy ending, but Hrabal persuaded him to retain the novel's tragic conclusion. The film is outstanding for its kindly, perceptive view of human foibles; never lapsing into sentimentality, it knits a range of recognizable characters into a narrative which ranges from hilarious to touching. It earned a well-deserved international success and was awarded an OSCAR, only the second given to a Czech film.

*O'SULLIVAN*, MAUREEN (1911– ), Irish-born actress who has worked almost exclusively in Hollywood where she made her first film in 1931. She became famous as Jane opposite Johnny WEISSMULLER in the first TARZAN sound films. She also appeared in a number of WARNER BROS' major productions, including THE THIN MAN (1934), DAVID COPPERFIELD (1934), and ANNA KARENINA (1935), and even found herself in the company of the MARX BROTHERS in A DAY AT THE RACES (1937). She has appeared less frequently since the fifties, but did much to enliven a predominantly mediocre comedy, *Never Too Late* (1965). She was married to the director John Farrow and is the mother of Mia FARROW.

*OTHELLO*, SHAKESPEARE's tragedy, has always appealed to film-makers. Some sources claim that VITAGRAPH issued a version in 1902: the first authenticated *Othello* is a CINES production of 1907. Other adaptations came from the US in 1908, one of several Shakespeare films issued by Vitagraph in that year; from Italy, two in 1909 and one in 1914; and from Austria (using an early sound process 'sung and spoken by Erik Schmedes', implying that the source was Verdi's opera rather than the play). In 1923 a German *Othello* was directed by Dmitri Buchovetzki, with Emil JANNINGS in the title role and Werner KRAUSS as Iago: Jannings conveyed the savage animal quality of Othello but lacked the essential nobility; Krauss played Iago as a power for mindless destruction, portrayed in constant restless movement.

The first sound version (GB, 1946) was to be the initial film of a series of self-styled 'tabloid' versions of Shakespeare's plays produced by Marylebone Film Productions, short, small-budget films fitting into the general release DOUBLE FEATURE programme. The idea was not successful and was not followed up. The version produced, directed, and adapted by Orson WELLES (Morocco, 1951) was the first attempt to interpret the play in truly cinematic terms. If Shakespeare's intentions were not fully realized, Welles nevertheless evoked the passion and tragedy of the original. 1955 brought a faithful adaptation from the USSR, directed and adapted by Sergei YUTKEVICH, with music by Aram Khatchaturian, and with Sergei BONDARCHUK concentrating more on the gentleness and nobility of Othello than on the power that both Jannings and Welles had emphasized. The film was visually striking, using the hot tones of SOV-COLOR to create a brilliant Mediterranean ambience. The version released in GB and the US was marred by English-language DUBBING using the original text, while the songs remained in the original Russian. *Othello* (1965), starring Laurence OLIVIER, was a valuable record of the production mounted by the National Theatre of Great Britain in 1964.

The basic theme of *Othello* has often been used. Modern versions of the story provided the plot for *Men Are Not Gods* (1937), a star-studded Alexander KORDA production; *Jubal* (Delmer DAVES, 1955), a Western; and *All Night Long* (Basil DEARDEN, 1961), set among jazz musicians. In *A Double Life* (George CUKOR, 1948) Ronald COLMAN played an actor whose stage portrayal of Othello enters his private life.

**O'TOOLE, PETER** (1932– ), Irish actor. A distinguished stage actor, his first film role of importance was in *The Day They Robbed the Bank of England* (1960). His striking facial resemblance to T. E. Lawrence, particularly the icy blue eyes, made him an appropriate choice for the title role of LAWRENCE OF ARABIA (1962), and the film's success brought him international fame. His own company, Keep Films, co-produced *Becket* (1964), in which he played Henry II, and *Lord Jim* (1964), with O'Toole in the title role. His roles since, in films which include *Night of the Generals* (1966), another view of Henry II in *The Lion in Winter* (1968), *Murphy's War* (1971), and *Under Milk Wood* (1971), have usually been of the type of eccentric visionary in which he excels. Under authoritative direction he can give performances of striking intensity.

***OTTO E MEZZO*** (*8½*), Italy, 1963. Wide screen; 3hr. *Dir* Federico Fellini; *prod* Cineriz; *scr* Fellini, Ennio Flaiano, Tullio Pinelli, Brunello Rondi, from a story by Fellini and Flaiano; *ph* Gianni Di Venanzo; *des* Piero Gherardi; *mus* Nino Rota; *cast* Marcello Mastroianni (Guido Anselmi), Anouk Aimée (Luisa), Claudia Cardinale (the Ideal, Claudia), Jean Rougeul (Daumier-Fabrizio Carini), Sandra Milo (Carla), Mario Pisu (Mezzabotta), Rossella Falk (Rossella), Edra Gale (Saraghina), Guido Alberti (Pace, the producer).

*Otto e mezzo* (Federico Fellini, 1963)

Guido, a film director in whom FELLINI creates a deliberate self-portrait, cannot find inspiration to make a start on his new film. He is harried on every side by the people involved with him in his life and in the supposed film, and he escapes from these pressures through flights of imagination into childhood memories. The title, characteristically light-hearted, represented the number of films Fellini had made to date.

Through a precise and luminous insight into conflicting processes of creative work, Fellini produced a cogent statement about the nature of inspiration and creativity, as well as a sharply-observed comment on society. Its visual excitement and complexity, its intellectual and emotional range, and the rich quality of its music, make $8\frac{1}{2}$ a masterly and memorable work. It won first prize at the MOSCOW Festival, 1963.

**OUR DAILY BREAD** (*The Miracle of Life* in GB), US, 1934. 1¼hr. *Dir, prod* King Vidor; *scr* Elizabeth Hill; *ph* Robert Planck; *ed* Lloyd Nossler; *cast* Karen Morley (Mary), Tom Keene (John).

The story of *Our Daily Bread* was based by King VIDOR on an article by a college professor proposing co-operatives as a solution to the acute problem of unemployment during the Depression. Its theme, the struggles of a farming co-operative started by a destitute young city couple (who had appeared in Vidor's *The Crowd*, 1928), was rejected by commercial backers and the film was made with minimal funds and complete independence. It was well received critically and at the box-office, perhaps in part because of its political ambiguity: the HEARST press labelled it 'pinko' (left-wing), while the second prize it was awarded at the first MOSCOW film festival (1935) might well have been first prize if it had not been considered 'capitalistic propaganda'. However, Vidor's awareness of the potential of cinema is evident, particularly in the sequence of the digging of an irrigation ditch, and the film maintains its reputation as a rare attempt to present contemporary problems on the commercial screen.

**OUTRAGE, The,** US, 1964. Panavision; 1½hr. *Dir* Martin Ritt; *prod* Harvest/February/Ritt/Kayos; *scr* Michael Kanin, from the play *Rashomon* by Fay and Michael Kanin; *ph* James Wong Howe; *cast* Paul Newman (Juan Carrasco), Laurence Harvey (husband), Claire Bloom (wife), Edward G. Robinson (con-man), William Shatner (preacher), Howard da Silva (prospector).

*The Outrage* is adapted from the Broadway play which in turn was based on KUROSAWA's film RASHOMON (1950). The story is of the killing of a Southern gentleman and the rape of his wife by a bandit, told through the eyes of each protagonist and then by an independent witness, each version differing.

The subject, an unusual one for RITT, has been transferred from twelfth-century Japan (the setting of both Kurosawa's film and the stage play) to the south-west United States in the 1870s. The script remains faithful to the original, but the events unfold uneasily in the different time and setting. The debt to Kurosawa is acknowledged even in the film's visual quality: James Wong HOWE's photography recurrently reproduces with meticulous accuracy the pictorial effects of the original film. *The Outrage* was harshly received by the critics; only Edward G. ROBINSON's performance was widely appreciated.

**OVERLANDERS, The,** GB/Australia, 1946. 1½hr. *Dir, scr* Harry Watt; *prod* Michael Balcon for Ealing Studios; *ph* Osmond Borrodaile; *mus* John Ireland arranged by Charles Mackerras; *cast* Chips Rafferty (Dan McAlpine), John Nugent Hayward (Bill Parsons), Daphne Campbell (Mary Parsons), Helen Grieve (Helen Parsons).

Inevitably known as the first British WESTERN, *The Overlanders* gave Harry WATT the opportunity to use his experience in documentary in his first large-scale fiction feature. Drawn from a true account of the movement of cattle overland from north-west Australia to Queensland following the threat of Japanese invasion in 1942, action and spectacle were authoritatively combined, although the obligatory romantic interest was grafted with some unease on to the main theme of man against nature.

**OX-BOW INCIDENT, The** (*Strange Incident* in GB), US, 1943. 1¼hr. *Dir* William Wellman; *prod* Twentieth Century-Fox; *scr* Lamar Trotti from the novel by Walter Van Tilburg Clark; *ph* Arthur Miller; *cast* Henry Fonda (Gil), Dana Andrews (Martin), Anthony Quinn (Mexican).

Often described as the first 'psychological' Western, *The Ox-bow Incident* can justly be classed as a forerunner of the increasingly complex Westerns of the fifties and sixties. In its handling of the lynching of three innocent men it was certainly one of the earliest Westerns to display social conscience and awareness. WELLMAN, probably because of budget limitations, dispensed with the wide open locations and sweeping action conventionally associated with the form, and by restricting the drama to confined studio settings such as the camp and the bar brilliantly generated an atmosphere of hysteria and claustrophobia. The film earned an enthusiastic critical reception and was awarded several prizes. A 43-minute remake was filmed in 1955, for showing on American television.

**OZU, YASUJIRO** (1903–63), Japanese director, joined Shochiku in 1923 as a scriptwriter and assistant director and remained with the company for his entire working life. His first film as director, *Zange no Yaiba* (*Sword of Penitence*, 1927), was written by Kogo Noda who worked on all Ozu's pre-war films including *Hitori Musuko* (*The Only Son*, 1936) which already shows Ozu's delicate presentation of family relationships. He was mobilized in 1937 and served in China and Singapore. Unlike many Japanese directors of the time he did not fully cooperate with the military régime; he completed only two films between 1937 and 1948, *Toda-ke no Kyodai* (*The Toda Brothers*, 1941) and *Chichi Ariki* (*Dear Dad*, 1942), and neither were on subjects particularly connected with the war.

In 1949 Kogo Noda worked with him again on *Banshun* (*Late Spring*) and they collaborated until the end of Ozu's life. They agreed on everything, including their method of working which often consisted of sitting up together all night over *sake*. This kind of long-standing close collaboration extended to Ozu's repeated use of other colleagues, especially the actor Chishu Ryu who played in all but two of Ozu's fifty-four films. He often treated the same theme in different films and twice remade silent films in sound versions, *Umarete wa Mita Keredo* (*I Was Born But . . .*, 1932) as *Ohayo* (*Good Morning*, 1959) and *Ukigasa Monogatari* (*Floating Weeds*, 1934) with the same title, also in 1959, as a guest director for Daiei.

Ozu never married and lived with his mother all the time that she was alive. This is interesting when considering the quiet accuracy with which so many of his films, notably TOKYO MONOGATARI (*Tokyo Story*, 1953), SOSHUN (*Early Spring*, 1956), and SAMMA NO AJI (*An Autumn Afternoon*, 1962), analyse family life and personal relationships. He appears to have been an eccentric by Western standards. He was a perfectionist technically and thought hard before committing himself to any new technique: his first sound film was in 1936, his first in colour was not until 1958, and he never used the wide screen.

Ozu's work is difficult to appreciate outside Japan, but his films are instantly recognizable. They are slow in tempo, with long-held shots composed with deliberate formal beauty, and with little physical movement within the frame. His camerawork is refined, with few panning shots, and from 1930 he never used a dissolve. Nearly all the indoor sequences are shot from a very low camera angle, approximating to the eye level of people sitting on the floor. (This caused grave discomfort to some of his colleagues:

*Tokyo monogatari* (Yasujiro Ozu, 1953)

Shigehara, the cameraman on nearly all Ozu's silent films, spent so much time flat on his stomach on cold ground that he finally developed a stomach ailment that forced him to retire. Yushun Atsuta, who succeeded Shigehara until the end of Ozu's life, was said to be a man with a cast-iron stomach.) Ozu's methods were also very demanding on his actors, from whom throughout his career he seems to have been able to extract fine performances. As far as possible he avoided using stars.

Ozu's later films are less socially conscious than those of his early career. Nevertheless, all his work falls within the tradition of the *shomingeki*, a genre concerned with middle-class family relationships. The seasonal references of many of his titles is an indication of the time of life of the main characters. He gradually abandoned the light or ironic comedy of his early work for the traditional concept of *mono no amare*— sympathetic sadness. The Japanese themselves regard him as their most traditional and Japanese director and as such, until recently, unsuitable for export, unlike others such as KUROSAWA, ICHIKAWA, and SHINDO. This may, however, be a misconception. To the Western eye his detailed depiction of an exotic domestic culture can be fascinating, and the universality of his view of humanity shows him to be one of the most perceptive and sensitive of film-makers.

# P

**PABST,** GEORG WILHELM (1887–1967), Austrian director born in Bohemia, began as a stage actor and director, travelling widely in Europe and visiting the US. In 1914 he was interned in France, returning to work in the Austrian theatre after the war. He played in Carl FROELICH'S *Im Banne der Kralle* (1921), was assistant director to Froelich on two films in 1922, then made his first film *Der Schatz* (*The Treasure*, 1923), very similar in style to DER GOLEM (1920).

With his third film, DIE FREUDLOSE GASSE (*Joyless Street*, 1925), Pabst began to develop the realism and social comment that characterized his best work: the film's objective depiction of human degradation, the result of a corrupt economy, shocked contemporary audiences. He was, in addition, already displaying his skill in choosing and directing actresses, disclosing their individual types of eroticism.

*Geheimnisse einer Seele* (*Secrets of a Soul*, 1926) was planned as an exposition of Freudian analysis, and Pabst was assisted on the story by two of Freud's collaborators, although the finished film was repudiated by Freud himself. The subject, and especially the hero's guilt-laden dreams, temporarily turned Pabst back to formal EXPRESSIONISM. In contrast, *Die Liebe der Jeanne Ney* (*The Love of Jeanne Ney*, 1927) is distinguished by an airy naturalism, with sequences shot in the streets of Paris. The film was a romanticized version of Ilya Ehrenburg's novel, and Pabst's sympathetic view of the Red Army appeared to confirm his increasing left-wing allegiance. His view of the decadence of the German moneyed classes was given full expression in DIE BÜCHSE DER PANDORA (*Pandora's Box*, 1928), full of coolly observed depravity and containing a performance of extraordinary eroticism by Louise BROOKS; it was heavily censored in many countries, and his next, *Tagebuch einer Verlorenen* (*Diary of a Lost Girl*, 1929) again with Louise Brooks, suffered even greater mutilation.

As right-wing nationalism gained ground in Germany, Pabst became aligned with the progressive left. In 1930 he succeeded Lupu PICK as president of Dacho, the main organization of German film workers, and with Piscator, Heinrich Mann, and others he helped to found the Volksverbund für Filmkunst. WESTFRONT 1918 (1930) was furiously attacked by the National Socialists for its internationalist, anti-war message; DIE DREIGROSCHENOPER/*L'Opéra de quat' sous* (*The Threepenny Opera*, 1931) identified him with BRECHT and WEILL (although they rejected his softening of their play's political comment); and KAMERADSCHAFT (1931) again pleaded the cause of international brotherhood. Politics apart, these early sound films display a remarkable command of the new technique, in particular *Westfront 1918* and *Kameradschaft*, where French and German are freely combined in the dialogue to naturalistic effect. *Die Dreigroschenoper* was, more conventionally, shot in two versions, French and German, with separate casts, as was *Die Herrin von Atlantis/L'Atlantide* (1932), an escapist romance.

In France he directed *Don Quichotte* (1934) in French and English versions, chiefly remarkable for being the only surviving film record of CHALIAPIN. Pabst spent a brief period in Hollywood (*A Modern Hero*, 1934, was a total failure) then worked in France until 1939, when he returned to his home in Vienna. He made three films during the war, the last uncompleted. His post-war films include *Der Prozess* (*The Trial*, 1948), an attack on anti-Semitism which won the prize for best direction at VENICE, and *Der letzte Akt* (1955) about the last days of Hitler.

**PACIFIC 231,** France, 1949. 10min. *Dir* Jean Mitry; *prod* Tadié-Cinéma; *mus* Arthur Honegger.

In 1923 Arthur HONEGGER, who loved railway engines, composed a 'symphonic movement' depicting in musical terms the start, journey, and final halt of a large French locomotive. The piece is derived from Honegger's score for GANCE's film LA ROUE (1922). MITRY's film essay is something more than a visual interpretation of the score: its variety of railway shots, dynamic motion, and disciplined editing result in an astonishing counterpoint of sound and image. The film won a prize at the CANNES festival in 1949. The title refers to the axle arrangement of a Pacific-type locomotive (i.e. with four bogie, six driving, and two trailing wheels).

Honegger's music was also the basis for a short film of the same title directed by M. Tsekhanovsky (USSR, 1931).

**PAGLIERO,** MARCELLO (Marcel) (1907– ), London-born Italian actor and director whose first important film role was in ROSSELLINI'S ROMA, CITTÀ APERTA (1945). In 1946 he directed *Roma città libera*, co-starring Vittorio DE SICA and Valentina Cortese, and he later settled in France. He there appeared in several films, including Yves ALLÉGRET'S *Dédée d'Anvers* (1948), and soon concentrated on direction. His earlier films have remained best known: *Un Homme marche dans la ville* (1949), *Les Amants de Bras-Mort* (1950), and the adaptation of Sartre's *La P . . . respectueuse* (1952) co-directed with Charles Brabant and co-scripted by Alexandre ASTRUC.

**PAGNOL,** MARCEL (1895–1974), French playwright, film writer, and director, born near Marseilles. The success of his play *Topaze*, which began its still legendary run in Paris in 1928, helped him to obtain backing for MARIUS which opened in Paris in 1929 and was filmed in 1931. A sequel, *Fanny* (see MARIUS), followed on the stage in 1931 and was filmed in 1932; *César* (see MARIUS), the third film in the trilogy, was filmed in 1936 without having been produced on the stage.

The great success of his works on stage and screen enabled Pagnol to set up his own company in 1934. He built studios near Marseilles, complete with laboratories, learned all the processes himself, and during the thirties devoted himself almost entirely to making films which included *Joffroy* (1933), *Angèle* (1934), *Merlusse* (1935), *Le Schpountz* (1938), and LA FEMME DU BOULANGER (1938). He scripted, produced, and directed from his own or other people's work, especially the writings of Jean GIONO, also a native of Provence. The setting of all his films is Provençal, with dialogue written for the accent of the south. His casts include several distinguished actors, Pierre FRESNAY, FERNANDEL, and CHARPIN among them, but the actor who contributed most to his success and the development of his work was undoubtedly RAIMU.

Pagnol never gave any sign of political commitment in his work. In the one film he made during the German occupation of France, *La Fille du puisatier* (1940), a radio broadcast by Pétain was part of the background: after 1945 a speech by de Gaulle was quietly substituted. He made several films after the war, including a remake in 1951 of *Topaze* (first filmed by Louis GASNIER in 1933) and a version of *Les Lettres de mon moulin* by Alphonse Daudet (again a fellow Provençal) in 1954.

Pagnol's use of sound in its earliest years was the subject of sharp controversy at the time: he was castigated for making 'canned theatre' rather than cinema. His originality as a writer has perhaps not been sufficiently recognized: *Marius* in particular contained a note of realism virtually unknown in the French theatre of the twenties. DE SICA saw in *Angèle* the first seeds of NEO-REALISM, and ROSSELLINI has acknowledged a similar debt to Pagnol.

**PAINLEVÉ,** JEAN (1902– ), French director, a pioneer of scientific film. He came under the influence of the AVANT-GARDE and discovered in the microscopic life of ponds and rivers a strange, abstract beauty comparable with the current experiments in ABSTRACT film. The imagery of his films was enhanced by remarkable music written at first by Maurice JAUBERT (*La Pieuvre*, 1928; *Les Oursins*, 1928), and later composed of the best contemporary jazz. Gradually the creatures of his films became humanized, heroes with metaphoric significance (*Bernard l'hermite*, 1930; *L'Hippocampe*, 1937): according to Georges SADOUL, he was at this time a 'sub-aquatic FLAHERTY'. He later experimented, with René Bertrand, on a *Barbe-bleue* (now thought to be lost) using animated sculptured figurines. Painlevé was an active militant during the Occupation; after the Liberation he became Directeur-Général du Cinéma and Chairman of the Fédération Française des Ciné-Clubs. Since 1950 he has made very few films, devoting his time to the International Scientific Film Association.

*PAISÀ* (*Paisan*), Italy, 1947. 2hr. *Dir* Roberto Rossellini; *prod* OFI, Foreign Film Production Inc, Capitani film; *scr* Federico Fellini, Sergio Amidei, Rossellini, from stories by Victor Haines, Marcello Pagliero, Amidei, Fellini, Rossellini, and Vasco Pratolini (uncredited); *ph* Otello Martelli; *ed* Eraldo Da Roma; *mus* Renzo Rossellini; *cast* Carmela Sazio, Robert Van Loon, Dots Johnson, Maria Michi, Bill Tubbs, Dale Edmonds.

ROSSELLINI was partly backed in making *Paisà* by Rod Geiger, who had introduced ROMA, CITTÀ APERTA (1945) to America; Geiger provided film stock and the American actors for the film. For the rest of the cast Rossellini characteristically used non-professionals. The film consists of six episodes, united sequentially by the progress of the Allied forces up the Italian peninsula, from the first landings in Sicily to the day before victory. The episodes, however, are tales of individuals, not armies, and Rossellini, who shot the film with the real background of Lombardy, Rome, and newly-liberated Naples, succinctly fuses the fragments of individual human experience with the general process of Italy's liberation.

With *Roma, città aperta*, *Paisà* introduced NEO-REALISM to Britain and the US, creating a sensation with the freshness and passion of the new movement.

**PAKISTAN.** Before independence and partition in 1947, Lahore was the third largest film production centre of the Indian subcontinent, operated by a Hindu monopoly. With the founding of Pakistan as a separate state the Hindus moved to Bombay, but the Moslem countermigration provided the basis for a new industry. By 1954 there were six studios functioning in Lahore and fifty features had been produced, forty in Urdu and ten in Punjabi. Competition from Indian films has handicapped the new industry from the beginning, in spite of government taxation intended to discourage their import; only the Punjabi-language films avoid this competition. Although over a thousand features have been made in Pakistan since 1947, the need to compete with flashy Bombay productions has resulted in work of little artistic merit, often using predictable triangle melodramas which denounce high society and Westernized women while glorifying the poor. The few directors who have attempted to infuse artistic and social values into popular entertainment include W. Z. Ahmed, Anwar Kamel, S. Suleman, Sharif Nayyar, Ahmed Bashir, and Hassan Tariq.

**PAKULA,** ALAN J. (1928–   ), US producer and director who in 1949 became assistant to the head of WARNER BROS cartoons. He became a producer for PARAMOUNT with *Fear Strikes Out* (1957), for which he chose television director Robert MULLIGAN, with whom he formed a company and remained in partnership through seven films in eleven years.

After the success of their *To Kill a Mockingbird* (1962), Pakula surrendered his interests in Broadway stage production to concentrate on films. He came late to direction with *The Sterile Cuckoo* (1969, *Pookie* in GB), consolidating his analytical style and preoccupation with people under stress in *Klute* (1971) and *The Widower* (1972).

**PALANCE,** JACK (1921–   ), US actor, owes much of the peculiarly menacing effect of his film roles to the war injuries which severely scarred his face. This apparent handicap for an actor has proved of value in playing villainous characters such as the plague-stricken gangster of Elia KAZAN's *Panic in the Streets* (1950) and the archetypal hired gunman in SHANE (1953); he had particular success in Clifford ODETS's *The Big Knife* (1955). Since the late fifties he has worked frequently in Europe, notably in LE MÉPRIS (1963).

**PALLETTE,** EUGENE (1889–1954), US actor, entered films in 1913. He appeared as a Union soldier in THE BIRTH OF A NATION (1915) and as Prosper Latour (the sweetheart of Brown Eyes) in the Huguenot episodes of INTOLERANCE (1916). His many other silent films included *The Three Musketeers* (Fred NIBLO, 1921), and for a time he appeared in Hal ROACH comedy shorts. But he came into his own in the thirties when his corpulent appearance, heavy jowls, and rasping voice made him in constant demand for character roles, particularly in comedy; he was the American tycoon in René CLAIR's *The Ghost Goes West* (1935), the rich head of the zany family in MY MAN GODFREY (1936), and an entertaining Friar Tuck in *The Adventures of Robin Hood* (1938).

**PALM BEACH STORY, The,** US, 1942. 1½hr. *Dir* Preston Sturges; *prod* Paramount; *scr* Sturges; *ph* Victor Milner; *cast* Joel McCrea (Tom Jeffers), Claudette Colbert (Gerry Jeffers), Rudy Vallee (J. D. Hackensacker III), Mary Astor (the Princess), Sig Arno (Toto), Robert Warwick (Mr Hinch), William Demarest (1st member of the Ale and Quail Club), Robert Dudley (Weinie King), Franklin Pangborn (manager).

After a quarrel with her husband Tom, Gerry sets out for Palm Beach to get a divorce and look for a rich husband. On the way she is adopted by the eccentric members of the Ale and Quail Club (among STURGES's happiest creations and led by William Demarest who acted in almost all Sturges's films) and meets millionaire J. D. Hackensacker III, who takes her to stay on his yacht. The film is a brilliant comedy, full of inventive humour and impeccably played by all concerned, not least Rudy Vallee as the unfortunate J.D.

**PALMER,** LILLI (1914–   ), German-born British actress, real name Maria Lilli Peiser. After stage experience in Germany and France, she moved to Britain, making her first screen appearance in *Crime Unlimited* (1934). She acted in a number of films including HITCHCOCK's *Secret Agent* (1936), *A Girl Must Live* (1938), and *Thunder Rock* (1942), and from 1938 established a career on the British stage. She married Rex HARRISON in 1943; after appearing together in *The Rake's Progress* (1946), they went to Hollywood where she appeared in Fritz LANG's *Cloak and Dagger* (1946). With Harrison she made *The Four Poster* (1952), in which they were the only characters. After a return to the London stage she appeared in films in France and Germany, winning awards for her performances in *Teurel in Seide* (1956) and *Montparnasse 19* (1957). She was divorced from Harrison in 1957. Her sister Maria Palmer (1924–   ) has played in a number of American films and another sister, Irene Pravda, is a television actress.

**PAN,** a CAMERA MOVEMENT in which the camera is rotated in a horizontal plane so that it moves panoramically across the subject to the right or left. A pan can be used to follow a moving object, to allow the camera to look at a different area, or simply to encompass a wider scene than the static FRAME permits. There is no normal movement of the human eye corresponding to the pan (the effect of a sideways glance is created by a cut rather than a pan); it can easily become annoying or artificial in unskilled hands. In the classic tradition of the well-made film, a pan was rarely used without 'motivation' in the form of action within the scene to 'lead' the camera in the required direction.

The tilt, in which the camera rotates up or down in a vertical plane, is often incorrectly called a pan. 'Pan' is also used in photographic terminology as an abbreviation of PANCHROMATIC film.

**PANAVISION** is known to the public primarily for its process of motion photography and printing, now widely adopted in professional production. The image is photographed on 70mm negative, and either printed normally for projection on 70mm or squeezed anamorphically on to 35mm positives for projection in theatres not equipped for 70mm projection. Purer definition is gained by this process than by anamorphic photography directly on to 35mm negative. (See also ANAMORPHIC LENS, WIDE SCREEN.)

**PANCHROMATIC FILM,** black-and-white film stock which is sensitive to light of all colours, producing a reasonably correct rendering of coloured objects as seen by the eye. Early silent films were shot on ORTHOCHROMATIC stock, totally insensitive to red; but in 1926 Robert FLAHERTY'S MOANA, the first feature on panchromatic stock, revolutionized cinematography with its soft gradations and realistic flesh tones. However panchromatic film stocks were slower—less sensitive to light—and in some ways their introduction marked a step backwards (see DEPTH OF FIELD). Modern black-and-white camera films are still panchromatic, but orthochromatic stock survives for printing and special EFFECTS.

*PANDORA'S BOX* see BÜCHSE DER PANDORA, DIE

**PAPAS, IRENE** (1926– ), Greek actress, began her professional career singing and dancing in a variety show and playing straight roles on the stage. Her first film was *Necropolitia*

(1951), and she made some films in Italy before signing a contract with METRO-GOLDWYN-MAYER. Her first American film was *Tribute to a Bad Man* (1955). She appeared in *The Guns of Navarone* (1961), and for Michael CACOYANNIS in *Electra* (1961) and *Zorba the Greek* (1965), which established her internationally, her dramatic beauty and uninhibited passion stimulating comparisons with Anna MAGNANI. Her recent appearances include *The Brotherhood* (1968), z (1968), and *Anne of the Thousand Days* (1969).

**PAPER PRINTS.** Under the US Copyright Act in force in 1894, motion pictures could be registered for protection only as a sequence of still photographs. Thomas EDISON and W. K. L. DICKSON secured the first such copyright by filing a contact paper print of *The Sneeze*, or as the copyright entry on 9 January 1894 described it: 'Edison Kinetoscopic Record of a Sneeze, January 7, 1894'. Almost all the early producers followed their example and by 1912, when the Copyright Act was amended to allow the deposit of the nitrate film itself as evidence of registration, more than 3,500 titles had been acquired by the Library of Congress as paper prints.

In 1956 the Library, in a programme sponsored by the ACADEMY OF MOTION PICTURE ARTS AND SCIENCES, began to transfer the 35mm rolls of paper prints to 16mm film. The work was carried out by the Renovare Film Company of Los Angeles under the direction of Kemp R. Niver and by 1964 over half a million feet of 16mm film had been added to the Library's collection. The original paper prints are still preserved by the Library and they constitute an invaluable record of American film production in the formative years.

See Kemp R. Niver, *Motion pictures from the Library of Congress paper print collection, 1894–1912*, Berkeley, 1967.

**PARAMOUNT PICTURES CORPORATION,** US production company, formed in 1927 after the merging of W. W. Hodkinson's Paramount Pictures distribution company and the Famous Players-Lasky production company (see FAMOUS PLAYERS) owned by Adolph ZUKOR, Jesse L. LASKY, and Cecil B. DEMILLE. Hodkinson was responsible not only for the name but also for the trademark, a snow-capped mountain peak encircled by stars.

Zukor was head of the new company and remained chairman of the board for over thirty years. Management of the studio was in the hands of Lasky, who was head of production until 1932, and others, including B. P. SCHULBERG, Barney Balaban, and Y. Frank Freeman. Zukor concentrated on acquiring cinema chains (the Publix Corporation in 1930) and developing overseas production. Judging that FOREIGN VERSIONS of sound films would be better made and received if made in a European studio rather than in Hollywood, he took over studios for this purpose at Joinville, near Paris, as early as 1930. Paramount also had a London-based subsidiary, Paramount British, which produced some films of note but which was primarily concerned with QUOTA production.

Paramount's studio style had a characteristic glitter; its films dealing with sophisticated, often risqué, themes. In the early years a number of European directors and actors heightened this quality: STROHEIM, STILLER, LUBITSCH, STERNBERG, MAMOULIAN; Pola NEGRI, Marlene DIETRICH, Maurice CHEVALIER, and Adolphe MENJOU, all worked at Paramount for brief or longer periods. Mae WEST contributed a home-grown version of the saucy entertainment that founded the company's fortunes.

In spite of some financially difficult years in the mid-thirties, Paramount was able to survive and to maintain its position by producing a steady diet of light, family entertainment films as well as DeMille's consistently popular spectaculars. The company's contract players included VALENTINO, Gloria SWANSON, Gary COOPER, W. C. FIELDS, Bing CROSBY, Bob HOPE, Dorothy LAMOUR, John WAYNE, Barbara STANWYCK, and Montgomery CLIFT; at various times it employed directors of the calibre of Frank CAPRA, George STEVENS, Billy WILDER, and Preston STURGES. 'If it's a Paramount Picture, it's the best show in town' was their slogan; their 'best shows' included films such as The Sheikh (1921), The Ten Commandments (1923 and 1956), the 'Road' series, the early MARX BROTHERS comedies, THE LOST WEEKEND (1945), SUNSET BOULEVARD (1950), A PLACE IN THE SUN (1951), and, appropriately enough, The Greatest Show on Earth (1952).

In 1950 Paramount was forced by the anti-trust laws to split into two separate companies; Paramount Pictures continued the business of producing and distributing films, while United Paramount Theaters Inc was formed to manage their theatre holdings. Three years later, Paramount was the only production company which refused to accept TWENTIETH CENTURY-FOX's anamorphic wide-screen system, CINEMASCOPE; their technicians developed an alternative system called VISTAVISION.

The last twenty years have witnessed the gradual decline of the epic tradition of film-making at Paramount which was so evident during DeMille's reign. More recently, the studio has been able to maintain a continuous flow of Westerns, thrillers, and sex-spectaculars, mostly through its ties with producers like Hal WALLIS

and Joseph E. LEVINE. International prestige productions, though apparently not a great concern at Paramount, have been occasionally attempted: Becket (1964), ROMEO AND JULIET (1968), and ROSEMARY'S BABY (1968).

Like other major Hollywood companies, Paramount was absorbed into a large industrial conglomerate with its takeover by Gulf and Western in 1966. Attempts to resist the crises that beset the industry in the late sixties included lavish productions such as Paint Your Wagon and Darling Lili (both 1969), which incurred large losses. These were counterbalanced by the remarkable success of Love Story (1970) and by THE GODFATHER (1971), which broke all box-office records.

**PARAPLUIES DE CHERBOURG, Les** (Umbrellas of Cherbourg), France/West Germany, 1964. Eastman Color; 1½hr. Dir, scr Jacques Demy; prod Parc Film/Madeleine Films (Paris)/Beta Film (Munich); ph Jean Rabier; des Bernard Evein; mus Michel Legrand; cast Catherine Deneuve (Geneviève), Nino Castelnuovo (Guy), Anne Vernon (Mme Emery), Ellen Farner (Madeleine), Marc Michel (Roland Cassard).

DEMY's spellbinding love story for a time aroused questioning as to whether Hollywood's supremacy in the film MUSICAL was at last to be seriously challenged. His nostalgic sweetness (in contrast to Hollywood's exuberance) does not always avoid sentimentality but is supported by ravishing and adventurous use of colour. The dialogue is all sung—there are no large-scale production numbers—and Michel LEGRAND's score entirely suits the film's delicate artificiality.

**PARENTS TERRIBLES, Les,** France, 1948. 1¾hr. Dir, scr Jean Cocteau, from his own play; prod Ariane (Alexandre Mnouchkine and Francis Cosne); ph Michel Kelber; des Christian Bérard; ed Jacqueline Sadoul; mus Georges Auric; cast Josette Day, Jean Marais, Yvonne de Bray, Marcel André, Gabrielle Dorziat.

The complex plot revolves around the possessiveness of the domineering mother who cannot accept the adulthood of her children. COCTEAU effectively retains the intense theatricality of the stage play, making few cuts from the original and using only two settings, while making the most of close-ups to sustain the drama. Three members of the cast of the original stage production provide the acting that is one of the film's most distinguished features.

**PARIS 1900,** France, 1948. 50min. Dir, scr Nicole Védrès; ed Myriam; mus Guy Bernard.

A documentary COMPILATION of old newsreels and other films, a nostalgic glance at the famous and unknown people and places of Paris at the turn of the century. It was one of the first of its kind produced after the Second World War, and won the Prix Louis DELLUC on its first appearance. Its enduring worth was confirmed by an award at the Edinburgh Film Festival in 1972.

**PARIS NOUS APPARTIENT,** France, 1960. 2½hr. *Dir* Jacques Rivette; *prod* AJYM/Films du Carrosse; *scr* Rivette, Jean Gruault; *ph* Charles Bitsch; *mus* Philippe Arthuys; *cast* Betty Schneider (Anne), Giani Esposito (Gérard), Françoise Prévost (Terry), Daniel Crohem (Philip), François Maistre (Pierre), Jean-Claude Brialy (Jean-Marc), with Claude Chabrol, Jacques Demy, Jean-Luc Godard.

In summer, in deserted Paris, a group of young amateurs are preparing a production of Shakespeare's *Pericles*; suddenly their composer dies, their producer commits suicide, they are threatened by a world-wide conspiracy which turns out to be the fantasy of one of their number. With an austerity of style characteristic of RIVETTE, the film attempts to reveal another plane of reality such as exists also in *Pericles*.

One of the first films of the NOUVELLE VAGUE, *Paris nous appartient* was shot over the years 1952–9: internal references to the problem of financing the production of *Pericles* reflect Rivette's own difficulties in finding backers.

**PARLO,** DITA (1906–71), German actress, real name Grethe Gerda Kornstadt, trained as a ballerina and at the UFA acting school. Her first film was *Die Dame mit den Maske* (1928). She made two films in Hollywood, *The Honour of the Family* and *Mr Broadway* (both 1933). She then went to France where she did some of her most fruitful work, including VIGO's L'ATALANTE (1934), in which she delicately played the young bride, PABST's *Mademoiselle Docteur* (1936), and RENOIR's LA GRANDE ILLUSION (1937). She was active in the attempts to restore *L'Atalante* to its original form and bring it before a wider public. As a German citizen she was arrested and deported to Germany in 1940 and did not return to the cinema until she made *Justice est faite* (1950); after which she appeared only occasionally.

**PARSONS,** LOUELLA (1890–    ), US columnist, real name Oettinger, whose work was syndicated through the HEARST group of newspapers. By virtue of this connection she spent the early part of her career supporting the popularity of Marion DAVIES. She became known as one of the most powerful gossip reporters in Hollywood, although estimates of her influence in making or destroying careers through exposure of stars' private lives have probably been exaggerated. She made several film appearances

as herself, notably in *Hollywood Hotel* (1937) and *Starlift* (1951), and wrote two autobiographies, *The gay illiterate* (1944) and *Tell it to Louella* (1962). Her chief rival was Hedda HOPPER: a joint biography *Hedda and Louella* was written by George Eells (New York, 1972).

**PARTIE DE CAMPAGNE, Une,** France, 1936, released 1946. 35min. *Dir, scr* Jean Renoir from a story by Maupassant; *prod* Pierre Braunberger for Films du Panthéon; *ph* Claude Renoir; *des* Robert Gys; *ed* Marguerite Renoir, Marinette Cadix; *mus* Joseph Kosma, Germaine Montero; *cast* Jeanne Marken (Mme Dufour), Sylvie Bataille (Henriette), Gabriello (M Dufour), Georges Danoux (Henri), Jacques Brunius (Rodolpho), Paul Temps (Anatole), Gabrielle Fontan (grandmother).

*Une Partie de campagne* forms an interlude in RENOIR's career, a return to the sources of his inspiration in the landscape in which he grew up and in French literature. His original idea was for a film of about fifty-five minutes involving about a week's shooting of exteriors, but the summer of 1936 was unusually rainy and the tense atmosphere among cast and crew—cooped up from mid-July until the beginning of September—was almost intolerable even before Renoir abandoned the film in order to begin *Les Basfonds* (1936). Subsequent abortive attempts to extend the film to feature length included a new script written by Jacques PRÉVERT. In fact Renoir had shot all the footage needed to tell Maupassant's story with great fidelity except for two interior sequences, and in 1946 the editor Marguerite RENOIR, who herself played a small acting role in the film, assembled it, using two titles to replace the missing scenes.

The film's serenity in no way reflects the difficulties of the production. A bourgeois family makes a rare country excursion and in the course of a summer's day both mother and daughter are expertly seduced by two young holidaymakers. While the sense of an idyll is perfectly captured the two seductions are ironically counterpointed: humorous caricature on the one hand and tender concern on the other run parallel and end leaving the young girl with a life-long regret for love enjoyed and lost. The images of the river and its banks captured by Claude RENOIR's camera blend with Joseph KOSMA's music to help in creating one of the screen's most nostalgic love stories.

**PARTY AND THE GUESTS, The,** see O SLAVNOSTI A HOSTECH

**PASAŻERKA** (*The Passenger*), Poland, 1963. Standard and Dyaliscope; 1hr. *Dir* Andrzej

*Une Partie de campagne* (Jean Renoir, 1936)

Munk, completed by Witold Lesiewicz; *prod* WFF Łódź; *scr* Munk, Zofia Posmysz-Piasecka, from her television play; *ph* Krzysztof Winiewicz; *mus* Tadeusz Baird; *cast* Aleksandra Slaska (Lisa), Anna Ciepielewska (Marta), Marek Walczewski (Tadeusz), Jan Kreczmer (Walter), Irena Malkiewicz (woman commandant).

Work on *Pasażerka* was halted in September 1963, two days after MUNK's death in a car crash. The material completed was assembled by his friends as a tribute, but with a warning that the director had left no clear indication of his final plan. It was known that he was dissatisfied with the sequences set in the present on the liner *Batory* and a solution was devised whereby this part of the film was arranged in a montage of still photographs with commentary over. These sections, in standard format, contrast with three episodes set in Auschwitz, shot in 'scope. In these episodes Liza, justifying to her husband her record as a camp guard, re-examines her relationship with Marta, a prisoner, revealing in each episode successive levels of memory and further truths about human actions and moral responsibility.

It seems likely that the power of the deeply moving sequences from Auschwitz upset the balance of Munk's original conception of the film. The present form is so effective that it is hard to imagine an improvement, the 'present' sequences on the liner providing a poignant and enigmatic counterpoint to the 'past' in its various, increasingly appalling, versions. The construction of the film was daring in its time and place, and the result deserves to rank with the best in world cinema.

**PASCAL,** GABRIEL (1894–1954), Hungarian-born producer, served in the Hussars and was an actor in Vienna. After the First World War he produced films in Italy, France, and Germany, migrating to Britain in 1935. He will be remembered chiefly for persuading George Bernard Shaw to sell the film rights of his plays, in spite of Shaw's previous refusal to countenance the filming of his work. Pascal produced PYGMALION (1938) and produced and directed MAJOR BARBARA (1941). CAESAR AND CLEOPATRA (1945), which he produced and directed, created something of a scandal. It was by British standards an extravagant and lengthy production, and Pascal's flamboyance was disliked by his colleagues: the ACTT passed an unprecedented resolution stating that Pascal should not be allowed to make films in England unless 'subject to special control'. He produced one more adaptation from Shaw,

*Androcles and the Lion* (1953), made in Hollywood.

Valerie Pascal, *The disciple and his devil: Gabriel Pascal, Bernard Shaw*, New York, 1970; London, 1971.

**PASOLINI,** PIER PAOLO (1922–75), Italian director, studied at Bologna, first art history and, after the war, literature. During the war he lived in Friuli where, in the peasants' struggle against the wealthy land-owners, he first encountered the Marxism which became the ideological basis of his creative work. During the fifties he worked extensively in both literature and cinema. His first novel, *Ragazzi di vita*, completed in 1954, led to work on the script of *La donna del fiume* (*Woman of the River*, SOLDATI, 1955) and two years later he worked for FELLINI on LE NOTTI DI CABIRIA, writing the low-life parts. He collaborated on three scripts for Mauro Bolognini including *La notte brava* (1959), the film version of *Ragazzi di vita*. In 1962 his second Roman novel, *Una vita violenta* (published 1959), was filmed and BERTOLUCCI made *La commare secca* from one of Pasolini's short stories.

ACCATONE (1961) was Pasolini's first film as director, with Bertolucci as his assistant. In 1962 he directed *Mamma Roma*, which starred Anna MAGNANI as a Roman prostitute who fails in an attempt to reform, and 'La ricotta', a section of *RoGoPaG* (other episodes by ROSSELLINI, GODARD, and Gregoretti), starring Orson WELLES. 'La ricotta' was temporarily banned in Italy, and Pasolini was given four months' suspended sentence for 'public defamation'.

Many of Pasolini's friends acted in his IL VANGELO SECONDO MATTEO (1964), among them the director's mother: this preference for non-actors has been a consistent feature of his work. The film was greeted with some astonishment for the proclaimed Marxist recounted the story of Christ with simplicity and sobriety. A similar directness was brought to a pagan myth in his version of EDIPO RE (*Oedipus Rex*, 1967).

TEOREMA (*Theorem*, 1968) marked a change in Pasolini's work, concentrating on several characters rather than on a single protagonist. The ultimate 'meaning' of the film is an open question, as it is in IL PORCILE (*Pigsty*, 1969). *Medea* (1969) was shot in Turkey, from the Euripides text. It contains a powerful performance in the leading role by Maria Callas, in spite of the dubbing of her voice by an unknown Italian woman.

Pasolini's work took another new direction with *Il Decamerone* (*The Decameron*) and *I racconti di Canterbury* (*The Canterbury Tales*), both 1971, in which his visual sense created a rich evocation of the medieval world, although he failed to place the separate stories (chosen from the most scatological in Boccaccio and Chaucer) in a convincing narrative framework; his violent death deprived the cinema of a many-sided artist.

*PASSENGER, The,* see PASAŻERKA

**PASSER,** IVAN (1933– ), Czech director, as the son of wealthy parents suffered calculated interruptions to his career. He spent two years at FAMU, the Prague film school, but was not allowed to finish. Directors who gave him a chance to persist in film-making as assistant include Brynych, Jasný (with whom he worked on several films, including *Až přijde kocour*, *That Cat*, 1963), and RADOK on the LATERNA MAGICA. A school-friend of Miloš FORMAN, he was drawn into the group which worked on Forman's films from *Konkurs* (1963) to *Taking Off* (1971). Passer's own first film was *Fadni odpoledne* (*A Boring Afternoon*), about football fanaticism, made in 1964: it was intended originally as an episode for *Perličky na dně* (*Pearls of the Deep*, 1965), but was withdrawn by Passer as the film became too long and won recognition on its independent release as a medium-length film. His gentle philosophy and sharp observation, developed during his experience with Forman, found full expression in the charming, apparently artless INTIMNÍ OSVĚTLENÍ (*Intimate Lighting*, 1966). He did not make another film of his own in Czechoslovakia: he was invited by PONTI to film in western Europe, and, like Forman, made his way to the USA, where he made *Born to Win* in 1971.

*PASSION DE JEANNE D'ARC, La,* France, 1928. 2hr. *Dir* Carl Dreyer; *prod* Société Générale de Films; *scr* Dreyer, Joseph Delteil; *ph* Rudolph Maté; *des* Hermann Warm, Jean Hugo; *cast* Renée Falconetti (Joan), Eugene Silvain (Cauchon), Maurice Schutz (Loyseleur), Michel Simon (Lemaître), Antonin Artaud (Massieu).

Having achieved a reputation in France with *Du skal aere din hustru* (*Master of the House*, 1925), DREYER was invited to direct his own choice of subject and was given a free hand in the treatment. The script, based on the actual records of Joan of Arc's trial, as well as the historical accuracy of the sets and costumes, testify to his characteristic preoccupation with authenticity; but his concern was not primarily with the dramatic reconstruction of history.

Dreyer later denied that he had hoped to use sound, although the essentially verbal, indeed polemical, nature of the source material makes it an apparently unsuitable choice for a silent film. Dialogue is uncompromisingly inserted in long and frequent titles, and there is little attempt by the actors to mime the actual lines. The narrative, compressed from the original eighteen months to

*Intimní osvětlení* (Ivan Passer, 1966)

a single day, is divided between the titles and images that illustrate the emotions behind the objective record. Using PANCHROMATIC film to strengthen the harsh contrasts of features and dark costumes against cold, plain backgrounds, Dreyer cruelly exposes these emotions. No member of the cast was allowed to wear make-up, and the texture of skin, facial blemishes, sweat, are bleakly recorded. Long-held close-ups, expressionistic camera angles, extending tracking shots, and pans, are brought to bear on the malice of the judges, the compassion of Massieu, and Joan's agony.

Renée FALCONETTI, in her only film role, memorably conveys Dreyer's conception of religious obsession and the indignity of suffering: during the making of the film she in fact submitted to harsh treatment in achieving the required intensity. The conception itself is not wholly successful: instead of pity and reverence, this interpretation of Joan is capable of arousing repugnance.

*La Passion de Jeanne d'Arc* was a commercial disaster, but has always been highly esteemed by critics. GODARD used parts of it to parallel the heroine's victimization in VIVRE SA VIE (1962). (See also JOAN OF ARC.)

***PASSPORT TO PIMLICO***, GB, 1949. 1½hr. *Dir* Henry Cornelius; *prod* Michael Balcon for Ealing Studios; *scr* T. E. B. Clarke; *ph* Lionel Baines; *mus* Georges Auric; *cast* Stanley Holloway (Arthur Pemberton), Barbara Murray (Shirley), Paul Dupuis (Duke of Burgundy), Margaret Rutherford (Prof Hatton-Jones).

A basically slender idea, the discovery that a small district of London is by ancient law a Burgundian possession, was developed into a vintage EALING comedy containing the typical ingredients of modesty (in both attitude and outlay), good humour, and detailed social observation.

**PASTRONE, GIOVANNI** (1883–1959), Italian director and producer, pseudonym Piero Fosco, worked in an administrative capacity in several fields before joining Rossi, one of the first Turin film companies, in 1905. By 1907, when Rossi became ITALA FILM, Pastrone had become managing director, thereafter pursuing an unusual parallel career as both organizer and film director. In 1910 he made two films, *Agnese Visconti* and *La caduta di Troia* (*The Fall of Troy*), the latter an exuberant and imaginative one-reel version of the Trojan War, notable for his skilled handling of crowds. Pastrone's next film was *Padre* (1912), and while making films and running Itala Film he worked on improving equipment and techniques. In 1912 he patented a DOLLY and a new, brighter projection lamp. He also improved projectors by experimenting with the perforation spacing on prints. Possibly his most historically significant innovation was that, realizing the financial importance of a tied outlet for his product, he created a chain of cinemas throughout Italy to exhibit Itala Film productions.

In 1913–14 he was occupied in making CABIRIA. Pastrone was almost the sole author of this huge film, but it was not until much later that he received even pseudonymous recognition. All his other films are attributed to Piero Fosco, but this could not appear on *Cabiria* because, for reasons of prestige, Gabriele d'Annunzio's name had been bought. *Cabiria*'s cost was unprecedented at the time and the film was six months in the shooting. In 1915, to demonstrate that he was not just a maker of spectacle films, Pastrone directed the romantic love story *Il fuoco* (*The Fire*), with two characters only. He also made the first of a series of films with MACISTE, the character he had created in *Cabiria*, as the central figure. An adaptation of Giovanni Verga's novel *Tigre reale* followed in the same year, and in 1919 he directed a film version of Ibsen's *Hedda Gabler*, after which he left Itala Film. He directed one other film, *Povere bimbe* (*The Orphans*, 1923), then retired from direction. Except for supervising the sound dubbing of a condensed version of *Cabiria* in 1931, which had a title crediting direction to Piero Fosco, he devoted himself to studying medicine and trying to find a cure for cancer.

**PATHÉ, CHARLES** (1863–1957), French industrialist who made a fortune by exploiting the phonograph in fairground booths. In 1895 he developed a Kinetoscope (see KINETOGRAPH) with four viewers instead of one, thereby quadrupling profits. In 1896 he marketed his own version of LUMIÈRE's Cinématographe and made a number of short films including an inevitable *Arrivée du train de Vincennes* in imitation of Lumière. In the same year he set up, with his brothers, the PATHÉ FRÈRES company which was to develop into the biggest film organization of the day. The First World War began the decline in Pathé's fortunes. In 1929 he was forced to sell out and retire.

**PATHÉ FRÈRES,** French film company, founded in 1896 by Charles PATHÉ and his brothers Émile, Jacques, and Théophile. Charles Pathé had made his money by astutely exploiting EDISON's phonograph in a fairground booth at Vincennes, near Paris. In 1897 a manufacturer of electrical motors, Claude Grivolas, bought himself into Pathé Frères and was instrumental in turning the organization's attention firmly towards film production. In 1900 Pathé took on

Ferdinand ZECCA to direct films for the company. Zecca began by imitating MÉLIÈS and the British pioneers before discovering his forte in comedy films. By 1907 Pathé Frères had thoroughly established itself, with several factories in France, and studios in England, Italy, Spain, Germany, Russia, and the US.

Having industrialized film production Pathé turned his attention to the marketing of films. Comfortable and permanent cinemas had begun to replace the draughty fairground booths where films were first shown. Pathé captured this new area of the market by effacing his weaker competitors, introducing the practice of renting, rather than selling, copies of films. This innovation was ratified at the CONGRÈS DES DUPES in February 1909.

As Pathé Frères virtually monopolized the French market they produced a great diversity of films, from naïve comic subjects for fairground consumption to the pompous and theatrical FILM D'ART. From this melting-pot emerged talents like Max LINDER, André DEED, and Rigadin, as well as directors like Lucien Nonguet, Gaston Velle, and Louis GASNIER.

In 1910 profits and production were soaring. Pathé Frères had broken EASTMAN's monopoly on raw stock and in that year the company began to manufacture cameras and projectors. The outbreak of the First World War disrupted the company, which was also beginning to feel the weight of opposition to its monopoly, especially in the US. In France the cost of production had risen sharply. American films were cornering a large section of the French market: in 1917 30 per cent of film programmes were still home-produced, but in 1918 the proportion had dropped to 10 per cent.

To try and hold back this tide Pathé Frères divested itself of a number of concerns: in 1918 the phonographic section was sold; in 1920 the Pathé-Exchange in New York and Pathé Limited in London were liquidated; in 1926 Kodak bought the film-stock factory. The final blow came in 1929 when Bernard Natan, director of Rapid Films, bought out Pathé-Cinéma, which became Pathé-Natan. In 1939 this company collapsed, but soon afterwards a group of financiers attempted to resuscitate it, this new company becoming, in 1944, the Société Nouvelle Pathé-Cinéma, orientated primarily towards distribution.

Charles Pathé, *De Pathé Frères à Pathé Cinéma*, Lyons, 1970.

***PATHER PANCHALI,*** India, 1955. 2hr. *Cast* Kanu Bannerjee (Harihar), Karuna Bannerjee (Sarbojaya), Subir Bannerjee (Apu), Uma Das Gupta (Durga), Chunibala ('Auntie').
*Aparajito* (*The Unvanquished*), India, 1956. 1¾hr.

*Cast* Kanu Bannerjee, Karuna Bannerjee, Pinaki Sen Gupta (Apu as a boy), Sumiran Ghosjal (Apu as an adolescent).

*Apur Sansar (The World of Apu)*, India, 1959. 1¾hr. *Cast* Soumitra Chatterjee (Apu), Sharmila Tagore (Aparna), Shapan Mukerjee (Pulu).

Production team for the trilogy: *dir* Satyajit Ray; *prod* Government of West Bengal; *scr* Ray, from the novels *Pather Panchali* and *Aparajito* by Bhibuti Bashan Bannerjee; *ph* Subrata Mitra; *des* Bansi Chandragupta; *ed* Dulal Dutta; *mus* Ravi Shankar.

Satyajit RAY's discovery of the films of DE SICA and FLAHERTY inspired him to film this account of a boy growing up in a rapidly changing society. Unable to find backing for the project, he set out with Subrata Mitra, like Ray an absolute beginner, as cameraman and Bansi Chandragupta, who had worked with RENOIR on *The River* (1950), as art director to shoot test material; but lack of funds forced them to abandon the project. In 1952 Ray raised enough money (by selling various possessions including his mother's and his wife's jewellery—a very last resort in Indian families) to complete a forty-minute silent ROUGH CUT: a year later Dr B. C. Roy, Prime Minister of Bengal, arranged government backing. (*Pather Panchali* may be translated as 'Little Song of the Road', and the subsidy was charged to road improvements, there being no official source of funds.) In 1955 *Pather Panchali* opened in Calcutta where it was an immediate success.

The individual quality of Ray's earliest films is perhaps less surprising than the accomplishment displayed by virtual novices working with very limited resources. In the first two parts of the trilogy dialogue is largely replaced by action and physical expression. Rural life provides an evolving background against which family and social relationships are observed with a rare quality of warmth and insight; the pace is leisurely, and there are no important events that do not spring naturally out of the villagers' way of life. *Apur Sansar*, in which the boy Apu, now grown up, has been separated from his family by death and from village life by education and economic factors, has a more conventionally structured plot and a fairly elaborate script.

*Pather Panchali* was awarded the prize for 'best human document' at CANNES in 1956 and *Aparajito* won the Golden Lion at VENICE in 1957.

**PATHS OF GLORY**, US, 1957. 1½hr. *Dir* Stanley Kubrick; *prod* James B. Harris for Bryna; *scr* Kubrick, Calder Willingham, Jim Thompson, based on the novel by Humphrey Cobb; *ph* George Krause; *cast* Kirk Douglas (Col Dax), Adolphe Menjou (Gen Broulard), George Macready (Gen Mireau), Ralph Meeker (Corp Paris), Timothy Carey (Pte Ferol).

This harshly uncompromising account of an incident in the First World War is not so much anti-war like THE BIG PARADE (1925) or ALL QUIET ON THE WESTERN FRONT (1930), as anti-militarist. Its chief concern is with the gulf between officers and men, unbridgeable even by the conscientious attempts of Colonel Dax (Kirk DOUGLAS) to defend three men against a patently unjust court-martial charge; there is savage irony in the cutting from the officers bargaining for promotion in the comfort of their quarters in a requisitioned castle to the men in the squalor of the trenches. On its first release the film was banned in parts of France, throughout Switzerland, and in US military cinemas in Europe.

LOSEY's *King and Country* (1964) dealt with a closely similar subject.

**PAUL, ROBERT WILLIAM** (1869–1943), British inventor and maker of scientific instruments, became one of the most important of pioneer English film producers. In 1899 he opened a studio at Muswell Hill, London, and until 1905 maintained an output of some fifty films a year, including a number of trick subjects mostly directed by Walter Booth. Of his surviving productions, typical titles are *A Railway Collision* (c. 1900), *The Waif and the Wizard* (1900), *The Haunted Curiosity Shop* (1901), *A Chess Dispute* (1903), and *Drat That Boy* (c. 1904), a tale of a mischievous boy who uses a bellows to cover his mother with soot. Perhaps the most famous is *The ? Motorist* (1906) with its car which goes up a house, into the sky, around the moon, and on to the rings of Saturn. Paul's films were popular with the public of the time, but in 1910 he abandoned production and returned to scientific pursuits.

**PAWNSHOP, The**, US, 1916. 30min. *Dir*, *scr* Charles Chaplin; *prod* Mutual; *ph* Rollie Totheroh, William C. Foster; *cast* Charlie Chaplin (clerk), Albert Austin (customer), Henry Bergman (boss), Edna Purviance (his daughter), Eric Campbell (thief), James T. Kelley.

A typically accomplished example of CHAPLIN's dozen titles for MUTUAL, this seems—with THE ADVENTURER (1917)—to be a particular favourite for children's parties. This is perhaps because it contains one of his most inventive mime sequences, in which an alarm clock is rapidly transformed from a patient, whose heart Charlie listens to with a stethoscope, to a can of peas on which he uses a tin-opener, to a mouth from which he extracts bad teeth, and so on. When he has finished, of course, the clock is quite ruined.

PAXINOU, KATINA (1900–72), Greek stage actress, a powerful and distinguished tragedienne, who won international acclaim (and an OSCAR) for her performance in *For Whom the Bell Tolls* (Sam WOOD, 1943). None of her subsequent parts quite reached comparable heights, but she appeared in several notable films including *Mourning Becomes Electra* (Dudley NICHOLS, 1947), *Confidential Report* (Orson WELLES, 1955), and ROCCO E I SUOI FRATELLI (*Rocco and his Brothers*, Luchino VISCONTI, 1960). She also appeared in a British film, *Uncle Silas* (1947).

PEARSON, GEORGE (1875–1973), prolific British producer, director, and writer, a leading and thoughtful figure in British films of the silent period and the earlier days of sound. He was thirty-seven when he gave up his career as a schoolmaster to enter films, initially making travel pictures, then features including *A Study in Scarlet* (1914), *John Halifax, Gentleman* (1915), and the *Urtus* serials (1915–17). He was prominent as a director for the Samuelson company, and is probably best remembered now for creating in Betty Balfour the first internationally-recognized British film star, making eleven films with her, including four about the Cockney character Squibs. She also starred in his most celebrated comedy-dramas *Love, Life and Laughter* (1923) and *Reveille* (1924), a film remarkable for its editing innovations.

Pearson was much in demand as a lecturer and contributor to periodicals and acted as spokesman for the industry during the campaign which led to the introduction of the Film Quota legislation of 1927. His own company, Welsh Pearson, was a major force in the British film industry of the period, and in the early thirties he was co-producer of some notable films including *Journey's End* (1930) and *The Good Companions* (1933). From then until the outbreak of war, he directed a number of minor films, and for several years after 1940 he was active as a producer of documentaries for the COLONIAL FILM UNIT. He wrote an interesting account of his years in film, *Flashback* (London, 1957).

PECK, GREGORY (1916– ), US actor who began his film career in 1944 in *The Keys of the Kingdom*. His many appearances include leading roles in *Spellbound* (1945), DUEL IN THE SUN (1946), *Twelve O'Clock High* (1949), THE GUNFIGHTER (1950), *Captain Horatio Hornblower* (1951), ROMAN HOLIDAY (1953), *The Big Country* (1958), which he co-produced, and *Arabesque* (1966), but only the ageing, disillusioned gunman in *The Gunfighter* gave full scope to his talent. His affable personality and engaging, relaxed manner possibly tended to obscure his acting ability, and his work seemed to promise a new dimension under Robert MULLIGAN's direction in *To Kill a Mockingbird* (1962) and *The Stalking Moon* (1968).

Peck produced *The Trial of the Catonsville Nine* (1972), about the radical priest Daniel Berrigan, and *The Dove* (1974).

PECKINPAH, SAM (1926– ), US director, worked in the theatre and then in television where he wrote and directed several Western series, notably 'Gunsmoke', 'The Westerner', and 'The Rifleman'. His first film script was for Don SIEGEL's *The Invasion of the Body Snatchers* (1956) and his first film as director was *The Deadly Companions* (1961). RIDE THE HIGH COUNTRY (1962, *Guns in the Afternoon* in GB) was followed by *Major Dundee*, released in 1964 after considerable difficulties which included extensive cutting of Peckinpah's original version. It resulted in several barren years before he attracted wide attention with THE WILD BUNCH (1969). Like *Ride the High Country* and his next film *The Ballad of Cable Hogue* (1970), this was an evocation of the Western myth at odds with the progress of history and technology. Its lyrical disenchantment, embodied in Lucien BALLARD's fine camerawork, captivated audiences even while the extreme violence provoked criticism.

Peckinpah's answer to these strictures was his first non-Western film *Straw Dogs* (1971), made in England, a grotesque compendium of horrors set uneasily in a Cornish village. He returned to the West with *Junior Bonner* (1972), about modern rodeo riders, a wry observation on the contemporary cheapening of the cowboy's skills. After *The Getaway* (1973) he returned to the old West with *Pat Garrett and Billy the Kid* (1973); this again suffered from cutting not authorized by the director, but its account of the last days of BILLY THE KID brought psychological insight to semi-mythological figures.

PENN, ARTHUR (1922– ), US director, after war service and college, studied at the ACTORS' STUDIO and from 1953 directed plays for television and on Broadway. Paul NEWMAN played BILLY THE KID in Penn's first film, THE LEFT-HANDED GUN (1958), which although uneven in quality gave Penn his preferred subject: a historical figure around whom simple myths have accrued as the focus for a study in human psychology. His next film was an adaptation of *The Miracle Worker* (1962), which he had also directed for television and on Broadway, with Anne BANCROFT and Patty Duke repeating their striking performances as Annie Sullivan and Helen Keller. *Mickey One* (1965), an elliptical study of paranoia, was less successful on all counts. THE CHASE (1966) powerfully showed an escaped convict at the mercy of society, with Marlon BRANDO as the honest sheriff providing a victim for the explosion of violence in a corrupt community.

BONNIE AND CLYDE (1967), which brought Penn international acclaim, again dealt with historical figures viewed from a contemporary standpoint. *Alice's Restaurant* (1969) was entirely up to date, using a ballad by Arlo Guthrie to cast an affectionate, regretful eye over the hippy life, but still frequently reverting to the Depression years with songs by Woody Guthrie and references to his life. The legends of the American West are the subject of *Little Big Man* (1970), the picaresque saga of a white child brought up by the Cheyenne and, as an adult, pulled between two cultures. As in all his period films, Penn's sense of historical perspective is acute and complex: he views his characters with a mixture of cool hindsight and affectionate nostalgia. All his films contain themes of violence, stemming from the difficulty of integrating particular individuals into accepted codes, but the violence is balanced by the humour and irony and is never introduced gratuitously.

**PENNEBAKER, DONN ALAN** (1930– ), US documentary film-maker, developed his style in the DREW ASSOCIATES school of DIRECT CINEMA film-makers working for television in the early sixties. Like Richard LEACOCK and Al MAYSLES he combines an extremely acute cameraman's eye with a zealot's belief in the moral and aesthetic superiority of working methods that interfere as little as possible in the situations being filmed.

After working on films like *Primary* (1960) and THE CHAIR (1963) he left Drew Associates in 1963. His best-known film, *Don't Look Back* (1967), was made independently; he has since reverted to collaborating with Leacock on informal projects like *One PM* (1969) and on big-budget feature documentaries including *Monterey Pop* (1968) and *Sweet Toronto* (1970).

**PEOPLE ON THE MOUNTAIN** see EMBEREK A HAVASON

**PEOPLE ON SUNDAY** see MENSCHEN AM SONNTAG

**PÉPÉ-LE-MOKO,** France, 1937. 1½hr. *Dir* Julien Duvivier; *prod* Paris Film; *scr* Henri Jeanson, Roger D'Ashelbe, Duvivier, from a novel by D'Ashelbe; *ph* Kruger, Marc Fossard; *des* Jacques Krauss; *mus* Vincent Scotto, Mohamed Ygner Buchen; *cast* Jean Gabin (Pépé), Mireille Ballin (Gaby), Lino Noro (Ines), Charpin (Régis), Saturnin Fabre (grandfather), Gabriel

Gabrio (Carlos), Lucas Gridoux (Slimane), Dalio (L'Arbi).

Pépé is a notorious French outlaw living in Algiers, within the confines of the Casbah where he is safe from the law. He falls in love with a Parisian girl visiting the city, and is tempted out of his refuge.

Made in the tradition of early American gangster films, glorifying the outlaw at the expense of society, the film did much to consolidate the myth of GABIN as the doomed outcast, and represents one of the best examples of the 'poetic realism' style current in France in the thirties.

A Hollywood remake in 1938, *Algiers*, starring Charles BOYER and Hedy LAMARR and directed by John CROMWELL, completely failed to capture the force and integrity of DUVIVIER's film, while causing the temporary withdrawal of the original in all countries except France (see COPYRIGHT).

**PERFORATIONS,** the regularly spaced holes along one or both edges of the film by means of which it is transported and registered. At the gate of the camera (or, *mutatis mutandis*, the projector) a claw engages each perforation, pulls the unexposed film into position, holds it steady during exposure, and finally moves it on. Magnetic sound film is perforated identically so that it can be driven in absolute SYNCHRONIZATION with the picture. In OPTICAL printing and EFFECTS work, specially precise perforations are used to register each frame accurately, since tiny errors of position in one part of the composite picture would be obvious.

**PÉRIER, FRANÇOIS** (1919– ), French actor, played a minor role in CARNÉ's *Hôtel du Nord* (1938). He quickly developed from shy, romantic parts in AUTANT-LARA's *Sylvie et le fantôme* (1945), CHRISTIAN-JAQUE's *Un Revenant* (1946), and CLAIR's *Le Silence est d'or* (1947), to stronger characterizations: as the chauffeur Heurtebise in ORPHÉE (1950), the drunken husband in *Gervaise* (René CLÉMENT, 1956), and the ignoble Oscar in LE NOTTI DI CABIRIA (1957). He remains a busy and highly professional character actor: his more recent appearances include MELVILLE's *Le Samourai* (1967), Z (1968), and JUSTE AVANT LA NUIT (1971).

**PÉRINAL, GEORGES** (1897–1965), French cameraman who entered the film business as a projectionist in 1913. He worked as lighting cameraman with some of France's most distinguished directors, including FEYDER (*Les Nouveaux Messieurs*, 1929), COCTEAU (LE SANG D'UN POÈTE, 1930), and CLAIR (SOUS LES TOITS DE PARIS, 1930; A NOUS LA LIBERTÉ, 1931; LE

MILLION, 1932; *Quatorze juillet*, 1933), and was invited to England by Alexander KORDA. His controlled camerawork was a constant element in a wide variety of Korda productions, from THE PRIVATE LIFE OF HENRY VIII (1933), REMBRANDT and THINGS TO COME (both 1936), through to *An Ideal Husband* (1947) and THE FALLEN IDOL (1948). In the late fifties he worked in France and Hollywood, retiring to England.

**PERKINS, ANTHONY** (1932– ), US actor, whose first film was *The Actress* (1953), co-starring Jean SIMMONS. He then spent some time on Broadway, returning to Hollywood to appear in *Friendly Persuasion* (William WYLER, 1956). He has since specialized in tense, sometimes neurotic roles, as in PSYCHO (1960), Orson WELLES's LE PROCÈS (*The Trial*, 1963), Mike NICHOLS's *Catch-22* (1970), *WUSA* (1970), and CHABROL's *La Décade prodigieuse* (1971).

**PERRAULT, PIERRE** (1927– ), Canadian writer, broadcaster, and film-maker, a leading figure in the Québecois movement for the recognition of French-Canadian culture. He is best known for his extraordinary exploration of the lives of fishermen in the St Lawrence estuary in *Pour la suite du monde* (1963, with Michel BRAULT), *La Règne du jour* (1966), and *Les Voitures d'eau* (1969), filmed in a style deriving from CINÉMA-VÉRITÉ.

**PERSISTENCE OF VISION,** a property of the human eye which causes the successive individual still pictures comprising a film to be seen as a continuous picture. In 1824, long before motion pictures and even photography, it was discovered that the eye retains the impression of an image for a brief moment after the image is removed. If a new image is presented quickly enough, the eye will not perceive the interval between them. The motion picture projector takes advantage of this phenomenon to black out the screen with a rotating shutter while the film is being advanced to the next frame. But if this happens at too slow a rate the eye perceives the intervals as flicker; early silent films suffered from this, which accounts for their nickname 'the FLICKERS'. At about 50 blackouts per second, flicker disappears.

Persistence of vision is only one of the principles underlying the motion picture. The illusion of *movement* from successive still pictures is attributed to the so-called 'phi phenomenon', a psychological effect occurring in the brain, not the eye. The individual pictures seem to fuse into continuous action at a much lower rate, about 16 frames per second, which is still the standard projection speed for silent films.

**PERSONA,** Sweden, 1966. 1¼hr. *Dir, scr* Ingmar Bergman; *prod* Svensk Filmindustri; *ph* Sven Nykvist; *ed* Ulla Ryghe; *cast* Liv Ullmann (Elisabet Vogler), Bibi Andersson (Nurse Alma), Margaretha Krook (doctor), Gunnar Björnstrand (Vogler).

Elisabet Vogler, a famous actress, is stricken with psychosomatic dumbness and is placed in the care of Nurse Alma in an isolated seaside house. Enclosed in mutual dependence, they pass through shifting stages in their relationship, ranging from hysterical aggression to total intimacy: at moments the two women become indistinguishable. Images of cool beauty convey the stripping of identity, the self-exposure which is imperative but ultimately destructive. Powerful performances by Liv ULLMANN and Bibi ANDERSSON draw the spectator into their personal anguish.

A prologue which rushes through a historical succession of film images and culminates in the film 'burning' in the projector would appear to intend an effect of alienation. The narrative itself, however, is so absorbing as to counteract such an effect.

**PETE SMITH SPECIALTIES,** probably the best known of the many series of short programme-fillers issued by Hollywood studios.

Pete Smith entered films as a publicist: for five years he was director of publicity for PARAMOUNT, moving to METRO-GOLDWYN-MAYER in 1925. He began writing and speaking the narrations for short films, notably *Goofy Movies*, a series consisting of clips from early films, and his own series which originated as *Pete Smith Oddities*. Sports subjects were favourite material in the early days; later the range of subjects widened considerably, but whatever the theme, the principal appeal was in the bright, and often amusing, narration. In the fifties the *Pete Smith Specialties* became mainly comedy anecdotes featuring Dave O'Brien, but unlike all other short-subject series they were not pinned down to a stereotyped formula—one issue could deal with demolition, rough weather, and early aviation (topped by the swaying and disintegration of the Tacoma suspension bridge four months after its completion), another could include Polly Patterson demonstrating economical savoury and sweet dishes, and another the technique and requirements of rodeo riding.

**PETIT SOLDAT, Le** (*The Little Soldier*), France, 1960, released 1963. 1½hr. *Dir, scr* Jean-Luc Godard; *prod* Georges de Beauregard; *ph* Raoul Coutard; *ed* Agnès Guillemot; *mus*

Maurice Leroux; *cast* Michel Subor (Bruno For-estier), Anna Karina (Veronica Dreyer), Henri-Jacques Huet (Jacques), Paul Beauvais (Paul), Laszlo Szabo (Laszlo).

During the Algerian war Bruno Forestier is a secret agent working against the FLN; but in a situation where Left and Right have become indistinguishable in their methods he feels a sense of nostalgia for the 'simpler' issues of the thirties, like the Spanish Civil War.

It was almost certainly the torture scenes, as much as the political content of the film, which resulted in its being banned by the French Cen-sor Board and Minister of Information until January 1963. The horror of those scenes lies in their matter-of-fact presentation and the every-day banality of the implements of pain and of their location. The film was also criticized for its confused plot which some felt reduced the Al-gerian crisis to a witless game of cops and robbers played out by Arab terrorists and Poujadist reactionaries all over Geneva, but this very con-fusion was a mirror of a time when, according to the opinion polls, three-quarters of the French population were undecided about the Algerian question. This objective presentation of the com-plexities of the situation also laid GODARD open to accusations of unfeeling neutrality.

*PHILADELPHIA STORY, The,* US, 1940. 1¾hr. *Dir* George Cukor; *prod* Joseph L. Man-kiewicz for MGM; *scr* Donald Ogden Stewart; *ph* Joseph Ruttenberg; *cast* Katharine Hepburn (Tracy Lord), Cary Grant (C. Dexter Haven), James Stewart (Macaulay Connor).

Tracy, a wealthy, dominating divorcée, on the eve of her second marriage has various romantic tussles with her first husband (Dexter) and a gossip-column journalist (Connor). She ends by surrendering some at least of her domination and remarrying Dexter. Stewart's elegant script, from Philip Barry's play, and CUKOR's direction succeed in integrating three very different types of performance: HEPBURN's polished stridency, GRANT's gentle mockery, and STEWART's throw-away acidity.

The musical remake HIGH SOCIETY appeared in 1956.

*PHILIPE,* GÉRARD (1922–59), French actor. His first film was Marc ALLÉGRET's *Les Petites du Quai aux Fleurs* (1943), but he came to pub-lic attention in the role of the adolescent lover, François, in AUTANT-LARA's LE DIABLE AU CORPS (1947). The blend of harshness and ten-derness, of boyishness and latent maturity, which he brought to the part established him as an actor of elegance and abundant talent. He played a series of more or less romantic leads, in, for example, CHRISTIAN-JAQUE's *La Chartreuse de*

*Parme* (1948), Allégret's *Une si jolie petite plage* (1948), and *Tous les chemins mènent à Rome* directed by Boyer in 1949, and became im-mensely popular with the French public. After playing in OPHULS' LA RONDE (1950), he made one of his most celebrated appearances as the hero of Christian-Jaque's robust historical bur-lesque, *Fanfan la Tulipe* (1951).

One of his most controversial roles was the title part in René CLÉMENT's KNAVE OF HEARTS (1954); Philipe played the part of the French Don Juan in London with a reticence and inscrutability which disturbed many critics, although for others it was one of his greatest performances, contrasting finely with his hard-edged and lucid portrayal of Valmont in VADIM's LES LIAISONS DANGEUREUSES (1959).

Philipe worked with many of the directors prominent in France during the forties and fifties. His other films include *La Beauté du diable* (1950) and *Les Grandes Manoeuvres* (1955) directed by René CLAIR; *Juliette ou la clef des songes* (1951) by Marcel CARNÉ; *Le Rouge et le noir* (1954) and *Le Joueur* (1958) by Autant-Lara; *Si Versailles m'était conté* (1954) and *Si Paris nous était conté* (1955) by Sacha GUITRY; *Les Orgueilleux* (1953) and *La Meilleure Part* (1956) by Yves ALLÉGRET; *Les Aventures de Till l'espiègle* (1956), which he co-directed with Joris IVENS; and *La Fièvre monte a El Pao* (1959) directed by BUÑUEL.

He also worked extensively in the theatre, mainly with Jean Vilar at the Théâtre National Populaire, where his successes included *Le Prince de Hombourg, On ne badine pas avec l'amour,* and, above all, *Le Cid.*

His early death at the age of thirty-six deprived the French cinema of a consider-able actor, as well as a dearly loved popular hero. Tribute was paid to his memory when he was depicted on a French postage stamp in 1961.

*PHILO VANCE.* William POWELL was the screen exponent *par excellence* of S. S. Van Dine's detective hero. His first appearance in the role was in PARAMOUNT's *The Canary Murder Case* (1928); the cast also included Louise BROOKS and Jean ARTHUR. It was followed by *The Green Murder Case* (1929), with Jean Arthur again in the cast. METRO-GOLDWYN-MAYER made a Philo Vance film, *The Bishop Murder Case* (1930), starring Basil RATHBONE, while the Paramount series with William Powell ended with *The Benson Murder Case* (1930). It was taken up by WARNER BROS with *The Kennel Murder Case* (1933), in which Powell was sup-ported by Mary ASTOR and Eugene PALLETTE. After Powell changed his allegiance to MGM and the successful THIN MAN series, Philo Vance reappeared occasionally on the screen up to the late forties.

*PIATKA Z ULICY BARSKIEJ* (*Five Boys from Barska Street*), Poland, 1953. Agfacolor; 2hr. *Dir* Aleksander Ford; *prod* Film Polski; *scr* Ford, Kazimierz Kozniewski, from the latter's novel; *ph* Jaroslav Tuzar, Karel Chodura; *cast* Tadeusz Janczar (Kazek), Aleksandra Slaska (Hanka), Mieczyslaw Stoor (Marek), Andrzej Kozak (Jacek), Tadeusz Lomnicki (Lutek).

Poland's first major production in colour is a sometimes uneasy blend of propagandist social realism and melodrama, a blend characteristic of pre-Gomulka days. Post-war reconstruction parallels the social rehabilitation of five delinquents. In its concern for youth, the film is thematically linked with FORD's *Legion ulicy* (*The Legion of the Street*, 1932) and *Ulica Graniczna* (*Border Street*, 1948).

**PICCOLI**, MICHEL (1925– ), French actor often associated with urbane bourgeois roles, became a stage actor in the late forties and made his first film appearance in 1949. After a number of routine 'policiers', interrupted by BUÑUEL's *La Mort en ce jardin* (*Evil Eden*, 1956), he achieved his first major part in MELVILLE's *Le Doulos* (1962). He has worked with many distinguished directors including HITCHCOCK, in *Topaz* (1969), CHABROL, in *La Décade prodigieuse* (*Ten Days' Wonder*, 1971) and *Les Noces rouges* (*Red Wedding*, 1973), and, most frequently, Buñuel, notably in *Belle de jour* (1966) and LE CHARME DISCRET DE LA BOURGEOISIE (*The Discreet Charm of the Bourgeoisie*, 1972). He turned to producing with Claude Faraldo's *Themroc* (1973) in which he also played the lead.

**PICK**, LUPU (1886–1931), German actor and director, of Romanian origin. Opposed to the principles of EXPRESSIONISM, he made SCHERBEN (1921), with his wife Edith Pasca as the daughter, and SYLVESTER (1923), both KAMMERSPIELFILMS, written by Carl MAYER. To these two films the first use of flexible camera movement is often wrongly ascribed. Pick was intended as director for the third film in the trilogy, DER LETZTE MANN (1924), but differed with Mayer over the character of the doorman, whose part Pick was to have taken. In LANG's *Spione* (1928) he played a Japanese diplomat. His *Napoleon auf Sankt Helena* (1929), was scripted by Abel GANCE. *Gassenhauer* (1931) was his only sound film.

**PICKFORD**, MARY (1893– ), Canadian-born US actress, real name Gladys Mary Smith, was a professional stage actress from the age of five. By 1909 she had had extensive stage experience on tour and on Broadway: it was only a period of unemployment that induced her to apply for work in films. She approached the BIOGRAPH studio, where she was taken on by D. W. GRIFFITH. In her early films her roles were varied, but she soon settled into one the public adored—a ringleted *ingénue* who brought an individual vitality to conventionally sentimental tales. Although she had no personal screen credit, she became known to audiences as 'Little Mary' or, following Florence LAWRENCE, the 'Biograph Girl'.

Her immense popularity could have made her a pawn in the battle for supremacy between producers, but she moved between companies with a shrewd awareness of her own commercial value. From Biograph she went to Carl LAEMMLE's Independent Motion Pictures Company (as the 'IMP Girl'), then to Majestic, back to Biograph, and, after a brief return to the stage, to FAMOUS PLAYERS, greatly increasing her salary with each change. At Famous Players, Adolph ZUKOR was forced to raise her pay from $500 to $2000 a week between 1913 and 1915, and then lost her to the AMERICAN FILM COMPANY's offer of $4000 a week. He tempted her back in 1916 with a two-year contract which guaranteed a total of over a million dollars, and created two subsidiary companies, the Mary Pickford Studio to produce, and Artcraft to distribute, her films. Some of her best films were made at this time, including *The Little American* (1917), a PROPAGANDA piece directed by Cecil B. DEMILLE, *Rebecca of Sunnybrook Farm* (1917), and *M'liss* (1918), both directed by Marshall NEILAN.

At the expiry of her contract, FIRST NATIONAL outbid Zukor with an offer of $350,000 for each of three films, including another children's classic directed by Neilan, *Daddy-Long-Legs* (1919). Her enormous following, based on her touching conviction in playing adolescents, even survived her divorce from Owen Moore (with whom she had appeared in several earlier films) and her remarriage to Douglas FAIRBANKS in 1919. In that year, with Fairbanks, Charles CHAPLIN, and Griffith, she set up UNITED ARTISTS, taking an active part in the management of the company. Its first successes, in fact, were more Mary Pickford films, tailored to the audience she had already acquired—*Pollyanna* (1920) and *Little Lord Fauntleroy* (1921) among them; in *Little Lord Fauntleroy* she played both the boy hero and his mother. Not unnaturally she was tiring of *ingénue* roles and used her independence to try a new image. She engaged Ernst LUBITSCH, newly arrived in Hollywood, to direct her in *Rosita* (1923) as a fiery Spanish beauty, but the public refused to accept the change. Even after she had bobbed her famous ringlets, she was forced to bow to her fans' preferences and wear a curly wig for *Sparrows* (1926).

Her first sound film, *Coquette* (1929), was a moderate success, but THE TAMING OF THE SHREW (1929) was a failure; perhaps surprisingly, for her Katharine, although light-weight, has considerable wit. She made two more sound films, returned briefly to the stage, and worked in radio during the thirties. In 1935 she divorced Fairbanks and married Charles 'Buddy' Rogers. In later years she lived as a total recluse at her palatial Hollywood home 'Pickfair'.

Her autobiography *Sunshine and shadow* (New York, 1955; London, 1956) is usefully supplemented by Robert Windeler's *Sweetheart* (London, 1973).

***PICKUP ON SOUTH STREET***, US, 1952. 1¼hr. *Dir, scr* Samuel Fuller, from a story by Dwight Taylor; *prod* Twentieth Century-Fox; *ph* Joe MacDonald; *ed* Nick de Maggio; *cast* Richard Widmark (Skip McCoy), Jean Peters (Candy), Thelma Ritter (Moe), Richard Kiley (Joey).

A pickpocket is instrumental in cracking a Communist spy-ring, helped by a girl who has unwittingly been a courier. FULLER'S complex film is more concerned with accurately portraying the world of the petty criminal, and the testing of his physical and mental strength, than with making an anti-Communist statement. In fact the political device is consistent with much of Fuller's other work, and when Skip—convincingly played by Richard WIDMARK—does finally break up the spy-ring, it is for personal motives of revenge, rather than from righteous political fervour.

**PIDGEON**, WALTER (1897–   ), US actor born in Canada, appeared in films from 1926 but made little impression until the introduction of sound. As an experienced stage actor he then became much in demand as a leading man in musicals and straight romances. In the forties he became very successful in variations on the role of an honest, attractive embodiment of domestic virtue, as in *How Green was my Valley* (1941), *Mrs Miniver* (1942), *Madame Curie* (1943), *That Forsyte Woman* (1950, *The Forsyte Saga* in GB), and *The Miniver Story* (1950). In eight films he played (often as an Englishman) opposite Greer GARSON, a partnership that was immensely successful. His career has continued with polished character performances, but his only outstanding films of recent years are *Advise and Consent* (1961), in which he played an elderly Senator, and *Funny Girl* (1968), in which he made a brief appearance as Florenz Ziegfeld.

***PIERROT-LE-FOU***, France, 1965. Techniscope; 1¾hr; Eastman Color. *Dir, scr* Jean-Luc Godard, based on the novel *Obsession* by Lionel White; *prod* Georges de Beauregard; *ph* Raoul Coutard; *ed* Françoise Collin; *mus* Antoine Duhamel; *cast* Jean-Paul Belmondo (Ferdinand), Anna Karina (Marianne), Dirk Sanders (Marianne's brother), Raymond Devos (the man on the pier), Graziella Galvani (Ferdinand's wife), Samuel Fuller (himself).

In his adaptation and treatment of Lionel White's story about a married man who gives up everything to run off with a seventeen-year-old baby-sitter and becomes inextricably involved with her criminal associates, GODARD makes many of his characteristic concerns apparent. There are didactic interpolations and unassimilated references (to Vietnam, the Yemen, Angola, and the Kennedy assassination); stylization of violence and symbolic use of colour; the rivalry of the contemplative and the active life represented by Ferdinand and Marianne respectively; and the impossibility of establishing lasting relationships. This last theme dominates the film, and an evocation of natural beauty rare in Godard's work, particularly in the depiction of the island idyll, provides the clue to an authentic sense of human tragedy surprising in so cerebral a director. BELMONDO and KARINA beautifully portray the relationship which exists in tensions between *désinvolture* and inevitable disaster.

**PIETRANGELI**, ANTONIO (1919–68), Italian critic, screenwriter, and director, began his film career as a critic, writing for BIANCO E NERO and campaigning for the revival of the Italian cinema. He came to particular prominence in the postwar years as an active supporter of the neorealist movement, and is in fact credited with coining the term NEO-REALISM. He began scriptwriting with OSSESSIONE (1942), on which he was also assistant director to VISCONTI, and scripted such films as *Fabiola* (BLASETTI, 1947), ROSSELLINI's *Europa 51* (1952), *La lupa* (LATTUADA, 1953). In 1953 he directed *Il sole negli occhi* for which he received a special Nastro D'Argento award, and in 1955 *Lo scapolo* starring Alberto SORDI. During the period to 1966 he made a further eight films dealing with the problems and perspectives of ordinary people. He was drowned while directing *Come, quando e con chi* on location.

***PIGSTY*** see PORCILE, IL

**PILBEAM**, NOVA (1919–  ), British actress, made her first stage appearance at the age of five. Her later experience includes appearances with the Old Vic and a good deal of work in radio.

The difficult role of the child in *Little Friend* (1934) was her first screen success, her intelligent, sensitive face and natural manner striking a fresh and welcome note. Next came HITCH-COCK'S THE MAN WHO KNEW TOO MUCH (1934) and, in 1936, *Tudor Rose*, in which she gave a fine performance as Lady Jane Grey. Later films include *Young and Innocent* (Hitchcock, 1939), *The Next of Kin* (Thorold DICKINSON, 1941), *This Man is Mine* (1946), *Counterblast* and *Three Weird Sisters* (both 1948). Gifted with an exceptionally beautiful speaking voice, she has perhaps been one of the neglected talents of the British cinema.

**PILGRIM, The,** US, 1923. 1hr. *Dir, scr* Charles Chaplin, assisted by Chuck Riesner; *prod* First National; *ph* Rollie Totheroh; *cast* Charlie Chaplin (the escaped convict), Edna Purviance (the girl), Kitty Bradbury (the mother), Mack Swain (the deacon), Dinky Dean [Dean Riesner] (the boy), Sydney Chaplin (his father), May Wells (his mother), Lloyd Underwood (the Elder), Chuck Riesner (the crook), Tom Murry (the Sheriff).

The last of CHAPLIN'S eight films for FIRST NATIONAL (billed as 'the Million Dollar Movies'—the sum which the company guaranteed him for them) deserves to be as well known as SHOULDER ARMS (1918) and THE KID (1920). As in THE ADVENTURER (1917), Chaplin is an escaped convict but this time he disguises himself as a priest, justifying one of his most memorable sequences, a sermon which consists of a mime rendering of the story of David and Goliath; at the end, he responds to the congregation's approval by taking several curtain calls. Once again, Chaplin was on thin ice, but only the State of Pennsylvania refused to let the film be shown because 'it made the ministry look ridiculous'.

**PINEWOOD,** British film studios, formally opened in September 1936, two years after the formation of Pinewood Studios Ltd, with J. Arthur RANK as chairman. Herbert WILCOX completed *London Melody* (1936) at the newly opened studios, and the first film made in its entirety there was Carol REED's *A Man With Your Voice* (1936). Gabriel PASCAL's PYGMALION was completed in 1938, but war the following year disrupted production, and the Royal Mint moved in to make copper coins; in 1941 the RAF and CROWN FILM UNIT began production there. In 1945 the RANK ORGANISATION resumed full control, producing POWELL and PRESSBURGER's *Black Narcissus* (1947) and THE RED SHOES (1948), David LEAN's GREAT EXPECTATIONS (1946) and OLIVER TWIST (1948), Noël COWARD's *The Astonished Heart* (1950), *Malta Story* (1953), *Genevieve* (1953), *Battle of the River Plate* (1955), *Reach for the Sky* (1956). Despite a period of inactivity around

1950, the studio maintained a consistent output until 1960, when it began a policy of renting its technicians and facilities to independent producers: the result was films such as *The Ipcress File* (1965), *Goldfinger* (1964), *You Only Live Twice* (1967), *Chitty Chitty Bang Bang* (1968), *The Battle of Britain* (1969). The later sixties saw an increasing orientation towards television production; four new stages that are suited to both film and television production represent an investment of over a million pounds by the Rank Organisation in the space of four years. The result is one of the best equipped studios in Europe.

**PIN SCREEN** see ALEXEÏEFF, ANIMATION

**PINTER, HAROLD** (1930–   ), British writer, started as a stage actor and has developed into one of the most influential British playwrights to have emerged since the Second World War. His plays, which are largely plotless and which reveal an uncannily sensitive ear for the rhythms and peculiarities of spoken language, include *The Caretaker*, *The Dumb Waiter*, *The Birthday Party*, and *The Homecoming*. He has written scripts for several films: Clive DONNER's film of *The Caretaker* (1963), *The Pumpkin Eater* (1964), *The Quiller Memorandum* (1966), and three Joseph LOSEY films, THE SERVANT (1963), ACCIDENT (1967), in both of which he had a small part, and THE GO-BETWEEN (1971). *The Birthday Party* was filmed by William Friedkin in 1968. Pinter is married to the actress Vivien MERCHANT.

**PINTOFF, ERNEST,** see UNITED PRODUCTIONS OF AMERICA

**PITTS, ZaSu** (1900–63), US actress, played small parts in films from about 1917. In her earlier career she was above all noted for her performances in GREED (1923) and other films by Erich von STROHEIM (THE WEDDING MARCH, 1926; HALLO SISTER, 1933). From the thirties she was famous as a character actress, with a distinctive wailing voice and perpetually fluttering hands; her last appearance was in *It's a Mad, Mad, Mad, Mad World* (Stanley KRAMER, 1963). Much of her later career had been devoted to stage and television work.

**PIXILLATION,** the use of a stop frame camera to speed up and distort the movement of actors, creating roughly the effect of ANIMATION with live people. The best-known example is Norman MCLAREN's *Neighbours* (1952).

**PLACE IN THE SUN, A,** US, 1951. 2hr. *Dir, prod* George Stevens for Paramount; *scr* Michael

Wilson, Harry Brown, from the novel *An American Tragedy* by Theodore Dreiser and the play by Patrick Kearney; *ph* William C. Mellor; *des* Hans Dreier, Walter Tyler; *cast* Montgomery Clift (George Eastman), Shelley Winters (Alice Trapp), Elizabeth Taylor (Angela Vickers), Ann Revere (Hannah Eastman), Raymond Burr (Marlowe).

Dating from a time when George STEVENS's work was becoming weighty in contrast with his earlier scintillating comedies, his version of Dreiser's AN AMERICAN TRAGEDY unhurriedly depicts the basic immorality of American society. The uncompromising ending made little concession to the box-office, but its principal interest lay in the acting. Montgomery CLIFT gave one of his more sensitive performances as George Eastman; Elizabeth TAYLOR as the society girl, and Shelley WINTERS as the factory girl whom George is morally guilty of murdering were both excellent.

**PLANET OF THE APES,** US, 1968. Panavision; 1¾hr; De Luxe Color. *Dir* Franklin J. Schaffner; *prod* Twentieth Century-Fox; *scr* Michael Wilson, Rod Serling, based on the novel *Monkey Planet* by Pierre Boulle; *ph* Leon Shamroy; *make-up* John Chambers; *cast* Charlton Heston (Taylor), Roddy McDowall (Cornelius), Kim Hunter (Zira), Maurice Evans (Dr Zaius), Lou Wagner (Lucius), Linda Harrison (Nova).

SCHAFFNER evoked with extraordinary feeling the alien culture of a highly civilized ape society ruling the earth in the future, in which HESTON's astronaut is changed from an arrogant human into an anthropological specimen. The film developed its basic paradoxical situation well, and the inventive make-up of fully flexible masks allowed for simian character development and gentle humour. Several sequels followed; *Beneath the Planet of the Apes* (1969), *Escape from the Planet of the Apes* (1971), *Conquest of the Planet of the Apes* (1972), *Battle for the Planet of the Apes* (1973), but none equalled the original. A television series was also based on the idea.

**PLAN-SÉQUENCE,** French critical term without a precise English equivalent (although it is sometimes clumsily rendered as 'plan sequence'), used by critics to describe a protracted shot in which development takes place through movement within the frame rather than by cutting together different shots. The term is applied mainly to the work of RENOIR, who developed the technique during the thirties in spite of technical difficulties (see DEEP FOCUS), and to such directors as VISCONTI and ANTONIONI who followed his lead. For technical and aesthetic reasons, protracted shots with or without movement are very common in recent cinema, but scarcely qualify as *plan-séquences*.

**PLATEAU,** JOSEPH ANTOINE FERDINAND (1801–83), Belgian physicist, became an important figure in cinema prehistory when, after publishing the results of his investigation into the PERSISTENCE OF VISION, he built in 1832 an optical toy which gave the illusion of movement. This device, popularly known as the Magic Disc, is also known under several other names, the most widely employed being Phantascope. A similar device was developed, contemporaneously and independently, by the Austrian physicist Stampfer.

**PLATTS-MILLS,** BARNEY (1944– ), British director, who began working as an editor's assistant at the age of sixteen, later forming an independent company with several friends (Maya Films). After directing two short films he made the low-budget feature BRONCO BULLFROG (1970).

This was followed by *Private Road* (1971), which like his first film dealt with adolescents in a situation of impasse. Maintaining the sensitive observation and warm humour which characterized his first film, *Private Road* was more tightly scripted, and was the first time Platts-Mills worked with professional actors.

A vigorous critic of the way the British film industry is structured, he distributed his second feature independently, hiring a cinema for an opening run of several weeks.

**PLAYBACK,** a production technique in which musical sequences are photographed with artists miming to a previously-recorded sound track. Speech and other sounds can usually be recorded live as each shot is photographed, but musical tempo and performance would vary noticeably between the many shots comprising a complete number. In addition the recording of music demands more stringent placing of microphones than speech, and quality would suffer if the microphones had to be always kept out of camera range. Musical sequences are therefore recorded first in a sound studio and played back while the various shots are photographed. Audiences are rarely aware of the technique, since the fragmented shooting allows the artists to rehearse each bit of miming to perfection. (See DUBBING, POST-SYNCHRONIZATION.)

**PLAYTIME,** France, 1967. 70mm; 2hr; Eastman Color. *Dir* Jacques Tati; *prod* Specta Films; *scr* Tati, Jacques Lagrange; *ph* Jean Badal, Andreas Winding; *des* Eugene Roman; *mus* Francis Lemarque; *cast* Jacques Tati (Monsieur Hulot), Barbara Dennek (American girl),

Jaqueline Lecomte (her friend), Valerie Camille (secretary), France Romilly (sales girl), Erica Dentzler (Madame Giffard), Yvette Crucreux (cloakroom girl), Jack Gautier (guide), Léon Doyen (doorman), Billy Kearns (Monsieur Schultz).

A group of American tourists arrive in Paris, only to find its mass of skyscrapers and office blocks indistinguishable from those of any other big city. Monsieur Hulot, the hero of two previous TATI films, features episodically as he crosses the path of the tourists. The characters are finally united in a restaurant where everything is so brand new that the floor tiles stick to the customers' feet, while the serving hatches are so small that the plates cannot be passed through them.

With its superbly designed sets of concrete and glass, where the only glimpses of traditional Paris are fleeting reflections in plate glass doors, and its luxurious use of colour and the wide screen, *Playtime* is the most visually exciting of Tati's films, and probably his subtlest comedy.

**PLEASENCE,** DONALD (1919– ), British actor, worked in repertory from 1939 and, after war service with the RAF, acted in television as well as the theatre. He has appeared in many films, specializing in evil characters such as the harsh market inspector in LOOK BACK IN ANGER (1959), the cold-eyed killer in *Dr Crippen* (1962), and the master villain Blofeld in *You Only Live Twice* (1967). He played a calculating prisoner-of-war in John STURGES's *The Great Escape* (1962) and 'the embodiment of evil' in George STEVENS's *The Greatest Story Ever Told* (1965). He was the tramp in Harold PINTER's *The Caretaker* on the stage in both London and New York before appearing in the film version directed by Clive DONNER (1963); POLAŃSKI cast him as the middle-aged neurotic and pathetic husband in CUL-DE-SAC (1966).

**PLOW THAT BROKE THE PLAINS, The,** US, 1936. 30min. *Dir, prod, scr, ed* Pare Lorentz for the Resettlement Administration Film Unit; *ph* Paul Strand, Ralph Steiner, Leo Hurwitz, Paul Ivan; *mus* Virgil Thomson; *narr* Thomas Chalmers.

Pare LORENTZ's first film was made for the Resettlement Administration, an agricultural relief agency primarily concerned with the drought which had hit the Great Plains, resulting in the infamous Dust Bowl. The film was beset by difficulties, including political differences among the production team, refusal by the big Hollywood companies to supply STOCK footage, Lorentz's own inexperience, and an attempted distribution boycott by commercial interests who resented government competition. However, Lorentz succeeded in making a documentary of notable conviction and beauty, effectively edited to Virgil THOMSON's first film score.

**POITIER,** SIDNEY (1927– ), US actor from a poor family and virtually self-educated, gained his early acting experience with the American Negro Theater, New York. His first film was *No Way Out* (MANKIEWICZ, 1950). He was outstanding in *Edge of the City* (Martin RITT, 1956, *A Man is Ten Feet Tall* in GB) and he won the award for best actor at the BERLIN film festival in THE DEFIANT ONES (Stanley KRAMER, 1958). Apart from Hattie MCDANIEL, he is the only black actor to have won an OSCAR—for *Lilies of the Field* (1963). He has shown himself a sensitive actor, notably in *Guess Who's Coming to Dinner?* (Kramer, 1967) and *For Love of Ivy* (1968), which he also wrote. His charm and acceptability have been to an extent exploited by Hollywood as a concession to black rights, particularly with IN THE HEAT OF THE NIGHT (1967) and its successors.

*POKOLENIE* (*A Generation*), Poland, 1954. 1½hr. *Dir* Andrzej Wajda; *prod* Film Polski; *scr* Bohdan Czeszko, from his own novel; *ph* Jerzy Lipman; *ed* Czeslaw Raniszewski; *mus* Andrzej Markowski; *cast* Tadeusz Lomnicki (Stach), Urszula Modrzynska (Dorota), Tadeusz Janczar (Jasio), Janusz Paluszkiewicz (Sekula), Ryszard Kotas (Jacek), Roman Polański (Mundek).

The title refers to Poland's 'lost generation', WAJDA's own. This remarkable first feature (for director, cameraman, scriptwriter, composer, and most of the cast), the first in Wajda's wartime resistance trilogy, reflects the restrictions of pre-Gomulka cinema in its over-simplistic idealism and the harsh polarization of nationalist villains and communist heroes—interesting to compare with Wajda's characterization of nationalists in KANAL (1957) and POPIÓL I DIAMENT (1958); but perhaps Aleksander FORD's presence as artistic supervisor granted the filmmakers a greater freedom (in depth of characterization and scope of conflict) than most of their contemporaries. Zbigniew CYBULSKI made his film début in the minor role of Kostek.

**POLAND.** Until 1914 Polish cinema was dominated by Russia, under whose rule part of Poland lay. Most of the indigenous production came from Aleksander Hertz who by 1918 was making five to twelve features a year. His pioneering spirit was reinforced by a happy gift for discovering stars, including Appolonia Chalupek, who was to become famous as Pola NEGRI. Most of the early films were derived from national literature, and after independence in

1918 a wave of anti-Tsarist films appeared, By 1919 the annual output had risen to twenty-two features: this level was maintained until the introduction of sound. Then production dropped, partly because taxes took 42 per cent of profits. In 1930–9 about 146 production companies were set up, of which there were only six whose total output exceeded ten features. Many films were exported to Polish communities in the US and Palestine.

An avant-garde film society, START (Stowarzyszenie Miłośników Filmu Artystycznego—Society of the Devotees of the Artistic Film) was founded in 1929 by a group of students including Wanda JAKUBOWSKA and Eugeniusz Cekalski, later joined by Jerzy BOSSAK, Aleksander FORD, and Jerzy Toeplitz. This group was to have a profound influence on Polish cinema in the post-war years.

Although Polish films of the thirties were popular at home, they achieved little artistic success; Ford's Legion ulicy (The Legion of the Street, 1932) is the only one of any distinction. A number of modest co-productions in Germany and Austria and PARAMOUNT's American-Polish films made at Joinville (see FOREIGN VERSIONS) met with little response. Ford's Przebudzenie (Awakening, 1934) and Jozef Lejtes's Róża (1936) fared better and demonstrated the strongly national flavour of Polish cinema. After the outbreak of the Second World War, filmmaking was permitted by the German Occupation in other countries, but not in Poland for fear of the subtle use of patriotic references.

Polish film was kept alive during the war years by the Polish Army Film Unit, functioning under the Russians and manned by some distinguished directors including Bossak and Ford. In 1944 production of short films began at a small studio in Lubiń and in 1945 general production started again under the state-owned Film Polski organization. Ford, as a colonel of the film unit, commandeered a gymnasium at Lódź which by 1946 had been enlarged to three sound stages. In 1947 BUCZKOWSKI directed the first feature since 1939—Zakazane piosenki (Forbidden Songs), which had documentary overtones and no individual hero. In 1948 Toeplitz opened the Film School at LÓDŹ, which was to become for a time the goal of young film-makers from many countries. Production was concentrated at Lódź with two studios, for feature and educational films; a third studio for puppet films was at nearby Tuszyn. Later developments included an animation studio at Bielsko, a features studio at Wroclaw, and three studios in Warsaw, for features, documentary, and animation, on the same site as the national film archive.

The first post-war films were directly concerned with the war, including Bossak's Powodz (The Flood, 1947), Jakubowska's OSTATNI ETAP (The Last Stage, 1948), on Auschwitz, and Ford's Ulica Graniczna (Border Street, 1948), on the Warsaw Ghetto, all international prize-winners. More general subjects came gradually into focus, Leonard Buczkowski launching happily into comedy with Skarb (The Treasure, 1949) and the indefatigable Ford making Młodość Chopina (Chopin's Youth, 1952) and PIATKA Z ULICY BARSKIEJ (Five Boys from Barska Street), CANNES prize-winner in 1953.

During the years of Stalinism film-makers worked under the extreme bureaucratic and ideological pressure of the 'Court System', by which the Central Committee on Films strictly planned the projects and censored the completed films. By 1956, three years after Stalin's death, the system had given way to a much more flexible network of production units, modelled on the plan originally introduced in Czechoslovakia, and scripts no longer had to be submitted for censorship. By 1958 there were seven of these groups making 18–21 films a year of a highly personal kind: bitter, brilliant, and intellectually tough. The inability of the individual to find a place in the post-war community was a recurrent theme, but the national preoccupation with heroism was the main characteristic.

WAJDA's POKOLENIE (A Generation, 1954) and KANAL (1957) first alerted the world to Polish cinema when they were shown at Cannes; the heroic trilogy was completed with POPIÓL I DIAMENT (Ashes and Diamonds, 1958). The wave included MUNK's EROICA, Czlowiek na torze (Man on the Track) (both 1957), Zezowate szczeście (Bad Luck, 1960), and PASAŻERKA (Passenger, 1963), which he did not live to complete; Witold Lesiewicz's Dezerter (1958); Wojciech HAS's Pożegnania (Farewells, 1958); a comedy, Ewa chce spać (Eve Wants to Sleep, 1958), from the young team of Tadeusz Chmielewski and W. A. Czekalski; Wajda's Niewinni czarodzieje (Innocent Sorcerers), Lotna (both 1959), and Samson (1961). The wildly popular actor Zbigniew CYBULSKI was closely associated with these years.

By 1960 the country was more stable politically and economically and intense examination of contemporary problems began to diminish. In that year Ford made a period piece Krzyzacy Granwald (Knights of the Teutonic Order) to commemorate the 550th anniversary of the Battle of Grunwald. Roman POLAŃSKI's brilliant examination of sexual conflict, NÓŻ W WODZIE (Knife in the Water), appeared in 1962. Like Polański, Jerzy SKOLIMOWSKI went abroad after a promising start in Rysopis (Identification Marks—None, 1964), Walkower (Walkover, 1965), and Bariera (Barrier, 1966). Jerzy KAWALEROWICZ made some shrewd comments on restrictive societies in MATKA JOANNA OD ANIO-ŁÓW (*Mother Joan of the Angels*, 1961), but in *Rekopis znaleziony w Saragossie* (*The Saragossa Manuscript*, 1964) Has was content with a lively romp starring Cybulski.

In spite of Wajda's *Wszystko na sprzedaz* (*Everything for Sale*, 1968) and *Polowanie na muchy* (*Hunting Flies*, 1969), the impetus of Polish film had weakened by the late sixties. The political crisis and the purges which followed the student demonstrations of March 1968 hit the cinema harder than any other art or industry. Every aspect of cinema came under official attack and almost everyone in a key position was either dismissed or demoted; the anti-Semitic campaign was particularly distressing. Ford emigrated to Israel; Toeplitz, rector of the Film School since 1949 (with some intervals), and Dr Roman Wajdowicz, one of his deputies and also a Jew, were dismissed, as was Bossak, despite the distinction he had brought to documentary. All the artistic directors, literary directors, and production managers of the eight existing units were dismissed, and a complete overhaul of the film system began. Since this severe dislocation of the industry, little of note has emerged from Poland with the exception of two films by Wajda, *Krajobraz po bitwie* (*Landscape after the Battle*, 1970) and *Wesele* (*The Wedding*, 1972).

**POLAŃSKI,** ROMAN (1933– ), Polish director, was born in Paris of Polish parents who returned three years later to live in Kraków. When Polański was eight the Germans sent his parents to a concentration camp where his mother died. Left entirely alone, he lived with a succession of Polish families. This unsettled childhood developed in Polański a severely pessimistic outlook which has underlined his work from his student days.

Polański was only fourteen when he started acting in the theatre, later appearing in films which included WAJDA's POKOLENIE (*A Generation*, 1954), *Lotna* (1959), *Niewinni czarodzieje* (*Innocent Sorcerers*, 1959), and *Samson* (1961). He studied painting, sculpture, and graphics at Kraków and spent five years at LÓDŹ film school, making *Dwaj ludzie z szafa* (*Two Men and a Wardrobe*, 1958), in which he also appeared, as his senior thesis. This surrealistic short film won international recognition, and in France Polański made *Le Gros et le maigre* (*The Fat and the Lean*, 1961), a parable about a tyrant and a slave with marked Beckett—indeed Godot—overtones. On his return to Poland in 1962 he made *Ssaki* (*Mammals*), another short of a similar kind.

His first full-length film, and the only one made in his own country, was NÓŻ W WODZIE (*Knife in the Water*, 1962), on the theme of sexual rivalry. REPULSION (1965), on sexual disgust, and CUL-DE-SAC (1966), a black comedy of sexual humiliation, were both made in Britain. Before leaving Britain for Hollywood he also directed *Dance of the Vampires* (1967), a stylish and mischievous horror piece. ROSEMARY'S BABY (1968), an effectively direct tale of witchcraft and Satanism, received the widest distribution of all Polański's films so far.

He returned to Britain to direct MACBETH (1971), again using a lucid, naturalistic style to convey the presence of evil forces. *Che? (What?*, 1972) gleefully conducted a latter-day Alice through a Wonderland of assorted perversions. *Chinatown* (1974) was his most commercially viable film since *Rosemary's Baby*, a thriller set in the thirties but still coloured by his characteristic vision.

Strongly influenced by both SURREALISM and the theatre of the absurd, Polański has developed a personal aura of association with the macabre which was intensified by the murder of his wife, Sharon Tate, in particularly horrifying circumstances in 1969.

**POLONSKY,** ABRAHAM (1910– ), US director, worked on radio and as a journalist before writing the script for *Body and Soul* (Robert ROSSEN, 1947). His first film as director, *Force of Evil* (1949), made a wide impression and great hopes were entertained for his future work; however, his blacklisting by the Hollywood studios following the hearings of the UNAMERICAN ACTIVITIES Committee led to a long absence from the US followed by a period of writing television scripts under an assumed name. *Tell Them Willie Boy is Here* (1969) marked his return as director. Willie Boy, an outsider from his Indian tribe and from white society, is hunted down as the focus of an unfounded fear of an Indian uprising. *Romance of a Horse Thief* (1971), a nostalgic Jewish tale of pre-revolutionary Russia, confirmed Polonsky as a polished and thoughtful film-maker.

**POLYVISION,** MULTI-SCREEN system set up for the climax of NAPOLÉON (1927) by Abel GANCE, working with André DEBRIE. It consisted of three linked projectors and three standard-size screens. The three images were sometimes different but complementary; at other times they joined to form a vast panorama.

**POMMER,** ERICH (1889–1966), German producer who contributed effectively to the great decade of German cinema after the First World War. From his own company, DECLA, he launched DAS CABINETT DES DR CALIGARI (1919); the next year Decla joined with Bioscop, forming for a brief time the only serious competitor to UFA. In 1921 Decla-Bioscop merged with UFA and Pommer became UFA's chief producer.

He excelled in bringing together creative teams, and usually supervised production himself. His name is associated with many of the enduring films and names of the period. He produced LANG'S DIE NIBELUNGEN (1924) and MURNAU'S DER LETZTE MANN (1924) and in the same year invited STILLER to make a film with GARBO; in 1925 he produced E. A. DUPONT'S VARIÉTÉ. In 1926 he was drawn, like many Germans, to Hollywood, but returned to Germany to make *Asphalt* (1929) and carried UFA into sound production. He showed concern for artistic development in sound, engaging STERNBERG for DER BLAUE ENGEL (1930), as well as developing the popular musical (DER KONGRESS TANZT, 1931).

The rise of Nazism made him leave Germany like many other Jewish artists. He worked as an independent producer in France, the US, and Britain where, with Charles LAUGHTON, he formed Mayflower Pictures. He spent the war years in Hollywood, becoming a US citizen in 1944.

**PONTECORVO, GILLO** (1919–  ), Italian director. First an assistant director, then a documentary maker, he contributed 'Giovanna', a neo-realist episode about the life of a servant girl, to Joris IVENS and Alberto CAVALCANTI'S *Die Vind Rose* (1956). After *La grande strada azzura* and *Squarcio* (both 1958), he directed *Kapo* (1960) with Emmanuele RIVA, chosen because Italian audiences were thought to be unacquainted with her. For *Kapo* Pontecorvo tried the process he was to use for LA BATTAGLIA DI ALGERI (1965) of duping copies of the film not from the negative but from a positive itself taken from a positive (see DUPE NEGATIVE). The resultant grainy effect did not disguise a sentimental strain in the film. Pontecorvo gained an international reputation with *La battaglia di Algeri*, a startling and convincing treatment of Algeria's struggle for independence, which was kept off French screens for five years.

He next made *¡Queimada!* (1968), starring Marlon BRANDO. Though he was again exploring the clash of interests inherent in colonialism, this time in nineteenth-century Antilles, his employment of Hollywood stars and styles failed to convey the intended irony, instead diluting the film's impact.

**PONTI, CARLO** (1910–  ), Italian producer who started in Milan in 1940. In 1945–9 he worked for Lux Films in Rome, producing nearly all the work of that period of ZAMPA, LATTUADA, and CAMERINI. In 1950 he joined with Dino DE LAURENTIIS; for their company he produced ROSSELLINI'S *Europa 51* (1952), FELLINI'S LA STRADA (1954), and DE SICA'S *Oro di Napoli* (1955), as well as several American BLOCKBUSTERS such as Camerini's *Ulysses* (1954) and King VIDOR'S *War and Peace* (1956). Producing Comencini's *Schiave bianche* in 1952, Ponti discovered Sophia LOREN whom he later married. His collaboration with De Laurentiis was wound up after 1954 when Ponti established himself as an independent producer working in Paris and Hollywood as well as Italy, increasingly undertaking international co-productions including collaborations with the film industry of Czechoslovakia. He has latterly concentrated on promoting Sophia Loren's career with films such as *Matrimonio all'Italiano* (1964) and *I Girasoli* (*Sunflower*, 1969); his other successful ventures include DOCTOR ZHIVAGO (1966).

**POPESCU-GOPO, ION** (1923–  ), Romanian animator, made his first animation films for children in 1951. *Saerta istorie* (*A Short History*, 1956) introduced his little nude character who acts out whimsically didactic explanations of history or short visual jokes. This has been the basis of Popescu-Gopo's subsequent work, which includes *Sapt arte* (*The Seven Arts*, 1958), *Homo Sapiens* (1960), *Kiss Me Quick* (1969), and the Mamaia Festival prologues, 1966.

**POPEYE**, cartoon character adapted by Dave FLEISCHER from a popular comic-strip, enjoyed great success in 1933–47. An ugly little sea captain, with a nutcracker jaw and creaking voice (spoken by William Costello), he was passionately devoted to the etiolated Olive Oyl. His adventures always took the pattern of some setback, usually at the hands of his arch-enemy Bluto, overcome with ease after he had fortified himself with a tin of spinach. Popeye had renewed success on television, but a new series initiated in 1959 lacked the Fleischer brand of cheerful brashness.

**POPIÓL I DIAMENT** (*Ashes and Diamonds*), Poland, 1958. 1¾hr. *Dir* Andrzej Wajda; *prod* Kadr Unit, Film Polski; *scr* Wajda, Jerzy Andrzejewski, from the latter's novel; *ph* Jerzy Wójcik; *ed* Halina Nawrocka; *cast* Zbigniew Cybulski (Maciek), Ewa Krzyanowska (Krystyna), Adam Pawlikowski (Andrzej), Bogumil Kobiela (Drewnowski), Waclaw Zastrzezynski (Szczuka).

The third film of WAJDA'S wartime resistance trilogy is still the work by which both director and leading actor are best known, dominated by CYBULSKI'S enigmatic portrayal of the young nationalist assassin ordered to kill a leading communist at the dawn of peace. In both direction and performance, personal, national, and universal symbols unite to bring out the individual yet eternal conflict beyond the immediate political division. KANAL (1957) had revealed to Western audiences the cinematic promise of the new Poland; *Popiól i diament* fulfilled that promise.

*PORCILE, Il* (*Pigsty*), Italy/France, 1969. Eastman Color; 1½hr. *Dir, scr* Pier Paolo Pasolini; *prod* Film Dell'orso/Idi Cinematografica/INDIEF (Rome)/CAPAC (Paris); *ph* Tonino Delli Colli; *mus* C. A. M. Ghiglia; *cast* Pierre Clementi (cannibal), Franco Citti (second cannibal), Jean-Pierre Léaud (Julian), Anna Wiazemsky (Ida), Ugo Tognazzi (Herdhitze), Alberto Lionello (Klotz).

PASOLINI's most pessimistic film intercuts two separate stories, one set in medieval Italy, the other in modern Germany. In the first, a group of cannibals struggles for survival in a volcanic landscape; in the second, an industrialist is blackmailed into a merger by a rival who has discovered that the industrialist's son can have sexual intercourse only with pigs. At the end the two tales overlap: in both, men become sacrificial victims of the society that formed them.

*PORTE DES LILAS*, France/Italy, 1957. 1½hr. *Dir* René Clair; *prod* Filmsonor/Cinetel/Seca (Paris)/Rizzoli Films (Rome); *scr* Clair, Jean Aurel from the novel *La Grande Ceinture* by René Fallet; *ph* Robert le Fèbvre; *des* Léon Barsacq; *mus* Georges Brassens; *cast* Pierre Brasseur (Juju), Georges Brassens (the Artist), Henri Vidal (the Gangster), Dany Carel (Maria), Raymond Bussières, Annette Poivre.

Juju, a drunk, persuades his friend the Artist to harbour a criminal who repays him by stealing his girl-friend; finally Juju kills him.

Setting the film in one of the poorest, greyest districts of Paris, CLAIR deliberately rejected a realistic approach in favour of poetic obliqueness, the dialogue in particular steering a delicate course between argot and formality. The cruder emotions are sensitively blended with gaiety, generosity, and pathos, reminiscent of Clair's great films of the thirties.

**PORTEN,** HENNY (1890–1960), German actress whose stage career began in 1903. She appeared in films from 1906, including a version of *Lohengrin* (1907) with her father, Franz Porten, in the title role. Under contract to Oskar MESSTER she became immensely popular as the 'Messter girl' and was soon credited in her own name. Ideally blonde and blue-eyed, she was Germany's most successful actress of the silent era. She appeared in LUBITSCH's *Anna Boleyn* (1920), Jessner's *Hintertreppe* (1921), and DUPONT's

*Das alte Gesetz* (1923) among many others, and in 1924 formed her own production company, personally producing many of her films. Her career survived the introduction of sound, although on a smaller scale. Her last success was FROELICH's *Familie Buchholz* (1943).

**PORTER,** COLE (1891–1964), US songwriter from a wealthy family, published his first song at the age of eleven and staged his first Broadway show, *See America First*, in 1916. During the twenties he was a leader of hedonistic New York social life and became famous in America and Europe with a succession of witty, sophisticated stage musicals.

In 1934 two of his shows were filmed, *Wake Up and Dream* (staged 1929) and *The Gay Divorcée* (staged 1932 as *The Gay Divorce*); the latter retained only one of Porter's songs, but it was the one written for and always associated with Fred ASTAIRE—'Night and Day'. *Anything Goes* (1936) included 'I Get a Kick Out of You', 'You're the Top', 'Anything Goes', and 'The Gipsy in Me'. Also in 1936 he wrote an original film score, *Born to Dance* starring Eleanor POWELL and James STEWART and including 'Easy to Love', 'I've Got You Under My Skin', and 'It's De-Lovely'.

In 1937 Porter suffered a serious riding accident which crippled both his legs, but he remained active both socially and artistically. His stage successes regularly became films, including *Dubarry Was a Lady* (1943, staged 1939) which contained 'Do I Love You, Do I?' and 'Well, Did You Evah' (revived in his score for HIGH SOCIETY, 1956). He wrote the original film score for BROADWAY MELODY *of 1940* which introduced 'I Concentrate on You', 'I've Got My Eyes On You', and 'Begin the Beguine'. In *Hollywood Canteen* (1944) Roy ROGERS had a hit with 'Don't Fence Me In' which Porter had written for an unproduced film in 1935. His filmed biography *Night and Day* (1946), starring Cary GRANT, revived the popularity of his earlier music. He wrote the original film score for MINNELLI's *The Pirate* (1948); meanwhile *Kiss Me Kate* was on Broadway (filmed 1953). *Silk Stockings*, a musical version of NINOTCHKA (1939), was staged in 1955 and filmed in 1957.

Porter's extraordinary output of popular classics is probably unparalleled. He invariably wrote both music and lyrics; and not only are his melodies at once original and memorable but his lyrics are distinguished by a wit, perceptiveness, and literacy equalled only by Noël COWARD, almost his exact contemporary.

**PORTER,** EDWIN S. (1870–1941), US director, born in Scotland, who introduced many cinematic concepts to the American film. He was employed by the EDISON company, and made, among many other films, *The Life of an American Fireman* (1903), which included uses of close-up and cross-cutting, THE GREAT TRAIN ROBBERY (1903), *The Dream of a Rarebit Fiend* (1906) with double exposures and stop-motion photography, and *Rescued from an Eagle's Nest* (1907), D. W. GRIFFITH's screen début—as an actor. Porter left Edison in 1911 to form his own producing company (Rex Films), but shortly afterwards joined FAMOUS PLAYERS. He added little of interest to cinema technique after his first few films; his last was *The Eternal City* (1915) with Pauline FREDERICK.

**PORTUGAL** has never had a large indigenous film industry. Most of the few films produced have been strictly for home consumption and the failure of the one serious attempt to break into world markets by the Invicta Company, formed in 1918 to specialize in adaptations of Portuguese literary classics, brought about the company's collapse in 1924. Throughout the thirties, forties, and fifties, with cinemas in Portugal showing mainly foreign films, the home industry restricted itself to innocuous comedies, literary adaptations, and historical romances. One exception was *Douro, faina fluvial*, an experimental documentary made in 1931 by Manuel de Oliveira, one of the few Portuguese directors to achieve some recognition outside his own country.

More recently something of a revival has occurred with the emergence of a new generation of more ambitious film-makers such as Antonio de Macedo (*Domingo a tarade*, 1964; *Nojo aos caes*, 1970) and Fernando Lopes (*Belarmino*, 1964; *Uma Abelha na chuva*, 1969), although opportunities for directing films of intelligence and originality remain sparse. Not only is the annual output very low (in 1970 only four features were made compared to 221 shorts, mainly government propaganda) but under the Caetano régime the censorship laws were extremely severe. The independently produced *Nojo aos caes*, which deals with student unrest, was banned outright and it was not until 1970 that Portuguese audiences were allowed to see LA DOLCE VITA (1960) and L'AVVENTURA (1960). There was a relaxation of censorship following the military coup of 1974.

**POSTMAN ALWAYS RINGS TWICE, The,** US, 1946. 1½hr. *Dir* Tay Garnett; *prod* MGM; *scr* Harry Ruskin, Niven Busch, based on the novel by James M. Cain; *ph* Sidney Wagner; *cast* Lana Turner (Cora Smith), John Garfield (Frank Chambers), Cecil Kellaway (Nick Smith).

James M. Cain's novel, published in 1934, was adapted for the stage in 1936. RENOIR, who

had wanted to film it, suggested it to VISCONTI, who made it the basis of OSSESSIONE (1942); in the meantime a French version, *Le Dernier Tournant* (1939), was directed by Pierre Chenal. The producers of neither European version settled the rights in the novel (see COPYRIGHT), which were bought by METRO-GOLDWYN-MAYER.

Tay GARNETT's adaptation of the sordid story of adultery and murder gave American parochial justice a grim touch of truth, in spite of lapsing into a sentimental ending.

***POSTO, Il,*** Italy, 1961. 1½hr. *Dir, scr* Ermanno Olmi; *prod* Titanus; *ph* Lamberto Caimi; *cast* Loredana Detto (Antonietta), Sandro Panzeri (Domenico).

The film tells the story of a shy young man from the provinces in search of a job in one of Milan's large industries, and the moral support he receives from a young city girl, also applying for a job. It was filmed in the business quarter of Milan, and the leading part was played by a young man who later started work as an office boy. The office block where Domenico works is the Edison building in which OLMI himself worked; the entirely non-professional cast is made up of Edison employees. Loredana Detto is Olmi's wife.

The film, which gained international recognition in the VENICE and London festivals of 1961, is remarkable for its tender, unpretentious examination of the grey beginning of the boy's career; the dehumanizing impersonality of big business, with its frustration of human feelings, is counterbalanced by the gentle humour of Olmi's observation.

**POST-SYNCHRONIZATION,** the process of adding new or changed dialogue in the original language to the sound track of a film after the picture itself has been shot. See DUBBING.

***POTE TIN KYRIAKI*** (*Never on Sunday*), Greece, 1959. 1½hr. *Dir, prod, scr* Jules Dassin for Lopert Pictures/Melinafilm; *ph* Jacques Natteau; *mus* Manos Hadjidakis; *cast* Melina Mercouri (Ilya), Jules Dassin (Homer), Georges Foundas (Tonio), Tito Vandis (Jorgo).

Homer, the ironically-named pedantic rationalist, attempts to re-educate the popular and independent prostitute Ilya, but is defeated by her exuberant hedonism. This light-hearted fable was immensely successful, chiefly by reason of Melina MERCOURI's vitality and HADJIDAKIS's theme music for bouzouki which became widely popular in its own right.

***POTOMOK CHINGIS-KHANA*** (*The Heir to Jenghis Khan* or *Storm over Asia*), USSR, 1928. 2¼hr. *Dir* V. I. Pudovkin; *prod* Mezhrabpom-

*Potomok Chinghis-khana* (V. I. Pudovkin, 1928)

Film; *scr* Osip Brik; *ph* Anatoli Golovnya; *des* Sergei Kozlovsky, M. Aaronson; *cast* Valeri In-kizhinov (Bair), A. Dedintsev (commander of the occupying forces), Paulina Belinskaya (his wife), V. Tzoppi (Smith, fur company agent), A. P. Khristiakov (partisan commander).

PUDOVKIN's last great silent film has an enduring appeal in many ways greater than that of his earlier, more political, films: MAT (*Mother*, 1926) and KONYETS SANKT-PETERBURGA (*The End of St Petersburg*, 1927). It tells the story of Bair, a Mongolian nomad, who joins a resistance group, is captured by the occupying British interventionist troops, and is discovered to be the bearer of an ancient document declaring the owner to be the heir of Jenghis Khan. He is cured of the effects of a botched execution and set up as a puppet monarch, but realizing his national and social identity he rouses the Asian hordes against the oppressors. The film ends with an impressive storm symbolizing the irresistible force of revolution. It has great visual beauty, a degree of humour unprecedented in Pudovkin's work, and an almost ethnographic quality in the detailed depiction of the life of the Mongolian herdsmen and in the long sequence showing ceremonial in a lamasery. A new version, re-edited and with a

sound track added under the director's supervision, was issued in 1950.

**POWELL, ELEANOR** (1912– ), US dancer and actress, remembered mainly for her accomplished tap-dancing. Her first appearance was a small part in *George White's Scandals* (1934) but her first big roles were in BROADWAY MELODY *of 1936* and *Born to Dance* (1936) in which she played opposite James STEWART. She replaced Jeanette MACDONALD as Nelson EDDY's partner in *Rosalie* (1939), and in *Broadway Melody of 1940* was the first to replace Ginger ROGERS as Fred ASTAIRE's partner. After *Lady Be Good* (1941) she teamed with Red Skelton in *Ship Ahoy* (1942) and *I Dood It* (1943, *By Hook or By Crook* in GB). She made a guest appearance in *The Duchess of Idaho* (1950).

**POWELL, MICHAEL** (1905– ), British director, worked first for Harry Lachman, then for Alfred HITCHCOCK on *Champagne* (1928) and BLACKMAIL (1929). His first success as director was a thriller, *Rynox* (1931). *The Edge of the World* (1938), made on location in the Shetland Islands with a supporting cast of local people, reveals the desire to experiment that characterizes his work.

In 1939 he first collaborated with Emeric PRESSEURGER—on *The Spy in Black*, and in 1941 they formed Archer Films, working together on all its productions until 1956. There were interesting experiments in the use of sound in *49th Parallel* (1941, *The Invader* in US), for which VAUGHAN WILLIAMS composed the music; in *One of Our Aircraft is Missing* (1942), which has no music; and in *The Small Back Room* (1948), where natural sound is skilfully used to counterpoint the action. Working with Hein HECKROTH and Alfred JUNGE as designers, Powell made expressive use of colour in *A Matter of Life and Death* (1946, *Stairway to Heaven* in US), *Black Narcissus* (1947), and THE RED SHOES (1948). This last, with *The Tales of Hoffman* (1951), which was suggested by Sir Thomas Beecham, aimed at a fusion of various art forms; but *The Tales of Hoffman* suffered from over-opulence.

The Powell/Pressburger working relationship was unusually close. They collaborated on the writing, production, and direction of their joint films, and even those of their films which are artistically unsuccessful testify to their high standards of professional craftsmanship.

Powell's later work as sole director includes *Peeping Tom* (1959) and *Age of Consent* (1969), further examples of the diversity of his approach.

**POWELL, WILLIAM** (1892–   ), US actor who had a suave, urbane charm that worked especially well against the light-hearted qualities of Myrna LOY, with whom he was often teamed. He began as a cowboy villain in silent films, progressing to the engaging 'con' man in *High Pressure* (LEROY, 1932). Powell found his form as a private detective who used cunning and deceptive sophistication to outwit criminals, first as PHILO VANCE in six films in the early thirties and especially as Dashiell HAMMETT's Nick Charles in THE THIN MAN (1934) and five sequels. Perhaps his most resourceful performance was as the butler who outwits a family of millionaires in the SCREWBALL comedy MY MAN GODFREY (1936). He also played the Broadway showman Florenz Ziegfeld with elegance and penetration in *The Great Ziegfeld* (1936). He was the outrageous title character in *Life With Father* (CURTIZ, 1947), and lent strong comic support to Henry FONDA in *Mister Roberts* (FORD and LeRoy, 1955).

**POWER, TYRONE** (1913–58), US actor who was little more than a handsome, rather wooden, romantic lead for the greater part of his career. He was best in colourful, swashbuckling roles, particularly under Rouben MAMOULIAN's direction in *The Mark of Zorro* (1940) and *Blood and Sand* (1940), and made a valiant attempt at a serious dramatic part in *The Razor's Edge* (1946). He died of a heart attack in Spain while working on King VIDOR's *Solomon and Sheba* (1959).

**POWER AND THE GLORY, The** (*Power and Glory* in GB), US, 1933. 1½hr. *Dir* William K. Howard; *prod* Fox; *scr* Preston Sturges; *ph* James Wong Howe; *cast* Spencer Tracy (Tom Garner), Colleen Moore (Sally), Ralph Morgan (Henry), Helen Vinson (Eve), Clifford Jones (Tom Garner Jr).

A railroad magnate has committed suicide and his life story is told by his secretary and friend who seeks to vindicate the dead man's character. The flashbacks were presented out of chronological order, a treatment considered bold in 1933; the term 'narratage' was coined by the producer, Jessie L. LASKY, to dignify the innovation. It presaged the narrative construction of CITIZEN KANE seven years later. Other parallels between the two films are the use of an important figure whose biography is built up piecemeal and out of sequence, and the striking similarity of camera technique.

**PRÉJEAN, ALBERT** (1893–   ), French actor and stuntman, first appeared in film in *Les Trois Mousquetaires* (1921). Many of his films involved his acrobatic abilities, particularly René CLAIR's *Paris qui dort* (1924). *Le Fantôme du Moulin Rouge* (1924), *Le Voyage imaginaire* (1924), UN CHAPEAU DE PAILLE D'ITALIE (1927), and SOUS LES TOITS DE PARIS (1930), all by Clair, display his almost balletic grace and timing. He continued active film-making until 1957.

**PREMINGER, OTTO** (1906–   ), US director, born in Vienna, worked for a time as an actor and assistant producer with Max REINHARDT, taking over the direction of the Josefstadt Theatre in 1933. In 1935 he went to the US where he continued his career in theatre, and made several films. In 1943 he became a naturalized American and signed a contract with TWENTIETH CENTURY-FOX as a producer-director. *Laura* (1944) marked the real beginning of his work as a film director. Throughout his film career Preminger has drawn his subjects from a wide variety of sources, ranging from best-selling thrillers to writers like Shaw and WILDE, but his predominant interest has been the evolution and analysis of character. Several of his early works had historical settings, notably *Forever Amber* (1947), a romance set in the reign of Charles II. Other films of this period include *Daisy Kenyon* (1947), *That Lady in Ermine* (1948), which had been begun by LUBITSCH, *The Fan* (1949, *Lady Win-dermere's Fan* in GB), an adaptation from Oscar Wilde, *Where the Sidewalk Ends* (1950), and *Angel Face* (1953).

In 1953 he left Fox to produce independently, forming Carlyle Productions for this purpose. His first independent production, *The Moon Is Blue* (1953), was refused a seal by the MOTION PICTURE PRODUCERS ASSOCIATION OF AMERICA because of the frankness of its dialogue, and was the first of his several battles with the system of American CENSORSHIP. *Carmen Jones* (1954) was based on the stage musical of Bizet's opera, with the action transferred from Spain to the southern states of America and with an all-black cast. In a completely different vein was *The Court Martial of Billy Mitchell* (1955, *One-Man Mutiny* in GB), which was drawn from the true story of a courageous one-man revolt in the army. Preminger again challenged the MPPAA with THE MAN WITH THE GOLDEN ARM (1955), a study of a drug addict. In 1957 he adapted *Saint Joan* from Shaw (see JOAN OF ARC), and he made a film of Françoise Sagan's *Bonjour Tristesse* (1958), both of which starred his new discovery Jean SEBERG. The musical *Porgy and Bess* (1959) was followed by a tense drama *Anatomy of a Murder* (1959).

In 1960 he made the epic EXODUS using the wide screen for the first time. He further explored the possibilities of the wide screen in a series of large-scale productions; *Advise and Consent* (1961) dealt with the machinery of American democracy through the story of power struggle among a group of politicians; *The Cardinal* (1964) explored through the central figure of the priest the larger themes of racialism and Nazism. *In Harm's Way* (1965) examined the aftermath of the bombing of Pearl Harbor. In *Bunny Lake Is Missing* (1965), he returned to the smaller scale of his earlier personal dramas, with a psychological suspense story about the disappearance of a small child. His later films include *Hurry Sundown* (1967), *Skidoo* (1968), and *Tell Me That You Love Me Junie Moon* (1969).

**PRESLE, MICHELINE** (1922–  ), French actress whose career began under the direction of G. W. PABST and Abel GANCE in 1939, developed in eight films in occupied France, and blossomed in *Boule de suif* (1945). She won critical acclaim opposite Gérard PHILIPE in LE DIABLE AU CORPS (1947), and scored again in the Sartre story *Les Jeux sont faits* (1947). In 1948, in the US, she starred with John GARFIELD in *Under My Skin*, and married Michèle MORGAN's ex-husband, William Marshall, with whom in 1949 she was involved in the production of an unsuccessful swashbuckling epic that starred her with Errol FLYNN. In 1952 she worked for Fritz

LANG in *An American Guerilla in the Philippines*, then returned to France for *La Dame aux camélias* (1952). She had a cameo role as GABIN's mistress in *Le Baron de l'écluse* (1959), made *Blind Date* (Joseph LOSEY, 1959) in England, and *L'assassino* (1961) in Italy. She has recently played in *Le Roi de coeur* (Philippe DE BROCA, 1966), *Le Bal du Comte d'Orgel* (1969) as the hero's mother, and as the queen in Jacques DEMY's fairy-tale *Peau d'âne* (1970).

**PRESLEY, ELVIS** (1935–  ), singer and guitarist, was already a major pop star when he appeared in his first film, *Love Me Tender* (1956). His many films lack almost any individual distinction, but none the less all were great commercial successes, largely because the magnetism of Presley's surly, deep-voiced, hip-swinging style drew into the cinemas the phenomenal following his records had already captured.

**PRESSBURGER, EMERIC** (1902–  ), director, scriptwriter, and producer of Hungarian birth. He came to Britain after working as a story writer for UFA and was introduced by Alexander KORDA to Michael POWELL in 1939. Together they formed Archer Films in 1941 and Pressburger worked on all the company's productions until 1956. His unusually close working relationship with Powell resulted in a number of films which, although not exceptionally successful commercially, had high artistic aims and were technically extremely distinguished.

**PRÉVERT, JACQUES** (1900–  ), French scriptwriter. After a period of involvement with SURREALISM in 1925–8 he began his career as a writer, contributing plays to the GROUPE OCTOBRE, and quickly achieved recognition as both poet and scriptwriter. He worked with various directors, including AUTANT-LARA, GRÉMILLON, RENOIR, and his brother Pierre PRÉVERT, but is known mainly for his collaboration with Marcel CARNÉ which resulted in some memorable films including LE JOUR SE LÈVE (1939), LES VISITEURS DU SOIR (1942), and LES ENFANTS DU PARADIS (1945). He also worked anonymously on the script and dialogue of *La Marie du port* (1950). There seems however to be a certain conflict between the innate warmth and optimism of Prévert and the cold visual perfection of Carné's films. Certainly there is a marked contrast between the rich, ornate dialogue he wrote for Carné and the biting satire and spontaneous wit which can be seen in some of his poetry and in scripts for films such as Renoir's LE CRIME DE MONSIEUR LANGE (1936): this Prévert is perhaps more appealing to modern taste. He was certainly one of the most important figures in the cinema of his time, ranking with Carl MAYER in Germany and ZAVATTINI in Italy.

Since 1950 Prévert has not written any major film script, although he has worked on various documentaries, short films, and radio programmes.

**PRÉVERT, PIERRE** (1906–    ), French director, actor, and scriptwriter. Although he acted in various films including BUÑUEL's L'ÂGE D'OR (1930), and wrote some scripts, his main interest was directing. He worked as assistant to a number of people, CAVALCANTI, CARNÉ, Marc ALLÉGRET among them. His own films are L'AFFAIRE EST DANS LE SAC (1932), *Adieu Léonard* (1943), *Voyage-Surprise* (1946), and two short films, *Paris mange son pain* (1956) and *Paris la belle* (1959), which includes material shot in 1928 for an uncompleted film *Paris-Express*. He has also made a number of films for television, including *La Maison du passeur* (1965).

His films were usually made in collaboration with his brother Jacques PRÉVERT, who wrote the scripts, and their actor friends from the GROUPE OCTOBRE. His work is characterized by a vital and almost surrealist style of comedy, and despite his very small output of films he has a place as one of the few real creators of farce in the French cinema.

**PREVIEW.** In general terms, a screening of a film prior to its public presentation, normally for trade, press, and publicity purposes. As a rule, in Britain, the TRADE SHOW follows the press preview and is itself sometimes followed by a preview for suburban cinema-managers. A particular species, associated mainly with the halcyon days of Hollywood, is the *sneak preview*, in which a completed, or substantially completed, film is 'sneaked' unheralded into a cinema programme to sound public reaction. The final version of the film often contained changes based on its reception by the preview audience.

**PREVIN, ANDRÉ** (1929–    ), German-born conductor, composer, and jazz pianist who had a distinguished career in Hollywood before settling in Britain as principal conductor of the London Symphony Orchestra. As musical director, he won OSCARS for GIGI (1958), *Porgy and Bess* (1959), *Irma La Douce* (1963), and MY FAIR LADY (1964), and also worked in this capacity on various other films including *Three Little Words* (1950), *Bells Are Ringing* (1960), *Thoroughly Modern Millie* (1967), *The Way West* (1967), and *Paint Your Wagon* (1969). He composed songs for *Pepe* (1960), *Harper* (1966, *The Moving Target* in GB), *The Swinger* (1966), *Valley of the Dolls* (1967), among other films. Since 1949 he has composed background scores,

including *Bad Day at Black Rock* (1954), *Elmer Gantry* (1960), *One, Two, Three* (1961), *Long Day's Journey into Night* (1962), *Kiss Me Stupid* (1964), *Inside Daisy Clover* (1966), and *The Fortune Cookie* (1966, *Meet Whiplash Willie* in GB). He is married to Mia FARROW.

**PRÉVOST, FRANÇOISE** (1930–    ), French actress, whose dramatic talents have served many a fledgling European director, such as Pierre KAST (*Le Bel Âge*, 1959; *La Morte Saison des amours*, 1960), Jean-Gabriel Albicocco (*La Fille aux yeux d'or*, 1961), Giuseppe Patroni Griffi (*Il mare*, 1962), Roger Fritz (*Häschen in der Grube*, 1969). She was also in PARIS NOUS APPARTIENT (1960), *L'Une et l'autre* (1967), the English-speaking *The Enemy General* (1960) and *Payroll* (1962), and she gave a notable performance in LIZZANI's *Il processo di Verona* (1962).

**PRICE, DENNIS** (1915–73), British actor, real name Dennistoun Rose-Price, played several romantic leading roles in films before his impeccable performance in KIND HEARTS AND CORONETS (1949). He continued to appear regularly, usually in light comedies and in similar urbane roles, and had particular success as P. G. Wodehouse's immortal Jeeves in the television series 'The World of Wooster'.

**PRICE, VINCENT** (1911–    ), US actor, appeared in suavely villainous roles in many screen dramas, including *Laura* (Otto PREMINGER, 1944), and *The Long Night* (Anatole LITVAK, 1947), a remake of LE JOUR SE LÈVE (1939), before making the series of horror films for which he is best known. To Roger CORMAN's adaptations from Poe, in particular, he brought a welcome element of polished irony.

**PRINTEMPS, YVONNE** (1895–    ), French actress, real name Luignolle, star of French operetta, with a charming singing voice. She was married to Sacha GUITRY, then from 1934 to Pierre FRESNAY, with whom she appeared in eight films in 1934–51, including *La Dame aux camélias* (1934), *Trois Valses* (1939), *Le Duel* (Fresnay, 1940), and *La Valse de Paris* (1949), in which she appeared as Hortense Schneider to Fresnay's Offenbach.

**PRIVATE LIFE OF HENRY VIII, The,** GB, 1933. 1½hr. *Dir, prod* Alexander Korda for London Film Productions; *scr* Lajos Biro, Arthur Wimperis; *ph* Georges Périnal; *des* Vincent Korda; *cast* Charles Laughton (Henry), Merle Oberon (Anne Boleyn), Robert Donat (Culpeper), Elsa Lanchester (Anne of Cleves), Binnie Barnes (Catherine Howard), Wendy

Barrie (Jane Seymour), Everly Gregg (Catherine Parr).

Alexander KORDA's first important British film dealt with five of Henry VIII's six marriages: Catherine of Aragon was omitted as being too respectable. The script (the first English film script to be published) reveals the poverty of the dialogue: in spite of this, and the fact that the film was quickly and cheaply made, the apparent lavishness and Charles LAUGHTON's vigorous performance helped to achieve a commercial success unprecedented in the British industry. The film broke all house records when it had its world première in New York and its reception internationally was no less astounding.

Unfortunately, this success led to two unhappy results: an immediate series of imitations of its popularized historical style; and a boom period of British production on far too costly a scale (see GREAT BRITAIN).

**PRIZMA,** two-colour ADDITIVE colour process introduced in the US in 1918. In its first form alternate frames were photographed through a rotating orange and blue-green filter on black-and-white stock with the camera running at double speed. The print, coated with emulsion on both sides, was chemically toned orange and blue-green and projected at double speed.

This was replaced in 1922 by a two-colour process in which two black and white positives, toned red and blue-green, were cemented back to back and projected at the normal speed. The best-known film made in this process was *The Glorious Adventure* (1921) directed by James Stuart BLACKTON.

*PROCÈS, Le (The Trial),* France, 1963. 2hr. *Dir, scr* Orson Welles, from the novel by Franz Kafka; *prod* Paris/Europa, FI-C-IT, HISA-Films; *ph* Edmond Richard; *cast* Anthony Perkins (Joseph K), Jeanne Moreau (Frl Burstner), Madeleine Robinson (Mme Grubach), Elsa Martinelli (Hilda), Romy Schneider (Lei), Orson Welles (the Advocate).

Kafka's infinite subtlety in conveying implicit menace is perhaps impossible to convey in visual terms. WELLES, fulfilling a long-cherished project, made a number of changes in an attempt to give *The Trial* more impact; but, apart from providing himself with a powerful role as the Advocate, he was less than successful in dramatizing the novel's depiction of man's isolation.

*PROCÈS DE JEANNE D'ARC, Le (The Trial of Joan of Arc),* France, 1962. 1hr. *Dir* Robert Bresson; *prod* Agnès Delahaie; *scr* Bresson, from the records of the trial; *ph* Léonce-Henry Burel; *des* Pierre Charbonnier; *ed* Germaine Artus;

*mus* Francis Seyrig; *cast* Florence Delay, alias Carrez (Joan), Jean-Claude Fourneau (Cauchon), Marc Jacquier (Lemaître), Roger Honorat (Jean Beaupère), Michel Herubel (Brother Isambart), Richard Pratt (Warwick).

BRESSON wrote his script from the minutes of the last three months of Joan's trial, between 21 February and 30 May 1431, and except for the opening scene (the petition for her rehabilitation, twenty-five years later) the film follows strictly the sequence of the trial. Bresson imposed on himself the formidable task of making cinematic the essentially verbal framework of question and answer. He resolved it by developing an almost staccato interchange of shots of Joan and her questioners, and of the court-room and Joan's journeys to and from her cell. The sound-track is almost devoid of music, but the film itself was consciously structured rhythmically, like a piece of music.

Joan's heroism emerges from her tenacity, and from the simplicity and lucidity with which she answers her sophisticated interrogators. At the same time, Bresson allows glimpses of her vulnerability and humiliation which he accords to none of the subjects of his other films, except perhaps MOUCHETTE (1966). Because of this, *Le Procès de Jeanne d'Arc*, besides being a powerful drama of moral and spiritual forces, is also deeply moving on the psychological and emotional levels, in a way uncharacteristic of Bresson. Among the long list of films about Joan, his film stands out, together with DREYER's very different LA PASSION DE JEANNE D'ARC (1928), as a major work of cinema.

**PRODUCER,** member of the production team responsible for the control of expenditure and therefore involved to a greater or lesser extent with such matters as casting, selection of personnel, and adherence to the planned work schedule. In Britain, especially in the early days of cinema, the terms producer and director were sometimes confused, using the terminology of the theatre. This confusion recurred when television began, cinema practice finally being adopted.

In commercial film-making, roles within the production team were at first relatively undefined. Mack SENNETT, D. W. GRIFFITH, and Thomas INCE were in effect producers as well as directors; once their work had proved their commercial worth, they were allowed to spend their budgets as they thought fit. Ince is generally credited with creating the role of the executive producer, supervising every stage of the work of a team of directors. The financial disaster of INTOLERANCE (1916) was instrumental in making the producer an accepted necessity, to curb the possible excesses of wild creative talents. By the mid-twenties the major Hollywood studios were operating as factories, with a production line that demanded efficient specialization at each stage, and the producer became, like the director, the cameraman, or any other member of the team, a functionary with clearly defined responsibilities. He was generally a member of the studio staff, assigned to a particular film and required to see that the production was completed within budget and schedule, and that it was up to a given standard. The producer's role in this sense was often regarded as a stepping-stone: satisfactory results could help a budding writer or director to more creative work. Stanley KRAMER, Richard FLEISCHER, and Albert LEWIN all began as producers.

Irving THALBERG, Louis B. MAYER, Samuel GOLDWYN, and David O. SELZNICK brought creative flair to the Hollywood producer's role. They had a shrewd understanding of audience taste and satisfied it by combining the talents and box-office appeal of director, stars, and other members of the production team. They supervised the overall quality of each production at every stage, besides controlling the balance-sheets. On occasion the work of a particular director would prove so successful that he would be trusted with budget control and thus become his own producer. An early example is Ernst LUBITSCH; others who have attained this status include Frank CAPRA, George CUKOR, Howard HAWKS, and Billy WILDER. With increasing recognition of the director's importance, his say in the allocation of funds has become accepted, but until he is a box-office draw in his own right it is still rare for a major company to give him the freedom that the term 'director-producer' implies.

Similarly, a star of sufficient commercial popularity might become a producer. This was often a matter simply of floating a company for tax purposes, but Gloria SWANSON, an outstandingly talented and businesslike woman, was—at the height of her popularity—a producer in the complete sense. This tendency has increased of late years, with stars like Robert REDFORD and Paul NEWMAN claiming the right to choose their subjects and production teams and taking personal responsibility for the financial risks.

Outside the US, film production never became the efficient industry it was in Hollywood, except perhaps in Germany where Erich POMMER at UFA and Seymour NEBENZAL at NERO-FILM became the only European equivalents of Mayer and Goldwyn. In Britain, Alexander KORDA attempted to play a similar role with varying success. But the European producer has usually been satisfied with the role of entrepreneur, bringing together money and talent, gambling with smaller sums than the Hollywood giants and therefore prepared to interfere less with the production process. Functioning in this way, Michael BALCON and Filippo DEL GIUDICE earned a considerable reputation for providing facilities for some of the best talents in British cinema, and Pierre BRAUNBERGER was instrumental in backing some of the early films of the NOUVELLE VAGUE. This ability to balance profitability with artistic freedom makes the good producer an invaluable support to the production team. In recent years large-scale commercial success has been achieved by, notably, Carlo PONTI and Dino DE LAURENTIIS, using co-production agreements with various Eastern European countries to combine the box-office appeal of popular stars with the cheaper film-making facilities of nationalized industries.

**PRODUCTION CODE** see CENSORSHIP, US

*PROFESSOR MAMLOCK*, USSR, 1938. *Dir* Adolf Minkin, Herbert Rappoport; *prod* Lenfilm; *scr* Friedrich Wolf, Minkin, Rappoport, from the play by Wolf; *ph* G. Filatov; *des* P. Betani; *mus* Y. Kochurov, N. Timofeyev; *cast* S. Mezhinski (Professor Mamlock), E. Nikitina (his wife), O. Zhakov (Rolf Mann), V. Chesnokov (Dr Hellpach), B. Svetlov (Dr Karlsen), N. Shaternikova (Dr Inge), V. Kiselev (Werner Seidel).

The rise of Nazism in 1933 is depicted through the experiences of a brilliant Jewish surgeon who, after being publicly degraded, is gunned down while making an impassioned speech against the régime. The Berlin setting was minutely reconstructed, and the taut and understated style of direction made this one of the most interesting Soviet films for some time; it was one of the rare Russian films of the epoch to deal with a subject other than national affairs. In France it was received with enthusiasm, but banned after the Soviet-German pact of 1939; in Britain it was at first banned because of the anti-German content, but shown after the outbreak of war.

In 1961, Konrad Wolf, son of the author of the original play, made a new version of the film in East Germany, which won international awards.

**PROJECTION**, the presentation of a film by forming an image in light upon a screen.

The early technical problem was to find a way of presenting successive frames rapidly, first for exposure in the camera, then to the eye for viewing. The first step in solving this problem was the use of flexible continuous film with images about an inch wide. These images had to be magnified; projection, already popular in magic lantern shows, was the logical answer. Short programmes of sensational subject matter were shown in converted stores ('nickelodeons' in the US, where a nickel was the price of admission, 'penny gaffs' in Britain) and the success of these sideshows established projection before groups of viewers in preference to individual peepshows. The subsequent development of the film medium can be seen as an exploration of forms acceptable to audiences comfortably seated in darkened rooms, confronted by rectangular moving images projected on to large screens.

The motion picture projector is essentially the inverse of the motion picture camera: light, instead of originating at the subject and travelling to the film to register an exposure, originates behind the film and travels to the screen where it recreates an image of the subject. The intermittent movement which presents successive frames is similar to that of the camera (see MALTESE CROSS), but despite its size and apparent complexity a projector is usually less sophisticated and less precise in operation than its corresponding camera.

Modern cinemas sport an array of projection equipment designed to cope with a changing variety of film forms. Most 35mm projectors have 20-minute spools, a few take 60-minute spools; thus two projectors side by side is the usual minimum for continuous showing of a feature film, the projectionist 'changing over' from one machine to another at the end of each spool. (Recently large cinemas have installed large disc-like spools on which an entire programme can be placed horizontally and shown without breaks.) Each projector carries a selection of lenses and apertures for the variety of formats now in use (see ASPECT RATIO). Major cinemas may also be equipped for showing 70mm prints, with reproducers for magnetic tracks in STEREOPHONIC sound. Projection rooms may also include 16mm projectors, slide projectors, effects projectors, and disc or tape players for interval music. Projectionists also control the entire presentation of the film: dimming of house lights, operation of stage curtains, size and shape of screen masking to suit each aspect ratio. A recent trend is to automate all the functions of projection and presentation; automatic timers and foil 'cues' on the film itself start projectors, dim lights, change lenses, and even operate buzzers to alert sales staff that the interval is approaching.

Projection rooms are designed to strict fire safety standards and a special licence is needed to show NITRATE prints.

Early projectors, like early cameras, were hand-cranked; the projectionist or cinema manager could determine how long a film would run by the speed of projection, even to the extent of fitting in an extra showing of a popular attraction. With mechanization, however, and

especially after the introduction of sound, it became essential to adhere to an agreed standard. Special effects are incorporated in the film itself, not created by the projectionist. Thus slow motion is achieved by filming with the camera speeded up, producing action which appears slow when the film is projected at normal speed. Nevertheless there have been frequent attempts to create unusual effects through non-standard forms of projection. In the fifties many cinemas linked pairs of projectors mechanically to show STEREOSCOPIC (3-D) films. Others installed special horizontal projectors to accommodate horizontal-format VISTAVISION. Loudspeakers were placed beside, above, and behind the audience to provide 'surround sound'; aromas were piped into the auditorium (see AROMARAMA): and recently subsonic frequencies physically shook the audiences during *Earthquake* (1975). These short-lived devices failed not because of imperfect execution by film-makers but because of the difficulty of reproducing them consistently to audiences everywhere. Projection and presentation remain passive technologies whose sole purpose is to transmit the film-maker's work as he intended it to be seen. (See also DOUBLE HEAD.)

**PROKOFIEV**, SERGEI (1891–1953), Soviet composer, apart from his distinguished and prolific output of opera, ballet, and orchestral works, wrote the scores for several important films. Outstanding among them are *Poruchik Kije* (*Lieutenant Kije* in GB, *The Tsar Wants to Sleep* in US, 1934), the music for which was later used for *The Horse's Mouth* (1958); ALEXANDER NEVSKY (1938), IVAN GROZNYI (*Ivan the Terrible*, 1944, 1958). Prokofiev arranged several of his film scores for concert performance.

**PROPAGANDA.** It has been held that almost all films intended for public viewing partake of the nature of propaganda. Both state-owned industries and commercial production companies may be said to have an interest in preserving the *status quo*, on the one hand to perpetuate a political system or on the other to maintain a social climate that will ensure a mass audience. Such arguments depend on a high degree of instinctive motivation among film producers: the term propaganda is more usually applied to films made with the conscious intention of either strengthening national or group solidarity or changing or subverting opinion in a hostile or neutral group. These aims are naturally at their strongest in times of war.

The persuasive power of film, although difficult to assess and quantify, was recognized from the earliest days of cinema. Part of its effectiveness stems from the conviction that 'the camera cannot lie', deeply held in spite of repeated proofs to the contrary, allied to the power of editing, by the timing, duration, and juxtaposition of shots, to convey a meaning extrinsic to those of the images themselves.

Early film classifiable as propaganda, like Albert SMITH and J. Stuart BLACKTON's *Tearing Down the Spanish Flag* (1898), were commercial ventures designed to please a jingoistic public. Georges MÉLIÈS, however, undoubtedly intended to strike a blow for justice with *L'Affaire Dreyfus* (1899). Such films were usually reconstructions: although some actuality film emerged from the Boer War, film-makers like R. W. PAUL and Charles URBAN cheerfully staged scenes from the war to provide audiences with topical, patriotic entertainment.

Propaganda film came of age during the First World War. Every major belligerent power commissioned official films and most ended the war with some kind of government department responsible for co-ordinating film propaganda.

At first Germany and Austria gained an impressive lead. German and neutral cameramen were allowed by the German High Command to film at the front from the beginning of the war, while the British and French authorities refused access to cameramen until 1915–16 (see NEWSREEL). Consequently the war was for a time represented almost entirely from the German point of view in neutral countries. In 1916 BUFA (Bild- und Filmamten) was set up to make propaganda films employing a team of combat cameramen assembled by Oskar MESSTER for his newsreels. The following year BUFA became a part of the newly-created UFA, still largely under government control.

The importance of winning the sympathy of neutrals, especially America, as well as encouraging and informing home audiences, quickly became apparent to the Allies. The British and French reversed their decision to bar cameramen from the front lines, and film became an integral part of the propaganda effort.

The French Service Photographique et Cinématographique de l'Armée provided the footage for battle films like *La Bataille de Verdun* (1916) and official COMPILATIONS such as *La Guerre anglaise* (1917). It also produced short featurettes, employing film-makers of the calibre of Marcel L'HERBIER and Abel GANCE. Gance made a number of typical melodramas with revealing titles such as *L'Heroïsme de Paddy*, *Strass et Compagnie*, *Le Gaz mortel*, and *La Zone de la mort* (all 1916). They were coolly received, but the experience enabled Gance to make his effective plea for peace, *J'ACCUSE* (1919).

The British government's propaganda effort got under way with *Britain Prepared* (1915), supervised by Charles Urban, showing the training of Kitchener's New Army, the Grand Fleet in the North Sea, and the vast expansion of munitions manufacture. Urban himself took the film to America, overcoming the commercial renters' lack of interest by personally handling the distribution and pulling in capacity audiences in New York, Boston, and Philadelphia. British battle films achieved similar success, both in Britain and the US. *The Battle of the Somme* (1916), *Battle of the Ancre* (1916), *The Battle of Arras* (1917), *St Quentin* (1917) seem today curiously lacking in propaganda elements: the takes are long, editing is minimal, and the titles are mostly factual. Later official compilations were more emotional in tone, attacking 'the Hun' as an inhuman monster, not just an enemy.

The Cinematograph Section of the Department of Information (later the Ministry of Information) dealt with newsreels and war documentaries for both home and overseas distribution and produced 'informational' films for British civilian and military audiences. These ranged from featurettes and short documentaries to the two-minute TRAILER which came at the end of newsreels. The trailers, calculated to have reached about ten million people, had titles like *Give 'Em Beans* and, ominously, *Don't Waste Diseased Potatoes*, and exhorted the public to save money, buy war bonds, and economize on food. The longer documentaries, each made at the request of a particular ministry, include *The Women's Land Army* (1917) and *Whatsoever a Man Soweth* (1917), shown to the troops as part of a campaign to contain venereal disease.

Commercial feature films in the war's early stages dwelt on the regenerative effect of active service: alcoholics were cured, social outcasts rehabilitated, and cowards shamed into heroism. However, the industry soon turned to providing the escapist entertainment which was badly needed as the war lengthened. There was also a wave of spy stories featuring ungentlemanly Germans who could be relied upon to attack innocent English girls, shoot from behind, and indulge in generally caddish behaviour while being stupid enough to be easily outwitted by English Secret Servicemen, Boy Scouts, or Girl Guides.

The commercial cinema in all combatant countries made every effort to denigrate the enemy. German films showed French Senegalese troops butchering German children; the French and British had the brutal Hun shooting civilians, hell-bent on world conquest; the Americans, when they entered the war, were even more savage, producing films like *The Kaiser Beast of Berlin* (1917) and subjecting fragile heroines like Mary PICKFORD and Lillian GISH to the threat of 'a fate worse than death' at the hands of bestial Germans.

The change from isolationism to involvement by the United States was clearly reflected in films. Thomas H. INCE preached pacifism in the hugely successful CIVILIZATION (1916) and Herbert BRENON directed the great NAZIMOVA in the film version of her stage hit *War Brides* (1916), in which the women of a nation at war resist their ruler under the slogan 'no more children for war'. Before the end of 1916, however, the pro-war lobby had succeeded in having Brenon's film banned and J. Stuart Blackton had returned to patriotic tracts with *The Battle Cry of Peace* (1915) followed by a succession of similarly nationalistic efforts. Public opinion was outraged when *Spirit of '76* (1917), celebrating America's victory over the British, was released on the eve of the American entry into the war on the British side: the film was banned and its producer, Robert Goldstein, was sentenced to ten years' imprisonment under the Espionage Code. Directors who had expressed pacifist views turned in their tracks with the declaration of war. Both D. W. GRIFFITH and Brenon were invited to make films in Britain: Griffith's visit resulted in HEARTS OF THE WORLD and *The Great Love* (both 1918), the latter portraying the effect of war on British society; Brenon's *The Invasion of Britain* was not completed until just after the war and was not released. Back at home commercial directors put out a flood of anti-German films, including Cecil B. DEMILLE with *Joan the Woman*, a tribute to France; *The Little American*, with Mary Pickford as the victim of attempted rape by Germans; *You Can't Have Everything*, a plea for self-denial; and *'Till I Come Back To You*, demanding vengeance on the despoilers of Belgian villages, all released between 1917 and early 1918.

On the official side, the handling of film propaganda was organized much faster in America than in any of the original combatant nations; a division of films was created within the Committee of Public Information, most of the footage being provided by the Photographic Section of the US Signal Corps. Feature-length documentaries like *Pershing's Crusaders*, *America's Answer to the Hun*, and *Under Four Flags* were released in the US almost as soon as the first American troops reached Europe and were distributed to as many Allied and neutral countries as possible. From mid-1918 the films division also had an arrangement with the commercial studios, providing scenarios free of charge and giving all distribution rights on the finished film, once approved, to the producing company. This encouraged the exhibition of propaganda shorts not otherwise commercially viable.

In Russia the film industry rallied behind the war, initially without government intervention: patriotism may have been a contributing cause, but producers certainly welcomed the commercial advantage which derived from the lack of foreign competition. As in other belligerent countries, a succession of hysterically nationalistic films in the war's early stage was followed by escapist films unrelated to the war. To stiffen morale during the winter of 1915–16, the Entente powers bombarded Russian audiences with atrocity films and anti-German feature films.

Signs of the importance film was to have in the SOVIET UNION became evident as early as September 1917, when a resolution was passed by the central council of workers' committees emphasizing the power of cinema as an educative force; LENIN himself recognized and formulated this. The great Soviet films of the first decade after the Revolution are all inspired propaganda; film-makers were almost unanimous in their political commitment and enthusiastically applied their art to winning over the masses and strengthening the new social system. The silent films of EISENSTEIN, PUDOVKIN, and DOVZHENKO are by design as propagandistic as VERTOV's KINO-PRAVDA newsreels or later documentaries on industrial development and agrarian reform. The stylistic experiments and innovations during the period of revolutionary art in the Soviet Union affected both the commercial cinema and the AVANT-GARDE and DOCUMENTARY fields throughout the western world.

The elusive relationship between documentary film and propaganda has been the basis for considerable discussion. The poetic, descriptive work of FLAHERTY, RUTTMANN, and of CAVALCANTI in his early years added richness and flexibility to the documentary form, but did not attempt persuasion. John GRIERSON and his group of film-makers were committed to social change, although they were in the singular position of working for the British government at the Empire Marketing Board (see CROWN FILM UNIT). Films like *Housing Problems* (1935) and *Coal Face* (1936) were low-key political propaganda against the establishment which financed the films. Pare LORENTZ's THE PLOW THAT BROKE THE PLAINS (1936) was backed by US government funds, but the New Deal administration was attempting to explain and alleviate the distress attributed to the failings of previous governments. Joris IVENS, on the other hand, worked independently and indeed at some personal risk of official action to make MISÈRE AU BORINAGE (1933), protesting against the suffering of Belgian miners. Ivor MONTAGU also worked independently: he was instrumental in bringing many Soviet films to the FILM SOCIETY and later distributed films about the Spanish Civil War through his Progressive Film Institute; he filmed in Spain himself during 1938. One of the most uncompromisingly political films made in Britain is Montagu's *Peace and Plenty* (1939), produced for the Communist Party, which was a savage attack on the National government.

The emotions aroused by the Spanish Civil War are evident in the large number of committed films it inspired. Films supporting the Republicans, including Montagu's *The Defence of Madrid* (1936), Sidney Cole's *Behind the Spanish Lines* (1938), Ivens's THE SPANISH EARTH (1937), Thorold DICKINSON's *Spanish ABC* (1938), André MALRAUX's ESPOIR (1939), and Esther SHUB's *Ispaniya* (*Spain*, 1939), a compilation of footage shot by Roman KARMEN, are best known. However, the Nationalists also had their advocates on film, a German–Spanish co-production *Helden in Spanien* (1938), the Italian *L'assedio dell' Alcazar* (1939), and the German *Im Kampf gegen den Weltfeind* (1941) among them. The debate was revived in the sixties by Frédéric ROSSIF's pro-Republican MOURIR A MADRID (1962), the success of which stimulated an answer from Spain, *Morir en España* (1965), which aimed to dissociate Franco from the other Fascist leaders. The East German *Unbändiges Spanien* (*Untameable Spain*, 1962) accused the democracies of having betrayed Spain by failing to depose Franco at the end of the Second World War.

In Germany the cinema was an integral part of the National Socialist government's propaganda machine. The confusion and inflation of the twenties had generated a nationalistic reaction and many patriotic films appeared before the Nazi victory in 1933. There was also a strong left-wing movement in the cinema, given force by the Volksverbund für Filmkunst set up by men like PABST, Piscator, and Heinrich Mann. Key films were *Mutter Krausens Fahrt ins Gluck* (Piel Jutzi, 1929) and KÜHLE WAMPE (Slatan DUDOW, 1932); Piscator's *Der Aufstand der Fischer von Santa Barbara* (*Revolt of the Fishermen*, 1934), although produced and released in the Soviet Union, belongs with this group. There was little the NSDAP could do to counter these films until its own film output was established, but vigorous action was taken against the anti-war and anti-nationalist films that were appearing: Pabst's WESTFRONT 1918 (1930) survived Nazi interference, but Lewis MILESTONE's ALL QUIET ON THE WESTERN FRONT (1930) was banned as a result of a staged riot outside the cinema. The Propaganda Ministry under Dr Goebbels was established immediately after the elections of 1933 and by June of that year its film section, the REICHSFILM-KAMMER, was in existence. The rapid hold gained

by the Nazis over the German film industry was in fact based on the repressive legislation passed during the Weimar period in an attempt to maintain order, and the Lichtspielgesetz (Motion Picture Act) of 1934 was a logical extension of the existing legal framework.

Much of the overtly propagandistic film output of the Nazis during the thirties, such as *SA Mann Brand* and HITLERJUNGE QUEX in 1933, met with a spectacular lack of enthusiasm from the public, but the work of Leni RIEFENSTAHL represents a considerable achievement in combining aesthetic quality with effective political propaganda. Goebbels quickly realized that propaganda must be judiciously balanced against entertainment; he particularly advocated the use of popular stars and well-known directors, as in OHM KRÜGER (1941). The acquisition of specific targets—the Jewish scapegoat and, after the outbreak of war, the Allied nations—helped give force to the arguments expressed. Anti-Semitism was all-pervading, cropping up in anti-British films like *Gentlemen* (1940) or anti-American and anti-Soviet films like *Rund um Freiheitstatue* and *Das Sowjetparadies* (both 1941): in each society the root evil is failure to control the Jews. Anti-Semitic films reached a peak with the full implementation of Hitler's 'final solution' to the Jewish 'problem'. Veit HARLAN's skilfully emotive JUD SÜSS was regarded at the time as more pernicious than Fritz Hippler's documentary DER EWIGE JUDE and Harlan was the only film-maker actually put on trial by the Allies; but the two films were released close together in 1940 and were probably intended to have a complementary effect. Closely related to the anti-Semitic films were the euthanasia films, fictional or documentary in presentation, which argued the justification for state-authorized sterilizations and killings in Germany and in the occupied territories.

Nazi Germany's most impressive achievements in the field of film propaganda were undoubtedly in the newsreel and in the great campaign films produced during their early military successes. Special units of combat cameramen, the Propaganda Kompanie, were attached to the fighting units for the Propaganda Ministry, and each of the armed services also had its own film production units. Their material was sent back to Berlin for editing and the resulting films were something entirely new in war reporting. Films produced by the service units avoided the extreme bias that was injected by the Propaganda Ministry into identical material; *Sieg im Westen* (1940), for example, an account of the campaign that led to the fall of France, is nationalistic without being clearly National Socialist: the French Army is not denigrated and even the now famous sequence of French colonial African troops dancing is presented without comment. In a Deutsche Wochenschau newsreel the same sequence carries a commentary sneering at the barbarians who are defending western civilization. Deutsche Wochenschau was regarded by Goebbels as his single most important propaganda weapon, and he took special interest in each issue. The swift cutting emphasized the blitzkrieg advance of the German armies and by moving rapidly between the war and home fronts without intervening titles it conveyed the impression of a nation totally united. As part of the highly organized undertaking, special UFA Auslandtonwoche were made for distribution in occupied and neutral territories, while cinema programmes in Germany were arranged so that it was extremely difficult to avoid seeing the newsreel.

Of the campaign films made during the first months of the war, perhaps the most effective was *Feuertaufe* (*Baptism of Fire*, 1941) on the invasion and defeat of Poland, with particular emphasis on the air attack and the virtual obliteration of Warsaw; the final sequences are still chilling today.

Alexander KORDA launched the British war effort in the cinema with *The Lion Has Wings* (1939), a disappointing film which is reputed to have been screened in Berlin as a comedy. The first GPO Film Unit production showed a more hopeful direction: *The First Days* (1939), by Humphrey JENNINGS and Harry WATT, opened a remarkable series of films conveying the mood of ordinary people under the impact of war. Meanwhile the Ministry of Information rapidly gained the wholehearted co-operation of the commercial studios: EALING, DENHAM, and PINEWOOD produced short anti-'careless talk' films and HALAS AND BATCHELOR made effective animation shorts aimed at the home front. As in the First World War, exhortatory trailers were appended to newsreels. For Ealing, Cavalcanti made *Yellow Caesar* (1941), a direct attack on Mussolini. Other commercially-made features, including Leslie HOWARD's *The First of the Few* (1942) and Noël COWARD's IN WHICH WE SERVE (1942), expressed an assurance which could not be interpreted simply as a propaganda exercise. One of the commonest criticisms now levelled at British war-time feature films is that they display a class-consciousness which appears at best ridiculous in a nation united in a common effort. Certainly most film-makers would appear to have accepted the social order, skirting the problem of class as though embarrassing questions were out of place; in fact, some of the films to which the criticism most applies were extremely successful both as propaganda and at the box office.

Films made directly for the British government included Watt's *Target for Tonight* (1940), noted for its undramatic realism, Dickinson's *The Next of Kin* (1941), a fictional story vividly demonstrating the dangers of 'careless talk' which, originally intended for instructional use with the forces, received public release, and Pat Jackson's *Western Approaches* (1944), one of the few colour films sponsored by the ministry. The ministry also produced numerous shorts for distribution in factories, including Richard MASSINGHAM's cheerful homilies, and special newsreels which stressed the dependence of front-line troops on factory workers. The personal tone of these films is in striking contrast to their German equivalents; RUTTMANN's *Deutsche Panzer* (1941), for example, is perhaps a finer film but its subject is the end product of the assembly line rather than the workers involved. The nearest British equivalent to the German campaign films was the series *Desert Victory* (1943), *Tunisian Victory* (1943), and *Burma Victory* (1945), all made by John BOULTING and David Macdonald of the Army Kinematograph Unit with Frank CAPRA collaborating on the second of the series. The films gave the British a much-needed chance to indulge in self-congratulation, but again their tone is far removed from the cold aggressiveness of their German counterparts.

Many film-makers who worked in the field of propaganda in its widest sense were forced to reconcile distaste for conscious manipulation of the audience with the imperatives imposed by a state of war. Manipulation was the enemy of freedom, democracy, free expression, and epitomized the practices of the Nazis, but the democracies found it necessary to employ at least some of the methods of the enemy. One striking contrast with the attitudes of the First World War was in the presentation of the enemy. Fascism was the abhorrent object, not Germany: the authorities were aware that, once the war ended, European reconstruction must not again be handicapped by the vindictiveness that had isolated Germany in the twenties.

The Soviet cinema moved on to a war footing with amazing rapidity. On the day Germany invaded Russia, three major studios embarked independently on producing short, sharp information films. During 1941–2 these were organized by an editorial committee into regular monthly issues as *Fighting Film Albums*. Newsreel cameramen in Moscow recorded the battle of December 1941; their material was released early in 1942 as *Razgrom nemetskikh voisk pod Moskvoi* (*The Defeat of the German Armies near Moscow*; *Moscow Strikes Back* in US). *Leningrad v borbe* (*Siege of Leningrad*, 1942) was the next major documentary, filmed under even more gruelling conditions. As these films reached the

West they helped to strengthen feelings of solidarity with the beleaguered Russians. *Stalingrad* (1943) received blanket distribution in the Allied countries and was later re-edited by the British for exhibition in the liberated territories: the immense psychological significance of Germany's first great defeat added to the film's power.

Typical feature film titles were DONSKOI's *Kak zakalyalas stal* (*How the Steel Was Tempered*, 1942), from a novel about Ukrainian resistance to the Germans during the First World War; ERMLER's *Ona zashchishchayet rodinu* (*She Defends her Country*, 1943), later dubbed in English as *No Greater Love*; and Pudovkin's *Vo imya rodini* (*In the Name of the Fatherland*, 1943). Many of the most important Soviet directors spent the war years working on newsreel footage: DOVZHENKO, in particular, placed his personal stamp on material shot by various cameramen in *Bitva za nashu Sovietskuyu Ukrainu* (*The Fight for Our Soviet Ukraine*, 1943).

As the last of the Allies to enter the war, America was late in organizing full-scale official propaganda, but as in the First World War both commercial and independent film-makers began to take sides long before December 1941. Herbert KLINE, who had already encountered Fascism in Spain, made *Crisis* (1938), with Alexander Hammid, examining the Munich Settlement and its real effect on the Czechs, and the same team followed this up with *Lights Out in Europe* (1940). THE MARCH OF TIME continually prodded the American conscience with issues like *Inside Nazi Germany* (1938), *Canada at War* (1939), *The Ramparts We Watch* (1940), *Britain's RAF* (1940), and *America Speaks Her Mind* (1941), an edition in which various points of view, including the isolationist, are expressed, but which is ultimately potently persuasive in arousing sympathy for Britain. Hollywood naturally took up an anti-Nazi stance, with Nazis as the villains in Anatole LITVAK's *Confessions of a Nazi Spy* (1939) and HITCHCOCK's *Foreign Correspondent* (1940). Overt attack on Germany was still, however, not wholly acceptable: CHAPLIN's THE GREAT DICTATOR (1940) shared with *Inside Nazi Germany* the honour of being banned by the Chicago local censorship committee for political bias. During 1941 a number of films appeared which swayed American feelings against Germany. The most important was probably Howard HAWKS's *Sergeant York* (1941), set in the First World War, in which Gary COOPER played a conscientious objector who becomes a hero in a just war without rejecting the ideal of pacifism. With America's entry into the war the commercial studios threw themselves into the war effort. One of the most suc-

cessful commercially-made propaganda films on any terms was William WYLER's *Mrs Miniver* (1942) which meticulously reproduces the social and emotional flavour of British films of the same period. *Mission to Moscow* (1943) went so far as to condone the Stalinist trials of the thirties in the cause of Soviet–American friendship. Almost every Hollywood personality at some time did his bit for Uncle Sam, including DONALD DUCK in *Der Führer's Face* (1943) and TARZAN, who took on the German army in *Tarzan Triumphs* (1943); in *The Desert Song* (1944) the villains were abruptly transformed into Nazis.

Hollywood directors of the calibre of Capra, John FORD, William Wyler, William WELLMAN, and John HUSTON served with the American Office of War Information. As executive producer of the WHY WE FIGHT series (1942–5), Capra made what is probably America's most enduring contribution to the propaganda film. The series represents the first attempt to present on film a unified account of the events leading up to the war, and it marked a new departure in the editing of compilation films in its juxtaposition of word and image. Capra also collaborated with Boulting and Macdonald on *Tunisian Victory*. Important American combat films included Ford's *The Battle of Midway* (1942) and *December Seventh* (1943) and Wyler's *Memphis Belle* (1944).

Official films played their part in post-war re-education and reconstruction, especially in occupied Germany. The Allied Control Commission's newsreel *Welt in Film* (1945–51) devoted its first five issues almost entirely to revealing the horrors of the concentration camps, showing groups of local citizens being conducted around the sites; the early issues now look uncomfortably self-righteous in their insistence on German collective guilt.

After the First World War, propaganda films had been rapidly abandoned. After 1945, however, there was little diminution in the output of propaganda films by the main combatants; while this reflects a continuing state of hostility, it also demonstrates official acceptance of the cinema as a means of political education. Britain virtually dropped out of the field: the Crown Film Unit lingered on until 1951, hampered by limited funds and lack of government interest, although the Central Office of Information continues to commission films on prestige subjects mostly for foreign and Commonwealth distribution; but America and the Soviet Union backed up their positions in the Cold War with a steady flow of cinematic self-justification. Official propaganda in the US, handled by the United States Information Service, reached overseas audiences of 100 million a year by 1950. Extreme anti-Soviet films with titles like *Red Nightmare, Why Korea?*,

*Why Vietnam?*, were to prove embarrassing in the more liberal climate of the seventies and were suppressed. Hollywood spy dramas followed the official line, their Nazi villains transformed into Communists. John WAYNE made a personal patriotic statement with *The Green Berets* (1968), supporting American intervention in Indo-China, and John Ford again worked for the USIS, making the compilation film *Vietnam Vietnam* (1971).

Comparatively little propaganda film percolated through to the west from Russia during the Cold War, but examples that have been seen give striking evidence of the Russian skill in rewriting history, with major battles completely restaged to support the official line on the war. Russian archivists have acknowledged their expertise in frame-by-frame 'correction' of archive footage so that, for example, Trotsky never appears in compilations on the revolutionary period. Mikhail Chiaureli became a specialist in deifying Stalin—*Klyatva* (*The Vow*, 1946) and *Padeniye Berlina* (*The Fall of Berlin*, 1950) —but in *Velikaya otechestvennaya voina* (*The Great Patriotic War*, 1965) Roman Karmen depicted the current official Russian view of the Second World War with minimal references to the discredited Stalin.

As in the inter-war years, film became the tool of radical film-makers and revolutionary governments. Vietnam was a rallying-point, the Spain of the sixties, with the official American view countered by films like *Inside North Vietnam* (Felix Greene), *Hanoi, martes 13* (Santiago ALVAREZ), and *Loin du Viet-nam* (RESNAIS, LELOUCH, VARDA, GODARD, Ivens, and MARKER), all in 1967. Chris Marker became a successor to Ivens, making his contribution to left-wing causes with *Dimanche à Pékin* (*Sunday in Peking*, 1955), CUBA SI! (1961), and *La Sixième Face du Pentagone* (1968). Film-makers of the THIRD WORLD have employed film in the tradition of revolutionary Russia, especially in CUBA where AGIT-PROP cinema continues to be a major force.

**PROTAZANOV,** YAKOV (1881–1945), Russian director, entered cinema as an actor in 1905. He directed a great many films before the Revolution, many of which had historical settings and tended towards sentimentality. His best films in this period were his literary adaptations,

*Aelita* (Protazanov, 1924)

which included *Pikovaya dama* (*Queen of Spades*, 1916) and *Otets Sergii* (*Father Sergius*, 1918). He also collaborated with GARDIN on several films. After the Revolution he went abroad and made films in Germany and France. One of these, *Le Sens de la mort* (1922), had René CLAIR in the cast. Returning to Russia in 1924 he made *Aelita*, a science-fiction fantasy with constructivist sets and costumes. This was followed by some comedies and the less characteristic SOROK PERVYI (*The Forty-first*, 1927). In 1930 he made a satire on religion, *Prazdnik svyatovo Iorgena* (*The Feast of St Jorgen*); his last film *Nasreddin v Bukhare* (*Nasreddin in Bukhara*, 1943) was about the folklore and legends surrounding Nasreddin, protector of the poor.

Protazanov's best films are distinguished by a strong narrative exposition and penetrating psychological interpretation.

**PSYCHO**, US, 1960. 1¾hr. *Dir, prod* Alfred Hitchcock for Paramount; *scr* Joseph Stefano, from the novel by Robert Bloch; *ph* John L. Russell; *des* Joseph Hurley—titles by Saul Bass; *mus* Bernard Herrmann; *cast* Janet Leigh (Marion Crane), Anthony Perkins (Norman Bates), Vera Miles (Lila Crane), John Gavin (Sam Loomis), Martin Balsam (Milton Arbogast), John McIntire (Sheriff), Simon Oakland (Dr Richmond).

Marion absconds with 40,000 dollars, and, en route to join her lover, stops for the night at a motel where she is brutally murdered, apparently by the motel-keeper's aged mother. After another murder, the crimes are finally solved by a psychiatrist's explanation. Combining horror, mystery, and grotesque comedy, *Psycho*, with its long and misleading introduction about the theft of the money, and its central hoax concerning the murderer, exemplifies the way in which HITCHCOCK manipulates not only the film, but the spectator too.

It is one of the first films for which the exhibitor, by contract, guaranteed to refuse admission after projection had begun. By the use of skilful advertising, this apparent liability was turned into an asset.

**PUBLIC ENEMY**, US, 1931. 1½hr. *Dir* William Wellman; *prod* Warner Bros; *scr* Harvey Thew, from the story by Kubec Glasmon and John Bright; *ph* Dev Jennings; *cast* James Cagney (Tom Powers), Jean Harlow (Gwen), Edward Woods (Matt Doyle), Joan Blondell (Mamie), Mae Clarke (Kitty).

The story of an urban gangster, recognizable to contemporaries as Hymie Weiss, told in episodes from his childhood to his ruthless death at the hands of rival mobsters, *Public Enemy* is a prime representative of the succession of GANG-STER FILMS made by WARNER BROS in the thirties. The economical script and spare visual style effectively indicate the roots of crime in social deprivation; the implication that defiance of the law may be a substitute for sexual achievement foreshadows the psychology of BONNIE AND CLYDE (1967). James CAGNEY's screen personality—arrogant, edgy, truculent—was fully exploited in the role of Tom Powers; the status of the anti-hero in the cinema was immeasurably enhanced by the brief moment when Cagney pushed a grapefruit into Mae Clarke's face.

**PUDOVKIN**, VSEVOLOD ILARIONOVICH (1893–1953), Russian director, studied chemistry at Moscow University. After military service he joined the State Film School in Moscow where he learned acting and filmmaking under Lev KULESHOV. His first film as director, *Shakhmatnaya goryachka* (*Chess Fever*, 1925), was an effective exercise in editing, using straightforward shots of the chess champion Capablanca cut into narrative material to produce a short comedy. *Mekhanika golovnovo mozga* (*Mechanics of the Brain*, 1926) was a direct account of the experimental work of the biologist Pavlov. These apprentice pieces were followed by Pudovkin's first fiction feature MAT (*Mother*, 1926), concerned with the abortive revolution of 1905. While *Mat* was still in production he was commissioned to make a film for the anniversary celebrations of 1927, just as EISENSTEIN had to interrupt his work on STAROYE I NOVOYE (*Old and New*, 1929) to make OKTIABR (*October*, 1928). Pudovkin's KONYETS SANKT-PETERBURGA (*The End of St Petersburg*, 1927) was completed before *Oktiabr*, and it was not involved with troubles (as Eisenstein's film was, with the sudden need to remove Trotsky). It was warmly received, although there was criticism of extravagance in some scenes and charges not only of corruption in production but also of neglect of genuine proletarian society at the film's presentation. Pudovkin was able, however, to go on to another success with his last great silent film POTOMOK CHINGIS-KHANA (*The Heir to Jenghis Khan* or *Storm over Asia*, 1928). In spite of official protests from abroad—particularly Britain where it was banned—this spirited film had great international success.

Pudovkin's early interest in acting continued throughout his career as a director. He often played small parts in his own and other films—his last appearance was in Eisenstein's IVAN GROZNYI (*Ivan the Terrible*, 1944)—and this understanding of the actor gave his three major silent films a warmth which provides their great contrast with the concurrent work of Eisenstein. Working from the same ideological standpoint and with similar methods and facilities, Pudovkin concentrated the audience's sympathy on the individuals involved in political issues, rather than on the issues themselves. His editing aimed at supporting the narrative by the linking of images in a meaningful way: his theory of MONTAGE was formulated in his lectures to the Moscow Film Institute in 1926 and published in *Film technique and film acting*, London, 1929. It was probably their human interest which gave his films their immediate popular appeal and saved him from the official disapproval which Eisenstein suffered during the thirties.

As a thoughtful film-maker, Pudovkin was ready in theory for the coming of sound but in practice was not very successful. His first sound film, *Prostoi sluchai* (*A Simple Case*, 1932), was misunderstood at home. His next, *Deserter* (1933), originally planned as a comment on the struggle of a Hamburg dock-worker and interrupted by Hitler's accession to power, was too experimental to meet with popular or official approval in the Soviet Union. The political atmosphere was hardening and the artistic straitjacket of SOCIALIST REALISM was already in operation.

Pudovkin was severely injured in a car crash in 1935 and was unable to work for some years. On his recovery he returned to directing, making films following the official line of grand historical reconstructions. He died in 1953, when censorship had brought Soviet film production almost to a halt.

***PUGNI IN TASCA, I*** (*Fists in the Pocket*), Italy, 1966. 2hr. *Dir, scr* Marco Bellocchio; *prod* Ezio Passadore; *ph* Alberto Marrama; *mus* Ennio Morricone; *cast* Lou Castel (Sandro), Paola Pitagora (Giulia), Marino Mase (Augusto), Liliona Gerace (the mother), Pier Luigi Troglio (Leone).

In a middle-class Italian family, made up of a blind widow with four children, three of whom are epileptics, only Augusto has a normal life and the family prevents him from living it fully. Sandro kills his mother and youngest brother in an attempt to free Augusto; as a result, his sister, Giulia, becomes semi-paralysed and thus unable to help him during his climactic attack, with which the film closes.

BELLOCHIO's first film is enigmatic. Those politically inclined see it as an analysis of the stagnation of present-day Italian society; others see in it only the story it tells. Acted by amateurs or student actors, it conveys the claustrophobia of the family and its relationships with a power and intensity remarkable in a first feature film.

**PUPPET FILM.** The costliness of the form and the availability of efficiently-marketed American cartoons have inhibited the production of puppet films, even in countries where there is a strong tradition of puppet theatre. One of the earliest films to use puppets was made by the energetic Giovanni PASTRONE, *La guerra e il sogno di Momi* (*The War and Momi's Dream*, 1916), but apart from the experimental work of STAREVITCH and PAINLEVÉ, the form was little explored until the mid-forties.

The sudden emergence of both puppet and drawn animation film in Eastern Europe after the Second World War was caused in part by the long gap in American imports and in part by an upsurge of patriotism and striving for national identity. Folk-lore and traditional modes of graphic expression offered stimulus to animators: in Poland and especially in Czechoslovakia, where marionette theatre has been a part of popular culture since the seventeenth century, puppet film became a new, exciting medium. As in the traditional puppet theatre, it has frequently offered a means of political and satirical comment, couched in allegorical form, when such criticisms could not be made openly.

The technique of filming puppets is basically that of graphic animation: stop-motion photography is used to record successive fractional changes in the figures to create the illusion of movement when the film is run continuously. For a five-minute sequence, each figure must be posed 7,200 times. The three-dimensional nature of the subject creates problems not encountered in conventional animation. Lighting is similar to that of live-action films and the materials used for both puppets and sets must be capable of resisting the heat of powerful lamps.

Much of the film's visual quality lies in the variety of textures used in faces, costumes, and sets. Painlevé animated 300 plasticine figures for *Barbe-bleue* (*Bluebeard*, 1938). The most common, and usually the most satisfying, material is wood: Katarzyna Latallo emphasized the chisel-cuts on wooden figures to great effect in *Sad Krolewski* (*The King's Sentence*). Serafinowicz and Wieczorkiewicz's *Przygoda z Bazyliszkien* (*The Basilisk*) and TRNKA's *Špalíček* (*The Czech Year*, 1947) played on the textures of coarse cloth and wool. The figures in Hermina Tyrlová's *Snowman* (1966) were made of bunched or curled wool, imparting a delicate, finely-lit effect of fragile beauty. ZEMAN animated glass figures for *Inspirace* (*Inspiration*, 1949). Paper sculptures, awkward to animate, were successfully brought to life in Bretislav Pojar's *Cat Talk*, *Cat Painting*, and *Cat School* (1960). Colin Hoedeman achieved fluid movement with figures of plastic wire in *La Boule magique* (1969) and Kotowski used a similar technique in his beautifully schematized *The World in Opera* (1969). In contrast is the use of *objets trouvés*: Edward Sturlis animated the statuettes from an old-fashioned piano in *A Little Quartet*, Etien Raik's metal nutcrackers marched with musical instruments in *14 juillet à Nutsville* (1969), and in a more experimental film, *Stones and Life* (1965), Garik Seko populated the screen with smooth river-stones, impressively life-like. Sets are usually formalized, even abstract, but Trnka's full-length *Sen noci svatojanské* (A MID-SUMMER NIGHT'S DREAM, 1958) used lavish settings in a film of splendid visual beauty, rich almost to excess in its intricate detail.

Apart from the straightforward use of puppets to tell a story of greater or lesser sophistication, they have been extensively used in mixed-media films. Live actors may be introduced, posed, and photographed in exactly the same manner as the puppets, a technique known as pixillation. As early as 1935, Ptushko's *Novyi Gulliver* (*The New Gulliver*) used tiny, grotesque puppets in conjunction with an actor; in Lidia Hornicka's *Olimpiada* (*The Olympic Games*) puppets made of chestnuts come to life beside a real boy; and Jan Svankmajer's *Coffin Factory* has a fight between two puppet clowns over a live guinea pig. The combination of drawn animation and puppets requires particular discretion in resolving the incompatibility between two- and three-dimensional objects. Zeman has attained remarkable accomplishment in this field. Jerzy Kotowski has used the technique in children's films like *Czarny Krol* (*The Black King*). Perhaps the most apt application was in Zenon Wasilewski's *Zbrodnia przy Ulicy Kota Brzuchomowcy* (*Crime on Cat Ventriloquist Street*) where the central figure is a two-dimensional man who uses this characteristic to escape from the puppet police.

Puppet films directed at adult audiences usually carry an allegorical meaning, for they operate most effectively on the symbolic level. Outstanding films in this vein are Trnka's *Ruka* (*The Hand*, 1965), in which a giant hand forces a sculptor to submit to its will and finally kills him, and Kotowski's macabre *Shadows of Time* (1964), in which two skeleton hands crawl out of a Nazi helmet, attempt to destroy a household, and are electrocuted. With their combination of fantasy and reality, puppet films are also an ideal medium for folk legends and fairy-tales, and their chief use has been for children's films. Some of the best have come from Poland's Tuszyn Puppet Studios, near Lódź, including Hornicka's *O Janku co psom szyl buty* (*About Johnny, Who Made Shoes for Dogs*), Teresa Badzian's *Muzycza* (*A Little Music*), and *Dwie Lampy* (*Two Lamps*) by Tadeusz Wilkosz. The massive demand for children's television programmes has stimulated the production of puppet series in France, Britain, and the US, the best including *The Magic Roundabout, The Clangers, Camberwick Green, Trumpton, Thunderbirds, Fireball XL5*, and *The Wombles*.

The comparatively recent emergence of puppet film as a viable cinematic form has shown it to be a neglected field: published material is sparse and no historical account is as yet available in English.

**PURVIANCE**, EDNA (1894–1958), US actress who was discovered by CHAPLIN at seventeen, when she was visiting his studios. *A Night Out* (1915) was the first of over thirty films in which she co-starred with him in a variety of parts, but invariably as the charming object of his affections. They include THE TRAMP (1915), THE IMMIGRANT (1917), SHOULDER ARMS (1918) and THE KID (1920). Later Chaplin directed her in A WOMAN OF PARIS (1923) in the part of an elegant prostitute, but it was not successful commercially, and Chaplin suppressed *The Sea Gull* (1926) which he had hired STERNBERG to direct as her come-back picture. Her acting career then came to a halt, but she and Chaplin remained life-long friends and she made a brief appearance as an extra in his LIMELIGHT (1952).

**PYGMALION**, GB, 1938. 1½hr. *Dir* Anthony Asquith, Leslie Howard; *prod* Gabriel Pascal; *scr* W. P. Lipscomb and Cecil Lewis from the play by George Bernard Shaw; *ph* Harry Stradling; *ed* David Lean; *mus* Arthur Honegger; *cast* Leslie Howard (Henry Higgins), Wendy Hiller (Eliza Doolittle), Wilfrid Lawson (Doolittle), Marie Lohr (Mrs Higgins), Scott Sunderland (Colonel Pickering), Jean Cadell (Mrs Pearce).

With a cast largely drawn from the English stage (only Leslie HOWARD was well known to film audiences), Anthony ASQUITH established himself as a master of elegant comedy, and Wendy HILLER's performance as Eliza made her a star. *Pygmalion* had an enthusiastic reception in Europe and the US: its wit and polish are enduring, in spite of the incongruity of updating the action. *Pygmalion* was withdrawn from circulation when the musical version, MY FAIR LADY (1964), was released.

# Q

**QUAI DES BRUMES,** France, 1938. 1½hr. *Dir* Marcel Carné; *prod* Rabinovich; *scr* Jacques Prévert from the novel by Pierre MacOrlan; *ph* Eugen Schüfftan; *des* Alexander Trauner; *mus* Maurice Jaubert; *cast* Jean Gabin (Jean), Michèle Morgan (Nelly), Michel Simon (Zabel), Pierre Brasseur (Lucien), Aimos (the tramp).

An army deserter commits a murder in a fit of temper. As he is fleeing from the police he meets and falls in love with a young girl, but their plan to escape together is foiled by the girl's guardian. Set in the mist-shrouded port of Le Havre, *Quai des brumes* blended realistic detail with a poetic quality which was to become the distinctive feature of the work of PRÉVERT and CARNÉ, and the film marks the crystallization of their collaboration. It was also the first to co-star Jean GABIN and Michèle MORGAN, subsequently one of the most famous acting couples in the French cinema.

**QUAI DES ORFÈVRES,** France, 1947. 1¾hr. *Dir* Henri-Georges Clouzot; *prod* Majestic-Film; *scr* Clouzot, Jean Ferry; *ph* Armand Thirard; *des* Max Douy; *cost* Jacques Fath; *cast* Simone Renant (Dora), Suzy Delair (Jenny), Bernard Blier (Maurice), Charles Dullin (Brignon), Louis Jouvet (Chief Inspector Antoine).

Coming between the biting *Le Corbeau* (1943) and the outré *Manon* (1948)—and before CLOUZOT achieved real international renown with LE SALAIRE DE LA PEUR (1953) and *Les Diaboliques* (1955)—this was a traditional *policier* with a complicated plot concerning a married pair of music-hall artists and the murder of a film company director, a lecherous old roué who has been making advances to the wife.

It was chiefly notable for Louis JOUVET's characteristically subtle performance as the gruff, slouching, but perceptive Inspector, for its music-hall scenes and costumes, and for Suzy Delair as the wife and Simone Renant as another music-hall performer, the couple's friend, who becomes implicated in the crime.

**QUARANTA,** LYDIA (1891–1928) and LETIZIA (1892–    ), Italian actresses. During her brief career Lydia achieved enormous popularity: her most famous appearance was in the title role of CABIRIA (1914). Her last film was CAMERINI's *Voglio tradire mio marito* (1925). Letizia's career was longer, starting with *Addio giovinezza* (1913), in which Lydia also appeared, and *Ma l'amore mio non muore* (CASERINI, 1913); she later specialized in thrillers such as *La nave dei morte* (1919), *La signora delle miniere*, and *Un simpatico mascalzone* (both 1920). She spent the years 1923–7 in Argentina and Brazil, working under the direction of her husband Carlo Campogalliani. Finding the transition to sound difficult, she retired in the early thirties but has occasionally played small parts in her husband's films. Letizia's twin sister Isabella also had a short career in films.

**QUARTERLY OF FILM RADIO AND TELEVISION** see FILM QUARTERLY

**QUATRE CENTS COUPS, Les,** France, 1959. Dyaliscope; 1½hr. *Dir* François Truffaut; *prod* Les Films du Carrosse; *scr* Truffaut, helped with dialogue by Marcel Moussy; *ph* Henri Decaë; *ed* Marie-Josèphe Yoyotte; *mus* Jean Constantin; *cast* Jean-Pierre Léaud (Antoine Doinel), Albert Rémy (his step-father), Claire Maurier (his mother), Patrick Auffay (René), Robert Beauvais (headmaster), Guy Decomble (teacher).

Fourteen-year-old ANTOINE DOINEL lives in a cramped apartment with his mother and step-father, neglected by them and unlucky at school. Living an intense imaginative life of his own, he gets into a series of scrapes (the nearest equivalent to 'faire les 400 coups' is 'to sow wild oats') in which he is supported only by his friend René. Finally he is committed to reform school for stealing a type-writer. He escapes and runs towards the sea, which he has never seen.

In his first feature film, dedicated to the memory of André BAZIN, TRUFFAUT was clearly drawing on the experiences of his own adolescence, and was giving expression to one of his principal preoccupations, his care and concern for children. To find a boy to play the crucial part of Antoine, he filmed with a group of boys, and from them chose the most committed and enthusiastic, Jean-Pierre LÉAUD, whose spontaneity and engaging wistfulness in the film correspond perfectly to Truffaut's sympathetic view of Antoine's truant-playing, lying, stealing, and dreaming.

Many of the elements distinguishing the films of the NOUVELLE VAGUE as well as Truffaut's own later films are present. Technical effects are used with daring and grace, the camera (brilliantly directed by Henri DECAË) moving with a new freedom in and around the streets of Paris or statically confronting the boy as he sits face-to-face with a psychiatrist. The last haunting shot of the film, a frozen close-up of Antoine's face, has become one of the most memorable in cinema. There are many references to film culture, which include overt homage to VIGO'S ZÉRO DE CONDUITE (1933) and a visit to a cinema at which RIVETTE'S PARIS NOUS APPARTIENT (1960, being shot at the time) is billed.

*Les Quatre Cents coups* won the Grand Prix for direction at CANNES in 1959, in competition with GODARD'S A BOUT DE SOUFFLE and RESNAIS'S HIROSHIMA MON AMOUR. The success of these films fairly launched the *nouvelle vague*, and *Les Quatre Cents coups* deservedly went on to win many prizes and sustained popular and critical success.

**QUEEN CHRISTINA**, US, 1934. 1¾hr. *Dir* Rouben Mamoulian; *prod* Walter Wanger for MGM; *scr* Salka Viertel, Margaret F. Levin; *ph* William Daniels; *cast* Greta Garbo (Queen Christina), John Gilbert (Don Antonio), Lewis Stone (Oxenstierna), C. Aubrey Smith (Aage), Ian Keith (Count Magnus).

*Queen Christina* gave GARBO her ideal role as the seventeenth-century Swedish ruler who, brought up to think and dress as a man, discovers her womanhood through love. The film endures only through her performance; but MAMOULIAN handled the historical spectacle with panache and he takes credit for establishing the definitive Garbo image in her final poignant close-up standing at the prow of her dead lover's ship.

**QUEEN ELIZABETH** see REINE ELISABETH, LA

**QUEEN KELLY**, US, 1928. 2hr (but see below). *Dir, scr* Erich von Stroheim; *prod* Joseph P. Kennedy for MGM; *ph* Ben Reynolds; *des* Stroheim, Robert Day; *cast* Gloria Swanson (Patricia Kelly), Walter Byron (Prince Wolfram), Seena Owen (Queen Regina), Sidney Bracey (valet), William von Brincken (adjutant).

In spite of the many conflicts STROHEIM had encountered in his previous projects, he embarked on *Queen Kelly* with his usual uncompromising attitude. Although deprived of his favourite actors and forced to frame the film around a star (Gloria SWANSON who, with Joseph P. KENNEDY, was financing it), his basic conception uses themes that recurred in his earlier work: pure love across class barriers opposed to

carnal desire, European decadence, and an ironically sophisticated attitude to sex. The lavishly detailed settings which in all his films give force and depth to character were here of astonishing costliness, particularly in the palace scenes where the jealous Queen's erotic obsessions are illustrated by décor of spectacular luxuriousness. Stroheim's flair for making silent films rich in implication by purely visual means here reached a peak of assurance.

With only a third of the shooting completed, about four hours of film had been amassed and the producers called a halt. Their ostensible reason was the disruption which the introduction of sound had caused in the industry, but Stroheim's intransigent extravagance was undoubtedly a major factor. The film was hastily edited, an arbitrary ending and a music track were added, and it was released in Europe but never commercially in the US. Surviving RUSHES indicate that the action was to move from Europe to Africa for the second half of the film: an interesting innovation in Stroheim's work, where physical surroundings are always of the utmost importance.

There are parallels to be drawn between *Queen Kelly* and SUNSET BOULEVARD (1950): these are fully examined in Joel Finler's useful *Stroheim*, London, 1967.

**QUEEN OF SPADES, The**, GB, 1948. 1½hr. *Dir* Thorold Dickinson; *prod* Anatole de Grunwald/Associated British; *scr* Rodney Ackland, Arthur Boys, from the story by Alexander Pushkin; *ph* Otto Heller; *des* Oliver Messel; *mus* Georges Auric; *cast* Edith Evans (the Countess), Anton Walbrook (Herman), Yvonne Mitchell (Lizaveta Ivanovna), Ronald Howard (Andrei), Mary Jerrold (Varvarushka), Miles Malleson (Tchybukin), Athene Seyler (Princess Ivashin).

Thorold DICKINSON displayed enormous skill in conjuring up richness and spaciousness from simple sets, properties, and sound effects, and made fluid and creative use of the camera. He showed himself, too, a master of concentrated atmosphere, reacting stylishly and convincingly to the supernatural elements in Pushkin's story. He achieved a fine sense of period with the support of Otto HELLER's photography, Oliver Messel's designs, and an authoritative performance from Edith EVANS in her first appearance in sound film.

**QUENEAU, RAYMOND** (1903–   ), French writer, closely associated with the Surrealist group in the twenties (see SURREALISM), has been preoccupied since the early thirties with exposing the gulf between spoken French and the written, academic language. A writer of insight and lively

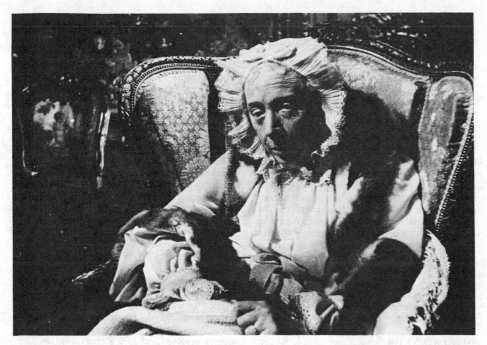

*The Queen of Spades* (Thorold Dickinson, 1948)

wit, he has since the early fifties enjoyed an appreciative flirtation with the cinema. His role has varied from that of subject-writer and actor (*Le Lendemain*, 1950, a silent short, and *Arithmétique*, an episode in Pierre KAST's *L'Encyclopédie filmée*, 1951) to dialogue-writer for René CLÉMENT (for KNAVE OF HEARTS/ *Monsieur Ripois*, 1954, and a song for *Gervaise*, 1956), for BUÑUEL (*La Mort en ce jardin*, 1956), for Nicholas RAY (*Bitter Victory/Amère victoire*, 1958), and for Jean-Pierre MOCKY (*Un Couple*, 1960, in which he also acted). He wrote the commentary for several short films, among them Alain RESNAIS's *Le Chant du styrène* (1958). Of his own works, two have been filmed: *Le Dimanche de la vie*, directed by Jean Herman in 1967, and ZAZIE DANS LE MÉTRO, directed by Louis MALLE in 1960. Queneau's delightful bombardment of the conventions of communication is best represented in cinema by the disruptive Zazie.

*QUE VIVA MEXICO!* see EISENSTEIN

**QUINE,** RICHARD (1920), US actor and director, was first a Hollywood juvenile and later a leading actor—in *For Me and My Gal* (Busby BERKELEY, 1942), for example. His films as director have included enjoyable musicals like

*My Sister Eileen* (1955) and excellent comedies such as *The Solid Gold Cadillac* (1956), *Bell, Book and Candle* (1959), and *How to Murder Your Wife* (1964). His style is variable: of his later films, *Paris When It Sizzles* (1963) was undistinguished but *Hotel* (1967), although routine, was a box-office success.

**QUINN,** ANTHONY (1915– ), Mexican-born US actor with some experience as a child player, made his first adult appearance in *Parole* (1936). Prolific but, except for THE OX-BOW INCIDENT (1943), unremarkable work finally led to an OSCAR as best supporting actor in VIVA ZAPATA! (Elia KAZAN, 1952). After working in Italy, notably in FELLINI's LA STRADA (1954), he returned to America to win a second Oscar for his performance as Gauguin in *Lust for Life* (Vincente MINNELLI, 1956): the flamboyance of this character set the tone for his later performances. During the filming of *The Buccaneer* (1959) he volunteered to take over direction on the illness of Cecil B. DEMILLE, whose adopted daughter Katherine he had married in 1937. *Zorba the Greek* (Michael CACOYANNIS, 1965) renewed his popularity and confirmed his ability to sustain the role of an earthy, disreputable character with innate dignity; but more recent films, *The Shoes of the Fisherman* (Michael Anderson, 1968), *The*

*Secret of Santa Vittoria* (Stanley KRAMER, 1969), and *Flap* (Carol REED, 1970, *The Last Warrior* in GB), have had less box-office success.

**QUOTA,** one of the commonest measures taken by national governments to support a country's film industry by specifying the proportion of indigenous films to be exhibited in relation to imported films. The pervasive influence of Hollywood in the twenties and thirties was a major factor in stimulating quota legislation, particularly in Europe and Latin America: it has never been needed in countries with either a thriving industry or a nationalized system. Quota legislation has rarely given any real aid to a commercially unhealthy industry as it makes no attempt to encourage a high standard of film-making; in fact, further exploitation by American producers was aided, as 'quota quickies'—cheap programme-fillers made with local personnel and technical resources but financed from the US—kept standards down while fulfilling legal requirements. As a token of government support without requiring any actual investment in the cinema it has had little more than a conscience-salving function.

*QUO VADIS?* The best-selling novel (published in 1896) by the Polish Nobel Prize winner Henryk Sienkiewicz has been filmed three times to date. An eight-reel version, made in Italy in 1913 for CINES, was directed by Enrico Guazzoni. The greatest spectacular of its day, it was an immense success in Europe and America, from both financial and artistic points of view—the sculptor Rodin declared it a masterpiece—and it established Italy briefly as the leading maker of feature films. Billed as having a cast of 5,000 people and thirty lions, it was the first film to be auctioned publicly in Britain, when it was sold to Jury's Imperial Pictures for £6,700.

An Italian-German co-production made in 1925, produced by Arturo AMBROSIO and directed by Georg Jacoby and Gabriellino d'Annunzio, was very much less successful, in spite of a strong international cast of 20,000 including Emil JANNINGS, Lilian Hall-Davies, and Bruto Castellani (repeating his role in the earlier version).

METRO-GOLDWYN-MAYER's production of 1951, directed by Mervyn LEROY, is reputed to have cost some $8,250,000, and occupied the CINECITTÀ studios near Rome for no less than two years. The enormous sets, break-neck chariot races, burning of Rome, and assorted circus blood-lettings remain less in the memory than Peter USTINOV's exquisitely effete Nero. Others involved included Robert TAYLOR, Deborah KERR, Buddy Baer, Leo Genn, and Maria Berti.

# R

**RABIER**, JEAN (1927– / ), French cameraman who worked for some time as assistant to
Henri DECAË. He has photographed all Claude
CHABROL's films since *Les Godelureaux* (1960),
Rabier's first feature film. He has developed a
striking mastery in the use of colour, contributing much to the sense of social and geographical
background characteristic of Chabrol's best
work: outstanding examples are the sun-
drenched Dordogne settings which heighten the
psychological drama of LE BOUCHER (1969), the
angular, wintry compositions of JUSTE AVANT LA
NUIT (1971), and the tense action sequences of
*Nada* (1974). Rabier also photographed CLÉO DE
5 A 7 (1962) and, with Claude Beausoleil, LE
BONHEUR (1964) for Agnès VARDA and LES
PARAPLUIES DE CHERBOURG (1964) for Jacques
DEMY.

**RACHEL, RACHEL**, US, 1968. Technicolor;
1¾hr. *Dir, prod* Paul Newman for Kayos
Productions; *scr* Stewart Stern, from the novel
*Jest of God* by Margaret Laurence; *ph* Gayne
Rescher; *cast*: Joanne Woodward (Rachel
Cameron), Estelle Parsons (Calla), Kate Har-
rington (Mrs Cameron), James Olson (Nick Kaz-
lik), Bernard Barrow (Leighton Siddley), Terry
Kiser (Preacher), Geraldine Fitzgerald (Rever-
end Wood).

In her thirty-fifth year, Rachel, trapped between a demanding mother and a frustrating job
as primary school teacher, has drifted into spin-
sterhood. Repressed by her small world, living
through her fantasies, she becomes deeply
involved with a casual acquaintance. He ends the
affair gracelessly, and, with few illusions but new
respect for herself, Rachel moves away with her
mother to a fresh start in a new town.

Paul NEWMAN's first film as director was a
remarkable accomplishment, his perceptiveness
and depth of direction matched by Joanne WOOD-
WARD's delicately balanced portrayal of Rachel.
Fine supporting performances, especially that by
Estelle Parsons, add a convincing dimension to
Rachel's world.

**RADEMAKERS**, FONS (1920– ), Dutch
director and actor, worked with Jean RENOIR,
Vittorio DE SICA, and Charles CRICHTON before
returning to Holland in 1956 to divide his time

between stage and screen. His friendship with
Ingmar BERGMAN influenced his first film *Dorp
aan de riveir* (*Doctor in the Village*, 1958) which
was nominated for an OSCAR as best foreign film.
*Makkers staakt uw wild geraas* (*That Joyous
Eve*), *Het Mes* (*The Knife*, both 1960), *Als twee
druppels water* (*The Spitting Image*, 1963), *De
Dans van de reiger* (*The Dance of the Heron*,
1966), shot in Yugoslavia, and *Mira* (1971), a
Dutch/Belgian co-production, show his insight
into folk tradition and psychological conflicts,
which he depicts in a powerful, sometimes
macabre, style.

**RADFORD**, BASIL (1897–1952), British
actor, who made his screen reputation in the late
thirties. He played in a Will HAY comedy, *Convict 99*, and in THE LADY VANISHES (both 1938)
in which he and Naunton WAYNE portrayed a
foolish pair of imperturbable Englishmen, setting
the pattern for numerous subsequent appearances together as similar characters. The two
made a popular combination and were effectively
complementary as a team; nevertheless Radford
often acted independently and is especially
remembered as the pompous English commander
in WHISKY GALORE! (1949, *Tight Little Island* in
US).

**RADOK**, ALFRED (1914– ), Czech director,
having become one of Prague's most distinguished theatrical directors, became actively
involved in film in 1947, first as art consultant
and then as director with *Daleká cesta* (*The
Long Journey*, 1949). This was the first Czech
film about Jewish sufferings at the hands of the
Nazis, and for several years remained the only
one. It caught the attention of young film
enthusiasts with its nightmarish atmosphere and
unorthodox camera work: it was officially labelled 'existentialist' and 'formalist', and was withdrawn. Radok's next film, three years later, was
quite different in tone but no less innovatory in
style. *Divotvorný klobouk* (*The Magic Hat*,
1952), based on a classic stage play, like his next
and last film, *Dĕdeček automobil* (*Old Man
Motor-Car*, 1956), wittily experimented with
film form, stimulating the young film-makers and
outraging the authorities.

He carried his experimentation with form

much further in the LATERNA MAGICA, which he developed for the Brussels Exhibition of 1958, inspiring those who worked with him (including FORMAN and Papoušek) and a much wider circle of film-makers with his daring and inventiveness. A film that he made for the second programme was criticized and banned, and Radok was unable to go on working for the Laterna Magica. He went on working in the theatre, but left Prague for Sweden in 1968. His influence in Czech cinema has been much greater than the sum of his films would suggest: almost a lone experimenter during the days of socialist realism, he inspired the new generation to go further and experiment with content as well as form.

**RAFFERTY, CHIPS** (1909–71), Australian actor, real name John Goffage, appeared in films from 1939. His laconic manner and rangy, outback charm became widely known through his leading role in THE OVERLANDERS (1946), which led to a contract with EALING STUDIOS. He established two independent companies in an unsuccessful attempt to stimulate Australian film production.

**RAFT, GEORGE** (1903–   ), US actor, played supporting roles in gangster films, first drawing attention in SCARFACE (1932). His gunmen, shady night-club owners, and other variations on standard criminal types are remembered for their suavity. His breach with WARNER BROS in 1943 led to unmemorable starring roles; however his self-parody in SOME LIKE IT HOT (1959) was notable. Two films based on his life, *Broadway* (1942) in which he played himself and *Spin of a Coin* (1961) in which he was played by Ray Danton, gave currency to popular beliefs about his youth in the New York underworld. He has long been associated with the gaming milieu and in 1967 the British Home Office stated that his entry permit to the UK would not be renewed because his presence was 'not conducive to the public good'.

**RAIMU** (1883–1946), French actor, full name Jules Muraire Raimu. Born in Toulon, Raimu started at the age of fifteen performing in *café-concerts* in the south of France. He graduated to the Paris stage, and by the end of the twenties had won a high reputation, excelling especially in comedy and revue. His role in the stage production (1929) of PAGNOL's *Marius* and his parts in Pagnol's plays and films, with their archetypal embodiment of Marseillais character, humour, and speech, set him among the most popular actors in France throughout the thirties. He was persuaded to make his first film appearance in Sacha GUITRY's *Le Blanc et le noir* (Robert FLOREY, 1931). His earlier resistance to films

was replaced by a corresponding enthusiasm: during the thirties he acted in thirty-four films and in only two stage plays; among the films were MARIUS (1931), *Fanny* (1932), *César* (1936), *Faisons un rêve* (Guitry, 1936), *Un Carnet de bal* (DUVIVIER, 1937), *Les Nouveaux Riches* (1938), with Michel SIMON, LA FEMME DU BOULANGER (1938). These preserve his best performances, vigorous and richly idiomatic, with brilliant switches from rumbustious humour to dramatic intensity.

Raimu continued acting in films and on the stage during the Occupation. He received the accolade of a contract with the Comédie Française in 1943. His later appearances include *Le Duel* (Pierre FRESNAY, 1940), *La Fille du puisatier* (Pagnol, 1940), *L'Arlésienne* (Marc ALLÉGRET, 1942). A 35-minute film of extracts, *La Vie de Raimu*, with commentary by Pagnol, was made in 1948.

**RAINER, LUISE** (1912–   ), Austrian actress who after working in Max REINHARDT's company in Berlin went to Hollywood in 1935. Her opportunity came when she replaced Myrna LOY (who had walked out) as William POWELL's co-star in *Escapade* (1935). She won an OSCAR for her performance in *The Great Ziegfeld* (1936), again opposite Powell, and in her next film, THE GOOD EARTH (1937), her performance as the Chinese peasant-wife won her a second Oscar. Her later performances were less impressive, with the exception of Julien DUVIVIER's film about Strauss, *The Great Waltz* (1938). She broke her virtual retirement from the screen with *Hostages* (1943).

**RAINS, CLAUDE** (1889–1967), British actor who first acted as a child, and had a long career on the London stage before going to America in 1926. His film career began in the thirties: he created a sensation almost entirely by means of his voice in THE INVISIBLE MAN (1933), and gave an outstanding performance in CRIME WITHOUT PASSION (1934). Occasional returns to England included the leading roles in *The Clairvoyant* (1935), CAESAR AND CLEOPATRA (1945), and *The Passionate Friends* (1949). For many years after 1936 he was under contract to WARNER BROS, appearing in a number of the company's famous films of the period, among them *The Adventures of Robin Hood* (1938), *They Made Me a Criminal* (1939), *The Sea Hawk* (1940), *Now Voyager* (1942), and *King's Row* (1943). His cynical police chief in CASABLANCA (1943) vies for fame with his Invisible Man. He was also associated with remakes of classic silents, in the Lon CHANEY part in *The Phantom of the Opera* (1943) and as Wallace BEERY's successor in *The Lost World* (1960). His last roles, both small, were in LAWRENCE OF ARABIA (1962) and *Twilight of Honor* (1963), after which he briefly returned to the stage. Rains was a subtle and expressive actor, and his speaking voice was justly renowned.

**RANK, J[OSEPH] ARTHUR** (1888–1972), began working in his father's prosperous flour business and became interested in films when, as a Methodist Sunday School teacher, he realized they could be an ideal medium for spreading the Gospel. In addition, his patriotic sense was offended by American domination of the British film industry.

Rank's main motivation in building up the RANK ORGANISATION was, however, the profitability of such an empire during the thirties and forties. His concern with the production side was always small and, as a shrewd financier, he was quick to diversify his interests when investment in the cinema became less attractive during the fifties. He was raised to the peerage in 1957, five years before his retirement.

Alan Wood, *Mr Rank*, London, 1952.

**RANK ORGANISATION,** British production, distribution, and exhibition company, trademark a muscular man beating an outsize gong (Bombardier Billy Wells dubbed by James Blades). In 1935, J. Arthur RANK founded General Film Distributors which, handling British distribution of UNIVERSAL pictures together with an increasing proportion of British-made films, rapidly grew into a powerful distribution concern. Rank acquired control of two leading cinema circuits, GAUMONT BRITISH and ODEON, and widened his activity to embrace almost all aspects of commercial cinema, studios and production, advertising and children's films, and film processing laboratories. The Organisation itself dates from March 1946 when the J. Arthur Rank Organisation Ltd was incorporated. It reached its peak in the following few years when the British film industry was at its most prosperous.

In the late forties, the Rank Organisation owned the two largest British film studios, DENHAM (seven sound stages) and PINEWOOD (five sound stages), appreciably big studios at Islington and Lime Grove (Shepherd's Bush), and several smaller ones—the Gate Studios at Elstree (used mainly for religious and specialized productions), Highbury Studios, Imperial Studios at Elstree (principally for the production of Gaumont British Instructional and children's films), and Moor Hall Studios at Cookham in Berkshire (for animated films); in addition EALING STUDIOS effectively came into Rank's orbit. In the production sphere, it controlled Cineguild (notably for films directed by David LEAN and Ronald Neame), Wessex Film Productions, GAINSBOROUGH Pictures, and TWO CITIES; and working for it was a large proportion of leading British directors, including Charles CRICHTON, Basil DEARDEN, Robert HAMER, Charles FREND, Harry WATT, and Peter USTINOV. The long-established General Film Distributors was renamed Jarfid (a name made up from J. Arthur Rank Film Distributors), before assuming its current title Rank Film Distributors. Briefly in the mid-forties some Rank-produced films were released by another distribution company owned by the Organisation, Eagle-Lion.

The Rank Organisation made a determined bid to compete on the American market, but with limited success. In Britain, its prestige in the film industry has gradually diminished since the fifties, but despite its share of closures, the Rank cinema circuit remains a dominant factor in exhibition. The famous trademark remains extant, though production has declined with the dwindling output of the film industry generally: only the seemingly inexhaustible CARRY ON films continue to enjoy a certain commercial success. The Rank Organisation has meanwhile developed conspicuously in non-cinematic areas.

**RÁNODY, LÁSZLÓ** (1919– ), Hungarian director, born in Sombor, Yugoslavia. After studying at the Budapest Academy for Dramatic Art, he became artistic director of the Hungarian Film Studios during the formative years after the Second World War. He was adviser on the first Hungarian colour film, Kálmán Nádasdy's *Ludas Matyi* (*Mattie the Goose-Boy*, 1949), making his own first film as director the following year, although *Csillagosok* (*Stars*) was one of the many films at that time never publicly shown. He co-directed with Nádasdy and Mihály Szemes *Föltámadott a tenger* (*The Risen Sea*, 1953), which encountered script difficulties with the authorities, and finally emerged as a director in his own right in 1954. As a middle-generation director, his works lack the aggressive questioning of his younger colleagues and show more compassion for his subjects, particularly in *A tettes ismeretlen* (*Danse Macabre*, 1957), *Akiket a pacsirta elkisér* (*For Whom the Larks Sing*, 1959), and *Pacsirta* (*Skylark*, 1964).

*RASHOMON*, Japan, 1950. 1½hr. *Dir* Akira Kurosawa; *prod* Daiei; *scr* Shinobu Hashimoto, Kurosawa; *ph* Kazuo Miyagawa; *cast* Toshiro Mifune (Tajomaru, the bandit), Masayuki Mori (Takehiro, the samurai), Machiko Kyo (Masago, his wife), Takashi Shimura (the woodcutter), Minoru Chiaki (the priest), Kichijiro Ueda (the commoner), Daisuke Kato (the police agent), Fumiko Homma (the medium).

Based on two short stories by Ryonosuke Akutagawa, *Rashomon* examines four conflicting yet equally credible accounts of the same crime in a brilliant cinematic questioning of the nature of truth. The film's striking visual qualities, created by KUROSAWA's constantly active camera, and the energetic conviction of the performances, contributed to its immense success at the 1951 VENICE festival, where it was awarded the Grand Prix, and awakened Western interest in Japanese cinema. *Rashomon* was remade by Martin RITT as THE OUTRAGE (1964).

**RATHBONE**, Basil (1892–1967), US actor, born in South Africa and educated in England. During the thirties he appeared in many films, in both Hollywood and Britain, specializing in suavely villainous types. Few of his roles were memorable apart from the Jew in *Loyalties* (1934), his best British performance, Mr Murdstone in DAVID COPPERFIELD (1934), and Karenin in ANNA KARENINA (1935). He was Errol FLYNN's opponent in swashbuckling sword play in *Captain Blood* (1935) and *The Adventures of Robin Hood* (1938) and Tyrone POWER's in *The Mark of Zorro* (1940); he only escaped type-casting with excellent performances as SHERLOCK HOLMES in *The Hound of the Baskervilles* and *The Adventures of Sherlock Holmes* (both 1940). A succession of standard rogues followed, concurrently with a series of poor quality Sherlock Holmes 'B' features. He continued to work regularly, both in films and the theatre, until his death, but except for *The Last Hurrah* (1958) with Spencer TRACY, his performances were routine.

**RATTIGAN**, TERENCE (1911– ), British playwright with a long and successful career, adapted many of his stylish and well-made plays for the screen including *The Winslow Boy* (1948) and *The Browning Version* (1951), both directed by Anthony ASQUITH. For Asquith he also wrote several screenplays including *The Way to the Stars* (1945), *The VIPs* (1963), and *The Yellow Rolls-Royce* (1964). His other film scripts include *Brighton Rock* (in collaboration with Graham GREENE, 1947) and the remake of *Goodbye Mr Chips* (1969). He was knighted in 1971.

*RAVEN'S END* see KVARTERET KORPEN

**RAWSTHORNE**, ALAN (1905–73), distinguished British composer whose work included film music. From 1937 to 1945 he composed for a number of documentaries before turning to features with *The Captive Heart* (1946). Other scores include *School for Secrets* (1946), *Pandora and the Flying Dutchman* (1951), *Where No Vultures Fly* (1951), *The Cruel Sea* (1952), and *The Man Who Never Was* (1955).

**RAY**, ALDO (1926– ), US actor in the HEAVY tradition with an effective gravel voice. His chance entry into films—*Saturday's Hero* (1951)—was the result of a visit by the director David Miller to Crockett, California, where Ray was standing for sheriff. Initially credited under his real name Aldo Da Re, he worked for CUKOR—*Pat and Mike* and *The Marrying Kind* (both 1952); Michael CURTIZ—*We're No Angels* (1955); and Raoul WALSH—*Battle Cry* (1955) and *The Naked and the Dead* (1958), among others, before moving to England in 1959 to appear in *The Siege of Pinchgut*. His work has also included *What Did You Do in the War, Daddy?* (Blake EDWARDS, 1966).

**RAY**, MAN (1890– ), US graphic artist, at first a member of the Dada group, later allied to SURREALISM. His earlier films, *Retour à la raison* (1923) and *Emak-Bakia* (1927), were abstract but nevertheless provocative. *Le Mystère du Château de Dès* (1929) was based on Mallarmé's 'Un coup de dès jamais n'abolira le hasard' ('A throw of the dice will never abolish chance'); *L'Etoile de mer* (1929), while more surrealist in form, displays a gentler humour. Ray also collaborated on two films by Hans RICHTER. He is best known for his Rayograms, still 'photographs' made by controlled exposure of photo-sensitive materials without the use of a camera, comparable with the Photograms of MOHOLY-NAGY.

**RAY**, NICHOLAS (1911– ), US director, real name Raymond Nicholas Kienzle, after studying at the University of Chicago under the architect Frank Lloyd Wright, worked in the theatre as director and actor, notably with Elia KAZAN, Martin RITT, and John Houseman. He was chosen by Kazan to assist on his first commercial film *A Tree Grows in Brooklyn* (1945), afterwards working with Houseman on television drama, then at a pioneering stage. In 1947 Houseman moved to film production at RKO; asked to produce *Your Red Wagon*, he named Ray as director and the film developed into the crime thriller *They Live by Night* (1947).

During the next eight years several of Ray's films—*Knock On Any Door* (1948), *In a Lonely Place* (1950), *On Dangerous Ground* (1950), the baroque Western *Johnny Guitar* (1954)—pursued the themes of violence and adolescent revolt which culminated in REBEL WITHOUT A CAUSE (1955). *The True Story of Jesse James* (1956), another study of violence, caused Ray's most serious clash with Hollywood and he walked out before the end of shooting; the editing was carried out contrary to his plan. He shot *The Savage Innocents* (1959) in Canada and Europe, where he stayed to make *King of Kings* (1961) and *Fifty-five Days at Peking* (1963), though he failed to find the artistic freedom for which he had left Hollywood.

Ray has attracted a devoted following and his work has been closely examined along AUTEUR lines. His use of the wide screen, in particular, has been subjected to much critical analysis.

**RAY**, SATYAJIT (1921–  ), Indian director born in Calcutta, studied fine arts at 'Tagore University', founded by Rabindranath Tagore, at that time still living. Working in advertising, Ray established himself as a respected commercial artist, developing a style that combined traditional Bengali graphic conventions with modern elegance and wit.

At this time the cinema became his hobby: in 1947 he was one of the founders of the Calcutta Film Society. In 1950 RENOIR visited Calcutta to film *The River* and from him Ray was able to gain a little knowledge of film-making. Renoir also encouraged him in his dream of filming PATHER PANCHALI, a popular book by the Bengali writer Bhibuti Bashan Bannerjee. Ray at first found it impossible to raise backing for his project, which he was determined to film in natural surroundings with a non-professional cast after the manner of NEO-REALISM. It took

over three years to complete the first part, Ray and his collaborators working on an amateur basis, but the completed film betrays little of the poverty and inexperience of its makers. Its immediate success throughout Bengal when it was eventually shown in 1955, and the acclaim with which it was received at CANNES the following year, ensured financing for his future work, enabling him to become a professional director.

*Aparajito* (*The Unvanquished*, 1956), the second part of *Pather Panchali*, was less successful locally than its predecessor, and Ray interrupted his work on the trilogy to make *Paras Pathar* (1957), his first urban film, full of compassionate observation of the city worker's drab life. In *Jalsaghar* (*The Music Room*, 1958) he returned to rural Bengal, this time to the decaying mansion of a provincial land-owner who, having outlived the society in which his class flourished, escapes from modern life by squandering his dwindling fortune on performances of classical music. *Jalsaghar* illustrates a theme basic to Ray's work, the transitional state of Indian society and the effect of rapid change on individuals. In the *Pather Panchali* trilogy, completed by *Apur Sansar* (*The World of Apu*, 1959), the progression from a tightly-knit family in a traditional rural community, through the

*Apur Sansar* (Satyajit Ray, 1959)

migration to the cities, ending with the son in his educated isolation, gives a microcosmic view of the changing society of modern India. *Devi* (1960) is about the collision of ancient and modern beliefs. An old man becomes convinced that his beloved daughter-in-law is an incarnation of the goddess Kali; the girl is helplessly drawn along on the upsurge of superstition which her husband, although educated and leaning towards free-thinking, is unable to defeat.

*Kanchenjunga* (1962) marked new departures in Ray's work: it was his first colour film and he for the first time wrote his own scenario. It was also his first film made outside Bengal, in the foothills of the Himalayas where the subtlety of colour in the natural surroundings was used as an integral background to a low-key, naturalistic story of complex relationships, observed with austere delicacy. Ray also wrote his own background score. Music was from the beginning an important element in his films, and he used some of India's finest classical musicians—Ravi Shankar in the Apu trilogy, Vilayat Khan in *Jalsaghar*, Ali Akbar Khan in *Devi*—before beginning to write his own scores. He also wrote the music for James IVORY's *Shakespeare-Wallah* (1965).

*Mahanagar* (*The Big City*, 1963) was perhaps weakened by an uncharacteristic dependence on plot rather than the development and interaction of characters; but the problems that emerge from a young wife's attempt to combine her traditional submissive role with that of a' career woman, and her husband's difficulty in accepting the new order, are at once moving and humorous. A sequence in the home of an Anglo-Indian girl shows Ray's scrupulous attention to social detail. This is the nearest he comes to including Europeans in his films: the influence of British colonial rule is pervasive, but as people Europeans have no part to play.

CHARULATA (1964), adapted from a story by Tagore, is an exquisite and melancholy study of a middle-class marriage in the early 1900s. *Nayak* (1966) observes the phenomenon of the Indian film star; *Chiriyakhana* (1968) is a detective story; and *Gopi Gyne Bagha Byne* (1969) is a very superior version of the traditional Indian musical film. *Aranyer din Ratri* (*Days and Nights in the Forest*, 1970) is a delicate exploration of social interaction, and particularly the relationships between women, fragile, poised, imperturbably in command, and men, blustering, posturing, and ultimately sheepish. The minimal story has Chekhovian overtones, and Ray's handling of groups of people in leafy surroundings is reminiscent of some films by Renoir. It may be considered the first of a modern trilogy, completed by *Pratidwandi* (*The Adversary*, 1970) and *Seemabadha* (*Company Ltd*, 1971). These, with *Ashanti Sanket* (*Distant Thunder*, 1972), are more politically conscious in tone while maintaining Ray's humanistic perception.

Ray is the only Indian director to have gained a considerable following abroad; his films express an appealing humanism as well as an engaging love of cinema and he has evolved a personal style in which an assured yet sensitive synthesis of Eastern and Western values assures him an audience in both cultures.

**REAGAN,** RONALD (1912– ), US actor who began his career as a sports journalist and broadcaster. He made his first film appearance in 1937 and was an agreeable leading man in numerous pictures for WARNER BROS. Among the most notable were *Dark Victory* (1939), *Kings Row* (1942), *The Voice of the Turtle* (1948), and *The Hasty Heart* (1950). In 1951 he moved to UNIVERSAL for a few films; he retired from the screen to devote himself to politics. Originally a Democrat deeply involved in Hollywood liberal causes, Reagan became more conservative in the fifties, was elected Republican governor of California in 1966 on a right-wing platform, and was resoundingly re-elected in 1970. In his political campaigns he deftly projected his screen image of sincerity and boyish honesty, making particular reference to his role as the legendary football star George Gipp in *Knute Rockne, All American* (1940).

**REAR PROJECTION** see BACK PROJECTION

**REAR WINDOW,** US, 1954. Technicolor; 2hr. *Dir, prod* Alfred Hitchcock for Paramount; *scr* John Michael Hayes, from a short story by Cornell Woolrich; *ph* Robert Burks; *cast* James Stewart (Jeff), Grace Kelly (Lisa), Wendell Corey (Doyle, the detective), Thelma Ritter (Stella), Raymond Burr (Thorwald).

Jeff, a news photographer, immobilized by a broken leg, passes the time spying on his neighbours from his window. He becomes convinced that a murder has been committed and with his fiancée's help unravels the crime.

With the exception of one climactic scene, the action is shown throughout from Jeff's viewpoint: HITCHCOCK brilliantly overcomes this self-imposed limitation. The basic idea is given substance by a variety of minor stories taking place among the families being watched, with the murder story gradually becoming dominant. Hitchcock's humour is well to the fore, particularly in the dénouement, where James STEWART repels the murderer's attack by exploding flash bulbs to dazzle him and survives at the cost of breaking his other leg.

**REBECCA,** US, 1940. 2¼hr. *Dir* Alfred Hitchcock; *prod* David O. Selznick; *scr* Robert E.

Sherwood, Joan Harrison from the novel by Daphne du Maurier; *ph* George Barnes; *cast* Laurence Olivier (Maxim de Winter), Joan Fontaine (Mrs de Winter), Judith Anderson (Mrs Danvers), George Sanders (Jack Favell), Nigel Bruce (Major Lacey), C. Aubrey Smith (Colonel Jolyon).

Alfred HITCHCOCK's first Hollywood film gave a new light on his talents: *Rebecca* was his first essay in the psychological mystery story, rather than the thriller, and he used camera mobility to create suspense instead of his usual disciplined cutting. The film had a formal stylishness usually attributed to the British origin of director, original author, and most of the cast. Joan FONTAINE's sensitive performance was particularly admired: the OSCAR she won the following year for SUSPICION is generally recognized as having a retrospective application.

**REBELLION** see JOI-UCHI

**REBEL WITHOUT A CAUSE**, US, 1955. CinemaScope; 1¾hr; Warner Color. *Dir* Nicholas Ray; *prod* Warner Bros; *scr* Stewart Stern, adapted by Irving Shulman from a story by Ray; *ph* Ernest Haller; *cast* James Dean (Jim Stark), Natalie Wood (Judy), Jim Backus (Jim's father), Ann Doran (Jim's mother), Rochelle Hudson (Judy's mother), William Hopper (Judy's father), Sal Mineo (Plato).

Nicholas RAY's best-known film, very much a product of its time, charts twenty-four hours in the life of three adolescents, whose inarticulate frustration is expressed in violence and foolhardiness.

The film was closely documented by Ray and Stern, who interviewed judges, police officers, youth workers, and teenagers. With hindsight, the problem of juvenile delinquency seems naïvely treated, the relationships between parents and children schematically drawn, and the preoccupation with psychological fixations superficial. The film's strength lies in its admirably sustained pace and tension, in the effective use of the wide screen (particularly in the cliff-hanging sequence), and in the performance of James DEAN, in the role which did most to create his image and posthumous myth and which gave the film an almost legendary reputation.

**RED AND THE WHITE**, The, see CSILLA-GOSOK, KATONÁK

**RED BADGE OF COURAGE**, The, US, 1951. 1hr. *Dir* John Huston; *prod* MGM; *scr* Huston, from the novel by Stephen Crane, adapted by Albert Brand; *ph* Harold Rosson; *des* Cedric Gibbons, Hans Peters; *ed* Ben Lewis; *mus* Bronislau Kaper; *cast* Audie Murphy (the Youth), Bill

Mauldin (the Loud Soldier), Royal Dano (the Tattered Soldier), John Dierkes (the Tall Soldier), Douglas Dick (the Lieutenant), Andy Devine (the Talkative Soldier).

John HUSTON's film version of Stephen Crane's novel was so untimely as to risk failure from the outset. The tale of a callow youth soldiering in the Civil War, who runs away until he learns to control his fear, was antipathetic to the emotional climate of America in the early fifties; and the casting of Audie Murphy, a celebrated war hero, in such a role showed little understanding of likely audience reactions. The many commercial intrusions, from casting to final editing, that were disastrous to the director's conception were meticulously described by Lilian Ross in *Picture* (first published in the *New Yorker*, 1952) and the film is probably better known through her account than through screenings. Among the strong points that emerge from what is undoubtedly an interesting failure are the large-scale battle scenes (reminiscent of GRIFFITH and effectively directed by Andrew Marton) and Harold ROSSON's accomplished photography, remarkable for its DEEP FOCUS.

**REDBEARD** see AKAHIGE

**RED DESERT, The,** see DESERTO ROSSO, IL

**REDFORD, ROBERT** (1936– ), US actor, first made an impression as an accomplished performer with open good looks in THE CHASE (1966). He played an arrogant individualist in *Inside Daisy Clover* (Robert MULLIGAN, 1966). In 1969 he appeared in two Westerns, Abraham POLONSKY's *Tell Them Willie Boy is Here* and George Roy HILL's BUTCH CASSIDY AND THE SUNDANCE KID: the latter, in which he co-starred with Paul NEWMAN, shot him to popularity. In the same year he set up a production company to make *Downhill Racer* (1969), about ski racing, directed by the untried Michael RITCHIE, and they followed this with *The Candidate* (1972), a powerful story of American politics. In Hill's *The Sting* (1973) Redford and Newman repeated their earlier joint success, and in Jack CLAYTON's much-vaunted *The Great Gatsby* (1974) Redford played the title role.

**REDGRAVE, LYNN** (1944– ), British actress, daughter of Michael REDGRAVE, apart from her stage career has made occasional film appearances. She has mainly been cast in sturdily unglamorous roles, with particular success in *Girl with Green Eyes* (1963) and *Georgy Girl* (1966).

**REDGRAVE, MICHAEL** (1908– ), British actor, a major figure in the British theatre who has also appeared in films, his first being THE LADY VANISHES (1938). He was outstanding as the possessed ventriloquist in DEAD OF NIGHT (1945), and he gave stylish performances under Anthony ASQUITH's direction in *The Browning Version* (1951) and *The Importance of Being Earnest* (1952). His thoughtful characterizations and beautiful speaking voice have distinguished a number of films including *The Innocents* (Jack CLAYTON, 1961), *The Loneliness of the Long Distance Runner* (1962), and THE GO-BETWEEN (1971), and he was one of the all-star cast of OH! WHAT A LOVELY WAR (1969). He was knighted in 1959 for his services to the theatre. He is married to the actress Rachel Kempson: their children Vanessa, Lynn, and Corin are actors.

**REDGRAVE, VANESSA** (1937– ), British actress, daughter of Michael REDGRAVE, was a successful stage actress before her first important film role in MORGAN . . . A SUITABLE CASE FOR TREATMENT (1966), in which her somewhat mannered charm helped her portrayal of a pixilated socialite. Her later appearances, including ANTONIONI's BLOW-UP (1967), Tony RICHARDSON's *The Charge of the Light Brigade*, Karel REISZ's *Isadora* (both 1968), OH! WHAT A LOVELY WAR (1969), and Ken RUSSELL's *The Devils* (1971), have not always given scope to the outstanding talent she has shown on the stage. She has recently been increasingly occupied with left-wing political activities.

**RED RIVER,** US, 1948. 1¾hr. *Dir, prod* Howard Hawks for Monterey Productions; *scr* Borden Chase, Charles Schnee, from Chase's story 'The Chisholm Trail'; *ph* Russell Harlan; *mus* Dmitri Tiomkin; *cast* John Wayne (Tom Dunson), Montgomery Clift (Matthew Garth), Joanne Dru (Tess Millay), Walter Brennan (Groot).

Howard HAWKS took an archetypal WESTERN situation—the first Texas cattle-drive to the newly-opened railhead—to present a characteristic examination of the effects of danger and endurance on the male group. Perhaps more importantly, his story is tautly structured with visually beautiful climaxes drawing the spectator into the action (the cattle stampede, handled by the SECOND UNIT director Arthur Rosson, and the river crossing, while the pioneering frontier spirit is admirably sensed. There are excellent performances by John WAYNE as the tough, ageing leader and by Montgomery CLIFT in his first screen role as his sensitive adopted son.

**RED SHOES, The,** GB, 1948. Technicolor; 2¼hr. *Dir, prod, scr* Michael Powell, Emeric Pressburger; *ph* Jack Cardiff; *des* Hein Heckroth; *mus* Brian Easdale, Royal Philharmonic Orchestra conducted by Sir Thomas Beecham; *cast* Anton Walbrook (Lermontov), Marius Goring (Julian Craster), Moira Shearer (Victoria Page), Leonide Massine (Ljubov), Ludmilla Tcherina (Boronskaya), Robert Helpmann (Boleslawsky), Marie Rambert (herself).

A superb attempt at fusing music, ballet, painting, and film into one form, the film has as its climax a full-length ballet that moves from the stage into a fantasy world. The synthesis is not entirely successful and the plot (a young dancer is torn between her lover and her profession) is sentimentally handled; but technically the film was remarkable and is still looked on proudly by TECHNICOLOR.

**REDUCTION PRINT,** a print made from a negative or original which was photographed on film of a larger gauge. Feature films, for example, are usually shot on 35mm film, but 16mm reduction prints are made in limited numbers for release to rural cinemas, film clubs, and some television stations. Eventually some films may be further reduced to 8mm for sale as home movies. When economy is a major consideration it is more usual to make a reduction DUPE negative in the smaller gauge and turn out contact prints from that. (See OPTICAL PRINTING.)

**REED, CAROL** (1906– ), British director, was a stage actor and producer, working for Edgar Wallace until 1932 when he was made dialogue director at EALING STUDIOS. He became assistant director to Basil Dean, who gave him an opportunity to direct with *Midshipman Easy* (1934); this was well received, as were *Bank Holiday* (1938) and *The Stars Look Down* (1939). He directed *Night Train to Munich* (1940), *Kipps* (1941), and *The Young Mr Pitt* (1942) before being appointed in 1942 a director with the rank of captain in the Army Kinematograph Service. He directed military training films and, with the Ministry of Information and the Director of Army Psychiatry, made *The Way Ahead* (1944).

After co-directing the campaign documentary *The True Glory* (1945) with Garson KANIN, Reed emerged from wartime film-making with ODD MAN OUT (1947), a critical and commercial success that led to a contract with Alexander KORDA. For him Reed directed THE FALLEN IDOL (1948), THE THIRD MAN (1949), *The Outcast of the Islands* (1951), *The Man Between* (1953), and *A Kid for Two Farthings* (1955). *The Third Man*, in particular, demonstrates Reed's accomplished handling of actors, his skill at evoking a milieu, and his story-telling ability.

Reed's later films have perhaps suffered from the exigencies of the commercial film industry: they include *Trapeze* (1956), *The Key* (1958),

*Our Man in Havana* (1959), *The Running Man* (1963), *The Agony and the Ecstasy* (1965), *Oliver!* (1968), an extremely popular musical for which Reed won an OSCAR as best director, and *Flap* (1970, *The Last Warrior* in GB). He was knighted in 1952 for his services to British films.

**REED,** Oliver (1938–   ), British actor, nephew of Carol REED, who rose to prominence in a number of HAMMER productions, among them *The Damned* (Joseph LOSEY, 1961), and in several Michael WINNER films. Ken RUSSELL's *Women in Love* (1969) liberated him from the confines of type-casting in sullen or vicious roles and since then he has been able to prove himself a versatile and accomplished actor, notably in *The Devils* (1971), again for Russell.

**REEL,** a film spool and, hence, the length of film wound on one spool. A 'reel' is also traditionally used as a rough measure of running time. The standard 35mm reel, based on the capacity of the standard studio camera MAGAZINE, holds 1000 feet of film (305 m), therefore at the silent running speed of 60 feet (18 m) per minute a full reel would theoretically last 15 minutes; at sound speed, 90 feet (27·5 m) per minute, the full reel length is 11 minutes. However, the overall length of film on the reel includes the LEADER, comprising not less than 20 feet at the beginning and 10 feet at the end of each reel, so in practice the viewing length becomes some 950 feet (290 m).

Early short films were sold as 'split-reelers' (two six- or seven-minute films combined on one reel, as in the first KEYSTONE issues), 'one-reelers', 'two-reelers', etc. Such descriptions can be used to calculate only very approximately a given film's actual running time; but there was a gentleman's agreement between producers and exhibitors on minimum reel lengths, so that, for instance, a two-reeler was expected to run to not less than 1400 feet.

Before cinemas were equipped with two projectors, intervals were necessary to effect reel changes. This affected the structure of many early films, notably in the USSR, where the action was broken into sections or 'acts' of reel length.

In current practice reel lengths vary to avoid breaking the flow of action, and modern cinemas can in any case project an entire programme from one oversized spool. (See CAMERA, PROJECTION.)

**REGGIANI,** SERGE (1922–   ), French actor born of Italian parents who moved to France in 1928. He began work as an extra and had his first success in CARNÉ's *Les Portes de la nuit* (1946). Of slight build, he was often cast as the mean little villain, notably in CLOUZOT's *Manon* (1948) and LITVAK's *Act of Love* (1953); but he played the hero in CAYATTE's *Les Amants de*

*Vérone* (1948) and the much weightier leading role in Thorold DICKINSON's *Secret People* (1951). He was one of the thirteen stars in LA RONDE (1950) in which he partnered Simone SIGNORET, and he played opposite her again in CASQUE D'OR (1952), his best role. He worked for VISCONTI in IL GATTOPARDO (1963) and played telling roles for Jean-Pierre MELVILLE in *Le Doulos* (1962) and *L'Armée des ombres* (1969). In recent years he has become a singer, much appreciated in France.

**RÈGLE DU JEU, La** (*The Rules of the Game*), France, 1939. 1¾hr. *Dir, scr* Jean Renoir; *prod* Nouvelles Editions Françaises; *ph* Jean Bachelet; *des* Eugène Lourié; *ed* Marguerite Renoir; *mus* Joseph Kosma, Mozart, Monsigny, Saint-Saëns, Johann Strauss, arranged by Robert Desormières; *cast* Marcel Dalio (La Chesnaye), Nora Gregor (Christine), Roland Toutain (André Jurieu), Jean Renoir (Octave), Mila Parély (Geneviève), Paulette Dubost (Lisette), Gaston Modot (Schumacher), Julien Carette (Marceau).

RENOIR was forty-four when he made *La Règle du jeu*, the culmination of a decade's activity which had already produced fourteen films in quick succession. It was shot with almost complete artistic and financial freedom: Renoir was producer, director, scriptwriter, and actor, working with colleagues of long standing. The result was a total commercial disaster and the film was progressively cut from the original 113 to 85 minutes before being banned as demoralizing shortly before the outbreak of war. Banned also by the Occupation authorities, it was re-released, largely to film clubs, in 1945 in no less than three separate mutilated versions lasting 90, 85, and 80 minutes respectively. The master negative had been lost through Allied bombing; but, thanks to devoted work by two young enthusiasts who in 1956 laboriously pieced together surviving fragments of the excised passages according to Renoir's memories of the original version, it is now possible for the film to be recognized as one of the supreme works of French cinema.

*La Règle du jeu* was shot between the Munich agreements and the outbreak of war, but Renoir chose to respond to the serious mood of the country by telling an apparently frivolous story and to reflect the times by recourse to the classical writers Beaumarchais and Musset. Rejecting the naturalistic basis of the majority of his films of the thirties, he found in Musset's *Les Caprices de Marianne* (1833) the model for the particular intermixture of realism and poetry, farce and profundity, which he was seeking.

The generally accepted view that Renoir began shooting without a script and that the film was largely improvised is misleading. In fact careful planning from the stage of shooting script did take place, but several changes had to be made. Simone SIMON was not available for the part of the Countess originally intended for her and Renoir introduced instead Nora GREGOR: from this change stemmed his growing interest in the character of Octave (central to *Les Caprices de Marianne*), and he decided to play the role himself instead of giving it to his brother Pierre. The lack of Simone Simon also decided him against his original choice of Fernand Ledoux for the Count; and he chose Marcel DALIO, who had worked with him so brilliantly in LA GRANDE ILLUSION (1937). (The fact that Dalio was Jewish was in this case irrelevant, but provided ammunition for the film's detractors.)

Such improvisation as there was took shape within Renoir's original conception, in response to his faith in the contribution his actors could make. As shooting progressed and the real difficulties of Nora Gregor's lâck of professionalism, for all her innate dignity, emerged, the role of Geneviève became a more positive force in the human mixture. The general result was a much more complex web of relationships than had originally been planned, and a much richer work.

It outraged contemporary audiences and created a furore. Renoir showed a society which functions according to the rules of a particular game, putting its faith in the maintenance of civilized appearances at the very moment when its fabric is being destroyed from within. Most of the characters are content within their elaborate structure of compromise and deceit, but two innocents from outside are unable to conform to the rules: the gamekeeper Schumacher and the aviator Jurieu. After the shooting of the one by the other following a series of jealous misunderstandings, society urbanely reconstitutes itself; but this time there is no room for Octave, whose tentative efforts to move in the worlds of both masters and servants has helped to precipitate the catastrophe.

There are no heroes and no villains in Renoir's world, but beneath the merry-go-round of love and caprice there is a savage reality, glimpsed in the hunt sequence and when the skeletons dance at the masquerade. *La Règle du jeu* is—however unacceptable to his contemporaries—a fine expression of a great artist's view of his society at a certain point.

**REICHENBACH, FRANÇOIS** (1922– ), French director, particularly of short films for which he was his own cameraman. One of the early exponents of CINÉMA-VÉRITÉ, he brought back from the United States some disturbing pictures of American life: *New York Ballade*

*La Règle du jeu* (Jean Renoir, 1939)

(1955), *Les Marines* (1957), *L'Amérique lunaire* (1962). He was cameraman for Chris MARKER on *La Sixième Face du Pentagone* (1968). His feature films, including *L'Amérique insolite* (1960), *Un Coeur gros comme ça* (1961), *Treize jours en France* (co-directed with Claude LELOUCH, 1968), and *L'Indiscret* (1969), are generally conventional commercial projects but demonstrate his sharp observation.

**REICHSFILMKAMMER** (Reich Chamber of Film) was founded by Goebbels in June 1933 with a view to imposing gradual state control over the whole of the film industry. Its formation so soon after the Nazis came to power was the direct result of several years of preparatory work in the National Socialist Party. It consisted of ten major sections which covered all aspects of film production and distribution, and had divisional offices throughout Germany. Professional and industrial organizations, as well as individual production companies, were not disbanded but absorbed by the Filmkammer. A state bank was established to make loans to producers.

In September 1933 the Reichskulturkammer (Reich Chamber of Culture) was set up with Goebbels as president and the Filmkammer automatically became part of this larger organization. The first president was Dr Fritz Scheuermann who made all other appointments and examined the racial and political backgrounds of its members. Every worker in the cultural field was expected to belong to the appropriate section of the Kulturkammer.

In 1934 stricter controls were introduced so that only members could make films. A film *Dramaturg* was appointed to advise the industry and examine all scripts. By the same law any film (German or foreign) made before 1933 could be censored. A system of grading films as culturally or politically valuable was begun and prizes were instituted.

The following year the Filmkammer organized an International Film Congress in Berlin which led to the formation of an International Film Chamber which was joined by eighteen European countries (not including Great Britain and the Soviet Union). This marked the beginning of Nazi manipulation of European film industries. In the same year the Filmkammer began to take control of the export industry.

Among the more positive activities during this time were the setting up of a film archive in 1935 and the foundation of a film academy in 1937.

State control of the film industry through the Filmkammer increased steadily until 1942 when nationalization was complete.

***REINE ELISABETH, La*** (*Queen Beth* in GB; *Queen Elizabeth* in US), GB/France, 1912. 1hr.

*Dir* Louis Mercanton, Desfontaines; *scr* Eugène Moreau; *cast* Sarah Bernhardt (Queen Elizabeth), Maxudian, Decoeur, Harmeroy, Marie-Louise Dorval.

Sarah BERNHARDT's most famous film appearance gives only a slight idea of her powers. The ageing actress's performance is exaggerated and the film itself, made in the style of the FILM D'ART, made no attempt to adapt stage conventions to cinematic form. Its great success lay in the novelty of bringing an international household name to a wide audience. The American rights were bought by Adolph ZUKOR for $28,000; he marketed the film with characteristic acumen, showing it in reputable theatres and implying in his publicity that Bernhardt would be present in the flesh. He recouped $80,000 on which he founded his career as a producer.

**REINHARDT,** MAX (1873–1943), Austrian theatrical producer and director, real name Goldmann, became a director of the Deutsches Theater in Berlin in 1903, his swift, colourful production of *A Midsummer Night's Dream* in 1905 drawing world attention. Although he is remembered as a master showman his productions ranged from Shakespeare, Greek drama, Expressionist plays, Molière, Shaw, Ibsen, Goldoni, Goethe, to Maugham and musicals. Among the most famous of his spectacular productions were *Oedipus Rex* in the Zirkus Schumann in 1910 and two years later at the Royal Opera House, Covent Garden, and *Jedermann* (*Everyman*), adapted by Hugo von Hofmannsthal from the medieval morality play, staged in front of the cathedral at the annual Salzburg Festival which Reinhardt and Hofmannsthal founded in 1920.

Although Reinhardt attained little importance as a film director in Germany, EXPRESSIONISM in the German cinema owed much to his handling of lighting, sets, and crowd movements in the theatre. Many major actors and directors worked in his company before entering films, including WEGENER, VEIDT, KRAUSS, JANNINGS, MURNAU, LENI, DIETERLE, PREMINGER, LUBITSCH, Elisabeth BERGNER, Luise RAINER, Marlene DIETRICH, Paula WESSELY.

He left Germany for the US in 1933. The following year he mounted a characteristically extravagant production of A MIDSUMMER NIGHT'S DREAM in Los Angeles and in 1935, with Dieterle, directed a film version for WARNER BROS. His last stage production was *The Eternal Road* in Chicago and at the Manhattan Opera House in 1937.

His son Gottfried Reinhardt (1914–   ) was a producer for METRO-GOLDWYN-MAYER (1940–54) later directing several films in the US and Europe.

**REINIGER,** LOTTE (1899–   ), German film-maker and creator of silhouette films. She worked initially for Paul WEGENER and cut the title vignettes for his *Der Rattenfänger von Hameln* (*The Pied Piper of Hamelin*, 1918). The next year she made a short film, *Das Ornament des verliebten Herzens*. Her first feature was *Die Abenteuer des Prinzen Achmed* (*The Adventures of Prince Ahmed*, 1926) for which Walter RUTT-MANN painted the backgrounds.

With the introduction of sound she was able to branch out from fairy-tale themes to musical ones: *Carmen* (1933) and *Papageno* (1935), using themes from Mozart's *Die Zauberflöte*. She also contributed a shadow play to RENOIR's *La Marseillaise* (1938), on which her husband and frequent collaborator Carl KOCH also worked.

Her films expertly adapt the technique of the Chinese shadow theatre to the film medium and all her work bears the mark of a true craftsman. (See ANIMATION.)

She is the author of *Shadow theatres and shadow films* (London, 1970).

**REISZ**, KAREL (1926– ), British director born in Czechoslovakia, moved to Britain as a child. He allied himself with the SEQUENCE group in the early fifties, and was for some time co-editor with Lindsay ANDERSON. Before making any films professionally, he published the excel-lent *The technique of film editing* (London, 1953). His first publicly shown film, *Momma Don't Allow* (1955), co-directed with Tony RICHARDSON, was shown in the opening FREE CINEMA programme; while associated with Free Cinema he became Films Officer for the Ford company, where he helped develop the sponsor-ship of film-making by industrial companies. His own sympathetic and entertaining *We Are the Lambeth Boys* (1959), financed by Ford, was one of the most attractive contributions to Free Cinema. SATURDAY NIGHT AND SUNDAY MORNING (1960), his first feature film, was also a percep-tive treatment of British working-class life, and it won critical and public acclaim. Reisz produced THIS SPORTING LIFE (1963) for Lindsay Ander-son, directing NIGHT MUST FALL the same year; made on the rebound from a Ned Kelly project, it was not up to his earlier work. MORGAN . . . A SUITABLE CASE FOR TREATMENT (1966) tackled a difficult subject with charm and humour; it was followed by *Isadora* (1968).

A lover of the practical business of film-making, Reisz has earned a living making adver-tising films with less resentment than some of his colleagues. He has, too, worked generously to improve the status of film in his adopted country. He is married to Betsy BLAIR.

*Rembrandt* (Alexander Korda, 1936)

**RELEASE PRINT,** the copy of the film which is distributed for exhibition. Such prints combine picture and sound on the same film and for commercial reasons are usually made from duplicate negatives (see DUPE NEGATIVE). This practice, although it means that an extra generation of printing is added to the process, permits the preservation of the original master from which only a small number of dupes need be made to provide large quantities of release prints.

*REMBRANDT,* GB, 1936. 1½hr. *Dir, prod* Alexander Korda for London Film Productions; *scr* Carl Zuckmayer, Arthur Wimperis, June Head; *ph* Georges Périnal, Richard Angst; *des* Vincent Korda; *cast* Charles Laughton (Rembrandt), Elsa Lanchester (Hendrikje), Gertrude Lawrence (Geerte).

One of Alexander KORDA's more neglected achievements, *Rembrandt* is a rich study of the painter's life, philosophy, and working methods, with a period setting lucidly evoked by Vincent KORDA's designs and PÉRINAL's photography. The film is distinguished by Charles LAUGHTON's complex characterization, and by uncompromising reliance on dialogue rather than action.

**REMICK,** LEE (1935– ), US actress, was chosen by Elia KAZAN for a supporting role in A FACE IN THE CROWD (1957). She has since been somewhat type-cast as a victim—of rape in Otto PREMINGER's *Anatomy of a Murder* (1959) and Tony RICHARDSON's *Sanctuary* (1960), and of alcoholism in Blake EDWARDS's *Days of Wine and Roses* (1962); she had more varied parts in *The Hallelujah Trail* (John STURGES, 1965), with Frank SINATRA in *The Detective* (1968), and in *A Severed Head* (1970).

**RENOIR,** Claude (1914– ), French cameraman, son of the actor Pierre RENOIR. He made his début as director of photography with two of the finest films of his uncle, Jean RENOIR: TONI (1935) and UNE PARTIE DE CAMPAGNE, shot in 1936. They also collaborated on some of the same director's most noteworthy post-war films: *The River* (1950), *Le Carrosse d'or* (1953), and *Éléna et les hommes* (1956). The sensitive use of colour in these films is typical of Claude Renoir's later work. He has become something of a specialist in this field, in his work with Alexandre ASTRUC (*Une Vie*, 1958) and Roger VADIM (*Et mourir de plaisir*, 1960; *La Curée*, 1966; *Barbarella*, 1968; etc), as well as a number of international co-productions.

**RENOIR,** Jean (1894– ), French director, the second son of the great Impressionist painter

Jean Renoir (right) in *La Règle du jeu* (1939)

Auguste Renoir. Though born in Paris he spent much of his childhood in the Provençal countryside, developing a love of nature which is a constant feature of his work, as well as a view of women derived directly from his father's influence. The circle of family, friends, and models which surrounded the painter also had a lasting effect on him: many of his finest films are the collective product of a group of friends and collaborators sharing his ideals and aspirations. He wrote a vivid account of his earliest years and his father's strong personality, published in English as *Renoir, my father* (1962).

In 1913 Renoir joined a regiment of dragoons and he served during the First World War as both cavalry officer and pilot, being wounded several times. Shortly after his father's death in 1919 he married one of the painter's models, Andrée Heuschling, and together they worked in ceramics for four years. But both were fascinated by the cinema, by CHAPLIN and the American serials in particular, and in 1924, after seeing MOZHUKIN in *Le Brasier ardent* (1923) and STROHEIM's FOOLISH WIVES (1921), Renoir decided to become a film-maker. He set up a production company with his own money and resolved to make his wife, now renamed Catherine HESSLING, into a star.

*Une Vie sans joie*, made in 1924, was written and produced by Renoir and he played an important secondary role, complete with monocle. A fairly conventional piece of work, with a GRIFFITH-style heroine and a climax of closely averted disaster, it was directed by Albert Dieudonné who was to make his reputation as Napoleon in Abel GANCE's NAPOLÉON (1927). *Une Vie sans joie* was later re-edited by Dieudonné and released in 1927 with the alternative title *Catherine*, after Renoir had completed two strongly contrasting films which in a sense represent the basic polarities of his style.

*La Fille de l'eau* (1924), like *Un Vie sans joie*, has a strong melodramatic narrative featuring an orphan heroine. What is new is Renoir's eclectic visual style, not only in the famous dream sequence but throughout the film. Themes he developed in later films are present: the use of landscape, the triumph of love over class barriers, the intermingling of joy and sorrow, dream and reality. He was already establishing a trusted group of collaborators: his wife Catherine, Pierre Lestringuez who wrote the script and played the villain (under the pseudonym Pierre Philippe), Pierre Champagne, actor, friend, and assistant, and the cameraman Jean Bachelet.

*Nana* (1926) is a very different and much more ambitious film, despite the presence of the same collaborators. A big-budget, Franco-German co-production adapted from Zola's novel, it had impressive sets designed by Claude AUTANT-LARA. The film placed Catherine Hessling's typically fantastical playing against the solemn, mannered style of Werner KRAUSS as her lover and principal victim. Further characteristic themes are apparent: a love of theatrical spectacle, seen from both backstage and the gods, and the parallel worlds of servants and masters. *Nana* has a heaviness more typical of Stroheim and the German school than of Renoir's subsequent work, and Catherine Hessling's puppet-like performance clashes with the inherent tragedy, setting up curious resonances even today.

Renoir directed two more purely personal films in the twenties—*Sur un air de Charleston* (1927) and *La Petite Marchande d'allumettes* (1928). Both were vehicles for the balletic charm of Catherine Hessling, with her white face, dark lips, and perpetual agitation. Renoir's lack of involvement with the AVANT-GARDE movement in French cinema at this time is strange; in these two films he came closest to acknowledging the influences at work among his contemporaries, although his experiments with trick shots and models, his play with varying speeds, optical effects, and superimpositions, hint more at a delight in the technical possibilities of cinema than deliberate formal experiment.

*Tir au flanc* (1928) was Renoir's first film with Michel SIMON, their first joint exploration of comic satire on established values. The two films he directed in 1929 for Les Grands Films Historiques, *Le Tournoi dans la cité* and *Le Bled*, express his enjoyment in innocent spectacle.

His first sound film, *On purge bébé* (1931), was essentially an exercise designed to prove to producers that he could work quickly and efficiently. It was successful and allowed him to go on to two films of merit, *La Chienne* (1931) and BOUDU SAUVÉ DES EAUX (1932). Both starred Michel Simon as an anarchic figure who rejects the hypocrisies of bourgeois life and ends up contentedly as a tramp. Two literary adaptations of this period show Renoir's skill in capturing atmosphere. In *La Nuit du carrefour* (1932) narrative continuity is sacrificed in order to convey the dark and rainy setting of Simenon's novel, and in *Madame Bovary* (1934) the portrait of nineteenth-century Normandy dominates Flaubert's story. TONI (1935) introduced a new social concern which was to develop strongly in Renoir's films of the late thirties. LE CRIME DE MONSIEUR LANGE (1936), made in collaboration with Jacques PRÉVERT and the left-wing GROUPE OCTOBRE, and *La Vie est à nous* (1936), commissioned by the French Communist Party, mark the climax of his political involvement during the years of the Popular Front.

UNE PARTIE DE CAMPAGNE (shot in 1936 but not released until ten years later) forms a delicate interlude before two films scripted by Charles

*Une Partie de campagne* (Jean Renoir, 1936)

SPAAK for all-star casts, *Les Bas-fonds* (1936) and LA GRANDE ILLUSION (1937). A collectively financed tribute to the popular movement, *La Marseillaise* (1938), was followed by two masterly and contrasting films scripted by Renoir himself, LA BÊTE HUMAINE (1938), based on Zola's novel, and LA RÈGLE DU JEU (1939), the director's undoubted masterpiece.

Renoir's claim to greatness rests securely on this succession of films which reflects the evolution of a nation's mood during the thirties, from anarchy to commitment, through disillusion to the brink of war. His increasing mastery is apparent in his direction of a variety of actors—the unknown players of *Toni*, rising or established stars like GABIN, FRESNAY, and SIMON, the fading giant Stroheim, whose presence in *La Grande Illusion* was Renoir's affectionate tribute to Stroheim's early work as a director in Hollywood. His revival of the use of DEEP FOCUS, in part stimulated by his admiration of Stroheim's films, was also aimed at enriching the performances of his actors and heightening the sense of human interaction which is at the core of his greatest films. His collaboration with some of the best scriptwriters of the period, as well as the scripts he wrote himself, also show how his understanding of the medium developed over this period.

The scandal and abuse that followed the appearance of *La Règle du jeu* was turned to good effect by the French government's cultural policy-makers. In accordance with the rapidly adopted plan of trying to cement the Latin nations against Germany, Renoir was sent to Rome early in 1940 to direct a co-production of *La Tosca*, a project proposed by VISCONTI who had been a supernumerary assistant on *Une Partie de campagne* and *Les Bas-fonds*. After Italy's declaration of intent of joining Germany in the Axis, Renoir had no alternative but to make his way to the US, accepting American citizenship as a means of entering the country (in contrast to, for instance, CLAIR, who was invited to work in Hollywood but was at this time a much less controversial figure). He found a welcome in Hollywood and made every effort to adapt himself to American production methods, finding excellent collaborators such as Dudley NICHOLS, who scripted *Swamp Water* (1941) and *This Land is Mine* (1943), and ideal subjects—*The Southerner* (1945) and Mirbeau's *The Diary of a Chambermaid* which he made with Paulette GODDARD in 1946. But a sense of cultural exile pervades his films of the forties and is particularly evident in *The Woman on the Beach* (1947).

Renoir went to India to make *The River* (1950). For the first time he used colour, exquisitely realized by the camera of his nephew Claude RENOIR, and he was able to recreate the relaxed but authoritative tone of his great French films. His stay in India was incidentally to have a crucial effect on the future career of Satyajit RAY. Returning to Europe he made three colourful period spectacles, all containing reflections on the relationship of art and life and built around the personalities of star performers—Anna MAGNA-NI in *Le Carrosse d'or* (*The Golden Coach*, 1953), Jean Gabin in *French Can-can* (1955), and Ingrid BERGMAN in *Éléna et les hommes* (1956). Always open to new methods, he formed his own production company in 1959 and shot two films in that year using fast television techniques, *Le Testament du Docteur Cordelier*, a version of DR JEKYLL AND MR HYDE released in 1961, and *Le Déjeuner sur l'herbe*, disconcertingly conveying a somewhat acrid view of modern life while using sensually sunlit images directly derived from Impressionist painting.

*Le Caporal épinglé* (1962) was an attempt on Renoir's part to recapture the charm and appositeness of his pre-war films: Jean-Pierre CAS-SEL gave a performance which encapsulated for admirers of Renoir his attempts to express the mood of a particular epoch. His farewell to the cinema was *Le Petit Théâtre de Jean Renoir*, shot for television and shown in 1970.

In addition to many unrealized film projects Renoir wrote plays, a novel, *Les Cahiers du Capitaine Georges* published in 1966, and an autobiography, *Les Films de ma vie*, published in English as *My life and my films* (London, 1974). The autobiography is dedicated to the filmmakers of the NOUVELLE VAGUE, a compliment to the younger generation of French directors whose appreciation of his work helped to confirm his post-war standing. A personality of great warmth, ebulliently combining enthusiasm and impulsive lack of discipline, has made Renoir deservedly the best-loved director in French cinema.

André Bazin, *Jean Renoir* (edited by François Truffaut), Paris, 1971; London, 1974.

**RENOIR, MARGUERITE,** French film editor. She was Jean RENOIR's companion throughout the thirties, taking his name and editing all his films from *La Chienne* (1931) to LA RÈGLE DU JEU (1939). Subsequently she edited all but one of the films directed by Renoir's former assistant Jacques BECKER. She made a brief acting appearance as a servant in Renoir's UNE PARTIE DE CAMPAGNE, the unfinished footage of which she edited for release in 1946.

**RENOIR, PIERRE** (1885–1952), French actor, eldest son of the Impressionist painter Auguste Renoir. He had a long career on the stage, par-ticularly with Louis JOUVET's company. Some of his finest roles on the screen were in films directed by his brother Jean RENOIR: as Inspector Maigret in *La Nuit du carrefour* (1932), as Charles Bovary in the adaptation of *Madame Bovary* (1934), and as Louis XVI in *La Marseillaise* (1938). Among the forty or so other films in which he appeared are Julien DUVIVIER's *La Bandéra* (1935) and Marcel CARNÉ's LES ENFANTS DU PARADIS (1945).

**RENOIR, RITA,** stage-name of actress and strip-dancer who was one of the leading artists at the Crazy Horse in Paris in the fifties. She has appeared in several small parts in films, and came to international attention with her part as one of the central quartet in ANTONIONI's IL DESERTO ROSSO (*The Red Desert*, 1964).

**RENTER,** British term for a film company engaged in the business of hiring and distributing films (see DISTRIBUTION). It has been largely supplanted by 'distributor', but still survives in trade circles and in the title of the appropriate association—the KINEMATOGRAPH RENTERS' SOCIETY.

**REPUBLIC PICTURES,** US production company, trade-mark an eagle on a mountain peak, established in 1935 by Herbert J. Yates (who had founded Republic Laboratories in 1918). The company concentrated on a large output of 'B' pictures, especially Westerns, until the early fifties. A flying start was made with two main stars John WAYNE and Gene AUTRY. *The Three Mesquiteers* (1936) was the first of a popular Western series. Noted bands, such as Cab Calloway's and Ted Lewis's sometimes appeared in Republic musicals, and both the Duke Ellington and Eddie Duchin orchestras were featured in *The Hit Parade* (1937). On the comedy side there were Alison Skipworth and Polly Moran.

By the forties John Wayne had progressed to major productions like *Flame of the Barbary Coast* (1945), and, while Gene Autry was away on war service, Roy ROGERS kept the Western going with William (Wild Bill) Elliott and Rex Allen as Republic's new cowboy stars. Herbert J. Yates's wife Vera (Hruba) Ralston became the company's most ubiquitous actress, often costarring with John Wayne: in *The Fighting Kentuckian* (1949) they were joined by Oliver Hardy (see LAUREL AND HARDY).

In the fifties there was a decline in production although there was an increase in the proportion of main features, including *Johnny Guitar* (Nicholas RAY, 1954) and two directed by John FORD and starring John Wayne, *Rio Grande* (1950) and *The Quiet Man* (1952), probably Republic's best productions. Film production was abandoned after 1958, although the company continued to exist for other purposes, changing its name to Republic Corporation in 1960.

**REPULSION,** GB, 1965. 1¾hr. *Dir* Roman Polański; *prod* Compton/Tekli; *scr* Polański, Gerald Brach; *ph* Gilbert Taylor; *mus* Chico Hamilton; *cast* Catherine Deneuve (Carol), Yvonne Furneaux (Helen), John Fraser (Colin), Ian Hendry (Michael), Patrick Wymark (landlord), Roman Polański (a spoons player).

POLAŃSKI's first English-language film, a psychological drama of a girl's mental breakdown culminating in murder. Sharp black-and-white photography and precise use of sound create a surrealist study of madness, in spite of awkward handling of dialogue; his unfamiliarity with London gave the city a fresh and frightening look. *Repulsion* won the Silver Bear at the BERLIN festival, 1965.

**RESNAIS,** ALAIN (1922–  ), French director, studied acting before attending classes in editing at the INSTITUT DES HAUTES ÉTUDES CINÉMATOGRAPHIQUES (IDHEC) and first worked in the professional cinema as an editor. In 1948 Pierre BRAUNBERGER commissioned him to remake his independent 16mm *Van Gogh* in 35mm, and in 1950 Resnais made two more art films, *Gauguin* and GUERNICA, for which Paul Éluard wrote the commentary. He collaborated with Chris MARKER on *Les Statues meurent aussi* (1953), an anti-colonialist study of the decline of African art which has never been shown in uncensored form, and with Jean CAYROL on NUIT ET BROUILLARD (1955), about Nazi concentration camps. A film on the Bibliothèque Nationale, *Toute la mémoire du monde* (1957), was followed by *La Mystère de l'atelier quinze* (1957), dealing with the problem of industrial illness. His last documentary, *Le Chant du styrène* (1958) on the production of polystyrene, used a commentary by Raymond QUENEAU.

This fine body of short films was a revealing prelude to Resnais's feature films, showing his creative style of editing, his predilection for the exploratory tracking shot, and his instinct for formal composition. From the beginning he chose to work with established writers of an avant-garde' persuasion, and for his first feature film he invited Marguerite DURAS to write the script. HIROSHIMA MON AMOUR (1959) contained striking innovations in the balance between words, music, and image and even more in the treatment of narrative, past and present fluidly intermingling and subjective time being undifferentiated from the story's 'now'. In L'ANNÉE DERNIÈRE A MARIENBAD (1961), scripted by Alain ROBBE-GRILLET, Resnais abandoned traditional conceptions of filmed reality, creating an engrossing mystery of glacial beauty.

MURIEL, OU LE TEMPS D'UN RETOUR (1963), another collaboration with Cayrol, is more realistic in subject-matter, but Resnais's fragmentary editing, with overlapping sounds and images, reflects the disorientation of a group of characters haunted by memories. In LA GUERRE EST FINIE (1966), scripted by the political writer Jorge Semprun, a middle-aged revolutionary encounters a crisis in his beliefs, and images of his memories and hopes are poignantly projected into the flow of real events. In 1967 Resnais contributed an episode to the collective protest film *Loin du Viet-nam*, working with the Belgian writer Jacques Sternberg with whom he made his next film, JE T'AIME, JE T'AIME (1968). He collaborated with Semprun again on *Stavisky* (1974), a study of the legendary swindler.

Unlike his contemporaries of the NOUVELLE VAGUE with their free-wheeling spontaneity, Resnais has created a new, stylized formality to carry his revolutionary conception of narrative. His films are decidedly literary: the writer works with remarkable freedom and Resnais then integrates word and image, but in spite of the variety of writers he has used his films express the attitudes of a single individual. Several of his scriptwriters have gone on to make their own films, bringing French literature and cinema into a mutually enriching dialogue.

***RETOUR, Le,*** France, 1947. 30min. *Dir* Henri Cartier-Bresson; *prod* Les Services Américaines d'Information; *comm* Claude Roy; *mus* Robert Lannoy.

*Le Retour* shows the post-war liberation and repatriation of displaced persons, assembled from newsreel footage and newly-shot material. One of the great film documents on the subject of war, it embodies the compassionate vision of CARTIER-BRESSON's still photography. Although his crediting varies (technical adviser or editor) he was in fact playing the creative role which came to be called director in a COMPILATION film.

**REVERSAL STOCK,** a film stock which after exposure is processed to produce a positive image on the original film base, the reverse of the usual negative image.

Negative film used by professionals must be printed on to a separate positive stock to produce a normal viewable image: the positive print is screened and edited while the negative is kept safe against wear and damage. But for amateurs, who have little need of such safeguards, reversal film provides a quicker and cheaper form of film-making, allowing them to project (and, if they wish, edit) the original film. Because of its amateur origin, reversal stock has been made almost exclusively in 16MM and smaller gauges. However professionals now frequently use reversal, particularly for television, where its fine grain, high sensitivity, and ability to conceal minor wear and damage are highly valued. In professional use, a reversal print is nevertheless made from the original, which is preserved just as negatives are.

**REYNAUD,** Émile (1844–1918), French inventor, important in the sphere of cinema prehistory for his Praxinoscope, an improvement on the Zoetrope, and especially for his optical show which he presented from 1892 at the Musée Grévin in Paris. Using perforated film, this exhibition of moving drawings was a forerunner of the animated cartoon.

**REYNOLDS,** DEBBIE (1932–   ), US actress, whose career began in 1948 when she won a beauty contest as Miss Burbank. Under contract to WARNER BROS, she had her first part in *The Daughter of Rosie O'Grady* (1950). Small, full of charm and exuberance, she became a popular star in musicals after her winning appearances in SINGIN' IN THE RAIN (1952) and *The Tender Trap* (1955), in comedies, and in romantic trifles like *Tammy* (1957); but *The Singing Nun* (1966) over-sentimentalized her appeal. She used her tremendous energy to good effect in *The Unsinkable Molly Brown* (1964) and demonstrated a flair for bitter-sweet comedy in *Divorce American Style* (1967). After *How Sweet It Is* (1968) she appeared in a television series entitled 'Debbie'.

**RICHARDSON,** RALPH (1902–   ), British actor with a distinguished stage career in both classical and modern roles. His acting has great nervous tension, although sometimes tending to be mannered. He has appeared in many films, giving outstanding performances for Carol REED in THE FALLEN IDOL (1948), *An Outcast of the Islands* (1951), and *Our Man in Havana* (1959); among his best roles were Buckingham in *Richard III* (OLIVIER, 1955) and the father in *Long Day's Journey into Night* (LUMET, 1962). Richardson has directed one film, *Home at Seven* (1952), in which he also starred. He was knighted in 1951.

**RICHARDSON,** TONY (1928–  ), British stage and film director. His first stage production, *Look Back in Anger* (1956) at the Royal Court Theatre, London, marked the beginning of a fruitful partnership with John OSBORNE as well as a radical change of direction in British drama. The following year Richardson directed Laurence OLIVIER in Osborne's *The Entertainer*. He had already co-directed with Karel REISZ a short film *Momma Don't Allow* (1955), which was part of the first FREE CINEMA programme.

Reisz and Osborne set up their own company, WOODFALL, to film LOOK BACK IN ANGER (1959) and *The Entertainer* (1960). Richardson went to Hollywood to direct *Sanctuary* (1960), from FAULKNER's novel, which had the merit of starring Lee REMICK. and the blues singer Odetta, meanwhile producing Reisz's SATURDAY NIGHT AND SUNDAY MORNING (1960); he followed this with his own best work, A TASTE OF HONEY (1961). *The Loneliness of the Long Distance Runner* (1962) showed him at his most eclectic; based on a story by Alan Sillitoe, author of the novel *Saturday Night and Sunday Morning*, the film borrowed freely from TRUFFAUT's LES QUATRE CENTS COUPS (1959).

With TOM JONES (1963) Richardson moved away from socially conscious themes and working-class settings into large-scale production. It was a considerable commercial success and he returned to Hollywood to make *The Loved One* (1965), based on Evelyn Waugh's book. *Mademoiselle* (1966) and *The Sailor from Gibraltar* (1966) both starred Jeanne MOREAU. His latest films have included *The Charge of the Light Brigade* (1968, starring Vanessa REDGRAVE, then his wife), HAMLET (1970), and *Ned Kelly* (1970), with Mick Jagger. Richardson has continued to direct for the stage, and in spite of a wide-ranging appreciation of cinematic effects and a steady output of films he remains essentially a theatrical director.

**RICHTER,** HANS (1888–   ), German filmmaker, was at first a painter successively involved with Cubism, Futurism, and, particularly, Dada. From 1918 he collaborated with Viking EGGELING on long paper scrolls which presented sequential variations of an abstract design; both, working independently, extended their experiments into film.

In *Rhythmus 21, 22, 23* (1921–3) Richter elaborated the rhythmic development of a single shape: rejecting the camera's ability to create the illusion of depth, he asserted the two-dimensional nature of both the screen and his chosen formal elements, creating perspective by the apparent movement of the units in relation to the frame. *Filmstudie* (1926) is a further development of the idea. *Vormittagspuk* (*Ghosts before Noon* or *Ghosts before Breakfast*, 1927) abandoned total abstraction for a Dadaist portrayal of objects in revolt: beards melt away at a touch and bowler hats fly about in search of heads.

From 1932 to 1940 Richter lived in Switzerland and France, then moved to the US. He took charge of the Institute of Film Techniques at the City College of New York in 1942 and taught there for nearly fifteen years. He made *Dreams That Money Can Buy* (1944), a surrealist film made up of sequences by himself, Fernand

LÉGER, Man RAY, Marcel Duchamp, Max Ernst, and Alexander Calder. *8 × 8* (1956) is composed of eight chess games, poetic and fantastic, and *Alexander Calder* (1963) examines the work of America's most important creator of mobile sculpture.

Richter's key role in the fusion of graphic art and film, and his own work, particularly in its early stages, have had a vital influence on the development of ABSTRACT film in both Europe and the US.

**RIDE THE HIGH COUNTRY** (*Guns in the Afternoon* in GB), US, 1962. CinemaScope; 1¼hr; Metrocolor. *Dir* Sam Peckinpah; *prod* MGM; *scr* N. B. Stone Jr; *ph* Lucien Ballard; *cast* Randolph Scott (Gil Westrum), Joel Mc-Crea (Steve Judd), Ronald Starr (Heck Long-tree), Mariette Hartley (Elsa Knudsen), James Drury (Billy Hammond), R. G. Armstrong (Joshua Knudsen), Edgar Buchanan (Judge Tolliver).

PECKINPAH's study of two ageing gunfighters, useless anachronisms in the society they helped to build as frontier lawmen, captures perfectly the spirit of the dying West. The yellowing, autumnal landscapes are superbly captured by Lucien BALLARD's camera; Joel MCCREA and Randolph SCOTT, both veterans of the WESTERN, play their roles with touching conviction.

**RIEFENSTAHL**, LENI (1902–   ), German director, studied painting in Berlin and trained as a ballet dancer. She collaborated with Arnold FANCK on his mountain films and acted in *Der heilige Berg* (*The Holy Mountain*, 1927), *Die weisse Hölle von Pitz Palü* (*The White Hell of Pitz Palü*, 1929), and the comedy *Der weisse Rausch* (*The White Frenzy*, 1931). With Béla BÁLAZS and the photographer Hans Schneeberger she directed and took the leading role in *Das blaue Licht* (*The Blue Light*, 1932), based on a legend of the Italian Dolomites, bearing a resemblance to the Fanck films. The co-operative group developed into her company Leni Riefenstahl Produktion. She was appointed by Hitler to make the short film *Sieg des Glaubens* (*Victory of Faith*, 1933) for the National Socialist Party, which featured the Party rally in Nuremberg.

After an abortive attempt to make a feature in Spain she was again approached by Hitler to film the 1934 Party rally in Nuremberg. She was at first unwilling, partly because of enmity between her and Goebbels, and passed the commission to Walter RUTTMANN. She finally agreed under certain conditions, one being that her own company should finance the film. The title TRIUMPH DES WILLENS (*Triumph of the Will*) was suggested by Hitler, and the film placed Riefenstahl in the front rank of German directors. *Tag der Freiheit*

(*Day of Freedom*, 1935) was a short film made after a complaint that the army did not feature in the film of the rally. Her next film was the famous OLYMPIA (1938), an even bigger undertaking than *Triumph des Willens*, which was given a gala première on the occasion of Hitler's forty-ninth birthday.

After several unrealized projects she began a film based on Eugene D'Albert's opera *Tiefland*. She spent the war years in Austria, was blacklisted by the Allies in 1945, and not allowed to work again until 1952 when she completed *Tiefland*. Her unfinished *Schwarze Fracht* (*Black Cargo*), begun in 1956 in Ethiopia, was ostensibly planned as an anthropological study, but in its treatment of human beings as objects it harks back to her films of the thirties.

**RIFIFI** see DU RIFIFI CHEZ LES HOMMES

**RIN-TIN-TIN** (1918–1932). The original Alsatian sheepdog was found in a deserted German dugout by an American Air Force officer, Lieutenant Lee Duncan, in the last months of the First World War. He became one of the great stars of the silent screen, earning $400 a week and having his own five-roomed bungalow at the peak of his career. He starred in more than forty films, many written by Darryl F. ZANUCK, including *Find Your Man* (1924) and *The Night Cry* (1925), in which he reputedly fought and killed a huge vulture on a cliff edge. After his death his film work was continued by five successors.

**RIO BRAVO**, US, 1959. Technicolor; 2¼hr. *Dir, prod* Howard Hawks for Armada Productions; *scr* Jules Furthman, Leigh Brackett from the story by B. H. McCampbell; *ph* Russell Harlan; *cast* John Wayne (John T. Chance), Dean Martin (Dude), Ricky Nelson (Colorado), Angie Dickinson (Feathers), Walter Brennan (Stumpy).

HAWKS's use of stock characters and conventional settings makes *Rio Bravo*, his counter to the self-consciously serious HIGH NOON (1952), seem comparatively slight; but his stripping of all social and historical significance from the framework focuses attention on the all-important inter-relation of characters. Deeply rooted in the small-town WESTERN tradition, *Rio Bravo* is a spirited and unpretentious compendium of Hawks themes.

**RISKIN**, ROBERT (1897–1955), US scriptwriter, originally a playwright, who went to Hollywood in the early sound era and wrote *Illicit* and *The Miracle Woman* (both 1931). He became particularly famous as Frank CAPRA's scriptwriter. Among the earlier and best of their films was IT HAPPENED ONE NIGHT (1934) which won Riskin an OSCAR; others include MR DEEDS GOES TO TOWN (1936), *Lost Horizon* (1937), and *You Can't Take It With You* (1938). His later work included *The Thin Man Goes Home* (1944) and *Riding High* (1950). For many years one of Hollywood's most eligible bachelors, he became the second husband of Fay WRAY.

**RISO AMARO** (*Bitter Rice*), Italy, 1949. 1¾hr. *Dir* Giuseppe De Santis; *prod* Lux Films; *scr* Corrado Alvaro, De Santis, Carlo Lizzani, Carlo Mussi, Ivo Perillo, Gianni Puccini; *ph* Otello Martelli; *ed* Gabriele Barriale; *mus* Goffredo Petrassi; *cast* Vittorio Gassman (Walter), Silvana Mangano (Silvana), Doris Dowling (Francesca), Raf Vallone (Marco), Checcho Russone (Aristide), Nico Pepe (Beppe).

Set in the rice-growing district of the Po valley, where city women come each year to work in groups, wading in the flooded fields, the film's neo-realist aspirations are somewhat offset by the melodramatic plot in which Silvana, bemused by gangster movies and magazines, falls for a small-time crook who plans to steal the rice crop. Silvana MANGANO, in her first major part, attracted international attention for her 'exceptional physique' and competent acting.

**RITCHIE,** MICHAEL (1936–   ), US director, was introduced to the cinema by Robert RED-FORD with their *Downhill Racer* (1969). For the striking skiing sequences, Ritchie experimented successfully and inventively with handheld and 16mm cameras. His second film, *Prime Cut* (1972) with Lee MARVIN and Gene HACKMAN, again showed his ability to handle movement (in this case motor vehicles), and was a tight, if conventional, thriller. *The Candidate* (1972), with Redford as a Kennedy-style politician who wins a Senate seat against all odds, has a forceful realism.

**RITT,** MARTIN (1920–   ), US director, began his career as a stage actor after studying with Elia KAZAN. He first became involved in the cinema in a role in the US Army Air Force's *Winged Victory* (1944), directed by George CUKOR, but after the war he returned to Broadway. He also acted and directed for television which gave his work considerable scope as well as a knowledge of camera technique. He acquired added experience in handling actors teaching at the ACTORS' STUDIO, his students including Paul NEWMAN, Joanne WOODWARD, and Rod STEIGER. In 1956 his stage production of Robert Aurthur's *A Very Special Baby* led to a Hollywood contract and his first film *Edge of the City* (1956, *A Man is Ten Feet Tall* in GB) was scripted by Aurthur; it starred Sidney POITIER and John CASSAVETES.

*No Down Payment* (1957) featured Joanne Woodward in a study of four couples in a Los Angeles suburb. With THE LONG HOT SUMMER (1958), scripted by Irving Ravetch from two stories by FAULKNER and starring Newman and Woodward, Ritt came together with the group with whom he was to do his best work. He returned to Faulkner, though less successfully, with *The Sound and the Fury* (1959). *Paris Blues* (1961) again starred Newman and Woodward. HUD (1963), Ritt's next film, was again written by Ravetch. Fine performances by Newman and Patricia NEAL were matched by James Wong HOWE's photography, a striking expression of Ritt's sense of place. THE OUTRAGE (1964), a remake of RASHOMON (1950), was as ravishingly photographed by Howe as the original.

In England Ritt made *The Spy Who Came in from the Cold* (1965), an uncompromisingly seedy and complex thriller; his skilful handling of actors is apparent in Richard BURTON's nicely understated performance. Returning to Hollywood he made his first Western, HOMBRE (1967), again showing the strength of his team, Ravetch, Newman, and Howe. His films since, including *The Molly Maguires* (1969), *The Great White Hope* (1970), and *Sounder* (1972), have not matched the force of his best work, although all show his professionalism and his adept direction of actors.

**RITTER,** THELMA (1905–   ), US actress who began her film career for TWENTIETH CENTURY-FOX, starting with *Miracle on 34th Street* (1947, *The Big Heart* in GB). After playing a droll housemaid in *Father Was a Fullback* (1949) she gave a scene-stealing performance as the star's individualistic dresser and general factotum in ALL ABOUT EVE (1950). Her films often exploited her talent for delivering lines of caustic wit or scathing comment in her cracked, Brooklyn voice. One of her most amusing comedy performances was as the hamburger-shop proprietress in *The Mating Season* (1951). In PICKUP ON SOUTH STREET (1952) she played a character part as a high-principled informer. The masseuse in REAR WINDOW (Alfred HITCHCOCK, 1954), the aunt in *A Hole in the Head* (Frank CAPRA, 1959), the landlady in THE MISFITS (John HUSTON, 1961), and the possessive mother in *Bird Man of Alcatraz* (John FRANKENHEIMER, 1962) were among her other notable performances.

**RITZ BROTHERS, The,** Al (1901–65), Jim (1903–   ), and Harry (1906–   ), formed a popular night-club act before and after appearing in several musicals, notably *Goldwyn Follies* (1938). Their attempts to compete with the MARX

BROTHERS' offbeat humour, as in *The Three Musketeers* (1939), were less successful.

**RIVA,** EMMANUELE (1932– ), French actress, was already an established stage actress when she made her first film appearance as the memory-enslaved heroine of HIROSHIMA MON AMOUR (1959). Her success in this crucial role led to parts in other films of distinction: outstandingly the frustrated young widow in LÉON MORIN, PRÊTRE (1961), the title role in THÉRÈSE DESQUEYROUX (1962), for which she won the best actress award at VENICE, and the hauntingly beautiful Princesse de Bormes in THOMAS L'IM-POSTEUR (1965). Her voice and diction are strikingly beautiful.

*RIVER, The,* US, 1937. 30min. *Dir, scr, ed* Pare Lorentz; *prod* Farm Security Administration Film Unit; *ph* Floyd Crosby, Willard Van Dyke, Stacy Woodard; *mus* Virgil Thomson; *narr* Thomas Chalmers.

After the success of THE PLOW THAT BROKE THE PLAINS (1936), LORENTZ received White House backing to make a film about the Mississippi and the social conditions of its great valley. The river's flooding during production provided unexpected drama and heightened the film's political pertinence. Much praised for its incantatory commentary, the fine score by Virgil THOMSON, and Floyd CROSBY's photography, *The River* won the best documentary award at VENICE in 1938 in competition with Leni RIEFEN-STAHL's OLYMPIA.

The enthusiastic critical reception which led PARAMOUNT to distribute *The River* also encouraged Roosevelt to set up the short-lived US Film Service in 1938.

**RIVETTE,** JACQUES (1928– ), French director, was one of CAHIERS DU CINÉMA's original group of critics. His first short film, *Le Coup du berger* (1956), was a light, stylish piece: his uncompromising seriousness became apparent in his first feature film PARIS NOUS APPARTIENT (1960). *La Religieuse* (1965), from the novel by Diderot, was received with considerable disapproval in official circles.

Rivette's preoccupation with the classical theatre runs constantly through his films. *Paris nous appartient* is centred on an amateur production of *Pericles*; in *L'Amour fou* (1968) a professional director prepares to stage Racine's *Andromaque*; and rehearsals of Aeschylus' *Seven Against Thebes* and *Prometheus* form a strand in his complex, $4\frac{1}{2}$-hour *Out One: Spectre* (1973). *Céline et Julie vont en bateau* (1974) is a surreal fantasy in a more light-hearted vein.

Rivette's films are long, cerebral, and intensely personal. Frequent references in them to money problems echo his difficulties in financing his work. He also directs for television: his *Renoir* (1966) was one of the series 'Cinéastes de notre temps' produced by Eric ROHMER, and *Out One: Spectre* originated as a 12-hour television film.

*RIVIÈRE DU HIBOU, La (Incident at Owl Creek),* France, 1961. 25min. *Dir, scr* Robert Enrico, from the story 'An Occurrence at Owl Creek Bridge' by Ambrose Bierce; *prod* Paul de Roubaix, Marcel Ichac; *ph* Jean Boffety; *cast* Roger Jazquet, Anne Cornaly, Anker Larsen.

During the American Civil War a man is hanged without trial. He is shown escaping and returning to his wife, but this happens only in his imagination: the tightening noose returns him and the audience to reality. Enrico's modest and lyrical rendering of the story won several awards including the OSCAR for best short subject in 1964. He combined it with two other stories by Bierce in a feature film *Au coeur de la vie* (1962).

Among other versions is *An Occurrence at Owl Creek Bridge* (1959), by students at USC. Another of Bierce's Civil War stories, 'One of the Missing', has been filmed twice: a British version in 1969 by Anthony Scott and an American version in 1970 directed by Julius D. Fugelson.

*RKO RADIO PICTURES INCORPORATED,* US production and distribution company (Radio-Keith-Orpheum), trademark a pylon on a terrestrial globe. In the twenties Joseph P. KENNEDY amalgamated his Film Booking Office of America with the production firm American Pathé, of which he was president, and with the Keith, Albee, and Orpheum theatre chain. In 1928 this group was joined by Radio Corporation of America, a Rockefeller concern attracted to film by the coming of sound. The resulting production and distribution company was known as RKO Radio Pictures and for twenty years owned one of the five major Hollywood studio complexes.

RKO was operated by men as diverse as film censor Joseph Breen, millionaire Howard HUGHES, and producers George J. Schaefer, Dore SCHARY, Jerry Wald, and Norman Krasna. Its policy was to produce low-budget films and cofeatures, capitalizing on its contract stars. RKO produced nine Fred ASTAIRE–Ginger ROGERS MUSICALS from *Flying Down to Rio* (1933) to *The Story of Vernon and Irene Castle* (1939), and all the early Katharine HEPBURN films, including *Morning Glory* (1933), *Mary of Scotland* (1936), and BRINGING UP BABY (1938), which also starred Cary GRANT. The company was responsible for *Cimarron* (1931), Merian C. COOPER and Ernest SCHOEDSACK'S KING KONG

(1933), *Of Human Bondage* (1934), John FORD's THE INFORMER (1935), and *The Hunchback of Notre Dame* (1939).

RKO had an active distribution branch, for years releasing all the films of Walt DISNEY, Samuel GOLDWYN, and David O. SELZNICK: FANTASIA (1940), THE LITTLE FOXES (1941), and THE BEST YEARS OF OUR LIVES (1946), for instance, went out under the RKO label. The distribution section of RKO was seriously affected when Disney, Goldwyn, and Selznick set up their own releasing companies.

Despite successful thirties productions, RKO found itself in financial difficulties by 1940. Looking for quick returns Schaefer took a chance on Orson WELLES. An artistic triumph, CITIZEN KANE (1941), brought litigation rather than funds and led to Welles's dismissal before completion of THE MAGNIFICENT AMBERSONS (1942). RKO had more success with Val LEWTON who produced a series of low-budget psychological thrillers including CAT PEOPLE (1942), *The Body Snatchers* (1945), *Bedlam* (1946), whose profits together with those of thrillers such as Alfred HITCHCOCK's SUSPICION (1941) and NOTORIOUS (1946) kept the studio afloat.

In 1948 Howard Hughes bought the studio for $9m, later paying $23m for ownership of all the RKO subsidiaries. Unable to run the studio himself and unwilling to delegate complete authority to his production managers, Hughes allowed the studio to die. By 1953 RKO had ceased production, and two years later the entire company was sold to the General Tire and Rubber Company. Thirty years' output of RKO features were immediately sold to television, and the studio itself was sold in 1957 to Lucille BALL's television company, Desilu Productions.

**ROACH,** HAL (1892–   ), US producer who, after prospecting for gold in Alaska, settled in Los Angeles where he began his film career as a cowboy for UNIVERSAL in 1912. In 1914, with Harold LLOYD, he formed the Rolin production company. By 1919 he was producing two-reel comedies rivalling Mack SENNETT's films in popularity, and more sophisticated in quality. He discovered and helped develop the talents of Lloyd, LAUREL AND HARDY, Mickey ROONEY, Charlie CHASE, Thelma Todd, and ZaSu PITTS, the directors Leo MCCAREY, George STEVENS, and Gordon Douglas. His most notable productions are *Safety Last* (1923), with Harold Lloyd; *From Soup to Nuts* (1928), with Laurel and Hardy; the *Our Gang* series; the *Topper* comedies starring Roland YOUNG; and one memorable drama, *Of Mice and Men* (Lewis MILESTONE, 1939). In 1948 he set up the Hal Roach Television Corporation, producing a series for American television called 'Screen Director's Playhouse', on which directors such as McCarey, John FORD, and Tay GARNETT collaborated.

**ROAD SHOW,** a term used mainly in the US, denoting a method of extended-run (often of many months) pre-release presentation of a major film production, usually involving higher admission prices, bookable seats, and separate performances. As a rule, it is not until the possibilities of this type of presentation are exhausted that a road-shown film is generally released.

**ROARING TWENTIES, The,** US, 1939. 1¼hr. *Dir* Raoul Walsh; *prod* Warner Bros; *scr* Jerry Wald, Richard Macaulay, Robert Rossen, from a story by Mark Hellinger; *ph* Ernest Haller; *cast* James Cagney (Eddie Bartlett), Priscilla Lane (Jean Sherman), Humphrey Bogart (George Halley), Gladys George (Panama Smith), Jeffrey Lynn (Lloyd Hart), Frank McHugh (Danny Green).

A First World War veteran turns to crime when unable to find work and soon rises to be a Prohibition bootlegging king.

The film stands as the culmination of the Hollywood GANGSTER FILM cycle. Its sets, costumes, and musical production numbers were consciously based on Prohibition era models, and there was even a comic sequence showing how 'bathtub gin' was made. HELLINGER based his original story on Broadway characters he had known: CAGNEY's role closely paralleled the career of the gangster Larry Fay, and Gladys George's that of the speakeasy hostess 'Texas' Guinan. The confrontations between WARNER BROS' two gangster stars, Cagney and BOGART, are memorable, and Bogart's ruthless killer more than compensates for Cagney's change of heart in the film's sentimental ending.

**ROBBE-GRILLET,** ALAIN (1922–   ), French novelist, scriptwriter, and director, published his first novel *Les Gommes* in 1953 and rapidly established himself in the forefront of the *nouveau roman* movement. He contributed a substantial body of theoretical writings, now collected under the title *Pour un nouveau roman* (Paris, 1962), as well as writing several more novels, including *Le Voyeur* (1955), *La Jalousie* (1957), and *Dans le labyrinthe* (1959).

In 1961 he was invited by RESNAIS to write the script for L'ANNÉE DERNIÈRE A MARIENBAD, in which he further explored the themes of his experimental novels and showed an immediate appreciation of cinematic possibilities. While continuing to work on novels he has written and directed several films—*L'Immortelle* (1963), *Trans-Europ-Express* (1966), *L'Homme qui ment* (1968), *L'Eden et après* (1970), and *Les*

*Gommes* (1972)—which are striking for their thematic consistency and technical polish. In his films as in his novels, he repudiates both objective reality and conventional narrative structure to create a formalized world of ambiguous relationships and sexual fantasy. Objects are an integral part of this subjective world, and this obsession, reflected in the novels in minutely detailed verbal description, is carried into the films in the slow-moving exploratory shots and statuesque images which characterize his style.

**ROBBINS**, JEROME (1918– ), US choreographer, real name Rabinowitz, whose career first as a dancer and then as a choreographer has been divided between ballet (the American Ballet Theatre, Ballets:USA, and New York City Ballet) and Broadway musicals. His ballet *Fancy Free* (1944) inspired the stage musical *On the Town*, which he also choreographed. In the cinema he has been responsible for the dances in *The King and I* (1956) and the choreography and co-direction of WEST SIDE STORY (1961), for which he won a special OSCAR for choreography.

*ROBE, The,* US, 1953. CinemaScope; 2¼hr; Technicolor. *Dir* Henry Koster; *prod* Twentieth Century-Fox; *scr* Philip Dunne from the novel by Lloyd C. Douglas; *ph* Leon Shamroy; *cast* Richard Burton (Marcellus Gallio), Jean Simmons (Diana), Victor Mature (Demetrius), Michael Rennie (Peter).

The first film to be commercially released in CINEMASCOPE, *The Robe* proved generally disappointing. In itself a routine, heavily reverent Biblical epic, it was not redeemed by the perhaps inevitable failure to explore the cinematic potential of WIDE SCREEN.

**ROBERTS**, RACHEL (1927– ), British actress on the stage and in the cinema, at her finest in dramatic roles where her deeply emotional qualities can be best used. She first appeared on the screen in *Valley of Song* (1952), and she gave outstanding performances in SATURDAY NIGHT AND SUNDAY MORNING (1960) and THIS SPORTING LIFE (1963). She was married to Rex HARRISON.

**ROBERTSON**, E. ARNOT (1903–61), British novelist, broadcaster, and critic, wrote several novels: *Four Frightened People* was filmed by Cecil B. DEMILLE in 1934. Her unguarded review of *The Green Years* (1946) led to her being barred from METRO-GOLDWYN-MAYER press shows and to that company's attempt to influence the BBC against employing her. She brought a libel suit against MGM and was awarded £1500 damages in the first instance, but the company successfully appealed and, although she fought

the case to the House of Lords (with the aid of a Critics' Circle grant), she eventually lost. She continued to be a popular broadcaster until her death.

**ROBESON**, PAUL (1898– ), US actor and singer, studied law and qualified at the New York Bar. While a student he earned money by singing: his rich voice and emotional delivery began to gain him professional engagements in New York and London. His first film was *The Emperor Jones* (1932), based on Eugene O'Neill's play in which Robeson had appeared. He was dissatisfied with the film's conventional treatment of the negro character and his constant struggles against such stereotyping limited his film appearances. Although he became a popular star with *Sanders of the River* (1935), made for Alexander KORDA in London, and *Show Boat* (1936), the only film to give him the serious part he aimed for was *The Proud Valley* (1940) in which he played the hero of a Welsh mining disaster. His Communist affiliations and his outspoken support of black civil rights caused the temporary withdrawal of his American passport but in 1958 he visited London to play Othello with the Royal Shakespeare Company.

**ROBEY**, GEORGE (1869–1954), British actor, although associated primarily with the English music-hall and known as 'The Prime Minister of Mirth', was active in British films during the First World War period and intermittently thereafter. In films he is best remembered for his Sancho Panza opposite CHALIAPIN in the English-language version of G. W. PABST's *Don Quichotte* (1934) and as Ali Babi in *Chu Chin Chow* (1934). He featured in several films of the forties, including *Salute John Citizen* (1942) and HENRY V (1944), and last appeared in a small role in *The Pickwick Papers* (1953). He was knighted in 1953.

**ROBIN HOOD**, legendary outlaw allegedly living *c.*1190, and referred to in documents from the thirteenth century. From his original territory of Yorkshire he was transferred ultimately to Sherwood Forest in Nottinghamshire. Probably the earliest screen version of the legend was *Robin Hood and his Merry Men* (GB, 1909), followed by several silent films using episodes from the many tales.

Douglas FAIRBANKS embarked on *Robin Hood* on a large scale in 1922. Extreme care was given to historical detail by the art director, Wilfrid Buckland, and the sets, designed on the principles of Gordon CRAIG and REINHARDT, included a castle said to be the biggest Hollywood set ever. Allan DWAN directed; the script is credited to Elton Thomas, a pseudonym for

Fairbanks, although thought to be the joint work of Fairbanks, Dwan, and Lotta Woods, a regular Fairbanks scriptwriter. The story line has more to do with the struggle for power between Richard the Lion-Heart, played by Wallace BEERY, and Prince John than with the greenwood frolics of a band of merry outlaws.

*The Adventures of Robin Hood* (1938) displayed Errol FLYNN's dash and vigour, and OSCARS were awarded for music, art direction, and editing. Maid Marian was played by Olivia DE HAVILLAND, and Little John by Alan Hale, as in the Fairbanks version; Michael CURTIZ co-directed with William Keighley. At a budget of $2m this was the most expensive WARNER BROS production to date: it was commercially very successful, both on first appearance and on re-issue in 1948.

Among later versions, COLUMBIA's *Rogues of Sherwood Forest* (1952) was notable chiefly for the third appearance of Alan Hale as Little John. Walt DISNEY's *The Story of Robin Hood* (1952), directed by Ken ANNAKIN, was made in England and Sherwood was used for location work; it starred Richard Todd. *Robin Hood* (1973), an animated feature-length cartoon from the Disney studios, turned the characters into animals.

**ROBINSON,** EDWARD G. (1893–1972), Romanian-born US actor, real name Emanuel Goldenberg, began his career in amateur theatricals and vaudeville, then on the legitimate stage, before making his first screen appearance in *The Bright Shawl* (1923). His gangster Cesare Bandello in Mervyn LEROY's LITTLE CAESAR (1930) was outstanding, and he remained particularly associated with racketeer or tough-guy roles in the thirties, playing, for example, an arrogant but likeable Portuguese sea captain in *Tiger Shark* (1932), an ex-gangster with social ambitions in *The Little Giant* (1933), a brutal and ambitious bandit-boss of San Francisco in gold rush days in *Barbary Coast* (1935), a rugged fight promoter in *Kid Galahad* (1937), and an eminent surgeon who becomes a jewel thief in *The Amazing Dr Clitterhouse* (1938).

In spite of this tendency to type-casting, Robinson was always an intelligent and versatile actor with a flair for comedy that showed up well in *The Whole Town's Talking* (1935) and *A Slight Case of Murder* (1938). With the end of the classic period of GANGSTER FILMS he played a wider range of roles, contributing to the WARNER BROS cycle of biographies with *Dr Ehrlich's Magic Bullet* (1940) and achieving particular success as the probing insurance agent in DOUBLE INDEMNITY (1943). Striking among his performances of the forties were those in two emotional dramas directed by Fritz LANG and co-starring Joan BENNETT: *The Woman in the*

*Window* (1944) and *Scarlet Street* (1945). He agreeably parodied his earlier gangster type in John HUSTON's *Key Largo* (1948) and returned to outright comedy in *A Hole in the Head* (1959). In THE OUTRAGE (1964), Martin RITT's strange remake of RASHOMON (1950), his blustering, seedy con-man was a striking characterization. For forty years this eminently likeable personality with his distinctive, dead-pan voice, remained among the most reliable of Hollywood actors.

**ROBINSON CRUSOE,** Mexico, 1952. Pathécolor; 1½hr. *Dir* Luis Buñuel; *prod* Ultramar Films; *scr* Buñuel, Philip Roll, from the novel by Daniel Defoe; *ph* Alex Phillips; *des* Edward Fitzgerald; *mus* Anthony Collins; *cast* Dan O'Herlihy (Robinson Crusoe), Jaime Fernandez (Friday), Felipe de Alba (Captain Oberzo), Chel Lopez (Bosun), Jose Chavez, Emilio Garibay (mutineers).

BUÑUEL's castaway, braving near-derangement and spiritual suffering, emerges from his long exile with a new moral force. Photographed on location in the Mexican jungle, the film lacks the imaginative extravagance characteristic of Buñuel, but, despite the constraints of cheap commercial production, it retains interest as an investigation of man divested of civilization and Christian faith.

Other films based more or less loosely on Defoe's novel include: *Robinson Crusoe en vingt-cinq tableaux* (1902) by Georges MÉLIÈS; *Robinson Crusoe* (1910), made in Denmark by August Blom; two American versions in 1922 and 1927, the latter managing to include 'a slight love interest'; *Mr Robinson Crusoe* (1932), starring Douglas FAIRBANKS; a Soviet version in 1946, claimed to be the first full-length STEREOSCOPIC film; and an excellent science fiction film, *Robinson Crusoe on Mars* (1964) directed by Byron Haskin.

**ROBISON,** ARTHUR (1888–1935), American-born director who made nearly all his films in Germany. He qualified in medicine and worked as an actor before entering the cinema in 1914 as literary manager, scriptwriter, and director. His first film was *Nacht des Grauens* (1916) in which Emil JANNINGS appeared. His next film *Schatten* (1923) was a remarkable achievement. Similar in many ways to the KAMMERSPIELFILMS, with nameless characters and no titles, it achieved greater psychological intensity; smooth development from one sequence to another created complete filmic unity. *Manon Lescaut* (1926), his next significant film, was a costume drama, much dependent on close-ups for establishing the passion between the two lovers. Forming a strange contrast to the rest of his work *Looping the Loop*

(1928) was set in a circus, then a popular milieu. The following year Robison went to England to make THE INFORMER, based on Liam O'Flaherty's novel of the Irish troubles, also the basis of John FORD's film.

Robison made several sound films, the last being a third, rather lame, version of DER STUDENT VON PRAG (1935).

**ROBSON, FLORA** (1902– ), British actress, has been associated with character parts, rather than glamorous leading roles, throughout her career—she was impressive as the ageing Queen Elizabeth in *Fire over England* (1937) while still in her mid-thirties and her ancient Empress in Josef von STERNBERG's unfinished *I, Claudius* (1937) showed extraordinary strength. Although her stage career is outstanding, her beautiful voice and unusual capacity for indicating suppressed passion have been under-used in films, but she gave memorable performances in CAESAR AND CLEOPATRA (1945) and John FORD's *Seven Women* (1965). She became a DBE in 1960.

**ROBSON, MARK** (1913– ), Canadian-born US director-producer, started in Hollywood as an editor, and at RKO he cut CITIZEN KANE (1941) with Robert WISE. His first films as director included two of the distinctive horror films in the series produced by Val LEWTON, both starring Boris KARLOFF: *Isle of the Dead* (1945) and *Bedlam* (1946). *Bedlam*, a truly horrific tale set in the nineteenth-century London madhouse, was banned outright in Britain. More characteristic of his work are two notable boxing dramas, *Champion* (1949) and *The Harder They Fall* (1956). A workmanlike, proficient director, his range extends from 'problem' films (*Home of the Brave*, 1949) through war stories (*The Bridges at Toko-Ri*, 1955) to blatant sensationalism (*Valley of the Dolls*, 1967). Among his best films are those starring Paul NEWMAN: the powerful *From the Terrace* (1960) and the lightly diverting *The Prize* (1963).

**ROBSON, MAY** (1865–1942), Australian-born actress, real name Mary Robison. She emigrated to England, studied in England, France, and Belgium, went to America in 1879, and began her acting career on the New York stage in *The Hoop of Gold* (1883). She made her film début in 1915, at the age of fifty, in VITAGRAPH's *Night Out* and, after a break from filming 1920–6, continued to play character roles up to her death. Her films include *King of Kings* (1927), CAPRA's *Lady for a Day*, in which she had her best role as Apple Annie, *Men Must Fight*, DINNER AT EIGHT (all 1933), ALICE IN WONDERLAND (1934), ANNA KARENINA (1935), A STAR IS BORN (1937), BRINGING UP BABY (1938), and *Daughters Courageous* (1939). Her last film was *Joan of Paris* (1942).

***ROCCO E I SUOI FRATELLI*** (*Rocco and his Brothers*), Italy, 1960. 3hr. *Dir* Luchino Visconti; *prod* Titanus/Films Marceau; *scr* Visconti, Suso Cecchi d'Amico, Pasquale Festa Campanile, Massimo Franciosa, Enrico Medioli, from the book *Il ponte della ghisolfa* by Giovanni Testori; *ph* Giuseppe Rotunna: *mus* Nino Rota; *cast* Alain Delon (Rocco), Renato Salvatori (Simone), Annie Girardot (Nadia), Katina Paxinou (Rosaria), Spiros Focas (Vincenzo), Rocco Vidolazzi (Luca), Max Cartier (Ciro), Claudia Cardinale (Ginetta).

VISCONTI's study of the Pafundi family and the problems facing them as immigrants from the depressed south of Italy to Milan was hailed as a return to the preoccupations of NEO-REALISM. His treatment of the subject, however, and the sensational events chosen to illuminate this tragedy of disorientation, make the film more a drama of personal conflict than a comment on political injustice.

**ROCHA, GLAUBER** (1938– ), Brazilian director who worked as a journalist and film critic and directed his first short film in 1958. A major figure in the Brazilian CINEMA NUOVO, he acted as producer, director, and proponent of a movement reflecting authentic Brazilian culture: among his best-known essays is 'The Aesthetics of Violence'. *Barravento* (1962) was his first attempt on film to examine the cultural roots of his country, the traditions of mysticism and primitivism and their contradictions. Far more successful were *Deus e o Diabo na Terra do Sol* (*Black God, White Devil*, 1964) and *O Santo Guerreiro contra o Dragano da Maldate* (*Antonio das Mortes*, 1969), both set in the barren north-east of Brazil and dealing with a starved peasantry gripped in the contrasting mythologies of the 'cangaceiros', the bandits, and the 'beatos', the millenarian holy men. Rocha's treatment reflects that 'permanent state of madness' which he considers characteristic of Brazilian culture; it is theatrical, almost operatic, with ritualized acting and stylized violence. *Terra em Transe* (1967) is perhaps Rocha's most personal work, examining the confusion of the city intellectual caught up in the political struggles of the Brazilian élite. *Antonio das Mortes* was the last film Rocha made in Brazil and for political reasons he has since worked in Europe and Africa. *Der Leone Have Sept Cabezas* (*Lions Have Seven Heads*, 1970) and *Cabezas Cortadas* (*Severed Heads*, 1970) continue the examination of the complex problems of Third World culture, of political action within it, and of the possibility of an authentic cinema in underdeveloped countries. He has written a history of the Brazilian cinema, *Revisao critica do cinema Brasiliero* (Rio de Janeiro, 1963).

**ROCK-'N-ROLL,** popular term for ROLL-BACK sound mixing.

**RODGERS,** RICHARD (1902–   ), US composer for stage and films, at first in collaboration with Lorenz HART. Having established a successful joint career in the theatre, they wrote their first film score for *The Hot Heiress* (1931), although some of their shows had already been filmed—*Spring is Here, Melody Man, Heads Up* (all 1930), and *A Connecticut Yankee* (1931). They found the demands of screen and stage very different, and the film was not a success; they returned to Broadway and wrote *America's Sweetheart* (1931), satirizing Hollywood. However, they returned to films and wrote LOVE ME TONIGHT (1932), *The Phantom President* (1932), and *Hallelujah I'm a Bum* (1933, *Hallelujah I'm a Tramp* in GB), a musical with rhythmic dialogue set in the Depression, with Al JOLSON and Harry LANGDON and a brief appearance by Rodgers and Hart themselves.

Many of the songs they wrote for films in the next few years ended on the cutting-room floor, and often in films based on their stage shows only a few of their numbers were used. One song cut from *Hollywood Party* (1934), after rewriting, became the classic 'Blue Moon', their only popular song intended neither for stage nor film. The British-made film of *Evergreen* (1934) fortunately retained 'Dancing on the Ceiling'; *Babes in Arms* (1939) kept only the title song and 'Where or When'; *On Your Toes* (1939) cut most of their numbers, but used Rodgers's music for 'Slaughter on Tenth Avenue'. Meanwhile they were also writing for Broadway, including *The Boys from Syracuse* (filmed 1940) and *Pal Joey* (filmed 1957). In 1943 they were invited to score *Oklahoma!* Owing to Hart's illness, Rodgers collaborated with Oscar HAMMERSTEIN II and when Hart died the new association continued. The Rodgers and Hammerstein score for the film STATE FAIR (1945) included 'It's a Grand Night for Singing' and won an OSCAR for 'It Might As Well Be Spring'. They wrote several memorable stage shows which were later filmed, including *Oklahoma!* (1955), *The King and I* (1956), *South Pacific* (1958), *Flower Drum Song* (1962), and THE SOUND OF MUSIC (1965). In 1952 Rodgers wrote the background music for a television series about the Second World War, *Victory at Sea*. His other solo work has included music for the television series *Winston Churchill—The Valiant Years* (1960), music and lyrics for the stage show *No Strings* (1962), and the theme music for the television production

*The Great Adventure* (1963). A somewhat dire film biography of Rodgers and Hart, *Words and Music* (1948), starring Tom Drake and Mickey ROONEY, had some good production numbers. Very full details of Rodgers's work may be found in *The Richard Rodgers fact book* (New York, 1968).

**ROEG,** Nicholas (1928–   ), British cameraman and director, after working with Clive DONNER on *The Caretaker* (1963) and *Nothing but the Best* (1964), photographed the magnificently baroque *The Masque of the Red Death* (Roger CORMAN, 1964). For TRUFFAUT he created the chilly, controlled colour of *Fahrenheit 451* (1966), but the lush beauty of John SCHLESINGER's *Far from the Madding Crowd* (1967) is more typical of his work. He co-directed, with Donald Cammell, and photographed *Performance* (1970), a strange allegory of confused identity, and directed and photographed *Walkabout* (1971), which contrasts the society of Australian aboriginals with 'civilized' life. *Don't Look Now* (1973), from a short story by Daphne du Maurier, is a tense psychological tale of horror. Like all his films as director it is distinguished by its visual strength.

**ROGERS,** GINGER (1911–   ), US actress, real name Virginia McMath, played second leads in MUSICALS, notably 42ND STREET (1933) and GOLDDIGGERS OF 1933, specializing in wisecracking blondes with a tough exterior and a soft heart. Her memorable partnership with Fred ASTAIRE started with *Flying Down to Rio* (1933); it starred Dolores DEL RIO, but the Astaire–Rogers number 'Carioca' was the film's high spot. Among the many musicals featuring their singing and dancing (she excelled in putting over a number with style as well as in the polish and versatility of her dancing) were TOP HAT (1935), SWING TIME (1936), and *Follow the Fleet* (1936). In spite of her success in this field, she preferred straight acting. She won an OSCAR for *Kitty Foyle* (1940), in which she played a money-hunting salesgirl whose ambition leads to unhappiness; but was at her best as a *comédienne* in films like *Bachelor Mother* (1939) and *The Major and the Minor* (Billy WILDER, 1942), in which her strikingly beautiful eyes with their clear candid gaze helped to make her a convincing child impersonator. She made one more film with Astaire, *The Barkleys of Broadway* (1949), playing a part originally intended for Judy GARLAND. Recently she has returned to stage musical comedy, notably in the title role of *Mame*.

**ROGERS,** ROY (1912–   ), US cowboy star, real name Leonard Slye, changed his name to Dick Weston and formed a singing cowboy group. Following another change of name—to Roy Rogers—and a couple of small parts, he performed his first starring role in *Under the Western Stars* (1938). With his veteran sidekick, Gabby HAYES, and his faithful horse, TRIGGER, he starred in a long series of Westerns which eventually made him 'King of the Cowboys'. He retained his popularity until his retirement in the early fifties.

**ROGERS,** WILL (1879–1935), US comedian whose homespun humour had a satirical edge: it was not always possible to tell how seriously he took his persona of simple cowboy philosopher. Discovered by Florenz Ziegfeld cracking jokes on stage while spinning a lariat, he achieved considerable fame before his first screen appearance in *Laughing Bill Hyde* (1918). Other films included *One Glorious Day* (1922) directed by James CRUZE, Frank BORZAGE's *A Connecticut Yankee at the Court of King Arthur* (1930), Henry KING's STATE FAIR (1933), and John FORD's *Steamboat round the Bend* (1935). His death in an aeroplane accident was mourned in America as a national disaster.

**ROGOSIN,** LIONEL (1924–   ), US documentary film-maker, made a considerable impression with his first film ON THE BOWERY (1954), a study of down-and-outs in New York. COME BACK AFRICA (1959), made clandestinely in South Africa, recorded the inhuman effects of apartheid. Although based on a structured narrative, the films used non-actors and were shot entirely on location, often with a concealed camera. Rogosin's social conscience as well as his attempt to record the lives of real people were influential on the early development of both DIRECT CINEMA in the US and FREE CINEMA in Britain. His films since, including *Good Times, Wonderful Times* (1966), setting the reality of war against remembered experience, and *Woodcutters of the Deep South* (1973), about black and white workers co-operating in the southern US, continue to opt for individual authorship rather than the non-intervention claimed for direct cinema: but they convey a deep concern for the sufferings of people neglected or rejected by rich societies.

Rogosin has also been involved in running an ART HOUSE cinema in Greenwich Village, New York.

**ROHMER,** ERIC (1920–   ), French director, real name Maurice Scherer. In 1950, with GODARD and RIVETTE, he founded *La Gazette du cinéma* which ran for only a year. From 1951 he wrote for CAHIERS DU CINÉMA under his own name, and after the death of André BAZIN in 1958 he became chief editor until ousted in 1963

owing to disagreements on the journal's aesthetic policies.

Rohmer made his first film *Le Journal d'un scélérat* in 1950, and in 1959 his first feature, *Le Signe du lion,* which finely captures the atmosphere of Paris in August. He then embarked on six *contes moraux, La Boulangère de Monceau* (1963), a short, *La Carrière de Suzanne* (1963), *La Collectioneuse* (1966), MA NUIT CHEZ MAUD (1968), LE GENOU DE CLAIRE (1970), and L'AMOUR, L'APRÈS-MIDI (1972), each concerning the temptation of a man able to take advantage of the absence of a woman he supposedly loves. The overriding fascination of the films, and Rohmer's predominant interest, lies less in the characterization of moral choice than in the discrepancies, affectionately and humorously observed, between the words—hence the importance of even the most desultory conversation—and the actions of the two or three central characters in each film. Always working in natural surroundings and assisted by the delicate camerawork of Nestor ALMENDROS, Rohmer draws the audience into an intimate relationship with the characters, enabling it to participate on an equal footing in the questioning of motives and feelings. The settings provide the dimension of chance (a snowstorm in *Ma Nuit chez Maud,* a freak rain shower in *Le Genou de Claire,* a friend's unexpected visit to the office in *L'Amour, l'après-midi*) essential to genuine temptation. Rohmer's perceptiveness, the sensitivity of his dialogue, the quality of the acting, together with his modest scale of working with a small, consistent team, have somewhat masked the originality of his achievement; but his films have attributes equivalent to those of the best short stories.

Since 1964 Rohmer has also worked for French television, producing a series 'Cinéastes de notre temps' beginning with *Carl Dreyer* (1964), and has made educational films, including *Le Celluloid et le marbre* (1964), and shorts, among them *La Fermière de Montfaucon* (1968).

**RÖHRIG,** WALTER (1893–   ), German painter, associated with EXPRESSIONISM, who worked as a set designer on DAS CABINETT DES DR CALIGARI (1919) and other classic German films of the silent period, including Fritz LANG's *Der müde Tod* (*The Weary Death* or *Destiny,* 1921) and von Gerlach's *Zur Chronik von Grieshuus* (*The Chronicles of the Grey House,* 1923). He was particularly associated with films directed by F. W. MURNAU: *Schloss Vogeloed* (*The Haunted Castle,* 1921), DER LETZTE MANN (*The Last Laugh,* 1924), *Tartüff* (1925), *Faust* (1926), and (in US) *Four Devils* (1928).

**ROLL-BACK MIXING,** popularly called 'rock-'n-roll', a method of MIXING sound-tracks to produce a master track, in which errors can be corrected by stopping the recording, rolling back the picture and sound-tracks in synchronization, and starting to record again from a point just before the error. This method, introduced in the sixties, allows the mixer to concentrate on a difficult portion by 'rocking and rolling' back and forth past a short section of the film until he finds the perfect balance of sound. (See SOUND.)

***ROMA, CITTÀ APERTA*** (*Rome, Open City*), Italy, 1945. 1¾hr. *Dir* Roberto Rossellini; *prod* Excelsa Film; *scr* Sergio Amidei, Federico Fellini, Rossellini; *ph* Ubaldo Arata; *ed* Eraldo Da Roma; *mus* Renzo Rossellini; *cast* Anna Magnani (Pina), Aldo Fabrizzi (Don Pietro Pellegnini), Marcello Pagliero (Manfredi), Maria Michi (Marina), Harry Feist (Major Bergmann), Francesco Grandjacquet, Giovanna Galletti.

The film was secretly planned by ROSSELLINI and his colleagues during the German occupation of Rome, but production was not begun until after the entry of the Allies. Originally intended as a short documentary of the sacrifice of Don Morosini, a priest shot by the Germans in 1944, *Roma, città aperta* tells the story of a Resistance leader, Manfredi, who is hunted by the Gestapo. A friend's fiancée, Pina, gives him shelter, but when she is shot, Manfredi takes refuge with his mistress, Marina, who betrays him to the Gestapo; Manfredi and the priest Don Pietro are arrested and killed.

Its intensity and immediacy derived principally from its depiction of war in terms of human values and relationships, from its subtle blend of documentary and fiction, and from the anger which informs it and still gives it power today. Apart from Anna MAGNANI and Aldo FABRIZZI the cast was non-professional, but they all give superbly authentic performances against the backdrop of Rome's dismal topography. (See also NEO-REALISM.)

***ROMANCE SENTIMENTALE,*** France, 1930. 30min. *Dir* Eisenstein and Alexandrov; *prod* Sequana Films; *ph* Edvard Tissé; *des* Lazare Meerson; *mus* Alexis Archangelski; *with* Mira Giry.

Passing through Paris in 1929, EISENSTEIN, ALEXANDROV, and TISSÉ accepted a commission from a jeweller to make a film featuring his wife singing. Eisenstein worked only briefly on the project, then left his companions a free hand in applying some of the ideas that the Russians had theoretically developed on the use of sound. The result is a zestful charivari of visual and aural effects, quite uncharacteristic of Eisenstein's

Aldo Fabrizzi in *Roma, città aperta* (Roberto Rossellini, 1945)

work; his name was attached to the film only at the insistence of the producer.

***ROMAN HOLIDAY***, US, 1953. 2hr. *Dir, prod* William Wyler for Paramount; *scr* Ian McLellan Hunter, John Dighton; *ph* Fritz Planer, Henri Alekan; *des* Hal Pereira, Walter Tyler; *mus* Georges Auric; *cast* Gregory Peck (Joe Bradley), Audrey Hepburn (Princess Ann), Eddie Albert (Irving Radovich), Margaret Rawlings (Countess), Harcourt Williams (Ambassador).

WYLER's most engaging excursion into light comedy was a variation on the theme of romance between royalty (Audrey HEPBURN's princess) and commoner (Gregory PECK's journalist). The substance was necessarily slight, but the film's freshness and charm were never forced, and the romantic sentiment of the bitter-sweet finale was nicely judged.

**ROMANIA.** The first film projection in Bucharest took place in 1896, and some films of the Romanian countryside were projected in 1897, but there were no resources for the development of an industry, and production remained sparse and sporadic. The poverty of production in fact caused several talented Romanians, such as Lupu PICK and NEGULESCO, to work abroad. Several feature films were produced during the silent era, with Jean Georgescu beginning his long and distinguished career in comedies. His sound films made some impact abroad during the thirties; and in 1938 international attention was drawn to the other *doyen* of Romanian cinema, Paul Călinescu, who won a documentary prize at VENICE. Documentary production had been encouraged by a Cinematographic Section set up by the National Touring Office in 1936, which later became the National Cinematographic Office, but only some fifty full-length films had been produced in Romania by the end of the Second World War.

The country became a socialist republic in 1945, and in 1948 the film industry was nationalized and reorganized. The socialist pattern of specialized studios and group production was gradually adopted, a film section started in the I. L. Caragiale Institute of Theatrical Art in Bucharest, and an important fillip given to production with the building of an impressive set of studios at Buftea, just outside Bucharest (begun 1950, completed 1957). The first film after 1945 was Călinescu's *Răsună valea* (*The Valley Resounds*, 1949), about young volunteers building a mountain road. Devotedly socialist realist in theme, the film also has many refreshing touches of elegant slapstick which are characteristically Romanian. Production built up slowly during the fifties, with most films based on novels about the changing national life: outstanding among them were *Mitrea Cocor* (Victor Iliu, 1952) and Călinescu's *De sfăşurarea* (*In a Village*, 1954). In *Directorul nostru* (*Our Manager*, 1955), Georgescu achieved a considerable breakthrough in acting technique, made possible by the emergence of actors trained alongside the directors in the film school.

The new directors, too, began to make their impact by the beginning of the sixties: Mircea Drăgan with *Setea* (*Thirst*, 1960) and *Lupeni '29* (1962); Lucian Bratu with *Tudor* (1962); and, from the theatre, Liviu Ciulei with *Valurile Dunării* (*The Danube Waves*, 1959). Themes of socialist struggle and historical epics dominated until the emergence of a more personal approach in Ciulei's *Pădurea spinzuraţitor* (*Forest of the Hanged*, 1964), which won the prize for best direction at CANNES, and Lucian Pintilie's first film, *Duminica la ora 6* (*Sunday at Six O'Clock*, 1965). Iulian Mihu continued this trend with *Procesul Alb* (*The White Trial*, 1965) and Andrei Blaier with *Diminiţile unui băiat cuminte* (*The Mornings of a Sensible Youth*, 1966). Production has now steadied at around seventeen features a year, in a cheerful atmosphere in which a sense of national cinematic tradition is emerging.

As in the other Eastern European countries, documentary and animated film have been nurtured, with Ion POPESCU-GOPO and Bob Călinescu outstanding among the strong school of animators. The pre-eminence of Romania's contribution to animation is attested by the fact that, since 1966, the annual international festival of animated film alternates between Annecy and Mamaia, on Romania's Black Sea coast. Romania also, like the other Balkan countries, has succeeded in building up foreign co-productions because of its good facilities and attractive scenery.

***ROMEO AND JULIET*** has been by far the most popular of SHAKESPEARE's plays with film-makers. Although some sources cite a VITAGRAPH *Romeo and Juliet* of 1903, well-authenticated versions did not appear until 1908, when a production by CINES directed by Mario CASERINI was followed by a Vitagraph version starring Paul Panzer and Florence LAWRENCE, and a British film with Godfrey Tearle and Mary Malone as the lovers. None of these exceeded one reel.

In 1911 Film d'Arte of Italy brought out a two-reel *Giulietta e Romeo* whose extra length allowed for a more elaborate treatment. The American Thanhouser Company also produced a two-reeler in the same year, but each reel was released independently, part 2 appearing a week after part 1. When in 1916 Metro announced it was to film the play with Francis X. BUSHMAN and Beverly Bayne, William FOX replied with a version starring Harry Hilliard and Fox's discovery, Theda BARA. After a good deal of wrangling both films were premièred on 22 October, the Metro version gaining the more general acclaim from reviewers.

*Romeo and Juliet* burlesques flourished in the twenties. LUBITSCH's *Romeo und Julia im Schnee* (1920) was a winter sports comedy; Clarence Badger's *Doubling for Romeo* (1921) starred Will ROGERS as a gauche cowboy and would-be lover; and Ben Turpin played a cross-eyed Romeo in a SENNETT parody of 1924.

Norma SHEARER played Juliet twice. In *Hollywood Revue of 1929* she appeared with John GILBERT in an excerpt from the play and in 1936 she starred with Leslie HOWARD in METRO-GOLDWYN-MAYER's *Romeo and Juliet* directed by George CUKOR. Though Shearer and Howard looked far too mature for the roles, they did bring some authority to their delivery of Shakespeare's poetry. The magnificent sets were designed by Cedric GIBBONS.

The late thirties and early forties saw adaptations of the play in Argentina, Spain, Mexico, Egypt, and India. In André CAYATTE's celebrated adaptation *Les Amants de Vérone* (1948), from a script by Cayatte and Jacques PRÉVERT, Anouk AIMÉE and Serge REGGIANI played two stand-ins who fall in love while filming Shakespeare's play.

In 1954 Renato CASTELLANI's *Giulietta e Romeo* won the Grand Prix at VENICE. The text was freely adapted by the director, who encouraged his young stars, Laurence HARVEY and Susan Shentall, to play as naturalistically as possible. Where Cukor had paid attention to the poetry, Castellani strove for a rich visual texture, perhaps to the detriment of the spoken word.

Two films have been made of the *Romeo and Juliet* ballet by Prokofiev; a Russian film of 1954 with Ulanova, and Paul CZINNER's of 1966 with Fonteyn and Nureyev. In 1961 Peter USTINOV made *Romanoff and Juliet*, a light political satire, which was followed a year later by Robert WISE's WEST SIDE STORY, a musical which up-dated the family feud to gang warfare in the streets of New York.

Franco ZEFFIRELLI, in his 1968 *Romeo and Juliet*, followed the naturalistic lead of Castellani by casting the 15-year-old Olivia Hussey and the 16-year-old Leonard Whiting as the lovers and laying great emphasis on the colour and bustle of Verona.

**ROMM,** MIKHAIL (1901–71), Russian director and scriptwriter. After serving in the Red Army 1918–21 and studying sculpture in Moscow, Romm began writing film scripts and was Macheret's assistant for *Dela i lyudi* (*Men and Jobs*, 1932). His first film, which he also

scripted, was *Boule de suif* (1934), from Maupassant's short story; it was the last Russian silent film. Following *Trinadtsat* (*The Thirteen*, 1937) Romm was required to make a film for the twentieth anniversary of the Revolution: LENIN V OCTIABRYE (*Lenin in October*, 1937) and *Lenin v 1918 godu* (*Lenin in 1918*, 1939) was the two-part result. Despite the tight schedule allotted, the films have both depth and warmth.

During the war Romm made *Chelovek No 217* (*Registration No 217*, 1944), about the ill-treatment of a Russian slave acquired by a German family. In 1948 he directed the anti-American *Russkii vopros* (*The Russian Question*), from a play by Simonov. The next year he made *Vladimir I. Lenin*.

In 1954 Romm became artistic director of a studio for film actors, and later he was artistic director of studies at Mosfilm and a professor at VGIK. His films of the sixties include *Devyat dnei odnovo goda* (*Nine Days of One Year*, 1960), a study of young scientists, and *Obiknovennyi fashizm* (*Ordinary Fascism*, 1965), a COMPILATION depicting the rise of Nazism from the point of view of the complaisant contemporary.

**RONDE, La,** France, 1950. 1½hr. *Dir* Max Ophuls; *prod* Sacha Gordine; *scr* Jacques Natanson, Ophuls, based on Arthur Schnitzler's play *Reigen*; *ph* Christian Matras; *des* Jean d'Eaubonne, Marpaux, M. Frederix; *cost* Georges Annenkov; *mus* Oscar Straus, Joë Hajos; *cast* Anton Walbrook (Narrator), Simone Signoret (Whore), Serge Reggiani (Soldier), Simone Simon (Chambermaid), Daniel Gélin (Young Man), Danielle Darrieux (Married Lady), Fernand Gravey (Husband), Odette Joyeux (Grisette), Jean-Louis Barrault (Poet), Isa Miranda (Actress), Gérard Philipe (Lieutenant).

*La Ronde*, France, 1964. Franscope; 1¾hr; Eastman Color. *Dir* Roger Vadim; *prod* Hakim brothers for Paris Film Production and Interopa Film; *scr* Jean Anouilh, based on Schnitzler's play; *ph* Henri Decaë; *des* François de Lamothe; *cost* Marc Doelnitz; *cast* Marie Dubois (Prostitute), Claude Girard (Soldier), Anna Karina (Maid), Valérie Lagrange (Friend), Jean-Claude Brialy (Young Man), Jane Fonda (Married Woman), Maurice Ronet (Husband), Catherine Spaak (Midinette), Bernard Noël (Author), Francine Bergé (Actress), Jean Sorel (Young Officer).

Schnitzler's play consists of a series of episodes in which each of the ten characters forms one half of two couples until the last character to be introduced brings the story full circle by sleeping with the first to appear. The first film version by OPHULS initiated the last, French, portion of his career. He brought a skilful light touch to the rather bitter original, and the resulting witty confection, with Oscar Straus's insidious waltz theme, became an enormous success. Probably Ophuls' best-known film, although not his best, it contained a splendidly stylish performance by Anton WALBROOK as the Narrator, commenting on the action and providing a distancing effect; of the remaining members of the star-studded cast, Danielle DARRIEUX and Fernand Gravey were particularly effective. The film became a *cause célèbre* in America, where it was the most explicit sex comedy that had so far been publicly screened. It was banned in New York and elsewhere and showings were finally permitted only by a decision of the US Supreme Court.

VADIM's version was generally considered less successful with the exception of the final episodes. It was beautifully photographed in colour by Henri DECAË, but most of the actors seemed ill-cast, although Catherine Spaak and Francine Bergé distinguished themselves. Vadim took full advantage of the possibilities of the bedroom sequences, but he failed to find an overall tone and the film was uneven in quality.

**RONET, MAURICE** (1927–  ), French actor, had his first screen role in BECKER's *Rendezvous de juillet* (1949). He has become one of France's best-known contemporary actors and has worked for several leading directors including MALLE, for whom he appeared in *L'Ascenseur pour l'échafaud* (1957) and gave a magnificent portrayal of an alcoholic suicide's last day in LE FEU FOLLET (1963). He was one of the many stars in VADIM's LA RONDE (1964) and for CHABROL he played in *Le Scandale* (1966) and in *La Femme infidèle* (1968), as the lover.

**ROOM, ABRAM** or **ALEXANDER** (1894–  ), Russian director, worked as a dentist, journalist, and theatre director before entering the film industry as assistant director on *Starets Vasili Gryaznov* (*Elder Vasili Gryaznov*, 1924). The next year he made his first films as director, the melodrama *Bukhta smerti* (*Death Ray*) and *Predatel* (*Traitor*). His best-known film, *Tretya Meshchanskaya* (*Third Meshchanskaya* or *Bed and Sofa* as it was called by its Berlin distributors, 1927), dealt with the human side of the Moscow housing shortage. *Privideniye, kotoroye ne vozvrashchayetsya* (*The Ghost That Never Returns*, 1930), set in Latin America, showed workers mounting an armed revolt against the oil companies. In the same year he was chosen to direct with Dziga VERTOV *Plan velikikh rabot* (*Plan for Great Works*), a series of documentary episodes about the first Five-Year Plan, mostly using footage from films by Vertov and Esther SHUB. The use of sound was relatively simple.

During the thirties and forties Room directed educational and documentary films, including one about Tito's wartime activities, *V gorakh Iugoslavii* (*In the Mountains of Yugoslavia*, 1946) photographed by Edvard TISSÉ, which was withdrawn when relations between the two countries became strained. His later films include *Serebristaya pyl* (*Silver Dust*, 1953), also filmed by Tissé, *Serdtse byotsya vnov* (*The Heart Beats Again*, 1956), and *Yakov Bogomolov* (1970), from an unfinished play by Maxim GORKY.

**ROOM AT THE TOP**, GB, 1958. 2hr. *Dir* Jack Clayton; *prod* Remus; *scr* Neil Paterson, from the novel by John Braine; *ph* Freddie Francis; *cast* Laurence Harvey (Joe Lampton), Simone Signoret (Alice), Heather Sears (Susan Brown), Donald Wolfit (Mr Brown), Donald Houston (Charles).

*Room at the Top*, closely following John Braine's best-selling novel, describes Joe Lampton's fight to force himself into the ranks of the socially privileged by mainly sexual manoeuvres. The film's realistic treatment of cluttered provincial dreariness and its frankness (which owed much to Simone SIGNORET's unreserved sensuality) were a welcome innovation in British cinema.

**ROONEY, MICKEY** (1922–  ), US actor and comedian, real name Joe Yule. Coming from a family of stage troupers, he appeared in vaudeville as a small child and began his film career in the popular series of Mickey McGuire comedy shorts. After a return to vaudeville, he began appearing in feature films as Mickey Rooney in 1932. His Puck in A MIDSUMMER NIGHT'S DREAM (1935) was among earlier successes. He won a special OSCAR for *Boys' Town* (1938), partnered the young Judy GARLAND in two memorable musicals (*Babes in Arms*, 1939; *Strike Up the Band*, 1940), and became particularly popular as the exuberant teenager Andy Hardy in the HARDY FAMILY series beginning with *A Family Affair* (1937). His screen adolescence was unusually long but he eventually survived the difficult transition into adult roles, including that of Lorenz HART in *Words and Music* (1948) and other attempts to break out of type such as *Baby Face Nelson* (1958), *The Big Operator* (1959), and *Skidoo* (1968). He scored a minor triumph in *Pulp* (1972).

**ROSAY, FRANÇOISE** (1891–1974), French actress, real name Françoise de Nalèche, studied acting and singing, intending a career in opera. She first appeared on the stage in 1908 and on film in *Falstaff* (1913), but retired in 1917 on her marriage to Jacques FEYDER. Her acting career began in earnest in 1923 in *Crainquebille*, directed by her husband. In 1929 she visited the US where she appeared in *The Trial of Mary Dugan*, then becoming immensely active in both America and France. Her best-known films include LA KERMESSE HÉOÏQUE (1935), her most notable collaboration with Feyder, CARNÉ's *Drôle de drame* (1937), and DUVIVIER's *Un Carnet de bal* (1937), all displaying her characteristic blend of mature charm, wit, and dignity. She spent the war years in Switzerland, where she taught film acting at the Conservatoire de Genève while filming *Une Femme disparaît* (1941), and in Britain, where she acted in the theatre and in films. Her numerous other films include *Saraband for Dead Lovers* (1948), *The Thirteenth Letter* (1950), *L'Auberge rouge* (1951), *Les Sept Péchés capitaux* (1951), *The Sound and the Fury* (1959), and *The Longest Day* (1962). She is a Chevalier de la Légion d'honneur. *Le Cinéma notre métier* (Geneva, 1944) is a memoir of her working collaboration with Feyder.

**ROSEMARY'S BABY**, US, 1968. Technicolor; 2¼hr. *Dir* Roman Polański; *prod* Paramount; *scr* Polański, from the novel by Ira Levin; *ph* William Fraker; *mus* Krzysztof Komeda; *cast* Mia Farrow (Rosemary), John Cassavetes (Guy), Ruth Gordon (Minnie), Sidney Blackmer (Roman), Ralph Bellamy (Dr Sapirstein), Maurice Evans (Hutch).

Rosemary, a young pregnant wife, believes she is in the clutches of a coterie of witches led by the splendidly grotesque Minnie and Roman Castevet. Within a totally realistic New York setting POLAŃSKI succeeds in creating his usual personal world of ambiguous menace. While entirely viable as a polished representative of the horror genre, *Rosemary's Baby* is also unusually rich in levels of interpretation.

**ROSI**, FRANCESCO (1922– ), Italian director, worked in the theatre for two years, then as assistant to VISCONTI on LA TERRA TREMA (1948). For the next ten years he gained experience as assistant to Luciano EMMER and ANTONIONI, as well as co-scripting Visconti's BELLISSIMÀ (1951) and ZAMPA's *Processo alla città* (*Town on Trial*, 1952). His first feature as director, *La sfida* (*The Challenge*, 1957) set in Naples, was in the tradition of American GANGSTER FILMS.

The two films that made Rosi's reputation, SALVATORE GIULIANO (1962) and LE MANI SULLA CITTÀ (*Hands Over the City*, 1963), also used Naples as their setting. They demonstrate a keen understanding of the social problems of southern Italy, extending the style and political commitment of NEO-REALISM into consideration of the processes of a corrupt society rather than the sufferings of its victims.

*Il momento della verità* (*The Moment of Truth*, 1964), about the rise of a bullfighter, lacked persuasive power, but *C'era una volta* (*Once Upon a Time*, 1967) with Sophia LOREN and Omar SHARIF, a departure from Rosi's social themes, is a charming and neglected film. After various unrealized projects, including one on Che Guevara, *Uomini contro* (1970), set in the First World War, reasserted Rosi's political and social concerns in its examination of the relationship between the individual and authority.

**ROSSELLINI**, ROBERTO (1906– ), Italian director, worked in editing and dubbing from the mid-thirties and made two short independent films, *Daphne* (1936) and *Prélude à l'après-midi d'un faune* (1938), banned as indecent by the Fascist censor. His first work in the commercial cinema was on the script of *Luciano Serra, pilota* (1938), directed by Goffredo Alessandrini and supervised by Vittorio Mussolini. After making short documentaries, Rossellini was commissioned by Francesco DE ROBERTIS, as head of the Centro Cinematografico del Marine, to direct *La nave bianca* (1941) in semi-documentary style with non-professional actors. It established Rossellini with the editor Eraldo Da Roma, who was to edit some of the major neo-realist films; Renzo Rossellini composed the somewhat overblown music, as he was to do for most of his brother's films.

ROMA, CITTÀ APERTA (1945) gained Rossellini international recognition as a director of originality and integrity; it also gave Anna MAGNANI her first role of real scope. The first film to draw attention to NEO-REALISM as an exciting new style, it forms with PAISÀ (1947) and GERMANIA, ANNO ZERO (1947) a trilogy in which Rossellini's belief in the importance of the individual within the social context is finely articulated. *Germania, anno zero* was the least successful, partly because Rossellini seemed ill at ease in an unfamiliar environment. Since the trilogy his work, although prolific, has sometimes betrayed an uncertainty of direction and tone.

*L'amore* (1948), a renewal of Rossellini's fruitful partnership with Magnani, was censored in New York for blasphemy (see MAGNANI). He then made his first film with Ingrid BERGMAN, *Stromboli, terra di Dio* (1949); like his next film, FRANCESCO, GIULIARE DI DIO (1950), it treats faith as an essential part of life. *Europa '51* and *Viaggio in Italia* (both 1952) were vehicles for Ingrid Bergman, by then his wife.

In 1953 Rossellini directed *Dov'è la libertà*, favourably comparing prison with the outside world, and produced on the stage Verdi's *Otello* and HONEGGER's oratorio *Giovanna d'Arco al rogo* (*Joan of Arc at the Stake*), making a film version of the latter. After visiting India he made *India* (1958), a rather diffuse documentary, and a series for television, then returned to the theme of the Resistance in *Il Generale della Rovere* (1959) and *Era notte a Roma* (1960): the former starred Vittorio DE SICA and won the Grand Prix at VENICE. After *Viva l'Italia* (1960), about Garibaldi, *Vanina, Vanina* (1961), and an episode in *RoGoPaG* (1962), he has worked only in the theatre and television.

**ROSSEN,** ROBERT (1908–66), US director, originally wrote and directed for the theatre. The success of his play *The Body Beautiful* (1934) and his evident social and political commitment led to a contract with WARNER BROS, who were currently specializing in socially aware films. Rossen scripted two such subjects, *Marked Woman* (Lloyd BACON, 1937), with BOGART as a racket-busting attorney based on Thomas E. Dewey, and *They Won't Forget* (Mervyn LEROY, 1937), about lynch law in the Deep South; his liberal attitude was also apparent in THE ROARING TWENTIES (1939). After writing three MILE-STONE films, *Edge of Darkness* (1943), *A Walk in the Sun* (1945), and *The Strange Love of Martha Ivers* (1946), Rossen was invited by Harry COHN to work for COLUMBIA on *Johnny*

*O'Clock* (1947) which he was also allowed to direct. He then made *Body and Soul* (1947) for Enterprise Pictures.

Rossen returned to Columbia on condition he could make ALL THE KING'S MEN (1949), which he had urged Cohn to buy when the novel was published in 1946, but he was released from his contract when he was called before the UNAMERICAN ACTIVITIES Committee. He formed his own company and made *The Brave Bulls* (1951), *Mambo* (1955), and *Alexander the Great* (1956), with Richard BURTON.

By 1957 he was working for Hollywood again with *Island in the Sun* (1957). His last two films, THE HUSTLER (1961) and *Lilith* (1964), showed that he was still, given the opportunity, a director of considerable originality and courage.

**ROSSI,** FRANCO (1919– ), Italian director, first worked as assistant to CAMERINI, CASTELLANI, Aldo Vergano, and others, before directing *I falsari* (1952). Since then he has worked on more than twenty films, including *Amici per la pelle* (*Friends for Life*, 1955), a remarkably sensitive study of childhood, and *Morte di un amico* (*Death of a Friend*, 1960), which display his gentle psychological awareness.

*Roma, città aperta* (Roberto Rossellini, 1945)

**ROSSIF,** FRÉDÉRIC (1922–    ), French director born in Yugoslavia, best known for his COMPILATION films. They include *Le Temps du ghetto* (1961), made up of footage shot before the Warsaw uprising, MOURIR A MADRID (*To Die in Madrid*, 1962), on the Spanish Civil War, and *Révolution d'octobre* (1967) about events in Russia 1896–1924, which includes sequences from VERTOV'S CHELOVEK S KINOAPPARATOM (*Man with a Movie Camera*, 1929). Rossif's films, although sometimes glib, occasionally attain considerable emotional power.

**ROSTRUM** see ANIMATION

**ROTA,** NINO (1911–    ), Italian composer who became active in writing music for films during the mid-forties and has since been constantly in demand. VIVERE IN PACE (1946) and *Mio figlio professore* (*My Son the Professor*, 1946) were among his early film scores. His music for a British film, *The Glass Mountain* (1948), with its miniature concerto-like piece for piano and orchestra in a style popular at the time, was an enormous success. He wrote the scores for I VITELLONI (1953) and almost all FELLINI's later films, including a notable contribution to LA DOLCE VITA (1960). Also outstanding was his music for IL GATTOPARDO (*The Leopard*, 1963) and THE GODFATHER (1971).

**ROTHA,** PAUL (1907–    ), British director, producer, and writer, was a painter, designer, and art critic before joining GRIERSON's Empire Marketing Board Film Unit (see CROWN FILM UNIT) for six months. In 1930 Rotha published *The film till now* (London, revised 1949, 1960, 1967), the first comprehensive survey of world cinema, still a standard reference book. Working independently for commercial sponsors, his films included *Contact* (1933) and *Shipyard* (1935). *The Face of Britain* (1935) reported on housing in the current sociological style. He began to function increasingly as a producer particularly during the wartime boom; Paul Rotha Productions was formed in 1941. *The Fourth Estate* (1940), which he directed for *The Times* newspaper, was never publicly shown, but a new and widely influential internationalism dominated two COMPILATION films concerning food strategy, *World of Plenty* (1943) and *The World is Rich* (1947), and a later film for UNESCO *World Without End* (co-director Basil WRIGHT, 1953). Rotha was BBC television's Head of Documentary, 1953–5. *No Resting Place* (1950), *Cat and Mouse* (1958), and *The Silent Raid* (1962) creditably brought documentary's low-budget realism to the feature film, but were less successful than his important compilation *Das Leben von Adolf Hitler* (*The Life of Adolf Hitler*, 1961).

More chronicler than critic, his prolific writings include *Documentary film* (London, 1936, revised 1939 and 1952), still the standard work, *Movie parade* (London, 1936, revised 1950), and a two-volume autobiographical history of British documentary, *Documentary diary* (the first volume published in London and New York, 1973; the second volume in preparation).

**ROUCH,** JEAN (1917–    ), French director and ethnographer, was a director of research studies at the CNRS (Paris). In connection with his work at the Musée de L'Homme he set up with Professor Leroi-Gourhan an International Ethnographic Film Committee in 1952.

Rouch started using film in 1947, initially as a means of recording his ethnographical work in Africa: he produced a number of short films on African customs and rites, some of which were collected together in 1955 to form *Les Fils de l'eau*.

However, Rouch became more interested in the film medium itself and in MOI, UN NOIR (1958), the first of his feature films, the subject's participation and response to the camera's presence became an essential component of the film. In *La Pyramide humaine* (1961), the camera was consciously used as a stimulant or catalyst. CHRONIQUE D'UN ÉTÉ (1961), made with the sociologist Edgar MORIN, aroused considerable controversy and gave rise to the term CINÉMA-VÉRITÉ. It was, moreover, the first time that a light-weight synchronized film unit was used in France.

After a few experimental short films which include *La Punition* (1963), and *Les Veuves de quinze ans* (1964), Rouch returned to documentary filming in Africa. He also finished *La Chasse au lion à l'arc* (1965), and *Jaguar* (1967), which he had left incomplete in the fifties. In *Petit à petit* (1970), Rouch's main thematic interests, the fusion of reality with fiction and the confrontation of Africans with Europeans, are prominent.

**ROUE, La,** France, 1922. 2hr. *Dir, scr* Abel Gance; *prod* Pathé; *asst dir* Blaise Cendrars; *ph* Burel, Bujard, Duverger; *ed* Marguerite Beaugé; *cast* Séverin-Mars (Sisif), Ivy Close (Norma), Gabriel de Gravone (Elie).

The story of the unhappy rivalry of a father and son in love with the same girl, shot on location in a railway yard.

Using rapid cutting, GANCE evolved a style of long sequences in which powerful images are rhythmically intercut, with consequent dramatic impact. Few critics appreciated the technical innovation, and the film came under strong attack. HONEGGER's accompanying music was later used as the basis for his PACIFIC 231.

A remake of *La Roue* was directed by André Haguet in 1956.

**ROUGH CUT,** the stage in EDITING at which the excess footage included in the ASSEMBLY has been removed. The rough shape of the film is by now evident, but the exact cutting points or OPTICAL devices intended may not have been determined. In practice, any cutting copy up to the final form can be said to be a rough cut.

*ROUND-UP, The,* see SZEGÉNYLEGÉNYEK

**ROUQUIER,** GEORGES (1909– ), French director, made his first film, *Vendanges,* an impressionistic study of the grape harvest in the south of France, in 1929. He worked for some years as a linotype operator and did not return to film-making until 1942, when he made a short film, *Le Tonnelier,* on the craft of coopering, followed in 1943 by *Le Charron,* on wheel-wrighting. Both films show Rouquier's understanding of the craftsman and his world, and his feeling for the traditions involved. This sensitivity reached its peak in his best-known film, FARREBIQUE; OU, LES QUATRE SAISONS (1946). Other documentaries include *L'Oeuvre biologique de Pasteur* (1947), co-directed by Jean PAINLEVÉ, and *Le Chaudronnier* (1949), about tin-smelting. Rouquier made two unsuccessful feature films, *Sang et lumière* (1953) and *SOS Noronha* (1956). He published *Album de Farrebique* in 1946.

**ROZIER,** JACQUES (1926– ), French director, after training at the INSTITUT DES HAUTES ÉTUDES CINÉMATOGRAPHIQUES (IDHEC), worked as an assistant to Jean RENOIR on *French Can-can* (1955). He directed two short films, *Rentrée des classes* (1955) and the very successful *Blue Jeans* (1958), about the exploits of two teenage boys girl-hunting on the beaches at Cannes. He made his first feature, ADIEU PHILIPPINE (1962), after GODARD had introduced him to the producer Georges de Beauregard. The film in many ways epitomized the youthful freshness of the NOUVELLE VAGUE and seemed a very promising début: but it was expensive by current standards, Rozier became involved in a dispute with de Beauregard, and eventually other backers took over the project.

In 1963 Rozier completed *I Paparazzi,* a documentary on Brigitte BARDOT made while she was filming in Godard's LE MÉPRIS. Since then he has worked mainly in television.

**ROZSA,** MIKLOS (1907– ), Hungarian-born composer, worked with Alexander KORDA in London on his first film score, for *Knight without Armour* (1937), and went to Hollywood with

him to work on THE THIEF OF BAGHDAD (1940). He became one of the most prolific film composers, writing in various styles from the eerie and haunting mood music for thrillers such as *Spellbound* (Alfred HITCHCOCK, 1945) and THE LOST WEEKEND (Billy WILDER, 1945), to his majestic scores for epics, among them QUO VADIS (1951), BEN-HUR (1959), and EL CID (1961). Rozsa's music began the vogue for recorded film scores, and he remains the most-recorded film composer. He has won three Oscars, for *Spellbound, A Double Life* (George CUKOR, 1948), and *Ben-Hur.*

**RUGGLES,** CHARLES (Charlie) (1890– ), US character actor who began his stage career at the age of fifteen. Chosen by PARAMOUNT for a part in *Gentlemen of the Press* (1929), he became a familiar figure on the Hollywood screen. He was especially adept at dithery, diffident, or dilatory parts, with an acute sense of timing in comedy. He played the leading role in the 1930 version of *Charley's Aunt,* but was mainly in demand as a top-grade supporting actor. He appeared in numerous Paramount successes of the thirties, including TROUBLE IN PARADISE (1932), LOVE ME TONIGHT (1932), and *Ruggles of Red Gap* (1935), and such comedy classics as BRINGING UP BABY (1938). During the forties he played in routine comedies; a notable exception was *A Stolen Life* (1946) with Bette DAVIS. For the next decade he worked mainly on stage and for television, returning to films in the sixties.

**RUGGLES,** WESLEY (1889–1972), US director, brother of Charles RUGGLES, began his film career in 1914 as one of Mack SENNETT'S KEYSTONE Kops. As a director he came to the fore in the early sound era with a number of films for RKO. He was with PARAMOUNT for several years, becoming particularly associated with romantic comedies featuring such players as Claudette COLBERT, Jean ARTHUR, Carole LOMBARD, Fred MACMURRAY, and Melvyn DOUGLAS; they include *The Bride Comes Home* (1935), *I Met Him in Paris* (1937), and *True Confession* (1937). *Invitation to Happiness* (1939) was an emotional drama and featured the director's brother in a straight role as a boxing trainer. For METRO-GOLDWYN-MAYER he directed *Somewhere I'll Find You* (1942), co-starring Clark GABLE and Lana TURNER, which continued the more dramatic trend, but he returned to comedy with *You Belong to Me* (1941, *Good Morning, Doctor* in GB), with Barbara STANWYCK and Henry FONDA, and *Slightly Dangerous* (1943), with Lana Turner and Robert YOUNG. In 1944 he was appointed director of MGM British productions: and for RANK he directed the Sid Field musical comedy *London Town* (1946). Ruggles occasionally produced his own films, including *Sing You Sinners* (1938) and *Arizona* (1940).

**RUMAN,** SIG (*c.*1884–1967), German character actor, who also appeared as Siegfried Rumann. He began his career on the stage in Germany, then on Broadway, and made his first film appearance in *Marie Galante* (1934). Over a period of more than thirty years, he played in numerous Hollywood films, and was particularly adept as a comedy foil demanding injured pride or ruffled dignity. He was a male counterpart to Margaret DUMONT in several MARX BROTHERS films (A NIGHT AT THE OPERA, 1935; A DAY AT THE RACES, 1937; *A Night in Casablanca*, 1946); but above all, perhaps, he is remembered for his performance as one of the three Russian trade officials in NINOTCHKA (1939).

**RUSHES,** a print of one day's unedited filming, quickly prepared for viewing and evaluation on the following day. In the US they are sometimes called 'dailies'.

Exposed film is usually processed overnight at the laboratory and the takes identified by the director as good are printed and returned to the editor. He synchronizes each take with its soundtrack (on a separate magnetic film) and the rushes are then viewed by the director and others in a screening room close to the studio, often during the lunch break. It is an unwritten rule, often broken, that rushes are never viewed by persons outside the production staff, since embarrassing errors have yet to be removed. As soon as the editor begins to cut them, the rushes are re-named the CUTTING COPY or work print. (See also DOUBLE HEAD.)

**RUSPOLI,** MARIO (1925–   ), French director, has become known, along with Jean ROUCH, as one of the major exponents of CINÉMA-VÉRITÉ.

His first film, *Les Hommes de la baleine* (1956), was scripted by Chris MARKER and depicted the life of men aboard a whaler. In *Les Inconnus de la terre* (1961) he observed the Lozère peasantry, their living and working conditions; *Regards sur la folie* (1961) examined various aspects of life in a psychiatric hospital. All his films bear witness to a hope that from patient and minute observation, with the conscious participation of the subject, as in *Le Dernier Verre* (1964), the truth will emerge.

**RUSSELL,** JANE (1921–   ), US actress, made famous by Howard HUGHES's exploitation of her generous physical proportions in *The Outlaw* (made 1940/1; released 1949) which achieved notoriety through its battle against the censors; its victory initiated the fifties vogue for films built around large-bosomed stars. But Jane Russell had other resources as an actress and her tough wise-cracking style was used to good effect in two comedy Westerns with Bob HOPE, *The Paleface* (1948) and *Son of Paleface* (1952), and in GENTLEMEN PREFER BLONDES (1953); more recent appearances on television confirm her aimiability and professionalism.

**RUSSELL,** KEN (1927–   ), British director, a former ballet dancer, actor, and photographer, made three amateur films in 1958, notably *Amelia and the Angel*. He then worked for BBC television, initially concentrating on films about contemporary artists, then embarked on his justly admired series on composers, each film increasingly conveying a personal conception of the subject's psychology. In *Prokofiev* (1961) only the composer's hands were seen, in *Elgar* (1962) an actor portrayed the composer in several scenes, and *The Debussy Film* (1965) was a fully dramatized biography. Meanwhile Russell had made his first cinema film, *French Dressing* (1963), a frothy comedy with a gaiety largely created by visual tricks derived from television commercials, adeptly employed by Russell some time before Richard LESTER gave them currency in feature films. Returning to television, Russell furthered his reputation with biographies of *Isadora Duncan* (1966) and Dante Gabriel Rossetti, *Dante's Inferno* (1967). His second feature, *Billion Dollar Brain* (1967), involving politics and espionage, was unsuited to his particular talent. For television Russell made a beautiful and restrained film on the last years of Delius, *A Song of Summer* (1968), and *Dance of the Seven Veils* (1970), a deliberately tendentious view of Richard Strauss.

The commercial success of Russell's film version of D. H. Lawrence's *Women in Love* (1969) established him in cinema and he thereafter produced his own films. *The Music Lovers* (1970), a voyeuristic account of Tchaikovsky's marriage and death, was followed by a sporadically brilliant if overblown interpretation of Aldous Huxley's *The Devils of Loudun*, *The Devils* (1971). The same year he transformed a modest English stage musical into an extravagant homage to Busby BERKELEY in *The Boy Friend*, and he gave explosive treatment to the life of the artist Gaudier-Brzeska in *Savage Messiah* (1972). He returned to the subject of musical composition in *Mahler* (1974), a somewhat morbid fictionalized biography.

Russell's taste for deliberate sensationalism has perhaps obscured his considerable originality and flair. His excursions into the psychology of artists have become increasingly exaggerated: at the same time his work provides acute comments on the cruelties arising from sexual inadequacies.

He has also shown a happy aptitude for picking unlikely actresses and drawing remarkable performances from them—Vivien Pickles in *Isadora Duncan*, Eleanor Bron in *Women in Love*, Twiggy in *The Boy Friend*, for example. However controversial he makes himself, his originality and talent are unusually refreshing in British cinema.

**RUSSELL, ROSALIND** (1912–    ), US actress whose first starring role was in *The Casino Murder Case* (1935). *The Women* (1939) revealed her talent for biting, incisive comedy which she developed further as the wise-cracking reporter battling with her ex-husband (Cary GRANT) in HIS GIRL FRIDAY (1940). Her real wit and drive, fast pace, and brittle humour led to a number of sophisticated comedy roles in films like *My Sister Eileen* (1942), which later became a successful stage musical for her. Ventures into more serious roles, in *Sister Kenny* (1946) and *Mourning Becomes Electra* (1947) for example, have been less happy. Her best performances of recent years were in *Auntie Mame* (1958) and *Gypsy* (1962).

**RUTHERFORD, MARGARET** (1892–1972), British actress, coming comparatively late to the stage, always specialized in character roles. Outstanding among her screen portrayals of eccentric Englishwomen are those in *Blithe Spirit* (1945), PASSPORT TO PIMLICO (1949), and Anthony ASQUITH's elegant version of *The Importance of Being Earnest* (1952). She played the detective Miss Marples in several Agatha Christie adaptations and was serious and moving as Mistress Quickly in Orson WELLES's CAMPANADAS A MEDIANOCHE (*Chimes at Midnight*, 1966). She was awarded the DBE in 1967.

**RUTTMANN, WALTER** (1887–1941), German director, studied architecture in Zürich and Munich, then painting with Angelo Jank and Übelohde. He worked for a short time as a poster designer before becoming interested in films and a leading member of the AVANT-GARDE. His first film, *Die tönende Welle* (1921), was an experiment with sound. His next work *Opus I, II, III, IV* (1921–4), consisting partly of a display of shapes vaguely reminiscent of X-ray photographs, created a kind of visual music and revealed Ruttmann's musical inclinations. For Fritz LANG he directed the dream sequence (Falkentraum) in Part I of DIE NIBELUNGEN (1924), and he collaborated with Lotte REINIGER on *Die Abenteuer des Prinzen Achmed* (1926).

BERLIN, DIE SYMPHONIE EINER GROSSSTADT (1927) marked the beginning of a transition from ABSTRACT film to DOCUMENTARY; it was the first of a number of film studies of various towns by Ruttmann and others. But after MELODIE DER WELT (*World Melody*, 1929), his first sound film, and *Feind im Blut* (1931), he assembled his ultimate experiment *Wochenende* (*Weekend*, 1931), a montage of sounds without images. He followed this with an unsuccessful attempt at a fiction film, *Acciaio* (1933), made in Italy and scripted by Pirandello. Thereafter he devoted himself to documentary, remaining in Germany under the Nazis and directing powerful PROPAGANDA-style films on armaments, including *Deutsche Panzer* (*German Tanks*, 1940), as well as on towns. He also acted as adviser to Leni RIEFENSTAHL on the editing of OLYMPIA (1938) and published some articles on film theory. He was killed in action.

Almost all Ruttmann's work, abstract or documentary, relies on the patterns of movement created by editing images which are chosen for their formal qualities rather than their literal meaning.

**RYAN, ROBERT** (1913–73), US actor, made his first film appearance in *Golden Gloves* (1940) and was featured in a number of RKO films, including several directed by Edward DMYTRYK, such as *Crossfire* (1947). Among other leading roles were those in *The Woman on the Beach* (Jean RENOIR, 1947), *The Boy with Green Hair* (Joseph LOSEY, 1948), and *The Set-Up* (Robert WISE, 1949). His performance in the latter particularly attracted attention: possibly his earlier boxing experience stood him in good stead. He could be chilling in a villainous role, as in *Bad Day at Black Rock* (1954), or as evil incarnate in *Billy Budd* (1962), and displayed laconic but assertive masculinity in *The Professionals* (Richard BROOKS, 1966), *The Dirty Dozen* (Robert ALDRICH, 1967), and THE WILD BUNCH (Sam PECKINPAH, 1969).

# S

**SABOTAGE** (*A Woman Alone* in US), GB, 1936. 1¼hr. *Dir* Alfred Hitchcock; *prod* Michael Balcon, Ivor Montagu for Gaumont-British; *scr* Charles Bennett, from *The Secret Agent* by Joseph Conrad; *ph* Bernard Knowles; *cast* Sylvia Sidney (Sylvia Verloc), Oscar Homolka (Verloc), Desmond Tester (Sylvia's brother), John Loder (Ted, the detective).

Verloc, ostensibly a cinema manager, sends his young brother-in-law to deliver a parcel which is in fact a disguised bomb. The plan is mistimed and the bomb explodes in a bus, killing the boy. Verloc's wife realizes the truth and stabs her husband: the manner of his death is concealed by an explosion at the cinema and Sylvia finds consolation with the detective.

Although HITCHCOCK considers *Sabotage* one of his less successful films, largely because of deficiencies in the casting, it demonstrates his unusual skill at creating tension by building up single images with camera movements and cutting.

His previous film *The Secret Agent* (1936) has no connection with the Conrad novel on which *Sabotage* is based; confusion may also arise between *Sabotage* and *Saboteur*, filmed in Hollywood in 1942.

**SABU** (1925–63), Indian actor who scored popular success after being discovered by Robert FLAHERTY for the title role in ELEPHANT BOY (1936). He maintained this popularity in further Alexander KORDA productions, *The Drum* (1938), THE THIEF OF BAGHDAD (1940), and *The Jungle Book* (1942); but as he grew up and gained weight his fame declined, and apart from *Black Narcissus* (1947) most of his later appearances were in minor films.

**SADOUL**, GEORGES (1904–67), French critic and historian. An early member of the Surrealist group with Aragon and Breton (see SURREALISM), he remained their close friend although by the mid-thirties he had taken up a firmly Marxist stance which coloured his critical approach to the end of his life. In 1945 he became general secretary of the Fédération Française de Ciné-Clubs and began his weekly film review in *Les Lettres françaises*, which he continued until his death. He also contributed to

*L'Écran français*. From 1945 until the mid-fifties (when CAHIERS DU CINÉMA changed direction) Sadoul stood with André BAZIN as the main figure and inspiration of French film criticism: his chief contribution in later years was in calling attention to the newly-emerging cinema of Third World countries. Even those who reject his critical bias recognize his role as a historian of cinema. Concurrently with a number of books on various special areas, he wrote the first large-scale history, *Histoire générale du cinéma* (Paris, 1946–52) in six volumes, left unfinished. Two small paperbacks, *Dictionnaire des films* and *Dictionnaire des cinéastes* (Paris, 1965), invaluable tools for any student of film, were the precursors of many larger encyclopedias.

**SAFETY FILM** (commonly known as acetate) was introduced for narrow gauge amateur film STOCKS before the First World War but failed to gain acceptance for professional 35mm film-making until 1937. NITRATE, despite its high flammability, was cheaper and generally stronger than cellulose tri-acetate. It took until 1951 for safety bases to replace nitrate base for all types and gauges of film stock.

**SAFETY SHOT,** an extra TAKE of a scene, made to protect the production against damage to the good take already shot; or an extra angle or viewpoint of a scene, made when there is some doubt that the existing angles will cut together properly. The 'danger' against which the safety shot protects is that of having to spend a great deal of money to re-shoot after sets have been destroyed and actors' contracts have expired.

**SAGAN**, LEONTINE (1899–1974), German director, trained as a stage director with Max REINHARDT and Barnovsky and worked as a teacher in Reinhardt's school. She became the head of the English Theatre in Berlin and played the leading role in many of its productions. Her first film, MÄDCHEN IN UNIFORM (1931), adapted from the play *Gestern und Heute* which she had produced on the stage, met with a *succès de scandale* chiefly by reason of its subject-matter. She directed a second film, *Men of Tomorrow* (1932) for KORDA in England, then returned to stage direction and production in England, South Africa, and Rhodesia.

***SALAIRE DE LA PEUR, Le*** (*The Wages of Fear*), France/Italy, 1953. 2¼hr. *Dir, scr* Henri-Georges Clouzot, from the novel by Georges Arnaud; *prod* Filmsonor-CICC/Vera Film-Fono Roma; *ph* Armand Thirard; *mus* Georges Auric; *cast* Yves Montand (Mario), Charles Vanel (Jo), Vera Clouzot (Linda), Folco Lulli (Luigi), Peter van Eyck (Bimba).

Four down-and-outs in a sleazy South American town agree to risk transporting two lorry-loads of nitro-glycerine, needed to blow up a burning oil-well three hundred miles away. CLOUZOT, working in the South of France, created perfectly the impression of tropical heat and filth, and used the sustained tension of the journey to examine his characters and their shifting relationships. The film was very successful: it won the Grand Prix at the 1953 CANNES festival and went on general release outside France.

***SALT FOR SVANETIA*** see DJIM CHUANTE

***SALT OF THE EARTH***, US, 1953. 1½hr. *Dir* Herbert J. Biberman; *prod* Paul Jarrico; *scr* Michael Wilson; *ph* Simon Lazarus; *cast* Rosaura Revueltas (Esperanza), Juan Chacon (Ramon), Will Geer (Sheriff).

A semi-documentary in which Mexican-American miners recreate their strike for equal pay and status with white workers, *Salt of the Earth* echoes the themes of NATIVE LAND (1942) and HURWITZ's *Strange Victory* (1949). It was sponsored by the International Union of Mine, Mill, and Smelter Workers, and director, producer, and writer were all victims of McCarthyism—BIBERMAN imprisoned as one of the Hollywood Ten, Jarrico and Wilson blacklisted (see UNAMERICAN ACTIVITIES). Few professional actors were used. The film met formidable opposition in both production and distribution, and Revueltas, a leading Mexican actress, was imprisoned.

***SALVATORE GIULIANO***, Italy, 1962. 2hr. *Dir* Francesco Rosi; *prod* Lux/Vides/Galatea; *scr* Rosi, Suso Cecchi d'Amico, Enzo Provenzale, Franco Solinas; *ph* Gianni Di Venanzo; *mus* Piero Piccioni; *cast* Frank Wolff (Pisciotta), Salvo Randone (judge), Federico Zardi (defence counsel), Pietro Cammarata (Giuliano Salvatore).

Giuliano Salvatore, a Sicilian outlaw who evaded the authorities for several years, was finally hunted down in 1950. ROSI's film takes the form of an investigation into his life and death, cutting flashbacks, reconstructions, interviews, and documentary evidence into his obsequies. It takes an objective yet severely critical stand in its analysis of the violence and corruption of Sicilian society, totally involving the spectator by means of DI VENANZO's probing camera. In the manner of NEO-REALISM (to which Rosi adhered after its full impetus had slackened) most of the actors were non-professionals.

The film's outspoken denunciation of officialdom created a furore in Italy and there were reports of threats against those concerned with

*Salvatore Giuliano* (Francesco Rosi, 1962)

its production. Certainly it was instrumental in securing a public inquiry by the government of Palermo into the activities of the Mafia.

**SAMMA NO AJI** (*An Autumn Afternoon*), Japan, 1962. Agfacolor; 2hr. *Dir* Yasujiro Ozu; *prod* Shochiku; *scr* Ozu, Kogo Noda; *ph* Yushun Atsuta; *des* Tatsuo Hamada; *mus* Takanobu Saito; *cast* Chishu Ryu (Shuhei Hirayama), Shima Iwashita (Michiko Hirayama), Shinichiro Mikami (Kazuo Hirayama), Keiji Sada (Koichi Hirayama), Mariko Okada (Akiko Hirayama), Nabuo Nakamura (Shuzo Kawai), Kuniko Miyake (Nobuko Kawai).

One of OZU's last films which demonstrates the refinement of his spare technique, *Samma no aji* concerns three widowers, one happily remarried to a much younger wife, one unhappily clinging to his equally discontented daughter, and one allowing himself to drift into the same miserable position.

The theme is developed by Ozu's characteristic method of examining minutely, in very formalized compositions, the interaction of the characters involved. Dramatic crises are avoided: the film's power lies in its patient, sympathetic, and absorbing observation.

**SAMOILOVA,** TATIANA (1934–    ), Russian actress, the daughter of the actor Yevgeni Samoilov (who played the lead in SHCHORS, 1939), she originally trained for ballet and her particular beauty and approach to acting are reminiscent of this. In LETYAT ZHURAVLI (*The Cranes are Flying*, 1957) her moving performance made her one of the few Soviet actresses to achieve international fame. She also appeared in the title role of ANNA KARENINA (1967).

**SANDERS,** GEORGE (1906–72), US actor, born in Russia and brought up in Britain, went to Hollywood in 1937 and, with the help of his English accent, established himself as a valuable supporting actor with an effective, if limited, flair for playing attractive, supercilious cads. His success as a romantic hero in *Rage of Heaven* (1941), opposite Ingrid BERGMAN, and in a serious drama, *The Moon and Sixpence* (1942), did not materially affect his routine casting as stylishly villainous Nazis or witty rakes. His particular forte was most successfully deployed in ALL ABOUT EVE (1950). Apart from the musical *Call Me Madam* (1953), his later films gave him little opportunity to do more than repeat his usual elegant type, but, speaking the role of Shere Khan the tiger in Walt DISNEY's *Jungle Book* (1967), he was again an impeccable villain.

**SANG DES BÊTES,** Le, France, 1949. 20min. *Dir, scr* Georges Franju; *prod* Forces et Voix de la France; *ph* Marcel Fradetal; *comm* Jean Painlevé, spoken by Nicole Ladmiral and Georges Hubert; *mus* Joseph Kosma, 'La Mer' sung by Charles Trenet.

FRANJU's first film uses the ritual of a slaughterhouse interspersed with aspects of Paris and the recently exposed atrocities of the Second World War to comment on modern city existence, and, by extension, the whole human condition. The juxtaposition of imagery establishes the constant presence of death beneath the daily surface of life.

**SANG D'UN POÈTE,** Le, France, 1930. 1¼hr. *Dir, scr, ed* Jean Cocteau; *prod* Vicomte de Noailles; *ph* Georges Périnal; *des* Jean d'Eaubonne; *mus* Georges Auric; *cast* Lee Miller, Pauline Carton, Odette Talazac, Enrique Rivero, Jean Desbordes, Barbette, Lucien Jager.

COCTEAU's first film is an allegorical fantasy that explores the process of artistic creation. The opening shot of a collapsing building is arrested, to be completed at the end of the film: the events within this metaphor are, it is implied, taking place in a split second of exterior time. The poet recognizes his muse, denies and flees it, dies and is resurrected twice, becomes one with it: the work of art is autonomous and inescapable.

*Le Sang d'un poète* has often been critically considered alongside BUÑUEL's UN CHIEN ANDALOU (1928) and L'ÂGE D'OR (1930); the contemporaneity of the three films, and their dealing with subconscious urges and dream-like imagery, links them, but Cocteau disavowed the influence of SURREALISM, and the Surrealists rejected his conscious structuring of the apparently irrational.

**SANJINES,** JORGE (1936–    ), Bolivian director whose first film, *Revolucion* (1963), was a documentary celebrating the social changes being made in Bolivia by the nationalist government of Paz Estenssoro. In 1965 Sanjines was appointed director of the National Film Institute where, with his collaborators Oscar Soria and Ricardo Rada, he continued to make films. *Ukamau* (1966) passionately depicted the exploitation of the Indian peasant majority by the rich white minority via the mestizo middle class: official outrage caused the disbanding of the Institute and Sanjines with his group set up an independent production company, Ukamau Films.

*Yawar Malku* (*Blood of the Condor*, 1969) attacked an alleged campaign of sterilization carried out on the Quechua Indians by a detachment of the US Peace Corps. Using a blend of documentary and neo-realist techniques, the film makes an emotionally charged plea for the preservation of Indian national and cultural independence. *La Noche de San Juan, o el Cor-*

*aje del Pueblo* (*The Night of San Juan, or The Pueblo's Courage*, 1971) reconstructed the bloody siege of the Siglo XX mines by the army under General Barrientos. Soon after the film's release, the government again shifted to the right, film-making in Bolivia came to a halt, and Sanjines took refuge in Chile.

***SANSHO DAYU*** (*Sansho the Bailiff*), Japan, 1955. 2hr. *Dir* Kenji Mizoguchi; *prod* Daiei; *scr* Yohiro Fuji, Yoshikata Yoda, from a story by Nori Ogai; *ph* Kazuo Miyagawa; *des* Kisaku Itoh; *mus* Fumio Hayasaka; *cast* Eitaro Shindo (Sansho), Kinuyo Tanaka (mother), Yoshiaki Hanayaki (Zushio), Kyoko Kagawa (Anjo), Ichiro Sugai (Sansho's son), Masao Chimizu (father).

Zushio and his sister, children of a noble family, are abducted, sold into slavery, and ruthlessly exploited by the tyrannical bailiff Sansho. Their mother is sold into prostitution. Zushio grows up to accept the brutality of society, but his sister adheres to the humane principles of their father and sacrifices herself to aid her brother's escape from slavery. The mother, blind, crippled, and living alone in abject poverty, is finally reunited with Zushio.

MIZOGUCHI unerringly re-creates the beauty and savagery of feudal Japan seen from his characteristically humanist viewpoint. As so often in his films, the patient love of women is the grace that will redeem men's cruelty; his steady compassion is conveyed through his unique style: limited use of close-ups, extended sequences where a delicately mobile camera obviates the need for cutting, and a fastidious withdrawal to the middle-distance view in scenes of violence. His painter's eye endows eleventh-century Japanese society with a richness that avoids opulence, the refinement of his vision producing an impression of total authenticity.

**SÁRA**, SÁNDOR (1933– ), Hungarian cameraman, a founder member of the BÁLASZ BÉLA STUDIO, whose lucid and controlled camerawork is closely identified with the Hungarian 'new wave' of the late sixties. He photographed István GAÁL's *Pályamunkások* (*Surfacemen*, 1957) and has maintained a strong association with this director. Sára has also worked with István SZABÓ, on APA (*Father*, 1967), with Ferenc KÓSA on TÍZEZER NAP (*Ten Thousand Suns*, 1967), and with Ferenc Kardos. In 1962 Sára made *Cigányok* (*Gipsies*), one of the most successful of the Studio's output of shorts, and he wrote, directed, and photographed the imaginative *Feldobott kő* (*The Upthrown Stone*, 1968) and the shorter *Pro patria* (1970), but he has continued to work as cameraman for other directors, notably on the colourful *Szinbád* (*Sinbad*, 1971).

**SARNE**, MIKE (1940– ), British actor and director, studied acting at the Max REINHARDT Seminar in Vienna, and appeared in German, French, and Italian films. His first British film was *No Kidding* (1960). He returned to films after a period in pop music, with *Every Day's a Holiday* (1964). In 1965 he directed his first film *Road to St Tropez*, since when he has directed *Joanna* (1968) and, in Hollywood, *Myra Breckinridge* (1970).

**SARRIS**, ANDREW, American film critic and teacher. In 1955 he joined the editorial board of FILM CULTURE, and led the American revaluation of the Hollywood film through his application of the AUTEUR THEORY, which resulted in the erection of a hierarchy of directors on the model of CAHIERS DU CINÉMA. He has been a film critic for *The Village Voice*, and edited *Cahiers du Cinéma in English*, 1965–7.

**SATIE**, ERIK (1866–1925), French avant-garde composer whose accompanying score for ENTR'ACTE (1924) is typical of his ironical declarations about music as ephemeral, emotionless, and without meaning. His piano piece 'Gymnopédies', used by Louis MALLE on the sound-track of LE FEU FOLLET (1963), highlights the hero's despair by its very emptiness and links the modern adaptation to the twenties setting of the original novel.

***SATURDAY NIGHT AND SUNDAY MORNING***, GB, 1960. 1½hr. *Dir* Karel Reisz; *prod* Harry Saltzman, Tony Richardson for Woodfall Films; *scr* Alan Sillitoe from his novel; *ph* Freddie Francis; *des* Ted Marshall; *ed* Seth Holt; *mus* Johnny Dankworth; *cast* Albert Finney (Arthur), Shirley Anne Field (Doreen), Rachel Roberts (Brenda), Hylda Baker (Aunt Ada).

Alan Sillitoe's realistic story of a Nottingham factory worker brought a freshness of approach to the British cinema. Albert FINNEY, in his first major film role, played the rebellious Arthur Seaton with energy and humour, and REISZ's sympathetic direction finely evoked the industrial setting and its effect on human relations.

**SAVILLE**, VICTOR (1897– ), British director-producer, entered films in 1916 as a salesman. As a director for GAUMONT-BRITISH he was responsible for a number of the company's successes, covering a wide range from musicals including *Sunshine Susie* (1931) and Jessie MATTHEWS vehicles (*Evergreen*, 1934; *First a Girl*, 1935; *It's Love Again*, 1936), to dramas such as *I Was a Spy* (1933) and *The Iron Duke* (1935) with George ARLISS. There followed a period with KORDA's LONDON FILM PRODUCTIONS for which he produced and directed *Storm in a*

*Teacup, Action for Slander* (both 1937), and *South Riding* (1938). He next became a producer with METRO-GOLDWYN-MAYER British Studios and was associate producer of *The Citadel* (1938) and *Goodbye Mr Chips* (1939) before going to Hollywood where he made a number of films for MGM, occasionally returning to Britain, where he produced *The Greengage Summer* (1961, *Loss of Innocence* in US). For a time he was an independent producer.

**SCARFACE,** US, 1932. 1½hr. *Dir* Howard Hawks; *prod* Howard Hughes; *scr* Ben Hecht, W. R. Burnett, John Lee Machin, Seton I. Miller, from the novel by Armitage Trail; *ph* Lee Garmes, L. W. O'Connell; *cast* Paul Muni (Tony Camonte), Ann Dvorak (Cesca Camonte), Karen Morley (Poppy), Osgood Perkins (Johnny Lovo), Boris Karloff (Gafney), C. Henry Gordon (Guarino), George Raft (Rinaldo).

'Scarface' rises from working as bodyguard to Prohibition ganglord Johnny Lovo to being his second-in-command, then orders Lovo's killing and takes over his rackets and his mistress. Eventually he is cornered and shot, and only the mistress survives the gangland murders.

Except for the ending, the film is based closely on the career of Al CAPONE, whose nickname was 'Scarface'. It depicts actual gangland incidents such as the killing of Jim Colismo (opening sequence) and the bloody St Valentine's Day Massacre. Intended by Howard HUGHES to be the 'gangster film to end all gangster films', it was not only more elaborately produced but also contained greater destruction, more gunplay, acts of cruelty, and gang deaths than any other early GANGSTER FILM.

The film got into immediate CENSORSHIP trouble, for public resentment against the amorality and violence of gangster films had reached its height, and the film seemed the most extreme example of the cycle. New York censors would not approve the film's release until certain violent scenes had been cut, moral judgements emphasized, and a subtitle 'The Shame of the Nation' added, while a number of cities banned showings altogether. Furthermore, critics found it inferior to its predecessors, LITTLE CAESAR (1930, also based on Al Capone's career) and PUBLIC ENEMY (1931). Hughes quickly withdrew the film from circulation, and it has rarely been seen in the US since.

In France the film made an instant impression, and after the war it exerted strong influence on NOUVELLE VAGUE film-makers. Today it stands as one of the classic gangster films; MUNI's vicious Scarface has an energy and arrogance that commands interest throughout. George RAFT gives a strong portrait of a killer, and incessant coin-flipping was to remain his characteristic gesture.

**SCARLET EMPRESS, The,** US, 1934. 1½hr. *Dir* Josef von Sternberg; *prod* Paramount; *scr* Manuel Komroff, based on a diary of Catherine the Great; *ph* Bert Glennon; *des* Hans Dreier; *mus* arranged by John M. Leipold and W. Frank Harling, from Tchaikovsky and Mendelssohn; *cast* Marlene Dietrich (Sophia Frederica/Catherine II), John Lodge (Count Alexei), Sam Jaffe (Grand Duke Peter), Louise Dresser (Empress Elizabeth).

Marlene DIETRICH, in the most bizarre of her STERNBERG performances, played Sophia Frederica, brought from Germany to Russia to become the wife of the mad Grand Duke Peter, gradually hardening in nature until she assumes the throne as Catherine II. A film of pictorial splendour and quasi-symphonic movement, it is an extraordinary achievement, particularly remarkable for the grotesquerie of its imagery, the array of statuary by Peter Ballbusch, and the Byzantine-style icons and portraits by Richard Kollorsz.

**SCEICCO BIANCO, Lo** (*The White Sheikh*), Italy, 1952. 1½hr. *Dir* Federico Fellini; *prod* OFI and PDC; *scr* Fellini, Tullio Pinelli from a story by Fellini, Pinelli, and Antonioni; *ph* Arturo Gallea; *des* Fellini; *mus* Nino Rota; *cast* Alberto Sordi (the White Sheikh), Leopoldo Trieste (Ivan), Brunella Bovo (Wanda), Giulietta Masina (Cabiria).

Wanda and Ivan, newly married, arrive in Rome to attend a papal audience with Ivan's family. Wanda becomes infatuated with the White Sheikh, hero of a photo-strip cartoon. She nearly misses the papal audience to go and see him, but is rapidly disillusioned.

This satire on the strip-cartoons published in the *fumetti* was FELLINI's first film as sole director and his only farce, but his ambiguous blend of humour and sympathy is already apparent.

**SCHAFFNER, FRANKLIN L.** (1920– ), US director, who following five years' war service became assistant editor of a series of short documentaries on the war for THE MARCH OF TIME. After working in the theatre and for television, directing several television documentaries, including a much acclaimed version of *The Caine Mutiny Court Martial* and Jacqueline Kennedy's tour of the White House, and making the 'Defenders' series, Schaffner turned to cinema. His first feature, *The Stripper* (1963, *Woman of Summer* in GB), starred Joanne WOODWARD in a sensitive study of an unsuccessful showgirl's affair with a younger man. *The Best Man* (1964), written by Gore Vidal and starring Henry FONDA, dealt with the less publicized aspects of a political convention. Schaffner's professionalism is evident in his ability to handle a variety of themes with energy and skill. His other films include *The War Lord* (1965), PLANET OF THE APES (1968), *Patton: Lust for Glory* (1969), and *Nicholas and Alexandra* (1971).

**SCHARY,** DORE (1905– ), US writer and producer, with a varied background as actor, journalist, and playwright, became a scriptwriter in 1932 and won an OSCAR for *Boys' Town* (1938). He ran a low-budget production unit at METRO-GOLDWYN-MAYER 1942–5 and was then lent by David O. SELZNICK to RKO where he was production head until Howard HUGHES took over the company in 1948. He returned to MGM as a vice-president and was made studio head after Louis B. MAYER's resignation in 1951. Schary's economical film-making was in striking contrast to Mayer's lavish style, but he was unable to save MGM from the decline common to Hollywood studios in the early fifties. Dismissed in 1956, he returned to writing plays, including *Sunrise at Campobello* (1958), has made occasional films as an independent, and wrote a book, *Case History of a Movie*, on the making of *The Next Voice You Hear* (William WELLMAN, 1950).

**SCHENCK,** JOSEPH (1877–1961), US executive. A Russian immigrant, Schenck worked as a pharmacist before he and his brother Nicholas began acquiring amusement parks. Both brothers joined the Loew's exhibition company, but Joseph left in 1917 to produce films for Lewis SELZNICK. After being president of UNITED ARTISTS, Schenck started his own production company, Twentieth Century Pictures, in 1933 with Darryl F. ZANUCK and served as board chairman of TWENTIETH CENTURY-FOX following the 1935 merger. Schenck was jailed in 1941 on income tax charges, but was pardoned in 1947 and re-established himself in Hollywood, winning an OSCAR in 1952 for 'services to the industry'. In 1953 he became a partner with Mike TODD in his Magna theatre and production company.

**SCHENCK,** NICHOLAS (1881–1969), US executive, Russian-born, went with his brother Joseph to America, where they operated several amusement parks. Their associations with film exhibitors led to their joining Marcus LOEW's theatre-owning group, later called Loew's Incorporated. Nicholas became company secretary in 1910, ascending to the presidency in 1927 and finally to the board chairmanship in 1955, shortly before his retirement. As the major power at Loew's Incorporated, Schenck had an important influence over the output of METRO-GOLDWYN-MAYER, specifying the films which would be acceptable for exhibition in Loew's

theatres and controlling the business side of the studio's operations.

***SCHERBEN*** (*Shattered Fragments*), Germany, 1921. 1hr. *Dir, prod* Lupu Pick; *scr* Carl Mayer; *ph* Friedrich Weimann; *cast* Werner Krauss (father), Hermine Strassmann Witt (mother), Edith Bosca (daughter), Paul Otto (inspector).

A railway worker's family on a remote part of the track receive a visit from an inspector. His seduction of the railwayman's daughter has fatal consequences.

*Scherben* exemplifies both the principles and the limitations of the KAMMERSPIELFILM, using a conventionally melodramatic plot to convey psychological tension through images alone. Only one title is used, in the originally red-tinted closing sequence, and objects are burdened with powerful significance. An attempt is made to place the story in a wider social context with shots of rich train passengers enjoying a meal.

**SCHLESINGER,** JOHN (1925– ), British director, worked for BBC television on 'Tonight' and 'MONITOR' and in 1961 made the award-winning documentary *Terminus* for British Transport Films. His first major film was *A Kind of Loving* (1962), an urban social drama adapted from Stan Barstow's novel. *Billy Liar* (1963), although uneven in its transposition to the screen of Keith Waterhouse's north-country comedy, drew excellent performances from Tom COURTENAY and from Julie CHRISTIE, who also starred in Schlesinger's next two films. *Darling* (1965), set in the gilded world of fashionable society, parodied various cinematic styles—social reportage, newsreels, commercials; *Far from the Madding Crowd* (1967) failed to capture the tone of Hardy's tale. Schlesinger then went to America to make MIDNIGHT COWBOY (1970), a critical and commercial success, with a memorable performance by Dustin HOFFMAN and some compelling images of New York life. *Sunday, Bloody Sunday* (1971), set in London, was a fairly superficial examination of a triangular sexual relationship, redeemed in part by Peter FINCH's performance and in part by Schlesinger's presentation of a *barmitzvah*, a marvellous set-piece.

Schlesinger has a fine eye for the mood of the time and if he does not always fully penetrate its surface, he nevertheless achieves outstanding passages in all his films. The acting, too, is usually of the highest calibre.

**SCHLÖNDORFF,** VOLKER (1939– ), West German director, studied in Paris and worked for French television. He was assistant director to RESNAIS, MALLE, and MELVILLE before making his first film in Germany, *Der junge Törless* (1966). Adapted from the novel by Musil, the story deals with the reactions of a sensitive boy to the sadistic persecution of his boarding-school contemporaries. *Mord und Totschlag* (*A Degree of Murder*, 1967) was an uneasy blend of thriller and social comment, and *Michael Kohlhaas* (1969), adapted from a short story by Kleist, is an attempt to give a contemporary slant to a sixteenth-century story of a man's fight for justice. *Der plötzliche Reichtum der armen Leute von Kombach* (*The Sudden Fortune of the Poor People of Kombach*, 1971) is characteristic of Schlöndorff's work in being elegant and technically accomplished.

**SCHNEIDER,** ROMY (1938–    ), Austrian actress, real name Rosemarie Albach, achieved popularity in the 'Sissi' series (1955 onwards) and caught international attention in the VISCONTI episode of *Boccaccio '70* (1962). Notable among her films are LE PROCÈS (*The Trial*, Orson WELLES, 1963), *The Victors* (Carl FOREMAN, 1963), *The Cardinal* (Otto PREMINGER, 1964), *What's New, Pussycat?* (Clive DONNER, 1965), *10.30 pm Summer* (Jules DASSIN, 1966), and *The Assassination of Trotsky* (Joseph LOSEY, 1972). Her appeal to English and American directors lies in an unusual blend of exotic sensuality and intelligent toughness.

**SCHOEDSACK,** ERNEST B. (1893–    ), US cameraman/director, started as a cameraman at the KEYSTONE studios in 1914. He served in the Signal Corps film unit during the war, often filming in the front line, and after 1918 he travelled on documentary assignments. In Poland he met Merian C. COOPER and in 1925 they worked together on a full-length documentary *Grass*, which included spectacular though hardly compassionate footage of migrating tribesmen and their herds crossing a torrential river. Following on the success of NANOOK OF THE NORTH (1922), PARAMOUNT distributed *Grass* with comparable financial reward and commissioned CHANG (1927), which was equally successful. From 1931 Cooper and Schoedsack jointly directed KING KONG (1933); Schoedsack directed alone thereafter, producing little of note except *Mighty Joe Young* (1949), a successor to *King Kong*.

**SCHORM,** EVALD (1931–    ), Czech director, began his artistic career as a singer in the Czechoslovak army opera. He went to FAMU, the Prague film school, and after graduating in 1962 started working in the documentary studios. He made several short films which established a reputation for him as an intellectual and philosophical force in the new generation of filmmakers. His first feature film, *Každý den odvahu* (*Everyday Courage*, 1964), revealed many of the characteristics of his later work. The CINÉMA-VÉRITÉ style which so profoundly influenced his generation was almost entirely dispensed with; but he did not replace it with formal innovations. Using professional actors and a serious, traditional dramatic form, he dealt with the story of a working family and the betrayal of ideals within it. The film aroused violent official criticism and condemnation: then it was awarded a critics' prize, which Schorm for a time was forbidden to receive. Finally, acclaim abroad forced its acceptance at home.

The theme of betrayal was taken up in his next feature film, *Návrat ztraceného syna* (*The Return of the Prodigal Son*, 1966), dealing with the dangerous topic of an attempted suicide, in which he again concerned himself less with formal considerations than with a philosophical inquiry into the causes of betrayal. In *Pět Holek na krku* (*Five Girls to Deal With/Saddled with Five Girls*, 1967), about the apparently close friendship of five teenagers, he returned to the question of human motivation. In 1966 he met the writer Josef Skvorecky while they were both taking part in NĚMEC'S O SLAVNOSTI A HOSTECH, and together they devised *Farářuv konec* (*End of a Priest*, 1969). Described by Skvorecky as a morality-farce, it was delayed by the authorities, but released later in the year. Schorm's next film, however, also completed in 1969, *Den sedmý, osmá noc* (*Seventh Day, Eighth Night*), was banned in the spring of 1970.

Together with Němec and CHYTILOVÁ, Schorm won a place as leader of one wing of Czechoslovakia's new wave of the sixties. His subtlety and seriousness, his lanky figure and prematurely grey hair have earned him the title of Grey Eminence among his contemporaries. It seems appropriate that his role in *O Slavnosti a hostech* should have been that of the Guest Who Refused to be Happy.

**SCHÜFFTAN,** EUGEN (1893–    ), German cameraman, first studied architecture, painting, and sculpture. He began working in films about 1920, concentrating on special effects, and developed the SCHÜFFTAN PROCESS first used in Fritz LANG'S METROPOLIS (1927). He photographed several more films, including MENSCHEN AM SONNTAG (1929), before leaving Germany in 1932. He became a respected, cosmopolitan figure of cinema (credited in France as Eugène Schuftan, in the US as Eugene Shuftan), particularly admired for the subtlety of his lighting effects. Notable films on which he has worked include *L'Atlantide* (1932), QUAI DES BRUMES (1938), *Le Drame de Shanghai* (1938), LA TÊTE CONTRE LES MURS (1958), LES YEUX SANS VISAGE (1959), THE HUSTLER (1961), for which he was awarded an OSCAR, and *Lilith* (1964).

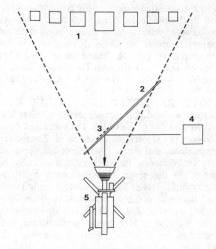

1 Full-size set
2 Semi-reflective mirror
3 Mask
4 Model
5 Camera

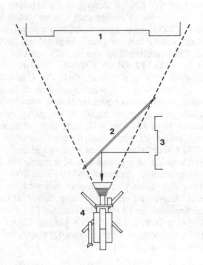

1 Full-size set lower floor only
2 Fully silvered mirror with silvering scraped
  away to allow camera view of set 1
3 Model of upper floors placed to align in
  mirror with set 1
4 Camera

**SCHÜFFTAN PROCESS,** a means of combining life-size action with models or artwork, named after its inventor, Eugen SCHÜFFTAN. A mirror mounted in front of the camera at an angle of 45 degrees to the optical axis both reflects light and allows light to pass through. Beyond the mirror, in line with the camera axis, is placed the model or artwork, which could be painted or photographic. A full-size detail of the set is placed at 90 degrees to the camera so that it is reflected into the camera lens by the mirror. A mask is placed on the back of the mirror over that area from which only the reflected image is required; the rest of the model or artwork remains visible through the mirror.

Thus, the complete scene is shot as a composite at the shooting stage rather than being combined optically by, say, travelling MATTE processes. The disadvantage of Schüfftan shots, especially when using the alternative method of a fully-coated mirror from which part of the silvering is scraped away to allow the model to show through, is that it is very time-consuming. It is therefore now obsolete, having been replaced by optical processes and other special EFFECTS. Well-known films in which it was employed include LANG's METROPOLIS (1927) and HITCHCOCK's BLACKMAIL (1929).

**SCHULBERG,** B. P. (1892–1957), US executive. Former reporter and studio publicity director, Schulberg became famous as an independent film producer and discoverer of the 'It' girl, Clara BOW. From 1925 to 1932 he was studio general manager of PARAMOUNT and, in later years, produced films for COLUMBIA and David O. SELZNICK.

**SCHULBERG,** BUDD (1914– ), US author and scriptwriter, son of B. P. SCHULBERG. He satirized the Hollywood in which he was brought up in *What Makes Sammy Run?* (1941), a novel about a dynamic but vulgar movie mogul. *The Disenchanted* (New York, 1950; London, 1969) is a fictional account of the last Hollywood years of F. Scott FITZGERALD. Schulberg's other works include *The Harder They Fall* (filmed in 1956), a musical, novels from his own film scripts, and stories, several of which have been adapted for the screen. Among his most important work in the cinema are the scripts for ON THE WATERFRONT (1954) and A FACE IN THE CROWD (1957).

**SCIUSCIÀ** (*Shoeshine*), Italy, 1946. 1½ hr. *Dir* Vittorio De Sica; *prod* Paolo W. Tamburella; *scr* Cesare Zavattini, Adolfe Franci, Sergio Amidei, C. G. Viola, De Sica; *ph* Anchise Brizzi; *mus* Alessandro Cicognini; *cast* Rinaldo Smordoni (Giuseppe), Franco Interlenghi (Pasquale), Aniello Mele, Bruno Ortensi, Claudio Ermelli.

Set in Rome during the Allied occupation, the story traces the gradual deterioration of two young shoeblacks, Pasquale and Giuseppe, through black-market racketeering, to their experiences in jail, from which they escape; in a fit of bitter rage Pasquale kills his friend. Shot mainly in the streets and one of the jails of Rome, the film attracted critical attention both for the astonishingly naturalistic acting of the cast of schoolchildren and for its wrathful yet humane tone; it was also awarded an OSCAR. It is one of the major achievements of NEO-REALISM in its early stages.

**SCOFIELD, PAUL** (1922–    ), British actor whose reputation rests on a succession of striking performances in the British theatre since the mid-forties. He entered films in 1955 in *That Lady* and was in *Carve Her Name with Pride* (1958). In 1966 he repeated his stage role of Sir Thomas More in Fred ZINNEMANN's *A Man for All Seasons*, successfully adapting his characteristic nervous intensity to the screen and winning several awards including an OSCAR. His occasional film appearances also include *The Train* (John FRANKENHEIMER, 1964), *Bartleby* (1970), and Peter BROOK's *King Lear* (1970).

**SCOPE** see ASPECT RATIO, WIDE SCREEN

*SCORPIO RISING*, US, 1964. Ektachrome; 30min. *Dir, prod, scr, ph* Kenneth Anger.

ANGER's study of a motor-cycle gang injects black humour into his obsession with homosexual sado-eroticism by structuring the narrative around thirteen rock songs, whose banal lyrics underline the film's quality of nightmare. Lush imagery—motor cycles, leather suits, Nazi symbols, occultism—are intercut with sequences of Marlon BRANDO in *The Wild One* (1953) and of the life of Christ from Cecil B. DEMILLE's *King of Kings* (1927), and Anger's usual brilliant editing produces implications beyond what is directly seen and heard.

In 1964 a court case in Los Angeles found *Scorpio Rising* obscene, shortly after Anger had been awarded a $10,000 Ford Foundation fellowship on the basis of his achievement in this film.

**SCOTT, GEORGE C.** (1927–    ), US actor, after ten years' stage experience which included some important Shakespeare roles—the title part in *Richard III*, Antony in *Antony and Cleopatra*, Shylock in *The Merchant of Venice*—made his first film appearance in *The Hanging Tree* (Delmer DAVES, 1959). He was the malevolent prosecutor in *Anatomy of a Murder* (Otto PREMINGER, 1959) and gave another memorable performance as a big-time gambler in THE HUSTLER (1961). He refused the subsequent OSCAR nomination, a gesture he repeated after *Patton: Lust for Glory* (Franklin SCHAFFNER, 1969); but he was this time nevertheless awarded the prize

in just acknowledgement of his powerful conviction in the title role. His tremendous versatility has enabled him to give life to such different characterizations as General Turgidson in DR STRANGELOVE (1963), Rochester in *Jane Eyre* (Delbert MANN, 1970), and Dr Herbert Bock in *The Hospital* (1971). He directed *Rage* (1972).

**SCOTT, RANDOLPH** (1903–    ), US actor, real name Randolph Crane, played his first film part in *The Far Call* (1929). The success of *Lone Cowboy* (1931) led to a series of Zane Grey adaptations, and since 1947 Scott has appeared only in Westerns. Between 1956 and 1960, he starred in the seven Westerns made by Budd BOETTICHER (co-producing several with Harry Joe Brown), notably *Seven Men from Now* (1956) and *The Tall T* (1957), both written by Burt Kennedy. His finest performance was undoubtedly as the veteran gunman, Gil Westrum, in Sam PECKINPAH's classic, GUNS IN THE AFTERNOON (1962, *Ride the High Country* in GB).

**SCOTT'S EXPEDITION TO THE SOUTH POLE.** As part of his activity as official photographer of the British Antarctic Expedition of 1910–13, Herbert Ponting shot a large quantity (at least 40,000 feet) of motion-picture negative, the first 8,000 feet reaching England in May 1911. The resulting film was initially released in parts in 1911–12 (*With Captain Scott to the South Pole*; *Epic of the South Pole*; *The Undying Story of Captain Scott*), when these first shots of a distant, strange, unknown landscape must have been electrifying to the audience; the parts were re-issued in 1924 in a feature-film version, revised and with additional footage, under the title *The Great White Silence*. A new and further revised version as a sound film with music track and commentary appeared in 1933 as *Ninety Degrees South*; this in turn was followed by a revised, shortened version, using tinted stills, which appeared in 1936 under the title *The Story of Captain Scott*. John MILLS played Captain Scott in the feature film *Scott of the Antarctic* (Charles FREND, 1948).

*SCOUNDREL, The*, US, 1935. 1¼hr. *Dir, prod, scr* Ben Hecht, Charles MacArthur for Paramount; *ph* Lee Garmes; *cast* Noël Coward (Anthony Mallare), Julie Hayden (Cora Moore), Stanley Ridges (Paul Decker).

A powerful publisher who has used and insulted his friends, colleagues, and mistresses is killed in an air crash. Following an old Jewish legend, his soul can find rest only when he is sincerely mourned.

The black brilliance of Ben HECHT and Charles MACARTHUR's script admirably suited

Noël COWARD's talent, and he gave a memorable portrayal of a cynical egotist; the film inevitably loses momentum with the main character's death, but it remains a prime example of the particular gifts of the main participants.

## SCREEN RATIO see ASPECT RATIO

**SCREWBALL COMEDY** was a unique creation of Hollywood in the thirties: its main elements were irreverent humour, vernacular dialogue, fast pace, and eccentric characters. The comic style was derived from Broadway farces of the late twenties, with the addition of physical humour bordering on the SLAPSTICK of silent films.

Screwball comedies were intended and received as escapist entertainment, improbable stories set among the irresponsible, often hard-drinking, rich. But they reflect the era of the Depression and the social disorientation of the thirties with their depiction of a crazy world of uncertain values. Some touched on actual Depression conditions: the shanty town scenes in MY MAN GODFREY (1936), the destitutes overwhelming Deeds when he tries to give his money away in MR DEEDS GOES TO TOWN (1936), or the pandemonium when the doors of the automat fly open in EASY LIVING (1937). The antics of the rich often placed them in ridiculous positions, giving an acceptably ambivalent viewpoint. If the hero was a serious, sensible man, he might be propelled into anarchic adventures by a beautiful, bewildered woman: Cary GRANT in BRINGING UP BABY (1938), Gary COOPER in *Ball of Fire* (1941). Jean HARLOW in BOMBSHELL (1933), Carole LOMBARD in *My Man Godfrey*, and Katharine HEPBURN in *Bringing up Baby* epitomized the highly-strung, 'wacky' heroine.

Frank CAPRA was the most highly regarded director in the form at the time, and other key directors of screwball comedy were Gregory LA CAVA (*My Man Godfrey*), Leo MCCAREY (THE AWFUL TRUTH, 1937), George CUKOR (HOLIDAY, 1938); but it is now recognized that Howard HAWKS's four classic screwball comedies— TWENTIETH CENTURY (1934), *Bringing up Baby*, HIS GIRL FRIDAY (1940), and *Ball of Fire*—best embody the essential elements of breakneck pace, confrontation between the sexes, and dialogue bristling with wise-cracks.

With the advent of the Second World War, frivolity and social ridicule became inappropriate and Preston STURGES's more broadly based social satires replaced screwball comedy. A generation later Peter BOGDANOVICH's *What's Up, Doc?* (1972) effectively re-created elements of the style in an affectionate pastiche.

## SCRIPT GIRL see CONTINUITY GIRL

**SEARCHERS, The,** US, 1956. 2hr. *Dir* John Ford; *prod* Merian C. Cooper, C. V. Whitney for Warner Bros; *scr* Frank Nugent, from the novel by Alan Lemay; *ph* Winton Hoch, Alfred Gilks; *mus* Max Steiner; *cast* John Wayne (Ethan Edwards), Jeffrey Hunter (Martin Pawley), Vera Miles (Laurie Jorgensen), Ward Bond (Captain Rev Samuel Clayton), Natalie Wood (Debbie Edwards).

After the Civil War, Ethan Edwards, a lonely, unregenerate Confederate officer, finds a mission in the ten-year search for his two nieces, kidnapped by Indians. *The Searchers* marks a new strain in FORD's work, showing the frontier myth in a sober, even disenchanted, light: John WAYNE's performance as the brutal, embittered survivor of the pioneering age outstandingly supports this mood. The film demonstrates Ford's major strengths as a film-maker: vigour, economy, down-to-earth humour, and authoritative handling of actors.

## SEASTROM, VICTOR, see SJÖSTRÖM

**SEBERG, JEAN** (1938– ), US actress who was 'discovered' by Otto PREMINGER for the title role in his *Saint Joan* (1957, see JOAN OF ARC). The film was a critical and commercial failure, and she fared little better in his *Bonjour Tristesse* (1958), from the novel by Françoise Sagan. She moved to France and re-emerged with her first real success as GODARD's selfish heroine in A BOUT DE SOUFFLE (1960). Many French films followed, including one directed by her sometime husband Romain Gary, *Les Oiseaux vont mourir à Péru* (1968). Outside France, she gave one of her best performances as the destructive *Lilith* (1964) in Robert ROSSEN's fine film.

**SECOND UNIT.** Term denoting an auxiliary group substantially working independently of a film's main production unit and usually responsible for LOCATION, stuntwork, action, or special EFFECTS sequences. Second unit work in its simplest forms is in effect directed by a cameraman, invariably different from the cameraman credited for the main substance of the film. Where more substantial second unit work is required, the subsidiary unit is headed by its own director. Films of modest dimensions and budget seldom demand an auxiliary production team, although a second unit director may be called in for location-action sequences on a film which has fallen behind schedule; but generally only films which are large in scale, budget, and resources demand a supplementary unit. Larger productions often credit two second unit directors, and occasionally may enjoy the luxury of three (e.g. BEN-HUR, 1959; *Catch-22*, 1970).

The importance of the second unit in saving

time, and therefore money, presumably increased as films became more costly and complex, but little attention was paid to the work of subsidiary technicians. One of the few second unit directors to achieve recognition in the silent era was B. Reeves EASON, whose handling of the action sequences, and particularly the chariot race, in BEN-HUR (1925) added immeasurably to the film's impact. Yakima CANUTT's contribution to many of John FORD's Westerns has been recognized, and he remains almost the only second unit director widely known in his own right. In more recent years, particularly since the growth of large-scale spectaculars in the late fifties, a number of specialists in the field have made names for themselves. Among those particularly notable are James Havens (THE MUTINY ON THE BOUNTY, 1962; THE CHASE, 1966; *The Silencers*, 1966); Richard Talmadge (*The Magnificent Showman*, 1964; *The Greatest Story Ever Told*, 1965); Andrew Marton (*Ben-Hur*, 1959; *55 Days at Peking*, 1963; CLEOPATRA, 1962; *Catch-22*); André Smagghe (LAWRENCE OF ARABIA, 1962; *Paris brûle-t-il?*, 1965); Noel Howard (*55 Days at Peking*; *Lawrence of Arabia*); Cliff Lyons (*Major Dundee*, 1964; *The Green Berets*, 1968); Ray Kellogg (STAGECOACH, 1966; HOMBRE, 1967; *Tora! Tora! Tora!*, 1970); Arthur Vitarelli (various 'live' features made by Walt DISNEY); and the versatile and ubiquitous Yakima Canutt (EL CID, 1961; *Cat Ballou*, 1965; *Khartoum*, 1966; *Rio Lobo*; *Song of Norway*, both 1970). Bob Simmons, a specialist in action sequences, is often credited as such (*Goldfinger*, 1964; *Thunderball*, 1965; *Shalako*, 1968).

**SECRET LIFE OF WALTER MITTY, The,** US, 1947. Technicolor; 1½hr. *Dir* Norman Z. McLeod; *prod* Sam Goldwyn for RKO Radio; *scr* Ken Englund, Everett Freeman, after James Thurber; *ph* Lee Garmes; *ed* Monica Collingswood; *cast* Danny Kaye (Walter Mitty), Virginia Mayo (Rosalind van Hoorn), Boris Karloff (Dr Hollingshead), Fay Bainter (Mrs Mitty), the Goldwyn Girls.

Danny KAYE scored a great success as Walter Mitty, enacting the daydreams of Thurber's short story with additions in the form of extravagant musical numbers. With Kaye hardly off-screen and at his exuberant best, especially in his brilliant 'scat' songs, the film is an outstanding example of the gifted comedian's screen work at the peak of his popularity.

**SEDMIKRÁSKY** (*Daisies*), Czechoslovakia, 1966. Eastman Color; 1¼hr. *Dir* Věra Chytilová; *scr* Chytilová with Ester Krumbachová, from a story by Chytilová and Pavel Juráček; *ph* Jaroslav Kučera; *ed* Miroslav Hajek; *mus* Jiří Šlitr

and Jiří Šust; Charleston sung by Eva Pilarová; *cast* Jitka Cerhová (Marie I, brunette), Ivana Karbonavá (Marie II, blonde).

Two bored girls (the 'daisies' of the title), finding the world has spoilt them, decide to set about spoiling the world. They play a series of increasingly outrageous and meaningless pranks, becoming more and more destructive until they find themselves symbolically destroyed. A briefly-offered possibility of recantation and return to 'useful' lives proves no solution.

This was CHYTILOVÁ's first collaboration with Ester KRUMBACHOVÁ, whose contribution is evident in the brilliance of the design as well as in the script, and her second collaboration with her (then newly-married) husband, Jaroslav KUČERA: already one of the most accomplished and adventurous Czech cameramen, he achieved in *Sedmikrásky* a range of extraordinary effects—prismatic fragmentation, distortions, floods of colour, double exposures. Chytilová wanted to avoid professional actors for the main parts: she had a long search for her two Maries, and her final choice was inspired. They pick their way with éclat along the delicate line between hilarity and outrageousness. In gag after gag, accepted social values, especially male ones, are ridiculed. Wit, satire, sharp observation, are combined with a daring use of cinematic tricks and an impeccable eye for beauty. Chytilová's absorption of film tradition is apparent in her style and in the many affectionate and mocking references she makes.

Of course the film caused an immediate official storm. It was withheld from circulation, and released in 1967 only after it had been shown to selected groups of workers who, unfortunately for officialdom, liked it. Enthusiastically received by Czech audiences and international critics alike, it remains outstanding among the Czech films of the sixties and in world cinema.

**SELDES, GILBERT** (1893–   ), US writer and critic, was a war correspondent in Europe, and on his return to America was a journalist, drama critic, and editor of *The Dial* (1920–3). His books and other writings are mainly concerned with American social history; those involving cinema are *The seven lively arts* (1924), *The movies and the talkies* (1929), *The movies come from America* (1937), and *The great audience* (1950). He has written detective stories under the pseudonym Foster Johns.

**SELIG,** US production company founded in 1896 by William N. Selig (1864–1948), the inventor, with Andrew Schustek, of a film projector and camera. In the cut-throat competition and continual lawsuits that characterized American motion picture production before 1909,

Selig moved to Los Angeles where he made pioneer Westerns in natural locales. He engaged Tom MIX to direct and act in one-reel Westerns. In 1909 Selig was one of the founding members of the MOTION PICTURE PATENTS COMPANY and pioneered the making of long films. The company's outstanding success was *The Spoilers* (1914), an eight-reel production directed by Colin Campbell, which included a classic fight, lasting a full reel, between William Farnum and Tom Santschi. Selig was also noted for its SERIALS; one of the most celebrated was *The Adventures of Kathlyn* (1913), starring Kathlyn Williams, which used wild animals for its thrills. In 1915 Selig merged with VITAGRAPH, LUBIN, and ESSANAY to form VLSE.

**SELLERS, PETER** (1925–   ), British actor from a theatrical family. His frenetically active film career during the fifties and early sixties resulted in performances of varying quality, the best being a small-time crook in *The Ladykillers* (1955), a sharply-observed shop steward in *I'm All Right Jack* (1959), and a refined Indian doctor in *The Millionairess* (1960). Sellers's talent for vocal mimicry can overbalance into caricature, but within the confines of a strong plot and a well-defined social milieu he can develop wickedly accurate satirical characterizations. Under the direction of Stanley KUBRICK, in LOLITA (1962) and DR STRANGELOVE (1963), in which he played three contrasting roles, he produced a remarkable variety of eccentrics. He created the character of the inept Inspector Clouseau in *The Pink Panther* (1963) and *A Shot in the Dark* (1964) and was one of the many stars in *What's New, Pussycat?* (1965). He has directed one film, *Mr Topaze* (1961), in which he also starred. Since a serious heart attack in 1964 his film parts have been less remarkable, although hardly diminished in frequency.

**SELZNICK, DAVID O.** (1902–65), US producer. The son of Lewis SELZNICK and brother of the agent Myron Selznick, David left the East Coast where he had been making short documentaries and became a Hollywood producer, working for PARAMOUNT, RKO, and for his father-in-law Louis B. MAYER, at METRO-GOLDWYN-MAYER. In 1935 he established his own independent film-making company, Selznick International Pictures, which released its output through RKO and UNITED ARTISTS, and later through its own distribution branch.

Like his contemporary Samuel GOLDWYN, Selznick was to become one of Hollywood's independent producers and star-makers on the grand scale. His lavish productions included DINNER AT EIGHT (1933), DAVID COPPERFIELD (1934), A STAR IS BORN (1937), NOTHING SACRED (1937), GONE WITH THE WIND (1939), for which Selznick should have received directing credit since, as well as controlling every aspect of the production, he planned every shot, and REBECCA (1940). His impressive financial position also enabled him to undertake international co-productions, including THE THIRD MAN (1949). He spent his later years nursing the acting career of Jennifer JONES, his second wife, who starred in several of his last films including DUEL IN THE SUN (1946), *A Farewell to Arms* (1957), and *Tender is the Night* (1962). Selznick's meticulous, almost neurotic, attention to detail is displayed in a collection of his memos, *Memo from David O. Selznick* (New York, 1972), and an excellent biography is *Selznick* by Bob Thomas (New York and London, 1971). The David O. Selznick Golden Laurel Trophy is awarded annually to an outstanding film producer.

**SELZNICK, LEWIS** (1870–1932), US executive, after his jewellery business failed, became a Broadway entrepreneur, eventually appointing himself to a job in the New York office of UNIVERSAL. He left Universal to found his own film-making company, World Special Film Corporation, producing a series of features starring Clara Kimball YOUNG and the TALMADGE sisters. Selznick later became a partner with Adolph ZUKOR in the short-lived Select Pictures company. He was soundly beaten by Zukor for control of the company and retired, embittered, in 1925.

**SEMON, LARRY** (1889–1928), US comedian, began his career as a cartoonist on a New York newspaper. In 1916 he joined VITAGRAPH for whom he directed and appeared in a large number of comedies until 1923. He used a stock company, including four stuntmen who doubled for him (see STUNTMAN), who could execute and contribute to the range of wild, acrobatic gags that formed the backbone of his films. He went into independent production, making seven features between 1924 and 1927, notably THE WIZARD OF OZ (1925), in which Semon played the Scarecrow and Oliver Hardy the Tin Man (see LAUREL AND HARDY), *The Perfect Clown* (1925), *Stop Look and Listen* (1926), and *Spuds* (1927). In spite of the acrobatic richness of these films, they failed to make a sufficient return on their production costs and he was heavily in debt when he died of pneumonia.

**SENNETT, MACK** (1884–1960), US producer and director of comedy, real name Michael Sinnott. Canadian-born, of Irish extraction, and possessed of a powerful bass voice, he left his job in a steelworks to seek his fortune on the New York stage. After several parts in burlesque plays, in 1909 he joined the BIOGRAPH company, where he began his long, close association with Mabel NORMAND. Sennett could not persuade D. W. GRIFFITH, then dominant at Biograph, to share his own predilection for burlesque, but he learnt rapidly from Griffith's methods of directing and editing and from Billy BITZER's experiments with camera technique. He was influential in developing a comedy troupe at Biograph, where by 1911 he was directing as well as acting in comedies. In 1912 he went to Los Angeles to make films for the newly-founded KEYSTONE company, and during the next five years was the mainspring of the company. Leaving Keystone in 1917, he went to Jesse L. LASKY's Artcraft, later PARAMOUNT, where he produced some of Fatty ARBUCKLE's best comedies and the first shorts featuring Buster KEATON. He remained with Paramount as an independent producer until 1935, and from 1939 until his death was an associate producer with TWENTIETH CENTURY-FOX.

Sennett's name and achievement are chiefly associated with Keystone, and justly so. His genial and rumbustious personality, his zest for fun as well as his shrewdness in organization, made him the key to the crazy world of Keystone from which emerged one of cinema's original creations in visual humour.

His (dictated) autobiography, *King of comedy*, New York, 1954, is an appealing and racy account of his career, to which a useful corrective is supplied by *Kops and custard* by Kalton C. Lahue and Terry Brewer, Oakland, 1968.

**SENSO**, Italy, 1954. Technicolor; 2hr. *Dir* Luchino Visconti; *prod* Lux Film; *scr* Visconti, Suso Cecchi d'Amico, from a novella by Camilla Boito; *ph* G. R. Aldo, Robert Krasker; *des* Ottavio Scotti, Gino Brosio; *mus* Bruckner's Seventh Symphony, Verdi's *Il Trovatore*; *cast* Alida Valli (Livia Serpieri), Farley Granger (Franz), Massimo Girotti (Roberto Ussoni), Heinz Moog (Count Serpieri), Rita Morelli (Laura).

Livia, passionately in love with an Austrian lieutenant, betrays her husband and country during Italy's third war of independence. She denounces her lover after his infidelity and goes mad at seeing him executed. VISCONTI parallels the sexual and political conflicts, setting them against a lavish evocation of a society in transition. His first film in colour, *Senso* shows complete authority in its rich yet controlled compositions.

A cut version, with dubbed dialogue co-written by Tennessee WILLIAMS, appeared in Britain under the misleading title *The Wanton Countess*.

**SEPMAG,** a word coined to describe a film with its MAGNETIC sound-track on a separate film, not combined on to a single film as in cinema practice. During editing, all films are 'sepmag'; they can be viewed by running them DOUBLE HEAD, on separate reels locked in synchronization, a method known as 'interlock' in the US. For television, films are often left in sepmag form for transmission, to save making a MARRIED PRINT. (See COMOPT, COMMAG.)

**SEPOPT,** a term describing picture and OPTICAL sound on separate reels, not combined on a single film as is normal procedure. (See COMMAG, COMOPT, SEPMAG.)

**SEPPUKU** *(Hara-Kiri)*, Japan, 1962. Grandscope; 2¼hr. *Dir* Masaki Kobayashi; *prod* Shochiku; *scr* Shinodu Hashimoto, from a novel by Yasuhiko Takiguchi; *ph* Yoshio Miyajima; *cast* Tatsuya Nakadai (Hanshiro Tsugumo), Shima Iwashita (Miho Tsugumo), Akira Isahama (Motome Chijiiwa), Rentaro Mikuni (Kageya Saito).

According to the samurai code a member of the order who has fallen into poverty can only kill himself, preferably with due ceremonial. From this practice KOBAYASHI builds a tragic story of despair and revenge, using FLASHBACKS with great skill to unfold his tale. As in JOI-UCHI *(Rebellion,* 1967), he faithfully adheres to the conventions of the period film while making a stand for humanity against system and for true honour against meaningless forms.

The film bears Kobayashi's characteristic hallmarks: extraordinary visual beauty, with particularly accomplished composition for the wide screen; rhythmic control of narrative, with beautifully paced formal rituals broken by intimate domestic moments and sequences of relentless slaughter; finely calculated use of natural sound to heighten tension.

*Seppuku* was acclaimed in Japan and won the Jury Prize at CANNES in 1963. It was, however, rejected by Western critics, puzzled by its unusual combination of gravity and violence, and has been unjustly neglected in comparison with other Japanese films.

**SEQUENCE.** A magazine of the Oxford University Film Society of which there were fourteen quarterly issues from 1946 to 1952. Under the editorship of various Film Society members including Gavin Lambert and Penelope Houston (later to become professional film critics and in turn editors of SIGHT AND SOUND), and Lindsay ANDERSON, *Sequence* carried film and book reviews, articles on the historical and aesthetic aspects of film, and pungent comment on the structure of the industry and the social implications of the medium. The esteem in which the journal was held is attested to by the appearance of several distinguished contributors, among them Helen VAN DONGEN, William WYLER, and John HUSTON, and two later to become widely known: Satyajit RAY and Karel REISZ. *Sequence* had a lasting effect on young film-makers and audiences and was important in disseminating the ideas which were later developed in FREE CINEMA.

**SERIAL,** a film in short episodes, with simple characterization and plot, each episode ending with a CLIFF-HANGER and beginning with the resolution of the last. Serials, which usually had ten, twelve, or fifteen episodes, were filmed at a low cost, often using actors between films, and sets which had been constructed for higher budget features. Cheap to produce and to hire, the serial was easily understood by all. The source of the genre was in the newspaper serial (the film version often being complemented by publication in a newspaper) and in the popular novel, with the emphasis on adventure, mystery, and excitement.

The forerunner of the serial was the SERIES, which had a continuity of characterization but did not have the serial's continuity of narrative. The series appeared simultaneously in 1908 in France (Victorin Jasset's Nick Carter), the US (ESSANAY's Broncho Billy), and Norway (Nordisk's Raffles). A year later production of the series began in England (James Williamson's The Dandy Detective) and Germany (Nick Carter). In 1913 Louis FEUILLADE began a new series with FANTÔMAS.

The first true serial was the SELIG company's *The Adventures of Kathlyn* (1913), although the year before EDISON had released *What Happened to Mary* in twelve one-reel 'chapters', to coincide with the publication in a magazine of a group of short stories having the same plot. The PATHÉ company, which was to dominate the silent serial market under the supervision of Louis GASNIER, entered the American arena with *The Perils of Pauline* (1914) starring Pearl WHITE which had a prodigious success. Pathé, who planned to produce six serials a year, followed with THE EXPLOITS OF ELAINE (1914), again with Pearl White in the leading role.

In Europe, the success of *The Perils of Pauline* prompted other producers to turn to the serial. In France Feuillade made LES VAMPIRES (1915–16) and JUDEX (1916); in Germany Otto Ripert made HOMUNCULUS (1916) and Fritz LANG made *Die Spinnen* (1919–20); in Italy Emile Ghione made *Za-la-mort*.

However, the serial met with its greatest popularity in the US. This eventually led to an American monopoly of the genre. In 1914 the US produced six serials, in 1915 thirteen, in 1916 eighteen, and in 1920 twenty-eight. The latter part of the silent era saw little development in the genre with the release of such serials as Pathé's *The Adventures of Ruth* (George MARSHALL, 1919), FIRST NATIONAL's *The Adventures of Tarzan* (1920), Pathé's *Plunder* (1923), *The Green Archer* (1925), and *The Masked Menace* (1927).

The serial was not slow to utilize the possibilities of sound, of which the immediate effect as in other kinds of cinema was to force many actors to bow out, while allowing others to bow in. New recruits included John WAYNE, Boris KARLOFF, and Bela LUGOSI. Studios such as COLUMBIA, REPUBLIC, UNIVERSAL, and RKO continued to produce mystery stories and WESTERNS, but science-fiction began to hold the stage. The popularity of the comic strip, the emergence of which coincided with that of the cinema (1896), provided the serial with new heroes, and further cemented the alliance between the newspaper and the serial that had existed from the start. The popular heroes of the comic strip appeared on the screen in such serials as *Flash Gordon* (1936), *Dick Tracy*, *Jungle Jim* (both 1937), *The Lone Ranger* (1938), and *Buck Rogers* (1939).

With the advent of the Second World War the American serial became patriotic: anti-Nazi (*Jungle Queen*, 1941) and anti-Japanese (*Drums of Fu Manchu*, 1940).

In the post-war period the standard of the serial fell. There was a change in characterization, with the hero swapping brains for brawn (*Superman*, 1948; *Batman and Robin*, 1950). By this time plots had become routine and predictable. The serial was made on an even smaller budget than its predecessors (often using STOCK material to save costs) and it showed. By the mid-fifties the serial was obsolete. The feature film had grown in length making the serial, which had served as a convenient programme filler, superfluous, and television had taken over the genre.

**SERIES.** Light-weight films, each complete in itself but centred on the same character or group of characters, became popular even before the SERIAL and long outlasted it in drawing power. G. M. ANDERSON as Broncho Billy and Wallace BEERY as Swedie in the US, Onésime, Max LINDER, and Bout-de-Zan in France, were among the early successes in the field. In feature films, the series provided a significant proportion of the Hollywood 'B' PICTURE output; given a popular key figure and guaranteed distribution as programme fillers, they could be produced with speed and economy. WESTERNS, thrillers, and situation comedies were, in that order, the most popular subjects for series presentation.

Apart from the ubiquitous TARZAN, UNIVERSAL's Cohens and Kellys (1926–33) led the way. The gang of boys in DEAD END (1937) attracted such attention that WARNER BROS featured them as the Dead End Kids in other films with slum backgrounds. In 1938 Universal attempted competition with the Little Tough Guys, then acquired the Dead End Kids themselves. MONOGRAM's East Side Kids gained a following and took in some of the Dead End team, their comedy angle increasing until they were concentrating on knockabout humour as the Bowery Boys.

COLUMBIA's Blondie series, with Penny Singleton, began in 1938 and developed into the Bumstead Family in the mid-forties. Most of the main studios had their 'family' series, with METRO-GOLDWYN-MAYER's HARDY FAMILY in the lead. MGM also led in the hospital drama series with Dr Kildare (Lew AYRES) succeeded by Dr Gillespie (Lionel BARRYMORE).

The hundreds of Westerns featuring regular cowboy stars were a major part of series production. PARAMOUNT's Hopalong Cassidy with William BOYD and REPUBLIC's Three Mesquiteers were among the longest-running. Roy ROGERS and Gene AUTRY also starred in Republic series.

The thriller series was particularly taken up by TWENTIETH CENTURY-FOX, with MR MOTO (Peter LORRE) and CHARLIE CHAN (Warner Oland succeeded by Sidney Toland), and Columbia, with the Lone Wolf (Warren Williams), Ellery Queen (Ralph Bellamy), Boston Blackie (Chester Morris), and Crime Doctor (Warner Baxter). Warner Bros had Perry Mason (Warner William), and the girl reporters Torchy Blane (Glenda Farrell) and Nancy Drew (Bonita Granville). MGM produced THE THIN MAN (1934) and its successors, RKO had The Saint (George SANDERS) and the FALCON (Sanders succeeded by Tom Conway), and Universal specialized in Basil RATHBONE's excellent SHERLOCK HOLMES.

Apart from FERNANDEL's Don Camillo films, there was no real equivalent to the series film in Europe. Britain had a few attempts at instituting the series—Betty Balfour as Squibs, Ernie Lottinger as Josser, Old Mother Riley (Arthur Lucan) in the thirties, the Huggetts (Jack Warner and Kathleen HARRISON) in the forties. The only comparable phenomenon in Britain has been the CARRY ON films which, beginning after the decline of the Hollywood series, have flourished remarkably, although they exploit a team of actors rather than carrying the same characters from film to film.

The disappearance of the series has been an inevitable part of changes in audience patterns and programming since 1950. The convention has been taken up almost unchanged by television Westerns, thrillers, and situation comedies, which play a precisely similar role to the series films of the thirties and forties.

**SERVAIS, JEAN** (1910–   ), Belgian actor with a career in French films beginning in 1931. In his earlier days he worked with such directors as Raymond Bernard (LES MISÉRABLES, 1934), Marcel PAGNOL (*Angèle*, 1934), and Fedor Ozep (*Amok*, 1934). Until the fifties he remained comparatively little known outside France. Then, after appearing in Max OPHULS' *Le Plaisir* (1952) and Jacques BECKER's *Rue de l'estrapade* (*Françoise Steps Out*, 1952), he clinched his international reputation in Jules DASSIN's DU RIFIFI CHEZ LES HOMMES (*Rififi*, 1955) as a mature actor similar in style and demeanour to the latter-day performances of his near-contemporary Jean GABIN.

**SERVANT, The,** GB, 1963. 2hr. *Dir* Joseph Losey; *prod* Springbok/Elstree; *scr* Harold Pinter, from the novel by Robin Maugham; *ph* Douglas Slocombe; *des* Richard MacDonald; *mus* John Dankworth; *cast* Dirk Bogarde (Barrett), James Fox (Tony), Wendy Craig (Susan), Sarah Miles (Vera).

Tony, an effete young man-about-town, engages a manservant, Barrett, who gradually dominates him.

One of LOSEY's favourite themes, a process of moral dissolution instigated by an intruder, was greatly enriched by Harold PINTER's script, full of sardonic ambiguities. Losey's preoccupation with English social classes here lacks conviction, to some extent weakening the film, and *The Servant* was criticized for its ornate visual style, in both the oppressive décor and the elaborate camerawork: the baroque elements, however, set up an effective tension with the terse dialogue and understated performances.

**SEVEN BRIDES FOR SEVEN BROTHERS,** US, 1954. CinemaScope; 1¾hr; Ansco Color. *Dir* Stanley Donen; *prod* MGM; *scr* Albert Hackett, Frances Goodrich, Dorothy Kingsley, based on *Sobbin' Women* by Stephen Vincent Benet; *ph* George Folsey; *choreog* Michael Kidd; *mus* Gene de Paul; *lyr* Johnny Mercer; *cast* Howard Keel (Adam), Jane Powell (Milly), Russ Tamblyn (Gideon), Tommy Rall (Frank), Jacques d'Amboise (Ephraim), Jeff Richards (Benjamin), Marc Platt (Daniel), Matt Mattox (Caleb).

The rape of the Sabine women transferred to the Oregon backwoods acted as a framework for an inventive musical with enormous zest. Michael Kidd's creative choreography produced some fine set-pieces, including the beautiful, snowbound 'Brothers' Lament', and Jane Powell's etiquette lesson in 'Goin' Co'tin''. DONEN's intelligent use of the CINEMASCOPE screen, at that time still an innovation, was especially notable in the dance sequences, all of which were neatly integrated into the plot.

**SEVEN DAYS IN MAY,** US, 1964. 2hr. *Dir* John Frankenheimer; *prod* Seven Arts, Joel Productions, Frankenheimer; *scr* Rod Serling, from the novel by Fletcher Knebel and Charles W. Bailey II; *ph* Ellsworth Fredericks; *cast* Burt Lancaster (Gen James M. Scott), Kirk Douglas (Col Martin 'Jiggs' Casey), Fredric March (President Jordan Lyman), Ava Gardner (Eleanor Holbrook), Edmond O'Brien (Senator Raymond Clark), Martin Balsam (Paul Girard), George Macready (Christopher Todd), Whit Bissell (Senator Prentice).

Casey stumbles on an Army plot to depose the President and assume power, and further realizes that the brain behind the plot is his superior, General Scott, whom he has always admired and respected. FRANKENHEIMER's film begins slackly, slow in tempo and with an abundance of dialogue and detail, but becomes increasingly taut and tense. A splendid cast is dominated by Kirk DOUGLAS as the Colonel, Burt LANCASTER as the purposeful General, and Fredric MARCH as the burdened President. It is a rare example of a really exciting political thriller.

**SEVEN SAMURAI, The,** see SHICHININ NO SAMURAI

**SEVENTH SEAL, The,** see SJUNDE INSEGLET, DET

**70MM,** the widest film gauge in normal use, often shown under trade names such as Super PANAVISION or Super TECHNIRAMA 70. This gauge, twice as wide as standard 35mm, provides about $2\frac{1}{2}$ times the picture area and room for four stereophonic sound tracks, affording perhaps the highest quality available on the screen today. It was developed in the late fifties in an attempt to give the cinema a competitive edge over television's small screen, but has recently fallen into disuse, perhaps because of its high cost, and is now used only for re-release of existing films. (The professional trend is to smaller gauges; see 16MM, SUPER-8.)

**SEVEN YEAR ITCH, The,** US, 1955. Cinema-Scope; $1\frac{3}{4}$hr; De Luxe Color. *Dir* Billy Wilder; *prod* Twentieth Century-Fox; *scr* Wilder, George Axelrod, based on the play by Axelrod; *ph* Milton Krasner; *cast* Marilyn Monroe (the girl), Tom Ewell (Richard Sherman), Evelyn Keyes (Helen Sherman), Oscar Homolka (Dr Brubaker).

George AXELROD's successful stage play con-centrated on the gentle humour of a grass widower (played on Broadway as in the film by Tom Ewell) and his fantasies of sexual freedom. Using the film as a star vehicle for Marilyn MONROE radically altered the balance, making it simply a blatantly funny sex comedy.

**SFTA** see SOCIETY OF FILM AND TELEVISION ARTS

**SHADOWS,** US, 1960. $1\frac{1}{2}$hr. *Dir* John Cassavetes; *prod* Cassavetes–McEndree–Cassel; *ph* Erich Kollmar; *mus* Charles Mingus; *cast* Leila Goldoni (Leila), Ben Carruthers (Ben), Hugh Hurd (Hugh), Anthony Ray (Tony), Rupert Crosse (Rupe), Tom Allen (Tom).

CASSAVETES's first film as director was made on location in New York and shot on 16mm with a technical crew of four. Its use of improvisation gained attention: there was no script and the actors were free to explore with tact, poignancy, and humour the social and emotional stresses of colour prejudice.

Although at first classified as an underground film, *Shadows* was more a manifestation of rebellion against Hollywood's domination of commercial film-making. It gave impetus to the production of low-budget features outside the studio system.

**SHAKESPEARE, WILLIAM** (1564–1616), English poet and dramatist. Most of the thirty-three plays firmly attributable to Shakespeare have at some time appeared on the screen, the most popular for adaptation being those with a large element of romance or violence: ROMEO AND JULIET, THE TAMING OF THE SHREW, HAMLET, OTHELLO, and MACBETH. His work has attracted film-makers from the very early days of cinema: there are references to an 1899 film of Sir Herbert Beerbohm Tree's stage production of *King John*, but the three-minute film of Sarah BERNHARDT in the duel scene from *Hamlet* shown at the Paris Exhibition in 1900 is almost certainly the first Shakespeare film. From then on films based on his plays poured out from all film-producing countries, particularly from the American VITAGRAPH company which in 1908 embarked on a series of one-reel Shakespeare adaptations.

The appeal of Shakespeare sources to early film-makers is at first sight difficult to explain. The poetry of the plays could not be conveyed and it would appear impossible to condense complex plots to acceptable length without reducing them to complete absurdity. But an aura of respectability was thought to be cast over a still raffish trade by the reference to great literary classics; this striving for artistic acceptability is sometimes discernible in later adaptations, when cinema was no longer regarded merely as entertainment for the poorer classes.

REINHARDT'S A MIDSUMMER NIGHT'S DREAM (1935), decked out with every technical resource and endowed with a star cast of wild improbability, was surprisingly successful in conveying the original poetic fantasy but was a resounding commercial failure. METRO-GOLDWYN-MAYER'S *Romeo and Juliet* (1936), directed by George CUKOR and starring Norma SHEARER and Leslie HOWARD, came near to sinking under the sheer weight of art direction and studio solemnity.

The desire to shine in famous dramatic roles may have been responsible for some of the less fortunate appearances of well-known stars—Theda BARA as Juliet (1916) among them. But the honest aim of re-creating the work of the greatest English-language dramatist in a new, resourceful medium has undoubtedly been the impulse behind more recent adaptations. Their varying degree of success can largely be attributed to a desire to succeed in both cinematic and Shakespearian terms—two objects which seem so far to have been irreconcilable.

The human values expressed in the plays, the basic emotions and motivations, are certainly communicable in film terms. The USSR *Othello* (1955) and *Hamlet* (1964) are outstanding examples of this, while HENRY V (1944), because of its timing, made a special impact as an expression of patriotism. On the whole, however, the more successful adaptations have been those which deliberately held back from exploring the full potential of film; an interesting comparison may here be made between two versions of JULIUS CAESAR—US, 1953 and GB, 1970. Tony RICHARDSON's *Hamlet* (1970) concentrated on the text almost to the exclusion of background detail, with considerable success.

The readiness with which Shakespeare's work lends itself to a variety of modern interpretations was illustrated in 1970 by two film versions of the same play. Peter BROOK's *King Lear*, starring Paul SCOFIELD, was a study of old age; Grigori KOZINTSEV's *Korol Lir* placed emphasis on a decaying feudal society.

In spite of the literary purists, very free adaptations can be successful in conveying the spirit of the original in cinematic terms; ZEFFIRELLI's *Romeo and Juliet* (1968) is an example. CAMPANADAS A MEDIANOCHE (*Chimes at Midnight*, *Falstaff* in the US, 1966) is another.

A valuable use of film, recording great stage performances and productions, has hardly been exploited. OLIVIER's *Richard III* (1956) and *Othello* (1965), though this was not the declared intention, may be considered in this light, but surprisingly little attempt has been made to produce direct transcriptions of memorable stage productions as has been done for OPERA and BALLET.

Many films have used Shakespeare's themes transposed to other times and settings. Among the most popular plays for this kind of treatment are *Romeo and Juliet* (*Les Amants de Vérone*, 1948; WEST SIDE STORY, 1961; and many others), *Othello* (*A Double Life*, 1948; *All Night Long*, 1961), and *Macbeth* (KUMONOSU-JO, 1957). *Broken Lance* (1954), a Western starring Spencer TRACY, was loosely based on *King Lear*, and *Forbidden Planet* (1954) effectively turned *The Tempest* into a science fiction story.

Robert Hamilton Ball, *Shakespeare on silent film*, London, 1968; ed. Max Lippman, *Shakespeare-Film*, Wiesbaden, 1964; Roger Manvell, *Shakespeare and the film*, London, New York, 1971.

**SHAMROY,** LEON (1901–74), US cameraman, a lifelong innovator who has worked in most genres, particularly epics and musicals. In 1928 he shot two experimental films: *The Last Moment* (Paul FEJOS) and *Acoma, the Sky City* (Robert FLAHERTY, unreleased), and in 1932 signed with PARAMOUNT, where his first feature was *Three Cornered Moon* (1933). He moved to TWENTIETH CENTURY-FOX in 1940 and stayed there for the rest of his career, working with Henry KING and Walter Lang particularly. In the forties, he was awarded three OSCARS: for *The Black Swan* (1942), *Wilson* (1944), and *Leave Her to Heaven* (1946). In 1947 he worked with Otto PREMINGER on *Forever Amber* and *Daisy Kenyon*, and was then closely involved in the development of CINEMASCOPE—shooting the first film in the new process, THE ROBE (1953). *Love is a Many-Splendored Thing* (1955) and *The King and I* (1956) were important works in colour, and Preminger was the only director to attract Shamroy away from Fox—for *Porgy and Bess* (1959) and *The Cardinal* (1964). He won a fourth Oscar for his joint work on CLEOPATRA (1962). Other films on which Shamroy worked include the amusing and light-hearted *The Glass Bottom Boat* (1966), *Caprice* (1967)—in which Shamroy appeared—and the brilliant PLANET OF THE APES (1968).

**SHANE,** US, 1953. Technicolor; 2hr. *Dir*, *prod* George Stevens for Paramount; *scr* A. B. Guthrie Jr, from the novel by Jack Schaefer; *ph* Loyal Griggs; *des* Hal Pereira, Walter Tyler; *ed* William Hornbeck, Tom McAdoo; *mus* Victor Young; *cast* Alan Ladd (Shane), Jean Arthur (Marion Starrett), Van Heflin (Joe Starrett), Brandon De Wilde (Joey Starrett), Jack Palance (Wilson).

Using stereotyped characters and basic plot elements of the genre—the conflict between rugged homesteader and unscrupulous cattle owners resolved by the intervention of a lonely hero—*Shane* is both a conventional WESTERN and a human drama in a Western setting: this may be attributable to the excellence of Jack Schaefer's novel. The film's mixed reception was a reflection of this ambiguity: non-adherents of the Western were delighted by the thoughtfulness and realism of the characters and their conflict; many Western-lovers were enraged by the slow pace and deliberate restriction of vigorous action.

Today, *Shane* is regarded with considerable respect. The slowness characteristic of George STEVENS's work in the fifties is well controlled, aiding the narrative suspense, and the occasional outbursts of violence are vivid and exciting. The performances are uniformly excellent.

*SHANGHAI EXPRESS*, US, 1932. 1½hr. *Dir* Josef von Sternberg; *prod* Paramount; *scr* Jules Furthman, from a story by Harry Hervey; *ph* Lee Garmes; *des* Hans Dreier; *cast* Marlene Dietrich (Madeline, known as Shanghai Lily), Clive Brook (Capt Donald Harvey), Anna May Wong (Hui Fei), Warner Oland (Henry Chang), Eugene Pallette (Sam Salt).

The melodramatic story of Shanghai Lily and her former lover, Captain Harvey, on an express train held up by revolutionaries was unusual for its time in having most of its action set aboard the train. STERNBERG used the restricted setting to advantage, and was able legitimately to indulge in one of his favourite compositional devices, the light and shade of slatted blinds. The exotic costumes designed for Marlene DIETRICH by Travis Banton, no less than the fine performances given by the four principal actors, made *Shanghai Express* the greatest popular success of Sternberg's classic films of the early thirties.

**SHARIF**, OMAR (1932– ), Egyptian actor, appeared in many Egyptian films before being chosen by David LEAN for LAWRENCE OF ARABIA (1962). Since then he has acted in several large-scale western productions including DOCTOR ZHIVAGO (1966), *Night of the Generals* (1966), and *Funny Girl* (1968).

*SHCHORS*, USSR, 1939. 1¼hr (orig. running time 2¼hr). *Dir, scr* Alexander Dovzhenko; *co-dir* Yulia Solntseva; *ph* Yuri Yekelchik; *mus* Dmitri Kabalevsky; *cast* Yevgeni Samoilov (Nikolai Shchors), Ivan Skuratov (Bozhenko).

The Civil War activity of the Ukrainian hero, Nikolai Shchors, was a subject suggested by Stalin. Nevertheless, DOVZHENKO's work on the film was severely hampered by the strict requirements of leadership-cult. The character to suffer most from this was Shchors himself, a somewhat unreal, godlike figure. The other characters,

notably Bozhenko, who were invented by Dovzhenko and based upon people he knew, are much more successful, and so too are the military actions, for which Dovzhenko was able to draw on his own experience. The film is loosely constructed and moves at a breathless pace, yet it has a poetic, lyrical feeling which is enhanced by the shimmering, luminous quality of the camerawork.

**SHEARER**, NORMA (1904– ), US actress born in Canada, worked in Hollywood from 1920. By 1924 she was a popular star, playing romantic, sometimes daring, roles: among her most popular films was *He Who Gets Slapped* (1924), in which she was a circus rider. In 1927 she married Irving THALBERG who controlled her career for the rest of his life. She successfully negotiated the changeover to sound and had particular success in *A Free Soul* (1931), in which she was roughly handled by Clark GABLE, and in *Private Lives* (1931), in which she tussled with Robert MONTGOMERY. Thalberg's determination to change her image resulted in some prestigious, but not very successful, films including *The Barretts of Wimpole Street* (1934), ROMEO AND JULIET (1936), and, after Thalberg's death, *Marie Antoinette* (1938). She worked out her contract with METRO-GOLDWYN-MAYER and retired in 1942.

**SHELL FILM UNIT** was set up following a report by John GRIERSON in 1933. Edgar ANSTEY became the Unit's first producer in 1934. Their first film was *Airport* (Roy Lockwood, 1935), but *Power Unit* (D'Arcy Cartwright, 1937) pointed the way forward—a celebrated tradition of concise, effective exposition which includes *Transfer of Power* (Geoffrey Bell, 1939), the six-part *How an Aeroplane Flies* (1947), and *The Cornish Engine* (Philip Armitage, 1948), all produced by Arthur ELTON. Francis Rodker's animated diagrams have made an important contribution to Shell films. *Shell Cinemagazine* ran for twenty issues between 1938 and 1952, interrupted by the war, when the Unit worked, with Anstey again producer, for the Ministry of Information and the Admiralty. The Unit's wide range of subjects includes the classic COMPILATION *Powered Flight* (1953), *The Rival World* (Bert HAANSTRA, 1955) on the insect menace, *Song of the Clouds* (John Armstrong, 1956), and *Unseen Enemies* (Michael Clarke, 1959) on disease control, all produced by Stuart LEGG.

**SHERLOCK HOLMES.** The renowned detective creation of Sir Arthur Conan Doyle has appeared in individual films and series, in adaptations of the original stories and in manufactured plots which would certainly have surprised Doyle.

A series of fifteen British two-reelers, each a complete story, appeared in 1921 under the general title of *The Adventures of Sherlock Holmes*. Their considerable success led to the production in the same year of another fifteen plus a feature-length version of *The Hound of the Baskervilles* and by a further fifteen two-reelers, *The Last Adventures of Sherlock Holmes* (1923). These were all directed by Maurice ELVEY, with Eille Norwood as Holmes.

In America, Clive Brook starred in *The Return of Sherlock Holmes* (1929). *The Hound of the Baskervilles* was remade in Britain in 1931 with Robert Rendell (Holmes) and Fred Lloyd (Watson), with dialogue by Edgar Wallace. *The Missing Rembrandt* (1931) had Arthur Wontner as Holmes and Ian Fleming as Watson; the two re-appeared in *The Sign of Four* (1932). Clive Brook re-assumed the role in *Sherlock Holmes* (1932) with Reginald Owen as Watson: Owen played Holmes in *A Study in Scarlet* (1933) which had Warburton Gamble as Watson and Anna May Wong as the sinister Chinese villainess.

For a time Holmes's popularity was usurped by other detective series. Only the feeble *Silver Blaze* (1937), with Arthur Wontner and Ian Fleming, kept the Holmes flag flying. He was brought back to favour by Basil RATHBONE's famous characterization backed by Nigel Bruce as Watson. A new version of *The Hound of the Baskervilles* and *Sherlock Holmes* (both 1939) were made by TWENTIETH CENTURY-FOX, then Rathbone and Bruce moved to UNIVERSAL to appear in twelve low-budget Holmes features which used new stories even more improbable than those originally written by Doyle. The series petered out in 1946, having been made enjoyable mainly by the performances of the co-stars.

In the hands of Billy WILDER, the great detective unexpectedly emerged from screen retirement with *The Private Life of Sherlock Holmes* (1970), starring Robert Stephens (Holmes) and Colin Blakely (Watson), an affectionate if uneven send-up of the Holmes mythology.

**SHERLOCK JUNIOR**, US, 1924. 1hr. *Dir* Buster Keaton; *prod* Joseph M. Schenck; *scr* Jean C. Havaz, Joseph A. Mitchell, Clyde Bruckman; *ph* Elgin Lessley, Byron Houck; *cast* Buster Keaton (the Boy), Katherine McGuire (the Girl).

The Boy is a cinema projectionist with aspirations to being a famous detective. He falls asleep at work: in a dream he sees on the screen the Girl suffering at the hands of the Villain, climbs up and enters the film. He is rushed through abrupt changes of scene—snow to jungle, desert to a rock in the sea—and is transmuted into Sherlock Junior, the World's Greatest Detective. The viewer's perspective changes from that of the screen and proscenium into that of the frame of the dream film: we are now within the dream. This section, the greater part of the film, contains some of KEATON's finest tricks and stunts, including a leap through a window straight into a set of old lady's clothes put there ready as a disguise.

*Sherlock Junior* is probably Keaton's most complex film. It separates his usual divided persona, the effete and helpless hero who becomes supremely capable in the face of adversity, into two roles, in real life and in the dream. The Boy does win through, but only through the efforts of the Girl. The film displays his awareness of the interaction between film, dream, and reality while maintaining the intrinsic logic of all his work: his character and the resources of cinema, far from being imposed on the narrative, are integral to it. As an example of his superbly surreal imagination it has never been surpassed.

**SHE WORE A YELLOW RIBBON**, US, 1949. Technicolor; 1¾hr. *Dir* John Ford; *prod* Argosy Pictures/RKO; *scr* Frank Nugent, Laurence Stallings, from the story *War Party* by James Warner Bellah; *ph* Winton C. Hoch, Charles P. Boyle; *mus* Richard Hageman; *cast* John Wayne (Capt Nathan Brittles), Joanne Dru (Olivia), John Agar (Cohill), Ben Johnson (Tyree), Harry Carey Jr (Pennell), Victor McLaglen (Quincannon).

The second of FORD's unofficially-named 'cavalry trilogy' is substantially an account of the last days in uniform of Nathan Brittles. John WAYNE gave a remarkable performance, in spite of some sentimental lapses, as the ageing captain simultaneously trying to avert war with the Indians and to face solitary retirement after a lifetime in the army. The film, shot in Monument Valley, won an OSCAR for the photography which frequently evokes the visual style of the painter Frederic Remington.

**SHICHININ NO SAMURAI** (*The Seven Samurai*), Japan, 1954. 2½hr (original version 3¼hr). *Dir* Akira Kurosawa; *prod* Toho; *scr* Shinobu Hashimoto, Hideo Oguni, Kurosawa; *cast* Takashi Shimura (Kambei, leader of the samurai), Toshiro Mifune (Kikuchiyo), Yoshio Inaba (Gorobei), Seiji Miyaguchi (Kyuzo), Minoru Chiaki (Heihachi), Damike Kato (Schichiroji), Ko Kimura (Katsushiro), Kamatari Fujimara (Manzo), Yoshio Tsuchiya (Rikichi), Keiko Tsushima (Shino, Manzo's daughter).

Seven itinerant samurai protect a village against the depredations of bandits. KUROSAWA's best-known film is also a key example of the JIDAI-GEKI, a genre which in its most popular form, the CHAMBARA, has much in common with the WESTERN including a similar dependence on stock characters and situations placed in a historically inaccurate setting. Kurosawa's awareness of these faults led to the film's strong sense of history and to the human qualities of the samurai, usually portrayed as grimacing puppets. The astonishing vitality of this true *jidai-geki* is largely due to its narrative economy, athletic camerawork, and the tempo of the editing.

John STURGES directed a Western remake of *Shichinin no samurai*, THE MAGNIFICENT SEVEN (1960).

**SHIMURA, TAKASHI** (1905–  ), Japanese actor, entered films in 1941. An actor of striking presence, he has appeared in more than sixty films, but he is best known in the west for his work for KUROSAWA, notably as the oafish woodcutter in RASHOMON (1950), the dying civil servant in IKIRU (*Living*, 1952), the tough leader of masterless samurai in SHICHININ NO SAMURAI (*The Seven Samurai*, 1954), and Toshiro MIFUNE's dignified, ruthless opponent in KAKUSHI TORIDE NO SAN-AKUNIN (*The Hidden Fortress*, 1958).

**SHINDO, KANETO** (1912–  ), Japanese director, entered films as a scriptwriter in 1934. He worked for KUROSAWA at Kyoto, then moved to Shochiku at the beginning of the Second World War. At Shochiku he worked with MIZOGUCHI and began a long collaboration with YOSHIMURA: they left Shochiku in 1950 to set up their own production company Kindai for whom Shindo directed his first film, *Aisai Monogatari* (1951). In 1952 he made *Genbaku no Ko* (*Children of Hiroshima*), which won prizes and notoriety. *Dobu* (1955) dealt again with the effects of the atomic bomb, this time on fishermen exposed to fall-out from tests near their fishing grounds. *Hadaka no Shima* (*The Island*, 1960) gained international recognition of a sort; practically silent and self-consciously beautiful, it was either loved or hated. Since then he has made many films, often showing a predilection for a combination of violence and sentimentality; but his films have been little seen in the west with the exception of *Onibaba* (1964), a weird and brutal folktale. His reputation varies widely, from that of a serious, sometimes sentimental film-maker to that of a sensational wide-screen titillater.

***SHOOT THE PIANIST*** see TIREZ SUR LE PIANISTE

**SHOSTAKOVICH, DMITRI** (1906–75), Russian composer, essentially a symphonist, whose works include many film scores, in which field he was particularly active in the thirties. He composed for several of the films directed separately or together by YUTKEVICH and ERMLER: *Zlatiye gori* (*Golden Mountains*, 1931); VSTRECHNYI (*Counterplan*, 1932); *Chelovek s ruzhyom* (*The Man with a Gun*, 1938); *Velikii grazhdanin* (*The Great Citizen*, 1939); and by KOZINTSEV and TRAUBERG: *Odna* (*Alone*, 1931); *Yunost Maksima* (*The Youth of Maxim*, 1935); *Vozvrashcheniye Maksima* (*The Return of Maxim*, 1937); *Vyborgskaya storona* (*The Vyborg Side*, 1939); and Kozintsev's HAMLET (1964). Among his other film scores were those for Dziga VERTOV's TRI PESNI O LENINYE (*Three Songs of Lenin*, 1934); Mikhail Chiaureli's *Padeniye Berlina* (*The Fall of Berlin*, 1950) and *Nezabyvayemyi: 1919 god* (*Unforgettable Year 1919*, 1952); the VASILIEVS' *Volochayevskiye dni* (*Volochayevsky Days*, 1938); DOVZHENKO's *Michurin* (1948); and Joris IVENS's *Das Lied der Ströme* (*The Song of the Rivers*, 1954). His opera *Katerina Ismailova*, first performed in 1934 under the title *Lady Macbeth of Mtsensk*, was filmed in 1966, directed by Mikhail Shapiro.

***SHOULDER ARMS***, US, 1918. 30min. *Dir, scr* Charles Chaplin; *prod* First National; *ph* Rollie Totheroh; *cast* Charlie Chaplin (American soldier), Edna Purviance (French girl), Sydney Chaplin (sergeant and Kaiser).

Like THE IMMIGRANT, made in the previous year, *Shoulder Arms* is placed very firmly in a real-life setting—the trenches and battlefields of the First World War. CHAPLIN had been much criticized because he had not enlisted in the armed forces and his friends urged him not to release a film making fun of the army. But he did, a few weeks before the war ended, and it immediately became his most popular success to date, especially with the troops themselves. Keeping just to the right side of the line that divided its comedy from the possible bad taste of making fun of the men in the front line, it is still one of the best war comedies ever made, and one of the most convincing revelations of what it must have felt like to be in the First World War trenches.

The version issued is shorter by two reels than originally planned. The rejected sections included scenes of Charlie at home before the war and again afterwards being congratulated by King George V; a final banquet with many dignitaries was planned but not filmed.

**SHUB, ESTHER** (1894–1959), Russian COMPILATION film-maker, began work in 1922 editing and titling foreign and pre-revolutionary films. The lack of production facilities in the Soviet Union and the limited supply of films from abroad necessitated the reissue of old titles, with requisite adjustments to revolutionary principles: she completely re-edited CARMEN (1916), CHAPLIN's first film to be seen in Russia, and worked on a range of subjects from Pearl WHITE serials to INTOLERANCE (1916). She progressed to cutting new films and worked with EISENSTEIN on the shooting script of STACHKA (*Strike*, 1925). BRONENOSETS POTEMKIN (*The Battleship Potemkin*, 1925) gave her the idea of recounting history by means of contemporary actuality film, and after three years' research among newsreels of 1912–17 as well as the Tsar's domestic collection of films she completed *Padeniye dinasti Romanovikh* (*The Fall of the Romanov Dynasty*, 1927) followed by *Velikii put* (*The Great Road*, 1927) drawn from newsreels of 1917–27; the latter brought intimate scenes of LENIN before Russian audiences for the first time. Film material being scarce for *Rossiya Nikolaya II i Lev Tolstoy* (*The Russia of Nicholas II and Leo Tolstoy*, 1928), she aimed for a flavour of the period rather than a chronological account.

Like Dziga VERTOV, working concurrently with newly-shot material, Shub used skilful and imaginative MONTAGE for ideological purposes. *Ispaniya* (*Spain*, 1939) used archive footage, fresh documentary sequences shot by Roman KARMEN, scenes from THE SPANISH EARTH (1937), and captured Fascist film to make a passionate statement of the Republican cause. The playwright Vishnevsky wrote and spoke the narrative, and words, music, and images are integrated to powerful emotional effect. In 1940 Shub co-directed with PUDOVKIN *Kino za dvadtsat let* (*Twenty Years of Soviet Cinema*) and during the war she worked on conventional newsreels.

Shub's accomplished editing, and particularly her use of pre-existing material to create ironic or didactic effects, was influential on later documentary and compilation film-makers, but perhaps as important was her insistence on the importance of tracing, identifying, and preserving historic film.

**SIDNEY, SYLVIA** (1910–  ), US actress, real name Sophia Kosow, who made her stage début under the direction of George CUKOR and embarked on her film career in *Thru Different Eyes* (1929). She worked with a number of notable directors including Rouben MAMOULIAN (CITY STREETS, 1931), Josef von STERNBERG, William WYLER (DEAD END, 1937), and, in England, Alfred HITCHCOCK (SABOTAGE, 1936). She was particularly associated with Fritz LANG in his earlier Hollywood films (FURY, 1936; *You Only Live Once*, 1937; *You and Me*, 1938). Her success at playing sensitive downtrodden heroines made her popular throughout the thirties especially with film-makers dealing with the

Depression; but she has appeared only occasionally since 1941. She could be excessively mannered, and her habitually strained expression limited her range, but her best roles prove her an accomplished dramatic actress.

**SIEGEL, DON** (1912–  ), US director, after studying at Cambridge University, England, and at RADA, returned to the US and in 1933 became assistant film librarian at WARNER BROS. As an assistant editor he organized a MONTAGE department and directed all the montage sequences for Warners' productions including HUSTON's *Across the Pacific* (1942). After directing two OSCAR-winning documentaries, *Star of the Night* and *Hitler Lives?* (both 1945), he made his first feature film, *The Verdict* (1946). During the fifties he directed a number of thrillers, Westerns, and action dramas notable for their drive and objectivity, among them *Riot in Cell Block 11* (1954), *Baby Face Nelson* (1957), *The Line Up* (1958). In *Invasion of the Body Snatchers* (1956), showing a world taken over by mindless 'pods' yet appearing terrifyingly normal, Siegel gave his own view of Hollywood, although the film has been interpreted as a parable of America dominated by McCarthyism.

THE KILLERS (1964), originally made for television, maintained the terse power of HEMINGWAY's story, and *Madigan* (1968), a racy and economical police drama, was a considerable box-office success. Siegel was now able to move from tight schedules and low budgets to large-scale productions, earning particular popularity with films starring Clint EASTWOOD—*Coogan's Bluff* (1968), *Two Mules for Sister Sara* (1969), and *Dirty Harry* (1971). Cynical about 'the system' while compelled to work within it, Siegel expertly defines the conflict between his heroes, criminals, lawmen, or ordinary citizens, and the authoritarian structures that rule their lives.

*SIEGFRIED* see NIBELUNGEN, DIE

*SIGHT AND SOUND,* quarterly film magazine, sponsored and published by the BRITISH FILM INSTITUTE. It was first issued in 1932, as the *Quarterly Review of Modern Aids*, under the auspices of the British Institute for Adult Education. Its publication arose directly out of exhibitions in London in 1930 and 1931 of mechanical aids for learning—dealing with the educational uses of film, radio, music, and television—which showed the need for a publication concerned with audio-visual aids. The first issue included an article on 'The Case for a National Film Institute', by A. C. Cameron, and in the winter of 1934, three months after the Institute was founded, *Sight and Sound, a Review of Modern Aids to Learning*, became officially published by the British Film Institute. Its content was still mainly concerned with educational aspects of the uses of film. The scope has widened over the years to encompass an international, critical approach to the cinema. Each issue contains authoritative signed articles of criticism and theory, film reviews, book reviews, interviews, and reports of film festivals. Editors since 1945 have included Gavin Lambert and Penelope Houston.

**SIGNORET,** SIMONE (1921–   ), French stage and film actress, real name Simone Saminker, whose first film appearance was a small role in LES VISITEURS DU SOIR (1942). After the war she appeared in *Les Démons de l'aube* (1945) by Yves ALLÉGRET, to whom she was then married. At this time she adopted the name Signoret. Her first featured role was in *Macadam* (*The Back Streets of Paris*, 1946). In 1950 she married Yves MONTAND, and in the same year appeared in LA RONDE. Her first starring role came in Jacques BECKER's CASQUE D'OR (1952) in which she gave a performance of attractive spontaneity. In Marcel CARNÉ's THÉRÈSE RAQUIN (1953) she was powerfully convincing as Zola's sensual heroine, tortured by guilt.

In 1956 she co-starred with Montand in the stage production of Arthur MILLER's *The Crucible*, and again in the film version, *Les Sorcières de Salem* (*The Witches of Salem*, 1956). For her performance in ROOM AT THE TOP (1958) she received an OSCAR. Her many other films include: *Dédée d'Anvers* (1948), *Les Diaboliques* (1955), *Ship of Fools* (1965), *Le Rose et le noir* (1970). Her most successful roles, usually sensuous, mature, worldly women, display her characteristic qualities of sensitivity and warmth.

**SILLY SYMPHONIES**, a series of DISNEY animated cartoons, the first of which was *The Skeleton Dance* (1928) and the last *The Ugly Duckling* (1938). Distributed successively by COLUMBIA, United States, UNITED ARTISTS, and RKO, more than seventy of these cartoons appeared in ten years. *Flowers and Trees* (1933) was the first TECHNICOLOR cartoon film, which gave the series the edge over MICKEY MOUSE, which was still in black and white. Half the films were based on traditional folk material (such as Aesop's fables), the remainder being original scripts, but it was not until *The Three Little Pigs* (1935) that they became financially rewarding. (See ANIMATION.)

**SIMMONS,** JEAN (1929–   ), British actress, made her début in *Give Us the Moon* (1944). She made a great impression as the young Estella in David LEAN's GREAT EXPECTATIONS (1946) and as Ophelia opposite Laurence OLIVIER in HAMLET (1948). After several more British films she went

to the US in 1952; her first Hollywood films were *Androcles and the Lion* and Otto PREMINGER's *Angel Face* (both 1953). She starred in a number of films including *The Actress* (1953), THE ROBE (1953), *Desirée* (1954), GUYS AND DOLLS (1955), *The Big Country* (1958), *Elmer Gantry* and SPARTACUS (both 1960). She returned to Britain to star in *Say Hello to Yesterday* (1970), directed by her second husband, Richard BROOKS.

**SIMON,** MICHEL (1895–   ), Swiss-born actor, began his stage career with the Pitoëff company in Geneva in 1918. He acted in the classical repertoire, including *Measure for Measure*, and in Shaw's *Androcles and the Lion* in which he had his first success as Caesar. He followed the Pitoëffs to Paris, but at first had little success on the French stage, mainly because of his Swiss accent. He made a living in minor comic roles and appeared in silent films including Marcel L'HERBIER's *Feu Mathias Pascal* (1925) and DREYER's LA PASSION DE JEANNE D'ARC (1928). In the same year he was in Jean RENOIR's *Tir au flanc*, which marked the beginning of great friendship and mutual admiration between the two men.

Simon's first public triumph was in 1929 in the play *Jean de la lune*. He repeated his role of Clo-Clo in his first sound film, made in 1931 and nominally directed by Jean Choux: Simon himself was in fact in control. His success as the comical, unscrupulous parasite who pulls faces, sings, tells jokes, could have secured him a series of similar parts, but he refused to restrict his range. In Renoir's *La Chienne* (1931) he played the seedy bank-clerk Legrand with convincing simplicity; in BOUDU SAUVÉ DES EAUX (1932), far from repeating his performance as Clo-Clo as the producer expected, he created a completely new anarchic tramp. The role of Père Jules in VIGO's L'ATALANTE (1934) is closely associated with his own personality: a grumbler and dreamer who, surrounded by animals in his collector's den, communicates a child-like happiness.

By now Simon was constantly in demand. He appeared for Marcel CARNÉ in QUAI DES BRUMES (1938) and for CHRISTIAN-JAQUE in *Les Disparus de Saint-Agil* (1938), opposite Erich von STROHEIM. In DUVIVIER's *La Fin du jour* (1938) he was remarkable as a mediocre actor grown old and childish but still dreaming of success. At the outbreak of war he was in Italy with Renoir, playing Scapin in *La Tosca* (1940).

During the war Simon was subjected to various kinds of persecution. He was suspected first of being a Jew, then a Communist: later there were rumours that he had been a collaborator. Duvivier's *Panique* (1946) was a kind of allegory of his career: in the end he is lynched by a crowd

Michel Simon in *L'Atalante* (Jean Vigo, 1934)

which resents his refusal to adapt to society's norms. In René CLAIR's *La Beauté du Diable* (1950) he dominated the film in a role which combined Mephistopheles and Faust, angel and demon. From the mid-fifties his appearances became infrequent owing to skin poisoning caused by an accident with make-up, but he contributed an intensely alive and authentic performance to Claude Berri's *Le Vieil Homme et l'enfant* (1966). At the age of seventy-six he scored another triumph in BOROWCZYK's *Blanche* (1971), playing a cruel and bitter seigneur of medieval times, the oddity of his square face accentuated by deep wrinkles, his body, as ever, at once agile and awkward.

Simon's career comprises more that 140 feature films and many short films such as Georges FRANJU's HÔTEL DES INVALIDES (1951) for which he spoke the narration. His ability to exploit his own extraordinariness and to transfer to the screen the intensity of his own experience has resulted in a wide range of characterizations of unusual coherence and integrity.

**SIMON, SIMONE** (1911– ), French actress, began as a fashion designer in Paris. She studied singing, making her first film appearance in *Le Chanteur inconnu* (1931), and continued an active but unremarkable film career until 1934, when she appeared in Marc ALLÉGRET's *Lac aux dames*. In 1936 she went to Hollywood and made *Girls' Dormitory* (1936), *Ladies in Love* (1936), *Seventh Heaven* (1937) with James STEWART, *Love and Kisses* (1937), and *Josette* (1938). She then returned to France for RENOIR's LA BÊTE HUMAINE (1938) and Raymond Bernard's *Cavalcade d'amour* (1940). On the invasion of France she once again went to the US where her most famous films, including *All That Money Can Buy* (1941), CAT PEOPLE (1942), *The Curse of the Cat People* (1944), and *Mademoiselle Fifi* (1944), showed off her lively Parisian style. She returned to France in 1946 where her film appearances included Allégret's *Petrus* (1946) and OPHULS' LA RONDE (1950) and *Le Plaisir* (1952). She has also worked in Italy, Germany, and Britain.

**SINATRA, FRANK** (1915– ), US singer and actor, was first noticed in an amateur group, the Hoboken Four. During the late thirties he sang with some of America's big name bands, including those of Harry James and Tommy Dorsey. In spite of his lack of conventional good looks he became nationally famous in 1942, with a phenomenally successful eight-week engagement at the Paramount Theater, New York.

In most of Sinatra's early films he performed only as a singer; his first acting role was in *Higher and Higher* (1943) and this was followed by several METRO-GOLDWYN-MAYER musicals, notably *Anchors Aweigh* (1945) and ON THE TOWN (1949) in which he played Gene KELLY's sidekick. Meanwhile his records had made him an international singing star with a large and devoted following, but by the early fifties his meteoric rise had given way to an equally rapid decline. He fought persistently to play Private Maggio in FROM HERE TO ETERNITY (1953), accepting half his usual salary, and his moving performance, which won an OSCAR for best supporting actor, revitalized his career. He starred in several popular musicals—*Young at Heart* (1954), *The Tender Trap* (1955), GUYS AND DOLLS (1955), HIGH SOCIETY (1956), *Pal Joey* (1957). His serious acting included THE MAN WITH THE GOLDEN ARM (1955), in which he gave a harrowing performance as a drug addict, and THE MANCHURIAN CANDIDATE (1962). He established a coterie of fellow performers including Dean MARTIN, Peter LAWFORD, and Sammy DAVIS Jr who became known as the 'Sinatra Clan' and as such made some undistinguished films—*Ocean's Eleven* (1960), *Sergeants Three* (1961), and *Robin and the Seven Hoods* (1964).

Sinatra directed one film *None but the Brave* (1965) and became a successful producer with action films such as *The Naked Runner* (1967), *The Detective* (1968), and *Lady in Cement* (1968). Throughout his acting career he also maintained his position as one of America's finest vocalists. He received the Jean Hersholt Humanitarian Award at the 1971 Academy Awards presentation and soon after announced his retirement, but he has continued to make concert appearances all over the world.

He has been married to Nancy Barbato, Ava GARDNER, and Mia FARROW and his children by his first marriage, Nancy, Frank Jr, and Tina, have become professional entertainers.

**SINCLAIR,** UPTON (1878–1968), US author and political activist. He wrote over a hundred works of fiction, including *The Jungle* (1906, filmed 1914), socialist polemic, drama, and journalistic biography, including *Upton Sinclair presents William Fox* (1933). Films based on his work include CHAPLIN'S THE ADVENTURER (1917), *The Money Changers* (1920), *Marriage Forbidden* (1938), and *The Gnome-Mobile* (1967). In 1932 Sinclair was involved with EISENSTEIN on the abortive *Que Viva Mexico!*; the course of this unfortunate relationship is carefully traced in *The making and unmaking of 'Que Viva Mexico!'* (Bloomington and London, 1970) edited by Harry M. Geduld and Ronal Gottesman.

**SINGIN' IN THE RAIN,** US, 1952. Technicolor; 1½hr. *Dir, choreog* Stanley Donen, Gene Kelly; *prod* Arthur Freed for MGM; *scr* Betty Comden, Adolph Green; *ph* Harold Rosson; *des* Cedric Gibbons, Randall Duell; *mus* Lennie Hayton; *cast* Gene Kelly (Don Lockwood), Donald O'Connor (Cosmo Brown), Debbie Reynolds (Kathy Selden), Jean Hagen (Lena Lamont), Millard Mitchell (R. G. Simpson), Cyd Charisse (guest artist), Rita Moreno (Zelda Zanders).

The film brings a delightful mixture of satire and nostalgia to its story of Hollywood during the transition to talkies. Songs written by Herb Nacio Brown and Arthur FREED for early BROADWAY MELODY films strengthen the period feel, and the numbers are integrated with dramatic scenes to provide mounting interest. Debbie REYNOLDS makes a charming leading lady for Gene KELLY (co-directing with Stanley DONEN for the second time) especially in the 'You Were Meant for Me' number set on an empty sound stage. The title song provides the music for one of Kelly's most inspired routines in which he sings and dances his way through the pouring rain. The film's only real flaw is the ballet, which is enjoyable in itself but except for its score has no real relationship with the rest of the film, and even has a different leading lady in the stunning Cyd CHARISSE; but Donald O'CONNOR had his best role as Kelly's sidekick, and his 'Make 'Em Laugh' is one of the film's high spots.

**SIODMAK,** ROBERT (1900–   ), American-born director who studied in Germany and became an actor and stage director there. In 1929 he joined UFA as an actor, scriptwriter, editor, and director and in that year he worked with the group who made MENSCHEN AM SONNTAG. His first sound film *Abschied* (1930) made imaginative use of the medium. He directed several more films in Germany, including *Voruntersuchung* (1931) which dealt with the insufficiency of circumstantial evidence, and in 1933 he went to Paris where he mainly directed adaptations of plays.

Between 1940 and 1952 he made films in Hollywood, mostly thrillers with a strong Teutonic flavour. Among the best known are *Phantom Lady* (1944), *Spiral Staircase* (1945), THE KILLERS (1946). After *The Crimson Pirate* (1952) he made *Le Grand Jeu* (1953) in France and then returned to Germany where he made *Die Ratten* (1955), an adaptation from Hauptmann, and *Nachts wenn der Teufel kam* (1959).

His recent work includes *Custer of the West* (1967) on which he was co-director.

**SIR ARNE'S TREASURE** see HERR ARNES PENGAR

**SIRK,** DOUGLAS (1900–   ), Danish-born stage and film director, real name Detlef Sierck. After working as a journalist, Sirk went in 1923 to Germany, where he became well known in the theatre, first as an actor, then as producer and director. In 1934, in spite of his left-wing reputation, he was engaged by UFA. He directed several successful films, including *Stützen der Gesellschaft* (1935), adapted from Ibsen's *Pillars of Society*, *Schlussakkord* (*Final Accord*, 1936), and *Zu neuern Ufern* (*To New Shores*, 1937).

In 1937 Sirk went to America, where, after some frustrating years as a contract writer-director loaned to various studios, he made his first US feature *Hitler's Madman* (1942), about the destruction of Lidice, which METRO-GOLDWYN-MAYER drastically altered before release. His next, *Summer Storm* (1944), an adaptation of Chekhov's *The Shooting Party*, had originally been planned for UFA. Sirk soon began to demonstrate a remarkable ability to make films which conformed to Hollywood studio conventions, while at the same time projecting his own view of the world. He notably studied stress within the family structure in *All I Desire* (1953), *There's Always Tomorrow* (1955), *Written on the Wind* (1956), and the gap between reality and delusion in *First Legion* (1950) and *Imitation of Life* (1959). His many other films include: *La Habañera* (1937), *Magnificent Obsession* (1953), *Taza, Son of Cochise* (1953), *A Time to Love and a Time to Die* (1957).

For a detailed study see *Sirk on Sirk*, by Jon Halliday (London, 1971).

**SISTERS OF THE GION** see GION SHIMAI

**16MM,** the standard non-theatrical film width used for most educational, sponsored, and television work. It was introduced by Kodak in 1923 as a cheaper material for amateur use than the 28mm SAFETY FILM available since 1918; a 17·5mm gauge was considered but, owing to fears that unscrupulous dealers might split the highly inflammable 35mm NITRATE theatrical stock and pass it off as suitable for home movies, a gauge of 16mm was arbitrarily adopted. Its origin as a safety film gave 16mm its peculiar status with regard to CENSORSHIP in Britain. Although it has virtually been replaced in the amateur market by SUPER-8, 16mm has become a professional medium with a greater variety of film stocks and cameras than any other gauge.

As an amateur film gauge, 16mm was given its greatest impetus by the introduction in 1933 of Kodachrome, a colour REVERSAL film better in many ways than the TECHNICOLOR of its day. In the Second World War, several films were shot on location in 16mm Kodachrome and enlarged to 35mm for cinema release, notably *The Fighting Lady* (1944), a documentary filmed by William WYLER on board an aircraft carrier. The relatively low costs of 16mm supported the post-war AVANT-GARDE and UNDERGROUND. Television in the post-war decade adopted 16mm for news and documentaries and still uses it for nearly all filmed programmes. Throughout its history, 16mm has been used for sponsored industrial films and educational films, principally because of the wide availability of 16mm sound projectors in schools and industry.

Equipment and services for 16mm developed over the same period and advanced the medium with each development. For pre-war professionals and skilled amateurs there were a few spring-driven cameras with facilities for making DISSOLVES and other effects while filming. Gradually laboratories began to offer such professional effects through processing. The spread of tape-recording after the war led to 16mm sound nearly as good as 35mm, recorded at first on perforated MAGNETIC film and played back from STRIPED prints. Shortly afterwards the ARRIFLEX 16mm reflex camera brought similarly high standards in the picture. Reversal film stocks, original to 16mm and not available in 35mm, extended the cameraman's range and made grain and dirt less visible in the small image. With the availability of EASTMAN COLOR negative on 16mm from 1958, 16mm filmmakers had at their disposal almost every facility common to 35mm work.

From the early sixties the facilities offered by 16mm equipment—lightness, compactness, unobtrusiveness—became an important factor in the development of DOCUMENTARY. Film-makers from American television, some of the most important of whom came together under the banner of DREW ASSOCIATES, explored the field of DIRECT CINEMA: using hand-held equipment, they followed their subjects, filming in long continuous takes without imposing preconceived requirements. In France, CINÉMA-VÉRITÉ film-makers led by Jean ROUCH were simultaneously adopting similar methods. Both movements were marked by a radical social consciousness in the presentation of their material, however objectively it was amassed. As improvements in 16mm equipment affected the techniques of direct cinema and *cinéma-vérité*, so the demands of the new approach led to further im-

provements: noiseless portable cameras, radio-
and rifle-microphones, crystal sync systems. The
ZOOM lens became standard, and special lighting
was made unnecessary by force-processing film
stocks to a higher sensitivity.

Production techniques in 16mm are different
from usual studio methods, partly because of the
less cumbersome equipment but also because,
as 16mm is usually concerned with filming
actuality, the studio craftsmen whose job is to
create an illusion of reality are not required. The
camera crew is reduced to two: the cameraman,
who operates the camera, adjusts focus, and arranges the lighting where necessary, and his assistant, who loads magazines, keeps the report
sheet, and holds a SLATE or clapper-board where
needed. The three-man sound crew is reduced to
two: one to operate the recorder and one to hold
the microphone. For extreme flexibility the crew
can be reduced to a cameraman and a sound man
only, and the development of audio cassette
recorders promises the eventual one-man crew.
In this context, even the director ceases to be a
separate functionary. Once editing and post-
production work begins, 16mm production follows the general lines of 35mm, but many innovations providing greater versatility and ease
in 16mm editing have been adapted to 35mm
equipment. Of recent years most significant
advances in film style and technique have been
pioneered in 16mm.

**65MM,** a wide professional film gauge, used for
original photography of films which are later
released on 70MM stock. The additional width is
occupied by stereophonic sound tracks on
release prints.

**SJÖBERG,** ALF (1903–   ), Swedish director,
studied at the Royal Dramatic Theatre, Stockholm, and in 1930 became its head director. The
most distinguished theatre director of his generation, he has also made important contributions to
the Swedish cinema, not least in his very first
film, *Den Starkaste (The Strongest,* 1929). Dealing with human relationships against a background of seal-hunting in a primitive natural
setting, it is a powerfully poetic drama,
beautifully photographed by Axel Lindblom and
showing a debt to EISENSTEIN in the mastery of
its editing.

Repelled by the frivolity that took over films
in SWEDEN on the introduction of sound, Sjöberg
confined himself to the theatre for the next ten
years. His second film, *Med livet som insats
(They Staked their Lives,* 1940), showed that his
skill was unimpaired by his long absence; the
film, about an underground resistance group in
an unnamed occupied country, also bears the
stamp of pessimism that runs through his work.

After two less memorable features he directed
the first of his films to use a historical setting.
Based on an allegorical play by Rune Lindström,
*Himlaspelet (The Road to Heaven,* 1942) uses
the medieval folk art of Sweden as strikingly as
BERGMAN's DET SJUNDE INSEGLET (*The Seventh
Seal,* 1957), but to very different effect with its
affirmation of simple faith. *Kungajakt (The
Royal Hunt,* 1943) is also in its way a deeply
patriotic work, using a historical attempt to
overthrow the Swedish throne as its basis. Here,
as in his other historical films, Sjöberg's evocation of period is entirely convincing.

HETS (*Frenzy,* 1944) brought the name of Sjöberg before international audiences; it was also
the first evidence to be seen abroad of the re-
birth of Swedish cinema. A deep impression
was made by the powerful imagery and the
strength of the performances, an impression
which was reinforced by Sjöberg's later films,
notably *Bara en mor (Only a Mother,* 1949) and
FRÖKEN JULIE (1951), adapted from Strindberg's
play.

With *Barabbas* (1953), and *Karin Månsdotter*
(1954), which was based on Strindberg's *Erik
XIV,* Sjöberg returned to the historical themes
with which he has been most successful. His
affinities with the theatre, apparent in all his
work except *Den Starkaste,* are here less disconcerting than in his films with a modern setting.
Latterly he has directed less frequently, but after
a five-year absence returned to films with another
Strindberg adaptation, *Fadren (The Father,*
1969).

**SJÖMAN,** VILGOT (1924–   ), Swedish director. Already an accomplished novelist, he wrote
the scripts for *Trots (Defiance,* Gustaf MOLAN-
DER, 1952), *Lek på regnbågen (Playing on
the Rainbow,* 1958), and, in collaboration with
Ulla Isaksson, *Siska* (1962). A close friend
and admirer of Ingmar BERGMAN, he was assistant director on *Nattvardsgästerna (Winter
Light,* 1963) and acted in *Skammen (Shame,*
1968).

Sjöman's first film as director, *Älskarinnan
(The Mistress,* 1962), shows some debt to Bergman in its account of a girl emotionally torn by
her love for an older and a younger man. His
subsequent films have tended to emphasize his
interest in social or sexual taboos: incest in
*Syskonbädd (My Sister, My Love,* 1966),
homosexuality, violence, and bestiality in *491*
(1964), explicit depictions of sexual intercourse
in *Jag är nyfiken—gul (I Am Curious—Yellow,*
1967), and lesbianism in *Jag är nyfiken—blå (I
Am Curious—Blue,* 1968). The last two films
examine contemporary Swedish social mores,
but their reputation outside Sweden rests, unfortunately, not on their intelligent observation and

polished film-making but on their more sensational passages.

**SJÖSTRÖM, VICTOR** (1879–1960), Swedish director and actor, at the age of sixteen became a professional actor like his mother and her brother, Victor Hartmann, whom he greatly admired. He rapidly gained popularity and developed into an actor of much strength; he also directed at the Swedish Theatre in Helsinki and at the Royal Theatre, Copenhagen, where he met his second wife Lili BECH.

It was not until 1912 that Sjöström was persuaded by Charles MAGNUSSON to work in films. He joined Svenska Bio (later SVENSK FILMINDUSTRI) and after appearing in Garbagny's *I livets vår* began his long and friendly collaboration with Mauritz STILLER in the latter's *Vampyren* (1913). He started directing films in the same year. Sjöström's early work was largely concerned with social problems. *Ingeborg Holm* (1913), basically a savage attack on the current Swedish poor law system, already showed signs of his adventurous use of camera technique and his preference for outdoor filming. By 1917 he had directed 32 features: *Terje Vigen* (1917), adapted from a poem by Ibsen, shows him at his peak of achievement as the most influential direc-

tor of the early Swedish cinema. The bereaved and embittered fisherman, Terje, lives against a landscape of great beauty and cruelty which takes an active part in the unfolding of the story and is integrated with the development of the character in a masterly and poetic style. Here, and even more in *Berg-Evind och hans hustru* (*The Outlaw and his Wife*, 1917), can be seen the beginnings of the animistic element that runs strongly through Swedish films up to the present day: the equating of summer with hope and happiness and of winter with despair and the death of love.

*Tösen från Stormyrtorpet* (*The Woman He Chose*, 1917) was the first of several adaptations which Sjöström made from the works of Selma LAGERLÖF and marked the début of Lars HANSON. KÖRKALEN (1921), also from one of Selma Lagerlöf's novels, while widely regarded as Sjöström's masterpiece, lacks the close relation with natural surroundings of other films of his pre-Hollywood years. It does however show an adventurous use of special effects for the period and a scrupulous attention to social detail; Sjöström gave an impressive performance in the leading role.

In 1923 METRO-GOLDWYN-MAYER brought him to Hollywood, where (under the name of

Victor Sjöström with Bibi Andersson in *Smultronstället* (Ingmar Bergman, 1957)

Seastrom) he directed nine films during his six-year stay. *The Scarlet Letter* (1926) and THE WIND (1928), both starring Lillian GISH and Lars Hanson, are memorable for the typically Swedish integration of landscape and climate with the inner life of the characters. But like many other artists imported from Europe, he seems to have been unhappy in Hollywood; he returned to Sweden in 1928 and remained there until his death. He made one sound film in Sweden, *Markurells i Wadköping* (1930), but the frivolity that dominated Swedish films during the thirties had no interest for him and he returned to acting; apart from a historical romance made in London for Alexander KORDA, *Under the Red Robe* (1937), he directed no more films. His last appearance was his moving and authoritative performance as Isak Borg in SMULTRON-STÄLLET (*Wild Strawberries*, 1957), a fitting farewell.

**SJUNDE INSEGLET, Det** (*The Seventh Seal*), Sweden, 1957. 1½hr. *Dir, scr* Ingmar Bergman; *prod* Svensk Filmindustri; *ph* Gunnar Fischer; *ed* Lennart Wallén; *mus* Erik Nordgren; *cast* Max von Sydow (Knight), Gunnar Björnstrand (Squire), Bengt Ekerot (Death), Nils Poppe (Jof), Bibi Andersson (Mia), Erik Strandmark (Skat), Gunnel Lindblom (Girl).

The Knight, Antonius Blok, returns from the Crusades with his squire Jöns to find Sweden ravaged by plague. He meets each encounter—with strolling players, a witch-burning, suffering and sinning peasants, flagellating penitents—as a stage in his search for knowledge of God; but at each step faces only Death, a monk-like figure against whom he plays chess for his own life and the lives of humanity.

The film is based on BERGMAN's own play *Trämalning* (*Wood Painting* or *Fresco*) published in 1954. The imagery is clearly derived from early church paintings of northern Europe, especially the Dance of Death motif, and with an unerring sense of period Bergman powerfully conveys the brutal squalor of medieval life. Only the lyrical interludes with the tumblers, limpidly beautiful in contrast to the dark, threatening compositions used elsewhere, offer a faint hope of survival for simple, unquestioning people.

With SMULTRONSTÄLLET (*Wild Strawberries*, 1957), *Det sjunde inseglet* firmly established Bergman's international reputation and that of his regular team of actors. All the performances are distinguished but particularly those of Max VON SYDOW as the austere Knight and Gunnar BJÖRNSTRAND as the robustly pragmatic squire.

**SKOLIMOWSKI, JERZY** (1938– ), Polish director, entered the LÓDŹ film school after working as writer and actor on WAJDA's *Niewinni czarodzieje* (*Innocent Sorcerers*, 1959). In 1962 he co-scripted POLAŃSKI's NÓŻ W WODZIE (*Knife in the Water*). Skolimowski's first film was *Boxing* (1961), a documentary about his own sport. His first feature, *Rysopis* (*Identification Marks: None*, 1964), was assembled from four yearly film school exercises. In it he played the main character, as he did in *Walkower* (*Walkover*, 1965). Skolimowski's subsequent Polish films, *Bariera* (*Barrier*, 1966) and *Rece do góry* (*Hands Up*, 1967) firmly established him as a spokesman for his generation, deeply concerned with the problems of youth. Like Polański, he has become an itinerant international, moving quickly and surely from *Le Départ* (Belgium, 1966) to one episode of *Dialog* (*Dialogues*, Czechoslovakia, 1968), and ably encompassing the picaresque humour of *The Adventures of Gerard* (GB/Switzerland, 1970) and the adolescent sexuality of *Deep End* (USA/FDR, 1970).

**SKOURAS, SPYROS** (1893–1971), US film executive. A Greek immigrant to the United States, Skouras was one of three brothers who, from a single NICKELODEON in 1914, built up a chain of cinema theatres in the mid-west. In 1932 Skouras took over the management of Fox Metropolitan Theaters in New York and, ten years later, became president of the parent company, TWENTIETH CENTURY-FOX. Considered an innovator among Hollywood studio heads, he was responsible for promoting Twentieth Century-Fox's venture into WIDE SCREEN entertainment, producing the first CINEMASCOPE film, THE ROBE (1953). After the disastrous CLEOPATRA (1962), however, Skouras was replaced as president by Darryl F. ZANUCK, although he remained as honorary board chairman until 1969.

**SLAPSTICK,** term usually applied to low or knockabout comedy. Origin of the term's use is attributed to the US: it derives from the slap stick or flexible lath, used like the bladder by the harlequin in a pantomime to make the maximum noise with the minimum injury, or alternatively to give a signal for scene-changing. The term thus indicates that the kind of essentially physical comedy it designates derives from the *commedia dell' arte* through Harlequinade, pantomime, music-hall, and, in the US, vaudeville and burlesque. In the context of cinema and particularly in the US it is often used more indiscriminately to describe any form of physical humour, from the boisterous fooling of LAUREL AND HARDY to the reticent elegance of Max LINDER or Buster KEATON.

A more specific usage may be discerned, describing knockabout comedy as it was developed with the resources that cinema offered. Slapstick in this sense is discussed by James AGEE in an essay, 'Comedy's Greatest Era' (see *Agee on Film*, New York, 1958). As it developed in the decade 1910–20, mainly through Mack SENNETT and his KEYSTONE company, slapstick depended on frenzied, often disorganized, motion that increased in tempo as visual gags proliferated. Every gesture was exaggerated, and every part of the actor's body was used to punctuate these over-emphasized gestures. Inanimate objects became the source of constant frustration, as actors became entangled in ladders, rugs, chairs; mechanical objects in particular, such as automobiles and locomotives, developed an apparent malignancy towards humans.

Two other important elements in the Keystone slapstick were the CUSTARD PIE and the chase. Virtually every Keystone comedy ended in a chase, in which police, girls, cars, objects, often animals as well, were hurled into violent motion, dashing about in a kind of organized chaos that increased in tempo as the climax approached.

The great comedians of the twenties developed more sophisticated comic styles involving an emotional response, but they all continued to use slapstick to a greater or lesser degree, and became adept at piling one gag on top of another to enhance the comic effect. When sound came, verbal humour largely replaced visual humour, and the heyday of slapstick was over. This was in part because of the rigid camera speed that synchronization with the sound track required. Although it remains an element in the repertoire of many screen comedians, it has diminished the further film has grown from its silent roots: the slapstick tradition has had to wait for television to push it a stage further, as in *The Laugh-In* and *Monty Python's Flying Circus*, where once again slow and speeded-up motion are freely used.

Most great slapstick occurred in a specific time and place—Hollywood in the silent film era. In its fast action, its split-second timing, and its distortions of reality, it created a special kind of comedy that remains as fresh today as when it was created.

**SLATE,** the generic name for any board which indicates the number of a shot. This normally takes the form of a CLAPPERBOARD, although other forms of marking both the shot numbering information and the synchronizing point are used. During production, shots are numbered sequentially; the first shot taken is 'slate one, take one', the word 'slate' being used to avoid confusion with 'scene', which is the number of the shot in the script. Thus every shot has two numbers: the slate number, indicating its place in the shooting schedule, and the scene number, indicating the place in the script.

**SMELLIES** see AROMARAMA

*SMILES OF A SUMMER NIGHT* see SOMMARNATTENS LEENDE

**SMITH,** GEORGE ALBERT (1864–1959), British photographer and film pioneer who began making films in 1897. A leading member of the BRIGHTON SCHOOL, he pioneered the use of basic camera movements and such editing devices as the close-up. His use of big close-ups is illustrated by *Grandma's Reading Glass* (*c.* 1900) and especially *The Big Swallow* (*c.* 1900). He was the inventor of the first commercial cinematographic colour process, KINEMACOLOR, in 1908.

**SMITH,** JACK (1932– ), US underground film-maker, collaborated with Ken Jacobs on *Blonde Cobra* (1959–62) and played the central role. His *Flaming Creatures* (1962–3), an orgiastic transvestite fantasy, and the ironically titled *Normal Love* (1963, uncompleted) display deliberate technical primitivism, especially in the use of stale film stock to achieve murky or bleached effects. Highly regarded by Jonas MEKAS and the FILM CULTURE group, Smith's small body of work has had considerable influence on the mythopoeic school of American UNDERGROUND films.

*SMULTRONSTÄLLET* (*Wild Strawberries*), Sweden, 1957. 1¼hr. *Dir, scr* Ingmar Bergman; *prod* Svensk Filmindustri; *ph* Gunnar Fischer; *ed* Oscar Rosander; *mus* Erik Nordgren; *cast* Victor Sjöström (Professor Isak Borg), Bibi Andersson (Sara), Ingrid Thulin (Marianne), Gunnar Björnstrand (Evald), Max von Sydow (Åkerman), Folke Sundquist (Anders), Björn Bjelvenstam (Viktor), Naima Wifstrand (Isak's mother).

With DET SJUNDE INSEGLET (*The Seventh Seal*, also 1957), *Smultronstället* established BERGMAN as a director of international stature: the two films are in fact complementary. Professor Borg, like the medieval Knight, pursues a quest, not here expressly for God but for self-understanding. The car journey taken by the seventy-eight-year-old physician to receive an honorary doctorate, functions as a pilgrimage into his own personality, exposing his effect on the people around him. The action flows between past and present, fantasy and reality: a dream sequence early in the film is loaded with mysterious significance. The old man enters into flashbacks unobserved by the people of his past; these passages are handled with a gentle pace and lyrical camerawork that contrasts with the harsh

*Smultronstället* (Ingmar Bergman, 1957)

cutting and bleak lighting of the present time. Performances of complete conviction by Bergman's regular team are headed by Victor SJÖ-STRÖM, impressive in his last acting role as the selfish old man.

**SNOW,** MICHAEL (1929–   ), Canadian director, painter, sculptor, and jazz musician, a leading figure in the American UNDERGROUND. His *Wavelength* (1966–7) is in effect a single ZOOM shot lasting forty-five minutes, which finally focuses on a photograph of the sea; in *Back and Forth* (1968–9) the camera constantly pans and tilts within a classroom. A camera mounted on a machine capable of moving in multiple directions was set up in the open country of Northern Canada for the three-hour *La Région centrale* (1970–1). Snow has exploited the inherent properties of film—filters, film stocks, light flares, splice marks, etc—echoing contemporary trends in the other arts.

***SNOW WHITE AND THE SEVEN DWARFS,*** US, 1937. Technicolor; 1½hr. *Prod* Walt Disney; *supervising dir* Hamilton Luske; *animation supervisor* David Hand; *mus* Frank Churchill, Leigh Harline, Paul J. Smith, Larry Morey.

The first of DISNEY's feature-length cartoons,

*Snow White* advanced the possibilities of the cartoon from its previous role of simple diversion or programme support. Its original budget of $250,000 had to be increased sixfold, but its immediate and continued success at the box-office has realized over $25 million. The names of the Seven Dwarfs (Doc, Grumpy, Sleepy, Happy, Bashful, Sneezy, Dopey) were chosen from a public poll. Perhaps the most famous of children's films, it has unusual pace and rhythmic control. It continues to enchant through the joyous simplicity of its narrative, its animal sketches, tuneful music, and gentle humour, although some genuinely frightening passages (those concerning the witch in particular) caused disquiet and the film was in some countries banned for very young children. (See ANIMATION.)

**SOCIALIST REALISM** in the Soviet Union was a reaction against formalism in all the arts. The Communist Party criticized directors like those from the FEKS group, EISENSTEIN, PUDOVKIN, DOVZHENKO, and VERTOV for aesthetic intellectualism and absorption in the medium for its own sake, which was making their work unintelligible to the majority of film-goers.

By 1928 the Party had already begun to limit

the unprecedented freedom which film-makers had enjoyed during the New Economic Policy. Scripts and final versions of films were supervised, to ensure that content was not obscured, as far as the masses were concerned, by unorthodox structures and non-naturalistic treatment. With the consolidation of Stalin's position, the film industry, previously under the enlightened leadership of Lunacharsky, came under the control of a Stalinist bureaucrat, Shumyatsky, and its burden of mass propaganda and education became greater. Thirty per cent of studio budgets were allocated to the production of documentaries. Concern with abstract film theory was considered to be self-indulgence. In 1932 the government dissolved all Leftist art organizations, and freedom of expression came to an end.

Some directors found it easier to conform than others. Among them ERMLER, YUTKEVICH, Macheret, and the VASILIEVS were able to come to grips with social and political matters and to show class characters struggling with the problems of the new society. Their films were usually optimistic and positive in outlook and the introduction of sound was an aid to such realism. The so-called formalists found it more difficult

and their work of this period, as well as their earlier films, came in for much criticism. The Kino Conference before the MOSCOW Film Festival of 1935 was highly critical of Vertov's TRI PESNI O LENINYE (*Three Songs of Lenin*, 1934), Dovzhenko's *Ivan* (1932), Pudovkin's *Prostoi sluchai* (*A Simple Case*, 1932), and Eisenstein's STAROYE I NOVOYE (*Old and New*, 1929); and extolled the Vasilievs' CHAPAYEV (1935), Ermler's VSTRECHNYI (*Counterplan*, 1932), and Alexander Macheret's *Dela i lyudi* (*Men and Jobs*, 1932) as supreme examples of the new style. Fictional plots, use of actors, psychological portrayal of individuals were all recommended as being methods easily grasped by the new cinema public. This went hand in hand with a narrow moral code and a slick visual style.

Although under socialist realism films did at first cope with contemporary life, there was an increasing tendency to fall back on historical subject matter which combined entertainment with political simplicity. The Soviet cinema was effectively put in a straitjacket which greatly influenced its further development. (See SOVIET UNION.)

*Chapayev* (S. & G. Vasiliev. 1935)

**SOCIETY OF FILM AND TELEVISION ARTS** (SFTA) was formed in 1959 by the amalgamation of the British Film Academy and the Guild of Television Producers and Directors. The BFA had existed since 1947, the Guild since 1954, with similar aims to raise standards in their respective fields. Until 1967 the Academy and the Guild continued to present awards separately: since 1968 the SFTA awards are presented annually for achievement in various areas of film and television. Membership of the Society is by election: those eligible are senior creative workers in British film and television. Honorary membership may be awarded to outstanding persons outside the creative field. The Society's first Fellowship (1971) was awarded to Alfred HITCHCOCK.

**SOCIETY OF MOTION PICTURE AND TELEVISION ENGINEERS** (SMPTE) was founded in 1916 in the United States to bring together engineers (the word applies in the broadest sense) working in all branches of the film industry. As the motion picture world has expanded, other areas of activity have been added: sound recording, television, and photoinstrumentation. Its work in the exchange of ideas and information is pre-eminent and has led to the establishment of many technical standards, most of them accepted by the AMERICAN STANDARDS ASSOCIATION (ASA). The Society's Journal is highly respected, read throughout the world and is perhaps the most authoritative technical publication in film and television engineering. The head office in Scarsdale, New York, administers a membership of more than 7,000, of whom about 600 are outside the US, and organizes two major exhibitions and conferences a year.

**SOLDATI, MARIO** (1905–   ), Italian writer and director, began his work in films with scripts for CAMERINI including *Gli uomini, che mascalzoni!* (1932), *Cento di questi giorni* (1933), and *Il Signor Max* (1937). He co-directed *La Principessa Tarakanova* (1937) with Fedor Ozep, and went on to direct a number of moderately successful light-hearted films including *OK Nerone* (1951), *La provinciale* (1952), and *Il sogno di Zorro* (1952), as well as working as SECOND UNIT director on *War and Peace* (1956) and BEN-HUR (1959). He considers himself, however, primarily a writer: his best-known books are *America, primo amore* (1935) and *Lettere da Capri* (1954).

**SOL SVANETII** see DJIM CHUANTE

**SOME LIKE IT HOT**, US, 1959. 2hr. *Dir* Billy Wilder; *prod* Mirisch; *sc.* Wilder, I. A. L.

Diamond; *ph* Charles Lang Jr; *cast* Marilyn Monroe (Sugar Kane), Tony Curtis (Joe), Jack Lemmon (Jerry), George Raft (Spats Colombo), Joe E. Brown (Osgood Fielding), Pat O'Brien (Mulligan), Joan Shawlee (Sue).

Tony CURTIS and Jack LEMMON, as out-of-work musicians, inadvertently witness the St Valentine's Day Massacre, and their attempts to avoid elimination take them into a girls' jazz band dressed as women. The dialogue—fast, funny, and delivered with impeccable timing—is aided by dexterous cutting to make the most of fine comic invention, both visually and verbally. Comedy in the film is brilliantly manipulated over levels varying from the most sophisticated to an uproarious evocation of primitive slapstick. It is full of references to earlier films, those of George RAFT, Joe E. BROWN, and Pat O'BRIEN in particular, and there is an entertaining take-off of Cary GRANT by Tony Curtis. The performances of the three leading actors, and particularly Jack Lemmon, combine with WILDER's unerring control of pace to make it engagingly nostalgic as well as riotously funny from the beginning to the memorable pay-off line. In spite of the financial crises created during shooting by Marilyn MONROE it was a great commercial success.

**SOMEWHERE IN EUROPE** see VALAHOL EURÓPÁBAN

**SOMMARNATTENS LEENDE** (*Smiles of a Summer Night*), Sweden, 1955. 1¾hr. *Dir, scr* Ingmar Bergman; *prod* Svensk Filmindustri; *ph* Gunnar Fischer; *ed* Oscar Rosander; *mus* Erik Nordgren; *cast* Eva Dahlbeck (Desirée Armfeldt), Ulla Jacobsson (Anne Egerman), Harriet Andersson (Petra), Margit Carlquist (Charlotte Malcolm), Gunnar Björnstrand (Frederick Egerman), Jarl Kulle (Count Carl-Magnus Malcolm), Naima Wifstrand (Mrs Armfeldt).

Set in 1901, *Sommarnattens leende* uses the style of operetta to weave a complicated intrigue of romances in which upper-class characters and their servants are involved in a comedy of manners. Beneath the frothy comedy lies a vein of astringency as BERGMAN exposes the foibles and pretensions of the combatants in the game. Polished performances from his regular troupe admirably sustain the sense of milieu and Gunnar FISCHER's accomplished camerawork is particularly striking in the luminous lighting of the Midsummer Eve sequence.

**SONG OF CEYLON**, GB, 1934. 40min. *Dir, scr, ph* Basil Wright; *prod* John Grierson and the GPO Film Unit for the Ceylon Tea Propaganda Board; *narr* Lionel Wendt; *mus* Walter Leigh.

*Song of Ceylon* is composed in four 'movements': The Buddha; The Virgin Island;

The Voices of Commerce; The Apparel of a God. The GPO (see CROWN FILM UNIT) received facilities for sound in 1934, and CAVALCANTI's experimentation contributed to this film's original use of the soundtrack as counterpoint rather than complement to the visuals, most notably in the third section. The commentary is taken from Buddhist gospels and Robert Knox's account of Ceylon, written in 1680. The film has acquired a considerable reputation for its lyrical treatment of the subject.

**SONTAG, SUSAN** (1933–    ), US critic, best known for the essays collected in *Against Interpretation* (New York, 1966). With reference to a variety of contexts—fiction, theatre, film, etc—she argues that criticism should not postulate a 'meaning' for a work of art, i.e., translate it into terms other than its own, but concentrate on 'how it is what it is', an approach she has adopted with marked effect in discussing Ingmar BERGMAN'S PERSONA (1966) or the films of Robert BRESSON and Jean-Luc GODARD. She wrote and directed an experimental film in Swedish, *Duett för kannibaler* (*Duet for Cannibals*, 1969), sponsored by SVENSKA FILMINSTITUTET.

**SORDI, ALBERTO** (1920–    ), Italian comic actor, at the age of thirteen won a competition held by METRO-GOLDWYN-MAYER to discover a voice suitable for DUBBING Oliver Hardy into Italian (see LAUREL AND HARDY). In the late thirties he became a variety comedian and from 1938 played minor film roles. A gentle comedian of unforced pathos, he has become immensely popular in Italy over the course of nearly 100 films; he is best known abroad for two films by FELLINI, LO SCEICCO BIANCO (1952) and I VITELLONI (1953). Since the mid-sixties he has also directed films, including two episodes of *Le coppie* (1970).

**SOROK PERVYI** (*The Forty-First*), USSR, 1927. 1½hr. *Dir* Y. Protazanov; *prod* Mezhrabpom-Russ; *scr* Boris Lavrenyov, Boris Leonidov; *ph* P. Yermolov; *cast* Ada Voitsik (Mary), Ivan Koval-Samborsky (officer), I. Strauch (commissar).

A girl from the Red Army finds herself alone on an island with a lieutenant of the White Guard. They fall in love, but when a detachment of the White Guard arrives, she remembers her duty and kills her lover.

Set in Turkestan, and shot on location in the record time of two months, the film evokes with great skill the desert and the island where the action takes place, but it is less certain in its portrayal of the growing love between the girl and the lieutenant. Nevertheless it was clearly the romantic rather than the political aspect of the theme which appealed to PROTAZANOV, as well as to his audience.

The film was remade by CHUKRAI in 1956.

**SOSHUN** (*Early Spring*), Japan, 1956. 2¼hr. *Dir* Yasujiro Ozu; *prod* Shochiku; *scr* Ozu, Kogo Noda; *ph* Yushun Atsuta; *des* Tatsuo Hamada; *mus* Takayori Saito; *cast* Ryo Ikebe (young office worker), Chikage Awashima (his wife), Keiko Kishi (office girl), Chishu Ryu (family friend).

The film explores the relationships between people who work in offices and how these relationships affect their home lives. A young man is slightly bored with his work and his wife, and on an office outing starts a brief liaison with the firm's flirt. His wife hears of this and leaves him. OZU delineates the couple's reconciliation with masterly economy and clarity. It is a slow film, characteristically formal in composition.

**SOTHERN, ANN** (*c.* 1912–    ), US actress, began as a singer and from 1934, when she starred opposite Edmund Lowe in *Let's Fall in Love*, spent much of her career in 'B' pictures. Her engaging screen personality made her particularly successful as a light *comédienne*, especially as a scatterbrained blonde in the title role of the 'Maisie' series which started in 1939 and remained popular for almost a decade. After a successful television career in the fifties she returned to films to make some memorable appearances in character roles, notably in *Lady in a Cage* (1964), *The Best Man* (1964), *Sylvia* (1965), and *Chubasco* (1968).

**SOUFFLE AU COEUR, Le** (*Dearest Love* in GB; *Murmur of the Heart* in US), France/Italy/West Germany, 1971. Eastman Color; 2hr. *Dir* Louis Malle; *prod* Nouvelles Editions de Films/Marianne (Paris)/Vides Cinematografica (Rome)/Franz Seitz Filmproduktion (Munich); *scr* Malle; *ph* Ricardo Aranovich; *des* Jean-Jacques Caziot, Philippe Turlure; *ed* Suzanne Baron; *cast* Lea Massari (Clara, the mother), Benoît Ferreux (Laurent), Daniel Gélin (father), Michel Lonsdale (Père Henri), Marc Wincourt (Marc), Fabien Ferreux (Thomas), Ave Ninchi (Augusta), Gila von Weiterhausen (Freda).

In setting his story of an adolescent boy in 1954, the year of Dien Bien Phu, and in the milieu of the *haute bourgeoisie*, MALLE was clearly drawing on experiences of his own. His observation of the boy and his family is characteristically acute, his cinematic handling deceptively simple. He drew from Benoît Ferreux, who had never acted before, a fine performance as the spontaneous and sensitive Laurent. The potentially scandalous effect of incest is rigorously excluded by the delicacy and warmth of Malle's treatment, and by the beautiful performance given by Lea Massari as the boy's mother. Many of Malle's preoccupations are assimilated in the film, from the tension between the eroticism of the mother and the boy's anarchic innocence to the organization of the structure in a manner reminiscent of the fifties. Even critics hitherto alienated by Malle's apparent inconsistencies were ready to hail the film as a masterpiece.

**SOUND.** The screen has never been truly 'silent'; the earliest film shows had some form of aural accompaniment, usually MUSIC, as much to counteract the noise of the projection apparatus as to enhance the visual impression. EDISON originally conceived his Kinetoscope (see KINE-TOGRAPH) as a visual complement to his successful talking machine, and many other moving picture pioneers experimented with forms of sound reproduction. During the so-called 'silent era' films were rarely exhibited in silence: a musical backing would be provided by a piano, small instrumental ensemble, or cinema organ, and in major cinemas by a full symphony orchestra playing specially composed scores.

The 'sound era' is usually dated from 1929, when the synchronized talking picture achieved commercial success, but attempts at synchronization had gone on for decades—the German Synchroscope, Edison's Kinetophone, and Lee DeForest's Phonofilm among them. Commercial production interests were in the main hostile to sound processes, conscious that their worldwide markets must contract when they could no longer use easily translated titles for dialogue and narrative. As so often in commercial cinema a financial recession drove producers to back a technical innovation: the financially ailing WARNER BROS adopted VITAPHONE, developed by Bell Telephone Laboratories, which reproduced sound from large discs precariously synchronized with the film by a mechanical linkage. Public reaction to the presentation in 1926 of a silent feature film with synchronized music plus short films of singers and violinists, convinced Warner Bros that the time was ripe to profit from sound. The following year, in THE JAZZ SINGER, Al JOLSON both sang and spoke (including the possibly prophetic phrase 'You ain't heard nothin' yet!') and in 1928 they released *Lights of New York*, the first all-talking feature film. By 1929 thousands of cinemas were equipped for sound and dozens of films were in release, either all-talking or with talking sequences hastily added. Competing reproduction systems flourished and the unsatisfactory Vitaphone discs were soon replaced by OPTICAL SOUND on the film itself, mostly based on the German TOBIS patents.

In Europe and the US talkies were the accepted norm by the early thirties. Some fine films suffered in consequence: the arrival of sound was the ostensible reason for abandoning STROHEIM'S QUEEN KELLY (1928); SJÖSTRÖM'S THE WIND (1928) and Junghan's TAKOVÝ JE ŽIVOT (1930) were both unjustly neglected. Elsewhere, notably in the Soviet Union and Japan, economic factors perpetuated the silent film for another five years.

In spite of the capital cost of the new device, the introduction of sound restored the flagging industry. An important factor was an influx of new subjects, writers, and actors, mostly from the theatre. Successful stage shows, both straight dramas and MUSICALS, could now be filmed virtually unchanged, and the theatre provided a pool of actors with trained voices, so far unnecessary in films. By the same token the cinema lost some popular stars, like John GILBERT, whose voices were not suited to early recording techniques, while imported actors like Emil JANNINGS and Pola NEGRI, unable to master the English language, returned to Europe.

Stage plays, comparatively static, offered a solution to the initial technical problems which immobilized the camera in a sound-proof booth. Film-makers were, however, unwilling to surrender camera mobility and soon the BLIMP was standard equipment, silencing the mechanism by enveloping the camera in a padded casing. Camera and projection speeds were standardized at 24 frames per second; a side-effect of this necessary step was to limit the scope of screen comedy as it had so far evolved (see SLAPSTICK). The resources of EDITING became for a time more limited, especially in the early stages when all dialogue, sound effects, and music had to be recorded simultaneously on a single track while the picture was being shot. Lewis MILESTONE, in ALL QUIET ON THE WESTERN FRONT (1930) and THE FRONT PAGE (1931), PABST, in WESTFRONT 1918 (1930), and CLAIR, in SOUS LES TOITS DE PARIS (1930), all demonstrated great skill in the use of single track sound; but this demanding technique was soon bypassed with the development of sound MIXING by means of which various sound elements could be separately recorded and combined on the final sound-track.

Sound (dialogue or effects) which simply accompanied action on the screen was dismissed by thoughtful film-makers—EISENSTEIN, Clair, and many others—as a kind of tautology. The power of off-screen sounds to convey information or atmosphere quickly became an integral part of film technique and aesthetics and the use of sound editing, sound mixing, DUBBING, and POST-SYNCHRONIZATION has made it possible to create awareness of conditions in the whole scene, irrespective of the framing that limits a particular shot. Only the recording quality of film sound tracks has lagged behind advances in creating the tracks, and has in general been greatly inferior to professional tape or disc recording: the recently introduced DOLBY SYSTEM promises improvements in this field.

**SOUND CAMERA,** term applied to a machine for recording optical sound tracks (by analogy with the picture-recording camera). Like a camera, it is a light-tight box containing film and a transporting mechanism; unlike a camera, its film is exposed by light originating *inside* the sound camera. A galvanometer in the light beam varies the width of the beam as the sound signal varies, recording a continuously varying track on the film passing it. (See VARIABLE AREA, VARIABLE DENSITY.) The exposed film is then removed and processed similarly to picture film.

Optical sound cameras are now used only to produce negatives for making MARRIED PRINTS of finished films. Tape recorders or magnetic film recorders are now used for virtually all original recording, although they are sometimes called sound cameras from habit. (See SOUND, OPTICAL SOUND.)

**SOUND MANIFESTO** see EISENSTEIN

**SOUND OF MUSIC, The,** US, 1965. Todd-AO; 3hr; De Luxe Color. *Dir, prod* Robert Wise for Twentieth Century-Fox; *scr* Ernest Lehman; *ph* Ted McCord; *ed* William Reynolds; *choreog* Marc Breaux, Dee Dee Wood; *mus, lyrics* Richard Rodgers, Oscar Hammerstein II; *cast* Julie Andrews (Maria), Christopher Plummer (Von Trapp), Eleanor Parker (Baroness), Peggy Wood (Mother Abbess).

RODGERS and HAMMERSTEIN's stage musical, which opened in New York in 1959 and ran for four years, was based on the true story of a postulant in a convent who became governess to Captain von Trapp's seven children, and later his wife, during the Nazi annexation of Austria. The film rights were bought by TWENTIETH CENTURY-FOX in 1960 for $1 million, with the proviso that filming could not begin until the play closed on Broadway. Production began in 1963 with William WYLER as director, but delays caused him to withdraw.

The film was shot in and around Salzburg and its final cost amounted to $8–10 million. Critical reaction was lukewarm, but it was an immediate and overwhelming box-office hit, winning five OSCARS and grossing in North America alone $20 million in the first ten months. Within two years, with earnings of $42½ million, it overtook GONE WITH THE WIND (1939). Reports came in of people (usually women) who had seen it dozens of times, responding to its unashamed escapism and retreat from the harshness of both the contemporary world and contemporary cinema. It

was undoubtedly a highly professional production, exuberantly combining panoramas of Tyrolean scenery with a homespun concern for family and religion; Julie ANDREWS's brisk charm was generally acclaimed, and the score contained several hit numbers.

In 1971 *Gone with the Wind* was again top earner (although only just), but in 1973 THE GODFATHER (1971) overtook both. *The Sound of Music*, despite incredible earnings in North America alone of $72 million slipped into third place.

**SOUND-ON-FILM** see MARRIED PRINT

**SOUS LES TOITS DE PARIS,** France, 1930. 1½hr. *Dir, scr* René Clair; *prod* Tobis; *ph* Georges Périnal; *des* Lazare Meerson; *mus* Armand Bernard, songs by Raoul Moretti; *cast* Albert Préjean (Albert), Pola Illery (Pola), Gaston Modot (Fred), Edmond Gréville (Louis).

A slight and sentimental story of the Paris underworld, with boulevard songs integrated into the action. In spite of CLAIR's open misgivings, his first venture with sound was an unqualified success both critically and commercially. To avoid the stultifying effect that dialogue at first imposed on the cinema he cut natural speech to a minimum, using it only to convey information not readily attainable through images. His use of background noise to drown the actors' voices and of the view of characters seen in unheard conversation through a window was daringly novel. *Sous les toits de Paris* influenced the balancing of sound and imagery in subsequent films.

**SOUTH AFRICA.** Cinema first appeared in South Africa with EDISON's Kinetoscope in 1895 in Johannesburg, which was later to become the centre of the organized film industry. Film was for many years a part of vaudeville shows, and included early productions of local views. Distribution on any major scale began with the South African Bioscope and Mutoscope Company in 1899. The Boer War, although a divisive factor in many ways, provided both national and foreign film-makers with the opportunity to develop the topical film, and with the curtailment of variety shows during the war cinema began to be taken more seriously.

The post-war depression hampered further progress, and it was only through the efforts of itinerant showmen that film was accessible to large parts of the country. The first attempt to establish permanent cinemas was made in 1908, with circuits eventually being created. American films were increasingly imported, but hostility to this dominance, and the unacceptable moral content of many of the films, prompted attempts to break it; from 1927 British films were increasingly shown. Exhibition was for some years a monopoly of African Theatres Trust Ltd and foreign distributors did not begin to operate until 1930, led by METRO-GOLDWYN-MAYER.

Production continues on a comparatively small scale; the films do not have any international appeal, partly because of their poor technical and artistic quality, and partly because censorship inevitably inhibits creativity. Few films have been made outside the established industry; ROGOSIN's COME BACK AFRICA (1959) is a notable exception, and *Phela-Ndaba* (1970), a political film made by Africans showing their lives under the South African régime, was smuggled out and shown in the UK. Censorship has been applied since early days on a local basis, particularly in Cape Province, and in 1931 the National Censor Board was instituted. Its application has become increasingly rigid, particularly as regards racial and sexual matters, and comparatively few foreign films are passed for exhibition uncut. Film societies are also subject to this law, which in 1934 forced the closure of the Cape Town Society, the only society in existence at that time: a film society movement as such did not begin until 1945.

**SOVCOLOR,** a colour REVERSAL film developed in the USSR from about 1950 and based on AGFACOLOR, Agfa's factory at Wolfen (now East Germany) having been taken over by the Russians towards the end of the Second World War. The bias towards the red/yellow end of the spectrum apparently inherent in Sovcolor has been turned to advantage by Russian art directors and cameramen, for example in YUT-KEVICH's OTHELLO (1955). (See COLOUR.)

**SOVIET UNION.** Cinema reached Russia in May 1896, when LUMIÈRE cameramen filmed the coronation in Moscow of Tsar Nicholas II, and in the same month set up the country's first film theatre in St Petersburg. Other foreign companies, among them GAUMONT and PATHÉ, established branches in Russia, but it was only in 1907 that the first Russian production company was set up by A. Drankov. Ermoliev and Khanzhonkov were also prominent producers in the pre-revolutionary period. By 1917 there were over twenty Russian companies, including Neptune, Kharitonov, and Russ, as well as the government-sponsored Skobelev Committee. At the outset Moscow dominated the industry, producing 90 per cent of films, the rest being made in studios in St Petersburg, Kiev, Odessa, and Yalta. Until the outbreak of the First World War foreign films dominated the Russian market.

There was little outstanding work produced in the pre-revolutionary era. As it was impossible to deal with contemporary issues under strict Tsarist censorship, film-makers concentrated on romantic historical drama, baroque supernatural tales, and 'modern' dramas which imitated popular Danish films. Films depended heavily on adaptation from literature or the theatre, Pushkin and Tolstoy being favourite sources.

STAREVITCH's exciting puppet films, and films by the theatrical producer Meyerhold, notably his *Portret Doriana Greya (The Picture of Dorian Gray*, 1915), were exceptions to the general mediocrity. Yevgeni Bauer was another talented director, working at the Khanzhonkov studios. He was particularly successful with actors, and discovered Vera Kholodnaya who played the lead in his version of Turgenev's *Pesn torzhestvuyushchei lyubvi (Song of Triumphant Love*, 1915). He was an important influence on the actor MOZHUKIN, to whom he gave an important role early in his career.

Many successful directors—Buchovetsky, GRANOVSKY, PROTAZANOV, Tourjansky, and Volkov—emigrated after the Revolution, as did actors such as Mozhukin, Nikolai Kolin, Nikolai Rimsky, Natalie Kovanko, and Natalie Lissenko. The emigrés formed little colonies in exile, adapting themselves more or less successfully to the film world of Paris, Berlin, or Hollywood. Some, notably Protazanov, subsequently returned to the Soviet Union. Alexander Sanin, Vladimir GARDIN, and Chardynin were other old-school directors who continued to make a contribution to Russian cinema after the Revolution.

Significant changes began to occur in the Russian cinema during the first months of 1917, after Kerensky's provisional government came to power; the Skobelev Committee was reorganized, and censorship was temporarily abolished. This stimulated the production of a crop of anti-Romanov films, which, in their use of authentic historical backgrounds, took the first step away from the predominantly theatrical style of cinema. Protazanov's anti-clerical *Otets Sergii (Father Sergius)*, released the following year, had an impressively realistic performance by Mozhukin. Lev KULESHOV was already beginning to publish theoretical articles at this time.

In September 1917, a conference of workers' educational organizations—the post-revolutionary Proletkult in embryo form—discussed the aspirations of a Socialist culture with respect to each of the arts. A resolution on the cinema proposed its transformation into 'a real and potent weapon for the enlightenment of the working class and the broad masses of the people, and one of the most important means in the sacred struggle of the proletariat away from the narrow path of bourgeois art'. During the first difficult years of Soviet power, with the country beset by civil war, foreign intervention, acute famine, and shortage of materials, the cinema could grow only slowly towards this goal.

In their first days of power, the Bolsheviks established a State Commission on Education, headed by the playwright Lunacharsky, and including an important sub-section devoted to cinema. Film producers, fearing nationalization, began closing down studios, destroying precious raw stock (none was manufactured in Russia at this time), and migrating southward. The reactionary film-makers union, 'Tenth Muse', prepared to resist nationalization by boycotting cinemas taken over by the Bolsheviks. However, certain studios continued to work alongside the State Committee, and many of the first Soviet films were privately produced. Although there was a radical change in subject matter—almost all films dealt with the recent revolutionary struggle, or with historical events seen in a revolutionary context—there was as yet little innovation in form.

The Mos-Kino branch of the State Cinema Committee released its first film in June 1918, *Signal*, directed by A. Arkatov, and photographed by TISSÉ and Novitsky. The first anniversary of the Revolution saw the release of two further films sponsored by the Committee: *Podpolye* (*Underground*, 1918), directed by Kasyanov and scripted by the Bolshevik novelist Serafimovich, and the semi-documentary *Vosstaniye* (*Uprising*, 1918), directed by Razumni. In the same year the Russ Studios released *Khleb* (*Bread*), directed by Sushkevich and Boleslawski, and the Petrograd committee released an 'agitcomedy', *Uplotneniye* (*Congestion*), scripted by Lunacharsky and directed by Panteleyev.

Soviet leaders realized from the outset the immense value of film as PROPAGANDA, and early Soviet cinema had an important role to play in keeping up the morale of the hard-pressed Red Army and in bringing the reality of the Revolution to outlying parts of the Soviet Union. The first agit-train was created in 1918, and its staff included a film-crew led by Tissé. The film they sent back to the Mos-Kino Committee was edited by the young Dziga VERTOV.

Early in 1919, a new kind of agitational-revolutionary film, known as the 'agitka', began to appear. With titles such as *Smelchak* (*Daredevil*), *Za krasnoye znamya* (*For the Red Banner*), both released in 1919, these films drew on the events of a year of civil war. Revolutionary content was still not matched by any radical change of form, but new influences were beginning to make themselves felt.

A new generation of cameramen, exemplified by Tissé, were learning their art not in the studios, but in the front line of battle, and the newsreel was becoming a vital form. The film schools, set up in Moscow and Petrograd in 1918, were already training the first post-revolutionary generation of film workers.

The showing of GRIFFITH's INTOLERANCE (1916), which found its way through the blockade early in 1919, was an exciting revelation of the possibilities of cinematic expression and proved a seminal work for young Soviet film-makers.

The winter of 1919–20 was a difficult period for the blockaded Soviet Union, and film production was severely affected. Among the few films was *Polikushka*, made by the Artistic Collective of Russ, a film co-operative from the Russ company, which concentrated on the production of artistic rather than purely political films. Ivan Moskvin, fresh from STANISLAVSKY's Moscow Art Theatre, made his film début in the title role. Finally released in 1922, it was one of the first Soviet films shown abroad, where it was very well received.

Nationalization of the film industry was decreed in August 1919, and effected the following January. VGIK, the national film school, was functioning in Moscow by 1919. However, by the end of the civil war (early 1921), the film industry, like the rest of the Soviet economy, was virtually in ruins, and half the cinemas had closed down. With the temporary re-introduction of private enterprise, under LENIN's New Economic Policy, and fresh possibilities of foreign trade, the film industry began to recover and gather strength. Popular foreign films (through which companies earned the money to finance their own productions) began to be imported in large quantities, even by State companies such as Petrograd's enterprising Sevsapkino, whose own successful productions included *Skorb beskonechnaya* (*Infinite Sorrow*, 1922), which dealt with the terrible famine of the previous year, and the anti-religious *Chudotvorets* (1922), both directed by Panteleyev.

At the end of 1922, the government began to regain control over the industry, both economically and politically, by re-organizing it under a central co-ordinating company Goskino (State Cinema Enterprise). This became the Sovkino Trust in 1925. Sovkino controlled with State finance the whole industry in the Russian republic, and was also responsible for the import and export of film, in both Russia and the autonomous republics. Certain companies retained their identity under the new structure, including Sevsapkino, which became Leningradkino, and the former Russ collective which became Mezhrabpom-Russ in 1924, when a controlling interest was bought by the International Workers' Aid in Berlin. The Ukrainian industry was reorganized as VUFKU in 1922, and subsequently came under the control of the veteran director Chardynin. Other non-Russian republics also had their own studios, under the control of local educational commissariats.

The period 1921–4 was not only a successful stage of economic reconstruction (production rose from 11 films in 1921 to 157 in 1924); it was also an important phase of artistic transition, in which the Soviet cinema gathered strength for its creative fulfilment in the second half of the decade. The first of Vertov's new-style newsreels, KINO-PRAVDA, was released in 1922. In 1923 Kuleshov made important MONTAGE experiments, and the following year released his *Neobychainiye priklucheniya Mistera Vesta v stranye Bolshevikov* (*The Extraordinary Adventures of Mr West in the Land of the Bolsheviks*), made with members of his workshop, among whom were the actress Alexandra Kokhlova, and PUDOVKIN, already active as actor, scriptwriter, and assistant director. EISENSTEIN, a producer at the Proletkult Theatre, made his first short film to incorporate into an Ostrovsky play in 1923.

Proletkino, concentrating on a political cinema, released its first films in 1923. These included Razumni's *Kombrig Ivanov* (US title *Beauty and the Bolshevik*) and Bassaglio's *Borba za 'Ultimatum'* (*The Fight for the 'Ultimatum' Factory*). Protazanov's expressionistic fantasy *Aelita* and Ivanovsky's *Dvorets i krepost* (*Palace and Fortress*) were among the successful films of the following year.

Some of the national cinemas began to come into their own, with VUFKU releasing *Slesar i kantsler* (*Locksmith and Chancellor*, 1923), directed by Gardin, and the Georgian Kino section achieving a popular success with Perestiani's *Krasniye diavolyata* (*Red Imps*, 1923).

These years saw a proliferation of film magazines, which became the theoretical debating ground for the growing avant-garde. *Kino-Phot* and *Kino*, with MAYAKOVSKY and Pudovkin as early contributors, were important, as was the extreme leftist *Lef*, where Eisenstein published his first articles.

The year 1925, which began with the release of Eisenstein's STACHKA (*Strike*), and ended with his BRONENOSETS POTEMKIN (*The Battleship Potemkin*), opened one of the most exciting and original periods in the history of cinema. The silent masterpieces of Pudovkin, DOVZHENKO, Vertov, and Eisenstein, were the richly individual responses to the stimulus offered by a young revolutionary society.

Other influential members of the avant-garde were Kuleshov, who considered his *Luch' smerti* (*The Death Ray*, 1925) a pioneer 'film-grammar', and TRAUBERG and KOZINTSEV, who came to films via the experimental theatre workshop, 'Factory of the Eccentric Actor' (FEKS); their best-known film of the period was NOVYI VAVILON (*New Babylon*, 1929). Esther SHUB, like

Vertov a pioneer in the documentary field, developed the COMPILATION film in such works as *Padeniye dinasti Romanovikh* (*Fall of the Romanov Dynasty*, 1927), and *Rossiya Nikolaya II i Lev Tolstoy* (*The Russia of Nicholas II and Leo Tolstoy*, 1928).

Alongside the avant-garde, a more conservative, theatrically orientated cinema continued to flourish. At the Mezhrabpom-Russ studios older directors continued in their traditional manner—Gardin and Eggert with *Medvezhya svadba* (*The Bear's Wedding*, 1926), and Zheliabuzhsky with *Kollezhskii registrator* (*The Station Master*, 1925).

Between these poles of experimentalism and conservatism, there developed a naturalistic movement which foreshadowed some of the aspects of the socialist realist style which evolved in the thirties. Olga Preobrazhenskaya's *Babi ryazanskiye* (*Women of Ryazan*, 1927), and Stabavoi's *Dva dnya* (*Two Days*, 1927), were works in this vein. Abram ROOM was another of the naturalist film-makers. His *Tretya Meshchanskaya* (*Bed and Sofa*, 1927), an unromantic picture of the relationship between a woman, her husband, and their lodger, was internationally successful. Friedrich ERMLER showed his future promise with the sensitive *Katka—bumazhnyr anyot* (*Katka's Reinette Apples*, 1926).

Among documentaries of this period, Turin's TURKSIB (1929), and KALATOZOV'S DJIM CHUANTE (*Salt for Svanetia*, 1930), were outstanding. More national cinemas also began functioning. The first Uzbek film, *The Starving Steppe Revives*, was released in 1925, when the Azerbaijan and Chuvash studios also opened.

The experimental vitality which characterized the Russian cinema of the late twenties was sadly short-lived. The later silent films of the avant-garde incurred increasingly severe criticism from the party establishment, whether for formalism or historical unorthodoxy. Stalin's first Five-Year Plan was implemented in 1928. This decisive move towards a totalitarian state was reflected in the cinema, as in the other arts, by the gradual imposition of the doctrine of SOCIALIST REALISM, which was to drive the Soviet film into a creative cul-de-sac and effectively stifle the film industry until Stalin's death in 1953.

The arrival of sound, which increased the possibilities of naturalism, was an important factor in the development of the socialist realist aesthetic. Sound-recording in Russia had been pioneered by Tager and Shorin from 1926, but was not fully developed until two or three years after its arrival in the West. The first full-length sound films, released in 1931, included EKK's *Putyovka v zhizn* (*Road to Life*), Kozintsev and Trauberg's *Odna* (*Alone*), and YUTKEVICH's *Zlatiye gori*

(*Golden Mountains*). Ermler's influential VSTRECHNYI (*Counterplan*, 1932), was an early model for socialist realism. SHOSTAKOVICH composed the music for many of these films.

Dovzhenko's first sound film, *Ivan*, came out in 1932, and Kuleshov and Pudovkin followed suit the following year, with *Velikii uteshitel* (*The Great Consoler*) and *Deserter* respectively. These films were disappointing in comparison with their directors' earlier work, probably a reflection of the increasing political difficulties as much as the inherent problems of the transition to sound. There was a resurgence of literary adaptations, such as V. Petrov's *Groza* (*The Storm*, 1934), from an Ostrovsky play, Roshal's *Peterburgskaya noch* (1934), from Dostoevsky, and *Pepo* (1935), directed by the pioneer of Armenian cinema, Bek Nazarov, and adapted from Sundukian's play. Musicals were another form to be exploited, particularly by Eisenstein's collaborator, ALEXANDROV, as in *Vesyoliye rebyata* (*Jazz Comedy*, 1934), and *Tsirk* (*Circus*, 1936).

An unusual feature of the Soviet cinema was that the silent film did not become obsolete with the advent of sound, but continued for a time as a valid and popular form, notably in the productions of the film train. This descendant of the agit-trains was created in 1931, and for two years the unit, under the direction of MEDVEDKIN, toured the country making instructional films and critical satires. Medvedkin made one of the last silent films in the Soviet Union, *Styazhateli* (*Snatchers*, 1935), a daringly unorthodox treatment of the delicate theme of collectivization.

Socialist realism emerged fully fledged in the VASILIEVS' CHAPAYEV (1935), which dealt with a popular Red Army hero. This film, with its naïve glorification of a 'positive hero' of socialism, its strictly ideological interpretation of history, and its unimaginative and straightforward style, delighted Stalin, and set the dominant tone for well over a decade. Thus Kozintsev and Trauberg directed the *Maxim* trilogy, which, in its successive parts (released 1935, 1937, and 1939), traced the hero's progress from young revolutionary to experienced party worker, to finance minister during the civil war. The adventurous style of their earlier films was eliminated, and their cameraman, Andrei MOSKVIN, renounced his elegant expressionism for a sober realistic style. After *Krestyanye* (*Peasants*, 1935), Ermler made *Velikii grazhdanin* (*The Great Citizen*), a two-part work appearing in 1938 and 1939, which based its hero, Shakhov, on the Bolshevik leader Kirov. Yuli Raizman also contributed two popular films in the socialist realist vein, *Lyotchiki* (*Airmen*, 1935), on the routine life at an aerodrome, and *Podnyataya tselina* (*Virgin Soil Upturned*, 1940), yet another

film on collectivization. Sergei GERASIMOV specialized in films about young people, and gathered round him a permanent group of actors, including Tamara Makarova, Oleg Zhakov, and Peter Aleinikov. His works include *Komsomolsk* (1938), and *Uchitel* (*The Teacher*, 1939).

The twentieth anniversary of the Revolution produced a crop of commemorative films, of which *Deputat Baltiki* (*Baltic Deputy*, 1937), directed by Zarkhi and HEIFITS, was the most interesting. Stalin's notorious 'cult of personality' was reflected in the number of films, often grossly sycophantic, depicting himself and Lenin. The actors Shchukin and Strauch became famous as impersonators of Lenin, the former in Mikhail ROMM's LENIN V OKTIABRYE (*Lenin in October*, 1937) and *Lenin v 1918 godu* (*Lenin in 1918*, 1939), the latter in Yutkevich's *Chelovek s ruzhyom* (*The Man with a Gun*, 1938) and *Yakov Sverdlov* (1940). The Georgian actor, Gelovani, was the most successful Stalin impersonator, appearing in Chiaureli's *Great Dawn* (1938), Kuleshov's *Sibiryaki* (*Siberians*, 1940), Kalatozov's *Valeri Chkalov* (1941), and the Vasilievs' *Oborona Tsaritsina* (*The Defence of Tsaritsin*, 1942). Dovzhenko was entrusted with making a Ukrainian equivalent of *Chapayev*, in SHCHORS (1939).

When Russia entered the Second World War, the emphasis turned to the documentary film. Verlamov and Kopalin's *Razgrom nemetskikh voisk pod Moskvoi* (*The Defeat of the German Armies near Moscow*, 1942) was the first full-length war documentary. Others were *Leningrad v borbe* (*Leningrad in Combat*, 1942), directed by Roman KARMEN, and *Den voini* (*Day of War*, 1942), a compilation film made by M. Slutsky, from material by a hundred front-line cameramen. In an effort to improve the war output, the documentary studios were reorganized early in 1944, and put under the supervision of Gerasimov. Many feature-film directors were then drafted to this section: Raizman made *Berlin* (1945), Polesky *Vienna* (1945), Dovzhenko *Pobeda na pravoberezhnoi Ukrainye* (*Victory in the Ukraine*, 1945), and Zarkhi and Heifits *Razgrom Japoni* (*Defeat of Japan*, 1945).

Feature-film production continued on a limited scale, often with several directors working simultaneously on different parts of a film, to speed up production. Feature films released during the war include Eisenstein's IVAN GROZNYI (*Ivan the Terrible*, Part 1, 1944), Pudovkin's *Vo imya rodini* (*In the Name of the Fatherland*, 1943), Room's *Nashestviye* (*Invasion*, 1945), *Chelovek 217* (*Man No 217*, 1944), and DON-SKOI's *Raduga* (*Rainbow*, 1944).

At the end of the war, Stalinist repression returned with a vengeance. Among films severely criticized, and in some cases banned, were

Kozintsev and Trauberg's *Prostiye lyudi* (*Plain People*, 1945, released 1956), Pudovkin's *Admiral Nakhimov* (1946), Lukov's *Bolshaya zhizn* (*A Great Life*, Part 2, 1946, released 1958), and *Ivan Groznyi*, Part 2 (1946, released 1958). The most successful film in a bleak year was Chiaureli's *Klyatva* (*The Vow*), a flattering review of Stalin's work. *Kamennyi tsvetok* (*The Stone Flower*, 1946), was the first Soviet film to be made with the captured German AGFA colour system.

Production declined still further during the last years of Stalinism (19 features released in 1945, 6 in 1950). With the new era of relative freedom ushered in by Khrushchev's 'secret speech' at the Twentieth Party Congress in 1956, a renaissance of the industry began.

CHUKRAI's *Sorok pervyi* (*The Forty-first*, 1956), a new version of Protazanov's 1927 classic, heralded the return of individual expression to the cinema. The film was an overnight success, particularly with the younger generation. Chukrai followed this with BALLADA O SOLDATE (*Ballad of a Soldier*, 1959), and the anti-Stalinist *Chistoye nebo* (*Clear Skies*, 1961). Kalatozov's LETYAT ZHURAVLI (*The Cranes are Flying*, 1957), with its emphasis on personal feelings, and its flamboyant camerawork, was another significant landmark in the resurgence of a personal cinema. This developed further in the films of the sixties, which were characterized by a more uninhibited critical approach to the problems of Soviet society, and a refreshing individualism in style.

BONDARCHUK began a successful career with SUDBA CHELOVEKA (*Destiny of a Man*, 1959); the tradition of literary adaptation was honourably maintained by Heifits with Chekhov and by Kozintsev with Cervantes and SHAKESPEARE. Among young directors emerging in the sixties were several from the autonomous republics, the Ukrainian Larissa Shepitko who made her first film, *Znoi* (*Heat*), in 1963, the Armenian Paradjanov, best known for his exotic *Teni zabytykh predkov* (*Shadows of our Forgotten Ancestors*, 1964), and the Georgian Khutsiev, who made a controversial film on Soviet youth, *Mne dvadtsat let* (*I am Twenty*, 1961, released 1963).

Many of the bolder young film-makers continue to encounter grave problems of censorship. Klimov's deft satire on Khrushchev and Soviet society, *Dobro pozhalovat* (*Welcome*, 1964), was indefinitely shelved, and TARKOVSKY, probably the greatest among the young directors, was accused of lack of historical truth in his *Andrei Rublev*, which was acclaimed abroad, but had its release in the USSR delayed from 1966 until 1971.

Other young and progressive film-makers are Mikhail Bogin, Pavel Lubimov, Alexander Mitta, Vladimir Fetin, Vassili Shukshin, and Gleb Panfilov.

By 1970 there were twenty studios producing 134 films between them. Every director is assigned to a specific studio. Films are rated by a special commission, and the director's salary is influenced by the rating awarded. Films not approved by the commission are remade until acceptable, or else shelved.

Jay Leyda, *Kino: a history of the Russian and Soviet film*, London, New York, 1960; Jeanne Vronskaya, *Young Soviet film makers*, London, 1972.

**SPAAK, CHARLES** (1903–    ), French scriptwriter, born in Belgium, came to Paris in 1928 as secretary to his fellow-countryman, FEYDER, and wrote the script for the latter's *Les Nouveaux Messieurs* (1929). The collaboration continued, with Spaak writing the scripts for *Le Grand Jeu* (1934), *Pension Mimosas* (1935), and LA KERMESSE HEROÏQUE (1935). Other directors with whom he worked include GRÉMILLON on *La Petite Lise* (1931), *L'Étrange Monsieur Victoire* (1938), *Le Ciel est à vous* (1943); RENOIR on *Les Bas-fonds* (1936), LA GRANDE ILLUSION (1937); ALLÉGRET on *Les Beaux Jours* (1935); CAYATTE on *Justice est faite* (1950) and *Nous sommes tous des assassins* (1952); CHRISTIAN-JAQUE on *L'Assassinat du Père Noel* (1941), *Premier Bal* (1941); and CARNÉ on THÉRÈSE RAQUIN (1953).

He is the father of actresses Catherine and Agnes Spaak and brother of the Belgian politician, Paul-Henri Spaak.

**SPACING,** material used during the tracklaying process of EDITING to fill in the gaps between sections of MAGNETIC sound film in each track. As there are often upwards of half a dozen separate tracks even for the shortest of films, with much of each track being silent, it is cheaper to use old film material in these silent sections than virgin magnetic STOCK. Spacing is also patched into work prints or cutting copies to maintain synchronization where short sections are missing.

**SPAIN.** Exhibition and film-making both took place in Spain from 1896 and the country produced one of the most distinguished early film-makers in Segundo de CHOMÓN. However, the early period of Spanish cinema was characterized by a proliferation of production companies turning out mediocre adaptations from literary or historical sources. This situation continued in general through the silent period, although critical awareness was fostered by the creation of the first Spanish ciné-club in 1928; at the same time the *Gaceta Literaria* began to devote a section to cinema, with Luis BUÑUEL among its contributors.

The arrival of sound coincided with the election of a democratic government in 1931, and an attempt was made to support and consolidate the film industry. Several new studios were built and the first big production and distribution company, CIFESA, was founded in 1934. But many of the more talented film-makers went to Hollywood to work on Spanish-language versions of American films and the home industry failed to develop. The Civil War reduced production to documentaries made with footage from the combat areas, such as the Republican *España leal en armes* (1937) to which Buñuel contributed. (His LAS HURDES, 1932, probably the most outstanding Spanish film of the thirties, had been banned immediately on release.) Joris IVENS's THE SPANISH EARTH (1937) was the most distinguished film of the war period.

The victorious Nationalists immediately began to bring the film industry under government control, introducing prizes and, from 1941, subsidies and QUOTA legislation, while imposing strict 'guidance' on the content of both newsreels and feature films. Spanish films of the forties reflected the sterility of moral and political repression, but in the fifties a distinctive Spanish cinema began to emerge. Co-productions helped financially, and a new generation of young directors was headed by BARDEM and BERLANGA, graduates of the Madrid film school, Instituto de Investigaciones y Experiences Cinematograficas, founded in 1947. Strongly influenced by Italian NEO-REALISM, they rejected as far as possible the values of the Franco régime: Berlanga's BIEN-VENIDA MR MARSHALL (*Welcome Mr Marshall*, 1953) and Bardem's MUERTE DI UN CICLISTA (*Death of a Cyclist*, 1955) won prizes at CANNES and had considerable success abroad. Other fresh and vigorous films came from Nieves Conde: *Surcos* (*Furrows*, 1951), *Los Peces rojos* (*The Red Fish*, 1955), *El Inquilino* (*The Tenant*, 1958), and from Cesar Fernandez de Ardavin: *Lazarillo de Tormes* (1959). The Italian Marco Ferrari directed several successful satirical films and at Bardem's instigation Buñuel returned to Spain to direct VIRIDIANA (1961), which was immediately banned there: his next visit was in 1970, when he made *Tristaña*.

International recognition stimulated extensive reorganization of the industry and the sixties saw a period of expansion, although young directors were increasingly in trouble with the censors. Berlanga's EL VERDUGO (*The Executioner*, 1964) demonstrated continuing resistance to the official suppression of a sharp view of Spanish life. The early seventies saw a gradual relaxation in the field of censorship—prior submission of scripts was made voluntary, although strict surveillance of the finished film was maintained. Foreign films which would earlier have been banned outright or severely cut were now passed for exhibition in the Salas Especiales, small art houses in the larger cities.

The vanguard of contemporary Spanish cinema is represented by Carlos Saura, director of *Peppermint Frappé* (1967) and *La Prima Angélica* (1974) as well as other, more conventional, films, and Victor Erice, whose *El espiritu de la colmena* (*The Spirit of the Beehive*, 1973), deals with the effects of the Civil War in a manner at once lyrical and honest.

**SPANISH EARTH, The**, US, 1937. 50min. *Dir, scr* Joris Ivens; *prod* Contemporary Historians Inc; *comm, narr* Ernest Hemingway; *ph* John Ferno; *ed* Helen van Dongen; *mus* Marc Blitzstein, Virgil Thomson.

Contemporary Historians, a group of American writers and intellectuals (HEMINGWAY, John Dos Passos, Archibald MacLeish, Lillian HELLMAN) sponsored this documentary to inspire support and publicity for the Spanish Republican cause. Hemingway, present in Spain as a journalist, had previously worked with the novelist Prudencio de Pereda on a propagandist documentary called *Spain in Flames* (1937). His understated commentary for *The Spanish Earth* is a milestone in documentary form, a continuing influence heard, for example, in the commentaries of *London Can Take It* (WATT and JENNINGS, 1940) by Quentin Reynolds, and *The Anderson Platoon* (Pierre Schoendoerffer, 1967). The version of *The Spanish Earth* released in France had a narration written and spoken by Jean RENOIR.

**SPARTACUS**, US, 1960. Technirama; 3$\frac{1}{4}$hr; Technicolor. *Dir* Stanley Kubrick; *prod* Kirk Douglas for Bryna; *scr* Dalton Trumbo, based on the novel by Howard Fast; *ph* Russell Metty; *cast* Kirk Douglas (Spartacus), Laurence Olivier (Marcus Crassus), Jean Simmons (Varinia), Charles Laughton (Gracchus), Peter Ustinov (Batiatus), John Gavin (Julius Caesar), Tony Curtis (Antoninus).

After the critical acclaim that greeted his small-budget films *The Killing* (1956) and PATHS OF GLORY (1957), KUBRICK, taking over the direction of *Spartacus* from Anthony MANN, proved more than capable of handling the large-scale, wide-screen epic with skill and intelligence. The film is a rare example of a spectacular with some awareness of artistic values: much of its strength lies in the script (Dalton TRUMBO's first after being blacklisted—see UNAMERICAN ACTIVITIES) which adheres closely to the liberal views expressed in Howard Fast's novel.

The subject of the slaves' revolt was also dealt with in a small-budget Italian production, *Spartaco* (1952), directed by Riccardo Freda.

**SPIEGEL,** SAM (1904– ), Polish-born US producer who first went to America in 1927 and worked as a reader at METRO-GOLDWYN-MAYER. He transferred to UNIVERSAL and was placed in charge of their European headquarters in Berlin. Fleeing Hitler in 1933 he went to Vienna, Paris, London, Mexico City, and New York before settling back in Hollywood in 1941. His first film as producer was *Tales of Manhattan* (1942) under the name S. P. Eagle which he used until ON THE WATERFRONT (1954). For six years from 1947 he was in partnership with John HUSTON in Horizon Films, during which time they made THE AFRICAN QUEEN (1952). His more recent films have been large-scale co-productions, including THE BRIDGE ON THE RIVER KWAI (1957), LAWRENCE OF ARABIA (1962), *Night of the Generals* (1966), and *Nicholas and Alexandra* (1971).

*SPIVS* see VITELLONI, I

**SPLIT SCREEN,** a photographic technique in which two independent images are displayed on the screen divided by a sharp line. It is typically seen in telephone sequences where both sides of the conversation are seen and heard simultaneously. The effect is similar to a WIPE and is produced in the same way—not in the camera but as an OPTICAL effect made in the laboratory. The two shots are made independently and need not even be framed to place the actors at screen right and left; the optical printer can shift them to their correct positions. The dividing line need not be a simple half-and-half vertical split; the screen may be split in any shape and into as many parts as the designer wishes. The split screen had a fashionable revival in the sixties when MULTI-SCREEN effects were adapted from spectacular demonstrations at various world's fairs and expositions, as in *Grand Prix* (1966) and *The Thomas Crown Affair* (1968).

When the dividing line between images moves, the effect is called a wipe; when the dividing line is deliberately made unnoticeable, the effect is called a MATTE shot and is used to combine separate images into a believable whole. However, in each case the technical process is very similar.

**SPOLIANSKY,** MISCHA (1898– ), Russian-born composer who began film work with UFA in the early thirties but settled in Britain in 1934, composing for Alexander KORDA's LONDON FILMS, beginning with *The Private Life of Don Juan* (1934) and *Sanders of the River*

(1935). Numerous other scores include *The Ghost Goes West* (1935), *King Solomon's Mines* (1937), *The Happiest Days of Your Life* (1950), PREMINGER's *Saint Joan* (1957, see JOAN OF ARC).

**SPOTTISWOODE,** RAYMOND (1913–70), British documentary film-maker and writer on technical aspects of the cinema. After a period with John GRIERSON's documentary production group, he worked for METRO-GOLDWYN-MAYER in Hollywood before the war, then produced some Canadian war films before becoming technical supervisor of the NATIONAL FILM BOARD of Canada. He returned home during the Festival of Britain in 1951 and was technical director of the stereoscopic film programme at the Telekinema. Principal works: *A grammar of the film*, London, 2nd ed, 1955; *Film and its techniques*, London, 1951; *The theory of stereoscopic transmission* (with Nigel Spottiswoode), Berkeley, 1953.

**SRI LANKA.** A film industry in Ceylon began in 1903, but only with the import and exhibition of foreign films. These films came from all over the world, but the introduction of sound created a diminution of sources and a dominance of Madras, Bombay, and American films, a situation which still holds today. Exhibition did not come under Sinhalese control until 1928 with the formation of Ceylon Theatres Ltd, an organization which maintained a monopoly until the late forties, when Ceylon Entertainments Ltd and Cinemas Ltd were established. Spasmodic attempts at production were made, unsuccessful except for *Royal Adventure* (1925) which was screened in India and Singapore but never seen in Ceylon as the print was accidentally destroyed abroad. It was not until after independence that another attempt was made—*Kadavunu Poronduva* (1947)—which had to rely on independent cinemas for exhibition. Further production was attempted, but unfortunately films were processed in South India and although the actors were Sinhalese, the directors and technicians were largely Indian and excessively influenced by the Indian cinematic tradition of remote historical subjects and musical interludes.

Despite the establishment of the Government Film Unit in 1947 (a miserably unsuccessful venture), the creation of local studios, and increasing attempts by independents to produce indigenous films, exhibition is still dominated by imports. Unfortunately the film society movement is also limited, as most societies were formed to conduct their business in English and still aim their work at English-speaking audiences. In 1962 a Commission reported on the situation of the Sinhalese film industry but none of its recommendations have been carried out, with the exception of the establishment of the State Film Corporation (Sri Lanka) in 1972 to undertake the import and distribution of all foreign films. Censorship, particularly in sexual matters, has been strict, and political censorship is increasing.

Recently the situation has improved slightly, largely with the success of Lester Peries, who began independent Sinhalese production in 1956 with *Rekava* which was shown at CANNES. Since then, against all odds, he has continued to produce films and establish his work abroad, but until proper national training facilities are established and wholehearted support given towards the creation of a genuinely Sinhalese industry he will unfortunately remain as a remarkable figure in an otherwise sterile cinematic culture.

Ceylon has also been the subject and location of many films, notably Basil WRIGHT's SONG OF CEYLON (1934).

*STACHKA* (*Strike*), USSR, 1925. 1¾hr. *Dir, ed* S. M. Eisenstein; *prod* Goskino; *scr* Proletkult Theatre team under V. Pletniev; *asst dir* Grigori Alexandrov; *ph* Edvard Tissé; *cast* Maxim Straukh (detective), Grigori Alexandrov (manager), M. Gomorov (factory worker), I. Ivanov (chief of police), members of the Proletkult Theatre.

EISENSTEIN's first film sprang directly from his work with the Proletkult Theatre and was a co-operative venture in the same style as their stage productions, with wild caricature, absurd humour, and a blunt political message. The director's hand is most clearly seen towards the end of the film, where the slaughter of the strikers and their families by mounted cavalry hints at the power of the massacre on the Odessa Steps in his next film BRONENOSETS POTEMKIN (1925); and the shock cutting between the mowing down of the workers and shots of a slaughterhouse are early experiments in the visual metaphor which characterizes all his films.

*STAGECOACH*, US, 1939. 1½hr. *Dir* John Ford; *prod* Walter Wanger for United Artists; *scr* Dudley Nichols, from Ernest Haycox's story 'Stage to Lordsburg'; *ph* Bert Glennon, Ray Binger; *cast* John Wayne (the Ringo Kid), Claire Trevor (Dallas), John Carradine (Hatfield), Thomas Mitchell (Dr Josiah Boone), Andy Devine (Buck), Donald Meek (Samuel Peacock), Louise Platt (Lucy Mallory), Tim Holt (Lt Blanchard), George Bancroft (Sheriff Curly Wilcox), Berton Churchill (Henry Gatewood).

This 'powerful story of nine strange people', adapted by Dudley NICHOLS from a story by Ernest Haycox, which was itself a Western relative of Maupassant's 'Boule de Suif', is a milestone in the history of the WESTERN.

*Stagecoach* was FORD's first Western for thirteen years, and the first to be shot in Monument Valley; it includes some fine SECOND UNIT work under the direction of Yakima CANUTT. It raised John WAYNE from 'B' pictures to stardom, and such was its success in all quarters that it brought about a Western revival and gave the genre new artistic standing. The 1966 remake led to the withdrawal of prints (see COPYRIGHT).

**STAMP**, TERENCE (1940–  ), British actor, selected from stage repertory to play the title role in Peter USTINOV's *Billy Budd* (1962) and immediately cast as the young thug in *Term of Trial* (1962). Rejecting the dangers of type-casting inherent in his surly good looks and laconic manner, he did not appear again until *The Collector* (William WYLER, 1965). Like Julie CHRISTIE, he struck a jarringly modern note in *Far from the Madding Crowd* (John SCHLESINGER, 1967); his best work was as the itinerant hero in *Poor Cow* (1967) and as the mystic stranger in PASOLINI's TEOREMA (*Theorem*, 1968). He replaced Robert REDFORD in *Blue* (1968) and gave a strong performance in *The Mind of Mr Soames* (1969).

**STANISLAVSKY**, KONSTANTIN SERGEY-EVICH (1863–1938), Russian stage director, real name Alexeiev, was the pioneer of modern character interpretation in acting. During his time as director of the Moscow Art Theatre, which he founded in 1898, he instituted an approach which combined simplicity and truth founded on an understanding of the author's intentions through self-exploration and extrapolation of the actor's own experience. Later self-styled disciples of the Stanislavsky 'Method', as it came to be known, often tended to overlook his insistence on the necessity of developing to a high degree the physical techniques needed to convey the results of intellectual understanding; improvisation, which he encouraged as a means of training the actor's mental and physical capacities, is still often regarded as an end in itself.

A desire for naturalism at all costs is often attributed to him: in fact he was fully aware of the dangers of naturalism in acting—incoherence and obscurity among them—and his aim was to produce the appearance of reality within the accepted non-realistic conventions of the theatre: in this he and his company brilliantly succeeded. Stanislavsky's attitude towards cinema was indifferent, if not absolutely hostile, but the influence of his ideas on acting in films as well as in the theatre has been immeasurable. These ideas are lucidly set out in his autobiography *My life in art* (1924) and in his other books including *An actor prepares* (1926) and *Building a character* (1950). (See also ACTORS' STUDIO.)

**STANWYCK,** BARBARA (1907– ), US actress who came to films from the stage. Her likeable directness made her one of Hollywood's most popular stars, and together with her acting ability gave quality to a number of otherwise undistinguished films. She is particularly successful at playing tough, strong women who are also sympathetic, for example in *Golden Boy* (1939), but THE LADY EVE (1941) is one of several films which demonstrate that she is a fine *comédienne* as well as a good dramatic actress. Despite this, her most famous part is probably the blonde vamp-murderess in DOUBLE INDEMNITY (1943). In recent years she has worked mainly for television, where she continues to demonstrate her ability to bring interest to second-rate material.

**STAREVITCH,** LADISLAS (1892–1965), animator, who studied art in St Petersburg before founding a Museum of Natural History in Kovno at the age of twenty. Not having the means to realize his ambition of making documentary films about insects, he turned to ANIMATION, his first important work being *Le Cigale et la Fourmi* (*The Grasshopper and the Ant*, 1913), after the fable by La Fontaine. During the same period (1914–18) he directed several fiction films with MOZHUKIN, notably *Ruslan i Ludmila* (1915), and photographed films for Chardynin and PROTAZANOV. In 1919 he left Russia for France where, with the help of his two daughters, he dedicated himself to developing the technique of puppet-animation, patiently turning out twenty or so films over the period 1923–50. His principal films, which reflect his passionate love of fantasy as well as of animals, are *La Voix du rossignol* (1923) and *Le Roman de Renart* (1930).

**STAR-FILM,** trademark used by Georges MÉLIÈS. In an attempt to curtail the illicit copying of his films by American distributors Méliès introduced into every décor a black plaque lettered in white reading: 'Copyrighted by Geo. Méliès [date]. Paris, New York. Trade Mark [a five-pointed star] Star'. This measure did not prevent the counterfeiting of his films, because the pirates quickly developed a method of eradicating the 'Star-Film' label. In 1903 Méliès opened an office in New York directed by his brother Gaston, under whose management the sales of 'Star-Film' expanded considerably. Unable, however, to keep pace with developing audience demands, the company foundered by 1914.

**STAR IS BORN, A,** US, 1954. CinemaScope; 2½hr; Technicolor. *Dir* George Cukor; *prod* Warner Bros; *scr* Moss Hart based on a screen-play by Dorothy Parker, Alan Campbell, and Robert Carson; *cast* Judy Garland (Vicki Lester–Esther Blodgett), James Mason (Norman Maine), Jack Carson (Matt Libby), Charles Bickford (Oliver Niles).

This successful remake of William WELLMAN's 1937 film, starring Janet GAYNOR and Fredric MARCH, tells the story of the disintegration of a marriage between two Hollywood stars, one whose career is just beginning, the other's just ending. The film marked a come-back for Judy GARLAND after four years' absence from the screen, and the quality of her dramatic acting impressed many critics used only to her talents as a musical star. James MASON gave a striking performance as a talented screen idol sliding into alcoholism. A lavish production, it was WARNER BROS' most expensive film to date, costing over $2 million; it was finally backed by Judy Garland herself with her husband Sidney Luft.

**STAROYE I NOVOYE** (*Old and New*), USSR, 1929. 2hr. *Dir, scr, ed* S. M. Eisenstein; *prod* Sovkino; *ph* Edvard Tissé; *asst dir* Grigori Alexandrov; *cast* Marfa Lapkina (Marfa), Vasya Buzenkov (a komsomol), Kostya Vasiliev (tractor driver), Chukhmarev (a kulak).

Commissioned as a propaganda tract, *Staroye i novoye* shows the conversion of a peasant woman to socialist principles in agriculture and her fight to maintain collective farming in her community. The film met with a hostile reception in the USSR: EISENSTEIN's treatment of the peasantry has a satirical, detached humour which was found offensive and his brilliant, cerebral MONTAGE led to accusations of 'formalism'. His ambiguous attitude to religion is also apparent, in the lengthy examination of a rain-making ceremony conducted by priests and in the semi-mystical adoration inspired by the operation of a new milk separator. But it is the only film by Eisenstein to centre on a warm, identifiable character: Marfa Lapkina's performance transcends the principle of 'typage' on which she was chosen and endows the political message with attractive human qualities.

*Staroye i novoye* was originally to be called *Generalnaya linya* (*The General Line*) and is often known by this title.

**STAR SYSTEM,** a phenomenon created by, and effectively confined to, the Hollywood film industry, although attempts have been made to apply it elsewhere, notably in Britain.

Although several names qualify for consideration as the first film star, the first player to be accorded the treatment that developed into the star system was Florence LAWRENCE. Like the other actors at BIOGRAPH, she received no screen credit, but when she was at the height of her popularity as the 'Biograph Girl' Carl LAEMMLE persuaded her to sign with him, part of the deal being the promise of credits in her own name. He even set up a publicity stunt involving a rumour that the new 'IMP Girl' had been killed in a car crash, which necessitated a personal appearance to reassure her public.

The promotion of a popular screen personality by publicity stunts, strict management of personal life, supervision of wardrobe, hairstyles, and even diet, and the careful selection of roles to conform with the desired public image were key factors in creating and maintaining star status. Theda BARA was one of the first examples of the full treatment, and one of its first casualties: the mythical personality constructed around her was more powerful than her own talent and when her type became unfashionable her career was effectively finished. Mary PICKFORD's combination of real talent and business acumen enabled her to retain her star status, but even she rebelled unsuccessfully against the winsome image to which the public had become accustomed in her early work for D. W. GRIFFITH.

Publicity campaigns often preceded the star's first appearance on the screen. But no amount of expert salesmanship could make an enduring star of inadequate material: Anna STEN flopped with the American public and Pola NEGRI was a success only in silent films. Greta GARBO was one of the really gifted actresses whose personality was sold, but not created, by the star system.

Male stars were somewhat less liable to the full star treatment than women, but Rudolph VALENTINO had a name and past life invented by publicity men, and Douglas FAIRBANKS cheerfully played out his athletic, wholesome screen image in his private life.

Fan magazines were encouraged to support and amplify the approved versions of stars' lifestyles, which changed in the thirties from the unreal luxury that had surrounded earlier stars like Gloria SWANSON and Clara BOW to a more cosy, domestic flavour. Irene DUNNE, Walter PIDGEON, and others embodied the conventional virtues which Hollywood had hastily taken up in deference to the power of the Legion of Decency, formed in 1934 (see CENSORSHIP, US). Often a 'morality clause' was included in a star's contract to guard against loss of popularity by indiscreet behaviour. Scandal was inevitably rife, and influential gossip writers like Hedda HOPPER and Louella PARSONS were natural by-products of the system. One late, and prime, example of a star's private life radically affecting her career was the ostracizing in America of Ingrid BERGMAN when her relationship with Roberto ROSSELLINI became known.

METRO-GOLDWYN-MAYER, which claimed to have 'more stars than there are in the heavens', formalized its control of stars to an unparalleled extent. Louis B. MAYER played the role of paterfamilias to a 'family' of actors and actresses, all closely supervised. The junior ranks, which included Judy GARLAND (one of the most notorious victims of the 'commodity' attitude to stars), Elizabeth TAYLOR, and Mickey ROONEY, were intended to graduate in time to the roles played by their seniors like Joan CRAWFORD, Robert TAYLOR, and Clark GABLE.

Although the salaries paid to stars were high, reports often exaggerated them, and producers made handsome profits out of their contracted big names, not only from their own films but by renting them out, often at inflated prices, to other producers; the star rarely had any say in these deals. Apart from direct interference in their private lives, the chief source of frustration for stars of any calibre as actors was the lack of choice in their roles: TYPE-CASTING was thought to be a guarantee of box-office success, and stars who refused to play the parts chosen for them were suspended from work until they came to heel. Bette DAVIS fought constantly on this issue, and in 1944 Olivia DE HAVILLAND won a legal action against WARNER BROS who had added her periods of suspension to her term of contract, an important step in eroding the studios' authority over their players. That casting 'against type' could be both intriguing and profitable was proved by Ray MILLAND in THE LOST WEEKEND (1945), but by this time the full force of the star system was beginning to flag, along with the decline of Hollywood as a major industry. Increasing sophistication in audiences and an insistence on greater independence among the stars themselves were other factors in the disappearance of a true star system. At this time an attempt was made in Britain to copy the Hollywood star system, particularly by GAINSBOROUGH, with Stewart GRANGER, Margaret LOCKWOOD, and other contract players, and by the RANK ORGANISATION which set up a 'charm school' and tried to transmute its starlets into big box-office names, with little success. As late as the mid-fifties Harry COHN at COLUMBIA gave the full star build-up to Kim NOVAK. The magic of Hollywood was already beginning to fade when the exploitation of Marilyn MONROE became apparent, but the public sympathy engendered by her vulnerability may have hastened disillusionment with the highly commercialized film industry.

A few outstanding stars like Bette Davis, Katharine HEPBURN, Cary GRANT, and John WAYNE have held the public's imagination and outlasted the star system itself; some later ones, notably Elizabeth Taylor, have carried the values of stardom into a new era, where a popular player can display all the glamour and excitement of the star image without submitting to the autocratic management of a studio. But generally the stars of the thirties and forties have been replaced by actors like Paul NEWMAN, Marlon BRANDO, and Barbra STREISAND, who can retain a faithful public while preserving their independence.

Films inspired by the star system and its effects include A STAR IS BORN (1937 and 1954), *Vie privée* (Louis MALLE, 1962), *Inside Daisy Clover* (Robert MULLIGAN, 1966), and *The Legend of Lylah Clare* (Robert ALDRICH, 1968).

**START** (Society of the Devotees of the Artistic Film), a film society inaugurated in Poland in 1930. Its purpose was twofold, covering theory and practice. It set out to spread knowledge of film and to keep up with progressive cinema in other countries, while its members were also engaged in active film-making.

Their progressive films were made despite the reactionary attitude of the government of the time, and ignored the conventions of commercial cinema. Those who founded START included Eugéniusz Cekalski, Mieczyslaw Choynowsky, Wanda JAKUBOWSKA, Tadeusz Kowalski, Stanislaw Wohl, and Jerzy Zarzycki. Among others associated with it were Jerzy BOSSAK, Aleksander FORD, Ludwig Perski, and Jerzy Toeplitz.

Although START was terminated in 1935 and its work carried on by SAF (Co-operative of Film Authors), the revival of film production after the war was initiated by a group of its founder members (see POLAND).

**STATE FAIR**, US, 1933. 1½hr. *Dir* Henry King; *prod* Fox; *scr* Sonya Levien, Paul Green from the novel by Philip Stong; *ph* Hal Mohr; *cast* Will Rogers (Abel Frake), Louise Dresser (Melissa Frake), Janet Gaynor (Margy Frake), Norman Foster (Wayne Frake), Lew Ayres (Pat Gilbert), Sally Eilers (Emily Joyce).

1945. 1½hr. *Dir* Walter Lang; *prod* Twentieth Century-Fox; *scr* Sonya Levien, Paul Green, Oscar Hammerstein II; *ph* Leon Shamroy, Fred Sersen; *ed* J. Watson Webb; *mus* Alfred Newman, Charles Henderson; *songs* Richard Rodgers, Oscar Hammerstein II; *cast* Dick Haymes (Wayne), Vivian Blaine (Emily), Jeanne Crain (Margy), Charles Winniger (Abel), Fay Bainter (Melissa), Dana Andrews (Pat).

1962. CinemaScope; 2hr; De Luxe Color. *Dir* José Ferrer; *prod* Twentieth Century-Fox; *scr* Richard Breen, from the previous screenplay; *ph* William C. Mellor; *ed* David Bretherton; *mus* Alfred Newman; *songs* Richard Rodgers, Oscar Hammerstein II; *cast* Pat Boone (Wayne), Bobby Darin (Jerry Dundee), Pamela

Tiffin (Margie), Ann-Margret (Emily), Tom Ewell (Abel), Alice Faye (Melissa), Wally Cox (Hipplewaite).

A simple story of a family's visit to the Iowa State Fair: the parents win prizes and the brother and sister each fall in love. Philip Stong's novel is regarded as a minor American classic and Henry KING's quiet and visually beautiful film was very successful in retaining the charm and simplicity of the original, with Will ROGERS particularly successful as the father whose beloved pig wins a first prize. The 1945 version is notable for the RODGERS and HAMMERSTEIN score (the only one they wrote directly for the screen) which includes numbers like 'It's a grand night for singing' and 'It might as well be Spring'. Jeanne Crain in one of her first films made a charming heroine, with songs dubbed for her by Louanne Hogan. José FERRER, who directed the third version in 1962, is not a musical director and despite five new songs by Richard Rodgers, including the attractive 'Never say no to a man' for Alice FAYE (making a brief come-back as the mother), both direction and cast are generally inferior to the 1945 film.

**STAUDTE, WOLFGANG** (1909– ), German director, played small parts in films, then became a director during the war. He became widely noticed with DIE MÖRDER SIND UNTER UNS (1946), the first feature film to emerge from postwar Germany, and *Der Untertan* (*The Underdog*, 1951), an anti-militaristic tragi-comedy. In spite of tensions with the DEFA management he stayed in East Germany until 1955 when he left for the west, but his reputation as a critical and committed film-maker made it difficult for him to find backing, leading to the unfortunate neglect of a competent and intelligent artist.

**STEAMBOAT WILLY** (1928), the third of DISNEY'S MICKEY MOUSE cartoons, and his first in sound, which demonstrated Disney's appreciation of the force of music, not as background accompaniment, but as an element intrinsic to the film's structure and visual rhythm. The animal concert (a cow's teeth being played like a xylophone, its udder becoming a bagpipe), is the first memorable example of the intricate visual orchestration that was to be an important factor in the Disney studio's subsequent success.

**STEIGER, ROD** (1925– ), US actor, started in small theatre groups, progressing to the ACTORS' STUDIO and first appearing on Broadway in Clifford ODETS's *Night Music*, playing a man of fifty-five while still in his twenties. Several successes on the stage and on television included the title role in the original television production of MARTY. After his first film, *Teresa* (Fred

ZINNEMANN, 1951), he appeared as the powerful union boss in ON THE WATERFRONT (1954) then in his only musical *Oklahoma!* (1955). He played the archetypal gangster in *Al Capone* (1959) and worked in Italy, where he was brilliantly convincing as a corrupt property speculator in LE MANI SULLA CITTÀ (*Hands over the City*, 1963); he also appeared in *E venne un uomo* (*A Man Called John*, Ermanno OLMI) and *Gli indifferenti* (*A Time of Indifference*, both 1965). He played a tragic misanthrope in Sidney LUMET's *The Pawnbroker* (1964), the opportunist Komarovsky in DOCTOR ZHIVAGO (1966), and won an OSCAR as the coarse, gum-chewing sheriff in IN THE HEAT OF THE NIGHT (1967). *The Sergeant* (1968), in which he gave a moving performance as a lonely, sadistic latent homosexual, has perhaps been unjustly neglected; in the same year his gift for mimicry was squandered in an uneasy black comedy, *No Way to Treat a Lady*. He starred opposite Claire BLOOM, then his wife, in a marital drama, *Three into Two Won't Go* (1969), and played Napoleon in BONDARCHUK's *Waterloo* (1970).

Steiger's career has been built entirely on character roles: lacking conventional good looks, he has concentrated on a range of intelligent characterizations, and if his talent occasionally lacks discipline he has contributed with distinction to a wide range of films.

**STEINBECK, JOHN** (1902–68), US novelist who was awarded the Nobel Prize in 1962. Works adapted for the screen include *Of Mice and Men* (1937; filmed by Lewis MILESTONE, 1939), THE GRAPES OF WRATH (1939; filmed 1940), and EAST OF EDEN (1952; filmed 1955). Steinbeck's own film scripts include *The Forgotten Village* (1941) and VIVA ZAPATA! (1952).

**STEINER, MAX** (1888–1971), Viennese-born composer and conductor who became the doyen of Hollywood film composers. He joined RKO in 1929, and his early scores included those for *Cimarron* (1931), KING KONG (1933), and THE INFORMER (1935, for which he won an OSCAR). He wrote the music for GONE WITH THE WIND (1939) and for many of the most famous WARNER BROS films of the forties, including *Now Voyager* (1942, Oscar) and CASABLANCA (1943). He won another Oscar for *Since You Went Away* (1944).

**STEN, ANNA** (1910–   ), Russian actress, appeared in a few silent films in Russia including *Devushka s korobkoi* (*The Girl with the Hat Box*, Boris BARNET, 1927); she was at this time married to Grigori ALEXANDROV. She went to Germany where her most notable success was as Gruschenka in *Der Mörder Dimitri Karamasoff*

(*The Brothers Karamazov*, Fedor Ozep, 1931). Signed by GOLDWYN, her first Hollywood film *Nana* (Dorothy ARZNER, 1934, *Lady of the Boulevards* in GB) was a disaster. Goldwyn tried strenuously to make her a star comparable with GARBO, using the manipulation and flamboyant publicity typical of the STAR SYSTEM; but in spite of her undoubted talent and beauty she failed to attract a following. She starred opposite Fredric MARCH in *We Live Again* (Rouben MAMOULIAN, 1934) and Gary COOPER in *The Wedding Night* (King VIDOR, 1935), followed by one film in Britain, but the rest of her Hollywood career was spent in supporting roles or 'B' pictures.

**STEP-PRINTING**   see   OPTICAL   PRINTING, STRETCHING

**STEREOPHONIC,** a form of sound reproduction in which individual sounds seem to come from a particular point rather than from a single loudspeaker. The method is similar to the two-channel principle used in stereo record players and cassettes, but for film applications there may be three, four, or more tracks contributing to the sound. Each track carries the sound from a single microphone and plays back through a single loudspeaker; the listener's ear and brain combine to create the impression of sounds coming from the spaces between the loudspeakers.

For music recording (other than pop) the best stereophonic effects are produced by rigid application of the basic principle, each microphone recorded on its own track and played through its own speaker. But for film sounds such as dialogue and sound effects artificial techniques are added to provide greater flexibility. The sound mixer can shift the apparent source of a sound by use of a 'pan pot' analogous to the balance control of a hi-fi amplifier. Dialogue recorded monophonically by a single microphone can thus be moved to match the actor's movements; a stock sound effect of a train in motion can be panned across the screen to match the passing of another train in the picture. However, experience has shown that sounds which correspond to a visible object, such as dialogue, are easily placed by the viewer without the aid of stereophony; it is off-screen sounds with no visible counterpart that benefit most from stereophonic placement.

Stereophonic sound was first used commercially in Walt DISNEY's FANTASIA (1940). Leopold Stokowski, who conducted the score, had also conducted the earliest public demonstrations of stereophony (in the early thirties under Bell Telephone Laboratories' sponsorship), and he collaborated with the Disney artists in making the music swoop across the screen in synchronization with their drawings. Stereo reappeared in the cinema with CINERAMA and CINEMASCOPE in the mid-fifties, where the very wide screens demanded an equally wide sound perspective. Either stereo or some approximation of it (such as Perspectasound) has remained, with colour and 'scope, an expected component of large-scale epics and musicals; but for less ambitious films (and in less well-equipped cinemas) its absence is hardly noticed by the average cinemagoer. (See DOLBY SYSTEM.)

**STEREOSCOPIC,** or 3-D, terms describing a photographic technique for producing a convincing appearance of depth and three-dimensional roundness in films. 3-D (the term 'stereoscopic' is more often applied to stills) depends upon the fact that much of our perception of depth comes from viewing with two eyes, spaced about $2\frac{1}{2}$ inches apart. The 3-D film simulates our two eyes with two cameras or two lenses, also spaced $2\frac{1}{2}$ inches apart, records the two viewpoints separately on film, and presents them separately to the viewer's two eyes.

Stereoscopic photography is almost as old as photography itself, and was well-known to the Victorians in the form of the parlour stereoscope. However, the motion picture developed as a projected image shown to large audiences (see PROJECTION), and all attempts to establish stereoscopy in film have been frustrated by the difficulty of presenting the necessary two images at this stage. One such early attempt was the *anaglyph*, in which left- and right-eye images coloured blue-green and red were viewed through spectacles coloured similarly. Another approach, still used in the Soviet Union, was the complex *integral screen*, in which a grid of vertical slats at the screen blocks the left-eye portions of the image from the right eye and vice versa.

No 3-D method achieved commercial success until the introduction of polarized projection, made possible by the invention of Polaroid in the late thirties. In this method the left- and right-eye images are admitted to the correct eye by Polaroid spectacles, which block rays of light polarized at right angles to the spectacle lens and admit rays polarized at the same angle. Under the trade name Natural Vision this system achieved brief popularity in the mid-fifties, first with Arch Oboler's *Bwana Devil* (1952). Cinemagoers became accustomed to donning cheap cardboard glasses (perching them precariously over their own spectacles) and watching lions leap out of the screen or having blazing torches thrown in their faces. (It was at this time that the term 3-D was coined by the US trade paper VARIETY, noted for its showbiz neologisms.) But the system was imperfect, from both the audience's and the exhibitor's point of view; the

spectacles were an increasing annoyance, and headaches were common when, as often happened, the two mechanically linked projectors went out of step and the left- and right-eye images failed to coincide. 3-D acquired a reputation for sensationalism rather than realism, and many reputable films already shot in 3-D (*Kiss Me, Kate*, 1953, and HITCHCOCK's *Dial M for Murder*, 1954) were released as ordinary 'flat' films. (Such films can still be identified by a perverse tendency to throw things at the audience.) Since then 3-D has only been revived occasionally for such purposes as near-pornography, where the illusion of roundness has obvious advantages.

If there is a future for stereoscopic films, it probably lies in the infant science of HOLOGRAPHY, which permits fully three-dimensional images to be photographed on a single film and viewed with the naked eye.

**STERNBERG,** JOSEF VON (1894–    ), Austrian-born US director, real name Jonas Sternberg, who worked in Hollywood, beginning in films as an editor, writer, and assistant director. He wrote, produced, and directed *The Salvation Hunters* (1925), a low-budget feature largely shot in the mud flats of San Pedro in California: the film immediately revealed the flair for pictorial composition that marked all Sternberg's work. He directed *The Exquisite Sinner* (1926) for METRO-GOLDWYN-MAYER, then quarrelled with the company and left to direct Edna PURVIANCE in *The Sea Gull* (1926, also known as *The Woman of the Sea*) for Charles CHAPLIN; although the film was completed, Chaplin decided not to release it.

The artistic and commercial success of UNDERWORLD (1927) began the association with PARAMOUNT during which Sternberg's best films were made. *The Last Command* (1928), with Emil JANNINGS as an aristocratic Russian émigré who has sunk to working as a film extra, and THE DOCKS OF NEW YORK (1928), had already confirmed his stature when he went to Berlin to make the sensational DER BLAUE ENGEL (*The Blue Angel*, 1930) for UFA. He returned to Paramount and embarked on his celebrated succession of films starring Marlene DIETRICH, who had become an overnight success in *Der blaue Engel*: *Morocco* (1930), DISHONORED (1931), SHANGHAI EXPRESS (1932), *Blonde Venus* (1932), THE SCARLET EMPRESS (1934), and *The Devil is a Woman* (1935). In addition to the Dietrich films, he made a version of Theodore Dreiser's AN AMERICAN TRAGEDY (1931) starring Phillips Holmes and Sylvia SIDNEY. His eight years at Paramount established Sternberg as an almost legendary figure surrounded by the flavour of vaguely perverse eroticism that characterized his preferred subjects: bizarre plots played out by exotic characters in settings of dreamlike extravagance, enhanced by his typical play of light and shadow. He cultivated a pose of egotistical arrogance: he claimed to have written and virtually photographed all his films, although the contribution of Jules FURTHMAN and Lee GARMES to Sternberg's best work was not insubstantial.

Sternberg's subsequent films bear little comparison with those he made for Paramount. He directed a version of CRIME AND PUNISHMENT (1935) with Peter LORRE as Raskolnikov and visited Britain to direct Alexander KORDA's unluckily abortive production of *I, Claudius* in 1937. Only *The Shanghai Gesture* (1941), the most successful of his later films, is reminiscent of his distinctive style. He acted as photographic consultant on David O. SELZNICK's production DUEL IN THE SUN (1946), but made no more films until he directed a Howard HUGHES production, *Jet Pilot* (1951) starring John WAYNE, and the feeble *Macao* (1952) starring Robert MITCHUM and Jane RUSSELL. His last film, *Anatahan* (1953, *The Siege of Anatahan* in GB), made in Japan, was no fitting postscript to his work, although Sternberg himself rated it as his best film, a typically eccentric opinion.

Sternberg wrote an idiosyncratic and unreliable autobiography, *Fun in a Chinese laundry* (New York, 1965, London, 1966). John Baxter's *The cinema of Josef von Sternberg* (London, 1971) is a useful survey.

**STEVENS, GEORGE** (1904–75), US director, made his first film—one of the Cohens and Kellys comedy series—in 1933. During the thirties and forties he established a reputation as a polished and professional craftsman with an unusually wide range: his best films of this period include *Alice Adams* (1935) starring Katharine HEPBURN, *Annie Oakley* (1935) with Barbara STANWYCK in the title role, and two Fred ASTAIRE musicals, SWING TIME (1936) and *A Damsel in Distress* (1937). He directed *Gunga Din* (1939), an adventure story adapted from Kipling, and *Penny Serenade* (1941), a poignant emotional drama starring Irene DUNNE and Cary GRANT; then came three outstanding comedies, WOMAN OF THE YEAR (1942), the first film in which Hepburn co-starred with Spencer TRACY, *The Talk of the Town* (1942), and *The More the Merrier* (1943), both with Jean ARTHUR. His first post-war film was the charming *I Remember Mama* (1948).

Stevens's work after the fifties was more personal, both in his chosen subjects and in style. A PLACE IN THE SUN (1951), his version of Theodore Dreiser's AN AMERICAN TRAGEDY; *Something to Live For* (1952), a drama of alcoholism; SHANE (1953), his only Western; *Giant* (1956); and *The Diary of Anne Frank* (1959)—all show a preoccupation with sombre aspects of human relationships. They have a thoughtful and lingering tempo, frequently using slow dissolves and frozen action. In the sixties he made two films, a weighty Biblical epic *The Greatest Story Ever Told* (1965) and the stagey *The Only Game in Town* (1969).

George Stevens Jr (1932– ), producer, was in charge of film production at USIA for five years and became executive director of the AMERICAN FILM INSTITUTE in 1967.

**STEWART, JAMES** (1908– ), US actor, as an architecture student at Princeton became a member of the college's famous theatre group, the Triangle Club, and joined a professional company as soon as he graduated. After numerous starring roles on Broadway in the early thirties, he went to Hollywood to appear in *Murder Man* (1935).

His versatility quickly made him a favourite with several of America's best directors, particularly for films where his engaging clumsiness and apparently inarticulate drawl added comically endearing effect to his roles. Frank CAPRA used him in such comedy classics as *You Can't Take It With You* (1938) and MR SMITH GOES TO WASHINGTON (1939), George MARSHALL in DESTRY RIDES AGAIN (1939), and LUBITSCH in *The Shop around the Corner* (1940). His performance in George CUKOR's THE PHILADELPHIA STORY (1940)—opposite such veteran scene-stealers as Cary GRANT and Katharine HEPBURN—confirmed his star stature and brought him an OSCAR. During the war he served in the Army Air Force and won a Distinguished Flying Cross.

Stewart has worked with other major directors including John FORD, for whom he starred in *Two Rode Together* (1961), THE MAN WHO SHOT LIBERTY VALANCE (1962), and *Cheyenne Autumn* (1964), and Alfred HITCHCOCK, with whom he worked on the classic thrillers *Rope* (1948), REAR WINDOW (1954), THE MAN WHO KNEW TOO MUCH (1956), and *Vertigo* (1958). His biographical film portrayals include *The Glenn Miller Story* (1953) and *The Spirit of St Louis* (1957) about Lindbergh, but he is best remembered for his comedy roles such as the eccentric, often inebriated, Elwood P. Dowd in *Harvey* (1950) or the humorous, shrewd country lawyer in Otto PREMINGER's *Anatomy of a Murder* (1959).

More recently Stewart has limited his appearances to more light-weight Westerns such as *Shenandoah* (1965), *The Rare Breed* (1966), and *Bandolero* (1968), and numerous television appearances. He has received many awards, both in the US and in Europe, and has remained one of Hollywood's most engaging stars throughout a long career of thirty-five years and over seventy films.

**STILLER,** MAURITZ (1883–1928), Swedish director born in Helsinki, first went to Sweden to avoid military service in the Imperial Russian Army and worked in the theatre there before, in 1912, joining Svenska Bio (later SVENSK FILM-INDUSTRI) as actor and director. The wit and elegance of his early films brought him popular success, in particular the sparkling comedies *Kärlek och journalistik* (*Love and Journalism*, 1916), *Thomas Graals bästa film* (*Thomas Graal's Best Film*, 1917), and EROTIKON (1920). Possibly owing to the influence of his friend and colleague Victor SJÖSTRÖM, Stiller moved away from sophisticated sexual comedy to themes closer to the Swedish literary tradition; *Sången om den eldröda blomman* (*Song of the Scarlet Flower*, 1919) was shown throughout the world and he had particular success with films based on novels by Selma LAGERLÖF. HERR ARNES PENGAR (1919) and GÖSTA BERLINGS SAGA (1924) show Stiller at his most mature, setting strong nordic themes in close relation to the natural landscape.

*Gösta Berlings saga* brought Stiller's talent, and also that of Greta GARBO, to the notice of Louis B. MAYER who invited them both to Hollywood in 1925. Stiller's career there was disappointing: his autocratic manner was unpopular and he completed only two films, *Hotel Imperial* (1927) and *The Woman on Trial* (1927), both for PARAMOUNT and both starring vehicles for Pola NEGRI. He died soon after his return to Sweden.

*Mauritz Stiller och hans filmer* by Gösta Werner, Stockholm, 1970, is a thoroughly researched work on Stiller's early career.

**STILLS,** illustrations from a particular film, as opposed to publicity photographs of actors. *Production stills* are taken while shooting is in progress. A scene may be re-staged for the still camera and lighting and composition adjusted to give the best results for a still photograph; or they may be taken during rehearsal. They are generally used for press release and foyer displays. *Frame stills* are reproductions of single frames from the film itself. They are almost invariably inferior in quality to production stills, depending on the grain and state of preservation of the print used, and in effect suffer from the problems of duping; but they convey the true feeling of a film more exactly than can a posed production still.

**STOCK,** or film stock, the actual film material in reel form. The word is used to describe all types of film materials: shooting stock (i.e. that which goes into the camera), print stock, or duplicating stock. Film stock is made up of several layers. The EMULSION is the layer which, by reacting to light, forms the photographic image when chemically treated. Colour film usually has several such layers, each recording a different part of the light spectrum. The emulsion is bonded to the base which is a transparent strip. Early film stock base was made of cellulose NITRATE which was highly flammable, even to the point of spontaneous combustion; this was replaced from 1937 by more stable materials such as cellulose tri-acetate, the use of which has been universal for both professional and amateur film since 1951 (see SAFETY FILM). Experiments with newer plastics continue. Substances such as mylar are often much tougher and more scratch-resistant and can be made very much thinner than previous base materials, making the film lighter and more compact in reel form. The film is manufactured in wide rolls, which are then slit to the gauge required and perforated.

**STOCK SHOT,** or library shot, a shot, incorporated into a film, which was originally made for an earlier film. Wars and battles, for example, are expensive to stage and shoot; where only a few shots are required it is cheaper to purchase stock shots from a library and intercut them with new shots made for the film. Stock shot libraries offer newsfilm of actual events, spectacular scenics from feature films, historical reconstructions, scientific subjects, and more: a DUPE negative is supplied and the original remains with the library. A clever EDITOR can integrate the stock shots imperceptibly; sometimes the cast of the film are even filmed performing in front of a stock shot (see BACK PROJECTION, FRONT PROJECTION, MATTE). A recent feature film (*Hennessy*, 1975) caused a political outcry in Britain by intercutting stock shots of the Queen at the State Opening of Parliament with a fictional plot to blow up Parliament.

**STONEY,** GEORGE, US documentary filmmaker, best known for *All My Babies* (1952), a half-hour teaching film commissioned by the State of Georgia's Public Health Department for use with black midwives. While satisfying his technical advisor's demand for 118 clearly set out teaching points Stoney managed to make his film a fluent and loving study of one particular black midwife. His working method—detailed research, location shooting, and re-enactment of events by people playing themselves—contributed to the development of an American documentary style in the FLAHERTY tradition.

Stoney became director of the Alternative Media Centre at New York University after spending two years (1968–70) as guest Executive Producer for the National Film Board of Canada's CHALLENGE FOR CHANGE programme organizing the use of film in community development.

**STORCK,** HENRI (1907– ), Belgium's leading documentary film-maker, has always worked in a widely diversified area. His films range from the avant-garde of the twenties to social and political topics, industrial and promotional films, and films on art in which he broke away from the usual static and formal presentations. Storck began his career by shooting material for the newsreel *Eclair Journal* in the twenties. In 1928, he founded the Club de Cinéma d'Ostende, where he showed avant-garde films until the club closed two years later. At this time, he began to make short impressionistic films such as *Images d'Ostende* (1929) and *Une Idylle à la plage* (1931, sound added in 1932), which he shot mainly with a hand-held camera and edited himself. In 1932, he compiled *Histoire du soldat inconnu* (*Story of an Unknown Soldier*) from newsreels and still photographs, an experimental satire in which he tried to draw attention to the dangers of the new militarism and re-armament in Europe. In the following year he worked as assistant to Jean VIGO on ZÉRO DE CONDUITE and collaborated with Joris IVENS on MISÈRE AU BORINAGE. Among Storck's films on social problems, this had the most stylistic influence on the British documentary movement's treatment of slum conditions. His other films in this vein include *Les Maisons de la misère* (1937) and *Au carrefour de la vie* (1949), the first a detailed study of slum conditions and a strong plea for housing reform, the other, sponsored by the United Nations, a dramatization of the problems of juvenile delinquency in post-war Belgium.

Storck's deep interest in the arts was first shown in his work in 1933, when he made a short film, *Métiers d'art*, about tapestry and furnishings. In 1947 he made the first of two films about the Belgian painter Paul Delvaux, *Le Monde de Paul Delvaux*, which had as commentary a poem written and spoken by the French surrealist poet, Paul Éluard. Storck took his audience inside Delvaux's dream world, making the paintings a subjective experience. His second film on this painter, *Paul Delvaux, ou les femmes défendues*, was made in 1971. In 1948, Storck made *Rubens*, in collaboration with Paul Haessarts, a study of the life and work of the Flemish painter, in which he was able, by highlighting details and setting them in their right context and by emphasizing elements of Rubens's technique, to convey the artist's ideas and emotions.

Outside these two main areas of interest

Storck is probably best known for producing *Les Seigneurs de la forêt* (*Lords of the Forest*, 1959; directed by Heinz Sielmann and Henry Brandt), which recorded in detail the animal life and native customs of the Belgian Congo.

***STORM OVER ASIA*** see POTOMOK CHINGHIS-KHANA

***STRADA, La,*** Italy, 1954. 1½hr. *Dir* Federico Fellini; *prod* Carlo Ponti, Dino De Laurentiis; *scr* Fellini, Ennio Flaiano, Tullio Pinelli; *ph* Otello Martelli; *des* Mario Ravasco; *mus* Nino Rota; *cast* Giulietta Masina (Gelsomina), Anthony Quinn (Zampanò), Richard Basehart (Il Matto).

The simple-minded Gelsomina is 'bought' by Zampanò, a travelling entertainer, to help him in his act. Zampanò fights and kills the gentle tightrope walker, Il Matto, and abandons Gelsomina, whose feeble brain is finally overcome by the shock. After she is dead, Zampanò realizes his need for her.

The film established the world reputation of Giulietta MASINA, and achieved wide popularity, greatly helped by the music. In its developed use of FELLINI's personal imagery (e.g. water as a sign of grace), and in its insistence that an understanding of private feeling is basic to an understanding of society, the film marked an absolute break with the concepts and practice of NEO-REALISM, and was bitterly attacked on that score by ZAVATTINI and other left-wing critics. It occupies a key position in Fellini's work as a whole.

**STRADLING,** HARRY (1910–70), British-born cameraman who first achieved distinction as a lighting cameraman in France, working on films directed by Jacques FEYDER, *Le Grand Jeu* (1934) and LA KERMESSE HÉROÏQUE (1935). He returned to England to work with Feyder on *Knight without Armour* (1937) and remained for further notable films (including PYGMALION, 1938; *The Citadel*, 1938; *Jamaica Inn*, 1939) before going to the US where he photographed SUSPICION (1941) for Alfred HITCHCOCK. He became a specialist in musicals, including *The Pirate* (1948), *The Barkleys of Broadway* (1949), *The Eddy Duchin Story* (1956), GUYS AND DOLLS (1955), *Pajama Game* (1957), *Funny Girl* (1968), and *Hello Dolly* (1969). He won OSCARS for *The Picture of Dorian Gray* (1944) and MY FAIR LADY (1964).

**STRAND,** PAUL (1890– ), US photographer and documentary film-maker, began to work in still photography as a student of Alfred Steiglitz. In 1921, with the painter Charles Sheeler, he made his first film, a lyrical study of

New York City called *Mannahatta*, based on a poem by Walt Whitman. After a long period of free-lance work for PATHÉ News, FOX News, FAMOUS PLAYERS, and METRO-GOLDWYN-MAYER he was joined by Fred ZINNEMANN to make *Redes* (*The Wave*, 1934) in Mexico. In 1935 he was recruited by Pare LORENTZ, along with Ralph Steiner and Leo HURWITZ, to shoot THE PLOW THAT BROKE THE PLAINS (1936). Then, as president of FRONTIER FILMS, he produced, directed, and shot *Heart of Spain* (1937) and NATIVE LAND (1942), both with Hurwitz.

Since Frontier Films was dissolved in the early forties Strand has gone back to still photography, specializing in studies of European regions.

***STRANGERS ON A TRAIN***, US, 1951. 1¾hr. *Dir, prod* Alfred Hitchcock for Warner Bros; *scr* Raymond Chandler, Czenzi Ormonde, from the novel by Patricia Highsmith; *ph* Robert Burks; *cast* Farley Granger (Guy Haines), Ruth Roman (Ann Morton), Robert Walker (Bruno Anthony), Leo G. Carroll (Senator Morton), Patricia Hitchcock (Barbara Morton).

Guy Haines, a wealthy and successful tennis star, wishes to marry a senator's daughter but has been refused a divorce by his estranged wife. On a train journey he meets Bruno, a spoilt psychopathic playboy, who strikes a bargain: he will murder Guy's wife if in return Guy will murder Bruno's domineering father. The plan for the perfect crime naturally goes awry.

One of HITCHCOCK's most successful suspense films, *Strangers on a Train* uses an implausibly symmetrical plot to support some virtuoso achievements in the creation of suspense. Recurrently, urgency is used to manipulate the audience's response, as in the tennis match which Guy must not only win, but complete in a certain time. There are many impressive technical feats, including a murder scene reflected in the victim's fallen spectacles, and the film is full of Hitchcock's particular brand of quirky humour. Robert WALKER gave the performance of his career, a chilling *tour de force*. ·

**STRAUB**, JEAN-MARIE (1933– ), French director born in Lorraine who, for political reasons, has worked mainly in Germany and Italy. His first two films *Machorka-Muff* (1963) and *Nicht Versöhnt* (*Not Reconciled*, 1965) were elliptical adaptations of stories by Heinrich Böll. Straub's austere 'minimal' style accompanied by a Brechtian treatment of his source material and frequently non-professional actors, developed further and most lyrically in *Chronik der Anna Magdalena Bach* (*The Chronicle of Anna*

*La strada* (Federico Fellini, 1954)

*Magdalena Bach*, 1967). All the roles were played by professional musicians (notably Gustave Leonhardt as Johann Sebastian Bach); this allowed the use of direct sound and extremely long takes. Straub's later films, including *Othon* (1972) and *Geschichtsunterricht* (*History Lessons*, 1973)—versions of plays by Corneille and BRECHT respectively—are also determinedly avant-garde in their approach to narrative and other aspects of film form. Straub's particular concern is the interrelation of formal invention with a political dimension, placing his characters (and his films) within the society that shapes them.

Richard Roud, *Jean-Marie Straub*, London, 1971.

***STREETCAR NAMED DESIRE, A***, US, 1951. 2hr. *Dir* Elia Kazan; *prod* Warner Bros; *scr* Oscar Saul, from the play by Tennessee Williams; *ph* Harry Stradling; *mus* Alex North; *cast* Vivien Leigh (Blanche Dubois), Marlon Brando (Stanley Kowalski), Kim Hunter (Stella), Karl Malden (Mitch), Rudy Bond (Steve Hubbel).

Tennessee WILLIAMS's play, set in the steamy squalor of New Orleans, tells of a neurotic woman's mental collapse through exposure to her brother-in-law's animal magnetism. The film drew its cast from KAZAN's New York stage production, except for Vivien LEIGH who had starred in the play in London.

The screen adaptation retained the play's spatial confinement, most of the action being set in the Kowalskis' apartment, contributing to the necessary sense of claustrophobia. The film is memorable for the acting, especially Vivien Leigh's ravaged Blanche and Marlon BRANDO's brutal, inarticulate Stanley, and for its relatively daring and novel use of a strongly sexual theme.

**STREET FILMS,** a term coined by Siegfried KRACAUER for a group of German films made in 1923–30 in which middle class individuals were enticed from the dull monotony of their homes by the lurid and forbidden attractions of the street. Occasionally the street was shown to harbour virtues which were absent in these homes. Examples of the type are: *Die Strasse* (*The Street*, Karl GRÜNE, 1923), DIE FREUDLOSE GASSE (*Joyless Street*, G. W. PABST, 1925), and *Dirnentragödie* (*Tragedy of a Street*, Bruno Rahn, 1927). (See also KAMMERSPIELFILM.)

**STREISAND,** BARBRA (1942– ), US singer and actress, won an OSCAR in her first film *Funny Girl* (William WYLER, 1968), based on the life of Fanny BRICE. After vivid performances in *Hello Dolly* (Gene KELLY, 1969) and *On a Clear Day You Can See Forever* (Vincente MINNELLI, 1970), she broke away from musicals to prove

an accomplished comic actress in *The Owl and the Pussycat* (1970), and her precise, Jewish humour was brilliantly exploited in Peter BOGDANOVICH's hilarious pastiche *What's Up, Doc?* (1972). In *Up the Sandbox* (Irving KERSHNER, 1972) she acted out the fantasies of a bored housewife and she played a dowdy left-wing enthusiast in *The Way We Were* (1973), reverting to outright farce in *For Pete's Sake* (1974).

**STRETCHING,** a method of OPTICAL PRINTING used principally to convert old film shot at silent camera speeds into new copies which run properly on modern projectors.

Before 1929 films were shot at 16 frames per second and projected at roughly the same speed; with the coming of SOUND the speed of cameras and projectors was standardized at 24 frames per second. Thus if an old film is shown on a modern projector the action appears speeded up by one-third. This can be corrected by stretching. A copy of the old film is made on an optical printer which automatically copies every other frame twice, so that the copy contains three frames for every two in the original. The process is fairly expensive, and is complicated by the fact that not all silent films were shot at exactly 16 frames per second, so that varying degrees of stretch may be needed. For these reasons makers of COMPILATION films often incorporate old footage without stretching it, with the result that modern audiences have come to regard all silent film as comic because of the jerky gestures and waddling walks.

**STRICK,** JOSEPH (1923– ), US director, worked on the *Los Angeles Times* while shooting his first film, *Muscle Beach* (1949), at weekends on the beaches of California. In the same year he made a short film, *Jour de fête*, in France. Working in his spare time over the next eight years he made *The Savage Eye* (1959), a bleak study of urban America which won several awards. He directed *The Balcony* (1963) from Genet's play; *Ulysses* (1966) from Joyce's novel; and a film for BBC television *The Hecklers* (1966), dealing with (and also provoking) heckling in British election meetings. After beginning work on *Justine* (1969) he was replaced by George CUKOR and went on to direct *Tropic of Cancer* (1969) from Henry Miller's novel. His *Interviews with My Lai Veterans* (1970) was awarded an OSCAR for best documentary short. His reputation rests more on a controversial choice of subjects, which inevitably invite CENSORSHIP problems, than on the intrinsic quality of his films.

**STRIPED PRINT,** a MARRIED print to which sound has been added by placing a thin stripe of magnetic oxide in the usual sound track position alongside the picture. The sound is later recorded on this stripe. (More usually the sound track on a married print is an OPTICAL track, printed photographically at the same time as the picture.) Sound striping can be applied to film of any gauge, and on 8mm and 16mm it produces the best quality sound. However, unlike an optical track, it requires two extra operations in addition to printing, and is therefore more expensive. In the cinema STEREOPHONIC sound is reproduced from 70mm prints with four stripes, two on each side of the picture. (See COMMAG.)

**STROBING,** a disturbing effect peculiar to the motion picture, in which rapidly-moving objects appear to 'jitter' rather than move smoothly. Normally, such an object would be photographed on each FRAME as a short blur, so that the successive positions blend together to give the impression of continuous motion. But under certain conditions the object photographs too sharply; the successive positions do not blend, and the movement is perceived as what it really is, a series of discontinuous frames. The effect is particularly annoying when the entire frame strobes, as when the camera is panned too quickly across a landscape. Strobing is also responsible for the effect sometimes seen in Westerns in which spoked stagecoach wheels appear to turn backwards.

**STROHEIM,** ERICH VON (1885–1957), US actor and director, was born in Vienna. His family was middle-class; it was after he entered films that he added the prefix 'von' to his name and encouraged the story that he was an army officer of noble descent. He emigrated to the US in about 1906 and from 1914 played small parts in films, including THE BIRTH OF A NATION (1915) and INTOLERANCE (1916). He became one of D. W. GRIFFITH's assistants and began to specialize in roles embodying the popular idea of the brutal Prussian officer, promoted as 'the man you love to hate'.

For UNIVERSAL he wrote, designed, and directed *Blind Husbands* (1918) and *The Devil's Passkey* (1919), his only films to be released without interference. They already display the themes and methods more fully developed in FOOLISH WIVES (1921). The attempted seduction of an American wife by a cynical European aristocrat (played by Stroheim himself in *Blind Husbands* and *Foolish Wives*) sets American simplicity against European decadence; these sophisticated, mordantly witty tales are played out against lavish décors. From his first film Stroheim began to assemble the actors who were to appear in his most important work, including Gibson Gowland, Maude George, Cesare Gravina, Dale Fuller, and ZaSu PITTS. His char-

acteristic visual style was also apparent early in his career: he depended little on conventional editing, achieving a singular density of dramatic effect by piling up detail within extended shots in a way which was profoundly to influence RENOIR and others (see PLAN-SÉQUENCE).

*Foolish Wives* gave rise to Stroheim's first major clash with his producers, but he attempted one more film for Universal, *Merry-go-round* (1922), a characteristic tale of love across class barriers in nineteenth-century Europe. His battles with Irving THALBERG now developed into open warfare and, on the grounds of extravagance, he was replaced as director by Rupert Julian. While little of Stroheim's original footage remained in the version finally released, his story, sets, and favourite actors give a strong impression of his typical work.

The Goldwyn Company (see METRO-GOLDWYN-MAYER) was the next to take on the Stroheim problem. GREED (1923) brought him once more into conflict with Thalberg: although Stroheim was allowed to shoot the film according to his original plan, his intentions are virtually unrecognizable in the truncated version finally released. MGM tried him again on THE MERRY WIDOW (1925) but imposed two stars on him (John GILBERT and Mae MURRAY), insisted on story changes, and battled unceasingly over his inability to observe either a shooting schedule or a budget. His relations with PARAMOUNT, for whom he directed THE WEDDING MARCH (1926) were no better: he was dismissed before the film was completed and at one stage Josef von STERNBERG had the task of editing it to acceptable length. A similar pattern occurred with QUEEN KELLY (1928), an independent production by Gloria SWANSON and Joseph P. KENNEDY, although the introduction of sound provided an excuse for stopping production. Even the distorted final version bears the authentic Stroheim touch; it also embodies his problems in completing a film without studio interference. With all his brilliance at conveying character, social patterns, and sexual manoeuvres (with particularly skilled use of décor, meticulously designed to support and round out the performances of his carefully chosen actors), Stroheim was unable to tailor his ideas to commercial demands. His projects, to a producer's eye extravagant and egotistical, have resulted in some enduring artistic achievements even when truncated, but they could never have been profitable in a mass medium.

During his remaining years in Hollywood he wrote scripts, made occasional acting appearances, notably opposite Greta GARBO in *As You Desire Me* (1932), and directed one sound film, *Walking Down Broadway* for FOX, released in 1933 as HALLO, SISTER. Although he behaved

Erich von Stroheim in *La Grande Illusion* (Jean Renoir, 1937)

impeccably during shooting, completing the film on schedule at a modest budget, the plot was changed and a new ending added; his name was removed from the credits at his own wish. Most of the footage in the release version was Stroheim's and might have indicated new directions for his talent, had there been a chance for him to pursue them.

In 1936 he left for France, spending the rest of his working life as an actor. Most of the films in which he appeared were undistinguished, but he gave three memorable performances: in LA GRANDE ILLUSION (1937), *Five Graves to Cairo* (Billy WILDER, 1943), in which he played Rommel, and SUNSET BOULEVARD (1950).

**STUDENT VON PRAG, Der** (*The Student of Prague*), has been the subject of three German films.

1913. 1¼hr. *Dir* Stellan Rye; *prod* Bioscop; *scr* Hanns Heinz Ewers; *ph* Guido Seeber; *des* Robert A. Dietrich, Kurt Richter; *cast* Paul Wegener (Baldwin), John Gottowt (Scapinelli), Lyda Salmanova (flower girl), Grete Berger (Countess).

The story, which is close to the favourite themes of German Romantic literature, concerns the student Baldwin, who is offered by the demonic Scapinelli wealth and a good marriage in exchange for his reflection. The reflection then takes on an independent existence and begins to do harm. Baldwin, unable to control his second self, finally shoots it, thereby causing his own death.

It is likely that Paul WEGENER, who worked closely with Rye and Ewers on this film, influenced the supernatural theme and atmosphere. The film evokes the dreamlike anguish of its hero and makes good use of the medium in its presentation of the Doppelgänger, a motif frequently used by German Expressionist films (see EXPRESSIONISM). Unlike these later films, however, it does not rely entirely on sets for its unreal atmosphere, but uses locations which are successfully integrated into the eerie tale.

1926. 2hr. *Dir* Henrik Galeen; *prod* H. R. Sokal; *scr* Galeen, Hanns Heinz Ewers; *ph* Günther Krampf, Erich Nitzschmann; *des* Hermann Warm; *cast* Conrad Veidt (Baldwin), Werner Krauss (Scapinelli), Agnes Esterhazy (Countess), Eliza La Porta (flower girl).

This version placed more emphasis on psychology, interpreting Baldwin's fight with his double much more clearly as a fight with his other self. The supernatural atmosphere is derived from a studio landscape, which reflects and highlights Baldwin's fears and inner conflicts. The sets and lighting are outstanding and the film is marked by an excellent performance from Conrad VEIDT.

1935. 1½hr. *Dir* Arthur Robison; *ph* Bruno Mondi; *des* Hermann Warm; *mus* Theo Mackeben; *cast* Adolf Wohlbrück (later Anton Walbrook) (Baldwin), Theodor Loos (Carpis [Scapinelli]), Dorothea Wieck (Countess).

The sound version toned down the supernatural elements and turned the demonic sorcerer into a jealous lover, thus giving psychological motivation to his actions. It failed, therefore, to exploit the theme's potential and although it makes good use of shadows in some effective sequences, it is inferior to the other two versions. ROBISON died during the production.

**STUDIO DES URSULINES,** founded by two actors, Armand Tallier and Laurence Myrga, like the VIEUX COLOMBIER and STUDIO 28, specialized in showing AVANT-GARDE films to a Parisian public eager for them. The cinema's first showing was PABST'S DIE FREUDLOSE GASSE (*Joyless Street*, 1925). Subsequently, such films as Man RAY'S *L'Étoile de mer* (1929), René CLAIR'S ENTR'ACTE (1924), and DULAC'S LA COQUILLE ET LE CLERGYMAN (*The Seashell and the Clergyman*, 1928) were shown. (See also ART HOUSE.)

**STUDIO 28** was founded in 1928 and directed by the doctor and journalist Jean Mauclaire. Like the STUDIO DES URSULINES and VIEUX COLOMBIER it was a cinema devoted to exhibiting contemporary AVANT-GARDE films; Luis BUÑUEL'S UN CHIEN ANDALOU (1928) and L'ÂGE D'OR (1930) were shown there, as was Jean COCTEAU'S LE SANG D'UN POÈTE (1930). (See also ART HOUSE.)

**STUNT MAN,** actor specializing in dangerous and spectacular feats. His work may include fights, car, motorcycle, aircraft, and speedboat crashes, horse-riding, work with dangerous animals, sequences involving fires, explosions, or collapsing buildings, jumps or falls from considerable heights. He works slowly, planning each stage of a stunt with great precision, himself arranging protective measures such as padded clothing and resilient landing material. To avoid injury to the star a stunt man will double for him in dangerous scenes; to save time and money these are often shot by a SECOND UNIT. Stunt men also double for female stars, but there is a small élite of stunt women. Stunting is highly paid: the varieties of stunt are strictly defined and paid according to a precise scale, but the fee for an unusually dangerous feat may be specially negotiated.

Stars who took a pride in planning and executing their own stunts include Buster KEATON, Harold LLOYD, Douglas FAIRBANKS, Burt LANCASTER, Steve MCQUEEN; but with increased production costs and insurance premiums the practice is no longer encouraged.

John Baxter, *Stunt* (London, 1973).

**STURGES, JOHN** (1911–   ), US director, began his career at RKO. He became a production assistant for David O. SELZNICK and at the outbreak of the Second World War was working as an editor. He joined the Signal Corps, transferring later to the Air Corps, and made a number of documentaries, among them the much praised *Thunderbolt* (with William WYLER). After the war he returned to Hollywood as a director.

In 1949 he made *The Walking Hills*, the first of a number of Westerns, including *Escape from Fort Bravo* (1953), *Bad Day at Black Rock* (1954), GUNFIGHT AT THE OK CORRAL (1956), *Last Train from Gun Hill* (1959), THE MAGNIFICENT SEVEN (1960), and *The Hallelujah Trail* (1965), on which his reputation is largely based, although one of his most successful films, *The Great Escape* (1962), is a war drama. His cool, unemotional style, which makes use of pans and long shots to relate characters to their environment is particularly well-suited to the Western, traditionally concerned with the isolation of the individual in a vast landscape, but has also provided striking moments in *Ice Station Zebra* (1968) and *Marooned* (1969), extreme permutations of the same theme. His best Westerns reveal a personal quality not always felt in his other work.

**STURGES, PRESTON** (1898–1959), US writer and director real name Edmond P. Biden. After some success as a playwright he worked as a scriptwriter in Hollywood from 1930. He wrote the scripts of all the twelve films he directed, beginning with THE GREAT MCGINTY (1940, *Down Went McGinty* in GB), typically a satire on American politics, which won an OSCAR for the best original screen story. A satirist with a fine sense of comic timing, Sturges constructed his films around witty lines, brilliant visual gags, and marvellous eccentrics, often played by actors (like Franklin Pangborn and Raymond Walburn) who formed a stock company in Sturges's films.

His view of the world and his fellow men seemed to be sour and often contemptuous, but the characters are usually presented with a certain affection and this, together with the pervading humour, gives the films a rather ambiguous tone. Several of his heroes and heroines are not particularly admirable, but he used actors of charm and skill to counteract this: Barbara STANWYCK's performance in THE LADY EVE (1941), for example, together with the film's pace and wit, masks the vindictiveness of the character she is playing. In UNFAITHFULLY YOURS (1948), Sturges's black vision seems to be inviting the audience to laugh at Rex HARRISON's day-dream of slashing his wife to death with a razor. His great period was between 1940 and 1944, when he made eight films including SULLIVAN'S TRAVELS (1941), THE PALM BEACH STORY (1942), and two satires on small town America starring Eddie Bracken—THE MIRACLE OF MORGAN'S CREEK (1944) and HAIL THE CONQUERING HERO (1944). He died in Paris, three years after making his last and unsuccessful film, *Les Carnets du Major Thompson* (*The Diary of Major Thompson*, 1956).

**SUBTITLES,** dialogue translations printed directly on to the film and appearing at the base of the frame; sometimes used for narrative and dialogue inserts in a silent film which are properly termed inter-titles.

A working print of the film is studied on a viewing machine and 'spotted' with crayon to mark the position and duration of each subtitle. The titles are set up in the laboratory, photographed, and combined with the negative to produce a release print. Alternatively, the titles are mounted in metal type which is applied to the release print itself, cutting through the emulsion to create a translucent image: each letter is outlined by a fine ridge of emulsion which may give the effect of hollow lettering. Both methods have drawbacks: subtitles printed photographically are low in contrast and are difficult to decipher on a pale background, although this may be corrected in the laboratory by careful GRADING of selected scenes; etched subtitles are often so brilliant as to throw a visual composition off balance or, in a dimly-lit scene, distract the eye from the dramatic action.

Foreign films shown on television are subtitled electronically to achieve a satisfactory size and position of lettering: the subtitles are projected separately, the print itself remaining unmarked.

The maximum duration of one subtitle is usually accepted as six seconds (144 frames or nine feet of 35mm film); the minimum length is variable, depending on the nature of the dialogue: routine phrases such as conventional greeting will be registered by the audience with great rapidity, but a quick exchange of important dialogue will need careful judgement of the speed at which an audience will follow it. The titler is restricted on the one hand by the audience's ability to receive printed information within a limited time and on the other by the duration of the section of speech being translated. Considerable condensing of the original script is inevitable; indeed, over-meticulous subtitling can be irritating when the action is self-explanatory. But with all its inherent limitations, subtitling is generally accepted as aesthetically preferable to DUBBING foreign-language films: the loss of detailed understanding of the dialogue is amply compensated by retaining the quality and expression of the original voices and avoiding the distraction of non-synchronized speech and lip-movement.

**SUBTRACTIVE COLOUR.** What the eye sees as 'white' light is made up of a mixture of all the colours of the spectrum. If white light is projected on to a screen and a dyed filter is inserted in the beam to absorb, or subtract, some of these colours, the eye sees only the colours which remain. A yellow-coloured filter, for example, subtracts all colours except yellow. Any colour can be produced on the screen by three filters of varying strengths coloured yellow, cyan, and magenta—the subtractive primary colours. All modern colour films, such as TECHNICOLOR and EASTMAN COLOR, are based on this principle. An Eastman Color print, for example, is simply clear film carrying three layers of dye which subtract colours from the white light projected through it. (See also ADDITIVE COLOUR, COLOUR.)

*SUCH IS LIFE* see TAKOVÝ JE ŽIVOT

**SUCKSDORFF,** ARNE (1917– ), Swedish documentary film-maker, first studied natural history and painting and in the late thirties spent some time in Berlin, studying film under Klein-Rogge. Among his early films *En sommarsaga* (1941) showed clearly the direction in which his talent was to develop, especially his involvement with wild animals in their natural surroundings, filmed with great visual beauty. *Vinden från väster* (*The West Wind*, 1942), made for SVENSK FILMINDUSTRI, deals with the annual northward migration of the Lapps: the theme is treated with sensitivity, communicating by almost entirely visual means the stunning impact of the arrival of spring in the far north.

Except in the case of *Sarvtid* (1943), which was supervised by Gunnar Skoglund, Sucksdorff continued to work with complete independence, even when working for commercial producers. *Människor i stad* (*Rhythm of the City*, 1946) and two films made in India, *Indisk by* (*Hindu Village*) and *Vinden och floden* (*The Wind and the River*, both 1951), demonstrate that his talent is not confined to his home ground. His first full-length documentary *Det stora äventyret* (*The*

*Great Adventure*, 1953) won wide recognition for his very individual gifts. The touching story of a boy who tames an otter provides the framework for exquisitely detailed observation of wild life, and it earned acclaim for its visual beauty and freshness. After this success Sucksdorff widened his approach, using colour and wide screen for the first time in *En djungelsaga* (*The Flute and the Arrow*, 1957) and allowing human beings to play a greater part: in *Pojken i tradet* (*The Boy in the Tree*, 1961) there is scripted dialogue and *Mit hem ar Copacabana* (*My Home is Copacabana*, 1965) uses a fictional scenario.

**SUDBA CHELOVEKA** (*Destiny of a Man*), USSR, 1959. 1½hr. *Dir* Sergei Bondarchuk; *prod* Mosfilm; *scr* Y. Lukin, F. Shakhmagonov, from the story by Mikhail Sholokhov; *ph* Vladimir Monakhov; *mus* V. Basnov; *cast* Sergei Bondarchuk (Andrei Sokolov), Zinaida Kirienko (Irina), Pavlik Boriskin (Vanyusha), P. Volkov (Ivan Timofeyevich).

For his début as director (he was already a distinguished film actor) BONDARCHUK was with some reluctance entrusted with the adaptation of Sholokhov's well-loved story of a man's triumph over the sufferings and deprivations inflicted by war. The film's compassion and integrity vindicate the choice of director. Human tragedy is depicted without sentimentality and the potentially startling visual style is firmly integrated into the tone of the narrative. As well as directing, Bondarchuk played the leading role with complete authority.

*Sudba cheloveka* is one of the few Russian features to have been generally released in Britain, but the version circulated was marred by DUBBING into English and by the cutting of twenty minutes from the original running time of 98 minutes.

**SULLAVAN,** MARGARET (1911–60), US actress popular in the thirties following her first film *Only Yesterday* (1933). *Little Man What Now?* (1934) and other films directed by Frank BORZAGE emphasized her romantically innocent quality, and she was a charming *ingénue* in *The Shop around the Corner* (Ernst LUBITSCH, 1940). Her last film was *No Sad Songs for Me* (1950).

**SULLIVAN,** C. GARDNER (1885–1965), US scriptwriter. In 1912–24 he worked with Thomas H. INCE and wrote numerous scripts for films supervised or directed by Ince, including *The Battle of Gettysburg* (1914), *The Wrath of the Gods* (1914), *The Aryan* (1916), CIVILIZATION (1916), and *Carmen of the Klondike* (1918). In 1929 he co-directed *Alibi* with Roland West. He continued scriptwriting during the thirties and forties, on occasion for Cecil B. DEMILLE.

**SULLIVAN'S TRAVELS,** US, 1941. 1¼hr. *Dir*, *scr* Preston Sturges; *prod* Paramount; *ph* John Seitz; *ed* Stuart Gilmore; *cast* Joel McCrea (John L. Sullivan), Veronica Lake (the girl), Robert Warwick (Mr LeBrand), William Demarest (Mr Jones), Franklin Pangborn (Mr Casalsis), Porter Hall (Mr Hadrian), Byron Foulger (Mr Valdelle), Margaret Hayes (secretary), Robert Grieg (butler), Eric Blore (valet).

A successful Hollywood comedy director pretends to be a tramp in order to make a convincing social drama. Initially he is frustrated by the studio caravan which trails ludicrously behind him with every conceivable comfort, but comedy turns to possible tragedy when amnesia leads to a sentence of hard labour, while his friends believe him dead. In an abrupt and unconvincing happy ending, Sullivan returns to Hollywood determined to give people enjoyment by making comedies. It is a strange and interesting film combining STURGES's usual comedy with near-tragedy and direct social comment and with attractive performances from Joel MCCREA (in one of his three starring parts for Sturges) and Veronica LAKE. It provides a very funny satire on Hollywood and some insight into the director's own attitudes.

**SUNA NO ONNA** (*Woman of the Dunes*), Japan, 1964. 2hr. *Dir* Hiroshi Teshigahara; *prod* Teshigahara Productions; *scr* Kobo Abe from his novel; *ph* Hiroshi Segawa; *ed* F. Susui; *mus* Toru Takemitsu; *cast* Eiji Okada (the man), Kyoko Kishoda (the woman).

An entomologist spends the night in a hut at the bottom of a sandpit; next day he cannot escape. His captivity is shared by an attractive widow, and TESHIGAHARA builds up the erotic tension between them with extreme close-ups that transform the human body into landscape, at one with the glittering sand. In the man's surrender to circumstance the film presents an intelligent, absurdist view of humanity in relation to environment.

**SUNRISE,** US, 1927. 2hr. *Dir* F. W. Murnau; *prod* Fox Film Co; *scr* Carl Mayer, from Hermann Sudermann's 'Die Reise nach Tilsit' ('A Trip to Tilsit'); *ph* Charles Rosher, Karl Struss; *des* Rochus Gliese; *mus* Dr Hugo Reisenfeld; *cast* George O'Brien (the Man), Janet Gaynor (the Wife), Margaret Livingston (the Woman from the City), Bodil Rosing (the Maid).

MURNAU had for some time wished to film Sudermann's short story; when he was given an almost free hand by FOX for his first American film, he chose to make of its drama of infidelity, attempted murder, and repentance a universal poetic tragedy epitomized by the sub-title 'A Song of Two Humans'. His aims were not entirely realized. A conventional happy ending was ordered, and broad comedy scenes injected into the city sequence consort oddly with the lyrical conception.

But the film has memorable visual qualities, notably in the farmhouse scenes which are composed and lit to resemble Dutch interiors, in the night scene by the lake where a low-angle view of the action is extended in long unbroken shots, and in the justly famous journey by trolley car, filmed without BACK PROJECTION. The film's visual distinction is greatly enhanced by using PANCHROMATIC stock: it was the first commercially made film to do so. The remarkable city set gave Murnau the opportunity for unusual action shots; these, together with back projection and other special effects, demonstrate a masterly combination of the technical resources of Germany and Hollywood. The leading actors contributed performances of high quality, in particular Janet GAYNOR who gave radiance to a potentially colourless role.

Made as a silent film, *Sunrise* was also issued in a sound version with a synchronized music track.

A German version of *Die Reise nach Tilsit* was made in 1939 by Veit HARLAN, again using the happy ending of the Murnau film.

**SUNSET BOULEVARD,** US, 1950. 1¾hr. *Dir* Billy Wilder; *prod* Charles Brackett for Paramount; *scr* Wilder, Brackett, D. M. Marshman Jr; *ph* John F. Seitz; *cast* Gloria Swanson (Norma Desmond), William Holden (Joe Gillis), Erich von Stroheim (Max von Mayerling), Nancy Olson (Betty Schaefer), Cecil B. DeMille, Hedda Hopper, Buster Keaton, H. B. Warner, Ray Evans, Jay Livinston, Anna Q. Nilsson (themselves).

Joe Gillis, down on his luck, stumbles into the bizarre *ménage* of Norma Desmond, a forgotten star of silent films who lives out a fantasy existence in a palatial house with her former director acting as major-domo.

Billy WILDER's choice of Gloria SWANSON to play the monomaniac movie queen was inspired: her performance was a fitting climax to a remarkable career. The evocation of her great days is brilliantly sustained with the aid of Erich von STROHEIM and other film personalities of the era playing themselves. A ruthlessly black comedy, the film displays an intimacy with the Hollywood of the twenties which has won it a unique place among films on the subject.

The film sequences screened by Norma Desmond at home are from QUEEN KELLY (1928), and Wilder's film contains many allusions to Stroheim's unfinished masterpiece.

**SUPER-8,** the current standard amateur and educational film gauge, introduced in 1965. It is the same width as the original 8MM film which it supersedes, but the perforations have been made smaller to permit a 50 per cent larger frame and thus better definition. Space has been allowed for a magnetic or OPTICAL sound track. Amateurs have been slow to change to Super-8 because of its greater cost over standard 8mm; but it is coming into wide use for educational and scientific films and even for television news coverage. Professionally, Super-8 approaches 16mm in definition and costs less; cameras of considerable sophistication are available. Several video cassette systems use Super-8 film as their recording medium.

**SUPERIMPOSITION,** the effect of making one image, such as a title, appear over another, such as a background. At its simplest a superimposition can be simply a double-exposure; but for professional purposes the background shot and the title to be superimposed are photographed separately and combined in the optical printer. Where the title lettering is in white, the procedure is simple, since the brightness of the letters 'burns out' any background detail. Where the lettering is coloured or complex, the technician must first produce a negative image of the lettering to 'hold back' the background in the areas where the letters are to appear.

The familiar superimposition of SUBTITLES on foreign films is not a photographic, but a mechanical process.

**SURREALISM,** a movement in the arts which flourished mainly in France in the twenties. Its principal theorist and spokesman was André Breton, who despotically laid down the lines the movement was to follow, first in his *Manifeste de Surréalisme* of 1924 and in later published statements. Breton's wartime service in the psychoanalytic ward of a military hospital presumably influenced his theories, which leaned heavily on the truth of the irrational (*l'acte gratuit*), the importance of dream states, the emotional power of incongruous juxtapositions, and the unswerving pursuit of personal gratification, particularly in the sexual field (*l'amour fou*). The movement took over from Dada, making aesthetic and political formulations of that movement's random attempts to shock. (Dada is well represented in cinema by ENTR'ACTE, 1924.) With their declared aim of liberating the individual from social and religious restrictions, the Surrealists took up a left-wing stance in politics, but their disruptive aims cut short their various alliances with formal Communism. Their influence on the arts, however, was crucial, affecting painting (Ernst, Magritte, Miró, DALI), poetry (Éluard, Peret, Breton himself), and theatre (Vitrac, ARTAUD). By the end of the thirties the movement as such was in decline, kept alive only by the vigorous Breton until his death in 1966.

The cinema appealed strongly as a means of surrealist expression, its photographic nature lending verisimilitude to the most extravagant fantasies and its fragmentation offering the means of making the most extraordinary juxtapositions seem real. In the movement's early days members of the group experimented with the medium, making films of an experimental, esoteric nature. Although Germaine DULAC's LA COQUILLE ET LE CLERGYMAN (1928) is usually considered the first surrealist film, it was rejected by the group. They enthusiastically endorsed the two films which best represent Surrealism in the twenties, Luis BUÑUEL's UN CHIEN ANDALOU (1928) and L'ÂGE D'OR (1930), the former an exposition of automatism, the latter about the subversive nature of *l'amour fou*. Other surrealist film-makers include Man RAY and Jacques BRUNIUS.

The appropriateness of cinema to surrealist modes of expression has given general currency to many of their ideas. Among the many popular films which share common ground with the group's preoccupation with incongruity, sexuality, and irrationality, the anarchic comedy of the MARX BROTHERS and the puckishness of HITCHCOCK; the differing erotic qualities of Louise BROOKS and Mae WEST; and the uneasy, humorous menace of the films of James WHALE and, outstandingly, THE NIGHT OF THE HUNTER (1955), all carry influences from Surrealism. In the more esoteric field this influence may be seen in the work of Hans RICHTER, Georges FRANJU and Jean COCTEAU (although Cocteau's aims and methods have always been disclaimed by the Surrealist group). The only film-maker to have remained declaredly and definitively a Surrealist is Buñuel. The extent to which the movement's intentionally shocking and disruptive ideas have become generally accepted may be seen in the reception of Buñuel's LA VOIE LACTÉE (1969), a film which encapsulates all the surrealist aims and yet was widely viewed with enjoyment, comprehension, and (ironically) respect.

An exhaustive account of the movement's connections with film is to be found in *Le Surréalisme au cinéma* by Ado Kyrou, Paris, 1953.

**SURTEES,** ROBERT (1906– ), US cameraman, joined UNIVERSAL as an assistant cameraman in 1927 and was later on the staff of WARNER BROS and METRO-GOLDWYN-MAYER. His first solo credit was in 1942 with *This Precious Freedom* and his work since has shown increasing distinction; he is now regarded as one of America's leading cinematographers. His many notable films include *Intruder in the Dust* (1949),

*King Solomon's Mines* (1950) for which he received an OSCAR, QUO VADIS (1951), THE BAD AND THE BEAUTIFUL (1952, Oscar), *Mogambo* (1953), *Oklahoma!* (1955), *Les Girls* (1957), BEN-HUR (1959, Oscar), THE GRADUATE (1967), *Sweet Charity* (1968), *Summer of '42* (1971), *The Last Picture Show* (1971), and *The Sting* (1973), the last remarkable for its combination of period visual style and zestful humour.

**SUSPICION,** US, 1941. 1¾hr. *Dir* Alfred Hitchcock; *prod* RKO; *scr* Samson Raphaelson, Joan Harrison, Alma Reville, from the novel *Before the Fact* by Francis Iles; *ph* Harry Stradling; *cast* Cary Grant (Johnnie), Joan Fontaine (Lina MacKinlaw), Sir Cedric Hardwicke (General MacKinlaw), Nigel Bruce (Beaky), Dame May Whitty (Mrs MacKinlaw).

General disillusionment with her husband's character increases to the point where Lina begins to suspect him of planning to kill her. The tension holds throughout, and *Suspicion* contains many of HITCHCOCK's most effective moments of suspense, notably the sequence of Cary GRANT impassively mounting a shadowed staircase carrying a glass of (poisoned?) milk. Grant's first role for Hitchcock showed him to be one of the perfect actors for the director's special demands on his players. Joan FONTAINE won an OSCAR for her performance as the distraught wife.

**SVENSKA FILMINSTITUTET,** the Swedish film institute, was established in 1963, chiefly at the instigation of Harry Schein, a film collector and enthusiast. It absorbed the Filmhistoriska Samlingarna, the museum and archive which had been organized on minimal funds by Einar Lauritzen in 1933. Its basic aim was to underwrite Swedish film production generally and especially to support quality films by guaranteeing any box-office losses. To this end the entertainment tax was replaced by a 10 per cent levy on ticket sales. The scheme has succeeded admirably, helping to maintain a thriving industry in the face of competition from television and a world recession in the cinema; and other countries, notably Denmark, Yugoslavia, and the US, have shown interest in its operation. The Institutet also manages a system of quality awards and supports the national film school and film clubs. (See SWEDEN.)

**SVENSK FILMINDUSTRI,** the major Swedish production and exhibition company, is a development from Svenska Bio, founded in 1907. Charles MAGNUSSON, who joined the company in 1909, was the driving force behind its success: he brought directors of the calibre of Mauritz STILLER and Victor SJÖSTRÖM on to his staff and managed Bio's amalgamation with its chief competitor AB Skandia to form Svensk Filmindustri in 1919. Magnusson retired in 1928 and the general decline in Swedish cinema was reflected in the company's fortunes. Svenska's studios at Lindingö were destroyed during the forties and new ones were built at Stocksund. Carl Anders Dymling, head of production 1942–61, was largely responsible for the company's revival and for recalling world attention to Swedish films. He deliberately sought out new talent, supporting the early work of Ingmar BERGMAN and Arne SUCKSDORFF and the return to films of Alf SJÖBERG. He was succeeded by Kenne Fant, himself an actor and director.

**SWANSON,** GLORIA (1898–    ), US actress, started in films with ESSANAY where she met and married Wallace BEERY. She joined Mack SENNETT's company in 1916 and appeared in several comedies but not, as is often said, as one of his Bathing Beauties. In 1918 she signed with Cecil B. DEMILLE who, in the course of several films including *Male and Female* (1919) and *Why Change Your Wife?* (1920), established her as the embodiment of the voluptuous luxury that became his hall-mark. During the twenties she was a symbol of Hollywood glamour with her well-publicized romances and extravagant spending: she became one of the highest-paid stars during her contract with PARAMOUNT (1922–6). Joseph P. KENNEDY backed her own production company, releasing the films through UNITED ARTISTS, which almost foundered on STROHEIM's QUEEN KELLY (1928). Her first sound film was *Rain* (1928) in which she played Somerset Maugham's Sadie Thompson with striking conviction. It was a considerable success, but she was still unable to recover from the losses incurred by *Queen Kelly*. She produced and starred in five more films, including *Perfect Understanding* (1933) made in Britain and co-starring Laurence OLIVIER, then gave up independent production. Her following had diminished; she made a musical, *Music in the Air* (1934), then made no more appearances until 1941 when she was in a comedy, *Father Takes a Wife*, with Adolphe MENJOU. Her next film was SUNSET BOULEVARD (1950) in which she gave a brilliant performance as an ageing silent star living on her forgotten reputation; after two less memorable appearances she retired from films.

**SWEDEN.** The first film shows in Sweden were in 1896, when the LUMIÈRE system was demonstrated at the Malmö Trade Fair followed a few weeks later by EDISON's Kinetoscope, shown in Stockholm and including in the programme short sequences shot in the city by Max Skladanowsky. The first cinema proper was in a pavilion of the 1897 exhibition of Stockholm in the Middle Ages. It was opened by Numa Peterson under licence from Lumière, who sent Georges Promio to supervise the installation and to film in the locality. Promio trained Ernest Florman, one of Peterson's employees, in the use of the camera and by 1898 Florman's programmes of actuality shorts and brief comic scenes were touring Sweden. In that year extracts from the production of Ibsen's *När vi döde vakna (When We Dead Awaken)* by the Kungliga Dramatiska Teatern (the Royal Dramatic Theatre in Stockholm) were filmed: this recognition of cinema by the artistic establishment has continued to be an important factor in the development of film culture in Sweden.

By 1905 most towns had their own cinema, but in the early years of the century home production was negligible, the Swedish market being dominated by imported films, mostly those of MÉLIÈS, PATHÉ, and GAUMONT. However, in the small provincial town of Kristianstad an energetic complex of small production companies was springing up. In 1907 two young businessmen founded Svenska Bio which had become a thriving company owning over twenty cinemas by the time that Charles MAGNUSSON joined as production manager in 1909. His first projects were adaptations of popular classics directed by well-known artists from the theatre, such as *Värmlänningarna (The People of Varmland*, 1910), which has so far been filmed five times. Svenska's justified reputation for films of high artistic quality stems from 1911 when Julius Jaenzon joined them. Although trained, like Magnusson, as a cameraman and best remembered for his work in that field, Jaenzon was also at first a director, chiefly of social dramas. In 1912 he co-directed with Magnusson the ambitious *Kolingens galoscher (The Vagabond's Galoshes)*, based on a fairy-tale by Hans Andersen. This had sequences shot on location in France and America and included one of the earliest dramatic uses of the tracking shot, with the camera mounted in a New York tram to follow a car containing the actors down Broadway.

In 1911 four more small companies were founded including Svea, which was responsible for the first film versions of Strindberg, *Fröken Julie (Miss Julie)* and *Fadren (The Father)*, both 1912, and for the film unit of the Salvation Army. Statens biografbyrå, one of the first State film censorship offices, also originated in 1911; censorship had until this time been arbitrarily handled by the local police authorities.

Magnusson's skill at discovering new talent brought three important directors to Svenska Bio in 1912. Georg af Klercker (1877–1951) stayed with them for only a few months before going to work for Pathé in France, but Victor SJÖSTRÖM and Mauritz STILLER remained for ten years and their work did much to establish the reputation of early Swedish films.

The First World War gave the film industry of neutral Sweden a considerable advantage, for with no competition from imported films and much inducement to export there was freedom to develop along independent lines. During the war Stiller perfected his early style of ironic comedy, outstandingly in *Kärlek och journalistik* (*Love and Journalism*, 1916), which reached its peak with EROTIKON (1920). Sjöström, meanwhile, worked on a line of social comment combined with intense observation of human nature and relationships. By 1917, with *Terje Vigen*, his peculiar capacity for relating human emotion to natural forces is well developed: this animistic linking of man and nature, recurrent in Swedish literature and drama, has run through Swedish films up to the present day. Jaenzon became Sjöström's frequent collaborator and his camera-work helps to give these early films much of their lyrical naturalism. Extensive use was made of the rich literature of Sweden, particularly the earthy, dramatic novels of Selma LAGERLÖF.

Silent cinema in Sweden reached its peak in the immediate post-war years with HERR ARNES PENGAR (*Sir Arne's Treasure*, 1919), KÖRKALEN (*The Phantom Chariot*, 1921), and GÖSTA BERLINGS SAGA (*The Atonement of Gosta Berling*, 1924). The Danish directors Carl DREYER and Benjamin CHRISTENSEN were invited to Sweden to make *Prästänkan* (*The Parson's Widow*, 1920) and HÄXAN (*Witchcraft through the Ages*, 1922). But the resurgence of the other European industries, particularly in Germany, and the increasing expansion of American companies began to threaten domestic production, and the creaming off of talent by Hollywood producers caused the loss of some of the Swedish cinema's greatest talent including Sjöström, Stiller, Lars HANSON, and Greta GARBO. In the face of this competition Swedish producers were forced to make compromises with popular taste and from the mid-twenties Swedish films lost the intensity and poetry that derived from their roots in national culture. Trivial comedies and, with the introduction of sound, operettas were the staple product, appealing ephemerally only to a local audience.

A workable sound-on-film process was developed in Stockholm as early as 1921, but its exploitation was resisted by the Swedish production companies. Their silent films were well received abroad and they not unreasonably foresaw the complete loss of foreign audiences if they made films depending on a knowledge of Swedish. The introduction of sound films from America proved them right: without the financial resources to make FOREIGN VERSIONS and before the development of SUBTITLES or DUBBING, Swedish producers were forced to give up any thoughts of an export market. In the thirties their output was restricted to parochial and undistinguished films now mostly forgotten. Production figures, however, remained stable: the annual output averaging 25–30 feature films has remained remarkably constant since 1930 except when the first impact of television affected film production in 1961 (18 features) and 1962 (17 features). Also during the years of artistic lethargy two new companies were formed: Sandrews (1926), at first exhibitors, which became a production company in 1938 under Rune WALDEKRANZ, and Europa Film (1930). Both companies were to play an important part in the revival of Swedish cinema from the forties.

The only director of note to survive this period was Gustaf MOLANDER who had written the scripts for some of the great films of Sjöström and Stiller and who became much respected as a director by the new generation of Swedish film-makers. Molander's INTERMEZZO (1936) indicated a stirring of new life in Swedish films. In itself a rather slight romance, it was directed with sensitivity, and the performance of Ingrid BERGMAN drew international attention and won her a Hollywood contract. Also in 1936, Swedish film workers held a meeting in the Stockholm concert hall to protest against the low artistic standards of Swedish films. In response to this unease improvements in quality quickly became noticeable, the most remarkable changes of emphasis coinciding with the outbreak of the Second World War. As in 1914, the inevitable interruption of film imports must be regarded as a major factor in this renewal; but the consciousness of neutrality in a war affecting most of the world may well be considered influential in the urge to re-assert a national identity through films.

The return of Alf SJÖBERG to the cinema, with *Med livet som insats* (*They Staked Their Lives*, 1940), was an important event in the Swedish film renaissance. Although his films now appear emotionally weighty, his sense of composition and rhythm set a fine example to young film-makers. HETS (*Frenzy*, 1944) remains a striking film in its own right, as well as for introducing Mai ZETTERLING to foreign audiences and for bringing Ingmar BERGMAN, as scriptwriter, into films.

From his début as director with *Kris* (*Crisis*, 1946), Bergman's striking talent was recognized, as well as the unusual intensity of his personal vision. For nearly twenty-five years his personality has dominated the Swedish film, particularly in foreign eyes, but a solid body of work was meanwhile produced by important if lesser artists, among them Anders Henrikson (1896–1965) with sombre studies of family life such as *Ett brott* (*A Crime*, 1940) and *Giftas* (*Married Life*, 1955), and Erik 'Hampe' Faustman (1919–61) with Marxist films combining political commitment with visual poetry in the manner of DOVZHENKO and DONSKOI, as in *När ängarna blommar* (*When Meadows Bloom*, 1946) and *Gud fader och tattaren* (*God and the Gipsyman*, 1954). Hasse EKMAN, a popular film actor, was also a prolific director during the fifties, showing particular sensitivity to feminine psychology, notably in *Flicka och hyacinter* (*Girl with Hyacinths*, 1950). Arne MATTSSON, a master of suspense who acknowledges his debt to HITCHCOCK, is best known abroad for *Hon dansade en sommar* (*One Summer of Happiness*, 1951), which satisfyingly encapsulated the popular myth of Swedish sexuality. His other films of the fifties are more in the vein of Sjöström, depicting human life in conflict or accord with the demands of nature. Arne SUCKSDORFF, an isolated figure whose personal approach gives his documentaries a poetic objectivity, reached his greatest heights in 1953 with *Det stora äventyret* (*The Great Adventure*).

The Swedish film institute (SVENSKA FILMINSTITUTET), founded in 1963, has done much to aid film production in Sweden by its system of quality awards which have also encouraged coproductions, notably VARDA's *Les Créatures* (1965), GODARD's *Masculin-Féminin*, and RESNAIS's *LA GUERRE EST FINIE* (both 1966). In 1964 a national film school (Filmskolan) was set up under the auspices of the institute.

Also in the early sixties, strongly influenced by the NOUVELLE VAGUE and made explicit in Bo WIDERBERG's writings, a feeling arose among young critics and film workers that Swedish film, under the dominating influence of Bergman, had for too long been concerned with intense exploration of the individual psyche. Their aim of integrating film art into the context of social awareness has developed into a generally humanist view, varying in emphasis according to each director's preoccupations: lyrical (Widerberg), overtly political (Vilgot SJÖMAN), moralistic (Jörn DONNER), stridently feminist (Zetterling). In many cases the new consciousness of the artist's political and social responsibility has been informed with the sensitivity to nature and climate which has for long been associated with the Swedish character and endows the best recent films with the richness of the silent Swedish classics.

The early growth of a distinctive cinema and the maintenance, even in the years of artistic languor, of a flourishing film industry, is unusual in a country with a small population. The strength of the indigenous film in Sweden is in large part attributable to the existence of a healthy dramatic tradition and the acceptance of cinema by directors, actors, and other theatre artists. Working in the theatre during the winter and in films (often on location) during the long daylight hours of summer is a recognized arrangement among them, and consorts well with the Swedish response to climate and the changing seasons.

Jean Béranger, *La Grande Aventure du cinéma suédois*, Paris, 1960; Peter Cowie, *Sweden 1 & 2*, London, 1970; *Image et Son* no. 236, February 1970, 'Le Cinéma suédois'; Svenska Filminstitutet, *Swedish silent pictures and sound pictures 1896–1966*, Stockholm, 1967.

**SWEET,** BLANCHE (1896–    ), US actress who worked in the theatre from the age of 18 months. She first appeared on screen as one of the wives in *The Man with Three Wives* (1909). A strikingly beautiful girl with large, wide-set eyes, she worked regularly for D. W. GRIFFITH in a series of one- and two-reelers including *The Lonedale Operator* (1911) and *The Massacre* (1913) and later played the title role in his first four-reeler, *Judith of Bethulia* (1914). In the same year, Griffith encouraged her to accept a contract with the LASKY Company where she was directed by both Cecil and William DEMILLE. Her parts were usually dramatic ones, although *The Thousand Dollar Husband* (1916) gave her a chance to play comedy. Her last three films for Lasky were directed by Marshall NEILAN whom she later married, but her finest performance was probably in *Anna Christie* (1923) for Thomas INCE. Her film career did not long survive the coming of sound and her last part was a small one in *The Silver Horde* (1930).

***SWEET SMELL OF SUCCESS, The,*** US, 1957. 1½hr. *Dir* Alexander MacKendrick; *prod* Harold Hecht; *scr* Clifford Odets, Ernest Lehman, from a short story by Lehman; *ph* James Wong Howe; *mus* Elmer Bernstein; *cast* Burt Lancaster (J. J. Hunsecker), Tony Curtis (Sidney Falco), Susan Harrison (Susan Hunsecker).

The machinations of a powerful newspaper columnist, helped by a toadying press agent, provide a mordant study of corruption. MACKENDRICK's cool, penetrating view of the New York publicity world was supported by James Wong HOWE's camerawork which endowed the film with an appropriately brittle sheen.

***SWING TIME,*** US, 1936. 1¾hr. *Dir* George Stevens; *prod* Pandro S. Berman for RKO; *scr* Howard Lindsay, Allan Scott; *ph* David Abel; *mus* Jerome Kern; *lyr* Dorothy Fields; *dance dir* Hermes Pan; *cast* Fred Astaire (Lucky Garnett), Ginger Rogers (Penny), Victor Moore (Pop), Eric Blore (Gordon).

A dancer and inveterate gambler, needing money to get married, forms a cabaret act with a dance instructress and falls for her instead. In one of the classic ASTAIRE and ROGERS MUSICALS, this slender romantic plot serves as a framework for some memorable musical numbers, including 'The Way You Look Tonight', the flowing 'Waltz in Swingtime', the gently mocking 'A Fine Romance', and a sparkling display of dancing virtuosity in 'Pick Yourself Up'.

**SWITZERLAND.** The film industry in Switzerland was for many years based almost entirely on foreign imports, with little or no indigenous production; the only Swiss film-maker to achieve some international repute was the Austrian-born Leopold Lindtberg (b. 1902) whose best film, *La Dernière Chance* (1945) about a group of refugees making their escape into Switzerland during the Second World War, won a prize at CANNES. The State support granted to producers since 1958 has helped to encourage new talent. Two promising directors are Alain Tanner and Claude Goretta who, after experience with the FREE CINEMA movement in Britain, worked for Swiss television before moving on to feature film direction. Tanner's *La Salamandre* (1971) and *Le Retour d'Afrique* (1973) and Goretta's *L'Invitation* (1973) show a basic consistency of aim: all three films view the provincial and bureaucratic aspects of contemporary Switzerland with a shrewd and witty scepticism. The two latter films were in part financed by Swiss television and by a co-production agreement with France. Young film-makers are also beginning to emerge from German-speaking Switzerland.

*SYLVESTER* (*New Year's Eve*), Germany, 1923. 1hr. *Dir* Lupu Pick; *scr* Carl Mayer; *ph* Karl Hasselman (interiors), Guido Seeber (street scenes); *des* Robert A. Dietrich; *cast* Eugen Klöpfer (café owner), Edith Posca (his wife), Frieda Richard (his mother).

This KAMMERSPIELFILM deals with a café-owner who suffers from the discord between his wife and mother. The situation reaches crisis point on New Year's Eve and he commits suicide while the crowds celebrate outside.

The film is noteworthy for its shots of natural phenomena (the sea, a storm, a heath) which participate symphonically in the action and act as symbols reinforcing and amplifying the given facts. Some of these shots are missing from modern prints.

**SYLVIE** (1883–1970), French actress, real name Thérèse Sylvie, began her stage career in 1902 and appeared frequently in films from 1912. She was a popular *ingénue*, noted for her wistful blue eyes, and played many leading stage roles, but she had only supporting roles in films until nearly the end of her life. Major films in which she appeared include *Un Carnet de bal* (1937), *Les Anges du péché* (1943), LE DIABLE AU CORPS (1947), THÉRÈSE RAQUIN (1953), and *Cronaca familiare* (1962). René ALLIO's LA VIEILLE DAME INDIGNE (1965) at last gave her a starring part; she will undoubtedly be remembered for the charm and conviction with which she portrayed the old lady on her brief career of gentle subversion.

**SYNCHRONIZATION,** the process of aligning picture and sound, which are usually recorded on separate strips of film, so that they coincide as in reality. The creative and technical demands of film require that sound and picture be handled independently throughout production; thus at every stage the two must be synchronized so that the final relationship of picture to sound is intentional and not random. The viewer is only aware of synchronization when it fails—as in television newsfilm, for example, where tight deadlines sometimes require that sound and picture be screened DOUBLE-HEAD: separately, but in synchronization. (See MARRIED PRINT.)

**SZABÓ,** ISTVÁN (1938–   ), Hungarian director, entered the Academy for Film Art in 1956 and graduated in 1961. His diploma short *Koncert* (*Concert*, 1961) was well received at many festivals and revealed a lively, strongly personal style. After confirming this original promise with two more shorts for the BÁLAZS BÉLA STUDIO— *Variációk egy témára* (*Variations on a Theme*, 1961) and the lyrical *Te* (*You*, 1963)—he made his first feature *Álmodozások kora* (*The Age of Daydreaming*) in 1964. Szabó has remained the leading figure in the Hungarian 'new wave', his works containing the same blend of charm and sincerity as TRUFFAUT's. His prize-winning second feature, APA (*Father*, 1967), showed to dazzling effect his technical mastery of the medium and his interest in his own generation— qualities further pursued in *Szerelmesfilm* (*Love Film*, 1970).

*SZEGÉNYLEGÉNYEK* (*The Round-Up*), Hungary, 1965. Agascope; 1½hr. *Dir* Miklós Jancsó; *prod* Mafilm Studio 4; *scr* Gyula Hernádi; *ph* Tamás Somló; *des* Tamás Banovich; *cast* János Görbe (Gajdor), Tibor Molnár (Kabai), András Kozák (his son), Gábor Agárdy (Torma), Zoltán Latinovits (Veszelka).

A group of hardened peasants are rounded up by troops of the Austro-Hungarian monarchy in an attempt to weed out Sándor, leader of a partisan group in the Kossuth revolution twenty years earlier (1848); by chess-like games of psychological humiliation and suspicion the authorities try to break the silent solidarity of the peasants.

First exported under the title *The Hopeless Ones* and later renamed *The Round-Up* (the Hungarian translates as *Outlaws*), JANCSÓ's fourth feature astonished audiences at CANNES in 1966 with its daring cinematic style. *Így jöttem* (*My Way Home*, 1964) had already shown his powerful use of the tracking camera and open spaces to conjure up menace: *Szegénylegények* marked his first complete attempt to heighten basic conflicts by suppressing outward emotion and depersonalizing his characters. Although he characteristically took an actual historical event as his subject, the costumes and buildings are deliberately timeless and the setting, the vast Hungarian plain, strips the narrative of everyday physical detail.

The originality of the film, its cold beauty and accomplished craftsmanship, confirmed Jancsó for foreign audiences as the major figure of the post-fifties Hungarian cinema.

**SZERELEM** (*Love*), Hungary, 1971. 1½hr. *Dir* Károly Makk; *prod* Mafilm Studio 1; *scr* Tibor Déry; *ph* János Tóth; *mus* András Mihály; *cast* Lili Darvas (old lady), Mari Törőcsik (daughter-in-law), Iván Darvas (son).

Adapted by Déry from two of his own short stories ('Two Women' and 'Love'), *Szerelem* showed a triumphant return to form by MAKK after much undistinguished work during the sixties. An old woman and her daughter-in-law both await the return of the former's son; the daughter-in-law sustains the old lady's weakening spirits by elaborate lies of his success in America; but the mother dies a few days before her son comes home—from prison. *Szerelem* is one of the finest examples of chamber cinema (exquisitely photographed in blacks and whites by János Tóth), and represents Makk's most direct examination of people trapped both by outside events and by their own dreams and fantasies. The repressive atmosphere of Budapest in 1953 is left largely to the audience's imagination, but the film shows an honest awareness of the personal problems engendered by such government. The work's optimism is quietly but powerfully vindicated in a moving scene of reunion between husband and wife.

# T

***TABU,*** US, 1931. 1½hr. *Dir, prod, scr* F. W. Murnau, Robert Flaherty; *ph* Floyd Crosby, Flaherty; *mus* Dr Hugo Reisenfeld; *cast* Reri (Anna Chevalier, the girl), Matahi (the boy), Hitu (the chief), Jean (the policeman), Jules (the captain), Kong Ah (the Chinaman).

MURNAU and FLAHERTY, equally disenchanted with commercial production, formed Murnau-Flaherty Productions in 1928. Each intensely admired the other's work but this, and their mutual aim of independent film-making, was insufficient to reconcile their radically different ideas. Flaherty wished to make an ethnographic film of the quality of NANOOK OF THE NORTH (1922) about the pearl fishers of the South Seas; Murnau's object was a narrative feature film, using the people and settings of Tahiti as he had attempted to use those of Dakota in *Our Daily Bread* (1929). As Murnau had found the finance for the project, Flaherty had to yield. He had little to do with the actual shooting and the film is essentially Murnau's.

The tabu of the title is that placed on the young virgin dedicated to the gods and the story deals with the violation of the interdict when she and a young pearl fisher fall in love. The film is romantic and intensely beautiful visually. The only film in which Murnau was able to express himself with total freedom, it demonstrates his strength as an individual artist.

As a silent film, *Tabu* was difficult to sell, but it was released a week after Murnau's death with a synchronized music score by Dr Hugo Reisenfeld, who had written the score for SUNRISE (1927). It was Murnau's only film to be an immediate popular success.

***TAIHEIYO HITORIBOCHI*** (*Alone on the Pacific*), Japan, 1963. CinemaScope; 1¾hr; Eastman Color. *Dir* Kon Ichikawa; *prod* Isahara Productions/Nikkatsu; *scr* Natto Wada; *ph* Yoshihiro Yamazaki; *mus* Yasushi Akatagawa, Tohru Takemitsu; *cast* Yujiro Ishihara (Kenichi Horie), Masayuki Mori (father), Kinuyo Tanaka (mother), Ruriko Asaoka (sister), Hajime Hana (friend).

For another of his masterly studies of individual obsession, ICHIKAWA took the true story of the 23-year-old Kenichi Horie who in 1962 sailed alone from Osaka to San Francisco in a nineteen-foot yacht. The film describes not only the lonely, dangerous three-month voyage but also, through skilfully integrated flashbacks, the young man's home life, his resistance to parental and official opposition, his often comical difficulties in achieving his ambition. The visual beauty is also characteristic of Ichikawa's work: spacious, leisurely sequences of the tiny boat in a vast ocean and the Golden Gate Bridge materializing from the pearly mists are contrasted with crowded interiors which demonstrate the director's total command of wide screen composition.

**TAKE,** the shortest unit of film shot; it may last up to ten minutes (the approximate running time of a roll of camera stock) if there are no cuts. If a particular shot is repeated, the takes are numbered in sequence (see SLATE), each take having a discrete number.

Alfred HITCHCOCK shot *Rope* (1948) as if the whole film were a single take; he was of course limited by the length of reels in the camera, but there was no editing within the reels. The style of shooting in long, continuous takes was used increasingly by GODARD, most notably Lemmy Caution's entry into the hotel in *Alphaville* (1965) and the whole of *One Plus One* (or *Sympathy for the Devil,* 1968). Other directors, such as Jean-Marie STRAUB in *Chronik der Anna Magdalena Bach* (*The Chronicle of Anna Magdalena Bach,* 1967), have used long, static takes to develop a style known as minimal cinema.

***TAKOVÝ JE ŽIVOT*** (*Such Is Life*), Czechoslovakia, 1930. 1½hr. *Dir* Karl Junghans, from his own script and story; *ph* Laszlo Schäffer; *des* Ernst Meiwers; *cast* Vera Baranovskaya (washerwoman), Theodor Pištěk (husband), Máňa Zeniškova (daughter), Wolfgang Zilzer, Jindřich Plachta, Manja Kellerova, Eman Fiala (pianist), Valeska Gert.

Junghans, a left-wing German journalist and novelist, was unable to find backing in Germany to film his story of the life of a washerwoman with her daughter and unemployed, alcoholic husband, and her tragic death from scalding. He managed to interest the famous Czech actor, Theodor Pištěk, in the subject, and Pištěk's influence brought backing. The film passionately reflects working-class conditions in Prague in the twenties. The principal actors, especially Baranovskaya, who had played the title role in PUDOVKIN's MAT (*Mother*, 1926), gave direct, moving performances, and the style of direction has a simplicity informed by bitterness. The film's authority derives from this bitterness and lack of sentimentality, which place it in the tradition of socially conscious Czech films of the twenties and as a spiritual precursor of NEO-REALISM. Made silent, like most Czech films until 1930 (it was made in a few weeks in 1929 but not released until May 1930), it was a victim of the introduction of sound, and has never been as widely known as it deserves.

**TALAZAC,** ODETTE (d. 1948), French actress whose first film was *Le Collier de la reine* (1929). She was a favourite character player of some of France's most distinguished directors of the thirties, including COCTEAU (LE SANG D'UN POÈTE, 1930), CLAIR (LE MILLION, 1932), L'HERBIER (*Nuits de feu*, 1938), PABST (*L'Esclave blanche*, 1938), and especially RENOIR (LE CRIME DE MONSIEUR LANGE, 1936; LA RÈGLE DU JEU, 1939). Although her physique tended to limit her to comic or almost burlesque parts, as in *Le Million*, she played them with intelligence and could ably sustain a straight characterization, as in *La Règle du jeu*.

**TALMADGE,** CONSTANCE (1899–     ), US actress whose vivacious personality made her a very popular comedy star. She began film work as an extra at VITAGRAPH in 1914 and became known as the Vitagraph Tomboy. Later she displayed a similar personality as the Mountain Girl in INTOLERANCE (1916). When her sister Norma married Joseph M. SCHENCK, Constance appeared for him in a successful series of farcical comedies, many of them written by Anita LOOS and John Emerson, with titles like *A Virtuous Vamp* (1919) and *Learning to Love* (1925). She apparently lost interest in acting and retired on her marriage in 1929.

**TALMADGE,** NORMA (1897–1957), US actress whose two sisters, Constance and Natalie, also acted in films, although the latter's only starring role was opposite Buster KEATON, then her husband. Norma began her acting career with VITAGRAPH at the age of thirteen and with the help of Maurice Costello had her first big success in a key role in *A Tale of Two Cities* (1911). She left Vitagraph after appearing in over a hundred films, mainly comedies, but after a short spell in Hollywood with D. W. GRIFFITH, she returned to New York where she met and married Joseph M. SCHENCK, who set up a company to produce her films. She became one of America's most popular stars as she loved and suffered through a series of dramas, including *Smilin' Through* (1922), *Secrets* (1924), CAMILLE (1927), and *The Dove* (1928). She was a good actress of moderate range, but had only indifferent success in sound films. After *Du Barry, Woman of Passion* (1930) she retired with a large personal fortune.

***TAMING OF THE SHREW, The.*** There were at least eight silent films of SHAKESPEARE's rumbustious comedy. These include one directed by D. W. GRIFFITH for BIOGRAPH, starring Florence LAWRENCE (1908), and the production by Sir Frank Benson's company at the Shakespeare Memorial Theatre, Stratford, which was filmed in 1911.

The first sound version was in 1929, and is notable as the only film in which Douglas FAIRBANKS and Mary PICKFORD co-starred. Fairbanks's broad characterization and physical agility were well suited to the role of Petruchio; Pickford's Katharina was, in contrast, somewhat prim. The film had the lavish and detailed sets and costumes usual in the Fairbanks costume spectaculars.

A French/Spanish co-production was made in 1955, *La Megère apprivoisée* or *La Fierecilla domada*. The stage production by the Soviet Army Theatre was filmed in the USSR in 1961, *Ukroshcheniye stroptivoi*. Franco ZEFFIRELLI directed the American/Italian co-production of 1967 which starred Richard BURTON and Elizabeth TAYLOR, both co-operating vigorously in the director's interpretation of the story as noisy farce. This rollicking version was visually brilliant, photographed with great virtuosity in soft yellows, browns, and reds.

The stage musical *Kiss Me, Kate* (1948), which incorporates into a modern version of the play a stage production of the play itself, was filmed by METRO-GOLDWYN-MAYER in 1953. It was originally issued in a STEREOSCOPIC process.

**TAMIROFF,** AKIM (1899–1972), Russianborn US actor, made his first film, *Sadie McKee* (1934), for METRO-GOLDWYN-MAYER and soon appeared in other MGM films including *Naughty Marietta* (1935) and *China Seas* (1935). But he was at this time principally associated with PARAMOUNT—LIVES OF A BENGAL LANCER (1935), *The General Died at Dawn* (1936), *For Whom the Bell Tolls* (1943)—and he had particular success in two of Preston STURGES's satirical comedies, THE GREAT MCGINTY (1940, *Down Went McGinty* in GB) and THE MIRACLE OF MORGAN'S CREEK (1944). Rotund and roundfaced, with a gravelly, strongly accented voice, he was constantly in demand for character parts. Orson WELLES gave him cameo roles in *Confidential Report* (1955), TOUCH OF EVIL (1958), LE

PROCÈS (*The Trial*, 1963), and CAMPANADAS A MEDIANOCHE (*Chimes at Midnight*, 1966), and he was in GODARD's *Alphaville* (1965).

**TARADASH,** DANIEL (1913– ), US scriptwriter, came into the film industry after winning a play-writing contest in 1938. He was hired by COLUMBIA to collaborate with Lewis Meltzer on *Golden Boy* (1939), then went to UNIVERSAL and worked on various films including *A Little Bit of Heaven* (1940). During his war service he wrote several training and documentary films. He returned to Hollywood after the war and continued his writing with *Knock On Any Door* (1948) and *Rancho Notorious* (Fritz LANG, 1952). His screenplay for FROM HERE TO ETERNITY (1953) won an OSCAR. In 1955 Taradash wrote and directed *Storm Center*, starring Bette DAVIS, a story of a small town librarian persecuted during the McCarthy era. The following year came *Picnic*, which he adapted from William Inge's prize-winning Broadway play. His other screenplays include *Don't Bother to Knock* (1952), *Desirée* (1954), *Bell, Book and Candle* (1959), *Hawaii* (1966). Taradash was Vice-President of the Writers' Guild of America 1956–9, and has been a trustee of the AMERICAN FILM INSTITUTE.

**TARKOVSKY,** ANDREI (1932– ), Russian director, studied at VGIK under Mikhail ROMM. His first feature was *Ivanovo detstvo* (*Ivan's Childhood*, 1962) which deals with an orphan working with a group of partisans. After assisting Konchalovsky with the script for *Pervyi uchitel* (*The First Teacher*, 1965), Tarkovsky directed *Andrei Rublev* (1966, shown at CANNES 1969, Russian release 1971), about the medieval icon painter who, faced with the horror and cruelty of his time, abandons his art. *Solaris* (1971) is a science fiction film remarkably bare of special effects. The cosmonauts find themselves unwillingly subjected to a process of self-exploration and forced to recognize the errors of their earlier lives.

Tarkovsky's films are distinguished by powerful visual composition, rich in realistic detail. They are intense, personal works, often disconcerting in the violence they portray, and although they have earned much praise abroad they have had only limited circulation in the Soviet Union.

**TARZAN,** the literary creation of Edgar Rice Burroughs (1875–1950), was first played on the screen by Elmo Lincoln in *Tarzan of the Apes* (1914). There were four other silent Tarzans before Johnny WEISSMULLER introduced the famous jungle cry in *Tarzan the Ape Man* (1932). Partnered by Maureen O'SULLIVAN as Jane, Weissmuller effectively monopolized the

role until 1948, to be succeeded in turn by Lex Barker, Gordon Scott, Denny Miller, and Bruce Bennett. Ron Ely played Tarzan in a television series in the late sixties which, like the later film versions, substituted pure action drama for Burroughs's romantic blend of Rousseau and Kipling. Tarzan has become a part of pop art and comic-strip iconography: Andy WARHOL made *Tarzan and Jane regained sort of* in 1963, and one of Tarzan's loincloths was sold at the auction of METRO-GOLDWYN-MAYER property in 1970.

**TASHLIN,** FRANK (1913– ), US writer and director, worked in various ANIMATION departments from 1928. He was an animator and cartoon story-writer as well as a gag-writer for various live-action shorts and took charge of COLUMBIA's Screen Gems cartoon department in 1941. From the mid-forties he wrote feature film scripts including *The Paleface* (1948), a spoof Western starring Bob HOPE, and he wrote and directed its successor, *Son of Paleface* (1952). Frenetic comedy became his speciality, including two vehicles for Jayne MANSFIELD, *The Girl Can't Help It* (1957) and *Will Success Spoil Rock Hunter?* (1957), and *Caprice* (1966), a headlong comedy-thriller starring Doris DAY. Tashlin's skills were best used in his films starring Jerry LEWIS: *Artists and Models* (1955), *Rockabye Baby* (1958), *Cinderfella* (1960), and *The Disorderly Orderly* (1964).

**TASTE OF HONEY, A,** GB, 1961. 1¾hr. *Dir, prod* Tony Richardson for Woodfall; *scr* Shelagh Delaney, Richardson, from the play by Delaney; *ph* Walter Lassally; *mus* John Addison; *cast* Dora Bryan (Helen), Rita Tushingham (Jo), Robert Stephens (Peter), Murray Melvin (Geoffrey), Paul Danquah (Jimmy).

*A Taste of Honey* was closely adapted from the successful stage play which had been introduced to London by Joan LITTLEWOOD. While it did not entirely shake off its theatrical origins, the film was visually appealing, Walter LASSALLY's camera endowing sleazy surroundings with a melancholy innocence. Tony RICHARDSON's direction drew moving and comic performances from his players, in particular Rita TUSHINGHAM and Murray Melvin as the lonely, pregnant girl and the homosexual waif who befriends her.

**TATI,** JACQUES (1908– ), French actor and director, real name Tatischeff, discovered his talent for entertaining at rugby club suppers and went into music hall, where his speciality was a comic mime of sportsmen. He acted in several comic shorts during the thirties, among them *Oscar champion de tennis* (1932), *Gai dimanche* (1935), and *Soigne ton gauche* (1936). After playing small roles in AUTANT-LARA's *Sylvie et le fantôme* (1945) and LE DIABLE AU CORPS (1947) he directed his own short *L'École des facteurs* (1947). The theme of this was expanded and developed in his first full-length film JOUR DE FÊTE (1947). This showed Tati to be a startlingly original new talent, his delightful handling of the visual gags which dominate the film recalling the great comics of the silent era. LES VACANCES DE MONSIEUR HULOT (1951) saw the creation of a new comic hero, as distinctive and endearing as CHAPLIN's Charlie.

*Jour de fête* was shot in a new colour process which was unsuccessful, but fortunately a black-and-white negative had also been made. His first film to be seen in colour was MON ONCLE (1958), which brought back Monsieur Hulot in a gently satirical observation of some of the incongruities and absurdities of modern life. Ten years later, his next film, PLAYTIME (1967), contains some interesting innovations and developments while retaining the distinctive qualities of his earlier work. In *Trafic* (1971) Monsieur Hulot, entrusted with taking a newly invented camping car to Amsterdam, encounters unprecedented misfortunes, and Tati explores yet another example of the absurd in modern life, the motor car.

Apart from himself, Tati has tended throughout his films to use non-actors as part of his attempt to re-invest film comedy with the spontaneity and realism which has been largely lost in the artificiality of the sound film comedy. His style has been compared with that of NEO-REALISM, for the comic element grows out of the collision of his hero with everyday reality: perhaps the greatest charm of his films is the natural manner in which the gags evolve. An almost exclusive use of the long shot gives an unforced quality to the comedy, and shows the intimate relation of the comic character to his surroundings; in the same way, although dialogue itself is minimal, the sound-track is rich in subtle absurdities. Tati spends up to four years preparing each film, and spends much of his time walking about Paris, going to football matches, and generally observing people. His passionate perfectionism is probably comparable only to that of BRESSON.

**TAUBER,** RICHARD (1892–1948), Austrian tenor, in his prime a distinguished opera singer, particularly in Mozart, but popularly associated with operetta and musical comedy. He appeared in several musical films on the Continent, in Britain, and in Hollywood, notably *Blossom Time* (1932) and *Pagliacci* (1937). An Austrian film of his life, *Du bist die Welt für mich* (*The Richard Tauber Story*, 1953), starred Rudolf Schock.

**TAYLOR,** ELIZABETH (1932– ), actress now holding British nationality, born in London of American parents. With the outbreak of war her family moved to Los Angeles where she became a CHILD STAR under long-term contract to METRO-GOLDWYN-MAYER. She attracted notice in *Lassie Come Home* (1943) and even more as the girl heroine of *National Velvet* (1944). After the light entertainment films of her adolescent years she embarked on more dramatic roles, in A PLACE IN THE SUN (1951) and *Giant* (1956) among others, often playing women older than herself and making with ease the transition from juvenile to mature parts.

At this time she began to acquire a distinct star personality, that of a beautiful and passionate woman easily swept away by emotion and living out the glamorous fantasies of ordinary people. This image was fully exploited by studio promotion and helped by her own penchant for husbands and high living. At the same time her ability as an actress was developing and she had particular success as Tennessee WILLIAMS's neurotic heroines in *Cat on a Hot Tin Roof* (1958) and *Suddenly Last Summer* (1960). Her fourth nomination, for her portrayal of a nymphomaniac in *Butterfield 8* (1961), won her the first of two OSCARS.

Her partnership with her fifth husband, Richard BURTON (the others being Conrad Hilton Jr, Michael WILDING, Mike TODD, and Eddie Fisher), constituted the most highly-paid acting team in cinema. Starting with the disastrous CLEOPATRA (1962) it produced several box-office successes and one remarkable virtuoso performance—the blowzy, shrewish Martha in *Who's Afraid of Virginia Woolf?* (Mike NICHOLS, 1966). She entered with gusto into the baroque fantasies by Joseph LOSEY, *Boom!* and *Secret Ceremony* (both 1968). She displays an unconcern with ageing, surprising in one of the few remaining Hollywood stars, and in spite of recurrent ill-health she has remained in constant demand by producers. (See also STAR SYSTEM.)

**TAYLOR,** ROBERT (1911–69), US actor, real name Spangler Arlington Brough, whose film career began in 1934. His handsome features made him a favourite with women filmgoers and his charm largely compensated for limited acting ability. For almost his entire career he was a prize possession of METRO-GOLDWYN-MAYER, with whom he remained for a record twenty-five years. He specialized in romantic leads, and his leading ladies included GARBO (CAMILLE, 1936) and Vivien LEIGH (WATERLOO BRIDGE, 1940). One of his best performances was as BILLY THE KID (1941); later he played knightly heroes (*Ivanhoe*, 1953; *Knights of the Round Table*, 1954; *Quentin Durward*, 1955), ending his career in television ('The Detectives' 1959–61). During the thirties he was married to Barbara STANWYCK.

**TECHNICOLOR** has been so successful a colour cinematography process that it has almost become the generic name for any colour film. It is, in fact, the trade name of a process which has existed in four different versions since its introduction around 1915. The first system was invented by Daniel F. Comstock who, with his partner Herbert T. Kalmus, formed the Technicolor Motion Picture Corporation after demonstrating the prototype of their first camera. The company was so named because both Comstock and Kalmus had doctorates from the Massachusetts Institute of Technology.

The first camera used two negatives which recorded light split by a prism into red and green components. A special projector with two apertures—one with a red filter, the other with a green filter—was needed to show early Technicolor films. This required the projectionist to maintain registration between the two, which proved very difficult. To demonstrate the quality of the process, Technicolor themselves made a film at Jacksonville, Florida, in 1916, *The Gulf Between*. It was processed in the first Technicolor laboratory which was built into a railway carriage in Boston and towed to the location. Florida was chosen because of the sunlight; indoor shooting was not yet possible. Apart from projection problems, the acclaim for the film was great enough to encourage further developments.

Technicolor process number two was a very complicated procedure. The two images, red and green, were now recorded on a single film. The camera pulled down two frames at a time of a special PANCHROMATIC black-and-white film and two exposures were made simultaneously, again using a beam-splitting prism to separate the red and green components. One of the images was inverted so that the lower edges of each pair of frames touched. During processing, all the 'red' frames were printed to make a relief image on one strip of film and the 'green' frames were similarly treated. The two films were then welded back-to-back in accurate register and each side skimmed over a bath of red or green dye. Again difficulties occurred in projection. The prints had a tendency to buckle in the heat of the projector lamps and, because both sides were coated with emulsion, scratching was a major problem.

However, several films were made in this second Technicolor process. Metro made *The Toll of the Sea* (1922), starring Anna May Wong and Kenneth Harlan, and the first interiors shot in Technicolor appeared in George Fitzmaurice's *Cytherea* in 1923. The best known film in this process was *The Black Pirate*, produced by

Douglas FAIRBANKS in 1926. Four of the eleven Technicolor cameras then in existence were used in the production, which was a considerable success.

Process number three introduced a principle which remains basic to Technicolor printing: dye transfer or 'imbibition'. Two separate black-and-white negatives were shot for the red-orange and blue-green areas of the spectrum. From these were made positive relief images on rolls of gelatine which were then treated as type is in printing. The relief 'matrices' were dyed red or green and brought into contact with a single strip of clear film coated with a dye-absorbent emulsion. Thus accurate registration was achieved—and with emulsion on one side of the film only. A further advantage was that the original negatives would be used to make only a few matrices, thereby conserving their quality, and many prints could be made from each matrix. Film speeds had increased considerably, thereby reducing the light levels necessary for shooting, but the absence of blue, the third primary colour, prevented true 'natural' colour from being achieved.

By now sound had arrived and WARNER BROS, after risking all on talkies with enormous success, made the first Technicolor all-talking picture, *On with the Show*, in 1929. Other musicals in colour followed: *Golddiggers of Broadway* (1929), *King of Jazz* (1930), and *Whoopee* (1930).

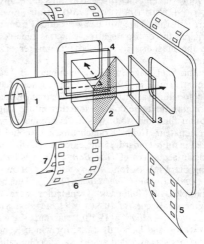

1 Lens
2 Beam splitter
3 Green filter
4 Magenta filter
5 Film receiving green image
6 Film (red filter sub-coated) receiving blue image
7 Film receiving red image

Three-strip Technicolor process

The third primary colour was included by 1932 in the famous 'three-strip' camera, designed by Technicolor's researcher, Joseph Arthur Ball, who had photographed *The Gulf Between*, and George Alfred Mitchell. The principles of the new process were essentially the same as those of the previous system, but three separate negatives replaced the single camera film, each recording one primary colour. A beam-splitter reflected light to an aperture to the left of the lens; over the prism was placed a magenta filter, which excluded green light from a panchromatic negative. Directly behind the aperture were two films: the front one, being ORTHOCHROMATIC, recorded only blue components and carried a red-orange dye which prevented blue light from reaching the back (panchromatic) film, which recorded the red components. An aperture in the normal position behind the lens, and covered with a green filter, recorded the green components on the back film. The three films were then processed to make separate relief matrices from which prints were made as in the previous process.

Another film-maker who was always ready to try something new, Walt DISNEY, used the three-strip Technicolor process to make his animated *Flowers and Trees* in 1933. Kenneth MACGOWAN was the first to use the system for live action in the two-reeler *La Cucaracha* (1934) and the first three-strip feature was Rouben MAMOULIAN's *Becky Sharp* (1935), which rather overdid the colour. But all other three-strip films are eclipsed by GONE WITH THE WIND (1939). Prints (in wide screen formats) are still being produced from the original three-strip negative, which is reputed to be the most heavily insured film master of all time.

The final stage in the development of Technicolor came in 1941 when Monopack Technicolor film was introduced by Eastman Kodak. Bringing the three colours together in one single 35mm film, the stock was a development from the amateur 16mm Kodachrome and could be used in any standard 35mm camera. The first use was in sequences of *Dive Bomber* in 1941 starring Errol FLYNN, followed by METRO-GOLDWYN-MAYER's *Lassie Come Home* (1943). The best examples of Monopack Technicolor were the Agincourt scenes of HENRY V (1944) and *King Solomon's Mines* (1950) starring Stewart GRANGER and Deborah KERR, for which Robert SURTEES was awarded an OSCAR for colour cinematography.

EASTMAN COLOR, introduced in 1949, changed the whole nature of colour filming and from 1951 onwards Technicolor prints were made, still by dye transfer, almost exclusively from Eastman Color negative.

The Technicolor Company has also introduced several photographic formats, such as the short-lived TECHNIRAMA and the much more useful TECHNISCOPE. It has also developed one SUPER-8 cassette format.

**TECHNIRAMA,** process developed by the TECHNICOLOR company, similar to PARAMOUNT's VISTAVISION, using a double frame on 35mm, anamorphically printed. Super Technirama-70, using the same process but on 70mm stock, superseded the original Technirama process. (See also WIDE SCREEN.)

**TECHNISCOPE,** process devised by the TECHNICOLOR company to produce a wide-screen image more economically than by photographing with an ANAMORPHIC lens. Two consecutive images are photographed, one below the other, on to the area of one 35mm frame, thereby producing an ASPECT RATIO of $2 \cdot 35 : 1$ while halving the cost of negative. Each is then enlarged, and printed anamorphically on to 35mm positive. (See also WIDE SCREEN.)

**TEDESCO,** JEAN (1895–1958), French director and writer. At the age of twenty-eight, Tedesco took over Louis DELLUC's revue *Cinéa*, renamed it *Cinéa-Ciné pour tous* and ran it until its demise in 1930. In 1924 he founded the first AVANT-GARDE cinema in Paris, the VIEUX COLOMBIER. He made films from 1932 until his death. Best known are *Mort ou vif* (1948) and *Napoléon Bonaparte* (1951). He was a founder and vice-president of the CINÉMATHÈQUE FRANÇAISE.

**TELECINE,** process of showing films on television. A great deal of film material is used in television, including considerable amounts shot for original television production, such as location inserts for plays and news programmes. Film equipment is still more portable than videotape recorders, television cameras, and all the associated accessories, and film also has an advantage in that it transcends the problems of recording programmes which are to be shown on different television systems and standards.

Film pictures can be translated into television pictures in two basic ways. A television camera is pointed into the lens of a normal film projector and transmits the picture as it would any other scene. The other method, known as flying spot telecine, does not use a television camera as such, nor does it require the film to be illuminated by a projector. Instead, very bright, constant light from a cathode ray tube is projected on to the film. Light which passes through the film, in accordance with the density of the film image, is detected by a photocell and converted into the television signal. The sound track is replayed and transmitted in the normal way.

As television has a 4 : 3 ASPECT RATIO, films shot on wide screen or ANAMORPHIC systems are rarely transmitted with the full frame in view. This would leave a space above and below the picture, which is regarded as unacceptable. Instead, the telecine machine PANS back and forth across the width of the frame selecting the most suitable section for transmission—a method which often leaves something to be desired, resulting as it does in awkward framing and jumps from one side of the frame to the other.

*TELEFTEO PSEMMA, To* (*A Matter of Dignity*), Greece, 1957. 1¾hr. *Dir, scr* Michael Cacoyannis; *prod* Finos; *ph* Walter Lassally; *mus* Manos Hadjikakis; *cast* Ellie Lambetti (Chloe), George Pappas (Cleon Pellas), Athena Michaelidou (Roxane), Elena Zafiriou (Katerina), Minas Christides (Dritsas).

When her father becomes bankrupt, Chloe steels herself to save the family's fortunes by marrying a wealthy nobody, but finally rejects the pride of social standing and devotes herself to the child of the family's faithful servant. CACOYANNIS here reached a peak in his precise depiction of social groupings and relationships: his penetrating analysis of family pride is equalled by his unsentimental observation of the servant's loyalty. Ellie LAMBETTI's perfect conviction is achieved through an unusual blend of passion and melancholy. As in TO KORITSI ME TA MAVRA (*The Girl in Black*, 1955), the whole effect is greatly enhanced by Walter LASSALLY's loving, observant camera.

**TELEPHOTO LENS,** a term commonly used to describe any LENS with a focal length longer than usual. Such lenses are the cinematographer's equivalent of a telescope: they produce a large image of a distant subject, and are most often used in applications such as wildlife films and investigative documentary, where the camera cannot physically approach the subject. Telephoto lenses also produce an apparent flattening of perspective, in which the distant subject appears to have little or no depth; this effect is sometimes used creatively, as when an actor runs frantically towards the camera but seems to come no nearer.

In a strict technical sense, not all 'long' lenses are telephotos—only those which, by a particular optical construction, achieve long focal length without correspondingly long physical length. (See WIDE-ANGLE LENS, ZOOM.)

**TELERECORDING,** UK term for a television recording made on motion picture film which can be shown on ordinary projectors. A camera photographs the image from the face of a special television tube. (The technical name of the tube is 'kinescope tube'; in the US a telerecording is called a KINESCOPE.) Before the introduction of videotape around 1955, telerecordings were the only means of preserving television programmes for re-broadcast or reference. They are still much in use for international distribution.

**TEMPLE,** SHIRLEY (1928–    ), US child star, appeared in minor roles from 1932. She played leading parts from 1934, enjoying phenomenal popularity in a succession of winsome stories often adapted from children's classics and usually with expertly performed songs and tap-dancing interpolated. *Bright Eyes* (1934), *The Little Colonel* (1935), *Wee Willie Winkie* (John FORD), *Heidi* (Allan DWAN, both 1937), *Rebecca of Sunnybrook Farm* (Dwan, 1938), *The Little Princess* (1939), were among her money-spinning successes, and she was TWENTIETH CENTURY-FOX's biggest asset until she retired from child roles after *The Blue Bird* (1940). She made a few attempts at *ingénue* parts, including Ford's *Fort Apache* (1948), then retired from films altogether. As Shirley Temple Black, after her second marriage, she has been active in politics for the Republican party, and in 1974 she was appointed US ambassador to Ghana. (See CHILD STARS.)

*TEN DAYS THAT SHOOK THE WORLD* see OKTIABR

*TEN THOUSAND SUNS* see TÍZEZER NAP

*TEOREMA* (*Theorem*), Italy, 1968. Eastman Color; 1½hr. *Dir, scr* Pier Paolo Pasolini; *prod* Aetos Film; *ph* Giuseppe Ruzzolini; *mus* Ennio Morricone; *cast* Terence Stamp (the visitor), Silvana Mangano (Lucia), Massimo Girotti (Paolo), Anna Wiazemsky (Odetta), Andrès José Cruz (Pietro), Laura Betti (Emilia).

PASOLINI began *Teorema* as a verse tragedy for the stage; this idea did not work, partly because of the minimal dialogue, so he transformed it into a film script and, later, a novel. An industrialist's family is visited by a young man who instantly arouses the desire of father, mother, daughter, son, and maid. He gratifies them all and leaves. Each is in turn liberated from his role in bourgeois society, but retreats into madness. In a prefatory sequence a reporter states that whatever the middle classes do, they are always wrong. Pasolini invests this bleak theorem with cool beauty, punctuating his elegantly composed scenes with shots of pale dust blowing across the action.

The film characteristically aroused controversy. The Italian government banned it and charged Pasolini with obscenity (he was acquitted on artistic grounds), while it was awarded the special prize of the International Catholic Bureau of Cinema.

**TERRA TREMA, La,** Italy, 1948. 2¾hr. *Dir, scr* Luchino Visconti; *prod* Universalia; *asst dir* Francesco Rosi, Franco Zeffirelli; *ph* G. R. Aldo; *operator* Gianni Di Venanzo; *ed* Mario Serandrei.

VISCONTI planned an epic trilogy, to be made in Sicily, describing the depressed economic conditions among the local fishermen, peasants, and workers in the sulphur mines. Only the first part, *Episodio del mare (Episode of the Sea)*, was completed, and it assumed the title of the whole project, *La terra trema*. The story of the Valastro family was inspired by Verga's novel *I malavoglia*, and additional tragic meaning is given to the film by the realization that social conditions in Sicily had hardly changed since 1881, when the novel was written.

*La terra trema* was conceived as a revolutionary document, an exposé of humiliation and injustice, and to this end Visconti used the documentary techniques adopted by the adherents of NEO-REALISM. The film was shot entirely on location and all the actors are local people playing roles close to their own lives: their unselfconsciousness and response to direction demonstrates Visconti's extraordinary *rapport* with his players. The beautiful visual imagery of the film, with great attention paid to tonal and plastic composition, may tend to jar against the cruel reality of the events depicted, but it is a memorable achievement by the great G. R. ALDO. The dialogue is spoken in the actors' own Sicilian dialect, with a commentary in Italian spoken by Visconti himself.

**TERRE SANS PAIN** see HURDES, LAS

**TESHIGAHARA,** HIROSHI (1927– ), Japanese director. Son of a flower arranger, he studied painting before making a short film, *Hokusai*, in 1953. Six years later, in New York, he made *Jose Torres*, a short on the Puerto-Rican boxer, before founding his own production company to make in Japan his first feature, *Otoshi Ana (Pitfall*, 1962), for about $50,000. The film had little exhibition, and it was not until SUNA NO ONNA *(Woman of the Dunes*, 1964), that Teshigahara made clear the possibilities of independent production to Japan's major companies (the film cost only $100,000). The successful experimentalism of his first two films did not evolve in his subsequent *Tanin no Kao (The Face of Another*, 1966), and *Moetsukita Chizu (The Man without a Map*, 1968).

**TESTAMENT DES DR MABUSE, Das** *(The Last Will of Dr Mabuse)*, Germany, 1932. 1¼hr.

*Dir, prod* Fritz Lang for Nero-Film; *scr* Lang, Thea von Harbou; *ph* Fritz Arno Wagner; *des* Karl Vollbrecht, Emil Hasler; *cast* Rudolph Klein-Rogge (Dr Mabuse), Otto Wernicke (Inspector Lohmann), Gustav Diesl, Oscar Beregi, Vera Liessem.

LANG'S second sound film reverted to the allegorical concerns of DIE NIBELUNGEN (1924) and METROPOLIS (1927), but in a contemporary setting. The arch-criminal of DR MABUSE DER SPIELER (1922), confined in a lunatic asylum, uses his hypnotic powers to suborn the hospital's director and puts into operation his plan to master the world. He is finally defeated by the same Inspector Lohmann created by Lang in M (1931). The parallels between Hitler and the insane demagogue Mabuse were overt enough to incur the anger of the Nazi Party, and soon after the film's completion Lang left Germany.

The film was shot in two versions, German and French. In the French version Rudolph Klein-Rogge again played Mabuse and Lohmann was played by Jim Gérald.

**TESTAMENT D'ORPHÉE, Le,** France, 1960. 1½hr. *Dir, scr* Jean Cocteau; *prod* Les Éditions Cinégraphiques; *ph* Roland Pontoizeau; *des* Pierre Guffroy; *mus* Georges Auric *et al*; *cast* Jean Cocteau (the Poet), Edouard Dermithe (Cégeste), Henri Crémieux (the Scientist), Maria Casarès (the Princess), François Périer (Heurtebise), Yul Brynner (the Doorman), Jean-Pierre Léaud (the Child), Jean Marais (Oedipus).

A recapitulation of COCTEAU's life and work, *Le Testament d'Orphée* contains numerous references to his previous films, especially ORPHÉE (1950). It has been dismissed by some critics as merely a facetious coda to the earlier film and hailed by others as one of the cinema's great confessional documents. Shot on a minimal budget using convenient locations, with Cocteau and his personal friends as actors, the film is certainly packed with private allusions. Subjective and objective reality are fused to a far greater degree than in, for instance, *Orphée*. Recurrent Cocteau characters like Heurtebise and Cégeste jostle with figures from mythology and with such visitors as Pablo Picasso and Charles AZNAVOUR.

The film represents the culmination of the director's preoccupation with himself as Orpheus, the poet. Clearly Cocteau intended *Le Testament d'Orphée* to be both his farewell to the screen and a personal monument which, like the many resurrections in the film, would transcend the fact of death. In a key scene Cocteau makes repeated attempts to draw a hibiscus flower but succeeds only in producing his own likeness, a demonstration of his statement that 'a film, whatever it may be, is always its director's portrait'.

**TÊTE CONTRE LES MURS, La** (*The Keepers*), France, 1958. 1¾hr. *Dir* Georges Franju; *prod* Atica-Sirius-Elpenor; *scr* Jean-Pierre Mocky, from the novel by Hervé Bazin; *ph* Eugen Schüfftan; *mus* Maurice Jarre; *cast* Jean-Pierre Mocky (François), Pierre Brasseur (Dr Valmont), Paul Meurisse (Dr Emery), Anouk Aimée (Stéphanie), Charles Aznavour (Hertevent), Edith Scob (madwoman).

François, a young delinquent committed by his father to a mental home, escapes but is returned to the institution before he can prove his sanity. FRANJU made much of the film in an actual mental hospital, which gives it an alarming authenticity. In spite of this, and SCHÜFFTAN's outstanding photography, the ambiguity of the leading character (whose real mental state is never established) weakens the finished work.

**TEXICAN,** originally a variant of Texan which enjoyed wide popular usage during the ten years of the Republic of Texas but lapsed during the next generation. It was revived in the film of THE ALAMO (1960), and began to regain a limited usage; but it was used in this case to designate Americans who were citizens of Texas before the state joined the Union. In *The Texican* (1966) it denotes a Texan citizen on the run in Mexico.

**THALBERG,** IRVING (1899–1936), US producer, the model for the hero of F. Scott FITZGERALD's unfinished novel *The Last Tycoon*. A delicate child with a weak heart, who was not expected to live beyond the age of thirty, he drove himself to succeed early in life and at twenty was in charge of production at UNIVERSAL Studios. Here he crossed swords for the first time with Erich von STROHEIM, removing him from the direction of *Merry-go-round* (1922); he was later to supervise the cutting of GREED (1923). In 1923 he became Vice-President of the Mayer Company, which was later absorbed into METRO-GOLDWYN-MAYER. At the height of his career at MGM he was the head producer overseeing and controlling all productions, responsible for building up a remarkable company of stars, which included GARBO, GABLE, HARLOW, and his future wife Norma SHEARER, and famous for his script factory which gave employment to many of the leading writers of the time. His particular involvement with each film came after the first PREVIEW, when he ordered re-editing and re-shooting until he was satisfied. He once said, 'Movies aren't made, they're re-made'.

Following a serious illness and a long trip to Europe, he returned to find he had been demoted from production head to running a production unit within MGM. This was a blow to him, but some of his most famous films were to follow including *The Barretts of Wimpole Street* (1934), THE MUTINY ON THE BOUNTY (1935), CAMILLE (1936), THE GOOD EARTH (1937). Before the last two were released, Thalberg's health finally gave way, and he died of pneumonia at the age of thirty-seven.

**THEATER** see CINEMA

**THEODORAKIS,** MIKIS (1925–  ), Greek composer and nationalist whose work includes a quantity of film music. Among his earlier film scores were *The Barefoot Batallion* (1954) and *Ill Met by Moonlight* (1956), but he gained international fame in the sixties when his film scores included *Mikhali* (1960); DASSIN's *Phaedra* (1961); CACOYANNIS's *Electra* (1961), *Zorba the Greek* (1965), and *The Day the Fish Came Out* (1967); and COSTA-GAVRAS's Z (1968). He was imprisoned by the Greek military junta in 1967 and he worked in exile from his release in 1970 until his return to Greece in 1974.

**THEOREM** see TEOREMA

**THÉRÈSE DESQUEYROUX,** France, 1962. 1¾hr. *Dir* Georges Franju; *prod* Filmel; *scr* François Mauriac, Claude Mauriac, Franju, from the novel by Mauriac; *ph* Christian Matras; *cast* Emmanuele Riva (Thérèse), Philippe Noiret (Bernard), Edith Scob (Anne de la Trave), Sami Frey (Jean Azavedo).

FRANJU's adaptation of Mauriac's novel, with the action transferred to the present day, retains the claustrophobic atmosphere of the original. Thérèse, stifling in her bourgeois marriage, attempts to poison her husband. Although she is acquitted in court, her punishment is effected by the family. Emmanuele RIVA is outstanding in the title role.

**THÉRÈSE RAQUIN,** Zola's powerful story of two lovers who kill the woman's husband and became prey to pathological guilt which drives them to mutual hatred and eventual suicide, has been filmed three times. The first version was made in Italy in 1915, directed by Nino Martoglio and starring Giacinta Pezzano and Dillo Lombardi. Jacques FEYDER's adaptation was a French/German co-production of 1928 (German title *Du sollst nicht ehebrecher*) starring Gina Manès and Wolfgang Zilzer. It emphasized the grotesque elements of the novel, with an Expressionist style of direction and stark contrasts of black and white. Marcel CARNÉ directed a French/Italian co-production in 1953. He gave the story a modern setting and introduced a blackmailing sailor as the agent of the lovers' downfall, thereby destroying much of the coherence of Zola's work; but he effectively captured the claustrophobia of the novel and Simone

SIGNORET and Raf Vallone gave a fine display of tortured sensuality.

**THIEF OF BAGDAD, The,** US, 1924. 2½hr. *Dir* Raoul Walsh; *prod* Douglas Fairbanks Pictures, for United Artists; *scr* Lotta Woods, Elton Thomas; *ph* Arthur Edeson; *des* William Cameron Menzies; *ed* William Nolan; *mus* Mortimer Wilson ; *cast* Douglas Fairbanks (Thief of Bagdad), Snitz Edwards (His Evil Associate), Charles Belcher (Holy Man), Julanne Johnston (Princess), Anna May Wong (Mongol Slave).

The Thief of Bagdad falls in love with the Princess, and in order to court her poses as a prince. Confessing to his deception, he is sent by the Holy Man in quest of a magic chest reputed to bring happiness. He succeeds in his mission, rescues the city from the Mongols, and wins the Princess.

Perhaps the most opulent of all FAIRBANKS's films, this exotic fairy-tale fantasy set a new Hollywood standard with the magnificence and grandeur of William Cameron MENZIES's settings and costumes and the technical accomplishment of its 'magic' and 'flying carpet' effects.

*The Thief of Baghdad*, GB/US, 1940. Technicolor; 1¾hr. *Dir* Ludwig Berger, Michael Powell, Tim Whelan; *prod* Alexander Korda for United Artists; *assoc prod* Zoltan Korda, William Cameron Menzies; *scr* Lajos Biro, Miles Malleson; *ph* Georges Périnal, Osmond Borrodaile; *des* Vincent Korda; *sp eff* Lawrence Butler; *ed* William Hornbeck, Charles Crichton; *mus* Miklos Rozsa; *cast* Conrad Veidt (Jaffar), Sabu (Abu), June Duprez (Princess), John Justin (Ahmad), Rex Ingram (Djinni), Miles Malleson (Sultan).

Even more spectacular than the FAIRBANKS–WALSH version, KORDA's beautifully designed and costumed production is equally enjoyable as an elaborate fantasy. The special EFFECTS were outstanding, notably in the flying horse and magic carpet sequences and in the scenes featuring the monstrous djinn, played with stentorian magnificence by Rex INGRAM. Miles Malleson's fussy, infantile Sultan obsessed by automatons and Conrad VEIDT's evil vizier are strikingly coherent characterizations.

The film was begun at DENHAM STUDIOS in 1939, and location shooting was planned in Baghdad; but owing to the outbreak of war it was completed in Hollywood and 'old Baghdad' was constructed in the Mojave Desert.

A third version was made in Italy, *Il ladro di Bagdad* (1960) starring Steve Reeves.

**THIELE, WILHELM** (1890–    ), Austrian-born director; made his début in Austrian films with *Märchen aus alt-Wien* (1923). He worked for UFA as literary manager and scriptwriter and then began to direct films, which included *Orient-express* (1927) and *Die Dame mit der Maske* (1928). His first sound film was the operetta *Drei von der Tankstelle* (1930), which made imaginative use of the new medium. He followed this success with *Liebeswalzer* (1930), enjoyed for its 'Viennese flavour'. Of Jewish extraction, Thiele was forced to leave Germany in 1933 and went to the US, where he worked as a director, making *Beg, Borrow or Steal* (1938) and several TARZAN films. After the war he directed some films in Germany.

**THINGS TO COME,** GB, 1936. 1¾hr. *Dir, des* William Cameron Menzies; *prod* Alexander Korda for London Film Productions; *scr* H. G. Wells; *ph* Georges Périnal; *mus* Arthur Bliss; *cast* Raymond Massey (John and Oswald Cabal), Ralph Richardson (the Boss), Margaretta Scott (Roxana and Rowena), Cedric Hardwicke (Theotocopulos).

H. G. Wells's prophetic novel *The Shape of Things to Come* was faithfully translated into a film about an apocalyptic world war and the strange society which results. KORDA brought William Cameron MENZIES from Hollywood to direct the film because of his skill in production design; and the intriguing visual style owes much to the futuristic effects designed by Menzies and executed by Harry Zech and Ned Mann. The film's popular success can be in part attributed to its timely prediction of global war; strong performances by Raymond MASSEY and Ralph RICHARDSON and the symphonic score by Arthur Bliss add to its enduring quality.

**THIN MAN, The,** US, 1934. 1½hr. *Dir* W. S. Van Dyke; *prod* MGM; *scr* Albert Hackett, Frances Goodrich, from the novel by Dashiell Hammett; *ph* James Wong Howe; *cast* William Powell (Nick), Myrna Loy (Nora), Maureen O'Sullivan (Dorothy), Nat Pendleton (Guild).

This hugely successful adaptation of Dashiell HAMMETT's classic of detective fiction (first published in 1932) gave a new twist to the genre on the screen by its light-hearted treatment. The public enjoyed the comic byplay which, though prominent, never engulfed the pursuit of the mysterious criminal, the Thin Man: the climactic stages built up some good suspense, though even this was tinged with humour.

Equally responsible for the film's popularity was the inspired casting of William POWELL and Myrna LOY: although they had made previous films together, this set the seal on their popularity as a co-starring team. Also competing in the popularity stakes was the dog, Asta, who completed the Nick Charles *ménage*. Sequels were inevitable, and both stars and director went on to make *After the Thin Man* (1937), *Another Thin*

*Man* (1939), and *Shadow of the Thin Man* (1941). *The Thin Man Goes Home* (1944) was directed by Richard Thorpe, and in later years the characters had a new lease of life in a television series which could not compensate for the lack of Powell and Loy.

**THIRD MAN, The,** GB, 1949. 1¾hr. *Dir, prod* Carol Reed for Alexander Korda and David O. Selznick; *scr* Graham Greene; *ph* Robert Krasker; *mus* Anton Karas; *cast* Orson Welles (Harry Lime), Joseph Cotten (Holly Martins), Alida Valli (Anna), Trevor Howard (Major Calloway), Bernard Lee (Sgt Paine).

Following THE FALLEN IDOL (1948), Carol REED and Graham GREENE enlarged on that successful collaboration with *The Third Man*, an effective thriller set in post-war occupied Vienna. The sense of locale is thoroughly established by making the shattered city an integral part of the action, aided by a polyglot soundtrack: Anton Karas's original zither music added atmosphere and became justly popular in its own right. Reed's usual accomplished direction of actors is evident here in the unemphatic performances which heighten the tension of the plot. Only the wilfully independent playing of Orson WELLES tends to unbalance the low-key acting, although his name certainly contributed to the film's commercial success. Welles himself wrote into the script the famous 'cuckoo clock' speech.

**THIRD WORLD CINEMA,** term used loosely to embrace films made in countries which have until recently been unable to sustain an indigenous film culture because of poverty, domination by foreign powers, or political oppression. Latin America has nurtured some of the most promising developments in national cinema, starting with CUBA and BRAZIL in the late fifties and spreading rapidly to BOLIVIA, CHILE, COLOMBIA, ARGENTINA, URUGUAY, and VENEZUELA. ALGERIA and Senegal have also demonstrated a lively sense of the importance of cinema in confirming national identity. The films themselves vary widely both in technical accomplishment and in primary aims, from the AGIT-PROP newsreels of Santiago ALVAREZ (Cuba), via the barbaric beauty of Glauber ROCHA's depictions of the sufferings of peasants (Brazil), the social observations of Tomás Gutiérrez ALEA (Cuba), and the documentary-style reconstructions of Jorge SANJINES (Bolivia), to the humanist narratives of Ousmane Sembene (Senegal); but they are generally characterized by a left-wing political stance, anti-imperialist (especially anti-American) intentions, rejection of the values of escapist entertainment, and energetic freedom in the use of cinematic conventions. When sufficient financial resources and political stability can be created, allowing continuity of output, the emergent nations promise an exciting and vigorous contribution to world cinema.

**35MM,** the standard film width used for professional film production (other than television or educational). Although early film workers used many different gauges and forms of perforations, the 35mm gauge introduced by Thomas EDISON about 1889 quickly became a world-wide standard and remains so with very few alterations. It has the appearance most commonly visualized by the layman: a wide strip of film, perforated down both sides, with each frame four perforations high. When sound-on-film was introduced in 1929, the only change in 35mm film was to reduce the picture size slightly to accommodate the sound track (see ASPECT RATIO); when CINEMASCOPE arrived in the mid-fifties, the larger images were literally squeezed into the same 35mm gauge.

**THIRTY-NINE STEPS, The,** GB, 1935, 1½hr. *Dir* Alfred Hitchcock; *prod* Michael Balcon for Gaumont British; *scr* Charles Bennett, Alma Reville, from the novel by John Buchan; *ph* Bernard Knowles; *des* Otto Werndorff, Albert Jullion; *mus* Louis Levy; *cast* Robert Donat (Richard Hannay), Madeleine Carroll (Pamela), Lucie Mannheim (Miss Smith/Annabella), Godfrey Tearle (Professor Jordan), Peggy Ashcroft (crofter's wife), John Laurie (crofter), Helen Haye (Mrs Jordan), Frank Cellier (the sheriff), Wylie Watson (Mr Memory).

A young Canadian, Richard Hannay, makes the acquaintance of an international spy. When he finds her murdered in his flat, he takes over her mission, to go to Scotland to prevent important defence secrets being sold. However, the police, suspecting him of the murder of the spy, give chase. Pursued by the police, trapped by the gang he is after, alternately captive and fugitive, Hannay undergoes a variety of escapades before finally achieving his goal, when a climax of immense ingenuity unravels the whole complicated intrigue.

The absurd plot, elaborated around an impossible web of coincidences, gave free reign to HITCHCOCK's imaginative powers. The film evolves through an ever-changing variety of settings, from a densely crowded music hall to the (studio-made) desolation of the Scottish moors, maintaining a vital sense of pace and rhythm throughout. Robert DONAT's urbanity is admirably matched by the cool, blonde charm which Hitchcock drew from Madeleine CARROLL: the couple give a polished performance which earns the film a place among the best British comedy-thrillers of the thirties.

**THIS MODERN AGE,** a monthly newsreel financed by the RANK ORGANISATION as Britain's answer to THE MARCH OF TIME, ran for forty-one issues between September 1946 and November 1950. After a comparatively parochial beginning, the series quickly broadened its social and political platform with *Palestine* (no 6), *Coal Crisis* (no 7) and subsequent appraisals of Britain in the post-war world: *Will Britain Go Hungry?* (no 13), *Women in Our Time* (no 22), *Fight in Malaya* (no 40). Although directed at the British public, the series was distributed widely abroad. Stylistically, *This Modern Age* represented little advance upon *The March of Time*, lacking the latter's controversial journalistic approach.

**THIS SPORTING LIFE,** GB, 1963. 2¼hr. *Dir* Lindsay Anderson; *prod* Karel Reisz for Independent Artists; *scr* David Storey, from his own novel; *ph* Denys Coop; *ed* Peter Taylor; *mus* Roberto Gerhard; *cast* Richard Harris (Frank Machin), Rachel Roberts (Mrs Hammond), Alan Badel (Weaver), William Hartnell (Johnson), Colin Blakely (Maurice Braithwaite).

The story of a Rugby League footballer and his affair with his widowed landlady functions as a study of the ambiguities of human nature, in particular the conflict of aggression and tenderness. The film unsentimentally captures the Northern industrial setting of the book, only losing conviction when it over-exploits the flashback.

Karel REISZ, after his success with SATURDAY NIGHT AND SUNDAY MORNING (1960), was originally invited to direct *This Sporting Life*, but suggested instead that he should produce and ANDERSON direct. David Storey wrote the script from his novel (published in 1960), working closely with Reisz and Anderson. Their experiences, Storey's of playing Rugby League football and Anderson's of making documentary films in the North, combined in a piece of powerful, stylized realism.

Anderson's chance to contribute to the 'new wave' he had done so much to promote (see also FREE CINEMA) came ironically late. Comparative inexperience, moreover, caused producer and director to lose control of the budget; the film was moderately successful and brought Anderson critical acclaim, but did not make him a reassuringly employable figure in the eyes of the industry.

**THOMAS L'IMPOSTEUR,** France, 1965. 1½hr. *Dir* Georges Franju; *prod* Filmel; *scr* Jean Cocteau, Michel Worms, Franju, from the novel by Cocteau; *ph* Marcel Fradetal; *cast* Emmanuele Riva (Princesse de Bormes), Fabrice Rouleau (Guillaume alias Thomas), Jean Servais (Presquel-Duport).

COCTEAU's concern with the fusion of fiction and reality, embodied in the wish-fulfilling masquerades of the adolescent Thomas, is successfully integrated with FRANJU's spare and horrific vision of the wanton destructiveness of war. As in HÔTEL DES INVALIDES (1951), the use of an objective commentary heightens the effect of horrifying imagery.

**THOMPSON,** J. LEE (1914– ), British director whose early career was as a playwright and screenwriter. From 1950 he directed a variety of thrillers and comedies, tackling a more serious theme, the topical question of capital punishment, in *Yield to the Night* (1956). After *The Good Companions* (1956) he concentrated for a time on dramatic subjects, notably *Woman in a Dressing Gown* (1957) with its strong performance by Yvonne MITCHELL. *Northwest Frontier* (1959), an action drama with an agreeably light touch, and the large-scale *The Guns of Navarone* (1961) set the course of his subsequent work: popular adventures and thrillers marked by his best attributes, a good visual sense and a flair for the creation of suspense.

**THOMSON,** VIRGIL (1896– ), American composer, is best known in the cinema for his musical contributions to four classic documentaries: LORENTZ's THE PLOW THAT BROKE THE PLAINS (1936), the score of which he later developed into a concert work, and THE RIVER (1937), IVENS's THE SPANISH EARTH (1937, with Marc Blitzstein) and FLAHERTY's LOUISIANA STORY (1948). Thomson frequently uses hymn tunes, popular melodies, and folk songs to establish a common cultural language with his audience. His other film works have included the score for *Power Among Men* (1958), an episodic documentary produced by Thorold DICKINSON for the United Nations Film Service, and for *The Goddess* (John CROMWELL, 1958).

**THORNDIKE,** ANDREW (1909– ) and ANNELIE (1925– ), German COMPILATION directors who together, after their marriage in 1955, compiled dossiers on living Nazis for a series *Archive sagen aus* (*The Archives Testify*) suggested by Andrew's earlier experience as DEFA documentary director. In *Urlaub auf Sylt* (*Holiday on Sylt,* 1957) and *Unternehmen Teutonenschwert* (*Operation Teutonic Sword,* 1958) they put photographs and letters with archive and contemporary footage into a popular detective format. Their best-known film *Das russische Wunder* (*The Russian Miracle,* 1963), a study of Russia since the Revolution, combines detailed research with many of SHUB's ideas to produce a rhapsody on the achievements of Soviet Russia.

**3-D** see STEREOSCOPIC

**THREE SONGS OF LENIN** see TRI PESNI O LENINYE

**3.10 TO YUMA**, US, 1957. 1½hr. *Dir* Delmer Daves; *prod* Columbia; *scr* Halsted Welles, from a story by Elmore Leonard; *ph* Charles Lawton Jr; *cast* Van Heflin (Dan Evans), Glenn Ford (Ben Wade), Felicia Farr (Emmy), Leora Dana (Alice Evans), Henry Jones (Alex Potter).

A classically schematic WESTERN in which an apparently ineffectual rancher (HEFLIN) must guard an outlaw until he can be put on the train that will take him to prison in Yuma. DAVES's handling of this economical story has earned considerable respect; dramatic interest is developed through the clash of personalities in confined settings and suspense is built up by pacing the second half of the film according to 'real' time as both characters and audience wait for the arrival of the train and the resolution of the drama. Glenn FORD's muted performance takes full advantage of the humour inherent in the confrontation.

**THRONE OF BLOOD, The**, see KUMONOSU-JO

**THULIN,** INGRID (1929– ), Swedish actress, attended theatre schools in Norrköping and Stockholm before becoming a stage actress. From 1948 she starred in a number of unremarkable films, but became internationally known in films directed by Ingmar BERGMAN. Since SMULTRONSTÄLLET (*Wild Strawberries,* 1957) she has appeared in most of his films and for her performance in *Nära livet* (*So Close to Life,* 1957) she won the award for best actress at CANNES. A less successful role was in Vincente MINNELLI's remake of THE FOUR HORSEMEN OF THE APOCALYPSE (1961). Her unusual and unsettling beauty as well as her subtle acting have been used to advantage by other directors including RESNAIS in LA GUERRE EST FINIE (1966) and VISCONTI in *La caduta degli dei* (*The Damned,* 1970). She is married to Harry Schein, the founder of SVENSKA FILMINSTITUTET.

**THUNDER OVER MEXICO** see EISENSTEIN

**THY SOUL SHALL BEAR WITNESS** see KÖRKALEN

**TILLIE'S PUNCTURED ROMANCE**, US, 1914. 1½hr. *Dir* Mack Sennett; *prod* Keystone; *scr* Hampton del Ruth, from the stage play *Tillie's Nightmare* by Edgar Smith; *cast* Marie Dressler (Tillie), Mack Swain (her father), Charles Bennett (her rich uncle), Charlie Chaplin (the city slicker), Mabel Normand (his partner), the Keystone Kops.

Not only CHAPLIN's first feature-length comedy (his only one for KEYSTONE), but the first ever, took fourteen weeks to shoot, as against the standard Keystone schedule of one week. Chaplin's role is really to support Marie DRESSLER, who had played Tillie in the stage musical on which the film is based, but he rose so superbly to the challenge of sustaining a long comic part against much typical Keystone SLAPSTICK that he got almost as good reviews as the star herself.

**TIME FOR BURNING, A**, US, 1966. 1hr. *Dir, ed* William C. Jersey, Barbara Connell; *prod* Quest Productions for Lutheran Film Associates; *ph* Jersey; *sd* Connell.

When a Lutheran pastor in Omaha, Nebraska, decided to involve his all-white congregation in efforts to contact a neighbouring black community, Lutheran Film Associates commissioned William Jersey, already well known for NBC News features like *Manhattan Battleground* (1964), to film the events that followed. 75,000 feet of 16mm film—committee meetings, confrontations with church elders anxious about property values, the bitter comments of a black barber—were edited down to a rhythmic, coherent 2,000 feet culminating in the forced resignation of the young minister. The film remains a fine example of DIRECT CINEMA effectively used.

**TIME IS**, GB, 1963. Kodachrome 5269; 30min. *Dir, scr, ed* Don Levy; *prod* June Goodfield, Fotis Mesthenos; *ph* Levy, Mesthenos; *mus* Ravi Shankar, Ali Akbar Khan.

One of a short series of films produced by a Nuffield Unit in an attempt to demonstrate that concepts can be expressed by images rather than words, *Time Is*, brilliantly edited by LEVY, demonstrates that man's conception of time is emotional as well as intellectual. The first European film to use Ravi Shankar's music, it was the only one of the Nuffield series to gain wide circulation.

**TIME-LAPSE**, a method of filming in which the action on screen appears much faster than in life. A plant, for example, which takes 30 days to sprout and blossom, can be shown on film covering the entire growth in 30 seconds. The effect is produced by filming the natural action one frame at a time, and allowing a considerable lapse of time—in the case of the plant, one hour—between frames. The camera is triggered automatically by a clock, and the environment of the subject is controlled to avoid sudden movements, such as wind, between frames. When the film is shown at the normal speed of 24 frames per second the action can be appreciated and studied in detail. Time-lapse filming is analogous to ANIMATION, but the movement between frames is controlled by nature rather than by an animator. The technique is most often seen in scientific films but has been used effectively in narrative films, notably ROUQUIER'S FARREBIQUE (1946).

When human movements are to be speeded up for comic effect, the term time-lapse is not used, since the time between frames may be only slightly greater than normal—$\frac{1}{12}$ second instead of $\frac{1}{24}$. However, Stanley KUBRICK used something like time-lapse filming in the orgy sequence of A CLOCKWORK ORANGE (1971), where by shooting about one frame per second he condensed several minutes of simulated sex into one chorus of the *William Tell Overture*.

**TIME OUT OF WAR, A,** US, 1954. 20min. *Dir, scr* Dennis Sanders, from the story 'Pickets' by Robert W. Chambers; *prod* Sanders Brothers Productions; *mus* Frank Hamilton; *cast* Barry Atwater (Craig), Robert Sherry (Alden), Alan Cohen (Connor).

*A Time Out of War* was made by an all-student cast and crew as a thesis for a master's degree in Theater Arts at the University of California at Los Angeles. The story of a day in the American Civil War when two Union soldiers and a Confederate arrive at a temporary truce recalls a similar episode poignantly dealt with by John HUSTON in THE RED BADGE OF COURAGE (1951). The film's striking freshness and eloquence won it several awards, including an OSCAR. It was given the unusual recognition of limited theatrical release in the US and Britain and stimulated interest in student film-making.

**TIME TO LIVE AND A TIME TO DIE, A,** see FEU FOLLET, LE

**TIMING,** a term generally used in the US for GRADING, the process of balancing the negative and correcting a print for colour and brightness. The term applies to both colour and black-and-white film.

**TINTING,** the process of artificially applying an overall colour to a black-and-white print, used extensively in the silent era and again for a time in the late thirties. The effect can be produced either by immersing an ordinary print in a dye solution or by printing on a pre-tinted film base. Tinting produces colour in the light areas of the picture; TONING, a similar process, colours only the dark areas. Successful tinting can only be achieved in prints made from a negative with strong contrast. During the late twenties, PARA-

MOUNT in the US often printed on a steely-blue tinted base to counteract the effects of bad arc projection. (See COLOUR.)

**TIOMKIN, DMITRI** (1899–    ), Russian-born US composer, wrote his first film score for ALICE IN WONDERLAND (1934). After *Lost Horizon* (Frank CAPRA, 1937), which allowed him to use his feeling for Oriental colouring and Slavonic melancholy, his work was in steady demand. During the war he worked with Capra on Army training films. RED RIVER (1948) is typical of Tiomkin's music for Westerns, with insistent rhythms, melodic sweep, and large-scale orchestration. In 1950 he was made head of music for Stanley KRAMER Productions, and won his first OSCAR for HIGH NOON (1952). He also won Oscars for *The High and the Mighty* (1954) and *The Old Man and the Sea* (1958). His most original score was for *Rhapsody in Steel* (1959), an animated film commissioned by the US Steel Company in which the action was totally dependent on the music, allowing the composer more than usual freedom. In the late sixties Tiomkin moved to Britain and turned to production, making *McKenna's Gold* (1969) with Carl FOREMAN and pioneering US/USSR co-operation as executive producer and musical supervisor on *Tchaikovsky* (1970). He has published an autobiography, *Please don't hate me* (New York, 1969).

**TIREZ SUR LE PIANISTE** (*Shoot the Pianist*), France, 1960. Dyaliscope; 1$\frac{1}{4}$hr. *Dir* François Truffaut; *prod* Pierre Braunberger for Les Films de la Pléiade; *scr* Truffaut, Marcel Moussy, from the novel *Down There*, by David Goodis; *ph* Raoul Coutard; *ed* Cécile Decugis, Claudine Bouché; *mus* Georges Delerue; *cast* Charles Aznavour (Edouard Saroyan–Charlie Kohler), Marie Dubois (Léna), Nicole Berger (Thérèse), Albert Rémy (Chico), Claude Mansard (Momo).

TRUFFAUT's second feature film, in which he began his fruitful collaboration with Georges DELERUE, again reflects many of the elements which distinguished the films of the NOUVELLE VAGUE. Based on the novel by David Goodis, it reflects the influence of the FILM NOIR, and is full of the references to cinema to which Truffaut and his contemporaries first gave currency. A gaily mobile camera, admirably directed by Raoul COUTARD, follows the adventures of Charlie Kohler, the café pianist who gets involved in the dealings of a gang of petty crooks. Technical tricks and jokes lend light-heartedness to a film which has the basic sadness characteristic of Truffaut, well caught by the wistful charm of Charles AZNAVOUR as Charlie, the pianist whose past is revealed in flashback. Movement and action culminate in an open, snowy scene in which Charlie's girl, Léna, beautifully portrayed by Marie Dubois, is killed by a bullet from the gangsters.

**TISSÉ,** EDVARD (1897–1961), Russian cameraman of Swedish parentage, studied painting before becoming an official war photographer in 1914. In 1918 he joined VERTOV'S KINO-GLAZ group, for which, in the following year, he made a film about Soviet Latvia. After work on the agit-trains (see PROPAGANDA) and with other directors he was invited by EISENSTEIN to shoot the latter's first film, STACHKA (*Strike*, 1925). They were well suited in their daring and eagerness to experiment and their next film, BRONENOSETS POTEMKIN (*The Battleship Potemkin*, 1925), confirmed the originality of their talents. Much of the power of the sequence on the Odessa steps comes from Tissé's ingenuity. He devised a camera trolley to run the length of the steps (at a time when DOLLY shots were almost unknown in Russia); he strapped the camera to the waist of a somersaulting acrobat; and he changed lenses instead of moving the camera, so that the extras did not become camera-conscious. He also created the montage sequence of the stone lions.

After photographing OKTIABR (*October*, 1928) and STAROYE I NOVOYE (*Old and New*, 1929), Tissé went with Eisenstein and ALEXANDROV to Europe and America. In Switzerland he made a film campaigning for the legalization of abortion, with Alexandrov he made ROMANCE SENTIMENTALE (1930) in France, and he shot the ill-fated

*Que Viva Mexico!* (see EISENSTEIN). On their return to the Soviet Union he continued to work with Eisenstein, on *Bezhin lug* (*Bezhin Meadow*, 1937), ALEXANDER NEVSKY (1938), and the exteriors of IVAN GROZNYI (*Ivan the Terrible*, 1944, 1958). Eisenstein came to rely on Tissé, whose understanding of filters and lighting, and skill in the use of different lenses for dramatic effects was invaluable to his vision.

After the completion of *Ivan Groznyi*, Tissé worked with Alexandrov. He filmed ROOM'S *V gorakh Iugoslavii* (*In the Mountains of Yugoslavia*, 1946) and his later work includes *Kompositor Glinka* (1952), *Serebristaya pyl* (*Silver Dust*, 1953), and *Bessmertnyi garnison* (*Deathless Garrison*, 1956), about the defence of the Brest fortress in the Second World War.

**TÍZEZER NAP** (*Ten Thousand Suns*), Hungary, 1967. Agascope; 1¾hr. *Dir* Ferenc Kósa; *prod* Mafilm Studio 3; *scr* Sándor Csoóri, Imre Gyöngyössy, Kósa; *ph* Sándor Sára; *mus* András Szöllősy; *cast* Tibor Molnár (István), Gyöngi Bürös (wife), András Kozák (son), János Koltai (Fülöp).

KÓSA's first feature was in fact presented as his diploma film at the Academy of Film Art in 1963 and introduced a young director who was concerned more with the experiences of his parents' generation than with the problems of his contemporaries. The Hungarian title has the double meaning of Ten Thousand Suns or Ten Thousand Days; in a series of flashbacks the film traces the life of István from the thirties through

Charles Aznavour in *Tirez sur le pianiste* (François Truffaut, 1960)

all the social changes up to the Russian intervention of 1956: in particular, the effects of collectivization on the peasant community are examined. The result of several years' detailed research, *Tízezer nap* is strengthened by its documentary basis without yielding any of its quality as a complex and beautiful narrative feature film. With the aid of SÁRA's brilliant photography, Kósa makes eloquent use of the wide screen.

The presentation of István, member of a socialist community, as an erring human being, earned official disapproval and the film was held back until 1967 when it deservedly won the prize for best director at CANNES. In Britain it was cut from 112 minutes to 97 minutes.

**TOBIS** (Tonbild Syndikat AG), German production company founded in 1928 by the Swiss Tri-ergon-Musik AG (owners of sound patents of the three inventors Vogt, Masolle, and Engel), Küchenmeister Kommendit Gesellschaft (Dutch), Deutsche Tonfilm AG (German), Messter Ton (German), together with German banks. Most of the capital was from outside Germany. Tobis took over the European rights of the Tri-ergon sound system from UFA, which had held them since 1923 without making use of them. The first head of Tobis was Guido Bagier, a German composer, who became a major influence in the development of sound films and also a theoretician of note.

In 1929 Tobis amalgamated with Klangfilm (AEG, Siemens, and Polyphone), setting up a parent office in Amsterdam. Klangfilm took over the production of sound equipment and the standardization of apparatus; Tobis was in charge of distribution and licensing. Their first full-length sound feature was RUTTMANN's MELODIE DER WELT (*World Melody*, 1929).

The new company was faced with opposition from America for the market rights in sound, but at the Paris Sound Film Conference of 1930 Tobis-Klangfilm was awarded the rights for most of Europe. A French offshoot later became Films Sonores Tobis; their monopoly of sound facilities brought, among others, René CLAIR to work for them until he incurred German displeasure with his left-wing satire A NOUS LA LIBERTÉ (1931). Tobis also floated a British company which equipped the Wembley Studios in 1930. The first production was a successful musical in three language versions, *City of Song* directed by Carmine Gallone.

In Germany Tobis soon became a serious rival to UFA. By 1933 it owned several studios which formed a subsidiary, Tobis Rota AG. It then began to rent studios already equipped for sound from other companies, compelling these to use the Tobis-owned laboratories for the processing of Tobis negative stock. Tobis Europa, a distribution company, was also formed in 1933, from the old Suedfilm AG. By the end of 1936 Tobis, now consisting of Tobis Rota (production), Tobis Syndikat (production), Tobis Magna (production), Tobis Europa (distribution), and Tobis Cinema (export), was an important force in the German film industry.

At this time Goebbels was engineering ever-increasing government control of film production (see GERMANY). An ostensibly private group, financed entirely by the government, had for some time been buying shares in Tobis; at the end of 1936 it gained stock control of the German arm and in 1937 the company was entirely reorganized. The script division, casting office, and advertising were put under one head and production was reduced. At the end of the year the government took total control, leaving the Dutch parent company, whose only income was now from sound film patents, with a debt of RM2½ million.

Tobis continued production under strict official control, their films of this period including OLYMPIA (1938), *Feuertaufe* (1941), and OHM KRÜGER (1941). Production ceased in 1945.

**TODD,** ANN (1909–    ), British actress whose first film was *Keepers of Youth* (1931). She appeared in many British films of the thirties, but without attracting particular attention until she appeared opposite James MASON in *The Seventh Veil* (1945). HITCHCOCK's *The Paradine Case* (1948), *Madeleine* (1951), and *The Sound Barrier* (1952), the last two directed by David LEAN, then her husband, gave her roles of a similar nervous intensity. Owing to an assault in which she sustained facial injuries her acting career came to an abrupt end, but in recent years she has produced and directed travel documentaries.

**TODD,** MIKE (1907–58), US stage and film producer, real name Avrom Goldbogen or Goldenborgen. One of America's most flamboyant impresarios, Todd made and lost several fortunes during his lifetime—the first in 1933 when he exhibited the 'flame dancer' at the Chicago World's Fair. From 1936 Todd co-authored and produced a series of burlesque revues on Broadway, again making a financial killing when he took these shows to the 1939 New York World's Fair.

He ventured into the film business in 1953, setting up a theatre chain (Magna Theaters) with Joseph SCHENCK and George Skouras and founding a film-making company, Magna Productions. Todd later sold out his share in the theatre interests following a disagreement with his associates. His main contribution to films, however, was his promotion of a new 70mm WIDE SCREEN process, called TODD-AO, in the mid-fifties. He produced AROUND THE WORLD IN EIGHTY DAYS (1956); his lavish investment, notably on the cast of star players in cameo roles, was rewarded by enormous financial returns. He married Elizabeth TAYLOR in 1956: their stormy marriage was cut short when Todd and his biographer, Art Cohn, were killed in a plane crash. Cohn's book, *The nine lives of Mike Todd*, was published in 1959.

**TODD-AO,** process developed during the early fifties to produce a wide-screen image by photographing on 65mm negative and printing on to 70mm positive. The remaining space at the side of the print allows room for six soundtracks for STEREOPHONIC sound. The process was developed by the American Optical Co (hence the AO) for Mike TODD, who aimed at simplifying the cumbersome process of enlarging the screen and using stereophonic sound by having 'everything coming out of one hole'. The success of Todd's *Oklahoma!* (1955) and AROUND THE WORLD IN EIGHTY DAYS (1956), both in his new process, demonstrated its effectiveness. (See also WIDE SCREEN.)

*TO DIE IN MADRID* see MOURIR A MADRID

*TO HAVE AND HAVE NOT,* US, 1944. 1¾hr. *Dir, prod* Howard Hawks for Warner Bros; *scr* Jules Furthman, William Faulkner, from the novel by Ernest Hemingway; *ph* Sidney Hickox; *cast* Humphrey Bogart (Harry Morgan), Walter

Brennan (Eddie 'The Mummy'), Lauren Bacall (Slim), Dolores Moran (Hélène de Bursac), Sheldon Leonard (Coyo), Marcel Dalio (Frenchy), Dan Seymour (Captain Renard).

As the owner of a fishing boat plying out of Martinique, BOGART created another of his classic loners, a man without allegiance except to his own standards. Persuaded to help the escape of Free French activists after the island has been brought under Vichy rule, he is forced to take a moral stand; the presence of Lauren BACALL as another independent spirit is crucial to his decision.

The film was at first coolly received. Bacall, a new discovery in her first film, was over-sold in the pre-release publicity: critics dismissed her idiosyncratic charm and attacked the cavalier treatment of HEMINGWAY's work. It now appears a characteristic HAWKS film, demonstrating his grasp of narrative and controlled vein of sentimentality, uniquely illuminated by the developing relationship between the two stars.

**TOHOSCOPE,** ANAMORPHIC WIDE SCREEN process developed in Japan and adopted by the Toho Company. It is patterned on CINEMASCOPE and has the same ASPECT RATIO, 2·35 : 1.

*TOKYO MONOGATARI,* (*Tokyo Story*) Japan, 1953. 2½hr. *Dir* Yasujiro Ozu; *prod* Shochiku;

*Tokyo monogatari* (Yasujiro Ozu, 1953)

*scr* Ozu, Kogo Noda; *ph* Yushun Atsuta; *mus* Senji Ito; *cast* Chishu Ryu (Shukichi), Chiyeko Higashiyama (Tomi), Setsuko Hara (Noriko), Satoshi Yamamura (Koichi).

An elderly couple visit their grown-up children in Tokyo, but find themselves an encumbrance. They return home, and the mother dies, leaving the father to face the future alone.

The film develops several themes: the generation gap (subject to even more stresses in Japan than in Europe), the tensions within the family, the discomfort of city life, but they are all events viewed *sub specie aeternitas*. OZU said that this was his most melodramatic film; although the measured pace seems slow to many Westerners, it is one of the more accessible of his later films, sharp in its observation and moving in its wide implications.

***TOKYO ORINPIKKU*** (*Tokyo Olympiad*), Japan, 1965. Tohoscope; 2¼hr; Eastman Color. *Dir* Kon Ichikawa; *prod* Suketaru Taguchi for Tokyo Olympic Film Association; *scr* Natto Wada, Yoshio Shirasaka, Shuntaro Tanikawa, Ichikawa; *des* Yusaku Kamekura; *mus* Toshiro Mayuzumi.

An imaginative documentary of the 1964 Olympic Games, ICHIKAWA's film shows with comic insight the human sweat and struggle involved in Olympic competition (quite unlike Leni RIEFENSTAHL's OLYMPIA, 1938). To capture the fifteen days of events, he employed a production unit of 556 people, over 100 cameras, and 232 different camera lenses. In all 400,000 feet of film were exposed; the original 70 hours was brilliantly edited by Ichikawa into its present running time. Several versions have been prepared with the emphasis favouring different national markets; these vary from 90 to 180 minutes.

***TOL'ABLE DAVID***, US, 1921. 1½hr. *Dir* Henry King; *prod* First National; *scr* Edmund Goulding, from the novel by Joseph Hergesheimer; *ph* Henry Cronjager; *cast* Richard Barthelmess, Ernest Torrence.

Drawing on his small-town background, Henry KING provided this simple story with a refreshingly 'real', rural atmosphere. It is King's finest achievement in the silent cinema, and, striking as it does the vein of affection and nostalgia for rural America, had immediate and widespread commercial success. David was the prototype for the All-American boy hero who reappeared in so many films.

**TOLAND,** GREGG (1904–48), US cameraman, began work at the age of twelve as an office-boy with FOX, becoming an assistant cameraman a year later. From 1926 he was assistant to the cameraman George Barnes at the GOLDWYN studios. He worked with Robert FLOREY and Slavko VORKAPICH on *The Life and Death of 9413, a Hollywood Extra* (1927–8) and received a joint credit with Barnes for *Bulldog Drummond* (1929), on which they eliminated the camera booth and substituted the soundproof BLIMP; they also devised a method of maintaining focus during a moving shot which is still in use. Toland's first solo credit was *Palmy Days* (1931) which was followed by a variety of films distinguished by their camerawork and lighting: they include *We Live Again* (1934), *Mad Love* (1935), LES MISÉRABLES (1935), *The Road to Glory* (1936), DEAD END (1937), *Kidnapped* (1938), WUTHERING HEIGHTS (1939), for which he won an OSCAR, THE GRAPES OF WRATH (1940), *The Long Voyage Home* (1940), and *The Westerner* (1940). Throughout his career he developed many innovations that gave his work a distinctive quality including the low-key effects that he became noted for, but it is on his work on CITIZEN KANE (1941), and particularly his use of DEEP FOCUS, that his reputation largely rests. His later films include THE LITTLE FOXES (1941), THE MAGNIFICENT AMBERSONS (1942), *December 7th* (1943) a campaign film he shot for John FORD while both were in the US Navy and for which Toland received another Oscar, *The Outlaw* (1946), *Song of the South* (1946) a DISNEY film with live action and animation, and THE BEST YEARS OF OUR LIVES (1946). Toland's early death from heart disease deprived Hollywood of one of its most polished and resourceful craftsmen.

***TO LIVE IN PEACE*** see VIVERE IN PACE

**TOM AND JERRY,** cat and mouse team of cartoon characters, created by Joe Barbera and William HANNA. In their first film, *Puss Gets the Boot* (1939), they were unnamed: they were christened in *The Milky Way* (1940). At first the pace was slow and the drawing over-detailed, but the series gained pace and polish, in its fast cutting and racy narrative style anticipating later feature film developments. In its prime it was notable for distinctive 'zazz' sound effects, well-chosen jazz scores, and plaintive theme music; dialogue has never had a part in Tom's eternally frustrated pursuit of the indomitable Jerry. Their cheerful violence, contrasting with the blandness of DISNEY cartoons, made Tom and Jerry continually popular for twenty years: outstanding titles were *Yankee Doodle Mouse* (1943), a satire on war, *Mouse Trouble* (1944), in which the bulldog first appeared, *The Little Orphan* (1948), using off-screen violence as Tom sadistically lashes a baby mouse, *Johann Mouse* (1952), a comic biography of Johann Strauss, and *Good Will to Men*

(1955), an anti-war cartoon. After 1955, when METRO-GOLDWYN-MAYER replaced Barbera and Hanna, the series degenerated into crude violence, losing its original saving qualities of style. In their best years from 1940 to 1957 Tom and Jerry appeared in 212 cartoons as well as in *Anchors Aweigh* (1945), in which Jerry danced with Gene KELLY, and *Dangerous When Wet* (1953), in which they both performed water ballet with Esther WILLIAMS. (See ANIMATION.)

**TOM JONES**, GB, 1963. Eastman Colour; 2¼hr. *Dir, prod* Tony Richardson for Woodfall; *scr* John Osborne, from the novel by Henry Fielding; *ph* Walter Lassally; *mus* John Addison; *cast* Albert Finney (Tom Jones), Susannah York (Sophia Western), Hugh Griffith (Squire Western), Edith Evans (Miss Western), Joan Greenwood (Lady Bellaston), David Warner (Blifil).

After the critical and commercial success of his earlier 'kitchen sink' films, A TASTE OF HONEY (1961) and *The Loneliness of the Long Distance Runner* (1962), Tony RICHARDSON had considerable difficulty in finding finance for his next, and far more costly, project. UNITED ARTISTS finally backed and distributed *Tom Jones*, a high-spirited romp based on a picaresque and distinctly improper eighteenth-century novel. At a cost of £500,000 it was one of the most expensive British productions to date; it had world-wide commercial success, particularly in the US.

**TONE**, FRANCHOT (1906–68), US actor, a prominent Broadway actor who first appeared on the screen in *The Wiser Sex* (1932). He attracted attention for his acting in *Gabriel over the White House* (1933), THE LIVES OF A BENGAL LANCER (1935), and THE MUTINY ON THE BOUNTY (1935). He achieved considerable popularity and made many films during the later thirties and forties, after which he worked in the theatre for some years before returning to the screen in the sixties to play character roles, notably the stubborn American president in Otto PREMINGER's *Advise and Consent* (1961).

**TONI**, France, 1935. 1½hr. *Dir* Jean Renoir; *prod* Films d'aujourd'hui; *scr* Renoir, Carl Einstein; *ph* Claude Renoir; *des* Leon Bourelly, Marius Brauquier; *ed* Marguerite Renoir, Suzanne de Troyes; *mus* Paul Bozzi; *cast* Charles Blavette (Toni), Jenny Hélia (Marie), Célia Montalvan (Josépha), Edouard Delmont (Fernand), Andrex (Gaby), Max Dalban (Albert).

The account in a Marseilles newspaper of the unhappy story of an immigrant worker caught RENOIR's attention and, aware of the resounding success of PAGNOL's tales of Marseilles life, he approached Pagnol, who lent him the facilities of his studios in Provence.

*Toni* is often cited as a forerunner of NEO-REALISM but was in fact unknown to the Italian directors of the forties. Renoir undoubtedly aimed at authentic settings, costumes, and performances and recounted a loosely woven succession of events in a laconic manner which carries a considerable degree of implicit social comment. But rather than the defined political commitment which is the mark of neo-realism, it reveals an impulse akin to that of certain Impressionist painters who sought the casual air of the snapshot in opposition to the formal posing of academic art.

**TONING**, the process of chemically staining a black-and-white print to produce an overall colour in the dark areas of the picture. Toning combined with TINTING (which colours only the light areas) was sometimes used in silent films to produce a remarkable two-colour effect. THE GOOD EARTH (1937) was, like other films with serious artistic aspirations, issued in sepia-toned prints. Modern films printed entirely on colour stock sometimes have black-and-white sequences which are subtly toned, intentionally or not, by slight imbalances in GRADING. (See COLOUR.)

**TOP HAT**, US, 1935. 1¾hr. *Dir* Mark Sandrich; *prod* Pandro S. Berman for RKO; *scr* Dwight Taylor, Allan Scott; *ph* David Abel; *mus, lyr* Irving Berlin; *dance dir* Hermes Pan; *cast* Fred Astaire (Jerry), Ginger Rogers (Dale), Edward Everett Horton (Horace Hardwick), Helen Broderick (Madge Hardwick), Eric Blore (Bates), Erik Rhodes (Beddini).

A tale of romantic complications hopping from London to Venice and attractive supporting performances (including Eric Blore as the valet who finally resolves the complications) help to make *Top Hat* one of the most delightful and enduring ROGERS–ASTAIRE musicals. Hermes Pan and Astaire created some fine dance numbers to Irving BERLIN's songs, especially the elegant 'Top Hat', 'Cheek to Cheek' developing from a dance floor into a romantic, flowing duet, and 'The Piccolino', danced to catchy Italian rhythms.

**TORRE-NILSSON**, LEOPOLDO (1924–  ), Argentinian director, son of the director Leopoldo Torres Rio for whom he started working at the age of fifteen. He was a scriptwriter and assistant director on several of his father's films before his first independent production *Días de odio* (1954), an adaptation of a short story by Jorge Luis Borges. His sixth feature *La Casa del angel* (*The House of the Angel*, 1957) was a turning-point in his career and in the history of the Argentinian cinema: a break with the traditional pallid comedies and melodramas produced for a market dominated by foreign products. Significantly, Torre-Nilsson first gained recognition abroad, particularly at European festivals, where his work sat comfortably within the category of 'art' cinema and could stand comparison in mood and intensity of feeling with that of BUÑUEL and BERGMAN. His vision of an isolated, Europeanized bourgeoisie stifled by a repressive Catholic morality is best expressed through the adolescent girls confronted by sin and its consequences in his three major films *La Casa del angel*, *La Caida* (*The Fall*, 1959), and *La Mano en la trampa* (*The Hand in the Trap*, 1961). All were adaptations of novels by Beatriz Guido, Torre-Nilsson's wife and frequent collaborator. Torre-Nilsson again attracted wide attention with *Boquitas pintadas* (*Painted Lips*, 1974), another study of false middle-class sentimentality.

**TOUCH OF EVIL**, US, 1958. 1½hr. *Dir* Orson Welles; *prod* Universal; *scr* Welles, from the novel *Badge of Evil* by Whit Masterson; *ph* Russell Metty; *mus* Henry Mancini; *cast* Charlton Heston (Vargas), Janet Leigh (Susan Vargas), Orson Welles (Quinlan), Marlene Dietrich, Mercedes McCambridge.

The investigations of Vargas, a narcotics inspector, in a Mexican border town, reveal the corrupt practices of the police chief, Quinlan. Directed with great virtuosity by WELLES, the deliberately confusing plot is laced with violence and perversion, as though parodying the 'B' picture genre. Welles's overpowering performance as Quinlan consistently threatens to slip into caricature, but Charlton HESTON's authoritative acting stands out even among the film's other felicities. *Touch of Evil* has been both widely attacked and hailed as a masterpiece. It has become something of a cult film among admirers of the FILM NOIR.

**TOURNEUR,** JACQUES (1904– ), US director, son of Maurice Tourneur, began his career as a director in France before going to Hollywood in 1935 and making a number of short subjects for METRO-GOLDWYN-MAYER, followed by his first American feature films for the same company, including *Nick Carter, Master Detective* (1940) with Walter PIDGEON in the title role. His fame rests primarily on the macabre films he made for RKO, mostly in partnership with the producer Val LEWTON. (The two first worked together in 1935, when they collaborated on the revolution sequences for MGM's *A Tale of Two Cities*.)

The first and best of Tourneur's horror films was CAT PEOPLE (1942), a new variation on lycanthropy, with Simone SIMON effective in the leading role. *I Walked with a Zombie* (1943) was a strange, sometimes eerie, and for its time unusual excursion into zombie lore; and *The Leopard Man* (1943) established an atmosphere of terror and foreboding, with a museum curator finally unmasked as the villain. Also notable were *Experiment Perilous* (1945), a more orthodox type of chiller in which Hedy LAMARR played the wife of a madman, and *Out of the Past* (1947, *Build My Gallows High* in GB), a sombre thriller which some consider to be Tourneur's masterpiece.

His later work, which included a number of Westerns, tended to be less distinguished; but he made an effective return to the macabre with *Night of the Demon* (1957, *Curse of the Demon* in GB) and a burlesque of the genre in the enjoyable *Comedy of Terrors* (1965) which assembled a formidable collection of horror-film veterans: Vincent PRICE, Peter LORRE, Boris KARLOFF, and Basil RATHBONE.

**TOURNEUR,** MAURICE (1876–1961), French-born director, real name Maurice Thomas, worked as an interior designer and book illustrator before, in 1900, entering the theatre as an actor. The following year he was combining acting and direction and in 1911 went over to directing films for Éclair, moving in 1914 to the Éclair studio in New Jersey. During the next ten years he became one of America's most respected directors: in 1918 he ranked behind only GRIFFITH and INCE in popularity.

Tourneur's films had a distinctive aestheticism, with meticulous décors and pictorial compositions. He was particularly successful with fantasy films: *The Wishing Ring* (1914), *Trilby* (1915), *The Blue Bird*, and *Prunella* (1918) are outstanding examples of his ability to create a fairy-tale world. His adaptations of literary classics, including *Victory* (1919), from Joseph Conrad, *Treasure Island* (1920), *The Last of the Mohicans* (1921), and *Lorna Doone* (1922), were also notable for their visual perfectionism.

In 1926 Tourneur quarrelled with his current producers, METRO-GOLDWYN-MAYER, and returned to Europe. He made one film in Germany, *Das Schiff der verlorene Menschen* (1927), then lived in France until his death. He continued to direct until 1949, when he was crippled in a car crash. His sound films are polished and effective, including thrillers such as *Accusée, levez-vous* (1930) and *Au nom de la loi* (1932) and historical romances like *Koenigsmark* (1936), *Katia* (1938), and *Mam'zelle Bonaparte* (1941). Probably the best is *La Main du diable* (1942), a Faust-like story that harks back to the fantasies of his most important work.

**TRACY, SPENCER** (1900–67), US actor, gave up his study of medicine to become an actor in New York. He appeared in a number of Broadway plays and after catching the notice of Hollywood with his portrayal of Killer Mears in *The Last Mile*, he appeared in John FORD's *Up the River* (1930). Because of his rugged looks he was at first type-cast as a HEAVY and appeared in several GANGSTER FILMS such as *Quick Millions* (1931) and *20,000 Years in Sing-Sing* (1933). *Man's Castle* (1933) gave him a change to sympathetic roles and FURY (1936), in which he played the innocent victim of mob violence, confirmed this new tendency. He won best acting OSCARS two years running for his warm-hearted, resourceful characterizations in *Captains Courageous* (1937) and *Boys' Town* (1938).

During the thirties and forties Tracy was one of METRO-GOLDWYN-MAYER's major stars. WOMAN OF THE YEAR (1942) was the first of nine films he was to make with his famous screen partner Katharine HEPBURN: among the others were ADAM's RIB (1949), *Pat and Mike* (1952), *Desk Set* (1957, *His Other Woman* in GB), and his last film *Guess Who's Coming to Dinner* (1967). Although very different personalities they were perfect foils, Tracy's steady unpretentiousness and dry humour contrasting delightfully with Hepburn's highly-strung elegance and flashing wit. George CUKOR directed a number of their films and the three were close friends. It was generally recognized that Tracy and Hepburn were for many years a devoted couple in their private life and the relationship is affectionately described in Garson KANIN's book *Tracy and Hepburn* (New York, 1970).

In his later years Tracy developed another screen image—the wise but strict father, statesman, or judge who was always dignified and honest without being stuffy or humourless. His films of this period include *Father of the Bride* (1950), *Bad Day at Black Rock* (1954), *The Old Man and the Sea* (1958), *The Last Hurrah* (1958), in which he played an Irish-American politician closely based on James Curley, the famous mayor of Boston, *Inherit the Wind* (1960), and *Judgement at Nuremburg* (1961).

**TRADER HORN**, US, 1931. 2hr. *Dir* W. S. Van Dyke; *prod* MGM; *scr* Dal Van Every, John Thomas Neville, from the book by Aloysius Horn and Ethelreda Lewis; *ph* Clyde De Vinna; *ed* Ben Lewis; *cast* Harry Carey (Trader Horn), Edwina Booth (Nina T), Duncan Renaldo (Peru), Olive Golden (the missionary).

Based on a once-famous book concerning an old river trader's adventures in Africa, the film version became an improbable novelette of the trader's encounter with a widowed missionary, and, following her death, his search for her daughter, seized as a young girl by hostile natives and now their tribal goddess. Nevertheless, the film initially made a great impact for its photography and extensive location work. Edwina Booth, playing her first major role, contracted a rare tropical disease during the making of the film.

A classic of its time, *Trader Horn* has not weathered the years well. The animal sequences, the jungle, river, and waterfall settings, the tribal dances and celebrations, remarkable for their authenticity in 1931, have become the stock items of jungle films.

**TRADE SHOW,** a private performance to introduce a new film to exhibitors and trade press reviewers. In Britain the trade show has been obligatory since the Cinematograph Films Act of 1909 which, as well as setting up regulations for the licensing of cinemas, sought to provide equitable opportunities for exhibitors to select films: distributors could not offer a film for hire, or exhibitors book it, until it had received its trade show. After the setting up of the BRITISH BOARD OF FILM CENSORS in 1912, the police were authorized to forbid any trade show if the film did not carry the censor's certificate, but this authority is not necessarily exercised.

Although the statutory obligation to hold trade shows still applies, the growth of monopolistic circuits has made its original purpose obsolete and the trade show has declined from a crowded, exciting occasion to an anachronistic formality.

Under British law the trade show is accepted as the act of publication in the country concerned. A film should not be altered in any way (shortened, lengthened, or rearranged) once the trade show has taken place, although this rule is regularly broken.

In the US the term has little currency: there is no statutory obligation to hold trade shows and the act of publication has not been legally defined.

**TRAILER,** short (3–4 minute) film advertising a forthcoming cinema programme, usually by presenting high spots from the film promoted. Variations on this pattern have included appearances by stars describing and recommending their new films.

Trailer-making is usually contracted out to a company specializing in this and similar work. Considerable skill is needed to select and cut together the best moments and to mount titles and commentary so as to create the desired impression of a film. Optical effects may be used with great resourcefulness to heighten the impact of the material: but, like all advertising, the result may be over-strained. The trailer should ideally convey the particular flavour of a film while attracting the widest possible audience.

In Britain trailers are subject to certification by the BRITISH BOARD OF FILM CENSORS. As the restrictions applying to 'x' CERTIFICATE films operate for the whole of a programme which includes such a film, trailers are generally designed to qualify for 'U' or 'A' CERTIFICATES, enabling them to be shown to any category of audience

Brief information or PROPAGANDA spots, shown in Britain at the end of NEWSREELS by government order during the two world wars, were also called trailers. In fact, any very short film which is not a paid advertisement is known to the trade as a trailer, and the term may be applied to subjects as diverse as the promotion of ice cream sales and the visual accompaniment to the playing of the National Anthem.

*TRAMP, The*, US, 1915. 30min. *Dir, scr* Charles Chaplin; *prod* Mutual; *ph* Rollie Totheroh; *cast* Charlie Chaplin (the Tramp), Fred Goodwins (the farmer), Edna Purviance (his daughter), Lloyd Bacon (her lover), Bud Jamison (tramp), Paddy McGuire (farm hand).

In CHAPLIN's later films, the comedy seems sometimes to be overwhelmed by pathos. This element can perhaps first be observed in *The Tramp* which, though critics see it as a landmark in his career, Chaplin did not even mention in his autobiography. When Charlie finally realizes that he cannot possibly win the farmer's beautiful daughter, he walks sadly away from the camera down a long straight road. Just before the final fade-out, he kicks his heels in the air and scampers joyfully off into the distance. It is one of the most familiar images of the twentieth century, and Chaplin's trademark.

**TRANSIT,** German distributors, set up in 1949 by the West German government to handle the feature films and newsreels of the Third Reich which remained in Germany after Allied confiscations. Recently, however, their right to ownership of COPYRIGHT has been challenged.

**TRAUBERG,** ILYA (1905 or 1907–48), Russian director, brother of Leonid, entered cinema as a writer. His first film was *Leningrad sevodniya* (*Leningrad Today*, 1927). He was assistant to EISENSTEIN on OKTIABR (1928). The following year he made *Colubi Ekspress* (*China Express*, 1929), an effective melodrama about the colonial powers in China. *Syn Mongolii* (*Son of Mongolia*, 1936) was an attempt to find a film method to reflect folklore. The entire film is sung and acted by the hero,

telling of all the strange people and places he has encountered. Trauberg's later films include *My zhdyom vas s pobedoi* (*We Expect Victory There*, 1941), his contribution to the war effort, and *Aktrisa* (*The Actress*, 1943).

**TRAUBERG,** LEONID (1902–  ), Russian director, brother of Ilya, met Grigori Kozintsev in 1921 and worked mostly in collaboration with him. (For details of their joint career see KOZINTSEV.) The work he did alone includes the scenario for *Zhizn v tsitadeli* (*Life in the Citadel*, 1947).

**TRAUNER,** ALEXANDER (1906–  ), French designer of Hungarian origin, studied painting in Paris. He was Lazare MEERSON's assistant on several films including René CLAIR's A NOUS LA LIBERTÉ (1931) and LE MILLION (1932) and Jacques FEYDER's *Pension Mimosas* (1935) and LA KERMESSE HÉROÏQUE (1935). He had collaborated on the set designs for L'AFFAIRE EST DANS LE SAC (1932) and went on to form part of the CARNÉ/PRÉVERT team, working on QUAI DES BRUMES (1938), *Hotel du Nord* (1938), LE JOUR SE LÈVE (1939), LES VISITEURS DU SOIR (1942), and LES ENFANTS DU PARADIS (1945), made in Nice during the Occupation. He worked for Orson WELLES in Morocco on OTHELLO (1951) and in Paris for Billy WILDER on *Love in the Afternoon* (1957). Since 1960 he has worked in both Hollywood and Europe and has been particularly associated with films directed by Wilder, Fred ZINNEMANN, and Anatole LITVAK.

**TRAVELLING MATTE** see MATTE

*TREASURE OF THE SIERRA MADRE, The*, US, 1948. 2hr. *Dir* John Huston; *prod* Warner Bros; *scr* Huston, from the novel by B. Traven; *ph* Ted McCord; *mus* Max Steiner; *cast* Humphrey Bogart (Dobbs), Walter Huston (Howard), Tim Holt (Curtin), Bruce Bennett (Cody), Barton MacLane (McCormick).

John HUSTON's uncompromising film on a theme of gold lust and greed represents a peak of his achievement. It was the one occasion on which he directed his father who, only two years before his death, was memorable in the role of an experienced old prospector. It is arguable that both Walter HUSTON and Humphrey BOGART gave the performances of their careers, and Bogart's cumulative study in human disintegration proved that he was not only a star but also an accomplished actor. Climactic irony has seldom been used to greater effect: the deranged and treacherous Dobbs is attacked by bandits and killed for his boots and his mules, while the valuable gold dust is scattered in the wind.

**TRENKER,** LUIS (*c.* 1892–      ), Austrian actor and director, worked first as a stunt man for Arnold FANCK and then starred in some of his films. He went on to direct his own films in which he also acted, the most famous being *Der Rebell* (1932), a strongly nationalistic film about the Tyrol's revolt against Napoleon. Under the Nazis he was at first in favour and made his finest film *Der verlorene Sohn* (1934), but he was blacklisted in 1940. He returned to directing after the war and his films include *Flucht in die Dolomiten* (1955) which he also scripted with PASOLINI.

**TREVOR,** CLAIRE (1909 or 1912– ), US actress, real name Wemlinger, entered films in 1933. Among the unluckier of Hollywood actresses, she was usually relegated to roles of the hard-shell-with-a-soft-centre type in 'B' pictures or routine films. However, her performance in John FORD's STAGECOACH (1939) and her playing of the drink-sodden moll in John HUSTON's *Key Largo* (1948), for which she won an OSCAR, are convincing evidence that for most of her long career her talent was wasted.

**TRIAL, The**, see PROCÈS, LE

**TRIANGLE,** US distribution company founded in 1915 by H. E. Aitken. Adam Kessel and Charles O. Baumann, vice-presidents, whose New York Motion Picture Company produced under the trade-marks BISON, K-B, and KEYSTONE, had joined Aitken and others in the MUTUAL distribution consortium. Aitken's successful gamble in backing THE BIRTH OF A NATION (1915) against the resistance of the other Mutual executives prompted him to form the new company. He brought D. W. GRIFFITH with him as Kessel and Baumann brought their most valuable properties, Thomas INCE and Mack SENNETT: the name 'Triangle' was based on these three striking assets, who also became company vice-presidents.

It was at first a marketing organization, handling the films of the constituent companies in specified programmes released by exclusive contract with exhibitors in the main cities. Aitken's aims were grandiose and ill-judged: he calculated on repeating the staggering profits made by *The Birth of a Nation* with all his 'quality' productions made under the Fine Arts mark and supervised by Griffith. He engaged well-known stage actors at unusually high salaries, in spite of the comparative failure of a similar policy attempted by Adolph ZUKOR a few years before (see FAMOUS PLAYERS). Although the first Triangle programme, shown at the Knickerbocker Theater on Broadway (the first of his projected chain of 'Theaters of Science and Artifice'), did

not meet with the acclamation he expected, he built large studios at Culver City and made much of the large sums spent on each production.

Exclusive distribution and high production costs were not supported by a product popular enough to attract audiences at the high admission prices demanded by Triangle programmes. The only stage actor to achieve stardom through his association with Triangle was Douglas FAIRBANKS: his polished comedies, Westerns starring W. S. HART, and Sennett's established comic team provided the main appeal. Ince's films were of a consistently high standard, but Griffith's creative energies were absorbed by INTOLERANCE (1916), an independent production. Triangle was undercapitalized for such an ambitious project and, in spite of the array of founding talents, the complex financial juggling needed to make the company viable was beyond the optimistic Aitken.

In 1917 Ince, Sennett, Fairbanks, Griffith, Hart, and Anita LOOS went to Zukor at PARAMOUNT and the following year the new studios were leased to Samuel GOLDWYN. Triangle lingered on, producing modest films at the old Inceville studios (which had been retained when the new ones were built) and leaning for a time on re-issuing old W. S. Hart films under new titles, a shady practice that was stopped by the threat of an injunction by the Federal Trade Commission. In 1921 a suit was brought against Aitken which exposed sharp dealings between the various companies under his management, and the final winding up of Triangle took place in 1923.

Kalton C. Lahue, *Dreams for sale*, New York, London, 1971.

**TRICKWORK** see EFFECTS

**TRIGGER,** a golden Palomino, 'the smartest horse in the movies', bought for less than $300, carried Roy ROGERS through most of his films. Trigger died at the age of twenty-eight, having been replaced by an identical Trigger Jr.

**TRINTIGNANT,** JEAN-LOUIS (1930–   ), French actor, began his career in Paris in 1950, entering films in 1955. His first major role was in ET DIEU CRÉA LA FEMME (1956). An unusually cryptic actor, with pale, expressionless eyes and a habitually repressed manner, who nevertheless conveys a variety of characterizations through very economical means, he worked consistently in France and Italy and eventually achieved an international reputation with *Un Homme et une femme* (Claude LELOUCH, 1966). Since then he has gained increasing recognition with such striking films as *Trans-Europ-Express* (ROBBE-GRILLET, 1966), *Les Biches* (CHABROL, 1968), z

(1968), MA NUIT CHEZ MAUD (1968), IL CONFOR-
MISTA (1970), *Le Voyou* (Lelouch, 1970), and
*L'Attentat* (*Plot*, 1972). He has appeared in films
directed by his wife Nadine and in 1973 directed
his first film, a black comedy *Une Journée bien
remplie*.

**TRI PESNI O LENINYE** (*Three Songs of
Lenin*), USSR, 1934. 1½hr. *Dir* Dziga Vertov;
*ph* Surensky, Magidson, Monastyrsky; *mus*
Shapovin.

The film links progress in Russia and change
in Spain and China with LENIN's teachings. VER-
TOV used images suggested by three folk songs
from Uzbekistan in Soviet Central Asia with the
songs themselves determining the structure of
the film, paralleling form and content. More
emotional than his other work, it is not a COM-
PILATION: it employs only one section of archive
footage, cut into fresh material. Technically
advanced, the film is built on contrasts of past
and present, and uses the countryside and
industry for symbolic and almost abstracted effect, heightened by an emotional sound-track of
funeral marches and Lenin's one recorded
speech.

**TRIUMPH DES WILLENS** (*The Triumph of
the Will*), Germany, 1934. 2hr. *Dir, ed* Leni
Riefenstahl; *prod* Leni Riefenstahl Produktion;
*ph* under the supervision of Sepp Allgeier; *mus*
Herbert Windt.

RIEFENSTAHL's film was commissioned by Hitler as the official Nazi record of the Nuremberg
Party Rally of 1934. Preparations for the Rally
were made in conjunction with preparations for
the camerawork. A staff of 120 was employed
which included about 40 cameramen with assistants. The film was intended as an important
piece of political propaganda, to introduce the
new leaders to the nation and to impress foreign
audiences.

In its manipulation of people as ornaments
and its use of monumental architecture for
dramatic effect, the film is clearly influenced by
Fritz LANG's DIE NIBELUNGEN (1924). The buildings of the old town of Nuremberg are used to set
the National Socialist Party against the backdrop of ancient German tradition.

*Triumph des Willens* is a masterpiece of EDIT-
ING. The atmosphere of the event is intensified by
the rhythmic cutting and the carefully contrived
sequences. From the arrival of Hitler by aircraft

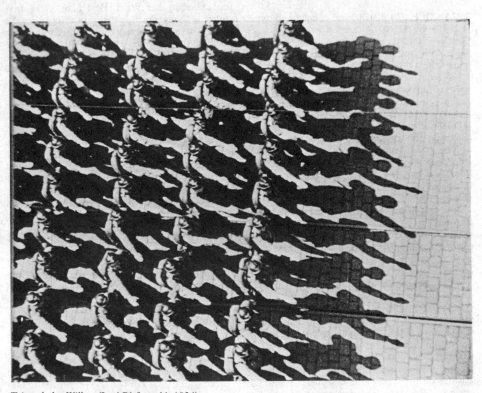

*Triumph des Willens* (Leni Riefenstahl, 1934)

to the close of the Rally both the cameras and the people seem to be in perpetual motion. The camera records the ecstatic faces, the marching columns, the waving banners, and the ornamental effect of the representatives of German workers massed together in the huge stadium. Little time is devoted to the speeches; the power comes almost entirely from the images.

After the war, a copy was taken to the US and distributed in a cut and re-edited version that was disowned by Riefenstahl. Rights to the original film were taken over by TRANSIT: Riefenstahl, claiming that the film was made independently and was never the property of the National Socialist Government, has fought several cases to gain personal control of the copyright.

**TRNKA, JIŘÍ** (1912–69), Czech puppet animator, was introduced to marionettes at an early age by the puppeteer Josef Skupa. In 1935 he became an illustrator, particularly of tales by Grimm, Andersen, and Hauff, and a stage designer. The following year, inspired by Maeterlinck's puppet plays, he established a puppet theatre, but it was only mildly successful and he returned to his successful career as a book illustrator.

After the war he made several colourful animated films, drawing on fairy-tale and Czechoslovak tradition: they include *Zasadil dědek řepu* (*Grandpa Plants Beet*, 1945), *Zvířátku a Petrovšti* (*The Animals and the Brigands*, 1946), and *Dárek* (*The Gift*, 1946). An anti-Nazi comment, *Pérak a SS* (*The Devil on Springs*, 1946), invoked the bitter feeling of the time. He returned to his first love with the puppet film *Špaliček* (*The Czech Year*, 1947) which won a prize at VENICE. He reconsidered the design of puppets for the camera, limiting the range of movement, enlarging the head, and concentrating expression around the eyes. He also suited the appearance to the subject: in *Císařův slavik* (*The Emperor's Nightingale*, 1948), for example, the characters have mysterious, translucent masks.

Two characteristic themes of Trnka's work are the harmony of rural life, represented by *Árie prérie* (*Song of the Prairie*, 1949), and the importance of the individual, expressed in his three-part version of *Dobrý voyák Švejk* (*The Good Soldier Schweik*, 1954). He departed from social comment for the intricate richness of *Sen noci svatojánské* (A MIDSUMMER NIGHT'S DREAM, 1958), then made two savage allegories, *Ruka* (*The Hand*, 1965) and *Archangel Gabriel a pani Husa* (*Archangel Gabriel and Mother Goose*, 1965).

Trnka was a restless and wide-ranging artist: painter, sculptor, draughtsman, and author of fantastic fairy-tales. He remains the pre-eminent figure in the strong tradition of Czech puppet film making. (See also PUPPET FILM.)

**TROU, Le** (*The Hole*), France/Italy, 1960. 2hr. *Dir* Jacques Becker; *prod* Play-Art/Filmsonor (Paris)/Titanus (Rome); *scr* Becker, José Giovanni, Jean Aurel, from the novel by Giovanni; *ph* Ghislain Cloquet; *cast* Philippe Leroy (Manu), Mark Michel (Gaspard), Jean Kéraudy (Roland), Michel Constantine (Geo), Raymond Meunier ('Monseigneur').

Five long-term convicts (played by non-actors) plan an escape which entails digging a tunnel through the prison vaults and into the Paris sewers. With painful realism BECKER shows every detail of their life in prison and the execution of their plan, together with the differing personalities of the men themselves. The characters are penetratingly explored and the development of their relationship up to the final betrayal is revealed with compassionate intensity. The sound-track uses only natural noises, and the film's stylistic austerity (contrasting with the richness of Becker's earlier work) aids the concentration on essentials which is the film's strength.

**TROUBLE IN PARADISE,** US, 1932. 1½hr. *Dir, prod* Ernst Lubitsch for Paramount; *scr* Samson Raphaelson and Grover Jones, from the play *The Honest Finder* by Laszlo Aladar; *ph* Victor Milner; *des* Hans Dreier; *mus* W. Franke Harling; *cast* Miriam Hopkins (Lily), Kay Francis (Marianne), Herbert Marshall (Gaston), Charlie Ruggles (the Major), Edward Everett Horton (François), C. Aubrey Smith (Giron).

The sophisticated tale of an amoral couple who fall in love and merge their talents as thieves until disaster threatens in the shape of a wealthy businesswoman was directed by LUBITSCH with deftness and originality. The film's other outstanding features were the adroit characterizations, flippant dialogue, and most of the acting performances (including characteristic contributions from Charlie RUGGLES, Edward Everett HORTON, and C. Aubrey Smith); and Hans Dreier's imaginative sets which at the time were regarded as the height of modernism.

**TROUBLE WITH HARRY, The,** US, 1955. Technicolor; 1½hr. *Dir, prod* Alfred Hitchcock for Paramount; *scr* John Michael Hayes from the novel by Jack Trevor Story; *ph* Robert Burks; *cast* Edmund Gwenn (Capt Wiles), John Forsythe (Sam), Shirley MacLaine (Jennifer), Mildred Natwick (Miss Gravely), Jerry Mathers (Tony).

The macabre story of a peripatetic corpse and various people who suspect they may be responsible for its state is depicted in autumnal settings of delicate and inapposite charm. HITCHCOCK's famous sly humour is here more like whimsy, but the film's engaging nonchalance is well sustained.

Shirley MACLAINE made a notable film début as the unfortunate Harry's widow.

**TRUFFAUT, FRANÇOIS** (1932– ), French director. His early life included a spell in a reformatory, desertion from military service, and consequent time in various prisons. His passion for cinema, nurtured by the programmes of the CINÉMATHÈQUE FRANÇAISE, brought him to the notice of André BAZIN, co-editor of CAHIERS DU CINÉMA. From 1951, for eight years, Truffaut wrote for *Cahiers* and earned the reputation of wielding its most acid pen. His first step in film-making was *Une Visite* in 1955, made on 16mm with Jacques RIVETTE and Alain RESNAIS. In 1956 he worked for a spell with ROSSELLINI, and formed his own company, Les Films du Carrosse (named from RENOIR's *Le Carrosse d'or*, 1953), to make *Les Mistons* in 1958. A short film of considerable if insubstantial charm, it sketches in what were to become two abiding characteristics of Truffaut's work: enjoyment of the medium itself, expressed here as admiration for some favourite directors, and sympathy for behaviour usually regarded as anti-social.

Another short film, *Histoire d'eau*, made with Jean-Luc GODARD, followed in 1959. In the same year, Truffaut's first feature film, LES QUATRE CENTS COUPS, won the prize for direction in the particularly challenging competition at CANNES. This, and the film's great success at home and abroad, established a reputation for Truffaut and the emerging NOUVELLE VAGUE with which his early career was associated. Recognition of cinematic influences and an unselfconscious freedom of expression combined with gentleness and clarity of observation to make a film of great charm yet hard-hitting authenticity.

Truffaut was associated during the same year, 1959, with Godard's first feature, A BOUT DE SOUFFLE (1960). He is usually credited with the non-existent script: certainly he lent his prestige to help Godard find financial backing for the film. Truffaut, who has collaborated on the scripting of all his own films, has also written scripts for three other films, including Jean-Louis Richard's *Mata Hari* (1964). He has the habit of using his company to help friends and colleagues by producing or co-producing their films, from Rivette's first feature, PARIS NOUS APPARTIENT (1960) to Eric ROHMER's MA NUIT CHEZ MAUD (1968).

In his next film, TIREZ SUR LE PIANISTE (*Shoot the Pianist*, 1960), Truffaut continued his exploration of what existing genres (in this case the American 'B' feature thriller) could offer as a framework for his own point of view. In JULES ET JIM (1961) he achieved a perfect balance of his qualities. With an assured ease and grace he used almost every cinematic device to produce a work of exhilaration and enduring charm. The film

repeated the critical and commercial success of *Les Quatre Cents coups*, and left Truffaut among the handful of directors who remained outstanding as the new wave subsided. In 1962 he was offered an episode in an international production, *L'Amour à vingt ans* (*Love at Twenty*), and used it for 'Antoine et Colette', a second instalment in the life of ANTOINE DOINEL, hero of *Les Quatre Cents coups*, once again played with diffident charm by Jean-Pierre LÉAUD. In *La Peau douce* (*Silken Skin*, 1963), Truffaut's concern with the fragmentation and isolation of modern city life made for an uncharacteristically cold-hearted film, which nevertheless frequently erupts with patches of spontaneous warmth.

Truffaut failed to find a French backer for a long-cherished project of filming *Fahrenheit 451*, Ray Bradbury's science fiction novel. Finally in 1966 American money enabled the film to be made in England, but in conditions of stress and strain which make it seem, alone of his films, lacking in zest and conviction. In *La Mariée était en noir* (*The Bride Wore Black*, 1967), he worked again with Jeanne MOREAU in a triumphant return to the FILM NOIR formula. *Baisers volés* (*Stolen Kisses*, 1968) continued the life and amorous adventures of Antoine Doinel in familiar light-hearted, wistful vein. *La Sirène du Mississippi* (1969), with Jean-Paul BELMONDO and Catherine DENEUVE, was perhaps more consciously aimed at the glossy international market than any other of Truffaut's films, but it retains his enjoyment of using conventional formulae and turning the apparently predictable to his own ends. In L'ENFANT SAUVAGE (1970) he returned to the theme of childish innocence and the conflict of adapting to the demands of society. The film, in which he also plays a leading role, is spare, shapely, and visually very beautiful: it breathes the spirit of elegance and reason of the age from which its story is taken, tempered by Truffaut's characteristic compassion. *Domicile conjugale* (*Bed and Board*, 1970) is another chapter in the story of Antoine Doinel, whose unfolding saga represents a form of autobiography rare in cinema. He chose Léaud to play another fey young lover in *Les Deux Anglaises et le continent* (*Anne and Muriel*, 1971). In LA NUIT AMÉRICAINE (*Day for Night*, 1973) Truffaut again acted a leading role, as a film director, and created a witty, loving celebration of cinema.

Truffaut has achieved in his work what many film-makers seek in vain, a distinctive personal expression within the accepted formulae of mass cinema. Impelled in the first place by an intoxication with the medium which he has never lost, he acknowledges a wide range of masters, from VIGO and Renoir to HITCHCOCK. Their influence and his own flair have been developed to a high degree of ease and accomplishment. His exhilarating use of camera movements and cutting are widely acknowledged: the care and effectiveness with which he uses dialogue and music have attracted less attention. For an advocate of the AUTEUR THEORY, he has drawn surprisingly often on literary sources, but (with the exception, perhaps, of *Fahrenheit 451*) has always reconceived the material in cinematic terms. His own work reflects all the qualities he admired in the early films of the *nouvelle vague*: grace, lightness, modesty, elegance, pace. The virulence of his critical writing has been conspicuously missing from his films. It is indeed precisely his gentleness and lack of condemnation that make him one of the most attractive among the masters of cinema.

Truffaut's *Le Cinéma selon Hitchcock* was published in Paris in 1966; and in English as *Hitchcock*, New York, 1967; London, 1968. *Les Films de ma vie*, Paris, 1975, is a collection of his critical writings. Graham Petrie's *The cinema of François Truffaut*, New York and London, 1970, is a perceptive and useful guide.

**TRUMBO,** DALTON (1905– ), US scriptwriter, made his name with a novel, *Johnny Got His Gun*, published in 1939. During the forties he was one of Hollywood's highest-paid writers: his films of this time include *Kitty Foyle* (1940), *A Guy Named Joe* (1943), *Thirty Seconds over Tokyo* (1944), and *Our Vines Have Tender Grapes* (1945). In 1947 he was blacklisted as one of the Hollywood Ten (see UNAMERICAN ACTIVITIES). He worked pseudonymously on several films, winning an OSCAR for the script of *The Brave One* (1957) under the name of Robert Rich, until 1960 when his name reappeared on the screen with EXODUS and SPARTACUS. He has since become re-established as an accomplished screenwriter with several films including *Lonely Are the Brave* (1962), *The Sandpiper* (1965), and *The Fixer* (1968); *Johnny Got His Gun* was filmed to his own script in 1971.

*Additional dialogue*, Trumbo's letters edited by Helen Manfull, New York, 1970, sheds new light on the careers of the Hollywood Ten.

**TRUST,** see MOTION PICTURE PATENTS COMPANY. The struggle between this group and smaller independent companies for control of the US industry between 1909 and 1913 is known as the Trust war.

**TURKEY.** Despite the potential audience offered by its population of approximately 25 million, local film production began only after the Second World War, and even now films are technically and artistically of poor quality. Actors are drawn mainly from the theatre. There is no state assistance (unlike the other arts) although an admission tax is levied. Imported films account for the greater proportion of exhibition. Attempts are currently being made by British interests to promote Turkey for location shooting, for which the variety of its countryside would be suitable. Labour is cheap, and on completion of a studio complex at Adana it could well take over from Italy and Spain. Censorship is applied, particularly in sexual matters; even kissing is not allowed on the screen.

**TURKSIB,** USSR, 1929. 1½hr. *Dir* Victor Turin; *prod* Vostok-Kino; *scr* Turin, Alexander Macheret, Viktor Shklovsky, Y. Aron; *ph* E. Slavinski, B. Frantzisson.

For propaganda reasons, the film, a documentary dramatizing the construction of the Turkestan–Siberian Railway, was completed before the railway itself. The film was presented to English audiences in a version prepared by John GRIERSON in consultation with Turin (the widely held belief that Grierson re-edited it is unfounded); and *Turksib* was undoubtedly an important influence upon the British documentary movement.

**TURNER,** LANA (1921– ), US actress, epitomized Hollywood glamour during the forties by the combination of intensive studio promotion (as 'The Sweater Girl') and her well-publicized private life. Her performances were rarely more than routine, one exception being the young wife in THE POSTMAN ALWAYS RINGS TWICE (1946). Her only other box-office success was *Imitation of Life* (Douglas SIRK, 1959), chiefly because of the plot's similarity to sensational events that had occurred in her own life.

**TUSHINGHAM,** RITA (1942– ), British actress, was born in Liverpool and educated at a convent there. Her first stage appearance was at the Royal Court Theatre in 1960 in *The Knack*. Her first film role, in A TASTE OF HONEY (1961), was an international success, winning several awards. Her subsequent films have included Sidney FURIE's *The Leather Boys* (1963), *Girl with Green Eyes* (1963), THE KNACK (1965), DOCTOR ZHIVAGO (1966), and *The Bed Sitting Room* (1969). A *jolie laide* character actress with a wistful air, she is capable at her best of touchingly naturalistic performances.

**TUTIN,** DOROTHY (1930– ), British actress best known for her stage career. In spite of a fragile appearance, she has given many strong, perceptive performances in both the classics and contemporary plays. Her occasional film roles are invariably striking; outstanding among them are her subtly witty Cicely in *The Importance of Being Earnest* (Anthony ASQUITH, 1952), Polly Peachum in THE BEGGAR'S OPERA (1953), and a steely Sophia Brzeska in *Savage Messiah* (Ken RUSSELL, 1972).

**TWELVE ANGRY MEN,** US, 1957. 1½hr. *Dir* Sidney Lumet; *prod* Henry Fonda, Reginald Rose for Orion-Nova Productions; *scr* Rose, from his own television play; *ph* Boris Kaufman; *cast* Henry Fonda (Juror No 8), Lee J. Cobb (No 3), Ed Begly (No 10), Martin Balsam (No 1).

Almost the whole film takes place in a jury-room where one man stands out against the majority assumption of guilt and insists on a full discussion of the evidence. The claustrophobic atmosphere leads to violent clashes of personality; a verdict of not guilty is ultimately returned.

LUMET had directed the play on television and he successfully transposed it to the large screen with very few changes. Like Delbert MANN, whose MARTY had scored an immense success the year before, John FRANKENHEIMER, and Arthur PENN, he helped to bring intimate subjects into the American cinema, in contrast with the large-scale epics then in vogue.

**TWENTIETH CENTURY,** US, 1934. 1½hr. *Dir* Howard Hawks; *prod* Columbia; *scr* Ben Hecht, Charles MacArthur, Charles Milholland from the play by Hecht and MacArthur; *ph* Joseph H. August; *cast* John Barrymore (Oscar Jaffe), Carole Lombard (Lily Garland), Walter Connolly (Webb), Roscoe Kearns (O'Malley).

The action is dominated by John BARRYMORE, playing an outrageous Broadway producer. Through imagination, zest, and superb comic timing, Barrymore turns what could have been a disastrous self-parody into a classic comic performance. He is matched by Carole LOMBARD's Hollywood star, who effectively counters every acting trick employed against her. Howard HAWKS kept the zany elements moving at break-neck pace.

**TWENTIETH CENTURY-FOX FILM CORPORATION,** US production and distribution company, a latecomer among the major Hollywood studios formed in 1935 by a merger of the two older companies, Twentieth Century Pictures Corporation and Fox Film Corporation. William FOX's company (see FOX FILM CORPORATION) had been in the film production business since 1915, but had been in a dire financial position since Fox himself was ousted in 1931. Twentieth Century Pictures had been set up in 1933 by Darryl F. ZANUCK and Joseph SCHENCK, who were responsible for negotiating the merger two years later with the floundering Fox company.

The company's imposing trademark—searchlights scanning the heavens above futuristic sky-scraping letters spelling the company's name—was soon to become synonymous in the public's mind with the type of 'big' feature entertainment possible only in Hollywood. The two men most responsible for the particular Fox formula of film-making were Zanuck, who had immediately taken over as head of production, a position he was to hold until 1956, and Spyros SKOURAS, who was company president for twenty years (1942–62). Their tight financial control and their own preferred subjects determined the output of the studio which consisted mainly of Westerns, musicals, religious epics, and, in later years, social message pictures. The best-remembered of these include John FORD's DRUMS ALONG THE MOHAWK (1939), THE GRAPES OF WRATH (1940), *How Green Was My Valley* (1941), MY DARLING CLEMENTINE (1946), and Henry KING's THE GUNFIGHTER (1950); musicals starring Betty GRABLE, Alice FAYE, Shirley TEMPLE, and, much later, Julie ANDREWS; epics such as *The Song of Bernadette* (1943), *David and Bathsheba* (1951), and Zanuck's own *The Longest Day* (1962); and controversial postwar dramas like *Gentleman's Agreement* (1947), *The Snake Pit* (1948), and *Pinky* (1949). The Fox roster of film-makers and stars included other major talents, notably directors Elia KAZAN, Joseph L. MANKIEWICZ, Jean NEGULESCO, and stars Marilyn MONROE, Tyrone POWER, Gregory PECK, Jennifer JONES, and Richard BURTON.

Early in 1953 Twentieth Century-Fox initiated the commercial development of wide screen film-making by taking an almost bankrupting chance on the ANAMORPHIC process originally discovered by Henri Chrétien which was rechristened CINEMASCOPE. Skouras himself was responsible for this venture which he hoped would be the solution to the drop in audience attendance caused mainly by the advent of television. The company's first wide-screen feature THE ROBE (1953) was received with more enthusiasm than the film itself merited, but Fox deserves praise for having taken the first major step in advancing film technology since the introduction of sound.

Fox also took an active part in furthering overseas productions of Hollywood companies, among other things financing most of the later British endeavours of Alexander KORDA. Elaborate overseas location shooting was a standard feature of many Fox films—an expensive habit which in 1962 almost destroyed the company. The disastrous CLEOPATRA (1962) not only cost Fox forty million dollars but also cost Skouras the presidency. Brought back from Europe, Zanuck was once again put in charge of Fox, although he put the studio in the hands of his son, Richard.

The overwhelming financial success of Robert WISE'S THE SOUND OF MUSIC (1965) put the studio back on its feet, but also led to an over-confidence which produced such expensive failures as *Dr Doolittle* (1967) and *Star!* (1968). To recoup costs Richard Zanuck countered with modestly budgeted successes like PLANET OF THE APES (1967) and M*A*S*H (1970) and with ex-ploitation movies such as *Valley of the Dolls* (1967), its sequel *Beyond the Valley of the Dolls* (1970), and *Myra Breckinridge* (1970). These latter films so outraged the Fox establishment that Zanuck was forced in 1971 to oust his son.

Like many of the major studios, Twentieth Century-Fox has had to depend on television films and series in recent years in an attempt to maintain its position as the only remaining Hollywood studio still run by the type of people who founded it.

John Gregory Dunn, *The studio*, New York, 1969, London, 1970.

**TWO CITIES,** British production company (the 'cities' being London and Rome), based at DEN-HAM STUDIOS in the halcyon days of the RANK ORGANISATION. Although it did not evolve an individual style comparable with EALING STUDIOS, under the control of Filippo DEL GIUDICE the company was for some fifteen years responsible for entertainment films of consider-able distinction. Versions of reputable novels included Compton Mackenzie's *Carnival* (1946), Stefan Zweig's *Beware of Pity* (Maurice ELVEY, 1946), Daphne du Maurier's *Hungry Hill* (1947), F. L. Green's ODD MAN OUT (Carol REED, 1947), Howard Spring's *Fame is the Spur* as scripted by Nigel Balchin (Roy BOULTING, 1947), Hugh Walpole's *Mr Perrin and Mr Traill* (1948), F. Anstey's *Vice Versa* (Peter USTINOV, 1948), and H. G. Wells's *The History of Mr Polly* (1949).

OLIVIER'S HENRY V (1944) and HAMLET (1948) were Two Cities productions, and the company co-produced with Cineguild David LEAN's *This Happy Breed* (1944) and *Blithe Spirit* (1945); but the director particularly associated with Two Cities over a long period was Anthony ASQUITH, from *French without Tears* (1939) and *The Demi-Paradise* (1943) to *The Importance of Being Earnest* (1952) and *The Net* (1953).

In later years, the company showed a notice-able predilection for adaptations of short stories: *The Rocking-Horse Winner* (1949) from D. H. Lawrence; *Prelude to Fame* (1950) from Aldous Huxley; and *Encore* (1951) with T. E. B. CLARKE crossing from Ealing to Denham to script one

of the episodes in this third and best of the W. Somerset Maugham EPISODE films. Other dis-tinguished films under the Two Cities banner included IN WHICH WE SERVE (1942), *The Way Ahead* (Reed, 1944), *Men of Two Worlds* (Thor-old DICKINSON, 1946), and *School for Secrets* (Ustinov, 1946).

**TWO OR THREE THINGS I KNOW ABOUT HER** see DEUX OU TROIS CHOSES QUE JE SAIS D'ELLE

**2001: A SPACE ODYSSEY,** GB, 1968. Super Panavision; 2½hr; Metrocolor. *Dir, prod* Stanley Kubrick for MGM; *scr* Kubrick, Arthur C. Clarke, based on Clarke's 'The Sentinel'; *ph* Geoffrey Unsworth; *des* Tony Masters, Harry Lange, Ernest Archer; *mus* Richard Strauss, Johann Strauss, Ligeti; *cast* Keir Dullea (Bow-man), Gary Lockwood (Poole), William Syl-vester (Floyd), Douglas Rain (Voice of Hal 9000).

*2001* marks a milestone in the use of photo-graphic special effects: most of the techniques used are not new, but they are here brought to a remarkably accomplished peak. Sequences of the travelling space-ship with the actions of the crew members visible through a window were con-structed by the very precise use of double ex-posure: the model ship was photographed first, in very slow motion so as to achieve maximum depth of focus without great increase of lighting, and with the window area blacked out, then the action scenes were projected separately and filmed on the same negative. The strictly con-trolled camera movements necessary were achieved by the use of a specially constructed camera animating device, with which the camera could be moved in any direction with absolute accuracy. Front-projection techniques were greatly improved, and the problems of conveying the illusion of weightlessness were overcome with greater success than ever before. KUBRICK'S concern with the special effects, which he designed and directed himself, led him to make *2001* in Britain, where he found technical facilities for his very ambitious requirements.

This brilliantly controlled venture into science fiction is not however merely a display of film technique: it expresses Kubrick's typically wry view of the human condition. The characters are all but extinguished by the wealth of tech-nological detail, and the unconscious subjection of man to exterior manipulation is ironically juxtaposed with the opulent technical skill of the film.

**TWO WEEKS IN ANOTHER TOWN,** US, 1962. CinemaScope; 1¾hr; Metrocolor. *Dir* Vin-cente Minnelli; *prod* John Houseman for MGM; *scr* Charles Schnee, from the novel by Irwin

Shaw; *ph* Milton Krasner; *des* George W. Davis, Urie McCleary; *mus* David Raksin; *cast* Kirk Douglas (Jack Andrus), Edward G. Robinson (Kruger), Cyd Charisse (Carlotta), George Hamilton (Davie Drew), Dahlia Lavi (Veronica), Claire Trevor (Clara Kruger).

Jack Andrus, a former star recovering from a breakdown, flies to Rome to resume his career and finds himself drawn into the old world of lies and illusion. A potentially fascinating study of people who have lost touch with the reality outside the movie business, the film was, in MINNELLI's opinion, marred by studio cutting. It is nevertheless an appropriately brash view of a synthetic, chaotic world.

**TYLER**, PARKER (d.1974), American film theorist who, since the publication of *The Hollywood hallucination* (1944) and *Magic and myth of the movies* (1947), has been one of America's best-known film critics. His early analyses of Hollywood cinema in terms of its unconscious, mythic aspects latterly gave way to a concern with film aesthetics (*The three faces of film*, 1960, and his writings in FILM CULTURE), and with the experimental film-makers (*Underground film: a critical history*, 1969). His disenchantment with Hollywood did not lead to adulation of the experimentalists; but he claimed that any future cinematic achievement will stem from the avant-garde, not from the commercial establishment.

**TYPE-CASTING.** The limitations imposed by an actor's physical characteristics will inevitably restrict his range of roles: even an actor of the versatility of Alec GUINNESS would be unlikely to undertake Othello, for example. The rationale of type-casting lies on the one hand in easing the actor's task by matching a role to his inherent characteristics and on the other in directing the audience's response by providing a clearly identifiable character. EISENSTEIN recognized the advantages of 'typage', as he termed it, but usually selected his type for òne specific role. True type-casting—the repeated use of an actor in variations on one basic role—dates from the early years of film-making: Mary PICKFORD had a long struggle to break away from the childish roles she had played for GRIFFITH. The practice reached its peak in Hollywood films of the thirties and forties and has since been taken up virtually unchanged by the television series.

In light-entertainment films type-casting had the considerable advantage of saving time in establishing a character. A glimpse of supporting players such as Margaret DUMONT, ZaSu PITTS, Billie BURKE, Eugene PALLETTE, or Edward Everett HORTON, was sufficient to place them in the narrative, and their predictability made a large contribution to their popularity.

The type-casting of stars was more directly a commercial matter. Having pleased the public with a certain kind of role—Bette DAVIS as a soured spinster, Clark GABLE as a romantic cad, James CAGNEY as an arrogant criminal, Gary COOPER as a laconic man of action—they were expected by producers to capitalize on their success by repetitions of such parts. Most stars accepted this condition of continuing employment: some, notably Bette Davis and Olivia DE HAVILLAND, fought for the right to choose and vary their roles (see STAR SYSTEM).

Although type-casting will probably continue to be a factor in the cinema, as in any other dramatic medium, the breakdown of the studio system, with teams of contract players available for each production, has led to increased variety in casting both leading and supporting actors.

# U

**'U' certificate,** category instituted by the BRITISH BOARD OF FILM CENSORS soon after it was established in 1912 to designate films particularly suitable for children. By 1916 the category had expanded to take in any film suitable for 'universal' viewing. (See CENSORSHIP, GB.)

**UFA** (Universum Film Aktiengesellschaft), German production company founded in 1917 at the instigation of the German government which provided DM eight million to launch it. It was a result of a merger of the major production companies, Messter Film, Davidsons Union, the Nordisk group, and BUFA, the government-sponsored newsreel company; its purpose was to promote German culture and, by raising the standard of production, to improve Germany's image abroad. Artists like Emil JANNINGS, Ernst LUBITSCH, and Pola NEGRI joined the company.

With Germany's defeat in 1918 the Deutsche Bank acquired most of the government's shares and although the basic nationalist ideology was not relinquished, commercial considerations began to play a larger part. Among the company's earlier films were Joe MAY's *Veritas Vincit* (1918), a historical costume film inspired by CABIRIA (1914), *Die Augen der Mumie Ma* (1918), and CARMEN (1918), both directed by Lubitsch and starring Pola Negri. These films set the style for many of the UFA films to come. In the same year UFA set up its Kulturabteilung (education department) and also began to secure the rights to cinemas in neutral countries in order to overcome the post-war boycott of German films.

In 1919 the company's huge Film Palast am Zoo in Berlin was opened with the première of Lubitsch's *Madame Dubarry*, and in the ensuing years it acquired a large number of cinemas, as well as setting up its own distribution network. The same year also saw the founding of the important association of the German film industry, known as SPIO, in which UFA played an influential role.

In 1923 Erich POMMER became chief of production and merged his own company DECLA BIOSCOP with UFA. Through this merger UFA gained the large studios at NEUBABELSBERG. At this time Germany was facing increasing competition from Hollywood. The accompanying financial crisis led to UFA's specializing in Kulturfilme (documentary films), which were cheaper to make. The first to achieve success was *Wege zur Kraft und Schönheit* (*Ways to Strength and Beauty*, 1925), which was made with financial support from the government and shown in German schools. All the UFA films of this type were skilfully made but tended to emphasize the exotic at the expense of realism. Increased financial losses, however, forced UFA to sign contracts with PARAMOUNT and METRO-GOLDWYN-MAYER (the Parafumet Verleih), under which, in return for a loan, UFA put its QUOTA certificates and many of its cinemas at the disposal of the two companies, terms which were to prove disastrous. However, distinguished films were coming from UFA at this period, including DER LETZTE MANN (1924), VARIÉTÉ (1925), and METROPOLIS (1927).

By 1927 UFA was again near financial ruin. Dr Alfred Hugenberg, a powerful financier with pronounced National Socialist sympathies, bailed out the company and became head of the board of directors. His influence was to increase the nationalist direction of the company, partly through the newsreels, of which UFA owned four-fifths, and by the distribution of some of the party films. In the late twenties the grand style of the feature films had been abandoned for the more fashionable social films. PABST's *Die Liebe der Jeanne Ney* (1927), which UFA censored, and May's *Asphalt* (1929) were produced by the company.

The coming of sound brought with it one outstanding film DER BLAUE ENGEL (1930) and many musicals and operettas, made with superb craftsmanship and technical perfection. The most famous were *Drei von der Tankstelle* (1930) and DER KONGRESS TANZT (1931). Pommer left during this period to be replaced by Hugo Corell.

When the Nazis came to power UFA was gradually coerced into producing National Socialist films. One of the earliest was HITLER-JUNGE QUEX (1933). In 1935 the UFA Lehrschau was founded which had departments for film history plus a library and production archives. It was incorporated into the film school which opened in Berlin in 1938 (see REICHS-FILMKAMMER). In spite of increasing attendances, rising costs and the loss of the export market owing to Nazi policies led to large deficits in the years 1933–6. In 1937 the government anonymously bought up all the stock on the market and gained control, although the company retained its name. In 1941 the first German colour film was made, *Frauen sind doch bessere Diplomaten* by Georg Jacoby. In 1942 Liebeneiner became head of production. To mark UFA's 25th anniversary in 1943 the large spectacular *Münchhausen* was made. The company ceased production in 1945 and the Neubabelsberg studios became the centre of the East German production company DEFA.

A new company under the name of UFA was launched after the war but went bankrupt.

***UGETSU MONOGATARI*** (*Tales of the pale moon after rain*: but known in the West by its original title), Japan, 1953. 1½hr. *Dir* Kenji Mizoguchi; *prod* Daiei; *scr* Matsutaro Kawaguchi, Giken Yoda; *ph* Kazuo Miyagawa; *mus* Fumio Hayasaka; *cast* Masayuki Mori (Genjuro), Kinuyo Tanaka (Miyagi), Sakae Ozawa (Tobei), Mitsuko Mito (Ohama), Machiko Kyo (Princess Wasaka).

One of the most perfect films in the history of Japanese cinema, *Ugetsu monogatari* blends the traditions of the JIDAI-GEKI with modern observation of human emotions and with MIZOGUCHI's recurring study of the contrasting destructive and redeeming aspects of woman's love. In spite of the importance of the supernatural in the story, Mizoguchi's poetic approach never becomes fantasy: the quality of his vision is built up by the use of long-held camera set-ups, long shots, and gentle, deliberate camera movements, making a lyrical affirmation of human values against a background of war and suffering. As in many of his films the women are of vital importance, and the performances of Machiko KYO as the ghost princess and Kinuyo Tanaka as the potter's wife are of the highest quality.

**ULLMAN, LIV** (1938–   ), Norwegian actress born in Tokyo, studied drama in London and Stavanger, and appeared on the stage and in films in Norway before moving to Sweden. Her first important film role was the intensely difficult one of Elisabet Vogler in PERSONA (1966); since then she has worked regularly for Ingmar BERGMAN to whom she was for a time married. In *Vargtimmen* (*Hour of the Wolf*, 1968), *Skammen* (*Shame*, 1968), *En Passion* (*A Passion*, 1969), all directed by Bergman, and in *Utvandrarna* (*The Emigrants*, Jan Troell, 1970), she played

*Ugetsu monogatari* (Kenji Mizoguchi, 1953)

opposite Max VON SYDOW, conveying the physical and mental stress of the characters with a powerfully anguished conviction. Three Hollywood films in 1972–4 failed to provide rewarding roles: Bergman's *Scener ur ett aektenskap* (*Scenes from a Marriage*, 1974) gave her a part more suited to her particular talent.

***UMBERTO D,*** Italy, 1952. 1½hr. *Dir* Vittorio De Sica; *prod* Dear Films (Rizzoli–De Sica–Amata); *scr* Cesare Zavattini, De Sica; *ph* G. R. Aldo; *ed* Eraldo Da Roma; *mus* Alessandro Cicognini; *cast* Carlo Battista (Umberto D), Maria Pia Casilio (the maid), Lina Gennari (the landlady).

Dedicated by DE SICA to his father, this study of an old pensioner's struggle against destitution, loneliness, and indignity was a critical success and a box-office failure. The film has only two characters of importance, both played by non-professional actors: Umberto D (played by an elderly professor of philology) and the little pregnant servant girl, with whom he tries unsuccessfully to communicate. Flawed by its sentimentality, the film was nevertheless a sincere and courageous attempt by De Sica and ZAVATTINI to carry on the social comment of NEO-REALISM in the face of mounting reaction. The authors earned a public reproof from the Minister of the Interior.

***UMBRELLAS OF CHERBOURG*** see PARAPLUIES DE CHERBOURG, LES

**UNAMERICAN ACTIVITIES,** House Committee on, set up in 1938, continued its attacks on New Deal measures and personalities as 'Communist' even during the war years, when America's deep-rooted antipathy to Soviet Russia was necessarily glossed over. In 1945, under John E. Rankin and J. Parnell Thomas, the Committee became permanent, and spear-headed in America a resurgence of fear and hostility towards Communism which erupted after the war and culminated in the early fifties in McCarthyism.

Hollywood became the subject of a full-scale investigation by the Committee in 1947. 'Friendly' witnesses (i.e. friendly to the purposes of the Committee) included Adolphe MENJOU, Robert TAYLOR, Ronald REAGAN, Gary COOPER, Jack WARNER. Nineteen 'unfriendly' witnesses were subpoenaed: ten of them, rather than refuse to testify on the grounds that they might incriminate themselves (under the Fifth Amendment), chose to regard the Committee as unconstitutional. 'The Unfriendly Ten', later known as 'The Hollywood Ten', were indicted and imprisoned for contempt of Congress. They were: Alvah Bessie, Herbert BIBERMAN, Lester Cole,

Edward DMYTRYK, Ring LARDNER Jr, John Howard LAWSON, Albert Maltz, Samuel Ornitz, Adrian Scott, Dalton TRUMBO. The investigation unleashed a witch-hunt in Hollywood. Dozens of people 'blacklisted' found their contracts terminated, their careers broken or able to be pursued only through shabby deals, under assumed names, or abroad, among them Robert ROSSEN, Joseph LOSEY, and Carl FOREMAN. The existence of a blacklist was always denied by the producers, but mere refusal to co-operate with the constantly probing UnAmerican Activities Committee was officially enough, for instance, to preclude nomination for an OSCAR until 1959. Very few of the indicted ten or the blacklisted dozens have been able to work in Hollywood under their own names.

Alvah Bessie, in his *Inquisition in Eden*, New York, 1965, and *Additional dialogue*, the letters of Dalton Trumbo (New York, 1970), shed new light on the processes involved and the hardship and loss to individuals and to Hollywood.

**UNDERGROUND FILM,** term originating in the US in the late fifties and applied to the area of film-making hitherto described as experimental, personal, independent, or avant-garde.

The movement is rooted in the European AVANT-GARDE and ABSTRACT film and their successors in America during the twenties and thirties. A second, more concerted period of experimental film-making began in the forties on the West Coast, aided by the increased availability of cheap, good-quality 16MM stock and equipment. Intellectual influence and encouragement were provided by a number of artists and film-makers from Europe, among them Hans RICHTER and Marcel Duchamp in New York and Oskar FISCHINGER in Los Angeles. An increasing number of European films were screened and circulated by the Museum of Modern Art, including those of Jean COCTEAU.

A major obstacle was the lack of outlets. Maya DEREN was one of the first film-makers to tackle this problem by screening and distributing her own work and by campaigning for a new cinema. Her *Meshes of the Afternoon* (1943), made on the West Coast, was one of the first films to mark the renewed surge of activity and was a prime example of the 'trance' film, subjective and dream-like. Other important examples of this surreal style were James Broughton and Sidney Peterson's *The Potted Psalm* (1946) and Peterson's *The Lead Shoes* (1949); the latter made particularly effective use of the distorting potential of the ANAMORPHIC LENS. In the late forties a younger generation was emerging on the West Coast, working in the same mode; Kenneth ANGER (*Fireworks*, 1947), Gregory MARKOPOULOS (*Psyche*, 1948), and Curtis Harrington

(*Fragment of Seeking*, 1946) were more directly concerned with sexual dreams and adolescent visions. Together with Stan BRAKHAGE's early work, also appearing at this time, they are often described as 'psychodramas'.

In complete contrast to this Freudian approach was the development—still on the West Coast—of a sophisticated abstract cinema inspired at least in part by the presence of Fischinger. Harry Smith created his first three hand-painted films in 1939–47, working frame by frame with richly coloured abstract imagery. The WHITNEY brothers also used abstract imagery in *Five Film Exercises* (1943–5) but drew more on the Constructivist tradition, attempting to attain the emotional condition of music with their hard-edged forms.

In 1947 an important series of screenings and symposia entitled 'Art in Cinema' was started in San Francisco by Frank Stauffacher—who made *Sausalito* (1948), a film striving towards a visual equivalent of poetry—and Richard Foster. The meetings provided a centre for all the West Coast work to date and brought the new generation in touch with older film-makers, familiarizing them with past activity in Europe such as that of EGGELING and Richter.

On the East Coast too, activity was encouraged by increased screening facilities. Deren, now in New York, set up public screenings of her work and her success led to the foundation by Amos Vogel of Cinema 16 which became a showcase for films by Deren, Brakhage, Anger, Broughton, Harrington, and others. In 1950 it developed a distribution side, an important step since experimental film-makers had until then no similar outlet for their work. A second such organization was the Gryphon Group, set up by Willard Maas and his wife Marie Menken. Both were film-makers: Maas's *Geography of the Body* (1943) explored the human body in extreme close-up and Menken, with *Glimpse of the Garden* (1957) and *Go! Go! Go!* (1963), was one of the first to work in a simple, diary-like film form. Gryphon also helped produce films by Brakhage, Markopoulos, Charles Henri Ford, and Charles Boultenhouse.

The fifties was thus a period of mounting activity, particularly in New York where Hans Richter was now teaching, working on *8 × 8* (1952–3) with Duchamp, Hans Arp, and Cocteau, and polemicizing on behalf of the new developments. FILM CULTURE, a magazine of crucial importance to the growth of the New American Cinema was founded in 1955. Its principal editor Jonas MEKAS, assisted by his co-editors, made *Guns of the Trees* (1961). It was one of a number of feature-length experimental films that appeared at this time, taking some of

their inspiration from the French NOUVELLE VAGUE but in their style and subject matter more related to the American beat generation, then at its height. Other important examples were SHADOWS (John CASSAVETES, 1960), *The Connection* (Shirley CLARKE, 1961), and *Pull My Daisy* (Robert Frank and Alfred Leslie, 1959).

Towards the end of 1960 these directors and those of other low-budget films founded the New American Cinema Group, to be mainly concerned with the finance and distribution of independent feature films. The group denounced censorship and favoured films that were 'rough, unpolished, *but alive*'. The Film-makers Co-operative was founded in 1962, but it could offer a financial return only for the experimental short-film maker; there were insufficient funds to support even the cheapest features. As a result, small-scale, personal work became increasingly the object of enthusiastic support by Mekas and *Film Culture*.

The term 'underground film' became current towards the end of the fifties. Screenings of even innocuous films were often necessarily clandestine since the authorities consistently harassed the movement's major showcase, the film-makers Cinematheque in New York, on one occasion seizing Jean Genet's *Un Chant d'amour* (1950) and Jack SMITH's *Flaming Creatures* (1963) and arresting Mekas and other organizers of the screening.

Smith's film and others like it, such as Ron Rice's *Chumlum* (1964), reflected a post-Beat life style, a world of homosexuality, transvestism, drag, and sad city decadence that was transformed in *Chumlum* into a lyrical dream world by the use of a fluid camera and flowing veils of superimposition. *Flaming Creatures*, more static and a parody of Hollywood archetypes, was one of the first films to exploit the vogue for 'camp', the elevation of cheap fantasy into an elaborate, semi-serious genre. This direction was to be notably exploited by Andy WARHOL, who was partly inspired by Smith in making his immobile studies *Kiss* (1963), *Blow Job*, and *Couch* (both 1964).

The blatant sexual content and apparent nihilism of Smith's and Warhol's films tend to distract attention not only from the aesthetic innovations of their work but also from the importance of the experimental or avant-garde film in the wider context of modern art. The first half of the sixties saw major works by several of the central figures of the New American Cinema, including Brakhage's *Dog Star Man* (1959–64) and *The Art of Vision* (1965), Markopoulos's *Twice a Man* (1963), Anger's SCORPIO RISING (1964) and *Inauguration of the Pleasure Dome* (1954–66), and Harry Smith's feature-length surrealistic animation *Heaven and Earth Magic*

(1958–61). Although each film-maker's style is distinctive, they came together as a movement determined to approach cinema as a modernist art, frequently deriving their inspiration from advanced work in painting, poetry, and music rather than from film. They introduced new subject matter to film, usually very personal and often at this stage couched in mythic terms, creating new narrative and temporal structures and, particularly in the case of Brakhage, breaking down the inherently illusionist nature of cinema as based on Renaissance perspective. Other underground film-makers active at this time in New York included Robert Breer, a sculptor and painter, who was working in animation, creating rushing collages of frame-by-frame images (*Fist Fight*, 1964) and drawn abstracts (*Breathing*, 1963); the Kuchar brothers who were producing heavy parodies of Hollywood; Ken Jacobs; Stan Van Der Beek; Ed EMSHWILLER; and Peter Goldman.

On the West Coast the underground took distinctive forms, either lyrical or in a more earthy, pop, frequently collage, style. Bruce Baillie is the prime exponent of the lyrical underground. Using sensually beautiful and technically immaculate imagery, his most successful films are compressed into a brief, *haiku*-like form (*All My Life*, 1966), or are combined with the recurrent American metaphors of travel and space as in *Mass* (1963–4), a hymn to the Dakota Sioux, *Castro St* (1966), or *Quixote* (1965). A different spatial quality is evoked by Jordan Belson, another respected West Coast figure. His *Allures* (1961), *Re-Entry* (1964), and *Samadhi* (1967) make use of fluid, soft-edged, and highly abstracted imagery to convey a meditative yet very physical sense of a spatial 'trip'.

In the pop vein, Bruce Conner and Robert Nelson have both made collages of 'found' footage. Conner is primarily an editor with a strong sense of the texture of his material, including film LEADER. *A Movie* (1958) is a black, humorous parody of violent scenes—colliding cars, collapsing bridges. In *Report* (1965) he re-examines footage of the Kennedy assassination through varying re-looping. Nelson's *Confessions of a Black Mother Succuba* (1964–5) is a satire on exploitation, cutting violence and brash television commercials into soft-core pornography. Another satire, *Oh Dem Watermelons* (1965), is a play on assumptions about blacks and movies. *The Great Blondino* (1967) and *Blue Shut* (1970) are his most intriguing films, the latter an elaborate parody of a television panel game.

The growth of distribution co-operatives in Los Angeles and San Francisco encouraged West Coast creativity. Younger film-makers became involved, as few had in the East, in processing methods. Pat O'Neill, for example, often works with found footage but transforms it, as in *Runs Good* (1969–70), by work with an optical printer. Scott Bartlett, with *Off/On* (1967) and *Moon 69* (1969), a subjective impression of a trip to the moon, has exploited the potential of the printer to rework contrast and colour to an impressive richness. He has also used video processes to mix in colour and superimpose layers of imagery.

Michael SNOW's *Wavelength* (1967) signified a new trend in the New York underground, breaking away from the work of Anger, Brakhage, Smith, etc, and from the other currently prominent style, the diary film typified by Mekas's *Diaries, Notes and Sketches* (1964–9) or Andrew Noren's erotic *Kodak Ghost Poems* (1969). The new development again found support in *Film Culture*, where the critic P. Adams Sitney defined its formal style as 'structural'. Brakhage and Warhol were important predecessors, and again there were many parallels with the other contemporary New York arts, many of them formally 'minimal'. New spatio-temporal concepts were explored and the physical properties of film, its basic processes and syntax, became dominant. Tony Conrad's *The Flicker* (1966) and George Landow's *Film in which there appear lettering, sprocket holes, dirt particles etc* (1966) were two early examples; Landow has continued to make important contributions to the field, including *Institutional Quality* (1969) and *What's Wrong with this Picture* (1970), and Snow's *Back and Forth* (1969) was in effect a continuous exploration of the ZOOM shot.

Ken Jacobs, whose *Blonde Cobra* (1962) starring Jack Smith was a milestone of an earlier era, worked on found footage in *Tom, Tom the Piper's Son* (1969). He took a short film (shot, apparently, by Billy BITZER in 1905) and made a feature-length film by repeating brief sections, playing on the original's grain by re-filming from the screen. Hollis Frampton's *Zorns Lemma* (1970) and *Hapax Legomena* (1972–3) adopt current structuralist theories of linguistics; in the former film, arbitrary images are regularly substituted for letters of the alphabet, erecting a visual code of some complexity.

From the mid-sixties underground film became prominent in Western Europe, particularly Germany, Italy, Holland, and Britain, coinciding with tours made by Mekas and Sitney to show programmes from America. Two festivals at Knokke-le-Zoute in Belgium, in 1963 and 1967, were devoted to experimental cinema. The London Film-makers Co-operative was founded in 1966.

Most of the significant European films have been in the 'structural' style; major figures are Wilhelm and Birgit Hein and Werner Nekes in Germany (a fertile country for independent cinema, although political film has recently become dominant), and Malcolm Le Grice in England. Kurt Kren and Peter Kubelka from Austria have been influential in the new formal film, both in Europe and the US. Kren has been active since 1960, Kubelka, who is frequently considered part of the New American Cinema, since 1955.

Other important European film-makers include David Larcher whose *Mare's Tail* (1968) uses a lyrical, diary-like form to elaborate on the nature of film and perception. Steve Dwoskin, an American now working in England, is noted for the bleak eroticism of, among others, *Chinese Chequers* (1964) and *Trixie* (1969–70). In Germany, Dore O, Werner Schroeter, and Rosa Von Praunheim work outside the 'structural' film, the latter two in a curious style combining the 'camp' and the Brechtian.

Sheldon Renan, *The underground film*, London, 1968; David Curtis, *Experimental cinema*, London, 1971; P. Adams Sitney (ed), *Film culture: an anthology*, London, 1971; Gregory Battock (ed), *The new American cinema*, New York, 1967; Jonas Mekas, *Movie journal*, New York, 1972; P. Adams Sitney, *Visionary film*, New York and London, 1974; Gene Youngblood, *Expanded cinema*, London, 1970; *Form and structure in recent film,* Vancouver, 1972, including writings by Frampton, Sharits, Snow.

**UNDERWORLD** (*Paying the Penalty* in GB), US, 1927. 1½hr. *Dir* Josef von Sternberg; *prod* Paramount; *scr* Jules Furthman, Robert N. Lee, from a story by Ben Hecht; *ph* Bert Glennon; *des* Hans Dreier; *cast* Clive Brook ('Rolls Royce'), Evelyn Brent ('Feathers' McCoy), George Bancroft ('Bull' Weed), Larry Semon ('Slippy' Lewis).

Organized crime was a new theme in the cinema when *Underworld* appeared: the film's commercial success initiated the cycle of classic GANGSTER FILMS which lasted throughout the thirties. Few, however, attempted to emulate STERNBERG's baroque vision, which endows squalid urban settings with a perverse poeticism.

**UNFAITHFULLY YOURS,** US, 1948. 1¾hr. (96min. in GB). *Dir, scr* Preston Sturges; *prod* Twentieth Century-Fox; *ph* Victor Milner; *des* Lyle Wheeler, Joseph C. Wright; *mus* Alfred Newman; *cast* Rex Harrison (Sir Alfred de Carter), Linda Darnell (Daphne de Carter), Barbara Lawrence (Barbara), Rudy Vallee (August Henschler), Kurt Kreuger (Anthony), Lionel Stander (Hugo), Edgar Kennedy (Sweeney).

Sir Alfred de Carter, a famous orchestral conductor, mistakenly believes his wife to be unfaithful. His jealousy reaches fever pitch while he is conducting a concert of music by Rossini, Wagner, and Tchaikovsky, during which he imagines himself dealing with the situation in three different but equally drastic ways.

By common consent the best of Preston STURGES's later films, this burlesque comedy was original in conception and imaginative in execution. The disturbing undertones typical of Sturges's humour, however, produced confused reactions from both public and critics. In the role of the temperamental conductor, Rex HARRISON was given one of the most rewarding acting opportunities of his career.

**UNFRIENDLY TEN/NINETEEN** see UN-AMERICAN ACTIVITIES

**UNITED ARTISTS CORPORATION,** US production and distribution company formed in 1919 by Charles CHAPLIN, Douglas FAIRBANKS, Mary PICKFORD, and D. W. GRIFFITH. Unhappy with the lack of independence entailed in working under contract to others, the four founders set up the company to finance 'quality' films by independent film-makers and to negotiate distribution agreements outside the arbitrary system whereby a film was available only to cinemas linked to its production company (see DISTRIBUTION). Oscar Price, who had instigated this merging of talent, was named president of United Artists, a position held subsequently by Hiram Abrams and, from the mid-twenties, Joseph SCHENCK.

The uniqueness of United Artists was quickly apparent. The company owned no studio of its own, instead renting the studio space required for each production. Apart from stars who made their own films for UA release, the company existed without the elaborate star contract system which was already beginning to make a costly impact on the other Hollywood companies. UA had no cinema holdings and had to arrange distribution of its products, each film on its own merits, with cinemas or circuits. These methods while having obvious drawbacks—the main one being the lack of a permanent studio team—were to prove the most flexible and, in time, the healthiest formula for film production.

The early UA successes were the work of the four founders: Fairbanks's *His Majesty the American* (1919), Griffith's BROKEN BLOSSOMS (1919) and WAY DOWN EAST (1920), Pickford's *Pollyanna* (1920), Chaplin's THE GOLD RUSH (1925). The early departure of Griffith from the company and the slow rate at which Chaplin worked severely restricted the output of features, and it was the infusion of talent brought to UA by Joseph Schenck that temporarily saved the company. VALENTINO, Gloria SWANSON, Buster

KEATON, and most importantly Samuel GOLDWYN were added to UA's roster. Howard HUGHES added to its success with *Hell's Angels* (1930) and SCARFACE (1932).

UA now began to look overseas for contracts with foreign film concerns. Fairbanks was instrumental in bringing Alexander KORDA into the UA fold, first by distributing in America Korda's THE PRIVATE LIFE OF HENRY VIII (1933) and then by setting up a long-term contract with Korda's LONDON FILMS. By 1935 Korda and Goldwyn were both partners in UA; within two years they were planning to take over control of the company, a plan which was later abandoned although Korda retained his partnership until 1944.

In spite of foreign agreements the number of UA products declined during the thirties and forties owing mainly to the steady rise of the other big Hollywood companies who could offer long-term security to directors and stars, leaving UA with a small number of independents on which to draw. The continual turnover of the UA management contributed to the general malaise. By 1950 the two remaining founders—Chaplin and Pickford—had sold out to a short-lived syndicate which the following year gave way to another syndicate run by Arthur Krim from Eagle-Lion, Robert Benjamin from the RANK ORGANISATION, Matthew Fox, William Heinemann, Max Youngstein, and Arnold Picker. Six years later UA became a public corporation, able to take full advantage of the current upsurge in independent production. A contract with MIRISCH BROTHERS which backed independent directors like Billy WILDER, John STURGES, Robert WISE, and Norman JEWISON secured UA release for their films, popular successes including MARTY (1955), THE MAGNIFICENT SEVEN, THE APARTMENT (both 1960), WEST SIDE STORY (1961); in 1963 a stock transfer gave ownership of Mirisch to UA. Stanley KRAMER, Fred ZINNEMANN, and Richard LESTER provided more films and, therefore, financial security for the company, and UA increased its support of overseas production, lavishly backing such films as TOM JONES (1963), Italian Westerns, and the JAMES BOND series beginning with *Dr No* (1962). The subsidiaries Artistes Alliés in France and Europa Film (formerly Dear Film) in Italy coproduced films by RESNAIS and TRUFFAUT among others.

In 1967 UA became part of the Transamerica Corporation of San Francisco. Two years later David Picker succeeded Krim as president while his brother Arnold became chairman of the board (prompting VARIETY's announcement 'Pickers Pluck Plum UA Posts'). Without huge studio overheads or star salaries UA was able to make profits during the late sixties when most studios were heavily in debt or closing down. UA now owns a small chain of cinemas, mostly showcase theatres, and continues to provide diverse entertainment ranging from Jewison's *Fiddler on the Roof* to John SCHLESINGER's *Sunday, Bloody Sunday* (both 1971).

**UNITED PRODUCTIONS OF AMERICA (UPA).** A group of animators from the DISNEY studios discovered, while working on wartime instructional films, that complicated concepts could be expressed in line and colour with extreme economy. Reacting against the exuberant picture-book detail of the Disney style, the rebels, led by Stephen Bosustow, formed UPA in 1945: by 1948 the UPA studios at Burbank, California, had a production staff of 175 and regular distribution had been arranged through COLUMBIA.

The films had an immediate and far-reaching effect on animation. The overall impression was of spare, elegant drawing matched by formalized movement, but the company's democratic organization allowed its members to explore their individual styles, as in John HUBLEY's *The Magic Flute* (1949), Robert Cannon's *Madeline* (1952), Hurtz's *The Unicorn in the Garden* (1954, based on James Thurber's drawings, with a delicate music backing by the Modern Jazz Quartet), and two films for Terry Toons, Deitch's *The Juggler of Notre Dame* (1957), which used tiny line drawings based on those of R. O. Blechman in a vast wide screen, and Ernst Pintoff's *Flebus* (1957). UPA's major successes were Cannon's *Gerald McBoing-Boing* (1951) and Pete Burness's MR MAGOO who, ironically, contributed to the decline of UPA as a major influence: the short-sighted little man lent himself to a limited but endless formula in the manner of Disney's own popular characters.

Unhappily, by the mid-fifties the economical vivacity of the UPA style was as much of a convention as the sweet naturalism of Disney. Some of the more individual talents—like Hubley, Pintoff, Sturm, and Deitch—found their creative freedom again curtailed within a large commercial set-up and left to work independently. Although UPA maintains a healthy output, its early influence has been dissipated. (See ANIMATION.)

**UNITED STATES OF AMERICA.** Questions of precedent on the development of cinema apparatus and on the application of the new technology to mass entertainment are still very much open amid rival national claims. The LUMIÈRE brothers are generally credited with the first demonstration of *projected* moving images before a *paying* audience (28 December 1895), but the American contributions were substantial in both technology and exploitation. Heyl, for example, was projecting a series of photographs (each stage in the action photographed separately by a still camera) before paying audiences in Philadelphia as early as 1870, and in 1873 Eadweard MUYBRIDGE developed a technique for instantaneously photographing action. Muybridge later transferred his series of photographs to the rim of a large glass disc and by rotating the disc in front of a light source produced the illusion of motion he styled the Zoopraxiscope.

In 1888 Thomas Alva EDISON (probably inspired by the Zoopraxiscope), conceived the idea for a device which would do for visual information what his phonograph already did for aural information: capture it and reproduce it at the will of the user. Armed with the concept, and with very little practical guidance, Edison's associate, W. K. L. DICKSON perfected the KINETOGRAPH (the camera) by 1890, and the Kinetoscope (a peepshow viewing device) a year later. Key elements were the celluloid roll film first developed by George EASTMAN in 1884 and ready to be manufactured in bulk for cinematography in 1888, and the sprocket-driven perforations—the 'American Perforation' which became universally accepted. By 1893 the Edison laboratories in West Orange, New Jersey, could boast the world's first film studio, the 'Black Maria'—a rotating tar paper stage able to follow the sun—to produce films for the proliferating Kinetoscopes. On 14 April 1894, the Holland brothers (Canadian entrepreneurs who had become Eastern agents for the Edison device) opened the first Kinetoscope Parlour at 1155 Broadway in New York. The Kinetoscope (which now offered thirty seconds of motion in return for a nickel dropped in the slot) was an immediate success, but the commercial possibilities were limited while the one machine/one viewer relationship held. The Lumières led the way in Paris while Edison was purchasing and incorporating the patents of Thomas J. Armat (who had developed the MALTESE CROSS mechanism essential for intermittent movement) and Charles F. Jenkins (who had devised a projecting apparatus he called the Phantascope) and refining a motion picture projector he christened the Vitascope. In April 1896, Edison gave the first public demonstration of true motion picture projection in America, at Koster and Bial's Music Hall, New York.

Despite Edison's control of the crucial patents, vigorous competition, the most striking characteristic of this early period in America, came from the American Mutoscope and Biograph Company, and the VITAGRAPH, KALEM, and SELIG companies, among others. The great lure was the substantial and almost instantaneous return possible from the 'nickelodeons', as the earliest moving picture theatres were called. Given a projector and several strips of film, each lasting a minute or so and purchased outright on a per foot basis, any storefront could be converted into a theatre whose first week's takings could cover the initial investment. By 1903 it was no longer necessary to purchase the films: 'exchanges' had sprung up to service the theatres with changes of programmes on a rental basis. Within five years there were more than a hundred theatres across America. Exchanges shared their profits with the production companies and thus the basic elements of the motion picture industry—a division by function into production, distribution, and exhibition—were in existence before the first story film made its appearance.

The earliest films were 'actualities', the results of the camera recording life around it. Any motion alone on the screen was enough to thrill the first audiences. The novelty quickly wore off, however, and the producers began to stage the action for the camera. It was Edison who actually initiated this line of development because the Edison camera was too bulky to move about easily. The first film copyrighted by Edison in 1896 was in fact a re-enactment of a key moment in a contemporary stage romance starring May Irwin and John C. Rice. Called *The Kiss* it shocked and titillated audiences with thirty seconds of osculation taking place before their eyes and ten times larger than life. Edison also brought personalities of the day such as sharpshooter Buffalo Bill CODY, dancer Annabelle, and boxer James J. Corbett to his 'studio' to perform their specialties for the camera. From there it was an easy progression to staging a series of actions and assembling the scenes into films. By Easter 1898 there were at least two versions of *The Passion of Our Lord* manufactured in that way for circulation. Each scene was a *tableau vivant* representing a complete action; the next step in the evolution of film technique was the recognition that the basic building block was not the scene but the individual shot. This was achieved as early as 1903 by an employee of Edison's, Edwin S. PORTER. In *The Life of an American Fireman* Porter not only assembled a series of shots to tell a story, but he also demonstrated how staged shots, the family threatened by fire, the fireman perceiving their predicament in a dream sequence, could be combined with actuality footage of fire engines in service on the streets of New York to tell a story. Porter elaborated on these basic principles of EDITING (intercutting two parallel actions, intercutting close shots and medium shots) in THE GREAT TRAIN ROBBERY the same year. This film, with development of parallel stories culminating in an exciting gun battle shot out of doors, was a great success and a great influence on the development of film technique.

Porter, however, never progressed much beyond this point, nor did his contemporaries. They made short films (usually limited to one reel, or less than ten minutes, in length) full of action, but never exploiting the emotional power of the medium through genuine human conflict. It was at this stage that D. W. GRIFFITH began his career in films. An actor and aspiring playwright he approached Porter to sell him a story idea, and was instead invited to act in *Rescued from an Eagle's Nest* (1907). Griffith was typical of the legitimate actors of his day in scorning the movies for their crude plots and simplistic characters and he consented to appear only under an assumed name. He began selling scenarios to the BIOGRAPH Company, however, and in 1908 he was asked to direct his first film *The Adventures of Dolly*. It was obvious from this first effort that Griffith had a feeling for the medium, and from the first he expanded the repertoire of filmic devices. Between 1908 and 1913 he directed more than 500 one-reel films for Biograph and in the process he revolutionized the medium. His literary aspirations broadened the content of films, his total mastery of film technique allowed him to concentrate on narrative thrust and character development, and his instinctive grasp of the essential differences between stage and screen acting enabled him to define and elicit natural performances of unparalleled intensity. By 1911 Griffith was finding the one-reel format too restrictive, and against the opposition of his employers he made his second version of *Enoch Arden* in two reels. The great success of Sarah BERNHARDT in the French-made LA REINE ELISABETH, in eight reels, the following year proved that audiences would accept longer films, and in 1914 Griffith made the grandiose historical spectacle *Judith of Bethulia* in four reels, an unprecedented one hour's running time for American films.

The resistance of the Biograph Company to Griffith's efforts to vary the length of his films in accordance with artistic imperatives was indicative of the attitude of the early producers towards the product of their industry. Edison attempted to rationalize the entire industry, and protect his patents, by forming the MOTION PICTURE PATENTS COMPANY in 1909. This grouped the major producers of the day (Edison, Biograph, Vitagraph, LUBIN, ESSANAY, Selig, MÉLIÈS, and Kalem) together with the major distributor Kleine, into a monopoly trust which could negotiate with George Eastman for the exclusive use of his stock, license exhibitors to use Edison's apparatus, and coerce exhibitors to show only films produced by Trust members.

In 1910 the Trust set up the General Film Company to monopolize the film exchanges.

In theory Edison's Trust had achieved an almost total stranglehold on the motion picture industry, but in practice independent producers, distributors, and exhibitors successfully evaded the Trust at every level of the industry. By 1913 William FOX, a distributor turned producer, could launch a suit against the Trust for restraint of trade under anti-trust legislation, and by the end of the following year, for all practical purposes, the Trust was broken.

The intense and conspiratorial rivalry the Trust had, however, provoked left its mark on the industry: the film-makers moved west, to HOLLYWOOD, as much to flee the machinations of Edison and his colleagues as to seek the sun, essential for both interior and exterior filming. The popularity of the players, hitherto anonymous or identified only by the company for which they worked (the Vitagraph Girl, the Biograph Girl, etc) began to be exploited in a series of well publicized talent raids (the defection of Florence LAWRENCE, the Biograph Girl to the IMP Company was the first such sensation) that resulted in precisely the vast increase in salaries that the early producers had feared; and the superior strength of the bigger companies in the fight for a share of the vast profits to be earned from the control of production, distribution, and exhibition was clearly established.

As the First World War brought film production to a halt overseas, the American independents that broke the Trust began to cluster into the conglomerates that were to dominate the industry. Carl LAEMMLE, William Fox, Adolph ZUKOR, Jesse LASKY, Marcus LOEW, Samuel Goldfish (later GOLDWYN), Lewis J. SELZNICK, Jack L. WARNER, and Louis B. MAYER became industrial giants steering the fortunes of UNIVERSAL, PARAMOUNT, WARNER BROS, METRO-GOLDWYN-MAYER, and TWENTIETH CENTURY-FOX. Along the way they refined and developed the STAR SYSTEM to dominate world film markets in the immediate post-war period. CHAPLIN, PICKFORD, and FAIRBANKS became household names throughout the world, and were so well rewarded for their efforts that they could combine with Griffith in 1919 to form their own distribution company, UNITED ARTISTS.

American directors and producers had already begun to mould film aesthetics, and to influence the acceptance of film as an art form. The foremost achievements were Griffith's THE BIRTH OF A NATION (1915) and INTOLERANCE (1916)—two towering masterpieces that consolidated the aesthetic and technical discoveries of the previous fifteen years. At the same time Mack SENNETT, an Irish-Canadian who had learned the directing craft with Griffith, was introducing a new genre, the slapstick comedy, with his series of one- and two-reelers featuring the Keystone Kops; and Thomas INCE, as executive producer, was developing the studio system, insisting for the first time on complete scenarios emphasizing strong narrative values, and on accurate budget forecasts in which all the mechanics of production were worked out in advance.

Given the economics of scale they had introduced, the American studios could also benefit from artistic advances made in Europe, whether Swedish naturalism or German EXPRESSIONISM, by buying up talent as it emerged to feed their own growth. In the early twenties such imported talent included Ernst LUBITSCH, F. W. MURNAU, E. A. DUPONT, Erich POMMER, Alexander KORDA, Michael CURTIZ, Mauritz STILLER, and Victor SJÖSTRÖM. Many brought along their leading players to enrich the star system such as Pola NEGRI, Conrad VEIDT, and the incomparable Greta GARBO, and these in turn helped the Hollywood film to dominate world screens.

As the industry solidified the studio structure that was to endure until the early fifties, American films in the post-war economic boom began to explore themes and develop genres with the confidence bred of constantly expanding markets. The studio system early recognized the value of repetitious themes and TYPE-CASTING, so that the persona of the stars was clearly identified by the audience with the roles they played. In the buoyant optimism and rampant materialism of the twenties, 'Hollywood' as a type of film and as a point of view began to typify a glamorous defiance of conventional morality, sometimes leading, more often reflecting, the changes in American society. Clara BOW, Coleen Moore, and Joan CRAWFORD as free-wheeling symbols of the jazz age began to replace the post-Victorian ideals of womanhood exemplified by Mary PICKFORD, Lillian and Dorothy GISH, and Bessie LOVE. Griffith's celebrated and successful tragedies BROKEN BLOSSOMS (1919) and WAY DOWN EAST (1920) mark the end of that era, while the sophisticated comedies and realistic dramas of Cecil B. DEMILLE, Lubitsch, and Erich von STROHEIM embodied the new social values. DeMille in particular, working for Paramount, set the tone for a raft of successors with provocative titles such as *Don't Change Your Husband* (1919), *Why Change Your Wife?* (1920) and *Fool's Paradise* (1921). DeMille also demonstrated that the lure of arrant sensuality could be carried by Biblical spectaculars such as *The Ten Commandments* (1923) and *King of Kings* (1927) that would dazzle audiences with sinful display while maintaining a high moral tone overall.

Whatever the genre the studio system, operating in fairly rigid compartments on each stage of production—scripting, shooting, editing—and tending to follow a cyclical pattern based on box-office success, worked to smooth out problems, homogenize productions, and maintain a constant flow of films to the theatres. Within the system, however, strong directors could still impose their will and their individual style on their films. In WESTERNS, for example, in a genre dominated by stars who seldom deviated from their established screen roles—W. S. HART, Tom MIX, Ken Maynard, Hoot GIBSON—individual efforts such as James CRUZE'S THE COVERED WAGON (1923) and John FORD'S THE IRON HORSE (1924) explored traditional themes with a new awareness of their infinite possibilities.

If any genre typified the Hollywood product and explained the universal acceptance of the American movie in the twenties it was the comedy. A quartet of comic geniuses—Charles Chaplin, Buster KEATON, Harry LANGDON, and Harold LLOYD—each in his own way harnessed the technology of film-making to create a new kind of physical comedy, at once magical in its seeming defiance of the laws of physics and the limitations of human anatomy, and realistic in its appraisals of society and the fragility of social relationships. In films such as *Safety Last* (Lloyd, 1923), THE GOLD RUSH (Chaplin, 1925), THE GENERAL (Keaton, 1926), and *The Strong Man* (Langdon, 1926) they also demonstrated the humanistic appeal of the clown, that easily overcame language barriers and cultural differences.

Along with the exotic phenomena Hollywood spawned in the twenties—Rudolph VALENTINO (*The Sheikh*, 1921), Gloria SWANSON (*Prodigal Daughters*, 1923), Greta Garbo (*Flesh and the Devil*, 1927)—a corps of talented directors were emerging from the studios, many of whom were to make their lasting contribution in the sound era. Henry KING, King VIDOR, Frank CAPRA, Howard HAWKS, William WYLER, and Frank BORZAGE were all nurtured by the studio system but managed to place their personal stamp on their films. Despite outstanding exceptions, however, American motion picture production was generally unremarkable in the late twenties, and box-office returns were failing to keep pace with the vast investment in 'picture palaces', the exotically decorated and cavernous theatres resulting from intense competition between the major studios to find an audience for their product (see CINEMA).

Conditions were ripe for radical innovation, and Warner Bros, ailing financially and owning fewer theatres requiring costly conversion than the other major studios, launched the first commercially successful sound feature film, THE JAZZ SINGER, starring Al JOLSON, in October 1927.

Warners' VITAPHONE system was sound-on-disc, mechanically synchronised with the film, but it was a cumbersome system and was quickly replaced by sound-on-film, first introduced commercially by William Fox. Both systems relied on the amplification of sound made possible by Lee DeForrest's audion tube, although the inventor's efforts to market a sound-on-film process as early as 1922 had failed owing to studio unwillingness to undertake the re-equipping involved. The Warners' breakthrough, followed by the all-talking *The Lights of New York* (July 1928), literally forced the other studios to change over to sound. The audience would no longer tolerate silent pictures. By the end of 1929 almost half of the 20,500 theatres in America were wired for sound.

The immediate artistic effect of the coming of sound was to immobilize the camera and to freeze the action in the studio. The immediate financial effect was to stabilize the industry and to protect it from the worst excesses of the Depression that followed the crash of 1929. Directors and studio technicians gradually learned how to mask off camera noise while freeing the camera and how to mobilize the microphones and sound recording equipment so that the technology was subservient to direction and not vice versa. Under such competent hands as Rouben MAMOULIAN (*Applause*, 1929) and Lewis MILESTONE (ALL QUIET ON THE WESTERN FRONT, 1930), they were to demonstrate that dialogue and sound effects need not interfere with the visual flow nor be allowed to dominate the action. The new technique soon brought MUSICALS into enormous popularity. Fred ASTAIRE at RKO and Busby BERKELEY at Warner Bros set the main styles, but all the major studios profited by the large following for operetta, backstage shows, or witty musical comedy. Some of America's best song-writers worked on Hollywood musicals in the thirties, including Harold ARLEN, Jerome KERN, RODGERS and HART, and Cole PORTER.

As in the silent era, producers and directors of vision and enterprise flourished as individual artists within the studio system, although one of the long-term effects of sound technology was a sharp increase in the cost of film-making which rigidified studio practices. The heads of the studios could, to some extent, impose a house style, although this could be interpreted as a tendency to concentrate on previous box-office successes. Jack L. Warner, for example, who with his brothers Harry and Albert ran Warner Bros, concentrated on sparse naturalistic dramas dealing more often than not with social issues such as juvenile delinquency, unemployment, civic corruption, and racketeering. Their major gangster successes, LITTLE CAESAR (1930), *I Am*

*a Fugitive from a Chain Gang* (1932), both directed by Mervyn LEROY, established the genre in the sound era; their small, but prolific team of directors included Michael Curtiz and William DIETERLE. They in turn were ably served by contract players such as Bette DAVIS, Barbara STANWYCK, Humphrey BOGART, James CAGNEY, and Paul MUNI.

In sharp contrast MGM, driven by Louis B. Mayer and, until his early death, inspired by Irving THALBERG, operated on a lavish budget in making 'beautiful pictures for beautiful people'. Garbo, Norma SHEARER, Jean HARLOW, Clark GABLE, Spencer TRACY, and William POWELL were among the expansive roster of star names under contract to the studio, and many of the great directors of the thirties worked there: Clarence BROWN, who directed many of Garbo's great successes (*Anna Christie*, 1930; ANNA KARENINA, 1935); Howard Hawks (*A Tale of Two Cities*, 1935); Victor FLEMING (GONE WITH THE WIND, 1939; THE WIZARD OF OZ, 1939); and Lubitsch (*The Merry Widow*, 1934; NINOTCHKA, 1939).

Paramount, controlled by Adolph Zukor, took the middle ground with sophisticated Lubitsch comedies (TROUBLE IN PARADISE, 1932), Biblical spectacles and epic Westerns by DeMille (*The Sign of the Cross*, 1932; *The Plainsman*, 1937; *Union Pacific*, 1939) and romantic dramas by Josef von STERNBERG (SHANGHAI EXPRESS, 1932; THE SCARLET EMPRESS, 1934). Players under contract included Marlene DIETRICH (Sternberg's discovery), Claudette COLBERT, Miriam HOPKINS, Gary COOPER, and Fredric MARCH.

Despite the studio system a handful of directors earned the independence to place their name and their mark on their films. Almost alone at Columbia, for example, Frank Capra (IT HAPPENED ONE NIGHT, 1934; MR DEEDS GOES TO TOWN, 1936) wrested that right from Harry COHN, who ran the studio. John Ford (THE INFORMER, 1935; STAGECOACH, 1939) and Howard Hawks (BRINGING UP BABY, 1938; *Only Angels Have Wings*, 1939) were tough-minded and successful enough at the box-office to demand that right as they moved from studio to studio. Along with other important directors in the thirties, such as George CUKOR, Lewis Milestone, and William Wyler, they were laying the groundwork for the 'one man, one picture' (Capra's celebrated catch-phrase) principle that was to emerge as the studio system broke down. In the thirties and forties new talent also surged in from Europe—LANG, HITCHCOCK, CLAIR, RENOIR—to be quickly absorbed into the Hollywood structure.

As America entered the war the studio system reached its height. With 80,000,000 admissions a week in the US, American films could earn back their investments at home and regard foreign earnings as excess profits. Markets abroad shrank, of course, with the German occupation of Europe, but in their place Hollywood secured a military audience numbering millions and complete domination of allied screens. Amid a plethora of war melodramas (Alfred Hitchcock's *Lifeboat*, 1943; Fritz Lang's *Hangmen Also Die*, 1943; and Milestone's *A Walk in the Sun*, 1945, are distinguished exceptions) Hollywood continued to produce escapist, albeit technically brilliant, fare: Westerns, Musicals, literary adaptations, and mysteries. The list of important films of the period, given the captive market, is nevertheless lengthy. Among the impressive accomplishments are: THE GRAPES OF WRATH (John Ford, 1940); CITIZEN KANE (1941) and THE MAGNIFICENT AMBERSONS (1942), two incontestable masterpieces by Orson WELLES; THE MALTESE FALCON (John HUSTON, 1941); THE OX-BOW INCIDENT (William WELLMAN, 1943); HAIL THE CONQUERING HERO (Preston STURGES, 1944); CASABLANCA (Michael Curtiz, 1943); THE BIG SLEEP (Howard Hawks, 1946); and THE BEST YEARS OF OUR LIVES (William Wyler, 1946).

Hollywood emerged from the war unscathed as to the structure of the studio system. MGM had by now taken the lead in musicals: Vincente MINNELLI was their strongest property in the forties, with Esther WILLIAMS carrying on the tradition of nonsensical Hollywood extravagance. But the effects of war were meanwhile becoming evident in the style and content of films like THE LOST WEEKEND (Billy WILDER, 1945); *Gentleman's Agreement* (Elia KAZAN, 1947); *Crossfire* (Edward DMYTRYK, 1947); and *Intruder in the Dust* (Clarence Brown, 1949). Ironically this tough new naturalism—a willingness to engage in serious confrontations with social problems and religious and racial bigotry —emerged just as the House of Representatives UNAMERICAN ACTIVITIES Committee, spurred on by Senator Joseph McCarthy, began its investigations into alleged Communist infiltration of the motion picture industry. By the end of the forties the right-wing reaction had resulted in the imprisonment of the 'Hollywood Ten', the exile of film-makers like Dmytryk, Joseph LOSEY, and Carl FOREMAN, and the notorious blacklist, the effects of which lasted into the sixties.

Although the investigations and the reprisals that followed had a drastic effect on attempts to deal with serious social issues within the studio system, it was the application of anti-trust legislation and the advent of television in the early fifties that signalled the end of the old Hollywood. Forced by law to divest themselves of financial control of the theatres, the major studios lost the guaranteed outlets for their products just as the audience began to decline in numbers. By 1968 only 20,000,000 Americans were going to the cinema every week, less than ten per cent of the population, and production had declined from a peak of over 500 in 1946 to less than 175. Lavish production values in colour and wide screen systems appeared to be the answer to the challenge of the television set (THE ROBE, 1953, launched the trend), and to add to the financial woes of the studios, the cost of an average production more than tripled between 1945 and 1965.

Hollywood also found itself, by the end of the fifties, with a relatively new audience brought up on television, increasingly drawn from the 16 to 24 age bracket, with new tastes, detectable primarily as an insatiable appetite for sensation, liberally dosed with sex and violence. The first institution to fall was the old Production Code that had remained unchanged since it was established by the Hays Office in the early thirties (see CENSORSHIP, US). New standards for permissible language and behaviour were adopted by the MOTION PICTURE ASSOCIATION OF AMERICA, and producers and directors immediately began testing those limits in order to satisfy the market. Film-going had ceased to be a habit: each film had to lure its own audience, and the advertising campaigns, hawking sensation, reflected this fact. Multi-million-dollar spectaculars, with multi-million-dollar advertising budgets became the norm in the industry—BEN-HUR (1959), SPARTACUS (1960), and above all CLEOPATRA (1962), which almost bankrupted Twentieth Century-Fox. Most of these blockbusters were shot in Spain or Italy and further diminished the significance of Hollywood as a production centre.

With the dramatic decline in the fortunes of the studios in the early sixties, independent producers became the dominant force in the industry. The studios became administrative centres organizing production facilities, financing, and distribution. The creative contribution came from outside, usually in the form of a production package consisting of a literary property (or a script or writers), a producer–director combination, and marketable stars. In many genres the films that resulted owed much to the patterns the studios had initiated. Musicals grew more lavish, and occasionally top heavy with décor and costume, but where stage adaptations like *South Pacific* (Joshua LOGAN, 1958), MY FAIR LADY (George Cukor, 1964), THE SOUND OF MUSIC (Robert WISE, 1965), and CABARET (Robert FOSSE, 1972) succeed they are a direct development of the stylish vitality characteristic of the Hollywood musical tradition. For directors like Alfred Hitchcock (REAR WINDOW,

1954; NORTH BY NORTHWEST, 1959; PSYCHO, 1960), John Ford (THE SEARCHERS, 1956; THE MAN WHO SHOT LIBERTY VALANCE, 1962), and George STEVENS (*Giant*, 1956; *The Diary of Anne Frank*, 1959), there was little change in their normal pattern of production, but for the myriad of lesser talents and hordes of studio craftsmen there was only work in television—or unemployment.

For those directors who found work, or hyphenated their roles doubling as producer–directors or writer–directors, there was always the law of the market place (with individual production deals you were not only 'as good as your last picture' you were only as solvent as your last picture), but also the freedom to shift directions or stretch the genre in which they worked. The Western, for example, proved it could accommodate Indians as heroes (BROKEN ARROW, Delmer DAVES, 1950), Arcadian myth-making (SHANE, George Stevens, 1953), critical self-analysis (*Lonely are the Brave*, David Miller, 1962), and unabashed sentimentality (*True Grit*, Henry HATHAWAY, 1969). Social dramas, on the other hand, tackled hitherto forbidden themes with such gusto that they constituted a frontal attack on traditional studio censorship. Richard BROOKS (THE BLACKBOARD JUNGLE, 1955; *Sweet Bird of Youth*, 1961), Otto PREMINGER (THE MAN WITH THE GOLDEN ARM, 1955; *Anatomy of a Murder*, 1959), and Billy Wilder (SOME LIKE IT HOT, 1959; THE APARTMENT, 1960) seemed to base their careers on challenging the Production Code.

This increasing refusal to submit to traditional restrictions in subject matter was in part a reflection of the current social climate. Nowhere was this more vigorously represented than in the so-called UNDERGROUND cinema which, from roots in the experimental work of the silent period, fed by the influx of refugee artists in the thirties, reached its peak in the sixties. American independent film-makers like Andy WARHOL, Stan BRAKHAGE, and Michael SNOW demonstrated an expressive freedom in the use of the medium which stimulated the growth of non-commercial 'personal' film-making in all the developed countries.

Personal cinema, in so far as it can exist in a corporate art that is still entirely dependent on large-scale distribution mechanisms (the factor that makes true independence largely a myth in Hollywood), also revolved around actors in the sixties, many of whom produced their own films. Burt LANCASTER, Kirk DOUGLAS, Marlon BRANDO, John WAYNE, Paul NEWMAN, and Warren BEATTY are among those who extended their control over the films in which they appeared, although by the mid-sixties it was obvious that no name could guarantee financial success in either the domestic market or the increasingly crucial international market from which American films now drew more than sixty per cent of their returns. With the end of vertical integration in the industry each project was judged on its own merits, even to attract a distributor, and it became impossible to predict success. Beatty, for example, failed financially with *Mickey One* (1965) but scored a resounding success with BONNIE AND CLYDE (1967), both directed by Arthur PENN.

In the past ten years American films have continued to dominate world screens, despite restrictive legislation in several countries designed to limit the number of titles that can be imported. The decline in the world-wide audience levelled out in the early seventies and, with the sharp increase in ticket prices, total dollar earnings are generally keeping pace with the costs of production. Instability is still a prime characteristic of the industry, however, with the solvency of a company frequently depending on a single film. With gross revenues on a runaway success frequently topping one hundred million dollars, the 'boom or bust' pattern of one smash success carrying twenty box-office failures has become standard. The result has been the emergence of a somewhat chaotic marketing system, that has on the one hand opened the door to unconventional productions (EASY RIDER, 1969) and on the other sealed off controversial (aesthetic as well as thematic) films from their potential audiences.

In the last decade American films have continued to demonstrate technical virtuosity (William Friedkin's *The French Connection*, 1971, and *The Exorcist*, 1974); a mastery of genres that continuously redefines the form (PECKINPAH'S THE WILD BUNCH, 1969, and *The Ballad of Cable Hogue*, 1970); a willingness to tackle complex social issues in unconventional narrative modes (NICHOLS'S THE GRADUATE, 1967, and *Carnal Knowledge*, 1971; ALTMAN'S M*A*S*H, 1971, and *McCabe and Mrs Miller*, 1972); and a capacity to generate entertainments whose artistic merits may be in doubt but whose broad, popular appeal can be precisely measured at the box-office (*Airport*, George Seaton, 1969; THE GODFATHER, 1971; *The Sting*, George Roy HILL, 1973). Films continue to attract the young, both as consumers and increasingly as practitioners as the number of university courses in cinema testify. The new directors who have emerged in the decade affirm the vitality of American film-making which gives assurance that American production will continue to make its contribution to world cinema.

**UNIVERSAL PICTURES,** US production company formed in 1912 by Carl LAEMMLE's amalgamation of his Independent Motion Picture

Company with a number of smaller concerns including Nestor and Powers. Laemmle moved his new company from New York to Los Angeles, not merely for its favourable climate and scenery but also for its proximity to the Mexican border where independents standing out against the monopolistic MOTION PICTURE PATENTS COMPANY could evade prosecution for infringement of patent rights. His studio was set up on a 230-acre chicken ranch in the San Fernando Valley and in 1915 became Universal City, the first incorporated city devoted entirely to film production.

Universal's success was founded on Laemmle's faith in the STAR SYSTEM. (He had been the first producer to identify a star by name—Florence LAWRENCE—in film credits.) Erich von STROHEIM directed his first films for Universal, but the company's prolific output was usually of a more modest type: Westerns, romantic adventures, horror films, comedies. Their Western heroes included popular figures such as Harry Carey, Johnny Mack Brown, Ken Maynard, and exotic romances brought world attention to stars like VALENTINO and Maria Montes. Almost all the famous early horror classics directed by James WHALE and starring Lon CHANEY, Boris KARLOFF, and Bela LUGOSI were Universal products, as well as the later comedies of W. C. FIELDS and Mae WEST. ALL QUIET ON THE WESTERN FRONT (1930) was a notable high point.

Laemmle was forced out of the studio management in 1936 and Universal was taken over by two Americans, J. Cheever Cowdin and Nate Blumberg, and a group of British financiers including L. W. Farrow and J. Arthur RANK. The association with Rank was profitable, since Universal acquired the distribution rights in the western hemisphere of all Rank's British films and secured the distribution of its own products in the English market. With the exception of a few Rank/Universal co-productions, the American studio rarely ventured into overseas production and most of their attempts at prestige production abroad were unsuccessful.

Unlike WARNER BROS, PARAMOUNT, or METRO-GOLDWYN-MAYER, Universal was never closely allied with a large cinema chain, and had therefore to rely solely on its own films for income. During the early forties, dependence on Deanna DURBIN, ABBOTT and COSTELLO, and Francis the Talking Mule seriously weakened the company, necessitating in 1946 a merger with International Pictures owned by Leo Spitz and William Goetz. The studio operated for six years as Universal-International, reverting to its original name just before its purchase in 1952 by Decca Records who gained a majority share in the company by buying out Rank's interest. In 1959 Decca was consolidated with the Music Corporation of America (MCA), a talent agency and television production company which has since taken over the management of Universal Studios.

In the fifties and early sixties Universal held its own chiefly by the efforts of its most successful single producer Ross Hunter, who specialized in 'women's pictures' such as lugubrious remakes of melodramas, usually directed by Douglas SIRK, and sex-war romps starring Rock HUDSON and Doris DAY. Universal also backed independent productions including SPARTACUS (1960) and Robert MULLIGAN's *To Kill a Mockingbird* (1962).

In the mid-sixties Lew Wasserman, as president, managed to make Universal one of the more successful Hollywood studios by concentrating almost entirely on the television market, producing both series and feature-length films for American television, and by organizing a profitable tourist centre at Universal City where visitors can take part in videotaped 'programmes' as well as viewing the remnants of Hollywood in its great days.

**URBAN,** CHARLES (1871–1942), American-born pioneer of British films, came to London about 1898 to manage the agency for EDISON's films and soon reorganized it into the flourishing Warwick Trading Company. Early in 1903 he abandoned it to found his own concern, the Charles Urban Trading Company, taking with him some of Warwick's best and most enterprising cameramen. Urban himself was more an astute businessman and entrepreneur than a filmmaker, but he was broadly responsible for the development of newsreel-style reportage, expeditionary, scientific, and educational films, and scored a particular success as the promoter of G. A. SMITH's KINEMACOLOR.

**URUGUAY.** Although the cinema has always had a large following in Uruguay, domestic production has never become established, owing to lack of financial and technical resources. Mario Handler, a Uruguayan of Hungarian descent who became head of the Instituto Cinematografica Uruguayo in the mid-sixties, has made the country's only significant contribution to Latin American political cinema with a series of documentaries. These include *Me gustan los estudiantes* (1967), an AGIT-PROP for students, *El problema de la carne* (1969), about a strike in the meat industry, and *Liber arce—Liberarse* (1969), on the funeral of a student killed in a demonstration, all necessarily made with the utmost economy. In 1970 Handler was dismissed from the Institute; Uruguay continues, however, to provide a base for the Cinemateca del Tercer Mundo, which shows films and publishes the journal *Cine del 3er Mundo.*

**US FILM SERVICE** see LORENTZ

**USTINOV, PETER** (1921–  ), British actor, director, and writer of Russian descent. His first film appearance was in *Mein Kampf* (1941). During war service he co-scripted *The Way Ahead* (Carol REED, 1944) with Eric AMBLER; he wrote and directed *School for Secrets* (1946) and *Vice Versa* (1948), the latter with costumes by Ustinov's mother, Nadia Benois. He scored his first major acting success in films as Nero in QUO VADIS (1951) and in 1955 he appeared in Max

OPHULS' LOLA MONTÈS and opposite Humphrey BOGART in Michael CURTIZ's *We're No Angels.* He won an OSCAR for his performance in SPARTACUS (1960).

Ustinov returned to directing with *Romanoff and Juliet* (1961) which he adapted from his stage play. He played a leading role in *Billy Budd* (1962), which he co-adapted from Herman Melville and directed. It is his most ambitious film but met with little response.

Large, ebullient, a brilliantly witty impersonator and raconteur, Ustinov has displayed a multiplicity of talents, but his particular vein of satirical fantasy has been expressed more pungently in his stage plays than in his films.

# V

**VACANCES DE MONSIEUR HULOT, Les,**
France, 1951. 1½hr. *Dir* Jacques Tati; *prod* Cady
Films/Discina; *scr* Tati, Henri Marquet; *ph* J.
Mercanton, J. Mouselle; *des* Henri Schmitt; *mus*
Alain Romans; *cast* Jacques Tati (M Hulot),
Nathalie Pascaud (Martine), Michèle Rolla
(aunt), Valentine Camax (old maid), Louis Per-
rault (boatman), André Dubois (colonel), Lucien
Frégis (hotel proprietor), Raymond Carl
(waiter).

Monsieur Hulot, an amiable character who
innocently causes chaos all around him, particularly when he is trying to be helpful, arrives
on holiday in a seaside village. The film is an
acute and delightful observation of the absurdities inherent in any seaside holiday, deriving its
humour from the conflict between Monsieur
Hulot and everyday reality. A marvellous
display of visual gags works up to a classic slapstick finale, when Hulot manages, characteristically, to set fire to a shed full of fireworks.
Dialogue plays very little part in the film, but the
sound-track, with its evocative seaside sounds,
contributes considerably to the realistic feel of
the film, and was even re-recorded some years
after the film was first made, when TATI had
better facilities available.

**VADIM,** ROGER (1928–   ), French director,
real name Roger Vadim Plemmiankov, had a
cosmopolitan upbringing and first worked as a
journalist on *Paris-Match* where he met Brigitte
BARDOT when she was featured as a cover girl. In
1947 he became scriptwriter and assistant to
Marc ALLÉGRET. His first film as director, ET
DIEU CRÉA LA FEMME (*And Woman ... Was
Created*, 1956), starred Bardot, by now his wife.
The film was considered sensationally erotic at'
the time, and the publicity and scandal which
surrounded it won international fame for both
Vadim and Bardot. It also attracted the attention
of producers to the potential profitability of the
NOUVELLE VAGUE with which Vadim is often, if
unconvincingly, associated.

It was followed by the less successful *Sait-on
jamais?* (1957) and *Les Bijoutiers du clair de
lune* (1958) which was a failure in spite of Bardot's presence. LES LIAISONS DANGEUREUSES
(1959) revived his fortunes: its visual elegance
and ironical tone, together with fine leading per-

formances by Gérard PHILIPE and Jeanne MOR-
EAU, give it an outstanding place in Vadim's
work. It featured his second wife Annette Stroy-
berg, who appeared again in *Et Mourir de plaisir*
(1960). At Bardot's request he took over direction from Jean Aurel on *Le Bride sur le cou*
(1961) and his next feature was again with Bardot, *Le Repos du guerrier* (*Warrior's Rest*,
1962). *Le Vice et la vertu* (*Vice and Virtue*,
1962), a transposition of Sadeian themes into a
Nazi setting, is notable, apart from its bad taste,
for the presence of Vadim's new protégée Catherine DENEUVE. *Château en Suède* (1963), with
Monica VITTI, was followed in 1964 by a remake of the Max OPHULS classic LA RONDE
(1950). *La Ronde* featured Jane FONDA who later
became Vadim's third wife and who appeared in
his next two films, *La Curée* (1966) and the
comic-strip fantasy *Barbarella* (1968). *Pretty
Maids All in a Row* (1971) was his first American film.

Vadim is a thoroughly professional director
whose gift for elegant and often beautiful visual
effects has attracted such talented cameramen as
Henri DECAË and Claude RENOIR to work with
him. His undoubted intelligence and wit are
usually put at the service of ephemeral material,
but his work reflects his unaffected enjoyment of
film-making.

**VAGHE STELLE DELL'ORSA** (*Of a Thous-
and Delights* in GB; *Sandra* in US), Italy, 1965.
1¾hr. *Dir* Luchino Visconti; *prod* Vides; *scr*
Suso Cecchi d'Amico, Visconti, Enrico Medioli;
*ph* Armando Nannuzzi; *mus* Prelude, Chorale,
and Fugue by César Franck; *cast* Claudia Cardinale (Sandra), Jean Sorel (Gianni), Michael
Craig (Andrew), Marie Bell (the mother), Renzo
Ricci (Gilardini).

The title ('misty stars of the Great Bear') is
the opening line of a poem, 'Le ricordanze'
('Memories'), by Leopardi, which describes a
return to the poet's childhood home. In the film,
Sandra, revisiting her family home, recalls the
war; her Jewish father's betrayal to the Germans,
perhaps by her mother, and her probably in-
cestuous relationship with her brother, Gianni.
The film's debt to the Electra myth is overt, but
not laboured. VISCONTI's brilliantly composed
handling of strong blacks and whites enhances

the mythic quality of the story, but the account of corruption and betrayal is wholly contemporary and deeply moving.

**VALAHOL EURÓPÁBAN...** (*Somewhere in Europe* or *Kuksi*), Hungary, 1947. 1½hr. *Dir* Géza Radványi; *scr* Radványi, Béla Bálazs, Judit Fejér, Félix Máriássy; *ph* Barnabás Hegyi; *des* József Pán, Miklós Benda; *mus* Dénes Buday; *cast* Arthur Somlay (conductor), Zsuzsa Bánki (girl), Miklós Gábor (Ossup), Laci Horváth (Kuksi), György Bárdy.

After the post-war collapse of production Radványi's film brought Hungarian cinema some much needed international prestige. His portrayal of a band of thieving and begging orphans who take refuge in a castle inhabited by an orchestral conductor, posed the question of the quality of life possible for the post-war generation—an issue still preoccupying present-day directors. Co-scripted by the returned exile Béla BÁLAZS, the film contained neo-realist influences which were developed into the semi-lyrical style of the fifties.

**VALENTINO,** RUDOLPH (1895–1926), US actor of Italian birth, real name Rodolfo Guglielmi di Valentino, was a professional ballroom dancer who in his first films was usually cast as an over-elegant gigolo. With THE FOUR HORSEMEN OF THE APOCALYPSE (1922) his star potential was recognized, and for the rest of his short career he held an unrivalled place in the imagination of female audiences. The dismissive description 'Latin lover' fails to convey the audacious, yet fundamentally romantic, sexuality which won him an unprecedented following, particularly in *The Sheikh* (1921), *Blood and Sand* (1922), and *Son of the Sheikh* (1926), his last film. He died suddenly and unromantically of a ruptured ulcer; at his funeral there were remarkable scenes of mass hysteria and his death was said to be the cause of several suicides.

**VALLI,** ALIDA (1921–  ), Italian actress of Austrian origin, real name Alida Maria Altenburger. From the mid-thirties until 1946 she appeared in numerous Italian films, few of which, excepting *Piccolo mondo antico* (1941), acquired an international reputation. After *Eugénie Grandet* (Mario SOLDATI, 1946), she pursued a cosmopolitan career, initially going to Hollywood where she appeared in *The Paradine Case* (Alfred HITCHCOCK, 1948). Outstanding among her subsequent films were THE THIRD MAN (Carol REED, 1949), SENSO (Luchino VISCONTI, 1954), IL GRIDO (Michelangelo ANTONIONI, 1957), *Une Aussi Longue Absence* (Henri COLPI, 1961), and *Strategia del ragno* (*The Spider's Stratagem*, Bernardo BERTOLUCCI, 1970).

**VAMP** see BARA, Theda

**VAMPIRES, Les,** France, 1915–16. Nine episodes, total running time 7hr. *Dir* Louis Feuillade; *prod* Gaumont; *cast* Musidora (Irma Vep), Edouard Mathé (Philippe Guérande), Marcel Lesque (Oscar Mazamette), Jean Aymé (the Grand Vampire).

The success in America of PATHÉ's series *The Mysteries of New York* (1915) prompted GAUMONT's *Les Vampires* (see SERIAL), the adventures of a journalist, Guérande, in pursuit of a band of audacious criminals led by Irma Vep (an anagram of vampire), thrillingly portrayed by MUSIDORA. Probably FEUILLADE's best work, *Les Vampires* differed from contemporary American serials in its combination of visual lyricism and cheerful inconsequentiality.

**VAMPYR,** France/Germany, 1932. 1½hr. *Dir* Carl Dreyer; *prod* Dreyer Filmproduktion; *scr* Dreyer, Christen Jul, from the story 'Carmilla' by Sheridan Le Fanu; *ph* Rudolph Maté, Louis Née; *des* Hermann Warm, Hans Bittmann, Cesare Silvagni; *mus* Wolfgang Zeller; *cast* Julian West (David Gray), Henriette Gérard (Marguerite Chopin, the Vampire), Jan Hieronimko (the doctor), Maurice Schutz (the owner of the castle).

Thanks to the enthusiasm of the Dutch Baron Nicolas de Gunzberg, an amateur actor, who financed the film in order to play the leading role under a pseudonym, DREYER had complete control in making *Vampyr*, his first sound film. It was made entirely on location, near Paris, and in three languages, French, German, and English; dialogue was therefore minimal, adding to the eerie effect of the horror story. Comparisons have been made with NOSFERATU (1922), and the contribution of Rudolph MATÉ and Hermann WARM reflects the influence of German EXPRESSIONISM. The leading performance was ineffective and the film failed to attract the public, although it has recently attracted critical attention.

**VAN CLEEF,** LEE (1925–  ), US actor, had had only amateur acting experience when given a small part in Joshua LOGAN's stage production of *Mr Roberts* in 1950. His first film was HIGH NOON (1952), and from then on Van Cleef's eagle-like features made him the instantly recognizable villain in over two hundred film and television parts. He achieved international fame in Sergio LEONE's Italian Westerns *Per qualche dollari in più* (*For a Few Dollars More*, 1965) and *Il buono, il bruto, il cattivo* (*The Good, the Bad, and the Ugly*, 1966). His other films include SHANE (1953), GUNFIGHT AT THE OK CORRAL (1956), *The Young Lions* (1958), THE MAN WHO SHOT LIBERTY VALANCE (1962).

**VAN DONGEN,** HELEN, Dutch documentary editor. Acknowledged primarily as the gifted editor who worked with Joris IVENS and Robert FLAHERTY, she also produced American wartime COMPILATION films—*Russians at War* (1943) and *News Review 2* (1943). Her skilled contributions to the works of Ivens and Flaherty can best be seen in NIEUWE GRONDEN (*New Earth,* 1934), THE SPANISH EARTH (1937), THE LAND (1941), and LOUISIANA STORY (1948).

**VAN DYKE,** WILLARD (1906–   ), US documentary film-maker, began his career as a stills photographer. He entered the film industry as a cameraman in 1935 and in 1937 was an assistant cameraman on Pare LORENTZ'S THE RIVER. In 1939 he co-founded with Ralph Steiner American Documentary Films which in the same year made *The City,* with music by Aaron COPLAND, which he co-directed with Steiner.

During the Second World War Van Dyke made several films for the American government, including *The Bridge* (1942), on trade relations with South America, and *Steeltown* (1943), about American steel workers. In 1945 he made *San Francisco,* the official film record of the establishment of the United Nations. In the forties and fifties he made short films on a variety of subjects, including *Working and Playing to Health* (1953), about recreational therapy in a mental institution, *Cabos blancos* (1954), a dramatized documentary on Puerto Rican farm co-operatives made for the Puerto Rican government, and *Land of White Alice* (1959), about radio communications in Alaska. In the sixties, Van Dyke worked increasingly for television, directing several films for Walter Cronkite's series 'The Twentieth Century', such as *Sweden* (1960), which tried to show the effects of the country's welfare policies on national morality, and *Depressed Area, USA* (1963), which examined the reasons for poverty in the Appalachians.

Van Dyke was director of the Department of Film at the Museum of Modern Art in New York, 1966–73.

**VAN DYKE,** W. S. (1899–1943), US director, originally a child actor, became one of GRIFFITH'S assistants on INTOLERANCE (1916). His early work as a director included Ruth Roland serials and Buck Jones Westerns. He leapt into prominence with exotic location films, WHITE SHADOWS IN THE SOUTH SEAS (1928), *The Pagan* (1929, *Pagan Love Song* in GB), and TRADER HORN (1931), and he made the first sound TARZAN film, *Tarzan the Ape Man* (1932) which launched Johnny WEISSMULLER'S screen career. *Eskimo* (1933, *Mala the Magnificent* in GB) ended his 'location' period.

His prolific work in the thirties, most of it for METRO-GOLDWYN-MAYER, included THE THIN MAN (1934) and some of its sequels; Jeanette MACDONALD and Nelson EDDY musicals; and a contribution to the HARDY FAMILY series. Also notable were *Manhattan Melodrama* (1934) with the popular team of William POWELL and Myrna LOY plus Clark GABLE, *Personal Property* (1937), with Jean HARLOW and Robert TAYLOR, and *It's a Wonderful World* (1939), with Claudette COLBERT and James STEWART.

A typical Hollywood professional, Van Dyke made several films which are far from negligible, and as a mainstream director has perhaps received something less than his due.

***VANGELO SECONDO MATTEO, Il*** (*The Gospel According to St Matthew*), Italy/France, 1964. 2½hr. *Dir, scr* Pier Paolo Pasolini; *prod* Arco Film (Rome)/Lux (Paris); *ph* Tonino Delli Colli; *mus* Bach, Mozart, Prokofiev, Webern, the *Missa Luba*; *cast* Enrique Irazoqui (Christ), Margherita Caruso (Mary as a girl), Susanna Pasolini (Mary as a woman), Marcello Morante (Joseph), Mario Socrate (John the Baptist), Settimio Di Porto (Peter), Otello Sestili (Judas Iscariot).

As a declared Marxist, PASOLINI might have been expected to use the life of Christ as a vehicle for an attack on superstition and on the Church's abuse of power. This film is in fact an objective re-telling of St Matthew's Gospel. The script uses only direct quotation from the Bible and speech is therefore minimal, greatly adding to the film's effectiveness. Realizing that his audience's familiarity with the story would make detailed exposition redundant (a source of weakness in more extravagant film versions of the subject), Pasolini enriches each episode with lingering contemplation of the faces of his amateur actors responding to events with awe, passion, pain, or incomprehension.

The drama, unfolding against an arid landscape (the film was shot in Calabria), is underlined by the use of sacred music from various periods and cultures: the imagery, too, evokes sacred and secular works in painting, sculpture, and film. By weaving many associations into a story central to the consciousness of his audience, Pasolini created a work of subtle complexity which succeeds in avoiding both sentimentality and didacticism.

**VAN PARYS,** GEORGES (1902–71), French composer of popular songs such as 'Si on ne s'était pas connu' and 'Ça s'est passé un dimanche'; he also wrote the music for over two hundred films. His most successful work includes the scores for René CLAIR'S LE MILLION (1931), *Le Silence est d'or* (1947), LES BELLES DE NUIT (1952), *Les Grandes Manoeuvres* (1955), and for CHRISTIAN-JAQUE's *Fanfan la Tulipe* and RENOIR's *French Can-can* (1955).

**VARDA, AGNÈS** (1928– ), French director. After working as a still photographer for the Théâtre National Populaire, she made her first film, *La Pointe courte* in 1955, having scarcely ever been to the cinema, and lacking any technical experience. Following the structure of William FAULKNER's novel, *The Wild Palms*, in which two stories are dealt with in alternating chapters, *La Pointe courte* counterpoints two themes in a highly stylized and abstract manner, and Alain RESNAIS, who edited it, found that it anticipated his own ideas.

Varda had no opportunity of making a second feature film for seven years, but she made three prize-winning shorts in the interval. *Ô Saisons ô châteaux* (1957) and *Du côté de la côte* (1958) were commissioned by the French Tourist Office, and despite the limiting nature of the subjects, Varda infused them with originality and visual stylishness. *Opéra Mouffe* (1958) is a portrait of the Mouffetard district of Paris seen through the eyes of a pregnant woman. Her second feature, CLÉO DE CINQ A SEPT (1962) examines two hours in the life of a woman awaiting the result of a vital medical test. A short documentary, *Salut les cubains* (1963), made up of her own still photographs, was followed in 1965 by her most controversial film, LE BONHEUR, an abstract reflection on happiness, clothed in the lyrical and quite unrealistic story of a young carpenter. In *Les Créatures* (1965), the worlds of fantasy and reality intermingle, when a writer encounters in real life characters that he has imagined. In 1967 Varda contributed an episode to the collective film *Loin du Viet-nam* and the following year made two documentaries in the US, *Uncle Janco* and *Black Panthers*, as well as a feature, *Lions Love*.

Varda is one of the few successful women directors; her films combine a rich visual texture and elegance with deliberate coldness and a disconcerting quality of abstraction. She married Jacques DEMY in 1962.

**VARIABLE AREA,** the form of OPTICAL sound track most often used for MARRIED prints. A variable area track appears along the edge of the film as a single or double white line with serrations corresponding to the variations of the sound signal. (Its appearance provided the model for the comic sound track interlude in FANTASIA, 1940.) It is slightly superior to the alternative, VARIABLE DENSITY, in its reproduction of extreme high- and low-frequency sounds. (See SOUND.)

**VARIABLE DENSITY,** a form of OPTICAL sound track used on MARRIED prints. A variable density track appears along the edge of the print as a narrow band laterally striped with bright and dark bands corresponding to the variations of the sound signal. (Its appearance may have originally inspired the term 'track'.) It resists the ill effects of wear and projector misalignment better than its alternative, VARIABLE AREA, but is now rarely used. (See SOUND.)

**VARIÉTÉ** (*Variety* in US; *Vaudeville* in GB), Germany, 1925. 2½hr. *Dir, scr* E. A. Dupont, from the novel by Friedrich Hollander; *prod* Erich Pommer for UFA; *ph* Karl Freund; *cast* Emil Jannings ('Boss' Huller), Lya de Putti (Berthe-Marie), Warwick Ward (Artinelli).

The story of passion and revenge among trapeze artists is given substance by the remarkable quality of its visual exposition. Building on his experience with MURNAU, particularly in DER LETZTE MANN (*The Last Laugh*, 1924), Karl FREUND used full camera mobility, reflected images, effects of light and movement, to create involvement with the action. The film was an enormous success and brought DUPONT an invitation to Hollywood.

Murnau directed an American remake, *Four Devils* (1928).

**VARIETY,** American weekly trade paper, started in December 1905 in New York, by Sime Silverman. From the very start *Variety* set out to create an original style of its own, dedicated to printing with complete impartiality news of all aspects of show-business, including vaudeville,

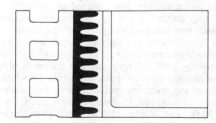

Variable area sound track (simplified)

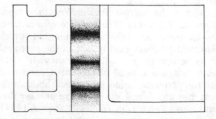

Variable density sound track (simplified)

theatre, radio, film, and later television. Its wide coverage includes gossip, obituaries, advance production news, reviews, box-office figures, and festival reports.

Apart from its honest approach and news reputation, *Variety* is probably best noted for its headline captions in an abbreviated language of its own: a piece on the box-office success in Chicago of the film *Sands of Iwo Jima* (1949) screamed 'Chi Socko Hits New B.O. Mark' and the observation that outlying areas no longer appreciated films emphasizing rural subjects was contracted to 'Stix Nix Hix Pix'. The original style continues even in the columns, where important studio personnel become 'Veeps' (VIPs), premières—preems, actors—thesps.

*Variety* continues to be the all-powerful newspaper of show business and mass-media; honest, international in scope; and consistently forward-looking. Yearly anniversary editions, giving annual reports from principal centres of production and distribution and of a table of 'grossers'—films earning the highest takings—have been published since 1948.

**VASILIEV, SERGEI** (1900–59) and **GEORGI** (1899–1946), Russian directors, generally referred to as brothers, although they were unrelated. Before entering films Sergei fought in the Red Army and studied at the Leningrad Institute of Film Art, where he became interested in the problems and aesthetics of film editing; his views are contained in his book *Montage* (1929). Georgi worked first as a journalist. Both worked as editors and in this capacity they made their first film *Ice-Breaker Krasin* (1928) from newsreel footage. *Spyashchaya krasavitsa* (*Sleeping Beauty*, 1929), scripted by ALEXANDROV, was the first of many films on the subject of war. After *Lichnoye delo* (*A Personal Affair*, 1931) they directed CHAPAYEV (1935), which was welcomed officially for its ideological content and was also widely popular for its warmth and humanity in tracing the rise of its peasant hero during the Civil War. *Volochayevskiye dni* (*Volochayevsky Days*, 1938) deals with the struggle of the Soviet people against invaders from the Far East, and uses folk songs as part of the authentic setting.

During the Second World War they made *Oborona Tsaritsina* (*The Defence of Tsaritsin*, 1942), about the defence of Stalingrad, which displayed psychological insight in the portrayal of its heroes, in spite of its militancy. In 1944 Sergei was made head of Lenfilm. Georgi died before agreement could be reached about their next film and Sergei did not make another film until *Geroi Shipki* (*The Heroes of Shipka*, 1954), which depicts, on a massive scale, the struggle of the Russians and Bulgarians against the Turks in

1877. He was working on a remake of OKTIABR when he died.

**VAUGHAN WILLIAMS,** RALPH (1872–1958), British composer, a prolific writer of symphonic and vocal music, who towards the end of his life wrote a number of film scores. His first was *49th Parallel* (1941, *The Invader* in US), followed by *Stricken Peninsular* (1945), *The Loves of Joanna Godden* (1947), *Scott of the Antarctic* (Charles FREND, 1948), from which Vaughan Williams developed his *Sinfonia Antarctica* (1952), *Dim Little Island* (Humphrey JENNINGS, 1949), *Bitter Springs* (1950), *The England of Elizabeth* (1956), and *The Vision of William Blake* (1958).

**VÁVRA,** OTAKAR (1911–   ), Czech director, studied architecture and made his way into film through publicity work. In the early thirties he made several experimental short films, and after working as scriptwriter and assistant to several directors made his own first feature, *Gaudeamus Igitur*, in 1937. In this film and the two others which followed it in 1937 and 1938, Vávra set standards of organization new to the Czech industry, and earned for himself the reputation of the first professional Czech film-maker. His *Cech panen Kutnohorských* (*Guild of the Maidens of Kutná Hora*, 1938) won the Golden Lion at VENICE, and was banned by the Nazis promptly on their arrival in Czechoslovakia. Vávra continued to work during the Occupation, however, using the tactic of adapting literary work. He took an active lead during the war in the preparation of plans for the nationalization of the industry, which took place as early as August 1945. FAMU, the Film Academy, was particularly his brain-child, and in the years immediately after the war he was heavily engaged with directing its Department of Direction as well as with other organizational work. He continued to make films, however, and solved the problem of meeting the socialist realist requirements imposed after 1948 by going on making adaptations of literary and historical subjects.

At FAMU he encouraged the viewing of western films which could not be seen anywhere else in the country, and fostered an atmosphere of open discussion and free artistic development which resulted, eventually, in the emergence of the new wave of the sixties. Vávra's own films were consistently distinguished by workmanlike scripting, good dialogue, and fine craftsmanship, but he was slow to make films himself which offered any comment on the present: his massive trilogy about the Hussite rebellion, *Jan Hus* (1954), *Jan Žižka* (1955), and *Proti všem* (*Against All*, 1957), was a characteristically non-committal recourse to the past. He did, however, surprise his pupils in the mid-sixties with two films of more direct contemporary relevance, *Zlatá Reneta* (*The Golden Rennet*, 1965) and *Romance pro křídlovku* (*Romance for the Fluegelhorn*, 1966).

Late in 1969, Vávra became the only leading director to sign a pledge of loyalty to the new régime, but in the same year he also made (working with Ester KRUMBACHOVÁ) *Kladivo na čarodějnice* (*Witchhammer*), a condemnation of the cruelty and injustice of witch-hunting. In 1970, one of his pupils made a film which displeased the authorities, and Vávra was dismissed from the post at FAMU which he had distinguished for twenty-five years. He returned to international attention with *Dny zrady* (*Days of Betrayal*, 1973), a sober reconstruction of the Munich crisis.

**VEDRÈS,** NICOLE (1911–65), French documentary director and screenwriter. Her first film, which she directed and wrote, was PARIS 1900 (1948), a COMPILATION for which she received the Prix Louis DELLUC and on which Alain RESNAIS was assistant. She also directed *La Vie commence demain* (1949) and *Aux frontières de l'homme* (1953) which received the Louis Lumière award.

**VEIDT,** CONRAD (1893–1943), German actor who after appearing with Max REINHARDT's company was in German films from 1917. The best known of his early performances was as the somnambulist Cesare in DAS CABINETT DES DR CALIGARI (1919). Among other famous films of this period in which he appeared were *Nju* (Paul CZINNER, 1924), *Der Januskopf* (F. W. MURNAU, 1920), DIE WACHSFIGURENCABINETT (*Waxworks*, Paul LENI, 1924), ORLACS HAŇDE (Robert WIENE, 1925), and DER STUDENT VON PRAG (Henrik GALEEN, 1926). He worked in Hollywood for a time (*The Man Who Laughs*, Leni, 1928; *The Last Performance*, Paul Féjos, 1929), then returned to Germany where he scored a triumph as Metternich in DER KONGRESS TANZT (*Congress Dances*, 1931). He attracted a following in British films of the thirties, bringing intelligence and finesse to essentially romantic roles in *Rome Express* (1932), *I Was a Spy* (1933), *Jew Süss* (1935), SJÖSTRÖM's *Under the Red Robe* (1937), *Contraband* (1940). He went back to Hollywood for KORDA's production of THE THIEF OF BAGHDAD (1940) and appeared in several more films there, the last being CASABLANCA and *Above Suspicion* (both 1943).

**VENEZUELA** has managed to sustain a small commercial film industry, but the great majority of features has always been imported, chiefly from the US. Recent developments in political cinema in Latin America have stimulated the growth of two radical movements. Cine Urgente, a group organized by the painter Jacobo Borges, aims to place the means of film-making in the hands of impoverished communities, somewhat in the manner of community action groups in North America. The Centro de Cine Documental at the University of Merida, working more conventionally, has produced several documentaries, mostly of a pamphleteering character. Notable examples are *Santa Teresa*, a CINÉMA-VÉRITÉ study of a priest heckled by students, and *TVenezuela*, directed by Jorge Sole, which effectively uses animation, titles, snatches from commercials, newsreels, and sequences from soap operas to attack false values and foreign control in the country's commercial television service.

**VENICE FILM FESTIVAL.** The first international film festival in the world was held as part of Venice's Biennale in 1932. The festival remained part of the Biennale in 1934, becoming thereafter an annual event in its own right, held in late summer. Since 1937 the main events have taken place at the cinema palace especially built on Venice Lido. During the years of Fascist government there were many complaints of political bias in the distribution of awards, but all film-producing countries were eager to compete for the gold cups awarded by Mussolini. The lavish parties which were an intrinsic part of film festivals until the late sixties were inaugurated by the British contingent at Venice in 1937. The festival was suspended in 1943–5 and no prizes were offered in 1946, but since then its importance and splendour has been restored and maintained.

The main competition at Venice is for feature films and the principal prize is the Leone d'Oro (Golden Lion). There are also awards for best direction, best actor and actress, best script, etc. Retrospectives of the work of important directors are included in the main programme and a prestigious week of short films follows the main festival. The first of the festivals, and still one of the world's most important (with CANNES, MOSCOW, and BERLIN), Venice has provided the archetype. It has always retained an artistic influence contrasting with the commercial glitter of Cannes, but has unhappily often been hampered by political strife. The festival was non-competitive in 1972, with no awards made, and it was cancelled in 1973 and 1974.

**VERDUGO,** *El* (*The Executioner*), Spain/Italy, 1964. 1¾hr. *Dir* Luis Garcia Berlanga; *prod* Naga Films Madrid/Zebra Films Rome; *scr* Berlanga, Rafael Azcona, Ennio Flaiano; *ph* Tonino Delli Colli; *cast* Nino Manfredi (José Luis),

Emma Penella (Carmen), José Isbert (Amedeo), José Luis Lopéz Vázquez (Antonio), Angel Alvarez (Alvarez).

José Luis, an undertaker's assistant, wishing to marry the daughter of the local hangman, agrees to become her father's apprentice and successor in order to qualify for a municipal flat. BER-LANGA handles this black humour with gusto, especially in the scene where the reluctant novice executioner is forcibly dragged to perform his duty on a calm and dignified political prisoner. The film carries sharp comments on Spanish life; it was severely cut by the censor.

**VERTOV,** DZIGA (1896–1954), Russian director, real name Denis Kaufman. His family fled from Russian-held Poland when the Germans invaded in 1915, taking with them three sons who were later famous in the cinema—Denis, Mikhail, and Boris (see KAUFMAN). Denis adopted the name Dziga Vertov (in Russian the word 'vertov' evokes the image of a turning wheel) while still a student and was at first a Futurist poet, experimenting with recorded sounds. At twenty he began to work with the Revolutionary Cinema Committee and from June 1918 was editor of its newsreel *Kino-Nedelya*, made up of footage sent back by cameramen working on the agit-trains (see SOVIET UNION). Two years later he used some of the off-cuts to make an experimental film-montage *Godovshchina revolutsii* (*The Anniversary of the Revolution*). The main idea embodied in this and in much of his later work is that a film-maker should think in visual rather than verbal or literary terms, even at the script or planning stage, and should strive to impose his own structure on filmed actuality material. He later identified six separate theoretical points at which such structuring should take place, from the first view of a subject by the cameraman's naked eye to the final version projected on a cinema screen.

His main collaborators were his wife Elizaveta Svilova and his brother Mikhail and the three formed the nucleus of a group which adopted the name *Kinoki* or, more usually, KINO-GLAZ (Film Eye); the name was also used for one of their films made in 1924. KINO-PRAVDA (*Film Truth*), their series of twenty-three newsreels issued in 1922–5, was built up from thousands of shots taken by hundreds of cameramen: footage taken from different angles, at different times, and even

*Chelovek s kinoapparatom* (Dziga Vertov, 1929)

in different places, was often assembled into one sequence. They used varied techniques—slow and reverse motion, composite and still photography, animation—as a practical demonstration of Vertov's theories.

From 1924 as head of a new studio, Kultkino, Vertov made information films about the achievements of Socialist industry and agriculture, including *Leninskaya Kino-Pravda* (*Leninist Film Truth*, 1925), issued as no 21 of the *Kino-Pravda* series, *Shagai, Soviet* (*Stride, Soviet*), *Shestaya chast mira* (*A Sixth of the World*, 1926), and *Odinnadtsatyi* (*The Eleventh*, 1928). He constantly held to LENIN's dicta on the function of cinema in maintaining revolutionary fervour, while using every opportunity to continue his experiments with editing for emotional effect.

Vertov's first full-length film incorporating his theories, CHELOVEK S KINOAPPARATOM (*The Man with a Movie Camera*, 1929), is also his best known, at least in the West (he toured Europe with it in 1931). It is a pyrotechnic display of editing and special effects which EISENSTEIN called 'just formal spillikins and purposeless camera hooliganism'. A more sober vein emerged in his first sound film *Entusiazm* (*Enthusiasm* or *Symphony of the Don Basin*, 1931), about miners fulfilling their Five-Year Plan, and TRI PESNI O LENINYE (*Three Songs of Lenin*, 1934), where the brilliance of his technique is matched by genuine warmth and emotion. With the rise of Stalinism he was bitterly attacked for 'formalism' and he made only one more full-length film, *Kolibelnaya* (*Lullaby*, 1937).

During the thirties, most of Europe's documentary film-makers—including GRIERSON, IVENS, RUTTMANN, VIGO—acknowledged Vertov's influence. He continued to work on newsreels during the forties but the war deprived him of opportunities for experiment just as it deprived the West of opportunities to see his films. In the sixties, a decade after his death, his work, and its influence, regained recognition.

*Soviet cinema* by Thorold Dickinson and Catherine de la Roche, London, 1948, and *Kino* by Jay Leyda, London, 1960, are the best surveys of Russian cinema in English and both contain personal reminiscences of Vertov.

**VGIK** (Vsesoyuznyi Gosudarstvenyi Institut Kinematografii), the All-Union State Institute of Cinematography in Moscow, is the earliest film school, set up at the personal instigation of LENIN in 1919 when the Russian film industry was nationalized. In spite of a critical shortage of equipment and film stock, artistic enthusiasm and a fervent belief in cinema as an instrument of revolution kept the school alive. KULESHOV's pioneering experiments, including short 'films' performed live to conserve materials, had a vital influence on the innovatory style of early Soviet cinema.

From this difficult beginning VGIK has become one of the world's major film schools, providing a model for film schools in most other Socialist countries. It is regarded as one of the best examples of well-planned professional training, with a paternal care for the student's general well-being; general education and a social science course are part of the curriculum. Courses also include direction, camerawork, acting, history and theory of cinema, and scriptwriting. (VGIK and FAMU in Prague are the only film schools offering scriptwriting courses.) The course lasts five years: foreign students, who mostly come from Socialist and Third World countries, may have to spend a preliminary year learning Russian.

The Institute's distinction stems from the quality of the teachers: EISENSTEIN, PUDOVKIN, KOZINTSEV, DOVZHENKO, YUTKEVICH, and TISSÉ, have worked there. Practical work is the basis of the teaching, and students start working with 35mm in their second year, in teams supervised by an established film-maker; they also have the opportunity of working in commercial studios. Their diploma films may be feature-length and are sometimes of full professional standard; they are often shown on the commercial circuits. (See FILM SCHOOLS.)

**VIDOR, CHARLES** (1900–59), US director, born in Budapest, studied in Berlin. He began his career with UFA, progressing to assistant director. His first few years in the US were spent singing with a Wagnerian opera company, but he eventually went to Hollywood, and in 1929 financed his own short film *The Bridge*, as a result of which he was signed on by METRO-GOLDWYN-MAYER. His first (uncredited) film was *The Mask of Fu Manchu* (1933) which he co-directed with Charles Brabin. His work, for several studios, includes *The Sensation Hunters* (1934), *The Lady in Question* (1940), *Cover Girl* (1944), a stylish musical starring Gene KELLY, *Gilda* (1946), and *A Farewell to Arms* (1957). He died of a heart attack while on location in Vienna directing *Song without End* (1960).

**VIDOR, KING** (1896–    ), US director of Hungarian extraction, showed an early interest in films. He worked as a projectionist in a local cinema, then set himself up with a cine camera as Texas correspondent of a newsreel company. In 1918 he went into independent production, making shorts and features starring his wife, Florence Vidor. After joining Metro he directed *Three Wise Fools* (1923), and gained critical acclaim with THE BIG PARADE (1925), one of the earliest films to deal realistically with the First

World War and its aftermath. *The Patsy* (1927) and *Show People* (1928) both starred Marion DAVIES; the latter dealt with life in Hollywood, and featured CHAPLIN, FAIRBANKS, W. S. HART, and Vidor playing themselves.

Vidor's first sound film, HALLELUJAH (1929), with an all-black cast, confirmed his originality; OUR DAILY BREAD (1934), influenced by the Depression, took an anti-urban stand, preaching a return to rural values and communal life. It has episodes of visual beauty reminiscent of some Soviet films of the period: it won a prize at the first MOSCOW film festival. In *Northwest Passage* (1939) Vidor attempted a brutally realistic appraisal of the pioneering experience, but only the first half of the projected film was completed.

*An American Romance* (1944) was intended to be a history of the US in the first forty years of this century, seen through the eyes of a European immigrant; but the film was so drastically cut before release by METRO-GOLDWYN-MAYER that Vidor's plan is unrecognizable.

His later films include *The Fountainhead* (1952), *War and Peace* (1956), and *Solomon and Sheba* (1959).

*VIEILLE DAME INDIGNE, La,* France, 1965. 1½hr. *Dir* René Allio; *prod* Claude Nedjar for SPAC; *scr* Allio, from the short story by Bertolt Brecht, 'Die unwürdige Greisin', from *Kalendergeschichten* (1948); *ph* Denys Clerval; *ed* Sophie Coussein; *des* Hubert Monloup; *mus, songs* Jean Ferrat; *cast* Sylvie (Madame Berthe), Malka Ribovska (Rosalie), Victor Lanoux (Pierre), Etienne Bierry (Albert), François Maister (Gaston), Jean Bouise (Alphonse).

ALLIO's version of BRECHT's story, about an old lady whose behaviour during her widowhood runs counter to all expectations, was not calculated to appeal to producers: it was Allio's first feature film and a seventy-year-old heroine lacks box-office appeal. The production was undertaken with modest means and a great deal of cheerful co-operation and improvisation of equipment. The story is transposed to Marseilles, where the traditions of family life against which the old lady stages her gentle but decisive revolt are beautifully observed in incisive and haunting images. In a fine cast without star roles, SYLVIE's performance is a *tour de force*: Madame Berthe rejects her quiet servitude with shrewdness, humour, and grace. A shapely and delightful film, *La Vieille Dame indigne* insists unobtrusively that all human situations must be questioned, and that happiness may be achieved through change.

VIERNY, SACHA (1919–   ), French cameraman, was an assistant director on *L'Ombre* (1948) and directed three short films in 1948–

51. He was first credited as cameraman on Chris MARKER's *Lettre de Sibérie* (1958), but has since worked almost exclusively for Alain RESNAIS: *Le Chant du styrène* (1958), HIROSHIMA MON AMOUR (1959), L'ANNÉE DERNIÈRE A MARIENBAD (1961), and MURIEL, OU LE TEMPS D'UN RETOUR (1963). He also photographed BUÑUEL's *Belle de jour* (1966).

VIEUX COLOMBIER, Paris ART HOUSE, originally a theatre famous as a showcase for experimental plays, which in 1924 was taken over by Jean TEDESCO to become a cinema specializing in AVANT-GARDE films. The opening night's programme included films by Abel GANCE and Arthur ROBISON; new work by VIGO, RENOIR, and GRÉMILLON was also launched there. A silent studio was constructed at the rear of the Vieux Colombier where Renoir and Tedesco made *La Petite Marchande d'allumettes* (*The Little Match Seller*, 1928).

VIGO, JEAN (1905–34), French director. The circumstances of Vigo's life markedly affected his work as a film-maker. His father, who took the name of Almereyda (an anagram of '*Y'a la merde*'), played a conspicuous part in anarchist politics before the First World War. In 1917 he was imprisoned on a charge of treason and died in prison in the same year amid great scandal. Although Almereyda had abandoned the austerities of the left wing in his last years, his career and death naturally made a deep impression on his son.

After an uneven school and college career Vigo tried in 1925 to get work with Abel GANCE on NAPOLÉON (1927). It was found that he had tuberculosis, and he went to a sanatorium in the Pyrenees, where he met his wife, Lydou, daughter of a Polish industrialist. From this time, the poor health of both of them forced Vigo to spend most of his time in the south of France. In 1928 he was engaged as assistant cameraman in a newly-opened studio in Nice. Later in the year he met Boris KAUFMAN, and their first film, A PROPOS DE NICE, was completed early in 1930.

There was no commercial response to the film, but it gave Vigo the opportunity of meeting other film enthusiasts. A screening in Brussels widened the circle, and led to an enduring friendship with Henri STORCK. Vigo had in the meantime begun a film club in Nice, Les Amis du Cinéma, and in 1931 he won a commission to make a series of short films about sport for GAUMONT. The first, early in 1931, was about the champion swimmer, Taris. Later in the year he made another film about tennis. In real financial difficulties at this time, he continued to scrape a living from his film club, helped by his wife and by Storck. In 1932 he was introduced to J. L. Nounez, an

*A propos de Nice* (Jean Vigo, 1930)

industrialist with great enthusiasm for the cinema, who financed ZÉRO DE CONDUITE (1933). Before it was completed, Nounez began pressing Vigo on to the next subject, a film about penal servitude in which doubtless Vigo would have taken the opportunity of vindicating his father's life and attitudes as he had his own in *Zéro de conduite*; but the banning of the latter film materially altered the prospect. In spite of his alarm at the censors' decision and the financial disaster, Nounez gave Vigo another chance, and himself picked the subject of L'ATALANTE (1934), a banal script from an obscure author which should have been commercially safe—in any other hands than Vigo's.

The exceptionally severe weather in which the exteriors were shot caused what was to be the final breakdown in Vigo's health. A few days after *L'Atalante* finished its first short run, under its commercial title of *Le Chaland qui passe*, Vigo died.

Vigo's work stands between the AVANT-GARDE surrealism of the twenties and the NEO-REALISM of the forties, with on the one hand his beautiful trickery and fantasy and on the other his unselfconscious use of actors and non-actors. His output was tiny, and in his short lifetime it made no impression in commercial terms. As he had earned his living by running a film club, so his films slowly came to life within the film society movement, finally earning Vigo one of the brightest reputations in cinema. Sensitive, abrasive, unrepentantly rebellious against injustice and inhumanity; above all assured in expressing these qualities on film, he showed himself in the few thousand feet which he did complete to be one of the few directors who has achieved mastery of his own created world in terms uniquely cinematic.

P. E. Salès Gomès, *Jean Vigo*, Paris, 1957 (English translation, London and Berkeley, 1972), is an outstanding work; Marcel Martin, *Jean Vigo*, Paris, 1966, and P. Lherminier, *Jean Vigo*, Paris, 1967, are both useful.

*VIRIDIANA*, Spain/Mexico, 1961. 1½hr. *Dir* Luis Buñuel; *prod* Gustavo Alatriste (Mexico)/Uninci Films 59 (Madrid); *scr* Buñuel, Julio Alejandro; *ph* José A. Agayo; *mus* Handel; *cast* Silvia Pinal (Viridiana), Fernando Rey (Don Jaime), Francisco Rabal (Jorge), Margarita Lozano (Ramona), Victoria Zinny (Lucia).

The convent novice, Viridiana, is cheated and abused at every turn. Her attempts at an unworldly life and her cousin's materialistic concerns sum up BUÑUEL's anti-clerical and anti-establishment attitudes. *Viridiana* contains probably his most famous set-piece—the evocation of Leonardo's *Last Supper* enacted by an assortment of repulsive cripples and beggars.

Buñuel's growing international reputation after NAZARÍN (1958) and two French productions was presumably the reason why the authorities in Spain countenanced his filming there for the first time since LAS HURDES (1932). The script was passed by the censor with only a few alterations, but the completed film was banned outright in Spain and an attempt was made to suppress it completely. However, after winning the Palme d'or at CANNES, 1961, it was widely circulated by the Mexican distributor and acknowledged as one of Buñuel's most powerful and subversive films.

**VISCONTI,** LUCHINO (1906–   ), Italian director of aristocratic family background, who is also a professed Marxist. As a boy he received a musical education. He worked as an amateur stage designer and race-horse trainer, then saw RENOIR'S TONI (1935) while on a visit to Paris and enthusiastically worked with Renoir in 1936 on UNE PARTIE DE CAMPAGNE. After a brief visit to Hollywood he returned to Italy to work in the theatre and was Renoir's assistant again on *La Tosca* (1940). From Renoir Visconti learned to direct actors, to portray character, and to relate individuals to their surroundings: the debt is apparent in his first film OSSESSIONE (1942), from a subject suggested by Renoir. Visconti's experience in France, during the formation of the Popular Front, sharpened his political views and during the early forties he was associated with the radical group who found a voice in the journal CINEMA.

After *Ossessione* Visconti worked in the theatre for six years. His next film LA TERRA TREMA (1948) is a drama of economic conflict made with some of the methods NEO-REALISM had borrowed from the documentary tradition. BELLISSIMÀ (1951), an attack on cinema stereotypes, is remarkable chiefly for the vigour of Anna MAGNANI's performance. SENSO (1954) was his first film in colour, which he used with authority and richness; he had proposed a contemporary treatment of the subject of divorce which was rejected by the Italian censors, and turned instead to the examination of political and sexual conflicts during the *Risorgimento* of the 1860s. His next film, LE NOTTI BIANCHI (*White Nights*, 1957), met with a hostile reaction from many critics, who found its nostalgic romanticism anomalous from a director who had been identified with the neo-realist movement. ROCCO E I SUOI FRATELLI (*Rocco and his Brothers*, 1960) returned to contemporary concerns and is, in a sense, a sequel to *La terra trema*.

'Il lavoro', an episode in *Boccaccio '70* (1962), was followed by IL GATTOPARDO (*The Leopard*, 1963). Like *Senso* and *Rocco*, this was an international co-production and Visconti again demonstrated his mastery of the dramatic and aesthetic use of colour. VAGHE STELLE DELL' ORSA (*Of a Thousand Delights*, 1965; *Sandra* in US) was a return to black-and-white photography, which he used with a similarly sensitive virtuosity. *Lo straniero* (*The Stranger*, 1967) again attempted the re-creation of another time and place, but was less successful in this than *Senso* or *Il gattopardo*. Visconti seemed less at ease in the Algiers of 1938 than in nineteenth-century Italy, and Marcello MASTROIANNI was inappropriately cast as Albert Camus's isolated anti-hero.

The effects of Nazism which Visconti had observed in *Vaghe stelle dell'orsa* were traced back in *La caduta degli dei* (*The Damned*, 1970), a baroque study of the Essenbeck family of steel barons in pre-war Germany. The film is overtly an extravagant attack on Nazism, but shows Visconti's ambivalent attitude towards corruption—an attitude which comes to the fore in MORTE A VENEZIA (*Death in Venice*, 1971), a rich evocation of an elegant society symbolically plagued by cholera.

Throughout his career in films Visconti has continued to work in the theatre, directing socially committed plays (in particular those of Arthur MILLER) in his early years, innovatory interpretations of the classics, and, of recent years, many operas.

His best work in the cinema has been characterized by a distinctive visual richness and formality which has developed as his theatrical experience has tended more towards the grandiose. The influence of his early contact with Renoir's naturalism and with neo-realism has gradually given way to a concern with visual textures and compositions, in which he is one of the undoubted masters of cinema.

*VISITEURS DU SOIR, Les,* France, 1942. 1¾hr. *Dir* Marcel Carné; *prod* André Paulvé; *scr* Jacques Prévert, Pierre Laroche; *ph* Roger Hubert; *des* Trauner, G. Wakhevitch; *mus* Maurice Thiriet, Joseph Kosma; *cast* Alain Cuny (Gilles), Arletty (Dominique), Marie Déa (Anne), Marcel Herrand (Renaud), Jules Berry (the devil), Fernand Ledoux (Baron Hugues).

In 1485 Baron Hugues is celebrating the betrothal of his daughter Anne and the Knight Renaud. Gilles and Dominique, servants of the devil, arrive disguised as minstrels. Dominique infatuates the baron and Renaud, and Gilles seduces Anne; but, forgetting the devil's work, falls in love with her. The devil himself arrives in a thunderstorm, and in his rage against Anne and Gilles turns the embracing lovers into statues. The power of their love is so great, however, that their hearts continue to beat.

This strange fairy-tale film was released during the German occupation and undoubtedly part of its success was due to the fact that French audiences saw in it an allegorical reference to their fight against the Nazis.

**VISTAVISION,** a process developed by PARA-MOUNT to produce a wide-screen image, using a camera with 35mm film running horizontally instead of vertically. One image was photographed on to two frames of negative, and was thus increased by more than one half in width and was also doubled in area. The image was then printed horizontally, or, to avoid the special projectors this involved, reduced and printed anamorphically in the normal position across 35mm film, thus having the advantages of enhanced sharpness and of being higher as well as wider than the ACADEMY FRAME. The process had been tried out in 1919, the patents bought by Paramount in 1926, and the process then shelved. During the search for a bigger image in the face of television's threat, the process was revived in 1953 under the name of VistaVision. It was, however, discontinued after some years because it proved too expensive. (See also WIDE SCREEN.)

**VITAGRAPH,** US production company founded in 1899 by James Stuart BLACKTON, Albert E. Smith, and W. T. Rock. Blackton, a newspaper cartoonist, acquired a Kinetoscope from EDISON in 1896 and went into the exhibition business with Smith, a conjuror, who shortly afterwards adapted the machine to make, as well as to project, films. They opened a roof-top studio in New York, making brief dramas with Blackton as sole protagonist and Smith as the entire crew, notably *The Burglar on the Roof* and *Tearing down the Spanish Flag* (both 1898). They also had considerable success with short actuality films, including the assassination of President McKinley in 1901; many of these contained faked sequences.

Vitagraph quickly became a major force in the American industry, amassing huge profits and taking a leading role in the formation of the MOTION PICTURE PATENTS COMPANY. Blackton was the controlling force behind Vitagraph's output and he shrewdly estimated his audience's capacity to accept increasingly complex subjects. By 1908 Vitagraph was issuing SHAKESPEARE adaptations and historical dramas as well as the usual romantic subjects and domestic comedies; from 1913 they were producing features of five or more reels. *The Battle Cry of Peace* (1915) initiated a series of war films that contrasted with the isolationist or pacifist tendencies of American films before the United States entered the war.

In 1915 Vitagraph formed a consortium with LUBIN, SELIG, and ESSANAY. Each company continued to produce independently until 1917 when

Vitagraph, always the strongest member, bought out the others and was renamed VLSE. At this time Blackton, although retaining a financial interest, became an independent producer/director, and the company undoubtedly suffered from the loss of his supervision. It continued to operate with moderate success until 1925 when it was taken over by WARNER BROS.

**VITAPHONE,** sound process introduced in 1926 by WARNER BROS. The sound track was recorded on discs which were played in synchronization with the projected film. The first presentation was the silent film *Don Juan* (1926), starring John BARRYMORE, with synchronized background music; the only voice in the programme was that of Will H. HAYS in a filmed introduction to the process. THE JAZZ SINGER (1927) was the first feature to use Vitaphone for a snatch of spoken dialogue and for songs, and the film's success gave impetus to the installation of sound recording and projection equipment in studios and cinemas. The cumbrous process was superseded by 1930 by the more flexible sound-on-film recording processes.

**VITARAMA,** a MULTI-SCREEN system using eleven interlocked films projected on to a curved arc. Demonstrated only once, in 1939, it was refined by its inventor, Fred Waller, into the successful CINERAMA.

***VITELLONI, I,*** Italy/France, 1953. 1¾hr. (First released in GB as *Spivs*; released in US as *Vitelloni* and *The Young and the Passionate*.) *Dir* Federico Fellini; *prod* Peg Films/Cité Films; *scr* Fellini, Ennio Flaiano, Tullio Pinelli; *ph* Otello Martelli; *des* Mario Chiari; *mus* Nino Rota; *cast* Alberto Sordi (Alberto), Franco Interlenghi (Moraldo), Franco Fabrizi (Fausto), Leopoldo Trieste (Leopoldo), Riccardo Fellini (Riccardo), Eleonora Ruffo (Sandra).

*I vitelloni* deals with a group of layabouts in a provincial town and the gradual emergence of one of them as less irresponsible than the others. They make their way through various scrapes, alternating between boredom and high spirits; until Moraldo, who alone shows any sense of concern, breaks up the group by leaving for Rome to make a fresh start. Marcello, in LA DOLCE VITA (1960), may be considered to represent what he became when he arrived there.

The film is notable for its delicate and precise social observation and by the affectionate humour with which the characters are portrayed. It established FELLINI as a director of international standing.

**VITTI, MONICA** (1931–   ), Italian actress, real name Maria Luisa Ceciarelli, studied at the

Rome Accademia d'Arte Drammatica, and started acting in classical roles on the stage. She gradually developed a comic vein, and won a considerable reputation in comedy and review. During the mid-fifties she was a member of a stage company directed for a time by ANTONIONI, who in 1957 directed a version of *I Am a Camera* in which Vitti's performance as Sally Bowles was acclaimed by the critics for its finesse and elegance. She made several film appearances in the late fifties, and was also employed in DUBBING other film actresses' voices, a routine job in Italy (she dubbed the voice of Dorian Gray in IL GRIDO, 1957).

Her association with Antonioni was fruitful for them both artistically: her beauty, eroticism, and spontaneity lit up Antonioni's subtle and sombre themes in L'AVVENTURA (1960) and contributed decisively to his first commercial success. Her parts in his next two films, LA NOTTE (1961) and L'ECLISSE (1962) confirmed her international standing, and in 1963 VADIM starred her in *Château en Suède*. In the same year she acted in Baratier's *Dragées au poivre* (*Sweet and Sour*), parodying her own alienated image as created in Antonioni's films. IL DESERTO ROSSO (1964) was the last of his films in which Vitti acted.

She returned to her preferred vein of comedy, making a bid for international recognition as a comic actor in the title role of LOSEY's *Modesty Blaise* (1966). The free, physical kind of comedy at which she excels is particularly popular in Italy, and she has acted regularly in Italian comedies, winning several awards for her performance in *La ragazza con la pistola* (1969), and playing opposite Alberto SORDI in *Le coppie* (1970). She had also appeared in several Italian romances, and returned to a dramatic role in JANCSÓ's *La pacifistà* (1971). Her reputation as an international star rests undoubtedly on the four films she made with Antonioni, but her reputation at home has grown steadily since she left the international scene.

*VIVA MARIA!*, France/Italy, 1965. Panavision; 2hr; Eastman Color. *Dir* Louis Malle; *asst dir* Volker Schloendorff, Manuel Munoz, Juan-Luis Buñuel; *prod* Nouvelles Editions de Films/ Artistes Associés/Vides Cinematografica; *scr* Malle, Jean-Claude Carrière; *ph* Henri Decaë; *ed* Kenout Peltier, Suzanne Baron; *mus* Georges Delerue; *cast* Brigitte Bardot (Maria II), Jeanne Moreau (Maria I), George Hamilton (Florès), Gregor von Rezzori (Diogène), Paulette Dubost (Madame Diogène), Claudio Brook (Rodolfo), Francisco Reiguera (Father Superior).

MALLE and CARRIÈRE began writing the story of *Viva Maria!*, about a revolution in an indeterminate Central American state, when they were inspired by the sense of spectacle aroused by Malle's production of *Der Rosenkavalier* at Spoleto in 1964. Moreover, Malle wanted to break with the introspection of LE FEU FOLLET (1963), and to try his hand at a superproduction. His decision to co-star Jeanne MOREAU and Brigitte BARDOT (rather sourly criticized by some reviewers) shows a characteristic sense of audacity and fun on his part, and also on the part of the two stars. Bardot's considerable potential as a *comédienne* came nearer realization in this role than in any other, with Moreau's superb professionalism as an admirable foil. Malle was perfectly at ease in a lavish production, handling crowds with assurance, playing technical tricks with his usual zest, and spoofing the super-production conventions even as he moved confidently within them. The sense of adventure and fun which pervaded the shooting in Mexico is apparent in the finished film; with its verve, gaiety, and accomplishment it deservedly won wide popular success.

*VIVA ZAPATA!*, US, 1952, 1½hr. *Dir* Elia Kazan; *prod* Darryl F. Zanuck for Twentieth Century-Fox; *scr* John Steinbeck, from the story *Zapata the Unconquered* by E. Pichon; *ph* Joe MacDonald; *mus* Alex North; *cast* Marlon Brando (Emiliano Zapata), Jean Peters (Josefa Espejo), Anthony Quinn (Enfemio Zapata), Joseph Wiseman (Fernando Aguirre), Arnold Moss (Don Nacio), Frank Silvera (General Huerta).

The film is based on the life of the Mexican revolutionary, Emiliano Zapata. KAZAN chronicles his early struggles against General Diaz, his guerrilla campaigns, his rise to the presidency, and, finally, his betrayal by a friend. Although individual sequences are tightly directed, the pace of the film as a whole lacks variety and dynamism and the elliptical rendering of the narrative tends to be confusing. The film does however develop a certain dramatic momentum through BRANDO's performance (which won him the best actor award at CANNES) and through good playing in the minor roles, especially that of Frank Silvera as General Huerta.

*VIVERE IN PACE* (*To Live in Peace*), Italy, 1946. 1½hr. *Dir* Luigi Zampa; *prod* Carlo Ponti for Lux Pao Film; *scr* Suso Cecchi d'Amico, Aldo Fabrizzi, Piero Tellini, Zampa; *ph* Carlo Montuori; *mus* Nino Rota; *cast* Aldo Fabrizzi (Uncle Tigna), Gary Moore (Ronald), Mirella Monti (Silvia), John Kitzmiller (Joe), Ave Ninchi (Corinna).

Two American soldiers take refuge in a remote Italian village, giving the community a chance to express its resistance to the contagion of war.

Appearing at the height of NEO-REALISM, *Vivere in pace* was hailed as a masterpiece. Although time has modified that judgement, the film is distinguished by Aldo FABRIZZI's acting as well as by ZAMPA's feeling for comedy (in spite of the tragic finale) and by his neo-realist concern for the human predicament.

*VIVRE SA VIE* (*It's my Life* in GB; *My Life to Live* in US), France, 1962. 1½hr. *Dir* Jean-Luc Godard; *prod* Pierre Braunberger for Films de la Pléiade; *scr* Godard, documentation from *Où en est la prostitution?* by Marcel Sacotte; *ph* Raoul Coutard; *ed* Agnès Guillemot; *mus* Michel Legrand; *cast* Anna Karina (Nana), Sady Rebbot (Raoul), André-S. Labarthe (Paul), Brice Parain (the philosopher).

*Vivre sa vie* marks a return to the probing, objective style of LE PETIT SOLDAT (1960), and all that is retained from the experiment of *Une Femme est une femme* (1961) is the use of direct sound, which gives GODARD's examination of prostitution an almost documentary tone. The film, which more than any of its predecessors gives the impression of careful construction and attention to its formal characteristics, was in fact made extremely rapidly in long takes of which very few were re-shot. The scenes were shot in order and simply joined together with as little editing as possible. The sound-track was recorded with similar simplicity on a single tape, with MIXING restricted to what could be done on location. The division of the film into twelve episodes was influenced by Brechtian practice, to maintain the distancing of the spectator. A similar effect is achieved by the frequent inclusion of 'texts': the story of the theft of 1,000 francs which Nana relates to the policeman, the little girl's essay about the chicken, told by Paul, the magazine story recited by the salesgirl, the extract from Poe's 'The Oval Portrait', all quotations which, being words not belonging to the speaker, impose a further barrier to audience involvement.

*VOIE LACTÉE, La* (*The Milky Way*), France/Italy, 1969. Wide screen; 1¾hr; Eastman Color. *Dir* Luis Buñuel; *prod* Greenwich Film Production (Paris)/Medusa (Rome); *scr* Buñuel, Jean-Claude Carrière; *ph* Christian Matras; *cast* Paul Frankeur (Pierre), Laurent Terzieff (Jean), Delphine Seyrig (the prostitute), Edith Scob (Virgin Mary), Bernard Verley (Jesus), Alain Cuny (man with the cape).

BUÑUEL's anti-clericalism is expressed in a picaresque narrative of two tramps on a pilgrimage, their various encounters serving as an examination of different elements of Christian dogma. The film is imbued with Buñuel's characteristic mischievousness, particularly in the refer-

ences to L'ÂGE D'OR (1930), LOS OLVIDADOS (1950), and VIRIDIANA (1961), and the discussion of abstruse theological questions often becomes hilarious in contrast with the inappropriateness of the participants and settings.

**VOIGHT, JON** (1939–   ), US actor, attracted wide attention in an off-Broadway production of *A View from the Bridge* in 1967. In the same year he appeared in two films, *Frank's Greatest Adventure* and *Out of It*. His brilliant performance in MIDNIGHT COWBOY (1970) won him an OSCAR nomination. He has proved both versatile and positive: in *Catch-22* (Mike NICHOLS, 1970), *The Revolutionary* (1970)—a quiet, understated performance in an unusual film—and *Deliverance* (John BOORMAN, 1972).

*VOINA I MIR* (*War and Peace*), USSR. Part 1: *Andrei Bolkonsky*, Part 2: *Natasha Rostova* (1966); Part 3: *1812*; Part 4: *Pierre Bezukhov* (1967). 70mm; 8hr; Sovcolor. *Dir* Sergei Bondarchuk; *prod* Mosfilm; *scr* Bondarchuk, Vasily Solovyov, from the novel by Leo Tolstoy; *ph* Anatoly Petritsky, Dmitri Korzhikin, A. Zenyan; *des* Mikhail Bogdanov, Gennady Myasnikov; *mus* Vyacheslav Ovchinnikov; *cast* Ludmilla Savelyeva (Natasha), Sergei Bondarchuk (Pierre), Vyacheslav Tikhonov (Andrei), Anastasia Vertinskaya (Princess Liza), Vasily Lanovoi (Kuragin), Irina Skobotseva (Hélène), Kira Ivanov-Golovko (Countess Rostova), Boris Zakhava (Kutuzov), Vladislav Strzhelchik (Napoleon).

To convey Tolstoy's great novel to the screen required the expenditure of massive resources of time, finance, and creative energy. The resulting film escapes the dangers of mere size by reason of BONDARCHUK's capacity to control both large-scale action sequences and intimate human relationships. Fine performances in all the principal roles help to balance the overpowering effect of the battle scenes. The technical command is wholly authoritative, the temptation to over-exploit virtuoso effects having been rigorously avoided.

A shortened, dubbed version, shown in two three-hour parts, circulated in Britain and the US.

Two previous Russian versions were made, both in 1915. *Voina i mir* (2½hr, issued in two parts) was adapted and directed by Vladimir GARDIN and starred Olga Preobrazhenskaya as Natasha. *Natasha Rostova* (1¼hr) starred Vera Coralli and was directed by Pyotr Chardynin.

*War and Peace* (US, 1956) was directed by King VIDOR and starred Audrey HEPBURN (Natasha), Henry FONDA (Pierre), Mel FERRER (Andrei), and Vittorio Gassman (Kuragin). It ran for 3½ hours, and Vidor concentrated, to good effect, on the action sequences; but the film showed, with perhaps the exception of Audrey Hepburn's appealing Natasha, little understanding of the great novel's power in depicting humanity on a massive scale through the observation of individual characters.

**VON SYDOW**, MAX (1929– ), Swedish actor, real forenames Carl Adolf, trained at the Royal Dramatic Theatre School, Stockholm. His first film was Alf SJÖBERG's *Bara en mor (Only a Mother*, 1949), which was followed by FRÖKEN JULIE (1951). His first film for Ingmar BERGMAN, DET SJUNDE INSEGLET (*The Seventh Seal*, 1957), made his ascetic face internationally known and he has since become a regular member of the Bergman team of actors. Von Sydow excels in portraying characters forced by mental anguish into madness, as in *Jungfrukällen (The Virgin Spring*, 1960), *Vargtimmen (Hour of the Wolf*, 1968), *Skammen (Shame*, 1968), *En Passion (A Passion*, 1969). His films outside Sweden include *The Greatest Story Ever Told* (George STEVENS, 1965), in which he played Christ, *Hawaii* (1966), and *The Exorcist* (1973).

**VORKAPICH**, SLAVKO (1895– ), Yugoslav-born editor, studied painting in Belgrade, Budapest, and Paris, and in 1920 went to New York where he worked as a commercial artist and portrait painter. He moved to Hollywood where, with Robert FLOREY and Gregg TOLAND, he made the experimental film *The Life and Death of 9413, a Hollywood Extra* (1928) using miniatures on a table. In 1928–34 he worked on MONTAGE sequences for RKO and PARAMOUNT, including the furies segment in CRIME WITHOUT PASSION (1934). His distinguished work in Hollywood includes sequences in *Viva Villa* (1933), *A Tale of Two Cities* (1935), ROMEO AND JULIET (1936), THE GOOD EARTH (1937), *Maytime* (1937), *The Broadway Melody of 1938* (1937), *Boys' Town* (1938), and MR SMITH GOES TO WASHINGTON (1939).

In 1938 he lectured on montage theories at the Museum of Modern Art, and in 1941 he directed short films in PATHÉ's 'This is America' series. He was Head of the Cinema Department at the University of California, 1949–51. In 1952–6 he lectured throughout Europe, and made a film—*Hanka* (1955)—in Yugoslavia. He edited John Gunther's *High Road*, and in 1965 he gave a series of lectures on *The Visual Nature of the Film*, again at the Museum of Modern Art.

**VREDENS DAG** (*Day of Wrath*), Denmark, 1943. 1¾hr. *Dir* Carl Dreyer; *prod* Palladium Film; *scr* Dreyer, Mogens Skot-Hansen, Poul Knudsen, from the play *Anne Pedersdotter* by Hans Wiers-Jenssen; *ph* Karl Andersson; *des* Erik Ases; *ed* Edith Schlüssel, Anne Marie Petersen; *mus* Poul Schierbeck; *cast* Thorkild Roose (Absalon Pedersson), Lisbeth Movin (Anne), Sigrid Neiiendam (Merete, Absalon's mother), Preben Lerdorff Rye (Martin), Anna Svierkier (Marte Herlof), Albert Høberg (the bishop).

Set in the seventeenth century, *Vredens dag* tells the story of Anne, whose infidelity leads to the death of her husband and to her being burned as a witch. The film has DREYER's characteristic deliberate pace and formal style and the objective cruelty of LA PASSION DE JEANNE D'ARC (1928): it achieves a convincing and moving study of people caught in the inexorable meshes of superstition and fear. Anne's fate was popularly taken as an allegory of Denmark's persecution by the Nazis during the Occupation; although Dreyer disclaimed any such intentions he escaped to Sweden to avoid reprisals.

**VSTRECHNYI** (*Counterplan*), USSR, 1932. 1¾hr. *Dir* F. Ermler, S. Yutkevich; *co-dir* L. Arnstam; *asst* B. Poslavsky, G. Kazansky, V. Eisimont; *scr* L. Arnstam, D. Del, Ermler, Yutkevich; *ph* I. Martov, A. Ginsburg, W. Rappoport; *des* B. Dubrovsky-Eshke, N. Pavlov, A. Ushin; *mus* D. Shostakovich.

Made to celebrate the fifteenth anniversary of the October Revolution, this ambitious film was based on real-life rivalry in a Leningrad factory. It attempts to explore the attitudes and responsibilities of workers, and their role in the new society.

The work was divided between the two directors: YUTKEVICH worked on the scenes with young people, and ERMLER tackled the tougher problems of the older generations. The theme song, which later became a UN hymn, linked the separate sequences.

The film's comparatively subdued naturalism made it easily appreciated; it may be classed with CHAPAYEV (1935) and SHCHORS (1939) among the key films in the development of SOCIALIST REALISM.

# W

**WACHSFIGURENCABINETT, Das** (*Wax-works*), Germany, 1924. 2hr. *Dir* Paul Leni; *prod* Neptun-Film; *scr* Henrik Galeen; *ph* Helmar Lerski; *cast* Emil Jannings (Harun-al-Rashid), Conrad Veidt (Ivan the Terrible), Werner Krauss (Jack the Ripper), Wilhelm Dieterle (the poet).

In its use of sets and lighting, *Das Wachsfigurencabinett* is one of the last true examples of EXPRESSIONISM in films. Paul LENI deliberately set out to symbolize character, social elements, and plot in the designs: Rashid's surroundings mirror the pastrycook's dimensions and confections; Ivan the Terrible's oppressive régime is emphasized by restrictive architecture and the apparent reduction of human figures to ornament; most remarkable is the sinister fairground, created by moving lights and shapes, haunted by Jack the Ripper. A fourth part, featuring Rinaldo Rinaldini, was originally planned.

**WAGES OF FEAR, The,** see SALAIRE DE LA PEUR, LE

**WAGNER,** FRITZ ARNO (1889?–1958), German cameraman, worked at first as a newsreel reporter for PATHÉ in Paris. In 1919 he joined DECLA BIOSCOP in Berlin, where one of his first films was LUBITSCH's *Madame Dubarry* (1919, *Passion* in the US). In 1921 he filmed LANG's *Der müde Tod* (*Destiny*) and MURNAU's *Schloss Vogeloed* and in the following year NOSFERATU, EINE SYMPHONIE DES GRAUENS, for which he created several special effects. Wagner also filmed ROBISON's *Schatten* (1923), one of the most famous Expressionist films, notable for the use of chiaroscuro lighting and scenes staged totally in silhouette (see EXPRESSIONISM).

His longest association was with PABST, a demanding master under whom Wagner worked well. Their first film was *Die Liebe der Jeanne Ney* (1927); Wagner's smoothly mobile camera, constantly panning and tracking, and perfectly natural light values contributed largely to the film's technical accomplishment. In KAMERAD-SCHAFT (1931), his last film for Pabst, Wagner used a mobile camera at a time when cameras were generally enclosed in booths to facilitate sound recording. An article by Pabst, where he claimed that the director alone had total control over the screen image brought an end to the partnership.

Wagner continued to work in Germany until the late forties, his most notable films being M (1931), DAS TESTAMENT DES DR MABUSE (1932), and OHM KRÜGER (1941).

**WAGONMASTER,** US, 1950. 1½hr. *Dir* John Ford; *prod* Argosy Pictures/RKO; *scr* Frank Nugent, Patrick Ford; *ph* Bert Glennon; *ed* Jack Murray; *mus* Richard Hageman; *songs* Stan Jones, sung by The Sons of the Pioneers; *cast* Ben Johnson (Travis), Harry Carey Jr (Sandy), Ward Bond (Wiggs), Joanne Dru (Denver), Charles Kemper (Uncle Shiloh Clegg), Jane Darwell (Sister Ledyard), Alan Mowbray (Dr Locksley Hall), Ruth Clifford (Fleuretty), James Arness (Floyd Clegg), Francis Ford (Mr Peachtree).

This deceptively simple film, telling the story of a Mormon wagon train guided by two young horse-traders in search of new settlements in the West, is full of FORD's mastery of characterization and incident. Some of the characters parallel those in MY DARLING CLEMENTINE (1946) and the familiar faces of the Ford 'stock' company abound. What matters most, however, is the way Ford takes a standard story-line and endows it with a sweep of emotion that perfectly conveys the dedication of the pioneer community. Ward BOND later repeated his role in the long-running television series 'Wagon Train'.

**WAJDA,** ANDRZEJ (1926–  ), Polish director, son of a cavalry officer who was killed in the Second World War. Wajda fought with the Resistance from the age of sixteen while working in a succession of jobs including painting church interiors. After the war he studied painting at Kraców and film directing at LÓDŹ. He became Aleksander FORD's assistant on PIATKA Z ULICY BARSKIEJ (*Five Boys from Barska Street*, 1953), and Ford was artistic supervisor on Wajda's first feature, POKOLENIE (*A Generation*, 1954).

Wajda's trilogy—*Pokolenie*, KANAL (1957), and POPIÓŁ I DIAMENT (*Ashes and Diamonds*, 1958)—established him as a major European director and marked a turning-point in Polish cinema. The three films are imbued with bitter scepticism towards the national tradition of romantic heroism, exposing the conflicts suffered by the young men who took over as the older generation fell and the suicidal consequences of the Polish legend. *Lotna* (1959), his first film in colour, again used an episode in the war—a Polish cavalry attack on German tanks—to illuminate traditional heroism: the grey horse of the title symbolizes the spirit of Poland.

*Niewinni czarodzieje* (*Innocent Sorcerers*, 1959) abandoned the subject of war to view with rueful humour the pains of adolescent sexuality. After *Vrata raja* (*Gates to Paradise*, 1967), a Polish/Yugoslav co-production based on Jerzy Andrzejewski's book about the children's crusade in the Middle Ages, Wajda made his most personal film, *Wszystko na sprzedaz* (*Everything for Sale*, 1968), in reaction to the death of Zbigniew CYBULSKI, who had become a super-star after appearing in Wajda's trilogy. Wajda then made an outright comedy, *Polowanie na muchy* (*Hunting Flies*, 1969), and returned to the effects of war in *Krajobraz po bitwie* (*Landscape after Battle*, 1970). Like the trilogy, this hints at a poignant obsession with the generation that found no place in post-war society; a love affair between a poet and a Jewess reflects the political troubles that were disrupting Poland shortly before the film was made. *Wesele* (*The Wedding*, 1972) combines folk-lore, politics, and an investigation of the artist's role in a fluidly moving poetic fantasy.

Although acknowledged as Poland's leading director, Wajda has never been a popular figure; he examines sensitive areas of the national conscience, and his complex anti-literary visual style, combined with an ambiguous attitude to traditional values, gives his films a harsh and unsettling brilliance.

**WALBROOK,** ANTON (1900–67), Austrian actor, real name Adolf Wohlbrück, son of the Viennese clown Adolf Wohlbrück, won a scholarship to Max REINHARDT's acting school at the age of sixteen. In 1930 he went to Berlin and appeared in his first film *Salto mortale* (1931)—a circus story. In 1937 he settled in England, where he acted on stage and screen under his new name. Among his most popular successes were *Victoria the Great* (1937), *Sixty Glorious Years* (1938), GASLIGHT (1940), *Dangerous Moonlight* (1941), THE RED SHOES (1948), THE QUEEN OF SPADES (1948), LA RONDE (1950), and Otto PREMINGER's *Saint Joan* (1957). His reputation was built on an elegance and mystique both romantic and sinister, but his versatility also included a flair for light comedy.

**WALDEKRANZ,** RUNE (1911–   ), Swedish producer. As head of production at Sandrews 1942–64 he made a striking contribution to the revival of Swedish cinema (see SWEDEN). He produced notable films by Alf SJÖBERG and Gösta EKMAN, sometimes also working as scriptwriter. When Ingmar BERGMAN's reputation was temporarily in decline, his career was supported by Waldekranz who produced GYCKLARNAS AFTON (*Sawdust and Tinsel* or *The Naked Night*, 1953) and *Kvinnodröm* (*Journey into Autumn* or *Dreams*, 1954). He also produced Jörn DONNER's *Att älska* (*To Love*, 1964) and Mai ZETTERLING's first feature *Älskande par* (*Loving Couples*, 1964). On retiring from Sandrews Waldekranz became principal of the Swedish film school. He has published books on the Swedish cinema.

**WALKER,** ROBERT (1918–51), US actor, a leading man in Hollywood after stage and radio experience with his wife Jennifer JONES. His first film was *Bataan* (1943) and in the same year he appeared in Mervyn LEROY's *Madame Curie*. He displayed an appealing, youthful personality in MINNELLI's *The Clock* (1944, *Under the Clock* in GB) which co-starred Judy GARLAND; but his divorce in that year led to a spiral of personal problems which led to his early death from a drug injection. In his last and best film, HITCHCOCK's STRANGERS ON A TRAIN (1951), he was effectively cast against type as a charming psychotic.

His son Robert Walker Jr (1941–   ) made a number of minor film appearances in the sixties.

***WALKING DOWN BROADWAY*** see HALLO, SISTER

**WALLACH,** ELI (1915–   ), US actor, one of the early adherents of the ACTORS' STUDIO, had already achieved success in the theatre before his first film appearance in BABY DOLL (1956), in which his performance as the sly and terrifying seducer was outstanding. In later films his considerable acting skill has been under-used: THE MAGNIFICENT SEVEN (1960), THE MISFITS (1961), and many others have offered him less rewarding roles. He has continued his distinguished stage career, notably in plays by Tennessee WILLIAMS.

**WALLIS,** HAL (1898–   ), US producer, worked in exhibition and publicity before becoming a producer for WARNER BROS. In 1933 he succeeded Darryl F. ZANUCK as head of production at Warners, and ten years later set up his own independent production company basing his unit successively at Warners, PARAMOUNT, and UNIVERSAL. Wallis is credited with discovering several box-office stars—Errol FLYNN, Olivia DE HAVILLAND, Burt LANCASTER, Kirk DOUGLAS, Elvis PRESLEY— and has produced a number of major films including LITTLE CAESAR (1930), *I Am a Fugitive from a Chain Gang* (1932), *Captain Blood* (1935), *Jezebel* (1938), THE MALTESE FALCON (1941), CASABLANCA (1943), GUNFIGHT AT THE OK CORRAL (1956). Of recent years he has specialized in costume dramas: *Becket* (1964), *Anne of the Thousand Days* (1969), and *Mary Queen of Scots* (1971). He has twice received the Irving THALBERG Award presented by the ACADEMY OF MOTION PICTURE ARTS AND SCIENCES to outstanding producers.

**WALSH,** RAOUL (1892–    ), US director, started as an actor in 1910 and made his first film appearance at BIOGRAPH where D. W. GRIFFITH made him his assistant and supervised his first film as director, *The Life of Villa* (1912). During his early career Walsh often wrote his own scripts and he continued to act—he played Lincoln's assassin John Wilkes Booth in THE BIRTH OF A NATION (1915)—until he lost his right eye while directing *In Old Arizona* (1929). His long career, extending into the mid-sixties and resulting in some two hundred films, has made him a thoroughly respected figure. Particularly during his time with WARNER BROS (1939–51) he directed many examples of Hollywood's forte: unpretentious adventure films whose inexhaustible action makes them the staple of popular film entertainment. His best films include THE THIEF OF BAGDAD (1924), *What Price Glory?* (1926), *The Big Trail* (1930), *The Bowery* (1933), THE ROARING TWENTIES (1939), *High Sierra* (1941), *They Died With Their Boots On* (1942), *Gentleman Jim* (1942), *Pursued* (1947), *Colorado Territory* (1949), *White Heat* (1949), *Distant Drums* (1951), *The Tall Men* (1955).

**WALTHALL,** HENRY B. (1878/6?–1936), US actor who was brought into films in 1909 by D. W. GRIFFITH for whom he gave his finest performance as the Little Colonel in THE BIRTH OF A NATION (1915). His other silent films include *The Scarlet Letter* (Victor SJÖSTRÖM, 1926), in which he played the harsh husband. After the coming of sound his pleasant speaking voice made him much in demand. He was working on *China Clipper* at the time of his death.

**WALTON,** WILLIAM (1902–    ), British composer, wrote the music scores for three films starring Elisabeth BERGNER: *Escape Me Never* (1936), *As You Like It* (1936), and *Stolen Life* (1939). During the war he wrote only film music, composing for, among others, *The Next of Kin* (1941), *The Foreman Went to France* and *The First of the Few* (both 1942). The latter work provided the basis for Walton's *Spitfire Prelude and Fugue* which, like sections of his score for

HENRY V (1944), has become a standard concert work. He was knighted in 1951.

**WAMPAS** (Western Associated Motion Picture Advertisers), a Hollywood publicists' association formed *c.* 1920, to enhance the prestige of film industry press agents. In 1922–32 it made an annual selection of aspiring young actresses, and dubbed them the WAMPAS 'Baby Stars'. Studios and agents realized the possibilities of the scheme and gave it financial and professional backing. Some successful WAMPAS 'Baby Stars' were: 1922, Colleen Moore, Bessie LOVE; 1924, Clara BOW; 1926, Dolores DEL RIO, Mary ASTOR; 1929, Jean ARTHUR; 1931, Joan BLONDELL; 1932, Ginger ROGERS. No selections were made in 1930, partly owing to the Depression and producers' economies, partly because the coming of sound confused the selectors' requirements. After WAMPAS disbanded spasmodic attempts were made to continue the tradition, e.g. 'Paramount Protégées of 1935', but the WAMPAS phenomenon was never quite recreated.

**WANGER,** WALTER (1894–1968), US producer, an intelligent and perceptive filmmaker whose early achievements included QUEEN CHRISTINA (1934), *You Only Live Once* (Fritz LANG, 1937), STAGECOACH (1939), and *Scarlet Street* (Lang, 1945). In 1951 he served three months in prison for shooting the agent of his wife, Joan BENNETT. The experience inspired *Riot in Cell Block 11* (Don SIEGEL, 1954), and he also produced for Siegel *Invasion of the Body Snatchers* (1956). Wanger's career ended when he failed to maintain control of CLEOPATRA (1962) and was sacked as producer, although he is credited on the titles. With Joe Hyams he wrote his side of the story in *My life with Cleopatra* (London, 1963).

***WAR AND PEACE*** see VOINA I MIR

**WARHOL,** ANDY (1928–    ), US graphic artist and film-maker, a major figure in the American Pop Art movement. He brought to film a feeling for contemporary icons (his screenprints include series on Marilyn MONROE, Elizabeth TAYLOR, and Marlon BRANDO) combined with the formal exploration characteristic of twentieth-century art and a flair for publicity. More than eighty films have emerged from his New York 'factory': they are in general team efforts, Warhol's signature denoting a style and an attitude rather than individual authorship.

The first were completely static: *Sleep* (1963)—a man sleeping for six hours; *Empire* (1964)—an eight-hour view of the Empire State Building. Like *Kiss* (1963) and *Blow Job* (1964)

they were silent, projected at 16 frames per second although shot at 24 fps, and without editing apart from the ending of the reels. *Harlot* (1964), his first sound film, was still static, but *Hedy* (or *The Shoplifter*, 1965), with a drag queen playing out the life of a Hollywood star, used a mobile, zooming camera that in turn caught the action, emphasized it, or left it off-screen.

*My Hustler* (1965) and the three-hour two-screen *Chelsea Girls* (1966) gained Warhol widespread attention, chiefly for their voyeuristic concentration on sex and their revelation of New York 'underground' life. By now his bizarre stars had extended their function, acting out their own fantasies in the films. Nico, Taylor Mead, and Viva emerged as 'super-stars' in *Lonesome Cowboys* (1968), a parody of the Western in which the tradition of male friendship is carried further than the genre usually allows. Viva also starred in *Fuck* (*Blue Movie*, 1968) showing two hours of a sexual encounter. Later 'super-stars' like Candy Darling and Holly Woodlawn are in fact male transvestites.

Paul Morrissey is credited as director of the films made after the attempt on Warhol's life in 1968. *Flesh* (1968), *Trash* (1970), and *Heat* (1971) all star Joe Dalessandro. They are more conventionally structured than the earlier experiments, still improvisatory but with sequential narratives and purposeful technique. They have received wide commercial release; their free-wheeling, uncensorious depiction of sexual activity and drug abuse outraged some audiences, presenting problems for the British CENSORSHIP authorities in particular.

Warhol is perhaps the only UNDERGROUND film-maker well known to the general public. He is, however, unrepresentative of the American underground in his indifference to the technical possibilities of cinema and his detachment from the groups established in the field. Warhol's films, like his life-style, are rather an extension of his work in graphic art; but they have none the less influenced independent film-makers, particularly in their examination of the illusion of acting and of the resources of minimal film-making.

The large number of books on Warhol include *Andy Warhol*, ed J. Coplans, London, 1971; Peter Gidal, *Andy Warhol: paintings and films*, London, New York, 1971; Stephen Koch, *Stargazer*, London, 1973.

**WARM,** HERMANN (1889–    ), German designer, was trained at the Kunstgewerbeschule in Berlin. He worked in the theatre before entering films in 1912 when he became an important figure in the Expressionist movement (see EXPRESSIONISM). He was one of the designers for DAS CABINETT DES DR CALIGARI (1919) and also designed the sets for *Der müde Tod* (Fritz LANG, 1921), DER STUDENT VON PRAG (1926), *Die Liebe der Jeanne Ney* (G. W. PABST, 1927), LA PASSION DE JEANNE D'ARC (1928), and VAMPYR (1932). He worked in Britain and France in the thirties, and after spending the war years in Switzerland, he returned to Germany where one of his later films was *Hokuspokus* (1966).

**WARNER BROS PICTURES,** US production company; its trademark a badge bearing the initials 'WB'. Harry, Jack, Albert, and Sam Warner had together attempted various professions before setting up a film distribution concern in New York in 1917. Expanding into production on the West Coast, they established Warner Bros Pictures Inc in 1923, with Harry and Albert, the company's president and treasurer respectively, running the New York headquarters and Jack and Sam managing the Hollywood studio.

Warners' first years were not conspicuously successful. They built large theatres in Hollywood and New York and in 1925 acquired the old VITAGRAPH company, but remained in a state of financial insecurity which induced them to gamble on introducing SOUND. Sam Warner was responsible for developing with Western Electric and Bell Telephone Laboratories a sound-on-disc system named VITAPHONE. He never lived to see the far-reaching effects of the innovation; he died at the age of thirty-nine, twenty-four hours before the première of THE JAZZ SINGER (1927). Other production companies and exhibitors, reluctant to invest the sums needed to adapt their facilities, fought briefly against the introduction of sound; but the 'talkies' were enthusiastically welcomed by the public.

The enormous financial success of their early sound films allowed Warners rapidly to expand its interests, acquiring in 1932 a vast theatre chain (the Stanley Company of America) and taking over other production companies (among them FIRST NATIONAL). The acquisitions also led to overseas commitments; Warner Bros inherited First National's connection with ASSOCIATED BRITISH PICTURE CORPORATION which later resulted in the establishment of Warner studios at Teddington and the purchase in 1941 of a 25 per cent interest in ABPC. Warners managed to hold on to these shares until 1969 when they were bought out by British interests.

Warner Bros always prided themselves on making modestly budgeted, technically competent entertainment features. In the thirties these were exemplified by their successful GANGSTER cycle—LITTLE CAESAR (1930), PUBLIC ENEMY (1931), SCARFACE (1932), etc—which made stars of Humphrey BOGART, James CAGNEY, and Edward G. ROBINSON, and by their Busby BERKELEY MUSICALS, notably the GOLDDIGGERS series (1933–8), 42ND STREET (1933), and *Footlight Parade* (1933). They were also able to make a profit with prestige productions: the heavier 'social conscience' films, in particular *I Am a Fugitive from a Chain Gang* (1932) and *Confessions of a Nazi Spy* (1939), as well as earnest biographies of famous figures, especially *The Life of Emile Zola* (1937). The studio housed at various times the talents of Bette DAVIS, Olivia DE HAVILLAND, Errol FLYNN, Paul MUNI, Hal WALLIS, Michael CURTIZ, Mervyn LEROY, Raoul WALSH, and more recently Elia KAZAN, Mike NICHOLS, and Arthur PENN.

During the late fifties the studio spent much of its resources on television series, some quite successful; in the last twenty years, however, Warners have become increasingly dependent on contracts with independent producers for their feature film output. During the sixties the company backed big productions like MY FAIR LADY (1964) and *Camelot* (1967), but should also be given credit for investing in such unconventional Hollywood films as *Who's Afraid of Virginia Woolf?* (1966) and BONNIE AND CLYDE (1967).

In mid-1967 Warner Bros was merged with Seven Arts, a distributor of films to television, and was known for two years as Warner Brothers–Seven Arts (or W–7). In 1969 a large financial concern, Kinney National Service, acquired the studio and returned it to its original title. Jack L. Warner, the last of the brothers to be associated with the company, retired from the board, leaving the studio under the management of Ted Ashley and John Calley. COLUMBIA moved to the Warner Bros studio in 1972 and the amalgamation was named Columbia–Warner. The studio has weathered the recent financial crises of the film industry by renting out, rather than selling, studio space, by making drastic reductions in employment and projects, and by closing down altogether, sometimes for months at a time.

**WARNERCOLOR,** name used by WARNER BROS to identify films photographed in EASTMAN COLOR and processed by them. The stock is identical with Eastman Color.

**WARNER, DAVID** (1941– ), British actor, made his first film appearance in TOM JONES (1963). He joined the Royal Shakespeare Company in 1963 and has carried on a distinguished stage career concurrently with his increasing popularity with cinema audiences. He starred in MORGAN . . . A SUITABLE CASE FOR TREATMENT (1966) and *Work Is a Four Letter Word* (1967) in roles ideally suited to his gaunt and nervous charm. He played the lead in a German film, *Michael Kohlhaas* (Volker SCHLÖNDORFF, 1969) and has worked for US directors Sidney LUMET

(*The Seagull*, 1968) and Sam PECKINPAH (*The Ballad of Cable Hogue*, 1970).

**WARREN, HARRY** (1893– ), US songwriter, real name Harry Guaragna, was one of the most prolific and accomplished Hollywood songwriters. He wrote the memorable songs for most of the Busby BERKELEY production numbers of the thirties, including the famous GOLD-DIGGERS series ('Lullaby of Broadway' is his most dramatic song), many of the wartime TWENTIETH CENTURY-FOX musicals, including those featuring Glenn Miller's orchestra, and the melodic score for Judy GARLAND in *The Harvey Girls* (1945).

*WATERLOO BRIDGE*, US, 1940. 1¾hr. *Dir* Mervyn LeRoy; *prod* Sidney Franklin for MGM; *scr* S. N. Behrman, Hans Rameau, George Froeschel from R. E. Sherwood's play; *ph* Joseph Ruttenberg; *mus* Herbert Stothart; *cast* Vivien Leigh (Myra), Robert Taylor (Roy Cronin), Lucile Watson (Lady Margaret Cronin), Virginia Field (Kitty), Maria Ouspenskaya, C. Aubrey Smith.

One of several film versions of a tearful romance of the First World War in which Scottish aristocrat Roy Cronin meets and loves Myra, an orphaned ballet dancer who finally commits suicide from Waterloo Bridge. Vivien LEIGH is at her youthful best, but the London scenery, in which St Paul's can be seen from every window, is unconvincing to British eyes.

**WATKINS, PETER** (1935– ), British director, developed his characteristic reportage style involving newsreel techniques and non-professional actors in an amateur film, *The Forgotten Faces* (1961). Two films for BBC television established this style: *Culloden* (1964) was very successful but *The War Game* (1965), his horrific vision of nuclear warfare, was not broadcast. Distributed theatrically, it won an OSCAR in 1966. Following the artistic and commercial failure of his first feature *Privilege* (1967), Watkins went to Sweden to make *Gladiatorerna* (*The Peace Game*, 1969) and to the US to make *Punishment Park* (1970).

**WATT, HARRY** (1906– ), British director, joined the Empire Marketing Board film unit, later the CROWN FILM UNIT, in 1931. He was assistant director to Robert FLAHERTY on MAN OF ARAN (1934) and also directed some fine short documentaries including NIGHT MAIL (1936, with Basil WRIGHT), *The First Days* (1939, with Humphrey JENNINGS and Pat Jackson), and *London Can Take It* (1940, with Jennings). His feature films show the strong influence of his background in documentaries, especially *Target for Tonight* (1940) and those with an Australian setting: THE OVERLANDERS (1946), *Eureka Stockade* (1948), and *The Siege of Pinchgut* (1959). His autobiography *Don't look at the camera*, London, 1974, is a self-styled 'irreverent memoir' of many major figures in the British cinema.

*WAXWORKS* see WACHSFIGURENCABINETT, DAS

*WAY DOWN EAST*, US, 1920. 2½hr. *Dir, prod* D. W. Griffith for United Artists release; *scr* Anthony Paul Kelly, Joseph R. Grismer, Griffith, based on the play by Lottie Blair Parker; *ph* G. W. Bitzer, Hendrick Sartov; *cast* Lillian Gish (orphan girl), Richard Barthelmess (farmer's son), Lowell Sherman, Burr Mcintosh, Kate Bruce, Creighton Hale, Porter Strong, Mary Hay, Mrs Morgan Belmont.

A young orphan girl, movingly played by Lillian GISH, is seduced and has a baby which dies. She is taken on as a servant by a farming family, but when her guilty past is revealed the farmer turns her out of the house into the wintry countryside. The girl almost drowns, but is rescued by the farmer's son who marries her.

Despite the trite sentimentality of the original play (for which GRIFFITH paid an unprecedented $175,000), the film had great popular success and in terms of profit was second only to THE BIRTH OF A NATION (1915) among Griffith's films. It is particularly memorable for the last-minute rescue in the dramatic setting of the ice-floes, which was accompanied by formidable sound effects in large cinemas. This climactic sequence involved an ingenious blending of library and studio shots with actual location work which was executed in hazardous conditions. The sequence is said to have provided the inspiration for similar scenes in PUDOVKIN'S MAT (*Mother*, 1926).

WAYNE, JOHN (1907– ), US actor, real name Marion Michael Morrison, grew up in California where he became a football star, appearing with his team (which included Ward BOND) in John FORD's *Salute* (1929). He worked as a property man in Hollywood where Ford advised Raoul WALSH to star him in *The Big Trail* (1930); Walsh agreed on condition Morrison changed his name. Throughout the thirties Wayne played minor roles, or leads in minor films, until in 1939 Ford cast him as the Ringo Kid in STAGECOACH and the film's success marked a turning-point in his career.

Although he has played soldiers, aviators, big-game hunters, and adventurers of all kinds, Wayne has become the archetypal WESTERN hero, tough, self-sufficient, brutal where necessary but not vicious, frequently embodying Ford's conception of the pioneer spirit. The many fine films they made together include SHE WORE A YELLOW RIBBON (1949), THE SEARCHERS (1956), and THE MAN WHO SHOT LIBERTY VALANCE (1962). He has also given excellent performances for Howard HAWKS in RED RIVER (1948), RIO BRAVO (1959), and *El Dorado* (1966), and for Henry HATHAWAY in *True Grit* (1969), in which he was ideally cast as the hard-drinking, one-eyed, ageing law-man Rooster Cogburn. It gained Wayne his first OSCAR, in part an acknowledgement of his having 'licked the Big C', Wayne's euphemism for the lung cancer which nearly killed him in 1964.

His own company, Batjac, has produced many of his films and he has directed twice—an account of the fall of the ALAMO in which he played Davy CROCKETT, *The Alamo* (1960), and *The Green Berets* (1968), a violent and sentimental approbation of American action in Vietnam.

Wayne has for many years been an active supporter of the Republican Party, energetically assisting the presidential campaigns of Eisenhower and Nixon and the presidential nomination campaigns of Barry Goldwater and Ronald REAGAN.

WAYNE, NAUNTON (1901–70), British actor who had extensive theatrical experience, from concert party to legitimate stage, before starting to appear in films in the early thirties. He achieved success on the screen in tandem with Basil RADFORD notably in THE LADY VANISHES (1938). Wayne was the pinch-voiced and rather blasé member of the pair who epitomized (in caricature) the bumbling but undeterred and imperturbable old-school-tie type of Englishman. Although each frequently worked independently, Wayne was the less versatile of the two and more dependent on the complementary effect of the teaming. From *The Titfield Thunderbolt* (1953), following the death of Radford in 1952, the magic was missing in Wayne's solo appearances.

WEBB, JACK (1920– ), US director, producer, and actor, who began his career in radio. In 1949 he created, directed, and acted in the radio thriller series 'Dragnet'. Enormously popular, it became a television series in 1951 and in 1954 a feature film, starring Webb and directed by him in a distinctive style, using clipped dialogue, large close-ups, and a semi-documentary presentation. The series rarely dealt with large-scale crime, using instead cases and people with which its audience could identify. In 1955 Webb produced, directed, and acted in *Pete Kelly's Blues*, with Ella Fitzgerald, Peggy LEE, and Janet LEIGH. Set in Kansas City in the twenties, and involving a jazz musician embroiled with gangsters, it conveyed with rare authenticity for a fiction film both a feeling of the jazz life and an accurate reflection of the period. Webb has also done much television work as an executive, producer, and director. His other films include *Hollow Triumph* (1948), *The D. I.* (1957), *The Last Time I Saw Archie* (1961), *Purple Is the Color* (1964).

**WEDDING MARCH, The,** US, 1926. (Running time, see below.) *Dir* Erich von Stroheim; *prod* Famous Players-Lasky; *scr* Stroheim, Harry Carr; *ph* Ben Reynolds, Hal Mohr; *des* Stroheim, Richard Day; *cast* Erich von Stroheim (Prince Nicki), Fay Wray (Mitzi), George Fawcett (Prince Ottokar), Maude George (Princess Maria), Cesare Gravina (Mitzi's father), Dale Fuller (her mother), ZaSu Pitts (Cecelia).

STROHEIM planned *The Wedding March*, like GREED (1923) and QUEEN KELLY (1928), as a two-part film to be shown in one programme with an interval; it is likely that he envisaged a total running time of about six hours although the completed footage would have run to twelve or more hours of screen time. Before the shooting of the second part was finished he was removed from the direction of the film, on the usual grounds of wild extravagance, and Josef von STERNBERG was instructed to edit the material to acceptable length. The first part, running about $3\frac{1}{2}$ hours, was released as *The Wedding March* and probably approximated to Stroheim's intentions; the second, mutilated still further after leaving Sternberg's hands, was given a limited release in Europe in 1928 under the title *The Honeymoon* or *Mariage de prince* and ran to less than two hours.

What remains of the original conception shows that it would have fallen into the pattern of themes Stroheim worked on in FOOLISH WIVES (1921), THE MERRY WIDOW (1925), and *Queen Kelly*. Set in a Ruritanian princedom, the plot deals with the love of a poor girl, Mitzi, and a rich one, Cecelia, for the profligate but sympathetic Prince Nicki. A rich variety of subsidiary characters, played by many of Stroheim's favourite actors, populate the two social levels of the story and the lavishly detailed décors illuminate their behaviour and relationships in the typical Stroheim manner.

**WEEK-END,** France/Italy, 1967. Eastman Color; $1\frac{1}{2}$hr. *Dir, scr* Jean-Luc Godard; *prod* Comacico/Copernic/Lira Films (Paris)/Ascot Cineraid (Rome); *ph* Raoul Coutard; *ed* Agnès Guillemot; *mus* Mozart, Antoine Duhamel; *cast* Mireille Darc (Corinne), Jean Yanne (Roland), Jean-Pierre Léaud (Saint-Just/man in phone booth), Juliet Berto, Anna Wiazemsky (guerrillas).

In GODARD's most stringent attack on bourgeois materialistic values, a young Parisian couple's weekend drive becomes an immense regression into barbarism. The acts of murder and cannibalism committed by guerrillas are scarcely more violent than the methods used by the bourgeoisie in defence of its motor cars—arguments sparked off by minor incidents in traffic are resolved with starting-handles, aerosol paint sprays, and guns. The essence of the automobile age is captured in the justly famous ten-minute tracking shot along stalled cars, impatient and irate drivers, and bloody victims of a collision, with an ear-splitting accompaniment of car horns.

**WEGENER,** PAUL (1874–1948), German actor and director. A leading REINHARDT actor, who quickly saw the potential of film for conveying the supernatural, he produced and performed in the first version of DER STUDENT VON PRAG (1913), and directed and played the monster in DER GOLEM in 1914 and 1920. He acted opposite Asta NIELSEN in *Vanina* (1922), adapted from Stendhal by Carl MAYER, and with Wilhelm DIETERLE and Conrad VEIDT in *Lucrezia Borgia* (1927). Remaining in Germany, he took part in Veit HARLAN's spectacular *Kolberg* (1945) and PABST's abandoned *Der Fall Molander* (*The Molander Affair*). He received an honorary degree from East Germany's Rostock University for his stand against Nazism. From the beginning Wegener advocated restrained acting for cinema, and seldom lapsed from this style himself.

**WEILL,** KURT (1900–50), German composer, collaborated on a number of BRECHT's theatre pieces, including DIE DREIGROSCHENOPER which has been filmed twice. After staging a theatrical entertainment, *My Kingdom for a Cow*, with Muir Mathieson in London in 1935, he went to the US where he was mainly involved in theatrical work, but he also wrote the music for the film *You and Me* (Fritz LANG, 1938). Some of his stage works were filmed with his collaboration, including *Lady in the Dark* (1944), *Knickerbocker Holiday* (1944), and *Where Do We Go from Here?* (1945). He was married to Lotte LENYA.

**WEISS,** PETER (1916– ), German director, novelist, and playwright, trained at the Prague Art Academy and was a surrealist painter before making his first experimental short film in 1952. During the fifties he worked almost entirely in films—mainly independent 16mm shorts on which he was director, scenarist, editor, and soundman. *Hallucinations* (1952) consisted of twelve erotic tableaux; *Atel einterior* (*The Studio of Dr Faustus*, 1956) concerned a modern, mad central figure whose vision was expressed by means of distorting lenses, collages, and electronic music. *Hägringen* (*The Mirage*, 1958), Weiss's longest film, used the Kafkaesque theme of the hero oppressed by his urban environment; it drew on the film-maker's past surreal concerns but also reflected his increasing documentary interests. His play *The Persecution and Assassination of Jean-Paul Marat, as performed by the inmates of the asylum of Charenton under the direction of the Marquis de Sade* was staged then filmed by Peter BROOK in 1966 from Weiss's own screen adaptation.

**WEISSMULLER,** JOHNNY (1904– ), champion Olympic swimmer, became internationally known as TARZAN in nineteen films in 1932–48. He was the first Tarzan in talkies and created the famous yodelling call. His only conventional acting role was in *Swamp Fire* (1946). In the late forties and fifties he appeared in features and in a television series as 'Jungle Jim'.

*WELCOME MR MARSHALL* see BIENVENIDO MR MARSHALL

**WELLES,** ORSON (1915– ), US director and actor, studied at the Chicago Art Institute and for a short time worked as a journalist. In 1931 while he was in Ireland on a sketching trip he bluffed his way on to the professional stage at the Gate Theatre, Dublin. Encouraged by his successful start he stayed on in Dublin for a year, playing in productions at both the Gate and Abbey Theatres. He continued in the theatre on his return to the US and by his progressive productions began to acquire a considerable reputation. In 1936, as director of a branch of the Federal Theater, he put on a famous production of *Macbeth* with an all-black cast. With John Houseman he founded the Mercury Theater, which opened in 1937 with a modern-dress version of *Julius Caesar*. He and his company also did some broadcasting; the famous radio version of H. G. Wells's *The War of the Worlds* in October 1938—which caused a considerable panic—probably prompted RKO to invite Welles to Hollywood.

Welles's first Hollywood contract is deservedly one of the most famous in film history. 'I didn't want money: I wanted authority', Welles said of it, and he got absolute freedom to work as he chose; even so, the money side was impressive. The terms aroused considerable resentment and jealousy in Hollywood and Welles did not make his arrival any smoother by announcing his intention of causing 'some disturbance in the industry'. Unabashed at his hostile reception, Welles started work in 1940 on CITIZEN KANE; his contempt for existing conventions and his ebullient confidence were fully jus-

tified by the result, one of the most impressive first films made by any director.

He began work on THE MAGNIFICENT AMBERSONS in 1941, but RKO, already becoming alarmed at the feeble receipts from *Citizen Kane*, refused to allow him to finish the editing of *Ambersons*. Welles called in Norman Foster to finish directing his next film, *Journey into Fear* (1942), leaving detailed instructions for its completion, and went to Brazil to start work on a semi-documentary film *It's All True* which was never completed. He was recalled to Hollywood and fired by RKO. His next two films, *The Stranger* (1946) and LADY FROM SHANGHAI (1948), which starred Rita HAYWORTH, Welles's estranged wife (they had married in 1943), were both commissioned works. His next chance to work freely again—albeit on a small budget—came with his own production of MACBETH (1948). He spent eight years in Europe, where his first film was OTHELLO (1951). In *Confidential Report* (or *Mister Arkadin*, 1955) he returned to a contemporary theme and in some measure to his earlier creation of the hero in *Citizen Kane*. On his return to the US he made TOUCH OF EVIL (1958), a brilliant treatment of a frankly pulp-fiction subject. LE PROCÈS (*The Trial*, 1963) and CAMPANADAS A MEDIANOCHE (1966, *Chimes at Midnight/Falstaff* in the US and Europe) were made in France and Spain respectively.

He has continued throughout his career to stage theatre productions in the US and Europe, often with the aim of financing his film projects. He has to his credit a long list of distinguished stage performances as well as many on the screen. Films by other directors in which his wayward talents are best displayed include *Jane Eyre* (1944), THE THIRD MAN (1949), *Moby Dick* (1956), THE LONG HOT SUMMER (1958), and *Compulsion* (1959).

Welles's impact on the cinema was both immediate and lasting. His radio experience helped in his imaginative use of the sound-track; this, and his elliptical narrative construction, greatly enriched Hollywood films. Perhaps more importantly, he took advantage of Gregg TOLAND's experiments with wide-angle and deep-focus lenses to develop dramatic action within the frame, instead of cutting between fragments of action, and to emphasize the three-dimensional quality of the setting. This heightening of the tension between characters, by maintaining their spatial relationship, became a vital element in the mature use of the WIDE SCREEN by ANTONIONI and other European directors. His own career as a director has been brilliant and erratic. His personality has been the cause of much of his frustration and his chosen role of infant prodigy combined with *enfant terrible* has always promised more than he could perform. His course has been strewn with unfulfilled projects and his later films at best only echo his former brilliance. On the strength of *Citizen Kane*, however, and of the other peaks of his uneven achievement, he must be reckoned one of the giants of cinema.

**WELLMAN**, WILLIAM (1896–   ), US director, was in the French Foreign Legion and the Lafayette Flying Squadron before becoming a film actor in Hollywood. The first film he directed was a Dustin Farnum Western, *The Man Who Won* (1923). He made cinema history with *Wings* (1927), an epic of the Royal Flying Corps with aerial sequences that are still impressive. Gary COOPER, who attracted notice in a small part in *Wings*, starred opposite Fay WRAY in *Legion of the Condemned* (1928), another air force story, and in that year Wellman also directed *Beggars of Life* with Louise BROOKS and Wallace BEERY.

*Other Men's Women* (1931, *The Steel Highway* in GB), a spectacular railway drama, featured James CAGNEY who in the same year starred in PUBLIC ENEMY, Wellman's contribution to the WARNER BROS GANGSTER cycle. Tough action films continued to be Wellman's speciality—*Love is a Racket* (1932), *Call of the Wild* (1935), *Robin Hood of El Dorado* (1936)—until he changed course with A STAR IS BORN (1937) and NOTHING SACRED (1937), a finely controlled comic satire on the gutter press.

In 1938 Wellman again drew on his flying experience in *Men with Wings* and he again directed Gary Cooper in P. C. Wren's chivalrous romance *Beau Geste* (1939). *Roxie Hart* (1942) starred Ginger ROGERS in another sharp, stylish comedy in strong contrast to THE OX-BOW INCIDENT (*Strange Incident* in GB), a sombre Western which he directed the following year. *The Story of GI Joe* (1945, *War Correspondent* in GB) was also in Wellman's serious vein and made a star of Robert MITCHUM as a newspaperman reporting the Italian campaign. *Track of the Cat* (1954), a hunting story with symbolic overtones also starring Mitchum, was chiefly remarkable for its experimental use of minimal colour.

Wellman's directing career extended into the late fifties with more Westerns and air dramas predominating. His best work has an edgy style and a quality of moral fervour, even when couched in the Hollywood conventions of comedy or masculine adventure story.

**WERNER**, OSKAR (1922–   ), Austrian actor, real name Josef Bschliessmayer, who has worked chiefly in the theatre beginning at the Vienna Burgtheater in 1941. His first film was *Der Engel mit der Posaune* (*Eroica, the Angel with the Trumpet*, 1948). In 1955 he helped set up LOLA MONTÈS, Max OPHULS' last film, and appeared in it, and made an outstanding contribution to PABST's *Der letzte Akt*. His quality of suppressed nervous intensity was especially suited to the diffident Jules in TRUFFAUT'S JULES ET JIM (1961), but he appeared less happy in the same director's *Fahrenheit 451* (1966). He gave a remarkable performance in *Ship of Fools* (1965) as the melancholy ship's doctor, and in *The Spy Who Came in from the Cold* (Martin RITT, 1965) he created a bleak, brilliant characterization as an East German interrogator.

**WESSELY**, PAULA (1908–   ), Austrian actress, attended the REINHARDT school in Vienna and made her first film appearance in Willi FORST's musical romance *Maskerade* (1934) which made her immediately famous. Her next film, *Episode* (1935), was equally successful, and throughout the thirties she was justly renowned for her subtle sense of warm comedy and pathos. She had a leading role in Ucicky's *Heimkehr* (1941), an emotional attempt to justify the Nazi annexation of German-speaking areas of Poland. In 1949 she formed her own production company whose films include *Cordula* (1950) and *Reise in die Vergangenheit* (1954) in which she also starred.

**WEST**, MAE (1892–   ), US actress, played child parts in stock companies before embarking on a long career in vaudeville during which she perfected a unique image combining sexuality, suggestiveness, and humorous gusto. She wrote plays as vehicles for her standard role—a woman of easy morals, with a ready wit and a toughness that no man could either resist or counter—and had spectacular success on Broadway with *Sex* (1926) and *Diamond Lil* (1928).

She started her film career at a comparatively advanced age, signing with PARAMOUNT in 1932 when the Depression had made investment in the theatre precarious. Unlike other stars, whose image was created for them by the studios, she took her perfected style into films and refused to modify it.

After a small part in *Night After Night* (1932) she made *She Done Him Wrong* (1933), an adaptation of *Diamond Lil* nominally directed by Lowell Sherman. Her famous innuendo 'Come up and see me sometime' became almost immediately a part of the language, although the phrase does not in fact occur in the film. *Belle of the Nineties* (1934) gave her another success: in an era of slender, boyish women she adopted the flamboyant costumes of the nineties to emphasize her *risqué* plots and dialogue. Following the formation of the Legion of Decency in 1934 (see CENSORSHIP, US), panic measures were taken by the studio to tone down her racy style: *Klondike Annie* (1936) even made her a reformed character at the end of the film. Realizing that her popularity could not survive the dilution of her particular talents, she resumed her stage and cabaret appearances, making only three films after 1937. MY LITTLE CHICKADEE (1940) combined her scriptwriting and acting talents with those of W. C. FIELDS to remarkable effect; she re-emerged as the madam in *Myra Breckinridge* (1970). Her legend endured: airmen's inflatable life jackets were known as 'Mae Wests'. She wrote an entertaining autobiography *Goodness had nothing to do with it* (London, 1960).

**WESTERN** films constitute the oldest and most enduring genre in cinema. Their historical setting is traditionally the 1850s to 1890s—a period which saw the Californian and Dakota Gold Rushes, the Civil War, the building of the transcontinental railroads, the Indian wars, the opening up of the cattle ranges, the range wars, and the steady spread westwards of homesteaders, farmers, and immigrants. It also saw the virtual extermination of the buffalo and of most of the indigenous Indian tribes.

Before the beginning of cinema in 1895 there was already an established literature of the West, a thriving business in Wild West shows (the most famous being BUFFALO BILL Cody's), and a mass of dime novels and pulp fiction celebrating the efforts of the heterogeneous group of people who conquered a vast wilderness. Legends of the West quickly took root in the national consciousness, based on the exploits of characters such as Wild Bill HICKOCK, CALAMITY JANE, Wyatt EARP, BILLY THE KID, the JAMES brothers.

In 1894 EDISON produced KINETOGRAPH items of Wild West shows, and in 1898 he made a vignette, *Cripple Creek Bar-room*, which showed a reconstructed Western saloon scene. In 1900 the notorious Wild Bunch held up the Union Pacific Railroad, and in 1903 Edwin S. PORTER made *The Great Train Robbery*, based on the incident—the first narrative Western. It marked the film début of G. M. ANDERSON who, though at the time unable to ride a horse, was to create the first Western cinema hero. In 1908, after becoming a co-director of ESSANAY, Anderson went to California, where he made a short film called *Broncho Billy and the Baby*. It was an outstanding success and Anderson made over three hundred Broncho Billy films, all shot on location and using a regular stock company. Although overtaken by W. S. HART and Tom MIX, he remained popular until about 1915.

Two major influences on both the Western and the cinema in general were D. W. GRIFFITH and Thomas H. INCE. In 1908–14 Griffith made a number of strikingly successful one-reel Westerns, among them *The Redman and the Child* (1908), *The Squaw's Love Story* (or *Twilight Song*, 1911), *The Massacre* (1913), and *Battle at Elderbush Gulch* (1914). Ince made Westerns with an emphasis on authenticity and epic scope; with *The Bargain* (1914) he brought to the screen William S. Hart who became the embodiment of the strong, silent, romantic Western hero. Ince's promotional expertise, coupled with Hart's knowledge of the West and eye for detail, made Hart the first star of Western films. Hart directed most of his films, including *Hell's Hinges* (1916) and *The Testing Block* (1920). His last film was *Tumbleweeds* (1925), a spectacular reconstruction of the Cherokee Strip land rush.

By the twenties the Western was an internationally accepted convention. Directors already working in the genre included DEMILLE, Henry KING, John FORD; among the stars of the period were Douglas FAIRBANKS, Harry Carey, and William Farnum. James CRUZE's THE COVERED WAGON (1923) showed the epic and artistic capabilities of the Western, and though it now appears slow and staged its effect then was startling; its success led Ford to make THE IRON HORSE (1924), which went further in evoking the heroic pioneer spirit. Though Ford had been directing Westerns since 1914, this was his first major success in the genre with which he was to become identified. Short, action-packed comedy-dramas, with the emphasis on stunts, chases, and excitement, became a staple ingredient of cinema programmes. They featured clean-cut young heroes like Ken Maynard, Buck Jones, Jack Holt, moral young men who were friends to all—old ladies, small children, young girls, and especially horses.

With the introduction of sound it was feared that the Western, with its emphasis on action rather than words, would suffer a decline. But directors such as Ford, Raoul WALSH, Rouben MAMOULIAN, Victor FLEMING, and William WYLER showed that the tradition could be developed and enhanced, particularly by sound effects and background music. Fleming's *The Virginian* (1929) kept from the original novel the immortal words 'When you call me that—smile'; Walsh's *In Old Arizona* (1929) caught the imagination with the sound of bacon crackling over a camp fire, and his *The Big Trail* (1930), with John WAYNE in his first leading role, was made simultaneously in a German version for the international market (see FOREIGN VERSIONS) as well as in an experimental wide screen process. A cycle of grand-scale epics in the early thirties, including King VIDOR's *Billy the Kid* (1930), Wyler's *Hell's Heroes* (1930), and Wesley RUGGLES's *Cimarron* (1931), was comparatively short-lived, but it started a boom of second-feature Westerns which lasted over fifteen years.

From 1935 came the heyday of the SERIES Western, featuring among others HOPALONG CASSIDY, John Wayne, the Three Mesquiteers, and also that strange hybrid the singing cowboy—Gene AUTRY, Roy ROGERS, Tex Ritter. This offshoot of the traditional Western was enormously popular and soon most of the major studios were sitting singers on horses. The long-standing popularity of Country and Western music, particularly in rural areas, no doubt encouraged the vogue, and the public in the post-Depression years welcomed any cheerful novelty.

In the late thirties and early forties the Western reached maturity, again led by Ford with STAGECOACH (1939), his first film to star John Wayne. Directors now saw in the tradition a means of self-expression, examples being George MARSHALL's DESTRY RIDES AGAIN (1939), the best of many comedies satirizing the genre, Michael CURTIZ's Santa Fe Trail and Virginia City (both 1940), Wyler's The Westerner (1940), Fritz LANG's The Return of Frank James (1940) and Western Union (1941). The output of Westerns, even more than production in general, diminished during the war, but two films of interest did emerge. William WELLMAN's THE-OXBOW INCIDENT (1943, Strange Incident in GB) took the traditional theme of a lynching and viewed it from a socio-political angle involving a whole town, an unusual treatment for the time, and Howard HUGHES's The Outlaw (1946) was the first Western to gain publicity by being banned for displaying the ample assets of its star, Jane RUSSELL. In the immediate post-war period Ford returned to the classic Western with MY DARLING CLEMENTINE (1946), but was upstaged that year by King Vidor's DUEL IN THE SUN, a torrid saga which tentatively attempted an inter-racial theme. Howard HAWKS's fine exposition of the traditional Western, RED RIVER, appeared in 1948.

The seriousness of intent increasingly evident in the Western during the forties became a major element from the early fifties, the accepted modes of the genre providing a twentieth-century mythology within which a wide variety of ideas could be developed and allegories of topical problems created. Remarkable Westerns of the period include Delmer DAVES's BROKEN ARROW (1950), Lang's Rancho Notorious (1952), Ford's WAGONMASTER (1950) and THE SEARCHERS (1956), Anthony MANN's Winchester 73 (1950) and The Man from Laramie (1955), Fred ZINNEMANN's HIGH NOON (1952), Nicholas RAY's Johnny Guitar (1954), Samuel FULLER's Run of the Arrow (1956), Bud BOETTICHER's The Tall T (1957) and Ride Lonesome (1959), and Hawks's

RIO BRAVO (1959). In the 'adult' Western the traditional distinctions of Good and Bad became blurred; the leading character became less the immaculate folk-hero and more the complex human being, as in Henry King's THE GUNFIGHTER (1950)—although Alan LADD in SHANE (1953) was a reversion to the original mould. Younger directors, too, tried to study the psychology and motivation of legendary characters, as in Arthur PENN's treatment of Billy the Kid in THE LEFT-HANDED GUN (1958). Calamity Jane (1953) and SEVEN BRIDES FOR SEVEN BROTHERS (1954) successfully combined the Western and MUSICAL genres, and the introduction of CINEMASCOPE added to the visual quality of epic themes as in Wyler's The Big Country (1958).

A flood of television Westerns began around the mid-fifties, gradually replacing the low-budget second features produced for cinema distribution. A number of fading stars, including Hopalong Cassidy, Gene Autry, and Roy Rogers, renewed their careers in television, and bit players and aspiring leads found a flourishing new medium—and regular work—especially in the long-running series such as 'Wagon Train', 'Gunsmoke', 'Wyatt Earp', 'Bonanza', 'Cheyenne', and 'The Virginian' (in which the original villain Trampas now became one of the heroes). A few stars made the reverse transition, from television to films: Clint EASTWOOD came from 'Rawhide', James GARNER from 'Maverick', and Steve MCQUEEN from 'Wanted, Dead or Alive'.

But the appeal of Westerns to creative directors remained undiminished: Marlon BRANDO chose the genre for his first (and, to date, only) excursion into directing, ONE-EYED JACKS (1960). In the sixties a number of notable films portrayed men trapped by their own myths and life-styles while the world moved on, as in David Miller's Lonely Are the Brave (1962), Ford's THE MAN WHO SHOT LIBERTY VALANCE (1962), PECKINPAH's RIDE THE HIGH COUNTRY (1962, Guns in the Afternoon in GB), THE WILD BUNCH (1969), and The Ballad of Cable Hogue (1970). There was a change in the treatment of violence, echoing the general trend in the cinema and elsewhere. The Western no longer presented injury and death as simplified adjuncts to a romantic tale of action: their physical meaning—depicted with a 'realism' that was sometimes overstrained—and their brutalizing effects on the individual and society became of central importance. Sergio LEONE stylized blatant violence in his vastly successful trilogy of Italian Westerns made in 1964–6, using as his anti-hero the 'Man With No Name'—a cold-blooded killer with no allegiance but to himself.

Concern for the rights of ethnic groups was illuminated by several films dealing with the Indian cause: Don SIEGEL's Flaming Star

(1960), Ford's more stereotyped *Cheyenne Autumn* (1964), Elliot Silverstein's *A Man Called Horse* (1970), with Richard HARRIS undergoing initiation ceremonies. Ralph Nelson's *Soldier Blue* (1970) struck a liberal attitude mainly to show a gruesome massacre as a finale, but Penn convincingly re-created the lost Indian culture in *Little Big Man* (1970) which also allowed Dustin HOFFMAN a virtuoso performance. Westerns in the current vein of irreverent comedy included *Cat Ballou* (1965), *Support Your Local Sheriff* (1968), BUTCH CASSIDY AND THE SUNDANCE KID (1969), and *Blazing Saddles* (1974).

Elvis PRESLEY returned in *Charro* (1966) and John Wayne was still tall in the saddle in *Eldorado* (1966), *True Grit* (1969), and *Rio Lobo* (1971). Blake EDWARDS continued the theme of an unheroic West in *Wild Rovers* (1971) and newer directors attest to the continuing fascination of the genre, including Sydney Pollack with *Jeremiah Johnson* and Robert Benton with *Bad Company* (both 1973).

Italian (or 'spaghetti') Westerns are a thriving section of the industry, having virtually replaced the hokum period spectacular in popularity. The Western has captured the allegiance of both audiences and film-makers all over the world. As well as the many examples of the form made in Europe—Spain, West Germany, and Yugoslavia, as well as Italy—its conventions have influenced action films of other cultures, notably the samurai stories of KUROSAWA.

**WESTFRONT 1918**, Germany, 1930. 1½hr. *Dir* G. W. Pabst; *prod* Nero-Film; *scr* Laszlo Wajda, Peter Martin Lampel, from the novel *Vier von der Infanterie* by Ernst Johannsen; *ph* Fritz Arno Wagner, Charles Métain; *cast* Gustav Diessl (Karl), H. J. Moebis (the student), Fritz Kampers (the Bavarian), Claus Clausen (the lieutenant), Jackie Monnier (Yvette).

With his sensitivity to current trends, PABST made *Westfront 1918* at a time when general revulsion against the horrors and futility of war was gaining ground: it appeared almost simultaneously with ALL QUIET ON THE WESTERN FRONT. The German account of trench warfare has a deliberately drab realism where monotony and horror are subtly balanced, the only brightness being in the sentimental view of the ultimate prospects for universal brotherhood.

**WEST SIDE STORY**, US, 1961. Panavision 70; 2½hr; Technicolor. *Dir* Robert Wise, Jerome Robbins; *prod* Wise for Mirisch/Seven Arts; *scr* Ernest Lehman; *ph* Daniel L. Fapp; *chor* Robbins; *mus* Leonard Bernstein; *lyr* Stephen Sondheim; *cast* Natalie Wood (Maria), Richard Beymer (Tony), Russ Tamblyn (Riff), George Chakiris (Bernardo), José de Vega (Chino).

The enormously successful stage musical, which transferred the theme of ROMEO AND JULIET to New York's West Side with its gang warfare, was faithfully adapted for the screen. The dynamic dance sequences, derived from the style of the New York City Ballet and in part filmed on location, were the high points of the film as of the play; but the necessity of DUBBING the singing voices introduced a strongly artificial element.

George Chakiris had played Riff in the London stage production; the other principal actors were newly cast for the film, but the rest of the company was largely drawn from the New York and London stage productions.

**WEXLER, HASKELL** (1926–  ), US cameraman. His father financed a private studio for him and he made amateur films, teaching himself camera technique. He photographed a number of documentaries in Chicago for Irvin KERSHNER, then had his first feature assignment with *The Savage Eye* (Joseph STRICK, 1959). The film's visual techniques paralleled those developing in DIRECT CINEMA and indicated Wexler's preference for harshly realistic photography. He continued and developed this style in subsequent films: *America, America* (Elia KAZAN, 1963), *The Best Man* (Franklin SCHAFFNER, 1964), *The Loved One* (Tony RICHARDSON, 1965) (*co-ph*), and *Who's Afraid of Virginia Woolf?* (Mike NICHOLS, 1966), for which Wexler won an OSCAR. He is a fine craftsman: IN THE HEAT OF THE NIGHT (Norman JEWISON, 1967) showed interesting advances in overcoming the problems of depth of focus in colour photography.

Wexler directed and co-photographed *Medium Cool* (1969), which combines reportage-style use of the camera with controlled, and sometimes very beautiful, colour. As a fiction devised to be played out against the predicted violence at Chicago in 1968, it underlined growing doubts as to the use of film in exploiting real events for artistic or didactic ends.

**WHALE, JAMES** (1889–1957), British director. After working in the English theatre as a designer, actor, and director, he directed in Hollywood *Journey's End* (1930), a very successful film adaptation of R. C. Sherriff's play which he had directed on the London stage. After co-directing *Hell's Angels* (1930) with Howard HUGHES, he became chiefly identified with the horror genre through his films starring Boris KARLOFF: FRANKENSTEIN (1931), *The Old Dark House* (1932), and *The Bride of Frankenstein* (1935). That Whale was more than a horror merchant is shown by the mordant humour exhibited in these films and in THE INVISIBLE MAN (1933); his versatility also extended to a musical

(*Show Boat*, 1936), war films (*The Road Back*, 1937), and comedies (*Wives under Suspicion*, 1938). He died after a mysterious fall in his swimming pool.

***WHISKY GALORE!*** (*Tight Little Island* in US), GB, 1949. 1¼hr. *Dir* Alexander MacKendrick; *prod* Ealing Studios; *scr* Compton Mackenzie, Angus McPhail, from Mackenzie's novel; *ph* Gerald Gibbs; *mus* Ernest Irving; *cast* Basil Radford (Capt Paul Waggett), Catherine Lacey (Mrs Waggett), Joan Greenwood (Peggy Macroon), James Robertson Justice (Dr Maclaren), Compton Mackenzie (Capt Buncher).

A gentle comedy based on an actual event, a wartime crisis on an island in the Outer Hebrides where the inhabitants are faced with the worst of all possible disasters—a drought of whisky. The film gave Basil RADFORD his best role and made Alexander MACKENDRICK's name as one of the regular team of directors for EALING STUDIOS.

**WHITE,** PEARL (1889–1938), US actress. After her plans to go on the stage were thwarted by an unsympathetic father, she ran away from home and appeared in operetta before going into films in 1909. She made a number of Westerns for PATHÉ before appearing in *The Perils of Pauline* (1914), and more serials followed on the immediate success of this prototype including THE EXPLOITS OF ELAINE and *The Clutching Hand* (both 1914). With the athletic skill and indomitable personality she brought to her screen heroines she was the foremost SERIAL star of her day. Her last serial was *Plunder* (1923).

***WHITE NIGHTS*** see NOTTI BIANCHI, LE

***WHITE SHADOWS IN THE SOUTH SEAS,*** US, 1928. 1¼hr. *Dir* W. S. Van Dyke; *prod* MGM; *scr* Robert Flaherty and Ray Doyle, from the book by Frederick O'Brien; *ph* Clyde De Vinna, George Nogle, Bob Roberts; *cast* Monte Blue (Dr Lloyd), Raquel Torres (Fayaway).

Following the success of MOANA (1926), Robert FLAHERTY went with W. S. VAN DYKE to Tahiti to collaborate on this film, but they disagreed about the approach and Flaherty abandoned the project.

Although no prints are known to be extant, surviving stills confirm recollections of its exquisite photography and beautiful South Seas locations and cloud effects (see PANCHROMATIC FILM). It won the best photography OSCAR for Clyde De Vinna in 1929, but it is possible that some of the best location photography was the work of Bob Roberts who had worked on *Moana*. The film's slightly sour reputation is based on deficiencies in acting and story development and on

perhaps over-pious speculation on what Flaherty might have made of it with a free hand.

In Britain it was issued in the spring of 1929 both in its original silent form and in a version which, using the Movietone process, had a synchronized musical accompaniment. American sources usually quote the title as 'White Shadows *of* the South Seas'.

***WHITE SHEIKH, The,*** see SCEICCO BIANCO, LO

***WHITE TELEPHONE FILM,*** an unreal, glamorous tale set in elegant surroundings (hence the term) which constituted the greater part of film production in Fascist Italy during the thirties, when vigilant censorship precluded comment on current events. Lilia Silvi, Roberto Villa, Leonardo Cortese, or Adriano Rimoldi often starred; typical directors were Guido Brignone, Gennaro Righelli, and Carlo L. Bragaglia. (See ITALY.)

**WHITNEY,** JOHN and JAMES his brother, US directors. John had been a student of photography and music and James a painter. Their work was central to the development of abstract forms on film. In collaboration they first produced *Variations* (1941–3), using paper cutouts in an attempt to relate abstract images to music. They later invented a machine capable of producing electronic music directly on to the film sound-track with a light beam, and with this, plus optical printers, pantographs, and colour filters, they made *Film Exercise 1* (1943) fragments known as *Film Exercises 2 and 3* (1944) and the sophisticated *Film Exercises 4 and 5* (1944). Working separately, they continued to develop technical innovations. John's work included *Mozart Rondo* (1947–9) and *Celery Stalks at Midnight* (1951) (remade in colour in 1957) which were animation films made with the diffraction of light through an oil bath and set to existing musical works. By linking an optical printer to an analogue computer he achieved complex and striking visual effects which he assembled in *Catalogue* (1961); graduating to digital computers, he made *Permutations* (1970) and *Matrix* (1971). James made *Yantra* (1950–5)—abstract forms flowing in a series of pulsating movements—and *Lapis* (1963–6), a computer film. The association of artistic creativity with the instruments of advanced technology, pioneered by the Whitneys, has influenced a range of audio-visual fields and fathered 'Expanded Cinema', the peculiarly West Coast contribution to American avant-garde film. (See ABSTRACT FILM, UNDERGROUND.)

***WHY WE FIGHT,*** series of twelve 'orientation' films issued by the US War Department, 1942–5. All were made under the supervision of Frank

CAPRA and some were personally directed by him: other film-makers who participated were Anatole LITVAK and Joris IVENS; Walter HUSTON was among the narrators; and the music for the series was by Dmitri TIOMKIN. The primary aim was to educate members of the US armed forces in the causes of the war and the reasons for America's participation, but some of the films were publicly shown and four were distributed in Britain, the first with a spoken preface by Winston CHURCHILL. COMPILATION techniques, combining documentary and newsreel footage to increase the force of a persuasive commentary, were used with great skill and Capra is generally given personal credit for the sharpness of the editing. Several of the films are still admired, in the USSR as well as the West, for their effectiveness.

**WIDE-ANGLE LENS,** a lens of short focal length used by cinematographers to photograph a large subject where physical limitations prevent moving the camera back to capture it with a normal lens. If the TELEPHOTO or long focal length lens is the equivalent of a telescope, the wide-angle lens is the equivalent of 'looking through the wrong end' of the telescope: the subject appears to be far away and the frame consequently includes a wider area. Such lenses are often used for shooting in cramped quarters such as kitchens or cars. The wide-angle lens also produces an effect of increased depth and perspective—the exact reverse of the telephoto lens—which can be used creatively to emphasize distance, as when a ballet dancer moves from close-up to long shot in only two or three leaps. (See ZOOM.)

**WIDERBERG,** BO (1930–   ), Swedish director, who worked at various jobs after leaving school early, then began writing. He has written four novels, some short stories, and a radio play. He took up film criticism, at first in a Stockholm paper and later in a booklet, *Visionen i svensk film* (Stockholm, 1962), bitterly attacking post-war Swedish films and in particular the oppressive influence of BERGMAN, whom he accused of being absorbed in a black and private mythology unrelated to contemporary Sweden or even to human beings in general. Having co-directed with Jan Troell a short film for television, *Pojken och draken* (*A Boy and his Kite*, 1961), he had the opportunity to improve on the situation he castigated by directing *Barnvagnen* (*The Pram*, 1963), an observant and engaging film about a recognizable modern situation. His second feature, KVARTERET KORPEN (*Raven's End*, 1963), a sharp look at a working-class family during the Depression, the time of his own childhood, was one of the first films to benefit from the system of quality awards set up under the Swedish Film Institute (see SVENSKA FILMIN-STITUTET) and it brought Widerberg his first recognition abroad.

In *Kärlek 65* (*Love 65*, 1965) Widerberg experimented with a more fragmented style of narrative, mixing fantasy and reality almost in the style of FELLINI to explore his own creative and personal problems. He also introduced an element of improvisation which was further exploited in *Heja Roland!* (*Thirty Times Your Money*, 1967), based on one of his novels. ELVIRA MADIGAN (1967) was his most accomplished film to date, a judicious blend of joyous affirmation and romantic sadness.

In 1968 he organized with a group of young film-makers the filming of *Den vita sporten* (*The White Game*), showing the demonstrations against Swedish participation in the Davis Cup matches against South Africa. He then returned to the time of the Depression with ÅDALEN 31 (1969), treating a grim social theme with all the assurance and lyricism so happily developed in *Elvira Madigan*. *Joe Hill* (*The Ballad of Joe Hill*, 1971) used the same charm and visual beauty to celebrate a folk-hero of early socialism in America, and *Fimpen* (*Stubby*, 1974) engagingly told a fantasy story of a six-year-old football star.

**WIDESCOPE,** a MULTI-SCREEN system, patented by George W. Bingham in 1921. Using two 35mm projectors, each showing half of a 70mm original, it was revived under the name Thrillerama in 1956, but was never sufficiently developed for commercial operation.

**WIDE SCREEN.** The natural urge of showmen to enlarge the cinema screen led to experiments in the earliest days. In the Paris Exhibition of 1900, for instance, Louis LUMIÈRE projected images on to a gigantic screen, 63 feet wide by 45 feet high, and the French engineer GRIMOIN-SANSON introduced his CINÉORAMA. But the balconies in traditional theatres cut off the top area of any screen taller than normal for spectators in rear seats under the balconies, and this practical limitation led to the logical decision to make the screen wider.

The pioneer in wide screen production was the exuberant Abel GANCE, working with André DEBRIE. At the climax of NAPOLÉON (1927), the action was spread across three flat screens, with three projectors being used to give a contiguous image. Few cinemas could cope with this system, which Gance named Polyvision.

In 1927 Claude AUTANT-LARA made a silent film to demonstrate the ANAMORPHIC process developed by Henri Chrétien and known as

Hypergonar. In *Construire un feu*, from a story of Alaska by Jack London, alternate reels passed the lens first horizontally then vertically. Influenced by Gance, the horizontal reels contained one, two, or three contrasting images side by side. The process needed a gigantic screen in an auditorium with no balcony to obstruct the view. It was highly effective, but the coming of sound with all its attendant costs of installation killed the venture.

At the Paris Exhibition of 1937, Chrétien supplied an immensely wide screen in the open air with a film made for two hypergonar projectors synchronized.

In 1952, worried by the inroads of television on the dwindling cinema audiences, Spyros SKOURAS bought for TWENTIETH CENTURY-FOX the patent rights to Chrétien's invention, calling it CINEMASCOPE. The first film in the new system was a Biblical story, THE ROBE (1953), which was enormously successful commercially in spite of the cost of installing new screens on which to show it. The process continues in use in cinema projection, but in photography it has been superseded by the PANAVISION lenses with their greater precision.

A poor man's version of wide screen is achieved by masking off the top and bottom (one third of the area) of the frame in the camera, composing a wider image in the area that remains. The positive is printed normally, and the only adjustment in presentation is to alter the shape of the screen and to instal a lens to project a larger image to compensate for the loss of height on the screen. This gives a narrower image than the anamorphic. A third of the celluloid involved is wasted, and the grain and other imperfections in the emulsion are inevitably emphasized.

Other systems for widening the screen have been developed and tested. These include CINE-RAMA, CIRCARAMA, PANAVISION, VISTAVISION, TODD-AO, TECHNISCOPE, TECHNIRAMA. As usual, it is the least cumbersome which have survived and are being further developed. The most palatial theatres now show films photographed and projected in 70MM: the prints are reduced anamorphically and projected as CinemaScope in theatres equipped only with 35mm projection. 70mm projection is accompanied by six-track STEREOPHONIC sound either on the film or cn a separate synchronous sound film.

When the wide screen was finally adopted as a commercial proposition, conservative critics received it with a sneer, and most film-makers were themselves slow to grasp its aesthetic possibilities (COCTEAU, for instance, is reputed to have said when he first saw CinemaScope, 'Next time I write a poem, I shall use a wider piece of paper'). In fact it has had a strong and healthy influence on the development of the art, rivalling in importance the introduction of sound. The dramatic possibilities of conveying the interrelation of characters by following their movement within the frame, rather than by cutting from one snatch of action to another, was fruitfully explored by STROHEIM in the twenties, RENOIR in the thirties, and WELLES in the forties: the greater area offered by the wide screen has furthered and confirmed the aesthetic value of their approach. As lenses and film stocks are improved so that DEEP FOCUS can be achieved even on colour film, the range of expression available to the filmmaker becomes wider and more flexible. Extraordinary beauty and visual tension can be achieved by sensitive composition within the wide screen format, and the development of multiple images further extends this range. (See also ASPECT RATIO.)

**WIDMARK**, RICHARD (1915–  ), US actor, made an impression as the giggling psychopath in his first film KISS OF DEATH (1947). Although in danger of being type-cast in this kind of part, as in *No Way Out* (Joseph L. MANKIEWICZ, 1950) and *The Long Ships* (Jack CARDIFF, 1963), he has been successful in fuller characterizations such as the petty criminal in PICKUP ON SOUTH STREET (1952) and in more sympathetic parts in *Panic in the Streets* (Elia KAZAN, 1950), *Cheyenne Autumn* (John FORD, 1964), and *Madigan* (Don SIEGEL, 1968).

**WIENE**, ROBERT (1881–1938), German director and actor, began working for MESSTER in 1914 as a scriptwriter and shortly afterwards directed his first film *Arme Eva* (1914). After making several films with Henny PORTEN in leading roles, he achieved international fame with DAS CABINETT DES DR CALIGARI (1919), a film which overshadowed the rest of his career. His next film, *Genuine* (1920), used a similar Expressionist décor and was, like *Caligari*, scripted by MAYER; it did not meet with the same success, partly because of the muddled and overloaded sets. His adaptation of part of CRIME AND PUNISHMENT—*Raskolnikoff* (1923)—was a better film, for here the sets and characters were ideally suited to Dostoevsky's universe. *INRI* (1924) was a version of the life of Christ with a distinguished cast including Werner KRAUSS as Pontius Pilate, Asta NIELSEN as Mary Magdalen, and Henny Porten as the Virgin Mary. ORLACS HÄNDE (1925) was a mediocre melodrama distinguished only by the fine acting of Conrad VEIDT.

Wiene went on to more commercial work in Germany and later in France, where he lived after 1933. He planned to make a sound version of *Caligari* with COCTEAU but this never materialized. His last French film *Ultimatum* (1938), with STROHEIM, was completed by Robert SIOD-MAK.

**WILCOX,** HERBERT (1892– ), Irish-born producer and director, began his film career immediately after the First World War and directed numerous silent films including *Chu Chin Chow* (1923). He brought major Hollywood stars (Pauline FREDERICK, Dorothy GISH, Mae MARSH, and Betty Blythe) to work in Britain and initiated the screen series of Aldwych farces starring Tom Walls. In the early thirties he directed a series of films starring Anna NEAGLE, who became his wife. After *Nell Gwyn* (1934) and *Peg of Old Drury* (1935), Wilcox went into production on his own; his most celebrated films of this period featured Anna Neagle as Queen Victoria (*Victoria the Great*, 1937; *Sixty Glorious Years*, 1938). His films of the forties revealed his feel for public taste: if marked by naïvety and sentimentality, they were overtly and completely geared to popular box-office appeal. Particularly successful were the romances starring Anna Neagle and Michael WILDING: *Piccadilly Incident* (1946), *The Courtneys of Curzon Street* (1947), *Spring in Park Lane* (1948), and *Maytime in Mayfair* (1949). Wilcox's films of the fifties were more varied but still characteristic in their wholesome popular appeal.

**WILD BUNCH, The,** US, 1969. Panavision 70; 2½hr; Technicolor. *Dir* Sam Peckinpah; *prod* Warner Bros/Seven Arts; *scr* Walon Green, Peckinpah, from a story by Green and Roy N. Sickner; *ph* Lucien Ballard; *cast* William Holden (Pike Bishop), Ernest Borgnine (Dutch), Robert Ryan (Deke Thornton), Edmond O'Brien (Sykes), Warren Oates (Lyle), Ben Johnson (Tector), Jaime Sanchez (Angel), Emilio Fernandez (Mapache).

In 1914, against a background of Mexican revolution, motor cars, and machine guns, Pike Bishop and his gang try to live as outlaws of the pioneer West. PECKINPAH's nostalgia for the end of a legend is obscured by insistent symbolism and by lingering scenes of carnage which caused widespread offence and distracted attention from his recurrent theme, 'unchanged men in a changing land'. Lucien BALLARD's camerawork again evoked place and period with exceptional skill, and Peckinpah's 'stock company' satisfyingly embodied the wayward group of doomed lawbreakers.

**WILDE,** OSCAR (1854–1900), Irish playwright and wit whose plays, mostly written in the early 1890s, are elegantly spun webs of epigram. His work suffered an eclipse after his conviction and imprisonment in 1895 on a charge of homosexual practices, but after his death the plays again became popular and have remained classics of the English stage. They are in general too static and literary to reward the film-maker, but LUBITSCH made a stylish version of *Lady Windermere's Fan* in 1925 (without using any of the original lines in the dialogue titles); a second American version *The Fan* (1949, *Lady Windermere's Fan* in GB) directed by Otto PREMINGER was less successful. Anthony ASQUITH's *The Importance of Being Earnest* (1952) rightly made no attempt to disguise its theatrical origin; it is enduringly delightful for the performances of several distinguished British actors, including Edith EVANS, Joan GREENWOOD, Michael REDGRAVE, Margaret RUTHERFORD, and Dorothy TUTIN.

Short stories by Wilde that have been filmed include 'Lord Arthur Savile's Crime' (in DUVIVIER's *Flesh and Fantasy*, 1943, *Obsessions* in GB), *The Canterville Ghost* (1944), directed by Jules DASSIN, and the novel *The Picture of Dorian Gray* (Albert LEWIN, 1944).

Changes in public attitudes to homosexuality, which were helped by the publication of the Wolfenden Report in 1957, may have motivated two British productions of 1960, both dealing with the crucial period of Wilde's trial—*Oscar Wilde* (*dir* Gregory Ratoff), starring Robert MORLEY, and *The Trials of Oscar Wilde* (*dir* Ken Hughes), starring Peter FINCH. The latter was generally considered the more successful, chiefly for Finch's deeply-felt performance and for its evocation of turn-of-the-century London society.

**WILDER,** BILLY (1906– ), US director of Austrian origin, real forename Samuel, started work as a journalist in Vienna and Berlin. From an early age he was attracted to cinema and spent his spare time writing unsuccessful scripts, finally getting his first film job as a writer on the semi-amateur MENSCHEN AM SONNTAG (1929). He continued to work as a scriptwriter in Berlin until Hitler's accession to power in 1933; he then left for Paris where he wrote and co-directed *Mauvaise Graine* (1933) which starred Danielle DARRIEUX. Another script was bought by COLUMBIA (but never filmed) and this financed his departure for Hollywood.

Within two years Wilder had acquired a remarkable command of English and was taken on as a writer by PARAMOUNT. His Viennese background seemed to fit him for light, escapist comedies; on BLUEBEARD'S EIGHTH WIFE (Ernst LUBITSCH, 1938) he joined forces with Charles Brackett, an association which lasted for several years with striking success. They worked again for Lubitsch on the script of NINOTCHKA (1939), which revealed Wilder as heir to the particular blend of comedy and convention-flouting which had been hailed as 'the Lubitsch touch'. This formula, in Wilder's hands, although liable to lapse into vulgarity, at its best produced films of memorable wit and sophistication.

In 1942 he was given his first chance as director. *The Major and the Minor* was a return to light comedy, with Ginger ROGERS trying to pass as a little girl in order to make a train journey at half fare. It was polished, funny, and successful at the box-office, promising well for Wilder's future with Paramount. He next made an effective war story, *Five Graves to Cairo* (1943), which brought Erich von STROHEIM, as Rommel, back to public notice. DOUBLE INDEMNITY (1943) and THE LOST WEEKEND (1945), with their unsparingly realistic treatment of greed and alcoholism respectively, both shocked and attracted audiences, and Wilder, still in his late thirties, was set to be one of Hollywood's most consistently successful directors.

A not surprising failure with a Bing CROSBY musical, *The Emperor Waltz* (1947), was followed the next year by a typical Wilder product. *A Foreign Affair*, set and partly shot in post-war Berlin, develops its acid humour within an intrinsically tragic situation, an approach which reached impressive heights with SUNSET BOULEVARD (1950). ACE IN THE HOLE (1951) had less success. The critics and the public alike resented his barbs when they were aimed nearer home, but, unabashed, Wilder carried on to make a brassy comedy set in a prisoner-of-war camp, *Stalag 17* (1953), and then a charming romantic comedy with only hints of his usual acerbity, *Sabrina* (1954), starring Audrey HEPBURN and Humphrey BOGART.

In 1954 Wilder left Paramount and for a while moved between production companies, finally settling with MIRISCH in 1958. In spite of the problems he encountered in working with Marilyn MONROE in THE SEVEN YEAR ITCH (1955) and SOME LIKE IT HOT (1959), both films were deservedly successful at the box office. The latter was the first of Wilder's script collaborations with I. A. L. DIAMOND, who has taken the place of Brackett as his regular co-writer; it was also his first use of Jack LEMMON as leading actor. These two worked with Wilder on THE APARTMENT (1960), a telling comedy of sexual subterfuge.

The Wilder formula showed signs of coarsening during the sixties. In *One, Two, Three* (1961) the speed of the action has the apparent aim of bombarding the audience with jokes at such a speed that consideration of their tastelessness is impaired. Set again in Berlin, the film even attempts a comic treatment of the building of the Berlin Wall, but conscious irreverence was not in this case rewarded by commercial success. *Kiss Me Stupid* (1964), a brash sex comedy, and *The Fortune Cookie* (1966, *Meet Whiplash Willie* in GB), about insurance fraud, again bordered on

vulgarity, but his affectionate debunking of a myth in *The Private Life of Sherlock Holmes* (1970) showed a return of his old sophisticated mockery. *Avanti!* (1972), a tongue-in-cheek summary of American assumptions about Italy, starred Jack Lemmon, who was teamed with Walter MATTHAU in Wilder's 1974 remake of THE FRONT PAGE (1931), sharpened with topical allusions.

Wilder's refusal to abide by conventional standards of 'good taste' in his treatment of such subjects as sex, suicide, and politics has in his best films been justified by film-making of the highest quality. His love of, or at least intimacy with, cinema—and Hollywood in particular—is shown in his frequent use of stars of earlier years (Stroheim, Gloria SWANSON, James CAGNEY, George RAFT, Marlene DIETRICH) and in the frequent references to other films which appear in his work.

**WILDING**, MICHAEL (1912– ), British actor whose first film was *Tilly of Bloomsbury* (1940). His good looks and easy charm soon made him a popular favourite, especially when he and Anna NEAGLE formed a co-starring team (including *Piccadilly Incident*, 1946; *The Courtneys of Curzon Street*, 1947; *Spring in Park Lane*, 1948; *Maytime in Mayfair*, 1949). Other notable films included *An Ideal Husband* (1947) and, for HITCHCOCK, *Under Capricorn* (1949) and *Stage Fright* (1950). He remained active throughout the fifties and sixties; he retired from acting to become an agent but he occasionally appears in small roles. He was Elizabeth TAYLOR's second husband, and later married Margaret Leighton.

***WILD STRAWBERRIES*** see SMULTRONSTÄLLET

**WILD TRACK, WILD SHOT.** It is normal film practice to shoot picture and sound in synchronization; the motors driving the camera and sound recorder must operate at constant, related speeds to ensure exact synchronization throughout the shot. On occasions where either picture or sound is shot on its own, there is no requirement for synchronization, and the motor is allowed (in theory) to run wild. Thus a wild track may be an ordinary recording of city traffic to be used as a background effect, and it need not synchronize with any shot; a wild shot may be a close-up of a passive spectator watching an event, and it need not synchronize with the sound of the event. However, in both cases the film editor will later establish a precise position for the wild shot or wild track, and once established this artificial SYNCHRONIZATION will be maintained as rigidly as true 'sync' sound.

Wild shots are often used where it may not appear obvious to the viewer; entire films have been shot wild. One celebrated *tour de force* was Alfred HITCHCOCK's *Rope* (1948), apparently shot in a single continuous take without cuts. Here the camera moved so often and so widely that the microphone had to be dispensed with, and the sound was all added later. (In this film, and many others, even the walls of the set were 'wild'—made movable to allow the camera crane to pass through doors and turn 180° to view the wall it had just passed through.)

**WILLIAMS,** ESTHER (1923– ), US actress. A champion swimmer, she was signed by METRO-GOLDWYN-MAYER in 1942. She starred in *Bathing Beauty* (1944) and other MGM musicals and light entertainments of the following decade, her aquatic skill, attractive looks, and dazzling smile compensating for limited acting ability. Her best film was probably *Neptune's Daughter* (1949), in which she sang 'Baby, It's Cold Outside'. She retired from the screen in the early sixties.

**WILLIAMS,** RICHARD (1933– ), Canadian-born animator working in Britain. His first film *The Little Island* (1958), provoked critical interest for its attempt to deal with abstract ideas—the conflict between Goodness, Truth, and Beauty—and for its expressive combination of sound and image. Apart from his independent work, including *A Lecture on Man* (1962) to Christopher Logue's poem and the ironic *Love Me Love Me Love Me* (1962), he has gained respect for his commissioned pieces, notably *Guinness at the Albert Hall*, a television commercial, the credit titles for *What's New, Pussycat?* (Clive DONNER, 1965), and the continuity inserts in the style of Victorian caricature for *The Charge of the Light Brigade* (Tony RICHARDSON, 1968). Williams's *A Christmas Carol* (1972) is outstanding, particularly in the treatment of movement in perspective, and although made for television won an OSCAR for animation.

**WILLIAMS,** TENNESSEE (1914– ), US author, born in Mississippi. His major work has been for the stage but his output includes stories, poems, and a novella, *The Roman Spring of Mrs Stone* (1950; filmed 1961). The films based on his plays, which usually revolve around traumatic, sometimes sleazy, sexual situations, have proved extremely popular; for example, *Cat on a Hot Tin Roof* (1955) and *Sweet Bird of Youth* (1959), filmed by Richard BROOKS in 1958 and 1961 respectively. Williams has also written or co-scripted films adapted from his own plays. KAZAN directed A STREETCAR NAMED DESIRE in 1951 and BABY DOLL in 1956. *The Milk Train Doesn't Stop Here Anymore* (1962)

was filmed in 1968 by LOSEY as *Boom*. Williams's other adaptations include the sensitive *The Glass Menagerie* (1945; filmed 1950), *The Rose Tattoo* (1951; filmed 1955), and *Suddenly Last Summer* (1958; filmed 1960). The world of America's Deep South as seen through Williams's eyes has a distinctiveness which emerges in the film adaptations of his work, however diverse the directors and actors who have brought them to the screen.

**WILLIAMSON,** JAMES (b. 1855), Scottish-born chemist who became a pioneer British filmmaker. In 1898 he began filming local events and soon graduated to making story films of a 'fake actuality' kind in the back garden of his home in Hove. The most famous of these, *Attack on a China Mission* (1900), also known as *Attack on a Chinese Mission Station*, has earned a place in film history as one of the earliest story films with a true cinematic technique. His *Fire!* (1902), a miniature drama in five scenes, included a fire sequence described as 'sensational' by Williamson in his 1902 catalogue where he adds: 'To enhance the effect, portions of the film are stained red.' He also made a number of trick films, among which *A Big Swallow* (1901–2) is noted for its early use of the close-up. Williamson abandoned film production in 1909.

**WIND, The,** US, 1928. 1½hr. *Dir* Victor Sjöström; *prod* MGM; *scr* Frances Marion, from the novel by Dorothy Scarborough; *ph* John Arnold; *cast* Lillian Gish (Letty), Lars Hanson (Lige), Montagu Love (Roddy), Dorothy Cummings, Edward Earle.

Letty, transplanted from lush Kentucky to the windswept desert of Texas, survives the threat of an intruder whom she kills in self-defence, a duststorm, and a temporary descent into near-madness. Lillian GISH's performance was the most powerfully dramatic of her career. SJÖSTRÖM (credited as Seastrom as in all his American films) perfectly synthesized the forces of nature and those of human emotion. This fine film was a commercial failure in its own time—Louis B. MAYER's interference with the editing and the need to impose a sound-track on what was conceived as a silent film were in part to blame—but it is now highly regarded.

**WINNER,** MICHAEL (1939– ), British director and producer, began his career writing screenplays and worked for the BBC as an assistant director. He made independent short films, progressing to second features. His first major film was *Play it Cool* (1962), followed by such films as *West 11* (1963) and *You Must Be Joking* (1964), and he attracted wider attention with *The*

*Jokers* (1966) and *I'll Never Forget What's 'Is Name* (1967), similar in structure and style to Don LEVY's *Herostratus* (1966, released 1968). His career then progressed at a frenetic rate; since 1971 he has made two films a year with increasingly impressive casts, including *The Nightcomers* (1971) with Marlon BRANDO, and *The Mechanic* (1972) with Charles Bronson. This achievement, remarkable by any contemporary standards, is attributable mainly to his understanding of the film industry. His films are always completed under budget, their subjects follow current thinking as to what the audience wants, and they always make an acceptable profit.

**WINTERS,** SHELLEY (1922–   ), US actress, played in comedy and musicals on Broadway where she took over the part of Ado Annie in *Oklahoma!* from Celeste HOLM. She appeared in films from 1943, attracting attention in *A Double Life* (1948) and contributing striking performances to A PLACE IN THE SUN (1951), THE NIGHT OF THE HUNTER, *The Big Knife* (both 1955), *The Diary of Anne Frank* (1959), LOLITA (1962), and *The Balcony* (1963). Closely associated with the ACTORS' STUDIO, she became skilled in playing vulnerable women past their first youth and aware that their attractions are fading. More recently she has played with gusto in hokum crime sagas, notably as the matriarch of a gang of violent hoodlums in Roger CORMAN's *Bloody Mama* (1969) and as the Fascist lesbian boss of a drugs ring in *Cleopatra Jones* (1973).

**WIPE,** a visual effect used to link one picture with another. A line moves across the screen, literally wiping one picture off and revealing the other. Wipes may come in any shape, ranging from diagonal, circular, and V-shapes to more complex chequerboard and spiral wipes. Unlike the FADE and DISSOLVE, the wipe is an artificial, self-conscious effect, with no real-life counterpart, and it is used to call attention to a transition rather than to link scenes unobtrusively. Wipes are produced by optical printing, not in the camera, by the same method as the SPLIT SCREEN, which is simply a motionless wipe.

**WISE,** ROBERT (1914–   ), US director and producer, entered the film industry in 1933 as a sound cutter, assistant editor, and then editor for RKO where he edited CITIZEN KANE (1941) with Mark ROBSON, and THE MAGNIFICENT AMBERSONS (1942). His early experience as a director was gained in thrillers—*Curse of the Cat People* (1944), *The Body Snatchers* (1945), *Blood on the Moon* (1948)—in which he learned to use the camera economically and to build up suspense.

*The Set Up* (1949), about second-rate boxers, had a remarkable sense of milieu and won the Critics' Prize at CANNES. With *Odds Against Tomorrow* (1959) he began to produce his own films. WEST SIDE STORY (1961) and THE SOUND OF MUSIC (1965) were large-budget musicals which earned enormous commercial success for their energetic treatment of sentimental themes, but *Star!* (1968) did not equal their popularity. *The Andromeda Strain* (1971) was his first essay in science fiction.

**WISEMAN,** FREDERIC, US law professor from Boston, began in 1967 to make a series of feature-length documentaries about social institutions. *Titticut Follies* (1967), which examined a Massachusetts mental institution for the criminally insane, is still under an injunction not to be screened. *High School* (1968), *Law and Order* (1969) about the police, *Hospital* (1970), *Basic Training* (1971) about the army, and *Essene* (1972) about a monastic community, are all characterized by their episodic structure, lack of focus on individual personalities, and visual acuity.

***WITCHCRAFT THROUGH THE AGES*** see HÄXAN

**WITHERS,** GCOGIE (1917–   ), British actress, real forenames Georgette Lizette, progressed from the theatre chorus line and film extra work when Michael POWELL gave her a leading part in *The Girl in the Crowd* (1934). She went on to play dumb blondes in pre-war comedies, but Powell again gave her a chance to prove her dramatic abilities, this time in *One of Our Aircraft Is Missing* (1942), as a key member of the Dutch underground. She emerged as one of Britain's finest actresses in parts like the ruthless Victorian murderess in *Pink String and Sealing Wax* (1945) and the Cockney housewife who helps her former lover, a criminal on the run, in *It Always Rains on Sunday* (1947), followed by a witty performance as the wife whose husband brings a mermaid home from a fishing trip in *Miranda* (1948). She moved to Australia with her husband John McCallum in 1958, after a successful Shakespeare season at Stratford-upon-Avon. In 1971 she acted in *Nickel Queen* which McCallum directed.

***WIZARD OF OZ, The,*** US, 1939. Technicolor; 1¾hr. *Dir* Victor Fleming; *prod* Mervyn Leroy for MGM; *scr* Noel Langley, Florence Ryerson, Edgar Allan Woolf from the book by Frank L. Baum; *ph* Harold Rosson; *des* Cedric Gibbons; *mus* Harold Arlen; *lyr* E. Y. Harburg; *cast* Judy Garland (Dorothy), Frank Morgan (Professor Marvel), Ray Bolger (Hunk/the Scarecrow), Bert

Lahr (Zeke/the Lion), Jack Haley (Hickory/the Tin Man), Billie Burke (Glenda).

Made on a very large budget for the time, this blend of musical fantasy and comedy based on the American children's classic follows the dream adventures of Dorothy, who, after being knocked unconscious by a tornado, makes her way with some bizarre companions to the Emerald City to find the Wizard of Oz. The Wizard turns out to be a Kansas conjuror, but nevertheless is able to grant the wishes of Dorothy's friends.

Popular with adults and children alike, the film has had several re-issues, and owes much of its success to the songs, particularly 'We're off to see the Wizard' and 'Over the Rainbow', with which it is always associated. Judy GARLAND's wide-eyed performance is unforgettable.

*Journey Back to Oz* (1971), a cartoon film, was a sequel, with Liza MINNELLI speaking the role of Dorothy and Mickey ROONEY that of the Scarecrow.

**WOLFF, FRIEDRICH** (1888–1953), German dramatist and scriptwriter worked mainly in left-wing theatre. He scripted *Die Natur als Arzt und Helfer* (1929), an UFA Kulturfilm and FANCK's *SOS Eisberg* (1933). In 1933 he left Germany for the USSR, where his anti-Nazi plays PROFESSOR MAMLOCK and *Das trojanische Pferd* were filmed in 1938 and 1939 respectively. After the war he scripted for DEFA adaptations of several of his plays, including *Kolonne Strupp* (1946), which was directed by Slatan DUDOW.

**WOLFIT, DONALD** (1902–68), British stage actor particularly respected in Shakespeare. Excepting film appearances in 1934 (including *Death at Broadcasting House*) he did not turn to the screen until the early fifties, appearing in such films as *The Pickwick Papers* (1953) and *Svengali* (1954). Among numerous others were ROOM AT THE TOP (1958), LAWRENCE OF ARABIA (1962), *Becket* (1964), *Life at the Top* (1965), and, more surprisingly, a few horror films. His most distinguished work was on the stage; his performances on the screen often tended to be inflated or overpowering. He was knighted in 1957.

**WOMAN OF PARIS, A**, US, 1923. 2hr. *Dir, prod, scr* Charles Chaplin, assisted by Eddie Sullivan, Henry d'Abbadie d'Arrast, Jean de Limur, for United Artists; *ph* Rollie Totheroh, Jack Wilson; *des* Arthur Stibolt; *cast* Edna Purviance (Marie), Adolphe Menjou (Pierre), Carl Miller (Jean), Lydia Knott (his mother), Charles French (his father).

CHAPLIN had had ambitions to make a serious film ever since his year at ESSANAY: his chance came when he could choose his own first subject for UNITED ARTISTS. The story is a rather ordinary melodrama of a love triangle in French society but subtle direction and accomplished acting lift it above that level. Chaplin himself did not take a starring role in this 'drama of fate', as it was subtitled, but appeared briefly and unrecognizably as a railway porter. He tried to give Edna PURVIANCE the opportunity of branching out into a dramatic career but the public, used to her in thirty-four Chaplin comedies, did not like the new persona and it was her last starring role. For Adolphe MENJOU, on the other hand, it was the first of many.

Though *A Woman of Paris* was a critical success at the time and clearly influenced directors such as Ernst LUBITSCH, audiences stayed away and it has not been publicly screened for over forty years. The film has been highly praised by those modern critics who have seen archive copies, but Chaplin himself refuses to let it be shown.

**WOMAN OF THE DUNES** see SUNA NO ONNA

**WOMAN OF THE YEAR**, US, 1942. 1½hr. *Dir* George Stevens; *prod* Joseph L. Mankiewicz for MGM; *scr* Ring Lardner Jr, Michael Kanin; *cast* Katharine Hepburn (Tess), Spencer Tracy (Sam), Fay Bainter (Ellen), Reginald Owen (Clayton), William Bendix ('Pinkie' Peters).

Sam Craig, a sports-writer, falls for and marries Tess Harding, a cultivated columnist. Their clashes of temperament and habit, and their ultimate reconciliation, are the subject for a polished and astrigent comedy. This was the first of the many successful appearances of HEPBURN and TRACY together.

**WOOD, NATALIE** (1938–  ), US actress who appeared as a child in *Tomorrow Is Forever* (1946). Beginning with *The Ghost and Mrs Muir* (1947), she was in a succession of films for TWENTIETH CENTURY-FOX until 1955 when she moved to WARNER BROS. She immediately attracted serious attention as the vulnerable adolescent heroine in REBEL WITHOUT A CAUSE (1955), and she was the attractive, wide-eyed heroine of *Cry in the Night* (1956), THE SEARCHERS (1956), and numerous other films for the same company. She continued to be active in the sixties in such films as WEST SIDE STORY (1961), *Gypsy* (1962), *Love with the Proper Stranger* (1963), and *Inside Daisy Clover* (1966).

**WOOD, SAM** (1883–1950), prolific US director. Prominent among his earlier work for PARAMOUNT were films starring Gloria SWANSON: *The Impossible Mrs Bellew* (1922), *Beyond the Rocks* (1922), co-starring Rudolph VALENTINO, and *Bluebeard's Eighth Wife* (1923). He directed two MARX BROTHERS films, A NIGHT AT THE OPERA (1935) and A DAY AT THE RACES (1937), allowing their zany humour full play while injecting the element of sentimentality demanded by METRO-GOLDWYN-MAYER. Sentimentality became a major characteristic of his work, but his best films, including *Goodbye Mr Chips* (1939), *Our Town* (1940), *Kitty Foyle* (1940), *The Devil and Miss Jones* (1941), *King's Row* (1942), and *For Whom the Bell Tolls* (1943), which he also produced, offer a clean narrative structure, well-drawn characterizations, and a willingness to let dialogue and talented players sustain a scene without obtrusive camera movements and obvious cutting.

**WOODFALL FILMS,** British production company formed in 1958 by Tony RICHARDSON and John OSBORNE for the filming of their stage successes, LOOK BACK IN ANGER (1959) and *The Entertainer* (1960). Most of the company's productions have been directed by Richardson. He was also in the early days producer not only for his own films but also for those of some fellow directors in the FREE CINEMA movement as they made their way into feature production, notably Karel REISZ'S SATURDAY NIGHT AND SUNDAY MORNING (1960). Woodfall's productions include *Girl with Green Eyes* (Desmond Davis, 1963), THE KNACK (1965), and *The White Bus* (Lindsay ANDERSON, 1967). With the support of BALCON's Bryanston Films and UNITED ARTISTS, Woodfall has offered the opportunity for directors to make films with an unusual degree of independence.

**WOODWARD, JOANNE** (1930– ), US actress, has worked mainly in films since 1955. She won an OSCAR for her performance as the schizophrenic heroine of *The Three Faces of Eve* (1957) and her other films have included THE LONG HOT SUMMER (1958), *The Sound and the Fury* (1959), *From the Terrace* (1960), *The Fugitive Kind* (1960), *Paris Blues* (1961), *A New Kind of Love* (1964), *A Fine Madness* (1966). RACHEL, RACHEL (1968), in which she portrayed a lonely spinster, was directed by her husband Paul NEWMAN; she acted for him again as the slatternly, despairing widow in *The Effect of Gamma Rays on Man-in-the-Moon Marigolds* (1972).

Not of a stereotyped kind of beauty, she is an imaginative and intelligent actress, excelling in the portrayal of gauche, wry women. Particularly when working with Newman, she has given convincing and effective performances.

***WORLD IN ACTION,*** a monthly newsreel produced by the NATIONAL FILM BOARD of Canada as an international complement to its domestically orientated *Canada Carries On* series, modelled on THE MARCH OF TIME. Distributed by UNITED ARTISTS to the US (6,000 cinemas), Britain (1,000 cinemas), Australia, New Zealand, South Africa, India, and Latin America, the series was produced by John GRIERSON, written and directed (with three exceptions) by Stuart LEGG. Between January 1942 and December 1945, *World in Action* charted developments in military and political strategy, as with *Food—Weapon of Conquest* (March 1942) and *Food—Secret of the Peace* (July 1945). *The March of Time*'s range of topics was soon surpassed: *Geopolitik—Hitler's Plan for Empire* (May 1942) explained Haushofer's philosophy, and *The War for Men's Minds* (May 1943) compared Allied with Nazi propaganda. Later issues anticipated post-war problems. *Now—The Peace* (April 1945) assessed the United Nations' future. *World in Action*'s role ended with the hostilities, while *Canada Carries On* carried on.

**WRAY, FAY** (1907– ), Canadian-born US actress who entered films as an extra, graduating to Hal ROACH comedies and UNIVERSAL Westerns before STROHEIM gave her a leading role in THE WEDDING MARCH (1926). She played a Secret Service agent opposite Gary COOPER in *The Legion of the Condemned* (1928) and starred in films by such directors as Mauritz STILLER (*The Street of Sin*, 1928), Josef von STERNBERG (*Thunderbolt*, 1929), and Frank CAPRA (*Dirigible*, 1931). She is best remembered for her series of heroines victimized by madmen and sundry terrors in chillers like *Doctor X* (1932), *The Mystery of the Wax Museum* (1933), and *The Vampire Bat* (1933). She had already appeared in two films directed by Ernest B. SCHOEDSACK—*The Four Feathers* (1929) and *The Most Dangerous Game* (1932, *The Hounds of Zaroff* in GB)—before starring in another Schoedsack film with which her name will remain associated: playing the blonde half of the Beauty and the Beast relationship, she screamed her way magnificently through KING KONG (1933). She occasionally appeared in British films, notably opposite Jack Hulbert in *Bulldog Jack* (1935). Her second husband was Robert RISKIN whom she married in 1942 when she virtually retired, though making some screen appearances after his death in 1955.

**WRIGHT, BASIL** (1907– ), British producer and director of documentaries, joined John GRIERSON at the Empire Marketing Board (see CROWN FILM UNIT) in 1929. He stepped to the forefront of British documentary with SONG OF CEYLON (1934) and NIGHT MAIL (1936) which characteristically combined the lyricism of

FLAHERTY with the social observation of the Grierson school. In 1937 he formed the Realist Film Unit and directed *Children at School*, but otherwise functioned as a producer until he directed *Bernard Miles on Gun Dogs* (1948). Subsequent projects included *Waters of Time* (1951) and *World without End* (1953, co-directed with Paul ROTHA for UNESCO). More recently Wright has favoured art subjects, notably *The Stained Glass at Fairford* (1956) and *The Immortal Land* (1958). His prolific writings include *The use of the film* (1948), and he has taught at the University of California. He has written a history of film, *The long view* (London, 1974).

## WR—MISTERIJE ORGANIZMA (WR—Mysteries of the Organism)

*WR—MISTERIJE ORGANIZMA* (*WR—Mysteries of the Organism*), Yugoslavia/West Germany, 1971. Eastman Color; 1½hr. *Dir, scr* Dusan Makavejev; *prod* Neoplanta Film (Novi Sad)/Telepool (Munich); *ph* Pega Popović, Aleksander Petković; *cast* Milena Dravić (Milena), Jagoder Kaloper (Jagoder), Zoran Radmilović (Radmilović), Ivica Vidović (Vladimir Ilyich), Miodrag Andrić (soldier), Tuli Kupferberg (US soldier), Jackie Curtis, Betty Dodson, Nancy Godfrey (themselves).

Ostensibly concerned with the work of Wilhelm Reich and the practices he advocated, MAKAVEJEV turns a devastatingly sharp eye on the decadence and self-deception of capitalist society, without, however, failing to make brutally sharp comment on the rape of socialist ideals in Czechoslovakia. In a cheerful hotchpotch of styles, he contrives a cunning ambivalence towards both his subject and the processes of film-making. Hilarious and appalling, the film owes a great deal to CHYTILOVÁ's SEDMIKRÁSKY (*Daisies*, 1967). It was withdrawn from the official festival at Pula, caused an uproar at CANNES, and subsequently had great success in Europe and the US.

## WUTHERING HEIGHTS

*WUTHERING HEIGHTS* by Emily Brontë (1818–48), published in 1847, tells a sombre and imaginative love story against a vividly described natural setting. It was first filmed in 1920, starring Milton Rosmer as Heathcliff and Annie Trevor as Cathy.

In the 1939 version directed by William WYLER, with Laurence OLIVIER and Merle OBERON, the plot was radically simplified and thirty new scenes were written by the apparently unlikely team of Ben HECHT and Charles MACARTHUR.

BUÑUEL's *Abismos de Pasion* (Mexico, 1953) modernized the story and transferred the setting to Mexico. *Wuthering Heights* (GB, 1970) starring Anna Calder-Marshall and Timothy Dalton and directed by Robert Fuest ignored the poetic passion of the original.

**WYLER, WILLIAM** (1902–   ), US director, began work as a studio publicist, became an assistant director, and graduated in 1925 to directing short Westerns. He directed minor feature films until 1935, then completed *Come and Get It* (1936) which had been started by Howard HAWKS. In the period 1936–42 he directed a succession of films of high quality, notably *Dodsworth* (1936), *These Three* (1936), DEAD END (1937), *Jezebel* (1938), WUTHERING HEIGHTS (1939), *The Letter* (1940), *The Westerner* (1940), and THE LITTLE FOXES (1941). His sentimental tribute to the British way of life, *Mrs Miniver* (1942) starring Greer GARSON, was an immense box-office success. In 1942–5 he made documentaries for the US Air Force, including *Memphis Belle* (1944).

Wyler made a tremendous impact with his first post-war film, THE BEST YEARS OF OUR LIVES (1946), then directed another succession of outstanding films—*The Heiress* (1949), *Detective Story* (1951), *Carrie* (1952), ROMAN HOLIDAY (1953), *The Desperate Hours* (1955), and *Friendly Persuasion* (1956)—which culminated in the hugely enjoyable *The Big Country* (1958). He then undertook the massive remake of BEN-HUR (1959), which is less characteristic of his work. His recent films include a remake of *These Three*, *The Children's Hour* (1962, *The Loudest Whisper* in GB), *The Collector* (1965), *How to Steal a Million* (1966), *Funny Girl* (1968), and *The Liberation of L. B. Jones* (1969).

In his best work, Wyler combines the polish of an experienced Hollywood professional with a perceptive view of human relationships which is embodied in a clear and stylish mode of narrative.

**WYNYARD, DIANA** (1906–64), British actress, appeared in a few Hollywood films in the early thirties, including *Cavalcade* (1933), but is best remembered in the cinema in some notable British productions of the forties: *Freedom Radio* (Anthony ASQUITH, 1940), GASLIGHT (1940), *Kipps* (Carol REED, 1941), and *An Ideal Husband* (Alexander KORDA, 1947). She returned to Hollywood to appear in *Island in the Sun* (Robert ROSSEN, 1957). An accomplished and sensitive actress, her work in films was secondary to a distinguished career on the stage.

# X Y Z

**'X' certificate,** category introduced by the BRITISH BOARD OF FILM CENSORS in 1951 to designate films unsuitable for juvenile audiences. Initially the certificate prohibited entry (to any part of a programme which includes a film bearing an 'X' certificate) to persons under the age of sixteen; in 1970 the minimum age was raised to eighteen. (See CENSORSHIP, GB.)

**YATES,** PETER (1929–  ), British director, was a motor-racing driver and team manager, then worked as a film editor and as assistant to Guy Hamilton and Tony RICHARDSON. In 1962 he directed his first film, the pop musical *Summer Holiday*, which was followed by a black comedy *One Way Pendulum* (1964). After *Robbery* (1967), a thriller starring Stanley BAKER, Yates was invited to Hollywood where he directed Steve MCQUEEN in *Bullitt* (1968), a fast-paced detective story containing a masterly car chase. *John and Mary* (1969), about the tentative development of a modern love affair, and *Murphy's War* (1971) were less suited to his style; he returned to form with a stylish comedy-thriller, *The Hot Rock* (1972, *How to Steal a Diamond in Four Uneasy Lessons* in GB).

**YELLOW SUBMARINE,** GB, 1968. De Luxe Color; 1¼hr. *Dir* George Dunning; story Lee Minoff, from the song by John Lennon and Paul McCartney.

A lively series of episodes, each constructed on a BEATLES song, is loosely linked by a fantastic narrative. Formalized caricatures of the Beatles are set against the bright contrasts of pop art. DUNNING relates a specific style to each song: striking examples are the photomontage treatment of 'Eleanor Rigby' and the loose, vital colour patterns of 'Lucy in the Sky with Diamonds'.

**YEUX SANS VISAGE, Les** (*Eyes without a Face*), France/Italy, 1959. 1½hr. *Dir* Georges Franju; *prod* Champs Elysées/Lux; *scr* Jean Redon, from his own novel; *ph* Eugen Schüfftan; *mus* Maurice Jarre; *cast* Pierre Brasseur (Prof Génessier), Alida Valli (Louise), Edith Scob (Christiane), François Guérin (Jacques).

A distinguished surgeon kidnaps a succession of young women with the aim of grafting their features on to the face of his daughter, disfigured in a motor accident. The element of surreal fantasy discernible in FRANJU's short documentaries is expanded into a full-scale horror film notable for its haunting baroque imagery and allegorical resonances.

**YORDAN,** PHILIP (*c.* 1913–  ), US playwright, scriptwriter, and producer, wrote several stage plays including *Anna Lucasta* (1944). His first film work was with William DIETERLE, with whom he collaborated on *All That Money Can Buy* (1941) (uncredited), and *Syncopation* (1942). He became one of Hollywood's most prolific writers of scripts and original screenplays; for *Broken Lance* (1954) he was awarded an OSCAR. He scripted both screen versions of *Anna Lucasta* (1949, 1959) and has been both writer and producer on numerous films. His films as a writer include *Johnny Guitar* (1954), *The Man from Laramie* (1955), *Joe Macbeth* (1955), *No Down Payment* (1957), EL CID (1961); as writer and producer *The Harder They Fall* (1956), *Day of the Triffids* (1962), *The Royal Hunt of the Sun* (1969), *Captain Apache* (1971). His novel *Man of the West* was filmed in 1957 as *Gun Glory*.

**YORK,** MICHAEL (1942–  ), British actor, joined the National Theatre in 1964. His first appearance there was in *Much Ado About Nothing* directed by Franco ZEFFIRELLI, who also directed the film THE TAMING OF THE SHREW (1967) in which York made his screen début. A talented actor of considerable promise he has, in his film roles, tended to be stereotyped as the traditionally pleasant, mannerly young Englishman of good education, but within this limitation he has contributed excellent performances to ACCIDENT (1967), Zeffirelli's ROMEO AND JULIET (1968), CABARET and *England Made Me* (both 1972).

**YORK,** SUSANNAH (1941–  ), British actress, first appeared on the screen as Alec GUINNESS's stubborn daughter in *Tunes of Glory* (Ronald Neame, 1960). She then gave a captivating performance as a schoolgirl in *The Greengage Summer* (1961) and as a result John

HUSTON cast her in *Freud* (1962). TOM JONES (1963) established her name, but among a number of films over the next five years only *A Man for All Seasons* (Fred ZINNEMANN, 1966) demonstrated her growing confidence. She played a confused lesbian in *The Killing of Sister George* (Robert ALDRICH, 1968) and gave excellent performances in *They Shoot Horses, Don't They* (1969) and *Jane Eyre* (Delbert MANN, 1970); she finally broke away from being type-cast as a conventional *ingénue* when she brought complete conviction to the central role of a schizophrenic innocent in Robert ALTMAN's *Images* (1972).

**YOSHIMURA, KIMISABURO** (1911– ), Japanese director, entered the Shochiku studios as assistant to Yasujiro Shimazu and directed his first film *Nakiashi Sashiashi* in 1934. His early work was flawed by gratuitous stylistic experiment, but his post-war films display increasing control of a wide range of subjects. His satirical comedy *Zo o kutta Renchu* (*The Fellows Who Ate the Elephant*, 1947) was followed in the same year by *Anjo-ke no Butokai* (*A Ball at the Anjo House*).

This study of the decline of the Japanese aristocracy was written by Kaneto SHINDO who remained his frequent collaborator. In 1950 they formed an independent production company, Kindai, for which Yoshimura directed *Itsuwareru Seiso* (*Clothes of Deception*, 1951), a geisha film which like *Yoru no kawa* (*Night River*, 1956) shows his affinity with MIZOGUCHI; in 1957 he completed Mizoguchi's *Osaka Monogatari* (*Osaka Story*).

Yoshimura's skill in portraying women emerged again in films such as *Yoru no Cho* (*Night Butterflies*, 1957), *Onna no Saka* (*Women of Kyoto*, 1960), and *Daraku suru Onna* (*A Fallen Woman*, 1967). He has also specialized in the JIDAI-GEKI (period film), using its conventions to illuminate modern problems, as in *Mori no Ishimatsu* (*Ishimatsu of the Forest*, 1949), *Genji Monogatari* (*A Tale of Genji*, 1951), and *Bijo to Kairyu* (*The Beauty and the Dragon*, 1955), an interesting attempt to present the KABUKI in terms of cinema.

**YOUNG, CLARA KIMBALL** (1890–1960), US actress, began her career on the stage as a child. She joined VITAGRAPH in 1912; among her early films were *Cardinal Wolsey* (J. Stuart BLACKTON, 1912), versions of *Beau Brummell* (1913), *The Little Minister* (1913), and *Trilby* (1916), and several films directed by Albert Capellani, including *Camille* (1917). She was starred in many films of the twenties, and was seen occasionally in the thirties, mainly in character parts in serials and Westerns.

**YOUNG, F. A.** (Freddie), (1902– ), British cameraman, entered the film industry in 1917 and worked his way up to become one of the world's most distinguished cinematographers. He is outstanding for his control of lighting, particularly in mastering the problems of available light on location. His work has added distinction to many large-scale productions including CAESAR AND CLEOPATRA (1945), LAWRENCE OF ARABIA (1962), in which his creation of a mirage effect created a sensation, DOCTOR ZHIVAGO (1966), and the intensely beautiful *Ryan's Daughter* (1971). His book, *The work of the motion picture cameraman* (with Paul Petzold, London, 1972), has become a standard work.

**YOUNG, LORETTA** (1912– ), US actress, real name Gretchen Belzer, whose wide-eyed prettiness and gift for wearing elegant clothes was successfully used first by WARNER BROS, then by TWENTIETH CENTURY-FOX, during the thirties and forties. Few of her films are memorable, but as Jean HARLOW's rival in *Platinum Blonde* (1931), the orphan girl in *A Zoo in Budapest* (1933), the working-class heroine of *Man's Castle* (1933), and the Swedish farm worker in *The Farmer's Daughter* (1947) she gave performances demonstrating her considerable range. Her television series 'Loretta Young Presents' (1953–60) made her a symbol for gracious living.

**YOUNG, ROBERT** (1907– ), US actor chiefly remembered as one of METRO-GOLDWYN-MAYER's resident leading men in 1931–44. As such he appeared with competence and charm opposite Joan CRAWFORD (*Today We Live*, 1933), Janet GAYNOR (*Carolina*, 1933), Shirley TEMPLE (*Stowaway*, 1936), Jeanette MACDONALD (*Cairo*, 1936), among many others. After leaving MGM he had less consistent success, although two television series in the US, 'Father Knows Best' and 'Marcus Welby MD', were very popular.

**YOUNG, ROLAND** (1887–1953), British-born actor known chiefly for his supporting roles in Hollywood films. After four years' experience in the London theatre he went to the US where he quickly became a popular stage actor. He appeared in only two silent films, playing Dr Watson in SHERLOCK HOLMES and in *Moriarty* (both 1922), but with the introduction of sound he rapidly became a favourite with his easy, quizzical style of humour. His excellent performance as Uriah Heep in DAVID COPPERFIELD (1934) was an exception to his usual type-casting. His best films include *Ruggles of Red Gap* (Leo MCCAREY, 1935), *The Young in Heart* (1939), and THE PHILADELPHIA STORY (1940); he starred, opposite Billie BURKE, in the title role of *Topper* (1937), *Topper Takes a Trip* (1939), and *Topper Returns* (1941).

**YOUNG, TERENCE** (1915–   ), director, born in Shanghai of Irish descent. He entered films in 1936 and worked as an assistant and writer to Brian Desmond Hurst. From 1948 he directed features, and has worked in a variety of countries. His great commercial successes were the early JAMES BOND films. *Dr No* (1962) set the style of the Bond image and much of its tongue-in-cheek quality arises from Young's interpretation of the character. In 1967 he directed the intense and claustrophobic thriller *Wait until Dark* with Alan Arkin and Audrey HEPBURN. It was his first Hollywood film and helped establish his reputation in France, where he became something of a cult. His recent films include *Soleil rouge* (*Red Sun*, 1971), an eastern-Western, and *Cosa Nostra* (1972, *The Valachi Papers* in GB).

**YOUNG, VICTOR** (1889–1956), US composer. Originally a teacher, pianist, and accompanist, he spent eight years as musical director in EDISON's experimental laboratory in New Jersey, and later in his career wrote film music. Notable among his earlier scores was *For Whom the Bell Tolls* (1943), and shortly before his death he wrote the music for AROUND THE WORLD IN EIGHTY DAYS (1956). Among his other scores were those for several films by Cecil B. DEMILLE and John FORD.

*YOUNG AND THE DAMNED, The*, see OLVIDADOS, LOS

**YUGOSLAVIA.** In 1896 there were LUMIÈRE shows and Lumière cameramen soon began to film local events including the coronation of King Peter in Belgrade in 1903. In 1905 Milton Manaki, a Macedonian, started making films abroad. *Karadjordje* (1910) was the first feature made locally; its subject was the first rising against the Turks, but it was made by Jules Bairy for a French company. A few small production companies were established; Josip Hall of Zagreb and Slavko Jocanović of Belgrade both shot newsreels of the Balkan Wars of 1912, and newsreels continued to be produced until after the First World War.

Small production companies sprang up and collapsed during the twenties and thirties. The best of Yugoslavia's small output of feature films at this time is considered to be Mihailo-Miko Popović's *S verom v boga* (*With Faith in God*, 1934), a Serbian epic of the First World War. During the Second World War Dragoljub Aleksič, a strong man in a circus, clandestinely made the patriotic NEVINOST BEZ ZAŠTITE (*Innocence Unprotected*, 1942), which was shown in spite of the German occupation; it was later revived by Dusan MAKAVAJEV.

The State Film Enterprise was formed in 1945, as soon as the war ended. Growth was slow in comparison with the other Socialist countries: only six feature films had been made by 1949. Studios were well equipped, but there was a lack of trained personnel. War was the exclusive subject at first; no contemporary theme was attempted until 1957. The partisan film, perennially popular and stylized into a genre, is the Yugoslav equivalent of the Western; within the framework various current problems can be considered. They are executed with verve, skill, and a splendid lack of self-consciousness.

Partly for artistic reasons, but also as an expression of national resurgence, each of the six republics has followed a characteristic cultural line which is particularly apparent in films. Croatian films were the first to make an impact abroad, through the work of the Zagreb school of animation. Their lively experimentalism was carried into feature films directed by the former animator Vetroslav MIMICA, notably *Prometej sa otoka Viševece* (*Prometheus from the Island of Viševeca*, 1965).

The Slovenian Boštjan Hladnik has studied problems of emotional alienation in *Ples na kiši* (*Dance in the Rain*, 1961) and *Pescani grad* (*The Sand Castle*, 1963). Moral predicaments have formed the substance of films by other Slovenian directors, notably France Štiglic and Matjaž Klopčič.

Wide distribution abroad has been achieved by only one Yugoslav director, the Serbian Makavajev. Although they are useful currency earners, his films tend to encounter official disapproval at home: WR—MISTERIJE ORGANIZMA (*WR—Mysteries of the Organism*) was banned from the Pula festival in 1971 and has apparently never been shown in Yugoslavia.

Much of the increasing awareness abroad of developments in Yugoslav cinema is attributable to the annual film festival at Pula. It was initiated in 1956 to show each year's productions to a foreign audience: no foreign films are screened.

The climate and scenery, and the comparative cheapness of working there, have made international co-productions a regular part of the Yugoslav film industry and an important source of revenue.

*YUKINOJO HENGE* (*An Actor's Revenge*), Japan, 1963. DaieiScope; 1¾hr; Daiei Colour. *Dir* Kon Ichikawa; *prod* Daiei; *scr* Natto Wada, Daisuke Ito, Teinosuke Kinugasa; *ph* Setsuo Kobayashi; *des* Yoshinobu Nishioka; *mus* Yasushi Akutagawa; *cast* Kazuo Hasegawa

(Yukinojo/Yamitaro), Ayako Wakao (Lady Namiji), Fujiko Yamamoto (Ohatsu), Ganjiro Nakamura (Lord Dobe), Raizo Ichikawa (youngest thief), Shusha Ichikawa (Kikunojo), Saburo Date (Kawaguchiya).

Yukinojo is an *onnagata*—an actor of female roles in a KABUKI company—and a wildly successful star. During the company's visit to Edo he recognizes three rich merchants who were responsible for the death of his parents and sets in train a complicated and determined revenge. A sub-plot involves the exploits of a daring bandit Yamitaro.

ICHIKAWA's exploration of the oppositions of drama and life, love and hate, violence and gentleness, masculinity and femininity, has extraordinary richness and complexity. The visual quality is remarkable: images are composed which sometimes virtually eliminate perspective in the manner of Japanese prints, sometimes break up the wide screen into areas of concurrent action; thoughts are depicted above a character's head as in strip cartoons; or the screen may be entirely blacked out except for restricted areas spot-lighting a white face, a snaking rope, a pale, endless wall.

The film's other great strength is the dual performance by the veteran film actor Kazuo HASEGAWA, as the fluttering Yukinojo and the agile Yamitaro. Particularly memorable is the sequence where Yukinojo, dressed as a woman, is breathlessly wooed by the daughter of one of his intended victims, which encompasses all the film's many ambiguities.

**YUTKEVICH, SERGEI** (1904–    ), Russian director, studied painting at Kiev and Moscow. In 1921–2 he worked with the FEKS group set up by KOZINTSEV and TRAUBERG. He was an assistant on ROOM's *Predatel* (*Traitor*, 1926) and co-directed with him *Tretya Meshchanskaya* (*Bed and Sofa*, 1927).

After directing two silent films he scripted and directed his first sound film *Zlatiye gori* (*Golden Mountains*, 1931), an ambitious attempt to achieve the audio-visual counterpoint recommended by EISENSTEIN, PUDOVKIN, and ALEXANDROV. He became a major exponent of SOCIALIST REALISM with VSTRECHNYI (*Counterplan*, 1932), co-directed by ERMLER.

In 1934 he organized in Leningrad an official experimental studio where he supervised the production of a series of high-quality films, and four years later he began teaching at VGIK where he is still a professor. He continued directing films including *Yakov Sverdlov* (1940), *Noviye pokhozhdeniya Shveika* (*New Adventures of Good Soldier Schweik*, 1943), and *Svet nad Rossiei* (*Light over Russia*, 1947), one of the many films banned under the Stalin régime. Some work

in the theatre, including a play by MAYAKOVSKY, was followed by his magnificent screen adaptation of OTHELLO (1955). He made workmanlike documentaries of Yves MONTAND's successful tour of the Soviet Union in 1957 and of Khrushchev's state visit to France in 1960. His later films include *Lenin v Polshe* (*Lenin in Poland*, 1964) and a sensitive period piece *Syuzhet dlya nebolshovo rasskaza* (*Lika, Tchekhov's Love*, 1969). Over a long period fraught with difficulties for Russian film-makers Yutkevich has succeeded in balancing individual expression with official acceptance.

**Z,** France/Algeria, 1968. Eastman Color; 2hr. *Dir* Costa-Gavras; *prod* Reggane Film (Paris)/ONCIC (Algiers); *scr* Costa-Gavras, Jorge Semprun, from the novel by Vassili Vassilikos; *ph* Raoul Coutard; *mus* Mikis Theodorakis; *cast* Yves Montand ('Z'), Jean-Louis Trintignant (magistrate), Jacques Perrin (journalist), François Périer (public prosecutor), Irene Papas (Hélène).

Although shot in Algeria and ostensibly a fictitious account of events taking place in an unidentified country, *Z* is patently the story of the murdered Greek left-wing deputy Lambrakis. The film's passionate attack on the injustices inherent in totalitarianism is the basis for a polished but slightly incoherent thriller, largely sustained by the sensitive acting of MONTAND, TRINTIGNANT, and Irene PAPAS.

**ZABRISKIE POINT,** US, 1970. Panavision; 1¾hr; Metrocolor. *Dir* Michelangelo Antonioni; *prod* Carlo Ponti for MGM; *scr* Antonioni, Fred Gardner, Sam Shepard, Tonino Guerra, Clare Peploe; *ph* Alfio Contini; *prod des* Dean Tavoularis; *des* George Nelson; *sp eff* Earl McCoy; *mus* The Pink Floyd; *cast* Mark Frechette (Mark), Daria Halprin (Daria), Rod Taylor (Lee Allen).

For his second film made under contract to METRO-GOLDWYN-MAYER, ANTONIONI took a real event (the shooting of a student by the Los Angeles police) and strung on it a series of incidents and fantasies representing an aristocratic distaste for current cultural and material values. Although lacking coherence, his message is admirably exposed in the photography of Los Angeles and the closing sequence of a refrigerator blowing up which, if jejune in conception, is beautifully executed and conveys a sense of glee unusual in his work.

The film marks several stylistic developments which carried Antonioni further away from the world of his great Italian films: and in the opening scenes of the student riot and in his choice of non-actors for the principal roles there is an interesting reversion to his documentary roots.

**ZAMPA**, LUIGI (1904– ), Italian director. After working as a playwright he enrolled at the age of thirty-one at the CENTRO SPERIMENTALE in its first year of operation. His first film, *L'attore Scomparso* (1941), was followed by similar light-weight enterprises until VIVERE IN PACE (1946) introduced an element of moral concern into his work. After *L'onorevole Angelina* (1947), with Anna MAGNANI, Zampa collaborated with the Sicilian writer Vitaliano Brancati on *Anni difficile* (1948), *Anni facile* (1953), and *L'arte di arrangiarsi* (1954). In these and in other films such as *Processo alla città* (1952), *La romana* (1952), with Gina LOLLOBRIGIDA, and *La ragazza del palio* (1958), the neo-realist impulse of *Vivere in pace* was diluted to nothing stronger than ironic social comment.

**ZANUCK**, DARRYL F. (1902– ), US producer and executive. Beginning as a screenwriter of RIN-TIN-TIN stories for WARNER BROS, Zanuck became a producer and finally studio production head (1929–33). In partnership with Joseph SCHENCK, he founded Twentieth Century Pictures in 1933, and when this company merged with the FOX Film Corporation two years later Zanuck took over production. Apart from war service with the Signal Corps film unit, Zanuck remained at the helm of TWENTIETH CENTURY-FOX until the mid-fifties when he became an independent producer. He returned to Fox after Spyros SKOURAS was ousted in 1962 and ruled as chief executive until his retirement. Of the many films he produced the most outstanding are THE GRAPES OF WRATH (1940), ALL ABOUT EVE (1950), VIVA ZAPATA! (1952), *The Roots of Heaven* (1958), and *The Longest Day* (1962).

His biography, *Don't say yes until I finish talking* by Mel Gusson, was published in 1971.

**ZANUCK**, RICHARD (1934– ), US producer, was assistant to his father Darryl F. Zanuck at TWENTIETH CENTURY-FOX, and became a producer in his own right with such films to his credit as *Compulsion* (1959) and *Sanctuary* (1960). He was production head at Twentieth Century-Fox 1969–71, moved to WARNER BROS, then became an independent producer at UNIVERSAL.

**ZAVATTINI**, CESARE (1902– ), Italian scriptwriter, was a journalist and film critic in the thirties. He first worked in films when he scripted CAMERINI's *Darò un milione* (1936), an inoffensive comedy that barely suggested the crucial role he was later to play in the development of Italian cinema. During the next few years he worked with ZAMPA, Mario Bonnard, and, most notably, DE SICA on *Teresa Venerdi* (1941). The first real expression of his concern with daily life and social problems was in his script for BLASETTI's *Quattro passi fra le nuvole* (*Four Steps in the Clouds*, 1942).

In the same year Zavattini and De Sica made *I bambini ci guardano* which, in its use of natural locations and implicit criticism of Fascist attitudes, indicated the style which came to be known as NEO-REALISM and which characterized their work until the mid-fifties. During this period Zavattini also worked with Blasetti (*Un giorno nella vita*, 1946), René CLÉMENT (*Le mure de Malapago*, 1948), Luciano EMMER (DOMENICA D'AGOSTO, 1950), DE SANTIS (*Roma, ore 11*, 1952), and VISCONTI (BELLISSIMÀ, 1951), but his most important work was with De Sica. After *La porta del cielo* (1944), which examined the effect of the war and the Resistance on everyday life, they made SCIUSCIÀ (1946) and LADRI DI BICICLETTE (*Bicycle Thieves*, 1948); the latter's box-office success came in a year when a quarter of the Italian working population was, like the film's protagonist, unemployed. Two years later Zavattini adapted his own novel *Toto il buono* (first published in 1943) as MIRACOLO A MILANO. This was followed by the last distinctively neo-realist film, UMBERTO D (1952), which incurred the open displeasure of the Christian Democrat Government.

Later that year, Zavattini announced a new project, *Italia mia*, which he saw as the logical development of neo-realism: a scriptless film simply recording everyday life in various parts of Italy. Although it was never made, its conception was important in the evolution of the 'survey' film, composed of a group of related episodes by different directors, which began with AMORE IN CITTÀ (1953). He attempted to counter the romantic unreality of commercial cinema with *Le Italiane e l'amore* (1961), made up of sketches by young film and television directors. In 1963 he worked in collaboration with fifteen young directors on *I misteri di Roma*: shot in 35mm, 16mm, and even 9·5mm, it was intended simply as an image of a day's events in Rome and combined interviews with actuality footage in CINÉMA-VÉRITÉ style.

Throughout the fifties Zavattini had used journalism to propagate the neo-realist ideal. He visited Spain in 1954 to work on an unrealized project, similar in style to *Italia mia*, with some of the country's more progressive young filmmakers, and in 1960–1 he was production supervisor on two films made in Cuba.

At the same time, he continued to work with De Sica on *L'ore di Napoli* (1954), *Il tetto* (1956), *La Ciociara* (1961), and *Oggi, ieri, domani* (1965). Only *Il tetto* retains the feel of his earlier work: with increasing capitulation to commercial demands his later films may appear to indicate a falling off, but the significance of his achievement in the formulation and practice of neo-realism cannot be over-estimated.

**ZAZIE DANS LE MÉTRO,** France, 1960. Eastman Color; 1½hr. *Dir* Louis Malle; *prod* Nouvelles Editions de Films; *scr* Malle, Jean-Paul Rappeneau, from the novel by Raymond Queneau; *ph* Henri Raichi; *des* Bernard Evein; *artistic adviser* William Klein; *ed* Kenout Peltier; *cast* Catherine Demongeot (Zazie), Philippe Noiret (Gabriel), Carla Marlier (Albertine), Vittorio Caprioli (Pedro–Trouscaillon, etc), Hubert Deschamps (Turandot), Annie Fratellini (Mado), Yvonne Clech (Madame Mouaque).

QUENEAU's best-selling novel, published in 1959, the story of plain-speaking Zazie spending thirty-six hours in Paris with the sole desire of going on the Métro, immediately attracted MALLE. Undaunted by the difficulty of adapting Queneau's verbal fireworks for the screen, and using every technical trick with a freshness and relish worthy of MÉLIÈS, he succeeded in achieving a sort of visual equivalent, questioning cinematic modes as acutely as Queneau had questioned linguistic conventions. Catherine Demongeot gave a sparkling performance as the egregious Zazie pursuing her quest single-mindedly among the mounting confusion, in a Paris in which Malle's use of colour and sets enhanced the surrealistic view of the way a modern city distorts human lives. The public was confused by the film, and most critics short-sightedly dismissed it as no more than a bagful of tricks.

**ZECCA,** FERDINAND (1864–1947), French director and producer. After achieving some success in *café-concerts*, he appeared in *Les Mésaventures d'une tête de veau (Misfortunes of a Mutton-head*, 1898) for GAUMONT, then moved to PATHÉ in 1899 as a comic actor. He progressed to directing almost at once, making the usual short comedies and dramas, and supervising the work of Pathé's other directors, including Segundo de CHOMÓN, Louis GASNIER, and Capellani. His own taste appears to have run to 'realistic' melodramas such as *Histoire d'une crime* (1901) from Victor Hugo, and *Les Victimes de l'alcoölisme* (1902) from Zola's *L'Assommoir*. His main accomplishment was in keeping up a constant stream of films to meet public demand: in 1905–20 he was Pathé's head of production, spending the years after 1913 managing their American production branch. On his return to France he managed the subsidiary Pathé-Baby until his retirement in 1939.

**ZEFFIRELLI,** FRANCO (1923–  ), Italian director, studied architecture at Florence, then worked as actor and designer in the theatre. His important career as a director of opera commenced in 1953; he has also directed Shakespeare in London and at Stratford-upon-Avon.

His training in film was as assistant to such important directors as VISCONTI, DE SICA, ANTONIONI, and ROSSELLINI: his own films have shown aims far removed from theirs. His two screen adaptations from SHAKESPEARE, THE TAMING OF THE SHREW (1967) and ROMEO AND JULIET (1968), alarmed purists by their treatment of the text, but added a dimension of great visual richness, which was also the main appeal of *Fratello sole, sorella luna (Brother Sun, Sister Moon*, 1973) about Francis of Assisi.

**ZEMAN,** KAREL (1910–  ), Czech animator, moved from poster design to making animated films in 1945. His films were conventional in technique until *Inspirace (Inspiration*, 1949), for which he animated glass figures. Another short, *Poklad ptaciho ostrova (The Treasure of Bird Island*, 1952), combined drawn animation and puppets, indicating the direction of Zeman's developed style—a mixture of graphics, live action, puppets, and optical effects. He has used this complex form in four feature films which wittily combine fantasy and allegory to deal with themes officially unacceptable at the time: *Cesta do pravĕku (Prehistoric Journey*, 1954), *Vynález zkázy (The Invention of Destruction*, 1958) which attracted world-wide attention and won a Grand Prix at the Brussels Exhibition, *Baron Prášil (Baron Munchausen*, 1962), and BLÁZNOVA KRONIKA (*The Jester's Tale*, 1964). Zeman has also continued to make shorts and is the creator of Mr Prokouk, Czechoslovakia's most popular puppet character.

**ZEMLYA** (*Earth*), USSR, 1930. 1½hr. *Dir* Alexander Dovzhenko; *prod* VUFKU; *ph* Danylo Demutsky; *des* Vasili Krichevsky; *cast* Semyon Svashenko (Vasili), Stepan Shkurat (his father), Mikola Nademsky (grandfather), Yelena Maximova (Vasili's betrothed), Piotr Masokha (Foma), Nikolai Mikhailov (priest).

A village committee led by Vasili is trying to implement collectivization in the face of opposition from the erstwhile landowners. Vasili uses the new tractor to throw down the fences dividing the land but returning home, dancing absorbedly in the moonlight, he is murdered. The film ends with his burial, triumphantly asserting the unity of the workers and their ultimate victory.

Filmed in the rich farming country of his beloved Ukraine, *Zemlya* perfectly embodies DOVZHENKO's intense commitment and artistic sensibility. Measured in pace and passionate in tone, it is made up of exquisitely composed shots that linger wonderingly on the forms and tex-

*Zemlya* (Alexander Dovzhenko, 1930)

tures of the land, its people, and its produce. It created a sensation abroad, particularly affecting the DOCUMENTARY film-makers of Britain and the US. Less happily received by the Soviet authorities, already perturbed by EISENSTEIN's cerebral, comic treatment of the same topic in STAROYE I NOVOYE (*Old and New*, 1929), it was issued with two sequences cut, the scene where Vasili's betrothed, naked and hysterical, mourns his death and the only moment of light relief, when the peasants delightedly replenish the tractor's radiator by urinating into it. The film was not seen in its original form until 1958.

***ZÉRO DE CONDUITE*** (*Nought for Conduct*— but the film is always referred to by its original title), France, 1933. 40min. *Dir, scr* Jean Vigo; *prod* Gaumont-Franco-Film Aubert; *asst* Albert Riera, Pierre Merle; *dial* Charles Goldblatt; *ph* Boris Kaufman, *asst* Louis Berger; *mus* Maurice Jaubert; *cast* Jean Dasté (Huguet), Robert Le Flon (Pète-Sec), le Nain Delphin (principal), Larive (chemistry master), Louis Lefèvre (Caussat), Gérard de Bédarieux (Tabard), Coco Goldstein (Bruel), Gilbert Pruchon (Colin), Blanchar (Bec-de-Gaz).

Four schoolboys, suffering the usual petty injustices inflicted in many boarding schools, plan and execute an uprising: VIGO's comment on inhumanity and revolt has, of course, a much wider context than the school setting. Strong autobiographical elements, together with other sources, both literary and cinematic, produce an original and personal style which conveys an atmosphere of euphoric anarchy.

Apart from DASTÉ as the sympathetic *surveillant* (affectionately parodying CHAPLIN at one point), the only professional actors were Le Flon, Larive, and the dwarf DELPHIN. Among the smaller parts not receiving credits, Henri STORCK played the curé. The production team was assembled from Vigo's friends, and the production was run very much on a shoestring. One at least of the limitations was put to good use by Vigo. The poor recording facilities and the accents and behaviour of the schoolboys did not lend themselves to prepared dialogue: the systematic repetition which he used as a solution has a curious beauty of its own, and he later used it to even greater effect in L'ATALANTE (1934). JAUBERT's music plays an integral part in the film.

After a very mixed reception at its first showing, the film was banned on political grounds, not for indelicacy or the other reasons which are sometimes put forward. Its unevenness has been ascribed to cuts by the censors, but the film was banned in its entirety: defects in rhythm and structure are attributable partly to lack of time and money, but also to Vigo's inexperience.

The ban on *Zéro de conduite* was not lifted until 1945. From that time it has gained steadily in circulation among film enthusiasts. It is the acknowledged inspiration of Lindsay ANDERSON's IF ... (1968).

**ZETTERLING,** MAI (1925– ), Swedish actress and director, began her stage career in Stockholm in 1941 and had her first film success in HETS (*Frenzy*, 1944). Her fragile vulnerability made her well suited to act the German war bride in the British film *Frieda* (1947) and the child Hedvig in Ibsen's *The Wild Duck*, her début on the British stage in 1948. She has since worked in Hollywood, notably opposite Danny KAYE in *Knock on Wood* (1954) and appeared in a number of British films including *Only Two Can Play* (1961) opposite Peter SELLERS.

Her career has spanned acting and directing in the theatre and in films in both Britain and Sweden. She has collaborated with her husband, David Hughes, on a number of feature films and documentaries: their film *War Games* won Best Short Film prize at the 1963 VENICE Festival. A consistent theme of her theatre and film work is the role of women: *Älskande par* (*Loving Couples*, 1964), set in a maternity hospital, and *Nattlek* (*Night Games*, 1966), in which a house party brings together a diverse collection of characters; both use many variants of sexual behaviour to question and illustrate the limits of human relationships.

**ZINNEMANN,** FRED (1907– ), US director born in Vienna, studied music and law before training as an assistant director in Paris and Berlin. He visited Hollywood in 1929, returning to Berlin with Robert FLAHERTY to assist on a proposed documentary on a nomadic tribe in the Soviet Union; the project fell through and Zinnemann worked on MENSCHEN AM SONNTAG (1929) before returning to Hollywood.

He had various film jobs, even appearing as an extra in ALL QUIET ON THE WESTERN FRONT (1930), and he went with Paul STRAND to Mexico where they co-directed the semi-documentary *Redes* (*The Wave*, 1934). In 1937 he was taken on by METRO-GOLDWYN-MAYER to direct short documentaries and programme-fillers including some episodes of the *Crime Does Not Pay* series. His first feature, *Eyes in the Night* (1942), was an unremarkable crime story, but he attracted wide attention with *The Seventh Cross* (1944), an account of the escape across Europe of a group of Jewish refugees. *The Search* (1948) was a serious attempt to bring home to Americans the plight of displaced persons and particularly of orphans in post-war Europe.

Zinnemann's career flowered in the fifties with a number of distinguished films including *The Men* (1950), *Teresa* (1951), HIGH NOON (1952), FROM HERE TO ETERNITY (1953) for which he won an OSCAR, THE MEMBER OF THE WEDDING (1953), *Oklahoma!* (1955), and *The Nun's Story* (1959); his sincere and unaffected style of direction demonstrates his respect for a wide range of material with perhaps a bias towards social problems and moral conflict. He won a second Oscar for his sober film version of *A Man for All Seasons* (1966), with Paul SCOFIELD repeating his stage role of Cardinal Wolsey. *The Day of the Jackal* (1973) was less characteristic, a taut thriller handled with a flair for concentrated narrative.

**ZOOM,** the effect of moving smoothly towards or away from the subject produced optically by a zoom lens without physically moving the camera. The zoom lens, introduced in the midfifties, is essentially a single lens of variable focal length; at its best it replaces a range of fixed focal length lenses from WIDE-ANGLE (short focal length) to TELEPHOTO (long focal length) including every stage between. By turning a ring on the lens barrel the cameraman can enlarge or reduce the size of the sharply focused image at any speed as though the camera itself were moving; or he can select any given image size and film continuously without the need to select an appropriate lens.

For the first fifty years of film-making the effect of gradually approaching or retiring from a subject could be achieved only by moving the camera itself on a CRANE, DOLLY, or improvised vehicle (see CAMERA MOVEMENTS). 'Zooming in' is not visually identical to 'tracking in'; zooming in enlarges everything in view at the same rate, ignoring parallax, but the camera tracking in enlarges nearer objects more quickly, providing a life-like sensation of depth and dimension. In unskilled or insensitive hands the zoom lens can produce irritation amounting to discomfort in the viewer; nevertheless, it offers an unprecedented degree of flexibility in the selection and framing of images and its use has to a great extent replaced cutting between long, medium, and close-up shots.

**ZORRO,** a swashbuckling character derived from a novel, *The Curse of Capistrano* by Johnston McCulley, a masked avenger who champions the oppressed peasants of Old California against the tyrannical Spaniards, signing his exploits with the 'Z' which is his trademark.

Hollywood fought shy of the original title and